Campbell-Walsh UROLOGY

EDITORS

Louis R. Kavoussi, MD

Chairman
The Arthur Smith Institute for Urology
North Shore-Long Island Jewish Health System
Manhasset, New York
Professor of Urology
New York University School of Medicine
New York, New York

Andrew C. Novick, MD

Chairman
Glickman Urological Institute
Cleveland Clinic Foundation
Professor of Surgery
Cleveland Clinic Lerner College of Medicine of
Case Western Reserve University
Cleveland, Ohio

Alan W. Partin, MD, PhD

David Hall McConnell Professor and Director
James Buchanan Brady Urological Institute
Johns Hopkins Medical Institutions
Baltimore, Maryland

Craig A. Peters, MD

John E. Cole Professor of Urology
University of Virginia
Charlottesville, Virginia

Campbell-Walsh
UROLOGY

NINTH EDITION

EDITOR-IN-CHIEF

Alan J. Wein, MD, PhD(Hon)

Professor and Chair
Division of Urology
University of Pennsylvania School of Medicine
Chief of Urology
University of Pennsylvania Medical Center
Philadelphia, Pennsylvania

Volume 3

SAUNDERS

ELSEVIER

SAUNDERS
ELSEVIER

1600 John F. Kennedy Blvd.
Ste 1800
Philadelphia, PA 19103-2899

CAMPBELL-WALSH UROLOGY

ISBN 13: 978-0-7216-0798-6
ISBN 10: 0-7216-0798-5
E-dition ISBN 13: 978-1-4160-2966-3
ISBN 10: 1-4160-2966-4
International Edition ISBN 13: 978-0-8089-2353-4
ISBN 10: 0-8089-2353-6

Notice

Knowledge and best practice in this field are constantly changing. As new research and experience broaden
our knowledge, changes in practice, treatment, and drug therapy may become necessary or appropriate.
Readers are advised to check the most current information provided (i) on procedures featured or (ii) by
the manufacturer of each product to be administered, to verify the recommended dose or formula, the
method and duration of administration, and contraindications. It is the responsibility of the practitioner,
relying on his or her own experience and knowledge of the patient, to make diagnoses, to determine
dosages and the best treatment for each individual patient, and to take all appropriate safety precautions. To
the fullest extent of the law, neither the publisher nor the editors assume any liability for any injury and/or
damage to persons or property arising out of or related to any use of the material contained in this book.

Note that the term ESWL has been trademarked by Dornier MedTech in the United States. The generic
term for extracorporial shock wave lithotripsy is SWL. As the use of ESWL has become part of the
vernacular of urology, some of the authors have elected to use this term in their chapters.

The Publisher

Library of Congress Cataloging-in-Publication Data
Campbell-Walsh urology.—9th ed. / editor-in-chief, Alan J. Wein; editors, Louis R. Kavoussi . . . [et al.].
       p. ; cm.
     Rev. ed. of: Campbell's urology / editor-in-chief, Patrick C. Walsh; editors, Alan B. Retik . . . [et al.]. 8th
ed. ©2002.
     Includes bibliographical references and index.
     ISBN 0-7216-0798-5 (set)
       1. Urology.   I. Campbell, Meredith F. (Meredith Fairfax).   II. Wein, Alan J.   III. Kavoussi,
Louis R.   IV. Campbell's urology.   V. Title: Urology.
     [DNLM: 1. Urogenital Diseases.   2. Urology—methods. WJ 100 c192 2007]
RC871.C33 2007
616.6—dc22

2006041807

Acquisitions Editor: Rebecca Schmidt Gaertner
Developmental Editor: Anne Snyder
Publishing Services Manager: Tina Rebane
Project Manager: Norm Stellander
Design Direction: Ellen Zanolle

Printed in China
Last digit is the print number: 9 8 7 6 5 4 3 2 1

To our families, our teachers, and our residents, all of whom have suffered our behavior in various ways and are responsible for our ability to do what we do.

CONTRIBUTORS

Paul Abrams, MD, FRCS
Professor of Urology,
Bristol Urological Institute,
Southmead Hospital,
Bristol, United Kingdom
Overactive Bladder

Mark C. Adams, MD
Professor, Division of Pediatric Urology,
Vanderbilt Children's Hospital,
Vanderbilt University Medical Center,
Nashville, Tennessee
Urinary Tract Reconstruction in Children

Mohamad E. Allaf, MD
Assistant Professor,
James Buchanan Brady Urological Institute,
Johns Hopkins Medical Institutions,
Baltimore, Maryland
Diagnosis and Staging of Prostate Cancer

J. Kyle Anderson, MD
Assistant Professor,
Department of Urologic Surgery,
Veterans Affairs Medical Center,
University of Minnesota Medical School,
Minneapolis, Minnesota
*Surgical Anatomy of the Retroperitoneum, Adrenals,
Kidneys, and Ureters*

Karl-Erik Andersson, MD, PhD
Professor, Lund University;
Head Physician, Clinical Chemistry and Pharmacology,
Lund University Hospital,
Lund, Sweden
*Pharmacologic Management of Storage and
Emptying Failure*

Kenneth W. Angermeier, MD
Associate Professor,
Prosthetic Surgery and Genitourethral Reconstruction,
Glickman Urological Institute,
Cleveland Clinic Foundation,
Cleveland, Ohio
Surgery of Penile and Urethral Carcinoma

Rodney A. Appell, MD
Professor, Scott Department of Urology,
Baylor College of Medicine;
F. Bantley Scott Chair in Urology,
St. Luke's Episcopal Hospital,
Houston, Texas
Injection Therapy for Urinary Incontinence

Dean G. Assimos, MD
Professor,
Division of Surgical Sciences,
Head, Section of Endourology and Nephrolithasis,
Department of Urology,
Wake Forest University School of Medicine,
Winston-Salem, North Carolina
Pathophysiology of Urinary Tract Obstruction

Anthony Atala, MD
W. Boyce Professor and Chair,
Department of Urology,
Wake Forest University School of Medicine;
Director, Wake Forest Institute for Regenerative Medicine,
Winston-Salem, North Carolina
*Tissue Engineering and Cell Therapy:
Perspectives for Urology*

Darius J. Bägli, MDCM, FRCSC, FAAP, FACS
Associate Professor of Surgery,
Institute of Medical Science,
University of Toronto;
Director of Urology Research,
Research Institute,
The Hospital for Sick Children,
Toronto, Ontario, Canada
Reflux and Megaureter

John M. Barry, MD
Professor of Surgery,
Head, Division of Urology and Renal Transplantation,
The Oregon Health & Science University School
    of Medicine;
Staff Surgeon, Doernbecher Children's Hospital,
Portland, Oregon
Renal Transplantation

Georg Bartsch, MD
Professor and Chairman,
Department of Urology,
Medical University of Innsbruck,
Innsbruck, Austria
Surgery of Testicular Tumors

Stuart B. Bauer, MD
Professor of Surgery (Urology),
Harvard Medical School;
Senior Associate in Urology,
Children's Hospital,
Boston, Massachusetts
*Anomalies of the Upper Urinary Tract
Voiding Dysfunction in Children: Non-Neurogenic and
Neurogenic*

Clair J. Beard, MD
Assistant Professor, Harvard Medical School;
Vice-Chair, Division of Radiation Oncology,
Dana-Farber Cancer Institute,
Brigham and Women's Hospital,
Boston, Massachusetts
Radiation Therapy for Prostate Cancer

Arie S. Belldegrun, MD, FACS
Professor of Urology,
Chief, Division of Urologic Oncology,
Roy and Carol Doumani Chair in Urologic Oncology,
David Geffen School of Medicine,
University of California, Los Angeles,
Los Angeles, California
Cryotherapy for Prostate Cancer

Mark F. Bellinger, MD
Professor of Urology,
Children's Hospital of Pittsburgh,
University of Pittsburgh Medical Center,
Pittsburgh, Pennsylvania
Abnormalities of the Testes and Scrotum and Their Surgical Management

Mitchell C. Benson, MD
George F. Cahill Professor and Chairman,
J. Bently Squier Urological Clinic,
Columbia University Medical Center,
New York, New York
Cutaneous Continent Urinary Diversion

Sam B. Bhayani, MD
Assistant Professor of Surgery,
Department of Urology,
Washington University School of Medicine,
St. Louis, Missouri
Urinary Tract Imaging: Basic Principles

Jay T. Bishoff, MD
Associate Clinical Professor of Surgery,
University of Texas Health Science Center,
San Antonio, Texas;
Director,
Endourology Section,
Wilford Hall Medical Center,
Lackland AFB, Texas
Laparoscopic Surgery of the Kidney

Jerry G. Blaivas, MD
Clinical Professor of Urology,
Weill Medical College of Cornell University;
Attending,
New York-Presbyterian Hospital,
Lenox Hill Hospital,
New York, New York
Urinary Incontinence: Epidemiology, Pathophysiology, Evaluation, and Management Overview

Jon D. Blumenfeld, MD
Associate Professor of Medicine,
Weill Medical College of Cornell University;
Director of Hypertension,
Director of The Susan R. Knafel Polycystic Kidney Disease Center,
The Rogosin Institute;
Associate Attending Physician,
New York-Presbyterian Hospital,
New York, New York
Pathophysiology, Evaluation, and Medical Management of Adrenal Disorders

Michael L. Blute, MD
Professor of Urology,
Mayo Medical School;
Chairman, Department of Urology,
Mayo Clinic,
Rochester, Minnesota
Surgery of the Adrenal Glands

Joseph G. Borer, MD
Assistant Professor of Surgery,
Department of Urology,
Harvard Medical School;
Assistant in Urology,
Children's Hospital Boston,
Boston, Massachusetts
Hypospadias

George J. Bosl, MD
Chairman, Department of Medicine,
Patrick M. Byrne Chair in Clinical Oncology,
Memorial Sloan-Kettering Cancer Center,
New York, New York
Surgery of Testicular Tumors

Charles B. Brendler, MD
Professor and Chief, Section of Urology,
University of Chicago School of Medicine,
Chicago, Illinois
Evaluation of the Urologic Patient: History, Physical Examination, and Urinalysis

Gregory A. Broderick, MD
Professor of Urology,
Mayo Medical School,
Mayo Clinic,
Jacksonville, Florida
Evaluation and Nonsurgical Management of Erectile Dysfunction and Premature Ejaculation

James D. Brooks, MD
Associate Professor,
Department of Urology,
Stanford University Medical Center,
Stanford, California
Anatomy of the Lower Urinary Tract and Male Genitalia

Ronald M. Bukowski, MD
Professor of Medicine,
Cleveland Clinic Lerner College of Medicine of
    Case Western Reserve University;
Director, Experimental Therapeutics,
Cleveland Clinic Foundation,
Cleveland, Ohio
    Renal Tumors

Arthur L. Burnett, MD
Professor of Urology, Cellular and Molecular Biology,
Johns Hopkins University School of Medicine;
Staff Urologist, The Johns Hopkins Hospital,
Baltimore, Maryland
    Priapism

Jeffrey A. Cadeddu, MD
Associate Professor,
Clinical Center for Minimally Invasive Urologic
    Cancer Treatment;
Department of Urology,
University of Texas Southwestern Medical Center,
Dallas, Texas
    Surgical Anatomy of the Retroperitoneum, Adrenals,
    Kidneys, and Ureters

Anthony A. Caldamone, MD, MMS, FAAP, FACS
Professor of Surgery and Pediatrics,
Department of Urology,
Brown University School of Medicine;
Head of Pediatric Urology,
Hasbro Children's Hospital,
Providence, Rhode Island
    Prune Belly Syndrome

Steven C. Campbell, MD, PhD
Professor of Surgery,
Cleveland Clinic Lerner College of Medicine of
    Case Western Reserve University;
Section of Urological Oncology,
Glickman Urological Institute,
Cleveland Clinic Foundation,
Cleveland, Ohio
    Renal Tumors
    Non–Muscle-Invasive Bladder Cancer (Ta, T1, and CIS)

Douglas A. Canning, MD
Professor of Urology,
University of Pennsylvania School of Medicine;
Director, Division of Urology,
Children's Hospital of Philadelphia,
Philadelphia, Pennsylvania
    Evaluation of the Pediatric Urology Patient

Michael Carducci, MD
Associate Professor of Oncology and Urology,
Johns Hopkins University School of Medicine;
Staff Physician, The Sidney Kimmel Comprehensive Cancer
    Center at Johns Hopkins,
Baltimore, Maryland
    Treatment of Hormone-Refractory Prostate Cancer

Michael C. Carr, MD, PhD
Associate Professor of Surgery in Urology,
University of Pennsylvania School of Medicine;
Attending Surgeon, Pediatric Urology,
Children's Hospital of Philadelphia,
Philadelphia, Pennsylvania
    Anomalies and Surgery of the Ureteropelvic Junction in
    Children

Peter R. Carroll, MD
Professor and Chair,
Department of Urology,
University of California, San Francisco, School of Medicine;
Surgeon in Chief, Comprehensive Cancer Center,
University of California, San Francisco, Cancer Center,
San Francisco, California
    Treatment of Locally Advanced Prostate Cancer

H. Ballentine Carter, MD
Professor of Urology and Oncology,
James Buchanan Brady Urological Institute,
Johns Hopkins Medical Institutions,
Baltimore, Maryland
    Basic Instrumentation and Cystoscopy
    Diagnosis and Staging of Prostate Cancer

Anthony J. Casale, MD
Professor and Chairman,
Department of Urology,
University of Louisville;
Chief of Urology,
Kosair Children's Hospital,
Louisville, Kentucky
    Posterior Urethral Valves and Other Urethral Anomalies

William J. Catalona, MD
Professor of Urology,
Feinberg School of Medicine,
Northwestern University;
Director, Clinical Prostate Cancer Program,
Robert H. Lurie Comprehensive Cancer Center,
Northwestern Memorial Hospital,
Chicago, Illinois
    Definitive Therapy for Localized Prostate Cancer—
    An Overview

David Y. Chan, MD
Assistant Professor of Urology and Pathology,
Director of Outpatient Urology,
James Buchanan Brady Urological Institute,
Johns Hopkins Medical Institutions,
Baltimore, Maryland
    Basic Instrumentation and Cystoscopy

Michael B. Chancellor, MD
Professor of Urology,
McGowan Institute of Regenerative Medicine,
University of Pittsburgh School of Medicine,
Pittsburgh, Pennsylvania
    Physiology and Pharmacology of the Bladder and Urethra

C. R. Chapple, BSc, MD, FRCS (Urol)
Professor of Urology (Hon),
Sheffield Hallam University;
Consultant Urological Surgeon,
Royal Hallamshire Hospital,
Sheffield, United Kingdom
   *Retropubic Suspension Surgery for Incontinence
   in Women*

Robert L. Chevalier, MD
Benjamin Armistead Shepherd Professor and Chair,
Department of Pediatrics,
University of Virginia;
Pediatrician-In-Chief,
University of Virginia Medical School,
Charlottesville, Virginia
   *Renal Function in the Fetus, Neonate, and Child
   Congenital Urinary Obstruction: Pathophysiology*

Ben H. Chew, MD, MSc, FRCSC
Assistant Professor of Urology,
University of British Columbia,
Vancouver, British Columbia, Canada
   Ureteroscopy and Retrograde Ureteral Access

George K. Chow, MD
Assistant Professor,
Department of Urology,
The Mayo Clinic,
Rochester, Minnesota
   Surgery of the Adrenal Glands

Ralph V. Clayman, MD
Professor of Urology,
University of California, Irvine, Medical Center;
Chair of the Department of Urology,
University of California, Irvine, School of Medicine,
Orange, California
   Basics of Laparoscopic Urologic Surgery

Craig V. Comiter, MD
Associate Professor of Surgery/Urology,
Instructor of Obstetrics and Gynecology,
University of Arizona;
Chief, Section of Urology,
Director, Urology Residency,
University of Arizona Health Sciences Center,
Tucson, Arizona
   *Surgical Treatment of Male Sphincteric Urinary
   Incontinence: The Male Perineal Sling and Artificial
   Urinary Sphincter*

Michael J. Conlin, MD
Associate Professor of Surgery,
Director, Minimally Invasive Urologic Surgery,
Division of Urology and Renal Transplantation,
The Oregon Health & Science University School
   of Medicine,
Portland, Oregon
   Renal Transplantation

Juanita Crook, MD
Associate Professor of Radiation Oncology,
University of Toronto;
Radiation Oncologist,
University Health Network,
Princess Margaret Hospital,
Toronto, Ontario, Canada
   Radiation Therapy for Prostate Cancer

Douglas M. Dahl, MD
Assistant Professor of Surgery,
Department of Urology,
Harvard Medical School;
Assistant in Urology,
Massachusetts General Hospital,
Boston, Massachusetts
   Use of Intestinal Segments in Urinary Diversion

Anthony V. D'Amico, MD, PhD
Professor of Radiation Oncology,
Harvard Medical School;
Professor and Chief of Genitourinary Radiation Oncology,
Dana-Farber Cancer Institute,
Brigham and Women's Hospital,
Boston, Massachusetts
   Radiation Therapy for Prostate Cancer

John W. Davis, MD
Assistant Professor of Urology,
University of Texas MD Anderson Cancer Center,
Houston, Texas
   Tumors of the Penis

John D. Denstedt, MD, FRCSC
Professor of Urology,
Chairman, Department of Surgery,
Schulich School of Medicine and Dentistry,
The University of Western Ontario,
London, Ontario, Canada
   Ureteroscopy and Retrograde Ureteral Access

Theodore L. DeWeese, MD, PhD
Professor of Oncology,
Johns Hopkins University School of Medicine;
Radiation Oncologist-in-Chief,
Department of Radiation Oncology and Molecular
   Radiation Science,
Johns Hopkins Medical Institutions,
Baltimore, Maryland
   Radiation Therapy for Prostate Cancer

David A. Diamond, MD
Associate Professor of Surgery,
Department of Urology,
Harvard Medical School;
Associate in Urology,
Children's Hospital,
Boston, Massachusetts
   Sexual Differentiation: Normal and Abnormal

Roger R. Dmochowski, MD, FACS
Professor,
Department of Urologic Surgery,
Vanderbilt University Medical Center,
Nashville, Tennessee
Tension-Free Vaginal Tape Procedures

Steven G. Docimo, MD
Professor of Urology,
Vice Chairman of Urology,
University of Pittsburgh School of Medicine;
Director of Urology,
Division of Pediatric Urology,
Children's Hospital of Pittsburgh,
Pittsburgh, Pennsylvania
Pediatric Endourology and Laparoscopy

Marcus Drake, DM, MA
Consultant Urological Surgeon,
Bristol Urological Institute,
Southmead Hospital,
Bristol, United Kingdom
Overactive Bladder

James A. Eastham, MD
Associate Professor,
Department of Urology,
Memorial Sloan-Kettering Cancer Center,
New York, New York
Expectant Management of Prostate Cancer

Louis Eichel, MD
Clinical Associate Professor of Urology,
University of Rochester School of
  Medicine and Dentistry;
Director of Minimally Invasive Surgery,
Center for Urology,
Rochester, New York
Basics of Laparoscopic Urologic Surgery

Mario A. Eisenberger, MD
R. Dale Hughes Professor of Oncology and Urology,
The Sidney Kimmel Comprehensive Cancer Center at
  Johns Hopkins,
Johns Hopkins University School of Medicine,
Baltimore, Maryland
Treatment of Hormone-Refractory Prostate Cancer

Alaa El-Ghoneimi, MD, PhD
Professor of Pediatric Surgery,
University of Paris;
Senior Surgeon,
Hospital Robert Debré,
Paris, France
*Anomalies and Surgery of the Ureteropelvic Junction
in Children*

Jack S. Elder, MD
Professor and Vice Chairman,
Department of Urology,
Case Western Reserve University School of Medicine;
Division of Pediatric Urology,
Children's Hospital,
Cleveland, Ohio
*Abnormalities of the Genitalia in Boys and
Their Surgical Management*

Jonathan I. Epstein, MD
Professor of Pathology, Urology, and Oncology,
The Reinhard Professor of Urologic Pathology,
Johns Hopkins University School of Medicine;
Director of Surgical Pathology,
Johns Hopkins Medical Institutions,
Baltimore, Maryland
Pathology of Prostatic Neoplasia

Andrew P. Evan, PhD
Chancellor's Professor,
Department of Anatomy and Cell Biology,
Indiana University School of Medicine,
Indianapolis, Indiana
Surgical Management of Upper Urinary Tract Calculi

Robert L. Fairchild, PhD
Professor of Pathology,
Case Western Reserve University School of Medicine;
Staff, Department of Immunology,
Cleveland Clinic Foundation,
Cleveland, Ohio
Basic Principles of Immunology

Amr Fergany, MD, MB, BCh
Staff, Section of Urologic Oncology,
Section of Laparoscopic Surgery and Robotics,
Glickman Urological Institute,
Cleveland Clinic Foundation,
Cleveland, Ohio
Renovascular Hypertension and Ischemic Nephropathy

James H. Finke, PhD
Professor of Molecular Medicine,
Cleveland Clinic Lerner College of Medicine of
  Case Western Reserve University;
Staff, Department of Immunology,
Cleveland Clinic Foundation,
Cleveland, Ohio
Basic Principles of Immunology

John M. Fitzpatrick, MCh, FRCSI, FRCS(Glas), FRCS
Professor and Chairman,
Department of Surgery,
University College, Dublin;
Professor of Surgery and Consultant Urologist,
Mater Misericordiae University Hospital,
Dublin, Ireland
*Minimally Invasive and Endoscopic Management
of Benign Prostatic Hyperplasia*

Robert C. Flanigan, MD
Albert J. Jr. and Claire R. Speh Professor and Chair,
Department of Urology,
Stritch School of Medicine,
Loyola University;
Chair of the Department of Urology,
Loyola University Medical Center,
Maywood, Illinois
  Urothelial Tumors of the Upper Urinary Tract

Stuart M. Flechner, MD
Professor of Urology,
Cleveland Clinic Lerner College of Medicine of
  Case Western Reserve University;
Director of Clinical Research,
Section of Renal Transplantation,
Glickman Urological Institute,
Cleveland Clinic Foundation,
Cleveland, Ohio
  Basic Principles of Immunology

Tara Frenkl, MD, MPH
Assistant Professor of Urology,
Director, Female Urology and Reconstructive Surgery,
Robert Wood Johnson Medical School,
The University of Medicine and Dentistry of New Jersey,
New Brunswick, New Jersey
  Sexually Transmitted Diseases

Dominic Frimberger, MD
Assistant Professor of Urology,
University of Oklahoma Health Sciences Center;
Pediatric Urologist,
Children's Hospital of Oklahoma,
Oklahoma City, Oklahoma
  Bladder Anomalies in Children

John P. Gearhart, MD
Professor of Pediatric Urology,
Johns Hopkins University School of Medicine;
Chief of Pediatric Urology,
The Johns Hopkins Hospital,
Baltimore, Maryland
  Exstrophy-Epispadias Complex

Glenn S. Gerber, MD
Associate Professor,
Department of Surgery (Urology),
University of Chicago School of Medicine,
Chicago, Illinois
  *Evaluation of the Urologic Patient: History, Physical
  Examination, and Urinalysis*

Inderbir S. Gill, MD, MCh
Professor of Surgery,
Head, Section of Laparoscopic and Robotic Urology,
Glickman Urological Institute,
Cleveland Clinic Foundation,
Cleveland, Ohio
  Laparoscopic Surgery of the Urinary Bladder

Kenneth I. Glassberg, MD
Professor of Urology,
Columbia University College of Physicians and Surgeons;
Director, Division of Pediatric Urology,
Morgan Stanley Children's Hospital of
  New York-Presbyterian,
New York, New York
  Renal Dysgenesis and Cystic Disease of the Kidney

David A. Goldfarb, MD
Head, Section of Renal Transplantation,
Glickman Urological Institute,
Cleveland Clinic Foundation,
Cleveland, Ohio
  Etiology, Pathogenesis, and Management of Renal Failure

Irwin Goldstein, MD
Editor-In-Chief,
The Journal of Sexual Medicine,
Milton, Massachusetts
  *Urologic Management of Women With
  Sexual Health Concerns*

Marc Goldstein, MD, FACS
Professor of Urology and Reproductive Medicine,
Surgeon-In-Chief, Male Reproductive Medicine and Surgery,
Executive Director, Men's Service Center,
Cornell Institute for Reproductive Medicine,
Weill Medical College of Cornell University;
Senior Scientist, Center for Biomedical Research,
The Population Council,
New York, New York
  Male Reproductive Physiology
  Surgery of the Scrotum and Seminal Vesicles

Leonard G. Gomella, MD
Professor and Chairman,
Department of Urology,
Jefferson Medical College;
Director,
Jefferson Prostate Diagnostic Center,
Kimmel Cancer Center,
Thomas Jefferson University Hospital,
Philadelphia, Pennsylvania
  Ultrasonography and Biopsy of the Prostate

Mark L. Gonzalgo, MD, PhD
Associate Professor of Urology and Oncology,
Johns Hopkins Medical Center,
Baltimore, Maryland
  Management of Invasive and Metastatic Bladder Cancer

Richard W. Grady, MD
Associate Professor of Urology,
The University of Washington School of Medicine;
Director, Clinical Research,
Children's Hospital & Regional Medical Center,
Seattle, Washington
  *Surgical Techniques for One-Stage Reconstruction of
  the Exstrophy-Epispadias Complex*

Matthew B. Gretzer, MD
Assistant Professor of Clinical Surgery,
Department of Surgery/Urology,
University of Arizona Health Science Center,
Tucson, Arizona
Prostate Cancer Tumor Markers

Mantu Gupta, MD
Associate Professor,
Columbia University College of Physicians and Surgeons;
Director of Endourology, and Director of
  Kidney Stone Center,
Columbia University Medical Center New York-
  Presbyterian Hospital,
New York, New York
Percutaneous Management of the Upper Urinary Tract

Ethan J. Halpern, MD
Professor of Radiology and Urology,
Jefferson Prostate Diagnostic Center,
Thomas Jefferson University,
Philadelphia, Pennsylvania
Ultrasonography and Biopsy of the Prostate

Misop Han, MD, MS
Assistant Professor,
Department of Urology,
James Buchanan Brady Urological Institute,
Johns Hopkins Medical Institutions,
Baltimore, Maryland
*Retropubic and Suprapubic Open Prostatectomy
Definitive Therapy for Localized Prostate Cancer—
An Overview*

Philip M. Hanno, MD, MPH
Professor of Urology,
University of Pennsylvania School of Medicine;
Medical Director, Department of Clinical Effectiveness
  and Quality Improvement,
University of Pennsylvania Health System,
Philadelphia, Pennsylvania
*Painful Bladder Syndrome/Interstitial Cystitis and
Related Disorders*

Matthew P. Hardy, PhD
Professor, Department of Urology,
Weill Medical College of Cornell University;
Member, Population Council,
The Rockefeller University,
New York, New York
Male Reproductive Physiology

David M. Hartke, MD
Resident Physician,
Department of Urology,
University Hospitals of Cleveland;
Case Western Reserve University School of Medicine,
Cleveland, Ohio
Radical Perineal Prostatectomy

Jeremy P. W. Heaton, MD, FRCSC, FACS
Professor of Urology,
Assistant Professor Pharmacology and Toxicology,
Queen's University,
Kingston, Ontario, Canada
Androgen Deficiency in the Aging Male

Sender Herschorn, BSc, MDCM, FRCSC
Professor and Chairman, Division of Urology,
Martin Barkin Chair in Urological Research,
University of Toronto;
Attending Urologist,
Director, Urodynamics Unit,
Sunnybrook Health Sciences Centre,
Toronto, Ontario, Canada
*Vaginal Reconstructive Surgery for Sphincteric
Incontinence and Prolapse*

Khai-Linh V. Ho, MD
Endourology Fellow,
Mayo Clinic,
Rochester, Minnesota
Lower Urinary Tract Calculi

Thomas H. S. Hsu, MD
Assistant Professor of Urology,
Director of Laparoscopic and Minimally
  Invasive Surgery,
Department of Urology, Stanford University
  School of Medicine;
Director of Laparoscopic, Robotic, and Minimally
  Invasive Urologic Surgery,
Stanford University Medical Center,
Stanford, California
Management of Upper Urinary Tract Obstruction

Mark Hurwitz, MD
Assistant Professor,
Harvard Medical School;
Director, Regional Program Development,
Department of Radiation Oncology,
Dana-Farber/Brigham and Women's Cancer Center,
Boston, Massachusetts
Radiation Therapy for Prostate Cancer

Douglas Husmann, MD
Professor of Urology,
Vice Chairman,
Department of Urology,
Mayo Clinic,
Rochester, Minnesota
Pediatric Genitourinary Trauma

Jonathan P. Jarow, MD
Professor of Urology,
James Buchanan Brady Urological Institute,
Johns Hopkins Medical Institutions,
Baltimore, Maryland
Male Infertility

Thomas W. Jarrett, MD
Professor of Urology,
Chairman, Department of Urology,
George Washington University,
Washington, DC
Management of Urothelial Tumors of the Renal Pelvis

Christopher W. Johnson, MD
Clinical Instructor of Urology,
Weill Medical College of Cornell University,
New York, New York;
Assistant Attending,
North Shore-Long Island Jewish Health System,
Manhasset, and St. Francis Hospital, Roslyn, New York
Tuberculosis and Parasitic and Fungal Infections of the Genitourinary System

Warren D. Johnson, Jr., MD
B. H. Kean Professor of Tropical Medicine,
Chief, Division of Internal Medicine and Infectious Diseases,
Weill Medical College of Cornell University;
Attending Physician,
New York-Presbyterian Hospital, Cornell Campus,
New York, New York
Tuberculosis and Parasitic and Fungal Infections of the Genitourinary System

Deborah P. Jones, MD
Associate Professor of Pediatrics,
University of Tennessee Health Science Center;
Attending, Le Bonheur Children's Medical Center,
Children's Foundation Research Center,
Memphis, Tennessee
Renal Disease in Childhood

J. Stephen Jones, MD, FACS
Associate Professor of Surgery (Urology),
Vice Chairman, Glickman Urological Institute,
Cleveland Clinic Lerner College of Medicine of
    Case Western Reserve University,
Cleveland Clinic Foundation,
Cleveland, Ohio
Non–Muscle-Invasive Bladder Cancer (Ta, T1, and CIS)

Gerald H. Jordan, MD, FACS, FAAP
Professor of Urology,
Eastern Virginia Medical School,
Norfolk, Virgina
Peyronie's Disease
Surgery of the Penis and Urethra

Mark L. Jordan, MD
Harris L. Willits Professor and Chief,
Division of Urology,
University of Medicine and Dentistry of New Jersey,
New Jersey Medical School;
Chief of Urology, University Hospital,
Newark, New Jersey
Renal Transplantation

David B. Joseph, MD
Professor of Surgery,
University of Alabama at Birmingham;
Chief of Pediatric Urology,
The Children's Hospital of Alabama,
Birmingham, Alabama
Urinary Tract Reconstruction in Children

John N. Kabalin, MD
Adjunct Assistant Professor of Surgery,
Section of Urologic Surgery,
University of Nebraska College of Medicine,
Omaha, Nebraska;
Regional West Medical Center,
Scottsbluff, Nebraska
Surgical Anatomy of the Retroperitoneum, Adrenals, Kidneys, and Ureters

Martin Kaefer, MD
Associate Professor, Indiana University,
Riley Hospital for Children,
Indianapolis, Indiana
Surgical Management of Intersexuality, Cloacal Malformation, and Other Abnormalities of the Genitalia in Girls

Irving Kaplan, MD
Assistant Professor of Radiation Oncology,
Harvard Medical School;
Radiation Oncologist,
Beth Israel Deaconess Medical Center,
Boston, Massachusetts
Radiation Therapy for Prostate Cancer

Louis R. Kavoussi, MD
Chairman, The Arthur Smith Institute for Urology,
North Shore-Long Island Jewish Health System,
Manhasset, New York;
Professor of Urology,
New York University School of Medicine,
New York, New York
Laparoscopic Surgery of the Kidney

Mohit Khera, MD, MBA, MPH
Fellow, Division of Male Reproductive Medicine
    and Surgery,
Scott Department of Urology,
Baylor College of Medicine,
Houston, Texas
Surgical Management of Male Infertility

Antoine Khoury, MD, FRCSC, FAAP
Chief of Urology,
Senior Associate Scientist,
The Hospital for Sick Children;
Professor of Surgery,
The University of Toronto,
Toronto, Ontario, Canada
Reflux and Megaureter

Adam S. Kibel, MD
Associate Professor, Division of Urologic Surgery,
Washington University School of Medicine,
St. Louis, Missouri
Molecular Genetics and Cancer Biology

Roger Kirby, MD, FRCS
Professor and Director, The Prostate Centre;
Visiting Professor, St. George's Hospital,
Institute of Urology,
London, United Kingdom
*Evaluation and Nonsurgical Management of Benign
Prostatic Hyperplasia*

Eric A. Klein, MD
Professor of Surgery,
Cleveland Clinic Lerner College of Medicine of
Case Western Reserve University;
Head, Section of Urologic Oncology,
Glickman Urological Institute,
Cleveland Clinic Foundation,
Cleveland, Ohio
Epidemiology, Etiology, and Prevention of Prostate Cancer

John N. Krieger, MD
Professor of Urology,
University of Washington School of Medicine;
Chief of Surgical Urology,
VA Puget Sound Health Care System,
Seattle, Washington
Urological Implications of AIDS and HIV Infection

Bradley P. Kropp, MD
Professor of Urology,
University of Oklahoma Health Science Center;
Chief, Pediatric Urology,
Children's Hospital of Oklahoma,
Oklahoma City, Oklahoma
Bladder Anomalies in Children

John S. Lam, MD
Clinical Instructor in Urology,
David Geffen School of Medicine,
University of California, Los Angeles;
Attending Urologist,
University of California, Los Angeles, Medical Center,
Los Angeles, California
Cryotherapy for Prostate Cancer

Herbert Lepor, MD
Professor and Martin Spatz Chair,
Department of Urology,
New York University School of Medicine;
Chief of Urology,
New York University Medical Center,
New York, New York
*Evaluation and Nonsurgical Management of Benign
Prostatic Hyperplasia*

Ronald W. Lewis, MD
Witherington Chair in Urology,
Professor of Surgery (Urology) and Physiology,
and Chief of Urology,
Medical College of Georgia,
Augusta, Georgia
Vascular Surgery for Erectile Dysfunction

James E. Lingeman, MD
Director of Research,
Methodist Hospital Institute for Kidney Stone Disease;
Volunteer Clinical Professor,
Department of Urology,
Indiana University School of Medicine,
Indianapolis, Indiana
Surgical Management of Upper Urinary Tract Calculi

Richard E. Link, MD, PhD
Associate Professor of Urology,
Director, Division of Endourology and Minimally
Invasive Surgery,
Scott Department of Urology,
Baylor College of Medicine,
Houston, Texas
Cutaneous Diseases of the External Genitalia

Larry I. Lipshultz, MD
Professor of Urology,
Scott Department of Urology,
Lester and Sue Smith Chair in Reproductive Medicine,
Chief, Division of Male Reproductive Medicine
and Surgery,
Baylor College of Medicine,
Houston, Texas
Surgical Management of Male Infertility

Mark S. Litwin, MD, MPH
Professor of Urology and Health Services,
David Geffen School of Medicine,
University of California, Los Angeles;
University of California, Los Angeles, School of
Public Health,
Los Angeles, California
Outcomes Research

Yair Lotan, MD
Assistant Professor,
Department of Urology,
University of Texas Southwestern Medical Center;
Attending,
Parkland Health and Hospital Systems,
Zale Lipshy University Medical Center,
Veterans Affairs Medical Center,
Dallas, Texas
*Urinary Lithiasis: Etiology, Epidemiology,
and Pathogenesis*

Tom F. Lue, MD
Professor and Vice Chair,
Emil Tanagho Endowed Chair,
Department of Urology,
University of California School of Medicine, San Francisco,
San Francisco, California
  *Physiology of Penile Erection and Pathophysiology of
  Erectile Dysfunction*
  *Evaluation and Nonsurgical Management of
  Erectile Dysfunction and Premature Ejaculation*

Donald F. Lynch, Jr., MD
Professor and Chairman,
Department of Urology,
Professor of Obstetrics and Gynecology,
Eastern Virginia School of Medicine;
Urologic Oncologist,
Sentara Hospitals;
Consultant Urologist,
Jones Institute for Reproductive Medicine,
Norfolk, Virginia
  Tumors of the Penis

Michael Marberger, MD, FRCS(Ed)
Professor and Chairman,
Department of Urology,
Medical University of Vienna,
Vienna, Austria
  Ablative Therapy of Renal Tumors

Fray F. Marshall, MD
Professor and Chairman,
Department of Urology,
Emory University School of Medicine,
Atlanta, Georgia
  Surgery of Bladder Cancer

Brian R. Matlaga, MD, MPH
Assistant Professor of Urology,
Johns Hopkins University School of Medicine;
Director of Stone Disease,
Johns Hopkins Bayview Medical Center,
Baltimore, Maryland
  Surgical Management of Upper Urinary Tract Calculi

Ranjiv Mathews, MD
Associate Professor of Pediatric Urology,
James Buchanan Brady Urological Institute,
Johns Hopkins Medical Institutions,
Baltimore, Maryland
  Exstrophy-Epispadias Complex

Julian Mauermann, MD
Senior Resident,
Department of Urology,
Medical University of Vienna,
Vienna, Austria
  Ablative Therapy of Renal Tumors

Sarah J. McAleer, MD
Chief Resident, Department of Urology,
Brigham and Women's Hospital,
Boston, Massachusetts
  *Tuberculosis and Parasitic and Fungal Infections of the
  Genitourinary System*

Jack W. McAninch, MD
Professor of Urological Surgery,
Department of Urology,
University of California, San Francisco, School of Medicine;
Chief of Urology, San Francisco General Hospital,
San Francisco, California
  Renal and Ureteral Trauma

John D. McConnell, MD
Professor of Urology, Department of Urology,
Executive Vice-President for Health Systems Affairs,
University of Texas Southwestern Medical Center,
Dallas, Texas
  *Benign Prostatic Hyperplasia: Etiology, Pathophysiology,
  Epidemiology, and Natural History*

W. Scott McDougal, AB, MD, MA(Hon)
Walter S. Kerr, Jr. Professor of Urology,
Harvard Medical School;
Chief of Urology, Massachusetts General Hospital,
Boston, Massachusetts
  Use of Intestinal Segments in Urinary Diversion

Elspeth M. McDougall, MD, FRCSC
Professor of Urology,
Irvine Medical Center,
University of California, Irvine,
Irvine, California
  Basics of Laparoscopic Urologic Surgery
  Percutaneous Management of the Upper Urinary Tract

Edward J. McGuire, MD
Professor, Department of Urology,
University of Michigan,
Ann Arbor, Michigan
  Pubovaginal Sling

James M. McKiernan, MD
Assistant Professor, Department of Urology,
Herbert Irving Comprehensive Cancer Center,
Columbia University;
Assistant Attending Urologist,
New York-Presbyterian Hospital,
New York, New York
  Cutaneous Continent Urinary Diversion

Alan W. McMahon, MD
Associate Professor, Department of Medicine,
Division of Nephrology and Transplant Immunology,
University of Alberta,
Edmonton, Alberta, Canada
  Renal Physiology and Pathophysiology

Maxwell V. Meng, MD
Assistant Professor,
Department of Urology,
University of California, San Francisco,
San Francisco, California
Treatment of Locally Advanced Prostate Cancer

Edward M. Messing, MD
W. W. Scott Professor,
Chairman, Department of Urology,
Professor of Pathology and Oncology,
University of Rochester School of Medicine and Dentistry,
Rochester, New York
Urothelial Tumors of the Bladder

Michael E. Mitchell, MD
Professor and Chief of Pediatric Urology,
University of Washington School of Medicine,
Children's Hospital & Regional Medical Center,
Seattle, Washington
*Surgical Techniques for One-Stage Reconstruction of the
Exstrophy-Epispadias Complex*

Drogo K. Montague, MD
Professor of Surgery,
Cleveland Clinic Lerner College of Medicine of
    Case Western Reserve University;
Head, Section of Prosthetic Surgery and
    Genitourethral Reconstruction,
Glickman Urological Institute,
Cleveland Clinic Foundation,
Cleveland, Ohio
Prosthetic Surgery for Erectile Dysfunction

Alvaro Morales, MD, FRCSC, FACS
Emeritus Professor,
Queen's University;
Director, Center for Advanced Urological Research,
Kingston General Hospital,
Kingston, Ontario, Canada
Androgen Deficiency in the Aging Male

Allen F. Morey, MD
Clinical Associate Professor of Urology,
University of Texas Health Science Center;
Chief, Urology Service,
Brooke Army Medical Center,
San Antonio, Texas
Genital and Lower Urinary Tract Trauma

John Morley, MB, BCh
Dammert Professor of Gerontology,
    and Director of Geriatrics, St. Louis University Medical
    Center;
Director of GRECC, St. Louis Veterans Affairs Hospital,
    St. Louis, Missouri
Androgen Deficiency in the Aging Male

Michael J. Morris, MD
Assistant Member,
Memorial Sloan-Kettering Cancer Center;
Instructor in Medicine,
Weill Medical College of Cornell University;
Assistant Attending Physician,
Memorial Hospital for Cancer and Allied Diseases,
New York, New York
*The Clinical State of the Rising PSA Level after Definitive
Local Therapy: A Practical Approach*

M. Louis Moy, MD
Assistant Professor,
Division of Urology,
University of Pennsylvania Medical School;
University of Pennsylvania Health System,
Philadelphia, Pennsylvania
Additional Therapies for Storage and Emptying Failure

Ricardo Munarriz, MD
Assistant Professor of Urology,
Boston University School of Medicine,
Boston, Massachusetts
Vascular Surgery for Erectile Dysfunction

Stephen Y. Nakada, MD
Professor of Surgery,
University of Wisconsin School of Medicine and
    Public Health;
Chairman of Urology,
University of Wisconsin Hospital and Clinics,
Madison, Wisconsin
Management of Upper Urinary Tract Obstruction

Joseph V. Nally, Jr., MD
Staff, Department of Nephrology and Hypertension,
Cleveland Clinic Foundation,
Cleveland, Ohio
Etiology, Pathogenesis, and Management of Renal Failure

Joel B. Nelson, MD
Frederic N. Schwentker Professor,
Chair, Department of Urology,
University of Pittsburgh School of Medicine;
Chairman of Urology,
University of Pittsburgh Medical Center;
Co-Chair, Prostate and Urological Diseases Program,
University of Pittsburgh Cancer Institute,
Pittsburgh, Pennsylvania
Hormone Therapy for Prostate Cancer

Michael T. Nguyen, MD
Fellow, Pediatric Urology,
The Children's Hospital of Philadelphia,
Philadelphia, Pennsylvania
Evaluation of the Pediatric Urology Patient

J. Curtis Nickel, MD
Professor of Urology, Queen's University;
Staff Urologist, Department of Urology,
Kingston General Hospital,
Kingston, Ontario, Canada
  Inflammatory Conditions of the Male Genitourinary
  Tract: Prostatitis and Related Conditions, Orchitis,
  and Epididymitis

Peter T. Nieh, MD
Assistant Professor, Department of Urology,
Emory University School of Medicine,
Atlanta, Georgia
  Surgery of Bladder Cancer

Victor W. Nitti, MD
Associate Professor and Vice-Chairman,
Department of Urology,
New York University School of Medicine;
Attending Physician,
New York University Hospitals Center,
New York, New York
  Urinary Incontinence: Epidemiology, Pathophysiology,
  Evaluation, and Management Overview

H. Norman Noe, MD
Professor of Urology,
Chief, Pediatric Urology,
University of Tennessee,
Saint Jude's Children's Research Hospital,
Memphis, Tennessee
  Renal Disease in Childhood

Andrew C. Novick, MD
Chairman, Glickman Urological Institute,
Cleveland Clinic Foundation;
Professor of Surgery,
Cleveland Clinic Lerner College of Medicine of
  Case Western Reserve University,
Cleveland, Ohio
  Renovascular Hypertension and Ischemic Nephropathy
  Renal Tumors
  Open Surgery of the Kidney

Seung-June Oh, MD, PhD
Associate Professor, Department of Urology,
Seoul National University Hospital,
Seoul National University College of Medicine,
Seoul, Korea
  Pubovaginal Sling

Carl A. Olsson, MD
John K. Lattimer Professor and Chairman Emeritus,
Columbia University College of Physicians and Surgeons;
Attending, New York-Presbyterian Hospital,
New York, New York
  Cutaneous Continent Urinary Diversion

Michael C. Ost, MD
Fellow, Endourology and Laparoscopy,
Institute of Urology,
North Shore-Long Island Jewish Medical Center,
New Hyde Park, New York
  Percutaneous Management of the Upper Urinary Tract

Vernon M. Pais Jr., MD
Assistant Professor,
Department of Surgery,
Division of Urology,
University of Kentucky School of Medicine;
University of Kentucky Medical Center,
Lexington, Kentucky
  Pathophysiology of Urinary Tract Obstruction

John M. Park, MD
Associate Professor of Urology,
University of Michigan Medical School;
Chief of Pediatric Urology,
University of Michigan Health System,
Ann Arbor, Michigan
  Normal Development of the Urogenital System

Alan W. Partin, MD, PhD
David Hall McConnell Professor and Director,
James Buchanan Brady Urological Institute,
Johns Hopkins Medical Institutions,
Baltimore, Maryland
  Retropubic and Suprapubic Open Prostatectomy
  Prostate Cancer Tumor Markers
  Diagnosis and Staging of Prostate Cancer
  Anatomic Radical Retropubic Prostatectomy

Christopher K. Payne, MD
Associate Professor of Urology,
Director,
Female Urology and Neurourology,
Stanford University Medical School,
Stanford, California
  Conservative Managment of Urinary Incontinence:
  Behavioral and Pelvic Floor Therapy, Urethral and
  Pelvic Devices

Margaret S. Pearle, MD, PhD
Professor of Urology and Internal Medicine,
University of Texas Southwestern Medical Center,
Dallas, Texas
  Urinary Lithiasis: Etiology, Epidemiology, and Pathogenesis

Craig A. Peters, MD
John E. Cole Professor of Urology,
University of Virginia,
Charlottesville, Virgina
  Congenital Urinary Obstruction: Pathophysiology
  Perinatal Urology
  Pediatric Endourology and Laparoscopy

Andrew C. Peterson, MD, FACS
Assistant Professor of Surgery,
Uniformed Services University of the Health Sciences,
Bethesda, Maryland;
Program Director,
Urology Residency,
Madigan Army Medical Center,
Tacoma, Washington
Urodynamic and Videourodynamic Evaluation of Voiding Dysfunction

Curtis A. Pettaway, MD
Associate Professor of Urology, and
Associate Professor of Cancer Biology,
Department of Urology,
University of Texas MD Anderson Cancer Center,
Houston, Texas
Tumors of the Penis

Paul K. Pietrow, MD
Director of Minimally Invasive Surgery,
Hudson Valley Urology,
Poughkeepsie, New York
Evaluation and Medical Management of Urinary Lithiasis

Louis L. Pisters, MD
Associate Professor of Urology,
Department of Urology,
University of Texas MD Anderson Cancer Center,
Houston, Texas
Cryotherapy for Prostate Cancer

Elizabeth A. Platz, ScD, MPH
Associate Professor,
Department of Epidemiology,
Johns Hopkins Bloomberg School of Public Health,
Johns Hopkins Medical Institutions,
Baltimore, Maryland
Epidemiology, Etiology, and Prevention of Prostate Cancer

Jeannette Potts, MD
Senior Clinical Instructor,
Department of Family Medicine,
Cleveland Clinic Lerner College of Medicine of
Case Western Reserve University;
Staff Physician,
Glickman Urological Institute,
Cleveland Clinic Foundation,
Cleveland, Ohio
Sexually Transmitted Diseases

Glenn M. Preminger, MD
Professor of Urologic Surgery,
Duke University Medical Center,
Durham, North Carolina
Evaluation and Medical Management of Urinary Lithiasis

Raymond R. Rackley, MD
Professor of Surgery (Urology),
Cleveland Clinic Lerner College of Medicine of
Case Western Reserve University,
Co-Head, Section of Female Urology and Voiding
Dysfunction,
The Glickman Urological Institute,
Cleveland Clinic Foundation,
Cleveland, Ohio
Electrical Stimulation for Storage and Emptying Disorders

John R. Ramey, MD
Jefferson Prostate Diagnostic Center,
Departments of Urology and Radiology,
Kimmel Cancer Center,
Thomas Jefferson University,
Philadelphia, Pennsylvania
Ultrasonography and Biopsy of the Prostate

Robert E. Reiter, MD
Professor of Urology,
Member, Molecular Biology Institute,
Associate Director,
Prostate Cancer Program,
Geffen School of Medicine,
University of California, Los Angeles,
Los Angeles, California
Molecular Genetics and Cancer Biology

Neil M. Resnick, MD
Professor of Medicine,
Chief, Division of Gerontology and Geriatric Medicine,
Director, University of Pittsburgh Institute on Aging,
University of Pittsburgh and University of Pittsburgh
Medical Center,
Pittsburgh, Pennsylvania
Geriatric Incontinence and Voiding Dysfunction

Martin I. Resnick, MD
Lester Persky Professor and Chair,
Department of Urology,
Cleveland Clinic Lerner College of Medicine of
Case Western Reserve University,
Cleveland Clinic Foundation,
Cleveland, Ohio
Radical Perineal Prostatectomy

Alan B. Retik, MD
Professor of Surgery (Urology),
Harvard Medical School;
Chief, Department of Urology,
Children's Hospital,
Boston, Massachusetts
Ectopic Ureter, Ureterocele, and Other Anomalies of the Ureter
Hypospadias

Jerome P. Richie, MD
Elliot C. Cutler Professor of Urologic Surgery,
Chairman, Harvard Program in Urology,
Harvard Medical School,
Brigham and Women's Hospital,
Boston, Massachusetts
  Neoplasms of the Testis

Richard Rink, MD
Professor, Indiana University,
Riley Hospital for Children,
Indianapolis, Indiana
  *Surgical Management of Intersexuality, Cloacal
  Malformation, and Other Abnormalities of the
  Genitalia in Girls*

Michael L. Ritchey, MD
Professor of Urology,
Mayo Clinic College of Medicine,
Phoenix, Arizona
  Pediatric Urologic Oncology

Ronald Rodriguez, MD, PhD
Associate Professor of Urology, Medical Oncology, Radiation
  Oncology, Cellular and Molecular Medicine,
Johns Hopkins University School of Medicine,
Baltimore, Maryland
  *Molecular Biology, Endocrinology, and Physiology of the
  Prostate and Seminal Vesicles*

Claus G. Roehrborn, MD
Professor and Chairman, Department of Urology,
University of Texas Southwestern Medical Center,
Dallas, Texas
  *Benign Prostatic Hyperplasia: Etiology, Pathophysiology,
  Epidemiology, and Natural History*

Jonathan A. Roth, MD
Assistant Professor of Urology and Pediatrics,
Temple University Children's Hospital,
Temple University,
Philadelphia, Pennsylvania
  Renal Function in the Fetus, Neonate, and Child

Eric S. Rovner, MD
Associate Professor of Urology,
Department of Urology,
Medical University of South Carolina,
Charleston, South Carolina
  Urinary Tract Fistula
  Bladder and Urethral Diverticula

Thomas A. Rozanski, MD
Professor, Department of Urology,
The University of Texas Health Science Center;
Chief, Medical Operations,
University Hospital,
San Antonio, Texas
  Genital and Lower Urinary Tract Trauma

Arthur I. Sagalowsky, MD
Professor of Urology and Surgery,
Chief of Urologic Oncology,
Dr. Paul Peters Chair in Urology in Memory of Rumsey
  and Louis Strickland,
The University of Texas Health Science Center,
Dallas, Texas
  *Management of Urothelial Tumors of the Renal Pelvis
  and Ureter*

Jay I. Sandlow, MD
Associate Professor and Vice-Chair,
Department of Urology,
Medical College of Wisconsin;
Director of Andrology and Male Infertility,
Froedtert Memorial Lutheran Hospital,
Milwaukee, Wisconsin
  Surgery of the Scrotum and Seminal Vesicles

Richard A. Santucci, MD
Associate Professor and Chief of Urology,
Wayne State University School of Medicine,
Detroit, Michigan
  Renal and Ureteral Trauma

Peter T. Scardino, MD
Chair, Department of Surgery,
Head, Prostate Cancer Program,
Memorial Sloan-Kettering Cancer Center,
New York, New York
  Expectant Management of Prostate Cancer

Harriette Scarpero, MD
Assistant Professor,
Department of Urologic Surgery,
Vanderbilt University Medical Center,
Nashville, Tennessee
  Tension-Free Vaginal Tape Procedures

Anthony J. Schaeffer, MD
Herman L. Kretschmer Professor and Chair,
Department of Urology,
Northwestern University Feinberg School of Medicine;
Chief of Urology,
Northwestern Memorial Hospital,
Chicago, Illinois
  Infections of the Urinary Tract

Edward M. Schaeffer, MD, PhD
Department of Urology,
James Buchanan Brady Urological Institute,
Johns Hopkins Medical Institutions,
Baltimore, Maryland
  Infections of the Urinary Tract

Howard I. Scher, MD
Professor of Medicine,
Weill Medical College of Cornell University;
Member, Department of Medicine,
Memorial Sloan-Kettering Cancer Center;
Attending Physician,
Memorial Hospital for Cancer and Allied Diseases,
New York, New York
The Clinical State of the Rising PSA Level after Definitive Local Therapy: A Practical Approach

Peter N. Schlegel, MD
Professor and Chairman,
Department of Urology,
Professor of Reproductive Medicine,
Weill Medical College of Cornell University;
Staff Scientist, The Population Council;
Urologist-in-Chief, New York-Presbyterian Hospital;
Associate Physician, Rockefeller University Hospital,
New York, New York
Male Reproductive Physiology

Steven M. Schlossberg, MD
Professor, Eastern Virginia Medical School,
Norfolk, Virginia
Surgery of the Penis and Urethra

Richard N. Schlussel, MD
Assistant Professor, Department of Urology,
Columbia University;
Assistant Professor, Division of Pediatric Urology,
Morgan Stanley Children's Hospital of New York-
   Presbyterian,
Columbia University Medical Center,
New York, New York
Ectopic Ureter, Ureterocele, and Other Anomalies of the Ureter

Francis X. Schneck, MD
Associate Professor of Urology,
Children's Hospital of Pittsburgh,
University of Pittsburgh Medical Center,
Pittsburgh, Pennsylvania
Abnormalities of the Testes and Scrotum and Their Surgical Management

Mark P. Schoenberg, MD
Professor of Urology and Oncology,
Director of Urologic Oncology,
James Buchanan Brady Urological Institute,
Johns Hopkins Medical Institutions,
Baltimore, Maryland
Management of Invasive and Metastatic Bladder Cancer

Martin J. Schreiber, Jr., MD
Chairman,
Department of Nephrology and Hypertension,
Cleveland Clinic Foundation,
Cleveland, Ohio
Etiology, Pathogenesis, and Management of Renal Failure

Joseph W. Segura, MD
Consultant in Urology,
Carl Rosen Professor of Urology,
Department of Urology,
The Mayo Clinic,
Rochester, Minnesota
Lower Urinary Tract Calculi

Jay B. Shah, MD
Chief Resident,
Columbia College of Physicians and Surgeons;
Department of Urology,
Columbia University Medical Center,
New York, New York
Percutaneous Management of the Upper Urinary Tract

Robert C. Shamberger, MD
Robert E. Gross Professor of Surgery,
Harvard Medical School;
Chief of Surgery, Children's Hospital,
Boston, Massachusetts
Pediatric Urologic Oncology

David S. Sharp, MD
Fellow, Department of Urology,
Memorial Sloan-Kettering Cancer Center,
New York, New York
Surgery of Penile and Urethral Carcinoma

Joel Sheinfeld, MD
Vice-Chairman, Department of Urology,
Memorial Sloan-Kettering Cancer Center,
New York, New York
Surgery of Testicular Tumors

Linda M. Dairiki Shortliffe, MD
Professor and Chair, Department of Urology,
Stanford University School of Medicine;
Chief of Pediatric Urology,
Stanford Hospital and Clinics,
Lucile Salter Packard Children's Hospital,
Stanford, California
Infection and Inflammation of the Pediatric Genitourinary Tract

Daniel A. Shoskes, MD, FRCSC
Professor of Surgery, Cleveland Clinic Lerner College of
   Medicine of Case Western Reserve University;
Urologist, Glickman Urological Institute,
Cleveland Clinic Foundation,
Cleveland, Ohio
Renal Physiology and Pathophysiology

Cary L. Siegel, MD
Associate Professor of Radiology,
Division of Diagnostic Radiology,
Mallinckrodt Institute of Radiology,
Washington University School of Medicine,
St. Louis, Missouri
Urinary Tract Imaging: Basic Principles

Mark Sigman, MD
Associate Professor of Surgery (Urology),
Brown University,
Providence, Rhode Island
Male Infertility

**Jennifer D.Y. Sihoe, MD, BMBS(Nottm),
    FRCSEd(Paed), FHKAM(Surg)**
Specialist in Pediatric Surgery,
Division of Pediatric Surgery and Pediatric Urology,
The Chinese University of Hong Kong,
Prince of Wales Hospital,
Hong Kong, China
*Voiding Dysfunction in Children: Non-Neurogenic and
Neurogenic*

Donald G. Skinner, MD
Professor and Chair,
Department of Urology,
Keck School of Medicine of the University of Southern
    California, Norris Cancer Center,
Los Angeles, California
Orthotopic Urinary Diversion

Arthur D. Smith, MD
Professor, Department of Urology,
Albert Einstein School of Medicine,
New York, New York;
Chairman Emeritus, Department of Urology,
North Shore-Long Island Jewish Medical Center,
New Hyde Park, New York
Percutaneous Management of the Upper Urinary Tract

Joseph A. Smith, Jr., MD
Professor,
Department of Urologic Surgery,
Vanderbilt University School of Medicine,
Vanderbilt University Medical Center,
Nashville, Tennessee
*Laparoscopic and Robotic-Assisted Laparoscopic Radical
Prostatectomy and Pelvic Lymphadenectomy*

Jonathan Starkman, MD
Clinical Instructor,
Department of Urologic Surgery,
Vanderbilt University Medical Center,
Nashville, Tennessee
Tension-Free Vaginal Tape Procedures

David R. Staskin, MD
Director, Section of Voiding Dysfunction,
Female Urology and Urodynamics,
New York Hospital-Cornell;
Associate Professor, Urology and Obstetrics and Gynecology,
Weill Medical College of Cornell University,
New York, New York
*Surgical Treatment of Male Sphincteric Urinary
Incontinence: The Male Perineal Sling and Artificial
Urinary Sphincter*

Graeme S. Steele, MD
Assistant Professor of Surgery,
Harvard Medical School;
Urologist, Brigham and Women's Hospital,
Boston, Massachusetts
Neoplasms of the Testis

John P. Stein, MD
Associate Professor in Urology,
Keck School of Medicine of the University of Southern
    California, Norris Cancer Center,
Los Angeles, California
Orthotopic Urinary Diversion

John T. Stoffel, MD
Assistant Professor of Urology,
Tufts University School of Medicine,
Boston, Massachusetts;
Senior Staff Urologist, Department of Urology,
Lahey Clinic Medical Center,
Burlington, Massachusetts
Pubovaginal Sling

Jack W. Strandhoy, PhD
Professor, Department of Physiology and Pharmacology,
Wake Forest University School of Medicine,
Winston-Salem, North Carolina
Pathophysiology of Urinary Tract Obstruction

Stevan B. Streem, MD (*deceased*)
Head, Section of Stone Disease and Endourology,
Glickman Urological Institute,
Cleveland Clinic Foundation,
Cleveland, Ohio
Management of Upper Urinary Tract Obstruction

Li-Ming Su, MD
Associate Professor of Urology,
Director of Laparoscopic and Robotic Urologic Surgery,
James Buchanan Brady Urological Institute,
Johns Hopkins Medical Institutions,
Baltimore, Maryland
*Laparoscopic and Robotic-Assisted Laparoscopic Radical
Prostatectomy and Pelvic Lymphadenectomy*

Anthony J. Thomas, Jr., MD
Head, Section of Male Infertility,
Glickman Urological Institute,
Cleveland Clinic Foundation,
Cleveland, Ohio
Surgical Management of Male Infertility

Ian M. Thompson, MD
Glenda and Gary Woods Distinguished Chair in
    Genitourinary Oncology,
Henry B. and Edna Smith Dielman Memorial Chair in
    Urologic Science,
The University of Texas Health Science Center,
San Antonio, Texas
Epidemiology, Etiology, and Prevention of Prostate Cancer

Sandip P. Vasavada, MD
Associate Professor of Surgery (Urology),
Cleveland Clinic Lerner College of Medicine of
    Case Western Reserve University;
Co-Head, Section of Female Urology and
    Voiding Dysfunction,
Glickman Urological Institute,
Cleveland Clinic Foundation,
Cleveland, Ohio
    Electrical Stimulation for Storage and Emptying Disorders

E. Darracott Vaughan, Jr., MD
James J. Colt Professor and Chairman Emeritus of Urology,
Weill Medical College of Cornell University,
New York-Presbyterian Hospital,
New York, New York
    Pathophysiology, Evaluation, and Medical Management of Adrenal Disorders

Robert W. Veltri, PhD
Associate Professor,
Department of Urology
Johns Hopkins University School of Medicine,
Baltimore, Maryland
    Molecular Biology, Endocrinology, and Physiology of the Prostate and Seminal Vesicles

Patrick C. Walsh, MD
University Distinguished Service Professor of Urology,
James Buchanan Brady Urological Institute,
Johns Hopkins Medical Institutions,
Baltimore, Maryland
    Anatomic Radical Retropubic Prostatectomy

George D. Webster, MD
Professor of Urologic Surgery,
Department of Urology,
Duke University Medical Center,
Durham, North Carolina
    Urodynamic and Videourodynamic Evaluation of Voiding Dysfunction

Alan J. Wein, MD, PhD(Hon)
Professor and Chair,
Division of Urology,
University of Pennsylvania School of Medicine;
Chief of Urology,
University of Pennsylvania Medical Center,
Philadelphia, Pennsylvania
    Pathophysiology and Classification of Voiding Dysfunction
    Lower Urinary Tract Dysfunction in Neurologic Injury and Disease
    Pharmacologic Management of Storage and Emptying Failure
    Additional Therapies for Storage and Emptying Failure

Robert M. Weiss, MD
Donald Guthrie Professor and Chief,
Section of Urology,
Yale University School of Medicine,
New Haven, Connecticut
    Physiology and Pharmacology of the Renal Pelvis and Ureter

Howard N. Winfield, MD, FRCS
Professor, Department of Urology,
Director, Laparoscopy and Minimally Invasive Surgery,
The University of Iowa Hospitals and Clinics,
University of Iowa,
Iowa City, Iowa
Surgery of the Scrotum and Seminal Vesicles

J. Christian Winters, MD
Clinical Associate Professor,
Louisiana State University Health Sciences Center;
Vice-Chairman and Director of Female Urology and
    Voiding Dysfunction,
Ochsner Clinic Foundation,
New Orleans, Louisiana
    Injection Therapy for Urinary Incontinence

John R. Woodard, MD
Formerly: Clinical Professor of Urology,
Director of Pediatric Urology,
Emory University School of Medicine;
Formerly: Chief of Urology,
Henrietta Egleston Hospital for Children,
Atlanta, Georgia
    Prune Belly Syndrome

Subbarao V. Yalla, MD
Professor of Surgery (Urology),
Harvard Medical School;
Chief, Urology Division,
Boston Veterans Affairs Medical Center,
Boston, Massachusetts
    Geriatric Incontinence and Voiding Dysfunction

C. K. Yeung, MBBS, MD, FRCSE, FRCSG, FRACS, FACS, FHKAM(Surg), DCH(Lond)
Clinical Professor in Pediatric Surgery and
    Pediatric Urology,
Chinese University of Hong Kong,
Prince of Wales Hospital,
Hong Kong, China
    Voiding Dysfunction in Children: Non-Neurogenic and Neurogenic

Naoki Yoshimura, MD, PhD
Associate Professor of Urology and Pharmacology,
University of Pittsburgh School of Medicine,
Pittsburgh, Pennsylvania
    Physiology and Pharmacology of the Bladder and Urethra

PREFACE

For each discipline in medicine and surgery, there is generally an acknowledged authoritative text, otherwise known as "the bible." For virtually every urologist in current practice, *Campbell's Urology* has had that distinction. The text, first published in 1954 with Meredith Campbell as its sole editor, has seen the editor-in-chief position pass to J. Hartwell Harrison, and then to Patrick Walsh. Under Dr. Walsh's leadership as editor-in-chief for the past 20 years (4 editions), *Campbell's Urology* has changed as much as the field itself—in virtually every way possible except for its preeminence. The current editorial board felt strongly that Pat's contributions to urologic education through his continuing improvements and innovations to *Campbell's* should be recognized in perpetuity by renaming the text in his honor; thus the new title—*Campbell-Walsh Urology.*

Aside from the name, the 9th edition is quite different from its predecessors, continuing the tradition of a constant evolution paralleling the changing nature of the field and its relevant pertinent information. We have changed the editorial board and increased it by one. Louis Kavoussi, Andrew Novick, Alan Partin, and Craig Peters all have moved up from their associate editor positions. From the standpoint of organization, Volume 1 now covers anatomy; molecular and cellular biology, including tissue engineering; the essentials of clinical decision-making; the basics of instrumentation, endoscopy, and laparoscopy; infection and inflammation; male reproductive function and dysfunction; and sexual function and dysfunction in both men and women. Volume 2 covers all aspects of the upper urinary tract and adrenal, including physiology, obstruction, trauma, stone disease, and neoplasia. Volume 3 includes all topics related to lower urinary tract function and dysfunction, including calculi; trauma, bladder, and prostate disease; and all aspects of urine transport, storage, and emptying. Volume 4 remains a 900-page textbook of pediatric urology. There are 24 totally new chapters; an additional 19 chapters have new authors; and the remaining 89 chapters have all undergone substantial revision. All chapters contain the latest concepts, data, and controversies. Illustrations, algorithms (extensively used), and tables are now in color, as are clinical photographs. Extensive highlighting is utilized, as well as key point boxes. The complete reference list is now online and bound on a CD; a list of suggested key references appears at the end of each chapter. An **e**-dition includes a fully searchable online version with downloadable images (for powerpoint, papers, etc.) and video clips of the key portions of certain procedures, and it will include weekly content updates (summaries of key journal articles in all areas) for the life of the edition. The *Review*, with questions, answers, and explanations, will continue as a separate publication.

Each of us is grateful for the opportunity to be a part of the continuing tradition of *Campbell-Walsh Urology* and wish to express our immense appreciation to all of our superb authors and to those at Elsevier who facilitated our efforts in bringing the 9th edition to publication: Rebecca Schmidt Gaertner, Senior Acquisitions Editor, and Anne Snyder, Senior Developmental Editor.

ALAN J. WEIN, MD, PhD (Hon)
For the Editors

CONTENTS

SECTION XIV

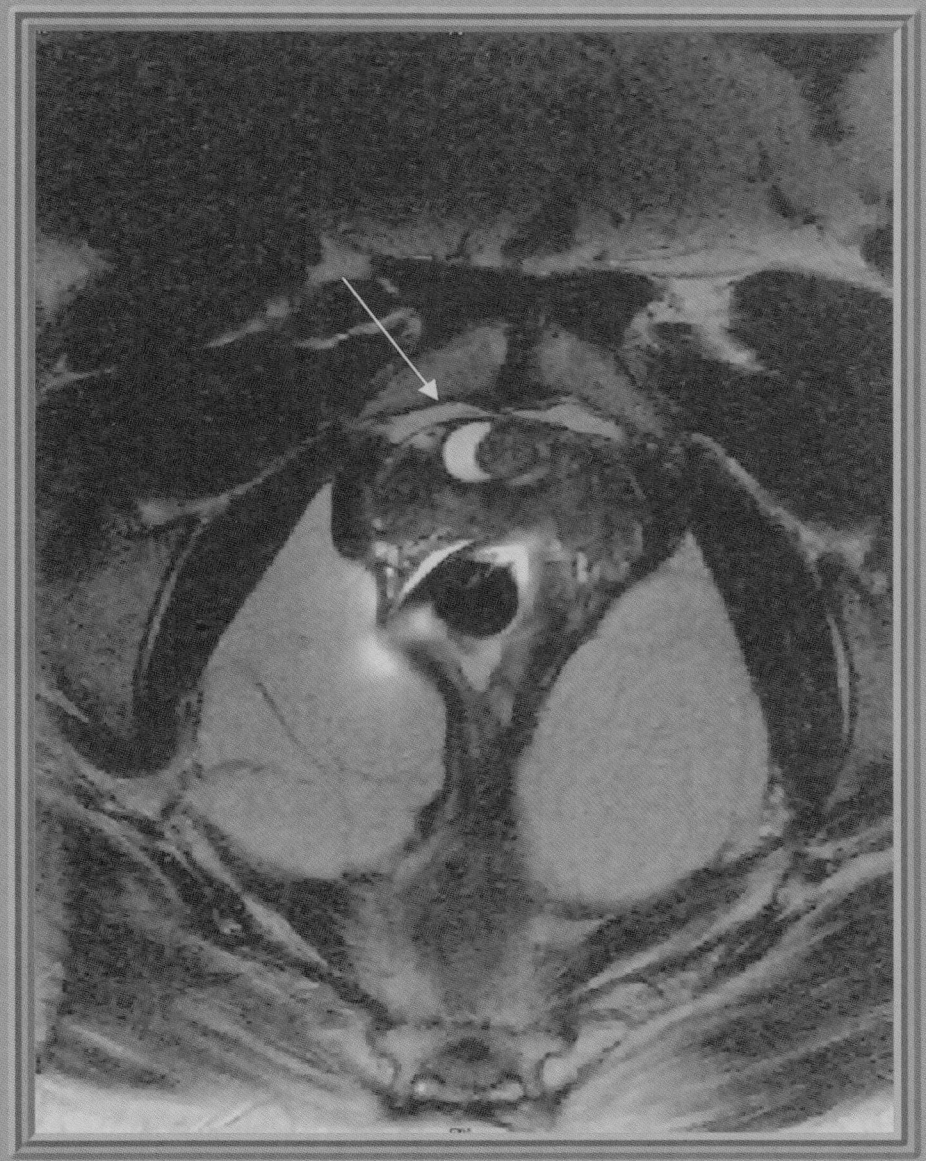

URINE TRANSPORT, STORAGE, AND EMPTYING

55 Physiology and Pharmacology of the Renal Pelvis and Ureter

ROBERT M. WEISS, MD

CELLULAR ANATOMY

The primary functional anatomic unit of the ureter is the ureteral smooth muscle cell. The cell is extremely small, approximately 250 to 400 μm in length and 5 to 7 μm in diameter. The **nucleus**, which is separated from the remainder of the cell by a nuclear membrane, is ellipsoid and **contains a darkly staining body, the nucleolus, and the genetic material of the cell. Surrounding the nucleus is the cytoplasm or sarcoplasm, which contains the structures involved in cell function.** Frequently in close relation to the nucleus, **mitochondria** in the cytoplasm **perform many of the nutritive functions of the cell. Endoplasmic reticulum and sarcoplasmic reticulum dispersed in the cytoplasm serve as Ca^{2+} storage sites.**

Dispersed in the sarcoplasm are the **contractile proteins, actin and myosin.** Depending on the local calcium ion (Ca^{2+}) concentration, they interact to produce contraction or relaxation. **Any process that leads to a significant increase in the Ca^{2+} concentration in the region of the contractile proteins results in contraction; conversely, any process that leads to a significant decrease in the Ca^{2+} concentration in the region of the contractile proteins results in relaxation.** The actin is dispersed throughout the sarcoplasm in hexagonal clumps and is interspersed with the less numerous clumps of the more deeply staining myosin. Dark bands along the cell surface are referred to as *attachment plaques*. Along with dense bodies dispersed in the cytoplasm, they serve as attachment devices for the actin.

Around the periphery of the cell are numerous cavitary structures, some of which open to the outside of the cell and are referred to as **caveolae.** Their exact function is not known, although they may serve a role in the nutritive functions of the cell or in the transport of ions across the cell membrane. **A double-layer cell membrane surrounds the cell. The inner plasma membrane surrounds the entire cell, but the outer basement membrane is absent at areas of close cell-to-cell contact, referred to as intermediate junctions.**

DEVELOPMENT OF THE URETER

The ureter, a 25- to 30-cm tube extending from the renal pelvis to the bladder, arises as an outpouching from the mesonephric duct. Formation of the ureteric bud and its subsequent branching is induced by glial cell line–derived neurotrophic factor (GDNF), derived from adjacent metanephrogenic mesenchyme (Pepicelli et al, 1997; Sainio et al, 1997). GDNF signals through the c-Ret receptor tyrosine kinase (Vega et al, 1996), which results in increased phosphatidylinositol 3-kinase (PI3K) activity and Akt/PKB phosphorylation (Tang et al, 2002). A number of other growth factors including transforming growth factor β (TGF-β), hepatocyte growth factor (HGF), and fibroblast growth factors (FGF 1, 2, 7, and 10) and matrix molecules such as heparin sulfate proteoglycans, laminins, integrins, and matrix metalloproteinases (MMPs) are involved in growth and branching of the ureteral bud

(Davies et al, 1995; Qiao et al, 1999, 2001; Pohl et al, 2000; Davies, 2001; Takemura et al, 2002; Sakurai, 2003; Bush et al, 2004; Chen et al, 2004). **Programmed cell death, or apoptosis, is involved in branching of the ureteric bud and subsequent nephrogenesis. Inhibitors of caspases, which are involved in the apoptotic signaling pathway, inhibit ureteral bud branching** (Araki et al, 1999). **At a point during development, the ureteral lumen is obliterated, and then it recanalizes** (Russo-Gil et al, 1975; Alcaraz et al, 1991). **It appears that angiotensin acting through the angiotensin II receptor is involved in the recanalization process** (Yerkes et al, 1998) and in the inhibition of aberrant ureteral budding (Oshima et al, 2001). Knockout mice for the *ATR2* gene have congenital anomalies of the kidney and urinary tract, including duplicated collecting systems with a hydronephrotic upper pole moiety, multicystic dysplastic kidneys, megaureters, and ureteropelvic junction (UPJ) obstructions. **Mutant mice lacking angiotensin II type I receptors fail to develop a renal pelvis and lack ureteral peristaltic activity** (Miyazaki et al, 1998). **Angiotensin II acting through angiotensin II type I receptors is also involved in ureteric bud cell branching** (Iosipiv and Schroeder, 2003).

Calcineurin, a Ca^{2+}-dependent serine/threonine phosphatase, also appears to be an essential signaling molecule in urinary tract development. Mutant mice in which calcineurin function is removed are noted to have reduced proliferation of smooth muscle and mesenchymal cells in the developing urinary tract with abnormal development of the renal pelvis and ureter and resultant defective pyeloureteral peristalsis (Chang et al, 2004).

ELECTRICAL ACTIVITY

The electrical properties of all excitable tissues depend on the distribution of ions on both the inside and the outside of the cell membrane and on the relative permeability of the cell membrane to these ions (Hodgkin, 1958). The ionic basis for electrical activity in ureteral smooth muscle has not been fully described; however, many of its properties resemble those in other excitable tissues.

Resting Potential

When a ureteral muscle cell is in a nonexcited or resting state, the electrical potential difference across the cell membrane, transmembrane potential, is referred to as the resting membrane potential (RMP). The RMP is determined primarily by the distribution of potassium ions (K^+) across the cell membrane and by the permeability of the membrane to K^+ (Hendrickx et al, 1975). In the resting state, the K^+ concentration on the inside of the cell is greater than that on the outside of the cell, that is, $[K^+]_i > [K^+]_o$, and the membrane is preferentially permeable to K^+. Because of the tendency for the positively charged K^+ ions to diffuse from the inside of the cell, where they are more concentrated, to the outside of the cell, where they are less concentrated, an electrical gradient is created, with the inside of the cell membrane being more negative than the outside (Fig. 55–1A). The electrical gradient that is formed tends to oppose the further movement of K^+ outward across the cell membrane along its concentration gradient, and an equilibrium is reached. There is a greater concentration of K^+ on the inside of the membrane than on the outside, with the inside of the cell membrane being negative with respect to the outside of the cell membrane.

If the membrane in the resting state were exclusively permeable to K^+, the measured RMP of the ureteral smooth muscle cell should approximate −90 mV, the K^+ equilibrium potential, as predicted by the Nernst equation:

$$E_k = -RT/nF \ln[K^+]_i/[K^+]_o$$

where E_k is the potential difference attributable to the concentration difference of K^+ across the cell membrane, R is the molar gas constant, T is the absolute temperature, n is the number of moles of K^+, and F is the faraday (Nernst, 1908). However, in the ureter and in other smooth muscles, the RMP is considerably less than the K^+ equilibrium potential, with values of −33 to −70 mV, the inside of the cell being negative with respect to the outside (Kuriyama et al, 1967). Studies of single isolated ureteral cells show spontaneous transient hyperpolarizations with the RMP transiently becoming more negative (Imaizumi et al, 1989). This phenomenon appears to be due to spontaneous release of Ca^{2+} from the sarcoplasmic reticulum with activation of tetraethylammonium (TEA)- and charybdotoxin-sensitive Ca^{2+}-dependent K^+ channels ($I_{K(Ca)}$). Although the low resting potential of ureteral cells may be explained in part by a relatively small resting K^+ conductance (Imaizumi et al, 1989), it may also be due to the contribution of other ions.

One such ion that could account for the relatively low RMP of the ureter and other smooth muscles is the sodium ion (Na^+) (Kuriyama, 1963). In the resting state, the Na^+ concentration on the outside of the cell membrane is greater than that on the inside, that is, $[Na^+]_o > [Na^+]_i$. If the resting membrane were somewhat permeable to Na^+, both the concentration and the electrical gradient would support an inward movement of Na^+ across the cell membrane, with a resultant decrease in the electronegativity of the inner surface of the cell membrane (Fig. 55–1B).

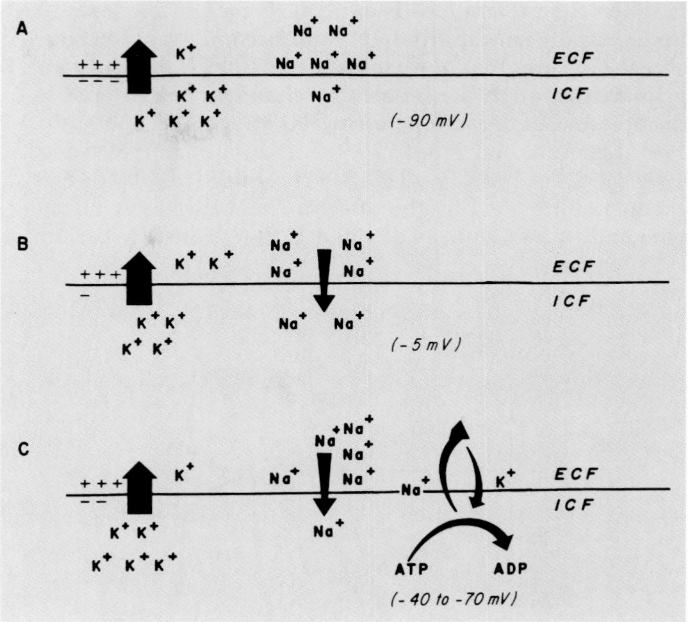

Figure 55–1. Ionic basis for the resting membrane potential (RMP) in smooth muscle. In the resting state, the K^+ concentration inside the cell is greater than the K^+ concentration outside the cell, and the Na^+ concentration outside the cell is greater than the Na^+ concentration inside the cell. **A,** Electrochemical changes that would occur if the membrane were solely permeable to potassium. Potassium would diffuse from the inside of the cell, where it is more concentrated, to the outside of the cell, where it is less concentrated. The outward movement of the positively charged K^+ ions would make the inside of the cell membrane negative with respect to the outside of the cell membrane. **B,** Electrochemical changes that would occur if the resting membrane were also permeable to sodium. An inward movement of Na^+ along its concentration gradient would make the inside of the cell membrane less negative with respect to the outside of the cell membrane than is depicted in A. **C,** Pump mechanism for extruding Na^+ from within the cell against concentration and electrochemical gradients. Inward movement of K^+ is coupled with outward movement of Na^+. This mechanism helps to maintain a steady state of ion distribution across the cell membrane and a stable RMP. ECF, extracellular fluid; ICF, intracellular fluid. (**A** to **C,** From Weiss RM: Ureteral function. Urology 1978;12:114.)

If such an inward movement of Na^+ went unchecked, the RMP would be expected to decrease to a level lower than that actually observed, and the concentration gradient for Na^+ might become reversed. In order to maintain a steady-state ion distribution across the cell membrane with $[K^+]_o < [K^+]_i$ and $[Na^+]_o > [Na^+]_i$ and to prevent the transmembrane potential from becoming lower than the measured ureteral RMP, an active mechanism capable of extruding Na^+ from within the cell against a concentration and electrochemical gradient is required (Fig. 55–1C). Such an outward Na^+ pump that is coupled with an inward movement of K^+ derives its energy requirements from the dephosphorylation of ATP (Casteels, 1970). Na^+-Ca^{2+} exchange may also play a role in Na^+ extrusion, especially when the Na^+ pump is inhibited (Aickin, 1987; Aickin et al, 1987; Lamont et al, 1998).

The dynamic processes illustrated in Figure 55–1 enable the ureter in its resting state to maintain a relatively low RMP. In addition to the mechanisms described, the distribution of chloride ions (Cl^-) across the cell membrane and the relative permeability of the membrane to Cl^- may be factors in the maintenance of the RMP in the ureter and other smooth muscles (Kuriyama, 1963; Washizu, 1966).

Action Potential

The transmembrane potential of an inactive or resting ureteral cell remains stable until it is excited by an external stimulus— electrical, mechanical (stretch), or chemical—or by conduction of electrical activity (action potential) from an already excited adjacent cell. **When a ureteral cell is stimulated, depolarization occurs, with the inside of the cell membrane becoming less negative than it was before stimulation. If a sufficient area of the cell membrane is depolarized rapidly enough to reach a critical level of transmembrane potential, referred to as the threshold potential, a regenerative depolarization, or action potential, is initiated.**

KEY POINT: URETERAL ACTION POTENTIAL

■ The RMP of the ureteral cell is approximately −33 to −70 mV and is determined primarily by the distribution of K^+ ions across the cell membrane and the relatively selective permeability of the resting cell membrane to K^+. When excited by a suprathreshold stimulus, the membrane becomes less permeable to K^+ and more permeable to Ca^{2+}, which moves inward across the cell membrane and provides the ionic mechanism for the development of the upstroke of the action potential. After reaching the peak of its action potential, the membrane maintains a depolarized state—plateau of the action potential— for a period of time before the membrane potential of the activated cell returns to its resting level (repolarization). The plateau appears to be related to a persisting inward Ca^{2+} current and to an influx of Na^+. Repolarization of the membrane is related to a renewed increase in permeability to K^+.

The changes that occur are diagrammatically depicted in Figure 55–2. If a stimulus is very weak, as shown by arrow a, the transmembrane potential may remain unchanged. A slightly stronger, yet subthreshold, stimulus may result in an abortive displacement of the transmembrane potential but not to such a degree that an action potential is generated (arrow b). If the stimulus is strong enough to decrease the transmembrane potential to the threshold potential, the cell becomes excited and develops an action potential (arrow c). The **action potential, which is the primary event in the conduction of the peristaltic impulse,** has the capability to act as the stimulus for excitation of adjacent quiescent cells **and through a complicated chain of events gives rise to the ureteral contraction.**

When the ureteral cell is excited, its membrane loses its preferential permeability to K⁺ and becomes more permeable to Ca²⁺ ions that move inward across the cell membrane primarily through fast L-type Ca²⁺ channels and give rise to the upstroke of the action potential (Fig. 55–3A) (Kobayashi, 1965; Kuriyama and Tomita, 1970; Imaizumi et al, 1989; Lang, 1989, 1990; Sui and Kao, 1997a, 1997b; Smith et al, 2002). This channel is inhibited by the calcium channel blocker nifedipine and by cadmium (Cd²⁺) and is potentiated by barium

(Ba²⁺). As the positively charged Ca²⁺ ions move inward across the cell membrane, the inside of the membrane becomes less negative with respect to the outside and may even become positive at the peak of the action potential, a state referred to as *overshoot*. Na⁺ ions may also play a role in the upstroke of the ureteral action potential (Kobayashi, 1964, 1965; Muraki et al, 1991). The rate of rise of the upstroke of the ureteral action potential is relatively slow, 1.2 ± 0.06 V/sec in the cat (Kobayashi, 1969). This compares with a 610 V/sec rate of rise in dog cardiac Purkinje fibers (Draper and Weidmann, 1951) and a 740 V/sec rate of rise in skeletal muscle (Ferroni and Blanchi, 1965). The slow rate of upstroke rise of the ureteral action potential accounts for the slow conduction velocity in the ureter.

After reaching the peak of its action potential, the ureter maintains its potential for a period of time (plateau of the action potential) before the transmembrane potential returns to its resting level (repolarization) (Kuriyama et al, 1967). The plateau phase of the guinea pig action potential is superimposed with multiple oscillations, a phenomenon not observed in the rat, rabbit, or cat (Fig. 55–4) (Bozler, 1938). The plateau phase appears to depend on the persistence of an inward Ca²⁺ current and on Na⁺ influx through a voltage-dependent Na⁺ channel (see Fig. 55–3A) (Kuriyama and Tomita, 1970; Imaizumi et al, 1989; Sui and Kao, 1997a). Also involved in the plateau formation is the maintenance of depolarization by an inward calcium-dependent chloride current ($I_{Cl(Ca)}$), which is countered by outward voltage-gated and Ca²⁺-activated K⁺ currents (Smith et al, 2002). There are species differences in the ionic currents involved in the formation of the action potential, with the Ca²⁺-activated chloride current being present in the rat but not in the guinea pig ureter. The inward Cl⁻ current can be inhibited by niflumic

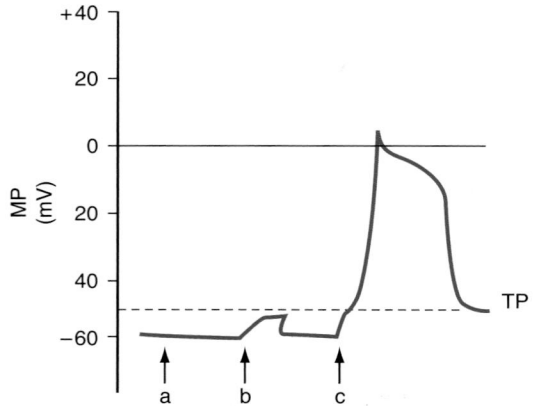

Figure 55–2. Response of ureteral transmembrane potential to stimuli. At *arrow a*, a weak stimulus is applied that does not alter the resting membrane potential (MP). At *arrow b*, a stimulus is applied that decreases the transmembrane potential but not to the level of the threshold potential TP (subthreshold stimulus). At *arrow c*, a stimulus is applied that decreases the transmembrane potential to TP, and an action potential is initiated (suprathreshold stimulus). (From Weiss RM: Ureteral function. Urology 1978;12:114.)

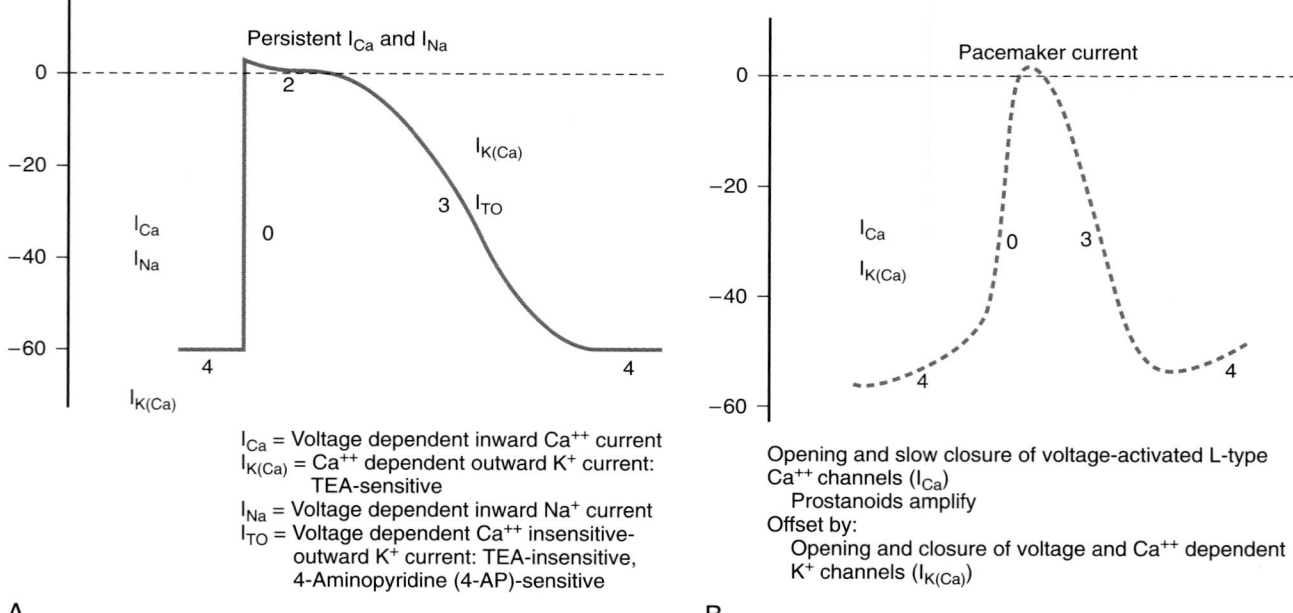

A

I_{Ca} = Voltage dependent inward Ca⁺⁺ current
$I_{K(Ca)}$ = Ca⁺⁺ dependent outward K⁺ current: TEA-sensitive
I_{Na} = Voltage dependent inward Na⁺ current
I_{TO} = Voltage dependent Ca⁺⁺ insensitive-outward K⁺ current: TEA-insensitive, 4-Aminopyridine (4-AP)-sensitive

B

Opening and slow closure of voltage-activated L-type Ca⁺⁺ channels (I_{Ca})
   Prostanoids amplify
Offset by:
   Opening and closure of voltage and Ca⁺⁺ dependent K⁺ channels ($I_{K(Ca)}$)

Figure 55–3. Schematic representation of ionic currents in (**A**) nonpacemaker *(solid line)* and (**B**) pacemaker *(dashed line)* action potentials: (0) upstroke or depolarization phase; (2) plateau phase; (3) repolarization phase; and (4) resting potential of the nonpacemaker cell and spontaneous depolarization phase of the pacemaker cell. A spontaneous decrease in the transmembrane potential of pacemaker cells accounts for their spontaneous activity. TEA, tetraethylammonium.

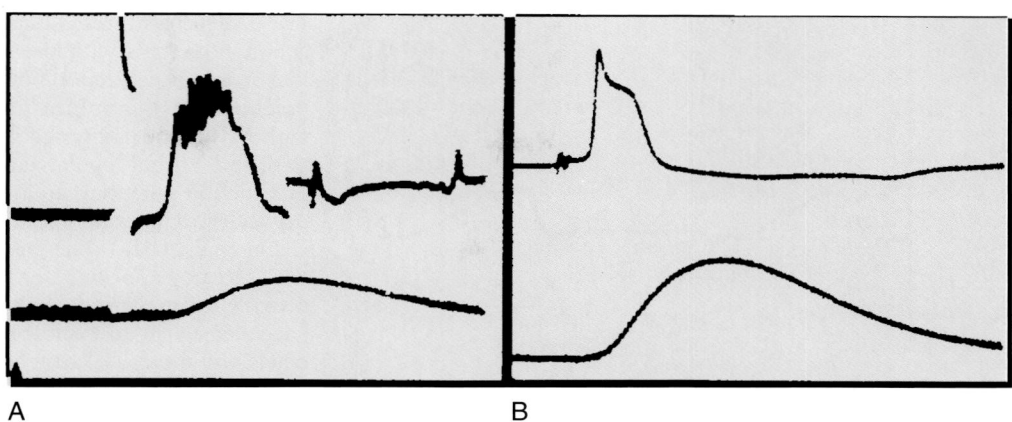

Figure 55–4. Intracellular recordings of ureteral action potentials *(upper tracings)* and isometric recordings of contractions *(lower tracings)* in response to electrical stimuli. Action potentials precede contractions. **A,** Guinea pig ureter; oscillations on the plateau of the action potential. **B,** Cat ureter; no oscillations on the plateau of the action potential. (**A** and **B,** From Weiss RM: Ureteral function. Urology 1978;12:114.)

acid and by Ba^{2+} (Smith et al, 2002). The oscillations on the plateau of the guinea pig action potential appear to depend on the repetitive activation of an inward Ca^{2+} current (Kuriyama and Tomita, 1970) and of a Ca^{2+}-dependent outward K^+ current (Imaizumi et al, 1989). Prolongation of the inward calcium current and the duration of the action potential correlates with an increased force of contraction (Burdyga and Wray, 1999b).

The activation of a Ca^{2+}-dependent K^+ current that is involved in repolarization is mainly due to Ca^{2+} release from the endoplasmic reticulum that is triggered by the influx of extracellular Ca^{2+} through voltage-dependent Ca^{2+} channels. The increase in intracellular Ca^{2+} concentration during the upstroke and plateau of the action potential finally may activate the outward Ca^{2+}-dependent K^+ current ($I_{K(Ca)}$) to such a degree that repolarization occurs with return of the transmembrane potential to its resting level (see Fig. 55–3A) (Imaizumi et al, 1989; Sui and Kao, 1997c). This $I_{K(Ca)}$ is sensitive to inhibition by TEA. A voltage-dependent, Ca^{2+}-insensitive outward K^+ current (I_{TO}) also appears to be involved in the repolarization (Lang, 1989; Imaizumi et al, 1990). These currents are TEA insensitive and 4-aminopyridine (4-AP) sensitive. In the rat but not the guinea pig ureter there is a late TEA-, Cd^{2+}-, and Ca^{2+}-insensitive outward K^+ current that is also involved in the repolarization process. The duration of the action potential in the cat ranges from 259 to 405 msec (Kobayashi and Irisawa, 1964).

Pacemaker Potentials and Pacemaker Activity

Electrical activity arises in a cell either spontaneously or in response to an external stimulus. If the activity arises spontaneously, the cell is referred to as a pacemaker cell. Pacemaker fibers differ from nonpacemaker fibers in that their transmembrane resting potential is lower (less negative) than that of nonpacemaker fibers (Lang and Zhang, 1996) and does not remain constant but rather undergoes a slow spontaneous depolarization (see Fig. 55–3B). If the spontaneously changing membrane potential reaches the threshold potential, the upstroke of an action potential occurs. The **ionic conduction underlying pacemaker activity in the upper urinary tract is due to the opening and slow closure of voltage-activated L-type Ca^{2+} channels, which are amplified by prostanoids** (Santicioli et al, 1995a). This is opposed by the opening and

closure of voltage- and Ca^{2+}-dependent K^+ channels. It has been suggested that prostaglandins and excitatory tachykinins, released from sensory nerves, help maintain autorhythmicity in the upper urinary tract through maintenance of Ca^{2+} mobilization (Lang et al, 2002a). **Tetrodotoxin and blockers of the autonomic nervous system, both parasympathetic and sympathetic, have little effect on peristalsis, suggesting that autonomic neurotransmitters have little role in maintaining pyeloureteral motility** (Lang et al, 2001, 2002a). Changes in the frequency of action potential development may result from a change in the level of the threshold potential, a change in the rate of slow spontaneous depolarization of the resting potential, or a change in the level of the resting potential.

Gosling and Dixon (1971, 1974) provided morphologic evidence of specialized pacemaker tissue in the proximal portion of the urinary collecting system and described species differences. **In species with a multicalyceal system, such as the pig, sheep, and human, the "pacemaker cells" are located near the pelvicalyceal border** (Dixon and Gosling, 1973). In species with a unicalyceal system, such as the dog, cat, rat, rabbit, and guinea pig, the pacemaker cells extend from the pelvicalyceal border to the UPJ. These atypical smooth muscle cells that give rise to pacemaker activity in the rat and guinea pig, in contrast to typical smooth muscle cells, have less than 40% of their cellular area occupied by contractile elements and demonstrate sparse immunoreactivity for smooth muscle and actin. (Klemm et al, 1999; Lang et al, 2001). These spindle-shaped cells are 90 to 230 μm in length and their electrical activity consists of simple waveforms of alternating depolarizing and repolarizing phases that occur at a relatively rapid frequency of 8 to 15/min (Fig. 55–5A) (Tsuchida and Suzuki, 1992; Klemm et al, 1999). Pacemaker potentials have a lower RMP, a slower rate of rise, and a lower amplitude than action potentials recorded from nonpacemaker cells. In the guinea pig, these atypical, presumably pacemaker cells constitute more than 80% of the cells at the pelvicalyceal junction and about 15% of the cells in the proximal renal pelvis but are not present in the distal renal pelvis or ureter (Klemm et al, 1999). Electrical recordings correlate with histologic findings in that pacemaker potentials were not observed in the distal renal pelvis or ureter (Klemm et al, 1999).

Driven action potentials that fire at lower frequency (3 to 5/min) than pacemaker potentials are recorded from longer (150 to 400 μm) spindle-shaped typical smooth muscle cells (Fig. 55–5B) (Klemm et al, 1999). Most muscle cells of the ureter (100%), distal renal pelvis (97.5%), and proximal renal

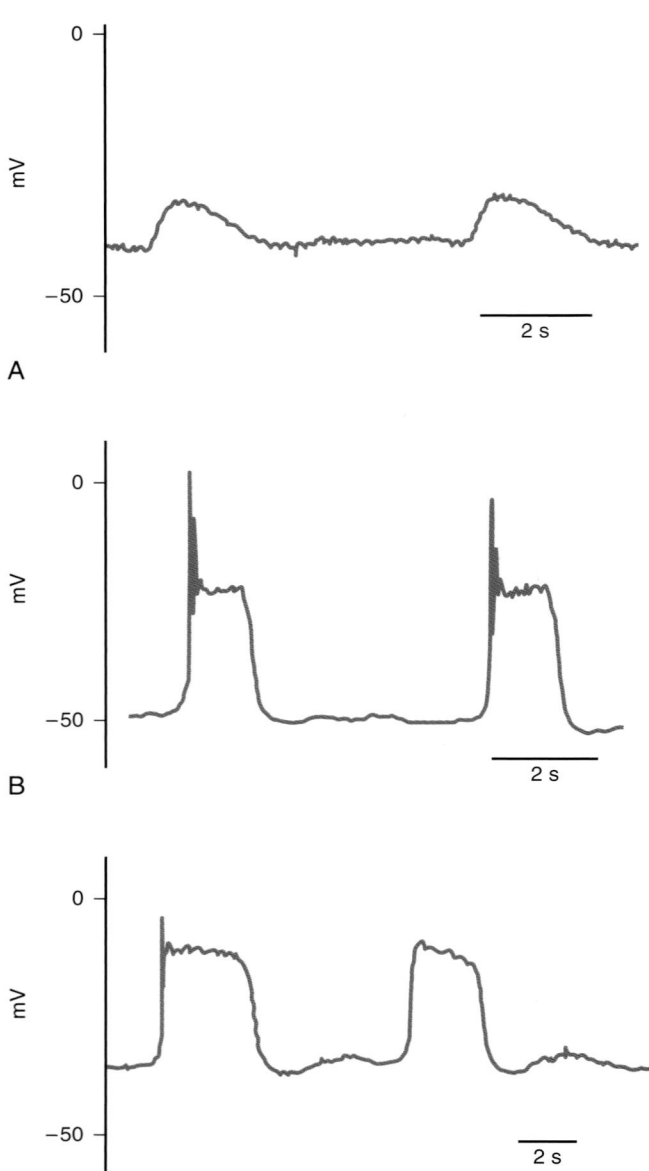

Figure 55–5. Action potentials in the upper urinary tract of the guinea pig. **A,** Pacemaker potentials; **B,** Driven action potentials; **C,** Intermediate action potentials. (Modified with permission from Klemm MF, Exintaris B, Lang RJ: Identification of the cells underlying pacemaker activity in the guinea pig upper urinary tract. J Physiol [Lond] 1999;519:867.)

pelvis (83%) are typical nonpacemaker smooth muscle cells with typical action potentials. Lang and colleagues (1998) described fibroblast-like cells resembling the interstitial cells of Cajal (ICC), which serve as pacemaker cells in the intestine, in the proximal portion of the guinea pig renal pelvis. These "ICC-like" cells are irregularly shaped with oval nuclei and many branching interconnecting processes and contain numerous mitochondria, caveolae, and prominent endoplasmic reticulum. The ICC-like cells are not immunoreactive for α-smooth muscle actin, which is present in typical smooth muscle cells, or for C-kit, a tyrosine kinase receptor that is expressed in intestinal ICC pacemaker cells (Klemm et al,

1999). Electrical recordings from these cells demonstrate action potentials with properties intermediate to the pacemaker and driven action potentials. These intermediate action potentials in the guinea pig have a single spike, a plateau without the superimposed spikes seen in driven action potentials, and a rapid repolarization phase (Fig. 55–5C). Intermediate action potentials are noted in 11% to 17% of cells at the pelvicalyceal junction and the proximal and distal renal pelvis (Lang et al, 2002a). These ICC-like cells in the upper urinary tract do not appear to be pacemaker cells but rather may provide for preferential conduction of electrical signals from pacemaker cells to typical smooth muscle cells of the renal pelvis and ureter (Klemm et al, 1999).

C-kit is a tyrosine kinase receptor that promotes cell migration and proliferation of melanoblasts, hematopoietic progenitors, and primordial germ cells (Fig. 55–6). Mice expressing mutant inactivating C-kit alleles lack intestinal ICC and have abnormal intestinal peristalsis and develop bowel obstruction, showing that **C-kit is important in the development of pacemaker activity and peristalsis of the gut** (Der-Silaphet et al, 1998). Pezzone and coworkers (2003) identified C-kit–positive cells in the mouse ureter. They suggested that the difference from previous studies in the guinea pig upper urinary tract in which C-kit positivity was not identified in ICC-like cells (Klemm et al, 1999) may be due to species differences, the C-kit antibody used, or the fixation methods. **C-kit expression** was noted to be **upregulated in the embryonic murine ureter prior to its development of unidirectional peristaltic contractions** (David et al, 2005). Incubation of isolated cultured embryonic murine ureters with antibodies that neutralize C-kit activity altered ureteral morphology and inhibited unidirectional peristalsis. C-kit–positive cells have been identified in the human ureter (Metzger et al, 2004) and in the human UPJ (Solari et al, 2003). In the presence of obstruction, C-kit–positive ICC-like cells at the UPJ were sparse or absent (Solari et al, 2003).

Bozler (1942), using small extracellular surface electrodes, demonstrated the characteristic slow spontaneous depolarization of pacemaker-type fibers in the proximal portion of the isolated ureter of a unicalyceal upper collecting system. In a multicalyceal kidney, Morita and associates (1981), using extracellular electrodes, recorded low-voltage potentials that appeared to be pacemaker potentials from the border of the pig minor calyces and the major calyx with the contraction rhythm varying between calyces. Multiple pacemakers fire simultaneously as coupled oscillators or individually as pacemaker activity shifts from one site to another along the renal pelvis of the unicalyceal kidney or the pelvicalyceal border of the multicalyceal pig and sheep kidney (Golenhofen and Hannappel, 1973; Constantinou et al, 1977; Constantinou and Yamaguchi, 1981; Lammers et al, 1996).

Although the primary pacemaker for ureteral peristalsis is located in the proximal portion of the collecting system, other areas of the ureter may act as **latent pacemakers.** Under normal conditions, the latent pacemaker regions are dominated by activity arising at the primary pacemaker sites. When the latent pacemaker site is freed of its domination by the primary pacemaker, it, in turn, may act as a pacemaker. To demonstrate latent pacemaker sites, Shiratori and Kinoshita (1961) transected the in vivo dog ureter at various levels. Before transection, peristaltic activity arose proximally from

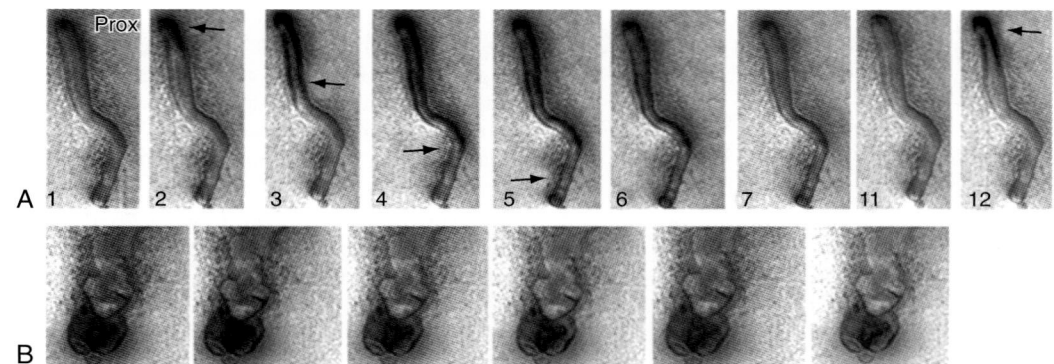

Figure 55–6. C-kit expression and the development of unidirectional peristaltic contractions in the embryonic murine ureter. **A,** After 72 hours of culture E15.5 ureteral explants develop contractions (arrows) that propagate in a proximal-to-distal direction. **B,** Explants cultured in the presence of inhibitory C-kit antibodies do not develop coordinated contractions. (Modified with permission from David SG, Cebrian C, Vaughan ED Jr, Herblinger D: C-kit and ureteral peristalsis. J Urol 2005;173:292.)

the primary pacemaker. When the ureter was transected at the UPJ, antiperistaltic waves of lower frequency than the previous normoperistaltic waves originated from the UVJ. Division of the ureter at the UVJ did not affect the normoperistaltic waves. After division of the midureter, the normoperistaltic waves in the upper segment remained unchanged, and the lower segment demonstrated antiperistaltic waves, which originated at the UVJ at a frequency less than that of the normoperistaltic waves in the upper segment. Thus, cells at the UVJ of the dog may act as pacemaker cells when freed of control from the primary proximally located pacemaker. **Latent pacemaker cells are present in all regions of the ureter** (Imaizumi et al, 1989; Meini et al, 1995).

Propagation of Electrical Activity

Excitable cells possess resistive and capacitative membrane properties similar to those of a cable or core conductor. The transverse resistance of the membrane is higher than the longitudinal resistance of the extracellular or intracellular fluid; this allows current resulting from a stimulus to propagate along the length of the fibers. The spread of current is referred to as *electrotonic spread* (Hoffman and Cranefield, 1960). The space constant (λ) determines the degree to which the electrotonic potential dissipates with increasing distance from an applied voltage. In a cable, this relation is expressed by

$$P = P_o \, e^{-X/\lambda}$$

where X is the distance from the applied voltage, P is the displacement of the membrane potential at X, P_o is the displacement of the membrane potential at the site of the applied voltage, e is the base of the natural logarithm, and λ is the space constant. Thus, the electrotonic potential decreases by 1/e in one space constant. The space constant of the guinea pig ureter measured by extracellular stimulation is 2.5 to 3 mm (Kuriyama et al, 1967).

The time constant τ_m is expressed by

$$\tau_m = RC$$

where R is the membrane resistance and C is the membrane capacity. The time constant τ_m signifies that a small displace-

ment of potential is decreased by 1/e of its value in 1 t_m. The time constant of the guinea pig ureter measured by extracellular stimulation is 200 to 300 msec (Kuriyama et al, 1967).

The ureter acts as a **functional syncytium**. Engelmann (1869, 1870) showed that stimulation of the ureter produces a contraction wave that propagates proximally and distally from the site of stimulation. Under normal conditions, **electrical activity** arises proximally and is **conducted distally from one muscle cell to another across areas of close cellular apposition referred to as intermediate junctions** (Uehara and Burnstock, 1970; Libertino and Weiss, 1972). The similarity of these close cellular contacts to nexuses, which have been shown to be low-resistance pathways for cell-to-cell conduction in other smooth muscles (Barr et al, 1968), suggests that a similar mechanism for conduction may be present in the ureter. **Gap junctions consisting of groups of channels in the plasma membrane of adjacent smooth muscle cells enable exchange of ions and small molecules and play a role in electrical coupling between adjacent cells and in electromechanical coupling** (Gabella, 1994; Santiciolli and Maggi, 2000). 18β-Glycyrrhetinic acid, a gap junction inhibitor, inhibits cell-to-cell electrical coupling in guinea pig renal pelvis and ureter and dissociates electrical and mechanical events (Santicioli and Maggi, 2000). **Conduction velocity in the ureter is 2 to 6 cm/sec** (Kobayashi, 1964; Kuriyama et al, 1967); it has been shown to vary with temperature, the time interval between stimuli (Van Mastrigt et al, 1986), and the pressure within the ureter (Tsuchiya and Takei, 1990). This is in comparison with conduction velocities ranging from 1.5 to 2 m/sec in cardiac Purkinje fibers (Rosen et al, 1981) and from 10 to 100 m/sec in the dorsal and ventral roots of the spinal cord (Biscoe et al, 1977). Conduction in the ureter is similar to that in cardiac tissue, even to the extent that the Wenckebach phenomenon (a partial conduction block) has been demonstrated in the ureter as it has been in specialized cardiac fibers (Weiss et al, 1968).

CONTRACTILE ACTIVITY

The contractile event is dependent on the concentration of free sarcoplasmic Ca^{2+} in the region of the contractile

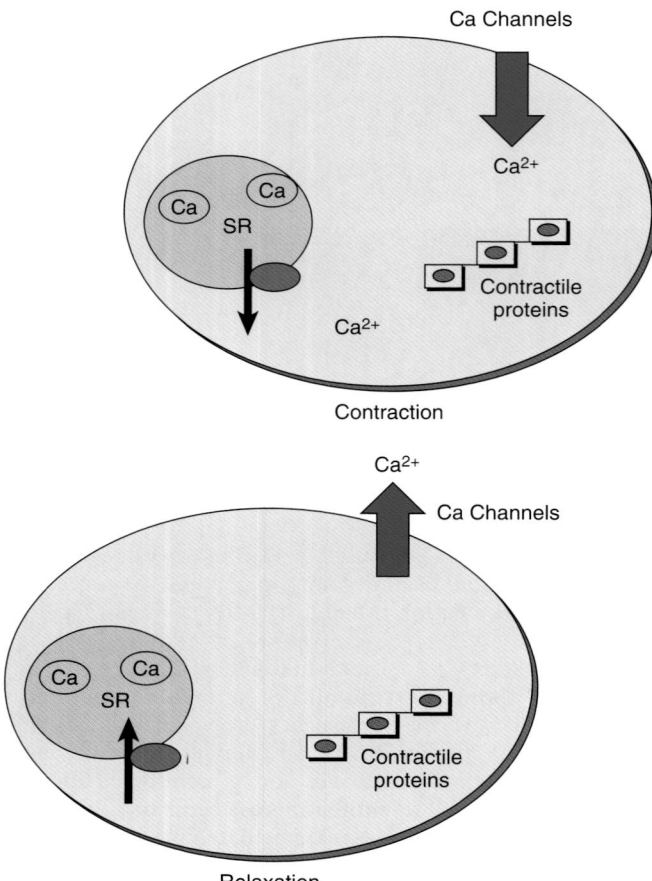

Figure 55–7. Schematic representation of calcium ion movements during contraction and relaxation. SR, sarcoplasmic reticulum.

proteins, actin and myosin. **Any process that results in a significant increase in Ca^{2+} in the region of the contractile proteins favors the development of a contraction; any process that results in a significant decrease in Ca^{2+} in the region of the contractile proteins favors relaxation** (Fig. 55–7).

Contractile Proteins

In skeletal muscle, Ca^{2+} appears to act as a derepressor. It is thought that in the relaxed state, a regulator system, consisting of the proteins troponin and tropomyosin, prevents the interaction of actin and myosin. In the relaxed state, the troponin that is attached to the tropomyosin is inactive, and the tropomyosin prevents the interaction between actin and myosin. With activation, there is an increase in the sarcoplasmic Ca^{2+} concentration. The Ca^{2+} binds to the troponin, producing a conformational change that results in the displacement of tropomyosin, thus allowing interaction of actin and myosin and the development of a contraction.

In smooth muscle, on the other hand, Ca^{2+} appears to act as an activator. The most widely accepted theory suggests that **phosphorylation of myosin is involved in the contractile process** and that a troponin-like system does not constitute the primary regulatory mechanism, as it does in skeletal muscle. **With excitation, there is a transient increase in the**

sarcoplasmic Ca^{2+} concentration from its steady-state concentration of 10^{-8} to 10^{-7} M to a concentration of 10^{-6} M or higher. At this higher concentration, **Ca^{2+} forms an active complex with the Ca^{2+}-binding protein calmodulin** (Watterson et al, 1976; Cho et al, 1988). Calmodulin without Ca^{2+} is inactive (Fig. 55–8). **The Ca^{2+}-calmodulin complex activates a calmodulin-dependent enzyme, myosin light-chain kinase** (see Fig. 55–8). **The activated myosin light-chain kinase, in turn, catalyzes the phosphorylation of the 20,000-dalton light chain of myosin** (Fig. 55–9). **Phosphorylation of the myosin light chain allows actin to activate myosin magnesium adenosine triphosphatase (Mg^{2+}-ATPase) activity, leading to hydrolysis of ATP and the development of smooth muscle tension or shortening** (Fig. 55–10). Actin cannot activate the ATPase activity of the dephosphorylated myosin light chain.

When the Ca^{2+} concentration in the region of the contractile proteins is low, the myosin light-chain kinase is not active because calmodulin requires Ca^{2+} to activate the enzyme. This prevents activation of the contractile apparatus because the myosin light chain cannot be phosphorylated, a process that must precede tension development. Furthermore, a phosphatase dephosphorylates the myosin light chain, thus preventing actin activation of myosin ATPase activity, and relaxation results.

Evidence indicates that phosphorylation of the enzyme myosin light-chain kinase by a cyclic adenosine monophosphate (cAMP)-dependent protein kinase decreases myosin light-chain kinase activity by decreasing the affinity of this enzyme for calmodulin (Adelstein et al, 1981).

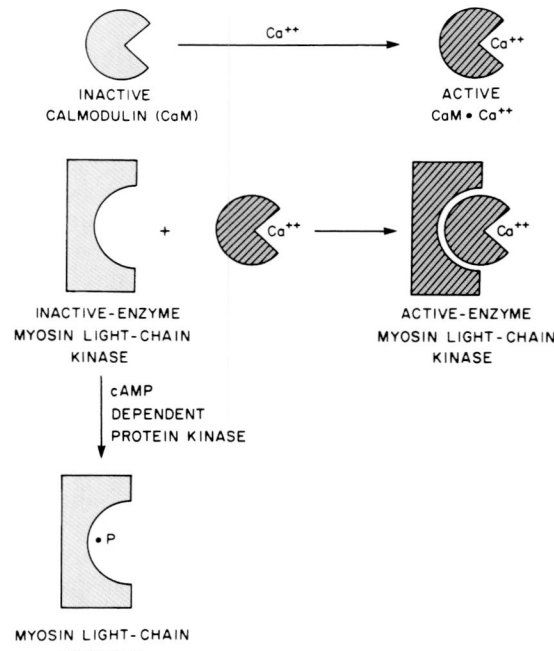

Figure 55–8. Schematic representation of the contractile process in smooth muscle. Calmodulin is activated by Ca^{2+}. The activated calcium-calmodulin complex activates the enzyme myosin light-chain kinase, which phosphorylates the light chain of myosin. Phosphorylation of myosin light-chain kinase decreases the rate of activation of the enzyme by the Ca^{2+}-calmodulin complex.

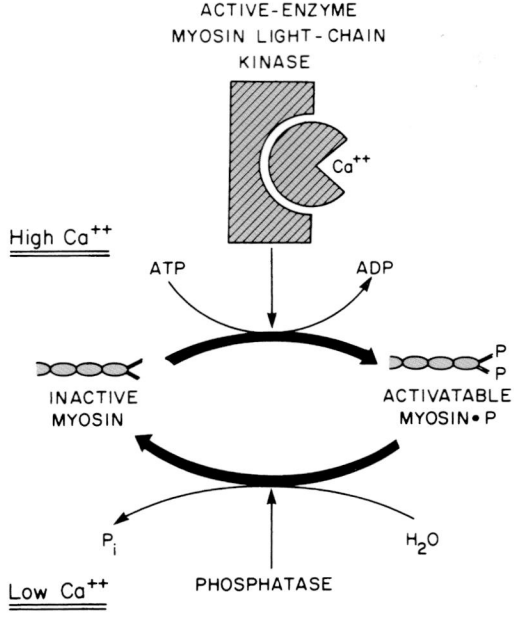

Figure 55–9. Schematic representation of the contractile process in smooth muscle. The activated enzyme myosin light-chain kinase catalyzes the phosphorylation of myosin. Myosin must be phosphorylated for actin to activate myosin adenosine triphosphatase.

Although Ca^{2+} is required for most smooth muscle contractile events, there is evidence in some smooth muscles, including rabbit and human bladder, that Ca^{2+}-independent contractions can occur (Yoshimura and Yamaguchi, 1997). Carbachol, a muscarinic cholinergic agonist, and phorbol ester, which activates protein kinase C (PKC), can induce contraction in Ca^{2+}-depleted bladder strips that can be inhibited by a PKC inhibitor, H7. It is suggested that activation of PKC coupled with agonist stimulation of the muscarinic receptor can induce a Ca^{2+}-independent contraction.

Calcium and Excitation-Contraction Coupling

The mechanical event of ureteral peristalsis follows an electrical event to which it is related. The Ca^{2+} involved in the ureteral contraction is derived from two main sources. Because smooth muscle cells have a very small diameter, the **inward movement of extracellular Ca^{2+} into the cell through L-type Ca^{2+} channels during the upstroke of the action potential provides a significant source of sarcoplasmic Ca^{2+}** (Brading et al, 1983; Hertle and Nawrath, 1989; Yoshida et al, 1992; Maggi et al, 1994a; Maggi and Giuliani, 1995) (see Fig. 55–7). This inward movement across the cell membrane is the major source of calcium used for contraction in most smooth muscles. Na^+-Ca^{2+} exchange, with an outward movement of Na^+ and an inward movement of Ca^{2+}, also plays a role in the ureteral contraction (Lamont et al, 1998). Furthermore, in response to an excitatory impulse, Ca^{2+} release from tightly bound storage sites (i.e., the endoplasmic or sarcoplasmic reticulum) also increases the Ca^{2+} concentration in the sarcoplasm (Burdyga et al, 1998; Burdyga and Wray, 1999a; Lang et al, 2002b). Calcium may be released from the sarcoplasmic

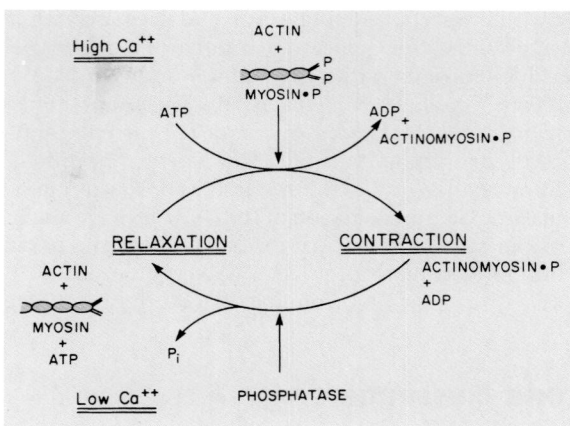

Figure 55–10. Schematic representation of the contractile process in smooth muscle. Actin activates adenosine triphosphatase activity of phosphorylated myosin. This allows interaction of actin and myosin with the development of a contraction.

reticulum (SR) of smooth muscle by an inositol trisphosphate (IP_3)–induced release mechanism or by Ca^{2+}-induced Ca^{2+} release (CICR) (Somlyo and Somlyo, 1994).

These processes appear to be species dependent. CICR that involves ryanodine receptors appears to be the sole mechanism for calcium release from the SR in the guinea pig ureter, whereas the SR store in the rat ureter appears to be exclusively under the control of IP_3 receptors (Burdyga et al, 1995). In addition to providing a source of calcium for contraction, Ca^{2+} released from the SR activates Ca^{2+}-sensitive surface membrane channels and modulates membrane excitability (Imaizumi et al, 1989; Carl et al, 1996). Both calcium-activated outward potassium currents (K_{Ca}) or STOCs (spontaneous transient outward currents) and calcium-activated inward chloride currents (Cl_{Ca}) or STICs (spontaneous transient inward currents) have been identified in smooth muscles. These currents affect membrane potential and thus affect calcium entry through L-type Ca^{2+} channels in the membrane. The Ca^{2+}-activated chloride currents are present in rat but not guinea pig ureteral smooth muscle. (Burdyga and Wray, 2002).

Support for utilization of a dual source of Ca^{2+} in the ureter has been provided by Vereecken and coworkers (1975), who noted that it took approximately 45 minutes for spontaneous contractions of isolated guinea pig ureters to cease when the tissue was placed in a Ca^{2+}-free medium. They interpreted this to indicate that some of the Ca^{2+} involved in the contractile process is derived from tightly bound intracellular stores. They also noted that recovery of the contractile response to electrical stimuli was almost immediate when the tissue was returned to a physiologic solution containing a normal concentration of Ca^{2+}. This suggests that free extracellular Ca^{2+} entering the cell during excitation also provides a source of Ca^{2+} for the contractile machinery. A similar conclusion was reached by Hong and associates (1985). There is, however, some evidence that Ca^{2+} release from the SR may not play a significant role in ureteral contractions, at least in the guinea pig (Maggi et al, 1994a, 1995, 1996), and some perturbations of contractility may be related to movements of ions other than Ca^{2+}. The increase in developed force in the guinea pig ureter with intracellular acidification and decrease with intracellular alkalinization appear to result from modulation of outward K^+ currents rather than effects on inward Ca^{2+} currents (Smith et al, 1998). That is, alkalinization (increasing intracellular pH) enhances outward K^+ currents and this reduces excitability, and acidification has the opposite effect. Relaxation results from a decrease in the concentration of free sarcoplasmic Ca^{2+} in the region of the contractile proteins. The decrease in sarcoplasmic Ca^{2+} can result from the uptake of Ca^{2+} into intracellular storage sites (Maggi et al, 1994a, 1995) or from extrusion of Ca^{2+} from the cell (Burdyga and Magura, 1988).

Second Messengers

The functional response to a number of hormones, neurotransmitters, and other agents is mediated by means of *second messengers*. The agonist, or first messenger, interacts with a specific membrane-bound receptor (Alquist, 1948; Furchgott, 1964); the agonist-receptor complex then activates or inactivates an enzyme that leads to alteration of an amount of a second messenger within the cell. These **second messengers include cAMP, cyclic guanosine monophosphate (cGMP), Ca^{2+}, inositol 1,4,5-trisphosphate (IP_3), and diacylglycerol (DG).** They mediate the functional response to the agonist (first messenger) through a process that frequently involves protein phosphorylation.

Although relaxation of smooth muscle may occur independently of changes in cyclic nucleotides (Vesin and Harbon, 1974), cAMP is believed to mediate the relaxing effects of β-adrenergic agonists in a variety of smooth muscles (Triner et al, 1971; Andersson, 1972). According to this concept, a β-adrenergic agonist, such as isoproterenol, serves as the first messenger and combines with a receptor on the outer surface of the cell membrane (Fig. 55–11). Isoproterenol itself does not enter the cell. The **β-adrenergic agonist-receptor** complex activates the enzyme adenylyl cyclase on the inner surface of the cell membrane in close morphologic relation to the receptor. **In the presence of magnesium (Mg^{2+}) and a guanine nucleotide (GTP), adenylyl cyclase catalyzes the conversion within the cell of ATP to cAMP.**

$$\text{ATP} \xrightarrow[\text{Mg}^{2+}, \text{GTP}]{\text{adenylyl cyclase}} \text{cAMP}$$

A stimulatory guanine nucleotide regulatory protein, or G protein (G_S), acts as a functional communication between the agonist-receptor complex and the catalytic or active unit of the enzyme adenylyl cyclase. cAMP acts as a second, or "internal," messenger of the response elicited by the β-adrenergic agonist. It has been suggested that the increase in cAMP through activation of an enzyme, that is, a protein kinase, and phosphorylation of proteins leads to the uptake of Ca^{2+} into intracellular storage sites (i.e., the endoplasmic reticulum or SR) with the resultant decrease of free sarcoplasmic Ca^{2+} in the region of the contractile proteins (Andersson and Nilsson, 1972). The decrease in sarcoplasmic Ca^{2+} in the region of the contractile proteins leads to relaxation of the smooth muscle.

cAMP levels may be increased within the cell in two ways. One is by increasing synthesis, which involves activation of the enzyme adenylyl cyclase; the other is by decreasing degrada-

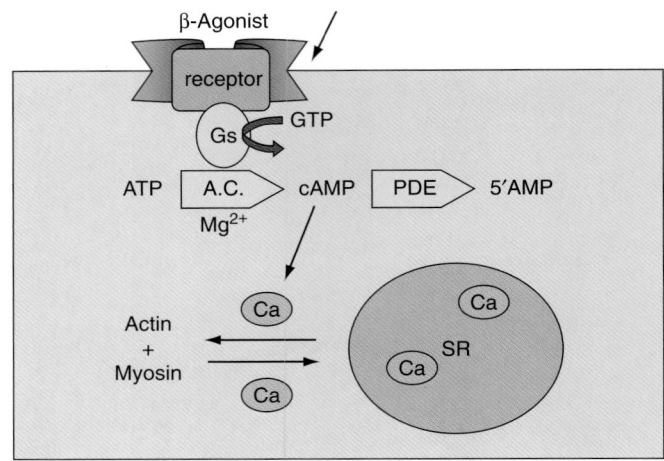

Figure 55–11. Schematic representation of the role of cyclic adenosine monophosphate (cAMP) in β-adrenergic agonist–induced relaxation of smooth muscle. Agonist combines with receptor on the outer side of the cell membrane. The receptor-agonist complex, in turn, through a stimulatory G protein, G_s, activates the enzyme adenylyl cyclase (A.C.) on the inner surface of the cell membrane, which in the presence of Mg^{2+} GTP results in the conversion of ATP to cAMP. cAMP is postulated to cause increased uptake of Ca^{2+} into intracellular storage sites with a resultant decrease in Ca^{2+} in the region of the contractile proteins that results in relaxation. cAMP may also have other actions (not shown) that inhibit the contractile process. The enzyme phosphodiesterase (PDE) degrades cAMP to 5'AMP. SR, sarcoplasmic reticulum.

tion. **The degradation of cAMP involves activation of an enzyme, a phosphodiesterase:**

$$\text{cAMP} \xrightarrow{\text{phosphodiesterase}} 5'\text{AMP}$$

Thus, agents that either increase adenylyl cyclase activity, such as the β-adrenergic agonist isoproterenol, or decrease phosphodiesterase activity, that is, phosphodiesterase inhibitors such as theophylline and papaverine, increase intracellular cAMP levels and cause smooth muscle relaxation.

Weiss and associates (1977) demonstrated the presence of both adenylyl cyclase and phosphodiesterase activities in the ureter. They showed in the ureter that isoproterenol stimulates adenylyl cyclase activity and theophylline inhibits phosphodiesterase activity. These two agents that relax ureteral smooth muscle would be expected to increase cAMP levels—isoproterenol by increasing synthesis and theophylline by decreasing degradation. Further support of **a role for cAMP in smooth muscle relaxation** can be derived from the finding that dibutyryl cAMP, which more readily diffuses into the intact cell and is less likely to be broken down by phosphodiesterase than is cAMP, has been shown to relax a variety of smooth muscles, including the ureter (Takago et al, 1971; Wheeler et al, 1990) and forskolin that activates the catalytic subunit of adenylyl cyclase relaxes the ureter (Wheeler et al, 1986; Hernández et al, 2004).

In addition to receptors and G proteins that are involved in stimulation of adenylyl cyclase and the formation of cAMP, as in the actions of β-adrenergic agonists, other receptors and G proteins inhibit adenylyl cyclase activity (Londos et al, 1981). Some actions of α_2-adrenergic and muscarinic cholinergic agonists involve stimulation of inhibitory G proteins (G_i) with subsequent inhibition of adenylyl cyclase activity.

Another cyclic nucleotide, **cGMP, can also cause smooth muscle relaxation. The cGMP is synthesized from GTP by the enzyme guanylyl cyclase and is degraded to 5'-GMP by a phosphodiesterase.** Phosphodiesterase activity that can degrade both cAMP and cGMP has been demonstrated in the canine ureter, and various inhibitors can preferentially inhibit the breakdown of one or the other cyclic nucleotide (Weiss et al, 1981; Stief et al, 1995). Insulin has been shown to activate cAMP phosphodiesterase activity in the ureter (Weiss and Wheeler, 1988), and 8-bromo-cGMP has been shown to cause relaxation of a number of smooth muscles (Schultz et al, 1979), including the ureter (Cho et al, 1984).

Nitric oxide (NO) stimulates soluble guanylyl cyclase activity and causes smooth muscle relaxation (Dokita et al, 1991, 1994). **Nitric oxide synthase (NOS) converts L-arginine to NO and L-citrulline in a reaction that requires reduced nicotinamide adenine dinucleotide phosphate (NADPH). There are three NOS isoforms. Neuronal NOS (nNOS) is present in neuronal tissues and is Ca^{2+} and NADPH dependent** (Bredt and Snyder, 1990). It is thought that with neuronal excitation, there is an increase in Ca^{2+} concentration within nerves that leads to the synthesis of NO from L-arginine. **NO released from the nerve activates the enzyme guanylyl cyclase in the smooth muscle cell with the resultant conversion of GTP to cGMP and smooth muscle relaxation** (Fig. 55–12). It also is possible that a yet-to-be-determined neurotransmitter is released from the neuron that stimulates NO production in the smooth muscle cell, which in turn leads to cGMP formation and smooth muscle relaxation. **Endothelial NOS (eNOS) is also Ca^{2+} and NADPH dependent** (Sessa, 1994). Like nNOS, eNOS produces small amounts of NO for prolonged periods of time. An **inducible NOS isoform (iNOS) is NADPH dependent but Ca^{2+} independent** and has been identified in ureteral smooth muscle (Smith et al, 1993). iNOS produces larger amounts of NO for short periods of time.

NOS-containing nerves have been demonstrated in the human ureter (Stief et al, 1993, 1996; Goessl et al, 1995), and NOS has been demonstrated in the pig UVJ (Phillips et al, 1995) and the upper ureter and calyces of pigs and humans (Iselin et al, 1998, 1999). NOS colocalizes with vasoactive polypeptide and neuropeptide Y (NPY) in nerves supplying the human ureter including the intravesical segment (Smet et al, 1994; Iselin et al, 1997). NOS appears to localize to parasympathetic and sensory nerves but not to adrenergic neurons. In primary cultures of rat ureteral cells, NO production was detected in urothelial but not in smooth muscle cells (Mastrangelo et al, 2003). These cells contain both eNOS and iNOS.

There is evidence that the NO pathway is involved in human ureteral relaxation (Stief et al, 1996; Iselin et al, 1997). The NO donor SIN-1 relaxes human ureteral segments, an action that is inhibited by the **guanylyl cyclase inhibitor methylene blue.** NO donors also inhibit agonist-induced contractions of isolated pig calyceal and rat, pig, and human intravesical ureteral segments, an action that is associated with an increase in cGMP. Furthermore, NO has been shown to be involved in nonadrenergic, noncholinergic–induced relaxation of the pig UVJ (Hernández et al, 1995). There is also evidence that adenosine relaxes the pig intravesical ureter through a process independent of NO (Hernández et al, 1999).

Some actions of **α₁-adrenergic and muscarinic cholinergic agonists** and a number of other hormones, neurotransmitters, and biologic substances are associated with an increase in intracellular Ca^{2+} and are related to changes in inositol lipid metabolism. These agonists **combine with a receptor on the cell membrane, and the agonist-receptor complex, in turn, activates an enzyme, phospholipase C, that leads to the hydrolysis of polyphosphatidylinositol 4,5-bisphosphate with the formation of two second messengers, IP_3 and DG** (Berridge, 1984) (Fig. 55–13). The activation of phospholipase C involves a G protein. **IP_3 mobilizes Ca^{2+} from intracellular stores (i.e., endoplasmic or sarcoplasmic reticulum)** with an initiation of a cascade of events through the calmodulin branch of the Ca^{2+} messenger system. In smooth muscles, **IP_3 is thought to be involved in brief contractile responses or in the initial phase of sustained responses** (Park and Rasmussen, 1985).

The other second messenger, **DG, binds to an enzyme, PKC,** translocates to the cell membrane, and, by reducing the concentration of Ca^{2+} required for PKC activation, results in an increase in this enzyme's activity. The **actions of PKC and thus DG involve the phosphorylation of proteins** (Nishizuka, 1984). The **PKC branch of the Ca^{2+} messenger system is thought to be responsible for the sustained phase of the contractile response in smooth muscle** (Park and Rasmussen, 1985) and is responsive to hormonally induced changes in intracellular Ca^{2+}. PKC has been implicated in Ca^{2+}-independent smooth muscle contractions (Yoshimura and Yamaguchi, 1997). Numerous PKC isoforms have been identified. The functional activity and specificity of function of these isoforms appear to be determined primarily by the state of phosphorylation of the isoenzyme and its subcellular localization (Dempsey et al, 2000).

DG also activates the enzyme phospholipase A, which serves as a source of arachidonic acid, the substrate for prostaglandin synthesis (Mahadevappa and Holub, 1983). Arachidonic acid, in turn, may stimulate guanylyl cyclase activity with the

CONSTITUTIVE NOS

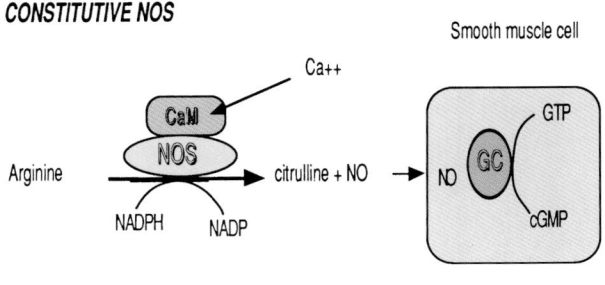

INDUCIBLE NOS

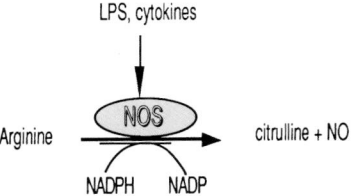

Figure 55–12. Schematic representation of inducible and constitutive nitric oxide synthase (NOS). CaM, calmodulin; GC; guanylyl cyclase; LPS, lipopolysaccharide.

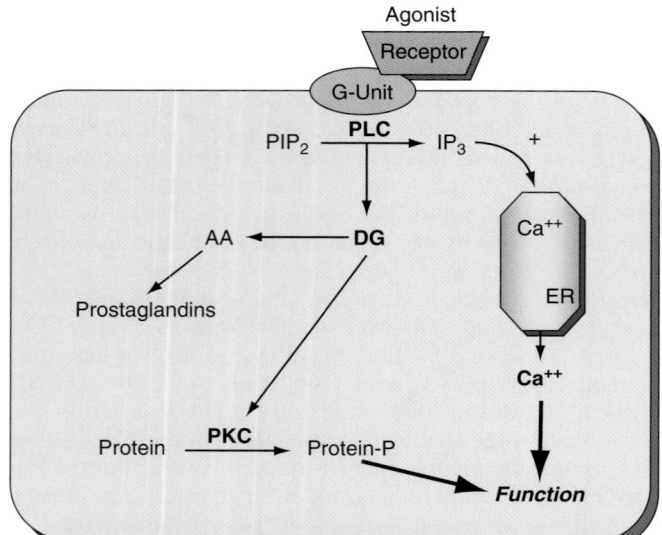

Figure 55–13. Schematic representation of the role of inositol lipid metabolism in smooth muscle function. The agonist combines with the receptor on the outer side of the cell membrane. The receptor-agonist complex in turn activates the enzyme phospholipase C (PLC), which leads to the hydrolysis of polyphosphatidylinositol 4,5-bisphosphate (PIP_2), with the formation of two second messengers, inositol 1,4,5-trisphosphate (IP_3) and diacylglycerol (DG). The activation of PLC involves a G protein. IP_3 mobilizes calcium from intracellular stores (i.e., endoplasmic reticulum), and this leads to a functional response. DG binds to an enzyme, protein kinase C (PKC), that results in phosphorylation of proteins and a subsequent functional response. AA, arachidonic acid; ER, endoplasmic reticulum.

subsequent formation of cGMP (Berridge, 1984), and this would explain the Ca^{2+}-dependent increase in cGMP levels associated with muscarinic cholinergic and α_1-adrenergic agonist–induced contractions in smooth muscle. The observed increases in cGMP levels follow, rather than precede, the onset of contractions induced by these agonists.

Thus, a group of second messengers are involved in the transduction of the signal that is initiated when an agonist combines with a specific receptor on the cell membrane of the smooth muscle. This process of **signal transduction** ultimately results in the functional response to the agonist.

MECHANICAL PROPERTIES

Mechanical characteristics of muscle are commonly assessed by defining force-length and force-velocity relations. Isometric force-length measurements depend on the number of linkages between the contractile proteins, actin and myosin, that are brought into action during contraction. Force-velocity relations depend on the rate of formation and breakdown of linkages between the contractile proteins. Interventions may affect force-velocity relations with or without affecting force-length relations. In addition to these methods of assessing mechanical properties of the ureter, the bidimensional nature of the ureter has lent itself to studies of pressure-length-diameter relations.

Force-Length Relations

Force-length relations express the relation between the force developed by muscle when it is stimulated under isometric

conditions and the resting length of the muscle at the time of stimulation. With stretching of the ureter (muscle lengthening), the resting force (i.e., the tension present when the muscle is not excited) increases at a progressive rate (Weiss et al, 1972). The force developed during isometric contraction also increases with elongation until a length is reached at which the maximal contractile force is achieved. With further lengthening, the developed force decreases (Weiss et al, 1972; Thulesius et al, 1989). The ureter at this length is overstretched or beyond the peak of its force-length curve. Ureteral resting tension is high at the length at which maximal contractile force is developed.

Because the ureter is a viscoelastic structure (Weiss et al, 1972), **the resting or contractile force developed at any given length depends on the direction in which the change in length is occurring and on the rate of length change** (Weiss et al, 1972; Vereecken et al, 1973). **This is referred to as hysteresis;** for the ureter, at any given length, the resting force is less and the contractile force is greater when the ureter is allowed to shorten than when the ureter is being stretched (Fig. 55–14).

When the ureter is stretched, the resting force increases. If the length is kept constant at its new longer length after a stretch, changes occur that result in a decrease in the resting force, or stress relaxation (Fig. 55–15) (Weiss et al, 1972). Within certain limits, when the ureter is stretched to a length beyond the peak of the force-length curve, that is, when the ureter is stretched to a length at which the contractile force declines in the presence of increasing muscle length, the degree of stress relaxation may be such that, within a period

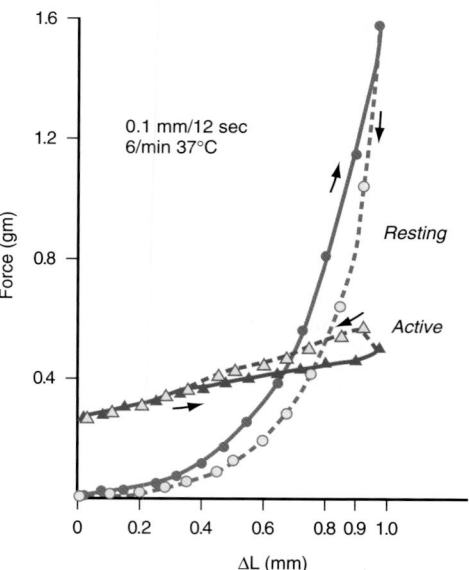

Figure 55–14. Hysteresis. Resting and contractile (active) force of cat ureter during muscle lengthening and shortening. Force is on the ordinate; change in length (ΔL) is on the abscissa. *Solid symbols* and *solid lines* show data obtained during muscle lengthening. *Open symbols* and *dashed lines* show data obtained during muscle shortening. *Circles* show resting force, and *triangles* show active or contractile force. Length and the direction of length change influence resting and contractile force. (From Weiss RM, Bassett AL, Hoffman BF: Dynamic length-tension curves of cat ureter. Am J Physiol 1972;222:388.)

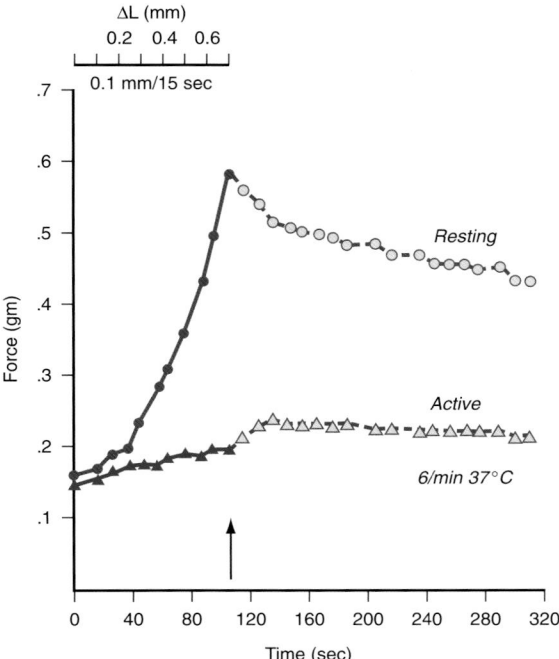

Figure 55–15. Stress relaxation. The resting and contractile (active) force of cat ureter is on the ordinate, the time from the onset of stretching is on the lower abscissa, and the change in length (ΔL) is on the left upper corner abscissa. Muscle is stretched by a given amount and then held at a fixed length. *Solid symbols* and *solid lines* show data obtained during muscle lengthening; *open symbols* and *dashed lines* show data obtained after stretching has ceased *(arrow)* and muscle is maintained at a constant length. Resting force decreases when muscle is held at a constant length after a stretch (stress relaxation). Contractile (active) force increases during this period of time. (From Weiss RM, Bassett AL, Hoffman BF: Dynamic length-tension curves of cat ureter. Am J Physiol 1972;222:388.)

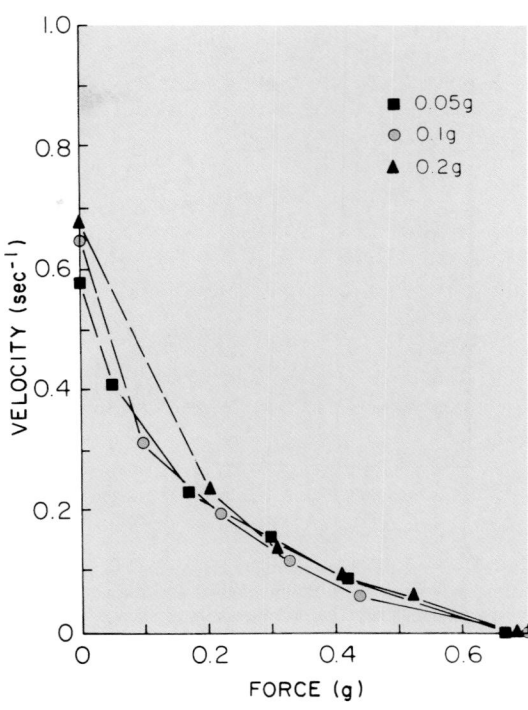

Figure 55–16. Force-velocity relation of guinea pig ureter. Specimens were stretched by three different preloads (0.05, 0.1, and 0.2 g). The velocity of shortening on the ordinate is plotted as a function of the total load lifted on the abscissa. V_{max} is obtained by extrapolating the experimental curves to intersect the ordinate. Isometric force is given by data points where velocity equals zero. (From Biancani P, Onyski JH, Zabinski MP, Weiss RM: Force-velocity relationships of the pig ureter. J Urol 1984;131:988.)

of time, the developed force no longer declines, even though the increased length is kept constant (Weiss et al, 1972). Stress relaxation can thus be considered a compensatory mechanism of a viscoelastic structure to stretch.

Force-Velocity Relations

Force-velocity curves depict the relation between the load and the velocity of shortening. A typical force-velocity curve, as predicted by Hill's equation for muscle shortening, has a hyperbolic configuration (Fig. 55–16) (Hill, 1938). From the force-velocity curve, one can extrapolate the **maximal velocity of shortening (V_{max}),** which **represents the velocity of shortening at zero load (i.e., at isotonic conditions).** V_{max} is determined by the level at which the force-velocity curve crosses the ordinate. V_{max} values in the ureter are in the range of 0.5 to 0.7 length per second (Biancani et al, 1984). The force-velocity curve intersects the abscissa at zero shortening, that is, at isometric conditions at which the load is great. Shortening depends on the total load lifted, with the ureter shortening to a lesser extent with heavier loads. At conditions near those of zero load, that is, conditions of free shortening (isotonic conditions), the in vitro guinea pig ureter shortens by 25% to 30% of its initial length (Biancani et al, 1984).

Pressure-Length-Diameter Relations

Because ureteral muscle fibers are arranged in a longitudinal, circumferential, and spiral configuration (Tanagho, 1971), longitudinal and diametral deformations of the ureter are interrelated. Simultaneous studies of length and diameter changes in response to an intraluminal pressure load are another means of assessing the mechanical properties of a tubular structure. After application of an intraluminal pressure, the ureter increases in both length and diameter, a process known as *creep* (Biancani et al, 1973). Deformation in response to a given intraluminal pressure load is greater in vitro than in vivo; this difference is partially negated if the in vivo preparation is pretreated with reserpine to suppress adrenergic influences (Fig. 55–17). Such data provide support for a role of the adrenergic nervous system in the control of ureteral function.

ROLE OF THE NERVOUS SYSTEM IN URETERAL FUNCTION

Some smooth muscles have a specific innervation of each smooth muscle fiber, whereas other, syncytial-type, smooth muscles lack discrete neuromuscular junctions and depend on a diffuse release of transmitter from a bundle of nerves with a subsequent spread of excitation from one muscle cell to another (Burnstock, 1970). **The ureter is a syncytial type of**

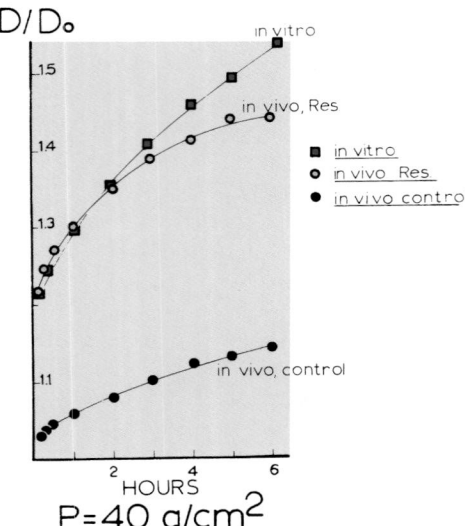

Figure 55–17. Pressure-diameter relations. An intraluminal pressure (p) load of 40 g/cm^2 is applied to rabbit ureters, and the change in diameter (D/D$_0$) is measured as a function of time. *Squares* show data obtained from in vitro ureters. *Closed circles* show data obtained in vivo. *Open circles* show data obtained in vivo from animals previously treated with reserpine. D$_0$, initial diameter; D, diameter during deformation.

smooth muscle without discrete neuromuscular junctions (Burnstock, 1970).

Because peristalsis may persist after transplantation (O'Conor and Dawson-Edwards, 1959) or denervation (Wharton, 1932), because spontaneous activity may occur in isolated in vitro ureteral segments (Finberg and Peart, 1970), and because normal antegrade peristalsis continues after reversal of a segment of ureter in situ (Melick et al, 1961), it is apparent that **ureteral peristalsis can occur without innervation.** However, analysis of the data in the literature clearly indicates that the **nervous system plays at least a modulating role in ureteral peristalsis.** Morita and colleagues (1987) have provided evidence that the autonomic nervous system may affect urine transport through the ureter by affecting both peristaltic frequency and bolus volume. Catecholamine fluorescence and acetylcholine (ACh) release studies indicate that the human ureter is supplied by sympathetic (noradrenaline-containing) and parasympathetic (ACh-containing) neurons (Duarte-Escalante et al, 1969; DelTacca, 1978).

Parasympathetic Nervous System

Although the role of the parasympathetic nervous system in the control of ureteral peristalsis has not been well defined, muscarinic cholinergic receptors have been demonstrated in the ureter (Latifpour et al, 1989, 1990; Hernández et al, 1993), and acetylcholinesterase-positive nerve fibers have been demonstrated in the equine ureter (Prieto et al, 1994). The cholinergic innervation is especially rich in the distal and intravesical ureter (Hernández et al, 1993). Furthermore, ACh has been shown to be released from isolated guinea pig, rabbit, and human ureters in response to electrical field stimulation (DelTacca, 1978), and this release is inhibited by the neural poison tetrodotoxin. These data suggest but do not prove that the parasympathetic nervous system has at least a modulatory role in the control of ureteral activity.

The prototypic cholinergic agonist is ACh, which serves as the neurotransmitter at (1) neuromuscular junctions of somatic motor nerves (nicotinic sites), (2) preganglionic parasympathetic and sympathetic neuroeffector junctions (nicotinic sites), and (3) postganglionic parasympathetic neuroeffector sites (muscarinic sites). ACh synthesis involves

$$\text{acetyl CoA} + \text{choline} \xrightarrow[\text{acetyltransferase}]{\text{choline}} \text{Ach}$$

where CoA is coenzyme A. The ACh is stored in vesicles within the synaptic terminal; its release depends on the influx of Ca^{2+} into the terminal, which presumably causes vesicle fusion with the presynaptic terminal membrane, thereby expelling ACh into the synaptic cleft. ACh is subsequently hydrolyzed by acetylcholinesterase. The muscarinic effects of cholinergic agonists can be blocked by atropine. The effects of nicotinic agonists can be blocked by nondepolarizing ganglionic blocking agents or by high concentrations of the nicotinic agonist itself, which may cause ganglionic blockade by desensitization of receptor sites after an initial period of ganglionic stimulation.

Cholinergic Agonists

Cholinergic agonists, including ACh, methacholine (Mecholyl), carbamylcholine (carbachol), and bethanechol (Urecholine), in general have been observed to have an excitatory effect on ureteral and renal pelvic function, that is, to increase the frequency and force of contractions (Vereecken, 1973; Longrigg, 1974; Rose and Gillenwater, 1974; Morita et al, 1986, 1987; Maggi and Giuliani, 1992; Hernández et al, 1993; Prieto et al, 1994). The excitatory effect of carbachol on isolated canine ureter has been thought to be mediated by the M3 receptor subtype, and carbachol-induced inhibition of KCl-induced contractions of longitudinal canine ureteral preparations appears to be mediated primarily by the M4 receptor subtype (Tomiyama et al, 2003b). ACh has also been shown to increase the duration of the guinea pig and rat ureteral action potential (Prosser et al, 1955; Ichikawa and Ikeda, 1960) and the number of oscillations on the plateau of the guinea pig ureteral action potential (Ichikawa and Ikeda, 1960). **The excitatory effects of cholinergic agonists may be related to an indirect release of catecholamines**—supported by the findings that the excitatory effects of bethanechol can be blocked by the α-adrenergic blocking agent phentolamine (Rose and Gillenwater, 1974) and that the increased frequency of canine ureteral peristalsis induced by ACh can be blocked by adrenalectomy (Labay et al, 1968)—or to a direct effect of the drug on muscarinic receptors (Vereecken, 1973; Hernández et al, 1993; Tomiyama et al, 2003b).

Nicotinic agonists, such as nicotine, tetramethylammonium, and dimethylphenylpiperazine, cause an initial stimulation of nicotinic receptors followed by desensitization of the receptor sites; the receptors then become unresponsive to nicotinic agonists and also to endogenous ACh, with a resultant transmission blockade. Nicotine, as would be expected, has been shown to have excitatory (Boyarsky et al, 1968), biphasic (Satani, 1919; Labay and Boyarsky, 1967), or inhibitory (Prosser et al, 1955; Vereecken, 1973) actions on the ureter that may be dose dependent.

Anticholinesterases

Anticholinesterases prevent the hydrolysis of ACh by cholinesterases and thus increase the duration and intensity of ACh action at both muscarinic and nicotinic receptor sites. With prolonged administration in high doses, they can result in desensitization blockade at nicotinic sites. The effects of **anticholinesterases**, such as **physostigmine and neostigmine**, parallel the excitatory effects of ACh and other parasympathomimetics on the ureter (Satani, 1919; Vereecken, 1973).

Parasympathetic Blocking Agents

Atropine is a competitive antagonist of the muscarinic effects of ACh. The inhibitory effects of atropine may be preceded by a transitory stimulatory effect on muscarinic receptors. Although atropine has been shown to inhibit the excitatory effects of parasympathomimetic agents (Vereecken, 1973; Longrigg, 1974) and physostigmine (Macht, 1916a) on a variety of ureteral and calyceal preparations, the majority of studies have shown that **atropine itself has little direct effect on ureteral activity in a number of species** (Gibbs, 1929; Gould et al, 1955; Butcher et al, 1957; Washizu, 1967; Vereecken, 1973; Reid et al, 1976), including humans (Kiil, 1957). **Even when atropine has been observed to inhibit ureteral activity, its effects are frequently minimal and inconsistent** (Ross et al, 1967), **thus providing little rationale for its use in the treatment of ureteral colic.**

Reports of the direct effects on ureteral activity of two other parasympathetic blocking agents, methantheline (Banthīne) and propantheline (Pro-Banthīne), have also been inconsistent (Draper and Zorgniotti, 1954; Kiil, 1957; Reid et al, 1976).

Sympathetic Nervous System

The sympathetic nervous system appears to modulate ureteral activity as evidenced by the demonstration of adrenergic receptors in the ureter (Latifpour et al, 1989, 1990), the identification of catecholaminergic neurons in the ureter as determined by labeling tyrosine hydroxylase as a marker (Edyvane et al, 1994), and the demonstration that catecholamines are released from the ureter (Weiss et al, 1978) and renal calyx (Longrigg, 1975) in response to electrical field stimulation.

The ureter contains excitatory α-adrenergic and inhibitory β-adrenergic receptors (McLeod et al, 1973; Rose and Gillenwater, 1974; Weiss et al, 1978) that have been demonstrated with receptor-binding techniques (Latifpour et al, 1989, 1990). **Norepinephrine, primarily an α-adrenergic agonist** (although it also can stimulate β-adrenergic receptors), increases the force of electrically induced ureteral contractions (Weiss et al, 1978). When administered in the presence of **phentolamine** (Regitine), **an α-adrenergic blocking agent,** norepinephrine decreases the force of ureteral contractions (Weiss et al, 1978). A similar reversal of action occurs in the in vivo ureter (McLeod et al, 1973) and can be explained by norepinephrine's primary action on inhibitory β-adrenergic receptors when the excitatory α-adrenergic receptors are blocked. Propranolol (Inderal), a β-adrenergic antagonist, potentiates the increase in contractile force induced by norepinephrine (Weiss et al, 1978). This can be explained by norepinephrine's acting more exclusively on excitatory α-

adrenergic receptors when the inhibitory β-adrenergic receptors are blocked. Furthermore, **isoproterenol, a β-adrenergic agonist**, depresses contractility (Weiss et al, 1978). These data provide evidence for excitatory α-adrenergic and inhibitory β-adrenergic receptors in the ureter and are in accord with the observations of McLeod and associates (1973) and Rose and Gillenwater (1974) on in vivo ureters.

Further support for the presence of excitatory α-adrenergic and inhibitory β-adrenergic receptors in the ureter includes the demonstration of adenylyl cyclase activity in the ureter (Weiss et al, 1977; Wheeler et al, 1986) and the finding that the ureters of rabbits depleted of catecholamines by the administration of reserpine undergo greater degrees of deformation when a given intraluminal pressure is applied than would result from the application of the same pressure load to the ureters of normal, non–reserpine-treated animals (see Fig. 55–17) (Weiss et al, 1974). Finally, electrical stimulation with high-intensity, high-frequency, short-duration stimuli has been shown to release neurotransmitter, presumably from intrinsic neural tissue within the wall of the ureter (Weiss et al, 1978) and renal calyx (Longrigg, 1975).

Adrenergic Agonists

Norepinephrine, the chemical mediator responsible for adrenergic transmission, is synthesized in the neuron from tyrosine. After its release from the nerve terminal, some of the norepinephrine combines with receptors in the effector organ, leading to a physiologic response. The greatest percentage of the norepinephrine is actively taken up (reuptake or neuronal uptake) into the neuron. Neuronal reuptake regulates the duration of norepinephrine contact with the innervated tissue and thus regulates the magnitude and duration of the catecholamine-induced response. Agents such as cocaine and imipramine (Tofranil), which inhibit neuronal uptake, potentiate the physiologic response to norepinephrine. The enzymes monoamine oxidase and catechol-O-methyltransferase provide degradative pathways for norepinephrine.

According to the general consensus, **agents that primarily activate α-adrenergic receptors, such as norepinephrine and phenylephrine, tend to stimulate ureteral and renal pelvic activity** (McLeod et al, 1973; Vereecken, 1973; Hannappel and Golenhofen, 1974; Rose and Gillenwater, 1974; Hernández et al, 1992; Rivera et al, 1992; Danuser et al, 2001), and **agents that primarily activate β-adrenergic receptors, such as isoproterenol and orciprenaline, tend to inhibit ureteral and renal pelvic activity** (Finberg and Peart, 1970; Ancill et al, 1972; McLeod et al, 1973; Vereecken, 1973; Hannappel and Golenhofen, 1974; Rose and Gillenwater, 1974; Weiss et al, 1978; Hernández et al, 1992; Rivera et al, 1992; Danuser et al, 2001). The β-adrenergic subtypes involved in ureteral relaxation are species specific: β_1-adrenoceptors in rat, β_2-adrenoceptors in rabbit, mainly β_3-adrenoceptors in dog, and β_2- and β_3-adrenoceptors in pig and human (Tomiyama et al, 1998; Park et al, 2000; Tomiyama et al, 2003a; Wanajo et al, 2004). In rabbit renal pelvis, β_2-adrenergic agonists inhibit contractile activity of the distal renal pelvis and β_1-adrenergic agonists potentiate contractile activity of the proximal renal pelvis (Kondo et al, 1989). Tyramine, whose adrenergic agonist effects are due primarily to the release of norepinephrine from adrenergic terminals, also has a stimulatory effect on the upper urinary tract (Boyarsky and Labay, 1969; Finberg and

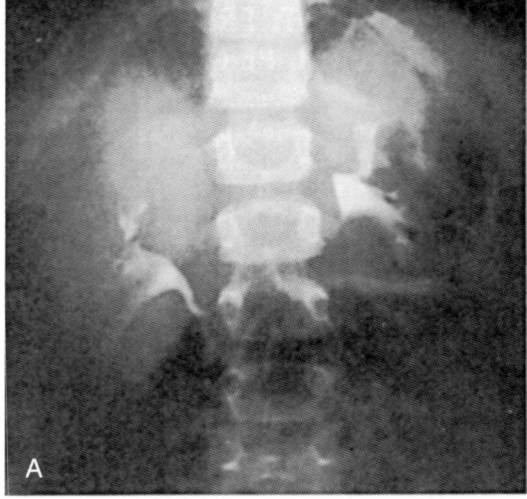

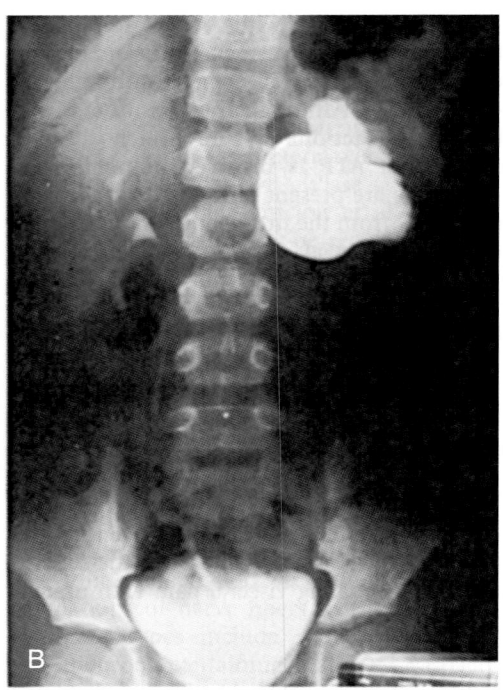

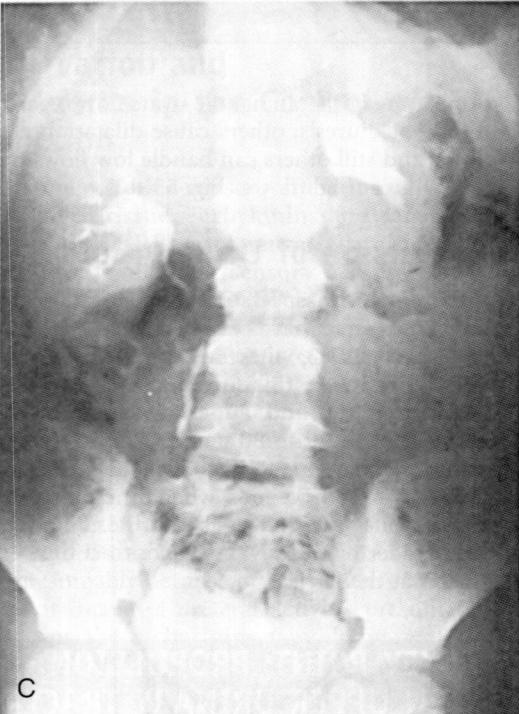

Figure 55–18. **A,** Intravenous pyelogram (IVP) shows essentially normal upper urinary tracts. **B,** Film from the same child taken immediately after a cardiac angiogram, which produces a massive diuresis. **C,** IVP 6 weeks after the angiogram. (**A** to **C,** From Weiss RM: Clinical implications of ureter physiology. J Urol 1979;121:401.)

As with any tubular structure, the ureter can transport a set maximal amount of fluid per unit time. Under normal flows, in which bolus formation occurs, the amount of urine transported per unit time is significantly less than the maximal transport capacity of the ureter. **At extremely high flows, as are employed in the standard perfusion studies** (Whitaker, 1973), **the ureteral walls do not coapt, and a continuous column of fluid, rather than a series of boluses, is transported.**

When transport becomes inadequate, stasis of urine occurs with resultant ureteral dilatation. Inadequate transport can result either from too much fluid entering the ureter per unit time or from too little fluid exiting the ureter per unit time. Both input and output must be considered in predicting whether or not ureteral dilatation will occur. For example, a

minor degree of obstruction to outflow causes more dilatation at high flow rates than at low flow rates. Even a normal nonobstructed ureter impedes urine transport if the rate of flow is great enough.

Changes in ureteral dimensions that occur in pathologic states may in themselves result in inefficient urine transport, even if the contractile force of the individual fibers is unchanged. The Laplace equation expresses the relation between the variables that affect intraluminal pressure:

$$\text{Pressure} = \frac{\text{tension} \times \text{wall thickness}}{\text{radius}}$$

An increase in ureteral diameter in itself can decrease intraluminal pressure and result in inefficient urine transport. Such dimensional changes may, at least theoretically, be deleterious

Anticholinesterases

Anticholinesterases prevent the hydrolysis of ACh by cholinesterases and thus increase the duration and intensity of ACh action at both muscarinic and nicotinic receptor sites. With prolonged administration in high doses, they can result in desensitization blockade at nicotinic sites. The effects of **anticholinesterases,** such as **physostigmine and neostigmine**, parallel the excitatory effects of ACh and other parasympathomimetics on the ureter (Satani, 1919; Vereecken, 1973).

Parasympathetic Blocking Agents

Atropine is a competitive antagonist of the muscarinic effects of ACh. The inhibitory effects of atropine may be preceded by a transitory stimulatory effect on muscarinic receptors. Although atropine has been shown to inhibit the excitatory effects of parasympathomimetic agents (Vereecken, 1973; Longrigg, 1974) and physostigmine (Macht, 1916a) on a variety of ureteral and calyceal preparations, the majority of studies have shown that **atropine itself has little direct effect on ureteral activity in a number of species** (Gibbs, 1929; Gould et al, 1955; Butcher et al, 1957; Washizu, 1967; Vereecken, 1973; Reid et al, 1976), including humans (Kiil, 1957). **Even when atropine has been observed to inhibit ureteral activity, its effects are frequently minimal and inconsistent** (Ross et al, 1967), **thus providing little rationale for its use in the treatment of ureteral colic.**

Reports of the direct effects on ureteral activity of two other parasympathetic blocking agents, methantheline (Banthīne) and propantheline (Pro-Banthīne), have also been inconsistent (Draper and Zorgniotti, 1954; Kiil, 1957; Reid et al, 1976).

Sympathetic Nervous System

The sympathetic nervous system appears to modulate ureteral activity as evidenced by the demonstration of adrenergic receptors in the ureter (Latifpour et al, 1989, 1990), the identification of catecholaminergic neurons in the ureter as determined by labeling tyrosine hydroxylase as a marker (Edyvane et al, 1994), and the demonstration that catecholamines are released from the ureter (Weiss et al, 1978) and renal calyx (Longrigg, 1975) in response to electrical field stimulation.

The ureter contains excitatory α-adrenergic and inhibitory β-adrenergic receptors (McLeod et al, 1973; Rose and Gillenwater, 1974; Weiss et al, 1978) that have been demonstrated with receptor-binding techniques (Latifpour et al, 1989, 1990). **Norepinephrine, primarily an α-adrenergic agonist** (although it also can stimulate β-adrenergic receptors), increases the force of electrically induced ureteral contractions (Weiss et al, 1978). When administered in the presence of **phentolamine** (Regitine), **an α-adrenergic blocking agent,** norepinephrine decreases the force of ureteral contractions (Weiss et al, 1978). A similar reversal of action occurs in the in vivo ureter (McLeod et al, 1973) and can be explained by norepinephrine's primary action on inhibitory β-adrenergic receptors when the excitatory α-adrenergic receptors are blocked. Propranolol (Inderal), a β-adrenergic antagonist, potentiates the increase in contractile force induced by norepinephrine (Weiss et al, 1978). This can be explained by norepinephrine's acting more exclusively on excitatory α-

adrenergic receptors when the inhibitory β-adrenergic receptors are blocked. Furthermore, **isoproterenol, a β-adrenergic agonist**, depresses contractility (Weiss et al, 1978). These data provide evidence for excitatory α-adrenergic and inhibitory β-adrenergic receptors in the ureter and are in accord with the observations of McLeod and associates (1973) and Rose and Gillenwater (1974) on in vivo ureters.

Further support for the presence of excitatory α-adrenergic and inhibitory β-adrenergic receptors in the ureter includes the demonstration of adenylyl cyclase activity in the ureter (Weiss et al, 1977; Wheeler et al, 1986) and the finding that the ureters of rabbits depleted of catecholamines by the administration of reserpine undergo greater degrees of deformation when a given intraluminal pressure is applied than would result from the application of the same pressure load to the ureters of normal, non–reserpine-treated animals (see Fig. 55–17) (Weiss et al, 1974). Finally, electrical stimulation with high-intensity, high-frequency, short-duration stimuli has been shown to release neurotransmitter, presumably from intrinsic neural tissue within the wall of the ureter (Weiss et al, 1978) and renal calyx (Longrigg, 1975).

Adrenergic Agonists

Norepinephrine, the chemical mediator responsible for adrenergic transmission, is synthesized in the neuron from tyrosine. After its release from the nerve terminal, some of the norepinephrine combines with receptors in the effector organ, leading to a physiologic response. The greatest percentage of the norepinephrine is actively taken up (reuptake or neuronal uptake) into the neuron. Neuronal reuptake regulates the duration of norepinephrine contact with the innervated tissue and thus regulates the magnitude and duration of the catecholamine-induced response. Agents such as cocaine and imipramine (Tofranil), which inhibit neuronal uptake, potentiate the physiologic response to norepinephrine. The enzymes monoamine oxidase and catechol-O-methyltransferase provide degradative pathways for norepinephrine.

According to the general consensus, **agents that primarily activate α-adrenergic receptors, such as norepinephrine and phenylephrine, tend to stimulate ureteral and renal pelvic activity** (McLeod et al, 1973; Vereecken, 1973; Hannappel and Golenhofen, 1974; Rose and Gillenwater, 1974; Hernández et al, 1992; Rivera et al, 1992; Danuser et al, 2001), and **agents that primarily activate β-adrenergic receptors, such as isoproterenol and orciprenaline, tend to inhibit ureteral and renal pelvic activity** (Finberg and Peart, 1970; Ancill et al, 1972; McLeod et al, 1973; Vereecken, 1973; Hannappel and Golenhofen, 1974; Rose and Gillenwater, 1974; Weiss et al, 1978; Hernández et al, 1992; Rivera et al, 1992; Danuser et al, 2001). The β-adrenergic subtypes involved in ureteral relaxation are species specific: $β_1$-adrenoceptors in rat, $β_2$-adrenoceptors in rabbit, mainly $β_3$-adrenoceptors in dog, and $β_2$- and $β_3$-adrenoceptors in pig and human (Tomiyama et al, 1998; Park et al, 2000; Tomiyama et al, 2003a; Wanajo et al, 2004). In rabbit renal pelvis, $β_2$-adrenergic agonists inhibit contractile activity of the distal renal pelvis and $β_1$-adrenergic agonists potentiate contractile activity of the proximal renal pelvis (Kondo et al, 1989). Tyramine, whose adrenergic agonist effects are due primarily to the release of norepinephrine from adrenergic terminals, also has a stimulatory effect on the upper urinary tract (Boyarsky and Labay, 1969; Finberg and

Peart, 1970; Longrigg, 1974). The reported stimulatory effects of cocaine on ureteral activity (Boyarsky and Labay, 1969) may be explained by blockage of norepinephrine reuptake into adrenergic nerve endings, with a resultant increase in the magnitude and duration of the effect of norepinephrine.

Adrenergic Antagonists

The α-adrenergic antagonists phentolamine and phenoxybenzamine (Dibenzyline) have been shown to inhibit the stimulatory effects of norepinephrine and other α-adrenergic agonists in a variety of preparations (Finberg and Peart, 1970; Gosling and Waas, 1971; McLeod et al, 1973; Vereecken, 1973; Hannappel and Golenhofen, 1974; Longrigg, 1974; Rose and Gillenwater, 1974; Weiss et al, 1978; Hernández et al, 1992). The β-adrenergic antagonist propranolol has been shown to block or attenuate the inhibitory effects of β-adrenergic agonists, such as isoproterenol, in a variety of preparations (McLeod et al, 1973; Vereecken, 1973; Longrigg, 1974; Rose and Gillenwater, 1974; Weiss et al, 1978).

Sensory Innervation and Peptidergic Agents in the Control of Ureteral Function

Sensory nerves can play both a sensory afferent and motor efferent role in a given tissue. Tachykinins and calcitonin gene–related peptide (CGRP) are neurotransmitters released from peripheral endings of sensory nerves (Maggi, 1995). **Tachykinins stimulate and CGRP inhibits electrical and contractile activity. Capsaicin-sensitive sensory nerves are located in the ureter** (Maggi et al, 1986; Maggi and Meli, 1988; Dray et al, 1989; Ammons, 1992) and contain the tachykinins substance P, neurokinin A, and neuropeptide K (Hua et al, 1985; Sann et al, 1992), as well as CGRP (Gibbins et al, 1985; Sann et al, 1992; Tamaki et al, 1992). Immunoreactivity for tachykinins and CGRP is less in the human than in the guinea pig ureter (Su et al, 1986; Hua et al, 1987; Edvyane et al, 1992, 1994). Capsaicin in low doses inhibits ureteral activity, presumably because of the release of CGRP, but in high doses it increases ureteral activity, presumably because of release of the tachykinins neurokinin A, neuropeptide K, and substance P (Hua and Lundberg, 1986). Neonatal capsaicin administration causes degeneration of CGRP-containing sensory nerves in the rat ureter, which is accompanied by an increase in sympathetic (noradrenergic) innervation (Sann et al, 1995). As nerve growth factor (NGF) is responsible for both increased sensory and noradrenergic innervation, capsaicin-induced degeneration of sensory nerves decreases NGF uptake into sensory neurons with a resultant increase in the amount of NGF available for stimulating sympathetic innervation (Schicho et al, 1998).

The excitatory effects of the tachykinins are more prominent in the renal pelvis than in the ureter, and the inhibitory effects of CGRP are more prominent in the ureter than in the renal pelvis (Maggi et al, 1992b). The excitatory effects of tachykinins involve excitation of NK-2 receptors in the human, pig, and guinea pig ureter; pig intravesical ureter; and guinea pig renal pelvis (Patacchini et al, 1998; Jerde et al, 1999; Bustamante et al, 2001; Nakada et al, 2001). The inhibitory actions of the neurotransmitter CGRP appear to involve multiple mechanisms (Maggi and Giuliani, 1991; Maggi et al,

1994c). By opening ATP-sensitive K^+ channels, CGRP causes membrane hyperpolarization with a resultant blocking of voltage-sensitive Ca^{2+} channels that are involved in generation of the ureteral action potential and ureteral contraction (Maggi et al, 1994b; Santicioli and Maggi, 1994; Meini et al, 1995). CGRP-induced ureteral relaxation may also result from stimulation of adenylyl cyclase activity with a resultant increase in cAMP (Santicioli et al, 1995b). The action of CGRP on the ureter may be regulated by an endopeptidase that degrades the CGRP released from the sensory nerves (Maggi and Giuliani, 1994).

Histochemical studies show that the tachykinins and CGRP co-localize in the same nerves in the ureter (Hua et al, 1987). Peptidergic neurons containing NPY and vasoactive intestinal polypeptide (VIP) are also present in the ureter (Allen et al, 1990; Edvyane et al, 1992; Prieto et al, 1997). VIP and pituitary adenylate cyclase–activating polypeptide (PACAP) have been shown to relax pig intravesical ureteral segments through a cAMP-dependent mechanism (Hernández et al, 2004). Edvyane and associates (1994) have provided evidence of at least four, and possibly six, different immunohistochemical populations of nerve fibers in the human ureter. The predominant types include noradrenergic nerves containing NPY, neurons containing NPY and vasoactive polypeptide, neurons containing substance P and CGRP, and neurons containing CGRP. NPY potentiates the excitatory effects of norepinephrine on the ureter (Prieto et al, 1997). Rare coexistences were also observed between CGRP and vasoactive polypeptide, CGRP and NPY, and CGRP and tyrosine hydroxylase, a marker of noradrenergic neurons. These investigators demonstrated regional differences in the innervation of the ureter, with a more extensive innervation noted in the lower than in the upper ureter.

Renal pelvic sensory nerves contain both substance P and CGRP. Increases in renal pelvic pressure result in the release of substance P with a subsequent increase in afferent renal nerve activity. CGRP potentiates the afferent renal nerve activity responses to substance P by retarding the metabolism of substance P, thus resulting in increased amounts of substance P available for potentiating afferent renal nerve activity (Gontijo et al, 1999). Prostaglandins also contribute to sensory receptor activation (Kopp et al, 2000).

Nonadrenergic, noncholinergic (NANC) excitatory neurotransmission is functional in the pig intravesical ureter (Bustamante et al, 2000, 2001). In the presence of agents that block adrenergic neurotransmission, muscarinic cholinergic receptors, NO synthase activity, prostaglandin synthesis, and A_1/A_2 adenosine receptors, electrical field stimulation (5 Hz) induced contractions that were potentiated by the tachykinins substance P and NKA, and that were inhibited by a sensory neurotoxin, capsaicin, and by an NK_2 receptor antagonist, GR94800. The electrical field stimulation–induced contractions were abolished by tetrodotoxin, providing evidence that the contractions were neurogenic in origin. It has been suggested that tachykinins, especially NKA, released from capsaicin-sensitive afferent nerves and activating NK_2 receptors are involved in NANC excitatory neurotransmission.

Purinergic Nervous System

Burnstock and associates (1972) postulated that ATP could act as an excitatory transmitter in the bladder. It was subsequently shown that ATP is released along with ACh in response to nerve stimulation (Kasakov and Burnstock, 1983) and that the excitatory response in the bladder is mediated through P2X receptors (Theobald, 1995). **Although there is no evidence for ATP mediating contractions in the ureter, there is evidence to suggest that ATP is involved in nociceptive processes.** P2X receptors are present in the ureter (Lee et al, 2000) and release of ATP from the urothelium, in response to ureteral distention (Knight et al, 2002), stimulates afferent terminals by interacting with multiple purinergic receptors (Rong and Burnstock, 2004).

Two classes of mechanosensitive afferent fibers have been identified in the guinea pig ureter (Cervero and Sann, 1989). It appears that one group of fibers are tension receptors that respond to normal ureteral peristalsis, whereas the others are involved in the signaling of noxious events such as kidney stones and increased intraluminal pressures. Both groups are chemosensitive, being excited by K^+, bradykinin, and capsaicin (Sann, 1998). As both ureteral distention and exogenous ATP increase afferent nerve discharge (Rong and Burnstock, 2004), ATP may be involved in signaling visceral pain with ureteral dilatation.

URINE TRANSPORT
Physiology of the Ureteropelvic Junction

With UPJ obstruction, there may be areas of narrowing or valvelike processes (Maizels and Stephens, 1980). In other instances, there is no gross narrowing at the UPJ, and abnormal propagation of the peristaltic impulse is a causative factor in the obstruction. In these instances, there appears to be a functional obstruction at the UPJ because a large-caliber catheter can be passed readily through the UPJ even though urine transport is inadequate. Murnaghan (1958) related the functional abnormality to an alteration in the configuration of the muscle bundles at the UPJ, and Foote and associates (1970) observed a decrease in musculature at the UPJ. Hanna (1978), in an electron microscopic study of severe UPJ obstructions, noted abnormalities in the musculature of the renal pelvis and disruption of intercellular relations at the UPJ itself. Increased accumulation of collagen has been described in the region of the UPJ with obstruction (Murakumo et al, 1997), and it has been suggested that differences in type I and type III collagen in the region of the obstructed UPJ may be age dependent (Yoon et al, 1998). Studies have also shown a decrease in nerves and in NGF messenger RNA (mRNA) expression in UPJ obstruction specimens compared with controls (Wang et al, 1995; Murakumo et al, 1997). A vessel or adhesive band crossing the UPJ may potentiate the degree of dilatation in any of the forms of UPJ obstruction.

The differences in the reported findings suggest a histopathologic spectrum in the group of cases referred to as *UPJ obstructions.* **It appears possible that, at least in some instances, disruption of cell-to-cell propagation of peristaltic activity results in impairment of urine transport across the UPJ.**

One must consider input and output when predicting whether or not dilatation will occur; the effects of diuresis and obstruction appear to be complementary and additive with respect to the development of renal pelvic and calyceal dilata-

KEY POINT: PROPAGATION OF URETERAL PERISTALSIS

■ At normal urine flows, the frequency of calyceal and renal pelvic contractions is greater than that in the upper ureter, and there is a relative block of electrical activity at the UPJ (Morita et al, 1981). At these flows, the renal pelvis fills; as renal pelvic pressure rises, urine is extruded into the upper ureter, which is initially in a collapsed state (Griffiths and Notschaele, 1983). Ureteral contractile pressures that move the bolus of urine are higher than renal pelvic pressures, and a closed UPJ may be protective of the kidney in dissipating backpressure from the ureter. As the flow rate increases, the block at the UPJ ceases and a 1:1 correspondence between pacemaker and ureteral contractions develops (Constantinou and Hrynczuk, 1976; Constantinou and Yamaguchi, 1981).

tion. Some UPJs can handle urine flow regardless of the magnitude of diuresis, others cause dilatation at even the lowest flows, and still others can handle low flows but cause massive dilatation at high flows (Fig. 55–18).

Propulsion of Urinary Bolus

The theoretical aspects of the mechanics of urine transport within the ureter have been described in detail by Griffiths and Notschaele (1983); these are depicted in Figure 55–19.

Baseline, or resting, ureteral pressure is approximately 0 to 5 cm H_2O, and superimposed ureteral contractions ranging from 20 to 80 cm H_2O occur two to six times per minute (Kiil, 1957; Ross et al, 1972). The urine traverses the UVJ to enter the bladder; when functioning properly, the UVJ ensures one-way transport of urine. The bolus is forced into the bladder by the advancing contraction wave that then dissipates at the UVJ.

KEY POINT: PROPULSION OF URINE IN UPPER URINARY TRACT

■ At normal flow rates, as the renal pelvis fills, a rise in renal pelvic pressure occurs, and urine is extruded into the upper ureter, which is initially in a collapsed state. The contraction wave originates in the most proximal portion of the ureter and moves the urine in front of it in a distal direction. The urine that had previously entered the ureter is formed into a bolus. In order to propel the bolus of urine efficiently, the contraction wave must completely coapt the ureteral walls (Woodburne and Lapides, 1972; Griffiths and Notschaele, 1983), and the pressure generated by this contraction wave provides the primary component of what is recorded by intraluminal pressure measurements. The bolus that is pushed in front of the contraction wave lies almost entirely in a passive, noncontracting part of the ureter (Fung, 1971; Weinberg, 1974).

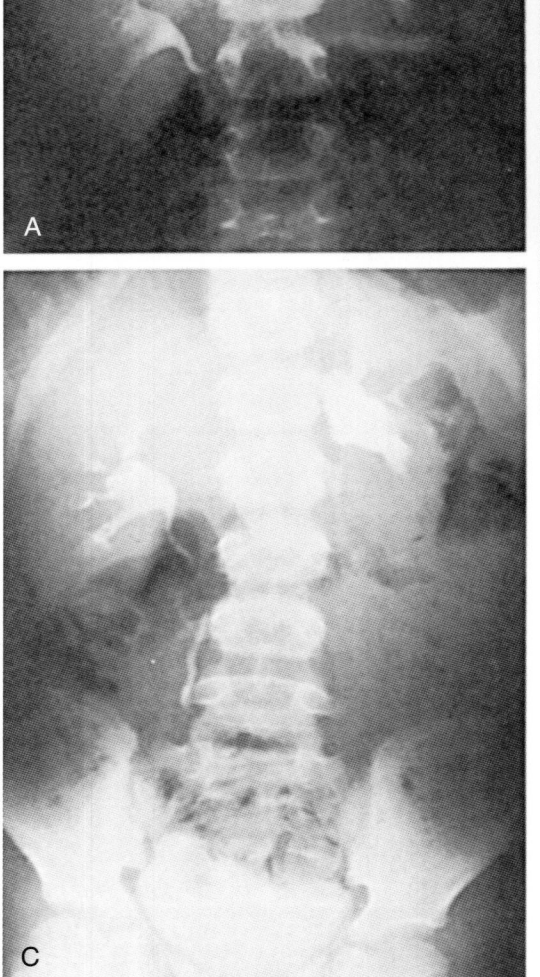

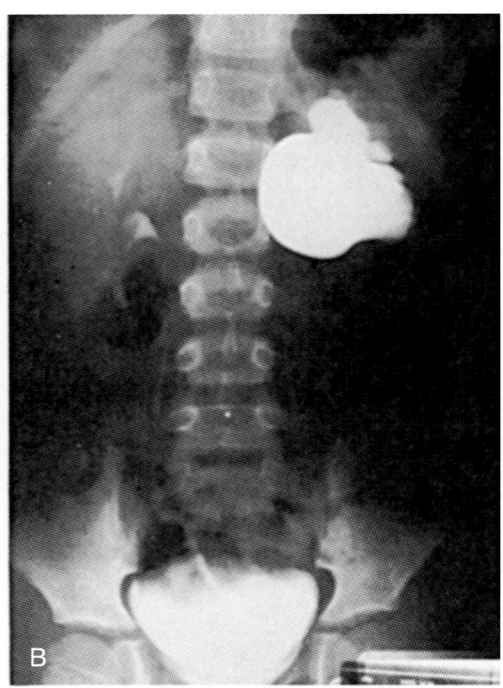

Figure 55–18. A, Intravenous pyelogram (IVP) shows essentially normal upper urinary tracts. **B,** Film from the same child taken immediately after a cardiac angiogram, which produces a massive diuresis. **C,** IVP 6 weeks after the angiogram. (**A** to **C,** From Weiss RM: Clinical implications of ureter physiology. J Urol 1979;121:401.)

As with any tubular structure, the ureter can transport a set maximal amount of fluid per unit time. Under normal flows, in which bolus formation occurs, the amount of urine transported per unit time is significantly less than the maximal transport capacity of the ureter. **At extremely high flows, as are employed in the standard perfusion studies** (Whitaker, 1973), **the ureteral walls do not coapt, and a continuous column of fluid, rather than a series of boluses, is transported.**

When transport becomes inadequate, stasis of urine occurs with resultant ureteral dilatation. Inadequate transport can result either from too much fluid entering the ureter per unit time or from too little fluid exiting the ureter per unit time. Both input and output must be considered in predicting whether or not ureteral dilatation will occur. For example, a

minor degree of obstruction to outflow causes more dilatation at high flow rates than at low flow rates. Even a normal nonobstructed ureter impedes urine transport if the rate of flow is great enough.

Changes in ureteral dimensions that occur in pathologic states may in themselves result in inefficient urine transport, even if the contractile force of the individual fibers is unchanged. The Laplace equation expresses the relation between the variables that affect intraluminal pressure:

$$\text{Pressure} = \frac{\text{tension} \times \text{wall thickness}}{\text{radius}}$$

An increase in ureteral diameter in itself can decrease intraluminal pressure and result in inefficient urine transport. Such dimensional changes may, at least theoretically, be deleterious

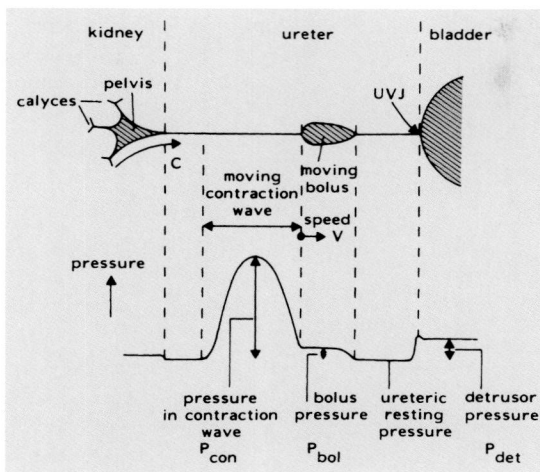

Figure 55–19. Schematic representation of a single bolus in the ureter moving away from the renal pelvis and toward the bladder. *Arrow* C indicates the direction of bolus transport. The corresponding distribution of pressure within the urinary tract is shown in the lower tracing. UVJ, ureterovesical junction. (From Griffiths DJ, Notschaele C: The mechanics of urine transport in the upper urinary tract. Neurourol Urodyn 1983;2:155.)

(Griffiths, 1983). Another factor may be the histologic composition of the dilated ureter, as evidenced by the description of different amounts of type I and type III collagen in primary obstructed and refluxing megaureters (Lee et al, 1998).

Effect of Diuresis on Ureteral Function

With increasing urine flow rates, the initial response of the ureter is to increase peristaltic frequency. After the maximal frequency is achieved, further increases in urine transport occur by means of increases in bolus volume (Morales et al, 1952; Constantinou et al, 1974). At relatively low flow rates, small increases in flow result in large increases in peristaltic frequency. At higher flow rates, relatively large increases in flow result in only small increases in peristaltic frequency. As the flow rate continues to increase, several of the boluses coalesce, and finally the ureter becomes filled with a column of fluid and dilates. At these high flow rates, urine transport is through an open tube.

Effects of Bladder Filling and Neurogenic Vesical Dysfunction on Ureteral Function

Ureteral dilatation can result either from an increase in fluid input or from a decrease in fluid output from the ureter. The relation between ureteral intraluminal pressure and intravesical pressure is important in determining the efficacy of urine passage across the UVJ into the bladder. In the case of the normal ureter under normal physiologic rates of flow, ureteral contractile pressure exceeds intravesical pressure, resulting in passage of urine into the bladder. In the dilated, poorly contracting ureter or in the normal ureter at extreme flow rates, the ureter does not coapt its walls to form boluses, and the baseline pressure in the column of urine within the ureter must exceed intravesical pressure for urine to pass into the bladder.

The pressure within the bladder during the storage phase is of paramount importance in determining the efficacy of urine transport across the UVJ. This is the pressure that the

ureter needs to work against for the longest period of time. During filling of the normal bladder, sympathetic impulses and the viscoelastic properties of the bladder wall inhibit the magnitude of the intravesical pressure rise, that is, the tonus limb. With filling, the normal bladder maintains a relatively low intravesical pressure (McGuire, 1983) that facilitates the transport of urine across the UVJ and prevents ureteral dilatation. In the noncompliant fibrotic bladder and in some forms of neurogenic vesical dysfunction, the bladder is autonomous, and relatively small increases in bladder volume result in large increases in intravesical pressure with resultant impairment of ureteral emptying. The ureter initially responds to its decreased ability to empty by increasing its peristaltic frequency (Zimskind et al, 1969; Rosen et al, 1971; Fredericks et al, 1972). Ultimately, stasis occurs with the development of ureteral dilatation. **The ureter has been shown to decompensate when intravesical pressure approaches 40 cm H_2O** (McGuire et al, 1981).

Physiology of the Ureterovesical Junction

Griffiths (1983) has analyzed the factors involved in urine transport across the UVJ. Under normal conditions and at normal flow rates, the contraction wave, which occludes the ureteral lumen, propagates distally with the urine bolus in front of it. When the bolus reaches the UVJ, the pressure within the bolus must exceed intravesical pressure for the bolus of urine to pass across the UVJ into the bladder. Under these conditions, in which the contraction wave is able to coapt the ureteral wall and move the urinary bolus distally, the pressure generated by the contraction wave exceeds the pressure within the urinary bolus. The contracted ureteral ring just proximal to the ureteral orifice at the UVJ is relevant in the antireflux mechanism (Roshani et al, 1996). As the bolus is ejected into the bladder, the distal ureter retracts within its sheaths; this telescoping of the ureter within its sheaths aids in decreasing UVJ resistance to flow and thus facilitates urine passage into the bladder (Blok et al, 1985). The UVJ does not relax (Weiss and Biancani, 1983). **Impediment of efficient bolus transfer across the UVJ into the bladder can occur when there is an obstruction at the UVJ, when intravesical pressure is excessive, or when flow rates are so high as to exceed the transport capacity of the normal UVJ. Under such conditions, in which the bolus of urine cannot pass freely into the bladder, the pressure within the bolus increases and may exceed the pressure in the contraction wave. This results in an inability of the contraction wave to occlude the ureter completely; there is retrograde flow of urine from the bolus, and only a fraction of the urinary bolus passes across the UVJ into the bladder.** Griffiths (1983) has presented theoretical evidence to show that a similar situation of impaired bolus transport across the UVJ would be expected if the ureter were wide or weakly contracting, even if the UVJ were perfectly normal. The wider and more weakly contracting the ureter, the lower the UVJ resistance must be in order not to interfere with bolus transport. The resistance to flow at the UVJ has been variously attributed to forces in the trigone (Tanagho et al, 1968) and to detrusor pressure (Coolsaet et al, 1982).

The theoretical considerations outlined by Griffiths (1983) have direct clinical implications. **If the UVJ is obstructed (i.e., has an abnormally high resistance to flow) or if the detrusor pressure is excessive, large boluses occurring at high-flow conditions would not be completely discharged into the bladder because the contraction wave pushing the bolus would be forced open and intraureteral reflux would occur.** Such obstruction at the UVJ would be detected by perfusion studies as popularized by Whitaker (1973) (i.e., the Whitaker test). On the other hand, Griffiths' (1983) theory suggests that a similar breakdown of bolus discharge into the bladder can occur in the wide or weakly contracting ureter at high flow rates even if the UVJ is normal and that such a condition would go undetected by a Whitaker perfusion test.

There is evidence that gravity may assist urine transport and that the erect position may aid urine transport across the UVJ, especially in individuals with dilated upper tracts (Schick and Tanagho, 1973). From a practical standpoint, George and associates (1984) suggested that bed rest may be deleterious to renal function in individuals with urinary retention and wide upper urinary tracts.

PATHOLOGIC PROCESSES AFFECTING URETERAL FUNCTION
Effect of Obstruction on Ureteral Function

General

The effect of obstruction on ureteral function depends on the degree and duration of the obstruction, on the rate of urine flow, and on the presence or absence of infection. After the onset of obstruction, a backup of urine occurs within the urinary collecting system, along with an associated increase in baseline (resting) ureteral intraluminal pressure and an increase in ureteral dimensions, that is, an increase in both length and diameter (Fig. 55–20) (Rose and Gillenwater, 1973; Biancani et al, 1976). **The increase in intraluminal pressure depends on the kidney's continued production of urine that cannot pass beyond the site of obstruction; the increase in ureteral dimensions results from the increased ureteral intraluminal pressure and the increased volume of urine retained within the ureter. A transient increase in the amplitude and frequency of the peristaltic contraction waves accompanies these initial dimensional and ureteral baseline (resting) pressure changes** (Rose and Gillenwater, 1978). **With time, as the ureter fills with urine, the peristaltic contraction waves become smaller and are unable to coapt the ureteral wall. Urine transport then becomes dependent on hydrostatic forces generated by the kidney** (Rose and Gillenwater, 1973). **Superimposed infection may result in complete absence of contractions in the obstructed ureter and contributes to impairment of urine transport** (Rose and Gillenwater, 1973).

Within a few hours after the onset of obstruction, the intraluminal baseline ureteral pressure reaches a peak and then declines to a level only slightly higher than the normal baseline pressure. This occurs at a time in which dimensional changes remain stable (Biancani et al, 1976). The decrease in ureteral pressure can be attributed to changes in intrarenal

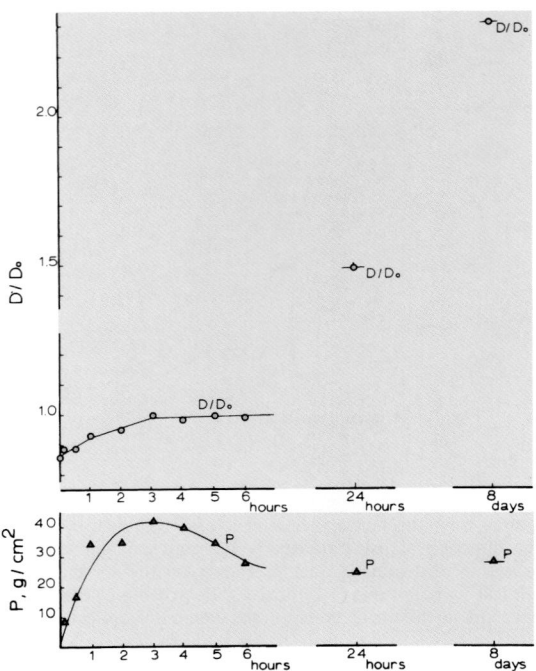

Figure 55–20. Intraluminal pressure and diameter changes after obstruction of rabbit ureter. The time from the onset of obstruction is on the abscissa. The change in diameter (D/D_0) is on the upper ordinate, and the intraluminal pressure is on the lower ordinate. During the initial 3 hours of obstruction, intraluminal pressure increased to reach a maximum and was associated with an increase in diameter. Between 3 and 6 hours after the onset of obstruction, pressure declined, although diametral deformation persisted. After 6 hours, pressure remained essentially unchanged, although the diameter continued to increase. Do, initial diameter; D, diameter during deformation; P, intraluminal pressure. (Adapted from Biancani P, Zabinski MP, Weiss RM: Time course of ureteral changes with acute and chronic obstruction. Am J Physiol 1976;231:393.)

hemodynamics, such as a reduction in renal blood flow (Vaughan et al, 1971), with resultant decreases in the glomerular filtration rate and intratubular hydrostatic pressure (Gottschalk and Mylle, 1956). Fluid reabsorption into the venous and lymphatic systems and a decrease in wall tension may also play a role in the reduction in baseline ureteral pressure (Rose and Gillenwater, 1978). The persistence of dimensional changes in the presence of a decrease in intraluminal pressure depends on the hysteretic properties of the viscoelastic ureteral structure (Fig. 55–21) (Weiss et al, 1972; Biancani et al, 1973, 1976; Vereecken et al, 1973).

As the obstruction persists, there is a gradual increase in ureteral length and diameter to considerable dimensions. This occurs even though ureteral pressure remains at a relatively low and constant level. This process, observed in viscoelastic structures, is referred to as creep (Biancani et al, 1973). Continued, albeit small, urine production is required for the continuing increase in intraureteral volume. Such changes account for the relatively low intrapelvic pressures clinically observed in the massively dilated, chronically obstructed upper urinary tract (Backlund et al, 1965; Struthers, 1969; Vela-Navarrete, 1971; Djurhuus and Stage, 1976) and in experimentally produced obstruction (Schweitzer, 1973; Koff and Thrall, 1981a). One could postu-

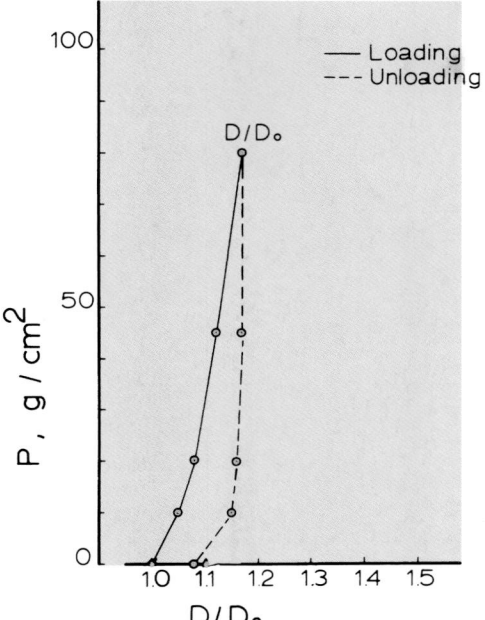

Figure 55–21. Demonstration of hysteretic properties of ureter show that dimensional changes depend on intraluminal pressure and on the direction of change of that pressure. At comparable pressures, deformations are greater during ureteral emptying than during ureteral filling. The *solid line* shows data obtained during loading; the *dashed line*, data obtained during unloading. D_0, initial diameter; D, diameter during deformation; P, intraluminal pressure in grams per square centimeter. (Adapted from Biancani P, Zabinski MP, Weiss RM: Time course of ureteral changes with acute and chronic obstruction. Am J Physiol 1976;231:393.)

late that with prolonged complete obstruction, total cessation of urine output ultimately occurs. A subsequent decrease in ureteral dimensions would depend on whether urine is reabsorbed and on the mechanical properties of the ureter at that time.

In order to determine the effect of obstruction on the contractile properties of the ureter, a rabbit model in which the ureter is totally obstructed for 2 weeks has been employed (Hausman et al, 1979; Biancani et al, 1982). After 2 weeks of obstruction, the cross-sectional muscle area increases by 250%, ureteral length by 24%, and ureteral outer diameter by 100%. In addition to undergoing **muscle hypertrophy**, in vitro segments from obstructed ureters develop greater contractile forces, in both longitudinal and circumferential directions, than do segments from control ureters (Fig. 55–22). With experimental obstruction at the UPJ there is also an increase in the frequency and amplitude of spontaneous mechanical contractions of the renal pelvis and an increase in the amplitude of phenylephrine- and 5-hydroxytryptamine (5-HT)-induced contractions (Ekinci et al, 2004). Determinations of stress (force per unit area of muscle) provide a means of determining whether the observed increases in developed force result from an increase in contractility or from an increase in muscle mass alone. The increases in force were associated with an increase in maximal active circumferential stress but no change in maximal active longitudinal stress (Fig. 55–23). Because there is an increase in circumferential stress and no change in longitudinal stress, the sum of the stresses (total stress) or overall contractility increases after 2 weeks of obstruction. For these differences in longitudinal and circumferential stresses to occur after obstruction, rotation of

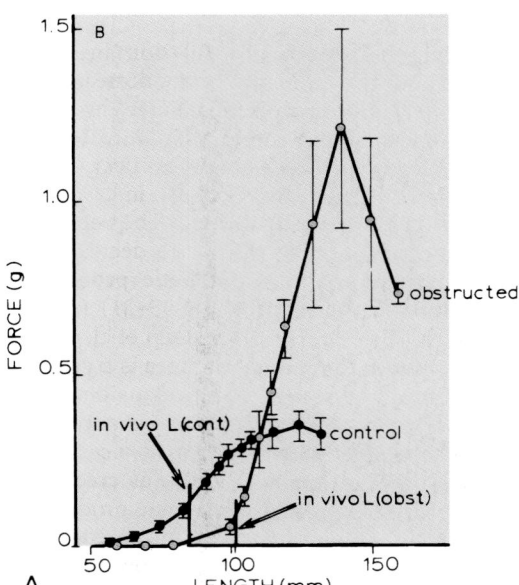
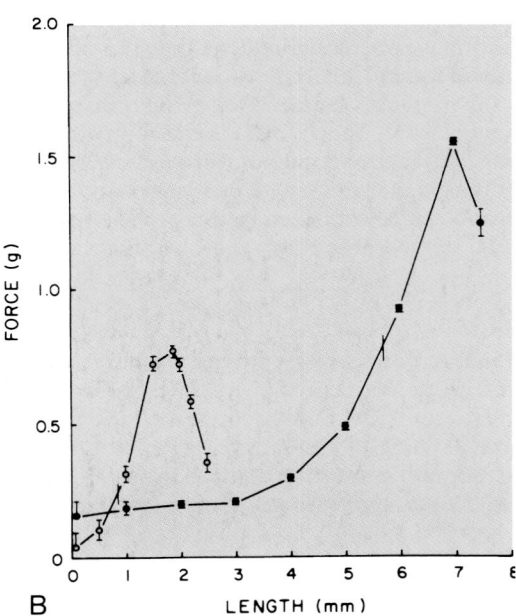

Figure 55–22. **A,** Active (contractile) longitudinal force-length relations of control *(closed circles)* and obstructed *(open circles)* rabbit ureters. Each data point represents mean ± SEM. **B,** Active (contractile) circumferential force-length relations of obstructed *(closed circles)* and control *(open circles)* ureteral rings. Vertical bars correspond to in vivo lengths of control and obstructed segments. (**A,** From Hausman M, Biancani P, Weiss RM: Obstruction induced changes in longitudinal force-length relations of rabbit ureter. Invest Urol 1979;17:223. **B,** From Biancani P, Hausman, M, Weiss RM: Effect of obstruction on ureteral circumferential force-length relation. Am J Physiol 1982;243:F204.)

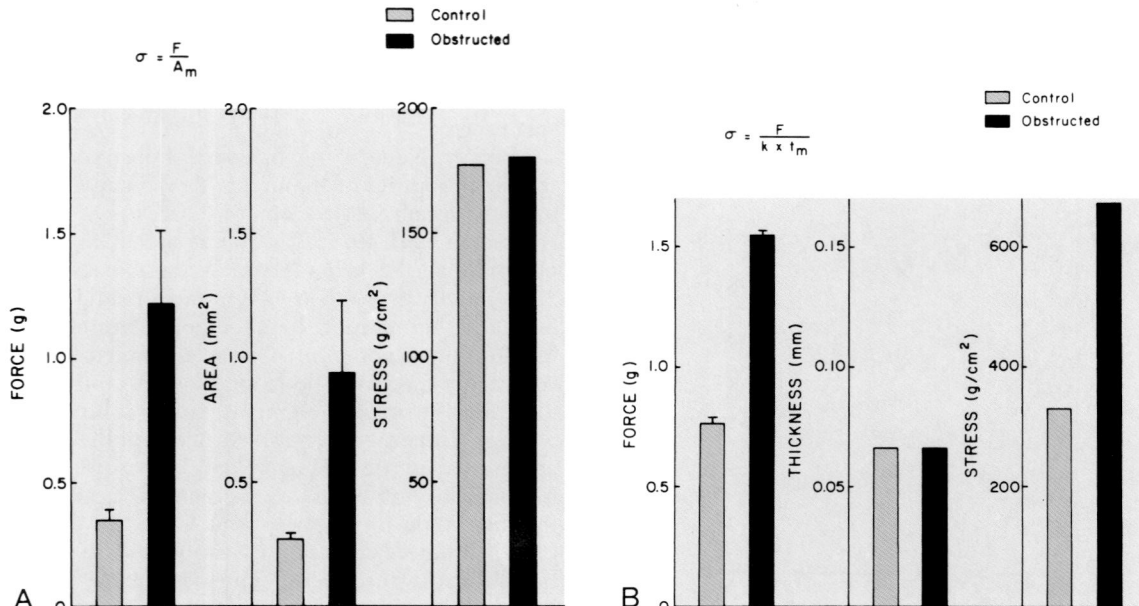

Figure 55–23. **A,** Longitudinal force, cross-sectional muscle area, and longitudinal stress at the length of maximal active force development. **B,** Circumferential force, average muscle thickness, and circumferential stress at the length of maximal active force development. σ, stress; F, force; A_m, cross-sectional muscle area; t_m, average thickness of muscle layer, a constant. (From Weiss RM, Biancani P: A rationale for ureteral tapering. Urology 1982;20:482.)

muscle bundles must occur; otherwise, longitudinal and circumferential stresses would increase equally. The rotation could result from the greater increase in diameter than in length after obstruction, from remodeling of the muscle fibers, or from both.

Thus, the ureter dilated after 2 weeks of obstruction is not mechanically decompensated but rather undergoes changes that result in an increase in contractility. **Despite both the muscle hypertrophy and the increase in contractility, it is clinically and experimentally evident that the obstructed, dilated ureter is less able than the normal ureter to generate the contractile pressures required for urine transport** (Rose and Gillenwater, 1973). The decrease in the ability to generate an intraluminal pressure despite an increase in contractility results from the increase in ureteral diameter that occurs after obstruction and can be explained by the **Laplace relation:**

$$\text{Pressure} = \frac{\text{stress} \times \text{wall thickness}}{\text{radius}}$$

Although contractility (stress) increases after 2 weeks of obstruction, the decrease in the wall's thickness-to-radius ratio resulting from the marked increase in intraluminal diameter and thinning of the muscle layer accounts for the decrease in pressure. It must be realized that a longer duration of obstruction or the presence of infection may alter these relations.

Estimates of intraluminal pressures as a function of diameter (pressure-diameter curves) can be calculated from in vitro circumferential force-length data (Fig. 55–24) (Biancani et al, 1982; Weiss and Biancani, 1982) and provide insight into how obstruction interferes with urine transport. The validity of such calculations is supported by their correspondence to actual in vivo measurements (Rose and Gillenwater, 1973;

Biancani et al, 1976). The obstructed ureter at in vivo dimensions has a higher resting (baseline) pressure and a lower contractile (active) pressure than a control ureter. In the control ureter, the total (active plus passive or resting) pressure developed at all diameters exceeds the passive pressure shown by the horizontal dotted line, and thus the generated active or contractile pressures are able to coapt fully the ureteral lumen and propel the urine bolus. In the obstructed ureter at diameters less than 3.3 mm, the passive pressure, as shown by the horizontal dotted line, exceeds the total pressure. The contraction ring therefore is incapable of contracting below this diameter, and the pressure in the whole ureter remains approximately uniform and equal to the passive pressure. The principal effect of the contraction wave in the obstructed dilated ureter is to reduce the ureteral volume slightly and thereby slightly raise the overall resting pressure. Thus, although the obstructed ureter is able to develop greater circumferential contractile forces than the control ureter, the expected intraluminal pressure generated by the obstructed ureter would be little different from baseline (resting) pressure, and the contraction wave occurring during propagation of peristalsis would be incapable of coapting the ureteral lumen and propelling the urine bolus in an effective manner.

It should be noted that the calculated active pressure in the obstructed ureter estimates the pressure that would develop if the whole ureter contracted simultaneously and uniformly throughout its whole length, rather than the pressure measured in a peristaltic contraction wave, which involves contraction of only a small segment of ureter at a given time. The fact that the calculated pressures in the obstructed ureter are, if anything, a slight overestimate of expected pressures only further supports the conclusion that **the obstructed ureter is incapable of coapting its lumen and efficiently propelling**

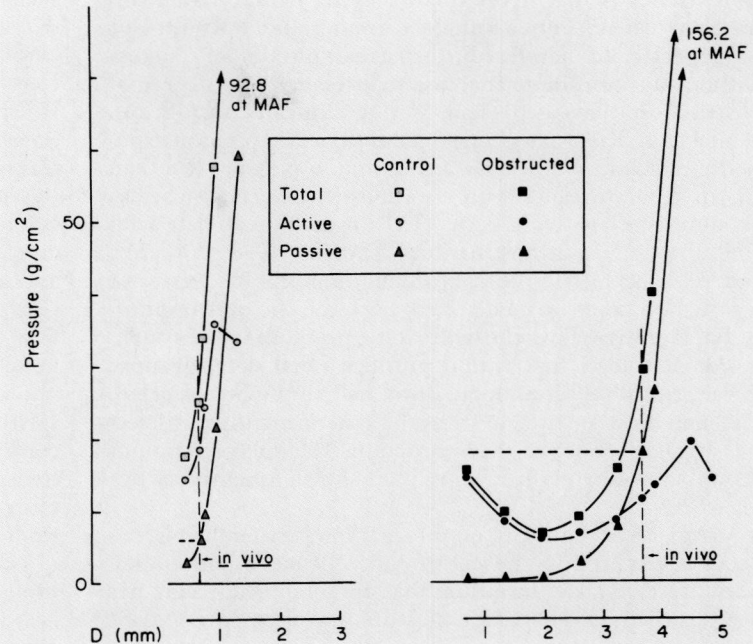

Figure 55–24. Pressure-diameter relationships of control and obstructed ureters. Calculated total, active, and passive pressures are shown as a function of intraluminal diameter (D). In vivo passive pressures are indicated by *horizontal dashed lines* and in vivo dimensions by *vertical dashed lines*. (Adapted from Biancani P, Hausman M, Weiss RM: Effect of obstruction on ureteral force-length relations. Am J Physiol 1982;243:F204.)

the urine bolus. If, however, the urine were removed from the lumen of the ureter (e.g., by relieving the obstruction), the ureter obstructed for 2 weeks would be able to coapt its lumen immediately and produce pressures comparable to those of control ureters. This can be appreciated from Figure 55–24, in which the total pressure in the obstructed ureter near zero diameter can be seen to be comparable to the total pressure in the control ureter at a similar diameter. Thus, **2 weeks of obstruction results in an increase in ureteral contractility but a decrease in contractile intraluminal pressures.** This decrease in the ability to generate an active intraluminal pressure and to coapt the ureteral lumen impairs urine transport in the obstructed ureter.

Obstruction of the fetal ureter is also accompanied by an increase in ureteral weight, smooth muscle mass, extracellular matrix, and the frequency and amplitude of spontaneous ureteral contractile activity (Santis et al, 2000). Obstructed and refluxing dilated ureters have an increase in type I and type III collagen and an increased ratio of collagen to smooth muscle (Gearhart et al, 1995; Lee et al, 1998). Hydrocortisone, verapamil (a calcium channel blocker), and D-penicillamine reduce collagen III production, which is increased in a variety of obstructed ureteral states and in ureteral cell cultures (Wolf et al, 1996). Obstruction has also been shown to alter the hierarchic organization of the multiple coupled pacemakers that normally coordinate peristaltic activity (Constantinou and Djurhuus, 1981; Djurhuus and Constantinou, 1982). Such disruption causes discoordination of pelvic contractility with resultant incomplete emptying of the renal pelvis that contributes to upper urinary tract dilatation.

Physiologic Methodologies for Assessing Clinical Obstruction

A variety of radiographic methodologies, the rationale for whose use is based on physiologic principles, are employed in the evaluation and differentiation of upper urinary tract dilatation and obstruction. Descriptions of these examinations, which include diuretic urograms, diuretic radionuclide renograms, pulsed Doppler sonographic assessment of renal vascular resistance, and ultrasonographic evaluation of ureteral peristalsis, are beyond the scope of this chapter. The best methods now available for differentiating obstructive from nonobstructive dilatation depend on assessing the efficacy of urine transport. When transport becomes inadequate, urine stagnates and dilatation occurs. **Dilatation depends on the compliance of the system and can result either from too much fluid entering the system per unit time or from too little fluid exiting the system per unit time.** The properly functioning upper urinary tract should transport urine over the entire range of physiologically possible flow rates without undergoing marked deformational changes or increases in intraluminal pressure of a magnitude that would be deleterious to the function of the ureter, renal pelvis, or kidney.

Measurement of basal or resting intraluminal pressures does not help in differentiating obstructive from nonobstructive dilatation because the pressures may be low even when obstruction is present (Backlund et al, 1965; Struthers, 1969; Vela-Navarrete, 1971). The values obtained vary with the state of hydration, the degree of renal function, the severity and duration of obstruction, and the compliance of the system. **Perfusion studies are used in an attempt to differentiate dilated systems that are obstructed from those that are not obstructed** (Backlund and Reuterskiöld, 1969a, 1969b; Reuterskiöld, 1969, 1970; Whitaker, 1973, 1978). The technique involves cannulating the dilated upper urinary tract and perfusing the system at a rate of 10 mL/min. Pressures are measured after the achievement of steady-state conditions, which occur when an equilibrium is reached between the flow into and out of the system. Fluoroscopic monitoring aids in the interpretation of the data. **The basic hypothesis in perfu-**

sion studies is that if the dilated upper urinary tract can transport 10 mL/min (a fluid load greater than it would ever be expected to handle during usual physiologic states) without an inordinate increase in pressure, any degree of obstruction that is present is not clinically significant. Whitaker and associates concluded from a large clinical experience that under these flow conditions, a pressure less than 15 cm H_2O correlates with a nonobstructive state, whereas pressures greater than 22 cm H_2O invariably correlate with clinically significant obstruction (Whitaker, 1978; Witherow and Whitaker, 1981). With this definition, minor degrees of obstruction could go undetected; however, **the presumption is that if at high flows the hydrostatic pressure in the system is not at a level that would produce renal deterioration, lower and more physiologic flows will surely be tolerated.** The high flows are used to stress the system and thus to detect the slightest propensity to obstruction. The interpretation of data obtained by perfusion studies is shown schematically in Figure 55–25.

In order to obtain relevant information, strict adherence to detail is required in the performance of perfusion studies. Care must be taken to ensure that an equilibrium state has been reached before making pressure measurements. Extrin-

sic factors that affect the resistance to flow, such as the needle size, length and compliance of extrinsic tubing, viscosity of the perfusion fluid, temperature, and flow rate, must be considered when quantitative data are obtained (Toguri and Fournier, 1982). Furthermore, the bladder should be continuously drained to eliminate the bladder's effect on urine transport.

When performed and interpreted properly, perfusion studies may provide clinically relevant information in selected cases. The basic problem in the interpretation of data with this and other diagnostic methods is the definition of "clinically relevant obstruction"—that is, just how much resistance to flow or increase in pressure is required to produce renal functional or anatomic deterioration as a function of time, taking into account the compliance of the system (Koff and Thrall, 1981b). Also, it is theoretically possible that the wide or weakly contracting ureter at high flow rates may interfere with bolus transport even if the UVJ is normal (Griffiths, 1983). Such an obstructive process would not be detected by perfusion studies.

These theoretical considerations provide a rationale for **ureteral tapering** (Hendren, 1970), a procedure that, to date, has been shown to improve radiographic appearances, although the question remains whether it aids in preserving renal function when anatomic or functional obstruction does not exist. The Laplace relation provides a possible explanation for anticipated improvement in function resulting from tapering. With ureteral tapering, muscle thickness and the ability of the ureteral fibers to contract (stress) are unchanged. The decrease in radius resulting from tapering itself, according to the Laplace relation, could account for higher intraluminal pressures, which could improve urine transport. Thus, the tapered ureter may coapt its walls more readily and generate higher intraluminal pressures even though the material itself has not changed (Weiss and Biancani, 1982). Although the possibility of deleterious effects of the wide "nonobstructed" ureter remains controversial, one should consider such effects when interpreting data obtained with the present modalities for diagnosing obstruction and when determining management.

Relation between Vesicoureteral Reflux and Ureteral Function

Factors that have been implicated in the development of vesicoureteral reflux include (1) anatomic and functional abnormalities at the UVJ, (2) inordinately high intravesical pressures, and (3) impaired ureteral function. The normal intravesical ureter is approximately 1.5 cm in length and takes an oblique course through the bladder wall. It is composed of an intramural segment surrounded by detrusor muscle and a submucosal segment that lies directly under the bladder urothelium (Tanagho et al, 1968). The relation between the length and the diameter of this intravesical segment of ureter appears to be a factor in the prevention of vesicoureteral reflux (Paquin, 1959). Reflux may occur when the intravesical tunnel is destroyed. Trigonal function may also be a factor in the prevention of vesicoureteral reflux. Tanagho and associates (1965) created vesicoureteral reflux in the cat by disruption of the trigone or by sympathectomy and, conversely, increased

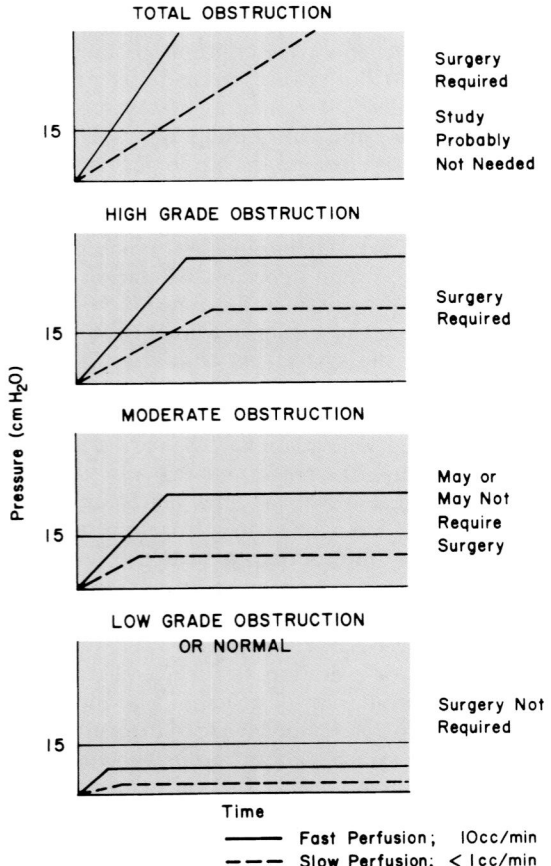

Figure 55–25. Schematic representation of data that can be obtained with perfusion studies. A fast perfusion rate, 10 mL/min, would be used in a standard Whitaker test. A slow perfusion rate, less than 1 mL/min, would be closer to more physiologic rates of flow. (From Weiss RM: Clinical implications of ureteral physiology. J Urol 1979;121:401.)

the pressure within the intravesical ureter by electrical stimulation of the trigone or by administration of intravenous epinephrine. The development of vesicoureteral reflux in individuals with bladder outlet obstruction and neurogenic vesical dysfunction provides evidence that increased intravesical pressures may also be a factor in certain instances of reflux.

Although an abnormality of the UVJ is the primary etiologic factor in most cases of reflux, there is evidence to suggest that decreased ureteral peristaltic activity can be a contributory factor. This may explain why a normal ureter may not reflux even when reimplanted into a bladder without a submucosal tunnel (Debruyne et al, 1978) or why a defunctionalized refluxing ureter may cease to reflux when a proximal diversion is taken down (Teele et al, 1976; Weiss, 1979). The observation that vesicoureteral reflux may temporarily cease after ureteral electrical stimulation (Melick et al, 1966) further supports this possibility.

Even the mildest forms of vesicoureteral reflux are associated with a decreased frequency of ureteral peristalsis (Kirkland et al, 1971; Weiss and Biancani, 1983). Although this may offer further evidence that decreased peristaltic activity is a possible etiologic factor in the development of reflux, an alternative interpretation is that the decreased peristaltic activity reflects changes in ureteral or renal function resulting from the reflux. Finally, the success rate of antireflux procedures is lower with poorly functioning dilated ureters, and, although this may be related to technical factors, decreased peristaltic activity may be another reason for failure in many instances.

Studies in normal and mildly refluxing systems have shown that there is a high-pressure zone in the distal ureter, with a resultant pressure gradient across the UVJ (Weiss and Biancani, 1983). Although the cause of the UVJ gradient is not known, the weight of the fluid within the bladder compressing the intravesical ureter may be a factor. Another causative factor may be bladder or trigonal tension involving myogenic or neurohumoral mechanisms. With bladder filling, there is an increase in the amplitude of the high-pressure zone that is greater in nonrefluxing than in refluxing systems. With bladder filling, the resultant UVJ-bladder pressure gradient increases in nonrefluxing systems, whereas it decreases and may disappear in refluxing systems (Fig. 55–26) (Weiss and

Biancani, 1983). This decrease in pressure gradient may correspond to the time when reflux occurs and may be related to lateralization of the ureteral orifice and shortening of the intravesical tunnel.

Effect of Infection on Ureteral Function

Infection within the upper urinary tract may impair urine transport. Pyelonephritis in the monkey has been associated with decreased peristaltic activity (Roberts, 1975). Furthermore, Rose and Gillenwater (1973) have shown that infection can potentiate the deleterious effects of obstruction on ureteral function. In 1913, Primbs showed that *Escherichia coli* and staphylococcal toxins inhibited contractions of in vitro guinea pig ureteral segments. A number of studies have confirmed that bacteria and *E. coli* endotoxin can inhibit ureteral activity (Grana et al, 1965; King and Cox, 1972), although these findings have not been universal (Struthers, 1976). Thulesius and Araj (1987) also failed to suppress ureteral activity with *E. coli* endotoxin but noted that growth supernatants from *E. coli*, *Pseudomonas aeruginosa*, and *Klebsiella pneumoniae* inhibited ureteral contractility. These investigators suggested that the inhibition of peristaltic activity is due to an exotoxin.

In humans, irregular peristaltic contractions with an often decreased amplitude have been recorded with infection, and an absence of activity has been noted in the more severe cases (Ross et al, 1972). Furthermore, ureteral dilatation has been reported to result from retroperitoneal inflammatory processes secondary to appendicitis, regional enteritis, ulcerative colitis, or peritonitis (Makker et al, 1972). Infection may also reduce the compliance of the intravesical ureter and permit reflux to occur in situations in which the UVJ is intrinsically of marginal competence (Cook and King, 1979).

Effect of Calculi on Ureteral Function

Factors that affect the spontaneous passage of calculi are (1) the size and shape of the stone (Ueno et al, 1977), (2) intrinsic areas of narrowing within the ureter, (3) ureteral peristal-

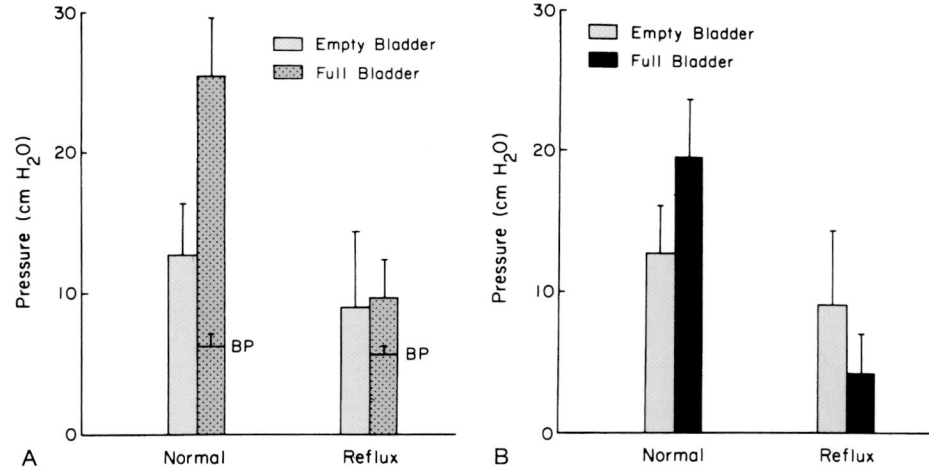

Figure 55–26. **A,** Ureterovesical junction pressures. Bladder pressure is approximately 0 cm H_2O with the bladder empty and is labeled BP with the bladder full. **B,** Pressure gradient across the ureterovesical junction, obtained by subtracting the bladder pressure from the ureterovesical junction pressure. (From Weiss RM, Biancani P: Characteristics of normal and refluxing ureterovesical junctions. J Urol 1983; 129:858.)

sis, (4) hydrostatic pressure of the column of urine proximal to the calculus (Sivula and Lehtonen, 1967), and (5) edema, inflammation, and spasm of the ureter at the site at which the stone is lodged (Holmlund and Hassler, 1965).

In an attempt to understand the physiologic processes that contribute to or hinder the passage of stones through the ureter, Crowley and associates (1990) created acute ureteral obstruction in the dog with an intraluminal balloon catheter and measured intraluminal ureteral pressures and peristaltic activity above and below the acutely obstructed site. The peristaltic rate and baseline, peak, and delta (peak minus baseline) pressures increased proximal to the site of obstruction. In contrast, the peristaltic rate remained unchanged distal to the obstruction, despite decreases in the baseline, peak, and delta pressures. It was suggested that failure of transmission of effective peristalsis across the site of obstruction may hinder stone passage; however, this remains to be proved. In a more recent study, implantation of an artificial calculus in a rat ureter resulted in an increase in the amplitude of contraction, a decrease in the rate of contractions, and a decrease in baseline pressure (Laird et al, 1997). These changes persisted for a period after spontaneous passage of the calculus. It was suggested that the increased motility caused by a stone contributes to the visceral pain associated with ureteral stone passage.

Two factors that appear to be most useful in facilitating stone passage are an increase in hydrostatic pressure proximal to a calculus and relaxation of the ureter in the region of the stone. In support of the theory that hydrostatic pressure facilitates stone passage, artificial concretions with holes were shown to move more slowly in the rabbit and dog ureter than those without holes (Sivula and Lehtonen, 1967). Furthermore, ureteral ligation proximal to a concretion, which decreases hydrostatic pressure by decreasing urine output and decreases peristaltic activity proximal to a stone, hampers stone passage (Sivula and Lehtonen, 1967).

With respect to the potential facilitative effect of ureteral relaxation on stone passage, spasmolytic agents phentolamine, an α-adrenergic antagonist, and orciprenaline and isoproterenol β-adrenergic agonists have been shown to dilate the ureteral lumen or decrease ureteral wall tension at the level of an artificial concretion and thus permit increased fluid flow beyond the concretion (Peters and Eckstein, 1975; Miyatake et al, 2001). In a human study, renal colic was relieved by meperidine in 83% of patients, by phentolamine in 63%, and by propranolol, a β-adrenergic antagonist that presumably would interfere with the β-adrenergic inhibitory actions of catecholamines, in 0% (Kubacz and Catchpole, 1972). Although these data suggest that drugs with spasmolytic effects on the ureter may relieve renal colic, whereas those with spasmogenic actions do not, no attempt was made to assess the efficacy of these agents in promoting stone passage.

Pharmacologic data can be interpreted to imply that ureteral relaxation in the region of a concretion could aid in stone passage. Agents such as theophylline (Weiss et al, 1977; Green et al, 1987) with strong relaxant effects on the ureter have potential value in facilitating stone passage, and oral theophylline appears to aid in the treatment of ureteral calculi (unpublished data). Interpretation of clinical data is difficult because of the marked variability of spontaneous stone passage in the clinical setting. In a rabbit in vivo model,

rolipram, a phosphodiesterase 4 inhibitor, caused more marked ureteral relaxation than the nonspecific phosphodiesterase inhibitors papaverine and theophylline and without the circulatory side effects seen with the nonspecific phosphodiesterase inhibitors (Becker et al, 1998). As the relaxant effect of rolipram was similar in human and rabbit in vitro ureteral segments, it was suggested that rolipram could potentially be of benefit in the treatment of renal colic and in the facilitation of stone passage (Becker et al, 1998). Rolipram has also been shown to relax pig intravesical ureteral segments (Hernández et al, 2004). In addition to the phosphodiesterase 4 inhibitor rolipram, phosphodiesterase 5 inhibitors relax in vitro human ureteral segments (Kuhn et al, 2000). Species differences in phosphodiesterase subtypes may exist. Although the nonspecific phosphodiesterase inhibitor papaverine decreased the frequency of ureteral peristalsis in the pig, the phosphodiesterase 4 inhibitor rolipram had no effect (Danuser et al, 2001).

A combination of the calcium channel blocker nifedipine, which causes ureteral relaxation, and the corticosteroid deflazacort, which reduces edema, was shown to facilitate spontaneous passage of 1-cm or smaller distal ureteral stones (Borghi et al, 1994; Porpiglia et al, 2000). Spontaneous expulsion of 79% of stones (average size 5.8 ± 1.8 mm) occurred in an average of 7 days in patients treated with nifedipine and deflazacort compared with spontaneous passage of 35% of stones (average size 5.5 ± 1.4 mm) within an average of 20 days in untreated patients (Porpiglia et al, 2000). In a subsequent study, the same group showed that both nifedipine and the α-adrenergic antagonist tamsulosin, when combined with deflazacort, increased the rate of spontaneous passage of lower ureteral calculi and that, in addition, tamsulosin reduced the time to spontaneous expulsion (Porpiglia et al, 2004).

With respect to treatment of ureteral calculi, it has been shown in a rabbit model that extracorporeal shock wave lithotripsy causes transient reversible histologic changes in the ureter, which are accompanied by a transient decrease in ureteral contractility (Kirkali et al, 1995). Clayman and associates showed that the duration and size of stents used after endoscopic incision of ureteral strictures may not be important (Moon et al, 1995; Gardner et al, 1996).

EFFECT OF AGE ON URETERAL FUNCTION

Clinically, the response of the ureter to pathologic conditions varies with age. **More marked degrees of ureteral dilatation are observed in the neonate and young child than in the adult.** Experimental data corroborating this clinical impression can be derived from observed age-dependent differences in the response of in vitro ureteral segments to an intraluminal pressure load. The neonatal rabbit ureter undergoes a greater degree of deformation in response to an applied intraluminal pressure than the adult rabbit ureter (Akimoto et al, 1977). Furthermore, norepinephrine decreases the diameteral deformation of the neonatal rabbit ureter in response to an applied intraluminal pressure but has little effect on the deformation of the adult rabbit ureter (Fig. 55–27). Thus, the in vitro neonatal rabbit ureter appears to be more compliant and more sensitive to norepinephrine than the adult rabbit ureter.

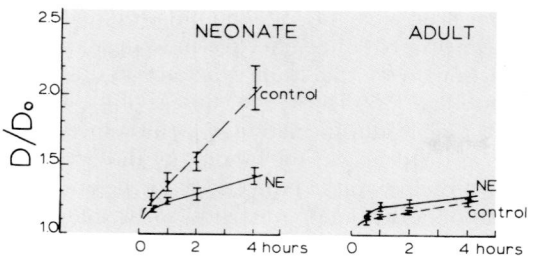

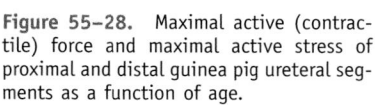

$$P = 20 \text{ g/cm}^2$$

Figure 55–27. Changes in diameter of neonatal and adult rabbit ureteral segments as a function of time after the application of a constant intraluminal pressure (P) of 20 g/cm². Diametral deformation (D/D₀) of control neonatal ureters was significantly greater than that of control adult ureters. Norepinephrine (10^{-5} M) decreased the diametral deformation of the neonatal ureters but had no significant effect on the deformation of the adult ureteral segments. D_0, initial diameter; D, diameter during deformation. (From Akimoto M, Biancani P, Weiss RM: Comparative pressure-length-diameter relationships of neonatal and adult rabbit ureters. Invest Urol 1977;14:297.)

Age also affects the response of the ureter to β-adrenergic agonists, with a decrease in the relaxant response to the β-adrenergic agonist isoproterenol with aging (Wheeler et al, 1990). The relaxant response to β-adrenergic agonists is related, in part, to cAMP levels. It has been shown that, with aging, there is a decrease in the enzymatic activities involved in the synthesis of cAMP (Wheeler et al, 1986) but no change in the enzymatic activities involved in cAMP degradation (Cho et al, 1988). These data suggest that the decrease in the ability of isoproterenol to relax the ureter with aging is due to a decrease in the ability of isoproterenol to activate adenylyl

cyclase, the enzyme involved in cAMP synthesis. Developmental differences in the response of the ureter to metabolic inhibitors are evident, with cyanide causing a larger decrease in force in the adult than in the neonatal guinea pig ureter (Bullock and Wray, 1998a, 1998b).

A progressive increase in ureteral cross-sectional muscle area is observed in the guinea pig between 3 weeks and 3 years of age. This is in accord with the findings of Cussen (1967), who noted in a human autopsy study in subjects ranging in age from 12 weeks of gestation to 12 years of age that there is a progressive increase in the population of smooth muscle cells and a small increase in the overall size of the individual smooth muscle cells. In addition, an irregular increase in the number of elastic fibers was observed with increasing age.

The contractility of the ureter is also affected by age. The maximal active force of isolated guinea pig ureteral segments increases between 3 weeks and 3 years of age (Fig. 55–28) (Hong et al, 1980). The increase in force developed between 3 weeks and 3 months of age seems to be attributable to an increase in contractility because there is an associated increase in active stress (force per unit area of muscle). The increase in force developed between 3 months and 3 years of age can be explained by an increase in muscle mass alone because there is no change in active stress between these two age groups (see Fig. 55–28).

Although changes in the force-length relations of guinea pig ureter occur with age, the force-velocity relations do not change with age (Biancani et al, 1984). Thus, although ureteral contractility increases during early development, as shown by an increase in force per unit area of muscle, or stress, no significant change is apparent in the rate of the driving reactions that control the contractile process, that is, no change in shortening, velocity, work, or power.

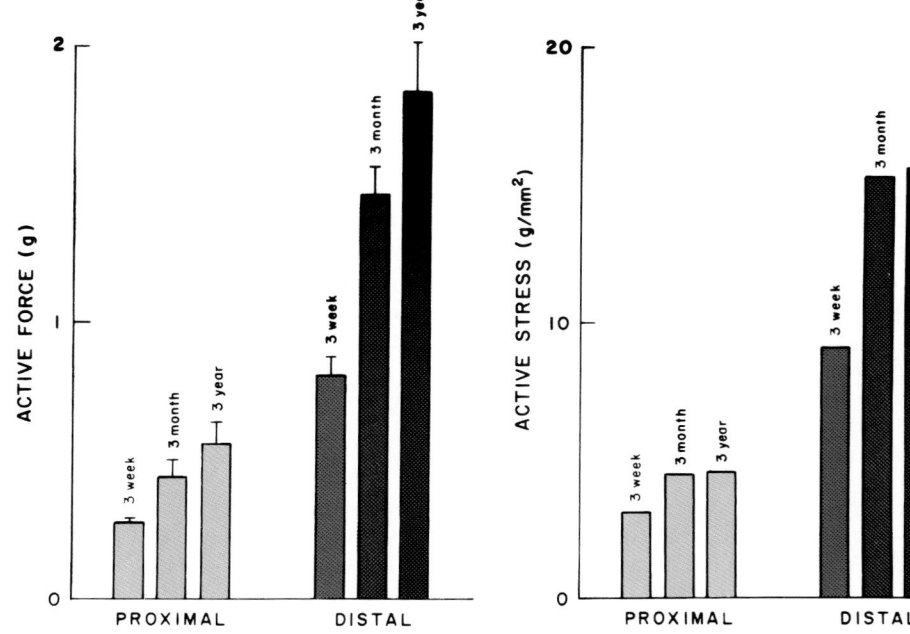

Figure 55–28. Maximal active (contractile) force and maximal active stress of proximal and distal guinea pig ureteral segments as a function of age.

EFFECT OF PREGNANCY ON URETERAL FUNCTION

Hydroureteronephrosis of pregnancy begins in the second trimester of gestation and subsides within the first month after parturition. It is more severe on the right side, and the ureteral dilatation does not occur below the pelvic brim. Roberts (1976) has presented a strong case in favor of obstruction as the etiologic factor in the development of hydrouretero-nephrosis of pregnancy, whereas other investigators have suggested a hormonal mechanism for the ureteral dilatation of pregnancy (Van Wagenen and Jenkins, 1939).

Roberts (1976) emphasized the following: (1) Elevated baseline (resting) ureteral pressures consistent with obstructive changes have been recorded above the pelvic brim in pregnant women, and these pressures decrease when positional changes permit the uterus to fall away from the ureters (Sala and Rubi, 1967). (2) Normal ureteral contractile pressures recorded during pregnancy suggest that hormonally induced ureteral atony is not the prime factor in ureteral dilatation of pregnancy. (3) Women whose ureters do not cross the pelvic brim (i.e., those with pelvic kidneys or ileal conduits) do not develop hydronephrosis of pregnancy. (4) Hydronephrosis of pregnancy usually does not occur in quadrupeds, whose uterus hangs away from the ureters (Traut and Kuder, 1938). (5) Elevated ureteral pressures in the pregnant monkey return to normal when the uterus is elevated from the ureters at laparotomy or when the fetus and placenta are removed from the uterus.

Observed hormonal effects on ureteral function have been used to implicate a hormonal mechanism in the ureteral dilatation of pregnancy, although difficulties in interpretation arise from inconsistencies in the data. Several studies have shown an inhibitory effect of **progesterone** on ureteral function (Kumar, 1962). Progesterone has been noted to increase the degree of ureteral dilatation during pregnancy and to retard the rate of disappearance of hydroureter in postpartum women (Lubin et al, 1941). Other studies, however, have failed to demonstrate an effect of progesterone on ureteral activity in animals (McNellis and Sherline, 1967) or in humans (Lapides, 1948), and still others have failed to induce changes in ureteral activity in women through the administration of estrogens, progesterone, or a mixture of these drugs (Clayton and Roberts, 1973; Marchant, 1972). Although some workers have noted that estrogens increase ureteral activity (Hundley et al, 1942), the majority of investigators have failed to observe an effect of estrogens in animal models (Abramson et al, 1953) or in humans (Kumar, 1962). Thus, **obstruction appears to be the primary factor in the development of hydronephrosis of pregnancy, although some evidence suggests that a combination of hormonal and obstructive factors is involved** (Fainstat, 1963).

EFFECT OF DRUGS ON THE URETER

To assess the effect of drugs on the ureter, it is necessary to understand the anatomic, physiologic, and biochemical properties of the ureter, in addition to understanding the principles of drug action. For a drug to elicit a given response, it is necessary to achieve and maintain an appropriate concentration of that drug at its site of action. Factors that can influence the achievement of an effective concentration of drug at a site of action are (1) the route of administration and cellular distribution of the drug; (2) the dosage of the drug administered; (3) the biotransformation, including metabolism and excretion, of the drug; (4) the binding of the drug to plasma and tissue proteins; and (5) the effects of age and disease on the absorption, distribution, metabolism, and elimination of the drug.

The literature contains considerable confusing and conflicting information concerning the effects of drugs on the ureter. To some extent, the discrepancies in the available data are due to poorly controlled experimental procedures or to attempts to compare dissimilar functional responses of the ureter with a given drug. To simplify the present section, no attempt is made to analyze the validity of each pharmacologic study or to rationalize discrepancies in the literature; rather, an overview is presented with an attempt to provide a consensus that, at times, may be prejudiced by personal bias. Furthermore, discussion of drugs related to the nervous system, pregnancy, and a variety of pathologic states is included in earlier sections of this chapter.

Histamine and Its Antagonists

Histamine has a dual action on smooth muscle; it may (1) release catecholamines from sympathetic nerve endings or (2) act directly on receptors within the smooth muscle. In addition, histamine may have excitatory or inhibitory effects on ureteral function. The majority of studies have shown an excitatory effect of histamine on ureteral function (Borgstedt et al, 1962; Sharkey et al, 1965; Vereecken, 1973; Benedito et al, 1991), a finding that may be species dependent (Tindall, 1972). **Histamine's excitatory effect on the ureter and UVJ appears to be mediated by H1 receptors** as it is inhibited by the H1 receptor antagonists mepyramine and dimethindene but not by the H2 receptor antagonist cimetidine (Benedito et al, 1991; Dodel et al, 1996). An H1 agonist, 2-(2-pyridyl)ethylamine, increases ureteral contractility (Dodel et al, 1996). The excitatory effect of histamine on the sheep UVJ is partially blocked by scopolamine, suggesting an indirect stimulatory action of histamine on intramural parasympathetic nerves. The antihistamines diphenhydramine (Benadryl) and tripelennamine have been shown to inhibit the effects of histamine on the ureter (Borgstedt et al, 1962; Sharkey et al, 1965). **The H2 receptor mediates inhibitory effects of histamine.** Histamine and the H2 receptor agonist impromidine relax precontracted ureteral segments, actions that are inhibited by the H2 receptor antagonist cimetidine (Dodel et al, 1996).

Serotonin

Serotonin (5-HT) has been reported to stimulate (Vereecken, 1973; Dodel et al, 1996; Hauser et al, 2002; Hernández et al, 2003), inhibit (Mazzella and Schroeder, 1960), or have no effect (Finberg and Peart, 1970) on a variety of ureteral preparations. In the pig ureter the contractile effects appear to be mediated by $5\text{-}HT_2$ receptors (Hauser et al, 2002; Hernández et al, 2003). Gidener and colleagues (1999) showed that 5-HT induces concentration-dependent contractions of isolated human ureteral segments. However, their studies suggested no involvement of 5-HT$_2$ receptors in the contractile effects of 5-HT. Tetrodotoxin, guanethidine, and phentolamine had an inhibitory effect on 5-HT–induced contractions of pig isolated intravesical ureteral segments, suggesting that some of the contractile effects of 5-HT are indirectly mediated through release of norepinephrine from sympathetic nerves (Hernández et al, 2003).

Kinins

The kinins—kallidin, eledoisin, and bradykinin—increase the frequency of contraction and baseline intraluminal pressure of the dog ureter (Boyarsky et al, 1966a, 1966b; Labay and Boyarsky, 1966), and bradykinin decreases the contractile force of the sheep ureter (Kaygisiz et al, 1995).

Angiotensin

Angiotensin has a stimulatory effect on the ureter. Angiotensin II and mRNA for angiotensinogen, a principal precursor of angiotensin II, renin, angiotensin-converting enzyme, and type I angiotensin receptor are expressed in the human ureter (Santis et al, 2003). Losartan, an angiotensin II receptor antagonist, decreases the amplitude and frequency of spontaneous contractions of human ureteral segments. Angiotensin II induces phasic contractions of rat ureteral segments, an effect that is inhibited by losartan (Fujinaka et al, 2000). The angiotensin II type I receptor also is expressed in the rat ureter (Paxton et al, 1993).

Narcotic Analgesics

Morphine has been reported to increase ureteral tone or the frequency and amplitude of ureteral contractions or both in a variety of experimental preparations and in humans (Macht, 1916b; Gruber, 1928; Ockerblad et al, 1935; Vereecken, 1973). Others, however, have failed to observe an effect of morphine on ureteral function (Gould et al, 1955; Kiil, 1957; Weinberg and Maletta, 1961; Ross et al, 1967).

Meperidine (Demerol) appears to have a similar excitatory effect on the activity of the intact dog ureter (Sharkey et al, 1968). Kiil (1957), however, failed to observe an effect of meperidine on ureteral peristalsis in humans. **If one considers only the effects on ureteral activity, there is no basis to favor morphine or meperidine in the treatment of renal colic. Both agents may have ureteral spasmogenic effects that theoretically would detract from their value in the management of ureteral colic. They certainly do not have potentially valuable spasmolytic actions.** Their efficacy in treating colic depends on their central nervous system actions, which decrease the perception of pain.

Prostaglandins

Prostaglandins are derived from fatty acids and have a variety of biologic actions in various systems of the body. Their effects vary with the species, type of prostaglandin, endocrine status of the tissue, experimental conditions, and origin of the smooth muscle. **The "primary" prostaglandins (PGs), PGE$_1$, PGE$_2$, and PGF$_{2\alpha}$, are synthesized from the fatty acid arachidonic acid by enzymatic reactions involving two**

cyclooxygenase (COX) isoforms, COX-1 and COX-2 (Vane, 1998). In most tissues COX-1 is constitutively expressed and is involved in the regulation of normal physiologic processes, whereas COX-2 is induced in response to processes such as inflammation and mitogenesis (Mitchell and Warner, 1999). **These enzymatic reactions can be inhibited by indomethacin and aspirin and by a number of COX-1 and COX-2 inhibitors.**

Indomethacin has been employed in the management of ureteral colic (Holmlund and Sjöden, 1978; Flannigan et al, 1983; Jönsson et al, 1987). The beneficial effects probably are due to indomethacin's inhibition of the PG-mediated vasodilatation that occurs subsequent to obstruction (Allen et al, 1978; Sjöden et al, 1982). The vasodilatation theoretically would result in an increase in glomerular capillary pressure and a subsequent increase in pelviureteral pressure. Indomethacin, by reducing pelviureteral pressure and thus pelviureteral wall tension, might eliminate some of the pain of renal colic that is dependent on distention of the upper urinary tract. An upregulation of COX-2 mRNA and protein supports the potential use of selective COX-2 inhibitors in the treatment of obstructive ureteral disease (Nakada et al, 2002). **A potential problem with the use of indomethacin for the treatment of renal colic is that PG-mediated vasodilatation aids in preserving renal function; thus, indomethacin may provide pain relief but it may be potentially deleterious to renal function** (Perlmutter et al, 1993; Kristova et al, 2000).

PGE$_1$ inhibits the activity of the dog (Boyarsky et al, 1966b; Wooster, 1971; Abrams and Feneley, 1976) and guinea pig ureter (Vermue and Den Hertog, 1987). PGE$_1$ inhibition of ureteral activity in the guinea pig is associated with an increase in cAMP levels (Vermue and Den Hertog, 1987). In the ureter, PGE$_1$ activates adenylyl cyclase, and this may account for the increase in cAMP (Wheeler et al, 1986). Johns and Wooster (1975) suggested that the inhibitory effects of PGE$_1$ on ureteral activity depended on the sequestration of Ca^{2+} at the inner surface of the cell membrane, with a resultant increase in outward K$^+$ conductance and hyperpolarization of the membrane. Although reports have indicated that PGE$_2$ relaxes the ureter (Vermue and Den Hertog, 1987), other reports describe an excitatory action of PGE$_2$ on sheep (Thulesius and Angelo-Khattar, 1985) and human (Angelo-Khattar et al, 1985; Cole et al, 1988) ureters and on renal pelvic smooth muscle (Lundstam et al, 1985). In contrast to the inhibitory effects of PGE$_1$, PGF$_{2\alpha}$ increases the frequency of ureteral peristalsis in the dog (Boyarsky and Labay, 1969). In human ureteral preparations PGE$_1$ and PGE$_2$ have been shown to decrease spontaneous contractions, whereas PGF$_{2\alpha}$ increased ureteral contractility (Abrams and Feneley, 1976). In human renal pelvis and ureter there is a higher concentration of PGF$_{2\alpha}$ than PGE$_2$ (Zwergel et al, 1991). The prostanoid PGI$_2$ is synthesized in the urothelium of the ureter (Ali et al, 1998). COX inhibitors such as indomethacin have been shown to inhibit the activity of rat (Davidson and Lang, 2000), guinea pig (Davidson and Lang, 2000), sheep (Thulesius and Angelo-Khattar, 1985), and human ureters (Angelo-Khattar et al, 1985; Cole et al, 1988) and renal pelvic smooth muscle (Lundstam et al, 1985; Zhang and Lang, 1994; Santicioli et al, 1995a; Davidson and Lang, 2000). The nonspecific COX inhibitor, diclofenac and the selective COX-2 inhibitor

NS-398 have been shown to be equipotent in inhibiting agonist-induced contractions of isolated pig and human ureter (Mastrangelo et al, 2000; Nakada et al, 2000) and diclofenac has also been shown to relax human ureteral segments that were precontracted with KCl (Sivrikaya et al, 2003). Species differences may exist with COX-2 being the primary enzyme involved in synthesizing PGs in the guinea pig upper urinary tract and COX-1 being the primary enzyme involved in PG synthesis in the rat upper urinary tract (Davidson and Lang, 2000).

Cardiac Glycosides

Ouabain, a cardiac glycoside, has an effect on ureteral activity that appears to be species dependent. In the isolated cat ureter, ouabain produces a marked increase in contractility, which is usually followed by a late decrease in excitability (Weiss et al, 1970). In the guinea pig ureter, ouabain inhibits activity without a preliminary potentiation of contractility (Washizu, 1968; Hendrickx et al, 1975). The inhibitory effects of ouabain are accompanied by a shortening of the action potential duration, a decrease of the number of oscillations on the plateau of the guinea pig action potential, and a decrease in the RMP.

Calcium Antagonists

As Ca^{2+} is necessary for the development of the action potential and contraction of the ureter, agents that block the movement of Ca^{2+} into the cell would be expected to depress ureteral function. Voltage-dependent Ca^{2+} channel antagonist binding sites (receptors) have been demonstrated in the ureter, and their density decreases with age (Yoshida et al, 1992). These dihydropyridine-sensitive, **L-type voltage-dependent Ca^{2+} channels appear to provide the main inward current for generation of the ureteral action potential and the phasic contractile response** (Shuba, 1977; Brading et al, 1983; Aickin et al, 1984; Imaizumi et al, 1989; Lang, 1989). Potassium-induced ureteral contractions depend on the inward movement of Ca^{2+} through L-type voltage-dependent Ca^{2+} channels (Maggi and Giuliani, 1995). The dihydropyridine Ca^{2+} channel agonist Bay K 8644 has an excitatory effect on ureteral activity (Maggi et al, 1994a) and potentiates K^+-induced contractions. The Ca^{2+} channel blockers verapamil, D-600 (a methoxy derivative of verapamil), diltiazem, and nifedipine have been shown to inhibit ureteral activity (Golenhofen and Lammel, 1972; Vereecken et al, 1975; Hertle and Nawrath, 1984; Hong et al, 1985; Sakanashi et al, 1985, 1986; Maggi et al, 1994a). These inhibitory effects are accompanied by decreases in the duration of the action potential, the number of oscillations on the plateau of the guinea pig action potential, excitability, and the rate of rise and amplitude of the action potential. High concentrations of verapamil and D-600 cause a complete cessation of electrical and mechanical activity.

Potassium Channel Openers

Potassium channel openers such as cromakalim, BRL 38227, and PFK217-744b hyperpolarize smooth muscle membranes and **inhibit renal pelvic and ureteral activity** (Kontani et al, 1993; Maggi et al, 1994b; Weiss et al, 2002). The inhibitory effects of cromakalim are prevented by glibenclamide, pro-

viding evidence that ATP-sensitive K^+ channels are involved in these processes (Maggi et al, 1994b). Activation of these K^+ channels may reduce the probability of the opening of voltage-sensitive Ca^{2+} channels, inhibit agonist-induced increases in IP_3, or reduce Ca^{2+} sensitivity of contractile elements, processes that are important in the generation of the ureteral action potential and the contractile response (Cook and Quast, 1990; Quayle et al, 1997).

The tricyclic antidepressant amitriptyline (Elavil) has been shown to relax isolated pig and human ureteral strips by opening potassium channels (Achar et al, 2003). This relaxation response is inhibited by 4-AP, a voltage dependent potassium channel blocker. Nicorandil, a K^+ channel opener and NO donor, stimulates guanylyl cyclase activity with formation of cGMP and hyperpolarizes the smooth muscle with resultant relaxation of rabbit, guinea pig, and human ureter (Klaus et al, 1989; 1990; Weiss et al, 2002). The relaxant effects of nicorandil can be inhibited by both the K_{ATP} antagonist glibenclamide and the guanylyl cyclase inhibitor methylene blue (Weiss et al, 2002).

Endothelins

Endothelins are potent vasoconstrictor peptides that exist in three isoforms: ET-1, ET-2, and ET-3. These peptides interact with their specific receptors: ET_A, ET_B, and ET_C. Endothelin binding sites (receptors) have been identified in the ureter and renal pelvis (Eguchi et al, 1991; Latifpour et al, 1995; Wada et al, 2001), where they are primarily of the ET_A subtype (Latifpour et al, 1995; Wada et al, 2001). Diabetes upregulates the expression of ureteral endothelin receptors (Nakamura et al, 1997). Endothelins have been shown to initiate contractions in isolated guinea pig and porcine ureters (Eguchi et al, 1991; Maggi et al, 1992a) and increase the contractile force of renal pelvis smooth muscle (Wada et al, 2001).

Antibiotics

Ampicillin causes relaxation of the ureter and antagonizes the stimulatory effects of barium chloride ($BaCl_2$), histamine, serotonin, and carbachol on the ureter, suggesting that its action is directly on the smooth muscle (Benzi et al, 1970b). Chloramphenicol, the isoxazolyl penicillins, and gentamicin also have spasmolytic effects on the ureter (Benzi et al, 1970a, 1971, 1973). The tetracyclines, on the other hand, potentiate the contractile effects of $BaCl_2$ on the ureter (Benzi et al, 1973).

KEY POINT: DRUG EFFECTS ON URETER

- This section has provided an assessment of the effects of the major classes of drugs on ureteral function. Many of the studies referred to were performed on animal models, and the extrapolation of the data to the intact human ureter is often difficult. In the clinical situation, the relatively sparse blood supply to the ureter limits the distribution of drugs to the ureter. In addition, many drugs with potential usefulness in the management of ureteral abnormalities have potential untoward side effects when used in concentrations required to affect the ureter.

SUGGESTED READINGS

Biancani P, Hausman M, Weiss RM: Effect of obstruction on ureteral circumferential force-length relations. Am J Physiol 1982;243:F204.

Biancani P, Zabinski MP, Weiss RM: Time course of ureteral changes with acute and chronic obstruction. Am J Physiol 1976;231:393.

Burdyga ThV, Wray S: The relationship between the action potential, intracellular calcium and force in intact phasic, guinea pig ureteric smooth muscle. J Physiol (Lond) 1999;520:867.

David SG, Cebrian C, Vaughan ED Jr, Herblinger D: C-kit and ureteral peristalsis. J Urol 2005;173:292.

Gosling JA, Dixon JS: Species variation in the location of upper urinary tract pacemaker cells. Invest Urol 1974;11:418.

Griffiths DJ: The mechanics of urine transport in the upper urinary tract: 2. The discharge of the bolus into the bladder and dynamics at high rates of flow. Neurourol Urodyn 1983;2:167.

Griffiths DJ, Notschaele C: The mechanics of urine transport in the upper urinary tract: I. The dynamics of the isolated bolus. Neurourol Urodyn 1983;2:155.

Klemm MF, Exintaris B, Lang RJ: Identification of the cells underlying pacemaker activity in the guinea pig upper urinary tract. J Physiol (Lond) 1999;519:867.

Koff SA, Thrall JH: The diagnosis of obstruction in experimental hydroureteronephrosis: Mechanism for progressive urinary tract dilation. Invest Urol 1981b;19:85.

Lang RJ, Davidson ME, Exintaris B: Pyeloureteral motility and ureteral peristalsis: Essential role of sensory nerves and endogenous prostaglandins. Exp Physiol 2002;87:129.

Maggi CA: Tachykinins and calcitonin gene-related peptide (CGRP) as cotransmitters released from peripheral endings of sensory nerves. Prog Neurobiol 1995;45:1.

McGuire EJ, Woodside JR, Borden TA, Weiss RM: Prognostic value of urodynamic testing in myelodysplastic patients. J Urol 1981;126:205.

Roberts JA: Hydronephrosis of pregnancy. Urology 1976;8:1.

Weiss RM: Clinical implications of ureteral physiology. J Urol 1979;121:401.

Weiss RM: Ureteral function. Urology 1978;12:114.

56 | Physiology and Pharmacology of the Bladder and Urethra

NAOKI YOSHIMURA, MD, PHD ·
MICHAEL B. CHANCELLOR, MD

Overactive bladder syndrome is an internationally "hot" topic. The tremendous number of patients with this problem is just now becoming recognized, and the potential economic impact is staggering (Yoshimura and Chancellor, 2002). In the United States, there are an estimated 34 million community-dwelling men and women with overactive bladder (Hu et al, 2004). It costs an estimated $19.5 billion and $12.6 billion a year in the United States to manage urinary incontinence and overactive bladder, respectively (Hu et al, 2003, 2004). With the continued aging of the populations in all developed countries, the problems associated with bladder control will certainly continue to increase. In this chapter, we review the neuromuscular physiology and pathophysiology of the bladder and urethra. We discuss what is new in pharmacology that may help us better treat our patients with voiding dysfunction. To conclude, we speculate about future treatment methods to conquer urinary incontinence, such as gene therapy.

The micturition process can be visualized as a complex of neural circuits in the brain and spinal cord that coordinate the activity of smooth muscle in the bladder and urethra (Torrens 1987; de Groat et al, 1993; Yoshimura and de Groat, 1997a). These circuits act as on-off switches to alternate the lower urinary tract between two modes of operation: storage and elimination.

Injuries or diseases of the nervous system in adults can disrupt the voluntary control of micturition, causing the re-emergence of reflex micturition and resulting in detrusor overactivity and urge incontinence (Fig. 56–1) (Torrens, 1987; Wein, 1992; de Groat et al, 1993; Yoshimura and de Groat, 1997a). Because of the complexity of the central nervous control of the lower urinary tract, urgency incontinence can result from a variety of neurologic disorders. In addition, urgency incontinence may be due to intrinsic detrusor myogenic abnormalities, resulting in detrusor overactivity (Brading, 1997). The morphology and function of the detrusor wall are reviewed, including new insights into the urothelium.

Urethral dysfunction can also be an important cause of urinary incontinence in both women and men. Many health care professionals who are not trained in urology erroneously believe that urethral dysfunction can be caused only by genuine stress urinary incontinence. This is not true. Urethral dysfunction can also cause urge incontinence. Increased bladder outlet urethral resistance in men with benign prostatic hyperplasia and in younger men and women with detrusor-sphincter dyssynergia (i.e., spinal cord injury, multiple sclerosis) causes secondary bladder changes. Increased bladder outlet resistance causes secondary bladder remodeling and can result in urgency incontinence. In addition, it can be speculated that in patients with mixed stress and urgency incontinence, stress incontinence can cause urgency incontinence. Leakage of urine into the urethra (stress incontinence) may stimulate urethral afferents that induce an involuntary voiding reflex (urge incontinence).

This chapter reviews studies in humans and animals that provide insights into
- **organization of neural pathways controlling the lower urinary tract;**
- **neurotransmitters involved in storage and voiding reflexes;**
- **function of the detrusor wall, including urothelium and smooth muscle;**

- contribution of the smooth and skeletal muscle urethral function and interaction of urethra with bladder function;
- action of drugs on the bladder; and
- mechanisms that contribute to overactive bladder.

Speculation about what the future holds in terms of research and treatment of lower urinary tract dysfunction ends the chapter. With the mapping of the human genome now completed, we believe that we are on the verge of a paradigm shift in clinical medicine. The future will bring molecular medicine into the hands of the practicing urologists.

RELEVANT ANATOMY AND BIOMECHANICS

The bladder can be divided into two parts: a body lying above the ureteral orifices and a base consisting of the trigone and bladder neck (Elbadawi and Schenk, 1966). Histologic examination of the bladder body reveals that myofibrils are arranged into fascicles in random directions (Donker et al, 1982). This architecture differs from the discrete circular and longitudinal smooth muscle layers in the ureter or gastrointestinal tract.

The bladder outlet is composed of the bladder base, urethra, and external urethral sphincter (Fig. 56–2). The bladder base has a laminar architecture with a superficial longitudinal layer lying beneath the trigone. A muscle layer deep to the superficial layer is continuous with the detrusor (Tanagho, 1982; Dixon and Gosling, 1987; Zderic et al, 1996). The smaller muscle bundles of the deep muscle layer in the bladder base exhibit a predominantly circular orientation.

The urethra begins at the internal meatus of the bladder and extends to the external meatus. In the male, four segments are readily identified. The first is the preprostatic portion, or the bladder neck. The prostatic urethra then extends throughout the length of the gland, terminating at its apex. The membranous urethra extends from the prostatic apex through the pelvic floor musculature until it becomes the bulbous and penile urethra (fourth segment) at the base of the penis. In women, the urethra extends throughout the distal third of the anterior vaginal wall from the bladder neck to the meatus. **The**

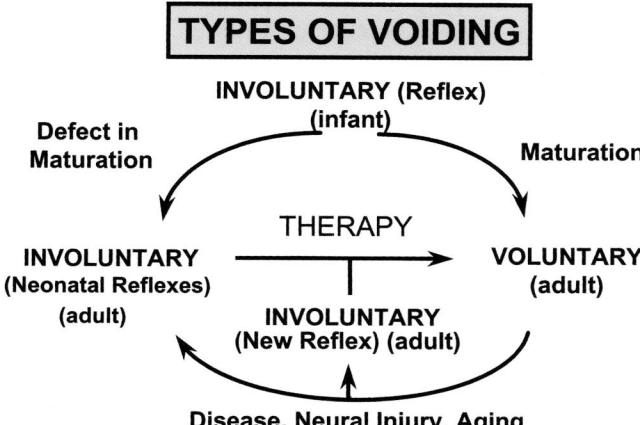

Figure 56–1. Bladder's "circle of life" by influence of maturation, pathologic processes, and aging. In infants, voiding is initiated and coordinated by reflex circuits. After maturation of central neural pathways, voiding is controlled voluntarily by neural circuitry in higher centers in the brain. A defect in neural maturation allows involuntary voiding to persist in adults. Aging, neural injury, or diseases such as benign prostatic hyperplasia can disrupt the central voluntary micturition neural pathways. Pathologic processes can lead to the formation of new reflex circuitry by reemergence of primitive reflex mechanisms that were present in the infant or that appear as the result of synaptic remodeling. The goal of therapy is to reverse the pathologic process and to reestablish normal voluntary control of voiding.

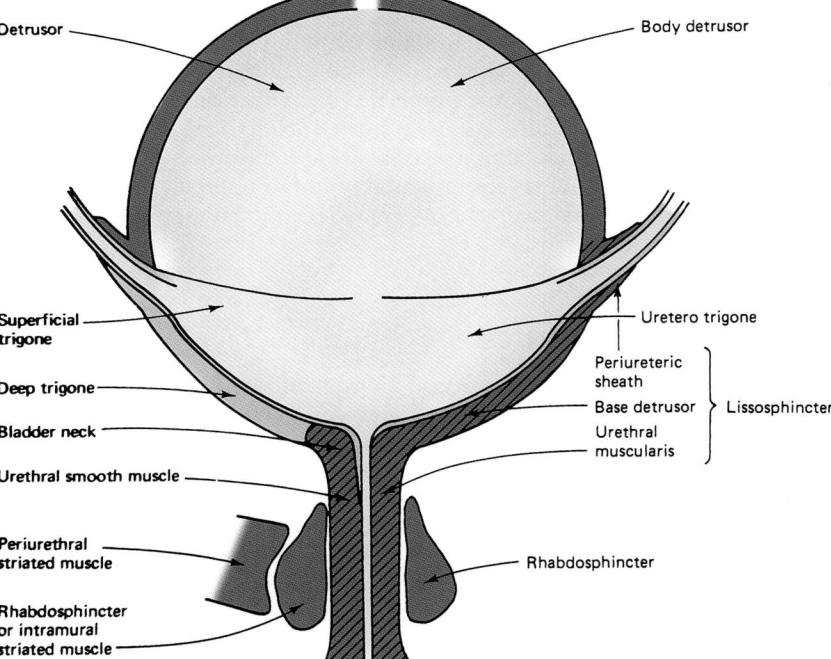

Figure 56–2. Anatomy of the bladder and its outlet as defined by Gosling and Dixon (left) versus Elbadawi and coworkers (right). (From Torrens M, Morrison JFB: The Physiology of the Urinary Bladder. Berlin, Springer-Verlag, 1987:1.)

urethra is composed of tissues that aid continence rather than a single discrete and visible "sphincter." A network of vascular subepithelial tissue in women contributes to a urethral seal effect.

It is debatable whether the detrusor or trigone muscles project into the proximal urethra (see Fig. 56–2). Embryologic data support the concept of a separate origin for muscles of the bladder and urethra (Dixon and Gosling, 1987; Zderic et al, 1996). Histologic studies show that the longitudinal muscle of the bladder base extends distally into the urethra to form an inner longitudinal layer (Hutch and Rambo, 1967; Tanagho, 1982). Examination of adult and fetal specimens shows that striated and smooth muscles coalesce in the urethra and interdigitate with the fibrous prostatic capsule (Oerlich, 1980). Conversely, a complete and competent ring of smooth muscle at the male bladder neck has been described (Gosling, 1999). No such collar of muscle is identified in the female. The maintenance of continence in men and some women with destruction or opening of the bladder neck argues that the bladder neck may not be the principal site of urinary continence (Chapple et al, 1989). **The importance of the bladder neck as the principal zone of maintaining continence remains controversial.**

The bladder neck serves an important function in reproduction. In men, closure of the bladder neck facilitates anterograde ejaculation. This is accompanied through a rich noradrenergic innervation by sympathetic nerves that actively contract the bladder neck during ejaculation. However, in women, the density of adrenergic innervation in the bladder neck is reportedly less than that in men (de Groat and Booth, 1993).

Understanding voiding and continence requires some working knowledge of the contractile properties of smooth and striated muscle. The contractile properties of bladder smooth muscle cells are well suited for either urine storage or release. Filling the bladder at a slow physiologic rate maintains an intravesical pressure of less than 10 cm H_2O (Klevmark, 1974). Acute denervation of the bladder does not appreciably alter this low filling pressure (Langley and Whiteside, 1951). This concept has been used to support the hypothesis that the intrinsic myogenic or viscoelastic properties of cellular and extracellular components are major contributors to low-pressure bladder filling and compliance (see "Mechanisms of Detrusor Overactivity"). Conversely, neural input is required for the rapid and sustained smooth muscle contraction accompanying voiding.

Bladder Biomechanics

What basic bladder hydrodynamics and biomechanical properties should practicing urologists know and why should they know them? These are some of the questions we attempt to answer in this section. We lay the foundation of the relationship between bladder shape, size, pressure, and tension as expressed by Laplace's law (Chancellor et al, 1996). Marquis Pierre-Simon de Laplace (1979-1827) has been called the Newton of France. Laplace made the keen observation that the tension in the wall of a container necessary to contain a given pressure is directly proportional to the radius of curvature at any point. This is Laplace's law.

It is intuitive to urologists that there is a relationship between intravesical pressure and the size of the bladder and that this affects the tension in the bladder wall. Increased wall tension activates bladder afferent nerves that evoke the sensation of bladder filling and also can evoke involuntary bladder contractions. Large increases in intravesical pressure, especially in a hypertrophic, small-capacity bladder, can dramatically elevate bladder wall tension, producing ischemia, vesicoureteral reflux, and bacterial emptying into the venous or lymphatic systems. Elevated wall tension and intravesical pressure may be the cause of bladder rupture sometimes seen after enterocystoplasty.

Laplace's equation states that there is a direct relationship between wall tension and intravesical pressure and bladder size. In this equation, T is tension, P is intravesical pressure, R is bladder radius, and d is wall thickness. During bladder filling, Pves is relatively constant. With a fully distended bladder, d, because of its relative thinness, is ignored relative to the other parameters unless a hypertrophied wall exists. Thus, T = P · R/2 approximates tension in the full normal bladder (Fig. 56–3).

Filling Mechanics

The viscoelastic behavior of the bladder and urethra depends on both neuromuscular and mechanical properties. Mechanical properties vary with the magnitude of stretch (distention), even in tissue deprived of adenosine triphosphate (ATP) (e.g., post mortem). Mechanical properties are extremely sensitive to tissue structure and composition. In the bladder and urethra, collagen and elastin content have a profound influ-

Laplace's Law $\qquad T = P_{ves}R/2d$

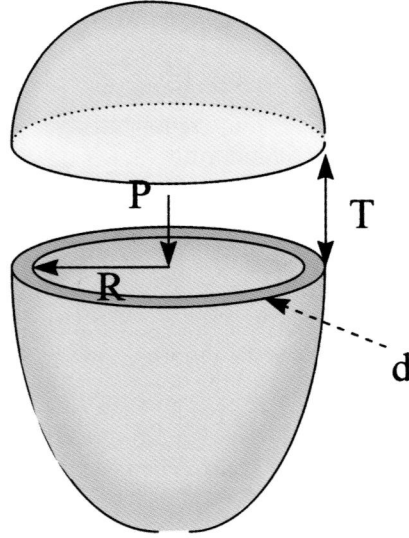

Figure 56–3. Laplace's equation describing wall tension (T) as a function of the bladder radius (R), intravesical pressure (P_{ves}), and wall thickness (d).

ence on the viscoelastic properties when these tissues are subjected to stress (force per area). Besides smooth muscle, the human bladder is composed of roughly 50% collagen and 2% elastin. With injury, obstruction, or denervation, collagen content increases (Macarak and Howard, 1999). When contractile protein content exceeds collagen, greater distensibility is achieved (compliance). Conversely, when collagen levels increase, compliance falls. Bladder compliance (C) is defined as the change in volume (V) relative to the corresponding change in intravesical pressure (P):

$$C = change \ V/change \ P$$

A decrease in compliance or efferent neural input can alter wall tension, cause afferent firing, and thereby change bladder sensations and the volume threshold for micturition. With increasing bladder volume, wall stress or tension (T) increases, as defined by Laplace's equation (see Fig. 56–3).

Bladder Accommodation

The bladder surface undergoes incredible change in size from empty to full. The percentage change is truly unmatched by any other organ in the body. The change is accommodated by both the urothelium and the bladder wall smooth muscle and connective tissue.

The changes in the thickness of the lamina propria and the detrusor are mechanical requirements for the bladder to accommodate increasing urine volume. During filling, the lamina propria thins at a faster rate than the muscle wall. It has been proposed that bladder wall thinning during filling is the result of a rearrangement of the muscle bundles and also alteration of collagen coil structure (Macarak and Howard, 1999). A combination of muscle and connective tissue spatial changes is required to accommodate urine at low intravesical pressures (Chang et al, 1999).

During filling, the detrusor reorganizes and muscle bundles shift position from a top-to-bottom to a side-to-side configuration. During reorganization, the coiled type III collagen fibers connecting the muscle bundles orthogonally become extended, longer, and taut and assume an orientation such that the fibers become oriented parallel to the lumen.

Voiding Mechanics

Intravesical pressure reflects the combined factors of abdominal (Pabd) and detrusor (Pdet) pressures. Therefore,

$$Pdet = Pves - Pabd$$

Micturition relies on a neurally mediated detrusor contraction, causing Pdet to rise without a significant change in Pabd. To assess the strength of a detrusor contraction, Pdet alone is an insufficient measure. A muscle can use energy either to generate force or to shorten its length. Because the bladder is a hollow viscus, the force developed contributes to Pdet, whereas the velocity of shortening relates to urine flow (Q). There is a trade-off between generating Pdet and urine flow. This has been nicely reviewed by Griffiths (1988). **If urethral resistance is low, as in women with sphincter insufficiency and even in normal continent women, Pdet may be almost undetectable; and yet, these women with modest Pdet would have normal flow rates. The trade-off between Pdet and Q**

resembles a curve for constant mechanical power (W) in which

$$W = Pdet \times Q$$

The equation explains why a woman could have normal detrusor contractility and normal detrusor power despite low voiding pressure. During micturition, Pdet reflects outlet resistance. When the urethra opens widely with a high flow (Q), one needs little Pdet to achieve the work necessary to empty the bladder. The key message is that low voiding pressure in a woman does not equate with impaired detrusor contractility; she may simply be able to open her urethra widely. Moreover, pressure-flow nomograms developed for men for diagnosis of obstruction should not be applied to women without validation.

Tissue Biomechanics and Bladder Function

In addition to important molecular and cellular parameters, tissue- and organ-level bladder properties are important to the function of the bladder during filling (Damaser, 1999). Fundamental mechanical properties include the stress-strain relationship, viscoelasticity, and deformation of bladder tissue. Whole-bladder properties include bladder shape, mass, and distention. Organ-level pressure-volume assessment is usually achieved by the cystometrogram. Although it is an essential tool for the urologist, the cystometrogram *alone* cannot rigorously distinguish between the effects of changes in tissue compliance and the shape and wall stress distribution of the whole organ. For example, changes in the cystometrogram in spinal cord injury could be a result of alterations in both bladder shape (Ogawa et al, 1988) and tissue properties. Thus, to assess intrinsic changes in bladder wall properties, proper assessment of the changes in bladder function requires an understanding of bladder wall biomechanical properties. The biomechanical components contributing to tissue mechanical responses have been studied in isolated detrusor tissue (Wagg and Fry, 1999). However, an ongoing problem is to determine whether clinically observed alterations in detrusor function are due to changes in the contractile apparatus or in the surrounding extracellular matrix.

The complexity of the bladder shape raises similar questions. The bladder can be mechanically idealized as a thin-walled shell. In the theory of thin shells, surface geometry is an integral part of how wall tensions are spatially distributed (Flugge, 1973). That is, a change in surface geometry can alter the stress distributions independent of changes in the mechanical properties. Thus, focal points of high curvature on the bladder surface (Fig. 56–4) can potentially induce regions of localized stress concentrations and may be related to bladder deformity, for example, during the spinal cord injury disease process. These phenomena have been underscored by the bladder shape modeling work of Damaser and Lehman (1995), who demonstrated the sensitivity of bladder wall stress distribution on bladder shape.

Although it is typically modeled as a spheroid, the bladder is clearly one of the more irregularly shaped anatomic structures. Irregularity in bladder shape, especially when it is full, is due to contact with surrounding pelvic structures. Note in

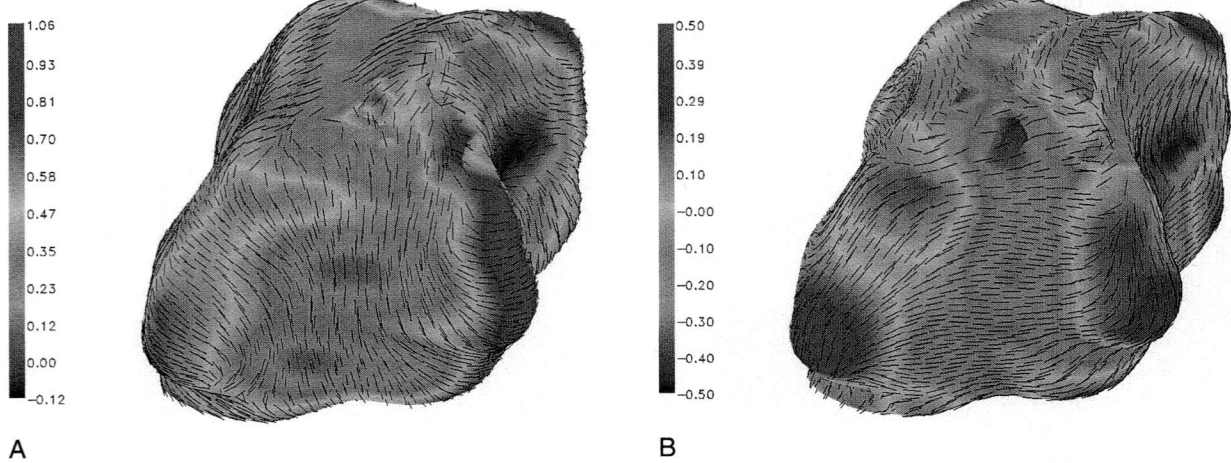

Figure 56–4. Major principal curvature (**A**) and minor principal curvature (**B**) for the bladder. Curvature magnitudes are indicated by gray scale and directions by vectors. When the bladder is full, as in this case, wide variations in curvature exist because of contact with the surrounding pelvic structures.

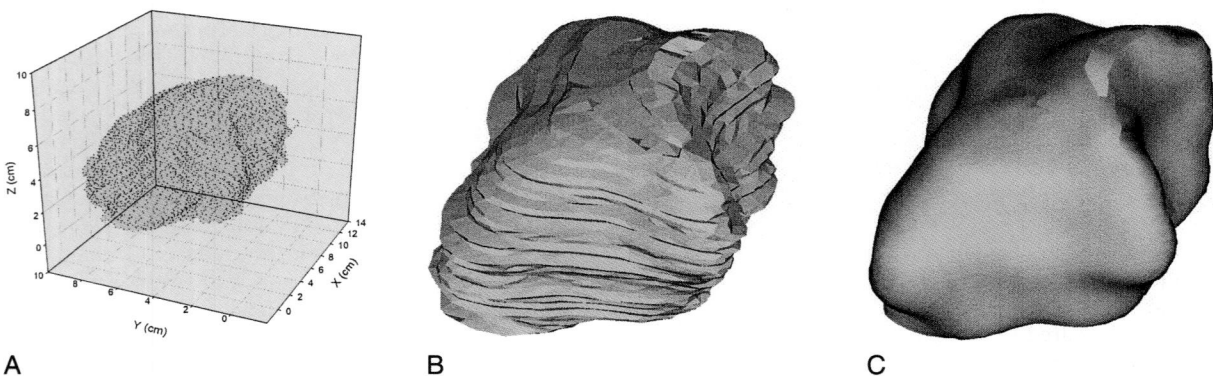

Figure 56–5. Three-dimensional reconstruction of the bladder. **A,** "Point cloud" of 3146 digitized surface points from a normal human bladder from computed tomographic images. **B,** The resulting reconstructed bladder surface, revealing a complex, nonspheroidal surface. **C,** Same surface as in **B** but with the surface roughness from imaging noise removed.

particular the complex spatial distribution of surface curvatures, including pointed regions of high curvature and rapid transitions between elliptical (both principal curvatures are positive) and hyperbolic (or saddle-shaped, where one principal curvature component is negative) regions (see Fig. 56–4). By use of the techniques developed by Sacks and colleagues (1993, 1999), this roughness can be removed and the original smooth in vivo surface recovered (Fig. 56–5).

THE URINARY BLADDER

The bladder performs several important functions. First, it must store a socially adequate volume of urine. The bladder wall must be able to stretch and rearrange itself to allow an increase in bladder volume without significant rise in pressure. In other words, the bladder wall must be extremely compliant. Second, the smooth muscle and intrinsic nerves have to be protected from exposure to urine by the urothelium, which itself must also expand readily during filling. Third, bladder emptying requires synchronous activation of all the smooth muscle, because if only part of the wall contracted, the uncontracted compliant areas would stretch and

prevent the increase in pressure necessary for urine to be expelled through the urethra. This is the problem often seen in an elderly man with benign prostatic hyperplasia who develops urinary retention and a bladder diverticulum.

In this section, we review the various components of the bladder, including smooth muscle, stroma, and blood vessels. First, we focus on the detrusor smooth muscle by contrasting the characteristics of smooth and striated muscle, the activation of smooth muscle contractility, the maintenance of bladder tone, and its neural regulation. In addition, we concentrate on the urothelium, because there is now a resurgence of research interest in this thin but complex membrane. Some exciting studies are presented that discuss the barrier, transport, and neurocommunication properties of the urothelium that are just beginning to be understood. Last, we briefly discuss ion channels and how they might contribute to detrusor dysfunction.

Smooth Muscle

There are several universal characteristics of smooth muscle:

Smooth muscle consists of a sheet containing many small, spindle-shaped cells linked together at specific junctions. Smooth muscle cells contain actin and myosin, but these proteins are not arranged in a regular sarcomere pattern. Instead, each smooth muscle cell consists of a more variable matrix of contractile proteins that is attached to the plasma membrane at the junctional complexes between neighboring cells.

Smooth muscle maintains a steady level of tension that can be modulated by circulating hormones, by local factors such as nitric oxide, or by activity in the autonomic nerves.

Smooth muscle is more adaptable than skeletal muscle and is able to adjust its length over a much wider range than skeletal muscle.

Based on the assumption of a spherical bladder, the circumference of a 400-mL capacity bladder is approximately 30 cm. If the bladder empties to a residual urine volume of 10 mL, the circumference would be only 8 cm. To accomplish this feat, the detrusor would have a change in muscle length of 75%. If the bladder were to be made of skeletal muscle instead, the maximum length change would be only about 30%. The maximum "skeletal muscle bladder" emptying would be only 70% of its contents, leaving a residual urine of 120 mL. Thus, the bladder requires the unique property of smooth muscle to accomplish its job. What is assumed to be the stronger skeletal muscle is not up to the job of bladder emptying (Gabella, 1995; Brading et al, 1996; Brading, 1999).

Morphology

The individual smooth muscle cells in the bladder wall are small spindle-shaped cells with a central nucleus; fully relaxed, they are several hundred micrometers long with a 5- to 6-μm maximum diameter. Skeletal muscle fibers are some 20 times wider and thousands of times longer (Smet et al, 1996).

Smooth muscle has a unique range of physiologic properties and consists of sheets containing many small spindle-shaped cells linked together at specific junctions. Each cell has a single nucleus. No cross striations are visible under the microscope, but like skeletal and cardiac muscle, smooth muscle cells contain actin and myosin. In addition, they contain cytoskeletal intermediate filaments that assist in transmission of the force generated during contraction to the neighboring smooth muscle cells and connective tissue. Although there are no Z lines in smooth muscle, they have a functional counterpart in dense bodies that are distributed throughout the cytoplasm and that serve as attachments for both the thin and the intermediate filaments. The thin and thick filaments of smooth muscle fibers are arranged as myofibrils that cross the fibers obliquely in a lattice-like arrangement. The filaments of contractile proteins are attached to the plasma membrane at the junctional complexes between neighboring cells (Fig. 56–6). A comparison of some of the properties of smooth and skeletal muscle is listed in Table 56–1 (Chacko et al, 1999).

Smooth Muscle Cellular Mechanics

Detrusor smooth muscle contracts and shortens by interaction between thin and thick filaments. The thin actin filaments are anchored at the membranes on the dense bands, or in the cytoplasm on the dense bodies, and interact with the thick

A) Relaxed smooth muscle cell

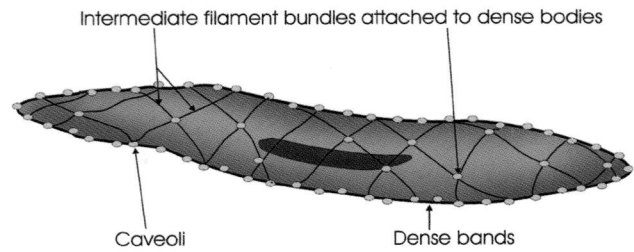

Intermediate filament bundles attached to dense bodies

Caveoli

Dense bands

B) Contracted smooth muscle cell

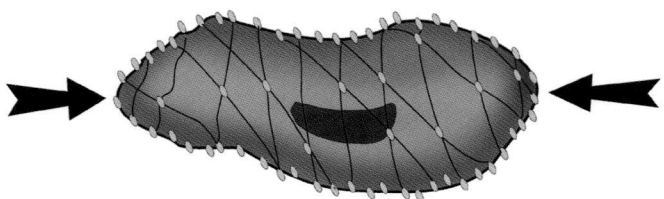

Figure 56–6. The organization of the contractile elements of smooth muscle fibers by a simple model of the contraction of smooth muscle. **A,** Relaxed smooth muscle cell. **B,** Contracted smooth muscle cell. Intermediate filaments, dense bodies, and dense bands of smooth muscle fibers harness the pull generated during myosin cross-bridge activity. Intermediate filaments attach to dense bodies scattered throughout the sarcoplasm and occasionally anchor to the dense bands situated between caveolae (invaginations of the sarcolemma). As the obliquely running contractile elements contract, the muscle shortens.

filaments through cross-bridges formed from the heads of myosin molecules. In both cases, the contractile mechanism is a myosin-activated system. Cross-bridge cycling is initiated when the ATPase activity of the myosin heads is switched on. This is achieved by phosphorylation of two light chains on the cross-bridge, through a specific enzyme, myosin light-chain kinase, that is activated by a rise in the intracellular calcium concentration (Hai and Murphy, 1989; Gunst et al, 1995; Andersson and Arner, 2004). Changes in the contractile proteins occur in developing bladders and also during bladder hypertrophy (Wang et al, 1995b; Wu et al, 1995; Sjuve et al, 1996).

The bladder muscle has a broad length-tension relationship, allowing tension to be developed over a large range of resting muscle lengths (Uvelius and Gabella, 1980). The tissue shows viscoelasticity that influences muscle tension and is manifested as total bladder wall tension (Venegas, 1991). Isolated detrusor strips show spontaneous mechanical activity to a variable extent. It is more frequently seen in bladders from small mammals (Sibley, 1984) but can also be seen in muscle strips from human detrusor. However, spontaneous fused tetanic contractions such as those commonly seen in smooth muscles from the gastrointestinal tract and uterus are almost never seen in normal bladders.

Membrane Electrical Properties and Ion Channels. The smooth muscle of the detrusor is able to support a regenera-

Table 56–1. Comparison of the Properties of Skeletal and Smooth Muscle

Property	Skeletal Muscle	Smooth Muscle
Cell characteristics	Very long cylindrical cells with many nuclei	Spindle-shaped cells with a single nucleus
Maximum cell size (length × diameter)	30 cm × 100 μm	200 μm × 5 μm
Visible striations	Yes	No
Ultrastructure	Sarcomere pattern / No immediate filaments	No sarcomere pattern / Intermediate filaments / Dense bodies
Motor innervation	Somatic	Autonomic
Type of contracture	Phasic	Mostly tonic, some phasic
Contractile activity	Disinhibition of tropomyosin / Sliding filaments / Rapid contraction	Active myosin phosphorylation / ? Sliding filaments / Formation of "latch state"
Calcium regulation	Rapid Ca^{2+} influx via T tubule	Voltage- and receptor-operated Ca^{2+} channels / Release from internal stores
Basic muscle tone	Neural activity	Intrinsic, extrinsic factors
Force of contraction regulated by hormone	No	Yes

tive action potential from a resting potential of −50 to −60 mV (Montgomery and Fry, 1992; Fry et al, 2002). The action potentials have marked after-hyperpolarizations, and several different K^+ channels, such as delayed rectifier and transient outward channels and both small and large calcium-activated K^+ channels (SKCa and BKCa, respectively), appear to be involved in determining their shape (Fujii et al, 1990; Brading and Turner, 1996; Heppner et al, 1997; Andersson and Arner, 2004). The upstroke is supported by calcium influx through L-type Ca^{2+} channels (Rivera et al, 1998). In addition, a K^+ channel opened by reduced intracellular ATP has been demonstrated (Bonev and Nelson, 1993a), which, on activation, is profoundly inhibitory to the spontaneous activity (Foster et al, 1989). Several other conductances, which include a nonspecific cation channel linked to the P2X receptor (Inoue and Brading, 1990) and stretch-activated cation channels (Wellner and Isenberg, 1993), have been demonstrated in detrusor smooth muscle.

In response to acetylcholine released from parasympathetic nerve terminals, muscarinic M_3 receptors are thought to induce detrusor muscle contractions by calcium entry through nifedipine-sensitive L-type Ca^{2+} channels (Schneider et al, 2004a, 2004b; Andersson and Arner, 2004; Andersson and Wein, 2004) in addition to increased polyphosphoinositide hydrolysis resulting in inositol 1,4,5-trisphosphate (IP_3) production and release of intracellular calcium stores (Iacovou et al, 1990; Eglen et al, 1994; Harriss et al, 1995; Fry et al, 2002; Hashitani et al, 2000; Braverman et al, 2006a), although the importance of L-type channel activation in muscarinic M_3 receptor–mediated detrusor

bladder contractions is still a matter of debate (Fry et al, 2002; Hashitani et al, 2000; Schneider et al, 2004a, 2004b; Braverman et al, 2006a, 2006b). **The calcium influx through L-type Ca^{2+} channels also triggers calcium-induced calcium release through ryanodine receptors and activates BKCa channels to generate the membrane after-hyperpolarization** (Hashitani and Brading, 2003). **The opening of the K^+ channel repolarizes the membrane potential by the efflux of positively charged potassium ions from the cell** (Mostwin, 1986). In addition, increased polyphosphoinositide hydrolysis after M_3 receptor activation can also generate diacylglycerol in the membrane; diacylglycerol can activate protein kinase C, which may be involved in generating the tonic element of the response through modulation of Ca^{2+} and K^+ channels (Zhao et al, 1993).

Calcium also activates a variety of cellular responses when it enters the cytoplasm of a cell by means of transmembrane channels. To be effective as a signal, its concentration must be returned to submicromolar levels, driven by ATP pumps. The Ca^{2+} pump is a membrane-bound, Ca^{2+}-activated ATPase, similar to the Na^+-K^+ pump that controls ion balance and membrane potential in all animal cells. These pumps belong to a superfamily of ATPases known as P type because they depend on the autophosphorylation—using ATP—of a conserved aspartic acid residue.

Excitation-Contraction Coupling in Smooth Muscle. Like skeletal and cardiac muscle, smooth muscle contracts when intracellular calcium concentration rises. Because smooth muscle does not possess the tubules of the "T system," the rise in calcium concentration occurs through calcium influx as the result of release from the sarcoplasmic reticulum after activation of receptors that increase the formation of IP_3 or voltage-gated Ca^{2+} channels in the plasma membrane. Although calcium serves the same triggering role in all muscle types, the mechanism of activation is different in smooth muscle. The contractile response is slower and longer lasting than that of skeletal and cardiac muscle. This can be explained by the slowness with which smooth muscle is able to hydrolyze ATP during the contractile process. A calcium-binding protein called calmodulin regulates the interaction between actin and myosin. The thin filaments lack troponin and are always ready for contraction. The slow and relatively steady generation of tension enables smooth muscle to generate and to maintain tension with relatively little expenditure of energy (Fig. 56–7 and Table 56–2).

The rise in cytoplasmic calcium concentration brought on by the action potential results in binding of calcium to

Table 56–2. Detrusor Smooth Muscle Contraction Sequence

Ca^{2+} binds to calmodulin, activating it.

Calmodulin activates the kinase enzyme.

Kinase enzyme catalyzes phosphate transfer from adenosine triphoshate to myosin, allowing myosin to interact with actin of the thin filaments.

Smooth muscle relaxes to widen intracellular decrease in Ca^{2+} levels.

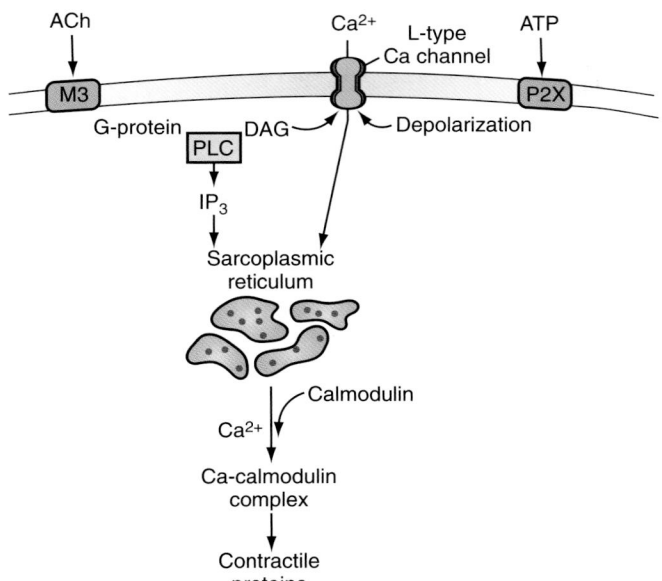

Figure 56–7. Acetylcholine (ACh) and adenosine triphosphate (ATP) pathway in the bladder. Acetylcholine interacts with M_3 muscarinic receptors and activates phospholipase C (PLC) through a G protein. Phospholipase activation leads to the production of inositol 1,4,5-trisphosphate (IP_3) and diacylglycerol (DAG). IP_3 elicits release of calcium from the sarcoplasmic reticulum through IP_3 receptors, and DAG may modulate voltage-sensitive Ca^{2+} channels in the plasma membrane. ATP acting through P2X purinergic receptors opens nonselective cation channels in the membrane, leading to depolarization that opens voltage-sensitive Ca^{2+} channels. Both lead to entry of calcium. This triggers release of more calcium from the stores through ryanodine receptors. The rise in intracellular free calcium concentration triggers contraction and may also open calcium-activated channels in the membrane, such as calcium-activated K^+ channels, that can modulate the response. (Redrawn from Brading AF: Cellular biology. In Abrams P, Khoury S, Wein A, eds: Incontinence. Plymouth, UK, Health Publications, 1999:73.)

calmodulin. Calcium-bound calmodulin is then capable of activating myosin light-chain kinase, permitting it to phosphorylate the myosin type II light chain. Phosphorylation of the light chain allows the myosin to interact with actin, leading to force generation (White et al, 1993; Chacko et al, 1994; Andersson and Arner, 2004). The actual geometric arrangement of the actin-myosin complex that permits force generation is unclear. Different isoforms of the myosin heavy chain have been defined by Chacko and associates (1994) as well as the components of the regulatory system linking cytoplasmic calcium levels to contraction (White et al, 1993). The smooth muscle myosin heavy chain is encoded by a single gene, and two heavy-chain variants formed by alternative splicing are identified (SM1 and SM2). Two additional myosin heavy chain isoforms, SM-A and SM-B, are then formed by alternative splicing in the amino-terminal region, enabling four possible isoforms: SM1-A, SM1-B, SM2-A, and SM2-B (Babu et al, 2000). Since the SM-B isoform is shown to propel actin at a faster velocity (Lauzon et al, 1998), the relatively high expression of SM-B isoform in the bladder shown at the mRNA level (Arafat et al, 2001) would contribute to a comparatively fast smooth muscle type of the bladder (Andersson and Arner, 2004).

Propagation of Electrical Responses. The lack of fused tetanic contractions in normal detrusor smooth muscle strips suggests that there is poor electrical coupling between smooth muscle cells (Uvelius and Mattiasson, 1986). **Measurements of tissue impedance support that the detrusor is less well coupled electrically than other smooth muscles** (Brading and Mostwin, 1989; Parekh et al, 1990). **Poor coupling could be a feature of normal detrusor to prevent synchronous activation of the smooth muscle cells during bladder filling.** Nevertheless, some degree of coupling within a muscle bundle clearly does exist because it is possible to measure the length constant of a bundle (Seki et al, 1992). There is also evidence for gap junction coupling between detrusor cells in humans and guinea pigs, detected by whole-cell patch clamp recordings (Wang et al, 2001) and Ca^{2+} imaging (Neuhaus et al, 2002), respectively. Significant expression of connexins 43 and 45, gap junction proteins, is found in human detrusor muscles (Wang et al, 2001; John et al, 2003). However, electrical couplings between detrusor cells seem to be reduced during postnatal development because coordinated, large-amplitude, low-frequency contractile activity seen in the neonate rat bladder declines and is replaced by low-amplitude, high-frequency, more irregular activity in older rats, which appears to depend on the disruption of the intercellular smooth muscle communication (Szell et al, 2003). It has also been suggested that a change in the properties of the cell coupling may underlie the generation of the uninhibited detrusor contractions occurring in overactive and aging bladders (Seki et al, 1992; Brading, 1997).

Smooth Muscle during Filling. As the bladder fills, the myocytes are stretched, leading to activation of nonselective cation channels that permit rapid entry of sodium and of some calcium (Wellner and Isenberg, 1993). Entry of cations depolarizes the smooth muscle membrane potential. If the extent of stretch is mild, there is low activation and the membrane potential rests at a more depolarized level, predisposing the cell to activation by lower levels of muscarinic agonists. If the extent of the stretch is more significant, the activation of cation channels may be sufficient to depolarize the cell sufficiently for initiation of an action potential. **Although individual cells may contract spontaneously, contraction of the bladder as a whole generally requires stimulation by parasympathetic nerves** (Andersson, 1993). **When the membrane is sufficiently depolarized, L-type Ca^{2+} channels open and Ca^{2+} channels in the sarcoplasmic reticulum open, flooding the cell with calcium and resulting in an action potential, thereby leading to spontaneous phasic activity in the bladder** (Mostwin, 1986; Kumar et al, 2005).

Between contractions, the sarcoplasmic reticulum accumulates calcium to levels far above those of the cytosol by means of a calcium ATPase (Wall et al, 1990). Calcium stores in the sarcoplasmic reticulum can be released in the absence of action potentials by exposure to caffeine, which renders the Ca^{2+} channels sensitive to normal ambient cytoplasmic calcium levels.

Interstitial Cells. Recent evidence suggests that the "normal" bladder may be spontaneously active and that exaggerated spontaneous contractions could contribute to the development of overactive bladder. In a rat model for detrusor overactivity, local areas of spontaneous contractions are increased and more coordinated in partial outlet-obstructed rat bladders (Drake et al, 2003). However, it is still not clear which cells generate spontaneous activity in the bladder. As mentioned before, detrusor myocytes could be spontaneously active, and electrical coupling through gap junctions could trigger spontaneous contractions. Alternatively, **another population of cells in the bladder known as interstitial cells or myofibroblasts has been proposed for a pacemaking role in spontaneous activity of the bladder** (Andersson and Arner, 2004; Kumar et al, 2005). Interstitial cells have been identified in human and guinea pig ureter, urethra, and bladder body (Kumar et al, 2005).

In the human bladder, subepithelial interstitial cells or myofibroblasts stain for vimentin and α-smooth muscle actin but not for desmin (Fry et al, 2004). These cells are linked by gap junctions consisting of connexin 43 proteins and make close appositions with C-fiber nerve endings in the submucosal layer of the bladder, suggesting that there is a network of functionally connected interstitial cells immediately below the urothelium that may be modulated by other nerve fibers (Fry et al, 2004) (Fig. 56–8). In addition, ATP can induce inward currents associated with elevated intracellular $[Ca^{2+}]$ in isolated suburothelial interstitial cells. Because ATP is known to be released during bladder stretch, it appears that suburothelial interstitial cells are in an ideal position between urothelium and nerve endings to modify a sensory feedback mechanism.

Interstitial cells found in the detrusor layer are shown to be spontaneously active (Kumar et al, 2005). These cells are stained for c-Kit and located along both boundaries of muscle bundles in the guinea pig bladder (McCloskey and Gurney, 2002; Hashitani, et al, 2004). These cells can fire Ca^{2+} waves in response to cholinergic stimulation and can be spontaneously active, suggesting that they could act as pacemakers or intermediaries in the transmission of nerve signals to smooth muscle cells (McCloskey and Gurney, 2002) (Fig. 56–9). However, Hashitani and colleagues (2004) have also suggested that interstitial cells in the detrusor may be more important for modulating the transmission of Ca^{2+} transients originating from smooth muscle cells rather than being the pacemaker of spontaneous activity because spontaneous Ca^{2+} transients occur independently in smooth muscles and interstitial cells. A study has demonstrated that the c-Kit tyrosine kinase inhibitor Glivec decreased the amplitude of spontaneous contractions in the guinea pig bladder, suggesting that targeting these receptors expressed in interstitial cells located at the detrusor layer may provide a new approach for treating overactive bladder (Kubota et al, 2004).

Further research is definitely required to fully understand the role of interstitial cells and their contribution to spontaneous contractions or detrusor overactivity.

Smooth Muscle Tone. The bladder smooth muscle maintains a steady level of contracture and tone. Tone is important in maintaining the capacity of the bladder. Smooth muscle tone depends on many factors, some intrinsic and some extrinsic. Extrinsic factors include activity in the autonomic nerves and circulating hormones; intrinsic factors include the response to stretch, local metabolites, locally secreted agents such as nitric oxide, and temperature. Consequently, smooth muscle tone does not depend solely on activity in the autonomic nerves or on circulating hormones.

The contraction of smooth muscle is slow, sustained, and resistant to fatigue. Smooth muscle takes 30 times longer to contract and relax than does skeletal muscle and can maintain the same contractile tension for prolonged periods at less than 1% of the energy cost.

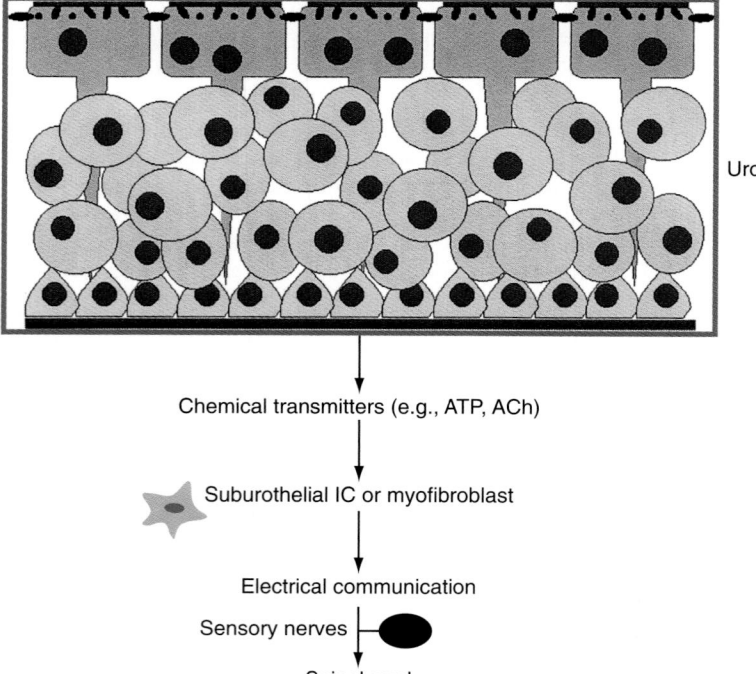

Urothelium

Chemical transmitters (e.g., ATP, ACh)

Suburothelial IC or myofibroblast

Electrical communication

Sensory nerves

Spinal cord

Figure 56–8. Schematic representation of suburothelial interstitial cells (IC) or myofibroblasts. Substances released from the basolateral surface during stretch, such as adenosine triphosphate (ATP) and acetylcholine (ACh), activate afferents in the suburothelial layer through the intermediation of suburothelially located interstitial cells or myofibroblasts.

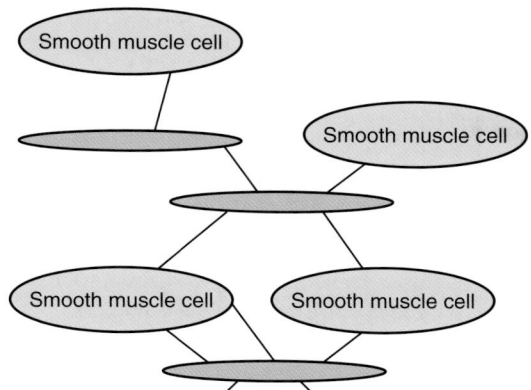

Interstitial cell (pacemaker, propagation, not contractile)

Figure 56–9. Schematic representation of interstitial cells in the detrusor muscle layers. These cells are not contractile but may be pacemakers with spontaneous activity and propagate signals between detrusor muscles.

Length-Tension Relationship. If a smooth muscle is stretched, there is a corresponding increase in tension immediately after the stretch. This is followed by a progressive relaxation of the tension toward its initial value. This property is unique to smooth muscle and is called stress relaxation (Chancellor et al, 1996).

Compared with skeletal or cardiac muscle, smooth muscle can shorten to a far greater degree. A stretched striated muscle can shorten by perhaps as much as a third of its resting length, whereas a normal resting muscle would shorten by perhaps a fifth. This is perfectly adequate for it to perform its normal physiologic role. In contrast, a smooth muscle may be able to shorten by more than two thirds of its initial length. This unusual property is conferred by the loose arrangement of the thick and thin myofilaments in smooth muscle cells. It is a crucial adaptation because the volume contained by the bladder depends on the cube of the length of the individual muscle fibers. The ability of the detrusor smooth muscle to change its length to such a large degree permits the bladder to adjust to much wider variations in volume than would be possible for skeletal muscle.

Stroma

The main constituents of bladder wall stroma are collagen and elastin in a matrix composed of proteoglycans. The main cells are fibroblasts. The passive mechanical properties of the bladder wall depend on the viscoelastic properties of the stroma and of the relaxed detrusor muscle (Cortivo et al, 1981). The stroma has commonly been considered a passive low metabolic tissue that fills out the space between muscle bundles, vessels, and nerves. In recent years, the important role of the stroma in the adaptation of the bladder to pathophysiologic conditions has been more appreciated (Macarak and Howard, 1999). Bladder hypertrophy is likely to involve an interaction of stroma and smooth muscle. In arteries, disruption of elastin in the stroma can stimulate proliferation of smooth muscle (Li et al, 1998). Although no such mechanisms are yet known in the bladder, it is possible that there could be a more intimate relationship between changes in the compo-

sition of the stroma and muscle function and growth than is appreciated at present.

Bladder Wall Collagen

Most of the bladder wall collagen is found in the connective tissue outside the muscle bundles. Changes in relation between the amount of muscle and nonmuscle tissue in the bladder wall would therefore influence collagen concentration. A number of different collagen types have been identified. In the bladder, types I, III, and IV are the most common (Macarak et al, 1995; Andersson and Arner, 2004). Landau and coworkers (1994) developed morphometric and histochemical techniques to determine the percentage volume of connective tissue in the bladder wall and to measure the two major types (I and III) of collagen. These methods quantitate three parameters of bladder ultrastructure: percentage volume of connective tissue, ratio of connective tissue to smooth muscle, and ratio of type III to type I collagen. These parameters have been shown to be abnormally elevated in patients with bladder disease compared with normals. They further studied the ultrastructural changes that occur in the wall of dysfunctional bladders to determine the ability of new urodynamic techniques to reliably detect the clinical effect of these histologic changes. The study included 29 consecutive patients undergoing bladder augmentation. Preoperative urodynamic evaluation included measurement of the total bladder capacity, pressure-specific bladder volume, and dynamic analysis of bladder compliance. Full-thickness bladder biopsy specimens were obtained from the dome of the bladders during augmentation. The percentage of connective tissue and the ratio of connective tissue to smooth muscle were determined for all patients. These histologic results were compared with previously established normal values. All 29 patients had decreased bladder compliance, even though 9 had a normal bladder capacity. **The ratio of connective tissue to smooth muscle was significantly increased in poorly compliant versus normal bladders. The ratio of type III to type I collagen was also significantly elevated. One can conclude that poor storage function of poorly compliant bladders is secondary to an alteration in the connective tissue content of the bladder wall, especially increased collagen type III.**

In the rat, infravesical obstruction or bladder denervation induces hypertrophy of the detrusor smooth muscle and, in turn, a decrease in the collagen concentration (Uvelius and Mattiasson, 1984, 1986). Aging is associated with a relative decrease in smooth muscle in both men and women relative to collagen content (Susset et al, 1978; Lepor et al, 1992). This could perhaps be related to the decreased packing density of submucosal collagen during aging (Levy and Wight, 1990).

Perhaps the most comprehensive work on bladder collagen has been performed by Macarak and Howard (1999), who have speculated that connections must exist between the tension-generating elements (i.e., the smooth muscle cells) and the other components of the bladder. In bladders that become noncompliant (e.g., from spinal cord injury), it is likely that there is some interference with the ability of the collagen fibers to alter their tortuosity. This, predictably, would reduce total bladder capacity. Further studies are required to establish the relationship between compliance changes and the passive mechanical elements of the bladder wall that make up its structural protein matrix.

Bladder Wall Elastin

Elastic fibers are amorphous structures composed of elastin and a microfibrillar component located mainly around the periphery of the amorphous component (Rosenbloom et al, 1995). In the mature fiber, the amorphous component composes about 90%. The microfibrils contain a number of glycoproteins. Elastin fibers are sparse in the bladder, compared with collagen, but are found in all layers of the bladder wall (Murakumo et al, 1995). A study by Nagatomi and associates (2005) has shown that increased expression of elastin occurs and is well correlated with increased bladder compliance due to bladder overdistention during a bladder areflexia phase after spinal cord injury in rats, suggesting a potential role of elastin in the modulation of bladder compliance.

Bladder Matrix

The nonfibrillar matrix in the stroma is largely composed of a gel of proteoglycans and water. Proteoglycans are glycoproteins with glycosaminoglycans covalently attached. The arrangement of the proteoglycans in the matrix creates a compartment of tissue water that has a viscous behavior when it is subjected to deformation.

Blood Vessels

The bladder has a multilayer vascular plexus, and this fact has morphologic as well as functional implications. When it is carefully examined, the underside of the epithelium is depressed by numerous grooves that are occupied by a dense network of blood capillaries. These vascular grooves allow a large number of capillaries to run at a distance of only a few tenths of a micron from the epithelium (Inoue and Gabella, 1991). The subepithelial capillary plexus may be associated with maintenance of the barrier function of the urothelium, reducing any exposure of the detrusor smooth muscle to substances diffusing from the urine (Hossler and Monson, 1995). It may also play a role in epithelial transport function and be necessary for urothelial metabolism.

Because of the large increase in surface area of the bladder wall during filling, the blood vessels need to be able to lengthen considerably. To maintain a good blood flow, mechanisms may have to be present to ensure that the overall resistance of the vessels as they lengthen does not increase sufficiently to reduce the effective perfusion of the tissue. Several groups have investigated the effects of bladder filling on the blood flow. The majority of reports have shown that the blood flow is reduced by distention (Batista et al, 1996; Greenland and Brading, 1996). In patients with a low compliant bladder, there is a marked increase in the intravesicular pressure and a more pronounced decrease in bladder blood flow compared with normal controls (Ohnishi et al, 1994). **The principal determinant of blood flow in the bladder wall seems to be intramural tension. During normal filling, the blood flow is able to adapt to the large increase in surface area until the pressure increases in the bladder** (Greenland and Brading, 1996).

When the detrusor is deprived of oxygen or a metabolic substrate, as would occur in ischemia, its contractile ability rapidly declines (Levin et al, 1983, 2003; Zhao et al, 1991; Pessina et al, 1997). It has been suggested that ischemia and

reperfusion might lead to damage to intramural neurons and result in the patchy denervation and altered smooth muscle function seen in bladders of people with detrusor overactivity (Brading, 1997).

Urothelium

The functions of the bladder are storage of urine, maintenance of urine composition, and facilitation of voiding at appropriate time intervals. The urothelium has physiologic functions in relation to all parts of these functions and, as such, can no longer be thought of as an inert barrier between urine and plasma.

Structure

The urothelium consists of a variable number of layers of cells, depending on the species (Fawcett, 1984). There are three distinct layers. A layer of basal cells are germinal in nature and 5 to 10 μm in diameter. Intermediate cells are superficial to these and approximately 20 μm in diameter, and a layer of umbrella cells forms the luminal surface of the urothelium (Lewis, 2000; Apodaca, 2004). These cells are the largest epithelial cells in the body, measuring 100 to 200 μm in diameter; they are polyhedral, are generally hexagonal, and can flatten and have more surface area with stretching. They may also be multinucleate (Kelly et al, 1984). The surface of the umbrella cells is covered with a glycosaminoglycan layer (Fig. 56-10).

Glycosaminoglycan Layer. The glycosaminoglycan (GAG) layer has been the controversial subject of urothelial barrier function. Parsons and associates (1990) reported that intravesical treatment of the rabbit bladder with protamine sulfate increased urothelial permeability, both in vivo and in vitro, to water, urea, and calcium. This effect was reversed with pentosan polysulfate. They concluded that the protamine sulfate affected the GAG layer and that this was repaired by pentosan polysulfate. However, no microscopic evidence of the anatomic changes was presented in this paper. This study was confirmed by Nickel and coworkers (1998), who compared pentosan polysulfate, heparin, and hyaluronic acid as treatments. The authors concluded that heparin was the best of the three agents in efficacy but pointed out that this may be due to its anti-inflammatory properties. Indeed, the role of the GAG layer may be more in line with an antibacterial adherence function as outlined by Hanno and coworkers (1981). The GAG layer may also be important for the formation and attachment of particulates to the urothelium and stone formation (Grases et al, 1966; Hurst, 1994). However, there are a number of problems with the theory that the GAG layer is the urothelial plasma barrier:

The GAG layer does not prevent small molecules such as amiloride from reaching the Na^+ channels expressed on the surface of the umbrella cells and interfering with them (Niku et al, 1994).

The polyene antibiotic nystatin can reach the urothelium, as evidenced by increases in the short-circuit currents and reduction in transepithelial resistance to insignificant values, as it generates nonspecific cation pores in the cholesterol-containing luminal membrane of the umbrella cells.

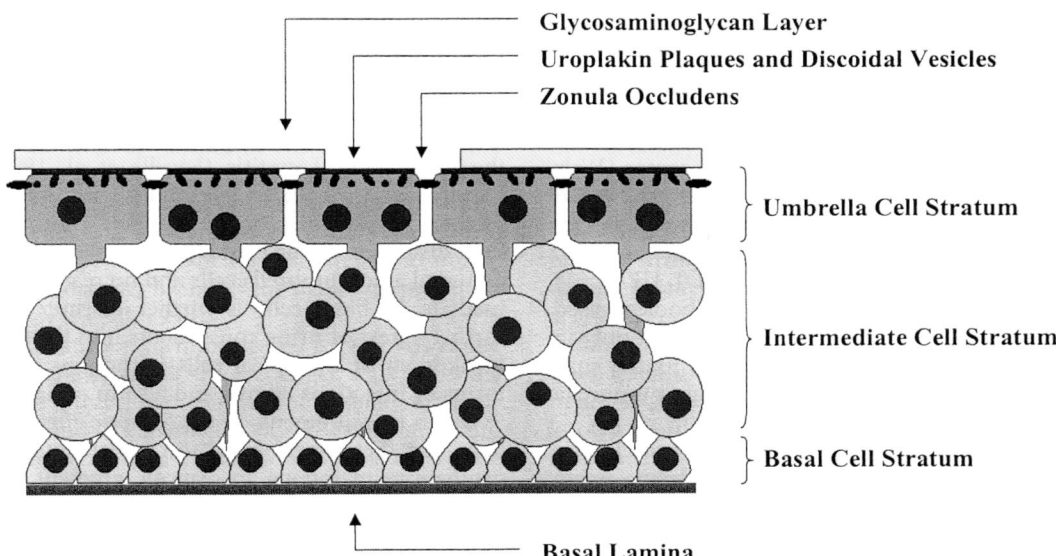

Glycosaminoglycan Layer
Uroplakin Plaques and Discoidal Vesicles
Zonula Occludens

Umbrella Cell Stratum

Intermediate Cell Stratum

Basal Cell Stratum

Basal Lamina

Figure 56–10. Diagrammatic representation of the bladder urothelium. The lumen of the bladder is on top and the lamina propria is below. The glycosaminoglycan layer is shown as discontinuous for illustrative purposes, enabling labeling of deeper structures.

With the use of microelectrodes, the first resistive barrier found is on entry into the cell. Addition of monomeric arginine or polyvalent cations does not alter transepithelial ion permeability based on electrical measurements.

Use of hydrolytic agents, such as neuraminidase, hyaluronidase, and chondroitinase, or of proteolytic agents, such as trypsin and kallikrein (to deliberately strip the urothelium of the GAG layer), does not alter the ability of protamine to increase the urothelial permeability (Lewis et al, 1995). This implies that the protamine acts not at the level of the GAG layer but rather at the surface of the luminal cells.

Protamine sulfate increases the apical membrane (luminal surface of umbrella cells) permeability to both monovalent cations and anions. This may be reversed on the basis of the concentration of the protamine, the composition of the bathing solution, and the exposure time of the urothelium to protamine. Prolonged exposure to protamine (>15 minutes) is poorly reversible and is thought to be caused by a decrease in paracellular resistance from cell lysis (Tzan et al, 1993, 1994).

In an indirect method of examining the GAG layer, Madin-Darby canine kidney (MDCK) cells were transfected with MUC-1, the major GAG of the bladder, with different tandem repeat units to vary the length of the glycosylated chain outside the cell. After this treatment, no difference in the transcellular water and urea permeability was found (Lavelle et al, 1997). **In summary, the GAG layer may have importance in bacterial antiadherence and in prevention of urothelial damage by large macromolecules. However, there is no definite evidence that the GAG layer acts as the primary epithelial barrier between urine and plasma.**

The Umbrella Cells. The large umbrella cells that form the primary urine-plasma barrier are unique in several ways. First, they have the ability to increase and to decrease considerably their surface area primarily at the apical (luminal) surface. Second, they may be multinucleate. Third, they have an unusual apical surface membrane, which is described as an asymmetrical unit membrane, with the outer leaflet consisting of protein plaques and lipid and with a lipid inner leaflet. Fourth, these cells maintain an extremely high gradient between the plasma and the urine in terms of water concentration, urea concentration, potassium concentration, osmolality, and pH.

Umbrella cells are so called for their shape, in that they look like umbrellas over the intermediate cell layer. They may cover several intermediate cells and have a stem that may extend to the lamina propria of the urothelium. They are capable of changing shape and can increase their surface area as the bladder fills and conversely decrease their surface area as the bladder empties. How this phenomenon occurs is still under debate. The primary theory is that there are a large number of subapical discoid vesicles with an asymmetrical membrane structure just under the apical membrane. These vesicles decrease in number with bladder stretch and increase the electrical capacitance of the luminal surface of the umbrella cells. This is consistent with the exocytosis of these vesicles to increase the cell surface area (Porter et al, 1965). Conversely, the discoid vesicles may be infoldings of membrane that stretch out and disappear with the requirement for increased surface area (Staehelin et al, 1972). These discoid vesicles are associated with a dense network of filaments (Hicks, 1965), which may be connected to the uroplakin plaques (Minsky and Chlapowski, 1978). The insertion of these vesicles into the apical membrane is a microfilament-dependent system requiring ATP for insertion but not collapse (Sarikas and Chlapowski, 1986) that does not require an intact microtubule system (Lewis and de Moura, 1982).

In membrane physiology, the primary determinant of the permeability of the lipid bilayer is the permeability of the individual leaflets. The leaflet that is least permeable will determine the overall permeability of the membrane (Negrete et al, 1996b). In the umbrella cell luminal membrane, there is

distal sphincteric muscles may contribute to urinary incontinence in females after resection of the bladder neck.

In women, urinary continence is maintained during elevations in intra-abdominal pressure by three processes. First, there is passive transmission of abdominal pressure to the proximal urethra. A guarding reflex involving an active contraction of striated muscle of the external urethral sphincter can transiently help continence (Enhorning, 1961; Tanagho, 1982). **However, mere transmission of abdominal pressure to proximal urethra does not account for the entire increase in urethral pressure** (Constantinou and Govan, 1982). **Urethral pressure rises before cough transmission** (Fig. 56–11). **These findings implicate an active urethral continence (neural) mechanism in women** (Constantinou and Govan, 1982). **DeLancey proposes the "hammock hypothesis" that abdominal pressure transmitted through the proximal urethra presses the anterior wall against the posterior wall. The posterior wall remains rigid if there is adequate pelvic support from muscle and connective tissues. More distally, based on morphologic data, DeLancey and colleagues** (DeLancey, 1989, 1997; Sampselle and DeLancey, 1998) **have postulated that the urethral attachments to the pubis (pubourethral) and vaginal connections to pelvic muscles and fascia actively change the position of the bladder neck and proximal urethra with voiding. This arrangement compresses the urethra against the pubis during bladder filling and straining. These attachments contain both fascia and smooth muscle** (Oerlich, 1983; DeLancey, 1988, 1989). **Thus, urinary continence results from the combination of active muscle tone and passive anatomic coaptation.**

Fiber Types of Urethral Striated Muscle

Striated muscles are characterized as slow type and twitch type. Twitch-type myofibrils can be further classified as slow and fast on the basis of functional and metabolic characteristics (Padykula and Gauthier, 1967). Slow-twitch fibers seem ideally suited to maintaining sphincter tone for prolonged periods, whereas fast-twitch fibers may be needed to add to sphincter tone rapidly to maintain continence when intra-abdominal pressure is abruptly increased. Like that of smooth muscle, contraction of striated muscle fibers is governed by intracellular calcium, through interactions with troponin.

The fast-twitch fibers can be recruited rapidly, tend to fatigue rapidly, and perform predominantly anaerobic metabolism (Markwardt and Isenberg, 1992). Fast-twitch fibers exhibit rapid bursts of contractile force and are rich in myosin ATPase that catalyzes the actin-myosin interaction. The speed of contraction may be correlated with the histochemical reaction of this ATPase and alkaline pH. In addition, fast-twitch muscles are supplied with a fast isoform of the Ca^{2+}-ATPase, which translocates the cytosolic calcium into the abundant sarcoplasmic reticulum to allow rapid relaxation.

In contrast, slow-twitch fibers are found in greater percentage in muscles that require sustained tension, such as the pelvic levators and urethral sphincter. These muscle fibers are recruited and fatigue slowly and can perform high rates of oxidative metabolism because they possess less of the myosin ATPase activity and contain an increased expression of a slow isoform of the Ca^{2+}-ATPase (Markwardt and Isenberg, 1992). These fibers give rise to the background electromyographic activity seen during a urodynamic evaluation.

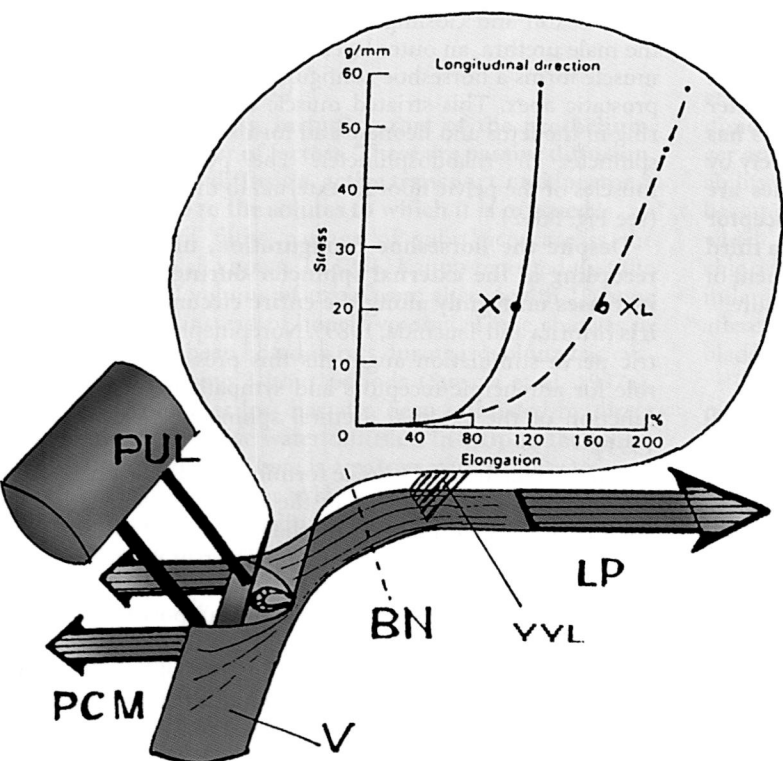

Figure 56–11.   Influence of vaginal laxity on muscle force transmission and urinary continence. *Inset,* Stress extension curve of vagina. BN, bladder neck; LP, levator plate; PCM, pubococcygeus muscle; PUL, pubourethral ligament; V, vaginal hammock; VVL, vaginal attachment to the bladder base; X, normal elasticity; XL, vaginal laxity. The authors propose that an increase in urethral pressure before cough transmission proves that an active continence mechanism is involved in preventing stress urinary incontinence. (From Petros PE, Ulmsten U: An integral theory and its method for the diagnosis and management of female urinary incontinence. Scand J Urol Nephrol 1993;27[suppl 153]:1-93. Copyright 1993 Scandinavian University Press, Stockholm, Sweden.)

The external urethral sphincter is composed of two parts. The periurethral striated muscle of the pelvic floor contains both fast-twitch and slow-twitch fibers. The striated muscle of the distal sphincter mechanism contains predominantly slow-twitch fibers (Elbadawi, 1984) and provides more than 50% of the static resistance (Tanagho et al, 1989). Gosling and colleagues (2000) presented histochemical evidence in humans that striated muscle within the distal urethra is composed primarily of slow-twitch myofibrils in contrast to the periurethral striated muscles of the pelvic floor, which contain fast-twitch and slow-twitch fibers. In the male, the rhabdosphincter consists of 35% fast-twitch and 65% slow-twitch fibers (Padykula and Gauthier, 1970). In the female, the ratio of slow-twitch to fast-twitch fibers is 87% slow-twitch and 13% fast-twitch.

The majority of the fast-twitch fibers and about a fourth of the slow-twitch fibers in the intramural striated muscle of the human membranous urethral sphincter show positive staining for nitric oxide synthase in the sarcolemma (Ho et al, 1998). Moreover, the striated periurethral muscles of the pelvic floor are adapted for the rapid recruitment of motor units required during increases in abdominal pressure. It has been speculated that the successful treatment of stress incontinence by pelvic floor exercises or electrostimulation is caused by the conversion of fast-twitch to slow-twitch striated muscle fibers (Bazeed et al, 1982).

In addition to striated muscle, the external sphincter appears to contain smooth muscle, which receives noradrenergic innervation. Investigators have shown that stimulation of the hypogastric nerve elicits myogenic potentials in the external urethral sphincter (Kakizaki et al, 1991). Whether this activity is the result of smooth or striated muscle is unclear. Because these potentials persist after α-adrenergic blockade, investigators postulate that it arises from striated muscle.

Lamina Propria and Paraurethral Tissue

Results are divergent regarding the clinical significance of connective tissue outside the urethra. Paraurethral tissue biopsy specimens from premenopausal women with stress incontinence contain 30% more collagen, and the diameter of the fibrils is 30% larger than in controls (Falconer et al, 1998a). Postmenopausal stress-incontinent women, on the other hand, have no difference in collagen concentration compared with their age-matched controls (Falconer et al, 1998b). Others, however, have found a decreased periurethral collagen concentration (Rechberger et al, 1993) and a decreased collagen I to collagen III ratio (Keane et al, 1997) in patients with stress incontinence.

NEURAL CONTROL OF THE LOWER URINARY TRACT
Peripheral Nervous System

The lower urinary tract is innervated by three sets of peripheral nerves involving the parasympathetic, sympathetic, and somatic nervous systems (Fig. 56–12). Pelvic

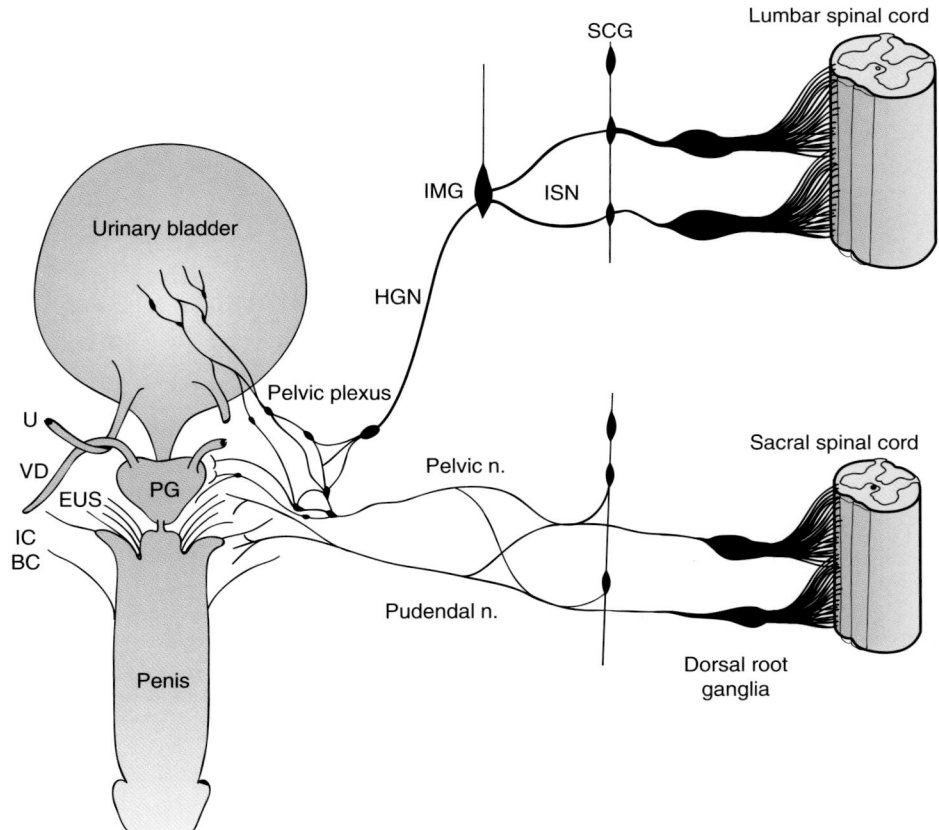

Figure 56–12. Diagram showing the sympathetic, parasympathetic, and somatic innervation of the urogenital tract of the male cat. Sympathetic preganglionic pathways emerge from the lumbar spinal cord and pass to the sympathetic chain ganglia (SCG) and then through the inferior splanchnic nerves (ISN) to the inferior mesenteric ganglia (IMG). Preganglionic and postganglionic sympathetic axons then travel in the hypogastric nerve (HGN) to the pelvic plexus and the urogenital organs. Parasympathetic preganglionic axons that originate in the sacral spinal cord pass in the pelvic nerve to ganglion cells in the pelvic plexus and to distal ganglia in the organs. Sacral somatic pathways are contained in the pudendal nerve, which provides an innervation to the penis and the ischiocavernosus (IC), bulbocavernosus (BC), and external urethral sphincter (EUS) muscles. The pudendal and pelvic nerves also receive postganglionic axons from the caudal sympathetic chain ganglia. These three sets of nerves contain afferent axons from the lumbosacral dorsal root ganglia. PG, prostate gland; U, ureter; VD, vas deferens.

parasympathetic nerves arise at the sacral level of the spinal cord, excite the bladder, and relax the urethra. Lumbar sympathetic nerves inhibit the bladder body and excite the bladder base and urethra. Pudendal nerves excite the external urethral sphincter. These nerves contain afferent (sensory) as well as efferent axons (Wein, 1992; de Groat et al, 1993; Sugaya et al, 1997b; Yoshimura and de Groat, 1997a).

Parasympathetic Pathways

Parasympathetic preganglionic neurons innervating the lower urinary tract are located in the lateral part of the sacral intermediate gray matter in a region termed the sacral parasympathetic nucleus (Nadelhaft et al, 1980; Morgan et al, 1981, 1993; de Groat et al, 1993, 1996). Parasympathetic preganglionic neurons send axons through the ventral roots to peripheral ganglia, where they release the excitatory transmitter acetylcholine (de Groat and Booth, 1993). **Parasympathetic postganglionic neurons in humans are located in the detrusor wall layer as well as in the pelvic plexus. This is an important fact to remember because patients with cauda equina or pelvic plexus injury are neurologically decentralized but may not be completely denervated. Cauda equina injury allows possible afferent and efferent neuron interconnection at the level of the intramural ganglia** (de Groat et al, 1993, 1996).

Sympathetic Pathways

Sympathetic outflow from the rostral lumbar spinal cord provides a noradrenergic excitatory and inhibitory input to the bladder and urethra (Andersson, 1993). Activation of sympathetic nerves induces relaxation of the bladder body and contraction of the bladder outlet and urethra, which contribute to urine storage in the bladder. **The peripheral sympathetic pathways follow a complex route that passes through the sympathetic chain ganglia to the inferior mesenteric ganglia and then through the hypogastric nerves to the pelvic ganglia** (Kihara and de Groat, 1997).

Somatic Pathways

The external urethral sphincter motoneurons are located along the lateral border of the ventral horn, commonly referred to as Onuf's nucleus (Fig. 56–13) (Thor et al, 1989). Sphincter motoneurons also exhibit transversely oriented dendritic bundles that project laterally into the lateral funiculus, dorsally into the intermediate gray matter, and dorsomedially toward the central canal.

Afferent Pathways

Afferent axons in the pelvic, hypogastric, and pudendal nerves transmit information from the lower urinary tract to the lumbosacral spinal cord (de Groat, 1986; Janig and Morrison, 1986; Yoshimura and de Groat, 1997a). The primary afferent neurons of the pelvic and pudendal nerves are contained in sacral dorsal root ganglia (DRG), whereas afferent innervation in the hypogastric nerves arises in the rostral lumbar DRG. The central axons of the DRG neurons carry the sensory information from the lower urinary tract to second-order neurons in the spinal cord (Morgan et al, 1981; de Groat, 1986; Thor et al, 1989; de Groat et al, 1996) (see Fig. 56–13). Visceral afferent fibers of the pelvic (Morgan et al, 1981) and pudendal (Thor et al, 1989) nerves enter the cord and travel rostrocaudally within Lissauer's tract.

Pelvic nerve afferents, which monitor the volume of the bladder and the amplitude of the bladder contraction, consist of myelinated (Aδ) and unmyelinated (C) axons (Table 56–3). During neuropathic conditions and possibly inflammatory conditions, there is recruitment of C fibers that form a new functional afferent pathway that can cause urge incontinence and possibly bladder pain.

Sensing bladder volume is of particular relevance during urine storage. On the other hand, afferent discharges that occur during a bladder contraction have an important reflex function and appear to reinforce the central drive that maintains the detrusor contraction. Afferent nerves that respond to both distention and contraction, that is, "in series tension

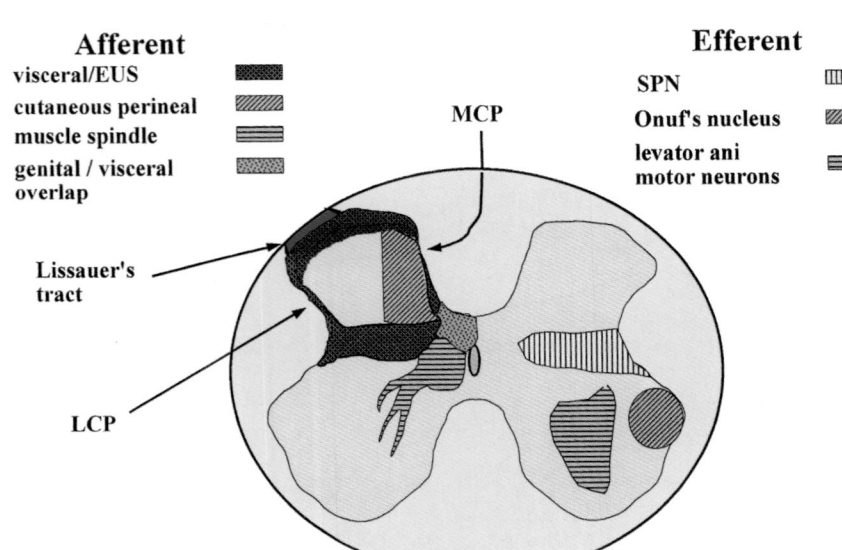

Figure 56–13. Cross section of sacral spinal cord; neuroanatomic distribution of primary afferent and efferent components of storage and micturition reflexes. For purposes of clarity, afferent components are shown only on the left, and efferent components are shown only on the right. Both components are, of course, distributed bilaterally and thus overlap extensively. Visceral afferent components represent bladder, urethral, and genital (glans penis or clitoris) afferent fibers contained in the pelvic and pudendal nerves. Cutaneous perineal afferent components represent afferent fibers that innervate the perineal skin contained in the pudendal nerve. Muscle spindle afferent components represent Ia/b afferent fibers contained in the levator ani nerve that innervate muscle spindles in the levator ani muscle. EUS, external urethral sphincter; LCP, lateral collateral projection; MCP, medial collateral projection; SPN, sacral parasympathetic nucleus.

Afferent
visceral/EUS
cutaneous perineal
muscle spindle
genital / visceral overlap

Lissauer's tract

LCP

MCP

Efferent
SPN
Onuf's nucleus
levator ani motor neurons

Table 56–3. Bladder Afferent Properties

Fiber Type	Location	Normal Function	Inflammation Effect
Aδ (finely myelinated axons)	Smooth muscle	Sense bladder fullness (wall tension)	Increase discharge at lower pressure threshold
C fiber (unmyelinated axons)	Mucosa	Respond to stretch (bladder volume sensors)	Increase discharge at lower threshold
C fiber (unmyelinated axons)	Mucosa muscle	Nociception to overdistention Silent afferent	Sensitive to irritants Becomes mechanosensitive and unmasks new afferent pathway during inflammation

receptors," have been identified in the pelvic and hypogastric nerves of cats and rats (see Table 56–3) (Iggo, 1955; Floyd et al, 1976; Morrison, 1997). Afferents that respond only to bladder filling have been identified in the rat bladder (Morrison et al, 1998) and appear to be volume receptors, possibly sensitive to stretch of the mucosa. In the cat bladder, some in series tension receptors may also respond to bladder stretch (Downie and Armour, 1992). In the rat, there is now evidence that many C bladder afferents are volume receptors that do not respond to bladder contractions, a property that distinguishes them from in series tension receptors (Morrison et al, 1998).

Species differences as well as differences of nomenclature might account for some of the variations in reported properties of bladder afferents. For example, the conduction velocity that differentiates Aδ and C fibers is 2 m/sec in the cat, whereas it is 1.3 m/sec in the rat (Waddell et al, 1989). In the cat, Aδ bladder afferents appear to be low-threshold mechanoreceptors (Häbler et al, 1993), whereas C bladder afferents (Häbler et al, 1990) are generally mechanoinsensitive ("silent C-fibers") (see Table 56–3). Some of the latter may be nociceptive and have been found to be sensitized by intravesical administration of chemicals such as high potassium, low pH, high osmolality, and irritants such as capsaicin (Fig. 56–14) (Maggi et al, 1987; McMahon and Abel, 1987; Häbler et al, 1990; Maggi, 1993; Wen et al, 1994; Wen and Morrison, 1994, 1996). After exposure to these substances, the sensitivity of bladder mechanoreceptors to distention increases and some "silent" afferents become mechanoreceptive.

Reflex Circuitry Controlling Micturition

Multiple reflex pathways organized in the brain and spinal cord mediate coordination between the urinary bladder and the urethra. The central pathways controlling lower urinary tract function are organized as simple on-off switching circuits (Fig. 56–15) that maintain a reciprocal relationship between the urinary bladder and the urethral outlet (de Groat, 1975; de Groat et al, 1993). The principal reflex components of these switching circuits are listed in Table 56–4 and illustrated in Figure 56–16. Some reflexes promote urine storage, whereas others facilitate voiding. It is also possible that individual reflexes might be linked together in a serial manner to create complex feedback mechanisms. For example, **the bladder to external urethral sphincter guarding reflex that triggers sphincter contractions during bladder filling could,**

KEY POINTS: AFFERENT PATHWAYS

- Studies of the properties of bladder afferents in the pelvic nerve, particularly in the rat, indicate that in series tension receptors, volume receptors and silent afferents (including nociceptors) are present.

- Intravesical irritant chemicals reduce the pressure thresholds of most of these endings, including the high-threshold receptors.

- A substantial proportion of the C-fiber afferent population is silent (i.e., insensitive to normal distention). However, these fibers become mechanosensitive after the action of various chemical mediators.

- During inflammation and possibly other pathologic conditions, there is recruitment of mechanosensitive C fibers that form a new functional afferent pathway. This is the rationale for intravesical C-fiber neurotoxin capsaicin and resiniferatoxin (RTX) therapy (Chancellor and de Groat, 1999).

in turn, activate sphincter muscle afferents that initiate an inhibition of the parasympathetic excitatory pathway to the bladder. Thus, a bladder to sphincter to bladder reflex pathway could in theory contribute to the suppression of bladder activity during urine storage. Alterations in these primitive reflex mechanisms may contribute to neurogenic bladder dysfunction. Direct activation of these reflexes by electrical stimulation of the sacral spinal roots very likely contributes to therapeutic effects of sacral nerve root neuromodulation (Dijkema et al, 1993; Chancellor and Chartier-Kastler, 2000).

The Storage Phase of the Bladder

Intravesical pressure measurements during bladder filling in both humans and animals reveal low and relatively constant bladder pressures when bladder volume is below the threshold for inducing voiding (Fig. 56–17). The accommodation of the bladder to increasing volumes of urine is primarily a passive phenomenon dependent on the intrinsic properties of the vesical smooth muscle and the quiescence of the parasympathetic efferent pathway (Torrens, 1987; de Groat et al, 1993; Yoshimura and de Groat, 1997a). **The bladder to sympathetic**

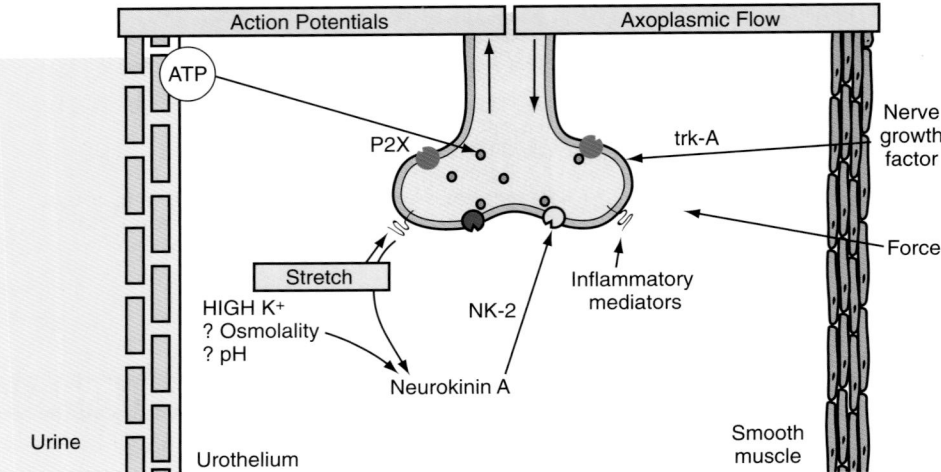

Figure 56–14. Actions of chemical mediators that may sensitize mechanosensory nerve endings in the bladder mucosa. Adenosine triphosphate (ATP) can be released from the urothelium and may sensitize the mechanoreceptors, which respond to stretch of the mucosa during bladder distention. Neuropeptides transported to the sensory ending by axoplasmic transport may be released during distention and chemical stimulation, and neurokinin A can act on NK$_2$ autoreceptors, which sensitize the mechanosensitive endings. This mechanism can be induced by high urinary potassium concentrations and possibly by other sensitizing solutions within the bladder lumen, such as those with high osmolality or low pH; the presence in the tissues of inflammatory mediators may also sensitize the endings. The smooth muscle can generate force that may influence some mucosal endings, and the production of nerve growth factor is another mechanism that can influence the mechanosensitivity of the sensory ending through the TrkA receptor.

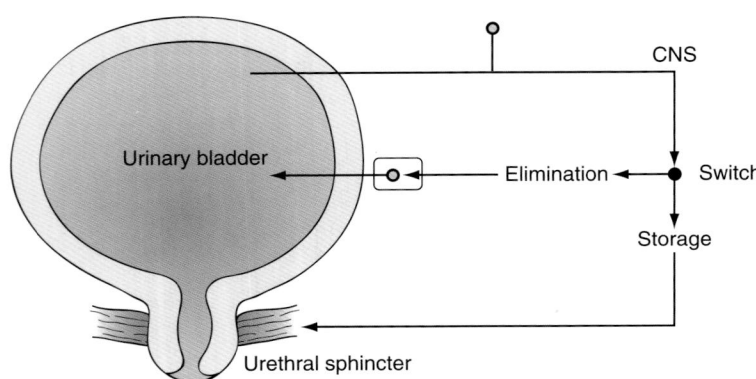

Figure 56–15. Diagram illustrating the anatomy of the lower urinary tract and the "switchlike" function of the micturition reflex pathway. During urine storage, a low level of afferent activity activates efferent input to the urethral sphincter. A high level of afferent activity induced by bladder distention activates the switching circuit in the central nervous system (CNS), producing firing in the efferent pathways to the bladder, inhibition of the efferent outflow to the sphincter, and urine elimination.

reflex also contributes as a negative feedback or urine storage mechanism that promotes closure of the urethral outlet and inhibits neurally mediated contractions of the bladder during bladder filling (de Groat and Theobald, 1976) (Table 56–4). Reflex activation of the sympathetic outflow to the lower urinary tract can be triggered by afferent activity induced by distention of the urinary bladder (de Groat et al, 1993; de Groat and Theobald, 1976). This reflex response is organized in the lumbosacral spinal cord and persists after transection of the spinal cord at the thoracic levels (Fig. 56–18). However, this bladder to sympathetic mechanism to suppress bladder contractions during urine storage may be weak in humans, given that bilateral retroperitoneal lymph node dissection, in which the sympathetic chains are destroyed, has no discernible alteration of filling or storage function in humans.

During bladder filling, the activity of the sphincter electromyogram also increases (see Fig. 56–17), reflecting an increase in efferent firing in the pudendal nerve and an increase in outlet resistance that contributes to the maintenance of urinary continence. Pudendal motoneurons are

Table 56–4.	Reflexes to the Lower Urinary Tract	
Afferent Pathway	**Efferent Pathways**	**Central Pathway**
Urine Storage		
Low-level vesical afferent activity (pelvic nerve)	External sphincter contraction (somatic nerves)	Spinal reflexes
	Internal sphincter contraction (sympathetic nerves)	
	Detrusor inhibition (sympathetic nerves)	
	Ganglionic inhibition (sympathetic nerves)	
	Sacral parasympathetic outflow inactive	
Micturition		
High-level vesical afferent activity (pelvic nerve)	Inhibition of external sphincter activity	Spinobulbospinal reflex
	Inhibition of sympathetic outflow	
	Activation of parasympathetic outflow to the bladder	
	Activation of parasympathetic outflow to the urethra	

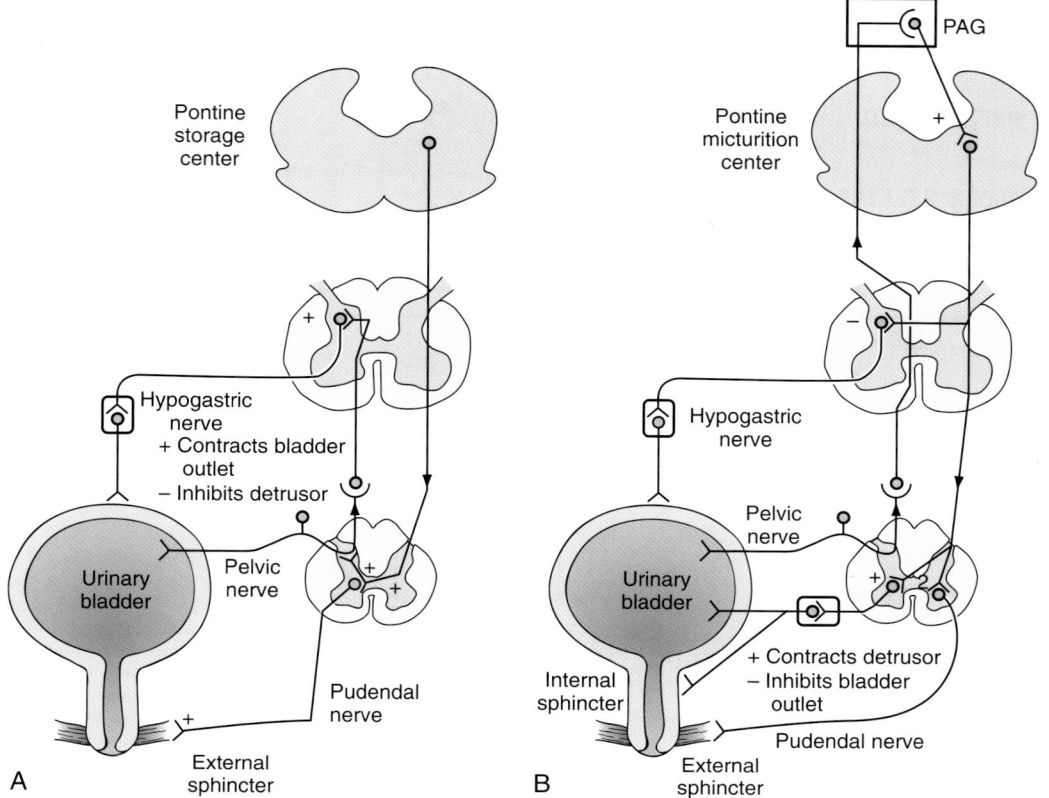

Figure 56–16. Mechanism of storage and voiding reflexes. **A,** Storage reflexes. During the storage of urine, distention of the bladder produces low-level bladder afferent firing. Afferent firing in turn stimulates the sympathetic outflow to the bladder outlet (base and urethra) and pudendal outflow to the external urethral sphincter. These responses occur by spinal reflex pathways and represent "guarding reflexes," which promote continence. Sympathetic firing also inhibits detrusor muscle and transmission in bladder ganglia. **B,** Voiding reflexes. At the initiation of micturition, intense vesical afferent activity activates the brainstem micturition center, which inhibits the spinal guarding reflexes (sympathetic and pudendal outflow to the urethra). The pontine micturition center also stimulates the parasympathetic outflow to the bladder and internal sphincter smooth muscle. Maintenance of the voiding reflex is through ascending afferent input from the spinal cord, which may pass through the periaqueductal gray matter (PAG) before reaching the pontine micturition center.

activated by bladder afferent input (the guarding reflex) (Park et al, 1997); whereas during micturition, the motoneurons are reciprocally inhibited (de Groat et al, 1993). External urethral sphincter motoneurons are also activated by urethral or perineal afferents in the pudendal nerve (Fedirchuk et al, 1992). This reflex may represent, in part, a continence mechanism that is activated by proprioceptive afferent input from the urethra or pelvic floor and that induces closure of the urethral outlet. These excitatory sphincter reflexes are organized in the spinal cord. Inhibition of external urethral sphincter reflex activity during micturition is dependent, in part, on supraspinal mechanisms because it is weak or absent in chronic spinal animals and humans, resulting in simultaneous contractions of bladder and sphincter (i.e., detrusor-sphincter dyssynergia) (Rossier and Ott, 1976; Blaivas, 1982).

Sphincter to Bladder Reflexes. It is well known that stimulation of somatic afferent pathways projecting in the pudendal nerve to the caudal lumbosacral spinal cord can inhibit voiding function. The inhibition can be induced by activation of afferent input from various sites including the penis, vagina, rectum, perineum, urethral sphincter, and anal sphincter (de Groat et al, 1979, 1993, 2001). Electrophysiologic studies in cats showed that the inhibition was mediated by

suppression of interneuronal pathways in the sacral spinal cord and also by direct inhibitory input to the parasympathetic preganglionic neurons (de Groat et al, 1982).

On the basis of experiments in our laboratory and the review of medical literature, we believe that contractions of the external urethral sphincter and possibly other pelvic floor striated muscles stimulate firing in muscle proprioceptive afferents, which then activate central inhibitory mechanisms to suppress the micturition reflex (Fig. 56–19). A similar inhibitory mechanism has been identified in monkeys by directly stimulating the anal sphincter muscle (McGuire et al, 1983). In monkeys, at least part of the inhibitory mechanism must be localized in the spinal cord because it persisted in T4 chronic paraplegic animals.

The Emptying Phase of the Bladder

The storage phase of the bladder can be switched to the voiding phase either involuntarily (reflexly) or voluntarily. The former is readily demonstrated in the human infant or in patients with neuropathic bladder when the bladder wall tension due to increased volume of urine exceeds the micturition threshold. At this point, increased afferent firing from tension receptors in the bladder reverses the pattern of

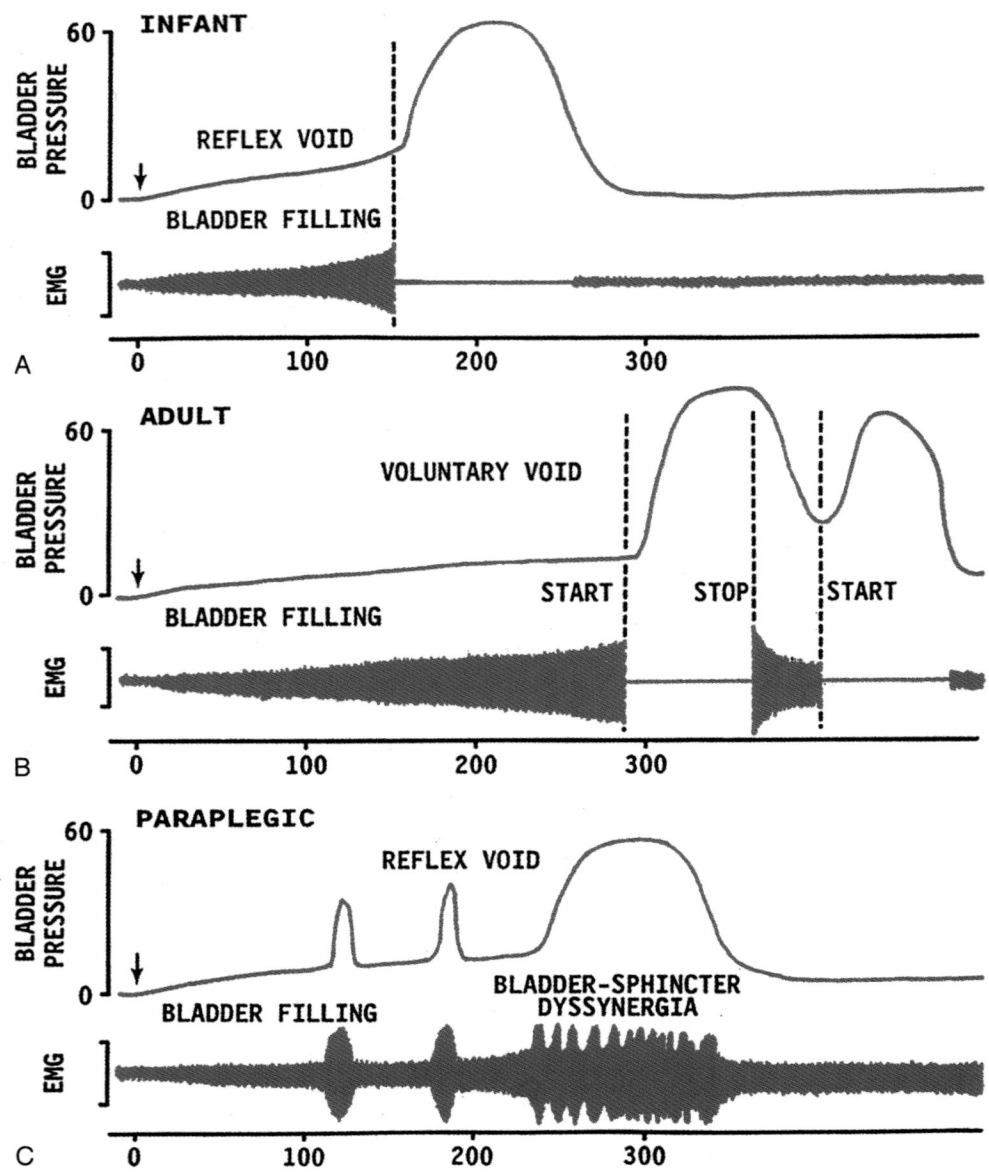

Figure 56–17. Combined cystometrogram and sphincter electromyogram (EMG) comparing reflex voiding responses in an infant (**A**) and in a paraplegic patient (**C**) with a voluntary voiding response in an adult (**B**). The x-axis in all records represents bladder volume in milliliters, and the y-axis represents bladder pressure in centimeters of water and electrical activity of the electromyographic recording. On the left side of each trace, the arrows indicate the start of a slow infusion of fluid into the bladder (bladder filling). Vertical dashed lines indicate the start of sphincter relaxation that precedes by a few seconds the bladder contraction in **A** and **B**. In **B**, note that a voluntary cessation of voiding (stop) is associated with an initial increase in sphincter electromyographic activity followed by a reciprocal relaxation of the bladder. A resumption of voiding is again associated with sphincter relaxation and a delayed increase in bladder pressure. On the other hand, in the paraplegic patient (**C**), the reciprocal relationship between bladder and sphincter is abolished. During bladder filling, transient uninhibited bladder contractions occur in association with sphincter activity. Further filling leads to more prolonged and simultaneous contractions of the bladder and sphincter (bladder-sphincter dyssynergia). Loss of the reciprocal relationship between bladder and sphincter in paraplegic patients interferes with bladder emptying. (From de Groat WC: Basic neurophysiology and neuropharmacology. In Abrams P, Khoury S, Wein A, eds: Incontinence. Plymouth, UK, Health Publications, 1999:112.)

efferent outflow, producing firing in the sacral parasympathetic pathways and inhibition of sympathetic and somatic pathways. The expulsion phase consists of an initial relaxation of the urethral sphincter (see Fig. 56–17) followed in a few seconds by a contraction of the bladder, an increase in bladder pressure, and the flow of urine. Relaxation of the urethral smooth muscle during micturition is mediated by activation of a parasympathetic pathway to the urethra that triggers the release of nitric oxide, an inhibitory transmitter (Andersson, 1993; Bennett et al, 1995), and by removal of excitatory inputs to the urethra. Secondary reflexes elicited by flow of urine through the urethra facilitate bladder emptying (Torrens, 1987; de Groat et al, 1993; Jung et al, 1999). These reflexes require the integrative action of neuronal populations at various levels of the neuraxis (see Fig. 56–16A). The parasympathetic outflow to the detrusor and urethra has

a more complicated central organization involving spinal and spinobulbospinal pathways passing through a micturition center in the pons (pontine micturition center) (see Fig. 56–16B).

Urethra to Bladder Reflexes. A landmark in the historical progress of neurourology is the contribution of Barrington. Using his keen observational skills, Barrington (1931, 1941) reported that urine flow or mechanical stimulation of the urethra with a catheter could excite afferent nerves that in turn facilitated reflex bladder contractions in the anesthetized cat (see Fig. 56–19). He proposed that this facilitatory urethra to bladder reflex could promote complete bladder emptying. Barrington identified two components of this reflex. One component was activated by a somatic afferent pathway in the pudendal nerve and produced facilitation by a supraspinal

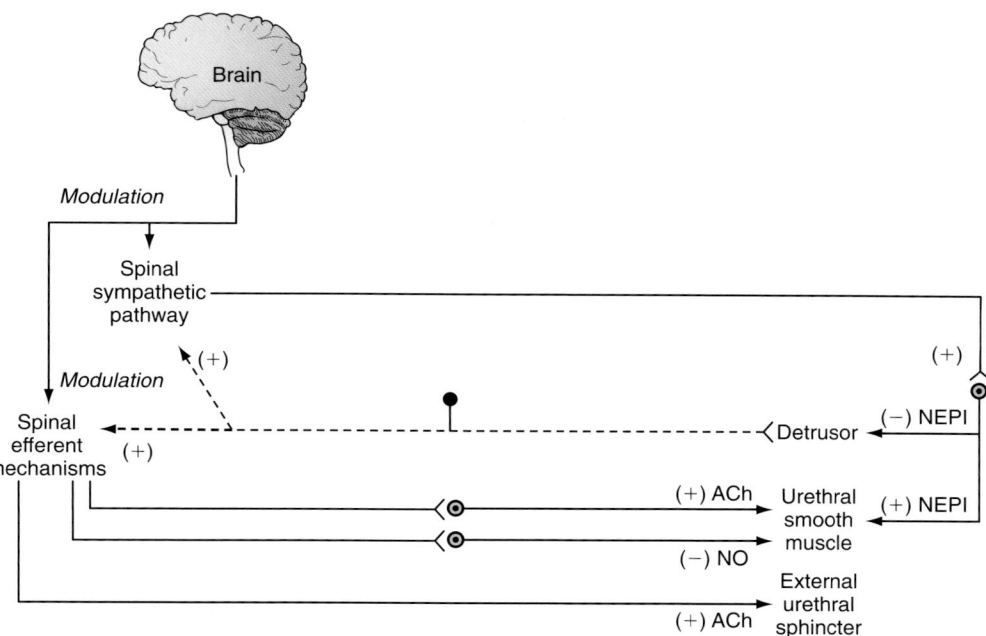

Figure 56–18. Diagram showing bladder to urethra reflex pathways. Afferent pathway *(dashed line)* from the detrusor activates spinal reflex mechanisms that induce firing in somatic cholinergic nerves to the external urethral sphincter, sympathetic adrenergic nerves to the urethral smooth muscle, and cholinergic and nitrergic nerves to the urethral smooth muscle. Bulbospinal pathways from the brain can modulate these spinal reflex mechanisms. ACh, acetylcholine; NEPI, norepinephrine; NO, nitric oxide; excitatory (+) and inhibitory (−) mechanisms.

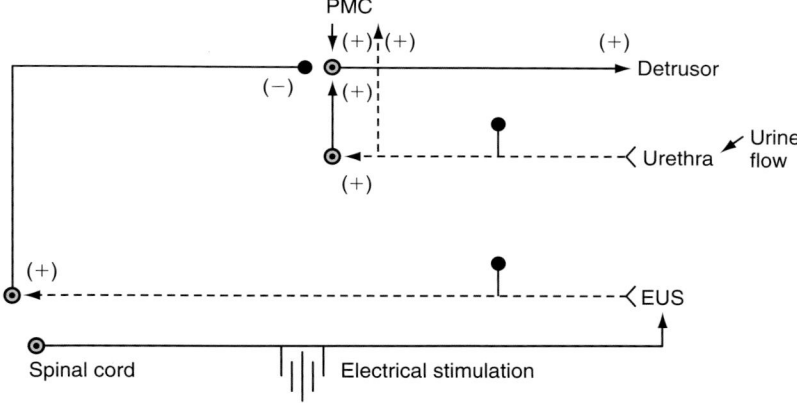

Figure 56–19. Urethra to bladder reflexes. Activity in afferent nerves *(dashed lines)* from the urethra can facilitate parasympathetic efferent outflow to the detrusor by means of a supraspinal pathway passing through the pontine micturition center (PMC) as well as a spinal reflex pathway. Afferent input from the external urethral sphincter (EUS) can inhibit parasympathetic outflow to the detrusor through a spinal reflex circuit. Electrical stimulation of motor axons in the S1 ventral root elicits an EUS contraction and EUS afferent firing that in turn inhibits reflex bladder activity; excitatory (+) and inhibitory (−) mechanisms.

mechanism involving the pontine micturition center (Barrington, 1931) (see Fig. 56–19). Studies have confirmed the existence of this type of reflex via the pudendal nerve since low-frequency electrical stimulation of afferent axons in the pudendal nerve in humans or the deep perineal nerve, a caudal branch of the pudendal nerve, in cats can initiate reflex bladder contractions and voiding (Shefchyk and Buss, 1998; Boggs et al, 2005). The other component was activated by a visceral afferent pathway in the pelvic nerve and produced facilitation by a spinal reflex mechanism (Barrington, 1941).

Studies (Jung et al, 1999) in the anesthetized rat have also provided additional support for Barrington's findings (Dokita et al, 1991). Measurements of reflex bladder contractions under isovolumetric conditions during continuous urethral perfusion (0.075 mL/min) revealed that the frequency of micturition reflexes was significantly reduced when urethral perfusion was stopped or after infusion of lidocaine (1%) into the urethra. Intraurethral infusion of

nitric oxide donors (S-nitroso-N-acetylpenicillamine [SNAP], or nitroprusside, 1 to 2 mM) markedly decreased urethral perfusion pressure (approximately 30%) and decreased the frequency of reflex bladder contractions (45% to 75%) but did not change the amplitude of bladder contractions (Fig. 56–20). Desensitization of the urethral afferent with intraurethral capsaicin also dramatically altered the micturition reflex (Fig. 56–21). It was concluded that activation of urethral afferents during urethral perfusion could modulate the micturition reflex in the rat. This may be an explanation of why stress incontinence and urge incontinence often occur together in women. Chancellor speculated that **in women with mixed incontinence, leakage of urine into the urethra can stimulate afferents and induce or increase detrusor overactivity. The theory is that stress incontinence can induce urge incontinence** (Lavelle and Chancellor, 2000). Surgical cure of the stress incontinence of women with mixed incontinence has resolved the urge incontinence in up to half of the patients.

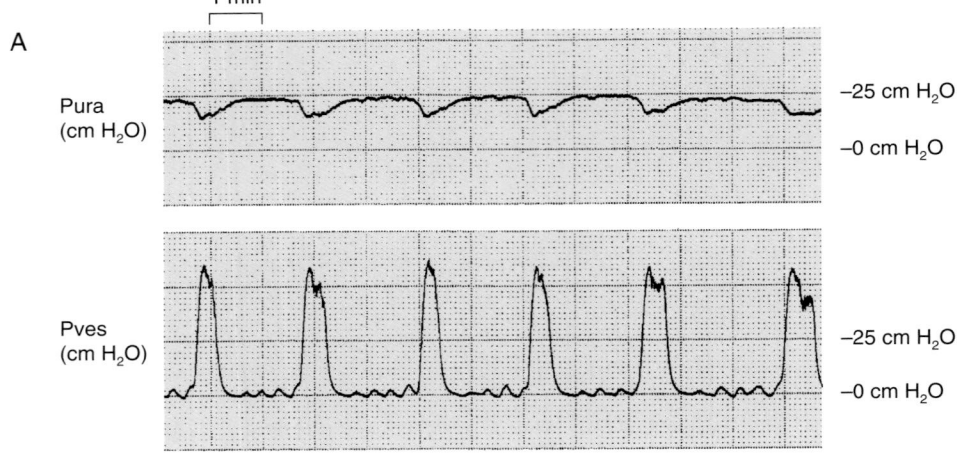

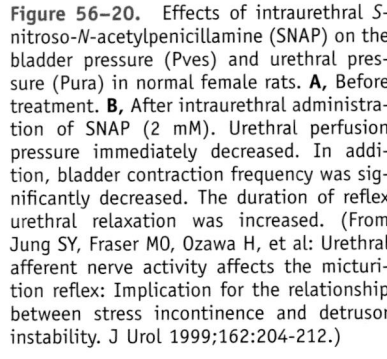

Figure 56–20. Effects of intraurethral *S*-nitroso-*N*-acetylpenicillamine (SNAP) on the bladder pressure (Pves) and urethral pressure (Pura) in normal female rats. **A,** Before treatment. **B,** After intraurethral administration of SNAP (2 mM). Urethral perfusion pressure immediately decreased. In addition, bladder contraction frequency was significantly decreased. The duration of reflex urethral relaxation was increased. (From Jung SY, Fraser MO, Ozawa H, et al: Urethral afferent nerve activity affects the micturition reflex: Implication for the relationship between stress incontinence and detrusor instability. J Urol 1999;162:204-212.)

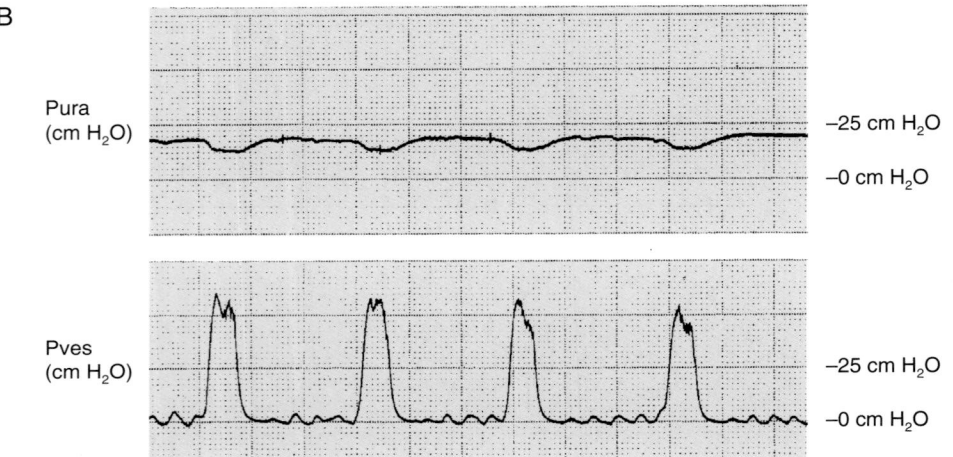

Spinal and Supraspinal Pathways Involved in the Micturition Reflex

Spinal Cord

In the spinal cord, afferent pathways terminate on second-order interneurons that relay information to the brain or to other regions of the spinal cord including the preganglionic and motor nuclei. Because disynaptic or polysynaptic pathways but not monosynaptic pathways mediate bladder, urethral, and sphincter reflex, interneuronal mechanisms must play an essential role in the regulation of lower urinary tract function. Electrophysiologic (de Groat et al, 1981, 1996; Araki and de Groat, 1997) and neuroanatomic (Birder and de Groat, 1993; Vizzard et al, 1995; Nadelhaft and Vera, 1996; Sugaya et al, 1997b) techniques have identified lower urinary tract interneurons in the same regions of the cord that receive afferent input from the bladder.

As shown in Figure 56–13, horseradish peroxidase labeling techniques in the cat revealed that afferent projections from the external urethral sphincter and levator ani muscles (i.e., pelvic floor) project into different regions of the sacral spinal cord. The external urethral sphincter afferent terminals are located in the superficial layers of the dorsal horn and at the base of the dorsal horn (laminae V to VII and lamina X), whereas the levator ani afferents project into a region just lateral to the central canal and extend into the medial ventral horn. The external urethral sphincter afferents overlap closely with the central projections of visceral afferents in pelvic nerve that innervate the bladder and urethra (Morgan et al, 1981). Intracellular labeling experiments also showed that the dendritic patterns of external urethral sphincter motoneurons (Sasaki, 1994) and parasympathetic preganglionic neurons (Morgan et al, 1993) are similar. **Pharmacologic experiments revealed that glutamic acid is the excitatory transmitter in these pathways.** In addition, approximately 15% of interneurons medial to the sacral parasympathetic nucleus in laminae V through VII make inhibitory synaptic connections with the preganglionic neurons (de Groat et al, 1996). **These inhibitory neurons release γ-aminobutyric acid (GABA) and glycine. Reflex pathways that control the external sphincter muscles also use glutamatergic excitatory and GABAergic and glycinergic inhibitory interneuronal mechanisms.**

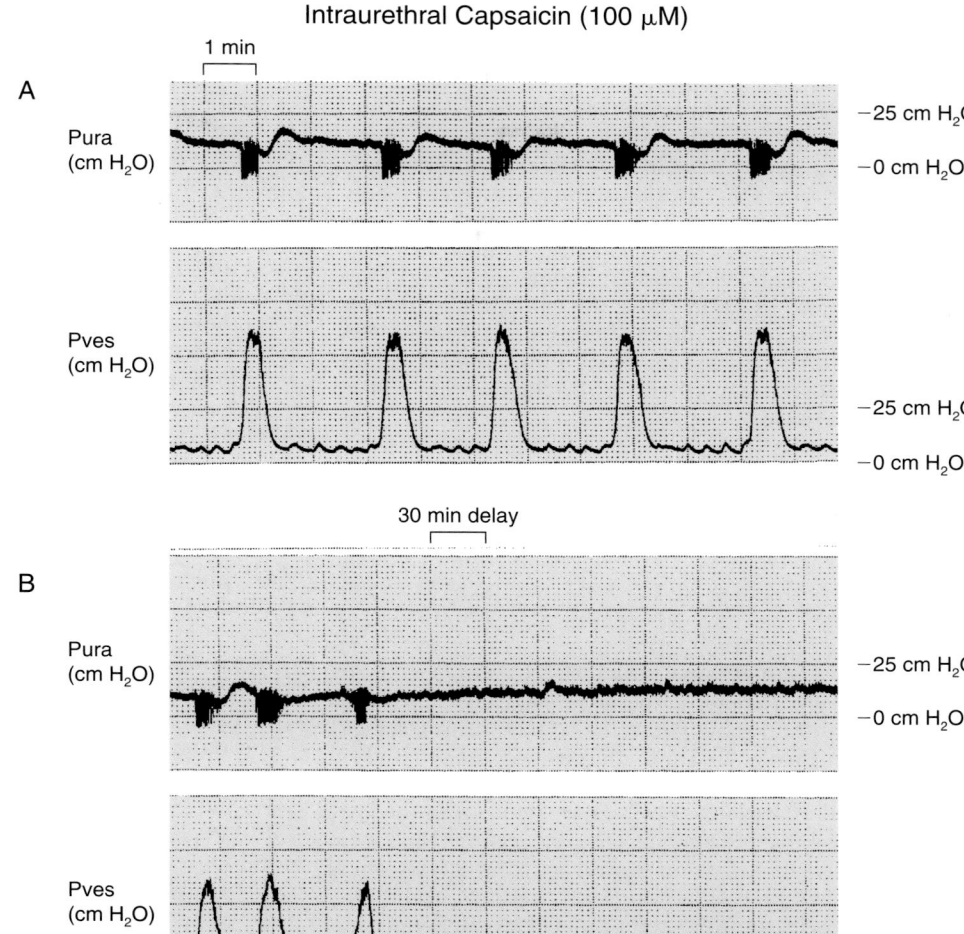

Intraurethral Capsaicin (100 μM)

Figure 56–21. Effects of intraurethral capsaicin on the bladder pressure (Pves) and urethral pressure (Pura) in normal female rats. **A,** Before treatment. **B,** After intraurethral administration of capsaicin (100 μM). Initially, intraurethral capsaicin instillation increased the bladder contraction frequency, but 30 minutes after continuous infusion, the activity was blocked. (From Jung SY, Fraser MO, Ozawa H, et al: Urethral afferent nerve activity affects the micturition reflex: Implication for the relationship between stress incontinence and detrusor instability. J Urol 1999;162:204-212.)

Tracing with neurotropic viruses such as pseudorabies virus has been particularly useful. Pseudorabies virus can be injected into a target organ and then move intra-axonally from the periphery to the central nervous system. In the nervous system, the virus can replicate and then pass retrogradely across synapses to infect second- and third-order neurons in the neural pathways (Vizzard et al, 1995; Nadelhaft and Vera, 1996; Sugaya et al, 1997b). Because pseudorabies virus can be transported across many synapses, it could sequentially infect all the neurons that connect directly or indirectly to the lower urinary tract. Interneurons identified by retrograde transport of pseudorabies virus injected into the urinary bladder are located in the region of the sacral parasympathetic nucleus, the dorsal commissure, and the superficial laminae of the dorsal horn (de Groat et al, 1996; Nadelhaft and Vera, 1996; Sugaya et al, 1997b). A similar distribution of labeled interneurons has been noted after injection of virus into the urethra (Vizzard et al, 1995) or the external urethral sphincter (Nadelhaft and Vera, 1996), indicating a prominent overlap of the interneuronal pathways controlling the various target organs of the lower urinary tract.

The micturition reflex can be modulated at the level of the spinal cord by interneuronal mechanisms activated by afferent input from cutaneous and striated muscle targets. Micturition reflex can also be modulated by inputs from visceral organs (de Groat, 1978; de Groat et al, 1975, 1981, 1993; McGuire, 1977; McMahon and Morrison, 1982; Torrens, 1987; Morrison et al, 1995; Yoshimura and de Groat, 1997a). Stimulation of afferent fibers from various regions (anus, colon-rectum, vagina, uterine cervix, penis, perineum, pudendal nerve) can inhibit the firing of sacral interneurons evoked by bladder distention (de Groat et al, 1981). This inhibition may be a result of presynaptic inhibition at primary afferent terminals or be due to direct postsynaptic inhibition of the second-order neurons. Direct postsynaptic inhibition of bladder preganglionic neurons can also be elicited by stimulation of somatic afferent axons in the pudendal nerve or visceral afferents from the distal bowel (de Groat and Ryall, 1969; de Groat, 1978). **Suppression of detrusor overactivity in patients by sacral root stimulation may reflect in part activation of the afferent limb of these visceral-bladder and somatic-bladder inhibitory reflexes** (Wheeler et al, 1992; Bosch and Groen, 1995; Chancellor and Chartier-Kastler, 2000).

Pontine Micturition Center

Various studies indicate that the micturition reflex is normally mediated by a spinobulbospinal reflex pathway passing through relay centers in the brain (see Fig. 56–16*B*) (de Groat, 1975; Torrens, 1987; de Groat et al, 1993; Yoshimura and de Groat, 1997a). Studies in animals by use of brain-lesioning techniques revealed that neurons in the brainstem at the level of the inferior colliculus have an essential role in the control of the parasympathetic component of micturition (Torrens, 1987; de Groat et al, 1993; Yoshimura and de Groat, 1997a). **Removal of areas of brain above the colliculus by intercollicular decerebration usually facilitates micturition by elimination of inhibitory inputs from more rostral centers. However, transections at any point below the colliculi abolish micturition.**

The dorsal pontine tegmentum has been firmly established as an essential control center for micturition in normal subjects. First described by Barrington (1921), it has subsequently been called Barrington's nucleus, the pontine micturition center (Blok and Holstege, 1997), or the M region (Blok and Holstege, 1996; Holstege et al, 1996) because of its medial location.

In addition to providing axonal inputs to the locus ceruleus and the sacral spinal cord (Ding et al, 1995; Otake and Nakamura, 1996; Valentino et al, 1996), neurons in the pontine micturition center (PMC) also send axon collaterals to the paraventricular thalamic nucleus, which is thought to be involved in the limbic system modulation of visceral behavior (Otake and Nakamura, 1996). Some neurons in the PMC also project to the periaqueductal gray region (Blok et al, 1998a), which regulates many visceral activities as well as pain pathways (Valentino et al, 1995). Thus, neurons in the PMC communicate with multiple supraspinal neuronal populations that may coordinate micturition with other functions of the organism. Although the circuitry in humans is uncertain, brain imaging studies have revealed increases in blood flow in this region of the pons during micturition (Blok et al, 1997b). This change presumably reflects increases in neuronal activity. Thus, the PMC appears critical for micturition across species.

Neurons in the PMC provide direct synaptic inputs to sacral preganglionic neurons (Blok and Holstege, 1997) as well as to GABAergic neurons in the sacral dorsal commissure region (Blok et al, 1997a). The former neurons carry the excitatory outflow to the bladder, whereas the latter neurons are thought to be important in mediating an inhibitory influence on external urethral sphincter motoneurons (Blok et al, 1998a). As a result of these reciprocal connections, the PMC can promote bladder-sphincter synergy. Studies in rats indicate that activation of bladder preganglionic neurons by input from the PMC can be blocked by inotropic glutamate receptor antagonists, suggesting that neurons in the PMC use glutamate as a neurotransmitter (Matsumoto et al, 1995a, 1995b).

Central Pathways That Modulate the Micturition Reflex

Various cortical areas are labeled after injection of pseudorabies virus into the lower urinary tract (Vizzard et al, 1995;

Nadelhaft and Vera, 1996; Marson, 1997; Sugaya et al, 1997b). Thus, cortical control of voiding is likely to be complex. The influence of the cortex on voiding function could be mediated by a number of pathways, including direct cortical projections from the prefrontal cortex and insular cortex to the PMC or projections through the hypothalamus and the extrapyramidal system (de Groat et al, 1993).

Studies in humans indicate that voluntary control of voiding is dependent on connections between the frontal cortex and the septal-preoptic region of the hypothalamus as well as on connections between the paracentral lobule and the brainstem (de Groat et al, 1993). Lesions to these areas of cortex appear to directly increase bladder activity by removing cortical inhibitory control. **Brain imaging studies (Fukuyama et al, 1996; Blok et al, 1997a) in human volunteers have implicated both the frontal cortex and the anterior cingulate gyrus in control of micturition and have indicated that micturition is controlled predominantly by the right side of the brain.**

Positron emission tomography (PET) scans were used to examine which brain areas are involved in human micturition (Blok et al, 1997c). Seventeen right-handed male volunteers were scanned during four conditions: (1) 15 minutes before micturition during urine holding, (2) during micturition, (3) 15 minutes after micturition, and (4) 30 minutes after micturition. Of the 17 volunteers, 10 were able to micturate during scanning. Micturition was associated with increased blood flow in the right dorsomedial pontine tegmentum, the periaqueductal gray, the hypothalamus, and the right inferior frontal gyrus. Decreased blood flow was found in the right anterior cingulate gyrus when urine was withheld. The other 7 volunteers were not able to micturate during scanning, although they had a full bladder and tried vigorously to micturate. In this group, during these unsuccessful attempts to micturate, increased blood flow was detected in the right ventral pontine tegmentum, which is consistent with the idea, arising from studies in cats (Blok and Holstege, 1996; Holstege et al, 1996), that this area controls the motoneurons of the pelvic floor. PET scan studies in humans have also confirmed that two cortical areas (the right dorsolateral prefrontal cortex and the anterior cingulate gyrus) are active during voiding (Blok et al, 1998b; Blok, 2002). Other PET studies that examined the changes in brain activity during filling of the bladder revealed that increased activity occurred in the periaqueductal gray, the midline pons, the mid–cingulate gyrus, and bilaterally in the frontal lobes (Athwal et al, 1999, 2001; Matsuura et al, 2002).

Increased blood flow also occurred in the right inferior frontal gyrus during unsuccessful attempts to micturate, and decreased blood flow occurred in the right anterior cingulate gyrus during the withholding of urine. The results suggest that the human brainstem contains specific nuclei responsible for the control of micturition and that the cortical and pontine regions for micturition are predominantly on the right side. The results are in accordance with the results of a clinical analysis that was performed to determine the individual contribution of the right and left cerebral hemispheres to the frequency and urgency of micturition in 134 chronic hemiplegic patients (Kuroiwa et al, 1987; Fukuyama et al, 1996). A mean frequency of micturition, nine times or more in 24 hours, was found more frequently in left than in right hemiplegics. Left hemiplegics also complained more often of urgency than did right hemiplegics (Kuroiwa et al, 1987).

A PET study (Blok et al, 1997c) was also conducted in adult female volunteers to identify brain structures involved in the voluntary motor control of the pelvic floor during four conditions: (1) rest, (2) repetitive pelvic floor straining, (3) sustained pelvic floor straining, and (4) sustained abdominal straining. The results revealed that the superomedial precentral gyrus, the most medial portion of the motor cortex, is activated during pelvic floor contraction and the superolateral precentral gyrus is activated during contraction of the abdominal musculature. In these conditions, significant activations were also found in the cerebellum, supplementary motor cortex, and thalamus. The right anterior cingulate gyrus was activated during sustained pelvic floor straining.

There is general agreement on the finding that patients with lesions in only the basal ganglia or thalamus have normal urethral sphincter function. These patients can voluntarily contract the striated sphincter and abort or considerably lessen the effect of the abnormal micturition reflex when an impending involuntary contraction or its onset is sensed. The patients with lesions in the cerebral cortex or internal capsule after a cerebrovascular accident are unable to forcefully contract the striated sphincter under these circumstances. Thus, these patients have a profound abnormality in the cerebral to corticospinal circuitry that is necessary for voluntary control of the striated sphincter (Yokoyama et al, 2000).

Hypothesis of Mechanism of Action of Sacral Neuromodulation

We hypothesize that the effects of sacral neuromodulation depend on electrical stimulation of afferent axons in the spinal roots that in turn modulate voiding and continence reflex pathways in the central nervous system. The afferent system is the most likely target because beneficial effects can be elicited at intensities of stimulation that do not activate movements of striated muscles (Vadusek et al, 1986; Thon et al, 1991; de Groat et al, 1997). **Sacral neuromodulation activates somatic afferent axons that modulate sensory processing and mic-**

turition reflex pathways in the spinal cord. Urinary retention and dysfunctional voiding can be resolved by inhibition of the guarding reflexes. Detrusor overactivity can be suppressed by direct inhibition of bladder preganglionic neurons. Inhibition of interneuronal transmission in the afferent limb of the micturition reflex can also block detrusor overactivity. Thus, the principles behind sacral neuromodulation can be summarized as somatic afferent inhibition of sensory processing in the spinal cord. Pudendal afferent input can also turn on voiding reflexes by suppressing the guarding reflex pathways. Pudendal afferent input to the sacral spinal cord can turn off supraspinally mediated hyperactive voiding by blocking ascending sensory systems.

How do sacral somatic afferents alter lower urinary tract reflexes to promote voiding? To understand these mechanisms, it should be recognized that in adults, brain pathways are necessary to turn off sphincter and urethral guarding reflexes to allow efficient bladder emptying. Thus, spinal cord injury produces bladder-sphincter dyssynergia and inefficient bladder emptying by eliminating the brain mechanisms (Fig. 56–22). This may also occur after more subtle neurologic lesions in patients with idiopathic urinary retention, such as after a bout of prostatitis or urinary tract infection. Before the development of brain control of micturition, at least in animals, the stimulation of somatic afferent pathways passing through the pudendal nerve from the perineum can initiate efficient voiding by activating bladder efferent pathways and turning off the excitatory pathways to the urethral outlet (de Groat et al, 1993; Kruse and de Groat, 1993). Tactile stimulation of the perineum in the cat also inhibits the bladder–sympathetic reflex component of the guarding reflex mechanism. We hypothesize that the sacral nerve stimulation can elicit similar responses in patients with urinary retention and turn off excitatory outflow to the urethral outlet and promote bladder emptying. Because sphincter activity can generate afferent input to the spinal cord that can in turn inhibit reflex bladder activity, an indirect benefit of suppressing sphincter reflexes would be a facilitation of bladder activity.

How do sacral afferents inhibit the overactive bladder? Several reflex mechanisms may be involved in the sacral neuromodulation suppression of detrusor overactivity. Afferent

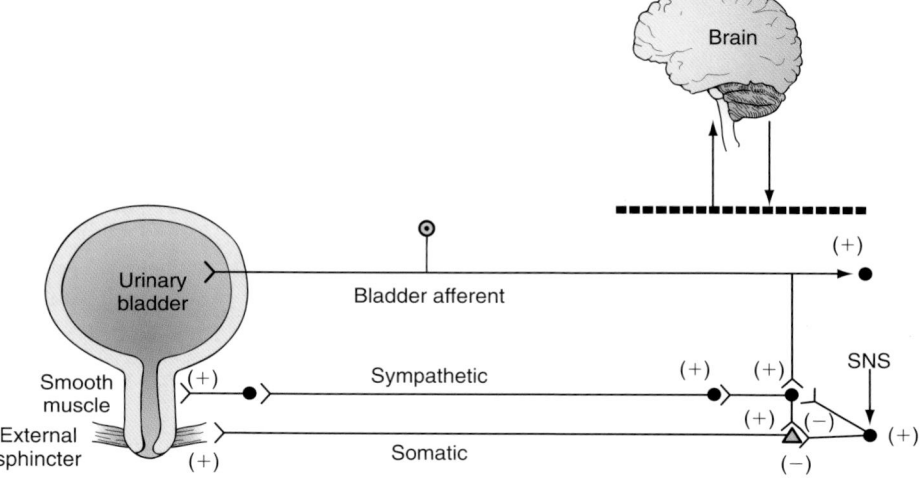

Figure 56–22. When there is a sudden increase in intravesical pressure, such as during a cough, the urinary sphincter contracts by means of the spinal guarding reflex to prevent urinary incontinence (guarding reflex). The spinal guarding reflexes can be turned off by the brain for urination. In cases of neurologic diseases, the brain cannot turn off the guarding reflex and retention can occur. The sacral nerve stimulation (SNS) restores voluntary micturition in cases of voiding dysfunction and urinary retention but inhibits the guarding reflex.

pathways projecting to the sacral cord can inhibit bladder reflexes in animals and humans. The source of afferent input may be from sphincter muscles, distal colon, rectum, anal canal, vagina, uterine cervix, and cutaneous afferents from the perineum (Fig. 56–23). As mentioned previously, two mechanisms have been identified in animals for somatic and visceral afferent inhibition of bladder reflexes. The most common mechanism is suppression of interneuronal transmission in the bladder reflex pathway (de Groat and Theobald, 1976; Kruse et al, 1990; Kruse and de Groat, 1993). It is assumed that this inhibition occurs in part on the ascending limb of the micturition reflex and therefore blocks the transfer of information from the bladder to the PMC. This action would prevent involuntary (reflex) micturition but not necessarily suppress voluntary voiding that would be mediated by descending excitatory efferent pathways from the brain to the sacral parasympathetic preganglionic neurons. A second inhibitory mechanism is mediated by a direct inhibitory input to the bladder preganglionic neurons. This can be induced by electrical stimulation of the pudendal nerve or by mechanical stimulation of the anal canal and distal bowel. It is not elicited by tactile stimulation of penile or perineal afferents; this mechanism would be much more effective in turning off bladder reflexes because it would directly suppress firing in the motor outflow from the spinal cord.

Developmental Changes of Bladder Reflexes

The neonatal bladder is a conduit of urine more than a storage organ. Without cerebral control, the bladder will reflexively empty into a diaper when it reaches functional capacity. Therefore, by definition, a normal toddler has detrusor overactivity. Neonatal animal bladder strips have repetitive spontaneous contraction, perhaps initiated by pacemaker cells within the bladder and propagated by gap junctions between cells (see Fig. 56–1) (Pezzone et al, 1999; Szell et al, 2003).

The bladder overactivity neonatal pathways do not disappear with growth and development; rather, increasing cerebral maturation actively inhibits them. Inhibition rather than resolution of neonatal reflexes may be difficult to grasp initially, but this concept holds true across most concepts of neuroscience. **With disease processes such as neurologic dis-** eases and aging, the neonatal reflexes are released and involuntary detrusor contractions recur (de Groat et al, 1975).

One of the most interesting clinical demonstrations of the reemergence of the primitive neonatal micturition reflex is the bladder ice-water test. The bladder ice-water cooling test is performed by quickly instilling up to 100 mL of 4° C sterile saline solution. The normal adult will sense cold but maintain a stable bladder. However, infants and neuropathic patients will develop involuntary detrusor contractions with this test (Chancellor and de Groat, 1999).

The bladder cooling response is triggered by activation of cold receptors within the bladder wall. The receptors are supplied by unmyelinated C-fiber afferent neurons (Chancellor and de Groat, 1999). The cooling response represents a neonatal reflex that may be unmasked by central neuropathologic processes, analogous to the appearance of the Babinski reflex in pyramidal tract lesions. The cooling response is present (development of involuntary detrusor contraction) in neurologically normal infants and children until about the age of 4 years. The reflex becomes absent with further maturation of the nervous system, but the response may be unmasked by pathologic processes that disturb the descending neuronal control of normal voiding (Geirsson et al, 1999). It has also been suggested that men with prostatic bladder outlet obstruction also have an ice-water test response. Chai and colleagues (1998) reported an ice-water test response in 12 of 17 patients (71%) with bladder outlet obstruction, but their method of ice-water infusion has been criticized (Geirsson et al, 1999). More recently, Hirayama and colleagues (2003) have also reported that an ice-water test response was found in 35 (27%) of 127 patients with benign prostatic hyperplasia and that the patients with the ice-water test response had detrusor overactivity and higher bladder outlet obstruction index than the nonresponders on the pressure flow study.

PHARMACOLOGY

Peripheral Pharmacology

Traditional teaching in uropharmacology is that if a drug works on the bladder or urethra, it is working on the postjunctional receptors. In this section, we present evidence for prejunctional as well as postjunctional actions of drugs.

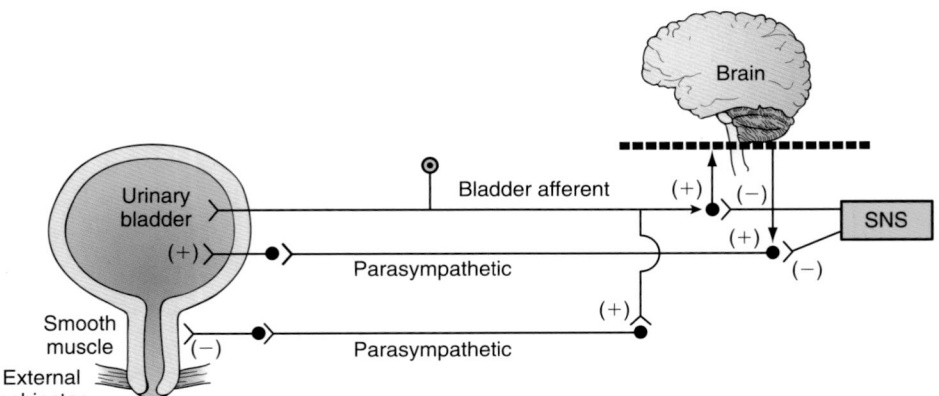

Figure 56–23. The voiding reflex involves afferent neurons from the bladder that project on spinal tract neurons that ascend to the brain. Descending pathways connect to parasympathetic efferent nerves to contract the bladder (bladder-bladder reflex). A spinal bladder-urethra reflex is activated by a similar bladder afferent innervation. In cases of supraspinal dysfunction, overactive micturition reflexes occur. The sacral nerve stimulation (SNS) inhibits urinary urgency, frequency, and urge incontinence by inhibiting the bladder-bladder and bladder-urethra reflexes.

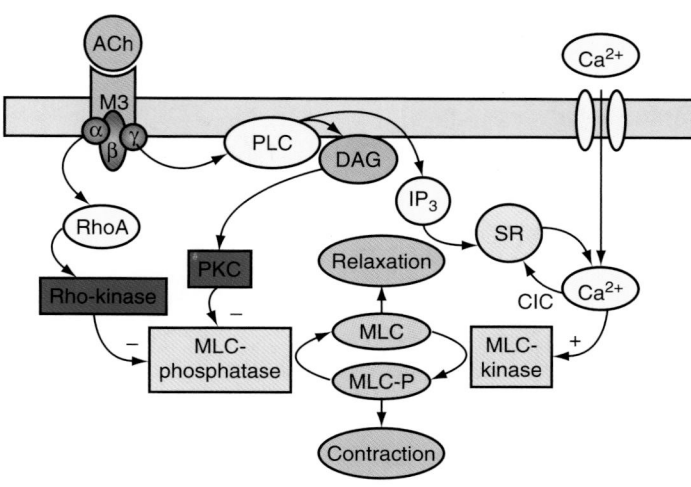

Figure 56–24. Transmitter signal pathways involved in activation of detrusor contractions through muscarinic M_3 receptors. ACh, acetylcholine; PLC, phospholipase C; DAG, diacylglycerol; PKC, protein kinase C; MLC, myosin light chain; SR, sarcoplasmic reticulum; CIC, calcium-induced calcium release. There seem to be differences between species in the contribution of the different pathways in contractile activation. (From Andersson KE, Wein AJ: Pharmacology of the lower urinary tract: Basis for current and future treatments of urinary incontinence. Pharmacol Rev 2004;56:581-631.)

Muscarinic Mechanisms

Detrusor strips from normal human bladders are contracted by cholinergic muscarinic receptor agonists and by electrical stimulation of intrinsic cholinergic nerves. Contractile responses can be completely abolished by atropine (Sibley, 1984). **There are at least five receptor subtypes based on molecular cloning and four different receptor subtypes based on pharmacology (M_1 to M_5)** (Somogyi et al, 1994; Yamaguchi et al, 1994; Wang et al, 1995a; Eglen et al, 1996; Hegde et al, 1997).

Pharmacologically, M_1, M_2, and M_3 receptor subtypes have been found in the human bladder by receptor binding assays (Kondo et al, 1995); all M_1 to M_5 receptor mRNAs are detected by reverse transcription–polymerase chain reaction assays (Andersson and Wein, 2004; Mansfield et al, 2005). **Although ligand receptor binding studies revealed that M_2 receptors predominate, M_3 receptors mediate cholinergic contractions** (Eglen et al, 1994; Harriss et al, 1995; Yamaguchi et al, 1996; Hegde et al, 1997; Lai et al, 1998). **Stimulation of M_3 receptors by acetylcholine leads to IP_3 hydrolysis due to phospholipase C activation and then to the release of intracellular calcium and a smooth muscle contraction** (Harriss et al, 1995; Fry et al, 2002) (Fig. 56–24). **The involvement of transmembrane flux of calcium ions through nifedipine-sensitive L-type Ca^{2+} channels has also been indicated in M_3 receptor–mediated detrusor muscle contractions** since the L-type Ca^{2+} channel inhibitor nifedipine strongly suppressed carbachol-induced detrusor contractions whereas the phospholipase C inhibitor or the store-operated Ca^{2+} channel inhibitor caused little inhibition in rats and humans (Schneider et al, 2004a, 2004b; Andersson and Arner, 2004; Andersson and Wein, 2004) (see Fig. 56–24). However, other studies have indicated the major contribution of the phospholipase C–mediated mechanism to M_3 receptor–induced detrusor contractions because phospholipase C inhibitors significantly suppressed carbachol-induced detrusor contractions in rats (Braverman et al, 2006a, 2006b), and intracellular calcium rises after carbachol application were observed without membrane depolarization, which is required for the opening of L-type Ca^{2+} channels, in human bladders (Fry et al, 2002). Hashitani and colleagues (2000)

have reported that the stimulation of muscarinic receptors activates both calcium influx through L-type Ca^{2+} channels and calcium release from intracellular calcium stores in guinea pig bladders.

It has also been proposed (Hegde et al, 1997; Ehlert et al, 2005) that **coactivation of M_2 receptors could enhance the response to M_3 stimulation by (1) inhibition of adenylate cyclase, thereby suppressing sympathetically mediated depression of detrusor muscle; (2) inactivation of K^+ channels; or (3) activation of nonspecific cation channels.** In addition, since the specific Rho kinase inhibitor Y-27632 reportedly suppresses carbachol-induced detrusor contractions in rats and humans, muscarinic receptor activation in detrusor smooth muscles is likely to stimulate the Rho kinase pathway, leading to a direct inhibition of myosin phosphatase that induces calcium sensitization to enhance the ability of the muscle to generate the same contractile force with lower levels of intracellular calcium (Andersson and Wein, 2004; Schneider et al, 2004a, 2004b). Although the involvement of M_3 receptors for the Rho kinase activation has been suggested (Andersson and Arner, 2004; Andersson and Wein, 2004; Schneider et al, 2004b) (see Fig. 56–24), a study has also suggested the participation of M_2 receptors in this mechanism because Y-27632 not only suppressed carbachol-induced muscle contractions but also increased the affinity of darifenacin, an M_3 receptor antagonist with approximately a 30-fold selectivity for M_3 over M_2 receptors, for inhibiting carbachol-induced contractions of rat bladders (Braverman et al, 2006a, 2006b). It has also been reported that the muscarinic receptor subtype–mediated detrusor contractions shift from M_3 to M_2 receptor subtype in certain pathologic conditions, such as obstructed or denervated hypertrophied bladders in rats (Braverman and Ruggieri, 2003; Braverman et al, 2006a, 2006b), as well as in bladder muscle specimens from patients with neurogenic bladder dysfunction (Pontari et al, 2004).

Studies using constructed mutant mice lacking the M_3 receptor or the M_2 and M_3 receptors have demonstrated that this subtype plays key roles in salivary secretion, pupillary constriction, and detrusor contractions (Matsui et al, 2000, 2002; Igawa et al, 2004). However, M_3-mediated signals in digestive and reproductive organs are dispensable, probably because of redundant mechanisms through other muscarinic

Table 56–5. **Drugs with Bladder Action**

Classification	Examples	Pharmacologic Action
Anticholinergic agents	Atropine Glycopyrrolate Oxybutynin Propantheline Tolterodine	Inhibit muscarinic receptors, thus reducing the response to cholinergic stimulation; used to reduce pressure during bladder filling and for the treatment of unstable bladder contractions
Smooth muscle relaxants	Dicyclomine Flavoxate	Direct smooth muscle relaxation reduces intravesical pressure during filling and reduces severity and presence of unstable bladder contractions; most of these agents have some degree of anticholinergic action
Calcium antagonists	Diltiazem Nifedipine Verapamil	Used in the treatment of unstable bladder contractions to reduce the magnitude of the spikes by reducing the entrance of calcium during an action potential
Potassium channel openers	Cromakalim Pinacidil	Act to increase the membrane potential and thus reduce the myogenic initiation of unstable bladder contractions
Prostaglandin synthesis inhibitors	Flurbiprofen	Prostaglandins have been implicated in increased smooth muscle tone and in the induction of spontaneous activity. Inhibition of prostaglandin synthesis could promote relaxation of the bladder during filling and decrease spontaneous activity of the bladder.
β-Adrenergic agonists	Isoproterenol Terbutaline	Stimulation of β receptors induces relaxation of the bladder body, resulting in a decrease in intravesical pressure during filling.
Tricyclic antidepressants	Amitriptyline Imipramine	These agents have anticholinergic, direct smooth muscle relaxant, and norepinephrine reuptake inhibition properties.
α-Adrenergic agonists	Ephedrine Phenylpropanolamine Midodrine Pseudoephedrine	Increase urethral tone and closure pressure by direct stimulation of α-adrenergic receptors
Afferent nerve inhibitors	DMSO Capsaicin Resiniferatoxin	Reduce the sensory input from bladder and thereby increase bladder capacity and reduce bladder instability
Estrogen	Estradiol	Direct application to the vagina or oral therapy may increase the thickness of the urothelial mucosa, making a better seal and reducing the incidence of incontinence. Other actions may include increasing adrenergic effects on the urethra and increasing blood flow.

DMSO, dimethyl sulfoxide.

acetylcholine receptor subtypes or other mediators (Matsui et al, 2000). In addition, it has also been found that male M_3 knockout mice had the distended bladder and larger bladder capacity compared with females, indicating a considerable sex difference in the micturition mechanism (Matsui et al, 2002; Igawa et al, 2004). Thus, M_3 or M_2 and M_3 double knockout mice should provide a useful animal model for the detrusor overactivity pathophysiology and pharmacology.

Muscarinic receptor antagonists tolterodine and oxybutynin (Table 56–5) are the most widely prescribed drugs for urinary incontinence. Oxybutynin is a nonspecific muscarinic antagonist with additional smooth muscle relaxant properties. The smooth muscle relaxation properties of oxybutynin may be clinically relevant only with intravesical instillation of the drug. Because new antimuscarinic drugs are such a hot topic for pharmaceutical development, all urologists should be aware of the existence of muscarinic receptor subtypes and their distribution in the lower urinary tract and other organs.

We wish to briefly present two additional issues regarding the effect of antimuscarinic drugs on the bladder and salivary glands that have clinical relevancy. First, antimuscarinic drugs are metabolized and their metabolites have pharmacologic effects. It has been shown that oxybutynin has less of a dry mouth effect than its metabolite desethyoxybutynin does (Gupta and Sathyan, 1999). Therefore, the controlled-release formulation of oxybutynin maintains the efficacy of immediate-release oxybutynin but with significantly fewer

side effects. Tolterodine and solifenacin have been shown in cats and rats, respectively, to have less activity on the salivary gland muscarinic receptors than on the bladder muscarinic receptors (Nilvebrant et al, 1997; Ohtake et al, 2004). Last, the site and speed of antimuscarinic metabolism appear to have profound effects in terms of clinical efficacy and side effects.

Muscarinic receptors are also located prejunctionally on cholinergic nerve terminals in the bladder (D'Agostino et al, 1986, 1997, 2000; Somogyi and de Groat, 1992; Somogyi et al, 1996; Braverman et al, 1998). Activation of M_1 prejunctional receptors facilitates acetylcholine release (Somogyi and de Groat, 1992; Somogyi et al, 1996), whereas activation of M_2-M_4 receptors inhibits the release (D'Agostino et al, 1997; Braverman et al, 1998). It has been proposed that inhibitory M_2-M_4 receptors are preferentially activated by autofeedback mechanisms during short periods of low-frequency nerve activity and thereby suppress cholinergic transmission during urine storage (Somogyi and de Groat, 1992). Conversely, M_1 receptors are activated during more prolonged, high-frequency nerve firing that would occur during voiding and thus participate in an amplification mechanism to promote complete bladder emptying. M_1-mediated facilitation of transmitter release involves the activation of a phospholipase C–protein kinase C signaling cascade that appears to facilitate the opening of L-type Ca^{2+} channels that are necessary for prejunctional facilitation of acetylcholine release from parasympathetic nerve terminals (Somogyi et al, 1996, 1997).

Inhibitory and facilitatory muscarinic receptors are also present in the central nervous system (de Groat et al, 1993; Yoshimura and de Groat, 1997a; Ishiura et al, 2001) and in bladder parasympathetic ganglia, where they modulate nicotinic transmission (de Groat and Booth, 1993). The ability to modulate neurotransmission in the bladder through the selective activation and inhibition of specific presynaptic receptors may lead in the future to novel forms of pharmacologic therapy for specific forms of lower urinary tract dysfunction.

Muscarinic Selectivity. Pharmacologically defined subtype-selective drugs have been developed. Darifenacin and vamicamide have been demonstrated to be relatively selective for the M_3 subtype (Newgreen et al, 1995; Yamamoto et al, 1995; Andersson, 1997). However, they are not necessarily tissue selective because salivary glands and other tissues also contain M_3 muscarinic receptors. Currently, several drugs are being tested for their tissue selectivity. Tolterodine appears to be a muscarinic antagonist that has selectivity for the bladder compared with the salivary gland, even though it may not be an M_3 subtype–selective antagonist (Nilvebrant et al, 1997; Andersson, 1998). More recently, solifenacin has also shown selectivity to the bladder over the salivary gland; the receptor selectivity of solifenacin to M_3 receptors over M_2 receptors (10-fold) is similar to that of oxybutynin (Ikeda et al, 2002; Ohtake et al, 2004). Thus, therapeutically, it is more important to be tissue selective than subtype selective (Nilvebrant et al, 1997; Andersson, 1998). A truly bladder-selective antimuscarinic drug with *no* dry mouth is the "holy grail" of overactive bladder drug therapy.

Purinergic Mechanisms

Purinergic contribution to parasympathetic stimulation in vivo, or field stimulation in vitro, has been proved to exist in a variety of species including rat, rabbit, and guinea pig (Burnstock et al, 1972; Chancellor et al, 1992; Burnstock, 1996). **However, there is less evidence that purinergic neurotransmission exists in humans, at least in regard to normal responses to stimulation, but it may play a role in pathologic conditions such as unstable bladders or bladder outlet obstruction** (Palea et al, 1993; Burnstock, 2000; O'Reilly et al, 2001a).

ATP acts on two families of purinergic receptors: an ion channel family (P2X) and a G protein–coupled receptor family (P2Y) (Inoue and Brading, 1990, 1991; McMurray et al, 1997). Seven P2X subtypes and eight P2Y subtypes have been identified. Analysis of the structure-activity relationships of a series of excitatory purinergic agonists on the guinea pig bladder revealed an order of potency consistent with $P2X_1$ or $P2X_2$ receptors (Burnstock, 2001; Zhong et al, 2001). In other species (rabbit, cat, and rat), various studies suggested that multiple purinergic excitatory receptors are present in the bladder (Burnstock, 2000). Immunohistochemical experiments with specific antibodies for different P2X receptors showed that $P2X_1$ receptors are the dominant subtype in membranes of rat detrusor muscle and vascular smooth muscle in the bladder (Lee et al, 2000). Clusters of $P2X_1$ receptors were detected on rat bladder smooth muscle cells, some of which were closely related to nerve varicosities. Northern blotting and in situ hybridization revealed the presence of $P2X_1$ and $P2X_4$ mRNA in the bladder (Valera et al, 1995). **The**

predominant expression of $P2X_1$ receptors has also been confirmed in the human bladder (O'Reilly et al, 2001a, 2001b). **Investigators also found that the amount of $P2X_1$ receptors was increased in the obstructed bladder compared with the control bladder, suggesting upregulated purinergic mechanisms in the overactive bladder due to bladder outlet obstruction** (O'Reilly et al, 2001a). In addition, ATP also seems to act through P2Y receptors in the smooth muscle to suppress cholinergic and purinergic contractions (Burnstock, 2001; Lee et al, 2000).

Purinergic nerves are likely to have other functions in the lower urinary tract because excitatory receptors for ATP are present in parasympathetic ganglia (Theobald and de Groat, 1989; Nishimura and Tokimasa, 1996; Zhong et al, 1998, 2001), afferent nerve terminals (Dmitrieva et al, 1998; Namasivayam et al, 1999; Burnstock, 2001; Lee et al, 2000), and urothelial cells (Buffington et al, 1999; Vlaskovska et al, 2001). Excitatory purinergic receptors in pelvic ganglia have been demonstrated in the cat (Theobald and de Groat, 1989), rabbit (Nishimura and Tokimasa, 1996), and rat (Zhong et al, 1998, 2001).

$P2X_3$ receptors that have been identified in small-diameter afferent neurons in DRG have also been detected immunohistochemically in the wall of the bladder and ureter in a suburothelial plexus of afferent nerves (Lee et al, 2000). Studies using patch clamp recordings in rats have also demonstrated that the majority (90%) of bladder afferent neurons projecting via pelvic nerves responded to α,β-methylene ATP and ATP with persistent currents, suggesting that bladder afferent pathways in the pelvic nerve express predominantly $P2X_{2/3}$ heteromeric receptors rather than $P2X_3$ homomeric receptors (Zhong at al, 2003; Dang et al, 2005). Intravesical or intra-arterial administration of ATP or 2-methylthio-ATP activated bladder afferent fibers and enhanced reflex bladder activity (Dmitrieva et al, 1998; Namasivayam et al, 1999; Pandita and Andersson, 2002; Zhang et al, 2003; Nishiguchi et al, 2005). On the other hand, desensitization of purinergic receptors by intravesical administration of α,β-methylene ATP, a purinergic receptor agonist, or administration of a receptor antagonist, suramin, depressed bladder afferent activity (Dmitrieva et al, 1998; Namasivayam et al, 1999). **In $P2X_3$ knockout mice, afferent activity induced by bladder distention was significantly reduced** (Burnstock, 2000; Cockayne et al, 2000; Cook and McCleskey, 2000; Souslova et al, 2000). Furthermore, deletion of the gene encoding $P2X_2$ and loss of heteromeric $P2X_{2/3}$ receptors also result in a marked urinary bladder hyporeflexia, as evidenced by increased thresholds for bladder contractions during bladder filling (Cockayne et al, 2005). These data indicate that purinergic receptors are involved in mechanosensory as well as nociceptive signaling in the bladder.

ATP is also released by afferent nerves and might act in an autofeedback manner to regulate afferent excitability. Two studies (Dmitrieva et al, 1998; Morrison et al, 1998) presented evidence for purinergic sensitization of bladder afferent nerve endings. Intra-arterial injection of ATP can activate bladder afferent nerves (Dmitrieva et al, 1998), whereas suramin, an antagonist of certain types of ATP receptors (P2X purinergic receptors), given intravesically reduced by 50% the firing of bladder mechanoreceptors induced by bladder distention (Morrison et al, 1998). Intravesical administration of α,β-

methylene ATP also reduced the firing of mechanosensitive afferents, presumably by desensitizing purinergic receptors on the afferent terminals.

In addition, adenosine, which can be formed by the metabolism of ATP, can depress parasympathetic nerve-evoked bladder contractions by activating P1 inhibitory receptors in parasympathetic ganglia (Akasu et al, 1984), in postganglionic nerve terminals, and in the bladder muscle (Burnstock, 2001; Cockayne et al, 2000). Adenosine P1 receptors have been further classified into a number of subtypes (i.e., A_1, A_{2A}, A_{2B}, and A_3) (Olah and Stiles, 1995). A study has demonstrated that adenosine reduces the force of nerve-mediated contractions by acting predominantly at presynaptic sites at the nerve-muscle junction through a subtype of an adenosine receptor (the A_1 receptor in guinea pigs), although these actions of adenosine are less evident in human detrusor muscles (Fry et al, 2004).

Adrenergic Mechanisms

β-Adrenergic. Stimulation of $β_2$- and $β_3$-adrenergic receptors that exist in the human detrusor results in the direct relaxation of the detrusor smooth muscle (Andersson, 1993; Morita et al, 1993; Levin and Wein, 1995; Nishimoto et al, 1995). In addition, β-adrenergic–stimulated relaxation is mediated through the stimulation of adenylate cyclase and the accumulation of cyclic AMP (cAMP) (Levin et al, 1986; Andersson, 1993; Andersson and Arner, 2004). Because β adrenoceptor–mediated relaxation of the human detrusor was not blocked by selective $β_1$ or $β_2$ adrenoceptor antagonists such as dobutamine and procaterol but was blocked by selective $β_3$ adrenoceptor antagonists, **the relaxation induced by adrenergic stimulation of the human detrusor is mediated mainly through $β_3$ adrenoceptor activation** (Igawa et al, 1999; Yamaguchi, 2002; Andersson and Arner, 2004). A quantitative analysis by reverse transcription–polymerase chain reaction has also confirmed that the $β_3$-adrenergic receptor is the most highly expressed subtype among α and β adrenoceptor subtypes at the mRNA level in human bladders (Nomiya and Yamaguchi, 2003). Therefore, $β_3$ receptor agonists have been proposed to be effective for treatment of detrusor overactivity, although no proof of concept studies have been performed (Andersson and Arner, 2004). β-Adrenergic blockers have also been advocated for urinary incontinence due to inappropriate reflex urethral relaxation because propranolol prevents the reduction in urethral pressure after sacral root stimulation (McGuire, 1978; McGuire and Herlihy, 1978). However, β-adrenergic antagonists are not particularly useful in treating bladder or urethral disorders (Castleden and Morgan, 1980; Naglo et al, 1981; Takeda et al, 1997).

A second pharmacologic method of increasing cAMP levels is with phosphodiesterase (PDE) inhibitors. PDE is the enzyme that catalyzes the degradation of cAMP to AMP and thus limits the action of cAMP (Andersson, 1997; Longhurst et al, 1997). There are several classes of PDEs that have individual substrate affinities, specific species and tissue distributions, and pharmacologic selectivities (Truss et al, 1996; Longhurst et al, 1997). **There is considerable research currently trying to identify the specific isoform of PDE present in the bladder as opposed to that in the penis** (Truss et al, 1996). **Selective inhibition of bladder PDE would result in both an increase in the basal levels of cAMP (and possibly**

relaxation of the detrusor) and enhancement of the sensitivity and efficacy of β-adrenergic agonists. In the isolated guinea pig bladder, the frequency of agonist-induced phasic activity is slowed by cAMP, and degradation of intracellular cAMP in the cells responsible for phasic activity appears to involve primarily PDE4** (Gillespie, 2004). Thus, a selective β agonist and a selective PDE inhibitor might be an effective combination for the relaxation of the detrusor in the future.

α-Adrenergic. Although α-adrenergic stimulation is not prominent in the normal bladder, recent evidence indicates that under pathologic conditions such as detrusor overactivity associated with bladder outlet obstruction, the α-adrenergic receptor density, especially the $α_{1D}$ receptor subtype, can increase to such an extent that the norepinephrine-induced responses in the bladder are converted from relaxation to contraction (Andersson and Arner, 2004). In rats with outflow obstruction, the proportion of $α_{1D}$ receptor subtype in the total $α_1$ receptor mRNA in the bladder is increased to 70% from 25% in the normal rat bladders (Hampel et al, 2002), and urinary frequency is suppressed by an inhibition of $α_{1D}$ and $α_{1A}$ receptors by tamsulosin whereas $α_{1A}$ receptor suppression by 5-methyl-urapidil has no effects. Moreover, $α_{1D}$ receptor knockout mice have larger bladder capacity and voided volumes than do their wild-type controls, supporting an important role of $α_{1D}$ receptors in the control of bladder function (Chen et al, 2005). However, in humans, there is the predominant expression of $α_{1D}$ receptors already in the normal bladder (Malloy et al, 1998), and the level of expression of α adrenoceptor mRNA, which is considerably low compared with $β_3$ adrenoceptors in normal bladders, was not increased in the bladder with outflow obstruction (Nomiya and Yamaguchi, 2003). Thus, the contribution of $α_{1D}$ receptors to detrusor overactivity observed in a variety of pathologic conditions including obstructive uropathy and incontinence still needs to be established (Andersson and Arner, 2004).

α-Adrenergic mechanisms are more important in urethral function. Substantial pharmacologic and physiologic evidence indicates that urethral tone and intraurethral pressure are influenced by α-adrenergic receptors. Radioligand binding reveals that $α_1$ and $α_2$ adrenoceptors are present in rabbit urethra (Yamaguchi et al, 1993). In female animals, the majority of α adrenoceptors are of the $α_2$ subtype (Andersson, 1993), whereas $α_1$ receptors predominate in the male. Isolated human urethral smooth muscle also contracts in response to α-adrenergic agonists (Yalla et al, 1977; Awad et al, 1978; Nordling, 1983; Mattiasson et al, 1984). $α_1$-Adrenergic antagonists block this contraction. Likewise, **hypogastric nerve stimulation and α-adrenergic agonists produce a rise in intraurethral pressure, which is blocked by $α_1$-adrenergic antagonists** (Awad et al, 1976; Yalla et al, 1977). These findings provide the rationale for use of α-adrenergic agonists to promote urine storage by increasing urethral resistance.

Conversely, α antagonists facilitate urine release in conditions of functionally increased urethral resistance, such as benign prostatic hyperplasia. However, side effects such as dizziness that may be due to block of $α_1$ adrenoceptors in the cardiovascular system limit their use. Because the $α_{1A}$ adrenoceptor is the major subtype in the prostate and urethra and all three $α_1$ adrenoceptor subtypes ($α_{1A}$, $α_{1B}$, $α_{1D}$) are present in blood vessels, selective α_{1A} antagonists are being tested clinically in patients with benign prostatic hyperplasia to determine whether side effects can be reduced while efficacy is maintained (Steers, 2000). Although the α_{1A}-selective drugs reduce outlet resistance, there are no reports indicating that they relieve symptoms such as urinary urgency, frequency, and nocturia. A failure of selective α_{1A} antagonists to reduce symptoms may reflect the contribution of other receptor subtypes to lower urinary tract dysfunction in benign prostatic hyperplasia (Steers, 2000).

α_2-Adrenergic antagonists increase the release of norepinephrine from urethral tissues through a presynaptic mechanism, but this does not affect the contractility of urethral smooth muscle in vitro (Mattiasson et al, 1984; Willette et al, 1990). The human urethra lacks postjunctional α_2-adrenergic receptors, although in vitro prejunctional activation of these receptors produces a feedback inhibition of norepinephrine release. Pharmacologic and electrophysiologic data suggest that adrenergic nerves influence excitatory cholinergic transmission in pelvic ganglia. de Groat and Booth (1980) have shown in the cat that hypogastric nerves inhibit excitatory cholinergic transmission in vesical ganglia by activation of α_2-adrenergic receptors (Fig. 56–25). Conversely, β-adrenergic agonists facilitate transmission in vesical ganglia.

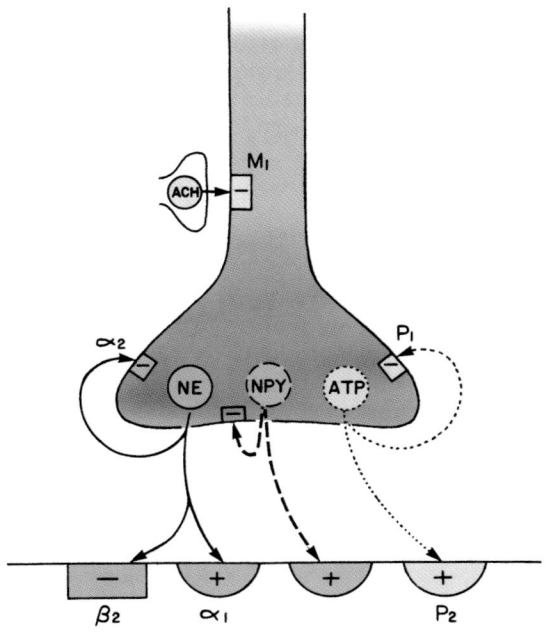

Figure 56–25. Diagram of possible transmitters in an adrenergic terminal supplying the bladder or urethra. Norepinephrine (NE) release can activate α_1-adrenergic receptors and produce contraction (+) or β receptors and cause relaxation (−) of the detrusor. Feedback inhibition of NE release through α_2 receptors can also occur. Neuropeptide Y (NPY) can produce smooth muscle contraction (+) or inhibit acetylcholine (ACH) release (not shown), or feedback can inhibit NE release. Adenosine triphosphate (ATP) can activate P2 receptors in the detrusor, which elicit contraction (+) or inhibit (−) further ATP release through P1 prejunctional receptors. ACH release from terminals in synaptic contact with an adrenergic varicosity can inhibit firing of adrenergic axons by activation of M_1 receptors.

Urethral Tone in Women. Taki and associates (1999) separated the entire length of the human female urethra into several parts and studied regional contractile effect to norepinephrine, clonidine, acetylcholine, and potassium chloride. Their findings suggest that sympathetic innervation helps maintain resting urethral tonus, mainly through α_1 adrenoceptors. With the recent identification of at least three distinct subtypes of α_1 adrenoceptors with distinct pharmacologic profiles, it may be possible to develop urethra-specific adrenergic agonists for the treatment of stress urinary incontinence. A small-scale, placebo-controlled clinical study has demonstrated that activation of the $\alpha_{1A/1L}$ adrenoceptor subtype, which is a pharmacologic isoform of the α_{1A} adrenoceptor gene product, was effective in reducing the number of incontinence episodes in women with mild to moderate stress urinary incontinence (Musselman et al, 2004), suggesting an important role of α_1 adrenoceptors in the urethral continence mechanism, although the data are still preliminary.

Nitric Oxide

Nitric oxide (NO) has been identified as a major inhibitory transmitter mediating relaxation of the urethral smooth muscle during micturition (Andersson et al, 1992; Andersson, 1993; Andersson and Persson, 1995; Bennett et al, 1995). In 1931, Barrington hypothesized that stimulation of the pelvic nerve, in addition to evoking a bladder contraction, produces urethral relaxation. Indeed, urodynamic studies document a reduction in urethral pressure just before a bladder contraction (Scott et al, 1964; van Waalwijk et al, 1991). In support of the contention that parasympathetic nerves mediate this urethral relaxation, sacral root stimulation reduces urethral pressure (McGuire and Herlihy, 1978; Torrens, 1978). Cholinergic innervation to the urethra has been supported by histochemical identification of acetylcholinesterase-staining fibers and ultrastructural data showing varicosities containing small clear vesicles in the human urethra (Ek et al, 1977; Gosling et al, 1977). Exogenous cholinergic agonists do not relax but rather contract urethral smooth muscle in vivo (Nergardh and Boreus, 1972; Yalla et al, 1977; Ek et al, 1978) and in vitro (Ek et al, 1978). Therefore, parasympathetic pathways mediating urethral relaxation must rely on a noncholinergic transmitter.

In the rat, NO is released by postganglionic nerves arising from neurons in the major pelvic ganglia (Fraser et al, 1995) (see Fig. 56–18). These neurons contain nitric oxide synthase (NOS), the enzyme that synthesizes NO, as well as nicotinamide adenine dinucleotide phosphate–diaphorase, a marker for NOS (Vizzard et al, 1994). Electrophysiologic studies in female rats showed that electrical stimulation of the lumbosacral (L6-S1) spinal roots elicits simultaneous bladder contractions and urethral relaxation (Fraser et al, 1995). The urethral relaxation was inhibited by NOS inhibitors, which did not alter the bladder responses. The inhibition was reversed by administration of L-arginine, a precursor of NO. The electrically evoked urethral relaxation was abolished by ganglionic blocking agents, indicating that it was mediated by stimulation of preganglionic parasympathetic axons in the lumbosacral roots.

NO is also involved in controlling bladder afferent nerve activity. Inhibitors of NOS, given systemically or intrathecally, do not affect normal micturition in conscious or anesthetized rats. However, detrusor overactivity that accompanies irritation with turpentine or acetic acid is ameliorated by spinal application of NOS inhibitors (Rice, 1995; Kakizaki and de Groat, 1996). However, intravesically administered capsaicin induces detrusor overactivity that is not influenced by an NOS inhibitor, although the behavioral effects of the irritation are reduced (Pandita et al, 1997). It is believed that NO is involved in mediating N-methyl-D-aspartate (NMDA) receptor–dependent effects but not those involving neurokinin 2 (NK$_2$) receptors. The inhibitory components of the somatovesical reflex elicited by electrical stimulation of the tibial nerve are also reduced by NOS inhibition (Morrison et al, 1996). One study also indicates that **intravesical application of NO can suppress detrusor overactivity due to cyclophosphamide-induced bladder irritation in rats. These effects are suggested to be mediated by suppression of bladder afferent activity** (Ozawa et al, 1999; Yoshimura et al, 2001).

Possible Gender Difference in Cholinergic and Nitrergic Innervation in the Urethra. A parasympathetic cholinergic excitatory input to the urethra (see Fig. 56–18) has been identified in male but not in female rats (Flood et al, 1995; Kakizaki et al, 1997). This was demonstrated by measuring intraurethral pressure during voiding after blockade of striated external urethral sphincter activity with a neuromuscular blocking agent. Under these conditions, urethral pressure increased during micturition in male rats. This urethral reflex was blocked by hexamethonium (a ganglionic blocking agent), markedly reduced by atropine, and increased by an NOS inhibitor. However, it was not changed by transection of sympathetic nerves or administration of an α_1-adrenergic blocking agent (prazosin). These results indicate that in male rats, parasympathetic nerve activity induces a predominant cholinergic muscarinic contraction of the urethra and a subordinate NO-mediated relaxation. These studies implicate possible gender differences in parasympathetic and especially nitrergic pathways in the human urethra.

Smooth Muscle Tone and Nitric Oxide. NO-mediated smooth muscle relaxation is due to increased production of intracellular cyclic guanosine monophosphate (cGMP). The second messengers cAMP and cGMP are synthesized from the corresponding nucleoside triphosphates by their respective membrane-bound or soluble adenylate or guanylate cyclases. cAMP and cGMP are inactivated by PDEs by hydrolytic cleavage of the 3' ribose phosphate bond. Therefore, the level of intracellular second messengers can be regulated by PDE isoenzymes (Truss et al, 1999, 2001).

Because of their central role in regulating smooth muscle tone and the considerable variation of PDE isoenzymes among species and tissues, PDEs have become an attractive target for drug development. So far, 7 PDE families, 16 genes, and 33 individual enzyme proteins have been defined. The hope is that bladder-specific PDEs can be developed.

Studies have reported that PDEs 1 to 5 exist in human detrusor smooth muscle (Truss et al, 1996). The PDE1-selective inhibitor vinpocetine has been tested in patients with detrusor overactivity who did not respond to conventional anticholinergic drugs with encouraging but preliminary results (Truss et al, 1997, 2001).

Afferent Neuropeptides

Immunocytochemical studies have revealed that bladder afferent neurons contain various neuropeptides, including substance P, neurokinin A, calcitonin gene–related peptide (CGRP), vasoactive intestinal polypeptide (VIP), pituitary adenylate cyclase–activating peptide (PACAP), and enkephalins (de Groat, 1989; de Groat et al, 1993; Yoshimura and de Groat, 1997a). **Many of these peptides, which are contained in capsaicin-sensitive, C-fiber bladder afferents, are released in the bladder by noxious stimulation and contribute to inflammatory responses by triggering plasma extravasation, vasodilation, and alterations in bladder smooth muscle activity** (Maggi, 1993; Ishizuka et al, 1994, 1995). **These agents also function as transmitters at afferent terminals in the spinal cord.**

Tachykinins. The tachykinins are a family of small peptides sharing a common C-terminal sequence Phe-Xaa-Gly-Leu-Met-NH$_2$ whose main members are substance P, neurokinin A, and neurokinin B. Tachykinins are found in both central and peripheral nervous systems. In the peripheral nerves, tachykinins are predominantly located in the terminals of nonmyelinated, sensory C fibers. The diverse biologic effects of the tachykinins are mediated through three receptors, designated NK$_1$, NK$_2$, and NK$_3$, which belong to the superfamily of seven transmembrane–spanning G protein–coupled receptors (Khawaja and Rogers, 1996). Substance P is the most potent tachykinin for the NK$_1$ receptor, whereas neurokinin A exhibits the highest affinity for the tachykinin NK$_2$ receptor and neurokinin B for the tachykinin NK$_3$ receptor (Table 56–6). All receptor subtypes have been identified in the bladder in humans and animals such as rats, mice, and dogs (Lecci and Maggi, 2001; Andersson and Arner, 2004).

Tachykinins released from capsaicin-sensitive sensory C fibers in response to irritation in the bladder can act on (1) NK$_1$ receptors in blood vessels to induce plasma extravasation and vasodilation, (2) NK$_2$ receptors to stimulate bladder contractions, and (3) NK$_2$ receptors on primary afferent terminals to increase the excitability during bladder filling or during bladder inflammation (de Groat, 1989; Andersson, 1993; Morrison et al, 1995; Lecci and Maggi, 2001). A study by Kamo and associates (2005) has also demonstrated that activation of NK$_3$ receptors on capsaicin-sensitive C-fiber afferents in the rat bladder can increase the excitability during bladder filling.

Intrathecal administration of NK$_1$ antagonists (RP 67580 and CP 96345) or systemic application of centrally acting NK$_1$ antagonists (GR 205171 and CP 99994) increased bladder capacity in normal rats and guinea pigs, respectively, without changing voiding pressure, whereas NK$_2$, NK$_3$, or peripherally acting NK$_1$ antagonists were ineffective (Lecci

Table 56–6. Tachykinins and Tachykinin Receptors	
Tachykinin	**Receptor**
Substance P	NK$_1$
Neurokinin A	NK$_2$
Neurokinin B	NK$_3$

et al, 1993; Yamamoto et al, 2003). Detrusor overactivity in rats induced by chemical cystitis, intravesical administration of capsaicin, or intravenous injection of L-dopa was also suppressed by intrathecal injection of NK_1 antagonists (Ishizuka et al, 1994, 1995; Lecci et al, 1994). Detrusor overactivity induced by capsaicin was reduced by an NK_2 antagonist (SR 48965) that did not influence normal voiding (Lecci et al, 1997). In the anesthetized guinea pigs, TAK-637, an NK_1 receptor antagonist, administered orally or intravenously, also increased the volume threshold for inducing micturition and inhibited the micturition reflex induced by capsaicin applied topically to the bladder (Doi et al, 1999). These results indicate that **sensory input to the spinal cord from non-nociceptive bladder afferents is mediated by tachykinins acting on NK_1 receptors, whereas input from nociceptive afferents in the bladder can be mediated by NK_1, NK_2, and NK_3 receptors.** In addition, tachykinin NK_3 receptor activation in the spinal cord can inhibit the micturition reflex through an activation of the spinal opioid mechanism (Kamo et al, 2005).

Autofeedback mechanisms may also be important at afferent nerve terminals (see Fig. 56–14). As mentioned earlier, some stimuli are known to release neuropeptides from afferent nerves, and these neuropeptides may in turn sensitize the afferents. NK_2 agonists were found (Wen and Morrison, 1996) to sensitize bladder mechanoreceptors by acting on NK_2 autoreceptors in the sensory endings in the bladder mucosa to produce the combination of effects found previously for other sensitizing agents (Morrison, 1998). The NK_2 receptor blocker SR 48968 decreases the sensitivity of bladder mechanoreceptors and also blocks the sensitization produced by NK_2 agonists and high urinary potassium levels. This suggests that the sensitization produced by intravesical chemical stimuli may be due to a mechanism using the NK_2 receptor. On the basis of these findings, it could be hypothesized that high urinary potassium concentration or higher levels of bladder distention release neurokinin A, from sensory endings, and that the sensitization is due to the action of the peptide on local NK_2 autoreceptors on the sensory endings. More recently, it has been shown that sensory neurons obtained from rat DRG can be excited by NK_2 agonists and inhibited by NK_3 agonists through modulation of Ca^{2+} channel activity mediated by protein kinase C activation (Sculptoreanu and de Groat, 2003).

Other Neuropeptides. Other afferent neuropeptides have effects on the peripheral organs or the central reflex pathways controlling the lower urinary tract. However, the effects can vary in different species and at different sites in the lower urinary tract. CGRP applied exogenously or released from primary afferents relaxes smooth muscle and produces vasodilation. The effect of CGRP on bladder is prominent in the guinea pig and dog but is absent in the rat and human bladder (Andersson, 1993). VIP, which is contained in C-fiber afferents as well as in postganglionic neurons (de Groat and Booth, 1993), inhibits spontaneous contractile activity in isolated bladder muscle from several species, including humans. However, VIP usually has little effect on bladder contractions induced by muscarinic receptor agonists or nerve stimulation (Andersson, 1993). In vivo studies in the cat revealed that VIP facilitates muscarinic but not nicotinic transmission in

bladder parasympathetic ganglia and also depresses neurally evoked contractions of the bladder (de Groat and Booth, 1993).

In the spinal cord, VIP-containing afferent pathways have been implicated in the recovery of bladder reflexes after spinal injury. In cats with chronic spinal injury, VIP immunoreactivity, which is a marker for C-fiber afferent terminals, is distributed over a wider area of the lateral dorsal horn, suggestive of afferent axonal sprouting after spinal injury (Yoshimura and de Groat 1997a; Doi et al, 1999). In addition, the effects of intrathecal administration of VIP are changed. In normal cats, VIP inhibits the micturition reflex; whereas in paraplegic cats, VIP facilitates the micturition reflex. These findings suggest that the action of a putative C-fiber afferent transmitter may underlie the emergence of C-fiber bladder reflexes in the paraplegic cat. In the normal rat, VIP and PACAP, another member of the secretin-glucagon-VIP peptide family, also facilitate the micturition reflex by actions on the spinal cord (Ishizuka et al, 1995). Patch clamp studies in the neonatal rat spinal slice preparation revealed that PACAP has a direct excitatory action on parasympathetic preganglionic neurons due in part to blockade of K^+ channels (Miura et al, 2001). In addition, PACAP has an indirect action by activating excitatory interneurons.

Prostanoids, Endothelins, and Hormones

Prostanoids. Prostanoids (prostaglandins and thromboxanes), which comprise a family of oxygenated metabolites of arachidonic acid via the enzymatic activity of cyclooxygenases 1 and 2, are manufactured throughout the lower urinary tract and have been implicated in bladder contractility, inflammatory responses, and neurotransmission. Biopsy specimens of human bladder mucosa contain prostaglandin (PG) I_2, PGE_2, $PGE_{2\alpha}$, and thromboxane A. In decreasing order of potency, $PGF_{2\alpha}$, PGE, and PGE_2 contract human detrusor (Andersson, 1993; Andersson and Arner, 2004). The actions of prostanoids are mediated by specific receptors on cell membranes. The receptors include the DP, EP, FP, IP, and TP receptors that preferentially respond to PGD_2, PGE_2, $PGF_{2\alpha}$, PGI_2, and thromboxane A_2, respectively. Furthermore, EP is subdivided into four subtypes: EP_1, EP_2, EP_3, and EP_4 (Breyer et al, 2001, 2003). The slow onset of action for these substances suggests a modulatory role for prostaglandins. Some prostaglandins may affect neural release of transmitters, whereas others inhibit acetylcholinesterase activity. These actions provide mechanisms whereby prostaglandins could potentially augment the amplitude of cholinergic-induced detrusor contractions (Borda et al, 1982).

Attempts to use prostaglandins to facilitate voiding have had mixed results. Intravesical PGE_2 has been shown to enhance bladder emptying in women with urinary retention and patients with neurogenic voiding dysfunction (Bultitude et al, 1976; Vadyanaathan et al, 1981; Tammela et al, 1987). Others have failed to find PGE_2 useful to facilitate complete evacuation of the bladder (Delaere et al, 1981; Wagner et al, 1985). Intravesical PGE_2 does produce urgency and involuntary bladder contractions (Schussler, 1990). Consistent with this finding, inhibition of prostaglandin synthesis with indomethacin reduces detrusor overactivity (Cardozo and Stanton, 1980).

Endothelins. Endothelins (ETs), a family of 21–amino acid peptides originally isolated from bovine aortic endothelial cells, include ET-1, ET-2, and ET-3, which are encoded by separate genes and mediate a variety of biologic actions through two distinct G protein–coupled receptor subtypes, the endothelin-A (ETA) and the endothelin-B (ETB) receptor (Yanagisawa et al, 1988; Masaki 2004). The ETA receptor subtype has a higher affinity for ET-1 and ET-2 than for ET-3; the ETB receptor subtype binds all ETs with equal affinity (Rubanyi et al, 1994). ET-1, which is known to be primarily produced by human endothelial cells, can induce prolonged contractile responses in isolated urinary bladder muscle strips in various species (Maggi et al, 1990b; Khan et al, 1999). In humans and rabbits, ET-like immunoreactivity is identified in almost all cell types in the bladder, including bladder epithelium, vascular endothelium, detrusor and vascular smooth muscles, and fibroblasts; it plays a role in control of bladder smooth muscle tone, regulation of local blood flow, and bladder wall remodeling in pathologic conditions (Saenz de Tejada et al, 1992). In a rabbit model of bladder outlet obstruction, ET-1 and ETA receptor binding sites in detrusor smooth muscle and urothelium as well as ETB receptor binding sites in detrusor smooth muscle were significantly increased (Khan et al, 1999). In addition, the endothelin-converting enzyme WO-03028719, which suppresses ET-1 production, can improve voiding efficiency and suppress detrusor overactivity in a rat model of bladder outlet obstruction (Schröder et al, 2004). These results suggest that **the increase in ET-1 expression and ET receptors could be involved in detrusor hyperplasia and overactivity seen in patients with bladder outlet obstruction resulting from benign prostatic hyperplasia.**

There is also evidence that ETs have a role in nociceptive mechanisms in the peripheral and central nervous system. The activation of ETA receptors in capsaicin-sensitive C-fiber afferents in the bladder can induce detrusor overactivity, whereas ETA receptor activation in the spinal cord can inhibit the micturition reflex through activation of a spinal opioid mechanism in rats, suggesting that modulation of ETA receptor activity in the bladder or the spinal cord could be effective in treating bladder overactivity or painful conditions (Ogawa et al, 2004).

Parathyroid Hormone–Related Peptide. Some locally released substances cause detrusor relaxation. Parathyroid hormone–related peptide is manufactured by bladder smooth muscle. Stretch in vivo (Yamamoto et al, 1992) and in vitro (Steers et al, 1998) increases parathyroid hormone–related peptide. Slow or gradual distention could release local relaxants, thereby maintaining low filling pressures.

Sex Steroids. Differences in responses of human and animal bladders to the effect of drugs suggest that sex steroids play a role in detrusor contractility. It is not unusual for women to note changes in voiding, bladder pain, or continence at different times of their menstrual cycle. **Sex steroids do not directly affect bladder contractility, but they modulate receptors and influence growth of bladder tissues.** Estrogen receptors are expressed by the trigone in women (Iosif et al, 1981). Levin and associates (1980) noted that bladder body muscle from young female rabbits treated with estrogens exhibits increased responsiveness to α-adrenergic, cholinergic,

and purinergic agonists. Others have seen a decreased density of adrenergic and muscarinic receptors in the bladder after estrogen administration (Shapiro, 1986; Batra and Andersson, 1989). In contrast to the study by Levin and coworkers (1980), Elliot and associates (1992) showed that bladder smooth muscle from estrogen-treated rats exhibited decreased contractions.

Estrogens also increase adrenergic receptors in the urethra (Callahan and Creed, 1985). Ekstrom and associates (1993) reported that estrogen administration to ovariectomized rabbits unmasked contractile responses to α-adrenergic agonists, whereas contracted and normal rabbit bladders demonstrated no response to these agents. Some clinicians have combined these agents to elevate urethral pressure in patients with stress incontinence (Wilson et al, 1987). However, the clinical efficacy of the combined use of estrogen with α agonists has been questioned (Walter et al, 1978). **The effect of estrogens on urinary continence in females probably reflects the multiple actions of this hormone on adrenergic receptors, vasculature, and urethral morphology. In addition, progesterone increases electrical and cholinergic contractions of the bladder.** Exogenous estrogens and progesterones also induce NOS activity in bladders of female guinea pigs (Ehren et al, 1995). This effect is postulated to contribute to relief of detrusor overactivity with hormonal treatment. However, the use of estrogens alone to treat either stress urinary incontinence or urgency incontinence has given disappointing results (Abrams et al, 2005), and studies have suggested that estrogen is associated with an increase in urinary incontinence in postmenopausal women (Hendrix et al, 2005).

Androgen treatment in the male rat has been reported to have similar effects on synaptic connections as well as effects on motoneuronal somatic and dendritic size in the androgen-sensitive motoneurons innervating the bulbocavernosus and levator ani muscles of the rat (Jordan, 1997; Matsumoto, 1997). Testosterone treatment can also influence the size of postganglionic neurons in the major pelvic ganglion of the male rat (Keast and Saunders, 1998). Thus, further studies are needed to evaluate the influence of changes in hormonal environment on the neural pathways controlling the lower urinary tract.

"Transducer" Function of the Urothelium

Whereas the urothelium has historically been viewed primarily as a "barrier," **there is increasing evidence that urothelial cells display a number of properties similar to sensory neurons (nociceptors and mechanoreceptors) and that both types of cells use diverse signal-transduction mechanisms to detect physiologic stimuli.** Examples of "sensor molecules" (i.e., receptors and ion channels) associated with neurons that have been identified in urothelium include receptors for bradykinin (Chopra et al, 2005), neurotrophins (TrkA and p75) (Murray et al, 2004), purines (P2X and P2Y) (Lee et al, 2000; Burnstock, 2001; Hu et al, 2002; Birder et al, 2004; Tempest et al, 2004), norepinephrine (α and β) (Birder et al, 1998, 2002a), acetylcholine (muscarinic) (Chess-Williams, 2002), protease-activated receptors (D'Andrea et al, 2003; Dattilio and Vizzard, 2005), amiloride and mechanosensitive Na$^+$ channels (Smith et al, 1998; Wang et al, 2003; Araki et al, 2004), and a number of TRP channels (TRPV1, TRPV2, TRPM8) (Birder et al, 2001, 2002b; Stein et al, 2004).

When urothelial cells are activated through these receptors and ion channels in response to mechanical as well as chemical stimuli, they can in turn release chemical mediators such as NO, ATP, acetylcholine, and substance P (Ferguson et al, 1997; Birder et al, 1998, 2003; Burnstock, 2001; Chess-Williams, 2004). These agents are known to have excitatory and inhibitory actions on afferent nerves that are close to or in the urothelium (Bean et al, 1990; Yoshimura and de Groat, 1997a; Dmitrieva et al, 1998; Birder et al, 2001). Thus, it has been speculated that **the urothelium may play a role in bladder sensation by responding to local chemical and mechanical stimuli and then sending chemical signals to the bladder afferent nerves, which then convey information to the central nervous system** (Ferguson et al, 1997).

NO can be released by the urothelium, particularly during inflammation (Birder et al, 1998). The release of NO may be evoked by the calcium ionophore A-23187, norepinephrine, and capsaicin. Substance P also acts on receptors on urothelial cells to release NO. The adrenergic release of NO from bladder strips was reduced by 85% after removal of the urothelium. Denervation of the bladder did not completely block the release of capsaicin-induced NO production, suggesting other sites of production. This is consistent with the observations that capsaicin released NO from cultured rat, cat, rabbit, and human urothelial cells and that the capsaicin receptor (VR1 or TRPV1) is expressed in cultured urothelial cells. NOS expression in afferent neurons is also increased in chronic bladder inflammation. Given that NO does not have much effect on the detrusor muscle but does inhibit Ca^{2+} channels in bladder afferent neurons, the role of NO in the urothelium has still to be clarified. Thus, **NO is likely to be involved in inflammatory and pain pathways and also to be part of the sensory signaling mechanisms involving the urothelium in the bladder.**

ATP released from urothelial cells during stretch can activate a population of suburothelial bladder afferents expressing $P2X_3$ receptors, signaling changes in bladder fullness and pain (Burnstock, 2001; Ferguson et al, 1997). Accordingly, **$P2X_3$ null mice exhibit a urinary bladder hyporeflexia, suggesting that this receptor as well as neural-epithelial interactions are essential for normal bladder function** (Cockayne et al, 2000). This type of regulation may be similar to epithelium-dependent secretion of mediators in airway epithelial cells, which are thought to modulate submucosal nerves and bronchial smooth muscle tone and may play an important role in inflammation (Homolya et al, 2000; Jallat-Daloz et al, 2001). Thus, it is possible that activation of bladder nerves and urothelial cells can modulate bladder function directly or indirectly by the release of chemical factors in the urothelial layer. ATP released from the urothelium or surrounding tissues may also play a role in the regulation of membrane trafficking. This is supported by studies in the urinary bladder in which urothelium-derived ATP release purportedly acts as a trigger for exocytosis—in part by autocrine activation of urothelial purinergic (P2X, P2Y) receptors (Wang et al, 2005). These findings suggest a mechanism whereby urothelial cells sense or respond to ATP and thereby translate extracellular stimuli into functional processes.

Prostaglandins are also released from the urothelium. These are assigned two possible functions: regulation of detrusor muscle activity and cytoprotection of the urothelium,

based on effective treatment of hemorrhagic cystitis by prostaglandins (Jeremy et al, 1987). The predominant forms found in human urothelium from biopsy specimens are 6-oxo-$PGF_{2\alpha}$ > PFE_2 > $PGF_{2\alpha}$ > thromboxane B_2. PGI_2 (prostacyclin) is also produced. These findings were confirmed and further developed in the guinea pig, in which it was found that the major production of prostaglandins occurred in the urothelium. The production of prostaglandins also increased greatly with inflammation (Saban et al, 1994). Prostaglandin synthesis also occurs in the ureter, where it is speculated to be important in the regulation of ureteral peristalsis and also in reducing the development of blood clots in the lumen of the ureter (Ali et al, 1998).

Evidence also suggests that the involvement of the muscarinic receptor in bladder function extends beyond detrusor contractility and into afferent sensory functioning. Muscarinic receptors are found on the urothelium at high density (Hawthorn et al, 2000), and there is a basal release of acetylcholine from the urothelium that is increased by stretch and aging (Yoshida et al, 2006). Thus, activation of the muscarinic receptors in the urothelium releases substances that modulate afferent nerves and smooth muscle activity (Hawthorn et al, 2000; de Groat, 2004).

The urothelium also releases substances called urothelium-derived inhibitory factors that decrease the force of detrusor muscle contraction in response to muscarinic stimulation (Hawthorn et al, 2000; Kumar et al, 2005). The molecular identity of this factor is not known; however, pharmacologic studies suggest that it is not NO, a prostaglandin, prostacyclin, adenosine, catecholamine, GABA, or one that acts through apamine-sensitive, small-conductance K^+ channels. It has been shown that an inhibitory response through this factor is attenuated in a fetal model of bladder outlet obstruction (Thiruchelvam et al, 2003). Further studies are required to clarify the identity of this substance and its role in bladder function.

Serotonin

Serotonin (5-HT) has been found in neuroendocrine cells along the urethra and in the prostate (Hanyu et al, 1987). In animals, $5\text{-}HT_2$ and possibly $5\text{-}HT_3$ agonists contract the urethra. If inflammatory conditions promote release of serotonin from paraurethral cells, irritative symptoms such as the urethral syndrome may arise because of serotonergic mechanisms. The $5\text{-}HT_2$ antagonist ketanserin has been shown to reduce urethral pressure in humans (Horby-Petersen et al, 1985). However, the reduction in urethral pressure after ketanserin administration can also be the result of blockade of α-adrenergic receptors (Thor and Katofiasc, 1995).

5-HT also has several pharmacologic effects on mammalian urinary bladders, both in vitro and in vivo. Human and pig isolated detrusor muscles are known to contract in a concentration-dependent manner in response to 5-HT (Klarskov and Horby-Petersen, 1986). In human isolated urinary bladder, there was potentiation of the contractions induced by electrical field stimulation, mediated by the $5\text{-}HT_4$ receptor subtype (Candura et al, 1996; Darblade et al, 2005). A similar response is present on guinea pig detrusor muscle through $5\text{-}HT_{2A}$ and $5\text{-}HT_4$ receptors, whereas in the rabbit and the rat, the receptors involved are the $5\text{-}HT_3$ and $5\text{-}HT_7$ subtypes, respectively (Palea et al, 2004).

Capsaicin, Resiniferatoxin, Vanilloid Receptor, and C-Fiber Pharmacotherapy

Capsaicin and its ultrapotent analog resiniferatoxin (RTX) are vanilloids that stimulate and desensitize a specific population of sensory nerves (unmyelinated C fibers) to produce pain and release neuropeptides. Because of the unique property to desensitize the C fibers, the vanilloids are undergoing intensive studies for treatment of pain not only in the bladder but also in other systems (Cheng et al, 1995; Chancellor and de Groat, 1999).

The normal sensations of bladder filling appear to be mediated by small myelinated Aδ fibers. In the cat, Aδ fibers have pressure thresholds in the range of those at which humans report the first sensation of bladder filling (Janig and Morrison, 1986). However, C-fiber afferents, which are small and unmyelinated, have high mechanical thresholds and do not respond to even high levels of intravesical pressure in the cat (Häbler et al, 1990). However, they are activated by noxious chemical irritation (Häbler et al, 1990) or by cold (Fall et al, 1990). Furthermore, in the irritated state, these fibers become responsive to low-pressure bladder distention like mechanoreceptive Aδ fibers. C fibers, therefore, are normally "silent" and appear to have a specific function, that is, signaling of inflammatory or noxious events in the bladder (Chancellor and de Groat, 1999) (Figs. 56–26 and 56–27).

The vanilloids capsaicin and RTX activate nociceptive sensory nerve fibers through an ion channel known as TRPV1 receptor subtype 1 or VR1 (Caterina et al, 1997), **which belongs to the superfamily of TRP (transient receptor potential) channels that can be subdivided into six subfamilies: TRPC, TRPM, TRPV, TRPA, TRPP, and TRPML** (Krause et al, 2005). The TRPV1 receptor is a nonselective cation channel and is activated by increases in temperature to within the noxious range and by protons, suggesting that it functions as a transducer of painful thermal stimuli and acidity in vivo. When it is activated, the channel opens, allowing an influx of calcium and sodium ions that depolarizes the nociceptive afferent terminals, initiating a nerve impulse that travels through afferent nerves into the central nervous system. Noxious temperature uses the same elements, which explains why the mouth feels hot when eating chili peppers

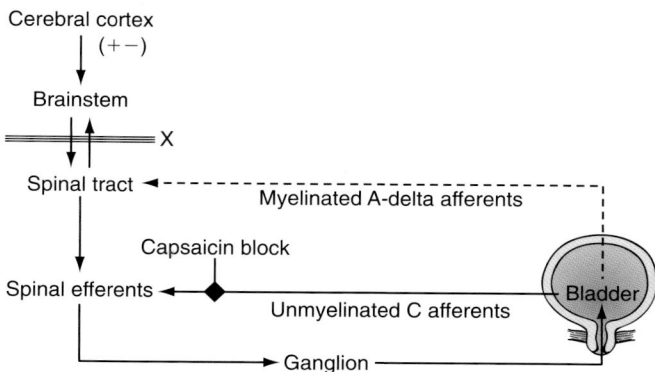

Figure 56–27. Illustration depicting the switch in afferent contribution to the micturition reflex from Aδ-fiber predominant to C-fiber predominant with neurologic diseases, aging, and possibly inflammatory disease. Note that capsaicin (and other vanilloids) can block the C-fiber contribution under these conditions.

(Clapham, 1997). Previously called the capsaicin receptor or VR1, TRPV1 has been localized in the spinal cord, DRG, and visceral organs, including the bladder, urethra, and colon. **Activation of TRPV1 results in spikelike currents** (Liu and Simon, 1996) **and selectively excites and subsequently desensitizes C fibers. Capsaicin desensitization is defined as long-lasting, reversible suppression of sensory neuron activity** (Craft et al, 1995). How fast and for how long the desensitization develops is related to the dose and time of exposure to capsaicin and to the interval between consecutive dosing (Szolcsányi et al, 1975; Maggi et al, 1988). The transient increase in intracellular concentration of calcium also leads to activation of intracellular enzymes, peptide transmitter release, and neuronal degeneration (Kawatani et al, 1989; Szallasi and Blumberg, 1990a).

RTX is the principal active ingredient in the drug euphorbium that is derived from the air-dried latex (resin) of the cactus-like plant *Euphorbia resinifera*. *E. resinifera* belongs to the Euphorbiaceae, commonly known as the spurge family, one of the most important families of medicinal plants. In 1975, the principal active ingredient in euphorbium was isolated and named resiniferatoxin (Hergenhahn et al, 1975). In 1989, **RTX was recognized as an ultrapotent analog of capsaicin; however, it has unique pharmacologic effects as well** (Szallasi and Blumberg, 1990a), **such as desensitization without prior excitation of the pulmonary chemoreflex pathway** (Szolcsányi, 1990). In 1990, specific binding of [³H]RTX provided the first direct proof for the existence of a vanilloid TRPV1 receptor shared with capsaicin (Szallasi and Blumberg, 1990b).

Pharmacologic Actions of Vanilloids at the Receptor Level

The TRPV1 receptor is a nonselective cation channel with a limited selectivity for calcium (Caterina et al, 1997). As a general rule, capsaicin and RTX induce slowly activating but persistent currents in DRG neurons, as measured under patch clamp conditions (Liu and Simon, 1994, 1996; Oh et al, 1996; Caterina et al, 1997; Szallasi et al, 1999a). RTX evokes a variety of currents in primary sensory neurons that differ in both peak value and duration from those of capsaicin (Liu and

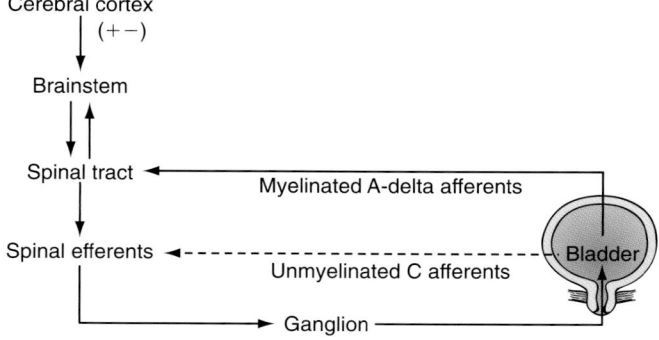

Figure 56–26. Illustration depicting the predominant Aδ afferent contribution to the normal micturition reflex.

Simon, 1996). This finding implies TRPV1 receptor heterogeneity. The available evidence suggests that TRP channels have a four-subunit combination, in either a homotetrameric or heterotetrameric complex, to form functional ion permeation complexes (Krause et al, 2005). It is not unlikely that regulatory proteins are associated with this receptor oligomer (Szallasi and Blumberg, 1999).

Excitation and Desensitization Effects of Vanilloid

Excitation; Release of Sensory Neuropeptides and Other Neurotransmitters. Capsaicin and RTX induce ^{45}Ca uptake in a subpopulation of dissociated cultured neurons from rat DRGs (Winter et al, 1990). Secondary to this calcium uptake, capsaicin and RTX evoke release of neuropeptides and other transmitters stored in vanilloid-sensitive nerves expressing TRPV1 receptors in a dose-dependent fashion.

Desensitization. The main difference between capsaicin and RTX is that desensitization predominates over excitation in response to RTX administration (Szallasi et al, 1999a; Szallasi and Blumberg 1999). It was believed that the divergence between the stimulatory and the desensitizing potencies of RTX reflects the existence of two distinct vanilloid receptors (referred to as C type and R type), responsible for excitation and desensitization, respectively (Szallasi and Blumberg, 1996; Bíró et al, 1998). This model was, however, discredited by the findings that RTX binding to the cloned rat vanilloid receptor TRPV1 and the subsequent calcium uptake mimic the C- and R-type responses described in DRG neurons (Szallasi et al, 1999a).

The divergence between excitation and desensitization by RTX predominantly lies in the kinetics of receptor gating. RTX opens the conductance after an initial delay, but then it provokes persistent currents. The slowly elevating intracellular calcium levels are not sufficient to cause action potential formation; nevertheless, they may activate various calcium-dependent mechanisms (e.g., calcineurin), leading to receptor desensitization. Furthermore, RTX may inhibit tetrodotoxin-insensitive Na$^+$ channels involved in action potential generation. This effect of RTX is probably mediated by TRPV1 receptors because it is prevented by co-application of the competitive TRPV1 receptor antagonist capsazepine (Kohane et al, 1999).

Mechanisms of Vanilloid-Induced Analgesia

Typically, vanilloids have a biphasic effect on thermal nociception. The early effect is believed to reflect conduction block (Holzer, 1991), presumably due to the inhibition of tetrodotoxin-insensitive Na$^+$ channels (Kohane et al, 1999). RTX treatment changes the phenotype of sensory neurons: the expression of a number of peptides and receptors is upregulated, whereas other neurotransmitters are, by contrast, downregulated (Szallasi and Blumberg, 1996). The former group includes galanin, VIP, and the enzyme NOS (Farkas-Szallasi et al, 1995); representatives of the latter group are substance P (Szallasi et al, 1999b) and CGRP (Szolcsányi, 1990).

Substance P has long been believed to play a central role in pain transmission. Depletion of substance P in capsaicin- and RTX-treated rats is important. The change in substance P expression is reversible and is due to a decrease in the steady-

state levels of mRNAs encoding substance P (Szallasi et al, 1999b). Capsaicin and RTX downregulate the expression of their own receptors (Goso et al, 1993; Farkas-Szallasi et al, 1995). Because TRPV1 represents a shared target for vanilloids, protons, and noxious heat (Caterina et al, 1997; Tominaga et al, 1998), the downregulation of TRPV1 expression might play a central role in the lasting vanilloid-induced analgesia in the hotplate test (Xu et al, 1997; Ossipov et al, 1999).

Botulinum Toxin

In recent years, there has been increasing evidence for the therapeutic efficacy of botulinum neurotoxin (BTX) for the treatment of various urethral and bladder dysfunctions (Smith and Chancellor, 2004).

Botulinum toxins act by inhibiting acetylcholine release at the presynaptic cholinergic nerve terminal, thereby inhibiting striated and smooth muscle contractions. The toxins are synthesized as single-chain polypeptides with a molecular weight of about 150 kD (DasGupta, 1994). Initially, the parent chain is cleaved into its active dichain polypeptide form, consisting of a heavy chain (approximately 100 kD) connected by a disulfide bond to a light chain (approximately 50 kD) with an associated zinc atom (Schiavo et al, 1992). Four steps are required for toxin-induced paralysis: binding of the toxin heavy chain to an as yet unidentified nerve terminal receptor, internalization of the toxin within the nerve terminal, translocation of the light chain into the cytosol, and inhibition of neurotransmitter release. Neurotransmitter release involves the ATP-dependent transport of the vesicle from the cytosol to the plasma membrane (Barinaga, 1993). Vesicle docking requires the interaction of various cytoplasm, vesicle, and target membrane proteins (i.e., synaptosome-associated membrane receptor [SNARE] proteins), some of which are specifically targeted with clostridial neurotoxins (Fig. 56–28). For example, BTX-A cleaves the cytosolic translocation protein SNAP-25, thus preventing vesicle fusion with the plasma membrane (Fig. 56–29) (Schiavo et al, 1993).

Seven immunologically distinct neurotoxins are designated types A, B, C, D, E, F, and G. Clinically, the urologic community has used commercial preparations of BTX-A to treat patients with spinal cord injury suffering from detrusor–external sphincter dyssynergia and detrusor overactivity (Dykstra et al, 1988; Dykstra and Sidi; 1990; Schurch et al, 1996, 2000; Petit et al, 1998). In addition, in basic research, botulinum toxins are shown to suppress not only efferent nerve activity by inhibition of the release of acetylcholine but also afferent nerve activity by release inhibition of neurotransmitters such as substance P and CGRP from sensory terminals (Chuang et al, 2004; Dressler and Adib Saberi 2005). There is also evidence that the toxin can reduce the release of ATP from urothelial cells in spinalized rats (Khera et al, 2004; Smith et al, 2005b). Thus, the use of the toxins has been expanded to treat women with pelvic floor spasticity as well as patients with non-neurogenic overactive bladder and even interstitial cystitis (Smith and Chancellor, 2004; Smith et al, 2003, 2004, 2005). The efficacy of botulinum toxins is also recently identified in patients with benign prostatic hyperplasia in whom BTX-A injection into the prostate induced an atrophy of the prostate by inducing apoptosis, inhibiting

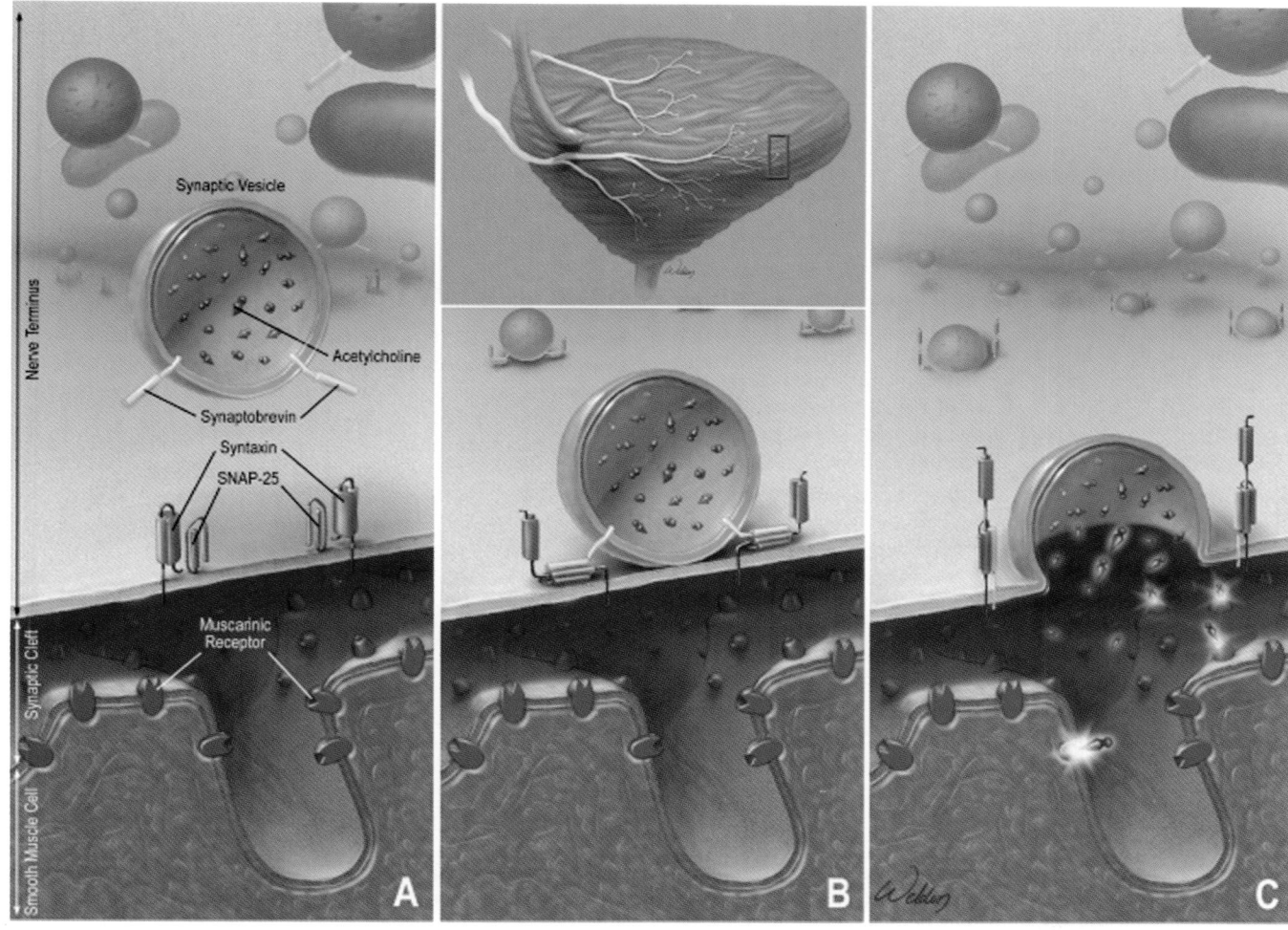

Figure 56–28. Schematic diagram demonstrating normal fusion and release of acetylcholine from nerve terminals through interaction of vesicle and membrane-bound (SNARE) proteins. Parasympathetic nerves innervate the urinary bladder *(inset)* with (**A**) nerve terminal in an unactivated state displaying numerous vesicles containing the neurotransmitter acetylcholine; (**B**) after nerve activation, assembly of the SNARE protein complex (e.g., synaptobrevin, SNAP-25, and syntaxin) leads to (**C**) release of acetylcholine and activation of postjunctional muscarinic receptors, resulting in bladder contraction.

proliferation, and downregulating α_{1A}-adrenergic receptors (Chuang et al, 2006).

Actions of Drugs on Bladder Smooth Muscle

Two major classes of pharmacologic agents that are used clinically to inhibit spontaneous activity of the bladder are calcium channel blockers, such as diltiazem and verapamil, and potassium channel openers, such as cromakalim and pinacidil (see Table 56–5) (Andersson, 1993, 1997; Andersson et al, 1999). Also, the direct effect of tricyclic antidepressants on the bladder is briefly discussed.

Calcium Channel Blockers

In the bladder smooth muscle, both spontaneous and evoked contractile activities are mediated by membrane depolarization and the movement of calcium into the smooth muscle cell through L-type Ca^{2+} channels (Brading,

1997; Fry and Wu, 1997). In addition, Ca^{2+} channels and nonselective stretch-activated divalent ion channels have been demonstrated in detrusor smooth muscle (Brading, 1997; Fry and Wu, 1997; Martin et al, 1997). The one thing in common is that all contractile activity involves the entrance of extracellular calcium. Some forms of contractile responses are mediated by both the entrance of extracellular calcium and the release of intracellular calcium from the sarcoplasmic reticulum (Levin and Wein, 1995; Zderic et al, 1996; Brading, 1997; Fry and Wu, 1997; Martin et al, 1997).

The relationship between various forms of contractile response and calcium translocation and release has been the subject of a large number of studies. Inhibition of the entrance of calcium can inhibit spontaneous and evoked contractile activity (Levin et al, 1991). L-type Ca^{2+} blocking agents, such as nifedipine, can reduce the level and severity of spontaneous myogenic contractile activity, which depends primarily on the entrance of extracellular calcium through L-type Ca^{2+} channels. Ca^{2+} channel blockers are less effective in suppressing nerve-mediated contractions, which are dependent on both

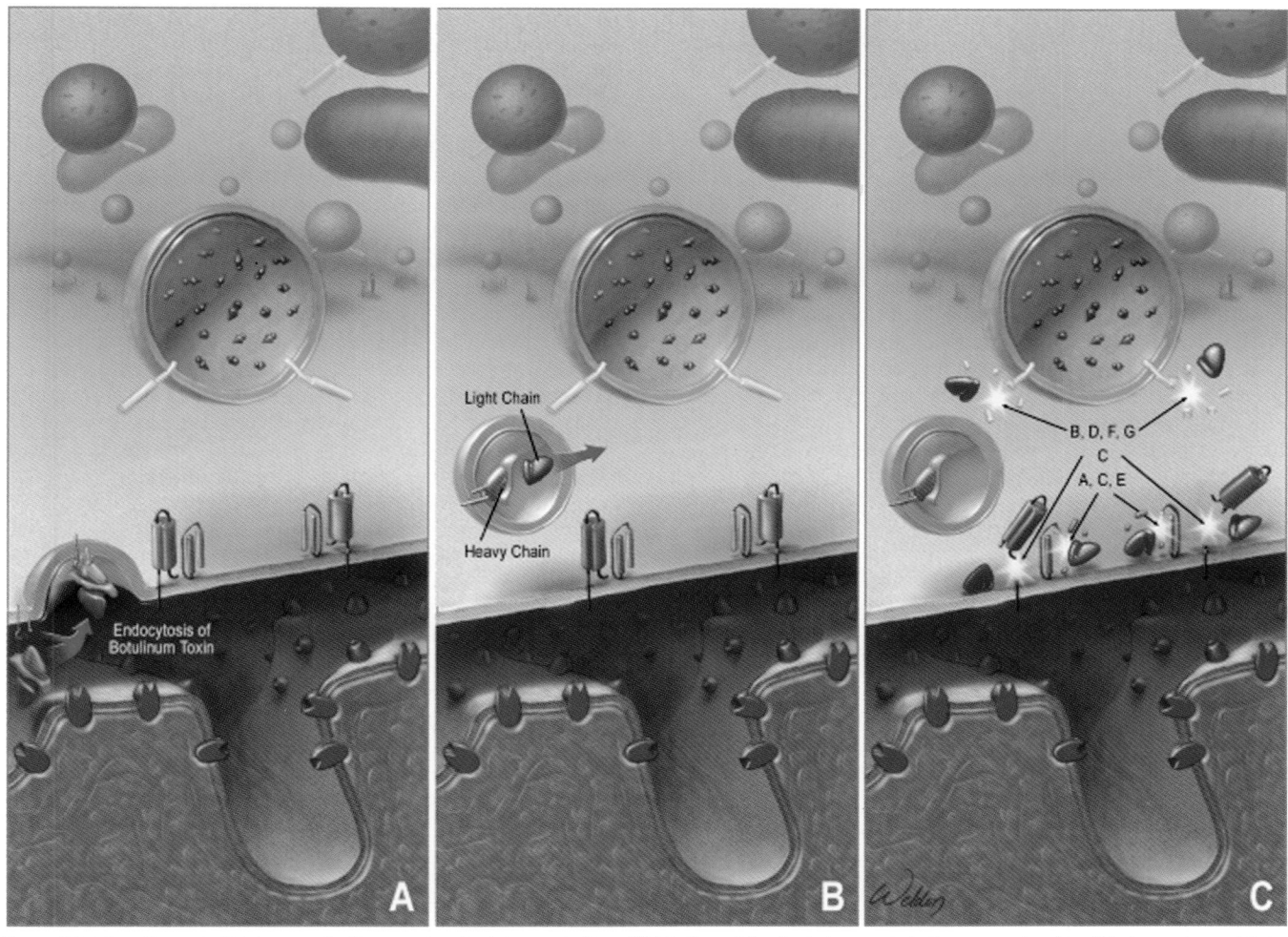

Figure 56–29. Diagram of parasympathetic nerve terminal demonstrating (**A**) binding of the toxin heavy chain to an as yet unidentified receptor and internalization of the toxin within the nerve terminal; (**B**) translocation of the light chain into the cytosol; and (**C**) inhibition of neurotransmitter release by cleavage of specific SNARE proteins. A to G represent different botulinum toxin serotypes.

the entrance of extracellular calcium and the stimulated release of intracellular calcium from the sarcoplasmic reticulum through IP_3-mediated mechanisms (Levin and Wein, 1995; Zderic et al, 1996; Brading, 1997; Andersson and Arner, 2004). This leads to the possibility of developing selective Ca^{2+} channel blocking agents that eliminate spontaneous contractions without affecting micturition contractions.

Potassium Channel Openers

K^+ channel openers such as cromakalim and pinacidil (see Table 56–5) stimulate the movement of potassium out of the cell, resulting in membrane hyperpolarization and a reduction in spontaneous contractile activity (Andersson, 1993, 1997; Andersson et al, 1999). In the detrusor, three types of K^+ channels have been identified: ATP-sensitive (K_{ATP}), calcium-dependent small conductance (SKCa), and calcium-dependent large conductance (BKCa) channels (Andersson, 1992; Trivedi et al, 1995; Andersson and Arner, 2004). It is currently still under investigation what the relationship is between each of these K^+ channels and the different forms of contractile activity (myogenic contractions, neurogenic con-

tractions, and micturition contractions). However, it is apparent that pharmacologic manipulation of both Ca^{2+} and K^+ channels can result in reduced spontaneous contractile activity (Levin et al, 1991; Andersson, 1992; Trivedi et al, 1995; Brading, 1997; Fry and Wu, 1997; Martin et al, 1997; Andersson and Arner, 2004). It has been documented that **intravesical instillation of the bladder-selective K_{ATP} channel opener ZD6169 significantly reduced detrusor overactivity in bladder outlet–obstructed rats. The mechanism of actions may be both direct smooth muscle action and action on the afferent nerve endings near the urothelium** (Hu and Kim, 1997; de Groat, 1999). Moreover, mice with the gene deletion of *mSlo1* for the pore-forming subunit of the BKCa channel exhibit increased urinary bladder spontaneous and nerve-evoked contractions as well as a marked elevation in urination frequency (Meredith et al, 2004). It has also been demonstrated that local injection of *hSlo* cDNA into the bladder lumen to increase BKCa channel activity eliminated detrusor overactivity in rats with bladder outlet obstruction (Christ et al, 2001), suggesting an important role of BKCa channels in urinary bladder function and overactive bladder. Thus, **there** is considerable interest in the development of specific K+ channel openers for therapeutic use in the treatment of bladder overactivity (Pandita and Andersson, 1999; Andersson and Arner, 2004).

Tricyclic Antidepressants

Tricyclic antidepressants, such as imipramine and amitriptyline, have been shown to be clinically effective in reducing the level of detrusor overactivity under specific conditions (Wein, 1998). Their effectiveness has been linked to antimuscarinic activity, inhibition of calcium translocation, and direct smooth muscle relaxant properties and possibly to an action on the central nervous system (Maggi et al, 1989). Each of these actions would relax the bladder and reduce the level of spontaneous activity. Because these are nonselective agents with multiple mechanisms of action, there is little research in the development of more bladder-selective tricyclic agents.

Spinal Ascending and Descending Pathways

It is possible to conjecture about the sites of action of drugs in the spinal cord on the basis of certain experimental designs. For example, alterations in the volume threshold for inducing micturition (in the absence of other changes of bladder activity) are interpreted as indicating an effect on the ascending limb of the micturition reflex. Alterations in the magnitude of bladder contractions (or pelvic nerve discharge) produced by PMC stimulation (Matsumoto et al, 1995a, 1995b) may be taken to indicate an action on the descending limb of the micturition reflex.

Glutamatergic Mechanisms

Intrathecal or intravenous administration of glutamatergic NMDA or α-amino-3-hydroxy-5-methylisoxazole-4-propionic acid (AMPA) antagonists in urethane-anesthetized rats depressed reflex bladder contractions and electromyographic activity of the external urethral sphincter in animals with an intact spinal cord as well as in animals with chronic spinal injury (Yoshiyama et al, 1994, 1997). These results indicate that spinal reflex pathways controlling bladder and sphincter function use NMDA and AMPA glutamatergic transmitter mechanisms. In spinal cord–injured rats, external sphincter muscle activity was more sensitive than bladder reflexes to glutamatergic antagonists, raising the possibility that the two reflex pathways might have different glutamatergic receptors (Yoshiyama et al, 1994). This was confirmed with in situ hybridization techniques, which revealed that sacral parasympathetic preganglionic neurons in the rat express high mRNA levels of GluR-A and GluR-B AMPA receptor subunits and NR1 but not NR2 NMDA receptor subunits (Shibata et al, 1999). Conversely, motoneurons in the urethral sphincter nucleus express all four AMPA receptor subunits (GluR-A, GluR-B, GluR-C, and GluR-D) in conjunction with moderate amounts of NR2A and NR2B as well as high levels of NR1 receptor subunits. It seems likely that this difference in expression accounts for the different sensitivity of bladder and sphincter reflexes to glutamatergic antagonists.

Glutamate also plays a role as an excitatory transmitter in the afferent limb of the micturition reflex. The c-*fos* expression induced in spinal interneurons by activation of bladder afferents is suppressed by the administration of both NMDA and non-NMDA glutamatergic receptor antagonists (Birder and de Groat, 1992; Kakizaki et al, 1996).

Inhibitory Amino Acids

Intrathecal injection of either GABA$_A$ or GABA$_B$ agonists increases bladder capacity and decreases voiding pressure and efficiency in rats (Igawa et al, 1993). Glycine and GABA inhibitory mechanisms have also been identified in the neonatal rat spinal cord in local interneuronal inhibitory pathways projecting directly to the preganglionic neurons (Araki, 1994). Clinical studies have revealed that intrathecal administration of a GABA$_B$ receptor agonist (baclofen) increased the volume threshold for inducing the micturition reflex (Bushman et al, 1993). Intrathecally administered baclofen also produced a phaclofen-sensitive inhibition of distention-evoked micturition in conscious rats that appears to be resistant to capsaicin (substance P depletion) or parachlorophenylalanine (5-HT depletion) pretreatment. Because baclofen also inhibits field stimulation–evoked release of CGRP from primary afferent terminals in dorsal horn slices, one possible site for this action is suppression of transmitter release from primary afferent terminals in the spinal cord. In addition, studies by Sugaya and colleagues have revealed that the level of glycine in the spinal cord is decreased by approximately 50% in rats with detrusor overactivity induced by chronic spinal cord injury compared with spinal intact rats (Miyazato et al, 2003, 2005) and that dietary supplement of glycine can restore bladder function along with an increase in the serum level of glycine in spinal cord–injured rats (Miyazato et al, 2005). These results suggest that downregulation of the spinal glycinergic mechanism may contribute to the emergence of neurogenic detrusor overactivity associated with spinal cord injury.

Adrenergic Mechanisms

In the spinal cord, α adrenoceptors can mediate excitatory and inhibitory influences on the lower urinary tract. In anesthetized cats, α_1 adrenoceptors were implicated in a bulbospinal noradrenergic excitatory pathway from the locus ceruleus to the sacral parasympathetic outflow to bladder (Yoshimura et al, 1988, 1990a, 1990b), although subsequent studies could not confirm these findings in conscious cats (Espey et al, 1992).

Experiments in conscious or anesthetized rats (Ishizuka et al, 1996b; de Groat et al, 1999) revealed that intrathecal administration of an α_1-adrenergic antagonist (doxazosin) decreased the amplitude of bladder contractions (Ishizuka et al, 1996b, 1997). The bladder inhibitory effect of intrathecal α_1-adrenergic antagonist was more prominent in animals with chronic outlet obstruction (Ishizuka et al, 1996b). It was also found that intrathecal administration of doxazosin suppressed detrusor overactivity (unstable bladder contractions) in spontaneously hypertensive rats (Persson et al, 1997). Although intrathecal injection of doxazosin suppressed the amplitude of reflex bladder contractions in anesthetized rats, it increased the frequency of isovolumetric contractions, indicating the presence of a tonic adrenergic inhibitory mechanism (de Groat et al, 1999). This was supported by the finding that phenylephrine, an α_1-adrenergic agonist, applied intrathecally, decreased the frequency of bladder contractions without changing contraction amplitude (de Groat et al, 1999). Thus, it appears that **efferent and afferent limbs of the micturition reflex receive excitatory and inhibitory input, respectively, from spinal noradrenergic systems.**

Evidence for a modulatory role of α_2 adrenoceptors in micturition is conflicting because both facilitatory and inhibitory roles of α_2 adrenoceptors have been documented (de Groat et al, 1999; Ishizuka et al, 1996a). Atipamezole, an α_2-adrenergic antagonist given intrathecally, can increase micturition pressure in the conscious rat, implying that there is a tonic inhibitory adrenergic control (Ishizuka et al, 1996a). However, yohimbine, an α_2-adrenergic antagonist, inhibits micturition in rats anesthetized with chloralose-urethane (Kontani et al, 1992). In paraplegic patients, intrathecal injection of clonidine suppressed detrusor overactivity (Denys et al, 1998). Conversely, in conscious spinal cats, clonidine, an α_2-adrenergic agonist, increased bladder pressures and facilitated voiding (Galeano et al, 1986).

Pharmacologic experiments showed that the bladder to sympathetic reflex pathway is modulated by central noradrenergic mechanisms (Danuser and Thor, 1995; de Groat, 1999; de Groat and Yoshimura, 2001). In the chloralose-anesthetized cat, prazosin or doxazosin, α_1 adrenoceptor antagonists, suppressed spontaneous firing (Ramage and Wyllie, 1995) or the reflex discharge recorded on the hypogastric nerve in response to pelvic nerve afferent stimulation (Danuser and Thor, 1995). Administration of α_2-adrenergic agonists also suppresses reflex sympathetic activity (Danuser and Thor, 1995). These observations suggest that bulbospinal noradrenergic pathways provide a tonic α_1-excitatory control of the bladder-sympathetic reflex in the spinal cord. α_2-Adrenergic inhibitory mechanisms are not active under control conditions in anesthetized animals but can be up-regulated by elevating endogenous norepinephrine levels with an inhibitor (tomoxetine) of norepinephrine reuptake (Danuser and Thor, 1995). These results suggest that the lumbar sympathetic outflow is controlled by α_1-excitatory and α_2-inhibitory mechanisms.

The activation of urethral sphincter motoneurons by stimulation of bladder (pelvic nerve) or urethral or perineal (pudendal nerve) afferents is part of a continence-maintaining mechanism. These reflexes recorded as efferent discharges on the pudendal nerve in chloralose-anesthetized cats were suppressed by the α_1 adrenoceptor antagonist prazosin (Gajewski et al, 1984; Danuser and Thor, 1995; Downie, 1999) but not by the α_2 blocker idazoxan (Danuser and Thor, 1995). Conversely, clonidine, an α_2 adrenoceptor agonist, suppressed the reflex in anesthetized cats (Downie and Bialik, 1988). The norepinephrine uptake blocker tomoxetine produced a slight inhibition alone and only a slightly greater inhibition after prazosin. However, it greatly facilitated the reflex when given after idazoxan (Danuser et al, 1995). These data indicate the existence of α_2 adrenoceptor–mediated inhibition and α_1 adrenoceptor–mediated tonic facilitation of sphincter function and that the α_2 adrenoceptor–dependent inhibitory mechanism is the dominant adrenergic modulator of the pudendal nerve reflex (Thor and Donatucci, 2004).

Serotonergic Mechanisms

Neurons containing 5-HT in the raphe nucleus of the caudal brainstem send projections to the dorsal horn as well as to the autonomic and sphincter motor nuclei in the lumbosacral spinal cord. In cats, activation of raphe neurons or 5-HT receptors in the spinal cord inhibits reflex bladder contractions and firing of the sacral efferent pathways to the bladder (McMahon and Spillane, 1982; Chen et al, 1993; de Groat et al, 1993; de Groat, 2002) and also inhibits firing of spinal dorsal horn neurons elicited by stimulation of pelvic nerve afferents (Fukuda and Koga, 1991). In rats, the administration of m-chlorophenylpiperazine, which is an agonist for 5-HT$_{2C}$ receptors, suppressed efferent activity on bladder nerves and reflex bladder contractions (Steers and de Groat, 1989). These effects were blocked by mesulergine, a 5-HT$_2$ receptor antagonist (Steers and de Groat, 1989; Guarneri et al, 1996). Intrathecal administration of methysergide, a 5-HT$_{1/2}$ antagonist, or zatosetron, a 5-HT$_3$ antagonist, decreased the micturition volume threshold in cats (Espey et al, 1998), implying that **descending serotonergic pathways tonically depress the afferent limb of the micturition reflex.**

8-OH-DPAT, a 5-HT$_{1A}$ agonist, administered intrathecally, facilitated bladder activity in both normal and spinal cord–injured rats but not in rats in which bladder afferents were damaged by treatment with capsaicin at birth (Lecci et al, 1992). Conversely, administration of the 5-HT$_{1A}$ receptor antagonist WAY 100635, which increases the firing rate of raphe neurons by blocking 5-HT$_{1A}$ inhibitory autoreceptors, inhibits reflex bladder contractions (Testa et al, 1999). The inhibition is antagonized by pretreatment with mesulergine, a 5-HT$_2$ receptor antagonist, indicating that 5-HT$_2$ receptors are involved in descending raphe and spinal inhibitory mechanisms (Testa et al, 1999). When the effects of intrathecal administration of WAY 100635 on the ascending and descending limbs of the micturition reflex pathway were examined in anesthetized rats, WAY 100635 depressed bladder contractions evoked by electrical stimulation of the PMC but did not alter the evoked field potentials in the region during electrical stimulation of afferent axons in the pelvic nerve, indicating that the drug suppresses the pathway from the brainstem to the spinal cord but does not alter the afferent pathway from the bladder to the PMC (Kakizaki et al, 2001; de Groat, 2002).

The sympathetic autonomic nuclei as well as the sphincter motor nuclei also receive a serotonergic input from the raphe nucleus (de Groat et al, 1979; Downie, 1999; Thor and Donatucci, 2004). Serotonergic activity mediated by 5-HT$_2$ and 5-HT$_3$ receptors enhances urine storage by facilitating sphincter reflexes (Danuser and Thor, 1996; Espey et al, 1998).

Duloxetine, a combined norepinephrine and 5-HT reuptake inhibitor (Sharma et al, 2000), **has been shown, in a bladder-irritated model, to increase the neural activity of both the urethral sphincter and the bladder** (Thor and Katofiasc, 1995; Thor and Donatucci, 2004). Duloxetine appears to have effects on both the bladder and the sphincter and has been proposed for treatment of both stress incontinence and urge incontinence (Cannon et al, 2003; Thor and Donatucci, 2004). Duloxetine increases the neural activity to the external urethral sphincter and decreases bladder activity through effects on the central nervous system (Thor and Donatucci, 2004). Clinical trials have also shown the efficacy of duloxetine for the treatment of stress urinary incontinence; the drug has been approved in Europe and is already available in several countries (Castro-Diaz and Amoros, 2005), although it has been withdrawn from the Food and Drug

Administration approval process in the United States by the manufacturer.

Opioid Peptides

Opioid peptides have an inhibitory action on reflex pathways in the spinal cord. In the cat spinal cord, inhibition of reflex bladder activity is mediated by δ receptors, whereas inhibition of sphincter activity is mediated by κ receptors (de Groat et al, 1993; Yoshimura and de Groat, 1997a; de Groat and Yoshimura, 2001). In the rat, both μ and δ receptors mediate bladder inhibition (Dray and Metsch, 1984a, 1984b, 1984c).

Purinergic Mechanisms

Adenosine A_1 (and perhaps A_2) receptor activation by intrathecal agonist administration has produced a caffeine-sensitive increase in volume threshold in conscious rats. Based on the known distribution of adenosine receptors in the spinal cord, excitatory interneurons are the presumed site of inhibitory action of adenosine A_1 agonist (Sosnowski et al, 1989).

Conclusion

Glutamate plays an important role in the spinal efferent circuitry supporting micturition. The spinal noradrenergic system, mediated by α_1 adrenoceptors, has a modulatory role in controlling micturition by inhibiting afferent inputs from the bladder and facilitating the descending limb of the spinal micturition reflex to increase bladder contractility. Transmitters such as 5-HT, purines, glycine, and GABA appear to selectively modulate the volume threshold by actions in the sacral spinal cord. These mechanisms seem to be favorable for development of novel drug therapies.

Pontine Micturition Center and Supraspinal Mechanisms

Glutamatergic Mechanisms

Glutamic acid also has a role in excitatory transmission at supraspinal sites in the micturition reflex pathway (Fig. 56–30). Exogenous L-glutamate or its analog injected at sites (locus ceruleus or parabrachial nucleus) in the brainstem of supracollicular decerebrate cats where electrical stimulation evoked bladder contractions elicited voiding or increased frequency and amplitude of rhythmic bladder contractions (Kruse et al, 1990; Mallory et al, 1991).

Administration of glutamatergic agonists into the region of the PMC in cats and rats elicits voiding or increases frequency

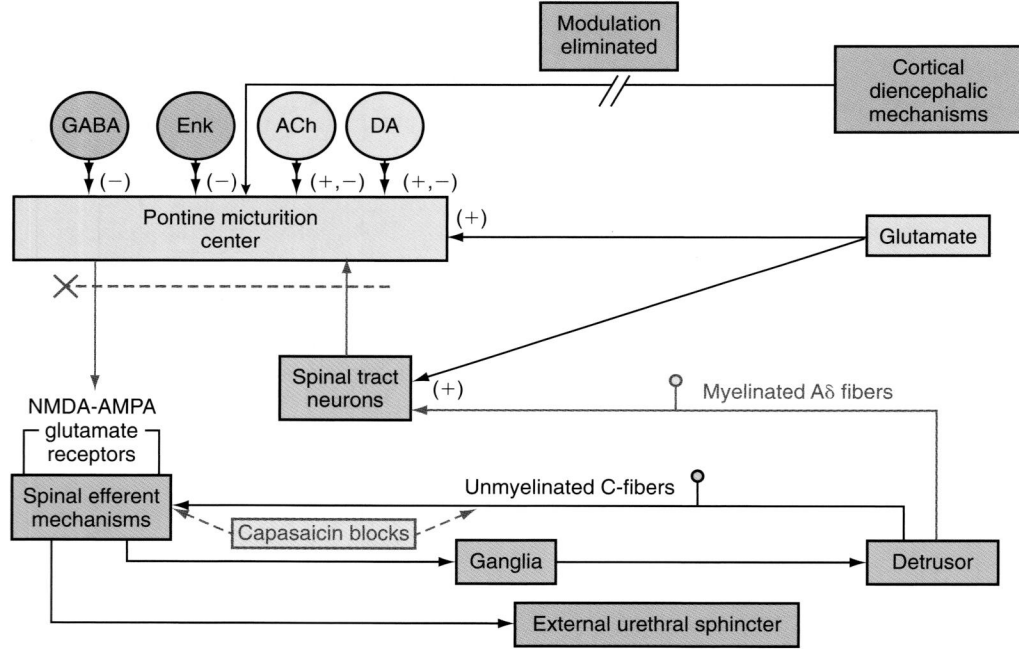

Figure 56–30. Diagram of the central reflex pathways that regulate micturition in the cat. Normally, micturition is initiated by a supraspinal reflex pathway passing through the PMC in the brainstem. The pathway is triggered by myelinated afferents (Aδ) connected to tension receptors in the bladder wall (detrusor). Spinal tract neurons carry information to the brain. During micturition, pathways from the PMC activate the parasympathetic outflow to the bladder and inhibit the somatic outflow to the urethral sphincter. Transmission in the PMC is modulated by cortical-diencephalic mechanisms. Interruption of these mechanisms leads to bladder instability. In spinal cord–transected animals, connections between the brainstem and the sacral spinal cord are interrupted and micturition is initially blocked. In animals with chronic spinal cord injury, a spinal micturition reflex emerges that is triggered by unmyelinated (C-fiber) bladder afferents. The C-fiber reflex pathway is usually weak or undetectable in animals with an intact nervous system. Stimulation of the C-fiber bladder afferents by instillation of ice water into the bladder (cold stimulation) activates voiding reflexes in patients with spinal cord injury. Capsaicin (20 to 30 mg/kg subcutaneously) blocks the C-fiber reflexes in cats with chronic spinal cord injury but does not block micturition reflexes in intact cats. Intravesical capsaicin also suppresses bladder instability and cold-evoked reflexes in patients with neurogenic bladder dysfunction. Glutamic acid is the principal excitatory transmitter in the ascending and descending limbs of the micturition reflex pathway as well as in the reflex pathway controlling sphincter function. Glutamate acts on both N-methyl-D-aspartate (NMDA) and α-amino-3-hydroxy-5-methylisoxazole-4-propionic acid (AMPA) glutamatergic receptors. Other neurotransmitters that regulate transmission in the micturition reflex pathway include γ-aminobutyric acid (GABA), enkephalins (Enk), acetylcholine (ACh), and dopamine (DA). Acetylcholine and dopamine have both excitatory and inhibitory effects on the pathway; excitatory (+) and inhibitory (−) synapse.

and amplitude of bladder contractions (Mallory et al, 1991; de Groat, 1999), whereas injection of agonists at other brainstem nuclei known to have inhibitory functions in micturition elicits inhibitory effects (Chen et al, 1993). Intracerebroventricular injection of AMPA or NMDA receptor antagonists blocks reflex bladder contractions in anesthetized rats, indicating that glutamatergic transmission in the brain is essential for voiding function (Yoshiyama and de Groat, 1996, 2005). Similarly, Yokoyama and colleagues (1999) have shown that glutamate plays an important role, especially through NMDA receptors, in the rat middle cerebral artery occlusion model of detrusor overactivity.

Cholinergic Mechanisms

Excitatory and inhibitory cholinergic influences on the micturition pathway have been identified at the supraspinal level. A decreased volume threshold and increased micturition pressure were detected after administration of bethanechol, a muscarinic agonist, into the central circulation of the cross-perfused dog (O'Donnell, 1990). One site of action can be localized to the midbrain-pons region because cholinergic agonists are effective after supracollicular decerebration in rats (Sillen et al, 1982). In the rat brain, muscarinic receptor–mediated cholinergic mechanisms may be involved in both inhibitory and facilitatory modulation of the micturition reflex (Ishiura et al, 2001; Yokoyama et al, 2001; Ishizuka et al, 2002), and the muscarinic inhibitory mechanism seems to involve an activation of M_1 muscarinic receptors (Yokoyama et al, 2001) and protein kinase C (Nakamura et al, 2003). In the brainstem, microinjection of acetylcholine to the PMC in cats increased or decreased the threshold volume for inducing a reflex contraction of the bladder (Sugaya et al, 1987; Yoshimura and de Groat, 1997a). These effects were blocked by atropine, indicating a role of muscarinic receptors. Nicotinic receptors are also involved in the control of voiding function since a nicotinic receptor agonist, epibatidine, injected into the lateral ventricle suppressed the micturition reflex in the rat (Lee et al, 2003).

GABAergic Mechanisms

GABA has been implicated as an inhibitory transmitter at supraspinal sites where it can act on both $GABA_A$ and $GABA_B$ receptors (de Groat and Booth, 1993; Yoshimura and de Groat, 1997a; de Groat et al, 1999; Kanie et al, 2000; de Groat and Yoshimura, 2001). Injection of GABA or muscimol, a $GABA_A$ receptor agonist, into the PMC of decerebrate cats suppressed reflex bladder activity and increased the volume threshold for inducing micturition (Mallory et al, 1991). These effects were reversed by bicuculline, a $GABA_A$ receptor antagonist. Because bicuculline alone stimulated bladder activity and lowered the volume threshold for micturition, the micturition reflex pathway in the PMC must be tonically inhibited by a GABAergic mechanism. Intracerebroventricular baclofen, a $GABA_B$ agonist, suppressed distention-evoked micturition in urethane-anesthetized rats, but the effect was not blocked by phaclofen, a $GABA_B$ receptor antagonist (de Groat et al, 1993; de Groat and Yoshimura, 2001).

Dopaminergic Mechanisms

In the central nervous system, dopaminergic pathways exert inhibitory and facilitatory effects, respectively, on the mic- turition reflex through D_1-like (D_1 or D_5 subtype) and D_2-like (D_2, D_3, or D_4 subtype) dopaminergic receptors (Albanease et al, 1988; Kontani et al, 1990; Yoshimura et al, 1992, 1993, 1998, 2003; Yokoyama et al, 1999; Seki et al, 2001; Hashimoto et al, 2003) (see Fig. 56–30). In anesthetized cats, activation of dopaminergic neurons in the substantia nigra inhibits reflex bladder contractions through D_1-like receptors (Yoshimura et al, 1992). A study also revealed that a D_1 dopaminergic antagonist (SCH 23390) facilitated the micturition reflex, whereas a D_1 agonist (SKF 38393) had no effect on the reflex bladder contractions in awake rats, suggesting that D_1 receptor–mediated suppression of bladder activity is tonically active in the normal awake state (Seki et al, 2001). Disruption of this tonic dopaminergic inhibition by destroying the nigrostriatal pathway with the neurotoxin MPTP produces Parkinson-like motor symptoms in monkeys accompanied by detrusor overactivity (Albanease et al, 1988; Yoshimura et al, 1993, 1998), as reported in patients with Parkinson's disease (Albanease et al, 1988; Yoshimura et al, 1993; Steers et al, 1996). Similarly, a rat model of Parkinson's disease induced by a unilateral 6-hydroxydopamine lesion of the nigrostriatal pathway also exhibits detrusor overactivity (Yoshimura et al, 2003). In these parkinsonian animals, detrusor overactivity was suppressed by stimulation of D_1-like receptors with SKF 38393 or pergolide (Yoshimura et al, 1993, 1998, 2003).

Conversely, activation of central D_2-like dopaminergic receptors with quinpirole or bromocriptine facilitates the micturition reflex pathway in rats, cats, and monkeys (Kontani et al, 1990; Yoshimura et al, 1993, 1998, 2003; Yokoyama et al, 1999). D_2-like receptor–mediated facilitation of the micturition reflex may involve actions on brainstem because microinjection of dopamine to the PMC reduced bladder capacity and facilitated the micturition reflex in cats (de Groat et al, 1993). D_2-like receptors are also involved in detrusor overactivity induced by middle cerebral artery occlusion in rats (Yokoyama et al, 1999). Thus, **central dopaminergic pathways exhibit different effects on micturition through actions on multiple receptors at different sites in the brain.**

Opioid Peptides

Intracerebroventricularly administered morphine suppressed isovolumic bladder contractions, and this effect was blocked by naloxone (Dray and Metsch, 1984a, 1984b, 1984c). Naloxone administered intracerebroventricularly also reversed the effects of systemically administered morphine. **Naloxone administered alone intracerebroventricularly or injected directly into the PMC facilitates the micturition reflex** (Hisamitsu and de Groat, 1984). Both μ and δ opioid receptors mediate inhibitory effects that are blocked by naloxone (Hisamitsu and de Groat, 1984; Mallory et al, 1991; Downie, 1999).

Conclusion

Glutamate appears to be involved as an excitatory transmitter in the supraspinal circuitry controlling micturition. Glutamate may also be a mediator of detrusor overactivity after neural injury. The role of other potential excitatory transmitters remains to be examined. Several substances can exert significant modulatory influences on the supraspinal

circuits (see Fig. 56–30) **and can have dramatic influences on micturition. The receptors for these substances therefore represent potential sites for therapeutic intervention.**

MECHANISMS OF DETRUSOR OVERACTIVITY

A variety of models have been used to explore the pathogenesis of detrusor overactivity and to formulate treatments for overactive bladder and urge incontinence. Models for detrusor overactivity in several species have been developed that are relevant to spinal cord injury, obstruction, denervation, Parkinson's disease, interstitial cystitis, diabetes, multiple sclerosis, and aging (de Groat et al, 1993; Dupont et al, 1994). In addition, the spontaneously hypertensive rat has provided a useful genetic model for detrusor overactivity (Steers et al, 1999). A common feature of many of these models is that changes in smooth muscle function can elicit long-term changes in nerves. Investigators are accustomed to examining short-term effects. However, there is now a greater appreciation that long-term events involving growth factors lead to plasticity in neural pathways with implications for disorders of micturition.

Neurotransmitters, prostaglandins, and neurotrophic factors such as nerve growth factor (NGF) are substances that provide mechanisms for communication between muscle and nerve. Disturbances in these mechanisms can cause detrusor overactivity by alterations in autonomic reflex pathways. This detrusor overactivity can in turn lead to urge incontinence. Cystometry and urinary frequency are commonly used to define detrusor overactivity and can be used to monitor responses to drugs or other therapies. A multidisciplinary approach incorporating biochemical, molecular, pharmacologic, physiologic, and behavioral methods can provide insight into the pathogenesis of detrusor overactivity. In addition, recent advances in constructing mutant mice lacking specific genes provide a useful tool to study the contribution of specific molecules to the lower urinary tract function or the emergence of detrusor overactivity. For example, bladder function has been investigated in knockout mice lacking muscarinic receptors (M_1 to M_5) (Matsui et al, 2002; Igawa et al, 2004), purinergic receptors ($P2X_2$, $P2X_3$) (Cockayne et al, 2000, 2005), TRPV1 (Birder et al, 2002b), *hSlo* for BKCa channels (Meredith et al, 2004), or serotonin reuptake transporter (Cornelissen et al, 2005).

Spinal Cord Injury and Neurogenic Detrusor Overactivity

Damage to the spinal cord above the sacral level results in detrusor overactivity (Kaplan et al, 1991; Chancellor et al, 1997). Acute spinal cord injury disrupts normal supraspinal circuits that control urine storage and release. After the spinal shock period of urinary retention that generally lasts a few weeks, hyperreflexic voiding develops. Electrophysiologic data reveal that this detrusor overactivity is mediated by a spinal micturition reflex that emerges in response to a reorganization of synaptic connections in the spinal cord (de Groat, 1975; de Groat et al, 1981, 1990; Araki and de Groat, 1997; Yoshimura, 1999). In addition, bladder afferents that are nor-

mally unresponsive to low intravesical pressures become more mechanosensitive, leading to the development of detrusor overactivity.

Normal micturition is associated with a spinobulbospinal reflex mediated by lightly myelinated Aδ afferents (de Groat, 1975; de Groat et al, 1993). **These fibers represent only 30% of bladder afferents in some species. Compared with Aδ-fibers, the more prevalent unmyelinated C-fibers are relatively insensitive to gradual distention of the urinary bladder, at least in the cat** (Häbler et al, 1990). Most C fibers in this species remain silent during normal filling of the bladder, although in the rat, some studies indicate that C fibers can fire at low pressures (Sengupta and Gebhart, 1994) whereas other studies (Morrison, 1998) showed firing at higher intravesical pressures of approximately 30 mm Hg. **After spinal cord injury, a capsaicin-sensitive C fiber–mediated spinal reflex develops** (see Fig. 56–30). **These C-fiber afferents are thought to play a role in the development of detrusor overactivity after spinal cord injury. Capsaicin-sensitive C fibers have also been implicated in detrusor overactivity after upper motoneuron diseases such as spinal cord injury, multiple sclerosis, and Parkinson's disease** (Fowler et al, 1992, 1994; Geirsson et al, 1995; Szallasi and Fowler, 2002).

Insight into the mechanism underlying the increased mechanosensitivity of C fibers after spinal cord injury has been gained by examination of the DRG cells supplying the bladder. Plasticity in these afferents is manifested by enlargement of these cells (Kruse et al, 1995) and increased electrical excitability (Yoshimura and de Groat, 1997a, 1997b; Yoshimura, 1999). A shift in expression of Na^+ channels from a high-threshold tetrodotoxin-resistant type to a low-threshold tetrodotoxin-sensitive type occurs after spinal cord injury (Yoshimura and de Groat, 1997a, 1997b; Yoshimura, 1999).

Plasticity in bladder afferents after spinal cord injury and upper motoneuron lesions may involve the retrograde transport of substances from either the spinal cord or the bladder to the DRG neuron. **NGF has been implicated as a chemical mediator of disease-induced changes in C-fiber afferent nerve excitability and reflex bladder activity** (Yoshimura, 1999; Vizzard, 2000c). It has been demonstrated that chronic administration of NGF into the bladder of rats induced bladder hyperactivity and increased the firing frequency of dissociated bladder afferent neurons (Yoshimura and de Groat, 1999) and that the production of neurotrophic factors including NGF increased in the bladder after spinal cord injury (Vizzard, 2000c). It has also been shown that the bladder hyperactivity and the hypertrophy in afferent and efferent neurons innervating the hypertrophic bladder in rats with partial urethral obstruction were antagonized in part by systemic autoimmunization against NGF (Steers et al, 1996). Thus, it seems that target organ–neural interactions mediated by neurotrophic factors such as NGF produced in the hypertrophied bladder muscle may contribute to changes in C-fiber bladder afferent pathways that induce detrusor overactivity and detrusor-sphincter dyssynergia after spinal cord injury. In addition, increased NGF in the spinal cord after spinal cord injury is also responsible for inducing hyperexcitability of C-fiber bladder afferent pathways, and intrathecal application of NGF antibodies, which neutralized NGF in the spinal cord, suppressed detrusor overactivity and detrusor-sphincter dyssynergia in spinal cord–injured rats (Seki et al, 2002, 2004).

Figure 56–31. Possible mechanisms underlying plasticity in bladder reflex pathways induced by various pathologic conditions. Bladders from rats with chronic spinal cord injury, urethral obstruction, chronic inflammation, and bladder denervation and those that are spontaneously hypertensive exhibit increased level of neurotrophic factors (NTF), such as nerve growth factor. NTFs can increase the excitability of C-fiber bladder afferent neurons and alter reflex mechanisms in parasympathetic excitatory pathways in the pelvic nerve (PN) as well as in sympathetic pathways in the hypogastric nerve (HGN). These reflex circuits are organized in the spinal cord as positive-feedback loops that induce involuntary bladder activity. In certain situations, such as the spontaneously hypertensive rat, peripheral efferent mechanisms are also altered: excitatory α_1 adrenoceptor mechanisms are upregulated, providing an additional excitatory input to the bladder.

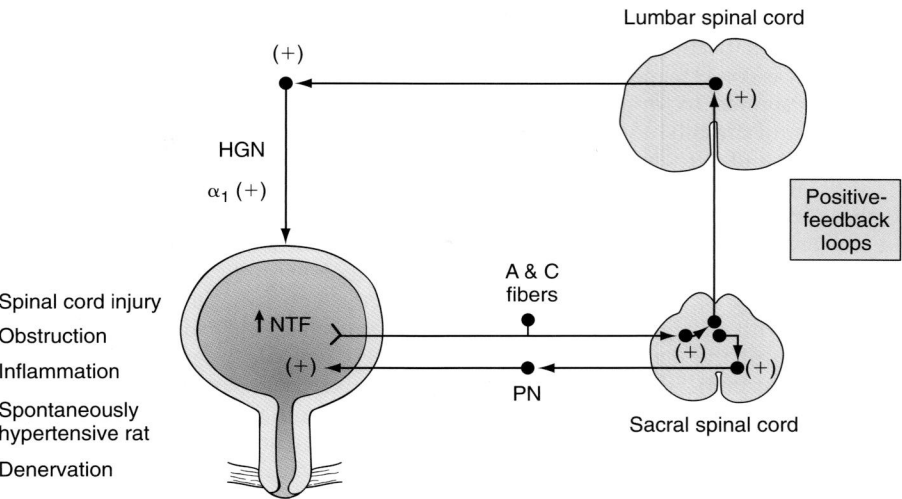

Intrathecal administration of NGF antibodies also reportedly blocked autonomic dysreflexia in paraplegic rats (Krenz et al, 1999). Thus, NGF and its receptors in the bladder or the spinal cord are potential targets for new therapies to suppress detrusor overactivity and detrusor-sphincter dyssynergia after spinal cord injury.

Other neurogenic disorders associated with urge incontinence respond to intravesical therapy with capsaicin or resiniferatoxin, suggesting that plasticity in C-fiber afferents could form the neurogenic basis for detrusor overactivity (Geirsson, 1993; Fowler et al, 1994; Geirsson et al, 1995; Szalasi and Fowler, 2002). The emergence of a spinal reflex circuit activated by C-fiber bladder afferents represents a positive feedback mechanism (Fig. 56–31) that may be unresponsive to voluntary control by higher brain centers and thereby be able to trigger involuntary voiding. **The bladder ice-water urodynamic test has been suggested as a method to assess the C fiber–mediated micturition reflex.** Although the ice-water test is consistent in a strictly controlled research environment, it has not been adequately sensitive or specific in routine clinical use (Chai et al, 1998; Chancellor et al, 1998).

Bladder Outlet Obstruction

It is important to understand that the bothersome symptoms of patients with urethral obstruction are in most cases caused by the bladder. Gosling and coworkers (2000) demonstrated that prolonged partial bladder outflow obstruction in the rabbit is accompanied by a progressive decrease in contractility of the detrusor smooth muscle.

Changes that occur in the rabbit detrusor muscle after outlet obstruction, including smooth muscle cell hypertrophy, reduction in myofilaments, and damaged mitochondria within the detrusor smooth muscle cells, are compatible with the reduced response of the detrusor to carbachol and field stimulation. This decompensation progressively increased up to 70 days after partial obstruction, indicating a continuous decline in bladder structure and function. The autonomic nerves are also vulnerable to partial obstruction, with documented axonal degeneration by day 7 and becoming more extensive thereafter. This type of research suggests that treatment of bladder outlet obstruction may need to focus on early intervention and on preventing and reverting the changes in the detrusor wall.

After chronic partial obstruction of the urethra, the bladder enlarges and is about 15 times heavier, but it has the same shape as in control subjects; the growth is mainly accounted for by muscle hypertrophy. The outer surface of the hypertrophic bladder is increased sixfold over that of the controls; the muscle is increased threefold in thickness and is more compact. Mitoses are not found, but there is a massive increase in muscle cell size. There is a modest decrease in percentage volume of mitochondria, an increase in sarcoplasmic reticulum, and no appreciable change in the pattern of myofilaments. Gap junctions between hypertrophic muscle cells are virtually absent. Intramuscular nerve fibers and vesicle-containing varicosities appear as common in the hypertrophic muscle as in controls (Gabella and Uvelius, 1990). There is no infiltration of the muscle by connective tissue and no significant occurrence of muscle cell death.

Bladder outlet obstruction often produces detrusor hypertrophy and detrusor overactivity (Gosling et al, 2000). **Obstruction-induced detrusor overactivity with irritative voiding symptoms has been attributed to denervation supersensitivity because increased contractile responses of the bladder smooth muscle to cholinergic agonists and electrical stimulation have been observed** (Speakman et al, 1987). **Molecular biologic techniques have also shown that alterations in detrusor contractility may result from changes in contractile proteins** (Uvelius et al, 1989; Cher et al, 1990; Chacko et al, 1999, 2004). After obstruction, a wide variety of structural, pharmacologic, and physiologic changes occur in the lower urinary tract (Levin et al, 1990). These changes include enlarged density of afferent and efferent nerve fibers, suggesting that changes are occurring in these nerves (Steers et al, 1991a). Brading and Turner (1994) proposed that all cases of detrusor overactivity have a common feature—detrusor smooth muscle change that predisposes it to unstable contraction. This change in detrusor muscle may be caused by reduction in the functional motor innervation of the bladder wall. It has been demonstrated that detrusor overactivity, as shown in a pig model of obstruction, may occur without participation of a micturition reflex. If this hypothesis is correct, and the functional change in the detrusor in response to outflow obstruction is an increased excitability of smooth muscle, drug development should focus on inhibition of detrusor excitability (Andersson et al, 1999).

Mills and coworkers (2000) have also implicated abnormalities in the detrusor muscle and its pattern of innervation in idiopathic detrusor overactivity. Compared with bladder wall in control subjects, there was evidence in the detrusor smooth muscle of altered spontaneous contractile activity consistent with increased electrical coupling of cells, patchy denervation of the detrusor, and potassium supersensitivity (Mills et al, 2000). This is similar to detrusor behavior in patients with detrusor overactivity secondary to bladder outlet obstruction (Harrison et al, 1987) and neurogenic detrusor overactivity (German et al, 1995). What is becoming increasingly evident is that there is a fundamental abnormality at the level of the bladder wall in many types of detrusor overactivity (Mills et al, 2000). One of the manifestations of this abnormality is a partial denervation of the detrusor smooth muscle. This does not preclude a role for a putative aberration in the micturition reflex but suggests that any such aberration may not necessarily be a prerequisite for the development of detrusor overactivity (Wang et al, 1995b). Changes in the cell-to-cell communication in detrusor muscles have also been indicated as a mechanism inducing detrusor overactivity because there is an upregulation of connexin 43, a gap junction protein, in rats with detrusor overactivity induced by bladder outlet obstruction (Christ et al, 2003), although the protein seems to be decreased when the decompensated bladder is developed as outlet obstruction persists (Mori et al, 2005). Increased expression of connexin 43 is also identified in the bladders from patients with neurogenic detrusor overactivity (Haferkamp et al, 2004).

However, **alterations also occur in neural networks in the central nervous system after obstruction of the lower urinary tract.** Bladder outlet obstruction in rats causes enhancement of a spinal reflex (Steers and de Groat, 1988). Similarly, in obstructed humans, a capsaicin-sensitive spinal reflex can be detected by the ice-water test (Chai et al, 1998; Hirayama et al, 2003, 2005). Within the spinal cord, obstruction stimulates an increased expression of growth-associated protein 43 that has been associated with axonal sprouting after injury (Steers and Tuttle, 1997). These observations suggest an enhancement or de novo development of new spinal circuits after obstruction. Similar to spinal cord injury, obstruction causes hypertrophy of bladder afferent and efferent neurons (Steers et al, 1990, 1991a). Conversely, relief of obstruction is associated with the reduction of urinary frequency and reversal of these neural changes (Steers and Tuttle, 1993). In animals that fail to revert to a normal voiding pattern after relief of obstruction, this neuroplasticity persists. Nevertheless, these findings are not mutually exclusive of changes in the bladder smooth muscle, which are also likely to participate in the development of detrusor overactivity (Turner and Brading, 1997).

Bladder outlet obstruction appears to initiate the morphologic and electrophysiologic afferent plasticity through a mechanism involving NGF (see Fig. 56–31). NGF is responsible for the growth and maintenance of sympathetic and sensory neurons and has been shown to be responsible for neuronal regrowth after injury. NGF content is increased in obstructed bladders in animals and in humans (Steers et al, 1991a). This increase in NGF content precedes the enlargement of bladder neurons and the developmental of urinary frequency (Steers et al, 1990, 1991b). Moreover, blockade of NGF action with autoantibodies prevents the neural plasticity and urinary frequency after obstruction (Steers et al, 1991a). In animals with persistent urinary frequency after relief of obstruction, NGF remains elevated in the bladder. These findings suggest a cause-and-effect relationship between NGF-mediated changes in bladder afferents and an enhanced spinal micturition reflex and urinary frequency associated with obstruction. Of interest, α adrenoceptor antagonists, administered intrathecally, can reduce unstable bladder contractions in obstructed rats (Ishizuka et al, 1997). This finding supports the notion that changes in the spinal cord, possibly related to alterations in the processing of afferent input, contribute to the bladder dysfunction after outlet obstruction.

A clinical association between hypertension and detrusor overactivity has also been noted in men with benign prostatic hyperplasia (Pool, 1994; Brock et al, 1996). Thus, it is of interest that there exists a direct correlation between urinary frequency and elevated blood pressure in rats, independent of urine output or osmolality (Clemow et al, 1998a). Taken together, the observations gained from spontaneous hypertensive rats provide evidence for an inborn error in NGF metabolism in smooth muscle that leads to increased sympathetic innervation (noradrenergic) and lower afferent thresholds than in controls (Fig. 56–32) (Chalfin and Bradley, 1982; Dupont et al, 1995; Clemow et al, 1997; Steers et al, 1998). On the contrary, it should not be assumed that all elderly men with detrusor overactivity must also have benign prostatic hyperplasia. Many younger men without any obstructive voiding symptoms have urgency and frequency. We have seen many older men without documented bladder outlet obstruction on pressure-flow urodynamics who complain of severe overactive bladder symptoms. We have all had patients with perfect surgical relief of prostatic urethral obstruction but who still have persistent irritative voiding symptoms.

Inflammation

Because NGF plays such a prominent role in the development and function of afferent neurons, it is no surprise that inflammation of the urinary bladder is accompanied by neuroplasticity in sensory nerves supplying the bladder (see Fig. 56–31) (Steers and Tuttle, 1997). Repeated inflammatory stimuli elicit neuronal hyperexcitability because of a reduced expression of A-type K^+ channel and somal hypertrophy in bladder DRG neurons (Dupont et al, 1995; Yoshimura and de Groat, 1999). After inflammation, a reduction in threshold for bladder afferents occurs (Dmitrieva and McMahon, 1996). Likewise, it has been shown that intravesical NGF can lower thresholds for bladder afferents and induce hyperreflexia (Dmitrieva and McMahon, 1996) and bladder hyperactivity (Chuang et al, 2001). Plasticity within the afferent pathways and spinal cord may also occur. After chemical or mechanical inflammation of the rat urinary bladder, increased expression of the early-immediate gene c-*fos* has been detected within the

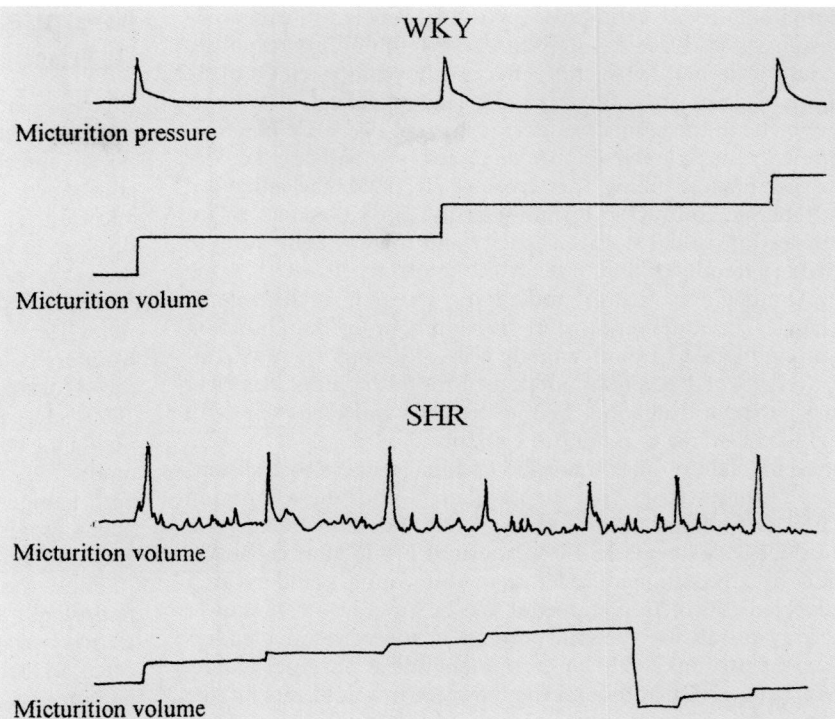

Figure 56–32. Awake cystometrograms in the Wistar-Kyoto normotensive rat (WKY) and the spontaneously hypertensive rat (SHR). Cystometrograms in the SHRs reveal frequent voiding contractions and small-amplitude contractions between voids consistent with unstable activity. SHRs void approximately three times more frequently than WKY controls. (From de Groat WC: Basic neurophysiology and neuropharmacology. In Abrams P, Khoury S, Wein A, eds: Incontinence. Plymouth, UK, Health Publications, 1999:138.)

lumbosacral spinal cord (Birder and de Groat, 1998; Birder et al, 1998), and increased expression of chemical markers such as NOS (Vizzard et al, 1996), growth-associated protein 43 (Vizzard and Boyle, 1999), pituitary adenylate cyclase–activating polypeptide (Vizzard, 2000a), neuropeptides such as substance P (Vizzard, 2001), protease-activated receptors (Dattilio and Vizzard, 2005), and cyclooxygenase 2 and prostaglandins (Hu et al, 2003) is increased in afferent neurons in lumbosacral DRG innervating the bladder.

With use of a rat model of chronic cystitis, increased expression of neurotrophic growth factors such as NGF, brain-derived neurotrophic factor, and ciliary neurotrophic factor in the bladder as well as phosphorylation of tyrosine kinase receptors (TrkA, TrkB) in bladder-innervating afferent neurons has been documented as direct evidence for neurotrophin-mediated signal transduction in chronic bladder inflammation (Vizzard, 2000; Qiao and Vizzard, 2002). Previous studies also demonstrated that exogenous NGF can induce bladder nociceptive responses and bladder overactivity in rats when it is applied acutely into the bladder lumen (Dmitrieva et al, 1997; Chuang et al, 2001) or chronically to the bladder wall or intrathecal space (Seki et al, 2003; Lamb et al, 2004). Moreover, it had been shown that an application of NGF-sequestering molecules (TrkA-IgG or REN1180) can reduce a referred thermal hyperalgesia elicited by bladder inflammation with turpentine oil (Jaggar et al, 1999) or bladder overactivity elicited by cyclophosphamide-induced cystitis (Hu et al, 2005), suggesting that increased NGF expression is directly involved in the emergence of bladder-related nociceptive responses in cystitis.

Vanilloid agonists and NK_1 receptor antagonists are being considered for bladder inflammatory conditions, including interstitial cystitis. However, these agents would be useful only if C-fiber afferent pathways mediate bladder inflammatory events. There is no definite proof that chronic bladder inflammation (or pain) is mediated by C-fibers in the human, although there is some experimental evidence in some models that says otherwise. The concept of using "sensory drugs" to treat bladder pain and inflammation is appealing but remains to be tested.

Aging

Contractility

Does aging result in diminished detrusor contractility? Many clinicians seem to implicitly believe this to be true because most patients who develop urinary retention are generally older. However, this clinical observation has not been completely substantiated by research. In fact, most experimental studies have not demonstrated a significant difference in detrusor contractile responses to cholinergic stimulation between young and old animals, nor a difference in bladder muscarinic receptor density (Chun et al, 1989; Longhurst et al, 1992a; Lieu et al, 1997; Lin et al, 1997). On the other hand, there are numerous reports of aging-related changes of the detrusor response to adrenergic stimulation (Latifpour et al, 1990). Most studies showed that detrusor contractile responses to α-adrenergic stimulation increased in old male and female rats (Saito et al, 1991, 1993; Lin et al, 1992a; Nishimoto et al, 1995).

The detrusor response to β-adrenergic stimulation is reduced in old male rats (Lin et al, 1992a; Nishimoto et al, 1995) along with a reduction in the density of β-adrenergic receptors and a decreased cAMP production (Nishimoto et al, 1995) in response to β-adrenergic stimulation. The combination of an increase in the α-adrenergic excitatory responses and decreased β-adrenergic inhibitory responses results in a net contracting effect of norepinephrine on the aged bladders in contrast to the relaxing effect of norepinephrine in the young bladders (Lin et al, 1992a). When norepinephrine is released by increased sympathetic activity during bladder filling (de Groat et al, 1993), the enhanced adrenergic contractile response in the aged bladders might reduce functional storage capacity and thereby contribute to urinary frequency and urgency in the older persons.

Another area that is undergoing research is the role of changes in innervation and development of gap junction among bladder smooth muscle cells. Although there is controversy whether a gap junction forms with aging, it is clear that structural changes in the detrusor muscle occur with aging (Elbadawi et al, 1997a, 1997b).

Many elderly have increased residual urine and a diminished uroflow rate. What is an explanation for these common clinical findings? Lin and coworkers demonstrated that bladders of old rats had lower energy production capability and became fatigued faster than did young bladders after repeated contraction (Lin et al, 1992a; Yu et al, 1997). Lower energy-producing capability found in the aged rat bladders has a close link with lower mitochondrial enzyme activity (Yu et al, 1997). Although the bladders from old rats fatigue faster, this is not due to a decreased release of neurotransmitters from nerve terminals. Several studies have shown that the frequency-response curve for electrically evoked bladder contractions was similar in young and old rat bladders (Yu et al, 1996), indicating that the release of neurotransmitters from presynaptic nerve endings was not altered during aging.

Bladder Sensation

Is there an alteration in bladder sensation with aging? The data are at present inconclusive (Collas and Malone-Lee, 1996). It was postulated that the decreased bladder sensation may prematurely terminate the reflex detrusor contraction, resulting in incomplete bladder emptying (Yu et al, 1997). A contradictory study demonstrated that the intravesical pressure during micturition was greater in old rats compared with young rats, but there were no age-related differences in the bladder volume threshold for inducing micturition (Chun et al, 1988). The pattern and density of CGRP-immunoreactive afferent nerves were also not changed in old rat bladders (Warburton and Santer, 1994).

Clinical studies reported a significantly lower pelvic floor position in the older females (Pinho et al, 1990) and a reduction in anorectal "squeeze" pressure. The altered pelvic floor muscle function was accompanied by an increase in the mean pudendal nerve terminal motor latency and an increase in the nerve fiber density in the striated anal sphincter as examined by single-fiber electromyography. It was concluded that these changes were due to damage to pudendal nerve and a later compensatory reinnervation in the sphincter muscle (Laurberg and Swash, 1989). Although these findings focused on anal sphincter physiology, in view of the close anatomic location and common innervation, such findings also imply a decreased innervation of the pelvic floor and urinary sphincter in the aged women.

Neurogenic Mechanisms Underlying Detrusor Overactivity

Changes in bladder innervation orchestrated by neurotrophins manufactured by detrusor smooth muscle are temporally linked with detrusor overactivity (see Fig. 56–31). The ability of local anesthetics, intravesical afferent neurotoxins, and destruction of afferent nerves in the bladder neck and prostate to reduce urgency, frequency, and urge incontinence indicates an important role for afferent evoked reflexes (Chalfin and Bradley, 1982). The development of a spinal reflex (ice-water test response) in patients with neurogenic bladders (Geirsson, 1993) as well as in patients with bladder outlet obstruction (Chai et al, 1998; Hirayama et al, 2003, 2005) suggests a common underlying plasticity in nerves supplying the bladder. Moreover, the association between elevated blood pressure and lower urinary tract symptoms in patients with benign prostatic hyperplasia (Pool, 1994; Sugaya et al, 2003) provides a link between changes in sympathetic tone and voiding complaints.

Thus, **the unifying story that is present in each of the pathologic conditions just discussed is neuroplasticity. Urinary frequency and possibly urge incontinence are often associated with elevated neurotrophin production, enhanced C-fiber afferent evoked bladder reflex, and noradrenergic function. The realization that nerves supplying the lower urinary tract can undergo long-term changes that lead to detrusor overactivity offers a novel avenue for therapeutic intervention.**

SUMMARY

This chapter began with the premise that the lower urinary tract has two main functions: storage and periodic elimination of urine. These functions are regulated by unique biomechanics of bladder and urethral muscles as well as by a complex neural control system located in the brain and spinal cord. The neural control system performs like a simple switching circuit to maintain a reciprocal relationship between the reservoir (urinary bladder) and the outlet components (urethra and urethral sphincter) of the urinary tract. The switching circuit is modulated by various neurotransmitters and is sensitive to a variety of drugs. In infants, the switching circuits function in a purely reflex manner to produce involuntary voiding; however, in adults, urine storage and release are subject to voluntary control (see Fig. 56–1).

Injuries or diseases of the nervous system in adults can disrupt the voluntary control of micturition, causing the re-emergence of reflex micturition, resulting in detrusor overactivity and incontinence. Because of the complexity of the central nervous control of the lower urinary tract, incontinence can result from a variety of neurologic disorders. Experimental studies indicate that detrusor overactivity occurs after a wide range of neurologic diseases, including interruption of cortical inhibitory circuits, disruption of basal ganglia function in models of Parkinson's disease, damage to pathways from the brain to the spinal cord (multiple sclerosis, spinal cord injury), and sensitization of bladder afferents. Various mechanisms contribute to the emergence of bladder dysfunction, including reorganization of synaptic connections in the spinal cord, changes in the expression of neurotransmitters and receptors, alterations in neural target organ interactions mediated by neurotrophic factors, and changes in smooth muscle function. An understanding of the physiologic events mediating micturition and continence provides a rational basis for the management of lower urinary tract dysfunction.

FUTURE RESEARCH

During the past few years, research in neurourology and female urology has led to the development of new concepts regarding the etiology of unstable bladder dysfunction and urinary incontinence. The breakthroughs outlined in this chapter have stimulated the development of new therapeutic approaches for incontinence, including the local administration of botulinum toxin and afferent neurotoxins, such as capsaicin and RTX. What are the research priorities for the future? It will be important to focus on the development of neuropharmacologic agents that can suppress the unique components of abnormal bladder reflex mechanisms and thereby act selectively to diminish symptoms without altering normal voiding function.

Neurourologic research with a clinical application is intensifying at major medical centers and also in the pharmaceutical industry. With the aging population across all the developed nations and public education that is demystifying the stigma of bladder control problems and urinary incontinence, more patients are seeking help. The dramatically expanding commercial markets and need for improved medications for the lower urinary tract have been recognized and publicized. We need better drugs and approaches to help the 85% of people with detrusor overactivity and urinary incontinence who have not yet sought medical help.

To end this chapter, we would like to look into our crystal ball and speculate on a few areas of research that we think may pay off within the next 5 years with new and better treatment of urinary incontinence:

1. Bladder-specific K^+ channel openers for treatment of overactive and hypersensitive bladder. Can truly bladder smooth muscle– or afferent nerve–specific K^+ channel openers be developed? This treatment may alleviate the unstable and sensitive bladder without side effects such as dry mouth.
2. Can the drug companies develop a truly bladder-specific and effective anticholinergic drug with *no* dry mouth?
3. Tachykinin antagonists are appealing in that they may be effective for unstable and painful bladder conditions without increasing residual urine volumes. Can clinically useful and safe NK antagonists be developed?
4. Urethral smooth muscle– or skeletal muscle–specific α agonist or 5-HT reuptake inhibitors that treat stress urinary incontinence. We need an effective drug for stress incontinence.
5. Although not as clinically obvious as the ideas just listed, we believe that drugs that can affect urothelial trafficking and permeability may be tremendously helpful. These types of drugs not only can aid the overactive and painful bladder but may have indications for bladder cancer and even urinary tract infection.
6. In addition, given that spontaneous activity in the detrusor muscle and interstitial cells in the bladder wall has

an important role in the regulation of bladder activity, targeting detrusor muscles or interstitial cells could be effective to treat detrusor overactivity, especially of myogenic origin.

Beyond the horizon of near-term advancement, we predict a brave new paradigm in neurourology. What has already started is the evolution of unstoppable forces of change in medicine that include pharmacogenomics, tissue engineering, and gene therapy. These will change how we practice urology:

Drug by Design (Pharmacogenomics). Medicine will be tailored to the genetic makeup of each individual. Through microarray gene chip technology, we will know how a patient metabolizes medication, receptor profile, and allergy risk. These factors can be used to screen against a list of medications before therapy. A urologist will then be able to always prescribe the best drug for each patient without the risk of side effects.

Tissue Engineering. Rapid advances are being made in tissue engineering (Atala, 2004) and organ reconstruction with autologous tissue and stem cells (Chancellor et al, 2000). We envision a day, in the not too distant future, when stress incontinence is cured not with a cadaver ligament and metal screws into the bones but rather with minimally invasive injection of muscle stem cells that will not only bulk up the deficient sphincter but actually improve the deficient sphincter's contractility.

Gene Therapy. Benign prostatic hyperplasia (Marcelli et al, 2000), diabetic neurogenic bladder (Phelan et al, 2000; Goins et al, 2001; Sasaki et al, 2004), and even interstitial cystitis (Franks et al, 2000) may be cured with one or more treatments with a gene vector that the urologist will inject into the bladder or prostate. The injection of a viral vector expression apoptotic factor can direct the hypertrophied prostate to shrink. Injection of NGF through a herpesvirus vector into the bladder of a diabetic person may promote the recovery of bladder sensation and innervation (Fig. 56–33). Last, what about the single condition most troubling to just about every urologist, interstitial cystitis? Can the introduction of a viral vector that is targeted to nerves and that carries a gene for an endogenous opioid peptide that blocks pain pathways be used to help alleviate pain, regardless of the cause of interstitial cystitis?

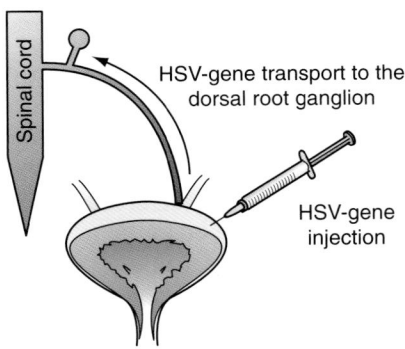

Figure 56–33. Illustration depicting the concept of gene therapy for neurogenic bladder, voiding dysfunction, and pain. Herpes simplex virus (HSV) is used as a vector for directed transfection of nerves that innervate the urinary bladder. Such an approach has interesting potential for the treatment of bladder dysfunction.

The **smooth sphincter** refers to the smooth musculature of the bladder neck and proximal urethra. This is a physiologic but not an anatomic sphincter and one that is not under voluntary control. The **striated sphincter** refers to the striated musculature that is a part of the outer wall of the proximal urethra in both the male and the female (this portion is often referred to as the **intrinsic or intramural striated sphincter**) and the bulky skeletal muscle group that closely surrounds the urethra at the level of the membranous portion in the male and primarily the middle segment in the female (often referred to as the **extrinsic or extramural striated sphincter**). The extramural portion is the classically described **external urethral sphincter** and is under voluntary control (for a detailed discussion see Chapter 56, Physiology and Pharmacology of the Bladder and Urethra; Zderic et al, 2002; DeLancey et al, 2002).

MECHANISMS UNDERLYING THE TWO PHASES OF FUNCTION: OVERVIEW

This section briefly summarizes pertinent points regarding the physiology and pharmacology of the various mechanisms underlying normal bladder filling/storage and emptying/voiding abnormalities, which constitute the pathophysiologic mechanisms seen in the various types of dysfunction of the lower urinary tract. The general information is consistent with that detailed by deGroat and associates (1993, 1999, 2001), Wein and Barrett (1988), Zderic and colleagues (2002), Steers 1998), Wein (1998, 2002), Andersson and Arner (2004), Andersson and Wein (2004), Morrison and colleagues (2005), and Mostwin and colleagues (2005). Other specific references are provided only when particularly applicable.

Bladder Response during Filling

The normal adult bladder response to filling at a physiologic rate is an almost imperceptible change in intravesical pressure. During at least the initial stages of bladder filling, after unfolding of the bladder wall from its collapsed state, **this very high compliance (Δ volume/Δ pressure) of the bladder is due primarily to its elastic and viscoelastic properties.** Elasticity allows the constituents of the bladder wall to stretch to a certain degree without any increase in tension. **Viscoelasticity** allows stretch to induce a rise in tension followed by a decay ("stress relaxation") when the filling (stretch stimulus) slows or stops. The viscoelastic properties are considered to be primarily due to the characteristics of the extracellular matrix in the bladder wall. Andersson and Arner (2004) cite references demonstrating that the main extracellular components are elastic fibers and collagen fibrils—present in the serosa, between muscle bundles, and between the smooth muscle cells in the muscle bundles. Brading and colleagues (1999) add that they believe that there is continuous contractile activity in the smooth muscle cells to adjust their length during filling but without the type of synchronous activity that would increase intravesical pressure, impede filling, and could cause urinary leakage. Clinically and urodynamically, therefore, the bladder seems "relaxed." The urothelium also expands but must preserve its barrier function while doing so.

There may also be a non-neurogenic active component to the storage properties of the bladder. Hawthorn and coauthors (2000) have suggested that an as yet unidentifiable relaxing factor is released from the urothelium during filling and storage, and some (Andersson and Wein, 2004) have suggested that urothelium-released nitric oxide may have an inhibitory effect on afferent mechanisms as well.

The viscoelastic properties of the stroma (bladder wall less smooth muscle and epithelium) and the urodynamically relaxed detrusor muscle thus account for the passive mechanical properties and normal bladder compliance seen during filling. The main components of the stroma are collagen and elastin. In the usual clinical setting, filling cystometry seems to show a slight increase in intravesical pressure, but Klevmark (1974, 1999) elegantly showed that **this pressure rise is a function of the fact that cystometric filling is carried out at a greater than physiologic rate and that, at physiologic filling rates, there is essentially no rise in bladder pressure until bladder capacity is reached.**

When the collagen component increases, compliance decreases. This can occur with chronic inflammation, bladder outlet obstruction, neurologic decentralization, and various types of injury. **Once decreased compliance has occurred because of a replacement by collagen of other components of the stroma, it is generally unresponsive to pharmacologic manipulation, hydraulic distention, or nerve section.** Most often, under those circumstances, augmentation cystoplasty is required to achieve satisfactory reservoir function.

Does the nervous system affect the normal bladder response to filling? At a certain level of bladder filling, **spinal sympathetic reflexes** facilitatory to bladder filling/storage are clearly evoked in animals, a concept developed over the years by deGroat and associates (deGroat et al, 1993; Zderic et al, 2002; deGroat and Yoshimura, 2001; Chancellor and Yoshimura, 2002; Yoshimura and Chancellor, Chapter 56, Physiology and Pharmacology of the Bladder and Urethra), who have also cited indirect evidence to support such a role in humans. This **inhibitory effect is thought to be mediated primarily by sympathetic modulation of cholinergic ganglionic transmission.** Through this reflex mechanism, **two other possibilities exist for promoting filling/storage.** One is neurally mediated stimulation of the predominantly α-adrenergic receptors in the area of the smooth sphincter, the net result of which would be to cause an increase in resistance in that area. The second is neurally mediated stimulation of the predominantly β-adrenergic receptors (inhibitory) in the bladder body smooth musculature, which would cause a decrease in bladder wall tension. McGuire and colleagues (1983) have also proposed a direct inhibition of detrusor motor neurons in the sacral spinal cord during bladder filling related to increased afferent pudendal nerve activity generated by receptors in the striated sphincter. **Good evidence also seems to exist to support a tonic inhibitory effect of other neurotransmitters (e.g., opioids) on the micturition reflex at various levels of the neural axis.** Bladder filling and consequent wall distention may also release autocrine-like factors that themselves influence contractility (e.g., nitric oxide, prostaglandins, peptides).

Outlet Response during Filling

There is a gradual increase in urethral pressure during bladder filling, contributed to at least by the striated sphinc-

teric element and perhaps by the smooth sphincteric element as well. The rise in urethral pressure seen during the filling/storage phase of micturition can be correlated with an increase in efferent pudendal nerve impulse frequency and in electromyographic activity of the periurethal striated musculature. This constitutes the efferent limb of a spinal somatic reflex, the so-called **guarding reflex**, which results in a gradual increase in striated sphincter activity during normal bladder filling and storage. Although it seems logical and certainly compatible with neuropharmacologic, neurophysiologic, and neuromorphologic data to assume that the muscular component of the smooth sphincter also contributes to the change in urethral response during bladder filling, probably through norepinephrine-mediated contraction, it is extremely difficult to prove this either experimentally or clinically. The direct and circumstantial evidence in favor of such a hypothesis has been summarized by Wein and Barrett (1988), Elbadawi (1988), Brading (1999), and Andersson and Wein (2004).

The **passive properties of the urethral wall** certainly deserve mention because these undoubtedly play a large role in the maintenance of continence (Zinner et al, 1983; Brading, 1999). Urethral wall tension develops within the outer layers of the urethra; however, urethral pressure is a product not only of the active characteristics of smooth and striated muscle but also of the passive characteristics of the elastic, collagenous, and vascular components of the urethral wall because this tension must be exerted on a soft or plastic inner layer capable of being compressed to a closed configuration—the "filler material" representing the submucosal portion of the urethra. The softer and more pliable this area is, the less pressure required by the tension-producing area to produce continence. Finally, whatever the compressive forces, the lumen of the urethra must be capable of being obliterated by a watertight seal. This "mucosal seal" mechanism explains why a very thin-walled rubber tube requires less pressure to close an open end when the inner layer is coated with a fine layer of grease than when it is not, the latter case being much like scarred or atrophic urethral mucosa.

Voiding with a Normal Bladder Contraction

Although many factors are involved in the initiation of micturition, in adults it is **intravesical pressure producing the sensation of distention that is primarily responsible for the initiation of normal voluntarily induced emptying of the lower urinary tract. Although the origin of the parasympathetic neural outflow to the bladder, the pelvic nerve, is in the sacral spinal cord, the actual coordinating center for the micturition reflex in an intact neural axis is in the rostral brain stem**, and the complete neural circuit for normal micturition includes the ascending and descending spinal cord pathways to and from this area and the facilitatory and inhibitory influences from other parts of the brain, particularly the cerebral cortex. **The final step in voluntarily induced micturition involves inhibition of the somatic neural efferent activity to the striated sphincter and an inhibition of all aspects of any spinal sympathetic reflexes evoked during filling. Efferent parasympathetic pelvic nerve**

activity is ultimately what is responsible for a highly coordinated contraction of the bulk of the bladder smooth musculature.

A decrease in outlet resistance occurs, with adaptive shaping or funneling of the relaxed bladder outlet. Besides the inhibition of any continence-promoting reflexes that have occurred during bladder filling, the change in outlet resistance may also involve an active relaxation of the smooth sphincter area through a nonadrenergic noncholinergic (NANC) mechanism, probably mediated by nitric oxide (Andersson and Arner, 2004; Andersson and Wein, 2004). **The adaptive changes that occur in the outlet are probably also due at least in part to the anatomic interrelationships of the smooth muscle of the bladder base and proximal urethra.** Longitudinal smooth muscle continuity (Chancellor and Yoshimura, 2002) would promote shortening and widening of the proximal urethra during a coordinated emptying bladder contraction. Other reflexes that are elicited by bladder contraction and by the passage of urine through the urethra may reinforce and facilitate complete bladder emptying. Superimposed on these autonomic and somatic reflexes are complex, modifying supraspinal inputs from other central neuronal networks. These facilitatory and inhibitory impulses, which originate from several areas of the nervous system, allow the full conscious control of micturition in the adult.

Urinary Incontinence during Abdominal Pressure Increases

During voluntarily initiated micturition, the bladder pressure becomes higher than the outlet pressure and certain adaptive changes occur in the shape of the bladder outlet with consequent passage of urine into and through the proximal urethra. One could reasonably ask, **why do such changes not occur with increases in intravesical pressure that are similar in magnitude but that are produced only by changes in intra-abdominal pressure, such as straining or coughing?** First, a coordinated bladder contraction does not occur in response to such stimuli, clearly emphasizing the fact that increases in total intravesical pressure are by no means equivalent to emptying ability. Normally, for urine to flow into the proximal urethra, not only must there be an increase in intravesical pressure but also the increase must be a product of a coordinated bladder contraction, occurring through a neurally mediated mechanism, and must be associated with characteristic conformational and tension changes in the bladder neck and proximal urethral area.

Assuming that the bladder outlet is competent at rest, a major factor in the prevention of urinary leakage during increases in intra-abdominal pressure is the fact that there is **at least equal pressure transmission to the proximal urethra (the midurethra as well as in the female) during such activity.** This phenomenon was first described by Enhorning (1961) and has been confirmed in virtually every urodynamic laboratory since that time. **Failure of this mechanism is an invariable correlate of effort-related urinary incontinence in the female and male. The increase in urethral closure pressure that is seen with increments in intra-abdominal pressure normally actually exceeds the intra-abdominal** pressure increase, indicating that active muscular function related to a reflex increase in striated sphincter activity or other factors that increase urethral resistance is also involved in preventing such leakage. Tanagho (1978) was the first to provide direct evidence of this. A more complete description of the factors involved in sphincteric incontinence can be found later in this chapter and in Chapter 60, Urinary Incontinence: Epidemiology, Pathophysiology, Evaluation, and Management Overview, and Chapter 66, Vaginal Reconstructive Surgery for Sphincteric Incontinence and Prolapse.

Sensory Aspects

Most of the afferent input from the bladder and urethra reaches the spinal cord through the pelvic nerve and dorsal root ganglia and some through the hypogastric nerve. Afferent input from the striated muscle of the sphincter and pelvic floor travels in the pudendal nerve. The most important afferents for initiating and maintaining normal micturition are those in the pelvic nerve, relaying to the sacral spinal cord. These convey impulses from tension, volume, and nociceptors located in the serosal, muscle, and urothelial and suburothelial layers of the bladder and urethra. In a neurologically normal adult, the sensation of filling and distention is what develops during filling/storage and initiates the reflexes responsible for emptying/voiding (deGroat and Yoshimura, 2001; Chancellor and Yoshimura, 2002; Morrison et al, 2005; Yoshimura and Chancellor, Chapter 56, Physiology and Pharmacology of the Bladder and Uretha). Alterations in this finely tuned pathway can be responsible for significant alterations in lower urinary tract function.

THE MICTURITION CYCLE: SIMPLIFICATION AND OVERVIEW

Filling and Storage

Bladder accommodation during filling is a primarily passive phenomenon dependent on the elastic and viscoelastic properties of the bladder wall and the lack of parasympathetic excitatory input. An increase in outlet resistance occurs by means of the striated sphincter somatic guarding reflex. In at least some species, a sympathetic reflex also contributes to storage by (1) increasing outlet resistance by increasing tension on the smooth sphincter, (2) inhibiting bladder contractility through an inhibitory effect on parasympathetic ganglia, and (3) causing a decrease in tension of bladder smooth muscle. Continence is maintained during increases in intra-abdominal pressure by the intrinsic competence of the bladder outlet (bladder neck and proximal/middle urethra) and the pressure transmission ratio to this area with respect to the intravesical contents. A further increase in striated sphincter activity, on a reflex basis, is also contributory.

Emptying/Voiding

Emptying (voiding) can be voluntary or involuntary and involves an inhibition of the spinal somatic and sympathetic reflexes and activation of the vesical parasympathetic pathways, the organizational center for which is in the rostral brain stem. Initially, there is a relaxation of the outlet musculature, mediated not only by the cessation of the somatic and sympathetic spinal reflexes but probably also by a relaxing factor, very possibly nitric oxide, released by parasympathetic stimulation or by some effect of bladder smooth muscle contraction itself. A highly coordinated parasympathetically induced contraction of the bulk of the bladder smooth musculature occurs, with shaping or funneling of the relaxed outlet, owing at least in part to a smooth muscle continuity between the bladder base and the proximal urethra. With amplification and facilitation of the bladder contraction from other peripheral reflexes and from spinal cord supraspinal sources, and in the absence of anatomic obstruction between the bladder and the urethral meatus, complete emptying occurs.

ABNORMALITIES OF FILLING/STORAGE AND EMPTYING/VOIDING: OVERVIEW OF PATHOPHYSIOLOGY

The pathophysiology of failure of the lower urinary tract to fill with or store urine adequately or to empty adequately must logically be secondary to reasons related to the bladder, the outlet, or both (Wein, 1981; Wein and Barrett, 1988).

Filling/Storage Failure

Absolute or relative failure of the bladder to fill with and store urine adequately results from bladder overactivity (involuntary contraction or decreased compliance), decreased outlet resistance, heightened or altered sensation, or a combination.

Bladder Overactivity

Overactivity of the bladder during filling/storage can be expressed as phasic involuntary contractions, as low compliance, or as a combination. Involuntary contractions are most commonly seen in association with neurologic disease or injury; however, they may be associated with increased afferent input related to inflammation or irritation of the bladder or urethral wall, bladder outlet obstruction, stress urinary incontinence (perhaps because of sudden entry of urine into the proximal urethra), or aging (probably related to neural degeneration) or may be idiopathic. Staskin (2001) and Mostwin and coworkers (2005) also hypothesized that decreased stimulation from the pelvic floor can contribute to phasic bladder overactivity. **Decreased compliance** during filling/storage may be secondary to neurologic injury or disease, usually at a sacral or infrasacral level, but may result from any process that destroys the viscoelastic or elastic properties of the bladder wall. **Bladder-related storage failure may also occur in the absence of overactivity because of increased afferent input from inflammation, irritation, other causes of hypersensitivity, and pain.** The causes may be chemical, psychologic, or idiopathic. One classic example is painful bladder syndrome, a term that is replacing "interstitial cystitis" (see Chapter 10, Painful Bladder Syndrome/Interstitial Cystitis and Related Disorders).

Outlet Underactivity

Decreased outlet resistance may result from any process that damages the innervation or structural elements of the smooth or striated sphincter, or both, or support of the bladder outlet in the female. This may occur with **neurologic disease or injury, surgical or other mechanical trauma, or aging. Classically, sphincteric incontinence in the female was categorized into relatively discrete entities:** (1) so-called **genuine stress incontinence** and (2) **intrinsic sphincter deficiency**, originally described as type III stress incontinence (DeLancey et al, 1994; Mostwin et al, 2005; Chapters 60, 66, and 67). **Genuine stress incontinence in the female** was described as associated with hypermobility of the bladder outlet because of poor pelvic support and with an outlet that was competent at rest but lost its competence only during increases in intra-abdominal pressure. **Intrinsic sphincter deficiency** (ISD) described a nonfunctional or very poorly functional bladder neck and proximal urethra at rest. **The implication of classic ISD was that a surgical procedure designed to correct only urethral hypermobility would have a relatively high failure rate, as opposed to one designed to improve urethral coaptation and compression. The contemporary view is that the majority of cases of effort-related incontinence in the female involve varying proportions of support-related factors and ISD.** It is possible to have outlet-related incontinence that is due only to ISD but not due solely to hypermobility or poor support—some ISD must exist.

Stress- or effort-related urinary incontinence is a symptom that arises primarily from **damage to muscles, nerves, or connective tissue, or a combination, within the pelvic floor** (DeLancey et al, 2002; Mostwin et al, 2005). Urethral support is important in the female, the urethra normally being supported by the action of the levator ani muscles through their connection to the endopelvic fascia of the anterior vaginal wall. Damage to the connection between this fascia and this muscle, damage to the nerve supply, or direct muscle damage can therefore influence continence. Bladder neck function is likewise important, and loss of normal bladder neck closure can result in incontinence despite normal urethral support. In older writings, the urethra was sometimes ignored as a factor contributing to continence in the female, and the site of continence was thought to be exclusively the bladder neck. However, in approximately 50% of continent women, urine enters the urethra during increases in abdominal pressure. The continence point in these women (highest point of pressure transmission) is at the midurethra.

Urethral hypermobility implies weakness of the pelvic floor supporting structures. During increases in intra-abdominal pressure, there is descent of the bladder neck and proximal urethra. If the outlet opens concomitantly, stress urinary incontinence ensues. In the classic form of urethral hypermobility, there is rotational descent of the bladder neck and urethra. However, the urethra may also descend without rotation (it shortens and widens), or the posterior wall of the urethra may be pulled (sheared) open while the anterior wall remains fixed. However, urethral hypermobility is often present in women who are not incontinent, and thus the mere presence of urethral hypermobility is not sufficient to make a diagnosis of a sphincter abnormality unless urinary incontinence is also demonstrated. The "**hammock hypothesis**" of John DeLancey (1994) proposes that for stress incontinence to occur with hypermobility, there must be a lack of stability of the suburethral supportive layer. This theory proposes that the effect of abdominal pressure increases on the normal bladder outlet, if the suburethral supportive layer is firm, is to compress the urethra rapidly and effectively. If the supportive suburethral layer is lax or movable, or both, compression is not as effective. **Intrinsic sphincter dysfunction** denotes an intrinsic malfunction of the urethral sphincter mechanism itself. In its most overt form, it is characterized by a bladder neck that is open at rest and a low Valsalva leak point pressure and urethral closure pressure (see Chapter 58) and is usually the result of prior surgery, trauma with scarring, or a neurologic lesion.

Urethral instability refers to the rare phenomenon of episodic decreases in outlet pressure unrelated to increases in bladder or abdominal pressure. The term urethral instability is probably a misnomer because many believe that the drop in urethral pressure represents simply the urethral component of what would otherwise be a bladder contraction/urethral relaxation in an individual whose bladder does not measurably contract, for either myogenic or neurogenic reasons. Little has appeared in the literature about this entity since the last edition of this text.

In theory at least, **categories of outlet-related incontinence in the male are similar to those in the female. Sphincteric incontinence in the male is not, however, associated with hypermobility of the bladder neck and proximal urethra but is similar to what is termed intrinsic sphincter dysfunction in the female.** There is essentially no information regarding the topic of urethral instability in the male.

> The treatment of filling/storage abnormalities is directed toward inhibiting bladder contractility, decreasing sensory output, or mechanically increasing bladder capacity and/or toward increasing outlet resistance, the latter either continuously or just during increases in intra-abdominal pressure.

Emptying/Voiding Failure

> Absolute or relative failure to empty the bladder results from decreased bladder contractility (a decrease in magnitude or duration), increased outlet resistance, or both.

Bladder Underactivity

Absolute or relative failure of bladder contractility may result from temporary or permanent alteration in one of the neuromuscular mechanisms necessary for initiating and maintaining a normal detrusor contraction. Inhibition of the voiding reflex in a neurologically normal individual may also occur; it may be by a reflex mechanism secondary to increased afferent input, especially from the pelvic and perineal areas, or may be psychogenic. Non-neurogenic causes also include impairment of bladder smooth muscle function, which may result from overdistention, various centrally or peripherally acting drugs, severe infection, or fibrosis.

Outlet Overactivity or Obstruction

Pathologically increased outlet resistance is much more common in men than in women. Although it is most often secondary to anatomic obstruction, it may be secondary to a failure of relaxation or active contraction of the striated or smooth sphincter during bladder contraction (see Chapter 59, Lower Urinary Tract Dysfunction in Neurologic Injury and Disease). Striated sphincter dyssynergia is a common cause of functional or nonanatomic (as opposed to fixed anatomic) obstruction in patients with neurologic disease or injury. A common cause of outlet obstruction in the female is compression or fibrosis following surgery for sphincteric incontinence.

> The treatment of emptying failure generally consists of maneuvers to increase intravesical/detrusor pressure, facilitate the micturition reflex, decrease outlet resistance, or a combination. If other means fail or are impractical, intermittent catheterization is an effective way to circumvent emptying failure.

CLASSIFICATION SYSTEMS

Based on the data obtained from the neurourologic evaluation, a given voiding dysfunction can be categorized in an ever-increasing number of descriptive systems. The purpose of any classification system should be to facilitate understanding and management and to avoid confusion among those who are concerned with the problem for which the system was designed. A good classification should serve as intellectual shorthand and should convey, in a few key words or phrases, the essence of a clinical situation. An ideal system for all types of voiding dysfunction would include or imply a number of factors: (1) the conclusions reached from urodynamic testing, (2) expected clinical symptoms, and (3) approximate site and type of a neurologic lesion or lack of one. If the various categories accurately portray pathophysiology, treatment options should then be obvious, and a treatment "menu" should be evident. **Most systems of classification for voiding dysfunction were formulated primarily to describe dysfunction secondary to neurologic disease or injury. The ideal system should be applicable to all types of voiding dysfunction.** Based on the data obtained from the neurourologic evaluation, a given voiding dysfunction can be categorized in a number of descriptive systems. **No one system is perfect.**

Most major systems or types of systems in use are reviewed, along with their advantages, disadvantages, and applicability. Understanding the rationale and shortcomings of each system significantly improves one's knowledge of voiding function and dysfunction.

The Functional System

Classification of voiding dysfunction can be formulated on a simple functional basis, describing the dysfunction in terms of whether the deficit produced is primarily one of the filling/storage or the emptying/voiding phase of micturition (Table 57–1) (Wein, 1981; Wein and Barrett, 1988). The genesis of such a system was proposed initially by F. Brantley Scott's group (Quesada et al, 1968). This simple-minded scheme assumes only that, whatever their differences, all "experts" would agree on the two-phase concept of micturition (filling/storage and emptying/voiding) and on the simple overall mechanisms underlying the normality of each phase (see previous discussion).

Storage failure results because of either **bladder or outlet abnormalities or a combination.** The proven **bladder abnormalities** very simply include only involuntary bladder contractions, low compliance, and heightened or altered sensation. The **outlet abnormalities** can include only an intermittent or continuous decrease in outlet resistance.

Emptying failure, likewise, can occur because of **bladder or outlet abnormalities or a combination.** The bladder side includes only inadequate or unsustained bladder contractility, and the outlet side includes only anatomic obstruction and sphincter dyssynergia.

There are indeed some types of voiding dysfunction that represent combinations of filling/storage and emptying/voiding abnormalities. Within this scheme, however, these become readily understandable and their detection and treatment can be logically described. Various aspects of physiology and pathophysiology are always related more to one phase of micturition than another. **All aspects of urodynamic and videourodynamic evaluation can be conceptualized in this functional manner as to exactly what they evaluate in terms of either bladder or outlet activity during filling/storage and emptying/voiding** (Table 57–2). In addition, **one can easily classify all known treatments for voiding dysfunction under the broad categories of whether they facilitate filling/storage and emptying/voiding and whether they do so by an action primarily on the bladder or on one or more of the components of the bladder outlet** (Tables 57–3 and 57–4).

Failure in either category generally is not absolute but more often is relative. Such a functional system can easily be "expanded" and made more complicated to include etiologic

Table 57–1. **The Functional Classification**
Failure to Store
Because of the bladder
Because of the outlet
Failure to Empty
Because of the bladder
Because of the outlet

Table 57-2. Urodynamics Simplified

	Bladder	Outlet
Filling/storage phase	Pves[1]Pdet[2] (FCMG[3]) DLPP[4]	UPP[5] VLPP[6] FLUORO[7]
Emptying phase	Pves[8]Pdet[9] (VCMG)[10]	MUPP[11] FLUORO[12] EMG[13]
		(_____)
		_____ FLOW[14] _____
		_____ RU[15] _____

This functional conceptualization of urodynamics categorizes each study as to whether it examines bladder or outlet activity during the filling/storage or emptying phase of micturition. In this scheme, uroflow and residual urine integrate the activity of the bladder and the outlet during the emptying phase.
[1,2]Total bladder (Pves) and detrusor (Pdet) pressures during a filling cystometrogram (FCMG).
[3]Filling cystometrogram.
[4]Detrusor leak point pressure.
[5]Urethral pressure profilometry.
[6]Valsalva leak point pressure.
[7]Fluoroscopy of outlet during filling/storage.
[8,9]Total bladder and detrusor pressures during a voiding cystometrogram (VCMG).
[10]Voiding cystometrogram.
[11]Micturitional urethral pressure profilometry.
[12]Fluoroscopy of outlet during emptying.
[13]Electromyography of periurethral striated musculature.
[14]Flowmetry.
[15]Residual urine.

or specific urodynamic connotations (Table 57–5). However, the simplified system is perfectly workable and avoids argument in the complex situations in which the exact etiology or urodynamic mechanism for a voiding dysfunction cannot be agreed upon.

Proper use of the functional system for a given voiding dysfunction obviously requires a reasonably accurate notion of what the urodynamic data show. However, **an exact diagnosis is not required for treatment.** It should be recognized that **some patients do not have only a discrete storage or emptying failure, and the existence of combination deficits must be recognized to utilize this system classification properly.** For instance, the classic T10 paraplegic patient after spinal shock generally exhibits a relative failure to store because of involuntary bladder contraction and a relative failure to empty the bladder because of striated sphincter dyssynergia. With such a combination deficit, to utilize this classification system as a guide to treatment, one must assume that one of the deficits is primary and that significant improvement will result from its treatment alone or that the voiding dysfunction can be converted primarily to a disorder of either storage or emptying by means of nonsurgical or surgical therapy. The resultant deficit can then be treated or circumvented. Using this example, the combined deficit in a T10 paraplegic patient can be converted primarily to a storage failure by procedures directed at the dyssynergic striated sphincter; the resultant incontinence (secondary to involuntary contraction) can be circumvented (in a male) with an external collecting device. Alternatively, the deficit can be converted primarily to an emptying failure by pharmacologic or surgical measures designed to abolish or reduce the involuntary contraction, and the

Table 57-3. Therapy to Facilitate Urine Storage/Bladder Filling

Bladder Related (Inhibiting Bladder Contractility, Decreasing Sensory Input and/or Increasing Bladder Capacity)

Behavioral therapy, including any or all of
  Education
  Bladder training
  Timed bladder emptying or prompted voiding
  Fluid restriction
  Pelvic floor physiotherapy ± biofeedback
Pharmacologic therapy (oral, intravesical, intradetrusor)
  Anticholinergic agents
  Drugs with mixed actions
  Calcium antagonists
  Potassium channel openers
  Prostaglandin inhibitors
  β-Adrenergic agonists
  α-Adrenergic antagonists
  Tricyclic antidepressants; serotonin and norepinephrine reuptake inhibitors
  Dimethyl sulfoxide (DMSO)
  Polysynaptic inhibitors
  Capsaicin, resiniferatoxin, and like agents
  Botulinum toxin
Bladder overdistention
Electrical stimulation and neuromodulation
Acupuncture and electroacupuncture
Interruption of innervation
  Very central (subarachnoid block)
  Less central (sacral rhizotomy, selective sacral rhizotomy)
  Peripheral motor or/and sensory
Augmentation cystoplasty (auto, bowel, tissue engineering)

Outlet Related (Increasing Outlet Resistance)

Behavioral therapy
  Education
  Bladder training
  Timed bladder emptying or prompted voiding
  Fluid restriction
  Pelvic floor physiotherapy ± biofeedback
Electrical stimulation
Pharmacologic therapy
  α-Adrenergic agonists
  Tricyclic antidepressants; serotonin and norepinephrine reuptake inhibitors
  β-Adrenergic antagonists, agonists
Vaginal and perineal occlusive and/or supportive devices; urethral plugs
Nonsurgical periurethral bulking
  Collagen, synthetics, cell transfer
Vesicourethral suspension ± prolapse repair (female)
Sling procedures ± prolapse repair (female)
Closure of the bladder outlet
Artificial urinary sphincter
Bladder outlet reconstruction
Myoplasty (muscle transposition)

Circumventing the Problem

Absorbent products
External collecting devices
Antidiuretic hormone–like agents
Short-acting diuretics
Intermittent catheterization
Continuous catheterization
Urinary diversion

resultant emptying failure can then be circumvented with clean intermittent catheterization. Other examples of combination deficits include impaired bladder contractility or overactivity with sphincter dysfunction, bladder outlet obstruction with detrusor overactivity, bladder outlet obstruction with

Table 57–4. Therapy to Facilitate Bladder Emptying/Voiding

Bladder Related (Increasing Intravesical Pressure or Facilitating Bladder Contractility)

External compression, Valsalva
Promotion or initiating of reflex contraction
  Trigger zones or maneuvers
  Bladder "training"; tidal drainage
Pharmacologic therapy (oral, intravesical)
  Parasympathomimetic agents
  Prostaglandins
  Blockers of inhibition
    α-Adrenergic antagonists
    Opioid antagonists
Electrical stimulation
  Directly to the bladder or spinal cord
  Directly to the nerve roots
  Intravesical (transurethral)
  Neuromodulation
Reduction cystoplasty
Bladder myoplasty (muscle wrap)

Outlet Related (Increasing Outlet Resistance)

At a site of anatomic obstruction
  Pharmacologic therapy—decrease prostate size or tone
    α-Adrenergic antagonists
    5α-Reductase inhibitors
    Luteinizing hormone–releasing hormone agonists/antagonists
    Antiandrogens
  Prostatectomy, prostatotomy (diathermy, heat, laser)
  Bladder neck incision or resection
  Urethral stricture repair or dilation
  Intraurethral stent
  Balloon dilatation of stricture/contracture
At level of smooth sphincter
  Pharmacologic therapy
    α-Adrenergic antagonists
    β-Adrenergic agonists
  Transurethral resection or incision
  Y-V plasty
At level of striated sphincter
  Behavioral therapy ± biofeedback
  Pharmacologic therapy
    Benzodiazepines
    Baclofen
    Dantrolene
    α-Adrenergic antagonists
    Botulinum toxin (injection)
  Urethral overdilation
  Surgical sphincterotomy
  Urethral stent
  Pudendal nerve interruption

Circumventing the Problem

Intermittent catheterization
Continuous catheterization
Urinary diversion (conduit)

Table 57–5. The Expanded Functional Classification

I. Failure to store
  A. Because of the bladder
    1. Overactivity
      a. Involuntary contractions
        Neurologic disease or injury
        Bladder outlet obstruction (myogenic)
        Inflammation
        Idiopathic
      b. Decreased compliance
        Neurologic disease or injury
        Fibrosis
        Idiopathic
      c. Combination
    2. Hypersensitivity
      a. Inflammatory/infectious
      b. Neurologic
      c. Psychological
      d. Idiopathic
    3. Decreased pelvic floor activity (?)
    4. Combination
  B. Because of the outlet
    1. Combination (GSI and ISD)
    2. Genuine stress urinary incontinence (GSI)
      a. Lack of suburethral support
      b. Pelvic floor laxity, hypermobility
    3. Intrinsic sphincter deficiency (ISD)
      a. Neurologic disease or injury
      b. Fibrosis
  C. Combination
II. Failure to empty
  A. Because of the bladder
    1. Neurogenic
    2. Myogenic
    3. Psychogenic
    4. Idiopathic
  B. Because of the outlet
    1. Anatomic
      a. Prostatic obstruction
      b. Bladder neck contracture
      c. Urethral stricture in the male
      d. Urethral compression, fibrosis in the female
    2. Functional
      a. Smooth sphincter dyssynergia
      b. Striated sphincter dyssynergia
      c. Dysfunctional voiding
  C. Combination

reasons for overactivity (see Table 57–5) further in terms of neurogenic, myogenic, or anatomic causes and further subcategorize neurogenic in terms of decreased inhibitory control, increased afferent activity, increased sensitivity to efferent activity, and so on. The system is flexible.

International Continence Society Classification

The classification system proposed by the International Continence Society (ICS) (Table 57–6) is **in essence an extension of a urodynamic classification system.** The storage and voiding phases of micturition are described separately, and, within each, various designations are applied to describe bladder and urethral function (Abrams et al, 1988, 1992). Some of the definitions were changed by the standardization subcommittee of the International Continence Society in 2002 and the relevant changes are indicated here (Abrams et al,

sphincter malfunction, and detrusor overactivity with impaired contractility.

One of the advantages of this functional classification is that it allows the clinician the liberty of "playing" with the system to suit his or her own preferences without an alteration in the basic concept of "keep it simple but accurate and informative." For instance, one could easily substitute the terms overactive or oversensitive bladder and underactive outlet for because of the bladder and because of the outlet under "Failure to Store" in Table 57–1. One could choose to categorize the bladder

Table 57–6. The International Continence Society Classification

Storage Phase	Voiding Phase
Bladder Function	*Bladder Function*
Detrusor activity	Detrusor activity
Normal or stable	Normal
Overactive	Underactive
Neurogenic	Acontractile
Idiopathic	Areflexic
Bladder sensation	
Normal	*Urethral Function*
Increased or hypersensitive	Normal
Reduced or hyposensitive	Abnormal
Absent	Mechanical obstruction
Bladder capacity	Overactivity
Normal	Dysfunctional voiding
High	Detrusor sphincter dyssynergia
Low	Nonrelaxing urethral sphincter
	dysfunction
Urethral Function	
Normal closure mechanism	
Incompetent closure mechanism	

Adapted from Abrams et al (1988, 1992, 2002).

Table 57–7. A Urodynamic Classification

Detrusor Hyperreflexia (or Normoreflexia)
Coordinated sphincters
Striated sphincter dyssynergia
Smooth sphincter dyssynergia
Nonrelaxing smooth sphincter

Detrusor Areflexia
Coordinated sphincters
Nonrelaxing striated sphincter
Denervated striated sphincter
Nonrelaxing smooth sphincter

Adapted from Krane RJ, Siroky MB: Classification of voiding dysfunction: Value of classification systems. In Barrett, DM, Wein AJ (eds): Controversies in Neuro-Urology. New York, Churchill Livingstone, 1984, pp 223-238.

2002, 2003). **Normal bladder function during filling/storage implies no significant rises in detrusor pressure (stability). Overactive detrusor function indicates the presence of "involuntary detrusor contractions during the filling phase which may be spontaneous or provoked."** If the condition is caused by neurologic disease, the term **neurogenic detrusor overactivity** (previously, detrusor hyperreflexia) is used; if not, the term **idiopathic detrusor overactivity** (previously, detrusor instability) is applied. **Bladder sensation** can be categorized only in qualitative terms as indicated. **Bladder capacity and compliance** (Δ volume/Δ pressure) are cystometric measurements. Bladder capacity can refer to cystometric capacity, maximum cystometric capacity, or maximum anesthetic cystometric capacity (Abrams et al, 2002). **Normal urethral function during filling/storage indicates a positive urethral closure pressure (urethral pressure minus bladder pressure) even with increases in intra-abdominal pressure, although it may be overcome by detrusor overactivity. Incompetent urethral function during filling/storage** implies urine leakage in the absence of a detrusor contraction. This may be secondary to genuine stress incontinence, intrinsic sphincter dysfunction, a combination, or an involuntary fall in urethral pressure in the absence of detrusor contraction (see Chapter 60).

During the voiding/emptying phase of micturition, normal detrusor activity implies voiding by a voluntarily initiated sustained contraction that leads to complete bladder emptying within a normal time span. An **underactive detrusor** defines a contraction of inadequate magnitude or duration, or both, to empty the bladder within a normal time span. An **acontractile detrusor** is one that cannot be demonstrated to contract during urodynamic testing. **Areflexia** is defined as acontractility due to an abnormality of neural control, implying the complete absence of centrally coordinated contraction. **Normal urethral function** during voiding indicates a urethra that opens and is continuously relaxed to allow bladder emptying at a normal pressure. **Abnormal urethra function**

during voiding may be due to either mechanical obstruction or urethral overactivity. Dysfunctional voiding describes an intermittent or fluctuating flow rate due to involuntary intermittent contractions of the periurethral striated muscle in neurologically normal individuals. **Detrusor sphincter dyssynergia** defines a detrusor contraction concurrent with an involuntary contraction of the urethral or periurethral striated muscle, or both. **Nonrelaxing urethral sphincter obstruction** usually occurs in individuals with a neurologic lesion and is characterized by a nonrelaxing obstructing urethra resulting in reduced urine flow.

Lower urinary tract dysfunction in a classic T10 level paraplegic patient after spinal shock has passed would be classified in the ICS system as follows:

- Storage phase—overactive neurogenic detrusor function, absent sensation, low capacity, normal compliance, normal urethral closure function
- Voiding phase—overactive obstructive urethral function, overactive detrusor function

The micturition dysfunction of a stroke patient with urgency incontinence would most likely be classified during storage as overactive neurogenic detrusor function, normal sensation, low capacity, normal compliance, and normal urethral closure function. During voiding, the dysfunction would be classified as normal detrusor activity and normal urethral function, assuming that no anatomic obstruction existed.

Urodynamic Classification

As urodynamic techniques have become more accepted and sophisticated, systems of classification have evolved based solely on objective urodynamic data (Table 57–7). Among the first to popularize this concept were Krane and Siroky (1984). When exact urodynamic classification is possible, such a system can provide a truly exact description of the voiding dysfunction that occurs. If a normal or hyperreflexic detrusor exists with coordinated smooth and striated sphincter function and without anatomic obstruction, normal bladder emptying should occur. **Detrusor hyperreflexia** (now termed **neurogenic detrusor overactivity** in ICS parlance) is most commonly associated with neurologic lesions above the sacral spinal cord. **Striated sphincter dyssynergia** is most commonly seen after complete suprasacral spinal cord injury, following the period of spinal shock. **Smooth sphincter**

dyssynergia is seen most classically in autonomic hyper-reflexia (see Chapter 59, Lower Urinary Tract Dysfunction in Neurologic Injury and Disease) when it is characteristically associated with detrusor overactivity and striated sphincter dyssynergia. **Detrusor areflexia** (actually this category includes acontractile and areflexia bladder) may be secondary to bladder muscle decompensation or to various other conditions that produce inhibition at the level of the brain stem micturition center, the sacral spinal cord, bladder ganglia, or bladder smooth muscle. Patients with a voiding dysfunction secondary to detrusor areflexia generally attempt bladder emptying by abdominal straining, and their continence status and the efficiency of their emptying efforts are determined by the status of their smooth and striated sphincter mechanisms.

This classification system is easiest to use when detrusor hyperreflexia (overactivity) or normoreflexia exists. Thus, a typical T10 level paraplegic patient after spinal shock exhibits detrusor hyperreflexia, smooth sphincter synergia, and striated sphincter dyssynergia. When a voluntary or a hyper-reflexic contraction cannot be elicited, the system is more difficult to use because it is not appropriate to speak of true sphincter dyssynergia in the absence of an opposing bladder contraction. There are obviously many variations and extensions of such a system. **Such systems can work well only when total urodynamic agreement exists among classifiers.** Unfortunately, there are many voiding dysfunctions that do not fit neatly into a urodynamic classification system that is agreed on by all experts. Compliance is not mentioned in this particular version, nor is sensation or the concept of deficient but not absent detrusor contractile function. As sophisticated urodynamic technology and understanding improve, this type of classification system may become more commonly used. The ICS system (see previous discussion) is in reality a logical and more complete extension of such a system.

Lapides Classification

Lapides (1970) contributed significantly to the classification and care of the patient with neuropathic voiding dysfunction by slightly modifying and popularizing a system originally proposed by McLellan in 1939 (Table 57–8). Lapides' classification differs from that of McLellan in only one respect, and that is the division of the group of "atonic neurogenic bladder" into sensory neurogenic and motor neurogenic bladder. This remains one of the most familiar systems to urologists and nonurologists because it describes in recognizable shorthand the clinical and cystometric conditions of many types of neurogenic voiding dysfunction.

A **sensory neurogenic bladder** results from disease that selectively interrupts the sensory fibers between the bladder and the spinal cord or the afferent tracts to the brain. **Diabetes mellitus, tabes dorsalis, and pernicious anemia** are most

commonly responsible. The first clinical changes are described as those of impaired sensation of bladder distention. Unless voiding is initiated on a timed basis, varying degrees of bladder overdistention can result with resultant hypotonicity. If bladder decompensation occurs, significant amounts of residual urine result, and at that time the cystometric curve generally demonstrates a large-capacity bladder with a flat, high-compliance, low-pressure filling curve.

A **motor paralytic bladder** results from disease processes that destroy the parasympathetic motor innervation of the bladder. **Extensive pelvic surgery or trauma** may produce this. **Herpes zoster** has been listed as a cause as well, but recent evidence suggests that the voiding dysfunction seen with herpes may be more related to a problem with afferent input (see Chapter 59). The early symptoms of a motor paralytic bladder may vary from painful urinary retention to only a relative inability to initiate and maintain normal micturition. Early cystometric filing is normal but without a voluntary bladder contraction at capacity. Chronic overdistention and decompensation may occur, resulting in a large-capacity bladder with a flat, low-pressure filling curve; a large residual urine may result.

An **uninhibited neurogenic bladder** was described originally as resulting from injury or disease to the "corticoregulatory tract." The sacral spinal cord was presumed to be the micturition reflex center, and this corticoregulatory tract was believed normally to exert an inhibitory influence on the sacral micturition reflex center. A destructive lesion in this tract would then result in overfacilitation of the micturition reflex. **Cerebrovascular accident, brain or spinal cord tumor, Parkinson's disease, and demyelinating disease** were listed as the most common causes in this category. The voiding dysfunction is most often characterized symptomatically by frequency, urgency, and urge incontinence and urodynamically by normal sensation with involuntary contraction at low filling volumes. Residual urine is characteristically low unless anatomic outlet obstruction or true smooth or striated sphincter dyssynergia occurs. The patient generally can initiate a bladder contraction voluntarily but is often unable to do so during cystometry because sufficient urine storage cannot occur before involuntary contraction is stimulated.

Reflex neurogenic bladder describes the post–spinal shock condition that exists after complete interruption of the sensory and motor pathways between the sacral spinal cord and the brain stem. Most commonly, this occurs in **traumatic spinal cord injury and transverse myelitis**, but it may occur with **extensive demyelinating disease or any process that produces significant spinal cord destruction.** Typically, there is no bladder sensation, and there is inability to initiate voluntary micturition. Incontinence without sensation generally results because of low-volume involuntary contractions. Striated sphincter dyssynergia is the rule. This type of lesion is essentially equivalent to a complete upper motor neuron (UMN) lesion in the Bors-Comarr system (see later).

An **autonomous neurogenic bladder** results from complete motor and sensory separation of the bladder from the sacral spinal cord. This may be caused by **any disease that destroys the sacral cord or causes extensive damage to the sacral roots or pelvic nerves.** There is inability to initiate micturition voluntarily, no bladder reflex activity, and no specific bladder sensation. This type of bladder is equivalent to a complete

Table 57–8. The Lapides Classification

Sensory neurogenic bladder
Motor paralytic bladder (motor neurogenic bladder)
Uninhibited neurogenic bladder
Reflex neurogenic bladder
Autonomous neurogenic bladder

lower motor neuron (LMN) lesion in the Bors-Comarr system and is also the type of dysfunction seen in patients with spinal shock. The characteristic cystometric pattern is initially similar to the late stages of the motor or sensory paralytic bladder, with a marked shift to the right of the cystometric filling curve and a large bladder capacity at low intravesical pressure. However, decreased compliance may develop, secondary either to chronic inflammatory change or to the effects of denervation/decentralization with secondary neuromorphologic and neuropharmacologic reorganizational changes. Emptying capacity may vary widely, depending on the ability of the patient to increase intravesical pressure and on the resistance offered during this increase by the smooth and striated sphincters.

These classic categories in their usual settings are generally easily understood and remembered, and this is why this system provides an excellent framework for teaching some fundamentals of neurogenic voiding dysfunction to students and nonurologists. Unfortunately, many patients do not exactly fit into one or another category. Gradations of sensory, motor, and mixed lesions occur, and the patterns produced after different types of peripheral denervation/defunctionalization may vary widely from those that are classically described. **The system is applicable only to neuropathic dysfunction.**

Bors-Comarr Classification

Bors and Comarr (1971) made a remarkable contribution by logically deducing a classification system from clinical observation of their patients with traumatic spinal cord injury (Table 57–9). **This system applies only to patients with neurologic dysfunction and considers three factors: (1) the anatomic localization of the lesion, (2) the neurologic completeness or incompleteness of the lesion, and (3) whether lower urinary tract function is *balanced* or *unbalanced*.** The last terms are based solely on the percentage of residual urine relative to bladder capacity. **Unbalanced** signifies the presence

Table 57–9. The Bors-Comarr Classification

Sensory Neuron Lesion

Incomplete, balanced
Complete, balanced

Motor Neuron Lesion

Balanced
Imbalanced

Sensory-Motor Neuron Lesion

Upper motor neuron lesion
   Complete, balanced
   Complete, imbalanced
   Incomplete, balanced
   Incomplete, imbalanced
Lower motor neuron lesion
   Complete, balanced
   Complete, imbalanced
   Incomplete, balanced
   Incomplete, imbalanced
Mixed lesion
   Upper somatomotor neuron, lower visceromotor neuron
   Lower somatomotor neuron, upper visceromotor neuron
   Normal somatomotor neuron, lower visceromotor neuron

of greater than 20% residual urine in a patient with a UMN lesion or 10% in a patient with an LMN lesion. This relative residual urine volume was ideally meant to imply coordination (synergy) or dyssynergia between the smooth and the striated sphincters of the outlet and the bladder during bladder contraction or during attempted micturition by abdominal straining or the Credé maneuver. The determination of the completeness of the lesion is made on the basis of a thorough neurologic examination.

The system erroneously assumes that the sacral spinal cord is the primary reflex center for micturition. LMN implies collectively the preganglionic and postganglionic parasympathetic autonomic fibers that innervate the bladder and outlet and originate as preganglionic fibers in the sacral spinal cord. The term is used in an analogy to efferent somatic nerve fibers, such as those of the pudendal nerve, which originate in the same sacral cord segment but terminate directly on pelvic floor striated musculature without the interposition of ganglia. **UMN** is used in a similar analogy to the somatic nervous system to describe the descending autonomic pathways above the sacral spinal cord (the origin of the motor efferent supply to the bladder).

In this system, **UMN bladder** refers to the pattern of micturition that results from an injury to the suprasacral spinal cord after the period of spinal shock has passed, assuming that the sacral spinal cord and the sacral nerve roots are intact and that the pelvic and pudendal nerve reflexes are intact. **LMN bladder** refers to the pattern resulting if the sacral spinal cord or sacral roots are damaged and the reflex pattern through the autonomic and somatic nerves that emanate from these segments is absent. This system implies that if skeletal muscle spasticity exists below the level of the lesion, the lesion is above the sacral spinal cord and is by definition a UMN lesion. This type of lesion is characterized by involuntary bladder contraction during filling. If flaccidity of the skeletal musculature below the level of a lesion exists, an LMN lesion is assumed to be present, implying that detrusor areflexia is present. Exceptions occur and are classified in a "**mixed lesion group**" characterized either by involuntary bladder contraction with a flaccid paralysis below the level of the lesion or by detrusor areflexia with spasticity or normal skeletal muscle tone neurologically below the lesion level.

The use of this system is illustrated as follows. A **UMN lesion, complete, imbalanced**, implies a neurologically complete lesion above the level of the sacral spinal cord that results in skeletal muscle spasticity below the level of the injury. Involuntary bladder contraction occurs during filling, but a residual urine volume of greater than 20% of the bladder capacity is left after bladder contraction, implying obstruction in the area of the bladder outlet during the involuntary detrusor contraction. This obstruction is generally due to striated sphincter dyssynergia, typically occurring in patients who are paraplegic or quadriplegic with lesions between the cervical and the sacral spinal cord. Smooth sphincter dyssynergia may be seen as well in patients with lesions above the level of T6, usually associated with autonomic hyperreflexia (see Chapter 59, Lower Urinary Tract Dysfunction in Neurologic Injury and Disease). An **LMN lesion, complete, imbalanced**, implies a neurologically complete lesion at the level of the sacral spinal cord or of the sacral roots, resulting in skeletal muscle flaccidity below that level. Detrusor areflexia results, and whatever measures the patient may use to increase intravesical pressure during attempted voiding are not sufficient to decrease residual urine to less than 10% of bladder capacity.

This classification system applies best to spinal cord injury patients with complete neurologic lesions after spinal shock has passed. It is difficult to apply to patients with multicentric neurologic disease and cannot be used at all for patients with non-neurologic disease. The system fails to reconcile the clinical and urodynamic variability exhibited by patients who, by neurologic examination alone, seem to have similar lesions. The period of spinal shock that immediately follows severe cord injury is generally associated with bladder areflexia, whatever the status of the sacral somatic reflexes. Temporary or permanent changes in bladder or outlet activity during filling/storage and emptying/voiding may occur secondary to a number of factors, such as chronic overdistention, infection, and reinnervation or reorganization of neural pathways following injury or disease; such changes make it impossible always to predict accurately lower urinary tract activity solely on the basis of the level of the neurologic lesion. Finally, although the terms balanced and imbalanced are helpful, in that they describe the presence or absence of a certain relative percentage of residual urine, they do not necessarily imply the true functional significance of a lesion, which depends on the potential for damage to the lower or upper urinary tracts and also on the social and vocational disability that results.

Hald-Bradley Classification

Hald and Bradley (1982) described what they termed a simple neurotopographic classification (Table 57–10). A **supraspinal lesion** is characterized by synergy between detrusor contraction and the smooth and striated sphincters, but defective inhibition of the voiding reflex exists. Involuntary bladder contraction generally occurs, and sensation is usually preserved. However, depending on the site of the lesion, detrusor areflexia and defective sensation may be seen. A **suprasacral spinal lesion** is roughly equivalent to what is described as a UMN lesion in the Bors-Comarr classification. An **infrasacral lesion** is roughly equivalent to an LMN lesion. **Peripheral autonomic neuropathy** is most frequently encountered in the diabetic patient and is characterized by deficient bladder sensation, gradually increasing residual urine, and ultimate decompensation, with loss of detrusor contractility. A **muscular lesion** can involve the detrusor itself, the smooth sphincter, or any portion, or all, of the striated sphincter. The resultant dysfunction is dependent on which structure is affected. Detrusor dysfunction is the most common and generally results from decompensation, following long-standing bladder outlet obstruction. In my opinion, this system is as confusing as the word neurotopographic and adds little to the understanding of lower urinary tract dysfunction.

Table 57–10. **The Hald-Bradley Classification**
Suprasacral lesion
Suprasacral spinal lesion
Infrasacral lesion
Peripheral autonomic neuropathy
Muscular lesion

Bradley Classification

Bradley's "loop system" of classification is a primarily neurologic system based on his conceptualization of central nervous system control of the lower urinary tract that identifies four neurologic "loops" (Hald and Bradley, 1982). Dysfunctions are classified according to the loop affected.

Loop 1 consists of neuronal connections between the cerebral cortex and the pontine mesencephalic micturition center; this coordinates voluntary control of the detrusor reflex. **Loop 1 lesions** are seen in conditions such as **brain tumor, cerebrovascular accident or disease, and cerebral atrophy with dementia.** The final result is characteristically **involuntary bladder contractions.**

Loop 2 includes the intraspinal pathway of detrusor muscle afferents to the brain stem micturition center and the motor impulses from this center to the sacral spinal cord. Loop 2 is thought to coordinate and provide for a detrusor reflex of adequate temporal duration to allow complete voiding. Partial interruption by spinal cord injury results in a detrusor reflex of low threshold and in poor emptying with residual urine. **Spinal cord transection of loop 2 acutely produces detrusor areflexia and urinary retention—spinal shock. After this has passed, involuntary bladder contractions result.**

Loop 3 consists of the peripheral detrusor afferent axons and their pathways in the spinal cord; these terminate by synapsing on pudendal motor neurons that ultimately innervate periurethral striated muscle. Loop 3 was thought to provide a neurologic substrate for coordinated reciprocal action of the bladder and striated sphincter. **Loop 3 dysfunction could be responsible for detrusor striated dyssynergia or involuntary sphincter relaxation.**

Loop 4 consists of two components. Loop 4A is the suprasacral afferent and efferent innervation of the pudendal motor neurons to the periurethral striated musculature. Loop 4B consists of afferent fibers from the periurethral striated musculature that synapse on pudendal motor neurons in Onuf's nucleus—the segmental innervation of the periurethral striated muscle. Bradley conceptualized that, in contrast to the stimulation of detrusor afferent fibers, which produced inhibitory postsynaptic potentials in pudendal motor neurons through loop 3, pudendal nerve afferents produced excitatory postsynaptic potentials in those motor neurons through loop 4B. These provided for contraction of the periurethral striated muscle during bladder filling and urine storage. The related sensory impulses arise from muscle spindles and tendon organs in the pelvic floor musculature. **Loop 4 provides for volitional control of the striated sphincter.** Abnormalities of the suprasacral portion result in abnormal responses of the pudendal motor neurons to bladder filling and emptying, manifested as detrusor striated sphincter dyssynergia, or loss of the ability to contract the striated sphincter voluntarily, or both.

The Bradley system is sophisticated and reflects the ingenuity and neurophysiologic expertise of its originator, himself a neurologist. For neurologists, this method may be an excellent way to conceptualize the neurophysiology involved, assuming that there is, in fact, agreement on the existence and significance of all four loops—a big assumption. Most urologists find this system difficult to use for many types of neurogenic voiding dysfunction and not at all applicable to non-neurogenic voiding dysfunction. Urodynamically, it may be extremely difficult to test the intactness of each loop system, and multicentric and partial lesions are difficult to describe.

SUGGESTED READINGS

Abrams P, Cardozo L, Fall M, et al: The standardization of terminology in lower urinary tract function: Report from the standardization subcommittee of the International Continence Society. Neurourol Urodyn 2002;21:167-178 and Urology 2003;61:37-49.

Andersson K-E, Arner A: Urinary bladder contraction and relaxation: Physiology and pathophysiology. Physiol Rev 2004;84:935-988.

Andersson K-E, Wein AJ: Pharmacology of the lower urinary tract: Basis for current and future treatments of urinary incontinence. Pharmacol Rev 2004;56:581-631.

Mostwin J, Bourcier A, Haab F, et al: Pathophysiology of urinary incontinence, fecal incontinence and pelvic organ prolapse. In Abrams P, Cardoyo L, Khoury S, Wein A (eds): Incontinence. Plymouth, UK, Health Publications, 2005, pp 423-484.

Wein AJ, Barrett DM: Voiding Function and Dysfunction: A Logical and Practical Approach. Chicago, Year Book Medical, 1988.

58 Urodynamic and Videourodynamic Evaluation of Voiding Dysfunction

ANDREW C. PETERSON, MD • GEORGE D. WEBSTER, MD

The term urodynamics was first defined by David M. Davis in 1953 to denote the study of the storage and emptying phases of the urinary bladder (Davis, 1953). Initially, the examiner simply observed the act of voiding and the strength of the stream in order to comment on the function of the bladder, but ultimately in 1897 instruments were devised to measure the function of the lower urinary tract (Rehfish, 1897). Such devices measured bladder pressure and urinary flow but had many limitations. Over the next 100 years there was much technical and procedural advancement of these original concepts and designs.

The cystometrograph, introduced in 1927 by D. K. Rose, was one of the earliest urodynamic instruments for measuring bladder pressure during filling and voiding (Rose, 1927). This was followed by the uroflowmeter by Drake in 1948. In the 1950s, the development of simultaneous radiographic imaging done in conjunction with physiologic studies was pioneered by Hinman and Miller (Hinman et al, 1954).

Today, the urodynamic armamentarium is extensive, including such simple tests as uroflowmetry and cystometry as well as more sophisticated studies such as pressure-flow studies, electrophysiologic studies, urethral pressure studies, and videourodynamic studies. **In performing urodynamics, the goal is to answer specific questions related to the patient's storage and voiding function** (Schafer et al, 2002).

The simplest and least invasive tests can be used initially with progression to more sophisticated testing when the clinical examination and more simple tests do not assist in making a diagnosis. It is imperative that during the urodynamic study the patient's presenting symptoms be reproduced. **With this concept in mind, Nitti noted three important principles in urodynamics: (1) a study that does not duplicate the patient's symptoms is not diagnostic, (2) failure to record an abnormality does not rule out its existence, and (3) not all abnormalities detected are clinically significant** (Nitti and Combs, 1998).

Good urodynamic practice includes three important elements (Schafer et al, 2002). These are a clear indication for the study, precise measurements with respect to quality control and complete documentation, and accurate analysis and critical reporting of the results. **The aim of clinical urodynamics is to reproduce symptoms while making precise measurements of the bladder physiology. Urodynamic measurements cannot yet be completely automated, and in order to fulfill these requirements, trained and experienced staff input is required during all phases of the study** (Schafer et al, 2002).

INDICATIONS

Clear indications for some type of urodynamic investigation include patients with persistent lower urinary tract symptoms (LUTS) despite presumed appropriate therapy and patients in whom potential therapy may have significant side effects (Table 58–1). **Urodynamics can also be invaluable in determining the impact of a known disease process on the lower urinary tract.** Specific examples of this include men with prostate outlet obstruction, children or adults being observed for spinal dysraphism or spinal cord injury, and others with suspected neurogenic bladder dysfunction including those with spinal disk disease, multiple sclerosis, Parkinson's disease and those who have undergone extensive pelvic surgery. It is also invaluable in establishing the cause of urinary incontinence in both men and women.

Table 58-1. Indications and Selection of Patients for Conduction of Urodynamics
Patients in whom potential therapy may be hazardous where one would want to be sure of the correct diagnosis before instituting therapy
Patients with recurrent incontinence in whom surgery is planned
Patients with incontinence and a confusing mix of stress and urge symptoms and those with associated voiding problems
Patients with neurologic disorders and those with a mismatch between symptoms and clinical findings
Patients with LUTS suggestive of bladder outlet obstruction
Patients with persistent LUTS despite presumed appropriate therapy
Patients with LUTS who have both obstructive and marked instability symptoms
Patients with obstructive LUTS and neurologic disease
Young men with LUTS
All neurologically impaired patients who have neurogenic bladder dysfunction
Children with daytime urgency and urge incontinence
Children with persistent diurnal enuresis
Children with spinal dysraphism

LUTS, lower urinary tract symptoms. (From Schafer W, Abrams P, Liao L, et al: Good urodynamic practices: Uroflowmetry, filling cystometry, and pressure-flow studies. Neurourol Urodyn 2002;21:261-274.)

PREPARATION OF PATIENTS AND PRECAUTIONS

Urodynamic studies are invasive and can be associated with morbidity such as urinary retention, hematuria, urinary tract infection, and pain, and prestudy discussion of the study technique and counseling about the risks are appropriate (Klingler et al, 1998). During the study, the patient should understand what information we are trying to collect sufficiently to be able to volunteer timely responses to changing events. We find that preparation of patients with handouts provided at the time of scheduling is invaluable. Some may have been started empirically on medication for their symptoms including anticholinergics, α blockers, bladder relaxation medications, and psychotropic medications. These affect urodynamic outcomes and should be stopped with an adequate washout period prior to the test.

Because micturition is normally a private act, the study setting should be quiet and clean with neatly placed lines and equipment so as to provide as little distraction as possible, allowing the patient to be able to replicate normal voiding habits. There should be as few observers as possible to minimize patients' embarrassment. An adequate history and physical examination should be performed before the test and a voiding diary completed to determine the functional capacity, daily urine output, and approximate filling volume.

Antibiotics

The use of antibiotic medications prior to or during the urodynamic study is controversial. Provided that the pretest urinalysis is negative for infection, it is probable that antibiotic coverage is unnecessary in most patients. However, parenteral antibiotic prophylaxis may be necessary in specific patients, such as those with cardiac valve abnormalities, orthopedic prostheses, genitourinary prostheses, pacemakers, and other electrical devices (Dajani et al, 1997).

An expert panel of urologists, orthopedic surgeons, and infectious disease specialists, convened by the American Urological Association (AUA) and the American Academy of Orthopaedic Surgeons (AAOS), developed guidelines for the use of antibiotic prophylaxis in patients with total joint arthroplasties. **They concluded that antibiotic prophylaxis is not indicated for urologic patients on the basis of pins, plates, and screws and not routinely indicated for most healthy urologic patients with total joint replacements. The panel did recommend prophylactic antibiotics in patients at potentially increased risk of hematogenous infection of joints.** These include patients with total joint replacements within 2 years after implant surgery, immunocompromised patients, and those with previous prosthetic joint infections (American Urological Association Advisory Statement, 2002).

Preparing for the Urodynamic Evaluation

All urodynamic procedures should be performed with a clear indication and with a specific question or questions that can be answered by the study. The procedure should be performed interactively with the patient and should include continuous and careful observation of the collected data. Artifacts should be corrected as they occur because they are often difficult to correct in retrospect (Schafer et al, 2002).

It is valuable for the investigator to have an understanding of the underlying physics of the measurements, practical experience with the equipment, an understanding of quality control, and the ability to analyze critically the results of the study. Understanding the pertinent anatomy and physiology of the lower urinary tract and the biomechanics and physics of the urodynamic study allows the clinician to analyze the data on a physical, biomechanical, and pathophysiologic clinical level (Schafer et al, 2002).

The Urodynamics Room

The room used for urodynamics does not have to be exclusively designed for this purpose but should be without distractions, quiet, and protected from unnecessary interruptions. This reduces the risk of "situational anxiety," which otherwise impairs patients' ability to function physiologically and reduces the likelihood that their symptoms will be reproduced or that they will be able to void. The room should be large enough for the physician to perform a physical and pelvic examination, to place catheters, and to move unencumbered within the room. One should always take into account the need for sufficient room to allow for wheelchairs and assist devices such as walkers (Fig. 58–1).

The importance of a well-trained, attentive, and supportive clinical staff to conduct the urodynamics cannot be overemphasized. Many companies offer formal training seminars for urology technicians and nursing staff. This, along with on-the-spot training by the physician, helps to ensure good data collection.

Signal Processing

The urodynamic parameters most commonly measured (pressures and urinary flow rate) are obtained with transducers.

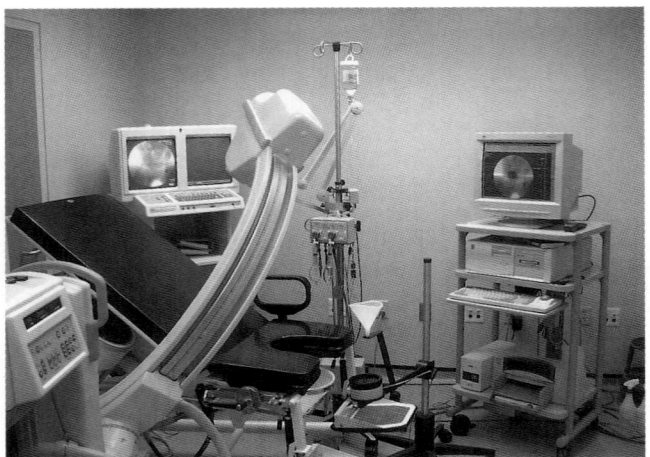

Figure 58–1. Videourodynamic study facility using a fluoroscopic C-arm and a purpose-made tilting chair.

Table 58–2. The International Continence Society Minimal Standards	
Accuracy:	±1 cm H$_2$O for pressure
	±5% of the full scale for flow
Detection ranges:	0 to 250 cm H$_2$O for pressure
	0 to 50 mL/sec for flow
	0 to 1000 mL for volume
Time constant:	0.75 seconds
Software:	No loss of data for pressures up to 250 cm H$_2$O and flow up to 50 mL/sec
Frequency:	Analog/digital frequency of 10 Hz per channel
	20 kHz minimum may be needed for EMG
Printout:	Line resolution better than 0.10 mm
Maximum deflection:	
Pressure:	200 cm H$_2$O
Flow:	50 mL/sec
Volume:	1000 mL
Minimum scaling:	
Pressure:	50 cm H$_2$O per cm
Flow:	10 mL/sec per cm
Time axis:	1 min/cm or 5 sec/mm for filling
	2 sec/mm for voiding

EMG, electromyography (Rowan, 1987; Schafer, 2002).

The transducers convert these data into an easily recordable electrical signal by *signal processing*. This is a process whereby the raw data from the transducer are amplified, filtered, and modified by a computer to produce readily interpretable data (Rowan et al, 1987).

URODYNAMIC EQUIPMENT

The International Continence Society (ICS) has developed recommendations for the minimum requirements for the equipment used to conduct urodynamics studies. **These include three measurement channels, two for pressure and one for flow; a display (on either a printer or a monitor); and a method for secure storage of the recorded pressures (abdominal, vesicle, detrusor) and flow measurements as tracings against time** (Schafer et al, 2002). **The infused volume and voided volume may be recorded graphically or numerically. There must be a method for event recording to mark information about sensation and additional comments during the study.**

For real-time analysis and troubleshooting, all measured and derived signals must be displayed continuously over time according to ICS standards, preferably with the following sequential position of tracings: from top down on the page Pabd (abdominal pressure), Pves (vesical pressure), Pdet (detrusor pressure), and flow (Q). Filling volume, electromyography (EMG), and voided volumes may be displayed in additional curves or numbers.

The ICS has also developed minimum technical specifications for equipment (Table 58–2). The software must ensure that information for pressures up to 250 cm H$_2$O and flow rates up to 50 mL/sec, even when not displayed, is not lost. Pressure transducers, flowmeters, and pumps must be able to be calibrated according to the specification of the manufacturer. New systems should be calibrated when first installed and then on a regular basis. If the expected error is small (e.g., less than 2 cm H$_2$O), calibration once a month is sufficient. More frequent calibration may be needed to ensure accurate measurements, however. Calibration is not the same as

"zeroing"; it must be possible to evaluate the amplitudes of all measurement channels in order to check, calibrate, and adjust them (Schafer et al, 2002).

Cystometry Transducers

A pressure transducer is a device that converts an applied pressure into an electrical signal (Rowan et al, 1987). The pressure to be measured may be transmitted to the transducer using either an open-ended or sealed catheter filled with liquid or gas or directly when the transducer is small and mounted on the tip of the catheter (microtip transducer). There are four basic types of transducers: resistive, capacitive, inductive, and optoelectronic. The customary unit of measurement for pressure during urodynamics is cm H$_2$O.

The transducer is normally calibrated against atmospheric pressure with the zero reference level being the superior edge of the symphysis pubis. The liquid-filled transducer system is subjected to two sources of hydrostatic pressure that negate each other. These are the pressure from the liquid in the catheter and the pressure from the depth of the catheter tip within a volume of fluid. This makes the measurement of bladder pressure independent of the location of the tip within the bladder, thus increasing reproducibility. Conversely, pressures measured by microtip and sealed gas system transducers are dependent on the position within the bladder, which introduces more variability.

Catheters

The standard catheter for routine urodynamics is a transurethral, double-lumen catheter (Schafer et al, 2002). Suprapubic placement has been used in patients with obstruction such as urethral stricture disease, but the potential morbidity of such placement must be justified by the importance of the information to be gained. The urethral catheters used should be as small as possible but not so small as to dampen pressure transmission or limit the desired filling rate. The smallest available is the 6 Fr double-lumen catheter. This allows the fill and void sequence to be repeated without recatheterization. Although good to limit interference with voiding, the 6 Fr double-lumen catheter can limit infusion rates. If the pump is set to fill at a higher rate but limited to a slower rate by the lumen of the catheter, an incorrect infusion volume may be recorded by the machine, throwing off all calculated volumes during analysis. It is essential that all systems be tested to measure the maximum filling rate that can be achieved by a specific catheter attached to a specific infusion pump. Further, similarly sized triple-lumen catheters are available that allow bladder filling, intravesical pressure measurement, and urethral pressure recording.

We prefer and continue to use the two-catheter technique for cystometry and subsequent voiding study. Using this technique, a 10 Fr filling catheter is inserted through the urethra together with a "piggy-backed" 4 Fr pressure-measuring catheter. When bladder filling and cystometry are completed through the larger catheter, it is withdrawn, leaving only the 4 Fr catheter in place to allow voiding without obstruction.

The use of a balloon catheter is best for the measurement of abdominal pressure. This is accomplished with an air-free balloon in the rectum or in the vagina in women. The balloon maintains a small fluid volume at the catheter opening to avoid fecal blockage preventing pressure transmission. This needs to be filled to only 10% to 20% of capacity because overfilling and distention of the balloon cause a high balloon pressure and artificially elevated abdominal pressure readings (Schafer et al, 2002).

Flowmeters

The flow rate is measured by a uroflowmeter with the SI unit for flow being cubic meters per second (m^3/sec) and for mass flow rate kilograms per second (kg/sec); however, most flow rates are reported in milliliters per second (mL/sec) (Rowan et al, 1987). The volumetric flow rate and the accumulated volume are related by the equations listed in Table 58–3. Most flowmeters are calibrated for water, which has a density of 1; therefore, the mass of the fluid in grams equals the volume in milliliters. **Variations in the specific gravity of the fluid therefore significantly affect the measured flow rate.** For instance, x-ray contrast medium, being much denser than water, may result in overestimation of the flow rate. This can be corrected

for by calibration of the machine and software. There is also a delay between initiation of voiding and the stream reaching the flowmeter. This should be from 1 to 1.4 seconds in females and 1.1 to 1.6 seconds in males (Schafer et al, 2002).

Gravimetric flowmeters operate by measuring the weight of the collected fluid or by measuring the hydrostatic pressure at the base of the collecting cylinder. The output signal is proportional to the mass of fluid collected. These meters therefore measure accumulated mass and mass flow rate is obtained by differentiation. *The electronic dip stick flowmeter* measures the electrical capacitance of a dipstick mounted in a collecting chamber. The output signal is proportional to the accumulated volume, and the volumetric flow rate is obtained by differentiation. In the *rotating disk flowmeter* the voided fluid is directed onto a rotating disk. The power required to keep the disk rotating at a constant rate is measured and proportional to the mass flow rate of the fluid. The accumulated mass is obtained by integration. Today, most available flowmeters are gravimetric or rotating disk transducers.

Electromyography Equipment

EMG is the study of the electrical potentials produced by the depolarization of muscle membranes. The depolarization must first be detected by an electrode placed close to the origin of the signal. These include intramuscular needle electrodes and surface electrodes placed on the skin or mucosa overlying the muscle of interest. Each type of electrode has advantages and disadvantages.

Types of Electrodes

Self-adhesive, skin patch electrodes provide good surface recordings and allow patients mobility. These electrodes are predominantly used in pediatric urodynamics. They are self-adhesive and contain a conductive gel. The skin should be shaved and prepared with alcohol to reduce surface resistance and the electrode placed directly on the skin overlying the muscle of interest (Barrett, 1980). They provide the least accurate representation of the activity of the underlying muscle. *Needle electrodes* provide better recording quality and specificity for certain muscle groups. However, patients' mobility may be restricted during the examination. *Wire electrodes* are made of stainless steel, platinum, or copper wire. The wire is placed into the muscle to be studied through a needle acting as a cannula. Wire electrodes permit better mobility of the patient because they can be secured in place well. *Monopolar electrodes* are thin needles coated with an insulating material with an exposed tip. These provide excellent recordings of very specific muscle potentials. They need a reference electrode, a small metal disk attached to the skin near the muscle being examined. *Concentric electrodes* consist of a wire inside an outer cannula, separated by insulating material. The outer, conductive portion serves as the ground. This can record from one to three motor units simultaneously (Siroky, 1996).

The selection of the type of electrode used is dependent on the urodynamic question to be answered. Although surface electrodes are easy to place, they provide only an average or summary of muscle activity and are used primarily for coordination or kinesiologic studies. The needle and

---

Table 58–3.	**Urodynamics Equations**

1. Flow rate: $Q = 1dm/p \, dt$. Flow is the change in volume over the change in time: $q = dV/dt$: flow rate (Q), volume (V), time (T), and mass of fluid (m) = density of fluid (p) × volume of fluid (V).
2. Compliance: C (compliance) = dV/dP_{det} (detrusor pressure).
3. Detrusor pressure: $p_{det} = p_{ves} - p_{abd}$, p_{det} (detrusor pressure), p_{ves} (vesical pressure), p_{abd} (abdominal pressure).
4. Physiologic filling rate for cystometry: rate = body weight (in kg)/4, expressed as mL/min.

wire electrode sense activity within a radius of 0.5 mm, permitting recording from a few or even a single motor unit. *Single-fiber electrodes* can make recordings from a single muscle fiber and are used, as are other needle electrodes, to diagnose neuropathic motor unit action potentials rather than simply to look at the coordination between bladder and sphincter (kinesiologic study).

Multiple factors must be considered when selecting the appropriate electrode to be used. These include the cooperativeness of the patient. Although very specific for recordings from muscle groups, wire and needle electrodes have several disadvantages. They need much greater technical expertise, they cause discomfort to the patient, and the small sampling area can be misleading. For instance, data measured from one single motor unit may not be representative of the muscle activity in general (Siroky, 1996).

CONDUCTING THE URODYNAMIC EVALUATION
Uroflow

Uroflowmetry is noninvasive, inexpensive, and invaluable in screening patients with voiding dysfunction. We feel this noninvasive test should precede any other urodynamic studies. It is easy to perform and quickly provides data on both storage

and voiding symptoms. These studies should be conducted with as much privacy as possible, and patients should be asked to void when they feel a normal desire. Ideally, two or more tests should be performed, and the addition of a noninvasive postvoid residual volume measurement by ultrasound adds to the value of the study.

Normal voiding includes a detrusor muscle contraction, coordinated bladder outlet relaxation, low voiding pressure, and a smooth, arc-shaped flow curve (Schafer et al, 2002). The flow pattern, that is, the shape of the flow tracing, can sometimes be used to make a presumptive diagnosis, although it cannot be used to make a definitive diagnosis. The normal flow pattern is a continuous, bell-shaped, smooth curve with a rapidly increasing flow rate (Fig. 58–2). An intermittent flow pattern is one that has one or several episodes of flow increasing or decreasing (or ceasing completely) and is commonly secondary to abdominal straining or external sphincter spasm (e.g., detrusor-sphincter dyssynergia). The typical obstructed flow pattern has a plateau-shaped curve with a prolonged flow time, sustained low flow rate, and increased time to Qmax. However, several studies have addressed the ability of uroflowmetry or corrected uroflowmetry (i.e., use of nomograms) to predict outflow obstruction. In general, the conclusion has been that **uroflowmetry alone is insufficient to diagnose bladder outlet obstruction because it cannot distinguish true obstruction from poor detrusor contractility** (Chancellor et al, 1991).

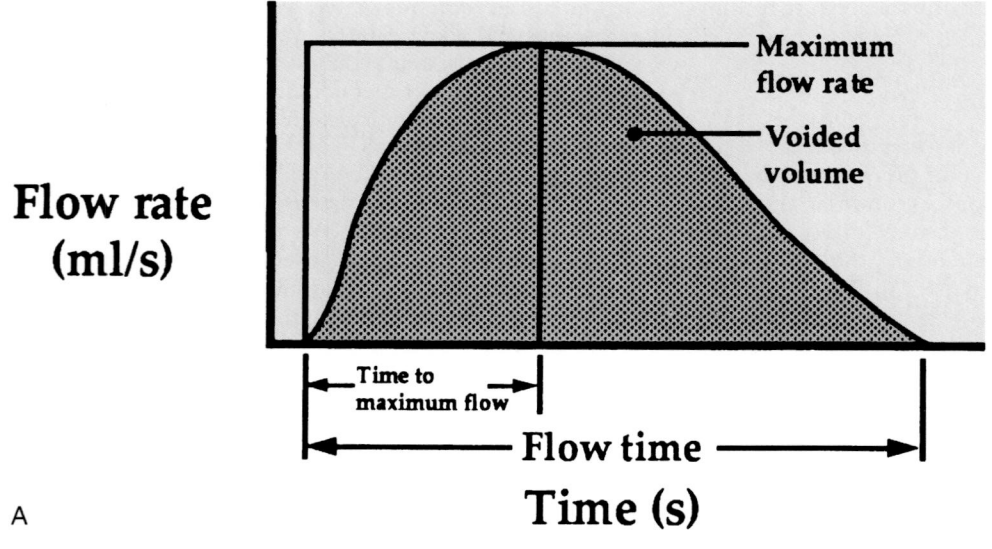

Figure 58–2. A, Schematic of a normal flow curve. Frequently measured variables are noted. **B,** Uroflow study in a 60-year-old man. Peak flow rate is 16 mL/sec. Total volume voided is 263 mL. Qura, urine flow rate; Qvol, voided volume.

The ICS has developed standards for the graphical scaling of flow curves (Schafer et al, 2002). Only flow rate values that have been smoothed either electronically or manually should be reported. Other valuable data from the uroflow curve include maximum flow rate, total voided volume, average flow rate, and the postvoid residual. **Because small voided volumes affect the curve shape and Qmax is volume dependent, only voided volumes of at least 150 mL should be interpreted** (Drach et al, 1979b; Drach and Steinbronn, 1986). The maximum flow rate should always be documented together with the total voided volume and postvoid residual volume with the following standard format: maximum flow rate/volume voided/postvoid residual volume.

Pitfalls

Electronic analysis of uroflowmetry may introduce errors because the electronic device reads the absolute maximum value recorded by the machine and may read spikes on the curve that do not represent true flow. Because of this, it has been demonstrated that visually determined flow values may be significantly lower than those determined electronically (Grino et al, 1993; Jorgensen et al, 1993b). It is important that the patient be appropriately instructed how to conduct the study. Disk flowmeters are susceptible to the direction with which the flow hits the device, and thus, depending on where the stream hits the disk, different flow rates are possible and may cause significant spikes or artifacts known as the wag artifact (Grino et al, 1993). Also, patients may sometimes strain to improve flow in order to do the "best they can."

Uroflow in Men. Normal uroflow parameters in young men are well established. **Most consider Qmax greater than 15 to 20 mL/sec as normal and less than 10 mL/sec abnormal. These numbers decline with age by 1 to 2 mL/sec per 5 years. There is a decline in peak flow with age resulting in a maximum flow of 5.5 mL/sec at 80 years** (Jorgensen et al, 1986, 1993a).

Uroflow in Women. Women have a very short urethra, minimal outlet resistance, and no prostate, and generally speaking the only factors influencing female uroflow are the strength of the detrusor muscle and the urethral resistance and the degree of relaxation of the sphincter mechanism. There is little information in the literature about normal uroflow values in women. However, **in the normal woman Qmax can be greater than 30 mL/sec, the flow curve is bell shaped as in men, and the flow time is shorter** (Susset et al, 1974; Drach et al, 1979a; Bottaccini and Gleason, 1980). **Maximum flow in women does not seem to be dependent upon age.**

The Cystometrogram

Cystometry is the term used to describe the urodynamic investigation of the filling component of bladder function. Although the fill rate used in the laboratory is artificially high and the circumstances surrounding the study do not closely duplicate the situations in which patients' storage problems may occur, it is still a valuable tool in diagnosis and as a guide to therapy. Patients' understanding and compliance with study goals are absolutely necessary to achieve interpretable data.

Because the data obtained are affected significantly by many technical variations, standardized study methods should be followed in order to optimize results.

The Procedure

Measurement of Intravesical and Abdominal Pressure. Zero pressure and reference height are often confused. Both are independent features of pressure and should follow the ICS methodology precisely. Zero pressure is the surrounding atmospheric pressure. This is measured with the transducer open or with the open end of a connected, fluid-filled tube positioned outside the bladder at the same level as the bladder. When external transducers are used, the reference point is the superior edge of the pubic symphysis (Schafer et al, 2002). All systems must be zeroed to atmospheric pressure, and it is crucial that there are no air bubbles in any of the transducers or tubing as these may cause pressure dampening or dissipation.

Fill Medium

A physiologic liquid medium is preferable. Gas cystometry is thought to be quicker and more hygienic if there is incontinence. However, it is compressible, not physiologic, and may evoke artifact (Gleason and Reilly, 1979). It is also impossible to detect leakage of gas; therefore, one cannot determine the presence of incontinence or obtain leak point pressures with stress maneuvers. Also, volumes are difficult to document with gas. When dissolved, CO_2 forms carbonic acid, which can irritate the bladder. Because CO_2 is compressible, subtle changes in bladder pressure may be missed and the rapid fill rates achieved with gas may artificially change the normal bladder response. Finally, voiding studies cannot be performed using gas.

Fluid cystometry uses more physiologic media such as sterile water, normal saline, or contrast material. These are not compressible and allow better assessment of voiding dynamics. Liquids allow easier detection of incontinence and are more physiologic. Other advantages include the ability to determine fluid loss and leak pressures and to serve as a medium for fluoroscopy.

The physical characteristics of the infused liquid may affect bladder behavior and urodynamic measurements. Acidic (pH 3.5) and alkaline (pH above 8.5) solutions may increase (Ashlund et al, 1988) or decrease (Sethia and Smith, 1987) overactivity in otherwise normal bladders. Temperature is also important. For instance, iced water may provoke overactivity, a characteristic often used for provocative testing (see later under Ice Water Testing). Therefore, the temperature should always be at or near body temperature.

Fill Rate

The fill rate is determined by the population being studied and the specific question to be answered. More rapid infusions may unmask involuntary bladder contractions but may also give the appearance of reduced compliance. **The ICS has established criteria for the standardization of filling rates during cystometry as follows** (Schafer et al, 2002):
- **Slow ("physiologic") fill—less than 10 mL/min**
- **Medium fill—10 to 100 mL/min**
- **Rapid fill—more than 100 mL/min**

Alternatively, bladder filling may be achieved by diuresis, allowing the bladder to fill itself at a normal physiologic rate.

Filling is most often performed at a medium fill rate with the slow rates reserved for second fills in patients who demonstrate significant detrusor overactivity at a faster fill rate. Provocative filling using the faster rates may be used to expose bladder overactivity in patients with a complaint of urgency.

Cystometry

The range of complexity in cystometry varies from the very simple to complex. In most cases the study is performed by placement of a bladder recording catheter transurethrally.

The simplest of these techniques is known as eyeball or bedside urodynamics. This is performed with only a syringe, urethral catheter, and sterile water. The catheter is placed in the bladder and the syringe attached. This is held above the symphysis pubis and fluid is infused by gravity. The need to elevate the syringe to maintain filling corresponds to an increase in bladder pressure (secondary to bladder contraction, reduced compliance, or abdominal straining). From this, bladder capacity, sensation, and information about detrusor overactivity may be obtained. This is a crude and relatively uninformative study.

A single-channel recording of bladder pressures is obtained by adding a transducer to this circuit. This setup measures vesical pressure only and does not account for the pressure-related events from abdominal strain or patients' activity. To delineate these factors requires the addition of abdominal pressure measurements (see section on "Multichannel Urodynamics").

Prior to filling, we prefer to conduct a noninvasive uroflow test as described earlier. The patient is then catheterized for a postvoid residual at the time of cystometry catheter placement. During cystometry, periodic coughing should be elicited to ensure accurate pressure recording in all channels being monitored (Pdet as derived from Pves and Pabd). A few common errors that result in inability to obtain a correct zero include pressure line displacement, kinking of the tubing, compression of the lumen of the tubing against the bladder or rectal wall, and the presence of air bubbles.

Filling

During the course of cystometry, information is gained regarding four bladder characteristics; *capacity, sensation, compliance, and the occurrence of involuntary contractions.* Historically the typical cystometrogram (CMG) tracing has been described as having four phases (Fig. 58–3):

(I) The immediate rise to resting bladder pressure occurring with initial filling, representing the response of the viscoelastic properties to the stretch of filling.

(II) The tonus limb, which reflects the viscoelastic properties of the bladder wall.

(III) The point at which bladder wall structures have achieved maximal elongation and a pressure rise is

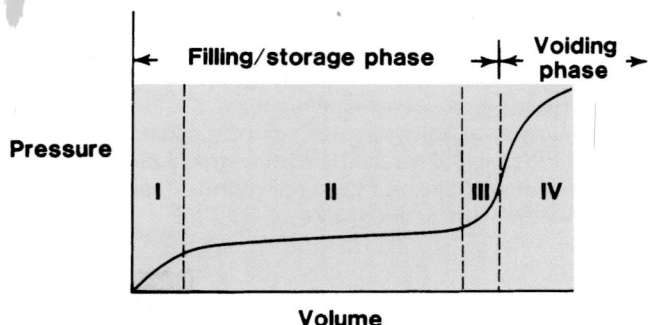

Figure 58–3. Schematically, the normal cystometrogram has four phases: (I) an initial pressure rise to achieve resting bladder pressure; (II) the tonus limb, which reflects the viscoelastic properties of the bladder wall; (III) bladder wall structures achieving maximal elongation and pressure rise caused by additional filling (this phase should not be encountered during cystometry); and (IV) the voiding phase, representing bladder contractility. (From Steers WD, Barret DM, Wein AJ: Voiding dysfunction: Diagnosis, classification and management. In Gillenwater JY, Grayhack JT, Howards SS, Duckett JW [eds]: Adult and Pediatric Urology, 3rd ed. St. Louis, Mosby–Year Book, 1996, Fig. 26B–1.)

caused by additional filling (i.e., exceeding the limit of compliance). This segment of filling is determined by failure of the viscoelastic accommodation of the bladder wall and normally cystometry does not challenge this zone.

(IV) The voiding phase consisting of a voluntary bladder contraction, which we consider to be part of the voiding study rather than the filling CMG.

From the clinical standpoint, we view the CMG in two components: the response to filling and then, when capacity has been achieved, the period of storage testing when there is no further fill but the patient stresses the full system with provocative maneuvers such as cough, Valsalva maneuver, and other provocative activities. In addition, one may try to provoke involuntary contractions by hand washing or running water.

Many factors can increase intravesical pressure including fast, supraphysiologic filling rates (Klevmark, 1980), increased bladder wall collagen from fibrosis associated with radiation, indwelling catheters, and specific infections (Dmochowski, 1996).

Capacity

Maximum cystometric capacity is the bladder volume at the end of the filling CMG when patients have a strong desire to void, feel they can no longer delay micturition, and are given permission to void (Abrams et al, 2002). This volume includes both the amount voided and the residual urine left after the void (postvoid residual). In contrast, **the functional bladder capacity** is the largest volume voided as determined by a voiding diary. The cystometric capacity is usually slightly greater than functional bladder capacity and in patients with impaired bladder sensation often cannot be determined; it is simply the point at which the examiner terminates the study. The maximal anesthetic capacity is the volume of the bladder after filling under anesthesia (general, spinal, epidural) and is not routinely measured.

Sensation

Bladder sensation is evaluated by questioning the patient about the feeling of the degree of bladder fullness and is the point at which cooperation between the patient and examiner becomes very important. Normal bladder sensation can be judged from three defined points noted during filling cystometry: the first sensation of bladder filling, the first desire to void, and a strong desire to void (Abrams et al, 2002). Urgency, pain, and multiple other sensations should be documented during filling as well (Table 58–4). These values help the clinician determine whether a patient has increased bladder sensation, reduced bladder sensation, absent bladder sensation, or nonspecific bladder sensation and help establish the vesical and urethral sensory threshold. It has been argued that the presence or absence of sensation may be more important than the volumes at which the sensations do or do not occur (Susset, 1991).

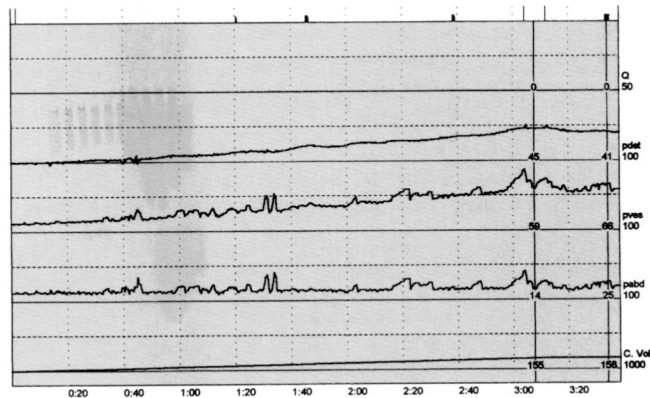

Figure 58–4. Filling cystometrogram shows low bladder compliance. At completion of fill (see vertical event line on the tracing), detrusor pressure (Pdet) is 45 cm H_2O at a capacity of 155 mL. This patient had neurogenic bladder dysfunction after abdominoperineal resection for rectal cancer. C Vol, volume infused; Pabd, abdominal pressure; Pves, intravesical pressure.

Compliance

During the filling and storage phase of the CMG, increasing intravesical volumes should occur with little or no change in intravesical pressure. **Bladder compliance is the relationship between change in volume and change in pressure. It is calculated by dividing the volume change (dV) by the change in detrusor pressure (dPdet) and expressed in mL/cm H_2O** (Abrams et al, 2002). It is generally calculated between two points: the Pdet with the bladder empty at the start of filling and the Pdet at either the maximal cystometric capacity or the start of a detrusor contraction (Abrams et al, 2002). **Normal bladder compliance should be less than 12.5 mL/cm H_2O** (Toppercer and Tetreault, 1979).

Compliance arises from the muscular, collagenous, and elastic components of the bladder wall (Fig. 58–4). Often a slight increase in pressure is seen and can be related to artifact such as fast filling rates. If this is suspected, the fill should be repeated at a slower rate. **Three variables come into play, intravesical pressure, wall tension, and bladder volume, all of which may be affected by multiple factors.**

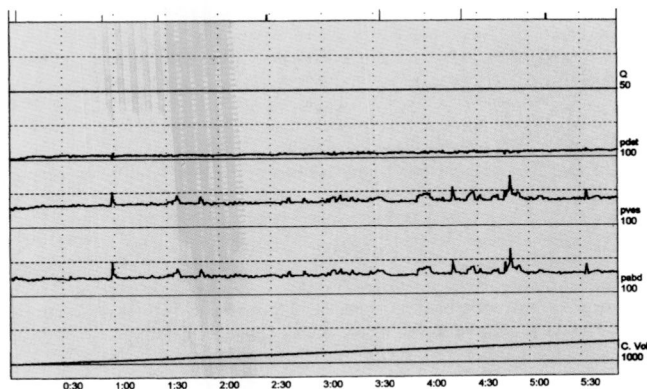

Figure 58–5. Multichannel normal-filling cystometrogram. At completion of fill, the detrusor pressure (Pdet) is 10 cm H_2O and there is no detrusor overactivity. C Vol, volume infused; Pabd, abdominal pressure; Pves, intravesical pressure.

Storage

Normally, bladder filling occurs with little or no change in pressure, and a "stable" bladder is a reflection of the integrity of the central nervous system control over bladder function. There should be no involuntary contractions during filling cystometry (Fig. 58–5). Detrusor overactivity, previously called bladder instability, is characterized by involuntary detrusor activity either spontaneously or with provocative maneuvers. In the past, these were documented as "unstable" only when they exceeded 15 cm H_2O. However, the ICS has determined that there is no lower limit for the amplitude and that any contraction during the study resulting in the patient's sensation of the need to void is detrusor overactivity. The term detrusor overactivity is further refined according to the underlying etiology of the event. **Idiopathic detrusor overactivity** is the term used when there is no identifiable cause and **neurogenic detrusor overactivity** when a relevant neurologic condition can be found. The term neurogenic detrusor over-

activity has replaced detrusor hyperreflexia, and idiopathic detrusor overactivity replaces detrusor instability (Abrams et al, 2002). **The mere absence of documented overactivity on a CMG does not rule out its existence. Up to 40% of patients with urge incontinence do not have detrusor overactivity on a CMG. This is probably due to the ability to inhibit the event consciously in the artificial setting of the urodynamics laboratory or the lack of a pertinent trigger for the event** (McGuire, 1995b).

When reporting detrusor overactivity, note should be made of the number of contractions, the volume at which they occur, the pressure amplitude, whether they are spontaneous or triggered by provocative maneuvers, and whether the patient is able to suppress them (Fig. 58–6).

In summary and simplistically, the normal bladder capacity is in the range of 300 to 500 mL; the bladder should have a constant, low pressure that usually does not reach more than 6 to 10 cm H_2O above baseline at the end of filling

Table 58–4. International Continence Society Cystometry Terms

There are two principal methods of urodynamic investigation:

Conventional urodynamic studies: Normally take place in the urodynamic laboratory involving artificial bladder filling.

Ambulatory urodynamic studies: A functional test of the lower urinary tract utilizing natural filling and reproducing the subject's everyday activities.

The following are required of both types of studies:

Intravesical pressure: The pressure within the bladder.

Abdominal pressure: The pressure surrounding the bladder; currently it is estimated from rectal, vaginal, or extraperitoneal pressure or a bowel stoma.

Detrusor pressure: The component of intravesical pressure created by forces on the bladder wall that are both passive and active.

Filling cystometry: The method by which the pressure and volume relationship of the bladder is measured during bladder filling.

Physiologic filling rate: A filling rate less than the predicted maximum. Predicted maximum is the body weight in kilograms divided by 4 and expressed as milliliters per minute.

Nonphysiologic filling rate: A filling rate greater than the predicted maximum.

Bladder sensation during filling cystometry:

Normal bladder sensation, defined by three points noted during filling cystometry and evaluated in relation to the bladder volume at that moment and in relation to the patient's symptomatic complaints.

First sensation of bladder filling: The volume at which the patient first becomes aware of the bladder filling.

First desire to void: The feeling during filling cystometry that would lead the patient to pass urine at the next convenient moment.

Strong desire to void: A persistent desire to void without the fear of leakage.

Increase that occurs at low bladder volumes and persists.

Reduced bladder sensation: Diminished sensation throughout bladder filling.

Absent bladder sensation: The individual has no bladder sensation.

Nonspecific bladder sensation: The individual is aware of bladder filling because of other sensations such as abdominal fullness or vegetative symptoms.

Bladder pain: A self-explanatory term that is abnormal.

Urgency: A sudden compelling desire to void.

Normal detrusor function: Allows bladder filling with little or no change in pressure, no involuntary contractions despite provocative maneuvers.

Detrusor overactivity: Involuntary detrusor contractions during the filling phase, spontaneous or provoked.

Phasic detrusor overactivity: A characteristic waveform that may or may not lead to urinary incontinence.

Terminal detrusor overactivity: A single involuntary detrusor contraction occurring at cystometric capacity that cannot be suppressed, resulting in incontinence with bladder emptying.

Detrusor overactivity incontinence: Incontinence related to involuntary detrusor contractions. This may be qualified according to cause:

Neurogenic detrusor overactivity: Overactivity accompanied by a neurologic condition; this term replaces the term detrusor hyperreflexia.

Idiopathic detrusor overactivity: Detrusor overactivity without concurrent neurologic etiology. This term replaces detrusor instability.

Provocative maneuvers: Techniques used during urodynamic border to provoke detrusor overactivity.

Cystometric capacity: The bladder volume at the end of the filling cystogram when permission to void is given.

Maximum cystometric capacity: The volume at which the patient feels he or she can no longer delay micturition and has a strong desire to void.

Maximum anesthetic bladder capacity: The volume to which the bladder can be filled under deep general or spinal anesthesia. This should be qualified as to what type of anesthesia is used, the rate of filling, the length of time of filling, and the pressure to which the bladder is filled.

Normal urethral closure mechanism: This maintains a positive urethral closure pressure during bladder filling even in the presence of increased abdominal pressure.

Incompetent urethral closer mechanism: This is defined as one allowing leakage of urine in the absence of detrusor contraction.

Urethral relaxation incontinence: Leakage related to urethral relaxation in the absence of raised abdominal pressure or detrusor overactivity.

Urodynamic stress incontinence: This is noted during filling cystometry and is defined as the involuntary leakage of urine during increased abdominal pressure in the absence of a detrusor contraction. This currently replaces genuine stress incontinence.

Urethral pressure measurements:

Urethral pressure: The fluid pressure needed to just open a closed urethra.

Urethral pressure profile: A graph indicating the intraluminal pressure along the length of the urethra.

Urethral closure pressure profile: The subtraction of intravesical pressure from urethral pressure.

Maximum urethral pressure: The maximum pressure of the measured profile.

Maximum urethral closure pressure (MUCP): The maximum difference between the urethral pressure and the intravesical pressure.

Functional profile length: The length of the urethra along which the urethral pressure exceeds intravesical pressure in women.

Pressure transmission ratio: The increment in urethral pressure on stress as a percentage of the simultaneously recorded increment in intravesical pressure.

Abdominal leak point pressure: The intravesical pressure at which urine leakage occurs because of increased abdominal pressure in the absence of a detrusor contraction.

Detrusor leak point pressure: The lowest detrusor pressure at which urine leakage occurs in the absence of either a detrusor contraction or increased abdominal pressure.

Pressure flow studies: The method by which the relationship between pressure in the bladder and urine flow rate is measured during bladder emptying.

Pressure measurements during pressure flow studies:

Premicturition pressure: The pressure recorded immediately before the initial isovolumetric contraction.

Opening pressure: The pressure recorded at the onset of urine flow.

Opening time: The elapsed time from original rise in detrusor pressure to onset of flow.

Maximum pressure: The maximum value of the measured pressure.

Pressure at maximum flow: The lowest pressure recorded at maximum measured flow rate.

Closing pressure: The pressure measured at the end of measured flow.

Minimum voiding pressure: The minimum pressure during measurable flow.

Flow delay: The time delay between a change in bladder pressure and the corresponding change in measured flow rate.

From Abrams P, Cardozo L, Fall M, et al: The standardisation of terminology of lower urinary tract function: Report from the Standardisation Subcommittee of the International Continence Society. Neurourol Urodyn 2002;21:167-178; and Schafer W, Abrams P, Liao L, et al: Good urodynamic practices: Uroflowmetry, filling, cystometry, and pressure-flow studies. Neurourol Urodyn 2002;21:261-274.

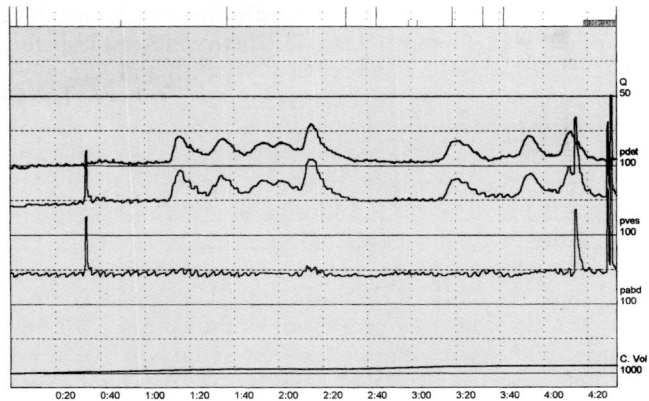

Figure 58–6. Multichannel filling cystometrogram shows detrusor overactivity with multiple contractions. Patient had idiopathic detrusor overactivity. C Vol, volume infused; Pabd, abdominal pressure; Pdet, detrusor pressure; Pves, intravesical pressure.

(end-filling pressure); and there should be no involuntary contractions.

Emptying

The voiding phase of the CMG is characterized by a coordinated decrease in outlet resistance (with opening of the bladder neck) and a simultaneous increase in bladder pressure (with detrusor contraction). Normally, the bladder neck remains closed during storage. However, during involuntary bladder contractions the bladder neck opens and continence must be maintained by contraction of the distal/external sphincter. Under testing circumstances, some may not be able to initiate voluntary voiding. This may not be an abnormal finding and may be related to the artificial testing environment.

Pitfalls in Cystometry

A number of causes of artifact in cystometry must be recognized. There are technical issues such as pressure measurement artifacts (the presence of air bubbles, kinked tubing, incorrect placement, migration of the pressure catheters) and infusion rate artifacts (especially in neurogenic bladder) and patient-related issues, including lack of cooperation, outlet incompetence, and vesicoureteral reflux. If bladder filling is too rapid, even a normal detrusor may appear to have low compliance; therefore, the identification of low compliance should be confirmed by repeated filling at a much slower fill rate. If the bladder outlet is incompetent, urine may leak around the filling catheter and a low bladder compliance may not be diagnosed because the bladder is never adequately filled (e.g., spinal dysraphism, severe intrinsic sphincter deficiency [ISD] in an older woman). In this scenario, the CMG may be repeated using a Foley catheter for bladder filling with the distended catheter balloon pulled down to occlude the bladder neck. In patients with reflux, large volumes of the filling solution may reflux into the dilated upper tracts and a low-capacity, low-compliance detrusor may be missed because of this "pop-off" mechanism. This problem is easy to identify during a videourodynamic study.

Special Testing

The *bethanechol supersensitivity test* was described by Lapides and modified by Glahn (1970). This test involves standard fluid infusion cystometry at a filling rate of 1 mL/sec until a bladder volume of 100 mL is achieved. Bladder pressures are recorded, and this is repeated two to three times for an average value. Bethanechol chloride (0.035 mg/kg) then is administered subcutaneously. Cystometry is repeated at 10, 20, and 30 minutes after injection. A neurologically intact bladder should have a pressure increase of less than 15 cm H_2O above the control value, whereas a "denervated" bladder shows a response greater than 15 cm H_2O. A positive test suggests an interruption in the afferent or efferent peripheral, or distal spinal innervation, of the bladder. However, Blaivas and associates found only 76% sensitivity of a positive test in diagnosing a neurogenic bladder and 50% specificity (Blaivas et al, 1980). Thus, a positive test by itself does not indicate a neurogenic bladder, and a negative test does not rule it out.

The *ice water test* was first described by Bors and Blinn as a way to differentiate "upper" from "lower" motor neuron lesions (Bors and Blinn, 1957). It is based on the principle that mucosal temperature receptors can elicit a spinal reflex contraction of the detrusor, a reflex that is normally inhibited by supraspinal centers. An upper motor neuron lesion interrupts these inhibitory pathways, resulting in manifestation of the reflex, whereas a lower motor neuron lesion does not. A positive test should therefore theoretically occur in patients with upper motor neuron lesions, whereas those with lower motor neuron lesions and neurologically normal patients should have a negative test (Geirsson et al, 1993, 1999). The original test involved rapidly injecting the bladder with ice water; if the ice water is expelled by the bladder within 1 minute, the test is positive. However, this test was susceptible to false-negative results because it is possible to have an involuntary bladder contraction without leakage. Raz remedied this by including the measurement of intravesical pressure in the protocol (Raz, 1973). The test is positive in approximately 97% of patients with complete suprasacral lesions and in 91% of those with incomplete suprasacral lesions; it is almost never positive in patients with lower motor neuron lesions.

Pressure-Flow Studies

Pressure-flow studies (PFSs) measure the relationship between pressure in the bladder and urine flow rate during bladder emptying (Abrams et al, 2002). These studies are **ideal to differentiate between patients with low flow because of obstruction and those with poor bladder contractility. They may also help identify patients with high-pressure obstruction and normal flow rates** (Gerstenberg et al, 1982). Obstruction may be structural, such as that caused by prostatic enlargement and stricture, or functional, caused by proximal or distal sphincter dyssynergia. PFSs alone cannot identify the location of the obstruction, but when combined with fluoroscopic screening or a sphincter EMG study, the site of obstruction may be determined.

PFSs are especially useful in the evaluation of men with LUTS because approximately one third of older men with LUTS do not actually have any urodynamic evidence of obstruction (Blaivas, 1990; Abrams, 1994). Similarly, a low flow rate is not diagnostic of bladder outlet obstruction because 25% to 30% of patients with low flow rates have detrusor hypocontractility as their main problem (Schafer et al, 1988; Rollema and Van Mastrigt, 1992), whereas a normal or high flow rate does not rule out obstruction because 7% of symptomatic men with a Qmax greater than 15 mL/sec have obstruction (Gerstenberg et al, 1982). PFSs should be performed when the information obtained will influence major therapeutic decisions. This is particularly true if surgery is being contemplated because there is evidence that the results of outlet reduction surgery are significantly improved when bladder outlet obstruction is confirmed by PFSs. This is especially true for older men with LUTS and any history of neurologic disease such as cerebrovascular accident, multiple sclerosis, or Parkinson's disease, which are known to affect detrusor or sphincter function. Also, younger men with LUTS benefit from PFSs to determine whether a functional disorder (e.g., bladder neck dysfunction) is present. PFSs are also helpful in men with benign prostatic hyperplasia (BPH) and Qmax over 10 mL/sec, a group making up 30% to 40% of BPH patients. Of these, PFSs would suggest that only 12% require surgery for obstruction (Jensen et al, 1988; Rollema and Van Mastrigt, 1992; Lim and Abrams, 1995).

Voiding dysfunction is relatively common in women, but there is considerable confusion about its cause and diagnosis. In retrospective reviews of women with LUTS, depending on the definition, obstruction was identified in 2.7% to 20% of cases (Farrar et al, 1975; Rees et al, 1975; Massey and Abrams, 1988; Lemack and Zimmern, 2000). Unfortunately, PFSs may be misleading in women with suspected obstruction. This is typified by women with postcystourethropexy voiding dys-

function who undergo successful urethrolysis. Only one third to one half of these women have obstructive PFS results before urethrolysis (Webster and Kreder, 1990; Nitti and Raz, 1994; Amundsen et al, 2000). This may be related partly to a lack of standardized criteria for diagnosing bladder outlet obstruction in women or a failure of the female detrusor to compensate in the presence of new outlet obstruction.

The ICS has defined the following terms in the interpretation of PFSs (Abrams et al, 2002; Schafer et al, 2002) (Fig. 58–7). The *premicturition pressure* is the intravesical pressure just before the onset of the isovolumetric detrusor contraction. The *detrusor opening pressure* is the detrusor pressure recorded at the onset of measured flow. It tends to be elevated in patients with infravesical obstruction, and pressures greater than 80 cm H_2O may indicate outflow obstruction. The *opening time* is the time that elapses from the initial rise in detrusor pressure to the onset of flow through the urethra. However, because the flow rate is measured at a downstream location (i.e., flowmeter outside the urethra), flow rate measurement is slightly delayed from the bladder pressure measurement. This flow delay is generally between 0.5 and 1 second and should be factored into the analysis (Griffiths et al, 1997). The *detrusor pressure at maximal flow* is the magnitude of the detrusor contraction at the time when the flow rate is at its maximum (Abrams et al, 2002). If this pressure is greater than 100 cm H_2O, it implies the presence of outlet obstruction even if the flow rate is normal (Gerstenberg et al, 1982). *Maximal detrusor pressure* is the maximal pressure recorded regardless of flow. This pressure can exceed the pressure at maximal flow if the bladder is contracting isometrically against a closed outlet. Isometric detrusor pressure is obtained by mechanical

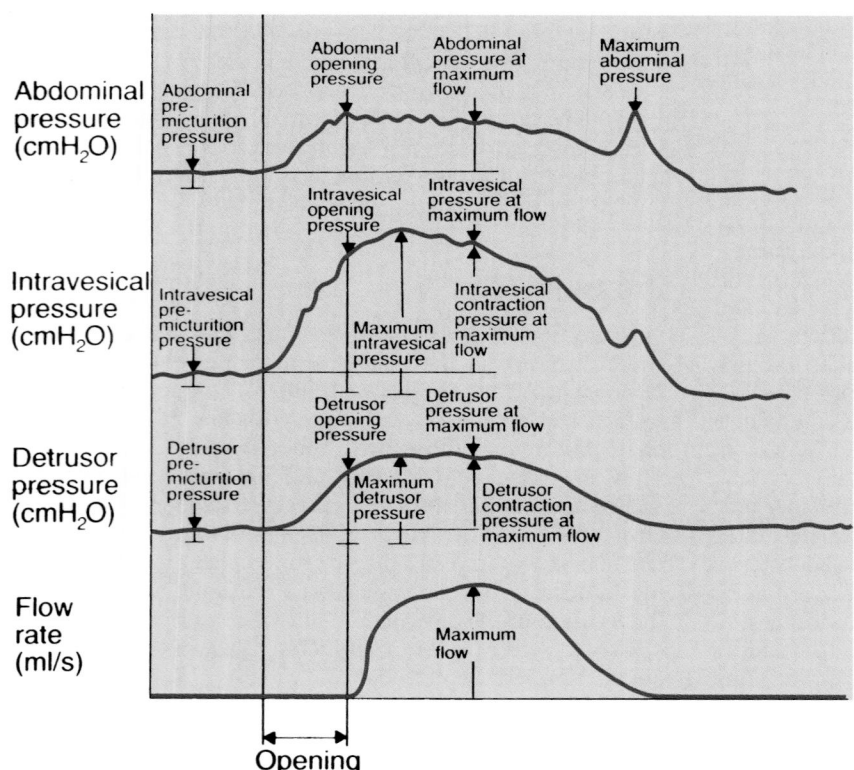

Figure 58–7. Schematic pressure-flow study labeled with recommended terminology.

obstruction of the urethra or by active contraction of the distal sphincter mechanism during voiding. The micturition pressure rises as the detrusor continues to contract isometrically, and the magnitude of this isometric spike is a reflection of the reserve strength of the detrusor. *Postmicturition contraction* (after-contraction) is a reiteration of the detrusor contraction after flow has ceased, and its magnitude is typically greater than that of the micturition pressure at maximal flow. After-contractions are not well understood, but they seem to be

more common in patients with unstable or hypersensitive bladders (Webster and Koefoot, 1983). The *postvoid residual* is the volume of urine remaining in the bladder immediately after voiding. Although the testing situation often leads to inefficient voiding and falsely elevated residual urine, **the absence of residual urine does not exclude infravesical obstruction or bladder dysfunction.** Examples of a typical obstructed PFS and a PFS showing detrusor dysfunction are depicted (Fig. 58–8).

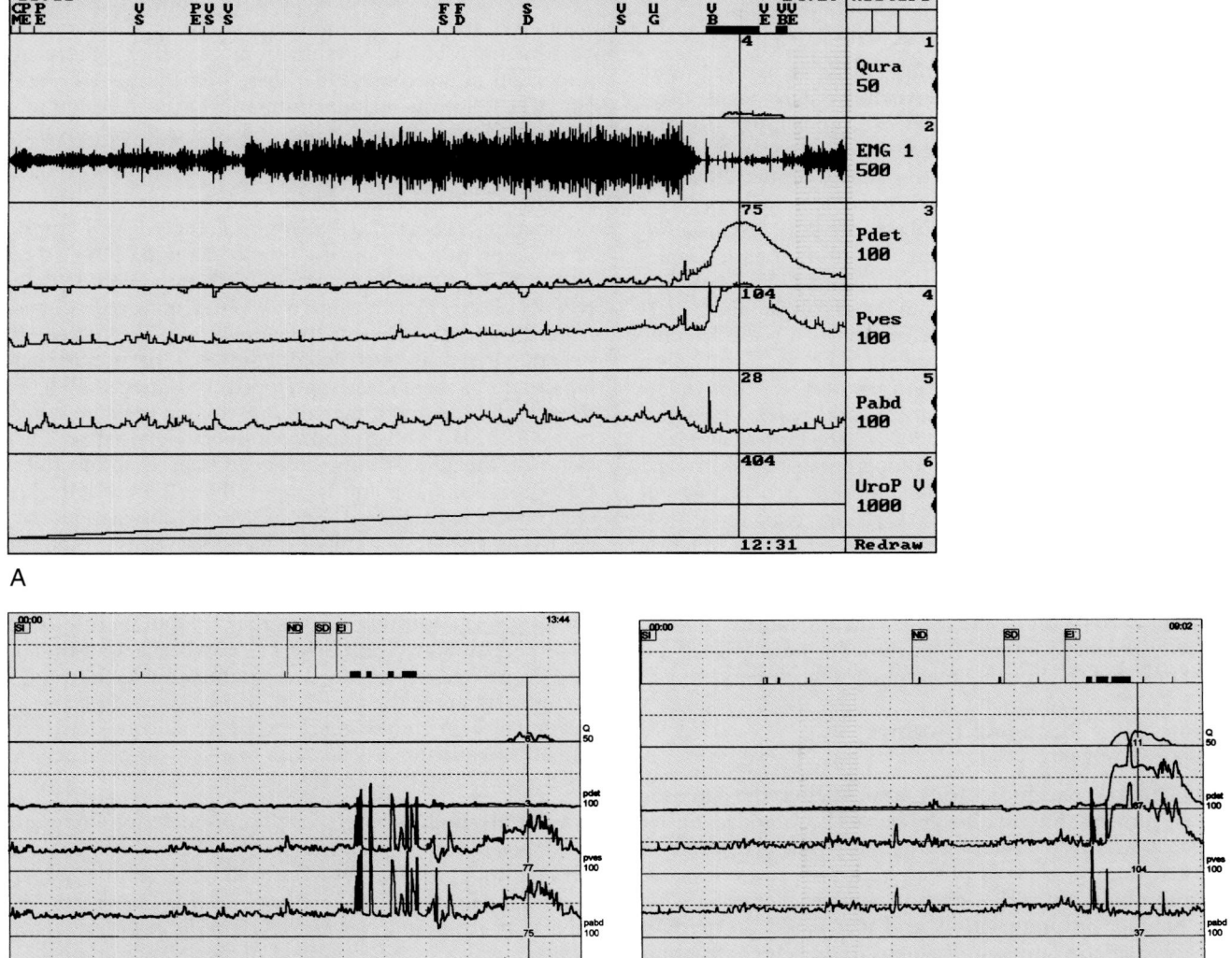

Figure 58–8. **A,** Typical micturition study shows an obstructed pressure-flow portion. The initial filling cystometrogram reveals a normal stable bladder. During micturition, a characteristic high-pressure (detrusor pressure [Pdet] 75 cm H_2O), low-flow (urine flow rate [Qura] 4 mL/sec) recording is obtained, indicating obstruction. EMG, electromyogram; Pabd, abdominal pressure; Pves, intravesical pressure; UroPV, filling volume. **B,** Multifunction filling and voiding study in a patient with poor detrusor contractility. The cystometrogram is normal during filling. During the micturition study (see vertical event marker), the patient achieves a peak flow rate of 6 mL/sec but with negligible identifiable detrusor contraction. Voiding is accomplished using Valsalva effort, as depicted by the elevation in intravesical pressure (Pves; 77 cm H_2O) and abdominal pressure (Pabd; 75 cm H_2O). The performance of subtracted pressure monitoring allows identification of poor detrusor contractility, which is otherwise masked in Pves. C Vol, volume infused; Pdet, detrusor pressure. **C,** Multichannel pressure-flow study in a 65-year-old man with storage and voiding symptoms. The pressure-flow study is suggestive of obstruction because detrusor pressure (Pdet) is 67 cm H_2O at a maximum flow rate (Qmax) of only 11 mL/sec. C Vol, volume infused; Pabd, abdominal pressure; Pves, intravesical pressure.

There is no consensus regarding a critical value for pressure and flow that is diagnostic for obstruction. The normal male generally voids with a Pdet of 40 to 60 cm H_2O, and women typically void with lower pressures (Stephenson, 1994). Although there would be little argument that obstruction existed in a patient with a Pdet of 100 cm H_2O at a Qmax of 10 mL/sec, there would be less agreement regarding a patient with a Pdet of 50 cm H_2O and a flow rate of 10 mL/sec. Recognizing this dilemma, Blaivas proposed that obstruction is suggested by a PFS in which low flow occurs despite a detrusor contraction of adequate force, duration, and speed, regardless of the actual numerical values (Chancellor et al, 1991).

Female Bladder Outlet Obstruction

Female bladder outlet obstruction is being recognized more frequently, but standardized urodynamic criteria for its diagnosis have been lacking. In the past, existing nomograms were not applicable to females because they were developed for use in men with bladder outlet obstruction (Griffiths, 1996). In addition, voiding dynamics in women are different (e.g., voiding with lower Pdet or voiding by pelvic floor relaxation and abdominal straining), making the values used for males inappropriate for females (Nitti et al, 1999). The fact that many women who benefit from urethrolysis after anti-incontinence surgery either have "normal" urodynamic studies or are unable to generate a detrusor contraction during the study calls into question the need for urodynamics in the obstructed female (Webster and Kreder, 1990; Nitti and Raz, 1994; Amundsen et al, 2000). However, Blaivas and Groutz (2000) have developed a nomogram for the obstructed woman. Using any pair of urodynamic values of maximum flow (Qmax) and detrusor pressure at maximum flow (Pdet.max), this nomogram defines obstruction in women as four types: no obstruction, mild obstruction, moderate obstruction, and severe obstruction. They also established a significant correlation between the patient's subjective sense of severity as defined by the AUA symptoms index score of the obstruction and the four nomogram classifications.

Pressure-Flow Plots and Urethral Resistance Models

A fundamental concept in urodynamics is that the detrusor pressure during micturition reflects the bladder outlet resistance. An inverse relation exists between pressure and flow such that for a given power, high pressure can occur only in combination with a low flow rate and vice versa. This is the bladder output relation, and it is based on the Hill model for depicting force and velocity of muscle contraction (Griffiths, 1977; Schafer, 1990). Therefore, the focus of the urodynamic analysis of outflow obstruction is the urethral resistance.

Early attempts to quantify the degree of outflow obstruction based on urodynamic pressure-flow data modeled the urethra as a rigid tube. This was a false assumption, and, therefore, these early systems were inaccurate. All modern PFS methods are based on Griffiths' model of flow through collapsible or elastic tubes (Griffiths, 1973). The basis of all techniques for pressure-flow analysis is the plotting of Pdet against flow rate at each point in time throughout micturition; this is the pressure-flow loop or the urethral resistance relation

(URR). It describes the pressure required to propel any given flow rate through the urethra. The important measurements from the pressure-flow loop include the opening pressure at the start of flow, the detrusor pressure at maximal flow (PdetQmax), the closing pressure at the end of flow, and the minimal voiding detrusor pressure (PdetQmin), which is usually at the end of voiding when the voiding pressure is at its least and the outlet at its most relaxed state.

Nomograms

Many nomograms have been developed in order to plot pressures against flow and allow the clinician to diagnose accurately the etiology of the voiding dysfunction, be it obstruction, detrusor dysfunction, or other causes. It is important to understand that these nomograms are sex specific. The following include summaries of the most commonly referred to nomograms, indications for use, and advantages and disadvantages of each.

Abrams-Griffiths Nomogram. The Abrams-Griffiths (AG) nomogram was based on "theoretical analysis and empirical observation" in symptomatic men undergoing PFSs (Abrams and Griffiths, 1979). This nomogram is constructed with three regions, and by plotting Qmax and PdetQmax measurements from a patient's PFSs on the nomogram, **the patient may be categorized as obstructed, equivocal, or unobstructed.** Further refinements were developed for patients falling into the equivocal group. If the minimal voiding pressure is higher than 40 cm H_2O, obstruction is present. Alternatively, if the slope of the line joining the PdetQmin location and the PdetQmax*Qmax point is more than 2 cm H_2O/mL/sec, obstruction is diagnosed. The degree of obstruction can be graded using the AG number. This is derived from the equation for the slope of the line that divides the obstructed group from the equivocal group on the AG nomogram and is calculated from the formula **AG number = PdetQmax − 2Qmax** (Lim and Abrams, 1995). The AG number is an estimate of PdetQmin, and it provides a constant variable, allowing the examiner to grade the degree of obstruction before and after treatment (Lim and Abrams, 1995). A value greater than 40 defines obstruction; a value less than 20, no obstruction. A range of 20 to 40 is designated as equivocal.

Schafer Method. Schafer's method for determining urethral resistance is based on consideration of the urethra as a distensible tube with a flow-controlling zone, the proximal urethra. In this model, the urethra is seen as a passive or elastic tube that requires a certain amount of pressure to open (Pmuo), which is the equivalent of the PdetQmin of the AG nomogram. Because the complete pressure-flow plot (i.e., URR) is too complex for detailed analysis, Schafer devised the PURR, which is a theoretical curve fitted to the lowest part of the URR (Schafer, 1990). It describes the relationship between pressure and flow during the period of lowest urethral resistance and thus reflects the passive anatomic factors responsible for the outlet resistance or flow-controlling zone and minimizes the effect of muscular activity, such as sphincter contraction.

Based on the position and slope of the PURR, two outlet parameters are characterized: (1) Pmuo (where the curve intersects the pressure axis), which reflects the collapsibility of the urethra or the degree of compressive obstruction, and (2) the cross-sectional area of the flow-controlling zone (represented by the slope of the PURR), which reflects the extensibility of the urethra or the degree of constrictive obstruction (Schafer, 1990, 1995). However, the nature of the PURR curve is such that it requires a computer for proper analysis. To simplify matters, Schafer developed the linear PURR (linPURR), which is a linear approximation of the PURR; the position and slope of the linPURR provide most of the clinically relevant information from the original PURR to define individual outflow conditions. The linPURR line is constructed by linking the Pmuo, the relative lowest detrusor pressure at which flow starts or stops, to the PdetQmax point.

Schafer constructed a linPURR nomogram that allows grading of the degree of obstruction from grade 0 (no obstruction) to 6 (severe obstruction) (Schafer, 1995). The linPURR line is plotted on the nomogram, and its location determines the grade of obstruction. To simplify matters even further, the PdetQmax*Qmax point from the pressure-flow plot can be plotted on the Schafer nomogram to determine the category of obstruction (Fig. 58–9). By projecting a line from this point to the pressure axis, parallel to the statistical linPURR lines, an estimate of Pmuo is obtained that can be used for continuous grading of obstruction (Schafer, 1995).

A further modification of this nomogram is the inclusion of detrusor contractility. Schafer added the "normal" detrusor strengths defined for typical BPH patients to his linPURR nomogram. These are essentially linearized forms of the bladder output relation and serve to eliminate the influence of variable detrusor contractility. The pressure value at which the linPURR line intersects the detrusor power line is called the detrusor adjusted mean PURR factor (DAMPF) and can be used for continuous grading of prostatic obstruction.

Group-Specific Urethral Resistance Factor. The group-specific urethral resistance factor (URA) nomogram was constructed from results obtained from a large group of adult patients with and without bladder outlet obstruction (Griffiths et al, 1989). The URA was derived from the recognition of a correlation between the minimal opening pressure

(Pmuo) and the curvature of the PURR, resulting in the ability to use one parameter, the URA, to define obstruction. A nomogram was created with a series of parabolic curves showing the average pressure-flow plots for different values of Pmuo. Each curve represents a different urethral resistance, and the value of Pmuo for the curve (where it intersects the pressure axis) is taken as the corresponding URA. By plotting the PdetQmax*Qmax point from a patient's PFSs onto the nomogram, a corresponding URA number is obtained. A URA greater than 29 cm H_2O is considered to represent obstruction. The URA nomogram is group specific in that it was derived for patients with a given type of obstruction (i.e., prostatic obstruction). It is not intended for use in patients with other types of obstruction (e.g., children) (Griffiths et al, 1989).

The ICS Provisional Nomogram. There is general agreement between all of the different models in the classification of obstruction. Lim and Abrams found 94% agreement between the AG nomogram/number and the URA in diagnosing obstruction (Lim and Abrams, 1995). Similarly, the line separating obstruction from equivocal in the AG nomogram corresponds to the line separating grade II from grade III obstruction in the Schafer nomogram, and the equivocal zone in the AG nomogram largely corresponds to milder degrees of obstruction in Schafer's nomogram. Khoury and coworkers similarly noted comparability between the AG nomogram and the Schafer nomogram (Khoury et al, 1998).

Recognizing the similarities between models and a need for a standardized analysis of pressure-flow data, the ICS has proposed a provisional standard nomogram (Griffiths et al, 1997; Abrams, 1999) (Fig. 58–10). It is very similar to the AG nomogram except that the boundary between unobstructed and equivocal has been moved to reduce the size of the equivocal region. When reporting pressure-flow results, it is recommended that this nomogram be used in addition to the method of choice of the investigator. As in the AG nomogram, the urethral resistance category (obstructed, equivocal, unobstructed) is determined by plotting the PdetQmax*Qmax value. In addition, a continuous grading of obstruction is

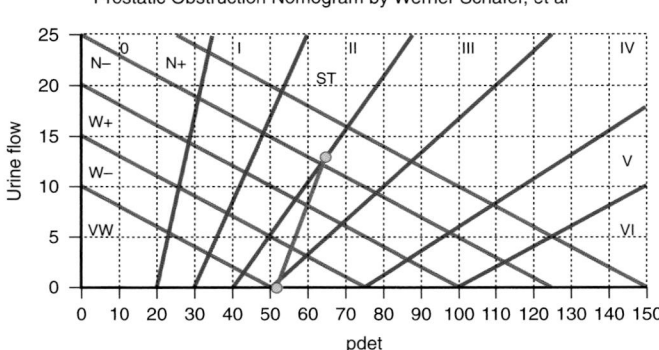

Figure 58–9. Pressure-flow data plotted on a Schafer nomogram. The plot indicates that the patient has a grade III severity of obstruction and that the patient has normal detrusor contractility. Pdet, detrusor pressure.

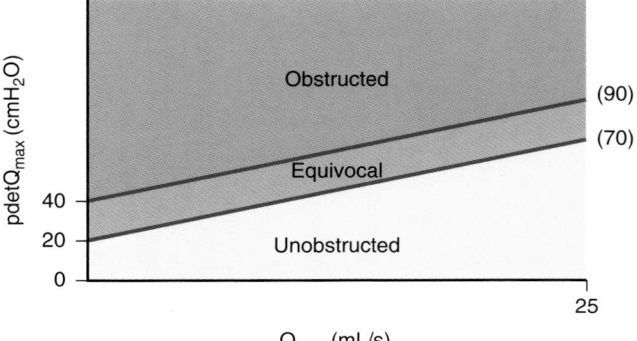

Figure 58–10. Provisional International Continence Society nomogram for analysis of voiding divides patients into three classes according to the bladder outlet obstruction index (BOOI) (PdetQmax – 2Qmax). The obstructed BOOI is greater than 40, equivocal findings are 20 to 40, and unobstructed patients have a BOOI of less than 20. Qmax, maximum flow rate.

possible by calculating the bladder outlet obstruction index (BOOI), which is essentially the AG number, given by the formula BOOI = PdetQmax − 2(Qmax). The patient is considered obstructed if the BOOI is greater than 40, unobstructed if the BOOI is less than 20, and equivocal if the BOOI is between 20 and 40. It is noteworthy that the equivocal region on this nomogram is similar to those of the AG and Spangberg nomograms and to the region defining linPURR grade II. As well, for voids with low to moderate flow rates, it is consistent with cutoff values used to define obstruction in the URA and CHESS methods (Griffiths et al, 1997).

An index of bladder contractility (**bladder contractility index [BCI]**) can be factored into the nomogram by incorporating Schafer's contractility groups. The slope of Schafer's lines is given by the formula **PdetQmax + 5Qmax**. Using this formula for the BCI (i.e., BCI = PdetQmax + 5Qmax), it is possible to define ranges of bladder contractility: **BCI greater than 150 is strong, BCI less than 100 is weak, and BCI of 100 to 150 is normal contractility** (Abrams, 1999). If this is plotted graphically on a nomogram, patients can be categorized into nine classes, according to three obstruction and three contractility categories (Abrams, 1999) (Figs. 58–11 and 58–12).

Videourodynamics

The simultaneous display of bladder and urethral pressures with fluoroscopic imaging of the lower tract is videourodynamics. It is the most sophisticated form of evaluation of patients with complex urinary tract dysfunction. This is desirable when simultaneous evaluation of structure and function is necessary to make a diagnosis (McGuire et al, 1996a; Keane et al, 1993). This study reduces the possibility of misinterpretation of findings because of artifacts. As McGuire has stated, **we also have found radiographic imaging in addition to urodynamic studies indispensable in situations including female and male incontinence, neurologic conditions, and the assessment of bladder compliance and bladder outlet obstruction** (McGuire et al, 1996a). **Because pressure-flow studies can diagnose only obstruction and not the actual location, videourodynamics is useful to identify the specific site of the obstruction** as being at the bladder neck, the prostatic urethra, or the distal sphincter mechanism (Fig. 58–13).

A *videourodynamic* evaluation is indicated when a diagnosis cannot be made with certainty without simultaneous evaluation of the structure and function of the urinary tract (McGuire et al, 1996a). Anatomic abnormalities that can also be identified or evaluated with videourodynamics include cystocele, diverticulum of the bladder or urethra, and abnormalities of the prostatic and proximal urethra, and it may also give information on the pelvic support and pelvic organ prolapse. Significant pelvic organ prolapse may cause changes in the urodynamic parameters measured, and the significance of this cause may go unrecognized unless fluoroscopy is added. It is helpful to place a pessary or use another prolapse support method to reduce the pelvic organ prolapse before performing urodynamics in order to reestablish the normal anatomy and exclude the effect of the prolapse. This is particularly important in women who have a significant central defect cystocele or other prolapse that may, by compression or distortion of the urethra, prevent incontinence from occurring. Because these defects may mask potential incontinence, they must be reduced during the study.

Videourodynamic studies can be performed using a variety of fluoroscopic units, a fluoroscopy table, and a radiographic

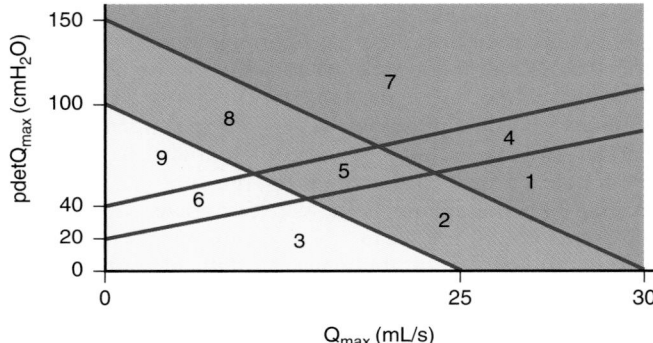

Figure 58–12. Composite nomogram allows categorization of patients into nine zones and therefore six groups according to the bladder outlet obstruction index and the bladder contractility index.

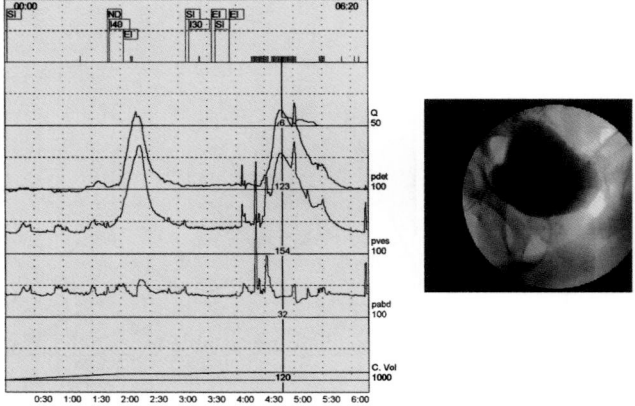

Figure 58–13. Videourodynamic study in a man with voiding and storage lower urinary tract symptoms. The filling cystometrogram (*left*) shows high-pressure detrusor overactivity. The micturition study (see vertical event marker) shows evidence of obstruction with detrusor pressure (Pdet) 123 cm H₂O at Qmax 6 mL/sec. The fluoroscopic image (*right*) at this instant shows a narrowed prostatic fossa. Qmax, maximum flow rate.

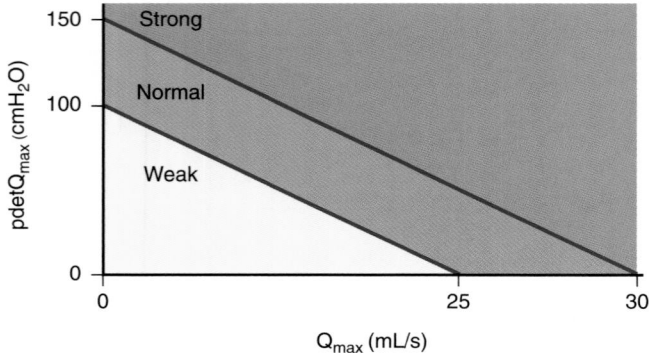

Figure 58–11. Bladder contractility nomogram divides patients into three categories according to the bladder contractility index (PdetQmax + 5Qmax). Qmax, maximum flow rate.

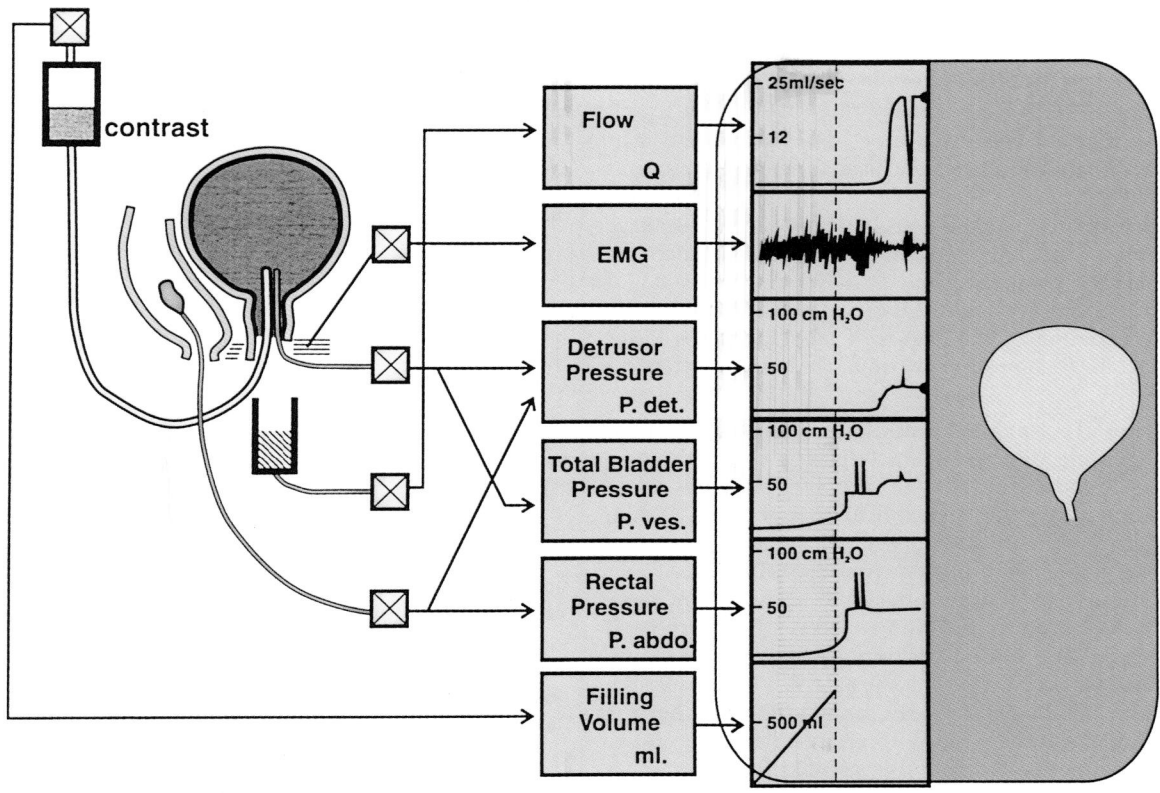

Figure 58–14. Block diagram depicts a videourodynamic evaluation. Electronic urodynamic data are projected onto the screen together with the simultaneously recorded cystogram. EMG, electromyogram; Pabdo, abdominal pressure; Pdet, detrusor pressure; Pves, intravesical pressure; Qmax, maximum flow rate.

contrast agent as the filling medium. A tilting fluoroscopy table is necessary as it allows supine placement of catheters with easy conversion to a sitting or standing position to conduct the study. A commode seat attached to the table facilitates fluoroscopic screening of voiding in the seated position, which is ideal for women. An alternative system, used currently by these authors, uses a fluoroscopic C-arm and a purpose-made tilting chair system (see Fig. 58–1). Figure 58–14 is a block diagram depicting the basic video and urodynamic setup that allows both urodynamic and radiologic imaging data to be projected simultaneously onto a television monitor for real-time viewing and for digital storage for later review. **Fluoroscopy time is limited by screening only points of interest (Valsalva and cough events during fill and sections of the voiding study) and should be less than 1 minute.** Many manufacturers make urodynamic equipment integrating the video and pressure flow data. The most important feature is the capability to measure urethral and bladder pressures while displaying them simultaneously with the corresponding fluoroscopic images (McGuire et al, 1996a).

Using this technique, the examiner is able to gain information on many aspects of the bladder and bladder function. Vesicoureteral reflux and the status of the bladder neck and sphincter may be identified. The anatomy of the bladder, including diverticula, shape, and bladder neck, may be determined as well. Also, it allows identification of dyssynergia of the proximal and distal sphincter mechanisms in neurogenic patients.

Particular Uses for Videourodynamics

Evaluation of Incontinence. Fluoroscopic screening of the incontinent woman in the standing position helps identify the presence and degree of urethral hypermobility, bladder neck competence, and the presence and grade of cystocele. Although each of these can be identified with a simple nonurodynamic cystogram, an open bladder neck could be due to urethral incompetence in a woman with ISD but it can also be a normal response to a bladder contraction during the study (Low, 1977). Hence, the open bladder neck could indicate bladder overactivity or ISD in an incontinent woman, and only simultaneous recording of the detrusor behavior with fluoroscopy makes the distinction (McGuire and Woodside, 1981). Video also improves the accuracy of a Valsalva leak point pressure (VLPP) measurement, making it is easier to observe the exact moment when leakage of contrast agent occurs rather than by trying to observe leakage from the urethral meatus, which can be exceedingly difficult in women in the standing position.

Bladder Neck Dysfunction. Bladder neck dysfunction is characterized by incomplete opening of the bladder neck during urination. This was first fully described by Turner-Warwick in 1973, and its exact etiology remains unknown. The disorder is most common in young men who complain of long-standing LUTS (Webster et al, 1980). Urodynamics alone can easily show evidence of bladder outlet obstruction. However, without the addition of videourodynamics the location of the obstruction is impossible to determine. The diagnosis of this disorder must be made with real-time, fluoroscopic imaging of the micturition event showing detrusor contraction in the absence of bladder neck relaxation.

Neurogenic Bladder Dysfunction. Although standard urodynamics adequately evaluates detrusor function for changes in compliance and for neurogenic detrusor overactivity, simultaneous video screening detects the presence of leakage per urethra or vesicoureteral reflux, which can artifactually increase bladder compliance, and shows the presence of bladder diverticula or calculus. Also, videourodynamics aids in the determination of the degree of hostility of the lower urinary tract by diagnosing proximal and distal sphincter dyssynergia.

Identification of Associated Pathology. Videourodynamics allows the identification and characterization of a pathologic process that can be associated with complex voiding dysfunction, including reflux, diverticula, fistulas, and stones. Again, simple radiography can also identify this process, but the simultaneous recording of bladder pressures allows the functional significance to be determined and management decisions made (Scholtmeijer and Nijman, 1994). For example, if reflux is detected on a voiding cystourethrogram, one does not know the bladder pressure or volume at which it is occurring; it is quite possible that the patient never achieves either the pressure or the volume needed to cause this reflux under normal circumstances, and, thus, the significance of the reflux may be minimal (McGuire et al, 1996a).

Electromyographic Studies

Clinical neurophysiologic studies, which include sphincter EMG, record the bioelectric potentials generated when the recorded muscle depolarizes. These enable the clinician to evaluate completely the striated sphincter complex and the activity of the pelvic floor during bladder filling, storage, and voiding. **Clinically, the most important information obtained from sphincter EMG is whether there is coordination or discoordination between the external sphincter and the bladder.**

Placement of Needle and Wire Electrodes

The reader is referred to our earlier discussion regarding types of electrodes. For studies measuring the activity of the external urethral sphincter in men, a 50- to 75-mm-long needle is used (Blaivas et al, 1977). The needle is placed through the perineum, advancing toward the apex of the prostate under guidance from a finger in the rectum. For women the needle is placed lateral to the urethral meatus and advanced parallel to the urethra a distance of about 1 to 2 cm. This may be difficult and painful for women, and transvaginal placement has been described as much less uncomfortable for the patient. Proper needle placement is confirmed by audio and oscilloscopic monitoring.

To obtain representative EMG studies of the perineal floor, needle and wire electrodes may be placed into the bulbocavernosus muscle in men and the superficial anal sphincter in women. The needle electrode is inserted through the perineum into the bulbocavernosus muscle without the need for local anesthesia as this is minimally painful. In women, the superficial anal sphincter is obtained with an electrode placed through the perineum at the 12 o'clock position. This is advanced just under the skin at the mucocutaneous junction to obtain the EMG signal (Siroky, 1996).

Kinesiologic Studies

Kinesiologic studies may be performed with the use of a variety of electrodes and display methods. Needle/wire electrodes are preferable because they are placed into the muscle of interest, allowing the detection of activity in individual motor units. **Although in many patients the recordings obtained from the periurethral pelvic floor and the perianal sphincter are the same, dissimilar information may be obtained, particularly in patients with lower spinal cord injury and in those who have had pelvic surgery or have demyelinating disease** (Perkash, 1980). Thus, it is always preferable to record from the periurethral area. The signal is usually recorded on a chart strip recorder or computer, or the signal is amplified and recorded as sound on an audio monitor. Many urodynamicists simultaneously monitor both visual and audio recordings for improved interpretability.

At the beginning of cystometry, before bladder filling begins, the patient is asked to demonstrate volitional control of the sphincter by actively contracting and relaxing it. The ability to do this implies intact pyramidal tracts. Next, the bulbocavernosus reflex (BCR) is tested by squeezing the glans penis or clitoris or pulling on the Foley catheter. A burst of EMG activity is a positive result and implies an intact sacral arc. Bladder filling is then begun, and, as it proceeds, there is progressive recruitment of sphincter activity, demonstrated by increased amplitude and frequency of firing (see Fig. 58–8A). Just before the onset of voiding, sphincter activity ceases and remains so for the duration of micturition. Once the bladder is empty, sphincter EMG activity resumes. **Failure of the sphincter to relax or stay completely relaxed during micturition is abnormal** (Abrams et al, 2002). When it occurs in patients with neurologic disease, it is termed *detrusor-sphincter dyssynergia*; this typically occurs in patients with suprasacral spinal cord injury in which there is an interruption of the spinobulbar-spinal pathways that normally coordinate the detrusor and the sphincter. The inappropriate sphincter activity during voiding has a variety of patterns, ranging from crescendo contraction to failure of relaxation (Fig. 58–15). In neurologic conditions, abnormal EMG waveforms, in addition to detrusor-sphincter dyssynergia, are seen. These include fibrillation potentials, complex polyphasic potentials, and complex repetitive discharges, but they require more specialized equipment for their demonstration. These are discussed later. **In the absence of neurologic disease, one cannot use the term detrusor-sphincter dyssynergia. Instead, the term** *pelvic floor hyperactivity* **or dysfunctional voiding is used.** Generally, this is a behavioral problem and is often seen in children with voiding dysfunction and neurologically normal women with voiding problems. It may have an inflammatory or pelvic pain etiology. In addition, if a patient has an unstable bladder contraction during filling cystometry, the normal response of the external sphincter is to contract in an attempt to prevent incontinence. This has the same appearance as detrusor-sphincter dyssynergia on an EMG study but is of different significance because it is a voluntary event. **Patients**

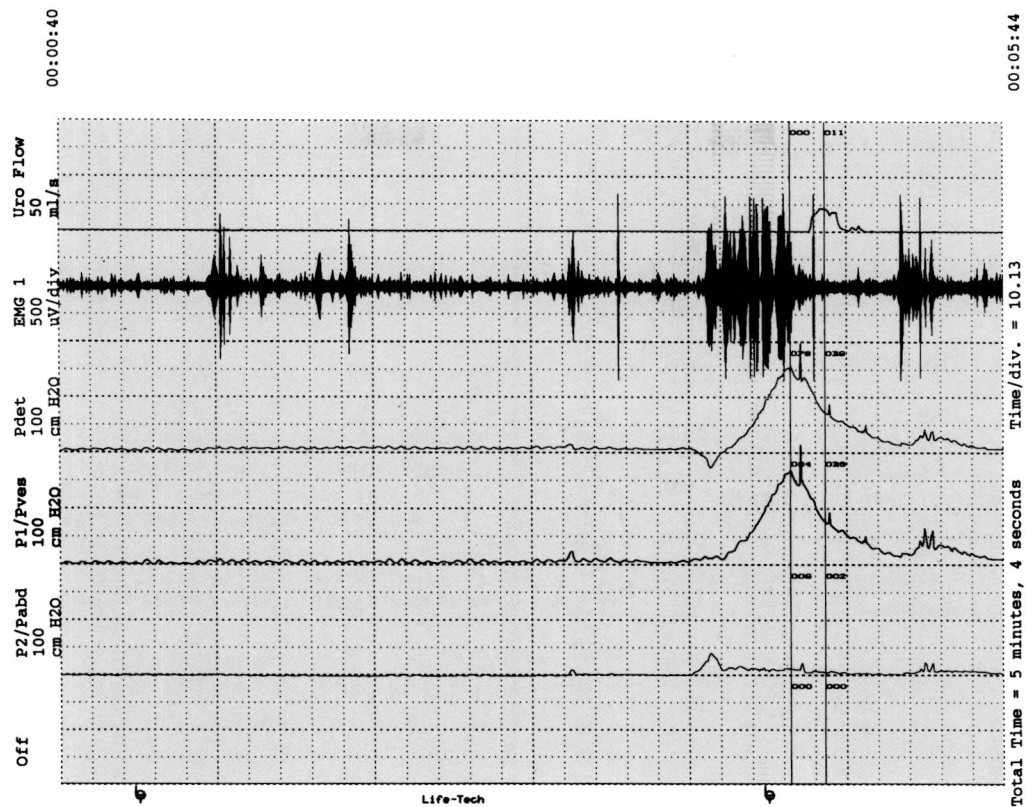

Figure 58–15. Filling cystometrogram in a man with complete suprasacral spinal cord injury. Neurogenic detrusor overactivity is demonstrated by the detrusor contraction, which is accompanied by a dyssynergic contraction of the external sphincter (see increased electromyographic activity). As the detrusor contraction is inhibited, the dyssynergic response in the sphincter decreases and flow occurs, but emptying is inefficient. EMG, electromyogram; Pabd, abdominal pressure; Pdet, detrusor pressure; Pves, intravesical pressure.

with Parkinson's disease may demonstrate a similar EMG picture that has been termed sphincter bradykinesia. There is a delay in the relaxation of the sphincter at the onset of voiding owing to skeletal muscle hypertonicity (Pavlakis et al, 1983).

Deviations from the normal EMG pattern during a kinesiologic study do not necessarily imply the presence of neurologic disease and may occur simply as a result of technical recording difficulties. Commonly, total electrical silence is not seen during the voiding study, and increases in EMG activity are often secondary to the patient straining during voiding.

Kinesiologic studies do not diagnose neuropathy but may characterize its effects. They are indicated in any patient in whom there is a suspicion of discoordination between the sphincter and the bladder. Thus, patients with spinal cord injury, with neurologic disorders (e.g., Parkinson's disease, spinal dysraphism, multiple sclerosis, and multiple system atrophy), or with voiding dysfunction after radical pelvic surgery or spinal surgery; children with voiding dysfunction and upper tract changes; and young women with urinary retention are appropriate candidates. In the last group, there is evidence that involuntary muscle fiber activity preventing sphincter relaxation may have a hormonal etiology associated with polycystic ovarian disease (Fowler et al, 1988). However, EMG should be interpreted in light of the patient's symptoms, physical findings, and urologic and urodynamic investigations

(Abrams et al, 2002). Except in patients with an unusual voiding history, a standard neurologic evaluation of the perineum and lower extremities is usually adequate to exclude most neurologic problems. Thus, there is limited role for kinesiologic studies in the routine urodynamic evaluation of incontinent or obstructed patients in whom neuropathy is not suggested by other clinical findings.

Neurophysiologic Studies

Neurophysiologic studies require more sophisticated instrumentation and investigator expertise and are **designed to diagnose and characterize the presence of neuropathy or myopathy.** Potentials generated during sphincter activity may be recorded with a specialized needle electrode inserted directly into the muscle to be tested. Motor unit action potentials (MUAPs) in health and disease differ, and, within certain limitations, the expert observer may use these studies to determine whether neuropathy is present.

Normally, the MUAP recorded from the distal urethral sphincter muscle has a biphasic or triphasic waveform with an amplitude of 50 to 300 mV and a firing frequency of 10 to 100 discharges per second (Fig. 58–16A). Simplistically, when the motoneuron or nerve to a muscle is damaged, the muscle fibers that have lost their innervation become reinnervated by adjacent healthy nerves. The resultant MUAP changes from a

Motor Unit Action Potentials

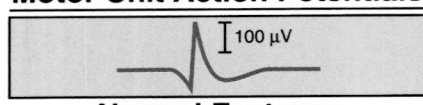

Normal Features

Characteristic configuration

Amplitude	50 - 300 µv
Duration	3 - 5 m.secs.
Frequency	1 - 4 per sec.

A

Motor Unit Action Potentials

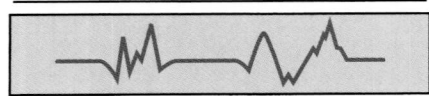

Abnormal Features

Increase in amplitude, duration, complexity of wave form.

    Polyphasic potentials (>5 deflections)
    Fibrillation potentials
    Positive sharp waves
B   Bizarre high frequency forms

Figure 58–16. **A,** Schematic of a normal motor unit action potential from the periurethral striated male sphincter. **B,** Schematic of an abnormal motor unit action potential shows complex form.

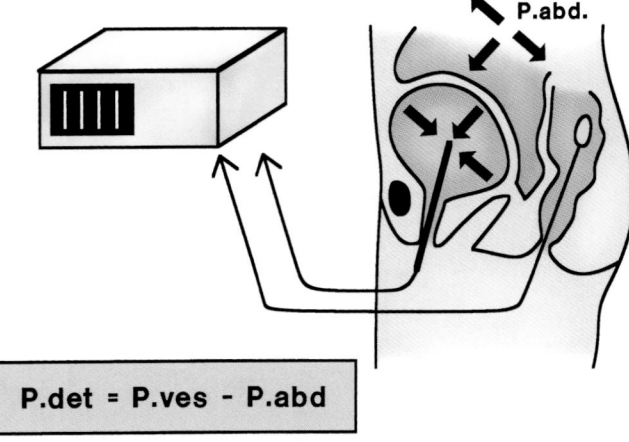

$$P.det = P.ves - P.abd$$

P.det (detrusor pressure/subtracted bladder pressure)
P.ves (intra-vesical pressure/total bladder pressure)
P.abd. (abdominal pressure/rectal pressure)

Figure 58–17. Schematic demonstrates the recording of detrusor pressure (Pdet). The detrusor contribution to micturition is recorded by subtracting the abdominal pressure (Pabd; recorded as rectal pressure) from the total intravesical pressure (Pves).

simple waveform to one that is larger in amplitude, complexity, and duration; these are termed polyphasic potentials (Fig. 58–16B). At least five deflections on the tracing must be present for an MUAP to be called polyphasic (Abrams et al, 2002). These are thought to represent the increased number of muscle fibers per motor unit that follows reinnervation. Normal muscle may have up to 15% of its activity in the form of such polyphasic potentials; however, when the amount of polyphasic activity is significantly greater than this, neuropathy is implied. Other findings that suggest neuropathy include fibrillation potentials, which are spontaneous, low-amplitude potentials of short duration, and positive sharp waves, which are biphasic potentials that are associated with fibrillation potentials.

Neurophysiologic studies are beyond the expertise of most urodynamic laboratories and are uncommonly indicated. Their role is in diagnosis of occult neuropathy or myopathy. **In the patient with overt neurologic findings who has bladder dysfunction, neurogenic bladder dysfunction can be deduced without further study. In such cases, a kinesiologic study to identify the pattern of dysfunction is all that is indicated. MUAP studies find their role in the evaluation of the patient with bladder dysfunction of unknown cause in whom neuropathy is suspected.** They are also used in medicolegal situations in an attempt to correlate voiding symptoms and sexual dysfunction with prior injuries.

Sources of Artifact

Artifacts can be very frustrating and difficult to deal with when performing EMG studies. They may be caused by multiple sources including the patient and the urodynamics suite itself. Electrical signals from other electrical equipment such as lights, transformers, electrocautery units, or the fluoroscopy equipment can all contribute. Other sources of artifact include improper grounding, defective insulation, and movement of the patient.

Multichannel Urodynamics

The preceding sections have described the individual components of the urodynamic evaluation. Here we discuss the use of multichannel urodynamics, incorporating these components into one all-inclusive study. **Multichannel urodynamics use simultaneous recording of total bladder pressure (Pves) and separate abdominal pressure (Pabd). Detrusor pressure (Pdet) is the component of intravesical pressure (Pves) created by both active (bladder contractions) and passive (elasticity) forces from the bladder wall** (Abrams et al, 2002; Schafer et al, 2002). Changes in passive forces may be caused by a loss of bladder compliance, and changes in active forces may result from muscular or neurogenic events.

The detrusor pressure (Pdet) is derived by subtracting the Pabd from Pves. Subtracted pressure readings assist in the identification of abdominal pressure events (such as straining to void) and provide true recording of what the detrusor itself is doing. A shortcoming of single-channel cystometry is that the measured intravesical pressure (Pves) represents a summation of the pressure caused by bladder wall events (e.g., detrusor contraction, Pdet) and the pressure caused by extravesical sources (e.g., abdominal straining, Pabd) (Fig. 58–17). Thus, when a rise in bladder pressure is recorded using single-channel cystometry (Pves), one cannot be sure whether this is due to a bladder contraction or to increases in intra-abdominal pressure that are transmitted to the bladder or both. **The use of multichannel cystometry allows the determination of the contributions of the individual components of Pves, Pdet, and Pabd.** Because Pdet is the component of

Pves that is created by the contractile forces within the bladder wall, it is the critical pressure to measure (see Fig. 58–17). However, it cannot be measured directly but rather is obtained by subtracting the abdominal pressure from the total vesical pressure (Pdet = Pves – Pabd). Pabd is most often recorded by a catheter placed in the rectum. The rectum is in close proximity to the bladder; therefore, the intra-abdominal pressure experienced by both is theoretically similar. The vagina (James et al, 1987) may be used in females or a colostomy/ileostomy in patients who have no anus (e.g., postabdominoperineal resection). However, in the latter case, there may be slight pressure transmission variations between these and the bladder. For rectal pressure monitoring, generally a partially fluid-filled balloon catheter is used and advanced well beyond the anal sphincter to try to avoid interference in pressure measurement caused by rectal contractions. Such contractions do occur and may be correlated with detrusor overactivity (Combs and Nitti, 1995).

The pressure transducers for the bladder and rectal catheters must be at the same reference level (at the upper edge of the pubic symphysis), and the rectal catheter should be zeroed to equal bladder pressure (which is zeroed to atmospheric pressure) at the start of the study. The lines should be flushed and the adequacy of pressure transmission checked by having the patient cough to demonstrate a rise in rectal pressure (Pabd), a rise in vesical pressure (Pves), and essentially no change in the subtracted detrusor pressure (Pdet). A change in either Pabd or Pdet should be accompanied by a change in Pves. If Pabd changes independent of Pves, the subtracted Pdet will also change, but this will be an artifact (poor pressure transmission, rectal contraction); **true detrusor pressure cannot change in the absence of a change in Pves.**

The measurement of Pdet is valuable in situations in which changes in Pabd would otherwise mask detrusor events (Webster and Older, 1980). An example is seen during provocative cystometry when coughing and jumping may lead to increases in intra-abdominal pressure that would otherwise mask any detrusor pressure response, thereby causing an involuntary detrusor contraction to be missed. The entity of stress-induced detrusor instability, in which a rise in intra-abdominal pressure (on Valsalva maneuver or cough) actually triggers an involuntary bladder contraction, can be diagnosed only by measuring the subtracted bladder pressure (Serels et al, 2000).

Leak Point Pressures

Two pressures obtained during urodynamics measure different aspects of lower urinary tract function, detrusor leak point pressure (DLPP) and abdominal leak point pressure (ALPP). **DLLP is defined by the ICS as the lowest detrusor pressure at which urine leakage occurs in the absence of either a detrusor contraction or increased abdominal pressure. ALPP is the intravesical pressure at which urine leakage occurs because of increased abdominal pressure in the absence of a detrusor contraction** (Abrams et al, 2002).

Detrusor Leak Point Pressure

The DLPP was first introduced by McGuire and associates for the evaluation of patients with low bladder compliance

secondary to myelodysplasia (McGuire et al, 1981). An important concept in urodynamics is the fact that bladder outlet resistance is the main determinant of detrusor pressure (McGuire et al, 1996b). Griffiths and Van Mastrier (1985) and Schafer (1976) also described this relationship, concluding that urethral outlet resistance at a moment of flow determines Pdet. If the outlet resistance is high, a higher bladder pressure is needed to overcome this resistance and cause leakage. This high pressure can be transmitted to the upper tracts, causing reflux and hydronephrosis. **McGuire found that in myelodysplastic patients with an elevated outlet resistance from a fixed external sphincter, those with a DLPP greater than 40 cm H_2O were at significantly higher risk for upper tract deterioration (hydronephrosis, reflux) than those with DLPPs less than 40 cm H_2O** (McGuire et al, 1981). However, while pressures >40 cm H_2O are important, the time over which an elevated pressure is exerted onto the system is also significant (McGuire et al, 1981, 1983).

Management aimed at bypassing or reducing outlet resistance (intermittent catheterization, urethral dilatation, sphincterotomy, vesicostomy) and relaxing the bladder (anticholinergic medication) is successful in preventing and reversing the dangerous effects of elevated urethral resistance on bladder compliance and the upper tracts (Wang et al, 1989; Bloom et al, 1990; Flood et al, 1994). The DLPP is the Pdet required to induce leakage but does not determine what is causing the elevated DLPP. The addition of fluoroscopy allows an accurate method for determining the presence and location of obstructive uropathy.

Technique for Measurement of DLPP. The test is performed during cystometry. The urethral meatus is observed for leakage while bladder pressure is measured. When leakage of urine is noted, the Pdet at that instant is recorded as the DLPP (Fig. 58–18). The Pves may serve as an alternative but then must be subtracted from the baseline Pves. Catheter size has not been standardized for this test but may have effects on the measurement. Therefore, use of the smallest catheter possible (6 Fr dual-lumen catheter) is recommended. Because of the presumed obstructive effect of the catheter, Combs and

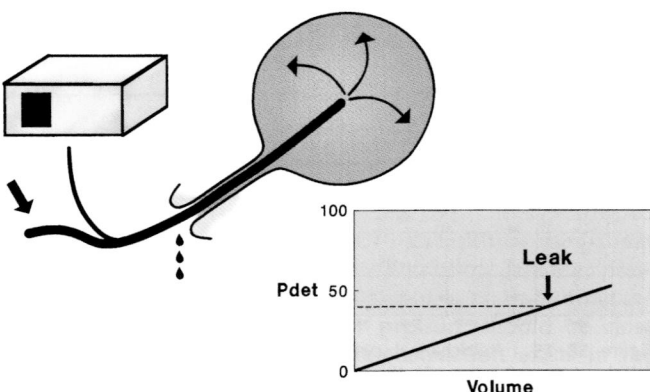

Figure 58–18. Schematic representation of the detrusor leak point pressure study. The urethral meatus is observed for urine leakage, and the pressure at which leakage occurs is the detrusor leak point pressure. Pdet, detrusor pressure.

Drake W: The uroflowmeter: An aid to the study of the lower urinary tract. J Urol 1948;59:650.

Griffiths DJ: Urodynamic assessment of bladder function. Br J Urol 1977;49:29-36.

Hinman F, Miller G, Nickle A, Miller E: Vesical physiology demonstrated by cineradiography and serial roentgenography. Radiology 1954;62:713.

Lim CS, Abrams P: The Abrams-Griffiths nomogram. World J Urol 1995;13:34-39

McGuire EJ: Diagnosis and treatment of intrinsic sphincter deficiency. Int J Urol 1995;2(Suppl 1):7-10.

McGuire EJ, Woodside JR: Diagnostic advantages of fluoroscopic monitoring during urodynamic evaluation. J Urol 1981;125:830-834.

McGuire EJ, Woodside JR, Borden TA, Weiss RM: Prognostic value of urodynamic testing in myelodysplastic patients. J Urol 1981;126:205-209.

Rose D: Determination of bladder pressure with the cystometer. JAMA 1927;88:151.

Schafer W, Abrams P, Liao L, et al: Good urodynamic practices: Uroflowmetry, filling cystometry, and pressure-flow studies. Neurourol Urodyn 2002;21:261-274.

Schafer W, Noppeney R, Rubin H, Lutzeyer W: The value of free flow rate and pressure/flow studies in the routine investigation of BPH patients. Neurourol Urodyn 1988;7:219-221.

Yalla SV, Sharma GV, Barsamian EM: Micturitional static urethral pressure profile: A method of recording urethral pressure profile during voiding and the implications. J Urol 1980;24:649-656.

Lower Urinary Tract Dysfunction in Neurologic Injury and Disease

ALAN J. WEIN, MD

OBJECTIVES

This chapter begins with a summary of the abnormalities of the micturition cycle produced by different types of neuromuscular disease, injury, or dysfunction. The source material for the central and peripheral factors involved in the physiology and pharmacology of lower urinary tract function (and dysfunction) are thoroughly discussed in Chapter 56, "Physiology and Pharmacology of the Bladder and Urethra." Most chronic voiding dysfunctions secondary to neurologic disease or injury are logical, meaning that they can be inferred from a knowledge of the normal physiology and pharmacology and the type(s) and location(s) of the pathologic process(es).

Certain secondary factors are considered that can modify the type of voiding dysfunction seen and that, once established, can cause persistence of a filling/storage or voiding/emptying abnormality, even after the initial precipitating factor or factors have disappeared or been corrected. The specific types of voiding dysfunction that occur secondary to the most common categories of neuromuscular disease, injury, or dysfunction are then described in detail. Ideally, in any such discussion, the expected states of the following parameters should be described (see Chapter 57, "Pathophysiology and Classification of Voiding Dysfunction" for specific definitions of terms):

Detrusor activity (normal, overactive, areflexic, impaired contractility)

Detrusor compliance (normal, decreased, increased)

Smooth sphincter activity (synergic, dyssynergic)

Striated sphincter activity (synergic, dyssynergic, bradykinetic, impaired voluntary control, fixed tone)

Sensation (normal, absent, impaired)

In Table 59–1 an attempt has been made to summarize many of these dysfunctions on the basis of the most common type of abnormal pattern that results from a given disease or injury, insofar as the parameters just listed are concerned. This abbreviated classification is not meant to be all inclusive but to simply indicate that, for the most part, an individual with a specific neurologic abnormality, and voiding dysfunction because of it, will, in general, have the type of dysfunction shown.

The chapter concludes with a general consideration of the principles that should guide the selection of therapy(ies) for the dysfunctions considered. The individual therapies are discussed in great detail in other chapters. The types and management of voiding dysfunction in the pediatric age group are specifically covered in Chapter 123, "Voiding Dysfunction in Children: Non-neurogenic and Neurogenic."

As an apology to others in the field whose works have not been specifically cited or not cited as frequently as they could have been, please note that citations have generally not been chosen, except where noted, because of initial publication or

intrinsic innervation of the bladder smooth muscle from a combination of pressure and ischemia (Turner and Brading, 1997; Mostwin et al, 2005). With all of these potential adverse changes occurring, it seems almost miraculous that the bladder is able to maintain its function, but it does for variable periods of time under different circumstances. However, there does come a point when the ability to fill/store and empty is adversely affected, but not necessarily to the same extent. Filling/storage changes seem related primarily to (1) changes in the extracellular matrix, leading to decreased compliance, and (2) to the appearance of phasic bladder overactivity. This overactivity could be myogenic in origin (caused by partial denervation—see Turner and Brading, 1997), or it could be neurogenic and related to another facet of plasticity. Afferent neuroplasticity mediated by nerve growth factors occurs experimentally in response to bladder outlet obstruction, a phenomenon that is inhibited by autoimmunization against nerve growth factor (Steers et al, 1996). The ability to empty can be adversely affected by factors related to neurogenic or myogenic mechanisms. The myogenic mechanisms could include a reversal of the compensatory changes that initially occur (see Chacko et al, 1999) or a breakdown of the structure and function of the proteins that enable the smooth muscle cells to take up, store, and release calcium, affecting the calcium activation of the contractile apparatus (Zderic et al, 1998; Chacko et al, 1999).

At this time, one cannot reverse certain precipitating factors for the initiation of voiding dysfunction, such as spinal cord transection and peripheral nerve injury.

Thus, the fact that the changes that result from the neuroplasticity induced by these insults are permanent is not surprising. However, **there are instances in which the initiating "cause" of a particular voiding dysfunction can be removed and yet the symptoms do not entirely disappear. This may be another instance in which neuroplasticity is a major factor.** For instance, irritative voiding symptoms fail to disappear in a certain percent of patients with outlet obstruction who undergo surgical correction. Chai and coworkers (1998) found an increased incidence of a positive ice water test in patients with bladder outlet obstruction, indicating the presence of a primitive reflex circuitry capable of mediating an abnormal micturition reflex. Because the ice water test is mediated by C-afferent fibers, the findings support the hypothesis that bladder outlet obstruction is associated with afferent neuroplasticity, detectable in this case by ice water cystometry. Furthermore, persistence of this afferent neural plasticity after relief of the obstruction could account for at least a proportion of the symptomatic treatment failures after urodynamically successful outlet reduction.

Vizzard (1999, 2000a-2000d; Qiao and Vizzard, 2004) has written prolifically about various aspects of neuroplasticity, specifically on the occurrence and potential role of such changes in altered lower urinary tract dysfunction after spinal cord injury (SCI) and irritant-induced cystitis. Changes in spinal cord protein expression from retrogradely transported bladder neurotrophic factors could play a role in the neurochemical, electrophysiologic, and organizational properties of the lower urinary tract seen in both of these conditions and could account, in the latter case, for persistence of symptomatic and/or urodynamic abnormalities after the irritating stimulus is removed (e.g., in patients with interstitial cystitis).

Those especially interested in this area should consult Vizzard's articles and associated references.

DISEASE AT OR ABOVE THE BRAIN STEM
Cerebrovascular Disease
Cerebrovascular Accident (Stroke)

Cerebrovascular accident (CVA) is a common cause of death and one of the most common causes of disability in the United States and Europe. CVA is the most devastating manifestation of cerebrovascular disease, with an **annual incidence in the United States that has been variably cited as approximately 550,000** (Blaivas et al, 1998a) **and 83 to 160 per 100,000** (Blaivas and Chancellor, 1995a). Approximately one third are fatal, and another third require long-term nursing care (Marinkovic and Badlani, 2001). The prevalence of stroke in persons older than 65 years has been cited as approximately 60 in 1000, and in persons older than 75, 95 per 1000 (Khan et al, 1990). Wyndaele and colleagues (2005) estimate that 1 in 200 individuals will suffer from a CVA. Although CVA is the third leading cause of death in the United States (Marinkovic and Badlani, 2001), approximately 75% of stroke victims survive (Blaivas et al, 1998a) and, of these, only 10% are unimpaired, 40% have a mild residual, 40% have a significant disability, and 10% require institutionalization (Arunable and Badlani, 1993). Thrombosis, occlusion, and hemorrhage are the most common causes of stroke, leading to ischemia and infarction of variably sized areas in the brain, usually around the internal capsule. Marenkovic and Badlani (2001) cite evidence that arterial occlusion is found in 80% of patients.

After the initial acute episode, urinary retention from detrusor areflexia may occur. The neurophysiology of this "cerebral shock" is unclear. After a variable degree of recovery from the neurologic lesion, a fixed deficit may become apparent over a few weeks or months. **The most common long-term expression of lower urinary tract dysfunction after CVA is phasic detrusor overactivity** (Wein and Barrett, 1988; Khan et al, 1990; Fowler, 1999; Wyndaele et al, 2005). **Sensation is variable but is classically described as generally intact, and thus the patient has urgency and frequency with detrusor overactivity. The appropriate response is to try to inhibit the involuntary bladder contraction by forceful voluntary contraction of the striated sphincter. If this can be accomplished, only urgency and frequency result; if not, urgency with incontinence results.**

The exact acute and chronic incidence of any voiding dysfunction after CVA, and specifically of incontinence, is not readily discernable. **The cited prevalence of urinary incontinence on hospital admission for stroke ranges from 32% to 79%, on discharge from 25% to 28%, and some months later, from 12% to 19%** (Brittain et al, 1998). Sakakibara and associates (1999), based on their on experience and that of others, estimate that some voiding dysfunction occurs in 20% to 50% of patients with focal brain lesions from tumor and CVA. They cite nocturnal frequency as the most common manifestation, affecting 36% of their patients. Urgency incontinence occurred in 29%, "voiding difficulty" in 25%, urgency without incontinence in 25%, diurnal frequency in 13%, and enuresis in 6%. Acute retention occurred in only 6%. Fowler (1999) cites studies showing that the presence of urinary incontinence within 7 days of a stroke is a more powerful prognostic indicator for poor survival and functional dependence than a depressed level of consciousness. Urinary incontinence at admission was found by Garibella (2003) to have a hazard ratio of 2.8 as a predictor of stroke death at 3 months. Stroke patients who were incontinent had an increased risk of infectious complications and were malnourished, possible confounders of the increased death risk. Patel and colleagues (2001) reported that urinary incontinence was associated with age older than 75 years, dysphagia, visual field defect, and motor weakness.

Previous descriptions of the voiding dysfunction after CVA have all cited the preponderance of detrusor overactivity with coordinated sphincter activity (Kolominski-Rabas et al, 2003; Wyndaele et al, 2005). **It is difficult to reconcile this with the relatively high incontinence rate that occurs, even considering the probability that a percentage of these patients had an incontinence problem before the CVA.** Tsuchida and coworkers (1983) and Khan and associates (1990) made early significant contributions in this area by correlating the urodynamic and computed tomographic (CT) pictures after CVA. They reported that patients with lesions in only the basal ganglia or thalamus have normal sphincter function. This means that when an impending involuntary contraction or its onset was sensed, these patients could voluntarily contract the striated sphincter and abort or considerably lessen the effect of an abnormal micturition reflex. The majority of patients with involvement of the cerebral cortex or internal capsule or both were unable to forcefully contract the striated sphincter under these circumstances. Although the authors and others have called this problem "uninhibited relaxation of the sphincter" (Marinkovic and Badlani, 2001), it really is not, but certainly the term does imply that a profound abnormality exists in these patients in the cerebral to corticospinal circuitry that is necessary for voluntary control of the striated sphincter.

Griffiths (2004) has summarized the evidence, obtained by electrical stimulation, positron emission tomography (PET), and functional magnetic resonance imaging (FMRI) implicating Barrington's nucleus, the so-called M-region, as responsible for coordinated striated sphincter relaxation followed by detrusor contraction, that is, normal voiding. He summarizes evidence that a second region in the pons—the L region—may be responsible for maintaining striated sphincter tone between voids, although the evidence for this is less convincing. Griffiths (1998), studying the results of single-proton emission computer tomography (SPECT) in a group of geriatric patients with established urinary incontinence, found urge incontinence in approximately 50%; and, in half of these there was reduced sensation of bladder filling, more so in men than in women. True urgency incontinence with reduced bladder sensation was associated with global underperfusion of the cerebral cortex, especially the frontal areas, especially on the right. **Thus, there are two possible mechanisms for the incontinence associated with involuntary bladder contractions in patients who have sustained a CVA: (1) impaired striated sphincter control and (2) lack of appreciation of bladder filling and impending bladder contraction.**

Smooth sphincter activity is generally unaffected (synergic) by CVA. Some authors describe striated sphincter dyssynergia in 5% to 21% of patients with brain disease and voiding dysfunction (Sakakibara et al, 1999). This is incompatible with accepted neural circuitry. I agree with those who believe that **true detrusor striated sphincter dyssynergia does not occur in this situation. Pseudodyssynergia may indeed occur** during urodynamic testing of these patients (Wein and Barrett, 1982). This refers to an electromyographic (EMG) sphincter "flare" during filling cystometry that is secondary to attempted inhibition of an involuntary bladder contraction by voluntary contraction of the striated sphincter. The guarding reflex is generally intact (Siroky and Krane, 1982).

Detrusor hypocontractility or areflexia may persist after CVA. The exact incidence of areflexia as a cause of chronic voiding symptoms after CVA is uncertain. In our patient population, this is rare, but some estimates place it as high as 20% (Arunable and Badlani, 1993). In a group of incontinent male stroke patients, Linsenmeyer and Zorowitz (1992) found 35% had involuntary bladder contractions with urodynamic evidence of bladder outlet obstruction and 6% had detrusor areflexia. In women in this group, 13% had involuntary contraction with a large residual urine volume and 19% had areflexia. **Poor flow rates and high residual urine volumes in a male with pre-CVA symptoms of prostatism generally indicate prostatic obstruction, but a full urodynamic evaluation is advisable before committing a patient to mechanical outlet reduction, primarily to exclude detrusor overactivity with impaired contractility as a cause of symptoms.**

KEY POINT: LOWER URINARY TRACT DYSFUNCTION AFTER CVA

- In the **functional system of classification** (see Chapter 57, "Pathophysiology and Classification of Voiding Dysfunction"), the most common type of voiding dysfunction after stroke would then be characterized as a failure to store secondary to bladder overactivity, specifically involuntary bladder contractions. In the **ICS Classification System,** the dysfunction would most likely be classified as overactive neurogenic detrusor function, normal sensation, low capacity, normal compliance, and normal urethral closure function during storage; during voiding the description would be normal detrusor activity and normal urethral function assuming that no anatomic obstruction existed. Treatment, in the absence of coexisting significant bladder obstruction or significantly impaired contractility, is directed at decreasing bladder contractility and increasing bladder capacity (see Tables 57–3 and 57–4).

Other important modifying factors should be considered in the case of these patients. This is generally a problem of the elderly, some of whom have preexistent lower urinary tract pathologic processes. Previously, the problems may have been manageable, but the additional difficulty may make the situation intolerable. As Andrews (1994) notes, other aspects of the brain damage can affect general rehabilitation and control of the lower urinary tract dysfunction. These may include cognitive impairment, dysphasia, inappropriate and aggressive behavior, impaired mobility, and low motivation. Finally, the entire voiding dysfunction may be adversely affected by treatment regimens that concentrate on detrusor overactivity alone (e.g., anticholinergic or antispasmodic therapy). Many such patients are depressed, and confusion and disorientation often result, which compounds the problem. Vigorous pharmacologic therapy of detrusor overactivity with agents that cross the blood-brain barrier and inhibit M_1 receptor function may make these associated problems of mentation worse.

The underlying basic mechanisms of bladder overactivity after CVA remain unclear. Experimental models of middle cerebral artery occlusion have been described, most recently followed by reperfusion to simulate the clinical condition (Pehrson et al, 2003). Shimizu and associates (2003) described the development of a rat model involving an electrolytic lesion of the right basal forebrain. Following at least middle cerebral artery occlusion the overactivity seems to involve glutaminergic, dopaminergic, and γ-aminobutyric acid (GABA)-ergic innervations (Yokoyama et al, 2002; Kanie et al, 2000). In addition, Fu and coworkers (2004) have shown upregulation of proinflammatory cytokines and neuronal nitric oxide synthetase gene in the spinal cord and bladder. Such findings raise interesting theoretical possibilities for pharmacologic management other than or in addition to antimuscarinic therapy.

Brain Stem Stroke

Sakakibara and associates (1996d) studied 39 patients with brain stem stroke. Nineteen of these had voiding symptoms. The major problems were nocturnal frequency and voiding difficulty in 6, urinary retention in 8, and urinary incontinence in 3. Problems were more common after damage from bleeding than from infarction. Symptoms did not occur in those with strictly midbrain lesions but occurred in 18% of patients with medullary stroke and in 35% of patients with pontine lesions. Eleven patients were symptomatic and underwent urodynamic study. Detrusor overactivity was found in 8 of the 11 and low compliance in 1. What was interpreted as striated sphincter dyssynergia was reported in 5 of the 11 patients, and what was called uninhibited sphincter relaxation occurred in 3. The authors concluded that lesions of the dorsolateral pons involving the pontine reticular nucleus, reticular formation, and the locus coeruleus were mainly responsible for the micturition disturbances in patients with brain stem lesions and that these findings corroborated the presence of a pontine micturition center in humans, corresponding to the pontine storage and micturition centers reported in animal studies.

Dementia

Dementia is a poorly understood disease complex involving atrophy and the loss of gray and white matter of the brain, particularly of the frontal lobes. Problems result with memory and the performance of tasks requiring intellectual mentation. Associated conditions include widespread vascular disease, Alzheimer's disease, Pick's disease, Jakob-Creutzfeldt disease, syphilis, heat trauma, and encephalitis. Alzheimer's disease is

the principal cause of dementia in the elderly (Wyndaele et al, 2005). **When voiding dysfunction occurs, the result is generally incontinence. It is difficult to ascertain whether the pathophysiology and considerations are similar to those in the stroke patient or whether the incontinence reflects a situation in which the individual has simply lost the awareness of the desirability of voluntary urinary control.** Even if the person has voluntary sphincter control, such individuals may void when and where they please, because mentation fails to dictate why they should not. Such activity may be caused by detrusor overactivity or an otherwise normal, but inappropriately timed, micturition reflex. An accurate estimate of the prevalence of dementia-associated incontinence is confounded by the difficulty in distinguishing this from age-related changes in the bladder and from other concomitant diseases, as pointed out by Wyndaele and colleagues (2005), who cite figures of 30% to 100%. Treatment is obviously difficult without a desire for improvement. Additionally, therapy that inhibits muscarinic brain receptors may be contraindicated in Alzheimer's disease if current theories about its etiology are valid (cortical cholinergic loss).

Traumatic Brain Injury

Traumatic brain injury has been cited as the most common form of severe neurologic impairment as a result of trauma (Blaivas and Chancellor, 1995a). **When voiding dysfunction occurs there may be an initial period of detrusor areflexia. With lesions above the pontine micturition center, involuntary bladder contractions are the most frequent manifestation of chronic lower urinary tract dysfunction. Coordinated sphincter function is the rule. In patients who have more isolated brain stem injuries with involvement below the pontine micturition center, detrusor striated sphincter dyssynergia may occur in addition.**

Brain Tumor

Both primary and metastatic brain tumors have been reported to be associated with disturbances of bladder function. When dysfunction results, it is related to the localized area involved rather than to the tumor type. **The areas that are most frequently involved with associated micturition dysfunction are the superior aspects of the frontal lobe** (Blaivas, 1985). **When voiding dysfunction occurs, it generally consists of detrusor overactivity and urinary incontinence.** These individuals may have a markedly diminished awareness of all lower urinary tract events and, if so, are totally unable to even attempt suppression of the micturition reflex. **Smooth and striated sphincter activity are generally synergic.** Pseudo-dyssynergia may occur during urodynamic testing. Fowler (1999) has reviewed the literature on frontal lobe lesions and bladder control. She cites instances of resection of a tumor relieving the micturition symptoms for a period of time, raising the question of whether the phenomenon of tumor-associated bladder overactivity was a positive one (activating some system) rather than a negative one (releasing a system from control). **Urinary retention has also been described** in patients with space-occupying lesions of the frontal cortex, in the absence of other associated neurologic deficits (Lang et al, 1996). Posterior fossa tumors may be associated with voiding dysfunction (32% to 70%, based on references cited by Fowler, 1999). Retention or difficulty voiding is the rule, with incontinence being rarely reported.

Cerebellar Ataxia

This group of diseases involves pathologic degeneration of the nervous system generally involving the cerebellum, but with a possible extension to the brain stem, spinal cord, and dorsal nerve roots (Leach et al, 1982). Poor coordination, depressed deep tendon reflexes, dysarthria, dysmetria, and choreiform movements result because of the cerebellar involvement. **Voiding dysfunction is generally manifested by incontinence, usually associated with detrusor overactivity and sphincter synergia. Retention or high residual urine volume may occur as well. Poor emptying, when present, is most commonly caused by detrusor areflexia, but it may be associated with detrusor striated sphincter dyssynergia, presumably secondary to spinal cord involvement.** Sakakibara and associates (1998b) reported micturitional symptoms in 184 patients with spinocerebellar degeneration. Twenty-nine (15.8%) showed stress urinary incontinence. Although 20 of these 29 also had detrusor overactivity and/or low compliance and/or residual urine, 9 had none of these findings. The authors speculate that in some such patients at least, spinal lesions affecting Onuf's nucleus and consequently pudendal nerve function were responsible.

Normal-Pressure Hydrocephalus

This is a disease of progressive dementia and ataxia occurring in patients with normal cerebrospinal fluid pressure and distended cerebral ventricles but with no passage of air over the cerebral convexities by pneumoencephalography (Blaivas, 1985). When voiding dysfunction occurs, it is generally incontinence secondary to detrusor overactivity with sphincter synergia.

Cerebral Palsy

Cerebral palsy (CP) is the name applied to a nonprogressive injury of the brain in the prenatal or perinatal or postnatal period (generally during the first year of life but some say up to 3 years) that produces neuromuscular disability and/or specific symptom complexes of cerebral dysfunction. The etiology is generally infection or a period of hypoxia. Affected children exhibit delayed gross motor development, abnormal motor performance, altered muscle tone, abnormal posture, and exaggerated reflexes. **Most children and adults with only CP have urinary control and what seems to be normal filling/storage and normal emptying.** The actual incidence of voiding dysfunction is somewhat vague, because the few available series report findings predominantly in those who present with voiding symptoms. Andrews (1994) estimates that a third or more of children with CP are so affected. Roijen and coworkers (2001) surveyed children and adolescents from six rehabilitation centers and cited the prevalence of "primary urinary incontinence" as 23.5%. The most important factors influencing the occurrence of incontinence were spastic tetraplegia and low intellectual capacity. Wyndaele and colleagues (2005) cite the occurrence of lower urinary tract

dysfunction as 36%. When an adult with CP presents with an acute or subacute change in voiding status, however, it is most likely unrelated to CP.

Reid and Borzyskowski (1993) described findings in 27 patients, aged 3 to 20 years, referred for voiding dysfunction. Incontinence (74%), frequency (56%), and urgency (37%) were the most common presenting symptoms, and detrusor overactivity was the most common urodynamic abnormality (87% of those undergoing urodynamics), with 25% of these exhibiting apparent striated sphincter dyssynergia. Mayo (1992) reported on 33 CP patients referred for evaluation, of whom 10 were older than 20 years. Difficulty urinating was the predominant symptom in about half the patients, but half of these also had overactivity and urgency when the bladder was full. The cause of the difficulty in voluntarily initiating micturition was thought to be a problem with relaxing the pelvic floor and not true striated sphincter dyssynergia. Incontinence was the major presenting symptom in the other half, associated in 14 of 16 with detrusor overactivity; all exhibited normal voiding otherwise. Decreased sensation was reported in 17 of 23 patients younger than 20 years of age and in 4 of 10 older than 20. The more serious manifestations, such as retention, were found only in the adults, prompting the author to suggest that difficulty urinating may progress in adulthood.

Reid and Borzyskowski (1993) note that incontinence can be significantly improved in most CP patients and that, in their experience, intellectual delay is not a barrier to successful management. However, one special problem that is encountered in some of these individuals that makes their management very difficult is a severe degree of mental retardation, such that any evaluation or treatment that requires cooperation is virtually impossible. With such individuals, sometimes the best that one can do is to check the upper tracts with renal ultrasonography, to measure serum creatinine levels, and to obtain an estimate of postvoid residual urine, either by catheterization or by ultrasound, and proceed accordingly. **In those individuals with CP who exhibit significant dysfunction, the type of damage that one would suspect from the most common urodynamic abnormalities seems to be localized anatomically above the brain stem. This is commonly reflected by phasic detrusor overactivity and coordinated sphincters. However, spinal cord damage can occur,** and perhaps this accounts for those individuals with CP who seem to have evidence of striated sphincter dyssynergia or of a more distal type of neural axis lesion.

Parkinson's Disease

Parkinson's disease (PD) is a neurodegenerative disorder of unknown cause that affects primarily the dopaminergic neurons of the substantia nigra but also heterogeneous populations of neurons elsewhere (Long and Lozano, 1998). The most important site of pathology is the substantia nigra pars compacta, the origin of the dopaminergic nigrostriatal tract to the caudate nucleus and putamen. **Dopamine deficiency in the nigrostriatal pathway accounts for most of the classic clinical motor features of PD.** The classic major signs of PD consist of tremor, skeletal rigidity, and bradykinesia, a symptom complex often referred to as *parkinsonism*.

There are causes of parkinsonism other than PD, and in an excellent review Long and Lozano (1998) discuss clinical distinguishing features of these other causes of parkinsonism from PD. These other causes consist of (1) multiple system atrophy (MSA: includes striatonigral degeneration, sporadic olivopontocerebellar atrophy, and Shy-Drager syndrome); (2) progressive supranuclear palsy; (3) cortical-basal ganglionic degeneration; (4) so-called vascular parkinsonism; and (5) dementia with Lewy bodies. **The combination of asymmetry of symptoms and signs, the presence of a resting tremor, and a good response to levodopa best differentiates PD from parkinsonism produced by other causes, although none of these is individually specific for PD.** Wyndaele and colleagues (2005) endorse additional criteria for distinguishing lower urinary tract symptoms caused by MSA from those caused by PD; the following suggest MSA: (1) urinary symptoms precede or present with parkinsonism; (2) urinary incontinence; (3) significant postvoid residual; (4) initial erectile failure; and (5) abnormal striated sphincter EMG.

The "gold standard" for the diagnosis of PD is the neuropathologic examination. In addition to the characteristic pattern of the loss of selected populations of neurons, there is the presence of degenerating ubiquitin-positive neuronal processes or neurites (Lewy neurites) found in all affected brain stem regions. The Lewy body is an intracytoplasmic eosinophilic hyaline inclusion consistently observed in selectively vulnerable neuronal populations, although these are not specific to PD, being found in small numbers in other neurodegenerative disorders. PD affects both sexes roughly equally. The prevalence is cited as 0.3% of the general population and 3% of people older than 65 years (Long and Lazano, 1998).

Voiding dysfunction occurs in 35% to 70% of patients with PD (Berger et al, 1990; Sotolongo and Chancellor, 1993; Blaivas et al, 1998a; Wein and Rovner, 1999; Wyndaele et al, 2005). Preexisting detrusor or outlet abnormalities may be present, and the symptomatology may be affected by various types of treatment for the primary disease. **When voiding dysfunction occurs, symptoms generally (50% to 75%) consist of urgency, frequency, nocturia, and urge incontinence.** The remainder of patients have "obstructive" symptoms or a combination. **The most common urodynamic finding is detrusor overactivity.** The pathophysiology of detrusor overactivity most widely proposed (Fowler, 1999) is that the basal ganglia normally have an inhibitory effect on the micturition reflex, which is abolished by the cell loss in the substantia nigra. Whether the dopamine D_1 or D_2 receptor (or both) is (are) primarily responsible does not seem to have been settled as yet. It has been suggested that loss of inhibitory D_1-like receptors causes detrusor overactivity, allowing D_2 receptors to facilitate micturition (Andersson, 2004). **The smooth sphincter is synergic. There is some confusion regarding EMG interpretation.** Sporadic involuntary activity in the striated sphincter during involuntary bladder contraction has been reported in as many as 60% of patients; however, this does not cause obstruction and cannot be termed *true* dyssynergia, which generally does not occur. **Pseudodyssynergia may occur, as well as a delay in striated sphincter relaxation (bradykinesia) at the onset of voluntary micturition, both of which can be urodynamically misinterpreted as true dyssynergia. Impaired detrusor contractility may also occur, either in the form of low amplitude or poorly sustained contractions or a combination. Detrusor areflexia is relatively uncommon in PD.**

It should be recognized, however, that **many cases of "PD" in the older literature may actually have been MSA, and cita-**

tions regarding symptoms and urodynamic findings may not therefore be accurate.** A good and important example of this is the inference from the publication by Staskin and coworkers (1988) that transurethral prostatectomy (TURP) in the patient with PD is associated with a high incidence of urinary incontinence (because of poor striated sphincter control). Retrospective interpretation (Fowler, 1999, 2001; Wyndaele et al, 2005) has shown that these were patients with MSA and not PD and that **TURP should not be contraindicated in patients with PD, because external sphincter acontractility is extremely rare** in such patients. However, one must be cautious with such patients, and a complete urodynamic or videourodynamic evaluation is advisable. Poorly sustained bladder contractions, sometimes with slow sphincter relaxation, should make one less optimistic regarding the results of outlet reduction in the male.

Christmas and coworkers (1988) demonstrated that subcutaneous administration of a dopamine receptor agonist (apomorphine) can reliably and rapidly reverse parkinsonian "off" periods (periods of worsening symptoms mainly caused by the timing of previous medication doses and the unpredictable nature of motor fluctuations). By repeating videourodynamic studies during the motor improvement after administration of apomorphine, bladder outlet obstruction secondary to benign prostatic hyperplasia (BPH) may be able to be distinguished from voiding dysfunction secondary to PD. The authors also point out that apomorphine might be useful in such patients who have severe off-phase voiding dysfunction, such as those with disabling nocturnal frequency and incontinence. **Voiding dysfunction secondary to PD defies "routine" classification within any system. It is most manifest by storage failure secondary to bladder overactivity, but detailed urodynamic evaluation is mandatory before any but the simplest and most reversible therapy.** The therapeutic menus (see Tables 57–3 and 57–4) are perfectly applicable, but the disease itself may impose certain limitations on the use of certain treatments (e.g., limited mobility for rapid toilet access, hand control insufficient for clean intermittent catheterization [CIC]).

Animal models of PD have been developed, utilizing injections of 1-methyl-4-phenyl-1,2,3,6-tetrahydropyridine or 6-hydroxydopamine into the nigrostriatal pathway (Yoshimura et al, 2003; Andersson, 2004; Wyndaele et al, 2005).

Multiple System Atrophy

Multiple system atrophy is a progressive neurodegenerative disease of unknown etiology. The symptoms encompass parkinsonism and cerebellar, autonomic (including urinary and erectile problems), and pyramidal cortical dysfunction in a multitude of combinations. The clinical features and the differentiation from PD are nicely described in a consensus statement by Gilman and associates (1999). These investigators advocate a designation of MSA-P if parkinsonian features predominate and one of MSA-C if cerebellar features predominate. Older names such as "striatonigral degeneration," "sporadic olivopontocerebellar atrophy," and "Shy-Drager syndrome" (Wein, 2002) should be discarded in favor of these.

The neurologic lesions of MSA consist of cell loss and gliosis in widespread areas, much more so than with PD, and this more diffuse nature of cell loss probably explains why

bladder symptoms may occur earlier than in PD and be more severe and why erection may be affected as well (Kirby et al, 1986; Beck et al, 1994; Chandiramani et al, 1997). Affected areas have been identified in the cerebellum, substantia nigra, globus pallidus, caudate, putamen, inferior olives, intermediolateral columns of the spinal cord, and Onuf's nucleus. Males and females are equally affected, with the onset in middle age. MSA is generally progressive and associated with a poor prognosis.

Shy-Drager syndrome has been described in the past as characterized clinically by orthostatic hypotension, anhidrosis, and varying degrees of cerebellar and parkinsonian dysfunction. Voiding and erectile dysfunction are common. Some consider this as late-stage MSA (Chandiramani et al, 1997).

Chandiramani and coworkers (1997) **compared the clinical features of 52 patients with probable MSA and 41 patients with PD.** Of patients with MSA, 60% had their urinary symptoms precede or present with their symptoms of parkinsonism. Of patients with PD, 94% had been diagnosed for several years before the onset of urinary symptoms. In patients with MSA, urinary incontinence was a significant complaint in 73% whereas 19% had only frequency and urgency without incontinence. Sixty-six percent of the patients with MSA had a significant postvoid residual volume (100 to 450 mL). In patients with PD, frequency and urgency were the predominant symptoms in 85%, whereas incontinence was the primary complaint in 15%. In only 5 of 32 patients with PD in whom residual urine volume was measured was it significant. Eleven men with MSA underwent TURP. Nine of these had deterioration of their urinary incontinence afterward. All 3 women with MSA were incontinent after pelvic floor repair. Five men with PD underwent prostatectomy, and 3 reported a good result. Ninety-three percent of the men with MSA questioned about erectile function reported erectile failure, and in 13 of 27 of these the erectile dysfunction preceded the diagnosis of MSA. Seven of the 21 men with PD had erectile failure, but in all these men the diagnosis of erectile dysfunction followed the diagnosis of PD by 1 to 4 years. Fowler (2001) lists the clinical urogenital criteria favoring a diagnosis of MSA as (1) urinary symptoms precede or present with parkinsonism; (2) male erectile dysfunction precedes or presents with parkinsonism; (3) urinary incontinence; (4) significant postvoid residual; and (5) worsening lower urinary tract dysfunction after urologic surgery.

The initial urinary symptoms of MSA are urgency, frequency, and urgency incontinence, occurring up to 4 years before the diagnosis is made, as does erectile failure. **Detrusor overactivity is frequently found, as one would expect from the central nervous system areas affected, but decreased compliance may occur, reflecting distal spinal involvement of the locations of the cell bodies of autonomic neurons innervating the lower urinary tract. As the disease progresses, difficulty in initiating and maintaining voiding may occur, probably from pontine and sacral cord lesions, and this generally is associated with a poor prognosis. Cystourethrography or video-urodynamic studies may reveal an open bladder neck (intrinsic sphincter deficiency), and many patients exhibit evidence of striated sphincter denervation on motor unit electromyography. The smooth and striated sphincter abnormalities predispose women to sphincteric incontinence and make prostatectomy hazardous in men.** Berger and coworkers (1990) described a

useful urodynamic differentiation of what was termed Shy-Drager syndrome (probable late stage MSA) from PD. Parkinsonian patients with voiding dysfunction generally have detrusor overactivity and normal compliance. An open bladder neck was seen only in patients with "Shy-Drager syndrome," excluding those patients with Parkinson's disease who have had a prostatectomy. EMG evidence of striated sphincter denervation was seen much more commonly in those diagnosed as having Shy-Drager syndrome.

The treatment of significant voiding dysfunction caused by MSA is difficult and seldom satisfactory. Treatment of detrusor overactivity during filling may worsen problems initiating voluntary micturition, or worsen impaired contractility during emptying. Patients generally have sphincteric insufficiency and, rarely, therefore, is an outlet-reducing procedure indicated. Drug treatment for sphincteric incontinence may further worsen emptying problems. Generally, the goal in these patients is to facilitate storage, and CIC would often be desirable. Unfortunately, patients with advanced disease often are not candidates for CIC.

DISEASES PRIMARILY INVOLVING THE SPINAL CORD
Multiple Sclerosis

Multiple sclerosis (MS) is primarily a disease of young and middle-aged adults with a twofold predilection for women. Litwiller and colleagues (1999) detailed current prevalence rates for MS as 1/1000 Americans, 2/1000 northern Europeans, and 20 to 40/100,000 first-degree relatives of patients with MS. **The disease is believed to be immune mediated and is characterized by neural demyelination, generally characterized by axonal sparing, in the brain and spinal cord** (Noseworthy et al, 2000). This demyelination causes impairment of saltatory conduction and of conduction velocity in axonal pathways, resulting in various neurologic abnormalities that are subject to exacerbation and remission. Lesions, known as plaques, range from 1 mm to 4 cm and are scattered throughout the white matter of the nervous system (Chancellor and Blaivas, 1993). **The demyelinating process most commonly involves the lateral corticospinal (pyramidal) and reticulospinal columns of the cervical spinal cord,** and it is thus not surprising that voiding dysfunction and sphincter dysfunction is so common. Autopsy studies have revealed almost constant evidence of demyelination in the cervical spinal cord, but involvement of the lumbar and sacral cord occurs in approximately 40% and 18%, respectively (Blaivas and Kaplan, 1988). Lesions may also occur in the optic nerve and in the cerebral cortex and midbrain, the latter accounting for the intellectual deterioration and/or euphoria that may be seen as well (Kirby, 1994; Noseworthy et al, 2000), ultimately in as many as 43% to 65% of patients (Litwiller et al, 1999).

The incidence of voiding dysfunction in MS is related to the disability status. Of patients with MS, **50% to 90% complain of voiding symptoms at some time; the prevalence of incontinence is cited as 37 to 72%** (Wyndaele et al, 2005). Litwiller and coworkers (1999), in their excellent review article, cite symptoms of frequency or urgency in 31% to 85% of patients in various series, with corresponding percentages of incontinence as 37% to 72% and of obstructive symptoms with urinary retention in 2% to 52%. Lower urinary tract involvement may constitute the sole initial complaint or be part of the presenting symptom complex in up to 15% of patients, usually in the form of acute urinary retention of "unknown" etiology or as an acute onset of urgency and frequency, secondary to overactivity (Wyndaele et al, 2005).

Detrusor overactivity is the most common urodynamic abnormality detected, occurring in 34% to 99% of cases in reported series (Blaivas and Kaplan, 1988; Chancellor and Blaivas, 1993; Sirls et al, 1994; Litwiller et al, 1999). **Of the patients with overactivity, 30% to 65% have coexistent striated sphincter dyssynergia. Impaired detrusor contractility or areflexia may also exist; estimates of prevalence range from 12% to 38%** (Wyndaele et al, 2005), **a phenomenon that can considerably complicate treatment efforts.** Generally, **the smooth sphincter is synergic.** Chancellor and Blaivas (1993) reviewed urodynamic findings in multiple series of patients with MS and voiding dysfunction and summarize the incidence of three basic patterns: (1) detrusor overactivity, striated sphincter synergia 26% to 50% (average 38%); (2) detrusor overactivity, striated sphincter dyssynergia 24% to 46% (average, 29%); and (3) detrusor areflexia 19% to 40% (average, 26%). Litwiller and coworkers (1999) tabularized 22 references, reporting approximately the same ranges. It is also possible to see relative degrees of sphincteric flaccidity caused by MS, a phenomenon cited as occurring in less than 15% of patients (Litwiller et al, 1999); this finding could predispose and contribute to sphincteric incontinence. DeRidder and associates (1998) reported weakness of pelvic floor contraction in nearly all 30 women they studied with MS. Spasticity of the pelvic floor was present in all patients with striated sphincter dyssynergia but in none with detrusor overactivity alone.

Because sensation is frequently intact in these patients, one must be careful to distinguish urodynamic pseudo-dyssynergia from true striated sphincter dyssynergia. Blaivas and associates (1981) subcategorized true striated sphincter dyssynergia in patients with MS and identified some varieties that are more worrisome than others. For instance, in a female with MS, a brief period of striated sphincter dyssynergia during detrusor contraction but one that does not result in excessive intravesical pressure during voiding, substantial residual urine volume, or secondary detrusor hypertrophy may be relatively inconsequential, whereas those varieties that are more sustained—resulting in high bladder pressures of long duration—are most associated with urologic complications. Giannantoni and colleagues (1998) reviewed 116 of their patients and likewise concluded that there was a significant relationship between the maximum amplitude of the involuntary bladder contractions and upper urinary tract deterioration. Chancellor and Blaivas (1993) emphasized what they believed were **the most important parameters predisposing patients with MS to significant urologic complications: (1) striated sphincter dyssynergia in men; (2) high detrusor filling pressure (>40 cm H_2O); and (3) an indwelling catheter. Interestingly, however, Wyndaele's committee (Wyndaele, 2005) concluded that progressive neurologic disease, MS included, rarely causes upper urinary tract damage, even when, in MS, severe spasticity and disability exist. The reason for this is unknown, but they believe that the situation and concerns with respect to this are unlike those for spinal cord injury.**

KEY POINT: MULTIPLE SCLEROSIS

■ The most common functional classification applicable to patients with voiding dysfunction secondary to MS would thus be storage failure secondary to detrusor overactivity. This is commonly complicated by striated sphincter dyssynergia, with varying effects on the ability to empty completely at acceptable pressures. Other abnormalities, and other combined deficits, are obviously possible, however. Once the dysfunction is broadly characterized, the treatment options should be obvious from the therapeutic menus (see Tables 57–3 and 57–4).

Aggressive and anticipatory medical management can obviate most significant complications. Sirls and associates (1994) reported that only 7% (I calculate 10.4%) of their patients required surgical intervention because of failure of aggressive medical management and that none developed hydronephrosis on such therapy. The regimens used were (1) drugs to decrease detrusor overactivity plus CIC (57%); (2) such drugs alone (13%); (3) CIC alone (15%); and (4) behavioral therapy. **A significant proportion of patients with MS with and without new symptoms will develop changes in their detrusor compliance and urodynamic pattern** (Ciancio et al, 2001). **Caution should therefore be exercised in recommending irreversible therapeutic options.**

A rat model for a demyelinating disease resembling MS has been described using myelin basic protein as an antigen for inducing experimental allergic encephalomyelitis (Mizusawa et al, 2000).

Spinal Cord Injury

Epidemiology, Morbidity, General Concepts

SCI may occur as a consequence of acts of violence, fracture, or dislocation of the spinal column secondary to motor vehicle, diving accidents or falls, vascular injuries or repair, infection, disk prolapse, or sudden or severe hyperextension from other causes. Altered lower urinary tract and sexual function frequently occur secondary to SCI and significantly affect quality of life; SCI patients are at risk urologically for urinary tract infection, sepsis, upper and lower urinary tract deterioration, upper and lower urinary tract calculi, autonomic hyperreflexia (dysreflexia), skin complications, and depression (which can complicate their urologic management). Failure to properly address the lower urinary tract dysfunction can lead to significant morbidity and mortality. There is great variation in urologic practice regarding initial evaluation, follow-up, and surveillance among spinal injury units (Bycroft et al, 2004), a problem that Boone (2004) properly attributes to a lack of evidence-based decision-making.

Complete anatomic transection of the spinal cord is rare, and the degree of neurologic deficit varies with the level and severity of the injury. **Spinal column (bone) segments are numbered by the vertebral level, and these have a different relationship to the spinal cord segmental level at different locations. One must be careful to specify cord or column** level when discussing SCI. The sacral spinal cord begins at about spinal column level T12 to L1. The spinal cord terminates in the cauda equina at approximately the spinal column level of L2. Multiple level injuries may occur, and, even with a single initial injury, cord damage may not be confined to a single cord segment and may extend cephalad, caudad, or both.

Stover and Fine (1987) reviewed the epidemiology and other general aspects of SCI. The annual rate was reported as 30 to 32 new SCIs per million persons at risk in the United States; the prevalence was approximately 906 per million. This coincides roughly with the estimate by DeVivo (1997) of approximately 10,000 new cases of SCI in the United States yearly and an estimate of 12,000 per year by Rabchevsky and Smith (2001). DeVivo (1997) reported the most common mechanisms of injury, as collected by the National Spinal Cord Injury Statistical Center, as motor vehicle accidents (35.9%), violence (29.5%), falls (20.3%), and sports-related injuries (7.3%). Males account for 71% to 80% of patients with SCI. The average age at injury is 31.5 years. Children comprise 3% to 5% of all patients with SCI (Generao et al, 2004). Stover and Fine (1987) reported that neurologically incomplete quadriplegics constituted the largest group of SCI patients at the time of hospital admission (28%), followed by complete paraplegics (26%), complete quadriplegics (24%), and incomplete paraplegics (18%). This seems to have changed little during the 1990s. The majority occur at or above the T12 spinal column (vertebral) level.

Although earlier data (Hackler, 1977) **indicated that renal disease was the major cause of death, at least in the paraplegic patient, a retrospective study of more than 5000 patients who sustained SCI between 1973 and 1980 revealed that the leading causes of death at that time were pneumonia, septicemia, heart disease, accidents, and suicide** (Stover and Fine, 1987; Soden et al, 2000). These figures seemingly indicate a distinct improvement in the urologic care of these patients.

Controlled and coordinated lower urinary tract function depends on an intact neural axis. Bladder contractility and the occurrence of reflex contractions depend on an intact sacral spinal cord and its afferent and efferent connections (see Chapter 56, "Physiology and Pharmacology of the Bladder and Urethra").

KEY POINT: SPINAL CORD INJURY

- Generally, complete spinal cord lesions above the sacral spinal cord, but below the area of the sympathetic outflow, result in detrusor overactivity, absent sensation below the level of the lesion, smooth sphincter synergia, and striated sphincter dyssynergia. Lesions at or above the spinal cord level of T7 or T8 (the spinal column level of T6) may result in smooth sphincter dyssynergia as well. However, although the correlation between neurologic and urodynamic findings is good, it is not perfect, and a neurologic examination is no substitute for a urodynamic evaluation in these patients when one is determining risk factors and treatment (see later).

There is an impressive amount of literature that is continuously building on the neurobiology of the spinal cord and its acute and chronic alteration after SCI. These topics are not specifically considered in detail here, nor are the ramifications of this information relative to potential improvement of spinal cord function after injury by stem cell implant or reinnervation. Earlier reviews can be found by Olson (1997), Fawcett (1998), and Kakulas (1999); later ones were presented by Rabchevsky and Smith (2001) (this also includes a discussion of pathophysiology and experimental models), Cao and coworkers (2002) (stem cell repair), Fawcett (2002) (repair of SCI), Rossi and Cattaneo (2002) (stem cell therapy), Mitsui and colleagues (2003) (stem cell repair), Kakulas (2004) (neuropathology and natural history of the spinal cord changes), and Livshits and associates (2004) (reinnervation). Sexual and reproductive dysfunction in the patient with SCI is a topic that deserves much attention in the overall rehabilitation plan. Pertinent general and specific concepts of sexual and reproductive dysfunction and their normalization in this special group of patients can be found in Chapter 21, "Physiology of Penile Erection and Pathophysiology of Erectile Dysfunction" and Chapter 23, "Prosthetic Surgery for Erectile Dysfunction" (male) and Chapter 28, "Urologic Management of Women with Sexual Health Concerns" (female). Other excellent reviews on the specifics of sexual function in SCI can be found by Bennett and coworkers (1988), Stone and MacDermott (1989), Smith and Bodner (1993), and Biering-Sorensen and Sonksen (2001), and on infertility by Linsenmeyer and Perkash (1991), Rajaskaran and Monga (1999), and Rutkowski and colleagues (1999).

Spinal Shock

After a significant SCI, a period of decreased excitability of spinal cord segments at and below the level of the lesion occurs, referred to as "spinal shock." There is **absent somatic reflex activity and flaccid muscle paralysis below this level.** Although classic teaching refers to generalized areflexia below the level of the lesion for days to months, Thomas and O'Flynn (1994) confirm that the most peripheral somatic reflexes of the sacral cord segments (the anal and bulbocavernosus reflexes) may never disappear or, if they do, may return within minutes or hours of the injury. However, functions proximal to the level of the injury may be depressed as well (Atkinson and Atkinson, 1996). Although the course of spinal shock is well known, the actual phenomenon remains poorly understood, with little or no basic research evident recently.

Spinal shock includes a suppression of autonomic activity as well as somatic activity, and the bladder is acontractile and areflexic. Radiologically, the bladder has a smooth contour with no evidence of trabeculation. The bladder neck is generally closed and competent unless there has been prior surgery or in some cases of thoracolumbar and presumably sympathetic injury (Sullivan and Yalla, 1992). **The smooth sphincter mechanism seems to be functional. Some EMG activity may be recorded from the striated sphincter, and the maximum urethral closure pressure is lower than normal but still maintained at the level of the external sphincter zone; however, the normal guarding reflex (striated sphincter response during filling) is absent and there is no voluntary control** (Fam and Yalla, 1988). Because sphincter tone exists, urinary incontinence generally does not result unless there is gross overdistention with overflow. In evolving lesions, every attempt should be made to preserve as low a bladder storage pressure as possible and to avoid any measures that might impair this. Urinary retention is the rule, and catheterization is necessary to circumvent this problem. Although virtually all would agree that CIC is an excellent method of management during this period and advocate its use, Lloyd and coworkers (1986) reported their own experience and cite that of others that indicate no differences in outcome when a small-bore Foley catheter or suprapubic tube is used at this stage.

If the distal spinal cord is intact but is simply isolated from higher centers, there is generally a return of reflex detrusor contractility. At first, such reflex activity is poorly sustained and produces only low-pressure changes, but the strength and duration of such involuntary contractions increase, producing involuntary voiding, usually with incomplete bladder emptying. This return of reflex bladder activity is generally manifested by involuntary voiding between catheterizations and occurs along with the recovery of lower extremity deep tendon reflexes. Spinal shock generally lasts 6 to 12 weeks in complete suprasacral spinal cord lesions but may last up to 1 or 2 years. It may last a shorter period of time in incomplete suprasacral lesions and only a few days in some patients.

Suprasacral Spinal Cord Injury

There is no unanimous agreement on the neurobiology of the development of reflex bladder contraction in response to bladder distention after suprasacral SCI. de Groat and colleagues (1997) have studied this phenomenon and related events extensively in cats and listed four potential mechanisms for the recovery of such micturition and the development of C-fiber afferent evoked bladder reflexes (see also the description by Yoshimura and Chancellor in Chapter 56, "Physiology and Pharmacology of the Bladder and Urethra"): (1) elimination of bulbospinal inhibitory pathways; (2) strengthening of existing synapses or formation of new synaptic connections from axonal sprouting in the spinal cord; (3) changes in synthesis, release, or actions of neurotransmitters, and (4)

alterations in afferent input (afferent axonal sprouting) from peripheral organs. Recent reports of specific alterations in animal models are summarized by Morrison and colleagues (2005) as (1) increased sensitivity of C-fiber afferents, possibly involving nerve growth factor; (2) enlargement of dorsal root ganglion cells; (3) increased electrical excitability of afferents associated with a shift in expression of sodium channels from a high-threshold tetrodotoxin-resistant type to a low-threshold tetrodotoxin-sensitive type. Other findings possibly related to the development of lower urinary tract dysfunction after SCI have been reported as (1) increased concentrations of glutamate, glycine, and taurine (Smith et al, 2002); (2) disruption of bladder epithelium barrier function (Apodaca et al, 2003); (3) change from low affinity M_1 to high affinity M_3 receptors at prejunctional cholinergic nerve endings (Somogyi et al, 2003); (4) increased release of adenosine triphosphate from bladder urothelium (Khera et al, 2004); (5) increased spinal cord nerve growth factor (Seki et al, 2004); and (6) alterations in smooth muscle myosin heavy chain gene expression (Wilson et al, 2005).

The characteristic pattern that results when a patient has a complete lesion above the sacral spinal cord is detrusor overactivity, smooth sphincter synergia (with lesions below the sympathetic outflow), and striated sphincter dyssynergia (Sullivan and Yalla, 1992; Thomas and O'Flynn, 1994; Chancellor and Blaivas, 1995b). **Neurologic examination shows spasticity of skeletal muscle distal to the lesion, hyperreflexic deep tendon reflexes, and abnormal plantar responses. There is impairment of superficial and deep sensation.** Figures 59–1 to 59–3 typify the cystourethrographic and urodynamic patterns. The guarding reflex is absent or weak in most patients with a complete suprasacral SCI. In incomplete lesions the reflex is often preserved but very variable (Morrison et al, 2005).

The striated sphincter dyssynergia causes a functional obstruction with poor emptying and high detrusor pressure. Occasionally, incomplete bladder emptying may result from what seems to be a poorly sustained or absent detrusor contraction. This seems to occur more commonly in lesions close to the conus medullaris than with more cephalad lesions. This may result from a second occult lesion or may be caused by

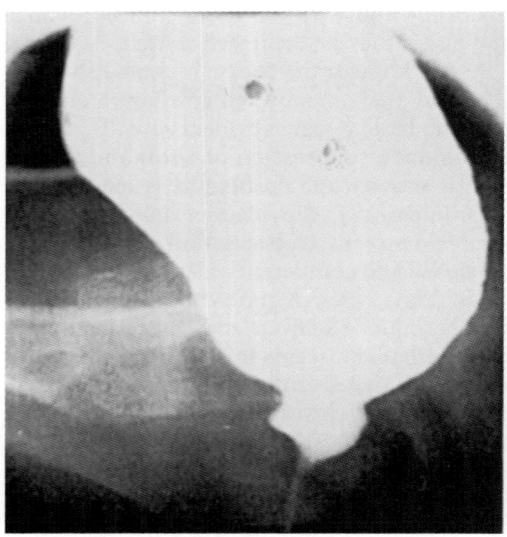 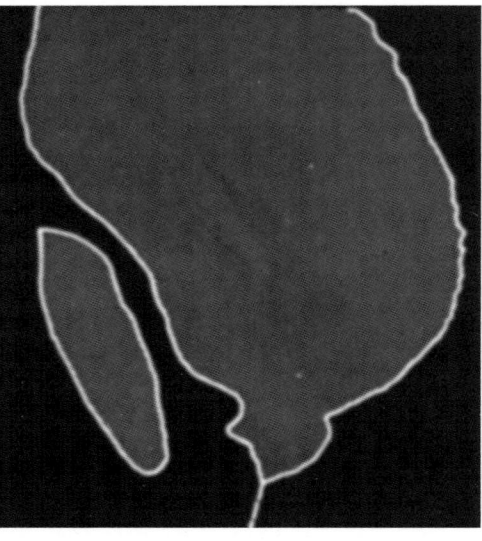

Figure 59–1. Cystourethrogram in a 19-year-old woman with detrusor-striated sphincter dyssynergia secondary to a complete spinal cord injury at vertebral level T11. Image was taken during an involuntary bladder contraction with exaggerated bladder neck opening caused by the obstruction below. (From Nordling J, Olesen KP: Basic urographic and cystourethrographic patterns. In Pollack HM [ed]: Clinical Urography. Philadelphia, WB Saunders, 1990, p 1953.)

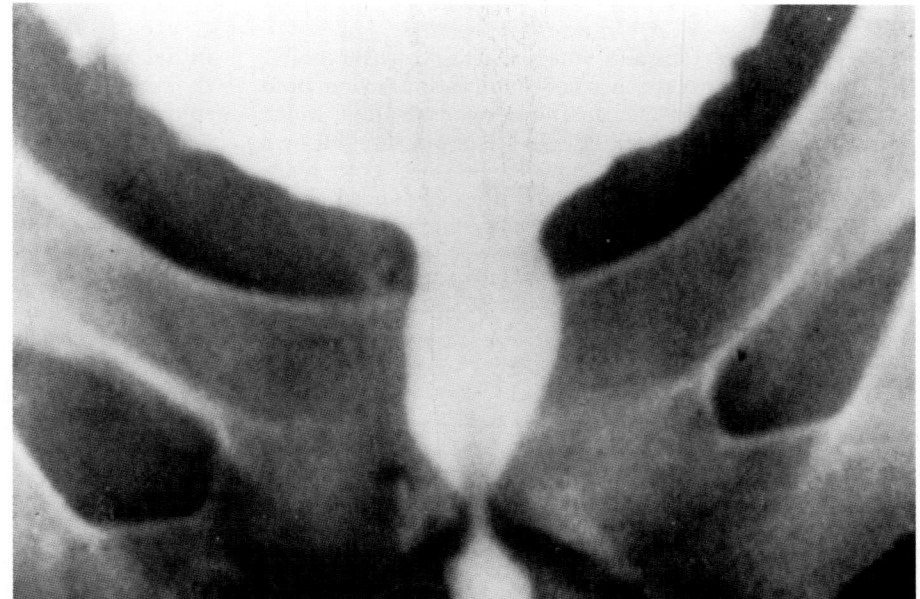

Figure 59–2. Typical cystourethrographic configuration of a synergic smooth sphincter and a dyssynergic striated sphincter in a man during a bladder contraction. (From Nanninga JB: Radiological appearances following surgery for neuromuscular diseases affecting the urinary tract. In Pollack HM [ed]: Clinical Urography. Philadelphia, WB Saunders, 1990, p 2003.)

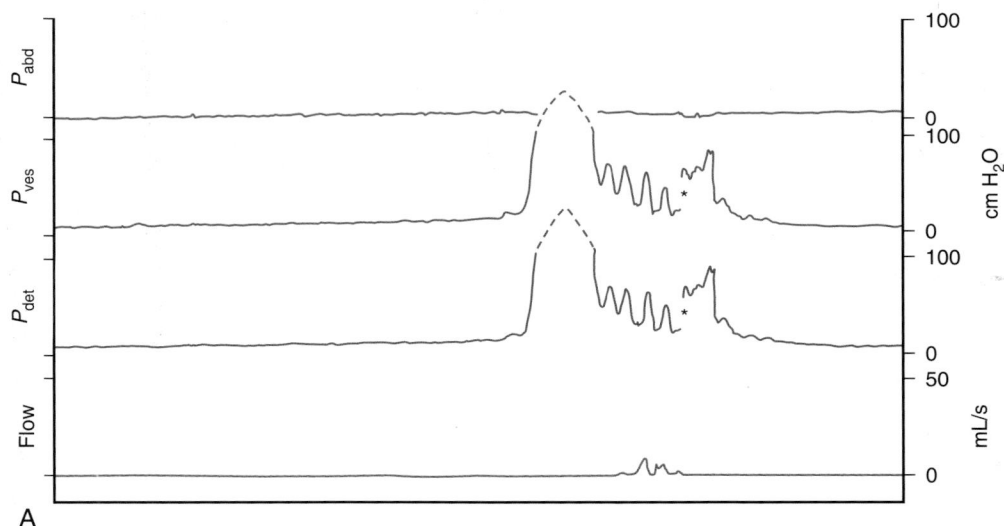

A

Figure 59–3. Video images in **B** at corresponding points of the urodynamic tracings in **A**. Detrusor hyperreflexia (P_{det} 150 cm H_2O), synergic bladder neck, dyssynergic striated sphincter. The *asterisk* represents a range change from a scale of 0 to 100 cm H_2O. (From Lawrence WT, Thomas DC: Urodynamic techniques in the neurologic patient. In O'Reilly PH, George NJR, Weiss RM [eds]: Diagnostic Techniques in Urology. Philadelphia, WB Saunders, 1990, p 360.)

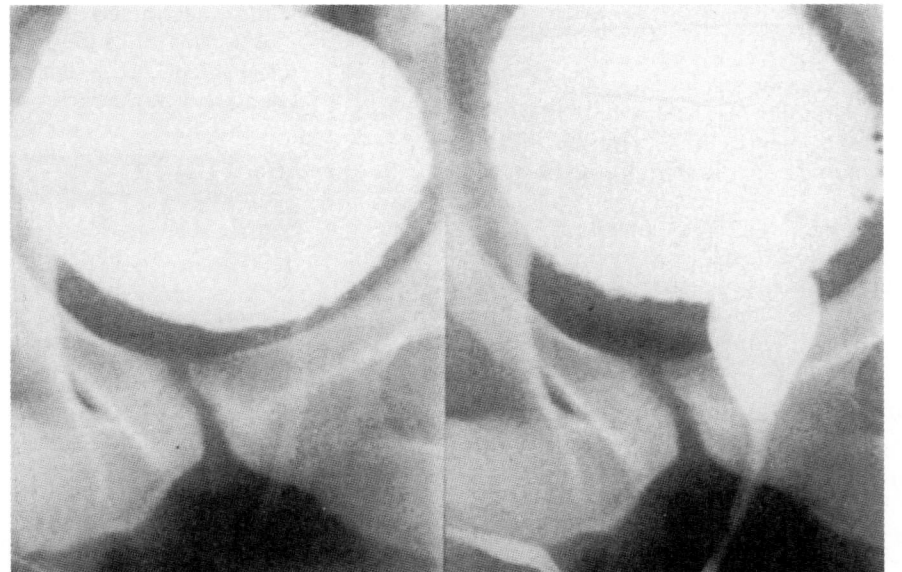

B

locally functioning reflex arcs, which result in detrusor inhibition from strong striated pelvic floor muscle contraction, or to a loss of higher center–mediated detrusor facilitation, which normally occurs after the initial increase in pressure during a bladder contraction (Thomas and O'Flynn, 1994). Once reflex voiding is established, it can be initiated or reinforced by the stimulation of certain dermatomes, as by tapping the suprapubic area. The urodynamic and upper tract consequences of the striated sphincter dyssynergia vary with severity (generally worse in complete lesions than in incomplete ones), duration (continuous contraction during detrusor activity is worse than intermittent contraction), and anatomy (male is worse than female) (Linsenmeyer et al, 1998).

KEY POINT: MANAGEMENT OF PATIENTS WITH SUPRASACRAL SPINAL CORD INJURY

■ From a functional standpoint the voiding dysfunction most commonly seen in suprasacral SCI represents both a filling/storage and an emptying failure. Although the urodynamics are "safe" enough in some individuals to allow only periodic stimulation of bladder reflex activity, many will require some treatment. If bladder pressures are suitably low or if they can be made suitably low with nonsurgical or surgical management, the problem can be treated primarily as an emptying failure; and CIC can be continued, when practical, as a safe and effective way of satisfying many of the goals of treatment. Alternatively, sphincterotomy, stenting, or intrasphincteric injection of botulinum toxin can be used in males to lower the detrusor leak point to an acceptable level, thus treating the dysfunction primarily as one of emptying. The resultant storage failure can be obviated either by timed stimulation or with an external collecting device. In the dextrous SCI patient, the former approach using CIC is becoming predominant. Electrical stimulation of the anterior sacral roots with some form of deafferentation is also now a distinct reality (Creasey et al, 2001; Seif et al, 2004). As with all patients with neurologic impairment, a careful initial evaluation and periodic follow-up evaluation must be performed to identify and correct the following risk factors and potential complications: bladder overdistention, high-pressure storage, high detrusor leak point pressure, vesicoureteral reflux (VUR), stone formation (lower and upper tracts), and complicating infection, especially in association with reflux.

Sacral Spinal Cord Injury

After the patient recovers from spinal shock, there **is generally a depression of deep tendon reflexes below the level of a complete lesion with varying degrees of flaccid paralysis. Sensation is generally absent below the lesion level. Detrusor areflexia with high or normal compliance is the common**

initial result, but decreased compliance may develop, a change seen in some neurologic lesions at or distal to the sacral spinal cord that most likely represents a complex response to neurologic decentralization probably involving reorganization and plasticity of neural pathways (Fam and Yalla, 1988; de Groat et al, 1997; Blaivas et al, 1998b). There is surprisingly little consensus on the evolution of the appearance or function of the bladder neck or smooth sphincter area after sacral spinal cord damage. **The classic outlet findings are described as a competent but nonrelaxing smooth sphincter and a striated sphincter that retains some fixed tone but is not under voluntary control. Closure pressures are decreased in both areas** (Sullivan and Yalla, 1992; Thomas and O'Flynn, 1994). However, the late appearance of the bladder neck may be "open" (Kaplan et al, 1991). Attempted voiding by straining or Credé's maneuver results in "obstruction" at the bladder neck (if closed) or at the distal sphincter area by fixed sphincter tone (Fam and Yalla, 1988; Thomas and O'Flynn, 1994). Figure 59–4 illustrates the typical cystourographic and urodynamic pictures of the late phases of such a complete lesion.

Neurologic and Urodynamic Correlation

Although generally correct, the correlation between somatic neurologic findings and urodynamic findings in suprasacral and sacral SCI patients is not exact. A number of factors should be considered in this regard. First, whether a lesion is complete or incomplete is sometimes a matter of definition, and a complete lesion, somatically speaking, may not translate into a complete lesion autonomically and vice versa. Multiple injuries may actually exist at different levels, even though what is seen somatically may reflect a single level of injury. Even considering these situations, however, all such discrepancies are not explained.

In a classic article, **Blaivas** (1982) **correlated clinical and urodynamic data from 550 patients with voiding dysfunction.** In 155 patients with complete and incomplete suprasacral neurologic lesions, physiologically normal voiding was reported in 41%. Detrusor striated sphincter dyssynergia was demonstrated in 34%, and, surprisingly (and seemingly paradoxically), detrusor areflexia was noted in 25%. Other authors have noted detrusor areflexia with suprasacral SCI or disease, and the causes have been hypothesized as a coexistent distal spinal cord lesion or a disordered integration of afferent activity at the sacral root or cord level (Light et al, 1985;

KEY POINT: MANAGEMENT OF PATIENTS WITH SACRAL CORD INJURY

■ **Potential risk factors and complications are those previously described, with particular emphasis on storage pressure, which can result in silent upper tract decompensation and deterioration in the absence of VUR. The treatment of such a patient is generally directed toward producing or maintaining low-pressure storage while circumventing emptying failure with CIC when possible.** Pharmacologic and electrical stimulation may be useful in promoting emptying in certain circumstances (see Tables 57–3 and 57–4).

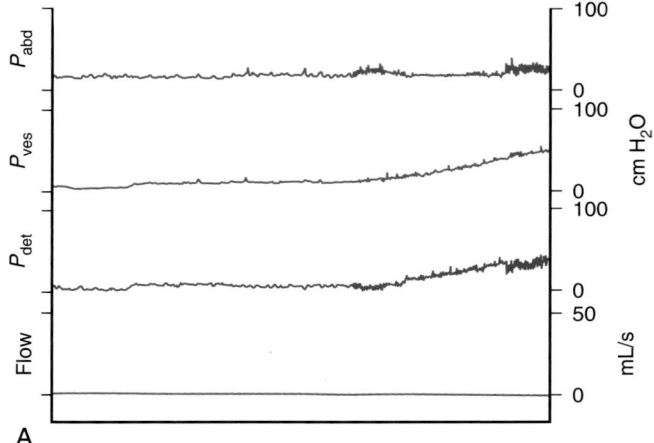

A

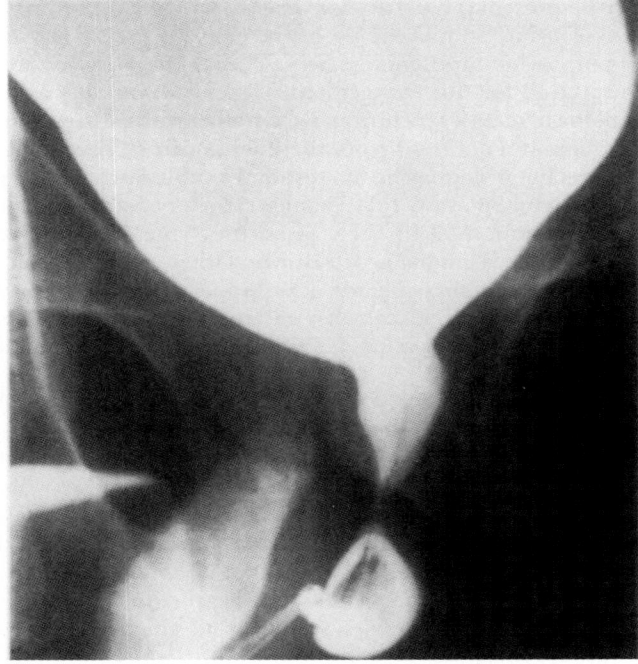

B

Figure 59–4. Simultaneous video (**B**) and urodynamic study (**A**) from a 28-year-old man whose bladder has been filled with 420 mL of contrast material. There is low compliance; the bladder neck is incompetent; and with straining the distal sphincter mechanism does not open—a pattern often seen in sacral spinal cord or efferent nerve root injury or disease. (From Lawrence WT, Thomas DC: Urodynamic techniques in the neurologic patient. In O'Reilly PH, George NJR, Weiss RM [eds]: Diagnostic Techniques in Urology. Philadelphia, WB Saunders, 1990, p 362.)

Beric and Light, 1992). Detrusor striated sphincter dyssynergia was reported in 45% of 119 patients with suprasacral spinal cord lesions. None of 36 patients with supraspinal neurologic lesions had striated sphincter dyssynergia. **These data certainly support prior conclusions that (1) coordinated voiding is regulated by neurologic centers above the spinal cord and (2) a diagnosis of striated sphincter dyssynergia implies a neurologic lesion that interrupts the neural axis between the pontine-mesencephalic reticular formation and the sacral spinal cord.** All 27 patients with neurologic lesions above the pons and who were able to void did so synergisti-

cally—with relaxation of the striated sphincter preceding detrusor contraction. Twenty of these patients had detrusor overactivity, but 12 of these 20 had voluntary control of the striated sphincter, supporting a thesis of separate neural pathways governing voluntary control of the bladder and of the periurethral striated musculature. Most of these patients with detrusor overactivity secondary to lesions above the pons were able to voluntarily contract the striated sphincter, but without abolishing bladder contraction. This seems to indicate that the inhibition of bladder contraction by pudendal motor activity is not merely a simple sacral reflex but, rather, a complex neurologic event. Twenty-two of these patients had evidence of either sacral or infrasacral neurologic impairment of bladder function with suprasacral control of striated sphincter function or vice versa; this provides a clinical correlate to the separate anatomic locations of the parasympathetic motor nucleus and the pudendal nucleus in the sacral spinal cord (see Chapter 56, "Physiology and Pharmacology of the Bladder and Urethra").

A subsequent study from the same center analyzed the results of urodynamic evaluation in 489 consecutive patients with either congenital or acquired SCI or disease and correlated these with the diagnosed neurologic deficit (Kaplan et al, 1991). Although there was a general correlation between the neurologic level of injury and the expected vesicourethral function, it was neither absolute nor specific. Twenty of 117 cervical lesions exhibited detrusor areflexia; 42 of 156 lumbar lesions, detrusor striated sphincter dyssynergia; and 26 of 84 sacral lesions, either detrusor overactivity or detrusor striated sphincter dyssynergia. The patients were further classified on the basis of the integrity of the sacral dermatomes (intact sacral reflexes or not). This helps to explain some, but not all, of the apparent discrepancies. Of the patients with suprasacral cord lesions who had detrusor areflexia, 84% also had abnormal sacral cord signs (absent bulbocavernosus reflex, lax anal sphincter tone, or sphincter EMG abnormalities indicative of lower motor neuron degeneration). All suprasacral cord lesion patients who had no evidence of sacral cord involvement had either detrusor overactivity or detrusor striated sphincter dyssynergia.

Patients were also classified according to the three most common neurologic causes for their lesion: trauma, myelomeningocele, and spinal stenosis. Of the 284 trauma patients, all with thoracic cord lesions had either detrusor overactivity or detrusor striated dyssynergia and negative sacral cord signs. In contrast, in patients with traumatic lesions affecting other parts of the spinal cord, there was a wide distribution of both urodynamic and sacral cord sign findings. For example, of patients with traumatic lumbar cord injury, 38% had detrusor areflexia and positive sacral cord signs, 25% had detrusor striated sphincter dyssynergia and negative sacral cord signs, 25% had detrusor overactivity and negative sacral cord signs, and 14% had either detrusor overactivity or detrusor striated sphincter dyssynergia and negative sacral cord signs. Of 25 patients with lumbar myelomeningocele, 20 had either detrusor areflexia or detrusor striated sphincter dyssynergia. All patients with lumbar myelomeningocele and detrusor areflexia had positive sacral cord signs. Of 48 patients with sacral myelomeningocele, 37 had detrusor areflexia and 35 had positive sacral cord signs. Of 54 patients with spinal stenosis, all those with cervical and thoracic cord lesions had either detrusor overactivity or detrusor striated sphincter dyssynergia and negative sacral cord signs. Patients with a lumbar cord stenosis had no consistent pattern of detrusor activity or sacral cord signs. An open bladder neck at rest was found in 21 patients. All had either lumbar or sacral SCI. Sixteen of these had sacral cord lesions and detrusor areflexia. Decreased bladder compliance was noted in 54 patients, 41 of whom had sacral cord injury and 43 of whom had detrusor areflexia.

Wyndaele (1997) correlated the neurologic and urodynamic data in 92 patients with SCI and came to the same general conclusion: **Although there was a general correlation between the neurologic level of injury and the expected vesicourethral function, it was neither absolute nor specific, especially in the group of patients with paraplegia resulting from spinal cord lesions at column level T10 to L2.** With reference to this latter group, Pesce and coworkers (1997) reported on 46 patients with complete SCIs from vertebral lesions between T11 and L2. Fifty percent of the patients had detrusor areflexia, and 50% had overactivity; 16 of the latter group also had striated sphincter dyssynergia. Of 22 patients with lesions above vertebral level L1, 8% showed areflexia and 14 showed overactivity, of whom 9 demonstrated sphincter dyssynergia. Of 9 patients with a lesion between T12 and L1, 3 showed detrusor areflexia and 6 overactivity, of whom 4 showed striated sphincter dyssynergia. Of 15 patients with a lesion at L1 or lower, 3% showed detrusor overactivity and striated sphincter dyssynergia.

Weld and Dmochowski (2000) agreed that the correlation between somatic neurologic findings or spinal imaging studies and urodynamic findings in patients with SCI is not exact, based on their review of 243 post-traumatic SCI patients who had complete spinal CT or MRI studies. It should be noted, however, that their correlation between level of injury and urodynamic findings was in fact better than those previously reported, most likely because of the more exact determination of the level of injury and the detection of multiple levels of injury, attributable to the precision of the radiologic imaging studies. Of 196 patients with suprasacral injuries, 94.9% demonstrated overactivity and/or striated sphincter dyssynergia, 41.8% had low bladder compliance (defined as 12.5 mL/cm H_2O), and 40.3% had detrusor leak point pressures greater than 40 cm H_2O. Of the 14 patients with sacral injuries, 85.7% demonstrated detrusor areflexia; 78.6%, low compliance; and 85.7%, high leak point pressures. Of 33 patients with combined suprasacral and sacral injuries, 68% demonstrated detrusor overactivity and/or detrusor dyssynergia; 27%, areflexia; 58%, low compliance; and 61%, high leak point pressures.

All these data make the point, as cogently as possible, that **management of the urinary tract in such patients must be based on urodynamic principles and findings rather than inferences from the neurologic history and evaluation. Similarly, although the information regarding "classic" complete lesions is for the most part valid, one should not make neurologic conclusions solely on the basis of urodynamic findings.**

Autonomic Hyperreflexia

First described by Guttmann and Whitteridge in 1947, autonomic hyperreflexia (autonomic dysreflexia) is a potentially fatal emergency unique to the SCI patient. Excellent sources of information include the reviews by Trop and Bennett (1991), Vaidyanathan and colleagues (1998), and Karlsson (1999). **Autonomic hyperreflexia represents an acute massive disordered autonomic (primarily sympathetic) response to specific stimuli in patients with SCI above the cord level of T6 to T8 (the sympathetic outflow).** It is more common in cervical (60%) than thoracic (20%) injuries. Onset after injury is variable—usually soon after spinal shock but may be up to years after injury. Distal cord viability is a prerequisite.

Symptomatically, autonomic hyperreflexia is a **syndrome of exaggerated sympathetic activity in response to stimuli below the level of the lesion. The symptoms are pounding headache, hypertension, and flushing of the face and body above the level of the lesion with sweating. Bradycardia is a usual accompaniment, although tachycardia or arrhythmia may be present. Hypertension may be of varying severity,** from causing a mild headache before the occurrence of voiding to life-threatening cerebral hemorrhage or seizure. **The stimuli for this exaggerated response commonly arise from the bladder or rectum and generally involve distention, although other stimuli from these areas can be precipitating.** Precipitation may be the result of simple lower urinary tract instrumentation, tube change, catheter obstruction, or clot retention; and, in such cases, the symptoms resolve quickly if the stimulus is withdrawn. Other causes or exacerbating factors may include other upper or lower urinary tract pathology (e.g., calculi), gastrointestinal pathology, long bone fracture, sexual activity, electrocoagulation, and decubiti.

Striated sphincter dyssynergia invariably occurs, and smooth sphincter dyssynergia is generally a part of the syndrome as well, at least in males. The pathophysiology is that of a nociceptive stimulation via afferent impulses that ascend through the cord and elicit reflex motor outflow, causing arteriolar, pilomotor, and pelvic visceral spasm and sweating. Normally, the reflexes would be inhibited by secondary output from the medulla, but because of the SCI this does not occur below the lesion level. Vaidyanathan and colleagues (1998) emphasized that the SCI disrupts control of the sympathetic preganglionic neurons because bulbospinal input has been lost, and the remaining regulation is accomplished by spinal circuits consisting of dorsal root afferent and spinal interneurons. Karlsson (1999), however, points out that the underlying pathogenic mechanisms may not be as simple as they first appear. The amplitude of the blood pressure reaction indicates involvement of a large vascular bed, perhaps larger than that of the skin and skeletal muscle. It may be that the splanchnic vascular bed is involved as well, either from the standpoint of active vasoconstriction or simply from a lack of the ability to exhibit compensatory vasodilatation. Afferent and efferent plasticity in the sympathetic nervous system may also be involved.

Ideally, any endoscopic procedure in susceptible patients should be done under spinal anesthesia or carefully monitored general anesthesia. Acutely, the hemodynamic effects of this syndrome may be managed with β- and/or α-adrenergic blocking agents. Ganglionic blockers had previously been the mainstay of treatment (Wein, 2000a), but their usage has essentially been abandoned. Sublingual nifedipine had been reported to be capable of alleviating this syndrome when given during cystoscopy (10 to 20 mg) and of preventing it when given orally 30 minutes before cystoscopy (10 mg) (Dykstra et al, 1987). The rationale was that this presumably prevented smooth muscle contraction through its calcium antagonist properties and thereby prevented the increase in peripheral vascular resistance normally seen with sympathetic stimulation. The use of sublingual nifedipine, however, has been prohibited in our particular medical center, and doubtless in some others as well. It has been reported that the sublingual absorption of nifedipine is negligible and that the favorable therapeutic results obtained from such administration are probably caused by swallowing the drug (van Harten et al, 1987). These particular authors believe that if a fast onset of action of nifedipine is desired, the patient should be instructed to bite the capsule and swallow the contents with water, thereby rapidly achieving therapeutic plasma levels of the drug. Prior to electroejaculation, Steinberger and colleagues (1990) recommended oral prophylaxis with 20 mg of nifedipine, finding this markedly lowered pressure rises during treatment.

Chancellor and colleagues (1994) reported on the use of terazosin (a selective α_1-adrenergic blocker) for long-term management (3-month study) and prophylaxis. A nightly dose of 5 mg reduced severity, whereas erectile function and blood pressure were unchanged. Vaidyanathan and colleagues (1998) affirmed the success of the prophylactic use of terazosin. They treated 18 adults with tetraplegia and 3 with paraplegia with graduated increasing doses of the drug, ultimately varying from 1 to 10 mg daily, and reported complete subsidence of dysreflexic symptoms in all patients. Only 1 patient, a tetraplegic, required discontinuation of the drug because of persistent dizziness. Such prophylaxis may be particularly important in view of the fact that significant elevations in blood pressure can occur without other symptoms of autonomic hyperreflexia (Linsenmeyer et al, 1996).

Prophylaxis, however, does not eliminate the need for careful monitoring during provocative procedures. There are patients with severe dysreflexia that is intractable to oral prophylaxis and correction by urologic procedures. For these unfortunate individuals, a number of neurologic ablative procedures have been used—sympathectomy, sacral neurectomy, sacral rhizotomy, cordectomy, and dorsal root ganglionectomy (Trop and Bennett, 1991). Hohenfellner and associates (2001) advocate sacral bladder denervation by sacral rhizotomy as a moderately invasive, relatively low risk procedure that, along with intermittent catheterization, produces good results in refractory patients.

Vesicoureteral Reflux

Surprisingly little is written about vesicoureteral reflux (VUR) in the SCI patient. **The reported incidence varies between 17% and 25% of such patients** (Thomas and Lucas, 1990) **and is more common in those with suprasacral SCI. Contributing factors include (1) elevated intravesical pressure during filling and emptying and (2) infection. Persistent reflux can lead to chronic renal damage and may be an important factor in the long-term survival of SCI patients.** In the series of SCI patients reported by Hackler and coworkers (1965), persistent reflux was present in 60% of patients of those dying

of renal disease. In patients with only transient reflux over a 5- to 15-year period, the urogram was normal in 83%, or calyceal changes were only minimal. It should be noted, however, that high storage and voiding pressures without reflux can be responsible for renal damage (McGuire, 1984; Vega and Pascual, 2001).

The best initial treatment for reflux in a patient with voiding dysfunction secondary to neurologic disease or injury is to normalize lower urinary tract urodynamics as much as possible. Depending on the clinical circumstances, this may be by pharmacotherapy, urethral dilatation (in the myelomeningocele patient), neuromodulation, deafferentiation, augmentation cystoplasty, or sphincterotomy (Flood et al, 1994; Perkash et al, 1998). If this fails, the question of whether to operate on such patients for correction of the reflux or to correct the reflux while performing another procedure (e.g., augmentation cystoplasty) is not an easy one, because correction of reflux in an often very thickened bladder may not be an easy task.

Transureteroureterostomy for unilateral reflux is feasible, but even experienced urologists had difficulties with ureteral calculi trapping, recurrent reflux, and obstruction at the vesicoureteral junction following such procedures in this difficult group of patients (Van Arsdalen et al, 1983). Submucosal trigonal injection of bulking substances may add a new dimension to the treatment of this difficult problem.

One must remember the potential artifact that significant reflux can introduce into urodynamic studies. Measured bladder capacity appears artifactually large, and measured pressures at given inflow volumes may appear lower than after reflux correction. The apparent significance of detrusor overactivity may thus be underestimated.

Urinary Tract Infection

Urinary tract infection (UTI) is relatively common in patients with SCI. Fifty-seven percent of patients with SCI experience UTI or bacteriuria in the first year after initial hospitalization (Morton et al, 2002). Recurrent infections may be a manifestation of upper or lower tract calculi, symptomatic or silent pyelonephritis, or lower urinary tract dysfunction causing persistent residual urine. In conjunction with poor urodynamic function, UTI can lead to high morbidity, poor quality of life, and decreased life expectancy in patients with SCI (Sauerwein, 2002). The use of antibiotics in SCI patients remains a topic of discussion. **Virtually all who have written on the subject agree that bacteriuria should be treated only when signs or symptoms present, a consensus reached by the National Institute on Disability and Rehabilitation Research Group (1992)** (Penders et al, 2003). Biering-Sorensen and coworkers (2001) authored a nicely organized, well-written, and referenced article on the subject. They recommended the following: (1) treat bacteriuria only if symptomatic; (2) use antimicrobial agents, if possible, with little or no impact on normal flora; (3) treat at least 5 days; those with reinfection or relapse, treat 7 to 14 days; (4) repair structural and functional risk factors; (5) use prophylaxis only in those with recurrent UTI when no underlying cause can be found and especially if the upper tracts are dilated; (6) do not use antibiotics to prevent UTI in patients with an indwelling catheter. They regard the use of prophylactic antibiotics in patients on CIC as controversial.

Morton and coworkers (2002) concluded from a meta-analysis of 15 controlled trials that prophylactic antibiotics were not generally helpful but added that they could not exclude a clinically important effect, especially in those who had recurrent UTI that limited their functioning and well-being. Sauerwein (2002) recommends beginning antibiotic prophylaxis in patients on CIC and stopping after 1 year if there has been one or fewer UTI. Some (Burns et al, 2001) believe that significant pyuria, defined as 8 to 10 or more white blood cells per high-power field, connotes tissue invasion and is an indication for antibiotic treatment. There are little evidence-based data in this area.

Spinal Cord Injury in Women

There are many aspects of management of the lower urinary tract affected by spinal cord injury that are specific to women (Yang and Cardenas, 2001). McColl (2002) summarized some of these. The problem of osteoporosis places women at a much increased risk of fracture. The symptoms of menopause (e.g., hot flashes) may be difficult to distinguish from those of autonomic dysreflexia. Incontinence and UTI become worse with age in women in the general population and particularly in those with SCI. Body composition of SCI women shows deficient protein and bone mass and excess fat, predisposing them to an increased incidence of fractures and the risk of skin breakdown. The incidence of SCI is highest among young men and older women. Psychological outcomes (e.g., depression) have been shown to improve after 30 years' duration of disability. Women injured at a modal age of 60 are unlikely to enjoy this benefit.

Special difficulty in this category of patients is encountered because of the lack of an appropriate external collecting device. Suitable bladder reservoir function can usually be achieved either pharmacologically or surgically, and paraplegic women can generally master CIC. Although a few quadriplegic women can be trained to self-CIC, for the majority there is no practical alternative to indwelling catheterization (Lindan et al, 1987). McGuire and Savastano (1988) point out that indwelling catheter drainage on a long-term basis in women may not be, however, as is sometimes written, well tolerated, because significant incontinence around the catheter and upper tract changes may develop.

For those SCI female patients who can assume CIC or who have around-the-clock medical or family care, creation of adequate bladder reservoir function is reasonable. For those not in this category, the alternatives are limited and difficult. Bennett and associates (1995) compared the incidence of major complications in a group of female SCI patients who were managed long term by (1) CIC; (2) reflex voiding and incontinence padding; and (3) an indwelling catheter. There were 10 major complications in the 25 patients in group 2 and 58 in the 22 patients in group 3, compared with only 4 major complications in group 1. Singh and Thomas (1997) looked at the results of treatment in a group of female tetraplegics. Twenty-three of 27 patients with complete lesions wound up using an indwelling catheter, 3 underwent diversion, and in 1 patient the caregiver performed CIC. In 20 patients with incomplete lesions, all with poor functional recovery, 14 had permanent indwelling catheters, 3 were able to perform CIC,

and 3 used reflex voiding by triggering. Of 37 patients with incomplete lesions with good functional recovery, only 3 required indwelling catheterization; 4 used CIC, and most were able to use reflex voiding by triggering. The authors noted also that 55% of the women with permanent catheters had bladder calculi, 35% had leakage around the catheter, and 33% had recurrent symptomatic infection. Although upper tract changes were seen in only 5%, it is obvious that the authors consider that, for the most part, female patients with voiding dysfunction secondary to cervical SCI who exhibit poor functional recovery represent urologic failures of management.

Spinal Cord Injury and Bladder Cancer

The development of carcinoma of the bladder in 6 of 59 patients with SCIs who had long-term indwelling catheters was reported by Kaufman and colleagues (1977). All were squamous cell lesions. Four of these patients had no obvious tumors visible at endoscopy, and the diagnosis was made by bladder biopsy. Five of these patients also had transitional cell elements in their tumor. Broecker and associates (1981) surveyed 81 consecutive SCI patients with an indwelling urinary catheter for more than 10 years. Although the investigators did not find frank carcinoma in any patients, they found squamous metaplasia of the bladder in 11 and leukoplakia in 1. Locke and coworkers (1985) noted two cases of squamous cell carcinoma of the bladder in 25 consecutive SCI patients catheterized for a minimum of 10 years. Bickel and colleagues (1991) reported eight cases of bladder cancer in SCI men, although the denominator was uncertain. Four of the men had been managed by indwelling catheterization for 7, 10, 14, and 19 years, respectively. All of these 4 had transitional cell carcinoma, whereas in the other 4, there were two cases of transitional and two of squamous cell carcinoma. In Chao and colleagues' series (1993), 6 patients developed bladder cancer, 3 of whom had indwelling catheters (of a total of 32) and 3 of whom (of 41) did not. Stonehill and associates (1996) retrospectively reviewed all bladder tumors in their SCI patients for 7 years and compared these with matched controls. They found 17 malignant and 2 benign bladder tumors. Indwelling catheters and a history of bladder calculi were statistically significant risk factors.

Hess and associates (2003) reported their own series and summarized one view of the literature regarding SCI and bladder cancer: (1) the relative risk in SCI patients is 16% to 28% greater than the general population; (2) the overall incidence is 2.3% to 10%; (3) there is a higher proportion of squamous cell than transitional cell carcinoma; (4) the prevalence peaks at an earlier age than in the general population; (5) diagnosis is made at a more advanced stage; (6) risk factors include chronic indwelling catheterization, bladder stones, and chronic UTI; (7) neither cystoscopy nor cytology is an entirely reliable diagnostic tool; and (8) those with multiple risk factors should have a more aggressive evaluation.

Tempering this are reports by Pannek (2002), who reviewed the data from 43,561 SCI patients in three countries and concluded the incidence of bladder cancer is comparable to that of the general population, but more than 60% of those affected presented initially with muscle invasive disease. Chronic indwelling catheters and persistent or recurrent UTI are suggested as the risk factors rather than the SCI itself. Subramoniam and associates (2004) reported similar conclusions regarding age-standardized incidence of bladder cancer relative to the general population. Seventy-five percent of the affected patients in the series had indwelling catheters for 18 to 32 years.

Follow-Up

Linsenmeyer and Culkin (1999) reported the American Paraplegic Society (APS) Guidelines for urologic care of SCI. **Annual follow-up is recommended for the first 5 to 10 years after injury. If the patient is doing well, then follow-up every other year is advised. Upper and lower tract evaluation should be done initially and yearly for 5 to 10 years, then every other year.** Burns and associates (2001) recommended at least plain films and nuclear renal scans, with a decrease of more than 20% in renal plasma flow warranting further investigation. **Urodynamic evaluation was recommended by the APS at the same intervals as upper and lower tract screening. Cystoscopy was recommended annually in those with an indwelling catheter.**

Cervical Myelopathy

Cervical myelopathy is generally caused by compression, secondary to either spondylosis, ossification of the posterior longitudinal ligament, or cervical disk herniation (Sakakibara et al, 1995a; Mochida et al, 1996). Sakakibara and associates (1995a) studied 128 affected patients, of whom 95 had voiding symptoms, 61 had irritative symptoms, 71 had obstructive symptoms, and 25 had urinary incontinence. Urodynamic studies revealed involuntary bladder contractions in 61 patients and detrusor sphincter dyssynergia (DESD) in 22. Mochida and colleagues (1996), on the other hand, reported on 60 patients undergoing surgery for cervical myelopathy, 22 of whom (37%) were found to have neuropathic bladder dysfunction on urodynamic study. Of these, 9 (41%) were found to have detrusor overactivity, but 13 (59%) were characterized as having an underactive detrusor. Because this is at odds with what one would expect with only cervical spinal cord pathology, this reinforces the need for urodynamic study to optimally guide therapy in patients with neurogenic bladder.

Acute Transverse Myelitis

Acute transverse myelitis is a rapidly developing condition with motor, sensory, and sphincter abnormalities, generally with a well-defined upper sensory limit and no signs of spinal cord compression or other neurologic disease (Kalita et al, 2002). It may result from a variety of mechanisms—parainfectious, autoimmune, vascular, or demyelinating (Ganesan and Borzyskowski, 2001). The condition usually stabilizes within 2 to 4 weeks, is not progressive afterward, and is followed by variable recovery with some residual neurologic deficits. Although recovery is more variable, and the prognosis, in general, is more favorable, the development and nature of voiding dysfunction has been reported to be similar, level by level, to that of SCI (Sakakibara et al, 1995b). Kalita and colleagues (2002), however, reported on 18 patients with acute transverse myelitis whose 6-month outcome included persistent retention in 6 and storage symptoms in 10, of whom 5 had emptying problems as well; 2 patients had regained normal voiding. In the acute state, urodynamics showed an areflexic or contractile bladder in 10, detrusor overactivity with poor compliance in 2, and DESD in 3. Seventeen had presented in urinary retention. As in SCI, because the activity of the bladder and outlet during filling/storage and emptying/voiding does not always correspond to what they "should" be, based on the level of pathology, urodynamic studies are necessary to guide irreversible therapy.

Neurospinal Dysraphism

These topics are covered primarily in Chapter 123, "Voiding Dysfunction in Children—Neurogenic and Non-neurogenic." However, certain considerations regarding the adult with these abnormalities should be mentioned. Spinal dysraphism refers to the malformation of the vertebral arches and, commonly, malformation of the neural tube. The term includes spina bifida occulta, which involves only a bony (vertebral) arch defect; and spina bifida cystica (aperta), which involves a bony defect and a neural tube (spinal cord) defect. The two primary subclasses of spina bifida cystica are myelomeningocele (the nerve roots or portions of the spinal cord have evaginated beyond the vertebral bodies) and meningoceles (contain only a herniated meningeal sac with no neural elements). If fatty tissue is present in the sac in either, the prefix "lipo-" is added (Churchill et al, 2001). **Myelomeningocele accounts for more than 90% of spina bifida cystica and is the most devastating condition in terms of sequelae. Of myelomeningoceles: 2% are cervical, 5% thoracic, 26% lumbar, 47% lumbosacral, and 20% sacral. The level(s) of the lesion correlates poorly with urodynamic findings** (Churchill et al, 2001). **Myelomeningocele occurs in approximately 1/1000 live births** (Wyndaele, 2005). **The incidence of lower urinary tract dysfunction is not absolutely documented, but most studies suggest an incidence of over 90%** (Wyndaele, 2005).

McGuire and Denil (1991) and Woodhouse (2005) point out that, secondary to progress in the overall care of children with myelodysplasia, urologic dysfunction often becomes a problem of the adolescent or adult with this disease. In McGuire and Denil's (1991) experience, **the "typical" myelodysplastic patient shows an areflexic bladder with an open bladder neck. The bladder generally fills until the resting residual fixed external sphincter pressure is reached, and then leakage occurs. Stress incontinence occurs also,** related to changes in intra-abdominal pressure. A small percentage (10% to 15%) of patients demonstrate detrusor striated sphincter dyssynergia, but these individuals show normal bladder neck function that, if detrusor reflex activity is controlled, is associated with continence. After puberty, most authors report that most myelodysplastic patients note an improvement in continence, but, at that age and after, they are less inclined than children to tolerate any degree of incontinence. In adult patients, the problems encountered in myelodysplastic children still exist but are often compounded by prior surgery, upper tract dysfunction, and one form of urinary diversion or another.

In adult females, the treatment strategy generally is to increase urethral sphincter efficiency without causing a major enough increase in urethral closing pressure that will result in a change in bladder compliance (McGuire and Denil, 1991). **Periurethral injection therapy to achieve continence may replace the pubovaginal sling and artificial sphincter in this circumstance. These authors also point out that continence in adult male myelodysplastic individuals follows the same general rules as in females, and injectable materials may give good results in this group as well. When the urethra is very widely dilated and somewhat rigid, and neither procedure alone will provide sufficient coaptation, it may be possible to combine a "prostatic sling" with periurethral collagen injection. Dry individuals, of course, will be on intermittent self-catheterization.**

"Classic" may imply different urodynamic findings to different groups of clinicians. **Nowhere is the failure of a neurologic examination to predict urodynamic behavior more obvious than in patients with myelomeningocele.**

Van Gool and colleagues (2001) summarized the urodynamic findings in 188 children with myelomeningocele and categorized these into five groups. Seven percent had normal detrusor and sphincter activity; 11% had detrusor overactivity and an inactive sphincter; 45% had detrusor overactivity and an overactive sphincter; 23% had an inactive detrusor and inactive sphincter; and 14% had an inactive detrusor and an overactive sphincter. Sakakibara and associates (2003) reported on urodynamic results in 16 adult patients with myelomeningocele. Detrusor overactivity was found in 38%, low compliance in 81%, impaired bladder sensation in 25%, DESD in 50%, low maximum urethral pressure in 56%, and silent sphincter EMG in 25%. Webster and colleagues (1986) urodynamically classified a large number of myelomeningocele patients as follows: 62% had detrusor overactivity, whereas 38% had detrusor areflexia, with 30 of 34 of these having low compliance with high terminal filling pressure. Striated sphincter behavior was characterized as follows: true detrusor striated sphincter dyssynergia in 15%, an apparently innervated but fixed nonrelaxing sphincter in 15%, and some evidence of striated sphincter denervation in 69%. **It is clear, however, that whatever the pattern of voiding dysfunction in the adult, all authors would agree that a prime directive of therapy is still the avoidance of high storage pressures** (McGuire and Denil, 1991; Persun et al, 1999; Woodhouse, 2005).

Voiding dysfunction secondary to occult spinal dysraphism may not present in childhood, and such patients may be referred as adults for symptoms as mundane as incontinence or recurrent urinary infection. Jakobsen and coworkers (1985) reported seven such patients ranging in age from 10 to 51 years; delayed diagnosis of such voiding dysfunction was also reported by Yip and colleagues (1985). There was no characteristic abnormality, and the specific dysfunction is dependent on the level and extent of the neurologic injury.

Tethered cord syndrome (TCS) is defined as a stretch-induced functional disorder of the spinal cord with its caudal part anchored by inelastic structures. Vertical movement is restricted. The anchoring structures can include scar from prior surgery, fibrous or fibroadipose filum terminale, a bony septum, or tumor (Yamada et al, 2004). Adults with TCS can be divided into those with a prior history of spinal dysraphism with a previously stabilized neurologic status who present with subtle progression in adulthood and those without associated spinal dysraphism who present with new subtle neurologic symptoms (Yamada et al, 2004). **Symptoms can include back pain, leg weakness, foot deformity, scoliosis, sensory loss, and bowel or lower urinary tract dysfunction** (Phuong et al, 2002). **TCS is reported to occur in 3% to 15% of patients with myelomeningocele. There is no typical dysfunction in TCS, and treatment must be based on contemporary urodynamic evaluation.** Voiding dysfunction may not be present until the teenage years or later (Kaplan WE et al, 1988; Husmann, 1995). Giddens and colleagues (1999) point out that, whereas children often develop symptoms of tethered cord after growth spurts, in adults presenting symptomatology often follows activities that stretch the spine, such as sports or motor vehicle accidents. In adults, urologic presentation can include irritative voiding symptoms, incontinence, or retention. These authors reported neurourologic and urodynamic findings in a group of adult patients. At presentation, urgency (67%) and urge incontinence (50%) were the most common findings. Pretreatment urodynamics in 18 patients revealed detrusor overactivity in 13 (72%), DESD in 4 (22%), decreased sensation in 4 (22%), decreased compliance in 3 (17%), and what was called a "hypocontractile" detrusor in 2 (11%). It is interesting that postoperative urodynamic findings were improved in only 4 patients (29%) and unchanged in 10 (71%).

Tabes Dorsalis, Pernicious Anemia

Although syphilitic myelopathy is disappearing as a major neurologic problem, involvement of the spinal cord dorsal columns and posterior sacral roots can result in a loss of bladder sensation and large residual urine volumes and therefore be a cause of "sensory neurogenic bladder" (see Chapter 57, "Pathophysiology and Classification of Voiding Dysfunction"). Although this represents the "classic" tabetic bladder (Wheeler et al, 1986), Hattori and coworkers (1990) reported on some patients with only tabes as an obvious cause of their voiding dysfunction who had low compliance or detrusor overactivity. Another spinal cord cause of the classic "sensory bladder" is the now uncommon pernicious anemia that produced this disorder by virtue of subacute combined degeneration of the dorsolateral columns of the spinal cord.

Poliomyelitis

When seen, voiding dysfunction in polio is that of a typical "motor neurogenic bladder" (see Chapter 57, "Pathophysiology and Classification of Voiding Dysfunction") with urinary retention, detrusor areflexia, and intact sensation. The reported incidence of voiding dysfunction in patients with polio was described as ranging from 4% to 42% by Bors and Comarr (1971).

DISEASE DISTAL TO THE SPINAL CORD

Disk Disease

Goldman and Appell (2000) nicely summarize the anatomic and neurologic considerations applicable to voiding dysfunction from lumbar disk disease. **In the adult, the sacral segments of the spinal cord are at the level of the L1 and L2 vertebral bodies.** In this distal end of the spinal cord, commonly called the *conus medullaris,* the spinal cord segments are named for the vertebral body at which the nerve roots exit the spinal canal. Thus, although the sacral spinal cord segment is located at vertebral segment L1, its nerve roots run in the subarachnoid space posterior to the L2 to L5 vertebral bodies until reaching the S1 vertebral body, at which point they exit the canal. Thus, all of the sacral nerves that originate at the L1 and L2 spinal column levels run posterior to the lumbar vertebral bodies until they reach their appropriate site of exit from the spinal canal. This group of nerve roots running at the distal end of the spinal cord is commonly referred to as the **cauda equina.**

Usually, disk prolapse is in a posterolateral direction, which does not affect the majority of the cauda equina. However, in 1% to 15% of the cases (Goldman and Appell, 2000a), central disk prolapse occurs and compression of the cauda equina may result. Thus, disk prolapse anywhere in the lumbar spine could interfere with the parasympathetic and somatic innervation of the lower urinary tract, striated sphincter and other pelvic floor musculature, and afferent activity from the bladder and affected somatic segments to the spinal cord. **Most disk protrusions compress the spinal roots in the L4-L5 or L5-S1 vertebral interspaces. Voiding dysfunction may result, and, when present, generally occurs with the usual clinical manifestations of low back pain radiating in a girdle-like fashion along the involved spinal root areas. Examination may reveal reflex and sensory loss consistent with nerve root compression. The most characteristic findings on physical examination are sensory loss in the perineum or perianal area (S2-S4 dermatomes), sensory loss on the lateral foot (S1-S2 dermatomes), or both.**

Goldman and Appell (2000a) also reviewed the literature on voiding dysfunction associated with lumbar disk disease. The incidence of such dysfunction in their review ranged from 27% to 92%. The true incidence is a bit difficult to ascertain, because many reported series on this subject describe findings only in patients who present with voiding dysfunction. Bartolin and colleagues (1998) reported on findings in 114 patients with lumbar disk protrusion who were prospectively studied. They found detrusor areflexia in 31 (27.2%) and normal detrusor activity in the remaining 83. **All 31 patients with detrusor areflexia reported difficulty voiding with straining. Patients with voiding dysfunction generally presented with these symptoms or in urinary retention. The most consistent urodynamic finding was that of a normally compliant areflexic bladder associated with normal innervation or findings of incomplete denervation of he perineal floor musculature.** In a later report, Bartolin and colleagues (2004) describe findings in 122 patients with lumbar disk protrusion. Detrusor areflexia was found in 32 (26%) and normal bladder urodynamic findings in 90 (74%). All with areflexia complained of difficulty voiding; 8 could not void at all, 14 had an interrupted flow, and 10 had a continuous but low

flow. Occasionally, patients may show detrusor overactivity, attributed to irritation of the nerve roots (O'Flynn et al, 1992).

The detrusor areflexia associated with lumbar disk protrusion shows a lower incidence of decreased compliance than in the voiding dysfunction caused by myelomeningocele. Sandri and coworkers (1987) offered two possible explanations for this difference: (1) the effect of the disk represents a more incomplete lesion of the preganglionic parasympathetic fibers and (2) the lesion is more sensory than motor, implying that the decreased compliance seen with the type of neural lesion in myelomeningocele is primarily caused by injury of the preganglionic parasympathetic motor fibers to the bladder.

Laminectomy may not improve bladder function, and prelaminectomy urodynamic evaluation is therefore desirable, because it may be difficult postoperatively in these cases to separate causation of voiding dysfunction owing to the disk sequelae from changes secondary to the surgery. Bartolin and colleagues (1999) reported on the results of surgery in a group of patients with lumbar disk protrusion. Of 27 patients with detrusor areflexia preoperatively, detrusor activity returned to normal in only 6. The patients were studied up to a year after surgery. Of the 71 patients with normal urodynamic findings preoperatively, 4 developed detrusor overactivity and 3 developed detrusor areflexia postoperatively. The medicolegal implications of a presurgical and postsurgical urodynamic evaluation are obvious.

Cauda equina syndrome **is a term applied to the clinical picture of perineal sensory loss with loss of voluntary control of both anal and urethral sphincter and of sexual responsiveness.** This can occur not only secondary to disk disease (severe central posterior disk protrusion) but to other spinal canal pathologic processes as well. Yamanishi and associates (2003) place the incidence of cauda equina syndrome at 1% to 5% of all prolapsed lumbar disks. They reported on 8 patients undergoing emergency corrective surgery for this entity. All had an acontractile detrusor with no bladder sensation and 4 of 7 had an inactive sphincter EMG. Follow-up urodynamics showed that all continued with an acontractile detrusor, 3 had normal EMG activity, and 3 had EMG activity but with denervation potentials in 2 and low activity in 2.

Spinal Stenosis

Spinal stenosis is a term applied to any narrowing of the spinal canal, nerve root canals, or intervertebral foramina. It may be congenital, developmental, or acquired. Compression of the nerve roots or cord by such a problem may lead to neuronal damage, ischemia, or edema. **Spinal stenosis may occur without disk prolapse. Symptoms may range from those consequent to cervical spinal cord compression to a cauda equina syndrome, with corresponding urodynamic findings** (Smith and Woodside, 1988). Back and lower extremity pain, cramping, and paresthesias related to exercise and relieved by rest are the classic symptoms of lumbar stenosis caused by lumbar spondylosis and are believed to result from a sacral nerve root ischemia. The urodynamic findings are dependent on the level and the amount of spinal cord or nerve root damage. Deen and coworkers (1994) reported subjective improvement in over 50% of such patients with bladder dysfunction who were treated by decompressive laminectomy. In cervical spondylitic spinal stenosis, detrusor overactivity or underactivity may occur, depending on whether the primary pathologic process affecting the micturition neural axis is compression of the inhibitory reticulospinal tracts or myelopathy in the posterior funiculus, which carries proprioceptive sensation (Tammela et al, 1992). Because there is no consistent pattern of dysfunction with any type of spinal stenosis, urodynamic studies again are the cornerstone of rational therapy.

Radical Pelvic Surgery

Voiding dysfunction after pelvic plexus injury occurs most commonly after abdominoperineal resection and radical hysterectomy. The true incidence of neurogenic vesicourethral dysfunction after various types of pelvic surgery is unknown, because there are few prospectively studied series of patients with preoperative and postoperative urodynamic evaluation. **The incidence has been estimated to range from 20% to 68% of patients after abdominoperineal resection, 16% to 80% after radical hysterectomy, 20% to 25% after anterior resection, and 10% to 20% after proctocolectomy** (Blaivas and Chancellor, 1995b). These are estimates drawn from past literature, and the current incidence is most likely significantly lower, owing to the use of nerve-sparing techniques during these types of pelvic surgery. It has been estimated, however, that **in 15% to 20% of affected individuals, the voiding dysfunction is permanent** (McGuire, 1984; Mundy, 1984). The injury may occur consequent to denervation or neurologic decentralization, tethering of the nerves or encasement in scar, direct bladder or urethral trauma, or bladder devascularization. Adjuvant treatment, such as chemotherapy or irradiation, may play a role as well. The type of voiding dysfunction that occurs is dependent on the specific nerves involved, the degree of injury, and any pattern of reinnervation or altered innervation that results over time (see Chapter 56, "Physiology and Pharmacology of the Bladder and Urethra" and the previous section on neuroplasticity).

Literature on the effects of parasympathetic decentralization on neuromorphology and neuropharmacology of the lower urinary tract in many animal models is abundant (Wein and Barrett, 1988). Parasympathetic decentralization has been reported to lead to a marked increase in adrenergic innervation of the bladder in some experimental models, with the resultant conversion of the usual β (relaxant) response of the bladder body in response to sympathetic stimulation to an α (contractile) effect (Sundin et al, 1977). Hanno and coworkers (1988) confirmed that, in the cat model, parasympathetic decentralization does result in adrenergic hyperinnervation of the detrusor but that pelvic plexus neurectomy alone or parasympathetic decentralization plus hypogastric neurectomy yields no detectable increase in adrenergic innervation. In their experimental model, decentralization did result in synaptic reorganization in bladder wall ganglia with new cholinergic excitatory inputs from the hypogastric nerves. Koyanagi was the first to call attention to what he referred to as supersensitivity of the urethra to α-adrenergic stimulation in a similar group of patients with neurologic decentralization of the lower urinary tract, implying a similar change in adrenergic receptor function in the urethra after parasympathetic decentralization (Koyanagi et al, 1988). Nordling and coworkers (1981) described a similar change in females after radical

hysterectomy and ascribed this change to damage to the sympathetic innervation of the lower urinary tract.

When permanent voiding dysfunction occurs after radical pelvic surgery, the pattern is generally one of a failure of voluntary bladder contraction, or impaired bladder contractility, with obstruction by what seems urodynamically to be residual fixed striated sphincter tone, which is not subject to voluntarily induced relaxation. Often, the smooth sphincter area is open and nonfunctional. Whether this appearance of the bladder neck/proximal urethra is caused by parasympathetic damage or terminal sympathetic damage or whether it results from the hydrodynamic effects of obstruction at the level of the striated sphincter is debated and unknown. **Decreased compliance is common in these patients, and this, with the "obstruction" caused by fixed residual striated sphincter tone, results in both storage and emptying failure. These patients often experience leaking across the distal sphincter area and, in addition, are unable to empty the bladder, because although intravesical pressure may be increased, there is nothing that approximates a true bladder contraction. The patient often presents with urinary incontinence that is characteristically most manifest with increases in intra-abdominal pressure.** This is usually most obvious in females, because the prostatic bulk in males often masks an equivalent deficit in urethral closure function. Alternatively, patients may present with variable degrees of urinary retention.

Urodynamic studies may show decreased compliance, poor proximal urethral closure function, loss of voluntary control of the striated sphincter, and a positive bethanechol supersensitivity test, findings similar to those in Figure 59–4. **Upper tract risk factors are related to intravesical pressure and the detrusor leak point pressure, and the therapeutic goal is always low-pressure storage with periodic emptying. The temptation to perform a prostatectomy should be avoided unless a clear demonstration of outlet obstruction at this level is possible.** Otherwise, prostatectomy simply decreases urethral sphincter function and thereby may result in the occurrence or worsening of sphincteric urinary incontinence. **Most of these dysfunctions will be transient, and the temptation to "do something" other than perform CIC initially after surgery in these patients, especially in those with little or no preexistent history of voiding dysfunction, cannot be too strongly criticized.** Our general practice in such patients is to discharge them on CIC and then have them return for a full urodynamic evaluation at a later date. Six to 12 months may elapse before detrusor function returns to an acceptable level (Blaivas and Chancellor, 1995b). Many of the changes after radical pelvic surgery are similar to those seen in sacral cord injury or disease. Sislow and Mayo (1990), in an excellent study on decreased bladder compliance after decentralization, noted a higher prevalence of this finding in patients who had undergone radical pelvic surgery than in those who had sustained conus medullaris or cauda equina injury.

Finally, to answer questions as to whether some types of nonradical pelvic surgery, such as simple hysterectomy, are ultimately responsible for filling/storage or emptying abnormalities on the basis of neurologic damage, more series that include sophisticated preoperative and early and late postoperative urodynamic evaluation are necessary.

Herpesvirus Infections

Invasion of the sacral dorsal root ganglia and posterior nerve roots with herpes zoster virus may produce urinary retention and detrusor areflexia days to weeks after the other primary viral manifestations (Ryttov et al, 1985). Generally, painful cutaneous eruptions secondary to the virus are also present, but initially there may be just fever and malaise with perineal and thigh paresthesias and obstipation. **Urinary incontinence secondary to detrusor overactivity may also occur, but the pathophysiology is uncertain.** It may be related to nerve root irritation, inflammation of the meninges or spinal cord, or "zoster cystitis" (Broseta et al, 1993). Cystoscopy may reveal vesicles in the bladder mucosa similar to those seen on the skin. **Spontaneous resolution generally occurs in 1 to 2 months.** Broseta and colleagues (1993) reported on 57 patients with herpes zoster infection whose records were reviewed retrospectively. Fifteen (26%) of these patients showed urologic manifestations, but in only 2 of these did frank urinary retention occur. Three patients demonstrated urinary incontinence; urodynamically, all of those showed involuntary bladder contractions. Ten patients demonstrated irritative voiding symptoms with dysuria and frequency.

Chen and colleagues (2002) reported on the incidence of voiding dysfunction in 423 patients admitted with a diagnosis of herpes zoster. Seventeen (4%) had voiding dysfunction. Excluding those with cranial rather than spinal nerve involvement, the incidence was 8.8%; when only lumbosacral dermatome patients were considered, the figure rose to 28.6%. The authors subdivided the bladder disorders into three types. The most common is associated with a herpetic cystitis. Patients in this group may present with dysuria, frequency, retention, pyuria, or hematuria. Twelve of the 17 affected patients (71%) were in this group; they presented with dysuria and frequency or retention. The second type is neuritis associated, presumably affecting the sacral motor neurons. Four of the 17 (24%) were in this group and presented in urinary retention and with a "flaccid bladder." Myelitis-associated voiding dysfunction is the third type, associated with spinal cord involvement and presenting with detrusor overactivity. One of their patients was in this group. All patients regained a normal or "balanced bladder" within 8 weeks, and no major urologic sequelae were noted.

Urinary retention has also been reported to occur in association with anogenital herpes simplex virus infection. Caplan and colleagues (1977) reported 11 such patients with the typical clinical picture of herpes genitalis, all of whom developed urinary retention 2 to 7 days after the genital eruption. Hemrika and associates (1986) reported 3 such patients, each of which showed pleocytosis of the cerebrospinal fluid, a finding that they believed was indicative of central nervous system involvement. They termed the coexistence of bilateral involvement of the sacral nerve roots of rapid onset accompanied by sphincteric incontinence with cerebrospinal fluid pleocytosis the *Elsberg syndrome* and tabulated 47 such cases reported before their article. Haanpaa and Paavonen (2004) added 2 cases, in both of which the patients had transient urinary retention but developed chronic neuropathic pain in the sacral area. The lower urinary tract dysfunction was transient, as with herpes zoster.

Diabetes Mellitus

Diabetes is the most common cause of peripheral neuropathy in Europe and North America. The exact prevalence of diabetes in the United States is somewhere between 1% and 6%, depending on whether one includes only diagnosed patients or diagnosed and undiagnosed patients and on what fasting blood glucose criteria one uses for inclusion (the higher estimate of prevalence represents a recent reduction in blood glucose criteria to 126 mg/dL) (Chancellor and Blaivas, 1995a; Goldman and Appell, 2000b). The clinical spectrum of voiding dysfunction thought to be caused by diabetes has been well reviewed by a number of authors, each of whom has cited the same historical articles up to their date of publication and added their personal experience at that time (Kaplan and Blaivas, 1988; Kaplan and Te, 1992; Beck et al, 1994; Kaplan et al, 1995; Chancellor and Blaivas, 1995a; Wein and Rovner, 1999; Goldman and Appell, 2000b). The exact incidence of voiding dysfunction caused by diabetes is, however, uncertain. Unselected patients generally do not complain of bladder symptoms. **If specifically questioned, anywhere from 5% to 59% of patients with diabetes report symptoms of voiding dysfunction.** However, the symptoms may or may not be caused by just the diabetes. In trying to come to conclusions regarding the incidence and types of voiding dysfunction specifically from diabetes, one has to carefully discriminate between articles that consider patients referred for voiding symptoms versus those that have evaluated unselected patients from a population known to have diabetes.

KEY POINT: DIABETES MELLITUS

- Cai Frimodt-Moller (1976) coined the term *diabetic cystopathy* to describe the involvement of the lower urinary tract by this disease. The classic description of voiding dysfunction secondary to diabetes is that of a peripheral and autonomic neuropathy that first affects sensory afferent pathways, causing the insidious onset of impaired bladder sensation. As the classic description continues, a gradual increase in the time interval between voiding results, which may progress to the point at which the patient voids only once or twice a day without ever sensing any real urgency. If this continues, detrusor distention, overdistention, and decompensation ultimately occur. Detrusor contractility, therefore, is classically described as being decreased in the end-stage diabetic bladder.

Current evidence points to both a sensory and a motor neuropathy as being involved in the pathogenesis, the motor aspect per se contributing to the impaired detrusor contractility. **The typically described classic urodynamic findings include impaired bladder sensation, increased cystometric capacity, decreased bladder contractility, impaired uroflow, and, later, increased residual urine volume.** The main differential diagnosis, at least in men, is generally bladder outlet obstruction, because both conditions commonly produce a low flow rate. Pressure/flow urodynamic studies easily differentiate the two. **Smooth or striated sphincter dyssynergia generally is not seen in classic diabetic cystopathy,** but these diagnoses can easily be erroneously made on a poor or incomplete urodynamic study—voiding may involve abdominal straining, which will produce an interference EMG pattern (pseudo-dyssynergia), and abdominal straining alone will not open the bladder neck area.

Other articles have appeared, however, suggesting that this "classic" diabetic cystopathy may not be the predominant form of lower urinary tract dysfunction. Starer and Libow (1990) reported on a group of 23 elderly diabetic nursing home patients who presented with symptoms of urinary dysfunction. In these 19 women and 4 men, 61% were found to have involuntary bladder contractions, 17% to have voluntary contractions of decreased magnitude, 13% to have normal detrusor contractility, and 9% were unable to initiate a detrusor contraction at all. Kaplan and coworkers (1995) reported on another group of patients with diabetes referred because of voiding symptoms. Fifty-five percent were found to have involuntary bladder contractions; 23%, impaired detrusor contractility; 10%, detrusor areflexia; and 11%, "indeterminate findings." In the 42 patients in this group with sacral cord neurologic signs, 50% had impaired detrusor contractility and 24% had detrusor areflexia. Chancellor and Blaivas (1995a) detailed the urodynamic findings in 43 diabetic patients at Chancellor's institution: 33% had involuntary bladder contractions with normal contractility; 23% had involuntary bladder contractions with impaired contractility but were able to void; 9% had impaired bladder contractility alone but were able to void; 23% had detrusor areflexia; and only 12% had a normal urodynamic study. Ueda and associates (1997) also found involuntary bladder contractions in a moderate percentage of diabetic patients (25%) but noted that all these patients had a history of cerebrovascular disease and that no patient had involuntary bladder contractions who did not have such a history. Although it is obvious that some (or even many) of the patients with diabetes who exhibited involuntary bladder contractions may have had factors other than diabetes to account for their bladder overactivity, the importance of urodynamic study in diabetic patients before the institution of therapy cannot be overemphasized.

Numerous articles describe potential pathophysiologic mechanisms that could account for the various types of voiding dysfunction seen in diabetes. Clark and Lee (1995) describe the basic mechanism of interference with physiologic mechanisms as increases in blood glucose increasing the intercellular accumulation of both glucose and its subsequent metabolic products. Hyperglycemia is then proposed to lead to microvascular and neurologic complications, the neurologic sequelae ultimately resulting in a loss of myelinated and unmyelinated fibers, wallerian degeneration, and blunted nerve fiber reproduction and function. The proposed mechanisms include increased accumulation of polyols (sorbitol) from glucose through the aldolase-reductase pathway, inhibiting both glomerular and neural synthesis of myoinositol. The decrease in myoinositol synthesis depresses phosphoinositide metabolism, decreasing Na^+,K^+-ATPase activity. Hyperglycemia also leads to the formation of advanced glycosylation end products, inhibition of the formation of which in animals has been shown to improve

response to functional and structural abnormalities of peripheral nerves.

In addition to this overall hypothesis, there are tantalizing "chunks" of data from various investigators that may or may not prove to be involved in the pathogenesis of voiding dysfunction secondary to diabetes. In streptozotocin-induced diabetic rats, Hashitani and Suzuki (1996) report reduced spontaneous spike activity, failure of neuromuscular transmission, reduced potency of the smooth muscle sodium-potassium pump, and the development of a postjunctional, muscarinic supersensitivity, but without alteration of the adenosine triphosphate receptor sensitivity. Tong and colleagues (1999) reported an upregulation of M2 receptor protein in the bladder of streptozotocin-induced diabetic rats and an upregulation of M2 receptor protein in bladder body tissue (Tong and Cheng, 2002). Presumably, this could be related to detrusor overactivity and conceivably account for a differential effect of various anticholinergic agents, depending on their receptor specificity. Mumtaz and coworkers (1999) reported an impairment of nitric oxide–mediated urethral smooth muscle relaxation in alloxan-induced diabetic rabbits along with a significant impairment of nonadrenergic noncholinergic nerve-mediated relaxation in this area. They hypothesize that nitric oxide may be functionally inactive and/or unavailable in this type of diabetes, and this lack may contribute to non–BPH-related outlet obstruction in patients with long-term diabetes and to detrusor overactivity, although it is a bit unclear as to how changes in only the outlet might influence overactivity. Gupta and colleagues (1996) and Gupta and Wein (1999) suggested that diabetes diminishes sodium pump activity, thereby inhibiting agonist-induced contractions in bladder smooth muscle by an increase in intracellular sodium concentration, the latter acting to diminish calcium influx. In abstract form, Chacko's group (2000) has hypothesized a translocation of protein kinase C isoforms as being involved in decreased detrusor contractility in alloxan-induced diabetes in rabbits. Cardozo and coworkers (2002) reported enhancement of bladder contractions to substance P and des-Arg-BK in a streptozotocin model. Sasaki and associates (2002) described decreased nerve growth factor in bladder tissue and L6 to S1 dorsal root ganglia. In alloxan-induced diabetic animals, Khan and colleagues (2002) noted decreased apoptosis of bladder urothelial cells. In this same model Su and associates (2004) reported increased myosin light chain phosphorylation and decreased sensitivity to activator calcium; Changolkar and coworkers (2005) reported decreased smooth muscle force associated with increased lipid peroxides and sorbitol and an overexpression of aldolase reductase and polyol pathway activation.

Early institution of timed voiding will avoid the proportion of the impaired detrusor contractility from chronic distention and detrusor decompensation. Experimental studies are currently directed at inhibiting the proposed mechanisms by which hyperglycemia produces neuropathy (Clark and Lee, 1995). Ayan and colleagues (1999) cite references showing that intensive therapy for diabetes can slow its progression and slow the development of abnormal autonomic tests. As a corollary, they showed on a short-term basis in alloxan-induced diabetic rabbits that insulin therapy prevented the urodynamic (increased bladder capacity and compliance) and histopathologic changes seen in a similar but non–insulin-treated group of animals. Insulin reversed most of the changes reported by Cardozo and coworkers (2002).

Guillain-Barré Syndrome

Guillain-Barré syndrome (GBS) is **an inflammatory demyelinating disorder of the peripheral somatic and autonomic nervous system** that may be life threatening. It is described as a recognizable clinical entity characterized by rapidly evolving symmetrical limb weakness, loss of tendon reflexes, absent or mild sensory signs, and variable autonomic dysfunctions (Hahn, 1998). It results from aberrant immune responses directed against peripheral nerve components (Hartung et al, 1995; Hahn, 1998). It is triggered by a preceding bacterial or viral infection, with the immune responses directed toward the infecting organisms cross-reacting with neural tissues. The immune reactions against Schwann cell surface membrane or myelin result in acute inflammatory demyelinating neuropathy (accounting for 85% of cases), whereas reactions against axonal membrane components cause acute motor-sensory axonal neuropathy, accounting for 15% of cases. Two-thirds of patients report an antecedent acute infectious illness, most commonly a respiratory tract infection or gastroenteritis, that has resolved by the time the neurologic symptoms begin. Several anecdotal case reports have linked GBS to vaccination by temporal association alone. About 75% of cases reach their nadir within 2 weeks and 94% within 4 weeks. After a brief plateau phase, improvement begins, with gradual resolution of paralysis over weeks to months. The outcome is generally favorable, but Hahn (1998) quotes a mortality rate of 5% to 8% despite the most aggressive management. **Autonomic neuropathy is a common complication.** Cardiac arrhythmia, hypertension and hypotension, and bowel, bladder, and sexual dysfunction may occur. **The prevalence of lower urinary tract dysfunction has been reported as ranging from 25% to over 80%** (Wyndaele, 2005). Zochodne (1994) reviewed multiple series and reported a urinary retention rate of 11% to 30%. Sakakibara (1997) reported 7 of 28 patients with voiding dysfunction. Of these, 3 had transient urinary retention, 2 had urgency, nocturia, and urge incontinence, 1 had stress incontinence, and 1 had voiding difficulty, otherwise unexplained. Many of these patients will have an indwelling catheter to monitor output while in the intensive care unit. Otherwise, **their voiding dysfunction should be managed by reversible therapy** (e.g., CIC, anticholinergic therapy) while waiting and hoping for resolution.

MISCELLANEOUS NEUROLOGIC DISEASES CAUSING VOIDING DYSFUNCTION
Lyme Disease

The associated neurologic symptoms of Lyme disease (neuroborreliosis) fall broadly into three syndromes: (1) encephalopathy, (2) polyneuropathy, and (3) leukoencephalitis. The Lyme spirochete can also (rarely) invade the bladder itself. Chancellor and colleagues (1991) described seven patients who also had lower urinary tract dysfunction.

Five had detrusor overactivity, none had dyssynergia, and two had detrusor areflexia. In two women, urinary retention was the presenting symptom of Lyme disease. Other subjective symptoms noted were urgency, frequency, nocturia, and urge incontinence. Follow-up at 6 months to 2 years after treatment revealed residual urgency and frequency in three patients.

Hereditary Spastic Paraplegia

Hereditary spastic paraplegia is a genetically transmitted disorder, generally autosomal dominant, less commonly autosomal recessive, and rarely sex linked. There is a pattern of central demyelination with axon loss and progressive lower extremity spasticity generally with muscle weakness. Bushman and coworkers (1993) reported three patients, two of whom had detrusor overactivity (one with striated sphincter dyssynergia), one who had significantly decreased compliance, and one who was urodynamically normal except for a high maximum urethral pressure of uncertain significance.

Jensen and colleagues (1998) reported the voiding characteristics of 11 patients with autosomal dominant pure spastic paraplegia linked to chromosome 2p21-p24. These were culled from six of eight families with the disorder, the authors commenting that lower urinary tract symptoms were present in 16 of 44 definitely affected family members. One patient had an indwelling catheter, and thus an accurate description of symptomatology was not possible. For the other patients, urinary urgency and frequency were the dominant complaints, with 6 of these 10 patients regularly experiencing urgency incontinence. Urodynamically, 3 patients showed detrusor overactivity, 6 demonstrated normal detrusor activity, and 1 demonstrated "hyporeflexia" with delayed first sensation. Satisfactory sphincter EMG recordings were obtained from 7 patients, and all were normal. Postvoid residual urine volumes were raised in 8 of 10 patients. The bulbocavernosus reflex was absent in 6 patients and was truly normal in only 1. The authors commented that the frequency of urinary symptoms in their patients (36%) correlated well with other reports in the literature. The authors proposed that the lower urinary tract symptoms (and bowel and sexual dysfunction) in patients with this disorder are caused by a combination of somatic and autonomic nervous system involvement, supporting a multisystem involvement.

Tropical Spastic Paraparesis

Tropical spastic paraparesis is primarily a spinal cord myelopathy caused by a retrovirus (human T-cell leukemia virus 1 [HTLV-1]) similar to HIV. Progressive lower limb weakness and back pain are typically the primary complaints, but voiding dysfunction occurs in up to 60% of those affected (Walton and Kaplan, 1993). Eardley and associates (1991) studied 6 such patients with voiding dysfunction. Two had detrusor areflexia, and 3 had overactivity, 1 of whom with dyssynergia. Walton and Kaplan (1993) found 4 of 5 consecutive patients had detrusor overactivity and striated sphincter dyssynergia, whereas 1 had overactivity and synergia. The type of voiding dysfunction depends on whether the damage is primarily to the descending spinal tracts, to the sacral nuclei, or to the sacral outflow. The disease must be distinguished from other myelopathic conditions associated with voiding dysfunction, such as MS.

Acquired Immunodeficiency Syndrome

Infection with HIV can affect both the central and the peripheral nervous systems, and so it is not unexpected that symptoms of lower urinary tract dysfunction occur, although there is some disagreement as to the overall prevalence of such symptoms in this population. Khan and coworkers (1992) were among the first to report on the types of voiding dysfunctions seen in patients with AIDS. They reported 11 such patients. Urinary retention occurred in 6. On urodynamic evaluation, 3 had detrusor overactivity, 4 had detrusor areflexia, 2 had a hypocontractile detrusor, and 2 had outlet obstruction secondary to BPH. Hermieu and associates (1996) prospectively studied 39 patients with HIV infection and voiding symptoms. Clinical symptoms included frequency, urgency, and incontinence in 41% of patients, acute urinary retention in 28%, dysuria and frequency in 18%, and decreased flow in 13%. Seventeen of the patients had involuntary bladder contractions; and, of these, 8 had striated sphincter dyssynergia or a lack of sphincter relaxation during micturition, 5 patients had detrusor areflexia, 4 patients had what was termed a "hypertonic urethra," 3 had "hypersensitivity," and 5 patients had a normal urodynamic evaluation. The authors characterized the voiding dysfunctions broadly as inability to void in 41% of the cases and frequency/urgency/incontinence in 41%. The authors comment that the appearance of neurogenic voiding disturbances heralds a poor prognosis. Eighteen HIV-positive patients, 13 with AIDS, who presented with voiding dysfunction were urodynamically characterized by Kane and coworkers (1996). Chief presenting complaints were daytime frequency in 8 patients; retention in 3; nocturia in 2; and having to strain to void, feeling incompletely empty, incontinence, split stream, and groin pain in 1 each. Five patients (28%) showed detrusor overactivity, 5 showed DESD, and 1 (6%) showed detrusor areflexia. The authors remark that there is a correlation between cytomegalovirus infection, polyradiculopathy, and detrusor areflexia, a phenomenon reported by others as well. Other common causes of voiding dysfunction exist as well, because 4 patients had outlet obstruction secondary to BPH and in 1 patient it was secondary to urethral stricture.

How common are voiding problems overall in patients with HIV infection and AIDS? Gyrtrup and associates (1995) prospectively investigated voiding function in 77 men and 4 women with HIV infection or AIDS consecutively attending an outpatient clinic. Eight of these (10%) had moderate subjective voiding problems, whereas 2 (2%) had severe problems. The authors believed that in only 4% of patients did the nature of the disturbance warrant urodynamic examination and concluded that urinary voiding symptoms are only a modest problem overall in an HIV/AIDS population and that neuropathic bladder dysfunction is rare and occurs mostly in the late stages of the disease.

Acute Disseminated Encephalomyelitis

Acute disseminated encephalomyelitis (ADEM) is an acute inflammatory demyelinating disorder of the CNS of unknown etiology. It is also sometimes known as parainfectious or postinfectious encephalomyelitis. The sites of lesions are multifocal and can include the cerebral white matter, cerebellum, brain stem, and spinal cord. The records of 11 patients with ADEM were reviewed and commented on by Sakakibara and associates (1996a). Nine patients had presented in urinary retention; the other 2 had urgency, frequency, nocturia, and difficulty voiding, 1 of whom had enuresis and urgency incontinence as well. The urodynamic findings are difficult to correlate with the presenting symptoms, because in 4 of the patients the studies were done considerably after the onset of the disease. During the follow-up period, 7 of the 9 patients who originally had retention became able to urinate. Five had difficulty voiding, and 4 developed irritative symptoms. Six of the patients ultimately had a near-complete neurologic recovery, but voiding symptoms persisted in 3. The authors concluded the supranuclear and nuclear types of pelvic and pudendal nerve dysfunction were primarily responsible for the micturitional disturbances in patients with this disease and that voiding dysfunction was very common in these patients.

Syringomyelia

Syringomyelia is a chronic disorder of the spinal cord characterized by dissociated sensory loss and brachial amyotrophy. It usually affects the cervical spinal cord but can extend caudally. Voiding dysfunction has been reported in 9% to 25% of patients. Fourteen patients with syringomyelia were studied urologically by Sakakibara and associates (1996c). Eleven of these had urinary symptoms: difficulty voiding in 8, retention in 3, nocturnal and daytime frequency in 3, incontinence in 2, and urgency and enuresis in 1. The urinary symptoms appeared from 2 months to 13 years after the initial neurologic symptoms. Urodynamic studies revealed detrusor overactivity in 7, detrusor-sphincter dyssynergia in 4, detrusor areflexia in 4, and "uninhibited sphincter relaxation" in 2. It is interesting that motor unit EMG recordings disclosed findings compatible with denervation of the striated sphincter in 5 of 6 patients. The authors concluded that both supranuclear and nuclear types of peripheral autonomic and somatic nerve dysfunction are responsible for the voiding dysfunctions seen. It is also interesting that the micturitional status gradually improved in 4 of 6 patients after syringosubarachnoid shunts.

Schistosomal Myelopathy

In addition to causing voiding dysfunction secondary to bladder neck obstruction and impaired muscle contractility as a result of infiltration of the bladder smooth muscle itself, schistosomiasis can rarely cause spinal cord involvement, either as a granulomatous intrathecal mass or as an acute transverse myelitis (Razdan et al, 1997). Two such patients were reported who presented with urinary incontinence as their chief urologic complaint. Both had detrusor overactivity: 1 without dyssynergia and with minimal motor weakness and 1 with striated sphincter dyssynergia and a T11 sensory level. It was believed that the findings in the former patient were characteristic of a partial spinal cord or cerebral lesion and that the second patient had a suprasacral transverse myelopathy. In the first patient, the urinary symptoms developed approximately 2 months after exposure and after the development of systemic symptoms; in the second case, symptoms developed some 5 years after the initial diagnosis. Gomes and associates (2002) reviewed the records of 14 patients with schistosomal myelopathy referred for voiding dysfunction. Of 5 patients with acute disease, 3 presented with retention and 2 had incontinence. Urodynamics were performed in 3 of these. Two (1 in retention, 1 with hesitancy and incontinence) demonstrated detrusor areflexia, and 1 (in retention) showed detrusor overactivity and striated sphincter dyssynergia. Of the 9 chronic patients, 5 showed detrusor overactivity with dyssynergia, 1 with decreased compliance; 2 showed overactivity with synergic sphincters; 25 showed detrusor areflexia, 1 with decreased compliance.

Systemic Lupus Erythematosus

Systemic lupus erythematosus (SLE) is a disease in which there is widespread inflammatory change in the connective tissues and small vessels of the skin and systemic organs, probably autoimmune in origin (Hahn cited by Sakakibara et al, 2003). The prevalence of nervous system involvement is cited from 18% to 75%. Myelopathy occurs in 1% to 3% of SLE patients. Sakakibara and associates (2003) reported on 8 patients with SLE who presented with voiding dysfunction, 6 with voiding difficulty (2 in retention) and 4 with urinary incontinence. Five exhibited decreased flow, 3 increased residual urine, 5 detrusor overactivity, 5 impaired detrusor contractility, 4 detrusor striated sphincter dyssynergia, and 2 of 4 studied exhibited abnormal striated sphincter EMG potentials. Sensation was impaired in 2. Although 3 patients had subacute encephalomyelopathy (1 subacute myelopathy, 4 chronic myelopathy), the lower urinary tract dysfunction seemed related mainly to the myelopathy.

Reflex Sympathetic Dystrophy

Reflex sympathetic dystrophy is a disabling syndrome characterized by severe pain with autonomic changes, such as vasomotor disturbances. The condition usually follows a traumatic injury. The exact etiology and pathogenesis are unclear. The prevalence of voiding dysfunction in patients with reflex sympathetic dystrophy is unknown, but it must be more than a rare occurrence, because Chancellor and colleagues (1996) were able to collect 20 consecutive patients with neurologically verified reflex sympathetic dystrophy who were referred for voiding symptoms, none of which existed before the initial trauma that induced the reflex sympathetic dystrophy. Seven of the patients presented with urinary retention, although some of these had had various types of surgery designed to treat the symptoms of the dystrophy. Five presented with urgency incontinence, 1 of whom also had stress incontinence. Six had urgency as a primary complaint, 1 had daytime frequency, and 1 had severe nocturia. Detrusor overactivity was demonstrated in 8 patients, DESD in 1, detrusor areflexia in 8, and hypersensitivity on filling in 3. Because the authors excluded patients with acute development of voiding dysfunctions after back surgery and with herniated discs and included only those in whom voiding symptoms developed concurrently with progressive symptoms of reflex sympathetic dystrophy, one must conclude that significant lower urinary

tract dysfunction can develop as a direct result of or an association with this problem, although the cause-and-effect relationship is unknown.

Other Conditions

A number of other conditions have been associated with voiding dysfunction, most of which have been reported as individual cases or small groups of cases. These are associated with neurologic symptoms typical of central or/and peripheral neural involvement. The interested reader is referred to relevant articles on amyloidosis (Sakamoto and Wheeler, 1997), adult polyglucosan body disease (Gray et al, 1988), Behçet's disease (Theodorou et al, 1999; Saito and Miyagawa, 2000; Sakakibara et al, 2000), neurofibromatosis (Brownlee et al, 1998), spinal muscular atrophy (Von Gontard et al, 2001), Duchenne muscular dystrophy (MacLeod et al, 2003), and familial dysautonomia (Saini et al, 2003).

MISCELLANEOUS CONDITIONS DEFINITELY, PROBABLY, OR POSSIBLY RELATED TO NEUROMUSCULAR DYSFUNCTION
Detrusor Sphincter Dyssynergia

Dyssynergia refers to the kinesiologic disassociation of two groups of muscles that generally work in harmony. Sphincter dyssynergia refers to an involuntary contraction or lack of relaxation of either the striated sphincter (the striated muscle surrounding the proximal urethra and the striated muscle that forms a part of the urethra for a variable distance from the "urogenital diaphragm" to the bladder neck) or the smooth sphincter (the smooth muscle of the bladder neck and proximal urethra). **Detrusor sphincter dyssynergia,** unless specified otherwise, refers to dyssynergia of the striated sphincter and is sometimes abbreviated DSD or DESD. This is discussed in Chapter 57, "Pathophysiology and Classification of Voiding Dysfunction" and in the earlier parts of this chapter, especially in the section on SCI. It is discussed as a separate entity here as well to emphasize its importance in terms of recognition and proper management in patients with neurogenic voiding dysfunction.

True DESD should exist only in patients who have an abnormality in pathways between the sacral spinal cord and the brain stem pontine micturition center, generally caused by neurologic injury or disease (Blaivas, 1982; Rudy, 1993; Chancellor and Rivas, 1995; Wein and Rovner, 1999). The diagnosis of DESD should be suspected in any patient with a neurologic lesion in this area. Common causes include traumatic SCI, multiple sclerosis, and the various forms of transverse myelitis. Conversely, **in patients without such a lesion, this diagnosis should always be viewed with skepticism,** and, without such apparent pathology, such a patient deserves exhaustive study to exclude a neural diagnosis. One exception to this precept is in infants and children with dysfunctional voiding or the Hinman syndrome (see later).

Blaivas and coworkers (1981) have described three main types of DESD. In type 1, there is concomitant increase in both detrusor pressure and EMG activity; at the peak of the detrusor contraction, the sphincter suddenly relaxes and unobstructed voiding occurs. In type 2, there are sporadic contractions of the striated sphincter throughout the detrusor contraction. In type 3, there is a crescendo-decrescendo pattern of sphincter contraction that results in outlet obstruction throughout the entire detrusor contraction. Schurch and colleagues (2005) have correlated neurologic status and DESD type after SCI. Those with an incomplete sensory and motor lesion generally present with type 1 DESD; those with complete sensory and motor lesions present with type 2 and type 3. Weld and associates (2000) prefer to classify DESD as intermittent or continuous but note that in their experience the clinical significance of DESD type is not crucial because both types require urodynamic surveillance and expedient treatment to minimize complications. No significant association between type and level of injury was found. Continuous DESD was more associated with complete injuries.

Sphincter EMG activity that increases simultaneously with intravesical or detrusor pressure does not always indicate true DESD, however. These other instances are referred to as pseudodyssynergia (Wein and Barrett, 1982), and such a misdiagnosis may be accompanied by adverse therapeutic consequences. **Common causes of pseudodyssynergia include (1) abdominal straining to either initiate or augment a bladder contraction or in response to discomfort and (2) attempted inhibition of a bladder contraction either because of its involuntary nature or because of discomfort.** Rudy (1993) has reported that pseudodyssynergia can reliably be differentiated from true DESD urodynamically by analyzing the patterns of detrusor and EMG activity, but others have not found this always to be the case.

Without proper treatment, over 50% of men with DESD will develop significant complications, such as VUR, upper tract deterioration, urolithiasis, urosepsis, and ureterovesical obstruction (Chancellor and Rivas, 1995). In women, these complications are much less common, probably because of the decreased detrusor pressures generated. Using Blaivas' categorization, type 1 DESD is generally managed with observation alone unless there is persistent reflux, hydronephrosis, or autonomic hyperreflexia. Types 2 and 3 are generally treated. In assessing success or failure of treatment, Kim and colleagues (1998) have used bladder leak point pressure greater than 40 cm H_2O as an indicator of the failure of at least sphincterotomy, because in their experience there was a significantly higher incidence of upper tract damage and persistent DESD in such patients. This most likely applies to other treatments as well. **Therapy for DESD is designed to either eliminate or significantly lessen the abnormal sphincter activity or to circumvent it. Oral medical therapy directed toward the striated sphincter has not enjoyed wide success, and the most common approaches currently are (1) CIC (usually combined with therapy to control detrusor overactivity), (2) sphincterotomy, (3) stent placement across the sphincter, (4) injection of botulinum toxin into the sphincter, (5) continuous catheterization, and (6) urinary diversion.**

Experimental small animal models of DESD have been reported by Burnett and colleagues (1997) in mice with targeted deletion of the gene for neuronal nitric oxide synthase and by Cheng and coworkers (1997) by instillation of cold water into the urinary bladder of rats.

Dysfunctional Voiding

This subject is more extensively considered in Chapter 123, "Voiding Dysfunction in Children—Neurogenic and Nonneurogenic," but is mentioned here because individuals with a history of unexplained lower urinary tract dysfunction symptomatology may not present to the urologist or be definitively diagnosed with this entity until adulthood. **This syndrome, also described by various authors as non-neurogenic neurogenic bladder, occult voiding dysfunction, occult neuropathic bladder, learned voiding dysfunction, and the Hinman syndrome, presents the unusual circumstance of what appears urodynamically to be involuntary obstruction at the striated sphincter level existing in the absence of demonstrable neurologic disease** (Hinman, 1986). It is very difficult to prove urodynamically that an individual has this entity, and it should further be noted that the diagnoses in many of the patients reported have been made on the basis of only history, isolated flowmetry, isolated measurements of total intravesical pressure, and pelvic floor EMG activity (Wein and Barrett, 1988). I believe unequivocal demonstration of this entity requires pressure-flow-EMG evidence of bladder emptying occurring simultaneously with involuntary striated sphincter contraction in the absence of any element of abdominal straining, either in an attempt to augment bladder contraction or as a response to discomfort during urination. Such reports do exist and confirm the existence of this syndrome. The etiology is uncertain and may represent a persistent transitional phase in the development of micturitional control or persistence of a reaction phase to the stimulus of lower urinary tract discomfort during voiding, long after the initial problem that caused this has disappeared (Jorgensen et al, 1982).

Bladder Neck Dysfunction

Bladder neck dysfunction is defined here as **an incomplete opening of the bladder neck during voluntary or involuntary voiding.** It has also been referred to as smooth sphincter dyssynergia, proximal urethral obstruction, primary bladder neck obstruction, and dysfunctional bladder neck. **The term** *smooth sphincter dyssynergia* **or** *proximal sphincter dyssynergia* **is generally used when referring to this urodynamic finding in an individual with autonomic hyperreflexia.** In male patients with autonomic hyperreflexia, the neurologic pathophysiology is clear. **The term** *bladder neck dysfunction* **more often refers to a poorly understood non-neurogenic condition first described over a century ago but first fully characterized by Turner-Warwick and associates in 1973. The dysfunction is found almost exclusively in young and middle-aged men, and characteristically they complain of long-standing voiding/emptying (obstructive) and filling/storage (irritative) symptoms** (Webster et al, 1980; Norlen and Blaivas, 1986; Wein and Barrett, 1988; Trockman et al, 1996; Yamanishi et al, 1997). **These patients have often been seen by many urologists and have been diagnosed as having psychogenic voiding dysfunction because of a normal prostate on rectal examination, a negligible residual urine volume, and a normal endoscopic bladder appearance.** The differential diagnosis also includes anatomic bladder neck contracture, BPH, dysfunctional voiding, prostatitis/prostatosis, neurogenic dysfunction, and low pressure/low flow (see later). **Objective evidence of outlet obstruction in these patients is easily obtainable by urodynamic study. Once obstruction is diagnosed, it can be localized at the level of the bladder neck by video-urodynamic study, cystourethrography during a bladder contraction, or micturitional urethral profilometry** (see Chapter 58, "Urodynamic and Videourodynamic Evaluation of Voiding Dysfunction"). The diagnosis may also be made indirectly by the urodynamic findings of outlet obstruction in the typical clinical situation in the absence of urethral stricture, prostatic enlargement, and striated sphincter dyssynergia. Involuntary bladder contractions or decreased compliance may occur; Noble and associates (1994) cite the incidence as 50%; this seems high. Trockman and colleagues (1996) quote it as 34%.

The exact cause of this problem is unknown. Some have proposed that there is an abnormal arrangement of musculature in the bladder neck region, so that coordinated detrusor contractions cause bladder neck narrowing instead of the normal funneling (Bates et al, 1975). The occurrence of this problem in young, anxious, and high-strung individuals and its partial relief by α-adrenergic blocking agents have prompted some to speculate that it may in some way be related to sympathetic hyperactivity. **When prostatic enlargement develops in individuals with this problem, a double obstruction results, and Turner-Warwick (1984) has applied the term** *trapped prostate* **to this entity.** The lobes of the prostate cannot expand the bladder neck and therefore expand into the urethra. A patient so affected generally has a lifelong history of voiding dysfunction that has gone relatively unnoticed because he has always accepted this as normal, and exacerbation of these symptoms occurs during a relatively short and early period of prostatic enlargement. Although α-adrenergic blocking agents provide improvement in some patients with bladder neck dysfunction, definitive relief in the male is best achieved by bladder neck incision. In patients with this and a trapped prostate, marked relief is generally effected by a "small" prostatic resection or ablation that includes the bladder neck or a transurethral incision of the bladder neck and prostate. Such patients often note afterward that they have "never" voided as well as after their treatment.

Bladder Outlet Obstruction in Women

The female counterpart of non-neurogenic bladder neck dysfunction in men does exist, although it is rare. **Bladder outlet obstruction in women in general is uncommon.** Diokno and coworkers (1984) were among the first to clearly define this entity in women on the basis of videourodynamic studies. Nitti and coworkers (1999) evaluated the videourodynamic studies of 261 of 331 women who underwent multichannel studies for non-neurogenic voiding dysfunction. **They defined** *bladder outlet obstruction* **as radiographic evidence of obstruction between the bladder neck and the distal urethra in the presence of a sustained detrusor contraction of any magnitude, which is usually associated with reduced or delayed urinary flow rate. Obstruction at the level of the bladder neck was diagnosed when the bladder neck was closed or narrowed during voiding. Obstruction of the urethra was diagnosed as a discrete area of narrowing, associated with proximal dilatation.** Strict pressure-flow

criteria were not used to classify cases as obstructed or not obstructed. Using these criteria they found 76, or 23%, of their cases to be obstructed. Of those obstructed, only 16% (12 patients) were diagnosed as having primary bladder neck obstruction (the counterpart to non-neurogenic bladder neck dysfunction in the male). Thirty-three percent of the cases of obstruction were caused by dysfunctional voiding (see earlier for description), 28% by cystocele, 14% by obstruction created by prior incontinence surgery, 4% by urethral stricture, 3% by uterine prolapse, and 1% each by urethral diverticulum and rectocele. Groutz and associates (2000) reviewed their urodynamic database of 587 consecutive women referred for evaluation of voiding symptoms. **They defined obstruction as a persistent low, noninvasive maximum flow rate less than 12 mL/s on repeated study combined with a detrusor pressure at maximum measured flow rate of more than 20 cm H_2O in a pressure-flow study.** Only 38 women (6.5%) met these criteria of bladder outlet obstruction. Of those, only 8% (3 women) were characterized as having primary bladder neck obstruction. Twenty-six percent (10 women) had obstruction on the basis of prior anti-incontinence surgery, 24% because of severe genital prolapse, 13% because of urethral stricture, 5% because of dysfunctional voiding, 5% because of true detrusor striated sphincter dyssynergia, and 3% because of urethral diverticulum; and in 16%, there was no definable etiology. **Most authors would agree that surgical treatment of this problem in women should be approached with caution, because sphincteric incontinence is a significant risk.**

Low-Pressure/Low-Flow Voiding in Younger Men: The Bashful Bladder

Low-pressure/low-flow voiding **can be the result of a number of causes, most notably a decompensating detrusor** (generally from bladder outlet obstruction—see Chapter 58, "Urodynamic and Videourodynamic Evaluation of Voiding Dysfunction" and Chapter 87, "Evaluation and Nonsurgical Management of Benign Prostatic Hyperplasia") or as a part of the syndrome known as detrusor hyperactivity with impaired contractility (DHIC—see Chapter 58, "Urodynamic and Videourodynamic Evaluation of Voiding Dysfunction" and Chapter 71, "Geriatric Incontinence and Voiding Dysfunction"). **When this occurs in a young man, it is generally characterized by frequency, hesitancy, and a poor stream.** The entity is readily demonstrated on urodynamic assessment and with no coexisting endoscopic abnormality. **The patient usually notes marked hesitancy when attempting to initiate micturition in the presence of others,** and some have therefore described this condition as an "anxious bladder" or a "bashful bladder." The estimate of the incidence of this problem in younger male patients referred for urodynamic assessment varies between 6% (Barnes et al, 1985) and 19% (George and Slade, 1979).

Barnes and associates (1985) suggested that these men are psychologically unusual but in the direction of being obsessional rather than anxious. They suggest that these individuals have a lifelong tendency to overcontrol the process of micturition and are thus vulnerable to lower urinary tract symptoms under stress, and they recommend that a behavioral modification program be considered. Rosario and colleagues (2000) performed ambulatory urodynamic studies on 40 consecutive symptomatic men with a mean international prostate symptom score of 19 who were unable to "perform" during conventional videourodynamic study. They concluded that a surgically correctable cause of the symptoms could be found in about 20% of men, but only in those older than 40 years. They believed therefore that the contribution of ambulatory urodynamic monitoring in such cases in men younger than 40 years was negligible. They also stated that they thought that evidence from the literature suggested that a significant proportion of such nonobstructed cases would respond to drug therapy or behavioral therapy. My own experience has been similar to that of others who have stated that, in the younger nonobstructed male with this condition, neither empirical pharmacologic treatment nor transurethral surgery has had any consistent beneficial effect.

Urinary Retention; The Fowler Syndrome in Young Women

Urinary retention is encountered fairly commonly by the urologist, especially in adult men secondary to anatomic obstruction from benign prostatic enlargement. Although unusual, urinary retention in women is not rare. As in the male, **the potential causes are classically cited as neurologic, pharmacologic, anatomic, myopathic, functional, and psychogenic.** A particularly excellent review of the various causes of urinary retention in women along with an algorithm for evaluation and treatment has been published by Smith and coworkers (1999).

The **Fowler syndrome** (Fowler et al, 1988; Noble et al, 1994; Fowler, 1999, 2003; Swinn and Fowler, 2001) refers particularly to **a syndrome of urinary retention in young women in the absence of overt neurologic disease. The typical history is that of a young woman younger than 30 years of age who has found herself unable to void for a day or more with no urinary urgency but increasing lower abdominal discomfort. A bladder capacity of over 1 liter with no sensation of urgency is necessary for the diagnosis. There are no neurologic or laboratory features to support a diagnosis of any neurologic disease.** MRI of the brain and the entire spinal cord is normal. **On concentric needle electrode examination of the striated muscle of the urethral sphincter, however, Fowler and associates described a unique EMG abnormality.** This abnormal activity, localized to the urethral sphincter, consists of a type of activity that would be expected to cause inappropriate contraction of the muscle. Sphincter activity consists of two components: complex repetitive discharges and decelerating bursts. This abnormal activity impairs sphincter relaxation. These patients often have polycystic ovaries, raising the possibility that the activity is linked in some way to impaired muscle membrane stability, allowing direct spread of electrical impulses throughout the muscle, owing possibly to a hormonal abnormality; and thus the disorder may possibly be the manifestation of a focal, hormonally dependent "channelopathy." This would explain why the condition is seen only in premenopausal women. Efforts to treat this condition by hormonal manipulation, pharmaco-

logic therapy, or injections of botulinum toxin have been unsuccessful. This condition is highly responsive to neuromodulation (success rate approaching 70%) even in women who have been in retention for many months or years.

The urodynamic problem is detrusor acontractility. The same EMG abnormality, however, is found sometimes in women with obstructed voiding. This type of EMG activity is not uncommon (Fitzgerald and associates [2000] cite an incidence of 8% in a series of women undergoing routine urodynamic and EMG studies), but its correlation with complete retention is relatively rare.

Postoperative Urinary Retention

Postoperative urinary retention is a well-recognized but poorly understood event. Its incidence is generally quoted overall as 4% to 25%. It occurs more frequently after lower urinary tract, perineal, gynecologic, and anorectal surgery. In the placebo arms of four trials of α-adrenergic blocker prophylaxis after these types of surgery, the incidence of postoperative retention ranged from 18.8% to 57% (Velanovich, 1992). **Contributing factors, which are not mutually exclusive, include the following eight factors:**
1. Traumatic instrumentation
2. Bladder overdistention
3. Diminished awareness of bladder sensation
4. Decreased bladder contractility
5. Increased outlet resistance
6. Decreased micturition reflex activity
7. Nociceptive inhibitory reflex
8. Preexistent outlet pathology (e.g., BPH)

Anesthesia and analgesia can contribute to factors 2, 3, 4, and 6. The idea of a nociceptive inhibitory reflex, initiated by pain or discomfort, is an attractive one, because a sympathetic efferent limb could directly affect factors 4, 5, and 6 (see Chapter 56, "Physiology and Pharmacology of the Bladder and Urethra").

Bladder decompression for 18 to 24 hours postoperatively decreased the incidence of retention in patients undergoing joint replacement surgery by 52% versus 27% (Michelson et al, 1988) and 65% versus 0% (Carpiniello et al, 1988), compared with CIC. The incidence of urinary infection with continuous catheterization was no different in the Michelson and colleagues' study (15% vs. 11%) and was less in the Carpiniello and coworkers' study (16% vs. 43%), in which straight catheterization was carried out in the recovery room as well. The avoidance of acute bladder overdistention to prevent postoperative urinary retention is supported by the experimental observation of a reduced bladder response to sacral neural stimulation during overdistention (>80% reduction) and, as well, after overdistention (19% reduction) (Bross et al, 1999).

α-Adrenergic blockade with phenoxybenzamine historically has seemed effective prophylactically in decreasing the incidence of postoperative retention. Velanovich (1992) performed a meta-analysis on the use of phenoxybenzamine (only randomized placebo-controlled studies) and concluded that this agent reduced the occurrence by 29.1%. In a retrospective review of colorectal patients treated with and without phenoxybenzamine, Goldman and colleagues (1988) found a 54.7% incidence of retention in patients not given this agent versus a 19.2% incidence in those who were. The regimen for those not catheterized preoperatively was 10 mg orally the evening before and 1 hour before surgery, 2 hours after, and 10 mg twice daily for 3 days. For those who were catheterized before the procedure, the regimen was 10 mg twice daily, initiated the day before catheter removal. The mechanism of action is uncertain. If an inhibitory nociceptive reflex is initiated, and this is similar to the sympathetic reflex elicited by bladder filling (see Chapter 56, "Physiology and Pharmacology of the Bladder and Urethra"), the mechanism is multifactorial. Alternatively, the drug may act only on the outlet to decrease resistance, which may be pathologically increased by anxiety, pain, and other factors related to surgery. Whether other α-adrenergic blockers are as effective is uncertain (Cataldo and Senagore, 1991).

Hyperthyroidism

Patients with thyrotoxicosis often present with symptoms caused by sympathetic overactivity and autonomic nervous system imbalance. Goswami and associates (1997) reported that 12 of 30 patients (40%) experienced the onset of voiding symptoms 1 to 6 months after the onset of the symptoms of thyrotoxicosis. Four of these patients had enuresis. Urodynamic studies were done in 5 patients; all had reduced flow rates, and 4 had a significant postvoid residual, 3 of whom had an enlarged bladder capacity and increased perineal EMG activity during voiding. The voiding dysfunction and urodynamic abnormalities resolved after resolution of the hyperthyroidism. The bladder symptoms were more common in females than in males. The authors hypothesize that increased β-adrenergic activity in thyrotoxicosis is responsible for a reduced flow rate and increased bladder capacity because of the inhibitory β-adrenergic activity on detrusor muscle contractility. Stoffer (1988) cited a much lower incidence of voiding dysfunction in thyrotoxicosis: a 7% prevalence of urgency and hesitancy and a 1% prevalence of enuresis.

Schizophrenia

Bonney and coworkers (1997) proposed that a significant subset of schizophrenic patients have involuntary bladder contractions secondary to brain pathology. In a previous study (Gupta et al, 1995), the same group demonstrated involuntary bladder contractions in 4 of 10 evaluable patients with schizophrenia who were referred for voiding dysfunction or incontinence. All of these patients had significant childhood incontinence, urge incontinence, bedwetting, and a small bladder capacity. In the later report (Bonney et al, 1997) the prevalence of urinary incontinence and related symptoms in a group of chronic schizophrenic patients was compared with a group of comparatively hospitalized patients with mood disorders. There was a significant difference in the prevalence of urge incontinence (34% vs. 17%) and bedwetting (46% vs. 20%). There were no significant differences in urinary urgency, overall voiding dysfunction, fecal incontinence, or sexual dysfunction. The hypothesis of a neurobiologic correlate between schizophrenic patients and the occurrence of involuntary bladder contractions in these patients is an intriguing one.

Gastroparesis

Gastroparesis is a condition characterized by symptoms from impaired transit of intraluminal gastric contents into the duodenum but in the absence of mechanical obstruction. It may be caused by diabetes, occur after gastric surgery, or be idiopathic. Goldman and Dmochowski (1997) characterized the voiding dysfunction of 17 patients with gastroparesis who were referred for voiding symptoms, 10 of whom had idiopathic gastroparesis and in 7 of whom the condition was secondary to diabetes. Seven patients had abnormal detrusor contraction and delayed sensation, 5 had poor detrusor function and normal sensation, 3 had normal detrusor function and poor sensation, and 2 had normal detrusor contraction and sensation. There was no difference between the occurrence of the dysfunctions in the two groups. Predominant symptoms were urinary frequency in 7 and difficulty emptying in 10. Patients with idiopathic gastroparesis were more likely to note difficulty emptying (70%), whereas those with diabetic gastroparesis were more likely to have urinary frequency (71%). The authors postulated an association between idiopathic gastroparesis and bladder dysfunction and proposed that a common autonomic neuropathic syndrome may account for the bladder dysfunction in both the idiopathic and the diabetic forms of this syndrome.

Myasthenia Gravis

Any neuromuscular disease that affects the tone of the smooth or striated muscle of the distal sphincter mechanism can predispose an individual patient to a greater chance of urinary incontinence after even a well-performed transurethral or open prostatectomy. Myasthenia gravis is an autoimmune disease caused by autoantibodies to acetylcholine nicotinic receptors. This leads to neuromuscular blockade and hence to weakness in a variety of striated muscle groups. The incidence of incontinence after prostatectomy is indeed greatly increased in patients with this disease (Greene et al, 1974; Khan and Bhola, 1989). Sandler and associates (1998), in addition, reviewed three cases of de novo voiding dysfunction in patients with myasthenia gravis (one woman with intrinsic sphincter deficiency, poor pelvic muscle contractility, and detrusor hyperreflexia; one male with detrusor hyporeflexia complaining of urgency and incontinence; and one young woman with an acontractile bladder); and add a personal report of a fourth patient with urinary retention from detrusor areflexia. They hypothesize that such autonomic dysfunction in a patient with myasthenia might indicate a unique subset with a worse prognosis.

Isaacs' Syndrome

Isaacs' syndrome is a rare neurologic disorder characterized by continuous muscle contraction, fasciculations, myokymia, excessive sweating, and elevated creatinine kinase level. It is shown to be secondary to antibodies possibly directed against potassium channels on peripheral nerves and is associated with peripheral neuropathy, autoimmune diseases, malignancies, and endocrine disorders. Tiguert and coworkers (1999) present a case with urinary retention associated with a picture of acute demyelinating neuropathy. Their patient was in painful urinary and fecal retention; the urinary retention was presumed to be caused by spasm of the periurethral striated sphincter, diagnosed by an inability to pass a catheter beyond this. Rectal sphincter spasm was also diagnosed. The condition was treated with plasmapheresis and pharmacologic agents to relax skeletal muscle. Suprapubic drainage was instituted. The condition subsided, and normal urinary function was ultimately restored.

Wernicke's Encephalopathy

Wernicke's encephalopathy is a rare but well-documented condition caused by a deficiency in thiamine (vitamin B_1) in both alcoholic and nonalcoholic populations. Pathologic lesions are characteristically distributed periventricularly at the levels of the third and fourth ventricles, including the mammillary body, medial thalamic nucleus, hypothalamus, superior cerebellar vermis, periaqueductal gray matter, and midbrain tegmentum. The two major clinical manifestations of thiamine deficiency involve the cardiovascular and neurologic systems. The latter manifests generally as peripheral neuropathy, the condition being known as Wernicke's encephalopathy. The initial symptoms of the polyneuropathy range from simply burning feet to muscle weakness. Sakakibara and associates (1997) report a case of a pregnant woman with multiple neurologic manifestations of central and peripheral neuropathy and with urge incontinence, manifested urodynamically by involuntary bladder contractions and a decreased bladder volume. **Resolution of the urinary symptoms occurred after thiamine replacement.** The authors hypothesize that lesions in the medial thalamic-hypothalamic area and periaqueductal gray matter were primarily responsible for the micturitional disturbance. Tjandra and Janknegt (1997) reported a case of a chronic alcoholic male with seemingly isolated erectile and voiding dysfunction, the latter consisting of complaints referable to emptying, correlated with flowmetry during a prolonged void with a peak flow rate of 6.4 mL/s with an interrupted pattern, suggesting poor detrusor contractility. The erectile dysfunction was determined to be neurogenic. Both resolved with thiamine replacement.

Systemic Sclerosis (Scleroderma)

Scleroderma is a disease of the connective tissue characterized by thickening and fibrosis of the skin, abnormalities of the small arteries, and involvement of the gastrointestinal tract, heart, lung, and kidneys. The pathogenesis is unknown but thought to be caused by overexpression of the collagen gene DNA, contributing to excessive production of collagen in these patients. Lazzeri and colleagues (1995) report the urodynamic assessment and histologic evaluation of 9 such women, of whom 5 had hesitancy; 4, decreased stream, 2, frequency and nocturia; and 2, suprapubic pain. Four patients had detrusor areflexia, 1 of whom also had decreased compliance. Another patient with decreased stream also had decreased compliance. Three of the patients with areflexia demonstrated collagen accumulation on histologic examination of bladder biopsies. The authors review five literature reports of various aspects of lower urinary tract function and histology in patients with scleroderma but fail to find a consistent pattern in these. They hypothesize that in their patients the areflexia resulted from impaired neurologic modulation owing to the histologic changes in the detrusor tissue.

Minervini and associates (1998), conversely, carried out urodynamic and bladder morphologic evaluations in 23 female patients with systemic sclerosis, 9 of whom complained of urinary symptoms, and found urodynamic alterations in only 3 cases. They were unable to correlate voiding symptoms, urodynamic changes, and the degree of bladder wall fibrosis or visceral involvement. Evidence of autonomic nervous system dysfunction was found outside the urinary tract in 13 of these patients. The authors speculate that voiding dysfunction, when it occurs, could be caused by the fibrotic replacement of bladder smooth muscle, but they did not exclude some degree of autonomic dysfunction as well.

Ehlers-Danlos Syndrome

Ehlers-Danlos syndrome refers to a heterogeneous group of disorders characterized by inherited abnormalities of connective tissue. The main clinical manifestations are skin fragility, skin hyperextensibility, and joint mobility. More than 10 subtypes of the syndrome have been defined based on clinical, genetic, and biochemical criteria. Bladder diverticula have been associated with this disorder, with operative repair characterized by an increased recurrence rate over that which would ordinarily be expected. Deveaud and associates (1999) reviewed the literature on this subject and reported on the intensive study of one such patient with a large left-sided diverticulum that did not empty, along with a greatly enlarged bladder capacity and residual urine. Simultaneously, they reported a second patient without Ehlers-Danlos syndrome who presented with a urinary tract infection and left pyelonephritis. This patient also reported decreased force of stream, and evaluation disclosed left VUR with a left (presumably congenital) periureteral diverticulum. The diverticulum enlarged with voiding, and the patient left a large postvoid residual. Both patients were treated surgically (successfully). The authors thought the tissue from the non-periureteral diverticulum was more closely related to the pathophysiology of Ehlers-Danlos syndrome, noting the tissue from that diverticulum to be more compliant, and attributed this to changes in the extracellular matrix protein caused by the Ehlers-Danlos syndrome.

Myotonic Dystrophy

Myotonic dystrophy is an autosomal dominant hereditary multiorgan disease characterized by myotonia and distal muscle atrophy, and in later stages by cataracts, endocrine disturbances, mental retardation or dementia, testicular atrophy and infertility, progressive frontal alopecia, and disturbances in cardiac conduction. Although myotonic activity has not been found in the sphincter or pelvic floor, many patients appear to have voiding complaints. Bernstein and coworkers (1992) reported on 10 patients, 8 of whom had urinary complaints by history (4 infrequent voiders, 1 with urge and stress incontinence, 1 with urge and urge incontinence, 1 with slight urgency without incontinence, and 1 with obstructive symptoms only in the morning). There were no characteristic urodynamic patterns observed, and urodynamic findings did not correlate particularly well with symptoms. Sakakibara and associates (1995b) also reported lower urinary tract symptoms in such patients, but the message seems to be that there is **no characteristic pattern of dysfunction,** and thus such patients need to be characterized urodynamically before making any assumptions regarding therapy based on symptoms alone.

Radiation

Vale and associates (1993) summarized their experience with the occurrence of voiding dysfunction after external-beam irradiation. **They describe an early radiation reaction most prominent at 4 to 6 weeks with an incidence as high as 70%. Symptoms are predominantly of the filling/storage type, and urodynamic studies have demonstrated reduced volume at first desire to void, reduced cystometric capacity, and reduced compliance. These parameters tend to return to pretreatment values by 6 months. Symptoms associated with later radiation effects are less common but may be progressive and intractable. Filling/storage symptoms predominate, and urodynamic studies, when positive, demonstrate reductions in first desire to void, maximum cystometric capacity, involuntary bladder contractions (in up to a third of patients), and an increase in maximum subtracted detrusor pressure during filling.** Historical explanations have concentrated on urothelial injury and ulceration with fibrosis. These authors attempted to develop an experimental model in rats. They found a biphasic reduction in compliance, the first reduction developing at 4 to 6 weeks after irradiation, followed by recovery. A second reduction phase in compliance started at 10 to 12 weeks and persisted. Interestingly, only half the irradiated bladders demonstrated fibrotic infiltration of muscle bundles, and there was no association between the presence of fibrosis and the magnitude of reduction and compliance. Mast cells were more abundant in irradiated bladders than in controls. Electron microscopic studies showed, in the irradiated bladders, the presence of areas displaying focal degeneration of smooth muscle cells, these cells showing disaggregation of filaments and in some cases cytoplasmic organelles free in the intracellular space. In scattered foci, selective degeneration of unmyelinated axon profiles was noted, ranging from marked to lesser degrees of axonal injury. The authors were thus unable to confirm a fibrosis-based hypothesis of postirradiation bladder dysfunction in their experimental model but did show other changes that could contribute to such dysfunction: neural degeneration and changes in the detrusor muscle itself.

Choo and colleagues (2002) reported on video-urodynamic parameters in 15 of 17 patients completing studies at baseline and at 3 and 18 months after external-beam irradiation for prostate cancer. Between baseline and 18 months there were no statistically significant changes in detrusor pressure, peak flow rate, voided volume, postvoid residual, compliance, occurrence of detrusor overactivity, or outlet obstruction. There was a mean reduction in bladder capacity of 100 mL in the supine position and 54 mL in the upright position. There was no change in self-assessed qualitative urological function (International Prostate Symptom Score, Quality of Life Assessment Index, and urinary frequency). There were, however, individual patients who developed decreased compliance (4 patients) and detrusor overactivity (2 patients), urgency (5 patients), and urgency incontinence (3 patients).

The Defunctionalized Bladder

The previously normal defunctionalized bladder will often show decreased capacity and involuntary bladder contractions and/or decreased compliance. Previously abnormal bladders will generally demonstrate their prior pathology, many times with these additional abnormalities. Rehabilitation of a defunctionalized bladder is certainly possible and should definitely be attempted by cycling with progressively increasing volumes. Serrano and associates (1996) considered this subject while evaluating the outcome of transplantation into five long-term defunctionalized bladders. Successful bladder rehabilitation was accomplished, and the transplantation was successful without bladder augmentation, although one patient required CIC. Normal compliance was inferred by the fact that there was no evidence of hydronephrosis after long-term allograft function up to 10 years. The authors recommend that transplantation can be accomplished into a previously defunctionalized bladder when a capacity greater than 100 mL and a voiding pressure less than 100 cm/H_2O are demonstrated during bladder rehabilitation.

Aging

Lower urinary tract symptoms and disorders are prevalent and bothersome in the elderly population. These problems are specifically and extensively considered in Chapter 71, "Geriatric Incontinence and Voiding Dysfunction." When considering the effects of aging on the lower urinary tract, one cannot separate the effects of chronologic age itself from the various anatomic, neuromorphologic, neurophysiologic, neuropharmacologic, metabolic, and hormonal changes that coexist with aging, along with the effects of other coexisting disease processes. In addition to the material contained in Chapter 71, there is an excellent review of this area that was carried out by the Committee on Pathophysiology of the Urinary Bladder and Obstruction and Aging for the 4th International Consultation on BPH (Nordling et al, 2001).

Other Conditions

Any neurologic disease or injury can affect lower urinary tract function. Many have been mentioned in this chapter, but case reports and small series exist that document many others. The dysfunction produced by some is logically deducible on the basis of similarity to other neurologic lesions; for others the lower urinary tract dysfunctions are inconsistent and seemingly at odds with what would be predicted on the basis of neuroanatomic and neurophysiologic principles. For those who wish to further pursue this subject, the following referenced list may be helpful:

Adrenoleukodystrophy (Silveri et al, 2004)
Adrenomyeloneuropathy (Sakakibara et al, 1998)
Brown-Séquard syndrome (Sakakibara et al, 2001)
Central cord syndrome (Newey et al, 2000; Smith et al, 2000)
Down's syndrome (Handel et al, 2003)
Intramedullary epidermoid cyst (Ferrara et al, 2003)

Lambert-Eaton myasthenic syndrome (Satoh et al, 2001)
Machado-Joseph disease (Sakakibara et al, 2004)
Sjögren's syndrome (Kovacs et al, 2003)
Spinal cord tumors (Uchiyama et al, 2004)

TREATMENT OF NEUROGENIC LOWER URINARY TRACT DYSFUNCTION: OVERVIEW

In later chapters, the various therapies available for the treatment of lower urinary tract dysfunction are considered. Only a discrete number of such therapies are available, and these are easily categorized on a functional "menu" basis according to whether they are used primarily to facilitate urine filling/storage or voiding/emptying and according to whether their primary effect is on the bladder or on the outlet (see Tables 57–3 and 57–4).

The initial choice of a mode of management for a given problem is multifactorial. Although many of us who lecture and write about the management of neurogenic lower urinary tract dysfunction are associated primarily with one approach or another, **all would doubtless agree on certain goals of management for voiding dysfunction** (Table 59–2). The fact that these goals have remained relatively unchanged over the past few editions of this text attest to their general validity. As a corollary, absolute or relative indications for changing or augmenting a particular regimen exist, and, likewise, there is general agreement on these, although the relative importance of the indication for change might be disputed (Table 59–3). It should be remembered that the term *inadequate*, when applied to storage and emptying, applies not only to volumes (capacity, voided volume, residual) but also to unacceptably high detrusor pressures during either or both of the two phases of the micturition cycle. In the planning of goals of therapy and reasons for change, the concept of a "hostility score," such as that of Galloway (1989), is attractive. His hostility score includes five urodynamic characteristics—bladder

Table 59–2. Voiding Dysfunction: Goals of Management

Upper urinary tract preservation or improvement
Absence or control of infection
Adequate storage at low intravesical pressure
Adequate emptying at low intravesical pressure
Adequate control
No catheter or stoma
Social acceptability and adaptability
Vocational acceptability and adaptability

Table 59–3. Reasons To Change or Augment a Given Regimen

Upper urinary tract deterioration
Recurrent sepsis or fever of urinary tract origin
Lower urinary tract deterioration
Inadequate storage
Inadequate emptying
Inadequate control
Unacceptable side effects
Skin changes secondary to incontinence or collecting device

Table 59–4. Patient Factors To Consider in Choosing Therapy

Prognosis of underlying disease, especially if progressive or malignant
General health
Limiting factors: inability to perform certain tasks (e.g., hand dexterity, ability to transfer, body habitus)
Mental status
Motivation
Desire to remain catheter or appliance free
Desire to avoid surgery
Sexual activity status
Reliability
Educability
Psychosocial environment, interest, reliability, and cooperation of family
Economic resources

compliance, overactivity, dyssynergia, outlet resistance, and VUR. Each is allocated a score of 0, 1, or 2. The best possible score is 0 and implies normal compliance, no inappropriate detrusor activity, a synergic sphincter, a low leak pressure, and no reflux.

The results of treatment of voiding dysfunction are rarely perfect, and they do not have to be. The goals are satisfaction and avoidance of adverse outcomes. A very flexible approach must be adopted in choosing therapy that takes into account the individual wishes of each patient and family and the practicality of each proposed solution for that particular patient (Table 59–4). The therapeutic decisions are thus made with the patient and with the family. In every case, within the limits of practicality, the following should be discussed: reversibility, side effects that occur with some regularity, ultimate best and worst possible scenario, frequency and extent of follow-up, and alternate methods of management. Treatment should always begin with the simplest most reversible form(s) of therapy, proceeding gradually up the ladder of complexity, but with the knowledge that it is only the patient (and/or family) who is (are) empowered to say when "enough is enough." Again, avoidance of adverse outcomes and satisfaction are the primary goals. A combination of therapeutic maneuvers can sometimes be used to achieve a particular end, especially if these modalities act through different mechanisms and their side effects are not synergistic or additive. There are circumstances and locales in which health care resources and hospital bed use must also be considered.

Acknowledgment

The author wishes to express his utmost appreciation to Rosemarie Larmer for her forbearance and expertise in assisting in the production of this chapter.

SUGGESTED READINGS

Abrams P, Cardozo L, Fall, M et al: The standardization of terminology in lower urinary tract function: Report from the Standardization Subcommittee of the International Continence Society. Urology 2003;61:37-49.

Blaivas JG: The neurophysiology of micturition: A clinical study of 550 patients. J Urol 1982;127:958-964.

Churchill BM, Abramson RP, Wahl EF: Dysfunction of the lower urinary and distal gastrointestinal tracts in pediatric patients with known spinal cord problem. Pediatr Clin North Am 2001;57:230-245.

Fowler C: Neurological disorders of micturition and their treatment. Brain 1999;122:1213-1231.

Kaplan SA, Chancellor MB, Blaivas JG: Bladder and sphincter behavior in patients with spinal cord lesions. J Urol 1991;146:113-117.

Serf C, Junenann KP, Braun PM: Deafferentation of the urinary bladder and implantation of a sacral anterior root stimulator (SARS) for treatment of the neurogenic bladder in paraplegic patients. Biomed Technik 2003;49:88-92.

Wein AJ, Barrett DM: Voiding Function and Dysfunction—A Logical and Practical Approach. Chicago, Year Book Medical, 1988.

Weld KJ, Dmochowski RR: Association of level of injury and bladder behavior in patients with post traumatic spinal cord injury. Urology 2000;55:490-494.

Woodhouse CRJ: Myelomeningocele in young adults. BJU Int 2005;95:223-230.

Wyndaele JJ, Castro D, Madersbacher H, et al: Neurogenic and faecal incontinence. In Abrams P et al (eds): Incontinence, ed 21. Paris, Health Publications Ltd, 2005, pp 1059-1162.

60 Urinary Incontinence: Epidemiology, Pathophysiology, Evaluation, and Management Overview

VICTOR W. NITTI, MD • JERRY G. BLAIVAS, MD

DEFINITION AND CLASSIFICATION OF URINARY INCONTINENCE

The International Continence Society (ICS) defines the symptom of urinary incontinence as **"the complaint of any involuntary loss of urine"** (Abrams et al, 2003). It is also recommended, when describing incontinence, to specify relevant factors such as type, severity, precipitating factors, social impact, effect on hygiene and quality of life, measures used to contain the leakage, and whether or not the individual experiencing incontinence desires help.

The definition of incontinence describes the symptom of incontinence as perceived by the patient or caregiver. **In addition, incontinence may be differentiated into signs and urodynamic observations** (Blaivas et al, 1997a; Abrams et al, 2003). **Signs** are observed by the physician by simple means (e.g., observation of the loss of urine with a cough) or by the use of diaries, pad **tests, symptoms scores, and validated quality of life instruments.** Urodynamic observations are made during urodynamic studies and reflect the definitive pathophysiologic condition that is causing the incontinence (e.g., detrusor overactivity or sphincter weakness). **When a condition cannot be documented by urodynamic observation, it may be "presumed" by clinical documentation.** The following terminology has been approved by the ICS (Abrams et al, 2003):

Stress urinary incontinence. The symptom is the complaint of involuntary leakage on exertion or on sneezing or coughing. The sign is the observation of involuntary urinary loss from the urethra synchronous with exertion, sneezing, or coughing. Urodynamic stress incontinence is noted during urodynamic testing (filling cystometry) and is defined as the involuntary leakage of urine during increases in abdominal pressure in the absence of a detrusor contraction.

Urge urinary incontinence. The symptom is the complaint of an involuntary leakage accompanied by or immediately preceded by urgency. The sign is the observation of involuntary urinary loss from the urethra that is accompanied by or immediately preceded by urgency. Detrusor overactivity incontinence is incontinence related to an involuntary detrusor contraction during urodynamics.

Mixed urinary incontinence. The complaint of an involuntary leakage of urine associated with urgency and also with exertion, effort, sneezing, or coughing.

In addition there are other symptoms of incontinence that cannot be classified as stress or urge incontinence, yet they may be caused by similar conditions:

Unconscious (unaware) incontinence is the complaint of involuntary loss of urine that is unaccompanied by either urge or stress.

Continuous urinary incontinence is the complaint of a continuous leakage.

Nocturnal enuresis is the complaint of loss of urine occurring during sleep.

Postmicturition dribble is the complaint of a involuntary loss of urine immediately after passing urine.

Overflow incontinence is not a symptom or condition but rather a term used to describe leakage of urine associated with urinary retention.

Extraurethral incontinence is the observation of urine leakage through channels other than the urethra (e.g., fistula or ectopic ureter).

EPIDEMOLOGY OF URINARY INCONTINENCE

Urinary incontinence is a significant health problem worldwide with considerable social and economic impact on individuals and society. It was estimated that urinary incontinence in women was the primary cause for more than 1.1 million office visits in 2000 in the United States (Litwin et al, 2005). Hu and associates (2004) estimated the total direct and indirect cost of incontinence in the United States in the year 2000 to be approximately $19.5 billion. Incontinence has a larger economic impact than many chronic conditions and diseases.

When discussing the epidemiology and impact of incontinence, it is important to distinguish its prevalence and incidence. **Prevalence is the probability of having a disease or condition, in this case incontinence, within a defined population at a defined point in time. Incidence, on the other hand, is the probability of developing a disease or condition during a defined period of time.** When determining social impact and allocation of health care resources, prevalence is the more important parameter. Incidence is important when discussing diseases or treatment where incontinence is a possible outcome—for example, the incidence of incontinence 1 year after radical prostatectomy or the incidence of incontinence in patients 1 year after stroke. The impact of incontinence on society and the number of patients who seek treatment depend not only on its prevalence but also on its impact on the individual patient. The severity of incontinence ranges from loss of drops to complete bladder emptying. It may occur daily, multiple times a day, or only occasionally. It may be fairly predictable (low-grade stress incontinence associated only with coughing or sneezing) or totally unpredictable (urge incontinence). These factors all play a role in how a patient is affected and whether he or she seeks or desires treatment.

An inherent limitation of large epidemiologic studies of incontinence is that they usually do not distinguish between the different types or conditions causing incontinence. Many of the large surveys rely on questionnaires as the primary tool for evaluating the presence of incontinence. In these studies it is often difficult, if not impossible, to determine the cause of incontinence. Even when patients are asked about specific symptoms, determining the etiology of the incontinence is only as reliable as the patients' own subjective reporting of symptoms. Another important factor to consider is how well established the symptom of incontinence is. Incontinence that is acute or of relatively new onset may be caused by a condition that can easily be corrected (e.g., urinary

tract infection, excess fluid mobilization, restricted mobility) (Resnick, 1984).

The epidemiology and natural history of urinary incontinence vary greatly between the genders. Causes and risk factors are different. Therefore, we feel that it is most practical to discuss the epidemiology of incontinence in men and women separately.

Urinary Incontinence in Women

Urinary incontinence is more prevalent in women than in men, making gender itself a risk factor. There are many epidemiologic studies on incontinence in women, but differences in definitions, measurement of incontinence, survey methodology, and cohort selection make comparisons difficult. In 10 such studies, **prevalence ranged from 5% to 72% among community-dwelling women** (Yarnell et al, 1981; Holst and Wilson, 1988; Brocklehurst 1993; Swithinbank et al, 1999; Bortolotti et al, 2000; Hannestad et al, 2000; Moller et al, 2000; Van Oyen and Van Oyen, 2002; Nygaard et al, 2003; Hunskaar, 2004). Hunskaar and colleagues (2005) summarized available epidemiologic data and concluded that **incontinence does show increasing prevalence during young adult life (20% to 30%), a broad peak around middle age (30% to 40%), and then a steady increase in elderly women (30% to 50%).** When one considers **the prevalence of severe incontinence** (as measured by frequency of leakage or pad weight), there is less variability among studies **with most estimates between 6% and 11%** (Broklehurst,1993; Samuelson et al, 1997; Bortolotti et al, 2000; Hannestad et al, 2000; Maggi et al, 2001). The proportion of types of incontinence varies considerably with age. **In young and middle-aged women, stress incontinence predominates** (Samuelsson et al, 1997), and **in older women mixed incontinence is most common** (Diokno et al, 1986; Hannestad et al, 2000). **Over all age groups, stress incontinence is most common (49%) followed by mixed incontinence (29%) and pure urge incontinence (21%)** (Hunskaar et al, 2002) (Fig. 60–1).

Most of the data regarding **risk factors for the development of urinary incontinence** are derived from cross-sectional studies of clinical and volunteer subjects. Age, parity, route of delivery, and obesity have been the most rigorously studied risk factors. Others such as menopause, smoking, chronic cough, constipation, and prior pelvic surgery have not (Brown et al, 2003; Hunskaar et al, 2005). As alluded to before, the risk of urinary incontinence increases with advancing age. **There is strong evidence to support the causal role of obesity and urinary incontinence.** A link between body mass and incontinence supports the concept that weight gain may increase susceptibility to incontinence and suggests that weight loss may decrease incontinence (Hunskaar et al, 2005). Subak and coworkers (2005) showed that in overweight women randomly assigned to a weight reduction program, weight loss reduced the number of stress and urge incontinence episodes compared with control women who did not lose weight. **Incontinence during pregnancy has a prevalence of 31% to 60%** (Mellier and Delille, 1990; Burgio et al, 1996), **but it resolves in most cases.** Some have speculated that incontinence during pregnancy predisposes women to developing the condition later in life. Both parity and the mode of delivery,

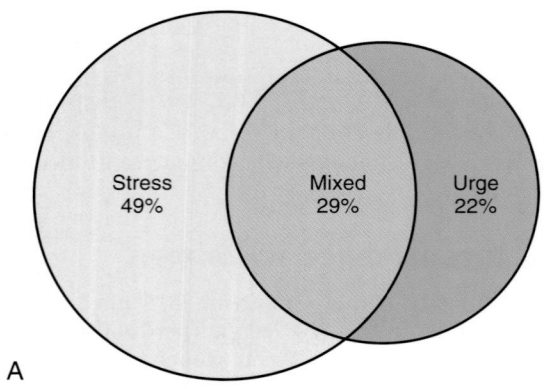

A

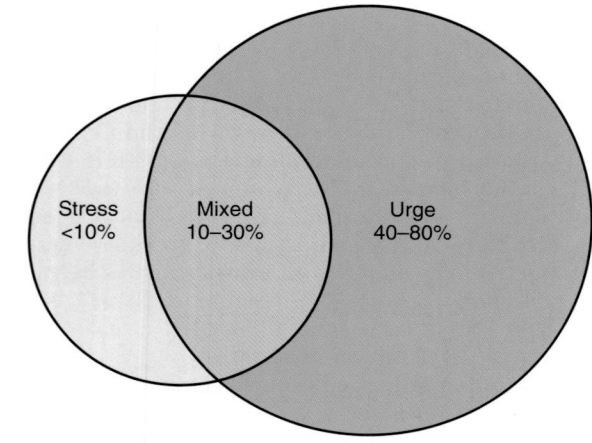

B

Figure 60–1. Prevalence of stress, urge, and mixed incontinence in (**A**) women and (**B**) men. (From Hunskaar S, Burgio K, Diokno AC, et al: Epidemiology and natural history of urinary incontinence [UI]. In Abrams P, Cardozo L, Khoury S, Wein A [eds]: Incontinence (2nd Edition) 2nd International Consultation on Incontinence. United Kingdom, Health Publications, 2002, pp 165-201.)

particularly **vaginal delivery and obstructed labor, have been implicated as a risk factor for the development of incontinence.** The Epidemiology of Incontinence in the County of Nord-Trondelag (EPINCONT) study conducted in Norway included a community-based cohort of 15,307 women younger than 65 years who were either nulliparous, delivered one to four children vaginally, or delivered one to four children by cesarean section (Rortveit et al, 2003). Compared with nulliparous women, those who underwent cesarean section had an age-adjusted odds ratio for incontinence of 1.5 and those who had vaginal delivery had an age-adjusted odds ratio of 2.3. The odds ratios for moderate and severe incontinence were similar. The attributable risk, or the proportion of incontinence among women who delivered vaginally that would be preventable by cesarean section, was 35%. This study did not take into account cesarean sections done after labor started (e.g., emergency, obstructed labor). Groutz and associates (2004) found that the prevalence of stress incontinence 1 year after first delivery was similar among women who had a spontaneous vaginal delivery (10.3%) and those who had a cesarean section for obstructed labor (12%) ($P = .7$) but was

significantly lower for those who had an elective cesarean section (3.4%, $P = .02$). **These data suggest that elective cesarean section reduces the incidence of incontinence.**

It has long been suspected that there is an association of urinary symptoms, including incontinence, with **menopause.** The prevalence of incontinence peaks in midlife in women, around the time of menopause. Furthermore, it seems reasonable to assume that estrogen loss contributes to the condition. However, the literature is inconsistent in this regard (Hunskaar et al, 2005). In addition, it was long thought that estrogen replacement improved symptoms of stress and urge incontinence, but two meta-analyses dispute that. Hextall (2000) concluded that when estrogen is used alone to treat incontinence, there is no objective improvement in urinary leakage. A Cochrane review assessing the effects of estrogen alone in treating urinary incontinence concluded that such treatment is associated with perceived improvement compared with placebo but that larger studies are needed (Moehrer et al, 2003). Two large-scale double-blind, placebo-controlled studies looking at (1) the effects of estrogen and progestin in the Heart and Estrogen/progestin Replacement Study (HERS) and (2) the effects of estrogen with and without progestin in the Women's Health Initiative (WHI) found that hormone replacement was not beneficial in treating or preventing incontinence. The HERS study found that daily oral estrogen plus progestin therapy was associated with worsening urinary incontinence in older postmenopausal women with weekly incontinence (Grady et al, 2001). In the WHI study, hormone replacement actually increased the risk of developing urinary incontinence in women who did not have incontinence at the start of the study and worsened the characteristics of preexisting symptoms (Hendrix et al, 2005).

Urinary Incontinence in Men

There is much less information on the epidemiology of urinary incontinence in men than in women. Incontinence in men of all ages is approximately **half as prevalent as it is in women. Incontinence in men increases with age and appears to rise more steadily than it does in women.** However, the estimate for severe incontinence in men in their 70s and 80s is still only about half of that in women (Hunskaar et al, 2005). Large studies have indicated that there is a **3% to 11% overall prevalence rate of incontinence in the male population** (Feneley et al, 1979; Yarnell and St. Leger, 1979; Thomas et al, 1980; Malmsten et al, 1997; Schulman et al,1997). Diokno and associates (1986) reported 19% prevalence in men older than 60. Urge incontinence is the prominent type of incontinence in men (40% to 80%), followed by mixed incontinence (10% to 30%) and stress incontinence (less than 10%) (Diokno et al, 1986; Herzog and Fultz, 1990; Schulman et al, 1997; Damian et al, 1998; Ueda et al, 2000) (see Fig. 60–1). The National Overactive Bladder Evaluation (NOBLE) program, initiated to better understand the prevalence and burden of overactive bladder in the U.S. population, found the prevalence of urge incontinence to be 2.6% in American men of all ages; however, after age 64, the prevalence rose sharply and was about 10% in men 75 years and older (Stewart et al, 2003). **Stress incontinence in men is rare unless attributable to prostate surgery, neurologic injury, or trauma.** Reported rates of incontinence after prostatectomy range from 1% after

Table 60–1.	Causes of Urinary Incontinence
Bladder dysfunction	Sphincter dysfunction
Detrusor overactivity	Intrinsic sphincter deficiency
Impaired compliance	Urethral support defect (hypermobility)

transurethral resection (Mebust et al, 1989; van Melick et al, 2003) to 2% to 57% after radical prostatectomy depending on the definition (Goluboff et al, 1998; Gray et al, 1999; Walsh et al, 2000; Moinzadeh et al, 2003; Lepor et al, 2004). A major consideration in the incontinent male patient, especially with urge incontinence, is the potential contribution of bladder outlet obstruction to bladder overactivity. Many men suffering from detrusor overactivity and urge incontinence also have bladder outlet obstruction, most often related to the prostate.

CONTINENCE AND THE PHYSIOLOGY OF MICTURITION

In order to understand the pathophysiology of urinary incontinence, it is important to be familiar with the micturition cycle and the physiology of normal storage and emptying of urine. The details of the physiology of micturition are provided in Chapters 56, "Physiology and Pharmacology of the Bladder and Urethra," and 57, "Pathophysiology and Classification of Voiding Dysfunction." Here we present a brief overview as it relates to incontinence. From a functional and anatomic perspective, it is intuitive to consider the lower urinary tract as a two-part system: the urinary bladder as a reservoir, and the bladder outlet as a sphincteric mechanism (Wein, 1981). Incontinence can occur when either part or both malfunction (Table 60–1).

Micturition is a complex series of finely tuned and integrated neuromuscular events that involve anatomic and neurologic mechanisms. Alterations in any of these events may result in abnormalities in emptying or urinary incontinence, or both. During bladder filling at physiologic rates, detrusor pressure remains nearly constant because of a special property of the bladder known as **accommodation** (Klevmark, 1974). Accommodation accounts for the nearly flat cystometric curve that is seen during normal bladder filling (Fig. 60–2). In experimental animals, accommodation is unaffected by acute neurologic impairment or by administration of cholinergic agonists or antagonists (Ruch and Tang, 1967; Klevmark, 1974, 1977). The viscoelastic properties of the bladder, based on its composition of smooth muscle, collagen, and elastin, normally produce a highly compliant structure. **When accommodation is impaired, low bladder compliance ensues. This is manifest as a steep rise in detrusor pressure during bladder filling** (Ghoniem et al, 1989; Zoubek et al, 1989; McGuire, 1994). In addition to the viscoelastic properties of the bladder, the neural control of the lower urinary tract and the anatomy and support of the sphincteric unit are important factors in the maintenance of urinary continence.

Neural Pathways

Normal storage of urine is dependent on (1) spinal reflex mechanisms that activate sympathetic and somatic path-

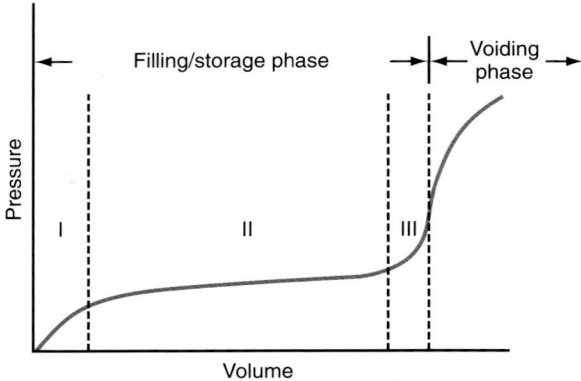

Figure 60–2. Idealized normal adult cystometrogram. Classically, the cystometrogram has been divided into four phases. Phase I reflects the bladder's initial response to filling. Phase II is the tonus limb and reflects bladder pressure during the majority of the filling phase. As the viscoelastic properties of the bladder reach their limit, phase III is entered, where pressures begin to increase just prior to phase IV, the voluntary contraction phase. This ideal description of the cystometry curve is often not seen, however. If filling rates are slow and a liquid medium is used, the pressure change from phase I to II is often imperceptible. Also, depending on how much the bladder is allowed to fill, phase III may not be appreciated as a significant pressure change. (From Wein AJ, English WS, Whitmore KE: Office urodynamics. Urol Clin North Am 1988;15:609-623.)

ways to the bladder outlet and (2) tonic inhibitory systems in the brain that suppress parasympathetic excitatory outflow to the bladder** (Morrison et al, 2005). Distention of the bladder walls during filling leads to sympathetic stimulation of the bladder outlet smooth musculature and pudendal outflow to the external urethral sphincter. Sympathetic stimulation also inhibits the bladder body musculature and transmission in the bladder parasympathetic ganglia (de Groat, 1997; Yoshimura and de Groat, 1997). These responses occur by spinal reflex pathways and represent **guarding reflexes** that promote continence. Damage to central inhibitory pathways, or sensitization of peripheral afferent terminals in the bladder, can unmask primitive voiding reflexes and trigger bladder overactivity (de Groat, 1997). Normal voiding is accomplished by activation of the micturition reflex (Fig. 60–3). **The micturition reflex is normally under voluntary control and is organized in the rostral brain stem (the pontine micturition center).** It requires integration and modulation by the parasympathetic and somatic components of the sacral spinal cord (the sacral micturition center) and the thoracolumbar sympathetic components (Bradley and Conway, 1966; Blaivas, 1982; Morrison, 1987a; de Groat and Steers, 1990).

At the initiation of micturition, intense bladder afferent activity activates the pontine micturition center, which inhibits the spinal guarding reflexes (de Groat, 1997). Relaxation of the urethral muscles is mediated in some species by activation of a parasympathetic pathway to the urethra that triggers the release of the inhibitory neurotransmitter nitric oxide (Anderson, 1993; Bennett et al, 1995) and by removal of adrenergic and somatic cholinergic excitatory inputs (Yoshimura and de Groat, 1997; de Groat et al, 2001). Thus, the first recorded event is sudden and complete relaxation of the striated sphincteric muscles, characterized by complete electrical silence of the sphincter electromyogram (Tanagho and Miller, 1970; Blaivas, 1982). This is followed almost

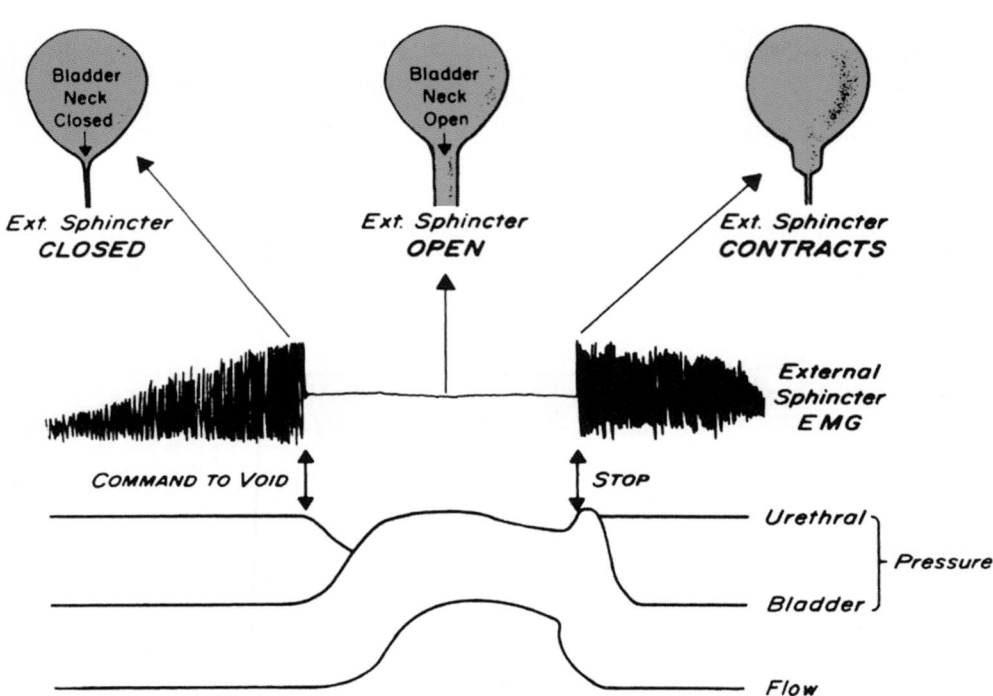

Figure 60–3. Physiology of micturition. See text for details. EMG, electromyogram. (From Blaivas JG: Pathophysiology of lower urinary tract dysfunction. Clin Obstet Gynaecol 1985;12:295-309.)

immediately by a rise in detrusor pressure and concomitant fall in urethral pressure as the bladder and proximal urethra become isobaric (Yalla et al, 1980; Blaivas, 1988a). The bladder neck and urethra open, and voiding ensues. Voluntary interruption of the stream is accomplished by a sudden contraction of the striated periurethral musculature, which, through a reflex mechanism, shuts off the detrusor contraction, aborting micturition. The sphincteric system is also designed to resist physiologic increases in abdominal pressure.

Sphincteric Mechanism and Anatomic Support

Traditionally, the urethral sphincter is considered to be composed of two components: the internal sphincter, which represents a direct continuation of the detrusor smooth muscle, and the striated external sphincter (Tanagho, 1992). From a clinical standpoint, the bladder neck–proximal urethra normally functions as a sphincter in both sexes, but anatomically there is no identifiable sphincter as such. Rather, a unique mixture of smooth and striated muscle, intracellular matrix, and mucosal factors accounts for the components of a functional sphincter (Wesson, 1920; Hutch, 1967; Woodburne, 1968; Zinner et al, 1980; Oelrich, 1983; Myers, 1991). **The principles underlying the function of a sphincter are (1) watertight apposition of the urethral lumen, (2) compression of the wall around the lumen, (3) structural support to keep the proximal urethra from moving during increases in pressure, (4) a means of compensating for abdominal pressure changes (pressure transmission), and (5) neural control.** Thus, normal sphincteric function is the result of an integrated interaction among all these factors.

The mechanism by which the urethra maintains a **watertight seal** has not been well defined. Zinner and associates

(1980), in a series of experiments performed on mechanical models of a urethra, concluded that there are at least three urethral wall factors that promote continence: (1) wall tension or external compression, (2) inner wall softness, and (3) a filler material beneath the mucosa that helps to deform the mucosal folds into apposition. The actual shape of the lumen of the sphincteric part of the urethra during bladder filling is difficult to define because there is no obvious way to look at it. Histologic cross sections of the urethra show that the urethra is not simply a closed tube; rather, there are numerous mucosal folds, between which are potential spaces for urine leakage. Zinner and associates (1980) proposed that a lining of mucus provides the stickiness that enables coaptation of these mucosal folds. The softer the lining, the better the apposition that can be achieved. In women, estrogen and a cushion effect of the submucosal vasculature have been suggested as ancillary factors (Raz et al, 1972; Tulloch, 1974). External compression of the urethral lumen is achieved by (1) smooth and striated muscle tone, (2) phasic contractions of the smooth and striated musculature, (3) elastic and viscoelastic properties of the extracellular matrix, (4) mechanical factors related to transmission of abdominal pressure, and (5) structural (anatomic) support of the posterior urethral wall.

The Sphincter in Women

For more than 50 years, the commonly held view has been that urethral support is critical to the maintenance of continence during increases in abdominal pressure. It was thought that loss of structural urethral support resulted in varying degrees of descent of the bladder neck and urethra, and it was thought that the resultant urethral hypermobility is the proximate cause of stress urinary incontinence (SUI) (Hodgkinson, 1953; Green, 1968; McGuire et al, 1976; Hodgkinson, 1978; Blaivas, 1988b; Walters and Jackson, 1990). It was also thought that the normally supported bladder neck and proximal urethra sit in a high retropubic position and that increased intra-abdominal pressure is transmitted equally to both bladder and urethra. In cases of stress-induced urethral descent, the urethra attains a low, dependent position. Increased intra-abdominal pressure is then transmitted unequally to the urethra and bladder; and when bladder pressure exceeds urethral pressure, SUI ensues (McGuire and Herlihy, 1977; Constantinou and Govan, 1982; Westby et al, 1982; Constantinou, 1985; Bump et al, 1988a; Rosensweig et al, 1991). However, the fact that many women are totally continent despite clinical evidence of urethral hypermobility somewhat refutes that theory. This implies that the normal urethra remains closed even during stress-induced descent (Walters and Diaz, 1987).

Today, **the most commonly held view of the pathophysiology of stress incontinence secondary to urethral hypermobility is based on DeLancey's theory of urethral support, the so-called hammock theory** (DeLancey, 1994). In anatomic specimens in which increases in abdominal pressure were simulated, he found that the urethra lies in a position where it can be compressed against a hammock-like musculofascial layer on which the bladder and urethra rest (DeLancey, 1994). **In this model, it is the stability of this supporting layer rather than the position of the urethra that determines stress continence.** Urethral support is supplied by connective tissue and muscle arranged to resist the downward pressure created by increases in abdominal pressure. The urethra is intimately connected to the anterior vaginal wall,

and the connections of these two structures to the levator ani muscle complex and arcus tendineus fascia pelvis (ATFP) determine the stability of the urethra. The ATFP is a fibrous fascial band that stretches from the pubic bone anteriorly to the ischial spine. The fascial covering of the levator ani consists of two leaves: the endopelvic fascia (abdominal side) and the pubocervical fascia (vaginal side). The two leaves fuse laterally to insert ATFP, creating a hammock of support under the urethra and bladder neck (Fig. 60–4). **Normally, with rises in intra-abdominal pressure, the urethra is compressed against the supporting structures, which act like a backboard and prevent loss of urine** (DeLancey, 1997) (Fig. 60–5). When the supporting structures fail, there can be rotational descent of the bladder neck and proximal urethra during increases in abdominal pressure. If the urethra opens concomitantly, SUI ensues. If this supporting layer establishes its stability, although at a lower level, continence may still be preserved. (DeLancey, 1996). **These findings have important clinical implications that support the contention that the primary goal of surgery for sphincteric incontinence in women is to provide a backboard against which the bladder neck and proximal urethra can be compressed during increases in abdominal pressure.** In fact, some of the most popular procedures for the treatment of stress incontinence do not change the position of the urethra or even correct mobility (Lo et al, 2001; Sarlos et al, 2003, Minaglia et al, 2005) An additional observation by DeLancey (1990) is that the medial portion of the levator ani muscle has a direct connec-

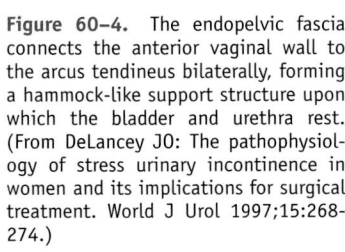

Figure 60–4. The endopelvic fascia connects the anterior vaginal wall to the arcus tendineus bilaterally, forming a hammock-like support structure upon which the bladder and urethra rest. (From DeLancey JO: The pathophysiology of stress urinary incontinence in women and its implications for surgical treatment. World J Urol 1997;15:268-274.)

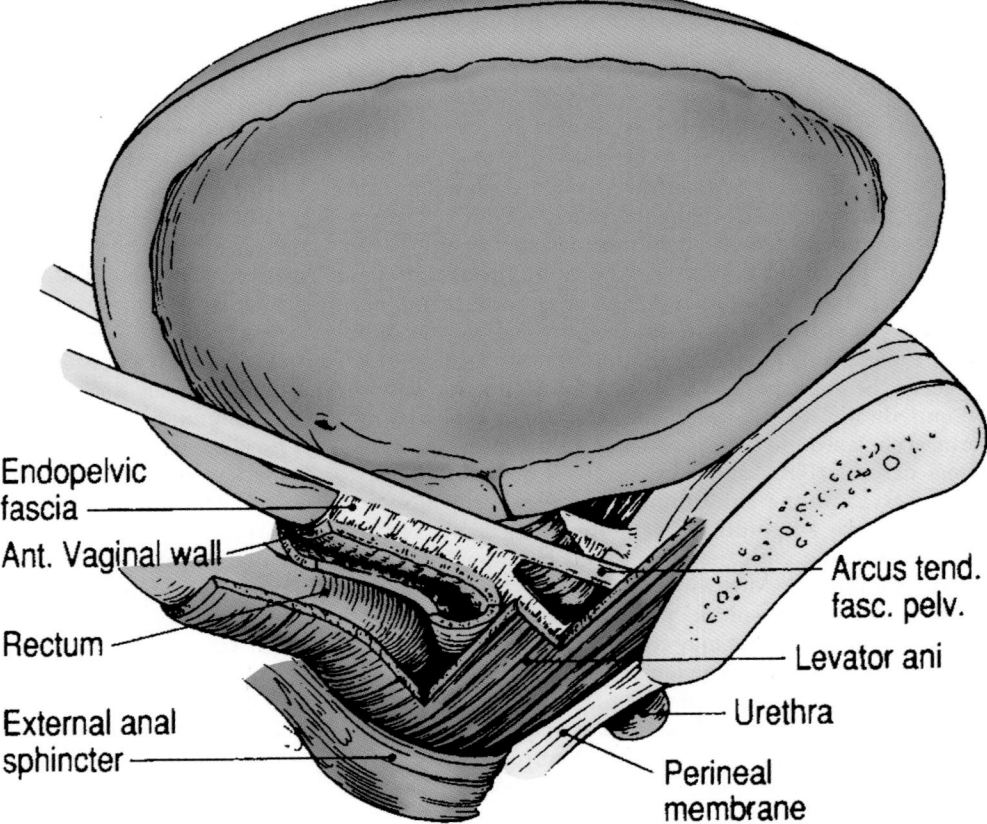

Endopelvic fascia

Ant. Vaginal wall

Rectum

External anal sphincter

Arcus tend. fasc. pelv.

Levator ani

Urethra

Perineal membrane

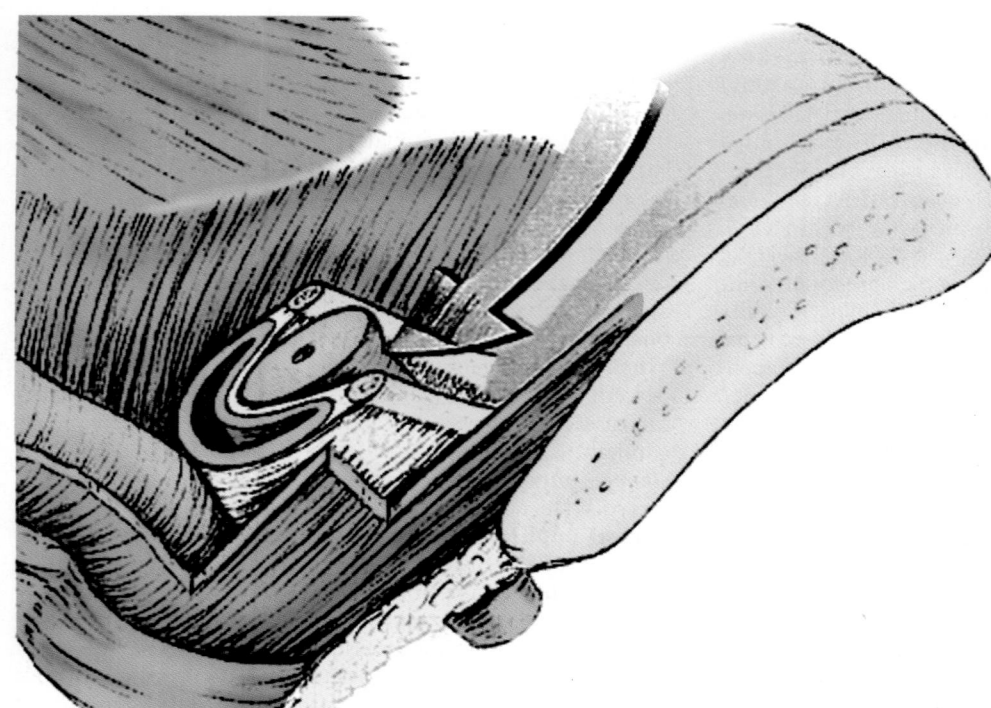

Figure 60–5. The hammock theory. With rises in intra-abdominal pressure, the urethra is compressed against the supporting structures, which act like a backboard. Stability of the supporting structures (not position or height) determines continence. When supporting structures are unstable, occlusive action is lost. (From DeLancey JO: The pathophysiology of stress urinary incontinence in women and its implications for surgical treatment. World J Urol 1997;15:268-274.)

tion to the endopelvic fascia and the vaginal wall and contraction of the levators contributes to stabilization of the urethra during sudden increases in abdominal pressure (e.g., a cough).

In a series of elegant magnetic resonance imaging studies of the pelvic floor, stress incontinence was found to occur when there was unequal movement of the anterior and posterior walls of the bladder neck and proximal urethra during stress; the urethral lumen is literally pulled open as the posterior wall moves away from the anterior wall (Yang et al, 1991, 1993; Mostwin et al, 1995). Furthermore, ultrasound imaging of the bladder neck and proximal urethra, in both normal and stress-incontinent patients, demonstrated that opening (funneling) of the bladder neck was the common denominator underlying stress incontinence, not urethral hypermobility. Anterior support of the urethra is provided by the pubourethral ligaments, attaching the midurethra to the inferior aspect of the pubic bone. These work in conjunction with the pubourethralis muscle of the levator ani complex, which forms a sling around the proximal urethra and prevents rotational descent (Plzak and Staskin, 2002). Together, the two structures form the **midurethral complex,** which is now thought to play a significant role in the maintenance of stress continence along with the suburethral hammock described earlier. According to Mostwin and colleagues (1995), **"It is the relative, not the absolute, position of the urethra with respect to the pubis that may contribute to urethral opening in stress incontinence. The length and strength of the suburethral complex may vary in patients. In those with shorter, stronger anterior fascial support, only a small loss of suburethral support may be sufficient to permit distraction (of the anterior and posterior urethral walls) during rotational descent."** In contrast to the explanation that proposes a pure transmitted pressure effect, the mechanism of shear force suggests that transmitted energy mechanically opens the proximal and middle urethra (Plzak and Staskin, 2002).

The exact point of continence in the urethra, if such a point exists, has been debated. For years it was thought to be the bladder neck; however, the work of Constantinou and Govan (1981) and Petros and Ulmstem (1990, 1998) **suggested that the midurethra supported anteriorly by the pubourethral ligaments is the most important zone of continence.** Constantinou and Govan (1981) showed that pressure change ratios in the urethra/bladder are highest at the midurethra in continent control patients and in postsurgical patients after endoscopic bladder neck suspension, whereas the high midurethral pressure is lost in women with stress incontinence. In 1990, Petros and Ulmstem published the **integral theory of stress and urge incontinence.** According to the theory, female stress incontinence and urge incontinence have a common etiology. They proposed that support of the anterior vaginal wall is provided by three separate but synergistic mechanisms. The anterior pubococcygeus muscle lifts the anterior vaginal wall to compress the urethra; the bladder neck is closed by traction of the underlying vaginal wall in a backward and downward fashion; and the pelvic floor musculature, under voluntary control draws the hammock upward, closing the bladder neck. Overall laxity of the anterior vaginal wall causes dissipation of all of these forces, resulting in stress incontinence. They further suggested that laxity of the anterior vaginal wall causes activation of stretch receptors in the bladder neck and proximal urethra that can trigger an inappropriate micturition reflex resulting in detrusor overactivity. These theories are not mutually exclusive, and there is probably a least some truth in each. The fact that both bladder neck and midurethral slings have been shown to be successful in treating stress incontinence supports all these theories (Ulmsten et al, 1998; Olsson and Kroon, 1999; Nilsson and Kuuva, 2001; Rezapour et al, 2001; Nilsson et al, 2004). Further reports of successful treatment of mixed incontinence with slings lend credence to the integral theory.

In 1980, **McGuire and colleagues first introduced the concept of intrinsic sphincteric deficiency (ISD)** when, in a retrospective analysis of the results of anti-incontinence surgery, they noted that some women who had undergone multiple retropubic operations had a deficient sphincteric mechanism characterized by an open bladder neck and proximal urethra at rest with minimal or no urethral descent during stress. They stated that ISD denotes an intrinsic malfunction of the urethral sphincter, regardless of its anatomic position. **Contemporary theories suggest that all patients with sphincteric incontinence have some degree of ISD.** Considerations that support this theory include the fact that the normal urethra is intended to remain closed no matter what the degree of stress or rotational descent. Furthermore, many women with urethral hypermobility remain continent (Versi, 1986). Finally, urethral hypermobility and ISD may (and often do) coexist in the same patient. Because urethral hypermobility and ISD often coexist, we believe that they do not necessarily define discrete classes of patients (Nitti and Combs, 1996; Fleischmann et al, 2003). Thus, these parameters may be used to characterize incontinence but not necessarily classify patients. Classification systems have been devised to characterize stress incontinence by the presence or absence of urethral mobility, the degree of mobility, and the presence of rotational descent (Green et al, 1962; McGuire et al, 1976; Blaivas and Olsson, 1988). However, we recommend that rather than "classifying" stress incontinence, it makes more sense simply to characterize it by two parameters—the degree of urethral mobility (i.e., as determined by the Q-tip test) and sphincter strength (i.e., the abdominal leak point pressure).

The Sphincter in Men

For simplicity, the normal male urinary sphincter mechanism may be divided into **two functionally separate** units, the proximal urethral sphincter (PUS) and the distal urethral sphincter (DUS) (Hadley et al, 1986). The PUS consists of the bladder neck, prostate, and prostatic urethra to the level of the verumontanum. It is innervated by autonomic parasympathetic fibers from the pelvic nerve. This portion of the continence mechanism is removed during prostatectomy, leaving only the DUS to prevent urinary leakage. The DUS extends from the verumontanum to the proximal bulb and is composed of a number of structures that help to maintain continence. The male DUS complex is composed of the prostatomembranous urethra, cylindrical rhabdosphincter (external sphincter muscle) surrounding the prostatomembranous urethra, and extrinsic paraurethral musculature and connective tissue structures of the pelvis. The rhabdosphincter is a concentric muscular structure consisting of longitudinal smooth muscle and slow-twitch (type I) skeletal muscle fibers that can maintain resting tone and preserve continence (Gosling et al, 1981; Turner-Warwick, 1983). Skeletal muscle fibers of the rhabdosphincter have been shown to intermingle with smooth muscle fibers of the proximal

urethra, suggesting a dynamic and coordinated interaction (Burnett and Mostwin, 1998). The rhabdosphincter is invested in a fascial framework and supported below by a musculofascial plate that fuses with the midline raphe, which is also a point of origin for the rectourethralis muscle (Burnett and Mostwin 1998). Superiorly, the fascial investments of the rhabdosphincter fuse with the puboprostatic ligaments (Steiner, 2000). This dorsal and ventral support probably contributes to the competence of the sphincter. The striated fibers of the extrinsic paraurethral muscle (levator ani complex), on the other hand, are of the fast-twitch (type II) variety (Gosling et al, 1981). During sudden increases in abdominal pressure, these fibers can contract rapidly and forcefully to provide continence. Continence has been showed to be maintained after inducing paralysis of the striated sphincter (Lapides et al, 1957; Krahn and Morales, 1965), indicating that this structure is not solely responsible for continence. **Unlike that in the female, where urethral support can be compromised as a result of childbirth and aging, in the male, compromise to the rhabdosphincter usually occurs after trauma or surgery (e.g., prostatectomy).**

ETIOLOGY AND PATHOPHYSIOLOGY OF URINARY INCONTINENCE

Urinary incontinence may be classified as urethral or extraurethral. **Urethral incontinence is caused by either an abnormality of the bladder, an abnormality of the bladder outlet (sphincter), or a combination of both** (Wein, 1981; Blaivas, 1985; Blaivas et al, 1997a). **Extraurethral incontinence is caused by either urinary fistula or ectopic ureter.**

Bladder Abnormalities
Urodynamic Observations

Bladder abnormalities that cause urinary incontinence include detrusor overactivity and low bladder compliance. Detrusor overactivity is a urodynamic observation characterized by involuntary detrusor contractions (Fig. 60–6). It is defined by the ICS as "involuntary detrusor contractions

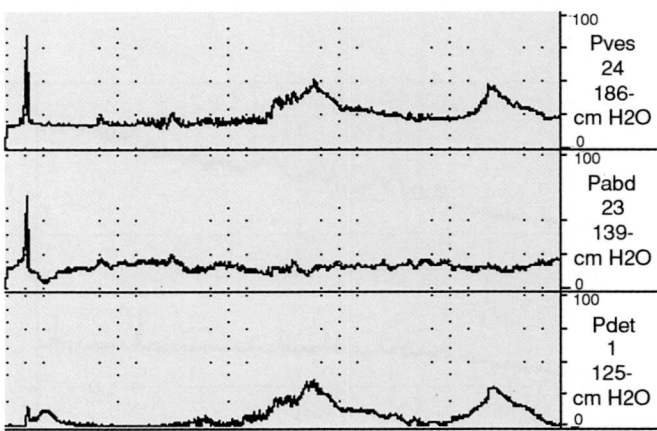

Figure 60–6. Detrusor overactivity. Note the two rises in bladder pressure during filling. The abdominal pressure remains unchanged, indicating a true detrusor contraction. p_{ves}, total vesical pressure; p_{abd}, abdominal pressure; p_{det}, detrusor pressure ($p_{ves} - p_{abd}$).

during the filling phase, which may be spontaneous or pro-voked" (Abrams et al, 2003). Although this is the current ICS terminology, there continues to be a lack of agreement about the optimal definition as well as basic techniques for measuring involuntary detrusor contractions (Artibani, 1997; Hampel et al, 1997). Detrusor overactivity may be phasic, ter-minal, or both (Abrams et al, 2003). Terminal detrusor over-activity is analogous to a normal micturition reflex except that it is involuntary. Terminal detrusor overactivity results in voiding without control. Detrusor overactivity can further be defined by its association, or lack thereof, with neurologic disease. When associated with neurologic disorders, it is termed neurogenic detrusor overactivity, and when not it is termed by the ICS idiopathic detrusor overactivity. The term idiopathic is a bit of a misnomer in that the cause of detrusor overactivity in a non-neurogenic patient may be readily apparent (e.g., bladder outlet obstruction, inflammatory process) or truly "unknown." Thus, from a practical stand-point, it makes more sense to classify detrusor overactivity as follows: idiopathic, neurogenic, and non-neurogenic detrusor overactivity.

Low bladder compliance denotes an abnormal volume-pressure relationship in which there is a high incremental rise in detrusor pressure during bladder filling. It, too, is a urody-namic observation (Fig. 60–7). The viscoelastic properties and neurologic innervation of the bladder allow it normally to store increasing volumes of urine at low pressure. Thus, with normal compliance there is little or no pressure change as the bladder fills. Compliance (Δ volume/Δ pressure) is expressed as mL/cm H_2O. Low bladder compliance may be caused by changes in the elastic and viscoelastic properties of the bladder, changes in detrusor muscle tone, or combinations of the two (Ghoniem et al, 1989; Zoubek et al, 1989; McGuire, 1994). Elastic and viscoelastic abnormalities are due primarily to changes in the extracellular matrix (ECM). The ECM is composed of four generic types of macromolecules: (1) colla-gens, (2) elastins, (3) proteoglycans, and (4) glycoproteins. The first two components, collagen and elastin, account for the structural support of the tissue; the proteoglycans and gly-coproteins fill interstices. Several collagen isoforms have been described, and with respect to passive mechanical properties types I and III are the most important (Macarak et al, 1995).

Both are arranged in banded fibrils and have different mechanical properties.

In the animal model, it has been shown that increased bladder compliance parallels a decrease in the ratio of type III to type I collagen and decreased compliance parallels an increase in the same ratio (Baskin et al, 1994). It has been shown that in noncompliant human bladders there is increased expression of type III collagen messenger RNA and a greater deposition of type III collagen mainly between the detrusor muscle bundles (Kaplan et al 1997; Macarak and Howard, 1997). In similar bladders, decreased elastin and elastin gene expression also occurs (Djavan et al, 1998). Although it is well established that high storage pressures can lead to incontinence and upper tract deterioration (McGuire et al, 1981; Comiter et al, 1997; Madersbacher et al, 1999; Leng and McGuire, 2003), at the present time there are no standard values to define normal, high, and low compliance (Toppercer and Tetreault,1979). **The calculated value of compliance is probably less important then the actual bladder pressure during filling.** This is because the compliance value can change depending on the volume over which it is calculated. For this reason, numeric values of compliance are rarely reported. For example, **absolute sustained detrusor pres-sures of 35 to 40 cm H_2O or greater during storage, regard-less of the bladder volume, can lead to upper tract damage** (McGuire et al, 1981; Churchill et al, 1987). When the detru-sor pressure exceeds the pressure capacity of the sphincter to resist that pressure, incontinence results.

Conditions Causing Bladder Abnormalities

Detrusor Overactivity. The ICS classifies detrusor over-activity as either idiopathic or neurogenic. By definition, neurogenic detrusor overactivity and idiopathic detrusor overactivity are distinguished not by specific symptoms or urodynamic characteristics but rather by the presence or absence of a neurologic lesion or disorder. We believe, however, that the term **idiopathic detrusor overactivity** is somewhat of a misnomer. Whereas in some cases the origin of the involuntary detrusor contractions is unknown (Hebjorn et al, 1976; Abrams et al, 2003), in other cases they are caused by, or at least are associated with, a variety of non-neurogenic clinical conditions, such as bladder outlet obstruc-

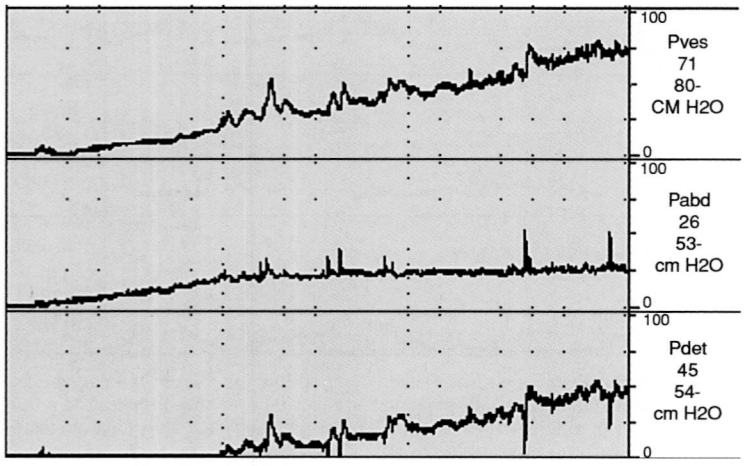

Figure 60–7. Impaired bladder compliance. Poorly compliant bladder with prolonged high-pressure storage and an end-filling pres-sure greater than 40 cm H_2O indicating potential for upper tract dete-rioration. p_{ves}, total vesical pressure; p_{abd}, abdominal pressure; p_{det}, detrusor pressure ($p_{ves} - p_{abd}$).

tion, dysfunctional voiding, and inflammatory reactions (Hebjorn et al, 1976; Awad and McGinnis, 1983; Blaivas, 1988b; Resnick et al, 1989; Fantl et al, 1990a; Brading and Turner, 1994; Carlson et al, 2001). For that reason, we prefer to classify detrusor overactivity in three ways—idiopathic, neurogenic, and non-neurogenic. **A list of specific causes of detrusor overactivity can be found in Table 60–2.**

Neurogenic detrusor overactivity (formally known as detrusor hyperreflexia) has been well categorized (Hebjorn et al, 1976; Blaivas et al, 1979a; Blaivas, 1982; Siroky and Krane, 1982; Morrison, 1987a, 1987b; Rudy et al, 1988; Kaplan et al, 1991; German et al, 1995; Ockrim et al, 2005). Neurologic lesions above the pons (e.g., cerebrovascular accident, brain trauma) usually leave the micturition reflex intact. Many affected patients have no voiding phase dysfunction at all. When micturition is affected, there is generally a loss of voluntary control of the micturition. In these patients, micturition is physiologically normal—there is a coordinated relaxation of the sphincter during detrusor contraction, but the patient has simply lost the ability either to initiate or to prevent voiding (Blaivas, 1982; Morrison, 1987a; Khan et al, 1990). There is great variability in the degree of the patient's awareness of, control of, and concern about micturition. Some patients have either no awareness or no concern and simply void involuntarily. Some patients can sense the impending onset of an involuntary detrusor contraction and are able to contract the sphincter voluntarily and abort the detrusor contraction before it starts. Such patients usually complain of urgency but not urge incontinence. Others are aware of the involuntary detrusor contraction and can contract the striated sphincter, but this does not abort the detrusor contraction and incontinence ensues. In addition to urinary urgency, these patients complain of urge incontinence. Still others can contract the sphincter during an involuntary detrusor contraction and abort the stream but not the detrusor contraction. As soon as they relax the sphincter, incontinence occurs. Some patients with supraspinal neurologic lesions develop detrusor areflexia or an acontractile detrusor, but the neurophysiologic pathways responsible for this have not been well described.

Interruption of the neural pathways connecting the "pontine micturition center" to the "sacral micturition center" also results in detrusor overactivity, which is often accompanied by detrusor external sphincter dyssynergia (DESD) or other manifestations of poor coordination of the micturition reflex, such as weak, poorly sustained detrusor contractions (McGuire and Brady, 1979; Blaivas, 1982; Rudy et al, 1988). DESD is characterized by involuntary contractions of the striated musculature of the urethral sphincter during an involuntary detrusor contraction. It is seen exclusively in patients with neurologic lesions between the brain stem (pontine micturition center) and the sacral spinal cord (sacral micturition center). DESD often results in high-pressure involuntary contractions because of the high outlet resistance. These lesions include traumatic spinal cord injury, multiple sclerosis, myelodysplasia, and other forms of transverse myelitis.

Elbadawi and colleagues (1993a, 1993b, 1993c) have proposed a possible explanation for age-related detrusor overactivity based on detailed ultrastructural studies of the bladder. They showed a characteristic structural pattern in bladder biopsy specimens obtained from elderly patients with detrusor overactivity. Electron microscopic changes (abundant, distinctive protrusion junctions and abutments) in patients with detrusor overactivity are thought to result in a diminished electrical resistance between detrusor muscle cells and, hence, a hyperexcitable state that results in involuntary detrusor contractions.

Data regarding the prevalence and urodynamic characteristics of involuntary detrusor contractions in various clinical settings, as well as in neurologically intact versus neurologically impaired patients, are scarce. In 1985, Coolsaet proposed a standardized method of evaluating detrusor overactivity in which the detrusor pressure during involuntary contraction, bladder volume at which the contraction occurs, awareness of and ability to abort the contraction, presence or absence of urinary incontinence during the contraction, and ability to abort contraction-related incontinent flow are assessed (Coolsaet, 1985). These parameters have been used to compare urodynamic characteristics of involuntary detrusor contractions in various clinical categories, and it has been found that all categories demonstrated involuntary contractions at approximately 80% of cystometric capacity (Romanzi et al, 2001). The ability to abort the contractions was significantly higher among continent patients with frequency/urgency (77%) compared with urge-incontinent patients (46%) and neurologically impaired patients (38%). It is possible that patients who are able to stop incontinent flow and abort the contraction may fare well with bladder retraining, pelvic floor exercises, and behavior modification alone, whereas those who are unable or partially able (i.e., can stop flow but cannot abort the contraction) might require anticholinergic medications to achieve continence. The true utility

Table 60–2. Causes of Detrusor Overactivity

Idiopathic Detrusor Overactivity

Neurogenic Detrusor Overactivity

Supraspinal neurologic lesions
  Stroke
  Parkinson's disease
  Hydrocephalus
  Brain tumor
  Traumatic brain injury
  Multiple sclerosis
Suprasacral spinal lesions
  Spinal cord injury
  Spinal cord tumor
  Multiple sclerosis
  Myelodysplasia
  Transverse myelitis
Diabetes mellitus

Non-neurogenic Detrusor Overactivity

Bladder infection
Bladder outlet obstruction
  Men—prostatic and bladder neck, strictures
  Women—pelvic organ prolapse, postsurgical, urethral, diverticulum, primary bladder neck, strictures
Bladder tumor
Bladder stones
Foreign body
Aging

of urodynamic evaluation may therefore lie in the assessment of these parameters rather than in the mere documentation of the presence or absence of detrusor overactivity.

A urodynamic classification of patients with overactive bladder (OAB) based on the presence of detrusor overactivity, patients' awareness, and ability to abort the involuntary contraction has been proposed (Flisser et al, 2003). They defined **four types of OAB. In type 1, the patient complains of OAB symptoms, but no involuntary detrusor contractions are demonstrated** (Fig. 60–8). **In type 2, there are involuntary detrusor contractions, but the patient is aware of them and can voluntarily contract the sphincter, prevent incontinence, and abort the detrusor contraction** (Fig. 60–9). **In type 3, there are involuntary detrusor contractions, the patient is aware of them and can voluntarily contract the sphincter and momentarily prevent incontinence, but the patient is unable to abort the detrusor contraction and when the sphincter fatigues, incontinence ensues** (Fig. 60–10) **In type 4, there are involuntary detrusor contractions, but the patient is not able to contract the sphincter voluntarily or abort the detrusor contraction and simply voids involuntarily** (Fig. 60–11). This classification system serves two purposes. First, it is a shorthand method of describing the urodynamic characteristics of the OAB patient. Second, it provides a substrate for therapeutic decision-making. For example, a patient with type 1 and 2 OAB exhibits normal neural control mechanisms and, at least theoretically, is an excellent candidate for behavioral therapy. It is likely that over time (with or without treatment), an individual patient can change from one type to another. Further, this classification relates only to the storage stage and can coexist with

normal voiding, bladder outlet obstruction, or impaired detrusor contractility.

Low Bladder Compliance. Incontinence related to low bladder compliance occurs when vesical pressure exceeds outlet resistance. Clinically, low bladder compliance is most commonly seen in a variety of neurologic conditions, especially lower motor neuron lesions such as spina bifida and cauda equina syndrome (McGuire et al, 1981, 1994; Weld et al, 2000; Shin et al, 2002). Obstructive uropathy, because of its effect on bladder ultrastructure (Kim et al, 1991; Peters et al, 1992, Karim et al, 1993), is known to cause low bladder compliance and has been identified as a urodynamic risk factor (Comiter et al,1997). Leng and McGuire (2003) showed that relief of obstruction by transurethral incision or resection of the prostate can improve compliance. **The clinical causes of low bladder compliance are listed in Table 60–3.**

Table 60–3.	Causes of Low Bladder Compliance

Neurogenic

Myelodysplasia
Shy-Drager syndrome
Suprasacral spinal cord injury/lesion
Radical hysterectomy
Abdominoperineal resection

Non-neurogenic (Increased Collagen)

Tuberculous cystitis
Radiation cystitis
Chronic indwelling catheter
Bladder outlet obstruction

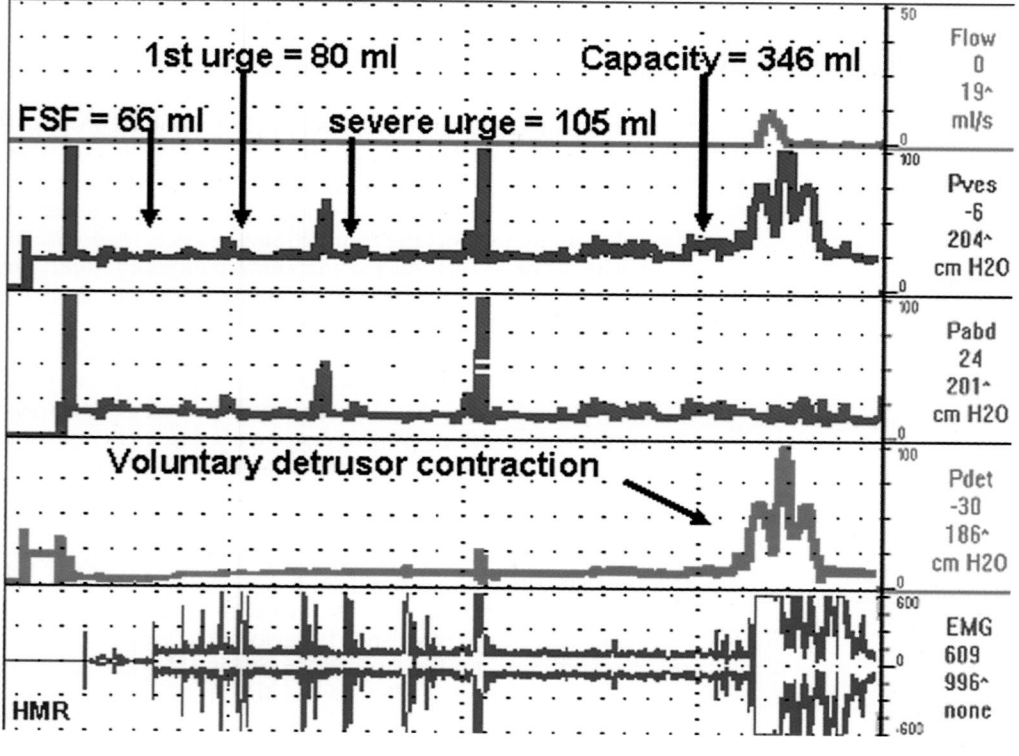

Figure 60–8. Type 1 overactive bladder. This represents a 54-year-old woman with mild exacerbating-remitting multiple sclerosis who complains of urinary frequency, urgency, and urge incontinence. Urodynamic tracing. FSF, first sensation of bladder filling (66 mL); 1st urge to void (80 mL); severe urge to void (105 mL); bladder capacity = 346 mL. Despite the fact that she complains of urge incontinence, there were no involuntary detrusor contractions and she voided normally with a voluntary detrusor contraction; thus, this is type 1 overactive bladder. EMG, electromyography.

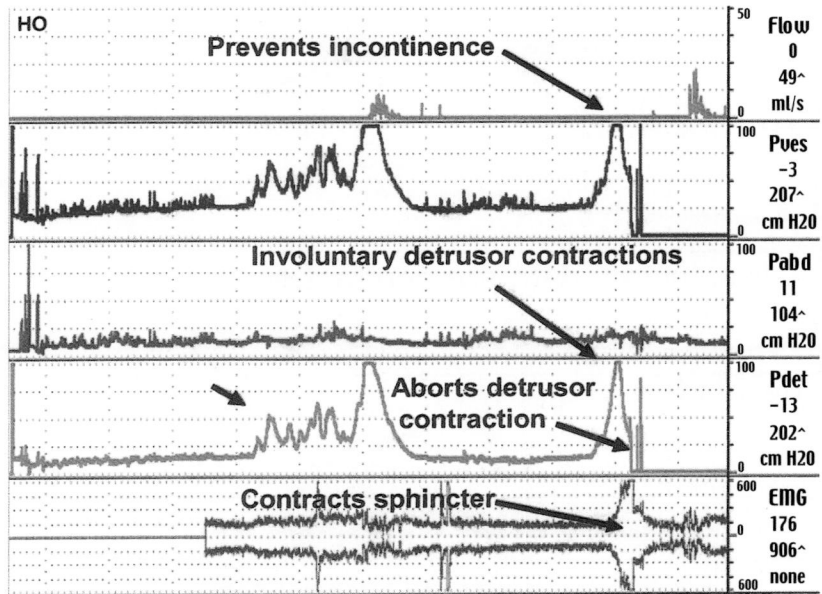

Figure 60–9. Type 2 overactive bladder in a 53-year-old man with prostatic obstruction. Urodynamic tracing. There is a series of poorly sustained involuntary detrusor contractions (*small arrow*) that he perceives as a severe urge to void, and then there is a sustained voiding contraction. He voluntarily relaxes his sphincter and voids. The pressure-flow data show Schafer grade 5 prostatic obstruction. (pdet@Qmax = 100 cm H_2O; Qmax = 8 mL/sec). The bladder is filled again and there is another involuntary detrusor contraction. This time he is instructed to try to hold. He contracts his sphincter, obstructing the urethra, the detrusor contraction subsides, and he is not incontinent. This characterizes type 2 overactive bladder.

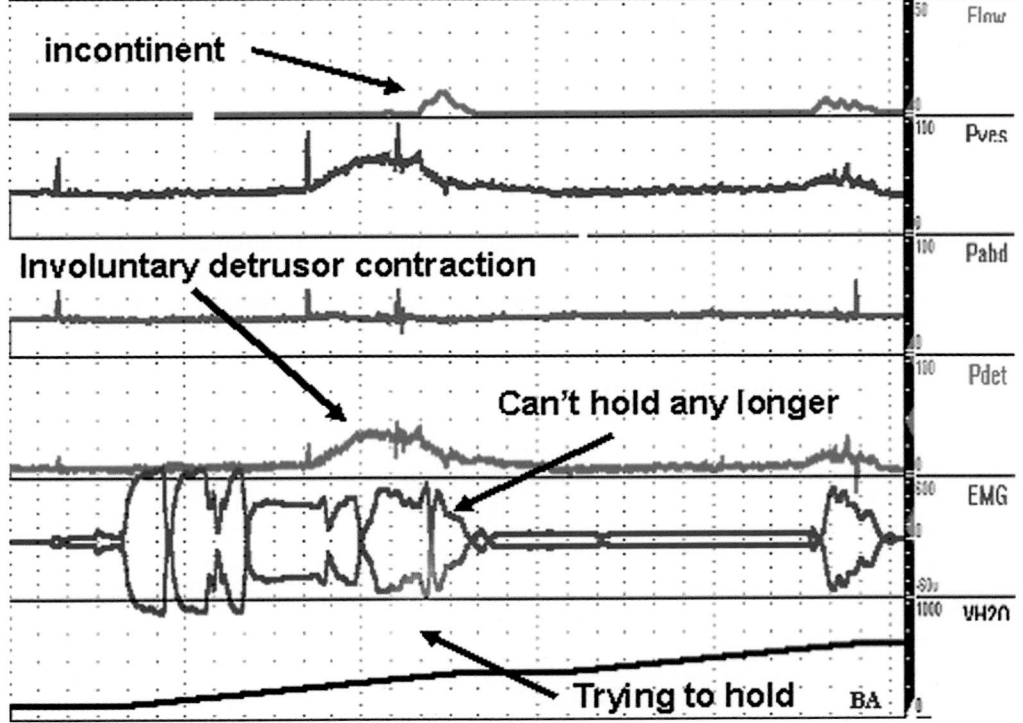

Figure 60–10. Type 3 overactive bladder in a 43-year-old woman with refractory idiopathic overactive bladder. Urodynamic tracing. A strong urge is felt at a bladder volume of 50 mL and she contracts her sphincter to prevent incontinence. At a volume of 275 mL, she develops an involuntary detrusor contraction and is able to continue contracting her sphincter, preventing incontinence, but does not abort the detrusor contraction. Once the sphincter fatigues, she voids involuntarily. This characterizes type 3 overactive bladder.

Sphincter Abnormalities

Urodynamic Observations

The ICS defines urodynamic stress incontinence as the **involuntary leakage of urine during increased abdominal pressure, in the absence of a detrusor contraction** (Abrams et al, 2003). There are various urodynamic measurements of sphincteric function (see section on "Urodynamic Testing"), but the diagnosis of urodynamic stress incontinence, per se, can be made without any such measurements.

Conditions Causing Sphincter Abnormalities

The causes of sphincteric dysfunction are different in men and women. **In men, sphincter abnormalities are most commonly caused by anatomic disruption after prostate surgery or, less commonly, by trauma or neurologic abnormalities. In women, sphincter abnormalities (as described previously) may be classified in two ways: from an anatomic viewpoint, urethral hypermobility (urethral support defect), or functional viewpoint, intrinsic sphincteric insufficiency**

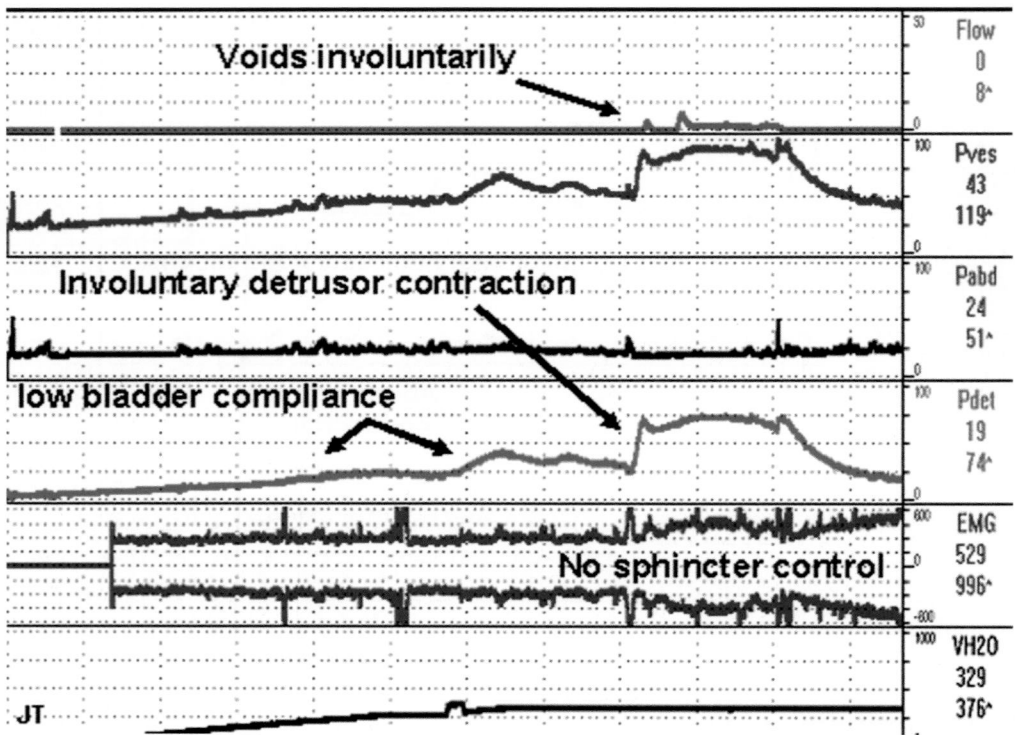

Figure 60–11. Type 4 overactive bladder in a 39-year-old woman with urge incontinence and urethral obstruction related to post-traumatic stricture. Urodynamic tracing. During bladder filling there is a steep rise in detrusor pressure that could be mistaken for an involuntary detrusor contraction, but when filling is stopped, the pressure does not fall, proving that the pressure rise is due to low bladder compliance. At a bladder volume of 329 mL, she experiences an involuntary detrusor contraction and is incontinent. She is unable to contract her sphincter or abort the stream. This is characteristic of type 4 overactive bladder. The pressure-flow data are indicative of grade 2 urethral obstruction on the Blaivas-Groutz nomogram (pdet@Qmax = 65 cm H_2O; Qmax = 8 mL/sec).

(ISD). Urethral hypermobility and support defects in women are most commonly associated with pregnancy and vaginal delivery, pelvic surgery, and chronic abdominal straining (e.g., chronic constipation). In some cases, loss of support many be secondary to neurologic injury. In such cases, nerve injury (e.g., pudendal nerve) can lead to muscle atrophy and subsequent failure of the support mechanism.

Sphincter Abnormalities in Women. Labor and delivery have long been thought to be risk factors for stress incontinence, urogenital prolapse, and anal incontinence. Vaginal delivery may be associated with direct injury to the pelvic soft tissues as well as partial denervation of the pelvic floor and thus may play a role in the etiology of SUI. On the basis of a thorough review of the literature, Mostwin and colleagues (2005) proposed four major mechanisms by which vaginal delivery might lead to sphincteric damage and incontinence: (1) injury to connective tissue support by the mechanical process of vaginal delivery; (2) vascular damage to the pelvic structures as a result of compression by the fetus; (3) damage to the pelvic nerves or muscles or both as a result of trauma during parturition, and (4) direct injury to the urinary tract during labor and delivery. Vaginal delivery can cause partial denervation with consequent reinnervation in most first deliveries (Allen et al, 1990). There is a growing body of evidence that multiparity; forceps delivery; increased duration of the second stage of labor, partially related to epidural anesthesia; third-degree perineal tear; and high birth weight (greater than 4000 g) are important factors leading to pudendal nerve injury (Snooks et al, 1986; Handa et al, 1996; Brown and Lumley, 1998; Rortveit et al, 2003). Snooks and associates (1984b) studied the postpartum innervation of the external anal sphincter and found that the external anal sphincter and its innervation might be damaged by vaginal delivery but not by cesarean section. The abnormalities found were most marked in multiparas and correlated most strongly with a prolonged second stage of labor and forceps delivery.

There are **several conditions associated with increased risk for ISD in women:**

1. **Previous urethral or periurethral surgery** (e.g., anti-incontinence surgery, urethral diverticulectomy) may result in postoperative ISD from periurethral fibrosis, scarring, or denervation (Haab et al, 1996). Prevalence of ISD after two or more failed anti-incontinence operations was found to be as high as 75% (McGuire, 1980).
2. **Neurologic insult** may cause ISD. Sacral neurologic lesions have a variable effect on micturition, depending on the extent to which the neurologic injury affects the parasympathetic, sympathetic, and somatic systems (Gerstenberg et al, 1980; Blaivas and Barbalias, 1983; Wheeler et al, 1986; McGuire et al, 1988). In complete parasympathetic lesions, the bladder is areflexic and the patient is in urinary retention. When, in addition to a parasympathetic lesion, there is a sympathetic lesion, the proximal urethra loses its sphincteric function. Clinically, this results in incomplete bladder emptying, caused by the acontractile detrusor, and sphincteric incontinence, caused by the nonfunctioning proximal urethra (Gerstenberg et al, 1980; Blaivas and Barbalias, 1983). Somatic neurologic lesions affect pudendal afferent and efferent nerves (Blaivas, 1982). In addition to loss of perineal and perianal sensation, these lesions abolish the bulbocavernosus reflex and impair the ability to contract the urethral and anal sphincters voluntarily. Sacral

neurologic lesions are caused by herniated disks, diabetic neuropathy, multiple sclerosis, and spinal cord tumors. They are also commonly encountered after extensive pelvic surgery such as abdominoperineal resection of the rectum and radical hysterectomy (Gerstenberg et al, 1980; Blaivas and Barbalias, 1983; Chang and Fan, 1983; McGuire et al, 1988).

3. **Pelvic radiation therapy** has been associated with damage to the mucosal seal coaptation of the urethra as well as local neurologic damage (Haab et al, 1996).

Sphincter Abnormalities in Men. Sphincter abnormalities in men are **caused by trauma or neurologic injury.** With **prostatectomy**, whether for benign disease or with radical prostatectomy, the DUS (particularly the rhabdosphincter) can be damaged by direct injury or injury to the nerve supply or supporting structures (Nitti, 2002). In some cases, there may be preexisting damage to the sphincter that cannot be accurately diagnosed preoperatively (Nitti, 2002). As in women (as noted earlier), **radiation** and **neurologic lesions** can cause sphincteric dysfunction. Finally, **pelvic trauma** or instrumentation that results in trauma to the DUS can result in incontinence, particularly when the PUS is absent or deficient.

DIAGNOSTIC EVALUATION

In the **initial assessment** of incontinence, a presumptive or condition-specific diagnosis is made and underlying organ-specific related or unrelated conditions that require further intervention are ruled out (Staskin et al, 2005). In addition, the level of bother and the desire for intervention are assessed. Based on the clinical situation, degree of bother, and the risks and benefits of the untreated condition, empirical (non-invasive reversible) treatment may be considered or a more detailed diagnostic assessment chosen before recommending treatment.

The initial evaluation of urinary incontinence begins with a thorough **history taking, physical examination, and routine laboratory studies, including urinalysis, urine culture, and, when indicated, renal function tests. All potential causes of "transient incontinence" such as urinary tract infection or medication effects should be addressed.** The causes of transient incontinence often lie outside the urinary tract. Conditions causing transient incontinence are more common in elderly persons and can be recalled using the mnemonic DIAPPERS (Resnick, 1984) (Table 60–4).

Table 60–4.	**Causes of Transient Incontinence**

Delirium
Infection (urinary tract infection)
Atrophic vaginitis/urethritis
Psychological (e.g., severe depression, neurosis)
Pharmacologic
Excess urine production
Restricted mobility
Stool impaction

From Resnick NM: Urinary incontinence in the elderly. Med Grand Rounds 1984;3:281-290.

In the **history**, there should be an assessment of the frequency and severity of incontinence, its degree of bother, and its effect on quality of life. This can be aided by the use of questionnaires and diaries. From the results of this initial assessment, certain secondary simple diagnostic tests may be recommended such as determination of postvoid residual (PVR) volume or specific laboratory testing (such as renal function tests). A more complex evaluation is recommended when a more precise diagnosis is required to treat the patient or rule out potentially harmful conditions. Such an evaluation may be prompted by findings in the initial assessment (e.g., suspicion of neurologic disease or an elevated PVR), a poor understanding of the condition based on the information obtained in the initial assessment, or failure of the patient to respond to empirical treatment. The more advanced diagnostic evaluation includes uroflowmetry, urodynamic testing, pad testing, endoscopic evaluation, and urinary tract imaging.

To be sure, the **sine qua non for a precise diagnosis is that the urinary incontinence is actually witnessed by the examiner.** It makes little difference whether the urinary loss is demonstrated during physical examination or diagnostic testing because the observations and measurements of an astute clinician are usually sufficient for establishing the presumed diagnosis. **A definitive diagnosis of the exact etiology of incontinence requires a full urodynamic evaluation, but this is not always necessary to treat patients.** However, it is axiomatic that **under ordinary circumstances no patient should undergo invasive or irreversible treatment until the cause of the incontinence has been clearly established.**

History

The patient's history is important in assessing the **characteristics and severity of incontinence as well as its impact on quality of life.** It is also important in identifying risk factors or transient causes of incontinence, or both. Acute symptoms may be further defined by documenting patterns of fluid intake and output, acute infection, and recent surgery or trauma. Insight into chronic symptoms may be obtained by eliciting a history of congenital anomalies, neurologic disease, prior surgery, or general health.

Patients should be queried specifically about **neurologic conditions** that are known to affect bladder and sphincteric function, such as multiple sclerosis, spinal cord injury, diabetes, myelodysplasia, stroke, and Parkinson's disease. In this regard, it is important to ask about double vision, muscular weakness, paralysis or poor coordination, tremor, numbness, and tingling sensation. A **history of prostate surgery, vaginal surgery, or previous surgical repair of incontinence** should suggest the possibility of sphincteric injury (McGuire, 1980; McGuire et al, 1987; Awad et al, 1988; Blaivas, 1988a; Blaivas and Jacobs, 1991). Abdominoperineal resection of the rectum (Gerstenberg et al, 1980; Mundy, 1982; Blaivas and Barbalias, 1983; Chang and Fan, 1983; McGuire et al, 1988) or radical hysterectomy (Mundy, 1982; Woodside and McGuire, 1982) may be associated with neurologic injury to the bladder and sphincter. **Radiation therapy** may adversely affect bladder capacity or compliance, or both.

In establishing an incontinence history, it is important to describe the character of the symptoms, their progression, any exacerbating or alleviating factors, impact on lifestyle, and possible risk factors. Each symptom should be characterized and quantified as accurately as possible. It is common for a patient to report multiple different lower urinary tract symptoms (LUTS) or even multiple incontinence symptoms (e.g., both stress and urge symptoms), and determining the most bothersome symptom can be important (Romanzi et al, 1995).

A **medication history,** especially with respect to medications that are known to cause alterations in urinary tract function, must be obtained. For example, sympatholytic agents such as clonidine, phenoxybenzamine, terazosin, doxazosin, and tamsulosin may cause or worsen stress incontinence. Sympathomimetics and tricyclic antidepressants such as ephedrine, pseudoephedrine, or imipramine may increase bladder outlet obstruction and contribute to urinary retention and overflow incontinence. Diuretics, although they do not cause incontinence, may exacerbate incontinence symptoms (Fantl et al, 1990b). The general medical history should also include questions regarding **bowel and sexual function as well as obstetric, menstrual, and hormone replacement history in women.**

It must be emphasized that the patient's history alone is not a completely accurate tool in the diagnosis of either sphincteric incontinence or detrusor overactivity and should not always be used as the sole determinant of diagnosis or treatment (Jensen et al, 1994). In cases in which the degree of certainty of the diagnosis is critical, further testing is appropriate, In a MEDLINE search of "urinary incontinence" and "urodynamics," Harvey and Versi (2001) found that the isolated symptom of stress incontinence has a positive predictive value (PPV) of 56% for the diagnosis of pure urodynamic stress incontinence and 79% for urodynamic stress incontinence with other abnormalities. A positive cough test had a PPV of 55% for the diagnosis of pure urodynamic stress incontinence and 91% for urodynamic stress incontinence plus other abnormalities. Similarly, Horbach (1990) found the PPV for the symptom of stress incontinence predicting urodynamic stress incontinence ranges from 64% to 90%. Summitt and colleagues (1992) reported that 53% to 71% of women with detrusor overactivity gave histories similar to those of women with urodynamic stress incontinence. The PPV of a history of pure urge incontinence has been shown to be as low as 37% for detrusor overactivity.

In men with incontinence, because of the association of benign prostatic obstruction with urge incontinence, a full assessment of all LUTS is important. In all cases of incontinence, structured, condition-specific questionnaires, either clinician or self-administered, may facilitate disclosure of symptoms and their effect of quality of life (Donovan et al, 2005). Table 60–5 lists important information and examples of information that should be obtained in an incontinence history.

Physical Examination

The physical examination should focus on detecting anatomic and neurologic abnormalities that contribute to urinary incontinence. The **neurourologic examination** begins by observing the patient's gait and demeanor as he or she first enters the examination room. A slight limp or lack of coordination, an abnormal speech pattern, facial asymmetry, or

Table 60–5. Examples of Important Information Obtained in an Incontinence History*

How often does the patient void during the day and night and how long can she or he wait comfortably between urinations?

Why does voiding occur as often as it does (urgency, convenience, attempt to prevent incontinence)?

How severe is incontinence (e.g., a few drops, saturate outer clothing)?

Are protective pads worn?

Do pads become saturated?

How often and why are pads changed?

Is the patient aware of incontinence occurring, or does the patient just find herself or himself wet?

Is there a sense of urgency before incontinence occurs? If so, how long can micturition be postponed?

Does stress incontinence occur during coughing, during sneezing, while the patient rises from a sitting to a standing position, or only during heavy physical exercise?

If the incontinence is associated with stress, is urine lost only for an instant during the stress, or is there uncontrollable voiding?

Is the incontinence positional? Does it ever occur in the lying or sitting position?

Is there difficulty initiating the stream, requiring pushing or straining to start?

Is the stream weak or interrupted?

Is there postvoid dribbling?

Has the patient ever had urinary retention?

*It is important to elicit not only the presence of the symptom but also the degree of bother and effect on lifestyle.

other abnormalities may be subtle signs of a neurologic condition. The **abdomen and flanks** should be examined for masses, hernias, and a distended bladder. **Rectal examination** discloses the size and consistency of the prostate. **Sacral innervation** (predominantly S2, S3, S4) is evaluated by assessing anal sphincter tone and control, genital sensation, and the bulbocavernosus reflex. With the physician's finger in the patient's rectum, the patient is asked to squeeze as if in the middle of urinating and trying to stop. A lax or weakened anal sphincter and the inability to contract and relax voluntarily are signs of neurologic damage, but some patients simply do not know or do not understand how to contract these muscles, whereas others may be too embarrassed to comply with the instructions. The **bulbocavernosus reflex** is checked by suddenly squeezing the glans penis or clitoris and feeling (or seeing) the anal sphincter and perineal muscles contract. Alternatively, the reflex may be initiated by suddenly pulling the balloon of the Foley catheter against the bladder neck. **The absence of this reflex in men is almost always associated with a neurologic lesion, but the reflex is not detectable in up to 30% of otherwise normal women** (Blaivas, 1981).

In women, the **pelvic examination** begins with inspection of the perineum and genitalia. The presence of any abnormal anatomic features, atrophy, excoriation, or erythema related to incontinence and pads should be noted. The **vaginal epithelium** should be observed for signs of atrophy. The well-estrogenized vagina has thick, pink epithelium with transverse rugae. The poorly estrogenized vagina has a paler, thinner epithelium with loss of rugae.

Ideally, a vaginal examination should be performed with the bladder both full (to check for incontinence and prolapse) and empty (to examine the pelvic organs). **With the bladder** comfortably full in the lithotomy position, the patient is asked to cough or strain in an attempt to reproduce the incontinence. The degree of urethral hypermobility may be assessed by the Q-tip test (Bergman and Bhatia, 1987; Walters and Diaz, 1987). The Q-tip test is performed by inserting a well-lubricated sterile cotton-tipped applicator gently through the urethra into the bladder. Once in the bladder, the applicator is withdrawn to the point of resistance, which is at the level of the bladder neck. The resting angle from the horizontal is recorded. The patient is then asked to strain and the degree of rotation is assessed. **Hypermobility is defined as a resting or straining angle greater than 30 degrees from the horizontal.**

A compartmentalized examination of the vagina follows, examining the anterior, apical, and posterior compartments as well as the perineal body. The **anterior vaginal wall** is examined first in the lithotomy position. The posterior blade from a split vaginal speculum is inserted and retracted posteriorly. The patient is instructed to strain and cough to assess for bladder, urethral, and cervical mobility and stress incontinence. Next, the **apex and its support** are examined. Normally this includes the cervix and uterus or the vaginal cuff in the posthysterectomy female. Reduction of the prolapse, if present, either manually or with a pessary in both positions may be necessary to demonstrate stress incontinence. Stress incontinence that is not present clinically or with a prolapse unreduced but is present after reduction of prolapse is termed **occult stress incontinence** (Barnes et al, 2002). After the anterior vaginal wall and apex have been examined, the blade is rotated and the anterior vagina gently retracted. The **posterior vaginal wall and vault** are examined for the presence of posterior prolapse (rectocele or enterocele). As the speculum is slowly withdrawn, a transverse groove separating an enterocele from a rectocele below may be visible. A finger inserted into the rectum can "tent up" a rectocele but not an enterocele. The **degree of prolapse** can be assessed by either the Baden-Walker system (grade 1 to 4) (Baden and Walker, 1992) or the pelvic organ prolapse quantification system (POP-Q), which assesses each compartment separately (Bump et al, 1996). The **perineal body and vaginal rectal septum** are examined by palpating the septum through the vagina and rectum. **Pelvic floor strength and the ability of the patient to contract her pelvic floor muscles voluntarily** are assessed.

If incontinence is not demonstrated with the patient in the lithotomy position and in a patient who has a history of stress incontinence, the examination is repeated in the standing position. The patient should be positioned standing in front of the examiner with one foot elevated on a short stool and again asked to cough and strain.

The physical examination of men with incontinence focuses on abdominal examination, digital rectal examination (DRE), and neurologic testing of the perineum and lower extremities. DRE includes palpation of the prostate to assess size, consistency, symmetry, and its relationship to surrounding structures. The external genitalia (penis, scrotum, testes, and epididymis) should be carefully examined. The man presenting with stress incontinence (e.g., after prostatectomy) should be examined in the standing position while performing Valsalva and coughing maneuvers. As in the female, the skin should be assessed for rashes and excoriation.

Urinalysis

Urinalysis is a fundamental test that **should be performed in all patients**. A complete urinalysis includes chemical and microscopic components. With respect to urinary incontinence, urinalysis is not a diagnostic test but rather a screening test to detect abnormalities such as hematuria, pyuria, bacteria, glucosuria, leukocyte esterase, and nitrates (Staskin et al, 2005). These may in turn be indicators of urothelial disease such as cancer, diabetes, and infection, all of which may be associated with incontinence. A urinalysis showing any of these is sure to prompt further testing. Although there is a lack of controlled studies indicating the usefulness of urinalysis in the incontinent patient, there is general expert consensus that the benefits of urinalysis clearly outweigh the costs involved (European Urinalysis Guidelines, 2000; Staskin et al, 2005). The importance of urinalysis in the evaluation of incontinence and LUTS is independent of age, gender, and etiology.

Postvoid Residual Volume

PVR is the volume of urine remaining in the bladder immediately following a representative void. It is usually measured by catheterization or ultrasonography. **Ultrasonography is the least invasive way of determining PVR** and its determination by bladder scanner is comparable to catheterization (Ding et al, 1996), especially at low volumes (less than 200 mL). **In a given patient, PVR may vary and one than one measurement may be necessary.** This intraindividual variability has been investigated mainly in male patients with obstruction and in elderly patients (Griffiths et al, 1996; Birch et al, 1998), but little information is available about its variability in incontinent patients. However, a nonrepresentative PVR is common when the patient's bladder is not sufficiently full to yield a normal urge to void. In interpreting the results, consideration should be given to the fact that voiding in unfamiliar surroundings may lead to unrepresentative results and an isolated finding of residual urine requires confirmation before being considered significant (Abrams et al, 1988). Furthermore, if results are "abnormal," tests should be repeated because the test-retest reliability of PVR measurements is poor (Stoller and Millard, 1989).

There is no evidenced-based specific maximum PVR that is considered normal, nor is there a minimal PVR that is considered abnormal (Staskin et al, 2005). The Agency for Health Care Policy and Research (AHCPR) guidelines state that, in general, a PVR less than 50 mL is adequate bladder empting and a PVR more than 200 mL is inadequate emptying (Fantl et al, 1996). It is clear that PVR is important for patients in whom decreased bladder emptying is known or suspected, especially if treatments to decrease bladder contractility or increase outlet resistance are being considered. One study questioned the value of routine use of PVR in the evaluation of incontinent women (Sander et al, 2002). In an analysis of 408 women, 4% had a PVR of 200 mL or greater and 6% had a PVR of 150 mL or greater. However, only 1.5% had management modified because of the results of PVR and uroflowmetry. Nevertheless the **third International Consultation on Incontinence recommends that PVR be determined in the initial assessment** (Tubaro et al, 2005).

Micturition Diary

The micturition diary records a patient's voiding (and incontinence) pattern in his or her own environment and during normal daily activities. In addition, close self-monitoring with a micturition diary may allow the patient insights into behavioral alterations that can decrease urge incontinence episodes (Burgio et al, 1998). Diary recordings have been shown to be reproducible and more accurate than patients' recall (Larsson and Victor, 1992; McCormack et al, 1992; Wyman et al, 1998; Blanker et al, 2000; Groutz et al, 2000b). Although there may be great variability in the actual data accumulated by these instruments, simply asking the patient whether the diary and pad test are representative of a "good" or "bad" day can be extremely useful.

Formal standardization of the structure, content, and duration of micturition diaries is lacking. Micturition diaries vary in duration from 24 hours to 14 days (Wyman et al, 1998; Larsson et al, 1992; Rabin et al, 1993; Abrams and Klevmark, 1996; Burgio et al, 1998; Groutz et al, 2000b). Prolonged complex charts yield more data, but they may be associated with a low compliance rate. Groutz and coworkers (2000b) studied the test-retest reliability of 24-, 48-, and 72-hour micturition diaries and found that both number of incontinence episodes and micturition episodes are reliable measures. However, lengthening the test period was associated with a decrease in patients' compliance (Groutz et al, 2000b). The nocturnal micturition episodes were found to have the lowest correlation value in the test-retest analysis. The inconsistency in reporting nocturnal micturition episodes may have several causes, such as recall capability (nocturnal micturition is occasionally reported the following morning), patterns and quality of sleep, the use of hypnotic medications, or actual variability in nocturnal diuresis.

Three different types of diaries have been described: (1) micturition time charts that record the number of voids (and incontinence episodes) in 24 hours, (2) frequency-volume charts in which the voided volumes are also recorded, and (3) bladder diaries in which additional information, such as the number, type, and degree of incontinence episodes, pad usage, fluid and food intake, and degree of urgency, is recorded (Abrams and Klevmark, 1996). The authors recommended the use of frequency-volume charts in routine clinical practice, keeping the more complex charts for research projects. They also pointed out that the reduced compliance associated with complex charts might be countered by giving more detailed instructions and encouragement in the research environment. In 1997, the Urodynamics Society (now known as the Society for Urodynamics and Female Urology) recommended that the following measurements be included in a micturition diary: time of micturition, time and type of incontinence, and voided volume (Blaivas et al, 1997b). No recommendations were given regarding the duration of the study. Schick and coauthors (2003) determined that a 4-day diary is as reliable as a 7-day diary. We believe that bladder diaries are extremely useful (for both the patient and the doctor) and recommend that they be part of not only the initial evaluation but also follow-up. **In the clinical setting, 24-hour diaries are adequate for the evaluation of lower urinary tract symptoms.** For research projects one may prefer the use of 72-hour studies, but care should be taken to ensure high compliance.

Symptom and Quality of Life Questionnaires

Symptoms of incontinence and their effect on quality of life can be assessed in a number of ways. Traditionally, clinicians have relied upon history obtained directly from the patient or caregiver, or both. Today there are a number of validated symptom and quality of life questionnaires that can help the clinician to better understand patients' symptoms and their impact and can aid in assessing the results of treatment. The third International Consultation on Incontinence has highly recommended several questionnaires for use in incontinence on the basis of validity, reliability, and responsiveness with rigor in one or several data sets (Donovan et al, 2005). Questionnaires are designed to assess symptoms, quality of life, or both. They are useful to obtain baseline information regarding incontinence and also to assess response to treatment. A list of recommended questionnaires is shown in Table 60–6. We believe that validated questionnaires can be extremely useful in clinical practice as well as research. Clinicians should choose the questionnaires that are most relevant to their group of patients and clinical setting.

Table 60–6. Questionnaires Highly Recommended by the Third International Consultation on Incontinence for the Evaluation of Urinary Incontinence (UI), Lower Urinary Tract Symptoms (LUTS), and Overactive Bladder (OAB)

I. Symptoms of UI	
A. Women	Urogenital Distress Inventory (UDI) (Shumaker et al, 1994)
	UDI-6 (Ubersax et al, 1995)
	Incontinence Severity Index (Sandvik et al, 1993)
	BFLUTS (Jackson et al, 1996)
B. Men	ISCmale (Donovan et al, 1996)
	DAN-PSS (Hald et al, 1991)
II. Quality of Life Impact of UI	
A. Men and women	I-QOL (Wagner et al, 1996; Patrick et al, 1999)
	SEAPI-QMN (Raz and Erickson, 1992; Stothers, 2004)
B. Women	King's Health Questionnaire (Kelleher et al, 1997)
	Incontinence Impact Questionnaire (Wyman et al, 1987)
	IIQ-7 (Ubersax et al, 1995)
	Urinary Incontinence Severity Score (UISS) (Stach-Lempinen et al, 2004)
	CONTILIFE (Amarenco et al, 2003)
C. Men	None
III. Combined Symptoms and Quality of Life Impact of UI	
A. Men and women	ICIQ (Avery et al, 2004)
B. Women	Bristol Female LUTS-SF (Brookes et al, 2004)
	SUIQQ (Kulseng-Hanssen and Borstad, 2003)
C. Men	ICSmaleSF (Donovan et al, 1996)
IV. Combined Symptoms and Quality of Life Impact of OAB	
A. Men and women	OAB-q (Coyne et al, 2002)

From Donovan J, Bosch R, Gotoh M, et al: Symptom and quality of life assessment. In Abrams P, Cardozo L, Khoury S, Wein A (eds): Incontinence (Edition 2005) 3rd International Consultation on Incontinence. United Kingdom (UK), Health Publications, 2005, pp 519-584.

Pad Testing

A pad test allows the detection and quantification of urine loss over a set period of time. It can be diagnostic of incontinence but not its cause. Pad tests have been described for multiple lengths of time from less than 1 hour to 48 hours (Jakobsen et al, 1987; Jorgensen et al, 1987; Hahn and Fall, 1991). Short-term pad tests (1 to 2 hours) are usually done in the physician's office under set conditions (activities or exercises). Pad tests of 1 hour or less are most reliable if done with a fixed bladder volume (Jorgensen et al, 1987; Kinn and Larsson, 1987; Lose et al, 1989; Hahn and Fall, 1991). Hahn and Fall (1991) described a 20-minute pad test done at 50% of maximum cystometric capacity where the patient climbs 100 steps, coughs 10 times, runs for 1 minute, washes hands for 1 minute, and jumps for 1 minute. In their study of women with stress incontinence they reported no false negatives, although there was a 12% discrepancy in the patients' perception of incontinence severity and pad test results. The 1-hour pad test has been extensively studied and is probably most reliable if done with a set bladder volume and with set exercises. It does not reflect daily incontinence nearly as well as a longer test (24 to 48 hours) and is probably best reserved for evaluation of stress incontinence. The ICS recommends a 1-hour test where the patient drinks 500 mL 15 minutes before the test and performs a number of set exercises (Abrams et al, 1988). A pad weight gain of more than 1 g on a 1-hour test suggests a positive test (Tubaro et al, 2005).

Longer duration pad tests are home based and are designed to diagnose and measure urine loss in a situation as close as possible to real life. Because it is not done under set conditions of exercise, the 24-hour test can be used to quantify both stress and urge loss. Lose and associates (1989) found a 90% correlation of the 24-hour pad test with a history of stress incontinence in 31 women, significantly better than with a 1-hour pad test. Mouritsen showed that a 24-hour home pad test is well tolerated and comparable to a 48-hour test in detecting incontinence. Similarly, Jorgensen and colleagues (1987) found the 24-hour home test to be more sensitive than a 1-hour test at a fixed bladder volume. The 24-hour pad test has good reproducibility but poorer compliance than shorter tests. **According to the third International Consultation on Incontinence, a pad weight gain of more than 1.3 g over 24 hours is considered a "positive" test** (Tubaro et al, 2005). **Others have stated that a weight gain of up to 8 g over a 24 hours is considered "normal"** (Lose et al, 1989; Mouritsen et al, 1989; Versi et al, 1996).

Groutz and colleagues (2000b) reported that weight gain and number of pads are reliable parameters over 24-, 48-, or 72-hour periods. They also recommended that once the test was completed, the patient be asked to state whether it was representative of his or her expected degree of incontinence or was better or worse than usual. If the patient states that the urinary loss was unusually large or small, that information is recorded and, if appropriate, the pad test is repeated. The literature suggests that pad testing for greater than 24 hours offers little advantage over 24-hour testing.

In conclusion, **pad tests are useful in the routine evaluation of incontinence and as an outcome measure in clinical trials and research studies.** If a short test is desired, a 20-minute to 1-hour office or ward test with a fixed volume in the bladder can be done. When a more precise "real life" test is desired, a 24-hour or longer test is preferred.

Dye Testing

In situations in which it is not possible to confirm a patient's complaint of urinary leakage, dye testing can be helpful. This test is **particularly useful when there is doubt about whether a discharge is truly urine** (e.g., vaginal discharge, peritoneal or serous fluid after pelvic surgery) or **when urine loss per urethra cannot be confirmed and extraurethral incontinence is suspected. Phenazopyridine (200 mg three times a day) can be given to stain the urine orange.** Confirmation of orange staining on a pad would confirm that leakage is actually urine. Alternatively, if a vesicovaginal fistula is suspected, methylene blue or indigo carmine can be instilled in the bladder and a tampon placed in the vagina. Blue staining of the inside portion of the tampon is suggestive of a fistula. If leakage is present but is clear and a ureteral-vaginal fistula is suspected, one can do a **two-dye test** in which phenazopyridine is given orally (to stain the renal urine) and blue dye is given intravesically (to stain the bladder contents) (Raghavaiah, 1974).

Uroflowmetry ("Free Flow")

The determination of urine flow rate and pattern with noninvasive uroflowmetry is useful in many patients with incontinence. **We believe it should be part of the initial evaluation of men (because of the high likelihood of bladder outlet obstruction) and in women at risk for obstruction** (grade 3 or 4 pelvic organ prolapse, prior vaginal surgery, dysfunctional voiders) and those with an elevated PVR. Urinary flow is described in terms of rate and pattern and may be continuous or intermittent (Abrams et al, 2003). The flow rate is a composite measure of the interaction between the pressure generated by the detrusor and the resistance offered by the urethra. Thus, **a low uroflow may be caused by either bladder outlet obstruction or impaired detrusor contractility** (Chancellor et al, 1991). Abnormal uroflow or PVR, or both, may prompt further testing such as multichannel urodynamics (see later).

Urodynamic Testing

For most incontinent patients there are two important fundamental questions that urodynamics should answer. The first is whether incontinence is being caused by bladder dysfunction, urethral dysfunction, or a combination of both. The second is whether the patient has exclusively a storage problem or whether there is also a problem with the voiding phase (obstruction, impaired contractility). In addition, urodynamic risk factors for the development of upper urinary tract deterioration can be identified. Urodynamic risk factors include DESD, low bladder wall compliance, bladder outlet obstruction leading to high storage pressures, and vesicoureteral reflux secondary to high intravesical pressures (McGuire et al, 1981; Blaivas and Barbalias, 1984; Ghoniem et al, 1989; Zoubek et al, 1989).

Urodynamic techniques range from simple "eyeball urodynamics" to sophisticated multichannel-pressure-flow-electromyography studies. Laboratory urodynamics relies on the same general principles as eyeball urodynamics; however, the measurements of pressure and flow are recorded electronically rather than visually. In addition, other physiologic parameters, such as sphincter electromyography, are impossible to evaluate without electronics. Fluoroscopic evaluation of the lower urinary tract is another valuable diagnostic tool that can be used simultaneously with urodynamics (videourodynamics) and provides the most precise evaluation of lower urinary tract function.

"Eyeball Urodynamics"

Eyeball urodynamics (or simple cystometry) is performed without any special urodynamic equipment through a urethral catheter, but we find it most useful to do at the time of cystoscopy in women. It has a more limited role in men. Its major disadvantage is that there is no real-time hard copy record of the study, but the cystometric tracing can be hand drawn to provide a permanent record. In elderly patients, Ouslander and colleagues (1988) found that the urodynamic information provided is often enough to aid in making a differential diagnosis. **In a cost-conscious environment, we believe that eyeball urodynamics, done at the time of cystoscopy, is perhaps the least expensive method of characterizing the urodynamic aspects of incontinence in women.** In fact, the only disposable items are the tubing and infusing fluid. In addition to cystoscopic findings, the following parameters can be assessed: (1) PVR, (2) bladder sensation, (3) bladder compliance, (4) bladder capacity, (5) involuntary detrusor contractions, and (6) urethral competence.

Eyeball urodynamics is performed with the patient in the lithotomy position immediately after voiding (preferably after uroflowmetry) (Fig. 60–12). A cystoscope or Foley catheter is inserted and PVR is measured. A 60-mL catheter-tip syringe is connected to the Foley catheter and its barrel removed. Water or saline solution is then poured in through the open end of the syringe and allowed to drip into the bladder by gravity. As the water level in the syringe falls, its meniscus represents the intravesical pressure, which can be estimated in centimeters of water above the symphysis pubis. When the water level in the syringe falls to the level of the catheter tip, it is refilled (usually 50- to 60-mL increments). When the urge to void is perceived, the patient is asked whether that is the usual feeling experienced when he or she needs to urinate.

Decreased sensations may be subtle signs of an underlying neuropathy (Wyndaele, 1993).

Changes in intravesical pressure are apparent as a slowing of the rate of fall or a rise in the level of the fluid meniscus. A rise in pressure may be caused by a detrusor contraction, an increase in abdominal pressure, or low bladder compliance. Any pressure high enough to cause fluid to rise above the level of the top of the syringe is a least 15 to 20 cm H_2O (see Fig. 60–12). As soon as a change in pressure is noted, the examiner should attempt to determine the cause. Visual inspection usually reveals if there is abdominal straining, but, in doubtful cases, the abdomen should be palpated. In most instances, the cause of the rise in intravesical pressure is obvious, but, when in doubt, formal cystometry with rectal or vaginal pressure monitoring is necessary. Any sudden rise in pressure that is accompanied by an urge to void or by incontinence is probably an involuntary detrusor contraction. In some instances, the etiology of the patient's incontinence is easily discernible as the patient voids uncontrollably around the catheter during an involuntary detrusor contraction. If involuntary detrusor contractions do not occur, the bladder is filled until the patient is comfortably full. The bladder is left full and the catheter removed. The presence or absence of gravitational urinary loss is noted. The patient is asked to cough and bear down with gradually increasing force to determine the ease with which incontinence may be produced. In women, the introitus is observed for signs of urethral mobility and pelvic organ prolapse.

Multichannel Urodynamics

Multichannel urodynamics provides a precise assessment of lower urinary tract function. There are many times when such precision is necessary to treat the incontinent patient effectively (Table 60–7). The urodynamic evaluation consists of several components including uroflowmetry, cystometry, abdominal pressure monitoring, electromyography (EMG), and voiding pressure-flow studies. Simultaneous fluoroscopic imaging of the entire urinary tract during urodynamics (i.e., videourodynamics) can be helpful when an anatomic correlate is desired. For practical purposes, it makes sense to divide the urodynamic study into the filling/storage phase and the voiding/emptying phase. **The filling/storage phase is assessed with a cystometrogram (CMG). During bladder filling,**

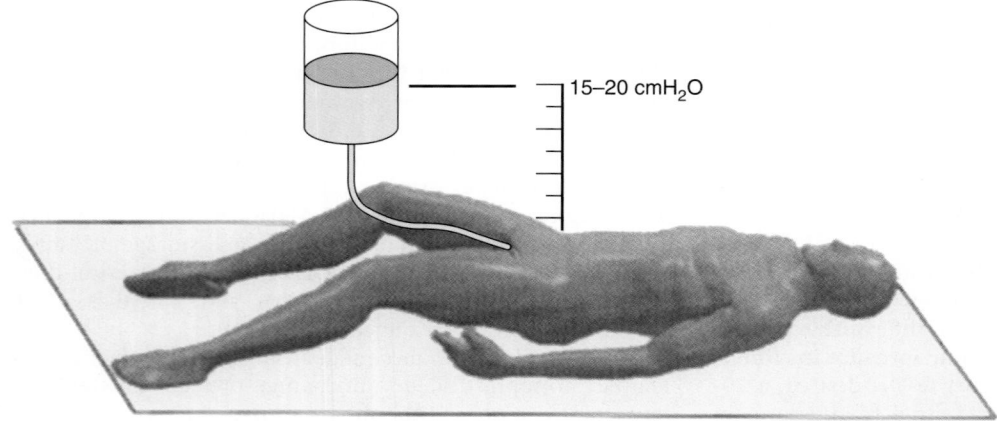

15–20 cmH₂O

Figure 60–12. Eyeball urodynamics —a urethral catheter is inserted into the bladder and raised vertically. A syringe (without its plunger) is connected to the end of the catheter and the bladder is filled. See text for details. (From Nitti VW: Cystometry and abdominal pressure monitoring. In Nitti VW [ed]: Practical Urodynamics. Philadelphia, WB Saunders, 1998, pp 38-51.)

provocative maneuvers to elicit detrusor overactivity can be performed (e.g., Valsalva, cough, change of position). The voiding/emptying phase is assessed with a detrusor pressure-uroflow study, in which detrusor pressure and urinary flow rate are simultaneously measured. In addition, one can assess external sphincter activity during voiding (and storage) using EMG. Urethral pressure can also be measured (urethral pressure profilometry) during storage, voiding, and provocative maneuvers. Herein, we present some of the essentials of urodynamic testing for the patient with incontinence. A comprehensive review is presented in Chapter 58, Urodynamic and Videourodynamic Evaluation of Voiding Dysfunction. For a complete reference to ICS terminology and good urodynamic practices, the reader is referred to the original monographs (Abrams et al, 2003; Schafer et al, 2002).

The Filling/Storage Phase

Cystometry. In simple terms, CMG is a measure of the bladder's response to being filled. It allows the clinician to determine the pressure-volume relationship within the bladder and ideally mimic the normal bladder filling and storage of urine. In addition, it provides a subjective measure of bladder sensation with the cooperation of the patient. The functions of the bladder are to store increasing volumes of urine at low pressure and to allow the voluntary and complete evacuation of urine. The CMG helps to assess these functions and correlate patients' symptoms with urodynamic abnormalities. Several parameters should always be evaluated when cystometry is performed:

1. Filling pressure
2. Sensation (e.g., first sensation of bladder filling, first desire to void, strong desire to void, urgency)
3. Presence of involuntary or unstable contractions
4. Compliance
5. Capacity
6. Control over micturition

In the incontinent patient it is important to document that abnormal findings on CMG (e.g., detrusor overactivity or impaired compliance) are associated with incontinence.

Cystometry can be performed as a single-channel study where the bladder pressure (p_{ves}) is measured and recorded during filling and storage or as a multichannel study where abdominal pressure (p_{abd}) is subtracted from p_{ves} to give the detrusor pressure (p_{det}). Subtracted detrusor pressure gives a much more accurate assessment of true bladder pressures as it allows one to differentiate between rises in p_{abd} and a true increase in p_{det} (whether by a contraction or decreased compliance) (Figs. 60–13 and 60–14). Therefore, it is recommended that simultaneous measurement of bladder pressure be done whenever possible (Schafer et al, 2002).

In the incontinent patient, **bladder dysfunction can by documented during CMG. Detrusor overactivity** (see Fig. 60–6) **and low bladder compliance** (see Fig. 60–7) **are causes of incontinence.** If such a finding is observed during urodynamics, it should be noted whether the patient has any sensation (e.g., desire to void, urgency, pain) and whether or not

---

Table 60–7. Indications for Multichannel Urodynamics in the Incontinent Patient

When results of simpler diagnostic tests have been inconclusive or in cases in which a more precise understanding of lower urinary tract function is desired

When empirical treatments have proved unsuccessful

In patients with known or suspected voiding phase dysfunction that could influence treatment of incontinence

When the patient complains of incontinence but it cannot be demonstrated clinically

When proposed therapy potentially can result in significant morbidity

In symptomatic patients who have previously undergone anti-incontinence or other lower urinary tract reconstructive surgery

In patients who have previously undergone radical pelvic surgery, such as abdominoperineal resection of the rectum or radical hysterectomy

In cases in which patients have received high-dose radiation to the pelvic region

In patients with known or suspected neurologic disorders that might interfere with bladder or sphincter function

---

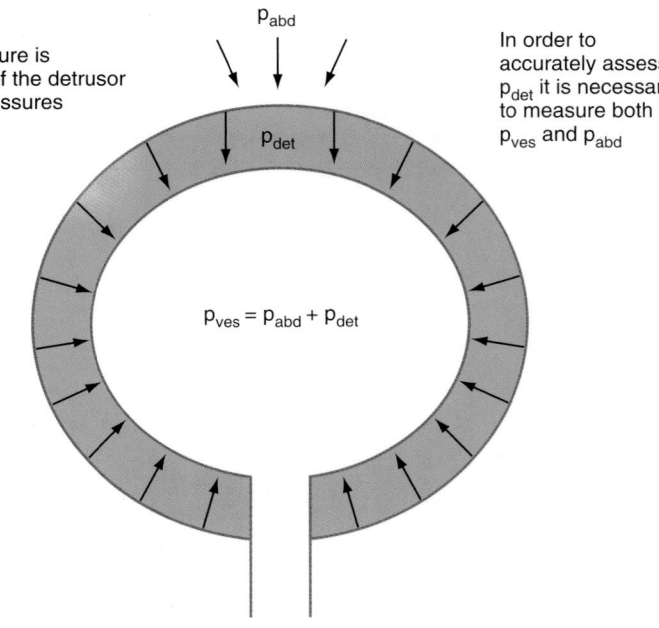

Total vesical pressure is made of the sum of the detrusor and abdominal pressures

p_{abd}

p_{det}

$p_{ves} = p_{abd} + p_{det}$

In order to accurately assess p_{det} it is necessary to measure both p_{ves} and p_{abd}

Figure 60–13. Schematic representation of total vesical pressure. The total pressure in the bladder (p_{ves}) is equal to the intra-abdominal pressure (p_{abd}) plus the pressure of the detrusor itself (p_{det}). Thus, a rise in p_{ves} may result from either a rise in p_{abd} (for example with coughing or Valsalva) or a rise in p_{det} (for example with a detrusor contraction or decreased compliance). (From Nitti VW: Cystometry and abdominal pressure monitoring. In Nitti VW [ed]: Practical Urodynamics. Philadelphia, WB Saunders, 1998, pp 38-51.)

A

Single Channel CMG

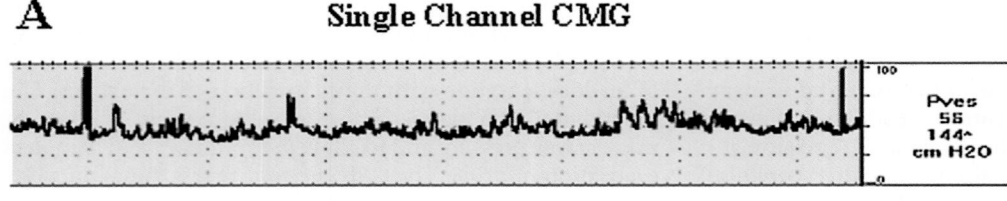

Pves
55
144^
cm H2O

B

Multichannel Urodynamics

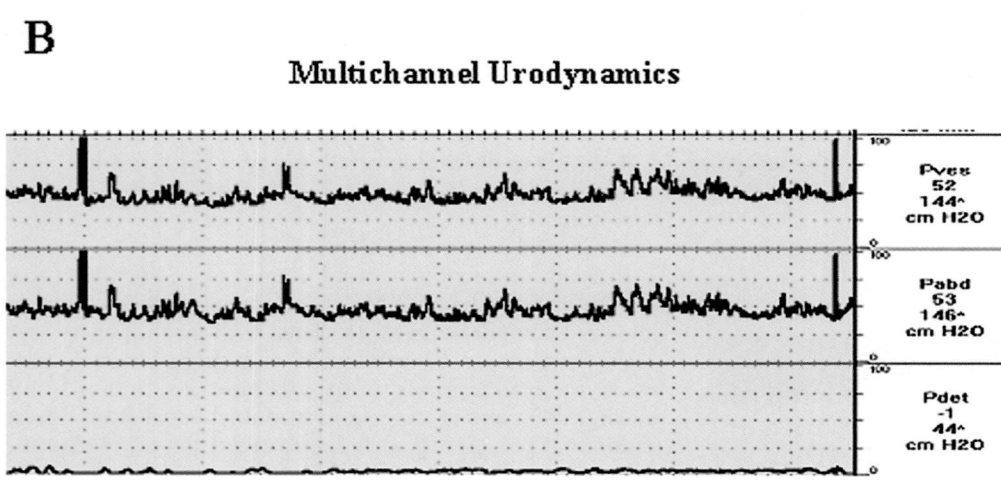

Pves
52
144^
cm H2O

Pabd
53
146^
cm H2O

Pdet
-1
44^
cm H2O

Figure 60–14. Adding intra-abdominal pressure monitoring gives a better representation of the true detrusor pressure. **A,** Single-channel cystometrogram (CMG) showing only vesical pressure. Without simultaneous monitoring of intra-abdominal pressure, it is impossible to determine whether these pressure spikes are due to a rise in detrusor or abdominal pressure. **B,** The same tracing with intra-abdominal pressure monitoring added. One can clearly see now that the changes in pressure were due to the changes in abdominal pressure. When one looks at the p_{det} curve, it is noted to be flat and without any rises in pressure. (From Nitti VW: Cystometry and abdominal pressure monitoring. In Nitti VW [ed]: Practical Urodynamics. Philadelphia, WB Saunders, 1998, pp 38-51.)

Leakage at arrow = ALPP = 109 cmH₂O

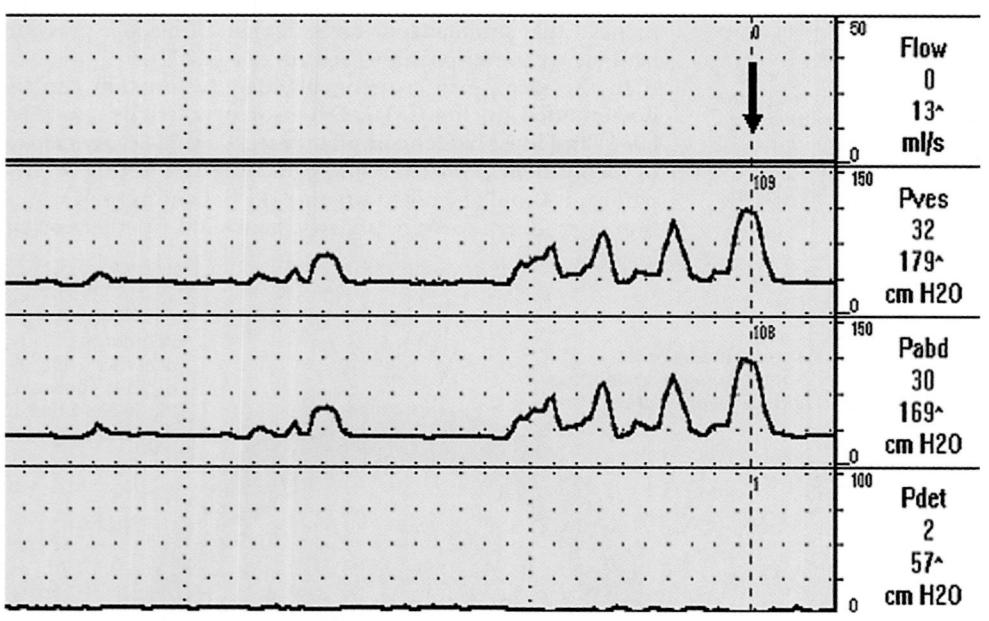

Flow
0
13^
ml/s

Pves
32
179^
cm H2O

Pabd
30
169^
cm H2O

Pdet
2
57^
cm H2O

Figure 60–15. Portion of a urodynamic tracing showing abdominal leak point pressure (ALPP) in a woman with stress incontinence. The rises in pressure on the p_{abd} and p_{ves} channels represent progressively stronger Valsalva maneuvers. Incontinence was demonstrated on the last Valsalva maneuver at a measured p_{ves} of 109 cm H₂0, which is the ALPP.

incontinence occurs with a rise in p_{det}. In addition, the p_{det} at which incontinence occurs may be noted (see the following regarding detrusor leak point pressure).

Leak Point Pressures. There are two distinct types of leak point pressures that can be measured in the incontinent patient. The two are independent of each other and conceptually measure completely different things. The first is the **abdominal leak point pressure** (ALPP), which is a measure of sphincter strength (its ability to resist changes in abdomi-

nal pressure) (McGuire et al, 1993). ALPP is defined as the **intravesical pressure at which urine leakage occurs because of increased abdominal pressure in the absence of a detrusor contraction** (Abrams et al, 2003) (Fig. 60–15). This measure of intrinsic urethral function is applicable to patients with stress incontinence. Conceptually, the lower the ALPP, the weaker the sphincter. **There is no normal ALPP as patients without stress incontinence do not leak at any physiologic abdominal pressure.**

The second type of leak point pressure is the **detrusor leak point pressure** (DLPP), which is a measure of detrusor pressure in patients with decreased bladder compliance. It is defined as the **lowest detrusor pressure at which urine leakage occurs in the absence of either a detrusor contraction or increased abdominal pressure** (Abrams et al, 2003) (Fig. 60–16). The higher the DLPP, the higher the urethral resistance. From a clinical perspective DLPP is most useful in patients with lower motor neuron disease affecting the bladder (spina bifida, spinal cord tumors, after abdominoperineal resection of the rectum or radical hysterectomy) and in non-neurogenic patients with low bladder compliance (after multiple bladder surgeries, radiation, and tuberculous cystitis). **The higher the DLPP, the more likely is upper tract damage as intravesical pressure is transferred to the kidneys.** McGuire and colleagues (1981) documented the deleterious effects that a high leak point pressure has on the upper urinary tracts; **leak point pressures greater than 40 cm H_2O result in hydronephrosis or vesicoureteral reflux in 85% of myelodysplastic patients.**

Urethral Pressure Profilometry. Despite an abundant literature on urethral profilometry, its clinical relevance is controversial; we do not perform urethral profilometry. Urethral pressure is defined as the fluid pressure needed to just open a closed urethra (Abrams et al, 2003). The urethral pressure profile (UPP) represents the intraluminal pressure along the length of the urethra in graphic form. Several parameters can be obtained from the UPP. The **urethral closure pressure profile** is given by the subtraction of intravesical pressure from urethral pressure. **Maximum urethral pressure** is the highest pressure measured along the UPP, and the **maximum urethral closure pressure** (MUCP) is the maximum difference between the urethral pressure and the intravesical pressure.

Functional profile length is the length of the urethra along which the urethral pressure exceeds intravesical pressure in women. **In most continent women, the functional urethral length is approximately 3 cm and the MUCP is 40 to 60 cm H_2O** (Steele et al, 1998), but normal values vary widely from study to study, probably because of its interdependence on age, hormonal status, degree of bladder filling, and type of catheter.

One caveat of UPP is that its measurement does not diagnose stress incontinence. For example, there is a difference between the urethra of an incontinent patient whose MUCP is 38 cm H_2O and that of a continent women with the same MUCP. One study showed that MUCP might offer prognostic information regarding outcomes of tension-free vaginal tape for stress incontinence (Rezapour et al, 2001). Several techniques that measure pressure transmission ratios from bladder to urethra during increases in intra-abdominal pressure have been described, but their clinical applicability has yet to be proved (Versi, 1990; Rosenzweig et al, 1991; Sorensen et al, 1991; Versi et al, 1991; Richardson and Ramahi, 1993). In 2002, the ICS standardization subcommittee concluded that the clinical utility of urethral pressure measurement is unclear (Lose et al, 2002). Furthermore, **there are no urethral pressure measurements that (1) discriminate urethral incompetence from other disorders, (2) provide a measure of the severity of the condition, and (3) provide a reliable indicator of surgical success and return to normal after surgical intervention** (Lose et al, 2002). **Based on the current understanding and application of UPP, we do not use it routinely in the evaluation of incontinence.** The micturitional static UPP as described by Yalla and associates (1980) is a useful means of pinpointing the site of urethral obstruction but is not necessary for routine evaluation.

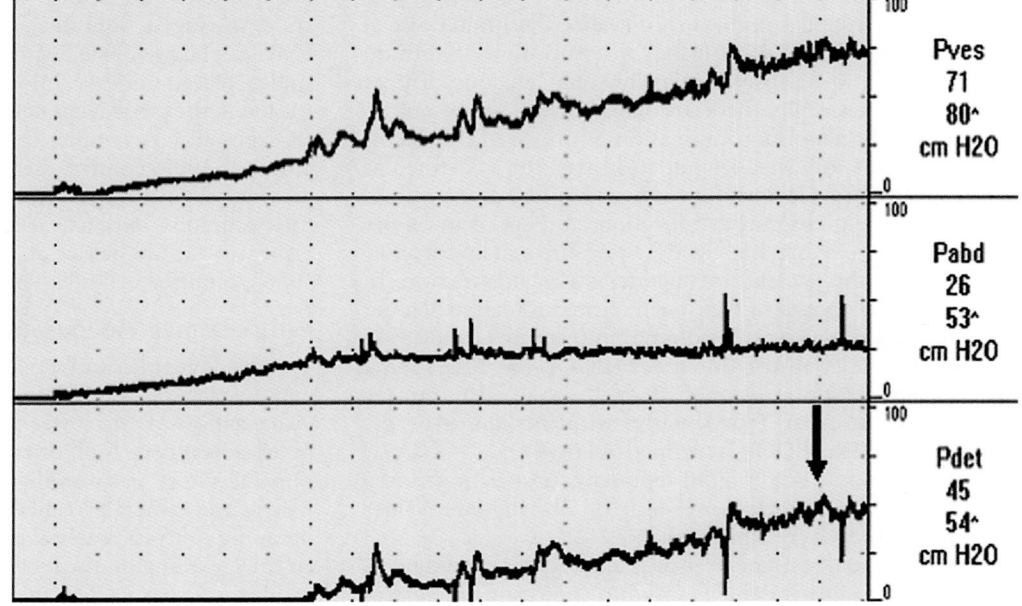

Leakage at arrow = DLPP = 45 cmH$_2$O

Figure 60–16. Demonstration of detrusor leak point pressure (DLPP) in a patient with neurogenic bladder. Impaired compliance is seen as p_{det} increases throughout filling. Leakage occurs when p_{det} reaches 45 cm H_2O, which is potentially harmful to the upper tracts.

The Voiding/Emptying Phase

Pressure-Flow Relation. Although incontinence is a problem related to abnormal storage of urine, events that cause incontinence (e.g., detrusor overactivity, impaired compliance) may be caused by abnormalities of the voiding phase. **Impaired contractility and outlet obstruction (anatomic or functional) are common abnormalities of the voiding phase that may be seen in incontinent patients.** For example, it is well known that bladder outlet obstruction is associated with detrusor overactivity and urge incontinence (Abrams et al, 1979; Fusco et al, 2001) and may also be associated with impaired compliance (Leng and McGuire, 2003). In patients with neurologic disease, incomplete bladder emptying related to DESD or impaired contractility may exist with incontinence. Stress incontinence and obstruction have been shown to coexist in women (Bradley and Rovner, 2004). Dysfunctional voiding (failure of the external sphincter to relax during voiding in a patient without neurologic disease) is associated with detrusor dysfunction and incontinence (Carlson et al, 2001). Although it is well known that urethral obstructions are common in men, it is not commonly known that 6% to 33% of women with persistent LUTS also have urethral obstruction (Groutz et al, 2000a; Carlson, et al, 2000). **In our opinion, all patients undergoing urodynamic testing should have both the storage and voiding phases evaluated whenever possible.**

The simultaneous measurement of detrusor pressure and urinary flow rate during voluntary voiding is the best way currently available to assess two critical parameters with respect to bladder and outlet function: detrusor contractility (normal versus impaired) and outlet resistance (obstructed versus unobstructed). Generally speaking, **pressure-flow studies identify three fundamental voiding states** (Kim and Boone, 1998):

1. **Low detrusor pressure and high flow rate (un-obstructed)**
2. **High detrusor pressure and low flow rate (obstructed)**
3. **Low detrusor pressure with low flow rate (impaired detrusor contractility)**

Although it is important to understand these three basic patterns, it is equally important to realize the limitations of such categorization. Unfortunately, pressure-flow studies do not always allow an absolute classification into one distinct category. For example, there are borderline cases as well as cases in which there is a combination of impaired contractility and obstruction. Bladder outlet obstruction is defined as the association of a low uroflow rate with a detrusor contraction of sufficient magnitude, duration, and speed to empty the bladder . Therefore, high voiding pressure and low uroflow rates identify the presence of bladder outlet obstruction. In men, several nomograms have been created to define bladder outlet obstruction. The ICS nomogram (Griffiths et al, 1997) and bladder outlet obstruction index (BOOI) combine several concepts to create a simplified method of determining obstruction in men (particularly with benign prostatic obstruction). The BOOI is defined as $p_{det}@Q_{max} - 2(Q_{max})$ (Abrams, 1999). A BOOI of 40 represents obstruction, and a BOOI less than 20 represents lack of obstruction. Values between 20 and 40 are equivocal.

The increased resistance encountered during voiding is directly responsible for the elevation of detrusor pressure as the bladder attempts to overcome such resistance. It is important that the external sphincter be relaxed during voiding to obtain an accurate measurement of voiding bladder pressure and flow rate. Voluntary or involuntary contraction of the external sphincter during voiding can have a dramatic effect on voiding pressure. Similar to the BOOI to evaluate obstruction, the bladder contractility index (BCI) has been derived from the work of Schafer (1995) to describe detrusor strength in men. BCI is defined as $p_{det}@Q_{max} + 5(Q_{max})$ (Abrams, 1999). A BCI greater than 150 represent strong contractility, 100 to 150 normal contractility, and less than 100 weak contractility. Thus, using the BOOI and BCI, one can evaluate obstruction and contractility, at least in men.

The Schafer nomogram describes six grades of urethral obstruction and five grades of detrusor contractility. For obstruction, grades 0 and 1 are unobstructed, grade 2 equivocal, and grades 3 to 6 represent increasing severity of obstruction. The five grades of detrusor contractility range from normal to very weak.

The nomograms and formulas used to diagnose obstruction and contractility in men are not fully applicable to women. Although the concepts are similar (high pressure–low flow = obstruction), the absolute values of pressure and flow differ greatly in normal and obstructed men and women. Blaivas and Groutz (2000) described a bladder outlet obstruction nomogram for use in women, and Nitti and coworkers (1999) based the diagnosis on low uroflow in the presence of a detrusor contraction of any magnitude coupled with the radiologic appearance of obstruction. Defreitas and colleagues (2004) used detrusor pressure–uroflow cutoffs for the diagnosis.

Sphincter Electromyography. EMG is the measurement and display of electrical activity recruited from the striated muscles of the urethral or anal sphincter or the perineal floor muscles. Sphincter EMG plays a dual role. In an indirect way, it provides kinesiologic information about the urethral sphincter and the pelvic floor muscles; it also provides objective data about the integrity of the innervation to these muscles and the synchronization between detrusor and external sphincter and is most useful to evaluate sphincter relaxation during a voluntary detrusor contraction. Sphincter EMG can be preformed with surface electrodes or needle electrodes placed directly into the urethral or anal sphincter. Although the most accurate and objective EMG is obtained by an experienced examiner using needle electrodes and oscilloscopic or audio control, the time, expense, requisite expertise, discomfort of the patient, and limited clinical utility render this technique impractical (Blaivas et al, 1979b; Blaivas and Fisher, 1981; Snooks et al, 1984a; Lose et al, 1985; Blaivas, 1988b; Smith et al, 1989; Fowler, 1991).

Multichannel Videourodynamics

Videourodynamics (VUDS) is the synchronous measurement and display of urodynamic parameters with radiographic visualization of the lower urinary tract. VUDS is the most precise diagnostic tool for evaluating disturbances of micturition (McGuire and Herlihy, 1977; Webster and Older, 1980; Blaivas and Fisher, 1981; Blaivas, 1988a). In these studies, radiographic contrast material is used as the infusant for cystometry. Depending on the level of sophistication required, other urodynamic parameters such as abdominal pressure, urethral pressure, uroflow, and sphincter EMG characteristics may be recorded as well. By simultaneously measuring multiple urodynamic variables, the clinician gains better insight into the underlying pathophysiologic process. Moreover, **because all variables are visualized simultaneously, it is possible to appreciate better their interrelationships and identify artifacts with ease, making VUDS the most precise diagnostic tool for voiding dysfunction.** Simultaneous fluoroscopic imaging of the bladder and bladder outlet during voiding can aid in the diagnosis and localization of obstruction in both men and women (Blaivas, 1988a, Nitti et al, 1999; Groutz et al, 2000). Also, external sphincter activity can be monitored fluoroscopically during voiding, which is helpful when EMG is equivocal. VUDS is also useful in cases of neurogenic voiding dysfunction and incontinence to assess the bladder outlet (e.g., detrusor–internal sphincter dyssynergia) and when vesicoureteral reflux is present as reflux volumes and pressures can be determined (Fig. 60–17).

Some clinicians prefer to use VUDS routinely, but there are specific circumstances in which this type of testing should always be employed. For example, in cases where routine multichannel urodynamics are equivocal or give an incomplete diagnosis, simultaneous fluoroscopic imaging can provide missing information. VUDS is useful in the evaluation of incontinence when incontinence cannot be demonstrated on routine urodynamic testing. VUDS is also helpful in cases in which it is important to visualize anatomy, such as in certain cases of pelvic prolapse. In the incontinent patient, VUDS also allows an accurate assessment of incontinence and leak point pressures when such measurements are difficult to obtain otherwise. Fluoroscopic monitoring during filling, voiding, and provocative maneuvers such as straining or coughing is far preferable to static films. In general, when these studies cannot be performed at the same time as urodynamic evaluation, it is better to perform the urodynamic studies first so that the functional status of the bladder and urethra is known at the time of radiologic examination.

Ambulatory Urodynamics

In ambulatory urodynamics, microtransducer catheters and a portable recording device are used to record bladder and abdominal pressures during natural bladder filling and emptying. The patient is able to move freely and to perform the activities that, according to his or her daily experience, provoke LUTS. Previous studies have shown a higher incidence of detrusor activity during ambulatory urodynamic monitoring compared with conventional cystometry. Up to 56% of patients with irritative LUTS and a stable bladder on conventional cystometry were found to have detrusor overactivity on ambulatory urodynamics (McInerney et al, 1991; Webb et al, 1991; Vereecken and Van Nuland, 1998; Swithinbank et al, 1999). The more physiologic filling and the lack of physical and behavioral restrictions during ambulatory urodynamics may explain this finding. Although ICS standards for terminology, methodology, analysis, and reporting of ambulatory urodynamic monitoring were suggested (Van Waalwijk van Doorn et al, 2000), **the use of this tool for routine clinical practice is limited by its potential artifacts, interpretation of findings, time consumption, techniques, and costs** (Heslington, 1997).

Endoscopy

Cystourethroscopy makes it possible to visualize the urethra and bladder and therefore facilitates the diagnosis of benign and malignant lesions. There are six specific areas pertaining to urinary incontinence where cystourethroscopy has been used (Tubaro et al, 2005): (1) observation of the female

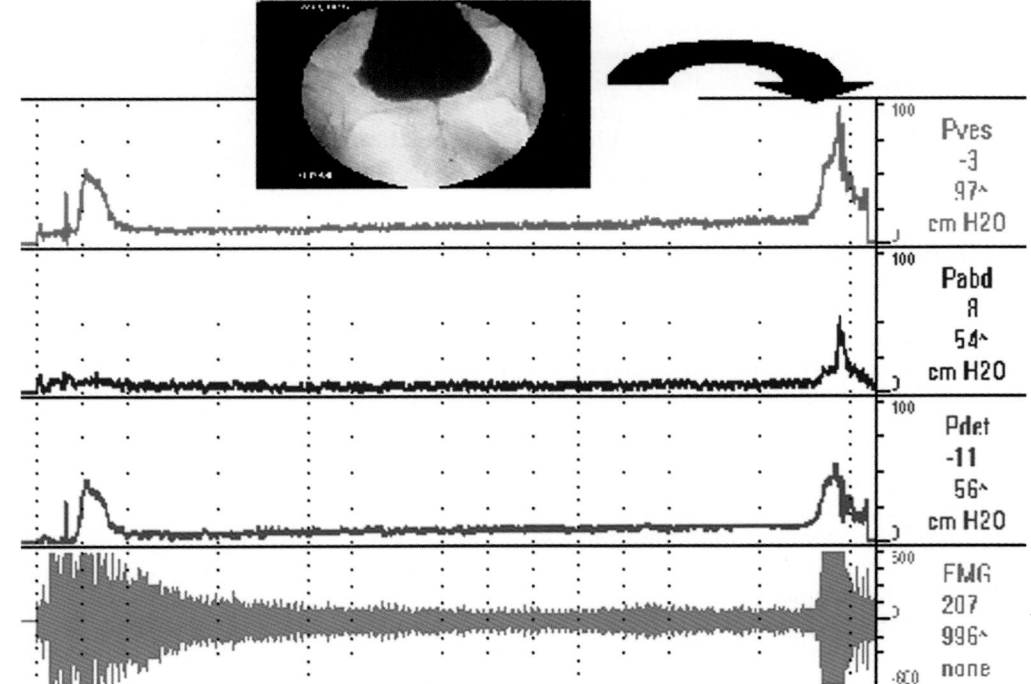

Figure 60–17. Videourodynamic evaluation of cervical spine–injured man with neurogenic voiding dysfunction with incontinence and incomplete bladder emptying. The urodynamic tracing clearly shows detrusor overactivity with detrusor–external sphincter dyssynergia (increased electromyographic [EMG] activity with involuntary contraction). However, it is only with the fluoroscopic view of the bladder outlet during an involuntary contraction that detrusor–internal sphincter dyssynergia is diagnosed (narrowed bladder neck).

SECTION XIV

sphincteric unit to assess its ability to coapt and close, (2) assessment of the bladder to rule out a concomitant condition that may cause or be associated with incontinence, (3) searching for extraurethral causes of incontinence, (4) intraoperative endoscopy during correction of stress incontinence, (5) evaluation of anatomy in postprostatectomy incontinence, and (6) assessment of the bladder outlet in men (e.g., prostate size, scarring and configuration, urethral stricture) with incontinence.

The literature does not support the use of urethroscopy to determine how well the female urethra functions or coapts (Aldridge et al, 1978; Sand et al, 1987; Scotti et al, 1990; Govier et al, 1994; Horbach and Ostergard, 1994). However, **those data did not take into account its utility in women with urethral diverticula, prior incontinence surgery, and radiation. In those instances we find cystourethroscopy useful** in assessing urethral and bladder neck scarring, caliber, mobility, and, in the case of diverticula, the location of the diverticular ostia. In men with urge incontinence and obstruction, it is useful to assess prostate size (for the purposes of planning surgery) and for the diagnosis of urethral and bladder neck strictures. **In men with postprostatectomy incontinence, endoscopy is helpful when anastomotic or other urethral stricture is suspected. Also, if surgical correction of incontinence is planned with either an artificial urinary sphincter or male perineal sling, it makes good clinical sense to perform endoscopy at some point prior to insertion** (Tubaro et al, 2005). With respect to evaluation of the male bladder outlet for urge incontinence associated with benign prostatic hyperplasia (BPH), the World Health Organization Third International Consultation on BPH (1995) considered cystoscopy to be an optional test in the standard patient with LUTS but recommended it as a guideline when surgical treatment is considered. We believe that cystourethroscopy will have its highest yield and should be considered in patients with persistent symptoms of urge incontinence despite proper treatment, failed anti-incontinence surgery, recurrent urinary tract infections, and hematuria (where it is essential) (Duldulao et al, 1997). **Endoscopy is also indicated in the evaluation of vesicovaginal fistula and extraurethral incontinence and should always be performed intraoperatively in incontinence surgery to rule out injury to the urinary tract.**

URINARY INCONTINENCE TREATMENT OVERVIEW

The approach to treating incontinence is predicated on a clear understanding of the underlying pathophysiology causing the symptom (i.e., whether it be caused by bladder or sphincteric dysfunction or a combination of both). As described in the previous sections of this chapter, the amount of information needed to decide on treatment varies depending on patients' characteristics and the type of treatment being considered. In this section, we present an overview of treatment options for urinary incontinence. Most of these treatments are discussed in greater detail in other chapters of this text. **Table 60–8 summarizes treatment guidelines for various causes of incontinence.** Many patients present with mixed symptoms (stress and urgency incontinence) and urodynamic findings (urody-

Table 60–8. Condition-Specific Treatments for Incontinence

Condition	Treatment
Detrusor overactivity	Treat underlying condition (e.g., UTI, bladder stone, urethral obstruction)
	Behavioral modification/lifestyle changes
	Pelvic floor muscle therapy
	Oral pharmacologic agents[*]
	Antimuscarinics
	Musculotropic relaxants
	Tricyclic antidepressants
	Intravesical agents[†]
	Oxybutynin
	Capsaicin
	Resiniferatoxin
	Botulinum toxin
	Neuromodulation
	Augmentation enterocystoplasty[*]
	Autoaugmentation[*]
	Denervation procedures
	Urinary diversion
Low bladder compliance	Oral pharmacologic agents[*]
	Antimuscarinics
	Musculotropic relaxants
	Tricyclic antidepressants
	Augmentation enterocystoplasty[*]
	Autoaugmentation[*]
	Denervation Procedures
Sphincteric dysfunction	Behavioral modification/lifestyle changes
	Pelvic floor muscle therapy
	Oral pharmacologic agents
	α-Adrenergic agonists
	Serotonin-norepinephrine reuptake inhibitors[‡]
	Urethral bulking agents
	Surgery
	Midurethral sling
	Pubovaginal sling
	Urethral/colposuspension
	Artificial urinary sphincter

[*]With or without intermittent self-catheterization.
[†]These treatments must be considered investigational and are "off label" in most countries.
[‡]Duloxetine is not approved by all regulatory agencies worldwide, including the U.S. Food and Drug Administration for the treatment of stress incontinence.

namic stress incontinence and detrusor overactivity). In such cases, treatment strategies must be individualized. Therapeutic decisions should be predicated by individual patients' preferences guided by their own risk-benefit analysis and expectation of outcomes. Although, in general, it makes good clinical sense to consider a stepwise algorithmic approach beginning with noninvasive treatments, many patients, when properly informed, opt for surgical treatment as an initial approach. This is especially true for conditions in which successful treatment is likely, for example, in women with uncomplicated sphincteric incontinence or men with severe prostatic obstruction.

Management with Continence Products

Not all incontinence can be cured, and some patients are not candidates for potentially curative treatments because of frailty, severity of incontinence, economics, personal preferences, or priorities or because they are awaiting treatment. In such cases, the goal of treatment is to minimize the effect on quality of life. A great variety of continence products can provide such "social continence" regardless of the etiology of the incontinence. Incontinence products include pads, sheaths, condom catheters, body-worn urinals and indwelling catheters to collect urine, occlusive devices and external clamps to prevent or reduce leakage, and intermittent catheterization to facilitate emptying (Cottenden et al, 2005).

Management of Incontinence Caused by Detrusor Overactivity or Low Bladder Compliance

Treatment of incontinence related to detrusor overactivity begins with a search for remediable causes including urinary tract infection, urethral obstruction, bladder stones, foreign bodies, and, in rare cases, bladder cancer. Neurologic causes are rarely remediable in the sense of treatment, but in some (multiple sclerosis, transverse myelitis) the disease process itself may remit. Occasionally, patients with herniated lumbar disks or tethered spinal cords respond to neurosurgical procedures. In men with prostatic obstruction and detrusor overactivity, OAB symptoms abate in approximately two thirds after transurethral resection of the prostate for benign prostatic obstruction (Cumming and Chisholm, 1992; Gormley et al, 1993). For bladder outlet obstruction caused by previous incontinence surgery in women, urethrolysis has been reported to be effective in treating symptoms of detrusor overactivity in 60% to 80% of patients (Foster and McGuire, 1993; Nitti and Raz, 1994; Austin et al, 1996; Petrou et al, 1999). There are no such data for women with urethral obstruction from prolapse, but in our experience the symptoms subside in the majority of patients who undergo prolapse repair. In women with mixed stress and urge incontinence, if the stress incontinence is the primary problem, successful treatment of stress incontinence has been associated with improvement or cure of the urge incontinence in 60% to 93% of patients (Chaikin et al, 1998; Morgan et al, 2000; Chou et al, 2003). More recent studies suggest that patients with the symptom of urgency incontinence with no demonstrable detrusor overactivity on CMG fare best with respect to treatment of urgency incontinence (Chou, 2003; Osman, 2003). Another study showed that low-pressure involuntary detrusor contractions responded better to treatment of stress incontinence than high-pressure involuntary detrusor contractions (Schrepferman et al, 2000).

When it is not possible to treat the underlying cause, the goal of therapy is to eliminate or suppress involuntary detrusor contractions. This may be accomplished by pharmacologic agents, behavior modification, pelvic floor rehabilitation, electrical stimulation, and neuromodulation or reconstructive surgery.

Rehabilitative Techniques: Behavior Modification, Pelvic Floor Muscle Training, Biofeedback, and Electrical Stimulation

Conservative techniques have been used for the treatment of both detrusor overactivity and sphincteric incontinence and are discussed in Chapter 63, Conservative Management of

Urinary Incontinence: Behavioral and Pelvic Floor Therapy, Urethral and Pelvic Devices. Briefly, behavioral therapy intends to teach the patient to regain control of the bladder and sphincter. It consists of a number of techniques including decreasing fluid intake, dietary and lifestyle changes, programmed voiding by the clock, and pelvic floor rehabilitation (Burgio and Goode, 1997; Fantl, 1998; O'Donnell, 1998; Payne, 1998; Wilson et al, 2005). With respect to lifestyle changes (weight loss, exercise or work, smoking cessation, diet), there is only a small amount of solid data that indicates an impact on incontinence (Wilson et al, 2005). Despite this, however, a commonsense approach to such changes, especially with respect to fluid intake, seems appropriate. Behavioral therapies have also been shown to work in concert with oral medications for urgency incontinence, at least in older women (Burgio et al, 2000).

Pelvic floor muscle training (PFMT) is an effective way to treat incontinence related to detrusor overactivity, although most of the data are in women. PFMT is defined as any program of repeated voluntary pelvic floor muscle contraction taught by a health care professional (Wilson et al, 2002). Biofeedback techniques may be used to assist in training. In addition, the use of vaginal cones on other devices as well as electrical stimulation that creates a "forced contraction" of the pelvic floor muscles may be considered in the realm of pelvic floor muscle rehabilitation. The biologic rationale is that a detrusor muscle contraction can be reflexly or voluntarily inhibited by a pelvic floor muscle contraction (Godec et al, 1975; Morrison, 1995; de Groat et al, 2001) and that single or repeated voluntary contractions can be used to control urgency and prevent urge leakage. PFMT can be conducted independently by the patient (usually with written instructions), with supervision and instruction, with weighted vaginal cones, with biofeedback techniques, and by using electrical stimulation. Although overall PFMT has been found to be effective for urgency incontinence (Wilson et al, 2005), the value of using different techniques is patient dependent. For example, although controlled studies have shown no advantage of biofeedback over supervised exercises (Burgio et al, 2003; Wilson et al, 2005), biofeedback is probably appropriate for the patient who cannot identify pelvic floor muscles on his or her own.

Oral Pharmacologic Treatment

Antimuscarinic agents are the mainstay of pharmacologic treatment of incontinence caused by detrusor overactivity. These agents are competitive inhibitors of acetylcholine that block the muscarinic effects. Some drugs have mixed actions, with a poorly defined "direct" action on bladder muscle (musculotropic relaxation) in addition to their predominant muscarinic action. If fully effective, antimuscarinics should result in abolition of the involuntary detrusor contractions; however, this rarely occurs. Partial efficacy results in an increase in the volume to the first involuntary detrusor contraction, a decrease in its amplitude, and an increase in bladder capacity. Five muscarinic receptor subtypes (M_1 to M_5) have been described. The M_2 and M_3 receptors are the most important for detrusor function. M_2 predominates over M_3 (about 4:1), but in the human detrusor M_3 receptors are thought to be the most important for contraction (Anderson, 1993; Chess-Williams et al, 2001); that is, stimulation of the

M_3 receptor causes muscle contraction. Stimulation of M_2 receptors has been shown to oppose sympathetically mediated smooth muscle relaxation mediated by β-adrenergic receptors (Hedge et al, 1997) and thus work indirectly to cause the detrusor to contract.

All of the active drugs must be given in an adequate dosage to ensure a physiologic effect. In practice, the dosage may be titrated until the patient is clinically improved or until untoward side effects occur. Common side effects consist of dry mouth, blurred vision, and constipation, corresponding to effects produced by muscarinic inhibition in other organ systems. Occasionally, supraventricular tachycardia may occur. Anticholinergic agents are contraindicated in certain patients with closed-angle glaucoma. In some patients, particularly those with neurologic disease and DESD, the drug may be so effective that the patient is unable to void at all and must be managed with intermittent self-catheterization. A list of antimuscarinic drugs used to treat incontinence related to detrusor overactivity is given in Table 60–9. A more detailed description of each agent can be found in Chapter 62, "Pharmacologic Management of Storage and Emptying Failure." Two commonly used antimuscarinics, oxybutynin and propiverine, have mixed actions.

Imipramine *is* a prototypical tricyclic antidepressant that has been used to treat incontinence. The exact mode of action has not been clearly demonstrated, but it exerts a direct relaxant effect on bladder smooth muscle and has sympathomimetic and central effects as well (Wein, 1995, 1998). The effects of imipramine on the bladder and urethra may be additive to those of anticholinergic agents. Consequently, a combination of the two may be useful. Most of the evidence for the use of imipramine to treat incontinence is based on retrospective studies and case series and not on randomized controlled trials (Anderson et al, 2005).

Table 60–9. Antimuscarinic Agents That Are Available Worldwide for the Treatment of Incontinence Secondary to Detrusor Overactivity

Antimuscarinic Drug	Grade of Recommendation*
Darifenacin	A
Oxybutynin[†]	A
Propiverine[†]	A
Tolterodine	A
Trospium	A
Solifenacin	A
Propantheline	B
Hyoscyamine	C

*Grade of recommendation is based on the finding of the third International Consultation on Incontinence (2005) according to the Oxford system. Grade A—depends on consistent level 1 evidence (good-quality randomized controlled trials [RTCs] or a meta-analysis of RTCs). Grade B—depends on consistent level 2 evidence (low-quality RTCs or meta-analysis of good-quality prospective cohort studies) or level 3 evidence (good-quality retrospective case-control studies or good-quality case series) studies or majority evidence from RTCs. Grade C—depends on level 4 evidence (expert opinion) or majority of evidence from level 2 or 3 studies.
[†]Mixed action drug.
Modified from Anderson KE, Appell R, Cardozo L, et al: Pharmacological treatment of urinary incontinence. In Abrams P, Cardozo L, Khoury S, Wein A (eds): Incontinence (Edition 2005) 3rd International Consultation on Incontinence. United Kingdom, Health Publications, 2005, pp 809-854.

Intravesical and Intradetrusor Therapies

Intravesical instillation of agents has been used to treat incontinence caused by detrusor overactivity. **Oxybutynin** has been administered in the bladder to decrease anticholinergic side effects. It must, however, be instilled regularly, usually two or three times a day. Intravesical oxybutynin has been shown to increase bladder capacity and produce clinical improvement in neurogenic and non-neurogenic detrusor overactivity with few side effects (Brendler et al, 1989; Kasabian et al, 1994; Palmer et al, 1997; Lose and Norgaard 2001).

Two intravesical agents, **capsaicin and resiniferatoxin (RTX)**, that block vanilloid receptors in the bladder have been used to treat detrusor overactivity. Vanilloids block C-fiber afferent nerves, which are implicated in the development of detrusor overactivity (by initiation of a reflex detrusor contraction) in certain pathologic conditions such as spinal cord injury. Blocking afferent stimulation can inhibit reflex contractions. Capsaicin is the main pungent ingredient in hot peppers of the genus *Capsicum*. On first contact with capsaicin, afferent neurons are stimulated, with no apparent gross difference whether the drug is applied to the peripheral or central endings or to the cell bodies of sensory neurons. Administration of capsaicin to peripheral nerve endings results in depolarization and discharge of action potentials, which in turn evokes burning pain. This stimulation produces an acute sensitization and then subsequently a prolonged period of desensitization, which blocks further stimulation and thus inhibits detrusor reflex contraction (Chancellor and de Groat, 1999). Capsaicin has been shown to reduce detrusor overactivity and improve symptoms in patients with multiple sclerosis and traumatic spinal cord injury. Most reports are case series (Fowler et al, 1992; Geirsson et al, 1995; Das et al, 1996; Cruz et al, 1997; De Ridder et al, 1997) with only limited randomized controlled studies available (de Seze et al, 1998, 2004). Widespread use has been limited by side effects of pain during and hematuria after instillation. RTX is a natural pungent principle from cactus-like plants of *Euphorbia resinifera* and has ultrapotent capsaicin-like activity. RTX is approximately 1000 times more potent than capsaicin but with minimal initial excitatory effects (Chancellor and de Groat, 1999). Its beneficial effects have been demonstrated in several controlled (Kim et al, 2003; de Seze et al, 2004; Giannantoni et al, 2004) and uncontrolled (Kuo, 2003; Watanabe et al, 2004) studies on neurogenic detrusor overactivity. RTX is an interesting alternative to capsaicin, but the drug is currently not in development because of problems in formulation (Anderson et al, 2005). The ideal dose, concentration, and duration interval between instillations have not been determined for either capsaicin or RTX.

Botulinum toxin (BTX) acts by inhibiting acetylcholine release at the presynaptic cholinergic junction in skeletal and smooth muscle, causing partial or complete paralysis. There are seven distinct serotypes (A, B, C, D, E, F, G) but only two, BTX A and B, are available for clinical use. There are several open-label reports showing efficacy of BTX-A injected into the detrusor of neuropathic (Schurch et al, 2000; Bagi and Biering-Sorensen, 2004; Reitz et al, 2004; Grosse et al, 2005) and non-neuropathic (Rapp et al, 2004; Smith et al, 2004; Kessler et al, 2005; Werner et al, 2005) detrusor overactivity patients. In addition, two randomized, controlled studies have shown efficacy in neuropathic patients (Giannantoni et al, 2004; Schurch et al, 2005). In the largest randomized, placebo-controlled study reported thus far, Schurch and colleagues (2005) showed that BTX-A at a dose of 200 or 300 units was superior to placebo injections in 59 patients with neurogenic detrusor overactivity from spinal cord injury or multiple sclerosis. Significant improvements over placebo were seen in urodynamic, incontinence episode, and quality of life parameters. Giannantoni and associates (2004) randomly assigned spinal cord–injured patients with detrusor overactivity to treatment with RTX versus BTX-A. Both groups had significant improvement in clinical and urodynamic parameters, with the patients receiving BTX-A showing more significant improvement.

BTX must be injected directly into the detrusor using an endoscopic technique. Most studies have used between 100 and 300 units of BTX-A injected at 20 to 30 different sites. However, the ideal concentration, dose, number, and location of injection sites have yet to be determined. A favorable response to BTX-A occurs in about 7 days (Anderson et al, 2005), although it can take up to 30 days to see a maximal response (Smith et al, 2005). A favorable response should last for 6 to 9 months (Anderson et al, 2005). Safety is satisfactory with most adverse events being related to hematuria, urinary tract infection, and urinary retention (which patients must be warned of). There are limited data on BTX-B for incontinence (Dykstra et al, 2003), and it is too early to determine whether it will have results similar to those with BTX-A. In summary, preliminary studies on the use of BTX to treat incontinence look promising. Further randomized, controlled studies on neuropathic and non-neuropathic detrusor overactivity will determine the efficacy, safety, and cost effectiveness of this novel treatment.

Surgical Treatment of Detrusor Overactivity Incontinence

When conservative and pharmacologic treatments for detrusor overactivity incontinence fail, there are a number of surgical procedures that can be performed for the patient who is significantly bothered by his or her symptoms. Surgical treatments include sacral nerve neuromodulation, bladder denervation, and bladder augmentation.

Sacral Nerve Neuromodulation. Sacral nerve stimulation (SNS) was introduced in the 1980s (Schmidt, 1988; Tanagho and Schmidt, 1988) and has **established itself as a second-line treatment for incontinence secondary to the overactive detrusor.** The underlying principle of neuromodulation for detrusor overactivity is **based on the induction of somatic afferent inhibition of sensory processing in the spinal cord.** Pudendal afferent input to the sacral cord is thought to inhibit or "turn off" supraspinally mediated hyperactive voiding. Technically, the treatment is done in two steps. Stage 1 is a "screening test" in which a stimulation lead (temporary or permanent) is placed next to the dorsal root of S3 and stimulated for a period of days (temporary) to weeks (permanent). If the patient has a positive response (usually defined as greater than 50% improvement in symptoms), the patient may go on to stage 2, in which a permanent neurostimulator or "pacemaker" is implanted in the soft tissue of the buttock after connection to the S3 lead. To date, most of the data on SNS

are for the non-neurogenic population, with limited data available on its effect in patients with neurogenic voiding dysfunction (Guys et al, 2004).

A number of reports show the efficacy of SNS for the treatment of urgency incontinence (Elabbady et al, 1994; Bosch and Groen, 1995; Shaker and Hassouna, 1998a). The initial report of a randomized controlled study of SNS for the treatment of refractory urge incontinence appeared in 1999. The study did not use a placebo or sham group, but rather 76 patients were randomly assigned to immediate versus delayed (6 months later) treatment. At 6 months, the patients assigned to immediate implantation showed a significant reduction in incontinence episodes, incontinence severity, and pad use compared with the delayed implantation group. Forty-seven percent were completely dry and another 29% had a greater than 50% reduction in incontinence episodes. Other nonrandomized studies, which included patients from a U.S. registry (Pettit et al, 2002) and an Italian registry (Spinelli et al, 2001), showed similar results. In the U.S. registry study (Pettit et al, 2002), 63% of patients had a greater than 50% reduction in incontinence episodes. In the Italian registry study (Spinelli et al, 2001), 39% of patients were completely dry and another 23% had less than one incontinence episode daily. Two reports have suggested that the effect of SNS may dwindle over time (Bosch and Groen, 2000; Elhilali et al, 2005). SNS is also used for frequency/urgency (Hassouna et al, 2000) and idiopathic urinary retention (Shaker and Hassouna, 1998b; Jonas et al, 2001).

Denervation Procedures. Denervation techniques include bladder transection and reattachment, either by open surgery or endoscopically; complete S2 to S4 rhizotomy; partial rhizotomy; and subtrigonal phenol or alcohol injections. **There is little documentation of long-term efficacy of these denervation procedures, and many of the techniques are associated with considerable morbidity, and, for practical purposes, they have been abandoned** (Nordling et al, 1986; Lucas and Thomas, 1987; Chapple et al, 1991; Ramsay et al, 1992). Furthermore, despite an initial short-term response, the long-term results are often dominated by the development of low bladder compliance or recurrent detrusor overactivity. Sacral rhizotomy is reserved for the paraplegic or quadriplegic population. Posterior rhizotomy may be combined with the placement of a neurostimulator on the anterior nerve roots to inhibit involuntary contractions and stimulate spontaneous voiding (Egon et al, 1998). In 1959, Ingelman-Sundberg described a transvaginal technique intended to accomplish partial denervation of the subtrigonal nerve supply to the bladder by selectively dividing the preganglionic nerves near the inferior surface of the bladder through a transvaginal incision. Several authors have reported success (Hodgkinson and Drukker, 1977; Cespedes et al, 1996; Westney et al, 2002), but outcome measures have included mostly patients' assessments done in a retrospective fashion. Thus, the procedure has never gained acceptance.

Augmentation Cystoplasty. Augmentation cystoplasty increases bladder capacity and decreases detrusor overactivity by enlarging the bladder with the addition of a bowel segment and possibly by disrupting the detrusor. In a large majority of patients with refractory detrusor overactivity, **augmentation enterocystoplasty is effective, provided that these basic prin-**

ciples are followed: (1) the intestinal segment is detubularized by incising the antimesenteric border, (2) the segment is reconfigured into the approximate shape of a half-sphere, (3) a wide anastomosis between the reconfigured bowel and the bladder is performed, and (4) a large bladder capacity is achieved. Classically, augmentation enterocystoplasty has been performed in patients with neurogenic voiding dysfunction, but it has been shown to be effective for patients with neurogenic (Luangkhot et al, 1991; Herschorn and Hewitt, 1998; Chartier-Kastler et al, 2000; Khastigar et al, 2003; Zachoval et al, 2003; Blaivas et al, 2005) and non-neurogenic detrusor overactivity (Mundy and Stephensen, 1985; Flood et al, 1995). Many patients, however, require intermittent self-catheterization after augmentation and need to be prepared to do this prior to consenting to the operation (Kockelbergh et al, 1991; Luangkhot et al, 1991; Robertson et al, 1991; Appell, 1998). Complications of augmentation cystoplasty include metabolic disturbances (hyperchloremic acidosis), urinary tract infections, stone formation, perforation, and malignancy.

Autoaugmentation of the bladder was initially described by Cartwright and Snow (1989) as an alternative to enterocystoplasty in children with neuropathic bladder. Autoaugmentation may be performed by incision (detrusor myotomy) or excision (detrusor myectomy) of a portion (usually the anterior, lateral, and superior surface) of the detrusor muscle (Stothers et al, 1994). Either technique creates a mucosal bulge or pseudodiverticulum, which should increase capacity and decrease storage pressure. There have been several reports of successful short-term outcomes after detrusor myectomy in children (Cartwright and Snow, 1989) and in adults with neuropathic bladder (Kennelly et al, 1994; Stohrer et al, 1995). However, longer term follow-up in children (MacNeily et al, 2003) and adults with non-neurogenic urge incontinence (ter Muelen et al,1997) showed disappointing results. One study compared a single-institution experience with autoaugmentation and enteroplasty in a mixed population (Leng et al, 1999). They concluded that detrusor myectomy is a safe method of bladder augmentation for most clinical indications and does not hinder future enterocystoplasty. Although it is a small series, careful review of the data would suggest that in the neurogenic population, enteroplasty is better.

In some patients with severe refractory incontinence, a urinary diversion by continent or incontinent means may serve as the best option. For example, in patients with overactive detrusor or impaired compliance secondary to radiation or in patients unable to catheterize through the urethra, diversion may be preferred over augmentation.

Management of Incontinence Caused by Sphincteric Dysfunction (Stress Incontinence)

Rehabilitative Techniques: Behavior Modification, Pelvic Floor Muscle Training, and Electrical Stimulation

As described previously, conservative techniques including decreasing fluid intake, dietary and lifestyle changes, and programmed voiding by the clock have been used to treat SUI

and seem to make common sense, especially in less severe and bothersome cases (Burgio and Goode, 1997; Fantl, 1998; O'Donnell, 1998; Payne, 1998; Wilson et al, 2005). After these techniques, PFMT is next in the line of conservative management for SUI. For some motivated patients who are willing to pursue the rigors of long-term treatment, a reasonable degree of improvement can be expected from behavioral therapy. Although there is a paucity of data on long-term therapy, effective treatment probably requires a lifetime commitment. As with the treatment of any other chronic condition that has an inevitable toll on lifestyle and self-perception, encouragement, close follow-up, and flexibility are as important to a successful treatment as any individual therapeutic method.

The rationale for PFMT in the treatment of SUI is to improve strength or timing, or both, of the pelvic floor muscle contraction. The end result should be (1) a stronger sphincteric unit that is better able to resist increases in abdominal pressure or (2) better voluntary use of a pelvic muscle contraction in anticipation of an event (e.g., a cough), or both. Since the original description of "Kegel's exercises" (Kegel, 1948), many studies have supported the use of PFMT in general for the treatment of SUI; however, no ideal exercise program has been established. Also, prior to beginning a program of PFMT, patients should be assessed to ensure that they are able to perform an adequate pelvic floor muscle contraction. Once this is established, patients can begin a regular program of exercises.

Several randomized studies have shown that PFMT is better than no treatment for women with SUI (Henalla et al, 1989; Burns et al, 1993; Bo et al, 1999). It appears that the most intensively supervised PFMT programs produce the best results, but there does not appear to be any benefit of biofeedback-assisted PFMT in the general population (Wilson et al, 2005). However, biofeedback-assisted PFMT may be useful on an individual basis for women who have difficulty identifying pelvic floor muscles and doing exercises properly. Conclusions from the third International Consultation on Incontinence (Wilson et al, 2005) state that PFMT and vaginal cones (weights) have similar efficacy and that PFMT appears to be superior to electrical stimulation for the treatment of SUI in women. Most would agree that when pelvic floor therapies are successful they are more likely to produce improvement than cure. Burgio and coauthors (2003) evaluated factors that predict success of a biofeedback-assisted PFMT program for women with SUI. In 60 women receiving such therapy with success defined as at least 75% reduction in incontinence episodes, they found that the variables that predicted success were degree of incontinence (10 or fewer episodes a week) and no prior evaluation or treatment of incontinence. Fifteen percent of women were cured in that study.

PFMT has been used in two ways in men with postprostatectomy stress incontinence: proactively and as a treatment method after such incontinence has been established. Two randomized studies show some benefit to starting a program of exercises immediately or shortly after catheter removal (Van Kampen et al, 2000; Parekh et al, 2003). When comparing treated and nontreated men, most of the benefit (or difference) is seen in the first 3 to 6 months. By 1 year the two groups are similar. Therefore, it appears that PFMT may get men to their ultimate level of continence faster but after 1

year does not affect that level of continence. With respect to treatment established of postprostatectomy incontinence, a Cochrane review of only five available randomized studies on different conservative managements was unable to find any definitive benefit as symptoms tended to improve over time irrespective of treatment (Moore et al, 2001).

Pharmacologic Treatment

Until recently, pharmacologic treatment has been largely confined to α-adrenergic agonists and estrogens. α-**Adrenergic agents** are thought to increase urethral muscle tone and resistance and thus improve the symptoms of SUI. Such agents include ephedrine, pseudoephedrine, midodrine, and phenylpropanolamine (PPA). However, a review of randomized and quasi-randomized studies by the Agency for Health Care Policy and Research (1992) and the Cochrane database (Alhasso et al, 2003) suggests that **there is only weak evidence to suggest that any α-adrenergic agent is better than placebo.** Questionable efficacy plus the side effects, which include hypertension, palpitations, sleep disturbances, headache, and tremor, have resulted in limited use of these compounds in the treatment of SUI. The future of α-adrenergic agents for the treatment of SUI is probably dependent on the development of a more "uroselective" agent.

Agents that inhibit the uptake of serotonin and norepinephrine have also been used to treat SUI. Imipramine, a tricyclic antidepressant, has been shown to have a positive effect on SUI in women in two open-label studies (Gilja et al, 1984; Lin et al, 1999). There are no randomized controlled trials of imipramine for SUI in women or men. **Duloxetine** is a combined serotonin-norepinephrine reuptake inhibitor that has been shown to decrease incontinence episode frequency versus placebo in women with SUI in several randomized, controlled trials (Norton et al, 2002, Dmochowski et al, 2003; Millard et al, 2004; Van Kerrebroeck et al, 2004). The proposed mechanism is stimulation of the pudendal nerve at the level of Onuf's nucleus in the sacral cord, causing increased urethral sphincter tone (Thor and Katofiasc, 1995). At a dose of 40 mg twice daily, duloxetine decreased incontinence episodes by about 51% versus 33% for placebo (Norton et al, 2002; Dmochowski et al, 2003; Millard et al, 2004; Van Kerrebroeck et al, 2004). Side effects include nausea, dry mouth, and fatigue (Norton et al, 2002; Dmochowski et al, 2003; Millard et al, 2004; Van Kerrebroeck et al, 2004). Duloxetine is approved for the treatment of SUI in women in several countries around the world. It is not approved in the United States for that indication at this time.

Estrogens have been used empirically to treat incontinence in women at least since the report of Salmon and colleagues (1941), but debate regarding their efficacy, site of action, route of administration, and dosage persists. Despite a plethora of animal and human data on the effects of estrogen on the lower urinary tract, its efficacy for the treatment of SUI has not been established. In both animals and humans, there is a high concentration of estrogen receptors in the urethra (Iosif et al, 1981; Batra and Iosif, 1983; Fantl et al, 1988). Estrogens appear to affect the lower urinary tract by enhancing α-adrenergic receptor density and sensitivity (Caine and Raz, 1975; Levin et al, 1981; Larsson et al, 1984), by enhancing neuronal sensitivity and transmitter metabolism, and by exerting trophic effects on urethral mucosa, submucosa, and pelvic floor/peri-

urethral collagen (Bump and Friedman, 1986; Bump et al, 1988b; Fantl et al, 1988; Versi et al, 1988). After menopause, urethral pressure parameters normally decrease somewhat (Rud, 1980; Versi et al, 1988), and although this is generally conceded to be related in some way to lower estrogen levels, whether the actual changes occur in smooth muscle, blood circulation, supporting tissues, or the mucosal seal mechanism is still largely a matter of speculation. Karram and Bhatia (1989) administered estrogens, either oral or vaginal, to women with premature ovarian failure and found a significant increase in the pressure transmission ratio to the proximal and middle sections of the urethra in women using vaginal estrogens only. **Although some researchers have noted a beneficial effect of estrogen for women with stress incontinence, the majority of data suggests that there is little if any effect on the symptom of stress incontinence whether estrogen is given systemically or topically** (Hextall, 2000). This, coupled with the data from the HERS (Grady et al, 2001) and WHI (Hendrix et al, 2005) trials showing no benefit and perhaps even a negative effect of systemic estrogen replacement on continence in postmenopausal women, suggests that **estrogen should no longer be considered part of the routine treatment armamentarium for women with SUI.**

Urethral Bulking Agents

Urethral bulking agents have been used for decades to treat SUI in women. Urethral bulking agents probably work by augmenting the submucosal layer of the urethra and increasing the compressive force inward toward the urethral lumen. They have no effect on urethral mobility. A variety of substances have been reported to be safe and effective including bovine glutaraldehyde cross-linked collagen (McGuire and Appell, 1994; Faerber, 1996; Herschorn et al, 1996; Khullar et al, 1997; Corcos and Fournier, 1999; Bent et al, 2001a), carbon-coated zirconium beads (Lightner et al, 2001; Chrouser et al, 2004), polytetrafluoroethylene (Politano et al, 1974; Politano 1982; Herschorn and Glazer, 2000), hyaluronic acid/dextranomer (Chapple et al, 2005), polydimethylsiloxane elastomer (Barranger et al, 2000; Tamanini et al, 2003), dimethyl sulfoxide in ethylene vinyl alcohol (Dmochowski and Appell, 2003), and autologous tissues such as fat and cartilage (Santarosa and Blaivas, 1994; Bent et al, 2001a). These agents are usually injected in a retrograde fashion using cystoscopic guidance or special delivery systems. In most cases, periurethral injections are simple office procedures, which may be accomplished with the patient under local anesthesia.

Most published trials on urethral bulking agents in women are of relatively short duration, with only a few reporting follow-up of more than 1 year (Smith et al, 2005). **To date, no one bulking agent has been shown to be consistently superior to another.** In general, early outcomes show a 25% cure, 50% improvement, and 25% failure rate. Duration of effect is not permanent and reinjections are required. Although bulking agents were originally indicated for ISD without urethral hypermobility, several studies using collagen suggest that outcomes are independent of urethral mobility (Herschorn et al, 1996; Corcos and Fournier 1999; Bent et al, 2001b). Given the durability of response, urethral bulking agents seem ideally indicated for patients who are not medically fit for surgery, those wishing to defer or avoid surgery, and those in whom surgery has failed. Patients and physicians must consider the expectations of treatment as well as potential morbidity (versus surgery) when deciding on bulking agents.

Urethral bulking agents have been used in men with post-prostatectomy SUI, but with less favorable results than in women. The experience as recorded in the literature is mostly with collagen and silicone macroparticles. For collagen, "success rates" vary from 36% to 69% with 4% to 20% of patients reported dry (McGuire and Appell, 1994; Aboseif et al, 1996; Cummings et al, 1996; Sanchez-Ortiz et al, 1997; Smith et al, 1998; Cespedes et al, 1999; Klutke et al, 1999; Tiguert et al, 1999). However, a critical review of the literature shows that in most studies endpoints are subjectively based, sustained total dryness rates are low, and multiple injections are required to achieve modest improvement (Herschorn et al, 2005). Polydimethyl-siloxane elastomer has also been used to treat postprostatectomy stress incontinence, but after initial improvement rapid deterioration was seen with success rates of 40%, 71%, 33%, and 26% at 1, 3, 6, and 12 months, respectively (Bugel et al, 1999). Thus, available data suggest that urethral bulking agents achieve only modest success rates, with low cure rates and relatively short duration of effect. It remains to be seen whether other agents will produce better, longer lasting results in men with postprostatectomy incontinence.

Surgery for Stress Incontinence in Females

The goal of surgical treatment for SUI in women is to restore urethral support and recreate a proper backboard to resist increases in abdominal pressure or to restore the coaptative forces of the urethra, or both. In cases of urethral hypermobility, it is important to restore support, whereas in the nonmobile urethra with a low ALPP, restoring compression and coaptation are important. A plethora of surgical procedures have been described over the past century, and there are few comparative data among the different procedures. It is only recently that specific objective and subjective outcome measures, collected in a prospective manner, have been utilized regularly in reporting results. Thus, one must be guarded in comparing data from procedures that are predominantly retrospective (even if quite good) with data that are prospective.

Surgical treatment of sphincteric incontinence may be divided into sling procedures, suspension procedures (transvaginal and retropubic), and sphincter prostheses. These surgical modalities are discussed in detail in their appropriate chapters. The choice of procedure depends upon several factors, including (1) the underlying condition—degree of urethral mobility and leak point pressure, (2) available outcome data on various procedures, (3) surgeon preference and expertise, and (4) patient-related factors such as age, comorbid conditions, desire for a fast recovery, and avoidance of potential complications.

In 1997, the AUA Stress Urinary Incontinence Clinical Guideline Panel analyzed published outcome data on surgical procedures to treat female SUI with the goal of producing practice recommendations based primarily on outcome data from the literature (Leach et al, 1997). With respect to general practice guidelines, the panel concluded that patients should be informed of the available surgical alternatives and the estimated risks and benefits of each procedure, including complications and how they would be treated. As far as evaluating individual procedures, **although much of the available data**

was inadequate, the panel concluded that retropubic suspensions (e.g., colposuspension) and slings were the most efficacious procedures for long-term success. These procedures had 84% and 83% cure/improvement rates at a minimum of 4 years of follow-up. The retropubic procedures reviewed consisted mainly of Marshall-Marchetti-Krantz urethropexy and the Burch colposuspension; the sling procedures were predominantly those done with autologous fascia or older synthetic materials.

More recent publications on longer-term outcomes of Burch colposuspension (Langer et al, 2001; Demirici et al, 2001) and autologous fascia pubovaginal sling (Chaikin et al, 1998; Morgan et al, 2000) support the findings of the AUA panel. A number of allograft and xenograft materials have been used for slings, including allograft fascia (Amundsen et al, 2000; Elliott and Boone, 2000; Flynn and Yap, 2002; Walsh et al, 2002), allograft dermis, (Crivellaro et al, 2004), porcine dermis (Barrington et al, 2002; Arunkalaivanan and Barrington, 2003), and small intestine submucosa (Rutner et al, 2003). These materials have shown some short-term success, but with longer followup some materials have shown higher failure rates (Brown and Govier, 2002; Fitzpatrick et al, 2004). At this time there is no high-level evidence to suggest that any biologic material should replace autologous fascia, and thus these materials should probably be used selectively (Smith et al, 2005).

In the decade since the AUA Stress Urinary Incontinence Panel guidelines were published, midurethral tension-free synthetic slings such as the tension-free vaginal tape (TVT) (Ulmsten et al, 1996) **have become the most popular procedures worldwide for the treatment of female SUI. Available short- and intermediate-term prospective data suggest that these procedures give comparable results to traditional pubovaginal sling and colposuspension with cure rates in the 80% to 94% range; however, there is some concern about serious complications during the learning curve and the long-term consequences of urethral and vaginal erosions of the sling material** (Ulmsten et al, 1998; Meschia et al, 2001; Nilsson et al, 2001; Tseng et al, 2005). A randomized, controlled trial of TVT versus Burch colposuspension showed comparable results at 2 years. Modifications of the original TVT procedure done by a transobturator approach to minimize morbidity have shown results similar to the traditional retropubic approach at 1 year (Fischer et al, 2005). Although longer-term data and selection criteria for patients are not yet available, this procedure seems to hold promise.

The artificial urinary sphincter (AUS) has been used to treat SUI in women. Although initially thought to be a procedure for failed prior surgery (Kowalczyk and Mulcahy, 2000), it has also been used successfully as a primary procedure for neurogenic (Thomas et al, 2002; Toh and Diokno, 2002) and non-neurogenic (Costa et al, 2001) SUI. Despite this, because of the high success rates of sling surgery and retropubic suspensions, the AUS is rarely used in women. In cases of refractory SUI with severe sphincteric damage, urinary diversion can be considered. This usually occurs in cases of multiple prior surgeries (often with complications) or pelvic radiation, or both.

In cases of mixed incontinence with a predominant stress component, successful surgical correction of stress incontinence has been shown to cure or improve urge incontinence in 50% to 93% of cases. This has been shown for Burch colposuspension (Osman, 2003), pubovaginal sling (McGuire et al, 1987; Chaikin et al, 1998; Chou et al, 2003; Osman, 2003), and TVT (Rezapour and Ulmsten, 2001a, 2001b; Segal et al, 2004). Certain urodynamic findings such as low- versus high-pressure detrusor overactivity (Schrepferman et al, 2000) and no demonstrable detrusor overactivity (Osman, 2003) may predict a better response of urge incontinence to surgery for SUI. In women who have concurrent pelvic organ prolapse with SUI, it is usually advisable to correct prolapse at the same time as SUI when surgical intervention is considered.

Surgery for Stress Incontinence in Males

SUI is most commonly a result of prostate surgery but may also result from trauma or neurologic injury. **The AUS has been the "gold standard" for the treatment of SUI in males for years.** In the last several years, nonmechanical compressive procedures have been reintroduced and male sling procedures are gaining popularity. However, the AUS remains the most effective long-term surgical treatment. Ultimately, the choice of AUS will be based upon patients' dexterity, economics, degree of incontinence, and patients' expectations from surgery. Success rates for AUS as defined by a continence status of zero to one pad per day range from 59% to 87% (Goldwasser et al, 1987; Montague, 1992; Perez and Webster, 1992; Martins and Boyd, 1995; Fleshner and Herschorn, 1996; Haab et al, 1997; Klijn et al, 1998, Gousse et al, 2001) and pad-free rates range from 10% to 72% (Perez and Webster, 1992; Martins and Boyd, 1995; Littewiller et al, 1996; Elliott and Barrett, 1998; Kuznetsov et al, 2000; Clemens et al, 2001; Gousse et al, 2001; Gomha and Boone, 2002). Nevertheless, very high satisfaction rates of patients of 87% to 90% are consistently reported, even without total continence (Fleshner and Herschorn, 1996; Littewiller et al, 1996; Haab et al, 1997). It must also be noted that most AUS series include patients with very severe and even total urinary incontinence. One caveat with the AUS is the potential need for periodic revisions or explantation because of mechanical failure, urethral atrophy, infection, and erosion. Revision and explantation rates vary considerably among studies with reports of 10.8% to 44.6% and 7% to 17%, respectively (Gousse et al, 2001). Actuarial freedom from revision at 5 years is estimated at 50% (Klijn et al, 1998). Despite this, long-term efficacy of the AUS was demonstrated by Fulford and colleagues, who reported that at 10- to 15-year follow-up, 75% of patients with an implanted AUS either still had or died with a functioning device (Fulford et al, 1997).

The male sling procedure utilizes the concept of passive external urethral compression originally described in the early 1970s by Kaufman (1970, 1972, 1973). At that time a high rate of failure, septic complications and pelvic pain, as well as the advent of the mechanical AUS led to the abandonment of the Kaufman prosthesis. More recently, with the higher prevalence of postprostatectomy incontinence and patients' wishes for less invasive surgery and a nonmechanical device, the concept has been revisited. Procedures have been developed that rely on compression from the ventral side of the urethra rather than the circular compression caused by a natural or artificial sphincter. Schaeffer and Stamey described the bulbourethral sling, which uses Dacron bolsters placed under the urethra and suspended to the anterior rectus fascia by sutures. In the initial report from two centers, 64 patients were included and 56% were "dry" and 8% "improved" at a mean follow-up of 22.4 months (Schaeffer et al, 1998). Almost one third needed secondary retightening procedures, and patients with radiation fared poorly. Subsequently, Clemens and coauthors (1999) reported a questionnaire-based study of 66 men from a single institution; 41% were cured and 51% improved, but mean follow-up was only 9.6 months. Other small series have described bulbourethral slings using a polypropylene mesh graft with or without a porcine dermis backing to reduce the risk of erosion, with similar short-term success rates (Migliari et al, 2003; John, 2004).

More recently, the bone-anchored perineal sling has been popularized. Comiter (2002) reported a 76% cure and 14% "substantially improved" rate in 21 men with postprostatectomy incontinence using polypropylene mesh with a mean follow-up of 12 months. An update, with a mean follow-up of 25 months in 36 men, reported that 67% were pad free and 14% used one pad per day (Ullrich and Comiter, 2004). Onur and colleagues (2004) used several different sling materials (biologic and synthetic) and reported 41% of 46 patients dry and 35% improved (50% reduction in the number of pads) with a mean follow-up of 17 months. Seventy-two percent of patients stated that postoperative urinary leakage was a small to no problem on the UCLA/RAND questionnaire, and 59% were completely satisfied with the procedure (Rajpurkar et al, 2005). In the short term, in a limited number of small series, the male sling appears to perform reasonably well. However, interpretation of results must be guarded as definitions of cure or success vary greatly. In addition, most studies include patients with less than 1 year follow-up. Selection criteria for who are the best candidates have not yet been defined, but preliminary data suggest that patients with lower to moderate grades of incontinence fare better (Onur et al, 2004; Huckabay et al, 2005).

As with the treatment of severe refractory incontinence related to bladder abnormalities, urinary diversion may be considered for severe cases of refractory sphincteric dysfunction in men. This usually occurs in cases of radiation and radiation plus surgery, where urethral strictures and urethral insufficiency can coexist.

SUGGESTED READINGS

Abrams P, Cardozo L, Fall M, et al: The standardisation of terminology in lower urinary tract function: Report from the standardisation sub-committee of the International Continence Society. Urology 2003;61:37-49.

Anderson KE, Appell R, Cardozo L, et al: Pharmacological treatment of urinary incontinence. In Abrams P, Cardozo L, Khoury S, Wein A (eds): Incontinence (edition 2005) 3rd International Consultation on Incontinence. United Kingdom, Health Publications, 2005, pp 809-854.

Blaivas JG: The neurophysiology of micturition: A clinical study of 550 patients. J Urol 1982;127:958-963.

Blaivas JG, Chancellor MB (eds): Atlas of Urodynamics. Baltimore, Williams & Wilkins, 1996.

Burgio KL, Goode PS, Locher JL, et al: Behavioral training with and without biofeedback in the treatment of urge incontinence in older women: A randomized controlled trial. JAMA 2002;288:2293-2299.

Chaikin DC, Rosenthal J, Blaivas JG: Pubovaginal fascial sling for all types of stress urinary incontinence: Long-term analysis. J Urol 1998;160:1312-1316.

Chou ECL, Flisser AJ, Panagopolous G, Blaivas JG: Effective treatment for mixed incontinence with a pubovaginal sling. J Urol 2003;170:494-497.

DeLancey JO: Structural support of the urethra as it relates to stress urinary incontinence: The hammock hypothesis. Am J Obstet Gynecol 1994;170:1713-1720.

DeLancey JO: The pathophysiology of stress urinary incontinence in women and its implications for surgical treatment. World J Urol 1997;15:268-274.

Fleischmann N, Flisser AJ, Blaivas JG, Panagopoulos G: Sphincteric urinary incontinence: Relationship of vesical leak point pressure, urethral mobility and severity of incontinence. J Urol 2003;169:999-1002.

Hextall A: Oestrogens and lower urinary tract function. Maturitas 2000;36: 83-92.

Hunskaar S, Burgio K, Clark A, et al: Epidemiology of urinary (UI) and faecal (FI) incontinence and pelvic organ prolapse (POP). In Abrams P, Cardozo L, Khoury S, Wein A (eds): Incontinence (edition 2005) 3rd International Consultation on Incontinence. United Kingdom, Health Publications, 2005, pp 255-312.

McGuire EJ, Fitzpatrick CC, Wan J, et al: Clinical assessment of urethral sphincter function. J Urol 1993;150:1452-1454.

McGuire EJ, Woodside JR, Borden TA, Weiss RM: Prognostic value of urodynamic testing in myelodysplastic patients. J Urol 1981;126:205-209.

Nitti VW (ed): Practical Urodynamics. Philadelphia, WB Saunders, 1998.

Osman T: Stress incontinence surgery for patients presenting with mixed incontinence and a normal cystometrogram. BJU Int 2003;92:964-968.

Petros PP, Ulmsten U: An integral theory of female urinary incontinence. Experimental and clinical considerations. Acta Obstet Gynecol Scand Suppl 1990;153:7-31.

Resnick NM: Urinary incontinence in the elderly. Med Grand Rounds 1984;3:281-290.

Schafer W, Abrams P, Limin L, et al: Good urodynamic practices: uroflowmetry, filling cystometry, and pressure-flow studies. Neurourol Urodyn 2002;21:261-274.

Ward KL, Hilton P: A prospective multicenter randomized trial of tension-free vaginal tape and colposuspension for primary urodynamic stress incontinence: Two-year follow-up. Am J Obstet Gynecol 2004;190:324-331.

Wein AJ: Classification of neurogenic voiding dysfunction. J Urol 1981;125: 605-609.

61 Overactive Bladder

PAUL ABRAMS, MD • MARCUS DRAKE, DM, MA

ETIOLOGY

PREVALENCE

CLINICAL ASSESSMENT

DISTINGUISHING OVERACTIVE BLADDER FROM PAINFUL BLADDER SYNDROME

URODYNAMIC CONFIRMATION OF DETRUSOR OVERACTIVITY

MANAGEMENT

In 1996, Wein and Abrams were asked to organize a consensus conference on the "unstable bladder" (Abrams and Wein, 1997). They were unhappy with the proposed title because this would, by the then current International Continence Society definitions, preclude discussion on the overactive detrusor, which owed its genesis to neurologic causes. The terms **unstable bladder/detrusor instability** and **detrusor hyperreflexia** were introduced 30 years ago. Their introduction has an interesting history: at that time the English-speaking world had adopted Patrick Bates' term *unstable bladder* to describe involuntary detrusor contractions seen during urodynamic studies, as the bladder was filled. At the same time the other major protagonists and innovators in urodynamics, the Scandinavians, were using the term *detrusor hyperreflexia*. How was this confusing situation to be resolved? The answer, a political one, was given by the International Continence Society's standardization committee under its first chairman, Tage Hald (Bates et al, 1980). The solution was to designate the term *unstable bladder* for involuntary detrusor contractions seen in patients with no obvious cause for the contractions and to use the term *detrusor hyperreflexia* for patients whose involuntary contractions had a neurologic cause, for example, multiple sclerosis. Although the two definitions had their specific roles, the International Continence Society standardization report used **overactive detrusor** as the generic, overarching term.

The terms *bladder instability* and *detrusor hyperreflexia* implied two different conditions, yet it was becoming clear that the more investigations performed on an individual patient the more likely a cause was to be found for involuntary detrusor contractions. Griffiths and coworkers (1996) had described reduced blood flow in the frontal lobes of elderly persons with urgency incontinence; Elbadawi and

colleagues (1993) had described the electron microscopic appearance of bladder tissue from patients with urgency incontinence, and Geirsson and associate (1993) had described the ice water test as being positive in patients who were apparently neurologically healthy. The ice water test had previously been thought to be positive (the test caused a detrusor contraction) only in overt neurologic dysfunction.

In addition, Wein and Abrams had grown tired of explaining the two existing terms to patients and, when teaching, to health care staff. In the English language, "unstable" has connotations of mental instability and physicians talking about the unstable bladder had always to be careful not to insult the sensibilities of the patient. Many individual clinicians had been in the habit of talking to patients about their overactive bladder, and, bearing in mind that the International Continence Society already used the term *overactive detrusor,* it seemed an excellent idea to propose "Overactive Bladder" as the title of the conference. There was some opposition to the suggestion, because regularity authorities, such as the Medicines Commissions Agency in the United Kingdom, only recognized the term *unstable bladder* as the therapeutic area. Nevertheless, Wein and Abrams persisted with their view and the term *overactive bladder* was used at the conference and in the subsequent publication (Abrams and Wein, 1997). The two authors proposed a definition for overactive bladder in 1999 (Abrams and Wein, 1999).

The International Continence Society committee produced its revised definition in 2002 (Abrams et al, 2002) as follows:

The overactive bladder (OAB) is defined as **urgency, with or without urge incontinence, usually with frequency and nocturia.**

- **Urgency incontinence** is the complaint of involuntary leakage accompanied by or immediately preceded by urgency.
- **Urgency** is the complaint of a sudden compelling desire to pass urine which is difficult to defer.
- **Frequency** is the complaint by the patient who considers that he/she voids too often by day.
- **Nocturia** is the complaint that the individual has to wake at night one or more times to void.

ETIOLOGY

The definition of OAB according to symptoms is a problem for investigation into its scientific basis, because the reliance on symptoms in the definition of the syndrome complicates the development of reliable animal models. Accordingly, research focus has particularly concentrated on abnormalities of afferent signaling and mechanisms underlying detrusor overactivity, the former as the presumed basis of urgency, the latter as it is likely to contribute in a large number of people with OAB. In addition, some hypothetical reasoning has been used to translate scientific observations into clinical reality.

Afferent Mechanisms in OAB and Detrusor Overactivity

The two major populations of afferents mediating the micturition reflexes are myelinated Aδ-fibers and unmyelinated C-fibers. As a general rule, **the Aδ-fibers are regarded as responding to passive bladder distention and active detrusor contraction ("in series" mechanoreceptors [Iggo, 1955]), thus conveying information about bladder filling** (Janig and Morrison, 1986). **They are probably responsible for the sensation of fullness and mediate the normal spinobulbospinal micturition reflex.** In contrast to the Aδ-fibers, **C-fibers are regarded as responding primarily to chemical irritation of the bladder mucosa** (Habler et al, 1990) **or to thermal stimulus** (Fall et al, 1990). Nonetheless, the transduction properties of the bladder wall receptors are not fully correlated with the conduction velocity of their centripetal fibers (Sengupta and Gebhart, 1994; Shea et al, 2000), and there is almost certainly considerable overlap in the sensory information carried by the myelinated and unmyelinated fibers. **Urothelial cells possess sensory and signaling properties that allow them to respond to their chemical and physical environments and to communicate with subjacent structures in the bladder wall** (Birder et al, 2001). Close by, there are numerous interstitial cells, some of which possess ultrastructural and other characteristics resembling interstitial cells of Cajal of the gastrointestinal tract (Sui et al, 2002; Wiseman et al, 2003). Suburothelial interstitial cells lie in close physical proximity to nerve fibers, suggesting a role in sensory transduction or regulation (Wiseman et al, 2003). The number of impulses fired by an afferent ending at any level of distension can be varied physiologically; that is, the gain of the sensory nerve endings can be changed to vary the "afferent sensitivity." Thus, the rate of firing in a particular afferent normally associated with a high vesical volume can occur at lower volumes if the afferent ending has been sensitized. Accordingly, a role for afferent dysfunction has been suggested in the pathogenesis of urgency incontinence (Klein, 1988) and detrusor overactivity (Cheng and de Groat, 2004; Schroder et al, 2003). In theory, **detrusor overactivity and OAB might arise in circumstances in which the afferent activity is inappropriately high for any given degree of bladder distention. This could arise if nerve endings are pathologically sensitized or if they are abnormally numerous.**

Hypotheses of Detrusor Overactivity

Three main hypotheses have been proposed to explain the pathophysiologic basis of detrusor overactivity: the neurogenic (de Groat, 1997), myogenic (Brading and Turner, 1994), and peripheral autonomy (Drake et al, 2001) hypotheses. Each of these puts forward a possible mechanism by which widespread contraction affects the bulk of the detrusor, explaining why this occurs without volitional control. Below is a distillation of the main threads of argument running through the three hypotheses.

The Neurogenic Hypothesis

The neurogenic hypothesis states that detrusor overactivity arises from generalized, nerve-mediated excitation of the detrusor muscle (de Groat, 1997; de Groat et al, 1998). There are several interdependent mechanisms by which this may arise. First, damage to the brain can induce detrusor overactivity by reducing suprapontine inhibition. Second, damage to axonal pathways in the spinal cord allows the expression of primitive spinal bladder reflexes. Third, synaptic plasticity leads to reorganization of sacral activity, with the emergence of new reflexes, which may be triggered by C-fiber bladder afferent neurons. Finally, sensitization of peripheral afferent terminals in the bladder can trigger detrusor overactivity.

The Myogenic Hypothesis

The myogenic hypothesis suggests that overactive detrusor contractions result from a combination of an increased likelihood of spontaneous contraction and enhanced propagation of activity between muscle cells (Brading and Turner, 1994; Brading, 1997). Patchy denervation is a common observation in detrusor overactivity, regardless of etiology (German et al, 1995; Charlton et al, 1999; Drake et al, 2000; Mills et al, 2000). A smooth muscle cell deprived of its innervation shows an upregulation of surface membrane receptors and may have altered membrane potential, which increases the likelihood of spontaneous contraction in that cell. Detrusor overactivity is also associated with characteristic changes in ultrastructure (Elbadawi et al, 1993; Haferkamp et al, 2003), which could facilitate the propagation of the contraction over a wider proportion of the body of the detrusor than normal. Thus, muscle strips from patients with detrusor overactivity can show altered responsiveness to nervous and pharmacologic stimuli; however, this is not invariably the case.

Peripheral Autonomous Activity

The peripheral autonomy hypothesis suggests that the normal bladder is modular, that increased bladder sensation results from exaggerated localized modular contraction, and that detrusor overactivity is due to enhanced coordination of modular activity through the myovesical plexus (Drake et al, 2001). The myovesical plexus comprises the intramural innervation and interstitial cells (Fig. 61–1), equivalent to the myenteric plexuses of the gut (Drake et al, 2001). The modules are circumscribed areas of muscle, each of which is defined by elements within the myovesical plexus, such as the area of supply of individual intramural bladder ganglia or by a node of interstitial cells. A module would be the smallest functional unit in the detrusor; contraction in isolation would generate localized activity, a property that has been clearly described in autonomous bladder activity in several species, including human (Van Os-Bossagh et al, 2001; Drake et al, 2003a, 2003b, 2005; Gillespie et al, 2003), and which may explain increased filling sensation including urgency (Coolsaet et al, 1993; Gillespie, 2004; Drake et al, 2005). Activity in individual modules would have very little effect on intravesical pressure, but synchronization of activity in neighboring modules would lead to contraction of a more substantial proportion of the bladder wall, resulting in measurable intravesical pressure effects (Drake et al, 2003b). There are thus two critical elements of the peripheral autonomy model. First, any change causing a shift in the balance of excitation and inhibition toward the former will predispose to local contraction, leading to increased bladder sensation. Second, any factor enhancing communication between modules will predispose to detrusor overactivity (Fig. 61–2).

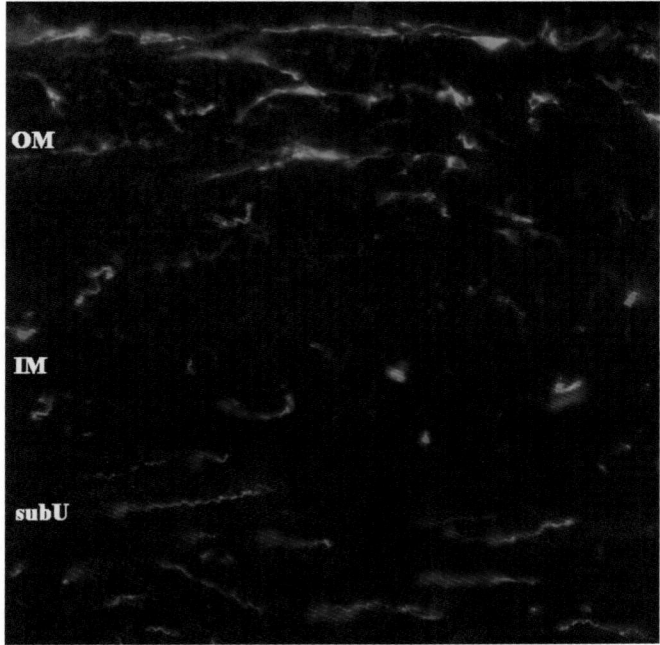

Figure 61–1. The myovesical plexus. Interstitial cells in the outer muscle (OM) of the mouse detrusor shown with cyclic guanosine monophosphate immunofluorescent histochemistry *(green)*, co-labeled with the general nerve marker PGP 9.5 *(red)*. In the mouse, the interstitial cells are lacking in the inner muscle (IM) and suburothelial region (subU), in contrast to other species.

PREVALENCE

One early prevalence study on OAB used an initial definition in which OAB symptoms "occurred singly or in combination" (Milsom et al, 2001). In this article, frequency alone or nocturia alone qualified as OAB. Because OAB is a syndrome, a single symptom would not usually be sufficient to describe that syndrome. The International Continence Society 2002 definition does not allow such patients to be included in the OAB group. Therefore, by the current definition, the prevalence of OAB in the Milsom study (16%) is too high; 9.2% of the population had urgency, and this is perhaps closer to the true prevalence of OAB in the community. However, whether the reader chooses to use the rate of 9% or 16%, it represents a huge number of individuals with OAB.

"OAB dry" is a term that emanated from the NOBLE study (Stewart et al, 2003) carried out in the United States to establish the prevalence of OAB in community-dwelling individuals (over 5000 were surveyed). In the NOBLE study a validated computer-assisted telephone interview was used to estimate the prevalence of OAB in a representative sample of adults aged 18 years or older. Of 5,204 individuals who participated, 857 (16.5%) were found to have OAB. In this survey, which used the current International Continence Society definition of OAB, the prevalence of OAB (16%) was identical to that in the European study in which 319 (6.1%) had OAB with urinary urgency incontinence and 538 (10.4%) had OAB without urinary urgency incontinence. Although men and women had the same prevalence of OAB overall (16.0% and 16.9%, respectively), **men were shown to have a higher prevalence of "OAB dry"** (13.4% as opposed to 7.6% in women) **and women had a higher prevalence of "OAB wet"** (9.3% as opposed to 2.6% in men). In both the European and the U.S. prevalence studies there were a proportion of individuals who had a significant problem with OAB symptoms but who did not have urgency incontinence. It is assumed that the difference in the proportion of "OAB dry" and "OAB wet," in men

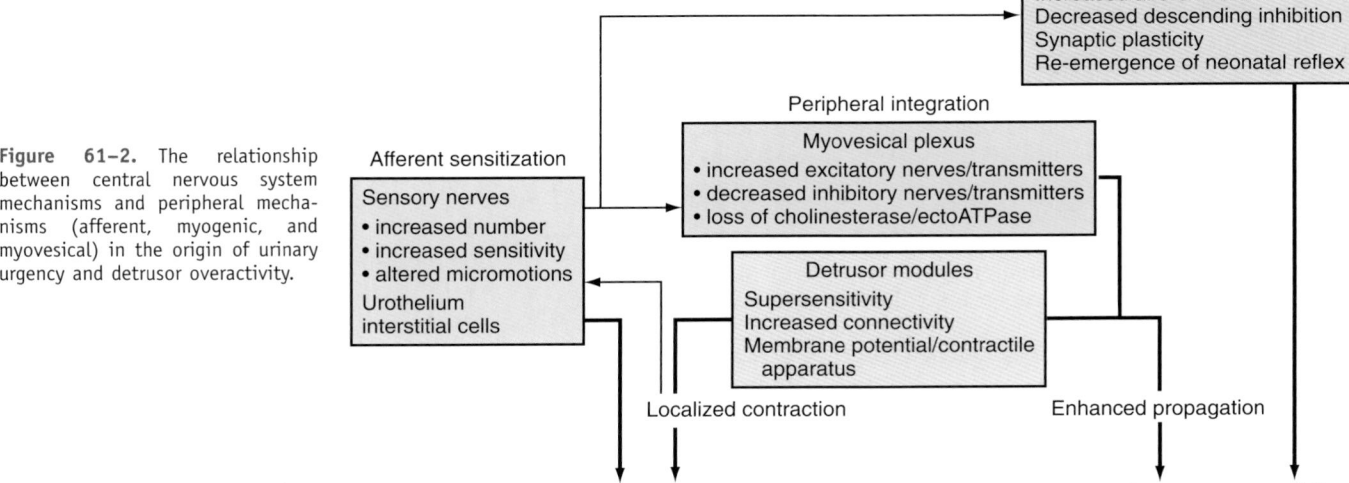

Figure 61–2. The relationship between central nervous system mechanisms and peripheral mechanisms (afferent, myogenic, and myovesical) in the origin of urinary urgency and detrusor overactivity.

and women, is due to the relative weakness of the bladder neck and urethral sphincter mechanism in women, particularly in those who have had children. Men may enjoy additional urethral support from the prostate gland, although 20% of older men with lower urinary tract symptoms suffer urgency incontinence due to detrusor overactivity (Abrams et al, 1978).

The prevalence of OAB rose similarly with age in both men and women, although in women the prevalence of "OAB wet" rose dramatically from 2.0% in the youngest group (ages 18 to 24) to 19.1% in those 65 to 74 years of age. Men, on the other hand, did not experience an increase in "OAB wet" until older: 8.22% for those 65 to 74 and 10.2% for those 75 years and older. Both types of OAB had a significant impact on the patients' quality of life, as measured by generic quality of life instruments, such as the SF-36 Health Survey (QualityMetric Inc., Lincoln, RI). It is not difficult to understand that being "OAB wet" has a profound impact, but the effect of "OAB dry" on quality of life can be equally dramatic: the difficulties of a long distance truck driver or someone working on a production line can be easily imagined.

CLINICAL ASSESSMENT

Patients with OAB may present to health care workers in either the community or to the hospital service. It is vital that whoever comes into contact with such individuals is both knowledgeable and sympathetic. OAB always requires management and often cannot be cured; therefore, it is important that both the sufferers and the therapists have reasonable expectations of each other. Because OAB has marked effects on the quality of life of both the individual and the family, the therapist needs to be prepared to consider the patient's psychosocial circumstances.

Clinical assessment may be carried out by a doctor or by a nurse. It is not important who sees the patient but, as intimated previously, the doctor or nurse must be trained to assess and manage an OAB patient and to safely exclude other causes of lower urinary tract symptoms. The clinical assessment may be carried out by a generalist (general practitioner/primary care physician) or by a specialist (urologist or gynecologist) or by a nurse. Continence nurses may work either in the community or within the hospital setting.

Each of the OAB symptoms requires assessment: its presence or absence, frequency, severity, bother, and effect on quality of life.

The definition of OAB also presumes that the clinician has excluded other causes for storage symptoms, such as urinary tract infection. The algorithm from the third International Consultation on Incontinence 2004 (Abrams et al, 2005b) defines the basic assessment necessary in the evaluation of lower urinary tract dysfunction, which includes a full history, physical examination, and appropriate investigations, the minimum of which are urinalysis and an assessment of bladder emptying (most simply by palpating the lower abdomen).

The key symptom of OAB is urgency. Urgency was also redefined by the International Continence Society (Abrams et al, 2002), after a good deal of debate, as **the complaint of a sudden compelling desire to void which is difficult to defer.**

As has been mentioned, urgency is the pivotal symptom of OAB. Although urgency has been defined by the International

Continence Society, much discussion still surrounds the term, and in the English language, there remains plenty of room for confusion. For example, in everyday English, *urge to void* is not synonymous with *urgency*. The International Continence Society in 2002 strongly recommended abandoning the term *urge to void* as being likely to create confusion in the minds of both patients and clinicians. The International Continence Society believed we would be better advised to use the term *desire to void* rather than *urge to void*. A recent article by Chapple and coworkers (2005) discusses the same issue and comes to the same conclusion. At the International Continence Society meeting in Paris in August, 2004, a terminology workshop (Abrams et al, 2005a) recommended that to be consequential the term *urge incontinence* should be replaced by the term *urgency incontinence*. This would also mean altering *urge syndrome,* an old term, to *urgency syndrome.*

Urgency with at least one other symptom is essential for the diagnosis of OAB: in approximately half of patients urgency incontinence also occurs (Fig. 61–3). However, the definition of incontinence has also produced problems. The original International Continence Society definition was that **urinary incontinence** is the involuntary loss of urine that is a social or hygienic problem.

The use of the words "social or hygienic problem" in the definition introduced the concept of quality of life impact before quality of life was a popular topic. However, we have all seen patients with incontinence they describe as "not troublesome," although it was considered a very significant problem by their caregivers or family. This particularly applies to children and the elderly who may be used to or unaware of their incontinence; nevertheless, with few exceptions, treatment proceeds according to the wishes of the individual patient. However, there are the horns of a dilemma in the old definition of incontinence. The definition that appears in the 2002 report acknowledges the dilemma and takes the purist view that "incontinence is incontinence" and therefore defines **urinary incontinence** as the complaint of any involuntary leakage.

In surveys it may be important to ask individuals about *any* involuntary leakage as well as about leakage that has an impact on quality of life. In their prevalence survey using the Bristol Female Lower Urinary Tract Symptoms (BFLUTS) question-

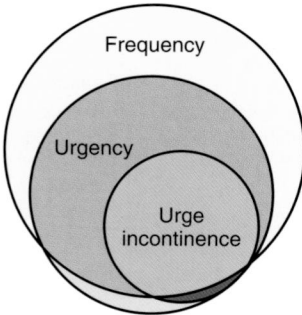

OVERACTIVE BLADDER
(SYMPTOMATIC DIAGNOSIS)

Figure 61–3. OAB rings: the diagram shows that approximately half of individuals with urgency have coexisting urge incontinence and almost all have coexisting frequency (day and night).

naire (sent by mail), Swithinbank and colleagues (1999) showed that of the 69% of women aged 18 to 92 who had "any incontinence," 30% had incontinence that produced a "social or hygienic problem" in that their incontinence had either an effect on their social functioning and/or they wore incontinence pads or changed underwear because of leakage. Also, 70% of those with "any incontinence" (48% of the total sample) reported no social impact, did not wear pads, and did not change clothes. However, identifying such individuals with incontinence that was not bothersome is likely to be important in longitudinal studies, which can be used to look at remission or worsening of urinary incontinence.

Many studies in women have shown that urgency incontinence is far more bothersome than stress incontinence. Indeed, the paradox often exists that, in an individual, stress incontinence may occur several times a day and urge incontinence only once or twice a week. However, the patient demands treatment for the urgency incontinence. Of course, this is because urgency incontinence occurs at unpredictable times and can involve complete bladder emptying with catastrophic and highly embarrassing results for the patient, as opposed to stress incontinence, which occurs predictably and can usually be well controlled by pads because each individual urine loss is relatively small.

An appropriate basic (initial) assessment gives a presumptive diagnosis and the basis for empirical treatment, having excluded common conditions such as urinary tract infection, and established the patient's desire for treatment and which therapies he or she is interested in. Empirical treatment may include lifestyle interventions, bladder training and pelvic floor muscle training, and drug treatments. Should these therapies fail and invasive treatment be contemplated by the patient and clinician, then urodynamic confirmation of detrusor overactivity is usually considered desirable.

Defining and Measuring Bladder Sensation Including Urgency

Those who work with OAB patients will be aware of the difficulty in being sure of the patient's meaning of urgency, the clinical definition of which is stated earlier. Normal individuals experience bladder sensation as the bladder fills, and the International Continence Society has endorsed the work of Wyndaele (1998), who described three sensations during cystometry, which were reproduced in his volunteers' everyday lives: (1) first sensation of filling, (2) normal desire to void, and (3) strong desire to void (Wyndaele and De Wachter, 2002).

Instruments for Measuring Bladder Sensations

Most of the work on measuring symptoms, apart from that of Wyndaele, has been done in patients with OAB, which poses a fundamental question "Does an individual with OAB also experience the three normal sensations felt by *normal* individuals during bladder filling?" The answer to this question is probably YES, although this has not been studied directly. However, in randomized controlled drug trials, participants have 10 to 12 micturitions per 24 hours but only approximately 5 are reported to be associated with urgency. This

implies that at least half of the micturitions are probably not accompanied by urgency. New evidence from a trial of tolterodine given in a night-time dose supports this. Patients were asked to grade their bladder sensation as follows (Abrams et al, 2005c):

1 No urgency : "I felt no need to empty my bladder but did so for other reasons."
2 Mild urgency: "I could postpone voiding as long as necessary without fear of wetting myself."
3 Moderate urgency: "I could postpone voiding for a short time without fear of wetting myself."
4 Severe urgency: "I could not postpone voiding but had to rush to the toilet in order not to wet myself."
5 Urgency incontinence: "I leaked before arriving at the toilet."

This instrument is known as the **urinary sensation scale.**

Freeman and associates (2003) used the **urgency percentage scale** (Cardozo et al, 2002) in a trial of tolterodine. It has three possible responses:

1 I am usually not able to hold urine.
2 I am usually able to hold urine until I reach the toilet if I go immediately.
3 I am usually able to finish what I am doing before going to the toilet.

Bowden and associates (2003) presented the Indevus **"Urgency Severity Scale,"** which was used in trials of trospium. There are four responses:

0 None, no urgency
1 Mild, awareness of urgency but easily tolerated
2 Moderate, enough urgency/discomfort that it interferes with usual activities/tasks
3 Severe, extreme urgency/discomfort that abruptly stops all activities/tasks

Oliver and associates (2003) described an **"urgeometer"** for use during cystometry in a study of patients being considered for neurostimulation for OAB. The patients were asked to press one of a series of five buttons during cystometry:

0 None
1 Mild
2 Moderate
3 Strong
4 Desperate

These scales are wrongly named. Each is a measure of the intensity of bladder sensation in differing parts of the sensation spectrum. None of the scales explains to the patient how urgency is defined. Such an explanation is essential if management is based on the assumption that OAB symptoms are secondary to involuntary detrusor contractions and characteristic of detrusor overactivity because all treatments are based on the concept of inhibiting detrusor overactivity. So far, no other treatment concepts have been advanced and there are no successful proofs of concept studies.

Defining *Urgency* to the Patient

The 2004 International Continence Society workshop (Abrams et al, 2005c) regretted the failure of the terminology committee to include "for fear of leakage" in the new definition of "a sudden compelling desire to void which is difficult to defer." The principal reason for its exclusion was because roughly half of OAB patients do not leak. Perhaps this was not

Table 61–1.	**Bladder Sensation Scale**

1 No sensation of needing to pass urine but passed urine for "social reasons" (e.g., just before going out, unsure where next toilet is); no urgency.
2 Normal desire to pass urine; no urgency.
3 Urgency but urgency passed away before had to visit bathroom; went later with normal desire to pass urine.
4 Urgency but managed to get to bathroom still with urgency but did not leak urine.
5 Urgency and could not get to bathroom in time so leaked urine.

Table 61–2.	**Cystometry Sensation Scale**

0 No bladder sensation: "I don't feel anything."
1 First sensation of filling: "I'm beginning to feel my bladder."
2 First desire to pass urine: "I feel like I want to pass urine."
3 Urgency is graded.
  Mild: "I think I can hold on."
  Moderate: "I don't know if I can hold on."
  Serious: "I have to go now or I will leak any moment."
4 Strong desire to pass urine: "I'm getting uncomfortable, I'd like to pass urine now."

entirely logical because many of these patients certainly feel as if they are going to leak even if they say they never have. A couple of phrases are often used by patients:

• "When I've gotta go, I've gotta go."
• "When I want to go, I have to rush because I think I may wet myself."

Hence "fear of leakage" is an important concept to patients.

What is needed is the production of instruments for use during everyday life in association with frequency volume charts and during urodynamics, which measure the range of sensations, including urgency, and are validated in a representative sample of the population. Two such scales have been suggested and are currently undergoing evaluation in nonselected populations. The **bladder sensation scale** for use with a frequency volume chart is shown in Table 61–1. The **cystometry sensation scale** for use during urodynamic study is shown in Table 61–2).

All other measures such as **"warning time"** (between first sensation of urgency and eventual voiding) also depend on the patients and the clinicians reaching a consensus as to the meaning of *urgency* (Cardozo et al, 2003).

Measuring Storage Symptoms

The frequency volume chart (Abrams and Klevmark, 1996) **remains the principal method of evaluating frequency and nocturia in an objective way. In OAB the pattern of voided volumes is characteristically erratic.** The bladder diary (Abrams et al, 2002) can be used when more data are required and to quantify both urgency and incontinence episodes. However, some caution needs to be exercised to ensure that the patient is not asked to deliver unrealistic amounts of data.

The symptoms can also be measured using validated questionnaires. There is now a range of questionnaires in a modular format that have been developed by the International Consultation on Incontinence (Abrams et al, 2005b), known as the ICIQ. The OAB-q (Coyne et al, 2002) has been adopted as one of the modules, all of which are fully validated.

In conclusion, if OAB symptoms are to be measured accurately then it will be necessary to use validated instruments capable of measuring the spectrum of bladder sensation in conjunction with either a frequency volume chart or during cystometry.

Mixed Urinary Incontinence

Mixed incontinence is the **complaint of involuntary leakage associated with urgency and with exertion, effort, sneezing, or coughing.** Figure 61–4 describes the relations between stress incontinence, mixed incontinence, "OAB wet," and "OAB dry" in women. In general, mixed incontinence is associated with more severe levels of leakage, although it is currently unclear which component, urgency or stress, is responsible: possibly either or both types will prove culpable.

DISTINGUISHING OVERACTIVE BLADDER FROM PAINFUL BLADDER SYNDROME

Painful bladder syndrome is defined **as the complaint of suprapubic pain related to bladder filling, accompanied by other symptoms,** such as increased daytime and night-time frequency, in the absence of proven urinary infection or other obvious pathology.

Urgency in the old International Continence Society terminology was defined in terms of "fear of leakage or pain." The new definition excludes urgency "for fear of pain." In the new definition "sudden compelling desire" has been added to the definition for clarification. The committee believed that the sensation (pain) associated with painful bladder syndrome (PBS) builds up more slowly through discomfort to pain. A useful question to ask patients is "if I paid you money, could you hold on longer?" Patients with detrusor overactivity cannot, whereas those who "go frequently for fear of pain" can hold on, albeit at the cost of greater pain. However, even this situation becomes confusing in those individuals with "OAB dry." A short article has been published that attempts to clarify and minimize any confusions between OAB and PBS (Abrams et al, 2005d).

STORAGE SYMPTOMS AND INCONTINENCE

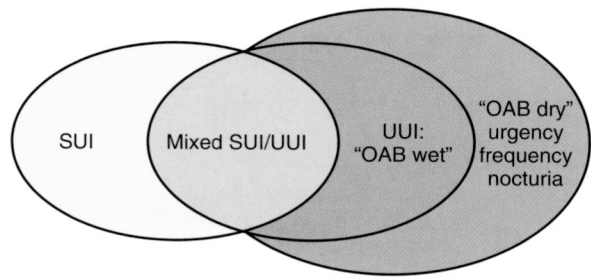

SUI: stress urinary incontinence
UUI: urge urinary incontinence

Figure 61–4. Incontinence in women may be urge, stress, or mixed in type. There is also a group with OAB syndrome who are dry: "OAB dry." Women with stress incontinence and OAB syndrome can be regarded as a spectrum.

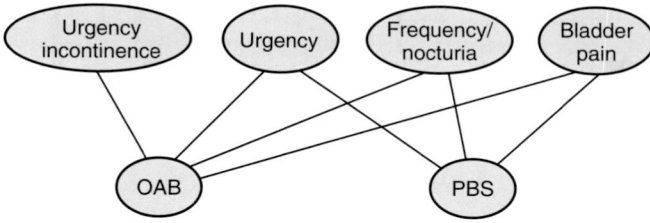

Figure 61–5. The difference in symptoms between OAB and painful bladder syndrome (PBS).

The diagram in Figure 61–5 illustrates that urgency and urgency incontinence are the key symptoms of OAB and that bladder pain is the key symptom of PBS.

The diagram in Figure 61–6 indicates the difference in bladder sensation/pain in the two conditions. The article goes on to state that **in PBS, sensation builds to discomfort and then to pain and is felt suprapubically even if the patient also has perineal (urethral/vaginal/penile) discomfort/pain. In OAB, urgency is usually described as being felt lower down than the sensations of bladder filling and the normal desire to void. In men it is felt in the perineum/base of penis and in women in the vagina/urethra. Urgency tends to come on quickly and resolve quickly if the patient can inhibit his or her bladder;** however, urgency may recur. The article then points out that **incontinence in PBS is rare, but voluntary (deliberate) leakage can occur because of great pain, whereas in OAB incontinence follows urgency and is involuntary, and much more common, with a prevalence of 30% to 50% in OAB sufferers.**

There are other differences that help to distinguish PBS from OAB. **In PBS the voided volumes are characteristically very similar throughout the 24-hour period, whereas in OAB they often differ widely** (Abrams and Klevmark, 1996).

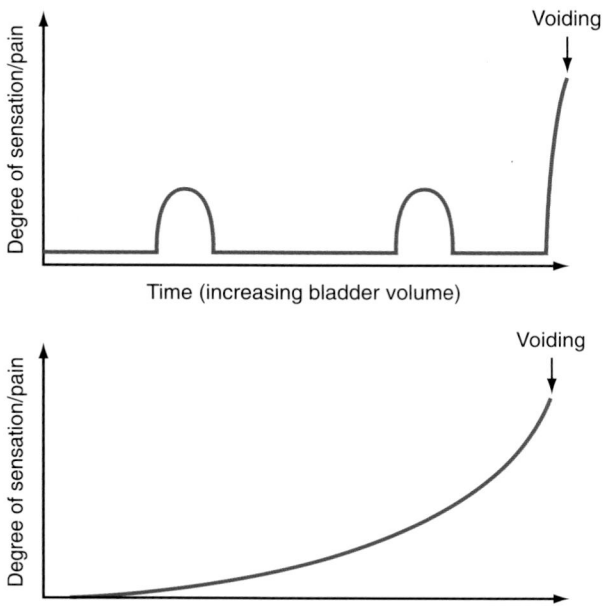

Figure 61–6. The differences in the development of bladder sensation in OAB and PBS.

URODYNAMIC CONFIRMATION OF DETRUSOR OVERACTIVITY

Most patients will be managed without having had urodynamic studies, which can be used to confirm that OAB is due to detrusor overactivity. There is a brief discussion of the treatments used in the management of OAB at the end of this chapter (see subsequent chapters for details). It is common practice to employ conservative management (lifestyle interventions) and oral pharmacotherapy (antimuscarinics) without a urodynamic diagnosis. This empirical practice is defensible from a number of viewpoints. First, OAB is so prevalent that the urodynamic facilities may be overwhelmed if it were necessary to confirm that OAB was secondary to detrusor overactivity in every case. Second, urodynamics are relatively invasive and costly and may not always confirm the presence of detrusor overactivity, even if subsequently the patient is proven to have detrusor overactivity by further studies. And third, the two broad categories of conservative and drug therapies are safe and relatively inexpensive—most patients chose to "try" nonsurgical treatments first before a urodynamic study.

Therefore, **the indication for routine specialist involvement is failure of conservative and drug therapy to adequately manage the patient's OAB.** If symptoms persist to the extent that the patient's quality of life is sufficiently compromised, then that individual is likely to seek further help. As the treatment synopsis shows, further management includes intravesical pharmacotherapy, including botulinum toxin and surgical procedures. Because these interventions are relatively "dangerous" and expensive, most patients and doctors believe that a confirmed diagnosis is essential.

When should specialist referral be made? There is no hard and fast rule, but trials of conservative and/or drug therapy for 6 to 12 weeks are regarded as reasonable by most patients. At this point, if the patient wishes, referral should be made to a specialist with particular training in lower urinary tract dysfunction. Most often this will be to a urologist with lower urinary tract dysfunction as his or her special interest. There are also some well-trained continence nurses and gynecologists who can perform this next level of assessment but who are likely to need to refer the patient to a specialist urologist for surgical treatment.

The 1988 International Continence Society terminology report (Abrams et al, 1988) differentiated types of detrusor storage function, as determined by filling cystometry:

- **Normal detrusor function** allows filling with little or no change in pressure; no involuntary phasic contractions occur despite provocation.
- **Overactive detrusor function** (as per the 2002 report, which retained the term *detrusor overactivity* but redefined it) is a urodynamic observation characterized by involuntary detrusor contractions during the filling phase which may be spontaneous or provoked.

The 1988 definition of overactive detrusor function (Abrams et al, 1988) contained the words "whilst the patient is attempting to inhibit micturition." This was always controversial because some believed it had large implications in the way urodynamic testing was conducted. A study by Romanzi and associates (2001) claimed that by using the International Continence Society definition, detrusor overactivity would be missed in a significant number of investigations. It is arguable whether any urodynamicist specifically told patients to inhibit voiding. During urodynamics, patients are apprehensive because of their "fear of the unknown" and need information as to the purpose and conduct of the tests. We tell patients that we will fill their bladders until they tell us that they need to void, which is the point when they would usually go to the toilet. The discussion as to whether the patient should be asked to inhibit micturition is thereby rendered superfluous. Furthermore, the argument may be entirely specious as we all spend 99% of our life inhibiting micturition until we are standing or sitting in the bathroom ready to micturate. If urodynamic testing is to mimic "everyday life," then we would expect the patient to inhibit micturition, albeit subconsciously, until he or she tells the urodynamicist that the patient is ready to, or "has to," pass urine. In ambulatory urodynamic studies, the situation is easier and more obviously similar to "everyday life" because the patient has to undress to void, which is not generally the case in conventional urodynamics.

The primary aim of urodynamic studies is to reproduce the patients' symptoms, and this has led to confusion around the diagnosis of detrusor overactivity. Figure 61–7 shows the relationship between OAB and the urodynamic demonstration of detrusor overactivity. It emphasizes that **whereas there is a good correlation between "OAB wet" and detrusor overactivity, that relation is not as strong in "OAB dry,"** and this is particularly the case in women. The correlation is further weakened in women with coexisting stress incontinence, that is, with mixed incontinence. On the other hand, Figure 61–7 also shows that **it is possible to have detrusor overactivity that is asymptomatic.**

It is vital that at the end of the urodynamic test the urodynamicist asks himself or herself:

- **Did I reproduce the patients' symptoms completely?**
- **Did I reproduce the patients' symptoms in part?**
- **Did I fail to reproduce the patients' symptoms?**

One of these three statements should appear in the urodynamic record.

Patient position during urodynamic studies is important; there is often the perverse habit of performing filling cystometry with the patient supine—perverse because most OAB sufferers experience their symptoms when in the vertical position. There is adequate literature to show that the symptoms of a higher proportion of OAB patients are shown to be due to detrusor overactivity if the patient is sitting or standing during bladder filling.

The advent of ambulatory urodynamics has complicated the discussion of the significance of detrusor overactivity. Detrusor overactivity has been shown to occur in 60% of asymptomatic women undergoing ambulatory urodynamics (Heslington and Hilton, 1996). What does this mean? Does detrusor overactivity in these circumstances have any clinical relevance? Because detrusor overactivity is a urodynamic diagnosis, in these individuals detrusor overactivity exists. It is not clear from the papers whether detrusor overactivity during ambulatory urodynamics, in normal individuals, is symptomatic or asymptomatic. If it were symptomatic, but this was a symptom the individual did not experience in everyday life, then the conclusion would be that the detrusor overactivity was artifactual. Even if it were asymptomatic one could not be sure that it was not an artifact and due to the presence of the pressure-measuring catheter "irritating" the bladder wall. Perhaps we would all have detrusor overactivity if we were catheterized for a period of 3 hours, the usual length of an ambulatory urodynamics study, but we would *not* have typical OAB symptoms!

Idiopathic and Neurogenic Detrusor Overactivity

Detrusor overactivity should be further qualified as:

- **Idiopathic detrusor overactivity,** when there is no defined cause, *or*
- **Neurogenic detrusor overactivity,** when there is a relevant neurologic condition.

Indeed there is the possibility to add further categories of detrusor overactivity in the future, if causation between another disease or pathophysiologic state is proven. Some believe that bladder outlet obstruction causes detrusor overactivity as it does in pigs, although this view has been disputed for many years by some (Abrams, 1984). It is of considerable interest that detrusor overactivity appears to return to a prevalence of 60% in men who have had transurethral resection of the prostate many years previously (Thomas et al, 2004), despite the fact that they remain unobstructed (Nitti et al, 1997).

Detrusor overactivity has a variety of patterns on urodynamic traces. The International Continence Society 2002 report describes two types:

- **Phasic detrusor overactivity** is defined by its characteristic waveform and may or may not lead to urinary incontinence.
- **Terminal detrusor overactivity** is defined as a single involuntary detrusor contraction occurring at cystometric capacity, which cannot be suppressed, and causes incontinence, which often results in complete bladder emptying (voiding).

In general, **phasic detrusor overactivity** tends to be characterized by contractions of increasing amplitude as the

OVERACTIVE BLADDER AND DETRUSOR OVERACTIVITY

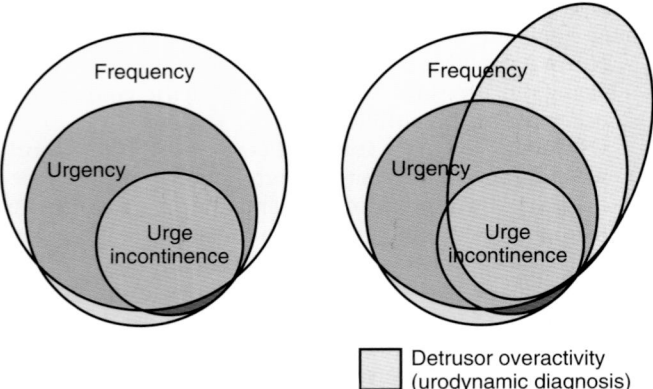

Detrusor overactivity (urodynamic diagnosis)

Figure 61–7. Correlation between the symptomatic diagnosis (OAB) and the urodynamic diagnosis (detrusor overactivity). The correlation is best for urge incontinence and least good for frequency (day and/or night)

bladder volume increases (Fig. 61–8) and is the characteristic pattern seen in most idiopathic detrusor overactivity, for example, in the middle-aged man or woman with overactive bladder syndrome. **Terminal detrusor overactivity** is most characteristically seen in the elderly person with "precipitant voiding," such as elderly patients who have suffered a cerebrovascular accident, who are incontinent, and who are shown on urodynamic studies to have terminal detrusor overactivity. Such patients appear to lose both warning of impending micturition and the ability to inhibit what turns out to be a voiding contraction. Incontinence is often disastrous as the patient empties the bladder on the way to the bathroom or even before he or she can get out of the chair or bed on the way to the toilet. This type of detrusor overactivity was first described by Geirsson and colleagues (1993). Such patients have a positive ice water test.

Some urodynamicists incorrectly include change in detrusor pressure during filling, which is not phasic, in the definition of detrusor overactivity. Sometimes this change in pressure occurs when the patient moves to the standing or sitting position, having had the bladder filled while supine. This "habit" of filling supine and asking the patient to void either sitting (women) or standing (men) appears to have come from the times when urodynamics were performed in the radiology suite and the patient had to lie on an x-ray table. However, if we are to mimic everyday life, then patients should be in the vertical position when most are troubled by their symptoms. Furthermore, technical artifacts are easily introduced by moving a patient during urodynamics and change of position may account for a change in detrusor pressure if pressure transmission to the transducers is altered by change in position. Nonphasic changes in detrusor pressure before micturition should be regarded as changes in bladder compliance rather than as detrusor overactivity.

Provocative maneuvers are popular in trying to demonstrate detrusor overactivity. Certainly the investigator should

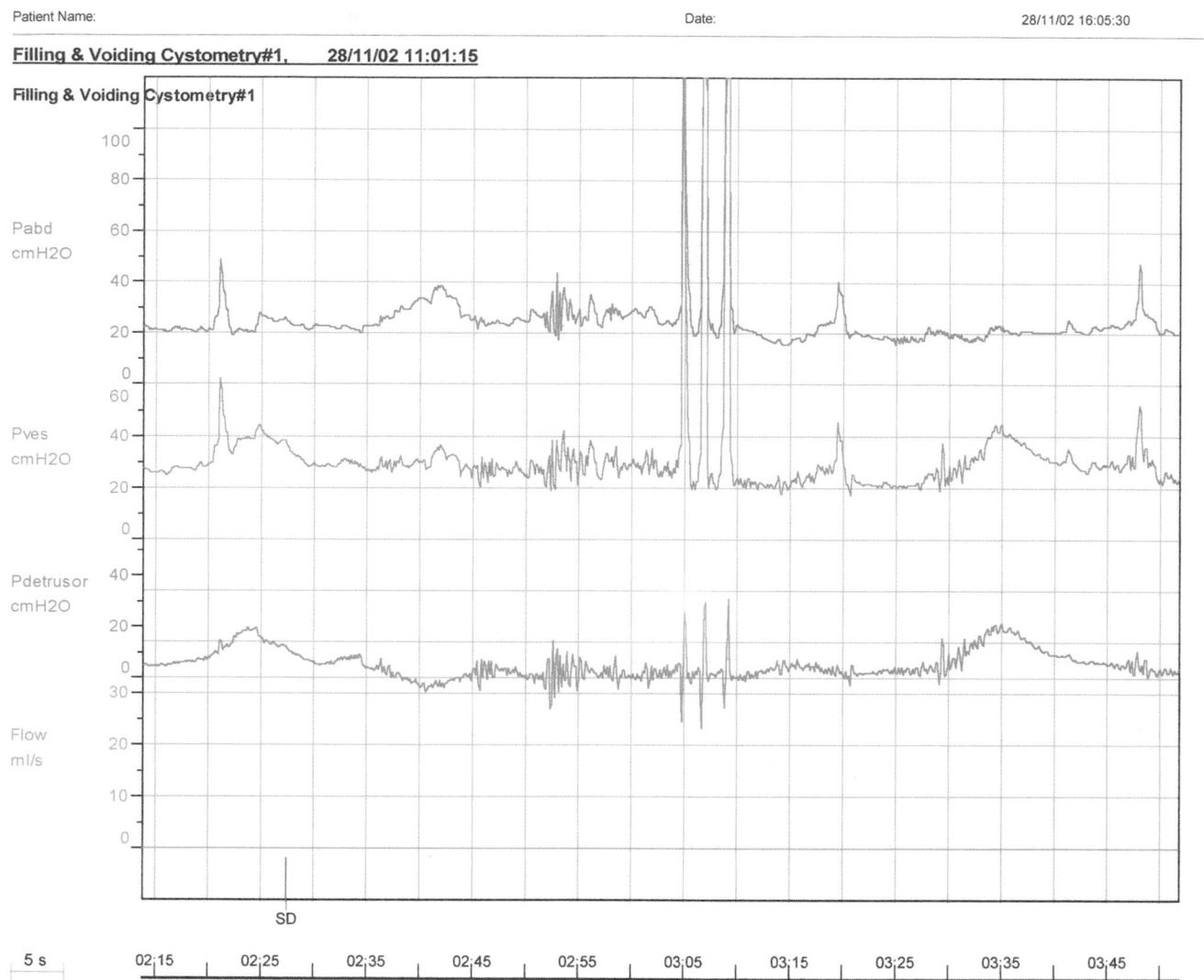

Figure 61–8. Detrusor overactivity trace. Phasic detrusor overactivity at either end of the lower trace. Three coughs are seen in the middle of the trace with the acceptable biophasic artifact on the lowest tract (Pdet).

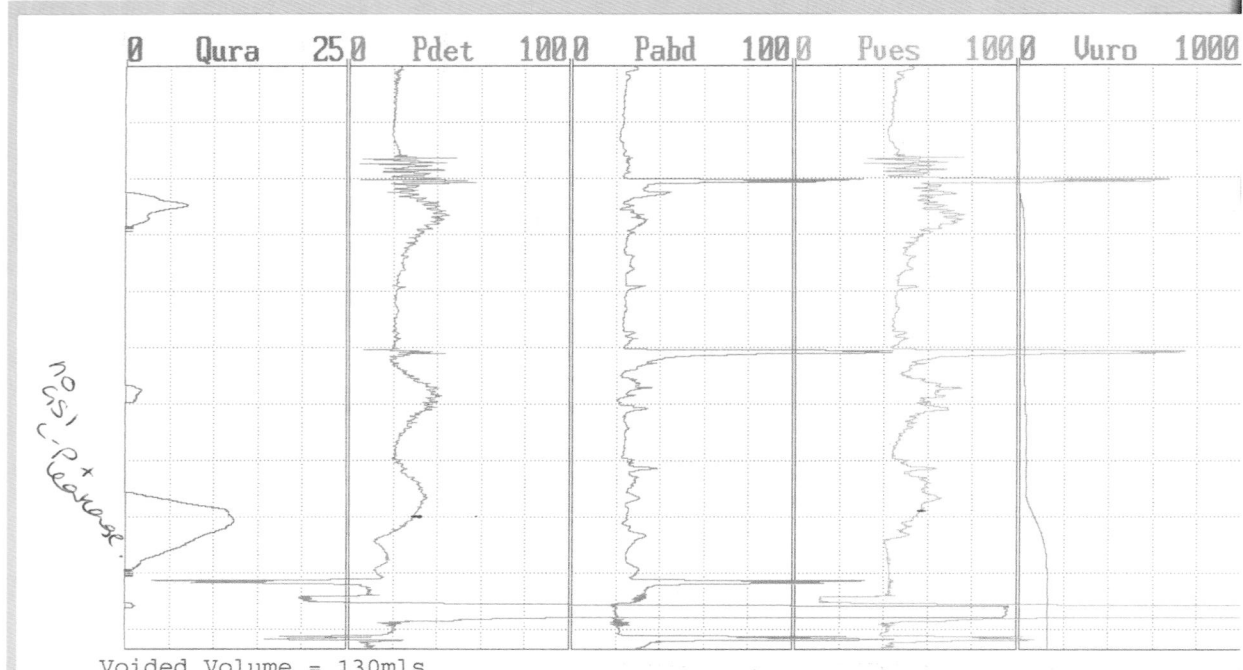

Voided Volume = 130mls

Figure 61–9. Cough-induced detrusor overactivity. The coughs (seen as spikes on Pves and Pabd traces) cause involuntary detrusor contraction on two instances, with resulting incontinence (seen on the lowest trace, Qura). This is followed by a normal void with a maximum flow rate of 12 mL/s.

try to use any provocations that the patient says lead to OAB symptoms: this might include change of posture or coughing. Figure 61–9 gives an example of cough-induced detrusor overactivity. Fast filling may mask detrusor overactivity in some patients and, in some individuals, causes low compliance, which disappears when the patient's bladder is filled slowly. On slow filling the compliance will often return to normal but phasic detrusor overactivity is demonstrated instead: this is particularly the case in neurogenic patients.

How "high" should an involuntary detrusor contraction be to qualify as detrusor overactivity? The first International Continence Society report (1980a, 1980b) stated that, in order to diagnose "detrusor instability," the contraction should be at least 15 cm H_2O. However, it was subsequently realized that involuntary detrusor contractions of less than 15 cm H_2O could cause significant symptoms. Therefore, in the 1988 International Continence Society Report (Abrams et al, 1988) and now in the 2002 International Continence Society Report (Abrams et al, 2002) **there is no proscribed minimum value.** In practice it may be difficult to be sure if an involuntary detrusor contraction has occurred if the phasic wave is less than 5 cm H_2O. Measurement of the heights of waves has been used as a way of describing the severity of detrusor overactivity. A variety of techniques have been used, including the "detrusor instability index" (expressed as cm H_2O per milliliters of bladder filling) (Abrams, 1984) (Fig. 61–10). Other more sophisticated methods involving computer analysis have been described (van Waalwijk van Doorn et al, 1997).

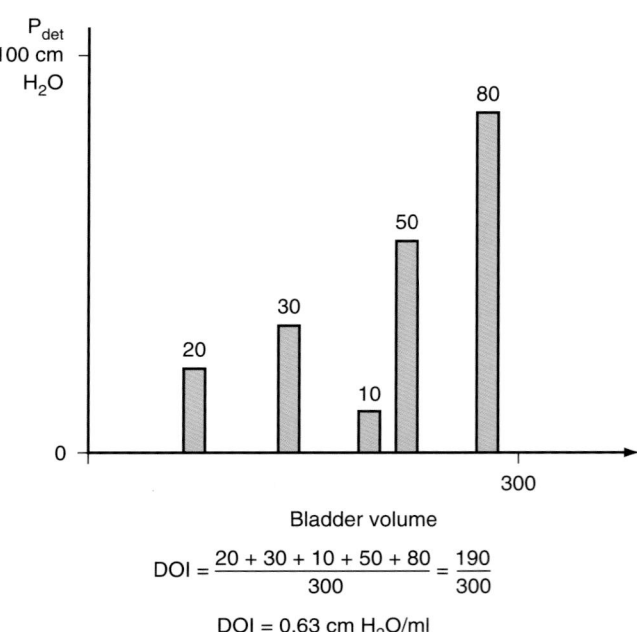

$$DOI = \frac{20 + 30 + 10 + 50 + 80}{300} = \frac{190}{300}$$

$$DOI = 0.63 \text{ cm } H_2O/ml$$

Figure 61–10. Detrusor overactivity index: a simple means of quantifying detrusor overactivity.

MANAGEMENT

The third International Consultation of Incontinence has produced a comprehensive review of the spectrum of management of incontinence, which ranges, for OAB and detrusor overactivity, from sensible fluid restriction to ileocystoplasty. The initial and specialized management algorithms for women show the care pathways for OAB and detrusor overactivity (Abrams et al, 2005b) (Figs. 61–11 and 61–12). Subsequent chapters deal with OAB treatment in detail.

The Consultation of Incontinence used the International Consultation on Urological Diseases' adaptation of the AHCPR/Oxford System of levels of evidence and grades of recommendation to evaluate the evidence from the scientific literature (Abrams et al, 2005b).

Therapy for OAB can be divided into four classes of treatment: (1) conservative management, (2) pharmacotherapy, (3) surgical therapy, and (4) treatment of intractable OAB.

Conservative Management

Conservative management includes weight loss, cessation of smoking, and dietary factors (decreased use of caffeine, decreased fluid intake, decreased alcohol intake, changes in food and drink). Lifestyle interventions include pelvic floor muscle training and bladder retraining.

Pharmacotherapy

Oral drugs include antimuscarinics, drugs acting on membrane channels, drugs with mixed actions, α-adrenergic antagonists, β-adrenergic agonists, antidepressants, prostaglandin synthesis inhibitors, arginine vasopressin analogs, and others. Intravesical agents include vanilloids and botulinum toxin.

Surgical Therapy

Neural stimulation/modulation, detrusor myectomy, and cystoplasty may be done.

Treatment of Intractable OAB

If the OAB is intractable, then the following can be used: catheters (urethral or suprapubic), appliances, urethral closure, and diversion.

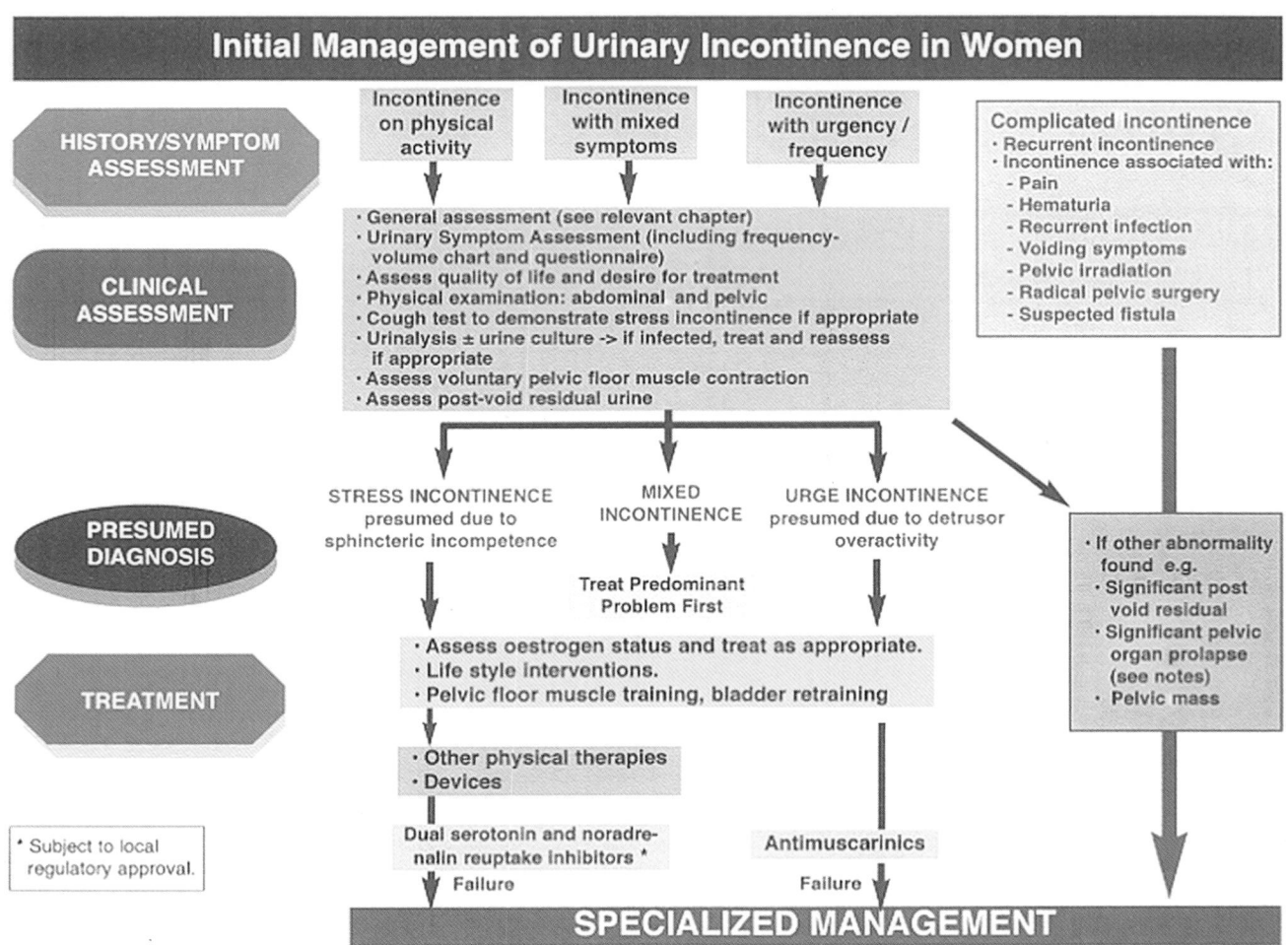

Figure 61–11. Algorithm for the basic management of female incontinence that includes OAB.

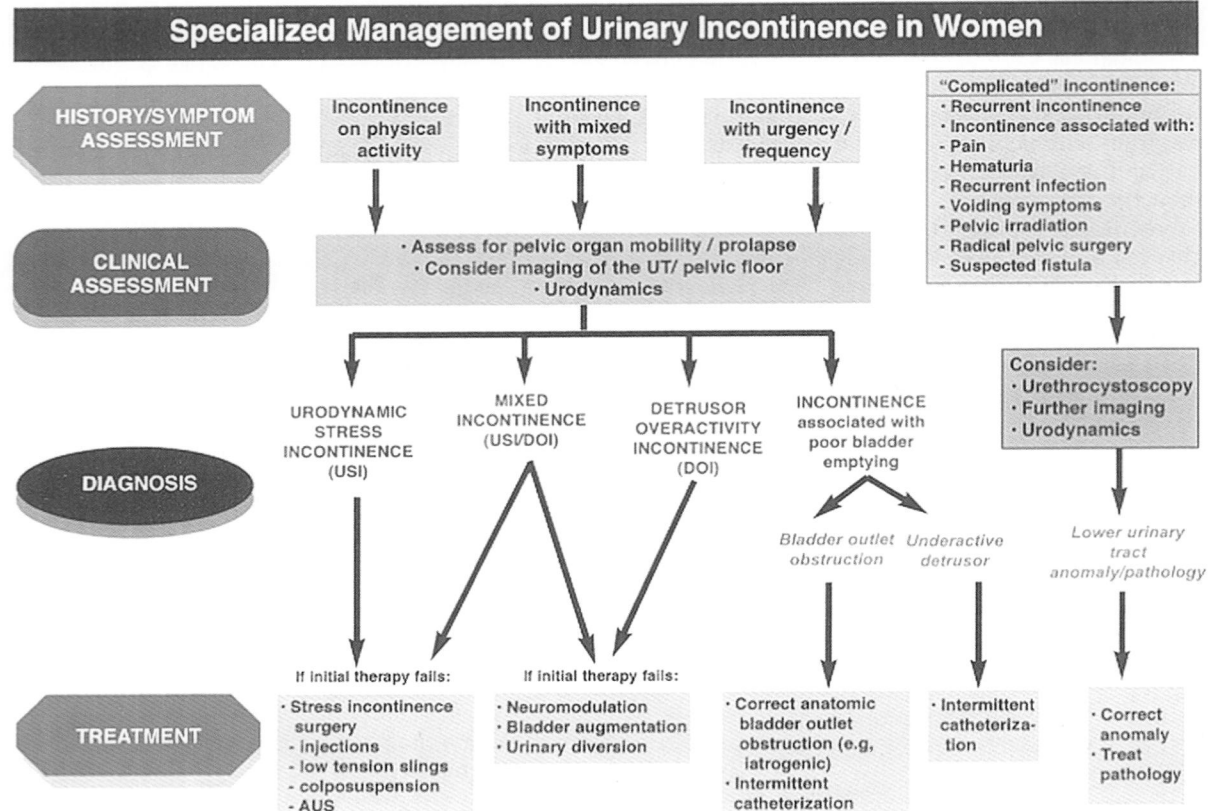

Figure 61–12. Algorithm for the specialized management of urinary incontinence in women that includes OAB and detrusor overactivity.

KEY POINTS: OVERACTIVE BLADDER

■ The International Continence Society updated its definitions for OAB and other lower urinary tract dysfunctions in 2002.

■ OAB is a symptomatic diagnosis but is assumed to be due to detrusor overactivity, which is a urodynamic diagnosis.

■ The quantification of OAB symptoms should be by frequency-volume chart and validated questionnaires.

■ If a definitive diagnosis for OAB is required, then urodynamic studies are indicated, and it should be stated whether OAB symptoms are reproduced during testing.

■ OAB and detrusor overactivity are associated with complex changes in the organization of the central nervous system and within the periphery.

■ The sensation of urgency may arise from enhancement of afferent activity or from localized contractions in the bladder wall.

■ Detrusor overactivity results when a large proportion of the bladder wall contracts outside volitional control.

SUGGESTED READINGS

Abrams P, Artibani W, Cardozo L, et al: Reviewing the ICS 2002 Terminology Report: The ongoing debate. Neurourol Urodyn 2005a, in press.

Abrams P, Cardozo L, Fall M, et al: The standardisation of terminology of lower urinary tract function: Report from the Standardisation Subcommittee of the International Continence Society. Neurourol Urodyn 2002a;21:167-178.

Abrams P, Cardozo L, Fall M, et al: The standardisation of terminology of lower urinary tract function: Report from the Standardisation Subcommittee of the International Continence Society. Am J Obstet Gynecol 2002b;187:116-126.

Abrams P, Cardozo L, Khoury S, Wein A: Incontinence. In: The Third WHO International Consultation on Incontinence. Health Publications, 2005b.

Abrams P, Hanno P, Wein A: Overactive bladder and painful bladder syndrome: There need not be confusion. Neurourol Urodyn 2005c;24:149-150.

Andersson K-E, Arner A Urinary bladder contraction and relaxation; physiology and pathophysiology. Physiol Rev 2004;84:935-986.

Brading AF: A myogenic basis for the overactive bladder. Urology 1997;50(Suppl 6A):57-67s.

de Groat WC: A neurologic basis for the overactive bladder. Urology 1997;50:36-52s.

Drake MJ, Mills IW, Gillespie JI: Model of peripheral autonomous modules and a myovesical plexus in normal and overactive bladder function. Lancet 2001;358:401-403.

Milsom I, Abrams P, Cardozo L, et al: How widespread are the symptoms of an overactive bladder and how are they managed? A population-based prevalence study. BJU Int 2001;87:760-766.

Wyndaele JJ, De Wachter S Cystometrical sensory data from a normal population: Comparison of two groups of young healthy volunteers examined with 5 years interval. Eur Urol 2002;42:34-38.

Pharmacologic Management of Storage and Emptying Failure

KARL-ERIK ANDERSSON, MD, PhD • ALAN J. WEIN, MD

PHARMACOLOGIC THERAPY TO FACILITATE BLADDER FILLING AND URINE STORAGE

PHARMACOLOGIC THERAPY TO FACILITATE BLADDER EMPTYING

PHARMACOLOGIC THERAPY TO FACILITATE BLADDER FILLING AND URINE STORAGE

Inhibiting Bladder Contractility, Decreasing Sensory Input, Increasing Bladder Capacity

Bladder Contraction and Muscarinic Receptors

The major portion of the neurohumoral stimulus for physiologic bladder contraction is acetylcholine-induced stimulation of postganglionic parasympathetic muscarinic cholinergic receptor sites in the bladder (detrusor smooth muscle and possibly other sites) (see Chapter 56, "Physiology and Pharmacology of the Bladder and Urethra"). **Atropine and atropine-like agents will depress normal bladder contractions and involuntary bladder contractions of any cause** (Andersson, 1993; Andersson and Wein, 2004). **In patients with involuntary contractions, the volume to the first involuntary contraction will generally be increased, the amplitude of the contraction decreased, and the total bladder capacity increased** (Jensen, 1981).

It has previously been stated (Wein, 1998) that bladder compliance in normal individuals and in those with neurogenic detrusor overactivity (DO), in whom the initial slope of the filling curve on cystometry is normal before the involuntary contraction, does not seem to be significantly altered by antimuscarinic agents and that the effect of pure antimuscarinics in those patients who exhibit only decreased compliance has not been well studied. Regarding the subject of bladder tone during filling, Andersson (1999a, 1999b, 2004;

Andersson and Yoshida, 2003) has pointed out that although it is widely accepted that there is no sacral parasympathetic outflow to the bladder during filling, **antimuscarinic drugs increase and anticholinesterase inhibitors decrease bladder capacity. Because antimuscarinic drugs do seem to affect the sensation of urgency during filling, this suggests an ongoing acetylcholine-mediated stimulation of detrusor tone** (see later). **If this is correct, agents inhibiting acetylcholine release or activity would be expected to contribute to bladder relaxation or the maintenance of low bladder tone during filling with a consequent decrease in filling and storage symptoms unrelated to the occurrence of an involuntary contraction. Outlet resistance, at least as reflected by urethral pressure measurements, does not seem to be clinically affected.**

Although the antimuscarinic agents usually produce significant clinical improvement in patients with involuntary contractions and associated symptoms, generally only partial inhibition results. In many animal models, atropine only partially antagonizes the response of the whole bladder to pelvic nerve stimulation and of bladder strips to field stimulation, although it does completely inhibit the response of bladder smooth muscle to exogenous cholinergic stimulation. This phenomenon, which is called atropine resistance, is secondary to release of transmitters other than acetylcholine (see Andersson, 1993; de Groat and Yoshimura, 2001; Andersson and Wein, 2004; see also Chapter 56, "Physiology and Pharmacology of the Bladder and Urethra"). Atropine resistance is the most common hypothesis invoked to explain the clinical difficulty in eradicating involuntary contractions with antimuscarinic agents alone, and it is also invoked to support the rationale of combined treatment of DO with agents that have different mechanisms of action.

Andersson and Wein (2004) cite references stating that atropine resistance seems to be of little importance in normal human bladder muscle but point out that atropine-resistant (nonadrenergic, noncholinergic) contractions have been reported in human detrusor smooth muscle and in morphologically or functionally changed bladders in individuals with various types of voiding dysfunction. Thus, the importance or nonimportance of an atropine-resistant component to detrusor contraction in the treatment of DO remains to be established.

Muscarinic Receptors. In the human bladder, mRNAs for all five of the pharmacologically defined receptors, M_1 to M_5, have been demonstrated (Sigala et al, 2002). **There is a predominance of M_2 and M_3 receptors** (Yamaguchi et al, 1996; Sigala et al, 2002), and this seems to be the case also in the animal species investigated (Hegde and Eglen, 1999; Chess-Williams, 2002; Andersson and Arner, 2004; Mansfield et al, 2005). **M_2 and M_3 receptors can be found not only on detrusor muscle cells, where M_2 receptors predominate at least 3:1 over M_3 receptors, but also on other bladder structures, which may be of importance for detrusor activation.** Thus, muscarinic receptors can be found on urothelial cells, on suburothelial nerves, and on other suburothelial structures, such as interstitial cells (Chess-Williams, 2002; Gillespie et al, 2003; Mansfield et al, 2005).

In human as well as in animal detrusor, the M_3 receptors are believed to be the most important for contraction (Andersson, 1993; Chess-Williams et al, 2001; Andersson and Wein, 2004). No differences between genders could be demonstrated in rat and human bladders (Kories et al, 2003). The functional role for the M_2 receptors has not been clarified, and even in M_3 receptor knockout mice, they seem responsible for less than 5% of the carbachol-mediated detrusor contraction (Matsui et al, 2000). Stimulation of M_2 receptors has been shown to oppose sympathetically (β adrenoceptor) mediated smooth muscle relaxation (Hegde et al, 1997). However, on the basis of animal experiments, **M_2 receptors have been suggested to directly contribute to contraction of the bladder in certain disease states** (denervation, outflow obstruction). Preliminary experiments on human detrusor muscle could not confirm this (Stevens et al, 2004a, 2004b). On the other hand, Pontari and colleagues (2004) analyzed bladder muscle specimens from patients with neurogenic bladder dysfunction to determine whether the muscarinic receptor subtype mediating contraction shifts from M_3 to M_2, as found in the denervated, hypertrophied rat bladder. They concluded that normal detrusor contraction is mediated by the M_3 receptor subtype, whereas contractions can be mediated by the M_2 receptors in patients with neurogenic bladder dysfunction.

Muscarinic receptors are coupled to G proteins, but the signal transduction systems may vary. In general, M_1, M_3, and M_5 receptors are considered to couple preferentially to $G_{q/11}$, activating phosphoinositide hydrolysis, which in turn leads to mobilization of intracellular calcium. M_2 and M_4 receptors couple to pertussis toxin–sensitive $G_{i/o}$, resulting in inhibition of adenylate cyclase activity. In the human detrusor, Schneider and coworkers (2004), confirming that the muscarinic receptor subtype mediating carbachol-induced contraction is the M_3 receptor, also demonstrated that the phospholipase C inhibitor U-73122 did not significantly affect carbachol-stimulated bladder contraction despite blocking inositol 1,4,5-trisphosphate generation. They concluded that carbachol-induced contraction of human urinary bladder is mediated by M_3 receptors and largely depends on calcium entry through nifedipine-sensitive channels and activation of the Rho kinase pathway. Thus, it may be that the main pathways for muscarinic receptor activation of the detrusor by M_3 receptors are calcium influx through L-type Ca^{2+} channels and

increased sensitivity to calcium of the contractile machinery by inhibition of myosin light-chain phosphatase through activation of Rho kinase.

The signaling mechanisms for the M_2 receptors are less clear than those for M_3 receptors. As mentioned, M_2 receptor stimulation may oppose sympathetically induced smooth muscle relaxation, mediated by β adrenoceptors through inhibition of adenylate cyclase (Hegde et al, 1997). In agreement with this, Matsui and associates (2003) suggested, on the basis of results obtained in M_2 receptor knockout mice, that a component of the contractile response to muscarinic agonists in smooth muscle involves an M_2 receptor–mediated inhibition of the relaxant effects of agents that increase cyclic adenosine monophosphate levels. M_2 receptor stimulation can also activate nonspecific cation channels and inhibit K_{ATP} channels through activation of protein kinase C (Bonev and Nelson, 1993; Kotlikoff et al, 1999).

Muscarinic receptors may also be located on the presynaptic nerve terminals and participate in the regulation of transmitter release. The inhibitory prejunctional muscarinic receptors have been classified as muscarinic M_2 in the rabbit (Tobin and Sjögren, 1998) and rat (Somogyi and de Groat, 1992) and M_4 in the guinea pig (Alberts, 1995) and human bladder (D'Agostino et al, 2000). Prejunctional facilitatory muscarinic receptors appear to be of the M_1 subtype in the bladders of rat, rabbit (Somogyi and de Groat, 1992; Tobin and Sjögren, 1998), and humans (Somogyi and de Groat, 1999). The muscarinic facilitatory mechanism seems to be upregulated in overactive bladders from chronic spinal cord–transected rats. The facilitation in these preparations is primarily mediated by M_3 receptors (Somogyi and de Groat, 1999).

The relative roles of the different presynaptic and postsynaptic receptor subtypes in normal and abnormal bladder function still require clarification, and thus **speculation regarding optimal drug therapy based only on in vitro receptor selectivity profiles represents, at the very least, a gross oversimplification of assumptions about the muscarinic regulation of bladder function.** The muscarinic receptor functions may be changed in different urologic disorders, such as outflow obstruction, neurogenic bladders, DO without overt neurogenic cause, and diabetes (Andersson, 2000b). However, it is not always clear what the changes mean in terms of changes in detrusor function.

In general, **drug therapy for lower urinary tract dysfunction is hindered by a concept that can be expressed in one word: uroselectivity** (Andersson, 1998). **The clinical utility of available antimuscarinic agents is limited by their lack of selectivity, responsible for the classic peripheral antimuscarinic side effects of dry mouth, constipation, blurred vision, and tachycardia and for the effects on cognitive functions.** Although M_3 receptor–selective agents have the potential to eliminate some of these side effects, it would appear that the M_3 receptors in tissues of the lower urinary tract are identical to those elsewhere in the body (Caulfield and Birdsall, 1998). It may be speculated, however, that there is some heterogeneity among M_3 receptors, and this has prompted many pharmaceutical companies to continue to search for the "ideal" antimuscarinic agent to treat DO, one that would be relatively selective for muscarinic receptors involved only or primarily in the regulation of bladder contraction. Receptor selectivity, however, is not the only basis on which a drug may be "uroselective." From a clinical standpoint, it would seem particularly important to be able to describe in relative terms the ratio between a drug dose required for a desired therapeutic action and the dose producing side effects. A differential effect could be based not only on receptor selectivity but also on other known and as yet undefined physiologic, pharmacologic, or metabolic characteristics. Organ selectivity would thus seem to be the "holy grail" of such therapy. The same problematic set of concepts applies to virtually all drugs used for the treatment of lower urinary tract dysfunction.

Drugs Used for Treatment of Overactive Bladder Symptoms and Detrusor Overactivity

It has been estimated that more than 50 million people in the developed world are affected by urinary incontinence. Even if it affects 30% to 60% of patients older than 65 years, it is not a disease exclusive to aging. It appears that overactive bladder–detrusor overactivity (OAB-DO) may be the result of several different mechanisms, both myogenic and neurologic (Morrison et al, 2002). Most probably, both factors contribute to the genesis of the disease.

An abundance of drugs have been used for the treatment of OAB-DO. It should be stressed that in many trials on OAB-DO, there has been such a high placebo response that meaningful differences between placebo and active drug cannot be demonstrated (Thüroff et al, 1998). However, drug effects in individual patients may be both distinct and useful.

The 3rd International Consultation on Incontinence, held in 2004 in Monaco, assessed drugs used for treatment of incontinence. The assessment criteria (Table 62–1) were based on the Oxford guidelines, and the drugs included are given in Table 62–2.

Antimuscarinic (Anticholinergic) Agents— Specific Drugs

Acetylcholine stimulates both muscarinic and nicotinic receptors. Antimuscarinics selectively block muscarinic receptors, and they are currently the mainstay of treatment of OAB-DO. **The common view is that in OAB-DO, the drugs act by blocking the muscarinic receptors on the detrusor muscle that are stimulated by acetylcholine, released from activated cholinergic (parasympathetic) nerves. Thereby,**

Table 62–1. International Consultation on Incontinence Assessments, 2004: Oxford Guidelines (modified)

Levels of Evidence

Level 1: Systematic reviews, meta-analyses, good-quality randomized controlled clinical trials
Level 2: Randomized controlled clinical trials, good-quality prospective cohort studies
Level 3: Case-control studies, case series
Level 4: Expert opinion

Grades of Recommendation

Grade A: Based on level 1 evidence (highly recommended)
Grade B: Consistent level 2 or 3 evidence (recommended)
Grade C: Level 4 studies or "majority evidence" (optional)
Grade D: Evidence inconsistent or inconclusive (no recommendation possible)

Table 62–2. Drugs Used in the Treatment of Detrusor Overactivity (assessments according to the Oxford system, modified)

	Level of Evidence	Grade of Recommendation
Antimuscarinic Drugs		
Tolterodine	1	A
Trospium	1	A
Solifenacin	1	A
Darifenacin	1	A
Propantheline	2	B
Atropine, hyoscyamine	3	C
Drugs with Mixed Actions		
Oxybutynin	1	A
Propiverine	1	A
Dicyclomine	3	C
Flavoxate	2	D
Antidepressants		
Imipramine	3	C
α Adrenoceptor Antagonists		
Alfuzosin	3	C
Doxazosin	3	C
Prazosin	3	C
Terazosin	3	C
Tamsulosin	3	C
β Adrenoceptor Antagonists		
Terbutaline	3	C
Salbutamol	3	C
Cyclooxygenase Inhibitors		
Indomethacin	2	
Flurbiprofen	2	C
Other Drugs		
Baclofen*		C
Capsaicin[†]	2	C
Resiniferatoxin[†]	2	C
Botulinum toxin[‡]	2	B
Estrogen	2	C
Desmopressin[§]	1	A

*Intrathecal.
[†]Intravesical.
[‡]Bladder wall.
[§]Nocturia.

they decrease the ability of the bladder to contract. However, antimuscarinic drugs act mainly during the storage phase, decreasing urgency and increasing bladder capacity, and during this phase, there is normally no parasympathetic input to the lower urinary tract (Morrison et al, 2002). Furthermore, antimuscarinics are usually competitive antagonists. This implies that when there is a massive release of acetylcholine, as during micturition, the effects of the drugs should be decreased; otherwise, the reduced ability of the detrusor to contract would eventually lead to urinary retention. Undeniably, **high doses of antimuscarinics can produce urinary retention in humans; but in the dose range needed for beneficial effects in OAB-DO, there is little evidence for a significant reduction of the voiding contraction.** The question is whether there are effects of antimuscarinics on other structures than detrusor muscle that can contribute to their beneficial effects in the treatment of OAB-DO (Andersson and

Yoshida, 2003). Muscarinic receptor functions may change in bladder disorders associated with OAB-DO, implying that mechanisms that normally have little clinical importance may be upregulated and contribute to the pathophysiologic process of OAB-DO (Andersson, 2004).

Muscarinic receptors are found on bladder urothelium-suburothelium, where their density can be even higher than in detrusor muscle (Chess-Williams, 2002; Mansfield et al, 2005). The role of the urothelium-suburothelium in bladder activation has attracted much interest (Andersson, 2002a; de Groat, 2004), but whether the muscarinic receptors on these structures can influence micturition has not yet been established. Yoshida and colleagues (2004) found that there is a basal acetylcholine release in human detrusor muscle. This release was resistant to tetrodotoxin and much diminished when the urothelium-suburothelium was removed; thus, the released acetylcholine was probably of non-neuronal origin and, at least partly, generated by the urothelium-suburothelium. There is also indirect clinical evidence for release of acetylcholine during bladder filling. Smith and coworkers (1974) found that in patients with recent spinal cord injury, inhibition of acetylcholine breakdown by use of cholinesterase inhibitors could increase resting tone and induce rhythmic contractions in the bladder. Yossepowitch and coworkers (2001) inhibited acetylcholine breakdown with edrophonium in a series of patients with disturbed voiding or urinary incontinence. They found a significant change in sensation and decreased bladder capacity, induction or amplification of involuntary detrusor contractions, or significantly decreased detrusor compliance in 78% of the patients with the symptom pattern of overactive bladder but in no patients without specific complaints suggesting DO. Thus, **during the storage phase, acetylcholine may be released from both neuronal and non-neuronal sources (e.g., the urothelium-suburothelium) and directly or indirectly (by increasing detrusor smooth muscle tone) excite afferent nerves in the suburothelium and within the detrusor. This mechanism may be important in the pathophysiologic process of overactive bladder and a possible target for antimuscarinic drugs** (Andersson, 2004).

In general, antimuscarinics can be divided into tertiary and quaternary amines (Guay, 2003). They differ with regard to lipophilicity, molecular charge, and, to less extent, molecular size. **Tertiary compounds generally have higher lipophilicity and less molecular charge than quaternary agents. Atropine, tolterodine, oxybutynin, propiverine, darifenacin, and solifenacin are tertiary amines. They are generally well absorbed from the gastrointestinal tract and should theoretically be able to pass into the central nervous system (CNS), dependent on their individual physicochemical properties. High lipophilicity, small molecular size, and low charge will increase the possibility of passing the blood-brain barrier. Quaternary ammonium compounds, like propantheline and trospium, are not well absorbed, pass into the CNS to a limited extent, and have a low reported incidence of CNS side effects** (Guay, 2003). They still produce well-known peripheral antimuscarinic side effects, such as accommodation paralysis, constipation, tachycardia, and dryness of mouth.

Many antimuscarinics (all currently used tertiary amines) are metabolized by the P-450 enzyme system to active or to inactive metabolites (Guay, 2003). The most commonly involved P-450 enzymes are CYP2D6 and CYP3A4. The metabolic conversion creates a theoretical risk for drug-drug interactions, resulting in either reduced (enzyme induction) or increased (enzyme inhibition, substrate competition) plasma concentration or effect of the antimuscarinic or interacting drug. Antimuscarinics actively secreted by the renal tubules (e.g., trospium) may theoretically be able to interfere with the elimination of other drugs by this mechanism.

Antimuscarinics are still the most widely used treatment for urgency and urgency incontinence (Andersson, 2004). However, currently used drugs lack selectivity for the bladder, and effects on other organ systems may result in side effects that limit their usefulness. For example, all antimuscarinic drugs are contraindicated in untreated narrow-angle glaucoma.

Theoretically, drugs with selectivity for the bladder could be obtained, if the subtypes mediating bladder contraction and those producing the main side effects of antimuscarinic drugs were different. Unfortunately, this does not seem to be the case. One way of avoiding many of the antimuscarinic side effects is to administer the drugs intravesically. However, this is practical only in a limited number of patients.

Several antimuscarinic drugs have been used for treatment of OAB-DO. For many of them, documentation of effects is not based on randomized, controlled clinical trials (RCTs) satisfying currently required criteria, and some drugs can be considered obsolete (e.g., emepronium). Information on these drugs has not been included but can be found elsewhere (Andersson, 1988; Andersson, 1999c).

Atropine. Atropine (*dl*-hyoscyamine) is rarely used for treatment of OAB-DO because of its systemic side effects, which preclude its use. However, in patients with neurogenic DO, intravesical atropine may be effective for increasing bladder capacity without causing any systemic adverse effects, as shown in open pilot trials (Ekström et al, 1993; Glickman et al, 1995; Deaney et al, 1998; Enskat et al, 2001).

The pharmacologically active antimuscarinic moiety of atropine is *l*-hyoscyamine. Although still used, few clinical studies are available to evaluate the antimuscarinic activity of *l*-hyoscyamine sulfate (Muskat et al, 1996).

Propantheline. Propantheline bromide is a quaternary ammonium compound, nonselective for muscarinic receptor subtypes, that has a low (5% to 10%) and individually varying biologic availability. It is metabolized (metabolites inactive) and has a short plasma half-life (less than 2 hours; Beermann et al, 1972). It is usually given in a dose of 15 to 30 mg four times daily, but to obtain an optimal effect, individual titration of the dose is necessary, and larger doses are often required. With use of this approach in 26 patients with uninhibited detrusor contractions, Blaivas and associates (1980) in an open study obtained a complete clinical response in all patients but one, who did not tolerate more than 15 mg four times daily. The range of doses varied from 7.5 to 60 mg four times daily. In contrast, Thüroff and coworkers (1991), comparing the effects of oxybutynin 5 mg three times daily, propantheline 15 mg three times daily, and placebo in a randomized, double-blind, multicenter trial on the treatment of frequency, urgency, and incontinence related to DO (154 patients), found no differences between the placebo and propantheline groups. In another randomized comparative trial with cross-over design (23 women with idiopathic DO) and with dose titration, Holmes and colleagues (1989) found no differences in efficacy between oxybutynin and propantheline.

There is a surprising lack of evaluable data on the effectiveness of propantheline for the treatment of DO. The Agency for Health Care Policy and Research (AHCPR) Clinical Practice Guidelines (1992) list five randomized controlled trials reviewed for propantheline, with 82% female patients. Percentage cures (all figures refer to percentage effect on drug minus percentage effect on placebo) are listed as 0% to 5%, reduction in urgency incontinence as 0% to 53%, and percentage side effects and percentage dropouts as 0% to 50% and 0% to 9%, respectively. Controlled randomized trials (n = 6) reviewed by Thüroff and coworkers (1998) confirmed a positive but varying response to the drug.

Although the effect of propantheline on OAB-DO has not been well documented in controlled trials satisfying standards of today, it can be considered effective and may, in individually titrated doses, be clinically useful.

Trospium. Trospium chloride is a quaternary ammonium compound with a biologic availability of less than 10% (Füsgen and Hauri, 2000). It is expected to cross the blood-brain barrier to a limited extent and seems to have no negative cognitive effects (Füsgen and Hauri, 2000; Todorova et al, 2001; Wiedemann et al, 2001). The drug has a plasma half-life of approximately 20 hours and is mainly (60% of the dose absorbed) eliminated unchanged in the urine by renal tubular secretion. It is not metabolized by the cytochrome P-450 enzyme system (Beckmann-Knopp et al, 1999).

Trospium has no selectivity for muscarinic receptor subtypes. In isolated detrusor muscle, it was more potent than oxybutynin and tolterodine to antagonize carbachol-induced contractions (Ückert et al, 2000).

Several RCTs have documented positive effects of trospium, both in neurogenic DO (Stöhrer et al, 1991; Madersbacher et al, 1995) and in non-neurogenic DO (Allousi et al, 1998; Cardozo et al, 2000; Jünemann et al, 2000; Halaska et al, 2003; Zinner et al, 2004a).

In a placebo-controlled, double-blind study of patients with neurogenic DO (Stöhrer et al, 1991), the drug was given twice daily in a dose of 20 mg during a 3-week period. It increased maximum cystometric capacity, decreased maximal detrusor pressure, and increased compliance in the treatment group, whereas no effects were noted in the placebo group. Side effects were few and comparable in both groups. In another RCT including patients with spinal cord injuries and neurogenic DO, trospium and oxybutynin were equally effective; however, trospium seemed to have fewer side effects (Madersbacher et al, 1995).

The effect of trospium in urgency incontinence has been documented in RCTs. Allousi and coworkers (1998) compared the effects of the drug with those of placebo in 309 patients in a urodynamic study of 3 weeks' duration. Trospium 20 mg was given twice daily. Significant increases were noted in volume at first unstable contraction and in maximum bladder capacity. Cardozo and associates (2000) investigated 208 patients with DO who were treated with trospium 20 mg twice daily for 2 weeks. Also in this study, significant increases were found

in volume at first unstable contraction and in maximum bladder capacity in the trospium-treated group. Trospium was well tolerated, with frequency of adverse effects similar to that in the placebo group. Jünemann and colleagues (2000) compared trospium 20 mg twice daily with tolterodine 2 mg twice daily in a placebo-controlled double-blind study of 232 patients with urodynamically proven DO, "sensory urgency" incontinence, or mixed incontinence. Trospium reduced the frequency of micturition, which was the primary endpoint, more than tolterodine and placebo did, and it also reduced the number of incontinence episodes more than the comparators. Dry mouth was comparable in the trospium and tolterodine groups (7% and 9%, respectively).

Halaska and associates (2003) studied the tolerability and efficacy of trospium in doses of 20 mg twice daily for long-term therapy in patients with "urgency syndrome." The trial comprised a total of 358 patients with urgency syndrome or urgency incontinence. After randomization in the ratio of 3:1, participants were treated continuously for 52 weeks with either trospium (20 mg twice daily) or oxybutynin (5 mg twice daily). Urodynamic measurements were performed at the beginning and at 26 and 52 weeks to determine the maximal cystometric bladder capacity. The frequency of micturition, frequency of incontinence, and number of urgency events were recorded in patient diary protocols in weeks 0, 2, 26, and 52. Analysis of the micturition diary clearly indicated a reduction of the micturition frequency, the incontinence frequency, and the number of urgencies in both treatment groups. Mean maximum cystometric bladder capacity increased during treatment with trospium by 92 mL after 26 weeks and 115 mL after 52 weeks ($P = .001$). Further comparison with oxybutynin did not reveal any statistically significant differences in urodynamic variables between the drugs. Adverse events occurred in 64.8% of the patients treated with trospium and in 76.7% of those treated with oxybutynin. The main symptom encountered in both treatment groups was dryness of the mouth. An overall assessment for each of the drugs reveals a comparable efficacy level and a better benefit-risk ratio for trospium than for oxybutynin because of better tolerability.

Zinner and colleagues (2004a) treated 523 patients with symptoms associated with OAB and urgency incontinence with 20 mg trospium twice daily or placebo in a 12-week, multicenter, parallel, double-blind, placebo-controlled trial. Dual primary endpoints were change in average number of toilet voids and change in urgency incontinent episodes per 24 hours. Secondary efficacy variables were change in average of volume per void, voiding urgency severity, urinations during day and night, time to onset of action, and change in Incontinence Impact Questionnaire score. Trospium significantly decreased average frequency of toilet voids and urgency incontinent episodes compared with placebo. It significantly increased average volume per void and decreased average urgency severity and daytime frequency. All effects occurred by week 1, and all were sustained throughout the study. Nocturnal frequency decreased significantly by week 4, and Incontinence Impact Questionnaire scores improved at week 12. Trospium was well tolerated. The most common side effects were dry mouth (21.8%), constipation (9.5%), and headache (6.5%). In a large U.S. multicenter trial with the same design and including 658 patients with OAB, Rudy and coworkers

(2005) confirmed the data of Zinner and colleagues (2004a) with respect to both efficacy and adverse effects.

Trospium is a well-documented alternative for treatment of OAB-DO and seems to be well tolerated.

Tolterodine. Tolterodine is a tertiary amine, rapidly absorbed and extensively metabolized by the cytochrome P-450 system (CYP2D6). The major active 5-hydroxymethyl metabolite has a pharmacologic profile similar to that of the mother compound (Nilvebrant et al, 1997a) and significantly contributes to the therapeutic effect of tolterodine (Brynne et al, 1997, 1998). The plasma half-life of both tolterodine and its metabolite is 2 to 3 hours, but the effects on the bladder seem to be longer lasting than could be expected from the pharmacokinetic data. The relatively low lipophilicity of tolterodine implies limited propensity to penetrate into the CNS, which may explain a low incidence of cognitive side effects (Hills et al, 1998; Clemett and Jarvis, 2001). Tolterodine has no selectivity for muscarinic receptor subtypes but is claimed to have functional selectivity for the bladder over the salivary glands (Stahl et al, 1995; Nilvebrant et al, 1997b). In healthy volunteers, orally given tolterodine in a large dose (6.4 mg) had a powerful inhibitory effect on micturition and also reduced stimulated salivation 1 hour after administration of the drug (Stahl et al, 1995). However, 5 hours after administration, the effects on the urinary bladder were maintained, whereas no significant effects on salivation could be demonstrated.

Tolterodine is available as both an immediate-release form (1 or 2 mg, twice daily dosing) and an extended-release form (2 or 4 mg, once daily dosing). The extended-release form seems to have advantages over the immediate-release form in terms of both efficacy and tolerability (van Kerrebroeck et al, 2001).

Several randomized, double-blind, placebo-controlled studies of patients with OAB-DO (both idiopathic and neurogenic DO) have documented a significant reduction in micturition frequency and number of incontinence episodes (Hills et al, 1998; Clemett and Jarvis, 2001; Andersson et al, 2002, 2005). Comparative RCTs, such as the OBJECT (Overactive Bladder: Judging Effective Control and Treatment) and the OPERA (Overactive Bladder: Performance of Extended Release Agents) studies, have further supported its effectiveness.

The OBJECT trial compared oxybutynin extended-release (ER), 10 mg once daily, with tolterodine immediate-release (IR), 2 mg twice daily, in a 12-week randomized, double-blind, parallel-group study including 378 patients with OAB (Appell et al, 2001). Participants had between 7 and 50 episodes of urgency incontinence per week and 10 or more voids in 24 hours. The outcome measures were the number of episodes of urgency incontinence, total incontinence, and micturition frequency at 12 weeks adjusted for baseline. At the end of the study, oxybutynin ER was found to be significantly more effective than tolterodine in each of the main outcome measures adjusted for baseline. Dry mouth, the most common adverse event, was reported by 28% and 33% of participants taking oxybutynin ER and tolterodine IR, respectively. Rates of CNS and other adverse events were low and similar in both groups. The authors concluded that oxybutynin ER was more effective than tolterodine IR and that the rates of dry mouth and other adverse events were similar in both treatment groups.

In the OPERA study (Diokno et al, 2003), oxybutynin ER at 10 mg/day or tolterodine ER at 4 mg/day was given for 12 weeks to women with 21 to 60 urgency incontinence episodes per week and an average of 10 or more voids per 24 hours. Episodes of incontinence episodes (primary endpoint), total (urgency and nonurgency) incontinence, and micturition were recorded in 24-hour urinary diaries at baseline and at weeks 2, 4, 8, and 12 and compared. Adverse events were also evaluated. Improvements in weekly urgency incontinence episodes were similar for the 790 women who received oxybutynin ER (n = 391) or tolterodine ER (n = 399). Oxybutynin ER was somewhat more effective than tolterodine ER in reducing micturition frequency, and 23.0% of women taking oxybutynin ER reported no episodes of urinary incontinence compared with 16.8% of women taking tolterodine ER. Dry mouth, usually mild, was more common with oxybutynin ER. Adverse events were generally mild and occurred at low rates, with both groups having similar discontinuation of treatment due to adverse events. The conclusions were that reductions in weekly urgency incontinence and total incontinence episodes were similar with the two drugs. Dry mouth was more common with oxybutynin ER, but tolerability was otherwise comparable, including adverse events involving the CNS.

In the ACET (Antimuscarinic Clinical Effectiveness Trial; Sussman and Garely, 2002) study, patients with OAB were randomized to 8 weeks of open-label treatment with either 2 mg or 4 mg of once-daily tolterodine ER and in the other trial to 5 mg or 10 mg of oxybutynin ER. A total of 1289 patients were included. Fewer patients prematurely withdrew from the trial in the tolterodine ER 4-mg group (12%) than in either the oxybutynin ER 5-mg (19%) or oxybutynin ER 10-mg (21%) groups. More patients in the oxybutynin ER 10-mg group than in the tolterodine ER 4-mg group withdrew because of poor tolerability (13% versus 6%). After 8 weeks, 70% of patients in the tolterodine ER 4-mg group perceived an improved bladder condition, compared with 60% in the tolterodine ER 2-mg group, 59% in the oxybutynin ER 5-mg group, and 60% in the oxybutynin ER 10-mg group. Dry mouth was dose dependent with both agents, although differences between doses reached statistical significance only in the oxybutynin trial (oxybutynin ER 5 mg versus oxybutynin ER 10 mg; $P = .05$). Patients treated with tolterodine ER 4 mg reported a significantly lower severity of dry mouth compared with oxybutynin ER 10 mg. The conclusion that the findings suggest improved clinical efficacy of tolterodine ER (4 mg) over oxybutynin ER (10 mg) is weakened by the open-label design of the study.

Zinner and colleagues (2002) evaluated the efficacy, safety, and tolerability of tolterodine ER in treating OAB in older (≥65 years) and younger (<65 years) patients in a 12-week double-blind, placebo-controlled clinical trial including 1015 patients (43.1% ≥ 65 years) with urgency incontinence and urinary frequency. Patients were randomized to treatment with tolterodine ER 4 mg once daily (n = 507) or placebo (n = 508) for 12 weeks. Efficacy, measured with micturition charts (incontinence episodes, micturitions, volume voided per micturition) and subjective patient assessments, safety, and tolerability endpoints were evaluated, relative to placebo, according to two age cohorts: younger than 65 years and 65 years and older. Compared with placebo, significant improvements in micturition chart variables with tolterodine ER showed no age-related differences. Dry mouth (of any severity) was the most common adverse event in both the tolterodine ER and placebo treatment arms, irrespective of age (<65 years: tolterodine ER 22.7%, placebo 8.1%; ≥65 years: tolterodine ER 24.3%, placebo 7.2%). Few patients (<2%) experienced severe dry mouth. No CNS, visual, cardiac (per electrocardiogram), or laboratory safety concerns were noted. Withdrawal rates due to adverse events on tolterodine ER 4 mg daily were comparable in the two age cohorts (<65 years: 5.5%; ≥65 years: 5.1%).

The central symptom in the OAB syndrome is urgency. Freeman and colleagues (2003) presented a secondary analysis of a double-blind, placebo-controlled study that evaluated the effect of once-daily tolterodine ER on urinary urgency in patients with OAB. Patients with urinary frequency (eight or more micturitions per 24 hours) and urgency incontinence (five or more episodes per week) were randomized to oral treatment with tolterodine ER 4 mg once daily (n = 398) or placebo (n = 374) for 12 weeks. Efficacy was assessed by use of patient perception evaluations. Of patients treated with tolterodine ER, 44% reported improved urgency symptoms (compared with 32% for placebo), and 62% reported improved bladder symptoms (placebo, 48%). The odds of reducing urgency and improving bladder symptoms were 1.68 and 1.78 times greater, respectively, for patients in the tolterodine ER group than for patients receiving placebo. In response to urgency, there was a more than sixfold increase in the proportion of patients able to finish a task before voiding in the tolterodine ER group. The proportion of patients unable to hold urine on experiencing urgency was also decreased by 58% with tolterodine, compared with 32% with placebo ($P < .001$).

Mattiasson and associates (2003) compared the efficacy of tolterodine 2 mg twice daily plus simplified bladder training with tolterodine alone in patients with OAB in a multicenter single-blind study. At the end of the study, the median percentage reduction in voiding frequency was greater with tolterodine plus bladder training than with tolterodine alone (33% versus 25%); the median percentage increase in volume voided per void was 31% with tolterodine plus bladder training and 20% with tolterodine alone. There was a median of 81% fewer incontinence episodes than at baseline with tolterodine alone, which was not significantly different from that with tolterodine plus bladder training (−87%). It was concluded that the effectiveness of tolterodine 2 mg twice daily can be augmented by a simplified bladder training regimen.

Millard and colleagues (2004a) investigated whether the combination of tolterodine plus a simple pelvic floor muscle exercise program would provide improved treatment benefits compared with tolterodine alone in 480 patients with OAB. Tolterodine therapy for 24 weeks resulted in significant improvement in urgency, frequency, and incontinence; however, no additional benefit was demonstrated for a simple pelvic floor muscle exercise program.

Tolterodine, in both the immediate-release and extended-release forms, has a well-documented effect in OAB-DO. It is well tolerated and is currently, together with oxybutynin, first-line therapy for patients with this disorder.

Darifenacin. Darifenacin is a tertiary amine with moderate lipophilicity, well absorbed from the gastrointestinal tract after oral administration and extensively metabolized in the liver by the cytochrome P-450 isoforms CYP3A4 and CYP2D6. The metabolism of darifenacin by CYP3A4 suggests that co-administration of a potent inhibitor of this enzyme (e.g., ketoconazole) may lead to an increase in the circulating concentration of darifenacin (Kerbusch et al, 2003). Darifenacin has been developed as a controlled-release formulation, which allows once-daily dosing. Recommended doses are 7.5 and 15 mg/day.

Darifenacin is a relatively selective muscarinic M_3 receptor antagonist. In vitro, it is selective for human cloned muscarinic M_3 receptors relative to M_1, M_2, M_4, or M_5 receptors. Theoretically, drugs with selectivity for the M_3 receptor can be expected to have clinical efficacy in OAB-DO with reduction of the adverse events related to the blockade of other muscarinic receptor subtypes (Andersson, 2002b). However, the clinical efficacy and adverse effects of a drug are dependent not only on its profile of receptor affinity but also on its pharmacokinetics and on the importance of muscarinic receptors for a given organ function.

The clinical effectiveness of darifenacin has been documented in several RCTs (Haab et al, 2004; Chapple et al, 2005a). Haab and associates (2004) reported a multicenter, double-blind, placebo-controlled, parallel-group study that enrolled 561 patients (19 to 88 years; 85% female) with OAB symptoms for more than 6 months and included some patients with prior exposure to antimuscarinic agents. After washout and a 2-week placebo run-in, patients were randomized (1:4:2:3) to once-daily oral darifenacin controlled-release tablets, 3.75 mg (n = 53), 7.5 mg (n = 229), or 15 mg (n = 115), or matching placebo (n = 164) for 12 weeks. Patients recorded daily incontinence episodes, micturition frequency, bladder capacity (mean volume voided), frequency of urgency, severity of urgency, incontinence episodes resulting in change of clothing or pads, and nocturnal awakenings due to OAB in an electronic diary during weeks 2, 6, and 12 (directly preceding clinic visits). Tolerability data were evaluated from adverse event reports.

Darifenacin 7.5 mg and 15 mg had a rapid onset of effect, with significant improvement compared with placebo for most parameters at the first clinic visit (week 2). Darifenacin 7.5 mg and 15 mg, was significantly superior to placebo for improvements in micturition frequency, bladder capacity, frequency of urgency, severity of urgency, and number of incontinence episodes leading to a change in clothing or pads. There was no significant reduction in nocturnal awakenings due to OAB.

The most common adverse events were mild to moderate dry mouth and constipation, with a CNS and cardiac safety profile comparable to that of placebo. No patients withdrew from the study as a result of dry mouth, and discontinuation related to constipation was rare (0.6% placebo versus 0.9% darifenacin).

A review of the pooled darifenacin data from the three phase III, multicenter, double-blind clinical trials in patients with OAB has been carried out (Chapple et al, 2005a). After a 4-week washout/run-in period, 1059 adults (85% female) with symptoms of OAB (urgency incontinence, urgency, and frequency) for at least 6 months were randomized to once-daily oral treatment with darifenacin 7.5 mg (n = 337) or 15 mg (n = 334) or matching placebo (n = 388) for 12 weeks. Efficacy was evaluated by electronic patient diaries that recorded incontinence episodes (including those resulting in a change of clothing or pads), frequency and severity of urgency, micturition frequency, and bladder capacity (volume voided). Safety was evaluated by analysis of treatment-related adverse events, withdrawal rates, and laboratory tests. Relative to baseline, 12 weeks of treatment with darifenacin resulted in a dose-related significant reduction in median number of incontinence episodes per week (7.5 mg, −8.8 [−68.4%]; 15 mg, −10.6 [−76.8%]). Significant decreases in the frequency and severity of urgency, micturition frequency, and number of incontinence episodes resulting in a change of clothing or pads were also apparent, along with an increase in bladder capacity. Darifenacin was well tolerated. The most common treatment-related adverse events were dry mouth and constipation, although together these resulted in few discontinuations (darifenacin 7.5 mg, 0.6% of patients; darifenacin 15 mg, 2.1%; placebo, 0.3%). The incidence of CNS and cardiovascular adverse events was comparable to that with placebo.

One of the most noticeable clinical effects of antimuscarinics is their ability to reduce urgency and allow patients to postpone micturition. A study was conducted to assess the effect of darifenacin on the "warning time" associated with urinary urgency. This was a multicenter, randomized, double-blind, placebo-controlled study consisting of 2 weeks of washout, 2 weeks of medication-free run-in, and a 2-week treatment phase (Cardozo and Dixon, 2005). Subjects with urinary urgency for more than 6 months before enrollment and episodes of urgency more than four times daily during run-in were randomized (1:1) to darifenacin controlled-release tablets 30 mg daily or matching placebo. Warning time was defined as the time from the first sensation of urgency to voluntary micturition or incontinence and was recorded by an electronic event recorder at baseline (visit 3) and study end (visit 4) during a 6-hour clinic-based monitoring period, with the subject instructed to delay micturition for as long as possible. During each monitoring period, up to three urgency-void cycles were recorded.

Of the 72 subjects who entered the study, 67 had warning time data recorded at both baseline and study end and were included in the primary efficacy analysis (32 on darifenacin, 35 on placebo). Darifenacin treatment resulted in a significant increase in mean warning time with a median increase of 4.3 minutes compared with placebo. Overall, 47% of darifenacin-treated subjects compared with 20% receiving placebo achieved an increase of 30% or more in mean warning time. There were methodologic problems associated with this study; it used a dose of 30 mg (higher than the dose recommended for clinical use), the treatment period was short, it was conducted in a clinic-centered environment, the methodology carried with it a significant potential training effect, and the placebo group had higher baseline values than the treatment group. However, this pilot study is the first study to evaluate changes in warning time, which is potentially important to individuals with symptoms associated with OAB. The observations suggest that darifenacin increases warning time compared with placebo, allowing subjects more time to reach a toilet and potentially avoiding the embarrassing experience of incontinence. It is likely that future studies with other antimuscarinic agents will demonstrate similar findings.

The effect of darifenacin on cognitive function was evaluated in elderly volunteers who did not present with clinical dementia (Lipton et al, 2005). This double-blind, three-period cross-over study randomized 129 volunteers (≥65 years, with no or mild cognitive impairment) to receive three of five tablets: darifenacin controlled-release, 3.75 mg, 7.5 mg, or 15 mg daily; darifenacin immediate-release, 5 mg three times daily; or matching placebo. Each 14-day treatment period was separated by 7 days of washout. Cognitive function tests and alertness, calmness, and contentment evaluations were completed at baseline and at treatment end. For the primary endpoints, memory scanning sensitivity, speed of choice reaction time, and word recognition sensitivity, there were no statistically significant differences for darifenacin versus placebo. Darifenacin treatment was not associated with changes in alertness, contentment, or calmness that are likely to be clinically relevant. Darifenacin was well tolerated, the most common adverse events being mild to moderate dry mouth and constipation. It was concluded from this study that in elderly volunteers, darifenacin did not impair cognitive function.

Darifenacin has a well-documented effect in OAB-DO, and the adverse event profile seems acceptable.

Solifenacin (YM905). Solifenacin (YM905) is a tertiary amine, well absorbed from the gastrointestinal tract (absolute bioavailability of 90%). It undergoes significant hepatic metabolism involving the cytochrome P-450 enzyme system (CYP3A4). The mean terminal half-life is approximately 50 hours (Kuipers et al, 2004; Smulders et al, 2004).

Two large-scale phase II trials with parallel designs were performed of men and women treated with solifenacin (Chapple et al, 2004a, 2004b; Smith et al, 2002). The first dose-ranging study evaluated solifenacin 2.5 mg, 5 mg, 10 mg, and 20 mg and tolterodine (2 mg twice daily) in a multinational placebo-controlled study of 225 patients with urodynamically confirmed DO (Chapple et al, 2004a). Patients received treatment for 4 weeks followed by 2 weeks of follow-up. Inclusion criteria for this and subsequent phase III studies of patients with OAB included eight or more micturitions per 24 hours and either one episode of incontinence or one episode of urgency daily as recorded in 3-day micturition diaries. Micturition frequency, the primary efficacy variable, was statistically significantly reduced in patients taking solifenacin 5 mg, 10 mg, and 20 mg but not in patients receiving placebo or tolterodine. This effect was rapid, with most of the effect observed at the earliest assessment visit, 2 weeks after treatment initiation. In addition, the 5-mg, 10-mg, and 20-mg dosing groups were associated with statistically significant increases in volume voided relative to placebo and numerically greater reductions in episodes of urgency and incontinence compared with placebo. Study discontinuations due to adverse events were similar across treatment groups, albeit highest in the 20-mg solifenacin group. As the 5-mg and 10-mg doses caused lower rates of dry mouth than did tolterodine and superior efficacy outcomes relative to placebo, these dosing strengths were selected for further evaluation in large-scale phase III studies.

The second dose-ranging study of solifenacin 2.5 mg to 20 mg was carried out in the United States (Smith et al, 2002). This trial included 261 evaluable men and women receiving solifenacin or placebo for 4 weeks followed by a 2-week follow-up period. Micturition frequency was statistically significantly reduced relative to placebo in patients receiving 10 mg and 20 mg of solifenacin. Number of micturitions per 24 hours showed reductions by day 7 and continued to decrease through day 28; day 7 was the earliest time point tested in solifenacin trials, and these findings demonstrate efficacy as early as 1 week. The 5-mg, 10-mg, and 20-mg dosing groups experienced statistically significant increases in volume voided, and the 10-mg solifenacin dose was associated with statistically significant reductions in episodes of incontinence.

Four pivotal phase III studies were conducted to evaluate the efficacy, safety, and tolerability of solifenacin in adult patients with OAB. The primary efficacy variable in all studies was change from baseline to endpoint in micturitions per 24 hours; secondary efficacy variables included change in mean number of daily urgency and incontinence episodes. Mean volume voided per micturition served as an additional secondary efficacy outcome and provided an objective measure of bladder function. Efficacy was assessed by patient diary recordings collected at four assessment points during the 12-week trial. Two studies used the King's Health Questionnaire to evaluate quality of life. Safety was evaluated on the basis of adverse events, clinical laboratory values, vital signs, physical examination findings, and electrocardiograms.

In the first of the double-blind multinational trials, a total of 1077 patients were randomized to 5 mg solifenacin, 10 mg solifenacin, tolterodine (2 mg twice daily), or placebo (Chapple et al, 2004b). This study was powered only to compare active treatments with placebo. Compared with placebo (−8%), mean micturitions per 24 hours were significantly reduced with solifenacin 10 mg (−20%), solifenacin 5 mg (−17%), and tolterodine (−15%). Solifenacin was well tolerated, with few patients discontinuing treatment. Incidences of dry mouth were 4.9% with placebo, 14.0% with solifenacin 5 mg, 21.3% with solifenacin 10 mg, and 18.6% with tolterodine 2 mg twice daily.

A second multinational trial reported efficacy outcomes in 857 patients randomized to placebo, 5 mg solifenacin, and 10 mg solifenacin (Cardozo et al, 2004). Primary efficacy analyses showed a statistically significant reduction in micturition frequency after treatment at both doses of solifenacin succinate compared with placebo. Secondary efficacy variables, including urgency, volume voided per micturition, and incontinence episodes per 24 hours, also demonstrated the superiority of solifenacin over placebo. Percentage reduction in urgency episodes per 24 hours was 51% and 52% with solifenacin (5 mg and 10 mg, respectively) and 33% with placebo. Percentage increase in volume voided per micturition was 25.4% (5 mg) and 29.7% (10 mg) with solifenacin compared with 11% for placebo. Percentage decreases in episodes of urgency incontinence were 62.7% (5 mg) and 57.1% (10 mg) for the solifenacin groups and 42.5% for the placebo group. Finally, all incontinence episodes were reduced by 60.7% (5 mg) and 51.9% (10 mg) with solifenacin compared with a 27.9% change with placebo. Most adverse events reported were mild. The proportion of patients who did not complete the study because of adverse events was low and comparable among treatment groups (i.e., 3.3% in the placebo group, 2.3% and 3.9% in the 5-mg and 10-mg solifenacin groups, respectively). Incidences of dry mouth were 2.3%, 7.7%, and 23.1% with placebo and solifenacin 5 mg and 10 mg, respectively. There were no clinically significant effects on electrocardiographic parameters, laboratory values, vital signs, physical examination findings, or postvoid residual volume. Solifenacin treatment was well tolerated and produced statistically significant reductions in quality of life domains including incontinence, sleep-energy, role limitations, and emotions.

Two additional double-blind pivotal trials with parallel study designs and similar baseline demographics were carried out in the United States, and results have been pooled for ease of reporting (Gittleman et al, 2003). Data collected from micturition diaries were analyzed for 1208 patients (604 placebo, 604 solifenacin). Reductions in the number of micturitions per 24 hours, the primary efficacy endpoint, were seen in the solifenacin group compared with the placebo group. Similar benefit was observed with solifenacin compared with placebo in three of the five secondary endpoints, including a decrease in the number of incontinence and number of urgency episodes per 24 hours as well as an increase in the volume voided per micturition (46.8 mL versus 7.7 mL). Among patients who were incontinent at baseline, a significantly greater number of patients in the solifenacin group than in the placebo group became continent by the end of the study (53% versus 31%, respectively).

Patients from the two phase III multinational trials described were invited to enroll in a year-long open-label extension trial of solifenacin 5 mg and 10 mg (Haab et al, 2005). The results from this extension trial suggested that solifenacin efficacy and tolerability continue to improve with long-term treatment.

In a prospective double-blind, double-dummy, two-arm, parallel-group 12-week study, the efficacy and safety of solifenacin 5 mg or 10 mg and tolterodine ER 4 mg once daily were compared in OAB patients (Chapple et al, 2005b). After 4 weeks of treatment, patients had the option to request a dose increase but were dummied throughout as approved product labeling allowed an increase only for those receiving solifenacin. Solifenacin, with a flexible dosing regimen, showed greater efficacy than tolterodine in decreasing urgency episodes, incontinence, urge incontinence, and pad use and increasing the volume voided per micturition. No difference was found in frequency of micturitions, the primary outcome variable. More solifenacin-treated patients became continent and reported improvements in perception of bladder condition assessments. The majority of side effects were mild to moderate in nature, and discontinuations were comparable and low in both groups. It was concluded that solifenacin, with a flexible dosing regimen, was superior to tolterodine ER with respect to the majority of the efficacy variables.

Solifenacin has a well-documented effect in OAB-DO, and the adverse event profile seems acceptable.

Calcium Antagonists

Activation of detrusor muscle, through both muscarinic receptor and nonadrenergic, noncholinergic pathways, requires influx of extracellular calcium through Ca^{2+} channels as well as mobilization of intracellular calcium (Andersson, 1993; Andersson and Arner, 2004). The influx of extracellular calcium can be blocked by calcium antagonists, blocking L-type Ca^{2+} channels, and theoretically, this would be an attractive way of inhibiting DO. Inhibitory effects have been demonstrated clinically in patients with DO (Andersson, 1988). However, **even though experimental data provide a theoretical basis for the use of calcium antagonists in the treatment of DO, there have been few clinical studies of the effects of calcium antagonists in patients with DO.** Naglie and associates (2002) evaluated the efficacy of nimodipine for geriatric urgency incontinence in a randomized, double-blind, placebo-controlled cross-over trial; 30 mg of nimodipine was given twice daily for 3 weeks in older persons with DO and chronic urgency incontinence. A total of 86 participants with a mean age of 73.4 years were randomized. The primary outcome was the number of incontinent episodes, as measured by the self-completion of a 5-day voiding record. Secondary outcomes included the impact of urinary incontinence on quality of life, as measured with a modified Incontinence Impact Questionnaire, and symptoms, as measured by the American Urological Association (AUA) symptom score. In the 76 (88.4%) participants completing the study, there was no significant difference in the number of incontinent episodes with nimodipine versus placebo. Scores on the Incontinence Impact Questionnaire and the AUA symptom score were not significantly different with nimodipine versus placebo, and the authors concluded that treatment of geriatric urgency incontinence with 30 mg of nimodipine twice daily was unsuccessful.

Available information does not suggest that systemic therapy with calcium antagonists, blocking L-type Ca^{2+} channels, is an effective way to treat OAB-DO.

Potassium Channel Openers

Opening of K^+ channels and subsequent efflux of potassium will produce hyperpolarization of various smooth muscles, including the detrusor (Andersson, 1992; Andersson and Arner, 2004). This leads to a decrease in calcium influx by reducing the opening probability of Ca^{2+} channels with subsequent relaxation or inhibition of contraction. **Theoretically, such drugs may be active during the filling phase of the bladder, abolishing DO with no effect on normal bladder contraction.** K^+ channel openers, such as pinacidil and cromakalim, have been effective in animal models (Andersson, 1992; Andersson and Arner, 2004), but clinically, the effects have not been encouraging. The first generation of openers of ATP-sensitive K^+ channels, such as cromakalim and pinacidil, were found to be more potent as inhibitors of vascular than of detrusor muscle, and in clinical trials performed with these drugs, no bladder effects have been found at doses already lowering blood pressure (Hedlund et al, 1990; Komersova et al, 1995). However, new drugs with K_{ATP} channel opening properties that may be useful for the treatment of bladder overactivity have been described (Andersson and Arner, 2004). K^+ channel opening is a theoretically attractive way of treating DO since it would make it possible to eliminate undesired bladder contractions without affecting normal micturition.

At present, there is no evidence from RCTs to suggest that K^+ channel openers represent a treatment alternative.

Drugs with "Mixed" Actions

Some drugs used to block DO have been shown to have more than one mechanism of action. **They all have a more or less pronounced antimuscarinic effect and, in addition, an often poorly defined "direct" action on bladder muscle. For several of these drugs, the antimuscarinic effects can be demonstrated at much lower drug concentrations than the direct action, which may involve blockade of voltage-operated Ca^{2+} channels. Most probably, the clinical effects of these drugs can be explained mainly by an antimuscarinic action.** Among the drugs with mixed actions was terodiline, which was withdrawn from the market because it was thought to cause polymorphic ventricular tachycardia (torsades de pointes) in some patients (Connolly et al, 1991; Stewart et al, 1992).

Oxybutynin. Oxybutynin is a **tertiary amine that is well absorbed and undergoes extensive upper gastrointestinal and first-pass hepatic metabolism via the cytochrome P-450 system (CYP3A4) into multiple metabolites.** The primary metabolite, N-desethyloxybutynin (DEO), has pharmacologic properties similar to those of the parent compound (Waldeck et al, 1997), but it occurs in much higher concentrations after oral administration (Hughes et al, 1992). It has been implicated as the major cause of the troublesome side effect of dry mouth associated with the administration of oxybutynin. **It seems reasonable to assume that the effect of oral oxybutynin to a large extent is exerted by the metabolite.** The occurrence of an active metabolite may also explain the lack of correlation between plasma concentration of oxybutynin itself and side effects in geriatric patients reported by Ouslander and coworkers (1995). The plasma half-life of oxybutynin is approximately 2 hours, but with wide interindividual variation (Douchamps et al, 1988; Hughes et al, 1992).

Oxybutynin has several pharmacologic effects, some of which seem difficult to relate to its effectiveness in the treatment of DO. **It has both an antimuscarinic and a direct muscle relaxant effect and, in addition, local anesthetic actions.** The anesthetic effect may be of importance when the drug is administered intravesically but probably plays no role when it is given orally. In vitro, oxybutynin was 500 times weaker as a smooth muscle relaxant than as an antimuscarinic agent (Kachur et al, 1988). **Most probably, when it is given systemically, oxybutynin acts mainly as an antimuscarinic drug.** Oxybutynin has a high affinity for muscarinic receptors in human bladder tissue and effectively blocks carbachol-induced contractions (Nilvebrant et al, 1985; Waldeck et al, 1997). The drug was shown to have slightly higher affinity for muscarinic M_1 and M_3 receptors than for M_2 receptors (Nilvebrant et al, 1996; Norhona-Blob and Kachur, 1991), but the clinical significance of this is unclear.

The immediate-release (IR) form of oxybutynin is recognized for its efficacy, and the newer antimuscarinic agents are all compared with it, once efficacy over placebo has been determined. In general, the new formulations of oxybutynin and other antimuscarinic agents offer patients efficacy roughly equivalent to that of oxybutynin IR, and the advantage of the newer formulations lies in improved dosing schedules and side effect profile (Appell et al, 2001; Dmochowski et al, 2002;

Diokno et al, 2003). An extended-release (ER) once-daily oral formulation gained approval by the U.S. Food and Drug Administration (FDA) in 1999. Oxybutynin ER uses a patented, push-pull, osmotic delivery system to deliver oxybutynin at a fixed rate during 24 hours and offers dosage flexibility between 5 and 30 mg/day. An oxybutynin transdermal delivery system (TDS) was approved by the FDA in 2003. This oxybutynin TDS offers a twice-weekly dosing regimen and the potential for improved compliance of patients and tolerability. Again, however, the data support these newer formulations of oxybutynin as effective in the treatment of OAB with significant reductions in urgency incontinence, but only a small number of patients reach total dryness. For this reason, in addition to side effects and cost, few patients continue to remain on the medications for a full year.

Immediate-Release Oxybutynin. Several controlled studies have shown that oxybutynin IR is effective in controlling DO, including neurogenic DO (see reviews by Yarker et al, 1995; Andersson and Chapple, 2001; Andersson et al, 2002). The recommended oral dose of the immediate-release form is 5 mg three or four times daily, although lower doses have been used. Thüroff and associates (1998) summarized 15 randomized controlled studies of a total of 476 patients treated with oxybutynin. The mean decrease in incontinence was recorded as 52%, and the mean reduction in frequency for 24 hours was 33%. The overall "subjective improvement" rate was reported as 74% (range, 61% to 100%). The mean percentage of patients reporting an adverse effect was 70% (range, 17% to 93%). Oxybutynin 7.5 to 15 mg/day significantly improved quality of life of patients suffering from overactive bladder in a large open multicenter trial. In this study, patients' compliance was 97%, and side effects, mainly dry mouth, were reported by only 8% of the patients (Amarenco et al, 1998). In nursing home residents (n = 75), Ouslander and colleagues (1995) found that oxybutynin did not add to the clinical effectiveness of prompted voiding in a placebo-controlled, double-blind, cross-over trial. On the other hand, in another controlled trial in elderly subjects (n = 57), oxybutynin with bladder training was found to be superior to bladder training alone (Szonyi et al, 1995).

Several open studies in patients with spinal cord injuries have suggested that oxybutynin, given orally or intravesically, can be of therapeutic benefit (Szollar and Lee, 1996; Kim et al, 1996).

The therapeutic effect of oxybutynin IR on DO is associated with a high incidence of side effects (up to 80% with oral administration). These are typically antimuscarinic in nature (dry mouth, constipation, drowsiness, blurred vision) and are often dose limiting (Baigrie et al, 1988; Jonville et al, 1992). Electrocardiographic effects of oxybutynin were studied in elderly patients with urinary incontinence (Hussain et al, 1994); no changes were found. It cannot be excluded that the commonly recommended dose of 5 mg three times daily is unnecessarily high in some patients and that a starting dose of 2.5 mg twice daily with following dose titration would reduce the number of adverse effects (Malone-Lee et al, 1992; Amarenco et al, 1998).

Extended-Release Oxybutynin. This formulation was developed to decrease metabolite formation of DEO with the presumption that it would result in decreased side effects, especially dry mouth, and improve patient compliance with oxybutynin therapy. **The formulation uses an osmotic system to release the drug at a controlled rate during 24 hours more distally into the large intestine, where absorption is not influenced as much by the cytochrome P-450 enzyme system in the liver.** This reduction in metabolism is meant to improve the rate of dry mouth complaints compared with oxybutynin IR. DEO is still formed during the first-pass metabolism through the hepatic cytochrome P-450 enzymes, but **clinical trials have indeed demonstrated improved dry mouth rates compared with oxybutynin IR** (Appell et al, 2003). Salivary output studies have also been interesting. Two hours after administration of oxybutynin IR or tolterodine IR, salivary production decreased markedly and then gradually returned to normal. With oxybutynin ER, however, salivary output was maintained at predose levels throughout the day (Chancellor et al, 2001).

The effects of oxybutynin ER have been well documented (Siddiqui et al, 2004). In the OBJECT study (Appell et al, 2001), the efficacy and tolerability of 10 mg of oxybutynin ER were compared with a twice-daily 2-mg dose of tolterodine IR. Oxybutynin ER was statistically more effective than tolterodine IR in decreasing weekly urgency incontinence episodes, total incontinence, and frequency, and both medications were equally well tolerated. The basic study was repeated as the OPERA study (Diokno et al, 2003), with the difference that this study was a direct comparison of the two extended-release forms, oxybutynin ER (10 mg) and tolterodine ER (4 mg), and the results were quite different. In this study, there was no significant difference in efficacy for the primary endpoint of urgency incontinence; however, tolterodine ER had a statistically lower incidence of dry mouth. Oxybutynin ER was only statistically better at 10 mg than tolterodine ER 4 mg in the reduction of the rate of urinary frequency. These studies made it clear that in comparative studies, immediate-release entities of one drug should no longer be compared with extended-release entities of the other.

Greater reductions in urgency and total incontinence have been reported in patients treated in dose-escalation studies with oxybutynin ER. In two randomized studies, the efficacy and tolerability of oxybutynin ER were compared with oxybutynin IR. In the 1999 study (Anderson et al, 1999), 105 patients with urgency or mixed incontinence were randomized to receive 5 to 30 mg of oxybutynin ER once daily or 5 mg of oxybutynin IR one to four times a day. Dose titrations began at 5 mg, and the dose was increased every 4 to 7 days until one of three endpoints was achieved: (1) the patient reported no urgency incontinence during the final 2 days of the dosing period; (2) the maximum tolerable dose was reached; or (3) the maximum allowable dose (30 mg for oxybutynin ER or 20 mg for oxybutynin IR) was reached. The mean percentage reduction in weekly urgency and total incontinence episodes was statistically similar between oxybutynin ER and oxybutynin IR, but dry mouth was reported statistically more often with oxybutynin IR. In another study (Versi et al, 2000), 226 patients were randomized between oxybutynin ER and oxybutynin IR with weekly increments of 5 mg daily up to 20 mg daily. As in the study of Anderson and coworkers (1999), oxybutynin ER again achieved a reduction of more than 80% in urgency and total incontinence episodes, and a significant percentage of patients became dry. A negative aspect of these studies is that there were no naive patients included, as all patients were known responders to oxybutynin. Similar efficacy results have been reported, however, with oxybutynin ER in a treatment-naive population (Gleason et al, 1999).

Transdermal Oxybutynin. **Transdermal delivery also alters oxybutynin metabolism, reducing DEO production to an even greater extent than oxybutynin ER does.** Davila and associates (2001) compared oxybutynin TDS with oxybutynin IR and demonstrated a statistically equivalent reduction in daily incontinent episodes (66% for oxybutynin TDS and 72% for oxybutynin IR) but much less dry mouth (38% for oxybutynin TDS and 94% for oxybutynin IR). In another study (Dmochowski et al, 2002), the 3.9-mg daily dose patch significantly reduced the number of weekly incontinence episodes while reducing average daily urinary frequency confirmed by an increased average voided volume. Furthermore, dry mouth rate was similar to that with placebo (7% versus 8.3%). In a third study (Dmochowski et al, 2003a), oxybutynin TDS was compared not only with placebo but with tolterodine ER. Both drugs equivalently and significantly reduced daily incontinence episodes and increased the average voided volume, but tolterodine ER was associated with a significantly higher rate of antimuscarinic adverse events. **The primary adverse event for oxybutynin TDS was application site reaction pruritus in 14% and erythema in 8.3%,** with nearly 9% thinking that the reactions were severe enough to withdraw from the study, despite the lack of systemic problems.

The pharmacokinetics and adverse effect dynamics of oxybutynin TDS (3.9 mg/day) and oxybutynin ER (10 mg/day) were compared in healthy subjects in a randomized, two-way cross-over study (Appell et al, 2003). Multiple blood and saliva samples were collected, and pharmacokinetic parameters and total salivary output were assessed. Oxybutynin TDS administration resulted in greater systemic availability and minimal metabolism to DEO compared with oxybutynin ER, which resulted in greater salivary output in patients taking oxybutynin TDS and fewer dry mouth symptoms than with oxybutynin ER.

Other Administration Forms. Rectal administration (Collas and Malone-Lee, 1997; Winkler and Sand, 1998) was reported to have fewer adverse effects than the conventional tablets. Administered intravesically, oxybutynin has in several studies been demonstrated to increase bladder capacity and to produce clinical improvement with few side effects, both in neurogenic and in other types of DO and both in children and in adults (see review by Lose and Norgaard, 2001), although adverse effects may occur (Kasabian et al, 1994; Palmer et al, 1997).

Oxybutynin has a well-documented efficacy in the treatment of OAB-DO and is, together with tolterodine, first-line treatment of patients with this disorder.

Dicyclomine. Dicyclomine has attributed to it both a direct relaxant effect on smooth muscle and an antimuscarinic action (Downie et al, 1977). An oral dose of 20 mg three times a day in adults was reported to increase bladder capacity in patients with neurogenic DO (Fischer et al, 1978). Beck and colleagues (1976) compared the use of 10 mg of dicyclomine, 15 mg of propantheline, and placebo three times a day in patients with DO. The reported cure or improved rates, respectively, were 62%, 73%, and 20%. Awad and associates

(1977) reported that 20 mg of dicyclomine three times a day caused resolution or significant improvement in 24 of 27 patients with involuntary bladder contractions.

Even if published experiences of the effect of dicyclomine on DO are favorable, the drug is not widely used, and controlled clinical trials documenting its efficacy and side effects are scarce.

Propiverine. Several aspects of the preclinical, pharmacokinetic, and clinical effects of propiverine have been extensively reviewed by Madersbacher and Mürz (2001). The drug is rapidly absorbed (t_{max}, 2 hours) but has a high first-pass metabolism, and its biologic availability is about 50%. Propiverine is an inducer of hepatic cytochrome P-450 enzymes in rats in doses about 100 times above the therapeutic doses in humans (Walter et al, 2003). Several active metabolites are formed (Haustein and Hüller, 1988; Muller et al, 1993). Most probably, these metabolites contribute to the clinical effects of the drug, but their individual contributions have not been clarified. The half-life of the mother compound is about 11 to 14 hours.

Propiverine has been shown to have combined antimuscarinic and calcium antagonistic actions (Haruno, 1992; Tokuno et al, 1993). **The importance of the calcium antagonistic component for the drug's clinical effects has not been established.**

Propiverine has been shown to have beneficial effects in patients with DO in several investigations. Thüroff and associates (1998) collected nine randomized studies of a total of 230 patients and found reductions in frequency (30%) and micturitions per 24 hours (17%), a 64-mL increase in bladder capacity, and a 77% (range, 33% to 80%) subjective improvement. Side effects were found in 14% (range, 8% to 42%). In patients with neurogenic DO, controlled clinical trials have demonstrated propiverine's superiority over placebo (Stöhrer et al, 1999). Propiverine also increased bladder capacity and decreased maximum detrusor contractions. Controlled trials comparing propiverine, flavoxate, and placebo (Wehnert and Sage, 1989) and propiverine, oxybutynin, and placebo (Wehnert and Sage, 1992; Madersbacher et al, 1999) have confirmed the efficacy of propiverine and suggested that **the drug may have efficacy equal to that of oxybutynin and fewer side effects.**

Madersbacher and coworkers (1999) compared the tolerability and efficacy of propiverine (15 mg three times daily), oxybutynin (5 mg twice daily), and placebo in 366 patients with urgency and urgency incontinence in a randomized, double-blind, placebo-controlled clinical trial. Urodynamic efficacy of propiverine was judged similar to that of oxybutynin, but the incidence of dry mouth and the severity of dry mouth were judged less with propiverine than with oxybutynin. Dorschner and colleagues (2000), in a double-blind, multicenter, placebo-controlled, randomized study, investigated the efficacy and cardiac safety of propiverine in 98 elderly patients (mean age, 68 years) suffering from urgency, urgency incontinence, or mixed urgency–stress incontinence. After a 2-week placebo run-in period, the patients received propiverine (15 mg three times daily) or placebo (three times daily) for 4 weeks. Propiverine caused a significant reduction of the micturition frequency (from 8.7 to 6.5) and a significant decrease in episodes of incontinence (from 0.9 to 0.3 per day). The incidence of adverse events was low (2% dryness of the mouth with propiverine, 2 of 49 patients). Resting and ambulatory electrocardiograms indicated no significant changes.

Propiverine has a documented beneficial effect in the treatment of DO and seems to have an acceptable side effect profile.

Flavoxate. Flavoxate is well absorbed, and oral bioavailability appeared to be close to 100% (Guay, 2003). The drug is extensively metabolized, and its plasma half-life was found to be 3.5 hours (Sheu et al, 2001). The main metabolite of flavoxate (3-methylflavone-8-carboxylic acid, MFCA) has been shown to have low pharmacologic activity (Cazzulani et al, 1988; Caine et al, 1991). The main mechanism of flavoxate's effect on smooth muscle has not been established. The drug has been found to possess a moderate calcium antagonistic activity, to have the ability to inhibit phosphodiesterase, and to have local anesthetic properties; no antimuscarinic effect was found (Guarneri et al, 1994). Überckert and colleagues (2000) found that in strips of human bladder, the potency of flavoxate to reverse contractions induced by muscarinic receptor stimulation and by electrical field stimulation was comparable. Tomoda and associates (2005) studied the effects of flavoxate on K^+-induced tension using strips prepared from human urinary bladder and also investigated the effects of flavoxate on voltage-dependent nifedipine-sensitive Ba^{2+} currents (i.e., L-type Ca^{2+} currents) in single freshly dispersed human detrusor smooth muscle myocytes by use of whole-cell patch clamp techniques. They found that flavoxate caused a concentration-dependent reduction of the K^+-induced contraction of the bladder strips and that in the human detrusor myocytes, flavoxate inhibited the peak amplitude of voltage-dependent, nifedipine-sensitive inward Ba^{2+} currents in a voltage- and concentration-dependent manner. They concluded that flavoxate caused muscle relaxation through the inhibition of L-type Ca^{2+} channels in human detrusor. It has been suggested that pertussis toxin–sensitive G proteins in the brain are involved in the flavoxate-induced suppression of the micturition reflex, since intracerebroventricularly or intrathecally administered flavoxate abolished isovolumetric rhythmic bladder contractions in anesthetized rats (Oka et al, 1996).

The clinical effects of flavoxate in patients with DO and frequency, urgency, and incontinence have been studied in both open and controlled investigations but with varying rates of success (Ruffmann, 1988). Stanton (1973) compared emepronium and flavoxate in a double-blind, cross-over study of patients with detrusor instability and reported improvement rates of 83% and 66% after flavoxate or emepronium, respectively, both administered as 200 mg three times daily. In another double-blind, cross-over study comparing flavoxate 1200 mg/day with oxybutynin 15 mg daily in 41 women with idiopathic motor or sensory urgency and using both clinical and urodynamic criteria, Milani and coworkers (1993) found both drugs effective. No difference in efficacy was found between them, but flavoxate had fewer and milder side effects. Other investigators, comparing the effects of flavoxate with those of placebo in RCTs, have not been able to show any beneficial effect of flavoxate at dosages up to 400 mg three times daily (Briggs et al, 1980; Chapple et al, 1990; Dahm et al, 1995).

In general, few side effects have been reported during treatment with flavoxate. On the other hand, its efficacy, compared with other therapeutic alternatives, is not well documented.

α Adrenoceptor Antagonists

Even if it is well known that α adrenoceptor antagonists can ameliorate lower urinary tract symptoms in men with benign prostatic hyperplasia (Andersson, 2002c), there are no controlled clinical trials showing that they are an effective alternative in the treatment of OAB-DO in this category of patients. In an open-label study, Arnold (2001) evaluated the clinical and pressure-flow effects of tamsulosin 0.4 mg once daily in patients with lower urinary tract symptoms caused by benign prostatic obstruction. It was found that tamsulosin produced a significant decrease in detrusor pressure, an increase in flow rate, and a symptomatic improvement in patients with lower urinary tract symptoms and confirmed obstruction. The α_1 adrenoceptor antagonists have been used to treat patients with neurogenic DO (Andersson et al, 2002; Abrams et al, 2003); however, the success has been moderate. In women, these drugs may produce stress incontinence (Dwyer and Teele, 1992). The use of α adrenoceptor antagonists in the management of benign prostatic hyperplasia and benign prostatic obstruction is covered in Chapter 87.

Although α adrenoceptor antagonists may be effective in selected cases of DO, convincing effects documented in RCTs are lacking.

β Adrenoceptor Agonists

In isolated human bladder, non–subtype selective β adrenoceptor agonists like isoprenaline have a pronounced inhibitory effect, and administration of such drugs can increase bladder capacity in humans (Andersson, 1993). However, the β adrenoceptors of the human bladder were shown to have functional characteristics typical of neither β_1 nor β_2 adrenoceptors since they could be blocked by propranolol but not by practolol or metoprolol (β_1) or butoxamine (β_2) (Nergårdh et al, 1977; Larsen, 1979). Atypical β adrenoceptor–mediated responses reported repeatedly in early studies of β adrenoceptor antagonists have been shown to be mediated by a β_3 adrenoceptor, which has been cloned, sequenced, expressed in model system, and extensively characterized functionally (Lipworth, 1996; Strosberg and Pietri-Rouxel, 1997). Both normal and neurogenic human detrusors were shown to express β_1, β_2, and β_3 adrenoceptor mRNAs, and selective β_3 adrenoceptor agonists effectively relaxed both types of detrusor muscle (Igawa et al, 1999, 2001; Takeda et al, 1999; Nomiya and Yamaguchi, 2003). Thus, **it seems that the atypical β adrenoceptor of the human bladder may be the β_3 adrenoceptor.**

On the other hand, early receptor binding studies using subtype-selective ligands suggested that the β adrenoceptors of the human detrusor are primarily of β_2 subtype (Levin et al, 1988), and favorable effects on DO were reported in open studies with selective β_2 adrenoceptor agonists.

Terbutaline (stimulating β_2 adrenoceptors), in oral doses of 5 mg three times a day, was reported to have a "good clinical effect" in some patients with urgency and urgency incontinence but no significant effect on the bladders of neurologically normal humans without voiding difficulty (Norlen et al, 1978). Although these results are compatible with those in other organ systems (β adrenoceptor stimulation causes no acute change in total lung capacity in normal humans, whereas it does favorably affect patients with bronchial asthma), few adequate studies are available on the effects of β adrenoceptor stimulation in patients with DO. Lindholm and Lose (1986) used 5 mg three times a day of terbutaline in eight women with motor urgency incontinence and in seven with sensory urgency incontinence. After 3 months of treatment, 14 patients claimed beneficial effects, and 12 became subjectively continent. In six of eight cases, the detrusor became stable on cystometry. Interestingly, the volume of the first desire to void increased in the patients with originally unstable bladders from a mean of 200 mL to 302 mL, but the maximum cystometric capacity did not change. Nine patients had transient side effects, including palpitations, tachycardia, and hand tremor; and in three of these, side effects continued but were acceptable. In one patient, the drug was discontinued because of severe adverse symptoms.

Gruneberger (1984) reported that in a double-blind study, **clenbuterol** (β$_2$ adrenoceptor agonist) had a good therapeutic effect in 15 of 20 patients with motor urgency incontinence. Unfavorable results of β adrenoceptor agonist use for DO were published by Castleden and Morgan (1980) and Naglo and coworkers (1981).

Treatment of OAB-DO with selective β$_2$ adrenoceptor agonists has not been successful. Whether β$_3$ adrenoceptor stimulation will be a more effective way of treating OAB-DO has yet to be shown in controlled clinical trials.

Antidepressants

Many clinicians believe that tricyclic antidepressants, particularly **imipramine,** are useful agents for facilitating urine storage, both by decreasing bladder contractility and by increasing outlet resistance (Wein, 1995a, 1995b). These agents have been the subject of a voluminous amount of highly sophisticated pharmacologic investigation to determine the mechanisms of action responsible for their varied effects (Maggi et al, 1989b; Richelson, 1994; Baldessarini, 1996). Most data have been accumulated as a result of trying to explain the antidepressant properties of these agents and are thus primarily from CNS tissue. The results, conclusions, and speculations inferred from the data are extremely interesting, but it is essentially unknown whether they apply to or have relevance for the lower urinary tract.

Tricyclic antidepressants possess varying degrees of at least three major pharmacologic actions: (1) they have central and peripheral antimuscarinic effects at some but not all sites; (2) they block the active transport system in the presynaptic nerve ending that is responsible for the reuptake of the released amine neurotransmitters norepinephrine and serotonin; and (3) they are sedatives, an action that occurs presumably on a central basis but is perhaps related to antihistaminic properties (at H$_1$ receptors, although they also antagonize H$_2$ receptors to some extent). There is also evidence that they desensitize at least some α$_2$ and some β adrenoceptors. Paradoxically, they also have been shown to block some α adrenoceptors and 5-hydroxytryptamine type 1 (5-HT$_1$) receptors.

As indicated before, **imipramine** has complex pharmacologic effects, and its mode of action in OAB-DO has not been established (Hunsballe and Djurhuus, 2001). Imipramine does not seem to possess a strong antimuscarinic effect directly on the detrusor smooth muscle. Even if it is generally considered that imipramine is a useful drug in the treatment of OAB-DO, no good-quality RCTs that can document this have been retrieved. However, it has been known for a long time that imipramine can have favorable effects in the treatment of nocturnal enuresis in children with a success rate of 10% to 70% in controlled trials (Hunsballe and Djurhuus, 2001; Glazener et al, 2003).

The risks (see later) and benefits of imipramine in the treatment of voiding disorders do not seem to have been assessed. Few studies have been performed during the last decade (Hunsballe and Djurhuus, 2001).

Doxepin is another tricyclic antidepressant that was found to be more potent, with use of in vitro rabbit bladder strips, than other tricyclic compounds with respect to antimuscarinic and musculotropic relaxant activity (Levin and Wein, 1984). Lose and coworkers (1989), in a randomized, double-blind cross-over study of women with involuntary bladder contractions and frequency, urgency, or urgency incontinence, found that this agent caused a significant decrease in urine loss (pad weighing test) and in the cystometric parameters of first sensation and maximal bladder capacity. The dosage of doxepin used was either a single 50-mg bedtime dose or this dose plus an additional 25 mg in the morning. The number of daytime incontinence episodes decreased in both doxepin and placebo groups, and the difference was not statistically significant. Doxepin treatment was preferred by 14 patients, whereas 2 preferred placebo. Three patients had no preference. Of the 14 patients who stated a preference for doxepin, 12 claimed that they became continent during treatment, whereas 2 claimed improvement; the 2 patients who preferred placebo claimed improvement. The AHCPR guidelines (1992) combine results for imipramine and doxepin, citing only three randomized controlled trials, with an unknown percentage of female patients. Percentage cures (all figures refer to percentage drug effect minus percentage effect on placebo) are listed as 31%, percentage reduction in urgency incontinence as 20% to 77%, and percentage side effects as 0% to 70%.

With use in the generally larger doses employed for antidepressant effects, **the most frequent side effects of the tricyclic antidepressants are those attributable to their systemic antimuscarinic activity** (Richelson, 1994; Baldessarini, 1996). Allergic phenomena, including rash, hepatic dysfunction, obstructive jaundice, and agranulocytosis, may also occur, but rarely. CNS side effects may include weakness, fatigue, parkinsonian effect, fine tremor noted most in the upper extremities, manic or schizophrenic picture, and sedation, probably from an antihistaminic effect. Postural hypotension may also be seen, presumably on the basis of selective blockade (a paradoxical effect) of α$_1$ adrenoceptors in some vascular smooth muscle. Tricyclic antidepressants can also cause excess sweating of obscure etiology and a delay of orgasm or orgasmic impotence, the cause of which is likewise unclear. They can also produce arrhythmias and interact in deleterious ways with other drugs, and so caution must be observed in their use in patients with cardiac disease (Baldessarini, 1996). Whether cardiotoxicity will prove to be a legitimate concern in patients receiving the smaller doses (than for treatment of depression) for lower urinary tract dysfunction remains to be seen but is a potential matter of concern. Consultation with a patient's internist or cardiologist is always helpful before instituting such therapy in questionable situations. It is well established that therapeutic doses of tricyclic antidepressants, including imipramine, may cause serious toxic effects on the cardiovascular system (orthostatic hypotension, ventricular arrhythmias). Imipramine prolongs QTc intervals and has an antiarrhythmic (and proarrhythmic) effect similar to that of quinidine (Bigger et al, 1977; Giardina et al, 1979). Children seem particularly sensitive to the cardiotoxic action of tricyclic antidepressants (Baldessarini, 1996).

With respect to the potential cardiovascular risks of antidepressant medication, two additional points need to be made. First, it is depression itself that is associated with an increased risk of myocardial infarction, cardiovascular disease, and all-cause mortality (see references in Cohen et al, 2000). Although treatments for depression, including antidepressive medications, are certainly a potential factor underlying this association, the separation from disease association and treatment association is difficult at best. The second point relates to whether there is a difference in this regard between the tricyclic antidepressants and the selective serotonin reuptake inhibitors. Data presented by Cohen and associates (2000) suggest, with respect to long-term adverse cardiovascular outcome, that there is an association with the tricyclic antidepressants but not with the selective serotonin reuptake inhibitors, a conclusion that differs from earlier data indicating no significant differences in the safety or efficacy of these two groups of agents (AHCPR report, cited by Cohen et al, 2000). As a closing statement on this subject, data in the literature refer to therapeutic doses of these medications for depression and not the relatively diminutive (in comparison) doses of imipramine used for the treatment of voiding dysfunction.

The use of imipramine is contraindicated in patients receiving monoamine oxidase inhibitors because severe CNS toxicity can be precipitated, including hyperpyrexia, seizures, and coma. Some potential side effects of the antidepressants may be especially significant for the elderly, specifically weakness, fatigue, and postural hypotension. Psychotropic drugs in general have been shown to increase the risk of falls and hip fractures in the elderly (Liu et al, 1998). If imipramine or any of the tricyclic antidepressants is to be prescribed for the treatment of voiding dysfunction, the patient should be thoroughly informed of the fact that this is not the usual indication for this drug and that potential side effects exist. Reports of significant side effects (severe abdominal distress, nausea, vomiting, headache, lethargy, and irritability) after abrupt cessation of large doses of imipramine in children would suggest that the drug should be discontinued gradually, especially in patients receiving large doses.

Duloxetine (see also later) is an agent that has nearly equal effect on the reuptake of serotonin and norepinephrine in vivo and shows no appreciable binding affinity for neurotransmitter receptors (Thor and Katofiasc, 1995). In a cat model, this agent had weak effects on bladder activity and urethral sphincter activity under normal conditions, but under conditions of "bladder irritation," it suppressed bladder activity through central serotonin receptor mechanisms and enhanced urethral sphincter activity through serotonergic (5-HT$_2$) and α_1 adrenoceptor mechanisms (Thor and Katofiasc, 1995). If the hypothesis regarding the serotonergic mechanism for depression of bladder contractility by tricyclic antidepressants is accurate, the selective serotonin reuptake inhibitors should

theoretically provide a more pronounced clinical effect with fewer side effects. At this time, these have not been systematically tested for treatment of OAB-DO.

Cyclooxygenase Inhibitors

Prostanoids (prostaglandins and thromboxanes) are generated locally in both detrusor muscle and mucosa (Jeremy et al, 1987; Khan et al, 1998). Synthesis is initiated by various physiologic stimuli, such as stretch of the detrusor muscle, but also by injuries of the vesical mucosa, nerve stimulation, and agents such as ATP and mediators of inflammation (e.g., bradykinin and the chemotactic peptide) (Downie and Karmazyn, 1984; Leslie et al, 1984; Andersson and Arner, 2004). Prostanoids are synthesized by cyclooxygenase in the bladder (Khan et al, 1998). This enzyme exists in two isoforms, one constitutive (cyclooxygenase 1) and one inducible (cyclooxygenase 2). It has been suggested that in the bladder, the constitutive form is responsible for the normal physiologic biosynthesis, whereas the inducible form is activated during inflammation.

Even if prostanoids cause contraction of human bladder muscle (Andersson, 1993), **it is still unclear to what extent they contribute to the pathogenesis of OAB-DO. More important than direct effects on the bladder muscle may be sensitization of sensory afferent nerves,** increasing the afferent input produced by a given degree of bladder filling. Involuntary bladder contractions can then be triggered at a small bladder volume. If this is an important mechanism, treatment with cyclooxygenase inhibitors could be expected to be effective. However, clinical evidence for this is scarce.

Cardozo and associates (1980) performed a double-blind controlled study of 30 women with DO using the nonselective cyclooxygenase inhibitor flurbiprofen at a dose of 50 mg three times daily. The drug was shown to have favorable effects, although it did not completely abolish DO. There was a high incidence of side effects (43%) including nausea, vomiting, headache, and gastrointestinal symptoms. Palmer (1983) studied the effects of flurbiprofen 50 mg four times daily versus placebo in a double-blind, cross-over trial in 37 patients with idiopathic DO (27% of the patients did not complete the trial). Active treatment significantly increased maximum contractile pressure, decreased the number of voids, and decreased the number of urgent voids compared with baseline. Indomethacin (nonselective cyclooxygenase inhibitor) 50 to 100 mg daily was reported to give symptomatic relief in patients with DO compared with bromocriptine in a randomized, single-blind, cross-over study (Cardozo and Stanton, 1980). The incidence of side effects was high, occurring in 19 of 32 patients. However, no patient had to stop treatment because of side effects. Sprem and colleagues (2000) administered ketoprofen (nonselective cyclooxygenase inhibitor) intravesically once a day for 4 weeks in a double-blind, placebo-controlled cross-over study to 30 women with urodynamically verified idiopathic DO. Both symptomatic improvement and urodynamic improvement were demonstrated. Eighteen of 30 patients became symptom free after treatment, and no side effects were observed.

The few controlled clinical trials on the effects of cyclooxygenase inhibitors in the treatment of OAB-DO and the limited number of drugs tested make it difficult to evaluate their therapeutic value.

Dimethyl Sulfoxide

Dimethyl sulfoxide is a relatively simple, naturally occurring organic compound that has been used as an industrial solvent for many years. It has multiple pharmacologic actions (membrane penetrant, anti-inflammatory, local analgesic, bacteriostatic, diuretic, cholinesterase inhibitor, collagen solvent, vasodilator) and has been used for the treatment of arthritis and other musculoskeletal disorders, generally in a 70% solution. The formulation for human intravesical use is a 50% solution. Sant (1987) has summarized the pharmacology and clinical use of dimethyl sulfoxide and has tabulated "good to excellent" results in 50% to 90% of collected series of patients treated with intravesical instillation for interstitial cystitis. **However, dimethyl sulfoxide has not been shown to be useful in the treatment of neurogenic or idiopathic DO or in any patients with urgency-frequency but without interstitial cystitis.** The subject of interstitial cystitis and its treatment is considered in Chapter 10, Interstitial Cystitis and Related Disorders.

Polysynaptic Inhibitors

Baclofen (Lioresal) is discussed primarily along with agents that decrease outlet resistance secondary to striated sphincter dyssynergia. Baclofen is a $GABA_B$ receptor agonist that depresses monosynaptic and polysynaptic motoneurons and interneurons in the spinal cord (Andersson et al, 1999c; Andersson, 2000a). It has also been shown to be capable of depressing neurogenic DO secondary to a spinal cord lesion (Kiesswetter and Schober, 1975). Taylor and Bates (1979), in a double-blind cross-over study, reported it to be effective also in decreasing daytime and nighttime urinary frequency and incontinence in patients with idiopathic DO. Cystometric changes were not recorded, however, and considerable improvement was also obtained in the placebo group. Effective intrathecal use of baclofen for treatment of neurogenic DO was reported by Kums and Delhaas (1991), Steers and associates (1992), and Bushman and coworkers (1993). Little on this subject has appeared during the last decade.

Botulinum Toxin

Seven immunologically distinct antigenic subtypes of botulinum toxin (BTX) have been identified: A, B, C1, D, E, F, and G. Types A and B are in clinical use in urology, but most studies have been performed with BTX-A. There are three commercially available products of type A (Botox and Dysport) and type B (Myobloc/NeuroBloc). It is important not to use these products interchangeably as they have different dosing and side effect profiles.

On a weight basis, botulinum toxin is the most potent naturally occurring substance known. The toxin **blocks the release of acetylcholine and other transmitters from presynaptic nerve endings by interacting with the protein complex necessary for docking vesicles** (Yokoyama et al, 2002; Smith et al, 2004; Simpson, 2004; Smith and Chancellor, 2004). **This results in decreased muscle contractility and muscle atrophy at the injection site. The produced chemical denervation is a reversible process, and axons are regenerated in about 3 to 6 months.** The botulinum toxin molecule cannot cross the blood-brain barrier and therefore has no CNS effects.

There are many open-label and a few double-blind studies and reports describing positive outcomes after treatment with botulinum toxin in many urologic conditions, including detrusor–striated sphincter dyssynergia, neurogenic DO (detrusor hyperreflexia) pelvic floor spasticity, and possibly benign prostatic hyperplasia and interstitial cystitis (Leippold et al, 2003; Cruz and Silva, 2004; Smith and Chancellor, 2004; Maria et al, 2005). However, toxin injections may also be effective in refractory idiopathic DO (Rapp et al, 2004; Smith et al, 2004).

Reitz and colleagues (2004a) reported in a retrospective study experiences of 200 cases treated with BTX-A injections into the detrusor muscle for urinary incontinence due to neurogenic DO. They concluded that treatment is safe and valuable and that significant improvement of bladder function corresponds with continence and the subjective satisfaction indicated by the treated patients.

Schurch and associates (2005) demonstrated in a multicenter, randomized controlled trial that treatment with a single dose of BTX-A combined rapid and sustained efficacy with a low incidence of side effects. They concluded that "this treatment represents a valuable option for managing urinary incontinence caused by neurogenic DO."

In a group of spinal cord–injured patients with neurogenic DO unresponsive to conventional antimuscarinic therapy, Giannantoni and coworkers (2004) compared intravesical resiniferatoxin and BTX-A in a prospective randomized study. They showed that both intravesical resiniferatoxin and BTX-A injections into the detrusor muscle provided beneficial clinical and urodynamic results with decreases in DO and restoration of urinary continence in a large proportion of patients. BTX-A injections provided superior clinical and urodynamic benefits compared with those of intravesical resiniferatoxin.

Grosse and associates (2005) confirmed that detrusor injections with BTX-A are an effective treatment of neurogenic DO, lasting 9 to 12 months. They also found that repeated injections with BTX-A are as effective as the first one.

Studies look promising with BTX-A. It seems too early to tell whether the same results will be seen with BTX-B. The safety of these products appears satisfactory. A good response rate appears to occur within 1 week and to last from 6 to 9 months before reinjection is necessary. It remains to be seen whether this treatment will be cost-effective for all of the diseases currently being studied.

Decreasing Sensory (Afferent) Input

By means of **capsaicin**, a subpopulation of primary afferent neurons innervating the bladder and urethra, the "capsaicin-sensitive nerves," has been identified. It is believed that capsaicin exerts its effects by acting on specific, "vanilloid" receptors on these nerves (Szallasi, 1994). **Capsaicin exerts a biphasic effect: initial excitation is followed by a long-lasting blockade, which renders sensitive primary afferents (C fibers) resistant to activation by natural stimuli.** In sufficiently high concentrations, capsaicin is believed to cause "desensitization" initially by releasing and emptying the stores of neuropeptides, then by blocking further release (Maggi, 1993). **Resiniferatoxin (RTX) is an analog of capsaicin, approximately 1000 times more potent for desensitization** than capsaicin (Ishizuka et al, 1995), **but only a few hundred times more potent for excitation** (Szallasi and Blumberg, 1996). Possibly, both capsaicin and RTX can have effects on Aδ fibers. It is also possible that capsaicin at high concentrations has additional, nonspecific effects (Kuo, 1997).

The rationale for intravesical instillations of vanilloids is based on the involvement of C fibers in the pathophysiologic mechanism of conditions such as bladder hypersensitivity and neurogenic DO. In the healthy human bladder, C fibers carry the response to noxious stimuli, but they are not implicated in the normal voiding reflex. After spinal cord injury, major neuroplasticity appears within bladder afferents in several mammalian species, including humans. C-fiber bladder afferents proliferate within the suburothelium and become sensitive to bladder distention. Those changes lead to the emergence of a new C fiber–mediated voiding reflex that is strongly involved in spinal neurogenic DO. Improvement of this condition by defunctionalization of C-fiber bladder afferents with intravesical vanilloids has been widely demonstrated in humans and animals.

Cystometric evidence that capsaicin-sensitive nerves may modulate the afferent branch of the micturition reflex in humans was originally presented by Maggi and coworkers (1989a), who instilled capsaicin (0.1 to 10 μM) intravesically in five patients with hypersensitivity disorders with attenuation of their symptoms a few days after administration. Intravesical capsaicin, given in considerably higher concentrations (1 to 2 mM) than those administered by Maggi and coworkers (1989a), has since been used with success in neurologic disorders such as multiple sclerosis and traumatic chronic spinal lesions (Fowler et al, 1992b; DeRidder et al, 1997; Andersson et al, 2002; Cruz, 2004; de Sèze et al, 2004). Side effects of intravesical capsaicin include discomfort and a burning sensation at the pubic-urethral level during instillation, an effect that can be overcome by prior instillation of lidocaine, which does not interfere with the beneficial effects of capsaicin (Chandiramani et al, 1996). No premalignant or malignant changes in the bladder have been found in biopsy specimens of patients who had repeated capsaicin instillations for up to 5 years (Dasgupta et al, 1998).

The beneficial effect of **RTX** has been demonstrated in several studies (Andersson, 2002a; Kim et al, 2003; Kuo et al, 2003; de Sèze et al, 2004; Giannantoni et al, 2004; Watanabe et al, 2004).

de Sèze and colleagues (2004) compared the efficacy and tolerability of nonalcohol capsaicin (1 mM) versus RTX (100 nM) in 10% alcohol in a randomized, double-blind, parallel-group study in 39 spinal cord–injured adult patients with neurogenic DO (hyperreflexia). Efficacy (voiding chart and cystomanometry) and tolerability were evaluated during a 3-month follow-up. On day 30, clinical and urodynamic improvement was found in 78% and 83% of patients with capsaicin versus 80% and 60% with RTX, respectively, without a significant difference between the two treated groups. The benefit remained in two thirds of the two groups on day 90. There were no significant differences in regard to the incidence, nature, or duration of side effects in capsaicin- versus RTX-treated patients. The data suggested that capsaicin and RTX are equally efficient for relieving the clinical and urodynamic symptoms of neurogenic DO and that glucidic capsaicin is as well tolerated as ethanolic RTX.

Available information (including data from RCTs) suggests that both capsaicin and RTX may have useful effects in the treatment of neurogenic DO. There may be beneficial effects also in non-neurogenic DO in selected cases refractory to antimuscarinic treatment, but further RCT-based documentation is desired. RTX is an interesting alternative to capsaicin, but the drug is currently not in clinical development because of formulation and supply problems.

Neither capsaicin nor RTX is approved in the United States for clinical use. It is obvious, however, that the intravesical use of such agents has the potential to significantly contribute to the treatment of DO in patients with neurogenic and other types of lower urinary tract dysfunction. Various techniques of administration of intravesical capsaicin and RTX differ slightly among experienced users and are described in detail in the articles by Chancellor and de Groat (1999), Fowler (2000), and DeRidder and Baert (2000).

Estrogens

There are a number of reasons that estrogens may be useful in the treatment of women with urinary incontinence (Hextall, 2000). As well as improving the "maturation index" of urethral squamous epithelium (Bergman et al, 1990), estrogens increase urethral closure pressure and improve abdominal pressure transmission to the proximal urethra (Hilton et al, 1983; Bhatia et al, 1989; Karram et al, 1989). The sensory threshold of the bladder may also be raised (Fantl et al, 1988).

There are a number of different causes of lower urinary tract disorders in postmenopausal women (Bent et al, 1983). It is well recognized that there is a poor correlation between a woman's symptoms and the subsequent diagnosis after appropriate investigation (Jarvis et al, 1980). Unfortunately, initial trials took place before the widespread introduction of urodynamic studies and therefore almost certainly included a heterogeneous group of individuals with a number of different pathologic processes. Lack of objective outcome measures also limits their interpretation.

Estrogen has been used to treat postmenopausal urgency and urgency incontinence for many years. **Even if it was concluded in a Cochrane review that "oestrogen treatment can improve or cure incontinence, and the evidence suggests that this is more likely with urge incontinence"** (Moehrer et al, 2003), **there have been few controlled trials performed to confirm that it is of benefit.** A double-blind multicenter study of 64 postmenopausal women with the "urge syndrome" has failed to confirm its efficacy (Cardozo et al, 1993). All women underwent pretreatment urodynamic investigation to establish that they had either sensory urgency or detrusor instability. They were then randomized to treatment with oral estriol 3 mg daily or placebo for 3 months. Compliance was confirmed by a significant improvement in the maturation index of vaginal epithelial cells in the active but not in the placebo group. Estriol produced subjective and objective improvements in urinary symptoms, but it was not significantly better than placebo.

In a prospective double-blind randomized placebo-controlled trial, Rufford and associates (2003) determined the effect of systemic estrogen (25 mg 17β-estradiol implant) on the urge syndrome in postmenopausal women. Serum estradiol levels and endometrial thickness were measured on entry to the trial and at 1, 3, and 6 months; the outcome measures employed were video cystourethrography, frequency volume chart, visual analog score of symptoms, and King's Health Questionnaire. Forty women were included. Subjectively, there was a significant improvement in urgency in both groups and in urge incontinence in the estradiol group, but there were no significant differences between the groups. Objectively, no significant differences were demonstrated between the groups. Nine women in the estradiol group had vaginal bleeding, and five had a hysterectomy during or after the study. The conclusion of the study was that the estradiol implant used did not produce a greater improvement in the urge syndrome than did placebo and had a high complication rate.

Grady and coworkers (2001) determined whether postmenopausal hormone therapy improves the severity of urinary incontinence in a randomized, blinded trial among 2763 postmenopausal women younger than 80 years with coronary disease and intact uteri. The study included 1525 participants who reported at least one episode of incontinence per week at baseline. Participants were randomly assigned to 0.625 mg of conjugated estrogens plus 2.5 mg of medroxyprogesterone acetate in one tablet daily (n = 768) or placebo (n = 757) and were observed for a mean of 4.1 years. Severity of incontinence was classified as improved (decrease of at least two episodes per week), unchanged (change of at most one episode per week), or worsened (increase of at least two episodes per week). The results showed that incontinence improved in 26% of the women assigned to placebo compared with 21% assigned to hormones, whereas 27% of the placebo group worsened compared with 39% of the hormone group ($P = .001$). This difference was evident by 4 months of treatment and was observed for both urge incontinence and stress incontinence. The number of incontinent episodes per week increased an average of 0.7 in the hormone group and decreased by 0.1 in the placebo group ($P < .001$). The authors concluded that daily oral estrogen plus progestin therapy was associated with worsening urinary incontinence in older postmenopausal women with weekly incontinence and did not recommend this therapy for the treatment of incontinence. It cannot be excluded that the progestin component may influence the effects found in this study.

Hendrix and associates (2005) reported the results of a large randomized study assessing the effects of hormone therapy (conjugated equine estrogen with and without progestin) on the incidence of stress, urge, and mixed incontinence in healthy postmenopausal women (27,347 women included). They found that estrogen therapy alone or in combination with progestin increased the risk of urinary incontinence among continent women and worsened the characteristics of incontinence among symptomatic women after 1 year. The outcome was similar in all types of incontinence. The authors concluded that conjugated equine estrogen with and without progestin should not be prescribed for the prevention or relief of urinary incontinence.

Estrogen has an important physiologic effect on the female lower urinary tract, and its deficiency may be an etiologic factor in the pathogenesis of a number of conditions. However, the use of estrogens alone to treat urinary incontinence has given disappointing results.

Other Pharmacologic Agents

Gabapentin. Gabapentin was originally designed as an anticonvulsant GABA mimetic capable of crossing the blood-brain barrier (Maneuf et al, 2003). The effects of gabapentin, however, do not appear to be mediated through interaction with GABA receptors, and its mechanism of action remains controversial (Maneuf et al, 2003). It has been suggested that it acts by binding to a subunit of the $\alpha_2\delta$ unit of voltage-dependent Ca^{2+} channels (Gee et al, 1996). Gabapentin is also widely used not only for seizures and neuropathic pain but for many other indications, such as anxiety and sleep disorders, because of its apparent lack of toxicity.

In a pilot study, Carbone and associates (2003) reported on the effect of gabapentin on neurogenic DO. These investigators found a positive effect on symptoms and significant improvement in urodynamic parameters after treatment with gabapentin and suggested that the effects of the drug should be explored in further controlled studies in both neurogenic and non-neurogenic DO. Kim and associates (2004) studied the effects of gabapentin in patients with OAB and nocturia not responding to antimuscarinics. They found that 14 of 31 patients improved with oral gabapentin. The drug was generally well tolerated, and the authors suggested that it can be considered in selective patients when conventional modalities have failed. It is possible that gabapentin and other $\alpha_2\delta$ ligands (e.g., pregabalin and analogs) will offer new therapeutic alternatives.

Other Mechanisms of Drug Delivery

Drug delivery often frustrates what would otherwise seem to be theoretically sound treatment of bladder disorders. Intravesical drug administration is one way to overcome this. Intravesical therapy optimizes drug delivery in the vicinity of the presumed primary pathologic process while theoretically reducing systemic availability. Most commonly, urologists are familiar with intravesical drug delivery for the treatment of malignant and premalignant conditions of the bladder. Agents to decrease bladder contractility can also be used, but such contemporary use requires clean intermittent catheterization for instillation. This has been mentioned previously in the sections on oxybutynin and other agents. There are devices that have been studied for intravesical delivery of a continuous predictable level of drug solution for up to several weeks.* Efficacy, systemic side effects, comfort of the patient, encrustation, infection, and stone formation are obviously all considerations in the potential use of such a device. The various pharmacokinetic and clinical considerations of intravesical drug delivery are discussed by Highley and colleagues (1999).

Drug Treatment of Overactivity in Augmented or Intestinal Neobladders

With regard to the subject of overactivity in bowel-augmented or intestinal neobladders, Andersson and coworkers (1992) reviewed this subject and its pharmacologic treatment. They noted a few instances of positive results with drugs given systemically, but locally applied agents were believed to offer more promise. Pure antimuscarinic agents had produced few good results, either locally or systemically. Oxybutynin had shown some good results with local therapy but poor results with systemic therapy. The α and β adrenoceptor agonists had shown little or no effects. Other possibilities mentioned

---

*UROS infuser, Situs Corporation, Solana Beach, Calif.

included opioid agonists (diphenoxylate—a component of Lomotil—and loperamide), calcium antagonists, potassium channel openers, and nitric oxide donors.

Increasing Outlet Resistance

Many factors are involved in the pathogenesis of stress urinary incontinence (SUI). Some of them, such as weak urethral support, vaginal prolapse, and severe vesical neck or urethral dysfunction (DeLancey, 1997), cannot be treated pharmacologically. Nonetheless, some studies reported cure or significant improvement of even severe incontinence with solely pharmacologic treatment (Lose et al, 1989). Women with SUI have lower resting urethral pressures than those of age-matched continent women (Henriksson, 1979; Hilton and Stanton, 1983), and the aim of treatment is often to increase intraurethral pressure.

Factors that may contribute to urethral closure include urethral smooth muscle tone and the passive properties of the urethral lamina propria, in particular the vascular suburothelial layer. The relative contribution to intraurethral pressure of these factors is still subject to debate. Rud and coworkers (1980) quantified the contribution of three major components of the female continence mechanism to intraurethral pressure. Patients underwent urethrocystometry including urethral pressure profile measurements before, during, and after curarization as well as after clamping of the arterial blood supply to the urethra. The contribution to the total intraurethral pressure of the striated muscle component in (1) urethra and pelvic floor, (2) urethral vascular bed, and (3) smooth musculature and connective tissues in urethra and periurethral tissues were found to be one third each.

Kuo (2000) found in a combined ultrasound and urodynamic study in 83 women that the size of the urethral striated muscle and the thickness of the urethropelvic ligaments decreased with increasing degrees of SUI. Nonetheless, the distinct role of striated urethral and pelvic floor muscles has not yet been established. A contributing factor to SUI, mainly in elderly women with lack of estrogen, may be insufficient mucosal "sealing" function.

There is ample pharmacologic evidence that a substantial part of urethral tone is mediated through stimulation of α adrenoceptors in the urethral smooth muscle by released norepinephrine (Andersson, 1993). However, the central nervous control of both the smooth and striated urethral muscle is important for the maintenance of continence. The nucleus of Onuf is the spinal target of reuptake inhibitors of serotonin (5-HT) and norepinephrine, which may increase the tone of the striated sphincter (see later).

Current Pharmacologic Treatment

The current pharmacologic treatments of SUI were recently evaluated by the 3rd International Consultation on Incontinence (Tables 62–3 and 62–4) (Andersson et al, 2005). The aims of most treatments are to increase intraurethral pressure by effects on the urethral smooth muscle or on the striated muscles in the urethra and pelvic floor (Zinner et al, 2004b).

α Adrenoceptor Agonists

The effects of α adrenoceptor agonists are believed to be exerted mainly by stimulation of postjunctional α_1 adrenoceptors on urethral smooth muscle (Andersson, 1993).

Table 62–3. Drugs Used in the Treatment of Stress Incontinence (assessments according to the Oxford system, modified)

Drug	Level of Evidence	Grade of Recommendation
Duloxetine	1	A
Imipramine	3	D
Clenbuterol		
Methoxamine	2	D
Midodrine	2	C
Ephedrine	3	D
Norephedrine (phenylpropanolamine)	3	D
Estrogen	2	D

However, effects on striated muscle by excitatory effects on the spinal cord level, leading to increased muscle tone through somatic motoneurons, have also been suggested (Thind et al, 1992).

Nonselective α Adrenoceptor Agonists. Ephedrine is a noncatecholamine sympathomimetic agent that enhances release of norepinephrine from sympathetic neurons and directly stimulates both α and β adrenoceptors. The oral adult dosage is 25 to 50 mg four times a day. Some tachyphylaxis develops to its peripheral actions, probably as a result of depletion of norepinephrine stores. **Pseudoephedrine,** a stereoisomer of ephedrine, is used for similar indications with similar precautions. The adult dosage is 30 to 60 mg four times a day, and the 30-mg dose form is available in the United States without prescription (Sudafed, others). Diokno and Taub (1975) reported a "good to excellent" result in 27 of 38 patients with sphincteric incontinence treated with ephedrine sulfate. Beneficial effects were most often achieved in those with minimal to moderate wetting, and little benefit was achieved in patients with severe SUI. Lose and Lindholm (1984) treated 20 women with SUI with **norfenefrine,** given as a slow-release tablet. Nineteen patients reported reduced urinary leakage; 10 reported no further SUI. Maximum urethral closure pressure increased in 16 patients during treatment, the mean rise being from 53 to 64 cm H_2O. It is interesting and perplexing that most patients reported an effect only after 14 days of treatment. The delay is difficult to explain on the basis of drug action, unless one postulates a change in the number of α adrenoceptors or in their sensitivity. It is obvious that there is a powerful placebo effect, for which the reasons are unknown, and therefore caution must be exercised in the evaluation of *all* modalities of therapy for sphincteric (and detrusor as well) incontinence.

Norephedrine (phenylpropanolamine, PPA) has classically been reported to share the pharmacologic properties of ephedrine and to be approximately equal in peripheral potency while causing less central stimulation. A dose of 75 to 100 mg of PPA (norephedrine chloride) has been shown to increase maximum urethral pressure and maximum urethral closure pressure in women with SUI (Ek et al, 1978). At a 300-mL bladder volume, maximum urethral pressure rose from 82 to 110 cm H_2O, and maximum urethral closure pressure rose from 63 to 93 cm H_2O. The functional profile length did not change significantly. Obrink and Bunne (1978), however,

Table 62–4. Drugs Used in the Treatment of Overflow Incontinence (assessments according to the Oxford system)

Drug	Level of Evidence	Grade of Recommendation
α *Adrenoceptor Antagonists*		
Alfuzosin	4	C
Doxazosin	4	C
Prazosin	4	C
Terazosin	4	C
Tamsulosin	4	C
(Phenoxybenzamine)	4	NR
Muscarinic Receptor Antagonists		
Bethanechol	4	D
Carbachol	4	D
Cholinesterase Inhibitors		
Distigmine	4	D
Other Drugs		
Baclofen	4	C
Benzodiazepines	4	C
Dantrolene	4	C

NR, not recommended.

noted that 100 mg of PPA twice daily did not improve severe SUI sufficiently to offer it as an alternative to surgical treatment. They further noted in their group of 10 such patients that the maximum urethral closure pressure was not influenced at rest or with stress at low or moderate bladder volumes.

PPA is available in 25- and 50-mg tablets and 75-mg timed-release capsules and is a component of numerous proprietary mixtures, some marketed for the treatment of nasal and sinus congestion (usually in combination with an H_1 antihistamine) and some marketed as appetite suppressants. With doses of 50 mg three times a day, Awad and coworkers (1978) claimed that 11 of 13 women and 6 of 7 men with SUI were significantly improved after 4 weeks of therapy. Maximum urethral closure pressure increased from a mean of 47 to 72 cm H_2O in patients with an empty bladder and from 43 to 58 cm H_2O in patients with a full bladder. With use of a capsule (Ornade) that then contained 50 mg of PPA, 8 mg of chlorpheniramine (an antihistamine), and 2 mg of isopropamide (an antimuscarinic), Stewart and colleagues (1976) reported that of 77 women with SUI, 18 were completely cured with 1 sustained-release capsule taken twice daily; 28 patients were "much better," 6 were "slightly better," and 25 were no better. In 11 men with post-prostatectomy SUI, the numbers in the corresponding categories were 1, 2, 1, and 7. The formulation of Ornade has now been changed, and each capsule of drug contains 75 mg of PPA and 12 mg of chlorpheniramine.

Collste and Lindskog (1987) reported on a group of 24 women with SUI treated with PPA or placebo with a crossover after 2 weeks. Severity of incontinence was graded 1 (slight) or 2 (moderate). Average maximum urethral closure pressure overall increased significantly with PPA compared with placebo (48 to 55 cm H_2O versus 48 to 49 cm H_2O). This was significant in grade 2 but not in grade 1 incontinence. The average number of leakage episodes per 48 hours was reduced significantly overall for patients receiving PPA versus placebo (5 to 1 versus 5 to 6). This was significant for grade 1 but not for grade 2 incontinence. Subjectively, 6 of 24 patients believed both PPA and placebo were ineffective. Of 18 of 24 patients reporting a subjective preference, 14 preferred PPA and 4 preferred the placebo. Improvements were rated subjectively as good, moderately good, and slight. Those obtained with PPA were significant versus placebo for the entire population and for both groups individually.

The AHCPR guidelines (1992) report eight randomized controlled trials with PPA, 50 mg twice daily, for SUI in women. Percentage cures (all figures refer to percentage effect on drug minus percentage effect on placebo) are listed as 0% to 14%, percentage reduction in incontinence as 19% to 60%, and percentage side effects and percentage dropouts as 5% to 33% and 0% to 4.3%, respectively. Siltberg and associates (1999) suggested that the cough-induced leak point pressure be adopted as a standard measure of the effects of treatment in patients with SUI. PPA in a dose of 100 mg significantly increased the cough-induced leak point pressure over placebo, and there was a moderate but statistically significant correlation between cough-induced leak point pressure and a short-term pad test.

There are potential complications of PPA. Baggioni and associates (1987) emphasized the possibility of blood pressure elevation, especially in patients with autonomic impairment. Liebson and coworkers (1987) found no cardiovascular or subjective adverse effects with doses of 25 mg three times a day or a 75-mg sustained-release preparation in a population of 150 healthy normal volunteers. Blackburn and colleagues (1989), in a larger series of healthy subjects and with multiple over-the-counter formulations, concluded that there was a statistically significant but clinically unimportant pressor effect in the first 6 hours after administration of PPA, and this was greater with a sustained-release preparation. Vick and associates (1994) reviewed literature on PPA side effects and carried out canine experiments at the U.S. FDA that looked at cardiovascular effects. They concluded that (1) individuals taking PPA might possibly show an initial increase in blood pressure that could be dangerous; (2) tachyphylaxis does occur with respect to this, and this could provide some degree of safety for individuals taking PPA on a repetitive basis; and (3) doses of PPA given in the range of 0.5 to 1 mg/kg are "reasonably safe," but the investigators cautioned that "this does not take into consideration the fact that some individuals taking PPA could be in poor cardiovascular health or that doses well in excess of 1 mg/kg could be ingested with potentially dangerous side effects."

The FDA has asked manufacturers to voluntarily stop selling PPA-containing drugs and to replace the ingredient with a safer alternative (Neergaard, 2000). This request, which, it was hinted, may be replaced by a ban, was based on a study reported by Kernan and associates (2000). They compared 702 adults younger than 50 years with subarachnoid or intracerebral hemorrhage with 1376 control subjects, reporting the risk of hemorrhagic stroke to be 16 times higher in women who had been taking PPA as an appetite suppressant and 3 times higher in women who had taken the drug for less than 24 hours as a cold remedy. This last finding was not statistically significant. PPA was reported not to be associated with an increased risk of stroke in men. In commenting on this article, Abramowicz and Zuccotti (2000) noted that no case-control studies were available on the safety of phenylephrine, ephedrine, or pseudoephedrine but did relate that case reports have associated ephedra alkaloids with hypertension, stroke, seizures, and death. Their article concluded, "Phenylpropanolamine may not be the only α-adrenergic agonist that can cause serious adverse effects when taken systemically in over-the-counter products marketed for nasal congestion or weight loss." Thus, extreme caution must be exercised in choosing patients, especially women, for α-adrenergic agonist therapy.

Selective α₁ Adrenoceptor Agonists. Midodrine is a relatively selective α_1-adrenergic agonist previously reported to be effective in alleviating SUI in doses ranging from 5 to 22.5 mg/day (see Weil et al, 1998, for references). Weil and colleagues (1998), however, reported no urodynamic improvement in such patients treated with 5 to 10 mg of this agent in a randomized, double-blind, placebo-controlled trial.

Radley and coworkers (2001) evaluated the effect of the selective α_1 adrenoceptor agonist **methoxamine** in a randomized, double-blind, placebo-controlled cross-over study of a group of women with genuine SUI while measuring maximum urethral pressure, blood pressure, heart rate, and symptomatic side effects. Methoxamine evoked nonsignificant increases in maximum urethral pressure and diastolic blood pressure but caused a significant rise in systolic blood pressure and a significant fall in heart rate at maximum dosage. Systemic side effects, including piloerection, headache, and cold extremities, were experienced in all subjects. The authors suggested that the clinical usefulness of direct, peripherally acting subtype-selective α_1 adrenoceptor agonists in the medical treatment of SUI may be limited by side effects.

Attempts have been made to develop agonists with selectivity for the human urethra. Among the three high-affinity α_1 adrenoceptor subtypes identified in molecular cloning and functional studies (α_{1A}, α_{1B}, α_{1D}), α_{1A} seems to predominate in the human lower urinary tract (Taniguchi et al, 1997; Nishimatsu et al, 1999; Andersson, 2002c). However, the receptor with low affinity for prazosin (the α_{1L} adrenoceptor), which has not been cloned and may represent a functional phenotype of the α_{1A} adrenoceptor, was found to be prominent in the human male urethra. In the human female urethra, the expression and distribution of α_1 adrenoceptor subtypes were determined by in situ hybridization and quantitative autoradiography. The mRNA for the α_{1A} subtype was predominant, and autoradiography confirmed the predominance of the α_{1A} adrenoceptor (Nasu et al, 1998). Fiduxosin, a novel α_{1A} adrenoceptor selective agonist, was shown to have an enhanced in vitro and in vivo profile relative to PPA and midodrine (Altenbach et al, 2002). However, there is so far no information available on its effects in humans, and the role of selective α_{1A} adrenoceptor agonists in the treatment of stress incontinence has yet to be established.

α Adrenoceptor Agonists in Combination. Several studies investigated the effect of a PPA in combination with estrogen or other nonsurgical treatments of SUI, such as pelvic floor exercises and electrical stimulation. Mostly a combination of either of the approaches was found beneficial, subjectively or objectively (Beisland et al, 1984; Kinn and Lindskog, 1988; Ahlström et al, 1990; Hilton et al, 1990). However, even if this

type of treatment can be effective in women with mild SUI or in those not suitable for surgery, the risks with PPA and related compounds (see earlier) do not seem to motivate their use as single-drug therapy or in combination with estrogen or conservative treatment.

Although some clinicians have reported spectacular cure and improvement rates with α adrenoceptor agonists and agents that produce an α adrenoceptor–mediated effect in the outlet of patients with sphincteric urinary incontinence, our experience coincides with that of those who report that such treatment with such agents may produce satisfactory or some improvement in mild cases but rarely total dryness in cases of severe or even moderate SUI. Such therapy, when it is used, should always be employed in conjunction with pelvic floor physiotherapy and biofeedback to achieve optimal results.

β Adrenoceptor Antagonists

The assumed mechanism of action of β adrenoceptor antagonists in the treatment of SUI is that blockade of urethral β adrenoceptors may enhance the effects of norepinephrine on urethral α adrenoceptors. Even if propranolol has been reported to have beneficial effects in the treatment of SUI (Gleason et al, 1974; Kaisary, 1984), there are no RCTs supporting such an action.

Antidepressants

Imipramine, among several other pharmacologic effects (see earlier), inhibits the reuptake of norepinephrine and 5-HT in adrenergic nerve endings. In the urethra, this can be expected to enhance the contractile effects of norepinephrine on urethral smooth muscle. Theoretically, such an action may also influence the striated muscles in the urethra and pelvic floor by effects at the spinal cord level (Onuf's nucleus).

Gilja and associates (1984) reported in an open study of 30 women with SUI that imipramine, 75 mg daily, produced subjective continence in 21 patients and increased mean maximum urethral closure pressure from 34 to 48 mm Hg. Lin and coworkers (1999) assessed the efficacy of imipramine (25 mg imipramine three times a day for 3 months) as a treatment in 40 women with genuine SUI. A 20-minute pad test, uroflowmetry, filling and voiding cystometry, and stress urethral pressure profile were performed before and after treatment. The efficacy of successful treatment was 60% (95% CI, 44.8 to 75.2).

As mentioned previously, imipramine can cause a wide range of potentially dangerous side effects, especially regarding the cardiovascular system, and should be used with caution. No RCTs on the effects of imipramine in SUI seem to be available.

Duloxetine hydrochloride, a combined norepinephrine and serotonin reuptake inhibitor, has been shown to significantly increase urethral sphincteric muscle activity during the filling-storage phase of micturition in the cat acetic acid model of irritated bladder function (Thor and Katofiasc, 1995; Katofiasc et al, 2002; Thor and Donatucci, 2004). Bladder capacity was also increased in this model, both effects mediated centrally through motor efferent and sensory afferent modulation (Fraser and Chancellor, 2003). The sphincteric effects were reversed by α_1-adrenergic (prazosin) and 5-HT₂ serotonergic (LY 53857) antagonism, and the bladder effects were blocked by nonselective serotonergic antagonism (methiothepin), implying that both effects were mediated by temporal prolongation of the actions of serotonin and norepinephrine in the synaptic cleft (Fraser and Chancellor, 2003). Duloxetine is lipophilic, well absorbed, and extensively metabolized (CYP2D6). Its plasma half-life is approximately 12 hours (Sharma et al, 2000).

There are several RCTs documenting the effects of duloxetine in SUI (Dmochowski et al, 2003; Millard et al, 2004b; van Kerrebroeck et al, 2004). Dmochowski and colleagues (2003) enrolled a total of 683 North American women 22 to 84 years old in a double-blind, placebo-controlled study. The case definition included a predominant symptom of SUI with a weekly incontinence episode frequency (IEF) of 7 or greater, the absence of predominant symptoms of urgency incontinence, normal diurnal and nocturnal frequency, a bladder capacity of 400 mL or more, and positive cough stress test and stress pad test results. After a 2-week placebo lead-in period, subjects were randomly assigned to receive placebo (339) or 80 mg of duloxetine daily (344) as 40 mg twice daily for 12 weeks. Primary outcome variables included IEF and an incontinence quality of life questionnaire. Mean baseline IEF was 18 weekly, and 436 subjects (64%) had a baseline IEF of 14 or greater. There was a significant decrease in IEF with duloxetine compared with placebo (50% versus 27%), with comparably significant improvements in quality of life (11.0 versus 6.8). Of subjects receiving duloxetine, 51% had a 50% to 100% decrease in IEF compared with 34% of those receiving placebo ($P < .001$). These improvements with duloxetine were associated with a significant increase in the voiding interval compared with placebo (20 versus 2 minutes), and they were observed across the spectrum of incontinence severity. The discontinuation rate for adverse events was 4% for placebo and 24% for duloxetine ($P < .001$), with nausea the most common reason for discontinuation (6.4%). Nausea, which was also the most common side effect, tended to be mild to moderate and transient, usually resolving after 1 week to 1 month. Of the 78 women who experienced treatment-emergent nausea while taking duloxetine, 58 (74%) completed the trial. The authors concluded that duloxetine 40 mg twice daily improved incontinence and quality of life.

Similar results were reported by Millard and colleagues (2004b) studying the effects of duloxetine 40 mg twice daily versus placebo in 458 women in four continents outside North America and by van Kerrebroeck and associates (2004) investigating 494 European and Canadian women.

The effectiveness of duloxetine for treatment of SUI is documented. Adverse effects occur but seem tolerable (Viktrup et al, 2004). **Duloxetine is available in Europe but was withdrawn from the FDA approval process; at the time of this writing, it has not been resubmitted.**

β Adrenoceptor Agonists. β Adrenoceptor stimulation is generally conceded to decrease urethral pressure (see Andersson, 1993, for references), but $β_2$ adrenoceptor agonists have been reported to increase the contractility of some fast-contracting striated muscle fibers and to suppress that of slow-contracting fibers from others (Fellenius et al, 1980). Some β adrenoceptor agonists also stimulate skeletal muscle hypertrophy—in fast-twitch more so than in slow-twitch fibers (Kim and Sainz, 1992). Clenbuterol has been reported to potentiate the field stimulation–induced contraction in rabbit isolated periurethral muscle preparations, an action that is suppressed by propranolol and greater than that produced by isoproterenol (Kishimoto et al, 1991). These authors were the first to report an increase in urethral pressure with clinical use of clenbuterol and to speculate on its potential for the treatment of SUI. Yamanishi and colleagues (1994) reported an inotropic effect of clenbuterol and terbutaline on the fatigued striated urethral sphincter of dogs, abolished by β adrenoceptor blockade.

Yasuda and coworkers (1993) described the results of a double-blind placebo-controlled trial with this agent in 165 women with SUI. Positive statistical significance was achieved for subjective evaluation of incontinence frequency, pad use per day, and overall global assessment. Pad weight decreased from $11.7 ± 17.9$ g to $6.0 ± 12.3$ g for drug and from $18.3 ± 29.0$ g to $12.6 ± 24.7$ g for placebo, raising questions about the comparability of the two groups. The "significant" increase in maximum urethral closure pressure was from $46.0 ± 18.2$ cm H_2O to $49.3 ± 19.1$ cm H_2O, versus a change of -1.5 cm H_2O in the placebo group. Of 77 patients in the clenbuterol group, 56 reported some degree of improvement versus 48 of 88 in the placebo group. The positive effects were suggested to be a result of an action on urethral striated muscle or the pelvic floor muscles. Ishiko and colleagues (2000) investigated the effects of clenbuterol on 61 female patients with SUI in a 12-week randomized study, comparing drug therapy with pelvic floor exercises and a combination of drug therapy and pelvic floor exercises. The frequency and volume of stress incontinence and the patient's own impressions were used as the basis for the assessment of efficacy. The improvement of incontinence was 76.9%, 52.6%, and 89.5% in the respective groups. In an open study, Noguchi and associates (1997) reported positive results with clenbuterol (20 mg twice daily for 1 month) in 9 of 14 patients with mild to moderate SUI after radical prostatectomy. Further well-designed RCTs documenting the effects of clenbuterol are needed to adequately assess its potential for treatment of SUI; it is possible that this agent may have a novel as yet undefined mechanism of action.

Estrogens

The role of estrogen in the treatment of SUI has been controversial, even though there are a number of reported studies (see Hextall, 2000). Some have given promising results, but this may be because they were observational, not randomized, blinded, or controlled. The situation is further complicated by the fact that a number of different types of estrogen have been used with varying doses, routes of administration, and durations of treatment. Fantl and associates (1996) treated 83 hypoestrogenic women with urodynamic evidence of genuine SUI or DO with conjugated equine estrogens 0.625 mg and medroxyprogesterone 10 mg cyclically for 3 months. Controls received placebo tablets. At the end of the study period, the clinical and quality of life variables had not changed significantly in either group. Jackson and coworkers (1999) treated 57 postmenopausal women with genuine SUI or mixed incontinence with estradiol valerate 2 mg or placebo daily for 6 months. There was no significant change in objective outcome measures, although both the active and placebo group reported subjective benefit.

There have been two meta-analyses performed that have helped clarify the situation further. In the first, a report by the Hormones and Urogenital Therapy committee, the use of estrogens to treat all causes of incontinence in post-menopausal women was examined (Fantl et al, 1994). Of 166 articles identified, which were published in English between 1969 and 1992, only 6 were controlled trials and 17 uncontrolled series. The results showed that there was a significant subjective improvement for all patients and those with genuine SUI. However, assessment of the objective parameters revealed that there was no change in the volume of urine lost. Maximum urethral closure pressure did increase significantly, but this result was influenced by only one study showing a large effect. In the second meta-analysis, Sultana and Walters (1990) reviewed 8 controlled and 14 uncontrolled prospective trials and included all types of estrogen treatment. They also found that estrogen therapy was not an efficacious treatment of SUI but that it may be useful for the often associated symptoms of urgency and frequency. Estrogen, when it is given alone, therefore does not appear to be an effective treatment of SUI. However, several studies have shown that it may have a role in combination with other therapies (for combination with α adrenoceptor agonists, see earlier). In a randomized trial, Ishiko and colleagues (2001) compared the effects of the combination of pelvic floor exercise and estriol (1 mg/day) in 66 patients with postmenopausal SUI. Efficacy was evaluated every 3 months on the basis of stress scores obtained from a questionnaire. They found a significant decrease in stress score in patients with mild and moderate SUI in both groups 3 months after the start of therapy and concluded that combination therapy with estriol plus pelvic floor exercise was effective and capable of serving as first-line treatment of mild SUI.

In the previously mentioned study by Hendrix and coworkers (2005), in which the effects of hormone therapy (estrogen therapy alone or in combination with progestin) were evaluated in healthy postmenopausal women, there was an increased risk not only of stress but also of urgency and mixed incontinence among continent women and worsened incontinence among symptomatic women.

Thus, reviews of recent literature agree that "estrogen therapy has little effect in the management of urodynamic SUI" (Al-Badr et al, 2003; Robinson and Cardozo, 2003).

Circumventing the Problem

Vasopressin Analogs: Desmopressin

Desmopressin (1-desamino-8-D-arginine vasopressin, DDAVP) is a **synthetic vasopressin analog with a pronounced antidiuretic effect but practically lacking vasopressor actions** (Andersson et al, 1988). **It is widely used for treatment of primary nocturnal enuresis** (Nevéus et al, 1999; Glazener and Evans, 2002). Studies have shown that one of the factors that can contribute to nocturnal enuresis in children, and probably in adults, is lack of a normal nocturnal increase in plasma vasopressin, which results in a high nocturnal urine production (Rittig et al, 1989; Matthiesen et al, 1996; Nørgaard et al, 1997; Hjälmås, 1999). By decreasing the nocturnal production of urine, beneficial effects may be obtained in

enuresis and nocturia. However, the drug may also have stimulatory effects on the CNS, as found in rats (DiMichele et al, 1996). Several controlled, double-blind investigations have shown intranasal administration of desmopressin to be effective in the treatment of nocturnal enuresis in children (Nevéus et al, 1999; Glazener and Evans, 2002). The dose used in most studies has been 20 μg intranasally at bedtime. However, the drug is orally active, even if the bioavailability is low (less than 1% compared with 2% to 10% after intranasal administration), and its efficacy in primary nocturnal enuresis in children and adolescents has been documented in randomized, double-blind, placebo-controlled studies (Janknegt et al, 1997; Skoog et al, 1997).

Positive effects of desmopressin on nocturia in adults have been documented (Månsson et al, 1980; Asplund and Åberg, 1993; Asplund et al, 1999). Nocturnal frequency and enuresis due to bladder instability responded favorably to intranasal desmopressin therapy even when previous treatment with "antispasmodics" had been unsuccessful (Hilton and Stanton, 1982). Also in patients with multiple sclerosis, desmopressin was shown in controlled studies to reduce nocturia and micturition frequency (Hilton et al, 1983; Kinn and Larsson, 1990; Eckford et al, 1994; Fredrikson, 1996; Ferreira and Letwin, 1998). Furthermore, desmopressin was shown to be successful in treating nocturnal enuresis in spina bifida patients with diurnal incontinence (Horowitz et al, 1997).

Oral desmopressin has also proved to be effective in the treatment of nocturia. In a randomized double-blind study, Mattiasson and associates (2002) investigated the efficacy and safety of oral desmopressin in the treatment of nocturia in men. A 3-week dose titration phase established the optimum desmopressin dose (0.1, 0.2, or 0.4 mg), and after a 1-week washout period, patients who responded in the dose titration period were randomized to receive the optimal dose of desmopressin or placebo in a double-blind design for 3 weeks. In all, 151 patients entered the double-blind period (86 treated with desmopressin, 65 with placebo). Twenty-eight patients (34%) in the desmopressin group and 2 patients (3%) in the placebo group had significantly fewer than half the number of nocturnal voids relative to baseline; the mean number of nocturnal voids decreased from 3.0 to 1.7 and from 3.2 to 2.7, respectively, reflecting a mean decrease of 43% and 12%. The mean duration of the first sleep period increased by 59% (from 2.7 to 4.5 hours) in the desmopressin group compared with an increase of 21% (from 2.5 to 2.9 hours) in the placebo group. The mean nocturnal diuresis decreased by 36% (from 1.5 to 0.9 mL/min) in the desmopressin group and by 6% (from 1.7 to 1.5 mL/min) in the placebo group. The mean ratio of night/24-hour urine volume decreased by 23% and 1%, and the mean ratio of night/day urine volume decreased by 27% and increased by 3% for the desmopressin and placebo groups, respectively. In the double-blind treatment period, similar numbers of patients had adverse events, 15 patients (17%) in the desmopressin group and 16 patients (25%) in the placebo group. Most adverse events were mild. Serum sodium levels were below 130 mmol/L in 10 patients (4%), and this occurred during dose titration. The authors concluded that orally administered desmopressin is an effective and well-tolerated treatment of nocturia in men.

Lose and coworkers (2003) found similar results in women. In the double-blind phase of their study, 144 patients were randomly assigned to groups (desmopressin, n = 72; placebo, n = 72). For desmopressin, 33 patients (46%) had a 50% or greater reduction in nocturnal voids against baseline levels compared with 5 patients (7%) receiving placebo. The mean number of nocturnal voids, duration of sleep until the first nocturnal void, nocturnal diuresis, and ratios of nocturnal/24 hours and nocturnal/daytime urine volumes changed significantly in favor of desmopressin versus placebo. In the dose titration phase, headache (22%), nausea (8%), and hyponatremia (6%) were reported.

Robinson and associates (2004) introduced antidiuresis as a new concept in managing female daytime urinary incontinence. In a multicenter, multinational, randomized, double-blind, placebo-controlled, cross-over exploratory study of women (aged 18 to 80 years) complaining of severe daytime urinary incontinence, 60 received study medication (safety population) and 57 completed the study. The primary efficacy endpoint was the number of periods with no leakage for 4 hours after dosing. There was a higher mean incidence of periods with no leakage in the first 4 hours on desmopressin, at 62 (35)%, than on placebo, at 48 (40)%, and during the first 8 hours, at 55 (37)% versus 40 (41)%. There was also a higher frequency of dry days on desmopressin than on placebo; 36% of patients had no leakage on virtually all treatment days (6 or 7) for 4 hours after dosing. The time from dosing to first incontinence episode was longer on desmopressin, at 6.3 (2.5) hours, versus 5.2 (3.3) hours, whereas the volume leaked per incontinence episode was lower on desmopressin than placebo. The total volume voided was consistently lower on desmopressin, at 1180 (58) mL versus 1375 (57) mL, during the 24-hour period after administration. There were no serious or severe adverse events reported, and it was concluded that desmopressin is an effective and safe treatment in women with daytime urinary incontinence.

Even if side effects are uncommon during desmopressin treatment, there is a risk of water retention and hyponatremia (Robson et al, 1996; Schwab and Ruder, 1997). **In elderly patients, it was recommended that serum sodium concentration be measured before and after a few days of treatment** (Rembratt et al, 2003).

Desmopressin is a well-documented therapeutic alternative in pediatric nocturnal enuresis and is effective also in adults with nocturia with polyuric origin. Whether it will be an alternative for managing female daytime incontinence requires further documentation.

Diuretics

Another circumventive pharmacologic approach is to give a rapidly acting loop diuretic 4 to 6 hours before bedtime. This, of course, assumes the nocturia is not caused by obstructive uropathy. A randomized, double-blind cross-over study of this approach using bumetanide in a group of 14 general practice patients was reported by Pederson and Johansen (1988). Control nocturia episodes per week averaged 17.5; this decreased with placebo to 12 (!) and with drug to 8. Bumetanide was preferred to placebo by 11 of 14 patients.

PHARMACOLOGIC THERAPY TO FACILITATE BLADDER EMPTYING
Increasing Intravesical Pressure and Bladder Contractility
Parasympathomimetic Agents

Because a major portion of the final common pathway in physiologic bladder contraction is stimulation of parasympathetic postganglionic muscarinic cholinergic receptor sites, **agents that imitate the actions of acetylcholine might be expected to be effective in treating patients who cannot empty because of inadequate bladder contractility.** Acetylcholine, which is a quaternary amine, cannot be used for therapeutic purposes because of its action at both muscarinic and nicotinic receptors; it is rapidly hydrolyzed by acetylcholinesterase and by butyrylcholinesterase (Brown and Taylor, 1996). Many acetylcholine-like drugs exist, but only bethanechol chloride exhibits a relatively selective in vitro action on the urinary bladder and gut with little or no nicotinic action (Brown and Taylor, 1996). Bethanechol is cholinesterase resistant and causes an in vitro contraction of smooth muscle from all areas of the bladder (Zderic et al, 1995) (see Chapter 56, Physiology and Pharmacology of the Bladder and Urethra).

Bethanechol, or agents similar to it, has historically been recommended for the treatment of postoperative or postpartum urinary retention, but only if the patient is awake and alert and if there is no outlet obstruction. The recommended dose has been 5 to 10 mg subcutaneously. For more than 50 years, bethanechol has been recommended for the treatment of the atonic or hypotonic bladder and has been reported as effective in achieving "rehabilitation" of the chronically atonic or hypotonic detrusor (Sonda et al, 1979). Bethanechol has also been reported to stimulate or to facilitate the development of reflex bladder contractions in patients in spinal shock secondary to suprasacral spinal cord injury (Perkash, 1975).

Although bethanechol has been reported to increase gastrointestinal motility and has been used in the treatment of gastroesophageal reflux, and although anecdotal success in specific patients with voiding dysfunction seems to occur, **there is little evidence to support its success in facilitating bladder emptying in a series of patients in whom the drug was the only variable** (Finkbeiner, 1985). In one set of trials, a pharmacologically active subcutaneous dose (5 mg) did not demonstrate significant changes in flow parameters or residual urine volume in (1) a group of women with a residual urine volume of 20% or more of bladder capacity but no evidence of neurologic disease or outlet obstruction; (2) a group of 27 "normal" women of approximately the same age; or (3) a group of patients with a positive bethanechol supersensitivity test result (Wein et al, 1980a, 1980b). This dose did increase cystometric filling pressure and also decreased bladder capacity threshold, findings previously described by others (Sonda et al, 1979). Short-term studies in which the drug was the only variable have generally failed to demonstrate significant efficacy in terms of flow and residual urine volume data (Barrett, 1981). Farrell and colleagues (1990) conducted a double-blind randomized trial that looked at the effects of two catheter management protocols and the effect of bethanechol on post-operative retention after gynecologic incontinence surgery. They concluded that bethanechol was not helpful at all in this setting. Although bethanechol is capable of eliciting an increase in bladder smooth muscle tension, as would be expected from in vitro studies, its ability to stimulate or to facilitate a coordinated and sustained physiologic-like bladder contraction in patients with voiding dysfunction has been unimpressive (Finkbeiner, 1985; Andersson, 1988).

It is difficult to find reproducible urodynamic data that support recommendations for the use of bethanechol in any specific category of patients. Most if not all "long-term" reports in such patients are neither prospective nor double blind and do not exclude the effects of other simultaneous regimens (such as treatment of urinary infection, bladder decompression, timed emptying, or other types of treatment affecting the bladder or outlet), an important observation to consider in reporting such drug studies. Whether repeated doses of bethanechol or any cholinergic agonist can achieve a clinical effect that a single dose cannot is speculative, as are suggestions that bethanechol has a different mode of action or effect on atonic or decompensated bladder muscle than on normal tissue. Bethanechol, administered subcutaneously, does cause an increased awareness of a distended bladder (Downie, 1984). This could facilitate more frequent emptying at lower volumes and thereby help avoid overdistention but, it would seem, only in a bladder that is capable of a contraction.

O'Donnell and Hawkins (1993) administered 5 mg of bethanechol subcutaneously to 10 neurologically intact men and made the following cystometric observations. Bladder volume at first desire to void decreased (220 mL to 85 mL), maximal bladder capacity decreased (380 mL to 160 mL), first desire to void occurred at a higher pressure (5 cm H_2O versus 28 cm H_2O), and compliance was reduced. They concluded that bethanechol affects the ability of the bladder to accommodate volume. Patients were comfortable at a resting bladder pressure of 20 cm H_2O (uncommon in their population), and the pressures at maximal bladder capacity were considerably higher than commonly seen under normal conditions. This suggested to them that either bladder pressure alone is not a significant factor in the perception of a sensation of first desire to void or bethanechol somehow alters the threshold at which perception of desire to void occurs (because these patients showed a tolerance for increased intravesical pressure before first desire to void and at maximal bladder capacity). De Wachter and Wyndaele (2001) determined the bladder electrical threshold in healthy volunteers receiving 5 mg of bethanechol subcutaneously. They found a marked decrease in the volume at which various filling sensations occurred and that the electrical threshold decreased after drug administration. De Wachter and coworkers (2003) treated 18 women with impaired detrusor contraction with subcutaneous bethanechol (5 mg four times daily) for 10 days. At the end of treatment, 61% of the patients voided without a postvoid residual volume. They also found that in these women, the sensation of filling and electrical sensitivity were significantly increased compared with before treatment. The authors suggested that patients likely to respond to bethanechol can be identified by determination of the bladder electrical perception threshold.

Riedl and associates (2000) investigated the effects of bethanechol in 45 patients with detrusor areflexia. The patients were tested with electromotive administration of intravesical bethanechol. Bethanechol 25 mg given orally once daily was then prescribed for 15 patients, and voiding control was assessed after 6 weeks of therapy. A mean pressure increase of 34 cm H_2O during the electromotive administration of bethanechol was found in 24 of 26 patients with areflexia and neurologic disease compared with only 3 cm H_2O in 3 of 11 with a history of chronic bladder dilatation. Oral bethanechol restored spontaneous voiding in 9 of 11 patients who had had a positive response to the electromotive administration of bethanechol, whereas all 4 without a pressure increase during the electromotive administration of bethanechol did not void spontaneously. Riedl and coworkers (2000) concluded that electromotive administration of intravesical bethanechol can identify patients with an atonic bladder and adequate residual detrusor muscle function who are candidates for restorative measures, such as oral bethanechol and intravesical electrostimulation. Those who do not respond to the electromotive administration of bethanechol do not benefit from oral bethanechol and are candidates for catheterization.

The question of whether bethanechol may be efficacious in a particular patient can be answered by a brief urodynamically controlled trial in which institution of therapy is the only variable. In the laboratory, a functioning micturition reflex is an absolute requirement for the production of a sustained bladder contraction by a subcutaneous injection of the drug (Downie, 1984). **Patients with incomplete lower motoneuron lesions constitute the most reasonable group for a trial of bethanechol** (Awad, 1985), although subcutaneous administration may be required. It is generally agreed that at least in a "denervated" bladder, an oral dose of 200 mg is required to produce the same urodynamic effects as a subcutaneous dose of 5 mg (Diokno and Lapides, 1977).

No agreement exists as to whether cholinergic stimulation produces an increase in urethral resistance (Wein et al, 1980a, 1980b). It would appear that pharmacologically active doses do, in fact, increase urethral closure pressure, at least in patients with neurogenic DO (Sporer et al, 1978). This would of course tend to inhibit bladder emptying. As to whether cholinergic agonists can be combined with agents to decrease outlet resistance to facilitate emptying and achieve an additive or synergistic effect, our experience with such therapy, even with oral administration of 200 mg of bethanechol daily, has been extremely disappointing. Certainly, most clinicians would agree that a total divided daily dose of 50 to 100 mg rarely affects any urodynamic parameter at all. In a prospective, single-blind randomized study comprising 119 patients with underactive detrusor, Yamanishi and associates (2004) studied the effect of combination of a cholinergic drug (bethanechol 60 mg daily or distigmine 15 mg daily) and an α-adrenergic receptor antagonist (urapidil 60 mg daily). The effectiveness of each therapy was assessed 4 weeks after initialization of the therapy by the International Prostate Symptom Score (IPSS). IPSS remained unchanged after the cholinergic therapy but was significantly lower after the α-adrenergic receptor antagonist treatment and the combination therapy. With regard to the total IPSS, there were significant differences between the cholinergic and the α-adrenergic receptor antagonist groups and also between the cholinergic and combination groups, in favor of the latter. The average and maximum flow rates did not increase significantly after monotherapy with either the cholinergic drug or the α-adrenergic receptor antagonist, but they significantly increased after combination therapy compared with baseline values. Postvoid residual volume did not decrease significantly after the cholinergic drug therapy but decreased significantly after the α-adrenergic receptor antagonist and the combination therapies. The authors concluded that combination therapy with a cholinergic drug and an α-adrenergic receptor antagonist appeared to be more useful than monotherapy for the treatment of underactive detrusor.

The **potential side effects of cholinomimetic drugs** include flushing, nausea, vomiting, diarrhea, gastrointestinal cramps, bronchospasm, headache, salivation, sweating, and difficulty with visual accommodation (Brown and Taylor, 1996). Intramuscular or intravenous administration can precipitate acute and severe side effects resulting in acute circulatory failure and cardiac arrest and is therefore prohibited. Contraindications to the use of this general category of drug include bronchial asthma, peptic ulcer, bowel obstruction, enteritis, recent gastrointestinal surgery, cardiac arrhythmia, hyperthyroidism, and any type of bladder outlet obstruction.

One potential avenue of increasing bladder contractility is cholinergic enhancement or augmentation. Such an action might be useful alone or in combination with a parasympathomimetic agent.

Metoclopramide (Reglan) is a dopamine receptor antagonist with cholinergic properties. It has a central antiemetic effect in the chemoreceptor trigger zone and peripherally increases the tone of the lower esophageal sphincter, promoting gastric emptying. Its effects seem to be related to its ability to antagonize the inhibitory action of dopamine, to augment acetylcholine release, and to sensitize the muscarinic receptors of gastrointestinal smooth muscle. Some data in the dog suggest that this agent can increase detrusor contractility (Mitchell and Venable, 1985), but there are no controlled studies documenting a useful clinical effect in the treatment of detrusor underactivity.

Cisapride is a substituted synthetic benzamide that enhances the release of acetylcholine in Auerbach's plexus (in the gastrointestinal tract). In 15 patients with complete spinal cord injury treated with 20 mg three times a day for 3 days, Carone and associates (1993) noted earlier and higher amplitude reflex contractions in those with overactive bladders; in those with hypoactive bladders, there was a significant decrease in compliance. There was also increased activity of and decreased compliance of the anorectal ampulla with no alteration in striated sphincter activity. In another study in paraplegic patients, cisapride was found to decrease colonic transit time and maximal rectal capacity; an incidental decrease in residual urine was also noted (although only 51.5 to 27.7 mL) (Binnie et al, 1988).

Steele and coworkers (2001) performed a randomized, double-blind, placebo-controlled trial of 20 patients without significant urinary incontinence who received either 20 mg of cisapride or an identical placebo. Urodynamic evaluation included uroflowmetry, multichannel filling cystometry, pressure-flow studies, and urethral pressure profile. There was a significant decrease in the maximum cystometric capacity

from 556 mL for placebo to 496 mL for cisapride; no difference in the detrusor pressure at maximum flow, the maximum detrusor pressure, the flow rate, or the percentage of maximum cystometric capacity voided was found. The authors concluded that in healthy women, cisapride caused a significant decrease in the maximum cystometric capacity but that there was no evidence the drug improved voiding function.

Cisapride has been associated with life-threatening arrhythmias in susceptible patients, meaning patients receiving a medication that inhibits cisapride metabolism or prolongs the QT interval or who have a disease that predisposes to such arrhythmias. The FDA issued a directive in 1998 contraindicating the use of cisapride in such patients (Smalley et al, 2000). The concept, however, remains attractive and awaits the development of a bladder-selective compound.

Prostaglandins

The reported use of prostaglandins to facilitate emptying is based on **hypotheses that these substances contribute to the maintenance of bladder tone and bladder contractile activity** (see Chapter 56, Physiology and Pharmacology of the Bladder and Urethra) (Andersson, 1993, 1999a, 1999b, 1999c; Zderic et al, 1995; Andersson and Wein, 2004, for a complete discussion). Prostaglandins and thromboxane A_2 have been shown to be present in human bladder in the following quantitative order: $PGE_2 > PGE_1 > PGF_{2\alpha} >$ thromboxane A_2; isolated detrusor muscle is contracted by $PGF_{2\alpha}$, PGE_1, PGE_2, and thromboxane A_2 (see references in Andersson and Wein, 2004). Prostanoids are synthesized locally in both bladder muscle and mucosa, with synthesis being initiated by various physiologic stimuli (such as detrusor muscle stretch, mucosal injury, and neural stimulation), by ATP, and by mediators of inflammation (Andersson and Wein, 2004). Prostanoids may affect bladder activity directly by effects on the smooth muscle or indirectly through effects on neurotransmission. Possible roles mentioned by Andersson (2000a) include (1) neuromodulators of efferent and afferent neurotransmission; (2) sensitization or perhaps (3) activation of certain sensory nerves; and (4) potentiation of acetylcholine release from cholinergic nerve terminals through prejunctional prostanoid receptors. PGE_2 seems to cause a net decrease in urethral smooth muscle tone; $PGF_{2\alpha}$ causes an increase.

Bultitude and associates (1976) first reported that instillation of 0.5 mg PGE_2 into the bladders of women with varying degrees of urinary retention resulted in acute emptying and improvement of longer term emptying (several months) in two thirds of the patients studied (n = 22). Desmond and coworkers (1980) reported results with intravesical use of 1.5 mg of this agent (diluted with 20 mL of 0.2% neomycin solution) in patients whose bladders exhibited no contractile activity or in whom bladder contractility was relatively impaired. Of 36 patients, 20 showed a strongly positive immediate response, and 6 showed a weakly positive one; 14 patients were reported to show prolonged beneficial effects, all but 1 of whom had shown a strongly positive immediate response. Stratification of the data revealed that an intact sacral reflex arc is a prerequisite for any type of positive response. Tammela and colleagues (1987) reported that one intravesical administration of 10 mg of $PGF_{2\alpha}$ facilitated voiding in women who were in retention 3 days after surgery for SUI. The drug was administered in 50 mL of saline solution as a single dose and retained for 2 hours. However, in these "successfully" treated patients, the average maximum flow rate was 10.6 mL/sec with a mean residual urine volume of 107 mL, and the authors stated that "bladder emptying deteriorated in most patients on the day after treatment." Koonings and associates (1990) reported that daily intravesical $PGF_{2\alpha}$ and intravaginal PGE_2 reduced the number of days required for catheterization after stress incontinence surgery compared with a control group receiving intravesical saline solution.

Others, however, have reported negative results. Grignaffini and Bazzani (1998) reported on instillation of 1.5 mg of PGE_2 in 50 mL of saline solution into the bladder of 50 patients on their fourth day after vaginal hysterectomy and cystourethropexy, with a control group of 60 patients. The results are presented in an interesting fashion. After catheter removal, following the PGE_2 or control treatment, 58% of the PGE_2-treated group voided spontaneously compared with 48.3% of the control group. This difference was not significant. Thus, 42% of the treated group and 51.7% of the control group were in retention. Of those who were in retention, the number who were in retention for less than 3 days was greater in the PGE_2 group (32%) versus the control group (25%), and this was statistically significant. Likewise, the number who remained in urinary retention for 3 days or longer after the initial treatment was 10% in the PGE_2-treated group versus 26.7% in the control group. Stanton and colleagues (1979) and Delaere and coworkers (1981) reported on success with use of intravesical PGE_2 in doses similar to those reported earlier; Delaere and coworkers (1981) similarly reported no success with use of $PGF_{2\alpha}$ in a group of women with emptying difficulties of various causes. Wagner and associates (1985) used PGE_2 in doses of 0.75 to 2.25 mg and reported no effect on urinary retention in a group of patients after anterior colporrhaphy.

In a prospective randomized double-blind study, Hindley and coworkers (2004) tested the hypothesis that intravesical PGE_2 and oral bethanechol are additive or synergistic in improving bladder emptying. Nineteen patients with detrusor underactivity (17 men and 2 women) were eligible and randomized to one of two treatments. One group (9 patients) received once-weekly intravesical PGE_2 (1.5 mg in 20 mL 0.9% saline) plus bethanechol 50 mg four times daily, for a total of 6 weeks. A second group of 10 patients received a once-weekly instillation of saline together with placebo tablets, again for 6 weeks. Although there was evidence of a pharmacologic effect, bethanechol and PGE_2 had a limited therapeutic effect compared with placebo. The authors did not recommend this treatment as routine but suggested that it may be considered for the occasional treatment of a patient with detrusor underactivity.

There has been little recent activity in this area, a fact that generally means clinicians have lost interest or the initial optimistic results have not been confirmed. Prostaglandins have a relatively short half-life, and it is difficult to understand how any effects after a single application can last up to several months. If such does occur, it must be the result of a "triggering effect" on some as yet unknown physiologic or metabolic mechanism. **Because of the number of conflicting positive and negative reports with various intravesical preparations, double-blind, placebo-controlled studies would obviously be helpful to see whether there are cir-** **cumstances in which prostaglandin use can reproducibly facilitate emptying or treat postoperative retention.** Potential side effects of prostaglandin use include vomiting, diarrhea, pyrexia, hypertension, and hypotension (Campbell and Halushka, 1996).

Blockers of Inhibition

de Groat and coworkers (see Chapter 56, Physiology and Pharmacology of the Bladder and Urethra) (de Groat and Booth, 1984; de Groat, 1993; de Groat et al, 1993, 1999; Zderic et al, 1995) have demonstrated a sympathetic reflex during bladder filling that, at least in the cat, promotes urine storage partly by exerting an α adrenoceptor–mediated inhibitory effect on pelvic parasympathetic ganglionic transmission. Some have suggested that α adrenoceptor blockade, in addition to decreasing outlet resistance, may in fact facilitate transmission through these ganglia and thereby enhance bladder contractility. On this basis, Raz and Smith (1976) were the first to advocate a trial of an α adrenoceptor–blocking agent for the treatment of nonobstructive urinary retention. A complete discussion of postoperative retention, including the use of α adrenoceptor antagonists for its treatment, is presented elsewhere (Chapter ***).

Opioid Receptor Antagonists

Recent advances in neuropeptide physiology and pharmacology have provided new insights into lower urinary tract function and its potential pharmacologic alteration. **Endogenous opioids have been hypothesized to exert a tonic inhibitory effect on the micturition reflex at various levels** (see Chapter 56, Physiology and Pharmacology of the Bladder and Urethra) (Zderic et al, 1995), and agents such as opioid receptor antagonists therefore may offer possibilities for stimulating reflex bladder activity.

Thor and associates (1983) were able to stimulate a micturition contraction with naloxone, an opioid receptor antagonist, in unanesthetized chronic spinal–injured cats. The effects, however, were transient, and tachyphylaxis developed. Vaidyanathan and colleagues (1981) reported that an intravenous injection of 0.4 mg of naloxone enhanced detrusor reflex activity in five of seven patients with neuropathic bladder dysfunction caused by incomplete suprasacral spinal cord lesions. The maximum effect occurred within 1 to 2 minutes after intravenous injection and was gone by 5 minutes. Murray and Feneley (1982) reported that the same dose of naloxone caused, in a group of patients with idiopathic DO, an increase in detrusor pressure at zero volume and at first desire to void, a decrease in the maximum cystometric capacity, and a worsening of the degree of instability. Galeano and coworkers (1986) reported that although naloxone increased bladder contractility in the cat with chronic spinal injury, it also aggravated striated sphincter dyssynergia and spasticity—a potential problem in the treatment of emptying failure. Wheeler and coworkers (1987) noted no significant cystometric changes in a group of 15 spinal cord–injured patients after intravenous naloxone, whereas 11 showed decreased perineal electromyographic activity.

Although an intriguing area, the concept of reversing an inhibitory opioid influence to stimulate reflex bladder activity is of little practical use at present.

Decreasing Outlet Resistance

α Adrenoceptor Antagonists

Whether one believes that there is significant innervation of the bladder and proximal urethral smooth musculature by postganglionic fibers of the sympathetic nervous system, one must acknowledge the existence of α and β adrenoceptor sites. **The smooth muscle of the bladder base and proximal urethra contains predominantly α adrenoceptors, although β adrenoceptors are present. The bladder body contains both varieties of adrenergic receptors, with β adrenoceptors (β₃ subtype) being more common** (see Chapter 56, Physiology and Pharmacology of the Bladder and Urethra) (Zderic et al, 1995; Andersson, 2000a). The human lower urinary tract contains more α_2 than α_1 adrenoceptors, but prostatic smooth muscle contraction and human lower urinary tract smooth muscle contraction are mediated largely, if not exclusively, by α_1 adrenoceptors. There are at least three subtypes of α_1 adrenoceptors, designated α_{1A}, α_{1B}, and α_{1D}. Smooth muscle contraction in the human lower urinary tract is mediated largely by the α_{1A} (and in the detrusor α_{1D}) subtype (Docherty, 1998; Harada and Fujimura, 2000; Michel et al, 2000; Schwinn, 2000; Andersson and Wein, 2004). In addition to the three cloned α_1 adrenoceptors, there is a possible fourth, α_{1L}, although the α_{1L} adrenoceptor is probably a variant of the α_{1A}. There is a tremendous amount of information and controversy in the literature regarding the selectivity of certain α adrenoceptor–blocking agents for these respective receptor subtypes. Conclusions are drawn regarding "the best" α_1 adrenoceptor antagonist for the treatment of at least benign prostatic hyperplasia on the basis of in vitro and in vivo pharmacologic selectivity, but many authors note that this does not necessarily translate into functional selectivity in a given patient (Andersson, 2002c; Djavan et al, 2004). The various α adrenoceptor antagonists are dealt with in more detail in Chapter 87.

Krane and Olsson (1973) were among the first to promote the concept of a physiologic internal sphincter partially controlled by tonic sympathetic stimulation of contraction-mediating α adrenoceptors in the smooth musculature of the bladder neck and proximal urethra. Furthermore, they hypothesized that some obstructions at this level during bladder contraction are a result of inadequate opening of the bladder neck or of inadequate decrease in resistance in the area of the proximal urethra. They also theorized and presented evidence that α adrenoceptor blockade could be useful in promoting bladder emptying in such a patient with an adequate detrusor contraction but without anatomic obstruction or detrusor–striated sphincter dyssynergia. They and many others (see Wein and Barrett, 1988) have confirmed the **usefulness of α adrenoceptor blockade in the treatment of what is now usually referred to as smooth sphincter or bladder neck dyssynergia or dysfunction.** Successful results, usually defined as an increase in flow rate, a decrease in residual urine, and an improvement in upper tract appearance (where pathologic), could often be correlated with an objective decrease in urethral profile closure pressure.

One would expect success with such therapy to be most evident in patients without detrusor–striated sphincter dyssynergia, as reported by Hachen (1980). Mobley (1976), however, reported a startling 86% subjective success rate in 21

patients with a reflex neurogenic bladder, with a corresponding success rate of 66% in what was called "flaccid" and 57% in what was called "autonomous" neurogenic bladder dysfunction, with success being defined as postvoid residual urine volume consistently less than 100 mL. Scott and Morrow (1978), on the other hand, noted excellent results with phenoxybenzamine therapy in 9 of 10 patients with a flaccid bladder and a flaccid external sphincter and in a single patient with an upper motoneuron bladder with intact sympathetic innervation, but in only 8 of 21 patients with hyperreflexia and autonomic dysreflexia, and in none of 6 patients with an upper motoneuron bladder and sympathetic denervation (lesion between T10 and L2).

Although most would agree that α adrenoceptor–blocking agents exert their favorable effects on voiding dysfunction by affecting the smooth muscle of the bladder neck and proximal urethra, **information in the literature suggests that they may decrease striated sphincter tone as well,** and other information suggests that they may exert some of their effects on at least the filling and storage symptoms of voiding dysfunction by decreasing bladder contractility (see previous discussion). Much of the confusion relative to whether α adrenoceptor–blocking agents have a direct (as opposed to indirect) inhibitory effect on the striated sphincter relates to the interpretation of clinical observations and experimental data referable to their effect on urethral pressure in the region of the urogenital diaphragm and on electromyographic activity in the periurethral striated muscle of this area. One cannot tell by pressure tracings alone whether decreased resistance in this area of the urethra is secondary to a decrease in smooth or striated muscle activity. Nanninga and associates (1977) found that the electromyographic activity of the external sphincter decreased after phentolamine administration in three paraplegic patients and attributed this effect to a direct inhibition of sympathetic action on the striated sphincter. Nordling and colleagues (1981) demonstrated that clonidine and phenoxybenzamine (both of which pass the blood-brain barrier) also decreased urethral pressure in this area and yet had no effect on electromyographic activity. They concluded that (1) the effect of phentolamine was from smooth muscle relaxation alone; (2) the effect of clonidine, and possibly of phenoxybenzamine, was elicited mostly through centrally induced changes in striated urethral sphincter tonus; and (3) these agents also had an effect on the smooth muscle component of urethral pressure. None of the three drugs, however, affected the reflex rise in either urethral pressure or electromyographic activity seen during bladder filling, and none decreased the urethral pressure or electromyographic activity response to voluntary contraction of the pelvic floor striated musculature. Gajewski and coworkers (1984) concluded that α adrenoceptor blockers do not influence the pudendal nerve–dependent urethral response in the cat through a peripheral action but that at least prazosin can significantly inhibit this response at a central level. Thind and colleagues (1992) reported on the effects of prazosin on static urethral sphincter function in 10 healthy women. They found a reduction—predominantly in the midurethral area—and hypothesized that the response was caused by a decrease in both smooth and striated sphincter activity, the latter as a result of a reduced somatomotor output from the CNS. Clinically, Chancellor and associates (1994) reported that terazosin, a selective α_1 adrenoceptor antagonist, had little or no effect on striated sphincter function in spinal cord–injured patients and had no effect on functional obstruction caused by sphincter dyssynergia in these patients.

The α adrenoceptor–blocking agents have also been used to treat both bladder and outlet abnormalities in patients with so-called autonomous bladders—such as those with myelodysplasia, sacral spinal cord or infrasacral neural injury, and voiding dysfunction after radical pelvic surgery (Wein and Barrett, 1988). Decreased bladder compliance is a common clinical problem in such patients, and this, along with a fixed urethral sphincter tone, results in the paradoxical occurrence of both storage and emptying failure. Such patients have been treated with α adrenoceptor blockers. In certain cases, bladder compliance has been reported to increase. Whether this represents a direct effect on the detrusor smooth muscle or is secondary to decreasing outlet resistance is uncertain.

Phenoxybenzamine was the α adrenoceptor antagonist originally used for the treatment of voiding dysfunction (see Te, 2002). Phenoxybenzamine has blocking properties at both α_1 and α_2 adrenoceptor sites. The initial adult dosage of this agent is 10 mg/day, and the usual daily dose for voiding dysfunction is 10 to 20 mg. After discontinuation, the effects of administration may persist for days because the drug irreversibly inactivates α adrenoceptors, and the duration of effect depends on the rate of receptor synthesis (Hoffman and Lefkowitz, 1996). Side effects affect approximately 30% of patients (Kirby, 1999) and include orthostatic hypotension, reflex tachycardia, nasal congestion, diarrhea, miosis, sedation, nausea, and vomiting (secondary to local irritation). It has mutagenic activity in the Ames test, and repeated administration to animals can cause peritoneal sarcomas and lung tumors (Hoffman and Lefkowitz, 1996). Furthermore, the manufacturer has indicated a dose-related incidence of gastrointestinal tumors in rats (see Physicians' Desk Reference, 2005), the majority of which were in the nonglandular portion of the stomach. Although this agent has been in clinical use for some 30 years without clinically apparent oncologic associations, one must now consider the potential medicolegal ramifications of long-term therapy, especially in younger persons. A reassessment of the use of phenoxybenzamine for treatment of urinary tract disorders was made by Te (2002).

Prazosin was the first potent selective α_1 adrenoceptor antagonist (Hoffman and Lefkowitz, 1996) used to lower outlet resistance. The duration of action is 4 to 6 hours; therapy is generally begun in daily divided doses of 2 to 3 mg. The dose may be gradually increased to a maximum of 20 mg daily, although seldom has anyone used more than 9 to 10 mg daily for voiding dysfunction. The potential side effects of prazosin are consequent to its α_1 adrenoceptor blockade. On occasion, there occurs a "first-dose phenomenon," a symptom complex of faintness, dizziness, palpitation, and, infrequently, syncope, thought to be caused by acute postural hypotension. The incidence of this can be minimized by restricting the initial dose of the drug to 1 mg and administering this at bedtime. Other side effects associated with chronic prazosin therapy are generally mild and rarely necessitate withdrawal of the drug.

Terazosin and **doxazosin** are two highly selective postsynaptic α_1 adrenoceptor antagonists. They are readily absorbed with high bioavailability and long plasma half-life, enabling their activity to be maintained for 24 hours after a single oral dose. Both of these agents have been evaluated with respect to their efficacy in patients with lower urinary tract symptoms and decreased flow rates presumed secondary to benign prostatic hyperplasia. Their efficacy in decreasing symptoms and raising flow rates has been shown to be superior to placebo and similar to that of prazosin (Kirby, 1999). Their safety profiles have been well documented as a result of their widespread use during several years for the treatment of hypertension. Side effects are related to peripheral vasodilatation (postural hypotension), and both drugs have to be started at a low dose and titrated to obtain an optimum balance between efficacy and tolerability. Dizziness and weakness are sometimes observed, and these are presumed secondary to CNS actions. These drugs are marketed for the treatment of hypertension as well as lower urinary tract symptoms presumed secondary to benign prostatic hyperplasia.

Most recently, **alfuzosin and tamsulosin,** both highly selective α_1 adrenoceptor blockers, have appeared and are marketed solely for the treatment of benign prostatic hyperplasia because of some reports suggesting preferential action on prostatic rather than on vascular smooth muscle (Kirby, 1999; Djavan et al, 2004). Marketing claims aside, whether there is any difference in the efficacy and side effect profiles of these individual agents remains a topic of controversy. Tamsulosin and alfuzosin have the advantage of being able to be administered once daily and without titration. Available data suggest that retrograde ejaculation and rhinitis are more common with tamsulosin, whereas dizziness and asthenia are more common with terazosin and doxazosin (Kirby et al, 2000; Djavan et al, 2004).

Thus, agents with α adrenoceptor–blocking properties at various levels of neural organization have been used in patients with varied types of voiding dysfunction—functional outlet obstruction, urinary retention, decreased compliance, and idiopathic and neurogenic DO. Our experience suggests that a trial of such an agent is certainly worthwhile because the effect or noneffect will become obvious in a matter of days, and any pharmacologic side effects are, of course, reversible. However, our results with such therapy for voiding dysfunction not related to benign prostatic hyperplasia have been somewhat less spectacular than those of at least some other investigators.

Nitric Oxide Donors

In the future, there may be other pharmacologic mechanisms that are explored to produce relaxation in the smooth muscle of the bladder neck, urethra, or prostatic stroma. **Nitric oxide is a neurotransmitter capable of producing smooth muscle relaxation, at least in the female rabbit urethra, pig urethra, and human bladder neck** (Andersson and Persson, 1993; Andersson and Wein, 2004). A selective nitrergic action on bladder neck and urethral smooth muscle is an interesting theoretical possibility, and Mumtaz and associates (2000) suggest that a topical intraurethral nitric oxide donor could induce urethral smooth muscle relaxation without affecting bladder smooth muscle function and that this is a possible clinical avenue of exploration. Mamas and colleagues (2001, 2003) hypothesized that augmentation of external sphincter nitric oxide could be an effective pharmacologic treatment for detrusor–striated sphincter dyssynergia.

In a functional urodynamic study, Reitz and coworkers (2004b) assessed the effect of the **nitric oxide donor** isosorbide dinitrate on the external urethral sphincter. Magnetic stimulation of the sacral roots was performed in eight healthy men to evoke reproducible contractions of the external urethral sphincter. Sublingual administration of isosorbide dinitrate (10 mg) could significantly reduce the resting pressure of the external urethral sphincter for at least 1 hour. The maximal contractile strength measured as the maximal urethral pressure during single-pulse and continuous magnetic stimulation of the sacral roots also decreased significantly. Nitric oxide did not induce a significantly faster fatigue of the external urethral sphincter during continuous magnetic stimulation of the sacral roots. The authors suggested that nitric oxide donors could offer a new pharmacologic approach to treat urinary retention due to overactive or nonrelaxing external urethral sphincter. In a later study of 12 male spinal cord–injured patients presenting with neurogenic DO and detrusor-sphincter dyssynergia, Reitz and coworkers (2004c) found that nitric oxide significantly reduced external urethral sphincter pressures at rest ($P < .05$) and during dyssynergic contraction ($P < .05$); bladder pressures at rest and during contraction as well as the reflex volume remained unchanged. In patients who used suprapubic tapping for bladder emptying, the mean post-triggering residual volume was significantly reduced ($P < .05$). They concluded on the basis of their findings that **nitric oxide donors could offer a potential pharmacologic option to treat detrusor-sphincter dyssynergia in spinal cord–injured patients.**

Benzodiazepines, Baclofen, and Dantrolene

There is no class of pharmacologic agents that will selectively relax the striated musculature of the pelvic floor. Three different types of drugs have been used to treat voiding dysfunction secondary to outlet obstruction at the level of the striated sphincter: the benzodiazepines, dantrolene, and baclofen. The benzodiazepines are classified both as antianxiety agents (Baldessarini, 1996) and as sedative-hypnotics, muscle relaxants, and anticonvulsants (Hobbs et al, 1996). Dantrolene and baclofen are characterized as antispasticity agents (Cedarbaum and Schleifer, 1990). Baclofen and diazepam exert their actions predominantly within the CNS, whereas dantrolene acts directly on skeletal muscle. Unfortunately, there is no completely satisfactory form of therapy for alleviation of skeletal muscle spasticity. Although these drugs are capable of providing variable relief in given circumstances, their efficacy is far from complete; troublesome muscle weakness, adverse effects on gait, and a variety of other side effects minimize their overall usefulness as treatments of spasticity (Cedarbaum and Schleifer, 1990).

γ-Aminobutyric acid (GABA) and glycine have been identified as major inhibitory transmitters in the CNS (Bloom, 1996; de Groat and Yoshimura, 2001; Andersson and Wein, 2004). GABA is the most widely distributed inhibitory neurotransmitter in the mammalian CNS. GABA receptors have been divided into three types. The $GABA_A$ receptor directly gates a chloride ionophore and has modulatory binding sites for benzodiazepines, barbiturates, neurosteroids, and ethanol (Bormann, 2000). The $GABA_B$ receptor couples to Ca^{2+} and K^+ channels by means of G proteins and second-messenger systems. The $GABA_B$ receptor is activated by baclofen and is resistant to drugs that modulate $GABA_A$ receptors. There is a third class of GABA receptor, the $GABA_C$, although some prefer to classify these as a subspecies of $GABA_A$ receptors (Bormann, 2000). GABA appears to mediate the inhibitory actions of local interneurons in the brain and presynaptic inhibition within the spinal cord (Bloom, 1996). Glycine receptors are prominent in the brainstem and spinal cord and have many features analogous to the $GABA_A$ receptor.

Benzodiazepines potentiate the action of GABA by facilitating neuronal hyperpolarization through the $GABA_A$ receptor (Baldessarini, 1996; Hobbs et al, 1996). Benzodiazepines are extensively used for the treatment of anxiety and related disorders (Shader and Greenblatt, 1993), although pharmacologically, they can also be classified as centrally acting muscle relaxants. The generalized anxiety disorder that is responsive to pharmacotherapy with these agents is characterized by unrealistic or excessive anxiety and worry about life circumstances. Specific symptoms can be related to motor tension, autonomic hyperactivity (frequent urination can be a manifestation of this, as well as nausea, vomiting, diarrhea, and abdominal distress), and excessive vigilance. Other common uses have included treatment of insomnia, stress-related disorders, muscle spasm, and epilepsy and as preoperative sedation (Lader, 1987). Side effects include nonspecific CNS depression—manifested as sedation, lethargy, drowsiness, a feeling of slowing of thought processes, ataxia, and decreased ability to acquire or store information (Shader and Greenblatt, 1993). Some believe that any muscle relaxation effect in clinically used doses is caused by the CNS depressant effects and cite a lack of clinical studies showing any advantages of these agents over placebo or aspirin in this regard (Baldessarini, 1996; Hobbs et al, 1996). Effective total daily doses of diazepam, the most widely used agent of this group, range from 4 to 40 mg. Other benzodiazepine anxiolytic agents include chlordiazepoxide, clorazepate, prazepam, halazepam, clonazepam, lorazepam, oxazepam, and alprazolam.

Few references are available that provide evaluable data on the use of any of the benzodiazepines in the treatment of functional obstruction at the level of the striated sphincter. Opinions, however, are commonly expressed, at least in regard to diazepam. We have not found the recommended oral doses of diazepam to be effective in controlling the classic type of detrusor–striated sphincter dyssynergia secondary to neurologic disease. If the etiology of incomplete emptying in a neurologically normal patient is obscure, and the patient has what appears to be inadequate relaxation of the pelvic floor striated musculature urodynamically (e.g., dysfunctional voiding, occult neuropathic bladder, the Hinman syndrome), a trial of such an agent may be worthwhile. The rationale for use is either relaxation of the pelvic floor striated musculature during bladder contraction or that such relaxation removes an inhibitory stimulus to reflex bladder activity. Improvement under such circumstances may simply be caused, however, by the antianxiety effect of the drug or by the intensive explanation, encouragement, and modified biofeedback therapy that usually accompany such treatment in these patients.

Baclofen (Lioresal) depresses monosynaptic and polysynaptic excitation of motoneurons and interneurons in the spinal cord by activating $GABA_B$ receptors (Cedarbaum and Schleifer, 1990). Baclofen's primary site of action is in the spinal cord, but it is also reported to have activity at more rostral sites in the CNS. Baclofen has been found useful in the treatment of skeletal spasticity from a variety of causes (especially multiple sclerosis and traumatic spinal cord lesions) (Cedarbaum and Schleifer, 1990). Determination of the optimal dose in an individual patient requires careful titration. Treatment is started at an initial dose of 5 mg twice daily, and the dose is increased every 3 days up to a maximum daily dose of 20 mg four times a day. With reference to voiding dysfunction, Hachen and Krucker (1977) found a daily oral dose of 75 mg ineffective in patients with striated sphincter dyssynergia from traumatic paraplegia, whereas they found a daily intravenous dose of 20 mg highly effective. Florante and colleagues (1980) reported that 73% of their patients with voiding dysfunction secondary to acute and chronic spinal cord injury showed lower striated sphincter responses and decreased residual urine volumes after baclofen treatment, but only with an average daily oral dose of 120 mg. Potential side effects of baclofen include drowsiness, insomnia, rash, pruritus, dizziness, and weakness. It may impair ability to walk or to stand and is not recommended for the management of spasticity caused by cerebral lesions or disease. Sudden withdrawal has been shown to provoke hallucinations, anxiety, and tachycardia; hallucinations during treatment, which have been responsive to reductions in dosage, have also been reported (Roy and Wakefield, 1986).

Drug delivery often frustrates adequate pharmacologic treatment, and baclofen is a good example of this. GABA's hydrophilic properties prevent its crossing the blood-brain barrier in sufficient amounts to make it therapeutically useful. For oral use, the more lipophilic analog, baclofen, was developed. However, its passage through the barrier is likewise limited, and it has proved to be a generally insufficient drug when it is given orally to treat severe somatic spasticity and micturition disorders secondary to neurogenic dysfunction (Kums and Delhaas, 1991).

Intrathecal infusion bypasses the blood-brain barrier; cerebrospinal fluid levels 10 times higher than those reached with oral administration are achieved with infusion amounts 100 times less than those taken orally (Penn et al, 1989). Direct administration into the subarachnoid space by an implanted infusion pump showed initially promising results not only for skeletal spasticity but also for striated sphincter dyssynergia and DO.

Nanninga and associates (1989) reported on such administration to seven patients with intractable spasticity. All patients experienced a general decrease in spasticity, and the amount of striated sphincter activity during bladder contraction decreased; six showed an increase in bladder capacity. Four previously incontinent patients were able to stay dry with clean intermittent catheterization. The action on DO is not unexpected, given its spinal cord mechanism of action, and this inhibition of bladder contractility when it is administered intrathecally may in fact prove to be its most important benefit. Loubser and colleagues (1991) studied nine spinal cord–injured patients with refractory spasticity by use of an external pump to initially test response. Eight showed objective improvement in functional abilities; three of seven studied urodynamically showed an increase in bladder capacity. Kums and Delhaas (1991) reported on nine paraplegic or quadriplegic men (secondary to trauma or multiple sclerosis) with

intractable muscle spasticity treated with intrathecal baclofen. After a successful test period through an external catheter, a drug delivery system was implanted and connected to a spinal catheter. Doses per 24 hours ranged from 74 to 840 µg. Patients were studied before and 4 to 6 weeks after initiation of therapy. Mean residual urine volume fell from 224 to 110 mL ($P = .01$), mean urodynamic bladder capacity rose from 162 to 263 mL ($P = .005$), and pelvic floor spasm decreased at both baseline and maximum bladder capacity ($P < .005$ and $< .025$, respectively). Three subjects became continent. In addition, clean intermittent catheterization was no longer complicated by adductor spasm. Bushman and associates (1993) reported an increase in bladder storage in three individuals with hereditary spastic paraplegia treated with intrathecal baclofen. Tolerance to intrathecal baclofen with a requirement for increasing doses may prove to be a problem with long-term use, and studies are under way to investigate this. Vaidyanathan and colleagues (2004) reported a case with insidious development of autonomic dysreflexia and hydronephrosis due to dyssynergic voiding after discontinuation of intrathecal baclofen therapy. They recommended that in spinal cord–injured patients in whom intrathecal baclofen therapy is terminated, close monitoring of the urologic status is needed.

Dantrolene (Dantrium) exerts its effects by a direct peripheral action on skeletal muscle (Cedarbaum and Schleifer, 1990). It is thought to inhibit the excitation-induced release of calcium ions from the sarcoplasmic reticulum of striated muscle fibers, thereby inhibiting excitation-contraction coupling and diminishing the mechanical force of contraction. The blockade of calcium release is not complete, however, and contraction is not completely abolished. It reduces reflex more than voluntary contraction, probably because of a preferential action on fast-type compared with slow-type skeletal muscle fibers. It has been shown to have therapeutic benefits for chronic spasticity associated with CNS disorders.

The drug has been reported to improve voiding function in some patients with classic detrusor–striated sphincter dyssynergia and was initially reported as being successful in doing so (Murdock et al, 1976). Therapy in adults is recommended to begin at a dose of 25 mg daily, and this is gradually increased by increments of 25 mg every 4 to 7 days to a maximal oral dose of 400 mg given in four divided doses. Hackler and coworkers (1980) achieved improvement in voiding function in approximately half of their patients treated with dantrolene but found that such improvement required oral doses of 600 mg daily. Although no inhibitory effect on bladder smooth muscle seems to occur (Harris and Benson, 1980), the generalized weakness that dantrolene can induce is often significant enough to compromise its therapeutic effects. Other potential side effects include euphoria, dizziness, diarrhea, and hepatotoxicity. Fatal hepatitis has been reported in 0.1% to 0.2% of patients treated with the drug for 60 days or longer, and symptomatic hepatitis may occur in 0.5% of patients receiving treatment for more than 60 days; chemical abnormalities of liver function are noted in up to 1%. The risk of hepatic injury is twofold greater in women (Ward et al, 1986).

One agreed-on use of dantrolene is acute management of malignant hyperthermia, a rare hereditary syndrome characterized by vigorous contraction of skeletal muscle precipitated by excess release of calcium from the sarcoplasmic reticulum, generally in response to neuromuscular blocking agents or inhalational anesthetics. Almost all hospital pharmacies stock parenteral dantrolene for this purpose. Virtually no one currently uses dantrolene for the treatment of voiding dysfunction.

Botulinum Toxin

Botulinum A toxin (Botox) is an inhibitor of the release of acetylcholine and other transmitters at the neuromuscular junction of somatic nerves in striated muscle and of autonomic nerves in smooth muscle (Simpson, 2004). It is interesting that it produces enough weakness of the muscle to prevent or considerably ameliorate spasm or involuntary contraction but not to completely block voluntary control, a phenomenon hypothesized to occur because more active neuromuscular junctions are more likely than less active junctions to be blocked by the effect of the drug (Hallett, 1999). Its **urologic use for the treatment of detrusor–striated sphincter dyssynergia** was first reported by Dykstra and colleagues (Dykstra and Sidi, 1990; Dykstra et al, 1998). Injections were carried out weekly for 3 weeks, achieving a duration of effect averaging 2 months. The only side effects reported in the Dykstra articles were transitory limb paresis and transitory exacerbation of autonomic hyperreflexia. Fowler and associates (1992a) injected six women with difficult voiding–urinary retention secondary to what is now called the Fowler syndrome (manifested by abnormal myotonus-like electromyographic activity in the striated urethral sphincter; Fowler et al, 1988). Although no patient had improved voiding characteristics (a fact attributed to the type of repetitive discharge activity), three women did develop transient stress incontinence, a positive effect of sorts, indicating that the sphincter muscle had indeed been weakened.

Petit and coworkers (1998) reported on the endoscopic injection of Botox (150 IU) into the striated urethral sphincter by a four-point injection technique (the medication was diluted to 4 mL with saline solution). Seventeen patients with spinal cord injury or spinal cord disease were treated, and evaluation 1 month after treatment disclosed the following positive results: a decrease in postvoid residual by an average of 176 mL; a decrease in bladder pressure during an emptying contraction by an average of 19 cm H_2O; and a decrease in urethral pressure during an emptying bladder contraction by an average of 24 cm H_2O. The authors judged voiding to be improved in 10 patients. Side effects included the new appearance of stress incontinence in two patients and exacerbation of preexisting incontinence in three. The duration of the effect was variable, but no less than 2 to 3 months. There were no adverse effects on striated muscle elsewhere. The authors concluded that Botox is a promising treatment for striated sphincter dyssynergia in certain patients refractory to clean intermittent catheterization or surgery.

Gallien and associates (1998) injected Botox transperineally in five men with traumatic quadriplegia and striated sphincter dyssynergia. Using a total initial dose of 100 units, divided into four injections of 25 units each, the authors noted what they called improved bladder function in all patients, with a significant decrease in residual urine volume (however, on examination of the figures, the mean reduction was only 14

mL, with one of the patients requiring a second set of injections). The maximum urethral pressure on average did not change, the maximum detrusor pressure during an emptying episode decreased 5 cm H_2O, and the functional detrusor capacity increased by an average of 89 mL. Urinary catheterization was able to be stopped in two patients, and autonomic hyperreflexia dramatically decreased in intensity in four patients. The time to improvement was 10 to 21 days, and the duration was 3 to 5 months. No patient had significant side effects.

Wheeler and colleagues (1998) reported on three men with spinal cord injury, all of whom had emptying problems related to striated sphincter dyssynergia. The sphincter was injected transperineally with botulinum toxin by use of electromyographic control for localization. Two of the patients reported excellent results.

Schurch and coworkers (1996) used both transurethral and transperineal injections in 24 male patients with spinal cord injury with voiding dysfunction secondary to striated sphincter dyssynergia. They judged that in 21 of these patients, striated sphincter dyssynergia was significantly improved with a concomitant decrease in postvoid residual urine volume in "most cases." Of 24 patients, 9 had a decreased postvoid residual volume from 450 to 50 mL; in 7 patients, the residual urine volumes were less than 50 mL to begin with and remained unchanged; and in 8 patients, the postvoid residual urine volumes were high and remained unchanged. The authors commented that transurethral injections appeared to be more effective, at least in reductions in maximum urethral pressure, than did transperineal injections. They noted no side effects.

de Sèze and colleagues (2002) performed a double-blind lidocaine-controlled study in 13 patients with spinal cord disease and detrusor-sphincter dyssynergia. They demonstrated the superiority of botulinum toxin compared with lidocaine in improving clinical symptoms and increased urethral pressure.

There are several reviews summarizing the uses of botulinum toxin injection (Münchau and Bhatia, 2000; Cruz and Silva, 2004; Rackley and Abdelmalak, 2004; Sahai et al, 2005). A potential side effect is the spread to nearby muscles, particularly when high volumes of Botox are injected. Distant effects can also occur, but distant weakness or generalized weakness due to the spread of toxins in the blood is very rare. Botulinum toxin should be used only under close supervision in patients with already disturbed neuromuscular transmission or during treatment with aminoglycosides.

Other Agents

Theoretically, any agent that promotes striated sphincter relaxation in a uroselective manner could be used to decrease outlet resistance and to facilitate voiding. Yoshiyama and associates (2000) described the laboratory use of intravenous α-bungarotoxin as improving voiding in spinal cord–injured rats. The drug is a toxin extracted from the venom of a Formosan snake; it selectively blocks nicotinic receptors without influencing transmission in autonomic ganglia. Although a long way from clinical use, nicotinic receptors in the striated sphincter have been shown to be a potential target of drug therapy for striated sphincter dyssynergia.

SUGGESTED READINGS

Andersson KE: The concept of uroselectivity. Eur Urol 1998;33(suppl 2):7-11.

Andersson KE: Antimuscarinics for treatment of overactive bladder. Lancet Neurol 2004;3:46-53.

Andersson KE, Arner A: Urinary bladder contraction and relaxation: Physiology and pathophysiology. Physiol Rev 2004;84:935-986.

Andersson KE, Wein AJ: Pharmacology of the lower urinary tract: Basis for current and future treatments of urinary incontinence. Pharmacol Rev 2004;56:581-631.

Andersson KE, Appell R, Cardozo L, et al: Pharmacological treatment of urinary incontinence. In Abrams P, Cardozo L, Khoury S, Wein A, eds: Incontinence, 3rd International Consultation on Incontinence. Plymouth, UK, Health Publications, 2005.

de Groat WC, Yoshimura N: Pharmacology of the lower urinary tract. Annu Rev Pharmacol Toxicol 2001;41:691-721.

Schurch B, de Sèze M, Denys P, et al, Botox Detrusor Hyperreflexia Study Team: Botulinum toxin type A is a safe and effective treatment for neurogenic urinary incontinence: Results of a single treatment, randomized, placebo controlled 6-month study. J Urol 2005;174:196-200.

Smith CP, Chancellor MB: Emerging role of botulinum toxin in the management of voiding dysfunction. J Urol 2004;171(pt 1):2128-2137.

63 Conservative Management of Urinary Incontinence: Behavioral and Pelvic Floor Therapy, Urethral and Pelvic Devices

CHRISTOPHER K. PAYNE, MD

GENERAL CONSIDERATIONS
Impact of Urinary Incontinence

Urinary incontinence (UI) affects people in all strata of society—the young and the old, male and female, rich and poor, all ethnic and racial backgrounds—although women and older individuals bear a disproportionate share of the burden. The impact is enormous. Total direct and indirect costs for UI in the United States alone are estimated at $19.5 billion (in year 2000 dollars; Hu et al, 2004). In the National Institutes of Health (NIH) compendium of diseases the direct cost of UI is estimated at $12.5 billion, a figure that is comparable to other important diseases such as Alzheimer's disease, chronic obstructive pulmonary disease, and human immunodeficiency virus infection/acquired immunodeficiency syndrome (Table 63–1). Although medical insurance will cover some expenses, UI patients bear a considerable percentage of the overall disease costs for protective pads, laundry, and other expenses not covered by individual insurance plans. **The consequences of UI lead to serious morbidity, including falls and fractures; urinary tract infections; skin breakdown, including pressure ulcers; and admission to nursing homes** as summarized in the Third International Consultation on Incontinence Economics Committee (Hu et al, 2005).

The Urologic Diseases in America project has published detailed analyses of expenditures by the U.S. health care system for UI in both men (Stothers et al, 2005) and women (Thom et al, 2005). Among the more interesting findings was a dramatic increase in Medicare expenditures for women from $128.1 to $234.4 million between 1992 and 1998, despite decreasing hospitalizations and length of stay. In men, the prevalence of incontinence was estimated at 17% for those older than 60 years of age (any incontinence over the past 12 months) and the **annual expenditures for privately insured male adults with UI were $7702 compared with $3204 for a man without UI.** Demographic trends producing increasing numbers of elderly individuals will make this problem a critical challenge to urologists for the coming decades.

The impact of UI cannot be measured in dollars alone. A "social cancer," incontinence impacts every facet of human life—work, home, social, physical, sexual, psychological, and medical. Numerous reports continue to document the serious impact of UI and overactive bladder (OAB) on quality of life using high-quality methodology (Coyne et al, 2003, 2004; Avery et al, 2004; Hajjar, 2004). Incontinent patients are more likely to have poor self-esteem, feeling shame and guilt, which may keep them from working effectively and partaking in social activities. **UI is associated with depression and vice versa** (Steers and Lee, 2001). Stress urinary incontinence (SUI) restricts the physical activity of patients, many of whom are otherwise healthy young women. The long-term

Conservative Management of Urinary Incontinence: Behavioral and Pelvic Floor Therapy, Urethral and Pelvic Devices **2125**

CHAPTER 63

Table 63–1. **Cost of Illness and NIH Support**				
Disease/Condition	*Year of Cost Data*	*Total Cost (in billions $)*	*Population*	*FY 1999 NIH Spending (in millions $)*
Asthma	1997	100.0	Total	140.4
Alzheimer's disease and other dementias	1996	14.0	Over 65	406.5
Cerebrovascular disease (stroke)	1998	43.3	Total	186.0
Chronic obstructive pulmonary disease	1998	37.3	Total	997.0
Diabetes	1997	98.2	Total	457.6
HIV infections/AIDS	1999	28.9	Total	1792.7
Incontinence	1995	26.3	Over 65	6.9

deleterious effects of exercise reduction on health are unclear but may be important. **Urinary urgency incontinence (UUI) affects quality of life even more than stress incontinence because of its unpredictable nature.** It may lead to loss of sleep as well as the limitations just mentioned. Sexual activity and interpersonal relationships suffer due to incontinence. Despite this, many and perhaps most still do not seek help for UI for a variety of reasons, including misguided perceptions that UI is a normal consequence of aging and that there is no effective treatment (Shaw, 2001). Even more importantly, **expenditures for UI research are a small fraction of that spent on other conditions; NIH-funded UI research is less than 2% that of stroke or Alzheimer's disease** (see Table 63–1).

KEY POINTS: GENERAL CONSIDERATIONS

- The consequences of UI lead to serious morbidity, including falls and fractures, urinary tract infections, skin breakdown including pressure ulcers, and admission to nursing homes.

- Urinary incontinence is not an inexorably progressive disease. Conservative therapies are effective, well tolerated, safe, and preferred by many patients. Thus, it is generally appropriate that the least invasive treatment that takes into account patient preferences and offers a reasonable chance for success be used first.

- Although it is important to rule out serious underlying or associated conditions, invasive testing is rarely required before initiating treatment with conservative measures.

Rationale for Conservative Therapies

This "silent" epidemic was brought to national attention with the 1988 NIH consensus conference (Consensus Conference, 1989) followed by the publication of the first Agency for Health Care Policy and Research (AHCPR) practice guideline on urinary incontinence in adults in 1992 (Urinary Incontinence Guideline Panel, 1992). Two of the principal recommendations of the guideline relate directly to improving the recognition of urinary incontinence and validating it as an important medical problem:

- "The guideline calls for vigorous efforts to educate health care professionals about this condition so that they are sufficiently knowledgeable to diagnose and treat it."

- "It recommends that the public be advised to report incontinence problems once they occur and be informed that incontinence is not inevitable or shameful but is a treatable or at least manageable condition."

A third recommendation of the 1992 AHCPR guideline applies directly to the focus of this chapter:

- "The guideline recommends that surgery, except in very specific cases, should be considered only after behavioral and pharmacologic interventions have been tried."

The rationale for a conservative approach is clear. **Urinary incontinence is not an inexorably progressive disease. A moderate delay in surgical therapy does not make such treatment more difficult. As will be amply documented, "conservative" therapies are effective, well tolerated, and safe. In addition, they are preferred by many patients.** In the fifth National Association for Continence (NAFC) survey of 130,000 members, 52% of men and 48% of women ranked conservative therapies in general as "most helpful" (NAFC, 1999). **Because the impact of incontinence varies greatly from patient to patient, the patient's feelings and goals must be taken into consideration in treatment planning. Thus, it is generally appropriate that the least invasive treatment that takes into account patient preferences and offers a reasonable chance for success be used first.**

Description: What Is "Conservative," Who Is It For?

Traditionally, treatments that are totally reversible have been considered "conservative." Depending on the reviewer, this may or may not include drugs. However, given the data just presented regarding the costs associated with UI, a more considered assessment is in order. It can no longer be acceptable to call all nonpharmacologic, nonsurgical therapy "conservative" and recommend that such treatments routinely be employed as initial therapy. "Conservative" therapies must be held to the same standards as pharmacologic and surgical treatments. Effectiveness and safety must be determined in the context of patient satisfaction—it does little good to identify a treatment as safe and effective if patients are ultimately not satisfied and go on to "second line" treatments. Ultimately, the clinician and patient need to know the long-term outcomes for continence, adverse events, and cost-effectiveness to develop appropriate treatment algorithms. Ultimately, specific patient factors should be identified that will help predict the likelihood of response to a given therapy. Only then will the precious resources spent on UI be used most effectively.

To this end, levels of evidence and grades of recommendation are used whenever possible and conclusions drawn from systematic literature reviews and the International Consultation on Incontinence (ICI) are highlighted. The AHCPR has used specified evidence levels to justify recommendations for the investigation and treatment of a variety of conditions, and the Oxford Centre for Evidence Based Medicine produced a widely accepted adaptation of the work of the AHCPR (Oxford Centre, 2001). The highest level of evidence (level 1) is based on systematic reviews and/or randomized controlled trials. The highest grade of recommendation (grade A) stems from consistent level 1 evidence. When possible these terms are used in the chapter, although there is a great need for further high-quality research and there is a notable lack of long-term follow-up of treatment effect for almost all of the therapies discussed.

Overview

The challenge to the urologist is to understand all of the treatments for incontinence, to be able to assess the patient efficiently yet thoroughly, and then to construct an appropriate treatment plan with the patient, taking into account the problem and the goals of the individual patient. This chapter reviews the basic nonsurgical tools used in treating urinary incontinence—behavioral therapy, pelvic floor muscle training and biofeedback, external devices, and peripheral electrical and magnetic stimulation. Pharmacologic therapy is discussed in Chapter 62, surgical therapy in Chapters 65 to 69 and 74, and neuromodulation in Chapter 64. The detailed evaluation of the incontinent patient is discussed in Chapters 60, 61, and 71; **although it is important to rule out serious underlying or associated conditions, invasive testing is rarely required before initiating treatment with the measures discussed here.** We focus here only on that part of the evaluation that directly relates to treatment planning. It is generally sufficient to have a working diagnosis classifying the patient as having stress, urgency, or mixed incontinence.

Patients with symptoms of OAB (the generic term for urgency and frequency with or without incontinence) are treated in the same manner as those with urgency incontinence. The chapter concludes with practical algorithms that provide a rational means of applying these varied treatments to an individual patient.

THE TOOLS OF CONSERVATIVE THERAPY
Behavioral Therapy

Behavioral therapy describes a group of treatments grounded in the concept that the incontinent patient can be educated about his or her condition and develop strategies to minimize or eliminate incontinence. It is sometimes erroneously reduced to the combination of fluid restriction and timed voiding but is actually a far richer therapy. In fact, one of the main problems with the term *behavioral therapy* is that it has been used so differently by various practitioners that its meaning has become diluted and vague. There is no one standard protocol or "best" methodology. The shared aims of behavioral therapy are illustrated in Figure 63–1 (Payne, 2000). Although various practitioners may have different emphasis, **the different treatment approaches are unified by education about normal urinary tract function.** The individual elements of behavioral therapies discussed here are centered on basic educational techniques such as operant learning, which is intended to model activity so as to reproduce normal behavior, in this case urinary continence (Palmer, 2004). All of the individual techniques discussed fall into this category, although pelvic floor muscle training is both a behavioral therapy (education about anatomy and function of the muscles, learning to use the muscles properly to control lower urinary tract function) and a physical therapy (strengthening the muscles to improve function). In any case, education binds the various techniques together and plays the central role in behavioral therapy.

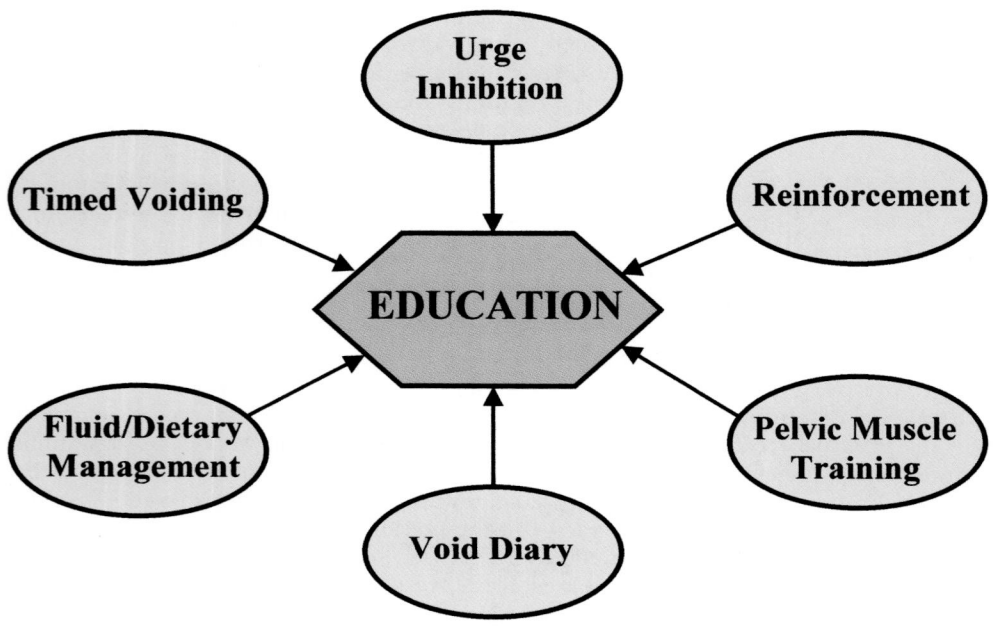

Figure 63–1. Behavioral therapy has many different components, all of which center on patient education. Education leads to understanding of normal lower urinary tract function and the patient's ability to self-regulate those functions.

Conservative Management of Urinary Incontinence: Behavioral and Pelvic Floor Therapy, Urethral and Pelvic Devices **2127**

CHAPTER 63

KEY POINTS: THE TOOLS OF CONSERVATIVE THERAPY: BEHAVIORAL THERAPY

- Behavioral therapy describes a group of treatments grounded in the concept that the incontinent patient can be educated about his or her condition and develop strategies to minimize or eliminate incontinence. There is no one standard protocol or "best" methodology. The different treatment approaches are unified by education about normal urinary tract function.

- Bladder training starts a patient voiding on a fixed time interval schedule with the intention that the patient will urinate before experiencing urgency and incontinence. It can be used with or without medical therapy. There is a level A recommendation that "bladder training is recommended as a first line treatment of UI in women."

- There have been no studies demonstrating a beneficial effect of smoking cessation on UI symptoms.

- There is scant level 1 evidence that decreasing caffeine improves continence.

- It would appear that it is best to recommend a normal fluid consumption, reserving fluid restriction for those patients with abnormally high fluid intakes.

- Epidemiologic data support a link between consumption of carbonated beverages with UI, with level 2 to 3 evidence.

- Epidemiologic studies provide consistent findings describing a linear relationship between obesity and incontinence that cumulatively provide strong evidence for obesity as an important modifiable risk factor for incontinence.

- There is level 2 evidence that weight loss in morbidly obese women decreases incontinence; there is scant level 1 evidence that moderately obese women who lose weight have less incontinence than those who do not.

- Although acknowledging that the optimal treatment package is unknown, combinations of conservative therapies are logical and appropriate, leading to a level A recommendation that, "women with stress, urge, or mixed incontinence should be offered a conservative management program as first line therapy for UI."

Pelvic Floor Education

In a pure form of behavioral therapy there would simply be education about the normal anatomy of the pelvic floor musculature and the function of these muscles in maintaining continence. In addition, pelvic muscle exercises could be explained. However, the literature includes sophisticated biofeedback techniques and treatment by physiotherapists in many trials of behavioral therapy. In most of these cases the purpose of the treatment is aimed at improving muscle strength and control; therefore, the detailed discussion of this approach is included in the section on pelvic floor rehabilitation (see later).

Bladder Training/Timed Voiding

The term *scheduled voiding* is the generic term preferred for describing voiding regimens used for home-dwelling cognitively intact patients as opposed to *prompted voiding* or *toileting,* terms properly applied to institutionalized or otherwise dependent patients. **The most commonly used technique for patients with OAB and UUI is "bladder training" (bladder drill, bladder retraining).** Bladder training starts a patient voiding on a fixed time interval schedule with the idea that, most of the time, the patient will urinate before experiencing urgency and incontinence. The interval is gradually increased with clinical improvement. **Early practitioners of bladder training first established the effectiveness of intensive inpatient bladder training temporarily supplemented by medications** (Frewen, 1978). **Next, outpatient treatment was proven to be effective** (Elder and Stephenson, 1980; Frewen, 1980). **Finally, the durability of response, with 85% initial and 48% three-year response rates was reported** (Table 63–2) (Holmes et al, 1983). **Bladder training should always be combined with urge inhibition techniques and is often combined with anticholinergic medical therapy, particularly for more severe cases and for patients with neurogenic bladder.** In contrast, **"timed voiding"** involves having a patient void on a fixed schedule, typically every 2 to 3 hours, and is intended to normalize frequency in a patient with infrequent voiding and/or diminished bladder sensation. **This technique can be employed for patients with SUI with the idea that leakage will be less if the bladder is less full when physical stress occurs. It can also be used in a variety of patients with UUI who have a good bladder capacity** (the classic example is that of patients with diabetic neurogenic bladder; they do not have proper bladder sensation and thus delay voiding inappropriately).

Although there is no evidence as to the optimal program of bladder training, typical programs start at an interval of approximately 1 hour (or more appropriate interval based on the patient's bladder diary) and increase the interval by 15 to 30 minutes when the patient achieves continence. The ultimate goal is a 2- to 4-hour interval between voids with continence—"retraining" the bladder. **Wilson and colleagues (2005) conclude that if no improvement is made after 3 weeks "the patient should be reevaluated and other treatment options considered."** The authors acknowledge that the quantity of evidence is low but still **make a grade A recommendation that "bladder training is recommended as a first**

Table 63–2. Long-Term Results of Behavioral Therapy

Patient Group	Cure/Improve	Relapse
Cystometrogram negative	15/16 (94%)	1 (6%)
Reduced compliance	19/21 (90%)	8 (42%)
Idiopathic instability	9/10 (90%)	4 (44%)
Neurogenic	3/6 (50%)	3 (100%)

line treatment of UI in women." Medical therapy is commonly employed initially, and there are rather limited studies comparing bladder training to anticholinergic medications for detrusor overactivity and UUI. One study demonstrated superior results with the combination of behavioral therapy and anorectal biofeedback in comparison to anticholinergic medication alone (oxybutynin chloride in titrated dosing) in a group of patients with urge and mixed incontinence (Burgio et al, 1998). Subsequent work by Burgio and colleagues (2000) confirms the clear truth that behavioral and drug therapy are complementary, not competitive treatments; the primary value of this research is to underscore the value of the behavioral component in the treatment plan. Logically, all patients should have behavioral therapy with medications used on an individualized basis.

Smoking Cessation

Aside from being a major risk factor for bladder cancer, smoking has been proposed as a risk factor for SUI by increasing coughing episodes and for OAB through bladder irritation from nicotine and toxins excreted in the urine. However, to date, epidemiologic studies of tobacco use have produced inconsistent findings. In women, some studies suggest that smoking increases the risk of UI, or at least severe UI, but others demonstrate no increased risk. A recent 1-year longitudinal study of 6424 women older then 40 years of age found that current smokers were at higher risk for both SUI and OAB than those who had never smoked, although statistical significance was seen only for OAB (Table 63–3). Ex-smokers had intermediate risk (Dallosso et al, 2004a). The same group also published a longitudinal study of 4887 men showing no association between smoking and OAB symptoms (Dallosso et al, 2004b). Another population-based study suggested that the risk of UI is limited to subjects with a history of more than 15 pack-years or current consumption of more than 20 cigarettes a day (Hannestad et al, 2003). **As of yet there have been no studies demonstrating a beneficial effect of smoking cessation on UI symptoms and the ICI committee could make no evidence-based recommendation** (Wilson et al, 2005). Despite these conflicting results, smoking cessation can logically be recommended as a general health measure, to reduce the risk of bladder cancer, and for those smokers with stress incontinence particularly related to coughing. More research, particularly on the effectiveness of smoking cessation in treating UI and on the relationship between smoking and OAB, would be welcomed.

Caffeine

Caffeine is well known as a nervous system stimulant and has demonstrable effects on detrusor muscle in vitro and in vitro, promoting unstable contractions. In one study of community-dwelling elderly women subjects who decreased caffeine and increased fluid intake, increased voiding volumes and fewer accidents were experienced (Tomlinson et al, 1999). High caffeine intake (>400 mg/day average) also correlated with urodynamic detrusor overactivity compared with stress-incontinent women (<200 mg/day average) (Arya et al, 2000). It has thus been postulated to be a cause of OAB symptoms, and caffeine reduction has been advised for OAB patients. Epidemiologic data are less clear. Reports usually break down consumption by type of beverage rather than actual caffeine consumption as is typically found in smaller studies of dietary intervention. Such small studies have typically shown a correlation between caffeine reduction and reduction of incontinence (Tomlinson et al, 1999; Bryant et al, 2002). Although larger studies would be helpful, it seems appropriate to recommend restriction, particularly in those patients with very high intake of caffeine. **The ICI Committee concluded that, "there is scant level 1 evidence that decreasing caffeine improves continence"** (Wilson et al, 2005).

Fluid Management

Fluid restriction has been advocated in the treatment of both SUI and OAB. The rationale is that abdominal leak pressures appear to be volume dependent; therefore, physical stress occurring at lower bladder volumes will be both less likely to cause incontinence and will be associated with lower volume loss when leakage does occur. **Similarly, OAB is believed to be a volume-driven phenomenon, and slower filling promotes bladder compliance and lower pressures.** This concept appears to be well accepted, as manifest by a recent U.S. study in which 38% of incontinent women had tried limiting fluids compared with 21% who tried Kegel exercises and 6% using prescription medications (Diokno et al, 2004a). On the other hand, extreme fluid restriction produces concentrated urine, which has been postulated to be a bladder irritant, leading to detrusor overactivity as well as constipation, which can negatively affect bladder function. Indeed, there is conflict regarding fluid management, with some investigators showing improvement with fluid reduction (Swithinbank et al, 2005), whereas others finding that increasing fluid intake improved incontinence (Dowd et al, 1996). **It would appear that it is best to recommend a normal fluid consumption, reserving fluid restriction for those patients with abnormally high fluid intakes** (Wilson et al, 2005).

The types of fluid intake may also be significant; caffeinated beverages, acidic juices, and alcohol have been suggested to be bladder irritants. Caffeine was discussed earlier. Tea consumption correlated with UI in the EPINCONT study, but alcohol and coffee consumption did not (Hannestad et al, 2003). Although it is possible that caffeine is not the critical component, there is no clear hypothesis as to why tea (which has less caffeine than coffee) would be a relevant dietary factor but not coffee. Unless confirmed in other studies this may turn

Table 63–3. Risk Factors for Stress Urinary Incontinence and Overactive Bladder (Multivariate Analysis)

Etiologic Factor	Overactive Bladder		Stress Urinary Incontinence	
	RR	CI	RR	CI
Smoking vs. Never Smoked				
Ex-smoker	1.24	0.97-1.44	—	—
Current smoker	1.44	1.05-1.63	—	—
Obesity vs. Acceptable Weight				
Underweight	0.69	0.38-1.26	0.82	0.46-1.44
Overweight	1.25	0.94-1.67	1.24	0.93-1.63
Obese	1.74	1.22-2.12	1.46	1.07-1.99

Conservative Management of Urinary Incontinence: Behavioral and Pelvic Floor Therapy, Urethral and Pelvic Devices **2129**

CHAPTER 63

out to be a statistical aberration. In a population of Chinese women, alcohol consumption correlated with SUI but not UUI (Song et al, 2005), but other studies have shown no link between alcohol use and UI symptoms. **Epidemiologic data support a link between consumption of carbonated beverages with both SUI and OAB** (Dallosso et al, 2003) **with level 2 to 3 evidence.** Data on the effects of other beverages are scarce.

Other Dietary Management

A variety of different dietary maneuvers have been recommended for incontinent patients, including avoidance of alcohol, carbonated beverages, acid foods, salt, and others. A detailed study examining dietary factors noted an association between intake of vegetables with lower risk of OAB and intake of fruit with lower risk of SUI (Dalosso et al, 2003). These observations have yet to be reproduced in other populations. A follow-up report (Dalosso et al, 2004a) examined details of the diet in relationship to SUI and found that "intakes of total fat, saturated fatty acids and monounsaturated fatty acids were associated with an increased risk of SUI onset one year later. Of the micronutrients studied, zinc and vitamin B_{12} were positively associated with SUI onset." Because these observations are not hypothesis driven, confirmation is mandated before any recommendation can be given. No similar connection was identified with alcohol consumption in the same or other studies, and one study actually suggested a lower risk of OAB in men who were beer drinkers (Dalosso et al, 2004b). Once again, the best advice for incontinent patients would seem to be to follow established guidelines for overall health with moderation in alcohol use and adequate intake of fruits and vegetables. Carbonated beverages should be restricted by patients with UI and OAB.

Obesity/Weight Reduction

There has long been an assumption that obesity is linked to UI, particularly SUI, by straining and potentially damaging the supportive structures of the bladder and pelvic organs. Weight loss has been empirically recommended as a treatment for incontinence and to improve the results of surgical therapy. However, until recently little has been known about the true risk of obesity, whether the risk relates to moderately obese or only those morbidly obese patients, or about the effectiveness of weight loss as a therapy for incontinence.

There are now epidemiologic data supporting a causal association between obesity and incontinence. In a 1-year longitudinal study of 6424 women older than 40 years of age there was a strong correlation between body mass index (BMI) and the risk of both OAB and SUI (Dallosso et al, 2003) (see Table 63–3). Work in other populations consistently confirms the relationship between obesity and UI (Thom et al, 1997; Brown et al, 1999; Fornell et al, 2004; Larrieu et al, 2004; Melville et al, 2005). **These and other studies provide consistent findings describing a linear relationship between obesity and incontinence that cumulatively provide strong evidence for obesity as an important modifiable risk factor for incontinence.**

However, data on treatment of incontinence through weight loss are less robust. There are positive case series of morbidly obese women but only one published, peer-reviewed

randomized study investigating the effect of weight loss on UI. Subak and colleagues (2005) randomized 48 women with UI and BMI between ages 25 and 45 to receive a liquid diet weight reduction program either immediately or after a 3-month delay. The median interquartile (25% to 75%) weight was 97 kg (87 to 106 kg), and the incontinence frequency was 21 episodes per week (11 to 33). At the end of 3 months women in the immediate treatment group lost an average of 16 kg compared with 0 kg in the delayed group. Incontinence episodes decreased 60% in the treatment group compared with 15% in the controls. Improvement was seen in both SUI and UUI. A similar response was then seen when the delayed group was treated. This study suggests that all types of UI may respond to moderate weight loss. The ICI committee concluded that, "there is level 2 evidence that weight loss in morbidly obese women decreases incontinence, and scant level 1 evidence that moderately obese women who lose weight have less incontinence than those who do not" (Wilson et al, 2005). **Given the other health problems associated with obesity it seems appropriate to work for weight loss in all overweight incontinent women.**

Urge Inhibition

Urgency is the predominant symptom for most patients with OAB and UUI. In many cases, incontinence has become a reflex as the patient has developed dysfunctional behavior in response to urgency. It is important to break the cycle of rushing to the toilet in response to urgency. The patient is instructed to stop, sit if possible, and use pelvic muscle contractions, distraction, or other techniques until urgency passes. There are no data on use of this practice as an isolated therapy, but it is a critical part of the overall treatment of patients with OAB; patients who learn to delay or overcome urgency may eventually be cured of their condition.

Other Lifestyle Issues

As summarized by the ICI report (Wilson et al, 2005), "there are many other lifestyle interventions suggested either by health care professionals or the lay press for the treatment of UI, including reducing emotional stress, wearing nonrestrictive clothing, utilizing a bedside commode, decreasing lower extremity edema, treating allergies and coughs, wearing cotton underwear, and increasing sexual activity. These interventions are, however, all anecdotal in nature."

It has been shown (level 2 evidence) that stress-induced urine loss can be reduced by positional changes, that is, having a woman cross her legs with coughing, although this was only examined in the acute urodynamic testing situation (Norton and Baker, 1994). **The ICI panel also concluded that constipation and chronic straining may be a risk factor for the development of urinary incontinence (level 2/3 evidence)** but that there were no data on the effect of intervention. There is even less known about the relationship of strenuous activity, sports, and work. Because women are universally advised to restrict activity after surgical treatment for stress incontinence, one might assume that the effect of postoperative activity on outcome had been investigated but there are actually no useful data. It is possible/probable that strenuous activity leads women to present with the symptom of UI but, within the realm of normal activities, does not actually play a role in the causation of UI.

CONCEPT OF "THERAPEUTIC PACKAGE"

It is, of course, logical and appropriate that these various behavioral treatments be used together in a therapeutic package. They are inherently complementary, are completely reversible, and lack significant adverse effects. They can also be (and typically are) combined with the pelvic floor rehabilitation techniques discussed later. Patients who are motivated to avoid surgical or pharmacologic interventions will be inclined to seek out such treatments; the problem remains as to the most efficient way to deliver therapy to the average patient.

Diokno and colleagues (2004b) demonstrated that two simple group sessions were effective in preventing incontinence. The trial randomized 359 continent women older than 55 years of age who were recruited and followed for 1 year. The treatment group received a single 2-hour group session teaching pelvic floor muscle training (PFMT) and bladder training as well as an audiotape on PFMT for reinforcement; the control group was not treated. There was one follow-up office visit with a nurse specialist in 2 to 4 weeks. At the end of 1 year, 56% of the treatment group reported the same or better continence compared with only 41% of controls; 37% of the treatment group reported "absolute continence" compared with 28% of the controls. Several other studies using various combinations of therapies led the ICI group (Wilson et al, 2005) to a **level A recommendation that, "women with stress, urge, or mixed incontinence should be offered a conservative management program as first line therapy for UI"** while acknowledging that there were inadequate data to define the optimal treatment package and that most of the data comes from trials in older women.

PELVIC FLOOR REHABILITATION

The term *pelvic floor rehabilitation* should be applied to any treatment intended to increase the strength, bulk, and function of the pelvic floor/levator muscles. Muscle rehabilitation can be achieved through a variety of tools, which can be classified as "basic" or "advanced," depending on the cost and complexity of the therapy. **Basic treatments (Kegel exercises, vaginal cones, and simple home perineometry) are used in the home setting, require no or inexpensive equipment, and can be administered by a relatively unskilled therapist. Advanced treatments are used in an office setting with a trained therapist or require more sophisticated equipment.**

Pelvic Floor Muscle Training

Pelvic floor exercises (PFE) or "Kegels" have been advocated in the treatment of urinary incontinence since the 1950s (Kegel 1948a, 1948b, 1956). Dr. Kegel taught his patients to forcefully contract the pelvic muscles to treat and prevent postpartum incontinence. **Unfortunately, half of patients are unable to perform a proper contraction with simple instructions** (Bump et al, 1991), **and up to one fourth will actually promote incontinence with their efforts.** Indiscriminant recommendation of this therapy to all incontinent patients has created a negative bias that PFE are just "something to do" before pharmacologic or definitive surgical treatment. It

should also be acknowledged that **Dr. Kegel routinely employed a perineometer with his patients in one of the first documented uses of biofeedback in medicine.** This implies that Kegel exercises alone should not be considered the standard treatment for pelvic floor rehabilitation.

Currently, PFMT is the currently accepted term, replacing Kegels and PFE. It is defined as "any program of repeated voluntary pelvic floor muscle contractions taught by a health care professional" (Wilson et al, 2005) and is advocated for both prevention and treatment of UI. **"Training" is preferred over "exercises" to emphasize the importance of a regimen of repeated exercise over time.** The therapy is intended to improve the function of the pelvic floor muscles; whether this happens primarily by increasing the strength, power, and speed and/or improving the timing and coordination of a contraction is not known. Much more is known about the clinical effectiveness of the therapy than the exact physiologic changes that produce the outcomes. **With repeated exercise a muscle will develop improved responsiveness that may lead to a faster and/or stronger contraction before any increase in actual bulk.** Over longer periods of time the muscle fibers will progressively hypertrophy, producing increased bulk (Wilson et al, 2005). **In any case, muscle bulk is clearly not a prerequisite for improved continence with PFMT, and many studies have failed to show a correlation between improved strength and improved continence.**

Although a huge number of studies have investigated PFMT it is challenging to draw clear conclusions for a variety of reasons:

1. Treatment regimens vary widely.
   a. Type of exercises
   b. Number and frequency of exercises
   c. Initial confirmation of correct technique
   d. Use of biofeedback in teaching
2. Patient types are often widely mixed.
   a. Type of incontinence
   b. Severity of incontinence
   c. Temporal relationship of therapy to childbearing
3. Outcome measures vary.
   a. Self-reported vs. objective
   b. "Cure" vs. "improved"
4. Duration of effect is not well defined.

When possible these issues are addressed in the following discussion. The interested reader is strongly encouraged to study the comprehensive review performed by the International Consultation on Incontinence committee (Wilson et al, 2005).

It is difficult to analyze the literature on PFMT because training is commonly combined with other modalities. The combination can range from general advice about incontinence management, specific strategies such as bladder diaries/timed voiding, and biofeedback training. It is important to realize how differently PFMT is applied in research trials and in European practice compared with standard U.S. clinical practice. **The definition of PFMT clearly states that it is "taught by a health care professional."** In clinical trials this is always the case; the instructor is usually a skilled physiotherapist who may apply a variety of techniques to promote learning as needed by an individual patient. In U.S. clinical practice a patient is often given only verbal instruction. In more ideal cases the patient will have written instruction after

Conservative Management of Urinary Incontinence: Behavioral and Pelvic Floor Therapy, Urethral and Pelvic Devices **2131**

CHAPTER 63

an initial assessment including a pelvic examination and assessment of and instruction in pelvic muscle contraction. Regular follow-up is all but impossible in most health care settings due to poor or absent reimbursement. This divergence in care means that results obtained in research trials may be difficult or impossible to obtain in standard clinical practice and that the difference between stand-alone PFMT and PFMT with adjunctive treatments may be much greater in U.S. clinical practice than in research studies. The following discussion of PFMT results is based on the published literature; it remains a challenge for the clinician to translate these somewhat idealized results into clinical practice.

Does PFMT Prevent UI in Childbearing Women?

PFMT has been used to prevent incontinence in pregnant women, because pregnancy and vaginal birth are strong risk factors for UI. Three prospective, randomized controlled trials have investigated this question (Sampselle et al, 1998; Reilly et al, 2002; Mørkved et al, 2003), **producing a grade B recommendation supporting the effectiveness of "sufficiently intensive and supervised antenatal PFMT" in primiparous women** (Wilson et al, 2005). In all three trials the PFMT group had less postpartum incontinence; and in one study (Reilly et al, 2002), the effect was still present at 4 years post partum, although only 100 of 268 patients were available for follow-up. The evidence reviewed by the ICI group for postpartum PFMT was less compelling, but it was concluded that **the evidence also supports a grade B recommendation for supervised intensive PFMT for women after instrumental delivery or delivery of a large infant** (Wilson et al, 2005).

Is PFMT an Effective Treatment for UI and Which Patients Are Good Candidates?

The most important question is whether PFMT is effective in the management of established incontinence and, if so, how to most effectively apply the therapy to the large population of incontinent women. Fifteen randomized controlled trials comparing PFMT to no intervention, placebo, sham, or control in childbearing women were summarized by Wilson and colleagues (2005). Although the magnitude and duration of the expected effect is not well defined, **the overwhelming majority of the trials showed effectiveness of PFMT leading to a grade A recommendation that "PFMT should be offered, as first line therapy, to all women with stress, urge or mixed incontinence."** This recommendation is, of course, based on the combination of demonstrable effectiveness with essentially no risk to the patient. It does not mandate that all patients undertake a formal course of PFMT before surgical treatment. However, there are as yet no studies that adequately define patient groups who are unlikely to respond to PFMT based on clinical factors such as age, obesity, and so on. In most cases studies have been too small to examine such predictive factors, and there may well be a role for individualized therapeutic recommendations if proper studies could be done.

The quality of the data for men with post-prostatectomy incontinence is less robust. Research has focused on use of pelvic floor therapies to hasten return of continence. Most of the evidence suggests that **there is no difference between routine preoperative and postoperative PFMT and that** although training may hasten return of continence after surgery (Filocamo et al, 2005), **it does not affect long-term outcome** (Wilson et al, 2005). **When PFMT is used for established post-prostatectomy incontinence, the results similarly do not establish long-term benefit of therapy, with or without biofeedback.** Interested readers are referred to a Cochrane review on the subject (Hunter et al, 2004).

Within these overarching categories it is likely that specific patient subgroups are more or less likely to benefit from PFMT (and probably other conservative techniques). However, studies have not been designed to specifically identify such groups and subgroup analysis of relatively small trials is fraught with error. In one retrospective series of 447 women with SUI, 49% of patients were "successfully treated." **Success appeared to be more likely in patients with milder degrees of incontinence (not using pads: 67% success; not having daily incontinence: 63% success; no leakage at first cough: 60% success). Independent risk factors for failure included two or more leaks per day, presence of leakage at first cough, and use of antidepressant/anxiolytic medications** (Cammu et al, 2004). Burgio (2004) argues that PFMT is equally effective in treating UI with stress, urge, and mixed incontinence, whereas Goode (2004) commented that there are as yet no reliable predictors of treatment outcomes.

Implementing PFMT in Clinical Practice

If PFMT is to be accepted as standard therapy one must also define how to implement training in clinical practice. Many articles have evaluated different regimens and use of ancillary tools, but in many cases quality is lacking. In evaluating the literature it is important to ensure that groups being compared are truly equivalent in all parameters other than that being tested. Key elements include the usual demographic characteristics, the degree of supervision (expertise and contact time), the intensity of the exercise program (number, frequency, and duration of contractions), use of ancillary tools, and, of course, the length of the program and follow-up. The ICI group (Wilson et al, 2005) concluded that:

1. **Clinicians should provide the most intensive PFMT supervision that is possible within service constraints.**
2. **No PFMT regimen has been proven most effective; treatments should be based on the exercise physiology literature.**
3. **There is no demonstrable benefit of biofeedback over PFMT alone, although properly powered quality trials are probably warranted to study this issue further.**

A representative strengthening program for PFMT used by the author suggests:

1. **Sets of 10 to 12 near-maximal contractions are recommended.**
2. **Each contraction is held 6 to 8 seconds with an equivalent rest period.**
3. **The exercises are repeated three to five times per day, every other day.**

In addition to the strengthening program **we recommend use of the "knack" maneuver to promote timing of the contraction coincident to coughing for SUI patients** (Miller et al, 2001) **and "quick flicks," short rapid contractions intended to inhibit urgency for those with OAB symptoms.** The need to practice PFMT is probably lifelong, and patients should be counseled to integrate exercise into their normal routines. Bo and colleagues (2005) reported 15-year follow-up of a randomized trial between intensive exercise therapy and home exercises in women with SUI. Ninety percent of the subjects were located and responded to a questionnaire. Half of the women in both groups eventually underwent surgical treatment. It is clear that exercises were not continued (28% exercise at least weekly and 36% never exercise). Although most women in both groups were satisfied with their current condition, "the marked benefit of intensive PFMT seen short-term was not maintained 15 years later." The author suggests that training one to two times a week at high intensity is enough to maintain muscle strength. On the other hand, Cammu and colleagues (2000) found that 16 of 24 patients (67%) originally satisfied with PFMT remained so after 10 years and only 2 of 24 (8%) went on to surgical therapy. They attributed sustained improvement to patients' use of a voluntary pelvic muscle contraction ("perineal lock" or "knack") before physical stress.

PFMT versus Other "Conservative" Modalities

PFMT has also been compared against other therapies, including various forms of vaginal cones, electrical stimulation, bladder training, and pharmacologic therapy. Again, most of the individual trials are relatively underpowered, often differ in the degree of therapist contact/supervision, and have a short follow-up. **In addition, there is always a selection bias because some women will not accept use of vaginal devices such as cones, biofeedback probes, or stimulators. The following conclusions were rated grade B by the ICI committee** (Wilson et al, 2005):

For women with SUI:
- PFMT and vaginal cones have similar effect.
- PFMT is superior to electrical stimulation.
- PFMT is less effective than surgery.

For women with all types of incontinence:
- PFMT and bladder training have similar effect.

For women with SUI with or without UUI:
- PFMT and adrenergic agonists have similar effect.

For women with detrusor overactivity with or without SUI:
- PFMT is superior to oxybutynin.

Although it is scientifically desirable to understand the relative value of each of these conservative treatments, the practical fact is that these are generally complementary tools. **In particular, bladder training and PFMT are useful for all types of incontinence and require no specialized equipment. Wyman and colleagues (1998) found that adding PFMT to bladder training produced superior short-term results. Another clinical trial demonstrated the feasibility of using a booklet to provide an initial "package" therapy to be used without ongoing supervision** (Goode, 2003). The standardized booklet was compared with one group receiving office behavioral training and another that used home vaginal electrical stimulation. Incontinence episodes were reduced by 52.5%, 68.6%, and 71.9%, respectively. While the booklet was inferior to the more intensive treatment, the results, including a statistically significant improvement in quality of life in all groups, suggest that the most cost-effective way to deliver therapy would be to begin with such a booklet, reserving office-based therapy requiring expert clinicians for those not satisfied with the initial results.

KEY POINTS: PELVIC FLOOR REHABILITATION: PELVIC FLOOR MUSCLE TRAINING (PFMT)

- The term *pelvic floor rehabilitation* should be applied to any treatment intended to increase the strength, bulk, and function of the pelvic floor/levator muscles.

- Basic treatments are used in the home setting, require no or inexpensive equipment, and can be administered by a relatively unskilled therapist. Advanced treatments are used in an office setting with a trained therapist or require more sophisticated equipment.

- *Pelvic floor muscle training* (PFMT) is the currently accepted term, replacing Kegels and pelvic floor exercises. It is defined as "any program of repeated voluntary pelvic floor muscle contractions taught by a health care professional."

- Evidence supports the effectiveness of routine PFMT to prevent UI in primiparous women and for supervised intensive PFMT for all women after instrumental delivery or delivery of a large infant (grade B recommendation).

- The overwhelming majority of the trials showed effectiveness of PFMT in treating established UI, leading to a grade A recommendation that "PFMT should be offered, as first line therapy, to all women with stress, urge or mixed incontinence."

- No role has been established for pelvic floor rehabilitation in the treatment or prevention of post-prostatectomy incontinence.

- Success with PFMT appears to be more likely in patients with milder degrees of incontinence. Independent risk factors for failure included two or more leaks per day, presence of leakage at first cough, and use of antidepressant/anxiolytic medications.

- The principles of a quality PFMT program include:
  - Clinicians should provide the most intensive PFMT supervision that is possible within service constraints.
  - No PFMT regimen has been proven most effective; treatments should be based on the exercise physiology literature.
  - There is no demonstrable benefit of biofeedback over PFMT alone, although properly powered quality trials are probably warranted to study this issue further.

- A representative strengthening program for PFMT could include: sets of 10 to 12 near-maximal contractions, with each contraction held 6 to 8 seconds with equivalent rest period and repeated three to five times per day, every other day.

Conservative Management of Urinary Incontinence: Behavioral and Pelvic Floor Therapy, Urethral and Pelvic Devices **2133**

CHAPTER 63

Biofeedback

Biofeedback is any method of training a patient to control a bodily function by providing him or her with information about that function. In this case, the patient hopes to gain control of, and strengthen, the pelvic muscles. The tools range from inexpensive vaginal cones to office systems costing thousands of dollars. One must remember, however, that no study has ever demonstrated that a particular device is responsible for restoring continence. On the contrary, **it is clear that the motivation of the patient and the experience and ability of the therapist are the critical factors for success** (Bo et al, 1990a). Published articles in the incontinence literature typically involve trained physical therapists specializing in incontinence and pelvic floor problems. In contrast, the biofeedback therapist in the "real world" setting is often a nurse or technician possessing only brief training in the subject. Finally, **biofeedback is only a tool, a teaching technique; real improvement in muscle strength and continence is dependent on the patient's work outside the office.** The bottom line with all of these pelvic floor therapies is that no piece of equipment is as important as the effort the patient puts into the program.

Palpation Only

Most of the literature on PFMT assumes at least initial basic evaluation and teaching by digital assessment of a pelvic floor muscle contraction during pelvic examination. This may or may not be performed at all follow-up visits. Although this is clearly an example of biofeedback, in the PFMT literature the term *biofeedback* is generally reserved for studies using sophisticated electronic or pressure devices to record pelvic floor activity.

Vaginal Cones

Sets of cones sold with varying numbers of cones ranging from 3 to 9, each of different weight, have been marketed for treatment of UI for many years (Fig. 63–2). The patient is instructed to insert a cone in the vagina above the levator muscles and hold it in for 15 to 20 minutes while in the erect

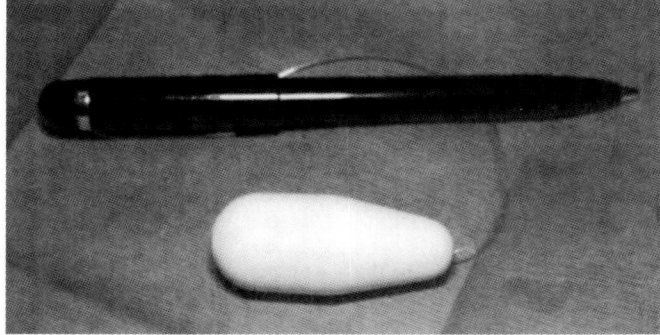

Figure 63–2. Small, weighted cones placed in the vagina provide biofeedback when the patient feels the cone slipping out and must tighten the pelvic floor muscles to retain it. They are typically sold in sets of five with progressively greater weight. (From Payne CK: Advances in nonsurgical treatment of urinary incontinence and overactive bladder. Campbell's Urology Update 1999;1[1]:6.)

position. The concept is that the sensation of the cones slipping down or falling out of the vagina will provide biofeedback to the patient to learn to identify and contract the pelvic muscles. As the patient gains the ability to retain the cone, she then progresses to the next heaviest. This provides additional biofeedback and may encourage the patient to continue with therapy. It is unlikely that this is equivalent to the effect of a skilled therapist, but this approach offers convenience at a very low cost. There are many limitations in the use of cones. **Many patients will not use any vaginal device, a substantial group will not even be able to retain the lightest cone, and some patients will retain the cones with use of thigh adductor muscles without proper levator contraction. They are obviously not useful for the male incontinent patient.**

The clinical effectiveness of vaginal cones has been examined in a Cochrane systematic review (Herbison et al, 2004). The authors identified 15 studies, involving 1126 women of whom 466 received cones. However, the trials were small, many were published only as abstracts, and "the quality was hard to judge." **Cones were believed to be better than no treatment but not clearly different from PFMT or electrical stimulation.** Wilson and colleagues (2005) concluded that there was grade A evidence that vaginal cones were equivalent to electrical stimulation for women with SUI but there were no data to evaluate the effectiveness of cones against other treatments such as bladder training, PFMT, or biofeedback.

Other Biofeedback Techniques

Most modern biofeedback units employ vaginal/anal sensors that display either pressure or electromyographic (EMG) activity on a computer screen for visual biofeedback (Fig. 63–3). In some cases auditory biofeedback corresponding to the muscle contraction is provided, and this can be beneficial for those patients with visual limitations. Perineometers measure vaginal or anal squeeze pressure—as per Arnold Kegel—are available for about $100 and, in theory, might be more effective in teaching a patient to identify the proper muscles than vaginal cones. In practice, however, **pressure-based biofeedback has been criticized because abdominal pressure is also transmitted to the probe** (Bo et al, 1990b). A patient may perform a Valsalva maneuver, which is counterproductive, because the pelvic muscles are contracting. The devices are more expensive and have the same problems with patient acceptance as vaginal cones. Pressure-based biofeedback has largely been supplanted by EMG systems, which are more expensive ($250 to $400 and up). These reduce the problem with Valsalva maneuvers but do not guarantee proper muscle isolation because they only register activity of one muscle group. Devices used with vaginal sensors, rectal sensors, and perineal patches are available. The ICI review data presented earlier (Wilson et al, 2005) made no effort to distinguish PFMT with and without biofeedback. In the United States, however, biofeedback is generally not considered a routine part of PFMT but a supplemental treatment. Although many randomized controlled trials have been performed examining exercises with and without biofeedback, the results are mixed, and a recent review concluded, **"The evidence for firm recommendations to include biofeedback in these conservative strategies is lacking, and further research is needed to clarify the role of biofeedback"** (Weatherall, 2000).

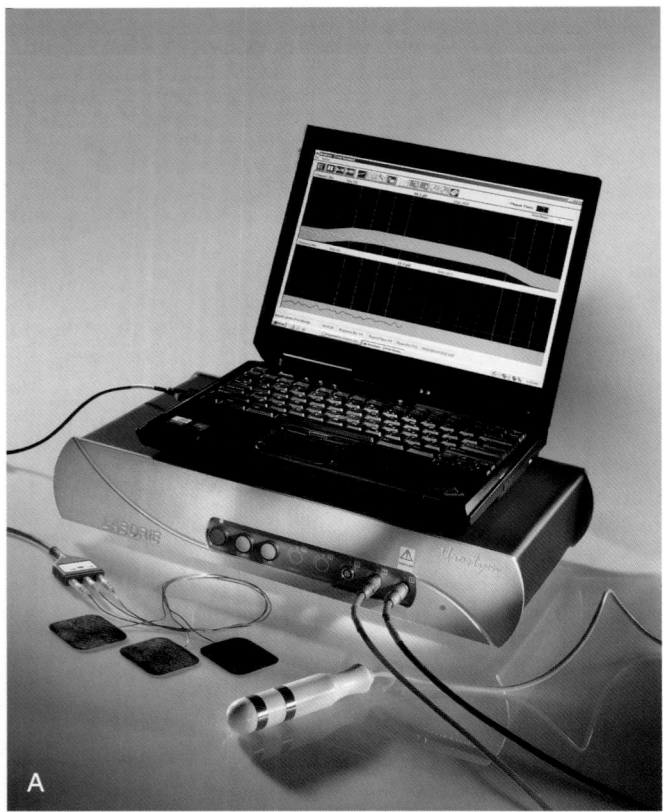

A

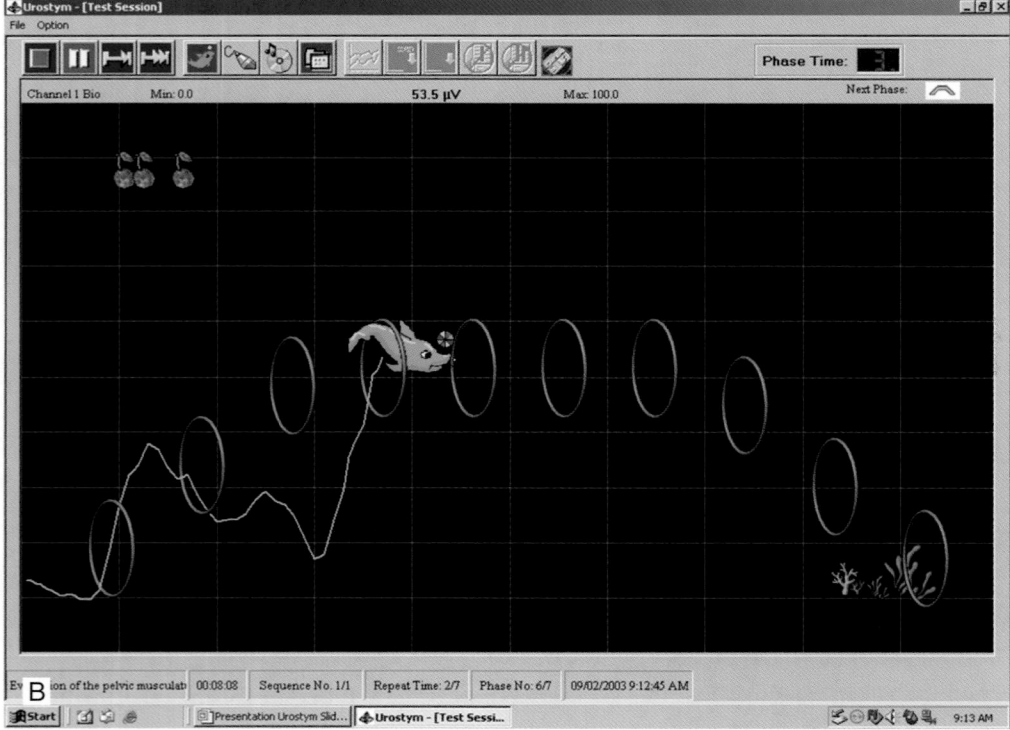

B

Figure 63–3. Tools for pelvic floor rehabilitation. **A,** Laptop-based office biofeedback system with probe and patches. **B,** Animated screen for pediatric biofeedback.

Continued

Conservative Management of Urinary Incontinence: Behavioral and Pelvic Floor Therapy, Urethral and Pelvic Devices **2135**

CHAPTER 63

C

Figure 63–3, cont'd. **C**, Typical home electrical stimulation unit. (**A** and **B**, Courtesy of Laborie Corporation [Williston, VT]; **C**, courtesy of Utah Medical Products [Midvale, UT].)

KEY POINTS: BIOFEEDBACK

■ Biofeedback is any method of training a patient to control a bodily function by providing him or her with information about that function. In this case, the patient hopes to gain control of, and strengthen, the pelvic muscles.

■ The simplest form of biofeedback is direct palpation by a skilled therapist.

■ Vaginal cones are inexpensive devices for home biofeedback. The evidence suggests that cones are better than no treatment but not clearly different from PFMT.

■ More sophisticated office biofeedback machines may be useful for certain subgroups of patients but have not been proven to be superior to PFMT.

Peripheral Stimulation

Dissatisfaction with the time, effort, and expertise required for office-based biofeedback has led to an interest in passive pelvic floor therapy. The two modalities used in this manner are peripheral electrical stimulation and magnetic stimulation.

Electrical Stimulation

There have been innumerable different devices used to assist and promote rehabilitation of the pelvic floor muscles. The type of stimulation varies by location, current type, waveform, and intensity. **High-frequency stimulation (50 to 200 Hz) has been used with vaginal or anal electrodes for SUI with an intention to directly stimulate the pelvic floor and urethral muscles with the intention of causing a contraction.** Exactly how this improves continence—by changing muscle reaction

or increasing bulk/strength—is not well documented in the literature. Electrical stimulation can also be used to treat patients with urge or mixed incontinence. **Low-frequency stimulation (5 to 20 Hz) is employed to activate inhibitory nerves to the bladder and reduce detrusor overactivity.** Although most devices employ vaginal or anal electrodes, the effect can also be achieved less invasively with peripheral stimulation using patch electrodes in the perianal or posterior tibial nerve distribution (McGuire et al, 1983; Hasan et al, 1996). Male patients find this mode of therapy much more acceptable than anal electrodes.

The advantage of this modality is that it is dependent only on patient compliance, not effort. The initial expense ($600 to $800) can be partially offset by home administration of treatments. Electrical stimulation can be combined with office biofeedback using the same probe on some systems.

Electrical stimulation has potentially wide applicability and reasonable cost. Unfortunately, the E-stim literature is characterized by case series with small numbers of patients using different devices and treatment algorithms, few of which provide any follow-up after the initial assessment of response. **In addition, the role of dual stimulation for mixed incontinence has not been adequately evaluated; this treatment would seem to be ideal for such patients using the high frequency for the sphincter and low frequency for the bladder.** The most clinically useful data come from three randomized controlled trials using the EMPI product (EMPI Corporation, St. Paul, MN). One study including 121 women with UI reported that 49% of the subset of patients with urodynamically proven detrusor overactivity converted to stable urodynamics ($P = .0004$) after active treatment compared with insignificant changes after sham treatment (Brubaker et al, 1997). However, there was no significant change in any of the clinical variables (frequency, incontinence, subjective improvement). **In the second study investigating women with SUI, E-stim was demonstrated to be significantly better than sham therapy.** Patients were treated with home vaginal stimulation for 15 minutes twice per day for 12 weeks. Leakage episodes decreased from 3.1 to 1.8 (42%) per day, and pad use decreased from 6.2 to 4.1 (34%) per week in the treatment group; there were small, statistically insignificant increases in the placebo group. Importantly, the clinical improvement correlated with improvement in pelvic muscle strength on perineometry (10.6 mm Hg baseline and 15.2 mm Hg at the end of treatment compared with a small decrease in strength in the placebo group) (Sand et al, 1995). The final study examined the optimal treatment regimen; **there was no difference in outcome between daily and every-other-day stimulation** (Richardson et al, 1996). In a literature review of 361 cumulative patients with urge incontinence, detrusor overactivity, and neurogenic detrusor overactivity, the overall results were 20% dry and another 37% significantly improved using a variety of definitions for outcome (Payne, 1996). Although the ICI committee (Wilson et al, 2005) identified 13 different trials comparing active stimulation to sham, the results were often conflicting and the authors could only conclude that **there was a "trend in favor of active stimulation" for women with detrusor overactivity.** Almost all of the relevant clinical questions about electrical stimulation will remain unanswered until the appropriate large-scale clinical trials are performed.

Magnetic Stimulation

One commercial device has been available in the United States to treat UI by extracorporeal magnetic innervation (ExMI) since 1998. The Neotonus (Neotonus Corporation, Marietta, GA) machine provides noninvasive, passive stimulation to the pelvic floor. The patient sits in the treatment chair, which emits electromagnetic waves focused on the expected area of the pelvic floor muscles. A typical treatment session lasts 20 minutes and includes both high- and low-frequency stimulation, regardless of the type of UI. The low-frequency stimulus elicits a pulselike contraction of the levators, whereas the higher frequency produces more of a tetanic contraction. There is some flexibility for the clinician to program the treatment, and the patient adjusts the intensity to comfort level. **The potential advantages of this therapy are increased patient acceptance in that no internal probe is required, a technician with minimal training can initiate it, and no supervision is required. The disadvantage is that the twice-weekly treatments must be administered in the clinician's office, which is quite inconvenient for many patients in comparison to home E-stim. The stimulation is nonspecific, and magnetic waves are not significantly attenuated by interaction with tissue. Thus, other muscles, nerves, and even the uterus could respond to stimulus, although most patients tolerate treatment well.** Although magnetic stimulation is usually thought to act by improving pelvic floor muscle function, acute stimulation has been shown to suppress detrusor overactivity in the acute setting (McFarlane, 1997).

There have been no controlled trials using the commercially available Neotonus device. Case series suggest that treatment may be effective for both SUI and UUI (Galloway et al, 1999; Yokoyama et al, 2004). Wilson and colleagues (2005) identified five trials (Fujishiro et al, 2000; 2002; Yamanishi et al, 2000; But, 2003; But et al, 2005) comparing magnetic stimulation to sham or control therapy. The quality and quantity of data limited the authors to concluding that **magnetic stimulation "might be effective" (grade C recommendation) in the treatment of UI, although they did also note that "there were no reported adverse events."** The first two studies investigated a novel portable magnetic stimulation unit placed in the pocket of specially designed underwear and used continuously day and night for 2 months. One study included 52 women with undifferentiated UI treated with stimulation at 10 Hz (But, 2003). Modest but statistically significant improvements were seen in pad use and pad tests in the treatment group only. Subjects with active stimulation rated their symptoms improved 56% on Visual Analog Scale compared with 26% in the placebo group. The second trial included 39 women with urge-predominant mixed UI (But et al, 2005) treated at 18.5 Hz. Those receiving active treatment had statistically significant improvements in several outcome variables, and symptoms improved 42% with active therapy compared with 23% in the placebo-treatment group. Fujishiro and colleagues (2000) studied the acute effect of a single session of magnetic stimulation using a 90-cm circular coil at 15 Hz for 30 minutes with the patient prone. In patients with mild SUI (mean pad test weights <15 g), active stimulation appeared superior to placebo based on a 3-day bladder diary and on a pad test performed 1 week after the stimulation. The same protocol was used to investigate 37 women with OAB, and again trends favored effectiveness of active therapy.

Electromagnetic therapy would seem to be a natural competitor to electrical stimulation systems. Only one head-to-head study has been reported (Yamanishi et al, 2000). This trial included 15 men and 17 women with detrusor overactivity. A single session of acute therapy was administered, either with an external magnetic coil, a vaginal electrical stimulation probe (women), or surface electrodes (men); urodynamic studies were performed before and after stimulation. Both magnetic and electrical stimulation was given at 10 Hz. Most urodynamic parameters were significantly improved in both groups, but the increase in maximal cystometric capacity was significantly better with magnetic stimulation.

It is clear that more randomized clinical trials with pragmatic design and standard clinical outcome measures are needed before the role of magnetic stimulation can be defined. **The most important question is whether any of the advanced pelvic floor rehabilitation techniques provide more consistent or better durability of response than PFMT. Until such data exist, biofeedback, E-stim, and electromagnetic therapy are all potential competitive treatment options to rehabilitate the pelvic floor when PFMT is insufficient.**

KEY POINTS: PERIPHERAL STIMULATION

- High-frequency stimulation (50 to 200 Hz) has been used with vaginal or anal electrodes for SUI, and low-frequency stimulation (5 to 20 Hz) is employed to reduce OAB/UUI.

- There is no convincing evidence to define a specific role for electrical or magnetic stimulation in the treatment of UI.

- Both electrical and magnetic stimulation are passive treatments that offer an opportunity to treat patients who may not be motivated to perform regular PFMT.

DEVICES

A variety of devices have been used to ameliorate lower urinary tract dysfunction: vaginal support devices (pessaries), urethral meatal occlusive devices, and urethral inserts. Permanently implantable devices are not discussed here. Many patients are attracted to and will actively seek out safe, effective nonsurgical, nonpharmacologic therapy. Some are fearful of the risks, potential complications, and inconvenience of surgical therapy; others are reluctant to commit to an indefinite course of drug therapy and possible attendant complications. These patients may see a device as an improvement over no treatment or protective pads. At the same time there are also many patients who have "taboos" or strong negative feelings regarding use of devices. For instance, devices are often associated with the infirm and elderly, a "last resort" option for those who cannot be treated by conventional means. Thus, as with much of the literature on pelvic floor therapies, there

Conservative Management of Urinary Incontinence: Behavioral and Pelvic Floor Therapy, Urethral and Pelvic Devices   **2137**

CHAPTER 63

is a significant selection bias involved in interpreting clinical research on devices.

Despite these limitations, there remains considerable interest in the area and ample room for innovation. It is thus worthwhile to review the devices that have been recently available to understand their strengths, weaknesses, and roles. Devices have been divided into "supportive" and "occlusive" categories. Occlusive devices include the urethral meatal-based devices and urethral stents or inserts. Only the devices inserted into the urethra have been required to show any significant long-term safety record, so the literature regarding the other types of devices is totally inadequate.

Vaginal Support (Pessaries) for SUI

Although vaginal support prostheses are among the oldest of medical devices, there has been a strong interest in developing products specifically for UI within the past few years. Although the concept of a vaginal support device has long been appreciated and many patients anecdotally report less SUI when using a tampon, the first device specifically designed, tested, and approved for the management of SUI was developed only recently. Older devices, some initially developed for low-grade cystoceles or uterine prolapse, such as the Smith and Hodge pessaries, have been used in treating SUI for many years, but there are very little clinical data as to their effectiveness (Bhatia et al, 1983; Bergman and Bhatia, 1984). **Any device that supports the bladder neck may be used to estimate the response to surgical therapy in a patient with mixed incontinence, although the predictive value is not established.**

Advantages of vaginal support devices include:
- They are potentially applicable to the majority of the incontinent population (those with pure stress or mixed incontinence and urethral hypermobility).
- They do not require specific testing, such as urodynamics.
- They can be used "as needed" for predictable SUI (as can the other devices).
- They have mild side effects limited to occasional vaginitis and minor local discomfort.
- Some devices can be used to treat both pelvic prolapse and SUI.

Disadvantages of vaginal support devices include:
- They do not correct intrinsic sphincter deficiency and thus are not likely to help those without hypermobility.
- They do not definitively treat potentially curable problems. If the problem worsens over time, the patient's health may make surgical therapy less attractive and, in rare cases, impossible.

Only one device, the Introl bladder neck support prosthesis, was approved specifically for SUI, and it has subsequently been withdrawn from the market. The Introl was a simple device to mechanically support the hypermobile bladder neck (Fig. 63–4). It was studied in several centers since its initial description (Biswas, 1988), always with good results. **In the clinical trials performed to test the device, significant improvements in diary reported incontinence events (10 to 3 per week), provocative pad test (49.8 to 18 g), Q-tip test (42 to 20 degrees), urethral length (2.46 to 2.73 cm), and pressure transmission ratio (76% to 88%) were reported. There**

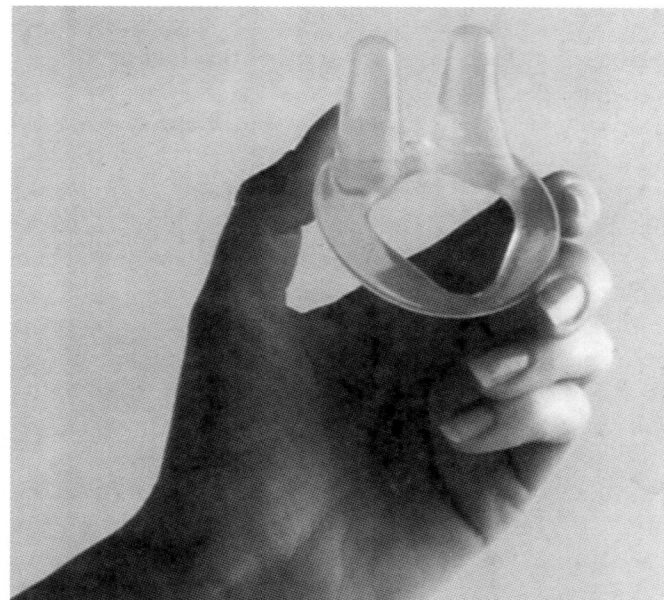

Figure 63–4. The Introl bladder neck support prosthesis. (Courtesy of UroMed Corporation, Needham, MA.)

was no change in residual urine (Davilla and Ostermann, 1994). The Introl came in 25 sizes, whereas traditional pessaries come in about 10 sizes. The device was intended to be inserted each morning and removed each evening (as stress incontinence is not a problem during sleep), although I typically allowed patients to use the device for 3 to 7 days initially as a test and did not see any local problems. The device must be removed for intercourse, and thus does not help the woman who suffers from leakage during coitus. It seemed to be somewhat more difficult for the patient to properly position than other pessaries and clearly more difficult for physicians to fit because of the large number of sizes. It could not be retained when significant pelvic organ prolapse was present. Eventually, despite demonstrable effectiveness, the device was discontinued. Perhaps an improved product could play an expanded role in the future.

Vaginal Support (Pessaries) for Prolapse (Overflow/Bladder Outlet Obstruction/UUI)

Pessaries have been used for years as a treatment for pelvic organ prolapse and diseases of the uterus (Miller, 1991). In fact, since withdrawal of the Introl, the only devices currently available are pessaries primarily designed for pelvic organ prolapse. The Milex Corporation (Chicago, IL) and the Mentor Company (Santa Barbara, CA) offer a full range of pessaries for prolapse and have developed devices intended for SUI alone (Fig. 63–5) or that associated with pelvic organ prolapse (Fig. 63–6). These devices include a "knob" oriented anteriorly in the distal vagina at the level of the proximal urethra to improve closure. In contradistinction to the Introl, these devices put pressure directly on the urethra and are thus more likely to be obstructive. **Pessaries used for prolapse only should be fitted with an empty bladder for patient comfort.**

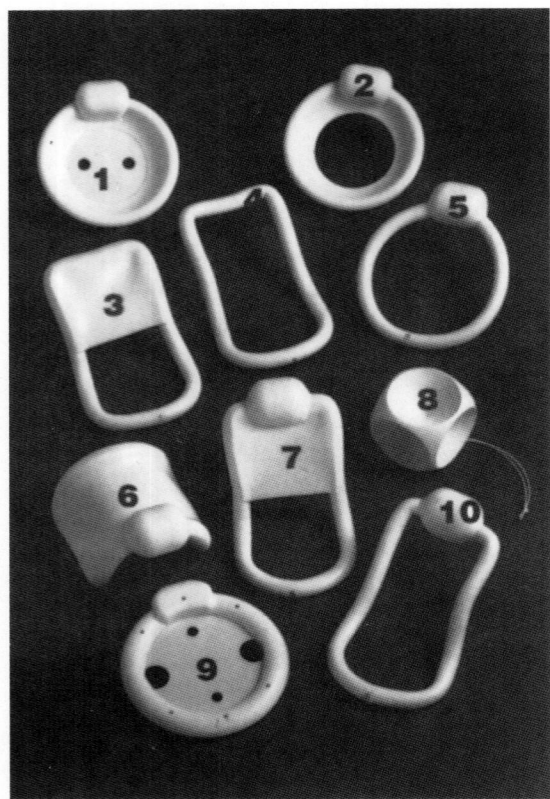

Figure 63–5. Pessaries available from Milex Corporation, Chicago. All provide varying anatomic support; those with "knobs" apply direct pressure to close the urethra to manage stress incontinence. 1, Incontinence dish with support; 2, Incontinence dish; 3, Hodge with support; 4, Hodge; 5, Incontinence ring; 6, Gehrung with knob; 7, Hodge with support and knob; 8, Cube; 9, Ring with support and knob; 10, Hodge with knob.

However, all pessaries intended for use in SUI should be fitted with the bladder at a comfortable fullness. The patient can then cough and strain to get an immediate assessment of effectiveness, and the patient should always urinate adequately before leaving the clinic because obstruction and retention can be a problem. This design could at least theoretically be useful for the patient with intrinsic sphincter deficiency because there is direct compression of the urethra. No direct comparison has ever been made between any of the various pessaries for any indication.

Vaginal pessaries have specific roles in diagnosis and treatment of lower urinary tract symptoms in at least three distinct situations:

1. Identification of "occult" SUI in a patient with cystocele
2. Identification/treatment of symptomatic prolapse causing OAB symptoms
3. Identification/treatment of symptomatic cystocele causing voiding symptoms and/or urinary retention

Prolapse, primarily from the anterior compartment, can impair voiding by mechanically obstructing the urethra through local pressure or by a kinking effect. This same mechanism could prevent clinical manifestations of SUI, and prolapse further diminishes SUI by dissipating abdominal pressure on the bladder neck and proximal urethra. Many authors have advocated using a vaginal pack or pessary test during preoperative evaluation before prolapse surgery (Fianu et al, 1985; Bergman et al, 1988; Ghoneim et al, 1994; Cross, 1998; Hextall et al, 1998; Chaikin et al, 2000; Klutke and Ramos, 2000). Despite this, there is as yet no body of evidence to prove that any preoperative test has adequate predictive value to be universally recommended. Still, it seems reasonable to encourage all prolapse patients considering surgery to undergo a trial of a pessary and evaluate the clinical response to the device. If "de novo" stress incontinence is uncovered, it would seem foolish not to perform an anti-incontinence procedure during the prolapse repair so long as adequate emptying was documented. **If OAB or other lower urinary tract symptoms resolve with the pessary, the patient may elect to use the device either temporarily until a convenient time for surgery or as a long-term solution. Similarly, if symptoms do not resolve after appropriate support with a pessary the patient should be counseled that they are more likely to persist even after successful repair of the anatomic defect. A pessary trial has an advantage over the packing tests during urodynamics in that the patient can be evaluated chronically and during day-to-day activities.** However, many patients with high-grade prolapse cannot retain any pessary and surgical decisions must be made using common sense, urodynamic data, and best clinical judgment.

Urethral Meatal Occlusive Devices

At least three devices have been marketed for female SUI that were applied directly to the urethral meatus. The exact mechanism of action for these devices is not clear. The devices generally have a small reservoir or some absorptive capacity. They may create a "dam" to prevent leakage, work through absorption, or increase urethral closure by eliminating "pop-off." The Capsure, Femassist, and Impress devices were approved for marketing, but all have been withdrawn from the market.

These devices were very uncomplicated and might be more attractive to patients than a pad because they actually prevent leakage rather than simply absorbing the fluid. This would reduce odor and skin irritation. They are simple to use and noninvasive. Good effectiveness was demonstrated for mild to moderate SUI, as detailed by Dmochowski (1998):

- Capsure: 84/100 completed 3 months, 48% dry/97% improved by pad test
- Femassist: 20/56 improved, 15 would use long term
- Impress: 17/19 cured/improved by a pad test

On the other hand, application was not uniformly easy and patients did not always have resources to help them get through initial problems in utilization. For some types of body habitus it was simply not possible to apply the device. The devices have a limited ability to oppose leakage and were not effective for severe stress leakage or any urge leakage. Finally, local tissue irritation was a minor but common problem. Second-generation devices have been developed for testing, and it is hoped that improved products will be available in the future.

Urethral Inserts

Sometimes referred to as urethral stents or plugs, the urethral inserts for SUI passively occlude and/or coapt the urethra and

Conservative Management of Urinary Incontinence: Behavioral and Pelvic Floor Therapy, Urethral and Pelvic Devices   **2139**

CHAPTER 63

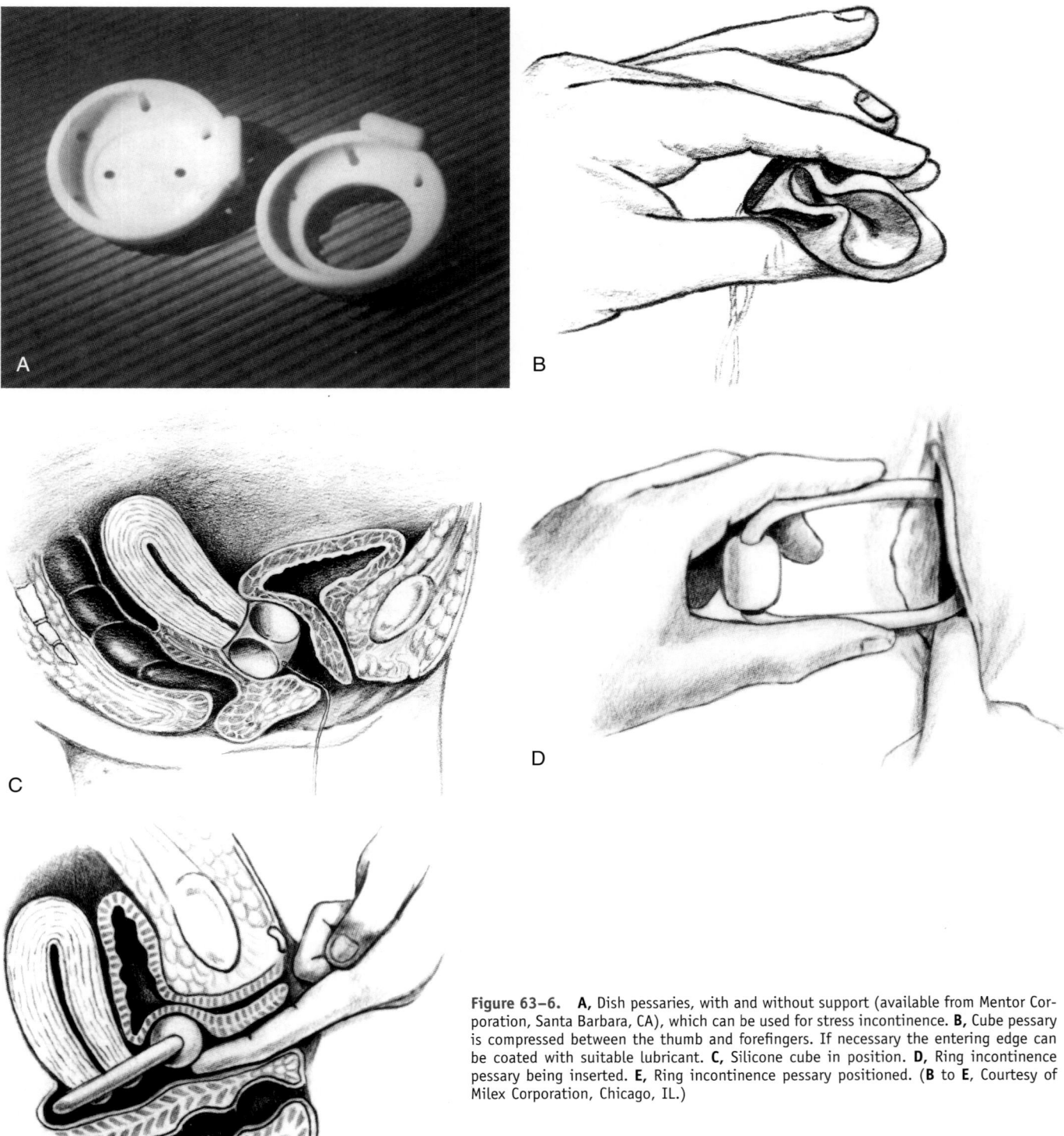

Figure 63–6.   A, Dish pessaries, with and without support (available from Mentor Corporation, Santa Barbara, CA), which can be used for stress incontinence. **B,** Cube pessary is compressed between the thumb and forefingers. If necessary the entering edge can be coated with suitable lubricant. **C,** Silicone cube in position. **D,** Ring incontinence pessary being inserted. **E,** Ring incontinence pessary positioned. (**B** to **E,** Courtesy of Milex Corporation, Chicago, IL.)

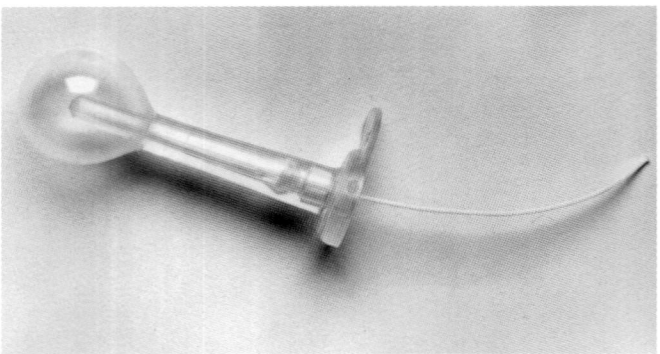

Figure 63–7. Reliance urethral insert. (Courtesy of Uromed Corporation, Needham, MA.)

must be removed for voiding. The first urethral insert to be approved for marketing by the U.S. Food and Drug Administration (FDA), the Reliance (UroMed, Inc., Needham, MA) (Fig. 63–7), has been withdrawn from the market. The second-generation FemSoft stent (Rochester Medical Corporation, Stewartville, MN) (Fig. 63–8) was FDA approved in 1997 and is currently available. No catheter has yet been approved. The discussion here focuses on devices for SUI (urethral plugs/stents), although many of the principles are equally applicable to the investigational catheters.

The multicenter study that led to the approval of the Reliance device enrolled 255 patients from eight centers. Of these, 135 completed at least 4 months with the device and were considered evaluable. The results were unquestionably good, with **80% of the subjects dry using the device and 95% improved** (Staskin et al, 1998). **At 1-year follow-up, the efficacy was maintained and there were significant but mostly minor complications, including urinary tract infection (30%), gross hematuria (24%), and local changes on cystoscopy (9%)** (Miller and Bavendam, 1996).

In comparison, the one published study of the newer FemSoft insert was a 5-year, multicenter trial involving 150 women with mean follow-up of 15 months (Sirls et al, 2002). Pad testing and bladder diaries demonstrated efficacy. This device appears to be useful for a wide spectrum of the incontinent population, including those with urgency, low leak point pressure, failed surgery, and advanced age. In contrast, the Reliance was believed to be applicable only for pure SUI; if urgency was present it tended to be exacerbated by the device, resulting in loss of both urine and the device with an involuntary bladder contraction. Adverse events with the FemSoft were again common but not severe, including symptomatic urinary tract infection in 31.3%, mild trauma with insertion in 6.7%, hematuria in 3.3%, and migration in 1.3% of women.

Although urethral inserts are potentially applicable to almost all women with pure SUI and possibly some of those with mixed incontinence, it must be remembered that the device must be removed and replaced for each void. Despite the new soft, hydrophilic materials, only a small percentage of the SUI population seems to be willing to instrument the urethra to be dry. The highest patient acceptance seems to be among those with very predictable, episodic SUI, such as during sports or dancing. Such patients might use a device several times each week and have complete elimination of leakage. Many of these patients believe that their problem is too mild to undergo a surgical procedure but are happy to have this minimally invasive alternative.

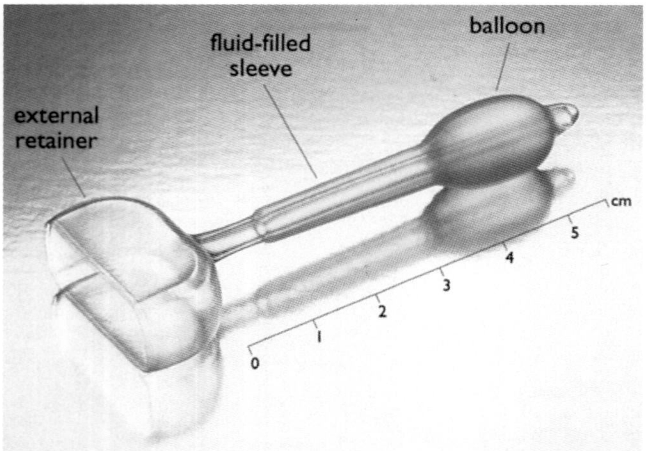

Urethral Stents

Urethral stents that allow for intermittent voiding through the device have been tested in both men and women with urinary retention/overflow incontinence. None has ever been approved in the United States. Most of the catheters that have been designed have internal motors that allow the patient to expel urine without removing the device, but one device, the ContiCath (ContiMed Corporation, Minneapolis, MN), works by allowing urine to pass around the catheter through three deep grooves. In contrast to the motorized stents, this device will be effective only for retention due to obstruction with intact detrusor function. In a preliminary trial (Corujo et al, 1999) 33 of 37 patients (90%) with a non-neuropathic cause and retention 1 week or less were able to establish controlled voiding. The device was ineffective for neurogenic and chronic retention.

PRACTICAL APPROACH TO TREATMENT
General Issues—Patient Goals

Treatment of UI is more challenging and potentially more rewarding than many of the tasks facing the urologist because it requires a true partnership with the patient. In most instances there is no one "best" treatment for the particular problem. **Even when there is a superior treatment option, the nature of the disorder—not directly threatening to life and not necessarily progressive—not only allows but also mandates an individualized approach to therapy.** The patient's personal goals should always be the prime concern. A 40-year-old aerobics instructor may be highly motivated to be completely dry, whereas another woman might only want to attend church without fear of leakage; an incontinent man might be much more bothered by getting up three to four times at night than by daytime incontinence. Brubaker and Shull (2005) point out that it is "the patient's perspective that drives

balloon

fluid-filled
sleeve

external
retainer

Figure 63–8. FemSoft urethral insert. (Courtesy of Rochester Medical Corporation, Stewartville, MN.)

Conservative Management of Urinary Incontinence: Behavioral and Pelvic Floor Therapy, Urethral and Pelvic Devices **2141**

CHAPTER 63

KEY POINTS: DEVICES

- Bladder neck support devices are potentially applicable to the majority of the incontinent population (those with pure stress or mixed incontinence and urethral hypermobility).

- Devices do not require specific testing such as urodynamics.

- Devices can be used "as needed" for predictable SUI.

- Supportive and occlusive devices have mild, reversible side effects limited to occasional vaginitis and minor local discomfort.

- Some supportive devices can be used to treat both pelvic prolapse and SUI.

- Support devices do not correct intrinsic sphincter deficiency and thus are not likely to help those without hypermobility.

- Devices do not definitively treat potentially curable problems. If the problem worsens over time, the patient's health may make surgical therapy less attractive and, in rare cases, impossible.

- Short-term trials using supportive devices can be a useful method to predict response to surgical therapy for prolapse and mixed incontinence.

decisions about further treatment [in quality of life disorders]" in a review describing the term EGGS, which has been coined to facilitate communication about patient-centered treatment outcomes. **EGGS—Expectations, Goal setting, Goal achievement and Satisfaction—describes a process in which the patient's point of view is explored to develop an individualized treatment plan.** This process is equally relevant for medical, surgical, and physical therapies; the importance of the patient perspective in surgical treatment has been demonstrated in prospective clinical trials. In a surgical series, **patient satisfaction was moderately correlated to goal achievement but was not related to objective cure of SUI or prolapse** (Elkadry et al, 2003), **and goal achievement appeared to be durable at longer-term follow-up** (Hullfish et al, 2004). Although less is known about expectations and goals as they relate to nonsurgical therapy, a clinician will do well to be aware of the patient's goals lest he or she lose the patient or find an unsatisfied customer. The very nature of conservative therapies—safe, reversible, and effective—means that most patients will choose these options for first-line treatment. When the treatments are skillfully delivered, most patients will be very satisfied with the results.

Treatment Planning—Data Collection

The clinician needs three primary pieces of information to develop a treatment plan for a given patient: the type of incontinence, the baseline voiding diary, and an assessment of anatomy with particular emphasis on pelvic floor muscle strength and function. In most cases, a clinical diagnosis of

stress, urge, or mixed incontinence is easily made but detailed evaluations are sometimes necessary before beginning treatment. The voiding diary is important for four reasons. First, it is a reasonable substitute for cystometry, as **the largest voided volume on a diary has been shown to correlate with the cystometric capacity defined by urodynamic testing** (Diokno et al, 1987). Given the high false-negative rate for cystometry and detrusor overactivity, determining a general sense of the bladder's capacity to store urine is at least as valuable as knowing whether involuntary contractions are present on cystometry. Second, the voiding diary allows the clinician to objectively determine a "safe" voiding interval to begin a program of bladder training. Third, the "baseline" diary becomes the comparison for the clinician to objectively measure change with therapy. Finally, the process of keeping the voiding diary involves the patient in the treatment program, starting the education essential to behavioral therapy. The assessment of baseline pelvic muscle strength is critical because that allows the clinician to intelligently prescribe pelvic floor rehabilitation therapy.

Pelvic floor rehabilitation has a unique role in incontinence therapy in that all types of incontinence can benefit and, potentially, be cured. Pelvic floor rehabilitation has long been identified as a treatment for SUI. It has been variously proposed that such treatments increase the resting tension, the contractile force, or the speed of recruitment of the voluntary sphincter. Such changes could increase resting urethral closure and improve the reflex closure that occurs with increases in abdominal pressure. Pelvic floor rehabilitation has been relatively overlooked in treating bladder-related incontinence. Pelvic floor therapy is theoretically valuable to the patient with OAB in these ways. First, the simple mechanics of voluntary sphincter closure oppose the unstable bladder contraction and prevent or minimize urine leakage. Second, there are inhibitory local reflexes between the pelvic floor muscles and the bladder. At least in theory, increased muscle tone and strength should decrease overactivity. Finally, many patients can use repeated quick, active contractions ("quick flicks") to inhibit an involuntary contraction once it starts. Thus, improved muscle function can improve continence for the patient with OAB through both passive and active mechanisms. Although pelvic floor therapy is of unquestioned value, it has not been properly appreciated, perhaps owing to confusion about the inappropriate use of the various tools described previously and improper referrals for therapy. A simple assessment of pelvic floor muscle function at physical examination may be useful in triaging UI patients.

Patients are classified into three groups based on the assessment of pelvic floor muscle strength at baseline examination: (1) those with no or minimal ability to isolate and contract the levator muscles, (2) those who can isolate the correct muscles with poor strength, and (3) those with good pelvic floor muscle strength and isolation on the initial examination. There is no universally accepted objective method of evaluating pelvic muscle strength by digital vaginal examination. It is principally important that the clinician be internally consistent in his or her assessment. I have used a convention proposed by Laycock (Tries and Eisman, 1995). A 6-point scale is used for contraction strength: 0, absent; 1, flicker; 2, weak; 3, moderate; 4, good; 5, strong. A second score is given to indicate the endurance time in seconds. Romanzi

Table 63-4. Functional Assessment of Pelvic Muscle Contraction

	0	1	2	3
Pressure*	None	Weak	Moderate	Strong
Duration	None	<1 s	1-5 s	>5 s
Displacement†	None	Slight anterior	Whole anterior	Gripped

*Resistance of contraction against digital opposition.
†Evaluates elevation and anterior rotation of the examiner's fingers on bimanual examination.
Data from Romanzi LK, Polaneczky M, Glazer HI: Simple test of pelvic muscle contraction during pelvic examination: Correlation to surface electromyography. Neurourol Urodyn 1999;19:603-612.

and associates (1999) examined a similar system (Table 63–4). Patients can have a maximum score of 9; score less than 4 correlated with self-reported incontinence in a small test group. Scores correlated well (r values ~ 0.8) for both intra-rater and inter-rater observations. There was also a reasonable correlation to surface EMG determinations (r values ~ 0.5).

Regardless of which system a clinician chooses to score pelvic muscle strength, it is proposed that patients be stratified into three clinically relevant groups by the physical examination as described earlier. It is possible to assign treatment to patients in the three clinical groups by applying these basic principles. **It seems illogical to prescribe home exercises in the first group (inappropriate or absent baseline function), and anecdotal experience suggests that significant improvement is uncommon. These patients need some form of biofeedback (or passive stimulation) just to get started.** Office-based training should be considered to be superior to other forms of biofeedback until proved otherwise. Many of these patients are older and will not accept home therapy. Our strategy has been to offer weekly office sessions and convert the patient to a home unit once there is consistent objective and subjective response. Alternatively, passive treatment with peripheral E-stim or magnetic stimulation can be investigated.

The second group of patients demonstrate weak contractions but appropriate isolation and should be good candidates for some form of pelvic muscle rehabilitation; biofeedback has not yet been conclusively proved to be better than PFMT alone in this general population. The lesson learned from biofeedback in SUI is that results are primarily dependent on the motivation of the patient and the skill and enthusiasm of the therapist. We recommend exercise therapy for most of these patients. They are given written instructions and a follow-up office appointment with a nurse to review their progress. Home therapy with cones or simple EMG/pressure devices is a practical option that is generally well accepted by patients who have a basic knowledge and comfort about their bodies. Definitive clinical trials focusing on this patient population would be welcome.

In the final category (strong baseline pelvic contraction) the value of pelvic floor "rehabilitation" is unclear. If these patients have significant incontinence, there is generally severe urethral incompetence and/or severe bladder dysfunction; and they require more aggressive treatment. My general practice is to instruct the patient in "quick flicks" to inhibit urgency and offer vaginal cones to motivated patients. With these patients the onus is on the clinician to demonstrate effectiveness of more complex and expensive treatment.

Treatment of Female Stress Urinary Incontinence

The two principal treatments of pure female SUI are pelvic floor rehabilitation and surgery. These options have been compared in three trials with similar results. Klaskov and coworkers (1986) randomized 50 consecutive females with SUI to immediate surgery versus 5 weekly visits with a physical therapist, without complex biofeedback. Ten of 24 (42%) patients treated initially with pelvic floor therapy were satisfied and declined surgery after the training program. Tapp and associates (1989) followed 81 consecutive patients with SUI who were randomized to three groups: PFE, PFE + e-stim, or immediate surgery. The group treated with pelvic floor therapy again had a 43% satisfaction rate (19/44), although only 4 (9%) were cured of incontinence. Finally, in a group of 39 women awaiting surgery for SUI, 30 completed 1 month of therapy using vaginal cones for home biofeedback. Seventy percent were considered cured or improved, 11 of 30 chose surgery, and thus 49% of the initial group avoided an operation (Peattie et al, 1988). **It thus seems proper to counsel women who might appropriately choose surgery that, although surgery is the single most effective treatment for SUI there is a 40% to 50% chance that they can avoid an operation and be satisfied with the outcome by going through PFMT.**

In practice, it seems that one could do better than simply giving the same advice to all patients. **Certain patients might logically benefit from immediate surgery. These would include those who have significant associated prolapse (beyond the hymenal ring) that may be corrected at the same time, those who are highly motivated to be completely dry or who have high levels of physical stress due to lifestyle or occupation, those with relatively severe stress incontinence, and especially those with good pelvic floor function on initial examination (group 3 above).** On the other hand, patients with poorer pelvic floor function might reasonably be expected to have even better odds of improvement than those cited earlier; thus a trial of pelvic floor therapy should be strongly encouraged. Those with weak muscles and good isolation may benefit from Kegel exercises alone, but those with absent voluntary contractions or poor isolation are probably best treated by immediate use of one of the advanced techniques: biofeedback or pelvic floor stimulation. Even those patients who eventually go on to surgery may be pleased with progress and may have better surgical outcomes because they will be better able to manage postoperative irritative bladder symptoms.

Surgery and pelvic floor therapy are the leading treatments for SUI because they are potentially curative. However, some patients will prefer other options for a variety of reasons. The devices mentioned previously are particularly attractive to the patient who really only needs "PRN therapy," that is, a patient whose leakage is infrequent but predictable and bothersome. An example would be a patient who only leaks during twice-a-week exercise classes or sports. She may feel that surgery would be too much treatment for such a problem but is not really satisfied with protective pads. Similarly, a patient may really prefer surgery but for personal or financial reasons may need to delay definitive treatment. The devices can provide good palliation of symptoms during the interim. Devices are

Conservative Management of Urinary Incontinence: Behavioral and Pelvic Floor Therapy, Urethral and Pelvic Devices **2143**

CHAPTER 63

also, of course, indicated for the nonsurgical patient with severe comorbidities. It is simply uncommon that a patient is too ill to undergo one of the minimally invasive operations yet still is active enough to have significant SUI. When such a patient has significant hypermobility, a vaginal support device may be used. Patients without hypermobility can usually be treated with periurethral injection therapy. Improved urethral stents or meatal occlusive devices will broaden the role for device therapy.

Finally, the role of behavioral therapy in SUI should not be overlooked. Fantyl and associates (1991) demonstrated **more than 50% improvement in leakage episodes and volume of urine lost with their program, getting essentially equal results in patients with both SUI and UUI.** This is enough improvement to satisfy many patients.

Overactive Bladder and Detrusor-Related Incontinence

Successful treatment of the OAB patient mandates a complete understanding of the pathophysiology. **Although anticholinergic medications are quite effective for most patients with OAB, medical therapy should not be a reflexive initial treatment and should rarely be used in isolation.** Abnormal bladder activity is often central to the problem, but it is inappropriate to focus only on the bladder. Dysfunctional behaviors and physical limitations strongly impact and can be the primary cause of OAB symptoms. The OAB patient with incontinence almost always has poor pelvic floor muscle function (or the symptoms would be limited to urge-frequency without incontinence). Thus, most patients can benefit from multimodality therapy (Fig. 63–9).

Once underlying causes for OAB have been ruled out in the initial history, physical examination, and testing as required, treatment planning should begin with a review of the voiding diary and the patient's behaviors. The diary reveals the maximum functional bladder capacity, which gives a strong indication as to the severity of the underlying bladder dysfunction. **A low functional capacity (less than 150 to 200 mL) typically correlates with more severe bladder dysfunction, whereas a good functional capacity (>300 mL or more) indicates better potential bladder function.** The clinician may find an unusually large fluid intake aggravating urge-frequency. A timed voiding regimen is prescribed based on a time interval determined by the patient's baseline diary. **Usually a patient is instructed to void at the longest consistently dry interval. When the patient becomes dry, the interval is increased by 15 to 30 minutes/week until a normal voiding pattern is established.** Some patients will benefit from use of a watch with a timing alarm for prompted voiding. Finally, the patient's response to urge should be reviewed. Inappropriate behaviors such as running to the bathroom must be replaced by proper urge inhibition techniques.

One of the key methods of urge inhibition is use of the pelvic muscle contraction and particularly "quick flicks," short rapid contractions. The advantage of quick contractions is that the muscles are less likely to fatigue. If the patient can inhibit the urge for about 30 seconds it is likely to pass. Few incontinent patients can hold a maximal contraction that long; therefore, they leak when the muscles fatigue. Some

therapists recommend teaching the patient to practice half-strength contractions for the same reason. In any case, pelvic floor therapy will be the appropriate second step for the vast majority of OAB patients who have suboptimal muscle function. The same classification system discussed in the context of SUI is also useful for triage of OAB patients.

The key question in the treatment of OAB is when to introduce pharmacologic therapy. Unfortunately, most patients have been given drugs as first-line therapy without supplementing treatment with behavioral and pelvic floor therapy. This approach has the tandem problems of exposing many patients to expense and side effects unnecessarily. More importantly, drug therapy is rarely curative alone, whereas the other conservative measures can cure many patients, especially those who start with a reasonable bladder capacity and no underlying neurologic abnormality. While the **newer medications have greatly improved patient acceptance of medical therapy, it still seems appropriate to use drugs selectively and with an eye toward ultimately rehabilitating the bladder and titrating the patient off of medicine. Early use of medication is particularly indicated for patients with a low maximal voided volume on the diary, patients with underlying neurologic disease, and patients who seem uninterested or unable to participate in behavioral techniques. Medications are relatively contraindicated in patients with a very large bladder capacity, medical reasons to avoid anticholinergics, the very old, and the very young.** Some clinicians prefer to start anticholinergic therapy on all patients (along with behavioral techniques) as in the original British bladder training protocols (Frewen, 1978; Holmes et al, 1983). This is reasonable because it improves the odds of the patient making an immediate improvement. However, whether drugs are used on all patients or selectively, consideration should be given to the ultimate goal of bladder retraining. Patients who become completely continent with good capacity on the voiding diary probably have approximately a 50% chance of being able to go off medication and stay dry in long-term follow-up (Holmes et al, 1983). **Titration off medication should be suggested after 3 to 6 months when drug therapy is successful.**

Refractory OAB

A small group of OAB patients will prove to be refractory to the basic methods described previously. These patients should have further evaluation with sophisticated urodynamic testing and cystoscopy to carefully define the nature of the lower urinary tract dysfunction and to rule out other causes for the symptoms. The patient who truly has refractory detrusor overactivity should be tried on combination medical therapy with a standard anticholinergic plus imipramine. When satisfactory continence is not achieved at the maximal tolerable medical therapy, the options are sacral neuromodulation or surgical reconstruction (e.g., augmentation, diversion). It has been my practice to move directly to staged implantation of a sacral nerve stimulator when the refractory patient has a bladder capacity greater than 150 mL on urodynamics. When the bladder capacity is less than 150 mL we have employed a lidocaine suppression test by anesthetizing the bladder with 2% alkalinized lidocaine and repeating cystometry. If the capacity increases dramatically,

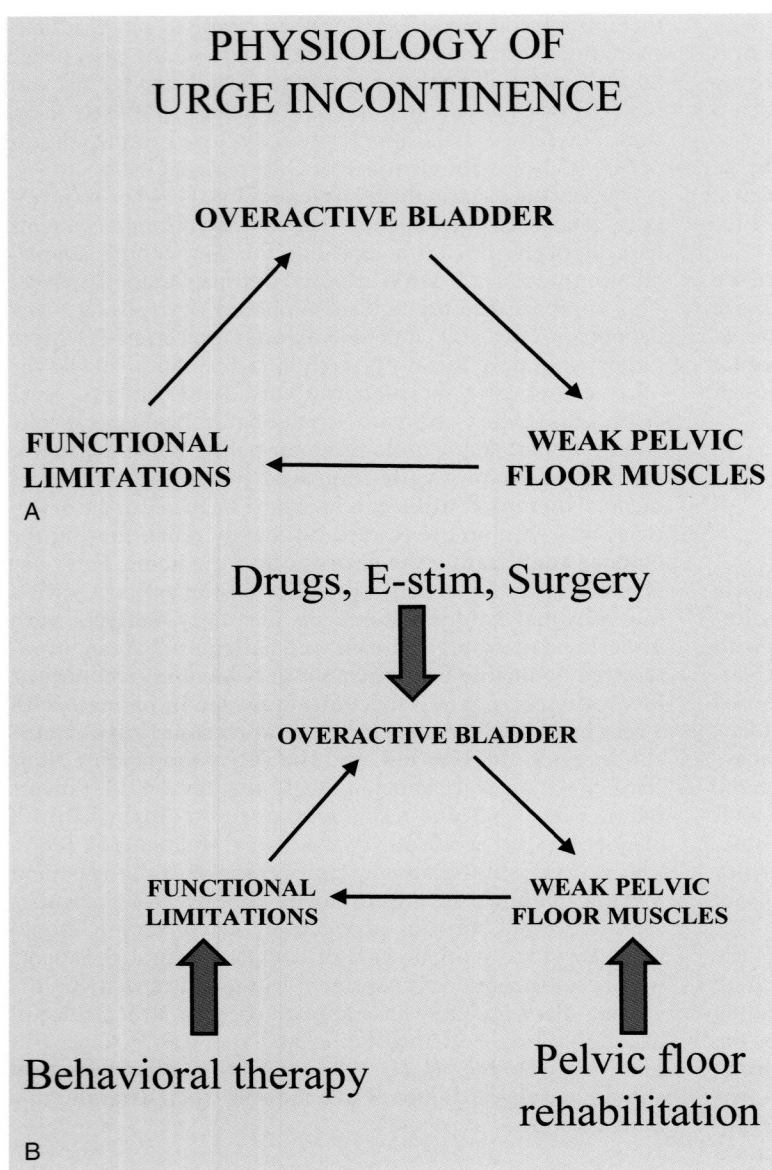

**PHYSIOLOGY OF
URGE INCONTINENCE**

OVERACTIVE BLADDER

**FUNCTIONAL
LIMITATIONS**

**WEAK PELVIC
FLOOR MUSCLES**

A

Drugs, E-stim, Surgery

OVERACTIVE BLADDER

**FUNCTIONAL
LIMITATIONS**

**WEAK PELVIC
FLOOR MUSCLES**

Behavioral therapy

Pelvic floor
rehabilitation

B

Figure 63–9. **A,** The clinical manifestation of urge incontinence is caused not only by bladder overactivity but also by poor pelvic floor muscle function, functional limitations, and dysfunctional behaviors. **B,** Multimodality treatment is the most effective approach to managing urge incontinence because each area can be addressed.

the bladder clearly still has the potential to store urine adequately. If not, neuromodulation is still an option, but these patients tend to have the most severe detrusor overactivity and surgical treatment is more likely to be required.

Advances with botulinum toxin type A (Botox-A) injection therapy for detrusor overactivity challenge this algorithm. Treatments are typically performed with cystoscopic techniques injecting a small amount of solution in 20 to 30 sites around the bladder. The procedure can be performed on an outpatient basis under local anesthesia or sedation. Botox-A injections have been proven effective for refractory neurogenic detrusor overactivity in one well-designed randomized controlled trial (Schurch et al, 2005). Fifty-nine patients with multiple sclerosis or spinal cord injury were randomized to receive injections with 200 units of Botox-A, 300 units of Botox-A, or a placebo. Dramatic improvements in bladder capacity and continence were seen in both active treatment

arms compared with placebo. The gains were maintained for 24 weeks of follow-up. A second prospective randomized trial demonstrated superiority of Botox-A injections to resiniferatoxin instillations in neurogenic detrusor overactivity (Giannantoni et al, 2004). More research is needed to define the optimal dose and the length of response; also, at this time there are no high-quality data to prove the effectiveness of Botox-A injections in the large population of patients with non-neurogenic detrusor overactivity and OAB.

When comparing neuromodulation to Botox-A injections, the most obvious difference is that the neuromodulation data are almost exclusively from the non-neurogenic population in contradistinction to the neurogenic patients treated with injections. The second key factor is that **neuromodulation is FDA approved for urgency incontinence, urge-frequency syndrome, and idiopathic urinary retention. Botox-A injections are not currently FDA approved for any application in**

Conservative Management of Urinary Incontinence: Behavioral and Pelvic Floor Therapy, Urethral and Pelvic Devices   **2145**

CHAPTER 63

the urinary tract. Nevertheless, some patients may prefer a trial of Botox-A injections, and it would seem reasonable to offer this therapy to a well-informed patient. The advantages of Botox-A include a lower initial cost, a somewhat simpler procedure, and elimination of the permanent implant (the implant precludes performing magnetic resonance imaging and can complicate travel). The disadvantages of Botox-A include the need for repeated injections indefinitely over time. Long-term response to neuromodulation is better established than Botox-A, but a great deal of research is needed in both areas and a head-to-head study would greatly advance this field.

The Problem of Mixed Incontinence

Mixed urinary incontinence presents a special challenge to the clinician. These patients have typically been approached by offering a trial of anticholinergic medication first and then operating on those who do not adequately respond. There are certainly clues that can be used to define the primary component of the incontinence in at least some of the patients and develop more individualized treatment strategies.

The history can be helpful; the primary problem in mixed incontinence is often that component (the stress or the urge) that occurred first chronologically. The voiding diary may show small daytime voids with little or no nocturia and a large first morning void. In such cases the urgency tends to be a manifestation of SUI as a few drops of urine leak into the proximal urethra with activity and trigger a sense of urgency. **Pelvic organ prolapse can have a similar effect. When SUI is suspected to be the primary component, a short-term trial of one of the vaginal support devices may clarify the picture.** If the symptoms are relieved by the device the patient may decide to continue using it or feel more confident that surgical intervention will be successful. **A pessary trial is doubly important before correcting pelvic organ prolapse (with or without incontinence). Elevation of a cystocele will unmask occult sphincteric incompetence in more than 50% of patients who are continent with the prolapse. If an ambulatory trial of a pessary is not performed, then a pessary or vaginal packing should be used during preoperative urodynamic testing as discussed in the pessary section previously.** The urethral stent/plug devices are relatively contraindicated in this patient population as clinical experience suggests that they typically aggravate the underlying urge and become totally ineffective.

The patient with mixed incontinence can usually benefit from each form of conservative treatment: behavioral, pelvic floor, and medical therapies. When medications are prescribed, it is particularly important to obtain voiding records before and during treatment. A patient who is not satisfied with treatment may be shown to have the same number of leaks but a significant improvement in bladder capacity. This would again argue for success with surgical therapy for residual SUI symptoms. **Pelvic floor rehabilitation is probably the most important treatment in this patient group, and there may be a special role for electrical stimulation because, at least theoretically, stimulation may specifically improve both urethral and bladder function.** The patient uses low- and high-frequency stimulation on alternate days. Any of the other therapies can be combined with stimulation.

KEY POINTS: PRACTICAL APPROACH TO TREATMENT

- The patient's personal goals should always be the prime concern. Patient satisfaction was moderately correlated to goal achievement but was not related to objective cure of stress incontinence or prolapse in prospective studies.

- The clinician needs three primary pieces of information to develop a treatment plan for a given patient: the type of incontinence, the baseline voiding diary, and an assessment of anatomy with particular emphasis on pelvic floor muscle strength and function. In most cases, a clinical diagnosis of stress, urge, or mixed incontinence is easily made but detailed evaluations are sometimes necessary before beginning treatment.

- The largest voided volume on a diary has been shown to correlate with the cystometric capacity defined by urodynamic testing.

- Patients are classified into three groups based on the assessment of pelvic floor muscle strength at baseline examination: (1) those with no or minimal ability to isolate and contract the levator muscles, (2) those who can isolate the correct muscles with poor strength, and (3) those with good pelvic floor muscle strength and isolation on the initial examination.

- Those with no voluntary pelvic muscle contraction should be offered biofeedback training and/or passive stimulation.

- Those with strong, coordinated muscle contractions will probably require medical or surgical therapy.

- Although surgery is the single most effective treatment for SUI, there is a 40% to 50% chance that women can avoid an operation and be satisfied with the outcome by going through PFMT.

- Early surgical intervention is more appropriate for patients with significant associated prolapse (beyond the hymenal ring) that may be corrected at the same time, those who are highly motivated to be completely dry or who have high levels of physical stress due to lifestyle or occupation, those with relatively severe SUI, and especially those with good pelvic floor function on initial examination (group 3 above).

- Most OAB patients can benefit from multimodality therapy including bladder training, PFMT, and medical therapy.

- When OAB symptoms are cured, a trial of titration off medication is warranted.

- After appropriate evaluation, sacral neuromodulation, botulinum toxin injections, and surgical reconstruction/diversion are options for refractory OAB.

SUMMARY

Urinary incontinence is a pervasive and increasing problem throughout all segments of our society that produces a severe impact on our health care system and patients' quality of life. The incontinence specialist of the 21st century must be familiar with all types of therapies: conservative/behavioral treatments, medical therapy, and surgical options. There is a great need for quality research that compares various treatment options to determine the initial effectiveness and durability, the adverse effects, and the advantages for specific groups of patients. In the meantime, the therapist must be able to match treatment to the problems and goals of individual patients. Nonsurgical treatments are unquestionably effective and are preferred by many patients. Mastering of all types of therapies will keep the urologist the recognized expert in incontinence. Ignoring nonsurgical therapies will pass the mantle, and the surgery, to other providers.

SUGGESTED READINGS

Burgio KL, Locher JL, Goode PS, et al: Combined behavioral and drug therapy for urge incontinence in older women. J Am Geriatr Soc 2000;48:370-374.

Cammu H, Van Nylen M, Blockeel C, et al: Who will benefit from pelvic floor muscle training for stress urinary incontinence? Am J Obstet Gynecol 2004;191:1152-1157.

Dallosso HM, McGrother CW, Matthews RJ, et al: The association of diet and other lifestyle factors with overactive bladder and stress incontinence: A longitudinal study in women. BJU Int 2003;92:69.

Diokno AC, Sampselle CM, Herzog AR, et al: Prevention of urinary incontinence by behavioral modification program: A randomized, controlled trial among older women in the community. J Urol 2004;171:1165-1171.

Dmochowski R: Occlusive and supportive devices. Lecture from panel discussion on "Female Urology: Non-surgical Management of Stress Incontinence" at 1998 AUA meeting, San Diego, CA. Available on CD-ROM Highlights of the 1998 American Urological Association Annual Meeting. Houston, AUA Office of Education, 1998.

Fantyl JA, Wyman JF, McLish DK, et al: Efficacy of bladder training in older women with urinary incontinence. JAMA 1991;265:609-613.

Goode PS, Burgio KL, Locher JL, et al: Effect of behavioral training with or without pelvic floor electrical stimulation on stress incontinence in women: A randomized controlled trial. JAMA 2003;290:345-352.

Hannestad YS, Rortveit G, Daltveit AK, Hunskaar S: Are smoking and other lifestyle factors associated with female urinary incontinence? The Norwegian EPINCONT Study. Br J Obstet Gynaecol 2003;110:247-254.

Hu TW, Wagner TH, Hawthorne G, et al: Economics of incontinence. In Abrams P, Cardozo L, Khoury S, Wein A (eds): Incontinence. Paris, Health Publications, 2005.

Payne CK: Behavioral therapy for the overactive bladder. Urology 2000;55:3-6.

Subak LL, Whitcomb E, Shen H, et al: Weight loss: A novel and effective treatment for urinary incontinence. J Urol 2005;174:190-195.

Tomlinson BU, Cougherty MC, Pendergast JF, et al: Dietary caffeine, fluid intake and urinary incontinence in older rural women. Int Urogyn J 1999;10:22-28.

Weatherall M: Biofeedback in urinary incontinence: Past, present and future. Curr Opin Obstet Gynecol 2000;12:411-413.

Wilson PD, Berghmans B, Hagen S, et al: Adult conservative management. In Abrams P, Cardozo L, Khoury S, Wein A (eds): Incontinence. Paris, Health Publications, 2005.

Wyman JF, Fantl JA, McClish DK, Bump RC: Comparative efficacy of behavioral interventions in the management of female urinary incontinence. Am J Obstet Gynecol 1998;179:999.

64 Electrical Stimulation for Storage and Emptying Disorders

SANDIP P. VASAVADA, MD • RAYMOND R. RACKLEY, MD

HISTORY OF ELECTRICAL STIMULATION

NEUROPHYSIOLOGY OF ELECTRICAL STIMULATION FOR STORAGE AND EMPTYING DISORDERS

ELECTRICAL STIMULATION FOR STORAGE DISORDERS

ELECTRICAL STIMULATION FOR EMPTYING DISORDERS

FUTURE RESEARCH AND CONCLUSIONS

For the past century, the development of electrical neurostimulation and neuromodulation to alter physiologic processes responsible for lower urinary tract symptoms and dysfunctions has largely been the result of important landmark discoveries in the clinical application of electricity and in the understanding of neuromuscular physiology. **In neurostimulation, the use of electrical stimuli on nerves and muscles has mainly been developed to achieve immediate clinical responses in neurogenic conditions of pelvic organ dysfunction; in neuromodulation, the application of electrical stimuli to nerves has been developed to alter neurotransmission processes in non-neurogenic and neurogenic conditions.** This chapter reviews the application (Table 64–1) and clinical outcomes of neurostimulation and neuromodulation therapies for pelvic organ dysfunction with respect to the development of our knowledge of pelvic neuromuscular physiology and its role in translational innovations.

HISTORY OF ELECTRICAL STIMULATION

Although the field of electrical simulation of nerves to achieve muscle contractions was not truly realized until the early 1800s, its roots can be traced into the 1700s, when inadvertent electrical impulses were found to generate strong muscle convulsions (Galvani, 1786; Bell, 1811). **Magendie (1822) was one of the first to conduct physiologic investigations of the spinal nerve roots, documenting in young dogs that tran-** section of the posterior (dorsal) segments resulted in a lack of sensation but persistence of motor function, whereas anterior (ventral) root transection yielded preservation of sensation yet abolishment of motor function. These important findings created the foundation for our understanding of basic neurophysiology of micturition and led to further discoveries on bladder function in the setting of selective rhizotomy of both the pelvic and hypogastric nerves (Giannuzzi, 1863; Langley, 1895). Ultimately, Saxtorph in 1878 used these principles to directly stimulate the bladder in patients with urinary retention via a metal transurethral catheter (Madersbacher, 1999). His early findings allowed others to develop enthusiasm for direct stimulation of the bladder through both transurethral and direct detrusor routes (see section on direct stimulation).

As Saxtorph had significant influence on the idea that direct bladder stimulation may lead to bladder contractility, McGuire used some of these same principles to perform direct bladder stimulation in dogs (Boyce et al, 1964). He concluded that multiple pairs of electrodes were required to achieve a more uniform pressure rise within the bladder during the stimulated contraction. Research continued throughout the late 1900s and moved toward development of new electrodes (Susset and Boctor, 1967) and differing wire configurations (Timm and Bradley, 1969; Tscholl et al, 1971).

Direct pelvic nerve stimulation and pelvic floor muscle stimulation were not well-known or well-studied concepts until the mid-1900s as emphasis was clearly on different areas of direct stimulation (i.e., bladder). Dees (1965) studied the bladder contraction state after stimulation to the pelvic nerve. He achieved contraction of both the detrusor muscle and urethral sphincter in a cat model and produced pain and hind leg contraction as well. Others demonstrated similar findings of nonspecific contraction of the bladder and pelvic floor and other areas with direct pelvic nerve stimulation and ultimately realized that direct pelvic nerve stimulation may not be suitable for treatment of bladder dysfunction (Burghele et al, 1962; Hald et al, 1966; Holmquist and Olin, 1968). It appears that direct pelvic nerve stimulation elicits pudendal nerve activity such that outlet resistance is increased, as is pain, through simultaneous hypogastric nerve stimulation. Thus,

Table 64–1. Potential Applications of Electrical Stimulation in the Treatment of Voiding Dysfunction

Purpose	Sites of Stimulation	Mechanism
Facilitate filling-storage		
Inhibit detrusor contractility	V, A, SP, PT	Neuromodulation
Increase bladder capacity	CP, SR, IV	
Decrease urgency and frequency		
Decrease nociception	V, A, SP, SR	Neuromodulation
Increase outlet resistance	V, A, SR	Direct stimulation (efferent nerves or roots)
Facilitate emptying		
Stimulate detrusor contraction (spinal cord–injured patient)	SAR	Direct stimulation (efferent nerves or roots)
Restore micturition reflex (idiopathic retention)	SR, IV	Neuromodulation

A, anal; CP, common peroneal; IV, intravesical; PT, posterior tibial; SAR, sacral anterior (ventral) roots; SP, suprapubic; SR, sacral roots; V, vaginal.

Table 64–2. Sacral Nerve Responses

Sacral Nerve	Motor and Sensory Response
S2	Motor: Plantar flexion of the entire foot with lateral rotation and clamp movement of the anal sphincter
	Sensory: Sensations in the leg and buttock
S3	Motor: Dorsiflexion of the great toe and a bellows reflex (anal wink)
	Sensory: Paresthesias or sensation of pulling in the rectum, scrotum, or vagina
S4	Motor: Bellows reflex only
	Sensory: Sensation of pulling in the rectum only

with the limited-potential clinical utility of the pelvic nerve for stimulation, efforts focused on the pelvic floor muscles, spinal cord, and sacral roots. Caldwell first reported experience with pelvic floor muscle stimulation with the goal of improving fecal continence and later urinary incontinence (Caldwell, 1963; Caldwell et al, 1965). Subsequently, interest increased and efforts toward external stimulation were described by anal, vaginal pessary, and direct vaginal stimulation (Hopkinson and Lightwood, 1967; Alexander and Rowan, 1968; Erlandson et al, 1977; Fall et al, 1977).

Spinal cord stimulation, by attempting to directly activate the micturition center, was thought to be a promising avenue of therapy (Nashold et al, 1971; Jonas and Tanagho, 1975). **Still, as in pelvic nerve stimulation, voiding was initiated; however, simultaneous sphincter activity precluded proper emptying.** The subsequent series of developments pursued therapy for incomplete emptying by affecting not only bladder stimulation but, in some way, sphincter relaxation as well.

In 1972, Brindley began experimentation of sacral root stimulation that led to implantation of sacral anterior root stimulators in paraplegic patients with urinary incontinence (Brindley, 1972, 1974, 1977). **Evolving data showed that for optimal bladder emptying to be achieved, sacral anterior root stimulation with posterior rhizotomies of S2, S3, and S4 would be required** (Sauerwein, 1990). **The posterior rhizotomy would decrease the reflex activity of the detrusor and improve bladder compliance.** Tanagho and coworkers then began further examining the sacral roots and their individual contributions to bladder and outlet function. In 1982, Tanagho and Schmidt presented initial experience in sacral root stimulation in paraplegic dogs. In this initial study, they realized the design of a spiral electrode to minimize nerve damage and fixed the lead wire to the sacral lamina, thereby preventing tension on the electrode itself. They ultimately attained good bladder contraction in these dogs, with minimal sphincteric response. From these initial good results, Tanagho then began human trials and characterized the sacral root

stimulation patterns and the corresponding muscle responses (Table 64–2). **In the course of the neurostimulation developments, they realized that sphincteric contraction abolished detrusor activity, and the role of the pudendal nerve and its modulation of bladder capacity began to evolve** (Tanagho and Schmidt, 1988; Schmidt, 1989). Thus, neuromodulation was introduced as a concept by which activation of the sacral roots may in fact modulate external sphincter function and in turn inhibit detrusor activity as a normal reflex. These early discoveries created the platform for the current and future concepts and technologies that are used for neurostimulation and neuromodulation.

NEUROPHYSIOLOGY OF ELECTRICAL STIMULATION FOR STORAGE AND EMPTYING DISORDERS

There is not a complete understanding of the exact mechanisms of how neuromodulation works, but several plausible theories with testable hypotheses are under investigation. Most are founded on the basic neurophysiologic mechanisms that result in the normal storage and emptying functions of the bladder. Although there is an expanding amount of information on our knowledge of micturition neurophysiology as discussed in this chapter, this section addresses the specifics of the micturition pathway in relation to neuromodulation.

Normal detrusor function appears to be a sacral balance under suprasacral influences of the sympathetic and parasympathetic nervous systems in their respective abilities to maintain continence. The sympathetic tone, for the most part, is dominant for the majority of time and thus provides continence or storage of urine; the parasympathetic nervous system allows detrusor contractions for emptying of the bladder. Thus, the micturition reflex pathway is activated by initial bladder afferent excitation that then results in a bladder efferent excitation leading to a detrusor muscle contraction. The acquired and unique ability to void volitionally is due to either negative feedback (inhibition of voiding) or positive feedforward (induction of voiding) influences of supraspinal inputs from the pontine micturition center of this sacral micturition reflex pathway. Any loss of either central supraspinal inhibitory influences or increased sensitization of bladder afferent signaling can lead to unmasking of involuntary voiding. There may be primitive reflexes that reside within the spinal cord that can be "awakened" by somatic and afferent nerve stimulation and may have something to do with the mechanism of action of neuromodulation (de Groat, 1975, 1976; de Groat and Ryall, 1968a, 1968b).

Bladder afferent nerve signaling sends information about pain and bladder fullness to the brain that will in turn initiate the micturition reflex. Bladder overactivity may be in part mediated by the loss of voluntary control of the voiding reflex and, furthermore, emergence of primitive voiding reflexes. In certain states of neurologic or inflammatory disease of the bladder, the previously silent C fibers may emerge and trigger the micturition reflex. Accordingly, blockade of this pathway by electrical neuromodulation, similar to pharmacologic blockade by capsaicin (a C-fiber blocker), may suppress detrusor overactivity.

Reflexes That Promote Bladder Storage. Two important reflexes may play an important role in modulation of bladder function, the guarding reflex and the bladder afferent loop reflex. Both reflexes promote urine storage (guarding reflex under somatic influence and bladder loop reflex under sympathetic tone). The guarding reflex guards or prevents urine loss from times of cough or other physical stress that would normally trigger a micturition episode. Suprapontine input from the brain turns off the guarding reflex during micturition to allow efficient and complete emptying. The bladder afferent reflex works through sacral interneurons that then activate storage through pudendal nerve efferent pathways directed toward the urethral sphincter. As such, the activity has truly been realized only in cats but has been postulated to exist in humans and to function the same. Similar to the guarding reflex, **the bladder afferent reflex promotes continence during periods of bladder filling and is quiet during micturition** (Fig. 64–1).

Reflexes That Promote Bladder Emptying. Signals from the bladder that may modulate the need to void with fullness, pain, pressure, or stretch may elicit bladder afferent activity through the Aδ or even C fibers. These bladder afferent nerve fibers then synapse with both parasympathetic efferents (bladder-bladder reflex) and parasympathetic urethral efferents (bladder-urethral) reflex. The urge to void may then be translated as an initial activity (inhibitory) of the bladder-urethral reflex to allow the pressure in the urethral outlet to drop immediately before a bladder contraction ensues and simultaneously permit the bladder-bladder reflex to allow a smooth bladder contraction to occur as the reflex is maintained throughout the entire void (de Groat, 1978; de Groat et al, 1981, 1996).

Putative Mechanism of Action of Sacral Neuromodulation

Although our knowledge of how neuromodulation works is evolving, two main theories exist: (1) direct activation of efferent fibers to the striated urethral sphincter reflexively causes detrusor relaxation and (2) selective activation of afferent fibers causes inhibition at spinal and supraspinal levels. **Accumulating evidence suggests that activation of somatic sacral afferent inflow at the sacral root level that in turn affects the storage and emptying reflexes in the bladder and central nervous system accounts for the positive effects of neuromodulation on both storage and emptying functions of the bladder** (Leng and Chancellor, 2005). Malaguti and coworkers (2003), using detection of somatosensory evoked potentials during sacral neuromodulation, concluded that sacral neuromodulation therapy works by sacral afferent activity and

Figure 64–1. The guarding reflex promotes continence and allows the outlet to contract the urinary sphincter during periods of stress (e.g., cough). The brain can turn this reflex off during voiding. (Modified from Leng WW, Chancellor MB: How sacral nerve stimulation neuromodulation works. Urol Clin North Am 2005;32:11-18.)

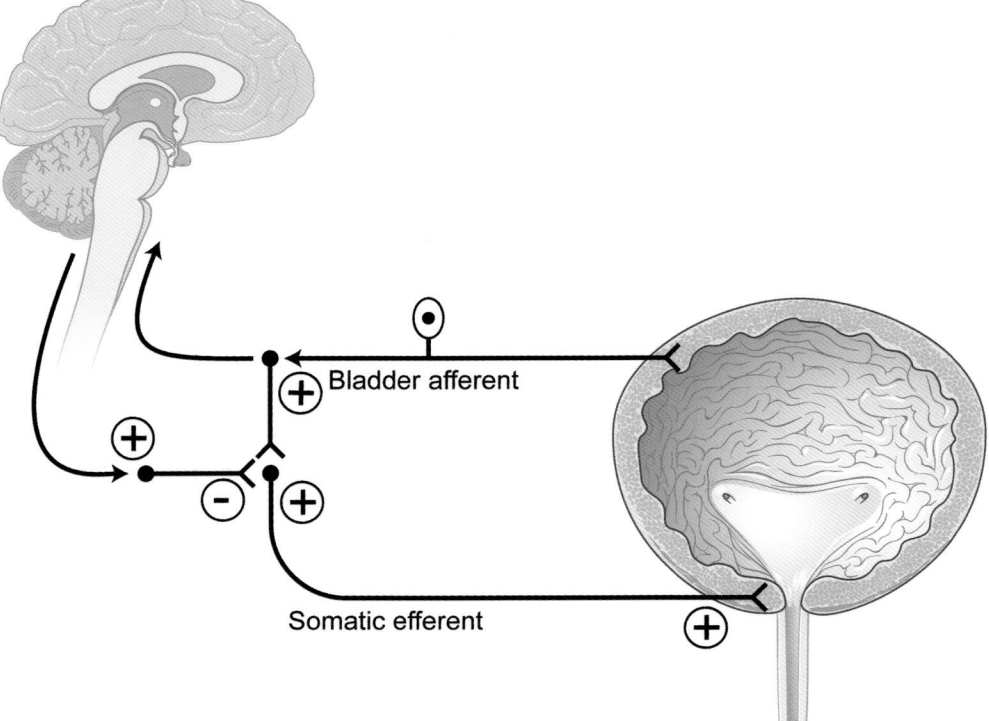

concomitant activation of the somatosensory cortex. Since sacral neuromodulation has been clinically proven for both storage (urgency-frequency and urgency incontinence) and emptying (nonobstructive urinary retention) dysfunctions of the bladder, isolating the mechanism of action to the micturition reflex pathway of sacral afferent and efferent pathways alone makes it a challenge for understanding. However, understanding the reflexes that influence the promotion of urine storage or emptying of the sacral micturition reflex pathway, one begins to realize how neuromodulation may affect these reflexes and elicit symptomatic and functional improvement of voiding function.

Putative Mechanism of Action of Sacral Neuromodulation in Overactive Bladder

The bladder storage and emptying reflexes are modulated by several centers in the brain and may be altered by neurologic injury that effectively unmasks involuntary bladder contractions. Thus, sacral neuromodulation of these primitive reflexes may restore normal micturition (de Groat, 1976). Animal data exist to support the fact that somatic afferent input to the spinal cord can affect the guarding and bladder-bladder reflexes (de Groat, 1978). It is believed that suppression of interneuronal transmission in the bladder reflex pathway may be how sacral neuromodulation affects detrusor overactivity (de Groat, 1976; Kruse and de Groat, 1993; Leng and Chancellor, 2005). **The inhibition by electrical neuromodulation may, in part, modulate the sensory outflow from the bladder through the ascending pathways to the pontine micturition center, thereby preventing involuntary contractions by modulating the micturition reflex circuit but allowing voluntary voiding to occur** (Fig. 64–2). The preservation of voluntary voiding may be due to selective avoidance of normal sensory ascending outflow pathways of the bladder from Aδ fibers to the pontine micturition center as well as initiation of the descending pathways from the pontine micturition center to sacral efferent outflow pathways. Therefore, as is seen in clinical practice, sacral neuromodulation may affect and improve the abnormal bladder sensations, involuntary voids, and detrusor contractions but still maintain normal bladder sensations and voluntary voiding patterns.

Putative Mechanism of Action of Sacral Neuromodulation in Urinary Retention

Sphincteric activity can be turned off by brain pathways to allow efficient and complete bladder emptying. **If the suprasacral pathways are altered, the guarding and urethral reflexes still exist and cannot be turned off. This may cause retention, as in the spinal cord–injured patient who in turn has detrusor-sphincter dyssynergia resulting in urinary retention. Thus, inhibition of the guarding reflexes may allow urinary retention states to be improved** (Fig. 64–3). Sacral neuromodulation may somehow turn off excitatory flow to the urethral outlet and facilitate bladder emptying.

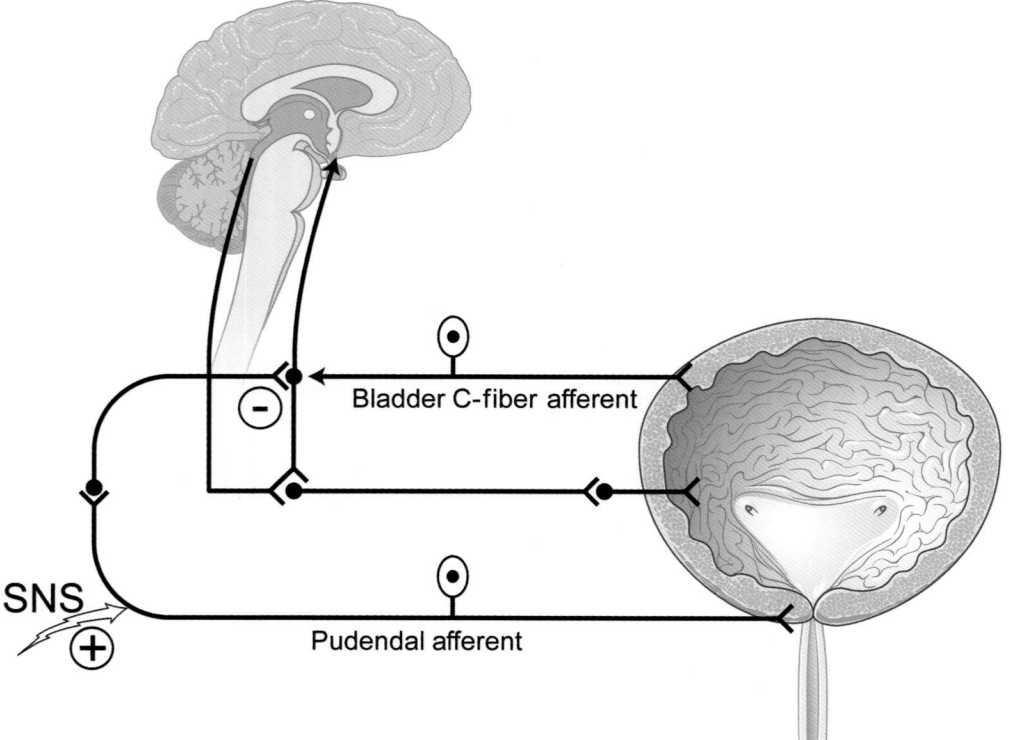

Figure 64–2. Pudendal nerve afferent firing can modulate and accordingly inhibit the bladder micturition reflex. SNS, sacral nerve stimulation. (Modified from Leng WW, Chancellor MB: How sacral nerve stimulation neuromodulation works. Urol Clin North Am 2005;32:11-18.)

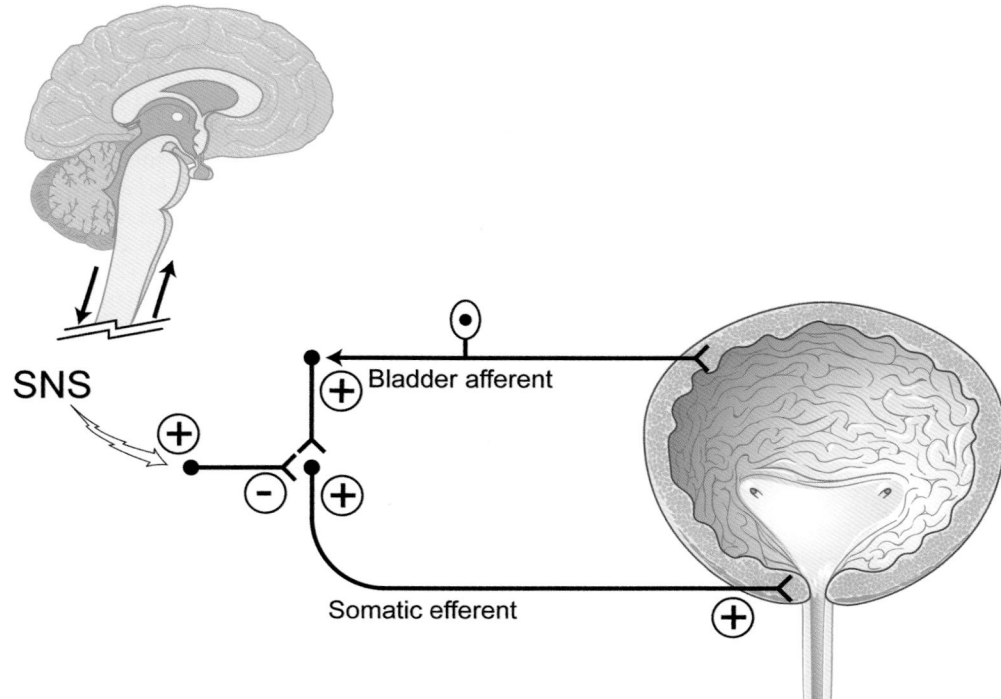

Figure 64–3. In neurologic disease, the supraspinal circuitry is "disconnected" and therefore cannot turn off the spinal guarding reflex, and thus retention occurs. Sacral neuromodulation (SNS) can restore the normal voluntary pattern of micturition by inhibition of the spinal guarding reflex. (Modified from Leng WW, Chancellor MB: How sacral nerve stimulation neuromodulation works. Urol Clin North Am 2005;32:11-18.)

ELECTRICAL STIMULATION FOR STORAGE DISORDERS
Criteria for Selection of Patients

Since many lower urinary tract symptoms and dysfunctions are secondary to a neuromuscular etiology, a thorough history and physical examination will often reveal the nature (acute versus chronic) and help classify the cause (neurogenic, anatomic, postsurgical, functional, inflammatory, or idiopathic). In addition to the unique evaluation of pelvic floor muscle dysfunction (Siegel, 2005), a urinalysis is routinely performed; urine cytology should be considered in patients who present with refractory symptoms of dysuria, urgency, or frequency of urination since carcinoma in situ and bladder tumors may present with irritative bladder symptoms without hematuria. Further assessment of the bladder function, urodynamic studies including cystometrogram, pressure-flow studies, and electromyography of sphincters and pelvic floor muscles are performed on a selected basis as most non-neurogenic assessments are completed routinely with the use of a voiding diary and a focused physical examination of the pelvis. Electromyography is recommended in suspected cases of neurogenic bladder dysfunction, detrusor-sphincter dyssynergia, or Fowler's syndrome and may be considered for evaluation of inappropriate pelvic floor muscle behavior (Dasgupta and Fowler, 2003). **The characteristics of neurogenic bladders, as seen in patients with multiple sclerosis and spinal cord injury, can change with time and disease progression. Therefore, re-evaluation with urodynamics and assessment of the upper urinary tracts may be needed when symptoms change despite active medical intervention.**

Cystourethroscopy may yield information helpful in making a diagnosis. Anatomic lesions such as urethral stricture, bladder neck fibrosis, trabeculation, and bladder lesions have been found even in women with bladder outlet obstruction. Baseline upper tract imaging is performed in patients with neurologic disease or, if indicated, by physical or baseline studies or a patient's history.

Sacral neuromodulation is frequently attempted in patients in whom traditional conservative measures (such as bladder retraining, pelvic floor biofeedback, and medications) have failed and before more invasive surgical procedures (such as enterocystoplasty and urinary diversion). **Despite all the studies done to date, there are no defined preclinical factors, such as urodynamic findings, that can predict which patients will or will not have a response to sacral neuromodulation.**

Whereas most patients are considered candidates for neurostimulation and neuromodulation therapies when more conservative treatment has failed, **there are some clinical considerations for excluding patients from this therapy. These include significant anatomic abnormalities in the spine or sacrum that may present challenges to gaining access; mental incapacitation of patients, who cannot manage their device or judge the clinical outcome; physical limitations that prevent the patient from achieving normal pelvic organ function, such as functional urinary incontinence; and noncompliance of the patient.**

Relative contraindications for patients who may be considering or who have an implantable electrical stimulation device are magnetic resonance imaging (MRI) and pregnancy. Magnetic fields produce currents in neuroelectrodes, and there is some concern that the magnetic field from MRI may damage the pulse generator, as discussed later. Many radiologists are reluctant to provide MRI services for patients with implantable electrical stimulation devices despite the anecdotal evidence that no adverse event has occurred when MRI has inadvertently or purposefully been done for emergent reasons or in small trials (Hassouna and Elkelini, 2005). For patients who have InterStim devices in place, we advocate removal of the neuroelectrode lead only with preservation of the pulse generator in preparation for elective MRI. After the MRI procedure, a new neuroelectrode may be placed and connected to the previously implanted and preserved pulse generator.

Because of the potential for teratogenicity or abortion from the effect of electrical stimulation, electrical stimulation has been considered contraindicated in pregnant women with various voiding dysfunctions. However, whether electrical stimulation can cause abortion or malformation is not known. Wang and Hassouna (1999) reported no adverse effects of electrical stimulation on pregnant rats and that termination of pregnancy is not advised for prospective mothers when electrical stimulation has been performed unknowingly in early pregnancy. Women with electrical stimulation devices for pelvic health conditions who become pregnant may simply turn off their devices during pregnancy.

Electrical Stimulation of the Bladder

Transurethral electrical bladder stimulation (TEBS) has been pursued not only for initiating sensory awareness of bladder filling and stimulating detrusor contractility (see later section) **but also for increasing bladder capacity at low pressure in pediatric patients with myelomeningocele** (Kaplan et al, 1989; Decter et al, 1994). The principals in these two cited references carried on an interesting point-counterpoint discussion in a publication regarding the practical benefit of TEBS (Kaplan, 2000; Decter, 2000). This remains a controversial area.

Both authors seem to be saying the same thing with respect to results but attach a totally different significance to the practical implications of the results. Kaplan (2000) points out that when the procedure was initiated, the goal was to provide children with neurogenic bladder dysfunction, mostly secondary to spina bifida, enough sensation to detect a filling or full bladder and to have them synergistically void or catheterize in a timely manner. As the results of treatment have been evaluated over the years, the real benefit of this program, to Kaplan at least, was the potential to increase bladder capacity while maintaining or decreasing end-filling bladder pressure (in essence, improving compliance). Decter (2000) gives what seems to be a reasonable summation of the largest multi-institutional report of this therapy involving 568 patients who underwent TEBS at 11 institutions, only 335 of whom had adequate pretreatment and post-treatment urodynamics for evaluation. Bladder capacity increased by 20% or more in 56% of the 335 patients, whereas pressure at bladder capacity decreased by 25% or more in 16% of those in whom the bladder capacity increased. Decter (2000) calculated that only 30 of 335 patients had both a 20% or more increase in bladder capacity and a 25% decrease in compliance. He reports his

experience with 25 patients during a 4-year period as showing that bladder capacity increased more than 20% (values referred to a comparison to age-adjusted bladder capacity) and end-filling bladder pressures showed clinically significant decreases in 29% of patients. Putting this in perspective, he believes "the practical benefits our patients derive seem limited . . . the urodynamic improvements we achieved after stimulation did not materially alter daily voiding routine (i.e., clean intermittent catheterization) of these children." Pugach and associates (2000) also reported the results of TEBS in a group of pediatric patients; only 7 of 44 (16%) had safe storage pressures with continence after treatment.

Sacral Rhizotomy

In most cases, **bilateral anterior and posterior sacral rhizotomy or conusectomy converts a hyperreflexic bladder to an areflexic one.** This alone may be inappropriate therapy because it also adversely affects the rectum, anal and urethral sphincters, sexual function, and the lower extremities. In an attempt to leave sphincter and sexual function intact, **selective motor nerve section was originally introduced as a treatment to increase bladder capacity by abolishing only the motor supply responsible for involuntary contractions.** The initial use of this procedure followed the observation that the third anterior (ventral) sacral root provided the dominant motor innervation of the human bladder. **To enhance the clinical response and to minimize side effects, differential sacral rhizotomy should always be preceded by stimulation and blockade of the individual sacral roots with cystometric and sphincterometric control.**

Although technique refinements, such as percutaneous radiofrequency selective sacral rhizotomy and cryoneurolysis, have occurred, **there is still controversy about the role of anterior rhizotomy procedures within a treatment plan for detrusor overactivity.** Torrens (1985) summarized successful results in collected groups of patients that ranged from 48% for idiopathic instability to 81% for patients classified as having a "paraplegic bladder." However, as he astutely pointed out, the definition of success varies from one series and from one patient to another. When these procedures are used, they should certainly be preceded by urodynamics and urologic evaluation of the effects of selective nerve blocks before performance, especially in patients without fixed neurologic disease or injury. Even then, **unintended effects on pelvic and lower extremity sensory or motor functions may occur with disastrous medical and legal sequelae.**

Both Tanagho and Schmidt (Tanagho and Schmidt, 1988; Tanagho et al, 1989) **and Brindley** (Brindley and Rushton, 1990) **have popularized the concept of sensory deafferentation by dorsal or posterior rhizotomy to increase bladder capacity as part of their overall plan to simultaneously rehabilitate storage and emptying problems in patients with significant spinal cord injury or disease. These are patients in whom they have also used electrical stimulation to alleviate emptying deficits** (see section on emptying disorders). **McGuire and Savastano** (1984) **also mentioned dorsal root ganglionectomy alone in such patients to increase bladder capacity.**

Gasparini and colleagues (1992) reported durability of the deafferentation response to selective dorsal sacral rhizotomy up to 64 months after section. The technique involves selecting nerve roots whose intraoperative stimulation provokes an adequate detrusor response. The dorsal and ventral components of these roots are then separated and the dorsal root or roots severed. An increase in bladder capacity of 259 mL to 377 mL was noted in 16 of 17 patients studied (24 in the original series), with an increase in the volume to the first contraction of 99 mL to 270 mL. A total of 14 patients were cured of incontinence, and two improved; the technique failed in one patient. Of seven potent men, two experienced a decrease in erectile frequency but were still able to achieve penetration. Bowel and sphincter function were unaffected. Koldewijn and associates (1994) reported on the effects of intradural bilateral posterior root rhizotomies from S2 to S5 with implantation of an anterior root stimulator in a group of patients with suprasacral spinal cord injury. All showed persistent detrusor areflexia afterward, although two required subsequent secondary rhizotomy at the level of the conus. A majority showed decreased bladder compliance up to 5 days postoperatively, followed by a rapid increase thereafter.

Brindley (1994) **summarized the advantages of bilateral posterior sacral rhizotomy in treatment of voiding dysfunction after spinal cord injury as abolishing reflex incontinence, improving compliance, and abolishing striated sphincter dyssynergia without altering resting tone. Partial or selective procedures are considered only in such patients who retain some sensation or have excellent reflex erections.** Madersbacher (2000) comments that posterior sacral rhizotomy for sacral deafferentation of the bladder is best achieved by the intradural approach, which has the advantage that in this location, motor and sensory fibers can easily be separated, whereas distal to the spinal ganglion, motor and sensory fibers are intermingled and a clear separation is no longer possible. If an intradural procedure is not possible, he believes that a deafferentation at the level of the conus medullaris is preferable to an extradural sacral approach. He mentions that he has treated 65 tetraplegic or paraplegic patients with post–spinal cord injury reflex urinary incontinence who were resistant to all other means of conservative treatment. Incontinence was abolished in 90% of these patients.

Sacral Neuromodulation

Neuromodulation is an innovative treatment of lower urinary tract symptoms and dysfunctions of bladder storage secondary to neuromuscular causes. In addition to the application of evolving technologies for sacral neuromodulation therapy, expanding clinical indications such as neurogenic detrusor overactivity, interstitial cystitis, pelvic pain, pediatric voiding dysfunction, and bowel disorders as well as novel forms of transcutaneous and implantable neuromodulation devices for different nerve roots are under investigation.

Technique

Sacral nerve stimulation (SNS) by the InterStim* procedure is performed in two stages: stage I, a clinical trial of a temporary or permanent lead for external stimulation; and stage II,

implantation of a subcutaneous implantable pulse generator (IPG). Each stage can be performed with monitored anesthesia care supplemented by local anesthesia. During the initial introduction of sacral neuromodulation therapy, patients underwent a percutaneous nerve evaluation by the placement of a unilateral percutaneous lead in the S3 foramen with use of local injectable anesthesia. The lead was connected to an external pulse generator and worn by the patient for several days. A large number of false-negative results with therapy are attributed to improper lead placement and migration. Whereas some physicians still prefer to perform the first stage by a percutaneous nerve evaluation approach, most have adopted a permanent tined lead placement for the first stage in an attempt to avoid the issues related to high false-negative results with the first stage and high false-positive results with the second stage. Changes in lower urinary tract symptoms and postvoid residuals are recorded in a detailed bladder diary. If improvement is minimal or absent, revision or bilateral percutaneous lead placement may be attempted. If more than 50% improvement in symptoms of urgency-frequency or urge incontinence is attained, a permanent IPG is implanted. The length of the trial with the external pulse generator may vary slightly from patient to patient, by the indication, and by the surgeon's practice preference. In patients with urgency-frequency syndrome and urge incontinence, a 2- to 4-week trial is generally adequate. For retention, a longer trial of 4 weeks or more may be necessary before a desired clinical response is obtained.

Previous lead placement required a more time-consuming surgical dissection of the layers above the sacral foramen and unreliable lead fixation with anchors. Recent technical advances have made implantation of the percutaneous lead easier and less prone to migration. Spinelli and colleagues (2003) were the first to present the advantages of the tined lead that used a percutaneous approach for placement and fixation (Fig. 64–4). Subsequent large-scale clinical experience worldwide confirms that the tined lead is less prone to migration and has decreased false-negative results with the screening trial. Furthermore, the false-positive rate of the screening trial

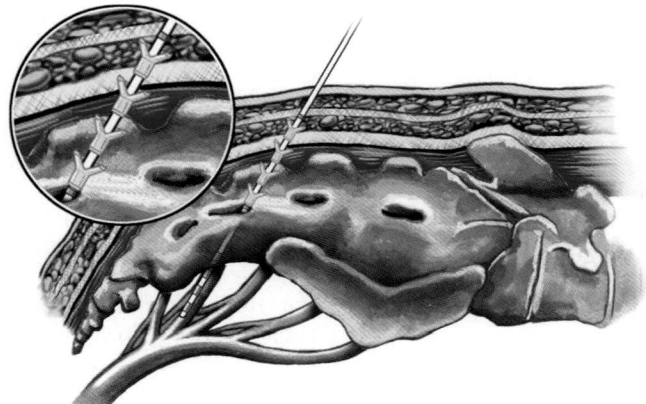

Figure 64–4. The tined lead is introduced typically into the S3 nerve foramen. The "tines" allow the lead to be fixed into the fascial layers above the sacrum. This lead has a quadripolar configuration (four contact points). (Courtesy of Medtronic Inc.)

*Medtronic, Minneapolis, Minn.

is reduced when placement of a permanent lead with reliable fixation during the screening trial ensures that the same location of stimulation is achieved when the IPG is implanted. With a percutaneous nerve evaluation or similar temporary lead electrode during the screening trial, a different clinical outcome may occur when the permanent lead is placed at the time of the IPG implantation.

For the first stage of the procedure, preoperative intravenous antibiotics are given before the procedure, and aseptic techniques of foreign body implants are implemented. The patient is placed in the prone position, and the buttocks are held apart by wide tape retraction so that the anus is visible during test stimulation. The anus and tape are prepared in a sterile fashion and then covered with a separate plastic drape until visualization is needed during the procedure. The sterile drape covering the feet must be folded back such that the feet can be visualized during the procedure as well.

The location of the S3 foramen is approximated by measuring approximately 9 cm cephalad to the drop-off of the sacrum and 1 to 2 cm lateral to the midline on either side. Alternatively, the site may also be localized by palpating the cephalad portions of the sciatic notches bilaterally and drawing a connecting line that intersects the midline of the sacrum; one fingerbreadth on either side of the midline of the sacrum at this intersection will define the location of the S3 foramen (Fig. 64–5). The foramen needle is then inserted into the S3 foramen. The pelvic plexus and pudendal nerve run alongside the pelvis, and therefore the needle should be placed just inside the ventral foramen. The position of the needle is confirmed by fluoroscopy. The nerve is tested for the appropriate motor response, which is dorsiflexion of the great toe and bellows contraction of the perineal area, which represents contraction of the levator muscles (bellows reflex). The foramen needle stylet is removed and replaced with the introducer sheath. The distal aspect of the lead consists of four electrodes numbered 0 through 3. The lead is placed into the introducer sheath as directed to expose the electrodes. Typically, electrodes are positioned such that electrodes 2 and 3 straddle the ventral surface of the sacrum (Fig. 64–6). Test stimulation is repeated on each electrode, and the responses are observed. An S3 response should be noted on at least two of the electrodes (see Table 64–2). Once the surgeon is satisfied with the position, the sheath is removed, releasing the tines that anchor the lead. A sensory response, sensation of stimulation in the perineum, is not needed to confirm proper placement if the correct S3 motor response is observed. However, when a motor response is absent, raising the conscious level of the patient during the procedure and detecting the correct sensory response will confirm proper localization, and a clinical response may still be obtained during the screening trial period despite the absence of the motor response.

A 3- to 4-cm incision into the subcutaneous tissues in the upper lateral buttock is made below the beltline or below the level of the ischial wings for connecting the permanent lead to the percutaneous extension lead wire. If the screening trial is successful, this connection site will be the site of implantation for the IPG. With use of the tunneling device provided in the commercial kit, the permanent lead is transferred to the medial aspect of the lateral buttock incision. The lead is then connected to the extension wire, and the tunneling device is used again to transpose the extension wire from the medial

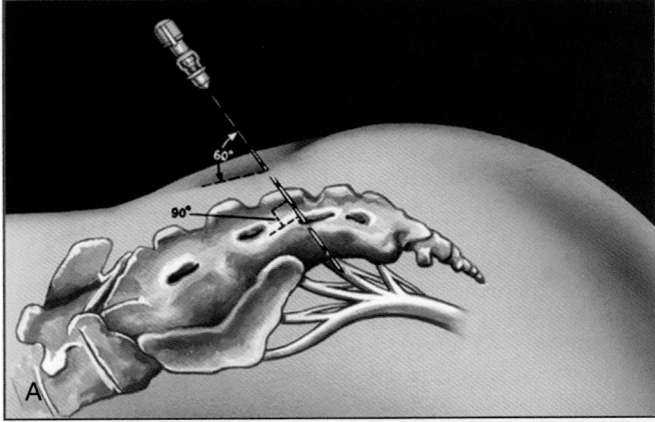

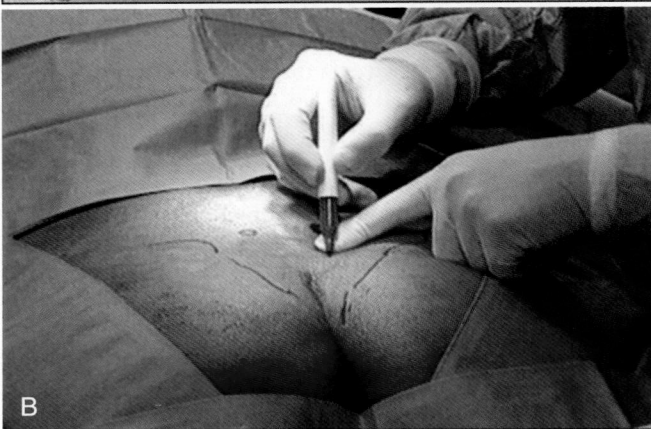

Figure 64–5. **A,** The percutaneous test stimulation is performed in an outpatient setting. A small lead wire is placed into S3 and connected to an external stimulator for 1 week to administer stimulation to the nerve roots. **B,** Measurement of the S3 nerve foramen is typically 9 cm to the coccyx and 11 cm to the anal verge. One measures 1 to 2 cm lateral to this mark to find the rough site of the S3 nerve foramen. One may use the "cross hair" technique to find the midline fluoroscopically and the lower aspect of the sacroiliac joints laterally to find the S3 nerve foramen as well. (Courtesy of Medtronic Inc.)

aspect of the incision to an exit point on the contralateral side of the back. This transfer and long tunnel reduce the occurrence of infection from the percutaneous exit site of the wire. The extension wire is connected to the external pulse generator. Patients are able to resume their normal activities immediately but are advised to limit excessive movement–related activities, such as high-impact exercises, for the duration of the trial period.

The external generator can be flexibly programmed for the duration of the intended trial while the patient records symptoms and bladder function in a voiding diary. If there is more than 50% improvement in the symptoms or voiding function, a stage II procedure is performed.

A stage II procedure entails placement of the IPG. No fluoroscopy is required during stage II when a permanent neuroelectrode has been placed for the stage I procedure; however, if a percutaneous nerve evaluation was performed for stage I, fluoroscopic confirmation of the neuroelectrode placement is advised. The patient may be placed in the prone position or a lateral position with the site of the previous

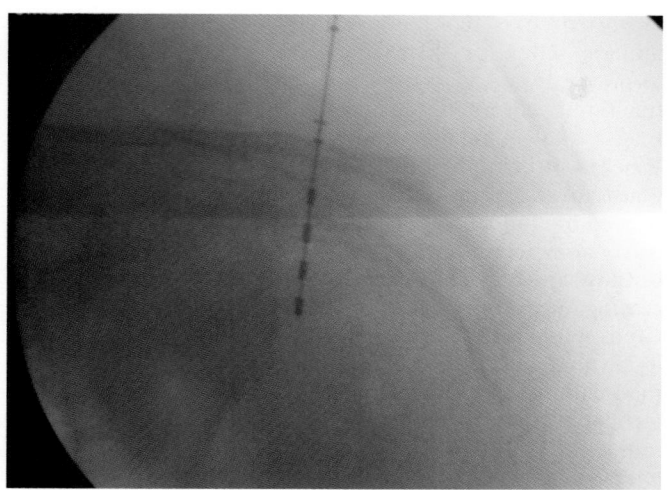

Figure 64–6. Fluoroscopy is used to confirm lead placement, typically with the lead configurations to obtain optimal muscle (bellows response and ipsilateral toe contractions) and sensory (vaginal, penile, or scrotal "pulsating" feeling) responses. The lead may then be deployed.

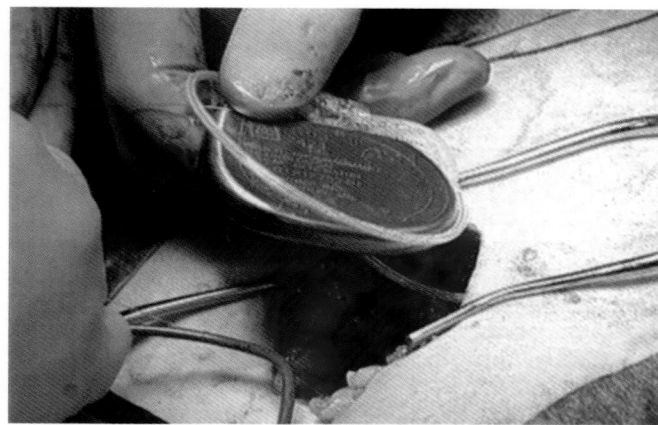

Figure 64–7. A 3- to 4-cm counterincision in the upper gluteal crease is made for a deep subcutaneous pocket to allow implantation of the IPG.

lateral incision for the lead connections placed upward (Fig. 64–7). The lateral position may improve ventilation during sedation. The previous buttock incision overlying the lead connections is opened, the percutaneous extension wire is removed, and the extension lead is secured to the permanent lead and subsequently to the IPG. A pocket is made in the subcutaneous tissue that is large enough to avoid tension on closure and at a depth to provide a covering layer of subcutaneous tissue anterior to the pulse generator to prevent erosion.

Outcomes

Urinary urgency, frequency, and urge incontinence have a significant impact on medical health and quality of life. Neuromodulation offers an alternative to patients who may be considering irreversible surgical options when pelvic floor muscle re-education and pharmacologic therapy have failed. Outcomes of SNS for the indications of idiopathic urgency-frequency and urge incontinence are derived from only two studies that have randomized patients to active or delayed therapy as well as reports from numerous prospective and retrospective reviews of case series and registry databases.

Schmidt and coworkers (1999) reported on SNS therapy in 76 patients with refractory urge incontinence from 16 centers worldwide randomized to active or delayed therapy (control group) during the study period of 6 months. Of the 34 patients receiving active SNS therapy compared with the delayed group, 16 (47%) were completely dry, and an additional 10 (29%) demonstrated more than 50% reduction in incontinence episodes. Complications were IPG site pain in 16%, implant infections in 19%, and lead migration in 7%.

In a similar study design, Hassouna and colleagues (2000) reported the outcomes of SNS on refractory urgency-frequency conditions in 51 patients randomized from 12 centers during an initial 6-month period that was extended to 2 years. Outcomes at 6 months in the active SNS group showed improvement in the number of daily voids (16.9 ± 9.7 to 9.3 ± 5.1), volume voided (118 ± 74 mL to 226 ± 124 mL), degree of urgency (rank score of 2.2 ± 0.6 to 1.6 ± 0.9), and SF-36

quality of life measures. At 6 months after implantation, stimulators in the active group were turned off and urinary symptoms returned to baseline values. After reactivation of SNS, sustained efficacy was documented at 12 and 24 months.

Limited but conformational results of the earlier randomized trials have been obtained from prospective series (Shaker and Hassouna, 1998; Siegel et al, 2000; Janknegt et al, 2001) and registry studies (Spinelli et al, 2001; Hedlund et al, 2002) evaluating efficacy, safety, and quality of life measures. The results for the U.S. registration trial that led to approval by the Food and Drug Administration (FDA) for SNS (Pettit et al, 2002) reveal that 37 of 62 patients (60%) with refractory urgency-frequency or urge incontinence achieved an improvement of 50% or more in their condition.

Special Populations

With the success of neuromodulatory therapies for refractory detrusor overactivity and urinary retention, it should be no surprise that indications are expanding. Despite the fact that there is no true FDA-approved indication for neuromodulation in select populations, these groups all have some component of the indicated symptom complex that includes urgency, frequency, urge incontinence, or urinary retention. The current expansion of indications for neuromodulation has developed into areas of neurogenic bladder (Parkinson's disease, multiple sclerosis, spinal cord injury), interstitial cystitis (painful bladder syndrome), pelvic pain, fecal incontinence and bowel disorders, and pediatric voiding dysfunction.

Neurogenic Bladder. Neurogenic bladder patients may have several urodynamic events that lead to their symptomatic voiding dysfunction. This may include neurogenic detrusor overactivity, detrusor-sphincter dyssynergia, and flaccid areflexia. Whereas neuromodulation has not been well examined in cases of obvious areflexia (possibly because of the need for some end-organ response for neuromodulation to have any benefit), it has been studied in small subgroups of patients with detrusor overactivity and possibly detrusor–external sphincter dyssynergia, although few published reports exist.

As the spectrum of neurologic diseases with potential bladder **manifestations is wide, one must be cognizant of a few important relative contraindications before contemplating current neuromodulatory therapies, as** follows: significant bone abnormalities in the spine or sacrum that may present challenges to gaining access; mental incapacity of patients, who cannot manage the device; physical limitations that prevent voiding (functional incontinence); future need of MRI; and noncompliance.

Multiple Sclerosis. Multiple sclerosis (MS) is a chronic demyelinating disease of the central and peripheral nervous system that can cause a variety of voiding dysfunction scenarios including neurogenic detrusor overactivity, detrusor-sphincter dyssynergy, areflexia, and combinations of these. As many patients have been refractory to standard therapies, neuromodulation or neurostimulation (to be addressed later in the section on neurostimulation for retention) may be considered a part of their treatment options. In an appropriately selected patient with MS, neuromodulation truly has some promise because it may balance the function of the bladder itself as well as that of the outlet (two of the main components of MS-related voiding dysfunction). This may be considered off-label use of neuromodulation as it is not approved specifically for MS-related voiding dysfunction, but approval may be based on symptoms such as urgency, frequency, or often urge incontinence and even nonobstructive urinary retention.

No prospective randomized trials exist on the use of neuromodulation in management of MS-related bladder dysfunction. Small series with encouraging results in patients with MS demonstrate that neuromodulation may have a role in treatment of MS-related voiding dysfunction (Bosch and Groen, 1996). It appears that the best candidates are ones with mild, nonprogressive MS, with few functional issues, who also have detrusor overactivity or even retention but not areflexia. One of the major issues that arises in the patient with MS in particular is the potential change in the disease state that may be potentiated by neuromodulation. Although this may be theoretical, it was one of the factors cited by the FDA in the original sacral neuromodulation trials and precluded MS patients from being enrolled (Hassouna et al, 2000).

A secondary issue that may arise if a patient with MS is implanted with the lead and IPG system is the potential need for MRI in the future. One should maintain close contact with the patient's neurologist as to the decision to place a neuromodulatory device to prevent any future need for MRI or selection of a patient in an active phase of disease that requires routine MRI. **The main concern with MRI and implantable stimulator or pacemaker-type devices is that heating of the leads has been demonstrated in vivo and in vitro** (Roguin et al, 2004; Martin, 2005). Whereas some question the clinical significance of the small temperature changes with the leads, the potential exists to elicit nerve damage with heating of the lead, and the magnetic field may change the generator itself (Gimbel and Kanal, 2004). At present, it is contraindicated to perform MRI of a patient with an implantable neurostimulator system.

Spinal Cord Injury. Many specialists who treat neurogenic disorders due to spinal injury realize that a patient may present with a variety of clinical and urodynamic findings. Many patients have neurogenic detrusor areflexic situations, but perhaps more often and sometimes more challenging is the subset who may be incontinent from neurogenic detrusor overactivity with or without concomitant sphincteric dyssynergy. Furthermore, the adverse sequelae of treated or untreated spinal cord injury may include infections, urolithiasis, reflux, or obstruction. Our goal, then, is not only to prevent these adverse events but to ensure a bladder that functions well, empties at a low pressure to protect the upper tracts, and maintains a good capacity and continence. **Whereas it is implied that an intact reflex arc should be in place for neuromodulation to work, this has not been proved in clinical studies. Basic science data suggest that at least some communication should exist between sacral outflow and the pontine micturition center to allow processing for the reflexes that may be inhibited by the brain** (de Groat et al, 1981). Thus, a patient with a complete spinal cord lesion may not have the same potential benefit from neuromodulation as does one with an incomplete lesion. Again, this fact has yet to be proved clinically in patients. Shaker and colleagues (2000) described their observations in a group of female rats that developed bladder hyperreflexia 3 weeks after spinal cord transection, associated with an increase in neuropeptide content of the dorsal root ganglion of L6. The spinal cord transections were at level T10. Electrostimulation of S1 was carried out and abolished hyperreflexia while still attaining the rise in neuropeptide content in the L6 dorsal root ganglion. This suggested that blockade of C-fiber afferent pathways may have been one of the mechanisms of action of neuromodulation of the sacral root. In addition, they believed the time course of the reduction in neuropeptide content may explain the long-term changes that occur with chronic neuromodulation and the time needed for detrusor overactivity to return toward baseline after neuromodulation is initiated.

From a clinical perspective, few studies exist in neurogenic patients alone for whom sacral neuromodulation was performed. Andrews described a T8 paraplegic with residual urinary urgency and urge incontinence who underwent percutaneous tibial nerve stimulation (see section in this chapter) for his problem (Andrews and Reynard, 2003). This patient experienced an almost twofold increase in bladder capacity; this was repeated, and again, increased cystometric capacity was demonstrated on follow-up.

It is clear that this is an emerging area of interest in current techniques, and some have postulated a role for selective stimulation in neurogenic patients as a means to achieve better results. Future research will clearly need to be done in this challenging subset of patients.

Interstitial Cystitis (Painful Bladder Syndrome). Chronic pelvic pain and interstitial cystitis are challenging and frustrating conditions for both the physician and the patient. Therapeutic options are limited and frequently ineffective. Whereas neuromodulation therapy in patients with interstitial cystitis has typically been reserved for patients considering major surgery (such as cystectomy and urinary diversion) when behavioral and pharmacologic therapies have failed, more innovative consideration has been given to earlier application of this therapy before chronic neuroplastic changes become irreversible.

Interstitial cystitis is not a true FDA-approved indication for neuromodulation; however, the symptom complex of urinary urgency and frequency is well within the standard approved criteria. **It may be realized that neuromodulation for interstitial cystitis may be best in combination with other therapies, as interstitial cystitis is thought to require a**

multimodal approach and neuromodulation should be considered only one part of the multimodal therapy.

Comiter (2003) performed a prospective evaluation of 25 patients with refractory interstitial cystitis. Seventeen of the 25 patients demonstrated more than 50% improvement in average pain score and voiding symptoms and therefore qualified for permanent IPG placement. At a mean of 14 months of follow-up, improvements were seen in frequency, nocturia, and mean voided volume. Average pain scores decreased from 5.8 to 1.6 on a 10-point scale, and Interstitial Cystitis Symptom Index (ICSI) and Problem Index (ICPI) scores decreased significantly. Furthermore, 94% of patients implanted had a sustained improvement in symptoms. Similar findings were noted by Whitmore and associates (2003) in 33 patients who had statistically improved parameters in frequency, pain, average voided volume, and maximum voided volume as well as ICSI and ICPI scores.

Peters and colleagues (2003) retrospectively evaluated 21 patients with refractory interstitial cystitis with pelvic pain who underwent permanent implantation of the IPG. The patients were contacted by mail and asked to respond to a questionnaire that addressed the use of narcotic pain medication. There was an average decrease in morphine dose-equivalents after implantation of 36%. In addition, subjects were asked to rate their pelvic pain complaints on a 7-point scale. Most patients reported a moderate to marked improvement in pain after sacral neuromodulation. Approximately one quarter of the patients were able to discontinue narcotics completely, and patients overall were satisfied with this form of therapy compared with previous ones.

Chai and coworkers (2000) have reported that perhaps some of the effects of neuromodulation in patients with interstitial cystitis may be due to changes in antiproliferative factor. His group has shown that antiproliferative factor and epidermal growth factor were elevated in the urine of patients with interstitial cystitis, and these factors subsequently normalized after a short trial of sacral neuromodulation.

Chronic Pelvic Pain. Pelvic pain, much like interstitial cystitis, has been investigated with therapy like neuromodulation; again, this is a challenging subset of patients that no other treatments seem to benefit. Bemelmans (1999) described the mechanism in pain inhibition as involving the gate control mechanism at the spinal segmental level. At this point, large somatic sensory fibers inhibit the activity in small Aδ or unmyelinated C fibers via sacral segmental interneurons or perhaps supraspinally by way of the spinobulbospinal reflex system. The hypothesis is that sacral root stimulation for the treatment of many disorders may result from decreasing pelvic floor spasticity.

Multimodal therapy is likely to benefit; however, results may not be optimal in all cases. **Spinal cord stimulation at higher centers has been used by pain therapists and with moderate success; however, trial design and consistent entry criteria are debated** (Feler, 2003; Mailis-Gagnon et al, 2004). Small series have looked at more selective stimulation, primarily at sacral roots. Aboseif and colleagues (2002) examined the effect of sacral neuromodulation on pelvic floor dysfunction in 41 of 64 patients thought to have chronic pelvic or perineal pain. Patients with chronic pelvic pain had decreased pain scores on average (5.8 to 3.7) after neuromodulation

based on validated pain scales. Siegel and associates (2001) examined patients with intractable pelvic or genitourinary pain in the absence of neurologic or pelvic disease. Sacral neuromodulation did benefit patients, and they described a decrease in severity of pain and quality of life improvements. Still, some form of placebo effect is likely to exist and is challenging to control in these small series.

Pediatric Voiding Dysfunction. Children experience voiding dysfunction in fairly high rates and may in fact have refractory bladder problems that require advanced management schemes. **Neuromodulation has been considered in this population because of the variety of lower tract dysfunctions that pediatric patients may have, including overactive bladder, urinary retention, and non-neurogenic neurogenic bladder (the Hinman bladder syndrome).** Since neuromodulation truly represents a minimally invasive option for refractory management, it follows that this may be an approach to be used in pediatric lower urinary tract dysfunction. **Still, sacral neuromodulation is not approved by the FDA for use in pediatric patients, perhaps owing to lack of data on what the sacral lead would do with concomitant growth of the spinal cord, nerve roots, and foramina. Accordingly, efforts in the past have been centered on alternative means of delivering electrical stimulation to the bladder and pelvic floor in these patients.** Few studies exist of pediatric patients and sacral neuromodulation. Guys and coworkers (2004) prospectively examined 21 patients aged 5 to 21 years with sacral neuromodulation in the setting of neurologic disease consisting predominantly of spina bifida. The neuromodulation implant group had improved compliance and bladder capacity at 6 and 9 months but not at 12 months. Of the 21 patients, nine improved their intestinal transit times, and one patient had complete disappearance of urinary incontinence. No patients in the control group improved.

Transcutaneous electrical nerve stimulation (TENS) has been used in pediatrics because it is noninvasive. One usually places a patch electrode on both sides of the S3 nerve foramen, and it is connected to a pulse generator and amplifier. Hoebeke and associates (2001) reported on this use in 41 children. In this case series, patients had urodynamically proven detrusor overactivity, and anticholinergic therapy had failed in all. Patients had daily therapy with the patch electrodes placed at S3, and stimulation was delivered at 2 Hz. A 76% response rate was observed, and this was due in part to increase in bladder capacity and reduction in urge incontinence and urge symptoms. Of 41 patients, 21 (51%) were definitively cured; the remainder relapsed in the ensuing 1 year of follow-up. Bower and colleagues (2001) reported a similar fairly high success rate with 17 children treated with S3 transcutaneous stimulation and demonstrated dryness in 73.3% of patients and improved urgency and bladder capacity based on visual analog scales and voiding diaries. Whereas this technology seems to have fairly good success, there has been no trial in a randomized prospective controlled fashion that may increase its acceptance.

Posterior tibial nerve stimulation (PTNS), much like TENS, has been studied in pediatric patients because of its lack of invasiveness. DeGennaro and colleagues (2004) reported on PTNS in children in a subset of patients with refractory non-neurogenic voiding dysfunction; 80% of patients had symptom improvement and 44% were totally dry, and 62.5% had improvement in bladder capacity. Furthermore, 71% had improvement in urinary retention symptoms. No patients had significant problems from the therapy, and it was overall thought to be both safe and well tolerated. Hoebeke and associates (2002), in a pilot study of PTNS, demonstrated similar success with 32 children. Of the 28 children with urgency before therapy, it disappeared after therapy in 7 and improved in 10. Of the 23 children with daytime incontinence before treatment, 4 became dry after stimulation, and in 12 patients, the incontinence decreased. Of the 19 patients who reported abnormal voiding frequency of either less than 4 or more than 8 voids per day, 16 of 19 achieved a normal frequency of 4 to 6 voids daily.

Fecal Incontinence and Bowel Disorders. Sacral neuromodulation was investigated for bowel disorders on the basis of some of the early experience in bladder patients who exhibited treatment benefits with regard to the bowel symptoms (Pettit et al, 2002). The use of sacral neuromodulation in bowel disorders is being actively examined, but it is not yet approved for use in the United States. **There exist two major areas of interest with regard to neuromodulation and bowel disorders: fecal incontinence and constipation.**

Fecal Incontinence. Several studies have been done to examine the utility of sacral neuromodulation in fecal incontinence (Kenefick, 2002a, 2002b; Uludag et al, 2002). It appears that patients with a variety of causes of the fecal incontinence seem to have benefited from sacral neuromodulation therapy in this setting. The Cleveland Clinic scoring system allows comparisons to be made with regard to outcome measures including incontinent episodes (solid, liquid, and flatus), pad use, and lifestyle changes. **Several studies have used this scoring system, and all have shown improvements in these assessed parameters** (Matzel et al, 2003; Jarrett et al, 2004). **The exact prognostic indicators for success have yet to be defined, particularly as they relate to etiology of the fecal incontinence (sphincter defect, neurologic, functional).**

Constipation. Constipation as such is a broad term, with the definition being in evolution. It is thought to be representative of difficult evacuation of feces and infrequent or inadequate defecation. Other refinements to the definition may include bowel frequency of fewer than three stools per week. The ROME II criteria categorize constipation into subtypes including constipation-predominant irritable bowel syndrome, functional constipation, and pelvic floor dyssynergia (Drossman and Corazziari, 2000). Sacral neuromodulation has been examined in this regard and has had favorable results on the basis of some of the criteria listed for improvement. Ganio and associates (2001) described 16 patients who underwent permanent implantation of sacral leads for constipation whereby they had more than 50% decrease in difficulty emptying the rectum and more than 80% improvement in the Cleveland Clinic constipation score that persisted during the course of 1 year of follow-up. Other series (Kenefick, 2002a, 2002b) have shown similar improvements although in smaller numbers. Still, with the small series available, it is difficult to make any meaningful analyses. The more important parameters, perhaps, in this setting relate to quality of life; these have been assessed with SF-36 questionnaires and have proved to be beneficial at least in the Kenefick study. **All of these results suggest, at least, that there is some benefit of sacral neuromodulation in refractory constipation cases. Further study is warranted to assess prognostic factors to better decide on future candidates for this therapy.**

Bilateral Stimulation and Neuromodulation

The current technique for sacral neuromodulation involves a unilateral lead at the S3 nerve foramen to achieve results in cases of urgency, frequency, urge incontinence, and idiopathic nonobstructive urinary retention. **Bilateral stimulation has been suggested as an alternative, particularly in failed unilateral lead placements, for potential salvage or added benefit as the bladder receives bilateral innervation** (van Kerrebroeck et al, 2005). The initial consideration of bilateral stimulation was based on animal studies demonstrating that bilateral stimulation yielded a more profound effect on bladder inhibition than did unilateral stimulation (Schultz-Lampel et al, 1998a, 1998b).

There has been only one clinical study to demonstrate the differences in unilateral versus bilateral stimulation (Scheepens et al, 2002). This study was a prospective randomized cross-over design in which all patients underwent unilateral as well as bilateral test stimulations to assess the benefits of bilateral stimulation. Both unilateral and bilateral test stimulation was continued for 72 hours, and the patients were randomly assigned to start with unilateral or bilateral stimulation. No significant difference was found in the unilateral versus bilateral group with regard to urge incontinence, frequency, or severity of leakage in the overactive bladder group, although overall, results were impressive in both categories. The retention group had better parameters of emptying (volume per void) in bilateral compared with unilateral stimulation. Still, the numbers were too small in the retention group for adequate conclusions to be made. **It appears that the data as presented, at least from a clinical perspective, do not suggest a large role for routine bilateral stimulation for most patients.** Perhaps there will be subgroups that may benefit more than others (e.g., retention patients), but larger scale studies with good methodology as shown in the Scheepens study will be required.

Selective Nerve Stimulation

Pudendal Nerve

Since the bladder afferent reflex works through sacral interneurons that then activate storage through pudendal nerve efferent pathways directed toward the urethral sphincter, the pudendal nerve is a logical target for developing neuromodulation therapies. The earliest attempts to manipulate this reflex through electrical stimulation were based on direct pelvic floor muscle stimulation by Caldwell (1963, 1965) and others with the development of the first implantable and external pelvic floor stimulators, anal plug stimulator (Hopkinson and Lightwood, 1966, 1967), and intravaginal pessary stimulation (Alexander and Rowan, 1968; Erlandson et al, 1977; Fall et al, 1977; Fall, 1985). To deliver optimal stimulation to the nerve directly, selective pudendal nerve stimulation was introduced by Vodusek and coworkers (1986) and shown to have an inhibitory effect on the micturition reflex.

Neurophysiologic studies reveal that SNS works for bladder storage disorders by a similar inhibition of the micturition reflex as a result of electrical stimulation of sensory afferent fibers, in particular by depolarization of Aα and Aγ somatomotor fibers that affect the pelvic floor and external sphincter and thus inhibit detrusor activity (Hohenfellner et al, 1992). Since many of the sensory afferent nerve fibers contained in the sacral spinal nerves originate in the pudendal nerve, the pudendal nerve afferents are important targets for neuromodulating the inhibitory reflex on the micturition reflex. Direct pudendal nerve neuromodulation stimulates more pudendal afferents than SNS provides and may do so without the side effects of off-target stimulation of leg and buttock muscles. Thus, techniques for direct pudendal nerve stimulation at alternative locations to the sacral foramen are being developed. Spinelli and associates (2005) modified existing sacral neuromodulation technology and adapted it to pudendal nerve stimulation and realized the need for more sensitive neurophysiologic guidance to better guide stimulation to the pudendal nerve target. Trials using different techniques and devices are under way for selective pudendal nerve stimulation within the ischial rectal fossa and the pure sensory afferent branch of the pudendal nerve at the level of the symphysis bone referred to as the dorsal genital nerve.

The Bion device* is a minimally invasive implantable ministimulator with an integrated electrode for nerve neuromodulation. Early feasibility trial results of the Bion device placed at the level of the pudendal nerve exiting Alcock's canal indicate that a considerable reduction in the degree of detrusor overactivity incontinence can be obtained in refractory cases, including those cases of failed SNS neuromodulation (Bosch, 2005). Clinical trials of the rechargeable Bion device are under way in the United States and Europe.

Dorsal Genital Nerve

The dorsal genital nerves (dorsal nerve of the penis in males, clitoral nerve in females) are the terminal and most superficial branches of the pudendal nerve found at the level of the symphysis pubis. The nerves are afferent nerves that carry sensory information from the glans of the penis or clitoris. Proximally, the dorsal genital nerves form a component of the pudendal nerve and then the sacral spinal roots. As a pure sensory afferent nerve branch of the pudendal nerve, the dorsal genital nerve contributes to the pudendal-pelvic nerve reflex that has been proposed as a mechanism of bladder inhibition. Whereas squeezing the glans penis or manipulation of the clitoris is clinically known to help suppress bladder contractions as observed in behaviors of voiding avoidance, direct electrical stimulation of these organs does not produce a significant effect on the micturition reflex as measured by urodynamics during the storage phase (Yalla et al, 1978; Kondo et al, 1982). However, direct dorsal genital nerve electrical stimulation in experimental and clinical studies appears promising in producing an inhibition of the micturition reflex.

Results in laboratory animals and in persons with spinal cord injury have demonstrated that electrical stimulation of

the dorsal genital nerves inhibits bladder contractions (Craggs and McFarlane, 1999). In anesthetized cats (Sundin et al, 1974; Jiang and Lindstrom, 1999) and in unanesthetized chronic spinal cord–injured cats, reflex bladder contractions could be inhibited by stimulation of the genital nerves (Walter et al, 1993). Conditioning stimulation of afferents in the dorsal clitoral nerves has also been shown to suppress reflex bladder contractions in anesthetized cats (Jiang and Lindstrom, 1999). Similarly, recent work in anesthetized cats has shown that low-amplitude electrical stimulation of the S1 dorsal root (which in the cat carries the dorsal genital afferents) inhibits or abolishes ongoing reflex bladder contractions (Jezernik et al, 2001), resulting in significantly shorter bladder contractions.

Stimulation of the dorsal penile nerve has been tested in humans to control incontinence in individuals with spinal cord injury and increase bladder volume and reduce bladder overactivity (Wheeler et al, 1992, 1994). Penile nerve stimulation was painless with no side effects, effective for inhibiting detrusor overactivity, and may be adaptable for chronic home use as an alternative to current therapy (Wheeler et al, 1992). Similar experiments have shown that stimulation of the dorsal nerve of the penis abolishes reflexive bladder contractions and increases bladder capacity in persons with spinal injury (Lee and Creasey, 2002). These results demonstrate that electrical stimulation of the dorsal genital nerves can abolish detrusor overactivity and increase bladder capacity in individuals with neurogenic detrusor overactivity due to spinal injury. Feasibility trials with MEDStim,* an implantable neuroelectrode and pulse generator, are under way to determine the optimal stimulation parameters that have limited its application in the past for increasing bladder capacity and treating the symptoms of idiopathic detrusor overactivity in otherwise healthy persons.

Posterior Tibial Nerve

The posterior tibial nerve is a mixed sensory and motor nerve containing fibers originating from spinal roots L4 through S3 that modulate the somatic and autonomic nerves to the pelvic floor muscles, bladder, and urinary sphincter. On the basis of translational findings of the traditional Chinese practice of using acupuncture points over the common peroneal or posterior tibial nerve to inhibit bladder activity, McGuire and associates (1983) used transcutaneous stimulation of the common peroneal or posterior tibial nerve for inhibition of detrusor overactivity. PTNS[†] as approved by the FDA currently consists of weekly 30-minute stimulation treatments provided by insertion of a small-gauge stimulating needle approximately 5 cm cephalad from the medial malleolus and just posterior to the margin of the tibia with the grounding electrode pad placed on the medial surface of the calcaneus (Govier et al, 2001; Cooperberg and Stoller, 2005).

Clinical trials of PTNS have been performed in detrusor overactive conditions with and without pelvic pain (Klingler, 2000; van Balken et al, 2003; Vandoninck et al, 2003; Congregado Ruiz et al, 2004) and urinary retention (van Balken et al, 2001; Vandoninck et al, 2003). Whereas clinical trials have produced variable results, PTNS is minimally invasive, demonstrates efficacy, and is easily applicable and well

---

*Boston Scientific, Natick, Mass.

*NDI Medical, Cleveland, Ohio.
[†]Urgent PC, CystoMedix, Anoka, Minn.

tolerated in all the lower urinary tract conditions studied. As with other neuromodulation therapies, there appears to be little evidence of producing improvements in urodynamic outcomes, and there does appear to be the need for chronic treatment that may be better derived from an implantable subcutaneous stimulation device (van Balken et al, 2003) and even conditional stimulation (Oliver et al, 2003).

Transcutaneous Electrical Stimulation

Other methods of electrical stimulation have been used that seem to occupy a place midway between anal, vaginal, or perineal stimulation and sacral root stimulation. TENS devices have been used to limited degrees to achieve better tolerability to bladder filling and may have some avenue for therapy in postponing voiding. Fall and associates (1980) described TENS use suprapubically in patients with interstitial cystitis, and subsequent studies have been done to gain wider use of this modality (Lindstrom et al, 1983; Fall and Lindstrom, 1991). The exact stimulation parameters are not agreed on as different frequencies have been used; 2 Hz may stimulate pudendal afferents, whereas 50 Hz may stimulate striated paraurethral musculature. Similarly, low-frequency TENS may have some use in abolishing detrusor contractility (Bower et al, 1998). As such, this technology is easy to do and apply, but it may be required for extended periods to gain treatment benefits. S2 or S3 TENS may make some sense, as direct stimulation transcutaneously of this area may yield better results than suprapubic stimulation. Positive results have been demonstrated on the basis of urodynamic data, with improved bladder capacity, delay in first urge to void, and reduced detrusor instability (Bower, 2001; Hoebeke et al, 2001). For adequate maintenance of the benefits of this therapy, it must also be continued for longer durations. McGuire and associates (1983) described 16 patients with involuntary bladder contractions of varying etiology who were treated with common peroneal or posterior tibial nerve patch electrode stimulation; 12 patients initially were dry, 3 were improved, and 1 was "possibly improved." Vereecker and colleagues (1984), however, were unable to suppress hyperactivity by this method in patients with suprasacral spinal cord injury or disease. Okada and associates (1998) reported a positive experience with transcutaneous stimulation of the thigh muscle in 19 patients with detrusor overactivity; the maximal cystometric capacity was increased by 57% in 11 of 19 patients.

Noninvasive magnetic stimulation of the sacral roots will also inhibit bladder contractions and cause effects that will persist for short times beyond the period of stimulation. This type of stimulation at present cannot be applied for prolonged periods and is currently unsuitable for long-term treatment, although it may be helpful for preliminary assessment of candidates for chronic sacral root neuromodulation. The extracorporeal magnetic stimulation provided by the "chair"* is under study for potential use in overactive bladder, stress incontinence, and pelvic pain. The exact mechanism of action, if effective, remains to be explained—namely, magnetic, nerve root or peripheral nerve, or intramural nerve stimulation.

---

*NeoControl Pelvic Floor Therapy System, Neotonus, Marietta, Georgia.

Complications and Troubleshooting of Sacral Neuromodulation

With the widespread adoption of sacral neuromodulation, an increasing need has developed to understand complications of this therapy and to learn how to troubleshoot the devices when responses change. It appears that the introduction of the tined lead concept has changed the frequency and profile of the complications that were once only technology related while keeping the patient-related complications at the same frequency.

Published Series

The SNS study group has published several reports on the efficacy and safety of the procedure for individual indications (Siegel et al, 2000). The complications were pooled from the different studies on the basis of the fact that the protocols, devices, efficacy results, and safety profiles were identical. The studies recruited 581 patients, 219 of whom underwent implantation of the InterStim system. The complications were divided into percutaneous test stimulation related and post-implant related problems. Of the 914 test stimulation procedures done on the 581 patients, 181 adverse events occurred in 166 of these procedures (18.2% of the 914 procedures). **Most complications were related to lead migration (108 events, 11.8% of procedures). Technical problems and pain represented 2.6% and 2.1% of the adverse events. For the 219 patients who underwent implantation of the InterStim system (lead and generator), pain at the neurostimulator site was the most commonly observed adverse effect at 12 months (15.3%). Surgical revision of the implanted neurostimulator or lead system was performed in 33.3% of cases (73 of 219 patients) to resolve an adverse event. This included relocation of the neurostimulator because of pain at the subcutaneous pocket site and revision of the lead for suspected migration. Explant of the system was performed in 10.5% for lack of efficacy. One should consider the fact that at the time, the generator was implanted in the lower abdomen.**

Everaert and associates (2004) reported specifically on the complications with SNS. This was a retrospective study of 53 patients who had undergone implantation of the quadripolar electrode (Medtronic InterStim, model 3886 or 3080) and subcutaneous pulse generator in the abdominal site (Medtronic Itrel 2 IPG) between 1994 and 1998. Device-related pain was the most frequent problem and occurred equally in all implantation sites (sacral, flank, and abdominal). This occurred in 18 of the 53 patients (34%) and was more frequent in patients with dysuria and retention or perineal pain. Pain responded to physiotherapy in 8 patients, and no explantation was done for pain reasons. Current-related complications occurred in 11%. They performed 15 revisions in 12 patients. Revisions for prosthesis-related pain (n = 3) and for late failures (n = 6) were not successful.

A review (Hijaz and Vasavada, 2005) of the tined lead approach was performed at the Cleveland Clinic from June 2002 to June 2004, when 167 patients underwent sacral neuromodulation for indications of refractory overactive bladder, idiopathic and neurogenic urinary retention, and interstitial cystitis. In this cohort, 180 stage I operations underwent the tined lead approach. After 2 to 4 weeks of test stimulation, 130 (72.2%) proceeded to stage II implantation of the IPG.

Stage I complications can lead to explantation or revision of the tined lead. The reasons for either fall under response related, mechanical, or infection related. In this series, 50 tined leads were explanted (27.8%). The majority of lead explantations were performed for unsatisfactory or poor clinical response (46 of 50; 92%). The rest of the explantations were done for infection (4 of 50; 8%). Explantation for response reasons is not truly considered a complication as much as it is an integral part of the procedure. Stage I revisions totaled 22 of the 180 operations (12.2%). Revisions were done for marginal response (13 of 22), frayed subcutaneous extension wire (6 of 22), lead infection (3 of 22), and improper localization of stimulus (1 of 22). Eleven (50%) of the revisions proceeded to stage II generator implantation. When the revision was done for a marginal response (13 of 22), the response was ultimately clinically satisfactory in 5 of 13 (38.5%), and patients proceeded to generator implantation. Typically, when the patient reported a marginal or equivocal response during the test stimulation in the absence of infection or mechanical problems, a lead revision was offered with intraoperative sensory testing. Because 38.5% of these revisions eventually were successful and patients proceeded to stage II, this is an option to keep in mind in motivated patients with equivocal response.

As in stage I, stage II complications can be divided into explantation (generator and lead) or revision. Explantation was performed in 16 of 130 (12.3%). Explantations were done

for infection and failure to maintain response in 56.3% and 43.7%, respectively. Revisions were done for infection, mechanical (generator related), and response causes. The revision rate of stage II in this series was 20% (26 of 130).

When infection at the generator site is diagnosed, the best management is explantation of the whole system.

Response-related complications necessitating revision are more common (18 of 26). The algorithm for management of a patient who presents with a decreased or absent response after a successful interval is outlined in Figure 64–8.

The outlined algorithm includes testing of impedances (Fig. 64–9). **Impedance describes the resistance to the flow of electrons through a circuit. Impedance or resistance is an integral part of any functioning circuit. However, if there is too much resistance, no current will flow (open). If there is too little resistance, excessive current flow results in diminished battery longevity (short). The electrical circuit that we are referring to starts at the neurostimulator's circuitry and goes through the connectors to the extension wires, through the extension connector to the lead wires, through the lead's electrodes to the patient's tissue, and back either through another electrode and up the same path to the circuitry (bipolar) or to the neurostimulator case and into the circuitry (unipolar).**

If the circuit is broken somehow, electrons cannot flow. **This is called an open circuit, and impedance measurements are high.** Open circuits can be caused by a fractured lead or extension wires and loose connections. Patients generally feel no stimulation if an open circuit is present. In measurement

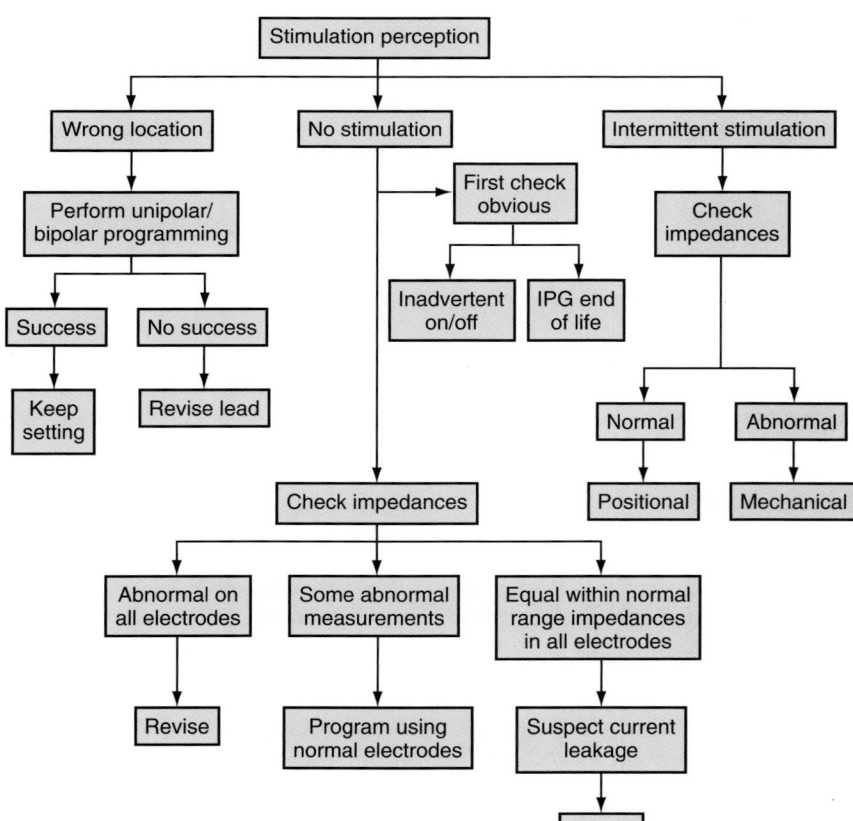

Figure 64–8. Diagnostic algorithm and troubleshooting for recurrent symptoms. IPG, implantable pulse generator.

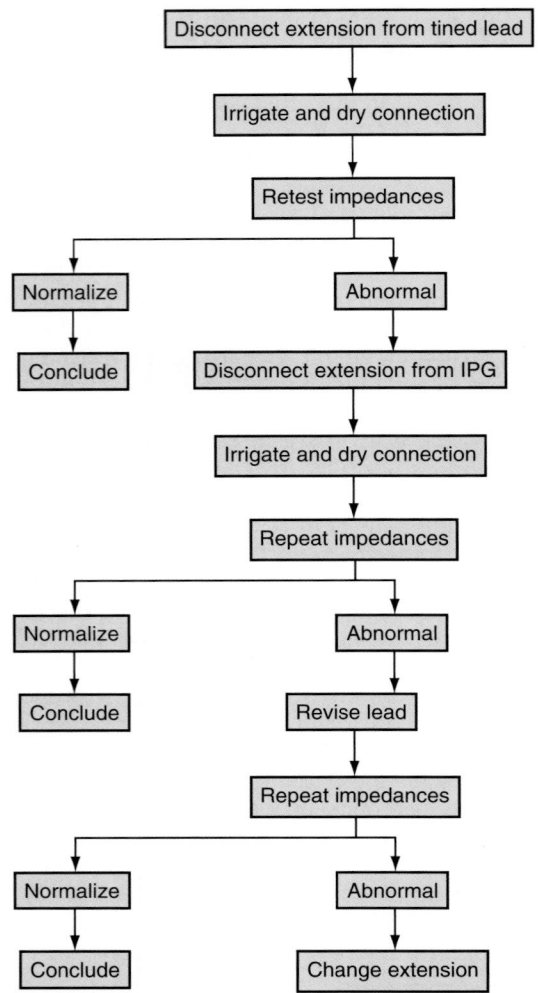

Figure 64–9. Intraoperative algorithm for impedance problem management. IPG, implantable pulse generator.

of impedances by the programmer, **unipolar measurements are most useful for identifying open circuits** because they take one lead wire measurement at a time, immediately identifying which connection or wire has the problem.

Short circuits, which are reflected in **low impedance measurements,** can be caused by body fluid intrusion into the connectors or crushed wires that are touching each other. The electrons will always follow the path of least resistance. Patients may or may not feel stimulation, or stimulation may not be present in the correct area (i.e., the generator site) or may vary in strength (i.e., a surging sensation). In measurement of impedances by the programmer, **bipolar measurements are most useful for identifying shorts between two wires.**

Therefore, impedance measurement is used as a troubleshooting tool to check the integrity of the system when a patient presents with a sudden or gradual disappearance of stimulation. Many measurements fall within the 400- to 1500-ohm range. High levels (>4000 ohms) identify open circuits, and low levels (<50 ohms) identify short circuits. Medtronic Corporation (manufacturer of the InterStim)

recommends performing the impedance measurements at the time of closure of the incision, at the first programming session, to get a baseline measurement and at any time a problem is suspected. These measurements will identify which electrodes, if any, are intact and allow the programmer to proceed with programming of only those with acceptable impedance measurements. If all electrode measurements read above 4000 ohms, a revision may be necessary.

The intraoperative algorithm for management of impedance problems includes initial testing of impedances (see Fig. 64–9). First, the tined lead is disconnected from the extension to the IPG and then dried. The connection may be irrigated with sterile water, and then the connection is dried with the 3-Fr ENT suction device before it is reconnected again. At this stage, the impedances are repeated. If they normalize, one can conclude the revision at this stage. If impedances continue to be abnormal, one can evaluate or change the 10-cm extension and retest impedances. If they continue to be abnormal, the lead is revised. It has been our experience that the connections to the IPG and the IPG itself seldom have anything to do with abnormal impedance values.

Troubleshooting Algorithm

After successful completion of stage II, a number of events can occur, and the treating physician should develop an algorithm to handle these events in a timely and efficient manner. These events with their probable causes and the troubleshooting algorithm are covered in this section.

Pocket (IPG Site) Discomfort. The probable causes of this symptom are pocket related or output related. Pocket-related causes of discomfort include infection, pocket location (waistline), pocket dimension (too tight, too loose), seroma, and erosion. Output-related causes include sensitivity to unipolar stimulation if this mode is used or current leak. To troubleshoot this problem, the evaluating specialist is advised to do the following (Fig. 64–10):

1. Turn off the device and ask the patient if the discomfort is still present to differentiate pocket-related from output-related causes.
2. If the discomfort persists, the cause is not related to the device output. In the absence of clinical signs of infection, pocket-related causes like pocket size, seroma, and erosion must be considered.
3. If the discomfort disappears, device output is probably causing discomfort. If the stimulation program is unipolar, switch to bipolar and see whether that eliminates discomfort. Some patients are sensitive to the unipolar mode of stimulation, as the positive pole is the neurostimulator itself. Another possibility is leakage of fluid into the connector. This somehow creates a short circuit whereby the current from the device now follows this fluid pathway out to the patient's tissue. Most patients report this as a burning sensation. One should keep in mind that even though current is following this fluid out to the patient's tissue, some of the current may also be getting to the electrodes as well, so some patients feel both burning in the pocket and stimulation in the perineum. Try reprogramming around this by using different electrode combinations. If reprogramming is unsuccessful, ask the patient if the "burning" sensation

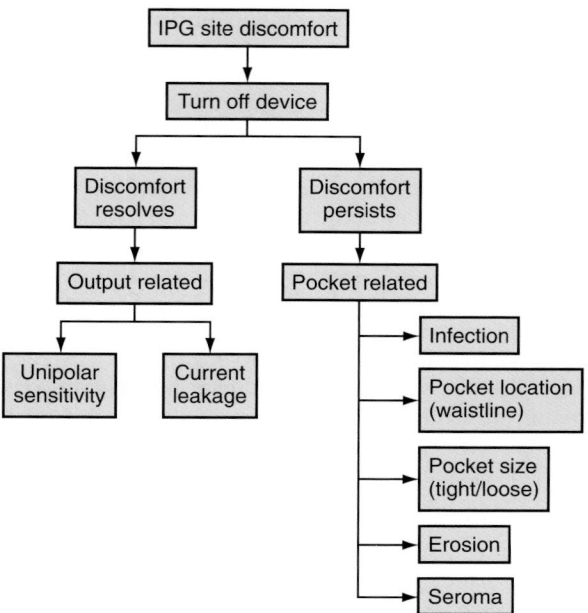

Figure 64–10. Troubleshooting algorithm for IPG site discomfort.

is tolerable (it will not harm the patient's tissues); if it is not tolerable, a revision may be necessary to dry out the connection sites.

Recurrent Symptoms. When the patient presents with recurrent symptoms, one should evaluate the stimulation perception. The possibilities are that the patient perceives the stimulation in a wrong location compared with baseline, has no stimulation, or has intermittent stimulation.

Wrong Location. If the patient reports that the stimulation location or pattern has changed, it is best to go back to each unipolar setting and "map" out where the patient feels the stimulation. Set the device to 0–, case+ and ask the patient where she or he feels the sensation; next set to 1–, case+ and ask the patient again; next set to 2–, case+ and finally 3–, case+. If these combinations do not confirm the target area, start programming bipolar combinations. If those are exhausted, sometimes increasing the pulse width widens the stimulation area. If one has exhausted the programming possibilities, revision for lead repositioning or relocation to the other side may be necessary.

No Stimulation. Check the obvious first. Make sure that the device parameters are set high enough, check for inadvertent on-off (set magnet switch off to avoid inadvertent magnet activations), and check whether the IPG is nearing the end of its life. Next perform impedance readings, paying close attention to unipolar impedances. These impedances measure one lead wire with the case, so it is easy to isolate a problem. Using unipolar impedances, one can tell which lead wires are still intact and which ones are not, as mentioned previously. Proceed with programming of the electrodes with acceptable impedance measurements. Check bipolar measurements to rule out short circuits as well (very low impedance measurements). If programming around the malfunctioning lead does not restore the stimulation, the patient will often need revision.

Intermittent Stimulation. Check for inadvertent on-off again. Intermittent stimulation can be caused by either a loose connection or positional sensitivity. If one suspects a loose connection, palpating the connection site and recreating the intermittency is a good clue as to where the problem lies. Taking impedances while the patient reports the stimulation intermittently determines whether the problem is positional (you still get acceptable impedances) or mechanical (when the patient feels stimulation go off, the impedances are high). With positional sensitivity, the lead position shifts when a patient moves in a certain direction (for instance, the patient reports that the stimulation goes away on standing). The lead position may have moved farther from the nerve during standing, and the amplitude may just need to be increased. Intermittent stimulation represents a challenging dilemma to troubleshoot.

ELECTRICAL STIMULATION FOR EMPTYING DISORDERS

There exists strong evidence to suggest that neuromodulation works through supraspinal pathways (see the section on neurophysiology of electrical stimulation). The question of how it works for refractory detrusor overactivity as well as for urinary retention is based on changes in supraspinal pathways and perhaps the guarding reflex. It is important to understand that before neuromodulation, neurostimulation was applied in different forms to achieve bladder emptying. Still, neurostimulation has a role today in management of disorders of bladder emptying and has evolved through many different versions before its current techniques.

Electrical Stimulation Directly to the Bladder or Spinal Cord

Clinical trials of direct electrical stimulation of the bladder to facilitate emptying originated in 1940 but have met with only partial success and intermittent enthusiasm since then (Wein and Barrett, 1988). **Direct electrical stimulation was most effective in patients with hypotonic and areflexic bladders.** Initial success, defined as low postvoid residual urine volume with sterile urine, was achieved in only 50% to 60% of patients, and **secondary failure often supervened, usually related to fibrosis, electrode malfunction, bladder erosion, or other equipment malfunction. The spread of current to other pelvic structures with a stimulus threshold lower than that of the bladder often resulted in abdominal, pelvic, and perineal pain; a desire to defecate or defecation; contraction of the pelvic and leg muscles; and erection and ejaculation in male patients. It was also noted that the increase in intravesical pressure was generally not coordinated with bladder neck opening or with pelvic floor relaxation and that other measures to accomplish these ends could be necessary.** Direct electrical stimulation of the sacral spinal cord was also performed as an attempt to take advantage of the remaining motor pathways to initiate micturition. Although some short-term success was noted, many of the side effects seen with direct bladder stimulation occurred as well because the stimulus applied in this way was also unphysiologic. **Enthusiasm** for both of these approaches has waned considerably, and resurrection seems unlikely.

Electrical Stimulation to the Nerve Roots

For the past 25 to 30 years, Brindley (1993) and (Tanagho and Schmidt, 1988; Tanagho et al, 1989) have pursued neurostimulation for the treatment of voiding dysfunction. The use of electrical stimulation for storage disorders and pelvic floor dysfunction has been covered. **This section concentrates exclusively on the use of anterior root electrical stimulation to facilitate emptying.**

The Brindley device is the one most commonly used. Prerequisites for such use are described by Madersbacher and Fischer (Fischer et al, 1993) as (1) intact neural pathways between the sacral cord nuclei of the pelvic nerve and the bladder and (2) a bladder that is capable of contracting. The chief applications are in patients with inefficient or nonreflex micturition after spinal cord injury. Simultaneous bladder and striated sphincter stimulation is obviated by sacral posterior rhizotomy, usually complete, which

eliminates reflex incontinence and improves low bladder compliance, if it is present (Brindley, 1994). The stimulation sequences and parameters themselves and their neurophysiologic consequences lead to less striated sphincter dyssynergia, even without posterior rhizotomy, than is seen in reflex micturition in a spinal cord–injured patient. Complete sacral deafferentation is usually performed, however, with the exception listed by Brindley as those patients who have genital sensation or useful reflex erections. **Electrodes are applied intradurally** to S2, S3, and S4 nerve roots, but the pairs can be activated independently (Fig. 64–11). **The detrusor is usually innervated primarily by S3 and to a smaller extent by S2 or S4. Rectal stimulation is by means of all three roots equally. Erectile stimulation is chiefly by S2 with a small contribution from S3 and none from S4.** Micturition, defecation, and erection programs are possible, with stimulus patterns set specifically for each patient (Brindley, 1994). The ventral sacral roots, however, carry both parasympathetic fibers to the bladder and somatic fibers to the striated sphincter. Ventral root stimulation therefore occasionally results in detrusor–striated sphincter dyssynergia.

The current Brindley stimulator uses the principle of post-stimulus voiding, a term first introduced by Jonas and

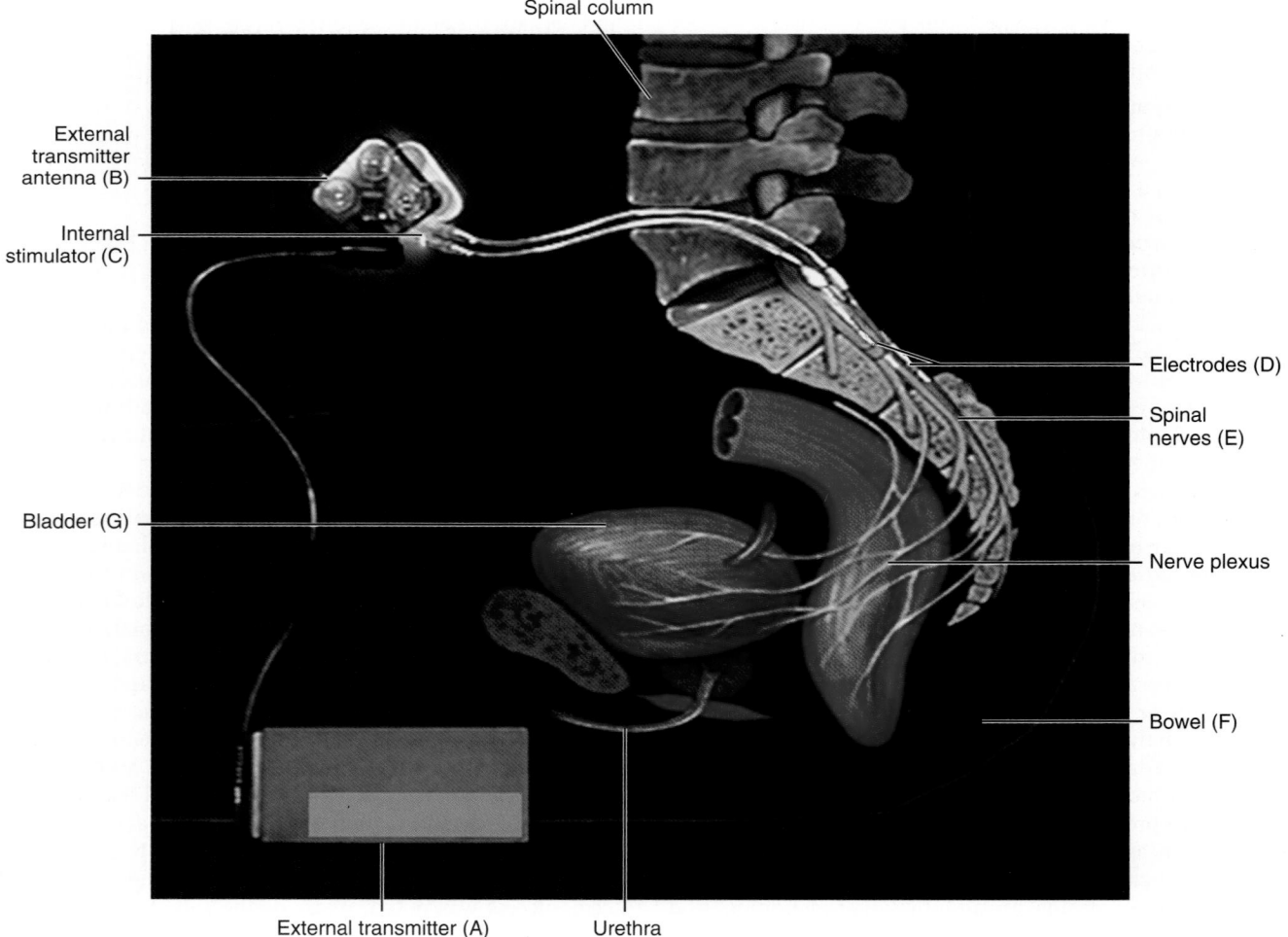

Spinal column

External transmitter antenna (B)

Internal stimulator (C)

Bladder (G)

Electrodes (D)

Spinal nerves (E)

Nerve plexus

Bowel (F)

External transmitter (A)   Urethra

Figure 64–11. Brindley-Finetech system for sacral root stimulation. (Courtesy of NDI Medical.)

Tanagho (1975) **to obviate this. Relaxation time of the striated sphincter after a stimulus train is shorter than the relaxation time of the detrusor smooth muscle. When interrupted pulse trains are used, voiding is achieved between the pulse trains because of the sustained high intravesical pressure.** This concept and other methods that are available to overcome the stimulation-induced sphincter dyssynergia and allow low-pressure emptying are nicely reviewed by Rijkhoff and colleagues (1997). **Post-stimulus voiding has a few shortcomings, described in this article as follows: voiding occurs in spurts at above-normal bladder pressures; when the stimulus parameters are not properly adjusted, the detrusor pressures can become too high, putting the upper tracts at risk; and movement of the lower limbs occurs during stimulation because the nerve roots also contain fibers innervating leg musculature, and this movement can be cumbersome for the patient.**

Brindley (1994) carefully reviewed the experience in the first 500 patients treated with his prosthesis with a total follow-up, at that time, of 2033.5 years. Of the total, 2 patients were lost to follow-up and 21 had died. Of the deaths, two were from septicemia (one definitely unrelated to the implant and the specifics of the other unmentioned) and one from related renal failure; the causes of five were unknown. Ninety-five reoperations were required for repair, six stimulators were removed (four infected), and two were awaiting repair. In 45 patients, the stimulator was believed to be intact but not used for various reasons. In all others, the stimulators were in use (411 for micturition and in most for defecation, and in 13 for defecation alone), and the users were believed to be "pleased." Upper tract deterioration was reported in only 2 of 365 patients with full deafferentation and in 10 of 135 with incomplete or no deafferentation. Two of these 10 had impaired renal function, and one died of this.

van Kerrebroeck and associates (1997) reported the results of use of the Finetech-Brindley stimulator in 52 patients. These patients were selected by screening 226 patients; complete posterior sacral root rhizotomies were performed in all. Thirty-seven of the patients had 6 months of follow-up; in these patients, complete daytime continence was achieved in 73% and nighttime continence in 86%. There were significant increases in bladder capacity and bladder compliance, and residual urine was reduced significantly. Complications included 23 patients with cerebrospinal fluid leaks, which resolved spontaneously; nerve damage that resolved in one patient; and one implant failure caused by a cable fracture, successfully repaired. Sauerwein and colleagues (2000) reported in abstract form the results of sacral deafferentation and implantation of an anterior sacral root stimulator in 294 patients with spinal cord injury. Bladder spasticity was relieved in all. In 50%, micturition was achieved by stimulating S4 and S5 sacral ventral roots; in the remaining cases, it was achieved by stimulating the S2 and S3 roots. **Variations in surgical approaches designed to achieve stimulation of only bladder contraction are described by Dahms and associates (2000), who also summarize overall success rates for sacral ventral root stimulation in spinal cord–injured patients at about 75%.**

Extradural stimulation has been used by the Tanagho group (Tanagho and Schmidt, 1988; Tanagho et al, 1989; Schmidt, 1989) in the treatment of 19 patients with serious

and refractory neuropathic voiding disorders. Extensive dorsal rhizotomy was performed, and a stimulator was implanted on the ventral component of S3 or S4 with selective peripheral neurotomy (Tanagho et al, 1989). In eight patients (42%), complete success was achieved with reservoir function, continence, and low-pressure/low residual voiding with electrical stimulation. Ten patients qualified as achieving partial success, regaining reservoir function and obtaining continence.

Electrical stimulation of the ventral sacral roots with some techniques to reduce detrusor hyperactivity and obviate striated sphincter dyssynergia has become an accepted treatment modality for lower urinary tract dysfunction in spinal cord–injured patients. Although more detailed follow-up is necessary, and further evolution will doubtless occur, these techniques have achieved remarkable improvements and success rates, which now seem to have stabilized at a high level.

Transurethral Electrical Bladder Stimulation

Intravesical electrotherapy is an old technique that has been resurrected with some interesting and promising results. The use of this technique to increase bladder capacity and to increase compliance has previously been discussed. This section deals with the use of TEBS **to facilitate bladder emptying by establishing conscious control of the initiation and completion of a micturition reflex.** Fischer and colleagues (1993) describe their concept of the basis for this use as follows. **In patients with incomplete central or peripheral nerve lesions**—and only these patients are suitable for this method—**at least some nerve pathways between the bladder and the cerebral centers are preserved but are too weak to be efficient under normal circumstances. TEBS in this situation is hypothesized to activate specific mechanoreceptors in the bladder wall.** With depolarization of these receptors, activation of the intramural motor system is said to occur, resulting in small local muscle contractions that further depolarize the receptor cells. As soon as this local motor reaction reaches a certain strength, "vegetative afferentation" begins, meaning that stimuli travel along afferent pathways to the corresponding cerebral structures with the occurrence of sensation. This, in time, reinforces efferent pathways, and their stimuli create centrally induced and more coordinated and stronger detrusor contractions. **Ebner and coworkers (1992) simply conceptualize the mechanism as involving an artificial activation of the normal micturition reflex and further suggest that repeated activation of this pathway may "upgrade" its performance during voluntary micturition.**

Children with congenital neurogenic bladder dysfunction who have never experienced the urge to void require a biofeedback system to realize the nature and meaning of this new sensation induced by TEBS. This exteroceptive stimulation is also important for other groups of patients because it signals detrusor contractions and whether and to what degree voluntary detrusor control is or has become possible and, by demonstrating progress, serves as positive feedback.

This technique involves direct intraluminal monopolar electrical stimulation with a special catheter equipped with a stimulation electrode. Saline solution is used as the current-leading fluid medium in the bladder. Exteroceptive reinforcement is achieved by visual recording of detrusor contractions on a water manometer connected to the stimulation catheter. An intensive bladder training program has to be combined with TEBS and must be highly individualized. **Only patients with an incomplete spinal cord lesion and with receptors still capable of reactivity and with a detrusor still capable of contractility will benefit from this technique. The achievement of conscious control requires, in addition, an intact cortex.**

Fischer and colleagues (1993) have used this technique in patients with incomplete spinal cord injury and other incomplete central or peripheral lesions of bladder innervation, in pediatric patients with congenital neurogenic lower urinary tract dysfunction, and in patients, especially children, with non-neurogenic dysfunction voiding. Only patients with preserved pain sensation in sacral dermatomes S2 through S4 improved with this technique. The technique is time-consuming because stimulation must be performed on a daily basis for weeks and months, with an individual treatment time of about 90 minutes. Kaplan and Richards (1988) reported on such therapy in myelodysplastic children, carrying out the treatment for 60 minutes (during a 90-minute catheterization), 3 to 5 days a week for 15 to 30 daily sessions. Of 62 patients evaluated, 42 completed at least one series of treatment. "Success" was defined differently for infants than for older children. For infants, this term implied a decrease in filling pressure, an increase in the quality of bladder contraction, and a decrease in residual urine. For older children, this type of result implied a heightened awareness of detrusor contractions before and during a contraction, maintenance of low-pressure filling, effectively emptying detrusor contractions with low residual, and either a conscious urinary control or timely enough sensory input to allow clean intermittent catheterization for continence. Of children who initially had some detrusor contraction on initial evaluation, 80% were said to have achieved some or all of the success parameters. Of those with no initial detrusor activity, 33% achieved some success.

Other reports have been less optimistic. Lyne and Bellinger (1993) **reported the results of TEBS treatment of 17 patients with neurologic dysfunction, 10 with myelomeningocele, and 2 with lipomeningocele. Ultimately, all patients showed detrusor contraction during therapy (12 did so initially), but results related to increased bladder capacity and improved continence were disappointing. Five patients showed minor positive changes in continence. After completion of therapy in 12 patients who had serial cystometry, 5 experienced an increase in capacity (14% to 158%) and 4 a decrease (7% to 37%).** Decter and associates (1994) used TEBS in 25 patients with neurogenic voiding dysfunction. TEBS was correlated with an increase from 18 to 24 in the number of patients who manifested contraction on stimulation and from 3 to 12 in the number who sensed contraction during stimulation. However, cystometry showed a more than 20% increase in the age-adjusted bladder capacity in only 6 of 18 patients with serial studies and clinically significant improvements in end-filling pressures in 5 of these. A telephone questionnaire revealed that 10 of 18 patients or parents perceived an improvement in bladder function, but the authors stated that "the limited urodynamic benefits our patients achieved have not materially altered the daily voiding regimen and, because of these factors, we are not enrolling any new patients in our . . . program." **This technique is certainly controversial.** Some question the theoretical basis and the definitions of "success" applied to patients treated. **Currently, even Kaplan (2000) does not seem enthusiastic about the use of this technique to attain the goal of volitional voiding, and Decter (2000), as previously pointed out, stated that in his opinion, TEBS is a modality with limited clinical efficacy for facilitation of filling-storage and emptying.**

Sacral Neuromodulation of Emptying Disorders

Sacral neuromodulation has been successful in patients with idiopathic nonobstructive retention, in patients with retention secondary to deafferentation of the bladder after hysterectomy, and in patients with Fowler's syndrome (Dasgupta et al, 2004). Patient factors predictive of success have been sought. Bross and coworkers (2003) evaluated the predictive ability of the carbachol test and concomitant diseases in patients with an acontractile bladder. Eighteen patients were subcutaneously injected with 0.25 µM of carbachol. A rise in detrusor pressure to more than 20 cm within 20 to 30 minutes after injection was considered a positive test result. Only 33% of patients had a successful bilateral percutaneous nerve evaluation, but a positive carbachol test result was not predictive of success. Percutaneous nerve evaluation appeared particularly effective in patients who developed retention after hysterectomy.

A large, prospective, randomized multicenter trial to evaluate the efficacy of SNS for urinary retention was performed by Jonas and colleagues (2001). After a percutaneous nerve evaluation period of 3 to 7 days, 68 patients (38% of those evaluated) with chronic urinary retention qualified for permanent implantation. Patients were randomly assigned to the treatment or control group in which treatment was delayed for 6 months. Successful results were initially achieved in 83% of patients who received the implant, with 69% able to discontinue intermittent catheterization completely. At 18 months, 71% of patients available for follow-up had sustained improvement.

Aboseif and coworkers (2002) evaluated the efficacy and change in quality of life in patients with idiopathic, chronic, nonobstructive functional urinary retention. Thirty-two patients with idiopathic retention requiring intermittent catheterization underwent percutaneous nerve evaluation. Permanent implants were placed in 20 patients (17 women) who showed more than 50% improvement in symptoms. Eighteen patients were subsequently able to void and no longer required intermittent catheterization; one patient required bilateral SNS implants. Average voided volumes increased from 48 mL to 198 mL, and postvoid residual volume decreased from 315 mL to 60 mL. Eighteen patients reported more than 50% improvement in quality of life, although the questionnaire used in the study was not described. Significant score improvements in the Beck Depression Inventory and SF-36 after sacral root neuromodulation for retention have been demonstrated by Shaker and Hassouna (1998). **Overall success rates of the percutaneous**

nerve evaluation range from 33.3% to 100% (Koldewijn 1994; Scheepens et al, 2002; Spinelli et al, 2003). Improvement in patients with retention may not be as rapid as in patients undergoing sacral root stimulation for other reasons. A percutaneous nerve evaluation period of at least 2 to 3 weeks and a permanent implant lead evaluation of 4 weeks or more have generally been recommended. **Furthermore, bilateral SNS for urinary retention may be considered initially or for unilateral SNS trial failures, although this technique is performed infrequently and is less studied to date** (Scheepens et al, 2002).

FUTURE RESEARCH AND CONCLUSIONS

During the last century, neurostimulation and neuromodulation that originated in the 19th century have been clinically adopted. Advances in electrical innovations and our understanding of neurophysiology have provided important discoveries for the care of people with neuromuscular causes of their pelvic organ dysfunctions. To date, influencing these dysfunctions at the level of the sacral roots appears to have stood the test of time and has become generalizable to physicians worldwide. At the start of our next century of using this expanding therapy, we will need to urgently focus on developing the supportive clinical research needed to drive further innovations and acceptance of wider clinical indications and applications. Long-term surveillance studies and randomized clinical trials to compare different techniques and nerve locations and to evaluate placebo effects are critically needed, as are more studies to elucidate modes of action to improve stimulation applications, selection of patients, and therapeutic results.

The introduction of new stimulation methods as well as application of these methods to different nerve locations will continue to provide improved treatment alternatives. In addition, these innovations will provide the ability to further develop testable hypotheses of more basic questions on electrical neurostimulation, neuromodulation, and neurophysiology of the autonomic, somatic, and central pathways that regulate pelvic organ function. Such questions need to address the observed lack of neural plasticity–induced changes with long-term neuromodulation and neurostimulation despite acute cellular changes identified in nerve signaling molecules secondary to magnetic and electrical field changes.

In their present form, neurostimulation and neuromodulation work acutely through continuous electrical activity without inducing long-term neuroplastic changes. Therefore, future technologies are likely to provide closed-loop conditional stimulation, much in the same manner as "on-demand" cardiac pacemakers and defibrillators do, as a means to obtain better efficacy without additional adverse electric field effects. The development of change from the present open-loop stimulation to closed-loop conditional stimulation will necessitate innovations in neurosensing of pathologic neuromuscular events of the pelvis that will lead to on-demand therapeutic electrical activity. These innovations will in turn have a profound effect on our diagnostic ability to predict clinical responses to neurostimulation and neuromodulation as we seek to maximize our benefit/risk and benefit/cost ratios in patient care.

> ## KEY POINTS: ELECTRICAL STIMULATION
>
> - Neuromodulation is a field clearly in its infancy.
>
> - Current techniques of sacral neuromodulation are indicated for treatment of refractory urgency-frequency, urge incontinence, and nonobstructive urinary retention.
>
> - Sacral neuromodulation has yielded successful stage I to stage II conversion rates based on 50% symptom improvement in more than 60% of patients for urge-frequency and urge incontinence.
>
> - The exact best nerves to stimulate have yet to be realized, but data seem to be focusing on more selective nerve stimulation, particularly in complex subgroups such as patients with neurogenic bladders.
>
> - Transurethral electrical stimulation has fallen out of favor for the most part.
>
> - Transcutaneous electrical stimulation, although demonstrating good efficacy, seems to have a more limited role because of the constant need to administer the therapy.
>
> - Expanding indications for neuromodulation are likely to dominate the literature in the coming years as comfort with neuromodulation increases and more challenging subgroups are addressed.

Acknowledgment

The authors acknowledge assistance from Dr. Ashwin Vaze and Ms. Natalie Butler for their help in preparation of this chapter.

SUGGESTED READINGS

Brindley GS: Emptying the bladder by stimulating sacral ventral roots. J Physiol 1974;237:15P-16P.

Chancellor MB, Chartier-Kastler E: Principles of sacral nerve stimulation (SNS) for the treatment of bladder and urethral sphincter dysfunctions. Neuromodulation 2000;3:15-26.

Hassouna MM, Siegel SW, Nyeholt AA, et al: Sacral neuromodulation in the treatment of urgency-frequency symptoms: A multicenter study on efficacy and safety. J Urol 2000;163:1849-1854.

Leng WW, Chancellor MB: How sacral nerve stimulation neuromodulation works. Urol Clin North Am 2005;32:11-18.

Siegel SW, Catanzaro F, Dijkema HE, et al: Long-term results of a multicenter study on sacral nerve stimulation for treatment of urinary urge incontinence, urgency-frequency, and retention. Urology 2000;56(suppl 1): 87-91.

Tanagho EA, Schmidt RA: Bladder pacemaker: Scientific basis and clinical future. Urology 1982;20:614-619.

Tanagho EA, Schmidt RA: Electrical stimulation in the clinical management of the neurogenic bladder. J Urol 1988;140:1331.

Wein AJ, Barrett DM: Voiding Function and Dysfunction—A Logical and Practical Approach. Chicago, Year Book, 1988.

Yoshimura N, de Groat WS: Neural control of the lower urinary tract. Int J Urol 1997;4:111.

Retropubic Suspension Surgery for Incontinence in Women

C. R. CHAPPLE, BSc, MD, FRCS (Urol)

Continence in the woman results from a complex interplay of the normal anatomic and physiologic properties of the bladder, urethra and sphincter, and pelvic floor acting under the coordinating control of an intact central and peripheral nervous system. The role of the pelvic floor is to provide support to both the bladder and urethra and to facilitate normal abdominal pressure transmission to the proximal urethra, thereby maintaining continence. There are different types of urinary incontinence, and the pathogenesis of incontinence is considered in detail elsewhere in this publication; but suffice it to say that it can be consequent to disorders of bladder, urethra, or pelvic floor, resulting from nerve damage or direct trauma. Stress incontinence is the symptom of involuntary loss of urine during situations of increased intra-abdominal pressure, such as coughing and sneezing. The International Continence Society defines urodynamic stress incontinence as the involuntary loss of urine during increased intra-abdominal pressure during filling cystometry, in the absence of detrusor (bladder wall muscle) contraction (Abrams et al, 2002). Thus, urodynamic evaluation is a prerequisite for the diagnosis of urodynamic stress incontinence. Therefore, in discussing stress incontinence, this review refers to women with stress urinary incontinence (SUI) diagnosed on the basis of symptoms alone or urodynamically proven, so-called urodynamic stress incontinence.

Treatment options for SUI include conservative techniques and both pharmacologic and surgical interventions. Surgical procedures to treat SUI generally aim to improve the support to the urethrovesical junction and to correct deficient urethral closure. There is a contemporary lack of consensus, however, regarding the precise mechanism by which continence is achieved in the "normal asymptomatic female" and therefore not surprisingly in how "normality" is restored by surgical manipulation. Anti-incontinence surgery is generally used to address the failure of normal anatomic support of the bladder neck and proximal urethra and intrinsic sphincter deficiency. **Anti-incontinence surgery does not necessarily work by restoring the same mechanism of continence that was present before the onset of incontinence. Rather, it works by a compensatory approach, creating a new mechanism of continence** (Jarvis, 1994a).

THERAPEUTIC OPTIONS

The surgeon's preference, coexisting problems, and anatomic features of the patient and her general health condition influence the choice of procedure. Numerous surgical methods have been described, but they essentially fall into seven categories (Table 65–1).

This wide variety of treatment options for stress incontinence indicates the lack of a clear consensus as to which procedure is the most effective. Several groups have reviewed the literature, often using systematic and methodical analyses of well-designed randomized controlled trials (Jarvis, 1994b; Black and Downs, 1996; Fantl et al, 1996; Leach et al, 1997;

Table 65–1.	**Surgical Methods**

Open retropubic colposuspension
Laparoscopic retropubic colposuspension
Suburethral sling procedure
Needle suspension
Periurethral injection
Artificial sphincter
Vaginal anterior repair (anterior colporrhaphy)

Table 65–2.	**Standardization Needed for Studies**

The patients under study (with regard to age, history of prior surgery, body mass)
The nature of the surgical technique, taking account of the surgeon's experience
Outcome measures and follow-up

Lapitan et al, 2003; Moehrer et al, 2000, 2003). **Most of these reviews, however, are hampered by the quality of the existing evidence base, and these reviews are based on studies of mixed quality with little standardization of the points in Table 65–2.**

A review of existing literature on confounding variables affecting outcome of therapy (Smith et al, 2005) concluded the following.

1. **Age may not be a contraindication to colposuspension,** with equivalent success rates in the elderly at long-term follow-up (Gillon and Stanton, 1984; Tamussino et al, 1999), although others reported less success with increasing age (Chilaka et al, 2002; Langer et al, 2001). Smith and associates (2005), from their review of the literature, concluded that there is level 3 evidence that older women respond to continence surgery as well as younger women do, although a decrement in satisfactory outcome cannot be ruled out. There is similar level evidence that the association of age with poorer outcomes has to do with other factors, such as urethral pressure.

2. The influence of the level of postoperative activity has been inadequately studied, so that no recommendations can be made (Smith et al, 2005).

3. There is level 4 evidence that medical comorbidity may have an impact on surgical outcomes, depending on the outcomes selected. There is level 3 evidence that psychological factors have an impact on subjective and objective outcomes in different ways (Smith et al, 2005).

4. **Obesity as a confounding variable is the subject of conflicting evidence in the literature and has not been studied in a prospective fashion.** Some studies have suggested increased failure rates in obese patients undergoing retropubic colposuspension (Brieger and Korda, 1992; Alcalay et al, 1995). Conversely, in a retrospective study of 198 women undergoing anti-incontinence surgery, cure rates were markedly better in those undergoing Burch colposuspension (Zivkovic et al, 1999).

5. **Surgery for recurrent stress incontinence has a lower success rate.** One study has reported that Burch colposuspension has an 81% success rate after one previous surgical procedure has failed, but this drops to 25% after two previous repairs and to 0% after three previous operations (Petrou and Frank, 2001). Other series report excellent results for colposuspension carried out after prior failed surgery. Maher and colleagues (1999) and Cardozo and associates (1999) have shown good objective (72% and 79%) and subjective (89% and 80%) success rates with repeated colposuspension at a mean follow-up of 9 months. Nitahara and coworkers (1999) reported a 69% subjective success at a mean follow-up of 6.9 years.

6. Berglund and associates (1996) reported that the duration of symptoms is a predictor of outcome, with a better response in those with a shorter history, which as a finding was independent of type of approach (e.g., vaginal versus retropubic). Ward and Hilton (2002), in a randomized comparison of colposuspension and tension-free vaginal tape, found no significant impact of symptom severity on outcomes for either procedure. Tamussino and coworkers (1999), in a review of 327 women assessed a minimum of 5 years postoperatively, noted that women with moderate or severe incontinence fared worse than those with milder symptoms. In their series, only Burch colposuspension was unaffected by the severity of preoperative symptoms.

7. It has been reported that as many as 23% of women undergoing urodynamics have mixed urodynamic stress incontinence and detrusor overactivity (Clarke, 1997). In a retrospective cohort study, Colombo and associates (1996b) compared 44 women with mixed incontinence with a matched group with urodynamic stress incontinence. The cure rate was 95% in the latter group compared with 75% in the former. Other studies report a less favorable outcome of 24% to 43% in those with detrusor overactivity combined with stress incontinence (Stanton et al, 1978; Milani et al, 1985; Lose et al, 1988).

8. The International Consultation on Incontinence, although allowing the fact that there is no consensus on the definition of intrinsic sphincter deficiency, concluded that there are no adequate evidence-based data to support that intrinsic sphincter deficiency influences either the outcomes of surgery or the type of surgical treatment (Smith et al, 2005).

CHOICE OF SURGICAL TECHNIQUE

Two types of stress incontinence have been suggested: one associated with a hypermobile but otherwise healthy urethra, a manifestation of weakened support of the proximal urethra; and one arising from a deficiency of the urethral sphincter mechanism itself, thereby compromising the ability of the urethra to act as a watertight outlet. **Hypermobility of the bladder neck and proximal urethra results from a weakening or loss of their supporting elements (ligaments, fasciae, and muscles), which in turn may be a consequence of aging, hormonal changes, childbirth, and prior surgery. It seems likely that the majority of women with SUI will also have an element of intrinsic sphincteric weakness with a variable degree of loss of the normal anatomic support of the bladder neck and proximal urethra, resulting in hypermobility. The compelling observation that one can cite for this is that a normal individual will not leak however much she strains.**

Differentiating Relative Contributions of Hypermobility and Intrinsic Sphincter Deficiency

A standardized test is not available to differentiate the relative contributions of intrinsic sphincter deficiency and hypermobility, and therefore few studies have been able to accurately separate their individual contributions to the development of incontinence (Chapple et al, 2005). Retropubic procedures act to restore the bladder neck and proximal urethra to a fixed, retropubic position and are used when hypermobility is thought to be an important factor in the development of that woman's stress incontinence. This may facilitate the function of a marginally compromised intrinsic urethral sphincter mechanism, but if significant intrinsic sphincter deficiency is present, SUI will persist despite efficient surgical repositioning of the bladder neck and proximal urethra.

In the normal continent woman, the bladder neck and proximal urethra are supported in a retropubic position, with the bladder base being dependent. Increases in intra-abdominal pressure are transmitted to both the bladder and the proximal urethra such that the pressure difference between the two is unchanged, promoting continence (Einhorning, 1961). A valvular effect at the bladder neck created by the transmission of abdominal pressure to the dependent bladder base may also be operative here (Penson and Raz, 1996). Furthermore, with proper bladder neck support, reflex contraction of the pelvic floor muscles during Valsalva maneuvers and coughing acts as a backboard for urethral compression (Staskin et al, 1985).

Surgical Procedures

This review deals with retropubic surgical procedures, usually chosen as surgical therapy for patients with stress incontinence in which there is a significant component of hypermobility.

Open retropubic colposuspension is the surgical approach of lifting the tissues near the bladder neck and proximal urethra into the area of the pelvis behind the anterior pubic bones. When it is an open procedure, the approach is through an incision over the lower abdomen. There are four variations of open retropubic colposuspension: Marshall-Marchetti-Krantz (MMK), Burch, vagino-obturator shelf (VOS), and paravaginal.

The term *colposuspension* was originally used to denote suspension of the urethra by the vaginal wall; however, by common usage, it now generally includes the paraurethral fascia and sometimes only this without the vagina. Retropubic colposuspension urethral repositioning can be achieved by three distinctly different procedures; these are all based on a similar underlying principle, but in a spectrum in relation to the degree of the support-elevation they achieve, and their outcomes differ somewhat in the longer term.

The Burch colposuspension (Fig. 65–1A) is the elevation of the anterior vaginal wall and paravesical tissues toward the iliopectineal line of the pelvic sidewall with use of two to four sutures on either side (Burch, 1961). The VOS repair (Fig. 65–1B) aims to anchor the vagina to the internal obturator fascia and is a modification of a combination of the Burch and

paravaginal defect repair, with placement of the sutures laterally anchored to the internal obturator fascia rather than hitching the vagina up to the iliopectineal line (Turner-Warwick, 1986), although a more recent modification does, where appropriate, insert stitches into both the internal obturator and iliopectineal line (Fig. 65–1C). The paravaginal defect repair (Fig. 65–1D) aims to close a presumed fascial weakness laterally at the site of attachment of the pelvic fascia to internal obturator fascia (Richardson et al, 1976). The MMK procedure (Fig. 65–1E) is the suspension of the vesicourethral junction (bladder neck) toward the periosteum of the symphysis pubis (Marshall et al, 1949) and was thought to act by buttressing the paraurethral area and bringing the vesicourethral junction into a more elevated "intra-abdominal" position.

The Degree of Urethral Elevation

The extent of the urethral elevation achieved by both the Burch (see Fig. 65–1A) and the VOS suspensions (see Fig. 65–1B and C) is higher than the arcus tendineus anchorage of the paravaginal defect repair (see Fig. 65–1D).

The Configuration of the Suspensions

A particular advantage of the horizontal urethral elevation achieved by both the VOS and the paravaginal repair suspensions is the significantly less susceptibility to tension on the urethra and to obstructive problems than with the V-shaped configuration of the Burch suspension (see Fig. 65–1A).

Tissue Approximation

Both the VOS and the paravaginal repair suspensions are anchored by tissue-approximating sutures; thus, unlike the Burch procedure, neither the VOS nor the paravaginal repair suspension is suture dependent in the longer term once the initial healing is complete because there is direct tissue adhesion. The VOS anchorage and suspension is significantly more robust than that of the paravaginal defect repair; the elevation it achieves can be further augmented by additionally including the iliopectineal ligament in the upper sutures (see Fig. 65–1C).

Laparoscopic colposuspension is the most popular of the laparoscopic incontinence procedures that were first introduced in the early 1990s (Vancaillie and Schuessler, 1991) with the premise that as minimally invasive procedures, they would benefit patients by avoiding the major incision of conventional open surgery and shorten the time for a return to normal activity. As in open colposuspension, sutures are inserted into the paravaginal tissues on either side of the bladder neck and then attached to the iliopectineal ligaments on the same side. There are, however, technical variations in surgery with respect to the laparoscopic approach (transperitoneal into the abdominal cavity or extraperitoneal) and in the number and types of sutures, the site of anchor, and the use of mesh and staples (Jarvis et al, 1999).

ASSESSING OUTCOMES OF THERAPY

Before the best procedure is determined, several issues regarding outcome reporting need to be addressed.

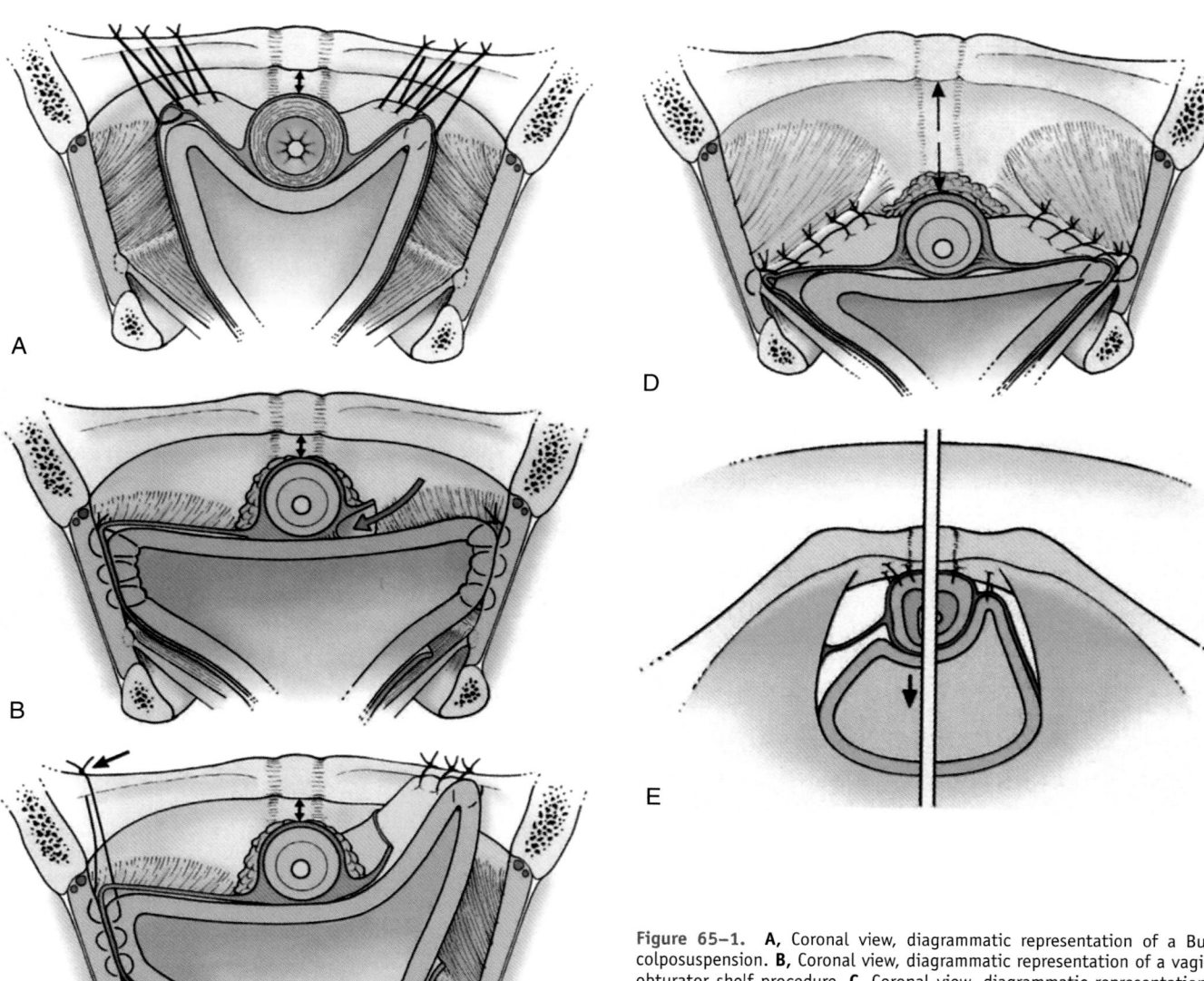

Figure 65–1. **A,** Coronal view, diagrammatic representation of a Burch colposuspension. **B,** Coronal view, diagrammatic representation of a vagino-obturator shelf procedure. **C,** Coronal view, diagrammatic representation of a vagino-obturator shelf procedure on the left, augmented by stitching to the iliopectineal line, and a Burch procedure on the right. **D,** Coronal view, diagrammatic representation of a paravaginal repair. **E,** Diagram demonstrating the sutures in a Marshall-Marchetti-Krantz procedure and their proximity to the urethra.

Duration of Follow-up

It is recognized that prolonged follow-up is required to assess the true benefit of an incontinence procedure. **Short-term follow-up should be considered to have begun in all studies after participants have reached 1 year of follow-up** (Abrams et al, 2005). In the short term (2 years), most procedures are successful, and success rates between procedures are similar (Leach et al, 1997). However, with longer follow-up (>5 years), failures become manifest, and the true benefit of the better procedures is realized. Most studies report outcomes after

short-term follow-up, and thus results must be interpreted with caution.

The Issue of Intrinsic Sphincter Deficiency

There are no data in the literature to support that intrinsic sphincter deficiency can influence either the outcomes or the type of surgical treatment. The main problem is that there is no uniform consensus on the meaning of intrinsic

sphincter deficiency and how to diagnose it (Smith et al, 2005).

The Definition of Cure

The definition of cure varies between studies. Some authors report cure of SUI only, whereas others define cure as complete continence postoperatively, implying the absence of urge incontinence as well. The assessment of cure may vary. Some authors report subjective cure based on patient history, questionnaire, bladder diary, or medical chart review; others use more objective measures, such as pad tests, stress tests, and urodynamics.

Finally, one must question whether the goal of complete continence is reasonable, given that the condition of SUI is generally a degenerative one and corrective surgery does not replace the defective components. As well, **even in normal healthy women, urinary continence is a spectrum of dryness; approximately 40% of nulliparous 30- to 49-year-olds experience some degree of incontinence with exercise** (Nygaard et al, 1990). It seems unreasonable to expect surgery for a degenerative condition to achieve results that are better than the nondegenerative state.

The Patient's versus the Physician's Perspective

A patient's satisfaction with treatment is often based on the difference between her expectations and her experiences (Sofaer and Firminger, 2005). Thus, fulfillment of positive expectations is a key element of a patient's satisfaction (Sitzia and Wood, 1997). Because expectations vary widely, satisfaction is not a standard concept. Consequently, treatment plans must be tailored to meet a nonstandard goal. An integral step in achieving this goal is the development of a patient-physician partnership that promotes the negotiation of realistic expectations.

Logically, agreement of patient and physician with respect to treatment plan and goals should improve outcomes. When a diagnosis has been made, asking patients what they already know about the condition may give clues to expectations for treatment. The "ask-tell-ask" method may be employed to mend the gaps between the physician's and the patient's expectations. The physician explains the proposed treatment plan and expectations for the outcome, then encourages the patient to ask questions. The physician provides the information requested and invites questions again, continuing the process until a mutual understanding of treatments and expectations is reached (Barrier et al, 2003). This approach may prevent "surprises" such as unexpected pain of treatment, adverse events of medication, and prolonged recovery time. Elkadry and associates (2003) emphasized this point by demonstrating a significant association between feeling unprepared for surgery and the patient's dissatisfaction after pelvic reconstruction. The same investigators also reported that achievement of patient-defined goals was more predictive of a patient's satisfaction than were objective measures of surgical success.

Clearly, one or more high-quality validated symptom and quality of life instruments should be chosen at the outset of a clinical trial representing the patient's viewpoint, accurately defining baseline symptoms as well as any other areas in which treatment may be beneficial, and assessing the objective severity and subjective impact of both. **Whereas many, including the author, think that urodynamic studies are helpful in defining the underlying pathophysiologic process in cases with incontinence, they have not been proved to have adequate sensitivity, specificity, or predictive value** (Chapple et al, 2005). **The International Consultation on Incontinence (ICI) meeting concluded that although urodynamic studies, such as frequency-volume charts and pad tests, are useful, there is inadequate evidence to justify pressure-flow studies for routine testing as either entry criteria or outcome measures in clinical trials. They recommended that most large-scale clinical trials enroll subjects by carefully defined symptom-driven criteria when the treatment will be given on an empirical basis** (Abrams et al, 2005).

INDICATIONS FOR RETROPUBIC REPAIR

The treatment of SUI in women must be tailored to the individual patient. Once evaluation has identified contributing factors, a trial of conservative therapy should be pursued and surgery considered for patients who fail to respond to this. Careful assessment of the patient is essential in making an accurate diagnosis (Fig. 65–2).

The selection of technique is largely based on the surgeon's preference and prior experience; bladder base and urethral hypermobility may be surgically corrected by either a vaginal or a retropubic approach. Although it has been suggested that a retropubic colposuspension should be considered in patients who frequently generate high intra-abdominal pressure (e.g., those with chronic cough from obstructive pulmonary disease and women in strenuous occupations) (Appell, 1993), it could also be argued that these patients may be better served by a pubovaginal sling as well.

Specific Indications

A retropubic approach for the correction of anatomic SUI is indicated (1) for a patient undergoing a laparotomy for concomitant abdominal surgery that cannot be performed vaginally and (2) where there is limited vaginal access.

Potential Contraindications

If there is a history of prior failed incontinence procedures, the existence of significant sphincteric deficiency must be suspected, even if hypermobility exists, and consideration given to performing a pubovaginal sling, although retropubic colposuspensions may be successful in this scenario as well (Cardozo et al, 1999; Maher et al, 1999; Nitahara et al, 1999). Clearly, when SUI exists solely due to intrinsic sphincter deficiency (i.e., a fixed, nonfunctional proximal urethra with intrinsic urethral sphincter dysfunction), a retropubic suspension procedure is not indicated because there is no hypermobility to correct and the patient is better served by a pubovaginal sling, collagen injections, or an artificial sphincter (Bergman et al, 1989a). This represents a personal view that is at variance with the ICI's conclusion statement.

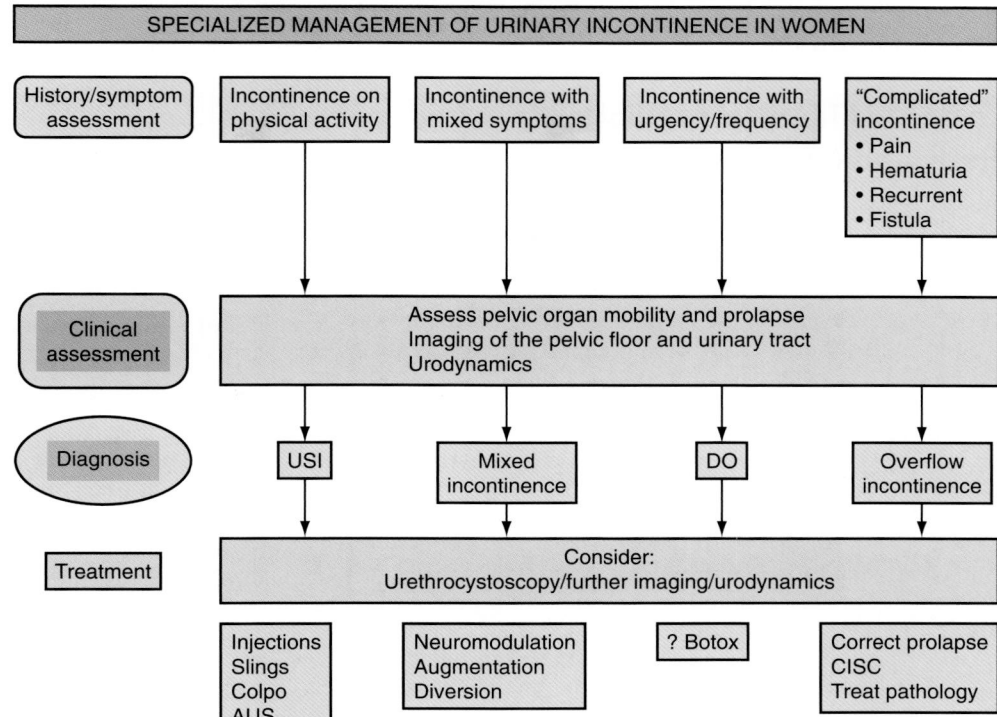

Figure 65–2. Algorithm for the specialized management of stress urinary incontinence (after the Third International Consultation on Incontinence, Monaco, 2004). USI, urodynamic stress incontinence; DO, detrusor overactivity; AUS, artificial urinary sphincter; CISC, clean intermittent self-catheterization.

In cases with a pan–pelvic floor weakness, a colposuspension should not be used in isolation but should be part of a comprehensive approach to the pelvic floor and combined as appropriate with other alternative pelvic floor repair procedures. A retropubic colposuspension does not always adequately correct the associated vaginal prolapse that frequently coexists with bladder neck hypermobility. Although lateral defect cystocele and enterocele lend themselves to retropubic repair, a central defect cystocele, rectocele, and introital deficiency do not.

A retropubic colposuspension is contraindicated **when there is an inadequate vaginal length or mobility of the vaginal tissues, for example, after prior vaginal surgery or radiotherapy or such as that after a prior vaginal incontinence procedure** (Appell, 1993). The lysis of retropubic adhesions can be performed adequately and safely by a vaginal approach in conjunction with a needle suspension procedure or pubovaginal sling.

Vaginal versus Retropubic Surgery

From a review of the literature, there is clearly a difference in the success rate of vaginal versus retropubic surgery alone with respect to correction of stress incontinence. An anterior colporrhaphy can certainly be efficacious for the correction of prolapse, with a reported efficacy in randomized controlled studies of 42% and 57% in the management of cystoceles (Sand et al, 2001; Weber et al, 2001). For the treatment of both a cystocele and stress incontinence, an anterior colporrhaphy should be combined with a sling procedure. Goldberg and colleagues (2001), in a case-control series, demonstrated that in women with a cystocele and SUI, the addition of a pubovaginal sling to an anterior colporrhaphy significantly decreased

the recurrence rate from 42% in the control group to 19% in the anterior colporrhaphy group.

Glazener and Cooper (2001) reviewed the literature on randomized or quasi-randomized trials that included anterior vaginal repair for the treatment of urinary incontinence. Nine trials were identified that included 333 women having an anterior vaginal repair and 599 who received comparison interventions. They concluded that anterior vaginal repair was less effective than open abdominal retropubic suspension on the basis of patient-reported cure rates in eight trials both in the medium term (failure rate within 1 to 5 years after anterior repair, 97 of 259 [38%] versus 57 of 327 [17%]; relative risk [RR], 2.29; 95% confidence interval [CI], 1.7 to 3.08) and in the long term (after 5 years, 49 of 128 [38%] versus 31 of 145 [21%]; RR, 2.02; 95% CI, 1.36 to 3.01). There was evidence from three of these trials that this was reflected in a need for more repeated operations for incontinence (25 of 107 [23%] versus 4 of 164 [2%]; RR, 8.87; 95% CI, 3.28 to 23.94). These findings held irrespective of the coexistence of prolapse (pelvic relaxation), although fewer women had a prolapse after anterior repair (RR, 0.24; 95% CI, 0.12 to 0.47), and later prolapse operation appeared to be equally common after either a vaginal (3%) or an abdominal (4%) operation.

Long-term follow-up beyond the first year is available in only three randomized controlled trials (Bergman et al, 1989b; Liapis et al, 1996; Colombo et al, 2000). There is a low morbidity with vaginal repair, but long-term success rates decrease with time to the extent that a 63% cure rate at 1 year fell to 37% at 5 years of follow-up (Bergman and Elia, 1995).

It can be concluded that with short-term follow-up, vaginal and open retropubic suspension procedures have similar success rates in the treatment of stress incontinence. However, with longer follow-up (and with the exception of

the pubovaginal sling), patients who have retropubic procedures fare better.

GENERAL TECHNICAL ISSUES
Retropubic Dissection

In open retropubic suspension procedures, good access to the retropubic space is crucial. This is best performed with the patient in the supine position with the legs abducted, in either a low or a modified dorsal lithotomy position with use of stirrups, allowing access to the vagina during the procedure and a perineal-abdominal progression. A urethral Foley catheter is inserted; the catheter balloon is used for subsequent identification of the urethra and bladder neck, and indeed, it is invaluable in allowing palpation of the edges of the bladder by appropriate manipulation. A Pfannenstiel or lower midline abdominal incision is made, separating the rectus muscles in the midline and sweeping the anterior peritoneal reflection off the bladder. It is essential to optimize the access to the retropubic space, and if a Pfannenstiel skin incision is made, it is advisable to use the suprapubic V modification described by Turner-Warwick and colleagues (1974). Likewise, whatever incision is made, extra valuable access to the retropubic space is obtained by extending the division of the rectus muscles down to the pubic bone and elevating the aponeurotic insertion of the rectus muscle off the upper border of the pubic bone.

The retropubic space is then developed by teasing away the retropubic fat and underlying retropubic veins from the back of the pubic bone. The bladder neck, anterior vaginal wall, and urethra are then easy to identify, often facilitated by the presence of the Foley balloon. In patients who have had previous retropubic surgery, the dissection is performed sharply, and it is important to take down all old retropubic adhesions, particularly in the face of a prior failed repair. If difficulty is encountered in the identification of the bladder neck, the bladder may be partially filled or even opened to identify its limits, and an examining finger in the vagina is invaluable in aiding the dissection (Symmonds, 1972; Gleason et al, 1976).

It is important to identify the lateral limits of the bladder as it reflects off the vaginal wall because only in this manner can one avoid inadvertent suturing of the bladder itself. Dissection over the bladder neck and urethra in the midline is to be avoided so as not to damage the intrinsic musculature. The lateral bladder wall may be "rolled off" medially and cephalad from the vaginal wall with a mounted swab and by use of countertraction with a finger in the vagina. In my experience, it is necessary to incise the endopelvic fascia. Occasional venous bleeding from the large vaginal veins is controlled by suture ligature, although it often resolves with tying of elevating sutures. To aid in the identification of the lateral margin of the bladder, it is helpful to displace the balloon of the Foley catheter into the lateral recess, where it can easily be palpated through the bladder wall.

Suture Material

Absorbable sutures were used in the original descriptions of the MMK procedure (chromic catgut), Burch procedure (chromic catgut), and VOS procedure (polyglycolic acid or polydioxanone), whereas the original paravaginal repair used nonabsorbable sutures (silicon-coated Dacron). Fibrosis during subsequent healing is likely to be the most important factor in providing continued fixation of the perivaginal fascia to the suspension sites (Tanagho, 1996); nevertheless, some surgeons believe that a nonabsorbable suture material is better because of the risk of suture dissolution before the development of adequate fibrosis (Penson and Raz, 1996). Clearly, the choice of suspension suture material is a personal choice, but erosion of nonabsorbent sutures into the lumen of the bladder is a not-uncommon complication and a not-uncommon source of medical litigation (Woo et al, 1995).

Bladder Drainage

Some degree of immediate postoperative voiding difficulty can be expected after retropubic suspensions (Lose et al, 1987; Colombo et al, 1996a). Immediately postoperatively, bladder drainage may take the form of a urethral or a suprapubic catheter, generally based on the surgeon's preference. A voiding trial is usually performed around the fifth day postoperatively. However, there is some evidence that a suprapubic catheter may be advantageous with respect to a lower incidence of asymptomatic and febrile urinary tract infection and earlier resumption of normal bladder function (Andersen et al, 1985; Bergman et al, 1987). In addition, the use of a suprapubic tube is generally more comfortable, allows the patient to participate in catheter management, and avoids the need for clean intermittent self-catheterization. Catheterization can be discontinued when efficient voiding has resumed, which is usually indicated by a postvoid residual either less than 100 mL or less than 30% of the functional bladder volume.

Drains

A tube drain may be placed in the retropubic space when there is concern about ongoing bleeding from perivaginal veins that may prove difficult to control with suture and electrocautery. Often, tying the suspension sutures is sufficient to stop this bleeding, but when it persists, drainage of the retropubic space is indicated. The drain is generally removed on the first to third day, when minimal output is noted.

MARSHALL-MARCHETTI-KRANTZ PROCEDURE
Technique

Marshall, Marchetti, and Krantz in 1949 described a retropubic approach for the elevation and fixation of the anterolateral aspect of the urethra to the posterior aspect of the pubic symphysis and the adjacent periosteum. Technically, the original description of the MMK procedure reported a double suture bite of the paraurethral tissue included with the vaginal wall; this may be generically entitled a cystourethropexy procedure. In 1949, Marshall and coworkers described their retropubic vesicourethral suspension in 50 patients; 38 of the patients had symptoms of SUI, 25 of whom had failed prior gynecologic operations for urinary incontinence. A simple suprapubic procedure was described by which the vesical outlet was suspended to the pubis (Marshall et al, 1949). In the original description, three pairs of sutures (taking double bites of tissue) were placed on each side of the urethra, incorporating full-thickness vaginal wall (excluding mucosa) and lateral urethral wall (excluding mucosa) (Marshall et al, 1949). Marchetti (1949) then modified the procedure to omit the tissue bite through the urethral wall because of concern about urethral injury. Apart from modifications in suture number and material over the years, the procedure remains the same today.

Cystourethropexy was often used as a secondary procedure for the resolution of persistent leaking after an anterior colporrhaphy. A cystourethropexy procedure does not support the posterior wall of the urethra unless the sutures include the paraurethral vaginal wall, nor does it positively reduce an anterior vaginal wall prolapse in the way that the true retropubic colposuspension procedures do. After cystourethropexy, if there is a significant urinary residual post-colporrhaphy with associated laxity of the anterior vagina wall, then with the descent, this applies traction to the posterior aspect of the bladder neck and tends to "tent" it open because the anterior aspect is tethered by sutures to the back of the pubis (see Fig. 65–1E). Sutures are placed on either side of the urethra (avoiding the urethral wall), taking bites through the paraurethral fascia and anterior vaginal wall (excluding mucosa). The most proximal sutures are placed at the level of the bladder neck. Each suture is then passed into an appropriate site in the cartilaginous portion of the symphysis (Fig. 65–3). However, the main technical problem relating to the MMK procedure is the difficulty of obtaining an adequately robust anchorage of the anterior wall of the urethra and the paraurethral fascia to the symphysis and the periosteum of the pubis where the suture bites are relatively insecure. As shown in Figure 65–3, these sutures can potentially either distort the bladder neck

and impair sphincter function (see Fig. 65–3A) or obstruct the bladder neck (see Fig. 65–3B). All sutures are inserted, and while an assistant elevates the anterior vaginal wall, each suture is individually tied, starting with the more distal pair. The proximal, or bladder neck, suture frequently needs to be passed through the insertion of the rectus abdominis muscle. Additional sutures may or may not be placed between the anterior bladder wall and the rectus muscles to pull the bladder farther anteriorly.

Results

Krantz described a personal series of 3861 cases with a follow-up of up to 31 years and a 96% subjective cure rate (Smith et al, 2005). Short- and medium-term results with the MMK procedure have been good. Mainprize and Drutz (1988) reviewed 58 articles (predominantly retrospective) published between 1951 and 1988 for treatment outcomes in 3238 cases. The cure rate, mostly based on subjective criteria, was 88%, with an improvement rate of 91%. Jarvis's meta-analysis of studies in the literature (1994b) noted subjective continence in 88.2% (range, 72% to 100%) of 2460 patients with 1- to 72-month follow-up and objective continence in 89.6% (range, 71% to 100%) of 384 patients with 3- to 12-month follow-up. Whether the procedure was being done primarily or secondarily affected the outcome, with subjective continence in 92% if it was done primarily versus 84.5% if it was done secondarily. Longer term data are limited in amount. McDuffie (1981) reported 75% success at 15 years. More recently, Clemens and coworkers (1998) noted subjective cure or improvement (SUI and urge urinary incontinence) in only 41% of patients with a mean follow-up of 17 years, and Czaplicki and colleagues (1998) noted decreasing continence rates from 77% at 1 year to 57% at 5 years to 28% at 10 years,

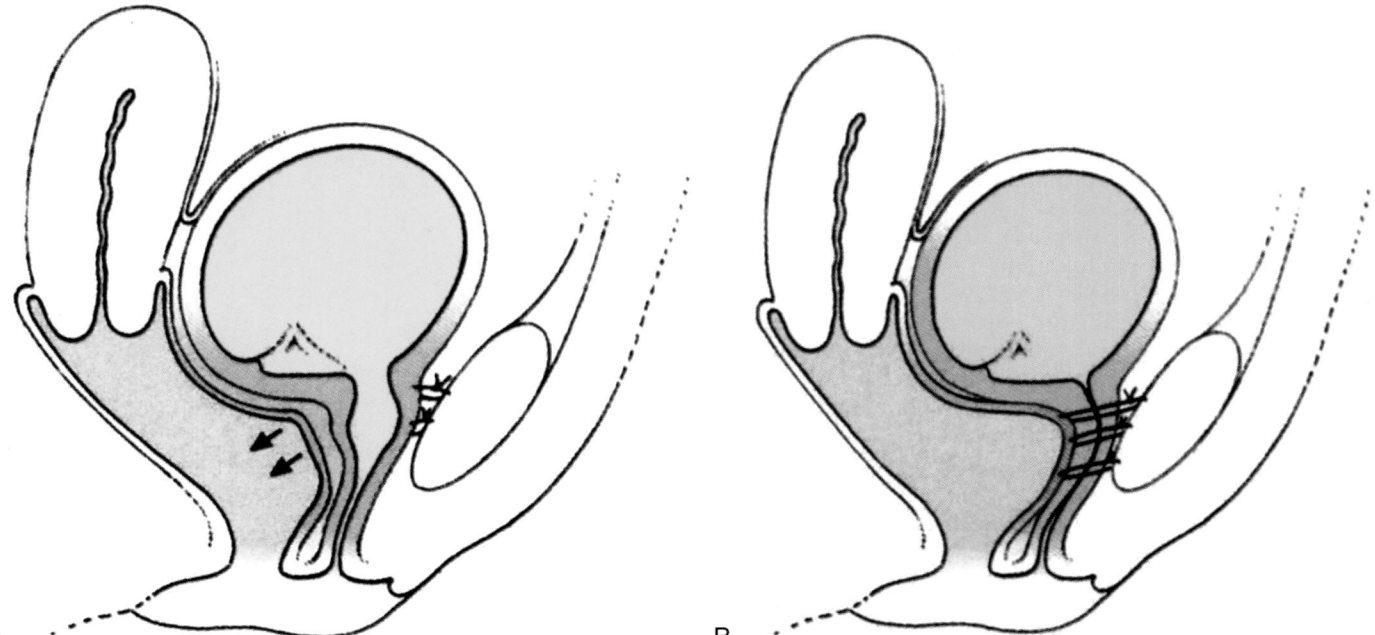

Figure 65–3. **A,** Potential risk of tethering the urethra with the MMK procedure, influencing the function of the urethral sphincter mechanism. **B,** Potential risk of obstruction of the urethra with the paraurethral sutures of the MMK procedure.

with a mean duration of continence of 78.5 months. There are significant limitations to the data since most series are retrospective, with preoperative assessment based mainly on history and physical examination and few studies using objective data as outcome measures.

Complications occur in up to 21% of cases (Mainprize and Drutz, 1988), and the **placement of sutures through the pubic symphysis incurs the risk of osteitis pubis, a potentially devastating complication of the MMK procedure that has been reported in 0.9% to 3.2% of patients** (Lee at al, 1979; Mainprize and Drutz, 1988; Zorzos and Paterson, 1996). Patients usually present 1 to 8 weeks postoperatively with acute pubic pain radiating to the inner thighs, aggravated by moving. Physical examination reveals tenderness over the pubic symphysis, and radiography demonstrates haziness to the borders of the pubic symphysis and possibly lytic changes. Treatment is with bed rest, analgesics, and possibly corticosteroids (Lee et al, 1979). Other specific complications of the MMK procedure have included the occasional erosion of nonabsorbable cystourethropexy sutures into the bladder lumen with stone formation. Also, the positioning of sutures in the endopelvic fascia close to the bladder neck can result in a significant outlet obstruction. **Whereas the MMK procedure produces a cure rate similar to that of colposuspension, the complication of osteitis pubis means that there is little to support its use instead of other colposuspension procedures.**

BURCH COLPOSUSPENSION
Technique

Burch's original description of the colposuspension in 1961 followed his original procedure, which was essentially a paravaginal repair attaching the paravaginal fascia to the white line of the pelvis, the arcus tendineus. The Burch colposuspension was a novel approach to restore the urethrovesical junction to a retropubic location by approximating the periurethral fascia to the tough bands of fibrous tissue running along the superior aspect of the pubic bone (Cooper's [iliopectineal] ligament) with three pairs of sutures. The original Burch retropubic colposuspension is appropriate only if the patient has adequate vaginal mobility and capacity to allow the lateral vaginal fornices to be elevated toward and approximated to Cooper's ligament on either side. This technique has been modified. Tanagho's modification (1978) approximated the vaginal wall to the lateral pelvic wall, with the sutures holding the anterior vaginal wall to Cooper's ligament being tied loosely so that two fingers could be placed between the symphysis and urethra. This achieved broad support for the urethra and bladder neck and potentially minimized the risk of postoperative voiding dysfunction. A more recent modification (Shull and Baden, 1989; Turner-Warwick and Chapple, 2002) involves a hybrid approach whereby the vaginal tissues are approximated to the internal obturator fascia with an anchoring bite to the iliopectineal ligament (see VOS repair later).

Suture placement is facilitated by the elevation of the dissected anterolateral vaginal wall into the field by the surgeon's left vaginal-examining fingers (Fig. 65–4). The bladder is retracted to the opposite side with a mounted swab. Two to

four sutures are placed on each side, each suture taking a good bite of fascia and vaginal wall, with care taken not to pass through the vaginal mucosa. Some recommend taking double bites of tissue to lessen the risk of suture pull-through (Jarvis, 1994a). The most distal suture is at the level of the bladder neck and placed no closer than 2 cm lateral to it, although some place distal sutures at the midurethral level (Tanagho, 1978). The suspension suture bites of the paraurethral fascia should not be positioned too close to the bladder neck and the urethra, as they are in the cystourethropexy procedures (MMK), because the unwanted effect of lateral traction-tension created by their anchorage to the iliopectineal ligaments may tether the sphincteric occlusive effect on the urethra or create a degree of obstructed voiding. Subsequent sutures are placed proximal to the level of the bladder neck, at about 1-cm intervals. The sutures are then placed into corresponding sites in Cooper's ligament, the emphasis being on a mediolateral direction for the sutures. The exact mechanism of continence of the Burch procedure is still unknown. Burch (1968) thought it to be secondary to elevation and stabilization of the bladder neck and urethra. In support of the suggestion regarding suture placement, Digesu and colleagues (2004) reviewed magnetic resonance imaging findings before and 1 year after open Burch colposuspension in 28 women to see if this would explain the mechanism. In the 86% who were cured, the distance between the levator ani muscle and bladder neck was significantly shorter than in those whose treatment failed. Their suggestion is that insertion of sutures in a medial-lateral direction as opposed to an anterior-posterior direction may better appose the levator ani muscle and bladder neck. The highly vascular vaginal wall may bleed profusely during

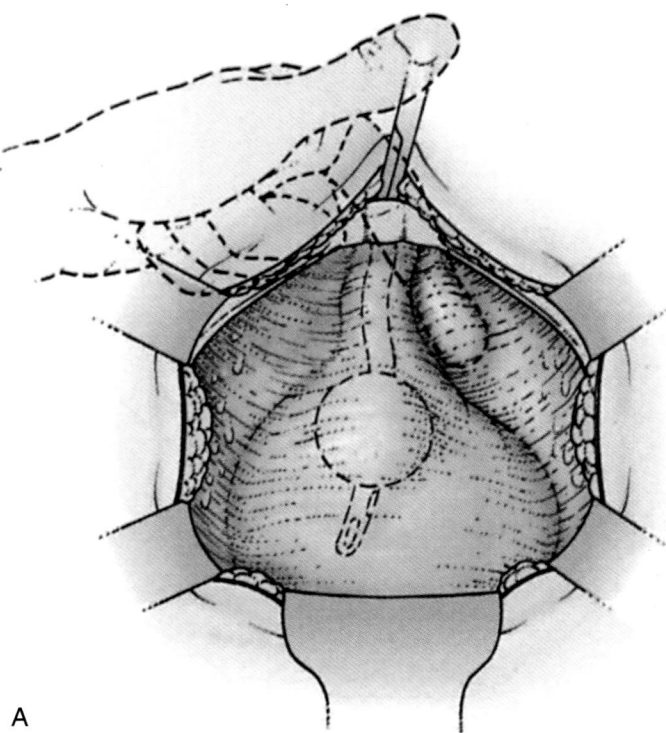

Figure 65–4. A, The use of a finger in the vagina when the pelvic tissues are dissected superomedially off of the vagina. *Continued*

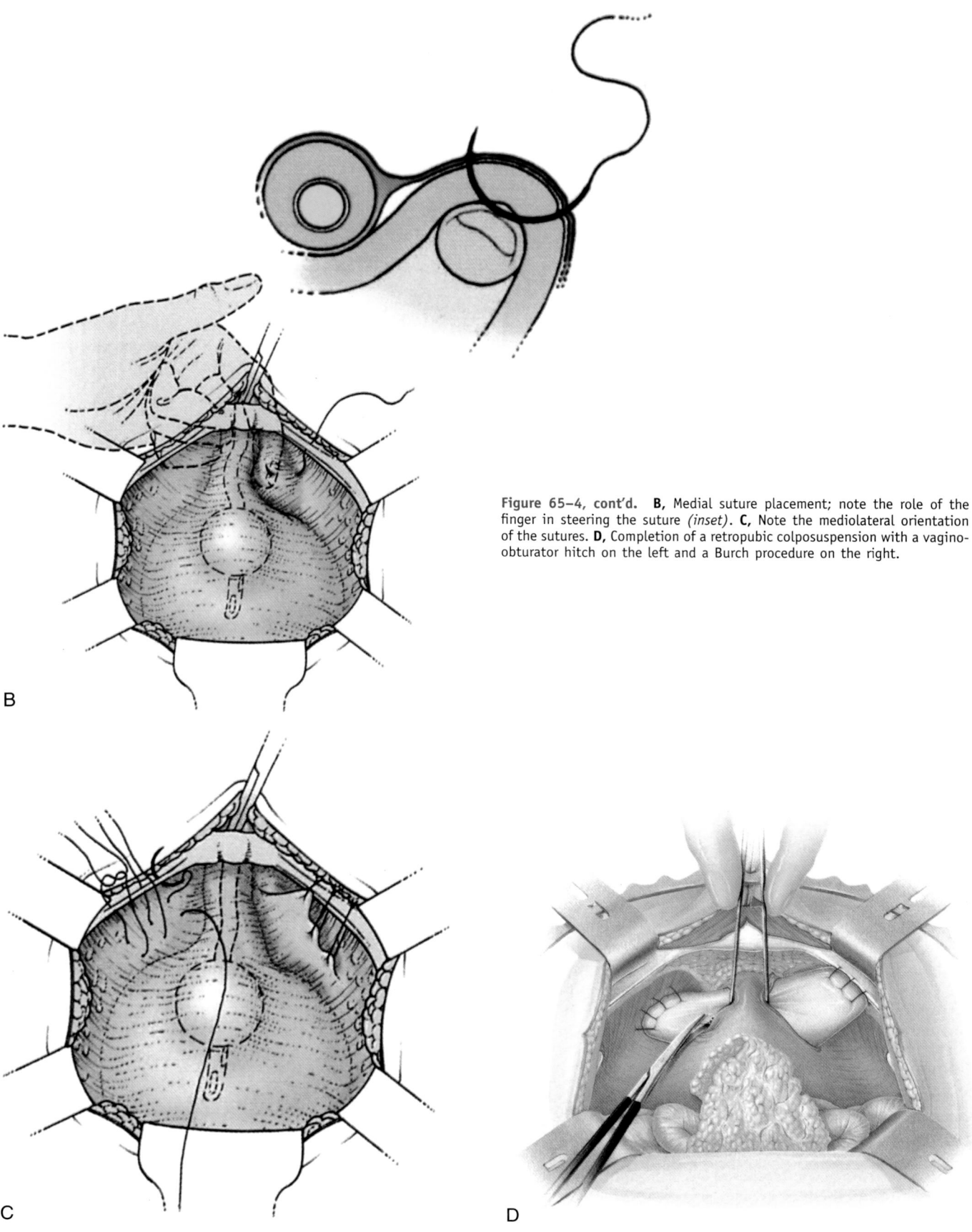

Figure 65–4, cont'd. **B,** Medial suture placement; note the role of the finger in steering the suture *(inset).* **C,** Note the mediolateral orientation of the sutures. **D,** Completion of a retropubic colposuspension with a vagino-obturator hitch on the left and a Burch procedure on the right.

B

C

D

suture placement, and large vaginal veins often need to be oversewn, but most bleeding ceases once the sutures are tied and the vagina is suspended. To facilitate tying of the sutures, the assistant elevates the appropriate portion of the vaginal wall as each suture is tied, commencing with the more distant pair.

No attempt should be made to tie the sutures tightly. Often, the vaginal wall does not approximate to Cooper's ligaments, and free suture material is seen between the vagina and the ligaments. The principle is to approximate the vaginal wall to the lateral pelvic wall, where it will heal and promote adhesion formation (Tanagho, 1978; Shull and Baden, 1989; Turner-Warwick and Chapple, 2002), **thereby creating a broad support for the urethra and bladder neck.**

Results

As in the MMK procedure, short- and medium-term outcomes with the Burch procedure have been good. In Jarvis's meta-analysis (1994b), subjective continence was achieved in 91% (range, 63% to 97%) of more than 1300 patients with 3 to 72 months of follow-up and objective continence in 84% of more than 1700 patients with 1 to 60 months of follow-up. Lapitan and associates (2003) reviewed 33 trials involving a total of 2403 women who underwent open colposuspension and found an overall cure rate between 68.9% to 88.0%, with a 1-year cure rate of approximately 85% to 90%. This decreased to 70% at 5 years. Although there may be a decline in the cure rate of only 15% to 20% beyond 5 years, Alcalay and colleagues (1995) noted a subjective and objective SUI cure rate of 69% with a mean follow-up of 13.8 years. Baessler and Stanton (2004) examined the impact of surgery on coital incontinence. Of the 30 women available for postoperative evaluation, 73% preoperatively had incontinence with penetration, 10% with orgasm only, and 17% with both. Postoperatively, 70% were cured of their coital incontinence. Moreover, in those who were subjectively cured of their stress incontinence, 87% were also cured of their coital incontinence.

Unlike with the MMK procedure, the good results with the Burch procedure appear to be durable with longer follow-up. Lapitan and associates (2003) reached the conclusion from a review of two trials comparing the Burch colposuspension and the MMK procedure that the Burch technique results in higher cure rates. Thus, it should be regarded as the *standard* **open retropubic colposuspension procedure.**

Open colposuspension is as effective as any other procedure in primary or secondary surgery at curing SUI with proven long-term success (level 1 evidence, grade A recommendation) (Smith et al, 2005).

Reoperative Surgery

Poorer results are likely to occur when the procedure is performed secondarily. Scarring and fibrosis from previous surgery can prevent adequate suspension in some cases, and suture cut-through is more likely. Furthermore, after failed surgery, patients may often have coexisting sphincteric weakness that places them at greater risk of recurrence after colposuspension (Bowen et al, 1989; Koonings et al, 1990).

Nevertheless, Maher and colleagues (1999) and Cardozo and associates (1999) have both shown good objective (72% and 79%) and subjective (89% and 80%) success with repeated colposuspension at a mean follow-up of 9 months. Nitahara and coworkers (1999) reported a 69% subjective success at a mean follow-up of 6.9 years. Urge incontinence and sphincteric weakness are the main causes of failure and dissatisfaction. Urge incontinence accounted for 63% (12 of 19) of failures; the remaining seven with persistent stress incontinence in Nitahara's series demonstrated sphincteric deficiency with mean Valsalva leak point pressures of 65 cm H_2O. The low-pressure urethra has often been quoted as an adverse risk factor for colposuspension (Haab et al, 1996; Bowen et al, 1989; Koonings et al, 1990), but this topic also remains controversial. Several authors have studied the urethral pressure profilometry changes after colposuspension and have noted a statistically significant increase in the postoperative pressure transmission ratio but minimal changes in the postoperative maximal urethral closing pressure (MUCP), functional urethral length, and continence area (Faysal et al, 1981; Weil et al, 1984; Feyersiel et al, 1994). Although a low-pressure urethra (MUCP $\leq$ 20 cm H_2O) is considered a contraindication to the Burch procedure, a modification of the standard Burch operation has had some success in managing SUI associated with the low-pressure urethra. Bergman and colleagues (1989c) combined a standard Burch procedure with the Ball procedure (Ball, 1963) whereby, before the Cooper ligament suspension is performed, two or three sutures are used to plicate the anterior urethral wall at the level of the proximal and middle urethra. They retrospectively noted greater success with this technique than with a standard Burch procedure for the low-pressure urethra, and this was comparable to the success obtained with a standard Burch procedure in patients with a normal-pressure urethra (MUCP > 20 cm H_2O). With longer follow-up, the Ball-Burch procedure continued to yield better results than the standard Burch procedure in patients with a low-pressure urethra, with a documented 5-year cure rate of SUI of 84% (Bergman et al, 1991; Elia and Bergman, 1995). However, there are no randomized studies addressing the issue, and whether these results can be extrapolated for the use of this technique in patients with intrinsic sphincter deficiency is debatable.

As with any major abdominal or pelvic surgical procedure, intraoperative and perioperative complications that may occur after a retropubic suspension include bleeding, injury to genitourinary organs (bladder, urethra, ureter), pulmonary atelectasis and infection, wound infection or dehiscence, abscess formation, and venous thrombosis or embolism. Other complications more specific to retropubic suspension procedures include postoperative voiding difficulty, detrusor overactivity, and vaginal prolapse. These are discussed in more detail along with other reported complications in a later section in this chapter.

PARAVAGINAL REPAIR
Technique

The origins of the paravaginal repair date to White (1909, 1912), who described the importance of the "white line" of the pelvis (arcus tendineus) as an integral structure supporting the proximal urethra and bladder base to the pelvic wall and the development of paravaginal fascial tears predisposing to cystocele formation. He performed the paravaginal repair by a vaginal approach but envisioned that it would be easier if it was performed abdominally (White, 1909, 1912). Later, in his original description, Burch attached the vaginal wall to the arcus tendineus in seven patients, only to realize that the attachment may not be secure, prompting him to use Cooper's ligament as an attachment site (Burch, 1961). In the 1970s, Richardson and coworkers (1976) reintroduced the concept of a lateral defect cystourethrocele as an etiologic factor in the genesis of SUI and popularized the paravaginal repair as a technique for management.

The patient is placed in a low lithotomy position, just as for the MMK procedure and Burch colposuspension. If there are retropubic adhesions resulting from prior surgery, they are sharply incised; the dissection is facilitated by placement of two fingers of the surgeon's left hand in the vagina. The bladder and urethra are not mobilized from the vaginal attachments. Richardson and colleagues (1981) describe an extensive reattachment of the lateral vaginal sulcus with its overlying fascia to the arcus tendineus fasciae pelvis from the back of the lower edge of the symphysis pubis to the ischial spine, using six to eight sutures placed at 1-cm intervals. The vaginal wall in the region of the bladder neck is identified, and these interrupted sutures are placed at approximately 1-cm intervals through the paravaginal fascia and vaginal wall (excluding vaginal mucosa) beginning at the urethrovesical junction. The sutures are then passed through the adjacent obturator fascia and underlying muscle at the site of the arcus tendineus fascia (Fig. 65–5). If the arcus is not visible, the obturator foramen may be used as a landmark. It is situated 1.5 to 2 cm above the white line.

The endpoint that should be achieved is the re-establishment of the urethral axis in an anatomic position, easily allowing three fingerbreadths between the pubic symphysis and the proximal urethra but providing secure fixation and preventing rotational descent. Consequently, it has been reported that postoperative voiding difficulties are uncommon (Richardson et al, 1981).

Results

Few reports on the use of this technique have been published. With variable follow-up, cure rates greater than 90% have been reported for the paravaginal repair (Richardson et al, 1981; Shull and Baden, 1989). There is only a single randomized comparison of colposuspension with paravaginal repair including 36 patients who were randomly allocated to treatment by either colposuspension or paravaginal repair with nonabsorbable suture material. At 6 months of follow-up, there was an objective cure rate of 100% for those undergoing colposuspension and 72% for those undergoing paravaginal repair (Colombo et al, 1996a).

Small series have reported on vaginal approach paravaginal repairs (Scotti et al, 1998; Mallipeddi et al, 2001). In particular, Mallipeddi and colleagues followed up 45 patients (21 with SUI) after this approach for a mean of 1.6 years, and 57% had persistent stress incontinence; their conclusion was that this technique had limited applicability for SUI. **It can be concluded that there is level 1/2 evidence that abdominal paravaginal repair is less effective than colposuspension. There are limited data (level 3/4) on laparoscopic and vaginal paravaginal repairs, but interpretation of these data is hampered by the small numbers of**

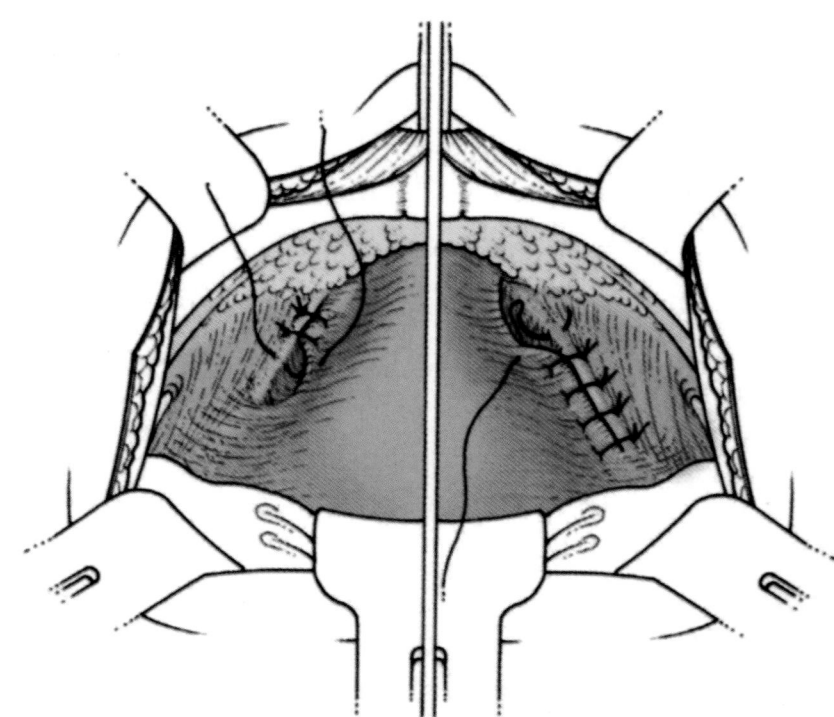

Figure 65–5. A paravaginal repair procedure.

patients, the short follow-up, and a combination of this procedure with other types of incontinence procedures (Smith et al, 2005).

VAGINO-OBTURATOR SHELF REPAIR

Technique

Turner-Warwick (1986; Turner-Warwick and Chapple, 2002) reported his variant of the paravaginal repair, which he called the vagino-obturator shelf (VOS) repair. The premise for this is that there should be no restriction to the intrinsic sphincteric function of the urethra by fixation or paraurethral tethering, and there should be no urethral compression (Turner-Warwick and Kirby, 1993).

Just as for other retropubic suspension procedures (Fig. 65–6), the anterior wall of the lower segment of the bladder wall is exposed and the position of the bladder neck is identified by gentle traction on a balloon catheter in the urethra. The surgeon's forefinger in the vagina elevates its anterior wall and the overlying endopelvic fascia on either side of the urethra. Lateral displacement of the catheter balloon with the finger in the vagina facilitates the identification of the inferolateral margin of the bladder, lateral to the bladder neck, and its separation from the paraurethral endopelvic fascia is achieved by simple blunt dissection with a sponge or scissor-tip retraction. This naturally exposes the surface of the obturator muscle and the arcus tendineus origin of the levator muscles deep in the sulcus below this, the site of suture placement in the paravaginal repair (which is well below the vaginal anchorage point in the VOS procedure). The obturator nerves lie superolaterally; their canals run high up in a groove under the superior pubic ramus so that once they are identified, injury to them can be avoided. The full thickness of the vagina and its overlying layer of endopelvic fascia are elevated by the surgeon's finger in the vagina and are approximated to the internal obturator muscle and anchored to the bulk of this with absorbable 0 or No. 1 sutures mounted on robust 35- to 40-mm half-circle needles. Slight flexion of the fingertip tents the vaginal wall and facilitates the full-thickness insertion of these suture bites through it, thus avoiding inclusion of the surgical glove. Three or four successive sutures are inserted. For knot security, these are best tied continuously, head to tail, as they are inserted, rather than separating them individually. Each tied suture bite facilitates the insertion of the next (unlike in the Burch procedure, in which the sutures are not tied until they have all been inserted). A similar obturator suspension of the elevated protrusion of the vagina and its overlying endopelvic fascia is achieved on the opposite side. Some additional elevation of the lateral anchorage of the VOS by the inclusion of a bite of the iliopectineal ligament within the suture bite approximating the vagina to the obturator muscle (like a Burch procedure) may be used to reinforce the repair (Shull and Baden, 1989). This modification is one the author favors and represents a hybrid with the Burch procedure, facilitating reattachment of the pubocervical fascia to the arcus tendineus fasciae pelvis, tissue apposition to the lateral pelvic wall, and nonobstructive elevation of the urethra and urethrovesical junction. In addition, obliteration of the pouch of Douglas (culdoplasty) may be needed to prevent enterocele (Shull and Baden, 1989; Turner-Warwick and Kirby, 1993).

Results

There are limited data available for the VOS repair, which has had reported cure rates of 60% to 86%, depending on whether the procedure was performed primarily or secondarily (Turner-Warwick, 1986; German et al, 1994). German and colleagues (1994) reported that the VOS procedure is less likely to be successful in those patients who had undergone previous surgery.

Ultimately, as with all such reconstructive surgery, the surgeon should select the correct procedure for the individual patient. Although the VOS, which is a synthesis of the principles of the paravaginal repair and the Burch colposuspension, is of interest, further clinical results are necessary before definitive conclusions can be drawn.

LAPAROSCOPIC RETROPUBIC SUSPENSION

Laparoscopic techniques for retropubic suspension were introduced by Vancaillie and Schuessler in 1991. They essentially performed an MMK urethropexy laparoscopically, and since that time, laparoscopic techniques have been applied to both the Burch procedure and the paravaginal repair. Subsequent modifications to the suspension suturing techniques have been introduced, including the use of mesh (Ou et al, 1993), staples (Lyons, 1994), and fibrin sealant (Kiilholma et al, 1995), but all adhere to the same principles of their open counterparts. Proposed advantages to the laparoscopic approach include improved intraoperative visualization, less postoperative pain, shorter hospitalization, and quicker recovery times (Liu, 1993). Disadvantages include greater technical difficulty with resultant longer operating times and higher operating costs (Paraiso et al, 1999).

The procedure may be performed extraperitoneally or transperitoneally, and each approach has its proponents. Although the extraperitoneal technique may be associated with shorter operating times, easier dissection, and fewer bladder injuries (Frankel and Kantipong, 1993; Raboy et al, 1995), the transperitoneal approach provides a larger operating space and the ability to perform concomitant intraperitoneal procedures and apical prolapse repair (Paraiso et al, 1999). The specifics of the different procedures are beyond the scope of this chapter.

Short- and medium-term outcomes with the laparoscopic retropubic suspensions have become available. In their review of 13 studies of laparoscopic retropubic suspensions, Paraiso and colleagues (1999) found cure rates to range from 69% to 100% with follow-up of 1 to 36 months. This is comparable to outcomes of the open procedures as already noted. Both retrospective (Polascik et al, 1995) and randomized, prospective comparisons (Summitt et al, 2000) between open and laparoscopic techniques have demonstrated similar short-term success. However, with longer follow-up, laparoscopic retropubic suspensions appear to fail more frequently. McDougall's group (1999) retrospectively noted only 30% cure of SUI and 50% cure or improvement by a laparoscopic Burch procedure with 45 months of follow-up, and this was no different from the results with a Raz procedure.

Five trials have compared laparoscopic with open colposuspension (Burton, 1997, 1999; Su et al, 1997; Carey et al,

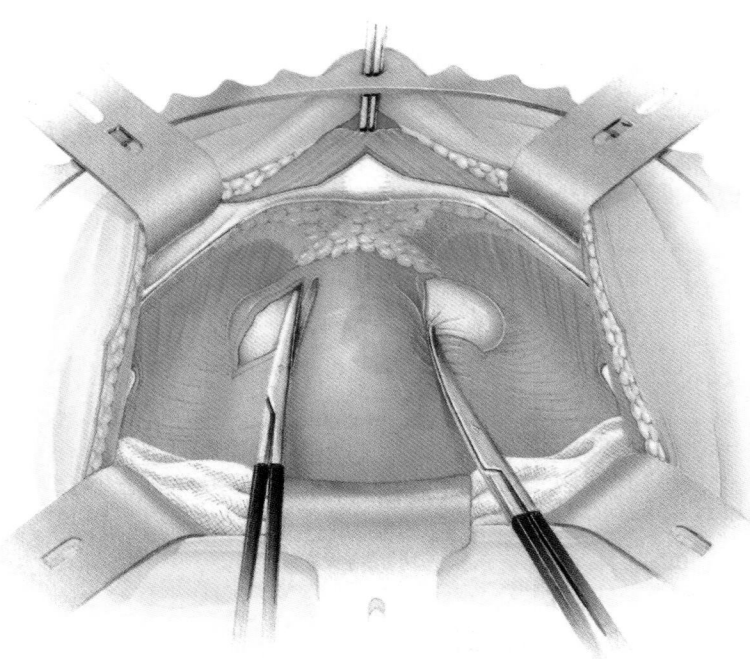

A

Figure 65–6. **A,** Mobilizing the tissues. The tissues should be stripped by blunt dissection with a mounted swab or the edge of a pair of scissors; only occasionally is sharp dissection necessary, provided the stripping action starts far laterally adjacent to the pubic bone. **B,** Completed vagino-obturator shelf procedure.

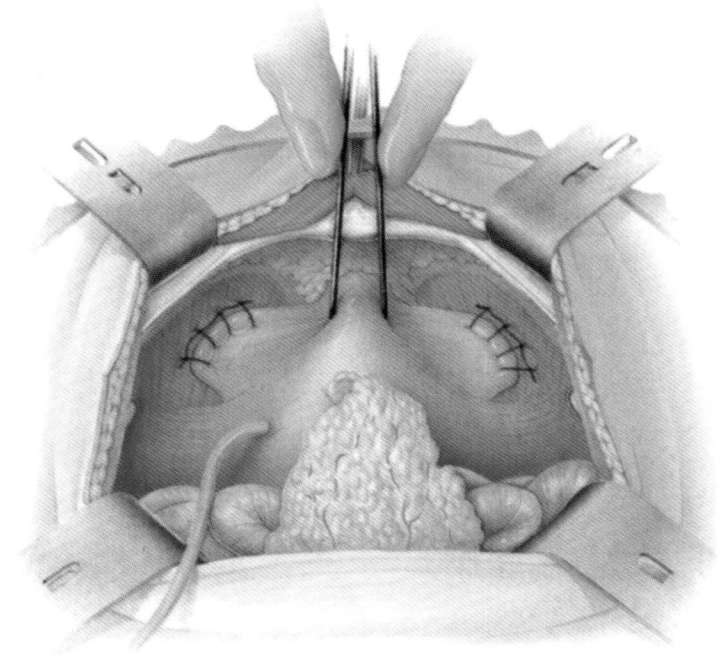

B

2000; Summitt et al, 2000; Fatthy et al, 2001). All different lengths of follow-up: 6 months (Carey et al, 2000); 1 year (Su et al, 1997; Summitt et al, 2000); 6 and 18 months (Fatthy et al, 2001); and 6 months, 1 year, 3 years, and 5 years (Burton, 1997, 1999). Outcome data for 6 months to 18 months were therefore available for all studies. Longer term data are currently available only for Burton's study. The ability to synthesize data was also limited by the variable tests and definitions used to measure subjective and objective outcomes across the trials (Moehrer et al, 2003). Moehrer and colleagues, in their meta-analysis, noted that a total of 233 women received a laparoscopic and 254 women an open colposuspension, and the confidence intervals are generally all wide as a consequence. Four trials comparing laparoscopic with open colposuspension were otherwise of good quality (Burton, 1997, 1999; Carey et al, 2000; Summitt et al, 2000; Fatthy et al, 2001). Burton's study had the potentially confounding factors of use of absorbable sutures and of the surgeon's having carried out only a relatively small number of laparoscopic colposuspensions (<20) before commencing the trial. These factors may have influenced his results, in particular since there is believed to be a definite albeit relatively steep learning curve associated with laparoscopic colposuspensions. The fifth trial had methodologic problems with corrupted randomization and confounding factors of performance of additional surgery in some patients and the use of a different number of sutures for laparoscopic (one suture) and open (three sutures) colposuspension (Su et al, 1997). The number of sutures used appears to have a significant influence on the cure rate, with more sutures resulting in a significantly higher success rate. Persson and Wolner-Hanssen (2000) compared different numbers of paravaginal sutures and found a significantly higher objective 1-year cure rate (dry on "ultrashort" pad test) for women randomized to two sutures compared with one suture, with a cure rate of 83% for two sutures and 58% for one suture. Only one trial currently has data beyond 18 months of follow-up (Burton, 1997, 1999). This suggested poorer long-term results after laparoscopic surgery. This finding should be interpreted cautiously, however, as there are concerns that the surgeon's laparoscopic performance may have been suboptimal because he had performed few laparoscopic colposuspensions when the trial started. Data from other larger trials with multiple operators are now needed to assess whether this is a real effect. All the other trials had data up to a maximum of 18 months. These show some inconsistencies. Outcome assessed by the women participating (arguably the most important outcome) appeared equally good in the two groups. Urodynamic investigations were used to assess cure objectively in all five studies. Overall, there was a significantly higher success rate after open colposuspension (RR, 0.89; 95% CI, 0.82 to 0.98) equivalent to an absolute difference of an additional 9% risk of failure after laparoscopic surgery. No significant differences between the two groups were observed for postoperative urgency, voiding dysfunction, or de novo detrusor overactivity. A trend was shown toward a higher complication rate, less postoperative pain, shorter hospital stay, and more rapid return to normal function for laparoscopic colposuspension. The operating time tended to be longer, the intraoperative blood loss less, and the duration of catheterization shorter for laparoscopic compared with open colposuspension (Moehrer et al, 2003).

In a previous review of laparoscopic colposuspension, Paraiso and colleagues (1999) noted major intraoperative and short-term complications in up to 25% of cases, with bladder injury being the most common complication and declining with experience; ureteric injury has also been reported (Aslan and Woo, 1997). The use of mesh and tacks or staples may be complicated by foreign body erosion (Arunkalaivanan and Arunkalaivanan, 2002; Kenton et al, 2002), and a randomized study (Ankardal et al, 2004) has reported that the use of sutures was superior to the laparoscopic mesh and staple technique.

Although it is possible that no difference exists between laparoscopic and open colposuspension, there appears to be a trend toward higher cure rates with open colposuspension. Another concern is how generalizeable the data are on laparoscopic colposuspension since the majority of reported studies are from expert laparoscopists. The evidence base on laparoscopic colposuspension is limited by short-term follow-up, small numbers, and poor methodology. No recommendation can be made on the use of laparoscopic colposuspension (Smith et al, 2005).

COMPLICATIONS OF RETROPUBIC REPAIRS

As with any major abdominal or pelvic surgical procedure, intraoperative and perioperative complications that may occur after a retropubic suspension include bleeding, injury to genitourinary organs (bladder, urethra, ureter), pulmonary atelectasis and infection, wound infection or dehiscence, abscess formation, and venous thrombosis or embolism. Other common complications more specific to retropubic suspension procedures include postoperative voiding difficulty, detrusor overactivity, and vaginal prolapse. Potentially, it is overcorrection of the urethrovesical angle that may be a major contributory factor in the development of the long-term complications of de novo urgency, voiding dysfunction, and enterocele formation.

Nevertheless, the reported incidence of these problems is relatively low. In their meta-analysis, Leach and associates (1997) noted a 3% to 8% transfusion rate for retropubic suspensions and no significant difference in the overall medical and surgical complication rates between retropubic suspensions, needle suspensions, anterior colporrhaphy, and pubovaginal slings. Mainprize and Drutz (1988), in their review of the MMK procedure literature (2712 patients), noted an overall complication rate of 21%, with wound complications and urinary infections making up the majority (5.5% and 3.9%, respectively). Direct surgical injury to the urinary tract occurred in only 1.6%, and genitourinary tract fistulas occurred in 0.3%. Ureteral obstruction has been reported rarely after Burch colposuspension, and it usually results from ureteral kinking after elevation of the vagina and bladder base, although direct suture ligation of the ureter can occur (Applegate et al, 1987). If it is identified intraoperatively, it is best remedied by removal of the offending ligature and temporary placement of a ureteral stent. The so-called post-colposuspension syndrome, which has been described as pain in one or both groins at the site of suspension, has been noted in up to 12% of patients after a Burch procedure (Galloway et al,

1987). More recently, Demirci and colleagues (2001) reported the occurrence of groin or suprapubic pain in 15 of 220 women (6.8%) after Burch colposuspension with a follow-up of 4.5 years.

Postoperative Voiding Difficulty

Postoperative voiding difficulty after any type of retropubic suspension is not uncommon, and undoubtedly its occurrence is more likely if there is preexisting detrusor dysfunction or denervation resulting from extensive perivesical dissection. In most cases, however, it is the result of overcorrection of the urethral axis from inappropriately placed or excessively tightened sutures. If the sutures are placed too medially, they may also transfix the urethra or distort it.

Preoperatively, at-risk patients may be identified by their history of prior voiding dysfunction or episodes of urinary retention. These women should be carefully counseled preoperatively about the potential for postoperative voiding difficulty and the possible need for self-catheterization intermittently. Their incontinence should be of sufficient magnitude that its correction offsets the risk of the need for self-catheterization.

Women with post-cystourethropexy voiding problems who have obstruction often do not exhibit the classic urodynamic features of obstruction. However, the history of postoperative voiding symptoms and associated new-onset bladder storage symptoms and a finding of a retropubically angulated and fixed urethra generally indicate that obstruction does exist (Carr and Webster, 1997). In such cases, revision of the retropubic suspension by releasing the urethra into a more anatomic position resolves voiding symptoms in up to 90% of cases (Webster and Kreder, 1990; Nitti and Raz, 1994; Carr and Webster, 1997).

The meta-analysis by Leach and coworkers (1997) noted that the risk of temporary urinary retention lasting more than 4 weeks postoperatively is 5% for all retropubic suspensions, and the risk for permanent retention is estimated to be less than 5%. These risks are not significantly different from those for needle suspensions or pubovaginal slings. Mainprize and Drutz's review of the literature (1988) yielded a 3.6% incidence of postoperative voiding problems after an MMK procedure, whereas the Burch procedure literature reports an incidence of postoperative voiding disorders ranging from 3% to 32% (Hilton and Stanton, 1983; Galloway et al, 1987; Eriksen et al, 1990; Alcalay et al, 1995; Colombo et al, 1996a). In more recent literature, voiding dysfunction may be persistent as noted in 3.5% of a series of 310 women with a mean follow-up of 36 months (Viereck et al, 2004). Nonpersistent voiding dysfunction has been reported in 12.5% (6% to 37.2%) after primary surgery (Smith et al, 2005). After colposuspension conducted as a secondary procedure, Bidmead and associates (2001) reported voiding difficulties requiring intermittent self-catheterization in 6% of cases.

Because the paravaginal repair aims to restore normal anatomy, there is theoretically little chance of overcorrection of the urethral axis, which should translate into a lower risk of postoperative obstruction. In Richardson and coworkers' study (1981), 80% of patients were able to void immediately after paravaginal repair, and "all patients had satisfactory bladder function at the time of discharge." However, temporary voiding difficulty has been noted in up to 17% of patients after a VOS procedure (German et al, 1994), and chronic (>2 years) voiding difficulty has been noted in up to 11% of patients after the paravaginal repair (Colombo et al, 1996a).

All patients should be counseled before surgery about the potential need for intermittent self-catheterization.

Bladder Overactivity

Bladder overactivity commonly accompanies anatomic SUI, and its incidence preoperatively has been reported to be as high as 30% in patients undergoing either first correction or repeated operations (McGuire, 1981). **Provided it is considered as a diagnosis, urodynamic evaluation is performed to show whether detrusor overactivity is present, an attempt at treatment of the related overactive bladder symptoms has been made (with or without success), and the patient has been advised that the presence of detrusor overactivity will increase the risk of continuing storage symptoms postoperatively, then preoperative bladder overactivity does not contraindicate a retropubic suspension procedure, provided that anatomic SUI has also been demonstrated.** In the majority of cases, the bladder overactivity symptoms resolve after surgical repair (McGuire, 1988). Leach and coworkers' meta-analysis (1997) found the risk of urgency after a retropubic suspension to be 66% if urgency and detrusor overactivity were present preoperatively, 36% if there was urgency but no documented overactivity preoperatively, and only 11% if there was neither urgency nor overactivity preoperatively. There was no significant difference in the incidence of postoperative urgency between retropubic suspensions, needle suspensions, and pubovaginal slings. Postoperative urgency was noted in only 0.9% of MMK procedures in Mainprize and Drutz's meta-analysis of 15 series (1988), although Parnell and associates (1982) reported that 28.5% of their patients developed postoperative storage symptoms. Jarvis's meta-analysis (1994b) of Burch procedures found the incidence of de novo bladder overactivity to be 3.4% to 18%. More recently, Smith and colleagues (2005) quoted a figure for postoperative detrusor overactivity of 6.6% for colposuspension (range, 1.0% to 16.6%), whereas the incidence of postoperative urgency or urge incontinence after the paravaginal/VOS repair has been reported to be 0% to 6% (Shull and Baden, 1989; German et al, 1994; Colombo et al, 1996a).

For those patients in whom postoperative storage symptoms persist, proven to be associated with detrusor overactivity and intractable to management with anticholinergic therapy and behavioral modification, surgical techniques including intravesical botulinum toxin therapy, neuromodulation, augmentation cystoplasty, or detrusor myectomy may be indicated.

Bladder storage symptoms arising de novo after retropubic suspension may be associated with bladder outlet obstruction. This premise is supported by the frequent coexistence of these symptoms with impaired voiding after suspension procedures and confirmed by the finding that urethrolysis, by freeing the urethra from an obstructed position, often resolves both storage and voiding symptoms (Raz, 1981; Webster and Kreder, 1990).

Vaginal Prolapse

Retropubic suspensions alter vaginal and bladder base anatomy, and thus postoperative vaginal prolapse is a potential complication. Genitourinary prolapse has been reported as a sequel to Burch colposuspension in 22.1% of women (range, 9.5% to 38.2%) by Smith and colleagues (2005) in their review of the literature. **The Burch procedure, because of lateral vaginal elevation, may aggravate posterior vaginal wall weakness, predisposing to enterocele.** The incidence varies between 3% and 17% (Burch, 1961, 1968; Galloway et al, 1987; Wiskind et al, 1992); **because of this, prophylactic obliteration of the cul-de-sac of Douglas is sometimes considered in performing retropubic suspensions** (Shull and Baden, 1989; Turner-Warwick and Kirby, 1993). However, simultaneous hysterectomy is not recommended prophylactically because it does not enhance the outcome of a retropubic suspension and should be performed only if there is concomitant uterine disease (Milani et al, 1985; Langer et al, 1988). Although the Burch procedure and paravaginal/VOS repair both correct lateral defect cystourethroceles, recurrent cystourethroceles were noted in 11% and 39% of Burch procedures and paravaginal repairs, respectively (Colombo et al, 1996a). In Mainprize and Drutz's review (1988), postoperative cystocele was noted in only 0.4% of patients after an MMK procedure.

Wiskind and coworkers (1992) noted that 27% of patients who had undergone a Burch colposuspension developed prolapse requiring surgery: rectocele in 22%, enterocele in 11%, uterine prolapse in 13%, and cystocele in 2%. More recently, it has been suggested that most women are asymptomatic, and less than 5% have been reported to request further surgery (Smith et al, 2005). Ward and Hilton (2004) reported that 4.8% of women needed a posterior repair, whereas Kwon and associates (2003) reported that 4.7% required subsequent pelvic reconstruction.

Because retropubic suspensions are unable to correct central defect cystoceles, patients must be carefully examined preoperatively to exclude their presence.

COMPARISONS BETWEEN INCONTINENCE PROCEDURES
Retropubic Repair versus Needle Suspension and Anterior Repair

Three articles that reviewed the literature on incontinence procedures all found retropubic suspensions to be more effective than either needle suspensions or anterior colporrhaphies (Jarvis, 1994b; Black and Downs, 1996; Leach et al, 1997). Cure rates were approximately 85% for the retropubic suspensions compared with 50% to 70% for the needle suspensions and anterior colporrhaphies. Results were more durable for the retropubic suspensions and better if the procedure was primary.

Retropubic Repair versus Pubovaginal Sling

Most studies in the literature have not demonstrated a significant difference in cure rates between retropubic

suspensions (generally a Burch procedure) and pubovaginal slings (Jarvis, 1994b; Black and Downs, 1996; Leach et al, 1997). However, often, selection bias exists in that the pubovaginal sling is generally reserved for patients with multiple prior failed incontinence procedures, with less prolapse, and the presence of presumed intrinsic sphincter deficiency (a fixed urethra with periurethral fibrosis) is often used in clinical practice as a contraindication to a retropubic suspension. In an interesting randomized study in patients with a prior failed incontinence procedure (anterior repair) but without a low-pressure urethra (i.e., MUCP > 20 cm H_2O), Enzelsberger's group (1996) found no significant difference in cure (subjective or objective) at 32 to 48 months between the Burch procedure and the Lyodura sling. However, they noted significantly more postoperative voiding difficulty with the pubovaginal sling (13% versus 3%) and more vaginal prolapse (enterocele or rectocele) with the Burch procedure (13% versus 3%).

Burch Colposuspension versus Marshall-Marchetti-Krantz Procedure versus Paravaginal Repair

Comparisons between the MMK and the Burch procedures have generally yielded similar results. Jarvis, in his meta-analysis of the literature (1994b), noted that overall continence rates were 89.6% and 83.9% for the MMK and the Burch procedures, respectively. When he looked at the effect of prior incontinence surgery, the continence rates were 92.1% and 94% when there was no prior surgery and 84.5% and 84% when there was a history of prior incontinence surgery for the MMK and Burch procedures, respectively. Similarly, Black and Downs (1996), in reviewing five studies (one randomized) that directly compared the MMK procedure with the Burch procedure, found that there was no significant difference in cure rates between the two procedures, although the Burch procedure generally yielded better results. However, they pointed out that overall, the studies were of poor quality with small sample sizes.

Two randomized studies that assessed urethral sphincteric function by urethral pressure profilometry had conflicting results. Quadri's group (1999) compared the MMK procedure with the Burch procedure in women with a hypermobile, low-pressure urethra (MUCP ≤ 20 cm H_2O) and noted significantly higher subjective and objective 1-year cure rates with the MMK procedure. They used urethroscopy to facilitate MMK suture placement. On the other hand, Colombo's group (1994) excluded women with a low-pressure urethra (MUCP < 30 cm H_2O) and performed a cystotomy to facilitate MMK suture placement. With 2- to 7-year follow-up (mean, 3 years), they noted higher subjective and objective cure rates with the Burch procedure, although these were not statistically significant. In addition, significantly more MMK patients had persistent postoperative voiding difficulties (28% versus 8%).

The literature on the paravaginal repair is sparse. The only randomized study that compared the Burch procedure with a paravaginal repair found significantly greater subjective and objective cure with the Burch procedure (Colombo et al, 1996a). Until large, randomized studies with prolonged follow-up are available, the issue of which is the best procedure will remain unresolved.

Tension-Free Vaginal Tape Procedure versus Colposuspension

Since its introduction in 1996 by Ulmsten, the tension-free vaginal tape (TVT) procedure has gained widespread acceptance for treatment of SUI, given its low morbidity, short-term success rates, and ability to be performed as an outpatient procedure under a local or regional anesthetic. The 7-year objective and subjective success rate for TVT is 81% (Nilsson et al, 2004). There have been a number of well-designed, prospective, randomized trials comparing the Burch colposuspension (two open and two laparoscopic) with TVT.

Liapis and coworkers (2002) reported a prospective randomized comparative study of Burch colposuspension (n = 35) and TVT (n = 36). They concluded that at 2-year follow-up, the TVT and Burch procedures were equally effective with an objective pad test cure rate of 84% and 86%, respectively. TVT had a shorter operative time and entailed less postoperative pain with a faster return to normal activity.

Ward and Hilton (2004) published a 2-year follow-up of their prospective randomized trial comparing TVT and open Burch colposuspension. At 2 years, 74% of the initial TVT and 69% of the open colposuspension patients completed the evaluation. The objective cure rates for the TVT (81%) and colposuspension (80%) were not significantly different. However, if the missing patients were evaluated by the last observation carried forward analysis, the cure rates would favor TVT (78% versus 68%). It is interesting that the subjective cure rates differ from the objective rates dramatically, with only 43% and 37% reporting subjective cure of stress incontinence after TVT and colposuspension, respectively. At 2 years, the colposuspension group still had significantly lower scores on mental and emotional health. The incidences of enterocele and vault prolapse were higher in the colposuspension group, requiring significantly more prolapse surgery. Likewise, the number of patients still requiring intermittent catheterization was higher in the colposuspension group. The intraoperative complications were higher in the TVT group, whereas the postoperative complications were higher in the colposuspension group. The authors' conclusion at 2 years, because of patients lost to follow-up, is unchanged from their conclusion at 6 months, namely, that TVT may be better than, worse than, or the same as colposuspension.

Persson and coworkers (2002) were one of the first groups to compare TVT and laparoscopic Burch colposuspension. At 1-year follow-up, there was no difference between objective and subjective cure rates. Valpas and associates (2004) conducted a prospective randomized trial comparing TVT and laparoscopic mesh colposuspension at 1-year follow-up. The objective cure rate (negative stress test, 86% versus 57%), satisfaction, and quality of life were statistically better for the TVT group.

Paraiso and colleagues (2004) prospectively randomized 72 patients into laparoscopic Burch colposuspension and TVT at a mean follow-up of 20 months, but only 17 and 16 patients were available in the laparoscopic and TVT groups, respectively. Whereas objective and subjective cure rates were significantly higher in the TVT group, satisfaction of patients was equal in each group, and no difference was reported in voiding dysfunction, urgency, or symptomatic pelvic prolapse. All these laparoscopic studies require longer follow-up with greater power to demonstrate a persistent difference between TVT and Burch colposuspension.

At this time, the TVT appears to be at least equivalent to the Burch colposuspension.

KEY POINTS: SURGERY FOR INCONTINENCE

- Anti-incontinence surgery does not necessarily work by restoring the same mechanism of continence that was present before the onset of incontinence. It works by a compensatory approach.

- The surgeon's preference, coexisting problems, and anatomic features of the patient and her general health condition influence the choice of procedure.

- There is lack of a clear consensus as to which surgical procedure for stress incontinence is most effective.

- A number of variables may influence surgical outcome: age, postoperative activity, medical comorbidity, obesity, duration of symptoms, coexistence of detrusor overactivity, prior surgery, intrinsic sphincter deficiency.

- There is no consensus on how to differentiate the relative contributions of hypermobility and sphincteric weakness.

- There remains no consensus on how to assess the outcomes of surgery, but this requires careful assessment with adequate follow-up and use of simple objective measures as well as taking particular account of patient-perceived outcomes.

- During short-term follow-up, vaginal and open retropubic suspension procedures have similar success rates. With longer follow-up (and with the exception of the pubovaginal sling), patients who have retropubic procedures fare better.

- With the MMK procedure, placement of sutures through the pubic symphysis incurs the risk of osteitis pubis in 0.9% to 3.2% of patients.

- Burch colposuspension is as effective as any other procedure in primary or secondary surgery at curing SUI, with proven long-term success. Thus, it should be regarded as the *standard* open retropubic procedure for incontinence.

- Abdominal paravaginal repair is less effective than other forms of colposuspension.

- As with any major abdominal or pelvic surgical procedure, intraoperative and perioperative complications that may occur after a retropubic suspension include bleeding, injury to genitourinary organs (bladder, urethra, ureter), pulmonary atelectasis and infection, wound infection or dehiscence, abscess formation, and venous thrombosis or embolism. Other common complications more specific to retropubic suspension procedures include postoperative voiding difficulty, detrusor overactivity, and vaginal prolapse.

- The risk of temporary urinary retention lasting more than 4 weeks postoperatively is 5% for all retropubic suspensions. The risk of permanent retention is estimated to be less than 5%. These risks are not significantly different from those of needle suspensions or pubovaginal slings.

- All patients should be counseled before surgery about the potential need for intermittent self-catheterization.

- Because retropubic suspensions are unable to correct central defect cystoceles, patients must be carefully examined preoperatively to exclude their presence. The Burch procedure, because of lateral vaginal elevation, may aggravate posterior vaginal wall weakness, predisposing to enterocele.

- Retropubic suspensions are more effective than either needle suspensions or anterior colporrhaphies.

- Most studies in the literature have not demonstrated a significant difference in cure rates between retropubic suspensions (generally a Burch procedure) and pubovaginal slings.

- Comparisons between the MMK procedure and the Burch procedure have generally yielded similar results.

- The literature on the paravaginal repair is sparse. The only randomized study that compared the Burch procedure with a paravaginal repair found significantly greater subjective and objective cure rates with the Burch procedure.

- At this time, the TVT appears to be at least equivalent to the Burch colposuspension.

ACKNOWLEDGMENT

I would like to thank Richard Turner-Warwick for allowing the use of figures from our book, in this chapter.

SUGGESTED READINGS

Abrams P, Cardozo L, Fall M, et al: The standardization of terminology of lower urinary tract function: Report from the standardisation subcommittee of the International Continence Society. Neurourol Urodyn 2002;21:167-178.

Abrams P, Andersson KE, Brubaker L, et al: 3rd International Consultation on Incontinence. Recommendations of the International Scientific Committee. Evaluation and treatment of urinary incontinence, pelvic organ prolapse, and faecal incontinence. In Abrams P, Cardozo L, Khoury S, Wein A, eds: Incontinence, vol 2. Management. Plymouth, UK, Health Publications, 2005:1589-1626.

Leach GE, Dmochowski RR, Appell RA, et al: Female Stress Urinary Incontinence Clinical Guidelines Panel summary report on surgical management of female stress urinary incontinence. The American Urological Association. J Urol 1997;158(pt 1):875-880.

Smith ARB, Daneshgari F, Dmochowski R, et al: Surgery for urinary incontinence in women. In Abrams P, Cardozo L, Khoury S, Wein A, eds: Incontinence, vol 2. Management. Plymouth, UK, Health Publications, 2005:1297-1370.

Turner-Warwick R, Chapple CR: Functional Reconstruction of the Urinary Tract and Gynaeco-Urology: An Exposition of Functional Principles and Surgical Procedures. Oxford, England, Blackwell Science, 2002.

66 Vaginal Reconstructive Surgery for Sphincteric Incontinence and Prolapse

SENDER HERSCHORN, BSc, MDCM, FRCSC

Urinary incontinence may be the primary symptom that brings the female patient to the urologist, but other complaints and findings of pelvic organ prolapse may also be present. To effectively manage these conditions, the urologist should be familiar with pelvic anatomy, clinical evaluation, and treatment of both incontinence and pelvic organ prolapse.

Incontinence and pelvic organ prolapse are very common. Approximately 50% of adults in the United States report "any" incontinence, whereas 5% to 25% note leakage at least weekly and 5% to 15% note it daily or most of the time (Nygaard et al, 2004b). The lifetime risk that a woman in the United States will have surgery for either of these conditions is 11%, with up to one third of surgeries representing repeat procedures (Olsen et al, 1997). The U.S. National Center for Health Statistics reported that in 2002 there were 188,000 operations performed for female stress incontinence and 266,000 operations for genital prolapse, apart from hysterectomy (Kozak et al, 2005). In 2000, there were 52.7 million women aged 45 years or older and 14.3% of women were age 65 years or older (U.S. Census Bureau, 2004). By the year 2020, it is estimated that there will be 73.6 million women aged 45 and older, an increase of almost 40%. Furthermore, 18% of women will be aged 65 or older. Part of this increase in numbers of aging people is also due to a steady increase in life expectancy, from 78 in 1982 to 80 in 2002 (U.S. National Center for Health Statistics, 2004). With the increase and aging of the population and the emphasis on quality of life issues in health care, these problems and their treatment will assume additional importance.

EPIDEMIOLOGY OF URINARY INCONTINENCE, ANAL INCONTINENCE, AND PELVIC ORGAN PROLAPSE

A large number of urinary incontinence studies have been published, and key factors that are evident from the literature are outlined. The *prevalence* of incontinence is defined as the number of cases within a population at a certain point in time. *Incidence* is the number of new cases over a period of time. **Estimates of prevalence vary widely depending on the epidemiologic methods used and the population studied.**

In their extensive review, Hampel and colleagues (1997) summarized the results of 48 studies and observed that epidemiologic studies of urinary incontinence suffer from lack of conformity with regard to the definition of incontinence, survey methods, and validation of results. They noted that generally three definitions of incontinence had been used: (1) any uncontrolled urine loss in the prior 12 months without regard to severity (Diokno et al, 1986); (2) more than two incontinent episodes per month (Thomas et al, 1980); and (3) the older International Continence Society (ICS) definition—a condition in which urinary incontinence is a social or hygienic problem and is objectively demonstrable (Abrams et al, 1988). Similar variability in prevalence has been reported from the Third International Consultation on Urinary Incontinence in a recent extensive review (Hunskaar et al, 2005).

Table 66–1 illustrates that with more stringent definitions of incontinence the prevalence is generally lower. Most of the studies were conducted with large population-based questionnaires. Prevalence estimates for the most inclusive definitions of incontinence ("ever," "any," or "at least once in the past 12 months") range from 5% among women 15 years and older in Belgium (Van Oyen and Van Oyen, 2002) to 69% among women 19 years and older in Wales (Swithinbank et al, 1999). Most studies are in the range of 25% to 45% (Hunskaar et al, 2005). Studies reporting daily urinary incontinence have been

Table 66-1. Prevalence of Urinary Incontinence in Relation to Definition

Authors	Definition	Age Group	Prevalence
Wolin, 1969	Sporadic episodes	17-25	51%
Nemir and Middleton, 1954	Occasional episodes	17-24	52%
Burgio et al, 1991	1 per month	42-50	58%
Kuh et al, 1999	Ever in past 12 months	48	55%
Moller et al, 2000b	Weekly or more	40-60	16%
Campbell et al, 1985	Any in previous year	65+	12%
Diokno et al, 1986	Any to 6 days in previous 12 months	60+	38%
Molander et al, 1990	Any, time not specified	65-85	25%
Thomas et al, 1980	>2 per episodes per month	35-75+	10%
Yarnell et al, 1981	Some degree of incontinence	18-75+	45%

Table 66-2. Incidence of Urinary Incontinence

Authors	Country	Age (yr)	Incidence
Diokno et al, 1986	US	≥64	22.4% in 1 year
Herzog and Fultz, 1990	US	≥60	20% in 1 year
Campbell et al, 1985	New Zealand	65-69	7% over 4 years
Koyano et al, 1986	Japan	>65	10% over 5 years
Elving et al, 1989	Norway	55-59	1.3% per year
Burgio et al, 1991	US	42-50	8% over 3 years
Molander et al, 1990	Sweden	65-85	11% over 20 years
Moller et al, 2000	Denmark	40-60	5.8% per year
Samuelsson et al, 2000b	Sweden	20-59	2.9% per year

fairly consistent, with estimates of 4% to 7% in women younger than the age of 60 years (Burgio et al, 1991; Moller et al, 2000b; Samuelsson et al, 2000a), and from 4% to 19% in women older than the age of 65 (Wetle et al, 1995; Nakanishi et al, 1997; Brown et al, 1999).

Studies conducted recently in the United States show similar prevalences, 16% (Nygaard et al, 2003) to 57% (Sampselle et al, 2002), to those conducted in European countries. However, the wide range of results makes it difficult to make meaningful comparisons between countries (Hunskaar et al, 2005).

Regarding age, some studies cover a wide span whereas others are focused on a specific group (see Table 66–1). In two studies of young nulliparous women (Nemir and Middleton, 1954; Wolin, 1969), which are often quoted to verify the magnitude of the problem, the prevalence of some degree of urinary incontinence was about 50% but was a problem in only 5% and 6% of respondents, respectively. The prevalence of urinary incontinence appears to increase up to middle age, with a leveling off or slight decrease between ages 50 and 70 and then another steady increase with aging (Hunskaar et al, 2005). The Norwegian EPINCONT (Epidemiology of Incontinence in the County of Nord Trøndelag) study involved 27,936 women aged 20 and older. This represented an 80% response rate (Hannestad et al, 2000). This study reported an increase from 10% at age 20 to 30% at age 50, a stabilization or slight decline until ages 60 to 65, and then a steady increase to 35% in those older than the age of 70. Nearly 7% of the respondents had moderate to severe bothersome incontinence. Hunskaar and coworkers (2004), in a study conducted simultaneously in France, Germany, Spain, and the United Kingdom involving 17,143 women, reported a similar prevalence pattern with 5% to 10% higher values at each peak.

When incontinence was classified by symptoms or urodynamics, in 21 of the 48 studies reviewed by Hampel and colleagues (1997), median prevalence of stress incontinence was 49% followed by mixed and urge incontinence at 29% and 22%, respectively. In the EPINCONT study, over 50% was stress, 36% was mixed, and 11% was urge incontinence (Hannestad et al, 2000). **However, proportions of types differ by age. Stress incontinence predominates in young and middle-aged women whereas mixed and urge incontinence predominate in surveys of older women** (Hunskaar et al, 2004, 2005).

Incidence rates have been more difficult to ascertain because they require repeated surveys of the same population. There is also variability in the reported rates from 11% over 20 years (Molander et al, 1990) to 22.4% in 1 year (Diokno et al, 1986), as seen in Table 66–2. Elving and colleagues (1989) found a steady increase in the incidence of incontinence with age from 45 to 59 years, using the previously given first and third definitions of incontinence, with a cumulative incidence of 18% to 28% over 15 years. However, the incidence of stress incontinence per year decreased from 0.55% to 0.43% whereas that of urge incontinence increased from 0.08% to 0.2%.

Longitudinal studies also show variable remission rates from 5.9% over 5 years (Samuelsson et al, 2000b) **to 30% over 1 year** (Moller et al, 2000a). **Remission rates may be affected by quality of the study and measures, test-retest reliability, increased awareness of the problem and seeking of treatment on the part of the subjects, as well as possible natural history of the condition.**

Anal incontinence is the involuntary loss of flatus or feces, and fecal incontinence is the involuntary loss of feces—solid or liquid. The prevalence of anal incontinence is difficult to ascertain because of nonstandardized definitions and embarrassment and reluctance on the part of patients to admit to the problem (Bump and Norton, 1998). In a systematic review of 16 qualifying studies, Macmillan and colleagues (2004) reported that the prevalence of anal incontinence varied from 2% to 24%, and the estimated prevalence of fecal incontinence varied from 0.4% to 18%. The degree of disability was not known. In select populations of women the prevalence appears to be higher. Nygaard and colleagues (1997) reported fecal incontinence in more than 25% of 118 women 30 years after vaginal delivery. Similarly, in other reports of women with pelvic floor problems and urinary incontinence, the prevalence of anal incontinence is 28% to 29% (Gordon et al, 1999; Leroi et al, 1999; Boreham et al, 2005).

Pelvic organ prolapse is defined as the downward descent of the pelvic organs resulting in protrusion of the vagina and/or uterine cervix and does not include rectal prolapse.

There are few prevalence reports since the inconsistency of symptoms, and the requirement for a vaginal examination have limited such studies (Hunskaar et al, 2005). In the Women's Health Initiative, with a nonvalidated physical examination to measure prolapse in 27,342 postmenopausal women, 41% of subjects with a uterus and 38% of those without a uterus had some degree of prolapse (Hendrix et al, 2002). A lower rate of 31% was reported in a younger community-based population in Sweden (Samuelsson et al, 1999), and a much higher rate of 94% was reported in a U.S. study (Swift, 2000). The variable rates may reflect the different populations studied.

Reports of incidence are limited to studies of surgical treatment. **Olsen and coworkers (1997), on the basis of chart reviews from a large managed care population in Oregon, reported a lifetime risk of undergoing a single operation for prolapse or incontinence by age 80 years was 11.1%.** The incidence increased steadily with age from 0.1% at ages 20 to 29 years. They found a reoperation rate of 29.2%. Mant and colleagues (1997) from the United Kingdom reported an annual incidence of hospital admission with prolapse of 0.204% in a 20- to 26-year follow-up study of 17,032 women. Surgically managed patients may represent only a small fraction of those affected because many women are managed conservatively, may be asymptomatic, or never present for evaluation.

It is common for urinary incontinence and pelvic organ prolapse to coexist in the same woman or to develop subsequently (Bump and Norton, 1998). In a Norwegian study of 105 women with urinary incontinence, 38% had significant genital prolapse (Seim et al, 1996). In other reports, pelvic organ prolapse requiring surgery occurred in 29% (Kjolhede et al, 1996) and 26.7% (Wiskind et al, 1992) of patients after Burch colposuspension. Incontinence and prolapse are now considered conditions associated with pelvic floor disorders or dysfunction and have shared risk factors.

Risk Factors for Stress Incontinence and Pelvic Organ Prolapse

Epidemiologic data have revealed several risk factors or contributing variables derived from cross-sectional studies of volunteer or clinical subjects. Little is known about their relative or absolute value ((Hunskaar et al, 1999). There is also overlap among causative factors (see Table 63–3).

Aging

In addition to the reported increased prevalence of urinary incontinence with advancing age, there are age-related lower urinary tract changes that may predispose to incontinence (Resnick et al, 1989). There may also be age-related extrapelvic changes that result in functional or cognitive impairment that precipitate incontinence. There is a rise in prevalence and incidence of pelvic organ prolapse with age (Hunskaar et al, 2005).

Menopause

The literature does not support a causative association between menopause and urinary incontinence. Although studies from the United States (Burgio et al, 1991) and United Kingdom (Jolleys, 1988) showed a lower prevalence of incontinence in postmenopausal compared with premenopausal women, studies from the Netherlands (Rekers et al, 1992), Sweden (Hording et al, 1986), and Denmark (Milsom et al, 1993) showed no difference between the two groups. Studies have also shown an increased risk of incontinence in postmenopausal women on estrogens (Hendrix et al, 2005). **Similarly, menopause has not been found to be a risk factor for pelvic organ prolapse** (Hunskaar et al, 2005).

Pregnancy and Parity

Urinary incontinence during pregnancy usually clears post partum, but its presence may portend subsequent onset (Hunskaar et al, 2005).

Vaginal delivery is a major factor for the development of pelvic floor dysfunction in the majority of women (Bump and Norton, 1998). Most studies demonstrate a link between urinary incontinence and parity (Thomas et al, 1980; Yarnell et al, 1982; Hording et al, 1986; Sommer et al, 1990; Foldspang et al, 1992; Rortveit et al, 2001), although the level of risk is variable and lessens with age (Burgio et al, 1991; Rortveit et al, 2001). Parity and vaginal delivery are strong risk factors in pelvic organ prolapse (Mant et al, 1997; Hendrix et al, 2002). The labor and delivery process may cause the pelvic floor dysfunction as a result of nerve damage (e.g., afferents, pudendal, pelvic), muscular damage, and direct tissue stretching and disruption.

The role of episiotomy in causing or preventing pelvic floor dysfunction is controversial. Although some investigators have demonstrated an association with pelvic floor weakness at 3 months post partum (Klein et al, 1994), others have found no association in young to middle-aged women with a history of episiotomy (Samuelsson et al, 2000a). In a systematic review of routine episiotomy Hartmann and coworkers (2005) noted that long-term follow-up of women who had episiotomies into an age when they have the problems is generally lacking. They also concluded that episiotomy does not prevent fecal or urinary incontinence or pelvic floor relaxation.

Obesity

Several studies have shown obesity with increased body mass index to be an independent risk factor for urinary incontinence (Burgio et al, 1991; Mommsen and Foldspang, 1994; Hannestad et al, 2000). There is also evidence that massive weight loss after bariatric surgery improves incontinence symptoms (Deitel et al, 1988; Bump et al, 1992). Similarly, obesity is a consistent risk factor for prolapse (Hendrix et al, 2002).

Surgery

Previous pelvic surgery has been reported to be a risk factor for urinary incontinence (Holtedahl and Hunskaar, 1998; Schmidbauer et al, 2001; Sherburn et al, 2001). **The role of hysterectomy in the onset of urinary incontinence is controversial. Although several large-scale population-based studies have shown hysterectomy to be a significant risk factor** (Milsom et al, 1993; Brown et al, 1996; van der Vaart et al, 2002), **other studies of patients after hysterectomy have not demonstrated a consistent effect** (Carlson, 1997; Vervest et al, 1988). The type of abdominal hysterectomy, whether complete or partial, has not been reported to affect the development of stress incontinence (Kilkku, 1985). In a systematic review of published data, Brown and coworkers (2000) reported increased odds for incontinence in women with hysterectomy, although the incontinence might not develop for many years.

The incidence of pelvic organ prolapse requiring surgery has been reported to be higher in patients who have undergone hysterectomy, especially if done for prolapse (Mant et al, 1997; Marchionni et al, 1999). As well, anterior and posterior compartment prolapse after retropubic urethropexy and sacrospinous vault fixation, respectively, have been well described (Shull et al, 1992; Wiskind et al, 1992; Kjolhede et al, 1996, 2005).

Constipation

Vaginal childbirth has been implicated in causing pelvic neuropathy (Bump and Norton, 1998), and constipation with repeated prolonged defecatory straining efforts has been shown to exacerbate the dysfunction (Lubowski et al, 1988). An association between constipation and incontinence in the elderly has been reported (Diokno et al, 1990), and constipation and straining at stool have been implicated as risk factors for later development of pelvic organ prolapse and stress incontinence (Spence-Jones et al, 1994). In the U.S. Women's Health Initiative, constipation modestly increased the risk of prolapse (Hendrix et al, 2002).

Chronic Respiratory Problems and Smoking

Chronic obstructive pulmonary disease and its symptoms have been linked to urinary incontinence in epidemiologic studies (Diokno et al, 1990; Brown et al, 1996). Cigarette smoking has also been implicated as a risk factor for incontinence in case-control studies (Bump and McClish, 1992; Tampakoudis et al, 1995). The mechanism may be through chronic coughing or interference with collagen synthesis (Hunskaar et al, 2005).

Exercise and Heavy Lifting

The prevalence of urinary incontinence has been noted in young nulliparous athletes and in those who exercise (Nygaard et al, 1994), but high-impact activity did not predispose to subsequent development of incontinence (Nygaard, 1997). In a large-scale Danish study, heavy lifting was suggested to predispose to pelvic organ prolapse surgery (Jorgensen et al, 1994).

Genetic Factors

Connective tissue weakness leading to anatomic defects as a result of biochemical alteration in affected patients has been identified (Kondo et al, 1994). Norton and colleagues (1992) found an increase in weaker type III collagen in women with pelvic organ prolapse, and Falconer and coworkers (1994) found a decrease in total amount of collagen in stress-incontinent women as compared with continent controls.

In the U.S. Women's Health Initiative, African American women had the lowest risk and Hispanic woman had the highest risk of prolapse compared with white women (Hendrix et al, 2002).

Women with bladder exstrophy have a propensity for pelvic organ prolapse, especially uterine prolapse post partum (Woodhouse and Hinsch, 1997). Pelvic organ prolapse may be seen in women with joint hypermobility and in those with the underlying connective tissue disorders such as Ehlers-Danlos syndrome (Norton et al, 1995). Prolapse may also be seen in patients with neuromuscular disorders such as spinal dysraphism (Loret de Mola and Carpenter, 1996).

KEY POINTS: EPIDEMIOLOGY OF URINARY INCONTINENCE, ANAL INCONTINENCE, AND PELVIC ORGAN PROLAPSE

- Estimates of incontinence and prolapse vary depending on the epidemiologic methods used and the population studies.

- Stress incontinence predominates in young and middle aged women, whereas mixed and urge incontinence predominate in older women.

- Remission rates may be affected by the quality of the study, test-retest reliability, increased awareness and treatment seeking, and natural history.

- Pelvic organ prolapse is the downward descent of the pelvic organs resulting in protrusion of the vagina and/or uterus. It does not include rectal prolapse.

- Major risk factors are aging, pregnancy and parity, obesity, previous pelvic surgery, constipation, chronic respiratory problems, exercise and heavy lifting, and genetic factors.

ANATOMY OF PELVIC FLOOR, SUPPORTING STRUCTURES, AND PATHOPHYSIOLOGY OF PELVIC ORGAN PROLAPSE

Different anatomic names are frequently applied to the same anatomic structure. The terminology used here represents the author's assessment of the most commonly used terms.

Bony Scaffolding

The maintenance of continence and prevention of pelvic organ prolapse rely on the support mechanisms of the pelvic floor. The bony pelvis consists of the two innominate or hip bones that are fused to the sacrum posteriorly and to each other anteriorly at the pubic symphysis. Each innominate (hip) bone is composed of the ilium, ischium, and pubis, which are connected by cartilage in youth but fuse in the adult (Soames, 1995). The pelvis has two basins, the major and minor (or greater and lesser). The abdominal viscera occupy the major basin, and the minor basin is the narrower continuation of it inferiorly. The inferior pelvic outlet is closed by the pelvic floor. **The female pelvis (Fig. 66–1) has wider diameters and a more circular shape than that of the male. The wider inlet facilitates head engagement and parturition. The wider outlet also predisposes to subsequent pelvic floor weakness.** Numerous projections and contours provide

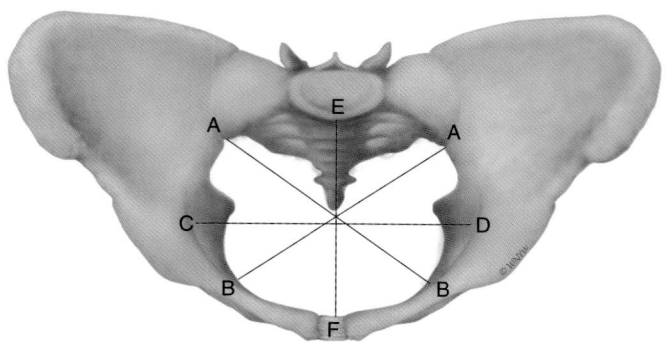

Figure 66–1. The diameters of the female minor pelvis. Lines A-B indicate superior aperture to inferior aperture. **A,** Sacroiliac joint. **B,** Iliopubic eminence. **C** and **D,** Middle of pelvic brim. **E,** Sacral promontory. **F,** Pubic symphysis.

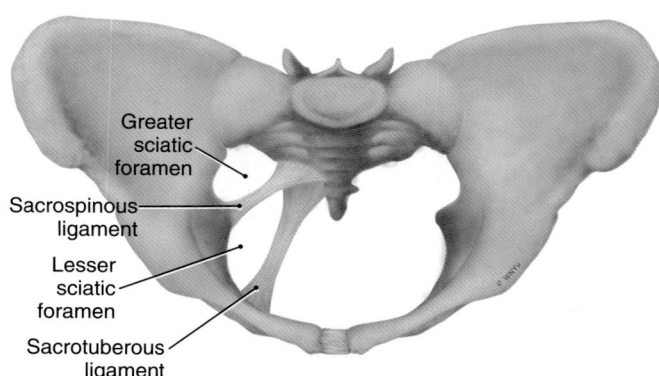

Figure 66–2. The female pelvis from above: the sacrospinous ligament extends from the ischial spines to the lateral margins of the sacrum and coccyx anterior to the sacrotuberous ligament, which extends from the ischial tuberosity to the coccyx. The sciatic foramina are above and below the sacrospinous ligament and anterior to the sacrotuberous ligament.

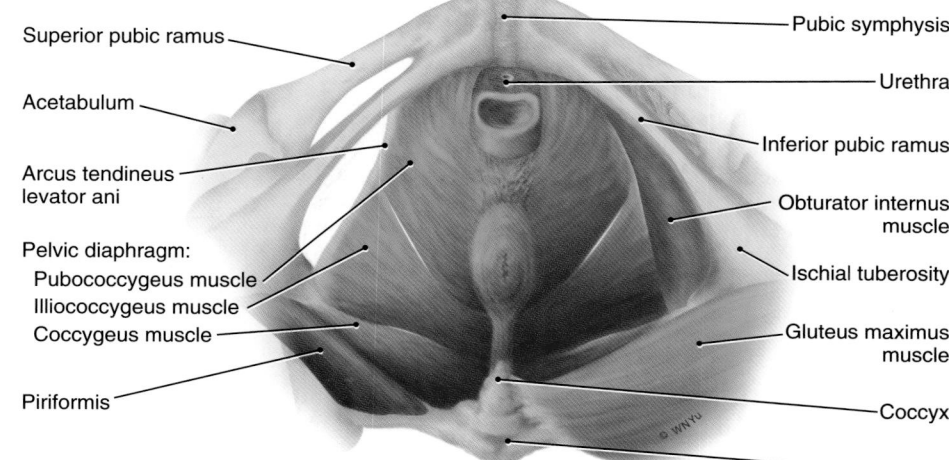

Figure 66–3. A caudal view of the levator ani muscles in the bony pelvis.

attachment sites for ligaments, muscles, and fascial layers. Of note is the thin and triangular sacrospinous ligament (Fig. 66–2), which extends from the ischial spines to the lateral margins of the sacrum and coccyx anterior to the sacrotuberous ligament. Its anterior surface is muscular and constitutes the coccygeus (also called the ischiococcygeus); the ligament is often regarded as the degenerate part of the muscle (Soames, 1995). The greater and lesser sciatic foramina are above and below the ligament.

Muscular Supports of the Pelvic Floor

Pelvic Diaphragm

The levator ani and coccygeus muscles that are attached to the inner surface of the minor pelvis form the muscular floor of the pelvis. With their corresponding muscles from the opposite side, they form the pelvic diaphragm (Fig. 66–3). The levator ani is composed of two major muscles from medial to lateral: the pubococcygeus and the iliococcygeus (Kearney et al, 2004).

The bulkier medial part is the pubococcygeus muscle that arises from the back of the body of the pubis and anterior portion of the arcus tendineus. **The arcus tendineus of the levator ani is a dense connective tissue structure that runs from the pubic ramus to the ischial spine and courses along the surface of the obturator internus muscle.** The muscle passes back almost horizontally to behind the rectum. The inner border forms the margin of the levator (urogenital) hiatus, through which passes the urethra, vagina, and anorectum. Various muscle subdivisions have been assigned to the medial portions of the pubococcygeus to reflect the attachments of the muscle to the urethra, vagina, anus, and rectum (Strohbehn, 1998). These portions are referred to as the pubovaginalis, puboanalis, and puborectalis, or, collectively, as the puboviscerialis (Lawson, 1974), because of its association and attachment to the midline viscera. The muscle attaches to the periurethral supports (DeLancey and Starr, 1990), and the vaginal and anorectal parts insert into the vaginal walls, perineal body, and external anal sphincter muscle (Salmons, 1995). The puborectalis portion passes behind the rectum and fuses with its counterpart from the opposite side to form a

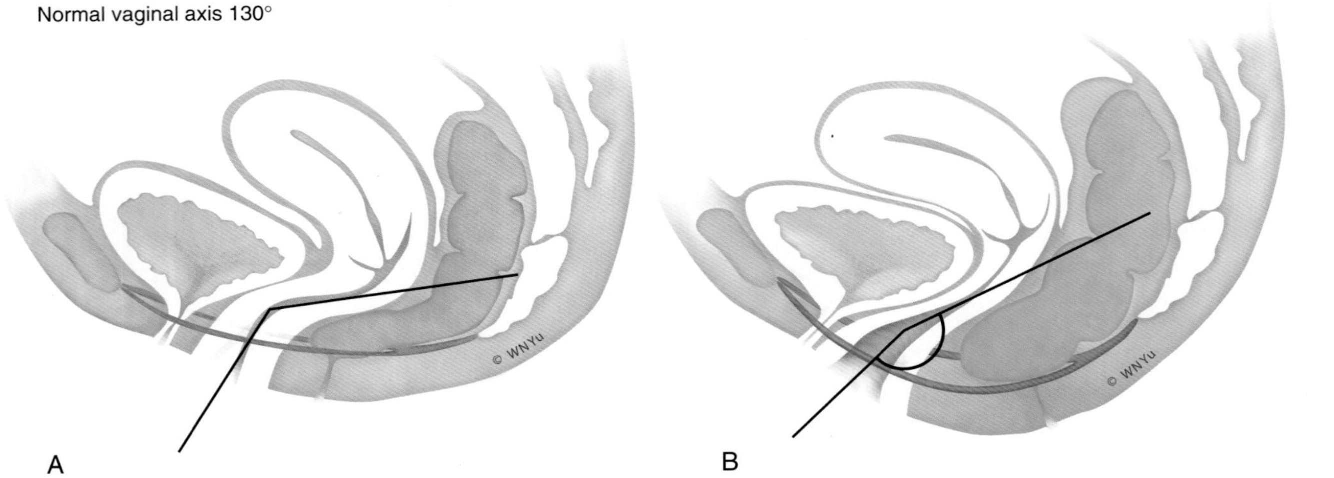

Normal vaginal axis 130°

A

B

Figure 66–4. Midsagittal section of the pelvis. **A,** Normal tone in the levator ani with acute anorectal angle and horizontal levator plate. Note the normal vaginal axis. **B,** With loss of tone in the levator ani there is change in the vaginal axis, sagging of the levator plate, and enlargement of the urogenital hiatus. Note the wider angle.

sling behind the anorectum. Other, more posterior parts of the pubococcygeus attach to the coccyx.

The pubococcygeus can be palpated during physical examination of the pelvis as a bulky muscular ridge on both right and left lateral side walls of the vagina, superior to the hymen. With contraction, it elevates the rectum, vagina, and urethra anteriorly and aids in compression of their lumina.

The thin lateral part of the levator ani is the iliococcygeus muscle that arises from the arcus tendineus of the levator ani to the ischial spine. Posteriorly, it attaches to the last two segments of the coccyx. The fibers from both sides also fuse to form a raphe that is continuous with the fibroelastic anococcygeal ligament. **This median raphe between the anus and the coccyx is called the *levator plate,* the shelf on which the pelvic organs rest. It is formed by the fusion of the iliococcygeus and the posterior fibers of the pubococcygeus muscles. In the standing position, the levator plate is horizontal and supports the rectum and upper two thirds of vagina above it.** Weakness of the levator ani may loosen the sling behind the anorectum and cause the levator plate to sag (Berglas and Rubin, 1953). This opens the urogenital hiatus and predisposes to pelvic organ prolapse (Fig. 66–4). Women with prolapse have been shown to have an enlarged urogenital hiatus on clinical examination (Delancey and Hurd, 1998).

The coccygeus muscle extends from the ischial spine to the coccyx and lower sacrum and forms the posterior part of the pelvic diaphragm. It sits on the pelvic surface of the sacrospinous ligament.

Three-dimensional magnetic resonance imaging (MRI) of the pelvic diaphragm (Fig. 66–5) shows its peripheral attachments and demonstrates the urogenital hiatus (Fielding et al, 2000).

Direct innervation of the levator ani muscles on its cranial surface is primarily from the third and fourth sacral nerve roots by means of the pudendal nerve (Gosling et al, 1999). The puborectalis may derive some of its innervation from a pudendal branch on the caudal side (Strohbehn, 1998). Regarding the type of striated muscle, it has been reported that the majority of the muscle fibers in the levator ani are slow-

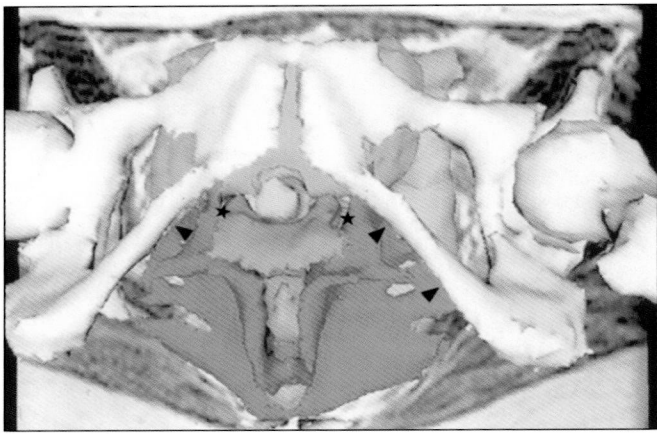

Figure 66–5. MR anatomy of 24-year-old healthy female volunteer. Color key: white = bones; pink = levator ani, yellow = bladder and urethra; blue = vagina; gray = rectum. View mimics that used by physicians when examining patients or performing surgery. Arcus tendineus is indicated by *arrowheads,* and levator hiatus is delineated by *stars.* (From Fielding JR, Dumanli H, Schreyer AG, et al: MR-based three-dimensional modeling of the normal pelvic floor in women: Quantification of muscle mass. AJR Am J Roentgenol 2000;174:657-660.)

twitch fibers that maintain constant tone (type I) (Gilpin et al, 1989), with an increased density of fast-twitch (type II) fibers distributed in the periurethral and perianal areas (Critchley et al, 1980; Gosling et al, 1981). This suggests that the normal levator ani maintains tone in the upright position to support the pelvic viscera. Furthermore, voluntary squeezing of the puborectalis may increase the tone to counter increased intra-abdominal pressure.

Urogenital Diaphragm (Triangle)

Another musculofascial structure is present over the anterior pelvic outlet below the pelvic diaphragm. **However, there is controversy over whether it contains a transverse sheet of muscle extending across the pubic arch (deep transverse perinei muscle) sandwiched between superior and inferior**

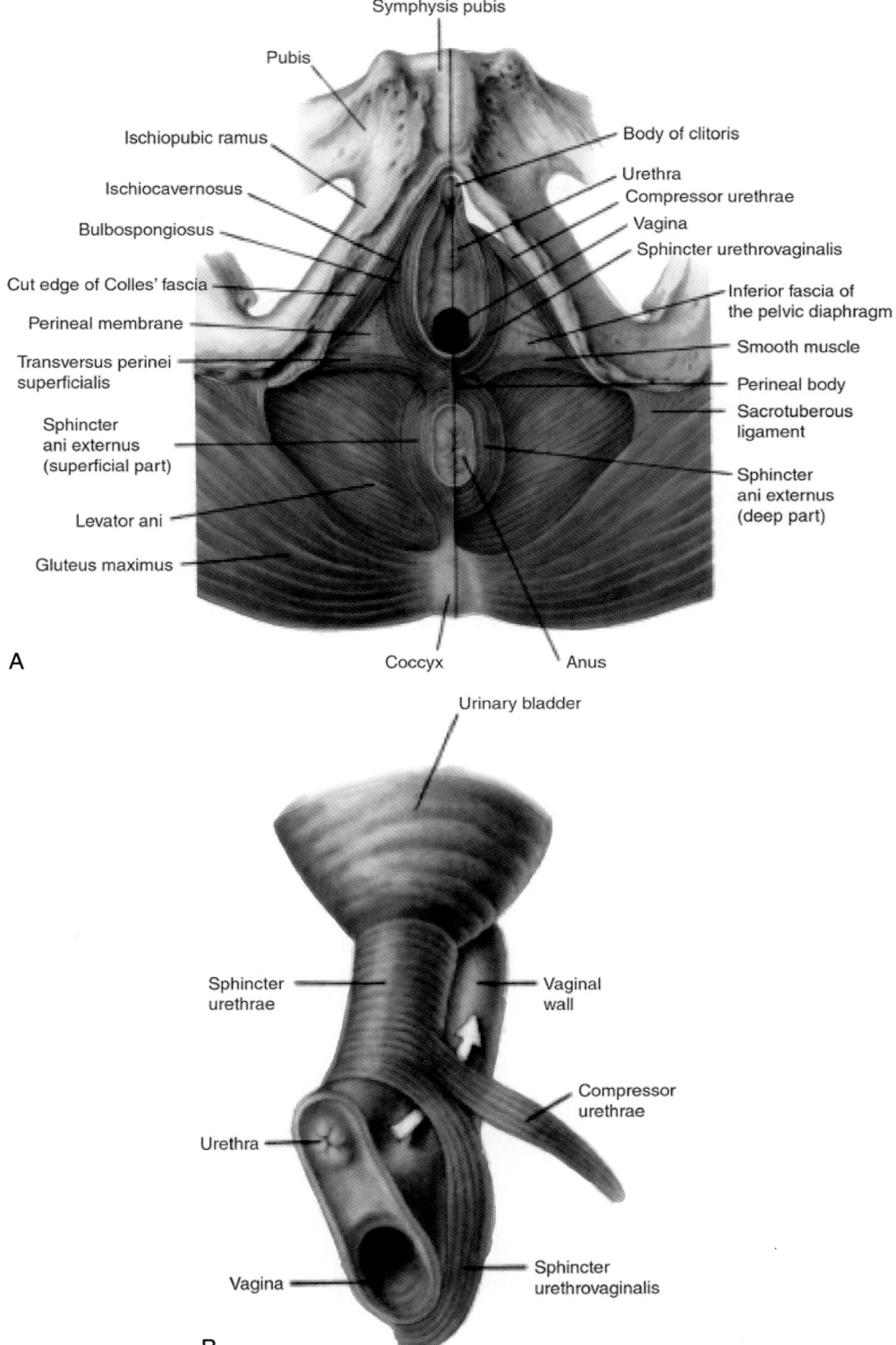

Figure 66–6. Muscles of the perineum. **A,** On the subject's right side, the membranous layer of the superficial fascia has been removed (note the cut edge). On the subject's left side, the symphysis pubis, pubis, part of the ischiopubic ramus, superficial perineal muscles, and inferior fascia of the urogenital diaphragm have been removed to show the deep perineal muscles. **B,** Drawing shows the continuity of the deep perineal muscles with the sphincter urethrae. (From Salmons S: Muscle. In Williams PL, Bannister LH, Berry MM, et al [eds]: Gray's Anatomy, 38th ed. New York, Churchill Livingstone, 1995, pp 737-900.)

fascia (Klutke and Siegel, 1995; Healy and Mundy, 2005) or three contiguous striated muscles (compressor urethrae, sphincter urethrae, and urethrovaginalis) and an inferior fascial layer called the **perineal membrane** (Oelrich, 1983; Salmons, 1995; DeLancey, 1999) (Fig. 66–6). Despite the controversy, MRI clearly depicts the structure (Klutke and Siegel, 1995; Strohbehn, 1998). The more superficial ischiocavernosus and bulbocavernosus muscles as well as the thin slips of superficial transverse perinei (DeLancey, 1999) complete the inferior aspect of the structure. It bridges the gap between the inferior pubic rami bilaterally and the perineal body. It closes the urogenital (levator) hiatus, supports and has a sphincter-like effect at the distal vagina, and contributes to continence because it is attached to periurethral striated muscles. It also provides structural support for the distal urethra. The posterior triangle around the anus does not have a corresponding diaphragm or membrane. The ischiorectal fossae are the spaces lateral to the anus below the pelvic diaphragm.

Perineal Body

The perineal body is a poorly defined pyramidal aggregation of fibromuscular tissue located in the midline between the anus and the vagina (Fig. 66–7; see also Fig. 66–6) with the rectovaginal septum at its cephalad apex (Healy and Mundy, 2005). Below this, muscles and their fascia converge and interlace through the structure. Attached to it are the rectum, vaginal slips from the pubococcygeus, perineal muscles, and anal sphincter. It also contains smooth muscle, elastic fibers, and nerve endings. During childbirth, it distends and then recoils (Klutke and Siegel, 1995). The perineal body is an important part of the pelvic floor because just above it are the vagina and the uterus. Acquired weakness gives rise to elongation and predisposes to defects such as rectocele and enterocele (Nichols, 1997; DeLancey, 1999).

Figure 66–7 demonstrates the pelvic organs with the two major levels of muscular support: the upper with the pelvic diaphragm and the lower with the perineal membrane anteriorly and anal sphincter posteriorly.

Endopelvic Fascia and Connective Tissue Supports

The bladder and urethra, vagina, and uterus are attached to the pelvic walls by a system of connective tissue that has been called the endopelvic fascia. It lies immediately beneath the peritoneum and is one continuous unit with various thickenings or condensations in specific areas. It is continuous with the visceral fascia that provides a capsule for organs and allows displacements and changes in volume. The distinct regions are given individual names, specifically, ligaments and fasciae, with variable internal structure. Endopelvic fasciae and ligaments are a meshlike group of collagen fibers interlaced with elastin, smooth muscle cells, fibroblasts, and vascular structures. The structures that attach the uterus to the pelvic wall, the cardinal ligaments, derive strength from the supportive collagen forming the walls of arteries and veins. Other structures such as the pelvic side wall attachment of the endopelvic fascia (arcus tendineus of the pelvic fascia) are predominantly fibrous collagen (Norton, 1993).

The term *endopelvic fascia* is controversial because it is imprecise and nonspecific. It refers to multiple areas of differing anatomic structure and implies that the fascia and its supports emanate from within the pelvis. The pelvic diaphragm has superior and inferior fascial layers. The thin inferior layer is continuous with the obturator fascia laterally, covers the medial wall of the ischiorectal fossa, and blends

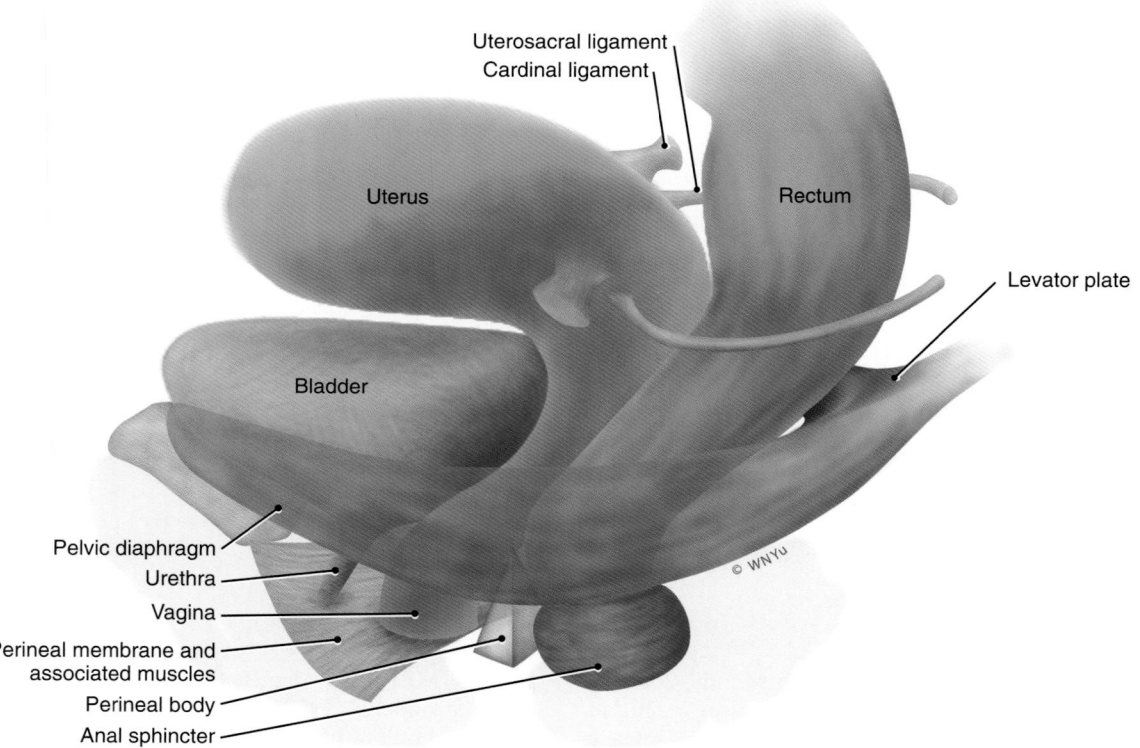

Figure 66–7. Diagram of pelvic organs. This shows the two major muscular supporting structures. The upper is the pelvic diaphragm, and the lower is the perineal membrane with associated muscles anteriorly and the anal sphincter posteriorly.

below with fascia of the sphincter urethrae, vaginal wall, and external anal sphincter (see Fig. 66–7). The superior fascia of the pelvic diaphragm is attached anteriorly to the back of the body of the pubis about 2 cm above the lower border and extends laterally along the pubis, blending with obturator fascia and continuing along a line to the ischial spine. Behind, it is continuous with pyriform fascia. Medially, it blends with the visceral pelvic fascia. **The arcus tendineus of the levator ani (ATLA), which runs from the pubic ramus to the ischial spine, is the thickening where the obturator fascia, superior and inferior diaphragmatic fasciae, and degenerated aponeurosis of the levator ani fuse. The ATLA attaches the posterior part of the pubococcygeus and the iliococcygeus muscles to the pelvic sidewall. Medial to it, within the superior fascia, is the arcus tendineus of the pelvic fascia or fasciae pelvis (ATFP), a thick white band extending from the lower part of the symphysis pubis to the ischial spine** (Salmons, 1995; Pit et al, 2003). The fascial supports of the bladder and upper parts of the urethra and vagina attach to the ATFP, on the surface of the superior pelvic diaphragmatic fascia. The white line of the endopelvic fascia usually refers to the ATFP. The ATFP and the ATLA can be seen together or diverging in retropubic dissections (Delancey, 2002; Pit et al, 2003). They are also palpable during a retropubic dissection.

Anterior Supports

There is agreement among authors that the connective tissue supports of the urethra, bladder, and vagina extend to the arcus tendineus of the pelvic fascia on the pelvic diaphragm (DeLancey, 1994; Klutke and Siegel, 1995; Weber and Walters, 1997; Strohbehn, 1998). There is also agreement that a "hammock" of anterior vaginal wall tissue, bridging the gap medially in the urogenital hiatus, supports the vesical neck and urethra (DeLancey, 1994). The controversies focus on the connective tissue structures that are associated with this hammock.

The pubourethral ligaments are connective tissue structures that extend from the urethra to the pubic bone. Some authors (Krantz, 1951; Zacharin, 1963; Milley and Nichols, 1971; Mostwin et al, 1995) have described them as structures responsible for supporting the urethra and keeping the vesical neck closed. Others have described connective tissue between the proximal urethra (and vesical neck) and the pubis as containing smooth muscle (Delancey, 1989) and cholinergic nerve supply (Wilson et al, 1983) that make the structures more suited to vesical neck opening during micturition than urethral support. It is postulated that there are two separate structures, one for support at the mid or distal urethra and one near the bladder neck that may open it during voiding. The distal support has been described (Delancey, 1989) as connective tissue that joins the vaginal wall and periurethral tissue to the ATFP and the levator muscles. Recently, Pit and coworkers demonstrated a structure that runs from the urethra to the inner surface of the pubic bone medial to the anterior attachment of the ATFP in cadaveric dissections (Pit et al, 2003). These ligaments appear to be important for urethral support (Mostwin et al, 1995).

There is controversy about the amount of supportive tissue or fascia in the anterior vaginal wall. Although the wall is composed of mucosa, muscularis, and adventitia and abuts a similar arrangement in both the urethra and the bladder,

various authors have attributed to it a vaginal fascial layer. Weber and Walters (1997) cited many articles on both sides of the controversy and showed no specific fascial layer, whereas DeLancey (1994) demonstrated a fascial layer suburethrally on the anterior vaginal wall. With or without the suburethral fascial layer, **the anterior vaginal wall supports the urethra by its lateral attachment to the levators (pubococcygeus) and to the endopelvic fascia from the ATFP** (Figs. 66–8 and 66–9). **In essence, it is a double hammock. Paradoxically, the more advanced the prolapse, the more thickened and hypertrophied is the vaginal submucosal layer** (DeLancey, 1994; Weber and Walters, 1997).

At the level of the bladder base, there is little actual endopelvic fascia between the bladder and the vaginal muscularis. Here the support comes from the lateral attachment of the vagina to the ATFP (DeLancey, 1994). The pubocervical fascia has been described as a trapezoidal layer extending from the symphysis along the anterior vaginal wall to blend with the fascia that surrounds the cervix. It is continuous laterally with the pubococcygeus and also suspended to the ATFP bilaterally. Its existence as a separate and discernible entity is in dispute (Weber and Walters, 1997), but the term is used commonly.

In cadaver dissections, Richardson and coworkers (1976) identified four basic problems that cause anterior vaginal wall prolapse. Weaknesses in the central part of the anterior vaginal wall or fascia give rise to cystocele from a central defect. Weakness in the lateral attachments to the arcus tendineus results in cystocele from a lateral or paravaginal defect. Combined defects with both central and lateral deficiency are also common (Fig. 66–10). These authors also identified a proximal transverse defect resulting from separation of the anterior wall fascia (pubocervical fascia) from the ring of fascia around the cervix. A distal defect was also described with separation of the pubocervical fascia from the pubis. The distal defect was rare in a study by Delancey (2002). Accompanying stress incontinence depends on associated weaknesses in urethral supports, pelvic floor muscles, and urethral function.

Middle Supports

The connective tissue surrounding the vagina and the uterus is the paracolpium and the parametrium, respectively. In the midvagina, the paracolpium fuses with the pelvic wall and fascia laterally (DeLancey, 1992). The cardinal ligaments (Fig. 66–11) (also called the transverse cervical ligaments of Mackenrodt) extend from the lateral margins of the cervix and upper vagina to the lateral pelvic walls. They originate over a large area from the region of the greater sciatic foramen over the pyriformis muscles, from the pelvic bones in the region of the sacroiliac joint, and from the lateral sacrum. They are condensations of the lowermost parts of the broad ligaments. Laterally, they are continuous with the connective tissue surrounding the hypogastric vessels. Medially, they are continuous with the paracolpium and parametrium as well as the connective tissue in the anterior vaginal wall (pubocervical fascia). The uterosacral ligaments are attached to the cervix and upper vaginal fornices posterolaterally. Posteriorly, they attach to the presacral fascia in front of the sacroiliac joint, although new MR data from asymptomatic women point to an insertion on the sacrospinous/coccygeus muscle complex

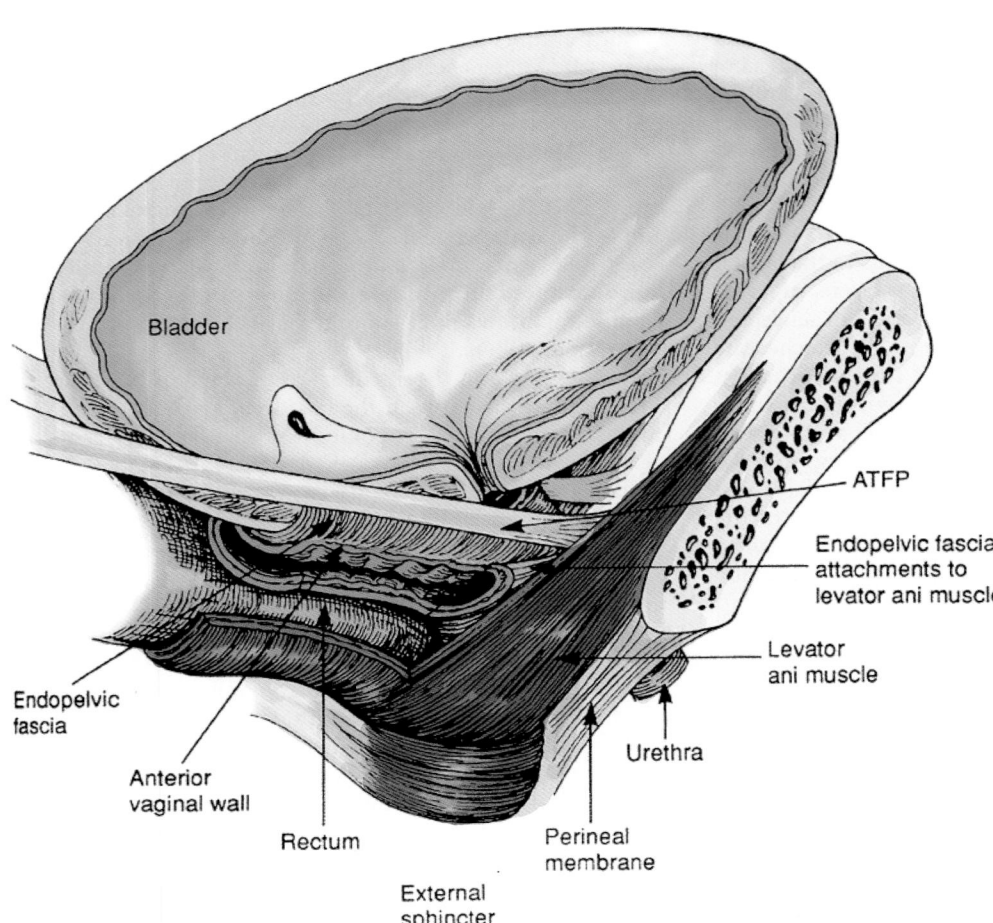

Bladder

ATFP

Endopelvic fascial
attachments to
levator ani muscle

Levator
ani muscle

Urethra

Endopelvic
fascia

Anterior
vaginal wall

Rectum

Perineal
membrane

External
sphincter

Figure 66–8. The "hammock" hypothesis. The anterior vaginal wall with its attachment to the arcus tendineus of the pelvic fascia forms a hammock under the urethra and bladder neck. (From DeLancey JOL: Structural support of the urethra as it relates to stress urinary incontinence: The hammock hypothesis. Am J Obstet Gynecol 1994; 170:1713-1723.)

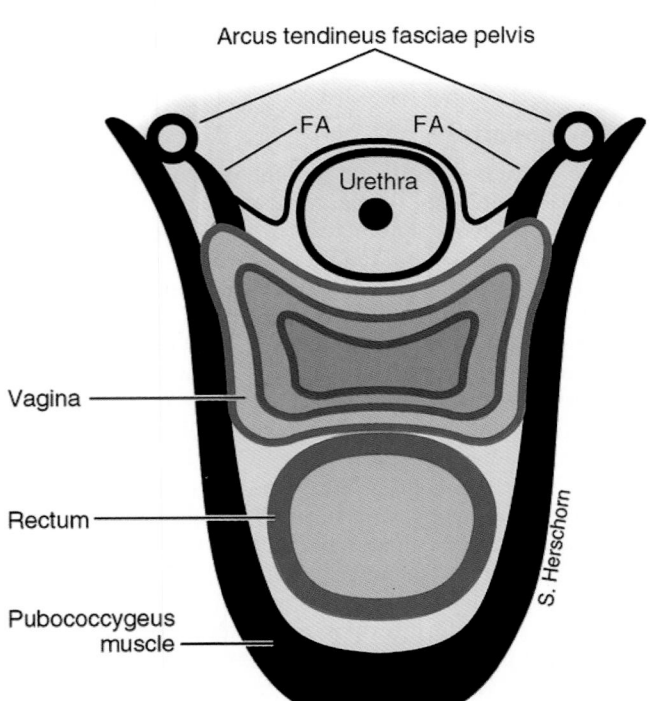

Arcus tendineus fasciae pelvis

FA   FA

Urethra

Vagina

Rectum

Pubococcygeus
muscle

S. Herschorn

Figure 66–9. Cross section of urethral supports below the bladder neck. The urethra is supported by a hammock of anterior vaginal wall suspended to the levators (pubococcygeus muscles) and the fascial attachments (FA) to the tendinous arch of the pelvic fascia. In essence it is a "double hammock."

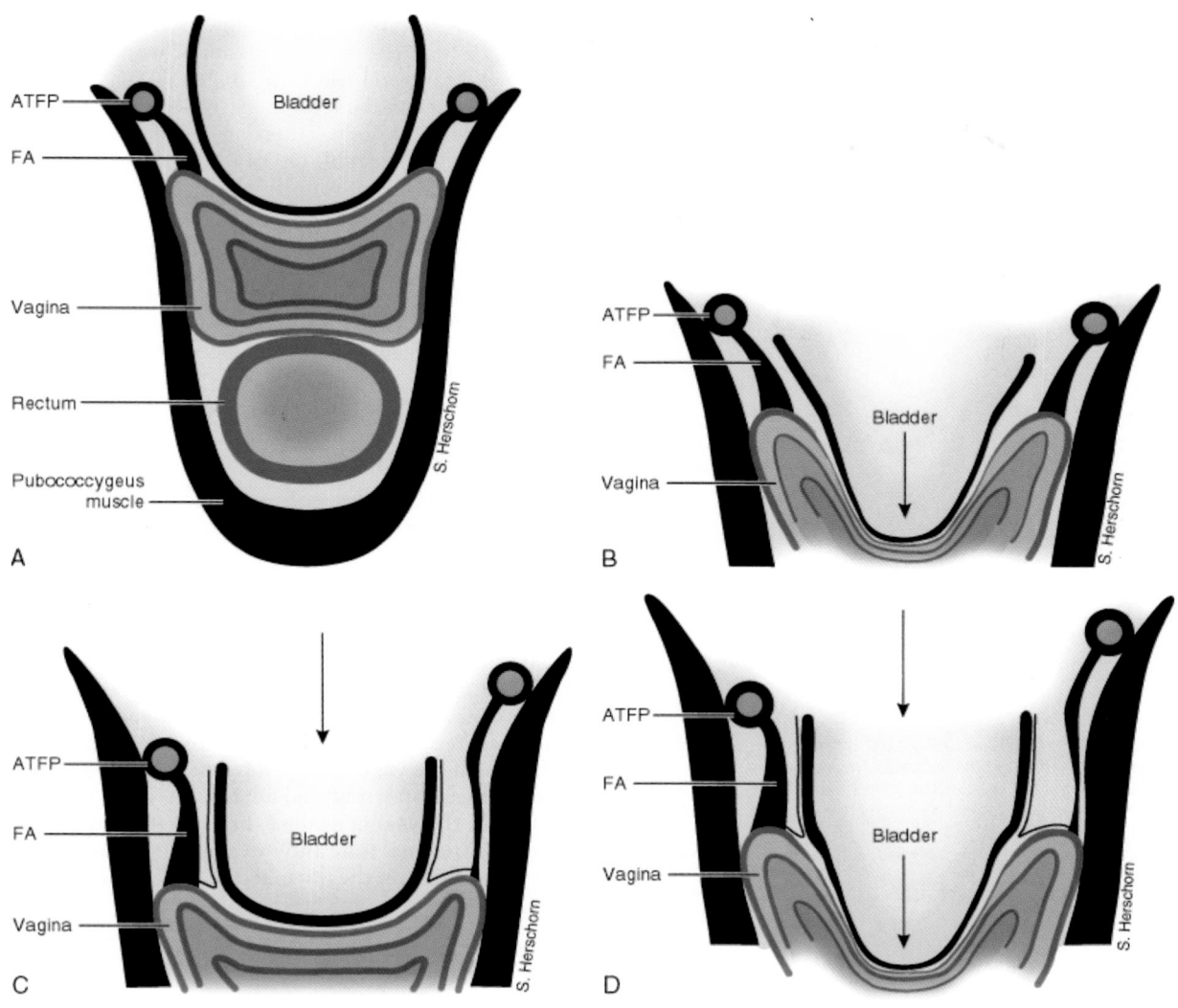

Figure 66–10. Illustrations of anterior vaginal wall defects. **A,** Normal bladder supported by suspension to arcus tendineus of the pelvic fascia (ATPF). The *arrows* on the diagrams show the amount of descent that occurs with the weakness of the supports. **B,** Cystocele from weakness of central vaginal wall supports. **C,** Cystocele from weakness of lateral supports, either separation of the ATPF from the fascia overlying the levator ani muscle on the right or stretching of the fascial layer. **D,** Cystocele from a combined central and lateral defect.

(Umek et al, 2004). The connective tissue of the uterosacral ligaments is continuous with that of the cardinal ligaments around the cervix. **The cardinal and uterosacral ligaments hold the uterus and upper vagina in their proper place over the levator plate** (Thompson, 1997). The arrangement is shown in Figure 66–11. The cardinal and uterosacral ligaments are not directly important for continence, but they do play a role in the support of the bladder base in the surgical correction of large cystoceles (Raz et al, 1998).

Posterior Supports

The posterior vaginal wall, below the cardinals, is supported from the sides by the paracolpium, which is attached to the endopelvic fascia (referred to as rectovaginal fascia in this area) and pelvic diaphragm. The rectovaginal fascia extends from the perineal body toward the ATPF, with which it converges approximately midway between the pubis and ischial

spine (Leffler et al, 2001). The anterior and posterior fascial layers unite along the sides of the vagina (Fig. 66–12).

According to DeLancey (1992), the rectovaginal fascia is mostly at the sides and is very thin in the midline of the vaginal wall. However, a posterior rectovaginal septum, consisting of fibromuscular elastic tissue extending from the peritoneal reflection to the perineal body, has been described (Milley and Nichols, 1969). In fetal life, the peritoneal cavity extends to the cranial part of the perineal body but becomes obliterated in early life. Its fused layers (Denonvillier's fascia) probably become part of the rectovaginal septum adherent to the undersurface of the posterior vaginal wall. This fascia forms the anterior margin of another potential space, the rectovaginal space. If intact and normal, the rectovaginal septum permits independent mobility of the rectal and vaginal walls.

In the distal vagina, 2 to 3 cm above the hymeneal ring, the vaginal wall is directly attached to surrounding structures

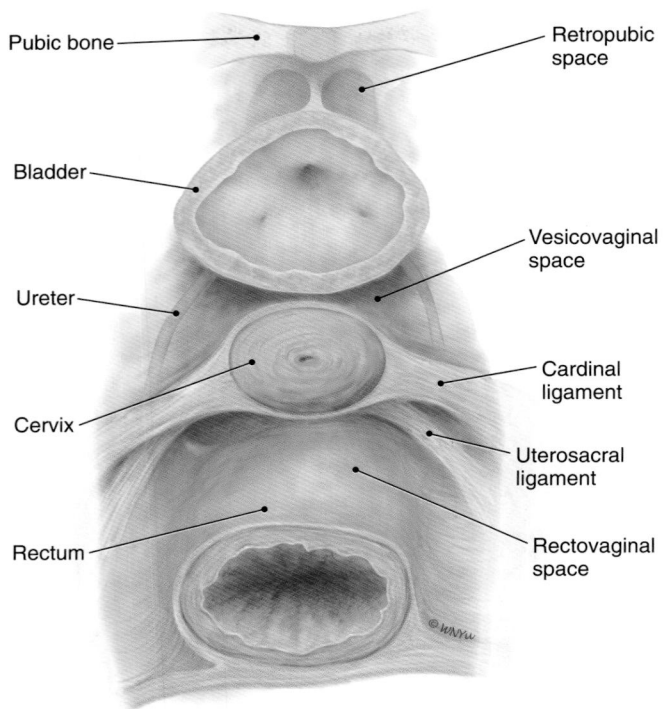

Figure 66-11. The cardinal and uterosacral ligaments provide support to the cervix and indirectly the bladder base. The retropubic, vesicovaginal, and rectovaginal spaces are seen at the level of the cervix. (Adapted from Raz S, Stothers L, Chopra A: Vaginal reconstructive surgery for incontinence and prolapse. In Walsh PC, Retik AB, Vaughan ED Jr, Wein AJ [eds]: Campbell's Urology, 7th ed. Philadelphia, WB Saunders, 1998, pp 1059-1094.)

without any intervening paracolpium. Anteriorly, the vagina fuses with the urethra and the connective tissue of the perineal membrane and muscles (urogenital diaphragm). Laterally, it blends with the levator ani muscles. Posteriorly, it fuses with the perineal body. The rectovaginal fascia is thickest in this region (Reiffenstuhl, 1993), and the vagina in the area has no mobility separate from its adjacent structures (DeLancey, 1992).

The fascial supports for the rectum, the lateral rectal ligaments, extend from the posterolateral pelvic side wall (level with the third sacral vertebra) to the rectum and surround the middle rectal arteries. Additional prerectal and pararectal fascial elements are frequently described (Raz et al, 1998).

PELVIC ORGAN PROLAPSE
Pathophysiology

The pelvic floor consists of innervated muscles with distinct connective tissue elements that support the pelvic organs. Delancey (DeLancey, 1993; Delancey and Hurd, 1998) has described protective mechanisms that are in place to prevent prolapse. **The uterus and vagina are attached to the pelvic walls by endopelvic fasciae and suspensory ligaments. The levator ani muscles constrict the lumen of these organs until they are closed, forming an occlusive layer on which the pelvic organs can rest. The closed and suspended organs rest on the surface of the posterior levator plate and act as a flap valve. With the vagina suspended in such a way that it rests against the supporting wall adjacent to it, increases in pressure force the vagina against the wall, thereby pinning it in place. The normal tone and integrity of the levators muscles may also maintain the normal dimensions of the urogenital**

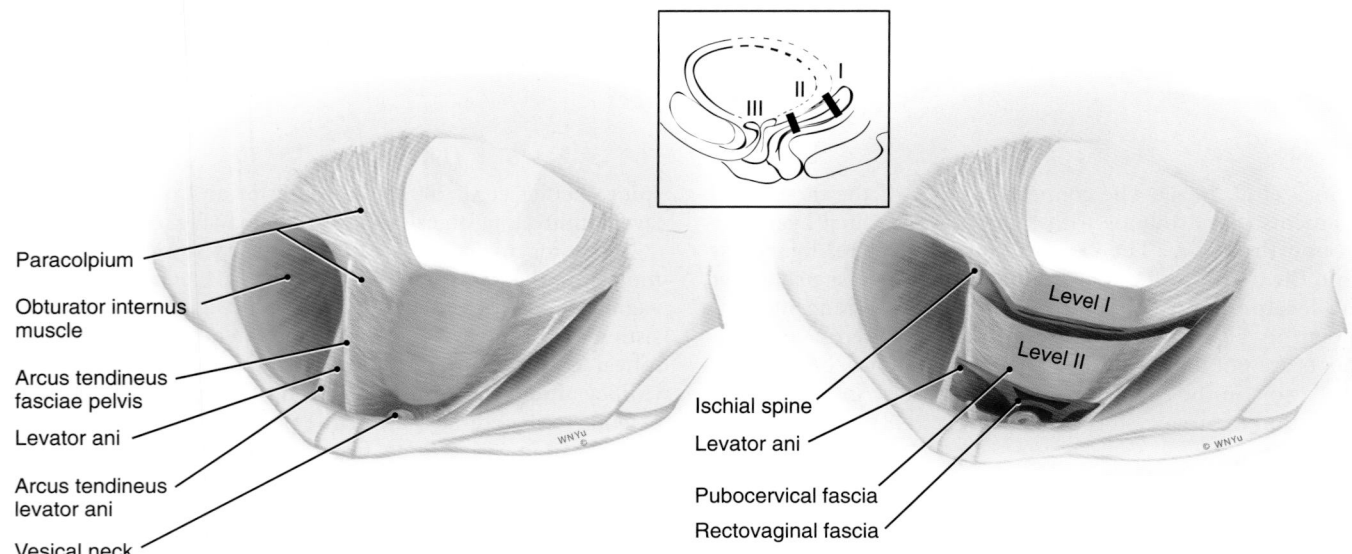

Figure 66-12. **A,** Vagina and supportive structures drawn from dissection of 56-year-old cadaver after hysterectomy. Bladder has been removed above the vesical neck. Paracolpium extends along lateral wall of vagina. **B,** In level I, paracolpium suspends vagina from lateral pelvic walls. In level II, vagina is attached to arcus tendineus of pelvic fascia and superior fascia of levator ani muscles. (Adapted from DeLancey JOL: Anatomic aspects of vaginal eversion after hysterectomy. Am J Obstet Gynecol 1992;166:1717-1728.)

hiatus. Factors that weaken the muscular and connective tissue supporting mechanisms may give rise to prolapse.

The risk factors for incontinence and pelvic organ prolapse are shown in Table 66–3. As was mentioned earlier, the labor and delivery process may cause the pelvic floor dysfunction because of nerve damage (e.g., afferents, pudendal, pelvic), direct muscle damage, and direct tissue disruption. The extent of birth-related levator injuries was shown in an MR study in which 20% of primiparas had defects primarily in the pubococcygeus muscle (DeLancey et al, 2003). Other risk factors, if present, may also contribute to the problem.

If levator ani muscle tone is lost or decreased, the support provided by the muscle to resist intra-abdominal pressures generated by standing or any other provocation is diminished. The connective tissue supports are then recruited to bear an even greater load of intra-abdominal pressure without the protective support of the pelvic muscular diaphragm. These connective tissue structures that may already be weakened may then undergo further damage, stretching, and breaking, resulting in pelvic organ prolapse and failure of continence mechanisms. Usually, there is a combination of both muscular and connective tissue weakness; however, it is occasionally possible for the cervix or vaginal wall to prolapse downward because of defective connective tissue supports without muscular damage or enlarged urogenital (levator) hiatus (Delancey and Hurd, 1998).

DeLancey (1992) has also characterized connective tissue supports into three levels, with levels I, II, and III representing apical, midvaginal, and distal vaginal supports (see Fig. 66–12B). Level I, or apical, defects are thought to be caused by loss of normal support of the upper paracolpium and parametrium and are associated with uterine prolapse, vaginal vault prolapse, and possibly enterocele. Level II, or midvaginal, defects anteriorly are associated with cystocele and/or hypermobile urethras. Midvaginal defects posteriorly are associated with rectocele. Level III, or lower vaginal and perineal, defects are associated with urethral hypermobility, perineal defects, and, frequently, rectocele (DeLancey, 1999). Although the adjacent levels are anatomically continuous, dividing them into levels provides an anatomic tool to correlate with clinical symptoms and signs and surgical approach.

Surgical Access

The vaginal approach to surgical management of stress incontinence may include surgical management of pelvic organ prolapse.

The vaginal wall is a fibromuscular tube that extends inward from the vestibule (Fig. 66–13) at a 45-degree angle and then ascends posterosuperiorly in a shallow S-shaped curve, at an angle of over 90 degrees to the uterine axis, but which varies with the contents of the bladder and rectum. The inner surfaces of the wall are ordinarily in contact with each other, and the lumen forms an H-shaped cleft seen on transverse section,

Table 66–3. Risk Factors for Development of Incontinence and Pelvic Organ Prolapse

Risk factor	Incontinence	Pelvic Organ Prolapse
Aging	+	+
Menopause	–	–
Pregnancy and parity	+	+
Episiotomy	?	?
Obesity	+	+
Surgery	+	+
Hysterectomy	?	+
Constipation	+	+
Chronic cough and respiratory disease	+	?
Exercise and heavy lifting	?+	?+
Genetic and neurologic conditions	+	+

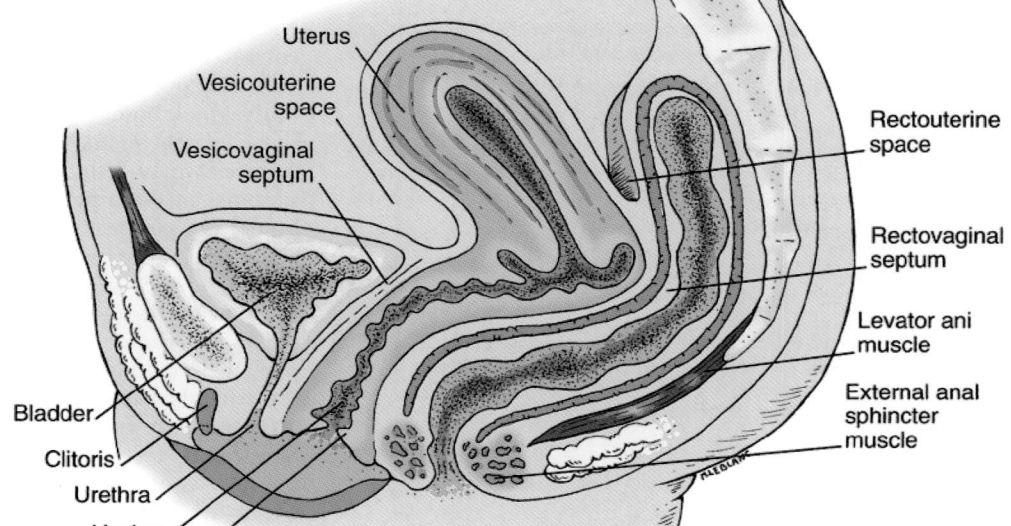

Figure 66–13. Median sagittal view of pelvic organs showing the potential spaces.

Uterus
Vesicouterine space
Vesicovaginal septum
Rectouterine space
Rectovaginal septum
Levator ani muscle
External anal sphincter muscle
Bladder
Clitoris
Urethra
Vagina
Hymen

as a result of the pattern of lateral attachment of the anterior and posterior fascia to the ATFP. The annular recess between the cervix and the vagina is the fornix; the anterior, posterior, and lateral parts are often given separate names, but the recess is essentially continuous (Bannister and Dyson, 1995).

The pelvic organs and peritoneal covered recesses are shown in Figure 66–13. The bladder base sits on the anterior vaginal wall. Surgical access to the various spaces has been described well by Brooks (2002). The bladder is connected to the cervix and vagina by smooth muscle fibers. The vesico-vaginal septum with a potential space between the bladder and the vagina is below. This potential space (vesicovaginal space) extends in the midline area down to the proximal urethra, where the urethra and vagina fuse. It is limited on the sides by the attachment of the bladder to the endopelvic fascia attachments (or pubocervical fascia). The space may be entered vaginally through an incision into the anterior vaginal wall distal to the cervix. Incision into the anterior vaginal wall on either side of the urethra leads into the retropubic space through the endopelvic fascia (or superior fascia of the pelvic diaphragm) (Fitzpatrick et al, 1996).

The posterior wall of the vagina, covered by peritoneum in its upper quarter (Bannister and Dyson, 1995), is separated from the rectum by the rectouterine pouch (cul-de-sac of Douglas) above and by moderately loose connective tissue in its middle half and fuses with the perineal body in the lower quarter, as mentioned earlier. Thus, the peritoneal cavity can be accessed through the upper posterior vagina. The potential rectovaginal space is behind the rectovaginal fascia. Incision into the posterior vaginal wall, below the peritoneal reflection, or cul-de-sac, provides access to the rectovaginal space, pararectal areas, and perineal body.

Anatomic Classification of Pelvic Organ Prolapse

The classification of prolapse is determined by which part of the vaginal wall is deficient (Table 66–4). **Anterior compart-ment prolapse includes two types of cystoceles.** If the weakness is in the lateral supports (pubourethral ligaments and pubocervical fascia attachment to the ATFP), the prolapse may involve the urethra and bladder. This is also called an *anterior cystocele* (Thompson, 1997). Central defects, resulting from anterior vaginal wall stretching and weakness, are also called posterior cystoceles (see Fig. 66–10). Combined defects are also seen, as mentioned previously. Urethrocele usually refers to urethral hypermobility (Weber and Walters, 1997).

Middle compartment defects involve the apical vaginal wall. Enteroceles are herniations of peritoneum-lined sacs containing abdominal contents such as small bowel or omentum (Fig. 66–14). The posterior type is located between the vagina and the rectum and is most common. Other types such as anterior or lateral (pudendal) enteroceles are less common. Enteroceles can occur with or without con-comitant vaginal vault prolapse or eversion. Vault eversions are accompanied by enteroceles about 75% of the time (Nichols, 1997).

Four types of enteroceles have been characterized by their suspected etiology (Waters, 1956). Congenital enteroceles, in the cul-de-sac, are thought to occur because of failure of fusion or reopening of the fused peritoneal leaves down to the perineal body. Post-hysterectomy vault enteroceles may be "pulsion" types that are from pushing with increased intra-abdominal pressure. They may occur because of failure to reapproximate the superior aspects of the pubocervical fascia and the rectovaginal fascia at the time of hysterectomy (Richardson, 1995). Enteroceles that are associated with cys-tocele and rectocele may be from "traction" or pulling down of the vaginal vault by the prolapsing organs. The last type may be iatrogenic after a surgical procedure that changes the vaginal axis, such as a Burch procedure that widens the entry into the cul-de-sac (Wiskind et al, 1992).

Uterine prolapse is part of the middle compartment and can vary from minimal to total procidentia. Massive eversion of the vagina can occur in young and old, although it is more common in older age groups (Hunskaar et al, 2005). If the uterus is present with the eversion, cystocele, enterocele, and rectocele may be seen concomitantly as a "general" prolapse. The most common type of general prolapse, according to Nichols (1997), involves a cystocele and a rectocele but not an enterocele, because the rectovaginal area remains intact.

In the posterior compartment, rectoceles may be low, midvaginal, high, or combinations. The supporting defects that cause the rectoceles also overlap the various levels. Low rectoceles may result from disruption of connective tissue supports in the distal posterior vaginal wall, perineal mem-brane, and perineal body (Fig. 66–15). Midvaginal and high rectoceles may result from loss of lateral supports (DeLancey, 1992) or defects in the rectovaginal septum (Nichols, 1993a). High rectoceles may also result from loss of apical vaginal sup-ports. Posterior or post-hysterectomy enteroceles may accom-pany the rectocele.

Perineal body defects are characterized by perineal relax-ation and are frequently seen with other organ prolapse. Surgical correction is part of the repair. An association between anorectal incontinence and "the descending peri-neum syndrome" from perineal body damage has been described (Henry et al, 1982) and is thought to be the result of chronic straining with defecation.

Table 66–4.	**Classification of Pelvic Organ Prolapse**

I. Anterior Vaginal Wall (Anterior Compartment)
   A. Cystocele
      1. Central (Posterior)
      2. Lateral (Anterior)
      3. Combined
   B. Urethrocele—uncommon
II. Apical Vaginal Wall (Middle Compartment)
   A. Enterocele
      1. Anterior
      2. Posterior*
   B. Uterine
   C. Uterovaginal with cystocele, enterocele, rectocele
   D. Vaginal vault eversion (post-hysterectomy) with cystocele, enterocele, rectocele
III. Posterior Vaginal Wall (Posterior Compartment)
   A. Rectocele
      1. Low
      2. Midvaginal
      3. High
IV. Perineal Body Defects

*Enterocele can also be seen in the posterior compartment.

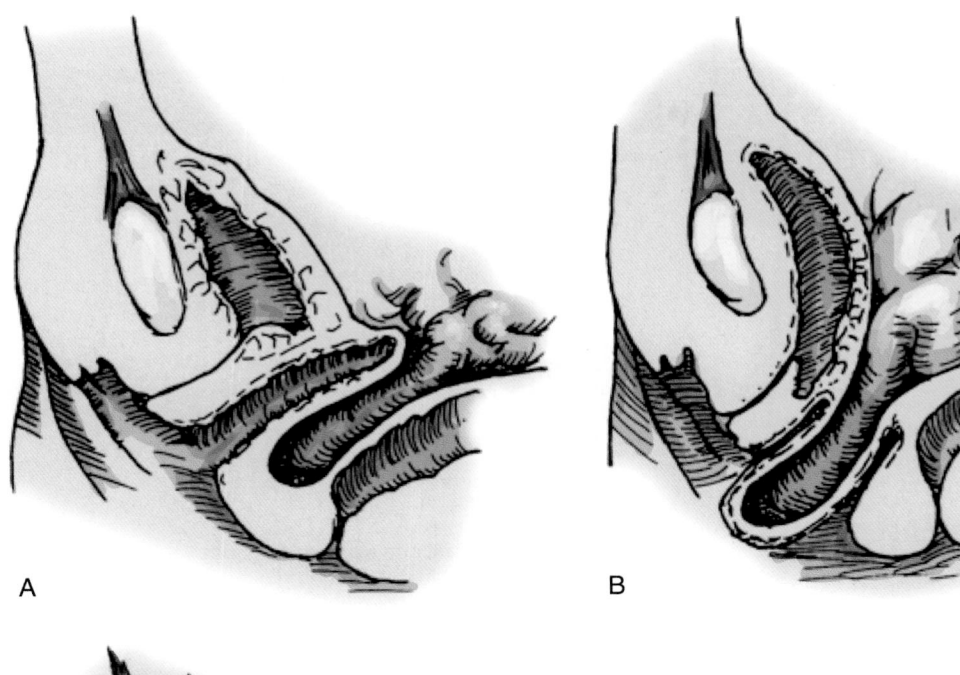

A

B

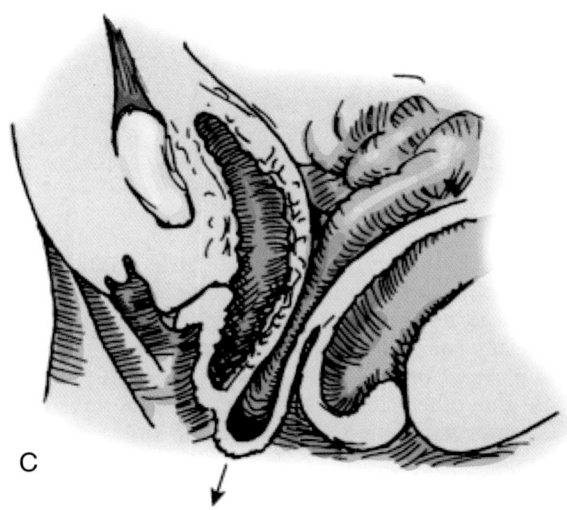

C

Figure 66–14. Different types of enteroceles. **A,** Posterior enterocele, probably congenital, without eversion of the vagina. **B,** The vagina is everted, and the pulsion enterocele follows the everted vaginal vault. Cystocele and rectocele are minimal. **C,** There is eversion of the vagina with traction enterocele, cystocele, and rectocele. The *arrow* indicates traction to the vault of the vagina. (From Nichols DH: Central compartment defects. In Nichols DH [ed]: Gynecologic and Obstetric Surgery. St. Louis, CV Mosby, 1993, pp 1006-1030.)

Figure 66–15. Large rectocele with perineal body defect. (From Nichols DH: Rectocele and perineal defect. In Nichols DH [ed]: Gynecologic and Obstetric Surgery. St. Louis, CV Mosby, 1993, pp 363-385.)

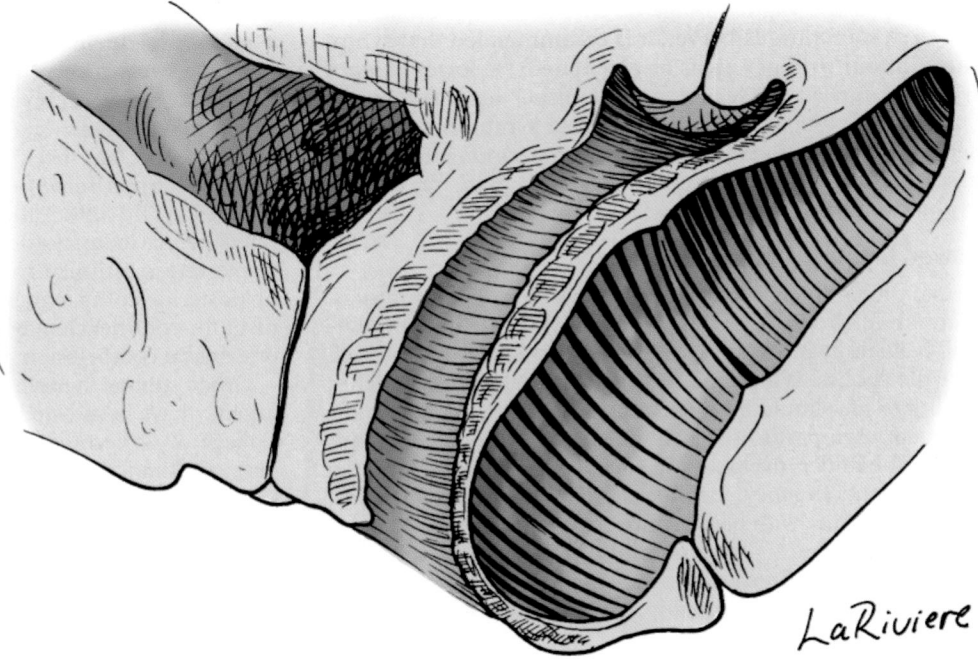

KEY POINTS: ANATOMY OF PELVIC FLOOR, SUPPORTING STRUCTURES, AND PATHOPHYSIOLOGY OF PELVIC ORGAN PROLAPSE

- The levator ani and coccygeus form the pelvic diaphragm.

- The pubococcygeus and iliococcygeus, from medial to lateral, are the two muscle groups of the levator ani.

- The levator plate, formed by the fusion of the levator muscles posteriorly, supports the rectum and upper two thirds of the vagina.

- The arcus tendineus levator ani (ATLA) and the arcus tendineus fasciae pelvis (ATFP) are the white fascial bands extending from the ischial spine to the pubis and are the lateral supports of the pelvic structures.

- Anterior wall defects can be central, lateral, or combined.

- The anatomic classification of pelvic organ prolapse is based on the part of the vaginal wall that is protruding.

Table 66–5. Clinical Evaluation of Incontinence/ Pelvic Organ Prolapse

History
  Clinical history
    Urinary symptoms
    Bowel symptoms
    Sexual symptoms
    Other local symptoms
  Questionnaires
  Voiding diaries
Pad test
Physical examination
  Abdominal: skin, incisions, hernias
  Neurourologic: cognitive status, mobility, focused neurologic examination if necessary
  Pelvic
    Position: dorsal lithotomy, semi-upright, upright
    External genitalia
    Full and empty bladder
    Bimanual examination to assess pelvic organs
    Urethral hypermobility—Q-tip test
    Anterior vaginal wall (Marshall or Bonney test)
    Cervix, uterus, vault (apical wall)
    Posterior wall
    Rectovaginal septum
    Perineal body
    Anal sphincter
    Assessment of pelvic floor muscle strength
Urinalysis
Postvoid residual urine

Clinical Evaluation

Symptoms caused by pelvic organ prolapse may or may not be specific to the prolapsing compartment(s), and the correlation of many pelvic symptoms with the extent of prolapse is weak (Mouritsen and Larsen, 2003; Burrows et al, 2004). **Many women with pelvic organ prolapse have no symptoms especially if the prolapse remains inside the vagina** (Swift et al, 2003). **Others present with symptoms in addition to the vaginal bulge, as a result of the associated organ dysfunction. However, it is recommended that symptoms in four primary areas be elucidated: (1) lower urinary tract, (2) bowel, (3) sexual, and (4) other local symptoms** (Bump et al, 1996b). **Documentation of symptoms not only serves as a guide to treatment but also permits an accurate assessment of post-treatment results. A plan for clinical evaluation is in Table 66–5.**

Lower Urinary Tract Symptoms

Urinary incontinence is one of the most common symptoms. Blaivas and Groutz (2002) have previously presented the clinical evaluation in detail. However, it should be emphasized that the specific symptoms and their impact on the patient's quality of life should be elucidated.

Urinary symptoms may include stress incontinence; symptoms of bladder overactivity, such as frequency, nocturia, urgency, and urgency incontinence; or voiding symptoms, such as difficulty with bladder emptying. The mechanisms for stress incontinence—hypermobility and intrinsic sphincter deficiency—have been discussed elsewhere in this volume. It is not unusual for patients to present with a combination of

urge and stress incontinence (McGuire, 1988; Fantl et al, 1990). When both symptoms are present, the incontinence is called *mixed incontinence* (Fantl et al, 1996). Mixed incontinence is especially common in older women. Often, however, one symptom (urge or stress) is more bothersome to the patient than the other. Identifying the most bothersome symptom is important in targeting diagnostic and therapeutic interventions.

Many women with severe prolapse recall that as the prolapse worsened, their stress incontinence symptoms improved. Reducing the vaginal prolapse with a pessary or a speculum during the examination by the clinician can produce stress incontinence in up to 80% of clinically continent patients with severe prolapse (Fianu et al, 1985; Bump et al, 1988; Rosenzweig et al, 1992; Romanzi, 2002). This phenomenon has been termed *latent, masked, occult, or potential stress incontinence* and should be elicited when considering therapy. Although the clinical experience reported refers primarily to cystocele, occult incontinence may also be unmasked in a similar manner in patients with severe middle or posterior compartment prolapse. The postulated mechanism for continence may be urethral kinking by the cystocele or external compression of the urethra (Romanzi et al, 1999).

Other storage symptoms such as frequency nocturia and urgency have been listed as symptoms of prolapse (American College of Gynecologists, 1995), although the mechanism is unknown and there are frequently other associated factors. Urgency incontinence may also be present. However, it is a common complaint in patients without organ prolapse, may or may not be the result of detrusor overactivity (Fantl et al, 1991), and becomes more prevalent with aging. Patients with advanced organ prolapse and urge incontinence have been shown to have detrusor overactivity (Romanzi et al, 1999) that may resolve after surgical correction of the prolapse (Rosenzweig et al, 1992; Nguyen and Bhatia, 2001). The mechanism is unclear; however, many of those patients may have outflow obstruction caused by the prolapse that is alleviated after repair. Nguyen and Bhatia (2001) reported resolution of urgency incontinence after pelvic prolapse repair in patients who had no obstruction preoperatively.

Symptoms of incontinence and/or the impact on quality of life can be assessed in a number of ways. The traditional and most frequently used way is questioning by the clinician. The important aspects of the incontinence history have been discussed in Chapter 60, "Urinary Incontinence: Epidemiology, Pathophysiology, Evaluation, and Overview of Management." Clinical histories, although extremely important, may be unstandardized; and evaluations have shown them to be unreliable and frequently not representative of the patient's perspective of the condition (Slevin et al, 1988). Early standardized questionnaires, the Boyarsky and Stamey, were very simple but not tested for validity or reliability (Donovan et al, 1999). A number of tools are now available to aid the clinician in elucidating the symptoms and their impact on quality of life to gain as accurate a picture as possible. These tools include questionnaires, voiding diaries, and pad tests, which are also used to evaluate treatment outcomes.

Self-administered questionnaires may be used to elicit both symptoms and impact on quality of life, and several are available (Table 66–6) **that have been shown to have validity, reliability, and responsiveness to change** (Donovan et al, 2005). An example of a simple symptom questionnaire is the Urogenital Distress Inventory Short Form (UDI-6) (Uebersax et al, 1995). It was produced by regression analysis, whereby six items that had a high correlation with the longer form (Urogenital Distress Inventory [UDI]) were chosen. It has been shown to have excellent psychometric properties in men and women (Donovan et al, 2005). Of quality of life questionnaires, the Incontinence Impact Questionnaire (IIQ)

Table 66–7. Self-administered Short Forms

Urogenital Distress Inventory—Short Form (UDI-6)
  Do you experience, and, if so how much are you bothered by:
  1. Frequent urination? (I)
  2. Urine leakage related to the feeling of urgency? (I)
  3. Urine leakage related to physical activity, coughing, or sneezing? (S)
  4. Small amounts of urine leakage? (S)
  5. Difficulty emptying your bladder? (OD)
  6. Pain or discomfort in the lower abdomen or genital area? (OD)
Incontinence Impact Questionnaire—Short Form (IIQ-7)
  Has urine leakage and/or prolapse affected your:
  1. Ability to do household chores (cooking, housecleaning, laundry)? (PA)
  2. Physical recreation such as walking, swimming, or other exercise? (PA)
  3. Entertainment activities (movies, concerts, etc.)? (T)
  4. Ability to travel by car or bus more than 30 minutes from home? (T)
  5. Participation in social activities outside your home? (SR)
  6. Emotional health (nervousness, depression, etc)? (EH)
  7. Feeling frustrated? (EH)

Item response levels are:
(0) Not at all
(1) Slightly
(2) Moderately
(3) Greatly
PA, physical activity; T, travel; SR, social/relationships; EH, emotional health; OD, obstructive/discomfort symptoms; I, irritative symptoms; S, stress symptoms.
From Uebersax JS, Wyman JF, Shumaker SA, et al: Short forms to assess life quality and symptom distress for urinary incontinence in women: The Incontinence Impact Questionnaire and the Urogenital Distress Inventory. Continence Program for Women Research Group. Neurourol Urodyn 1995;14:131-139.

(Wyman et al, 1987; Shumaker et al, 1994) is an example that has been validated and modified, and a seven-item shortened form has been constructed (Uebersax et al, 1995) and found to be reliable. The short-form questionnaires are found in Table 66–7.

A brief and robust 4-item questionnaire is the ICIQ (International Consultation on Incontinence Questionnaire). It was recently validated and translated into 27 languages (Avery et al, 2004; Donovan et al, 2005). Another example of a scoring system that was devised for the definition and standardization of the measurement of incontinence, analogous to the TNM classification for tumors, is the SEAPI QMM system (Raz and Erickson, 1992). Each letter of the classification represents an aspect of incontinence: Stress-related leak, Emptying ability, Anatomy, Protection, Inhibition, Quality of life, Mobility, and Mental status. Each is measured from 0 to 3, with "U" for unknown and "N" for not tested. The system includes a 15-item quality of life questionnaire, also scored 0 to 3, covering domains such as emotional well-being, interpersonal relationships, work, financial factors, physical health, recreation, and overall satisfaction, all as they relate to urinary incontinence. The system was shown to have good psychometric properties in men and women (Stothers, 2004).

Voiding diaries, also known as micturition or bladder diaries and incontinence or frequency-volume charts, are widely used to assess frequency, nocturia, and incontinent episodes. The intake and voided volumes can also be

Table 66–6. Recommended Self-administered Incontinence Questionnaires

Name	Reference
Symptom Assessment	
Urogenital Distress Inventory (UDI)	Shumaker et al, 1994
UDI-6 (short form)	Uebersax et al, 1995
ICIQ	Avery et al, 2004
Bristol Female Lower Urinary Tract Symptoms (BFLUTS and BFLUTS-SF)	Jackson et al, 1996; Brookes et al, 2004
Stress and Urge Incontinence QOL Questionnaire (SUIQQ)	Kulseng-Hanssen, 2003
Assessment of Impact on Quality of Life	
Quality of life in persons with urinary incontinence (I-QoL)	Wagner et al, 1996
Incontinence Impact Questionnaire (IIQ)	Wyman et al, 1987; Shumaker et al, 1994
IIQ-7 (short form)	Uebersax et al, 1995
King's Health Questionnaire	Kelleher et al, 1997
SEAPI-QMM	Stothers, 2004
Urinary incontinence severity score (UISS)	Stach-Lempinen et al, 2004
CONTILIFE	Amarenco et al, 2003

recorded. **They have been shown to exhibit test-retest relia-bility for incontinent episodes** (Wyman et al, 1988) and have been used to check the validity of questionnaires (Donovan et al, 1996). They are helpful because they can portray the patient's daily picture of lower urinary tract dysfunction. However, for accuracy they rely heavily on the patient's willingness and diligence to complete them. A 3-day diary has been suggested as optimal (Palnaes Hansen and Klarskov, 1998).

The pad test was first described as an objective measure of urine loss in 1981 (Sutherst et al, 1981), and many variations have been reported subsequently. Abrams and coworkers (1988) in the ICS Standardization Report described administering phenazopyridine (Pyridium) and then checking the pad after 1 hour of activity. A positive test has orange stain and a weight gain of 1.0 g or more. Wall and colleagues (1990) subsequently showed that continent volunteers had staining on pads, but a pad weight gain of more than 1.0 g was seen only in the incontinent subjects. They called into question the addition of Pyridium to the test, but it can be helpful in the occasional patient whose leakage is difficult to characterize. Pad weight testing can be done in the clinic setting for 1 to 3 hours or at home with 12-, 24-, or 48-hour testing (Tubaro et al, 2005). The short pad tests require a fixed bladder volume and a standard set of activities. The 24- and 48-hour tests have been shown to be reproducible and correlate well with other data (Versi et al, 1996). Pad weight testing has become a standard test in reporting outcomes of incontinence therapies.

Difficult voiding symptoms are common with severe prolapse and should be elicited. As mentioned earlier, patients with prolapse may have urethral kinking or external pressure on the urethra that not only prevents incontinence but also may cause difficult voiding (Romanzi et al, 1999). Patients occasionally have to digitally reduce the prolapse to void (splinting) or assume unusual positions to initiate or complete micturition (Bump et al, 1996b). Urinary splinting has been reported to be 97% specific for severe anterior prolapse (Tan et al, 2005).

Urodynamic abnormalities with decreased uroflow, increased postvoid residual urine (Coates et al, 1997), and bladder outlet obstruction have been reported (Chassagne et al, 1998; Nitti et al, 1999; Romanzi et al, 1999). The degree of obstruction may be related to the severity of the prolapse (Romanzi et al, 1999). The urodynamic definition of obstruction in women is different than in men. A cutoff value of 12 mL/s or less maximum flow rate and a detrusor pressure at maximum flow of 25 cm H_2O or more in conjunction with high clinical suspicion provides good predictive value (Defreitas et al, 2004). Acute urinary retention secondary to the prolapse is rarely seen (Klarskov et al, 1987). **The prevalence of hydronephrosis in patients with pelvic organ prolapse is also low. Beverly and coworkers (1997) reported mild to moderate hydronephrosis in 6.8% and severe hydronephrosis in 0.9% of 323 patients with pelvic organ prolapse. The severe cases were seen only with uterine procidentia.**

Bowel Symptoms

Anal incontinence is the involuntary loss of flatus or feces, and its prevalence and association with pelvic organ prolapse is up to 29% of patients (Gordon et al, 1999; Leroi et al, 1999; Boreham et al, 2005) and has been discussed earlier. The

most common cause of anal incontinence in healthy women is obstetric trauma. Vaginal delivery can damage the anal continence mechanism by direct injury to the anal sphincter muscles, damage to the motor innervation of the pelvic floor, or both (Womack et al, 1986; Toglia, 1998).

Other symptoms that are commonly attributed to rectoceles are from the stool getting trapped within the rectal bulge, difficult defecation with distal stool trapping, or excessive straining (tenesmus). The patient may have to manually splint the perineum or vagina to reduce the rectal reservoir and assist evacuation or manually evacuate the rectum (Kenton et al, 1999). Digital assistance with fecal evacuation is frequently associated with moderate to severe posterior prolapse (Tan et al, 2005). Constipation may be associated with a rectocele or may be one of the factors that predisposed the patient to prolapse. Either way it should be elicited and managed.

Sexual Symptoms

Female sexual dysfunction is a multicausal and multidimensional problem combining psychological, physiologic, and interpersonal factors. It progresses with age and affects 20% to 50% of women (Basson et al, 2000). It has been classified to include psychogenic and organic causes of desire, arousal, orgasm, and sexual pain disorders (Basson et al, 2000) (Table 66–8). A validated condition-specific questionnaire on sexual function in women with pelvic organ prolapse and urinary incontinence, the Pelvic Organ Prolapse/Urinary Incontinence Sexual Questionnaire (PISQ), has been shown to be reliable (Rogers et al, 2001).

The impact of incontinence and prolapse on sexual function is not entirely known. Sexual dysfunction, such as dyspareunia and decreased desire, has been attributed to prolapse and incontinence (Haase and Skibsted, 1988). Reported rates of sexual dysfunction in women with incontinence range from 32% to 49% (Sutherst and Brown, 1980; Iosif, 1988; Walters et al, 1990; Field and Hilton, 1993). Dyspareunia was the most common reason for reduced frequency of intercourse. In a study by Weber and colleagues (1995), the prevalence of dyspareunia and sexual dysfunction was similar in a population with prolapse with or without incontinence when compared with an age-matched population without those complaints. Only 17% of the subjects complained that the prolapse interfered with sexual activity. However, Laumann and coworkers (1999) in a population-based study of 1750 women reported that the presence of unspecified urinary tract symptoms

Table 66–8. Classification of Female Sexual Dysfunction: 1999 Consensus Classification System

I. Sexual Desire Disorders
    A. Hypoactive sexual desire disorder
    B. Sexual aversion disorder
II. Sexual Arousal Disorder
III. Orgasmic Disorder
IV. Sexual Pain Disorders
    A. Dyspareunia
    B. Vaginismus
    C. Other sexual pain disorders

From Basson R, Berman J, Burnett A, et al: Report of the international consensus development conference on female sexual dysfunction: Definitions and classifications. J Urol 2000;163:888-893.

appeared to affect sexual function (e.g., arousal and pain disorders). Furthermore, in a study of 1299 women about to undergo hysterectomy, Handa and colleagues (2004b) showed that sexual complaints were strongly associated with urinary incontinence but not with prolapse.

Sexual function may be affected by the underlying problem and its surgery, which can affect sensation, obstruct the vagina, or alter vaginal capacity. It is therefore important to address the problem with the patient during the evaluation so that any subsequent adverse effects can be recognized.

Other Local Symptoms

Other local symptoms may include vaginal pressure or heaviness, vaginal or perineal pain, sensation or awareness of tissue protruding from the vagina, low back pain, abdominal pressure or pain, and observation or palpation of a mass (Bump et al, 1996b). The complaint of a bulge or protrusion outside the vagina is very common with more severe prolapse (Tan et al, 2005). Women may also report they can no longer wear tampons with descent of the cervix into the vagina (Weber and Richter, 2005).

Physical Examination

The physical examination should provide information about the cause of the lower urinary tract and other symptoms and suggest additional management options. The general examination should include an abdominal examination to evaluate the skin, surgical incisions, and the presence of any hernias or abdominal masses, including a full bladder. It is also recommended to assess mobility and cognitive status and to perform a focused neurologic examination if necessary (Shull et al, 2002).

Pelvic Examination

The patient is placed in the lithotomy position. The external genitalia should be examined for dermatologic lesions and inflammatory conditions. The internal genitalia should be examined for estrogen deficiency, urine or abnormal vaginal discharge, pelvic organ prolapse, and abnormal pelvic masses. The poorly estrogenized vaginal wall has a thinned epithelium with loss of transverse rugae, which are normally present in its lower two thirds (Fantl et al, 1994). The patient should be examined with a full bladder to assess stress incontinence and, if necessary, with an empty bladder to assess other pelvic organ prolapse and masses.

Because incontinence and pelvic organ prolapse may not be evident, or its full extent demonstrated, in the dorsal lithotomy position, it has been recommended that the patient be examined in the semi-upright or even upright position (Walters and Karram, 1992). An important consideration is the variable abilities of patients to strain and cough. The patient can also be given a mirror to hold and verify the maximal extent of the prolapse. However, it has been shown that when the examination is done carefully, the clinical assessment of pelvic organ prolapse is similar in both the lithotomy and the upright positions (Swift and Herring, 1998). A bimanual pelvic examination is done to assess uterine size and position and adnexal masses.

The necessary instruments for assessment of prolapse are a Sims speculum or a standard bivalved Graves speculum that can be split and the posterior blade inserted into the vagina to assess the opposite wall. A measuring device, either a ruler or a ring (sponge) forceps with centimeter markings, can also be used. The examination is performed in a systematic fashion to assess the different components: urethral hypermobility; anterior, apical, and posterior prolapse; rectovaginal septum; perineal body; and anal sphincter. The levator ani muscles can also be assessed. It is important to have the patient strain forcefully while the examiner assesses each portion to avoid underestimating the degree of prolapse (Theofrastous and Swift, 1998). The hymenal ring, rather than the introitus, is defined as the fixed reference point for measuring the amount of prolapse (Bump et al, 1996b).

Patients with pelvic organ prolapse have been reported to have an enlarged urogenital (levator) hiatus (Delancey and Hurd, 1998). The boundaries are the pubic bones anteriorly, the medial margins of the levators laterally, and the perineal body dorsally. The hiatus can be assessed on pelvic examination.

Urethral mobility can be observed with the patient straining or by the cotton-swab or Q-tip test (Crystle et al, 1971). The angles of deflection of the Q-tip at rest and with straining are measured with a goniometer. Hypermobility is defined as a maximum strain axis of more than 30 degrees from the horizontal. Urethral axis testing does not diagnose any form of incontinence because continent women may demonstrate rotational descent of the urethra (Fantl et al, 1986) and incontinent women may have no descent. Although it has been shown to be reproducible (Fantl et al, 1986), it has not been compared with other radiologic methods. However, it may be helpful in assessing the amount of hypermobility. In women with large defects, the urethra may be compressed by the large bulge when the patient strains, impairing assessment of mobility and stress incontinence. In these women, it may be necessary to reduce the bulge with various devices, such as a pessary, ring forceps, or the posterior blade of bivalve speculum, to allow assessment of the hypermobility and to demonstrate incontinence.

The anterior vaginal wall and supports can be assessed by placing the posterior blade of the bivalve speculum in the vagina to depress the posterior wall. The degree of anterior vaginal wall relaxation with and without straining is assessed. Support defects may be midline (central), lateral or paravaginal, or combinations (Shull, 1993). Anterior defect assessment involves supporting a part of the vagina with the sponge forceps, with the speculum blade still in place, while the patient strains and observing whether this corrects the prolapse. A midline (central) defect is demonstrated by placing the sponge forceps against the bulge and by it not reappearing with the patient straining. Large central defects that extend superiorly are also associated with loss of the vaginal rugae along the base of the bladder (Shull, 1993). Bilateral paravaginal or lateral defects can be supported by the open sponge forceps holding the anterior wall laterally, simulating normal attachment of the wall to the ATFP (Fig. 66–16). Similarly, one-sided lateral defects may be demonstrated by holding up the affected side with the closed sponge forceps. Combined defects are present if the sponge forceps holding the vaginal walls laterally or in the midline fails to abolish the bulge.

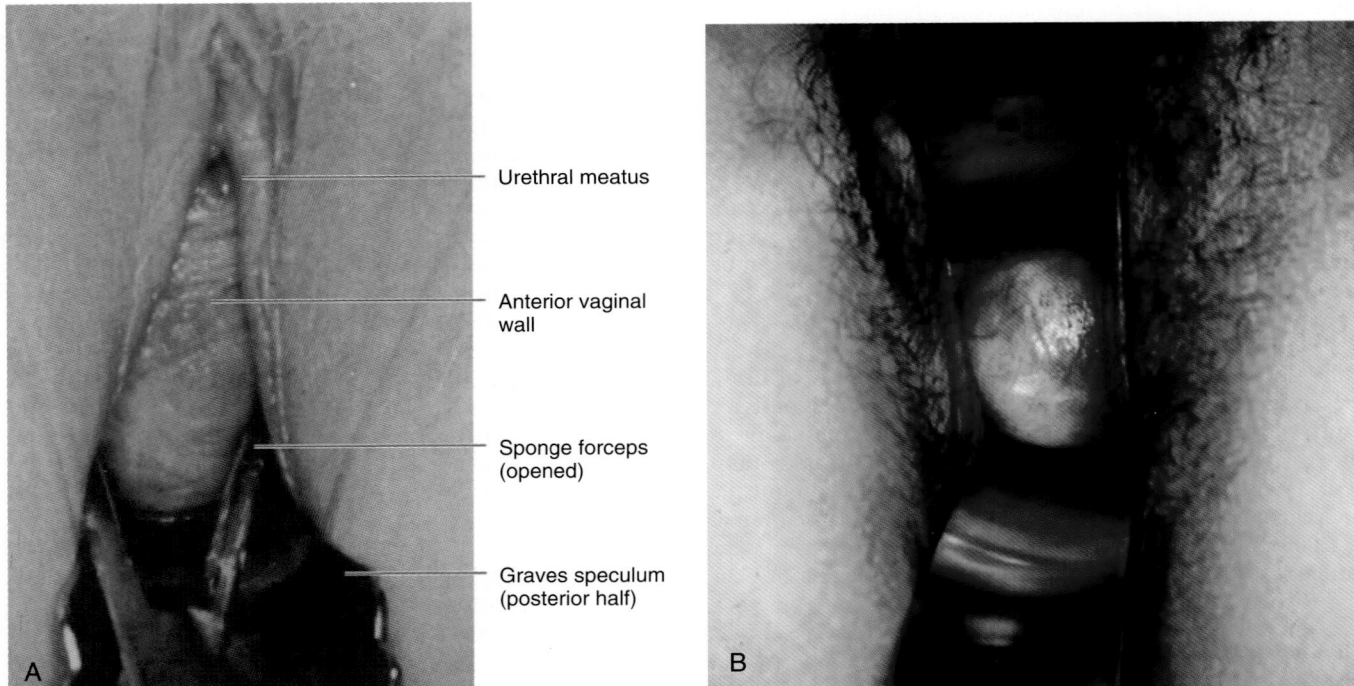

Urethral meatus

Anterior vaginal wall

Sponge forceps (opened)

Graves speculum (posterior half)

Figure 66–16. **A,** Lateral replacement of the anterior vaginal wall with the sponge forceps corrects part of the anterior defect but there is still a bulge centrally and the urethral meatus rotates anteriorly when the patient is straining. **B,** Stage II prolapse of the vaginal apex. With retraction of the anterior and posterior vagina, the prolapse can be seen to involve the vaginal apex, possibly with an enterocele. (**A,** from Shull BL: Clinical evaluation of women with pelvic support defects. Clin Obstet Gynecol 1993;36:939-951; **B,** from Weber AM, Richter HE: Pelvic organ prolapse. Obstet Gynecol 2005;106:615-634.)

The accuracy of clinical examination in assessing anterior defects has not yet been proved. Current understanding of anterior vaginal support is based on the work of Richardson and colleagues (1976), who popularized abdominal paravaginal repairs. They found paravaginal defects in 67% of their patients, with 75% having unilateral defects. In contrast, Barber and coworkers (1999) found paravaginal defects in only 42% of 70 patients, with 76% bilateral. Furthermore, they found that the sensitivity and negative predictive value for the clinical assessment for paravaginal defects were good on both the right and left sides whereas the specificity and positive predictive values were poor. Previous retropubic urethropexy significantly decreased the accuracy of the clinical examination. Midline defects were not assessed. Furthermore, Whiteside and colleagues (2004) showed poor intra-observer and inter-observer reliability in identifying specific anterior defects in a cohort of women with at least stage II anterior wall prolapse. Although physical examination is not perfect, it is a useful guide to further management.

A clinical test for stress incontinence is the Marshall (or Bonney) test in which the examiner places one or two fingers or an instrument next to the bladder neck and elevates the bladder neck or urethra after demonstrating stress incontinence. If repeat coughing or straining results in no leakage, the test is positive. The test was originally described to simulate the effect of surgery and to be of prognostic significance for stress incontinence repairs (Berkeley and Bonney, 1935). Subsequent investigators (Bhatia and Bergman, 1983; Bergman and Bhatia, 1987; Migliorini and Glenning, 1987) with urodynamic studies concluded that the Bonney test produced continence by direct urethral compression and was therefore an invalid test that should be discarded. Gleason and coworkers (1980) also described another test to simulate anterior wall support, the apical suspension test, in which pressure is applied at the vaginal apex toward the sacrum with a sponge stick and cotton swab when the patient is straining. No results were given. However, Miyazaki (1997) compared direct urethral compression to the Bonney test and to a modified Bonney test that involved lateral elevation with cotton swabs in 37 patients with stress incontinence. He found that the Bonney test and modified tests do not work by urethral compression but instead appear to produce continence by restoring the anterior vaginal wall hammock. The modified Bonney test did not prevent leakage in three patients with type III (nonmobile) urethras, implying a different cause of the stress incontinence, as expected. These tests may be useful but are not standardized.

The middle or apical compartment is examined next. With inadequate cardinal and uterosacral ligament support, the cervix may descend below the level of the ischial spines to all the way below the hymen (procidentia). In some women, the intravaginal portion of the cervix may become elongated and cause the cervix to extend into the lower vaginal canal, simulating prolapse, but the fundus has good support (Shull et al, 2002). **After hysterectomy, the vaginal cuff will have dimples at the 3 and 9 o'clock areas, at the locations of the cardinal uterosacral ligament attachments** (Shull, 1993). The vaginal cuff may be well supported or may prolapse outside the hymen with other vaginal segments. Although an enterocele may be obvious with severe degrees of prolapse, it may not be obvious with milder degrees. The cul-de-sac leading to the rectovaginal septum (see Fig. 66–13), where enteroceles most commonly appear, is normally at or above the level of the ischial spines and devoid of small bowel. With loss of support, the epithelium becomes shiny and thin and may be distended by intestine. Rarely palpation of small bowel or visible peristalsis helps to confirm the presence of enterocele. Distinction between an enterocele and a high rectocele is difficult. The discrete appearance of a bulge above a rectocele is indicative of an enterocele but is generally not present (Shull, 1993). **Other maneuvers to demonstrate a midvaginal prolapse involve the use of two speculum blades to retract the anterior and posterior vaginal walls simultaneously** (see Fig. 66–18B). Palpation of the rectovaginal septum with the index finger in the rectal ampulla and thumb in the vagina may indicate a bulge between the rectum and the vagina. Having the patient stand and strain may make the enterocele more obvious (Theofrastous and Swift, 1998).

The speculum can be rotated to support the anterior wall while the posterior wall is examined. The posterior bulge can be demonstrated with the patient straining. Defects in the rectovaginal septum can be palpated with a finger in the rectum. When a rectocele is demonstrated, it is possible to differentiate between a distal defect with or without involvement of the attachments to the perineal body and a higher defect with weakness of the lateral supports. The curved ring or sponge forceps can be used in similar fashion as in the anterior wall examination (Shull, 1993).

The perineal body is examined along with the rectovaginal septum. In women with severe prolapse, the perineal body may be thinned or expanded. The perineum may bulge or widen during straining and descends below the bony pelvis (Theofrastous and Swift, 1998). Severe perineal descent has been described as a clinical entity (Henry et al, 1982) and may have to be repaired.

Anal sphincter tone can be evaluated by subjective digital testing of the strength of contraction. Occasionally, defects in the anal sphincter can also be palpated. Women with disruption of the anal sphincter may have gross abnormalities of the perineal body in the area of the disrupted sphincter (Toglia and DeLancey, 1994).

The examiner can palpate the levator ani muscles with two gloved fingers in the posterior vagina 2 to 4 cm above the hymen (Toglia and DeLancey, 1994). **The muscles form a hammock around the rectum and insert anteriorly on the pubis. They can be palpated posteriorly and followed around bilaterally.** The examiner asks the patient to squeeze the muscles she normally uses to hold urine and avoid passing gas, without using other muscles such as the rectus abdominis or hip adductors. The examiner can also assess the strength according to different scales, which were discussed in Chapter 61, "Overactive Bladder."

Clinical Classification

A number of classification systems have been published to facilitate standardization of clinical findings and enable communication about patients among practitioners (Fig. 66–17) (Porges, 1963; Baden and Walker, 1972; Beecham, 1980). Until recently, none of the systems had been validated. The systems rely on a detailed pelvic examination and a presumptive diag-

---

KEY POINTS: CLINICAL ASSESSMENT

- In the clinical assessment, symptoms in the four domains should be elicited: lower urinary tract, bowel, sexual, and local prolapse symptoms.

- In patients with prolapse, it is necessary to check for occult or masked stress incontinence.

- Pelvic examination should include a standardized and systematic assessment of all zones of the vagina—anterior, apical, posterior, and perineum.

- The Pelvic Organ Prolapse Quantification (POPQ) system uses the hymenal ring as the principal reference point.

---

nosis of the organ that has prolapsed (e.g., cystocele, enterocele, or rectocele). Because there was a lack of an objective, universally accepted, and validated system for describing pelvic organ support, the ICS established an international, multidisciplinary terminology standardization committee for prolapse in 1993. The committee devised a site-specific quantitative description of support that locates six defined points around the vagina (two anterior, two posterior, and two apical) with respect to their relationship to the hymenal ring (Bump et al, 1996a). The classification system is known as the POPQ system for *pelvic organ prolapse quantification*. The instruments required and the technique using a part of the bivalve speculum to perform the examination have been described previously.

The POPQ system assigns negative numbers (in centimeters) to structures that have not prolapsed beyond the hymen and positive numbers to structures that protrude, with the plane of the hymen defined as zero (Fig. 66–18). The hymen was selected as the reference point rather the introitus because it is more precisely identified (Bump et al, 1996b). The terminology avoids assigning a specific label, such as cystocele or rectocele, to the prolapsing part of the vagina, acknowledging that the actual organ(s) above the prolapse frequently cannot be determined on physical examination. There are three reference points anteriorly (Aa, Ba, and C) and three posteriorly (Ap, Bp, and D) (see Fig. 66–18). Points Aa and Ap are 3 cm proximal to or above the hymenal ring anteriorly and posteriorly, respectively. Points Ba and Bp are defined as the lowest points of the prolapse between Aa anteriorly or Ap posteriorly and the vaginal apex. Anteriorly, the apex is point C (cervix), and posteriorly is point D (pouch of Douglas). In women after hysterectomy, point C is the vaginal cuff and point D is omitted. Three other measurements are taken: the vaginal length at rest, the genital hiatus (gh) from the middle of the urethral meatus to the posterior hymenal ring, and the perineal body (pb) from the posterior aspect of the genital hiatus to the midanal opening. An example of measurements is given in Figure 66–19.

Once the measurements are taken, the subjects are assigned to ordinal stages:

Stage 0—no prolapse is demonstrated.
Stage I—the most distal portion of the prolapse is more than 1 cm above the level of the hymen.

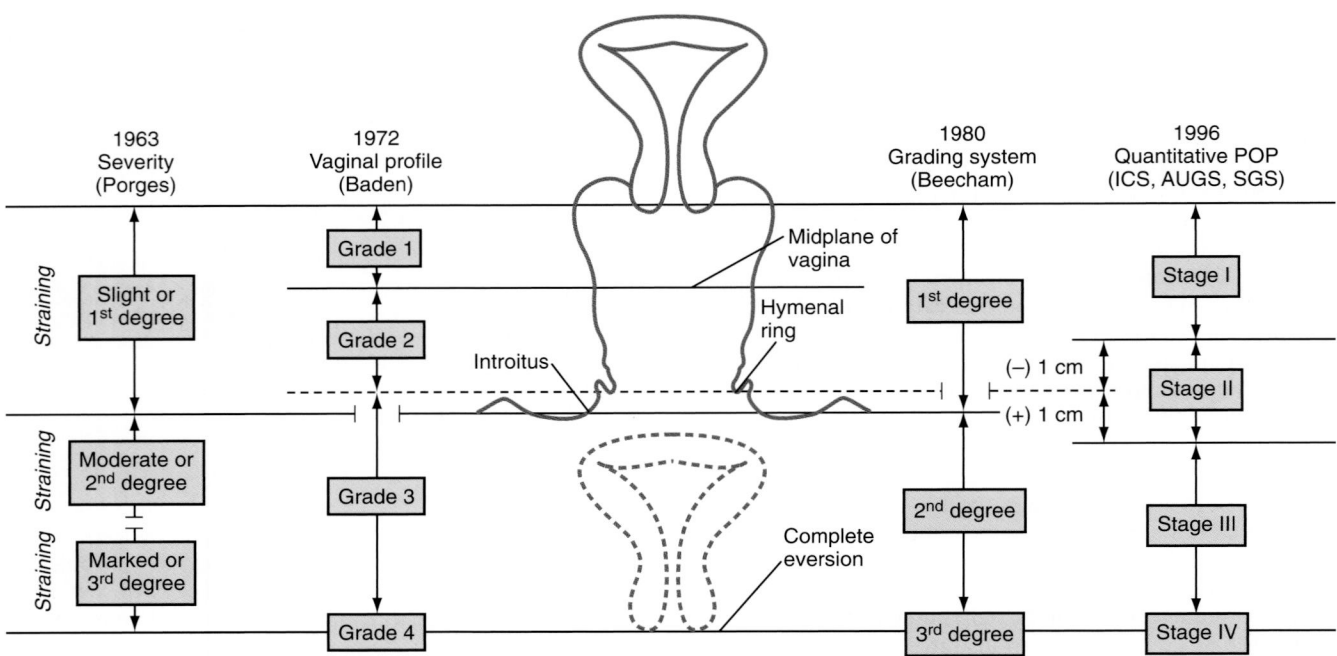

Figure 66–17. Comparison of classifications of pelvic organ prolapse. (From Theofrastous JP, Swift SE: The clinical evaluation of pelvic floor dysfunction. Obstet Gynecol Clin North Am 1998;25:783-804.)

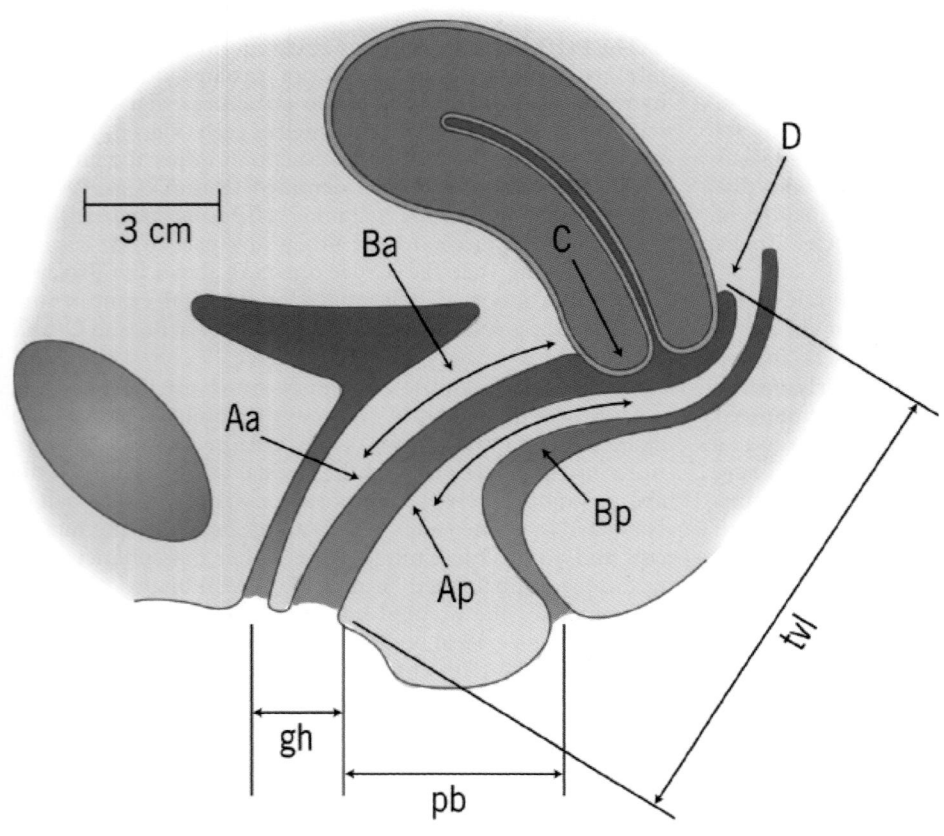

Figure 66–18. Landmarks for quantitative pelvic examination: Aa, point A anterior; Ap, point A posterior; Ba, point B anterior; Bp, point B posterior; C, cervix or vaginal cuff; D, posterior fornix (if cervix is present); gh, genital hiatus; pb, perineal body; tvl, total vaginal length. (From Bump RC, Mattiasson A, Bo K, et al: The standardization of terminology of female pelvic organ prolapse and pelvic floor dysfunction. Am J Obstet Gynecol 1996;175:10-17.)

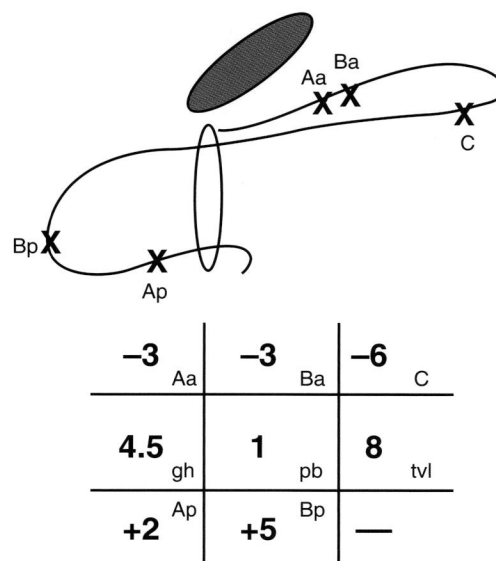

-3 Aa	-3 Ba	-6 C
4.5 gh	1 pb	8 tvl
+2 Ap	+5 Bp	—

Figure 66–19. Grid and line diagrams of predominantly posterior support defect. Leading point of prolapse is upper posterior vaginal wall, point Bp (+5). Point Ap is 2 cm distal to hymen (+2) and vaginal cuff scar is 6 cm above hymen (–6). Cuff has undergone only 2 cm of descent because it would be at –8 (total vaginal length) if it were properly supported. This represents stage III Bp prolapse. (From Bump RC, Mattiasson A, Bo K, et al: The standardization of terminology of female pelvic organ prolapse and pelvic floor dysfunction. Am J Obstet Gynecol 1996;175:10-17.)

Stage II—the most distal portion of the prolapse is 1 cm or less proximal or distal to the hymenal plane.

Stage III—the most distal portion of the prolapse protrudes more than 1 cm below the hymen but protrudes no farther than 2 cm less than the total vaginal length (i.e., not all of the vagina has prolapsed).

Stage IV—vaginal eversion is essentially complete.

Excellent inter-observer and intra-observer reliability has been shown (Hall et al, 1996; Kobak et al, 1996). It has been used for longitudinal follow-up of a population of women with prolapse (Bland et al, 1999) and extensively for outcome reporting after prolapse repair since 1996 (Muir et al, 2003). However, there are some caveats. The system is more difficult to learn than the traditional staging and overall adoption by specialists is about 40% (Auwad et al, 2004). Patient position also affects reproducibility. The measurements are taken with the patient in the dorsal lithotomy position, and the degree of prolapse is assessed with patient straining. Prolapse may be more severe with the table raised at the head to a 45-degree angle (Barber et al, 2000a). The system also does not identify unilateral or asymmetrical defects.

Additional Testing

The initial evaluation of urinary incontinence in women includes a history, physical examination, urinalysis, and measurement of postvoid residual urine (Abrams et al, 2005). The basic evaluation may be satisfactory for proceeding with treatment, including surgery, for patients with straightforward stress incontinence associated with hypermobility with normal postvoid residual volume (Fantl et al, 1996). However, the International Scientific Committee of the Third Interna-

tional Consultation on Urinary Incontinence advised that for women who desire interventional treatment urodynamic testing is highly recommended (Abrams et al, 2005). There is controversy over the need for urodynamic testing. Diokno and coworkers (1999) showed that systematic history, vaginal speculum examination, and postvoid residual urine were 100% accurate in identifying patients who had pure type II stress incontinence on urodynamic studies. Other groups have shown a positive correlation of symptoms and urodynamic findings (Nitti and Combs, 1996; Lemack and Zimmern, 1999) potentially bypassing the need for urodynamic studies in many patients (Lemack and Zimmern, 2000; Weber et al, 2002). On the other hand, investigators have shown that symptoms are not always related to the actual dysfunction causing the incontinence demonstrated on urodynamics (Bergman and Bader, 1990; Versi et al, 1991; Haeusler et al, 1995; Amundsen et al, 1999; Weidner et al, 2001). The actual role of urodynamics in case selection and predicting continence outcome of surgery is still unknown (Lemack, 2004).

There are many instances in which a basic clinical evaluation is insufficient. The Agency for Health Care Research and Quality (formerly the Agency for Health Care Policy and Research) published guidelines in 1996 that are still relevant (Fantl et al, 1996). Criteria for further evaluation of incontinence include uncertain diagnosis and inability to develop a reasonable treatment plan based on the basic diagnostic evaluation; uncertainty in diagnosis when there is lack of correlation between symptoms and clinical findings; failure to respond to the patient's satisfaction to an adequate therapeutic trial and the patient is interested in pursuing further therapy; consideration of surgical intervention, particularly if previous surgery failed or the patient is a high surgical risk; hematuria without infection; the presence of other comorbid conditions, such as incontinence associated with recurrent symptomatic urinary tract infection; persistent symptoms of difficult bladder emptying; history of previous anti-incontinence surgery or radical pelvic surgery beyond hymen and symptomatic pelvic prolapse; abnormal postvoid residual urine; and a neurologic condition, such as multiple sclerosis and spinal cord lesions or injury. Additional testing includes urodynamics, cystoscopy, and imaging, and the evaluation must be tailored to the question to be answered.

Urodynamic testing is discussed in Chapter 58, "Urodynamic and Videourodynamic Evaluation of Voiding Dysfunction." Pelvic organ prolapse, as mentioned earlier, may be associated with symptoms and urodynamic findings of obstruction demonstrable with flow rates and pressure/flow studies. The urodynamic definition of outflow obstruction in females is lower than that in men (Groutz et al, 2000; Defreitas et al, 2004). Video-urodynamic and fluoroscopic studies, in addition to demonstrating incontinence and degree of hypermobility, may also allow characterization of the type of cystocele (Fig. 66–20).

The role of routine cystoscopy in the evaluation of incontinence is controversial. Most agree that it is indicated for the evaluation of incontinent patients who have sterile hematuria or pyuria; recent (weeks to months) onset of storage symptoms such as frequency, urgency, and urge incontinence in the absence of any reversible causes; bladder pain; recurrent cystitis; or suspected intravesical foreign body. It is also used

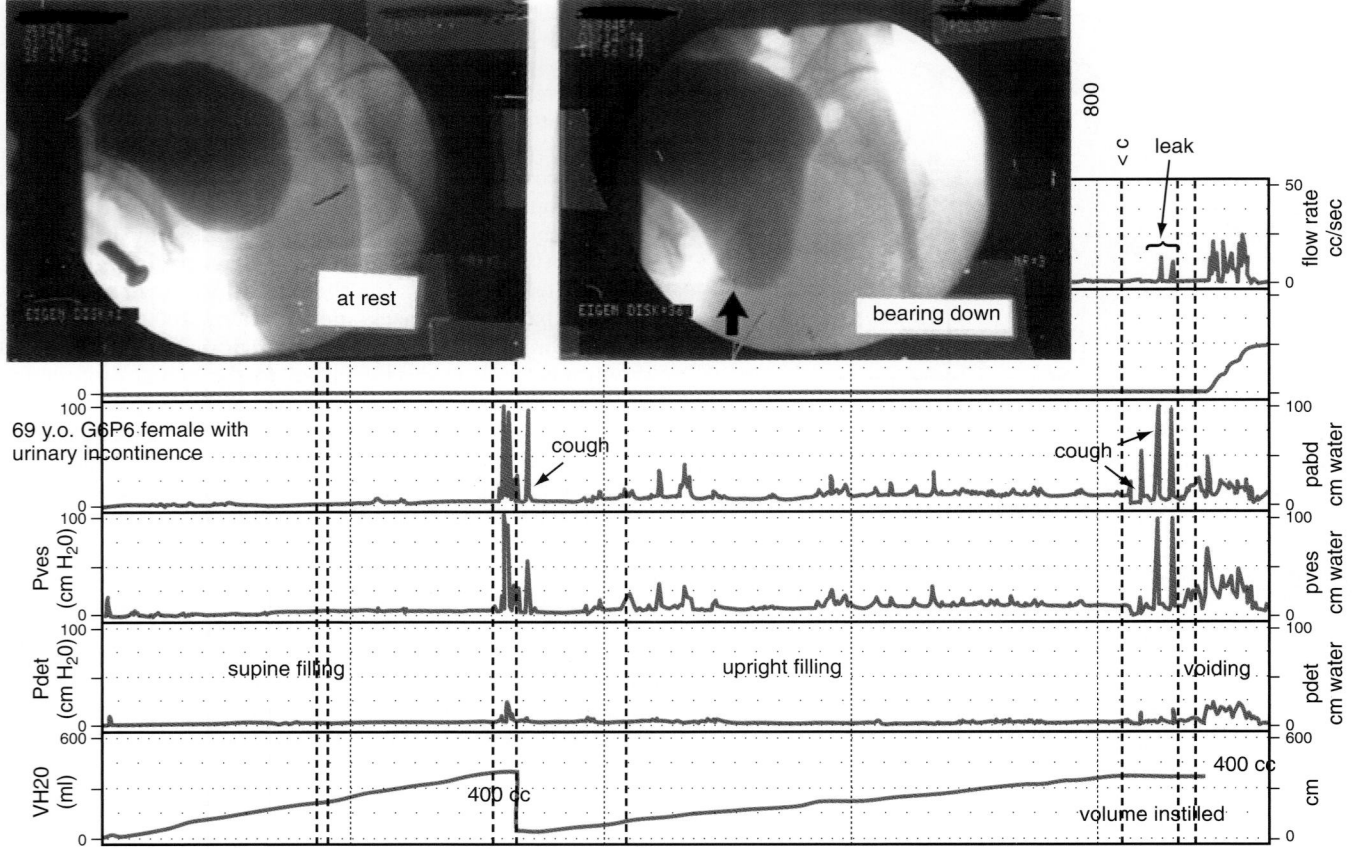

Figure 66–20. Video-urodynamic study of a 69-year-old woman with incontinence. Bearing down film shows descent of the bladder and proximal urethral *(arrow)*. This is consistent with a lateral defect.

when urodynamics fails to duplicate symptoms of incontinence (Fantl et al, 1996) or with a suspected fistula or ectopic ureter (Tubaro et al, 2005). Cystoscopy has also been reported to aid in the preoperative and intraoperative differentiation of the type of organ prolapse in patients with high-grade prolapse or multiple prolapsing organs (Vasavada et al, 1999). It is done simply by identifying the light transmitted through the bladder wall. Intraoperative cystoscopy is also necessary to assess for bladder or urethral perforation or ureteric obstruction during various pelvic procedures.

Ultrasound imaging of the bladder and urethra can be done by the transabdominal, transperineal, translabial, transvaginal, or transrectal route. The advantage of ultrasound is the ability to do real-time scanning without radiation exposure, but the major disadvantages are the variability introduced by the examiner with small changes in the transducer position and the availability of only a limited number of pictures after the examination. Earlier, Mostwin and coworkers (1995) demonstrated incontinence with bladder neck funneling and urethral rotational descent with a sagittal transrectal view. Transperineal sagittal scanning was used to measure bladder neck descent with straining (Peschers et al, 1996), and both translabial (Dietz et al, 1999) and transperineal ultrasound (Dietz and Wilson, 1998) were reported to compare favorably with video-urodynamics in the evaluation of stress incontinence.

Two-dimensional translabial scanning is now a standard technique and has been reported for assessing position and mobility of the bladder neck and proximal urethra, stress incontinence, bladder wall thickness (with transvaginal scanning as well), levator activity (with perineal scanning), and prolapse quantification (Dietz, 2004a). Multiple two-dimensional images can be combined, like slices of bread, to yield a three-dimensional image. Current transducers can acquire images by rapid oscillation of elements in a multitude of sectional planes within the transducer head. The images are integrated into a volume and displayed in various forms on a computer. Three-dimensional ultrasound has been used to image the urethra, levator ani complex, paravaginal supports, prolapse, and synthetic implant materials (Dietz, 2004b). Ultrasound is not recommended in the primary evaluation of women with incontinence and prolapse and is an optional test for complex problems (Tubaro et al, 2005).

MRI has been used to demonstrate the pelvic floor and organs in the normal and the pathologic states and has been proposed as a noninvasive modality that is more accurate than physical examination in identifying prolapsed organs. It provides multiplanar images, does not use ionizing radiation, usually does not requires contrast medium, and is relatively non–operator dependent. Various techniques provide imaging details of soft tissue structures. Endoanal and endovaginal magnetic coils produce high-resolution images of the anal sphincter and vagina, respectively, but other structures are not as clear. Imaging with a body coil produces a more global view of the pelvic floor and organs. Each imaging system and the choice of imaging sequences produce variable appearances of the soft tissue structures and differentiation between tissue planes (Weidner and Low, 1998). During the process, tissue responds to being stimulated by a radio signal in the presence of a strong magnetic field with two different response signals that vary in length: T1 and T2. Different tissues have different response times, both T1 and T2, thereby permitting construction of an image. T1-weighted sequences can be obtained in a shorter time, resulting in less motion artifact, and are used as the initial imaging sequence. T2-weighted images have clearer soft tissue contrast discrimination. Very fast single-shot MR sequences have been developed for the evaluation of pelvic prolapse, allowing excellent visualization of the pelvic floor.

The first report of fast MRI of the pelvic floor was from Yang and colleagues (1991). They were able to show a difference between control subjects and those with prolapse at maximal strain using the pubococcygeal line as a reference. Klutke and colleagues (1990) also described bladder neck anatomy in normal women compared with those with stress incontinence. MRI has been done in cadavers to complement anatomic dissections of the pelvic floor (Strohbehn et al, 1996). It has been used extensively for studying urethral anatomy, for levator ani imaging in normal subjects (see Fig. 66–5), and for evaluation of stress incontinence and pelvic organ prolapse (Tubaro et al, 2005).

MR images are routinely obtained in the axial, coronal, and sagittal planes. By convention, coronal slices are presented with the subject facing the observer and axial images are presented with the subject's feet closest to the observer. Sagittal images are presented with the subject facing to the left of the observer. Various protocols have been published with different coils applied. For pelvic organ prolapse resting and straining sagittal and coronal views are obtained. The easily interpretable view is a sagittal midline slice 10 mm in thickness that includes the symphysis, bladder neck, vagina, rectum, and coccyx (Fig. 66–21). Repeated straining attempts can be done because each image usually takes less than 3 seconds (Hoyte et al, 2001).

One of the criticisms of MRI is that it is done with the patient in the supine position. Fielding and coworkers (1998), using an open MR scanner, showed similar pelvic descent in incontinent women in both the supine and the sitting positions. An MR grading system has also been proposed by Comiter and coworkers (1999). This uses the size of the levator hiatus, the H line (from the pubis to the posterior anal canal), the amount of levator descent from the pubococcygeal line (the M line), and the amount of organ prolapse below the levator hiatus (see Fig. 66–21). They showed significant differences in patients with prolapse and controls. Singh and colleagues proposed another reference line at the midpubic level to correspond to the hymenal ring in the POPQ clinical staging system. They showed good correlation of MR images in prolapse patients with their POPQ stage (Singh et al, 2001). MRI has been compared with radiographic contrast imaging with cystocolpoproctography. MRI detects more enteroceles but fewer rectoceles, unless rectal opacification is used (Tubaro et al, 2005).

MRI may be helpful in patients with complex organ prolapse to supplement the physical examination. Its clinical utility in comparison with physical examination and in the decision for surgical management has yet to be demonstrated. MRI is not indicated in the evaluation of patients with incontinence or prolapse and is still considered an investigational tool (Tubaro et al, 2005).

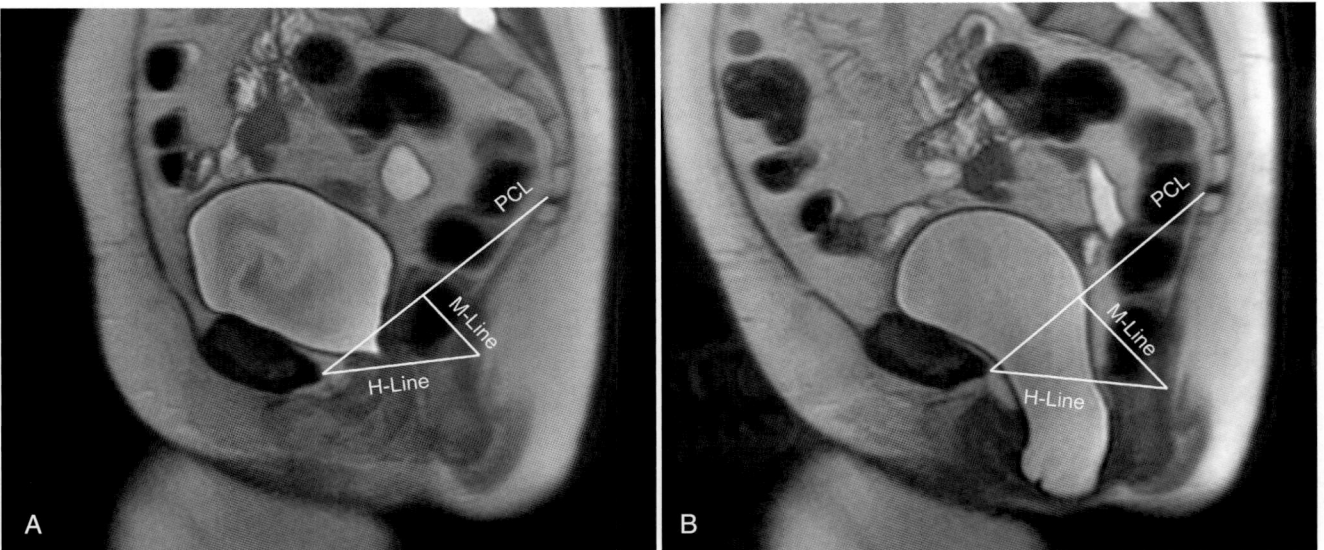

Figure 66–21. **A,** Dynamic sequence MR image in a patient with prolapse. T2-weighted image of a 57-year-old woman with anterior, midvaginal, and posterior prolapse. The patient's bladder is above the pubococcygeal line at rest. H-line, or puborectal line, measures size of levator hiatus. M-line measures pelvic floor relaxation (i.e., descent of levator plate from pubococcygeal line). **B,** With straining the patient's bladder descends markedly through the levator hiatus along with the posterior wall. On clinical examination, she had stage 3 vaginal vault prolapse.

VAGINAL SURGERY FOR STRESS INCONTINENCE

The first reports of surgical management of stress incontinence from the early part of the 20th century recommended a vaginal approach with plication of the periurethral tissue to narrow the urethral lumen and elevate the bladder neck (Kelly and Dumm, 1914). By the 1940s, concepts regarding etiology changed and procedures to address lateral support defects were published. Retropubic suspensions (Marshall et al, 1949) or slings (Aldridge, 1942) followed in an attempt to improve efficacy and durability. To achieve elevation as in the retropubic suspension with reduced morbidity, Pereyra introduced the vaginal needle suspension in 1959. There have been many subsequent modifications with regard to the extent of dissection, location of sutures, method of fixation, and types of ligature carrier. The most widely adopted procedures, the Modified Pereyra (Pereyra and Lebherz, 1967), Stamey (Stamey, 1973), Raz (Raz, 1981), and Gittes (Gittes and Loughlin, 1987) procedures, are discussed.

Although initial reports with relatively short-term follow-up showed success rates equivalent to retropubic suspensions, with less postoperative morbidity, longer-term outcomes have been worse (Elkabir and Mee, 1998; Kondo et al, 1998; Masson and Govier, 2000). **A review of published studies by the American Urological Association Female Stress Urinary Incontinence Clinical Guidelines Panel** (Leach et al, 1997) **showed a significantly lower cure (dry) rate beyond 4 years with transvaginal suspensions (67%) compared with retropubic suspensions (84%) or slings (83%). The review panel still considered transvaginal suspensions to be a good option for the appropriate women with stress incontinence, those with smaller volume incontinence, those with less intrinsic urethral sphincter deficiency, and those who are willing to accept worse long-term benefit in favor of lower immediate morbidity. With the advent of less invasive midurethral slings the role of needle suspensions is limited** (Bodell and Leach, 2002).

Because the needle suspension techniques form the basis for many procedures that are currently used they will be described here.

Preoperative and Intraoperative Management

Vaginal suspensions are routinely performed under general or regional anesthesia. Local anesthesia with sedation has been advocated for newer midurethral techniques (Ulmsten et al, 1998). Antibiotic prophylaxis is commonly employed, although there are no specific data supporting its use. Patients are placed in dorsal lithotomy with Trendelenburg positioning to optimize visibility and lower the chance of bowel injury with needle or suprapubic catheter passage. A weighted vaginal speculum, or Simms retractor, and pinning of the labia with sutures or a Scott retractor to spread the vaginal introitus improve access. A Foley catheter is inserted to allow identification of the bladder neck by palpation and to decompress the bladder to allow safe passage of the ligature carrier. With the vaginal incision, injection of sterile saline into the mucosa facilitates the development of the submucosal plane. Hema-

turia from the Foley catheter should alert one to suture penetration of the bladder (usually laterally, near the bladder neck). Stamey (1973) first introduced the idea of intraoperative cystoscopy to check suture placement and elevation and rule out bladder or urethral injury. This gave origin to the term *endoscopic suspension.*

A vaginal packing may be left at the end of the procedure depending on the amount of bleeding encountered. Postoperative bladder drainage is with either a urethral Foley or a suprapubic catheter. A urethral catheter avoids potential complications of blind insertion of a suprapubic catheter. However, with prolonged retention, women must master intermittent catheterization in the presence of adjacent surgical swelling and pain. Care must be taken with percutaneous insertion of a suprapubic catheter, especially if there is a history of previous lower abdominal surgery or radiation. The bladder must be very distended with the patient in exaggerated Trendelenburg positioning to minimize the risk of bowel penetration.

Surgical Techniques

Modified Pereyra

Pereyra's original description involved a T-shaped vaginal incision with minimal periurethral dissection and no penetration into the retropubic space (Pereyra, 1959). A single needle stylet and absorbable suture were used to suspend the periurethral tissue over the rectus fascia. The needle stylet was delivered into the vagina through a single midline lower abdominal incision. Pereyra and Lebherz (1967) subsequently modified the procedure by incorporating bladder neck plication but still using absorbable sutures. They reported a 94% cure rate with 1-year follow-up in 210 patients.

Stamey Needle Bladder Neck Suspension

Stamey's (1973) modifications to the transvaginal suspension incorporated three different aspects. Endoscopy was an adjunct to ensure sutures were placed at the bladder neck. Nonabsorbable suture was used with Dacron tube vaginal pledgets to buttress both sides of the urethra and prevent suspensory suture pull-through on the vaginal side. Stamey also designed a single-pronged blunt-tipped needle (Stamey needle) that is still commonly used in many versions of transvaginal suspensions. The procedure involved two lateral suprapubic incisions, and a suprapubic catheter was inserted for bladder drainage. Success has been reported in 72% to 91% of patients (Stamey, 1980; Walker and Texter, 1992) and tends to decrease with longer follow-up (Kondo et al, 1998) and in younger patients (Hilton and Mayne, 1991). Erosion of the Dacron pledgets has been reported at up to 3 years after surgery (Bihrle and Tarantino, 1990).

Gittes Bladder Neck Suspension

Gittes and Loughlin (1987) described a no-incision pubovaginal suspension. Two lateral suprapubic stab incisions are made and the Stamey needle is passed twice on each side from over the rectus fascia through the vaginal wall at the bladder neck (guided by the Foley balloon) to retrieve the ends of a No. 2 polypropylene stitch. A Mayo needle is used to take helical bites of vaginal mucosa before delivering the second end of the stitch to the abdominal wall. The sutures are tied over the rectus fascia without tension. Gittes postulated that the vaginal suspension sutures under slight traction will cut through the vaginal wall and become buried in scar, creating an "autologous pledget." A suprapubic catheter was also used.

Although favorable short-term results were published (Gittes and Loughlin, 1987; Kil et al, 1991; Conquy et al, 1993), this technique has the poorest reported long-term outcome of endoscopic suspensions. Kondo and coworkers (1998) compared their experience with 382 patients undergoing a Stamey or Gittes suspension with a mean follow-up of more than 5 years in both groups. The Kaplan-Meier cumulative continence rates were 71.5% for the Stamey at 14 years and 37% for the Gittes at 6 years postoperatively ($P < .0001$). Elkabir and Mee (1998) found a similarly low cure rate of 38.5% at 2 years with the Gittes technique.

Raz Procedures for Stress Incontinence

In 1981, Raz reported a modification of the Pereyra procedure (Fig. 66–22). The technique required an inverted U-shaped vaginal incision to improve access. It also was the first to enter the retropubic space sharply via the vaginal route by detaching the periurethral connective tissue and endopelvic fascia from the arcus tendineus and pelvic sidewall. Opening the retropubic space facilitates blind passage of the ligature carrier from the abdomen to the vaginal incision by allowing finger guidance, permitting urethrolysis if required, and allowing placement of helical sutures into the vaginal side of the periurethral connective tissue, which results in a more secure purchase of tissue. Another subsequent modification was the double-pronged ligature carrier that is passed twice via a midline suprapubic incision to retrieve the No. 1 nonabsorbable suture from each side. A suprapubic catheter was used.

A 15-month follow-up (Raz et al, 1992) showed a 92% success rate. Severity of incontinence was found to be a negative predictor for outcome. Golomb and coworkers (1994) have confirmed good early results and low morbidity for the procedure. However, there are reports of poor long-term results from this version of the Raz procedure (Korman et al,

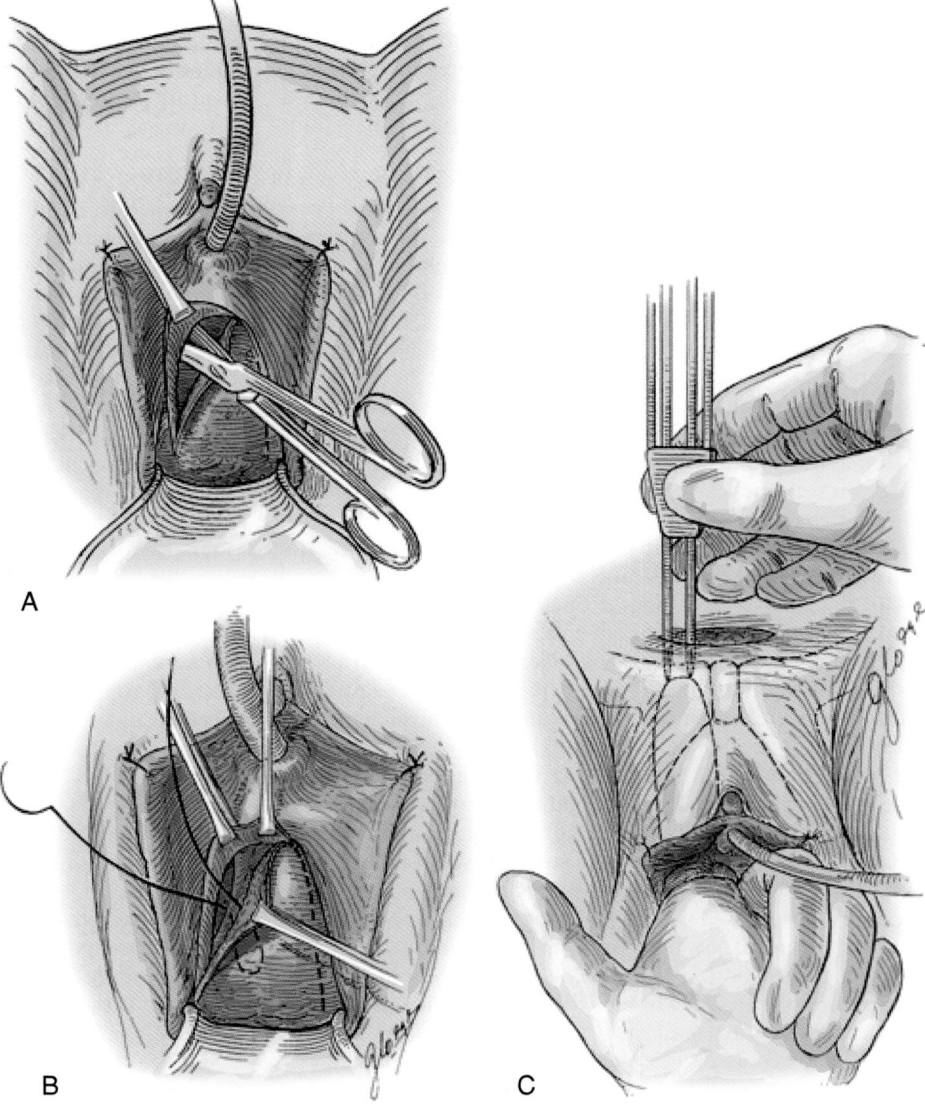

Figure 66–22. Raz bladder neck suspension. **A,** Inverted U-shaped incision is made in the anterior vaginal wall with the base of the U at a point midway between the bladder neck and the urethral meatus. The vaginal wall is dissected off the surface of the periurethral fascia. The retropubic space is entered by detaching the endopelvic fascia from the arcus tendineus. **B,** A No. 1 polypropylene suture is placed to include the endopelvic fascia and pubocervical fascia, which underlies the vaginal wall. A similar suture is placed on the opposite side. **C,** A midline transverse incision is made just above the pubis and carried down to the rectus fascia. The double-prong suture carrier is placed through the rectus fascia and muscle, and the tips are palpated with the index finger in the retropubic space. The suture carrier is guided down and out through the vaginal incision. The sutures are placed into the needle holes and guided back up through the rectus fascia. Cystoscopy is carried out. The vaginal incision is closed, and the sutures are tied suprapubically. The vagina is packed and the suprapubic incision is closed. (From Raz S: Female Genitourinary Dysfunction and Reconstruction. Philadelphia, WB Saunders, 1996.)

1994; Trockman et al, 1995; Das, 1998; Masson and Govier, 2000). Furthermore, Masson and Govier (2000) showed that of 135 patients with a mean follow-up of more than 4 years, only 14% were dry and 53% continued to wear pads.

Raz Vaginal Wall Sling

In 1989, Raz devised a vaginal technique to treat stress incontinence due to intrinsic sphincter dysfunction. A rectangular flap of vagina was buried at the bladder neck and suspended by nonabsorbable sutures at each corner by passage of a ligature carrier. In 1992, they reported on 54 patients with this procedure, showing a success rate of 94% after a mean follow-up of 24 months (Juma et al, 1992). Other investigators confirmed similar short-term success and low morbidity (Couillard et al, 1994).

Subsequently, Raz and coworkers modified the procedure in that the vaginal flap was no longer buried. The later technique is based on the importance of the midurethral mechanism to prevent incontinence. The surgical goals of the anterior vaginal wall "sling" were (1) to provide elastic support to the mid urethra and bladder neck and (2) to create a strong hammock of vaginal wall and underlying tissues, which provides a backboard against which the urethra can be compressed with increases in intra-abdominal pressure (Raz et al, 1996). It was applicable to all patients with stress incontinence. A similar technique of six-corner suspension is illustrated in Figure 66–24.

Two oblique incisions are made in the anterior vaginal wall extending from the level of the mid urethra to 3 cm beyond the level of the bladder neck. The incisions are 1 cm medial to the lateral margin folds of the anterior vaginal wall. Dissection to enter the retropubic space is then carried out. The proximal (bladder neck) sutures are placed in the same fashion as the modified Pereyra stitches using No. 1 nonabsorbable suture with the addition of several helical passes under the vaginal epithelium capturing further periurethral and perivesical tissue. The distal (midurethral) sutures are then placed again using No. 1 nonabsorbable suture. To facilitate multiple helical passes with a good purchase of periurethral tissue in this location, Russian forceps are opened widely in the retropubic space with gentle downward traction maintaining the forceps parallel to the ground. After this deep tissue is taken, several helical bites of anterior periurethral fascia underlying the vaginal epithelium are taken at the midurethral level. Care must be taken to avoid urethral perforation by maintaining the needle parallel to the vagina. The identical sutures are then placed on the contralateral side. These four sutures suspend a rectangle of support ("sling") for the bladder neck and mid urethra. The double-pronged ligature carrier is then passed in the same fashion as the Raz procedure through a midline suprapubic incision. It must be passed four times to transfer the sutures, which are then tied over the immobile portion of the rectus fascia. The vaginal incisions are closed using running, locking 2-0 delayed absorbable suture. Cystoscopy is used to rule out bladder or urethral penetration.

Initial results in 160 women with incontinence who underwent the Raz vaginal wall sling with a median follow-up of 17 months showed 152 to be cured of stress incontinence (Raz et al, 1996).

Complications of Vaginal Suspensions

Intraoperative Complications

The most commonly encountered intraoperative complications are bleeding, suture passage through the bladder, or laceration of the bladder or urethra during dissection. Bleeding from vaginal veins may be brisk but can usually be controlled by electrocautery or absorbable stitches. Bleeding from retropubic dissection may be more problematic and is often a result of dissection too far laterally into the obturator fossa. Temporary vaginal packing along with digital compression can slow bleeding. Suture ligatures may be required. Vaginal closure with packing may tamponade bleeding that is not too brisk or flowing freely into the retropubic space. Rarely, abdominal exploration may be required to control bleeding. Transfusion requirement for endoscopic suspensions is estimated at 1% (Leach et al, 1997).

When hematuria is identified after passage of a ligature carrier, bladder puncture is likely. Cystoscopy should be done and the suture removed. It is usually on the lateral side, near the bladder neck. Removal and replacement of the stitch along with catheter bladder decompression for 48 hours is generally sufficient. Finally, if dissection leads to urethral or bladder laceration, this should be repaired using multilayer absorbable suture closure and consideration given to longer-term bladder drainage.

Postoperative Complications

Postoperative voiding dysfunction can occur. The most commonly encountered problem is urinary retention. This persists beyond 2 weeks in 5% to 8% (Leach et al, 1997; Kondo et al, 1998; Elkabir and Mee, 1998; Tamussino et al, 1999). Permanent retention is a rare complication and may not be predicted by preoperative urodynamics. De novo detrusor overactivity or overactive bladder symptoms or worsening of preexisting storage symptoms such as frequency, urgency, and urge incontinence is estimated to occur in 4% to 16% (Raz et al, 1992; Trockman et al, 1995; Leach et al, 1997; Kondo et al, 1998). For some patients this is quite problematic and may not respond to anticholinergics. Both retention and de novo overactive bladder symptoms, if from obstruction, may respond to urethrolysis (Nitti and Raz, 1994; Carr and Webster, 1997). Cutting the suspensory sutures beyond the initial postoperative period may not be effective. Other complications that are less frequent but well recognized include persistent pelvic pain or dyspareunia in 5% (Elkabir and Mee, 1998; Raz et al, 1992), pelvic organ prolapse in 6% (Raz et al, 1992), and death in 0.05% (Leach et al, 1997).

Conclusions

In general, the long-term success of transvaginal endoscopic suspension is not as good as open retropubic repairs or sling procedures. Of the transvaginal suspensions, the Gittes procedure appears to be the least durable. However, the morbidity associated with transvaginal suspensions for stress incontinence is lower than that with open retropubic or sling surgery (Leach et al, 1997).

These results were reiterated in a recent Cochrane Database Systematic Review of bladder neck needle suspensions (Glazener and Cooper, 2004). Nine trials with 347 women with needle suspensions were compared with 437 women who received comparison interventions. The results showed that needle suspensions were more likely to fail after 1 year than open retropubic suspensions (29% vs. 16%), and the difference in perioperative complications was not significant (23% vs. 16%).

KEY POINTS: VAGINAL SURGERY FOR STRESS INCONTINENCE

- The long-term success of transvaginal needle suspension procedures is not as good as that of open retropubic suspensions or slings.

- Needle suspension techniques form the basis of newer stress incontinence procedures that are currently used.

VAGINAL SURGERY FOR PROLAPSE
Principles of Surgery for Prolapse

A glossary of terms used in vaginal surgery is found in Table 66–9. The goals of surgery are listed in Table 66–10. The primary goal of surgery for pelvic organ prolapse is to effect changes in anatomic structure that provide patients with relief of symptoms (Wall et al, 1998). The three main types of procedures, which can be combined, are repairing the tissue,

---

Table 66–9. Glossary of Terms for Vaginal and Pelvic Surgery

Colporrhaphy: repair of vaginal wall
Colpocleisis: obliteration of vaginal lumen (Le Fort—denudation of anterior and posterior vaginal mucosal strips with approximation of anterior and posterior walls [Thompson, 1997])
Colpectomy: resection of vagina
Colpopexy: suspension of vaginal wall
Culdotomy: incision into (posterior) cul-de-sac (pouch of Douglas)
Culdoplasty (culdeplasty): surgical obliteration of cul-de-sac to treat or prevent enterocele
  Abdominal
    Moschowitz (1912): multiple purse-string sutures picking up uterosacral ligaments laterally, posterior vagina wall, and shallow bites of rectal serosa
    Halban (1932): 3 to 4 parallel sagittal sutures starting on the posterior vaginal wall picking up peritoneum and rectal serosa
  Vaginal
    McCall (1957): transverse sutures placed into the cardinals, uterosacrals, pararectal fascia, peritoneum, and posterior vaginal wall
Perineorrhaphy: repair of perineal body

Table 66–10. Goals of Surgery for Pelvic Organ Prolapse

1. Relieve symptoms
2. Maintain or improve urinary, bowel, and sexual function
3. Reposition pelvic structures and supports to normal anatomy
4. Prevent new pelvic support defects and symptoms
5. Correct concomitant intrapelvic disease
6. Achieve a durable result

---

replacing it with grafts, and occasionally obliterating or closing the vagina (Weber and Richter, 2005).

There is still no consensus or guidelines regarding which tests constitute an adequate workup for patients before surgery, nor are the functional deficits and symptoms caused by pelvic organ prolapse and pelvic floor dysfunction totally specific or absolutely established (Mouritsen and Larsen, 2003; Burrows et al, 2004). It is therefore important for the surgeon to fully evaluate the patient clinically and record all of the symptoms and physical findings in a standardized manner, as discussed earlier. Because the various forms of organ prolapse are interrelated, owing to shared support mechanisms, it is generally recommended that all defects be repaired at the same time (Thompson, 1997; Raz et al, 1998; Kobashi and Leach, 2000) because occult weaknesses in other sites or new support defects may be acquired (Shull et al, 2002). Although this approach is supported by clinical experience and the reported occurrence of prolapse after retropubic urethropexy (Wiskind et al, 1992; Kjolhede et al, 1996) and vaginal vault suspension (Shull et al, 1992; Smilen et al, 1998), there are little data on the natural history of untreated pelvic organ prolapse and whether correction matters (Whiteside et al, 2004). Furthermore, Handa and coworkers (2004a) in a 2- to 8-year longitudinal study of 410 women as part of the Women's Health Initiative Study reported spontaneous regression in some women with low-stage prolapse.

Other important considerations are the risk factors outlined in Table 66–3. Age and general health status will affect the decision to operate and the choice of operation. Risk factor reduction in obesity, smoking and chronic cough, constipation, and heavy lifting may improve symptoms and postoperative outcomes. In addition, the preoperative discussion should address the patient's desire for preservation of coital, menstrual, and reproductive function when appropriate.

Nonsurgical treatment of prolapse may involve measures to improve the risk factors along with vaginal estrogen and pelvic muscle exercises (Thakar and Stanton, 2002). These may help alleviate symptoms and prevent worsening of the prolapse, but the actual hernia will not spontaneously disappear. **Pessaries are the mainstay of nonsurgical treatment and are of primarily two types: ring and support. Pessary use is widespread and may be successful in alleviating symptoms in the majority of women** (Clemons et al, 2004) **and occasionally improve the prolapse** (Handa and Jones, 2002). **Complications such as vaginal wall ulceration can be minimized by proper sizing, care, and cleansing and estrogen replacement therapy** (Cundiff et al, 1998b). **Stress incontinence may also be unmasked in about 20% of patients** (Clemons et al, 2004). **Sulak and coworkers (1993) reported that, despite effective management in women who refused surgery, there was a 20% discontinuation rate.**

In postmenopausal women, estrogen therapy has been widely proposed for the preparation of the vagina before surgery. Because the estrogen dose required to improve urogenital atrophy is lower than that required for endometrial proliferation, administration of unopposed low dose estrogen is safe and effective (Robinson and Cardozo, 2003). The vaginal route of administration also has been found to correlate with better urogenital atrophy symptom relief, greater improvement in vaginal cytologic findings, and higher serum estradiol levels than the oral, transcutaneous, or subcutaneous routes (Cardozo et al, 1998). A practical regimen is a 6-week preoperative course of vaginal estrogen cream (Kobashi and Leach, 2000). Long-term safety of various vaginal estrogen delivery systems has also been confirmed (Robinson and Cardozo, 2003).

The Use of Biologic and Synthetic Materials

In an attempt to improve the outcomes of incontinence and prolapse surgery surgeons have used a large variety of synthetic or biologic materials. The ideal prosthesis should be biocompatible, be inert, lack an allergic or inflammatory response, be sterile, be noncarcinogenic, be resistant to mechanical stress or shrinkage, and be available in a convenient and affordable format for clinical use (Birch and Fynes, 2002). For use in the vagina it should also not result in erosion or infection or limit elasticity.

Prostheses may be classified as autologous, allograft, xenograft, or synthetic. An understanding of their inherent strength, surgical handling, reaction within human tissues, and potential morbidity is required to allow appropriate selection.

Biologic Grafts

Autologous grafts may be harvested from the vagina, abdominal wall, or thigh. Perioperative morbidity with incisional hernias or unsatisfactory cosmesis may occur. Women with prolapse may have inherently weak tissue that may compromise the surgical result. Cadaveric donor fascia lata **allografts** avoid the morbidity of autologous harvesting and reduce the risk of graft erosion associated with synthetic meshes. These grafts are harvested with aseptic technique, soaked in antibiotics, freeze dried, and sterilized with gamma irradiation. Concerns have been raised about the small risks of antigenic expression and transmission of prion or human immunodeficiency virus. Human-derived dura matter is available in the United States but not in countries of the European Union owing to concerns over prion transmission (Brubaker et al, 2005).

The available **xenograft** products include acellular porcine small intestinal submucosa (SIS, Cook, Spencer, IN), porcine dermis (DermMatrix [InteXen], Carbon Medical Technologies, St. Paul, MN; Pelvicol, Bard Urological, Covington, GA) and bovine pericardium (Veritas Collagen Matrix, Synovis, St. Paul, MN). Strict U.S. Food and Drug Administration (FDA) guidelines regarding the animal sources, feed sources, BSE status, and processing of the tissue are in place. Laboratory and animals studies have shown that the graft material acts as scaffolding and induces host tissue cells to infiltrate its substance and to essentially replace it (Colvert et al, 2002). However, there are still some concerns about latent animal zoonoses (Brubaker et al, 2005).

Synthetic Grafts

Synthetic prostheses, both absorbable and nonabsorbable, are classified into four types according to the material, pore size, and whether they are monofilament or multifilament (Table 66–11). The important factors are flexibility and passage of leukocytes/macrophages. These cells are small enough to pass through pore sizes of less than 75 μm. However, multifilament grafts may have interstices of less than 10 μm that will allow passage of small bacteria (<1 μm) but not leukocytes, thereby increasing the risk of infection (Birch and Fynes, 2002).

Extrusion and erosion are the main risks of synthetic prostheses. Extrusion may occur with inadequate vaginal incision closure, superficial placement, atrophy, or infection. Erosion may occur at any time and present with no symptoms or with discharge, dyspareunia, or vaginal pain. The stiffness or flexibility of the graft also influences the likelihood of these complications. Local reaction to the graft may result in inflammation or fibrosis, causing vaginal pain. Most grafts will shrink about 20% over time so sufficient excess graft should be taken to allow for remodeling (Brubaker et al, 2005).

Type I polypropylene synthetic graft has the lowest rate of erosion (<3%) and is therefore the most commonly used (Cosson et al, 2003; Brubaker et al, 2005). However, there are great variations in the types of polypropylene and the surgeon must be aware of the different characteristics of thickness, flexibility, and stiffness. Combined absorbable and nonabsorbable as well as combined biologic and synthetic products are also available. However, there is no definite evidence yet demonstrating superiority of the combination products.

Type	Component	Trade Name (Manufacturer)	Fiber Type	Pore Size*
Type I	Polypropylene	Prolene (Ethicon) Surgipro (US Surgical)	Monofilament	Macro
		Marlex (Bard)	Monofilament	Macro
		Atrium (Atrium)	Monofilament	Macro
		Gynemesh (Ethicon)	Monofilament	Macro
	Polypropylene/Polyglactin 910	Vipro (Ethicon)	Mono/multifilament	Macro
	Polyglactin 910	Vicryl (Ethicon)	Multifilament	Macro
	Polyglycolic acid	Dexon (Syneture)	Multifilament	Macro
Type II	Expanded PTFE	Gore-Tex (Gore)	Multifilament	Micro
Type III	Polyethylene	Mersilene (Ethicon)	Multifilament	Micro/macro
Type IV	Polypropylene sheet	Cellgard (not used)	Monofilament	Submicro

Table 66–11. **Types of Synthetic Grafts**

*Macro, >75 μm; Micro, <75 μm.
Modified from Birch C, Fynes MM: The role of synthetic and biological prostheses in reconstructive pelvic floor surgery. Curr Opin Obstet Gynecol 2002;14:527-535.

Anterior Vaginal Wall (Anterior Compartment)

It has been noted earlier that anterior vaginal prolapse can result from weaknesses in four distinct areas of anterior wall (Richardson et al, 1976). Many different operations have been described, and the operative strategy can be determined by the pattern identified. Weaknesses in the central part of the anterior vaginal wall or fascia give rise to cystocele from a central defect and, according to Richardson and coworkers (1981), account for only 1% to 2% of patients. Weakness in the lateral attachments to the arcus tendineus results in anterior prolapse from a lateral or paravaginal defect and is seen in 80% to 85% of patients. Combined defects with both central and lateral deficiency are also common (see Fig. 66–10). A proximal transverse weakness results from the separation of the pubocervical fascia from the ring of fascia around the cervix, or the cardinal-uterosacral complex after hysterectomy, and is seen in 15% of patients. A distal transverse defect results from separation of the fascial attachments to the pubis.

Anterior Colporrhaphy for Central Defect

Anterior colporrhaphy, initially described by Kelly and Dumm in 1914 for the treatment of urinary incontinence, is applicable for treatment of cystocele from central defects. Most descriptions of the technique involve not only plication sutures in the pubocervical fascia underneath the cystocele but also sutures into the attenuated fascia at the level of the bladder neck and urethra to buttress the hypermobile urethra from below (Nichols, 1993b; Thompson, 1997). **Because the failure rate of anterior colporrhaphy for urinary incontinence has been up to 50%** (Black and Downs, 1996; Leach et al, 1997; Glazener and Cooper, 2000) **it is not recommended as a surgical procedure for stress incontinence. Its importance now is that it is has been incorporated into other transvaginal repairs that are done for incontinence to address the anterior midline support defect. Failure to address the urethral support defect may unmask stress incontinence; conversely, fixing only the urethral hypermobility and leaving a cystocele may create or exacerbate outflow obstruction** (Kobashi and Leach, 2000).

Technique, Results, and Complications. Injection of sterile saline solution just beneath the vaginal mucosa facilitates dissection in the proper plane. A midline incision is made through the vaginal mucosa extending from the apex of the vagina to within 1 cm of the meatus (Fig. 66–23). Placing Allis clamps, either proximally or distally, and lifting the vaginal mucosa, depending on the mobility of the anterior wall, can further facilitate the midline incision. Alternatively, a proximal longitudinal incision can be made near the cervix, which is grasped with a tenaculum; Metzenbaum scissors are inserted and advanced into the plane just underneath the vaginal mucosa, with the scissors spread in the vesicovaginal space. The incision near the cervix can also be transverse, at the junction of the cervix and the anterior vaginal wall, with the midline incision coming off like a T. The midline incision is then made in the mobilized mucosa. The flaps are dissected out laterally as far as possible, by sharp dissection, exposing the white endopelvic (or pubocervical) fascia. The underlying fascia is left attached to the bladder and intact after exposure.

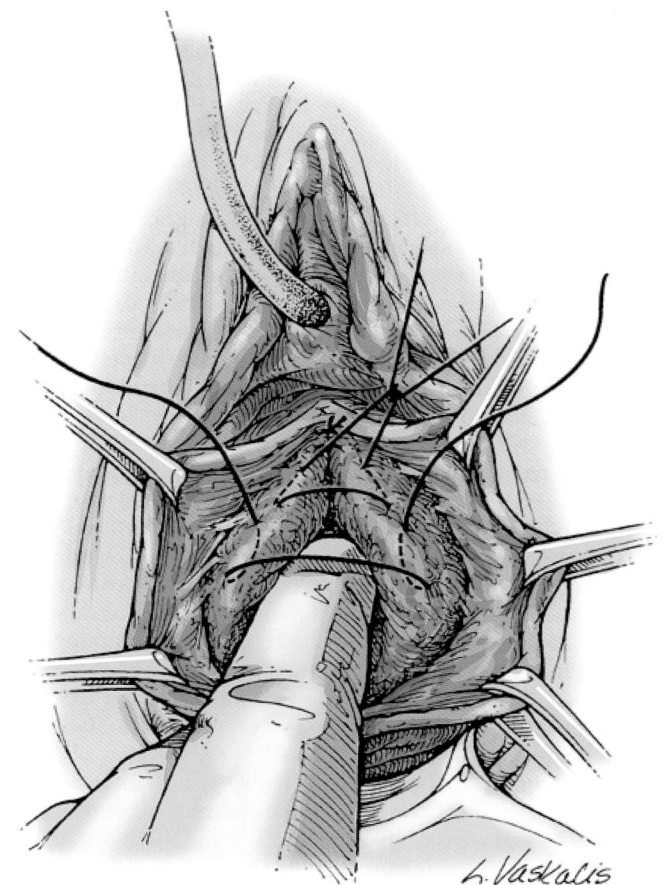

Figure 66–23. Anterior colporrhaphy. The anterior submucosal layer is imbricated with 2-0 delayed absorbable continuous or interrupted suture. (From Nichols DH Cystocele. In Nichols DH [ed]: Gynecologic and Obstetric Surgery. St. Louis, CV Mosby, 1993, pp 334-362.)

Plication sutures of interrupted 2-0 or 3-0 delayed absorbable material are then inserted. In the Kelly procedure for incontinence, the sutures are placed at the level of the urethra and bladder neck by taking lateral tissue and approximating it in the midline. To support and raise the bladder neck, the plication sutures approximate tissue from the posterior aspect of the symphysis bilaterally. (Because another procedure will most likely be done for urethral hypermobility or incompetence, these sutures are not necessary.) To support the cystocele, approximating vertical mattress sutures bring together the lateral aspects of the mobilized fascia. Upward pressure on the prolapsed bladder base with an instrument facilitates placement of the sutures and their subsequent tying, to reduce the cystocele. Large cystoceles may require an initial purse-string suture, the neck of which may be supported by additional side-to-side sutures. In the posterior aspect, approximating stitches can be placed in the pericervical fascia or cardinal-uterosacral ligament complex for additional support. Excess vaginal flaps may be trimmed and the mucosa approximated with continuous or interrupted 2-0 or 3-0 delayed absorbable sutures. Variations involve overlapping of opposite sides of vaginal fascia and "vest over pants" repairs.

Other modifications consist of the addition of biologic or synthetic materials to support the vagina. Reports have included full-thickness vaginal graft (Zacharin, 1992), collagen mesh (Friedman and Meltzer, 1970), absorbable polyglactin mesh (Safir et al, 1999), Mersilene mesh (Nichols, 1993b), Marlex mesh (Flood et al, 1998; Julian, 1996), and cadaveric fascia (Kobashi and Leach, 2000). Julian (1996) reported a 66% cure rate for a standard anterior colporrhaphy for recurrent anterior prolapse compared with a 100% cure rate when Marlex mesh was used to substitute for the vaginal fascia. However, there was a 25% incidence of mesh-related complications. **There have been two prospective randomized control trials comparing the use of polyglactin 910 absorbable mesh to anterior colporrhaphy alone.** Sand and coworkers (2001) reported that, after 1 year, 30 (43%) of 70 subjects without mesh and 18 (25%) of subjects with mesh had recurrent cystoceles beyond the midvaginal plane ($P < .02$). Weber and colleagues (2001) reported that at a median follow-up of 23.3 months, an optimal result was seen in 10 (30%) of 33 patients after standard anterior colporrhaphy, compared with 11 (42%) of 26 after standard colporrhaphy plus mesh and 11 (46%) of 24 with ultralateral colporrhaphy, that is, no significance differences among the groups. **Taken together these reports suggest improvement of 12% to 18% in the cure rate when polyglactin mesh is placed over the midline plication compared with standard colporrhaphy.**

The results of anterior colporrhaphy are in Table 66–12. Most series consist of patients who underwent other prolapse and incontinence procedures so the specific outcome of the anterior wall is sometimes difficult to ascertain. The reported recurrence of anterior vaginal prolapse after anterior colporrhaphy is lower than that of stress incontinence and ranged from 0% to 20% (see Table 66–12). However, in recent series higher recurrence rates have been reported (Sand et al, 2001; Weber et al, 2001).

High anatomic recurrence rates have also been reported when anterior colporrhaphy is combined with various other procedures (see Table 66–12). With vaginal needle suspension, Miyazaki and Miyazaki (1994) reported a recurrence rate of 59% and Kohli and coworkers (1996) reported a recurrence rate of 33%. This may be caused by worsening of the paravaginal defect by retropubic dissection (Kohli et al, 1996). The recurrence rate after sacrospinous ligament fixation ranges from 22% to 92% (Morley and DeLancey, 1988; Shull et al, 1992; Holley et al, 1995; Paraiso et al, 1996; Maher et al, 2001) and may be caused by altering the vaginal axis with exposure of the anterior wall to greater abdominal pressure or a neuropathy caused by the vaginal dissection (Benson et al, 1996). It should be noted that most patients reported with recurrences did not undergo additional surgery.

Complications of anterior colporrhaphy, apart from recurrent cystocele, may include de novo stress incontinence, especially if the patient had potential or masked stress incontinence before the procedure, and urge incontinence. The bladder may be injured during vaginal flap dissection or suture placement. Urinary retention, ureteral obstruction, and significant bleeding may rarely occur (Raz et al, 1998). Urethral injury is rare.

Table 66–12. Results of Anterior Vaginal Prolapse Repairs

Author	Recurrence	Follow-Up (yr)
Anterior Colporrhaphy (AC)	**Cystocele**	
Macer, 1978 (vaginal)	22/109 (20%)	5-20
Stanton et al, 1982	8/54 (15%)	Up to 2
Walter et al, 1982	0/86 (0%)	1-2.5 (aver. 1.2)
Porges and Smilen, 1994	10/388 (3%)	1-20 (aver. 2.6)
Smilen et al, 1998	23/245 (9.4%)	>6 mo
Colombo et al, 2000	1/33 (3%)	8-17
Sand et al, 2001	AC alone 30/70 (43%); AC + mesh 18/73 (25%)	1
Weber et al, 2001	AC alone 36/57 (63%); AC + mesh 15/26 (58%)	23 months
Anterior Colporrhaphy with Sacrospinous Ligament Fixation		
Morley and DeLancey, 1988	16/71 (22%)	1-11 (aver. 4.3)
Shull et al, 1992	20/81 (25%)	2-5
Holley et al, 1995	33/36 (92%)	1.2-6.6
Paraiso et al, 1996	91/243 (37.4%)	6.1
Maher et al, 2001	9/36 (25%)	1.6
Abdominal Repair		
Paravaginal Defect		
Richardson et al, 1981	10/213 (5%)	2-8
Shull and Baden, 1989	8/149 (5%)	0.5-4
Bruce et al, 1999	6/25 (24%)	1.4
Scotti et al, 1998	3/35 (8.6%)	3.25
Central Defect		
Macer, 1978	6/76 (8%)	5-20
Vaginal Paravaginal Repair		
White, 1909	0/19	Up to 3
Shull et al, 1994	4/56 (7%) severe 11/56 (20%) mild	0.1-5.6 (aver. 1.6)
Benson et al, 1996	12/46 (26%)	1-5.5 (aver. 2.5)
Farrell and Ling, 1997	6/27 (22%)	0.75
Mallipeddi et al, 2001	1/35 (3%)	1.6
Young et al, 2001	22/100 (22%)	11 months

Procedures for Lateral and Combined Defects

Abdominal Repairs. Lateral defects, causing mild to moderate cystoceles, can be repaired abdominally with a paravaginal repair or Burch colposuspension. The retropubic space is dissected to identify the arcus tendineus running from the posterior aspect of the pubic to the ischial spine. The obturator neurovascular bundle runs superolateral to it. In the paravaginal repair (Richardson et al, 1976), the endopelvic fascia and lateral vaginal sulcus are sutured to the arcus tendineus with four to six interrupted permanent sutures. In the Burch repair (Burch, 1961), the distal vaginal sutures are inserted into the pectineal (Cooper's) ligament.

Scotti and coworkers (1998) in a two-phase study reported on optimal suture placement in 13 cadavers and then clinical results in 40 patients. Paravaginal fixation to the ischial periosteum and obturator membrane was performed. The suspension suture was passed through the arcus tendineus and the obturator internus muscle, piercing the periosteum and obturator membrane after palpation of the ischial spine and sciatic foramina to ensure safe and anatomically correct suture placement. Two or three deep bites were taken extending from just anterior to the ischial spines along an oblique line anteriorly and caudally toward the pubic bone. The arcus tendineus was used as a superficial landmark after careful palpation of the bony pelvis before each suture was placed. Care was taken to avoid the obturator neurovascular bundle by means of gentle retraction with a vein retractor.

For the abdominal approach to central defects, Macer (1978) described opening the vesicouterine peritoneal reflection and mobilizing the bladder anteriorly. Redundant vaginal tissue is excised, and the wall is closed in layers with anchoring of the vaginal cuff to the cardinal ligaments. Bladder flap hematomas occurred in 4% of patients.

The results, in Table 66–12, show a recurrence rate of 5% to 24%. Complications of the paravaginal repair can include enterocele formation and vault prolapse (Shull and Baden, 1989). The paravaginal repair alone is not recommended for stress incontinence (Colombo et al, 1996).

Vaginal Paravaginal Repair. In 1912, White described the vaginal paravaginal repair on the basis of autopsy dissections showing that the cause of cystocele was weakness of the lateral vaginal attachments to the arcus tendineus (White, 1909). The concept fell into disfavor for many years until it was revived by Richardson and colleagues (1976). The approach has been illustrated in surgical textbooks (Nichols, 1993b; Shull, 1997). Richardson and colleagues (1976) popularized the abdominal paravaginal procedure, but the uncertainty of the location and integrity of the arcus tendineus for stabilization limited its popularity until recently (Scotti et al, 1998).

Technique, Results, and Complications. The vaginal procedure is done with the patient in the lithotomy position through a midline, inverted U or V, or bilateral parallel incisions (Nichols, 1993b). The retropubic space is entered through the endopelvic fascia that is separated from the inferior rami. The pubocervical fascia is separated from the sidewall of the pelvis, exposing the obturator fascia and the arcus tendineus. Four to six interrupted permanent sutures are placed between the arcus tendineus with underlying obturator membrane laterally and the pubocervical fascia medially. The sutures extend from the back of the pubis distally to the ischial spine proximally. Additional procedures such as anterior colporrhaphy can be done after the sutures are tied. Shull and coworkers (1994) described the use of a fiberoptic light retractor to facilitate the operation and pointed out that patients with a narrow pubic arch are not candidates.

The results can be found in Table 66–12. The rate of recurrence of anterior prolapse was 0% to 26%. In the series from Shull and coworkers (1994), most of the recurrences were mild and the prolapse was less than preoperatively. Benson and coworkers (1996) conducted a randomized trial of the abdominal versus vaginal approach for pelvic support defects and reported a 26% cystocele recurrence. **Complications are of some concern. Mallipedi's group** (Mallipeddi et al, 2001) **reported 1 patient with bilateral ureteric obstruction, 1 patient with retropubic hematoma requiring surgery, 2 patients with vaginal abscesses, and 2 patients requiring**

transfusions in a total of 45 patients. Young and coworkers (2001) reported 21 major complications in 100 patients with a transfusion rate of 16%. Shull and colleagues (1994) also reported intraoperative bleeding in 2 patients. Other complications included transient pyriformis muscle syndrome, femoral nerve paresis, and ureteric obstruction relieved after removal of a culdoplasty suture.

To date there are no long-term results published and there are no randomized trials comparing it to anterior colporrhaphy. Specific expertise is required to carry it out and to avoid complications. It is also not effective alone in the treatment of stress incontinence.

Four- and Six-Corner Suspensions. The four-corner suspension was devised by Raz and coworkers (1989) for patients with stress incontinence, urethral hypermobility, and mild to moderate lateral defect cystocele. It did not include anterior colporrhaphy. It was subsequently modified to a six-corner suspension (Albo et al, 1996). The difference between this and a simple needle suspension is the placement of additional proximal sutures to support the bladder.

Technique, Results, and Complications. Two oblique incisions are made from the midurethra to the proximal vagina (Fig. 66–24). The layer of pubocervical fascia is exposed under the vaginal mucosa. The endopelvic fascia is perforated into the retropubic space, and the pubocervical fascia holding the bladder to the arcus tendineus is separated from the pelvic sidewall anteriorly. The lateral attachments of the bladder base

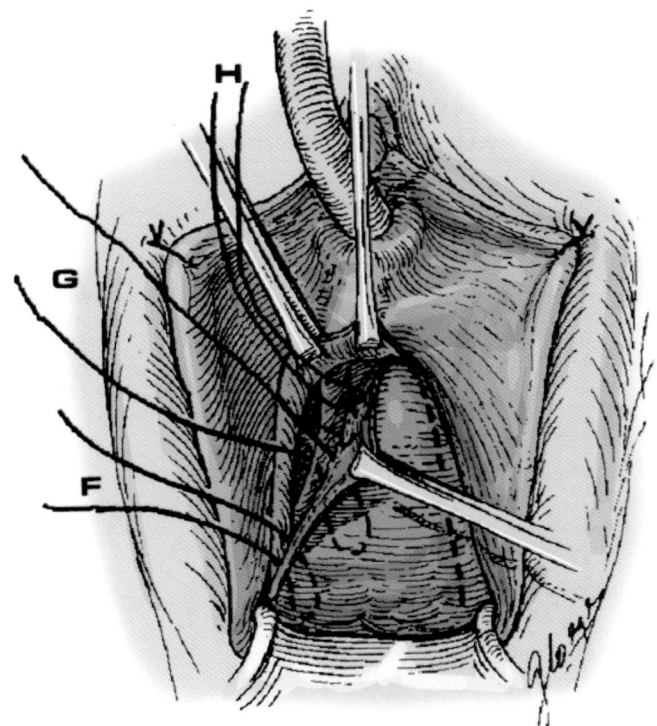

Figure 66–24. Six-corner bladder neck suspension. No. 1 polypropylene sutures are placed at level of vaginal cuff (F), bladder neck (G), and distal urethra (H). (From Albo M, Dupont MC, Raz S: Transvaginal correction of pelvic prolapse. J Endoruol 1996;10:231-239.)

are exposed proximally to the cardinal ligaments. Three sets of 1-0 polypropylene sutures are placed on each side. Each suture incorporates multiple passes through the tissue and is laterally placed to avoid periurethral scarring and outflow obstruction. The proximal suture is placed though the cardinal ligament and vaginal wall to support the bladder base. The middle suture is at the level of the bladder neck, and the distal suture is at the mid urethra. The sutures are passed up individually to a small suprapubic incision with the double-pronged ligature carrier. Indigo carmine is administered intravenously, and cystoscopy confirms ureteral patency and the absence of suture in the bladder or urethra. The sutures are lifted to ensure adequate anatomic reduction of the cystocele. The vaginal incision is closed with 2-0 delayed absorbable material, and then the suspension sutures are tied sequentially to themselves and to the corresponding one from the opposite side. It is important to avoid tension on the polypropylene sutures to prevent postoperative urinary retention.

Published results are in Table 66–13. Although needle suspension of the proximal urethra has frequently been incorporated into prolapse repairs, as discussed in the next paragraph, four- or six-corner suspension without colporrhaphy has not been widely reported. The initial good results from Raz and colleagues (1989) were not reproduced in subsequent reports (Miyazaki and Miyazaki, 1994; Dmochowski et al, 1997). The procedure was also modified. Atahan and associates (1998) coiled the bladder neck sutures and placed them into the pubis, and Migliari and Usai (1999) incorporated a mixed

Table 66–13. Results of Anterior Vaginal Prolapse Repairs with Suspensions

| | Recurrence | | |
Author	Prolapse	Incontinence	Follow-Up (yr)
Four or Six-Corner Suspension			
Raz et al, 1989	2/107 (2%)	5/89 (6%)	0.5-5 (aver. 2)
Miyazaki and Miyazaki, 1994	13/22 (59%)		3.5-4
Dmochowski et al, 1997	19/47 (40%) grade I	14/47 (30%) once per week	1.25-6.75
	8/47 (17%) grade II	8/47 (17%) daily	(aver. 3)
Atahan et al, 1998	0/26 (0%)	2/36 (8%)	2-4 (aver. 2.8)
Migliari and Usai, 1999 (mixed fiber mesh added)	1/15 (7%)	2/15 (13%)	1.5-3.25 (aver. 2)
Anterior Colporrhaphy and Needle Suspension			
Raz et al, 1991 (4-corner)	5/46 (11%)	3/26 (12%)	0.5-5.3 (aver. 2.8)
Gardy et al, 1991	3/29 (10%)	2/29 (7%)	0.75-5 (aver. 2)
Kelly et al, 1991	14/58 (24%)	9/58 (16%)	Average 5
Kohli et al, 1996 (4-corner)	13/40 (33%)	Not stated	0.25-3 (aver. 1.1)
Bump et al, 1996	7/14 (50%)	2/14 (14%)	0.5
Safir et al, 1999 (4-corner)	6/114 (5%) mild	5/49 (10%)	0.5-3.5 (aver. 1.75)
	5/114 (4%) severe		
Anterior Colporrhaphy with Sling Procedures			
Autologous Fascia			
Cross et al, 1997 (autologous fascia)	6/36 (17%) mild	4/36 (11%)	1-3.25 (aver. 1.7)
	3/36 (8%) severe		
TVT			
Gordon et al, 2001	0/30 (0%)	0/30 (0%)	1.2
Lo et al, 2003	2/55 (4%)	5/55 (9%)	1
Huang et al, 2003	4/50 (8%)	7/50 (14%)	1.5
Meschia et al, 2004 AC + TVT	6/25 (24%)	2/25 (4%)	2
AC alone	7/25 (28%)	11/25 (44%)	2
Graft Repairs			
Polypropylene Mesh			
Nicita, 1998	3/44 (7%) mild	0/44	Up to 2yr
Bader et al, 2004	2/40 (5%)		1.4
de Tayrac et al, 2004	6/48 (12.5%) mild, 4 erosions	1/26 (4%) after TVT	1.7
		6/22 (27%) no TVT	
Rodriguez et al, 2005	13/98 (13%) stage 1	3/98 (3%) stress	<5
	3/98 (3%) stage 2		
Cadaveric Fascia			
Groutz et al, 2001	0/21 (0%)	0/21 (0%)	1.7
Frederick and Leach, 2005	39/251 (16%) any	27/251 (10.8%) stress	0.5 to 5
	18/251 (7%) symptomatic	15/251 (6%) urge	
		17/251 (6.8%) mixed	
Porcine Dermis			
Gomelsky et al, 2004	6/70 (8.6%) stage 2	7/65 (9%)	2
	3/70 (4.3%) stage 3		

fiber mesh (60% polyglactin 910 and 40% polyester) into the repair. The durability of the procedure is not known. Complications may include bladder or urethral injury with suture passage, ureteral obstruction, and injury or entrapment of the genitofemoral or ilioinguinal nerve.

Anterior Colporrhaphy with Needle Bladder Neck Suspension. For moderate to large cystoceles, Raz and coworkers (1991) combined anterior colporrhaphy with the previously described four-corner suspension (Raz et al, 1989). They reported cystocele recurrence of 11% (see Table 66–13). The procedure was modified in a number of aspects, and a "goal post" incision was added to include a segment of vaginal wall to function as a sling (Safir et al, 1999) (Fig. 66–25).

Technique, Results, and Complications. The goal post incision is made with the distal limbs at the mid urethra and ending 1 cm proximal to the bladder neck (Safir et al, 1999). The crossbar incision joins the limbs, and the midline incision is carried from the crossbar to the vaginal cuff or the anterior fornix of the cervix. The vaginal mucosa is cleared laterally from the underlying fascial elements as in the six-corner suspension. Care must be taken to identify the posterior junction of the bladder with the cervix or midline peritoneal folds, if after hysterectomy. If there is an enterocele, repair should be done at this point. A 2-0 delayed absorbable figure-of-eight suture is placed into the diastatic cardinal ligaments and not tied. The retropubic space is then entered lateral to the goal post incisions. Two 1-0 polypropylene sutures with helical

bites are placed proximally and distally on both sides, as shown in Figure 66–25. The four sutures are then transferred to above the rectus fascia with the double-pronged suture carrier. The central defect is repaired by colporrhaphy with interrupted 2-0 delayed absorbable suture after an 8 × 4-cm crumpled delayed absorbable mesh is placed underneath the bladder and pushed upward. Indigo carmine is injected, and cystoscopy is performed. The colporrhaphy and cardinal ligament sutures are then tied, the vaginal wall is reapproximated, and the suspension sutures are tied, as in the six-corner suspension.

The published results (see Table 66–13) show a cystocele recurrence of 5% to 50% and incontinence recurrence of 7% to 15%. Kelly and coworkers (1991) reported a high cystocele recurrence in 24% of patients at a mean of 62 months. In a randomized trial of anterior colporrhaphy with or without four-corner needle suspension, Kohli and coworkers (1996) reported a recurrence rate of 33% versus 7% in patients who had not undergone needle suspension. They attributed this to worsening of the paravaginal defect by retropubic dissection. However, in a similar randomized trial of a bladder neck needle suspension, Bump and coworkers (1996a) reported no significant difference in cystocele recurrence. The difficulty in assessing and comparing results may stem from variations in the surgical procedures. As mentioned earlier, the group from the University of California, Los Angeles (Safir et al, 1999), substantially modified their earlier reported procedure (Raz et al, 1991) in the type

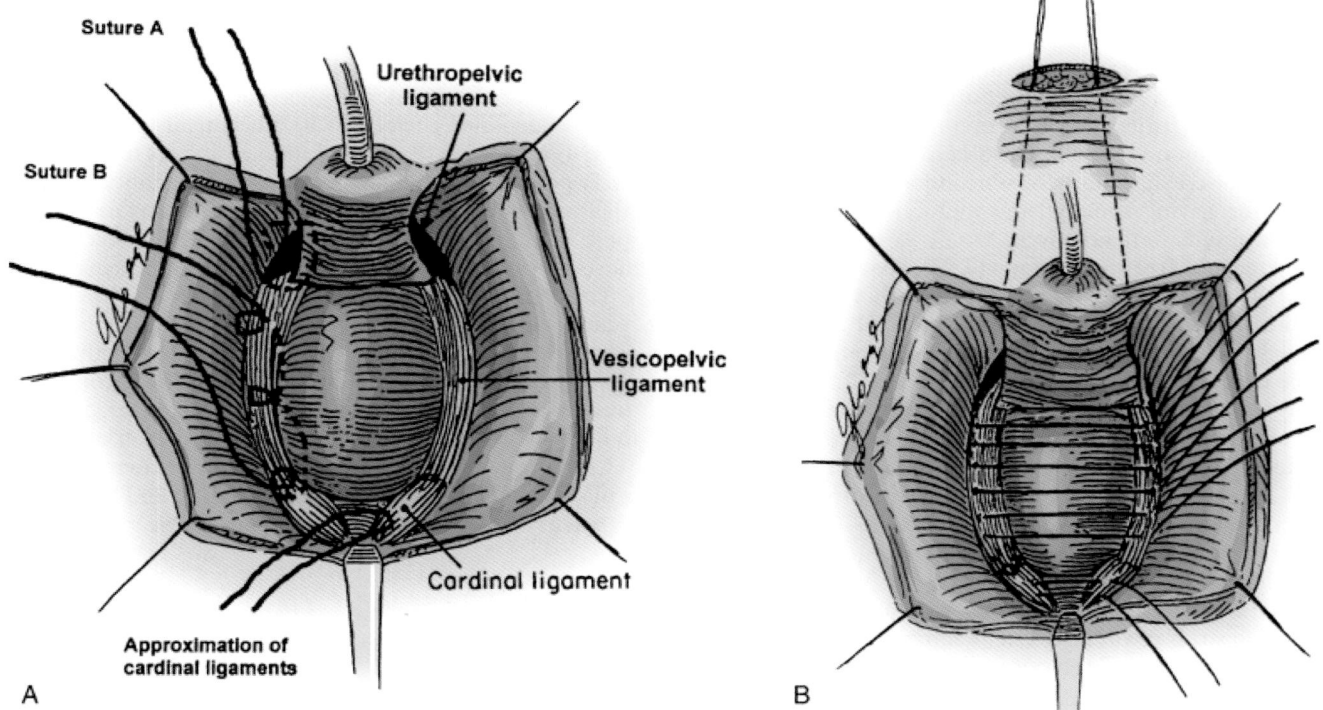

Figure 66–25. **A,** Four-corner suspension through goal-post incision. Suture A incorporates periurethral tissue at mid urethra. Suture B incorporates endopelvic fascia at bladder neck, perivesical fascia (attentuated pubocervical fascia), and ipsilateral cardinal ligament. **B,** Imbricating sutures placed to reduce the cystocele. Suspension sutures have been transferred suprapubically. (From Safir MH. Gousse AE, Rovner ES, et al: 4-Defect repair of grade 4 cystocele. J Urol 1999;161:587-594.)

of incision and by limiting the retropubic dissection to the level of the urethra rather than from the urethra to the ischial spine. They also modified the suspension suture placement and added in a piece of absorbable mesh above the colporrhaphy.

Possible complications are similar to those described for six-corner suspension and anterior colporrhaphy. Inadvertent cystotomy demands a two-layer closure with absorbable suture and may be protected by a suprapubic tube for 7 to 10 days (Kobashi and Leach, 2000). The tube may be removed after a cystogram.

Anterior Colporrhaphy With Sling Procedures. Various sling procedures have been combined with anterior colporrhaphy. The results are shown in Table 66–13.

Technique, Results, and Complications. If autologous fascia is used, it is harvested in the usual fashion. Through a midline vaginal incision extending from the mid urethra proximally to the vaginal cuff or apex, the vaginal mucosa is dissected laterally to expose the fascia overlying the urethra and bladder. The retropubic space is entered at the bladder neck bilaterally. The anterior repair is performed by plicating the fascia extending from the cardinal ligaments to the bladder neck with interrupted 2-0 delayed absorbable sutures. The Peyrera-Raz double-pronged needle is passed from the suprapubic incision out the vaginal incision by finger guidance and then is used to pass the sling sutures back up to the suprapubic incision. The sling sutures are tied without tension on the sling. The sling can also be sutured to the pubocervical fascia with interrupted 2-0 delayed absorbable suture material to prevent rolling or dislodgment. The vaginal mucosa is approximated with 2-0 delayed absorbable sutures.

Cross and coworkers (1997) reported a grade 3 and 4 cystocele recurrence rate of 8% and a grade 1 recurrence rate of 15% in 36 of 42 patients who returned for follow-up. The continence rate was 89%. New-onset urge incontinence was seen in 16%, and 1 patient required urethrolysis at 6 months for retention. Amundsen and coworkers (2000) reported on cadaveric fascia slings for stress incontinence in 104 patients, with some having simultaneous cystocele repairs; however, prolapse results were not given.

The tension-free vaginal tape (TVT) procedure (Ulmsten et al, 1996) **has also been combined with prolapse repair. Studies that have stratified results for TVT with prolapse repair versus TVT alone have found no difference in continence outcome or major complications** (Jeffry et al, 2001; Liapis et al, 2001; Rafii et al, 2004). **However, there is a higher rate of minor bladder perforation and early postoperative voiding dysfunction in combined procedures** (Tamussino et al, 2001). The results of studies that involved TVT with anterior colporrhaphy are listed in Table 66–13. The recurrence rate of anterior prolapse is 0% to 24% and that of stress incontinence is 0% to 14%. The study by Meschia and colleagues (2004) was done in patients with prolapse and occult or masked stress incontinence. The subjects were randomized to have either TVT or anterior wall plication for their occult incontinence. While the prolapse recurrence was similar, significantly more patients in the plication group developed postoperative incontinence. The study by Gordon and coworkers (2001) was also done in 30 women with prolapse and occult incontinence. After 12 to 24 months no patient had

symptomatic stress incontinence. These studies support the use of TVT in patients with prolapse for both overt and occult stress incontinence.

The factors still to be addressed are the sequence of procedures (i.e., TVT before or after anterior colporrhaphy) and whether one or two incisions are used. The author generally performs the tape procedure through a separate incision after the anterior colporrhaphy.

Vaginal Repairs with Graft Materials. To improve the failure rate of cystocele repair, various graft materials have been used not only to buttress the colporrhaphy but also to suspend the anterior wall to various parts of the lateral pelvic sidewall (see Table 66–13). Nicita (1998) first described the addition of polypropylene mesh, which he sutured bilaterally to the ATFP. Subsequent investigators (Bader et al, 2004; de Tayrac et al, 2004) reported on the use of a soft polypropylene mesh (Gynemesh; Ethicon) also fastened laterally to the ATFP. Similarly the ATFP was the lateral attachment of other graft materials, including cadaveric fascia (Groutz et al, 2001) and porcine dermis (Gomelsky et al, 2004). Another site of lateral attachment of the graft is the medial edge of the levators. In 2000, Kobashi and coworkers described using a T-shaped segment of cadaveric fascia. The ends of the T are placed retropubically and fastened to the pubis with vaginally introduced bone anchors. The remainder of the patch is secured up to the medial edges of the levator muscles bilaterally and back to the vaginal cuff or cervix proximally. The final site of lateral attachment, that has been described, is the obturator internus fascia below the levators (Rodriguez et al, 2005), with soft polypropylene mesh as the graft material. In most of these series stress incontinence, both symptomatic and occult, was treated with a sling simultaneously.

The surgical approach involves a similar dissection to the vaginal paravaginal procedure with perforation through the endopelvic fascia anteriorly if a sling is to be performed. The ATFP is identified laterally by its attachment to the obturator fascia (Fig. 66–26). Extending the incision in the endopelvic fascia posterolaterally may permit easier identification of the ATFP, especially if the dissection is to be carried to the ischial spine. The side wall for lateral attachment of the graft, either the levator muscle or obturator fascia, is readily palpable.

The results of graft repairs are in Table 66–13. Whereas recurrence of anterior prolapse may appear to be lower than other nongraft techniques, the series are not strictly comparable owing to different follow-up times and outcome measures. Furthermore, the question of optimal technique is still to be answered with a prospective randomized trial.

Complications apart from failure or recurrence of the prolapse or incontinence include bleeding and hematomas, transient ureteric obstruction, and synthetic graft erosion.

Apical Vaginal Wall (Middle Compartment)

Apical support defects may occur because of compromise of the cardinal uterosacral ligament complex or failure to reapproximate the superior aspects of the pubocervical and rectovaginal fascia at the time of hysterectomy (Richardson, 1995). **Ventral fixation of the vagina, such as a Burch proce-**

Enterocele Repairs

Vaginal Approach. An enterocele is a peritoneum-lined sac herniating through the pelvic floor, most commonly between the rectum and vagina. The vaginal epithelium overlying the sac may be thin or may have normal thickness with intact muscularis (Tulikangas et al, 2001). A vault enterocele has a hernial sac forming behind the vaginal wall that lacks underlying musculofascial support. **The goals of surgical repair of enterocele are (1) to recognize the entity and its probable cause; (2) to expose, dissect, mobilize, and then excise or obliterate the entire sac; (3) to occlude the orifice of the sac by ligation as high as possible; and (4) to perform all indicated repairs to provide adequate support from below for the occluded sac by reestablishing continuity of the anterior and posterior vaginal fascia at the vaginal apex and a normal upper vaginal axis** (Nichols, 1993c; Cundiff and Addison, 1998).

Technique, Results, and Complications. Transvaginal enterocele repair is done after vaginal hysterectomy or at the time of repair of other pelvic floor defects and before the other parts of the procedure (Nichols, 1997).

The patient is placed in the lithotomy position, and the table is placed in Trendelenburg position. A povidone-iodine–soaked rectal packing is used to aid in identifying the rectum. The vaginal apex is grasped with Allis forceps bilaterally (Fig. 66–27), and a vertical incision is made in the vaginal wall after infiltration of the mucosa with saline solution. The peritoneal sac is dissected free from the vaginal wall laterally, the bladder anteriorly, and the rectum posteriorly. Filling the bladder with a cystoscope in place and seeing the transmitted light may be helpful to distinguish the bladder from the enterocele (Vasavada et al, 1999). However, the enterocele sac can be distinguished from the bladder by palpating the Foley balloon or a metal sound within the collapsed bladder, by the presence of preperitoneal fat, and by the appearance of peritoneal contents within the sac. The sac is opened in the midline, and the contents are packed into the peritoneal cavity. A small moist laparotomy sponge is inserted to protect the bowel. A Deaver retractor is used to expose the areas in which to put the culdoplasty stitches. Two 0 delayed absorbable purse-string sutures (proximal and distal) are placed that incorporate the anterior prerectal fascia posteriorly, the cardinal and uterosacral ligaments laterally, and the peritoneum overlying the bladder anteriorly. Two modified McCall sutures (McCall, 1957) of No. 1 delayed absorbable material are then placed from outside the proximal vaginal wall into both cardinal and uterosacral ligaments through the peritoneal sac and back out the vaginal wall (Fig. 66–28).

The proximal and distal purse-string sutures are then tied to obliterate the cul-de-sac and elevate the peritoneum. The peritoneal sac is ligated at the base and may be excised. The patient is given indigo carmine intravenously, and cystoscopy is done to confirm ureteral and bladder integrity.

To facilitate repair of other defects, the McCall sutures are tied after the anterior wall and upper posterior wall are repaired. It is also recommended to approximate the anterior and posterior fibromuscular connective tissue (Weber and Richter, 2005). Excess vaginal wall is excised, and the incision is closed with continuous 2-0 delayed absorbable sutures.

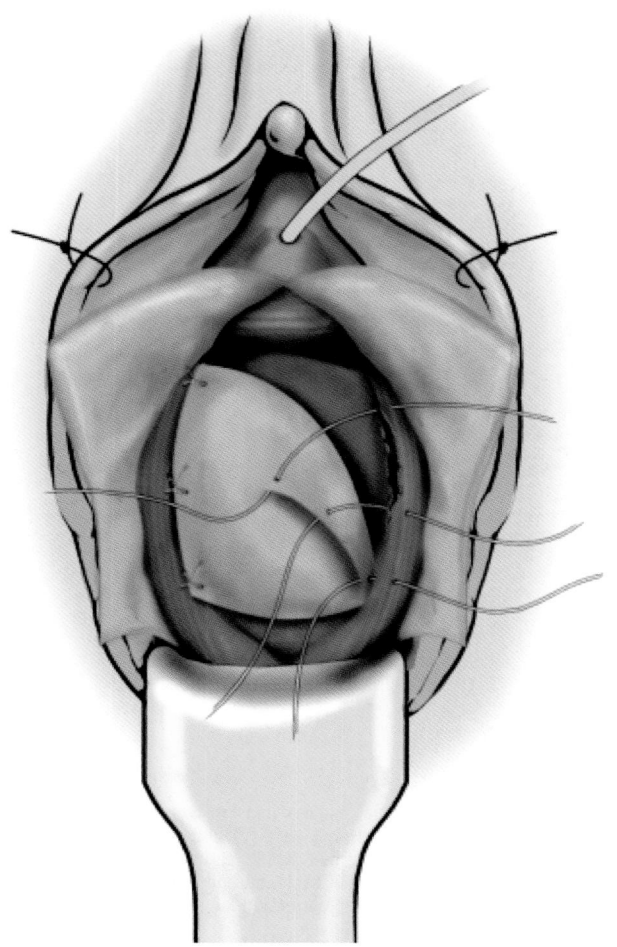

Figure 66–26. Surgical procedure showing a tailored patch of porcine dermis graft. Three pairs of sutures are inserted into the arcus tendineus fasciae pelvis (ATFP) under direct vision. (From Gomelsky A, Rudy DC, Dmochowski RR: Porcine dermis interposition graft for repair of high grade anterior compartment defects with or without concomitant pelvic organ prolapse procedures. J Urol 2004;171:1581-4.)

dure, may also cause widening of the cul-de-sac with resultant enterocele formation (Kjolhede et al, 1996; Wiskind et al, 1992).

Apical prolapse may include the uterus with or without enterocele and vaginal vault prolapse usually with enterocele. The standard treatment for symptomatic uterine prolapse is hysterectomy with procedure(s) to support the vaginal apex, address enterocele when indicated, repair coexisting anterior and posterior prolapse, and perform anti-incontinence procedures as needed. However, there is a lack of evidence suggesting that hysterectomy improves the outcome of prolapse surgery. Descent of the uterus is thought to be a result, not a cause of prolapse (Brubaker et al, 2005). When hysterectomy is performed for prolapse, hysterectomy alone, or with colporrhaphy, is insufficient; a specific vault suspension procedure must be performed in addition to the hysterectomy (Weber and Richter, 2005).

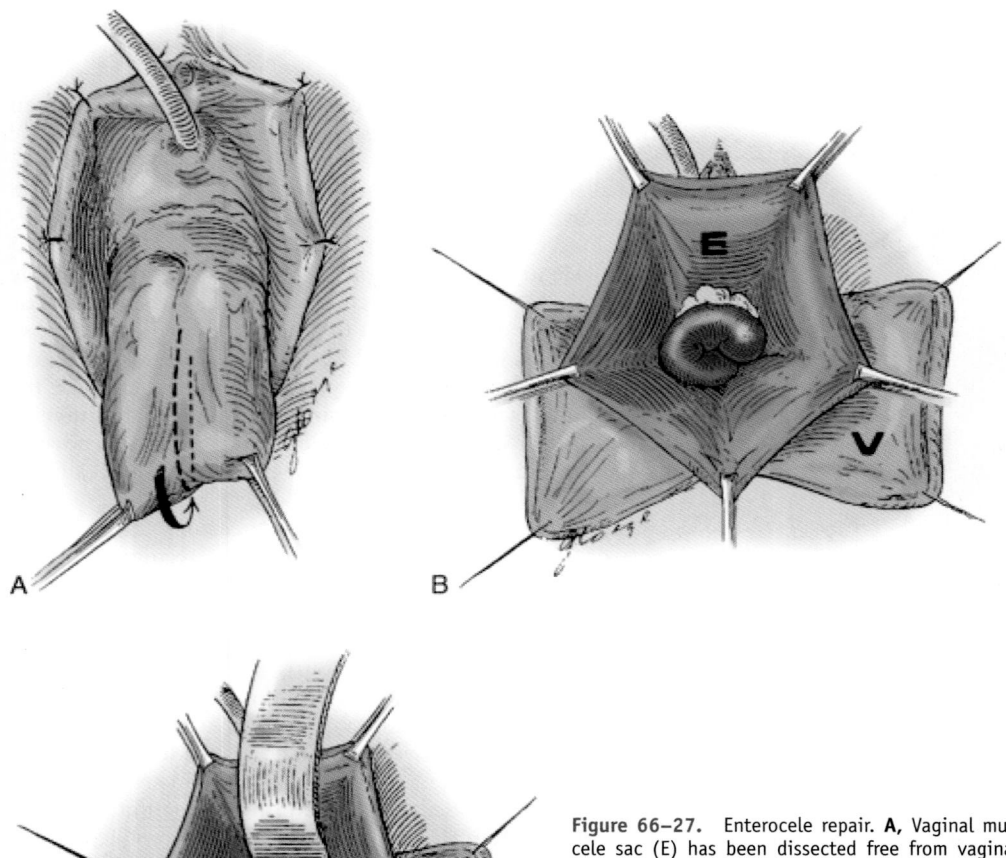

Figure 66–27. Enterocele repair. **A,** Vaginal mucosa incision over enterocele. **B,** Enterocele sac (E) has been dissected free from vaginal wall (V) and opened. **C,** Placement of purse-string suture, which will close sac. Modified McCall suture will be placed to bring together cardinal/uterosacral ligaments, prerectal fascia, and peritoneum at base of bladder. (From Albo M, Dupont MC, Raz S: Transvaginal correction of pelvic prolapse. J Endoruol 1996;10:231-239.)

Most reports of enterocele repair include repairs of other defects apart from the report of Raz and coworkers (1993). With this technique, 40 of 49 (82%) patients had a successful result after a mean follow-up of 15 months (range: 3 to 70 months). Complications such as rectal or small bowel injury may be avoided by careful insertion of the purse-string sutures, identification of the yellow prerectal fat, and avoidance of pressure with retraction. **Vaginal evisceration is a rare but life-threatening surgical emergency that can arise after vaginal or abdominal hysterectomy, enterocele repair, dilatation and curettage, brachytherapy, vault suspension, or colpocleisis** (Virtanen et al, 1996; Ginsberg et al, 1998; Verity and Bombieri, 2005). The evisceration repair operation can be done vaginally, abdominally, laparoscopically, or combined. Obliterating the cul-de-sac and firmly closing the vaginal vault can theoretically prevent it. Because the ureters traverse close to the uterosacrals,

precautionary measures with indigo carmine and cystoscopy to verify patency are important.

Abdominal Approach. Transabdominal repair of an enterocele is done only at the time of another abdominal procedure. The procedure includes approximation of the uterosacral ligaments, if the uterus has been removed, and obliteration of the cul-de-sac with circumferential sutures of the Moschowitz type (Moschowitz, 1912) or sagittal antero-posterior sutures of the Halban type (Halban, 1932). The circumferential stitches are started at the bottom of the cul-de-sac, and two to three are placed. They are prone to causing ureteral obstruction due to the ureter's course in close proximity to the uterosacrals. Neither type of stitch effectively anchors a poorly supported or unsupported vaginal vault. This requires separate colpopexy or a vaginal approach.

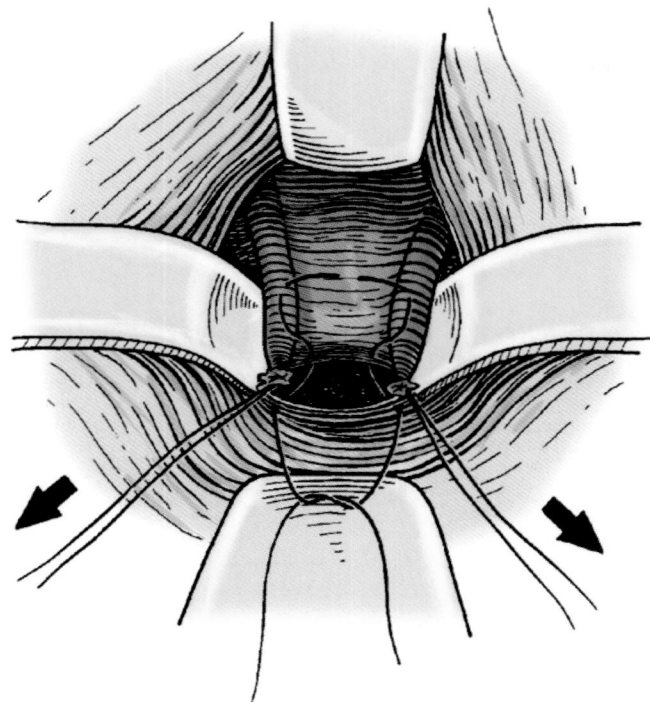

Figure 66–28. Modified McCall stitch. (From Nichols DH: Enterocele. In Nichols DH [ed]: Gynecologic and Obstetric Surgery. St. Louis, CV Mosby, 1993, pp 420-430.)

Apical Vaginal Prolapse Repairs

More than 40 different techniques have been described to treat vaginal vault prolapse (Sze and Karram, 1997). The vaginal reconstructive approach was first described in 1892 by Zweifel in Germany when he connected the vaginal vault to the sacro-tuberous ligament. Now there are a number of currently accepted techniques. **There have been a number of randomized trials comparing different procedures but controversy exists over the choice of vaginal procedure as well as the relative merits of vaginal versus abdominal suspension procedures.**

Sacrospinous Ligament Fixation. The sacrospinous ligament extends from the ischial spine to the lateral margins of the sacrum and coccyx (see Fig. 66–2). Its anterior surface is muscular and constitutes the coccygeus muscle; the ligament is regarded as the degenerate part of the muscle. The greater and lesser sciatic foramina are above and below the ligament. Many important structures are in close proximity and must be avoided during the procedure. The hypogastric vessels lie superior and medial. The sciatic nerve and inferior gluteal artery exit the pelvis through the lower part of the greater sciatic foramen (Soames, 1995). The pudendal vessels and nerve and the nerve to the obturator internus travel around the ischial spine and reenter the pelvis through the lesser sciatic foramen, below the pelvic diaphragm.

The procedure was first reported by Sederl in 1958 and became popular with subsequent reports (Randall and Nichols, 1971; Richter and Albrich, 1981; Nichols, 1982). The primary indication was to correct total procidentia or post-

hysterectomy vaginal vault prolapse with an associated weak or atrophied cardinal-uterosacral ligament complex (Sze and Karram, 1997). The indications have been expanded to include post-hysterectomy enterocele (Morley and DeLancey, 1988), and there is controversy about whether it should be used as a prophylactic measure after vaginal hysterectomy (Cruikshank and Cox, 1990; Colombo and Milani, 1998). It can be performed unilaterally or bilaterally, but most authors believe that unilaterally may be sufficient (Beer and Kuhn, 2005).

Technique, Results, and Complications. The position and preparation of the patient are identical to those for the enterocele procedure. **A surgical head lamp is highly recommended for this procedure.** A longitudinal incision is made in the vaginal mucosa over the enterocele sac and extending to the posterior wall. The vaginal wall is dissected away from the enterocele sac, as described earlier. The sac is opened; and after determining that there are no surgically useful cardinal-uterosacral supports, the surgeon mobilizes and closes the sac with high purse-string sutures and may excise the excess (Nichols, 1993c). It is also acceptable to expose the ligament and place the suspension sutures before opening and ligating the enterocele, because the manipulations around the ligament can tear out the enterocele stitches (Chapin, 1997).

The surgeon then palpates the ischial spine, with the index finger in the rectovaginal space, and traces the ligament that runs posteriorly to the hollow of the sacrum. (It is easier for a right-handed surgeon to use the right sacrospinous ligament.) The ligament must be exposed through a window in the soft tissue to allow suture placement. The rectal pillar, or lateral connective tissue between the rectum and the vagina, is penetrated either bluntly or with Mayo scissors to enter the pararectal space. The sacrospinous ligament/coccygeus muscle is palpated, and the window into the pararectal space is gently enlarged. Spreading the index and middle finger in the window can expose the pelvic diaphragm (iliococcygeus and pubococcygeus muscles), ischial spine, and coccygeus muscle. Because the ligament is covered by the coccygeus muscle it is not visible.

Flat long-blade retractors, such as the recommended Navratil-Breisky retractors, are placed to retract the peritoneum and bladder upward and the rectum medially, and a shorter retractor may compress the distal portion of the pelvic diaphragm laterally. **The sutures are placed 1.5 to 3 cm medial to the ischial spine, to avoid injury to the pudendal nerves and vessels, and through the substance of the ligament.** The ligament can be grasped with a long Allis or Babcock clamp, and/or the sutures can be placed directly with a long needle driver or Deschamps ligature carrier and retrieved with a nerve hook (Fig. 66–29). Two No. 1 or 2 delayed absorbable sutures are placed. A gentle tug on the ligature carrier or on the suture should move the patient a small amount and confirms proper placement in the ligament.

The sutures are then put aside on a clamp and held until completion of the enterocele. One end of each suture is then attached to the undersurface of the posterior vaginal wall at the apical area. If a posterior colporrhaphy is to be done, the suspension sutures are tied when the colporrhaphy closure reaches the midpoint of the vagina. The vaginal apex is then

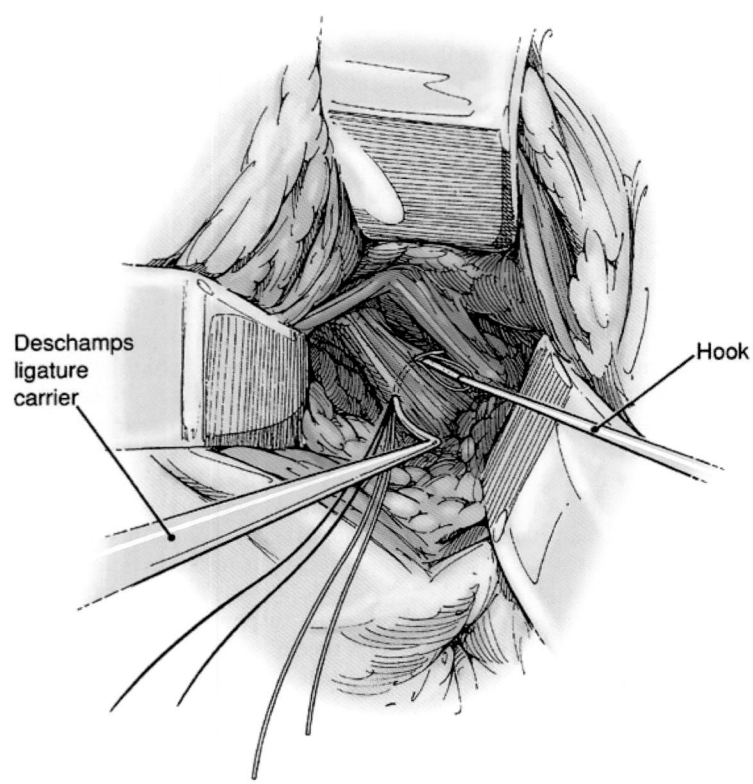

Deschamps
ligature
carrier

Hook

Figure 66-29. Sacrospinous ligament fixation. The right sacro-spinous ligament and coccygeus muscle have been penetrated by the blunt end of the Deschamps ligature carrier 2 to 3 cm medial to the ischial spine. The nerve hook is used to grasp the previously threaded sutures. (From Nichols DH: Enterocele. In Nichols DH [ed]: Gyneco-logic and Obstetric Surgery. St. Louis, CV Mosby, 1993, pp 420-430.)

tied firmly to the ligament with no intervening bridge of suture material.

Modifications to facilitate needle passage include the Miya hook (Miyazaki, 1987), the Shutt punch automatic suture retrieval system (Sharp, 1993), and the use of a laparoscopic suturing device (Schlesinger, 1997).

The results and complications from 22 reports involving a total of 1229 sacrospinous ligament fixations were summa-rized in a review by Sze and Karram (1997). Of the 1062 patients available for follow-up, the objective cure rate, defined as a complete restoration of normal pelvic anatomy at follow-up examination, ranged from 8% to 94%. Most of the studies involved patients who had multiple defects repaired simultaneously. Recurrent pelvic relaxation developed in 109 (18%) patients, including 81 anterior vaginal wall defects, 32 vaginal vault eversions, 24 posterior vaginal wall prolapses, and 56 defects at unspecified or multiples sites. Reoperations were performed in 7 of 81 patients with anterior defects, 20 of 32 with vault eversion, and 4 of 24 with posterior wall pro-lapse. The relatively high recurrence or new onset of anterior vaginal prolapse has been mentioned earlier and ranges from 22% to 92% (Morley and DeLancey, 1988; Shull et al, 1992; Holley et al, 1995; Maher et al, 2001). It may be caused by exaggerated retroversion of the vagina with exposure of the anterior wall to greater abdominal pressure or possibly a neu-ropathy caused by the vaginal dissection (Benson et al, 1996). However, the overall results appeared better in a recent review of 2390 patients from Beer and Kuhn (2005). They reported a subjective cure rate of 70% to 98% and an objective cure rate based on physical examination of 67% to 96.8%. Recurrent prolapse in 2256 patients was reported at the vault in 3.6%,

enterocele in 0.7%, cystocele in only 4.6%, and rectocele in 1.5% of patients.

Other complications in 1922 patients included hemorrhage with a transfusion rate of 2%. Perforation of the bladder, rectum, and small bowel occurred in 0.8%, ureteral kinking and micturition problems in 2.9%, vaginal adhesions and rec-tovaginal fistulas in 0.5%, and nerve damage to the femoral, peroneal, or sciatic nerves in 1.8% of patients (Beer and Kuhn, 2005). Gluteal pain may resolve within 6 weeks, but patients have required reoperation with removal and repositioning of the sutures for severe gluteal pain and pudendal, sciatic, or lumbar plexus neuropathy (Sze and Karram, 1997). Vaginal narrowing and shortening may occur after the operation. Sexual dysfunction has also been reported in up to 13% of the patients who are questioned (Holley et al, 1996; Beer and Kuhn, 2005), but its relationship to the change in vaginal anatomy has not been clearly established (Weber et al, 2000).

Uterosacral Ligament Suspension. Suspension of the vaginal vault to the uterosacral ligaments is another approach and is based on McCall's original description (McCall, 1957) that uses the uterosacrals as a support for the vaginal vault. It can be used prophylactically at hysterectomy or for treatment of vault prolapse (Shull et al, 2000). Its main advantages are a normal resultant vaginal axis and avoidance of suturing near neural or vascular structures. Some authors also describe using the fascial tissue lateral and posterior to the upper vagina and rectum.

Technique, Results, and Complications. Through a midline vaginal incision (Barber et al, 2000b; Shull et al, 2000), after reflection of the vaginal epithelium from the pubocervical fascia anteriorly, enterocele at the vault, and rectovaginal fascia posteriorly, the enterocele sac is entered and the bowel is packed away. The remnants of uterosacral ligaments are identified posterior and medial to the ischial spines at the 4- and 8-o'clock positions within the peritoneal cavity. An Allis clamp is used to apply traction to the tissue, and the contralateral index finger is used to trace the strong suspensory tissue of the uterosacral ligament toward the sacrum. A bayonet retractor is used to retract the rectum medially, and a Deaver retractor is used to hold the bowel and surgical pack cephalad.

With a long straight needle driver, a double-armed nonabsorbable suture is placed through the ligament on the sacral side of the ischial spine. One or two additional sutures are placed distal (on the sacral side) to the initial suture. The most distal suture that will exit the vaginal epithelium can be a delayed nonabsorbable one. Two or three similar sutures are placed on the opposite side. Once all the suspensory sutures are placed, any midline (central) defects in the pubocervical and rectovaginal fascia are repaired by side-to-side plication.

Cystoscopy is performed after intravenous administration of indigo carmine to ensure ureteral patency. The double-armed sutures are then used to secure the superior aspect of the transverse portion of pubocervical and rectovaginal fascia. When the sutures are tied, the anterior and posterior vaginal fasciae are approximated and the vault is suspended (Fig. 66–30). The ligaments can be approximated in the midline, as described by McCall, to close the cul-de-sac. Or the right and left vaginal apex can be suspended individually to the ipsilat-

eral uterosacral to leave the cul-de-sac open and avoid impinging on the rectum (Weber and Richter, 2005). A modification involves placing sutures into the levator muscle lateral to the rectum, plicating the muscle anterior to the rectum, and suspending the vault to this tissue (Lemack and Zimmern, 2000).

Sze and Karram (1997) reviewed the results of 322 reported patients followed for 1 to 12 years. The cure rate was 88% to 93%. Thirty-four patients (11%) developed recurrent prolapse, including 2 anterior, 9 apical, 11 posterior, and 12 multiple defects. Subsequent reports of a total of 881 patients (Webb et al, 1998; Lemack et al, 2001; Barber et al, 2000b; Shull et al, 2000) showed a similar success rate. Recurrent anterior prolapse was noted in 13% (Shull et al, 2000) and 15% (Lemack et al, 2001) of patients. Although the rate is less than that reported with sacrospinous ligament fixation, it is still noteworthy.

Complications may include hemorrhage, vault hematoma, bladder and rectal lacerations, and vaginal narrowing and shortening. Intraoperative ureteral injury has been reported as high as 11% (Barber et al, 2000b), underscoring the importance of performing intraoperative cystoscopy. If ureteral obstruction is suspected, the ipsilateral uterosacral stitch(es) should be replaced or additional maneuvers, such as retrograde and stent, may be required.

Iliococcygeus Suspension. Bilateral fixation of the vaginal apex to the iliococcygeus fascia was first described in 1963 by Inmon. The procedure involves an extraperitoneal exposure through a midline posterior incision. One or two suspension sutures are placed bilaterally into the fascia of the iliococ-

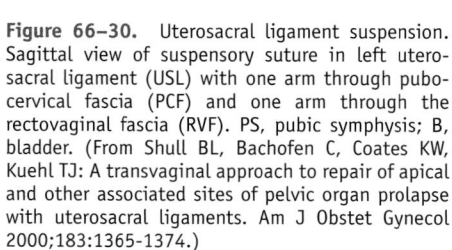

Figure 66–30. Uterosacral ligament suspension. Sagittal view of suspensory suture in left uterosacral ligament (USL) with one arm through pubocervical fascia (PCF) and one arm through the rectovaginal fascia (RVF). PS, pubic symphysis; B, bladder. (From Shull BL, Bachofen C, Coates KW, Kuehl TJ: A transvaginal approach to repair of apical and other associated sites of pelvic organ prolapse with uterosacral ligaments. Am J Obstet Gynecol 2000;183:1365-1374.)

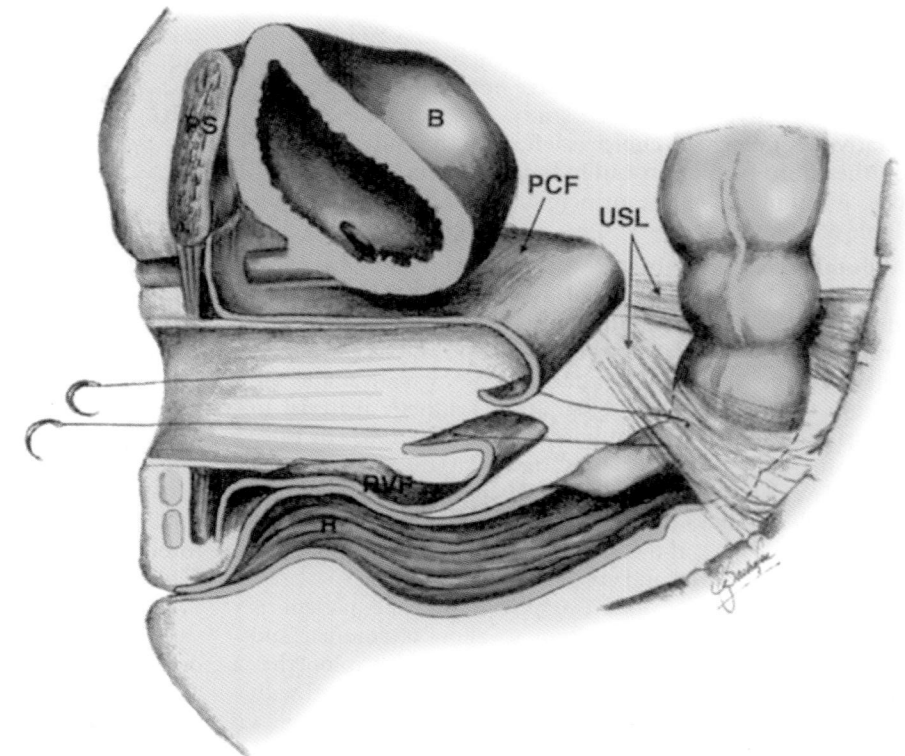

Table 66–14. Summary of Principal Risks and Benefits of Vaginal Apical Repairs

Procedure	Major Risks	Major Benefits
Sacrospinous ligament fixation	Postoperative anterior prolapse; injury to pudendal and inferior gluteal arteries and pudendal and sciatic nerves; ligament may be atrophied in elderly; more difficult to teach and learn	No ureteral injury; rectal injury rare
Uterosacral ligament suspension	Entry into peritoneum; may be adhesions; possible bowel and ureteral injuries; ligaments may not be apparent or usable	Normal vaginal supports; resultant vaginal axis may be most physiologic
Iliococcygeus suspension	Possible shortened vagina; fewest reported cases	No vital structures nearby

Adapted from Weber AM, Richter HE: Pelvic organ prolapse. Obstet Gynecol 2005;106:615-634.

cygeus muscle just anterior to the ischial spines and then attached to the vault. In reports with a total of 257 patients, the success rate ranges from 81% (Shull et al, 1993) to more than 90% (Meeks et al, 1994; Peters and Christenson, 1995; Koyama et al, 2005). Similar to the previously described suspensions, there was a slightly higher recurrence of anterior wall prolapse compared with other defects. A potential benefit is the absence of critical structures in the area. Although the suspension sutures maintain normal vaginal alignment, vaginal shortening may occur because the apex will lie anterior to the ischial spine (Cundiff and Addison, 1998).

The various vaginal repairs have not yet been compared in a prospective randomized study. The outcomes appear relatively similar. The choice is left up to the clinician based on the clinical situation and individual training and expertise. A summary of the principal risks and benefits is in Table 66–14.

Abdominal Sacral Colpopexy. The abdominal approach is indicated after failed vaginal repair, when concomitant abdominal surgery is required, or when the surgeon is unfamiliar with the vaginal approach (Kobashi and Leach, 2000). The procedure that involves attaching the vaginal vault to the sacrum using autologous, allograft, or synthetic material to bridge the gap was first proposed by Lane in 1962. In early series, the suspension mesh was attached to the sacrum at the S3-S4 level (Birnbaum, 1973), but significant hemorrhage prompted a change to the upper sacrum and promontory (Sutton et al, 1981), at the S1-S2 level, where blood vessels are more easily visualized and avoided.

Technique, Results, and Complications. The patient is placed in low lithotomy position to allow abdominal and vaginal access. If necessary, anterior and posterior colporrhaphy may be done first vaginally. The bladder is drained with a Foley catheter. The peritoneal cavity is entered through a midline or Pfannenstiel incision, laparotomy is performed, an abdominal ring retractor is inserted, and the bowels are packed out of the field after mobilization out of the pelvis. A suitable length of 3-cm-wide graft or mesh material is fashioned in a Y shape to extend from the anterior and posterior vaginal walls to the sacral promontory. Inserting an instrument into the vagina, such as a ring forceps or end-to-end anastomosis sizer, may identify the vaginal apex. The bladder and rectum may be dissected away to expose at least a 3 × 4-cm area of vaginal wall. With the instrument held in the vagina, four 1-0 monofilament almost full-thickness sutures, without mucosa, are placed in the anterior vaginal wall to the apex from one lateral fornix to the other (Fig. 66–31). The sutures are placed through the mesh and tied, and a second row of sutures is placed through the mesh into the posterior wall. The cul-de-sac may then be closed, especially if it is deep, with a Halban or Moschowitz technique that can be modified as a hemi-Moschowitz on each side of the sigmoid to avoid constriction (Hendee, 1997). The peritoneum over the sacral promontory is opened with care to expose the presacral fascia and avoid bleeding from presacral vessels. The mesh is cut to length and fastened to the promontory with either interrupted 1-0 monofilament or a laparoscopic (Autosuture Protac) device that inserts multiple coils. The sacral peritoneum and as much pelvic peritoneum as possible are closed over the mesh. When sacral colpopexy is planned for a concomitant high rectocele, the graft can be extended down the posterior vagina to address it (Cundiff et al, 1997).

In an extensive review of published articles from January 1966 to January 2004, Nygaard and colleagues (2004a) analyzed results from over 2000 patients. With a follow-up duration of 6 months to 3 years, the success rate, when defined as a lack of apical prolapse postoperatively, ranged from 78% to 100% and when defined as no postoperative prolapse, from 58% to 100%. The median reported reoperation rate for recurrent prolapse was 4.4% (range: 0% to 18.2%) and for stress incontinence was 4.9% (range: 1.2% to 30.9%). The overall rate of mesh erosion was 3.4% (70 of 2178). Some reports found mesh erosions when concomitant total hysterectomy was done; others did not. Concomitant culdoplasty was not found to decrease the risk of failure. Most authors recommended burying the graft under the peritoneum to decrease the risk of bowel obstruction. The median reported rate of small bowel obstruction requiring surgery was 1.1% (range: 0.6% to 0.8%). Few studies rigorously assessed pelvic symptoms, bowel function, or sexual function. In a similar review of apical prolapse procedures published between 1972 and 2002, Beer and Kuhn (2005) summarized results of 2008 patients who had undergone sacral colpopexy with mesh. The site of recurrent prolapse was the vault in 1.9%, enterocele in 1.2%, cystocele in 2.3%, and rectocele in 4.1% of patients. Significant complications reported in 1571 patients included hemorrhage and hematomas in 3%, damage to pelvic organs (bladder, rectum, intestine) in 1.6%, and secondary laparotomy for bowel problems, incisional hernia, vesicovaginal fistula, or other complication in 2.9%.

Although mesh erosion can frequently be managed by vaginal excision of all or part of the mesh, laparotomy or laparoscopy is occasionally required for removal (Begley et al, 2005). Some concern has also be raised about the durability of allograft fascia (FitzGerald et al, 2004; Culligan et al, 2005).

KEY POINTS: VAGINAL SURGERY FOR PROLAPSE

- The primary goal of prolapse surgery is to effect change in anatomic structures that provides patients with relief of symptoms.

- Nonsurgical treatment of prolapse involves measures to improve risk factors, vaginal estrogen if appropriate, pelvic muscle exercises, and pessaries.

- Surgical procedures for anterior wall prolapse should be applied to improve both the central and lateral defects, as required. Failure to improve the urethral support defect may unmask stress incontinence, and fixing only the urethral hypermobility and leaving a cystocele may create or worsen outflow obstruction.

- Anterior colporrhaphy results have been improved, in the short term, by the addition of a delayed absorbable graft.

- Transvaginal vault suspension may result in an increased risk of anterior support defect, so a preexisting defect should be addressed.

- A systematic review has shown that abdominal sacral colpopexy results in a lower prolapse recurrence rate than transvaginal sacrospinous fixation, but the benefits must be balanced against a longer operating time, recovery time, and increased cost.

- Although posterior colporrhaphy is effective for posterior prolapse, it has been associated with dyspareunia. The patient with asymptomatic mild to moderate rectocele may be better served by delaying surgery until specific symptoms need to be addressed.

SUGGESTED READINGS

Brubaker L, Bump R, Fynes MM, et al: Surgery for pelvic organ prolapse. In Abrams P, Cardozo L, Khoury S, Wein A (eds): Incontinence: 3rd International Consultation. Plymouth, UK, Health Publications, 2005, pp 1371-1401.

Bump RC, Mattiasson A, Bo K, et al: The standardization of terminology of female pelvic organ prolapse and pelvic floor dysfunction. Am J Obstet Gynecol 1996b;175:10-17.

DeLancey JO: Anatomic aspects of vaginal eversion after hysterectomy. Am J Obstet Gynecol 1992;166:1717-1724; discussion 1724-1728.

DeLancey JO: Structural anatomy of the posterior pelvic compartment as it relates to rectocele. Am J Obstet Gynecol 1999;180:815-823.

Delancey JO: Fascial and muscular abnormalities in women with urethral hypermobility and anterior vaginal wall prolapse. Am J Obstet Gynecol 2002;187:93-98.

Donovan J, Bosch R, Gotoh M, et al: Symptom and quality of life assessment. In Abrams P, Cardozo L, Khoury S, and Wein A (eds): Incontinence: 3rd International Consultation. Plymouth, UK, Health Publications, 2005, pp 519-584.

Glazener CM, Cooper K: Bladder neck needle suspension for urinary incontinence in women. Cochrane Database Syst Rev 2004;(2):CD003636.

Hendrix SL, Clark A, Nygaard I, et al: Pelvic organ prolapse in the Women's Health Initiative: Gravity and gravidity. Am J Obstet Gynecol 2002; 186:1160-1166.

Hunskaar S, Burgio KL, Clark A, et al: Epidemiology of urinary (UI) and faecal (FI) incontinence and pelvic organ prolapse. In Abrams P, Cardozo L, Khoury S, Wein A (eds): Incontinence: 3rd International Consultation. Plymouth, UK, Health Publications, 2005, pp 255-312.

Maher C, Baessler K, Glazener CM, et al: Surgical management of pelvic organ prolapse in women. Cochrane Database Syst Rev 2004a;(4):CD004014.

Nichols DH: Central compartment defects. In Rock JA, Thompson JD (eds): Te Linde's Operative Gynecology. Philadelphia, Lippincott-Raven, 1997, pp 1006-1030.

Raz S: Atlas of Transvaginal Surgery. Philadelphia, WB Saunders, 1992.

Romanzi LJ: Management of the urethral outlet in patients with severe prolapse. Curr Opin Urol 2002;12:339-344.

Weber AM, Richter HE: Pelvic organ prolapse. Obstet Gynecol 2005;106:615-634.

67 Pubovaginal Sling

SEUNG-JUNE OH, MD • JOHN T. STOFFEL, MD •
EDWARD J. MCGUIRE, MD

KEY POINTS: INDICATIONS FOR FASCIAL SLINGS

- Autologous pubovaginal sling is probably the best option for treating loss of proximal urethral closure function due to decentralizing neuropathic conditions or acquired causes, including tissue loss after urethral diverticulectomy, erosion of an artificial sphincter or a synthetic material sling, pelvic trauma with fracture, urethral erosion related to chronic catheterization, and urethral fistula.

- Autologous pubovaginal sling is an effective option for managing weakness of proximal urethral closure caused by genuine stress urinary incontinence or incontinence after prior failed anti-incontinence surgery.

BRIEF HISTORICAL NOTE

Autologous material used to suspend the urethra as a sling is a relatively old technique. German surgeons at the turn of the last century were using slings fashioned from muscle and fascia (Goebel, 1910). Price (1933) probably described the first rectus fascia sling; Millen (1947), a urologist, used slings for recurrent stress incontinence. In the United States, Ridley (1966) described a large series of patients with stress incontinence treated with a variation of the Goebel sling.

SPECIFIC INDICATIONS FOR FASCIAL SLINGS

Autologous pubovaginal sling is indicated for the treatment of loss of proximal urethral closure function and in the management of weakness of proximal urethral closure.

Loss of Proximal Urethral Closure

Urethral Failure and Nonfunction

Partial or total urethral sphincteric failure can be congenital or acquired. Stress incontinence associated with these conditions is severe and often complicated by abnormal bladder function and other conditions, for example, spinal cord injury or disease, pelvic radiation therapy, and multiple prior oper-

ations on the bladder or urethra. Autologous fascia provides a strong nonreactive material for urethral closure that can be used in surgical reconstruction of a nonfunctional urethra, even a urethra that will be subjected to lifelong intermittent catheterization. The conditions illustrated here require a degree of compression of the urethra for continence function to be regained (Chancellor et al, 1994; Ghoniem, 1994).

Neuropathic Conditions

Prototypical neuropathic urethral dysfunction occurs in patients with myelodysplasia. The bladder is decentralized and the proximal urethra nonfunctional. Upright cystography demonstrates an open bladder outlet from the bladder neck to the distal sphincter mechanism (Fig. 67–1). Stress testing during videourodynamics confirms low-pressure leakage driven by abdominal pressure. Identical loss of proximal urethral closing function is associated with T12-L1 spinal cord injury (Fig. 67–2). The deficit in urethral function is the result of loss of cells in the intermediolateral cell columns at this cord level providing preganglionic motor innervation to the urethra. It is feasible to close an open urethra of this type and restore stress competence with fascial slings constructed to compress the urethra (Woodside, 1987; Gormley et al, 1994; Austin et al, 2001).

Abdominoperineal resection for carcinoma of the rectum and radical hysterectomy for carcinoma of the cervix can injure the pelvic plexus, resulting in loss of proximal urethral

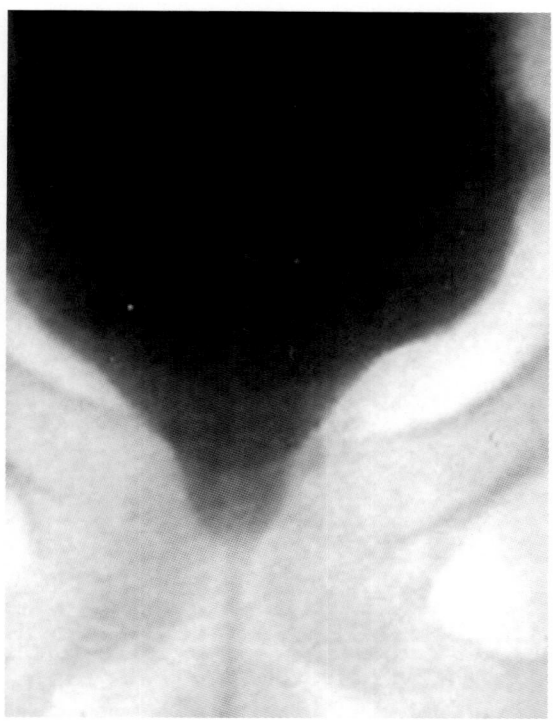

Figure 67–1. Spot photograph from a video-urodynamics study in an 18-year-old man with myelodysplasia. The subject is relaxed and at rest (i.e., not straining). This is the filling phase of the study. The bladder is decentralized and trabeculated. The urethra is wide open from the bladder outlet to the distal sphincter. The wide dilation of the prostatic urethra is related to the closure of the distal sphincter and the detrusor pressure required to overcome that urethral resistance, which is fixed. He has severe stress incontinence.

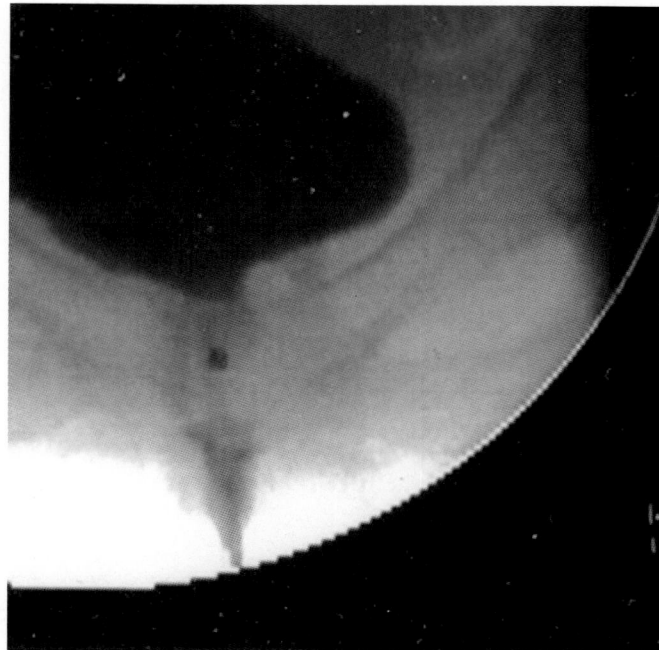

Figure 67–2. Stress incontinence associated with a low thoracic spinal cord injury. The patient is resting, not straining. The proximal sphincter does not function, and severe stress incontinence is present with straining and with transfers.

function (Fig. 67–3) and stress incontinence as well as decentralization of the bladder with gradual development of a low-compliance bladder. In these cases, abnormal and dangerous bladder storage function must be treated before the urethral resistance problem is addressed.

Acquired Severe Urethral Dysfunction

Urethral continence function can be adversely affected by surgery to repair a urethral diverticulum. In these cases, partial or complete loss of proximal urethral closure may occur, often with the development of a pseudo–urethral diverticulum and urethral-vaginal fistula formation (Leng and McGuire, 1998) (Fig. 67–4). Reconstruction of the urethra is complex when periurethral fascia is absent and a fistula present; autologous fascia is excellent material for a sling in these cases, both to reinforce the repair and to treat coexistent stress incontinence (Swierzewski and McGuire, 1993).

Erosion of synthetic slings into the urethra or bladder mandates total removal of the foreign material, but severe stress incontinence is often the long-term outcome (Fig. 67–5). Video-urodynamics shows total absence of any closing function of the urethra (Fig. 67–6). The loss of function may be accompanied by urethral-vaginal or combined vesicourethral-vaginal fistula formation, which further complicates repair. The problem is to gain closure where tissue loss has occurred

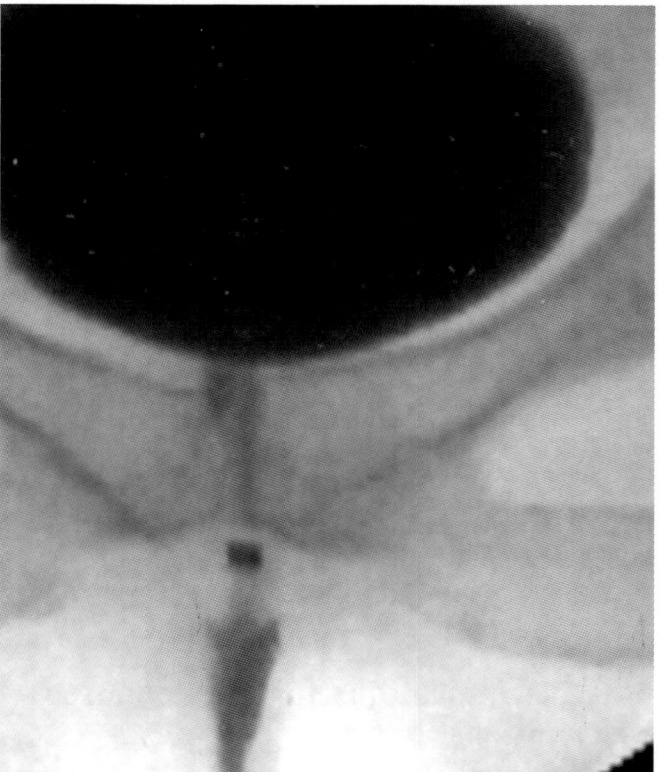

Figure 67–3. Loss of proximal urethral function associated with radical hysterectomy The subject is straining. The Valsalva leak point pressure is 14 cm H_2O. There is little urethral mobility.

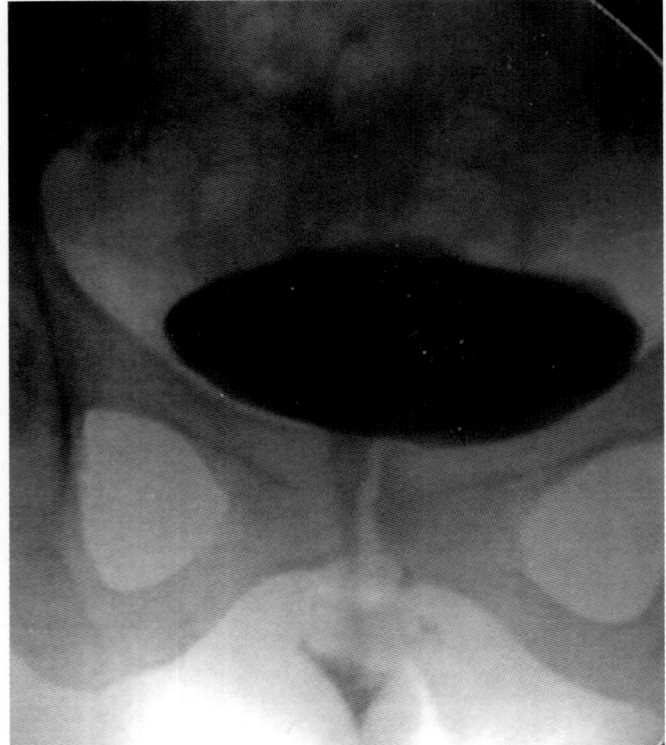

Figure 67–4. Upright video study from a 42-year-old woman with continuous urinary incontinence after a urethral diverticulectomy. There is total loss of urethral function and a large urethral-vaginal fistula. At the time of the photograph, the subject is straining.

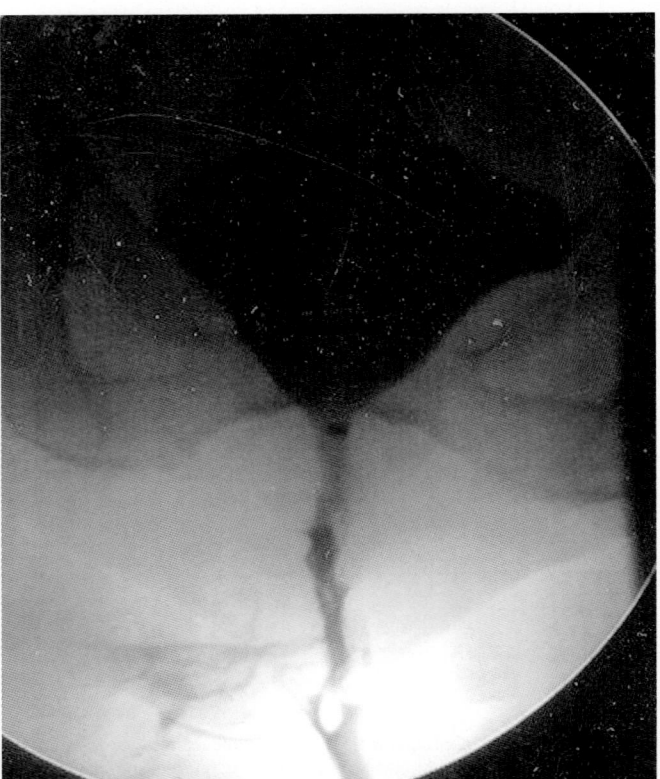

Figure 67–5. Upright photograph taken from a video study of a 78-year-old woman 1 year after removal of an eroded synthetic sling from the urethra and bladder. Several bulking agent injections failed. There is no urethral function. She is at rest, not straining.

and scarring incident to the erosion is inevitable. Compression of the urethra is an absolute requirement here.

Pelvic fracture with trauma to the fascia and muscles of the pelvis, especially where wide diastasis of the symphysis occurs, is often associated with severe stress incontinence. In these cases, fixation of a standard vector force sling to the endopelvic fascia or rectus fascia may not be possible. A circumferential wrap-type sling may be the best option here; but even then, adequate suspension of the urethra requires some ingenuity as the rectus fascia above the symphysis is also often destroyed (O'Donnell, 1992).

Chronic catheterization in neurogenic bladder dysfunction is usually initiated to treat incontinence. Unfortunately, urethral damage caused by the catheter often leads to loss of urethral function and severe incontinence (Fig. 67–7). This kind of total loss of urethral function can be associated with partial or total urethral erosion, requiring vaginal or bladder flap reconstruction of the urethra and a fascia sling (Blaivas, 1989; Blaivas and Jacobs, 1991). These types of complex reconstruction require a sling to achieve a stress-competent urethra.

Relative Indications for Autologous Fascia Slings

Weakness of Proximal Urethral Closure

Less than absolute loss of proximal urethral function is also associated with stress incontinence. There are three age groups

in which stress incontinence is likely to develop in women. One is during childbearing years, when stress incontinence develops in association with labor and delivery. Stress incontinence that develops immediately after labor and delivery is sometimes severe. Patients complain that even minor activity causes gross leakage. The video shows a partly open bladder outlet at rest and gross leakage with some mobility at a low pressure. In the perimenopausal years (45 to 65 years), the onset of stress incontinence tends to be more gradual but the problem progressive. In the majority of patients in this age group, mobility of the urethra is easily demonstrable. In later years, new-onset stress incontinence tends to be associated less often with urethral mobility and more often with some degree of intrinsic sphincter deficiency.

Patients in whom one or more operations for stress incontinence have failed may on video-urodynamics show urethral hypermobility with relatively high leak point pressures or rather severe low leak point pressure intrinsic sphincter deficiency. This video shows severe stress incontinence in a woman after a bone anchor donor fascia sling. There is little mobility, and the leak point pressure is 30 cm H_2O. If the urethra is immobile or nearly so as a result of a prior operation but nonetheless leaks, some degree of intrinsic sphincter deficiency is probably present.

Vaginal prolapse, especially a cystocele, complicates the assessment of urethral function. To some extent, grading the size of a cystocele, or any vaginal prolapse, with the patient in the usual position for a pelvic examination leads to

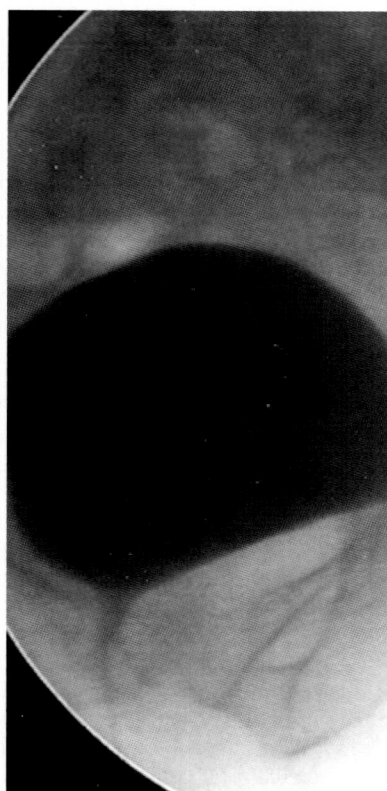

Figure 67–6. Lateral view of the bladder base and urethra taken from a video study of a 79-year-old woman with continuous leakage after erosion of a donor fascia sling fixed in place with bone anchors. The subject is not straining. The proximal urethra is nonfunctional, but there is also a vesicourethral-vaginal fistula involving the bladder neck and urethra. The nature of the problem here is difficult to determine with the video study alone because leakage is instantaneous and rapid, so that precise determination of urethral function and the associated presence of a fistula is difficult.

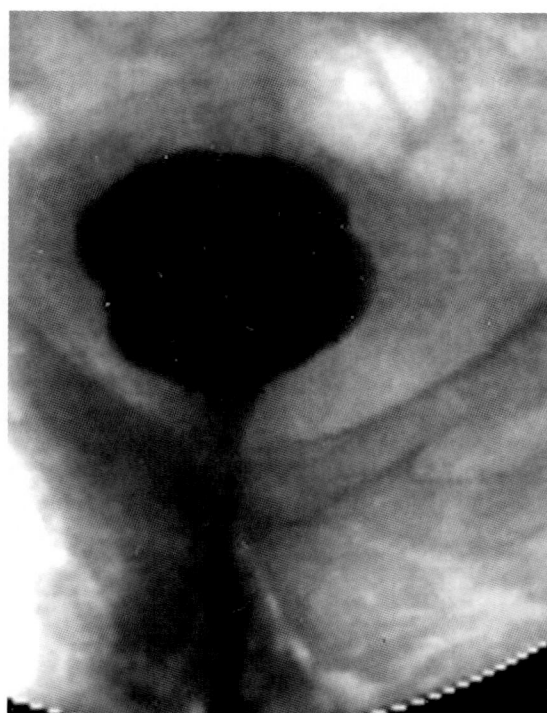

Figure 67–7. Upright cystourethrogram taken during a video study of a 54-year-old woman with paraplegia as a result of a schistosomiasis infection of the meninges. The subject is not straining. She was treated with Foley catheter for 9 years. The urethra is not functional.

SLING MATERIALS

Pubovaginal slings can be created from autologous tissue, allografts, xenografts, or synthetic materials. Although there is no "best choice" for treatment of stress incontinence, surgeons should understand the relative merits and disadvantages of each type of material. Synthetic materials for slings are discussed in detail elsewhere in this textbook.

KEY POINTS: SLING MATERIALS

- Pubovaginal slings can be created from autologous tissue, allografts, xenografts, or synthetic materials.

- Urethral erosion of autologous fascial slings, harvested from rectus or fascia lata, is extremely rare.

Autologous Tissue

Rectus fascia is harvested through a suprapubic incision (see "Operative Procedure"). One advantage of this material is complete biocompatibility without tissue rejection. **Urethral erosion of autologous rectus fascial slings is extremely rare** (Webster and Gerridzen, 2003). Disadvantages include increased operative time, relative increase in postoperative pain, and suprapubic tissue seromas.

Fascia lata is harvested from the iliotibial tract through skin incisions between the greater trochanter and the lateral

underestimation of the size and extent of the prolapse. When a definite cystocele is present, video-urodynamics helps select patients who actually have stress incontinence even if their symptoms related to that condition are absent or minor. Exactly the opposite can also occur. A woman may be treated by her gynecologist with a pessary for vaginal prolapse with the idea that occult stress incontinence might be obvious with the pessary in place.

Stress incontinence alone is not an indication for a sling procedure, although autologous fascia slings are successful in most kinds of stress incontinence. **In those cases where some compression of the urethra is required, in those circumstances where intermittent catheterization will be required indefinitely or prior procedures have failed, and after erosion of synthetic or natural materials into the bladder or urethra, autologous fascia is probably the best material to use. That is also true of reconstructive procedures, especially in children, in whom autologous fascial slings have been used for many years** (Herschorn and Radomski, 1992; Chancellor et al, 1994; Flood et al, 1995; Gosalbez and Castellan, 1998; Austin et al, 2001; Nguyen et al, 2001; Blaivas and Sandhu, 2004). Slings do not appear to be affected by growth in these cases, and long-term outcome in our hands in children as late as 20 years remains excellent.

epicondyle of the femur. Different harvesting techniques have been described, including use of a Crawford fascial stripper (Latini et al, 2004) and Metzenbaum scissors (Beck et al, 1988). After harvesting of the tissue, the fascia incision is usually left open and the epithelial incisions are closed with absorbable suture. The leg can also be wrapped to prevent postoperative hematoma. The advantage of this material is complete biocompatibility, similar to autologous rectus fascia. Disadvantages include increased operative time, the need to reposition the patient, and postoperative pain. In 24 patients undergoing open fascia lata harvest for ptosis surgery, Wheatcroft and colleagues (1997) noted that 67% had pain on walking for approximately 1 week after surgery. However, the method of fascia harvest may influence the severity of postoperative leg pain. Latini and coworkers (2004) noted that only 7% of their patients had pain at the incision site 1 week after harvesting of the tissue with a fascial stripper. Vaginal wall and rectus pedicle flaps can be used as sling materials. However, this is discussed elsewhere in this textbook.

Allografts

Cadaveric allografts have been used in orthopedic, ophthalmic, and neurosurgical procedures for the last 2 decades. However, this material has only recently been adopted for use in stress incontinence surgery as a readily available "off-the-shelf" material. Advantages of this material include shorter operative times and less postoperative morbidity.

Today, allograft slings can be made from cadaveric fascia lata and acellular dermis. **After harvesting, allografts are processed by solvent dehydration or by lyophilization (freeze-drying) to remove genetic material and to prevent the transmission of infectious agents. Gamma irradiation may also be used for secondary sterilization** (Gomelsky et al, 2003). No specific allograft material has demonstrated a clear clinical advantage in use. Acellular dermis rehydrates in 0.9% saline more rapidly than does cadaveric fascia lata (5 minutes versus 15 to 30 minutes), but each type is pliable, is easy to use, and comes in a variety of ready-made sizes (Gomelsky et al, 2003). Despite these similarities, some biomechanical studies suggest that solvent-dehydrated cadaveric fascia lata and acellular dermis have a higher maximal load failure compared with freeze-dried cadaveric fascia lata (Hinton et al, 1992; Lemer et al, 1999). However, the tissue thickness of these samples may not have been standardized before comparison, and the clinical significance of these tests is unknown.

There has been concern about potential disease transmission from allograft transplantations, particularly human immunodeficiency virus and Creutzfeldt-Jakob prion infection. Since 1985, the American Association of Tissue Banks required prospective donors to be screened for viruses. By 1987, banks were also required to treat donor tissue with sodium hydroxide to decontaminate potential prion infectivity. **The risk of iatrogenic infection from an allograft is estimated to be approximately 1 in 8 million for the human immunodeficiency virus** (Buck and Malinin, 1994) **and 1 in 3.5 million for the Creutzfeldt-Jakob prion** (Amundsen et al, 2000). Despite the low risk of disease transmission, human DNA has been detected in various allograft materials (Choe

and Bell, 2001; Hathaway and Choe, 2002). The clinical significance of this finding is unknown.

Xenografts

Like allografts, xenografts offer the advantage of an off-the-shelf material available for immediate use. Xenografts are also processed after harvest to remove genetic material and infectious agents. As a result, xenografts do not generate an intense host immune response after transplantation (Zheng et al, 2004). Although xenograft materials are generally considered safe for use as sling material, long-term efficacy has not been established for these products.

Porcine and bovine xenografts can be used as sling material. Porcine dermis has been used since 1987 (Iosif, 1987). Modern processing techniques using diisocyanate have made this material more pliable and safer to use. However, porcine dermis had a significant loss of tensile strength after implantation in a 12-week rabbit model (Dora et al, 2004). Bovine pericardium is also available, either cross-linked with glutaraldehyde or as a non–cross-linked acellular matrix (Gomelsky et al, 2003).

Porcine small intestinal submucosa has also been introduced for use as sling material. **Histopathologic analysis has shown small intestinal submucosa to contain growth factors that may reduce significant host-graft immunologic reaction and result in less tissue scarring** (Wiedemann and Otto, 2004). However, Kubricht and colleagues (2001) showed that small intestinal submucosa has less tensile strength than cadaveric fascia lata.

EVALUATION OF PATIENTS FOR SLINGS
Physical Examination

Both urethral and bladder function are evaluated, and a search is made for conditions that are associated with stress incontinence, such as vaginal prolapse or urethral diverticulum. Stress incontinence can be objectively identified by observation of a jet of urine from the meatus during pelvic examination or by sitting or standing stress testing when patients are asked to cough or strain and visible evidence of leakage is sought (Shull et al, 1999). Usually, the observed leakage is temporally related to the actual increase in intra-abdominal pressure, whereas a detrusor contraction can be generated in rare instances by an abrupt increase in abdominal pressure. In that case, the actual leakage occurs somewhat after the peak abdominal pressure is reached (Couillard and Webster, 1995; Shull et al, 1999). Unfortunately, the presentation of incontinence after stress maneuvers can also be delayed with a concomitant large cystocele or with considerable urethral hypermobility (Gardy et al, 1991). In these patients, it can be difficult to discern stress from urge incontinence.

Researchers have also attempted to correlate degree of urethral mobility with stress incontinence. To this end, cotton swab testing is commonly employed to determine the degree of urethral mobility and rotational descent during straining. However, the actual abdominal pressure attained is not measured, so the test is qualitative (Fedorkow et al, 1995). **No absolute relationship exists between the degree of urethral motion and the severity of stress incontinence symptoms** (Cross et al, 1997).

KEY POINTS: EVALUATION OF PATIENTS FOR SLINGS

- There does not seem to be any method to identify, with certainty, patients who will have persistent or new-onset urge incontinence symptoms after an operation for stress incontinence.

- It is not clear what the actual effect of incontinence due to detrusor overactivity is on outcomes. Satisfactory resolution of the condition stress incontinence is often associated with simultaneous resolution of these symptoms.

- A low-compliance bladder of any cause should be identified and treated before treatment of putative urethral dysfunction is undertaken. Cystometrography is a sensitive and accurate method to determine whether a low-compliance bladder is present.

- Urethral pressure profilometry and leak point pressure measurements do not correlate well. A low-pressure urethra is not always related to poor surgical outcome. Measurement of the leak point pressure has been used to characterize the degree of urethral dysfunction leading to stress incontinence.

Tests for Bladder Function

The Overactive Bladder and Overactive Detrusor

Evaluation of bladder function in patients with symptoms of stress incontinence was formerly directed at the detection of uncontrolled detrusor contractility by provocative cystometry (Abrams, 1984; Stanton, 1991). If the cystometrogram was "normal," then "genuine stress incontinence" was present. If uninhibited bladder contractility was detected during cystometry, then mixed incontinence was present and by definition genuine stress incontinence was not. The effect of uncontrolled detrusor activity seen during cystometry on the outcome of stress incontinence surgery was presumed to be negative (Cardozo et al, 1979). These terms, formerly used by the International Continence Society, still appear in the literature, but their meaning and significance are no longer obvious. The International Continence Society now uses the term *overactive bladder* for a loosely defined group of symptoms including urgency of urination, urge incontinence, and frequency of urination (Abrams et al, 2003). In part, this is because cystometry is grossly inaccurate in the identification of the overactive bladder. For example, Skorupski and coworkers (2003) studied 21 women with overactive bladder symptoms with a detailed micturition diary. All reported urinary loss with urinary urgency, but only eight had urodynamic evidence of uninhibited detrusor contractility provoked by filling. Malone-Lee and coworkers (2003) studied 352 women with overactive bladder symptoms. Of these, 76% had evidence of "detrusor instability" on urodynamic study. Both groups responded identically to treatment with antimuscarinic agents. However, the concept of detrusor instability as a clinical condition still exists. Bulmer and Abrams (2004)

suggested that detrusor instability, "a condition associated with urinary frequency and urgency and urge incontinence," can be diagnosed only by "urodynamic testing." Abrams, in another paper (2003), noted that the International Continence Society has adopted the term *overactive detrusor* as a replacement for detrusor instability but indicated that the new term designates a clinical diagnosis, not a urodynamic one. Estimates of the prevalence of these conditions in populations with stress incontinence are 60% to 75% for overactive bladder symptoms and 12% for overactive detrusor dysfunction. The latter is a urodynamic diagnosis, and the former a clinical one (Cardozo et al, 1979; McGuire and Savastano, 1985; Steel et al, 1986; Morgan et al, 2000).

The precise effect of an overactive bladder, or an overactive detrusor identified by cystometry, in patients with objectively identified stress incontinence who undergo surgery for that condition may actually be moot. Many prospective studies of outcomes in patients undergoing surgery for stress incontinence indicate that **satisfactory resolution of the stress incontinence symptom is often associated with resolution of overactive bladder symptoms as well** (Cross et al, 1998b; Koonings et al, 1988; Langer et al, 1998; Morgan et al, 2000). These older series involved slings, retropubic suspensions, and other operations for stress incontinence. The recent development of various synthetic sling procedures is remarkable for excellent outcomes and a lack of adverse effects of overactive bladder symptoms on those outcomes. For example, Al-Badr and coworkers (2003) noted that although transient voiding dysfunction occurred in a minority of women after a tension-free vaginal tape procedure, this had no effect on late outcome. Richter and associates (2003) noted an enduring beneficial effect on quality of life scores after a cadaveric fascial sling procedure. Abouassaly and coworkers (2004) reported late outcomes after tension-free vaginal tape procedures in 241 women with stress incontinence. Some 15% had de novo urgency symptoms after the procedure, but these were transient. Cindolo and colleagues (2004) reported a series of 80 women with stress incontinence treated by a transobturator sling procedure. Of these 80, 16 had recurrent incontinence, and 22 had overactive bladder symptoms. The objective cure rate for stress incontinence was 92%. Only two patients had urge incontinence. There are numerous reports of outcomes in the 80% to 95% range for various sling procedures, synthetic and natural, with little or no mention of problems related to overactive bladder symptoms or overactive detrusor dysfunction (Rardin et al, 2002; Abdel-Fattah et al, 2004a; Abdel-Hady and Constantine, 2005). Barnes and coworkers (2002) reported a series of 38 women who had a sling procedure in conjunction with a major pelvic prolapse repair. Existing urge incontinence resolved in 45%, whereas de novo urge incontinence developed in only two patients. There was no effect on voiding efficiency associated with the sling. Demirci and Yucel (2001) compared the outcome of a Burch urethropexy with an autologous fascial sling in 46 patients. Short-term outcomes were similar; one patient in the sling group had overactive bladder symptoms, as did one in the Burch group.

On the basis of the literature, neither overactive bladder symptoms nor objectively determined overactive detrusor dysfunction can be regarded as a risk factor for failure of operative therapy with any variety of sling procedure in

patients with clearly defined stress incontinence. The outcomes reported for synthetic and autologous and other natural material slings are similar with respect to overall success for stress incontinence as well as overactive bladder symptoms. Perhaps reflecting these data are the results of a survey of gynecologists reported by Duggan and coworkers (2003). They surveyed gynecologists in the United Kingdom, United States, Australia, and New Zealand to determine what urodynamic tests each used in patients with stress incontinence. The survey was restricted to those respondents who frequently operated on patients with stress incontinence. The authors suggested, on the basis of their results, that many gynecologists who operate frequently for stress incontinence do not use urodynamic investigations at all or often fail to use them "appropriately" if they do use them. This may be related to the fact that traditional urodynamic investigations are regarded as unnecessary by most gynecologists caring for patients with stress incontinence.

The Low-Compliance Bladder

The low-compliance bladder is another matter. This refers to a bladder that gradually gains pressure with volume. This creates a situation in which detrusor pressure approaches and then equals urethral resistance. At that point, type III stress incontinence exists, but the expulsive force is detrusor pressure and not abdominal pressure (O'Connell and McGuire, 1996). A treatment that only increases urethral resistance will actually make this situation worse, serving only to raise the detrusor pressure at which leakage occurs. This kind of bladder dysfunction occurs after pelvic irradiation for malignant disease, in neurogenic conditions, after chronic Foley catheter treatment, and after bladder decentralization syndromes, for example, those occasionally associated with radical pelvic extirpative surgery (Flood et al, 1995; McGuire and O'Connell, 1995; Leng and McGuire, 1999). **Cystometrography is a sensitive and accurate method to determine whether a low-compliance bladder is present.** If it is identified, this condition must be treated before treatment of putative urethral dysfunction is undertaken (Leng et al, 1999).

Assessment of Urethral Continence Function

How best to identify the condition stress incontinence and intrinsic sphincter deficiency or the various types of urethral dysfunction within the broader diagnosis of stress incontinence remains controversial. Gynecologists tend to use urethral pressure profilometry, whereas urologists use leak point pressures (Hilton and Stanton, 1983; Wolters and Methfessel, 1996; Bump et al, 1997; Cummings, 1997; Elser et al, 1999). The two measurements do not correlate well (Bump et al, 1995; Sultana, 1995; Swift and Ostergard, 1995a). A problem exists in this area in that comparisons of the maximum urethral closing pressure (MUCP) and the Valsalva leak point pressure (VLPP) have been done in populations of women with putative "genuine stress incontinence." At present, there is no established, standard method to make that diagnosis. Often one or the other test, the MUCP or the VLPP, is part of the diagnostic process (Swift and Ostergard, 1995b; Bump et al, 1997). VLPPs, at least, were correlated with video-

urodynamic findings (McGuire et al, 1993; Wan et al, 1993; Faerber and Vashi, 1998). Lose (1997), in a review article, noted that urethral pressure measurements were not useful in the diagnosis of stress incontinence and did not correlate with the severity of the condition; and even if urethral pressure measurements were abnormal preoperatively, they failed to return to normal after treatment.

There is a large overlap of urethral pressure profile values in women with and without stress incontinence (Khullar and Cardozo, 1998), whereas Nitti and Combs (1996) were able to correlate the severity of stress incontinence symptoms with VLPPs in a group of women with stress incontinence. Siltberg and coworkers (1996) have shown the cough leak point pressure to be useful in the evaluation of stress-incontinent patients and to accurately reflect the effects of treatment. Although pressure transmission to the upper urethra improves after successful surgery, Swift and colleagues (1996) found pressure transmission ratios difficult to duplicate in the same patient. Urethral pressure profile data have been used to select patients for a sling procedure of various types based on retrospective data (Sand et al, 1987). These studies suggest that persons with a low MUCP will have a high failure rate after retropubic suspension procedures. However, at least two groups have prospectively looked at whether a "low-pressure urethra" is a risk factor for failure of a suspension operation to cure stress incontinence. **Patients with a low-pressure urethra did not have a higher failure rate than did those without that problem** (Maher et al, 1999; Sand et al, 2000). Although urethral pressures are not now used to establish whether stress incontinence is present, gynecologists do continue to use MUCP data to identify intrinsic sphincter deficiency and to plan an appropriate surgical procedure for that condition (Bump et al, 1995).

Measurement of the Valsalva Leak Point Pressure

Measurement of the abdominal pressure required to produce leakage from an incompetent urethra (variously called the Valsalva, abdominal, or cough leak point pressure) has been used to characterize the degree of urethral dysfunction leading to stress incontinence. As originally described, total vesical pressure was measured, or detrusor pressure plus abdominal pressure, with the patient upright, under fluoroscopic monitoring at a bladder volume of 200 to 300 mL (McGuire et al, 1996). Normally, the detrusor pressure component is small, and the major force measured is abdominal pressure. Within broad limits, a urethra that leaks at low pressures, 0 to 60 cm H_2O, is severely dysfunctional (Fig. 67–8), whereas a urethra that leaks at higher pressures, 61 to 150 cm H_2O, is less dysfunctional (Figs. 67–9 and 67–10) (Nitti and Combs, 1996). A normal urethra will not leak (Ghoniem et al, 2002).

Obviously, leak point pressures vary with detrusor pressure changes. A low-compliance bladder combines the effect of detrusor pressure with abdominal pressure, and recorded leak point pressures do not accurately reflect the closing strength of the urethra vis-à-vis abdominal pressure as an expulsive force (Fig. 67–11). **Vaginal prolapse also makes leak point pressures inaccurate, either because the prolapse actually**

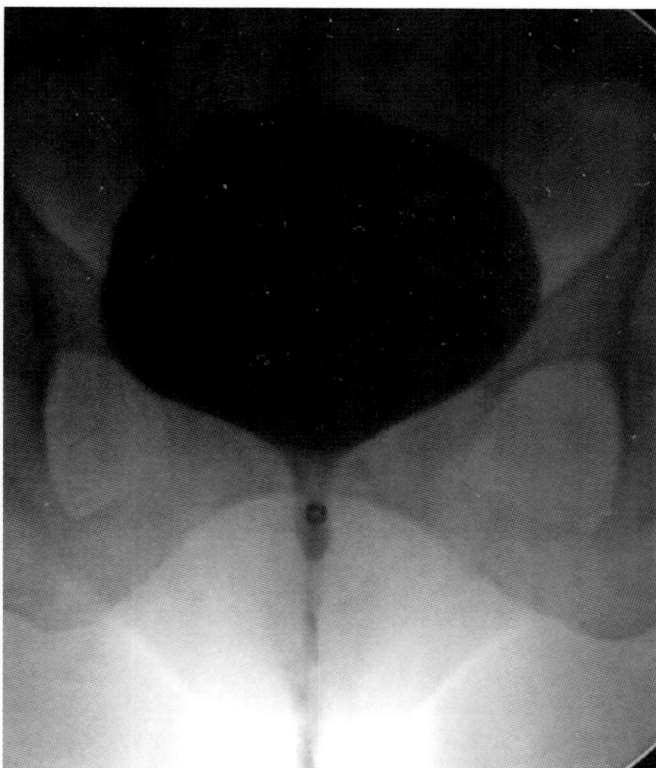

Figure 67–8. Spot photograph taken from an upright video study of a 34-year-old woman with severe stress incontinence that began immediately after labor and delivery. Two prior operative procedures have failed. As she strains, there is little urethral mobility but gross leakage at a Valsalva leak point pressure of 25 cm H_2O.

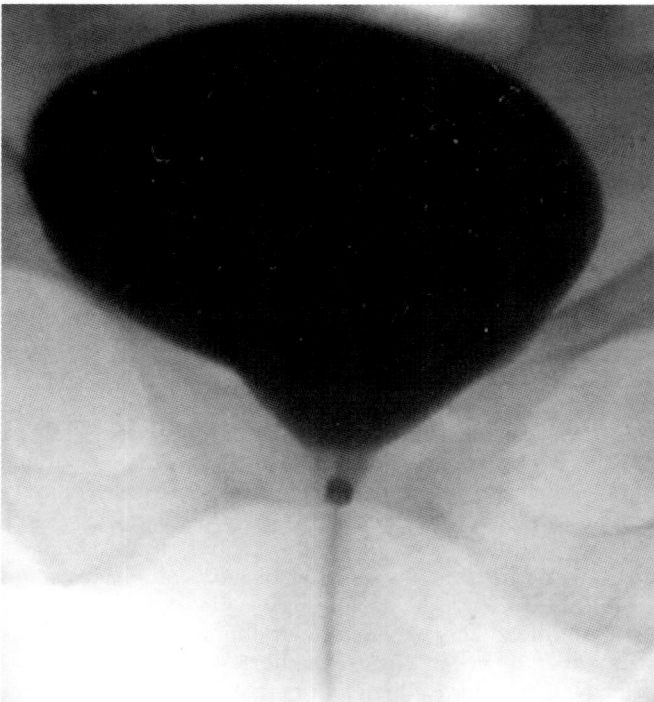

Figure 67–9. Spot photograph taken at the instant of leakage associated with straining from a 55-year-old woman. There is considerable urethral mobility, and the Valsalva leak point pressure at 260 mL is 102 cm H_2O.

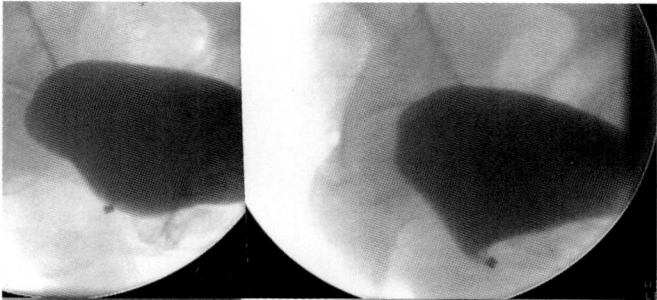

Figure 67–10. Spot photographs taken during a video study from a 47-year-old woman in the resting state on the left and during straining on the right. There is mobility of the bladder base and urethra. At a bladder volume of 288 mL, the Valsalva leak point pressure is 122 cm H_2O.

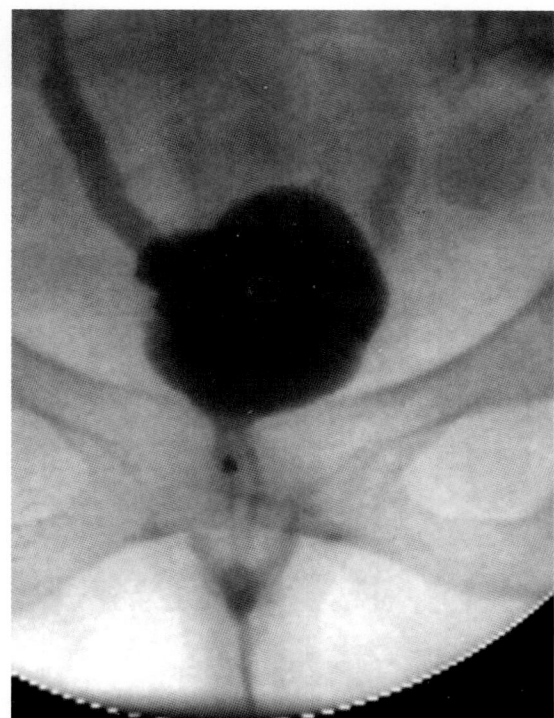

Figure 67–11. Spot photograph taken early during a video-urodynamics study from a 78-year-old woman with continuous incontinence treated by a Foley catheter. There is continuous leakage, bladder compliance is low, and there is bilateral vesicoureteral reflux. Obviously, there is a problem with bladder storage function here.

supports the urethra during stress or because abdominal pressure is dissipated in the prolapse, thus protecting the urethra (Fig. 67–12). Leak point pressure testing, with other data, helps to completely characterize urethral dysfunction and to select patients with conditions appropriately treated with an autologous fascial sling (Figs. 67–13 and 67–14) (Cummings et al, 1997; Paick et al, 2004).

Leak point pressures vary with subject position, catheter size, bladder volume, and subjective effort. As first described, a three-lumen No. 10 French catheter was used, the patients were upright on a fluoroscopy table, and the bladder was filled to 200 to 300 mL. The triple-lumen catheter was positioned so that the neutral-filling aperture was in the bladder together

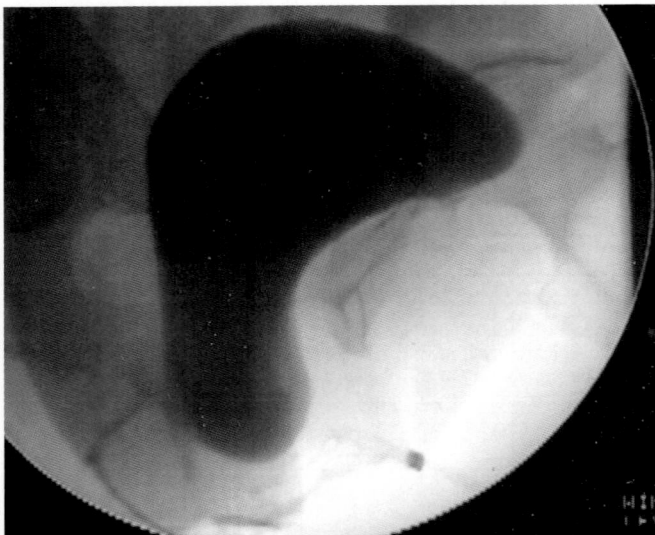

Figure 67–12. Spot film taken during a video study from a patient with a symptomatic cystocele. The patient is straining. There is gross urethral mobility in association with herniation of the "central" cystocele, but there is no actual stress leakage. The patient has the condition stress incontinence even if we cannot demonstrate that.

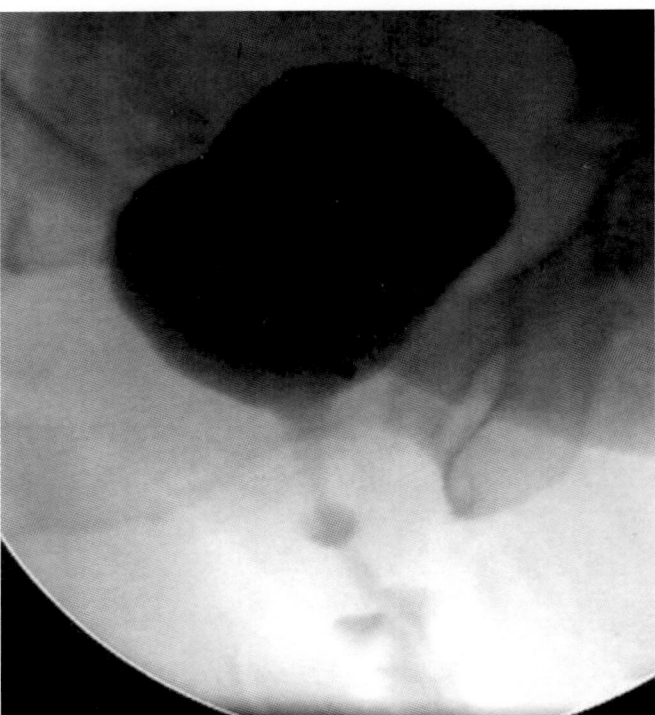

Figure 67–14. Upright photograph during a video study of a 78-year-old woman treated for incontinence with a Foley catheter. The urethra does not function. The Valsalva leak point pressure is not measurable as leakage begins at no pressure when the patient is placed in the upright position.

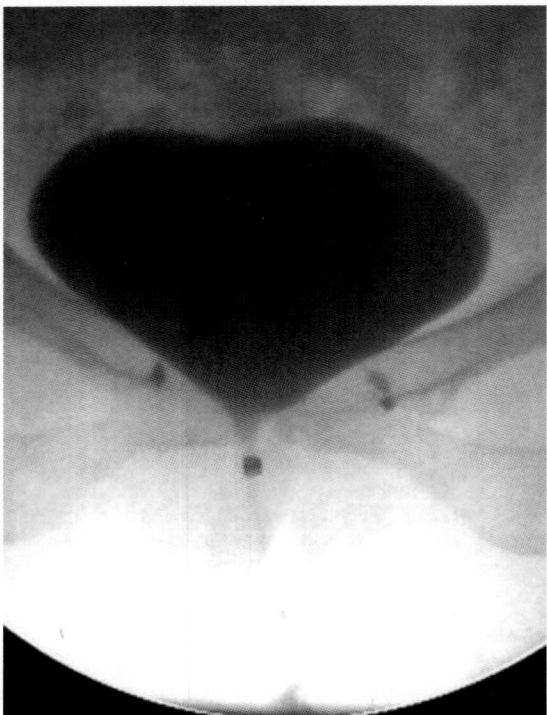

Figure 67–13. Upright study from a 49-year-old woman with stress incontinence persistent after a sling procedure with donor fascia and bone anchors. The patient is straining. The bladder neck and proximal urethra are open. The sling fails to compress the urethra. The Valsalva leak point pressure is 34 cm H_2O.

with one pressure-sensing aperture; the third aperture, also pressure sensing, was placed in the midurethral high-pressure zone. With the use of that technique, the test was found to be reproducible and to correlate with video-urodynamic findings that were gathered at the same time (McGuire et al, 1993).

Measurement of total vesical pressure has an advantage. If there is abnormal compliance, it can be identified (Wan et al, 1993). Others have measured abdominal pressure in the rectum, or in the vagina, during straining or coughing (Haab et al, 1996, 1997). The cough-induced leak point pressure, described by Siltberg and coworkers (1996, 1998), has been found useful to characterize stress incontinence and to determine changes induced by surgery.

Although leak point pressures have been used to diagnose stress incontinence, their accuracy in this regard had never been tested in a large population of patients. Vaginal prolapse, for example, interferes with leak point pressure testing, apparently because the abdominal pressure is dissipated in the prolapse; this makes the urethra appear better than it really is. Ghoniem and coworkers (1994) described a method to reduce a cystocele and then perform leak point pressure testing. In the absence of prolapse, leak point pressure testing can be valuable to establish at what pressure this occurs. Selection of patients whose urethral function is so poor as to be reparable only with a compressive operative procedure may not always require urodynamics, especially video-urodynamics, but the tests are useful in cases in which urethral failure is not so obvious and in cases in which low bladder compliance could be a problem. There are data to suggest that prospective identification of patients with low leak point pressure, or type III stress incontinence by video-dynamic testing, defines a subset of patients who have a high failure rate after standard operations for stress incontinence (Kondo et al, 1998; Kayigil et al, 1999). Similar prospective data do not exist for MUCP data (Maher et al, 1999; Sand et al, 2000).

OPERATIVE PROCEDURE
Preliminary Steps

General or regional anesthesia is administered according to the preference of the anesthesiologist and patient. A single dose of a broad-spectrum parenteral antibiotic such as cefazolin is given. The patient is placed in the modified dorsal lithotomy position with use of Yellofins lithotomy stirrups. The stirrups may be lowered for the abdominal portion of the procedure and raised for the vaginal portion. Foam supports are placed to prevent excessive pressure on the calf. The abdomen and vagina are prepared and draped as a single field; a No. 18 French urethral catheter is placed, the balloon is inflated with 10 mL, and the catheter is clamped with a Kelly clamp. The bladder is allowed to fill slightly to check for hematuria after passage of the sling sutures. A thorough vaginal examination is performed.

Abdominal Approach and Sling Harvest

The rectus fascia is exposed by making a 6- to 8-cm transverse incision 3 to 4 cm superior to the pubis. The leaves of the fascia are lifted with Kocher clamps and mobilized from the underlying rectus muscle with electrocautery. The sling is usually obtained from the lower fascial leaf, but the upper may also be used. **Scarred and thickened fascia is suitable for use as a sling as long as it can be passed from the vaginal incision into the retropubic space.** A scalpel is used to make a midline stab incision in the fascia so that the sling width is 1.0 to 1.5 cm. The incision is continued laterally with scissors, tapering the ends of the sling to 0.5 to 1.0 cm. The ends are transected at right angles. Final sling dimensions are 6 to 8 cm × 1.5 cm. Sling sutures are placed perpendicular to the direction of the sling fibers, approximately 0.5 cm from the ends and incorporating the full width of the sling. The sutures are tied and left long, and the sling is placed in a saline solution–filled basin for later use.

A variety of suture types and sling lengths may be used in performing a pubovaginal sling. The authors currently use absorbable 0 Vicryl (polyglactin 910) suture material owing to the belief that the sutures play no role in maintaining continence after the immediate postoperative period. The 6- to 8-cm length used by the authors is adequate for both ends of the sling to cross the endopelvic fascia, where it can be fixed in place by subsequent scarring.

Development of Retropubic Tunnels

At its insertion into the pubis, the rectus muscle is swept medially until the triangular space just lateral to the muscle is identified. The transversalis fascia is bluntly pierced with a finger to gain entry to the retropubic space. If a prior retropubic or transvaginal bladder neck suspension has been performed, this layer may be scarred, making blunt entry impossible. In this situation, a curved Metzenbaum scissors may be spread directly on the superior aspect of the pubis to sharply gain entry. A finger is then gently passed immediately adjacent to the pubis, sweeping the bladder medially until the endopelvic

fascia is encountered. A moist gauze pad is packed in the abdominal wound.

Vaginal Approach

The Yellofins lithotomy stirrups are adjusted to elevate the patient's legs. A Scherbeck weighted vaginal retractor is placed, and the anterior vaginal wall midway between the urethral meatus and the bladder neck is grasped with one or two long Allis clamps for superior retraction. Moderate Trendelenburg position and use of a headlight give optimal visualization of the anterior vaginal wall. The authors prefer an inverted U-shaped incision since it enables an adequate exposure of the proximal urethra and bladder without the aid of assistants.

The vaginal mucosa is dissected from the underlying white periurethral fascia with a scalpel and Church scissors. **Brisk bleeding may usually be avoided by staying superficial to the periurethral fascia,** although in young patients or those with prior vaginal surgery, bleeding may be unavoidable. Superficial dissection also avoids damage to the urethra or bladder. When adequate lateral mucosal flaps have been developed, the tips of the Metzenbaum scissors are placed medial to the ischiopubic ramus at the superior margin of the dissection, and the endopelvic fascia is perforated in a superolateral direction. The scissors are spread wide to facilitate subsequent sling passage, and blunt finger dissection further widens the entry into the retropubic space. This dissection leads to connection between the infrapubic and retropubic dissection planes. Simultaneous finger palpation from the abdominal and vaginal incisions is performed to ensure that the bladder is safely medial. **Any intervening tissue above the level of the endopelvic fascia is often the bladder, fixed to the pubis.** Gentle medial mobilization may be attempted, but vigorous blunt dissection will often result in bladder injury.

Sling Placement and Fixation

A McGuire suture guide or other choice of ligature carrier is placed from above through the defect in the transversalis fascia lateral to the rectus muscle. **The tip of the passer should be in contact with the pubis at all times to ensure that inadvertent bladder injury does not occur.** Use of a ligature carrier may facilitate sling passage in difficult cases. If a prior bladder neck suspension has been performed, the bladder may be densely adherent to the lateral pelvic sidewall, and carrier passage must then be subperiosteal. Depending on the operator's preference, passing the ligature carrier can be accomplished either from above downward or from below upward. In the latter situation, a ligature passer is preloaded with the sutures to the sling before passing. The Foley catheter is unclamped, and the bladder is drained to evaluate for hematuria. If a bladder injury is suspected, cystoscopy is performed with a 70-degree lens. The ligature carrier should be kept in place so that any injury will be obvious on cystoscopy. Bladder injuries occur near the dome of the bladder, at the 11-o'clock and 1-o'clock positions. In the event of a small bladder injury, the ligature carrier is removed and passed again, extravesical passage is confirmed with cystoscopy, and the procedure is completed. Larger injuries must be formally repaired before the procedure may continue.

After safe carrier passage is confirmed, the sling sutures are placed in the opening of the ligature carrier, which is then pulled back up. A degree of resistance will be felt as the sling passes through the defect in the endopelvic fascia. The sling is centered and sutured to the periurethral fascia with 3-0 polyglactin suture. One suture may be used to fix the sling in place. **The sling should be located at the level of the bladder neck and proximal urethra, and both ends of the sling should be in the retropubic space.** Accurate positioning of the sling at the bladder neck is generally not a problem because sling mobility is limited by the incision and by the sutures in the perforated endopelvic fascia. The vaginal mucosa is closed with a running 3-0 chromic or similar suture. At that point, all bleeding from the vagina usually stops.

KEY POINTS: SLING PLACEMENT AND TENSION

- The sling should be located at the level of the proximal urethra, and both ends of the sling should be in the retropubic space. The achievement of the correct amount of sling tension requires an individualized approach to each patient.

- When urethral function is poor and mobility is minimal in neuropathic conditions, the crossover sling technique can be performed to achieve circumferential compression. The amount of the tension varies according to the purpose of the procedure.

Determination of Sling Tension

The sling sutures are passed through the inferior leaf of the rectus fascia by use of a sharp clamp, and the rectus fascia is closed with a running 0 polyglactin suture. The vaginal retractor is removed, and the degree of urethral mobility is assessed. The sutures are tied down to the rectus fascia with the least amount of tension to prevent urethral motion. There may be room for two fingers to slide underneath the knot between the fascia and the knot at the end of the tie-down. There may be minimal urethral hypermobility when the Foley catheter is placed on traction under bimanual control.

The weakness of these standardized approaches is that **the degree of sling tension required to achieve continence is different in different types of patients.** Patients with urethral hypermobility and a reasonable degree of urethral function (VLPP > 90 cm H_2O) require slings that increase urethral support; these slings can be quite loose. Slings for patients with high-grade pelvic prolapse and occult stress incontinence also require no tension. For more severe intrinsic sphincter deficiency (VLPP < 90 cm H_2O) with periurethral and perivesical scarring, such as often occurs after a prior bladder neck suspension, a degree of tension on the sutures is required to prevent urethral mobility and to attain continence. When urethral function is poor (VLPP < 60 cm H_2O) and mobility is minimal, a compressive sling is required. In patients who desire the preservation of volitional voiding, this technique can be used to minimize the risk of urinary retention by avoiding excess upward tension on the sutures. Clearly, **the achievement of the correct amount of sling tension requires an individualized approach to each patient;** use of a single "no-tension" technique in every instance will result in suboptimal results.

Wound Closure

For better postoperative analgesia, 5 to 8 mL of 0.25% bupivacaine HCl, a local anesthetic, is infiltrated into the subcutaneous tissues. Scarpa's fascia is approximated with interrupted absorbable suture. The skin is closed with a running absorbable subcuticular stitch. A sterile dry dressing is applied. The urethral catheter is placed to gravity drainage, and a vaginal pack soaked with povidone-iodine (Betadine) is placed.

MODIFICATIONS OF THE STANDARD SLING
Crossover Variety

When urethral function is poor (VLPP < 60 cm H_2O) and mobility is minimal, a compressive sling is required. These characteristics are generally seen in patients with myelodysplasia or in those who have many failed prior attempts at surgical treatment of their incontinence. In these cases, the sling sutures can be crossed in the retropubic space before passing them through the rectus fascia. When tied, the crossed sutures exert a more circumferential force on the urethra, providing a compressive effect.

The procedure is largely based on that of the standard pubovaginal sling. After the sling is harvested, the rectus muscles are opened in the midline, and blunt and sharp dissection in combination is used to gently push the bladder back from the posterior surface of the symphysis and gain access to the endopelvic fascia on either side of the urethra. After the abdominal wound is packed, the vaginal incision and dissection are made as for a standard sling procedure. Under careful bimanual control, the sling sutures are pulled through the retropubic space by use of the ligature carrier on both sides. Once both sling ends are visualized in the retropubic space, both sling ends are crossed over so that the sling end that comes around the right side of the urethra is tunneled through the left side of the rectus fascia and vice versa. In addition, the sling sutures are tunneled more laterally than usual through the inferior leaf of the rectus fascia. In this manner, nearly circumferential compression of the urethra can be achieved. After closure of the rectus fascia, the sling sutures are tied down over the closed rectus fascia with sufficient tension to fix the urethra in position. **The amount of the tension varies according to the purpose of the procedure.** If the aim is total urethral closure and diversion, sufficient tension should be applied to prevent any leakage through the urethra. In the patients who need subsequent urethral catheterization, adequate tension around the urethral wall may be applied so that the passage of the catheter without incontinence can be achieved. The rest of the procedures are similar to the standard sling procedure.

Deliberate Closure of the Urethra in Combination with Other Reconstructive Procedures

Deliberate closure of the urethra with a sling is often done as part of a major reconstruction procedure including augmentation cystoplasty and neourethra construction. The objective is to achieve continence and to facilitate intermittent catheterization through an accessible abdominal stoma. Rather strong tension is placed on the urethra by the sling. The sling sutures are tied down over the closed rectus fascia with the Foley catheter removed to gain maximal compression. Urethral catheterization may be difficult after this type of sling.

POSTOPERATIVE CARE

All patients leave the operating room with vaginal packing and an indwelling urethral catheter. The vaginal packing is removed on postoperative day 1. A postoperative hematocrit is not checked unless the patient's blood pressure or urine output is abnormally low. Pneumatic compression boots are initially used for deep venous thrombosis prevention and are discontinued on postoperative day 1 when the patient begins ambulating. A general diet is resumed by postoperative day 1. All patients start aggressive pulmonary toilet with incentive spirometry after leaving the postoperative recovery unit, and it is continued until discharge. **Patients are usually discharged from the hospital on postoperative day 1 or 2 with instructions to avoid strenuous activity for approximately 5 to 6 weeks. Women can resume sexual intercourse 3 to 4 weeks after the surgery.** We also routinely reassess each patient's progress through a postoperative visit 3 weeks after the procedure.

A combination of oral and parenteral narcotics usually achieves adequate postoperative analgesia. Intravenous ketorolac is used for supplemental pain control in patients with adequate preoperative renal function. **Surgeons should judiciously use this medication if intraoperative blood loss was significant since ketorolac can increase bleeding times by 50% in normal patients** (Singer et al, 2003).

We remove the patient's urethral catheter on the morning of postoperative day 1. If an intraoperative cystotomy occurred, the catheter is left in place for 7 days and is removed after a cystogram confirms bladder integrity. All patients are taught clean intermittent catheterization with a 14 French coudé catheter during the hospital stay. Postvoid catheterization is continued until residual volumes fall below 100 mL. Our mean duration of postoperative intermittent catheterization has been 8 days. Only 2% of patients continued intermittent catheterization beyond 3 months (Morgan et al, 2000). Patients who are physically unable to perform intermittent catheterization may be treated with a temporary indwelling catheter or suprapubic tube. However, we do not advocate this approach because indwelling catheters can cause irritative bladder symptoms that are occasionally misinterpreted as urinary tract infections by health care professionals (Capewell and Morris, 1993).

COMPLICATIONS AND PROBLEMS
Retention

Transient retention is common after sling procedures (Morgan et al, 2000). Most surgeons who use slings extensively instruct their patients in the technique of intermittent catheterization preoperatively. This reduces the median length of stay for a sling to about 24 hours (Curtis et al, 1997; Webster and Gerridzen, 2003). The period of retention and intermittent catheterization, on average, is 8 days when a sling is the only procedure done. In those cases in which slings are done in conjunction with complex procedures for vaginal prolapse, intermittent catheterization may be required for longer periods (Barnes et al, 2002). Some reports suggest that retention can be a protracted problem. Borup and Nielson (2002) reported that one patient in a series of 32 women treated for stress incontinence by a sling developed partial retention requiring intermittent catheterization indefinitely. Groen and Bosh (2004) noted that 42% of their sling patients required intermittent catheterization at 3 months and 18% at 6 months postoperatively. Patients with retention, without urinary urgency, who have some urethral mobility on pelvic examination normally do resume low-pressure voiding within 30 to 40 days. Those with urgency and urge incontinence coupled with retention, so that volitional voiding is not possible, should be reevaluated frequently. This is a dynamic process in some patients, and not infrequently a patient who appears to be doing well and progressing toward voiding presents with a high fixed urethral position and severe motor urge incontinence despite nearly total retention as a new finding. **If the urethra appears hypersuspended, or higher than it was placed at the time of surgery, it is probably best to take the sling down.** Autologous fascia slings are no more likely to produce obstruction than are other procedures for stress incontinence, but a high index of suspicion and early takedown may prevent some of the long-term problems associated with obstructive uropathy. In a series of 15 patients who had a urethrolysis for obstruction after a sling, Leng and coworkers (2004) noted that persistent intractable urgency incontinence was much more common in those women experiencing a protracted delay between the sling and the urethrolysis. Most patients would rather have stress incontinence than an uncontrollable overactive bladder. After 5 to 6 weeks of retention, any sling procedure should probably be taken down.

> ### KEY POINTS: COMPLICATIONS
>
> ■ If the urethra appears hypersuspended, or higher than it was placed at the time of surgery, it is probably best to take the sling down. Autologous fascia slings are no more likely to produce obstruction than are other procedures for stress incontinence, but a high index of suspicion and early takedown may prevent some of the long-term problems associated with obstructive uropathy.
>
> ■ Erosion of an autologous fascial sling is relatively rare. Early sling failure within days of the procedure is rare, but when it occurs, the sling is simply not under enough tension. Late failure of a sling is also rare.

Methods of Sling Release

Simple release by cutting the sling under the urethra is usually enough if it is done within 6 weeks of the procedure (Goldman, 2003). Amundsen and colleagues (2000) reported a series of 32 patients with obstruction after various sling procedures. Of these 32, 30 had urge incontinence symptoms, 63% required intermittent catheterization, and 19% had an indwelling catheter. After sling takedown, which varied somewhat according to the material used for the sling, 93% achieved efficient voiding. Only 3% redeveloped stress incontinence. A lack of recurrent stress incontinence in the vast majority of patients subjected to sling takedown has been noted by several authors (Cross et al, 1998a; Goldman et al, 1999; Cespedes, 2001). **If the urethra is hypersuspended, complete removal of the sling under the urethra and takedown of the lateral sling attachments at the endopelvic fascia are usually required.** This is the situation if several months or more have elapsed since the sling procedure.

Erosion

Erosion of an autologous fascial sling is relatively rare. When this occurs early during a period of intermittent catheterization, it generally is associated with traumatic catheterization and a through-and-through urethral injury that exposes the sling (Handa and Stone, 1999; Webster and Gerridzen, 2003). Use of a coudé catheter obviates this problem in most patients. If erosion occurs with autologous fascia in association with difficult catheterization, a 10-day period of Foley catheter drainage will allow healing without sequelae. Amundsen and coworkers (2003) reported on a series of nine patients who developed erosion. In five of these, the eroded material was synthetic. The authors removed the entire sling, did a multilayer closure of the urethra, and covered that with a Martius flap. In the other four, the sling material was autograft or allograft; in these, the sling was incised and the urethra closed. Results were better in the nonsynthetic group. Blaivas and Sandhu (2004) reviewed the literature on urethral reconstruction after synthetic and nonsynthetic sling erosion.

Pain Syndromes

Most patients have pain in the area just above the abdominal wound on one side or the other, when upright, for 2 to 3 weeks after a sling. This goes away when the sling sutures dissolve. It can be relieved by lying down with the knees bent slightly upward.

Sling Failure

Early sling failure within days of the procedure is rare, but when it occurs, the sling is simply not under enough tension. This can occur if one or both of the sling ends are not well into the retropubic space, completely through the endopelvic fascia; if a suture pulls out of the sling; or because the slack in the sling was not taken out and proper tension for the specific urethral condition treated by the sling was not applied.

Late failure of a sling is also rare. When this occurs, it is often related to vaginal prolapse, which exerts a traction force on the sling and breaks the lateral fixation points of the sling to the endopelvic fascia and arcus tendineus fasciae pelvis.

If a vaginal prolapse does develop after a sling procedure, especially a cystocele, correction of the problem when that involves the arcus tendineus fasciae pelvis is likely to detach the sling from its fixation points with the development of recurrent stress incontinence. In these cases, a well-supported urethra and good sling at the beginning of the procedure mean nothing. If the cystocele repair seems to loosen the sling and produces new urethral mobility, it is best to redo the sling.

OUTCOME STUDIES

Defining Outcomes

In 1997, the American Urologic Association–sponsored Female Stress Urinary Incontinence Guidelines Panel reviewed the medical literature on surgical outcomes after stress incontinence surgery and performed a comparative meta-analysis to estimate cure rates for different techniques. Although the panel identified 5322 papers for review, only 282 articles provided enough outcomes data for analysis (Leach et al, 1997). **In general, surgical outcomes after stress incontinence surgery are difficult to compare because selection of patients varies widely between studies and study endpoints are not well defined.**

Patient Selection

The severity of incontinence symptoms before surgery is particularly difficult to compare between studies. During the past 20 years, researchers have classified incontinence severity through clinical history (Elser et al, 1995), physical examination (Bhatia and Bergman, 1983; Ferrari et al, 1986), pad use (Soroka et al, 2002; Abdel-Fattah et al, 2004b), urodynamics (Fleischman et al, 2003), and quality of life questionnaires (Karantanis et al, 2004). Although research definitions of stress incontinence exist (Weber et al, 2001), no recommendations have been made to standardize methodology for quantifying severity of the symptoms.

Other variables also make comparisons between patient samples challenging. Geographic and racial distributions influence the clinical impact of symptoms within specific study samples (Graham and Mallett, 2001; Bogner, 2004). Researchers may bias their studies by excluding patients with comorbidities, such as obesity, pelvic organ prolapse, and previous incontinence surgeries. Incomplete follow-up is also highly variable between studies.

Definition of Study Endpoints

Although the International Continence Society has published broad recommendations for comparing outcomes after incontinence surgery and measures for gauging surgical efficacy (Lose et al, 2001), researchers still use multiple different methods to determine the "cure rate" after pubovaginal sling surgery. Inconsistencies can thus arise, depending on who determines surgical success and how it is measured. Sirls and colleagues (1995) have shown that surgeons attributed higher levels of continence to patients after surgery compared with patients scoring their own symptoms. Furthermore, history does not always correlate with pad testing, voiding diaries, urodynamics, or other "objective" measurements of incontinence (Elser et al, 1995; Chaikin et al, 1998; Matharu et al, 2004). Quality control for individual tests within an institution also can become an issue (Sullivan et al, 2003).

Outcomes—Literature Review

The 1997 Female Stress Urinary Incontinence meta-analysis concluded that pubovaginal slings had an 83% cure rate at 48 months (Leach et al, 1997). Outcomes for each class of sling material are presented here and summarized in Table 67–1.

Autologous Rectus Fascia

Cure rates for rectus fascia pubovaginal slings range from 67% to 97% (Blaivas and Jacobs, 1991; Mason and Roach, 1996; Zaragoza, 1996; Chaikin et al, 1998; Hassouna and Ghoniem, 1999; Morgan et al, 2000; Groutz et al, 2001; Richter et al, 2001; Chou et al, 2003).

Morgan and coworkers (2000) described 247 patients treated with autologous pubovaginal slings. Patients with type II, type III, and mixed urinary incontinence were well represented. Concomitant vaginal procedures were performed in 48% of patients. Outcomes were determined through chart review and a condition-specific quality of life questionnaire. At a mean follow-up of 51 months, **88% were cured of symptoms. Cure rates were higher for type II incontinence than for type III (91% versus 84%).**

Chaikin and coworkers (1998) reported similar results for a series of 251 patients assessed with physical examination, voiding diaries, and standardized questionnaires. After a 36-month mean follow-up, 73% were cured of symptoms and 19% were improved. Previous analysis of 67 patients with complicated type III incontinence from this sample showed an 82% cure rate at 3.5 months (Blaivas and Jacobs, 1991). Several authors have published further subgroup analysis for treatment of patients with specific conditions or comorbidities. Mason and Roach (1996) reported a 93% cure rate in a patient sample with a high degree of pelvic organ prolapse. Chou and colleagues (2003) retrospectively evaluated 52 women with mixed urinary incontinence treated with an autologous sling and found that 93% were cured or improved of stress incontinence symptoms, a rate similar to that of patients with pure stress incontinence.

KEY POINTS: OUTCOMES FOR AUTOLOGOUS RECTUS FASCIA SLINGS

- Cure rates for rectus fascia pubovaginal slings are very good, ranging from 67% to 97%.

- Very high scores of quality of life have been reported after autologous rectus fascial slings.

High quality of life has also been reported after autologous rectus fascial slings. Richter and coworkers (2001) performed a retrospective analysis of 57 patients observed for a mean of 42 months. Of these patients, 88% indicated that the sling had improved their quality of life, and 82% would undergo the procedure again.

Autologous Fascia Lata

Less information is available to judge the efficacy of autologous fascia lata pubovaginal slings. Latini and colleagues (2004) retrospectively reviewed 100 patients treated with this modality. Outcomes were assessed by chart review and patient questionnaire responses. After a mean follow-up of 4.4 years, 85% of patients were cured of symptoms, and 83% would undergo the procedure again. Beck and coworkers (1988) evaluated 170 patients, all of whom had failed previous surgical procedures to correct incontinence. During a 22-year period, they reported that 98% of patients were cured on the basis of physical examination and urodynamic evaluation. Mean time to normal voiding was 59 days. Follow-up was not definitively specified for these patients.

Although subgroup analysis has not been extensively performed for autologous fascia lata slings, Govier and coworkers (1997) performed a chart review of 32 patients treated for intrinsic sphincter deficiency with autologous fascia lata sling and found that 87% did not need pads afterward. Interestingly, an independent patient survey showed that only 70% reported using no pads. Follow-up was not well defined in this study.

Cadaveric Fascia Lata

Outcomes for cadaveric fascia lata slings have been decidedly mixed. Cure rates have ranged from 33% to 93%, but sample sizes in these reports are smaller than in autologous sling studies (Lemer et al, 1999; Amundsen et al, 2000; Walsh et al, 2002; Richter et al, 2003; Carey and Leach, 2004).

Amundsen and coworkers (2000) evaluated 104 patients treated with a freeze-dried allograft fascia sling. The type of incontinence was not directly specified in this study, but patients' mean VLPP was 56 to 63 cm H_2O. Outcomes were determined through a validated questionnaire, physical examination, and chart review. At a mean follow-up of 19 months, 63% of patients were cured of incontinence symptoms, and 21% reported occasional stress urinary incontinence. Richter and colleagues (2003) prospectively evaluated 102 women treated with freeze-dried cadaveric fascia lata slings and determined outcomes with validated symptom-specific quality of life questionnaires. Type of incontinence was not specified, but 85% reported both stress and urge incontinence on the questionnaires. **Although 80% of patients reported significant improvement of symptoms at 12 months, only 33% had complete resolution of urine leakage.** Carbone and coworkers (2001) also reported a high rate of failure in a 154-patient study. At 11-month mean follow-up, 38% had moderate to severe stress incontinence as determined by chart review and a mailed patient questionnaire.

Little information is available on cadaveric fascia lata efficacy in treating intrinsic sphincter deficiency. Wright and colleagues (1998) reported that 58 of 59 patients with intrinsic sphincter deficiency were dry after a cadaveric fascia lata sling, but follow-up was limited to 11 months. There are no clinical data to suggest that the method of tissue preparation (freeze-dried versus solvent dehydration) influences the cure rate for patients treated with cadaveric fascia lata slings.

Cadaveric Dermis

Few data are available for the cadaveric dermal sling outcomes. Crivellaro et al (2004) studied 254 patients treated with this

Table 67-1. Outcomes for Sling Material

Author	Year	Sling Material	Sling Length (cm)	Study (n)	Previous Surgery (%)	Concomitant Prolapse (%)	Mixed Incontinence (%)	Evaluated (n)	Evaluation Method	Follow-up (mo)	Cure Rate (%)
Autologous Slings											
Beck et al	1988	AFL	NR	170	100	NR	NE	170	PE, U, C	NR	98
Zaragoza	1996	ARF	8	60	40	0	58	60	C	25	95
Mason and Roach	1996	ARF	4	63	0	76	NR	63	Q, U, C	12	93
Chaikin et al	1998	ARF	15	251	Yes*	Yes	NR	251	Q, VD, PE	36	73
Hassouna and Ghoniem	1999	ARF	7	112	Yes†	60	51	78	Q	41	78
Morgan et al	2000	ARF	8	247	Yes‡	87	44	247	Q, PE, C	51	88
Richter et al	2001	ARF, AFL	24	63	46	29	1	30	PE, C	42	85
Groutz et al	2001	ARF	NR	69	43	0	0	67	Q, VD, PT	34	67
Chou et al	2003	ARF	NR	131	22	NR	52	98	Q, VD, PT, PE	36	97
Latini et al	2004	AFL	18	100	NR	NR	NR	63	Q, C	52	85
Allografts											
Amundsen et al	2000	CFL-F	15	104	38	39	65	91	Q, VD, PE, C	19	63
Carbone et al	2001	CFL-F	7	154	24	63	NR	145	Q, PE, C	11	62
Walsh et al	2002	CFL-F	10	31	65	19	55	31	Q, VD, C	13	94
Richter et al	2003	CFL-F	25	102	NR	59	NR	100	Q, C	35	33
Carey and Leach	2004	CFL-S	7	234	NR	100	56	234	Q, PE, C	12	55
Crivellaro et al	2004	CD	4	253	57	77	62	234	Q, C	18	53
Owen and Winters	2004	CD	12	25	NR	52	28	25	C	15	32
Xenografts											
Pelosi et al	2002	BP	NR	22	23	NR	0	22	C	20	95
Rutner et al	2003	SIS	10	152	NR	NR	8	152	C	28	93
Arunkalaivanan and Barrington	2003	PD	NR	74	NR	NR	NR	74	Q, C	12	89
Wiedemann and Otto	2004	SIS	10	15	47	NR	20	15	C	NR	93

AFL, autologous fascia lata; ARF, autologous rectus fascia; BP, bovine pericardium; CD, cadaveric dermis; CFL-F, cadaveric fascia lata, freeze-dried; CFL-S, cadaveric fascia lata, solvent dehydrated; PD, porcine dermis; SIS, small intestine submucosa.

Evaluation types: C, chart review; PE, physical examination; PT, pad test; Q, questionnaire; VD, voiding diary; U, urodynamics.

*Patients with simple incontinence underwent 0.8 previous procedure/person; patients with complex incontinence underwent 3.1 previous procedures/person.

†Patients underwent 1.4 previous procedures/person.

‡Patients with type II stress urinary incontinence underwent 0.9 previous procedure/person; patients with type III underwent 2.4 previous procedures/person.

material. Patients with type II, type III, and mixed incontinence were well represented in the study. Outcomes were determined through patient response to symptom-specific validated questionnaires. **At a mean follow-up of 18 months, 57% and 55% of patients with type II and type III incontinence were completely dry.** In a different study, Owen and Winters (2004) reported that only 8 of 25 patients (32%) remained dry at 15 months of mean follow-up. More studies are needed to confirm outcomes for this material.

Xenograft

As with allograft dermal slings, few data are available for xenograft sling outcomes. Rutner et al (2003) studied 152 patients treated with porcine subintestinal mucosal slings during a 4-year period. Of these patients, 136 had type II, 4 had type III, and 12 had mixed incontinence. At a median follow-up of 2.3 years, 94% were defined as cured on the basis of patient questionnaire responses. There is a similar paucity of data regarding porcine dermal sling outcomes. In the largest series, Arunkalaivanan and Barrington (2003) reported a mean cure rate of 89% for 74 patients observed for a mean of 12 months after surgery. With the exception of a 2002 pilot study of 22 patients (Pelosi et al, 2002), no clinical data are available on the efficacy of bovine pericardium slings.

Slings Combined with Reconstructive Procedures

Slings and Pelvic Organ Prolapse

Pelvic organ prolapse represents a global or specific loss of tissue support within the female pelvis. Consequently, many patients with prolapse also have stress urinary incontinence. Bai and coworkers (2002) demonstrated an inverse relationship between degree of pelvic organ prolapse and the risk of stress incontinence. However, prolapsed pelvic organs can mask symptoms of incontinence by absorption of abdominal pressure during strain or by mechanically kinking the urethra (Bergman et al, 1988; Gardy et al, 1991). **Urodynamics can be useful to detect occult stress incontinence through examination of secondary signs, such as an open bladder neck, filling of the proximal urethra on Valsalva maneuver, or severe urethral hypermobility** (McGuire et al, 1991). Gardy and coworkers (1991) were able to demonstrate that up to 60% of patients who had cystoceles but no symptoms of stress incontinence actually had urodynamic evidence of urine leakage.

Pubovaginal sling procedures frequently accompany the surgical correction of pelvic organ prolapse. In Shah's series of 29 patients undergoing total pelvic reconstruction with synthetic mesh, 66% had symptomatic stress incontinence, 79% had anterior prolapse, and 45% had posterior prolapse. On follow-up evaluation at 12 weeks, 79% did not require pads for protection and 7% had recurrent prolapse (Shah et al, 2004). In 2000, Kobashi and colleagues described a combined cadaveric fascia lata sling and cystocele repair. A follow-up, multicenter study of this technique for 172 patients had a mean follow-up time of 12.4 months. Outcomes were determined by physical examination to grade the degree of prolapse and validated questionnaire to determine the severity of stress incontinence. Recurrent cystoceles were found in 13% and de

novo apical prolapse in 10%. Stress incontinence of any degree was present in 18% at follow-up. There are no data to suggest that the sling material type influences outcomes of combined procedures. Comparative studies are needed.

Slings and Reconstruction of the Eroded Urethra

Urethral destruction may occur from erosion of synthetic pubovaginal slings, obstetric or pelvic trauma, or indwelling catheter erosion. In a contemporary literature review, Blaivas and Sandhu (2004) noted that postoperative incontinence occurred in 44% to 83% of patients after urethral reconstruction for eroded sling material. When an anti-incontinence procedure is performed at the time of reconstruction, postoperative incontinence is present in 13%. For patients with loss of urethra length due to destruction of tissue, Blaivas and Heritz (1996) also described lengthening the urethra by use of lateral vaginal flaps. The proximal urethra is covered with an autologous rectus fascial sling to preserve continence, and a Martius labial pedicle graft is interposed between the sling and urethral reconstruction to prevent pressure necrosis from the sling. At a mean follow-up of 4 years, 42 of 49 patients were successfully treated with this technique.

Slings and Urethral Diverticula

Urinary incontinence and urethral diverticula occur within the same demographic of perimenopausal women. In a series of 14 patients with urethral diverticula, Swierzewski and McGuire (1993) reported that 10 had urinary incontinence as the chief complaint. Patients with diverticulum measuring larger than 4 cm and horseshoe-shaped diverticulum may be at greater risk for complications such as stress incontinence after repair (Porpiglia et al, 2002). Some series report the rate of postoperative stress incontinence to be as high as 25% (Lee, 1984; Porpiglia et al, 2002). Consequently, a pubovaginal sling is commonly performed at the time of urethral diverticulectomy, particularly for women with concomitant type II or type III stress incontinence. The sling may be placed directly over the repair, or a Martius labial pedicle graft can be interposed between the urethral suture line and the sling material to reduce tension on the repair site (Leach, 1991). **Outcomes for autologous pubovaginal sling at the time of urethral diverticulectomy, defined as no postoperative stress incontinence, approach a 90% cure rate** (Leng and McGuire, 1998).

Slings Associated with Bladder Reconstruction

Little information is available regarding the efficacy of pubovaginal slings when they are combined with surgery for bladder reconstruction. In a series of 101 female patients treated with orthotopic ileal neobladder reconstruction, Quek and coworkers (2004) found only 4 patients requiring surgical treatment of postoperative stress urinary incontinence. However, two of these women developed significant complications from the retropubic dissection, including one enteropouch fistula. Watanabe and colleagues (1996) collected information on 18 women with indwelling catheters, treated with pubovaginal slings and ileovesicostomy or bladder augmentation. Although the efficacy of the sling in treating incontinence is not well quantified, the authors found that pubovaginal sling surgery established "perineal dryness" in 13 patients. Most patients had improvement in body image or sexual quality of life after indwelling catheter removal.

SUGGESTED READINGS

Austin PF, Westney OL, Leng WW, et al: Advantages of rectus fascial slings for urinary incontinence in children with neuropathic bladders. J Urol 2001;165(pt 2):2369-2371.

Chou EC, Flisser AJ, Panagopoulos G, Blaivas JG: Effective treatment for mixed urinary incontinence with a pubovaginal sling. J Urol 2003;170(pt 1):494-497.

Govier FE, Kobashi K: Pubovaginal slings: A review of the technical variables. Curr Opin Urol 2001;11:405-410.

Groutz A, Blaivas JG, Hyman MJ, Chaikin DC: Pubovaginal sling surgery for simple stress urinary incontinence: Analysis by an outcome score. J Urol 2001;165:1597-1600.

Morgan TO Jr, Westney OL, McGuire EJ: Pubovaginal sling: 4-year outcome analysis and quality of life assessment. J Urol 2000;163:1845-1848.

Wilson TS, Lemack GE, Zimmern PE: Management of intrinsic sphincteric deficiency in women. J Urol 2003;169:1662-1669.

68 Tension-Free Vaginal Tape Procedures

ROGER DMOCHOWSKI, MD, FACS •
HARRIETTE SCARPERO, MD • JONATHAN STARKMAN, MD

THE TENSION-FREE VAGINAL TAPE PROCEDURE

TRANSOBTURATOR SLINGS

Since the inception of the pubovaginal sling approximately a century ago, experimentation has continued with multiple types of slings composed of different materials using different suspension techniques. Materials used as sling constituents have included autografts, allografts, xenografts, and, more recently, synthetic variants. Methods of anchoring these slings have also undergone development and advancement; however, the ideal method of suspension remains to be completely defined. **Sling placement was classically described at the level of the bladder neck in an effort to correct urethral hypermobility and enhance pressure transmission invoked by intra-abdominal straining.**

However, competing theories arose initially as espoused by Zaccharin in the 1960s and DeLancey in the 1990s (Zaccharin, 1968; DeLancey, 1994). In these theories, the importance of the pubourethral ligaments and their function in maintaining the integrity of urinary control **furthered the concept of the importance of the midurethral mechanism for preservation of urinary incontinence under stress circumstances. These findings further demonstrate the fact that hypermobility is a secondary finding noted in association with incontinence but not causative of the condition of effort-related urinary loss (stress incontinence).** Studies performed by Asmussen and Ulmsten (1983) demonstrated the importance of the distal components of the urethra for preserving urethral closure during stress events. They demonstrated that maximal urethral closure pressure occurs at the level of the midurethra and this closure mechanism is associated with intrinsic urethral function in continent women. Ingelman-Sundberg (1953) noted that the pubococcygeal muscles also played a role in the midurethral mechanism, inserting at the level of the midurethra just outside the vaginal epithelial wall, and propounded this anatomic finding as being important when considering methods to correct urinary incontinence. Westby and colleagues (1982) demonstrated that in continent women midurethral closure is associated with the area of maximum urethral closure pressures on pressure evaluation of the urethra and considered this phenomenon to be due to the confluence of anatomic structures in that area.

Petros and Ulmsten, using these theories, **proposed a unifying concept now known as the midurethra theory (previously the integral theory)** (Petros and Ulmsten, 1993). They postulated that **injury arising from surgery, parturition, aging, or hormonal deprivation led to weakening or damage of the pubourethral ligaments, impairing midurethral function and anterior urethral wall support, thus resulting in urinary incontinence. They theorized that this damage was not only a ligamentous injury but also a representation of weakening of the pubococcygeal muscles at the level of the midurethra.** It has been shown that weakness of soft tissue in this area and specifically connective tissue can contribute to urinary incontinence (Ulmsten et al, 1987).

THE TENSION-FREE VAGINAL TAPE PROCEDURE

Transvaginal taping was developed using the concepts of the integral theory. The provisions of this operation include a **minimally invasive approach, which would supplement the diminished midurethral mechanism and produce the ingrowth of new host tissues after implantation for purposes of further supplementing support introduced by the procedure.** As initially described, the procedure was performed under local anesthesia to allow ambulatory delivery of the intervention.

Initially, several types of material were evaluated until the final material was chosen, **a synthetic polypropylene monofilament mesh with pore size under 150 μm. Also, this material allowed optimal migration of host inflammatory components (leukocytes and macrophages) into the mesh for purposes of infectious surveillance and host wound healing (imbibition and inosculation). It was found that this material was optimal for inciting fibrous tissue ingrowth. This type of mesh is known as a type 1 mesh** and has previously been described in the general surgical literature as being favorable from the standpoints of its mechanical properties (stretch and elasticity) (Dietz et al, 2001, 2003). Efforts have been made to standardize the procedure by incorporating certain technical approaches and safety features for purposes of avoiding injury to surrounding structures. To date, more than 400,000 of these procedures have been performed worldwide.

The Procedure

The device consists of two specially curved 5-mm-diameter insertion needles that are attached to a 40-cm segment of polypropylene tape that is 11 mm wide. The tape is covered with a clear plastic sheath, which protects the tape from contamination and allows easy passage through host tissues. A rigid catheter guide is placed in the bladder with an 18 French Foley catheter to help deflect the bladder away from the locale of needle path insertion. An ergonomic handle is attached to the insertion needles for actual placement of the needles during the procedure. This handle is reusable and sterilizable.

The midurethra sling procedure (transvaginal tape) is performed with the patient in the dorsal lithotomy position with a significant degree of flexion (70 degrees or more) of the thighs. As heretofore described, the patient has received parenteral sedation and then local anesthetics are placed in the region of insertion of the device (vaginal wall and retropubic space). Approximately 5 mL of local anesthetic is injected into the vaginal area as well as into the planned suprapubic insertion skin sites. For placement of retropubic local anesthesia, another 20 mL of local anesthetic agent is injected into the area along the posterior aspect of the pubic bone to the level of the urogenital diaphragm. Additional vaginal infiltration includes approximately 10 mL injected on either side of the urethra to the level of the urogenital diaphragm.

After appropriate anesthesia, two small suprapubic stab incisions are created just above the level of the symphysis pubis, approximately 2 cm lateral to the midline. A third midline vaginal incision approximately 1.5 cm wide is created approximately 1.5 cm from the external meatus of the urethra, between that structure and the bladder neck. After the vaginal incision is created, minimal dissection is performed using Metzenbaum scissors under the vaginal flaps on either side to elevate the vaginal epithelium from the underlying periurethral tissue to the level of the pubocervical fascia, which is not perforated. The tension-free vaginal tape (TVT) needle is then placed in the dissection tunnel immediately beneath the vaginal epithelium on one side of the urethra with the needle tip situated in close proximity to the lower rim of the pubic ramus. Using controlled pressure, the needle is elevated through the endopelvic fascia, into the space of Retzius, through the rectus muscles and through the previously created suprapubic skin incision. During this maneuver, the needle is kept in close contact with the intrapelvic surface of the pubic bone in order to avoid perforation of the lower urinary tract and also to avoid intraperitoneal entry. Tactile contact ensures direct apposition of metal to bone, as does slow graded pressure during needle advancement.

Simultaneous deflection of the lower urinary tract is accomplished during insertion using the catheter guide and catheter with pelvic viscera deflected away from the side of needle insertion. The same maneuver is performed contralaterally so that each needle exits through the appropriate skin incision. Cystoscopy is performed to exclude needle penetration of the lower urinary tract. The use of a 70-degree lens is essential, as is complete distention of the bladder with irrigant to exclude subtle tangential injury. If perforation is noted, the needle is withdrawn and passed once more in the same area in an effort to avoid further perforation. Once cystoscopy has demonstrated no evidence of bladder injury, the tape is brought through the incisions and tension adjustment of the tape is performed. Tension adjustment is most commonly performed by inserting either a surgical instrument (clamp) or a metallic sound between the tape and urethra while the covering plastic sheath is removed from the field. The tape is set to tension such that with the bladder full to 300 mL of saline and the patient now aroused and asked to cough, no incontinence occurs during the stress maneuver. Redundant tape is then excised at the level of the suprapubic skin incisions and all incisions are closed (Fig. 68–1).

The procedure may also be performed under regional or general anesthesia according to the surgeon's preference. Outcome data support the incorporation of midurethral sling techniques with concomitant vaginal prolapse repairs.

Results

In reviewing the extensive results reporting for the midurethral sling, several caveats must be entertained. Outcomes are reported in varying fashions using different tools, lengths of follow-up, and overall definitions of success and failure. These factors should be kept in mind when attempting to cross-compare different groups and procedural nuances.

Initial results with the midurethral sling technique approximated 80% (author-defined) success rates (Ulmsten et al, 1996). A subsequent prospective multicenter trial that included 130 women with genuine stress incontinence (GSI) who were observed for 1 year revealed success rates of 91% (Ulmsten et al, 1998). Seven percent were considered improved and only 2% deemed failures. Complication rates were low, including one bladder perforation and one wound infection. Voiding dysfunction was also relatively low, with one patient experiencing retention for 12 days, which resolved spontaneously, and three patients with less than 3 days of voiding dysfunction (regarding catheterization), which the authors defined as a short-term voiding problem.

On the basis of these findings, further studies were then embarked upon. Nilsson and Kuuva (2001) evaluated 161 consecutive TVT operations in cases of which 28% had failed prior incontinence surgery, 11% had intrinsic sphincteric deficiency (ISD), and 37% had mixed incontinence. At 16 months mean follow-up, the overall objective cure rate was 87% with 7% significantly improved and another 5% considered failures. Bladder injury rate at the time of insertion was 3.7%, and 4.3% of women experienced short-term de novo voiding dysfunction. Urge symptoms arising after surgery occurred in 3% of women, yet 80% of the women who had preoperative urgency symptoms had relief of those symptoms at their 16-month visit. No serious complications were noted.

Long-term results mirror the short-term experience with this procedure. Success rates ranging from 81% to 90% have been reported at more than 3 years. Ulmsten (1999) reported an 86% success rate in 50 women at 3 years. Olsson reported 90% success in 51 women at 3 years (Olsson and Kroon, 1999). Nilsson reported success rates of 84.7% at 5 years (Nilsson et al, 2001) and 81.3% at 7 years (Nilsson et al, 2004)

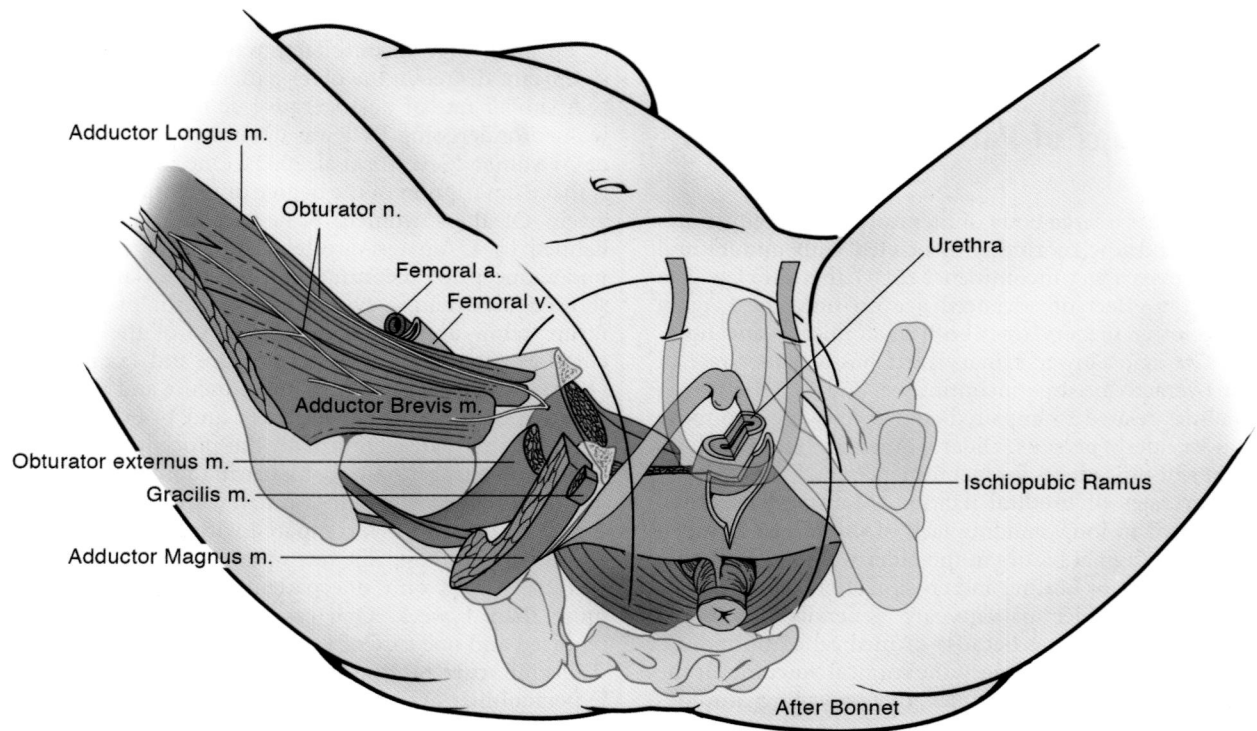

Figure 68–1. Midurethral sling as placed by the suprapubic approach (any technique).

in a consistent cohort of 90 women. These long-term studies have attempted to evaluate risk factors for declining effectiveness. **There does appear to be a tendency for higher failure rates to be associated with advancing age at the time of procedure and also with diminished urethral function (intrinsic sphincter deficiency).** Notable, **the long-term studies demonstrate an absence of signs of long-term tissue erosion or other complications related to material insertion.**

The most stringent evaluation of this technique has occurred in four randomized controlled clinical trials that have compared it with the colposuspension procedure. The most meticulously designed trial was that of the UK/Ireland cooperative group, which compared TVT with open colposuspension. One hundred seventy-five women underwent TVT and 169 underwent Burch suspension. Clinical follow-up was continued for 24 months. A variety of outcome measures including subjective and objective measures were utilized. Overall cure rates noted in the study were lower than other reported cure rates, with 63% of TVT patients and 51% of colposuspension patients being cured (Table 68–1) (Ward and Hilton, 2004).

Three other randomized trials have been performed: one that compared TVT with laparoscopic colposuspension using mesh (Valpas et al, 2004), another that used laparoscopic colposuspension with Gortex sutures as the comparator (Persson et al, 2002), and a third that used laparoscopic colposuspension with polyfilament polyester sutures as the comparator technique to TVT (Paraiso et al, 2004). Valpas and Persson reported results at 12 months, and Paraiso reported outcomes at 18 months. The results of the laparoscopic trials revealed TVT cure rates in the range of 86% to 97%, with colposus-

Table 68–1. **Comparator Tabulation of Outcomes Obtained with the Tension-Free Vaginal Tape and Burch Procedure in a Randomized Analysis**

	Tension-Free Vaginal Tape (%)	Colposuspension (%)
Urodynamics (UDS)	81	67
1-hour pad test	73	64
Objective cure		
Negative urodynamic studies + pad test	66	57
Subjective cure		
No stress incontinence	59	53
No incontinence	36	28
Response to procedure		
Satisfied	85	82
Recommend	84	82

From Ward K, Hilton P: A prospective multicenter randomized trial of tension-free vaginal tape and colposuspension for primary stress incontinence. Two-year follow-up. Am J Obstet Gynecol 2004;190:324-331.

pension rates ranging from 57% to 100%, depending on the reporting method. There was no apparent difference between procedures in the Persson trial, but Paraiso and Valpas noted significant differences in success in the two study groups. These trials noted no other apparent differences between techniques other than that the TVT group recovered more rapidly and had a lower need for subsequent urogenital prolapse procedures than the colposuspension group.

An expanding area of concern with any new technology is the cost effectiveness and impact on diminishing health care resources. The procedure is cost effective and superior in terms of impact on health care spending compared with open colposuspension (Manca).

Special Groups of Patients

Elderly

Although there is a large body of literature that demonstrates the efficacy and low morbidity associated with midurethral slings for stress urinary incontinence (SUI), there are few data evaluating the effect of advanced age on outcomes. Aging affects the lower urinary tract both anatomically and functionally. The aging lower urinary tract has a higher rate of detrusor overactivity, urge incontinence, and ISD. Emptying abnormalities related to impaired contractility are also more common in elderly persons. Older women are more likely to have had prior procedures for incontinence and therefore may have higher rates of urethral fixation. More severe vaginal atrophy related to long-standing lack of salubrious estrogen support of the vaginal tissues in the older woman could pose a greater risk of poor healing and erosion after vaginal incontinence surgery. Older patients are generally considered poorer surgical candidates because of medical comorbidities that could complicate the surgery, the surgical outcome, or the postoperative course. Prior studies and prevailing attitudes maintain that retropubic suspensions and vaginal procedures for stress incontinence in elderly patients have variable rates of success (Gillon and Stanton, 1984; Schmidbauer et al, 1986; Couillard et al, 1994; Chilaka et al, 2002).

Few studies of relatively small numbers of patients examine the safety and efficacy of midurethral slings in older women. In all these studies, "old" is defined as 70 years of age and older. The most robust of the studies is a prospective comparison of 460 consecutive women who underwent TVT surgery (Gordon et al, 2005); 157 (34%) were elderly, and all women underwent urodynamic evaluations preoperatively and 3 months postoperatively. Outcome measures were compared between elderly and younger patients with follow-up of at least 12 months, and mean follow-up was 26 months. Preoperatively, a statistically significant greater prevalence of mixed incontinence was noted in the older (31%) versus younger (23%) patients. Concomitant pelvic organ prolapse surgery was undertaken in 84% of older patients and 67% of younger patients. The main outcome measures evaluated were perioperative morbidity, postoperative SUI, persistent or de novo urge incontinence, and voiding dysfunction. Intraoperative complications were infrequent. The rates of blood loss were equal, and there were significantly fewer bladder perforations in the elderly patients. The incidence of postoperative fever, urinary tract infection, wound infection, and hematoma formation was similar in the two groups. Older patients did experience some age-related morbidities such as pulmonary embolism (two), cardiac arrhythmia (two), deep vein thrombosis (one) and pneumonia (one), whereas younger patients had only one case of cardiac arrhythmia. Older women experienced no increased risk of urethral erosion or vaginal extrusion. The rates of postoperative voiding dysfunction necessitating catheterization for more than 1 week were low and similar between groups. Only one patient, an older woman, required urethrolysis. Rates of persistent SUI were uniformly low and no higher in the older women. Rates of

urge incontinence were similar between groups, but the rate of de novo urge incontinence was greater to a statistically significant degree in the older patients (18% versus 4%).

A similar rate of postoperative de novo urgency in elderly women undergoing TVT was documented in a smaller study of 76 women (Sevestre et al, 2003). One strength of this study is that a description of the degree of urethral hypermobility is given. Of these women, 53% had urethral hypermobility defined by Q-tip test greater than 30 degrees, 28.9% had undergone prior incontinence procedures, and four (5.2%) showed urodynamic evidence of detrusor overactivity. At a mean follow-up of 24.6 months, 67% of the patients were cured as determined by questionnaire and examination. Ten (13.7%) had persistent stress incontinence and all of these had negative Q-tip tests preoperatively, and 14 (18.4%) had urge incontinence. Satisfaction with the procedure was 82% and rates of dissatisfaction were higher in those with de novo urge incontinence. For the older women with a negative Q-tip test, the cure rate was 71%, compared with 100% in women with a positive Q-tip test. The rate of immediate urinary retention was 26.3%, but only one patient had urinary retention for more than 1 week. One case of bladder perforation was reported and one case of vaginal erosion.

Overall, **cure rates at least in older women with urethral hypermobility are comparable to those in younger women.** Complication rates vary, with some studies citing a higher rate of age-related morbidities but no apparent increase in intraoperative complications. **Postoperative voiding dysfunction or increased de novo urgency does seem to be a complication of greater incidence and significant impact in older women.** Postoperative urgency symptoms in as many as 60% of women older than 70 years have been reported (Allahdin et al, 2004), and 44% developed the symptom de novo. A sensation of impaired emptying postoperatively has also been reported (Sevestre et al, 2003). Furthermore, one study documented a 4-fold increase in the need for repeated urodynamics in older women after TVT and an approximately 30-fold higher risk of further surgery to divide the tape.

Another important measure of the success of TVT in elderly patients is quality of life assessments. The outcome of TVT was assessed prospectively in older women at a mean follow-up of 22 months by a validated health-related quality of life instrument, the King's Health Questionnaire (Walsh et al, 2004). The improvement in stress incontinence was greater in the age group younger than 70, which is not clearly attributed to any preoperative factor. Rates of preoperative detrusor overactivity were 24% versus 9% in older and younger women, respectively. Older women had a history of prior surgery more often than younger women (67% versus 28%) and lower leak point pressures, but no specific comment on their physical examination and degree of urethral hypermobility was made. Although the outcome for TVT was successful, the hospital course may be longer, as found by Walsh and colleagues (2004). The mean hospital stay in their series was 6 days, indicating that the postoperative morbidity in this age group was significant. The reasons for the longer hospital stays were not given in this study.

Obesity

Whether obesity affects surgical outcome with TVT is controversial. A few small studies have examined the safety and efficacy of TVT in this population. In a prospective study of 242 women with GSI, women were stratified into three groups on the basis of body mass index (BMI) (Mukherjee and Constantine, 2001). The cure rate in obese women was 90% versus 95% in women with a BMI of 25 to 29 and 85% in those with a BMI less than 25. No women experienced a wound infection, and there was no higher rate of retropubic hematoma in obese women. In addition, obese patients undergoing TVT did not demonstrate a statistically significant difference in the incidence of voiding dysfunction: de novo urge symptoms, urge incontinence, or voiding disorders. Although few in number, studies with 6- to 12-month follow-up support equal efficacy and no difference in intraoperative or postoperative complication rate. No relation between obesity and the occurrence of bladder injury has been found (Lovastis et al, 2003; Rafii et al, 2003). Despite the success of TVT in obese women, there is a reported case of necrotizing surgical site infection after TVT placement in a 53-year-old obese woman (Connolly, 2004). Morbidly obese patients have a 44% increased risk of postoperative infectious morbidity (Forse et al, 1989). Obesity poses a greater risk for necrotizing fasciitis than diabetes in obstetric and gynecologic procedures (Gallup et al, 2002). Standard antibiotic prophylaxis and the time of surgery may need to be altered for the morbidly obese to provide adequate tissue levels, and infected tapes require complete removal. Obese women, like all women undergoing midurethral sling, should be counseled about the risk of infection.

Concomitant Pelvic Organ Prolapse

A large proportion of women with stress incontinence have associated pelvic organ prolapse that requires concurrent treatment. Many studies have explored the outcomes of TVT with concomitant surgery. **The advantage of using a synthetic sling with concomitant surgery is that operative time is reduced sizably and blood loss from the TVT portion is usually minimal compared with autologous slings or retropubic suspensions. Some of the theoretical risks of midurethral slings with concomitant transvaginal surgery are that the increased dissection will increase exposure of the graft, leading to greater rates of infection, erosion, or vaginal extrusion, or that increased blood loss or anatomic distortion from the concomitant procedures could increase the rate of sling migration and postoperative voiding dysfunction or obstruction. These studies tend to be small and have short followup, but results suggest that TVT can be added to prolapse surgery with minimal morbidity.** Success rates in combined TVT and prolapse repair vary from 88% to 93% (Jomaa, 2001; Huang et al, 2003; Meltomaa et al, 2004). Even in questionnaire-based assessments 3 years after surgery, the data do not show a statistical difference in the cure rate of SUI and incidence of urge symptoms after TVT alone or in combination with other vaginal surgery (Meltomaa et al, 2004). Transient urinary retention occurred more often in patients undergoing concomitant vaginal surgery, but urethrolysis rates were low and not statistically different between groups. Interpretations of rates of postoperative urinary retention are limited by variation in the definition of retention, and therefore caution must be exercised when reviewing outcomes.

Gordon and colleagues (2005) examined TVT as a prophylactic procedure for stress incontinence in prolapse repairs. None of the patients had undergone prior incontinence surgery. With a mean followup of 14 months, no patient developed symptomatic stress incontinence, but three had a positive stress test urodynamically. Six of nine patients with preoperative urgency had persistent symptoms, and four (13.3%) developed de novo urgency without evidence of obstruction. No woman had urinary retention lasting more than 2 weeks. Subsequent 5-year data from a prospective analysis of a large group of women undergoing TVT for occult stress incontinence combined with transvaginal repair of second or third-degree prolapse showed a low incidence of complications (Groutz et al, 2004). The authors reported that one case of bladder perforation was managed conservatively without consequence. Two patients experienced extended voiding difficulty requiring catheterization for more than 7 days, but urethrolysis was not necessary in any case. Three cases of vaginal erosion were documented. Two patients developed recurrent symptomatic stress incontinence, and another 15 patients were found to have asymptomatic urodynamically confirmed stress incontinence. Eight patients developed de novo urge incontinence, and 72% of the 18 patients with preoperative urge incontinence had postoperative persistent incontinence.

Although **concurrent surgery does not appear to alter success of TVT,** whether concurrent surgery alters the time to efficient voiding or incidence of urinary retention has been examined separately in a retrospective study of 267 women (Sokol et al, 2005). Without standard definitions of urinary retention, results are not comparable between studies. Sokol and coauthors found no difference in prolonged urinary retention rates between patients who had TVT alone or TVT with prolapse repair. Factors independently associated with a longer time to adequate voiding were increasing age, decreasing BMI, and presence of a urinary tract infection postoperatively. Preoperative urodynamic parameters did not predict postoperative urinary retention. No statistically significant difference in the rate of urethrolysis between TVT alone and TVT with prolapse repair was found.

Unlike most other authors, Partoll (2002) claimed that urinary retention is far more common after combined procedures than TVT alone. Results showed a 94% cure rate at 11 months and an alarming 43% rate of urinary retention after concurrent anterior or posterior repair. However, in her study urinary retention was defined as not meeting the criteria for catheter removal on postoperative day 2. The expectation of voiding efficiently within 48 hours of surgery, rather than the more lenient expectations in other studies, probably accounts for the higher rate of retention found in her study.

TVT performed with either transvaginal or laparoscopic-assisted vaginal hysterectomy and anterior/posterior colporrhaphy has been shown to have success rates similar to those in published series of TVT alone (Huang et al, 2005). Complication rates were also in accordance with other TVT series, with 2% bladder perforation, 11% postoperative urgency, and 11% postoperative voiding difficulty. A study specifically looking at the complications and cure rates of TVT performed with or without vaginal hysterectomy found that there was no overall difference (Darai et al, 2002). The TVT-hysterectomy group did have a trend toward more bladder perforation and lower postoperative urinary flow rates, but it was not statistically significant. Objective and subjective cures for this group were 92.5% and 75%, respectively, which was not significantly different from the TVT-alone group.

Secondary or Salvage Procedure

There are limited data regarding the efficacy of midurethral slings as secondary surgery in women with recurrent incontinence. Five small studies with relatively short follow-up could be found addressing the issue (Azam et al, 2001; Rezapour and Ulmsten, 2001; Kuuva and Nilsson, 2002, 2003; Lo et al, 2002a; Rardin et al, 2002b). Comparison of the studies is hampered by differences in the definitions used for cure, improved, and failed. The population of patients may be considered skewed by the inclusion of women in whom bulking agents failed. It is debatable whether women in whom bulking agents fail are the same as those in whom a surgical anti-incontinence procedure has failed. The methods of evaluating outcomes (objective, subjective, or both) also differ between studies. Despite these limitations between studies, cure rates of a midurethral sling after prior failed anti-incontinence surgery vary from 81% to 89.6%. Failure rates vary from 4.2% to 13%. In a review of these articles, several trends emerge: **the procedure can be performed in the same way as it is performed for primary GSI. The complication rate is similar to that of TVT done for primary SUI, but risk of bladder perforation appears to be higher in women who have had one or more prior retropubic suspensions. The failure rate is higher in women with immobile urethras, as is the case in primary surgery.**

The longest follow-up of women who underwent TVT for recurrent incontinence is 4 years in a study by Rezapour and Ulmsten (2001). The 34 women studied had undergone 64 different anti-incontinence surgeries. Any patient with significant prolapse, detrusor overactivity, or ISD defined as a maximal urethral closure pressure of less than 20 cm H$_2$O was excluded. By physical examination, 24 women had a hypermobile urethra. Ten had a less mobile urethra, but none had a fixed urethra. The procedure was performed using the standard TVT technique, and only one bladder perforation occurred in a patient with a prior Marshall-Marchetti-Krantz (MMK) urethroplasty. No significant complications were encountered. Twenty-eight (82%) were cured by objective and subjective parameters, three (9%) were improved based on failure to achieve more than 90% improvement in quality of life, and three were failures. Postoperative voiding dysfunction was negligible with no change in postvoid residual urine after 8 weeks. Long-term catheterization was not necessary in any patient. These results were durable up to 5 years.

The mechanism of failure in midurethral slings is typically misplacement of the suburethral tape or inadequate tension on the tape. Little is known about whether revision or repeated midurethral sling procedure is feasible after a failed primary midurethral sling, but it appears from a few reports of small numbers that recurrent incontinence after a midurethral sling may be treated with a repeated midurethral sling (Riachi et al, 2002; Villet et al, 2002). As for whether a revision or repeated midurethral sling is feasible after a failed primary midurethral sling, there are three case reports including nine patients in all that describe success. A new surgical technique of plication and shortening of a TVT tape by non-

absorbable 0 nylon suture was described. The author proposed that the technique also allows readjustment of tape position (Villet et al, 2002). Taking only 8 to 12 minutes, it was quick, easy, and without complication. The procedure was described as successful in three of four women on the basis of subjective report and a negative cough stress test.

Mixed Incontinence

Evidence suggests that TVT has successful outcomes for women with mixed urinary symptoms as well. However, interpretation of these studies should be judicious as many outcomes were reported on the basis of symptoms only, with no urodynamic substantiation.

In a retrospective analysis of 112 consecutive women with GSI and mixed incontinence, the objective cure rate as measured by clinical and urodynamic examination was 89.3% at a mean follow-up of 25 months. Objective cure was defined as no evidence of stress incontinence, a negative stress provocation test, and no urinary retention or residual greater than 150 mL. No difference was found in the objective cure rate between patients with GSI and those with mixed incontinence. The overall subjective cure rate determined by the Contilife questionnaire was 66%. Subjective cure was lower than objective cure in both GSI patients and patients with mixed incontinence, 69.3% and 54.2%, respectively. The type of incontinence did not alter the incidence of postoperative voiding difficulty. Ten of the 24 patients with mixed incontinence had persistence of the urge component (Jeffry et al, 2002).

Holmgren and colleagues (2005) evaluated the outcome of TVT in women with stress and mixed incontinence with mailed questionnaires 2 to 8 years postoperatively. This was a large cohort of 970 women, and the 78% response rate was remarkable. Five hundred eighty women with stress incontinence and 112 women with urge incontinence were eligible for analysis. However, urodynamics were not performed in these women pre- or postoperatively, and therefore categorization of their incontinence was based only on a positive stress test and a history of leakage immediately preceded by urgency. The questionnaire itself is not fully described in this article; therefore, it is not clear whether a validated instrument was used. Specific questions regarding stress and urge incontinence were posed, and respondents selected options including worsened, unchanged, improved, almost cured, and cured.

For analysis, the women were grouped into cohorts by the number of years since they had undergone TVT surgery. The mean age of women with mixed incontinence was greater than the age of women with stress incontinence (67 versus 61.2), and this was a statistically significant difference. Adjustment for age was made in the analysis. In addition, women with mixed incontinence had a statistically significant higher BMI, rate of cesarean delivery, and prevalence of urinary frequency than those with stress incontinence. More women with mixed incontinence had a history of radiation for gynecologic malignancy. Although the numbers were small, radiation may have had repercussions for bladder function that cannot be fully elucidated by questionnaire and could skew results.

Sixty percent of women with mixed incontinence were cured up to 3 years after surgery, but outcome declined steadily thereafter. By 6 to 8 years postoperatively, the cure rate in women with mixed incontinence was only 30%. Urgency and episodes of urge incontinence increased with time after the TVT. In the final analysis, the lower rate of cure in the patients with mixed incontinence may be due to the other variables in this population such as age, cesarean section, radiation, and higher BMI. These differences in the populations confound the ability to assess outcome and highlight the limitations of this study design. Overall, despite the population variables, early outcomes of TVT are good and equal in women with stress incontinence and those with urge incontinence. The diminishment of results over time needs to be confirmed by a prospective study (Holmgren et al, 2005).

In a similar Finnish study, 191 women who underwent TVT were evaluated by examination or telephone interview for outcome at a mean follow-up of 17 months. Sixty-four (34%) of these women had preoperative stress-predominant mixed urinary incontinence. None of the women had preoperative urodynamic evaluation; instead, the preoperative diagnosis was based on symptoms. Cure after TVT was judged as self-report of completely dry in any stress situation. At latest follow-up, 164 of the 187 patients were completely cured, for a cure rate of 87.7%. The cure rate in women with mixed incontinence was 69% compared with a cure rate of 97% in the women with pure stress incontinence. This outcome difference was statistically significant. No difference in cure rate was found between women who had concomitant surgery or TVT alone. Sixty percent of the women with mixed incontinence considered themselves improved from an urge incontinence perspective as well. The lower cure rate in the mixed incontinent patients is not fully known. No description of the preoperative physical examination is given, and it is not known how many of them were among the 149 (78%) who had urethral hypermobility. The authors suggested that on the basis of these results, preoperative urodynamics should be performed in women with mixed incontinence prior to anti-incontinence surgery (Laurikainen and Killholma, 2003).

Segal and colleagues (2004) evaluated 98 women after TVT explicitly to answer the question of what happens to the urinary urge incontinence. The outcome of TVT in women with mixed incontinence or significant stress incontinence with associated frequency and urgency was assessed retrospectively by a variety of methods: subjectively by patients' symptoms, by the rate of anticholinergic use before and after TVT, and by before and after quality of life questionnaires. One strength of this study is that patients with concomitant surgery were excluded in order to minimize the confounding effect of other causes on urinary urge incontinence or frequency and urgency. Sixty-five women were identified as having urge incontinence, and follow-up occurred at 3 months and 1 year. Several preoperative factors were looked at for risk of postoperative frequency, urgency, or urge incontinence requiring anticholinergics. On the basis of preoperative subjective symptoms, the urge component was found to be resolved in 63.1% after TVT. Two patients with complaints of urge incontinence only but stress incontinence identified on urodynamics had persistent urinary urge incontinence requiring anticholinergic drug treatment. Seventy-five patients had preoperative urinary frequency and urgency, which resolved in 57.3% after TVT.

Thirty (57.7%) of the 52 patients requiring anticholinergic medications preoperatively no longer needed medication after

surgery. Only four (8.7%) patients needed anticholinergics for the first time after TVT. Of all the variables assessed as possible risk factors for postoperative overactive bladder requiring an anticholinergic, only a history of prior anti-incontinence surgery was statistically significant. Patients with prior surgery were eight times more likely to have postoperative overactive bladder needing anticholinergics.

Overall, the resolution of preoperative urge incontinence was 63% and resolution of preoperative urinary frequency and urgency was 57.3%. Resolution based on no longer needing anticholinergic medication postoperatively was 57.7%. TVT surgery resulted in statistically significant improvement in quality of life scores postoperatively in women with stress-predominant mixed incontinence and stress incontinence with urinary frequency and urgency (Segal et al, 2004).

Rezapour and Ulmsten (2001) reported their 5-year data on the efficacy and safety of TVT in women with mixed incontinence. In all of these women the urge component was sensory, and no woman had urodynamic evidence of detrusor overactivity. Eighty women were evaluated and reported in a retrospective fashion. All had undergone urodynamic evaluation preoperatively and all were found to have stress incontinence as well as motor detrusor contractions during filling. At follow-up, 85% were reported as cured and an additional 4% had improved symptoms on the basis of pad testing and symptom questionnaire. They concluded that urodynamics were essential prior to surgery to analyze presenting symptoms. Only one patient had prolonged retention (6 weeks), but 8% were found to have small hematomas and one patient required exploration for bleeding.

Intrinsic Sphincteric Deficiency

In most evidence sources, intrinsic sphincteric deficiency (ISD) is defined urodynamically as a leak point pressure less than 60 cm H_2O or maximal urethral closure pressures less than 20 cm H_2O. However, several of these articles fail to describe the patients' physical examination or reveal whether any urethral hypermobility existed. What is clear from the current literature is that success of midurethral slings is less in the patient with a fixed urethra, and low leak point pressures seem to portend a poorer outcome, but this may be due to lack of urethral mobility in the same patient. Rezapour and associates (2001) published a prospective 4-year follow-up study of 49 women with ISD who underwent TVT. Forty-one of these women had hypermobility of the urethra; the other eight had immobile urethras. Postoperatively, 36 (74%) of patients were cured, 12% were improved, and 7 patients (14%) failed. None of the women with fixed urethras were cured: three improved and five failed. Other studies support lower cure rates of TVT in women with low leak point pressures when rates of urethral hypermobility are not statistically different (Paick et al, 2004). Urethral mobility before midurethral sling procedures has been shown to be predictive of success. The more the proximal urethra moves during Valsalva maneuvers, the better the cure rate for incontinence (Fritel et al, 2002). Leak point pressures alone have not been shown to predict outcome after a midurethral sling (Gutierrez Banos et al, 2004; Rodriguez et al, 2004); therefore, low leak point pressures are not necessarily a contraindication to TVT. Leak point pressures in the era of the midurethral sling should be correlated with the patient's physical examination and used to counsel patients about their risk for a reduced chance of success.

Mode of Anesthesia

In the original description of the midurethral sling, anesthesia was local so that the patient would be able to perform a cough as a method of adjusting sling tension intraoperatively. It was believed that this would minimize the incidence of obstruction; however, there is conflicting information in the literature regarding whether the mode of anesthesia affects the incidence of intraoperative and postoperative complication. Two studies have failed to show a difference in the efficacy or safety of TVT performed under local or spinal anesthesia (Wang and Chen, 2001; Adamiak et al, 2002). In a study of 103 women who underwent TVT procedures, a comparison of local and spinal anesthesia was made; 67 women underwent the procedure with local and 36 underwent TVT with spinal anesthetic (Adamiak et al, 2002). In the postoperative evaluation there was no difference in the success rate of the TVT performed; there was also no difference in the rate of complication between the groups. There was a difference in the patients' ability to perform a cough test effectively during the procedure because of spinal anesthesia, but this did not result in an increase in the rate of postoperative obstruction. It appears that tensioning the sling by cough stress test is not necessary. Lo and colleagues (2002b) demonstrated that vigorous manual pressure against the abdominal wall and intraoperative introital ultrasonography to set tension resulted in no obstruction in 45 patients at 1 year. No comparisons of tensioning techniques have been performed to our knowledge, and many different methods are used. Outcomes in women who undergo TVT in combination with a prolapse repair under general or spinal anesthesia are similar to those in women who undergo TVT alone.

KEY POINT: TVT RESULTS IN SPECIAL POPULATIONS

- The literature supports the use of midurethral slings in a variety of special populations of patients. Efficacy and safety of TVT are not compromised in the elderly, obese, those with recurrent incontinence, or those undergoing concomitant vaginal surgery. A few small studies suggest that concomitant vaginal surgery places a patient at higher risk for delayed return to normal voiding and urinary retention. However, limitations in the studies prevent comparison of the data. It is difficult to analyze the current sling data because of the lack of standard definitions of cure and improvement and lack of standard outcome measures. Absolute conclusions about the use of TVT in special populations should not be made until larger prospective multicenter studies can be performed.

Complications

Complications associated with TVT appear to be within the acceptable range for incontinence procedures. Quality of life is affected not only by the outcome of the incontinence

surgery from the standpoint of cure or improvement but also by the appearance of voiding difficulties, urinary tract infections, and other adverse consequences of the surgical procedure itself. The evidence appears to suggest that a minimally invasive procedure that is standardized can decrease rates of complications. **The Finnish TVT registry demonstrates a pronounced learning curve** for surgeons adopting this new technology (Kuuva and Nilsson, 2003). This registry is unique in that all TVT procedures are recorded in this data bank and therefore the data are reflective of an entire national experience with a new procedure. A second registry is currently maintained in Austria and includes somewhat over 3000 cases, but it does not involve all surgeons in the country (Tamussino et al, 2001). Overall, the rate of complications associated with the TVT procedure is relatively low. **Bladder injury in the two national registries ranges from 2.7% to 3.8%. Voiding dysfunction is reported as approximately 7.6%, and wound healing problems are less than 1%.** Other studies have also reported complication rates in smaller but still significant groups of patients (Table 68–2).

The definition of voiding dysfunction in these studies varies; however, the common definition is the need for catheterization, with short-term catheterization usually being defined as 2 days. The highest voiding dysfunction rate was reported by Abouassaly and colleagues (2004) at 48 hours. The highest urinary tract infection rates were reported in the Austrian National Registry (17%) (Tamussino et al, 2001). However, in this registry the infection rate may be reflective of the operative tendency to leave indwelling catheters in the majority of cases. Bodelsson and associates (2002) found that the risk of bladder perforation was three times higher in patients undergoing regional versus local anesthesia.

When urge incontinence and urgency symptoms are evaluated, patients with mixed incontinence experienced cure rates of approximately 80% with resolution in patients with urgency in approximately 50% to 80% of cases. The appearance of de novo urgency occurs in between 0.2% and 15% of patients without an apparent escalation of risk over time from the initial procedure. Long-term follow-up suggests approximately 6% of patients with de novo urgency postoperatively (Nilsson et al, 2001).

Intraoperative and postoperative bleeding are also variably defined, often by estimation of volume of blood loss. **Hemorrhage, however, is relatively rare.** Hemorrhage, defined as greater than 200 mL or postoperative hematoma occurs in approximately 2% of patients and can usually be managed by observation or local compression. Flock and coauthors (2004) reported a rate of 4.1% of 249 patients experiencing hemorrhage of 300 mL or more and requiring surgical intervention.

Although rare, vaginal, urethral, and intravesical erosion of the midurethral sling polypropylene mesh is a particularly feared complication of the technique, largely because of advances in materials science. Tape erosion has been reported in the literature with an incidence of 0.3% to 23%, and currently there is no clear consensus on the management of this particular complication. Given the extensive experience with the TVT device, the majority of reported complications have been associated with this device; however, given the similarity between the various devices, it is reasonable to assume that these results will be noted with other types

Table 68–2. **Complications as Reported by Recent Large Series (Two of Which Represent National Registries)***

Complication	Abouassaly et al, 2004 N = 241	Karram et al, 2003 N = 350	Kuuva and Nilsson, 2002 N = 1455	Levin et al, 2004 N = 313	Nilsson and Kuuva, 2001 N = 161	Tamussino et al, 2001 N = 2795
Bladder injury	5.8	4.9	3.8	5.1	3.7	2.7
Bleeding	2.5	0.9	1.9	NR	1.8	2.3
Defect healing	0.4	0.9	0.7	1.3	NR	NR
Hematoma	1.9	1.7	2.4	NR	1.2	NR
New-onset urge	15	12	0.2	8.3	3.1	NR
Urinary tract infection	NR	10	4.1	NR	6.2	17
Voiding difficulty	19.7	4.9	7.6	2.5	4.3	NR
Wound infection	0.4	NR	0.8	NR	1.8	NR

*Definitions of some entities vary, and voiding dysfunction specifically is defined differently between trials. NR, not reported.

of midurethral slings (Clemens et al, 2000; Volkmer et al, 2003).

The incidence of TVT erosion in the reported literature is extremely low. Many attribute this phenomenon to the macroporous characteristics of the polypropylene mesh. These characteristics allow excellent incorporation of fibroblasts, macrophages, white blood cells, collagen, and neovascular tissue within the interstices of the tape. The excellent tissue ingrowth facilitates integration of the mesh with the surrounding host tissues and decreases tape encapsulation, all of which minimize the risk of an erosion complication. The erosion rate reported in the literature for polypropylene mesh is 0.5% to 1.3% (Meschia et al, 2001; Kuuva and Nilsson, 2002; Karram et al, 2003; Levin et al, 2004).

Terminology

The term erosion implies that the polypropylene mesh has either entered the lower genitourinary tract (urethra or bladder) or has penetrated through the vaginal epithelium. The latter circumstance may better be termed exposure or extrusion (exposure may be preferable as the underlying causative mechanism may not be identifiable) and may arise from either mechanical or wound-related variables. The actual mechanism of erosion is still poorly understood. There are a number of theoretical possibilities, including subclinical infection, poor tissue ingrowth into the sling, disturbed wound healing, rolling or twisting of the tape, and excessive friction between host tissue and the tape. Also, iatrogenic injury and surgeon technical error should be considered as factors in the etiology of erosive complications (Kobashi and Govier, 2003a, 2003b; Domingo et al, 2005). Biomechanical properties of the sling material play a major role in the incidence of complications related to tape erosion. Although various materials have been historically utilized for sling implants, there has been a trend in the contemporary literature toward the use of macroporous polypropylene slings. The increased pore size allows excellent tissue ingrowth, promotes integration with the surrounding host tissues, and decreases encapsulation and infection (Dietz et al, 2001, 2003; Slack et al, 2005). Adherence to meticulous surgical technique and utilization of polypropylene tapes with favorable biomechanical properties may help the surgeon minimize this particular complication.

Vaginal Erosion

Vaginal tape erosion or extrusion is a rare complication after the TVT procedure. **In three large studies, the incidence was reported to be 1.1%, 1.3%, and 0.5%** (Meschia et al, 2001; Levin et al, 2004; Huang et al, 2005). Most cases present within a few weeks to a few months following the midurethral sling procedure. One case of delayed vaginal erosion at 18 months has been reported (Sharma and Oligbo, 2004). **Symptoms of vaginal erosion include vaginal discharge (with variable constituents and different amounts of blood and inflammatory components), a palpable rough surface in the vagina, sexual discomfort (including partner related), pelvic pain, inguinal discomfort, and lower urinary tract symptoms** (LUTS) (urgency, frequency, persistent incontinence, hematuria). Symptoms are often nonspecific, and therefore a high index of suspicion is required. Careful vaginal examination usually identifies an area on the anterior vaginal wall with separated epithelial edges and exposed mesh. **The management of this complication is not standardized, and there are various reports claiming successful outcomes with observation, partial tape excision, complete tape excision, and reapproximation of the vaginal mucosa over the exposed tape** (Table 68–3).

Historically, most authors have advocated removal of the exposed tape when a vaginal erosion occurs. Reports of conservative management in the literature are sparse. Kobashi and Govier (2003a) reported their experience managing four patients (three suprapubic arch sling [SPARC] and one TVT) with vaginal erosion in a conservative fashion. Two patients presented with persistent vaginal discharge and two were completely asymptomatic. All patients were observed with serial physical examinations and all patients had spontaneous reepithelialization of the mesh at 3 months, which they attributed to the macroporous characteristics of the polypropylene mesh facilitating excellent tissue ingrowth. This is less likely with other synthetic materials such as Gortex, polyester, and silicone, as epithelialization is not likely to occur (Leach et al, 1997; Kobashi et al, 1999).

In a review by Huang and associates (2005), six vaginal erosions and one bladder erosion following polypropylene synthetic slings were initially expectantly managed. In four patients with vaginal mesh erosion of less than 1 cm, conservative management was initiated for a 3-month period. One

Table 68–3. Vaginal Erosion and Management

Study	N	Location of Erosion	Management	Removal	Symptom Resolution	Continence
Huang et al, 2005	6	6 vaginal	6 transvaginal	Partial	6 asymptomatic	6 dry
Tsivian et al, 2004	5	5 vaginal	4 vaginal; 1 observation	Partial	5 asymptomatic	4 dry; 1 dry repeat TVT
Karram et al, 2003	3	3 vaginal	1 vaginal excision; 1 vaginal advancement flap; 1 antibiotics	Partial	3 asymptomatic	2 dry; 1 SUI
Levin et al, 2004	4	4 vaginal	4 vaginal excision		Not reported	Not reported
Kuuva and Nilsson, 2002	10	10 vaginal	4 resutured; 2 tape partially removed; 3 observation; 1 unknown	Partial		10 dry
Meschia et al, 2001	2	2 vaginal	Resuture vaginal mucosa		Yes	2 dry
Volkmer et al, 2003	1	1 vaginal	Transvaginal tape excision	Partial	Yes	Recurrent SUI
Sharma and Oligbo, 2004	1	1 vaginal–delayed 18 months	3 transvaginal tape excisions (same patient)	Partial	Yes	NA
Kobashi and Govier, 2003a	4	4 vaginal	Observation	NA	Yes	All 4 dry

SUI, stress urinary incontinence; TVT, tension-free vaginal tape.

of these patients was observed for 24 months without adverse sequelae. In contrast with the results seen by Kobashi and Govier, none of the patients in their series had vaginal epithelialization over the area of erosion. Therefore, all six patients underwent transvaginal tape excision in conjunction with excision of all fibrotic vaginal tissues. Symptoms resolved in all patients, and all patients were continent at their last followup. Although all patients ultimately required surgical intervention, the authors felt that a trial of conservative management in appropriately selected patients (i.e., erosion less than 1 cm) was reasonable, and if no epithelialization occurs at 3 months of followup, the tape should be surgically removed.

In a review of tape-related complications in a series of 200 patients, Tsivian and coworkers (2004) observed five vaginal tape erosions. Four patients required surgical excision of the exposed tape, and one asymptomatic patient was being observed conservatively without adverse outcomes. Four of the five patients were dry and one with recurrent stress incontinence was dry with repeated TVT. Symptoms resolved in all patients after partial tape excision and judicious vaginal débridement.

Furthermore, in a large series of 350 TVT procedures reported by Karram and colleagues (2003), three vaginal erosions were noted with one patient managed with local estrogen cream and antibiotics. This patient had done well without recurrence of symptoms or additional morbidity at last follow-up. In the same series, another patient underwent careful excision of the vaginal tissues with coverage of the tape with a vaginal advancement flap with satisfactory results. The third patient required partial excision of the exposed tape and redeveloped stress incontinence. In all patients, symptoms related to the tape erosion resolved after management.

In the Finish nationwide review of 1455 TVT procedures, 10 patients were identified with vaginal polypropylene tape exposure. Three of these patients were managed without surgical intervention with good results and maintenance of continence (Kuuva and Nilsson, 2002). Four patients had the vaginal mucosa resutured over the exposed tape, and two patients required partial tape excision. One patient was lost to follow-up and management was unknown at the time of their report. According to this national registry, continence was maintained in all patients, regardless of the management.

KEY POINT: TVT-VAGINAL EROSION

■ Conservative management seems to be a plausible option in well-selected patients who are relatively asymptomatic and have small-caliber erosions. Good results have also been observed in selected patients with vaginal advancement flaps and suture approximation of the débrided vaginal mucosa over the exposed tape (Meschia et al, 2001; Kuuva and Nilsson, 2002, 2003; Karram et al, 2003). Even with partial excision of the tape, continence is maintained in the majority of patients. Observation should never be considered when there is foreign body involvement of the urinary tract, as with urethral or intravesical erosion. Obviously, more data supporting specific management strategies are necessary before a given approach can be advocated for patients with this complication. The authors recommend initial judicious observation for small vaginal erosions (with use of topical estrogen cream when appropriate). Excision should be reserved for failure of conservative therapy or when local symptoms mitigate against observational management (i.e., bothersome dyspareunia).

Urethral Erosion

Urethral erosion is defined as presence of sling material within the urethral lumen. **A review of the published literature by the American Urological Association (AUA) guidelines panel found five cases of urethral erosion following 1715 autologous fascial slings (0.003%) and 27 cases of urethral erosion following 1515 synthetic pubovaginal slings (0.02%)** (Leach et al, 1997). **The exact incidence of urethral erosion following the newer tension-free midurethral sling procedures is, as yet, undetermined. Factors thought to contribute to urethral erosion include compromised urethral blood supply** (i.e., radiation therapy or estrogen deficiency), **excessive sling tension, extensive dissection too close to the urethra with subsequent urethral devascularization, iatrogenic urethral injury (at time of device** insertion), and traumatic catheterization/dilation. Furthermore, **twisting or rolling of the tape can create a ridge that leads to pressure necrosis and erosion through the urethra** (Dell and O'Kelley, 2005). Management of this complication is extremely challenging with the possibility of significant morbidity, as access to the tape is traditionally gained by incising the urethra, although endoscopic management has been attempted.

Presenting symptoms are varied. In almost all published cases, voiding dysfunction is predominant, with **typical symptoms including urgency, urgency incontinence, obstructive voiding, urinary retention, history of self-catheterization, urethral dilations, recurrent urinary tract infection, and persistent urinary incontinence** (Haferkamp et al, 2002; Madjar et al, 2002; Pit, 2002; Sweat et al, 2002; Lieb and Das, 2003; Vassallo et al, 2003; Glavind and Sander, 2004; McLennan, 2004; Tsivian et al, 2004; Wai et al, 2004). Diagnosis is often delayed in these patients for an extended period of time. In a review by Amundsen and associates (2003), the average time from placement of the initial pubovaginal sling to diagnosis of urethral erosion was 9 months.

Diagnosis is made by confirming the presence of the tape within the urethral lumen during cystoscopy. Voiding cystourethrography has also been useful adjunctively by documenting a dilated proximal urethra related to high-grade obstruction caused by the eroded tape (Lieb and Das, 2003). A review of urethral erosions is presented in Table 68–4.

Management of urethral tape erosion has typically involved transvaginal urethrotomy and excision of the exposed tape. In selected cases, an autologous fascial sling and Martius labial fat pad graft can be utilized at the discretion of the surgeon. Pit (2002) described two cases of urethral erosion. The urethra was incised and the tape was cut at the level of the mucosa. The tape was then dissected on its medial edge toward the inferior ischiopubic ramus and cut bilaterally, which allowed the tape to be removed from the periurethral fascia. A Martius graft was placed over the urethra in one case and a cadaveric fascia lata graft was used in the second case. A second TVT was then placed over the tissue

bolsters without complication. In a review by Sweat and colleagues (2002), transvaginal tape excision was accomplished by identifying and dividing the tape in the midline, followed by sharp lateral dissection along the medial border of the tape, freeing the mesh from the urethra and bladder neck. The endopelvic fascia was perforated and the tape cut in the retropubic space. A Martius fat pad graft was interposed over the urethral closure in one case and an autologous fascial sling placed over the graft in both cases. Both patients improved symptomatically and were continent during postoperative follow-up. Glavind and coauthors (2004) reported a urethrovaginal fistula caused by urethral erosion of the polypropylene tape. Transvaginal tape excision failed to resolve the fistula, and the patient required two transabdominal fistula repairs until closure was achieved and symptom resolution occurred. Persistent stress incontinence was managed by conservative means with satisfactory results. Four other additional case reports reported excellent results utilizing a midline transvaginal approach with partial tape excision and closure of the urethra (Haferkamp et al, 2002; Madjar et al, 2002; Lieb and Das, 2003; Wai et al, 2004).

In 2004, McLennan successfully managed a TVT urethral erosion endoscopically. Hysteroscopic scissors were used to transect the tape flush with the urethral mucosa. Catheter drainage was continued postoperatively for 72 hours. The patient remained symptom free and continent at 10 months of followup. In a case report by Wai and associates (2004), a combined endoscopic and transvaginal approach was used successfully to manage a difficult urethral erosion. Initially, the tape was cut in the midline transurethrally. Transvaginal periurethral dissection was performed and the tape was identified and removed from the dense fibrous attachments. An accidental urethrotomy was noted and closed without difficulty. The theoretical advantage of this technique is that with endoscopic transection of the tape, entry into the urethral lumen is unnecessary.

The postoperative results reported by each of these investigators were excellent, with all patients achieving symptom resolution following surgical intervention. In two cases, mild

Table 68–4. Urethral Erosion and Management

Study	N	Location of Erosion	Management	Removal	Symptom Resolution	Continence
McLennan, 2004	1	1 urethral	Endoscopic resection	Partial	Yes	Dry
Pit, 2002	2	2 urethral	TV resection, Martius with TVT; TV with dermis with TVT	Partial	Yes	Dry
Haferkamp et al, 2002	1	1 urethral	TV resection, urethral reconstruction	Partial	Yes	Dry
Lieb and Das, 2003	1	1 urethral	TV resection, urethral reconstruction	Partial	Not reported	Not reported
Vassallo et al, 2003	1	1 urethral	TV revision, urethrotomy closure	Partial	Yes	Dry with fascial PVS
Wai et al, 2004	1	1 urethral	Endoscopic and transvaginal	Partial	Yes	SUI treatment with biofeedback
Madjar et al, 2002	1	1 urethral	TV partial resection, closure of urethra	Partial	Yes	Dry
Glavind and Sander, 2004	1	1 urethral vaginal fistula TVT	Partial tape removal, two transabdominal repairs	Partial	Yes	SUI treatment with biofeedback
Sweat et al, 2002	3	2 urethral	TV excision, PVS, Martius; TV/retropubic	Near complete	Not reported	3 dry (1 with collagen)

SUI, stress urinary incontinence; TV, transvaginal; PVS, pubovaginal sling; TVT, tension-free vaginal tape.

recurrent stress incontinence was successfully managed with biofeedback (Wai et al, 2004; Glavind and Sander, 2004). In two cases continence was achieved by intraoperative fascial sling and in a single case, postoperative fascial sling resulted in satisfactory continence (Vassallo et al, 2003; Wai et al, 2004).

KEY POINT: TVT-URETHRAL EROSION

■ Overall, the incidence of urethral erosion is extremely low in the reported TVT literature. As the number of synthetic midurethral slings continues to increase, physicians need to be aware of the potential complications, have a high index of suspicion, and be aware of the management options available to treat the patient. Conservative observational treatment is not an option for urethral tape erosion. The success of endoscopic tape transection needs to be duplicated by others before it can be considered first-line management of urethral erosion. Currently, transvaginal excision of the polypropylene mesh with closure of the urethrotomy should be considered the first line of management and is the authors' preferred method if significant surface area of the sling is present within the urethral lumen. If the repair is tenuous, a vascularized Martius fat pad graft can bolster the repair. Furthermore, an autologous fascial sling can be placed at the time of surgery or in a delayed fashion to treat recurrent SUI.

Intravesical Tape Erosion

The finding of synthetic mesh within the lumen of the urinary bladder is another particularly distressing complication. This complication is also **exceedingly rare following the TVT procedure** with only case reports in the published literature. Bladder injury recognized at the time of cystoscopy is much more common, occurring with a frequency between 2% and 11% of cases (Nilsson et al, 2001). Recognition of this complication allows the surgeon to remove and reintroduce the trocar in a controlled fashion, with placement of the tape in the correct anatomic plane. The **vast majority of intravesical tape erosions are most likely due to unrecognized cystotomy and placement of the tape within the urinary bladder at the time of surgery. True erosion of the tape across the seromuscular wall of the bladder into the lumen is much less likely.** Thus, performing complete and thorough cystoscopic examination of the bladder with adequate hydrodistention is critical to minimize this complication. Occasionally, the insertion trocar may telescope the vesical wall during insertion and may obscure intravesical entry.

Patients typically present following their TVT procedure with a variety of symptoms. A review of seven reported cases in the literature was included in a case report by Negoro and colleagues (2005). **Typical symptoms can include lower abdominal pain, intermittent gross hematuria, recurrent urinary tract infection, urgency, frequency, dysuria, and urinary incontinence.**

Diagnosis is made with a high index of suspicion by the clinician and cystoscopic examination confirming the presence of the tape within the lumen of the urinary bladder.

Imaging including computed tomography scan and cystography may help in difficult cases but is not a substitute for cystoscopic examination. A review of intravesical polypropylene tape erosions is presented in Table 68–5.

Management goals are aimed at removing the portion of polypropylene tape from the urinary tract and reconstructing the lower urinary tract. Observational treatment is not recommended as the tape often becomes encrusted, leading to stone formation, persistent lower urinary tract storage/voiding symptoms, recurrent urinary tract infection, and intermittent gross hematuria. Different techniques and surgical approaches have been advocated with varying levels of invasiveness, complexity, and success.

In a report by Negoro and colleagues (2005), a retropubic approach was used to resect the intravesical portion of the tape. The bladder was closed with absorbable suture and catheter drainage was maintained postoperatively. The patient was symptom free and continent at 10-month follow-up. Volkmer (2003), Sweat (2002), and Huang (2003) used a combined transvaginal and abdominal approach to remove the tape in its entirety. One patient had residual urgency and frequency treated with anticholinergics; the other patients had resolution of symptoms but recurrent stress incontinence

---

Table 68–5. Intravesical Erosion and Management

Study	N	Location	Management	Removal	Symptoms	Symptom Resolution	Continence
Huang et al, 2005	1	1 bladder	Combined transvaginal/retropubic	Complete	F/U/UI/hem/pain	1 urge/UI	UI treatment anticholinergic
Tsivian et al, 2004	1	1 bladder	Combined endoscopic/suprapubic	Partial	UTI, perineal pain	Yes	1 dry
Levin et al, 2004	2	2 bladder	2 endoscopic excision	Partial	UTI, F/U/UI	Not reported	Not reported
Sweat et al, 2002	1	1 bladder	Combined transvaginal/retropubic	Complete	UTI, hematuria	Not reported	SUI (dry with collagen)
Wyczolkowski et al, 2001	1	1 bladder	Failed endo; retropubic with inguinal fixation	Partial	Abdominal pain	Yes	Dry
Volkmer et al, 2003	1	2 bladder	TV tape excision; sp tape resection	complete	UTI	Yes	2 SUI, PFMT, estrogen
Jorion, 2002	1	1 bladder	Endoscopic	Partial	UTI	Yes	Dry
Negoro et al, 2005	1	1 bladder	Retropubic	Partial	UTI	Yes	Dry

SUI, stress urinary incontinence; TV, transvaginal; sp, suprapubic; F, frequency; U, urgency; UI, urge incontinence; PFMT, pelvic floor muscle therapy.

managed with collagen in one and pelvic floor muscle training and estrogen in the remaining two.

Jorion (2002) excised the tape endoscopically using an offset nephroscope transurethrally and a 5-mm laparoscopic trocar placed suprapubically. Laparoscopic grasping forceps were used to grasp the tape and endoscopic shears excised the mesh flush with the bladder mucosa, allowing the tape to be easily removed. Cystoscopy at 1 month revealed healed mucosa and the patient was continent and symptom free. In a separate report by Tsivian and coworkers (2004), the tape was cut endoscopically. Because of dense adhesions and adherent calculus, the tape could not be extracted endoscopically. Therefore, a suprapubic approach was required to remove the stone and intravesical tape. Wyczolkowski and associates (2001) attempted to cut the tape endoscopically without success. Transabdominal exploration allowed the tape to be excised, and the cut ends were secured to the inguinal ligaments bilaterally. Holmium laser destruction (vaporization) of visible tape has been successfully used in two cases (Hodroff et al, 2004; Lane et al, 2005).

It is unclear from the literature whether complete or partial tape excision is preferred. The authors routinely use the open cystostomy approach for complete tape excision. This approach is necessitated by a large surface area of tape present in the vesical lumen or in the case of tape collocation near the bladder neck, trigone, or ureteral orifices. Only patients with complete tape removal had recurrent stress incontinence; the patients with partial excision maintained continence postoperatively. The significance of this, given the small number of cases, is unclear, but it may imply that suburethral support is maintained when the midurethral portion of tape is left in situ. The endoscopic approach is intriguing as it is minimally invasive and with the addition of the laparoscopic trocar achieved a satisfactory outcome. This should be duplicated by others before it is universally adopted to treat patients with this particular complication.

Voiding Dysfunction

Voiding dysfunction is a well-recognized complication of suburethral sling procedures for SUI. Although it is difficult to quantify objectively, a review by the AUA guidelines panel concluded that the incidence of permanent urinary retention following suburethral slings does not exceed 5% (Leach et al, 1997). **Anti-incontinence surgery, regardless of the technique, has some effect on outlet resistance. As a result, clinical symptoms of urethral obstruction have not been eliminated by the TVT procedure with an incidence in the literature of 1.9% to 9.9%** (Klutke et al, 2001; Meschia et al, 2001; Kuuva and Nilsson, 2002, 2003; Volkmer et al, 2003; Levin et al, 2004; Long et al, 2004).

Despite the fact that TVT is described as a tension-free procedure, there is controversy about whether tension or resistance is directed at the bladder outlet. In one study of 404 TVT procedures, urodynamics before and after surgery showed an increase in voiding time but no difference in flow rate, urethral closure pressure, or urethral functional length (Meschia et al, 2001). A study by Lo and colleagues (2001) showed no statistical difference in several urodynamic parameters (Q_{av}, Q_{max}, postvoid residual [PVR], maximum urethral closure pressure [MUCP], and functional urethral length) in 82 patients before and after TVT. In another study, Wang and

Chen (2001) looked at filling cystometry, uroflowmetry, and urethral pressure profile data before and after TVT and found the only statistically significant difference to be in resting maximal urethral closure pressure. Several other studies have also shown no statistical difference in urodynamic pressure flow variables following the TVT procedure (Wang and Chen, 2003a, 2003b; Lin et al, 2004; Wang, 2000).

In contrast, Gateau and associates (2003) analyzed pre- and post-TVT urodynamics in 112 patients and showed consistent decreases in Q_{max}, increased mean $Pdet_{Qmax}$, increased mean urethral resistance, and elevated postvoid residual urine. They concluded from their data that TVT leads to obstructive changes in the bladder outlet. Sander and colleagues (2002) evaluated the voiding phase before and 1 year after the TVT procedure. They found both subjective and objective changes in the voiding phase, with 78% of patients experiencing more difficult voiding and significant decreases in Q_{max}, corrected Q_{max}, and Q_{avg}. Postvoid residual urine was also significantly increased, although not greater than 25% capacity. Furthermore, in another study comparing TVT and Burch colposuspension, a significant decrease in the flow rate was observed following surgery (Atherton and Staton, 2000).

There are contemporary urodynamic data both supporting and refuting bladder outlet obstructive changes following the TVT procedure. The physician must therefore consider these issues when counseling patients with stress incontinence before surgical intervention with TVT.

It would be most helpful when selecting patients for the TVT procedure to identify preoperative factors predictive of voiding dysfunction and urinary retention following surgery. One study assessed differences in surgical outcome following TVT by subgrouping patients into two groups, those with dysfunctional voiding and those with normal voiding (Wang and Chen, 2003b). Dysfunctional voiding in this study was defined as having both a free Q_{max} of less than 12 mL/sec and a $Pdet_{Qmax}$ of greater than 20 cm H_2O as defined by Blaivas and Groutz (2000). Statistically significant differences in pressure-flow variables freeQ_{max} and $Pdet_{Qmax}$ between the two groups were observed, as well as a higher objective cure rate in the normal voiding group. In a separate study by Hong and colleagues (2003), 375 patients were analyzed to see which factors predicted urinary retention following the TVT procedure. Urinary retention, defined as the need to catheterize for 72 hours or longer following surgery, was identified in 32 patients. Twenty-eight patients resumed normal voiding within 3 months, and four patients required a transvaginal tape release procedure. Patients' age, parity, peak flow rate, and history of hysterectomy predicted urinary retention on univariate analysis, and only peak flow rate predicted urinary retention on multivariate analysis. Finally, a small study of 14 patients showed that low $Pdet_{Qmax}$ on the preoperative pressure-flow study correlated with elevated postvoid residual urine in three patients following TVT (Kawashima et al, 2004).

Urethral obstruction following suburethral sling surgery can arise in variety of ways. **Patients may complain of straining to void, incomplete emptying, urgency and frequency, hesitancy, urgency incontinence, elevated postvoid residual urine, recurrent urinary tract infection, and total urinary retention.** These symptoms usually cause patients bother and prompt evaluation and treatment after the initial surgical procedure.

The optimal evaluation for patients with postoperative voiding dysfunction is poorly defined in the literature. In a study by Carr and Webster (1997), there were no parameters (urodynamic, previous surgery, time from suspension to urethrolysis, and surgical approach) that predicted which patients would benefit from urethrolysis. The decision to perform urethrolysis was based on a clear temporal relationship between onset of symptoms and the surgical procedure. In a study by Petrou and coauthors (1999), there was no difference in urethrolysis outcomes with respect to patients with urodynamic obstruction versus those who had surgery based on clinical criteria. Under ideal circumstances, videourodynamics would differentiate patients with high-pressure, low-flow voiding consistent with obstruction and patients with detrusor hypocontractility. **At this time there does not appear to be enough evidence correlating urodynamic parameters with surgical outcomes. Therefore, urodynamics can be useful in selected cases at the physician's discretion; however, it appears that the temporal relationship correlating symptoms with an antecedent surgical procedure should be the primary criterion in selecting patients for urethrolysis and tape release procedures. Cystoscopy is useful to rule out bladder pathology, urethral tape erosion, and a hypersuspended bladder neck.**

In most cases, persistent postoperative voiding dysfunction is initially treated conservatively. Temporary catheter drainage, clean intermittent catheterization, timed voiding, biofeedback, pelvic floor muscle training, and selective medical therapy have all been successful to some degree in managing postoperative voiding dysfunction. Several reports have shown some benefit with urethral dilation (Hong et al,

2003; Mishra et al, 2005). **However, when these conservative measures fail, surgical intervention is usually indicated.** The urethrolysis literature is more mature and robust in the management of urethral obstruction secondary to traditional pubovaginal sling surgery. We discuss the results of surgical management of urethral obstruction following the TVT procedure (Table 68–6).

In a large review of 1175 TVT procedures, Rardin and colleagues (2002a) found 23 (1.9%) women with persistent voiding dysfunction. Twenty patients had urinary retention or incomplete emptying, three patients had symptoms of refractory urgency and urge incontinence, and seven had both. Symptoms of incomplete bladder emptying usually arose in the immediate postoperative period, and LUTS arose in delayed fashion some weeks later. All patients were refractory to conservative regimens and underwent transvaginal tape release at a mean time of 17.3 weeks following TVT. Tape release was performed in the majority (17 patients), with mild urethrolysis in 2 patients, and segmental tape excision (2 to 11 mm) in 4 patients. Relief of impaired bladder emptying was complete in 100%, and relief of urgency/urge incontinence was complete in 30% and partial in 70%. Fourteen patients (61%) maintained their baseline continence, six (26%) were improved over baseline, and three (13%) had recurrent stress incontinence.

Kuuva and Nilsson (2002) reviewed complications associated with the TVT procedure from the nationwide database in Finland. In their analysis of 1455 TVT procedures, 34 cases (2.3%) of urinary retention were reported and duration was recorded for 23 patients. A normal voiding pattern was resumed in 14 patients (2 days to 2 weeks), 2 patients (5 to 6

Table 68–6. Result of Therapy for Urethral Obstruction after Midurethral Sling Surgery

Study	N	Time to Sx	Management	Symptom Improvement	Continence
Rardin et al, 2002	23/1175 (1.9%)	17.3 wk (2-69)	Midline transection (17); urethrolysis (2); segmental excision (4)	Retention (100%); LUTS (30% c, 70% p)	14 dry; 6 improved; 3 SUI
Klutke et al, 2001	17/600 (2.8%)	64 days (6-228)	Midline transection or 1 cm downward traction	All patients symptom free	16 dry; 1 SUI
Long et al, 2004	7/71 (9.9%)	28 days (4-108)	Right-sided lateral transection ("J" sling)	6/7 symptom free	5/7 dry; 2 SUI
Meschia et al, 2001	17/404 (4%)	Not reported	Only 2 patients required midline tape release	17 patients resumed normal voiding	Not reported in data
Volkmer et al, 2003	3	14 mo, 6 mo, 6 wk	1 segmental tape excision; 2 tape cut in midline	All patients symptom free	2 dry; 1 SUI
Levin et al, 2004	8/313 (2.5%)	2 mo	Only 1 patient required transvaginal excision and urethrolysis	All patients symptom free	All dry
Kuuva and Nilsson, 2002	34/1455 (2.3%) 111/1455 Subset w "minor" v.d. (7.6%)	3 mo 1 mo and 4 mo	1 patient tape cut in midline 2 patients with persistent urgency/frequency tape cut midline	Symptom free Symptom free	All dry All dry
Tsivian et al, 2004	8	14 mo (5-46)	5 midline transection, 3 lateral segmental excision	Symptom free	6 dry; 2 SUI
Karram et al, 2003	17/350 (4.9%)	>6 wk	6 tape takedown/midline transection	Symptom free	4 dry; 2 SUI
Hong et al, 2003	32/375 (8.5%)	3 mo	4 transvaginal midline incision of tape	Symptom free	4 dry
Zubke et al, 2004	3	Not reported	3 transvaginal midline incision prolene mesh lengthening	Symptom free	3 dry
Abouassaly et al, 2004	15/241 (6.2%)		7 transvaginal tape release, 3 segmental tape excision	Symptom free	6 dry; 4 SUI

SUI, stress urinary incontinence; c, complete; p, partial; v.d., voiding dysfunction.

weeks), and 6 patients (within 24 hours) following surgery. One patient required that the tape be released by cutting it in the midline and normal voiding resumed.

In 111 cases the authors noted "minor" postoperative voiding difficulty (e.g., urgency, frequency) that resolved without intervention in the vast majority. Thirteen cases were identified that lasted up to 4 months, and two of these patients required surgical transection of the tape to achieve a normal voiding pattern (Kuuva and Nilsson, 2002, 2003).

In another large review by Klutke and colleagues (2001), 17 of 600 patients (2.8%) required reoperation secondary to urinary retention and persistent obstructive symptoms. In their series, tape release was performed at mean of 64 days after TVT. The tape was identified and either released with downward traction for 1 cm or cut in the midline. There was one urethral injury, which was repaired without sequelae. Symptoms resolved in all patients following tape release, all patients voided to completion, and 16 patients remained continent.

In a review by Long and associates (2004), 7 of 71 patients (9.9%), underwent lateral tape excision to treat patients with evidence of urethral obstruction. All patients had irritative symptoms or elevated residual urine and six patients voided with significant straining. Six of the patients had urodynamic obstruction (Pdet > 20 cm H_2O and Qmax < 12 mL/sec) and one patient had low-pressure, low-flow voiding. They described a technique transecting the tape lateral to the midline on the right side of the periurethral fascia, leaving the tape in the shape of a "J" underneath the urethra. Symptoms resolved in six patients, and five patients were continent. Of note, in the two patients who had recurrent stress incontinence after transection of the tape, the tape was cut on postoperative day 4 in both cases. In the other cases, the tape was cut after a minimum of 14 days after TVT. Therefore, on the basis of their experience, the authors recommended a minimum waiting period of 2 weeks prior to surgical intervention.

In a study reviewing outcomes and complications of 404 TVT procedures, Meschia and coworkers (2001) found 17 patients (4%) who had voiding difficulties defined as residual urine greater than 100 mL. At 1 month of follow-up, 15 patients resumed normal voiding patterns, and the remaining 2 patients required the tape to be cut in the midline to release tension. Normal voiding was observed thereafter.

A review by Volkmer and coauthors (2003) found three patients with permanent urinary retention following the TVT procedure. Urodynamics revealed high-grade obstruction in each patient utilizing the Abrams-Griffiths nomogram. Two patients had the tape cut in the midline transvaginally, and one patient had segmental excision of the entire suburethral portion of the tape. All three patients were able to resume normal voiding without significant residual urine, and two of the three patients remained continent. In the patient with recurrent stress incontinence, the suburethral portion of the tape was excised, and she underwent repeated TVT to restore continence.

Levin and colleagues (2004) reviewed a series of 313 patients who underwent the TVT procedure. They identified eight patients (2.5%) who had urinary retention with incomplete bladder emptying. Seven patients required temporary catheterization for a short period of time prior to resumption

of normal voiding at a follow-up of 1 month. The remaining patient had persistent urinary retention 2 months following TVT and urodynamics showed obstruction on the pressure-flow study. Transvaginal urethrolysis with tape excision was performed, and the patient thereafter resumed complete bladder emptying with complete continence.

Tsivian and associates (2004) found 8 of 12 patients who required repeated surgery following TVT to have urethral obstruction with complaints ranging from severe urge symptoms to straining to void. All patients had incomplete bladder emptying and five cases had objective evidence of obstruction on pressure-flow urodynamics. All eight women underwent corrective surgery with resolution of symptoms, and only two women suffered from recurrent stress incontinence symptoms.

Karram and coworkers (2003) reviewed their series of TVT procedures looking at the incidence of postoperative complications. Seventeen women (4.9%) were performing clean intermittent self-catheterization beyond 7 days. Another 42 women with irritative LUTS were taking anticholinergic medications more than 6 weeks after surgery. Twenty-eight patients underwent urethral dilation, which provided symptom relief in 23, and 6 patients with persistent urinary retention had transvaginal takedown and incision of the tape. Normal voiding resumed in all six of these patients, although two experienced recurrent stress incontinence.

Zubke and colleagues (2004) managed three patients with urethral obstruction following TVT with a novel surgical technique. They cut the tape in the midline with a transvaginal approach and sutured the edges of the tape to a Prolene mesh, thus lengthening the tape. All three patients were continent and resumed normal voiding following intervention.

KEY POINT: TVT-VOIDING DYSFUNCTION

■ Based upon these data, it appears that long-term urinary retention and obstructive voiding dysfunction is extremely rare following the TVT procedure. Although definitions of urinary retention and indications for management vary in the reported literature, most patients are initially managed conservatively. Anecdotal cases have shown modest benefit from urethral dilation. For patients with persistently elevated residual urine and bothersome symptoms refractory to conservative management, transvaginal tape release procedures consistently provide resolution of symptoms with maintenance of continence in the majority of cases. The authors recommend a waiting period of at least 4 weeks prior to any consideration of sling release. Sling release should be attempted through a small midline vaginal incision using minimal dissection.

Other Complications

A diverse group of complications have been reported with the midurethral sling, aside from those mentioned previously. These include vascular injury, bowel perforation, dyspareunia, pain (inguinal, suprapubic, pelvic), and infection-related complications. Mortality has also occurred after sling implant and been directly attributable to the procedure.

Wound-related complications include minor superficial cutaneous infections, pelvic abscesses, and urinary tract infection. A case of necrotizing fasciitis was reported in an obese, diabetic patient. This resolved after intensive resuscitation (Connolly, 2004). Interestingly, a review of necrotizing fasciitis in gynecologic surgery found that obesity (88%), hypertension (65%), and diabetes (47%) were all strong factors in the development of this infection after surgery (Gallup et al, 2002).

Serious complications such as vascular perforation or intestinal perforation remain relatively low. The rate of serious vascular complications in the Finnish registry was 0.07%, and the Austrian registry reported a bowel perforation rate of 0.04%.

Review of the Food and Drug Administration safety database for complications reported to that agency is noted in Table 68–7. Catastrophic complications do occur and may result in mortality, as seven reported deaths exist in the database from 1998 to August 2005.

Summary

Clinical experience with the TVT operation suggests that it is beneficial in the management of stress incontinence. In prospective trials, significant percentages of patients have been found to be cured or significantly improved compared with standard operations for the indication of SUI. There appears to be a relatively robust outcome expected from this procedure in patients with all types of incontinence, whether it be primary stress or mixed incontinence, or in patients who have prior failed procedures or who are undergoing simultaneous pelvic prolapse surgery. One group that appears to perform somewhat less well is patients with intrinsic sphincter deficiency, although the absolute reported rates of cure and improvement are within the range of reported results experienced with other types of procedure.

The risks of intraoperative and short-term postoperative complications are low, especially with trained physicians. There does appear to be a learning curve, which must be taken into account with new adopters and trainees. There do not appear to be any long-term adverse events.

TRANSOBTURATOR SLINGS

Subsequent to the development of the TVT, it was recognized that the transobturator (TOT) tape was a viable method for correction of SUI. Since Ulmsten's initial article in 1996, there has been extensive acceptance of the various midurethral sling technologies. In Europe, as of 2005, approximately 83.9% of

all procedures are midurethral-type synthetic slings, of which 26.9% are TOT (de Tayrac and Medelenat, 2004). Since the initial description of the TOT approach, numerous other similar TOT approaches have been noted.

The goal of the minimally invasive surgical procedure should be to provide acceptable long-term efficacy comparable to that of more standard methods as well as a relatively low incidence of long-term complications, again compared with these "gold standard" procedures. Retropubic midurethral slings have demonstrated robust outcomes in both primary and recurrent stress incontinence as well as in women with mixed incontinence and in those with intrinsic sphincter deficiency. Delorme (2001) initially described the placement of synthetic polypropylene mesh using the TOT approach. The technique was described as being relatively facile and associated with fewer complications than retropubic approaches. It was also thought that the procedure did not require cystoscopy.

Much of the understanding of the function of the TOT slings arises from that which has evolved from TVT-type procedures. Perineal ultrasonography has been used to assess the function of the TVT in patients who undergo successful incontinence procedures. In those individuals, a functional kinking of the urethra during stress events is noted to occur when the tape is placed at the midurethra (Lo et al, 2004).

In relatively long-term follow-ups (3 years), 92% of patients had ultrasonic demonstration of tape at the midurethra and evidence of urethra kinking that caused the "urethral knee angle." Of these patients, 92% were continent. Of the patients who had tape location either at the posterior urethra or bladder neck, only three of five (60%) were continent, presumably because of lack of a fulcrum-like effect at the midurethra. These ultrasound studies appear to underscore the importance of the midurethral location and also the ability of the TOT to accomplish this localization (Lo et al, 2001, 2004).

Similarly, Minaglia and colleagues (2004), using a variant of the TOT (ObTape), showed no difference in resting urethral angulation after tape insertion. These authors, however, did notice that there was a statically significant difference pre- and postoperatively in urethral angle with straining. They also noted that most women had persistent urethral hypermobility after the procedure, and they concluded that correction of hypermobility was not necessary to achieve continence. Their results documented that 90.4% of patients with documented hypermobility were continent, whereas only 50% of the patients without hypermobility were continent. They concluded that a persistently positive Q-tip test was predictive of a successful outcome. They found that concomitant prolapse surgery or previous incontinence surgery had no effect on outcome.

Table 68–7. Summary of All Significant Complications Reported to the Food and Drug Administration since 1998 with the Midurethral Sling

TVT Complications 1998-2005								
Bladder Erosion	Urethral Erosion	Vaginal Erosion	Bowel Perforation	Major Vascular	Blood Loss >200 mL	Plastic Sheath Malfx	Leg Pain	Needle Broken from Mesh
35	36	100	42	15	17	24	19	116

This analysis is limited by reporting inaccuracies and the incomplete nature of adverse event reporting in common practice.

Surgical Anatomy

For successful implantation of the TOT tape, an understanding of the surgical anatomy of the pelvic floor, including the surrounding neurovascular structures, pelvic and perineal anatomy, and the obturator foramen, is crucial to provide surgical success and minimize morbidity. Three reviews have demonstrated with cadaveric dissection the importance of landmarks and implantation technique for the success of the TOT.

Bonnet and colleagues (2005) performed the "inside-out" TOT technique as described by de Leval (2003) in 13 cadavers to determine tape path and proximity to surrounding structures. Cadaveric dissection was extended from the femoral triangle medially through the obturator externus muscle and adductor longus to the inferior pubic ramus. The perineal space was then entered and the pubic bone was sectioned to evaluate the relationship of the tape to various structures. Finally, the subfascial anterior perineum and pelvis were dissected to analyze the tape path fully. These authors demonstrated several significant points in their cadaveric dissection. They noted that the tape never penetrated the adductor longus muscle, thus being a safe distance from neurovascular structures. In approximately 70% of studied cases, the implanted material did traverse the adductor magnus, adductor brevis, and gracilis muscles during its path into the pelvis.

At the level of the obturator foramen, the tape was noted to traverse both the obturator externus and internus muscles as well as the obturator membrane. The relationship between the inserted tape and the obturator nerve showed that the closest proximity of the two was 22 mm with a distance as great as 30 mm (mean 26.2 ± 2 mm) at the level of the obturator foramen. The authors emphasized that an individual's thighs in hyperflexion and the rotational trajectory of the helical passer associated with this positioning ensured the separation of the insertion tool from the nerve during the actual implantation of the material. They also noted that regional vascular anatomy (anterior branch of the obturator) was protected from injury by the bony architecture of the inferior pubic ramus.

More medially, the tape entered the anterior compartment of the ischiorectal fascia, in the area of the levator ani membrane and obturator internus muscle. The tape remained outside the pelvic space and did not penetrate the levator ani muscular group. The tape remained above the perineal membrane at all times. The dorsal nerve of the clitoris was found to be consistently caudal to the perineal membrane and thus protected from injury during needle passage. They found these relationships to be consistently confirmed in each cadaveric specimen, felt that these observations represented highly reproducible anatomic positioning, and therefore concluded that the TOT technique is safe.

Delmas and associates (2003) utilized the "outside-in" approach on 10 female cadavers, again detailing the relevant pelvic anatomy in relationship to the tape insertion path. In this study, dissection demonstrated that the tape always consistently passed 4 cm opposite and caudal to the obturator canal, again confirming the relative safety of neurovascular structures. They also demonstrated that the tape traverses a plane between the perineal and levator antimusculature but above the neurovascular pedicle of the pudendal. They also

noted that in the pelvic component of their dissections, the tape courses medial to the obturator plexus. They concluded that tunneler passage anteriorly risks injury to the bladder and passage in posterior dissection demonstrated a risk of vaginal perforation.

A third study by Whiteside and Walters (2004) further evaluated the obturator anatomy in relationship to tape insertion in six female cadavers. These authors found that the mesh, on average, passed 2.4 cm inferior and medial to the obturator canal and that both divisions of the obturator (anterior and posterior) were 3.4 and 2.8 cm, respectively, separated from the path of the insertion tool. They also noted that the insertion tool passed within, on average, 1.1 cm proximity to the medial branch of the obturator vessels. These authors concluded that a risk of injury does exist and appropriate caution should be exercised.

Operative Technique

Operative technique varies with insertion method. Various procedures using similar insertion methods represent relatively similar technique (Fig. 68–2).

Not only does implantation technique affect overall success of the sling, but also the type of mesh or tape implanted has a substantive effect upon overall results. Mesh properties have been shown to have a significant effect upon local inflammatory response and ingrowth of local fibrous tissues (collagen, neovascularity) and subsequent integration of these tapes into host tissues. These differences in properties are felt to affect the risk of erosion and subsequent infection and other vaginal and local complications. There are intrinsic differences between the various meshes that have been used for the TOT approach. The ObTape and UraTape meshes are polypropylene material but are small-pore, knitted and thermally bonded with an approximately 15-mm silicone component that is immediately suburethral in location after implantation. A second-generation obturator tape developed by the Mentor Corporation is known as the Aris TOT; it has a larger 200-μm pore size that allows improved tissue ingrowth with less encapsulation. The ObTryx, TVT-O, Monarc, I STOP, and Urotex-TO are large-pore open knit polypropylene meshes. A unique obturator mesh is the BioArc, which, like the suprapubic variety, has a biologic graft material that is sutured on either end to the polypropylene tape. The biologic material actually occupies a suburethral position (deLeval, 2003; Delorme et al, 2003) (Table 68–8).

Transobturator Outside In

The patient is placed in the dorsal lithotomy position with legs in hyperflexion (120 degrees). A small vertical vaginal incision is created as with the TVT over the midurethra, and dissection is carried out laterally to the ischiopubic ramus. A puncture incision is made in the obturator foramen at the level of the clitoris in the leg using the tunneler; the obturator membrane is perforated, at which point resistance is noted by the operative surgeon. Using the nondominant index finger and identifying the landmarks of ramus and the obturator internus muscle, the tunneler is turned in a medial orientation and advanced on the tip of the index finger and brought out through the vaginal incision. Inspection is carried out at this point to exclude inadvertent penetration of the vaginal fornix

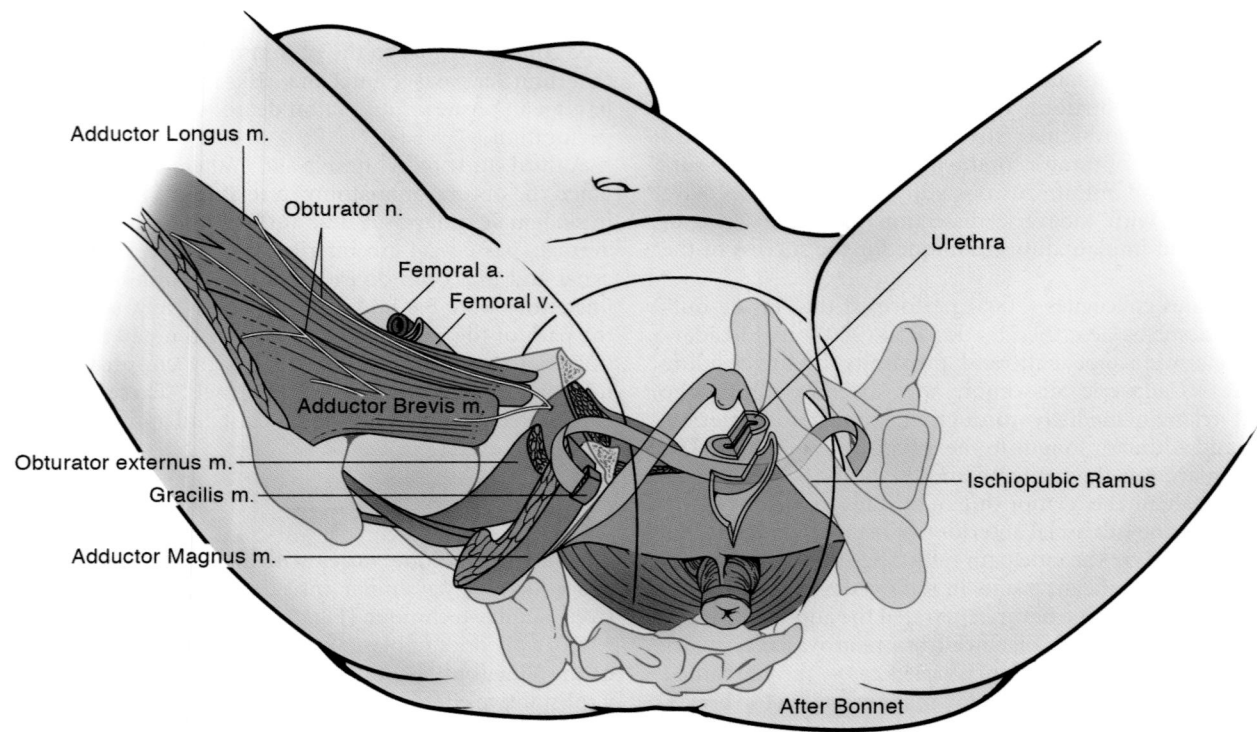

Figure 68–2. Midurethral sling as placed by the transobturator approach (any technique).

Table 68–8. Devices and Descriptions

Company	Brand Name	Mesh Material	Pore Size (μm)
Mentor	ObTape	Prolene, 15-mm silicone	50
	UraTape	Prolene, 15-mm silicone	50
	Aris	Polypropylene	200
AMS	Monarc	Knitted polypropylene	Large, open knit
	BioArc	Polypropylene with biologic suburethral component	Large, open knit
GyneCare	TVT-Obturator	Polypropylene	Large, open knit
Bard	Uretex-TO	Polypropylene	Large pore
Boston Scientific	ObTryx	Polypropylene with detangled suburethral segment	Large pore, >100 >75, low weight/area
CL Medical, France	I STOP	Monofilament prolene	weave

or associated urinary structures. The synthetic material is then attached to the tunneler and brought out through the inner thigh stab wound. The procedure is then repeated on the contralateral side. Tension is set on the tape by passing a clamp between the tape and urethra such that a surgical clamp can be passed easily between these two structures. Excess material is then cut at the skin puncture site and the incisions are closed according to the surgeon's preference.

This approach is used by the following devices: ObTape, UraTape, Aris TOT, Monarc, BioArc TO, Uretex-TO, ObTryx, I STOP.

Transobturator Inside Out

The vaginal component of the procedure is essentially the same as in the outside-in technique. Stab incisions are created approximately 2 cm superior to the horizontal line level with the urethra and 2 cm lateral to the labial folds, which will be the exit point for the helical passer. Once the device

is inserted through the urethra and the upper part of the ischiopubic ramus is reached with the device, the obturator membrane is perforated sharply with scissors. The introducer is then passed at a 45-degree angle relative to the midline sagittal plane until it reaches and perforates the obturator membrane. The open side of the introducer is passed out facing the surgeon. The more distal end of the tubing is then mounted on the spiral segment of the helical passer and slipped along the open gutter of the introducer. The passer is aligned parallel to the sagittal axis and rotated so that the tip of the tubing exits the inter-thigh stab incision. The tubing is then removed from the passer until the first few centimeters of the tape become externalized, and the procedure is repeated on the contralateral side. All plastic covering sheaths are then removed simultaneously from the tape while maintaining no tension upon the sling itself using the technique previously described.

Only one technique currently uses this method; TVT-O.

Results

Since the initial description by Delorme in 2001, continence rates have been reproducibly satisfactory although follow-up has, in general, been short (Table 68–9). Reported continence rates range from 80.5% to 96% on the basis of a variety of subjective (questionnaire and quality of life single-item assessment) and objective (cough stress test, uroflowmetry, physical examination) measures.

Efficacy

Efficacy analyses have included heterogeneous groups of patients including those in whom prior procedures failed, those who had concomitant prolapse, and those with mixed incontinence. Delorme (2001) noted that 15.6% of his patients had ISD, and Mellier and colleagues (2004) diagnosed 28% of their patients with ISD. Despite these diverse populations of patients, relatively similar results were obtained. However, no preoperative predictors of outcomes using either clinical or urodynamic parameters were established to determine overall results of these procedures. Therefore, the effect of mixed incontinence, ISD, and concomitant prolapse on surgical outcomes for this intervention are unknown. Prospective studies are needed to answer these questions.

Two nonrandomized studies have compared TOT with TVT procedures and have found no significant difference in postoperative voiding dysfunction, complications, or overall continence. There was a tendency toward more bladder injuries (10% versus 0%) and hemorrhage (10% versus 2%) with the suprapubic as compared with the TOT approach, but this did not reach statistical significance (de Tayrac et al, 2004; Mellier et al, 2004).

Complications of the Transobturator Approach

Despite the minimally invasive nature of these procedures, peri- and postoperative complications have been reported with a variety of techniques.

Bladder perforation appears to be the most common complication associated with any midurethral sling, with a 2% to 11% risk with the suprapubic approach. Although initial reports described the risk with the TOT approach as being negligible, the risk of bladder injury is now identified as associated with this sling insertion technique (Table 68–10) (Olsson and Kroon, 1999; Kobashi and Govier, 2003b; de Tayrac et al, 2004).

Minaglia and colleagues (2004) reported three cases of intraoperative bladder injury while performing the TOT insertion method. They identified all injuries intraoperatively because of their utilization of cystoscopy as an adjunct to all insertion procedures. All injuries were managed with catheter placement for 1 week postoperatively, and these authors noted no complications after sling removal and reinsertion at that same setting.

A single case of bladder laceration was reported by Cindolo and Costa that was also managed intraoperatively (Cindolo et al, 2004; Costa et al, 2004). This apparently was a more extensive injury than just trocar perforation. The tunneler passage

of the outside-in obturator approach has been shown to be associated with lower urinary tract injury. To date, no case of bladder injury when performing the TOT by the inside-out approach has been reported using the TVT-O (Hermieu et al, 2003; Whiteside and Walters, 2004).

Domingo and coauthors (2005) reported a relatively high incidence of vaginal erosion in their series using either the ObTape or UraTape. They attributed their erosion rate to the characteristics of the particular mesh that they utilized, with the reduced pore size and other mechanical properties of that particular material. They noted a slightly increased risk of erosion with the ObTape (15-mm silicone-coated portion), 19% versus 12% compared with the UraTape, and they felt that this was most likely due to reduction in pore size and higher degree of encapsulation. They also concluded that synthetic mesh with larger pore sizes facilitates vascular and tissue ingrowth, optimizing mesh incorporation.

Tape erosion was usually managed by removal by the transvaginal approach alone or combined with the transobturator approach. They noted continence rates of 78% (despite tape removal in their series) (Domingo et al, 2005).

Postoperative voiding dysfunction has been noted to occur in 0% to 20.6% of patients following TVT (Pesschers et al, 2000). **The incidence following TOT procedures varies between 2.1% and 6.7%.** There appears to be no significant difference in postoperative voiding dysfunction between the TVT and TOT in nonrandomized studies (Mansoor et al, 2003; de Tayrac et al, 2004). Urinary retention also appears to be not significantly different. The rate of obstructive symptoms after the TOT midurethral sling varies between 1.5% and 15.6% of patients. This phenomenon is usually transient and managed with short-term intermittent catheterization, although occasionally symptoms mandate tape release. Long-term retention after TVT is a rare complication (0.6% to 3.8%) and can be expected in the TOT population as well (deTayrac et al, 2004). Removal of the tape, in most cases, improves the patient's symptoms. There has been some anecdotal experience with downward displacement of the tape under local anesthesia to provide symptomatic relief in patients with persistent voiding dysfunction (Ozel et al, 2004). Nonetheless, the overall risk of postoperative voiding dysfunction after the TOT is relatively low.

Another bothersome complication, unique to the TOT approach, is that of postoperative leg pain. de Leval (2003) described 15.9% of patients with temporary groin pain that resolved after the second postoperative day. Similarly, Krauth and associates (2005) reported 14 cases (2.3%) of patients with postoperative perineal groin pain. They also noted it to be transient and responding to nonsteroidal anti-inflammatories in all but one case. They hypothesized that the etiology of the pain was either subclinical hematoma or a transient neuropathic phenomenon. They recommended that persistent leg pain that does not respond to conservative measures should prompt an investigation to exclude the possibility of erosion, which has been reported in several case reports (Mahajan et al, 2006).

Infection-related complications have included thigh abscess requiring drainage (Goldman, 2005) and an infected obturator hematoma also requiring exploration and drainage (Game et al, 2004).

Table 68–9. Outcomes with Transobturator Techniques

Study	N	Follow-up	Cured/Improved/Failed	Assessment of Outcome	Patients' Age	Pure SUI	Mixed UI	ISD	Previous Anti-Incontinence Surgery	Prehysterectomy	Concomitant Prolapse Repair
Delorme et al, 2003	150 (32 w/1 year f/u)	17 mo (13-29)	90.6%; 9.4%; 0	Cough stress test; uroflow	64 (50-81)	14 (44%)	18 (56%)	5 (15.6%)	5 (15.6%)	5 (15.6%)	0
Costa et al, 2004	183	7 mo (1-21)	80.5%; 7.5%; 12%	Cough stress test/questionnaire	56 yr (29-87)	53%	27.30%	10 (MUCP <20 cm H_2O); 5.4%	14.20%	25.70%	26 (14.2%)
de Tayrac et al, 2004	30	12 mo	90%; 3.3%; 6.7% 92% objective cure; 97% subjective;	Cough stress test/questionnaire	54.7	27	3	4	4	2 (4 previous prolapse sx)	None
Cindolo et al, 2004	80	4 mo (1-8)	96% overall satisfaction	Questionnaire/quality of life instrument	56 (39-79)	62 with + Q-tip test (78%)	22 (28%)	NA	16 (20%)	NA	None
Mellier et al, 2004	94	12.8 mo (2-20)	95% cured; 4%; 1%	Telephone based Questionnaire	58.1 (±9.3)	94 (100%) defined on three-grade scale	12 (13%) preop urgency	26 (28%) MUCP < 30	28 (30%)	17 (18%)	None
Queimadelos et al, 2004	47	18 mo	45/47 (96%)	Questionnaire	55 (40-69)	47	0	3	NA	NA	0
Krauth et al, 2005	604 (140 w/1 year f/u)	1-3 mo in 572; 1 yr in 140	85.5% satisfied at 1 yr	Subjective questioning	57	47.30%	52.70%	Not reported	Not reported	Not reported	8%

MUCP, maximal urethral closure pressure.

Table 68–10. Complications Associated With TOT Techniques

Study	N	Adverse Events
Delorme et al, 2003	32	None reported
de Leval, 2003	107	One superficial vein thrombosis with abscess; ?(27/107) 15.9% transient thigh pain
Domingo et al, 2005	65	Nine vaginal mesh erosion
Costa et al, 2004	183	Three vaginal erosion; two urethral erosion; one bladder perforation; one vaginal perforation; two urethral perforation
de Tayrac et al, 2004	30	Six uncomplicated UTI; one obturator hematoma
Cindolo et al, 2004	80	One vaginal erosion with inguinal abscess
Mellier et al, 2004	94	2% intraop hemmorhage (300 mL); one urethral perforation
Queimadelos et al, 2004	47	None reported
Krauth et al, 2005	604 (140 with 1-year Follow-up	0.3% vaginal erosion; 2.5% UTI; 0.5% bladder perforation; 0.33% vaginal perforation; 2.3% perineal pain

UTI, urinary tract infection.

KEY POINT: TRANSOBTURATOR-MIDURETHRAL SLINGS

■ The transobturator sling appears to have reproducible short-term continence results similar to those seen with the TVT. It does appear to mimic the suprapubic approach by stabilizing the midurethra, recapitulating the hammock support that is thought to be responsible for continence. Major vascular and bowel complications have not been reported, but lower urinary tract injury does occur, and this experience underscores the necessity of cystoscopy as an adjunct to this technique. Initial retrospective comparisons with the TVT show no significant difference in efficacy outcomes between these techniques. Longer term followup is necessary prospectively to evaluate these procedures.

SUGGESTED READINGS

Abouassaly R, Steinberg J, Lemieux M, et al: Complications of tension-free vaginal tape surgery: A multi-institutional review. BJU 2004;94:110-113.

deTayrac R, Deffieux X, Droupy S, et al: A prospective randomized trial comparing tension-free vaginal tape and transobturator suburethral tape for surgical treatment of stress urinary incontinence. Am J Obstet Gynecol 2004;190:602-608.

Klutke C, Siegel S, Carlin B, et al: Urinary retention after tension-free vaginal tape procedure: Incidence and treatment. Urology 2001;58:697-701.

Kuuva N, Nilsson C: Tension-free vaginal tape procedure: An effective minimally invasive operation for the treatment of recurrent stress urinary incontinence? Gynecol Obstet Invest 2003;56:93-98.

Mansoor A, Vedrine N, Darcq C: Surgery of female urinary incontinence using trans-obturator tape (TOT): A prospective randomized comparative study with TVT. Neurourol Urodyn 2003;22:488-489.

Meltomaa S, Backman T, Haarala M: Concomitant vaginal surgery did not affect outcome of the tension-free vaginal tape operation during a prospective 3-year follow up study. J Urol 2004;172:222-226.

Nilsson C, Falconer C, Rezapour M: Seven-year follow-up of the tension-free vaginal tape procedure for treatment of urinary incontinence. Obstet Gynecol 2004;104:1259-1262.

Petros P, Ulmsten U: An integral theory and its method for the diagnosis and management of female urinary incontinence. Scand J Urol Nephrol Suppl 1993;153:1-93.

Sokol A, Jelovsek J, Walters M, et al: Incidence and predictors of prolonged urinary retention after TVT with and without concurrent prolapse surgery. Am J Obstet Gynecol 2005;192:1537-1543.

Ward K, Hilton P: A prospective multicenter randomized trial of tension-free vaginal tape and colposuspension for primary stress incontinence. Two-year follow-up. Am J Obstet Gynecol 2004;190:324-331.

Injection Therapy for Urinary Incontinence

RODNEY A. APPELL, MD • J. CHRISTIAN WINTERS, MD

PATIENT SELECTION

INJECTABLE MATERIALS

INTRAURETHRAL INJECTION TECHNIQUES

POSTOPERATIVE CARE

EFFICACY OF INJECTABLE TREATMENT

COMPLICATIONS

SAFETY

PRESENT AND FUTURE OF INJECTABLES IN URINARY INCONTINENCE

The ideal injectable agent is one that is biocompatible, causes little inflammatory or foreign body reaction resulting in a lack of chronic tissue change, does not migrate, and maintains its bulking effect for a long period of time. Present experience suggests the technology to achieve a successful injection is currently at our disposal but that we are injecting agents that may be less than ideal.

Surgical procedures designed to correct stress urinary incontinence (SUI) raise the concern that increasing urethral resistance to abdominal pressure (Pabd) may result in a parallel increase in detrusor pressure (Pdet). This may have untoward effects on bladder compliance, leading to upper tract damage. **One does not wish to increase resistance to Pdet just to correct SUI that occurs with increases in Pabd. Injectable materials** can be used successfully in patients because they dramatically improve the ability of the urethra to resist increases in Pabd without changing voiding pressure or the Pdet at the time of leakage. The goal of injectables is to restore mucosal coaptation and its "seal effect" contribution to the continence mechanism. The intraurethral placement of a bulking agent creates a coaptive effect, which increases the urethral resistance at rest and restores continence. Bulking agents for the most part do not obstruct voiding, because the ability of the urethra to funnel and open without extrinsic compressive forces is preserved during normal micturition.

To achieve this desired effect, **most bulking agents are actually injected into the urethral smooth muscle at the level of the bladder outlet.** This means that phrases such as "periurethral" or "submucosal" may not be truly accurate. The injection is intraurethral. The techniques described that follow facilitate placing the needle into the muscle by beginning outside the urethra (periurethral approach) or transurethrally through a cystoscope, during which the needle is placed in a submucosal plane up to the bladder outlet and turned into the urethral muscle.

PATIENT SELECTION

Injectable agents represent one of the many treatment options in the management of SUI. Strict criteria for the consideration of injectables as a treatment modality have been ascertained, and they appear most suitable for patients with SUI secondary to intrinsic sphincteric deficiency (ISD) and normal detrusor muscle function.

The activity precipitating the urinary leakage is important. **Patients who leak in the supine position, have bed wetting, or leak with a sensation of urinary urgency do not have genuine SUI and need to be investigated for ISD.** Urodynamic studies are performed to evaluate possible bladder causes of incontinence and to evaluate urethral function, which is easily ascertained by measuring abdominal leak point pressure (ALPP), that is, the abdominal pressure (Pabd) required to drive urine through the continence mechanism. Previously, only a low ALPP (65 cm H$_2$O) with video-urodynamics revealing an open bladder outlet at rest (in the absence of a detrusor contraction) resulting in urinary leakage was thought to imply ISD. However, some have utilized a "clinical" definition of ISD as any leak point below 100 cm H$_2$O. This variance and other reported limitations in the testing process make the absolute ALPP value of less importance. *The ideal patient for the use of injectables has been described as one with poor urethral function (ISD), normal bladder capacity and compliance, and good anatomic support.* Many women, despite the presence of urethral hypermobility, may still do well after injectable therapy (Herschorn et al, 1992; Faerber, 1995; Winters et al, 2000). Therefore, it appears that all patients who present with isolated SUI and no evidence of detrusor causes of incontinence can be offered injectable agents to treat stress urinary incontinence. Contraindications to injectables include active urinary tract infection, untreated detrusor overactivity, and known hypersensitivity to the proposed injectable agent.

Adult Males

Leakage demonstrable with coughing, straining, or exercise is sufficient to judge that SUI, and more specifically ISD, is present in men. The concept of SUI in men is different, all men with SUI have ISD, and urodynamic investigation is performed to rule out detrusor causes of incontinence. Bladder neck contracture must be recognized and addressed before injectable therapy, and previous radiation therapy may limit the ability to do bulking without rupture of the urothelium, thus reducing the ability to coapt the walls of the urethra. In addition, microvascular damage from radiation may retard host tissue ingrowth into the implant, adversely affecting durability. **To be effective, injectable material must be injected in the urethra superior to the external sphincter.** Although no controlled studies have been completed, the placement of injectable materials below the sphincter is limited by the pliability and width of the bulbar urethra. This section of the urethra acts mainly as a conduit, and external compression (sling or artificial urinary sphincter) is probably needed to create effective coaptation at this level of the urethra. In addition, placement of the material into the external sphincter has been associated with sphincter spasm and failure (Appell, 1994a). **The depth of injection and the quality of the tissue is critical, because the injectable material must deform the urethral mucosa so that it closes the urethral lumen.**

Adult Females

Injectables are most suitable for patients with ISD and the absence of detrusor storage abnormalities (detrusor overactivity). A pelvic examination that demonstrates no urethral mobility in conjunction with a positive "stress test" when the patient strains in the upright position with 200 mL in the bladder constitutes presumptive evidence of ISD. The cotton-swab test can be useful, with an angle of greater than 30 degrees signifying urethral hypermobility (Chrystle et al, 1971; Appell and Ostergard, 1992). Radiographically, the presence of an open bladder neck and proximal urethra with the bladder at rest in the absence of a detrusor contraction during the filling phase implies the presence of ISD. Urodynamic investigation is performed to rule out possible detrusor causes of incontinence, as well as to obtain ALPP. This measurement of the abdominal pressure required to induce leakage is a confirmatory step. Today, we appear to be entering a new paradigm in the understanding of the pathophysiology of SUI. There are women with urethral hypermobility who do not leak urine with increasing abdominal pressure, implying that all patients with SUI have some degree of ISD whether associated with hypermobility or not (Appell, 1988). The occurrence of SUI appears to be a combined disorder of anatomy (urethral support) and function (intrinsic sphincteric resistance) that occurs to varying degrees. Very few women with SUI (if any) have pure anatomic-induced incontinence without some degree of sphincteric dysfunction. Those with fixed, nonmobile urethras have a deficiency of intrinsic urethral function as the predominant cause of urinary leakage

(Winters, 2004). A number of authors have noted that the presence of urethral hypermobility does not seem to have an adverse effect on outcome and intraurethral injections may be considered in these patients (Herschorn et al, 1992; Faerber, 1995; Winters et al, 2000). Although patients with combined ISD and hypermobility can be treated with injectables, they may be better served with alternative surgical endeavors such as the artificial urinary sphincters or pubovaginal or tension-free midurethral sling procedures.

Children

In these patients, although the etiology of the ISD may be different (e.g., myelodysplasia instead of postsurgical), the criteria of adequate bladder capacity, lack of detrusor dysfunction, and lack of anatomic abnormality (patulous, open bladder neck) in the presence of ISD again indicate the best candidates. Patients with isolated sphincteric deficiency are the best candidates for injection. Those with detrusor causes (detrusor overactivity) or impaired contractility of the bladder may be more prone to complications such as continued leakage, impaired compliance, or inability to empty. Those children with patulous bladder necks that appear fixed in the open position are not as likely to do well, based on the significant anatomic correction that is required. These children may also be better served with artificial sphincters or sling procedures.

KEY POINT: PATIENT SELECTION

- Urodynamic testing is mandatory in the evaluation of the patient to rule out any abnormalities in detrusor function.

INJECTABLE MATERIALS
Historical Chronology

The technique of intraurethral injection of material to increase outflow resistance in patients with urinary incontinence is not new. The first report (Murless, 1938) involved 20 patients and described the injection of a sclerosing solution (sodium morrhuate or cod-liver oil) into the anterior vaginal wall. An inflammatory response developed with secondary scarring and resultant compression of the incompetent urethra. Cure or improvement was reported in 17 patients; however, the complications included pulmonary infarction and cardiorespiratory arrest. Quackels (1955) reported two patients successfully treated with periurethral paraffin injection without complications. Sachse (1963) treated 31 patients with another sclerosing agent, Dondren, and 12 of 24 men with postprostatectomy incontinence and 4 of 7 women were reported as cured. Again, however, pulmonary embolization was the major drawback.

Polytetrafluoroethylene

The first report of the use of polytetrafluoroethylene (PTFE) paste in a glycerol base (Polytef, Urethrin) by Berg (1973) described three women with surgically induced ISD who experienced resolution of symptoms, although two thirds required a repeat injection. The only complication was asymptomatic bacteriuria in one patient. The use of PTFE injection for incontinence was promulgated in the United States by Politano and associates at the University of Miami for many years (Politano et al, 1974; Kaufman et al, 1984; Lewis et al, 1984; Vorstman et al, 1985). However, this procedure did not attain universal acceptance despite reports from various other centers demonstrating its efficacy (Heer, 1977; Lampante et al, 1979; Lim et al, 1983; Schulman et al, 1983; Deane et al, 1985; Appell, 1990a). These and other studies were extensively reviewed for efficacy and safety by the Department of Technology Assessment of the American Medical Association (Cole, 1993), which concluded that PTFE injection is a *reasonably* effective treatment for incontinence and technically easy to perform. However, particle migration (Malizia et al, 1984) and granuloma formation (Mittleman and Marraccini, 1983) raised concerns about the safety of the product. Despite these findings, there have been no reports of untoward sequelae in humans. A current investigation into the efficacy and safety of PTFE injections for incontinence caused by only ISD has begun under monitoring by the U.S. Food and Drug Administration (FDA), and it is hoped that this will clarify many of these concerns with respect to efficacy and safety.

Glutaraldehyde Cross-Linked Bovine Collagen (GAX-Collagen)

Bovine dermal collagen has long been recognized as a **biocompatible biomaterial** primarily in the form of resorbable sutures and hemostatic agents. Cross-linking with glutaraldehyde results in a fibrillar collagen with resistance to collagenase digestion and significantly enhances persistence, with stabilization preventing synerisis. For this reason, overcorrection is not necessary or desirable with GAX-collagen implants, because the volume does not undergo rapid shrinkage soon after injection, owing to the formation of this compact fibrous structure that promotes incorporation into surrounding host connective tissue with additional production and deposition of new host collagen within the implant (DeLustro et al, 1991). This material does not cause granuloma formation, and migration of particles to distant body sites does not appear at autopsy (DeLustro et al, 1991).

GAX-collagen is a highly purified 35% suspension of bovine collagen in a phosphate buffer containing at least 95% type I collagen and 1% to 5% type III collagen prepared by selective hydrolysis of the nonhelicoidal amino-terminal and carboxy-terminal segments (telopeptides) of the collagen molecules, which has the effect of decreasing the antigenicity (DeLustro et al, 1990) and increasing the duration of the implant within the human body by increasing its resistance to collagenase (McPherson et al, 1986).

GAX-collagen is biocompatible and biodegradable and elicits only a minimal inflammatory reaction without foreign body reaction (Canning et al, 1988). **GAX-collagen begins to degrade in 12 weeks and is completely degraded in 19 months,** yet the transformation of the injected material into living connective tissue (Remacle and Marbaix, 1988) explains its ability to maintain its effectiveness in nearly 80% of those who have attained continence (Appell, 1994a). Despite FDA

approval for the treatment of ISD in males and females in the later part of 1993, GAX-collagen does have the potential for eliciting an allergic reaction and, although it is more compatible than PTFE in biologic systems, it is considerably more expensive and requires more treatment sessions to attain continence; thus, the search continues for a better injectable.

Synthetic Materials

Durasphere and Durasphere EXP

Durasphere was approved by the FDA in 1999. This material consists of nonresorbable pyrolytic carbon-coated zirconium beads that are much larger (212 to 500 µm) than either PTFE or silicone polymers and are transferred in a 2.8% β-glucan water-based gel. The randomized, multicenter, double-blind study (Lightner et al, 2001) accepted by the FDA compared collagen to Durasphere and showed similar outcomes, with the original Durasphere offering a slight benefit. Durasphere is more viscous than collagen and its injection was more technically demanding until the introduction of Durasphere-EXP. Recently, renewed concern has been expressed about material migration after injection (Pannek, et al, 2001; Ritts, 2002), despite lack of clear evidence demonstrating any migration. Microcrystalline components of the bulking agent should be composed of uniform spheroidal particles with sizes above 80 µm (approximate size required to avoid migration, determined in studies involving PTFE [Teflon]). Migration is clearly influenced by the ability of host macrophages to phagocytize particles, and smaller particle sizes have been shown to migrate to distant locations with Teflon injection. However, direct embolization of material is caused by high-pressure injection, resulting in material displacement into vascular or lymphatic spaces. Injection technique should therefore rely on larger particle sizes administered with low-pressure injection instrumentation. This should not become a problem with Durasphere-EXP, because its smallest particle is 95 µm and ranges up to 200 µm, which is significantly smaller than the original Durasphere (200 to 550 µm) but still in the size greater than the 80-µm minimum needed for safety.

The beads encapsulate within the tissue and retain implant bulk for at least 2 years (Fig. 69–1). This use of carbon beads does not require skin testing because there is no associated antigenicity.

Ethylene Vinyl Alcohol

Tegress is a permanently implanted nonpyrogenic, injectable bulking agent composed of ethylene vinyl alcohol (EVOH) copolymer dissolved in dimethyl sulfoxide (DMSO). The resulting mixture is 8% EVOH in DMSO. This material is packaged in 3-mL glass vials and contains a corresponding 3-mL DMSO-compatible syringe. It is easily injected through a 25-gauge needle. After injection into tissue, the solution is exposed to blood or extracellular fluid at physiologic temperatures and the DMSO diffuses away, resulting in the EVOH precipitating into a complex cohesive spongiform mass. **This phase transformation takes place rapidly (within 60 seconds),** and this effect creates increased tissue bulk; however, the phase change requires diligent separation of the agent and body temperature fluids before implantation. Implantation of this material seems to elicit an acute

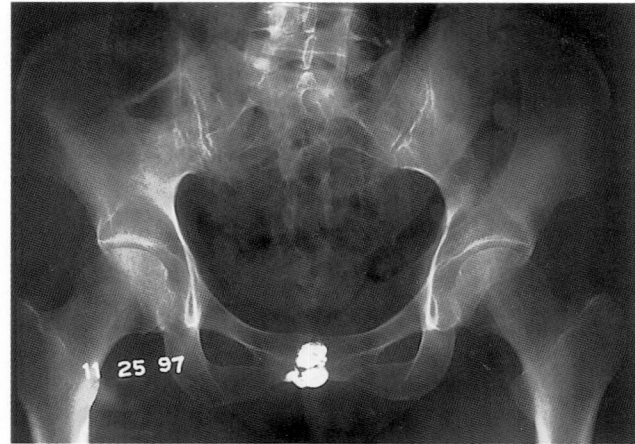

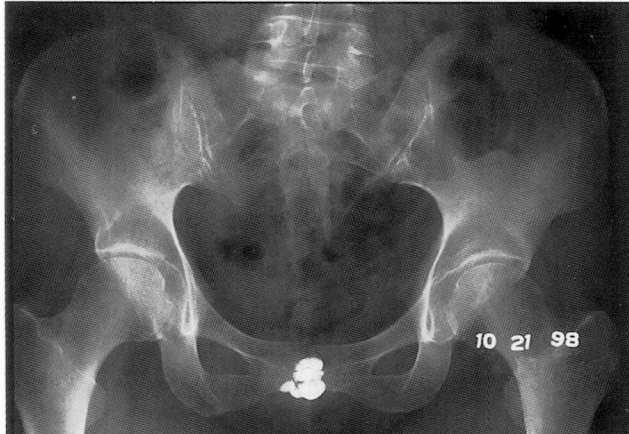

Figure 69–1. Radiographs demonstrating preservation of injected Durasphere material with appearance identical at 1 *(left)* and 2 *(right)* years after injection.

inflammatory response, with the greatest severity at 1 month. After 3 months, the severity of the inflammatory response stabilizes and decreases to a mild, localized foreign body response with some mineralization. There was no effect of the implant on tissues away from the implant site, nor any evidence of migration. In a multicenter prospective evaluation of patients injected with EVOH, adverse events, particularly exposed material, occurred more frequently after periurethral injection. Therefore, the only approved method of injection is via a transurethral approach (U.S. Food and Drug Adminstration, 2004).

Silicone Polymers

Macroplastique and Bioplastique are textured polydimethylsiloxane macroparticles (>100 µm) suspended within a bioexcretable carrier hydrogel of polyvinylpyrrolidone (povidone) in which the solid particle content is 33% of the total volume.

Henly and associates (1995) compared migratory and histologic tendencies of solid silicone macrospheres with smaller silicone particles in dogs in which nuclear imaging revealed small particles were disseminated throughout the lung, kidney, brain, and lymph nodes 4 months after injection, whereas only one episode of large particle migration to the

lung occurred without associated inflammation. The concerns over migration of particles and the adverse publicity over silicone gel implants will likely limit the use of this material in the United States.

Autologous Injectables

Autologous materials have been utilized as injectable agents in the treatment of SUI. **Autologous blood** appears to have no lasting quality. In one small study of 14 women (Appell, 1994b), 30 mL of blood from an antecubital vein in a heparinized syringe was used. Within two treatment sessions, each patient was rendered continent; however, the duration of continence lasted only between 10 and 17 days. **Autologous fat** provides the advantages of ready availability and biocompatibility and is easily obtainable via liposuction. The technique was first reported by Gonzalez de Garibay and coworkers (1989) in 10 women; and in a follow-up report at 1 year after a single injection in 15 women and 5 men, they noted "good" results in 33% of the women and none of the men (Gonzalez de Garibay et al, 1991). These results do not compare favorably with that of PFTE or GAX-collagen. The reason for this appears to be because the injected fat degrades: only a very small proportion remains viable because neovascularity is never adequately achieved at the center of the graft to maintain its long-term viability. Minimal fat integrates as a graft, with 60% lost in only 3 weeks after injection (Bartynski et al, 1990). This is probably the result of destruction of the normal adipocyte architecture (Nguyen et al, 1990). As the injected material is reabsorbed, it is replaced by inflammation and fibrosis, with connective tissue producing the final bulking effect (Santarosa and Blaivas, 1994). The use of autologous fat should be discouraged because of its potential association with systemic embolization and death (Sweat and Lightner, 1999).

KEY POINTS: INJECTABLE MATERIALS

- There are many materials that can be used for injection, and a continued look for the perfectly safe substance that is easy to inject and results in a durable response will and should continue.

- The unique aspects to each substance will also alter the techniques used to perform the actual injection, and it will be up to the surgeon to make certain that he or she feels adequately trained in the optimal technique for whatever substance is to be used.

INTRAURETHRAL INJECTION TECHNIQUES

The techniques used to inject the various materials are not difficult, even when the substance requires some special instrumentation, such as liposuction before autologous fat injection (Ganabathi and Leach, 1994) or specialized pressure injectors for more viscous material such as PTFE or silicone polymers. However, it is essential to perform precise placement of the material to ensure an optimal result. The injections (Appell,

1994a) can be performed suburothelially through a needle placed directly through a cystourethroscope (transurethral injection) or periurethrally with a spinal needle or specialty injector injected percutaneously and positioned in the urethral tissues while observing the manipulation endoscopically per urethra. Other possible routes of injection are by means of an ultrasound probe per vagina in females (Appell, 1996) or per rectum in males (Kageyama, et al, 1994), although these results are rarely if ever used in clinical practice. Regardless of technique used, the implant is placed within the wall of the urethra (intraurethral). The cause of the incontinence, the tissue at the injection site, and the plane of delivery of the injectable substance will affect the treatment results. Nearly every patient can be injected with the use of local anesthesia, which has the added advantage of allowing the patient to stand and perform a few provocative maneuvers immediately after the injection in an attempt to cause urinary leakage, which can then be addressed before the patient is released from treatment.

The methods of injection should not pose great difficulty to the urologist comfortable with transurethral surgery. Precise localization of the site of deposition of the collagen material is essential to ensure an optimal response. **Men are injected through the transurethral approach, and females are injected by either approach.** The periurethral approach decreases bleeding complications, which hamper visualization and extrusion of the injected material, but has a much longer learning curve than the transurethral approach. In a prospective randomized comparison of the transurethral and periurethral approaches to injection therapy in women, no differences in efficacy were seen. This suggests that each approach has similar success rates, but the rate of urinary retention and the volume of material injected was higher in the periurethral group (Schulz et al, 2004).

Males

Male patients are positioned in a semi-lithotomy position, and the surgical field is prepared in the usual sterile fashion. If local anesthesia is employed, which is preferred by the authors, it is used in the form of 2% lidocaine jelly intraurethrally 10 minutes before instrumentation. In some patients, preoperative sedation may also be of benefit. A 20- or 21-Fr cystoscopic sheath is employed using a 0-degree or 30-degree lens. GAX-collagen is provided in a 3.0-mL Luer-Lok syringe containing 2.5 mL of injectable material. The syringe attaches to a 5-Fr injection catheter containing a 1.5-cm 20-gauge needle at the tip. Durasphere is provided in a 1.0-mL Luer-Lok syringe and is injected with an 18-gauge needle. Most men are injected transurethrally under cystoscopic vision.

The **postprostatectomy** urethra is frequently scarred and less pliant; thus, several needle positions are frequently needed to deposit sufficient material to produce urethral coaptation. The injection is completed in four quadrants after localization of the appropriate level in the proximal urethra. The needle is advanced under the urethral mucosa with the beveled portion of the needle facing the urethral lumen to allow for layering of the material. The injectable material is then delivered, creating a bleb under the urethral mucosa that protrudes into the urethral lumen. This is performed in a circumferential manner in four quadrants, creating a bleb in each quadrant

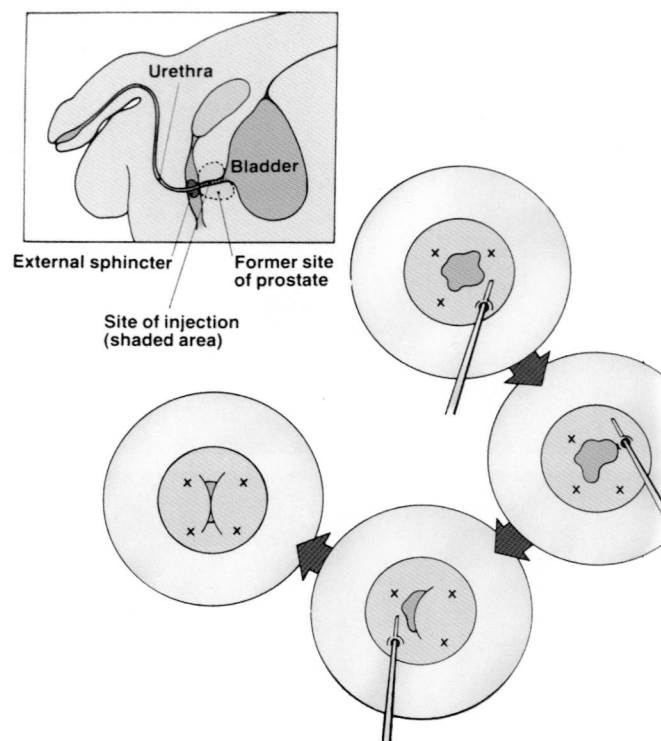

Figure 69–2. Schematic representation of transurethral circumferential injection in a male after prostatectomy. (From McGuire EJ, Appell RA: Collagen injection for the dysfunctional urethra. Contemp Urol 1991;3:11.)

(Fig. 69–2). After completion, the urethral mucosa should be completely coapted and creates the appearance of an obstructed urethra. Extrusion of the injectable agent into the urethral lumen as the needle is withdrawn may occur; however, loss of injected material is minimal and inconsequential with most substances, with the exception of PTFE and Durasphere, with which the loss may be significant. This may be prevented in most cases by leaving the needle in place for at least 30 seconds after the injection is completed or by flushing the material with saline. The loss of additional material is diminished by preventing advancement of the cystoscope proximal to the injection sites. If material extravasation occurs in all quadrants during injection, the procedure should be terminated and rescheduled after 4 weeks.

Because of the difficulty of localizing the injection by means of cystoscopy, an alternative method of injecting collagen in men was introduced using a **suprapubic antegrade approach.** This approach has been described employing a flexible cystoscope (Klutke et al, 1996) placed through a suprapubic cystotomy. The antegrade approach has the advantage of direct visualization of the bladder neck and the injection of material into more supple, less scarred urethra. We have described this technique using a 14-Fr pediatric endoscope used formerly for PTFE injections or a pediatric cystoscope (Winters and Appell, 1996). The patient is positioned in the modified lithotomy position, and flexible cystoscopy is carried out, simultaneously filling the bladder. After this, a percutaneous suprapubic punch allows placement of two guide wires into the bladder. The site is dilated to 16 Fr with Amplatz dilators.

A sheath may be used, but commonly the cystoscope can be advanced over one of the guide wires into the bladder. A small red rubber catheter or the flexible cystoscope can be used to assist in localization of the bladder neck.

This approach offers an excellent view of the bladder neck and proximal urethra (Fig. 69–3). In our experience, fewer injection sites are needed because the nonscarred bladder neck tissue readily remodels as the material is injected. Therefore, it is not uncommon to be able to complete an injection using two or three injection sites. The needle is placed just under the urethral mucosa at the level of the bladder neck and advanced proximally, meaning it is pulled back toward the bladder. The bladder neck closes off completely as the material is injected. Injection stops after the bladder neck closes off, the two sides meeting in apposition near the midline. It is optional to place a small suprapubic tube to avoid the possible necessity of urethral catheterization. As newer procedures emerge in the treatment of postprostatectomy incontinence, these antegrade techniques may reemerge as alternatives to improve upon less than satisfactory results.

To be effective, any injectable material must be injected in the urethra superior to the external sphincter. Most certainly, it should not be placed in the bulbous urethra where the cuff of the artificial sphincter is placed, because injectables work at the level of the continence zone at the neck of the bladder (i.e., the intra-abdominal urethral segment). In the treatment of postprostatic resection incontinence, the injection is in proximal membranous urethra and laterally beside the verumontanum to give the impression of replacing "apical" tissue, and it should visually appear obstructed at the conclusion of the injection. Injections in patients after radical prostatectomy are more difficult, especially in irradiated tissue or those with more scar tissue, and considerable practice is needed to reach correct tissue depth with the needle.

Females

Females may be injected by a transurethral technique (O'Connell and McGuire, 1995) or a periurethral technique with a

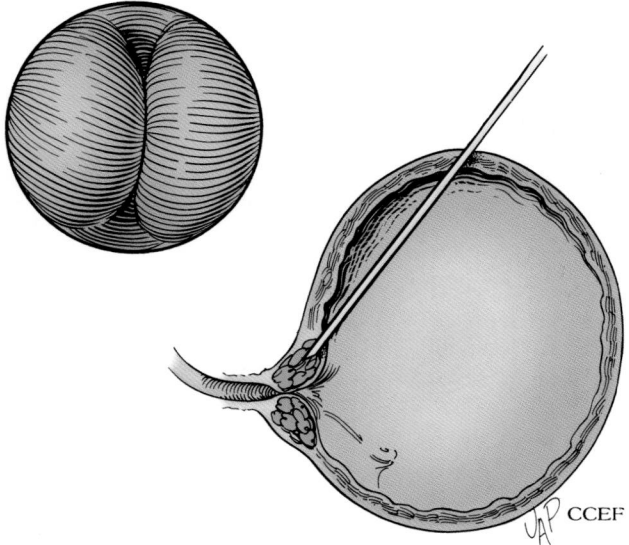

Figure 69–3. Antegrade injection in the male.

spinal needle inserted lateral to the meatus, which then traverses the wall of the urethra while the needle placement is observed by the surgeon directly by cystourethroscopy (Appell, 1990b) or transvaginally with the needle placed through the biopsy port of an ultrasound probe (Appell, 1996). Maneuvers to help in localization of the needle tip are useful, such as preinjecting the urethra during the periurethral technique with methylene blue to enable the surgeon to place the implant more accurately (Neal et al, 1995). In either case, the patients are placed in the lithotomy position and prepared in the usual sterile fashion. Topical 2% lidocaine jelly is used in the urethra, and 20% benzocaine is used in the vestibule. The periurethral tissues are infiltrated with 2 to 4 mL of 1% plain lidocaine injected at the 3- and 9- o'clock positions. **It is most important to emphasize that the material injected should be positioned at the bladder neck and proximal urethra.** Placement too distally will ultimately fail and cause irritative voiding symptoms.

In the **transurethral approach,** a 0-, 12-, or 30-degree lens is used. The endoscope is placed at the mid urethra, and the needle is advanced in the 4-o'clock position. The point of submucosal insertion is immediately beyond the mid urethra and advanced proximally to the level of the bladder neck into the urethral muscle closest to the submucosa. The material is then injected, and the urethral mucosa can be seen to gradually protrude to the midline. It is important to inject the material slowly to allow the tissue to adequately accommodate it. When the mucosal bleb reaches the midline, the needle is withdrawn while continuing to slowly inject. The needle is then repositioned in the 8 o'clock position, and the injection is performed until the urethral mucosal blebs again approximate into the midline, creating the appearance of an obstructed prostatic urethra in the male. A novel device called an "implacer" (Q-Med AB, Upsalla, Sweden) has been developed to facilitate the engagement of injectable agents without the use of a cystoscope (Fig. 69–4). This device utilizes four syringes preloaded with injectable material. These syringes are advanced into the urethral wall at the level of the mid urethra in four quadrants. The purpose is to place four quadrants of injectable material at the same level in the mid urethra. The urethral length is determined with the use of a urethral catheter, and the corresponding midurethral length is noted on the implacer. After advancing the device into the mid urethra, the outer sleeve is retracted, deploying the syringes into the urethra. The rationale of this device is to provide a reproducible method of material implantation without the need of a cystoscope. A periurethral block and intraurethral lidocaine is all the anesthesia that is necessary. Clinical trials are currently ongoing in the United States. A similar implantation device may also be used with silicone polymers (Macroplastique).

When performing the transurethral injection of EVOH, the technique is different. As the DMSO dissolves, the ethylene vinyl remains as a spongy mass. Injecting too much material is likely to elicit mucosal disruption and exposure of the material. To avoid this from occurring, the injection should occur in a more distal urethral location (1.5 cm distal to bladder neck) and the injection should occur slowly (30 seconds/injection site). **One does not wait for urethral coaptation and, in fact, it should not coapt during the injection process;** the injection is guided by location and the volume of material injected. In fact, urethral coaptation with

MIDURETHRAL INJECTION OF HYALURONIC ACID AND DEXTRANOMERS

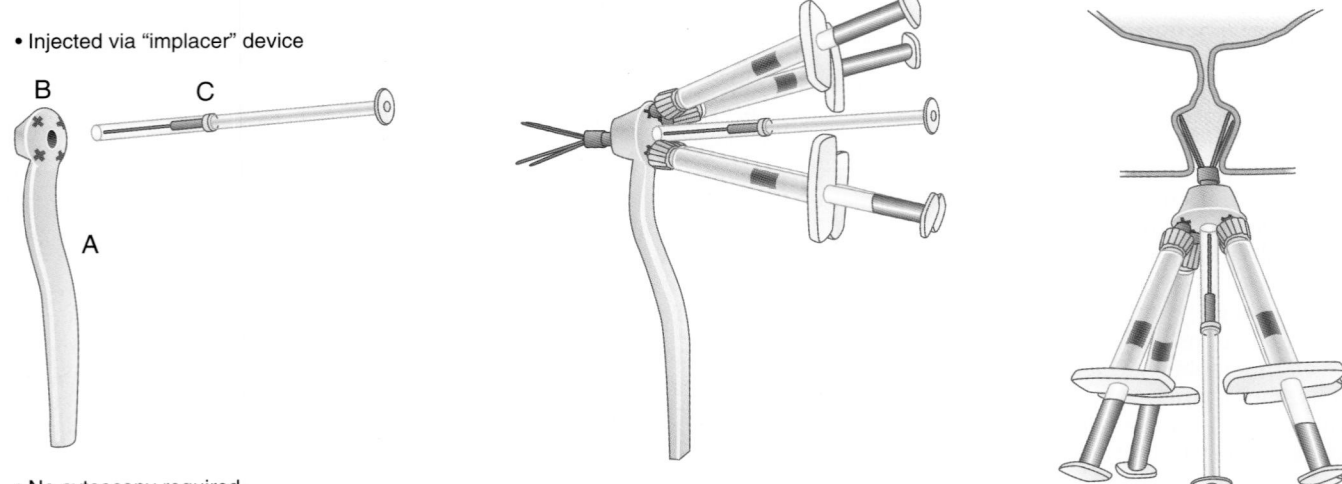

- Injected via "implacer" device

- No cytoscopy required
- Injection of all 4 syringes of material

Figure 69–4. Implacer for midurethral injection.

EVOH may signify overinjection (Dmochowski and Appell, 2003).

In the **periurethral approach** (which some prefer to minimize intraurethral bleeding and extravasation of the injectable substance), the goal of creating urethral mucosal coaptation is the same. After infiltration of the periurethral tissues, the appropriately gauged needle (with GAX-collagen, this is accomplished with a 20- or 22-gauge standard spinal needle) with the obturator in place is inserted into the periurethral tissue at the 4 o'clock position. The needle should be positioned within the lamina propria; in this plane, the needle advances with minimal resistance. During advancement of the needle, urethroscopy is performed to monitor placement of the needle at the level of the bladder neck.

It is quite easy to hold the endoscope with one hand while advancing the needle with the other hand. Gentle rocking of the needle assists in confirming the proper location and depth of the needle tip. Once this is confirmed, the material is injected, creating a mucosal bleb just as in the transurethral technique. Once the mucosal bleb meets the midline, the needle is repositioned in the 8-o'clock position and the injection carried out on the contralateral side (Fig. 69–5). If extravasation occurs, the needle is repositioned in a more anterior location and the injection repeated. Once the appearance of obstruction is created by urethral coaptation, the procedure is terminated (Winters and Appell, 1995). A "bent-tip" needle (Boston Scientific, Inc., Natick, MA) has been designed to ease placement of the needle within the proper

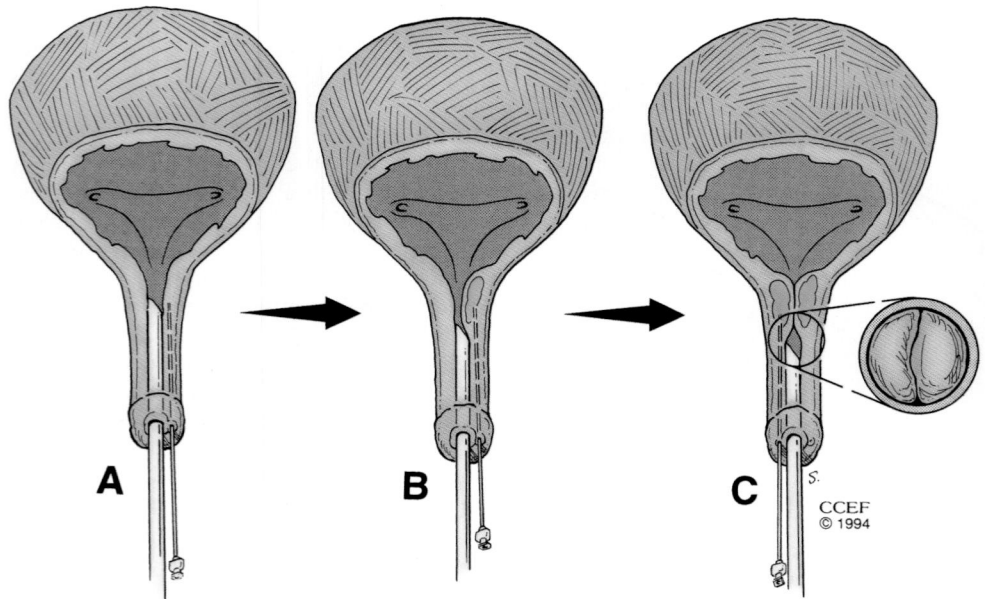

A

B

C

Figure 69–5. **A**, Appearance of urethra before treatment. **B**, Periurethral needle positioned in the proximal urethra below the bladder neck. **C**, Appearance of urethra after injection. (**A** to **C** from Winters JC, Appell RA: Periurethral injection of collagen in the treatment of intrinsic sphincteric deficiency in the female patient. Urol Clin North Am 1995;22:673.)

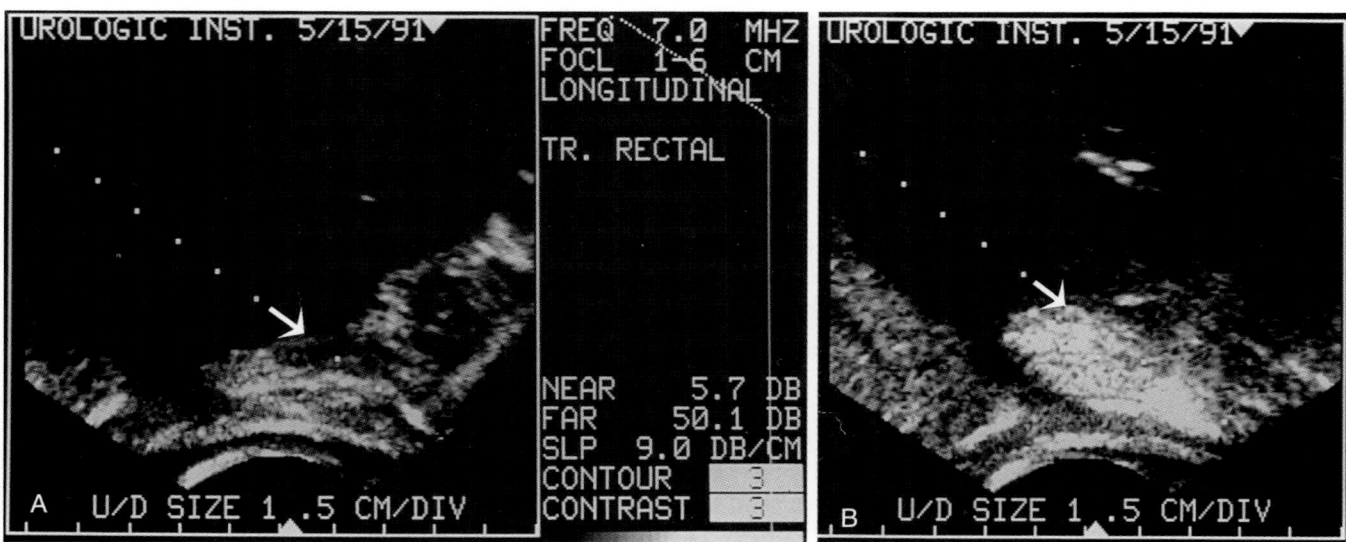

Figure 69–6. **A,** Transvaginal ultrasound identification of bladder neck *(arrow).* **B,** Ultrasound of bladder neck after injection (note hyperechoic appearance of injected GAX-collagen).

intraurethral plane. By placing the needle in the lateral sulci of the urethra, simple advancement of the bent-tip needle advances it medially and ultimately into the proper intraurethral position. This can be confirmed via urethroscopy. This has been particularly useful when injecting Durasphere, because larger-sized bent-tip needles have been created specifically to facilitate the periurethral injection of this material.

To avoid instrumenting the urethra and the risk of compressing the freshly placed implant by the endoscope, transvaginal ultrasound-guided injections have been used and have been demonstrated to work equally as well (Appell, 1996). A multiplanar probe with a biopsy port (the standard transrectal ultrasound probe for prostate examination and biopsy) passed vaginally is used to identify the open bladder neck (Fig. 69–6A). The needle (the same one used for transurethral injection) is placed accurately through the biopsy port, and the injection is followed through closure of the bladder neck (see Fig. 69–6B) by longitudinal (sagittal) scanning. This procedure is rarely utilized, but there are data to suggest that the ultrasound appearance of the periurethral collagen may be predictive of long-term outcome (Defreitas et al, 2003). These authors have demonstrated that the circumferential distribution of collagen around the urethra, verified by three-dimensional ultrasound, provides an objective, noninvasive

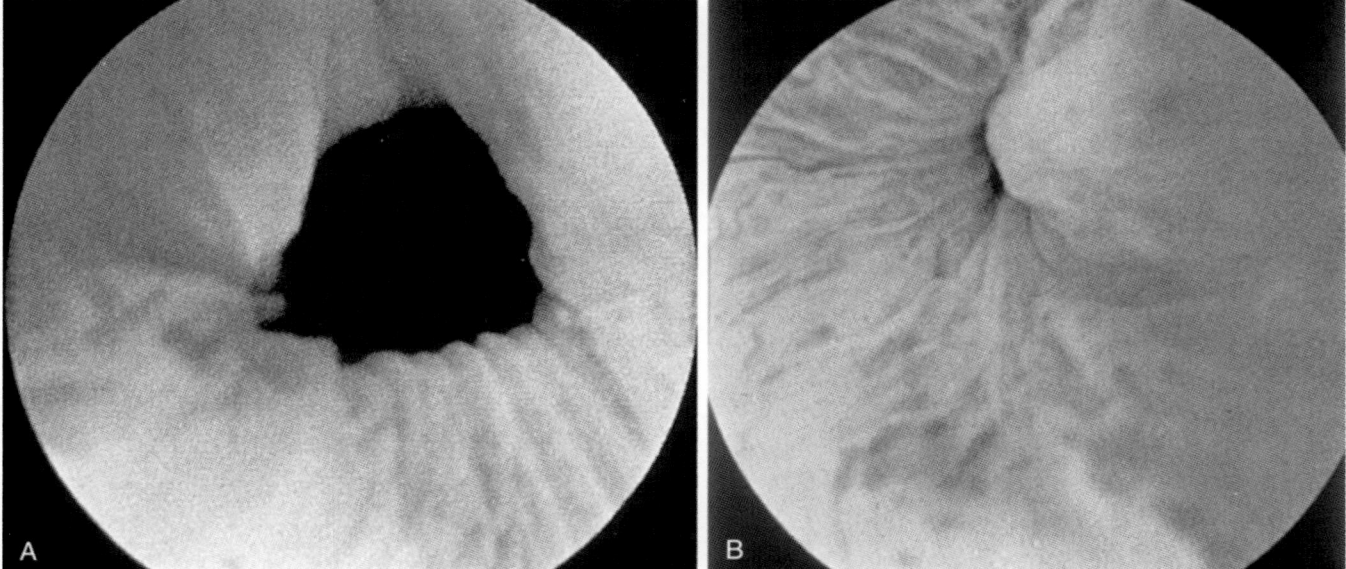

Figure 69–7. **A,** Endoscopic appearance of bladder neck from mid urethra in a female patient with intrinsic sphincter deficiency. **B,** Same view after injection. (**A** and **B** from Winters JC, Appell RA: Periurethral injection of collagen in the treatment of intrinsic sphincteric deficiency in the female patient. Urol Clin North Am 1995;22:673.)

outcome measure that may aid in further treatment planning. In later work, these authors demonstrated the long-term durability of periurethral collagen injections on serial three-dimensional ultrasound studies. They demonstrated that the volume of collagen and the appearance of collagen by ultrasound persisted and was associated with improved continence and quality of life. A circumferential or horseshoe configuration of collagen implants appears more desirable (Poon et al, 2005). **Regardless of the technique of injection chosen, the goal is closure of the bladder outlet such that there is mucosal apposition, as evidenced endoscopically, with the exception of EVOH injection** (Fig. 69–7).

Children

The techniques and principles of injection are identical to those used in adults. Williams needles as small as 3.7 Fr are available for the less viscous injectable implants (e.g., GAX-collagen). Systems that require higher-pressure delivery systems (Teflon, silicone) can be more cumbersome to inject in children.

KEY POINTS: INTRAURETHRAL INJECTION TECHNIQUES

- The best technique for injection is the one that is simplest, meaning it meets the required needs of the substance that is to be injected and helps to keep the surgeon comfortable and confident.

- It is imperative that the surgeon has been adequately trained in the technique required for the particular substance injected.

POSTOPERATIVE CARE

Perioperative antibiotic coverage is recommended for 2 to 3 days. **If urinary retention should occur, clean intermittent catheterization should be used with a small 10- to 14-Fr catheter.** Indwelling catheters should be avoided in patients undergoing implantation because this promotes molding of the intraurethral material around the catheter, although it has not been verified that short-term placement of a small caliber Foley catheter (overnight) adversely effects the outcome. However, most would agree a routine practice of placing a urethral Foley catheter after injection therapy should probably be avoided. Although rarely necessary, if long-term catheterization is needed, suprapubic cystotomy should be considered until voiding has again been initiated. Repeat injection treatment sessions for those requiring more implant should be scheduled based on the desired period of time for the substance used. For example, GAX-collagen can be reinjected within 1 week (however, we prefer to wait 4 weeks, as was the case in the original multicenter study), whereas with PTFE a wait of at least 4 months is recommended, owing to synersis possibly resulting in improved coaptation and continence with time.

KEY POINT: POSTOPERATIVE CARE

- Postoperative care should be minimal unless the patient cannot void post injection, in which case it is imperative to use short-term intermittent catheterization techniques and *not* leave an indwelling catheter in place.

EFFICACY OF INJECTABLE TREATMENT

Controlled, long-term follow-up reports are rare for any of the commonly injected substances. It is also quite difficult to compare data, because of variance in reporting techniques. It is difficult to compare the severity or etiology of stress incontinence. For example, many groups report their results of the use of injectables in SUI without differentiating between patients with hypermobility, those with ISD, and those with both. Males with incontinence after prostatic resection for benign prostatic hyperplasia often have not been distinguished from those who have had a radical prostatectomy, and for those with post–radical prostatectomy incontinence it is often unclear which approach (retropubic or perineal) was employed. There has been very little in the way of objective reporting, with mostly subjective patient statements of cure, improvement, or failure. Thus it is very difficult to accurately compare outcomes data. In addition, mixed techniques of injection and instrumentation are often intertwined. All of this means that results are really a combination of anecdotal reporting mixed with conjecture, speculation, and the hope that the truth is involved. Unfortunately, this clinical dilemma is common in all outcomes reported regarding incontinence treatment, a situation recognized by the American Urologic Association Stress Urinary Incontinence Clinical Guidelines Panel, which has called for standard criteria to be used in the reporting of all outcome studies (Leach et al, 1997).

Recognizing these limitations in the literature, when evaluating the results of intraurethral injections, these procedures are naturally compared with slings and the artificial sphincter. When assessing the existing data in a similar fashion it is clear that injectables are very helpful for some incontinent patients. Recently, primarily because it was used in the North American GAX-Collagen Study, a subjective grading of incontinence (Table 69–1) has been used in evaluating treatment success/failure. Improvement is noted when there appears to be a decrease in the grade of incontinence, as stated by the patient. Cure includes those patients with "social continence," a term coined by Scott and colleagues (1973), meaning that any perceived wetting by the patient is controlled with the use of tissues or a small minipad.

Table 69–1.	**Incontinence Grading System**
Grade 0	Continent
Grade I	Patient loses urine with sudden increase in Pabd but not supine
Grade II	Patient loses urine with physical stress (walking; changing from a reclining to a standing position; sitting up in bed)
Grade III	Patient with total incontinence; urine loss unrelated to physical activity and or position

Patients rendered dry or socially continent are considered as a treatment success in evaluation of these results. If one also includes as cured those dry individuals who must empty their bladders with self-catheterization, results may appear astounding for slings, the artificial sphincter, and injectables. With these criteria, **sling surgery is successful in 81% to 98%** (Blaivas, 1991); sphincter surgery in over 90% regardless of whether the abdominal (Light and Scott, 1985) or transvaginal (Appell, 1988) approach is used; PTFE injections in 70% to 95% (Appell, 1990a), GAX-collagen in 64% to 95% (Appell, 1990b), fat in 70% to 90% (Ganabathi and Leach, 1994), and silicone macrospheres in 70% to 82% (Buckley et al, 1992, 1993a).

Because all of these procedures appear to have comparable success rates, the question arises as to the reasons for lack of universal acceptance of injectables. There are **three major disadvantages** to the use of injectables (Appell, 1992): **(1) the inability to determine the quantity of material needed for an individual patient; (2) the safety of nonautologous products for injection with respect to migration, foreign-body reaction, and immunologic effects; and (3) the consistent lack of durability of these agents with time resulting in either lack of efficacy or the need for reinjection.**

Males after Prostatic Resection

PTFE has been shown to achieve improvement or dryness in 88% of males for treatment of incontinence after transurethral resection of the prostate for benign disease. Thus far, there has been a single report (Patterson et al, 1993) of the use of silicone polymers for postprostatic resection incontinence in which 43% were rendered continent, 19% improved, and 38% unchanged. The application of autologous fat injections has demonstrated very poor results in postprostatectomy incontinence, such that it cannot be recommended (Santarosa and Blaivas, 1994). Durasphere use in males has not been reported.

In the original North American **GAX-collagen** Study Group, there were only 17 men with post–transurethral resection incontinence, but 15 of 17 were dry at 1 year (C.R. Bard Company, personal communication, 1990).

Males after Radical Prostatectomy

PTFE has been shown to achieve improvement or dryness in 67% of males incontinent after radical prostatectomy (Politano, 1992). In this large series of 720 men, no major complications were noted. Three diabetics did develop a perineal abscess that required incision and drainage.

The first clinical trial of **GAX-collagen** was mentioned earlier in this chapter and involved 16 men with postprostatectomy incontinence (Shortliffe et al, 1989). Nine were reported as cured or improved, with an average injected volume of 28.4 mL per patient, which is of import considering the significant expense of this injectable agent. Results were reported in the North American GAX-Collagen Study Group (McGuire and Appell, 1994) for 134 postprostatectomy patients and 17 men rendered incontinent when treated with radiation for their malignancy. This study showed that only 22 men (16.5%) regained continence after GAX-collagen injections. Another 62.2 % were significantly improved at 1 year of follow-up. Of 60 of these men followed for 2 years,

47% were improved and 25% cured (Appell et al, 1994a). Once improved, the probability of remaining so for 1 year was 71% and for 2 years it was 60%. This demonstrates rather poor results with respect to attaining complete dryness in post–radical prostatectomy incontinence. Those attaining continence required an average of 33 mL and 2.7 injection sessions. In this trial, all patients with ISD were included, even those with other problems contributing to their incontinence, including detrusor dysfunction. Cured and improved rates appear slightly better than those with the use of GAX-collagen when silicone polymers have been used as the injectable agent in post–radical prostatectomy incontinence (Colombo et al, 1997; Strasser et al, 1999). Kylmala and associates utilized a 1-hour pad test and patient self-grading of incontinence to assess the results of Macroplastique injections in 50 men with postprostatectomy incontinence. They concluded that the initial results of this material were encouraging and did note dysuria occurred often after the injection process (Kylmala et al, 2003).

Females

In women, the results of **PTFE** paste for incontinence have been relatively good, at least in the short term (Cole, 1993). A recent report (Buckley et al, 1993b) of women followed for 21 to 72 months (mean: 49 months) is less encouraging, with a success rate of only 38% and the occurrence of late local side effects such as fibrosis in the urethra and bladder granuloma balls in 15%, indicating a need for a more inert substance.

Reports with **autologous fat** have had less than impressive results (Cervigni and Panei, 1993; Santarosa and Blaivas, 1994). Santarosa and Blaivas (1994) reported on 12 women with ISD in which 83% were improved subjectively, but this improvement appeared to drop precipitously at 1 year. Additionally, the role of autologous fat as an injectable in urethral hypermobility is not reliable or efficacious (Blaivas, et al, 1994). Therefore, although autologous fat injections seem to work reasonably well for ISD, the long-term follow-up requires further assessment, because it appears that autologous fat undergoes a rapid rate of reabsorption, owing to its high water content. Potentially fatal fat embolism should preclude the future use of this material.

The first report of **silicone polymers** used for incontinence in women appeared in 1992 and was encouraging, with a short-term cure rate of 82% in 84 patients (Buckley et al, 1992). This was supported by a second group with follow-up at 1 year post injection (Iacovou et al, 1993), but when Buckley and associates (1993a) observed the original group for 14 months, the cure rate was 70%. Radley and associates reported on a group of patients 19 months after Macroplastique injections and considered 19.6% cured and 41.1% significantly improved (Radley et al, 2001). Tamanini and associates (2003) utilizing validated quality of life questionnaires and the Stamey grading system concluded that after 12 months, 57.1% of patients were cured from the patient perspective and 38.1% were cured from the surgeon's perspective. These authors concluded that after 12 months, the Macroplastique implantation technique has an acceptable outcome for both patient and surgeon. More data are needed to define the potential role of this material, but present reports demonstrate cured and improved rates comparable with those of GAX-collagen in females (Adile et al, 1996; Harriss et al, 1996; Sheriff et al, 1997; Koelbl et al, 1998). In a direct comparison of Macroplastique to GAX-collagen, Anders and associates found that when 62 women were randomized to receive either injectable agent, the efficacy between the two agents was similar, although the mean volume of Macroplastique injected was less than that of GAX-collagen required (Anders, et al, 1999).

Regarding the results of Durasphere, in a head-to-head study with GAX-collagen injections at 1 year without limitations on re-treatment, the two injectable materials showed statistical equivalence on the two primary endpoints: (1) subjectively by improvement in continence grade and (2) objectively by reduction in leakage demonstrated on a pad weighing test (Lightner et al, 2001). Slightly more carbon-bead—treated patients were successfully managed with a single injection than those women treated with GAX-collagen. In a small group of 13 women, Pannek and colleagues (2001) reported that the success rate of Durasphere declined from approximately 77% at 6 months to 33% at 12 months. In addition, they reported that the Durasphere material does migrate to distant sites on follow-up radiographic study. As a result of reported technical difficulties in the injection of Durasphere, Madjar and colleagues reported on a modified technique of Durasphere implantation and its results at a mean follow-up of 9.4 months. Using a 1-site periurethral technique to achieve circumferential mucosal coaptation, 55.2% of patients considered themselves cured or improved and 50% had a urine loss of less than 8 g/24 hr via pad testing. These authors concluded that improved injection techniques may lead to more durable outcomes (Madjar et al, 2003). The long-term data from the multicenter, prospective comparative trial of Durasphere and GAX-collagen reported data up to 36 months. At 24 and 36 months Durasphere remained effective in 33% and 21% of patients compared with 19% and 9% for Contigen, respectively. After controlling for differences in follow-up time, there was no significant difference in time to failure between the treatment groups and only a third of patients in each group believed that treatment was a success (Chrouser et al, 2004).

The **results of EVOH injection in women** were evaluated in a prospective multicenter, randomized trial comparing EVOH with collagen. There were 253 patients enrolled in the study, and 177 completed 12 months of follow-up. Sixteen patients receiving EVOH were "training cases" to familiarize the surgeon with the implanting nuances noted previously. Therefore, the analyzable trial population consisted of 237 women. The efficacy of the agents at 12 months was assessed by Stamey grade, pad weight, and quality of life questionnaire. Of patients treated with EVOH 18.4% were dry via Stamey grade compared with 16.5% of patients receiving collagen. The pad weight was dry in 37.8% of patients after injection with EVOH compared with 32.1% with collagen. Among patients who actually had pad testing at 12 months after injection, the pad test was significantly improved when compared with collagen, implying better durability of EVOH when compared with GAX-collagen (U.S. Food and Drug Administration, 2004). **These analyses suggest superior performance of EVOH-implanted patients versus GAX-collagen controls, as evidenced by higher dry rates and higher overall dry and improved rates on the most objective study endpoint**

of pad weight and resulted in U.S. FDA approval for clinical use in the United States in December, 2004 (Dmochowski, 2005).

At present the most widely used injectable agent is GAX-collagen. To this end, more clinical data exist with this material. The summary of the North American multicenter clinical investigation was presented in 1994 (Appell et al, 1994b). One hundred twenty-seven women with ISD were observed for 1 year, and 88 were observed for 2 years. Of the patients observed for 2 years, 46% were dry and another 34% were "socially continent," meaning significantly improved with management for urinary leakage by a single minipad or tissues. This was accomplished with a rise in ALPP of 40 cm H_2O. Continent women received a mean volume of 18.4 mL of GAX-collagen implanted over a mean of 2.1 ($\pm$1.5) treatment sessions. Once attaining continence, 77% remain dry and do not require a repeat injection. It had previously been reported that 55% of women could regain continence after a single treatment session (Appell, 1990c). These multicenter results have been supported by other worldwide independent studies (Herschorn et al, 1992; Striker and Haylen, 1993; Swami et al, 1994; Goldenberg and Warkentin, 1994) and compare favorably with results obtained using slings and the artificial sphincter for ISD (Appell, 1992). Long-term data (>2 years) has been reported in several series. Gorton and associates (1999) evaluated 53 women 5 years after instituting collagen injection therapy and found that only 26% reported continued improvement 5 years after therapy. Corcos and Fournier (1999) noted that 40% of 40 women treated with collagen were improved, and 30% of those patients were dry 50 months after collagen implantation. Winters and coworkers (2000) reported that 45% of elderly women were improved at 24.4 months' follow-up. In this population approximately 40% required reinjection for lack of efficacy at an average of 7.9 months after the initial injection. Also, these authors noted that the continence was restored in only 42% of the women undergoing reinjection. Richardson and colleagues (1995) examined 42 patients with ISD and, after an average follow-up of 46 months, achieved a dry rate of 40% and an improved rate of 43%. Failure occurred in 17% of the patients.

Whereas the success and efficacy of collagen implantation for females with ISD has been reproduced in these series, considerable debate exists about the efficacy of GAX-collagen in patients with type II hypermobility of the vesicourethral junction, so-called genuine anatomic SUI. Kreder and Austin (1996) reported a significant difference in outcome when comparing patients with ISD and urethral hypermobility treated with a sling (81% cure rate) versus those who underwent a *single* collagen injection (25% cure rate). However, many subjects need an average of between two and three injection treatments to achieve continence (Smith et al, 1997). Herschorn and associates (1992) reported equal success rates among patients with type II SUI and patients with ISD; however, the number of injections and the amount of material injected were higher in patients with anatomic urinary incontinence. It has also been documented that elderly female patients with anatomic incontinence do well with the injections of GAX-collagen (Faerber, 1995; Winters et al, 2000). Herschorn and Radomski (1997) evaluated patients with and without hypermobility and demonstrated no significant difference in duration of effect by Kaplan-Meier survival curves, thus making a statement for injectable treatment for all types of SUI. This study also demonstrated the lack of durability of GAX-collagen. These findings contrast to those found in the 17 patients from the North American multicenter trial with hypermobility, in which the early 82.3% success was short-lived, because all of the patients required bladder neck suspension surgery within 2 years of the initial "dryness" (Press and Badlani, 1995). Bent and colleagues supported Herschorn and Radomski's (1997) earlier work by including only patients with anatomic SUI (hypermobility), as evidenced by radiographic findings in a multicenter, prospective trial of collagen injections. Fifty-eight patients were evaluated at 12 months, and the results were similar to existing data in patients with ISD (Bent et al, 2001). These findings appear to confirm previous anecdotal **reports of long-term clinical efficacy of GAX-collagen injection in women with hypermobility comparable with that observed in patients with classic ISD** (Monga et al, 1995; Swami et al, 1995). Interestingly, there has even been some suggestion that patients with hypermobility have a better result from GAX-collagen injection than patients with ISD alone (Gorton et al, 1999; Steele et al, 2000).

A search of the Cochrane Database reviewing randomized or quasi-randomized controlled trials in the treatment of urinary incontinence containing at least one arm involving injection therapy was completed in 2003. The authors concluded that periurethral injection results in subjective and objective short-term improvement of symptomatic SUI in adult women. In women with an extensive comorbidity precluding anesthesia, injections may present a useful option to manage symptoms for 1 year, although two to three injections may be needed (Pickard et al, 2003).

Children

Reports of the use of injectables in children are sparse. Vorstman and associates (1985) reported on 11 children (9 girls and 2 boys) injected with PTFE. Of the 4 girls with myelodysplasia or sacral agenesis, 50% were rendered dry and required intermittent catheterization to empty. The other 5 girls and the 2 boys had ISD due to previous surgery, and the success rate was 85.7%. Appell (1992) reported on 14 children treated with GAX-collagen in whom 75% of 6 boys and all of the 8 girls were rendered completely continent; however, the volume of material needed was significant (31.8 mL for the boys and 14.5 mL for the girls). The ALPP rose 56.5 cm H_2O in the boys and 23.6 cm H_2O in the girls.

Wan and colleagues (1992) treated 8 children with GAX-collagen with an 88% cure rate at 14 months, whereas, more recently, the Cleveland Clinic experience (Ross et al, 1995) in treating 7 children with GAX-collagen for ISD was presented in which 4 of 7 were dry but the other 3 had no benefit from multiple injections, and **it appears that the children who do benefit have large bladder capacities and moderate (as opposed to severe) ISD.** Perez and associates (1996) reviewed their experience with collagen injection therapy in children. Of children with neurogenic bladder, 20% became dry after 1 injection and 28% improved. These authors concluded that based on its minimally invasive nature, collagen therapy has a viable role in the treatment of select pediatric patients.

Kassouf and associates (2001) reported disappointing long-term results and suggested that this treatment is rarely effective in children. In a review of the outcomes of all pediatric continence procedures performed at one institution, Cole and associates (2003) reported that collagen was successful as primary therapy only 20% of the time, whereas it was successful as a secondary procedure after previously failed anti-incontinence surgery 100% of the time. There has been a positive report utilizing collagen in children with primary epispadias (Duffy and Ransley, 1998).

COMPLICATIONS

Perioperative complications associated with periurethral injections are uncommon. **The rate of *urinary retention*** in patients undergoing PTFE injections is 20% to 25% (Politano, 1982). These patients may require a transient period of catheterization. In the multicenter U.S. clinical trial of GAX-collagen injections, transient urinary retention developed in approximately 15% of patients (C. R. Bard Company, 1990).

<table>
<tr><td colspan="2">**KEY POINTS: EFFICACY OF INJECTABLE TREATMENT**</td></tr>
<tr><td>■</td><td>Attempts to improve results with newer substances will really depend on the durability of the substance placed into tissue, which is constantly changing as it ages, as well as the surgeon's experience with the technique required for whatever substance is used in a specific patient.</td></tr>
<tr><td>■</td><td>Current substances are safe and effective in about two thirds of patients, but it is the lack of durability and, therefore, the reinjection rate that disturbs both patient and surgeon.</td></tr>
</table>

Irritative voiding symptoms develop in 20% of patients after injection of PTFE but resolve after several days (Schulman et al, 1983), and urinary tract infection is stated at 2% (Lim et al, 1983). With GAX-collagen, only 1% of patients experienced irritative voiding symptoms whereas 5% had a urinary tract infection (C. R. Bard Company, 1990). More recent reports describe surprisingly high rates of irritative voiding symptoms. Corcos and Fournier (1999) demonstrated a 10% rate of de novo urgency and frequency, whereas Steele and colleagues (2000) stated that 50% of patients developed some degree of de novo detrusor overactivity.

When patients' complaints of persistent incontinence were investigated urodynamically, Cross and coworkers (1998) documented de novo urge incontinence in 28% of patients without evidence of ISD. In a prospective study to determine the complications of periurethral GAX-collagen injection in 337 women, Stothers and colleagues (1995) also noted that the most frequent and distressing complication was de novo urgency with urge incontinence that occurred in 12.6% of patients. They further noticed that 21% of these women did not respond to standard anticholinergic agents, suggesting that, in some of the patients, the urgency may be sensory.

During injection, **perforation and extravasation of the injected material can occur if the mucosa is disrupted.** This may also result in minor urethral bleeding. Whereas the transurethral technique is mandatory in the male and with EVOH in women, complications of bleeding and extrusion of the injectable material are lessened utilizing a periurethral approach in the female. With GAX-collagen, extravasation is generally not a problem, because the material is easily flushed away in the urinary stream. However, during injection of PTFE, any extrusion of material can be problematic, because it may be difficult to remove from the lumen. As noted earlier, exposed material has been described after injection of EVOH. Most often, this exposed material has no detrimental sequelae and will dissipate with time. There have been instances that have required debulking or endoscopic removal of this material without difficulty.

Regardless of the material, the act of repeated injection into the urethra may result in some other minor complications, all rapid to resolve. Sweat and Lightner (1999) reported three patients requiring drainage of sterile abscesses after transurethral injection of GAX-collagen and a patient injected periurethrally with autologous fat who suffered a pulmonary embolism. Expansion of the data from the multicenter GAX-Collagen study really covers all conceivable problems from injectables (Table 69–2).

KEY POINTS: COMPLICATIONS

- Fortunately, injectable agents used thus far have been safe and complications have been rare.

- The surgeon must be vigilant in follow-up of the patient in being cognizant of any unexpected urethral pain, swelling, or bleeding, because infection and erosion of material are possible.

SAFETY

When PTFE is injected, the acute reaction after injection is a histiocytic and giant cell response with an ingrowth of fibroblasts among the small PTFE particles. Although this creates a compression of the tissue at the injection site (Stone and Arnold, 1967), subsequently **foreign body giant cells and granuloma formation are seen at the site of injection with encapsulation of the material.**

After injection of PTFE, the particles are noted to be found within lymphatics and blood vessels. Particles have also been found 1 year after injection in the pelvic lymph nodes, lungs, brain, kidneys, and spleen of animal models (Malizia et al, 1984; Vandenbossche et al, 1994). Patients after PTFE have been noted to develop fever with negative blood and urine culture results at a rate of about 25%. This resolves after a few days and probably indicates a mild allergic response, especially in the 5% who also report perineal discomfort that spontaneously resolves (Politano, 1978, 1982).

In humans, reports of PTFE particle migration to the lungs have been documented in two patients. The first report by Mittleman and Marraccini (1983) described a PTFE granuloma in the lung of a patient 2 years after injection, and another case has been reported with an apparent clinically significant febrile response (Claes et al, 1989). A PTFE granuloma has also been reported to mimic a cold thyroid nodule several months after injection (Sanfilippo et al, 1980). No adverse clinical events were attributable to these findings by Mittelman and Marraccini or Sanfilippo and colleagues (1980).

However, the first clinically significant case of migration of PTFE after injection therapy involved the report by Claes and associates (1989). Their patient had received injections of PTFE for urinary incontinence 3 years before presenting with unexplained fevers associated with new lung lesions. A bronchial lavage and lung biopsy revealed PTFE granulomas with surrounding inflammation. **The major concern associated with the use of PTFE particles is that, after particle migration, there is foreign body granuloma formation,** and this has the potential to be carcinogenic, because sarcoma formation has been induced in rats and mice after implantation of material similar to PTFE (Oppenheimer et al, 1958) and chondrosarcoma of the larynx 6 years after PTFE injections for the treatment of vocal cord paralysis has been reported (Hakky et al, 1989). No case of carcinogenesis has been

Table 69–2. Adverse Events Reported during a Multicenter Study of 382 Patients Treated with GAX-Collagen				
	Treatment-Related		**Non–Treatment Related**	
Adverse Event	*Events, No. (%)*	*Patients, No. (%)*	*Events, No. (%)*	*Patients, No. (%)*
Urinary retention	36 (15)	31 (8)	2 (1)	1 (<1)
Urinary tract infection	14 96)	14 (4)	92 (38)	63 (16)
Hematuria	8 (3)	8 (2)	0	0
Injection site injury	5 (2)	5 (1)	0	0
Urinary outlet obstruction	2 (1)	2 (<1)	5 (2)	4 (1)
Accidental injury, urinary	3 (1)	3 (1)	0	0
Pain at injection site	3 (1)	3 (1)	0	0
Balanitis	1 (<1)	1 (<1)	4 (2)	3 (1)
Urinary urgency	1 (<1)	1 (<1)	1 (<1)	1 (<1)
Urethritis	1 (<1)	1 (<1)	0	0
Epididymitis	1 (<1)	1 (<1)	0	0
Bladder spasm	1 (<1)	1 (<1)	0	0
Abscess injection site	1 (<1)	1 (<1)	0	0
Vaginitis	1 (<1)	1 (<1)	0	0
Application site reaction	0	0	1 (<1)	1 (<1)
Vesicovaginal fistula	0	0	1 (<1)	1 (<1)

From CR Bard Company, Product Monograph, Submission of ISFDA for IDE G850010, 1990.

identified after widespread use of this material for over 30 years in laryngeal and urethral augmentation procedures.

A complete review (Dewan, 1992) concluded that PTFE does not have any carcinogenic potential, and there have been only three reported cases of malignancy adjacent to PTFE implants and no cause-and-effect has been demonstrated (Lewy, 1976; Montgomery, 1979; Hakky et al, 1989). However, the fear of this potential problem has caused many to reserve the use of PTFE for older patients. PTFE for injection has been removed from the marketplace by the FDA, although it has allowed a long-term study to begin comparing PTFE and GAX-collagen for efficacy and safety.

Although complications are rarely reported with **autologous fat** injections, a death has been reported secondary to a fat embolus after injection (Currie et al, 1997).

GAX-collagen, as stated, is both biocompatible and biodegradable. The low concentration of glutaraldehyde minimizes the immunoreactivity and cytotoxicity of the implant; therefore, this substance elicits no foreign body reaction because it becomes incorporated into the host tissue (Ford et al, 1984). A minimal inflammatory response has been associated with the injection of GAX-collagen, but no granuloma formation is present (DeLustro et al, 1986).

GAX-collagen begins to degrade in 12 weeks; however, neovascularization and deposition of fibroblasts with host collagen formation occur within the implant (Stegman et al, 1987). The GAX-collagen completely degrades within 10 to 19 months (Canning et al, 1988), and there are no reports of particle migration of the collagen material because it is transformed into living connective tissue (Remacle and Marbaix, 1988). Because of the minimal inflammatory response and no evidence of migration, GAX-collagen is the most widely used bulk-enhancing agent for the treatment of incontinence in adults and children.

Safety of GAX-collagen is further enhanced by the use of a **dermal skin test** with the more immunogenic non–cross-linked bovine collagen. Although those with a positive skin test could conceivably not suffer from injection with the less immunogenic GAX-collagen, this is not advised. Positive skin tests in the multicenter study amounted to less than 1% of males and less than 4% of females (Appell et al, 1994a, 1994b). This is important because there have been legal claims by patients who had collagen injections for soft tissue augmentation (facial plastic surgery techniques) of signs and symptoms of collagen vascular disorders such as dermatomyositis. Delayed hypersensitivity reaction at the skin test site with and without associated arthralgia has been reported but is extremely rare (Stothers and Goldenberg, 1998). Despite these claims, **there has been no evidence to link injections of bovine collagen with any disorder** (Appell, 1992). The patient population has, thus far, actually had a lower incidence of such disorders than would be expected in the general population (DeLustro et al, 1991), and no plaintiffs have been able to glean support during litigation.

With the exception of exposed material, the rates and severity of adverse events are similar between EVOH and collagen. With care taken to meticulous transurethral injection technique, the incidence of exposed material decreased. The exposed material was not associated with adverse consequences, and most commonly resolved. However, to avoid this problem, periurethral injection of EVOH is not recommended (U.S. Food and Drug Administration, 2004).

FUTURE OF INJECTABLES FOR STRESS URINARY INCONTINENCE

In the properly selected patient, periurethral injections offer excellent treatment results for patients with SUI. Patients with no significant anatomic hypermobility and ISD in the presence of a stable bladder of adequate capacity appear to be the most satisfactory candidates for periurethral injections. GAX-collagen is the most widely used injectable because it has been shown to be both biocompatible and biodegradable. There are no reports of particle migration with this material, and repeat injections can be performed safely with the patient under local anesthesia.

The treatment response in females with these procedures is similar to that for surgical procedures to correct ISD, and the complications are minimal. Although long-term results (>5 years) for all of these procedures are scarce in the literature and injected patients have been observed for only short periods of time and the data available do not take into consideration **reinjection rates, which run as high as 22% with collagen at 2 years after attaining dryness** (Winters and Appell, 1995), this factor affects the cost of this therapy. In addition, in males, the success rate of intraurethral injections does not approach that of the artificial urinary sphincter to date.

Treatment with GAX-collagen is not considered permanent, and there is a great deal of variability in published reports of treatment durability, as pointed out in earlier sections of this chapter. When time to failure analysis was used to measure GAX-collagen durability in one study (Tschopp et al, 1999), 50% of patients were classified as failures 4.7 months after the last injection. In contrast, Corcos and Fournier (1999) and Cross and coworkers (1998) noted an 11% to 33% reinjection rate because of decreased efficacy between 36 and 50 months after the initial treatment. Stothers and associates (1995) identified artificial sphincters as a more cost-effective method than collagen injections in treating postprostatectomy incontinence. Later work by Brown and colleagues (1998) comparing the cost of conservative versus surgical management of postprostatectomy incontinence supports the use of GAX-collagen in patients with mild to moderate incontinence. Collagen injections have not been compared with male sling procedures in the management of postprostatectomy incontinence. It appears, however, that many patients previously selected for injection therapy after radical prostatectomy are having the male sling procedure performed. Long-term data and cost comparisons of these two procedures are needed. In selected elderly and less mobile female patients with anatomic incontinence, recent data suggest that GAX-collagen may be useful. The use of periurethral injections in the treatment of ISD certainly has a role in treatment in the properly selected patient. **Intraurethral injections allow treatment of incontinence in patients who** are poor surgical candidates and may be denied other forms of therapy.

Injectables must be considered to be in the developmental stages, and their roles in the management of incontinence still need to be defined more precisely, as must development of new, nonmigrating, safe, and technically simple-to-use injectables. **The optimal substance has to be inert and nondegradable. It must encapsulate and remain where injected and neither lose bulk nor gain it** (syneresis). It must not be too viscous so that it can be injected with standard cystoscopic equipment used for other purposes under local anesthesia in an outpatient setting to help keep the procedure safe and cost effective. In addition, more accurate techniques for determining the quantity of material to inject in an individual must be developed to get the optimal result in a single treatment session. This "wish list" for injectable therapy is not beyond our ability to develop. Injectable agents currently undergoing investigation in the United States are discussed next.

Hylagel Uro

This is a cross-linked hyaluronic acid that is highly biocompatible and nonimmunogenic with enhanced residence time in tissues before absorption. Hyaluronic acid is a water-insoluble complex glycosaminoglycan composed of disaccharide units that form molecules of 8 to 23 million daltons molecular weight and is dissolved in normal saline solution for urethral bulking purposes. A stage I feasibility study (Biomatrix Corporation, 2000) has been completed with FDA approval given to proceed with a stage II multicenter trial in comparison with GAX-collagen.

Hyaluronic Acid and Dextranomer Microspheres

Both constituents of this material are complex sugar polymers. Dextranomer is a cross-linked dextran, and, as stated earlier, hyaluronic acid is a glycosaminoglycan. Both agents are biocompatible and biodegradable. Hyaluronic acid functions as the transport vehicle and is resorbed within 2 weeks after injection. Dextranomer microspheres, acting as the bulking agent, are very slowly biodegraded and remain in the injected location for up to 4 years (Stenberg et al, 1999). This material is easily injected and forms a framework for fibroblast infiltration and collagen deposition. Currently approved in Europe, this material is undergoing clinical trials in the United States, yet the material itself has been found safe and is already approved for the treatment of vesicoureteral reflux in children. Van Kerrebroeck and associates (2004) investigated the efficacy and safety of this material utilizing the "implacer" (see Fig. 69–4) tool to complete the injection procedure at the mid urethra. There was a significant reduction in the number of incontinent episodes, and 69% of the patients had improved in the 6-point patient perception scale. This study of 42 patients was carried on for 12 months. Stenberg and associates (2003) published long-term data from 20 patients originally injected with this material in 1994-1995. They concluded that only 3 (15%) of patients failed to respond to the treatment, and a sustained response was reported in 57% of the patients, leading them to conclude that the dextranomer/hyaluronic acid copolymer offers long-term

efficacy in women with SUI. This material has been extensively utilized in the United States in the treatment of vesicoureteral reflux in children.

Bioglass

This is a biologically inert mixture of calcium oxide, calcium silicone, and sodium oxide that has had no toxicity in animal models in which the inflammatory response has also been minimal. Tissue integration occurs between the patient's collagen and the surface of the composite material (Walker et al, 1992), but no human trial data are available.

Calcium Hydroxyapatite

This synthetic is identical to the same entity found in bone and teeth and consists of hydroxyapatite spheres in an aqueous gel composed of sodium carboxymethylcellulose, which has been previously used in dental restoration and bone healing. In animal studies, this material does not encapsulate and has been demonstrated to be biocompatible while causing adhesion to ingrowing collagen fibers of the patient with minimal chronic inflammatory infiltrate and can be identified on plain film radiography or ultrasound. This material is easily injected, not requiring pressurized administration. In an initial study of 10 women, 7 reported substantial improvement and the 24-hour pad weight decreased more than 90% at 1-year follow-up (Mayer et al, 2001). A multicenter randomized trial has been completed in the United States, and the data from the trial after FDA scrutiny has obtained approval in December, 2005.

Autologous Chondrocytes

Combining the technique of intraurethral injection with tissue engineering principles is used here as an interesting variant (Atala et al, 1993a). Chondrocytes are harvested from the patient's auricular surfaces, expanded by tissue culture techniques, submersed in an alginate polymer delivery vehicle, and then injected intraurethrally (Atala et al, 1993b). The clinical applicability is being assessed in a multicenter trial. Other bioengineering techniques are being considered, including myoblasts from biopsies of the biceps muscle (Yokoyama et al, 2000). The benefits of this type of product include biocompatibility and longevity. In addition, the use of muscle progenitor cells that can differentiate into smooth or striated muscle after urethral injection, with documented increases in urethral muscular activity appears quite promising as a potential human application (Cannon et al, 2003; Peyromaure et al, 2004). However, a concern exists regarding safety and confidentiality procedures to prevent the disastrous consequences of injecting the cell culture into the wrong patient or the potential expense involved in cell expansion, harvesting, packaging, and then reinjection into the patient. Considerable research is needed in this area to determine if this technology may eventually become clinically applicable.

Injectable Balloons

Early experience with implantable microballoons (called *Urovive*) placed intraurethrally by means of a periurethral approach was encouraging (Pycha et al, 2000); however, continued problems in the delivery system led to the demise of clinical trials in the United States. Another implantable balloon designed to have its volume adjusted once implanted via a completely periurethral approach (called ACT) is undergoing trials worldwide. This balloon is placed completely outside the urethra at the level of the bladder neck and then filled through a port that remains accessible in the patient's labium, much like a pump mechanism from an artificial urinary sphincter. A disadvantage thus far has been the requirement for general or regional anesthesia for implantation.

Treatment of SUI with endoscopic injections is an effective method and is the least invasive of all surgical procedures. New developments, either those discussed earlier or injectable materials or devices not yet on the scene, may yet become the primary treatment modality for SUI.

KEY POINT: PRESENT AND FUTURE OF INJECTABLES IN URINARY INCONTINENCE

■ The search for the "perfect" injectable will, and should, continue until we have a safe, easily injected, efficacious, and durable agent for the patient with intrinsic sphincteric deficiency.

SUGGESTED READINGS

Appell RA, Vasavada SP, Rackley RR, et al: Antegrade collagen injection therapy for urinary incontinence following radical prostatectomy. Urology 1996;48:769-772.

Chrouser KL, Fick F, Goel A, et al: Carbon coated zirconium beads in beta-glucan gel and bovine glutaraldehyde cross-linked collagen injections for intrinsic sphincteric deficiency: Continence and satisfaction after extended follow-up. J Urol 2004;171:1152-1155.

Cole HM (ed): Diagnostic and therapeutic technology assessment (DATTA). JAMA 1993;269:2975-2980.

Dmochowski RR: Tegress™ Urethral implant phase III clinical experience and product uniqueness. Rev Urol 2005;7(Suppl 1):S22-S26.

Winters JC, Appell RA: Periurethral injection of collagen in the treatment of intrinsic sphincteric deficiency in the female patient. Urol Clin North Am 1995;22:673-678.

Additional Therapies for Storage and Emptying Failure

M. LOUIS MOY, MD • ALAN J. WEIN, MD

TO FACILITATE BLADDER FILLING/URINE STORAGE

TO FACILITATE BLADDER EMPTYING

SUMMARY

The numerous treatment options that exist for storage and emptying failure range from noninvasive therapies to pharmacotherapy, minimally invasive surgery, and/or complex lower urinary tract reconstruction, which are discussed in other chapters (see Tables 57–3 and 57–4). In this chapter additional treatment options are presented for the treatment of storage and emptying failure not covered in the previous chapters. Some of these treatments have promising potential with the need for continued studies and research, whereas others have fallen out of favor and are of historic interest only.

TO FACILITATE BLADDER FILLING/URINE STORAGE
Bladder Overdistention

Therapeutic overdistention involves prolonged stretching of the bladder wall using a hydrostatic pressure equal to systolic blood pressure. Smith (1981) originally summarized the experience at his center and detailed the technique used, a modification of the original cystodistention procedure described by Helmstein. **Improvement, when it occurs, is generally attributable to ischemic changes in the nerve endings or terminals in the bladder wall. Potential complications include bladder rupture (5% to 10%), hematuria, and retention.** Good to excellent results have been reported in the treatment of detrusor overactivity by Ramsden and colleagues (1976), but our impression is that this procedure is of little use in patients with storage failure secondary to neurogenic detrusor overactivity. Even in patients with detrusor overactivity, Jorgensen and coworkers (1985) reported a success rate of 1 of 15 patients. In 27 patients with benign functional disease reported by

Lloyd and colleagues (1992) (none with neurogenic detrusor overactivity), only 6 had a good response (0/6 with idiopathic detrusor overactivity). Liapis and associates (2001) also report poor results from treatment with bladder distention. They retrospectively reviewed a series of 26 women with a history of urgency and frequency who underwent bladder distention for treatment. Although there was an increase in mean bladder capacity after treatment, of the 28 women treated only 4 (15%) had any improvement in symptoms at 9 months.

Overdistention is also discussed in Chapter 10, "Interstitial Cystitis and Related Disorders," as a therapy for interstitial cystitis.

Acupuncture

Acupuncture compositely describes a number of procedures involving stimulation of anatomic locations on the skin by a variety of techniques. It is thus **a form of somatic sensory stimulation,** the most common techniques of which involve stimulation of certain "acupuncture points" by means of penetration of the skin by thin solid metallic needles that are manipulated manually or electrically stimulated. **The techniques of classic acupuncture seem to merge with other forms of peripheral electrical stimulation to inhibit bladder contractility,** such as the posterior tibial nerve stimulation described by McGuire and coworkers (1983). Philp and colleagues (1988) reported on patients who underwent weekly acupuncture treatments for 10 to 12 weeks. Of 3 patients with "sensory urgency," none noted improvement. Sixteen patients had idiopathic detrusor overactivity. Three of these patients had enuresis, 1 of whom was cured and 2 experienced no change. Thirteen patients had overactivity and diurnal symptoms, and 10 showed what was considered significant symptomatic improvement, although cystometric bladder function changes were inconsistent.

Bergström and associates (2000) reported on the results of classic acupuncture performed twice weekly in a group of 15 elderly women with urgency or mixed incontinence. In this open uncontrolled study, subjective assessments of improvement and objective measurements in the form of grams of leakage for 48 hours were positive not only at the end of the study but also 1 and 3 months thereafter. This article contains a review of other articles in the literature dealing with the use of acupuncture in similar clinical situations and a discussion of the acupuncture points involved. **As possible mechanisms of action for acupuncture,** the authors hypothesize any one or a combination of (1) **endorphinergic effects at the sacral spinal cord level or above, (2) inhibitory somatovesical reflexes, and (3) increase in peripheral circulation.**

More recently, Emmons and Otto (2005) compared acupuncture versus placebo acupuncture in the treatment of women with overactive bladder and urinary urgency incontinence. The women underwent cystometric testing, completed a voiding diary and urinary distress inventory and incontinence impact questionnaire, and validated quality of life inventories before and after four weekly acupuncture treatments. The primary endpoint was the number of incontinent episodes over 3 days. The number of incontinent episodes decreased by 59% in the treatment group compared with 40% in the placebo group. The treatment group had a significant improvement in bladder capacity, urgency, frequency, and quality of life scores compared with the placebo group.

Interruption of Innervation

Many different techniques for denervation of the bladder, both centrally and peripherally, have been described over the past 50 years. We will briefly discuss some techniques here, because there is further discussion in Chapter 64, "Electrical Stimulation for Storage and Emptying Disorders." Only a few of these procedures have stood the test of time. Conservative therapy for detrusor overactivity has become much more effective, and, when this fails, denervation procedures compete with neuromodulation and augmentation cystoplasty. In general, peripheral denervation is more selective but less effective than central denervation. One significant problem with denervation is that neuroplasticity often results in restoration of neurologic function and sometimes with an even less desirable result than was present originally (Madersbacher, 2000).

Very Central (Subarachnoid Block)

Historically, this type of interruption was not used solely for urologic indications but, rather, to convert a state of severe somatic spasticity to flaccidity and to abolish autonomic hyperreflexia (see Wein and Barrett, 1988, for references). **As a by-product, neurogenic detrusor overactivity was converted acutely to areflexia.** The flaccid bladder that resulted generally required additional therapy to empty or required clean intermittent catheterization (CIC). The obvious disadvantage of this type of procedure is **a lack of selectivity,** with unintended motor or sensory loss other than related to the bladder. **Impotence was very common in males; and in those patients with some residual motor or sensory function, these functions were often significantly altered or lost. Additionally, the conceptually simple result of an areflexic bladder, although it may be produced acutely, very often was not maintained on a long-term basis after neurologic decentralization. Decreased compliance often developed in such patients,** resulting in significant storage problems.

Less Central (Sacral Rhizotomy, Selective Sacral Rhizotomy)

In most cases, **bilateral anterior and posterior sacral rhizotomy or conusectomy converts an overactive bladder to an areflexic one.** This alone may be inappropriate therapy because **it also adversely affects the rectum, anal and urethral sphincters, sexual function, and the lower extremities. Selective motor nerve sectioning was originally introduced as a treatment to increase bladder capacity by abolishing only the motor supply responsible for involuntary contractions** in an attempt to leave sphincter and sexual function intact. The initial use of this procedure followed the observation that the third anterior (ventral) sacral root provided the dominant motor innervation of the human bladder. **To enhance the clinical response and to minimize side effects, differential sacral rhizotomy should always be preceded by stimulation and blockade of the individual sacral roots with cystometric and sphincterometric control.**

Although technique refinements, such as percutaneous radiofrequency selective sacral rhizotomy and cryoneurolysis have occurred, **there is still much argument as to the place of these anterior rhizotomy procedures within a plan of treatment for detrusor overactivity.** Torrens (1985) summarized successful results in collected groups of patients that ranged from 48% for idiopathic detrusor overactivity to 81% for patients classified as having a "paraplegic bladder." However, as he astutely pointed out, what is meant by a success varies from one series and one patient to another. When these procedures are used, they should certainly be preceded by urodynamic and urologic evaluation of the effects of selective nerve blocks before performance, especially in patients without fixed neurologic disease or injury. Even then, **unintended effects on pelvic and lower extremity sensory or motor functions may occur, with disastrous medical and legal sequelae.**

Both Tanagho and Schmidt (1988), Tanagho and associates (1989), and Brindley (1990) have popularized the conception of **sensory deafferentation using dorsal or posterior rhizotomy to increase bladder capacity as part of their overall plan to simultaneously rehabilitate storage and emptying problems in patients with significant spinal cord injury (SCI) or disease. These are patients in whom they have also used electrical stimulation to alleviate emptying deficits.** McGuire and Savastano (1984) also mentioned **dorsal root ganglionectomy** alone in such patients to increase bladder capacity.

Gasparini and colleagues (1992) report durability of the deafferentation response to selective dorsal sacral rhizotomy up to 64 months after section. The technique involves selecting nerve roots whose intraoperative stimulation provokes an adequate detrusor response. The dorsal and ventral components of these roots were then separated and the dorsal root(s) severed. An increase in bladder capacity of 148 mL to 377 mL was noted in 16 of 17 studied patients (24 in the original series) with an increase in the volume to the first contraction of 99 mL to 270 mL. A total of 14 patients were cured of incontinence, 2 improved, and in 1, treatment failed. Of 7 potent men, 2 experienced a decrease in erectile frequency but were still able to achieve penetration. Bowel and sphincter function were unaffected. Koldewijn and associates (1994) reported on the effects of intradural bilateral posterior root rhizotomies from S2 to S5 with implantation of an anterior root stimulator in a group of patients with suprasacral SCI. All showed persistent detrusor areflexia afterward, although two required subsequent secondary rhizotomy at the level of the conus. A majority showed decreased bladder compliance up to 5 days postoperatively, followed by a rapid increase thereafter.

Brindley (1994) summarizes the **advantages of bilateral posterior sacral rhizotomy in treating voiding dysfunction after SCI as (1) abolishing reflex incontinence, (2) improving compliance, and (3) abolishing striated sphincter dyssynergia without altering resting tone. Partial or selective procedures are considered only in such patients who retain some sensation or have excellent reflex erections.** Madersbacher (2000) comments that posterior sacral rhizotomy for sacral deafferentation of the bladder is best achieved by the intradural approach, which has the advantage that, in this location, motor and sensory fibers can easily be separated, whereas distal to the spinal ganglion, motor and sensory fibers are intermingled and a clear separation is no longer possible. If an intradural procedure is not possible, he believes that a deafferentation at the level of the conus medullaris is preferable to an extradural sacral approach. He mentions that he has treated 65 tetraplegic or paraplegic patients with post-SCI reflex urinary incontinence, resistant to all other means of conservative treatment. Incontinence was abolished in 90% of these patients.

Peripheral and Perivesical Bladder Denervation

A number of procedures fall into the category of attempts to achieve a peripheral parasympathetic "denervation." As is evident from neuroanatomic considerations, **such attempts, at best, achieve primarily neurologic decentralization and, at most, partial peripheral denervation.** It is interesting, however, to consider at this juncture the fact that many authors report high success rates for various such procedures, so high that one wonders why they are not used more frequently. Considering just the problem of detrusor overactivity, there seems to be a number of reasons for this. First, many clinicians believe that more conservative methods (as opposed to surgery) are often successful in managing detrusor overactivity with fewer side effects. In their hands, the success rates of peripheral bladder denervation in patients who have failed vigorous but nonsurgical attempts at therapy are much lower. Second, in many articles, there is little description of what "success" actually means. Finally, there is very little long-term follow-up for any of these procedures, and "postoperative assessment" usually means within a few months of the procedure.

Mundy (1985) very nicely summarized surgical treatment of detrusor overactivity by peripheral "denervation" up to that point in time. It is sometimes difficult in reading the literature to ascertain exactly what variety of phasic hyperactivity (neurogenic or idiopathic detrusor overactivity) is being considered (or whether both are included in the treatment results). **Transvaginal partial denervation of the bladder was originally described by Ingelman-Sundberg in 1959.** This procedure has been used mostly for the treatment of refractory urge urinary incontinence; and in the originator's hands, success rates of up to 80% have been achieved. Mundy (1985) cites these reports and reports of the successes of others in 50% to 65% of cases. Torrens (1985) cites the original work

but simply states that "the technique has not found favor with other workers." Cespedes and associates (1996) described McGuire's modification of the Ingelman-Sundberg procedure, which they used in 25 women with urinary urgency incontinence and symptoms suggestive of detrusor overactivity who had failed behavioral and medical therapy. Transvaginal local anesthesia was used as a test to determine which patients would benefit from the procedure, and the 25 patients represent those with a positive test; the number of patients unsuccessfully tested was not mentioned. Sixty-four percent (16 patients) of these patients were cured of urgency incontinence at a mean follow-up of 14.8 months. Of the 16 patients cured, 9 additionally required one medication and 2 required two medications. Madersbacher (2000) comments that a follow-up period of 15 months is too short to determine long-term effects.

As a follow-up to this, Westney and associates (2002) retrospectively reviewed 28 patients with refractory urinary urgency incontinence who underwent the Ingleman-Sundberg procedure with a mean follow-up of 44.1 months. Of these, 68% were cured (54%) or improved (14%). The authors conclude that this is an effective procedure in a difficult-to-treat patient population and is a reasonable minimally invasive alternative.

Cystolysis is a term used to describe extensive perivesical dissection and mobilization with division of the superior vesical pedicle and the ascending branches of the inferior vesicle pedicle. Although some initial reports were very promising for relief of both pain and overactivity (see Wein and Barrett, 1988, for references), it is interesting that there has been essentially nothing in the literature on this procedure since 1983, perhaps because the short-term optimism was replaced by nonpublished long-term pessimism.

Bladder transection involves a complete circumferential division of the full thickness of the bladder wall at a level just above the ureteric orifices, although Mundy (1985) believed that only the posterior part of the transection was of importance. Initial encouraging reports in the early 1970s were followed by longer-term reviews of larger series, all reporting success rates in excess of 50% for at least detrusor overactivity, using varying criteria. Mundy (1985) reviewed his large experience with transection in patients with detrusor instability and reported that of 104 patients with a follow-up for 1 to 5 years, 74% were cured, 14% were improved, and 12% were failures. Between 20 and 32 months, 10% of the group initially judged to have a satisfactory response suffered a relapse, giving a long-term subjective success rate of 65%. Only 35% of those who claimed to be symptomatically cured had reverted to urodynamically stable detrusor behavior, however. Thus, Mundy wisely commented that a symptomatic cure does not necessarily mean a urodynamic one and a symptomatic failure does not necessarily mean a urodynamic failure.

Parsons and coworkers (1984) described endoscopic bladder transection in patients with phasic detrusor hyperactivity. Their early results were encouraging, but Lucas and Thomas (1987) reported essentially no change in 14 of 18 patients with intractable detrusor overactivity treated by this technique. Two achieved complete symptomatic relief, and 2 more were rendered continent but with the complaint of urgency and nocturia.

One of the more interesting juxtapositions in the literature is that of two articles reporting vastly different results using the same principle of therapy. Crooks and colleagues (1995) report on the results of open bladder transection in 12 of 19 patients who were available for follow-up. The indication was urinary frequency and nocturia unresponsive to more conservative measures. Three patients were deemed cured: 7 were better, and 2 were not better. Interestingly, 6 patients with preoperative enuresis were cured of at least this symptom by the procedure. Hasan and associates (1995) report on the results of endoscopic bladder transection in 50 patients with symptoms of urinary frequency, urgency, and urgency incontinence; all were unresponsive to anticholinergic therapy, and 45 had undergone hydrostatic distention with no lasting result. When a grading system for irritative symptom scores was used, there was no significant difference between preoperative and postoperative ratings. Subjective assessment revealed an overall symptomatic improvement in 12% of the patients. Objective urodynamic analysis demonstrated no significant improvement. Seventy-four percent of the patients on long-term follow-up had undergone alternative treatment. It is possible, of course, that endoscopic transection is simply not sufficient to produce the desired effect. Whether bladder transection remains a viable procedure for certain patients is still an issue.

Transvesical infiltration of the pelvic plexus with phenol aims to produce a chemical neurolysis whose results parallel the surgical approaches outlined earlier. Mundy (1985) and Torrens (1985) described the technique as being originated by Ewing and colleagues, who reported successful treatment of 19 of 24 patients with multiple sclerosis. Blackford and associates (1984) reported a satisfactory response in 82% of women with refractory neurogenic detrusor overactivity and in 69% of women with detrusor overactivity older than the age of 55. For some reason, the response rate was much less satisfactory for detrusor overactivity in females younger than 55 years of age (14%). Cameron-Strange and Millard (1988) reported a 70% success rate in 11 patients with neurogenic detrusor overactivity secondary to MS. Although they achieved a 58% success rate in 29 patients with detrusor overactivity, Wall and Stanton (1989) reported only a 29% significant response rate to therapy in a mixed group of 28 females with urinary urgency incontinence, only 2 of whom did not have detrusor overactivity or low compliance. **The potential risks of this procedure** include urinary retention and vaginal fistula. Chapple and coworkers (1991) reported success in only 2 of 18 patients with idiopathic detrusor overactivity observed for 6 months and in 2 of 6 with neurogenic detrusor overactivity. Two fistulas resulted, one vesicoureterovaginal and one vesicovaginal. They conclude, on reviewing their results and those of others, that subtrigonal phenol should be used in such cases only when no other treatment is possible.

To show how time tempers some views, in discussing the management of refractory urgency, **Stephenson and Mundy stated in 1994, "the procedures popularized in the early 1980s intended to partially or totally denervate (or more correctly decentralize) the bladder have been abandoned ... although some of these techniques had a high initial success rate in controlling incontinence and abolishing instability ... the relapse rate within 18 months approached 100%. The advent of clam enterocysto-** **plasty has revolutionized the treatment of the refractory group."**

Augmentation Cystoplasty

The fact that this topic has been accorded separate discussions (see Chapter 124, "Urinary Tract Reconstruction in Children"; Chapter 17, "Tissue Engineering and Cell Therapy: Perspectives in Urology"; and Chapter 80, "Use of Intestinal Segments and Urinary Diversion") emphasizes its importance in lower urinary tract reconstruction and in the treatment of refractory filling/storage problems of various causes. Suffice it to say here that **positive results have been obtained in up to 90% of patients with neurogenic lower urinary tract dysfunction and also in patients with bladders of limited capacity secondary to other problems,** such as tuberculous cystitis, for which the procedure was used initially. **Emptying failure afterward is a distinct possibility but can usually be predicted most of the time by careful preoperative urodynamic evaluation. The ability to perform CIC, or the means to have someone perform it, is essential.** By the time this point in the treatment "menu" for filling/storage problems has been reached, urinary retention at low pressure is generally not an unreasonable result, and the main issue is therefore one of patient and family informed consent. Specific issues regarding augmentation cystoplasty are explicitly considered in the other chapters mentioned and include the type of procedure to be carried out (enterocystoplasty, autoaugmentation, ureterocystoplasty), the amount (if any) of bladder to be removed in different disease states, the effect of the loss of the bowel segment on the individual patient's physiology, and the question of whether to perform a simultaneous procedure on the bladder outlet, generally to increase its resistance. New considerations include the possibility of creating new functional bladder segments by tissue engineering, using selective cell transplantation, expansion in culture, attachment to a support matrix, and reimplantation after expansion (see Chapter 17).

Nonsurgical Mechanical Compression

Vaginal and Perineal Occlusive and Supportive Devices; Urethral Plugs

Over the years, and especially more currently, there have appeared a number of nonsurgical urethral occlusive and supportive devices and urethral "plugs." Besides the time-honored penile clamp for postprostatectomy incontinence, these have been developed mostly for the treatment of female sphincter incontinence. This subject is further considered under the category of conservative management of incontinence in Chapter 63, "Conservative Management of Urinary Incontinence: Behavioral and Pelvic Floor Therapy, Urethral and Pelvic Devices." A few comments, based on personal experience, bear mention here.

Support of the bladder neck in the female resulting in improved continence is possible with intravaginal devices that have not been reported to cause significant lower urinary tract obstruction or morbidity. Tampons, traditional pessaries, and contraceptive diaphragms and intravaginal devices specifically designed for bladder neck support have been used. **Support devices** ideally would reduce any degree of vaginal prolapse and, by supporting the interior vaginal wall and therefore the urethrovesical junction and bladder neck, should theoretically control incontinence caused by hypermobility and poor pelvic support. Although most individuals agree that information about vaginal support devices should be included in the treatment options when counseling women with stress incontinence, most would also agree that studies performed on these devices in the acute laboratory setting demonstrate better performance than diary-based studies with respect to the amount and number of episodes of leakage. It has been our experience that **such devices work best in individuals with minimal to moderate leakage. True pessary usage seems most reasonable in the elderly woman with a major degree of anterior vaginal wall prolapse and hypermobility-related stress incontinence who is a poor surgical candidate.**

Occlusive devices can be broadly divided into external and internal devices, referring to whether the device itself occludes the urethra or bladder neck from the outside or has to be inserted per urethra. **There have been many patterns of external occlusive devices available for use in the male,** but all seem to take the form of a clamp applied across the penile urethra. **Soft tissue damage by excess compression can occur with these clamps, and thus their use is extremely risky in patients with neurologic disease and sensory impairment.** Their prime use is in patients with sphincteric incontinence, although if one applies them tightly enough, one can doubtless occlude the urethra under any circumstances, although with a distinct danger of retrograde damage from increased pressure.

Occlusive devices for female sphincteric incontinence have been mentioned since the late 1700s. Multiple **intravaginal occlusive devices** have been described, all of which historically consist of rather bizarre-looking configurations of silicone and plastic with a dual purpose: to stay in the vagina and to compress the urethra. None of these seems to have stood the test of time. The simplest of the most recent devices is a continence control pad **or external urethral occlusion device.** A hydrogel-coated foam pad is placed by the patient over the external urethral meatus. Another type of device is a meatal suction or occlusion device. The concept is to create, by suction, a measured amount of negative pressure, causing coaptation of the urethral wall. **Intraurethral devices** can be inserted to block urinary leakage as well. Similarities among these devices include (1) a means to prevent intravesical migration (generally a meatal plate or tab at the meatus); (2) a mechanism to maintain the device in its proper place in the urethra (spheres, inflatable balloons, or flanges on the proximal end); and (3) a device or mechanism to permit removal for voiding. Most patients utilizing external meatal occlusive devices or intraurethral devices have reported dryness or improvement in the laboratory and in diaries. Long-term results, however, are limited, and the exact place of this therapy in the algorithm of conservative management of female sphincteric incontinence has not yet been determined. **The characteristics of an ideal occlusive or supportive device would include** (1) efficacy, (2) comfort, (3) ease of application/insertion/removal, (4) lack of interference with adequate voiding, (5) lack of tissue damage, (6) lack of infection, (7) no compromise of subsequent therapy, (8) cosmetic acceptance (unobtrusive), and (9) lack of interference with sexual activity. Ideally, such a device could

be used continuously during waking hours (for the majority who do not have sphincteric incontinence after bedtime), but many people would be happy with a device that functioned well for use only during those activities most provocative of incontinence. **The ideal patient for such a device** would be one with pure sphincteric incontinence that is mild to moderate and without significant detrusor overactivity or decreased compliance who desires active involvement in her treatment program, who desires immediate results, and who has the body habitus, manual dexterity, and cognitive ability to apply or insert the device and remove it. **Reasons for failure of these devices in our experience have included** (1) the patient's reluctance to "put anything inside me or on me"; (2) inconvenience (frequent removal/self-insertion or requirement for periodic replacement by a health care provider); (3) real or perceived discomfort; (4) fear of infection and/or bleeding; (5) association of such devices by the patient with a remedy of last resort and the implications that that type of association raises; (6) nonwillingness to pay out of pocket for these devices, which are generally poorly covered by insurance; (7) perceived lack of long-term success; and (8) nonincentive for the health care provider to promote the devices except in a capitated environment. The various details surrounding particular devices are more thoroughly considered in Chapter 63, "Conservative Management of Urinary Incontinence: Behavioral and Pelvic Floor Therapy, Urethral and Pelvic Devices."

Periurethral Bulking Procedures

Chapter 69, "Injection Therapy for Urinary Incontinence," thoroughly considers the history, indications, techniques, and results of periurethral bulking procedures. A variety of periurethral bulking agents are now available that can be injected via a percutaneous, transurethral, or transvesical injection to increase urethral resistance in both women and men with sphincteric incontinence. In women, the results from various authors have ranged from quite good to not so good, with the best "success" and improvement rates ranging from 70% to 90%. Multiple therapy sessions may be required to achieve the desired results. The results obtained in men have not been as good, especially in patients with post–radical prostatectomy incontinence. Originally, this therapy was "approved" (for reimbursement) only for patients with intrinsic sphincter dysfunction, defined by a Valsalva leak point pressure of less than 60 cm H_2O. The technique has been used with success, however, in other categories of incontinent female patients, including those, especially the elderly, with what seems to be a combination of hypermobility-related incontinence and intrinsic sphincter deficiency. The procedures can be carried out under local anesthesia or sedation, making them simple and relatively noninvasive. None of the procedures seems to compromise further therapy.

Implantable Microballoons

Implantable microballoons have also been used in the adult female and in children of both sexes to increase outlet resistance. These balloons can be implanted by means of periurethral or transurethral procedures and are likewise discussed in Chapter 69, "Injection Therapy for Urinary Incontinence."

Surgical Compression or Closure of the Bladder Outlet

Vesicourethral Suspension ± Prolapse Repair (Female)

Fixation of the vesicourethral junction in a physiologic position in such a way as to prevent hypermobility (posterior and inferior rotational descent with abdominal straining) has been observed to "correct genuine stress incontinence" in the female in 85% to 90% of patients undergoing a first operation for this problem. There are over 150 varieties of this procedure, and the names attached to many of these read like a virtual honor roll of urologic and gynecologic authorities. Each practitioner has his or her favorite suspension procedure, generally based on the site of residency or fellowship training, or on some recent development or product that promises to achieve the same end with less time and morbidity. The use of bone anchors for suture fixation, stapling devices, and laparoscopic techniques have added to the seemingly endless variations available for vesicourethral suspension. If significant vaginal or rectal prolapse is present, this should be repaired at the same time, remembering that the pelvic floor in the female acts as a unit, and a surgical procedure should endeavor to correct, where practical and possible, all associated abnormalities. These techniques are thoroughly discussed in Chapter 66, "Vaginal Reconstructive Surgery for Sphincteric Incontinence."

Sling and Tension-Free Tape Procedures

These procedures are thoroughly discussed in Chapter 67, "Pubovaginal Sling," and Chapter 68, "Tension-Free Vaginal Tape Procedures." The senior author of Chapter 67 (Edward J. McGuire) is the individual who deserves credit for fully describing the concepts that relate to the use of the sling procedure and for popularizing the procedure. He was among the first to conceptualize, in logical fashion, the fact that there was a category of female patients who leaked with increases in abdominal pressure who were not well repaired by standard suspension procedures. These were women who had poor sphincter function, irrespective of hypermobility, and whose urethral function at that time could be semi-quantitated only with the urethral pressure profile. He later developed the concept of Valsalva leak point pressure to better quantitate sphincteric resistance in patients with stress incontinence. **The sling is optimal surgical treatment for women with sphincteric incontinence from poor urethral closure function and poor urethral smooth muscle function.** Success rates as high as 90% with the pubovaginal sling procedure have been reported. As individuals have come to believe that "genuine" stress incontinence (hypermobility related) and intrinsic sphincter dysfunction are but two ends of a spectrum and that the great majority of women with sphincteric incontinence have some combination of the two, the sling procedure became a logical choice for the correction of stress incontinence of all types. As concepts regarding the pathophysiology of effort-related incontinence have continued to evolve, "tension-free" vaginal tape procedures (see Chapter 68) have begun to supplant the classic sling procedure for all varieties of sphincteric incontinence in the female.

Closure of the Bladder Outlet

This is generally **an end-stage procedure whose indication is a totally incompetent outlet that is uncorrectable by medical or conventional surgical means. This is most commonly caused by urethral necrosis secondary to long-term urethral catheterization in the neurologically impaired woman.** Trauma, infection, and fibrosis may also be responsible for irreparable urethral damage in both the male and female. In an individual with adequate hand control who desires to be dry, bladder neck closure can be combined with the creation of a continent catheterizable abdominal stoma. Augmentation cystoplasty can also be carried out at the same time. For individuals lacking adequate hand control or the cognitive facilities necessary for CIC or for those who simply do not want to carry out catheterization, a "chimney"-type conduit of bowel can be created with an abdominal stoma that drains into an appliance. Our technique of combined abdominal and vaginal bladder neck closure was described by Levy and associates (1994), with success in 10 patients. Drainage was by a suprapubic tube. Eckford and coworkers (1994) reported an initial 54% continence rate using only a transvaginal closure (and suprapubic cystostomy) in women with multiple sclerosis; an additional 24% were rendered dry after a revision. Chancellor and colleagues (1994b) used a pubovaginal sling to close the outlet in 14 women; greater tension than usual was applied. In 5 of these patients an ileocystostomy and cutaneous urostomy (bladder chimney) were performed; in 2, a suprapubic tube was used; in 5, an augmentation cystoplasty was necessary; and in 2, only the sling was necessary.

Shpall and Ginsberg (2004) retrospectively reviewed a series of 39 patients who had neurogenic lower urinary tract dysfunction who were treated with transabdominal bladder neck closure and simultaneous lower urinary tract reconstruction. The additional procedures included ileovesicostomy (19 patients), augmentation enterocystoplasty with a continent catheterizable stoma (19 patients), and revision of a Mitrofanoff appendicovesicostomy. The mean follow-up was 36.9 months. The overall complication rate was 31%, with 15% (6/39) developing a vesicourethral fistula. O'Connor and associates (2005) reviewed their outcomes of 35 patients who underwent suprapubic bladder neck closures for intractable incontinence: 83% (28/35) of the bladder neck closures were successful, with 94% (33/35) being successful after one revision. The mean follow-up period was 79 months. Complications (excluding bladder neck fistula) were seen in 9% in the early period and 14% in the late periods. Therefore, **bladder neck closure and simultaneous lower urinary tract reconstruction seems to be a reasonable treatment option with acceptable risks in those with a completely incompetent bladder neck.**

In some females who may have a completely incompetent bladder neck and sphincter complex with intact anatomy, bladder neck closure can be performed by the use of an obstructing sling (Chancellor et al, 1994b). Typically, the sling is performed via a retropubic approach with the use of autologous fascia to minimize the chance of erosion because these slings are placed under tension to obstruct the urethra rather than simply support it. This may also be combined with other lower urinary tract reconstruction. Dik and associates (2003) treated 24 girls with neurogenic incontinence secondary to spina bifida with an obstructing autologous fascial sling and additional lower urinary tract reconstruction. Initially, 19 of the girls were completely dry and 3 more became dry with the addition of periurethral bulking agent.

Artificial Urinary Sphincter

Control of sphincteric urinary incontinence with implantable prosthetics has evolved over the past 30 years. Clearly, the most significant contribution was the introduction by Scott and coworkers (1974) of a totally implantable artificial sphincter mechanism that could be used in adults and children of both sexes. The biomechanical evolution of this device and its current indications and use are considered in Chapter 74, "Surgical Procedures for Sphincteric Incontinence in the Male." **Silent upper tract deterioration after genitourinary sphincter placement (or any procedure designed to increase outlet resistance) should be remembered as a potential adverse phenomenon for which post-treatment surveillance must be instituted.** This may occur even if involuntary bladder contractions or decreased compliance were not present preoperatively. The incidence of mechanical malfunction and infection, though initially high, is quite low in contemporary series.

Bladder Outlet Reconstruction

Reconstruction of the bladder outlet is one method of restoring sphincteric continence in patients with a fixed, open bladder outlet. This technique was introduced for the treatment of urinary incontinence by Hugh Hampton Young in 1907 and was subsequently modified by Dees, Leadbetter, and Tanagho. Procedures using the **Young-Dees principle** involve construction of a neourethra from the posterior surface of the bladder wall and trigone. In the male, the prostatic urethra affords additional substance for closure and increase in outlet resistance. The **Leadbetter modification** involves proximal reimplantation of the ureters to allow more extensive tubularization of the trigone. **Tanagho** (1981) has described a procedure based on a similar concept but using the anterior bladder neck to create a functioning neourethral sphincter. Long-term success rates of between 60% and 70% have been reported (Leadbetter, 1985), but it is difficult to know what success means and what the true rates of success are, using a contemporary definition.

Myoplasty for Functional Sphincter Reconstruction

Deming (1926) first reported the use of the **gracilis muscle, transposed around the urethra,** for the treatment of sphincteric incontinence. In this "unstimulated" myoplasty, reliance is placed on the patient's own voluntary contraction (adduction of the leg) to provide sphincteric continence. Stenzl (1998) describes unstimulated graciloplasty as an innovative idea but one that was associated with a number of problems: (1) the need for uncomfortable prolonged adduction of the leg to maintain sphincteric contraction; (2) unsatisfactory sustained muscle contraction caused by the high content of fast-twitch, non–fatigue-resistant fibers; (3) loss of resting tension after dissection of the muscle, resulting in reduced contractility; (4) passive obstruction; and (5) the risk of fibrosis because the minor pedicles supplying the caudal segment of the gracilis are severed.

To overcome these problems, electrical stimulation through electrodes implanted into the muscle was developed and reported on by Janknegt and associates (1995). The electrical stimulation program used parameters to transform fatigable type 2 skeletal muscle fibers to slow type 1 fibers, able to sustain a long-lasting contraction. Only three patients are described as having "good results," and a further patient is described as being dry at night. Chancellor and colleagues (1997) described the use of a gracilis muscle urethral wrap in 5 men with neurogenic bladder dysfunction and severe stress incontinence from striated sphincter control failure. Although the surgery was considered to be successful in 4 patients, 3 were managed with CIC and 1 with ileocystostomy. Of the 3 who were managed with intermittent self-catheterization, 2 had persistent stress incontinence and 1 required two subsequent periurethral collagen injections. One patient had a pulse generator implanted, connected to intramuscular electrodes, and apparently had a successful result. Stenzl (1998) comments that such electrical stimulation does not overcome the problems associated with what he calls the anatomic shortcomings of the gracilis muscle. The bulk of the gracilis muscle so transplanted seems to be a problem.

Palacio and coworkers (1998), using female dogs, described an interesting technique to avoid these problems by using a free but innervated flap of well-vascularized (only) proximal gracilis muscle that apparently is easily transposable to the urethra because of its smaller size. Stimulation of the sphincter is carried out through the graft's own motor innervation. The main vascular pedicle to the gracilis flap is divided, and thus the muscle becomes a free flap, but blood supply is restored by anastomosing the main artery and vein to the deep inferior epigastric vessels. They cite previous attempts at graciloplasty with implantable pulse generators as resulting in an approximately 50% failure rate, caused mostly by stricture of the outlet at the location of the gracilis neosphincter. They believe their technique has the potential to avoid these problems, and it remains to be seen whether this innovative idea can be translated into clinical success.

Catheterization

Clean Intermittent Catheterization

CIC has proved to be the most effective and practical means of attaining a catheter-free state in the majority of patients with acute spinal cord lesions. It is also an extremely effective method of treating the adult or child whose bladder fails to empty, especially when efforts to increase intravesical pressure and/or decrease outlet resistance have been unsuccessful. In those patients who have filling/storage failure caused by bladder hyperactivity and/or sphincteric incontinence with adequate or inadequate emptying, CIC may also be used if the dysfunction can be converted solely or primarily to one of emptying by nonsurgical or surgical means (see Wein and Barrett, 1988).

CIC has revolutionized the treatment of difficult cases of neuromuscular dysfunction of the lower urinary tract by providing a safe and effective method that preserves the independence of the patient to empty the lower urinary tract in cases in which continence has been produced

pharmacologically or surgically, producing total or partial urinary retention. Without CIC, the success of augmentation cystoplasty or continent urinary diversion would never have been achieved, and all of us should feel a great debt to Jack Lapides for promoting and popularizing CIC (Lapides et al, 1972). Lapides deserves enormous credit for first applying the concept of self-CIC to large groups of patients with voiding dysfunction. He and his coworkers demonstrated the long-term efficacy and safety of such a program and subsequently so have many others.

A cooperative, well-motivated patient or family is a requirement. The patient must have adequate hand control, or a family member must be willing to catheterize; in addition, adequate urethral exposure must be able to be obtained. An excellent consideration of factors involved in making a catheterization program work in the patient with functional limitation, as exists in many patients with neurogenic lower urinary tract dysfunction, is reported by Graham (1989). It is advantageous to have a special nurse who instructs the patients and families in the regimen; provides them with understandable written instructions to refresh their memory regarding technique, precautions, and danger signals; and provides continuing support for patients and families who call with questions or problems referable to their regimen. Teaching self-CIC requires an approach that communicates acceptance of the procedure by the instructor. Many patients are initially extremely reluctant to perform any procedure on themselves that involves the genitalia. Patients need a thorough explanation of the advantages of CIC along with assurances that it is simple and that it will not tie them to their houses or to an absolute time schedule. Additionally, proper selection of equipment for the patient's intelligence and financial level will increase patient acceptance of and compliance with a self-CIC program. Patients who are reticent initially are continually amazed by the ease with which such a regimen is established.

For adult male patients, a 14- or 16-Fr red rubber catheter is generally used. In patients with impaired fine-motor skills, stiffer plastic catheters may be easier for them to insert. A notable advantage to the red rubber catheters is their longevity. They can be reused indefinitely and boiled or microwaved for sterilization (Douglas et al, 1990). For female patients, disposable plastic catheters are recommended; they are inexpensive, are very convenient, and can be obtained under many insurance plans. Red rubber catheters may also be used.

Complications to be watched for, and which we have seen, can include urethral false passages, bladder perforation, and silent deterioration of the upper urinary tracts. Bacteriuria is common, but symptomatic infection is not. When this occurs, it should be treated with short-term antibiotic therapy. Antibiotic or antiseptic prophylaxis in this group of patients is considered in Chapter 8, "Infections of the Urinary Tract."

Continuous Catheterization

Indwelling urethral catheters are generally used for short-term bladder drainage, and careful use of a small-bore catheter for a short time, does not, in our opinion and that of others, seem to adversely affect the ultimate outcome, at least insofar as this applies to initial bladder management in SCI (Lloyd et al, 1986).

Occasionally, more often in females, an indwelling catheter is a last resort type of therapy for long-term bladder drainage. Virtually all such patients have bacteriuria after a certain period of time. A contracted fibrotic bladder may be the ultimate result. Bladder calculi may form on the catheter or on the retention balloon. Urethral complications are relatively uncommon in females when proper care is exercised, but bladder spasm may occur, producing urinary incontinence around the catheter. The temptation to use a larger-bore catheter with a larger-capacity balloon should be resisted, because the continuous use of such a drainage system combined with some pressure on the catheter may cause erosion of the bladder neck and urethra. A suprapubic catheter may be initially more comfortable and obviates urethral complications in the male, which is the main advantage of this type of continuous drainage over longer periods of time. **Use of a suprapubic catheter does not, however, obviate urethral leakage with detrusor contractions, nor does it provide better drainage or less leakage in patients with sphincteric incontinence.** When blockage or dislodgement occurs, nursing personnel may be reluctant to change this type of catheter without physician assistance.

There is controversy, much of it recent, over whether long-term indwelling catheterization in the neurologically challenged population is associated with a poorer outcome, with respect to either significant upper and lower urinary tract complications or quality of life. After CIC became a popular option, indwelling catheterization was discouraged for all but desperate situations, first on the basis of infection and then on the basis of the occurrence of other urologic complications. The article by Jacobs and Kaufman (1978) was often cited to show that removal of an indwelling catheter in men with SCI would prevent renal deterioration. What this article actually showed was that there were more renal and other urologic complications with long-term (>10 years) than short-term (removed just after injury) use. Hackler (1982) reported accelerated renal deterioration in patients with SCI managed with long-term suprapubic catheterization. McGuire and Savastano (1984) reported a poorer outcome in women with an indwelling urethral catheter than in those on CIC after 2 to 12 years. Of 13 in the former group, 54% had adverse changes on intravenous pyelography, as opposed to 0% in the latter group. Other urologic complications were also more frequent and severe in the former group.

Talbot and colleagues (1959) were among the first to suggest a relatively benign renal course for indwelling catheterization in the patient with SCI. Dewire and associates (1992) reviewed the course of 32 quadriplegic patients managed with, and 25 without, an indwelling catheter. The groups were roughly comparable, and follow-up was for 10 years or longer. The incidences of upper and lower urinary tract complications and renal deterioration were not significantly different. Chao and coworkers (1993) did a similar review on 32 patients with SCI with an indwelling urethral (14 patients) or suprapubic catheter (18 patients) versus 41 patients without. Follow-up was 20 years or longer. Although the catheterized group had a higher prevalence of upper tract scarring and caliectasis, no significant differences were found in other indices of renal function or in the prevalence of other urologic complications.

Jackson and DeVivo (1992) reported on the results of indwelling catheterization in 108 women after SCI followed for 2 to 5 years (56 women), 6 to 9 years (31 women), and 10 or more years (21 women) after injury. Compared with the male population, the majority of whom were managed by condom drainage, there was no difference in upper or lower tract complications. Renal function was assessed by effective renal plasma flow, quantitated on a renal scan. Barnes and associates (1993) concluded that long-term suprapubic catheters were well tolerated by patients with neuropathic bladders. Based on the replies of 32 of 35 who expressed an opinion, 84% were satisfied. However, the follow-up was short (3 to 66 months; mean, 23 months). In 2 of 12 patients assessable at over 2 years (exact length not specified), there was an increase in serum creatinine level. Other problems, however, were apparent in the entire group. Recurrent catheter blockage occurred in 38%, recurrent symptomatic urinary infections in 23%, and displaced catheters, requiring reinsertion in the operating room, in 15%. Urethral leakage occurred in 8 of 14 females with a suprapubic catheter alone and in 6 of 16 males.

MacDiarmid and colleagues (1995) reported on suprapubic catheterization in 44 patients with SCI, with follow-up ranging from 12 to 150 months (mean: 58 months). They reported that no patient had renal deterioration or vesicoureteral reflux and that the incidences of incontinence, infection, and calculi were acceptable. Eleven percent of the patients had leakage, 100% had bacteriuria, 41% developed bladder calculi, and 7% developed renal calculi. Thirty-six percent of patients developed episodes of catheter blockage, and gross hematuria resulting in hospitalization occurred in 5%. Sheriff and associates (1998) discussed the clinical outcome in a satisfaction survey of 185 patients with neuropathic bladder dysfunction treated with long-term suprapubic catheterization (follow-up: 3 to 68 months; mean: 24 months). There were only 8 patients who had a suprapubic catheter for longer than 2 years. The authors reported a general level of satisfaction (82% believed that suprapubic catheterization had improved their lives), but it should be noted that the main reason for this procedure was failed CIC from poor hand function. With this relatively short follow-up, 5 patients were noted to have had a small bowel injury on insertion of the catheter, 2 developed significant hemorrhage, 2 required catheter repositioning because of drainage failure, 1 required reinsertion because of dislodgement, and 8 had persistent incontinence. Recurrent catheter blockage occurred in 18%. Bacteriuria existed in 98% of the patients, but recurrent symptomatic infection occurred in only 4%. Only 103 of the 185 patients filled out the satisfaction questionnaire, and between 3% and 17% of these did not answer the main questions of the survey. The authors conclude that suprapubic catheterization is "an effective and well-tolerated method of management in selected patients with neuropathic bladder dysfunction for whom only major surgery would otherwise provide a solution to incontinence."

Sekar and coworkers (1997) reported on the effect of different bladder management methods in 1114 patients with SCI using total and individual kidney effective renal plasma flow as the primary outcome measure. Twenty percent of these patients were followed for at least 10 years, and 40% were followed for at least 5 years. However, the maximal follow-up in 51.3% of the patients was 0 to 3 years, hardly a long-term sample. It is difficult to ascertain the exact methods of urinary management at discharge, because discharge data from approximately 200 of the patients were not included in the study. In addition, the comment was made that most men who were discharged on CIC changed their method of management at a later date to condom catheter drainage. The authors concluded that there was very little change in renal function as the time from injury increased and that there were no clinically meaningful differences in renal function over time among persons using different bladder management methods.

More recently, Weld and Dmochowski (2000) reported a retrospective review of 316 post-traumatic patients with SCI with a mean follow-up of 18.3 years. Bladder management methods included chronic urethral catheterization in 114 patients, CIC in 92, spontaneous voiding in 74, and suprapubic catheterization in 36. Complications were recorded in terms of infectious complications (epididymitis and pyelonephritis), renal and bladder calculi, urethral complications (stricture and periurethral abscess), and radiographic abnormalities (vesicoureteral reflux and abnormal urographic findings). Overall, there were 398 complications recorded, of which 236 developed in 61 patients (53.5%) on chronic urethral catheterization, 48 in 16 patients (44.4%) on suprapubic catheterization, 57 in 24 patients (32.4%) who voided spontaneously, and 57 in 25 patients (27.2%) on CIC. Separate bar graphs for each type of complication seem to confirm the overall superiority of CIC as the least problematic form of management. These conclusions may be related to observations made by Weld and Dmochowski (2000) on the effects on bladder compliance in patients with SCI managed by CIC versus indwelling urethral catheterization. Logistical regression analysis of compliance versus bladder management and interval since injury revealed that CIC and spontaneous voiding were associated more with normal compliance than indwelling urethral catheterization. Low compliance was statistically associated with vesicoureteral, radiographic upper tract abnormalities, clinical pyelonephritis, and upper tract calculi.

Jamil and associates (1999) reported on ambulatory urodynamics in 30 patients with SCI whose bladders were managed with an indwelling urethral catheter. They found that the indwelling catheters on free drainage were not a guarantee of a constantly low intravesical pressure: detrusor contractions causing intravesical pressure rises greater than 40 cm H_2O for up to 4.5 minutes were observed in 11 of these patients. These patients had used an indwelling catheter for a mean of 14.3 years (range: 4 to 36 years). Renal scarring was observed in 9 patients; and of these, 6 were in the group with the abnormal bladder contractions whereas only 5 of 21 patients with normal kidneys had such pressure rises. The clinical correlate that the authors emphasize is their belief that maintenance of a compliant bladder and suppression of high-pressure contractions in such chronically catheterized patients may play a role in the prevention of renal deterioration.

Thus, **there is certainly some controversy about the classic teaching that long-term continuous bladder catheterization in patients with neurogenic bladder dysfunction should be avoided at all costs. There are obviously situations in which such management is desirable and necessary. Most of the studies that purport to compare methods of management** with respect to lower and upper tract complications are flawed in certain ways that prevent total acceptance of their conclusions. In the absence of a prospective randomized study or at least "cleaner" data, patient and family comfort, convenience, and quality of life must be strongly considered in this decision.

The Carcinoma Controversy

The development of carcinoma of the bladder in 6 of 59 patients with SCI who had long-term indwelling catheters was reported by Kaufman and colleagues (1977). All were squamous cell lesions. Four of these patients had no obvious tumors visible at endoscopy, and the diagnosis was made by bladder biopsy. Five of these patients also had transitional cell elements in their tumor. Broecker and associates (1981) surveyed 81 consecutive patients with SCI with an indwelling urinary catheter for more than 10 years. Although the investigators did not find frank carcinoma in any patients, they found squamous metaplasia of the bladder in 11 and leukoplakia in 1. Locke and coworkers (1985) noted two cases of squamous cell carcinoma of the bladder in 25 consecutive patients with SCI catheterized for a minimum of 10 years. Bickel and colleagues (1991) reported eight cases of bladder cancer in male patients with SCI, although the denominator was uncertain. Four of these had been managed by indwelling catheterization for 7, 10, 14, and 19 years, respectively. All of these had transitional cell carcinoma, whereas in the other 4, there were two cases of transitional carcinoma and two cases of squamous cell carcinoma. In Chao and colleagues' series (1993), 6 patients developed bladder cancer, 3 of whom had indwelling catheters (of a total of 32) and 3 of whom (of 41) did not. Stonehill and associates (1996) retrospectively reviewed all bladder tumors in their patients with SCI for 7 years and compared these with matched controls. They found 17 malignant and 2 benign bladder tumors. Indwelling catheters and a history of bladder calculi were statistically significant risk factors.

Should screening cystoscopy be done in chronically catheterized patients with SCI? Some believe that this will result in an earlier stage of diagnosis of bladder cancer and will therefore convey a survival advantage (Navon et al, 1997); some believe that cystoscopy does not fulfill the accepted criteria for screening for primary bladder cancer in patients with SCI (Yang and Clowers, 1999). Certainly, all would agree that such patients with new-onset gross hematuria should be evaluated with some upper tract imaging, urinary cytology, and cystoscopy, perhaps with random biopsy. We continue to screen patients on long-term indwelling catheter drainage with cystoscopy, bladder washings for cytology, and, when indicated, bladder biopsies.

Urinary Diversion

Although commonly employed in the past for the treatment of neurogenic voiding dysfunction, supravesical diversion is now rarely indicated in any patient with only voiding dysfunction. Indications may include (1) progressive hydronephrosis and intractable upper tract dilatation (which may be caused by obstruction at the ureterovesical junction from a trabeculated thick bladder or by vesicoureteral reflux

that does not respond to conservative measures); (2) recurrent episodes of urosepsis; and (3) intractable filling/storage or emptying failure when CIC is impossible.

Learning from the success of cutaneous vesicostomy in children, cutaneous incontinent diversion at the level of the bladder can be accomplished without the need for ureteral reimplantation by an **ileovesicostomy or "chimney" procedure.** Another advantage to the ileovesicostomy over a bowel conduit is that it is easier to reverse if such a situation arises.

Continent diversion requires that the patient be able to perform CIC or that dependable assistance is available for this. The potential advantages of continent reservoir diversion are obvious, but they introduce the potential of upper tract deterioration secondary to high-pressure storage, with or without vesicoureteral reflux. Continent diversion can be performed with anastomosis to a urethral stump, with at least the potential of less reliance on CIC. No further discussion of urinary diversion is presented here, and the reader is referred to Chapter 124, "Urinary Tract Reconstruction in Children"; Chapter 80, "Use of Intestinal Segments and Urinary Diversion"; Chapter 81, "Cutaneous Continent Urinary Diversion"; and Chapter 82, "Orthotopic Urinary Diversion" for a contemporary review.

The Artificial Bladder

Prosthetic organs have been successful in many regions of the body, and on the surface it would seem to be a simple matter to replace a biologic reservoir such as urinary bladder with a mechanical storage/emptying device. However, despite numerous attempts over the past 50 years, we do not seem to be very close to this goal. Desgrandchamps and Griffith (1999), in an excellent review that includes a consideration of all aspects of development of an artificial bladder, describe the **goals as a structure that will provide adequate urine storage with complete volitional evacuation of urine while preserving renal function. The structure of the artificial bladder must be biocompatible and resistant to urinary encrustation and tolerant to bacterial infection.** There have been numerous alloplastic materials (nonbiologicals) considered for such use along with the consideration of various (mostly failed) design concepts for total artificial bladder replacement. They describe what they believe are certain desirable **guidelines for future designs** as follows:

1. Direct anastomoses between living tissue and the prosthesis should be as limited as possible.
2. A composite structure reservoir is preferable, one that will prove resistant to long-term encrustation, allow tissue penetration to ensure watertight anastomoses, and reduce the risks of urinary leaks.
3. Active reservoir filling and emptying are necessary; ureteral peristalsis alone is unable to ensure reliable filling of an artificial flexible bladder; gravity alone is insufficient to ensure complete emptying.
4. New technologies will be necessary to resolve infection and encrustation problems, which will remain, in these authors' opinion, the limiting factors of a traditional alloplastic prosthetic bladder. They also mention the possibility of a tissue-engineered artificial bladder that would presumably avoid the risk of encrustation and

infection by avoiding the use of any alloplastic intraurinary material.

External Collecting Devices

Unfortunately, no optimal external collecting device has been yet approved for the female, primarily because of the difficulties of fixation and of leakproof collection. External collecting devices for the male (a condom or Texas catheter) are generally successful, insofar as urine collection is concerned, but are unacceptable to many patients because of the visible equipment required and the leaks of often foul-smelling urine that can result. Because many patients with neurogenic lower urinary tract dysfunction have impairment of sensation, it is easy for these devices to cause severe pressure necrosis of the penis down to and including the urethra (Golji, 1981). A collecting device without a single discrete roller band or application ring offers at least a theoretical advantage for this reason. Maintaining an external urinary collecting device is a major problem in some patients with SCI because of the inability to maintain a device during a vigorous voiding contraction, often associated with inadequate penile length, and because of recurrent lacerations of the penile skin, dictating temporary use of a Foley catheter. Van Arsdalen and coworkers (1981) described the use of noninflatable penile prostheses in this type of patient, with resultant ease of applying and maintaining such a device. This is particularly an advantage in those patients who are interested in a prosthesis for potency reasons as well. It should be noted, however, that the penile implant loss in these patients is much higher than in the general population (25% in this series). For similar problems resulting from a receding phallus, Binard and colleagues (1993) describe a "penoplasty."

Absorbent Products

Absorbent products, collection devices of sorts, represent a last resort for many patients. The ideal substance for absorptive padding is one that is highly permeable and absorbent. Immediately next to the patient is generally a layer of hydrophobic material, through which the urine passes into the absorbent pad, which is in turn surrounded by a waterproof material to keep clothing dry. Ideally, the hydrophobic material next to the skin keeps the patient relatively dry and reduces chafing as much as possible. An excellent review of the types of such devices available for males and females, as well as a review of external collecting devices and urethral compression devices and of skin care, can be found in the book by Newman (1999) and the catalogue available from the National Association for Continence (2004) or on their website (www.nafc.org).

TO FACILITATE BLADDER EMPTYING
External Compression, Valsalva Maneuver

The Credé maneuver (manual compression of the bladder) is most effective in patients with decreased bladder tone who can generate an intravesical pressure greater than 50 cm H$_2$O with this maneuver and in whom outlet resistance is borderline or decreased (Wein and Barrett, 1988). The technique of voiding by the openhanded Credé method involves placement of the thumbs of each hand over the area of the anterior superior iliac spines and of the digits over the suprapubic area, with slight overlap at the fingertips. The slightly overlapped digits are then pressed into the abdomen and, when they have gotten behind the symphysis, pressed downward to compress the fundus of the bladder. Both hands are then pressed as deeply as possible into the real pelvic cavity. At times, the compression can be accomplished more efficiently by the use of the closed fist of one hand or by a rolled-up towel.

A similar increase in intravesical pressure may be achieved by abdominal straining (Valsalva maneuver). The proper technique involves sitting and letting the abdomen protrude forward on the thighs. During straining in this position, hugging of the knees and legs may be advantageous to prevent any bulging of the abdomen. To increase intravesical pressure in this manner requires voluntary control of the abdominal wall and diaphragmatic muscles. The Credé maneuver obviously requires adequate hand control. Straining at the time the Credé maneuver is applied is generally counterproductive because this increases intra-abdominal pressure and causes bulging of the abdominal wall, which then tends to lift the compressing hands off the fundus of the bladder. If the proper reflex arcs are intact, this also causes striated sphincter contraction. The Credé maneuver is obviously much easier in a patient with a lax, lean abdominal wall than in a person with a taut or obese one, and it is more readily performed in a child than an adult.

Such "voiding" is unphysiologic and is resisted by the same forces that normally resist stress incontinence. Adaptive changes (funneling) of the bladder outlet generally do not occur with external compression maneuvers of any kind. As referred to previously, increases in outlet resistance (through a reflex mechanism) may actually occur. If adequate emptying does not occur, other types of therapy to decrease outlet resistance may be considered; however, these may adversely affect urinary continence. **Vesicoureteral reflux is a relative contraindication** to external compression or Valsalva maneuver, especially in patients capable of generating a high intravesical pressure by doing so.

The greatest likelihood of success with this mode of therapy (although some would say it should never be used) is in the patient with an areflexic and hypotonic or atonic bladder and some outlet denervation (smooth or striated sphincter or both). Such a patient not uncommonly has stress incontinence as well. The continued use of external compression or Valsalva maneuver implies that the intravesical pressure between attempted voidings is consistently below that associated with upper tract deterioration. This may be an erroneous assumption, and close follow-up and periodic evaluation are necessary to avoid this complication. **The most flagrant misuse of this form of management is in the patient with a decentralized or denervated bladder in whom decreased compliance during filling and storage has already developed.** In such a patient, increased intravesical pressures may develop silently that are greater than those necessary to cause upper tract deterioration with minimal filling, and then external compression and Valsalva maneuver under those circumstances simply aggravate an already dangerous situation.

Promotion or Initiation of Reflex Contractions

In most types of SCI or disease characterized by neurogenic detrusor overactivity, manual stimulation of certain areas within sacral and lumbar dermatomes may sometimes provoke a reflex bladder contraction (Wein and Barrett, 1988). Such **"trigger voiding"** is sometimes induced by pulling the skin or hair of the pubis, scrotum, or thigh; by squeezing the clitoris; or by digital rectal stimulation. According to the classic reference (Glahn, 1974), the most effective method of initiating a reflex contraction is rhythmic suprapubic manual pressure (seven or eight pushes every 3 seconds). Such activity is thought to produce a summation effect on the tension receptors in the bladder wall, resulting in an afferent neural discharge that activates the bladder reflex arc. Ideally, the contractions thus produced will be sustained and of adequate magnitude. Patients potentially able to induce bladder contraction in such a way should be encouraged to find their own optimal "trigger points" and position for urination. To accomplish this, manual dexterity and either the ability to transfer to a commode or the ability to use an external collecting device are required. If this type of patient has significant sphincter dyssynergia, such maneuvers may have to be combined with measures to decrease outlet resistance. This form of inducing bladder contraction is occasionally possible and desirable in patients with supraspinal disease and involuntary bladder contractions. If induced emptying can be carried out frequently enough to keep bladder volume and pressure below the threshold for activation of the micturition reflex and below the level dangerous for upper tract deterioration, incontinence can be "controlled." This actually amounts to a form of timed voiding.

Some clinicians still believe that the establishment of a rhythmic pattern of bladder filling and emptying by maintaining a copious fluid intake and by periodically clamping and unclamping an indwelling catheter or by CIC can "condition" or "train" the micturition reflex. Such regimens certainly are of benefit by focusing attention on the urinary tract and by ensuring an adequate fluid intake. It is also true that balanced lower urinary tract function can be achieved while a patient is on such a program (Opitz, 1984; Menon and Tan, 1992), but whether this is a cause-and-effect relationship is unknown and difficult to prove.

One fascinating set of experiments that relates to the concept of establishing or promoting a reflex pathway for micturition is that reported by Xiao and de Groat (1999). These individuals created a skin to central nervous system to bladder reflex pathway in cats by intradural microanastomosis of the left L7 ventral root to the S1 ventral root, leaving the L7 dorsal root intact to conduct cutaneous afferent signals. A detrusor contraction was able to be initiated by scratching the skin or by percutaneous electrical stimulation in the L7 dermatome. This new reflex pathway could initiate voiding without striated sphincter dyssynergia. This reflex could be elicited after transecting the spinal cord at the L2-L3 or L7-S1 levels. The pathway is mediated by cholinergic transmission at both ganglionic and peripheral levels, as shown by cholinergic blockade experiments. Thus, in this experimental model, somatic motor axons can innervate parasympathetic bladder ganglion cells and thus transfer somatic reflex activity to the lower urinary tract.

Reduction Cystoplasty

Myogenic decompensation of the bladder with persistently large amounts of residual urine may arise as a result of neurogenic problems or intravesical obstruction, may exist with megacystis, or may be of an unknown cause. **The anatomy and pathology of myogenic decompensation have suggested surgical treatment to some. Because the chronic overstretching affects mainly the upper "free" part of the bladder and because the nerve and vessel supply enters primarily from below, resection of the dome does not influence the function of the spared bladder base and lower bladder body** (Klarskov et al, 1988). **When the detrusor is underactive rather than acontractile, this type of partial cystectomy has been performed with some successful results** (Kinn, 1985; Klarskov et al, 1988). Because of limited success, Kinn (1985) recommends that such surgery be combined with radical incision of the bladder neck in males and rarely in females. Of Klarskov and coworkers' 11 patients, 3 were termed subjectively cured. One went on to supravesical diversion, and 5 were on CIC either regularly or periodically.

Hanna (1982) suggested a different concept in bladder remodeling that conceptually seemed to make more sense than just resection of the upper part of the detrusor. His procedure involved creating a laterally based mucosa-free detrusor pedicle flap and wrapping this flap around the body of the bladder, thus doubling the muscle bulk while reducing the bladder size. Bukowski and Perlmutter (1994) reported the results of a similar procedure in 11 boys with prune-belly syndrome. Interpretation of the data was complicated, but they concluded that the operation "has helped to improve voiding and minimize infection during early childhood but it does not seem to decrease bladder capacity or improve voiding dynamics in the long term." **Whether the risk/benefit ratio of these procedures, in view of their arguable success rate, justifies their use over CIC is debatable.**

Bladder Myoplasty

Transfer of an innervated free striated muscle flap has proved to be a valuable adjunct in the reconstructive repair of various types of functional deficits. Chancellor and associates (1994b) were among the first to report successful restoration of voluntary emptying of the bladder with a wrap of skeletal muscle, in this case rectus abdominis. Stenzl and colleagues (1998) reported on three patients with bladder acontractility who were treated with a microneurovascular free transfer of autologous latissimus dorsi muscle to the bladder to restore contractility. At the time of the report, the patients had been observed for 12 to 20 months. They all had an indwelling catheter initially and then were converted to CIC. Total postoperative catheterization time ranged from 16 to 30 weeks. At 12 months, their peak flow rates ranged from 18 to 26 mL/s with residual urine volumes of 0 to 90 mL. Maximum detrusor pressures during bladder emptying in two patients were 21 and 23 cm H_2O and, in a third, 82 cm H_2O. In this surgery, the main neural and vascular supply to the latissimus dorsi was anastomosed to the lowermost motor nerve supplying the rectus abdominis and to the inferior epigastric vessels. The transferred muscle was wrapped around the bladder with longitudinal tension and a slightly spiral configuration, ultimately covering about 75% of the mobilized bladder and leaving only the area of the trigone and the lateral pedicles uncovered. Patients were instructed to empty their bladders by actively contracting the lower abdominal musculature.

Interestingly, in that same year, von Heyden and colleagues (1998) reported on a similar procedure in dogs, anastomosing the thoracodorsal nerve to the obturator nerve and the vascular supply to the external iliac vessels. The graft was then stimulated by electrodes connected to the anastomosed neural supply and with direct muscle stimulation. Van Savage and colleagues (2000) studied the feasibility of performing detrusor myoplasty with rectus muscle in human cadavers. The deep inferior epigastric artery and veins and the two most caudal intercostal nerves were able to be preserved. They then carried out this procedure in a canine experiment, with stimulation being achieved with electrodes inserted into the muscle near the nerve entrance. Their later study looking at electrically stimulated myoplasty in dogs showed good results with acute stimulation generating bladder pressures adequate for bladder emptying. Unfortunately, in a chronic study, although compliance and flap viability were maintained, bladder emptying was not (Van Savage et al, 2002).

Another fascinating concept that falls under the rubric of myoplasty is the use of myoblasts as a vehicle for gene delivery to muscles. Yokoyama and coworkers (2000) describe a plan of research involving myoblast-mediated ex vivo gene transfer, with observations of long-term survival of the injected myoblasts in the bladder and with preliminary histochemical evidence that, after injection, these skeletal myoblasts can differentiate into smooth muscle. The question is whether such tissue engineering by cellular myoplasty can improve impaired bladder contractility. These investigators are also looking into the use of myoblast injection therapy for the treatment of stress urinary incontinence. Potential tissue engineering solutions for bladder failure are also discussed in Chapter 17, "Tissue Engineering and Cell Therapy: Perspectives for Urology."

Decreasing Outlet Resistance at a Site of Anatomic Obstruction

The topics here properly include the treatment of prostatic obstruction and urethral stricture disease, and their discussion is appropriately found in Chapters 87, "Evaluation and Nonsurgical Management of Benign Prostatic Hyperplasia"; 88, "Minimally Invasive and Endoscopic Management of Benign Prostatic Hyperplasia"; and 89, "Retropubic and Suprapubic Open Prostatectomy" and Chapter 33, "Surgery of the Penis and Urethra." Pharmacologic treatments are discussed in Chapters 62, "Pharmacologic Management of Storage and Emptying Failure," and 87, "Evaluation and Nonsurgical Management of Benign Prostatic Hyperplasia."

Transurethral Resection or Incision of the Bladder Neck

Emmett performed the first transurethral bladder neck resection for neurogenic lower urinary tract dysfunction in 1937, and for years this procedure represented the first line of surgical treatment in such patients with poorly balanced bladder function (Wein and Barrett, 1988). The operation was originally performed primarily in two types of neurogenic patients: (1) those with weak or absent detrusor contractions and (2) those with anatomic or functional obstruction at the level of the bladder neck and/or proximal urethra, which prevented emptying either with abdominal straining or with a sustained detrusor contraction.

More refined urodynamic techniques have resulted in the realization that **true dyssynergia at the level of the bladder neck or proximal urethra is uncommon, both in patients with neurologic disease and in those without. The prime indication for transurethral resection or incision of the bladder neck is the demonstration of true obstruction at the bladder neck or proximal urethra by combining urodynamic studies that demonstrate obstruction either with fluoroscopic demonstration of failure of opening of the smooth sphincter area or with a micturitional (urethral pressure) profile showing that the pressure falls off sharply at some point between the bladder neck and the area of the striated sphincter.**

In the past, it was believed by some that another category for whom this procedure was useful was that of a patient with a sacral spinal cord lesion and an areflexic bladder who could achieve a measurable increase in intravesical pressure by straining or Credé maneuver but who could not empty the bladder adequately with these methods (Wein et al, 1976). We believe such a procedure in this type of patient can at best create a form of graded stress incontinence and that other alternatives for adequate emptying should be sought first.

The preferred technique at this time is incision of the bladder neck at the 5 and/or 7 o'clock position: a single full-thickness incision extending from the bladder base down to the level of the verumontanum. As Turner-Warwick (1984) originally described this technique, it involves deepening the incision until pinpoints of reflected light reveal minute interstitial fat globules between the latticework of the residual prostatic capsule fibers. Turner-Warwick (1984) reports the incidence of diminished ejaculate volume to be only 10% with this technique, and in fewer than 5% of these patients does he report absent ejaculate. **Most people would place the incidence of retrograde or diminished ejaculation somewhere between the reported incidences of 15% to 50%.** Other techniques of resection include a limited resection of dorsal tissue from the 3 o'clock to the 9 o'clock position, a resection further limited to the posterior lip, and a thorough circumferential resection of all tissue in males between the internal orifice and the verumontanum.

YV-Plasty of the Bladder Neck

It would seem reasonable to recommend this procedure only when a bladder neck resection or incision was desired and an open surgical procedure was simultaneously required to correct a concomitant disorder. This procedure, although certainly an established one, is in reality a revision of only the anterior bladder neck, because the posterior bladder neck is untouched. Because it is rarely carried out at this time, there is little information on whether it actually achieved, or was capable of achieving, the same urodynamic results as transurethral resection or incision.

Decreasing Outlet Resistance at the Level of the Striated Sphincter

Pharmacologic Sphincterotomy

Botulinum A toxin (Botox) is an inhibitor of acetylcholine release at the neuromuscular junction of somatic nerves on striated muscle. Although it is one of the deadliest poisons known, causing death by muscle paralysis, the use of small injected doses has been successful in the management of focal dystonia, skeletal muscle spasms and spasticity, and, more recently, of wrinkles maintained by the contraction of small muscle fibers in the face. It is interesting that it produces enough weakness of the muscle to prevent or considerably ameliorate spasm or involuntary contraction but not to completely block voluntary control, a phenomenon hypothesized to occur because more active neuromuscular junctions are more likely than less active junctions to be blocked by the effect of the drug (Hallett, 1999). Its urologic use for the treatment of detrusor striated sphincter dyssynergia was first reported by Dykstra and colleagues (Dykstra and Sidi, 1990; Dykstra et al, 1998). Injections were carried out weekly for 3 weeks, achieving a duration of effect averaging 2 months. The only side effects reported by Dykstra and coworkers were transitory limb paresis and transitory exacerbation of autonomic hyperreflexia.

Fowler and coworkers (1992) injected six women with difficult voiding/urinary retention secondary to what is now called the Fowler syndrome (manifested by abnormal myotonus-like electromyographic activity in the striated urethral sphincter). Although no patient achieved improved voiding characteristics (a fact attributed to the type of repetitive discharge activity), three women did develop transient stress incontinence, a positive effect of sorts, indicating that the sphincter muscle had indeed been weakened. Petit and associates (1998) reported on the endoscopic injection of botulinum toxin, 150 IU, into the striated urethral sphincter, using a four-point injection technique (the medication was diluted to 4 mL with saline solution). Seventeen patients with SCI or spinal cord disease were treated, and evaluation 1 month after treatment disclosed the following positive results: (1) a decrease in postvoid residual by an average of 176 mL; (2) a decrease in bladder pressure during an emptying contraction by an average of 19 cm H_2O; and (3) a decrease in urethral pressure during an emptying bladder contraction by an average of 24 cm H_2O. The authors judged voiding to be improved in 10 patients. Side effects included the new appearance of stress incontinence in 2 patients and exacerbation of preexisting incontinence in 3 patients. The duration of the effect was variable, but no less than 2 to 3 months. There were no adverse effects on striated muscle elsewhere. The authors concluded that botulinum toxin was a promising treatment for striated sphincter dyssynergia in certain patients refractory to CIC or surgery.

Gallien and colleagues (1998) injected botulinum toxin transperineally in five men with traumatic quadriplegia and striated sphincter dyssynergia. Using a total initial dose of 100 IU, divided into four injections of 25 IU each, the authors noted what they called improved bladder function in all patients, with a significant decrease in residual urine volume (however, on examining the figures, the mean reduction was

only 14 mL, with one of the patients requiring a second set of injections). The maximal urethral pressure on average did not change, the maximal detrusor pressure during an emptying episode decreased 5 cm H_2O, and the functional detrusor capacity increased by an average of 89 mL. Urinary catheterization was able to be stopped in two patients, and autonomic hyperreflexia dramatically decreased in intensity in four patients. The time to improvement was 10 to 21 days, and the duration was 3 to 5 months. No patient had significant side effects. Wheeler and associates (1998) reported on three men with SCI, all of whom had emptying problems related to striated sphincter dyssynergia. The sphincter was injected transperineally with botulinum toxin, using electromyography control for localization. Two of the patients reported excellent results.

Schurch and associates (1996) used both transurethral and transperineal injections in 24 male patients with SCI with voiding dysfunction secondary to striated sphincter dyssynergia. They judged that in 21 of these patients, striated sphincter dyssynergia was significantly improved with a concomitant decrease in postvoid residual urine volume in "most cases." Nine of 24 patients had a decreased postvoid residual volume from 450 to 50 mL; in 7 patients, the residual urine volumes were less than 50 mL to begin with and remained unchanged; and in 8 patients, the postvoid residual urine volumes were high and remained unchanged. The authors commented that transurethral injections appeared to be more effective, at least in reductions in maximal urethral pressure, than did transperineal injections. They noted no side effects.

Kuo (2003) treated 103 patients, 45 in urinary retention and 58 with difficulty urinating, with periurethral injections of 50 to 100 IU of botulinum A toxin. The lower urinary tract dysfunction was due to a number of different causes including detrusor sphincter dyssynergia in 29, dysfunctional voiding in 20, nonrelaxing urethral sphincter in 19, cauda equina lesion in 8, peripheral neuropathy in 14, and idiopathic detrusor underactivity in 13. Subjective assessment was excellent in 39% and significantly improved in 46%. There was a significant decrease in mean voiding pressures, mean urethral closure pressures, and postvoid residual. Unfortunately, assessment was performed only 2 to 4 weeks after treatment.

Münchau and Bhatia (2000) summarized the uses of botulinum toxin injection. A potential side effect is the spread to nearby muscles, particularly when high volumes are injected. They comment that distant effects can also occur, but distant weakness or generalized weakness, owing to the toxins spreading in the blood, is very rare. They do advise it should be used only under close supervision in patients with already disturbed neuromuscular transmission or during treatment with aminoglycosides. Theoretically, any agent that promotes striated sphincter relaxation in a uroselective manner could be used to decrease outlet resistance and facilitate voiding dysfunction. Yoshiyama and associates (2000) describe the laboratory use of intravenously administered α-bungarotoxin as improving voiding in rats with SCI. The drug is a toxin extracted from the venom of a Formosan snake; it selectively blocks nicotinic receptors without influencing transmission in autonomic ganglia. Although a long way from clinical use, nicotinic receptors in the striated sphincter have been shown to be a potential target for drug therapy for striated sphincter dyssynergia.

Surgical Sphincterotomy

Therapeutic destruction of the external urethral sphincter was first performed in 1936, but the first large clinical series was not reported until 1958 by Ross and colleagues (Wein and Barrett, 1988). **The primary indication for this procedure was, and still is, detrusor striated sphincter dyssynergia in a male patient when other types of management have been unsuccessful or are not possible.** A substantial improvement in bladder emptying was classically reported in 70% to 90% of cases (Wein et al, 1976). Upper tract deterioration was rarely reported after successful sphincterotomy. Vesicoureteral reflux, if present preoperatively, often disappears because of decreased bladder pressures and a reduced incidence of infection in a catheter-free patient with a low residual urine volume. An external collecting device is generally worn postoperatively, although total dripping incontinence or severe stress incontinence should be unusual unless the proximal sphincter mechanism (the bladder neck and proximal urethra) has been compromised—by prior surgical therapy, by the neurologic lesion itself, or as a secondary effect of the striated sphincter dyssynergia (presumably a hydraulic effect on the bladder neck itself).

The **12-o'clock sphincterotomy,** originally proposed by Madersbacher and Scott (1975), **remains the procedure of choice for a number of reasons,** which have been confirmed and commented on by others. The anatomy of the striated sphincter is such that its main bulk is anteromedial. The blood supply is primarily lateral, and thus there is little chance of significant hemorrhage with a 12-o'clock incision. There is some disagreement about the rate of postoperative erectile dysfunction in those individuals who preoperatively have erections. Estimates using the 3- and the 9-o'clock technique vary from 5% to 30%, but, whatever the true figure is, it is clear that most would agree that this complication is far less common (approximately 5%) with incision in the anteromedial position. Other complications may include significant hemorrhage (5% to 20%) and urinary extravasation. Sphincterotomy can be performed by use of a knife electrode, resection with a loop electrode, or laser ablation. The incision must extend from the level of the verumontanum at least to the bulbomembranous junction. Gradual deepening of the incision allows good visual control and minimizes the chance of significant hemorrhage and extravasation. When early failure occurs, it is generally attributable to an inadequate surgical procedure (either not deep enough or not extensive enough), inadequate detrusor function, and bladder neck or prostatic obstruction.

More recent reports have questioned the long-term efficacy of sphincterotomy. Santiago (1993) reported late failure requiring reoperation in 10 of 25 patients with SCI. Vapnek and associates (1994) reported that, of 13 cervical and 3 thoracic patients with SCI undergoing sphincterotomy 3 months to 8 years previously, only 8 of 16 were still on condom catheter drainage, and these had a significantly shorter follow-up (average, 16 months) than those who converted to an indwelling suprapubic catheter (39 months). Late failure may occur because of fibrosis somewhere along the extent of the sphincterotomy, a change in detrusor function, the development of prostatic obstruction, or a change in neurologic status

such that smooth sphincter dyssynergia develops (Lockhart and Pow-Sang, 1989).

Yang and Mayo (1995) reported long-term follow-up in a group of 37 male SCI patients who had undergone sphincterotomy. The procedure was judged a failure because of any or all of (1) the presence of large postvoid residual urine volumes associated with urinary tract infections; (2) autonomic hyperreflexia symptomatology associated with bladder overdistention or high voiding pressures; and (3) progressive upper tract deterioration from persistent reflux or poor bladder emptying. Eighteen surgeries were judged failures. Causes for failure included recurrent striated sphincter dyssynergia in 6, the development of a poorly contractile bladder in 6, bladder neck contracture in 3, stricture in the area of the sphincterotomy in 1, incomplete sphincterotomy in 1, and from unknown causes in 1. Mean follow-up time was 49 months for the failure group and 26 months for the success group, indicating that perhaps some of the latter group would shift to the former over time. There was no predictor of failure among any of the following parameters: age at surgery, injury level or type, previous bladder neck or striated sphincter surgery, preoperative maximal detrusor contraction pressure, and rise time to maximal pressure.

Juma and associates (1995) likewise reported long-term follow-up (time from last sphincterotomy 2 to 30 years, mean 11 years) in a group of 63 patients. Nineteen patients had significant upper tract complications, half of which developed more than 2 years after sphincterotomy. Thirty patients had lower urinary tract complications (recurrent infection, calculi, urethral diverticula, stricture, bladder neck stenosis, recurrent epididymitis). The authors considered **detrusor leak point pressure as the most reliable urodynamic parameter to predict the risk of upper tract complications after sphincterotomy.** The risk was 25% with a leak point pressure of less than 40 cm H_2O and 50% when the leak point pressure was over 70 cm H_2O. Kim and coworkers (1998) likewise concluded that a detrusor leak point pressure of more than 40 cm H_2O is a valid indicator of failure of sphincterotomy, because in their series of 55 patients with SCI there was a significantly higher incidence of upper tract damage and persistent sphincter dyssynergia in patients in this category. Noll and colleagues (1995) reported on follow-up of transurethral sphincterotomy in quadriplegic patients at three separate centers, the mean follow-up ranging from 4.2 to 4.9 years. Their reoperation rate for maintenance of urodynamic success (judged by detrusor leak point pressure and residual urine) was 57%. This included procedures other than re-sphincterotomy. With respect to the necessity for additional sphincterotomies, laser sphincterotomy seems to be an advantage over a conventional diathermy procedure, because only 15.1% of laser-treated patients required re-sphincterotomy compared with 30% of those treated with conventional sphincterotomy.

Outcome parameters to judge success or failure of sphincterotomy should include detrusor leak point pressure, upper tract function (renal chemistries and imaging appearance), presence and severity of vesicoureteral reflux, frequency and severity of autonomic hyperreflexia, occurrence of urosepsis, the need for catheterization, residual urine volume, and sexual function. Residual urine volume per se, however, does not always indicate the success or failure of the procedure. One other factor to consider when determining "success" is urine collection. Some patients may not be able to maintain an external collecting device and require a penile prosthesis. The percent of patients requiring such a procedure is difficult to ascertain in some series. Problems consequent to a condom catheter or to any prosthesis inserted to make it easier to maintain a condom catheter should likewise be included in outcome parameters but rarely are.

Urethral Overdilatation

Urethral overdilatation to 40 to 50 Fr in females can achieve the same objective as external sphincterotomy in males (see Wein and Barrett, 1988) but is rarely performed because of the lack of a suitable external collecting device. In young boys, when sphincterotomy is contemplated, a similar stretching of the posterior urethra can be accomplished through a perineal urethrostomy, obviating or postponing the need for normal sphincterotomy. Wang and associates (1989) reported the results of urethral dilatation with sounds or balloon procedures to 22 to 28 Fr in 11 myelodysplastic children with high intravesical pressures refractory to other traditional forms of management. After dilatation, the intravesical pressures decreased and upper tract function and bladder compliance improved. There was no discernible effect on continence. These observations indicate that compliance in these patients can be improved by a decrease in outlet resistance, and producing a decrease in outlet resistance in this fashion did not result in any deterioration in urinary control over what was present preoperatively.

Balloon dilatation of the external urethral sphincter was reported by Werbrouck and associates (1990). Using balloon dilatation to 90 Fr at 3 atm, Chancellor and colleagues (1994) compared balloon dilatation (20 patients), sphincterotomy (15 patients), and stent placement (26 patients) (see later) in the treatment of striated sphincter dyssynergia. A significant decrease in detrusor leak point pressure and residual urine occurred in all three groups. Bladder capacity remained constant, renal function stabilized or improved, and autonomic hyperreflexia likewise improved. Balloon dilatation and stent placement were associated with a significantly shorter surgery and hospitalization and less of a decrease in hemoglobin. In the dilatation group, 3 developed recurrent obstruction (at 3, 8, and 12 months), 1 had bleeding requiring transfusion, and 1 developed a 1-cm bulbar stricture. In the surgical sphincterotomy group, there were 2 cases of bleeding requiring transfusion, 2 cases of stricture with obstruction, and 1 case of erectile dysfunction. In the stent group, 3 had migration requiring adjustment (1 replaced, 2 with a second overlapping stent), and 2 developed bladder neck obstruction requiring transurethral incision. McFarlane and colleagues (1997) reported on the use of balloon dilatation of the striated sphincter as an alternative to sphincterotomy in 14 patients followed for a mean of 55.5 months (8 to 68 months). Sphincter activity was initially abolished in all patients, and reflux, which was present in 1 patient, resolved. Long term, however, there was an 85% overall failure rate and a 62% failure rate within 1 year. The authors concluded that this is an ineffective long-term treatment for striated sphincter dyssynergia in the majority of patients, recommending either surgical sphincterotomy or stenting as the surgical treatments of choice for this condition.

Urethral Stent Prosthesis

Shah and associates (1990) suggested the use of a permanent urethral stent to bypass the striated sphincter area, drawing on the British experience with urethral stricture disease. Chancellor and Rivas, in 1995, reported the multicenter North American data to that point with the use of the UroLume stent (American Medical Systems, Minnetonka, MN) in 153 patients at 15 centers. A significant decrease in detrusor leak pressure and residual urine volume occurred. Eighteen percent of patients required more than one procedure to adequately cover the sphincter with the prosthesis. Three months after, hyperplasia within the lumen was seen in 42 patients (33.3%). Of these, the ingrowth was labeled minor in 36, moderate in 5, and marked in 1. Ten devices were removed (7 for migration), and 7 were replaced. Thirteen patients developed bladder neck obstruction requiring treatment (4 with a blockers, 7 with incision, 2 with CIC). When removal was required (in 4) this was not a problem up to 12 months. Rivas and coworkers (1994) concluded that, in comparison to sphincterotomy, a stent prosthesis is as effective, easier, less morbid, and less expensive.

Chancellor and colleagues (1999a) reported the long-term follow-up for the UroLume stent in the treatment of striated sphincter dyssynergia in a group of 160 men with SCI at 15 centers in North America. Mean voiding pressure decreased from 75.1 cm H_2O to 37.4 cm H_2O at year 1, and this decrease seemed to be maintained at up to 5 years (mean of 44.2 cm H_2O in 41 patients followed for that period). Residual urine volume decreased, and this decrease was maintained for 5 years. However, at no point up to 5 years was the residual urine volume less than 105 mL in any group. Mean cystometric bladder capacity did not change. In those patients evaluated 1 year after stent placement, 53 of 89 experienced resolution of symptoms of autonomic hyperreflexia; at 2 years after implant, corresponding numbers were 37 of 72. In the 1-year follow-up group, only 1 patient of 36 who did not have hyperreflexia to begin with developed this; in the 2-year group, the numbers were 3 of 30. One obvious advantage to a sphincter stent is that it is potentially reversible. Fifteen percent of patients (24 patients) required stent removal; another stent was implanted in 4 of these. Stent migration occurred in 12.4% of patients at 3 months after implantation and in 5% at 6 months, with correspondingly decreased percentages up to 4 and 5 years. Forty-seven patients (26.3%) were diagnosed with bladder neck obstruction subsequent to stent placement, and this was managed by bladder neck incision in 20, a blockade in 10, CIC in 8, and watchful waiting in 9. An additional 7.8% of patients had non–bladder neck obstruction diagnosed subsequent to stent insertion. The authors commented that in those patients who required stent removal, the procedure was able to be accomplished despite epithelialization but that a learning curve certainly exists before one becomes comfortable removing the stent. It will be interesting to follow the feasibility and ease of removal after longer time periods.

Chancellor also headed a group that carried out a prospective randomized multicenter trial of sphincteric stent placement versus external sphincterotomy (Chancellor et al, 1999b). Fifty-seven men were randomized; the primary outcome indicator was maximum detrusor pressure. At 12 months, there was no difference in this outcome indicator in the two groups. At 24 months, this outcome indicator had decreased from 90.6 cm H_2O to 41.6 cm H_2O in the sphincterotomy group and from 101.9 cm H_2O to 71.6 cm H_2O in the stent group. Whether this is meaningful is uncertain. At 24 months, residual urine volume had decreased from 218 to 112 mL in the sphincterotomy group and from 164 to 132 mL in the stent group. Cystometric capacities did not appear to change up to 24 months. Bladder neck obstruction requiring treatment developed in 6 patients in each group. Six of the 31 stent patients required stent removal, all without difficulty. **The authors conclude that sphincteric stent prosthesis is as safe and effective as sphincterotomy and that the simplicity of placement and minimal associated morbidity make it an attractive alternative for the treatment of striated sphincter dyssynergia.**

An intraurethral sphincter prosthesis with a self-contained urinary pump has been developed for use in women with a hypocontractile or acontractile bladder ("Inflow" intraurethral insert). Schurch and associates (1999) reported on the use of this device in 18 women with neurogenic voiding dysfunction and a hypocontractile bladder. All but 1 had been using CIC previously, 1 using the Credé maneuver. Sixteen months after placement, only 6 of the women were still using the implant and were satisfied. In 10 patients, major incontinence around the catheter or irritation necessitated removal. In 2 patients, the device was removed because the patients could not learn how to transfer to the toilet to empty their bladder. Fourteen of the devices had to be replaced early because of technical dysfunction, and 3 external remote control units malfunctioned. The authors considered the device at that time unsuitable for long-term use.

Madjar and colleagues (2000) reported on 92 women with the device followed for periods of longer than 1 year. They concluded that the device can serve as long-term treatment and that the women who continued treatment for a prolonged time were satisfied with the device. Early removal of the device (<14 days) was required in 56.5% of patients, mostly because of local discomfort and urinary leakage. In an additional 20.6% of patients, the device was removed between 2 and 16 months after placement, although it appeared that in only 10 of the 19 patients was a true problem with the device responsible. The authors were following 21 patients (only 22.8% of the original group) with the device still in place after more than 1 year (mean, 24.6 months). In these patients, there were 6 necessitated removals in 4 patients because of migration into the bladder, asymptomatic bacteriuria developed in 15

patients, and symptomatic urinary tract infections developed in 4 patients. The authors' conclusion that further studies are necessary to compare this treatment with CIC and other modalities seems justified.

Pudendal Nerve Interruption

Relief of obstruction at the level of the striated sphincter can also be achieved by pudendal neurectomy, first described in 1899 by Rocket (see Wein and Barrett, 1988). **This method is seldom used today because of the potential of undesirable effects consequent to even a unilateral nerve section.** Bilateral nerve section results in an extremely high rate of male impotence and may result in fecal and severe stress urinary incontinence. In the rare instance of use, therapeutic assessment of the results of a block should certainly precede the formal procedure, which should be performed only unilaterally.

SUMMARY

There are more treatment options than ever before for voiding dysfunction causing problems of bladder storage or emptying. Some of the currently available options may one day appear to have been misguided, whereas other current treatments will be seen as the beginning of breakthrough treatment. An improved understanding of the pathophysiology of voiding dysfunction will certainly continue to drive the development of better solutions.

SUGGESTED READINGS

Chancellor MB, Rivas DA: Current management of detrusor-sphincter dyssynergia. In McGuire E (ed): Advances in Urology. St. Louis, CV Mosby, 1995, pp 291-324.
Lapides J, Diokno A, Silber S, et al: Clean intermittent self-catheterization in the treatment of urinary tract disease. J Urol 1972;107:458-465.
Locke JR, Hall DE, Walzer Y: Incidence of squamous cell carcinoma in patients with long-term catheter drainage. J Urol 1985;133:1034-1038.
Schurch B, Hauri D, Rodic B, et al: Botulinum-A toxin as treatment of detrusor sphincter dyssynergia: A prospective study in 24 spinal cord injury patients. J Urol 1996;155:1023-1029.
Tanagho EA, Schmidt RA: Electrical stimulation in the clinical management of the neurogenic bladder. J Urol 1988;140:1331-1336.
Wein AJ, Barrett DM: Voiding Function and Dysfunction—A Logical and Practical Approach. Chicago, Year Book Medical, 1988.
Wein AJ, Raezer DM, Benson GS: Management of neurogenic bladder dysfunction in the adult. Urology 1976;8:432-438.

Geriatric Incontinence and Voiding Dysfunction

NEIL M. RESNICK, MD • SUBBARAO V. YALLA, MD

Urinary incontinence is a major problem for the elderly. **It afflicts 15% to 30% of older people living at home, one third of those in acute-care settings, and half of those in nursing homes** (Fantl et al, 1996; McGrother, 1998). It predisposes to perineal rashes, pressure ulcers, urinary tract infections, urosepsis, falls, and fractures (Fantl et al, 1996; Tromp et al, 1998; Brown et al, 2000). It is associated with embarrassment, stigmatization, isolation, depression, and risk of institutionalization (Fantl et al, 1996). And it cost more than $26 billion to manage in America's elderly in 1995 (Wagner and Hu 1998; Andersson et al, 1999), exceeding the amount devoted to dialysis and coronary artery bypass surgery combined.

Providers and older patients alike often neglect incontinence or dismiss it as a normal part of growing older (Branch et al, 1994; Mann et al, 2000), but **it is abnormal at any age** (Herzog and Fultz, 1990; Fantl et al, 1996; Resnick, 1988). Although its prevalence increases, at no age does incontinence affect the majority of individuals, even those older than age 85 (Wetle et al, 1995). Moreover, the reason for its increased prevalence in the elderly appears to be the diseases and functional impairments that become more likely with growing older rather than age itself (Resnick et al, 1988; Herzog and Fultz 1990; Resnick, 1995; Wetle et al, 1995). Regardless, **incontinence is usually treatable and often curable at all ages, even in the frail elderly** (Ouslander and Schnelle 1995; Resnick 1995; Wagg and Malone-Lee, 1998; Weinberger et al, 1999), **but the approach must differ significantly from that used in younger patients.**

THE IMPACT OF AGE ON INCONTINENCE

At any age, continence depends on not only the integrity of lower urinary tract function but also the presence of adequate mentation, mobility, motivation, and manual dexterity. Although incontinence in younger patients is rarely associated with deficits outside the urinary tract, such deficits are found commonly in older patients. It is crucial to detect them, both because they exacerbate and occasionally even cause incontinence in the elderly and because design of an efficacious intervention requires that they be addressed.

In addition, **the lower urinary tract changes with age,** even in the absence of disease. Data from continent elderly are sparse and longitudinal data are virtually nonexistent. However, it appears that although **bladder capacity does not change with age** (Pfisterer et al, 2006b), **bladder sensation, contractility, and the ability to postpone voiding decline in both sexes, whereas urethral length and maximum closure pressure, as well as striated muscle cells in the rhabdosphincter, probably decline with age in women** (Diokno et al, 1988; Resnick, 1988; Resnick et al, 1995a; Strasser et al, 1999; Pfisterer et al, 2006a, 2006b). The prostate enlarges in most men and appears to cause urodynamic obstruction in approximately half (Resnick et al, 1995a). **In both sexes, the prevalence of involuntary detrusor contractions increases whereas the postvoid residual volume (PVR) probably increases to no more than 50 to 100 mL** (Diokno et al, 1988; Resnick, 1988; Resnick et al, 1995a; Bonde et al, 1996). In addition, **the elderly often excrete most of their fluid intake at night,** even in the absence of venous insufficiency, renal disease, heart failure, or prostatism (Miller, 2000; Morgan et al, 2000). **This fact, coupled with an age-associated increase in sleep disorders, leads to one to two episodes of nocturia in the majority of healthy elderly** (Miller, 2000; Morgan et al, 2000). Finally, **at the cellular level, detrusor smooth muscle develops a "dense band pattern" characterized by dense sarcolemmal bands with depleted caveolae** (Elbadawi et al, 1993b, 1997a). This depletion may mediate the age-related decline in bladder contractility. **In addition, an "incomplete dysjunction pattern" develops,** characterized by scattered protrusion junctions, albeit not in chains; these changes may underlie the high prevalence of involuntary detrusor contractions (Resnick et al, 1995; Elbadawi et al, 1997a; Hailemariam et al, 1997).

None of these age-related changes causes incontinence, but they do predispose to it. This predisposition, coupled with the

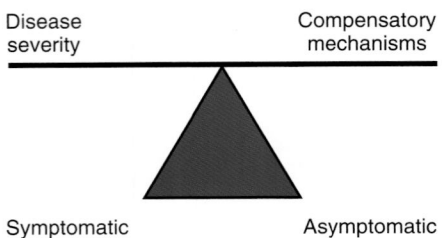

Figure 71–1. Incontinence results when the ability to compensate for bladder dysfunction is inadequate. For instance, in the intact older person, detrusor overactivity or sphincter weakness may not cause leakage if the patient is more attuned to bladder fullness, drinks less, voids more often, eliminates precipitants such as coughing, and stays close to a toilet. This explains how older patients may remain continent despite such abnormalities and also suggests alternate therapeutic approaches independent of the urinary tract. (From Resnick NM: An 89-year-old woman with urinary incontinence. JAMA 1996;276:1832-1840.)

increased likelihood that an older person will encounter an additional pathologic, physiologic, or pharmacologic insult, explains why the elderly are so likely to become incontinent. The implications are equally important. **The onset or exacerbation of incontinence in an older person is likely to be due to precipitant(s) *outside* the lower urinary tract that are amenable to medical intervention. Furthermore, *treatment of the precipitant(s) alone may be sufficient to restore continence, even if there is coexistent urinary tract dysfunction*.** For instance, flare of hip arthritis in a woman with age-related detrusor overactivity may be sufficient to convert her urinary urgency into incontinence. Treatment of the arthritis—rather than the involuntary detrusor contractions—will not only restore continence but also lessen pain and improve mobility. These principles, depicted in Figures 71–1 and 71–2 (Resnick, 1996; Resnick and Marcantonio, 1997), provide the rationale in the older patient for adding to the established lower urinary tract causes of incontinence a set of transient causes as well.

LUT ABNORMALITY VS. UI

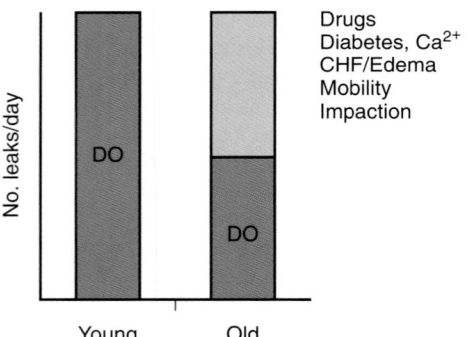

Figure 71–2. This graph shows why treatment of UI in older adults differs and is often easier than in younger adults. Both of these patients with detrusor overactivity (DO) have the same frequency of leakage. However, in the younger patient with intact compensatory mechanisms, such leakage reflects solely the contribution of the DO. In the older adult, other comorbid conditions make it more difficult to appreciate bladder fullness, adjust fluid output, and reach the bathroom. Such conditions magnify the impact of DO and will be unaffected by bladder relaxant therapy. But addressing them will result in a marked improvement in the UI even without treatment of the DO and will make DO therapy—if still required—more effective. LUT, lower urinary tract; UI, urinary incontinence. (From Resnick NM, Marcantonio ER: How should clinical care of the aged differ? Lancet 1997;350:1157-1158.)

Because of their frequency, ready reversibility, and association with morbidity beyond incontinence, the transient causes are discussed first.

CAUSES OF TRANSIENT INCONTINENCE

Incontinence is transient in up to one third of community-dwelling elderly and in up to half of acutely hospitalized patients (Resnick, 1988; Herzog and Fultz, 1990). Although most of the transient causes lie outside the lower urinary tract, **three points warrant emphasis.** First, the risk of incontinence developing from a transient cause is increased if, in addition to physiologic changes of the lower urinary tract, the older person also suffers from pathologic changes. Anticholinergic agents are more likely to cause overflow incontinence in individuals with a weak or obstructed bladder, whereas excess urine output is more likely to cause urge incontinence in people with detrusor overactivity and/or impaired mobility (Diokno et al, 1991; Fantl et al, 1990). Second, although termed "transient," these causes of incontinence may persist if left untreated and cannot be dismissed merely because incontinence is of long standing. Third, similar to the situation for established causes, identification of "the most common cause" is of little value. The likelihood of each cause depends on the individual, the clinical setting (community, acute hospital, nursing home), and the referral pattern. Moreover, geriatric incontinence is rarely due to just one of these causes. Trying to disentangle which of the multiple abnormalities is "the" cause is more useful for metaphysics than for clinical practice.

The causes of transient incontinence can be recalled easily using the mnemonic DIAPERS (Table 71–1). In the setting of *delirium* (an acute and fluctuating confusional state due to virtually any drug or acute illness), incontinence is merely an associated symptom that abates once the underlying cause of confusion is identified and treated. The patient needs medical rather than bladder management (Resnick, 1988).

Symptomatic urinary tract **infection** causes transient incontinence when dysuria and urgency are so prominent that the older person is unable to reach the toilet before voiding. Asymptomatic bacteriuria, which is much more common in the elderly, does not cause incontinence (Brocklehurst et al, 1968; Resnick, 1988; Baldassare and Kaye 1991; Ouslander et al, 1995b). Because illness can present atypically in older patients, however, incontinence is occasionally the only atypical symptom of a urinary tract infection. Thus, if otherwise asymptomatic bacteriuria is found on the initial evaluation, it should be treated and the result recorded in the patient's record to prevent future futile therapy.

Atrophic urethritis/vaginitis frequently causes lower urinary tract symptoms, including incontinence. As many as 80% of elderly women attending an incontinence clinic have atrophic vaginitis, characterized by vaginal mucosal atrophy, friability, erosions, and punctate hemorrhages (Robinson and Brocklehurst, 1984). Incontinence associated with this entity usually is associated with urgency and occasionally a sense of "scalding" dysuria that mimics a urinary tract infection, but both symptoms may be unimpressive. In demented individuals, atrophic vaginitis may present as agitation. Atrophic vaginitis also can exacerbate stress incontinence.

The importance of recognizing atrophic vaginitis is that it may respond to low-dose estrogen (Fantl et al, 1996; Cardozo

Table 71–1.	**Causes of Transient Incontinence**
Cause	**Comments**
Delirium/confusional state	Results from almost any underlying illness or medication; incontinence is secondary and abates once the cause of confusion has been corrected
Infection—urinary (only *symptomatic*)	Causes incontinence, but the more common asymptomatic bacteriuria does not
Atrophic urethritis/ vaginitis	Characterized by vaginal erosions, telangiectasia, petechiae, and friability; may cause or contribute to incontinence. Now controversial but may be worth a 3- to 6-month trial of estrogen, especially local (if not contraindicated by breast or uterine cancer)
Pharmaceuticals	Includes many prescribed and nonprescribed agents, because incontinence can be caused by diverse mechanisms (see Table 71–2)
Excess urine output	Results from large fluid intake, diuretic agents (including theophylline, caffeinated beverages, and alcohol), and metabolic disorders (e.g., hyperglycemia or hypercalcemia); nocturnal incontinence also may result from mobilization of peripheral edema (e.g., congestive heart failure, venous insufficiency
Restricted mobility	Often results from overlooked, correctable conditions such as arthritis, pain, postprandial hypotension, or fear of falling
Stool impaction	May cause both fecal and urinary incontinence that remit with disimpaction

Adapted from Resnick NM: Urinary incontinence in the elderly. Med Grand Rounds 1984;3:281-290.

et al, 2004). Moreover, as for other causes of transient incontinence, treatment has additional benefits; in the case of atrophic urethritis, treatment ameliorates dyspareunia and reduces the frequency of recurrent cystitis (Resnick, 1988; Raz and Stamm 1993; Cardozo et al, 1998; Eriksen, 1999).

Reports from two large-scale randomized prospective trials, however, have recently challenged long-standing assumptions about the benefits and risks of hormone therapy. The Women's Health Initiative (WHI) randomized more than 27,000 women aged 50 to 79 years to oral conjugated equine estrogen, 0.625 mg, with or without medroxyprogesterone, 2.5 mg (Hendrix et al, 2005). The Heart and Estrogen/ Progestin Replacement Study (HERS) randomized nearly 2800 postmenopausal women of the same age to the same regimen (Grady et al, 2001). Both studies found that hormone therapy was associated with worsening of preexisting incontinence. WHI investigators also found that hormone therapy, whether prescribed as conjugated equine estrogen alone or with medroxyprogesterone, was associated with increased incidence of new incontinence. Because both studies also found that hormone therapy did not protect against heart disease, they advised against using hormone therapy for urinary incontinence.

In trying to apply the results of the WHI and HERS trials, several caveats should be noted. Postmenopausal hormone levels differ substantially, and in some individuals they are similar to levels seen in the follicular phase of premenopausal women (Kuchel et al, 2001). Tissue sensitivity also varies. Thus, it is surprising that neither WHI nor HERS stratified results by the presence or absence of atrophic vaginitis, nor did investigators examine patients to determine whether the dose administered was sufficient to treat the condition if it was present. In addition, incontinence data were based on self-report, which can be problematic in older adults, both for reproducibility and for determining the type of incontinence (Resnick et al, 1994; Kirschner-Hermanns et al, 1998). Urodynamic testing was not performed. Moreover, although drugs used to treat heart disease in such patients can cause or exacerbate incontinence (e.g., diuretics, α-adrenergic blockers, calcium channel blockers, and angiotensin-converting enzyme inhibitors), their impact was not reported. Finally, other doses, hormone types, and routes of administration were not evaluated.

There is less evidence available from recent studies of nursing home patients but meaningful conclusions are precluded by limitations of sample size; selection bias; route, dose adequacy, and type of hormone used; and characterization and stratification by type of urinary incontinence (DuBeau, 2001; Ouslander et al, 2001).

The apparent lack of efficacy for conjugated equine estrogen demonstrated in these two studies, as well as the risks associated with long-term use of higher doses, must be balanced against the other benefits cited earlier, the lower doses and shorter duration of treatment advised for treatment of atrophic vaginitis, and the shorter life expectancy of many older women in whom the prevalence and severity of atrophic vaginitis are highest. Moreover, data from other randomized double-blind trials, which employed different estrogen preparations (estriol, estradiol, or quinestradol), demonstrated significant reduction in incontinence among nursing home residents (Judge, 1969) and among postmenopausal women with sensory urge incontinence (Walter et al, 1978). Thus, clinical judgment is warranted, and local administration of other types of estrogen may be best. Unfortunately, the use of vaginal estrogen has not yet been well studied.

With adequate treatment, symptoms of atrophic vaginitis remit in a few days to several weeks, but the intracellular response takes longer (Semmens et al, 1985). The duration of therapy has not been well established (Pandit and Ouslander, 1997). One approach is to insert a ring containing estradiol. The advantage is that it is small and delivers the dose locally. Because it does not increase systemic estrogen concentrations, it is often considered for women with past history of breast cancer. The disadvantage is that, despite its small size, it is not always feasible or well tolerated by frail older women, especially those with pronounced vaginal stenosis. Another option is to administer a low dose of estradiol orally or vaginally for 1 to 2 months and then taper it. Most patients probably can be weaned to a dose given as infrequently as two to four times a month. After 6 months, estrogen can be discontinued entirely in some patients, but recrudescence is common. Because the dose is low and given briefly, its carcinogenic effect is likely slight, if any. However, if long-term treatment is selected, a progestin probably should be added if the patient has a uterus. Hormone treatment (other than a vaginal ring) is contraindicated for women with a history of breast cancer. For those without such a history, mammography should be performed before initiating hormone therapy. There appears to be a slightly increased risk of breast cancer among women using oral estrogen daily for more than 5 years, but fortunately, such high-dose, frequent, and long-term therapy is rarely required.

Pharmaceuticals are one of the most common causes of geriatric incontinence, precipitating leakage by a variety of mechanisms (Table 71–2). Experts often cite dosages and serum levels below which side effects are uncommon. Unfortunately, such rules are of limited use in the elderly because they are generally derived from studies of healthy younger people who have no other diseases and take no other medications. Of note, many of these agents also are used in the treatment of incontinence, underscoring the fact that most medications are "double-edged swords" for the elderly.

Long-acting sedative/hypnotics, whose half-life can exceed 100 hours, are associated not only with incontinence but also with falling, hip fractures, driving accidents, depression, and confusion. Alcohol causes similar problems, but for a variety of reasons physicians frequently fail to identify alcohol use by older people as a source of symptoms, including incontinence. Sequelae of alcohol abuse are often absent or attributed to other causes. In addition, because of age-related alterations in the pharmacokinetics and pharmacodynamics of alcohol disposal, as well as interactions with other commonly used drugs, as few as one or two drinks can pose a problem for older individuals.

Because **anticholinergic agents** are prescribed so often for older people, and are used even without prescription (e.g., sedating antihistamines used for allergies, coryza, and insomnia), they are important to ask about. They cause or contribute to incontinence in several ways. In addition to provoking overt urinary retention, these agents often induce subclinical retention. The resultant decrease in available bladder capacity (i.e., total capacity minus residual) allows it to be reached more quickly, exacerbating incontinence due to detrusor overactivity as well as that due to functional impairment. By increasing residual volume, anticholinergic agents also can aggravate leakage due to stress incontinence. Additionally, many of these drugs decrease mobility (e.g., antipsychotics that induce extrapyramidal stiffness) and precipitate confusion. Finally, several agents intensify the dry mouth that many elderly already suffer owing to an age-related decrease in salivary gland function; the resultant increased fluid intake contributes to incontinence. Attempts should be made to discontinue anticholinergic agents or to substitute ones with less anticholinergic effect (e.g., a selective serotonin reuptake inhibitor for a tricyclic antidepressant; olanzapine or risperidone for chlorpromazine). Limited data suggest that bethanechol may be useful for nonobstructed patients whose urinary retention is associated with use of an anticholinergic agent that cannot be discontinued (Everett, 1975).

In men with asymptomatic prostatic obstruction, **α-adrenergic agonists** can provoke acute retention. Particularly problematic are **nonprescribed decongestants.** They often contain an (anticholinergic) antihistamine and are frequently taken with a nonprescribed hypnotic, all of which are also sedating antihistamines. Because older individuals often fail to mention nonprescribed agents to a physician, urinary retention due to use of a decongestant, nose drops, and a hypnotic may result in premature or even unnecessary prostatectomy.

By blocking receptors at the bladder neck, **α-adrenergic antagonists** (many antihypertensives) may induce stress incontinence in older women (Mathew et al, 1988; Marshall and Beevers, 1996) in whom urethral length and closure pressure decline with age. Since hypertension affects half of older people, use of these agents may increase. Before considering interventions for stress incontinence in such women, one

Table 71–2.	**Commonly Used Medications That May Affect Continence**	
Type of Medication	*Examples*	*Potential Effects on Continence*
Sedatives-hypnotics	Long-acting benzodiazepines (e.g., diazepam, flurazepam)	Sedation, delirium, immobility
Alcohol		Polyuria, frequency, urgency, sedation, delirium, immobility
Anticholinergics	Dicyclomine, disopyramide, antihistamines (sedating ones only, e.g., diphenhydramine [Benadryl])	Urinary retention, overflow incontinence, delirium, impaction
Antipsychotics	Thioridazine, haloperidol	Anticholinergic actions, sedation, rigidity, immobility
Antidepressants (tricyclics only)	Amitriptyline, desipramine; *not* selective serotonin reuptake inhibitors	Anticholinergic actions, sedation
Anti-parkinsonians	Trihexyphenidyl, benztropine mesylate (*not* L-dopa or selegiline)	Anticholinergic actions, sedation
Narcotic analgesics	Opiates	Urinary retention, fecal impaction, sedation, delirium
α-Adrenergic antagonists	Prazosin, terazosin, doxazosin	Urethral relaxation may precipitate stress incontinence in women
α-Adrenergic agonists	Nasal decongestants	Urinary retention in men
Calcium channel blockers	All dihydropyridines*	Urinary retention; nocturnal diuresis due to fluid retention
Potent diuretics	Furosemide, bumetanide (*not* thiazides)	Polyuria, frequency, urgency
NSAIDs	Indomethacin, cyclooxygenase-2 inhibitors	Nocturnal diuresis due to fluid retention
Thiazolidinediones	Rosiglitazone, pioglitazone	Nocturnal diuresis due to fluid retention
Parkinson's agents (some)	Pramipexole, ropinirole amantadine	Nocturnal diuresis due to fluid retention
Angiotensin-converting enzyme inhibitors	Captopril, enalapril, lisinopril	Drug-induced cough can precipitate stress incontinence in women and in some men with prior prostatectomy
Vincristine		Urinary retention owing to neuropathy

*Examples include amlodipine (Norvasc), nifedipine, nicardipine, isradipine, felodipine, and nimodipine.
Adapted from Resnick NM: Geriatric medicine. In Isselbacher KJ, Braunwald E, Wilson JD, et al (eds): Harrison's Principles of Internal Medicine. New York, McGraw-Hill, 2004, p 34.

should substitute an alternative agent and reevaluate the incontinence.

Calcium channel blockers also can cause incontinence. As smooth muscle relaxants, they may increase residual volume and may occasionally lead to overflow incontinence, particularly in obstructed men with coexisting detrusor weakness. The dihydropyridine class of these agents (e.g., nifedipine, nicardipine, amlodipine, nimodipine) also can cause peripheral edema, which can exacerbate nocturnal polyuria and nocturnal incontinence.

Angiotensin-converting enzyme (ACE) inhibitors are prescribed increasingly for age-associated conditions such as myocardial infarction, congestive heart failure, and hypertension. Because the risk of developing an ACE inhibitor–induced cough increases with age, these agents may exacerbate what otherwise would be minimal stress incontinence in older women.

A few reports impugn **cholinesterase inhibitors** such as donepezil (Aricept) as a cause of urinary incontinence (Hashimoto, 2000). The association is plausible because these agents block the breakdown of acetylcholine within the neuroeffector junctional cleft. However, the incontinence seems to cease even if donepezil is continued, the number of cases is small, and the descriptions and evaluations of these cases are sparse. In addition, prospective trials in which these agents were evaluated for their cognitive impact did not note an increase in incontinence. Moreover, these agents are prescribed for cognitive impairment, which also can fluctuate. Thus, the possible association is still speculative.

Excess urine output commonly contributes to or even causes geriatric incontinence. Causes include excessive fluid intake; diuretics (including theophylline-containing fluids, lithium, and alcohol); metabolic abnormalities (e.g., hyperglycemia and hypercalcemia); and disorders associated with fluid overload, including congestive heart failure, peripheral venous insufficiency, hypoalbuminemia (especially in malnourished debilitated elderly), and drug-induced peripheral edema associated with an increasing array of medications, including nonsteroidal anti-inflammatory drugs, dihydropyridine calcium channel blockers, thiazolidinediones ("glitazones"), ropinerol and pramipexole (for Parkinson's disease), amantadine (for Parkinson's disease and influenza), and β-adrenergic blockers. Fluid overload is a likely contributor when incontinence is associated with nocturia.

Restricted mobility commonly contributes to geriatric incontinence. It can result from numerous treatable conditions, including arthritis, hip deformity, deconditioning, postural or postprandial hypotension, claudication, spinal stenosis, heart failure, poor eyesight, fear of falling, stroke, foot problems, drug-induced disequilibrium or confusion, or being restrained in a bed or chair (Resnick, 2004). A careful review will often identify these or other correctable causes. If not, a urinal or bedside commode may still improve or resolve the incontinence.

Finally, *stool impaction* is implicated as a cause of urinary incontinence in up to 10% of older patients admitted to acute hospitals or referred to incontinence clinics (Resnick, 1988); the mechanism may involve stimulation of opioid receptors (Hellstrom and Sjöqvist, 1988). Patients present with urge or overflow incontinence and typically have associated fecal incontinence as well. Disimpaction restores continence.

These seven reversible causes of incontinence should be assiduously sought in every elderly patient. In one series of hospitalized elderly patients, when these causes were identified, continence was regained by most of those who became incontinent in the context of acute illness (Resnick, 1988). Regardless of their frequency, their identification is important in all settings because they are easily treatable and contribute to morbidity beyond incontinence.

ESTABLISHED INCONTINENCE
Lower Urinary Tract Causes

If incontinence persists after transient causes have been addressed, the lower urinary tract causes should be considered. These are similar to the causes in younger individuals, but there are several significant differences.

Detrusor overactivity is **the most common type of lower urinary tract dysfunction in incontinent elderly of either sex** (Resnick, 1988; Resnick et al, 1989). It is associated with increased spontaneous activity of detrusor smooth muscle and with specific changes at the cellular level. Termed the *complete dysjunction pattern,* these changes include widening of the intercellular space, reduction of normal (intermediate) muscle cell junctions, and emergence of novel "protrusion" junctions and "ultraclose abutments" connecting cells together in chains. These junctions and abutments may mediate a change in cell coupling from a mechanical to an electrical mechanism, which could facilitate propagation of heightened smooth muscle activity and provide the "final common pathway" by which such spontaneous cellular contractions result in involuntary contraction of the entire bladder (Elbadawi et al, 1993c, 1997a, 1997b; Hailemariam et al, 1997; Tse et al, 2000).

A distinction is generally made between detrusor overactivity that is associated with a central nervous system lesion and that which is not. In older patients the distinction is often unclear, because involuntary detrusor contractions may be due to normal aging, a past stroke (even if clinically unapparent), or urethral incompetence or obstruction, even in a patient with Alzheimer's disease. There is still no reliable way to determine the source of such contractions (Elbadawi et al, 2003). This obviously complicates treatment decisions. It also suggests that detrusor overactivity coexisting with urethral obstruction or stress incontinence is less likely to resolve postoperatively than in younger individuals without other reasons for detrusor overactivity (Resnick, 1988; Gormley et al, 1993).

Traditionally, detrusor overactivity has been thought to be the primary urinary tract cause of incontinence in demented patients. Although this is true, detrusor overactivity is also the most common cause in nondemented patients; the three studies that examined it failed to find an association between cognitive status and detrusor overactivity (Castleden et al, 1981; Resnick et al, 1989; Dennis et al, 1991). This lack of association likely reflects the fact that in the elderly there are multiple causes of detrusor overactivity unrelated to dementia, including cervical disk disease or spondylosis, Parkinson's disease, stroke, subclinical urethral obstruction or sphincter incompetence, and age itself. Moreover, demented patients also may be incontinent due to the transient causes discussed earlier. Thus, it is no longer tenable to ascribe incontinence in demented individuals a priori to detrusor overactivity (Resnick, 1995).

Detrusor overactivity in the elderly exists as two physiologic subsets: one in which contractile function is preserved and one in which it is impaired (Resnick and Yalla, 1987). **The latter condition is termed** *detrusor hyperactivity with impaired contractility* **(DHIC) and is likely the most common form of detrusor overactivity in the elderly** (Resnick et al, 1989; Elbadawi et al, 1993c). DHIC appears to represent the coexistence of detrusor overactivity and bladder weakness rather than a separate entity (Elbadawi et al, 1993c). Regardless of the cause, DHIC has several implications. First, because the bladder is weak, urinary retention develops commonly in these patients and DHIC must be added to outlet obstruction and detrusor underactivity as a cause of retention. Second, even in the absence of retention, DHIC mimics virtually every other lower urinary tract cause of incontinence. For instance, if the involuntary detrusor contraction is triggered by or occurs coincident with a stress maneuver, and the weak contraction (often only 2 to 6 cm H_2O) is not detected, DHIC will be misdiagnosed as stress incontinence or urethral instability (Resnick et al, 1996a); alternatively, because DHIC may be associated with urinary urgency, frequency, weak flow rate, elevated residual urine, and bladder trabeculation, in men it may mimic urethral obstruction (Brandeis et al, 1990). Third, bladder weakness often frustrates anticholinergic therapy of DHIC because urinary retention is induced so easily. Thus, alternative therapeutic approaches are often required (see "Therapy").

Stress incontinence is the second most common cause of incontinence in older women. As in younger women, it is **usually associated with urethral hypermobility. A less common cause is intrinsic sphincter deficiency (ISD)** or type 3 stress incontinence (McGuire, 1981; Blaivas and Olsson, 1988). The prevalence of ISD may be lower than thought, however, because the diagnosis is often based solely on documenting a very low leak point or urethral closure pressure. Because urethral pressure decreases with age, even a closure pressure less than 20 cm H_2O does not establish the presence of ISD. Moreover, because urethral pressure normally decreases with detrusor contraction, leakage coinciding with low urethral pressure can be observed in patients with DHIC in whom the low pressure contraction is missed (Resnick et al, 1996a).

When it occurs, ISD is usually due to operative trauma. But a milder form also occurs in older women, resulting only from urethral atrophy superimposed on the age-related decline in urethral pressure. Instead of leaking with any bladder volume, such women leak at higher amounts (e.g., >200 mL). *Many become dry if bladder volume is kept below this level.*

A rare cause of stress incontinence in older women is urethral instability, in which the sphincter paradoxically relaxes in the absence of apparent detrusor contraction (McGuire, 1978). However, most older women thought to have this condition actually have DHIC (Resnick et al, 1996a).

In men, stress incontinence is usually due to sphincter damage after prostatectomy. In both sexes, stress-associated leakage also can occur in association with urinary retention, but in this situation leakage is not due to outlet incompetence.

Outlet obstruction is the second most common cause of incontinence in older men, although most obstructed men are not incontinent. When obstruction is associated with incontinence, it generally presents as urge incontinence owing to the associated detrusor overactivity. In most women, urethral elasticity decreases with age. In a small proportion of older women, this reduced elasticity may be compounded by fibrotic changes associated with atrophic vaginitis and can result in moderate urethral stenosis. Frank outlet obstruction, however, is as rare in older women as in younger women. When present it is usually due to kinking associated with a large cystocele or to obstruction after bladder neck suspension. Rarely, bladder neck obstruction or a bladder calculus is the cause.

Detrusor underactivity is usually idiopathic. In the absence of obstruction or overt neuropathy, it is characterized at the cellular level by widespread degenerative changes of both muscle cells and axons, without accompanying regenerative changes (Elbadawi et al, 1993b). When it causes incontinence, detrusor underactivity is associated with overflow incontinence (<10% of geriatric incontinence) (Diokno et al, 1988; Resnick, 1988; Resnick et al, 1989). Owing to the age-related decline in sphincter strength, however, the postvoid residual (PVR) volume in women with overflow incontinence is often lower than in younger women. A mild degree of bladder weakness occurs quite commonly in older individuals. Although insufficient to cause incontinence, it can complicate treatment of other causes (see "Therapy").

Causes Unrelated to the Lower Urinary Tract ("Functional" Incontinence)

"Functional" incontinence is often cited as a distinct type of geriatric incontinence and attributed to deficits of cognition and mobility. This concept is problematic for several reasons (Resnick and Marcantonio, 1997). First, "functional incontinence" implies that urinary tract function is normal, but studies of both institutionalized and ambulatory elderly reveal that normal urinary tract function is the exception even in continent subjects and is rarely observed in incontinent elderly (Ouslander et al, 1986; Resnick, 1988; Resnick et al, 1989, 1995a). Second, incontinence is not inevitable with either dementia or immobility. We found that 17% of the most severely demented institutionalized residents (mean age = 89) were continent; more impressive, if they could merely transfer from bed to chair, nearly *half* were *continent* (Resnick et al, 1988). Third, because functionally impaired individuals are the most likely to suffer from factors causing transient incontinence (Resnick et al, 1988; DuBeau and Resnick, 1995; Skelly and Flint, 1995; Brandeis et al, 1997), a diagnosis of functional incontinence may result in failure to detect reversible causes of incontinence. Finally, functionally impaired individuals may still have obstruction or stress incontinence and benefit from targeted therapy (Resnick, 1988; Resnick et al, 1989; Gormley et al, 1993; DuBeau and Resnick, 1995).

Nonetheless, the importance of functional impairment as a factor *contributing* to incontinence should not be underestimated, because incontinence is also affected by environmental demands, mentation, mobility, manual dexterity, medical factors, and motivation. Although lower urinary tract function is rarely normal in such individuals, these factors are important to keep in mind because small improvements in each may markedly ameliorate both incontinence and functional status. In fact, once one has excluded causes of transient incontinence and serious underlying lesions, addressing causes of functional impairment often obviates the need for further investigation.

DIAGNOSTIC APPROACH
Evaluation

The evaluation should **identify transient and established causes of incontinence, assess the patient's environment and available support, and detect uncommon but serious conditions that may underlie incontinence,** including lesions of the brain and spinal cord, carcinoma of the bladder or prostate, hydronephrosis, bladder calculi, detrusor-sphincter dyssynergia, and decreased bladder compliance. **Assessment must be tailored** to the individual's clinical status and goals and **tempered by the realization that not all detected conditions can be cured, that simple interventions may be effective even in the absence of a diagnosis, and that, for many elderly persons, diagnostic tests are themselves often interventions.** Because the evaluation generally requires a comprehensive approach, it should be conducted over more than one visit to ease the burden and obviate further evaluation in those who respond to simple measures.

History

In addition to the assessment outlined in Chapter 60, "Urinary Incontinence: Epidemiology, Pathophysiology, Evaluation, and Overview of Management," evaluation of the older patient should search for transient causes of incontinence (including nonprescribed medications) and functional impairment. It should be augmented by medical records, as well as input from caregivers. Functional assessment focuses on both basic activities of daily living (ADLs: e.g., transferring from a bed, walking, bathing, toileting, eating, and dressing) and more advanced "instrumental" activities of daily living (IADLs: e.g., shopping, cooking, driving, managing finances, using the telephone). The assessment is accomplished by using a questionnaire, which can be completed by the patient or caregiver prior to the evaluation, and by objective evaluation of the patient from the beginning of the encounter, noting affect, mobility, ability to sit and rise from a chair, ability to provide a coherent history, and amount of time and assistance required to dress and undress.

Of course, as for younger individuals, it also is important to characterize the voiding pattern and the type of incontinence. Although the clinical type of incontinence most often associated with detrusor overactivity is urge incontinence, **"urge" is neither a sensitive nor specific symptom; it is absent in 20% of older patients with detrusor overactivity, and the figure is higher in demented patients** (Resnick et al, 1989). **"Urge" is also reported commonly by patients with stress incontinence, outlet obstruction, and overflow incontinence.**

A better term for the symptom associated with detrusor overactivity is **"precipitancy,"** which can be defined in two ways. For patients with no warning of imminent urination ("reflex" or "unconscious" incontinence), the abrupt gush of urine in the absence of a stress maneuver can be termed *precipitant leakage,* and it is almost invariably due to detrusor overactivity. For those who do sense a warning, it is of less value to focus on the leakage, because the presence and volume of leakage in this situation depend on bladder volume, amount of warning, toilet accessibility, the patient's mobility, and whether the individual can overcome the relative sphincter relaxation accompanying detrusor contraction (Dyro and Yalla, 1986). Instead, **precipitancy** should be defined as the *abrupt sensation* that urination is imminent, *whatever the interval or amount of leakage that follows;* defined in these two ways, precipitancy is both a sensitive and specific symptom (Resnick, 1990).

Similar to the situation for urgency, other symptoms ascribed to detrusor overactivity also can be misleading in the older person unless explored carefully. **Urinary frequency (>7 diurnal voids) is common** (Brocklehurst et al, 1968; Diokno et al, 1986; Resnick, 1988) and may be due to voiding habit, preemptive urination to avoid leakage, overflow incontinence, sensory urgency, a stable but poorly compliant bladder, excessive urine production, depression, anxiety, or social reasons (Resnick, 1990). **Conversely, incontinent individuals may severely restrict their fluid intake so that even in the presence of detrusor overactivity they do not void frequently.** Thus, the significance of urinary frequency, or its absence, can be determined only in the context of more information.

Nocturia also can be misleading unless it is first defined (e.g., two episodes may be normal for the individual who sleeps 10 hours but not for one who sleeps 4 hours) and then approached systematically (Table 71–3). The **three general reasons for nocturia—excessive urine output, sleep-related difficulties, and urinary tract dysfunction—can be differentiated by careful questioning and a voiding diary that includes voided volumes** (Fig. 71–3). One inspects the record of voided volumes to determine the available bladder capacity (the largest single voided volume) and compares it to the volume of each night-time void. For instance, if the available bladder capacity is 400 mL and each of three nightly voids is approximately 400 mL, the nocturia is due to excessive production of urine at night. If the volume of most nightly voids is much smaller than bladder capacity, nocturia is due to either (1) a sleep-related problem (the patient voids since she is awake anyway) or (2) a problem with the lower urinary tract. Like excess urine output, sleep-related nocturia may also be due to treatable causes, including age-related sleep disorders, pain (e.g., bursitis, arthritis), dyspnea, depression, caffeine, or a short-acting hypnotic (e.g., triazolam). Bladder-related causes of nocturia are displayed in Table 71–3. Whatever the cause, the nocturnal component of incontinence is generally remediable.

The symptoms of "prostatism" also warrant comment. Owing to the high prevalence of medication use, nocturnal polyuria (Reynard et al, 1998), constipation, and DHIC, as well as the impairment of bladder contractility that accompanies aging, "prostatic" symptoms are even less specific in older men than in younger men (DuBeau and Resnick, 1991).

Table 71–3. **Causes of Nocturia**

Volume Related

Age-related
Excess intake/alcohol
Diuretic, caffeine, theophylline, lithium
Endocrine/metabolic
    Diabetes mellitus/insipidus
    Hypercalcemia
Peripheral edema
    Congestive heart failure
    Low albumin states
    Peripheral vascular disease
    Venous insufficiency
    Drugs (e.g., NSAIDs [indomethacin, cyclooxygenase-2 inhibitors],
      nifedipine)

Sleep Related

Insomnia
Obstructive sleep apnea
Pain
Dyspnea
Depression
Drugs

Lower Urinary Tract Related

Small bladder capacity
Detrusor overactivity
Prostate related
Overflow incontinence
Decreased bladder compliance
Sensory urgency

Adapted from Resnick NM: Noninvasive diagnosis of the patient with complex incontinence. Gerontology 1990;36(Suppl 2):8-18.

SAMPLE VOIDING RECORD

Date	Time	Volume voided (mL)	Are you wet or dry?	Approximate volume of incontinence	Comments
4/5	3:50 PM	240	Wet	Slight	
	6:05 PM	210	Dry		
	8:15 PM	150	Dry		
	10:20 PM	150	Wet	15 ml	Running water
	10:30 PM	30	Dry		Bowel movement
4/6	3:15 AM	270	Slight		
	6:05 AM	300	Slight		
	7:40 AM	200	Dry		
	9:50 AM	?	Dry		
	11:20 AM	200	Dry		
	12:50 PM	180	Dry		
	1:40 PM	240	Dry		
	3:35 PM	160	Dry		
	6:00 PM	170	Dry		Running water
	8:20 PM	215	Wet	Slight	
	10:25 PM	130	Dry		

Figure 71–3. Voiding diary of an incontinent 75-year-old man. Urodynamic evaluation excluded urethral obstruction and confirmed a diagnosis of detrusor hyperactivity with impaired contractility (DHIC). However, note the 24-hour urine output of nearly 3 L, resulting from the belief that drinking 10 glasses of fluid per day was "good for my health." (He did not mention this until queried about the voiding record.) Given the typical voided volume of 150 to 250 mL and a measured postvoid residual (PVR) of 150 mL, excess fluid intake was overwhelming his usual bladder capacity of 400 mL (150 + 250 mL). Although uninhibited bladder contractions were present, the easily reversible volume component of the problem—coupled with the risk of precipitating urinary retention with an anticholinergic agent—prompted treatment with volume restriction alone. After daily urinary output dropped to 1500 mL, frequency abated and incontinence resolved. (Adapted from DuBeau CE, Resnick NM: Evaluation of the causes and severity of geriatric incontinence: A critical appraisal. Urol Clin North Am 1991;18:243-256.)

When asking about leakage with stress maneuvers, it is important to ensure that the absence of such leakage is not due to simply the lack of coughing or sneezing. For those without such precipitants, it is useful to inquire about instantaneous leakage with lifting or bending over to put on a shoe or stockings.

Finally, **patients or their caregivers should be asked which voiding symptom is most bothersome.** For example, although a woman may have both stress and urge incontinence, the urge component may be her worst problem and should become the focus of evaluation and treatment. A man with "prostatism" may be most bothered by nocturia (DuBeau et al, 1995), which may be remedied without any consideration of his prostate (see Fig. 71–3). Failure to address the symptom that causes the most bother can lead to frustration for patient and provider alike.

Voiding Diary

One of the most helpful components of the history is the voiding diary. Kept by the patient or caregiver for 48 to 72 hours, the diary records the time of each void and incontinent episode. No attempt is made to alter voiding pattern or fluid intake. Many formats have been proposed; a sample is shown in Figure 71–3.

To record voided volumes at home, individuals use a measuring cup, coffee can, pickle jar, or other large-mouth container. **Information regarding the volume voided provides an index of functional bladder capacity and, together with the pattern of voiding and leakage, can suggest the cause of leakage.** For example, incontinence occurring only between 8 AM and noon may be caused by a morning diuretic. Incontinence that occurs at night in a demented man with congestive heart failure, but not during a 4-hour nap in his wheelchair, is likely due to neither dementia nor prostatic obstruction but to postural diuresis associated with his heart failure. A woman with volume-dependent stress incontinence may leak only on the way to void after a full night's sleep, when her bladder contains more than 400 mL, more than it ever does during her continent waking hours. A patient with impaired mobility may become incontinent if polyuria develops.

The voiding diary should also guide therapy. For instance, in a patient with detrusor overactivity or prostatic obstruction, excess nocturnal excretion may result in nocturnal incontinence, which is more severe and troublesome than daytime leakage; successful therapy must address the excess excretion. By contrast, another patient with the same urinary tract dysfunction and excretion, but with the ability to hold more urine when asleep, might be bothered more by daytime leakage. Shifting nocturnal excretion to the daytime will *exacerbate* the problem.

Targeted Physical Examination

Like the history, the physical examination is essential to detect transient causes, comorbid disease, and functional impairment. In addition to the standard neurourologic examination, one should check for signs of neurologic diseases that are more common in the older person, such as delirium, dementia, stroke, Parkinson's disease, cord compression, and neuropathy (autonomic or peripheral), as well as for atrophic vaginitis and general medical illnesses, such as heart failure and peripheral edema. The rectal examination checks for fecal impaction, masses, sacral reflexes, symmetry of the gluteal creases, and prostate consistency and nodularity; as noted in Chapter 87, "Evaluation and Management of Benign Prostatic Hyperplasia," the palpated size of the prostate is unhelpful. Many neurologically unimpaired elderly patients are unable to volitionally contract the anal sphincter, but if they can it is evidence against a spinal cord lesion. The absence of the anal wink is not necessarily pathologic in the elderly, nor does its presence exclude an underactive detrusor (e.g., due to diabetic neuropathy).

Stress Testing and PVR Measurement

Several caveats apply to performing the stress test and measuring the PVR in older patients. Stress testing is performed optimally when the bladder is full and the patient is relaxed (check the gluteal folds to corroborate) and in as close to the upright position as possible. The cough or strain should be vigorous and *single*, so one can determine whether leakage coincides with the increase in abdominal pressure or follows it. Stress-related leakage may be missed if any of these conditions is not met. Delayed leakage typical of stress-induced detrusor overactivity should be differentiated from leakage typical of stress incontinence, which is instantaneous and ceases as soon as abdominal pressure declines. **To be useful diagnostically, leakage must replicate the symptom for which help is sought,** because many older women have incidental but not bothersome leakage of a few drops. The test should not be performed if the patient has an abrupt urge to void because this is usually due to an involuntary detrusor contraction that will lead to a false-positive stress test. False-negative tests occur when the patient fails to cough vigorously or to relax the perineal muscles, the bladder is not full, or the test is performed in the upright position in a woman with a large cystocele (which kinks the urethra). If performed correctly, the stress test is reasonably sensitive and quite specific (>90%) (Hilton and Stanton, 1981; Diokno, 1990; Kong et al, 1990).

After the stress test, the patient is asked to void into a receptacle and the PVR is measured. If the stress test was negative, the history suggests stress incontinence, *and* the combined volume of the void and PVR is less than 200 mL, the bladder should be filled with sterile fluid so that the stress test can be repeated at an adequate volume. There is no need to repeat a correctly performed positive stress test or to repeat it in a woman whose history is negative for stress-related leakage; the sensitivity of the history for stress incontinence, unlike its specificity, exceeds 90% (Diokno et al, 1987; Jensen et al, 1994), making the likelihood of stress incontinence remote in this situation.

Optimally, the PVR is measured within 5 minutes of voiding. Measuring it after an intentional void is better than after an incontinent episode, because many patients are able to partially suppress the involuntary contraction during the episode and more than the true PVR remains. In cognitively impaired patients this may not be possible. Nonetheless, because the resulting artifact will lead to a falsely elevated PVR, a low value is still useful. The PVR will also be spuriously high if measurement is delayed (especially if the patient's fluid intake was high or included caffeine), the patient was inhibited during voiding, or there is discomfort due to urethral inflammation or bladder infection. It will be spuriously low if the patient augmented voiding by straining (most important in women), if the catheter is withdrawn too quickly, and if the woman has a cystocele that allows urine to "puddle" beneath the catheter's reach. Of note, relying on the ease of catheterization to establish the presence of obstruction can be misleading, because difficult catheter passage may be caused by urethral tortuosity, a "false passage," or catheter-induced spasm of the distal sphincter, while catheter passage may be easy even in obstructed men (Klarskov et al, 1987).

Two other tests should be mentioned. The Q-tip (cotton swab) test for pelvic floor laxity is of little value in determining the cause of a patient's leakage and has a high false-negative rate in elderly women (DuBeau and Resnick, 1991). The Bonney (or Marshall) test is also of limited usefulness in the elderly because vaginal stenosis is common and may lead to a false-positive result by precluding accurate finger placement. Furthermore, even if the test is performed correctly, a false-positive result may occur if the first episode of leakage was due to a cough-induced detrusor contraction, which, having emptied the bladder, does not recur during bladder base elevation.

Laboratory Investigation

One should check the blood urea nitrogen and creatinine levels and order a urinalysis, urine culture, and PVR in all older patients (Resnick and Ouslander, 1990; DuBeau and Resnick, 1991; Fantl et al, 1996). Serum sodium, calcium, and glucose values should be measured in patients with confusion. If the voiding record suggests polyuria, serum glucose and calcium (and albumin, to allow calculation of free calcium levels in sick or malnourished patients) levels should be determined. Sterile hematuria suggests partially/recently treated bacteriuria, malignancy, or calculus; tuberculosis should also be considered, because the elderly, particularly institutionalized residents, are an unappreciated reservoir of this infection (Stead, 1985). Finally, it is important to recognize when evaluating renal function that the age-related decline in glomerular filtration rate (30% by the eighth decade) is not associated with an increase in creatinine because of a concomitant decrease in muscle mass; thus, *normal creatinine levels do not imply a normal glomerular filtration rate.*

Empirical Diagnostic Categorization

After transient and serious causes have been addressed, the optimal diagnostic strategy for persistent incontinence is unknown (Resnick and Ouslander, 1990; Fantl et al, 1996; Abrams et al, 2005; Fonda et al, 2005). "Bedside" cystometry has been proposed, but its utility is limited because it misses low pressure contractions of DHIC; its feasibility and accuracy are low in frail elderly (Ouslander and Colling, 1992); and detected detrusor overactivity may be either incidental and unrelated to leakage or due to urethral obstruction or incompetence and warrant different therapy. The following approach (Resnick, 1995), while still unproven, is relatively noninvasive, accurate, cost effective, and easily tolerated. A similar approach forms the basis for the Agency for Health Care Policy and Research (AHCPR) Clinical Practice Guideline (Fantl et al, 1996), the International Consultation on Incontinence (Fonda et al, 2005), as well as the Minimum Data Set/Resident Assessment Instrument, which we designed and validated for use in all American nursing homes (Resnick et al, 1996b).

The first step is to identify individuals with overflow incontinence (e.g., PVR > 450 mL). Because obstruction and underactive detrusor cannot be differentiated clinically (Resnick et al, 1996b; DuBeau et al, 1998; Sonke et al, 2000), **further assessment is warranted for those in whom it would affect therapy, whereas catheterization should be used for the rest. For the remaining 90% to 95% of patients, the next step depends on their sex. In women, the differential diagnosis is generally between stress incontinence and detrusor overactivity, because obstruction is rare in the absence of previous bladder neck suspension or prolapsing cystocele.** If the contemplated intervention is nonoperative, the diagnosis usually can be established on clinical grounds alone, informed by the caveats mentioned earlier.

In men, stress incontinence is uncommon and, when present, results in a characteristic drip (similar to a "leaky faucet") that is exacerbated by standing or straining. Thus, **the usual problem in men is differentiating detrusor overactivity from obstruction. Uroflowmetry is helpful but only if peak flow is normal (e.g., >12 mL/s for voided volume of 200 mL); the age-related decrease in bladder contractility means that a normal unstrained flow rate, together with PVR less than 100 mL, effectively excludes clinically significant obstruction in an older man** (DuBeau et al, 1998). **The next step is to search for hydronephrosis in men whose PVR exceeds 200 mL and to decompress those in whom it is found** (DuBeau and Resnick, 1992). Further evaluation is also reasonable for men without hydronephrosis who are appropriate candidates and would be amenable to surgery if obstructed. For the rest, **it seems sensible to treat those with urge incontinence for presumed detrusor overactivity, provided they are compliant and can be taught signs of incipient urinary retention;** bladder relaxants probably should be avoided in those with significantly elevated PVR (e.g., ≥150 mL). A similar approach is advocated for cognitively impaired men who can be closely observed (e.g., institutionalized residents) (Resnick et al, 1996b). **Men without urge incontinence, those who fail empirical therapy, and those who are cognitively impaired and less supervised should be evaluated further if findings would affect therapy.**

Urodynamic Testing

Although its precise role in the elderly is unclear, **multichannel urodynamic evaluation is probably warranted when diagnostic uncertainty may affect therapy and when empirical therapy has failed and other approaches would be tried.** Because conditions that closely mimic obstruction and stress incontinence are so common in the elderly, including altered fluid excretion (Reynard et al, 1998), medication use, detrusor hyperactivity, and DHIC (Brandeis et al, 1990; Resnick et al, 1996a), urodynamic corroboration of the diagnosis

is strongly recommended if surgery will be performed (Resnick et al, 1991, 1995a; Fantl et al, 1996). Whatever its role, however, urodynamic evaluation of even frail elderly patients is reproducible, safe, and feasible (Resnick et al, 1987, 1989).

THERAPY

Like the diagnostic approach, treatment must be individualized because factors outside the lower urinary tract so often impact on feasibility and efficacy. For instance, although both may have detrusor overactivity that can be managed successfully, a severely demented and bedfast woman must be treated differently from one who is ambulatory and cognitively intact. This section and Table 71–4 outline several treatments for each condition and provide guidance for their use. It is assumed that serious underlying conditions, transient causes of incontinence, and functional impairments have already been addressed.

It cannot be overemphasized that successful treatment of established incontinence, especially in the elderly, is usually multifactorial and requires addressing factors beyond the urinary tract. Figure 71–4, based on empirical data, illustrates the many factors that determine whether detrusor overactivity in an older adult will be associated with incontinence and, if so, the frequency of the related leakage (Miller et al, 2002; Rosenberg et al, 2005).

Detrusor Overactivity

The initial approach to detrusor overactivity is to identify and treat its reversible causes. Unfortunately, many of its causes are not amenable to specific therapy or a cause may not be found, so treatment usually must be symptomatic. **Simple measures, such as adjusting the timing or amount of fluid excretion** (see Fig. 71–3) **or providing a bedside commode or urinal are often successful. If not, the cornerstone of treatment is behavioral therapy.** If the patient can cooperate, bladder training regimens will extend the voiding interval (Fantl et al,

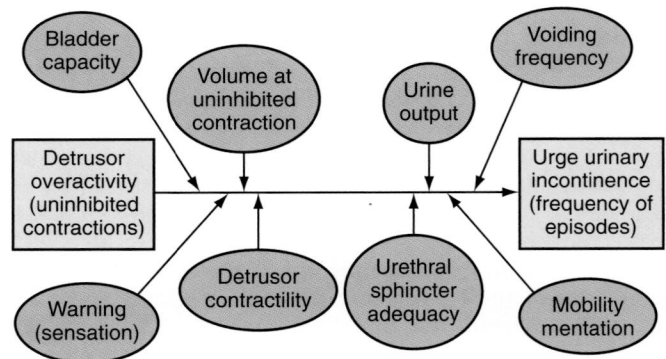

POTENTIAL DETERMINANTS OF
URGE URINARY INCONTINENCE

Figure 71–4. Factors that determine whether detrusor overactivity, found in nearly half of *continent* older adults, will be associated with urge incontinence and, if so, the frequency of the related leakage. (Data from Miller KL, DuBeau CE, Bergmann M, et al: Quest for a detrusor overactivity index. J Urol 2002;167:578-585; and Rosenberg LJ, Griffiths DJ, Resnick NM: Factors that distinguish continent from incontinent older adults with detrusor overactivity. J Urol 2005;174:1868-1872.

Table 71–4. Stepwise Approach to Treatment*

Condition	Clinical Type of Incontinence[†]	Treatment
Detrusor overactivity with normal contractility	Urge	1. Bladder retraining or prompted voiding regimens 2. ±Bladder relaxant medication if needed and not contraindicated 3. Indwelling catheterization alone is often unhelpful because detrusor "spasms" often increase, leading to leakage around the catheter 4. In selected cases, induce urinary retention pharmacologically and add intermittent or indwelling catheterization[‡]
Detrusor hyperactivity with impaired contractility	Urge[§]	1. If bladder empties adequately with straining, behavioral methods (as above) ± bladder relaxant medication (low doses; especially feasible if sphincter incompetence coexists) 2. If residual urine > 150 mL, augmented voiding techniques[¶] or intermittent catheterization (±bladder relaxant medication). If neither feasible, undergarment or indwelling catheter[‡]
Stress incontinence	Stress	1. Conservative methods (weight loss if obese; treatment of cough or atrophic vaginitis; physical maneuvers to prevent leakage [e.g., tighten pelvic muscles before cough, cross legs]; occasionally, use of tampon or pessary is useful) 2. If leakage threshold ≥ 150 mL identified, adjust fluid excretion and voiding intervals appropriately 3. Pelvic muscle exercises ± biofeedback/weighted intravaginal "cones" 4. (Imipramine [or doxepin] or α-adrenergic agonists ± estrogen, if not contraindicated) 5. Surgery (urethral suspension, or compression ["sling"], periurethral bulking injections, artificial sphincter)
Urethral obstruction	Urge/overflow[‖]	1. Conservative methods (including adjustment of fluid excretion, bladder retraining/prompted voiding) if hydronephrosis, elevated residual urine, recurrent symptomatic urinary tract infection, and gross hematuria have been excluded 2. α-Adrenergic antagonists and bladder relaxants if detrusor overactivity coexists, PVR is small, and surgery not desired/feasible; *monitor PVR!* 3. Finasteride, if not contraindicated and the patient either prefers them or is not a surgical candidate 4. Surgery (incision, prostatectomy)
Underactive detrusor	Overflow	1. If duration unknown, decompress for several weeks and perform a voiding trial 2. If cannot void, PVR remains large, or retention is chronic, try augmented voiding techniques[¶] ± α-adrenergic antagonist, but only if some voiding possible; bethanechol rarely useful unless, possibly, bladder weakness due to an anticholinergic agent that cannot be discontinued 3. If fails, or voiding is not possible, intermittent or indwelling catheterization[‡]

*These treatments should be initiated only after adequate toilet access has been ensured, contributing conditions have been treated (e.g., atrophic vaginitis, heart failure), fluid management has been optimized, and unnecessary or exacerbating medications have been stopped. For additional details, recommendations, and drug doses, see text.

[†]*Urge:* leakage in the absence of stress maneuvers and urinary retention, usually preceded by *abrupt* onset of need to void;

Stress: leakage that coincides *instantaneously* with stress maneuvers, in the absence of urinary retention or detrusor contraction;

Overflow: frequent leakage of small amounts associated with urinary retention.

[‡]Urinary tract infection prophylaxis can be used for recurrent symptomatic urinary tract infections, but only if catheter is not indwelling.

[§]But may also mimic stress or overflow incontinence.

[‖]Also can cause postvoid "dribbling" alone, which is treated conservatively (e.g., by sitting to void and allowing more time, "double voiding," and in men by gently "milking" the urethra after voiding).

[¶]Augmented voiding techniques include Credé (application of suprapubic pressure) and Valsalva (straining) maneuvers, and "double voiding." They should be performed only *after* voiding has begun.

Adapted and updated in 2005 from Resnick NM: Voiding dysfunction and urinary incontinence. In Beck JC (ed): Geriatric Review Syllabus, American Geriatrics Society, 1991, pp 141-154.

1991; Burgio et al, 1998, 2002; Berghmans et al, 2000; Payne, 2000). For instance, if the voiding record documents incontinence when the interval exceeds 3 hours, the patient is instructed to void every 2 hours and suppress urgency in between. Once dry the patient can extend the interval by half an hour and repeat the process until a satisfactory result or continence is achieved. Patients need not follow this regimen at night because night-time improvement parallels daytime success (Johnson et al, 2005). Biofeedback may be added (Berghmans et al, 2000), but its marginal benefit is unclear (Resnick, 1998; Payne, 2000; Burgio et al, 2002; Wilson et al, 2005).

For cognitively impaired patients, "prompted voiding" is used (Fantl et al, 1996; Tannenbaum and DuBeau 2004). Asked every 2 hours whether they need to void, patients are escorted to the toilet if the response is affirmative. Positive verbal reinforcement is employed and negative comments are avoided. Prompted voiding reduces incontinence frequency in nursing homes by roughly 50%, and leakage can be virtually eliminated during daytime hours in one third of residents (Hu et al, 1989; Engel et al, 1990; Schnelle, 1990). The latter group can be identified within 3 days. When prompted *hourly* to void, they urinate into a toilet or commode more than two thirds of the time that they indicate the need to do so, or they become continent on more than 80% of checks. Response is maintained when the prompting interval is increased to 2 hours. Half of the remaining patients also improve with prompting, but they are still wet more than once during the daytime. For the fourth of patients who do not respond to prompting at baseline, little benefit is obtained by further prompting. Importantly, response does not correlate with the degree of dementia. In addition, these results were obtained without drugs and urodynamic evaluations were not performed (Schnelle, 1990; Ouslander et al, 1995b). Tailoring the regimen to the cause and pattern of incontinence should further improve outcome.

The voiding record also can be helpful if it reveals that nocturnal incontinence correlates with nocturnal diuresis. If due to systolic congestive heart failure, it should improve with diuretic therapy. If due to peripheral edema in the absence of heart failure and hypoalbuminemia (i.e., venous insufficiency), it should respond to pressure gradient stockings. If not associated with peripheral edema, it may respond to alteration of the pattern of fluid intake or administration of a rapidly acting diuretic in the late afternoon or early evening (Pedersen and Johansen, 1988; Reynard et al, 1998). For patients with DHIC whose voiding record and PVR suggest that involuntary detrusor contractions are provoked only at high bladder volumes, augmented voiding techniques or catheterization at bedtime will remove the residual urine, thereby increasing functional bladder capacity and restoring both continence and sleep.

Drugs augment behavioral intervention but do not supplant it, because they generally do not abolish involuntary contractions. Timed toileting or bladder retraining in conjunction with a bladder relaxant is thus especially useful for older adults who have little warning before detrusor contraction (Wagg and Malone-Lee, 1998). There are few data on comparative efficacy or toxicity of standard drugs in the elderly, but available studies show similar efficacy for most agents except flavoxate, which fares poorly in controlled trials (Fantl et al, 1996); no controlled data are available for hyoscyamine in any adult age group.

Both oxybutynin and tolterodine have proved effective in well-conducted trials that included older adults, and these two agents should be considered first-line pharmacotherapy in this population. Healthy elderly patients appeared to respond as well as younger ones (Zinner et al, 2002; Ouslander, 2004; Andersson et al, 2005). Fewer data are available for extended-release oxybutynin in the elderly (Ouslander, 2004; Andersson et al, 2005), but our randomized and controlled data, in which *low doses* of immediate-release oxybutynin were given three to four times daily, suggest that the more constant serum concentrations achieved with extended-release oxybutynin should yield similar results to the immediate-release form. For instance, in our trial of community-dwelling patients, two thirds of patients (mean age = 73 years) became continent, including 71% whose bladder had normal contractility and 47% of those with DHIC, as compared with 17% on placebo (Miller et al, 2000). Immediate-release oxybutynin, which has a short half-life, can be employed prophylactically if incontinence occurs at predictable times. Intravesical instillation of several of these agents is also effective in younger patients, but the need for self-catheterization makes this strategy less useful in the elderly.

The only currently used agents that have been evaluated in the nursing home setting are the immediate-release formulations of tolterodine (1 to 2 mg twice daily) and oxybutynin (2.5 mg three to four times daily). Both have been evaluated during daytime hours when staff are available (7 AM to 7 PM). Overall, the reported reduction in leakage frequency is

roughly 25%; roughly one third of such patients experience a decrease of at least 33% and about 10% become continent during that time period (Ouslander et al, 2001; Fonda et al, 2002).

Both oxybutynin and tolterodine can induce confusion, but concern about the risk is related more to marketing strategies than to the frequency of such occurrences. Such impairment is rarely reported in clinical trials or seen in clinical practice. Only a handful of case reports with each agent have appeared in the past decade (see Tsao and Heilman, 2003; Andersson, 2004; Ouslander, 2004). Recent reanalysis of the OPERA trial, which included approximately 120 patients over age 75 years, disclosed only 1 of 390 patients on oxybutynin who reported confusion; it was judged "mild" because it did not interfere with activities or require intervention. None of the 399 patients on tolterodine reported confusion (Chu et al, 2005). Further research would be useful to delineate the type and frequency of more subtle effects. One published report found that darifenacin did not affect cognition (Lipton et al, 2005), but the study had several methodologic flaws and requires confirmation. Although the practitioner should be alert for the appearance or worsening of cognitive impairment when prescribing these bladder relaxants, their proven benefit generally exceeds their risk in the vast majority of older patients, even among those with concurrent dementia.

There is a theoretical concern with prescribing an anticholinergic bladder relaxant to a patient taking a cholinesterase inhibitor. Fortunately, it has not proved to be a problem in clinical practice, although a few case reports have documented a clinically relevant interaction (Siegler and Reidenberg, 2004). Moreover, in some situations, the clinician and caregiver will decide that the positive impact on the incontinence warrants continuation of both agents regardless.

Newer agents include darifenacin, solifenacin, and trospium. Each has theoretical benefits and drawbacks for older adults, but there are much less data regarding their actual efficacy and adverse effects in this population; Table 71–5 notes some of the relevant caveats. One of the calcium channel blockers, a class of agents long thought to be theoretically preferable for the elderly, was finally studied in a controlled trial and found to be ineffective (Naglie et al, 2002). There is no good evidence to support the use of flavoxate. For depressed patients, nortriptyline or imipramine may be tried (amitriptyline and doxepin should not be given to older patients) (Fantl et al, 1996), but only if the depression has not already responded to a selective serotonin reuptake inhibitor and there is no evidence of orthostatic hypotension; even so, such patients should be monitored for orthostasis and for falls.

Regardless of which bladder relaxant is used, urinary retention may develop. The PVR and urine output should be monitored, especially in DHIC in which the detrusor is already weak. Subclinical urinary retention also may develop, reducing available bladder capacity and attenuating or even reversing the drug's benefit. Thus, if incontinence worsens as the dose is increased, the PVR should be measured again. **Another reason for drug failure is excess fluid ingestion engendered by anticholinergic-induced xerostomia.** For patients whose incontinence defies other remedies (e.g., those with DHIC), inducing urinary retention and using intermittent catheterization may be viable if catheterization is feasible.

Table 71-5. Bladder Relaxant Medications Used to Treat Urge Incontinence*

Medication Class, Name, and Dosage	Comments
Anticholinergic agents Oxybutynin IR, 7.5-20 mg daily (2.5-5 mg PO tid-qid)[†] Oxybutynin XL, 5-30 mg daily (given once daily) Tolterodine, 2 mg twice daily Tolterodine LA, 4 mg daily Darifenacin, 7.5-15 mg qd[‖] Solifenacin, 5-10 mg qd[§‖] Trospium, 20 mg daily to twice daily[§¶]	These agents are now the drugs of choice for older adults. Both oxybutynin and tolterodine have proved effective for older patients in controlled trials when used continuously; less controlled data are not yet available for the other agents and still less for their use, side effects, and drug interactions in older adults. Benefits of M3 selectivity remains theoretical. Concerns re: central nervous system side effects of oxybutynin and tolterodine emanate primarily from rare case reports and are likely greatly overstated. Report of solifenacin's lack of central nervous system effect requires confirmation. Note caveats for use of solifenacin and trospium. Immediate-release oxybutynin has a rapid onset of action and can be tried prophylactically if incontinence occurs at predictable times.
Smooth muscle relaxant Flavoxate, 300-800 mg daily (100-200 mg PO tid-qid)	Has not proved effective in placebo-controlled trials.
Calcium channel blocker Diltiazem, 90-270 mg daily (30-90 mg PO qd-tid) Nifedipine, 30-90 mg daily (10-30 mg PO qd-tid)	Few data support their use, and there are no positive controlled trial data. *Potentially* useful for the patient with another indication for the drug (e.g., hypertension, angina pectoris, or abnormalities of cardiac diastolic relaxation).
Tricyclic antidepressants[‡] Imipramine, 25-100 mg daily (10-25 mg PO qd-qid) (Doxepin, 25-75 mg daily [10-25 mg PO qd-tid])	Older controlled trial data support their use, but they are not first choice. May be particularly helpful in women with coexistent stress incontinence. Orthostatic hypotension often precludes their use, but a tricyclic antidepressant may be preferred for a depressed incontinent patient without risk for orthostatic hypotension. Doxepin has more anticholinergic side effects than imipramine and can cause confusion.

IR, Immediate release; XL and LA, extended release. Adapted and updated in 2005 from Resnick NM: Urinary incontinence. Lancet 1995;346:94-99.
*All drugs should be started at the lowest dose and increased slowly until encountering maximum benefit or intolerable side effects.
[†]May also be applied intravesically in patients who can use intermittent catheterization.
[‡]May give as single daily dose of 25-100 mg after determining the optimal dose.
[§]Dose reduction required for creatinine clearance $\leq$ 30 mL/min (e.g., in an 85-year-old woman with serum creatinine of 1.2 mg/dL who weighs 50 kg).
[‖]Toxicity can occur with concurrent use of potent cytochrome p_{450} $3A_4$ inhibitors (e.g., amiodarone).
[¶]Levels may be affected by other drugs such as digoxin and metformin, which compete for renal tubular secretion.

Other remedies for urge incontinence, including electrical stimulation (see Chapter 64, "Electrical Stimulation for Storage and Emptying Disorders") and selective nerve blocks, are successful in selected situations but have not been studied adequately in the elderly. Trials of botulinum A toxin injection have included older adults, but further data are needed before its role in the treatment of geriatric detrusor overactivity can be established.

Recent studies have suggested that desmopressin is relatively safe for older adults. However, these studies have generally been short term, have included very few subjects older than age 75, have included still fewer with comorbidity or diuretic use, and have sedulously screened and monitored all subjects (Weatherall, 2004). Despite these precautions, hyponatremia developed in up to 22% of patients. Serum sodium levels decreased to less than 130 mmol/L in one fifth of these individuals, almost all of whom were older than 65 years old (Abrams et al, 2002; Weatherall, 2004). Moreover, **there is little evidence that vasopressin is effective for geriatric incontinence** (Dequecker, 1965; Asplund and Aberg, 1993; Cannon et al, 1999). Thus, **the high prevalence of contraindications to its use (e.g., hyponatremia, renal insufficiency, heart failure [even subclinical]), the risk of inducing serious hyponatremia and fluid retention** (Cannon et al, 1999), **and the considerable expense suggest that use of desmopressin in the elderly should await results of further studies.** These caveats are underscored by recent data that suggest that nocturnal polyuria may reflect more of a disordered release of atrial natriuretic peptide than of vasopressin (Carter et al, 1999). If corroborated, such increased atrial natriuretic peptide release could result in a natriuresis that would underlie the older patient's predisposition to hyponatremia when treated with vasopressin.

Adjunctive measures, such as pads and special undergarments, are invaluable if incontinence proves refractory. Many types are now available, allowing the recommendation to be tailored to the individual's problem (Brink and Wells, 1986; Snow, 1988; Brink, 1990; Cottenden et al, 2005). Most are included in an illustrated catalog (available from NAFC, PO Box 1019, Charleston, SC 29402; www.nafc.org). For bedridden individuals, a bed pad that can be laundered may be preferable, whereas for those with a stroke, a diaper or pant that can be opened using the good hand may be preferred. For ambulatory patients with large gushes of incontinence, wood pulp–containing products are usually superior to ones containing polymer gel, because the gel generally cannot absorb the large amount and rapid flow, whereas the wood pulp product can easily be doubled up if necessary. Optimal products for men and women differ because of the location of the "target zone" of the urinary loss. Finally, the choice will be influenced by the presence of fecal incontinence.

Condom catheters are helpful for men, but they are associated with skin breakdown, bacteriuria, and decreased motivation to become dry (Ouslander and Schnelle, 1995; Cottenden et al, 2005), and they are not feasible for the older man with a small or retracted penis. External collecting devices have been devised for institutionalized women, but whether they will adhere adequately in more active women remains to be determined. **Indwelling urethral catheters are not recommended for detrusor overactivity because they usually exacerbate it.** If they must be used (e.g., to allow healing of a pressure sore), a small catheter with a small balloon is preferable to avoid leakage around the catheter; such leakage almost invariably results from bladder contractions rather than from a catheter that is too small. Increasing catheter and balloon size only aggravates the problem and may result in urethral erosion and sphincter incompetence. If spasms persist, drugs such as oxybutynin can be tried. More potent anticholinergic agents, such as belladonna suppositories, should be avoided in the elderly.

Stress Incontinence

Urethral hypermobility, the most common cause of stress incontinence in older women, may be improved by **weight loss** if the patient is obese, **by postural maneuvers** (Norton and Baker, 1994), **by therapy of precipitating conditions such as atrophic vaginitis or cough** (e.g., due to an ACE inhibitor), **and (rarely) by insertion of a pessary** (Suarez et al, 1991; Zeitlin and Lebherz, 1992; Cottenden et al, 2005). If the voiding diary reveals that leakage is volume dependent, it may be improved by adjusting fluid excretion and voiding intervals to keep bladder volume below this threshold. However, if the threshold is less than 150 to 200 mL, this strategy is generally not alone sufficient.

Pelvic muscle exercises can decrease incontinence substantially in older women who are motivated, cognitively intact, and trained to perform them 30 to 200 times daily (Wells et al, 1991; Burns et al, 1993; Fantl et al, 1996; Goode et al, 2003; Wilson et al, 2005). Unfortunately, such exercises must be pursued indefinitely, efficacy is limited for severe incontinence, only 10% to 25% of women become fully continent, and many older women are unable or unmotivated to follow such regimens. **Adding vaginal cones, biofeedback, or electrical stimulation likely enhances efficacy, but the marginal benefit is unclear** (Burgio and Engel, 1990; Burns et al, 1993; Fantl et al, 1996; Berghmans et al, 2000; Goode et al, 2003; Resnick and Griffiths, 2003; Wilson et al, 2005). Urethral plugs are still under development (Junemann, 2001).

Estrogen monotherapy has not proved effective for stress incontinence (Al-Badr et al, 2003), but it can augment the response to an α-adrenergic agonist, although complete continence is rarely achieved (Wells et al, 1991; Fantl et al, 1996; Andersson et al, 2005). **Phenylpropanolamine,** the agent for which most data are available, was withdrawn from the American market owing to reports of a small risk of hemorrhagic stroke (Haller and Benowitz, 2000). **Pseudoephedrine** remains available, inexpensive, and obtainable without a prescription. Because it is also contained in nonprescribed remedies for coryza and allergy, however, the physician should prescribe the dose and guide the choice of preparation, because some capsules also contain agents such as chlorpheniramine in doses that can be troublesome for elderly patients. The physician should also closely supervise its use in patients with hypertension, if it is used at all. **Imipramine,** with beneficial effects on the bladder and the outlet, is a reasonable alternative for patients with evidence of both stress and urge incontinence, but it should be used only if symptoms

as well as signs of postural hypotension have been excluded. Duloxetine, for which clinical trial evidence in younger women suggests more promising results (Andersson et al, 2005), is not yet available for treatment of stress incontinence in the United States.

If these methods fail or are unacceptable, further evaluation of the urinary tract may be warranted. **If urethral hypermobility is confirmed, surgical correction is successful in the majority of selected elderly patients** (Resnick, 1988; Eriksen et al, 1990; Griffith-Jones and Abrams, 1990; Nitti et al, 1993; Carr et al, 1997; Sand et al, 2000; Hawkins et al, 2002; Smith et al, 2005). **If sphincter incompetence is diagnosed instead, it can be corrected with a different procedure (e.g., pubovaginal sling), but the morbidity is higher and precipitation of urgency and chronic retention is more likely than with correction of urethral hypermobility** (Litwiller et al, 1997; Carey and Leach, 2004; Walsh et al, 2004; Smith et al, 2005). Preliminary experience from three tension-free vaginal tape series suggests that older women fare approximately as well as younger individuals (Walsh et al, 2004; Smith et al, 2005). As for younger women, long-term success rates are lower. Epidemiologic survey data suggest a "real world" success rate of approximately 70% at 2 years and 40% at 10 years for women older than age 60 years (Diokno et al, 1989, 2003). The influence of coincident detrusor overactivity on outcome in older women has been inadequately investigated for either type of stress incontinence.

Other treatments for sphincter incompetence include periurethral bulking injections and insertion of an artificial sphincter. Experience with these approaches has proved less auspicious than originally thought, but older women appear to benefit as much as younger women, although both short-term and long-term data in women older than age 75 are still limited (Winters et al, 2000; Smith et al, 2005).

For men in whom these interventions fail, an artificial sphincter and "male sling" are potential options. Little data are available regarding their efficacy in older men (Herschorn et al, 2005), and the sphincter requires considerable cognitive capacity and manual dexterity. Prostheses such as condom catheters or penile clamps may be useful, but most of these require substantial cognitive capacity and manual dexterity as well and are often poorly tolerated. Penile sheaths (e.g., McGuire prosthesis or adhesive underwear liners) are an alternative. As discussed earlier, pads and undergarments are used as adjunctive measures. However, in these cases, polymer gel pads are frequently successful because the gel can more readily absorb the smaller amount of leakage. Some products can be flushed down the toilet, a convenient feature for ambulatory individuals.

Outlet Obstruction

For older men, **conservative management of outlet obstruction often suffices.** In the absence of urinary retention or upper tract damage, modification of fluid excretion and voiding habits may be effective. If not, **α-adrenergic antagonists** are useful and generally well tolerated; they are actually beneficial for men with systolic (not diastolic) congestive heart failure. However, their use requires caution. With age, cardiac output depends less on cardioacceleration than on adequate ventricular filling. Unfortunately, the left ventricle also becomes stiffer, necessitating higher filling pressure. Thus, α-adrenergic blockers, which decrease preload as well as afterload, can result in symptomatic hypotension in older men, particularly those whose age-related ventricular hypertrophy is exacerbated by hypertension or aortic stenosis. Medical consultation should be sought before prescribing an α-adrenergic blocker to such individuals. Although the newer agents tamsulosin and alfuzosin are more selective and appear to be less likely to cause orthostasis than terazosin and doxazosin in older patients (Mann et al, 2000; AUA Practice Guidelines Committee, 2003), further data are required. Because doxazosin was associated with an increased risk when used to treat older men with hypertension in the ALLHAT trial, it probably should be avoided.

Three recent studies have documented the safety of tolterodine in obstructed men with concomitant detrusor overactivity who have not responded well to treatment with an α-adrenergic blocker. Each study excluded men with severe obstruction, PVR greater than 150 mL, or evidence of renal disease (Abrams, 2002; Athanasopoulos et al, 2003; Lee et al, 2004). Particular caution should be exercised for men who take other agents with anticholinergic properties, for those with any degree of cognitive impairment, and for those in whom close follow-up is questionable. Preliminary data on botulinum toxin A suggest that it, too, may have a role as further data become available (Maria et al, 2003; Kuo, 2005).

The 5α-reductase inhibitors (finasteride or dutasteride) have also proved effective as monotherapy, but fewer men appear to benefit, the effect is more modest, and the response occurs over months (Gormley et al, 1992). By contrast, and particularly for men with larger glands, combined therapy with an α-adrenergic blocker for several years is more efficacious than therapy with either drug alone. It also reduces the risk of urinary retention, albeit not in the first year. Devices and surgical approaches, as well as the approach to obstruction in women, are discussed elsewhere. Of note, detrusor overactivity probably resolves less often after removal of obstruction in older patients than in younger ones, but incontinence may still improve, even in cognitively impaired individuals (Eastwood and Smart, 1985; Gormley et al, 1993). In addition, less extensive resection or ablation often suffices for frail elderly men, in whom recurrence of symptoms with adenoma regrowth years later is often not an issue. This fact, coupled with surgical techniques that now permit resection under local anesthesia, has made surgery increasingly feasible for this population.

Underactive Detrusor

Management of detrusor underactivity is directed at reducing the residual volume, eliminating hydronephrosis (if present), and preventing urosepsis. **The first step is to use indwelling or intermittent catheterization** to decompress the bladder for up to a month (at least 7 to 14 days), while reversing potential contributors to impaired detrusor function (fecal impaction and medications). **For patients presenting with acute retention, an α-adrenergic blocker should be considered as well.** Recent data suggest that such therapy increases the chances of success in men without another obvious cause of retention, even among men older than age 65 years and those with retained volume of 1000 to 1500 mL (Lucas et al,

2005; McNeill et al, 2005). Given the long-term success of combined therapy with an α-adrenergic blocker and a 5α-reductase inhibitor, addition of the latter should also be considered if the patient's life expectancy is estimated to exceed 1 year.

If an indwelling catheter has been inserted, it should then be removed (Table 71–6). If decompression does not fully restore bladder function, augmented voiding techniques (e.g., double voiding and implementation of the Credé [application of suprapubic pressure during voiding] or Valsalva maneuver) may help *if the patient is able to initiate a detrusor contraction or if there is coexistent stress incontinence,* especially in women. Bethanechol (40 to 200 mg/day in divided doses) is occasionally useful in a patient whose bladder contracts poorly because of treatment with anticholinergic agents that cannot be discontinued (e.g., a tricyclic antidepressant). In other patients, bethanechol may decrease the PVR if sphincter function and local innervation are normal, but evidence for its efficacy is

---

Table 71–6. Removing an Indwelling Urethral Catheter

1. Ensure that the bladder has been decompressed for at least several days, and 7 to 21 days if possible; the higher the residual volume, the longer the bladder should be decompressed.
2. Correct reversible causes of urinary retention: fecal impaction; pelvic/perineal pain; and use of anticholinergic, α-adrenergic agonist, or calcium channel blocker medications. If an anticholinergic antidepressant/antipsychotic agent cannot be stopped, consider switching to one with fewer or no anticholinergic side effects.
3. Treat delirium, depression, atrophic vaginitis, impaction, or urinary tract infection, if present.
4. An α-adrenergic blocker (e.g., alfuzosin or tamsulosin) increases the chances of success in men but is still unproved in women. It should be initiated several days before the catheter is removed. If a man's life expectancy is estimated to exceed a year, finasteride should be considered as well.
5. Record output at 6- to 8-hour intervals for 2 days to establish a pattern of baseline urine excretion.
6. Remove the catheter at a time that permits accurate recording of urine output and allows for postvoiding recatheterization; clamping the catheter before removal is unnecessary and can be dangerous.
7. Reinsert the catheter *only:*
   a. After the patient voids, to determine PVR volume; or
   b. After the expected bladder *volume* (based on records of urine output)—not the time since the catheter was removed—exceeds a preset limit (e.g., 600-800 mL); or
   c. If the patient is uncomfortable and unable to void despite ensured privacy and maneuvers performed to encourage voiding (e.g., running water, tapping suprapubic area, or stroking inner thigh).
8. If the patient voids and the PVR volume is:
   a. Greater than 400 mL—reinsert the catheter and evaluate further, if appropriate.*
   b. 100-400 mL—watch for delayed retention and evaluate further, if appropriate.*
   c. Less than 100 mL—watch for delayed retention.
9. If the patient is unable to void, evaluate further if appropriate.* If not, the patient requires permanent catheterization.

PVR, postvoid residual.

*Further evaluation is appropriate when the patient and physician believe that if a surgically correctable condition were found (e.g., urethral obstruction), an operation would be preferable to chronic catheterization or the other options described in the text.

Modified from Resnick NM: Incontinence. In Beck JC (ed): Geriatric Review Syllabus, American Geriatrics Society, 1991, pp 141-154.

Table 71-7. Principles of Indwelling Catheter Care

1. Maintain sterile, closed gravity drainage system:
   a. Secure the catheter to upper thigh or abdomen to avoid urethral irritation and contamination. Rotate the site of attachment every few days.
   b. Empty the bag every 8 hours.
   c. Do not routinely irrigate the catheter.
   d. Do not clamp or kink the drainage tubing, and keep the collection bag below bladder level at all times.
   e. Avoid frequent cleaning of the urethral meatus; washing with soap and water once daily is sufficient; periurethral application of antimicrobial creams is ineffective.
   f. Adding disinfectants to the catheter bag is ineffective.
2. If "bypassing" occurs in the absence of obstruction, it is likely due to a bladder spasm, which can be minimized by using the smallest balloon that will keep the catheter in place and by treating with a bladder relaxant medication if necessary.
3. Infection prophylaxis, as well as treatment of asymptomatic bacteriuria, is fruitless and usually leads to the emergence of resistant organisms.
4. Surveillance cultures are unnecessary and potentially misleading because bacteriuria is universal, frequently changing, and often polymicrobial.
5. If symptomatic urinary tract infection develops, change the catheter before obtaining a culture specimen, because cultures obtained through the old catheter may reflect organisms colonizing encrustations rather than the infecting organism. Pending culture results, antibiotic treatment should include coverage of common uropathogens, as well as uncommon ones such as *Providencia stuartii* and *Morganella morganii*.
6. If catheter obstruction occurs frequently, and urine cultures reveal *P. stuartii* or *Proteus mirabilis*, antibiotic treatment may reduce the frequency of obstruction but induces emergence of resistant organisms. In the absence of urea-splitting organisms, consider urine acidification if urine output is normal (at low output, acidification may increase blockage due to uric acid crystals). If frequent blockage persists, consider using a silicon catheter.
7. In the absence of obstruction and symptomatic urinary tract infection, there is no consensus on the best time to change the catheter. Some persons form material that frequently clogs the lumen; their catheter probably should be changed often enough to reduce such obstruction. Other individuals can use the same catheter for years, but it is customary to change it every 1 to 2 months. For patients who are difficult to catheterize, the catheter can be changed less frequently if it remains patent and complication-free.

Adapted from Resnick NM: Voiding dysfunction and urinary incontinence. In Beck JC (ed): Geriatric Review Syllabus, American Geriatrics Society, 1991, pp 141-154.

equivocal at best (Andersson et al, 1999) and residual volume should be monitored to assess its effect (Downie, 1984; Finkbeiner, 1985).

On the other hand, if after decompression the detrusor is acontractile, these interventions are likely to be fruitless, and the patient should be started on intermittent catheterization or an indwelling urethral catheter. For individuals at home, intermittent self-catheterization is preferable and requires only clean, rather than sterile, catheter insertion. The patient can purchase two or three of these catheters inexpensively. One or two are used during the day and another is kept at home. The catheters are cleaned daily, allowed to air dry at night, sterilized periodically, and may be reused repeatedly. Antibiotic or methenamine prophylaxis against urinary tract infection is probably warranted if the individual gets more than an occasional symptomatic infection or has an abnormal heart valve (Chawla et al, 1988; Warren, 1990; Cottenden et al, 2005). Intermittent catheterization in this setting is generally painless, safe, inexpensive, and effective and allows individuals to carry on with their usual daily activities. For debilitated patients, however, intermittent catheterization is usually less feasible, although sometimes possible (Hunt and Whitaker, 1990). If used in an institutional setting, sterile rather than clean technique should be employed until studies document the safety of the latter (Gammack, 2003).

Unfortunately, despite the benefits and proven feasibility of intermittent catheterization (Bennett and Diokno, 1984; Hunt and Whitaker, 1990; Bakke et al, 1992), most elderly patients choose indwelling catheterization instead. As in younger individuals, complications of chronic indwelling catheterization include renal inflammation and chronic pyelonephritis (Warren et al, 1994), bladder and urethral erosions, bladder stones and cancer, as well as urosepsis (Warren, 1990; Gammack, 2003; Cottenden et al, 2005). Principles of catheter care are summarized in Table 71-7.

When indicated, indwelling catheters can be extremely effective, but their use should be restricted. They are indicated in the acutely ill patient to monitor fluid balance, in the patient with a nonhealing pressure ulcer, for temporary bladder decompression in patients with acute urinary retention, and in the patient with overflow incontinence refractory to other measures. Even in long-term care facilities, they are probably indicated for only 1% to 2% of patients.

SUMMARY

Regardless of age, mobility, mentation, or institutionalization, incontinence is never normal. By attenuating physiologic reserve, aging increases the likelihood of becoming incontinent in the setting of additional physiologic, pharmacologic, or pathologic insults. Because many of these problems lie outside the urinary tract, so, too, must the diagnostic and therapeutic focus. However, such a strategy, coupled with a multifactorial, creative, persistent, and optimistic approach, will increase the chances of a successful outcome and generally reward patient and physician alike.

SUGGESTED READINGS

Andersson KE, Appell R, Cardozo L, et al: Pharmacological treatment of urinary incontinence. In Abrams P, Cardozo L, Khoury S, Wein A (eds): Incontinence, 3rd ed. Plymouth, UK, Health Publications, 2005, pp 809-850.

Cottenden A, Fader M, Getliffe K, et al: Management with continence products. In Abrams P, Cardozo L, Khoury S, Wein A (eds): Incontinence, 3rd ed. Plymouth, UK, Health Publications, 2005, pp 149-253.

Fonda D, DuBeau CE, Harari D, et al: Incontinence in the frail elderly. In Abrams P, Cardozo L, Khoury S, Wein A (eds): Incontinence, 3rd ed. Plymouth, UK, Health Publications, 2005, pp 1163-1239.

Gammack JK: Use and management of chronic urinary catheters in long-term care: Much controversy, little consensus. J Am Med Dir Assoc 2003;4(Suppl):S53-S59.

Herschorn S, Thuroff J, Bruschini H, et al: Surgical treatment of urinary incontinence in men. In Abrams P, Cardozo L, Khoury S, Wein A (eds): Incontinence, 3rd ed. Plymouth, UK, Health Publications, 2005, pp 1241-1296.

Resnick NM: An 89-year-old woman with urinary incontinence. JAMA 1996;276:1832-1840.

Resnick NM: Geriatric medicine. In Kasper DL, Braunwald E, Fauci AS, et al (eds): Harrison's Principles of Internal Medicine, 16th ed. New York, McGraw-Hill, 2004, pp 43-53.

Resnick NM, Baumann M: Urinary incontinence. In Morris JN, Lipsitz LA, Murphy K, Belleville-Taylor P (eds): Quality Care in the Nursing Home. St. Louis, CV Mosby, 1997, pp 376-406.

Smith ARB, Daneshgari F, Fynes M, et al: Surgery for urinary incontinence in women. In Abrams P, Cardozo L, Khoury S, Wein A (eds): Incontinence, 3rd ed. Plymouth, UK, Health Publications, 2005, pp 1297-1370.

Wilson PD, Berghmans B, Hagen S, et al: Adult conservative management. In Abrams P, Cardozo L, Khoury S, Wein A (eds): Incontinence, 3rd ed. Plymouth, UK, Health Publications, 2005, pp 855-964.

72 Urinary Tract Fistula

ERIC S. ROVNER, MD

A fistula represents an extra-anatomic communication between two or more epithelium- or mesothelium-lined body cavities or to the skin surface. **Although most fistulas in the industrialized world are iatrogenic, they may also result from congenital anomalies, malignant disease, inflammation and infection, radiation therapy, iatrogenic (surgical) or external tissue trauma, ischemia, parturition, and a variety of other processes.** The potential exists for fistula formation between a portion of the urinary tract (kidney, ureters, bladder, and urethra) and virtually any other body cavity including the chest (pleural cavity), gastrointestinal tract, lymphatics, vascular system, genitalia, skin, and reproductive organs. Classification is generally based on the organ of origin in the urinary tract and the termination point of the fistula (e.g., vagina, skin, gastrointestinal tract). The presenting symptoms and signs are variable and depend to a large degree on the involved organs, the presence of underlying urinary tract obstruction or infection, the size of the fistula, and the associated medical conditions (e.g., malignant neoplasm). Urinary tract fistulas may result in communication between adjacent viscera without symptoms of urinary incontinence or drainage (e.g., colovesical fistula) or, more commonly, present with external urine leakage (e.g., vesicovaginal fistula). **Vesicovaginal fistulas represent, by far, the most common type of acquired fistula of the urinary tract** (Gerber and Schoenberg, 1993) (Fig. 72–1) and therefore are the most widely discussed entity in this chapter.

GENERAL CONSIDERATIONS

Since acquired urinary tract fistulas in the industrialized world are almost universally unexpected and may result in a great deal of inconvenience, discomfort, and physical disability for the affected individual, and because they may be **acquired as a result of a medical or surgical intervention for an unrelated problem, considerable emotional and psychological distress often accompanies the diagnosis and subsequent treatment.** This may be expressed as anger, resentment, and disappointment on the part of the patient toward the physician. Not infrequently, the medicolegal aspects of these cases can be disturbing to the treating health care practitioner, with an increasing proportion of these cases being adjudicated in court (Thomas and Williams, 2000). Only the most naive surgeon would fail to recognize that many of these fascinating reconstructive cases often have significant medicolegal implications, especially in the setting of an iatrogenic fistula. Nevertheless, minimizing the patient's discomfort, maintaining a positive and honest physician-patient relationship while providing constant reassurance, and, perhaps most important, pursuing expeditious and successful treatment of the fistula will most often result in a satisfactory, nonconfrontational, mutually satisfying long-term outcome.

Notably, after the initial diagnosis of a urinary tract fistula that results in external urine leakage, immediate management or control of the leakage is vital. Addressing this quickly will reduce skin breakdown and related complications as well as alleviate much of the psychological distress on the part of the affected individual. The judicious use of catheters, pads, and appliances can be helpful in this regard. Skin care and odor control products are also adjunctive measures in minimizing the patient's distress until definitive therapy and repair of the fistula can be undertaken. The importance of these types of interventions on the patient's behalf should not be underestimated by the surgeon. These simple measures can often deflect or assuage the anger of an otherwise disaffected sufferer, thereby reducing the potential for further aggravating an already difficult medical and possibly litigious situation.

The principles of repair of urinary tract fistula are outlined in Table 72–1 and can be applied to virtually any type of fistula involving the urinary tract. **Prevention of urinary tract fistula is, of course, paramount; however, nutrition, infection, and malignant disease are important considerations not only in assessment of a patient for the risk of fistula formation during any given intervention but also on evaluation for the repair of an existing urinary tract fistula.** Although most urinary tract fistulas in the industrialized world occur in healthy, well-nourished individuals, a nutritional assessment may be an important factor in some patients with fistula. Ensuring adequate nutrition is integral to surgical healing in general but especially important in the setting of urinary tract fistula. Not uncommonly, the catabolic processes contributing to the lack of healing that may have been a contributing factor

Table 72–1. **Principles of Urinary Tract Fistula Management**

Adequate nutrition
Elimination of infection
Unobstructed urinary tract drainage or stenting
Removal or bypass of distal urinary tract obstruction
Beware of malignant etiology of fistula

in the initial fistula formation are often ongoing. This is especially relevant in fistulas related to radiation therapy or in debilitated patients.

Although some types of urinary tract fistulas will heal with conservative management, surgery often assumes a role in the definitive repair. Repair and reconstruction of urinary tract fistulas are sometimes complex. These should be approached on an individual case by case basis as repair may involve some innovative and even improvisational maneuvers in the operating room. The surgeon should be familiar with a variety of approaches and techniques because one approach will not be optimal for all patients with a given type of urinary tract fistula. Principles of surgical management of urinary tract fistula are outlined in Table 72–2. **The finding of a persistent fistula after presumably definitive treatment may suggest the existence of other contributing host factors, such as malignant neoplasm, nutritional issues, unrecognized foreign body, and tissue ischemia, or surgical factors, such as inadequate postoperative urinary tract drainage, persistent distal urinary tract obstruction, and technical problems with the surgery.**

KEY POINTS: URINARY TRACT FISTULAS

- Urinary tract fistulas are often associated with considerable physical and psychological distress for the patient.

- Nutrition, infection, malignant disease, urinary tract obstruction, and foreign body are important factors to be considered in the initial approach to urinary tract fistula as well as in those patients whose initial therapy has failed.

UROGYNECOLOGIC FISTULA
Vesicovaginal Fistula

Vesicovaginal fistula (VVF) is the most common acquired fistula of the urinary tract (Gerber and Schoenberg, 1993) and has been known since ancient times (see Fig. 72–1). However, it was not until 1663 that Hendrik von Roonhuyse first described surgical repair of VVF by denuding the fistula margins and then reapproximating them with sharpened stiff swan quills (Margolis and Mercer, 1994). Johann Fatio is generally credited with the first successful VVF repair in 1675 with use of von Roonhuyse's technique (Falk and Tancer, 1954). In 1838, by use of leaden suture, John Peter Mettauer was the first U.S. surgeon to claim a successful VVF closure (Kight, 1967).

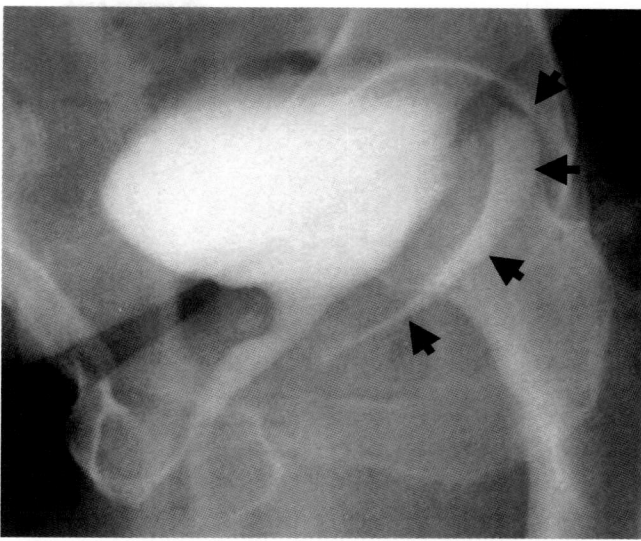

Figure 72–1. Voiding cystourethrogram demonstrates filling of the vagina with voiding due to a post-hysterectomy VVF.

Table 72–2. **Principles of Surgical Repair of Urinary Tract Fistula**

Adequate exposure of the fistula track with débridement of devitalized and ischemic tissue
Removal of involved foreign bodies or synthetic materials from region of fistula, if applicable
Careful dissection or anatomic separation of the involved organ cavities
Watertight closure
Use of well-vascularized, healthy tissue flaps for repair (atraumatic handling of tissue)
Multiple-layer closure
Tension-free, nonoverlapping suture lines
Adequate urinary tract drainage or stenting after repair
Treatment and prevention of infection (appropriate use of antimicrobials)
Maintenance of hemostasis

In 1852, James Marion Sims published his now famous surgical series describing his method of surgical treatment of VVF with silver wire in a transvaginal approach. Of note, it was not until his 30th attempt at closure of VVF that he achieved success. Sims was later to become one of the great figures in the history of operative gynecology. The first successful transabdominal approach to VVF repair was reported by Trendelenburg in 1888, and the concept of an interpositional flap was first proposed in 1928 by Martius, who used a labial fat pad.

Etiology and Prevalence

The etiology of VVF differs in various parts of the world. In the industrialized world, the most common cause (>75%) of VVF is injury to the bladder at the time of gynecologic, urologic, or other pelvic surgery (Symmonds, 1984; Lee et al, 1988; Tancer, 1992). **Surgical injury to the lower urinary tract most commonly occurs in the setting of hysterectomy** (Fig. 72–2); **most of the remainder are related to general surgery procedures in the pelvis, anterior colporrhaphy or cystocele repair, anti-incontinence surgery, or other urologic procedures** (Armenakas et al, 2004). Of 207 VVFs

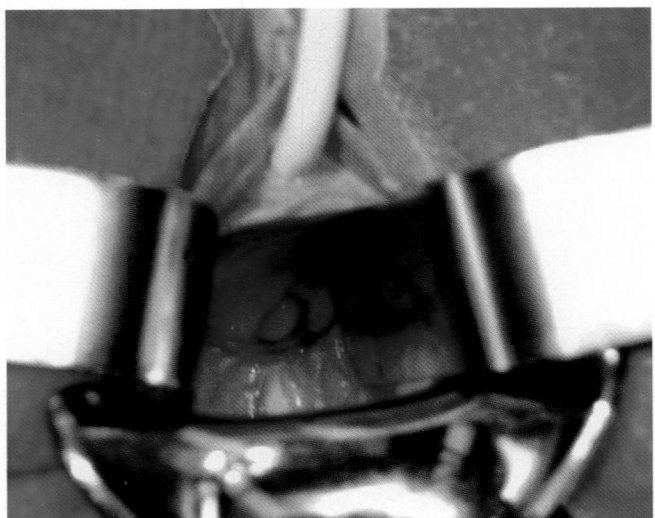

Figure 72–2. Post-hysterectomy VVF. Retraction with a weighted speculum and Heaney right-angled retractors to provide lateral retraction are needed to visualize this post-hysterectomy VVF in a nulliparous woman.

repaired at the University of California, Los Angeles, during a 10-year period ending in 2001, Eilber and colleagues (2003) reported the cause as abdominal hysterectomy in 83%, vaginal hysterectomy in 8%, irradiation in 4%, and miscellaneous in 5%. In 1964, Massee and associates from the Mayo Clinic reviewed the cause of urogenital fistulas in 262 patients and cited uterine operations as a proximate cause in 73.7%, vaginal wall operations in 6.5%, urinary tract operations in 6.9%, and obstetric operations in 6.5%, with the remainder being due to miscellaneous causes (Massee et al, 1964). A later series of more than 300 fistulas from the same institution cited the cause of VVF as gynecologic surgery in 82%, obstetric procedures in 8%, irradiation in 6%, and trauma or fulguration in 4% (Lee et al, 1988). **Other causes of VVF in the industrialized world include malignant disease, pelvic irradiation, and obstetric trauma including forceps lacerations and uterine rupture** (Everett and Mattingly, 1956; Gerber and Schoenberg, 1993). Although uterine ruptures are fortunately uncommon during labor, approximately 22% are associated with a bladder injury (Raghavaiah and Devi, 1975). Before 1900, the most common cause of VVF in the United States was obstructed labor (Stothers et al, 1996). However, obstructed labor and obstetric trauma in general now account for few VVFs in the United States and other industrialized nations, probably because of the widespread availability of excellent prenatal and perinatal obstetric care.

The rate of iatrogenic bladder injury during abdominal hysterectomy is estimated to be between 0.5% and 1.0% (Keettel et al, 1978). Mathevet and coworkers (2001) reported the incidence of bladder injury during vaginal hysterectomy to be 1.7% in 3076 cases, with all injuries being recognized and repaired intraoperatively. Despite the immediate intraoperative repair reported in this series, four VVFs were noted, giving a crude VVF rate during vaginal hysterectomy of 0.13%. The reported incidence of intraoperative bladder injury varies considerably in the literature, depending on whether routine cystoscopy was performed. In series in which

cystoscopy was not performed, the overall rate of bladder injury was reported to be approximately 2.6 per 1000 cases; in series in which cystoscopy was routinely performed, the overall rate of bladder injury was approximately 10.4 per 1000 cases (Gilmour et al, 1999). **The incidence of fistula after hysterectomy is estimated to be approximately 0.1% to 0.2%** (Harris, 1995). There are approximately 140 to 150 VVF repairs annually in England and Wales (Hilton, 1997).

Post-hysterectomy VVFs are thought to result most commonly from an incidental unrecognized iatrogenic cystotomy near the vaginal cuff (Kursh et al, 1988). If this is unrecognized intraoperatively, a pelvic urinoma may develop and ultimately drain out through the vaginal cuff. Ongoing urine drainage along this track results in a fistula. Other potential mechanisms for post-hysterectomy VVF include tissue necrosis from cautery and suture placement through both the bladder and vaginal wall during closure of the vaginal cuff or during an attempt to control pelvic bleeding by suture ligature. Tissue ischemia and then necrosis promote fibrosis and induration, finally resulting in an epithelial or mucosal lining and the development of a fistula track. It is possible that factors other than an isolated suture through the bladder and vagina are necessary for post-hysterectomy VVF formation; at least in an animal model, deliberate suture fixation of the bladder to the vagina did not invariably result in VVF in the absence of infection, urine extravasation, or other complicating factors (Meeks et al, 1997).

In the developing world, where routine perinatal obstetric care may be limited, VVF most commonly results from prolonged obstructed labor due to cephalopelvic disproportion, with resulting pressure necrosis to the anterior vaginal wall, bladder, bladder neck, and proximal urethra from the baby (Arrowsmith et al, 1996) (Fig. 72–3). **The constellation of problems resulting from obstructed labor is not limited to VVF and has been termed the obstructed labor injury complex, which includes varying degrees of each of the following: urethral loss, stress incontinence, hydroureteronephrosis, renal failure, rectovaginal fistula, rectal atresia, anal sphincter incompetence, cervical destruction, amenorrhea, pelvic inflammatory disease, secondary infertility, vaginal stenosis, osteitis pubis, and footdrop** (Arrowsmith et al, 1996). The obstructed labor injury complex occurs largely in developing countries in certain cultures because of several factors, including marriage and conception at a very young age, which results in childbearing in a relatively small and immature pelvis; poor nutrition resulting in stunted skeletal (e.g., pelvic) growth in the mother; and absence of qualified prenatal and obstetric care (Margolis and Mercer, 1994). Patients may suffer with obstructed labor for days in a rural environment, eventually traveling to a distant health care facility only to have a stillborn fetus and a VVF. In direct contradistinction to the epidemiology of VVF in the industrialized world, 96.5% of 932 VVFs seen at a single hospital in Nigeria during a 7-year period were temporally associated with labor and delivery (Wall et al, 2004). The incidence of obstetric fistula in developing countries has been estimated at approximately 0.3% to 0.4% of deliveries (Margolis et al, 1994) or between 1 and 4 per 1000 vaginal deliveries (Margolis et al, 1994; Danso et al, 1996). In sub-Saharan Africa, the incidence rate has been estimated at 10.3 per 100,000 deliveries (Vangeenderhuysen et al, 2001). Approximately 500,000

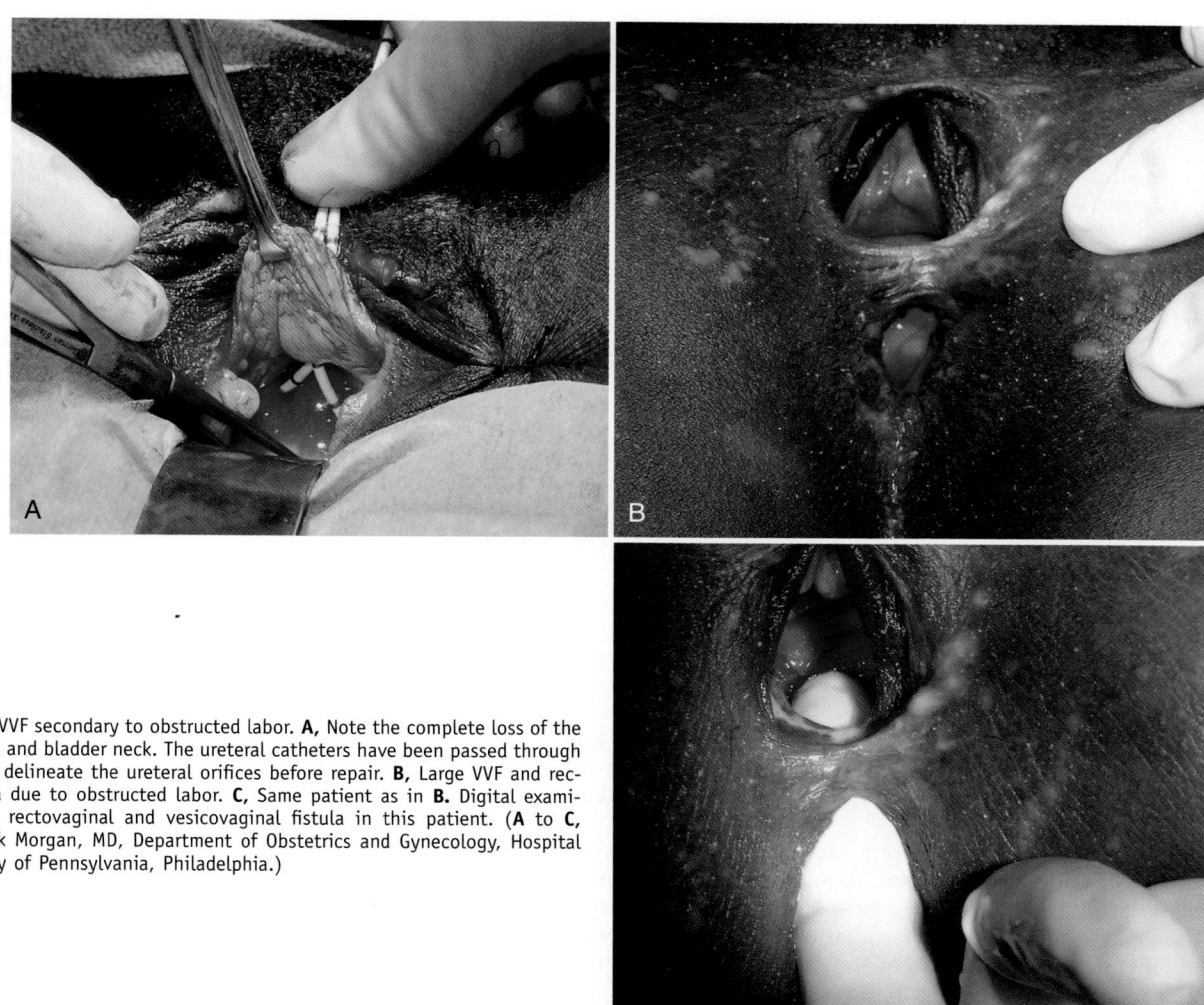

Figure 72–3.   VVF secondary to obstructed labor. **A,** Note the complete loss of the proximal urethra and bladder neck. The ureteral catheters have been passed through the urethra and delineate the ureteral orifices before repair. **B,** Large VVF and rectovaginal fistula due to obstructed labor. **C,** Same patient as in **B.** Digital examination confirms rectovaginal and vesicovaginal fistula in this patient. (**A** to **C,** courtesy of Mark Morgan, MD, Department of Obstetrics and Gynecology, Hospital of the University of Pennsylvania, Philadelphia.)

new cases of obstetric fistula occur throughout the world annually (Hilton, 2003), although the total morbidity from obstructed maternal labor has been estimated to be in excess of 5 million individuals annually (Kelly, 1991). Risk factors include young or old maternal age and primigravid status (Danso et al, 1996).

Obstetric fistulas tend to be larger, located distally in the vagina, and may involve large portions of the bladder neck and proximal urethra. Even in experienced hands, these are often difficult to repair because of the extensive soft tissue loss as well as the ischemia and fibrosis of adjacent tissues (Arrowsmith, 1994; Elkins, 1994). Obstetric fistulas are devastating injuries in the developing world with significant socioeconomic ramifications (Donnay and Weil, 2004; Wall et al, 2004). The affected individuals, commonly young teens, are often ostracized and shunned from family and friends and become permanent outcasts in society. Only rarely are these individuals able to get adequate care and repair because of the lack of organized health care in many countries in the developing world. Major efforts are under way to improve education, socioeconomic status of women, and access to health care in these regions (Tahzib, 1983, 1989; Kelly, 1991, 2004; Wall, 1996; Donnay and Weil, 2004). With improvements in the delivery of prenatal care in some areas of the developing world, it appears that the incidence of VVF due to obstetric causes may be decreasing as a subset of all VVFs, with a proportional increase in the rate of iatrogenic gynecologic fistulas approaching that in industrialized nations (Ayhan et al, 1995). Another important cause of VVF in some parts of the world is traditional folk treatments such as *gishiri* cutting, which may account for up to 13% of VVFs in some series (Tahzib, 1983). This ritual practice involves use of a knife to incise the anterior vagina for treatment of a variety of conditions, including infertility, dyspareunia, dysuria, and back pain.

Other causes of VVF are urologic or gynecologic instrumentation, including percutaneous procedures (Ramsay et al, 1992; Pruthi et al, 2000); **retroperitoneal, vascular, or pelvic surgery; infectious and inflammatory diseases** (Borjas and Rodriguez Diaz, 1949; Bland and Gelfand, 1970; Ba-Thike et al, 1992; Monteiro et al, 1995); **foreign bodies, including neglected pessaries** (Binstock et al, 1990; Goldstein et al,

Table 72–3. Etiology of Vesicovaginal Fistula

Traumatic
  Postsurgical
    Abdominal hysterectomy
    Vaginal hysterectomy
    Anti-incontinence surgery
    Anterior vaginal wall prolapse surgery (e.g., colporrhaphy)
    Vaginal biopsy
    Bladder biopsy, endoscopic resection, laser procedures
    Other pelvic surgery (e.g., vascular, rectal)
  External trauma (e.g., penetrating, pelvic fracture, sexual)
Radiation therapy
Advanced pelvic malignant disease
Infectious or inflammatory
Foreign body
Obstetric
  Obstructed labor
  Forceps laceration
  Uterine rupture
  Cesarean section injury to bladder
Congenital

1990; Grody et al, 1999); **congenital VVF** (Rousseau et al, 1996); **sexual trauma** (Roy et al, 2002); **vaginal laser procedures** (Colombel et al, 1995); **and external violence** (Table 72–3). **The three most common locally advanced malignant neoplasms that result in VVF are cervical, vaginal, and endometrial carcinomas, which in aggregate account for approximately 3% to 5% of VVFs in the industrialized world.**

VVF due to radiation therapy deserves special mention. **These VVFs may occur several decades after completion of the radiation treatment** (Zoubek et al, 1989). **The incidence of urinary tract fistula after radiation therapy varies with the type, dose, and location of the radiation.** Both external beam and interstitial (Aristizabal et al, 1983) radiation therapy may result in VVF. **An incidence of 1.6% of any type of urinary tract fistula was noted in one series of more than 2200 patients treated with a variety of different radiation modalities for cervical carcinoma** (Alert et al, 1980). Perez and coworkers (1999) reported a 0.6% to 2.0% incidence of VVF formation in 1456 patients undergoing combined external beam radiotherapy and brachytherapy for stage I to stage III cervical cancer. In a series of 2096 patients undergoing therapy for cervical cancer, there was an overall genital fistula rate of 1.8%, including rectovaginal fistulas. All patients diagnosed with fistula had received radiation therapy; the median interval from completion of radiation therapy to presentation of VVF was 8.7 months (Emmert and Kohler, 1996). Higher radiation doses seem to correlate with a greater risk for overall morbidity as well as with fistula formation (Perez et al, 1984, 1999). **An important consideration in any fistula after radiation therapy for malignant disease is the possibility that the fistula represents a recurrence of the malignant disease. Therefore, biopsy of the fistula track should be strongly considered before definitive repair is undertaken in these patients.**

Risk Factors

Intraoperative injury to the urinary bladder is clearly a primary risk factor for subsequent development of a post-operative VVF. Other risk factors for postoperative VVF

formation include **prior uterine surgery (cesarean section), endometriosis, infection, diabetes, arteriosclerosis, pelvic inflammatory disease, and prior radiation therapy** (Blandy et al, 1991). In a large series of VVFs, Tancer (1992) described several factors that increased the risk for VVF after hysterectomy, including prior uterine operation (especially cesarean section), endometriosis, recent cold-knife cervical conization, and prior radiation therapy. Nevertheless, almost 30% of the patients in this series had no identifiable risk factor. **The operative approach to hysterectomy is an important factor as bladder injuries are at least three times more common during abdominal hysterectomy compared with vaginal hysterectomy.**

Intraoperative recognition and repair of the bladder injury are paramount in prevention of VVF; however, despite intraoperative repair, VVF may still result in a substantial number of patients (Tancer, 1992). In 1969, Hutch emphasized five factors in the prevention of VVF during gynecologic surgery: (1) immediate detection of bladder injury with use of vital dyes, if necessary; (2) watertight closure of the bladder; (3) satisfactory extravesical drain placement; (4) avoidance of a vaginal incision, if possible, after recognition of the bladder injury; and (5) prolonged, uninterrupted postoperative bladder drainage (Hutch and Noll, 1970).

Clinical Features

Evaluation and Diagnosis. VVF must be distinguished from urinary incontinence due to other causes, including stress (urethral) incontinence, urge (bladder) incontinence, and overflow incontinence.

Presentation. **The most common complaint in patients with VVF is constant urine drainage per vagina.** The amount of urine leakage can vary considerably from patient to patient and may be proportional to the size of the fistula track. Patients may void a variable amount, depending on the size of the fistula and the volume of urine leakage. For example, when a large VVF is present, patients may not void at all and simply have continuous leakage of urine into the vagina. Small, pin-point fistulas may present with intermittent wetness that is positional in nature. In the supine position, when sleeping, the amount of leakage reported by the patient may be minimal; but on rising to a seated or standing position, the amount of leakage may increase precipitously. Patients may also complain of recurrent cystitis, perineal skin irritation due to constant wetness, vaginal fungal infections, or rarely pelvic pain. In fact, **pain is an uncommon finding in patients with VVF unless there is considerable skin irritation or the VVF resulted from radiation therapy.**

VVF after hysterectomy or other surgical procedures may present on removal of the urethral catheter or 1 to 3 weeks later with urine drainage per vagina. It may be possible to identify some patients at high risk for VVF in the immediate postoperative period. Kursh and associates (1988) noted that patients who developed VVF after hysterectomy more commonly had postoperative ileus, hematuria, bladder irritability, and elevated white blood cell count compared with a cohort of patients who did not develop VVF. On occasion, post-hysterectomy VVF may go undiagnosed for an extended time because postoperative clear or serosanguineous vaginal discharge is often attributed to the surgery itself. If a VVF is suspected, the fluid may be collected and analyzed for urea and creatinine, thereby providing a means of obtaining a timely and noninvasive diagnosis of VVF.

VVFs resulting from radiation therapy may not present for months to years after completion of radiation treatment. These tend to represent some of the most challenging reconstructive cases in urology because of their size and complexity and the associated voiding dysfunction due to the radiation effects on the urinary bladder. The endarteritis as a result of the radiation therapy may involve the surrounding tissues, limiting reconstructive options.

Physical Examination. **A pelvic examination with a speculum should always be performed in the evaluation of VVF. The bivalved speculum examination usually provides a precise assessment of VVF, including the location, size, and number of fistulas.** Vaginoscopy has been suggested as an adjunct measure in some cases with use of a modified endoscope to precisely visualize the fistula track (Redman, 1990). **Most commonly, VVFs after hysterectomy are located along the anterior vaginal wall at the level of the vaginal cuff** (Fig. 72–4). A visual and manual assessment of inflammation surrounding the fistula is necessary as it may affect timing of the repair. Significant inflammation, infection, or induration about the fistula may militate against immediate repair. Relevant vaginal anatomic features, including depth, associated prolapse, atrophy, and introital size, are carefully recorded as these may affect the surgical approach to repair. Fistulas high in the vagina at the level of the hysterectomy cuff in a deep narrow vagina may be best approached by some surgeons abdominally because a vaginal approach in these patients can be challenging. This may be especially relevant in nulliparous women, in whom there is usually limited pelvic floor laxity or vaginal prolapse. Postmenopausal vaginal atrophy may be treated with preoperative topical estrogen replacement, thereby optimizing the health and vascularity of potential

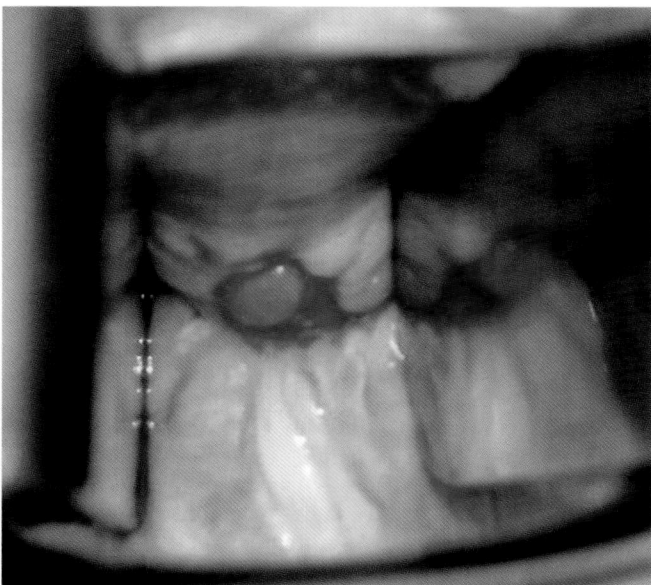

Figure 72–4. VVF on physical examination. A large VVF is seen at the apex of the vagina after hysterectomy. The VVF in this image is seen as reddish pink bladder mucosa prolapsing into the vagina. Hand-held Heaney right-angled retractors provide lateral retraction in this image.

reconstructive flaps. Palpation for masses or other pelvic disease that may need to be addressed at the time of fistula repair is also performed. Notation of prior incisions in the perineum, lower abdomen, and thigh is necessary as these tissues may be required for flap reconstruction when definitive repair is undertaken.

The presence of a VVF may be confirmed by instillation of a vital blue dye into the bladder per urethra and observing for discolored vaginal drainage. Small or occult fistulas may be identified in this fashion (Drutz and Mainprize, 1988). A dye such as methylene blue or indigo carmine is mixed into solution and infused into the bladder. The vagina may be packed with gauze or directly inspected for blue-tinged leakage. If blue-tinged leakage is not apparent and the diagnosis of VVF is in doubt, the sensitivity of this test may be improved by placement of a vaginal packing and ambulation of the patient for a short time. Staining at the introital (distal) end of the packing suggests urinary incontinence or a urethrovaginal fistula, whereas proximal staining suggests a VVF. **If the vaginal packing remains dye free with this maneuver, a ureterovaginal fistula should be excluded with a clean vaginal packing, the intravenous administration of indigo carmine (or other vital dye), and a repeated pad test. Blue staining at the proximal end of the pad after this maneuver suggests a ureterovaginal fistula.**

A double dye or tampon test may confirm the diagnosis of urinary tract fistula as well as suggest the possibility of an associated ureterovaginal or urethrovaginal fistula (Moir, 1973; Raghavaiah, 1974). In one variation of the double dye test, a tampon is placed per vagina. Oral phenazopyridine is administered, and vital blue dye is instilled into the bladder. If the tampon is discolored yellow-orange at the top, it is suggestive of a ureterovaginal fistula. Blue discoloration in the midportion of the tampon suggests VVF, whereas blue staining at the bottom suggests a urethrovaginal fistula.

Clear vaginal discharge after hysterectomy does not invariably represent a urinary tract fistula or incontinence. Other than normal vaginal secretions, less common causes include a peritoneovaginal fistula (Ginsberg et al, 1998), lymphatic fistula (Lau and Wong, 1994), vaginitis, and fallopian tube fluid (Leach, 1987). Incontinence after cesarean section in which a VVF has been excluded may suggest the possibility of a ureterovaginal or vesicouterine fistula.

Cystoscopy. **An endoscopic examination should be performed in patients in whom a VVF is suspected** (Fig. 72–5). An immature fistula may appear as an area of localized bullous edema without a distinct ostium. Mature fistulas may have smooth margins with variably sized ostia. In some cases, multiple pits and cavities along an area of the traumatized posterior bladder wall in the setting of a small VVF may make it difficult to identify the exact fistula track. In these cases, a guide wire or ureteral catheter may be placed through the working channel of the cystoscope and into the fistula track (Fig. 72–6). Visualization of the wire in the vagina confirms the exact location of the VVF on both the bladder and genital sides. Cystourethroscopy can confirm the presence of the fistula but also may assess the size of the track, the presence of collateral fistulas, and the location of the ureteral orifices in relation to the fistula. Small fistulas, usually less than 3 or 4 mm in diameter, may be amenable to simple fulguration, which can be performed at the time of cystoscopy (see later

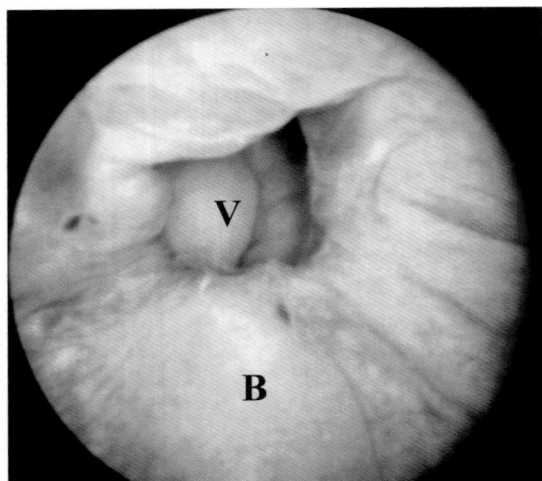

Figure 72–5. Endoscopic view of VVF. This is the same patient as in Figure 72–4. The fistula is now seen from the bladder side. This VVF is large enough to see directly into the vagina (V) through the bladder (B).

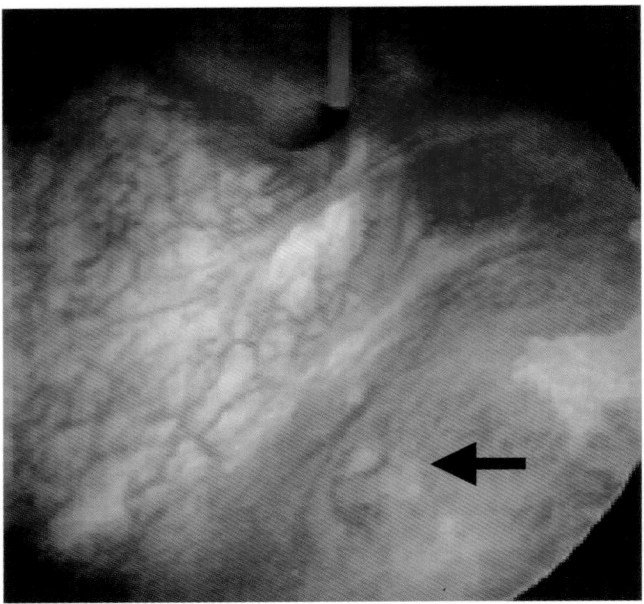

Figure 72–6. Confirmation of a VVF. A 4-Fr ureteral catheter traverses the fistula track in this endoscopic photograph. The VVF is high on the posterior bladder wall, the typical location for a post-hysterectomy VVF. The right ureter is seen *(arrow)*.

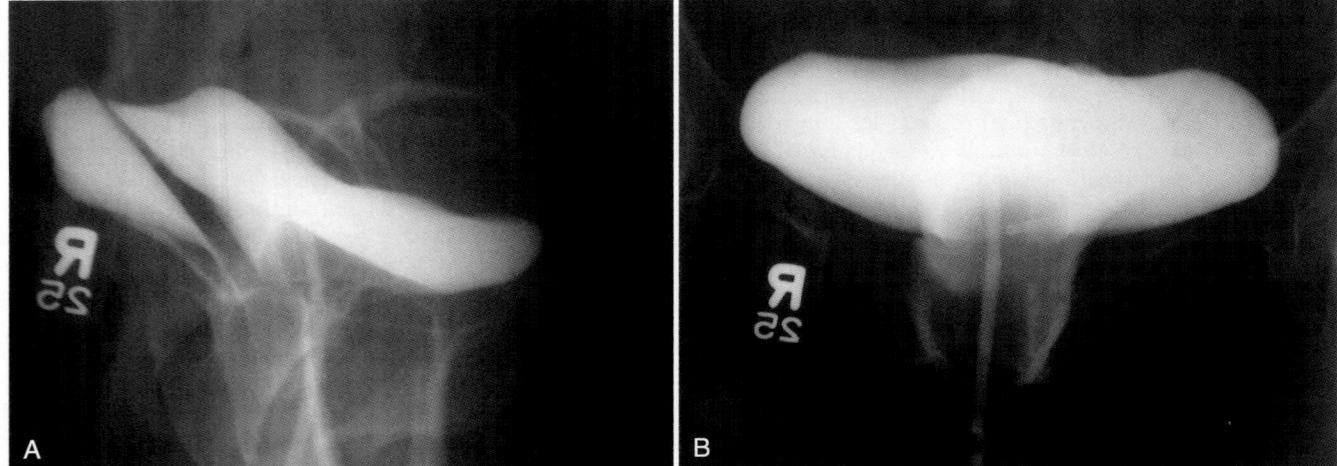

Figure 72–7. Cystogram demonstrating a VVF. **A,** Lateral image demonstrates a post-hysterectomy VVF. **B,** Anteroposterior view. The contrast agent is seen opacifying and outlining the vagina superimposed on the bladder.

discussion) (Stovsky et al, 1994). **Importantly, in the setting of a prior history of pelvic malignant disease, biopsy of the fistula is done to evaluate for the possibility of a recurrent malignant neoplasm.** Fistulas near or at the ureteral orifice may require ureteral reimplantation at the time of VVF repair. This type of requirement would usually mitigate against a completely transvaginal attempt at repair.

Imaging. **Cystography or voiding cystourethrography and an upper tract study should be performed in patients being evaluated for a VVF. The cystogram may objectively determine the presence and location of the fistula.** On filling of the bladder, contrast material often begins to opacify the vagina almost immediately, confirming the presence of a VVF.

VVFs are often best seen in the lateral projection (Fig. 72–7), in which the bladder and vagina are not superimposed. Often, the actual VVF track may be visible in the lateral projection (Fig. 72–8). **However, voiding images may be necessary in some patients with small fistulas to demonstrate the VVF.** The slight increase in intravesical pressure that accompanies micturition is usually adequate to demonstrate even very small fistulas. Importantly, a cystogram that fails to demonstrate a suspected VVF but lacks voiding images or postvoid images should be considered nondiagnostic. During voiding, care should be taken to exclude vaginal voiding or reflux of contrast material from the introital region cephalad into the vagina, which would produce a falsely positive image. An

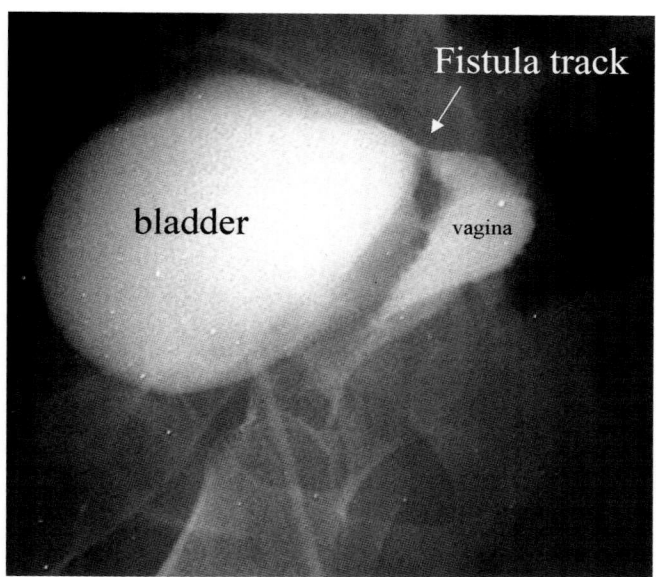

Figure 72–8. Lateral image during cystography demonstrates the VVF track.

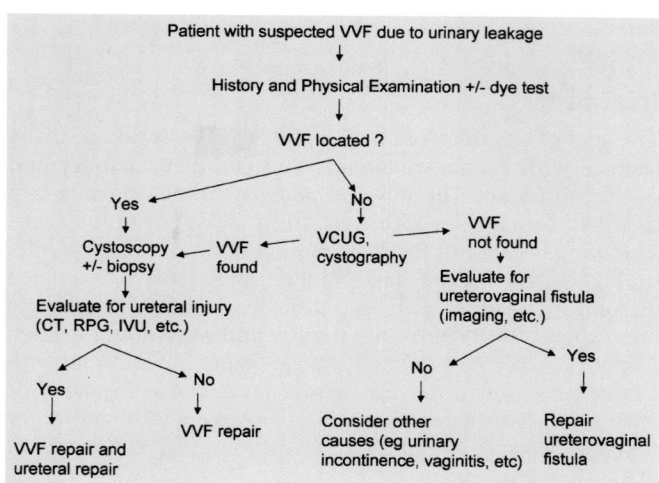

Figure 72–9. Algorithm for the diagnosis of VVF. CT, computed tomography; IVU, intravenous urography; RPG, retrograde pyelography; VCUG, voiding cystourethrography.

involuntary bladder contraction can be provoked with rapid filling during cystography, and if the intravesical pressure rises sufficiently, this may also be sufficient to demonstrate a VVF in a patient in whom the filling images of the cystogram failed to demonstrate it. In some instances, a cystogram can also make an assessment of bladder capacity (important in the setting of prior radiotherapy), cystocele, bladder neck competence, and vesicoureteral reflux, any of which may have an impact on operative repair.

Up to 12% of postsurgical VVFs have an associated ureteral injury or ureterovaginal fistula (Goodwin and Scardino, 1980); **thus, upper urinary tract evaluation is important.** Intravenous urography is usually sufficient for this purpose (Gerber and Schoenberg, 1993). In one series of 216 consecutive patients with VVF due to obstructed labor, almost 50% of patients were diagnosed with an upper tract abnormality on intravenous urography; caliectasis was found in 71% of those affected, but almost 10% were found to have a nonfunctioning renal unit (Lagundoye et al, 1976). If a ureterovaginal fistula is suspected or if the distal ureter is not well seen on intravenous urography, retrograde pyelography may be performed (Blandy et al, 1991) (Fig. 72–9).

Computed tomography (CT), ultrasonography, and magnetic resonance imaging have also been used in the evaluation of VVF (Kuhlman and Fishman, 1990; Outwater and Schiebler, 1993; Yang et al, 1994). Delayed CT visualization of contrast material within the vagina is considered highly suggestive of VVF in the majority of cases (Kuhlman and Fishman, 1990) (Fig. 72–10). In cases of suspected VVF, CT should be performed with only intravenous administration of a contrast agent, or alternatively a CT cystogram can be performed to isolate the bladder. A tampon placed per vagina during intravenous urography or CT scan may improve the sensitivity for finding small or occult VVFs in patients with an otherwise normal evaluation (Wesolowski and Meaney, 1977). **Cross-sectional imaging may also be**

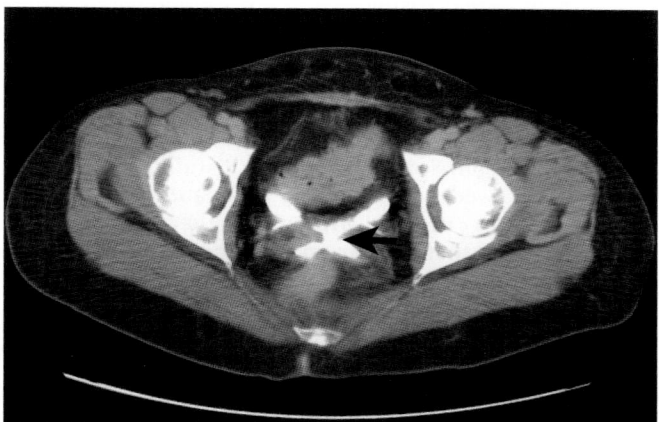

Figure 72–10. CT scan of VVF. After intravenous administration of the contrast agent, there is high-density material in both the bladder and vagina consistent with a VVF. The arrow demonstrates the fistulous connection between the underfilled bladder anteriorly and the vagina posteriorly.

helpful in assessment for recurrent malignant disease in those with such a history.

Other Studies. **Appropriate urine studies including culture and, when indicated, cytologic analysis are performed.** When infection is detected, appropriate antibiotic coverage is initiated. Urodynamic studies, including videourodynamics, are generally not necessary in the evaluation of routine post-hysterectomy VVF. However, in the setting of a prior history of radiation therapy or radical pelvic surgery (e.g., radical hysterectomy) and in those with preexisting neurogenic vesicourethral dysfunction, urodynamics can be used to evaluate for significant detrusor dysfunction including impaired bladder compliance. In patients with a history of significant symptoms of voiding dysfunction and incontinence preceding the VVF, urodynamic evaluation may help define these symptoms before repair of the VVF (Hilton, 1998), an important element in preoperative counseling regarding potential outcomes and preparation for the optimal operative plan.

Treatment

The goal of treatment of VVF is the rapid cessation of urine leakage with return of normal and complete urinary and genital function. The physical and psychological impact of constant urinary incontinence from a VVF can be overwhelming because of the burden of continual wetness, undesirable odors, vaginal and bladder infections, and related discomfort. Bladder catheterization may temporize some of these effects until definitive repair is undertaken, but it often will not completely eradicate leakage, especially in those with a large fistula or those with significant detrusor overactivity. Furthermore, catheterization may provoke additional irritation and pelvic pain and is a constant reminder to the patient of an iatrogenic insult.

Regardless of these limitations and drawbacks, **a trial of indwelling catheterization and anticholinergic medication for at least 2 to 3 weeks may be warranted in selected patients with newly diagnosed VVF as spontaneous healing may result** (Davits and Miranda, 1991). This is especially applicable in those patients in whom the initial placement of the catheter immediately resolves the vaginal leakage. Tancer (1992) described three patients with immature VVF tracks who were successfully treated expectantly with indwelling catheterization. All three patients were seen within 3 weeks of the initial surgery and were found to have nonepithelialized VVF tracks on physical examination. **Fistulous tracks that remain open 3 weeks or more after adequate Foley drainage are unlikely to resolve without further intervention, especially those that appear completely epithelialized on examination.**

Patients with small epithelialized fistulas may benefit from a minimally invasive treatment involving disruption of the epithelial layer of the fistula track (Fig. 72–11). Curettage of the fistula track with an ordinary screw followed by prolonged catheterization has been reported to be successful in a small series of patients (Aycinena, 1977). **Catheterization may be combined with minimally invasive electrocoagulation of the fistula track.** In this approach, a small cautery electrode is passed into the fistula track endoscopically as far as possible. The electrode is slowly withdrawn from the track with the electrode on coagulation. The edges of the fistula track should blanch. Care is taken not to overcoagulate as this can cause widespread tissue necrosis, sloughing, and enlargement of the fistula. This approach was advocated by O'Conor as far back as 1938 for small, highly situated fistulas (O'Conor and Sokol, 1951). Stovsky and colleagues (1994) demonstrated success with endoscopic electrocoagulation and bladder drainage in 11 of 15 cases. All patients had VVFs less than 3.5 mm in diameter and were drained for a minimum of 2 weeks after treatment. It was suggested that disruption of the epithelial component of the VVF track with subsequent fibrosis, scarring, and closure of the track is the mechanism by which electrocoagulation exerted its favorable effects. Falk and Orkin (1957) successfully treated eight patients with electrocoagulation and catheter drainage for 10 days. All successfully treated patients had VVFs less than 3 mm in diameter; this approach failed in two patients with 6-mm VVFs. Importantly, in patients with a thin vesicovaginal septum, a large VVF, or a

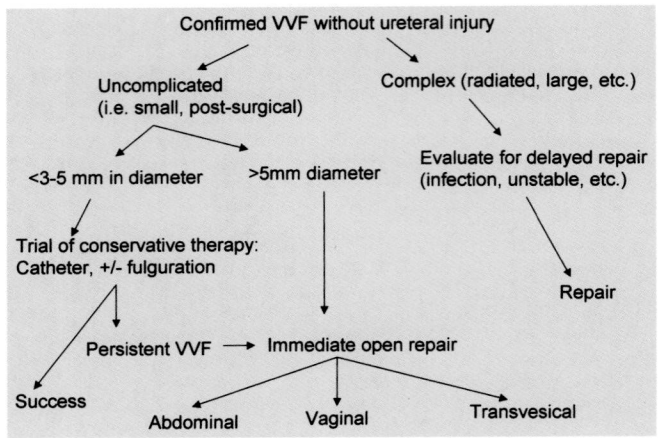

Figure 72–11. Algorithm for management of VVF.

nonoblique fistula track and in those with significant inflammation about the fistula track, fulguration risks failure and the possibility of enlarging the fistula. This approach may also devitalize adjacent tissues, thereby compromising their future utility as flaps. Fibrin sealant has been used as an adjunctive measure to treat VVF (Pettersson et al, 1979; Hedelin et al, 1982). The fibrin sealant may be injected directly into the fistula track after fulguration as described before. The bladder is then drained for several weeks. Presumably, the gel-like nature of the fibrin sealant plugs the hole until tissue ingrowth occurs from the edges of the fistula. Fibrin sealant has been used successfully in combination with (Morita and Tokue, 1999) and without (Evans et al, 2003b) bovine collagen as an additional "plug." **In general, these conservative measures are useful for small, oblique fistulas, usually less than 2 or 3 mm in diameter, in patients who are agreeable to this course of therapy.**

Surgical Repair. It has been stated that the best opportunity to achieve successful repair of VVF is with the initial operation (Elkins, 1994; Weed, 1978). Previous failed attempts at repair produce scar and anatomic distortion and may compromise potential reconstructive flaps. Therefore, careful preoperative planning is essential to maximize the chances for a successful result. **There is no "best" approach for all patients with VVF.**

Timing: Immediate versus Delayed Repair. The timing of VVF repair is somewhat controversial. **Repair of VVF should be as expeditious as possible to minimize the patient's suffering; however, optimal timing for repair should consider certain medical and surgical factors as well.** It is generally accepted that VVF resulting from obstructed labor should be associated with a 3- to 6-month delay before definitive repair (Wein et al, 1980a; Arrowsmith, 1994; Waaldijk, 1994) to allow maximum demarcation of ischemic tissue and resolution of the associated edema and inflammatory reaction. Longer periods, up to 6 to 12 months, have been advocated for radiation-induced fistulas (Wein et al, 1980a), which are often associated with a severe obliterative endarteritis and reduced tissue vascularity.

In the classic teaching of VVF, a minimal waiting period of several months is suggested from the inciting event before the definitive repair attempt to allow reduced tissue edema and inflammation and optimal pliability of the tissues (Persky and Rabin, 1973; Lawson, 1978; O'Conor, 1980; Wein et al, 1980a). O'Conor recommended a waiting period of 3 to 6 months for suprapubic VVF repairs (O'Conor et al, 1973). In this setting, the reduction of inflammation and edema permits easier identification of tissue planes and therefore flap development, less bleeding, and less tension on the reapproximated suture lines. **However, during the ensuing decades, the enthusiasm for delayed management has waned, and in general, uncomplicated postgynecologic urinary tract fistulas may be repaired as soon as they are identified and confirmed, thereby minimizing the patient's discomfort and anguish** (Collins et al, 1971; Persky et al, 1979; Fourie, 1983; Badenoch et al, 1987; Cruikshank, 1988; Wang and Hadley, 1990; Blandy et al, 1991; Blaivas et al, 1995; Kostakopoulos et al, 1998). This is especially true when they are a result of clean surgical trauma (Wang and Hadley, 1990). Nondelayed closure has also been applied to obstetric fistulas with good results (Waaldijk, 1994, 2004). Nevertheless, in some cases, the timing of a VVF repair is best tailored to the individual patient (Blaivas et al, 1995). Raz and associates (1993) suggested that uncomplicated VVFs after abdominal hysterectomy could and should be repaired as expediently as possible transvaginally; however, a 2- to 3-month waiting period may be warranted for some VVFs after vaginal hysterectomy. Conversely, if an abdominal approach is being considered after a particularly difficult or complicated abdominal surgery that resulted in the VVF (e.g., complicated by abscess, urinoma), a period of delay may be warranted to allow resolution of active inflammation. Another potential reason to delay repair is to treat ongoing infection or inflammation at the level of the vaginal cuff. Periodic reexamination of the vaginal tissues can be performed every 1 or 2 weeks and definitive repair scheduled when suitable pliability is noted (Carr and Webster, 1996).

A vaginal approach can be attempted as soon as 2 to 3 weeks after the initial injury if conservative therapy fails (i.e., the patient remains wet with a Foley catheter in place and providing adequate drainage of the bladder) and the patient is in good general health. The vaginal tissues are usually relatively undisturbed from the prior causative surgery, especially if the surgery was transabdominal. Wide healthy vaginal flaps can usually be obtained. In the rare circumstance when a VVF presents within the first 24 to 48 hours postoperatively, an immediate repair can be attempted (Margolis and Mercer, 1994); however, it is possible that these VVFs, especially if they are small in diameter, may heal spontaneously with catheterization during the course of several weeks. It is well documented that similar outcomes can be achieved with early versus delayed abdominal and vaginal repair (Collins et al, 1960; Persky et al, 1979; Zimmern et al, 1985; Badenoch et al, 1987; Wang and Hadley, 1990; Blandy et al, 1991), with success rates in excess of 90% for uncomplicated VVFs.

Approach: Abdominal versus Vaginal. VVF may be repaired through a transvaginal or transabdominal (transvesical) approach. Each approach has merits, depending on the particular circumstances of the fistula, and excellent outcomes can be expected with both approaches (Table 72–4). **Although factors such as size, location, and need for adjunctive procedures often have an impact on the choice of approach, the most important factor is commonly the experience of the operating surgeon. Thus, there is no preferred approach for all fistulas, and the "optimal" approach to the uncomplicated postgynecologic VVF is usually the one that is most successful in the individual surgeon's hands** (Gerber and Schoenberg, 1993; Akman et al, 1999). Although it has been a long-held belief that gynecologists prefer to fix VVF transvaginally and urologists prefer a transabdominal approach because of their respective training and experience (Edwards, 1982; Gerber and Schoenberg, 1993), this difference is becoming increasingly blurred as urologists gain more experience and comfort operating transvaginally for a number of different indications.

The majority of VVFs in the industrialized world are amenable to a transvaginal repair (Turner-Warwick, 1972; Margolis and Mercer, 1994). The relative advantages of a transvaginal approach compared with an abdominal approach are outlined in Table 72–5 and include shorter operative times, briefer hospital stay, and less blood loss (Goodwin and Scardino, 1979). The principal disadvantages of the transvaginal approach include the relative lack of familiarity of the vaginal cuff anatomy to many urologists; the potential for vaginal shortening, especially with the Latzko approach; and the difficulty in exposing high or retracted fistulas near the

Table 72–4. Abdominal versus Transvaginal Repair of Vesicovaginal Fistula

	Abdominal	Transvaginal
Incision	Abdominal incision	Vaginal incision
Timing of repair (elapsed time from fistula formation)	Often delayed 3-6 months	Can be done immediately in the absence of infection or other complications
Exposure	Fistula low on the trigone or near the bladder neck may be difficult to expose transabdominally	Fistula high at the vaginal cuff may be difficult to expose transvaginally
Location of ureters relative to fistula track	Fistula near ureteral orifice may necessitate reimplantation	Reimplantation may not be necessary even if fistula track is near ureteral orifice
Sexual function	No change in vaginal depth	Risk of vaginal shortening (e.g., Latzko technique)
Use of adjunctive flaps	Omentum, peritoneal flap, rectus abdominis flap	Labial fat pad (Martius fat pad), peritoneal flap, gluteal skin or gracilis myocutaneous flap
Relative indications	Large fistulas, location high in a deep narrow vagina, radiation fistulas, failed transvaginal approach, small-capacity bladder requiring augmentation, need for ureteral reimplantation, inability to place patient in the lithotomy position	Uncomplicated fistulas, low fistulas

Table 72–5. Potential Advantages of a Transvaginal Approach for Post-hysterectomy Vesicovaginal Fistula

Avoidance of a laparotomy and its associated morbidity
Short operative time
Brief inpatient stay
Quick convalescence and return to normal activities
Minimal postoperative pain
Minimal blood loss
Absence of the need for wide opening or bivalving of the bladder
Approach is not compromised by multiple prior abdominal or pelvic surgeries
Concomitant anti-incontinence or prolapse surgery may be performed
Local interpositional flaps are adjacent (e.g., Martius, peritoneal)
A three- or four-layer closure is possible
If failure occurs, a subsequent abdominal approach is not compromised

vaginal cuff, especially in deep, narrow vaginas or those without any apical prolapse, such as that found in nulliparous women (see Fig. 72–2). Patients who are unable to get into the high lithotomy position because of musculoskeletal conditions are not candidates for a transvaginal approach.

The abdominal approach to VVF repair is advantageous in several circumstances. If the VVF is associated with another intra-abdominal pathologic process requiring repair, such as an associated ureteral injury (i.e., ureterovaginal fistula) or a complex fistula involving another intra-abdominal organ, a transabdominal approach is indicated to address the problems simultaneously. If the VVF is adjacent to the ureteral orifice, some authors have suggested that this is an indication for an abdominal approach (Carr and Webster, 1996), whereas others have not (Dupont and Raz, 1996). In patients with a small-capacity or poorly compliant bladder (often secondary to irradiation) requiring augmentation cystoplasty, an abdominal approach is indicated as both procedures can be performed with the same incision. Complicated fistulas, including those associated with multiple prior failed attempts at repair (Kristensen and Lose, 1994) or those that are large (>5 cm), might be best approached abdominally as well. Nevertheless, a prior failed attempt at repair is not necessarily a contraindication to a transvaginal approach as excellent results can be achieved in this setting (Eilber et al, 2003).

Combined transabdominal-transvaginal approaches to VVF have been described (Clark and Holland, 1975; Taylor et al, 1980; Henriksson et al, 1982). This approach has been suggested in patients with large, complex, or recurrent VVFs after prior attempts at repair.

Handling of Fistula Track: Excision versus No Excision. A long-held tenet for successful fistula closure dating to Sims' original description in 1852 involved complete excision of the fistulous scar tissue and track (Fearl and Keizur, 1969; Persky et al, 1979; Wein et al, 1980a; Fourie, 1983). This approach ensures clean, well-vascularized viable edges to be approximated for the initial layer of repair. Simple excision of the scar in an inverted "funnel" shape with careful reapproximation of the defect edges has been shown to be an effective repair of VVF (Iselin et al, 1998; Flynn et al, 2004). **However, excision of the fistula track itself is not always thought to be necessary and may even compromise the repair in some patients** (Zimmern et al, 1985; Cruikshank, 1988; Tancer, 1992; Raz et

al, 1993; Margolis and Mercer, 1994). There are several potential disadvantages of excision of the fistula track. First, this results in a larger soft tissue defect to be repaired. Excision of the fibrous track may lead to bleeding, which, if cautery is used, may result in tissue necrosis and impede healing (Eilber et al, 2003). If the VVF is adjacent to the ureter, excision of the track may mandate reimplantation of the ureter. Alternatively, if the track is left in situ, the ureter may be catheterized for the repair and then left undisturbed during a transvaginal operation, obviating the need for reimplantation. In addition, in chronic fistulas, a strong fibrous ring forms outside the epithelialized track that maintains some strength through the repair if this layer is incorporated into the closure. This can be an important consideration in those patients with significant detrusor instability postoperatively from either the repair itself or the indwelling drainage catheters.

Use of Adjuvant Flaps or Grafts: Type and Application. Before embarking on surgical repair, the surgeon should be familiar with a variety of adjuvant flaps and grafts that allow the interposition of healthy tissue during VVF repair. It is not possible to predict which patients will require these procedures ahead of time. **The indications for tissue interposition are not well defined, but these measures are most commonly used in the setting of irradiated tissues, obstetric fistulas, failed prior repairs, large fistulas, and fistulas with tenuous repairs.** The various types of flaps are discussed in more detail later in the chapter.

Other Considerations. Preoperative estrogen supplementation may be beneficial in the postmenopausal patient with vaginal atrophy and VVF (Massee et al, 1964). There are few data in the literature beyond expert opinion to support this use. However, topical estrogen preparations may improve vascularity (Margolis and Mercer, 1994) and local tissue quality (Carr and Webster, 1996). Therefore, a trial of topical estrogens in individuals with postmenopausal vaginal atrophy and a post-hysterectomy VVF may be warranted, provided there are no contraindications to their use.

Perioperative intravenous antibiotics are often administered, although their utility in the post-hysterectomy VVF repair is questionable in the absence of infection. Whether antibiotics should be administered prophylactically before surgical repair is controversial, but at least one study suggests that preoperative antibiotics do not improve outcomes when they are administered before the repair of obstetric fistula (Tomlinson and Thornton, 1998). Treatment of existing infection based on preoperative urine culture is potentially beneficial in preventing bacteremia during surgery. However, prolonged use of broad-spectrum antibiotics postoperatively after repair may result in bacterial resistance and possibly fungal vaginal infections, which may compromise suture lines.

Sexual activity should be documented preoperatively. Patients should be specifically queried about sexual function and dyspareunia before the onset of the event that resulted in the fistula. Although these data are subject to recall bias, they may play an important role during choice of surgical approach as well as have medicolegal implications postoperatively. Some types of vaginal procedures for the repair of VVF, including the Latzko partial colpocleisis, may result in vaginal shortening and postoperative dyspareunia. Preoperative documentation of this preexisting condition can be invaluable. Furthermore, adjuvant procedures that may alter vaginal appearance or function, such as the harvesting of a Martius fibrofatty labial flap or an episiotomy, should be carefully discussed with the patient in advance, especially as regards sexual function.

Finally, postoperative drainage after VVF repair can be maintained by single or dual catheters. Some authors suggest that a urethral catheter alone provides satisfactory drainage (Collins et al, 1960; Fearl and Keizur, 1968; Tancer, 1980; Leng et al, 1998). Others advocate a suprapubic catheter (Blaivas et al, 1995; Carr and Webster, 1996; Iselin et al, 1998) alone to minimize bladder spasms and trauma to the surgical repair. Most commonly, both urethral and suprapubic drainage catheters (O'Conor et al, 1973; Wein et al, 1980a; Dupont and Raz, 1996; Eilber et al, 2003) are left postoperatively. The disadvantage to single-catheter drainage is principally the potential that the catheter will malfunction, clog, or kink, resulting in bladder filling, eventual overdistention, and disruption of the suture line.

Preoperative Counseling and Indications for Surgery. Surgical repair of a VVF is indicated after confirmation of the diagnosis. A trial of conservative management may be warranted in selected cases, especially in those with a newly diagnosed, small, uncomplicated fistula in which the vaginal leakage significantly improves or resolves with catheter drainage. When conservative measures fail or, after adequate counseling, the patient requests repair before a trial of conservative management, surgical treatment is pursued. Before surgery, patients should be counseled that most VVFs in the industrialized world are repaired on the first attempt in more than 90% of cases; however, prolonged postoperative urinary catheter drainage is necessary after surgery. Postoperative urgency and frequency are common for a time after removal of the catheter but are usually self-limited. Finally, the patient should be aware that it may be necessary to alter the surgical plan intraoperatively because of a variety of factors encountered during the operation and that interpositional flaps or grafts may be used.

Vaginal Techniques. Common vaginal approaches to the repair of uncomplicated VVF are described. The merits of the vaginal approach are reviewed in Tables 72-4 and 72-5.

Vaginal Flap or Flap-Splitting Technique. This approach popularized by Raz and colleagues (Zimmern et al, 1985; Raz et al, 1993; Stothers et al, 1996; Eilber et al, 2003) results in a three-layer closure without the use of an adjuvant flap and a four-layer closure if a flap is used (Fig. 72–12). It can be performed as an outpatient procedure and is applicable to most simple, uncomplicated VVFs.

Step 1 (positioning, preparation, and retraction): The patient is placed in the dorsal lithotomy position; rectal packing is placed (to aid in identification of the rectum), and the lower abdomen and perineum are prepared with a standard surgical preparation solution. Appropriate exposure is maintained with use of a vaginal weighted speculum, silk labial retraction sutures, and a ring retractor with hooks. A suprapubic tube is placed, cystoscopy with reassessment of the VVF location is performed, and ureteral catheters are placed if the fistula track is adjacent to or involves the ureteral orifices. A posterolateral episiotomy may be performed to improve exposure in patients with a narrow introitus. A urethral catheter is placed in addition to the suprapubic tube, maximizing postoperative urine

drainage (Fig. 72–13A). Any concomitant anti-incontinence or other vaginal surgery that is to be performed simultaneously with VVF repair should be done before reconstruction so that the repair is not disturbed once it has been completed.

Step 2 (incision): The fistula track is cannulated with a small Foley catheter (10 to 12 French); after inflation of the balloon, gentle downward traction is placed on the Foley catheter, pulling the VVF toward the introitus. On occasion, a small VVF requires dilation with metal sounds for placement of the Foley catheter; nevertheless, the gentle traction on the VVF provided by the Foley catheter greatly enhances exposure (see Fig. 72–8). The vaginal flaps are marked out (Fig. 72–13B). Saline is then injected into the anterior vaginal wall surrounding the fistulous track and along the lines of the vaginal flaps. The fistula track is carefully circumscribed. An inverted J-shaped or U-shaped incision that circumscribes the fistula track is made with the limbs of the J or U extending to the apex of the vagina. The circumscribed fistula is incorporated into the curved portion of the incision. The nature of this incision allows development of a vaginal wall flap that can be advanced and rotated over the fistula repair. This helps avoid vaginal shortening as well as overlapping suture lines during reconstruction. However, some surgeons have recommended that the long end of the incision be extended along the anterior vaginal wall toward the introitus (Wang and Hadley, 1990).

Step 3 (development of vaginal wall flaps): The vaginal wall flaps are developed by dissecting in a proximal, distal, and lateral direction away from the incision (Fig. 72–13C). Mobilization of the vaginal wall distal to the VVF is especially important because it will be necessary to advance the proximal vaginal wall flap beyond the fistula as the final layer of closure. Each flap is mobilized 2 to 4 cm from the fistulous track, exposing the underlying perivesical fascia. The ring of vaginal wall tissue where the initial incision circumscribed the fistula opening is left intact; thus, the flap is constructed in healthy tissue, avoiding dissection of the actual fistulous track. This technique facilitates dissection in proper tissue planes, avoids bleeding edges at the resected fistula track, ensures that closure of the fistula is done with healthy tissue (vaginal wall flaps), and decreases the risk of potential bladder perforation. In addition, adequate mobilization of the vagina off perivesical fascia and bladder allows easier construction of a tension-free closure.

Step 4 (fistula closure): Closure of the fistulous opening is now done. The catheter in the fistula track is removed, and the first layer of the repair is performed. Interrupted 2-0 or 3-0 absorbable sutures are placed in a transverse or vertical fashion across the fistula. These sutures incorporate bladder wall and the fistulous track itself, starting in healthy tissue approximately 0.5 cm away from the margin of the fistula (Fig. 72–13D). Inclusion of the fistulous track in the repair (and not resecting the fistula) provides a strong anchor of supporting tissue for the first layer of the repair. The second layer of the repair is placed with interrupted 2-0 or 3-0 absorbable sutures. These sutures are placed to invert the previous layer by imbricating the perivesical fascia and the deep musculature of the bladder over the first layer–fistula track (Fig. 72–13E). The sutures should be applied at least 3 to 5 mm from the prior suture line, free of tension and at a 90-degree angle from the first suture line to minimize overlapping of the two lines

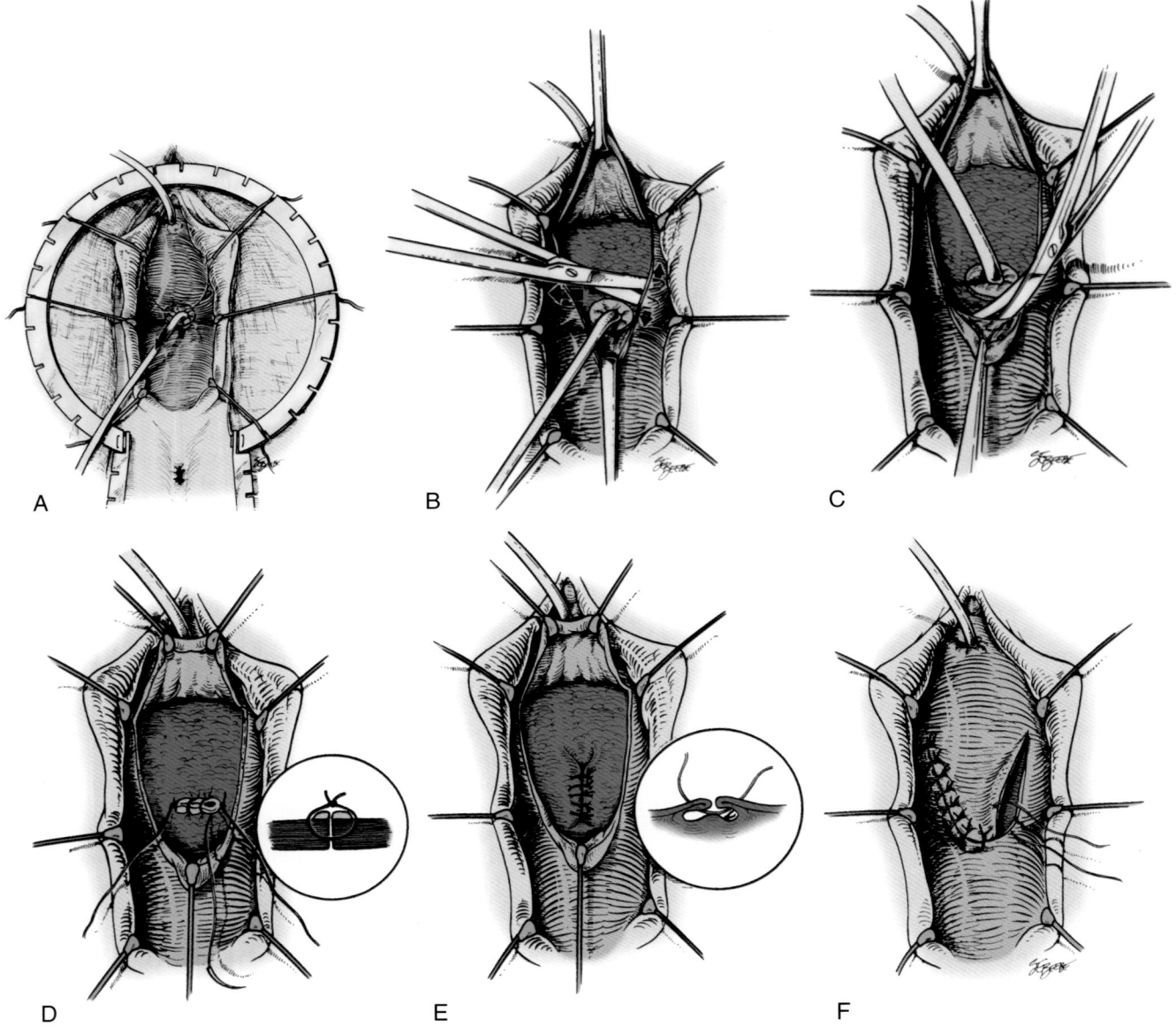

Figure 72–12. Technique of vaginal repair of a post-hysterectomy VVF. **A,** Retraction including ring retractor, vaginal speculum, and Foley catheter in the VVF track. A Foley catheter is seen in the VVF track providing traction on the vaginal cuff. **B,** Mobilization of anterior vaginal wall flap. Lateral flaps are developed as well, thereby isolating the VVF track. **C,** Mobilization of posterior vaginal wall flap. **D,** Initial layer of closure is performed without excising the edges of the fistula track. **E,** The perivesical fascia is closed with Lembert-type sutures. This line of closure is perpendicular to the initial suture line. **F,** The vaginal wall flaps are advanced to avoid overlapping suture lines. (From Ganabathi K, Sirls L, Zimmern P, Leach GE: Vesicovaginal fistulas: Reconstructive techniques. In McAninch J, ed: Traumatic and Reconstructive Urology. Philadelphia, WB Saunders, 1996:317.)

of repair. The integrity of the repair is confirmed by filling the bladder with 200 to 300 mL of saline mixed with indigo carmine and observing for vaginal staining. At this point, if it is desired, an interpositional peritoneal or Martius flap may be mobilized and secured over the existing suture line (Raz et al, 1993; Eilber et al, 2003).

Step 5 (advancement and closure of vaginal wall flap): The final and third layer of closure is done with the vaginal wall flaps that were previously constructed. The redundant, excess anterior (distal) vaginal flap is excised, and the posterior (proximal) vaginal flap is advanced beyond the fistula closure.

This covers the fistula site with fresh, healthy vaginal tissue, which helps avoid overlapping of suture lines.

Step 6 (closure of the vaginal wall): The flap is advanced at least 2 or 3 cm beyond the fistula closure and the vaginal wall is closed with a running, locking, absorbable 2-0 polyglycolic acid suture. An antibiotic-impregnated vaginal packing is placed for 24 hours postoperatively. The urethral Foley and suprapubic catheters are left to drainage for 10 to 14 days.

Postoperative urine drainage is essential, and the draining catheters are left in all patients postoperatively until cystography confirms successful repair of the fistula. In general,

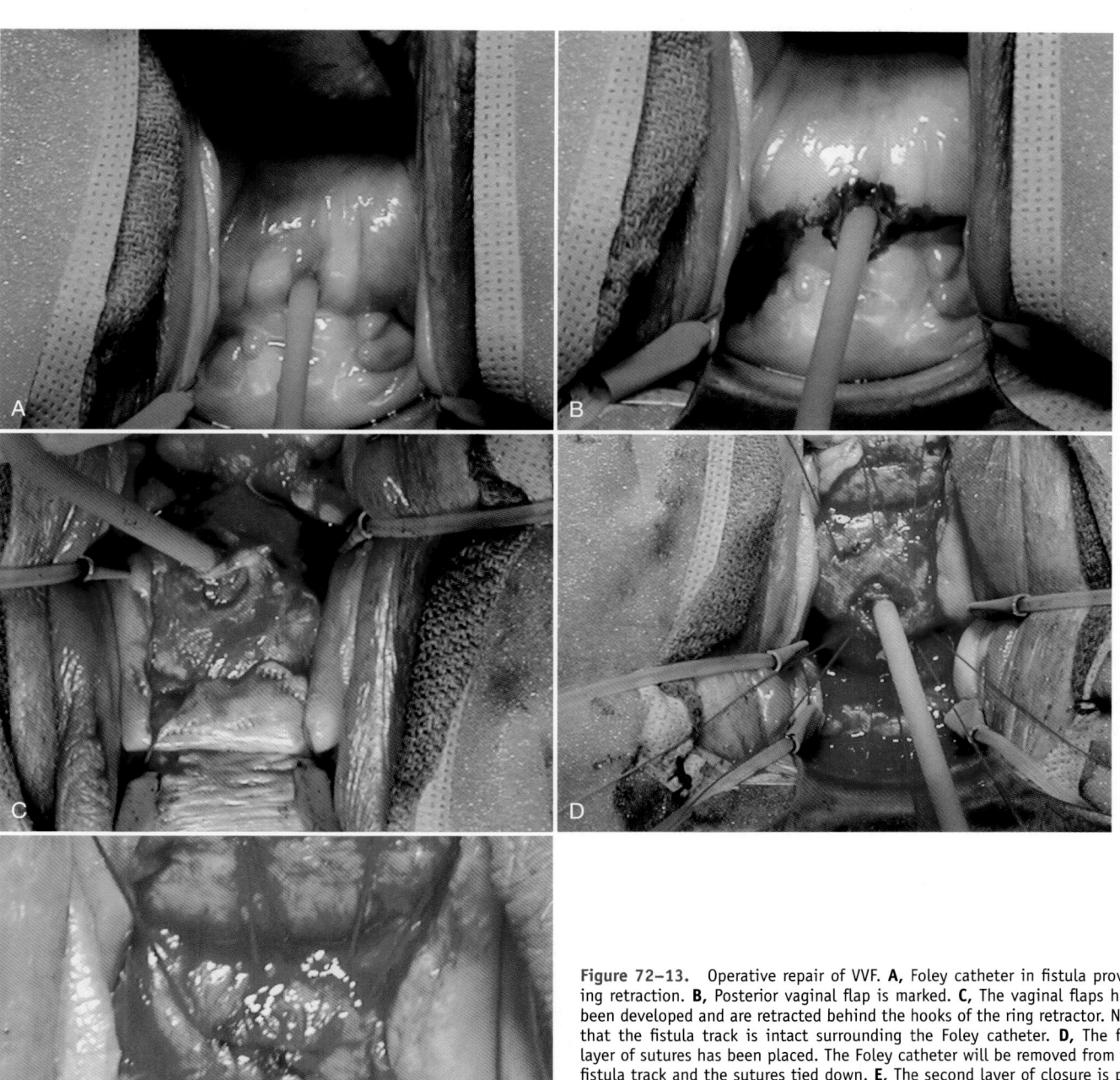

Figure 72–13. Operative repair of VVF. **A,** Foley catheter in fistula providing retraction. **B,** Posterior vaginal flap is marked. **C,** The vaginal flaps have been developed and are retracted behind the hooks of the ring retractor. Note that the fistula track is intact surrounding the Foley catheter. **D,** The first layer of sutures has been placed. The Foley catheter will be removed from the fistula track and the sutures tied down. **E,** The second layer of closure is performed by reapproximating the perivesical fascia over the first suture line.

imaging is obtained at between 10 and 21 days from the time of repair. If a persistent leak is noted, ongoing catheterization and repeated imaging at a 2- to 3-week interval may demonstrate eventual resolution (Schwab and Rovner, 2003). Anticholinergic agents are given to decrease bladder irritability. A cystogram is obtained before catheter removal to document integrity of the repair. Sexual intercourse is avoided for 3 months postoperatively.

Complications. Dissection in the proper surgical planes ensures minimal bleeding. When significant bleeding is encountered during the dissection, it is possible that an improper plane of dissection was entered. Careful intraoperative inspection and reevaluation of the surgical planes are warranted. Furthermore, excessive use of cautery may compromise the vascular supply of the tissue flaps used for repair. This may only become evident in the postoperative period with ischemic flaps and recurrence of the fistula. Intraoperative bleeding should be controlled with fine absorbable suture whenever possible. **The possibility of ureteral injury is a concern if the VVF is adjacent to the insertion of the ureter.** If there is doubt about a ureteral injury, cystoscopy should be performed after the intravenous administration of indigo carmine. Blue efflux from the ureteral orifice confirms ureteral patency.

Long-term complications from transvaginal VVF repair include vaginal shortening and stenosis. Careful attention to flap mobilization and reconstruction will minimize this complication. In addition, excessive resection of the vaginal wall should be avoided during reconstruction to prevent vaginal shortening or scarring.

The most important complication of VVF repair is recurrence of the fistula. A repeated transvaginal approach can be attempted with satisfactory success. A careful review of potential factors leading to failure of the initial repair is undertaken, and any remediable factors (inadequate nutrition, vaginal atrophy, excessive postoperative bladder spasms) are addressed. Strong consideration should be given to the use of adjuvant flaps in repeated VVF repairs.

Other Transvaginal Techniques. There are multiple variations to transvaginal fistula repair including that described by Latzko. Originally described in 1914 (Latzko, 1914), the Latzko high partial colpocleisis is a popular approach among some reconstructive surgeons, with reported success rates in excess of 90% (Kaser, 1977; Tancer, 1980). This approach may not be as successful as the vaginal flap technique for large obstetric fistulas (Elkins et al, 1988). In this procedure, the fistula track is isolated and the tissue surrounding the VVF track is denuded of vaginal "epithelium" circumferentially for a distance of 1 to 2 cm. Care is taken to avoid deeply "denuding" the vaginal tissues to avoid entry into the bladder or perivesical fascia. The denuded areas are then reapproximated over the fistula track with a series of interrupted absorbable sutures. Sutures are not placed into the bladder wall or vesical mucosa. The edges of the vaginal wall are then reapproximated as a second layer, with partial colpocleisis in some patients. Advantages of the Latzko procedure include minimal blood loss, no need for ureteral reimplantation (even for a fistula adjacent to the ureter as sutures are not placed through the bladder), and short convalescence. Potential disadvantages include the possibility of vaginal shortening (Enzelsberger and Gitsch, 1991) and directly overlapping suture lines.

Webster and colleagues reported excellent results with a transvaginal approach to VVF by vaginal cuff excision (Iselin et al, 1998; Flynn et al, 2004). In this approach, the fistula track is isolated and the entire epithelialized portion of the track is excised in a wide inverted cone fashion, leaving a funnel-shaped defect from the vesical to the vaginal side of the fistula. The defect is then closed in three or four layers with absorbable suture. Principal advantages of this technique are that mobilization of vaginal flaps is not required and vaginal shortening is minimal.

Abdominal Techniques. VVF may be repaired transabdominally, and this is the preferred approach in those cases requiring augmentation cystoplasty or ureteral reimplantation. Compared with the vaginal approach, the abdominal approach to VVF repair is associated with a longer recovery time and inpatient hospitalization, greater blood loss, more cosmetic deformity, and, in general, greater morbidity. Abdominal repair of VVF may be performed intraperitoneally or extraperitoneally as well as transvesically.

Suprapubic Intraperitoneal-Extraperitoneal Approach. The patient is placed in a low lithotomy position with access to the vagina in the sterile operative field. Ureteral catheters may be placed preoperatively to assist in identification of the ureters intraoperatively, especially if the VVF is close to the ureteral orifices. A lower midline incision is carried out. As classically described by O'Conor and colleagues (O'Conor and Sokol, 1951; O'Conor et al, 1973), the bladder is approached extraperitoneally; however, in some cases, the peritoneum will be entered. The bladder is opened vertically, and the cystotomy is extended down to the opening of the VVF (Fig. 72–14). As the dissection proceeds distally, stay sutures placed on the bladder edges greatly assist in retraction. In addition, a curved sponge stick placed per vagina with gentle upward traction can provide excellent exposure of the VVF. After the bladder has been bivalved down to the level of the VVF, the VVF track is excised, and the dissection is continued beyond the fistula track to develop the vesicovaginal space (Fig. 72–15). The vagina is carefully dissected and separated from the bladder for a distance of 2 or 3 cm beyond the VVF. The key to the operation is the mobilization of the bladder from the vagina caudal to (beyond) the VVF track. After wide mobilization from the bladder, the vagina is closed with a running absorbable suture. At this point, if an interpositional flap of

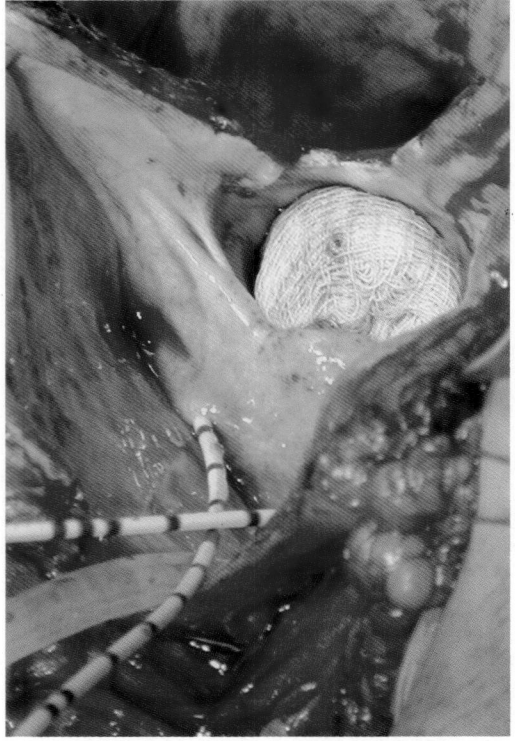

Figure 72–14. Intraoperative photograph from a suprapubic VVF repair. The bladder has been opened anteriorly and bivalved in the midline down to the level of a very large VVF. The gauze packing lies in the vagina. The ureteral catheters were placed to identify the ureters intraoperatively.

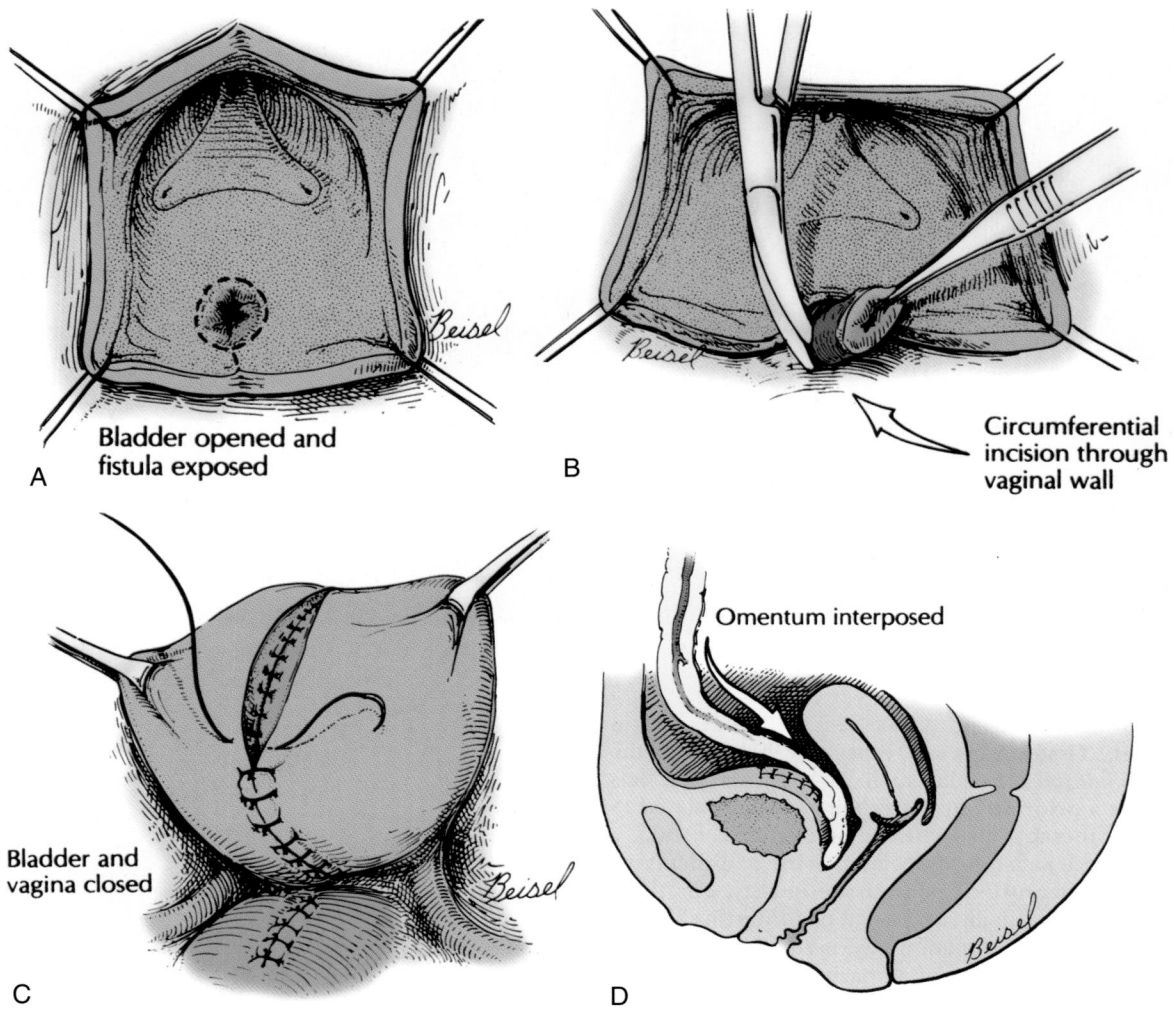

A, Bladder opened and fistula exposed

B, Circumferential incision through vaginal wall

C, Bladder and vagina closed

D, Omentum interposed

Figure 72–15. Diagrams of suprapubic repair of VVF. **A,** The bladder opened and bivalved down to the level of the VVF. **B,** The VVF track is excised. **C,** After closure of the vagina, the bladder is closed in multiple layers. **D,** Omentum is interposed between the bladder and vaginal closures. (From Ganabathi K, Sirls L, Zimmern P, Leach GE: Vesicovaginal fistulas: Reconstructive techniques. In McAninch J, ed: Traumatic and Reconstructive Urology. Philadelphia, WB Saunders, 1996:315.)

greater omentum is to be used, it is mobilized and then secured 1 to 2 cm distally beyond the excised VVF track (see later discussion) (Wein et al, 1980a). The bladder is then closed in several layers. A suprapubic tube and urethral catheter are usually left for postoperative drainage. Anticholinergic agents are used liberally in the postoperative period to minimize bladder irritability, which is often a problem.

Bladder augmentation or ureteral reimplantation, if necessary, can be incorporated into the suprapubic approach before closure of the bladder. Large or small bowel may be used for augmentation cystoplasty, depending on the clinical circumstances.

Transvesical. A suprapubic transvesical approach to VVF repair has also been described (Landes, 1979; Cetin et al, 1988; Gil-Vernet et al, 1989). In this approach, the bladder is opened through a vertical cystotomy but is not bivalved down to the VVF track. From a transvesical approach, the VVF track is circumscribed and excised transvesically. The vaginal edges are then carefully mobilized from the bladder. The vagina and

bladder are closed sequentially. A V-shaped flap of adjacent posterior bladder wall may be brought down as a flap to close a large gap or to minimize overlapping suture lines (Gil-Vernet et al, 1989). This approach has been successful in both simple and complex fistulas (Gil-Vernet et al, 1989).

Other Techniques for VVF Repair. Minimally invasive approaches to VVF repair would be ideal. Laparoscopic approaches to VVF have been reported (Nezhat et al, 1994; von Theobald et al, 1998; Miklos et al, 1999; Ou et al, 2004), but these consist largely of case reports and small series. In comparison to the minimally invasive nature of the transvaginal approach to VVF repair, it is unclear whether the laparoscopic approach will offer any distinct advantages. Laser tissue welding with a neodymium:yttrium-aluminum-garnet laser (Dogra and Nabi, 2001) and transurethral endoscopic suturing have been reported in the treatment of VVF (Okamura et al, 1997; McKay, 2001).

Adjuvant Techniques in the Repair of VVF: Tissue Interposition. The interposition of a healthy, well-vascularized

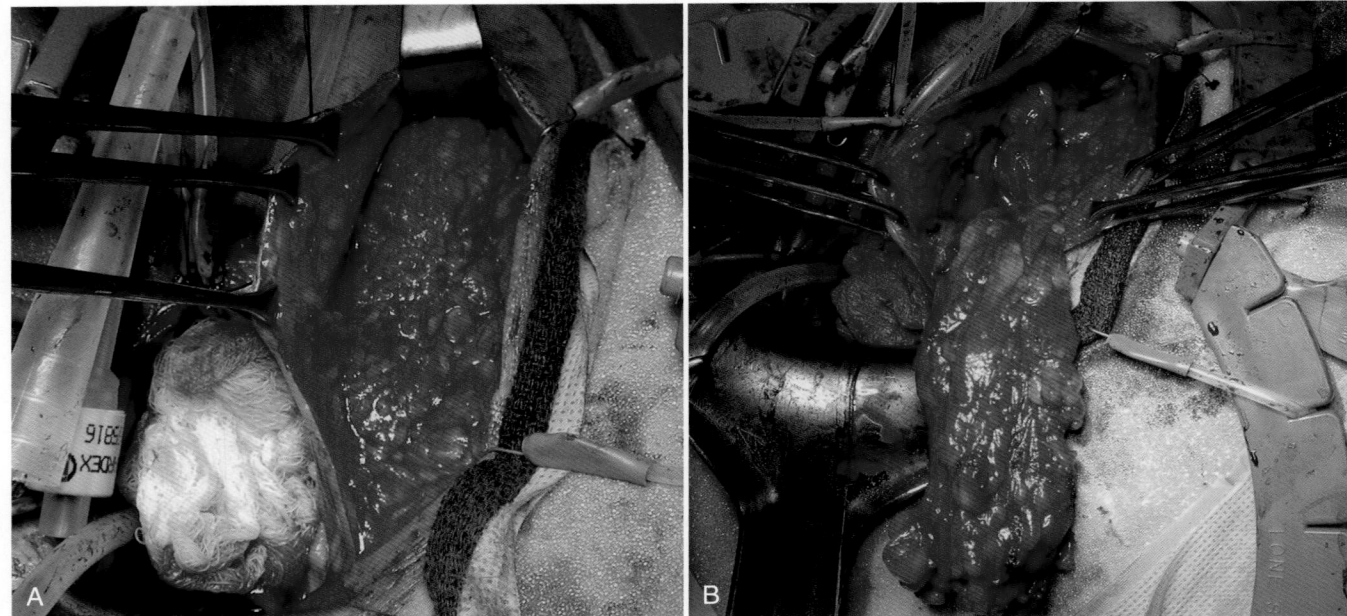

Figure 72–16. Harvesting of a Martius flap. **A,** The incision is made in the labia. **B,** A large flap may be obtained.

tissue flap during VVF repair may be beneficial under certain circumstances. **Tissue flaps are especially helpful in the setting of a complex fistula, such as a fistula that has recurred after a prior attempt at repair, a fistula related to previous radiotherapy, an ischemic or obstetric fistula, a large fistula, and a fistula associated with a difficult or tenuous closure because of poor tissue quality.** For those VVFs repaired transvaginally, a labial fat pad (Martius flap) or a peritoneal flap is most commonly used. From a transabdominal approach, omentum or peritoneum (Eisen et al, 1974) is often used as an interpositional flap.

Martius Flap. For low or distal fistulas, a Martius fibrofatty labial flap is a reliable source of tissue. The fibrofatty labial flap was first described by Heinrich Martius in 1928. **This flap consists of adipose tissue and connective tissue and is the preferential tissue for fistulas involving the trigone, bladder neck, and urethra** (Zimmern et al, 1986; Rangnekar et al, 2000). **The blood supply to the flap is provided inferiorly by the posterior labial vessels (off the internal pudendal artery), superiorly by the external pudendal artery, and laterally by the obturator artery.** The lateral blood supply is sacrificed during mobilization of the flap; the flap may be divided at either its most superior or inferior margin (basing the blood supply on the inferior or superior vascular pedicle, respectively), depending on where the flap will be transferred.

The flap is harvested after the first two layers of closure of the VVF but before the final vaginal wall flap is advanced over the repair (see earlier discussion). For harvesting of the flap, a vertical incision is made over the labia majora. The borders of dissection include the labiocrural fold laterally, the labia minora and the bulbocavernosus muscle medially, and Colles' fascia covering the urogenital diaphragm posteriorly. Flap harvest is accomplished in a lateral to medial fashion. Dissecting down to the adductor muscles laterally before coming around the width of the Martius flap facilitates the harvest of

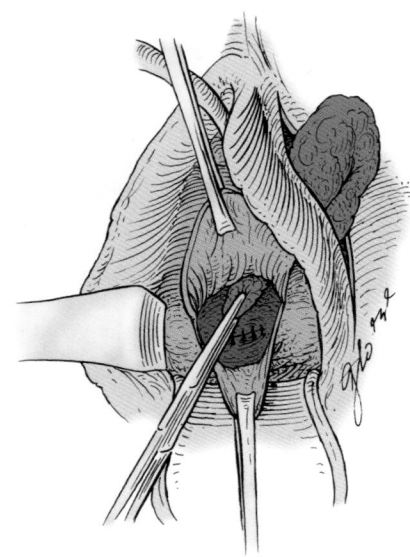

Figure 72–17. Tunneling of the Martius flap. (From Raz S: Vesicovaginal fistulas. In Raz S, ed: Atlas of Transvaginal Surgery. Philadelphia, WB Saunders, 1992:158.)

a thick, fatty segment for flap placement. The entire thickness of the fibrofatty flap is included in a small Penrose drain, and gentle downward traction is applied to aid in dissection superiorly. The main vascular supply to the flap is located at the base of the labia majora. The anterior segment is clamped and transected anterior to the pubic symphysis. The free segment of the flap is dissected from the underlying structures down to the posterior-based vascular pedicle (Fig. 72–16).

After the flap has been mobilized, a tunnel is developed from the labial incision to the site of the fistula repair (Fig. 72–17). A hemostat is used to transfer the fibrofatty pad from the harvest site, through the tunnel, to the level of the fistula repair. The flap is placed over the fistula repair and secured with interrupted absorbable sutures in a tension-free manner. The vaginal wall flap is advanced over the Martius flap and closed as previously described. A small Jackson-Pratt or Penrose drain may be left in the labial incision in the operative bed. The labial incision is closed, and a pressure dressing may be applied to the labial skin incision.

Rangnekar and colleagues (2000) reported on the utility of the Martius flap in both urethrovaginal and vesicovaginal fistulas, the majority of which (32 of 46) were due to obstetric trauma. Of the patients undergoing VVF repair, 4 of 21 repairs without a Martius flap failed compared with none in the 13 patients who underwent an adjuvant Martius flap. Eilber and coworkers (2003) reported that 33 of 34 patients (97%) undergoing repair of a distal VVF with a Martius flap were cured after the first operation.

For post-hysterectomy fistulas, the distance from the labial harvesting site of the Martius flap to the fistula at the apex of the vagina may be considerable. Mobilizing and then tunneling the Martius flap to reach this location may compromise its blood supply and viability. In these cases, a peritoneal flap is preferred (Raz et al, 1993).

Peritoneal Flap. The use of a peritoneal flap during transvaginal repair of a complex VVF is a simple procedure that does not require extravaginal harvesting of the flap. **This technique is primarily used in conjunction with repair of a high-lying, post-hysterectomy VVF** (Raz et al, 1993; Eilber et al, 2003). Notably, peritoneal flaps may also be used as an adjunctive measure during transabdominal repair of VVF, although the approach and technique are vastly different (Eisen et al, 1974).

After a two-layer closure as described previously, the peritoneum is identified posteriorly. The peritoneum and preperitoneal fat are identified, isolated, and mobilized from the caudal origin of the vaginal wall flap by sharp dissection. Usually, dissection just beyond the posterior wall of the bladder will expose the edge of the peritoneum in the anterior cul-de-sac (Raz et al, 1993). The peritoneum is identified as a distinct layer from the bladder. The peritoneum is not opened but is mobilized and then advanced over the fistula repair and secured with interrupted absorbable sutures in a tension-free manner (Fig. 72–18). If a peritoneotomy is made during dissection or mobilization, the peritoneal defect can be closed as the flap is secured to the perivesical fascia over the fistula repair. The vaginal flap is then advanced and closed as previously described.

Raz initially reported success in 9 of 11 patients with high VVF undergoing peritoneal flap placement (Raz et al, 1993). A later study from the same institution reported on the use of peritoneal flaps in 83 patients, of whom 80 were cured after the first operation (Eilber et al, 2003). Of the three patients whose repair failed, two were successfully repaired with a repeated transvaginal repair and peritoneal flap, whereas the one patient required a transabdominal repair with omental interposition.

Greater Omentum. The omentum is a particularly useful structure in the repair of VVF. **Although most commonly used as an adjunct during transabdominal VVF repair as an interpositional layer between the bladder and vagina,** it has occasional utility in transvaginal VVF repair if it had been

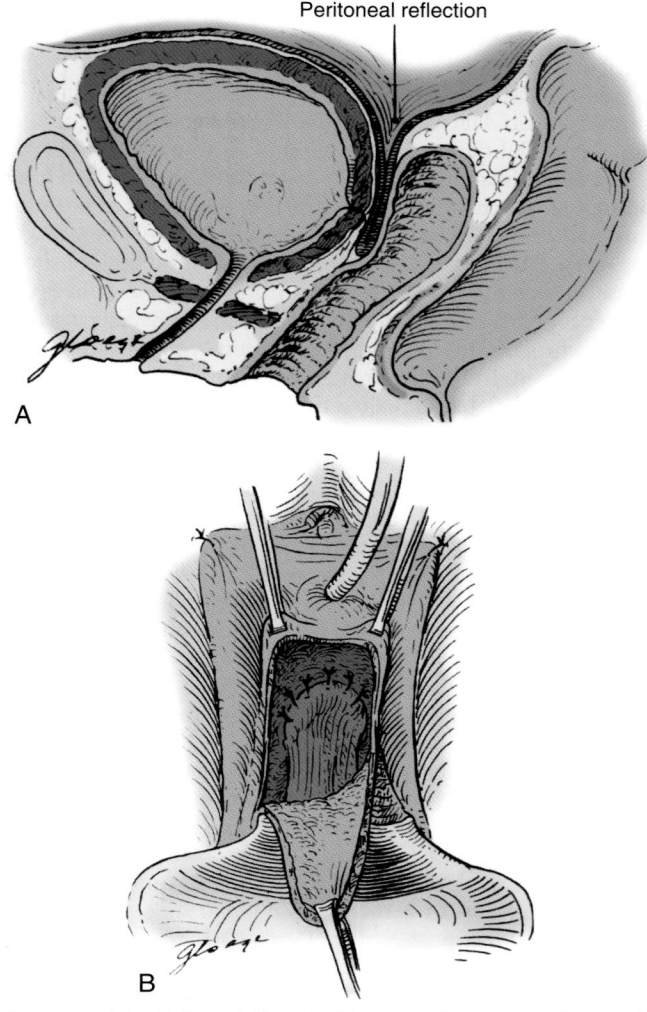

Peritoneal reflection

A

B

Figure 72–18. Peritoneal flap. **A,** Diagrammatic representation of the location of the peritoneal flap during VVF repair. **B,** Diagram of peritoneal flap advanced over fistula repair. (**A** and **B,** from Raz S: Fistulas: Transvaginal repair of vesicovaginal and urethrovaginal fistulas. In Raz S, ed: Atlas of Transvaginal Surgery, 2nd ed. Philadelphia, WB Saunders, 2002:242.)

brought down into the pelvis during a prior surgical procedure. **Favorable properties of the omentum include its ability to be mobilized on a well-vascularized pedicle into the deep pelvis without tension, its inherent lymphatic properties, its ability to contribute to healing even in the presence of infection, and the ease with which epithelialization occurs on its surface** (Turner-Warwick, 1976; Wein et al, 1980b).

The blood supply of the greater omentum derives principally from the right and left gastroepiploic arteries as well as the distal branches of the gastroduodenal and splenic arteries. The right and left gastroepiploic arteries join along the greater curvature of the stomach to form the gastroepiploic arch. The arterial anatomy within the greater omentum is variable but usually consists of a right and left omental artery and occasionally a middle omental artery, all of which run perpendicular to their origin off the gastroepiploic arch. The caliber of the right gastroepiploic is usually larger, which generally favors a pedicle based on this artery; however, in practice, a pedicle based on either artery may be used (Kiricuta and Goldstein, 1972; Bissada and Bissada, 1992). In addition, the origin of the right gastroepiploic artery is somewhat caudal compared with the left gastroepiploic, allowing a slight advantage in reaching into the deep pelvis.

The free distal end of the greater omentum is often long enough to reach into the deep pelvis tension free without any further mobilization. In some patients, however, it will not reach into the pelvis without tension, and therefore some mobilization may be necessary. Initially, to mobilize the greater omentum, it should be freed from the usually avascular attachments to the transverse colon. Mobilization may then proceed from the greater curvature of the stomach, usually in a left to right direction, with care taken to avoid injury to the vascular supply of the flap while the gastric branches from the gastroepiploic arch are ligated (Wein et al, 1980b). Mobilizing from left to right leaves the omental flap based on the right gastroepiploic artery with the advantages noted before. Once mobilized, the omental flap is secured with absorbable suture to healthy tissue at a location distal to and beyond the closed VVF track between the vagina and bladder. When it is secured beyond and between the suture lines of the closed viscera, it will prevent overlying or apposed suture lines.

Evans and colleagues (2001) reported retrospectively on the utility of an omental interpositional flap in 37 patients undergoing transabdominal VVF. Of the 29 patients with a benign etiology of VVF, all 10 patients in whom an omental flap was used were cured, compared with only 12 of 19 (63%) in whom an omental flap was not used. Orford and Theron (1985) reported a 93% cure rate with the use of an omental pedicle graft in 52 patients undergoing VVF repair. In addition to its utility in routine post-hysterectomy VVF, the omentum is reported to be a useful adjunct in complicated or complex cases, such as those associated with large VVFs (Kiricuta and Goldstein, 1972; Bissada and McDonald, 1983), obstetric VVFs (Baines et al, 1976; Sharma et al, 1980), and those associated with radiation therapy (Bissada and Bissada, 1992; Evans et al, 2001).

Other Flap and Graft Techniques. A variety of flaps including gracilis muscle flaps (Izes et al, 1992), labial myocutaneous flaps (Symmonds and Hill, 1978), seromuscular intestinal flaps (Mraz and Sutory, 1994), and rectus abdominis flaps (Menchaca et al, 1990; Viennas et al, 1995) have been used as adjunctive measures in the repair of complex VVF. Obstetric fistulas associated with significant urethral loss may be repaired in part with the use of anterior or posterior bladder flaps (Hanash and Sieck, 1983; Elkins et al, 1992; Khanna, 1992). The gracilis muscle in the medial thigh is a convenient adjunct to repair of large soft tissue defects, especially those associated with radiation therapy (Obrink and Bunne, 1978; Heckler, 1980). The gracilis muscle is close to the vagina and has a reliable blood supply. The muscle is mobilized through a thigh incision from its distal attachment on the tibial condyle with care to preserve its blood supply. It is tunneled cephalad into the vagina subcutaneously and secured over the fistula. Bilateral gracilis muscle flaps can be used for total vaginal reconstruction.

Bladder mucosa as a free graft has been used for repair of VVF (Brandt et al, 1998; Ostad et al, 1998; Sharifi-Aghdas et al, 2002). The bladder is approached extraperitoneally and a small cystotomy is performed. The fistula track is identified and denuded of mucosa circumferentially for approximately 1 cm. A free graft of bladder mucosa is harvested from the edge of the cystotomy and placed over the denuded VVF track and secured in place with absorbable suture. Brand and colleagues (1998) reported a 96.3% success rate in 80 patients. Ostad and coworkers (1998) described six patients with complex, high, irradiated, large, or recurrent VVFs, all of whom were cured by this technique.

Outcomes of VVF Repair. The success rate reported for a simple VVF repair in the modern era, through an abdominal or vaginal approach, is in excess of 90% (Table 72–6). Complicated VVFs, including those resulting from obstetric causes (Elkins et al, 1988; Arrowsmith, 1994), as well as those associated with radiation therapy have generally lower success rates (Massee et al, 1964; Hedlund and Lindstedt, 1987; Langkilde et al, 1999). Massee and colleagues (1964) reported a 93.8% cure of urinary-vaginal fistulas due to surgical trauma but only a 66.7% success with those due to radiation therapy. Some authors have suggested that urinary diversion should be strongly considered as primary therapy (Murray et al, 2002) for radiation-induced fistulas, as the results with surgical repair in this group are less than optimal (Langkilde et al, 1999). **In patients with obstetric fistulas associated with loss of the bladder neck and proximal urethra, relatively high rates of persistent severe sphincteric incontinence are noted despite successful repair of the VVF** (Murray et al, 2002; Browning, 2004), which is responsible for the majority of treatment failures (Kelly, 1992). Thus, despite a technically successful VVF repair, functionally, from the patient's perspective, some of these individuals may not be significantly improved after the repair. Pubovaginal slings and periurethral injectable agents are often beneficial in these patients once the VVF has been surgically closed (Arrowsmith, 1994).

VVF and Urinary Diversion. In some patients, repair of VVF is not possible or multiple surgical attempts have failed. This is probably most commonly associated with existing pelvic malignant disease, severe radiation damage, or large soft tissue loss, especially in the setting of obstetric fistula. However, some patients may simply not be candidates for repair because of coexistent medical morbidities that make them a prohibitive surgical risk. In the patient in whom VVF repair is not possible or has failed, urinary diversion in the form of either a urinary conduit (Kisner and Kesner, 1987) or a continent reservoir can be considered. Fistulas in patients who are not candidates for surgical intervention may be managed by percutaneous ureteral occlusion and permanent nephrostomy (Kinn et al, 1986; Stern et al, 1987; Hubner et al, 1992; Farrell et al, 1997).

In the developing world, where catheters and ostomy appliances are too expensive or completely unavailable, continent urinary diversion or incontinent urostomies are not practical. In these situations, internal urinary diversion with ureterosigmoidostomy has some application in patients with unreconstructable lower urinary tracts (Attah and Ozumba, 1993). This is clearly a last resort operation because of its significant metabolic and neoplastic potential.

KEY POINTS: VESICOVAGINAL FISTULA

■ VVF is the most common acquired fistula of the urinary tract.

■ The etiology of VVF in the industrialized world is very different from that in the developing world.

■ In the industrialized world, surgical injury to the bladder is the most common cause of VVF. This is most commonly seen after hysterectomy.

■ VVFs due to radiation therapy are usually complex.

■ VVF occurring in the setting of a history of pelvic malignant disease should undergo biopsy before repair to exclude recurrent malignant disease as a cause of the fistula.

■ Diagnosis of VVF can be confirmed on voiding cystourethrography. Voiding images should be obtained if the fistula was not demonstrated on the filling images of cystography.

■ Upper tract imaging should be obtained after a diagnosis of VVF to exclude injury to the ureter.

■ Small, oblique fistulas may respond to conservative therapy, including prolonged catheterization with or without fulguration of the fistula track.

■ There is no optimal method for the surgical repair of VVF. In the properly selected patient, transabdominal and transvaginal approaches to fistula repair have similar success rates.

■ Adjuvant tissue flaps may be useful to prevent surgical failure in the setting of a complex or recurrent fistula, a radiation fistula, an obstetric fistula, and the fistula with a tenuous repair.

Ureterovaginal Fistula

Ureteral fistulas to the genital tract in the female may connect with the vagina or much less commonly with the fallopian tube or uterus (Billmeyer et al, 2001). **Risk factors for the development of ureterovaginal fistulas include endometriosis, obesity, pelvic inflammatory disease** (Symmonds, 1976), **radiation therapy, and pelvic malignant disease.** Nevertheless, Symmonds (1976) has noted that the patient with a ureteral injury after gynecologic surgery is typically one who had an uncomplicated, technically easy hysterectomy for minimal disease. Thus, except for those oncologic cases in which a segment of ureter is deliberately excised, many ureteral injuries are likely to be due to technical or iatrogenic factors.

Etiology and Presentation

The most common etiology of ureterovaginal fistula is surgical injury to the distal ureter, with gynecologic procedures being by far the most common cause (Symmonds, 1976;

Dowling et al, 1986; Badenoch et al, 1987; Lee et al, 1988; Blandy et al, 1991). **Most ureterovaginal fistulas occur during procedures for benign as opposed to malignant indications** (Mandal et al, 1990), **including hysterectomy most commonly but also cesarean section, cystocele repair, and other pelvic surgery** (Table 72–7). With respect to the approach for hysterectomy, the risk of ureteral injury appears to be greatest during laparoscopic hysterectomy, followed by abdominal and then vaginal hysterectomy (Harkki-Siren et al, 1998). **The incidence of iatrogenic ureteral injury during major gynecologic surgery is estimated to be about 0.5% to 2.5%** (Symmonds, 1976; Payne, 1996; Gilmour et al, 1999).

The mechanism of injury resulting in iatrogenic postoperative ureterovaginal fistula includes ureteral laceration or transection, blunt avulsion, crush injury, partial or complete suture ligation, and ischemia due to operative devitalization of the ureteral vascular supply or cautery injury. **Overall, the ureter is most commonly injured during gynecologic surgery in the distal third or pelvic portion, which is accordingly the only location where a ureteral injury may result in a ureterovaginal fistula.** Not uncommonly, this occurs inadvertently during an attempt by the surgeon to control active bleeding or in the process of clamping large segments of tissue in an attempt to avoid bleeding.

The pelvic ureter is intimately related to the female genital tract throughout its course. In the deep pelvis, the ureter passes at the lateral edge of the uterosacral ligament and ventral to the uterine artery and then just lateral to the cervix and fornix of the vagina. In close apposition to these structures, it must be carefully avoided during any gynecologic procedure in the deep pelvis. **Any injury to the ureter that exposes the ureteral lumen (e.g., laceration) or results in delayed necrosis of a portion of the ureter (e.g., suture ligation) and subsequent urine extravasation may lead to a fistula.** A ureterovaginal fistula may result from a sequence of events including urine extravasation from the ureteral injury, urinoma formation, subsequent extension along nonanatomic planes developed during surgery, and eventual drainage through the vaginal incision or an ischemic area of the vaginal cuff. Infection, prior radiation therapy, or other factors that may impede healing probably promote the development of ureterovaginal fistulas under these circumstances.

The most common presenting symptom is the onset of constant urinary incontinence 1 to 4 weeks after surgery (Mandal et al, 1990). This may have been preceded by several days of flank or abdominal pain, nausea, and low-grade fever, presumably as a result of urinoma or obstruction of the kidney (Lee et al, 1988). Flank pain will often be masked in the postoperative period because of the use of postoperative narcotic analgesics. **Importantly, and in direct contrast to large VVF, in the setting of continuous urine leakage from a ureterovaginal fistula, patients will continue to report normal voiding habits as bladder filling is maintained from the contralateral, presumably undamaged upper urinary tract.**

Diagnosis and Management

Diagnosis of a ureterovaginal fistula can usually be accomplished with a combination of relevant history, physical examination, and appropriate radiologic studies including intravenous urography, retrograde pyelography, and cystogra-

Table 72–6. Outcomes for Vesicovaginal Fistula Repair

Author (Date)	No. of Patients	Success (%)	Approach	Comments
Eisen et al (1974)	29	90	Abdominal	Peritoneal flap
Kaser (1977)	38	92	Vaginal	Latzko
Keettel et al (1978)	168	94	156 vaginal, 6 abdominal, 6 combined	
Persky et al (1979)	7	86	6 abdominal, 1 vaginal	
Tancer (1980)	45	93	43 vaginal, 1 abdominal, 1 spontaneous closure	Latzko vaginal approach
O'Conor (1980)	42	88	Abdominal	
Wein et al (1980a)	34	88	Abdominal	
Lee et al (1988)	182	98	145 vaginal, 37 abdominal	100% success with abdominal approach
Gil-Vernet et al (1989)	42	100	Abdominal	
Wang and Hadley (1990)	16	94	Vaginal	
Blandy et al (1991)	25	100	Abdominal	Transvesical
Motiwala et al (1991)	68	94	Abdominal	58 transvesical, 10 transabdominal with omental flap
Raz et al (1993)	11	82	Vaginal	Peritoneal flap
Arrowsmith (1994)	98	96 (81% success after first attempt)	Multiple	All obstetric fistulas
Elkins (1994)	82	95 (88% success after first attempt)		All obstetric fistulas
Kristensen and Lose (1994)	18	94	Abdominal	5 ureteral reimplants required
Blaivas et al (1995)	24	96	15 vaginal, 8 abdominal, 1 spontaneous closure	
Ayhan et al (1995)	70	93	66 vaginal, 4 abdominal	
Brandt et al (1998)	80	96	Abdominal	Bladder mucosa autograft
Iselin et al (1998)	20	100	Vaginal	Vaginal cuff excision
Evans et al (2001)	37	76	Abdominal	Includes 8 malignant fistulas
Eilber et al (2003)	207	97	Vaginal	

Table 72–7. Etiology of Ureterovaginal Fistula

Gynecologic Surgery

Abdominal hysterectomy
Vaginal hysterectomy
Radical hysterectomy
Cesarean section
Anterior colporrhaphy (cystocele repair)

Other Pelvic Surgical Procedures

Vascular surgery
Urologic surgery including retropubic bladder neck suspensions
Colon surgery

Other

Locally advanced malignant disease
Radiation therapy
Pelvic trauma
Chronic inflammatory diseases (e.g., actinomycosis)

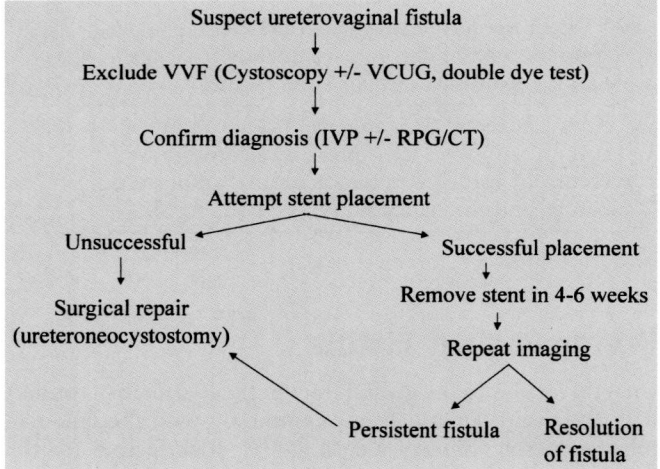

Figure 72–19. Algorithm for diagnosis and management of ureterovaginal fistula. CT, computed tomography; IVP, intravenous pyelography; RPG, retrograde pyelography; VCUG, voiding cystourethrography; VVF, vesicovaginal fistula.

phy (Mandal et al, 1990) (Fig. 72–19). **A double dye test may be of some value in differentiating between a ureterovaginal and vesicovaginal fistula as a cause of ongoing urine leakage** (Raghavaiah, 1974). Suspicion of a ureterovaginal fistula should prompt intravenous urography (Badenoch et al, 1987). **Intravenous urography most commonly will demonstrate some degree of ureteral obstruction and associated caliectasis or ureteral dilation** (Selzman et al, 1995). **These findings in the presence of constant vaginal drainage strongly suggest a ureterovaginal fistula.** Alternatively, if the fistula is mature and large, the upper urinary tract may appear completely unremarkable; however, urine will be seen opacifying the vagina before the postvoid image (Fig. 72–20). Antegrade

pyelography after nephrostomy tube decompression of a partially obstructed ureter may be associated with similar findings (Fig. 72–21). **A high oblique or lateral film may be necessary to differentiate the contrast in the bladder from that in the vagina.** A retrograde pyelogram may show the ureter and fistula well or may demonstrate an abrupt termination of the ureter 3 to 4 cm from the ureteral orifice. Retrograde pyelography may be the single best test for diagnosis of a ureteral injury (Payne, 1996). **If retrograde pyelography**

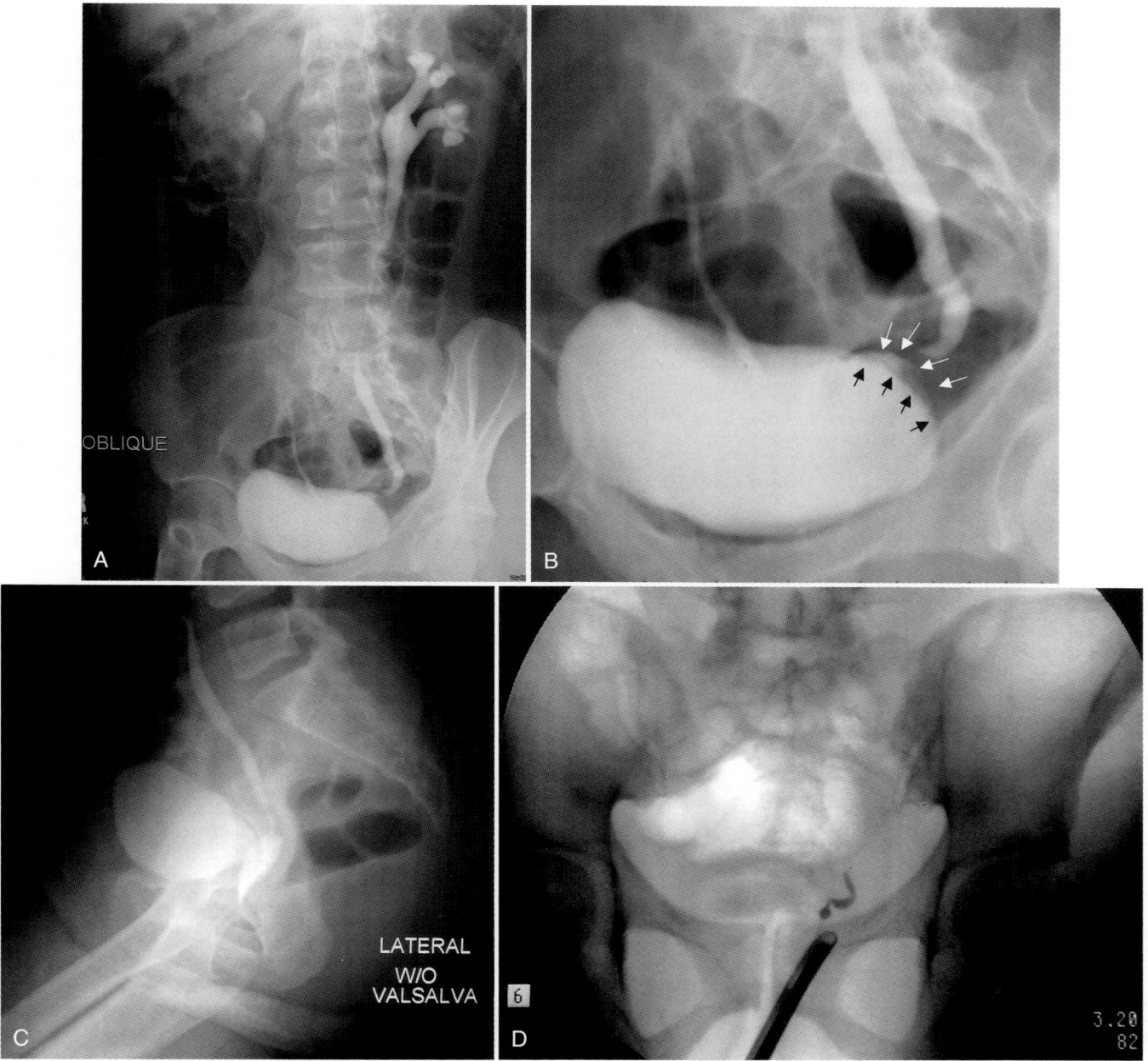

Figure 72–20. Ureterovaginal fistula. **A,** Oblique view on intravenous urography shows mild left-sided hydroureteronephrosis associated with a distal tapering of the ureter. **B,** Faint and subtle opacification of the vagina *(white arrows)* is somewhat obscured by bladder filling (bladder edge indicated by *black arrows*) on this oblique image. **C,** Lateral view demonstrates the ureter clearly entering the vagina. **D,** Retrograde pyelogram demonstrates abrupt termination of the distal ureter.

demonstrates the fistula as well as ureteral continuity, an attempt at stenting is warranted. **Cystography is performed primarily to exclude a coexistent VVF.** Most commonly, a cystogram is unremarkable unless there is preexisting vesicoureteral reflux. On occasion, a ureterovaginal fistula may be diagnosed on CT (Fig. 72–22); however, the central role of cross-sectional imaging in the setting of a ureterovaginal fistula is to evaluate for pelvic abscess or undrained urinoma.

The goal of therapy is the expeditious resolution of urine leakage, prevention of urosepsis, and preservation of renal function. Once the diagnosis is made, prompt drainage of

the affected upper urinary tract is essential (Gerber and Schoenberg, 1993) **as partial ureteral obstruction is often present.** An attempt at ureteral stenting or percutaneous nephrostomy tube decompression is warranted as soon as possible (Dowling et al, 1986; Kostakopoulos et al, 1998) if direct open surgical repair is not being immediately considered. Conservative management alone will occasionally result in fistula closure. Hulse and colleagues (1968) noted spontaneous resolution of ureterovaginal fistula in four patients in whom a ureteral stent could not be placed. Alonso Gorrea and coworkers (1986) noted that spontaneous resolution of ureterovaginal fistula is possible in patients with ureteral continuity and a normal-appearing ureter beyond the fistula; 11 fistulas were successfully managed under these criteria. Endoscopic management including ureteral stenting may be sufficient to promote closure of the fistula in some cases. Dowling and associates (1986) reported that 11 of 23 patients with ureteral injuries recognized postoperatively were successfully treated with nephrostomy tube drainage or ureteral stenting. Selzman and colleagues (1995) reported successful manage-

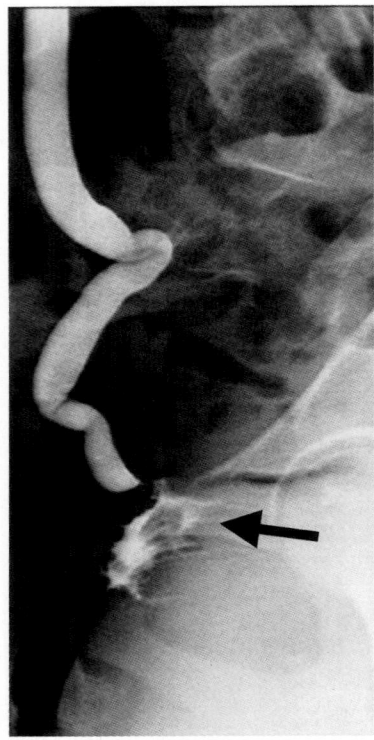

Figure 72–21. Ureterovaginal fistula. Antegrade nephrostogram demonstrates mild ureterectasis with opacification of the vagina *(arrow)*.

ment of 7 of 20 ureterovaginal fistulas with internal ureteral stenting alone. None of the seven patients in whom a ureteral stent was successfully placed required open surgery. In general, if ureteral continuity can be demonstrated on imaging, retrograde placement of a stent is often possible. In some cases, an antegrade stent placement will be successful when a retrograde attempt has failed.

If ureteral stenting is unsuccessful because of complete ureteral occlusion or prolonged leakage persists despite stenting, formal surgical repair is indicated. Timing of the repair of ureterovaginal fistula is controversial. Some authors advocate early repair (Talbert et al, 1965; Flynn et al, 1979; Badenoch et al, 1987; Blandy et al, 1991; Selzman et al, 1995); others recommend a delay of 4 to 8 weeks (Hulse et al, 1968; Lee and Symmonds, 1971). More recent literature suggests that early repair is preferred and is not associated with an increase in morbidity or higher failure rates (Payne, 1996). As noted previously, ureterovaginal fistula most commonly results from injury to the distal third of the ureter below the level of the iliac vessels. **The site of the injury and the surrounding fibrosis and inflammation usually preclude primary repair of the fistula by separation of the ureter from the vagina and closure of the involved organs. Therefore, open surgical repair most commonly involves ureteroneocystostomy.** The ureter is located and dissected as distally as possible in the pelvis. Care is taken to preserve the periureteral adventitial layer to prevent ureteral ischemia. The ureter is divided distally, and a ureteroneocystostomy is performed with or without a psoas hitch. A Boari flap may occasionally be necessary because of extensive ureteral injury. Rarely, transureteroureterostomy, ileal substitution of the ureter, or renal autotransplantation is required. In patients with a normal contralateral kidney in whom there is extensive renal damage due to obstruction or infection, nephrectomy may be the most expeditious method of management.

Successful repair of ureterovaginal fistulas is expected in more than 90% of cases. Blandy and associates (1991) reported on early repair of iatrogenic injury to the ureter in 43 cases including 30 ureterovaginal fistulas. All patients were cured by a combination of techniques including the Boari flap.

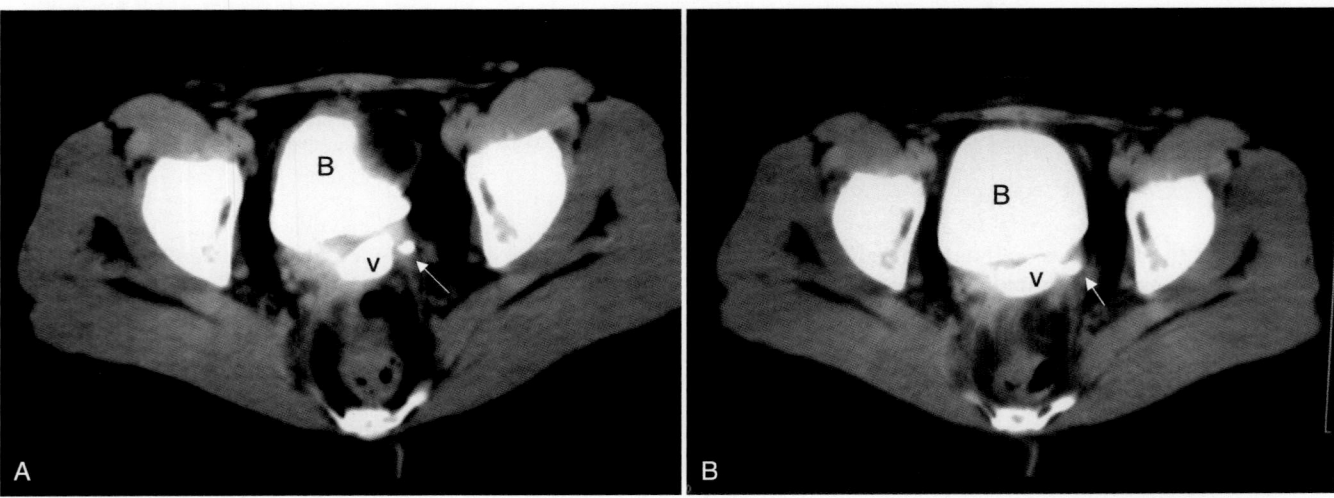

Figure 72–22. CT scan of ureterovaginal fistula. **A,** CT scan demonstrates contrast material within the bladder (B) and vagina (V). The ureter is seen *(arrow)* adjacent to the vagina. **B,** This image shows the ureter *(arrow)* entering the vagina.

Others have reported similar results (Lee and Symmonds, 1971; Flynn et al, 1979; Mandal et al, 1990).

Ureteral fistulas to other gynecologic organs have been reported. Ureterouterine fistulas may result from cesarean section, uterine malignant disease, and elective abortion (Keegan and Forkowitz, 1982; Lazarevski and Badiev, 1996; Wang and Hung, 1997; Sheen et al, 1998). Ureter–fallopian tube fistula has also been reported as a consequence of laparoscopic fulguration of endometriosis (Steckel et al, 1993).

Vesicouterine Fistula
Etiology and Presentation

Vesicouterine fistulas are among the least common urogynecologic fistulas. Fewer than 100 cases were reported in the world literature between 1908 and 1986, with no series having more than four patients (Tancer, 1986). However, the incidence of this condition is increasing in parallel with the rising numbers of low-segment cesarean sections being done worldwide (Porcaro et al, 2002). **Cesarean section is by far the most common cause of this unusual fistula** (Tancer, 1986; Miklos et al, 1995; Vu et al, 1995). Tancer (1986) related that of the 74 cases of vesicouterine fistula reported from 1947 to 1986, 57 followed low-segment cesarean section and 7 followed vaginal operative delivery; the remaining cases were related to a variety of disparate scenarios including induced abortion, hysterectomy, and dilatation and curettage. Jozwik and colleagues (1997) reported that 21 of 24 vesicouterine fistulas treated during a 12-year period followed cesarean section, the majority of which were repeated cesarean sections. Those undergoing vaginal birth after a prior cesarean section are also at risk for vesicouterine fistula (Gil and Sultana, 2001). Vesicouterine fistula may occur spontaneously as a result of a ruptured uterus during obstructed labor. In these cases, the posterior bladder wall may tear along the uterine rupture line, with the potential for a fistula. Bladder wall invasion by penetration of chorionic villi beyond the uterine serosa, placenta percreta, may also cause a vesicouterine fistula (Krysiewicz et al, 1988). A foreign body such as an intrauterine device (Schwartzwald et al, 1986), uterine artery embolization (Sultana et al, 2002), brachytherapy (Memon et al, 1998), and traumatic bladder catheterization (Futter and Baker, 1995) have been reported to cause vesicouterine fistula. Before 1947, the most common cause was high forceps vaginal delivery. In most cases, simultaneous injury to the bladder and uterus is the inciting event. An unrecognized and unrepaired ("occult") bladder injury or incorporation of a portion of the bladder during closure of the uterus after any number of operations may result in a vesicouterine fistula. The most common location of the fistula is along the posterior bladder wall in the midline or, from the genital side, just cephalad to the internal cervical os.

Unlike other types of urogynecologic fistula, **vesicouterine fistula may or may not present with constant urinary incontinence owing to the sphincter-like activity of the cervix; the exception is in the setting of an incompetent cervix, when urine leakage is constant.** In this clinical setting, which typically follows vaginal delivery, urine flows from the bladder through the fistula into the uterine cavity and then into the vagina through an incompetent cervical os. Tancer (1986) described 12 such patients with urinary incontinence as the presenting symptom of 15 patients with vesicouterine fistulas after vaginal operative delivery. However, in the setting of a relevant clinical history, vesicouterine fistula will also present with menouria and cyclic hematuria in the setting of urinary continence. **Youssef's syndrome describes the presenting symptom complex of vesicouterine fistula: menouria, cyclic hematuria with associated apparent amenorrhea, infertility, and urinary continence** (Youssef, 1957; Tancer, 1986) **in a patient who has undergone prior low-segment cesarean section.** Endometriosis of the bladder, in which cyclic hematuria may be present, must be differentiated from this condition.

Diagnosis and Management

Diagnosis of vesicouterine fistula can be made by a combination of cystoscopy and radiographic studies. Cystoscopy may demonstrate a midline lesion along the posterior bladder wall (Fig. 72–23). Urine cytology may reveal endothelial cells.

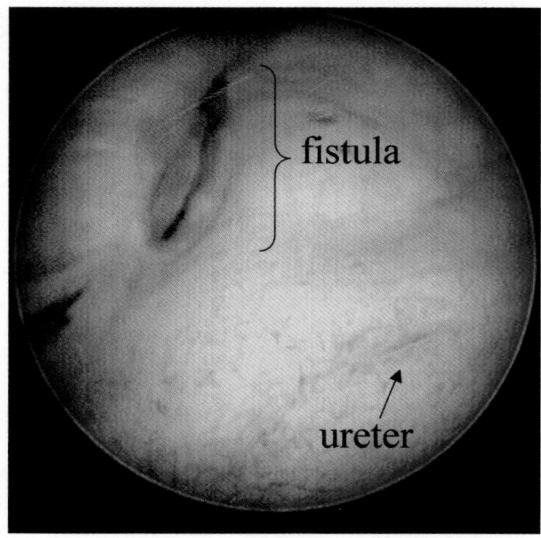

Figure 72–23. Cystoscopic view of vesicouterine fistula before repair.

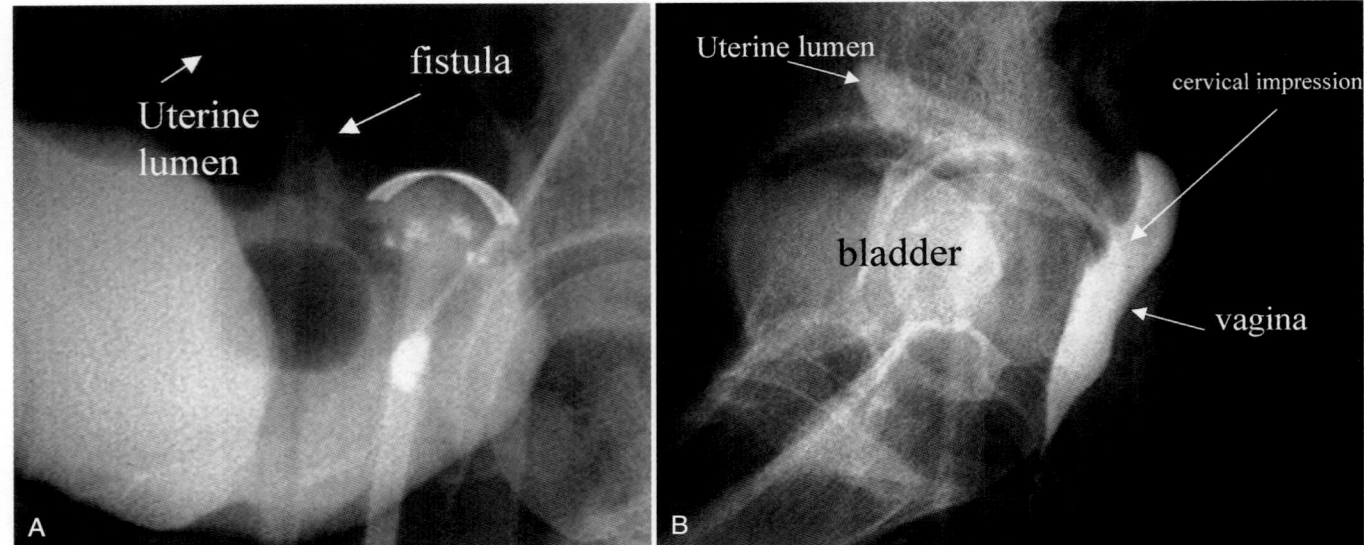

Figure 72–24. Cystogram demonstrating vesicouterine fistula in a postpartum woman. **A,** Filling of the bladder demonstrates a small amount of contrast material cephalad to the tip of the Foley catheter. The uterine cavity is faintly seen. **B,** Postvoid image demonstrates filling of the uterine cavity and cervical canal. The bladder is not well seen. This patient is immediately post partum. Contrast material in the vagina outlines the incompetent cervical canal and os.

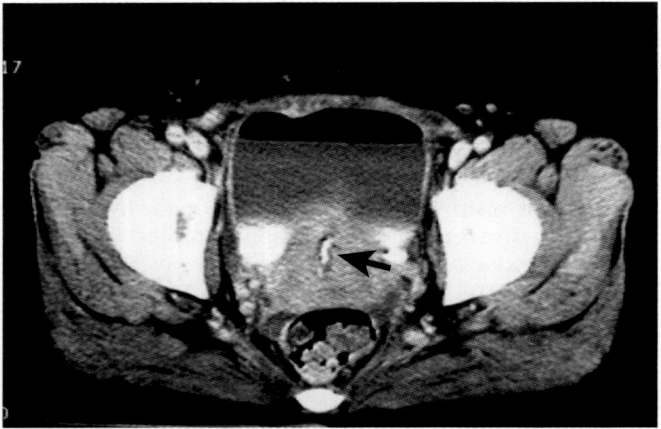

Figure 72–25. CT scan with contrast enhancement demonstrating a vesicouterine fistula. Contrast material is seen layering in the partially filled urinary bladder; contrast opacification of the uterine canal (arrow) suggests a vesicouterine fistula.

Instillation of contrast material into the bladder (cystogram) will outline the uterine cavity (Fig. 72–24), whereas a hysterosalpingogram will demonstrate filling of the bladder. Magnetic resonance imaging, CT (Fig. 72–25), and ultrasonography have been used in the diagnosis and evaluation of vesicouterine fistula as well (Mercader et al, 1995; Huang et al, 1996; Murphy et al, 1999). Intravenous urography or contrast-enhanced CT can be used to exclude concomitant ureteral injury.

Several different approaches have been advocated for the treatment of vesicouterine fistulas. Spontaneous resolution may occur, and Graziotti and associates (1978) noted that only five such cases including their case had previously been reported in the world's literature. Therefore, these authors recommend against a "precocious" surgical repair of these lesions as time may allow some fistulas to resolve without surgery. **Prolonged indwelling bladder catheterization or fulguration of the fistula track followed by bladder drainage may be successful in select cases, especially those with small, immature fistulas** (Graziotti et al, 1978; Molina et al, 1989; Ravi et al, 2003; Novi et al, 2004). **Hormonal induction of menopause will induce involution of the puerperal uterus, and this principle has been used with some success in treating this condition as well** (Hemal et al, 1994; Jozwik and Jozwik, 1999; Ravi et al, 2003). Jozwik and Jozwik (1999) reported successful treatment in eight of nine patients by hormonal manipulation.

Surgical therapy for vesicouterine fistula is contingent on the reproductive wishes of the patient. If there is no further desire for childbearing, transabdominal hysterectomy and bladder closure should be considered. Ureteral stents can be placed to facilitate identification of the ureters intraoperatively. After performance of the hysterectomy, the fistula track on the posterior bladder wall is excised and the bladder is closed primarily. An omental flap can be placed into the deep pelvis to buttress the bladder closure and to separate the bladder closure from the vaginal closure to reduce the possibility of a postoperative VVF. **For the patient who desires preservation of fertility, uterus-sparing surgery can be considered.** In a manner similar to an O'Conor transabdominal VVF repair, the bladder is opened and bivalved down to the fistula track. Careful dissection allows separation of the bladder from the uterus beyond the fistula track. The fistula track is excised from both structures, the uterus and bladder are closed individually, and an interpositional flap, usually omentum, is secured between the two organs. Fertility is possible after repair of vesicouterine fistula. Lotocki and associates (1996) reported five pregnancies with four full-term deliveries in a cohort of 16 patients who had undergone uterus-sparing surgery for vesicouterine fistula.

Urethrovaginal Fistula

Etiology and Presentation

In the industrialized world, urethrovaginal fistula most commonly results from vaginal surgery, including anti-incontinence surgery, anterior vaginal wall prolapse surgery, and urethral diverticulectomy (Henriksson et al, 1982; Webster et al, 1984; Blaivas, 1989; Glavind and Larsen, 2001). In the nonindustrialized world, similar to the etiology of VVF, obstructed labor is the most common cause of urethrovaginal fistula (Elkins, 1994) (Fig. 72–26). In the setting of obstructed labor, this lesion is due to extensive ischemic necrosis and often extends beyond the bladder neck, resulting in a combined urethral-vesicovaginal fistula. These are some of the most difficult cases to repair because of the size of the fistula, ischemia of the surrounding tissues, and implications for continence in those individuals with destruction of the bladder neck and proximal urethra. Fortunately, because of modern obstetric care in the industrialized world, these are rarely seen. **Other causes of urethrovaginal fistula include radiation therapy for pelvic malignant disease, trauma including pelvic fracture, and vaginal neoplasms.** Another important cause in the long-term care setting is urethral catheter erosion (Trop and Bennett, 1992; Andrews and Shah, 1998). In patients with poor sensation, especially the cognitively or otherwise neurologically impaired patient, pressure necrosis from a chronically indwelling catheter may result in traumatic hypospadias and urethrovaginal fistula. If this is not recognized, over time, the catheter may erode to the level of the bladder neck and beyond, effectively creating a bivalved urethra and a urethral-vesicovaginal fistula (Fig. 72–27).

Symptoms of urethrovaginal fistula are largely dependent on the size and location of the fistula along the urethral lumen. A small fistula may produce only minimal leakage, whereas a large urethrovaginal fistula can present with continuous urine drainage. **Proximal fistulas can be associated with stress incontinence, or if they are located at the bladder neck, continuous incontinence similar to that associated with VVF may result. Distal fistulas beyond the sphincteric mechanism may be completely asymptomatic or may be associated with a splayed urinary stream.** On occasion, distal

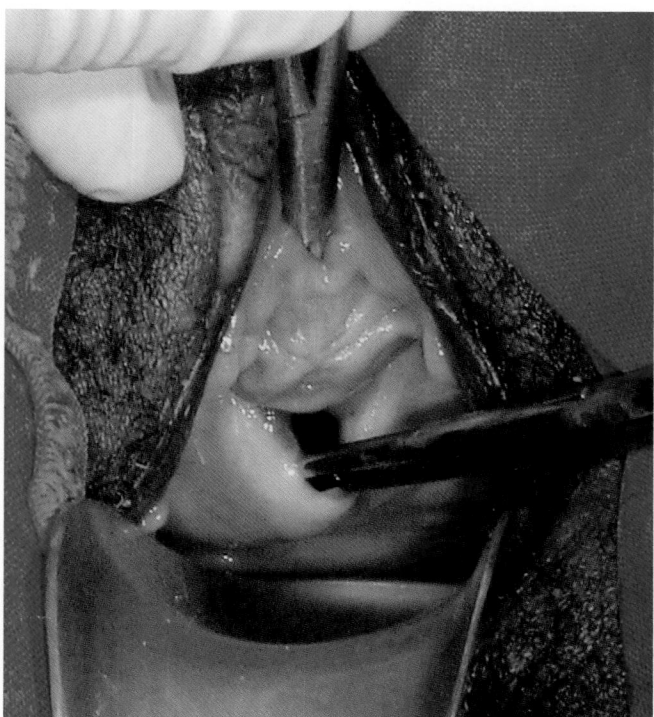

Figure 72–26. Urethrovaginal fistula at the bladder neck from obstructed labor. A hemostat is seen entering the urethral meatus. (Courtesy of Mark Morgan, MD, Department of Obstetrics and Gynecology, Hospital of the University of Pennsylvania, Philadelphia.)

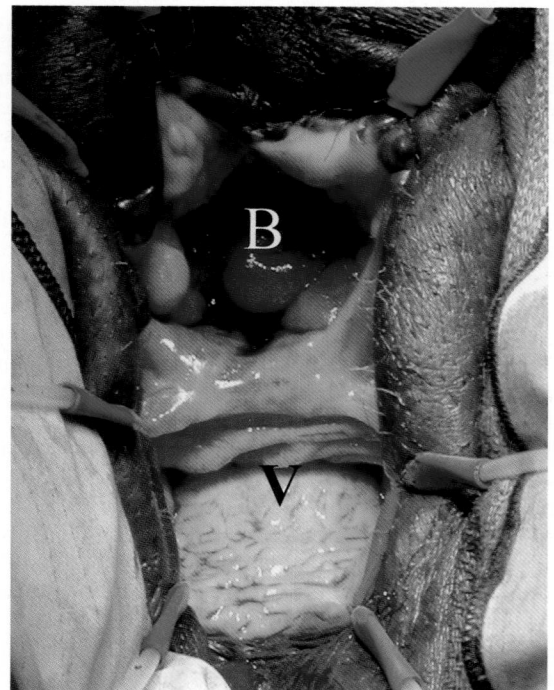

Figure 72–27. Severe complete erosion of the urethra secondary to chronic indwelling urinary catheter. This patient with advanced multiple sclerosis underwent surgical bladder neck closure and ileovesicostomy (ileal chimney). B, bladder; V, vagina.

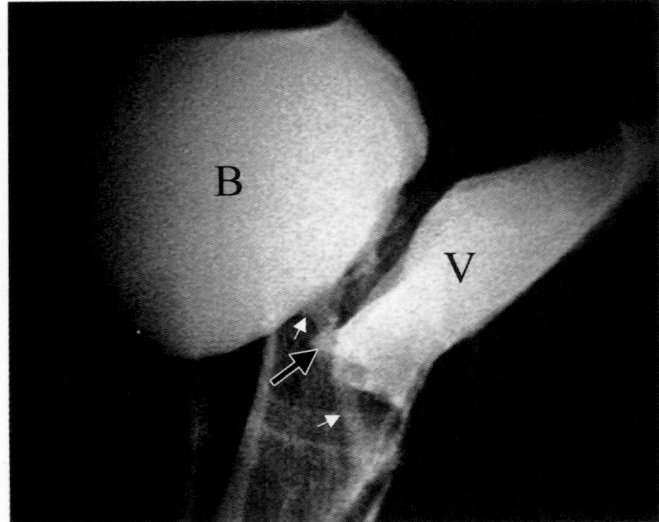

Figure 72–28. Urethrovaginal fistula on lateral voiding image from voiding cystourethrography. B, bladder; V, vagina; arrow demonstrates fistula *(black arrow)* in this patient with a primary symptom of vaginal voiding. The urethra proximal and distal to the fistula is well opacified *(white arrows)*.

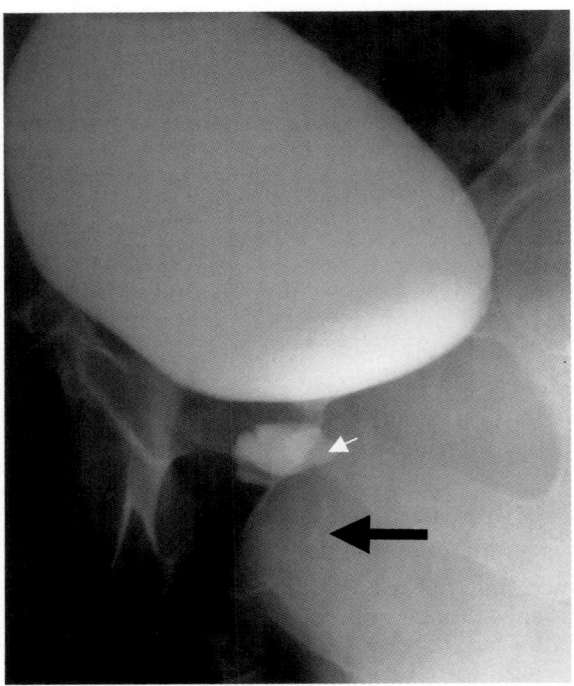

Figure 72–29. This patient was referred for the evaluation of persistent incontinence after urethral diverticulectomy. A voiding cystourethrogram demonstrates incomplete resection of the urethral diverticulum *(white arrow)* with a pinpoint postoperative urethrovaginal fistula *(black arrow* shows a small amount of contrast material faintly outlining the anterior vaginal wall). Resection of the residual diverticulum with repair of the fistula by a Martius flap was curative.

fistulas are associated with vaginal voiding and pseudoincontinence, so called because the patient complains of urinary incontinence only on arising from a seated position after voiding; this is a result of urine accumulation in the vagina during voiding that empties on standing (Fig. 72–28).

Diagnosis and Management

The diagnosis of urethrovaginal fistula can often be made on physical examination and cystourethroscopy; however, voiding cystourethrography is most useful (Fig. 72–29), especially in complex cases. Small fistulas may be difficult to locate on physical examination even with a speculum because of the surrounding vaginal rugation (Fig. 72–30). An associated VVF will be found in up to 20% of cases, and therefore a thorough evaluation of the entire lower urinary tract is warranted (Lee et al, 1988). **Endoscopic examination of the urethra should be performed.** Because of its short length, however, the female urethra may be difficult to fully examine with a standard rigid cystoscope as the irrigation fluid is discharged 1 to 2 cm proximal to the lens. A specially designed female cystoscope with a short beak is helpful in visualizing the entire urethral lumen as the irrigation fluid is discharged next to the lens, distending the adjacent urethral lumen (Fig. 72–31). Once the diagnosis is made on cystoscopy, the bladder is examined for additional fistulas. **Videourodynamics may accurately characterize any associated incontinence, including that associated with detrusor dysfunction. This study also assesses the anatomic relationship of the fistula to the bladder neck and urethra as well as examines for associated VVF.**

The surgical repair of urethrovaginal fistula is challenging and can often be more difficult than repair of VVF. This is due to several factors, including extensive soft tissue defects and the lack of local viable tissue for a multilayer repair (Keettel et al, 1978). Repair of urethrovaginal fistula usually involves the use of rotational vaginal wall flaps, but

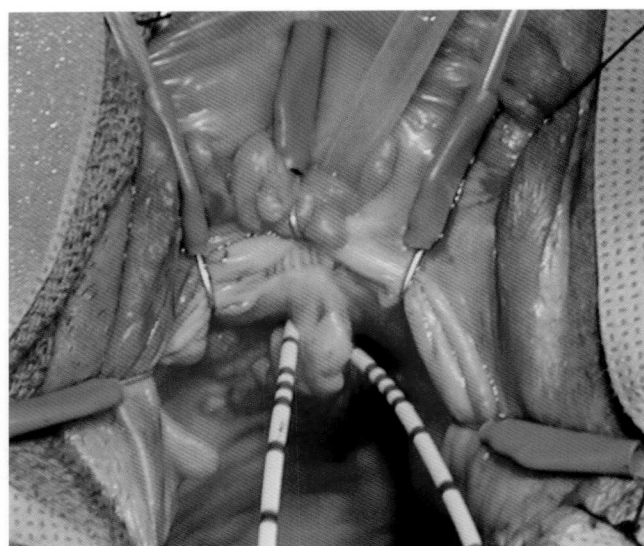

Figure 72–30. Urethrovaginal fistulas. The patient presented with complaints of ongoing urinary incontinence after multiple Marshall-Marchetti-Krantz retropubic suspensions. The ureteral catheters are seen identifying two small fistulas to either side of the midline.

anteriorly (Elkins et al, 1992) and posteriorly (Khanna, 1992) based bladder flap tubes have been used as well.

A number of factors should be considered before repair. Small fistulas may be managed by a multilayered closure, usually with an interpositional graft such as a Martius flap

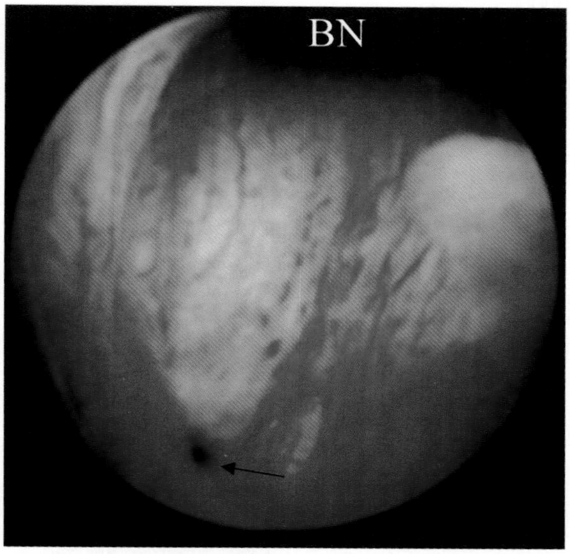

Figure 72–31. Endoscopic view of a urethrovaginal fistula *(arrow)*. This patient complained of ongoing urinary incontinence for 10 years after an endoscopic bladder neck suspension. BN, bladder neck.

(Webster et al, 1984; Leach, 1991). Larger fistulas, including those resulting from obstructed labor, may require extensive surgery with urethral reconstruction (Tehan et al, 1980; Blaivas, 1989; Khanna, 1992; Elkins et al, 1992; Wang and Hadley, 1993). **Distal fistulas without associated voiding symptoms or incontinence may be observed or, alternatively, can be managed with an extended meatotomy** (Lamensdorf et al, 1977). Quality of the vaginal tissues should be optimized before operative repair; this may include the use of antibiotics to treat associated infection or topical estrogen treatment in those patients with significant atrophic vaginitis. Similar to VVF repair, timing of repair is controversial. Some authors have suggested that a waiting time of 2 to 6 months is advisable in most patients, with a waiting period of up to 1 year in those with radiation fistulas (Webster et al, 1984; Zimmern et al, 1986). Other authors have advocated immediate repair as soon as the vaginal tissues are free of infection and inflammation (Blaivas, 1989; Blaivas et al, 1995).

Operative Technique. The repair of urethrovaginal fistula is conceptually similar to the vaginal flap repair of VVF described previously. The patient is placed in the dorsal lithotomy position, and urethral and suprapubic catheters are placed. A ring retractor is helpful for exposure. Allis clamps are used to reflect the vaginal wall cephalad, exposing the fistula. In some patients, an episiotomy may facilitate exposure to the fistula, improving visualization for repair (Webster et al, 1984). However, because of the distal (with respect to the vagina) location of these lesions, this is not usually necessary.

After infiltration of the fistula margins with injectable saline, the fistula track is circumscribed several millimeters from its edges (Fig. 72–32). The fistula track and immediate surrounding epithelium are not typically excised as this will make a larger defect in the urethra that will be more difficult to close without undue tension. However, the vaginal wall is dissected several millimeters from the edge of the circum-

scribed fistula track in a radial orientation. An inverted U- or J-shaped incision is marked out along the anterior vaginal wall with the base of the U or J at the margin of the circumscribed fistula track. This is infiltrated with injectable saline, and the anterior vaginal wall flap is developed, exposing the underlying periurethral fascia to the level of the bladder neck or beyond, depending on the size and location of the fistula. If a concomitant anti-incontinence procedure is planned, dissection may be carried laterally from the edges of the flap at the level of the bladder neck and the retropubic space entered.

The edges of the circumscribed track are reflected over the fistula and apposed with absorbable suture, the first layer of closure. The periurethral fascia is then reapproximated in a perpendicular suture to the first layer of closure, thereby minimizing overlap. At this point, a Martius flap or other adjuvant flap can be secured over the periurethral fascia. Finally, the anterior vaginal wall flap is brought over the repair, including a Martius flap if it is used, and secured beyond the original fistula track.

Adjuvant Flaps and Procedures in the Repair of Urethrovaginal Fistula. One of a variety of types of soft tissue flaps is often an important component of a successful urethrovaginal fistula repair as fistula excision and vaginal flap advancement have been historically associated with a high rate of failure (Birkhoff et al, 1977; Keettel et al, 1978; Davis et al, 1980; Patil et al, 1980; Leach, 1991; Fall, 1995; Bruce et al, 2000; Rangnekar et al, 2000). A variety of adjuvant procedures have been used in the repair of urethrovaginal fistula, including most commonly a Martius labial fat flap but also gracilis and rectus abdominis muscle, myocutaneous flaps, vaginal wall flaps, fibrin glue, and free labial skin grafts (Keettel et al, 1978; McKinney, 1979; Tolle et al, 1981; Webster et al, 1984; Krogh et al, 1989; Leach, 1991; Izes et al, 1992; Candiani et al, 1993; Fall, 1995; Rangnekar et al, 2000).

Webster and colleagues (1984) described 11 patients with urethrovaginal fistulas, of whom 10 underwent surgical repair. Of the 10 patients, 3 patients had recurrence of the fistula, all of whom were salvaged with a subsequent repair combined with a Martius labial fat pad interposition; 2 patients had primary repair with a Martius flap (see earlier section on VVF for a more complete discussion of Martius flap), and both were cured. These authors recommended a Martius flap for all patients undergoing urethrovaginal fistula repair. Bruce and colleagues (2000) reported on the use of a pedicled rectus abdominis muscle flap based on the inferior epigastric artery for complex and refractory urethrovaginal fistula in six patients. All patients had at least one failed attempt at repair with a Martius flap. Of the six patients, six remained successfully closed at a mean follow-up of 23 months; one patient had persistent urge incontinence postoperatively. The authors concluded that the rectus abdominis flap is a useful adjunct in the repair of complex or refractory urethrovaginal fistula.

Suprapubic as opposed to urethral catheterization has been suggested postoperatively for at least 14 days to allow adequate healing (Tehan et al, 1980; Webster et al, 1984), although the use of only a single drainage catheter postoperatively is not universally agreed on; other authors use both suprapubic and urethral catheters (Leach, 1991). Anticholinergics are

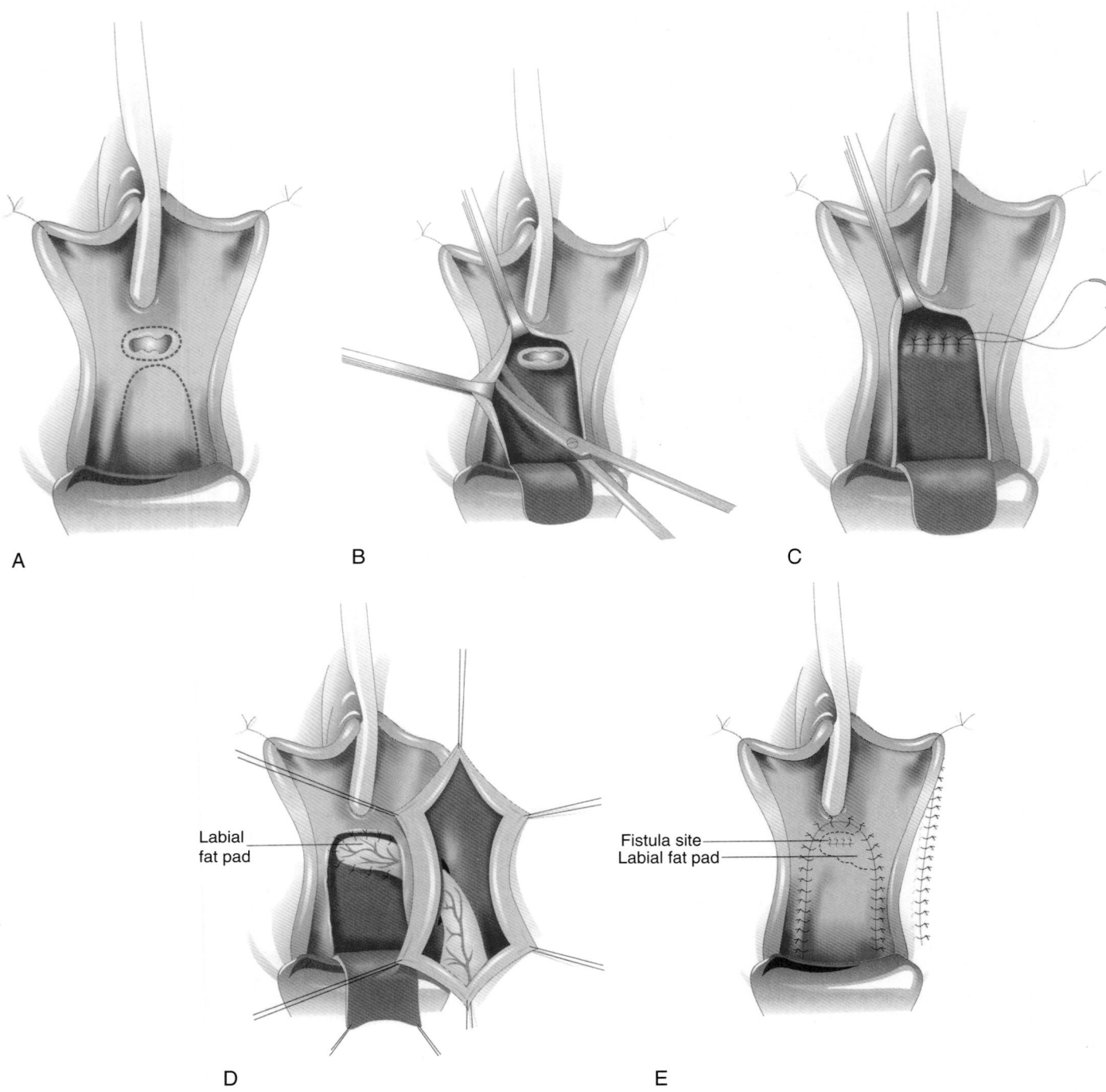

A

B

C

Labial
fat pad

D

Fistula site
Labial fat pad

E

Figure 72–32. Operative diagram of urethrovaginal fistula repair. **A,** Inverted U incision is made in the anterior vaginal wall with the base of the U at the proximal margin of the fistula. The fistula is circumscribed. **B,** The anterior vaginal wall flap is mobilized, exposing the periurethral fascia. Dissection is also carried out laterally and distally from the margins of the fistula. The edges of the fistula track are not excised. **C,** The epithelialized margins of the fistula track are reapproximated with absorbable suture for the initial layer of closure. The periurethral fascia may be closed as a second layer, imbricating the initial layer of closure (not shown). **D,** A Martius flap may be harvested from the labia majora and tunneled as an additional layer of closure. **E,** The anterior vaginal wall flap is advanced over the closure and secured with absorbable suture. (From Leach GE, Kobashi KC: Urethral diverticulum and fistula. In Cardozo L, Staskin D, eds: Textbook of Female Urology and Urogynecology. London, Isis Medical Media, 2001:721-745.)

administered liberally to reduce bladder irritability. Voiding cystourethrography with contrast material administered through the suprapubic tube is usually performed to document resolution of the fistula.

Stress incontinence may persist after repair of ure-throvaginal fistula. Whether repair of stress incontinence should be done concomitantly with the fistula surgery or deferred until after repair of the fistula is controversial. Blaivas (1989) argued that sphincteric incontinence should be repaired at the time of fistula surgery with a Martius flap interposed between the fistula repair and a pubovaginal fascial sling. Webster and colleagues (1984) suggested that stress incontinence associated with a proximal or mid urethral urethrovaginal fistula should not be corrected until the fistula is closed and the patient reassessed for persistent incontinence. These authors suggest, however, that stress incontinence associated with distal urethrovaginal fistula can be repaired concomitantly.

Overall, the success rate of urethrovaginal fistula repair is variable, but it is not generally considered to be as high as that for VVF repair (Gerber and Schoenberg, 1993). Not uncommonly, two or more procedures may be necessary for a satisfactory result (Webster et al, 1984).

Table 72–8. Causes of Vesicoenteric Fistula*

Diverticulitis	65%-75%
Malignant disease	10%-15%%
Crohn's disease	5%-6%
Other (trauma, appendiceal abscess, foreign body)	<5%

*Morse and Dretler, 1974; Amendola et al, 1984; Pollard et al, 1987; Schofield, 1988; Walker et al, 2002.

Table 72–9. Presenting Symptoms of Vesicoenteric Fistula*

Pneumaturia	52%-77%
Fecaluria	36%-51%
Urinary tract infection symptoms (frequency, urgency, dysuria)	44%-45%
Fever and chills	41%
Abdominal pain	25%
Nonspecific gastrointestinal symptoms	25%
Hematuria	5%-22%
Orchitis	10%
Urine per rectum	5%

*Morse and Dretler, 1974; Pontari et al, 1992; Najjar et al, 2004.

KEY POINTS: URETHROVAGINAL FISTULA

- Distal urethrovaginal fistulas are often asymptomatic, whereas proximal fistulas may present with intermittent or constant urine leakage.

- Urethrovaginal fistulas due to surgical trauma may be difficult to visualize on physical examination or cystoscopy.

- Diagnosis of a urethrovaginal fistula is best made with voiding cystourethrography.

- Repair of urethrovaginal fistula can be challenging and often involves an interpositional tissue flap because of the relative lack of surrounding connective tissue in the mid and distal urethra.

UROENTERIC FISTULA
Vesicoenteric Fistula

Etiology and Presentation

Vesicoenteric fistulas commonly occur in the setting of bowel disease, such as diverticulitis, colorectal carcinoma, and Crohn's disease. Less common causes include irradiation, infection, and trauma (external penetrating trauma as well as iatrogenic surgical trauma). Diverticulitis is the most common cause of colovesical fistula in most series, accounting for approximately 70% of cases (Mileski et al, 1987; Pollard et al, 1987; Walker et al, 2002; Najjar et al, 2004) (Table 72–8). The second most common cause of vesicoenteric fistula is cancer, followed by Crohn's disease. The peak incidence of vesicoenteric fistula is between 55 and 65 years of age, although fistulas due to Crohn's disease present much earlier (Badlani et al, 1980). Approximately 2% of patients with diverticulitis may experience a colovesical fistula as a complication of their disease (Hafner et al, 1962). In a multi-institutional retrospective review of 400 patients with Crohn's disease during a 10-year period, 8 patients (2%) were found to have enterovesical fistulas (Gruner et al, 2002) . Underlying gastrointestinal tract disease strongly influences the type of fistula; ileovesical fistulas are more common in Crohn's disease than in cancer, and colovesical fistulas are usually due to diverticulitis.

Symptoms of vesicoenteric fistula may originate from the urinary or gastrointestinal tract; however, in general, lower urinary tract symptoms are more common at presentation (Morse and Dretler, 1974; Ray et al, 1976). In the early stages, symptoms are nonspecific and relate to lower urinary tract dysfunction. Lower urinary tract symptoms include pneumaturia, frequency, urgency, suprapubic pain, recurrent urinary tract infections, and hematuria (Table 72–9). **Pneumaturia, noted in 50% to 70% of cases, is considered the most common presenting symptom** (Morse and Dretler, 1974; Pontari et al, 1992; Solem et al, 2002; Jarrett and Vaughan, 1995). Gastrointestinal symptoms may include fecaluria and tenesmus. **The classic presentation of vesicoenteric fistula is described as Gouverneur's syndrome and consists of suprapubic pain, urinary frequency, dysuria, and tenesmus** (Sans et al, 1986). Recurrent urinary tract infections or cystitis refractory to antibiotic therapy may suggest a colovesical fistula (Rao et al, 1987). Although it is rare for enterovesical fistula to present with sepsis (Woods et al, 1988), patients presenting with such signs are found to have urinary tract obstruction in approximately 70% of cases (Mileski et al, 1987).

Diagnosis

Many studies exist for the diagnosis of enterovesical fistula; however, there are significant problems with both false negatives and false positives among the diagnostic modalities, and thus the diagnosis is often made on clinical grounds. **Cystoscopy has the highest yield in identifying a potential lesion, with some type of abnormality noted on endoscopic examination in more than 90% of cases** (Morse and Dretler, 1974). **However, the findings on cystoscopy are often nonspecific and include localized erythema and papillary or bullous change; a definitive diagnosis by cystoscopy can be made in only 35% to 46% of cases** (Woods et al, 1988; Pontari et al, 1992). Cystoscopy and biopsy of abnormal-appearing tissue or an established fistula track in the setting of a history of malignant disease are indicated to evaluate for the possibility of a malignant fistula.

Cross-sectional imaging, especially CT scan, has become the imaging modality of choice (Goldman et al, 1984, 1985; Jarrett and Vaughan, 1995; Gruner et al, 2002). CT or magnetic resonance imaging (Haggett et al, 1995) may localize the fistula track as well as the involved segment of bowel. **The triad of findings on CT that are suggestive of colovesical fistula consists of (1) bladder wall thickening adjacent to a loop of thickened colon, (2) air in the bladder (in the absence of previous lower urinary tract manipulation), and (3) presence of colonic diverticula** (Labs et al, 1988). Labs and coworkers (1988) correctly diagnosed colovesical fistula on CT in 11 of 12 patients with surgically confirmed lesions. **CT is now generally considered to be the most sensitive and specific modality for the diagnosis of colovesical fistula** (Najjar et al, 2004), **with diagnostic accuracy as high as 90% to 100%** (Goldman et al, 1985; Jarrett and Vaughan, 1995). **The high diagnostic accuracy of CT in detecting enterovesical fistula relates to its ability to detect even a small amount of air in the bladder.** Although air in the bladder on diagnostic imaging is suggestive of colovesical fistula, false positives may be caused by recent instrumentation (catheterization, cystoscopy) or an active urinary tract infection with a gas-forming organism. CT scanning should be done after the administration of an oral contrast agent but before the intravenous administration of contrast material to permit detection of barium within the bladder. Ultrasonography has also been reported to be useful in the diagnosis of colovesical fistula. A characteristic "beak" sign may be noted; however, this study is not usually performed in the routine evaluation of the patient with a suspected enterovesical fistula (Chen et al, 1990).

Although commonly used, cystography and transrectal contrast studies (e.g., barium enema) are generally less likely to demonstrate the fistula. Rao and coworkers (1987) reported that 14 of 24 barium enemas either demonstrated or were suggestive of colovesical fistula in a series of surgically treated patients. Barium enema examination and colonoscopy may be valuable adjunctive studies in evaluating for colonic disease, such as malignant neoplasm, as a cause of the fistula; the preoperative knowledge of such a condition can considerably alter management decisions. Nevertheless, barium enemas have limited utility in the diagnosis of enterovesical fistula because of low sensitivity (Amendola et al, 1984). **The Bourne test, however, can be a useful adjunctive study in the evaluation of colovesical fistula** (Bourne, 1964). **As described, the Bourne test is performed after a nondiagnostic barium enema study. The first voided urine after the barium enema is immediately centrifuged and then examined radiographically. Radiodense particles in the urine are considered a positive test result and evidence for a vesicoenteric fistula.** Amendola and colleagues (1984) reported a positive Bourne test result in 9 of 10 patients with colovesical fistula; the Bourne test result was the only evidence for a colovesical fistula in 7 such patients who had an otherwise normal evaluation with a combination of other diagnostic studies.

The diagnosis of vesicoenteric fistula may be confirmed by the oral administration of activated charcoal, which in the setting of a fistula will appear in the urine as black particles (Geier et al, 1972). This test provides no anatomic information about the location of the fistula but is useful in confirming the diagnosis in suspected cases. Intrarectal administration of vital dyes has been advocated for the diagnosis of occult colovesical fistula; however, the dye may be absorbed and then excreted in the urine, giving a false-positive test result (Deshmukh et al, 1977).

Management

Nonoperative management is a viable option in selected patients with vesicoenteric fistula. Amin and colleagues (1984) described 4 of 30 patients with colovesical fistula secondary to diverticulitis who were observed without active intervention for between 3 and 14 years. There were no significant long-term sequelae in this select population of patients. **In nontoxic, minimally symptomatic patients with nonmalignant causes of enterovesical fistulas, a trial of medical therapy including intravenous total parenteral nutrition** (Dudrick et al, 1999), **bowel rest, and antibiotics may be warranted. This may be the preferred initial approach, especially in patients with Crohn's disease, in whom the notion of immediate exploratory laparotomy and bowel resection is often discouraged because of the chronic relapsing nature of the disease** (Evans et al, 2003a).

The goal of operative management is to separate and close the involved organs with minimal anatomic disruption and normal long-term function of both systems. Unfortunately, enterovesical fistula may be complicated by intense pelvic inflammation, pelvic abscess, and phlegmon formation in some cases. Bowel resection or partial cystectomy may be necessary to obtain viable tissue margins to ensure adequate, watertight closure of the involved viscera. An interpositional flap of greater omentum is often placed between the repaired bowel and urinary bladder, preventing overlapping suture lines and providing a well-vascularized surface for healing.

Both one- and two-stage procedures have been advocated, depending on the clinical circumstances (Morse and Dretler, 1974; Castro, 1975; Ray et al, 1976; Morrison and Addison, 1983; Mileski et al, 1987; Pollard et al, 1987; Rao et al, 1987; Walker et al, 2002; Najjar et al, 2004). A one-stage procedure involves removal of the fistula, closure of the involved organs, and primary reanastomosis of the bowel after resection of the involved bowel segment. A two-stage approach advocates removal of the fistula, closure of the involved organs, and construction of a temporary proximal diverting colostomy, with a later return to the operating room for colostomy takedown once the fistula track is demonstrated to be closed. **The choice**

of whether to proceed with a one-stage or two-stage repair is influenced by the location and cause of the fistula, the patient's general condition, the presence of a pelvic abscess, and the presence of colonic obstruction (McConnell et al, 1980). **Patients with an inflammatory cause of the fistula but without gross contamination can be treated with a one-stage procedure, whereas those with unprepared bowel, gross contamination, or abscess may require a two-stage procedure** (Mileski et al, 1987). However, most patients with colovesical fistula present electively with lower urinary tract symptoms, not emergently in extremis with sepsis (Mileski et al, 1987). Therefore, adequate preoperative support including bowel preparation and appropriate antibiotics can be used in the majority of cases, allowing an elective one-stage approach.

Laparoscopic management of colovesical fistula has been reported, albeit with a relatively high rate of conversion to open repair (Joo et al, 1997).

KEY POINTS: VESICOENTERIC FISTULA

- The most common cause of vesicoenteric fistula is diverticulitis.

- Presenting symptoms are usually urinary, most commonly pneumaturia.

- Diagnosis is generally made with a combination of cystoscopy and cross-sectional imaging, including CT scan.

- Repair of colovesical fistula involves a one- or two-stage procedure, depending on a number of clinical factors including the presence of gross fecal contamination, infection, and prepared bowel.

Ureteroenteric Fistula

Fistulas between the ureter and the bowel are most likely to occur in the setting of inflammatory bowel disease such as Crohn's disease. The segment of bowel most likely to be involved is the terminal ileum (Banner, 1987); **thus, most cases of ureteroenteric fistula are unilateral and right sided** (Sigel et al, 1977). Rarely, diverticulitis (Ney et al, 1986; Cirocco et al, 1994; Maeda et al, 1998) or ulcerative colitis will lead to a left-sided ureteroenteric fistula (Sigel et al, 1977). Involvement of the ureter is usually at the level of the sacral promontory (Sigel et al, 1977). Other causes of ureteroenteric fistula include calculous disease, tuberculosis, external and iatrogenic (surgical) trauma, radiation therapy, and transitional cell carcinoma (Javadpour et al, 1973; Sankaran et al, 1974; McElwee et al, 1983; Sumiya et al, 1985; Flood et al, 1992; Goetz et al, 1992; Toporoff et al, 1992; Oh et al, 2002). Unlike vesicoenteric fistula, ureteroenteric fistula is more likely to present with bowel as opposed to urinary tract symptoms. Pain may also be reported in the hip, flank, or anterior thigh.

The diagnosis is most often made by retrograde pyelography, although CT and intravenous urography are useful as well. Barium contrast studies of the small bowel will often show a diseased segment of bowel but will only rarely demonstrate the fistula. Treatment involves ureterolysis and possible bowel resection. Ureteral resection is not necessary if it can be separated from the involved bowel segment and stented. Unfortunately, in many of these cases, significant renal damage has occurred before the definitive diagnosis, and thus nephrectomy may be necessary for definitive management (Sigel et al, 1977).

Pyeloenteric Fistula

Pyelointestinal fistulas represent an epithelialized connection between the renal pelvis or collecting system of the kidney and the gastrointestinal tract. **Chronic inflammatory disease, such as xanthogranulomatous pyelonephritis or other infectious disease involving the kidney or bowel, has been historically the most common cause of this condition** (Schwartz et al, 1970; Greene et al, 1975; Bhargava et al, 1982; Cheatle et al, 1985; Desmond et al, 1989; Yildiz et al, 1993; Majeed et al, 1997). **However, iatrogenic surgical trauma, especially that related to percutaneous nephrolithotomy and lithotripsy, has been associated with an increasing number of such fistulas** (LeRoy et al, 1985; Culkin et al, 1990). Penetrating external trauma, malignant disease, ulcer disease, ingested foreign bodies, and complex calculous disease may also result in pyeloenteric fistula (Brust and Morgan, 1974; Mooreville et al, 1988; Ginsberg et al, 1996; Blatstein and Ginsberg, 1996; Chen et al, 2002). **Right-sided pyeloenteric fistulas most often involve the duodenum because of their close anatomic relationship, whereas left-sided pyeloenteric fistulas most commonly involve the descending colon.**

The majority of patients present with nonspecific symptoms including malaise, nonspecific gastrointestinal symptoms, urinary frequency, flank mass, or tenderness. Approximately 60% to 70% of patients present with flank pain, fever, and pyuria (Desmond et al, 1989). **Iatrogenic fistulas as a result of endourologic procedures may present with minimal symptoms.** In some cases, they are noted only incidentally on postoperative nephrostography (Culkin et al, 1990). Diagnosis can be made with a combination of urography, retrograde pyelography, and nephrostography. The gastrointestinal tract may be studied with barium swallow or enema.

Historically, pyeloenteric fistulas were treated by nephrectomy and closure of the gastrointestinal tract (Greene et al, 1975); however, given the changing nature of the cause of these lesions, in many cases the fistula may be initially treated conservatively, especially if it is associated with a normally functioning kidney. **A large nephrostomy tube, enteric suction or bowel rest, antibiotics, and removal of any foreign body (e.g., stone) may be attempted. Internal stenting of the urinary tract may be pursued for maximal drainage** (Desmond et al, 1989). **Fistulas associated with a poorly functioning kidney are best treated by primary closure of the bowel and nephrectomy.**

Urethrorectal (Rectourethral or Prostatorectal) Fistula

Acquired rectourethral fistula may occur in the male under a variety of clinical circumstances, including prostatectomy

for benign or malignant disease, cryotherapy, pelvic radiotherapy, anorectal surgery, external penetrating trauma (al-Ali and Kashmoula, 1997; Bukowski et al, 1995), **urethral instrumentation** (Thompson and Marx, 1990), **locally advanced prostatic or rectal malignant disease, infection such as tuberculosis** (Okaneya et al, 1988) **or ruptured prostatic abscess, and inflammatory disease such as Crohn's disease** (Fazio et al, 1987; Stamler et al, 1985). Congenital rectourethral fistula associated with imperforate anus is covered in Chapter 123, Voiding Dysfunction in Children: Non-Neurogenic and Neurogenic.

Etiology and Presentation

The incidence of rectourethral fistula after radical retropubic prostatectomy is low, but owing to the frequency with which the operation is performed, it is the most common cause of rectourethral fistula in most modern series (Stephenson and Middleton, 1996; Nyam and Pemberton, 1999; Renschler and Middleton, 2003). **Rectal injury during radical prostatectomy occurs in less than 1% to 2% of patients** (Igel et al, 1987; Borland and Walsh, 1992; McLaren et al, 1993; Guillonneau et al, 2003). In the Mayo retropubic prostatectomy series, there were 27 documented rectal injuries in 2212 patients (McLaren et al, 1993). In this series, 26 of 27 injuries were recognized intraoperatively and repaired; 6 patients underwent temporary colostomy, and 4 patients developed rectourethral fistula. In a community-based practice, Harpster and colleagues (1995) reported rectal injuries in 7 of 516 patients undergoing retropubic prostatectomy (1.4%) and 1 of 17 patients undergoing radical perineal prostatectomy. Five rectal injuries were recognized and repaired intraoperatively. There were three rectourethral fistulas reported in this series; none closed with conservative management, and all required formal repair. Rassweiller and associates (2003) reported 1 rectourethral fistula in a series of 219 patients undergoing retropubic prostatectomy but 7 rectourethral fistulas in 538 patients undergoing laparoscopic radical prostatectomy. All operations were performed by the same surgical team. Guillonneau and colleagues (2003) reported a 1.3% incidence of rectal injury in 1000 consecutive patients undergoing laparoscopic radical prostatectomy. Of 13 injuries, 11 were recognized and repaired intraoperatively with a two-layer closure; one of these patients subsequently underwent temporary colostomy for complications related to the injury. Both patients with rectal injuries recognized postoperatively underwent colostomy; one of the two patients presenting late with a rectal injury developed a rectourethral fistula requiring a primary surgical closure.

In the setting of radical prostatectomy, a prior history of pelvic radiation therapy, rectal surgery, or transurethral resection of the prostate is associated with an increased risk of rectourethral fistula (Thompson and Marx, 1990; McLaren et al, 1993). Rectourethral fistulas that occur after radical prostatectomy are usually seen at the vesicourethral anastomosis and are often due to an unrecognized rectal injury at the time of surgery. When a rectal injury is recognized and repaired intraoperatively, however, rectourethral fistula is extremely uncommon. Borland and Walsh (1992) reported 10 rectal injuries in 1000 nonirradiated patients undergoing radical prostatectomy at Johns Hopkins Hospital; however, no patient developed a rectourethral fistula. Of the

10 patients, 9 had a two-layer closure performed with an omental interpositional flap at the time of injury. One patient underwent a temporary diverting colostomy as the rectal injury was diagnosed and repaired on postoperative day two. All patients had an anal sphincter dilation performed and received 7 to 14 days of postoperative antibiotics.

The reported incidence of rectourethral fistula after cryosurgical ablation of the prostate is between 0.5% and 2% in patients undergoing primary therapy for localized carcinoma of the prostate (Zippe, 1996; Long et al, 2001), **whereas the rate of rectourethral fistula after cryotherapy as salvage therapy for prostate cancer is somewhat higher at approximately 3.3%** (Chin et al, 2001). **The incidence of rectourethral fistula after brachytherapy for prostate cancer is reported as 0.4%** (Theodorescu et al, 2000). Rectourethral fistulas have also been reported after high-intensity focused ultrasound treatment (Uchida et al, 2002; Blana et al, 2004), high-intensity focused ultrasound treatment combined with external beam radiotherapy (6% incidence) (Gelet et al, 2004), laparoscopic radical prostatectomy (Guillonneau et al, 2003; Katz et al, 2003; Rassweiler et al, 2003; Dafnis et al, 2004), and transurethral thermotherapy for benign prostatic hyperplasia (Norby and Frimodt-Moller, 2000). The incidence of rectourethral fistula in Crohn's disease is estimated to be approximately 0.3% (Stamler et al, 1985) (Fig. 72–33). Fistulas due to Crohn's disease are complex, and management should be individualized (Stamler et al, 1985; Fazio et al, 1987; Santoro et al, 1995; Cools et al, 1996; Rius et al, 2000).

The presentation of rectourethral fistula is variable. **Symptoms may include fecaluria, hematuria, urinary tract infection, nausea, vomiting, and fever.** Peritonitis and sepsis may

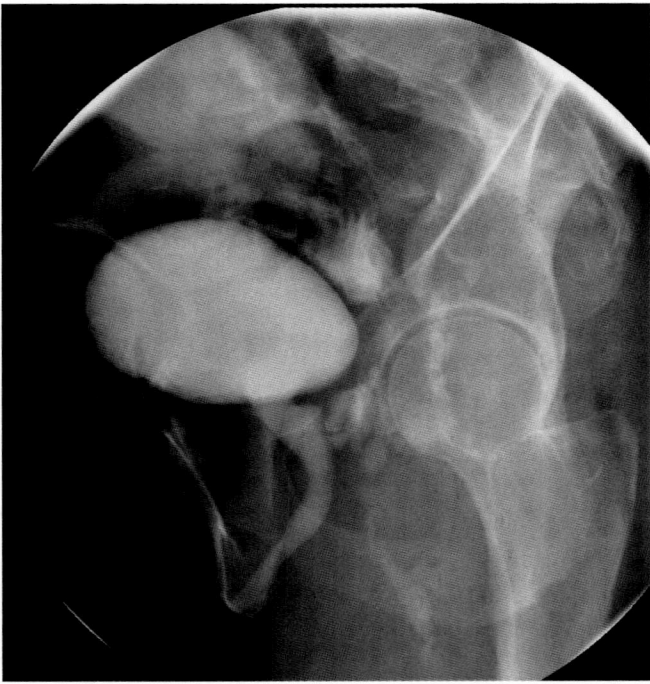

Figure 72–33. Rectourethral fistula due to Crohn's disease. Contrast material is seen posterior to the bladder on this voiding image from voiding cystourethrography. (Courtesy of Nancy Curry, MD, Department of Radiology, Medical University of South Carolina, Charleston.)

occur as well. Digital rectal examination often permits palpation of the fistula track along the anterior rectal wall. **Cystoscopy and sigmoidoscopy** (Shin et al, 2000) **visualize the fistula track in the majority of cases and provide a mechanism for biopsy. In patients with a history of pelvic malignant disease, biopsy of the fistula is suggested to evaluate for a local recurrence of the tumor** (Shin et al, 2000). Voiding cystourethrography or retrograde urethrography usually provides a definitive diagnosis of rectourethral fistula (Fig. 72–34). The exact anatomic location and size of the fistula are also usually well delineated on voiding cystourethrography or retrograde urethrography, providing important information for surgical planning. Lateral projections may be necessary to visualize small fistulas because contrast material in the rectum or urethra can sometimes obscure extremely thin fistulous tracks. **Upper tract imaging should be performed in patients with rectourethral fistulas to exclude a related ureteral injury. It is important to make an assessment of continence and sphincteric function in patients with rectourethral fistula after radical prostatectomy. Given the location of most rectourethral fistulas at or near the vesicourethral anastomosis and the membranous urethra, there is a risk for persistent severe stress incontinence postoperatively after rectourethral fistula repair in those patients with stress incontinence preoperatively.** In patients with rectourethral fistula and severe stress incontinence, closure of the rectourethral fistula may not be sufficient to bring about continence in many patients. Additional procedures may be needed to bring about a satisfactory result in these patients; this is an important issue to discuss in preoperative counseling of the patient.

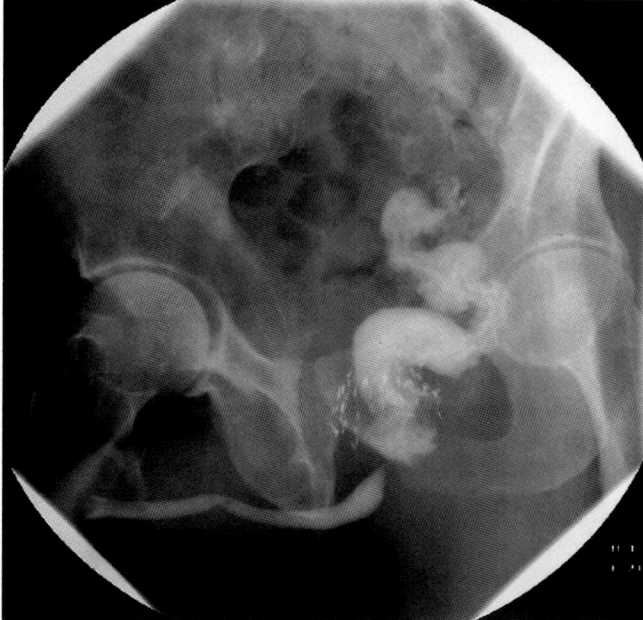

Figure 72–34. Rectourethral fistula after brachytherapy for carcinoma of the prostate. A retrograde urethrogram demonstrates filling of the rectum in this patient who presented several years after brachytherapy with fecaluria. The bladder is not opacified. The brachytherapy seeds are seen in the area of the prostate.

Management

Most rectourethral fistulas will require surgical repair (Bukowski et al, 1995; Stephenson and Middleton, 1996), although it is clear that some will close with conservative management. **Rectourethral fistula after open or laparoscopic prostatectomy may heal spontaneously with catheter drainage, bowel rest, and intravenous hyperalimentation. In some cases, fecal diversion is necessary.** Rassweiler and colleagues (2003) reported that six of eight patients with rectourethral fistulas were treated successfully in such a manner; two patients required a temporary colostomy. Noldus and associates (1999) reported closure with conservative management in 7 of 13 patients with rectourethral fistula after radical prostatectomy or cystoprostatectomy; 6 patients eventually were successfully closed with a transanal Latzko procedure (see later). Successful minimally invasive management has been reported as well with endoscopic suturing, fulguration of the fistula track, and application of fibrin glue (Wilbert et al, 1996).

Surgical repair of rectourethral fistula can be challenging, and the basic tenets of operative fistula repair are especially relevant in these cases (see Table 72–2). Several surgical approaches have been advocated and are outlined. **Single and staged repairs have been described for the repair of rectourethral fistula.** The controversy surrounding the staged repair centers on the issue of whether to perform fecal diversion at all or to perform it before or at the time of repair of the urinary tract. Some authors have advocated fecal diversion and staged repair of all rectourethral fistulas (Shin et al, 2000). This is considered the standard conservative approach and, in combination with an indwelling urethral catheter, permits a trial of spontaneous healing of the fistula without open manipulation of the urinary tract. In support of the single-stage repair, a successful one-stage approach limits the potential morbidity and cost of multiple procedures that, by design, accompany the staged repair. **Suggested guidelines for cases in which a one-stage approach might be appropriate include surgically induced, small rectourethral fistulas not associated with infection, abscess, or a poor bowel preparation** (Wood and Middleton, 1990). **Staged repairs might be considered in cases of large fistulas and those associated with radiation therapy, uncontrolled local or systemic infection, immunocompromised states, or inadequate bowel preparation at the time of definitive repair** (Stephenson and Middleton, 1996).

Transrectal approaches with and without division of the anal sphincter have been described for the operative repair of rectourethral fistula. **The York-Mason procedure is a transrectal, transsphincteric approach that has been shown to be effective with low morbidity** (Henderson et al, 1981; Prasad et al, 1983; Wood and Middleton, 1990; Stephenson and Middleton, 1996; Fengler and Abcarian, 1997; Renschler and Middleton, 2003). **Classically, this is a staged repair with fecal diversion performed before repair of the rectourethral fistula. However, in patients with small, nonirradiated fistulas, a single-stage approach can be employed, provided that a vigorous bowel preparation and broad-spectrum antibiotics are used** (Renschler and Middleton, 2003). For repair of the urinary tract, the patient is placed prone on the operating room table in the jack-knife position. A full-thickness incision through the posterior anus and dorsal rectal wall is performed and deepened down to the level of the coccyx through the external anal sphincter (Fig. 72–35). Care is taken to mark or tag each layer of the anal sphincter as it is divided. Later in the procedure during closure, careful anatomic reapproximation of the layers of the external anal sphincter is necessary to avoid the devastating complication of anal incontinence postoperatively. The anorectal incision as described provides excellent exposure of the fistula in the anterior rectal wall. The fistula track is excised, and the anterior rectal wall is mobilized circumferentially around the fistula margins. The urethra is closed and then the anterior rectal wall is closed. Finally, the rectal mucosa is reapproximated, providing a three-layer closure. Alternatively, after excision of the rectourethral fistula, an anterior rectal wall flap can be developed and advanced over the fistula (al-Ali et al, 1997) in a fashion similar to the transvaginal repair of VVF with use of the vaginal wall (see previous discussion under VVF repair). Closure of the incision is performed by reapproximating the posterior rectal wall and then sequentially closing the layers of the anal sphincter in an anatomic fashion. Results with the York-Mason procedure have been excellent. In the largest series of patients undergoing the York-Mason procedure, Renschler and Middleton (2003) reported a successful repair in 22 of 24 patients. One of the two failures was subsequently repaired with another York-Mason procedure. No serious complications were reported, and no patient developed anal incontinence or anal stenosis. Similar excellent results have been noted by other authors (Prasad et al, 1983; Bukowski et al, 1995; Fengler and Abcarian, 1997).

In contrast to the transrectal, transsphincteric approach, the transanal approach to rectourethral fistula repair does not involve division of the anal sphincter. Exposure of the fistula is provided by dilation of the anus and fixed retraction. The Latzko procedure is one such approach (Noldus et al, 1999; Hata et al, 2002). Similar to the Latzko method described previously for transvaginal VVF repair (see earlier discussion), the fistula track and surrounding rectal mucosa are denuded in all four quadrants. The fistula is then closed in three layers. The major disadvantages to this approach are the relatively poor exposure and the lack of maneuverability within the operative field. Rectal advancement flaps have also been used to successfully treat rectourethral fistula through a transanal approach (Fazio et al, 1987; Dreznik et al, 2003; Garofalo et al, 2003).

A perineal approach to rectourethral fistula has been advocated by some authors in selected cases (Bukowski et al, 1995; Nyam and Pemberton, 1999; Youssef et al, 1999; Zmora et al, 2003). This is a familiar approach for many urologists and has the added advantage of local access to a variety of potential interpositional flaps. Excellent results have been obtained with the perineal approach in combination with an interpositional flap including gracilis muscle (Ryan et al, 1979; Rius et al, 2000; Zmora et al, 2003), pedicled dartos muscle (Venable,

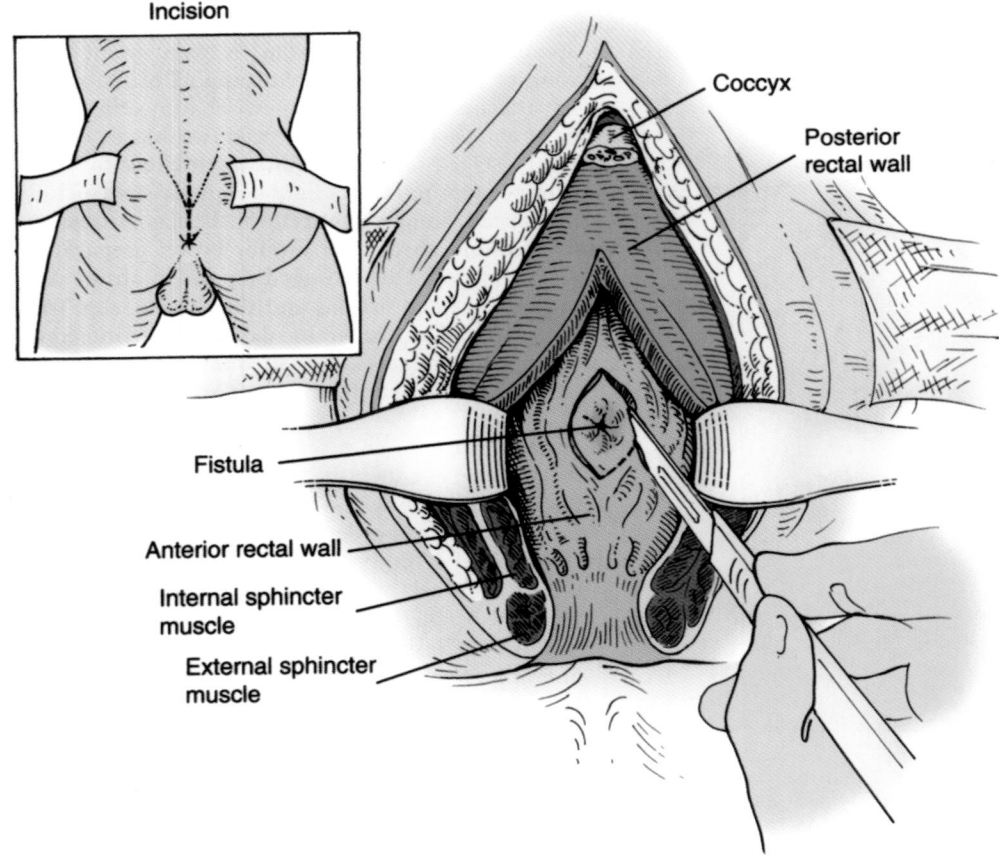

Figure 72–35. Diagram of York-Mason approach to the repair of rectourethral fistula. (From Middleton RG: Rectourethral fistula repair. In Krane RJ, Siroky MB, Fitzpatrick JM, eds: Operative Urology. Philadelphia, Churchill-Livingstone, 2000:286.)

Incision

Coccyx

Posterior rectal wall

Fistula

Anterior rectal wall

Internal sphincter muscle

External sphincter muscle

1989; Youssef et al, 1999; Yamazaki et al, 2001), penile skin (Morgan, 1975), levator muscle (Goodwin et al, 1958), and bladder (Kokotas and Kontogeorgos, 1983). Transabdominal approaches to rectourethral fistula have been described with limited success (Bukowski et al, 1995; Nyam and Pemberton, 1999; Shin et al, 2000). The principal advantage to this technique is the availability of greater omentum for an interpositional flap. Potential disadvantages include the morbidity and prolonged postoperative convalescence associated with a laparotomy incision, the poor exposure of the operative field with limited maneuverability in the deep pelvis, and the risk of urinary and fecal incontinence.

The repair of rectourethral fistulas after brachytherapy or cryosurgical ablation of the prostate can be especially difficult. These fistulas may be large and are associated with considerable induration, fibrosis, and ischemia for a variable distance around the fistula, limiting reconstructive options. Urinary tract reconstruction may not be possible in some of these cases, necessitating urinary diversion. Moreiera and colleagues (2004) described 11 patients with rectourethral fistula after brachytherapy for the treatment of prostate cancer, all of whom underwent diverting colostomy; 3 patients with satisfactory baseline continence underwent primary repair by a York-Mason approach with a gracilis flap, 7 patients underwent urinary diversion combined with radical pelvic surgery (6 cystoprostatectomy, 1 prostatectomy), and 1 refused repair. Izawa and coworkers (2000) reported on the management of severe complications of cryosurgical ablation of the prostate, including two cases of prostatopubic fistula and one rectourethral fistula; two of these patients underwent cystoprostatectomy, and one had a bladder neck closure and continent reconstruction.

KEY POINTS: RECTOURETHRAL FISTULA

- Rectourethral fistulas are an uncommon outcome that results most commonly from the surgical treatment of localized prostate cancer.

- Diagnosis of rectourethral fistula can be confirmed with voiding cystourethrography.

- Treatment of rectourethral fistula most commonly involves surgical repair; however, select patients may respond to conservative therapy, including Foley catheter drainage.

UROVASCULAR FISTULA

Fistulas between the urinary tract and the vascular system are rare but have increased in frequency with the rapid integration of minimally invasive interventions in the upper urinary tract, such as percutaneous access procedures (Clayman et al, 1984; Segura et al, 1985) **and indwelling ureteral stents** (Kar et al, 1984; Smith, 1984; Teuton et al, 1987; Sacks and Miller, 1988; Cass and Odland, 1990). These fistulas involve communications between the upper urinary tract including the collecting system or ureter and an artery or vein.

Renovascular and Pyelovascular Fistula

The most common cause of renovascular or pyelovascular fistula is a procedure in which percutaneous renal access is required, such as percutaneous nephrolithotomy (Clayman et al, 1984; Segura et al, 1985; Lang, 1987; Lee et al, 1987). Typically, these fistulas are caused by puncture of an intrarenal vascular structure during construction or dilation of the nephrostomy track. The damaged vessel may bleed on puncture or may not hemorrhage immediately because of external compression and tamponade from the catheter in the nephrostomy track. However, on removal of the catheter, brisk bleeding may be noted into the relatively lower pressure renal collecting system (Patterson et al, 1985). Alternatively, a long-term indwelling nephrostomy tube may lead to pyelovascular fistula formation. In this setting, a chronic indwelling large-bore nephrostomy tube may erode into an adjacent renal vessel with resulting hemorrhage after removal of the tube. Lee and associates (1987) reported an 11.2% incidence of bleeding requiring transfusion and a 1.2% incidence of bleeding requiring surgical or angiographic intervention after percutaneous nephrolithotomy in 582 patients. Patterson and colleagues (1985) reported a vascular injury in 0.9% of 1032 patients undergoing percutaneous renal stone surgery. Segura and coworkers (1985) reported a 3% transfusion rate in 1000 patients undergoing percutaneous nephrolithotomy. Other causes of renovascular fistula include external penetrating and blunt (Stower et al, 1989) trauma, infection, and open renal surgery including partial nephrectomy.

Renovascular fistula may present with life-threatening hemorrhage and hypovolemic shock or intermittent gross hematuria. After percutaneous nephrolithotomy, these fistulas may appear on removal of the nephrostomy tube with brisk bleeding out of the flank from the nephrostomy tube track in combination with brisk hematuria, or they may present several days to weeks later with only hematuria (Clayman et al, 1984; Patterson et al, 1985).

Treatment of renovascular fistula is contingent on the presentation, etiology, and hemodynamic stability of the patient. Patients with severe hemorrhage on removal of the nephrostomy tube can be temporized in some instances by replacement of the tube or, in large mature tracks, by placement of a Foley catheter to tamponade the bleeding. In patients with ongoing bleeding, transcatheter angiographic embolization of the lacerated vessel is recommended (Clayman et al, 1984; Patterson et al, 1985). Flank exploration is occasionally necessary with partial or simple nephrectomy to control hemorrhage.

Ureterovascular Fistula

Rarely reported before the advent of indwelling ureteral stents, ureterovascular fistula is becoming increasingly common. Most reported ureterovascular fistulas are ureter–iliac artery fistulas, although ureter–iliac vein fistulas have been reported as well (Teuton et al, 1987). Ureteroaortic fistulas are

---

of healthy tissue. **Iatrogenic fistulas due to percutaneous access procedures can be managed nonoperatively in some cases** (Lallas et al, 2004). For patients undergoing surgical exploration, a double-lumen endotracheal tube may be useful

2003;169:1033-1036.

Falk HC, Tancer ML: Vesicovaginal fistula; an historical survey. Obstet Gynecol 1954;3:337-341.

Gerber GS, Schoenberg HW: Female urinary tract fistulas. J Urol 1993;149:229-236.

Table 72–10. Predisposing Risk Factors in 37 Patients with Ureteroarterial Fistula

hematuria. **Intermittent gross hematuria or the sudden onset of massive hematuria in a patient with an indwelling stent and a history of previous iliac artery surgery or radia-**

Iselin CE, Aslan P, Webster GD: Transvaginal repair of vesicovaginal fistulas after hysterectomy by vaginal cuff excision. J Urol 1998;160(pt 1):728-730.

Lee RA, Symmonds RE, Williams TJ: Current status of genitourinary fistula. Obstet Gynecol 1988;72(pt 1):313-319.

Margolis T, Mercer LJ: Vesicovaginal fistula. Obstet Gynecol Surv 1994; 49:840-847.

McConnell DB, Sasaki TM, Vetto RM: Experience with colovesical fistula. Am J Surg 1980;140:80-84.

O'Conor VJ Jr, Sokol JK, Bulkley GJ, Nanninga JB: Suprapubic closure of vesicovaginal fistula. J Urol 1973;109:51-54.

Renschler TD, Middleton RG: 30 years of experience with York-Mason repair of recto-urinary fistulas. J Urol 2003;170(pt 1):1222-1225.

Tancer ML: Vesicouterine fistula—a review. Obstet Gynecol Surv 1986;41: 743-753.

Turner-Warwick R: The use of the omental pedicle graft in urinary tract reconstruction. J Urol 1976;116:341-347.

73 Bladder and Urethral Diverticula

ERIC S. ROVNER, MD

BLADDER DIVERTICULA

FEMALE URETHRAL DIVERTICULA

BLADDER DIVERTICULA

Bladder diverticula represent a herniation of the bladder urothelium through the muscularis propria of the bladder wall. This results in the typical finding of a variably sized, thin-walled, urine-filled structure adjacent to and connecting with the bladder lumen through a narrow neck or ostium. **On histologic examination, the diverticulum wall is composed of mucosa, subepithelial connective tissue or lamina propria, scattered thin muscle fibers, and an adventitial layer** (Fig. 73–1) (Peterson et al, 1973; Gil-Vernet, 1998). **A fibrous capsule or pseudocapsule outer shell is often present and may be a useful surgical plane for excision** (see later discussion). The outside wall of the bladder diverticulum may contain some residual scattered strands or bundles of smooth muscle; however, these are disorganized and nonfunctional. Therefore, bladder diverticula generally empty poorly during micturition, leaving a large postvoid residual urine volume that results in the characteristic findings on presentation and imaging.

Classification, Pathophysiology, and Etiology

Bladder diverticula may be classified as either congenital or acquired. Pathophysiologic features, presentation, and imaging may differentiate between these two types. **Congenital diverticula usually present during childhood, with a peak incidence in those younger than 10 years** (Boechat and Lebowitz, 1978). **These are usually solitary, occur almost exclusively in boys** (Stage and Tank, 1992; Sarihan and Abes, 1998), **and are located lateral and posterior to the ureteral orifice. The primary causation, in those without coexisting lower urinary tract conditions, appears to be a congenital weakness at the level of the ureterovesical junction and not bladder outlet obstruction** (Johnston, 1960; Hutch, 1961; Hutch et al, 1961; Stephens, 1979). Blane and colleagues (1994) reported the incidence of bladder diverticula in chil-

dren to be approximately 1.7% in a pediatric genitourinary database of more than 5000 cases. These authors suggested that the finding of more than one bladder diverticulum may warrant further investigation to rule out an underlying pathologic (i.e., neurogenic, anatomic) condition. Congenital bladder diverticula are usually solitary but larger in comparison with those associated with obstruction or neurogenic bladder dysfunction (Gearhart, 2002). Congenital bladder diverticula may occur in the presence of normal voiding dynamics in the absence of bladder outlet obstruction (Cendron and Alain, 1972; Barrett et al, 1976). However, there are reports of secondary bladder outlet obstruction when diverticula extend distally toward the bladder neck (Taylor et al, 1979) and even urinary retention (Epstein et al, 1982; Verghese and Belman, 1984; Oge et al, 2002). **Typically, congenital bladder diverticula are found in smooth-walled bladders and are not associated with significant trabeculation on cystoscopic examination** (Hutch, 1961). However, in patients with prune-belly syndrome or posterior urethral valves, bladder diverticula may be located at the dome and be associated with aberrant voiding dynamics or anatomy. These are to be distinguished from the urachal diverticula seen in some pediatric urologic conditions. Congenital bladder diverticula have been noted in association with a number of congenital syndromes, including Menkes syndrome (kinky-hair or copper deficiency syndrome) (Harcke et al, 1977; Daly and Rabinovitch, 1981), Williams syndrome (Babbitt et al, 1979; Blane et al, 1994; Schulman et al, 1996), Ehlers-Danlos syndrome (Breivik et al, 1985; Levard et al, 1989; Schippers and Dittler, 1989; Rabin et al, 1991; Bade et al, 1994; Cuckow et al, 1994; Burrows et al, 1998), and fetal alcohol syndrome (Lewis and Woods, 1994). Whether there is a genetic predisposition to the formation of bladder diverticula in individuals without congenital syndromes is unclear, although congenital bladder diverticula have been reported in twins (Beall and Berger, 1978) and possibly as an autosomal dominant trait in a family (Hofmann et al, 1984).

Acquired (also termed secondary) diverticula occur most commonly in the setting of bladder outlet obstruction or neurogenic vesicourethral dysfunction but may also be iatrogenic. Similar to the congenital type, these diverticula are also located most commonly at the ureterovesical hiatus (Van Arsdalen and Wein, 1992) but occur elsewhere in the bladder as well. **Acquired diverticula in men usually occur after the age of 60 years, which corresponds to the age at development**

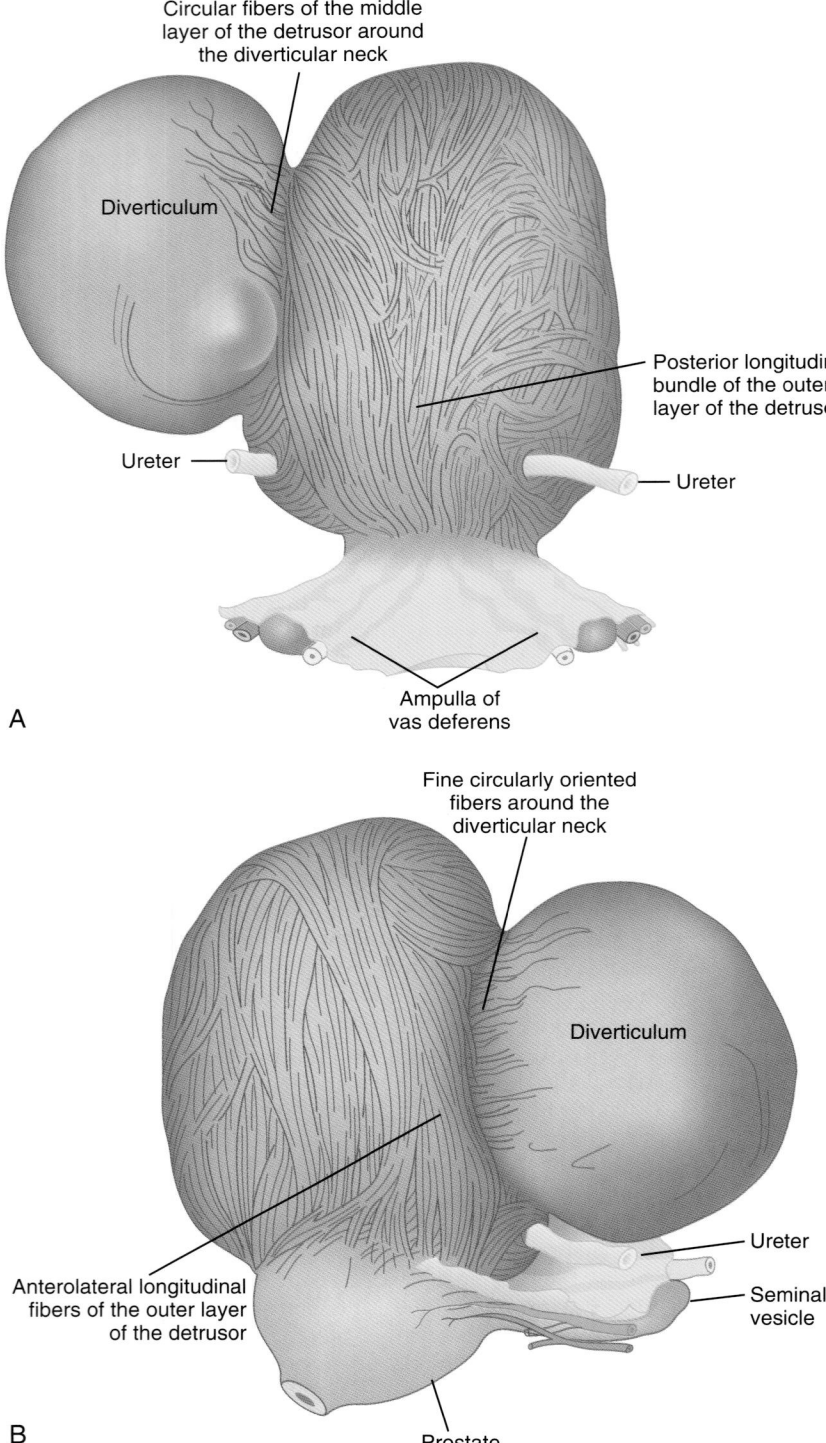

Circular fibers of the middle
layer of the detrusor around
the diverticular neck

Diverticulum

Posterior longitudinal
bundle of the outer
layer of the detrusor

Ureter

Ureter

Ampulla of
vas deferens

A

Fine circularly oriented
fibers around the
diverticular neck

Diverticulum

Ureter

Seminal
vesicle

Anterolateral longitudinal
fibers of the outer layer
of the detrusor

Prostate

B

Figure 73–1. Drawing of bladder and diverticulum. **A,** Posterior view: 1, ampulla of vas deferens; 2 and 2′, ureters; 3, posterior longitudinal bundle of the outer layer of the detrusor; 4, diverticulum; 5, circular fibers of the middle layer of the detrusor around the diverticular neck. **B,** Lateral view: 1, seminal vesicle; 2, ureter; 3, prostate; 4, anterolateral longitudinal fibers of the outer layer of the detrusor; 5, diverticulum; 6, fine circularly oriented fibers around the diverticular neck.

of prostatic enlargement (Fig. 73–2). Bladder outlet obstruction, including that due to benign and malignant disease of the prostate, and urethral stricture are the most commonly associated factors in adults, although obstruction is not considered to be present in all cases (Blacklock et al, 1983). **Acquired diverticula are usually multiple, typically found in** **association with significant bladder trabeculation** (Wesselhoeft et al, 1963), **and much more common in men than in women** (Senger et al, 1952; Pool and Hacker, 1966). Bladder diverticula in women are uncommon (Gillon et al, 1988) and in the absence of obstruction are rare (Safir et al, 1998) (Fig. 73–3). Historically, the reported prevalence of

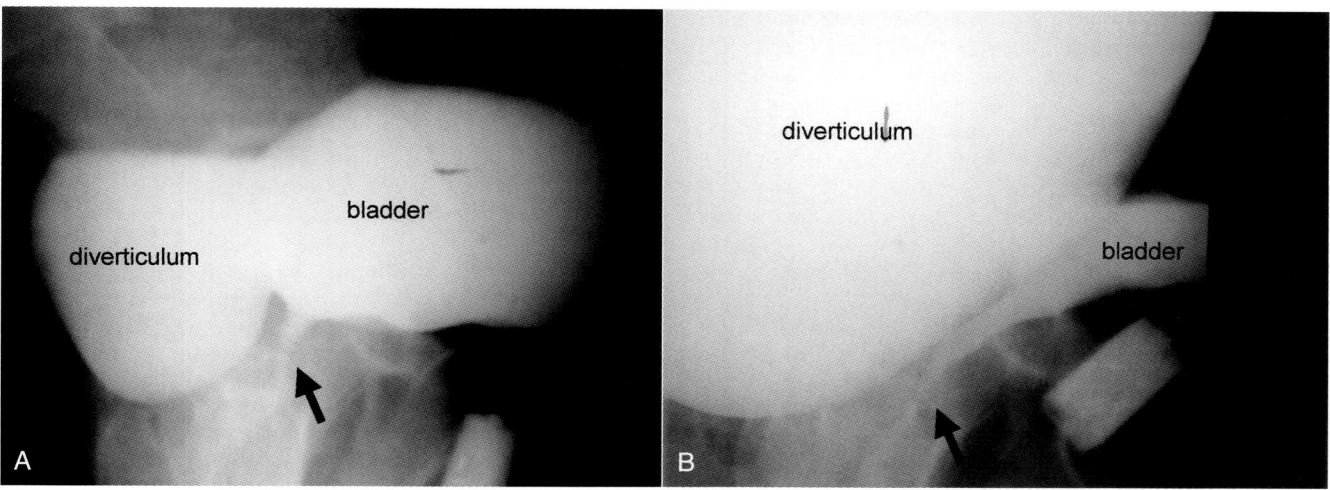

Figure 73–2. Voiding cystourethrogram demonstrating a bladder diverticulum in a man. **A,** The diverticulum is seen posterior to the bladder on this lateral voiding image (*arrow* points to urethra). There is a fluid-fluid level within the diverticulum representing the settling of relatively denser contrast medium below the urine. **B,** Later image demonstrates near-emptying of the bladder with enlargement of the diverticulum.

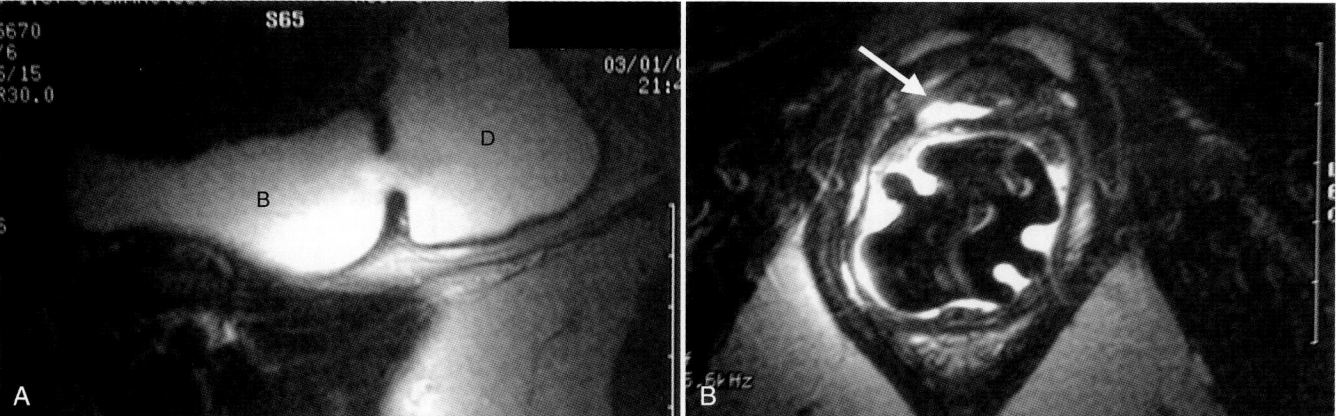

Figure 73–3. Bladder and urethral diverticulum in a female patient. **A,** MRI of a bladder diverticulum. B, bladder; D, bladder diverticulum. **B,** Endoluminal MRI demonstrating urethral diverticulum (*arrow* points to urethral diverticulum). Urodynamics revealed bladder outlet obstruction in this female patient, presumably due to the urethral diverticulum.

moderate-sized to large bladder diverticula in association with "prostatism" is approximately 1% to 6% (Burns, 1944). Acquired bladder diverticulum may also be found in children and young adults secondary to a number of conditions including bladder neck dysfunction, posterior urethral valves, and neurogenic vesicourethral dysfunction. **If the diverticulum encompasses the ureteral orifice in the setting of a neurogenic bladder and vesicoureteral reflux, it is termed a Hutch diverticulum** (Hutch, 1952). These diverticula may also occur in the setting of dysfunctional voiding.

Bladder diverticula may also be iatrogenic in nature (Hernandez et al, 1997; Suzuki et al, 2002). Inadequate closure of the muscle layers of the bladder wall after cystotomy for any indication may result in formation of a bladder diverticulum at a weak point of the suture line. Bladder diverticula may also occur after ureteral reimplantation surgery at the ureteroneocystostomy site (Ahmed and Tan, 1982; Sheu et al, 1998).

Diagnosis and Evaluation

Presentation

Acquired bladder diverticula do not typically produce specific symptoms. Because large bladder diverticula empty poorly or incompletely during voiding, symptoms and signs, if present, are usually attributed to urinary stasis within the diverticulum or, alternatively, to its mass effect in the lower abdomen and pelvis. When the patient is queried retrospectively, symptoms such as incomplete bladder emptying, lower abdominal fullness, and double voiding may be attributed to some large bladder diverticula. These symptoms, however, are nonspecific and can be due to prostatic enlargement, obstruction, or a number of other lower urinary tract conditions as well. **Most bladder diverticula are, in fact, diagnosed during the investigation of nonspecific lower urinary tract symptoms, hematuria, or infection or, alternatively, noted incidentally during radiographic or endoscopic investigation of**

these conditions. Congenital bladder diverticula most often present with urinary tract infection (Bauer and Retik, 1974; Pieretti and Pieretti-Vanmarcke, 1999), but hematuria, abdominal pain, or an abdominal mass may be present as well. Inguinal hernias containing bladder diverticulum have also been reported (Scardino and Upson, 1953; Bolton and Joyce, 1994; Buchholz et al, 1998; Schewe et al, 2000).

Urinary tract infection in the male patient has been associated with bladder diverticula; it is often an infection in a man that provides the impetus for further clinical investigation, which in part may uncover the diverticulum. Whether bladder diverticula result in a predisposition for urinary tract infection or whether the presence of a bladder diverticulum confers an increased difficulty in eradicating an existing infection is unclear (Shah, 1979; Taylor et al, 1979). Nevertheless, urine analysis and urine culture are important in the evaluation of bladder diverticulum. Abnormalities of the urine sediment are common in patients with bladder diverticula. Pyuria and hematuria are often present. In fact, relapsing or persistent pyuria unresponsive to antibiotic therapy may be an indication for bladder diverticulectomy. Urine cytology should be considered in most patients with bladder diverticula, especially when nonoperative management is being considered.

Imaging

The diagnosis of bladder diverticula relies on radiographic and endoscopic findings. Bladder diverticula are part of the radiologic continuum that includes cellules and saccules. Cellules, saccules, and bladder diverticula are thought to represent increasingly larger and therefore more severe manifestations of the same pathologic process involving elevated intravesical voiding pressure (Talner et al, 2000). **Cellules and saccules represent small outpouchings between hypertrophied bands of bladder muscle, with saccules generally being larger than cellules. However, there are no universally agreed on minimum size requirements between cellules, saccules, and bladder diverticula, and the differentiation between these three entities is often subjective and arbitrary** (Talner et al, 2000).

Bladder diverticula are often found incidentally in the radiographic investigation of recurrent urinary tract infections or other nonspecific lower urinary tract symptoms or signs. Fluoroscopically monitored voiding cystourethrography (VCUG) is an excellent study to detect bladder diverticula; however, false-negative results are possible (Hernanz-Schulman and Lebowitz, 1985). **VCUG with anterior-posterior, oblique, and lateral images provides information about anatomy, location, size, associated vesicoureteric reflux, and, importantly, emptying of the bladder diverticulum with voiding.** Anomalous voiding into the diverticulum during a detrusor contraction may result in paradoxical enlargement of the bladder diverticulum during micturition (Wesselhoeft et al, 1963) (see Fig. 73–2). This presumably occurs as the contrast material flows from an area of relatively high pressure in the bladder during the bladder contraction to the diverticulum, which represents an area of low pressure. In some instances, the bladder may empty partly into the diverticulum and partly through the urethra. After relaxation of the detrusor, continued fluoroscopic imaging may reveal relatively rapid refilling of the bladder as contrast material decompresses back into the bladder from the diverticulum.

VCUG may be more revealing than intravenous urography (Quirinia and Hoffmann, 1993) in the diagnosis of bladder diverticula; however, if the neck of the diverticulum is obstructed from tumor or otherwise not patent, cross-sectional imaging may be required for diagnosis (Dondalski et al, 1993). Cross-sectional imaging including computed tomography and magnetic resonance imaging (MRI) may also be useful for the evaluation of masses within the diverticulum (see later discussion of associated conditions). **Review of the radiographic films should accurately characterize the number, anatomy, and location of the diverticula.** Filling defects within the diverticula should prompt further investigation (Fig. 73–4). The amount of postvoid residual urine in the bladder diverticulum and bladder should be noted. Incomplete bladder emptying suggests that a urodynamic abnormality may be present, requiring further study.

Imaging of the upper urinary tract may include intravenous pyelography, ultrasonography, computed tomography, or MRI. **In the absence of hematuria or a known or suspected urinary tract malignant neoplasm, the goal of upper tract imaging is to evaluate for asymptomatic or silent hydroureteronephrosis related to the diverticulum** (Lebowitz et al, 1979; Sharma et al, 1997). Hydronephrosis may be related to obstruction of the ureter (Livne and Gonzales, 1985; Kwan and Lowe, 1992), an underlying urodynamic abnormality that results in the formation of the diverticulum, vesicoureteral reflux in association with the diverticulum, or inflammation (Bellinger et al, 1985), or it may be completely unrelated to the bladder diverticulum. A thorough multichannel urodynamic study in combination with VCUG or, alternatively, a video-urodynamic study is useful in this setting to differentiate upper from lower urinary tract causes of the hydronephrosis.

A bladder diverticulum may cause deviation with or without compression of the ipsilateral ureter. **On intravenous**

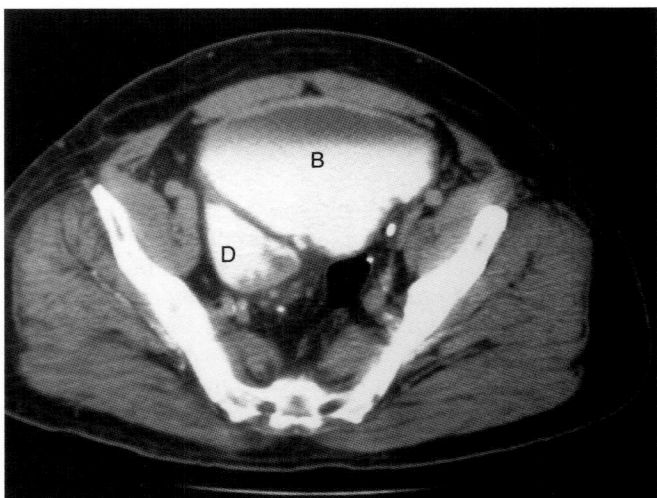

Figure 73–4. Computed tomographic scan demonstrating a bladder diverticulum with multiple filling defects. Cystoscopy and biopsy revealed transitional cell carcinoma. D, bladder diverticulum; B, bladder. Surgical exploration revealed invasive transitional cell carcinoma with extension to the pelvic sidewall and lymph node involvement. This underscores the potentially advanced presentation of transitional cell carcinoma when it is located in a bladder diverticulum.

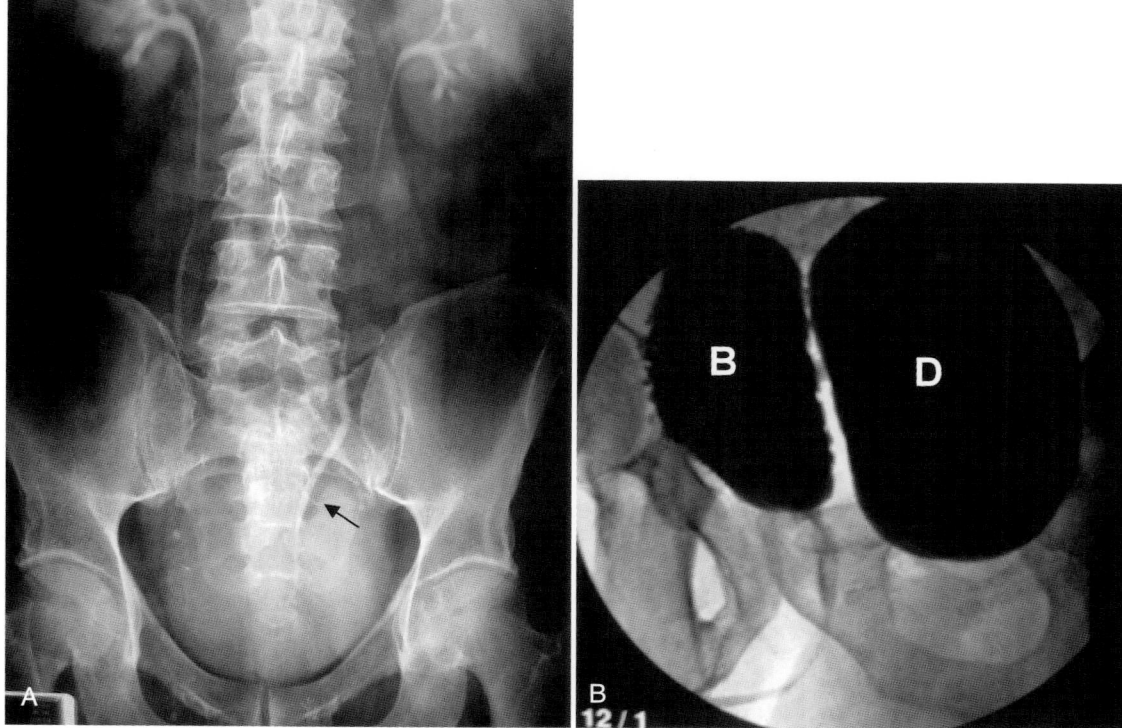

Figure 73–5. Bladder diverticulum with deviation of the ureter. This patient had a long history of recurrent urinary tract infections due to presumed prostatitis. **A,** The 10-minute film from intravenous urography demonstrates medial deviation of the pelvic ureter *(arrow).* **B,** Voiding image from VCUG revealed a large, smooth-walled bladder diverticulum (D) emanating from the trabeculated bladder (B).

urography, **medial deviation of the pelvic ureter is most commonly seen; however, lateral deviation may also occur** (Talner et al, 2000) (Fig. 73–5). Furthermore, a bladder diverticulum that encompasses the ureteral orifice may create a functionally shortened intramural ureteral segment and result in vesicoureteral reflux (see later discussion). In these patients, excision of the bladder diverticulum with ureteroneocystotomy may be necessary.

Urodynamics

Bladder outlet obstruction, impaired compliance, and neurogenic voiding dysfunction may result in the formation of bladder diverticula. Therefore, a urodynamic study can be helpful in the investigation of these patients. **Failure to identify and to treat an existing underlying urodynamic abnormality before or concomitantly with definitive surgical therapy for bladder diverticula may result in a high risk of recurrent diverticula or other problems after surgery.** Successful treatment of the urodynamic abnormality may improve bladder emptying and may potentially result in resolution of the symptoms or complications. Importantly, bladder contractility may appear to be diminished on urodynamics because of the "pressure sink" effect of the bladder diverticulum. This artifact occurs as the detrusor contracts and the intravesical contents are decompressed through the path of least resistance into the bladder diverticulum as opposed to the urethra (Wilson and Klufio, 1985). Videourodynamics may be helpful in assessing the significance of this possibility.

Endoscopic Examination

The entire interior of each bladder diverticulum should be thoroughly inspected endoscopically for stones or abnormal-appearing epithelium. Flexible fiberoptic endoscopes may be required to examine the entire interior of some diverticula. The location of the diverticulum relative to the ureters and bladder outlet is noted, and size of the diverticulum is carefully recorded (Fig. 73–6). Ideally, a specimen for urine cytology should be obtained from the diverticulum during endoscopic examination. **Any abnormal-appearing epithelium or lesions within the diverticulum are carefully sampled. Extreme care must be taken during the biopsy to prevent perforation, as the wall of the diverticulum is very thin due to the lack of a muscularis propria layer.** Patients who elect nonoperative management of bladder diverticula are usually observed closely with periodic endoscopic examinations and cytology. The natural history of untreated bladder diverticula is unknown, but the possibility of malignant transformation due to urinary stasis over time within the diverticulum should be considered.

Associated Conditions

Acquired bladder diverticula are commonly found to exist in the setting of bladder outlet obstruction. Common causes of bladder outlet obstruction in men include benign and malignant disease of the prostate and urethral stricture disease. Less common causes are bladder neck hypertrophy, vesicourethral

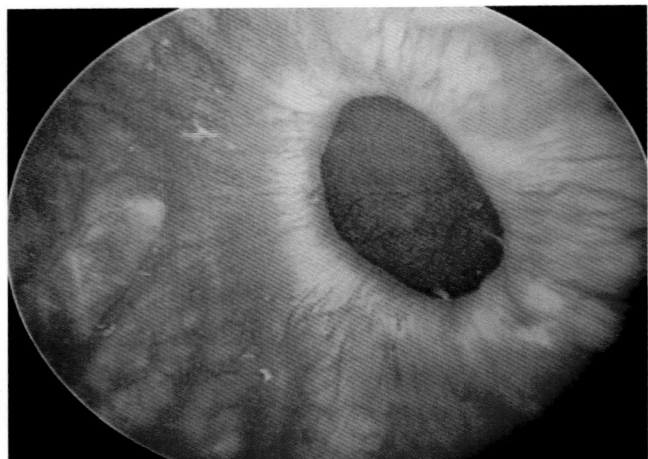

Figure 73–6. Endoscopic view of the ostium of a bladder diverticulum. The entire interior of a diverticulum should be examined endoscopically.

stricture after prostatectomy, and functional obstruction as a result of neurogenic vesicourethral dysfunction (bladder neck or striated sphincter dyssynergia). Both congenital and acquired bladder diverticula can result in urethral obstruction (Epstein et al, 1982; Verghese and Belman, 1984; Jarow and Brendler, 1988; Parrott and Bastuba, 1992; Zia-Ul-Miraj, 1999; Oge et al, 2002) and urinary retention. Strong consideration should be given to management of bladder outlet obstruction before or concomitant with treatment of the bladder diverticulum. **In some patients, treatment of bladder outlet obstruction alone may subsequently allow low pressure and complete emptying of the bladder diverticulum with micturition, thus reducing the potential for complications associated with these lesions and possibly avoiding the need for future operative intervention in the form of diverticulectomy.**

The finding of a neoplasm within a bladder diverticulum has particularly important diagnostic and therapeutic considerations. The overall prevalence of malignant tumors within a bladder diverticulum has been reported to range from 0.8% to 10% (Montague and Boltuch, 1976; Melekos et al, 1987; Baniel and Vishna, 1997; Golijanin et al, 2003). **The most common histologic type of malignant neoplasia seen within bladder diverticula is transitional cell carcinoma in approximately 70% to 80% of cases, followed by squamous cell carcinoma in 20% to 25% of cases** (Montague and Boltuch, 1976; Redman et al, 1976; Micic and Ilic, 1983; Van Arsdalen and Wein, 1992; Yu et al, 1993; Baniel and Vishna, 1997; Golijanin et al, 2003). Adenocarcinoma (Moinzadeh et al, 2003), carcinosarcoma (Nuwahid et al, 1994; Sousa et al, 2000; Bigotti et al, 2001; Omeroglu et al, 2002), and sarcoma (Ward, 1958; Sarno et al, 1991) represent the remainder. Tumors in bladder diverticula occur almost exclusively in adults with a peak occurrence between the ages of 65 and 75 years (Ostroff et al, 1973). The prognosis for patients with these tumors has historically been reported as poor (Faysal and Freiha, 1981; Micic and Ilic, 1983; Das and Amar, 1986; Melekos et al, 1987), although some reports may suggest otherwise in selected

patients (Montague and Boltuch, 1976; Baniel and Vishna, 1997). The reason for the poor prognosis has been attributed to delayed diagnosis and advanced stage at presentation (Ostroff et al, 1973; Fellows, 1978; Faysal and Freiha, 1981; Micic and Ilic, 1983) in some patients. The lack of a well-defined muscularis layer of bladder diverticula is likely to be an important factor. **Because bladder diverticula lack a muscle layer beyond the urothelium, there is theoretically a greater risk for early transmural involvement with local extension to the perivesical fat through the comparatively thinner diverticular wall compared with the normal bladder wall.** In addition, the lack of a defined muscle wall risks early dissemination of tumor cells into an extravesical location during transurethral resection of these lesions and makes precise pathologic staging difficult. Accurate identification of tumors within bladder diverticula has been demonstrated by a variety of radiographic techniques including computed tomography, MRI, and ultrasonography (Dragsted and Nilsson, 1985; Saez et al, 1985; Williams and Gooding, 1985; Lowe et al, 1989; Dondalski et al, 1993; Durfee et al, 1997; Mallampati and Siegelman, 2004) (see Fig. 73–4). Whether these modalities can reliably predict extravesical invasion and therefore affect staging and prognosis is not clear. It has been suggested that clinical stage at presentation is the most important prognostic factor for patients with tumors in bladder diverticula; 5-year actuarial survival ranges from 83% ± 9% in patients with superficial disease to 45% ± 14% in those presenting with extradiverticular disease (Golijanin et al, 2003). One small series suggests that aggressive individualized multimodal therapy in these patients including surgery, chemotherapy, and radiation therapy may improve prognosis (Garzotto et al, 1996). Since pathologic staging after transurethral resection is difficult and often inaccurate, some authors have suggested an aggressive approach to these tumors. This surgical staging approach involves an open exploration and partial or radical cystectomy without a prior transurethral resection (Redman et al, 1976). Others have advocated a selective individualized approach, taking into account the clinical stage and pathologic grade of the tumor (Golijanin et al, 2003). Low-grade, low-stage tumors may be successfully treated with diverticulectomy alone (Sulaiman et al, 1998). However, the ability to reliably predict stage and grade preoperatively is limited, and therefore this approach should be undertaken only with caution in select cases with adequate counseling and follow-up. In any case, close surveillance of these patients is warranted whether aggressive therapy is undertaken or not.

The location of many bladder diverticula at the level of the ureterovesical junction may explain the high incidence of associated ipsilateral ureteral abnormalities. For a ureter found within a diverticulum, the lack of a muscle backing to the diverticulum results in a functionally shortened intramural tunnel. **A high prevalence of ipsilateral vesicoureteral reflux has been noted in association with congenital bladder diverticula** (Amar, 1972). One study noted reflux in 83 of 89 diverticulum-associated ureteric units (Barrett et al, 1976). Other considerations in the evaluation and management of bladder diverticula include the potential development of stones within the diverticulum, ureteral obstruction (Lebowitz et al, 1979; Bellinger et al, 1985; Kwan and Lowe,

1992; Khan et al, 1994; Sharma et al, 1997), and even the rare but life-threatening complication of perforation or rupture of the bladder diverticulum (Mitchell and Hamilton, 1971; Keeler and Sant, 1990; Itoh and Kounami, 1994; Jorion and Michel, 1999).

Management

In general, if the etiology of the bladder diverticulum is thought to be consistent with bladder outlet obstruction, definitive treatment of the bladder outlet is indicated before or concomitant with treatment of the bladder diverticulum. If treatment of the obstruction is pursued initially and results in satisfactory emptying of the diverticulum postoperatively, and complicating factors such as reflux, infection, malignant disease, and stones are absent, ongoing surveillance of the diverticulum may be all that is required. Emptying of the diverticulum after relief of outlet obstruction may be assessed by ultrasonography, VCUG, or video-urodynamics.

Management options in the treatment of bladder diverticula include observation, endoscopic management, and surgical excision. However, there are many factors to consider during the evaluation of these lesions before deciding on appropriate therapy (Fig. 73–7).

Observation and Expectant Management

Patients who have poor bladder emptying after relief of obstruction or who are unable or unwilling to undergo surgical excision of the bladder diverticulum may be effectively treated with clean intermittent catheterization or an indwelling catheter. In this setting, and in the absence of future complicating factors, surveillance of the bladder diverticulum may be all that is required. Patients who demonstrate significantly impaired bladder contractility on preoperative urodynamics or who fail to empty the bladder (independent of emptying of the diverticulum) on preoperative VCUG or video-urodynamics after relief of obstruction may have persistent failure to empty the bladder even after successful diverticulectomy. Therefore, long-term clean intermittent catheterization may be a viable option in these patients.

Indications for Intervention

Once diagnosed, congenital or acquired bladder diverticula may require no further therapy unless they are associated with persistent symptoms, recurrent infections, obstruction, stones, malignant disease, or other complicating factors such as ipsilateral vesicoureteral reflux. Symptoms or complications related to bladder diverticula are most often due to poor emptying of the diverticulum and urinary stasis. Therefore, excision of the diverticula would be expected to improve emptying of the lower urinary tract, provided the primary problem that resulted in the formation of the bladder diverticulum (i.e., obstruction) has been adequately addressed. Bladder diverticulectomy therefore is indicated for the treatment of symptoms related to the diverticulum or for the major complications directly related to it, including chronic relapsing urinary tract infection, stones within the diverticulum, carcinoma or premalignant change, and upper urinary tract deterioration as a result of obstruction or reflux.

Bladder diverticula can vary tremendously in size and in some instances are larger than the bladder itself. Size of the diverticulum does not appear to correlate with symptoms or complications and therefore cannot be used as an absolute indication to proceed with surgery. As noted previously, rarely do individuals with bladder diverticulum present because of symptoms specific to the bladder diverticulum. Asymptomatic patients without complicating factors may be observed closely with endoscopic examination, urine cytology, and cultures. Controversy exists as to whether prophylactic excision of asymptomatic bladder diverticula should be carried out to prevent malignant transformation or whether close observation is sufficient. Cytologic techniques and endoscopic equipment allow excellent follow-up, but patients should be counseled that the treatment and prognosis of malignant lesions, should they develop in follow-up, remain variable and unpredictable.

Excision of bladder diverticula is most commonly elective. The relative merits of surgical excision versus surveillance should be carefully considered and discussed with each patient individually. The patient should be in relatively good health and have a reasonable surgical risk before the procedure is considered. Preoperative medical status should be assessed and reversible risk factors corrected or optimized (e.g., nutritional, renal, cardiac, pulmonary). Preoperative urinary tract infection should be treated. Patients who have a prohibitive surgical risk because of concurrent medical illness or other factors should not undergo surgical excision but may be candidates for endoscopic treatment.

Endoscopic Management

Endoscopic management of bladder diverticulum may be considered in patients who are aged or somewhat debilitated, those who are not good candidates for an open operative approach, or those undergoing transurethral resection of the prostate in whom there exists an associated poorly draining diverticulum (Orandi, 1977; Vitale and Woodside, 1979). Transurethral resection of the diverticular neck has been reported to be successful in select cases (Vitale and Woodside, 1979). This technique is performed with a standard resectoscope. The neck of the diverticulum is incised with the resectoscope loop or Collins knife. Incisions are carried down to the muscle fibers of the bladder at the level of the ostium of the diverticulum. Circumferential resection of the entire neck may be performed. When it is successful, this procedure enlarges the neck of the diverticulum, disrupting the narrow sphincter-like properties of its connection to the bladder lumen and thereby permitting improved emptying of the diverticulum during micturition. Although it is generally safe and well tolerated, this technique has resulted in urinary retention by a reversal of flow during micturition and "venting" of the bladder contents into the diverticulum postoperatively (Schulze and Hald, 1983). Transurethral resection of the diverticular neck may be combined with fulguration of the entire urothelial lining of the diverticulum (Clayman et al, 1984; Adachi et al, 1991a, 1991b; Yamaguchi et al, 1992). Fulguration of the lining of the diverticulum may result in obliteration of the diverticulum or a considerable reduction in size.

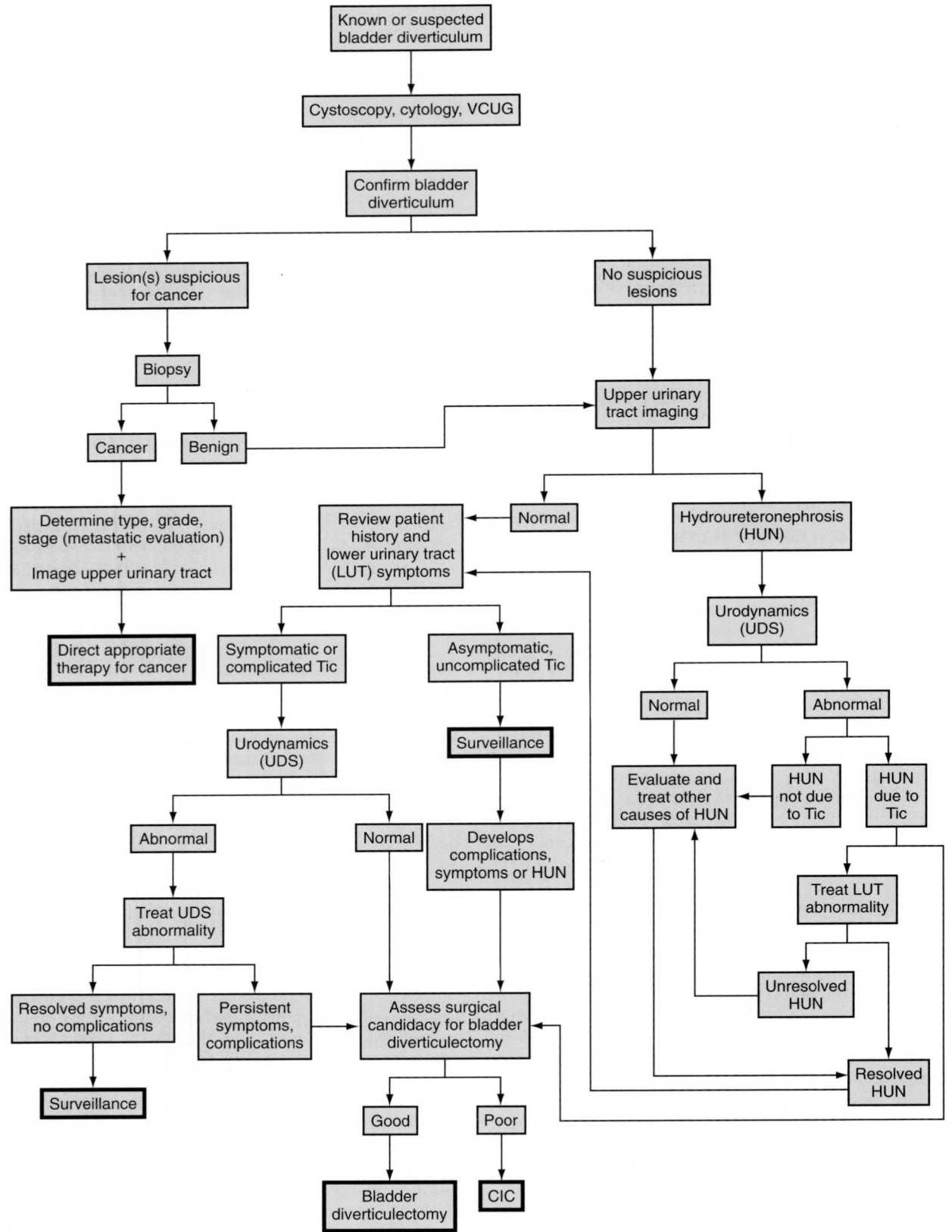

Figure 73–7. Algorithm for the evaluation and treatment of bladder diverticula. CIC, clean intermittent catheterization; VCUG, voiding cystourethrography. (Modified from Rovner ES, Wein AJ: Bladder diverticula in adults. In Resnick M, Elder JA, Spirnak JP, eds: Decision Making in Urology, 3rd ed. Hamilton, Ontario, BC Decker, 2004:260-263.)

Open Surgical Management

Open excision is usually performed through a transvesical approach, although extravesical and combined approaches have been described. In cases of marked prostatic enlargement and obstruction, open suprapubic prostatectomy and transvesical bladder diverticulectomy may be performed concomitantly. Adequate preoperative imaging and endoscopic evaluation should provide information about the size, number, and location of all bladder diverticula. Furthermore, the relationship of the adjacent anatomic structures, including the major pelvic vessels, ureters, and bowel, should be noted. The bladder is most commonly approached extraperitoneally through a low midline or transverse incision. The retropubic space is entered and developed. Regardless of the technique used, careful dissection is required during excision of the diverticulum to avoid ureteral injury; many bladder diverticula are located adjacent to the ureter or may be adherent to it. Ureteral stents are often placed preoperatively or intraoperatively to facilitate dissection and to avoid ureteral injury. Often, several bladder diverticula are noted preoperatively. Simultaneous resection of all existing bladder diverticula should be performed to optimize postoperative bladder emptying (Gil-Vernet, 1998).

Transvesical Bladder Diverticulectomy. The transvesical approach to bladder diverticulectomy was first reported by Hugh Hampton Young in 1906 (Gil-Vernet, 1998). The bladder is opened along the anterior wall, and suitable retraction is placed to visualize the neck of the diverticulum (Fig. 73–8). For the excision of small diverticula, a locking instrument such as an Allis-type clamp is passed through the neck of the diverticulum; the base or bottom of the diverticulum is grasped, pulled, and everted back into the bladder. **In the absence of extravesical adhesions or inflammation, a small diverticulum can be completely everted into the bladder and exposed in this manner.** The urothelium of the diverticulum at the level of the neck is incised circumferentially, and the

diverticulum is removed. The defect in the bladder wall is closed with absorbable suture in two layers. **Care must be taken in performing this technique to avoid injury to structures adherent or adjacent to the external surface of the diverticulum; they may be blindly pulled into the bladder with the diverticulum wall and inadvertently injured during resection.**

If eversion of the diverticulum is not possible because of adhesions or inflammation, or if the diverticulum is too large to permit complete exposure during eversion, submucosal excision of the diverticulum may be performed. An anterior cystotomy is performed, the bladder is opened, and suitable retraction is placed to visualize the neck of the diverticulum within the bladder. The neck of the diverticulum is then identified and mobilized initially similar to the technique used for the first part of the dissection of the ureter during ureteroneocystostomy. The diverticular neck is circumscribed sharply with scissors or electrocautery, and the plane between the wall of the diverticulum and the surrounding fibrous capsule is defined (Fig. 73–9). Traction is placed on the edges of the neck of the diverticulum with Allis clamps circumferentially, and the neck and then the exterior walls of the diverticulum are carefully mobilized from the surrounding tissues and delivered into the bladder lumen. Sharp and blunt dissection on the exterior wall of the diverticulum is performed in a well-defined periadventitial plane between the diverticulum wall and the fibrous pseudocapsule. Packing of the diverticulum with gauze may facilitate dissection and provide some countertraction (Fig. 73–10). The diverticulum is completely freed from its fibrous pseudocapsule and removed. The bladder wall defect is then repaired in two layers with absorbable sutures. Drainage of the potential space left by the pseudocapsule is not necessary (Firstater and Farkas, 1977).

Combined Intravesical and Extravesical Approach. For individuals with large diverticula or considerable peridiverticular inflammation, a purely transvesical approach may not be feasible. In addition, involvement of the ureter within the diverticulum or severe peridiverticular inflammation encompassing the ureter may have altered the usual course of the ureter and may incur a prohibitive risk of injury to the ureter with a transvesical approach. Therefore, a combined intravesical and extravesical approach may be warranted. Ureteral catheters are usually placed to prevent ureteral injury. The bladder is opened as if for a transvesical diverticulectomy. The diverticular neck is incised circumferentially. The surgeon's finger is then inserted into the diverticulum to identify the location of the rest of the diverticulum (Fig. 73–11). The diverticulum may be packed with gauze as well. If the neck of the diverticulum is sufficiently mobile, the anterior aspect of the neck is brought up into the operative field outside the bladder by use of the surgeon's finger. The overlying tissue is dissected free, and the anterior portion of the neck of the diverticulum is exposed and incised extravesically. The neck is circumferentially mobilized and then transected. The diverticular wall is then mobilized and dissected free of its attachments as described previously. In some cases, anterior reflection of the surgeon's finger allows opening of the diverticulum itself, and dissection can be carried out in the plane between the pseudocapsule and the urothelium in a

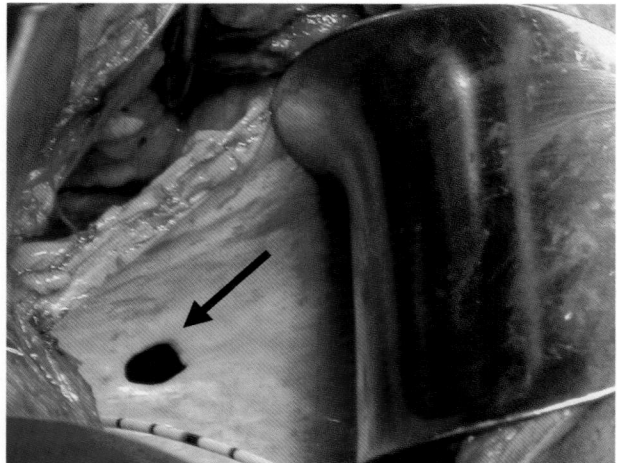

Figure 73–8. Intraoperative view of the neck *(arrow)* of a bladder diverticulum before transvesical submucosal diverticulectomy. The bladder has been opened and retraction placed. A ureteral catheter is seen emanating from the region of the left ureteral orifice.

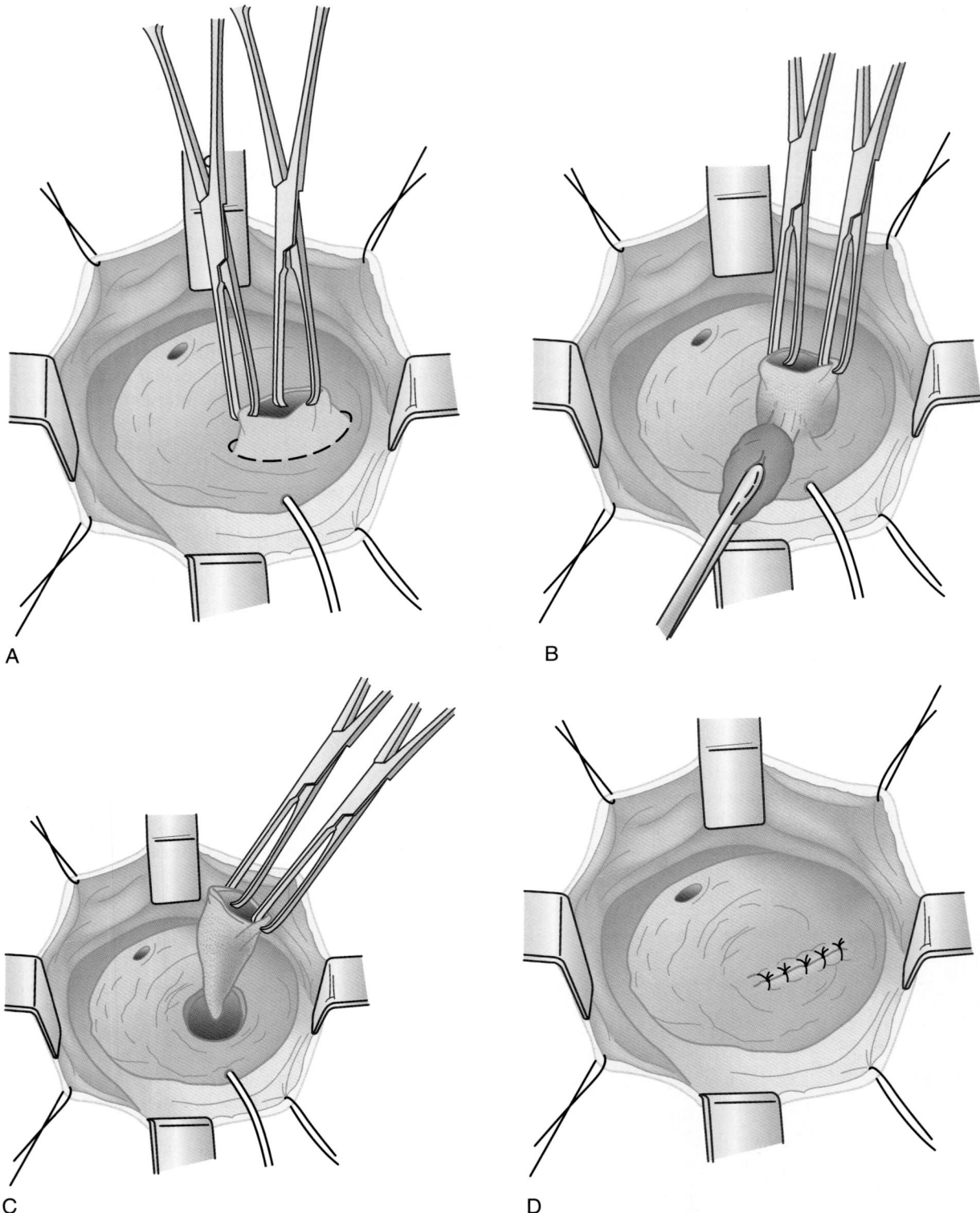

Figure 73–9. Intravesical submucosal bladder diverticulectomy. **A,** The neck of the diverticulum is grasped and circumscribed sharply. **B,** The adventitial tissue is dissected free from the diverticulum wall. **C,** The diverticulum is completely removed. **D,** The bladder is repaired.

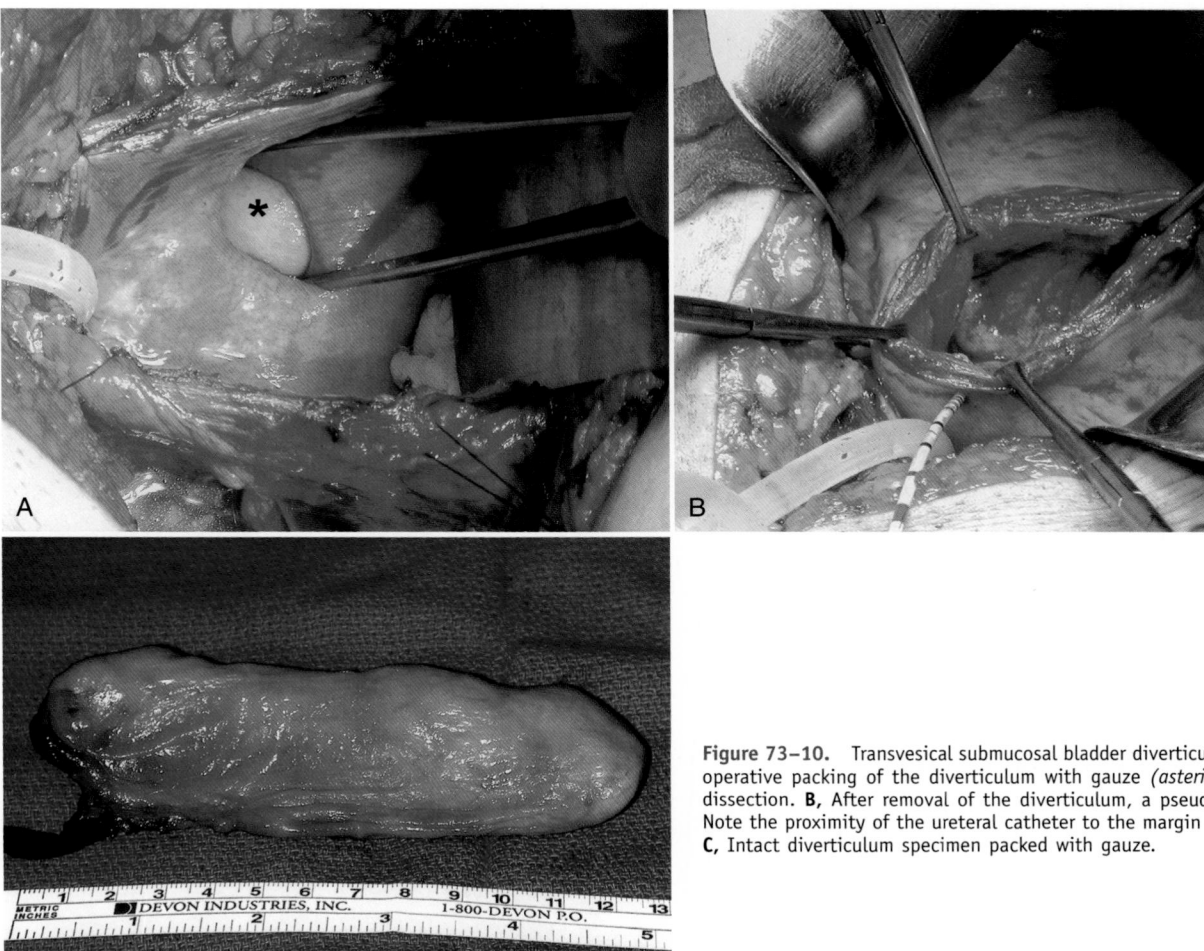

Figure 73–10. Transvesical submucosal bladder diverticulectomy. **A,** Intraoperative packing of the diverticulum with gauze *(asterisk)* may facilitate dissection. **B,** After removal of the diverticulum, a pseudocapsule is seen. Note the proximity of the ureteral catheter to the margin of the dissection. **C,** Intact diverticulum specimen packed with gauze.

completely extravesical fashion. In some cases, it may be necessary to divide the ipsilateral superior vesical pedicle to facilitate exposure and delivery of the diverticulum. If additional difficulty is encountered in exposing the diverticulum, the original cystotomy incision can be extended or enlarged in a T fashion over the neck of the diverticulum. This procedure generally removes the entire diverticulum including the mucosa and fibrous pseudocapsule. When considerable inflammation is encountered and the diverticulum is closely adherent to adjacent vital structures, it may be necessary to leave portions of the fibrous pseudocapsule in situ. The bladder is closed as described previously.

Other. A "tubeless diverticulostomy" approach has been described for the high-risk patient or elderly patient (Presman, 1965). In this procedure, the neck of the diverticulum is located and divided. The bladder is repaired, and the diverticulum is completely left in situ. The diverticular cavity may be drained or sclerosed.

Minimally invasive techniques such as laparoscopy have been applied to bladder diverticulectomy as well (Das, 1992; Parra et al, 1992; Jarrett et al, 1995; Faramarzi-Roques et al, 2004). The role of laparoscopy in the surgical management of this condition is evolving.

Complications

The most devastating complication during bladder diverticulectomy is ureteral injury. This is fortunately rare and can be avoided by careful attention to technique. Placement of a ureteral catheter can help in identifying the ureter during surgery. If it is identified intraoperatively, a partial transection may be repaired primarily and stented. Complete transection usually mandates ureteral reimplantation into the bladder with or without a psoas hitch. Other complications include urinary tract infection, bleeding, prolonged urinary extravasation postoperatively, urinary fistula, and bowel injury.

KEY POINTS: BLADDER DIVERTICULA

- Bladder diverticula do not contain a defined functional muscularis propria layer and therefore empty poorly with micturition.

- In the adult, bladder diverticula are often associated with bladder outlet obstruction or neurogenic vesicourethral dysfunction. Congenital bladder diverticula are usually solitary, are associated with a smooth-walled bladder, and occur in the absence of bladder outlet obstruction.

- Presenting symptoms of bladder diverticula are legion. Bladder diverticula are most often diagnosed incidentally in the evaluation of nonspecific lower urinary tract symptoms or infection.

- Patients with bladder diverticula should be evaluated for bladder outlet obstruction. If bladder outlet obstruction is present, it should be addressed in advance of or concomitantly with definitive treatment of the bladder diverticulum.

- Surgical diverticulectomy is often curative.

FEMALE URETHRAL DIVERTICULA

Diverticula of the female urethra present some of the most challenging diagnostic and reconstructive problems in female urology. These cases can be simultaneously fascinating and frustrating. Urethral diverticula are notable for a bewildering variety of clinical presentations ranging from completely asymptomatic, incidentally noted lesions on physical examination or radiography to debilitating, painful vaginal masses associated with incontinence, stones, or tumors. Anatomic variations between patients and in the location, size, and complexity of these lesions ensure that each case is unique. Diverticula of the male urethra are rare and are discussed in Chapter 33.

Although urethral diverticula were described as early as the 19th century (Hey, 1805), the modern era of female urethral diverticula began in 1956 with the advent of positive-pressure urethrography by Davis and Cian (Davis and Cian, 1952). During the next several years, there was a dramatic increase in the number of cases of urethral diverticula reported in the literature. Davis and TeLinde's series of 121 cases published in 1958 approximately doubled the number of cases reported during the previous 60 years (Davis and TeLinde, 1958). Development of adjuvant imaging techniques such as ultrasonography and surface coil and endoluminal MRI in the past 2 to 3 decades has contributed greatly to further understanding of urethral diverticula (Fig. 73–12). With the expanding use of these imaging modalities, the diagnosis and evaluation of this condition continue to evolve. Once the diagnosis is confirmed, definitive therapy often consists of operative excision and reconstruction. Successful surgical excision and reconstruction require a detailed knowledge of the relevant operative anatomy and adherence to basic surgical tenets as well as an ability to be creative and sometimes even improvisational in the operating room.

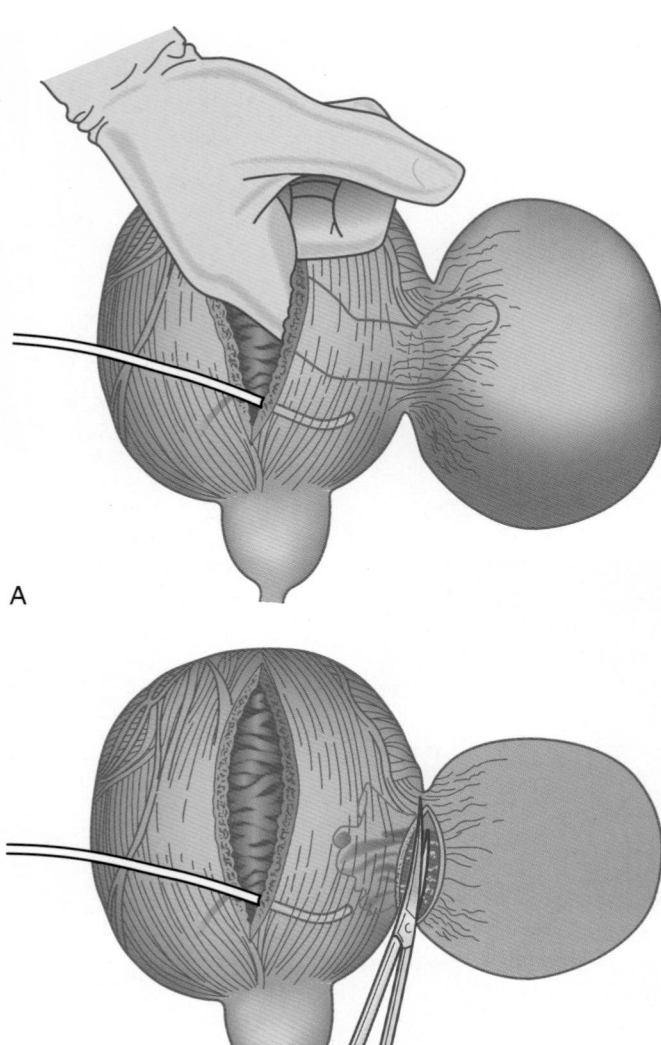

A

B

Figure 73–11. Combined intravesical-extravesical bladder diverticulectomy. **A,** The surgeon's finger is inserted into the diverticulum through a cystotomy, allowing identification of the diverticular neck. **B,** The diverticular neck is divided, and the remaining portion of the diverticulum is dissected free from the surrounding tissues.

Anatomy of the Female Urethra

The normal female urethra is a musculofascial tube approximately 3 to 4 cm in length extending from the bladder neck to the external urethral meatus. It is suspended to the pelvic sidewall and pelvic fascia (tendinous arc of the obturator muscle) by a sheet of connective tissue termed the urethropelvic ligament. The urethropelvic ligament is composed of two layers of fused pelvic fascia that extend toward the pelvic sidewall bilaterally (Fig. 73–13). This structure can be considered to have an abdominal side (the endopelvic fascia) and a vaginal side (periurethral fascia). **Within and between these two leaves of fascia lies the urethra, and it is the location of most urethral diverticula.**

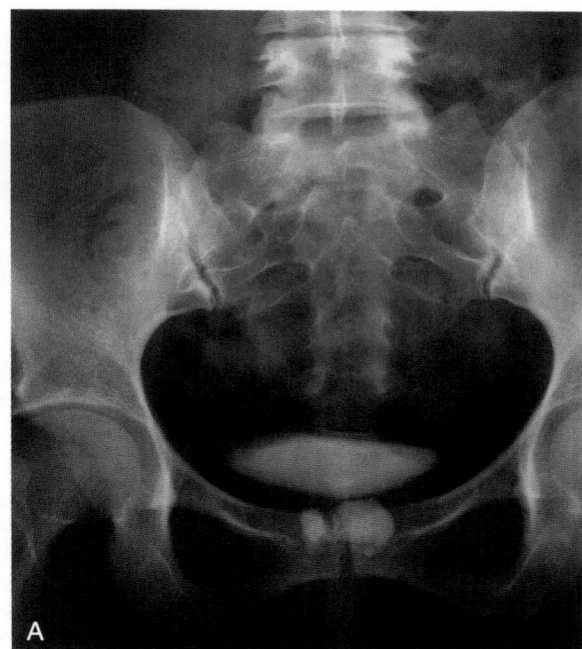

Figure 73–12. Imaging of urethral diverticula. **A**, Postvoid film from VCUG demonstrates a collection of contrast material below the bladder, suggesting a urethral diverticulum. **B**, Endoluminal MRI with both sagittal and axial T2 images demonstrates the relevant anatomy of a patient with a urethral diverticulum (UD).

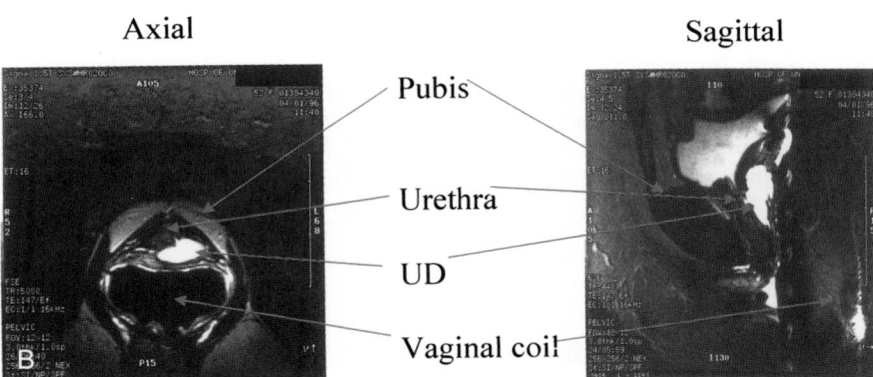

Axial   Sagittal

Pubis

Urethra

UD

Vaginal coil

The urethral lumen is lined by an epithelial layer that is transitional cell type proximally and nonkeratinized stratified squamous cell type distally. The urethra may be conceptualized as a rich vascular spongy cylinder surrounded by an envelope consisting of smooth and skeletal muscle

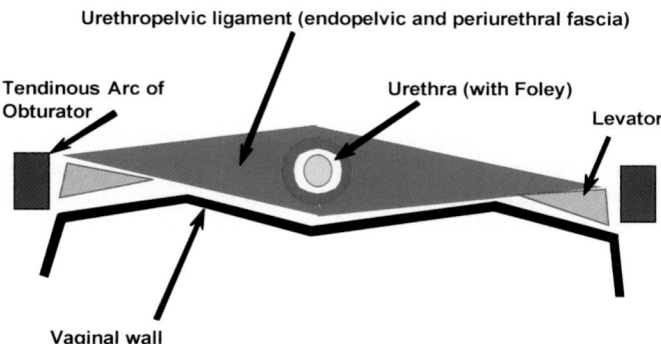

Urethropelvic ligament (endopelvic and periurethral fascia)

Tendinous Arc of Obturator

Urethra (with Foley)

Levator

Vaginal wall

Figure 73–13. Schematic diagram of the anatomy of the midurethra in a coronal plane.

and fibroelastic tissue (Young et al, 1996). Within the thick, vascular lamina propria–submucosal layer are the periurethral glands (Fig. 73–14). These tubuloalveolar glands exist over the entire length of the urethra posterolaterally; however, they are most prominent over the distal two thirds, with the majority of the glands draining into the distal third of the urethra. Skene's glands are the largest and most distal of these glands. These glands drain outside the urethral lumen, lateral to the urethral meatus. **It is from pathologic processes involving the periurethral glands that most acquired female urethral diverticula are thought to originate.**

The urethra has several muscle layers: an internal longitudinal smooth muscle layer, an outer circular smooth muscle layer, and a skeletal muscle layer. The skeletal muscle component spans much of the length of the urethra but is more prominent in the middle third. It has a U-shaped configuration, being deficient dorsally. Ventral to the urethra but separated from it by the periurethral fascia lies the anterior vaginal wall (see Fig. 73–13). **The location and competence of the urethral sphincters have important implications when**

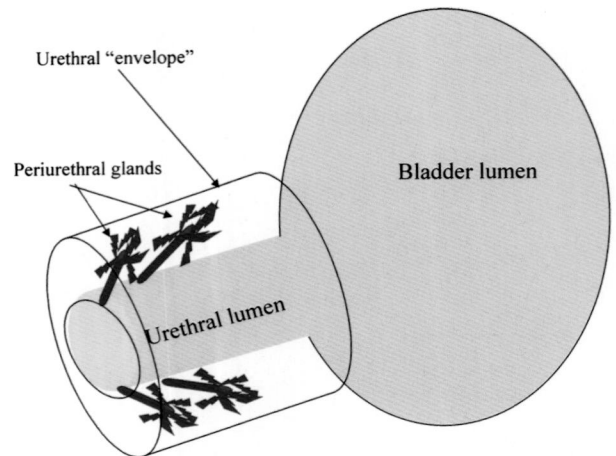

Figure 73–14. Periurethral glands are located within submucosa of urethra deep to the muscle envelope draining distally but arborizing proximally.

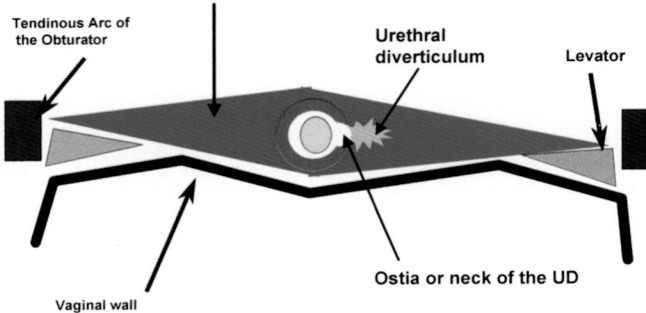

Figure 73–15. Diagram of urethral diverticulum. The urethral diverticulum forms within and between the layers of the urethropelvic ligament.

surgical repair of urethral diverticula is considered owing to the anatomic overlap of these two entities.

Arterial inflow to the urethra derives from two sources. The proximal urethra has a blood supply similar to that of the adjacent bladder, whereas the distal urethra derives its blood supply from the terminal branches of the inferior vesical artery via the vaginal artery that runs along the superior lateral aspect of the vagina (Hinman, 1993). Lymphatic drainage of the female urethra is to the external and internal iliac nodes from the proximal urethra and to the superficial and deep inguinal lymph nodes from the distal urethra. Innervation to the female urethra is from the pudendal nerve (S2-4), and afferents from the urethra travel via the pelvic splanchnic nerves.

Urethral Diverticula

Pathophysiology and Etiology

As conceptualized by Raz and colleagues, urethral diverticulum represents a cavity dissecting within the confines of the fascia of the urethropelvic ligament (Young et al, 1996). This defect is often an isolated cystlike appendage with a single discrete connection to the urethral lumen, termed the neck or ostium (Fig. 73–15). **However, complicated anatomic patterns may exist, and in certain cases the urethral diverticulum may extend partially ("saddlebag" urethral diverticulum) around the urethra, anterior to the urethra** (Vakili et al, 2003), **or circumferentially around the entire urethra** (Rovner and Wein, 2003) (Fig. 73–16).

The exact origin of urethral diverticula is still unproven. A major debate in the earlier part of the 20th century focused on whether urethral diverticula were congenital or acquired lesions (Johnson, 1938; Gilbert and Rivera Cintron, 1954; Pinkerton, 1963). Although this condition exists in children, the diagnosis may represent a clinical entity different from adult female urethral diverticula. Scattered reports of congenital urethral diverticula in female infants have been described (Glassman et al, 1975). Marshall (1981) reported five cases of urethral diverticula in young girls, of which three underwent spontaneous regression. Congenital anterior urethral divertic-

ulum is a well-described entity in boys (Kirks and Grossman, 1981; Lau and Ong, 1981; Kaneti et al, 1984), but this is considered to be a clinical entity entirely different from urethral diverticula in the female. Congenital Skene's gland cysts have been reported (Kimbrough and Vaughan, 1977; Lee and Kim, 1992) but are considered extremely rare. Diverticula in the pediatric population have been attributed to a number of congenital anomalies, including an ectopic ureter draining into a Gartner's duct cyst and a forme fruste of urethral duplication (Silk and Lebowitz, 1969; Vanhoutte, 1970; Boyd and Raz, 1993). The vast majority of urethral diverticula, however, are likely to be acquired and are diagnosed in adult women. In two large series of urethral diverticula, there were no patients reported who were younger than 10 years (Davis and TeLinde, 1958; Davis and Robinson, 1970), arguing against a congenital etiology for these lesions. Although it is possible that there exists a congenital defect in patients that results in or represents a precursor to urethral diverticulum, which then becomes symptomatic only later in life, it is as yet unproven.

There are multiple theories regarding the formation of acquired urethral diverticula. For many years, acquired urethral diverticula were thought to be most likely due to trauma from vaginal childbirth (McNally, 1935). It was postulated that mechanical trauma during vaginal delivery resulted in herniation of the urethral mucosa through the muscle layers of the urethra, with the subsequent development of a urethral diverticulum. However, up to 20% to 30% of patients in some series of urethral diverticula are nulliparous (Lee, 1984; Ganabathi et al, 1994), which may significantly discount parity as a risk factor. Trauma with forceps delivery, however, has been reported to cause urethral diverticula (Klyszejko et al, 1985), as has the endoscopic injection of collagen (Clemens and Bushman, 2001).

The periurethral glands are thought to be the probable site of origin of acquired urethral diverticula (Young et al, 1996). Huffman's anatomic work with wax models of the female urethra were critical to the early theories regarding the pathophysiology of urethral diverticula and the involvement of the periurethral glands (Huffman, 1948). By reviewing 10-μm transverse sections, he refuted earlier anatomic descriptions of the glandular anatomy of the female urethra. He characterized the periurethral glands as located primarily dorsolateral to the urethra, arborizing proximally along the urethra and yet draining into ducts in the distal third of the

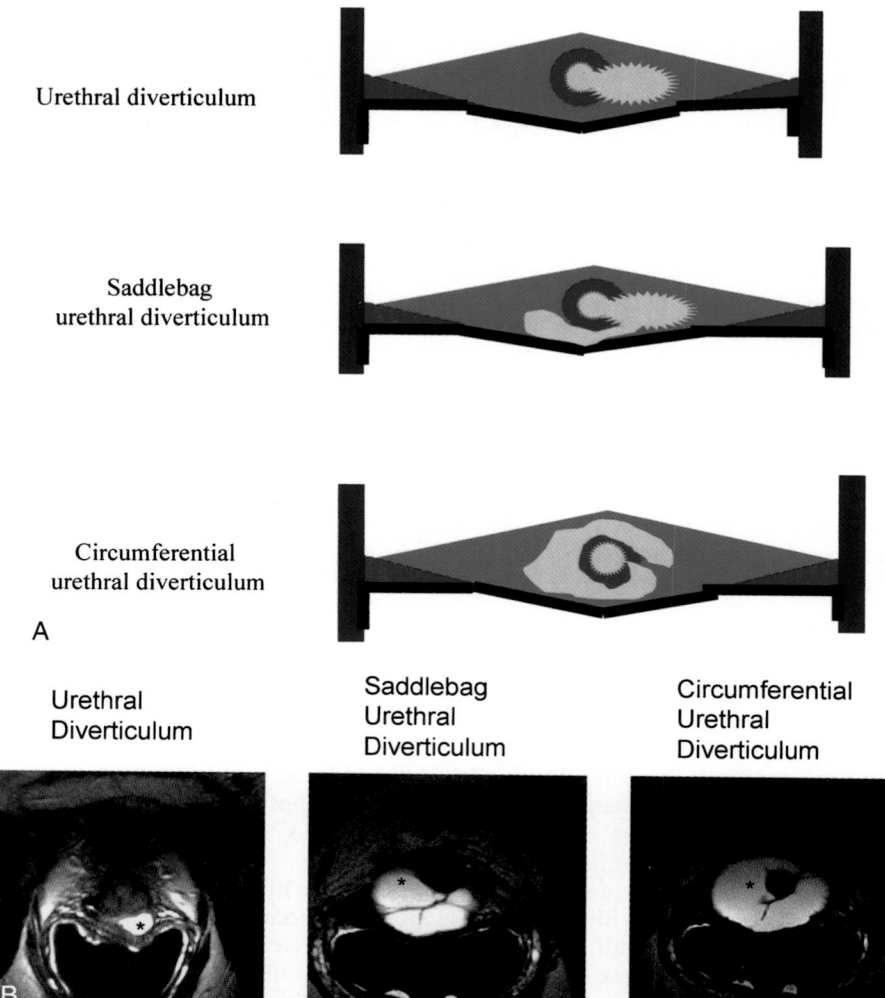

Urethral diverticulum

Saddlebag
urethral diverticulum

Circumferential
urethral diverticulum

A

Figure 73–16. Multiple different morphologic patterns of urethral diverticulum may exist. **A,** Schematic diagrams representing three different morphologic appearances of urethral diverticulum. **B,** Endoluminal MRI images corresponding to each of the configurations in three different patients. The asterisk demonstrates urethral diverticulum.

Urethral Diverticulum	Saddlebag Urethral Diverticulum	Circumferential Urethral Diverticulum

urethra (see Fig. 73–3). Furthermore, he noted that periductal and interductal inflammation was found commonly. **In support of these observations and an infectious (acquired) etiology of urethral diverticula, in more than 90% of cases, the ostium is located posterolaterally in the mid or distal urethra, which corresponds to the location of the periurethral glands** (Lang and Davis, 1959; MacKinnon et al, 1959).

Although there are probably other unknown factors that may facilitate the initiation, formation, or propagation of urethral diverticula, infection of the periurethral glands seems to be the most generally accepted common etiologic factor in most cases. Peters and Vaughn (1976) found a strong association with concurrent or previous infection with *Neisseria gonorrhoeae* and urethral diverticula. However, the initial infection and especially subsequent reinfections may originate from a variety of sources, including *Escherichia coli* and other coliform bacteria as well as vaginal flora. Nevertheless, urethral diverticula have historically been attributed to recurrent infection of the periurethral glands with obstruction, suburethral abscess formation, and subsequent rupture of these infected glands into the urethral lumen. Continual filling and

pooling of urine in the resultant cavity may result in stasis, recurrent infection, and eventual epithelialization of the cavity, forming a permanent urethral diverticulum. This concept was first popularized by Routh more than a century ago and has now become the most widely accepted theory regarding the formation of female urethral diverticula (Routh, 1890). Reinfection, inflammation, and recurrent obstruction of the neck of the cavity are theorized to result in the patient's symptoms and enlargement of the diverticulum. This proposed pathophysiologic process appears to adequately explain the anatomic location and configuration of most urethral diverticula and is supported by the work of Huffman noted previously. However, Daneshgari and colleagues (1999) have reported noncommunicating urethral diverticula diagnosed by MRI. Whether this lesion represents a forme fruste of urethral diverticulum or simply an obstructed ostium is unclear.

Raz and colleagues have formulated a modern hypothesis regarding the pathogenesis of urethral diverticula through an extensive clinical experience with this entity, including the diagnosis, imaging, and surgical repair of urethral diverticula (Young et al, 1996). These authors propose that acquired urethral diverticula result from infection and obstruction of the periurethral glands. These glands are normally found in the submucosal layer of the spongy tissue of the distal two thirds of the urethra. Repeated infection and abscess formation in these obstructed glands eventually result in enlargement and expansion. Initially, the expanding mass displaces the spongy tissue of the urethral wall and then enlarges to disrupt the muscle envelope of the urethra. This results in herniation into the periurethral fascia. The enlarging cavity can then expand and dissect within the leaves of the periurethral fascia and urethropelvic ligament. This expansion occurs most commonly ventrally, resulting in the classic anterior vaginal wall mass palpated on physical examination in some patients with urethral diverticula. However, these may also expand laterally or even dorsally about the urethra. Eventually, the abscess cavity ruptures into the urethral lumen, resulting in the communication between the urethral diverticulum and the urethral lumen. An appreciation of the anatomy and pathophysiology of urethral diverticula is important in understanding the surgical approach to the excision and reconstruction of these lesions.

Prevalence

Moore stated that urethral diverticulum as an entity is "found in direct proportion to the avidity with which it is sought" (Moore, 1952). Although it is not considered a rare lesion today, fewer than 100 cases of urethral diverticulum had been reported in the literature before 1950. With the development of sophisticated imaging techniques including positive-pressure urethrography in the 1950s, the diagnosis of urethral diverticula became increasingly common.

The true prevalence of female urethral diverticula is not known; however, urethral diverticulum is reported to occur in up to 1% to 6% of adult women in some series. Determining the true prevalence of urethral diverticula would require appropriate screening and imaging of a large number of symptomatic and asymptomatic adult female subjects in a primary care setting, which to date has not been done. Bruning (1959) found urethral diverticula in 3 of 500 female autopsy specimens. In 1967, Andersen reported the results of positive-pressure urethrography of 300 women with cervical cancer but without lower urinary tract symptoms and found urethral diverticula in 3%. Aldridge and colleagues (1978) reported a prevalence of urethral diverticula in 1.4% of women presenting with incontinence and related symptoms. Stewart and associates (1981) found urethral diverticula in 16 of 40 highly symptomatic women investigated with positive-

pressure urethrography. More recently, endorectal coil MRI was performed on 140 consecutive female patients with lower urinary tract symptoms, and the incidence of urethral diverticula was approximately 10% (Lorenzo et al, 2003). However, this represented a series of *symptomatic* women at a tertiary referral center and therefore is not likely to be reflective of the general population.

Some series have suggested a definite racial predilection, with blacks being as much as six times as likely to develop urethral diverticula as their white counterparts (Davis and Robinson, 1970). The reason for this racial distribution is not well understood. Furthermore, it has not been confirmed in some modern case series; it may be due to referral bias at the urban academic centers in the original reported series (Leach and Bavendam, 1987).

Diverticular Anatomy

Most commonly, urethral diverticulum represents an epithelialized cavity with a single connection to the urethral lumen. The size of the lesion may vary from only a few millimeters to several centimeters. In addition, the size may vary over time because of inflammation and intermittent obstruction of the ostium with subsequent drainage into the urethral lumen.

The epithelium of urethral diverticula may be columnar, cuboidal, stratified squamous, or transitional. In some cases, the epithelium is absent and the wall of the urethral diverticulum consists only of fibrous tissue. Urethral diverticula are found within the periurethral fascia bordered by the anterior vaginal wall ventrally. In the sagittal plane, urethral diverticula are most often located and centered at the level of the middle third of the urethra with the luminal connection or ostium located posterolaterally. They may extend distally along the vaginal wall almost to the urethral meatus or proximally up to and beyond the bladder neck underneath the trigone of the bladder (Fig. 73–17). A bewildering array of configurations can be noted on imaging and at surgical exploration (Table 73–1). In the axial plane, the urethral diverticulum cavity may extend laterally along the urethral wall and in some cases around to the dorsal side of the urethra or wrap circumferentially around the entire urethra. Urethral diverticula may be bilobed (dumbbell shaped), extending across the midline in a so-called saddlebag configuration (see Fig. 73–16). Multiple loculations are not uncommon, and at least 10% of patients have multiple urethral diverticula at presentation. Varying degrees of sphincteric compromise may exist because of the location of the diverticulum relative to the

Table 73-1. Diverticular Morphology and Characteristics

Series	No. of Patients	Size Range (cm)	Axial Location (%)			Number (%)		Coronal Location (%)		
			Anterior	Lateral	Posterior	Single	Multiple	Proximal	Mid	Distal
Lang and Davis, 1959	108	NA	NA	NA	NA	NA	NA	11 (10)	50 (46)	47 (44)
Hoffman and Adams, 1965	60	0.5-5.0	NA	NA	NA	NA	NA	4 (7)	29 (48)	23 (38)
Pavlica et al, 1988	47	0.5-6.0	3 (6)	6 (13)	38 (81)	41 (87)	6 (13)	3 (6)	39 (83)	5 (11)
Kim et al, 1993	16	0.9-4.5	5 (31)*	NA	11 (69)	NA	NA	4 (25)	10 (63)	2 (12)
Leach et al, 1993	61	0.2-5.0	NA	NA	NA	55 (90)	6 (10)	15 (25)	37 (60)	9 (15)

*Anterior and lateral.

Modified from Westney OL, Leng WW, McGuire EJ: The diagnosis and treatment of female urethral diverticulum. AUA Update Series, Lesson 37, vol 20. Houston, Texas, American Urological Association, 2001:291.

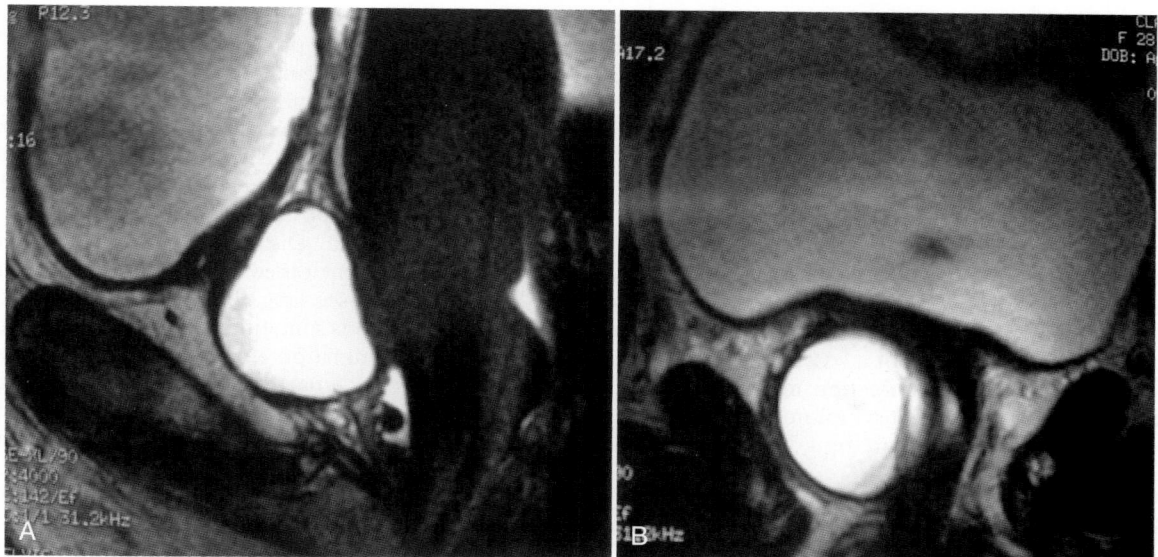

Figure 73–17. T2 MRI images demonstrating a large urethral diverticulum extending to the trigone of the bladder in the sagittal (**A**) and coronal (**B**) planes.

proximal and distal urinary sphincter mechanisms, or sphincteric compromise may coexist with urethral diverticula due to other factors. This is important to note when surgical repair is considered, as discussed later.

Presentation

The majority of patients with urethral diverticula present between the third and seventh decades of life (Johnson, 1938; Moore, 1952; Pathak and House, 1970; Ginsburg and Genadry, 1983; Ganabathi et al, 1994). The presenting symptoms and signs in patients with urethral diverticula are protean (Table 73–2). The classic presentation of urethral diverticula has been described historically as the "three Ds": dysuria, dyspareunia, and dribbling (postvoid). However, individually or collectively, these symptoms are neither sensitive nor specific for urethral diverticula. **Although presentation is highly variable, the most common symptoms are irritative (frequency, urgency) lower urinary tract symptoms, pain, and infection** (Davis and TeLinde, 1958; Davis and Robinson, 1970; Peters and Vaughan, 1976; Leach et al, 1986). **Dyspareunia will be noted by 12% to 24% of patients** (Davis and TeLinde 1958; Davis and Robinson, 1970). **Approximately 5% to 32% of patients will complain of postvoid dribbling** (Davis and Robinson, 1970; Ganabathi et al, 1994). **Recurrent cystitis or urinary tract infection is also a frequent presentation in one third of subjects** (Davis and Robinson, 1970; Ganabathi et al, 1994), **probably due to urinary stasis in the urethral diverticulum. Multiple bouts of recurrent cystitis should alert the clinician to the possibility of a urethral diverticulum. Other complaints include pain, vaginal mass, hematuria, vaginal discharge, obstructive symptoms or urinary retention, and incontinence (stress or urge).** Patients may also present with complaints of a tender or nontender anterior vaginal wall mass, which on gentle compression may reveal retained urine or purulent discharge per the urethral meatus. Although spontaneous rupture of these lesions is extremely rare, urethrovaginal fistula may result under these circumstances

Table 73–2. **Signs and Symptoms of Urethral Diverticula**
Symptoms
Vaginal or pelvic mass
Pelvic pain
Urethral pain
Dysuria
Urinary frequency
Postvoid dribbling
Dyspareunia
Urinary urgency
Incontinence
Urinary hesitancy
Vaginal or urethral discharge
Double voiding
Sense of incomplete emptying
Signs
Recurrent urinary tract infection
Hematuria
Vaginal or perineal tenderness
Urinary retention
Vaginal mass
Urethral discharge with stripping of anterior vaginal wall

(Nielsen et al, 1987). **Notably, up to 20% of patients diagnosed with urethral diverticula may be completely asymptomatic, having the lesions diagnosed incidentally on imaging or physical examination.**

The size of the urethral diverticulum does not correlate with symptoms. In some cases, very large urethral diverticula may result in minimal symptoms, and conversely, some urethral diverticula that are nonpalpable may result in a patient's considerable discomfort and distress. Finally, symptoms may wax and wane and even resolve for long periods. The reasons for these exacerbations and remissions are poorly understood but may be related to periodic and repeated episodes of infection and inflammation.

As many of the symptoms associated with urethral diverticula are nonspecific, patients may often be misdiagnosed and treated for years for a number of unrelated conditions before the diagnosis of urethral diverticulum is made. This may include therapies for interstitial cystitis, recurrent cystitis, vulvodynia, endometriosis, vulvovestibulitis, and other conditions. In one series of 46 consecutive women eventually diagnosed with urethral diverticula, the mean interval from onset of symptoms to diagnosis was 5.2 years (Romanzi et al, 2000). In this series, women consulted with an average of nine physicians before the definitive diagnosis was made despite the fact that 52% of women had a palpable mass on examination. This underscores the importance of a baseline level of suspicion and a thorough pelvic examination in female patients complaining of lower urinary tract symptoms or other symptoms that may be associated with urethral diverticula.

Evaluation and Diagnosis

The diagnosis and complete evaluation of urethral diverticula can be made with a combination of a thorough history, physical examination, appropriate urine studies including urine culture and analysis, endoscopic examination of the bladder and urethra, and selected radiologic imaging. A urodynamic study may also be helpful in selected cases.

Physical Examination. During physical examination, the anterior vaginal wall should be carefully palpated for masses and tenderness. The location, size, and consistency of any suspected urethral diverticulum should be recorded. **Most urethral diverticula are located ventrally over the middle and proximal portions of the urethra, corresponding to the area of the anterior vaginal wall 1 to 3 cm inside the introitus** (Fig. 73–18). However, urethral diverticula may also be located anterior to the urethra or extend partially or completely around the urethral lumen. These particular configurations may have significant implications when surgical

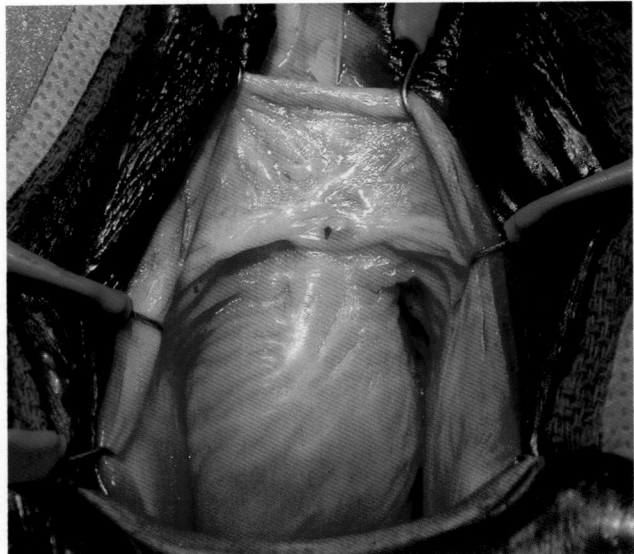

Figure 73–18. Large anterior vaginal wall mass. The urethral catheter is seen superiorly, and a weighted vaginal speculum is seen inferiorly. Scott retractor hooks are seen exposing the anterior vaginal wall in this intraoperative photograph.

excision and reconstruction are undertaken. Urethral diverticula may also extend proximally toward the bladder neck. These urethral diverticula may produce distortion of the bladder outlet and trigone of the bladder on cystoscopy or on radiographic imaging. Special care should be taken during surgical excision and reconstruction because of concerns for intraoperative bladder and ureteral injury as well as the potential development of postoperative voiding dysfunction and urinary incontinence. Distal vaginal masses or perimeatal masses may represent other lesions including abnormalities of Skene's glands (see later discussion). The differentiation between these lesions sometimes cannot be made on the basis of a physical examination alone and may require additional radiologic imaging. **A particularly hard anterior vaginal wall mass may indicate a calculus or malignant neoplasm within the urethral diverticulum and mandates further investigation. During physical examination, the urethra may be gently "stripped" or "milked" distally in an attempt to express purulent material or urine from within the cavity of the urethral diverticulum.** Although often described for the evaluation of urethral diverticula, this maneuver is not successful in producing the characteristic discharge per urethral meatus in the majority of patients (Leach and Bavendam, 1987).

The vaginal walls are assessed for atrophy, rugation, and elasticity. Poorly estrogenized, atrophic tissues are important to note if surgery is being considered for definitive treatment. These tissues are mobilized intraoperatively and may be used for flaps during excision and reconstruction. The distal vagina and vaginal introitus are also assessed for capacity. These factors may have an impact on surgical planning, as a narrow introitus can make surgical exposure difficult and may mandate an episiotomy or other measures. Finally, during physical examination, a provocative maneuver to elicit stress incontinence should be performed as well as an assessment of the presence or absence of any vaginal prolapse.

Urine Studies. Urine analysis and culture should be performed. The most common organism isolated in patients with urethral diverticula is *E. coli*. However, other gram-negative enteric flora as well as *N. gonorrhoeae*, chlamydia, streptococcus, and staphylococcus are often present (Davis and TeLinde, 1958; Hoffman and Adams, 1965). A sterile urine culture does not exclude infection as these patients are often receiving antibiotic therapy at presentation. In patients with irritative symptoms or when a malignant neoplasm is suspected, urine cytology can be performed.

Cystourethroscopy. Cystourethroscopy is performed in an attempt to visualize the ostium of the urethral diverticulum as well as to rule out other causes of the patient's lower urinary tract symptoms. A specially designed female cystoscope can be helpful in evaluating the female urethra. The short beak of the female cystoscope maintains the discharge of the irrigation solution immediately adjacent to the lens and thus aids in distention of the relatively short (compared with the male) urethra, permitting improved visualization. It may also be advantageous to compress the bladder neck while simultaneously applying pressure to the diverticular sac with an assistant's finger. Luminal discharge of purulent material can often be seen with this maneuver or with simple digital compression of the urethral diverticulum during urethroscopy. **The ostium of the urethral diverticulum is most often located posterolaterally at the level of the midurethra but can be difficult to identify in some patients** (Fig. 73–19). The success in identifying a diverticular ostium on cystourethroscopy is highly variable and is reported to be between 15% and 89% (Davis and Robinson, 1970; Leach and Bavendam, 1987; Ganabathi et al, 1994). As a note of caution, patients with urethral diverticula are often highly symptomatic, and endoscopic examination can be difficult to initiate or to complete without anesthesia. Notably, abnormal examination findings may help in surgical planning; however, the failure to locate an ostium on cystourethroscopy should not influence the decision to proceed with further investigations or surgical repair.

Urodynamics. For patients with urethral diverticula and urinary incontinence or significant voiding dysfunction, a urodynamic study may help in accurately characterizing these symptoms (Bhatia et al, 1981; Reid et al, 1986; Summitt and Stovall, 1992). Urodynamics may document the presence or absence of stress urinary incontinence before repair. **Approximately 50% of women with urethral diverticula will demonstrate stress urinary incontinence on urodynamic evaluation** (Bass and Leach, 1991; Ganabathi et al, 1994). A video-urodynamic study combines both a voiding cystourethrogram and a urodynamic study, thus consolidating the diagnostic evaluation and decreasing the number of required urethral catheterizations during the patient's clinical workup. **For patients undergoing surgery for urethral diverticula with coexistent symptomatic stress urinary incontinence demonstrated on physical examination or urodynamically demonstrable stress urinary incontinence, or for those found to have an open bladder neck on preoperative evaluation, a concomitant anti-incontinence surgery can be offered.** Multiple authors have described successful concomitant repair of urethral diverticula and stress incontinence in the same operative setting (Bass and Leach, 1991; Swierzewski and McGuire, 1993; Ganabathi et al, 1994; Faerber, 1998). Alternatively, a small number of patients may have evidence of bladder outlet obstruction on urodynamic evaluation due to the obstructive or mass effects of the ure-

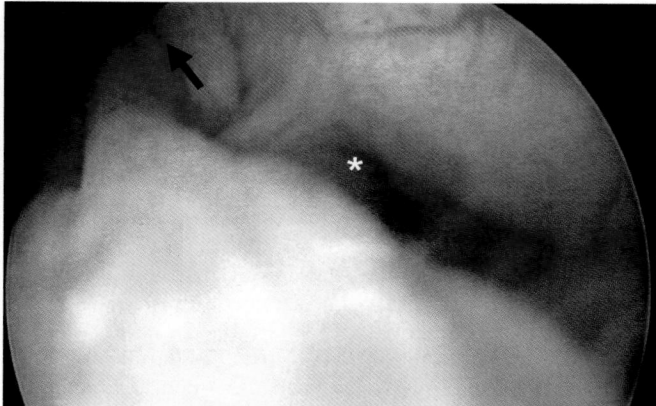

Figure 73–19. Intraoperative view of the ostium of a urethral diverticulum. The ostium is often difficult to visualize endoscopically. The asterisk represents the ostium of the diverticulum. The arrow shows the orientation of the lumen of the urethra.

thral diverticulum on the urethra. Stress urinary incontinence may coexist with obstruction (Bradley and Rovner, 2004), but nevertheless both conditions can be treated successfully with a carefully planned and executed operation. Urethral pressure profilometry has also been used by some authors to assess or to diagnose patients with urethral diverticula; a biphasic pattern or pressure drop is noted at the level of the lesion during the study (Bhatia et al, 1981; Wagner et al, 1986; Summitt and Stovall, 1992).

Imaging

High-quality preoperative imaging is important in the diagnosis and treatment of female urethral diverticula. **Aside from its utility as a diagnostic entity, radiologic imaging should also provide an accurate reflection of the relevant anatomy of the urethral diverticulum, including its relationship to the proximal urethra and bladder neck.**

A number of imaging techniques have been applied to the study of female urethral diverticula, and no single study can be considered the "gold standard" or optimal imaging study for the evaluation of urethral diverticula. Each technique has relative advantages and disadvantages, and the ultimate choice of diagnostic study in many centers often depends on several factors, including local availability, cost, and experience and expertise of the radiologist. Currently available techniques for the evaluation of urethral diverticula include double-balloon positive-pressure urethrography (PPU), voiding cystourethrography (VCUG), intravenous urography, ultrasonography, and magnetic resonance imaging (MRI) with or without an endoluminal coil.

Positive-Pressure Urethrography, Voiding Cystourethrography, and Intravenous Urography. Historically, double-balloon PPU had been considered the optimal study for the diagnosis and assessment of female urethral diverticula (Davis and Cian, 1952; Davis and TeLinde, 1958; Greenberg et al, 1981; Ganabathi et al, 1994). In this technique, a highly specialized catheter with two balloons separated by several centimeters is inserted into the female urethra (Fig. 73–20). This catheter contains a channel within the catheter that exits through a side hole between the two balloons. One balloon is positioned adjacent to the external urethral meatus, and the other balloon is situated at the bladder neck. Both balloons are inflated, creating a seal about the urethral lumen. Contrast material is then infused through the channel under slight pressure, distending the urethral lumen between the two balloons and forcing contrast material into the urethral diverticulum, thereby opacifying the cavity. **This highly specialized study provides outstanding images of the urethra and urethral diverticulum and, importantly, unlike VCUG, is not dependent on the patient's successfully voiding during the study.** However, PPU is not widely performed clinically. It is a complicated study requiring a specific type of modified urethral catheter as well as expertise in the performance and interpretation of the study by the radiologist. Furthermore, it is invasive, requiring catheterization of the female urethra, which in the setting of acute inflammation commonly seen with female urethral diverticula can cause considerable discomfort and distress for the patient. Finally, noncommunicating urethral diverticula (Daneshgari et al, 1999) and loculations within existing urethral diverticula cannot be visualized with PPU

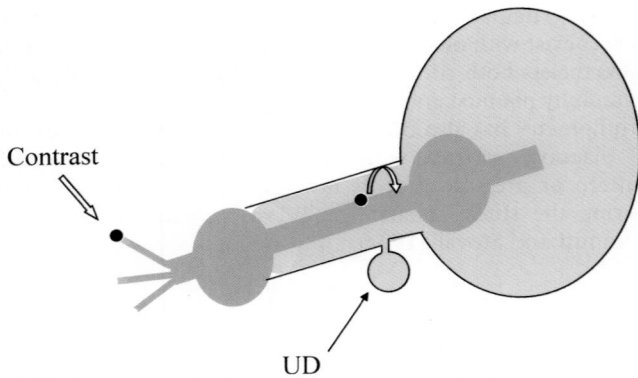

Figure 73–20. Schematic diagram of a double-balloon catheter. UD, urethral diverticulum. The curved white arrow represents flow of the contrast material as it enters the urethral lumen.

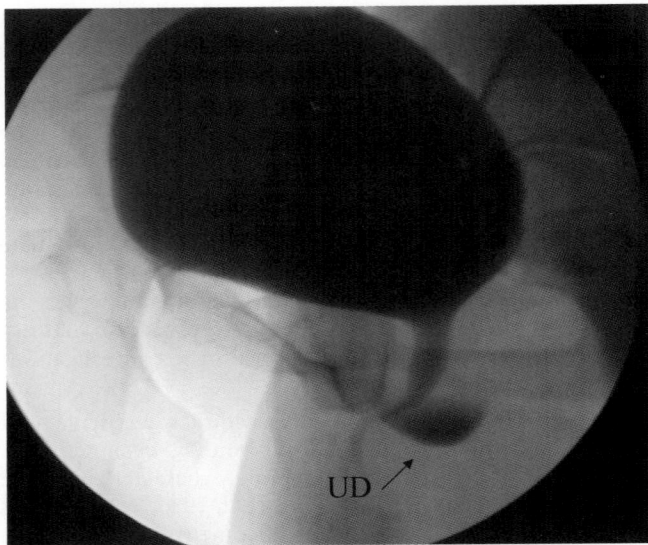

Figure 73–21. Voiding image from VCUG demonstrating a urethral diverticulum (UD).

because the contrast material will not enter and fill these areas in the absence of a connection to the urethral lumen.

As an alternative to PPU, VCUG may provide excellent imaging of urethral diverticula (Fig. 73–21). It is widely available and is a familiar diagnostic technique to most radiologists. Sensitivity for urethral diverticula with this technique varies from 44% to 95% (Ganabathi et al, 1994; Jacoby and Rowbotham, 1999). After a scout film, the bladder is filled through a urethral catheter. The catheter is removed at bladder capacity, and images of the bladder and bladder neck are obtained. Ideally, voiding images are obtained in the anterior-posterior, lateral, and oblique projections. Finally, a postvoid film is done. Patients will often have difficulty in initiating micturition in the radiology suite because of the pain associated with urethral catheterization, psychogenic inhibition due to voiding in the presence of others, or other factors. In the absence of voiding, the urethral diverticulum will not be seen. Therefore, VCUG that does not demonstrate a urethral diverticulum but did not contain voiding images or postvoid images is nondiagnostic. If the patient is unable to void under fluoroscopy during VCUG, an attempt should be made to void in the privacy of an adjacent bathroom. If voiding in private is successful, a postvoid film under these circumstances will likely show a collection of contrast material inferior to the bladder demonstrating the urethral diverticulum. **Whereas VCUG is probably the most widely used study for the diagnosis and evaluation of patients with known or suspected urethral diverticula, it has several limitations.** First, VCUG is invasive, requiring catheterization of the urethra for bladder filling. This can result in considerable discomfort for the patient and may risk translocation of bacteria from an infected urethral diverticulum into the bladder during catheterization, resulting in bacterial cystitis. This is also a risk of PPU. Importantly, successful imaging of the urethral diverticulum occurs only during the voiding phase of VCUG with subsequent filling of the urethra. On occasion, only the postvoid film demonstrates the urethral diverticulum (Houser and VonEschenbach, 1974; Stern and Patel, 1976; Goldfarb et al, 1981). As noted before, not uncommonly, patients are somewhat inhibited or otherwise unable to void during VCUG for a variety of reasons, including pain from the initial urethral catheterization. Unfortunately, in the absence

of contrast material entering the urethra, opacification of the diverticulum does not occur. Furthermore, an inability to generate an adequate flow rate during VCUG will result in suboptimal filling of the urethral diverticulum and an underestimation of its size and complexity (Fig. 73–22). Finally, similar to PPU, some urethral diverticula may not opacify after technically successful VCUG because of acute inflammation of the ostium or neck of the diverticulum or because the diverticulum does not otherwise communicate with the urethral lumen.

Three studies have compared VCUG with PPU and concluded that PPU is a more sensitive test for urethral diverticula than is VCUG (Jacoby and Rowbotham, 1999; Wang and Wang, 2000; Golomb et al, 2003). In one study of 32 patients, VCUG failed to demonstrate the urethral diverticulum in 69% of patients, whereas PPU failed to demonstrate the lesion in only 6% (Jacoby and Rowbotham, 1999).

Intravenous urography may be considered in patients in whom it is necessary to delineate the upper urinary tract or to evaluate for the possibility of a congenital ectopic ureteral anomaly as the cause of an anterior vaginal wall mass (Blacklock and Shaw, 1982). The postvoid film can be helpful for the diagnosis of urethral diverticula in some patients (Stern and Patel, 1976; Goldfarb et al, 1981).

Ultrasonography. This study has been advocated for the preoperative assessment of vaginal masses and urethral diverticula by multiple authors (Lee and Keller, 1977; Wexler and McGovern, 1980; Baert et al, 1992; Martensson and Duchek, 1994; Chancellor et al, 1995; Vargas-Serrano et al, 1997; Dmochowski, 2001; Fortunato et al, 2001; Lee et al, 2001; Gerrard et al, 2003). Abdominal, transvaginal, translabial, and transurethral techniques have been described. **Transvaginal imaging often provides information about the size and location of urethral diverticula.** On ultrasonographic imaging, the urethral diverticulum appears as an anechoic or hypoechoic area with enhanced through-transmission. Ultrasonog-

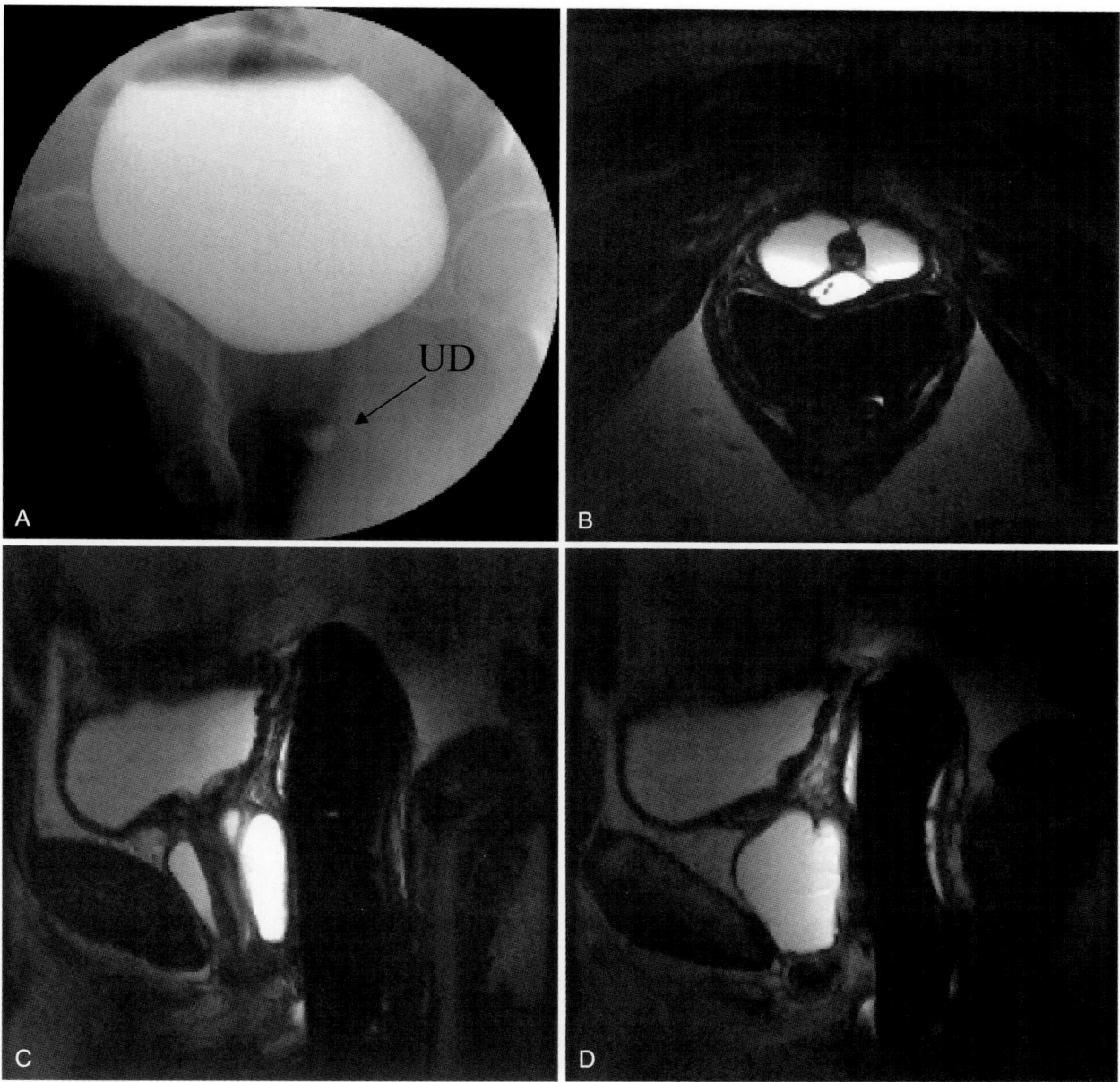

Figure 73–22. VCUG and MRI study of a patient with a large circumferential urethral diverticulum. The voiding image from VCUG (**A**) shows poor opacification of the proximal urethra with suboptimal distention of the urethral diverticulum (UD) due to a poor voiding effort. Endoluminal MRI demonstrates the full extent and complexity of the lesion on the T2 axial (**B**), midline sagittal (**C**), and parasagittal (**D**) images.

raphy is relatively noninvasive and does not expose the patient to radiation. Another significant advantage of ultrasonography is that successful imaging of urethral diverticula does not require voiding. However, ultrasonography may not produce detailed high-resolution images that demonstrate precise surgical anatomy. Furthermore, this study can be somewhat operator dependent. Transurethral ultrasound techniques are evolving and may provide an incremental improvement in resolution. However, similar to PPU and VCUG, the transurethral techniques are invasive as the ultrasound probe is placed per urethra and can cause discomfort to the patient and bacterial seeding of the lower urinary tract.

Magnetic Resonance Imaging. As an alternative to the radiologic investigations noted previously, MRI permits relatively noninvasive, high-resolution, multiplanar imaging of urethral diverticula. **Urethral diverticula appear as areas of decreased signal intensity on T1 images compared with the surrounding soft tissues and have high signal intensity on T2 images** (see Figs. 73–16, 73–17, and 73–22). **Additional advantages of MRI compared with PPU and VCUG are that successful imaging of urethral diverticula is wholly independent of voiding and that it is free from ionizing radiation.** Surface coil (Hricak et al, 1991; Kim et al, 1993) (Fig. 73–23) and endoluminal techniques (Blander et al, 2001; Siegelman et al,

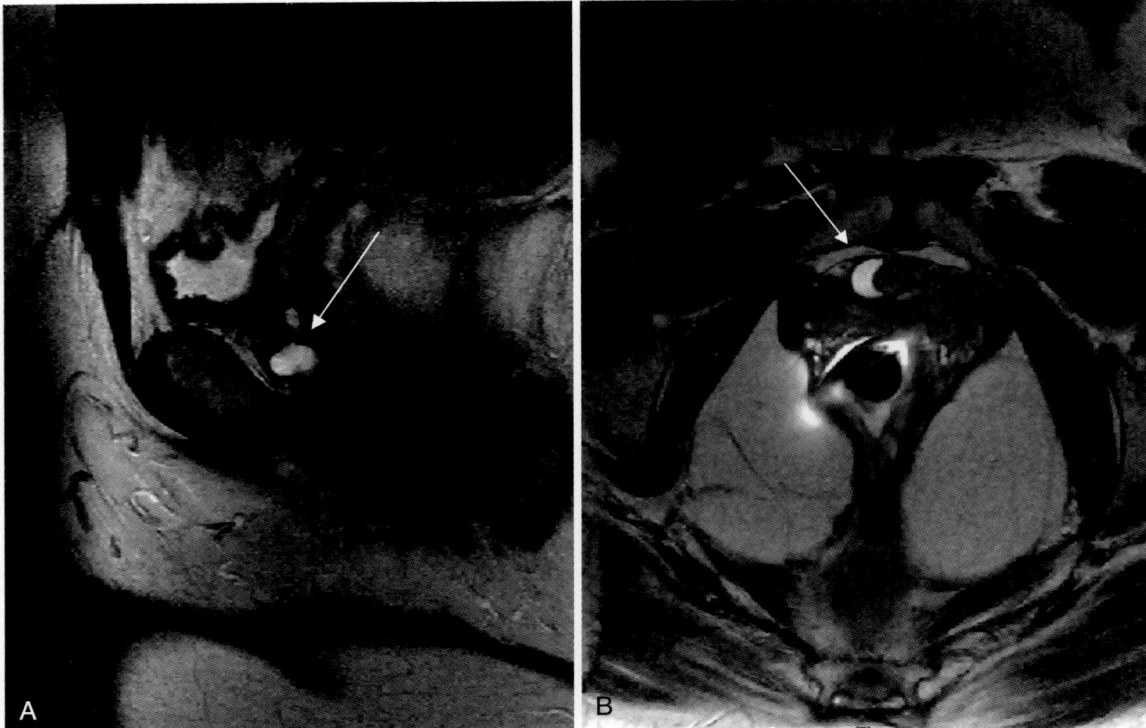

Figure 73–23. Surface coil T2 MRI demonstrating a urethral diverticulum in the sagittal (**A**) and axial (**B**) planes. The arrow shows the urethral diverticulum.

1997; Wang and Wang, 2000; Lorenzo et al, 2003) have been described. Endoluminal imaging places the magnetic coil into a body cavity adjacent to the area of interest. This location produces an improved signal-to-noise ratio and high-resolution imaging of these areas (Siegelman et al, 1997; Blander et al, 2001). For the evaluation of urethral diverticula, the coil is placed intravaginally or intrarectally (see Figs. 73–12, 73–16, 73–17, 73–22, and 73–23). Both surface coil MRI and endoluminal MRI appear to be superior to VCUG and PPU in the evaluation of urethral diverticula (Kim et al, 1993; Neitlich et al, 1998; Blander et al, 2001), but the technology is expensive and not widely available. Contraindications to MRI for urethral diverticula are few; these include metallic foreign body fragments, claustrophobia, and an inability to tolerate the endoluminal probe.

Differential Diagnosis: Periurethral Masses Other Than Urethral Diverticula

Periurethral masses other than urethral diverticula represent a wide spectrum of conditions that must be differentiated from each other and urethral diverticula. It may often be possible to make a definitive diagnosis on the basis of history and physical examination alone; in other cases, judicious use of radiographic and cystoscopic studies will be necessary to exclude urethral diverticula.

Vaginal Leiomyoma. Vaginal leiomyoma is a benign mesenchymal tumor of the vaginal wall that arises from smooth muscle elements. It commonly presents as a smooth, firm, round mass on the anterior vaginal wall (Fig. 73–24). It is an uncommon lesion with approximately 300 cases reported in

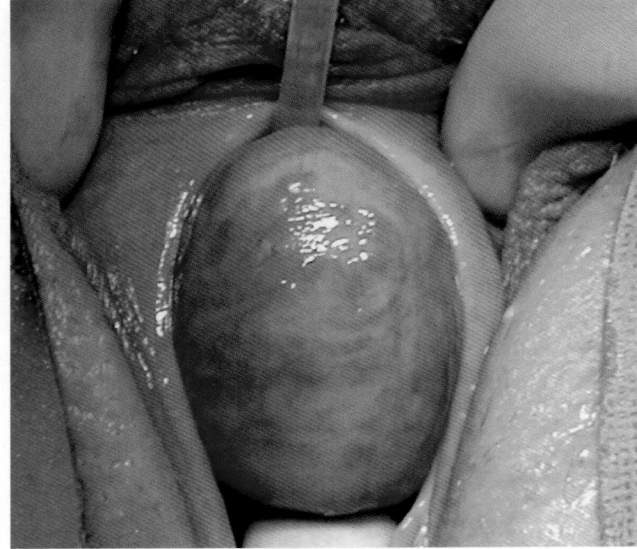

Figure 73–24. Large anterior vaginal wall leiomyoma.

the literature (Young et al, 1991). In a recent series of 79 patients with periurethral masses, 4 (5%) were found to have vaginal leiomyoma (Blaivas et al, 2004). These masses were all apparent on physical examination as freely mobile, firm, nontender masses on the anterior vaginal wall. They may be misdiagnosed as urethral diverticula (Shirvani and Winters, 2000). Symptoms, if they exist, are usually related to the size of the lesion and include a mass effect, obstruction, pain, and dyspareunia.

Vaginal leiomyomas commonly present in the fourth to fifth decade. Like uterine leiomyomas, these lesions are usually estrogen dependent and have been demonstrated to regress during menopause (Liu, 1988). Excision or enucleation (Young et al, 1991) through a vaginal approach is often curative and is recommended to confirm the diagnosis, to exclude malignant histology, and to alleviate symptoms.

Skene's Gland Abnormalities. Skene's gland cysts and abscesses are similar lesions that are differentiated on the basis of clinical findings (Fig. 73–25). Both lesions generally present as small, cystic masses just lateral or inferolateral to the urethral meatus. They may be lined with transitional or stratified squamous epithelium. Abscesses may be extremely tender and inflamed, and purulent fluid can be expressed from the ductular orifice in some cases. **Classically, in contrast to urethral diverticula, these lesions do not communicate with the urethral lumen.** Skene's gland cysts are not uncommonly noted in neonatal girls and young to middle-aged women (Lee and Kim, 1992). Symptoms may include dysuria, dyspareunia, obstruction, and pain. **Differentiation from urethral diverticula can often be made on physical examination as these lesions are located relatively distal on the urethra, often distorting the urethral meatus, compared with urethral diverticula, which most commonly occur over the mid and proximal urethra.** Various treatments for abnormalities of Skene's glands have been described, including aspiration, marsupialization, incision and drainage, and simple excision.

Adenocarcinoma arising in Skene's glands has been reported. Because of homology with the prostate, these patients may demonstrate elevated prostate-specific antigen levels, which normalize with treatment (Dodson et al, 1994).

Gartner's Duct Abnormalities. Gartner's duct cysts represent mesonephric remnants and are found on the anterolateral vaginal wall from the cervix to the introitus. Because these are mesonephric remnants, they may drain ectopic ureters from poorly functioning or nonfunctioning upper pole moieties in duplicated systems (Fig. 73–26). They have also been reported with single-system ectopia, although this is much less common in females (Gadbois and Duckett, 1974; Currarino, 1982). It is not clear what proportion of patients with Gartner's duct cysts will have ipsilateral renal abnormalities, but upper tract evaluation is recommended. In contrast, approximately 6% of subjects with unilateral renal agenesis will have a Gartner's duct cyst (Eilber and Raz, 2003). Up to 50% of patients with Gartner's duct cysts and renal dysplasia may also have ipsilateral müllerian duct obstruction (Sheih et al, 1998).

Treatment depends on symptoms and association with ectopic ureters. If the lesions are asymptomatic and are associated with a nonfunctioning renal moiety, they can be observed. Aspiration and sclerotherapy have been successful (Abd-Rabbo and Atta, 1991). Simple excision or marsupialization has also been recommended for symptomatic lesions. If the cyst is associated with a functioning renal moiety, treatment must be individualized.

Vaginal Wall Cysts. Vaginal wall cysts usually present as small asymptomatic masses on the anterior vaginal wall (Deppisch, 1975) but may enlarge to cause lower urinary tract symptoms or dyspareunia (Fig. 73–27). They may arise from multiple cell types: mesonephric (Gartner's duct cysts), paramesonephric (müllerian), endometriotic, urothelial, or epidermoid (inclusion cyst). A specific diagnosis cannot reliably be made until the specimen is removed and examined by a pathologist. The histologic subtype is usually of little consequence, although epidermoid cysts are usually associated with

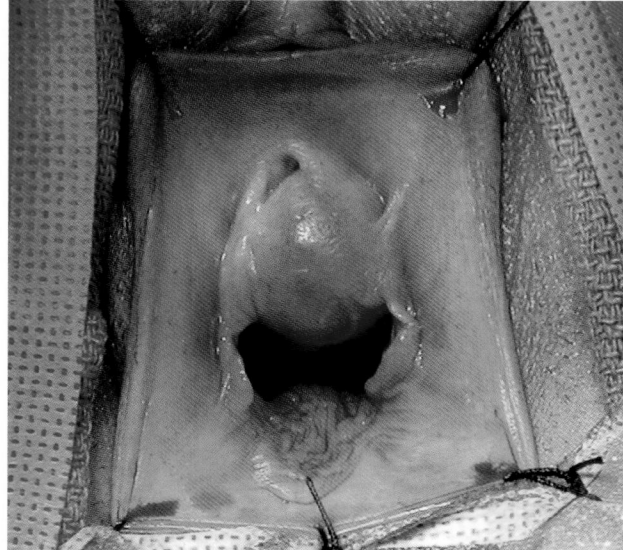

Figure 73–25. Skene's gland cyst in a 19-year-old woman. Note the large periurethral mass with displacement of the urethral meatus.

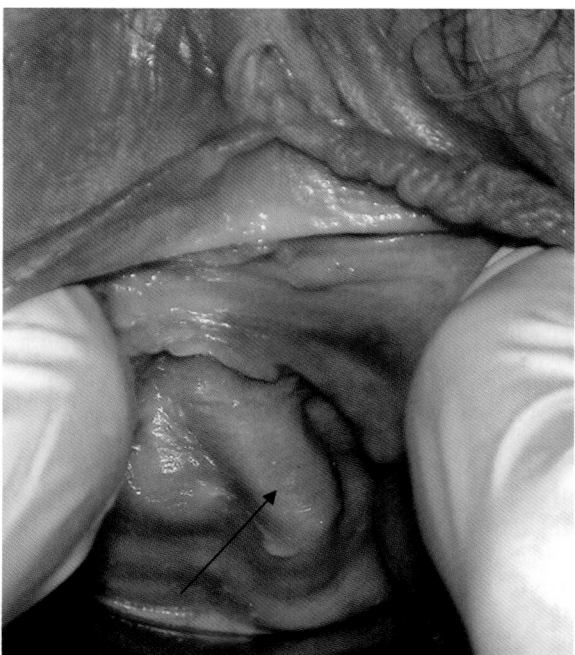

Figure 73–26. Upper pole ectopic ureter in a 39-year-old woman being evaluated for lifelong urinary incontinence and recurrent pyelonephritis. A tubelike structure *(arrow)* representing the turgid, debris-filled ectopic ureter is seen on the anterior vaginal wall.

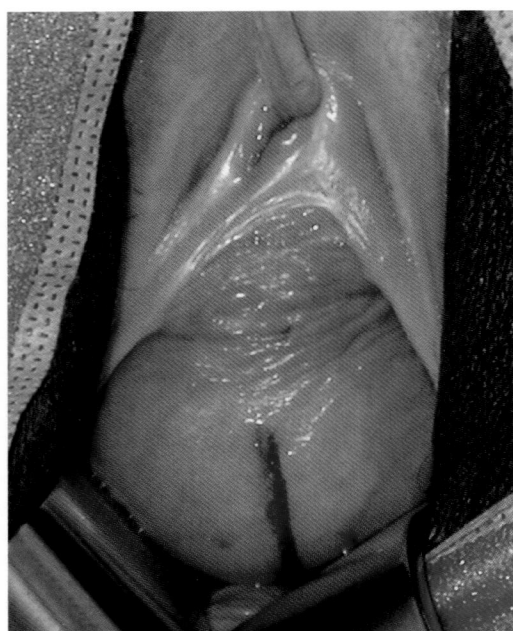

Figure 73–27. Anterior vaginal wall cyst before planned excision. This anterior vaginal wall mass was misdiagnosed as a cystocele and observed for many years in this patient with considerable lower urinary tract symptoms.

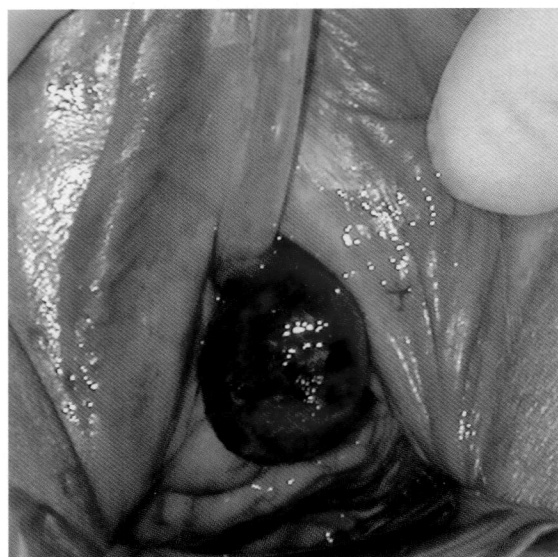

Figure 73–28. Thrombosed urethral caruncle in a postmenopausal woman. The Foley catheter is seen in the urethra. Simple excision was curative.

previous trauma or vaginal surgery. Pradhan and Tobon (1986) described the pathologic characteristics of 43 vaginal cysts in 41 women removed during a 10-year period. The derivation of the cyst was müllerian in 44%, epidermoid in 23%, and mesonephric in 11%. The remainder were Bartholin gland type, endometriotic, and indeterminate. As with other periurethral masses, they must be differentiated from urethral diverticula. Treatment is usually by simple excision in symptomatic patients.

Urethral Mucosal Prolapse. Urethral prolapse presents as a circumferential herniation or eversion of the urethral mucosa at the urethral meatus. The prolapsed mucosa commonly appears as a beefy red "doughnut"-shaped lesion that completely surrounds the urethral meatus. It may be asymptomatic or present with bleeding, spotting, pain, or urinary symptoms. It is commonly noted in two separate populations: postmenopausal women and prepubertal girls. Although thought to be more common in young African American girls, more recent series do not confirm this predilection (Fernandes et al, 1993; Rudin et al, 1997). In children, it is often causally related to a Valsalva maneuver or constipation. Eversion of the mucosa may then occur because of a pathologically loose attachment between smooth muscle layers of the urethra (Lowe et al, 1986). Etiology is much less clear for postmenopausal women, although it has been epidemiologically linked to estrogen deficiency.

Treatment may be medical or surgical. Medical treatment involves topical creams (estrogen, anti-inflammatory) and sitz baths. Various surgical techniques, including cauterization, ligation around a Foley catheter, and complete circumferential excision, have been described. Circumferential excision with suture reapproximation of the remaining urethral mucosa to the vaginal wall can be performed with few com-

plications. Rudin and colleagues (1997) reported outcomes in 58 girls with urethral prolapse. Medical treatment was initially successful in 20 patients, in whom there were five recurrences. Initial conservative management failed in the remaining 38 patients, who underwent surgical excision with four complications, including urethral stenosis in two. Jerkins and coworkers (1984) found superior results in surgically treated patients compared with medical management or catheter ligation.

Urethral Caruncle. Urethral caruncle is an inflammatory lesion of the distal urethra that is most commonly diagnosed in postmenopausal women. It usually appears as a reddish exophytic mass at the urethral meatus that is covered with mucosa. These lesions are often symptomatic and noted incidentally on gynecologic examination. When irritated, they may cause underwear spotting or become painful. Less commonly, they may cause voiding symptoms. Rarely, these lesions may thrombose, resulting in a discolored periurethral mass (Fig. 73–28). They are etiologically related to mucosal prolapse. Chronic irritation contributes to hemorrhage, necrosis, and inflammatory growth of the tissue, which corresponds to the histology of excised lesions. If the lesion is atypical in appearance or behavior, excision may be warranted to exclude other entities. Intestinal metaplasia, tuberculosis, melanoma, and lymphoma have been reported either to coexist with or to mimic urethral caruncles (Willett and Lack, 1990; Indudhara et al, 1992; Khatib et al, 1993; Lopez et al, 1993; Atalay et al, 1998).

There is a paucity of literature regarding optimal treatment of urethral caruncle. Most authors recommend initial conservative management with topical estrogen or anti-inflammatory creams and sitz baths. Large or refractory lesions may be managed with simple excision. The tip of the lesion should be grasped and traction employed to fully expose the base of the caruncle. The lesion can then easily be excised. If a large defect remains, the mucosa may be reapproximated with absorbable suture. In most instances, the urethral mucosa will heal around a Foley catheter that may be left in place for several days.

Classification of Urethral Diverticula

Although not yet widely adopted, a classification system for urethral diverticula has been proposed by Leach and colleagues (1993). This staging system, termed the L/N/S/C3 classification system, is similar to that used for cancer staging and is based on several characteristics of urethral diverticula including location, number, size, anatomic configuration, site of communication to the urethral lumen, and continence status of the patient. This system attempts to standardize description of urethral diverticula but has not been prospectively applied or validated by other authors. Another proposed classification scheme uses the location of the urethral diverticulum as the primary determinant of surgical approach, with distal lesions undergoing marsupialization and more proximal lesions undergoing excision and reconstruction (Ginsburg and Genadry, 1983).

Finally, a classification system proposed by Leng and McGuire (1998) divides urethral diverticula into two categories based on the presence or absence of a preserved periurethral fascial layer. In some patients with urethral diverticula who have undergone prior vaginal or urethral surgery, the periurethral fascial layer may be deficient, resulting in a pseudodiverticulum. These authors suggest that the recognition of this anatomic configuration has important implications for surgical reconstruction. These patients may require additional reconstruction or interposition of a tissue flap or graft for reconstruction.

Surgical Repair of Female Urethral Diverticula

Indications for Repair

Although often highly symptomatic, not all urethral diverticula mandate surgical excision. Some patients may be asymptomatic at presentation, with the lesion incidentally diagnosed on imaging for another condition or perhaps incidentally noted on routine physical examination. Other patients may be unwilling or medically unable to undergo surgical removal. **Little is known about the natural history of untreated urethral diverticula. Whether these lesions will progress in size, symptoms, or complexity with time is unknown.** For these reasons and because of the lack of symptoms in selected cases, some patients may not desire surgical therapy. However, there are multiple reports in the literature of carcinomas arising in urethral diverticula (Marshall and Hirsch, 1977; Prudente et al, 1978; Tesluk, 1981; Tines et al, 1982; Patanaphan et al, 1983; Gonzalez et al, 1985; Thomas and Maguire, 1991; Rajan et al, 1993; Seballos and Rich, 1995; Hickey et al, 2000), and it is possible that certain carcinomas arising in urethral diverticula are asymptomatic and may not be prospectively identified on radiologic imaging. Thus, counseling is necessary in patients who elect primary nonoperative management. Patients electing nonoperative management can be treated with low-dose antibacterial suppressants and digital stripping of the anterior vaginal wall after micturition to prevent postvoid dribbling and to reduce the risk of urinary tract infection due to stasis in the urethral diverticulum.

Whether long-term surveillance is required in these patients with periodic physical examinations, radiographic imaging, or endoscopic examination is unknown.

Symptomatic patients, including those with dysuria, refractory bothersome postvoid dribbling, recurrent urinary tract infections, dyspareunia, and pelvic pain in whom the symptoms can be attributed to the urethral diverticulum, may be offered surgical excision. Those with urethral diverticula and symptomatic stress urinary incontinence can be considered for a concomitant anti-incontinence procedure at the time of excision of the urethral diverticulum (see later discussion) (Fig. 73–29).

Techniques for Repair

Alternative Techniques. A variety of surgical interventions for urethral diverticula have been reported since 1805, when Hey described transvaginal incision of the urethral diverticulum and packing of the resulting cavity with lint (Hey, 1805). Approaches have included transurethral (Davis and Robinson, 1970) and open (Spence and Duckett, 1970; Roehrborn, 1988) marsupialization, endoscopic unroofing (Lapides, 1978; Spencer and Streem, 1987), fulguration (Saito, 2000), incision and obliteration with oxidized cellulose (Ellick, 1957) or polytetrafluoroethylene (Mizrahi and Bitterman, 1988), coagulation (Mizrahi and Bitterman, 1988), and excision with reconstruction. Most commonly, complete excision and reconstruction are performed as described in the following section. However, for distal lesions, a transvaginal marsupialization as described by Spence and Duckett may reduce operative time, blood loss, and recurrence rate (Spence and Duckett, 1969, 1970; Roehrborn, 1988). During this procedure, care must be taken to avoid aggressively extending the incision proximally, which could result in vaginal voiding or potentially damage the proximal and distal sphincteric mechanism, causing stress urinary incontinence. Therefore, this approach is probably applicable only to urethral diverticula in very select cases involving the distal third of the urethra. It is not commonly performed.

Excision and Reconstruction. The most common surgical approach to urethral diverticula in the modern era is probably excision and reconstruction. The principles of the urethral diverticulectomy operation have been well described (Table 73–3). There are only a few minor issues about which some surgeons may disagree, including the type of vaginal incision (inverted U versus inverted T), whether it is necessary to remove the entire mucosalized portion of the lesion, and the optimal type of postoperative catheter drainage (urethra only versus urethra and suprapubic).

Table 73–3. Principles of Transvaginal Urethral Diverticulectomy

Mobilization of a well-vascularized anterior vaginal wall flap
Preservation of the periurethral fascia
Identification and excision of the neck of the urethral diverticulum or ostium
Removal of entire urethral diverticulum wall or sac (mucosa)
Watertight urethral closure
Multilayered, non-overlapping closure with absorbable suture
Closure of dead space
Preservation or creation of continence

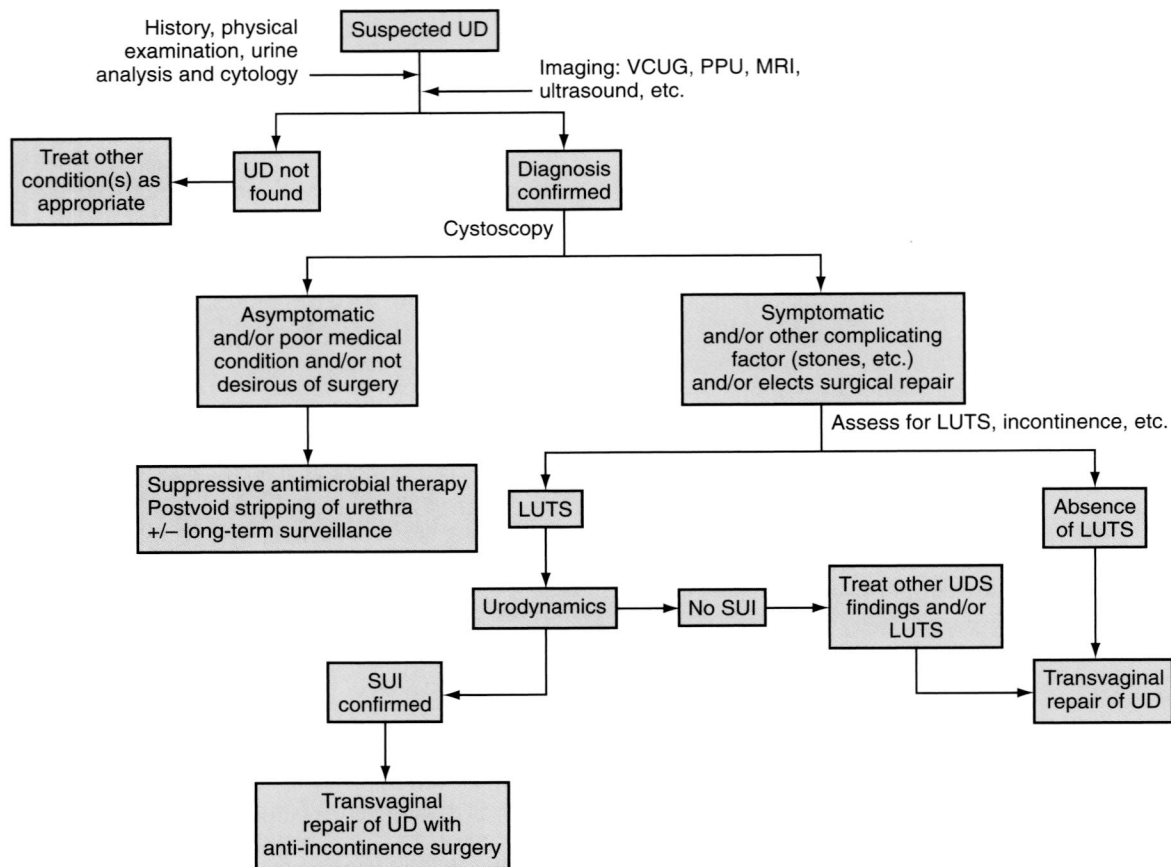

Figure 73–29. Algorithm for treatment of urethral diverticula. UD, urethral diverticulum; LUTS, lower urinary tract symptoms; MRI, magnetic resonance imaging; PPU, positive-pressure urethrography; SUI, stress urinary incontinence; UDS, urodynamics; VCUG, voiding cystourethrography.

Complex urethral reconstructive techniques for the repair of urethral diverticula have been described. Fall (1995) described the use of a bipedicled vaginal wall flap for urethral reconstruction in patients with urethral diverticula and urethrovaginal fistula. Laterally based vaginal flaps have also been used as an initial approach to urethral diverticula (Woodhouse et al, 1980; Appell and Suarez, 1982). Complex anatomic configurations may exist, and many novel approaches have been described for complicated anteriorly located or circumferential lesions (Clyne and Flood, 2002; Rovner and Wein, 2003; Vakili et al, 2003).

The technique described herein is similar to that described by Leach and Raz (Leach et al, 1986) based on earlier work by Benjamin and colleagues (1974) and Busch and Carter (1973).

Preoperative Preparation. Prophylactic antibiotics are often used preoperatively to ensure sterile urine at the time of surgery. Patients can also be encouraged to strip the anterior vaginal wall after voiding, thereby consistently emptying the urethral diverticulum and preventing urinary stasis and recurrent urinary tract infections. This may not be possible in those with noncommunicating urethral diverticula or in those who have significant pain related to the urethral diverticulum. Application of topical estrogen creams for several weeks before surgery may be beneficial in some patients with postmenopausal atrophic vaginitis in improving the overall quality of the tissues with respect to planned operative dissection and

mobilization. Preoperative parenteral antibiotics are often administered, especially for those with recurrent or persistent urinary tract infections.

Patients with symptomatic stress urinary incontinence can be offered simultaneous anti-incontinence surgery. Preoperative video-urodynamics may be helpful in evaluating the anatomy of the urethral diverticulum, assessing the competence of the bladder neck, and confirming the diagnosis of stress urinary incontinence. In patients with stress urinary incontinence and urethral diverticula, Ganabathi and others have described excellent results with concomitant needle bladder neck suspension in these complex patients (Ganabathi et al, 1994; Lockhart et al, 1990). More recently, pubovaginal fascial slings have been used in patients with urethral diverticula and stress urinary incontinence with satisfactory outcomes (Swierzewski and McGuire, 1993; Faerber, 1998; Romanzi et al, 2000).

Further complicating these cases may be associated symptoms such as pain, dyspareunia, voiding dysfunction, urinary tract infections, and urinary incontinence. These associated symptoms are often but not always improved or eliminated with surgical repair. Therefore, the importance of appropriate preoperative counseling of the patient about surgery and postoperative expectations of cure cannot be overemphasized.

Procedure. The patient is placed in the lithotomy position with all pressure points well padded. The use of padded adjustable stirrups for the lower extremities greatly enhances operative access to the female perineum. A standard vaginal antiseptic preparation is applied. A weighted vaginal speculum and Scott retractor with hooks aid in exposure. **A posterolateral episiotomy may be beneficial in some patients for additional exposure, although the midurethral (and therefore somewhat distal in the vaginal canal) location of most urethral diverticula usually precludes the need for this type of adjunctive procedure.** A Foley catheter is placed per urethra. If desired, a suprapubic tube is placed at the start of the procedure either by use of a Lowsley retractor or percutaneously under direct transurethral cystoscopic visual guidance. Placement of the suprapubic tube at the end of the case is not advisable as this will require traversing the fresh urethral suture line and risk disruption of the repair.

An inverted U is marked out along the anterior vaginal wall with the base of the U at the level of the distal urethra and the limbs extending to the bladder neck or beyond (Fig. 73–30A). Care is taken to make the limbs of the U progressively wider proximally (toward the bladder neck) to ensure adequate vas-

cularity at the distal lateral margins of the anterior vaginal wall flap. As opposed to the inverted T incision, the inverted U incision provides excellent exposure laterally at the level of the midvagina and can be extended proximally as needed for lesions that extend beyond the bladder neck. Injectable saline can be infused along the lines of the incision to facilitate dissection. An anterior vaginal wall flap is created by careful dissection in the potential space between the vaginal wall and the periurethral fascia. **The use of sufficient countertraction during this portion of the procedure is important in maintaining the proper plane of dissection. Care is taken to preserve the periurethral fascia and to avoid inadvertent entry into the urethral diverticulum.**

A distinct layer of periurethral fascia is usually interposed between the vaginal wall and the urethral diverticulum. Preservation and later reconstruction of this layer are of paramount importance to prevent recurrence, to close dead space, and to avoid urethrovaginal fistula formation postoperatively. Pseudodiverticula have been described where this layer of tissue is considerably attenuated or even absent (Leng and McGuire, 1998). In these patients, an interpositional

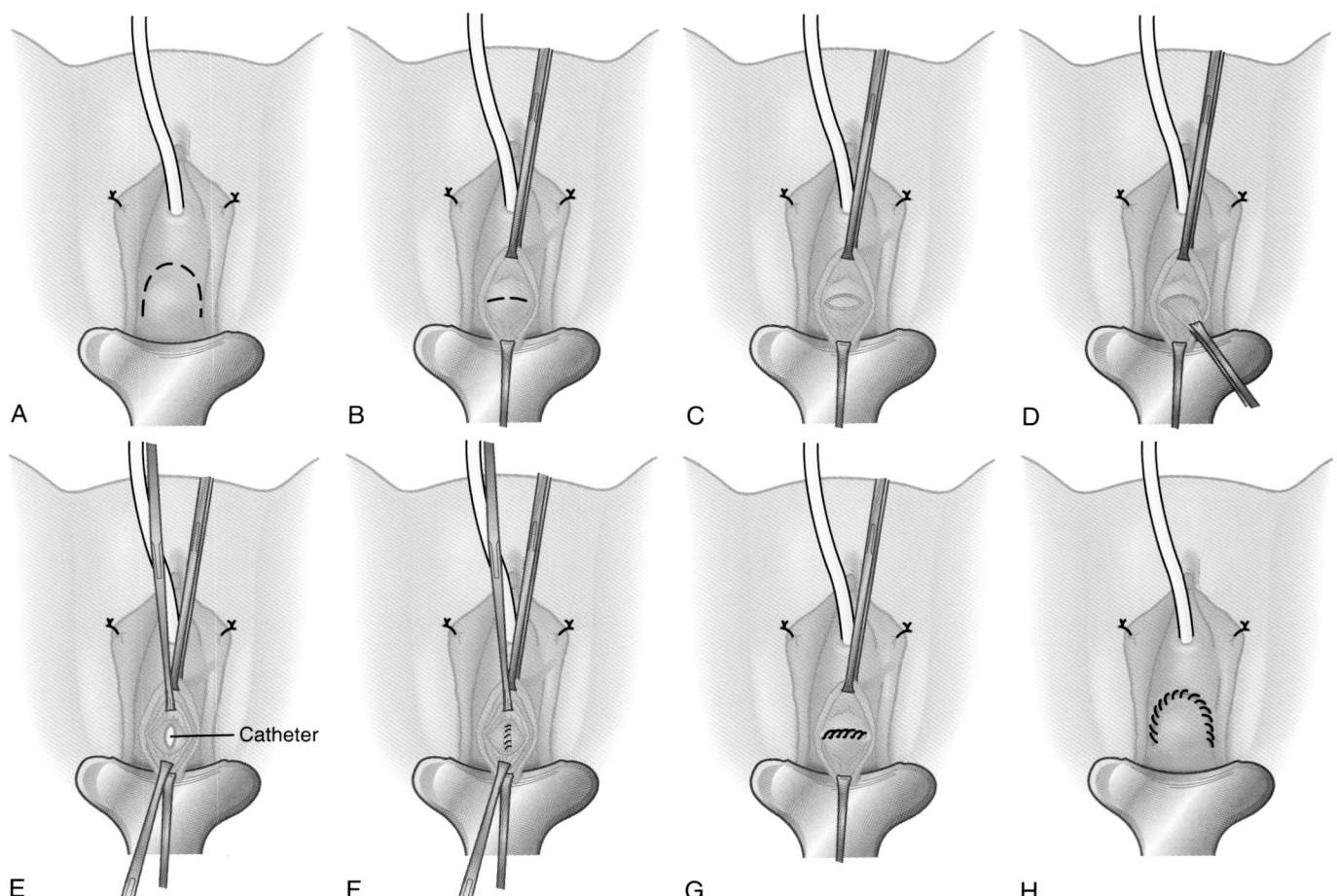

Figure 73–30. **A,** An inverted U incision is marked on the anterior vaginal wall. Retraction is aided by the use of Allis clamps and a ring retractor with hooks. **B,** After reflection of the anterior vaginal wall, a transverse incision is made in the periurethral fascia. The dotted line represents the intended incision line. **C,** The periurethral fascia is incised and dissected from the underlying urethral diverticulum. **D,** The diverticular sac is freed from the periurethral fascia. **E,** The urethral catheter is seen after complete excision of the diverticular sac. **F,** The urethra is closed with absorbable suture. **G,** The periurethral fascia is closed with care to obliterate any dead space. **H,** The anterior vaginal wall flap is advanced over the periurethral suture line and secured with running interlocking absorbable suture.

flap or graft, such as a pubovaginal sling, may be used for reconstruction.

The periurethral fascia is incised transversely (Fig. 73–30B). Proximal and distal layers of periurethral fascia are carefully developed, avoiding entrance into the urethral diverticulum. The urethral diverticulum is then grasped and dissected back to its origin on the urethra within the leaves of the periurethral fascia (Fig. 73–30C). In many cases, it is necessary to open the urethral diverticulum to facilitate dissection from the surrounding tissues. The ostium or connection to the urethra is identified, and the walls of the urethral diverticulum are completely removed. Every effort should be made to remove the entire mucosalized surface of the urethral diverticulum to prevent recurrence (Ganabathi et al, 1994; Fortunato et al, 2001). This may involve removal of small adherent or inflamed portions of the urethral wall, especially in the area of the ostium (Fig. 73–30D). All abnormal tissue in the area of the ostium should be removed if possible to ensure that no mucosal elements of the diverticular wall remain that could result in postoperative urine leakage and recurrence. Elaborate methods of identifying the full extent of the diverticular cavity have been described, including catheterization of the urethral diverticulum with urinary (Moore, 1952; Kohorn and Glickman, 1992) and Fogarty (Wear, 1976) catheters, packing the urethral diverticulum with gauze (Hyams and Hyams, 1939), infusing and staining the urethral diverticulum with methylene blue (Gilbert and Rivera Cintron, 1954), and using silicone (Hirschhorn, 1964) or cryoprecipitate (Feldstein, 1981) to create a solid mass and ease dissection. However, these measures are mostly of historical interest only and are usually not necessary in modern surgery for urethral diverticula (Leach and Bavendam, 1987; Ganabathi et al, 1994).

The Foley catheter is usually seen after complete excision of urethral diverticula (Fig. 73–30E). The urethra can be reconstructed over a Foley catheter as small as 12 French without long-term risk of urethral stricture (Young et al, 1996) and should be closed in a watertight fashion with absorbable suture (Fig. 73–30F). The closure should be tension free. Uncommonly, a urethral diverticulum may extend circumferentially around the urethra and require segmental resection of the involved portion of the urethra and complex reconstruction (Tamada et al, 2000; Rovner and Wein, 2003).

The periurethral fascial flaps are reapproximated with absorbable suture in a perpendicular orientation to the urethral closure line to minimize overlap and the risk of postoperative urethrovaginal fistula formation (Fig. 73–30G). Care is taken to secure the periurethral fascial flaps in such a way as to close all dead space.

If desired, a fibrofatty labial (Martius) flap can be harvested at this point and placed over the periurethral fascia as an additional layer of closure (Dmochowski, 2001). **Indications for such a flap are not universally agreed on. However, in those patients with poor-quality tissues, with attenuated periurethral fascia, or in whom significant inflammation is encountered intraoperatively, a well-vascularized adjuvant flap such as a Martius flap may reduce the risk of wound breakdown and subsequent complications such as urethrovaginal fistula.**

The anterior vaginal wall flap is then repositioned and reapproximated with absorbable suture (Fig. 73–30H). This completes a three-layer closure (four layers if a Martius flap is used). An antibiotic-impregnated vaginal pack is placed.

Table 73-4. Complications of Transvaginal Urethral Diverticulectomy

Complication	% Range of Reported Incidence
Urinary incontinence	1.7-16.1
Urethrovaginal fistula	0.9-8.3
Urethral stricture	0-5.2
Recurrent urethral diverticulum	1-25
Recurrent urinary tract infection	0-31.3
Other	
Hypospadias, distal urethral necrosis	
Bladder or ureteral injury	
Vaginal scarring or narrowing (e.g., dyspareunia)	

*Modified from Dmochowski R: Surgery for vesicovaginal fistula, urethrovaginal fistula, and urethral diverticulum. In Walsh PC, Retik AB, Vaughan ED Jr, Wein AJ, eds: Campbell's Urology, 8th ed. Philadelphia, WB Saunders, 2002:1214.

Postoperative Care. Antibiotics are continued for 24 hours postoperatively. The vaginal packing is removed and the patient discharged home with closed urinary drainage. Antispasmodics are used liberally to reduce bladder spasms. A pericatheter VCUG is obtained at 14 to 21 days postoperatively. If there is no extravasation, the catheters are removed. If extravasation is seen, repeated pericatheter VCUGs are performed weekly until resolution is noted. In most cases, extravasation will resolve in several weeks with this type of conservative management (Schwab and Rovner, 2003).

Complications. Careful adherence to the principles of transvaginal urethral diverticulectomy should minimize postoperative complications. Nevertheless, complications may arise (Table 73–4). One small series suggested that large diverticula (>4 cm) or those with a lateral or horseshoe configuration may be associated with a greater likelihood of postoperative complications (Porpiglia et al, 2002). **Common complications include recurrent urinary tract infections, urinary incontinence, and recurrent urethral diverticula. Urethrovaginal fistula is a devastating complication of urethral diverticulectomy and deserves special mention.** A urethrovaginal fistula located beyond the sphincteric mechanism should not be associated with symptoms other than perhaps a split urinary stream or vaginal voiding. As such, an asymptomatic distal urethrovaginal fistula may not require repair, although some patients may request repair. Conversely, a proximal fistula located at the bladder neck or at the midurethra in patients with an incompetent bladder neck will likely result in considerable symptomatic urinary leakage. These patients should undergo repair with consideration for the use of an adjuvant tissue flap such as a Martius flap to provide a well-vascularized additional tissue layer. The actual timing of the repair relative to the initial procedure is controversial. Meticulous attention to surgical technique, good hemostasis, avoidance of infection, preservation of the periurethral fascia (Fig. 73–31) and a well-vascularized anterior vaginal wall flap, and multilayered closure with nonoverlapping suture lines should minimize the potential for postoperative urethrovaginal fistula formation.

Persistence of Symptoms After Urethral Diverticulectomy. Some patients will have persistence or recurrence of their preoperative symptoms postoperatively. The finding of a urethral diverticulum after a presumably successful ure-

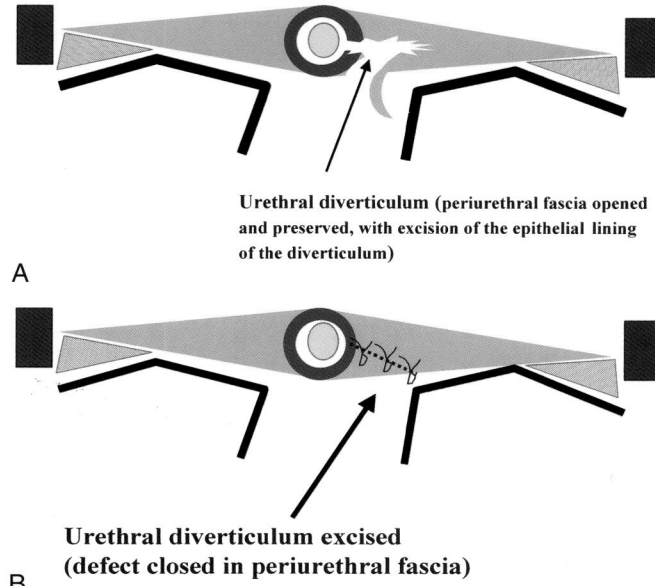

A

Urethral diverticulum (periurethral fascia opened and preserved, with excision of the epithelial lining of the diverticulum)

B

Urethral diverticulum excised (defect closed in periurethral fascia)

Figure 73–31. Diagrams demonstrating the importance of preserving and reconstructing the periurethral fascia. **A,** The periurethral fascia has been opened, and the urethral diverticulum has been excised. **B,** The periurethral fascia has been closed.

thral diverticulectomy may be a new medical problem (e.g., urinary tract infection), a new urethral diverticulum, or a recurrence of the original lesion. Recurrence of urethral diverticula may be due to incomplete removal of the urethral diverticulum, inadequate closure of the urethra or residual dead space, or other technical factors. Lee (1983) noted recurrent urethral diverticulum in 8 of 85 patients at follow-up between 2 and 15 years from the initial urethral diverticulum resection. **Repeated urethral diverticulectomy surgery can be challenging because of altered anatomy, scarring, and the difficulty in identifying the proper anatomic planes.**

Female Urethral Diverticula and Associated Conditions

Malignant and benign tumors may be found in urethral diverticula. Both are rare, and fewer than 100 cases of carcinoma within urethral diverticula have been reported in the English language literature (Rajan et al, 1993). **The most common malignant pathologic process in urethral diverticula is adenocarcinoma, followed by transitional cell and squamous cell carcinomas** (Rajan et al, 1993). This is in direct contrast to primary urethral carcinoma, in which the primary histologic type is squamous cell carcinoma. Some authors have suggested that urethral diverticulum is associated with the development of urethral adenocarcinoma in the female (Oliva and Young, 1996). If this is true, then nonexcisional therapy for urethral diverticula, such as marsupialization or endoscopic incision, should always be combined with a biopsy to rule out malignancy (McLoughlin, 1975). **There is no consensus on proper treatment in these cases, and recurrence rates are high with local treatment alone** (Rajan et al, 1993). The incidental finding of malignant change in these cases can be particularly troubling when it is found intraoperatively or even more disturbingly on the postoperative pathology report. Although it is interesting to speculate, it has not been conclusively demonstrated that any particular preoperative imaging modality, such as ultrasonography or MRI, can reliably and prospectively diagnose a small malignant neoplasm arising in a urethral diverticulum. In considering curative therapy, it is unclear whether extensive surgery including cystourethrectomy with or without adjuvant external beam radiotherapy is superior to local excision followed by radiotherapy (Patanaphan et al, 1983).

Multiple benign lesions including nephrogenic adenoma and endometriosis have been described within urethral diverticula (Palagiri, 1978; Peterson and Matsumoto, 1978; Piazza et al, 1987; Paik and Lee, 1997). On pathologic examination, nephrogenic adenoma can be difficult to differentiate from adenocarcinoma.

Calculi within urethral diverticula are not uncommon and may be diagnosed in 4% to 10% of cases (Ward et al, 1967;

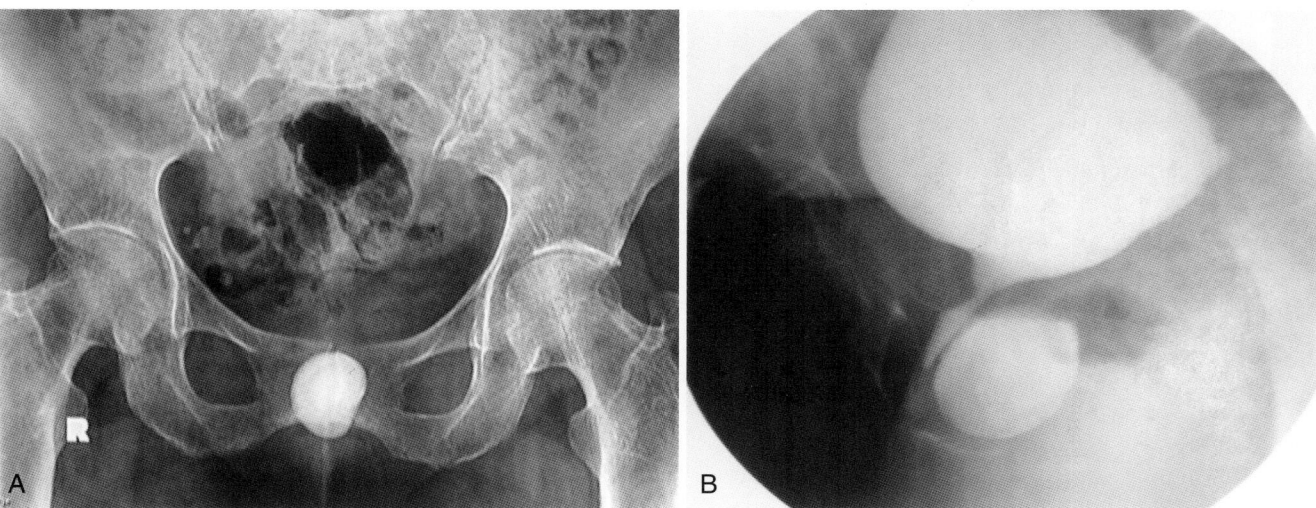

Figure 73–32. Calculi within a urethral diverticulum. **A,** Scout film shows a calcified density overlying the symphysis pubis. **B,** Voiding image from VCUG demonstrates that the density seen on the scout film represents a stone within a urethral diverticulum.

Ginesin et al, 1988; Romanzi et al, 2000); they are most likely due to urinary stasis or infection (Fig. 73–32). This may be suspected by physical examination findings or noted incidentally on imaging evaluation. The presence of a stone will not significantly alter the evaluation or surgical approach and can be considered an incidental finding. The stone is removed with the urethral diverticulum specimen at the time of surgery.

Urethral diverticulum has also been reported to present during pregnancy. Moran and colleagues (1998) reported four cases of urethral diverticula diagnosed during pregnancy. Conservative treatment included antibiotics and aspiration or incision and drainage. Two women delivered vaginally, and the other two delivered by cesarean section for unrelated reasons. In one patient, drainage was performed during labor to facilitate delivery. Three of the four women had definitive repair performed after delivery. It is not known if pregnancy is associated with formation of urethral diverticula, although patients may be more likely to become symptomatic during this period. Usually, conservative management with antibiotics may be desirable until after delivery to avoid precipitation of premature labor, although successful surgical treatment during pregnancy has been reported (Wittich, 1997).

KEY POINTS: FEMALE URETHRAL DIVERTICULA

- Female urethral diverticula are often diagnosed in the evaluation of nonspecific lower urinary tract symptoms including dysuria, pelvic pain, vaginal mass, dyspareunia, and recurrent urinary tract infections.

- Multiple imaging modalities may be used in the diagnosis and evaluation of female urethral diverticula, including positive-pressure urethrography, voiding cystourethrography, ultrasonography, and magnetic resonance imaging. Each of these techniques has inherent advantages and disadvantages.

- Concomitant urinary incontinence symptoms should be thoroughly investigated preoperatively, and strong consideration should be given to surgical treatment of stress urinary incontinence at the time of urethral diverticulectomy.

- The most common approach to the treatment of urethral diverticula in the female patient is transvaginal excision and urethral reconstruction.

SUGGESTED READINGS

Barrett DM, Malek RS, Kelalis PP: Observations on vesical diverticulum in childhood. J Urol 1976;116:234-236.

Bauer SB, Retik AB: Bladder diverticula in infants and children. Urology 1974;3:712-715.

Davis HJ, TeLinde RW: Urethral diverticula: An assay of 121 cases. J Urol 1958;80:34-39.

Eilber KS, Raz S: Benign cystic lesions of the vagina: A literature review. J Urol 2003;170:717-722.

Ganabathi K, Leach GE, Zimmern PE, Dmochowski R: Experience with the management of urethral diverticulum in 63 women. J Urol 1994;152(pt 1):1445-1452.

Garzotto MG, Tewari A, Wajsman Z: Multimodal therapy for neoplasms arising from a vesical diverticulum. J Surg Oncol 1996;62:46-48.

Gil-Vernet JM: Bladder diverticulectomy. In Graham SD Jr, ed: Glenn's Urologic Surgery, 5th ed. Philadelphia, Lippincott-Raven, 1998:205-209.

Lee RA: Diverticulum of the urethra: Clinical presentation, diagnosis, and management. Clin Obstet Gynecol 1984;27:490-498.

Spence HM, Duckett JW Jr: Diverticulum of the female urethra: Clinical aspects and presentation of a simple operative technique for cure. J Urol 1970;104:432-437.

Van Arsdalen K, Wein AJ: Bladder diverticulectomy. In Droller MJ, ed: Surgical Management of Urologic Disease: An Anatomic Approach. St. Louis, Mosby, 1992:629-639.

74 Surgical Treatment of Male Sphincteric Urinary Incontinence: The Male Perineal Sling and Artificial Urinary Sphincter

DAVID R. STASKIN, MD • CRAIG V. COMITER, MD

GENERAL INDICATIONS

PROSTHETICS FOR MALE INCONTINENCE

MALE PERINEAL SLING

ARTIFICIAL URINARY SPHINCTER

SUMMARY

Urinary incontinence is described symptomatically as the complaint of any involuntary leakage of urine. The etiology of urinary incontinence is described as "failure to store" urine secondary to dysfunction of the bladder-reservoir (the failure to maintain an adequate volume without a true rise in intravesical pressure) or dysfunction of the outlet-sphincter (the failure to maintain adequate resistance to prevent involuntary leakage).

The therapies described in this chapter, the male perineal sling (MPS) and the artificial urinary sphincter (AUS), are intended to prevent involuntary urinary loss during urinary storage by increasing outlet resistance. Bladder emptying is optimized when these implants do not significantly obstruct urinary flow and there is adequate detrusor contractility.

Broad utilization of these devices requires an acceptance of established indications and contraindications, a standardized implantation technique for simple cases, and surgical variations developed from sound principles for complicated cases. In addition, reasonable physician and patient expectations based on reproducible results of clinical efficacy, acceptable morbidity (severity, duration, and need for additional therapy), and the avoidance of serious complications are essential. The frequency, severity, social impact, and effect on hygiene and quality of life of the incontinence must be balanced against the ability of the patient to conservatively manage the condition. The patient must also be willing to undergo surgical intervention and manage the postoperative condition. The pathophysiology of urinary incontinence is discussed in Chapter 60, "Urinary Incontinence: Epidemiology, Pathophysiology, Evaluation, and Management Overview." In this chapter we consider the historical developments of the AUS and MPS, implantation techniques, and clinical outcomes.

GENERAL INDICATIONS

The MPS and AUS function by addressing the underactive outlet (inadequate resistance of the sphincter) by increasing the resistance to urinary flow during the storage phase. **The pathophysiology of the underactive outlet in the male is intrinsic sphincter deficiency (ISD),** manifesting as the symptom of stress urinary incontinence or loss of urine with effort. **These devices should be implanted cautiously in patients with an uncontrolled overactive bladder, elevated storage pressures secondary to detrusor contractions, or decreased compliance and/or vesicoureteral reflux** because the presence of an adequate reservoir and competent ureterovesical junction protects the upper tracts and minimizes continued postoperative urinary loss from uncontrolled detrusor contractions. Resistance to flow is a measure of the friction between the tube wall (the urethra) and the fluid (urine) and is dependent on the viscosity of the fluid and the radius and length of the tube. To improve continence, **the resistance to urinary leakage is created by applying pressure over a length of the urethra** utilizing the MPS mesh or the AUS cuff. Importantly, **these forces are also applied to the blood supply of the incorporated and compressed urethral segment and may result in urethral ischemia.** Therefore, device construction, component selection, and implantation technique must optimize urethral compression and coaptation while minimizing the risk to urethral viability.

Surgical intervention is indicated for the treatment of bothersome stress urinary incontinence in men due to ISD that fails to improve adequately with conservative management. The most common cause of ISD in men is iatrogenic injury during prostate cancer surgery, but it is also a well-known complication of transurethral resection of the prostate, simple open prostatectomy, traumatic and acquired myelopathy, pelvic trauma, urethral reconstructive surgery, and congenital disorders, including spinal dysraphism, sacral agenesis, and the exstrophy/epispadias complex.

Contraindications to surgical intervention include the inability to operate the device and those disorders that may jeopardize the upper urinary tract, the most prominent being diminished vesical compliance, frequent high pressure detrusor contractions, or vesicoureteral reflux at low intravesical pressure. **Additionally, urinary tract abnormalities that may require future transurethral management may be considered relative contraindications to outlet surgery,** especially if the AUS or MPS would impair transurethral access or if repeated instrumentation would put the devices at risk for infection or erosion (e.g., urolithiasis, recurrent transitional carcinoma, or stricture disease affecting the bladder neck or vesicourethral anastomosis). Finally, **stress incontinence surgery is not recommended in patients with untreated low-volume detrusor overactivity that would not permit adequate symptomatic improvement. Chronic infection of the urine or skin, anatomic abnormalities, immunosuppression, and poor tissue quality of the urethra are also relative contraindications.**

KEY POINTS: GENERAL INDICATIONS

- The resistance to urinary leakage is created by applying pressure over a length of the urethra.

- Forces applied to the blood supply of the urethral segment may result in urethral ischemia.

- Surgical intervention is indicated for stress urinary incontinence due to ISD that fails to improve adequately with conservative management.

- Contraindications to surgical intervention include the inability to operate the device, disorders that may jeopardize the upper urinary tract, untreated low-volume detrusor overactivity, chronic infection of the urine or skin, anatomic abnormalities, immunosuppression, and poor tissue quality.

PROSTHETICS FOR MALE INCONTINENCE
History and Development

The male sling for post-prostatectomy incontinence (PPI) is not a new idea. One of the first prosthetic devices in the modern era to increase urethral resistance was described by Berry in 1961. The Berry prosthesis was an acrylic device placed beneath the bulbocavernosus muscle, designed to kink and compress the bulbous urethra at a point just distal to the urogenital diaphragm (Berry, 1961). In an effort to avoid suture breakage, the procedure was modified to include the use of stainless steel sutures, which were passed through drill holes in the ischial and pubic rami (Kishev, 1975). Other modifications of the Berry prosthesis included replacement of acrylic with silicone rubber and use of Silastic strips rather than wire sutures (Watkins et al, 1964). However, high rates of perineal pain and fistula formation, in the presence of only modest success, led to the abandonment of the Berry prosthesis (Engel and Wade, 1969). In 1970, Kaufman published his initial description of a surgical method for compressing the urethra. In the Kaufman type I anti-incontinence procedure, the penile crura are crossed over the bulbous urethra to produce urethral compression (Kaufman, 1970). Success was reported in only 30% of patients, and the procedure was modified. In the Kaufman type II procedure, the crura are approximated in the midline using a polytetrafluoroethylene mesh tape (Kaufman, 1972). The synthetic tape was folded in such a manner as to compress the bulb of the urethra. Success rate increased to 50%. Further modification led to the Kaufman type III procedure, in which a silicone-gel–filled hemispherical prosthesis, surrounded by external velour of polyurethane and two polyurethane straps, was used to bolster the urethral compression by attaching the device to the corpora cavernosa (Kaufman, 1973). Early success rates for the Kaufman III device approached 70% (Kishev et al, 1972).

Kishev (1975) described a combined perineal-abdominal approach for correction of stress urinary incontinence utilizing a pliable prosthetic "wad" under the bulbar urethra, with tension provided by nylon sutures that are passed through the retropubic space and secured over small Marlex pledgets over the abdominal fascia. The Kaufman and Kishev prostheses ultimately fell out of favor because of high failure rates, infectious complications, and pelvic pain, concomitant with the emergence of the modern artificial urinary sphincter (AUS) (see later).

The modern male sling is based on concepts similar to those performed by Berry in the 1960s and by Kaufman and Kishev in the early 1970s (Kaufman, 1970, 1972, 1973; Kishev, 1975). Schaeffer and associates from Northwestern University described a novel bulbourethral sling procedure to treat postprostatectomy incontinence in 1997 (Schaeffer et al, 1998). **Similar to the Stamey needle suspension procedure in women, the "Northwestern" male bulbourethral sling procedure uses bolsters that are suspended from the rectus fascia by sutures. The bolsters are placed beneath the bulbar urethra to form a sling.** The surgeon adjusts the tension of the sling, aiming for an intraoperative leak point pressure (LPP) greater than 150 cm H_2O. Clemens and colleagues (1999a) reported a retrospective questionnaire-based study of 66 men from a single institution, and this innovative technique resulted in a 38% cure rate and a 49% pad-free rate. Furthermore, it was demonstrated that the bulbourethral sling did not cause significant outlet obstruction during micturition (Clemens et al, 1999b). However, despite these excellent continence rates, 21% of patients required revision of the sling and in 6% bolster removal was necessary secondary to infection or erosion. Moreover, 52% of patients experienced chronic perineal numbness or pain, with 26% rating this problem as moderate or severe. (Clemens et al, 1999a).

Surgical Treatment of Male Sphincteric Urinary Incontinence: The Male Perineal Sling and Artificial Urinary Sphincter   **2393**

CHAPTER 74

Such perineal discomfort was proposed to be due to high pressure compression of the bulbar urethra or entrapment of pudendal nerve branches during suprapubic suture passage (Comiter, 2002). A recent follow-up on 71 patients undergoing synthetic bolster slings reported that 36% of patients required no pads and 68% of patients used two pads or fewer (Stern et al, 2005).

Recent alterations of the Northwestern sling have been described. The concept of suburethral compression of the bulbar urethra was utilized, with modification of the sling material. Migliari and colleagues (2003) reported using a polypropylene mesh suspended via sutures over the rectus fascia to compress the corpus spongiosum and retrospectively reported that 5 of 9 patients had their incontinence cured and an additional 2 patients realized significant improvement at an average of 14 months. However, a revision rate of 33% was noted. John (2004) reported that with a composite graft of polypropylene and porcine skin collagen placed suburethrally and suspended over the rectus fascia, 11 of 16 patients were completely dry and 12 of 16 were dry or improved at an average of 14 months' follow-up.

Perhaps the most significant innovation affecting male sling surgery has been the use of bone screws. This modification is based on Berry's use of drill holes in the pubic bone and Kaufman's use of bone staples (Kishev, 1975). Currently, the most frequently utilized male sling is the bone-anchored perineal sling or In Vance procedure (American Medical Systems, Minnetonka, MN). Approximately 6500 In Vance procedures have been performed between 1999 and 2003. This purely perineal approach has transformed the surgery into a minimally invasive outpatient procedure. Reported success rates for this technique vary, according to the method of evaluation, the length of follow-up, and the sling material used.

KEY POINTS: PROSTHETICS FOR MALE INCONTINENCE

- The modern male sling is based on compression procedures performed by Berry, Kaufman, and Kishev.

- The "Northwestern" bulbourethral sling uses bolsters suspended from the rectus fascia by sutures.

- The most frequently utilized male sling is the bone-anchored perineal sling.

MALE PERINEAL SLING
Implantation Technique

The patient is given 1 g of intravenous cefazolin (unless allergic) 30 minutes before surgery. General or spinal anesthesia is recommended, and the patient is placed in lithotomy position and prepared and draped sterilely. A 14-Fr Foley catheter is introduced into the bladder to aid with urethral palpation. A 3.5-cm perineal incision is made, centered over the bulbous urethra; the bulbospongiosus muscle is exposed in the midline; and the medial aspects of the descending pubic rami are exposed bilaterally (Fig. 74–1A). Three titanium bone

screws preloaded with a pair of 1-0 polypropylene sutures are inserted in the anteromedial aspect of each descending pubic ramus utilizing a bone drill (see Fig. 74–1B). The proximal bone screws are placed just beneath the junction of the descending ramus and pubic symphysis, and the distal screws are inserted approximately 3 cm caudally, at the level of the bulbar urethra.

Retrograde leak point pressure (RLPP) is then measured via perfusion sphincterometry using a 14-Fr catheter with the balloon inflated with 1 mL H_2O in the distal penile urethra. Perfusion sphincterometry is performed by connecting a bag of saline to the catheter via sterile tubing. The bag is elevated until fluid flows from the bag, through the drip chamber, and into the urethra (Comiter et al, 1997). The RLPP is recorded as the height of the fluid column above the symphysis at which fluid flow begins.

A 4×7-cm sling composed of synthetic or organic material is used, and the bone-anchored sutures are passed through the sling with the aid of an 18-gauge needle, 0.5 cm from the left edge, equally spaced along the width of the sling, and tied down to the bone (see Fig. 74–1C). With the sling positioned over the bulbospongiosus muscle, the contralateral sutures are passed through the right side of the sling and secured with a single throw of the suture over a silk safety tie. RLPP is again measured, and sling tension is adjusted by moving the right sutures more medially (tighter) or laterally (looser) until an RLPP of 60 cm H_2O is achieved (see Fig. 74–1D). The wound is irrigated and closed in two layers. The catheter is removed in the recovery room or the following morning for a trial of voiding.

A value of 60 cm H_2O compression pressure was chosen based on the well-known success of the 61- to 70 cm H_2O reservoir balloon pressure of the AUS. Patients who achieve an RLPP of 60 cm (measured on postoperative urodynamics) have a better outcome than those who demonstrate a lower compression pressure (Ullrich and Comiter, 2004b). Additionally, there have been no instances of prolonged postoperative urinary retention in the cohort when using the 60 cm RLPP as an intraoperative guide to sling tensioning. Alternative methods of sling tensioning have been described, such as an intraoperative cough test to determine sling tensioning (Rajpurkar et al, 2005) and then adjust sling tension to 30 to 50 cm H_2O above baseline measurement (Madjar et al, 2001).

Results (Table 74–1)

Madjar and coworkers (2001) initially retrospectively reported on 14 patients with post-prostatectomy incontinence who underwent the procedure with a synthetic or cadaveric fascial sling. Preoperative pad use ranged from 2 to 6 per day (average: 3.7). At a mean follow-up of 12.2 months, 86% were wearing 1 or no pad. Defidio and associates (2002) reported similar success, with 86% "cure" in 15 patients at an average of 9 months' follow-up using a composite (polypropylene/fascia) graft. Bryan and Ghoniem (2001) reported in their retrospective analysis a 70% "cure" rate and 10% "improvement" rate using cadaveric fascia, with similar length of follow-up. Onur and colleagues (2004) reported on 46 men with a mean follow-up of 17 months (range: 6 to 26 months). Their results were not as favorable as those just mentioned, with 41% of patients being dry and 35% improved at an

Figure 74–1.   Dissection for male perineal sling implantation. **A,** Dissection and exposure of pubic ramus. **B,** Implantation of bone anchor. **C,** Mesh attached and tensioned. **D,** Anchor sutures placed before tying. (Photos by Craig Comiter, Tucson, AZ.)

average of 18 months' follow-up. The results are confounded by the use of a variety of sling materials (cadaveric fascia, dermis, porcine small intestine submucosal graft, synthetic mesh, and a composite of synthetic and dermis). However, in all patients in whom allograft or xenograft alone was used, the sling failed over time. A follow-up retrospective study from the same group utilizing a questionnaire-based outcome measure reported that 72% had only a small to no problem from incontinence and 59% were completely satisfied (Rajpurkar et al, 2005). Dikranian and colleagues (2004) also reported that a synthetic sling had a higher cure rate (87%) than did a dermal graft (56%) at 1-year follow-up, and

Surgical Treatment of Male Sphincteric Urinary Incontinence: The Male Perineal Sling and Artificial Urinary Sphincter **2395**

CHAPTER 74

Table 74-1. Results of the Male Perineal Sling Procedure

Study	No. Patients	Mean Follow-Up (mo)	Sling Material	Tensioning Method	Cure (%)	Cure/Improvement (%)	Failure (%)
Madjar et al, 2001	16	12	Synthetic or organic	RLPP			
Defidio et al, 2002	15	5	Synthetic	RLPP	87	93	7
Comiter et al, 2002	21	12	Synthetic	RLPP	70	95	5
Dikranian et al, 2004	36	12	Organic	RLPP	56	87	13
	20	12	Synthetic	RLPP	87	100	0
Ullrich and Comiter, 2004a	36	25	Synthetic	RLPP	67	92	8
Onur et al, 2004	46	18	Synthetic or organic	Cough	41	76	24
Rajpurkar et al, 2005	46	24	Synthetic or organic	Cough	37	74	26
Cespedes and Jacoby, 2001	9	13		RLPP	67	78	22
Migliari et al, 2003	9	14	Synthetic	Cough	56	78	22
Sousa-Escandon et al, 2004	6	18	Synthetic	Cough	83	100	0
John, 2004	16	14	Synthetic	Cough	69	75	25
Schaeffer et al, 1998	64	18	Synthetic	ALPP/MUCP	56	64	36

RLPP, Retrograde leak point pressure; ALPP, abdominal leak point pressure; MUCP, maximum urethral closure pressure.

Rajpurkar and associates (2005) published a confirmatory study demonstrating 96% success with synthetic slings versus only 8% with absorbable slings, which failed at an average of 6 months postoperatively.

A prospective study of the bone-anchored sling utilizing synthetic material, including rigorous preoperative and postoperative evaluation of the patients by pad score as well as by the self-administered validated UCLA Prostate Cancer Index, reported on patients using 3 or more pads preoperatively with severe incontinence (Comiter, 2002). At a mean of 1-year follow-up, 76% of patients had no leakage/no problem and 14% improved to 1 pad daily/small problem. The prospective cohort was expanded and followed further, and a recent update, with a mean follow-up of 25 months in 36 men, reported 67% were pad free and 14% used 1 pad/day (Ullrich and Comiter, 2004a). Additionally, 83% of men reported from small to no bother (UCLA/RAND questionnaire) from incontinence after the sling procedure. In a prospective urodynamic evaluation of a subgroup of 22 patients, studied both preoperatively and postoperatively, the sling had no significant adverse effects on voiding function and there were no instances of postoperative bladder outlet obstruction (Ullrich and Comiter, 2004b). In another series, at a mean follow-up of 24 months, 46 patients were evaluated objectively and with the help of the validated UCLA/RAND questionnaire. Patients were defined as "cured" if they were dry or "improved" if utilizing 1 to 2 pads/day: 1 patient developed infection and 2 developed short-lasting perineal/buttock pain and there was no urethral erosion. Reports of "dry" (17/46, 37%) or utilizing only 1 to 2 pads/day (17/46, 37%) provided a cure/improvement rate of 74%, and 72% of patients stated that urinary leakage and function were a "small to no problem" (Rajpurkar et al, 2005).

Complications

Bleeding. Bleeding complications have not been reported for the perineal bone-anchored sling, and infection is a relatively rare occurrence. In a cohort of 76 men, infection has occurred in 1 patient (1.3%) with neurogenic bladder dysfunction

(Comiter, 2002), and a similar infection rate, with an incidence of 1/46 (2.3%), has also been reported (Rajpurkar et al, 2005). Erosion of the sling into the urethra has been reported with the use of polypropylene (Hakim and Gignac, 2004), in the setting of prolonged urethral catheterization. However, there are no reports of urethral erosion of organic sling material. No instances of prolonged urinary retention have occurred, with 90% to 95% of patients voiding on removal of the catheter and the remaining patients voiding at the next trial without catheter (Comiter, 2002; Rajpurkar et al, 2005). There have been no instances of de novo urgency or urge incontinence reported (Ullrich and Comiter, 2004b) and no instance of bladder outlet obstruction. A minority of patients (5% to 10%) have been noted to complain of mild scrotal and perineal numbness and hyperesthesia, the vast majority of which resolves within 3 months (Rajpurkar et al, 2005). It is likely that with the relatively small number of publications (as compared with the AUS literature), especially with short follow-up and small cohort size, complications with this technique are underreported. However, the early results of the MPS demonstrate a relatively low complication rate.

Infection. Infection necessitates removal of the foreign body (sling). Nonabsorbable sutures should be removed as completely as possible. Bone anchors are difficult to remove, unless involved in a suppurative bony process. Similar to the case of an infected pubovaginal sling, unless osteomyelitis is evident, no extraordinary effort should be made to remove the well-secured titanium bone screws.

Urinary Retention. It is important that patients have a contractile bladder demonstrated on preoperative urodynamics, because detrusor underactivity is a relative contraindication for placement of a fixed resistance sling owing to the increased difficulty with long-term intermittent catheterization. Such patients are better suited for the artificial sphincter, which can be deflated to allow Valsalva voiding. Retention should be managed preferentially with clean intermittent catheterization or suprapubic tube placement to minimize the risk of pressure-induced erosion of the sling. If retention persists, sling removal is indicated, with consideration of placement of an AUS.

Pain. Unlike the Northwestern sling, persistent scrotal/perineal pain is a relatively unusual occurrence (10%) with the bone-anchored sling, probably owing to the lack of high-tension entrapment of pudendal nerve branches that can occur during blind suture transfer through the perineum to the suprapubic region. However, small pudendal branches do travel along the medial aspect of the descending pubic rami and may be injured during dissection or screw insertion. Complaints of pain (without evidence of infection) should be managed conservatively, with narcotics and anti-inflammatory medication. If bothersome pain persists after 6 to 8 weeks of conservative management, consideration should be given to sling removal. As is the case with pubic symphyseal bone anchors in women, bone anchor removal is a difficult procedure and usually recommended only in cases of bone infections.

Recurrent Incontinence. Recurrent incontinence may be due to insufficient resistance, and patients should be examined urodynamically. In cases of persistent stress urinary incontinence, a pelvic radiograph is indicated to rule out bone-anchor displacement. If a bone anchor has pulled out, revision of the sling with placement of additional bone screw(s) is indicated. If bone anchor migration is not the cause, then other options for treatment are recommended, ranging from pelvic floor exercises, periurethral injections, a repeat MPS if the mesh compression was inadequate, or artificial sphincter placement.

Special Circumstances

Radiation. Prior irradiation was the only factor that predisposed to failure of the Northwestern sling. The success rate following a single sling procedure was only 29% (2 of 7) for irradiated patients, and the corresponding rate for nonirradiated patients was 68% (39 of 57) (Schaeffer et al, 1998). To date, the success rate for the bone-anchored male sling surgery has not been reported to be adversely affected by adjuvant radiation for recurrent local prostate cancer or prophylactic radiation for positive surgical margins (Comiter, 2002). However, the bone-anchored procedure has not been reported for use in patients status post full-course pelvic irradiation for prostate cancer treatment. Theoretical drawbacks of MPS surgery after radiation include a poorly compliant/difficult to coapt bulbous urethra, as well as a potential increased risk of urethral erosion due to a compromised blood supply.

Previous and Subsequent Incontinence Treatment. Previous antegrade or retrograde collagen injection does not adversely affect the outcome of the bone-anchored sling (Comiter, 2002), because the sling is placed distal to the site of collagen injection. In those individuals who have had previous AUS explantation, the results of the bone-anchored sling appear somewhat inferior to those undergoing sling surgery as their initial surgical treatment (Comiter, 2002). This decrement in efficacy is likely due to urethral atrophy and poor compliance, rendering the urethra more difficult to coapt with a noncircumferential sling. In the case of suboptimal continence after sling surgery, it is our preference to leave the previously placed sling in situ and place the AUS cuff distal to the sling through a scrotal incision. This approach has two advantages: (1) avoiding the previous operative field, minimizing

dissection through potentially scarred tissue; and (2) leaving the proximally placed sling as a partially effective compressive device, similar to a tandem-cuff AUS. In cases where the surgeon elects to place the AUS cuff transperineally, the previous sling neither renders the operation more difficult nor decreases AUS efficacy. In our experience, the silicone-coated polyester is not well incorporated into the subcutaneous or periurethral tissue and is therefore easily removed. The bulbospongiosus may then be split and dissected off the underlying spongy urethra without difficulty.

Concomitant or Prior Penile Prosthesis. During concomitant implantation or in the presence of a previously placed penile prosthesis the exposure of the descending rami of the pubis can be cumbersome. The corporal implants lie directly adjacent to and anterior of the descending rami; and with an inflatable penile prosthesis, the proximal cylinders are at particular risk of perforation by the titanium bone screws. Therefore, a previously placed penile prosthesis is a relative contraindication to the bone-anchored male sling. With concomitant implantation of a penile prosthesis and male sling, it is recommended that the bone anchors are placed first, following exposure through a midline perineal approach. Then a separate penoscrotal incision is recommended for implantation of the penile prosthesis. After the penile prosthesis is placed (with balloon reservoir and pump if applicable), then the sling is positioned and appropriately tensioned utilizing the preplaced bone-anchored sutures. Rhee (2005) reports no decrease in success rates in such patients.

ARTIFICIAL URINARY SPHINCTER
History and Development

In 1947, Foley introduced an external occlusive pressurized cuff that surrounded the urethra and could be connected to a pump carried by the patient (Tse and Stone, 2003). Volume-dependent urethral compression was attempted by Kaufman and by Rosen. The Kaufman III was a silicone-gel–filled hemispherical prosthesis, surrounded by an external velour of polyurethane and two polyurethane straps, used to support urethral compression by attaching the device to the corpora cavernosa (Kaufman, 1973).

In 1976, Rosen designed an early model of an AUS. The Rosen device was composed of a three-pronged urethral clamp, two arms of which were parallel on one side with a single arm carrying a balloon opposing them. Urethral occlusion depended on fluid transfer from a scrotal reservoir to a perineal balloon that is fixed to the inside of the bulbocavernosus muscle. Unfortunately, hydraulic failure and fistula formation approached 100%, and this technique was abandoned (Fowler and Auld, 1985). In our opinion overzealous inflation of the cuff without an appreciation of the ischemic pressure to the urethra was the major contributing factor.

At approximately the same time as the Rosen prosthesis became popular, Scott presented his initial report of an implantable artificial sphincter in a patient with neurogenic bladder dysfunction, followed shortly by his series of 34 patients undergoing implantation of the AS 721 (American Medical Systems, Minnetonka, MN), noting a 79% success rate (Scott, 1978). Over the next 10 years, further developments in design of the AUS were made. The AMS 742 con-

Surgical Treatment of Male Sphincteric Urinary Incontinence: The Male Perineal Sling and Artificial Urinary Sphincter **2397**

CHAPTER 74

sisted of a single-cuff, balloon pressure reservoir, and peri-urethral cuff, allowing automatic cuff closure after pump-mediated cuff decompression. The AMS 791 and 792 utilized a silicone rubber cuff and a deactivation button, which permitted periods of reduced urethral pressure (Scott, 1989). The AMS 800 included the deactivation button within the control pump; and in 1987, the narrow-backed cuff was introduced, which, by improving pressure transmission from the cuff pressure to the underlying tissue, has greatly decreased the incidence of urethral erosion and tissue atrophy (Light and Reynolds, 1992) (Fig. 74–2). Fluid transfer from the cuff to the reservoir is accomplished by active "pumping" while refilling of the cuff occurs by the pressure gradient from the reservoir that traverses a resistor implanted in the pump mechanism. Acute pressure transmission from the reservoir to the cuff is prevented by this valve mechanism. Devices have been proposed that include a separate pressure-transmitting reservoir that allows for acute transfer of increased intra-abdominal pressure to the cuff but are not commercially available (Hussain et al, 2005).

Implantation Techniques

Variations in implantation technique are based on (1) the site of cuff placement—bulbar urethra or bladder neck (Fig. 74–3A); (2) the primary incision for cuff placement around the bulbar urethra—perineal or scrotal (see Fig. 74–3B) (Wilson et al, 2003); (3) the number of cuffs—single or double (see Fig. 74–3C) (Brito et al, 1993); and (4) the plane of cuff placement—periurethral or transcorporeal (see Fig. 74–3D) (Guralnick et al, 2002). In addition, the reservoir may be placed through a midline incision or through the inguinal canal, in either a perivesical space or in a more superficial pouch above the transversalis fascia (Wilson and Delk, 2005).

Bulbous Urethral Placement

In men with post-prostatectomy incontinence, the bulbous urethra is the classic route of implantation through a perineal incision. Preparation, positioning, and exposure of the bulbocavernosus muscle are similar to what was previously described for the sling. The bulbocavernosus muscle may be preserved or split, and the urethra is dissected circumferentially such that a 2-cm-wide segment of urethra is freed to accommodate the cuff. The circumference of the urethra is measured, and an appropriate-sized cuff is placed around the urethra—typically the cuff size is 4.5 cm. The connecting tubing is tunneled subcutaneously to the lower abdomen for connection to the balloon reservoir after the abdominal portion of the procedure is completed.

A 4-cm transverse incision is made over the lower rectus muscle, and a space is dissected bluntly either preperitoneally, intraperitoneally, or paravesically for placement of the balloon reservoir. Generally, a 61- to 70-cm H_2O pressure reservoir is chosen and filled with 22 mL of saline or a normo-osmotic mixture of radiocontrast medium and water. A suprafascial plane is developed from the abdominal incision down to the dependent scrotum (using a ringed clamp or Hagar dilators), and the sphincter pump is placed in a subcutaneous or dartos pouch in the dependent hemiscrotum ipsilateral to the balloon reservoir. The components are connected, and the

artificial sphincter is cycled to verify integrity and proper functioning of the device. The AUS is deactivated for 6 weeks to permit healing without undue periurethral pressure.

Placement of the cuff through a trans-scrotal incision has been advocated; the major advantage has been purported to be implantation without hip flexion, resulting in less stretch-tension on the bulbar urethra and thus providing improved ease of dissection of the spongiosum from the cavernosum. Double-cuff implantation with a Y-connector has been advocated for improved resistance in the cases of severe incontinence or cuff atrophy. Transcorporal implantation has been advocated for cases in which dissection of the spongiosum from the cavernosum is technically difficult secondary to inflammation, ischemia, or prior erosion.

Bladder Neck Placement

In the male patient with stress urinary incontinence who has not had previous radical prostatectomy, the cuff may also be placed around the bladder neck. Through a transabdominal incision, the retropubic space is developed and exposure down to the endopelvic fascia is obtained. In the female, a transabdominal approach was the most commonly utilized in France before the popularization of midurethral sling surgery, in which the urethra and bladder neck were dissected from the endopelvic fascia (Costa et al, 2001). A transvaginal placement in the female was popularized in the United States (Appell, 1988; Hadley, 1991). In the male, the posterior bladder neck is dissected off the rectum so that a 2-cm-wide cuff may be placed without restriction. An 8- to 14-cm cuff is usually used in the adult male. After the cuff is secured around the bladder neck, the tubing is passed through the rectus muscle and fascia, to be connected to the pump tubing.

Results

Success with the AUS for the treatment of PPI is generally excellent, with continence rates between 75% and 90% in most modern series and patient satisfaction rates of 85% to 95% despite revisions (Fishman et al, 1989; Light and Reynolds, 1992; Perez and Webster, 1992; Littwiller et al, 1996; Petrou et al, 2000; Wilson et al, 2003). Since the modification of the AMS 800 in 1987 to include the narrow-backed cuff, success has improved and complications have diminished, particularly with respect to urethral erosion and atrophy. The largest series to date was presented by investigators at the Mayo Clinic, who reported that in 323 patients with a mean follow-up of nearly 6 years, 90% of patients were alive with a well-functioning AUS. Revision rate was 42% prior to the development of the narrow-backed cuff (21% mechanical failure, 17% nonmechanical failure) but decreased to 17% when using the narrow-backed cuff (8% mechanical failure, 9% nonmechanical failure) (Elliott and Barrett, 1998). In a report of patients with at least 10-year follow-up, an excellent continence rate of 75% was realized, despite a revision rate of 80% (Fulford et al, 1997). Other groups have reported similar excellent continence at a minimum of 10 years' follow-up, with 84% of 100 patients remaining continent, with two thirds requiring at least one revision (27% due to mechanical failure and 21% due to nonmechanical failure) (Venn et al, 2000).

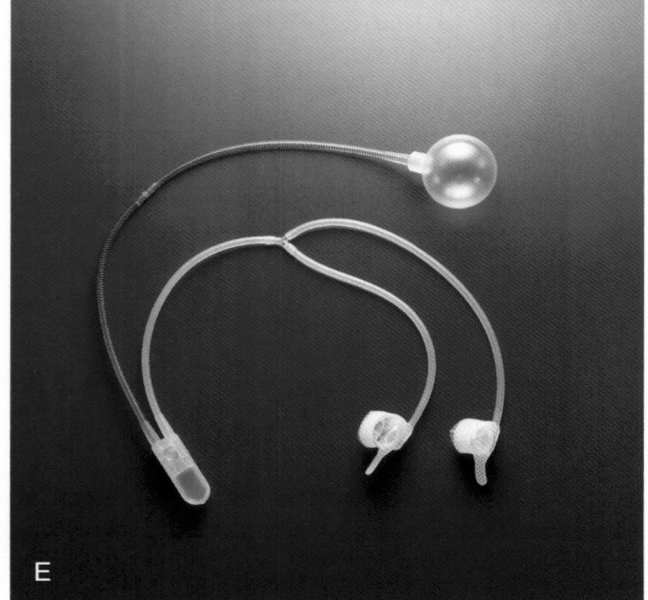

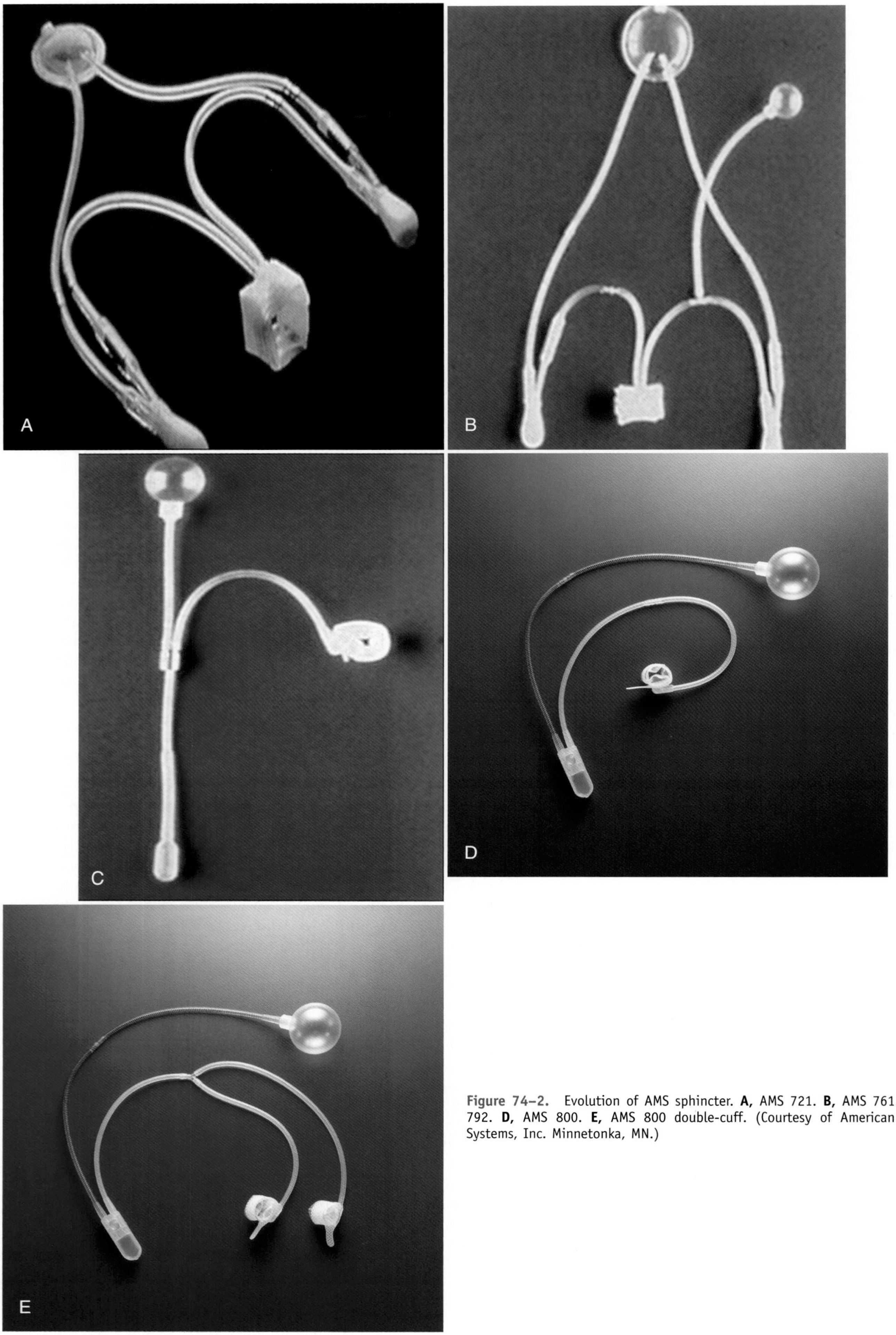

Figure 74–2. Evolution of AMS sphincter. **A,** AMS 721. **B,** AMS 761. **C,** AMS 792. **D,** AMS 800. **E,** AMS 800 double-cuff. (Courtesy of American Medical Systems, Inc. Minnetonka, MN.)

Surgical Treatment of Male Sphincteric Urinary Incontinence: The Male Perineal Sling and Artificial Urinary Sphincter **2399**

CHAPTER 74

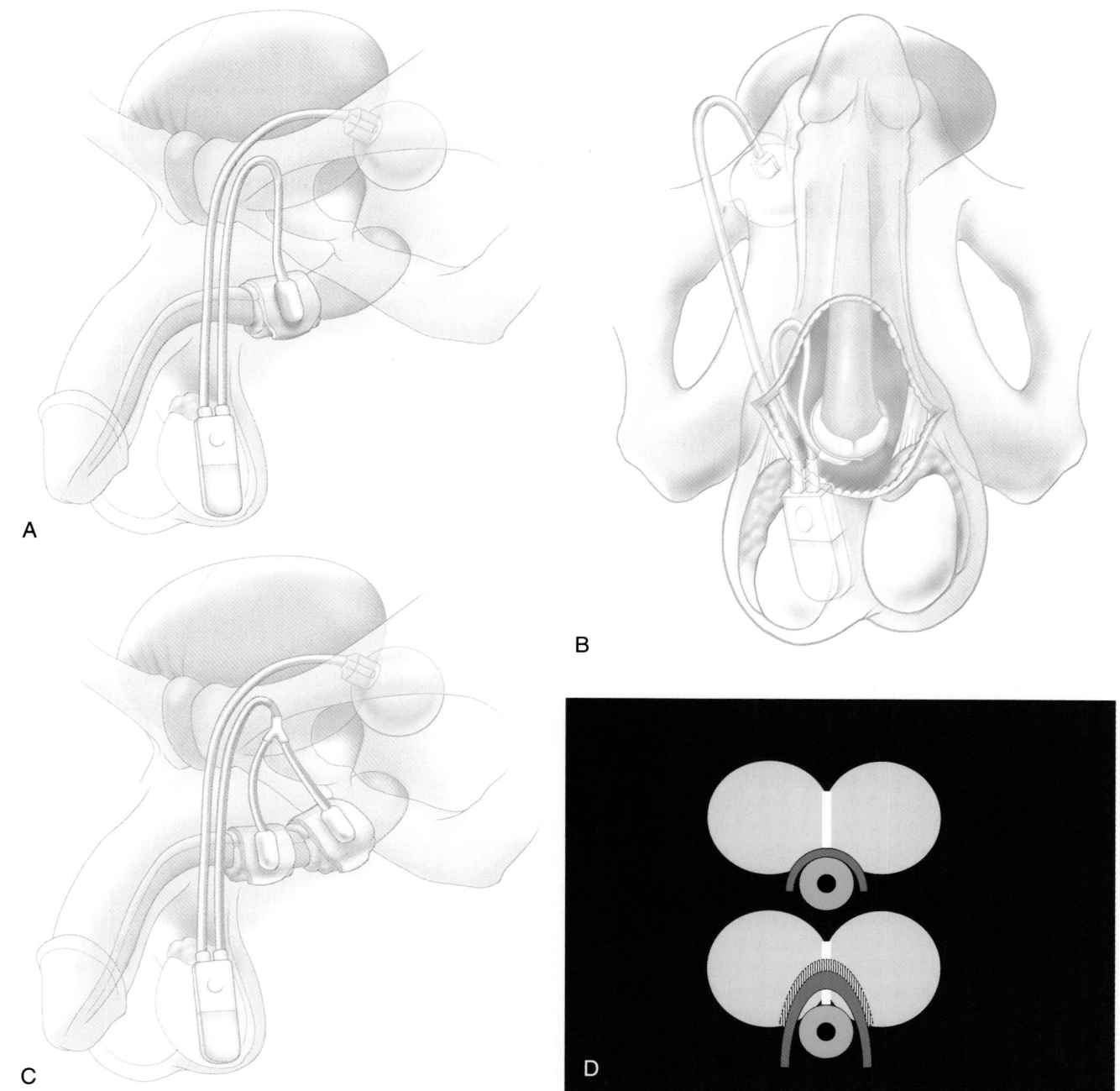

Figure 74–3. Variations in cuff approach and implantation. **A,** Bulbar urethral cuff. **B,** Trans-scrotal incision. **C,** Double-cuff sphincter. **D,** Transcorporal cuff. (Courtesy of American Medical Systems, Inc. Minnetonka, MN.)

Complications

Bleeding/Hematoma. Postoperative hematoma usually manifests as a purple discoloration of the scrotum or labia majora but may also present as an actual subcutaneous fluid collection. A gentle pressure dressing or scrotal support usually arrests the problem. In certain instances of a large collection of blood, evacuation and drainage is indicated.

Urinary Retention. Swelling is the most likely cause of urinary retention in the immediate postoperative period.

This should be managed by transurethral bladder drainage with a small (10 Fr or 12 Fr) catheter for 24 to 48 hours. Obviously, cuff deactivation should be confirmed before catheterization. If the patient fails a voiding trial at 48 hours, suprapubic drainage is recommended. Care must be taken to avoid perforating the balloon reservoir, and the use of ultrasound or fluoroscopic guidance is recommended. In cases of inaccurate intraoperative urethral circumferential measurement, upsizing the cuff may be required. Late-onset urinary retention mandates endoscopic and urodynamic evaluation to rule out proximal obstruction or detrusor failure. Prior to catheterization or cystoscopy, the cuff must be deactivated.

Infection and Erosion. Infection of the AUS and urethral erosion are often reported together and are usually related. The incidence of infection/erosion ranges from 0% to 25% (Webster and Sihelnik, 1984; Roth et al, 1986; Fishman et al, 1989; Marks and Light, 1989; Aprikian et al, 1992; Light and Reynolds, 1992; Montague, 1992; Simeoni et al, 1996; Leibovich and Barrett, 1997; Venn et al, 2000) when reported as a single entity. Regardless of whether an infection led to erosion or vice versa, the device should be explanted, usually in its entirety. A second system can be implanted 3 to 6 months subsequently, with equal success rates as first-time surgery (Motley and Barrett, 1990; Frank et al, 2000; Guralnick et al, 2002).

When reported by itself, the infection rate with initial AUS surgery is 1% to 3% (Blum, 1989; Carson, 1989; Gundian et al, 1989; Marks and Light, 1989; Litwiller et al, 1996; Singh and Thomas, 1996; Montague, 2000) but can be as high as 10% in patients status post pelvic radiation and in reoperations (Montague, 1992). Skin pathogens are the most commonly cultured organism with perioperative infections, usually from *Staphylococcus epidermidis* and *S. aureus* (Shandra and Thompson, 1994; Licht et al, 1995; Roberts and Barrett, 1999). Late infections (longer than after 4 months) are assumed to be hematogenously caused from other sources of bacteremia. Therefore, antibiotics are often administered before unsterile dental or surgical manipulation.

Although erythema, edema, and frank purulence may signify infection, the initial complaint is usually scrotal pain. Most surgeons traditionally elect removal of all three components (pump, cuff, and balloon reservoir), followed by attempted reimplantation after a 3- to 6-month waiting period. However, a salvage regimen for an infected but noneroded device has been reported. Using a regimen similar to that for penile prosthesis salvage, Mulcahy's group reported that 7 of 9 patients were successfully salvaged, with only one subsequent erosion, and the other patient was successfully resalvaged (Bryan et al, 2002).

In most recent reports, with the routine practice of delayed cuff activation (Motley and Barrett, 1990), erosion rates are in the range of 1% to 5% (Gundian et al, 1989; Marks and Light, 1989; Litwiller et al, 1996; Singh and Thomas, 1996; Elliot and Barrett, 1998; Montague, 2000) after initial surgery and usually occur within 4 months of surgery. Early erosion is usually ascribed to unrecognized urethral injury or compromise, whereas later erosions are usually due to urethral atrophy or urethral manipulation through an activated cuff. Erosion is often heralded by dysuria, scrotal pain and swelling (from urinary extravasation), hematuria, and recurrent incontinence. After cuff erosion, the entire device should be removed, as bacterial contamination of the entire device is common. The urethra should be allowed to heal over a small urethral catheter to minimize urinary extravasation and subsequent urethral stricture formation (Flynn and Webster, 2004). Similar to the case of infection, a previously eroded AUS can be replaced after 3 to 6 months, with expectations of success rates equal to that for first-time AUS placement (Motley and Barrett, 1990, Kowalczyk et al, 1996c; Frank et al,

2000). However, the new cuff should be positioned away from the erosion site.

A recent report of patients with one cuff erosion in a double-cuff AUS system advocates removal of the eroded cuff, with conversion of the remaining components into a single cuff system. Of 9 patients, only 2 required explantation of the remaining device (one erosion, one infection). In the remaining 7 patients, no further surgery was required. Not surprisingly, continence was better than before AUS placement but worse than with two cuffs (Bell and Mulcahy, 2000).

The introduction of the narrow-backed cuff in 1987 has led to substantial decreases in device failure—with nonmechanical failure decreasing from 17% to 9% and mechanical failure decreasing from 21% to 8%. The design change allows more even distribution of circumferential pressure on the urethra, leading to less urethral atrophy and a lower rate of cuff leakage secondary to kinking and fracturing (Light and Reynolds, 1992; Elliott and Barrett, 1998).

Recurrent Incontinence. Immediate failure of the device may be secondary to unrecognized detrusor overactivity, unrecognized fistula or surgical trauma, incorrect selection of components or incorrect assembly, device malfunction, or improper device activation. Delayed failure may be secondary to mechanical failure in 7.6% to 21% or to cuff atrophy, cuff erosion, or detrusor instability in 5% to 17% (Raj et al, 2005).

Just as the patient with post-prostatectomy incontinence or neurogenic voiding dysfunction requires a thorough evaluation to determine the precise etiology of the incontinence and direct rational treatment, a thorough diagnostic evaluation of recurrent incontinence after AUS placement is indicated. History and physical examination should rule out infection. System obstruction (fluid debris or tube kinking) or fluid loss will manifest as difficulty compressing the scrotal/labial pump. Fluid loss may be documented by pelvic radiography, after the system is filled with radiopaque solution (Taylor and Leibowitz, 1985; Lorentzen et al, 1987). However, the use of contrast material in the system may theoretically increase the risk of fluid obstruction due to crystallization. If fluid loss is evident, but the site of perforation is not obvious, intraoperative electrical testing, using an ohmmeter (Webster and Sihelnik, 1984; Kreder and Webster, 1991), has been described to determine the site of fluid leakage from the system, thereby obviating the need to change the whole system by allowing selective replacement of the damaged component.

If infection or fluid loss has been ruled out, then cystoscopy to rule out cuff erosion and urodynamics to rule out bladder overactivity or diminished compliance and assess for recurrent or persistent ISD are recommended. Approximately 10% of patients with severe post-prostatectomy incontinence due to ISD will not obtain sufficient control after AUS placement. In such patients, addition of a second cuff around the bulbar urethra can be expected to yield satisfactory continence in 80% of the patients with time (Brito et al, 1993; Kabalin, 1996; DiMarco and Elliott, 2003). The new cuff is placed 1.5 to 2 cm distal to the primary cuff and incorporated via a Y-connector. An additional 3 mL must be added to the balloon reservoir, and the entire device is left deactivated for 6 weeks postoperatively.

Primary double-cuff or tandem placement has been reported to yield excellent continence but may be associated

Surgical Treatment of Male Sphincteric Urinary Incontinence: The Male Perineal Sling and Artificial Urinary Sphincter **2401**

CHAPTER 74

with a higher rate of urethral erosion (Kowalczyk et al, 1996a; Montague and Angermeier, 2000). For this reason, Flynn and Webster (2004) at Duke University recommend reserving use of the double-cuff AUS for cases of recurrent or persistent incontinence secondary to cuff atrophy rather than as a primary procedure. Kowalczyk's group from Indiana University, on the other hand, does recommend double-cuff AUS as a primary treatment for the severely incontinent patient (Kowalczyk et al, 1996b), and a recent report from the University of Chicago supports the contention that patient satisfaction is superior without an increase in complications in such patients (O'Connor et al, 2003).

If urodynamic evaluation documents recurrent ISD due to urethral atrophy, then revision of the AUS is indicated. Increasing cuff pressure around the atrophied urethra may be accomplished by exchanging the balloon reservoir for one generating a higher pressure or downsizing the cuff diameter (Martins and Boyd, 1995; Petrou et al, 2001; Saffranian, et al 2003). Alternatively, the cuff may be downsized or repositioned proximally along the bulbar urethra. The group from the University of California at Davis reported that 5 of 6 patients had significant improvement in continence after proximal repositioning (Couillard et al, 1995).

A more recently described treatment for urethral atrophy or fibrosis or scarring of the plane between the urethra and corpora due to prior erosion consists of transcorporal cuff implantation. In cases in which a 4.0-cm cuff is already around the proximal bulbar urethra, then downsizing and/or proximal repositioning is not possible (Flynn and Webster, 2004). This technique involves vertical corporotomies, with creation of a tunnel leaving a cuff of tunica albuginea on the dorsal aspect of the urethra (Flynn et al, 2002; Guralnick et al, 2002).

Mechanical Failure. Mechanical failure includes loss of fluid from the system due to tube disconnection or perforation of the cuff or balloon reservoir or, less frequently, obstruction of the AUS system secondary to kinking of the connection tubing or to air lock or debris within the fluid (Leo and Barrett, 1993; Fulford et al, 1997; Diana et al, 1999). The incidence of mechanical failure varies in the literature from 0% to 52.5% (Light and Marks, 1992; Fulford et al, 1997; Diana et al, 1999) but has diminished substantially after improvements in the synthetic material and the introduction of the narrow-backed cuff. Elliott and Barrett (1998) and (Haab et al, 1997) have noted a greater than 50% decrease in mechanical failures, as design improvements have prevented kinking of the cuff, thereby minimizing the risk of cuff fracture.

Special Circumstances

Diminished Bladder Compliance. Diminished vesical compliance or de novo detrusor overactivity after AUS placement is unique to children with neurogenic voiding dysfunction, which may result in upper urinary tract deterioration in up to half of cases (Bauer et al, 1986; Light and Pietro, 1986; Roth et al, 1986; Scott, 1986; Churchill et al, 1987; Murray et al, 1988; Bitsch et al, 1990; Warwick and Abrams, 1990; O'Flynn and Thomas, 1991; Aprikian et al, 1992; Ghoniem et al, 1994; Simeoni et al, 1996). On the other hand, in adult men with

post-prostatectomy incontinence and women with ISD, upper tract deterioration is not a known complication (Litwiller et al, 1996; Montague and Angermeier, 2000). In those children with preexisting bladder compliance abnormalities, performing surgery that elevates urethral resistance is contraindicated until the elevated bladder storage pressure is addressed—with antimuscarinics, timed urination (or catheterization), or augmentation cystoplasty. Opinion varies whether simultaneous AUS placement and enterocystoplasty increases the risk of infection compared with staged surgery. Whereas some reports claim no difference in infection rates (Gonzalez et al, 1989), others note that the rate of infection may be halved with a staged procedure (Furness et al, 1999).

Urethral Atrophy. Circumferential compression of the urethra can lead to atrophy of the muscle and spongy tissue, thereby resulting in recurrent incontinence due to a relative reduction in urethral size under the cuff (Bosch et al, 2000). AUS revision due to urethral atrophy ranges from 3% to 9.3% (Fishman et al, 1989; Light and Reynolds, 1992; Montague, 1992; Simeoni et al, 1996; Haab et al, 1997; Leibovich and Barrett, 1997). Although the introduction of the narrow-backed cuff has improved urethral pressure transmission and reduced potentially harmful cuff kinking, urethral atrophy remains responsible for more than half of all revisions for nonmechanical reasons (Elliott et al, 2001; Raj et al, 2003). In patients who do not have bothersome nocturnal incontinence before surgery, nocturnal deactivation may be offered. In one report, in patients who deactivated their cuff at night, recurrent incontinence due to urethral atrophy was halved (Elliott et al, 2001). In addition to exploration and placement of a smaller cuff (4.0 cm), a double-cuff modification may be employed.

Female. Sphincteric incompetence in women is most commonly treated with a suburethral or pubovaginal sling or with periurethral bulking agents. The familiarity of these procedures, as well as their long track record of safety and overall excellent efficacy, has relegated AUS placement for the treatment of ISD in the non-neurogenic female patient (always placed at the bladder neck) as a "procedure of last resort." However, AUS surgery is relatively straightforward, can be performed via a transvaginal (Hadley, 1991; Appell, 1988) or transabdominal approach (Heitz et al, 1997; Costa et al, 2001), and in the properly selected patients has been associated with excellent outcome.

Appell (1988) reported that in a cohort of 34 patients, all were dry and only 3 (9%) required revision of their AUS after transvaginal placement. Hadley (1991) reported that 13 of 14 patients (93%) status post transvaginal placement of AUS improved to a satisfactory level, using no pad or 1 pad daily for stress incontinence.

Most investigators who perform this procedure regularly in women report that the transvaginal approach is relatively contraindicated in patients with previous surgery, owing to difficulty dissecting the plane between the vaginal wall and the urethra and bladder neck, and in patients with previous pelvic radiation, owing to an increased risk of cuff extrusion through the irradiated vagina. The transabdominal approach, on the other hand, allows better exposure, with placement of the cuff around the bladder neck between the periurethral fascia and the vagina (Webster et al, 1992; Heitz et al, 1997; Costa et al,

2001; Sanz Mayayo et al, 2003). Conversely, in our opinion, the greatest risk of vaginal cuff erosion into the urethra or vagina is during the dissection of this plane, which is exposed most easily with an inverted-U vaginal flap. Regardless, if a patient needs a revision-replacement, it is helpful to know the route of implantation to access the components effectively.

With the use of a transverse abdominal incision, the rectus muscle is cut and the retropubic space is dissected. The endopelvic fascia is entered 2 cm on either side of the bladder neck. The dissection through the periurethral fascia is facilitated by placing a sponge stick in the vagina. The bladder neck is dissected from the vagina below the periurethral fascia in both directions at the level of the Foley catheter balloon. In instances of difficult dissection, intentional cystotomy (cephalad to the cuff placement) can be helpful, to better allow discernment of the plan between the vagina and periurethral fascia. Typical cuff sizes range from 6 to 8 cm. The pump is placed in a subcutaneous pocket of the labia majora with the aid of a ringed forceps, and the balloon reservoir is placed in the laterovesical space ipsilateral to the pump.

Success rates generally range from 76% to 89% (Webster et al, 1992; Heitz et al, 1997; Costa et al, 2001), with lower success rates and a higher revision rate in patients with neurogenic bladder dysfunction. In the largest contemporary series from Costa and coworkers (2001), 207 women were followed for a mean of 4 years. Success was 89% and 82% in non-neurogenic and neurogenic patients, respectively, with an erosion/extrusion rate of 6%.

Children. As is the case with women, the AUS cuff in children is placed at the bladder neck and is typically 6 to 8 cm in circumference (Light et al, 1983; Gonzalez et al, 1989; Levesque et al, 1996). The indication in children is identical to that in adults, namely ISD. However, pediatric sphincteric incompetence is more likely to result from a neurogenic pathophysiology rather than postsurgical sphincteric injury. Contraindications to sphincter placement are more rigidly considered, owing to the increased susceptibility of the upper tracts to untoward changes. Therefore, patients with diminished vesical compliance should not have AUS placement if storage pressures will exceed 40 cm H_2O. Bladder augmentation (prior to AUS or concomitant with AUS surgery) is indicated in such cases.

Whereas continence rates for AUS placement are generally excellent in children, ranging from 62% to 90% (Decter et al, 1988; Barrett and Parulkar, 1989; Gonzalez et al, 1989; Bosco et al, 1991), infection and erosion are substantially more common than in adults (Adams et al, 1989; Bosco et al, 1991; Kryger et al, 2001; Herndon et al, 2003). These complications resulted in removal of devices in 13% to 25% of patients. The Indiana University group has demonstrated that, similar to the situation in adults, the infection and erosion rate has greatly diminished since the modifications introduced with use of the AMS 800 model AUS (Herndon et al, 2003). Interestingly, the continence rate and complication rates with long-term follow-up are similar between younger and older children (Kryger et al, 2001) and between boys and girls (Decter et al, 1988; Barrett and Parulkar, 1989; Gonzalez, et al, 1989; Bosco et al, 1991). However, success rates are generally half as good in patients with previous bladder neck surgery compared with those without prior surgery (Castera et al, 2001).

Previous or Simultaneous Placement of Penile Prosthesis. There are some men with post-prostatectomy incontinence who also suffer from erectile dysfunction unresponsive to nonoperative therapies who may elect placement of a penile prosthesis (Cooperberg et al, 2003). Just as previous AUS is not a contraindication to penile prosthesis placement, neither is penile prosthesis a contraindication to AUS placement. However, regardless of the order of surgery, the surgeon must be aware of the location of the previously placed components. For simultaneous procedures, Parulkar and Barrett (1989) recommend placing the sphincter first. The AUS balloon reservoir and scrotal pump are placed on one side; and if an inflatable penile prosthesis is being implanted, the inflatable penile prosthetic pump and balloon reservoir are placed in the contralateral perivesical space and hemiscrotum, respectively. In a review of combined implantation of an AUS and penile prosthesis, Parulkar and Barrett (1989) reported a satisfactory continence rate of 95%, with a functional penile prosthesis rate of 98%. The risk for mechanical or surgical problems did not appear to be higher in 65 patients, demonstrating the safety of dual implantation.

Recently a transverse scrotal approach has been described that is conducive to simultaneous placement of a penile prosthesis (inflatable or malleable) and the AUS through a single, upper transverse scrotal incision (Wilson et al, 2003). However, proximal bulbar urethral placement is more difficult and no long-term results are available at this time (Stone et al, 2003). Cost and time benefits have been demonstrated by dual simultaneous implantation through a single incision (Seftel, 2005).

Previous or Simultaneous Augmentation Cystoplasty. With AUS placement in children with neurogenic voiding dysfunction, one needs to monitor for upper tract deterioration, which can occur in up to 28% to 57% of cases (Bauer, et al, 1986; Light and Pietro, 1986; Roth et al, 1986; Scott et al, 1986; Churchill et al, 1987; Murray et al, 1988; Bitsch et al, 1990; Warwick and Abrams, 1990; O'Flynn and Thomas, 1991; Aprikian et al, 1992; Ghoniem et al, 1994; Simeoni et al, 1996). Augmentation cystoplasty in addition to artificial sphincter placement in children with neurogenic bladder dysfunction has the theoretical advantage of preventing upper urinary tract deterioration. Occasionally, in a patient with a small capacity, poorly compliant bladder, it is difficult to accurately evaluate the outlet, owing to excessively high bladder pressures. Such patients may undergo augmentation cystoplasty to address the vesical dysfunction and later elect artificial sphincter placement if stress urinary incontinence becomes a problem with significant bother.

In the patient with readily documented ISD and neurogenic bladder overactivity or high pressure storage, augmentation cystoplasty and AUS placement are both indicated. Some surgeons prefer a staged procedure, supported by two recent reports (Miller et al, 1998; Furness et al, 1999) in which it was found that staging the surgeries may lower the infection rate by as much as half. Others have reported excellent success with simultaneous augmentation cystoplasty and sphincter placement (Gonzalez et al, 1989; Abdel-Azim and Abdel-Hakim, 2003) with a cuff placed around the bladder neck.

Radiation. Previous pelvic irradiation is not an absolute contraindication to placement of an AUS. Although the risk of

Surgical Treatment of Male Sphincteric Urinary Incontinence: The Male Perineal Sling and Artificial Urinary Sphincter **2403**

CHAPTER 74

infection/erosion and the need for device revision is higher in irradiated versus nonirradiated patients (Wang and Hadley, 1992; Martins and Boyd, 1995; Litwiller et al, 1996; Manunta et al, 2000; Petrou et al, 2000; Gomha and Boone, 2002; Walsh et al, 2002), overall continence rates and patient satisfaction are similar (Gousse et al, 2001; Gomha and Boone, 2002; Walsh et al, 2002; Lai et al, 2003).

Previous Male Sling. In cases of infected or eroded sling, the synthetic material must be explanted and the urethra should be allowed to heal over a 12-Fr catheter, similar to the management of infected or eroded AUS. Reoperation with sling or AUS may be attempted 3 to 6 months later. In cases of recurrent incontinence after male sling, the authors recommend trans-scrotal AUS placement, with the resulting urethral cuff being slightly distal to the usual transperineal placement. In our experience, when the trans-scrotal approach is used for AUS surgery, the previously placed perineal sling is not encountered and acts similar to a "double cuff" placed more proximally. If the surgeon chooses to explant the sling and place an AUS, then reoperation through the midline perineal incision is recommended. The silicone-coated polyester does not incorporate well into the tissues and is therefore easily identified, divided, and explanted, leaving a relatively clean plane for dissection of the bulbar urethra.

SUMMARY

After appropriate diagnostic workup, surgery is often elected by those patients with bothersome sphincteric incompetence who fail conservative management. With the continuing popularity of prostate cancer screening, post-prostatectomy incontinence remains the most common indication for AUS placement. AUS has previously been the gold standard treatment for post-prostatectomy incontinence, with excellent patient satisfaction despite the common need for operative revision. However, recent modifications of the male sling, resulting in intermediate-term success rates equaling those of the AUS, have rendered the perineal bone-anchored male sling a viable alternative for the treatment of PPI.

SUGGESTED READINGS

Appell RA: Techniques and results in the implantation of the artificial urinary sphincter in women with type III stress urinary incontinence by a vaginal approach. Neurourol Urodyn 1988;7:613-619.

Brito CG, Mulcahy JJ, Mitchell ME, Adams MC: Use of a double cuff AMS800 urinary sphincter for severe stress incontinence. J Urol 1993;149:283-285.

Comiter CV: The male sling for stress urinary incontinence: A prospective study. J Urol 2002;167:597-601.

Elliott DS, Barrett DM: Mayo Clinic long-term analysis of the functional durability of the AMS 800 artificial urinary sphincter: A review of 323 cases. J Urol 1998;159:1206-1208.

Guralnick ML, Miller E, Toh KL, Webster GD: Transcorporeal artificial urinary sphincter cuff placement in cases requiring revision for erosion and urethral atrophy. J Urol 2002;167:2075-2078.

Kowalcyk JJ, Nelson R, Mulcahy JJ: Successful reinsertion of the artificial urinary sphincter after removal for erosion or infection. Urology 1996;48:906-908.

Leach GE, Raz S: Perfusion sphincterometry: Method of intraoperative evaluation of artificial urinary sphincter function. Urology 1983;21:312-314.

Leach GE, Trockman B, Wong A, et al: Post-prostatectomy incontinence: Urodynamic findings and treatment outcomes. J Urol 1996;155:1256-1259.

Raj GV, Peterson AC, Toh KL, Webster GD: Outcomes following revisions and secondary implantations of the artificial urinary sphincter. J Urol 2005;173:1242-1245.

Rajpurkar AD, Onur R, Singla A: Patient satisfaction and clinical efficacy of the new perineal bone-anchored male sling. Eur Urol 2005;47:237-242; discussion 242.

Schaeffer AJ, Clemens JQ, Ferrari M, Stamey TA: The male bulbourethral sling procedure for post-radical prostatectomy incontinence. J Urol 1998;159:1510-1515.

Stern JA, Clemens JQ, Tiplitsky SI, et al: Long-term results of the bulbourethral sling procedure. J Urol 2005;173:1654-1656.

Wilson SK, Delk JR 2nd, Henry GD, Siegel AL: New surgical technique for sphincter urinary control system using upper transverse scrotal incision. J Urol 2003;169:261-264.

sexes, rather than the longer female life expectancy, explain the roughly 50% higher lifetime likelihood of dying from this disease in women who contract it compared with men (SEER, 1973-1997). These sex differences have been observed in other countries as well (Mungen et al, 2000).

Age

Bladder cancer can occur at any age—even in children. However, it is generally a disease of middle-aged and elderly people, with the median ages at diagnosis for urothelial carcinoma being 69 years in males and 71 years in females (Lynch and Cohen, 1995). Moreover, **the incidence of bladder cancer increases directly with age—from roughly 142 per 100,000 men and 33 per 100,000 women age 65 to 69 years to 296 per 100,000 men and 74 per 100,000 women 85 years old or older.** Relatively similar trends are found for squamous carcinomas. Mortality from bladder cancer is also higher in elderly persons. For instance, the ratio of disease-related mortality to incidence for men and women in the United States age 65 to 69 years is 14% and 18%, respectively, whereas for men and women age 80 to 84 years it is 30% and 37%, respectively (SEER, 1973-1997). Again, whether this represents a more aggressive variant of the disease in elderly people, a relatively advanced stage at diagnosis (for both social reasons [patient and medical provider driven] and biologic reasons [such as impaired host defenses in the elderly]), or the offering and selection of less aggressive (or successful) therapies in the elderly patient is uncertain—but it is probably due to a combination of these factors.

In adolescents and in adults younger than 30 to 40 years, bladder cancers tend to express well-differentiated histologies and behave in a more indolent fashion (Linn et al, 1998). Intriguingly, the molecular and genetic aberrations in bladder tumors in this population do not share the fairly close correlation with histologic grade and clinical behavior that is seen in tumors in the middle-aged and elderly populations (Linn et al, 1998). Younger patients appear to have a more favorable prognosis because they present more frequently with superficial, low-grade tumors; however, the risk for disease progression is the same, grade-for-grade, in younger patients as in older ones (Wan and Grossman, 1989).

Regional and National Differences

Although the incidence rates of bladder cancer have been reported as somewhat higher in the northern United States than in the southern United States (Morrison, 1984), owing to migrations of elderly populations to southern states, these differences in incidence rates are diminishing (SEER, 1973-1997). Incidence rates in different countries also differ considerably, with higher rates in the United States than in Japan and Finland (Morrison, 1984). In Hawaii, the incidence is more than twice as high in whites as in those of Japanese descent (Waterhouse et al, 1982). These differences probably reflect the combined effects of environmental and hereditary factors. However, it also reflects national (and at times, regional) differences in case reporting. For instance, in the United Kingdom, in-situ and epithelium-confined (stage Ta) carcinomas are not reported in cancer statistics, whereas in the United States they are (Crow and Ritchie, 2003).

Autopsy Data

Unlike virtually all other common malignancies, bladder cancer has almost never been reported as an incidental finding at autopsy (Marshall, 1956; Resseguie et al, 1978; Kishi et al, 1981). This is distinctly different from carcinomas of the prostate (Franks, 1954), kidney (Hellsten et al, 1981), and many other sites, in which "autopsy cancers" actually occur more commonly than the clinically diagnosed entity. Although this may be explained in part by postmortem urothelial autolysis or by erosive effects of indwelling catheters, which may obscure the identification of small malignancies, and is at odds with the occasional experience of all urologists who may find incidental bladder tumors during cystoscopic examinations for other diseases (Kim and Ignatoff, 1994; Wasson et al, 1995), this remains a remarkable observation. It implies that at some point before demise, virtually everyone with bladder cancer has the disease diagnosed. Furthermore, it implies that reported differences in incidence rates among people of different sexes, races, ages, and locales cannot simply be explained by a failure to diagnose the disease in particular groups. Finally, it implies that the preclinical latency of this tumor (the time between when it is large enough to be seen cystoscopically [or at autopsy] and when it is actually symptomatic) must be relatively brief. The implications of this in terms of early detection strategies, including their potential advantages or disadvantages and how often they should be repeated, are considerable.

KEY POINTS: EPIDEMIOLOGY

- Bladder cancer is nearly three times more common in men in the United States than in women, but women have more than a 30% higher chance of dying of bladder cancer, if they develop it, than men do.

- Bladder cancer is rare in persons younger than the age of 50, with median ages at diagnosis of around 70 years for each gender. Incidence of and mortality from the disease increase further with age.

- Bladder cancer occurs roughly half as often in African Americans as in whites but is nearly twice as likely to be lethal in African Americans as in whites.

- In Hispanic Americans, bladder cancer also occurs about half as often as in whites but Hispanics are less likely to die of bladder cancer, if they develop it, than whites are.

- Bladder cancer is almost never found incidentally at autopsy, making it unlikely that differences in incidence between genders, races, and people of various ages are due to its underdiagnosis in some groups.

ETIOLOGY AND RISK FACTORS
Basic Biology

Factors reported to be causally related to bladder cancer's development and progression include occupational exposure to chemicals; cigarette smoking; coffee drinking; ingestion of analgesics or artificial sweeteners; bacterial, parasitic, fungal, and viral infections; harboring of bladder calculi, and receiving genotoxic chemotherapeutic agents. Data suggest that at least some bladder cancers are carcinogen induced. Carcinogens produce lesions in the DNA of target cells, both initiating and propagating the process of tumorigenesis. It is likely that multiple lesions are required to cause malignant transformation of cells. Additionally, because the transitional epithelium's microenvironment may affect exposure and/or sensitivity to carcinogens and mitogens, it may facilitate the development of different genetic alterations to relatively similar chemical insults. Epidemiologic, molecular, and histopathologic evidence confirming that this is often the response to some of the best-defined environmental carcinogens—cigarette smoke and industrial chemicals—is presented later.

Oncogenes

Despite these complexities, oncologic research dictates that genetic changes must occur for malignant transformation to result. Several different potential mechanisms can account for these genetic changes. One involves the induction of oncogenes—altered normal genes that encode for the malignant phenotype, primarily by permitting cells to escape from normal mechanisms of growth control. Oncogenes that have been associated with bladder cancer include those of the *RAS* gene family, including the *P21 RAS* oncogene (Czerniak et al, 1992), which has been found, at least in some studies, to correlate with a higher histologic grade. This is a guanosine triphosphatase, transducing signals from the cell membrane to the nucleus, affecting proliferation and differentiation (Barbacid et al, 1987). Although some reports have claimed that nearly 50% of TCCs have *RAS* mutations, others have reported a far lower level (Knowles and Williamson, 1993).

Tumor Suppressor Genes

Although oncogenes are easier to detect because they have a positive dominant effect, an equally important molecular mechanism in the process of carcinogenesis is the inactivation of genes coding for proteins that regulate cell growth, DNA repair, or apoptosis. Deletions or inactivation of these so-called cancer suppressor genes could encourage unregulated growth or fail to direct cells with damaged DNA to programmed cell death, ultimately resulting in uncontrolled proliferation of genetically altered clones. This results in genetic instability, with DNA copying errors appearing throughout affected cells' genomes. Because multiple short nucleotide sequence repeats are dispersed throughout the normal mammalian genome, searching for DNA replication errors in regions of known multiple repeating sequences can be used as a means to screen for malignant cells (Mao et al, 1994) and

also as a means of mapping deleted regions of DNA (Cairns et al, 1998; Hoque et al, 2003).

For a tumor to result from a suppressor gene alteration, the protein encoded by the gene (the gene product) must be nonfunctional. Hence, either both alleles of the gene are deleted, silenced, and/or mutated or the molecular product resulting from dimerization (or more) of a mutant and wild-type protein chain is nonfunctional (a so-called dominant-negative mutation). Historically, this has been most easily recognized by cytogenetic analysis, in which large chromosomal segments or entire chromosomes are found to be "missing" from karyotypes. However, even in the absence of deletions large enough to be identified cytogenetically, because many genes are polymorphic (i.e., the inherited maternal and paternal alleles differ slightly in genetic code), comparisons of DNA digests from malignant and normal tissues (where both alleles are retained) can be used to identify deletions of one allele of a specific genetic region (loss of heterozygosity of the alleles) in the malignant DNA. For many of the chromosomal regions known to be deleted from human bladder cancer in a nonrandom fashion (and hence presumably providing the cell with some selective advantage), a suppressor gene has been located in the deleted region, and, for several, molecular analysis of the retained gene copy has identified one or several mutations or silencing via hypermethylation of its promoter (Nakagawa et al, 2003; Tsutsumi, et al, 1998) that could render its product nonfunctional or absent.

Further confirmation has been done by demonstrating absent or abnormal expression of the gene with molecular studies. Similarly, proteins can be detected by immunoprecipitation or by immunoblotting a mixture of proteins run on gels with labeled antibodies to the protein of interest (Western blotting). Additionally, mass spectroscopy can be used to distinguish proteins in body fluids and tissues based primarily on size and other chemical characteristics, without having antibodies to them. Many of these molecular studies require relatively pure samples of DNA, RNA, and/or proteins from tumors uncontaminated by molecular materials from normal epithelial, stromal, inflammatory, and/or vascular cells. Harvesting such pure specimens of tumor molecules has been greatly facilitated by laser capture microdissection, in which histologically normal-appearing tissues and cells can be identified and deleted from the group of cells to be sampled (Cheng et al, 2003). Also, visual approaches (such as in situ hybridization that anneals labeled complementary DNA [cDNA] to specific sequences in tumor cell RNA or immunohistochemistry using labeled antibodies to antigens of interest) can be used to identify the gene's message (messenger RNA [mRNA]) or product (protein) in tissue sections. By having scores to hundreds of tissue specimens on a single slide (tissue array), the expression of a molecule in hundreds of specimens can now be determined. Additionally, owing to technologic advances, molecular assays can be performed on a computer chip or with a time-of-flight mass spectrometer and require far smaller samples of normal and tumor DNA, RNA, and proteins than previously needed. These advances, together with high through-put methodologies, enable simultaneous semiquantitative assessment of thousands of genes and gene products. These gene and protein arrays can be modified to identify deletions and mutations in genes and posttranslationally modified proteins (Hoque et al, 2003; Vettman et al, 2003). This exciting technology holds tremendous promise for both furthering our understanding of cancer biology (see later for examples) and providing clinically useful tools for risk assessment, prognosis, and predicting and assessing responses to various preventive and therapeutic interventions. Sophisticated bioinformatics, however, is required to analyze the huge amounts of data that are becoming available. Currently chip technology and mass spectroscopy are only beginning to be applied to the study of urothelial cancer, but within a few years it is possible that major breakthroughs in basic science and in clinical applications will occur because of their use.

By using traditional molecular and cytogenetic methods, several suppressor gene loci already have been closely associated with bladder cancer. These include that of TP53 (on chromosome 17p); the retinoblastoma *(RB)* gene on chromosome 13q; genes on chromosome 9, at least one of which is likely to be on 9p in region 9p21 where the genes for the P19 and P16 proteins reside; and another on 9q in region 9q32-33 (and perhaps genes in other regions of 9q).

TP53

The *TP53* gene is the most frequently altered gene in human cancers (Vogelstein, 1990; Harris and Hollstein, 1993). The normal protein, wild-type TP53, has a variety of functions, including acting as a transcription factor that suppresses cell proliferation (Vogelstein, 1990; Cote and Chatterjee, 1999), directing DNA damaged cells toward apoptosis before DNA replication (S phase of cell cycle) occurs (reviewed in Harris and Hollstein, 1993), contributing to the repair of damaged DNA by inducing the production of deoxyribonucleotide triphosphates in the nucleus (reviewed by Lozano and Elledge, 2000), and other mechanisms (Smith et al, 1994). Because of TP53's functions of repairing damaged DNA and directing cells with other genetic abnormalities toward apoptosis, *TP53* mutations have been associated with genomic instability— and hence progressive development of further mutations (Harris and Hollstein, 1993). Thus, it is not surprising that bladder cancers with *TP53* abnormalities appear to have more aggressive behaviors (Esrig et al, 1994; Cordon-Cardo, 1995).

For tumors to exceed 1 or 2 mm in diameter, new blood vessels must feed them. **Wild-type TP53 induces the expression of a potent inhibitor of angiogenesis, thrombospondin-1 (TSP-1), a normal constituent of the extracellular matrix, whereas mutant (or absent) TP53 does not.** A correlation of abnormal TP53 immunostaining with downregulation of TSP-1 and neoangiogenesis has been reported in bladder cancer (Grossfeld et al, 1997). Additionally, whereas wild-type TP53 may repair DNA damage caused by chemotherapeutic agents such as cisplatin (Hawkins et al, 1996), impaired TP53 function, although contributing to a more aggressive phenotype, may paradoxically enhance sensitivity to some chemotherapeutic agents (Hawkins et al, 1996; Cote and Chatterjee, 1999).

Considering the critical role TP53 has in controlling normal cell growth and the neoplastic process, it is not surprising that its own stability is under tight regulation. **MDM2, whose expression itself is induced by TP53, binds to TP53's amino-terminal, targeting it for ubiquitization and proteosomal degradation** (summarized in Carr, 2000). Failure of this process stabilizes TP53. Indeed, wild-type TP53 normally lasts only very briefly in the cell nucleus, whereas mutated forms often accumulate for longer times and hence are more easily detected by immunohistochemistry (Finlay et al, 1988). Several groups have closely correlated TP53 accumulation in cell nuclei (immunohistochemical detectability) with genetic mutations in the *TP53* gene and have employed immunohistology as a fairly simple means of screening cancers to assess whether *TP53* is mutated or not. Unfortunately, some important mutations in the *TP53* gene result in expression of a sufficiently truncated form of the protein (or no protein) so that no nuclear overexpression is seen—a circumstance that is indistinguishable immunohistochemically from one in which wild-type TP53 is expressed (Cordon-Cardo, 1995). Similarly, deletion of both alleles of the gene (homozygous deletion) or methylation of the promoters of both alleles (gene silencing) (Nakagawa et al, 2003) is also not detectable immunohistochemically. This may explain some of the discordance between immunohistochemical data and loss of heterozygosity data or other molecular data in some reports (Cote and Chatterjee, 1999). Additionally, because the wild-type TP53 protein functions as a tetramer, the altered product of a mutant allele stabilizes (permitting nuclear accumulation) but inactivates the tetrameric protein (resulting in tumorigenesis), even when the nonmutated allele is expressed normally. This dominant-negative effect offers a theoretical hurdle to genetic therapeutic strategies that attempt to insert a wild-type *TP53* gene into tumors with mutated *TP53* alleles.

Retinoblastoma Gene, Its Product, and Regulators P15, P16, P21, P27, and P19

The normal protein product of the *RB* gene (RB) is phosphorylated by several of the cyclin-dependent kinases, phosphorylating proteins residing in the cell nucleus, which "drive" various transition points of the cell cycle. Phosphorylated RB disassociates from another protein, the transcription factor E2F, to which it is normally complexed. This permits uncomplexed E2F to bind with promoting regions of several genes whose products induce cells to transit from G1 to S phase (Cordon-Cardo, 1995). Inactivation of RB through genetic deletion or mutation, therefore, permits cells to go through the G1 to S checkpoint more easily, stimulating cell proliferation.

Similarly, inhibitors of the cyclin-dependent kinases that phosphorylate RB, disassociating it from E2F, normally serve as regulators of the cell cycle themselves. **Such regulators include P15 and P16, proteins coded for on neighboring regions of chromosome 9p, which normally complex with cyclin-dependent kinases 4 and 6, inhibiting the phosphorylation of RB.** Additionally, two other nuclear proteins— P21, whose expression is induced directly by wild-type TP53 (Cordon-Cardo, 1995), and P27, whose level of expression is determined by proteosome-mediated degradation (Loda et al, 1997)—also inhibit phosphorylation by cyclin-dependent kinases of RB (Xiong et al, 1993; Loda et al, 1997). Alterations of any of these proteins thus would permit RB to become phosphorylated, resulting in uncomplexed E2F driving the G1 to S transition and cellular proliferation. Hence, reduced or abnormal expression/function of the products of genes coding for P15, P16, P21, P27, or RB would be expected to result in uninhibited proliferation and perhaps malignant transformation and tumor progression. It is not surprising, therefore, that these genes have all been noted to be bladder cancer suppressor genes.

This was demonstrated by nonrandom deletions of chromosomes 13q and 9 in bladder cancers (Babu et al, 1989; Atkin and Fox, 1990; Tsai et al, 1990) and subsequently confirmed by molecular studies. **Precise molecular analyses have been far more difficult for chromosome 9 than for 13q (RB) or 17p (TP53), because most often an entire chromosome is "missing"** (Wheeless et al, 1994). Furthermore, instead of point mutations in the *P15* or *P16* genes on the retained copy of chromosome 9 (region 9p21), the entire gene regions (often of both *P15* and *P16*) have been deleted (homozygous deletion), which is impossible to detect on loss of heterozygosity studies. Moreover, the promoter of *P16* may be hypermethylated in cytosine-phosphate-guanine (CpG)-rich regions, leading to transcriptional silencing without deletion or mutation of the allele. This occurs particularly in squamous carcinomas (Tsutsumi et al, 1998).

Sharing the same region of chromosome 9p21 is the gene that encodes both P16 and P19 *(ARF)* via an alternate reading frame. P19 (ARF) stabilizes TP53 by promoting MDM2 degradation (Tsutsumi, et al 1998). Thus, both gene products serve as tumor suppressors, and it is not surprising that deletion of this region is a common early event in bladder cancer development. Additionally, several authors have data indicating that additional bladder cancer suppressor genes may be located on chromosome 9, including those in the 9q region (Tsai et al, 1990; Knowles et al, 1994; Spruck et al, 1994; Habuchi et al, 1995; Lin et al, 1995; Bartlett et al, 1998; Takahashi et al, 1998, 2000; Czerniak et al, 1999; Simoneau et al, 1999).

Understanding the normal functions of the products of suspected deleted genes and particularly what their roles in regulating cellular proliferation are, investigators have tried to correlate identified deletions with the known differences in behaviors of the two major types of TCC: low-grade papillary superficial tumors and high-grade cancers that rapidly become invasive and metastasize. **Through such correlations, several groups have now identified chromosome 9** (Tsai et al, 1990; Spruck et al, 1994) **and particularly 9q losses** (Knowles et al, 1994; Habuchi et al, 1998; Simoneau et al, 1999; Czerniak et al, 1999) **as early events in the development of low-grade superficial tumors.** Alternatively, high-grade cancers are much more commonly associated with *TP53* abnormalities and chromosome 17p deletions (Spruck et al, 1994; Gruis et al, 1995). This again is not surprising, because accumulated genetic errors expected in a cell with a nonfunctioning TP53 protein encourage continued genetic instability and selection for aberrant (i.e., aggressive) behavior and anaplastic morphology. Such abnormalities are beginning to be used to predict future tumor behavior.

Abnormal expression of RB (deletion or overexpression) detected immunohistochemically also appears to occur primarily in aggressive TCCs (Cairns et al, 1991; Cote et al, 1998). Similarly, P21 deletions also correlate with more aggressive bladder cancers, and abnormal expression of either P21 or RB, along with mutated (or overexpressed) TP53, may

have additional adverse prognostic implications (Cote and Chatterjee, 1999). Although with many cancers and cell lines P16 and RB expression is inversely related, the exact tumor profile of P16 aberrations remains controversial, with some studies pointing to a more aggressive phenotype (Spruck et al, 1994; Reznikoff et al, 1996), whereas others are far less clear, revealing losses equally in nonaggressive and aggressive urothelial cancers (Friedrich et al, 2000).

Amplification and Overexpression

A third type of carcinogenic genetic mechanism is amplification or overexpression of normal genes that encode for growth factors or their receptors. Messing (1987, 1990) and Neal (1990) and their respective coworkers (Mellon et al, 1995) have independently shown **that abnormal expression of the receptor for epidermal growth factor (EGF) occurs in bladder cancer cells and that increased expression is associated with more aggressive biologic behavior.** Because a major ligand for this receptor, EGF, is excreted in urine in very high quantities in biologically active forms (Fuse et al, 1992; Messing and Murphy-Brooks, 1994), abnormally high expression of the EGF receptor may be an example of a cell taking advantage of its unique environment to provide it with a growth advantage. Additionally, EGF receptor signaling induces not only growth but also cancer cell motility (Theodorescu et al, 1998) and matrix metalloproteinase-9 (MMP-9) expression (Ocharocnrat et al, 2000), both steps necessary for invasion and metastasis. Mechanisms of its overexpression are uncertain, because even when the protein is overexpressed, amplification of the EGF receptor's gene has not commonly been seen in bladder cancer (Neal et al, 1989).

Alterations in the *ERBB2* oncogene that codes for a growth factor receptor functionally and anatomically related to that for EGF (also called *ERBB1*) have also been associated with a variety of malignancies, including bladder cancer (Wright et al, 1991; Swanson et al, 1992; Ding-Wei et al, 1993; Sauter et al, 1993). Sauter and associates (1993) found overexpression of the ERBB2 product, P185, in 61 of 141 bladder cancers, but in only 10 was amplification of the gene also encountered. Ding-Wei and colleagues (1993) found that 33% of 56 bladder tumors had increased expression of P185 by immunohistochemical detection that correlated with higher-grade, higher-stage, and tumor recurrence. However, not all authors (Wright et al, 1991; Mellon et al, 1996; Orlando et al, 1996) have found a significant correlation between P185 expression and aggressive bladder cancer behavior. Other ERBB-like molecules exist, and it is possible that by using real-time reverse transcriptase polymerase chain reaction (RT-PCR) analyses, quantification of the entire family of ERBB receptors (ERBB1-4) can be done to develop a profile of these receptors in each tumor (Junttila et al, 2003).

Genetic models in animals also are an excellent way of studying the individual and combined effects of putative suppressor genes, oncogenes, and molecules that facilitate urothelial cancer development and progression such as the EGF receptor, TP53, RB, and ERBB2. For example, the oncoviral protein, SV40 large T antigen, contains components that inactivate RB and TP53 (Reznikoff et al, 1996). Using a promoter to the urothelial specific gene, uroplakin II, tied to SV40 large T antigen, Zhang and coworkers (1999) have developed a mouse that expresses SV40 large T antigen in the urothelium only (tissue-specific gene expression) with diffuse carcinoma in situ eventually resulting from expression of a low copy number of SV40 large T antigen and invasive high-grade cancer resulting from a high copy number. Using the same system, Cheng and co-workers (2002), have developed a mouse that expresses the EGF receptor in all urothelial cells, a pattern that typifies what occurs in normal-appearing urothelium in patients with cancer elsewhere within the bladder (see "Patterns of Spread"—Messing et al, 1987, 1990). So far when the EGF receptor is abnormally expressed, only hyperplasia has predictably occurred, but when the urothelial EGF receptor mouse is crossed with the urothelial, low copy number SV40 large T antigen mouse, the EGF receptor accelerated tumor growth and converted the carcinomas in situ developing in the SV40 large T antigen mouse into high-grade invasive urothelial cancers (Cheng et al, 2003). This implies that abnormal expression of the EGF receptor can facilitate the progression of urothelial cancer but may not be capable of malignant transformation on its own, a finding supported by in vitro (Messing and Reznikoff, 1987) and clinical data (Messing, 1990; Rao et al, 1993; Mellon et al, 1995).

KEY POINTS: MOLECULAR "PLAYERS" IN BLADDER CARCINOGENESIS

- Inactivation of several tumor suppressor genes appears to be important in the development and progression of bladder cancer. The products of these genes are no longer able to inhibit tumor development because mutations and/or deletions of the genes have occurred or because the genes are no longer transcribed once their promoters have been methylated.

- The important tumor suppressor genes so far associated with bladder cancer include *TP53* (which normally inhibits cell cycle progression, repairs damaged DNA or directs cells with genetic abnormalities towards apoptosis, and inhibits angiogenesis, among other activities) and cell cycle inhibitors RB, P21, P27, and P16.

- Oncogenes are activated mutated genes that induce carcinogenesis, often by avoiding normal mechanisms of growth control. The one most closely associated with bladder cancer is *RAS*, a membrane-bound, mitogenic, signal transduction molecule.

- Overexpression of normal genes including those for the receptor of EGF *(ERBB1)* and *ERBB2* occur in most bladder cancers and also may facilitate cancer development and progression.

Occupational Exposure Risk Factors

Aniline dyes, introduced in the late 1800s to color fabrics, are urothelial carcinogens (Rehn, 1895). Other chemicals that have been shown to be carcinogens for bladder cancer include 2-naphthylamine, 4-aminobiphenyl, 4-nitrobiphenyl, 4-4-diaminobiphenyl (benzidine), and 2-amino-1-naphthol (Morrison and Cole, 1976); combustion gases and soot from coal; possibly chlorinated aliphatic hydrocarbons (Steinbeck et al, 1990); and certain aldehydes such as acrolein used in chemical dyes and in the rubber and textile industries (Stadler, 1993). It has been estimated that occupational exposure accounts for roughly 20% of bladder cancer cases in the United States (Cole et al, 1972), with long latency periods (i.e., 30 to 50 years) being typical. However, this is probably related to cumulative dose, and with more intensive exposures the latent period may well be shortened (Case et al, 1954). With manufacturing and chemical industries moving from North America to other regions, a reduction in cases of bladder cancer would be expected, but this has not (yet) been seen. Whether this means that other industrial/environmental carcinogens have replaced those no longer in North America (through economics or regulations), or that a very long latency effect exists, is not known.

Most bladder carcinogens are aromatic amines. Other potential sources of such compounds are dietary nitrites and nitrates that are acted on by intestinal bacterial flora (Chapman et al, 1981) and contaminants of ingested herbal remedies such as aristolochic acid (Nortier et al, 2000). Also, metabolites of the amino acid tryptophan have been reported, but not proved, to be potentially carcinogenic. Occupations reported to be associated with increased risk of bladder cancer include autoworker, painter, truck driver, drill press operator, leather worker, metal worker, and machiner, as well as those occupations that involve organic chemicals, such as dry cleaner, paper manufacturer, rope and twine maker, dental technician, barber or beautician, physician, worker in apparel manufacturing, and plumber (Silverman et al, 1989a; 1989b).

Cigarette Smoking

Cigarette smokers have up to a fourfold higher incidence of bladder cancer than do people who have never smoked (Morrison 1984; Burch et al, 1989). The risk correlates with the number of cigarettes smoked, the duration of smoking, and the degree of inhalation of smoke. This risk has been observed in both sexes. Former cigarette smokers have a reduced incidence of bladder cancer compared with active smokers (Augustine et al, 1988). However, the reduction of this risk down to baseline (age adjusted) takes nearly 20 years after cessation, a period far longer than that for the reduction of risk of cardiovascular disease and lung cancer after smoking has stopped. Other forms of tobacco use are associated with only a slightly higher risk for bladder cancer (Burch et al, 1989). Although it has been estimated that one third of bladder cancer cases may be related to cigarette smoking (Howe et al, 1980), this figure is clearly complicated by the knowledge that former smokers are also at risk and that the overwhelming majority of American men age 60 years or older (who represent 65% to 70% of all patients who develop bladder cancer) have strong smoking histories (Morrison and Cole, 1976). The evidence regarding an increased risk in individuals with high occupational (e.g., tavern workers) or social exposure to "second hand" smoke is not clear. However, Paz and coworkers (2002) recently reported such a risk in spouses of long-term cigarette smokers in Israel.

The specific chemical carcinogen responsible for bladder cancer in cigarette smoke has not been identified. Nitrosamines, 2-naphthylamine, and 4-aminobiphenyl are known to be present and increased urinary tryptophan metabolites have also been demonstrated in cigarette smokers (Hoffman et al, 1969).

It has long been noted that individuals with seemingly equal exposures to environmental carcinogens (either through occupational exposure or smoking) vary enormously in their risks of developing bladder cancer. Considerable effort for assessing this has focused not only on obtaining precise information about exposures but also on understanding mechanisms by which purported agents may be carcinogenic, how they reach the bladder, and how humans activate or detoxify them. **Much interest has focused on 4-aminobiphenyl, primarily because it is in several industrial chemicals and is in cigarette smoke. Because acetylation of this agent initiates a detoxifying pathway,** measurements of rates of acetylation of substrates metabolized in a similar way to 4-aminobiphenyl, such as sulfamethazine or caffeine, have been correlated with risk. Lower and colleagues (1979) showed that slow acetylators were more susceptible to development of bladder cancer. Similar findings have been reported in populations with industrial exposures (Cartwright et al, 1982; Hanke and Krajewska, 1990), although these results have not always been confirmed in studies using other populations, substrates, and techniques (Miller and Cosgriff, 1983; Horai et al, 1989). Complicating analyses are the presence of activating as well as detoxifying enzymes and that profiles of these enzymes in urothelium and hepatocytes differ (Pink et al, 1992; Fredrickson et al, 1994).

N-Acetyltransferase 2 (NAT2), a major acetylating enzyme, is polymorphic, with six genetic variants predominating in whites. Of these six alleles, only one produces an enzyme with rapid activity, and hence only individuals homozygous for two "rapid" alleles will be true rapid acetylators. **Using genetic analyses from white blood cells, Risch and colleagues (1995) were able to demonstrate that in bladder cancer patients with and without known industrial and/or smoking exposures, slow acetylator genotypes predominated, compared with non–bladder cancer controls.**

More recently, Taylor and associates (1998) have shown that another polymorphic N-acetyltransferase, NAT1, may actually be more predictive of bladder cancer development; those individuals homozygous for the NAT1* allele with more than a 30-year history of cigarette smoking have an 8.5-fold odds ratio of developing bladder cancer compared with wild-type NAT1. This tendency, however, is considerably greater in those NAT1* heterozygotes or homozygotes who are also homozygous for NAT2 genotypes associated with slow acetylation. Okkel and coworkers (1997) also found an increased association of slow acetylator NAT2 genotypes with risk for bladder cancer in smokers. Intriguingly, the relative frequency of NAT2 slow acetylating genotypes among male smokers of various races closely reflects the known risks for developing bladder cancer among whites, blacks, and Asian Americans (Yu et al, 1994).

In a separate analysis, Horn and colleagues (1995) looked at the role of another enzyme, cytochrome P450 1A2 (CYP 1A2), which is known to demethylate aromatic amines, thus activating potential carcinogens. As opposed to NAT2, CYP 1A2 is a highly inducible enzyme, and common environmental chemicals such as caffeine are known inducers. A phenotypic assay (caffeine breath test) allows the amount of $^{13}CO_2$ exhaled after ingestion of a known amount of ^{13}C-caffeine to be used to assess the relative activity of CYP 1A2. In a study of normal volunteers, men and parous women had significantly higher amounts of $^{13}CO_2$ in exhaled air on the caffeine breath test than did nulliparous women or parous women taking birth control pills. The authors concluded that excessive inducibility and activity of this enzyme in males might predispose them to a greater amount of carcinogen activation and hence a greater bladder cancer risk compared with women. Further studies of populations of bladder cancer patients are necessary to determine if this test has a predictive role. In a separate study, Brockmoller and associates (1998) reported that in German smokers, rapid metabolizing CYP 1A2 alleles, particularly in combination with a slow NAT phenotype, predicted susceptibility for bladder cancer. Researchers, however, have not found such a correlation between other alleles in the CYP family and bladder cancer risk (summarized in Bartsch et al, 2000).

Another enzyme family likely to be important in carcinogen detoxification is the glutathione transferases, particularly glutathione S-transferase M1, encoded for by the polymorphic gene GSTM1, which occurs in about 50% of the white population. Cigarette smokers who are homozygous for lacking this gene have a 1.8-fold greater risk of developing bladder cancer than do smokers who have one or two copies. However, nonsmokers who lack this gene have a similar risk of developing bladder cancer as do nonsmokers who have it, thus supporting the notion that this gene plays a role in development of smoking-induced bladder cancer (Bell et al, 1993). The roles of other isoforms in the glutathione S-transferase enzyme family are less certain (Berendsen et al, 1997; Pendyala et al, 1997; Sarkar et al, 1998).

Because the molecular adducts resulting from aromatic amine metabolism are believed to mutate DNA in specific ways that potentially affect all areas of the genome, determining the pattern of mutation occurring in known genes in bladder cancer patients may shed light on whether their malignancy arose spontaneously or was induced by a purported chemical carcinogen (Jones et al, 1991). Particularly, the TP53 gene has been studied both because its sequence is well established and because of its close association with bladder cancer. The hypothesis guiding these studies is based on the observation that most common mutations seen spontaneously are transitions at CpG dinucleotides. By assuming that CpG transitions are primarily spontaneous mutations, if these are most of the mutations found in the gene of interest, such mutations would be considered spontaneously induced. Alternatively, because specific carcinogens create specific mutational events, or genetic "footprints," finding other types of mutations may indicate a carcinogenic process involving specific agents. When one performs this analysis on tumors associated with TP53 mutations, colon carcinomas and leukemias have been shown to have a relatively high rate of predominantly spontaneous TP53 mutations, whereas small cell carcinomas of the lung appear to have a high proportion of nonspontaneous or exogenously induced mutations (Jones et al, 1991). When this analysis is applied to bladder cancer, an intermediate rate of mutations is seen in which roughly 50% of the mutations are thought to be exogenously produced. **However, when comparing *TP53* mutations in bladder tumors of smokers with those in bladder cancers of patients who have never smoked, differences in the types or sites of mutations have not been seen, although a higher number of mutations occurred in smokers** (Spruck et al, 1993). This suggests that smoking might increase the amount of mutations in urothelial cells without necessarily directing the site or type of mutation that occurs (Spruck et al, 1993). This type of analysis correlates closely with the elegant case-control study of Hayes and coworkers (1993), who found that although exposure to industrial carcinogens and smoking clearly correlated with an increased risk for developing bladder cancer, with the exception of young patients, these exposures did not correlate with any particular bladder cancer phenotype. Thus, assuming that low-grade superficial and high-grade rapidly invasive TCCs have different fundamental "genetic pathways" (Spruck et al, 1994; Gruis et al, 1995), the two best-described environmental carcinogenic exposures for bladder cancer predispose to the development of each of these genetic alterations in similar proportions to that seen in the non-exposed population.

Further complicating these analyses are data indicating that regardless of types of TCCs, hypermethylation of CpG "islands," particularly in the promoting regions (inhibiting transcription of the corresponding allele) and, at times, in the exons of genes shown to be relevant to urothelial carcinogenesis, such as *P16, P19 (ARF)* (Dominguez et al, 2002) and the gene deleted on 9q32-q34 (*DBCCR1*) (Habuchi et al, 1995), is quite common in tumors (Habuchi et al, 2000; Salem et al, 2000). This occasionally occurs in normal urothelium in the elderly (Habuchi et al, 2000) as well and has a debatable relationship with tumor aggressiveness and stage (Habuchi et al, 2000; Salem et al, 2000). Additionally, aging itself may have further confounding influences because mutations in genes highly relevant to bladder cancer, such as *TP53* and *HRAS*, were detected in peripheral blood leukocytes of 7 of 19 apparently normal individuals (Wilson et al, 2000). Many of these mutations, again, were in CpG islands, implying that there may be a subset of individuals with hypermethylation (and other mutational) tendencies that may serve as a background on which carcinogens act. Epidemiologic studies to assess whether such individuals and their relatives are at higher risk to develop bladder cancer, with or without environmental exposures, have not been conducted. Regardless of these factors, **from a clinical standpoint it is important to realize that not only does smoking increase the risk for developing bladder cancer but also failure to quit smoking once a diagnosis is made predicts a more ominous outcome, even in those diagnosed with noninvasive initial cancers** (Thompson et al, 1993; Fleshner et al, 1999).

Coffee and Tea Drinking

Although coffee and tea drinking has been implicated in some studies of the etiology of bladder cancer, when cigarette smoking is controlled for, no increased risk with coffee drinking has been found (Cohen and Johansson, 1992).

Analgesic Abuse

Consumption of large quantities (5 to 15 kg over a 10-year period) of analgesic combinations containing phenacetin (which has a chemical structure similar to that of aniline dyes) is associated with an increased risk for TCC of the renal pelvis and bladder (Piper et al, 1985). The latency period may be longer for bladder tumors than for renal pelvic tumors, whose latency period may be as long as 25 years (Steffens and Nagel, 1988). A correlation with the use of other analgesics has been debated (Wahlqvist, 1980; McCredie et al, 1983; DeBroe and Elseviers, 1998).

Artificial Sweeteners

Large doses of artificial sweeteners, including saccharin and cyclamates, have been shown to be bladder carcinogens in experimental studies of rodents. These studies are controversial because of the extremely high doses of sweeteners given, because cancer occurred only in animals exposed in utero or in the neonatal period (Sontag, 1980), and because urinary pH was markedly affected by the doses and the electrolyte composition of the saccharin given, which in turn, influenced susceptibility to carcinogenesis (Fukushima et al, 1990; Cohen et al, 1991). In contrast, case-control epidemiologic studies in humans show little evidence for increased risk of bladder cancer in consumers of artificial sweeteners (Morrison, 1984).

Chronic Cystitis and Other Infections

Chronic cystitis in the presence of indwelling catheters or calculi is associated with an increased risk for SCC of the bladder (Kunter et al, 1984; Locke et al, 1985). Between 2% and 10% of paraplegics with long-term indwelling catheters develop bladder cancer, 80% of which are SCCs. However, with means of managing these patients without chronic indwelling catheters, the incidence of bladder cancer and the preponderance of SCCs, appears to be decreasing (Pannek, 2002). Unfortunately, despite these favorable trends, well over half the patients have muscle-invading cancers at diagnosis (Pannek, 2002), a figure that more than doubles that found in the non–spinal cord–injured population (Messing et al, 1995b). Despite this high risk, periodic screening with cystoscopy and/or cytology for patients with long-term indwelling catheters (in the absence of gross hematuria) is not strongly supported (Bahnson, 1997; Hamid et al, 2003).

Similarly, ***Schistosoma haematobium*** cystitis appears to be causally related to the development of bladder cancer—often SCC. In Egypt, where schistosomiasis is endemic among males, SCC of the bladder (bilharzial bladder cancer) is the most common malignancy. However, there is also an increased incidence of TCCs in males with schistosomiasis. Cystitis-induced bladder cancer from all causes is usually associated with severe, long-term infections. The mechanisms of carcinogenesis are not understood but may involve formation of nitrite and *N*-nitroso compounds in the bladder (Tricker et al, 1989), presumably from parasitic or microbial metabolism of normal urinary constituents (Higgy et al, 1985). Intriguingly, *P16* silencing by hypermethylation of CpG islands in the promoter region of the gene is found in 20% of SCCs but in a far lower percentage of TCCs (Tsutsumi et al, 1998).

The role of exposure to the human papillomavirus (HPV) in bladder cancer has been evaluated by several groups, with widely divergent findings. Reports have indicated that as few as 2% (Maloney et al, 1994; Aynaud et al, 1998) to as high as 35% of human bladder cancers are contaminated by HPV DNA (LaRue et al, 1995). Reasons for disparate results are not apparent, although **Griffiths and Mellon (2000) concluded that this virus was more likely to play a role in transitional cell tumorigenesis in immunocompromised hosts rather than in cancers arising in immunologically competent individuals.** The role of other viral agents in the etiology of TCC has been investigated but not established by Fraley and colleagues (1976).

Pelvic Irradiation

Women treated with radiation for carcinoma of the uterine cervix or ovary have a twofold to fourfold increased risk of developing bladder cancer subsequently compared with women only undergoing surgery (Duncan et al, 1977; Kaldor et al, 1995). The incidence rises further if chemotherapy was also administered (with or without cyclophosphamide) or even if chemotherapy was used alone. The risks in all groups continued to rise after 10 years (Kaldor et al, 1995). These tumors are characteristically high grade and locally advanced at the time of diagnosis (Quilty and Kerr, 1987). In a fascinating report from Kiev in which ground contamination from the Chernobyl nuclear reactor accident is still endemic, patients undergoing evaluation or treatment of urinary retention or chronic abacterial cystitis from regions that were considered contaminated excreted far higher amounts of cesium-137 in urine over 15 years after the nuclear accident than those residing in uncontaminated areas, had significantly more proliferative and dysplastic lesions on select mucosal biopsies, and had a 52% incidence of histologic carcinoma in situ versus 0% in patients from uncontaminated areas. Moreover, there were 10 cancers (6.4%) immediately found in patients from contaminated areas and none in those from clean areas. Whereas increased expression of base excision repair enzymes was seen in the urothelium of patients from contaminated areas, none was seen in invasive cancers, indicating that there was disruption of the base repair mechanism when carcinoma develops. Perhaps this was because of mutations/inactivations of *TP53* (which repairs abnormal DNA or sends cells with abnormal DNA to apoptosis).

Cyclophosphamide

Patients treated with cyclophosphamide have up to a ninefold increased risk of developing bladder cancer, although the specific relationship has not yet been formally demonstrated in case-control epidemiologic studies (Morrison, 1984). Most of these tumors are high grade and muscle infiltrating at the time of diagnosis, occur in patients younger than those with sporadic urothelial cancer, and have an equal incidence in both sexes (Vlaovic and Jewett, 1999). A urinary metabolite of cyclophosphamide, acrolein, is believed to be responsible for both hemorrhagic cystitis and bladder cancer (Cohen et al, 1992); however, the development of hemorrhagic cystitis does not necessarily correlate with the development of bladder cancer (Pedersen-Bjergaard et al, 1988). The

latent period for cyclophosphamide-induced bladder cancer is relatively short, ranging from 6 to 13 years. Studies suggest that the uroprotectant mesna (2-mercaptoethanesulfonic acid) may reduce the risk of bladder cancer (Habs and Schmahl, 1983). Some authors suggest aggressive therapy on diagnosis (e.g., cystectomy), even when the tumor is still noninvasive, because of the unusually high rate of progression experienced by patients in whom cystectomy is withheld (Fernandes et al, 1996).

Other Risk Factors

***Blackfoot disease* is endemic in South Taiwan and is usually associated with vascular and cardiac disease and with the development of numerous malignancies, including TCC of the bladder** (Liou et al, 1999). This condition appears to be related to ingestion of large quantities of arsenic in artesian well water. Similar endemic pockets of bladder cancer are found in other regions with high arsenic concentrations in drinking water (Moore et al, 1997). In a nested case-control study, Liou and coworkers (1999) demonstrated that specific cytogenetic abnormalities, including chromosome-type breaks, gaps, exchanges, and other aberrations, were more frequent in peripheral blood cells of exposed patients who ultimately developed cancer over a 4-year period of observation compared with exposed individuals who did not. Regardless of the mechanisms of oncogenesis in this entity, the incidence appears to be declining with effective public health measures focused on avoiding contaminated water (see the section on prevention).

***Aristolochia fangchi* is a Chinese herb** (containing *Stephania tetrandra* and *Magnolia officinalis*) that was imported into Belgium as a popular weight-reduction aid primarily used by women and that became responsible for an epidemic of interstitial nephropathy—presumably from contamination with *A. fangchi,* which had been substituted for *S. tetrandra* (Vanhaelen et al, 1994). Subsequently, patients with Chinese herb nephropathy have been reported to be at much higher risk for developing urothelial carcinoma, primarily of the upper urinary tract but also of the bladder (Nortier et al, 2000). A major mechanism in this condition appears to be the development of aristolochic acid–related DNA adducts in the urothelium of both the upper tract and bladder (Nortier et al, 2000). Public health measures are restricting the distribution of these herbs in some countries (Kessler, 2000).

***Additional risk factors* include being a renal transplant recipient** (Buzzeo et al, 1997) and having a chronically low amount of fluid ingestion (Michaud et al, 1999). Transplant recipients are known to be at a higher risk for developing numerous tumors, presumably because of prolonged immunosuppression (Penn, 1998). Similarly, if certain chemicals are responsible for initiating mutational events (discussed previously), prolonged exposure to higher concentrations of them is likely to be more mutagenic/carcinogenic than exposure to lower concentrations.

Heredity

Strong epidemiologic evidence does not exist for a hereditary cause of most cases of bladder cancer. **Perhaps the most compelling evidence in this regard comes from the work of**

Klemeney and colleagues (1997), **who studied the records of more than 12,000 relatives of 190 patients diagnosed with TCC in Iceland between 1983 and 1992 and found that while the risk of developing TCC was slightly elevated in relatives (observed-to-expected odds ratio of 1.24, 95% confidence interval of 0.9 to 1.67), this ratio was greater among second- and third- than first-degree relatives. This argues strongly against a straightforward genetic mechanism being responsible.**

Familial clusters of bladder cancer have been reported (Aherne, 1974; McCullough et al, 1975; Lynch et al, 1987, 1990; Klemeney and Schoenberg, 1996). However, most of the authors did not report on whether this increased risk in the affected families was related to relatives of the index case being smokers (or having exposures to other putative carcinogens). This is important because Kantor and associates (1988) indicated that the increased familial risk was primarily in relatives who smoked. Correlation of familial predisposition and possible exposures and some of the genotypic/phenotypic analyses discussed earlier (e.g., of GSTM1, NAT1 and NAT2, and CYP 1A2) are required to permit identification of at-risk individuals who may be the best subjects for interventions such as avoidance, prevention, and early detection strategies.

KEY POINTS: RISK FACTORS

- Exposure to environmental carcinogens contributes strongly to the development of bladder cancer.

- Cigarette smoking is the most common exposure, with increased risk (fourfold compared with people who never smoked) only declining slowly after smoking is discontinued.

- Bladder cancers associated with smoking or industrial exposures have similar proportions of indolent and aggressive cancers as those occurring in the unexposed population, but recurrences are likely to be more aggressive in patients who continue to be exposed than those who stop the exposure.

- Inherited polymorphisms of enzymes that activate and inactivate putative carcinogens may predict which individuals out of many with equal exposures will develop bladder cancer. However, there is no strong epidemiologic evidence that there is an inherited cause for bladder cancer; second- and third-degree relatives of index cases are at greater risk than are first-degree relatives.

PATHOLOGY
Normal Bladder Urothelium

The urothelium of the normal bladder is three to seven layers thick. There is a basal cell layer on which rests one or more layers of intermediate cells. The most superficial layer is composed of large, flat, umbrella cells, which contain an asymmetric unit membrane on the luminal surface. Whether this structure is a major contributor to the urothelium's barrier function is still uncertain, but it is chiefly composed of uroplakins, which are urothelium-specific proteins (Wu et al, 1990; Moll et al, 1995; Wu et al, 1993). The urothelium rests on the lamina propria basement membrane. In the lamina propria is a tunica muscularis mucosa containing scattered smooth muscle fibers (Younes et al, 1990; Engel et al, 1992).

Epithelial Hyperplasia and Metaplasia

The term *epithelial hyperplasia* is used to describe an increase in the number of cell layers without nuclear or architectural abnormalities.

Urothelial *metaplasia* refers to the bladder lining, often in focal areas, demonstrating a nontransitional epithelial appearance, usually with epidermoid (squamous metaplasia) or glandular (adenomatous metaplasia) development. Squamous metaplasia in the absence of cellular atypia or marked keratinization is a benign condition.

Von Brunn's nests are islands of benign-appearing urothelium situated in the lamina propria. Cystitis cystica is von Brunn's nests in which urothelium in the center of the nest has undergone eosinophilic liquefaction. Cystitis glandularis is similar to cystitis cystica except that the transitional cells have undergone glandular metaplasia. Cystitis glandularis may be a precursor of adenocarcinoma (Edwards et al, 1972).

Urothelial Dysplasia
Preneoplastic Proliferative Abnormalities

Atypical hyperplasia is similar to epithelial hyperplasia, except that there are also nuclear abnormalities and partial derangement of the umbrella cell layer (Koss et al, 1974). The World Health Organization (WHO) and the International Society of Urological Pathology (ISUP) developed a consensus classification of urothelial neoplasms, including flat intraepithelial lesions (Epstein et al, 1998). Two lesions, overactive atypia and atypia of unknown significance, were believed to have very little malignant potential, as confirmed by Cheng and colleagues (1999a), who reported that none of the 60 patients with these lesions experienced grade progression to dysplasia, carcinoma in situ, or urothelial carcinoma over a median 3.5-year follow-up.

Dysplasia

The term *dysplasia* denotes epithelial changes that are intermediate between normal urothelium and carcinoma in situ (severe dysplasia). Dysplastic cells have large, round, notched, basally situated nuclei that do not exhibit the normal epithelial polarity. Dysplastic epithelium does not have an increased number of cell layers or mitotic figures (Murphy and Soloway, 1982). Cheng and colleagues (1999a) reported that 4 of 26 patients (15%) with moderate dysplasia developed high-grade urothelial cancer (median follow-up, 3.5 years), 3 with muscle invasion.

Inverted Papilloma

An *inverted papilloma* is a benign proliferative lesion associated with chronic inflammation or bladder outlet obstruction.

Papillary fronds project into the fibrovascular stroma of the bladder rather than into the bladder lumen. The lesion is usually covered by a thin layer of normal urothelium (Fig. 75–1). Inverted papillomas may contain an area of cystitis cystica or squamous metaplasia.

Rare cases of malignant transformation of inverted papillomas have been reported (Lazarevic and Garret, 1978). However, there is a more common association of inverted papilloma with coexistent TCC elsewhere in the urinary tract or with histories of such tumors (Cheon et al, 1995; Asano et al, 2003). This appears to be far more likely with inverted papillomas of the upper urinary tract than of the bladder (Asano et al, 2003). Mainly, because the overlying epithelium is normal, inverted papillomas appear as small raised nodules rather than as papillary or frondlike tumors on endoscopic inspection.

Nephrogenic Adenoma

Nephrogenic adenoma is a rare lesion that histologically resembles primitive renal collecting tubules. It is a metaplastic response of urothelium to trauma, infection, or radiation therapy and is often associated with dysuria and frequency. Edema and inflammatory cell infiltration are common, but there is little nuclear atypia or mitotic activity (Navarre et al, 1982). Mesonephric adenocarcinoma is the malignant counterpart of nephrogenic adenoma (Schultz et al, 1984).

Vesical Leukoplakia

Leukoplakia is characterized by squamous metaplasia with marked keratinization, downward growth of rete pegs (acanthosis), cellular atypia, and dysplasia. It is believed to be a response of the normal urothelium to noxious stimuli and is generally considered a premalignant lesion that may progress to SCC in up to 20% of patients.

Pseudosarcoma (Postoperative Spindle Cell Nodule)

Postoperative spindle cell nodule is a rare lesion resembling a sarcoma of the bladder. It consists of reactive proliferation of spindle cells occurring several months after a lower urinary tract procedure or infection. These lesions have been misinterpreted as being malignant, and radical surgery has been performed inappropriately. Usually, they are confused with leiomyosarcomas (Huang et al, 1990; Vekemans et al, 1990).

UROTHELIAL CARCINOMA
Carcinoma in Situ

Carcinoma in situ may appear as a velvety patch of erythematous mucosa, although quite often it is endoscopically invisible. Histologically, it consists of poorly differentiated TCC confined to the urothelium (Fig. 75–2). Carcinoma in situ may be asymptomatic or may produce severe symptoms of urinary frequency, urgency, and dysuria (Utz et al, 1970; Utz and Farrow, 1984). **Urine cytopathology is positive in 80% to 90% of patients with carcinoma in situ.**

Carcinoma in situ is present in 25% or more of patients with high-grade superficial tumors (Koss et al, 1974), and between 40% and 83% progress to muscle-invasive cancer (Althausen et al, 1976). Carcinoma in situ occurs in 20% to 75% of high-grade muscle-invasive cancers. Patients with marked urinary symptoms generally have a shorter interval preceding the development of muscle-invasive cancer. About 20% of patients treated with cystectomy for diffuse carcinoma in situ are found to have microscopic muscle-invading cancer (Farrow et al, 1976).

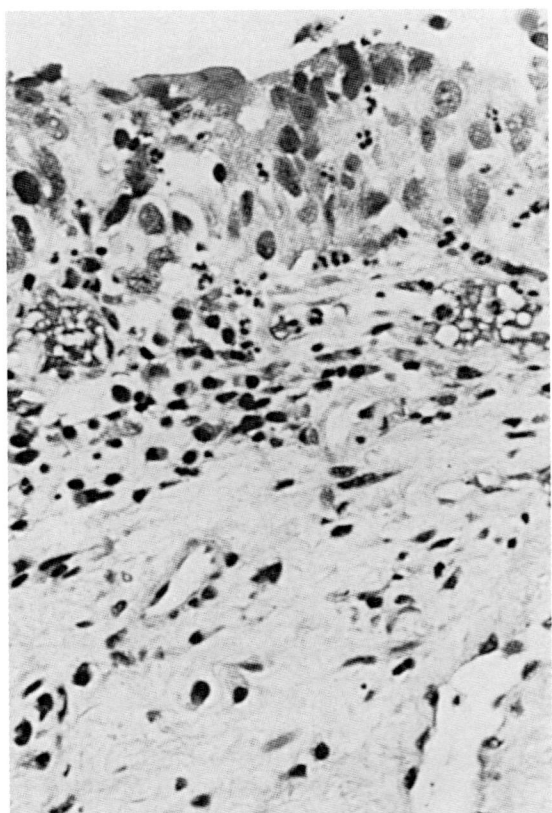

Figure 75–2. Carcinoma in situ. (Courtesy of Dr. Louis P. Dehner.)

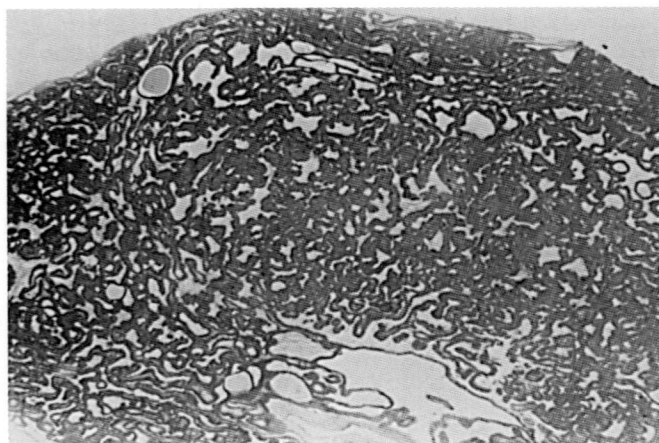

Figure 75–1. Inverted papilloma. (From Mostofi FK, Sobin LH, Torloni H: Histological Typing of Urinary Bladder Tumors, no. 10. International Histological Classification of Tumors. Geneva, World Health Organization, 1973.)

A variety of investigative approaches have confirmed carcinoma in situ's direct relationship to muscle-invading cancer. Cytogenetic (loss of chromosome 17p) (Olumni et al, 1990; Tsai et al, 1990; Knowles et al, 1994), molecular genetic (Sarkis et al, 1993), and immunohistologic (Sarkis et al, 1993, 1994; Esrig et al, 1994) studies have shown that high proportions of both carcinoma in situ and deeply invasive bladder cancer have deletions and/or mutations of the *TP53* gene and alterations of its protein product. This not only supports the contention that carcinoma in situ is a precursor lesion of invasive bladder cancer but also, to a large degree, eliminates it as a precursor of low-grade papillary tumors in which TP53 abnormalities are rarely found (except in extremely young patients) (Habuchi et al, 1992; Spruck et al, 1994; Linn et al, 1998).

Transitional Cell (Urothelial) Carcinoma

Tumor Architecture

More than 90% of bladder cancers are TCCs (Figs. 75–3 to 75–6; see also Fig. 75–2). At a consensus conference, the pathologists of the WHO and the ISUP preferred to term these *urothelial cancers* (Epstein et al, 1998); such a name may be confusing for nonpathologists because cancers of other histologic types, such as squamous cancers and adenocarcinomas, also arise in the urothelium. Regardless of name, urothelial (transitional cell) cancers differ from normal urothelium by having an increased number of epithelial cell layers with papillary foldings of the mucosa, loss of cell polarity, abnormal cell maturation from basal to superficial layers, increased nuclear-cytoplasmic ratio, prominent nucleoli, clumping of chromatin, and increased number of mitoses (Koss, 1975).

Urothelial carcinomas demonstrate a variety of patterns of tumor growth, including papillary, sessile, infiltrating, nodular, mixed, and flat intraepithelial growth (carcinoma in situ). **Cancer invasion between and through the smooth muscle cells of the tunica muscularis mucosa (within the lamina propria) can be mistaken for invasion of the bladder detrusor muscle** (Younes et al, 1990; Engel et al, 1992), a particular problem in specimens obtained by endoscopic biopsy or transurethral curettage.

Urothelium has great metaplastic potential; therefore, urothelial carcinomas may contain spindle cell (Young et al, 1988), squamous, or adenocarcinomatous elements. These elements are present in about one third of muscle-invasive urothelial bladder cancers, and several may be exhibited in a single cancer. Approximately 70% of bladder tumors are papillary, 10% are nodular, and 20% are mixed.

Tumor Grading

No uniformly accepted grading system for bladder cancer exists. Most commonly used systems are based on the degree of anaplasia of the tumor cells (Broders, 1922; Bergkvist et al, 1965; Mostofi et al, 1973; Koss, 1975). In a consensus conference, the WHO and the ISUP decided to classify many of these tumors as *papillary urothelial neoplasms* (Epstein et al, 1998).

A strong correlation exists between tumor grade and stage (Jewett and Strong, 1946), with most well-differentiated and moderately differentiated tumors being superficial and most poorly differentiated ones being muscle invasive. Stage for stage, there is a significant correlation between tumor grade and prognosis; however, the correlation between tumor stage and prognosis is even stronger. As several authors (Knowles et al, 1994; Spruck et al, 1994; Reznikoff et al, 1996; Cote and Chatterjee, 1999) have proposed, **there are now molecular and cytogenetic data to support the well-established clinical impression that low-grade (all well-differentiated and most moderately differentiated) tumors and high-grade (poorly**

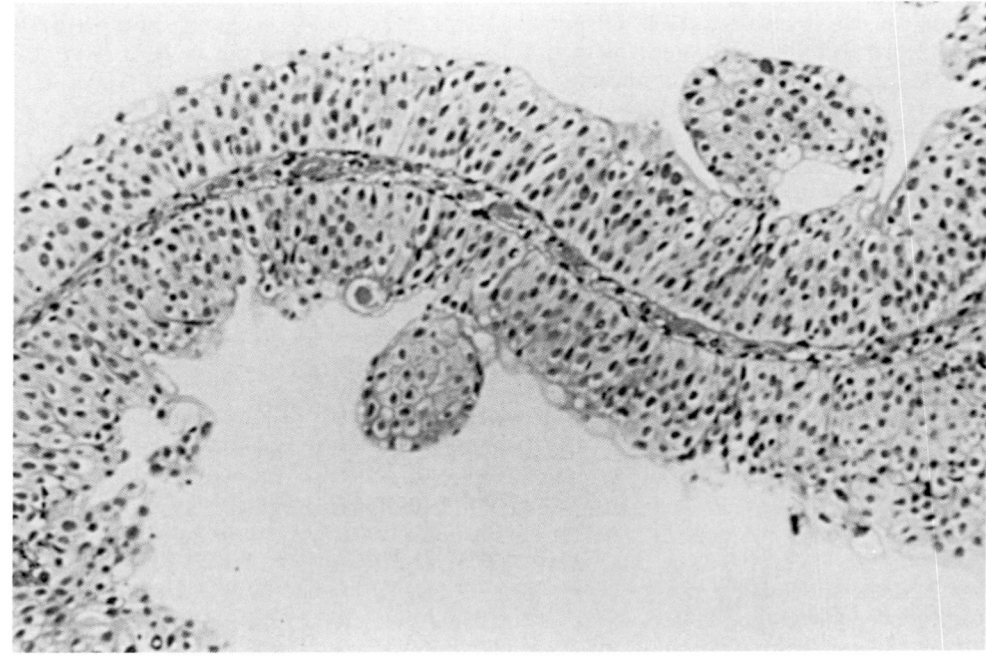

Figure 75–3. Transitional cell papilloma. (From Mostofi FK, Sobin LH, Torloni H: Histological Typing of Urinary Bladder Tumors, no. 10. International Histological Classification of Tumors. Geneva, World Health Organization, 1973.)

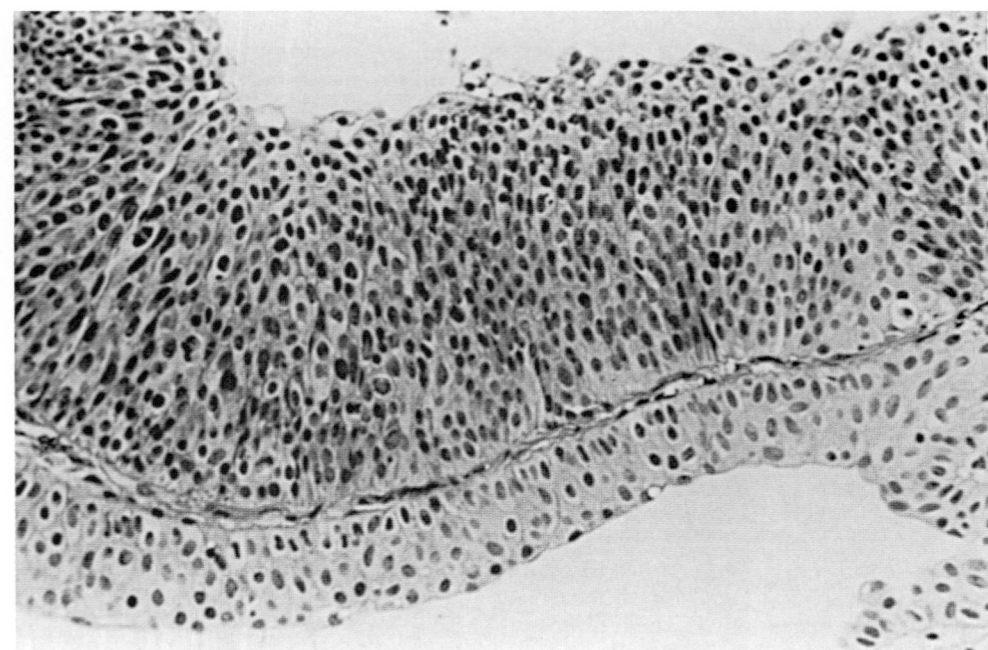

Figure 75–4. Well-differentiated transitional cell carcinoma. This lesion is now called *papillary urothelial tumor of low malignant potential*. (From Mostofi FK, Sobin LH, Torloni H: Histological Typing of Urinary Bladder Tumors, no. 10. International Histological Classification of Tumors. Geneva, World Health Organization, 1973.)

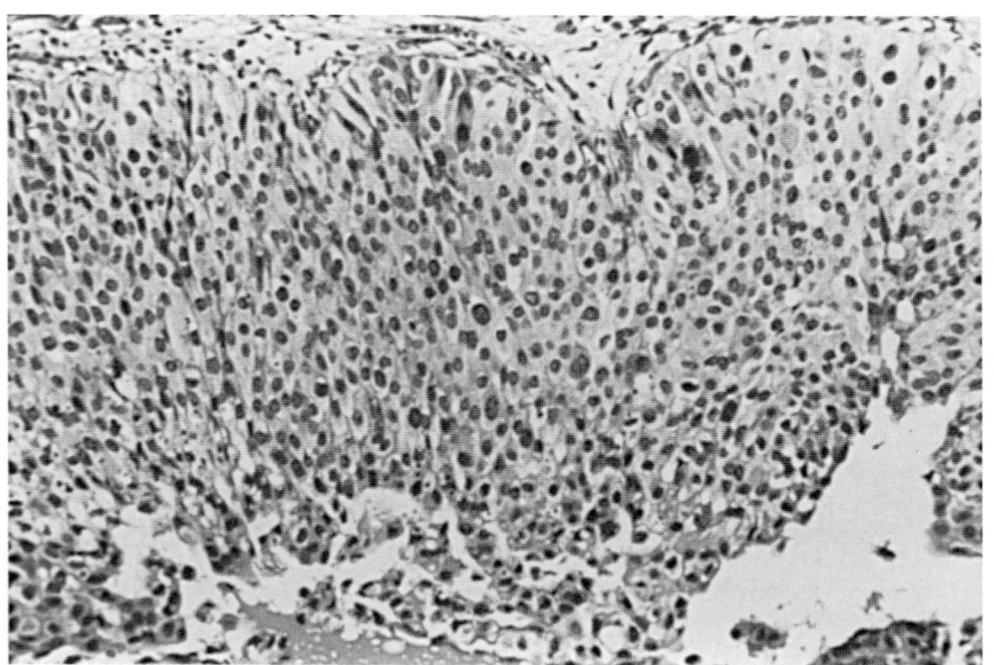

Figure 75–5. Moderately differentiated transitional cell carcinoma. This lesion is now called *low-grade urothelial cancer*. (From Mostofi FK, Sobin LH, Torloni H: Histological Typing of Urinary Bladder Tumors, no. 10. International Histological Classification of Tumors. Geneva, World Health Organization, 1973.)

differentiated) **tumors have fundamentally different origins, with the former losing one or more suppressor genes on chromosome 9q and the latter having TP53, RB, and/or P16 abnormalities as early events.**

A papilloma (grade 0) is a papillary lesion with a fine fibrovascular core covered by normal bladder mucosa (Friedell et al, 1976; Cheng et al, 1999c) (see Fig. 75–3). It does not have more than seven epithelial cell layers nor any abnormalities in histology. This is an extremely rare tumor that, unlike TCCs, almost never recurs after endoscopic resection,

so that if it occurs alone, it may legitimately be considered to be a benign neoplasm (Cheng et al, 1999c). However, it must be remembered that a histologic papilloma is often found in the same bladder as higher-grade urothelial cancer, clouding the certainty of its benignity. Molecular analyses of these lesions have not been reported.

Well-differentiated tumors (see Fig. 75–4) have a thin fibrovascular stalk with a thickened urothelium containing more than seven cell layers, with cells exhibiting only slight anaplasia and pleomorphism. The disturbance of the base-to-

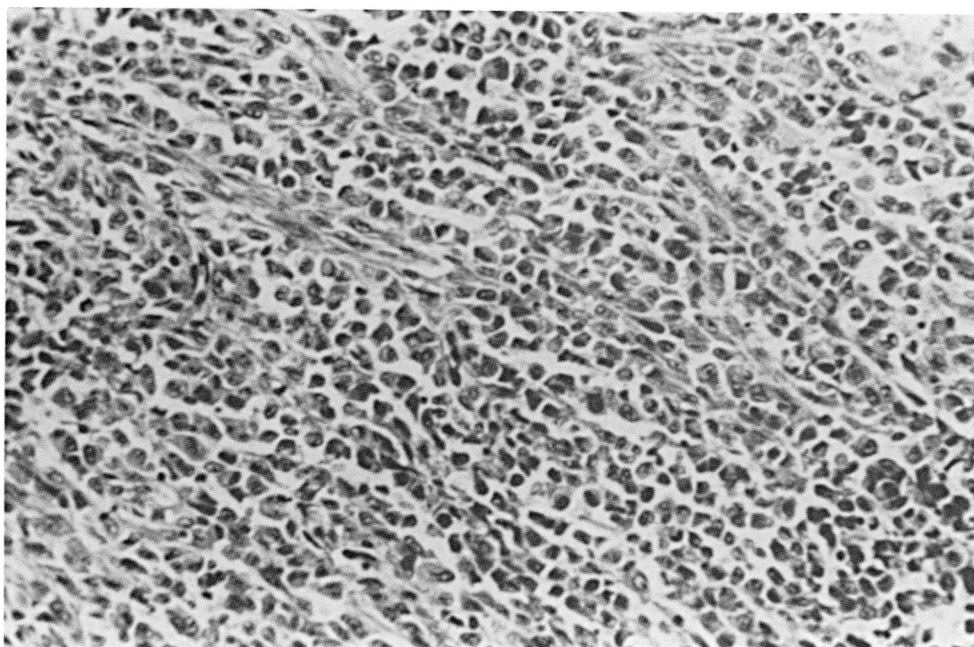

Figure 75–6. Undifferentiated transitional cell carcinoma. This lesion is now called *high-grade urothelial cancer.* (From Mostofi FK, Sobin LH, Torloni H: Histological Typing of Urinary Bladder Tumors, no. 10. International Histological Classification of Tumors. Geneva, World Health Organization, 1973.)

surface cellular maturation is mild, and there are only rare mitotic figures. When they are mucosally confined, these have been termed ***papillary urothelial tumors of low malignant potential*** by the WHO and the ISUP (Epstein et al, 1998). However, even when detected alone, they often recur, and recurrences may be of higher histologic grade and stage (Cheng et al, 1999c). Lesions with this appearance (similar to those formerly called grade 1) are urothelial cancers. They are found in the same bladders (and frequently in the same individual tumors) as higher-grade cancers (Cheng et al, 2000a), and share similar molecular (Cote and Chatterjee, 1999) and prognostic features with low-grade cancers (Cheng et al, 1999c; Cheng and Bostwick, 2000; Oyasu, 2000).

Moderately differentiated (low grade—old grade 2) tumors (see Fig. 75–5) have a wider fibrovascular core, a greater disturbance of the base-to-surface cellular maturation, and a loss of cell polarity. The nuclear-cytoplasmic ratio is higher, with more nuclear pleomorphism and prominent nucleoli. Mitotic figures are more frequent. These have been termed ***low-grade urothelial carcinomas*** in the new WHO and ISUP classification (Epstein et al, 1998). Murphy and colleagues (2002) point out the difficulties for even experienced practitioners to distinguish between low malignant potential and low-grade carcinoma lesions as defined in the current classification.

Poorly differentiated tumors (see Fig. 75–6), named ***high-grade urothelial carcinoma*** in the new WHO and ISUP system (Epstein et al, 1998) (old grade 3), have cells that do not differentiate as they progress from the basement membrane to the surface. Marked nuclear pleomorphism is noted, with a high nuclear-cytoplasmic ratio. Mitotic figures may be frequent (Friedell et al, 1980). The changes made in the new classification may allow grouping together of a larger number of patients who are at high risk for progression.

Metaplastic Elements

It is not unusual for different tumor types to coexist in the same bladder; however, all epithelial tumors are believed to have a common ancestry in the transitional epithelium. **The presence of these metaplastic elements (e.g., SCC and adenocarcinoma) in a lesion that is primarily a urothelial carcinoma does not change the principal classification of the tumor as a urothelial carcinoma.**

Squamous Cell Carcinoma
Etiology

Considerable variability is noted in the prevalence of SCC of the bladder in different parts of the world. It accounts for only 1% of bladder cancers in England (Costello et al, 1984), 3% to 7% in the United States (Koss, 1975; Lynch and Cohen, 1995), but as many as 75% in Egypt (El-Bolkainy et al, 1981). About 80% of SCCs in Egypt are associated with chronic infection with *S. haematobium.* **These cancers occur in patients who are, on the average, 10 to 20 years younger than patients with TCC. Bilharzial cancers are exophytic, nodular, fungating lesions that are usually well differentiated and have a relatively low incidence of lymph node and distant metastases. Whether the low incidence of distant metastases is due to capillary and lymphatic fibrosis resulting from chronic schistosomal infection** (Ghoneim and Awad, 1980) or to the relatively low histologic grade (El-Bolkainy et al, 1981) of these tumors is not clear.

Nonbilharzial SCCs are usually caused by chronic irritation from urinary calculi, long-term indwelling catheters, chronic urinary infections, or bladder diverticula. As many as 80% of paraplegics with chronic infections and/or indwelling catheters have squamous changes in the bladder, and about 5% develop SCC (Bahnson, 1997). Cigarette smoking has also been reported to be significantly associated with an increased risk of bladder SCC (Kantor et al, 1988). Male predominance is far less striking in SCC (1.3 : 1 to 1.7 : 1) (Lynch and Cohen, 1995). In general, its prognosis is poor because most patients have advanced disease at the time of diagnosis.

Histology

SCC consists, characteristically, of keratinized islands that contain eccentric aggregates of cells called squamous pearls. They may show varying degrees of histologic differentiation (Koss, 1975) (Fig. 75-7). Cytology has been of limited utility in the diagnosis of this tumor. In a small series of patients with SCC, urinary excretion of psoriasin, produced by the tumor, was found in all cases (Ostergaard et al, 1997). However, because this protein is also excreted in squamous metaplasia, it is unlikely that this test is specific enough to be used in the diagnosis or screening of SCC or in the monitoring of patients who have not undergone cystectomy.

Histologic differentiation more loosely correlates with prognosis, stage for stage, than it does with urothelial carcinomas, but grade and node status still predict subsequent metastases (Zaghloul, 1996). Particularly with bilharzial SCCs, bone is the most common site of distant metastases (Zaghloul, 1996). **As with aggressive urothelial cancer, SCCs often have P16 and TP53 abnormalities** (Cote and Chatterjee, 1999), although the mechanisms of gene silencing often differ between the two tumor types (Tsutsumi et al, 1998). Several reports suggest that, stage for stage, the prognosis of SCC is comparable to that of TCC (Johnson et al, 1976; Richie et al, 1976).

Adenocarcinoma

Adenocarcinomas account for less than 2% of primary bladder cancers (Kantor et al, 1988; Lynch and Cohen, 1995). They are classified into three groups: (1) primary vesical; (2) urachal; and (3) metastatic (Manunta et al, 2005). Adenocarcinomas also occur in intestinal urinary conduits, augmentations, pouches, and ureterosigmoidostomies (Husmann and Spence, 1990; Spencer and Filmer, 1991). They are discussed elsewhere in this book.

Primary Vesical Adenocarcinoma

Adenocarcinomas usually arise in the bladder base area or in the dome, but they can occur anywhere. It is the most common type of cancer in exstrophic bladders. These tumors develop in response to chronic inflammation and irritation (Nielsen and Nielsen, 1983; Bennett et al, 1984).

All histologic variants of enteric adenocarcinoma occur in the bladder. Most are mucin producing (Koss, 1975). Signet-ring carcinomas characteristically produce linitis plastica of the bladder (Choi et al, 1984; Sheldon et al, 1984; Blute et al, 1989a). Most adenocarcinomas are poorly differentiated and invasive. They are more commonly associated with cystitis glandularis than with carcinoma in situ.

The generally poor prognosis associated with adenocarcinomas is due primarily to their advanced stage at diagnosis. There is no evidence to indicate that, stage for stage, their prognosis is markedly different from that of urothelial carcinoma.

Urachal Carcinoma

Urachal carcinomas are extremely rare tumors that arise outside the bladder, and they are usually adenocarcinomas,

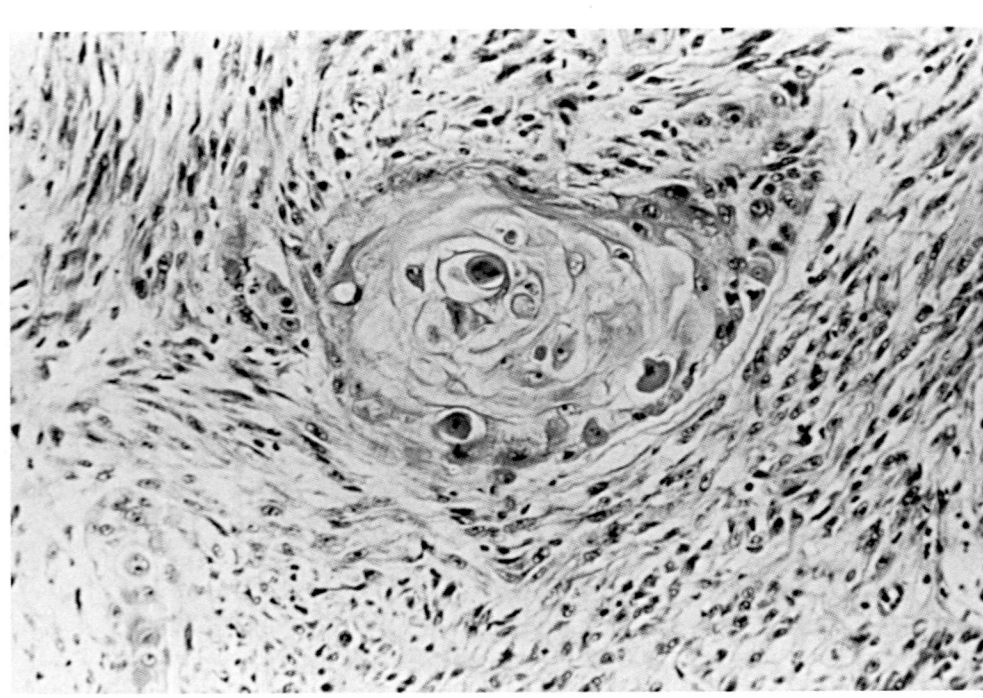

Figure 75-7. Squamous cell carcinoma. (From Mostofi FK, Sobin LH, Torloni H: Histological Typing of Urinary Bladder Tumors, no. 10. International Histological Classification of Tumors. Geneva, World Health Organization, 1973.)

although they may be primary TCCs or SCCs and, rarely, even sarcomas. Urachal carcinomas have a sharp demarcation between the tumor and the adjacent bladder epithelium, with the tumor being located in the bladder wall beneath the normal epithelium (Mostofi, 1954). They may appear with a bloody or mucoid discharge from the umbilicus or produce a mucocele, occurring as a palpable mass. Many urachal tumors have stippled calcifications on radiographs (Brick et al, 1988; Narumi et al, 1988). Tumors invading the bladder lumen may produce mucus in the urine.

Patients with urachal carcinomas have a worse prognosis than do those with primary bladder adenocarcinomas (Mostofi, 1954). **Histologically, these tumors exhibit wider and deeper infiltration of the bladder wall than expected, compromising the results of partial cystectomy** (Kakizoe et al, 1983; Sheldon et al, 1984). Urachal carcinomas metastasize to iliac and inguinal lymph nodes, omentum, liver, lung, and bone (Sheldon et al, 1984).

Metastatic Adenocarcinoma

One of the most common forms of adenocarcinoma of the bladder is metastatic (or invasive) adenocarcinoma (Choi et al, 1984). The primary sites for these tumors include the rectum, stomach, endometrium, breast, prostate, and ovary (Klinger, 1951).

KEY POINTS: PATHOLOGY

- Over 90% of bladder cancers in the United States are urothelial (transitional cell) cancers. Most are papillary well (urothelial tumor of low malignant potential) or moderately (low grade) differentiated cancers.

- Most high-grade (undifferentiated) urothelial cancers are deeply invasive at diagnosis.

- The two most common nonurothelial epithelial malignancies of the bladder are squamous cell cancers and adenocarcinoma. Both are usually diagnosed at advanced stages and have prognoses that are similar to high-grade invasive urothelial cancers.

ORIGIN AND PATTERNS OF DISSEMINATION OF UROTHELIAL CARCINOMA

Multicentric Origin

Traditionally, urothelial carcinoma has been considered a field change disease, with tumors arising at different times and sites in the urothelium (polychronotopicity). This suggests a polyclonal etiology of bladder cancer—particularly because recurrences often arise many years after the original tumors (Prout et al, 1992; Thompson et al, 1993; Holmang et al, 1995; Cheng and Bostwick, 2000; Oyasu, 2000). The phenomenon of late recurrences would be at odds with the competing theory, that recurrences represent clonal seedings of the original tumor, particularly in view of the known rapid growth of even low-grade papillary TCCs (Messing et al, 1995c) and their virtual absence as an incidental finding at autopsy (discussed previously). Similarly, immunohistochemical and immunocytochemical studies have confirmed that normal-appearing urothelium (histologically and cystoscopically) remote from tumors shares with those tumors altered expression of "tumor markers" such as G-actin, the receptor for EGF, and other tumor-associated antigens (Messing, 1990; Rao et al, 1993; Lee et al, 1997; Hemstreet et al, 1999).

Alternatively, molecular evidence using loss of heterozygosity or gene-sequencing analyses indicates, at least at times, a clonal etiology of multiple simultaneous (Sidransky et al, 1992; Takahashi et al, 1998; Hartmann et al, 2002) or sequential tumors in the upper tracts, bladder, and/or extraurinary sites (Harris and Neal, 1992; Lunec et al, 1992; Habuchi et al, 1993; Hruban et al, 1994; VanderPoel et al, 1998; Hoque et al, 2003). However, these molecular "fingerprinting" studies have focused primarily on high-grade invasive urothelial cancers, which provide the greatest amounts of tissue and in which *TP53* (for which the DNA sequence is well known) is often mutated. Indeed, similar fingerprinting analyses have rarely been performed on much more common types of bladder cancer. **Furthermore, even in the select group in which molecular analyses have been performed, examples of both uniclonal and multiclonal origins have been reported** (Jones, 1994; Takahashi et al, 1998; 2000; Hartmann et al, 2002). Whether the use of highly specific microsatellite mutational analyses, DNA methylation patterns, and/or "gene chip" methodologies will clarify these issues is uncertain (Habuchi et al, 2000; Muto et al, 2000; Salem et al, 2000; Takahashi et al, 2000; Hoque et al, 2003; Vettman et al, 2003). Certainly, in some cases, multiple tumors are derived from a single cell clone that has disseminated to other sites in the urinary tract. However, both epigenetic (Messing, 1990; Rao et al, 1993; Lee et al, 1997; Hemstreet et al, 1999) and genetic (Muto et al, 2000; Pan et al, 2000) changes characteristic of TCC occur throughout the urothelium of patients with bladder cancer(s) in locations remote from actual tumors. These findings are not consistent with implantation and migration mechanisms that would predict a higher density of such alterations adjacent to the tumor. Further clouding this issue is that a substantial percentage of stage T1 tumors are inadvertently incompletely resected (Klan et al, 1991), leading to the possibility that incomplete treatment, rather than spontaneous or iatrogenic implantation or transepithelial spread, is responsible for purported cases of clonal tumor recurrence. Several recent developments have shed further light on this question, if only to indicate how complex the biology of urothelial cancer's development and its propensity for recurrence is. First, the unquestionable success of a single intravesical instillation of chemotherapy immediately after transurethral resection (TUR) in preventing tumor recurrences (Oosterlinck et al, 1993; Solsona et al, 1999) would seem to indicate that clonal implantation is a major mechanism of recurrence. However, in many series, well fewer than 50% of recurrences are "prevented," implying that if the chemotherapy was very effective against implantation, many recurrences are due to field effect mechanisms. One of course could argue that existing lesions that were too small to see cystoscopically were also killed by the one-time exposure to chemotherapy, but this is at odds with other studies that indicate the superiority of multiple long-term courses of intravesical instillations of chemotherapy compared with shorter-term instillations initiated 1 to 2 weeks after TUR (at a time when implanted tumors should be somewhat established) in preventing recurrences (Bouffioux et al, 1995) or the superiority of single-dose immediate postresection instillations in preventing recurrences of solitary tumors compared with multiple ones (Rajala et al, 1999). Additionally, the success of fluorescent cystoscopy in identifying additional cancers (and the true size of visible ones) and reducing recurrence rates (by enabling destruction of these tumors) also indicates that multiple tumors exist at the time that one or a few are seen (Zaak et al, 2002; Filbeck et al, 2002; Schmidbauer et al, 2004), although it does not clarify whether the tumors are clonally derived.

Further complicating our understanding is the finding of Cheng and colleagues (2003), who used microdissection and X chromosome inactivation (which is determined early in utero in females) to study clonality in muscle-invading tumors (for which there is the strongest evidence for clonality). They found that many solitary-appearing bladder cancer lesions *must* be multiclonal. Finally, Borhan and coworkers (2003) found that roughly 50% of newly diagnosed, solitary high-grade superficial bladder cancers treated by endoscopic resection alone which recurred did so as lower-grade lesions and that nuclear overexpression of TP53, which was seen with most of the high-grade index lesions (and which correlates closely with molecular evidence of *TP53* mutation/deletion—see earlier), was lost in the low-grade recurrences. The return to normal TP53 status, given the selective advantage that a cancer cell with a mutated and nonfunctional *TP53* has, implies either that the low-grade recurrences were clonally distinct from the high-grade TP53 abnormal index tumors or that both the high-grade and low-grade tumors came from a common TP53 normal progenitor clone that subsequently diverged into a TP53 abnormal clone (the resected index tumor) and a retained normal TP53 daughter clone (the recurrence). However, because the recurrences often occurred many months or years after the index tumor was resected, this explanation is not consistent with data presented earlier concerning the very rapid growth rates of even well-differentiated urothelial cancers. Others have also reported finding grade regression in recurrences. **Suffice it to say that currently the clonal versus field change etiology of recurrences remains unsettled and it is likely that both mechanisms (and possibly others) take place. This is discussed in an excellent review of the topic by Duggan and colleagues (2004).**

Patterns of Spread

Direct Extension: Basic Biology

The process of tumor invasion, in which malignant transitional epithelial cells extend beneath the basal lamina into the connective tissue of the lamina propria and, subsequently, into muscularis propria and perivesical fat, represents the culmination of a variety of biologic processes, **including stimulation of neovascularization (angiogenesis), proteolysis resulting from elaboration of collagenases, increased cellular motility, proliferation, and escape from local surveillance mechanisms—primarily the immune system.** Additionally, because cellular adhesion molecules and other components of the extracellular matrix bind urothelial cells both to each other and to the underlying basal lamina, such connections have to be altered to permit some semblance of cellular disaggregation and local motility.

Angiogenic factors are excreted in the urine of bladder cancer patients (Chodak et al, 1988), and the substances responsible for such activity include autocrine motility factor (Guirguis et al, 1988), acidic and basic fibroblast growth factors (FGFs), and vascular endothelial growth factor (VEGF) (Chopin et al, 1993; Nguyen et al, 1993; Soutter et al, 1993; Crew et al, 1999). There is some evidence that FGFs are produced by urothelial cells (as well as other urinary sources). However, this is usually in lower concentrations than in the basal lamina of normal urothelium (O'Brien et al, 1997). It is thus likely that particularly basic FGF is released by degradation of the bladder's basement membrane and detrusor, from which it can diffuse into the tumor's microenvironment and bind to the endothelium of nearby vessels (O'Brien et al, 1997). The source of autocrine motility factor is even less certain. Endothelial cells and malignant transitional epithelial cells both appear to contain membrane-bound receptors for these substances (Chopin et al, 1993; Korman et al, 1996), thus making it likely that they are involved not only in the formation of new vessels but also, through juxtacrine/paracrine mechanisms, in the induction of motility in malignant urothelial cells. The mRNA for VEGF is upregulated in malignant compared with normal urothelium, but whereas VEGF protein levels increase further with increasing stage, there is not a corresponding increase in mRNA levels (reviewed in Crew, 1999). This suggests that post-transcriptional regulation of this cytokine may play a role in bladder cancer progression.

Malignant transitional epithelial cell lines elaborate proteases, primarily collagenase type IV, that are capable of digesting the connective tissue of the basal lamina and underlying lamina propria (Liu and Liotta, 1992). In specimens of human TCCs, expression of collagenase type IV has been associated with invasive histology (Liu and Liotta, 1992), thus providing clinical substantiation of implications drawn from experimental models.

Most of the type IV collagenases are MMPs, a family of proteases that chelate zinc and calcium (hence their name); are inhibited by tissue inhibitor of metalloproteinases (TIMP); are secreted in a proenzyme form that requires activation by other proteases (often other MMPs); and share overlapping substrate and sequence specificities (Liu, 1998). Measurements of these substances in tissue, serum, and urine have been correlated with clinical tumor behavior. For instance, Gohji and colleagues (1996) have found that a high ratio of MMP2 to TIMP2 in sera from patients with invasive urothelial cancer who have undergone complete resection predicted poor tumor-free recurrence and survival rates. Additionally, Ozdemir and associates (1999) found that tissue expression and urinary excretion of MMP9 were increased in all patients with bladder cancer and that levels reflected tumor grade and stage. Of note is that, at least in experimental systems, urothelial cancer MMP9 is upregulated both by interleukin-8, which is produced by inflammatory and neoplastic cells, and by EGF receptor signaling, and in turn MMP9 can upregulate VEGF (Inoue, et al 2000; Ocharocnrat et al, 2000).

Major intracellular adhesion molecules, such as E-cadherin and the transmembrane protein family of integrins, also appear to be important barriers against invasion that can become disrupted in invasive tumors. These molecules are necessary not only for anchoring epithelial cells to each other and to the basal lamina but also for cell-cell communication—often regulating the expression and function of membrane-bound growth factor receptors, in part through linkages to the cytoskeleton via catenins (Shimazui et al, 1996). Reduced expressions of E-cadherin and α, β, and/or γ catenins have been found in invasive tumors and have been associated with decreased survival of bladder cancer patients (Bringuier et al, 1993; Shimazui et al, 1996; Syrigos et al, 1998). Additionally, in carcinoma in situ, which requires intraepithelial spreading and motility as a prerequisite for nodular tumor development, expression of integrin $\beta4$ is reduced. This observation is in agreement with in vitro data demonstrating that lower expression of integrin $\beta4$ and replacement of the $\alpha6$-$\beta4$ complex with $\alpha6$-$\beta1$ integrin correlated well with intraepithelial spreading on laminin and that this behavior could be abrogated by transfection of cells with $\beta4$ integrin cDNA, which was then overexpressed (Harabayashi et al, 1999). Another molecule that affects adhesion and ability to bind extracellular matrix components is a member of the family of cell surface transmembrane glycoproteins, CD44. Gadella and colleagues (2004) reported finding reduced CD44 expression with increasing tumor grade and stage in urothelial cancers but not SCCs.

Another molecule that is likely to facilitate invasion of urothelial cancer cells is urokinase plasminogen activator (u-PA), which is a serum protease that cleaves plasminogen to plasmin and can be inactivated by plasminogen activator inhibitors 1 and 2. Plasmin degrades laminin, a major component of the basal lamina, and u-PA can directly degrade fibronectin in the extracellular matrix and activate type IV collagenase (reviewed in Hasui and Osada, 1997). The binding of u-PA to tumor cell surfaces by the urokinase receptor enhances plasmin generation (Ellis et al, 1992). Both in culture and in situ, human bladder cancer cells produce u-PA and u-PA receptor, and their expressions reflect urothelial cancer stage and grades (Dickinson et al, 1995; Hasui et al, 1996; Hudson and McReynolds, 1997). Furthermore, u-PA expression is an independent predictor of bladder cancer recurrence and progression (Hasui et al, 1996).

As discussed earlier, abnormal expression or function of receptors for growth factors can, of course, enhance proliferative capacity of malignant cells, a major component of the invasive process. Under normal circumstances, receptors for EGF are primarily confined to the basal layer of epithelial cells (Messing, 1990). **However, in both TCCs and SCCs, EGF receptors become expressed not only on basal cells but also on cells of all layers, including those at the luminal surface** (Messing, 1990). This abnormal distribution of the EGF receptor is also seen in dysplastic and normal-appearing urothelium, both near and remote from TCCs (Messing, 1990; Rao et al, 1993). Even tumor cells that invade deeply into the bladder wall still express the EGF receptor (Messing, 1990). Several groups have independently demonstrated that the degree of expression of the EGF receptor directly correlates with the invasive phenotype (Messing, 1990; Neal et al, 1990; Popov et al, 2004). Two independent groups with extensive follow-up have demonstrated that abnormally high expression of the EGF receptor in bladder cancer is a strong predictor of poor survival (Neal et al, 1990; Mellon et al, 1995; Popov et al, 2004).

Additionally, other ligands that work through EGF receptors, such as transforming growth factor-α (TGF-α) and heparin-binding EGF-like growth factor (HB-EGF), may also play a role in bladder tumor progression and proliferation and possibly in other processes (Cooper et al, 1992; Brown et al, 1993; Freeman et al, 1995b; Theodorescu et al, 1998). Indeed, **because ligands for the EGF receptor induce not only mitogenesis but also cellular motility, stimulation of the EGF receptor on malignant urothelial and normal endothelial cells may encourage angiogenesis and malignant cell motility, as well as proliferation—all processes important for invasion to occur.** This has been supported by the elegant transgenic mouse studies by Cheng and associates (2002) mentioned earlier.

Histopathology and Clinical Correlates

Local invasion of bladder cancer can occur by three mechanisms (Jewett and Eversole, 1960). The most common is en bloc spread, which occurs in about 60% of tumors and is characterized by cancer cells invading in a broad front directly beneath the primary mucosal lesion. Tentacle-like invasion occurs in about 25% of tumors, and lateral spread, with tumor cells growing under normal-appearing mucosa, is observed in only about 10%. Malignant urothelial cells entering the lamina propria and, much more commonly, the muscularis propria can gain access to blood vessels and lymphatics through which they may metastasize to regional lymph nodes or distant sites. **The very close correlation between muscle invasion and distant metastases was noted by Jewett and Strong in 1946 and has remained one of the hallmarks of classification, prognosis, and management of this disease.**

More than 40% of men undergoing cystectomy for muscle-invading bladder cancer have involvement of the prostate (Hardeman et al, 1988). In the majority of such cases, the prostatic urethra is the site of involvement, but 6% have stromal involvement without prostatic urethral involvement. Overall, about 40% with prostatic involvement have invasion of the stroma (Wood et al, 1989). In such patients, there is a high incidence (approximately 80%) of subsequent distant metastases despite seemingly complete local excision of all malignant tissue (e.g., cystoprostatourethrectomy). Tumors arising in bladder diverticula pose a special problem. They can invade directly from the epithelium into the perivesical tissues because bladder diverticula do not have muscular walls. Thus, wide excision or complete cystectomy, with a decision based on urothelial mapping studies, may be needed for cancers whose histologic characteristics would have permitted endoscopic management had they not arisen in a diverticulum (Faysal and Freiha, 1981; Golijanin et al, 2003).

Metastatic Spread

Roughly 5% of patients with well-differentiated or moderately differentiated superficial papillary cancer and approximately 20% with high-grade superficial disease (including carcinoma in situ) ultimately manifest vascular or lymphatic spread. These percentages do not indicate how many patients had metastases while their tumors remained superficial or that **almost all patients who develop metastases develop muscle-invasive recurrences before or at the time metastases are recognized.** Although, realistically, some patients with superficial malignancies have already developed latent metastases, the vast majority of such individuals have their bladder lesion pathologically understaged and already harbor muscle-invading lesions (Freeman et al, 1995a).

Lymphatic Spread

Lymphatic metastases occur earlier and independent of hematogenous metastases in some patients. This may be evidenced in patients with limited lymph node metastases who are apparently cured with radical cystectomy and pelvic lymphadenectomy (Lerner et al, 1993; Vieweg et al, 1999a; Fleshner et al, 2000). The **extent of the local tumor, as well as of the nodal metastases, directly affects survival after surgical excision** (Vieweg et al, 1999b). The most common sites of metastases in bladder cancer are the pelvic lymph nodes. Among these, the paravesical nodes are involved in 16%, the obturator nodes in 74%, the external iliac nodes in 65%, and the presacral nodes in roughly 25%. Juxtaregional common iliac lymph nodes are involved in about 20% of patients, but almost always with involvement of the previously mentioned regions as well (Smith and Whitmore, 1981). Autopsy studies have shown that 25% to 33% of patients dying of bladder cancer do not have pelvic lymph node metastases (Babaian et al, 1980).

Vascular Spread

The common sites of vascular metastases are liver, 38%; lung, 36%; bone, 27%; adrenal glands, 21%; and intestine, 13%. Any other organ may be involved (Babaian et al, 1980). Bone metastases are considerably more common with bilharzial bladder cancer (Zaghloul, 1996). Despite advances in treatment of systemic urothelial cancer, few patients with distant metastases survive 5 years (Loehrer et al, 1992; Jemal et al, 2005).

Implantation

Bladder cancer also spreads by implantation in abdominal wounds, denuded urothelium, resected prostatic fossa, or traumatized urethra (Weldon and Soloway, 1975). Implantation occurs most commonly with high-grade tumors. Tumor implantation into the resected prostatic fossa is an infrequent occurrence but, again, primarily occurs with high-grade and multiple tumors (Green and Yalowitz, 1972). Similarly, inadvertent bladder perforation during endoscopic resection can result in tumor seeding or metastases, but this appears to be an uncommon event (Mydlo et al, 1999). **Avoidance of iatrogenic implantation has been the impetus for use of** **immediate postresection intravesical therapy** (Oosterlinck et al, 1993; Solsona et al, 1999), development of experimental anti-adherence agents (See et al, 1992; Hyacinthe et al, 1995), and debate over the risks and benefits of performing random urothelial biopsies at the time of transurethral bladder tumor resection (Klemeney et al, 1994).

KEY POINTS: ORIGINS AND PATTERNS OF DISSEMINATION

- Evidence exists that the multifocal recurrences (polychronotopicity) that characterize urothelial cancer probably are due to multiple factors, including tumor cell implantation and spread (clonality), field change effects, and incomplete resection of the original tumor.

- A variety of molecules encourage invasive and metastatic behavior including those that stimulate angiogenesis (VEGF, bFGF), facilitate invasion (reduced expression of E-cadherin and increased expression of type IV collagenases, such as MMP9 and MMP2, and u-PA), and stimulate cell motility (the EGF receptor and its ligands EGF, TGF-α, and HB-EGF).

- In patients with positive lymph nodes, the local extent of the primary tumor (in addition to the extent of nodal metastases) strongly influences outcome after surgical resection.

- Metastases (nodal or hematogeneous) very rarely occur when there has not been a prior or concomitant muscle invading urothelial cancer.

NATURAL HISTORY

In Western countries, 55% to 60% of all newly diagnosed bladder cancers are well differentiated or moderately differentiated, superficial (confined to the urothelium or lamina propria) papillary TCCs (Messing et al, 1995b; Thorstenson et al, 2003). The majority of these patients develop tumor recurrences after endoscopic resection, 16% to 25% with higher-grade tumors (Althausen et al, 1976; Prout et al, 1992). Ten to 20 percent of patients with superficial papillary tumors subsequently develop invasive or metastatic cancer (Althausen et al, 1976; Lutzeyer et al, 1982). Important to understanding these data, however, is that late and invasive recurrences are not unheard of after a prolonged tumor-free remission (e.g., more than 5 years), even in those whose index tumors were well differentiated and superficial (Thompson et al, 1993; Holmang et al, 1995; Cheng et al, 1999c).

Forty to 45 percent of newly diagnosed bladder cancers are high-grade lesions, more than half of which are muscle invading or more extensive at the time of diagnosis (Messing et al, 1995b; Thorstenson et al, 2003). As discussed earlier, patients with high-grade superficial tumors have high likelihoods of recurrence and far higher chances of developing invasive and metastatic disease than do those with low-grade superficial tumors (Cookson and Sarosdy, 1992; Norming et al, 1992a; Freeman et al, 1995a; Messing et al, 1995b). Not withstanding the evidence presented earlier about solitary bladder cancer lesions being composed of multiple clones (Cheng et al, 2003) and the recurrences of high-grade cancers being clonally distinct (Borhan et al, 2003), **the preponderance of clinical evidence still would dictate that TCC has two major variants, low grade and high grade, which can be determined by routine cystoscopic examination (Herr et al, 2002b), TUR, and histopathologic analysis.**

Although the use of molecular probes to further assess prognosis remains under continued vigorous study, realistically only a few provide independent prognostic information over routine cystoscopic and pathologic evaluation. However, such "markers" may also give insight into the biologic processes underlying the dimorphic nature of TCC. Although the functions of the major deleted genes on chromosome 9q are unknown, because isolated chromosome 9q abnormalities have mostly been associated with papillary and superficial tumors (Tsai et al, 1990; Spruck et al, 1994; Wheeless et al, 1994; Simoneau et al, 1999; Takahashi et al, 1998; Cote and Chatterjee, 1999), it is unlikely that their deletion results in loss of control over processes regulating genetic stability, tumor motility, invasion, or metastases. However, processes controlling proliferation or angiogenesis (both of which are required for any tumor growth) could well be involved. Abnormalities in TP53 functioning, on the other hand, not only permit the cell cycle to continue but also prevent cells with abnormal DNA from having the DNA repaired or going into an apoptotic pathway, and hence foster progressive genomic instability (Harris and Hollstein, 1993); therefore, they are more commonly associated with high-grade lesions. These are more likely to continue to undergo further genetic and epigenetic alterations, promoting the processes of invasion and metastasis (discussed earlier) (Esrig et al, 1994; Spruck et al, 1994). **However, some patients with low-grade tumors eventually develop higher-grade recurrences** (Prout et al, 1992; Thompson et al, 1993; Cheng et al, 1999c), completely resected high-grade cancers frequently recur as low-grade ones (Borhan et al, 2003), and it is not uncommon to have low-grade and high-grade lesions simultaneously in the same patient's bladder. Such exceptions to the normally biphasic profile of urothelial carcinoma are not inconsistent with epidemiologic and molecular data indicating that there are similarities (and presumably common points of origin) between low-grade and high-grade disease (Messing, 1990; Sheinfeld et al, 1990; Tsai et al, 1990; Hayes et al, 1993; Rao et al, 1993; Golijanin et al, 1995; Borhan et al, 2003). That even TP53 abnormalities may not in themselves invariably be determinant of phenotype is demonstrated by the finding that in patients younger than 30 years, whose urothelial cancers are almost always low-grade noninvasive papillary ones and who generally have an excellent prognosis, nuclear accumulation of TP53 and chromosome 17p deletions are quite common (Linn et al, 1998). This would imply that an accumulation of genetic and/or epigenetic events that may be part of normal aging and/or prolonged carcinogen exposure, which have not been characterized yet, are necessary along with already defined

molecular alterations to permit the malignant urothelial phenotype to be fully expressed.

Almost 25% of patients with newly diagnosed bladder cancer have muscle-invasive disease, the vast majority being tumors of high histologic grade (Messing et al, 1995b; Thorstenson et al, 2003). **Most patients with muscle-invasive bladder cancer already have this level of invasion at the time of initial diagnosis** (Vaidya et al, 2001; Messing, 2001; Kaye and Lange, 1982; Hopkins et al, 1983). Almost 50% of patients with muscle-invasive bladder cancer already have occult distant metastases. This limits the efficacy of local or regional forms of therapy for invasive tumors. Most patients with occult metastases develop overt clinical evidence of distant metastases within 1 year (Babaian et al, 1980).

PROGNOSTIC INDICATORS

Clinical and laboratory tests have been examined as potential means of predicting the course of bladder cancer in individual patients. For these tests to be of prognostic value, they must add some predictive capacity beyond what standard clinical and pathologic parameters offer. This usually requires a multivariate analysis to determine each marker's prognostic independence, which in turn requires sufficient numbers of samples in the relevant staging and grading categories to permit appropriate statistical analyses.

Clinical and Pathologic Parameters in Superficial Bladder Cancer

The most useful prognostic parameters for tumor recurrence and subsequent cancer progression in the patient with superficial tumors are tumor grade, depth of tumor penetration (stage), lymphatic invasion, tumor size, urothelial dysplasia or carcinoma in situ in neighboring or distant urothelial areas, papillary or solid tumor architecture, multifocality, and frequency of prior tumor recurrences (Heney et al, 1983; Wolf and Hojgaard, 1983; Madgar et al, 1988). **The most important of these are grade, stage, and presence of carcinoma in situ** (Holmang et al, 1997; Millan-Rodriquez et al, 2000). In patients with lamina propria–invading, high-grade urothelial carcinomas, at least one third exhibit stage progression to muscle invasion (Jakse et al, 1987; Holmang et al, 1997), even with complete endoscopic resection and intravesical therapy with bacille Calmette-Guérin (BCG) (Cookson and Sarosdy, 1992; Waples and Messing, 1992).

Laboratory Parameters

Various laboratory parameters have also been evaluated for prognostic significance. Although significant correlations with tumor progression have been demonstrated, these tests have not yet been adopted into standard practice and do not influence treatment decisions in individual patients. However, in research settings the true prognostic values of the more established ones (e.g., TP53 nuclear accumulation) are being assessed in prospective randomized studies (reviewed by Grossman and Dinney, 2000).

Lewis Blood Group and Other Tumor Associated Antigens

Malignant urothelial transformation appears to be associated with enhanced expression of the Lewis[x] blood group antigen. This is a potentially useful diagnostic test (discussed later), although because it is abnormally expressed regardless of tumor grade or stage its prognostic utility is limited (Sheinfeld et al, 1990; Golijanin et al, 1995).

A variety of TCC-associated antigens detectable with monoclonal antibodies have shown promise as diagnostic or prognostic markers. Among these antigens, M344 is detectable in roughly 70% of superficial bladder tumors, is rarely found in invasive lesions (Fradet and Cordon-Cardo, 1993), and is detectable in exfoliated cells (Bonner et al, 1993). A second tumor-associated antigen, T138, also is expressed in exfoliated malignant cells but is associated with decreased survival (Fradet et al, 1990). Another antigen detected by a monoclonal antibody, 19A211, when seen on superficial tumors (it is also found on 25% of normal umbrella cells) predicts a lower likelihood of tumor recurrence, whereas expression of T138 predicts a significantly higher likelihood (Allard et al, 1995). Another antigen, epithelial membrane antigen (EMA), has more homogeneous staining in bladder tumors associated with poor survival and more heterogeneous expression in those associated with improved survival (Lopez-Altran et al, 1993). Hyaluronidase activity was elevated (10 mU/mg or more) in urine from 49 patients with grade 2 and 3 urothelial cancers but in only 9% and 12% of urine samples from patients with grade 1 tumors and controls, respectively (Pham et al, 1997). Hyaluronidase activity and hyaluronic acid excretion are being combined as a diagnostic test (discussed later).

Extracellular Matrix and Cell Adhesion Molecules

Fibronectin is a component of the bladder's extracellular matrix that appears primarily in the basement membrane and submucosa and is absent from the luminal surface of urothelial cells (Pode et al, 1986). Soluble fibronectin can inhibit BCG's adherence to the vesical wall, which is necessary for it to achieve its antitumor activity. Malmstrom and colleagues (1993) measured urinary fibronectin excretion and found little changed in superficial and superficially invading tumors but much higher levels for deeply invading malignancies. In the last group, 2 to 4 weeks after seemingly complete tumor resection, urinary fibronectin excretion decreased sixfold, down to normal levels. Patients receiving BCG therapy who had lower urinary fibronectin levels before the initiation of treatment (but after TUR) had a much higher likelihood of being tumor free at 1 year than did those with elevated fibronectin excretion. However, this may simply reflect persistence of tumor rather than known mechanisms of BCG action.

Another extracellular matrix component that is present in the basement membrane of the urothelium is laminin, a 950- to 1000-Da glycoprotein thought to be synthesized by the epithelial or endothelial cells resting on the basement membrane (Foydart et al, 1980). Focal interruption of basal membrane laminin correlated with tumor recurrence after endoscopic resection and with a shorter recurrence-free interval. Subsequent development of metastases correlated with disruption of subendothelial laminin in bladder vessels within the lamina propria.

As mentioned earlier, altered expression of two other extracellular adhesion molecules, E-cadherin (Bringuier et al, 1993; Shimazui et al, 1996; Syrigos et al, 1998) and integrin $\alpha6$-$\beta4$ (Liebert et al, 1994; Harabayashi et al, 1999); the cytoskeletal molecules α, β, and γ catenin (Shimazui et al, 1996; Syrigos et al, 1998); MMP9 and MMP2—particularly in association with reduced TIMP levels (Gohji et al, 1996; Liu, 1998; Ozdemir et al, 1999; Inoue et al, 2000); and the u-PA/u-PA receptor (Dickinson et al, 1995; Hasui et al, 1996) have also been associated with an invasive bladder cancer phenotype.

Growth Factors and Their Receptors

As discussed earlier, several groups have demonstrated that abnormal expression of the receptor for EGF on malignant urothelium correlates with increased tumor aggressiveness (Messing, 1990; Neal et al, 1990; Mellon et al, 1995; Popov et al, 2004) and is a predictor of poor survival from disease (Mellon et al, 1995; Popov et al, 2004). Quantification of EGF receptor expression, however, has not been standardized, and until it is this test cannot yet enter routine clinical practice because the cumbersome methods reported for research studies (Messing, 1990) are not easily adaptable to standard clinical settings. However, with the availability of several EGF receptor tyrosine kinase inhibitors, Popov and colleagues (2004) have suggested that despite these limitations staining for it may be justified to select patients for targeted therapeutic approaches. Enthusiasm for this approach, however, must be tempered with the understanding that specific EGF receptor polymorphisms and mutations, which can rarely be detected through immunohistochemistry, strongly influence susceptibility to specific EGF receptor inhibitors (Sordella et al, 2004; Mitsudomi et al, 2005). More information about specific EGF receptor mutations that are common in bladder cancer are needed to predict which, if any, EGF receptor targeted therapy(ies) is (are) likely to be effective (summarized in Baselga et al, 2005).

Transforming growth factor-βs (TGF-βs) compose a family of related proteins that include TGF-$\beta1$ to $\beta5$, müllerian inhibitory substance, inhibin, and activin (Sporn and Roberts, 1989). Whereas TGF-βs were originally found to assist the malignant transformation of rat fibroblasts (Sporn and Roberts, 1989), in most cases they are inhibitors of cellular proliferation, at least in part through stimulating P27 and P15, nuclear proteins that inhibit the phosphorylation of RB by various cyclin-dependent kinases (Cote and Chatterjee, 1999). It would therefore be expected that tumors with elevated expression of TGF-βs (particularly TGF-$\beta1$) would have slower proliferation and be more indolent than those with reduced expression. This has been found using Northern blotting to detect TGF-$\beta1$ and TGF-$\beta2$ mRNAs by Coombs and colleagues (1993). Alternatively, Miyato and coworkers (1995) reported that all types of TCCs had higher TGF-$\beta1$ expression than did normal urothelium, but as Coombs and colleagues (1993) had found, TGF-$\beta1$ expression was significantly higher in the more indolent tumors than in aggressive ones. However, TGF-βs also have potent angiogenic activity, and it is noteworthy that TGF-β1's concentrations in sera of patients with invasive and/or grade 3 tumors were significantly higher than those in normal patients and in patients with superficial grade 1 and 2 cancers (Eder et al, 1996). It is not clear what the source of TGF-β1 in the serum was, and it is quite possible that sites other than the tumors themselves were producing it. Indeed, this would seem likely because there were no differences in urinary TGF-β1 (or TGF-β2) concentrations between these same patient groups (Eder et al, 1996).

Amplification of the HER2/NEU oncogene is rarely found, but when detected, it has a strong association with progression of bladder cancer. However, overexpression of its normal counterpart ERBB2, which is far more common than amplification of its gene, has been unrelated to tumor recurrence or progression (Underwood et al, 1995). Underwood and coworkers (1995) concluded that expression of this gene may be more useful as a marker of disease than as a prognostic indicator. Other authors have found conflicting results as well, and its prognostic utility is uncertain (Mellon et al, 1996). However, because of the availability of clinically safe, immunologic reagents to this antigen, ERBB2 expression may be useful as a guide for therapy. Additionally, an intriguing recent report indicates that HER2/NEU expression predicts a better response to paclitaxel-based chemotherapy (Gandour-Edwards et al, 2002).

Platelet-derived endothelial cell growth factor (PDECGF) is a thymidine phosphorylase that is a potent angiogenic factor. Mizutani and colleagues (1997) showed that its concentrations in tumor tissues (determined biochemically and by immunoassay) correlated directly with tumor stage and grade. Although malignant cells can express PDECGF, this was not tested in the study (e.g., by immunohistochemistry), so the source of this molecule in bladder cancer tissue is uncertain. The biochemical and tissue-handling techniques required for its measurement also preclude its use in standard clinical settings.

Chromosomal and Genetic Abnormalities

Chromosomal abnormalities, including increased or decreased number of chromosomes (hyperdiploidy and aneuploidy), marker chromosomes, and chromosomes of abnormal size or configuration, have also been shown to correlate with an increased risk of tumor recurrence and cancer progression (Sandberg, 1986; Falor and Ward-Skinner, 1988). Waldman and colleagues (1991) have found that, particularly, an increased number of chromosome 7 correlates with tumor grade and labeling index (as a surrogate for proliferation).

One of the most commonly found chromosomal abnormalities is deletion of chromosome 9—including loss of an entire chromosome. This can be analyzed by image analysis using fluorescence in situ hybridization (FISH) (fluorescent DNA probes to various portions of the chromosome are applied and then examined microscopically using computer technology). Wheeless and associates (1996) have demonstrated that having only a single copy of chromosome 9 in cells from bladder wash specimens obtained immediately after a 6-week course of BCG correlated well with

tumor recurrence and predicted failure of BCG intravesical therapy. Using molecular probes, Bartlett and coworkers (1998) found that deletion of 9q12 predicted superficial tumor recurrence.

Deletions of chromosome 17p have been associated with tumor progression—presumably because *TP53* is lost with the section of 17p that is deleted. Others have looked at increased immunohistochemical detectability of TP53 in the nucleus as a surrogate for genetic deletion and/or mutation (Finlay et al, 1988). Esrig and colleagues (1994) demonstrated that increased nuclear expression of TP53 in formalin-fixed, paraffin-embedded sections of TCCs from patients undergoing cystectomy correlated with reduced survival and disease progression. As mentioned earlier, TP53 status may also predict responsiveness to chemotherapy (Cote and Chatterjee, 1999). Thus, because of its ability to predict tumor behavior as well as response to treatment, this characteristic is being tested to see if it can determine which patients with muscle-invading urothelial cancer should be randomized to post-cystectomy chemotherapy or observation. Other prospective clinical trials testing whether TP53 status will determine management are planned or under way (summarized in Grossman and Dinney, 2000). Alternatively, several studies have failed to find prognostic value for nuclear overexpression of TP53, independent of tumor grade and stage, in patients with superficial bladder tumors (Lipponen et al, 1993; Gardner et al, 1994; Thomas et al, 1994; Lebret et al, 1998; Linn et al, 1998; Pfister et al, 1998). In part, this reflects variations in reagents, tissue preparations, means of quantification, and thresholds of positivity that various researchers have employed. The lack of technologic consensus on these issues has significantly reduced widespread acceptance of the prognostic utility of TP53 status. Thus, although its role as a marker of adverse prognosis in superficial tumors is likely, it has not yet been established.

Nonrandom losses of chromosome 13q, where the *RB* gene is located, have been associated with bladder cancer (Ishikawa et al, 1991; Dalbagni et al, 1993). Mutations or deletions of the *RB* gene or its protein product lead to uninhibited proliferation by permitting the cell cycle to go through its G1 to S checkpoint. It has been recognized that intense overexpression or absence of expression of RB detected immunohistochemically has similar adverse prognostic implications (Cote et al, 1998). Others have independently confirmed the significance of RB overexpression or underexpression (Cordon-Cardo et al, 1997), although not all have found its abnormal expression, when analyzed either alone or with TP53 expression, to have independent prognostic value (Johnson and Karlsson, 1998). Therefore, although the biologic importance of RB deletions or mutations seems likely, the utility of their detection for clinical patient management, and particularly prognosis, remains in question.

Markers of Proliferation

It has long been recognized that a higher percentage of proliferating cells correlates with tumor aggressiveness. Counting mitotic figures per microscopic field has been a standard way of assessing tumor aggressiveness in almost all malignancies. Similarly, various laboratory parameters have been used to assess proliferation. These include nondiploid fractions in flow cytometric analysis (Wheeless et al, 1994), increased DNA-synthesizing S phase fraction on flow cytometry of both exfoliated and formalin-fixed cells (Nemoto et al, 1988), and immunohistochemical detection of antigens expressed during various phases of the cell cycle, including proliferating cell nuclear antigen (PCNA) (Waldman et al, 1993) and the antigen detected with antibody MIB-1, an analog of Ki67 (Cohen et al, 1993; VanderPoel, 1999; Popov 2004). Each roughly correlates with cell proliferation or at least DNA synthesis. Several groups have indicated that increased aneuploid population and proportion of S phase cells correlate with both tumor grade and stage and also with a higher likelihood of recurrence, progression, and reduced survival (Koss et al, 1989; Norming et al, 1992b; Wheeless et al, 1993). Increased expression of PCNA and/or Ki67's antigen has also been associated with worse prognosis of bladder cancer (Cohen et al, 1993; Waldman et al, 1993; Pfister et al, 1998; Popov et al, 2004). However, lack of consensus about appropriate cutoffs and areas of heterogeneity within tumors makes interpretation of results challenging and renders the applicability of these tests for individual patient management highly questionable.

Markers of Apoptosis

Survivin, an inhibitor for apoptosis, is upregulated in many cancers, including urothelial cancer (Smith et al, 2001). Detection of survivin in urine has had promising results as a diagnostic marker (see later). Hausladen and colleagues (2003) demonstrated that survivin levels in urine before TUR, after TUR, during BCG or mitomycin intravesical therapy, and particularly 1 month after intravesical instillations ended, correlated closely with when, and if, urothelial cancer recurred. Again, however, as with chromosome 9 deletion (see earlier) this may reflect quantities of remaining cancer rather than resistance to intravesical agents.

Combinations of Markers

For superficial and invasive cancers, expressions of multiple markers, particularly TP53 and either RB or P21, have been investigated with variable results (Cordon-Cardo et al, 1997; Johnson and Karlsson, 1998; Cote and Chatterjee, 1999; Cote et al, 1998; VanderPoel, 1999). Additionally, combinations of these markers with proliferative antigens (Pfister et al, 1998) and/or the apoptosis inhibitor BCL2 (Kirsh et al, 1998; Kong et al, 1998; Vollmer et al, 1998) and/or markers of angiogenesis (summarized in Cote and Chatterjee, 1999) have been performed with variable findings. **Further complicating these analyses is that even if abnormal expression of more than one antigen is found in a tumor, it is very difficult to determine if these multiple abnormal expressions are occurring in the same cell** (VanderPoel, 1999).

Genomics and Proteomics

The use of high throughput technologies to assess gene and protein expression patterns (Hoque et al, 2003; Vettman et al, 2003) in tissues, exfoliated cells in urine, or molecules in the serum or in circulating cells is being assessed for many malignancies, including bladder cancer. Similarly, the development of tissue and arrays and automated means of semiquantification has greatly improved the ability to assess expression of a variety of proteins in tumors and premalig-

nant and normal tissues. However, long-term results using these technologies have not been published, and currently none should be considered a useful tool in guiding clinical management decisions.

KEY POINTS: NATURAL HISTORY AND MARKERS OF PROGRESSION

- Fifty-five percent of newly diagnosed urothelial cancers of the bladder are low grade (or low malignant potential) non–muscle-invading cancers, and 45% are high-grade cancers, well over half of which are muscle invading at diagnosis.

- The majority of all patients with muscle-invading (or more advanced) bladder cancer have that level of invasion at their initial presentation.

- Molecular as well as clinical evidence indicates that there are two major forms of urothelial cancer: high-grade cancer with abnormalities in TP53 and possibly P21, P27, RB, and P16 contributing to aggressive behavior and low-grade cancer with deletions of yet unidentified genes on the long arm of chromosome 9 being the primary genetic abnormality.

- Many molecular markers are associated with tumor aggressiveness, but currently only altered TP53, detected by immunohistochemistry as nuclear overexpression, remotely approaches being ready for clinical application as a marker of prognosis and as a guide for therapy. Even this marker is only now being tested in a randomized prospective clinical trial.

DIAGNOSIS
Signs and Symptoms

The most common presenting symptom of bladder cancer is painless hematuria, which occurs in about 85% of patients (Varkarakis et al, 1974). In reality, nearly all patients with cystoscopically detectable bladder cancer have at least microhematuria if enough urine samples are tested (Messing and Valencourt, 1990). However, hematuria is often quite intermittent so that a negative result on one or two specimens has little meaning in ruling out the presence of bladder cancer (Messing and Reznikoff, 1987; Messing and Valencourt, 1990). Thus, if a patient in the bladder cancer age range has unexplained hematuria on a urine specimen (either microscopically or grossly evident) and a "confirmatory" second specimen is free of any hematuria, cystoscopic examination is still usually warranted (Messing, 1987; Messing et al, 1992; Khadra et al, 2000; Messing, 2000). Others have disagreed with this recommendation, suggesting a confirmatory microscopic urinalysis be done (Khan et al, 2002), but genders, age breakdowns, associated symptoms, and other characteristics were absent from their report. It is likely that several urine specimens must be negative if one is to safely forego cystoscopy.

Moreover, in individuals older than age 60 or younger people with smoking or other significant exposures, a very low threshold for performing cystoscopy is warranted. Of concern is that in two recent reports from Sweden and the United States, over 70% of patients with bladder cancer had macroscopic hematuria as their presenting finding rather than having their tumors detected during the evaluation of asymptomatic microhematuria (O'Donnell et al, 2004; Boman et al, 2002b).

The symptom complex of bladder irritability and urinary frequency, urgency, and dysuria is the second most common presentation and is usually associated with diffuse carcinoma in situ or invasive bladder cancer. However, these symptoms almost never occur without (at least) microscopic hematuria. Other signs and symptoms of bladder cancer include flank pain from ureteral obstruction, lower extremity edema, and pelvic mass. Very rarely, patients present with symptoms of advanced disease, such as weight loss and abdominal or bone pain.

Conventional Microscopic Cytology

Malignant urothelial cells can be observed on microscopic examination of the urinary sediment or bladder washings. Characteristically, tumor cells have large nuclei with irregular, coarsely textured chromatin. The limitations of microscopic cytology are due to the cytologically normal appearance of cells from well-differentiated tumors and because well-differentiated cancer cells are more cohesive, they are not readily shed into the urine. Therefore, **microscopic cytology is more sensitive in patients with high-grade tumors or carcinoma in situ. Even in patients with high-grade tumors, however, urinary cytology may be falsely negative in 20%.**

False-positive cytology may occur in 1% to 12% of patients and is usually due to urothelial atypia, inflammation, or changes caused by radiation therapy or chemotherapy (Koshikawa et al, 1989). These changes are frequently observed after several months of therapy and may persist for more than 1 year after the cessation of therapy. Despite these problems, **the specificity and positive predictive value of cytology are generally quite high, as long as only unequivocally malignant or highly suspicious samples are considered positive** (Schwalb et al, 1993). Cytology is not a cost-effective means of screening for bladder cancer unless high-risk populations alone are evaluated (Gamarra and Zein, 1984). As discussed later, because far more surface epithelial cells are present in specimens obtained from bladder washes than from voiding, the former have traditionally been more useful in the diagnosis of bladder cancer (Trott and Edwards, 1973). It has been estimated that the sensitivity of a single barbotage specimen is equivalent to that of three voided specimens (Badalament et al, 1987). However, in that study, irrigations were performed through a rigid cystoscope sheath, not through the flexible scopes with which most men are now cystoscoped. It is almost certain that the yield of epithelial cells is far lower when obtained through a flexible scope, perhaps making current lavage specimens less informative than they used to be. Tauber and colleagues (2003), in an intriguing report, took advantage of the concept of a fluorescent cystoscopy (see later) by performing a bladder lavage on patients who had 5-aminolevulinic acid (ALA) instilled into the bladder. A bladder lavage specimen (obtained through a rigid scope) was centrifuged and then promptly examined using blue-violet light (390 to 430 nm wavelength) to induce fluorescence. The red fluorescence of the malignant epithelial cells improved the sensitivity over white light standard cytology (with counterstaining and fixation) from 79% to 86%. This gain was exclusively for well-differentiated cancers (improved sensitivity from 53% to 82%), a lesion that is routinely overlooked by standard cytology. This technique, although promising, has some practical drawbacks, including the very rapid fading of fluorescence from malignant cells (requiring relatively immediate examination) and the loss of nuclear detail because nuclear counterstaining was not done, and the ALA, being a heme precursor, was concentrated in the cytoplasm because heme synthesis is associated with mitochondria. Thus, the same slide could not be examined for classic cytology's nuclear abnormalities, and the standard cytology specimen had to be prepared separately.

Flow Cytometry

Flow cytometry measures the DNA content of cells whose nuclei have been stained with a DNA-binding fluorescent dye. Therefore, it can quantitate the aneuploid cell populations and the proliferative activity (percentage of S phase cells) in a tumor. DNA diploid tumors tend to be of low grade and low stage, and patients have a favorable prognosis. Tumors with a triploid to tetraploid chromosome number have unfavorable pathologic characteristics, and patients have a poor prognosis. Patients with tumors that are tetraploid have a more favorable prognosis than those with triploid to tetraploid tumors but a worse prognosis than patients with diploid tumors (Tribukait, 1987; Winkler et al, 1989; Wijkstrom and Tribukait, 1990).

Flow cytometry can measure multiple parameters simultaneously. For example, cells can be stained for DNA and cytokeratins (a marker for epithelial cells). The flow cytometer can be programmed to measure DNA content only in cells that stain positively for cytokeratins (Hajazi et al, 1989). This multiparameter approach improves the accuracy of flow cytometry because it makes it possible to actually measure which cells are proliferating in specimens, thus avoiding attributing characteristics to tumor cells that actually belong to nonmalignant cells such as white blood cells. Studies that have exploited this approach demonstrate more prognostic significance than either DNA or antigen expression measurements alone (Fradet et al, 1990). A similar multiparameter approach is applicable for cytology as well (Fradet and Lockhart, 1997).

In general, flow cytometry has not been found to be more clinically valuable than conventional cytology, although some studies have reported that it is more accurate (Denovic et al, 1982). Low-grade superficial tumors, which are usually diploid, often produce false-negative results. Aneuploidy is a common feature of high-grade tumors, and thus flow cytometry is especially accurate in patients with carcinoma in situ or high-grade malignancies, in whom 80% to 90% of tumors can be correctly identified (Badalament et al, 1987). Flow cytometry has not supplanted conventional cytology in managing bladder cancer patients.

Image Analysis

Quantitative fluorescent image analysis is an automated cytologic technique that analyzes smears of cells on a microscope slide and quantitatively measures DNA content in each cell (Carter et al, 1987). It combines quantitative biochemical analysis and more subjective visual evaluation of individual cells (cytometry can analyze only a population of cells).

This technique uses a computer-controlled fluorescent microscope that automatically scans and images the nucleus of each cell on a slide. The computer quantitates the amount of emitted fluorescence, which is directly proportional to the nucleic acid content, and identifies each cell that contains an abnormal amount of DNA. Thus, a cytotechnologist can focus on each abnormal cell identified by an automatic analyzer for morphologic evaluation. **Because individual cells can be examined by image analysis, this technique can more easily use voided urine specimens than can flow cytometry, which requires large cell populations for its analysis.**

As with flow cytometry, multiparameter image analysis can also be performed. Labeled monoclonal antibodies to various tumor markers used in conjunction with DNA fluorescence can increase the specificity of image analysis for bladder cancer detection and monitoring of treatment response. This technique is more sensitive than either standard cytology or flow cytometry for detecting low-grade bladder tumors without reduced specificity (Parry and Hemstreet, 1988). Additionally, **image analysis can be performed using fluorescently labeled DNA probes to specific chromosomes of interest** and can, in conjunction with in situ hybridization, effectively demonstrate that tumors have trisomy of the centromeric region of chromosome 7 (Waldman et al, 1991), loss of various regions (or all) of chromosome 9 (Wheeless et al, 1994), or deletions of 17p.

Specimen Interpretation

Whether a voided specimen or bladder wash is examined, osmotic changes caused by contrast media, radiation therapy, and intravesical therapy can induce confusing abnormalities. **Perhaps the greatest utility of cytology, cytometry, or image analysis on voided specimens is the capacity to sample areas of the urinary tract other than the bladder, which may shed malignant transitional epithelium. Additionally, in the face of diagnosing a low-grade papillary superficial bladder tumor, positive cytology, cytometry, or image analysis (on either voided or barbotage specimens) for high-grade cells is likely to indicate the presence of cystoscopically invisible carcinoma in situ elsewhere in the patient's urinary tract.**

EARLY DETECTION

Rationale

All epithelial bladder tumors begin on the urothelial surface, and virtually all patients who succumb to this disease have distant metastases. **However, almost all patients who develop metastases have concomitant or prior muscle-invading bladder cancers** (Jewett and Strong, 1946; Freeman et al, 1995a). Because a high proportion of all patients who have muscle-invading bladder cancer have it at the time of their

---

> ### KEY POINTS: DIAGNOSIS
>
> - Hematuria is the most common presenting symptom or sign of bladder cancer, with over 70% of patients having episodes of macroscopic hematuria directly leading to their diagnosis.
>
> - Bladder cancer–induced hematuria (microscopic or macroscopic) is quite intermittent so in a middle-aged or elderly patient even a single episode of hematuria warrants evaluation (or several urine specimens must be negative to safely forego evaluation).
>
> - Cytology has a very high specificity (few false positives), a low sensitivity for low-grade tumors and, at most, an 80% sensitivity for high-grade ones. Voided urine cytology is particularly helpful in sampling the upper urinary tracts and prostate. Also, if cytology is positive for highly malignant cells when only a low-grade papillary tumor is seen cystoscopically, it is likely that carcinoma in situ resides somewhere in the urinary tract.

initial diagnosis (Vaidya et al, 2001; Messing, 2001; Kaye and Lange, 1982; Hopkins et al, 1983), management approaches for patients with superficial bladder cancers, although critically important to those individuals, are unlikely in themselves to significantly reduce mortality from bladder cancer unless they are combined with some form of early detection strategy. Conversely, if bladder cancers can be detected while they are still confined to the mucosa or lamina propria, they can be treated by relatively nonmorbid, highly successful means (e.g., endoscopic resection with or without intravesical therapy). Moreover, even highly selected patients with high-grade superficial cancers refractory to conservative treatments are almost always cured with localized therapies (Freiha, 1990; Malkowicz et al, 1990; Freeman et al, 1995a), indicating that distant metastases have rarely occurred in these patients. Furthermore, early detection is unlikely to hurt an individual in whom tumors are detected because they undoubtedly would have become symptomatic at some time during the patient's life, eventually leading to diagnosis and treatment. Were this not the case, far more tumors would be reported as incidental findings on autopsy.

The differences in mortality of bladder cancer between the sexes could be used as another argument for early detection (see "Mortality: Sex and Race"). **Women tend to be diagnosed later** (Mommsen et al, 1983; Mansson et al, 1993) and at more advanced stages (Mungen et al, 2000) than men. This, in part, may explain the poorer outcome from this disease occurring in women (Mungen et al, 2000; Jemal et al, 2004; Madeb and Messing, 2004).

Bladder Cancer Screening

Biases and Pitfalls

Early detection strategies for bladder cancer can be considered of value only if they actually reduce mortality or morbidity of this disease compared with what would happen in a comparable population that went unscreened. Ideally, demonstrations of efficacy require prospective studies in which survival from the disease is the major endpoint and in which participants are randomized to standard care or to an early detection intervention. By such a comparison, one can rule out biases in screening encountered by earlier diagnosis without reducing mortality in patients screened (lead time bias), tendencies to detect more indolent tumors with longer preclinical durations and clinical courses in the screened group (length bias sampling), tendencies toward overzealous diagnosis of malignancy in the screened population, and tendencies for participants in early detection programs to be more healthy and health conscious (selection bias) (Morrison, 1992). To date, no such prospective, randomized, controlled screening trial for bladder cancer has been performed.

For early detection to be effective, accurate instruments (screening tools) must be available. In general, particularly for an ostensibly healthy population (albeit at high risk for developing bladder cancer), the screening technique should be inexpensive and nonmorbid. However, instruments must be both sensitive (free of false negatives) and specific (free of false positives) and have acceptable positive and negative predictive values (if a test is positive or negative, there is a high likelihood of actually harboring or not having the disease, respectively). Unfortunately, most potentially useful tests for screening have had their performances assessed on highly biased populations: those with known bladder tumors or histories of tumors or with a small number of presumably normal controls often not matched with the bladder cancer population for age, sex, and exposure history. Such characteristics may have little to do with the actual performances of these tests in a more generalized population of whom only a small fraction actually have bladder tumors.

Reported Studies

Two major screening studies have been performed on relatively generalized, geographically defined populations (unselected middle-aged and elderly males), in which participants, solicited from primary care rosters, tested their urine at home repeatedly (10 to 14 times) using multiple hematuria home testings with chemical reagent strips. If a test was positive, the patient underwent a standard urologic evaluation that included urinary cytology and cystoscopy. Messing (1992; 1995b; 1995c) and Britton (1989; 1992) and their collaborators in studies in south central Wisconsin and Leeds, England, respectively, had very similar findings: roughly 20% of participants had hematuria at least once, and in those who underwent a thorough evaluation, 6% to 8% were found to have urothelial cancers. Overall, 1.2% to 1.3% of participants had bladder cancer. At 16 years after the initiation of the Wisconsin study, none of the 21 participants in whom bladder cancer was detected by screening had died of the malignancy. Neither study had a prospective, randomized, controlled population, but Wisconsin tumor registry data were used to compare outcomes and histopathologic findings of all Wisconsin men age 50 years or older having newly diagnosed bladder cancer in 1988 with those of patients having bladder cancer detected by hematuria screening. **Both screened and unscreened cases had similar proportions of low-grade (grade 1 and 2) and high-grade cancers (roughly 55% low grade and 45% high grade). However, although almost all low-grade tumors**

were confined to the epithelium or the lamina propria in both groups, more than half of high-grade cancers in unscreened men were not diagnosed until muscle (or deeper) invasion had occurred (about 24% of all unscreened cases), whereas only 10% of high-grade (under 5% of all) screening-detected cancers were muscle invading. Thus, screening had effected a shift of the high grade tumors to earlier (more superficial) stages at diagnosis. Not surprisingly, mortality was significantly reduced in the screened population.

The control group in these studies was not a randomized one, but biases such as self-selection for bladder cancer risk; overdiagnosis, especially of indolent tumors; or significant differences in care between the cohorts could not explain these findings (Messing et al, 1995b). Moreover, the grade and stage distribution was almost identical to that of newly diagnosed bladder cancer cases in the Stockholm, Sweden, region in 1995 and 1996, indicating that the Wisconsin control population was quite representative of how bladder cancer presents in Western countries (Thorstenson et al, 2003). Thus, in the absence of a prospective randomized trial, available information indicates that screening permits the diagnosis of bladder cancers destined to become invasive at preinvasive stages, which translates into reduced mortality from the disease. Furthermore, when compared with other screening modalities for chronic diseases that have been proven effective in prospective randomized studies and are well accepted and incorporated into standard medical care, repetitive reagent strip testing for hematuria offers a favorable cost-effectiveness profile that extends the longevity of the entire screening population, and particularly the bladder cancer patients within it (Lawrence et al, 1995). To maximize this benefit, because of the brief preclinical duration of this malignancy, screenings should be repeated on at least an annual basis (Messing et al, 1995c).

Besides hematuria home testing, other diagnostic technologies have been advocated for bladder cancer screening. **Unfortunately, conventional cytology, flow cytometry, image analysis, and marker tests commercially available in the United States have relatively poor sensitivities for well-differentiated and moderately differentiated tumors. This is a serious drawback, even though such lesions rarely pose a risk to patients' lives, because failure to detect a large proportion of bladder cancers would seriously undermine the confidence both the public and physicians have in the screening modality.** Furthermore, most of the marker tests are not sensitive for small tumors, even of high histologic grade, such as the ones one would want to find on screening (Boman et al, 2002a). More importantly is that missing more than 10% to 20% of high-grade cancers is likely to significantly compromise the major goal of screening, to reduce bladder cancer mortality. However, by combining phenotypic antigen expression and/or genetic abnormalities with cytology (Golijanin et al, 1995; Bonner et al, 1996; Fradet and Lockhart, 1997; Grossman and Dinney, 2000), multiparameter flow cytometry, or image analysis (Jung et al, 1999), specificity would clearly be enhanced, and sensitivity may be as well. Additionally, excretions of a variety of soluble factors in urine, including growth or motility factors (Guirguis et al, 1988; Nguyen et al, 1993; Messing and Murphy-Brooks, 1994), their receptors (Korman et al, 1996), DNA copying errors

(Mao et al, 1994; Steiner et al, 1997), enzymes that enhance cells' continued replicative capacity (Landman et al, 1998), and other substances (Sarosdy et al, 1995; Getzenberg et al, 1996; Senga et al, 1996; Ellis et al, 1997; Pariente et al, 1997; Sarosdy et al, 1997; Schmetter et al, 1997; Miyake et al, 1998; Stampfer et al, 1998; Pode et al, 1999; Sanchez-Carbayo et al, 1999; Lokeshwer et al, 2000; Nguyen et al, 2000) have been tested in preliminary studies, and some have promise. Although many of these methodologies have yet to reach clinical practice, examples of the more promising are discussed below.

The Lewis[x] blood group-related antigen is normally absent from urothelial cells in adults except for occasional umbrella cells. There is increased expression of Lewis[x] in urothelial carcinoma independent of secretor status, tumor grade, or stage (Sheinfeld et al, 1990). Furthermore, Sheinfeld and colleagues (1990) demonstrated that immunostaining of Lewis[x] antigen on epithelial cells from bladder washings could detect tumors with a sensitivity of 86% and specificity of 87%. Subsequently, Golijanin and coworkers (1995), using this test on cytologic preparations of cells from freshly voided urine specimens, reported a sensitivity in detecting cystoscopically evident bladder tumors on two voidings (considered positive if either one was positive) of 97%, a specificity of 85%, a positive predictive value of 76%, and a negative predictive value of 98%. Whether such outstanding results, particularly in terms of sensitivity, could be achieved in populations in which slightly more than 1% (as would occur in most screening studies using general populations) as opposed to 32% (as was present in the cohort of 101 patients, most of whom had histories of recurrent bladder tumors) had bladder cancer, is questionable. However, repetition in a larger screening cohort is clearly warranted.

Antigen M344 is expressed on 70% of superficial bladder tumors. A cocktail of antibodies to M344, another mucin-related antigen, and a high-molecular-weight form of carcinoembryonic antigen, marketed as ImmunoCyt (μCyt in Europe) and detected by immunofluorescent cytology, had been reported to have overall sensitivity of 95% and specificity of 76% and, depending on the cutoff of stained cells needed for a test to be positive, from 74% to 89% and from 96% to 100% sensitivities for grade 1 and 3 tumors, respectively (Fradet and Lockhart, 1997; see later).

Another antigen, DD23, which is expressed on roughly 80% of bladder tumors regardless of stage and grade and is not seen on normal urothelial cells, may again improve diagnostic performance when used in conjunction with immunocytology or multiparameter image analysis.

It should be noted that with several of these techniques, what are believed to be false-positive results may simply be the detection of tumors that are not yet cystoscopically visible but will become so within the next 3 to 6 months. This has particularly been found with immunocytologic stainings with M344 (Fradet and Cordon-Cardo, 1993), Lewis[x] (Sheinfeld et al, 1992), and even conventional cytology (Schwalb et al, 1993).

Excretions of soluble factors in urine, such as autocrine motility factor (Guirguis et al, 1988), autocrine motility factor receptor (Korman et al, 1996), basic FGF (Chodak et al, 1988; Nguyen et al, 1993), EGF (Fuse et al, 1992; Messing and Murphy-Brooks, 1994), human complement factor H–related

protein (BTA stat and BTA TRAK) (Ellis et al, 1997; Sarosdy et al, 1997; Pode et al, 1999), and hyaluronidase (HAase)/hyaluronic acid (HA) (Lokeshwar et al, 2000), have all been found to be abnormal in patients with bladder cancer, with sensitivities as high as 80% or higher. However, only two of these are currently commercially available in the United States (BTA stat and BTA TRAK). Furthermore, many have primarily been studied in patients with high-grade tumors, who are often overrepresented in populations available to academic medical centers. **Additionally, most of these trials have compared their data with that of voided urine cytology** (Sheinfeld et al, 1990, 1992; Nguyen et al, 1993; Golijanin et al, 1995; Sarosdy et al, 1995), which has been found to be insufficiently sensitive for routine screening. Indeed, when cytology is well prepared and performed by an expert with vast experience, it often outperforms more objective marker tests (Murphy et al, 1997).

Promising Marker Tests: Hyaluronic Acid/Hyaluronidase

Lokeshwar and colleagues (2000) demonstrated that HA, a bladder glycosaminoglycan often beneath the superficial layer of cells, and HAase, an HA-degrading enzyme, have potential roles in angiogenesis and bladder tumor progression. Both HA and HAase can be measured in the urine and can assist in the detection of bladder cancer (Lokeshwar et al, 1997; Pham et al, 1997). When these tests are combined, they have been reported to have an overall sensitivity of nearly 92%, a specificity of 84%, and 88% accuracy (Lokeshwar et al, 2000). In patients at high risk for recurrent bladder cancer, a similar sensitivity has been reported, but whereas the initial specificity was quite a bit lower (73%), 35% of the "false-positive" cases had tumor recurrence within 3 to 6 months, yielding a revised specificity of 81%. As with other assays, the performance of this test in patients with a low likelihood of bladder cancer remains uncertain.

Nuclear Matrix Proteins

The nuclear matrix, by presenting specific sections of DNA to the transcription and DNA-replicating machinery, by necessity regulates a number of critical nuclear processes. After using molecular separation and blotting techniques to identify nuclear matrix proteins associated with bladder cancer and not other malignancies, **one specific protein, termed BLCA4, was found to be expressed in 75% of tumor tissues, 100% of normal-appearing bladder epithelium from patients with bladder tumors elsewhere, and no normal bladders** (Nguyen et al, 1999). These findings support the presence of a field defect throughout the urothelium in individuals with bladder cancer (discussed earlier) (Nguyen et al, 1999; 2000). Moreover, by developing antibodies to various portions of the BLCA4 molecule, this group detected bladder cancer by detecting BLCA4 in urine of 52 of 55 patients with tumors (96.4% sensitivity) and in urine of 0 of 51 normal controls (100% specificity). Obviously, before this test can be used in a diagnostic screening setting, its performance on patients with pathologic conditions other than malignancy must be known. Intriguingly, BLCA4 was also expressed in the urothelium of Fisher 344 rats who received intravesical instillations of the carcinogen methylnitrosourea at various times after exposure but before the development of bladder malignancies (Konety et al, 2000). This implies that reversing BLCA4 expression may serve as a promising intermediate endpoint in bladder cancer prevention studies.

Another nuclear matrix protein, NMP22, has been commercially available as a bladder cancer marker test for several years in the United States. Results using an enzyme-linked immunosorbent assay have been reported for its detection of cystoscopically visible tumors, with sensitivities ranging from 51% (Casella et al, 2000a) to 100% (Zippe et al, 1999) in detection series. However, the latter series had few superficial and no low-grade cancers. It has been reported to have excellent performance (85% sensitivity, 91% specificity) in a population with a large number of participants with bilharzial bladder cancer and bilharzial cystitis (considered a "benign" condition for this study) (Eissa et al, 2002). Of perhaps greatest concern is that its sensitivity for small cancers, even those of high histologic grade, was low (e.g., <75% for grade 3 cancers) (Boman et al, 2002a), making it less certain how it could be used as the sole test in early detection efforts. Recently, a point-of-care version of this test (NMP22 Bladder Chek) has been approved for use with cystoscopy for the detection of bladder cancer and in the evaluation of hematuria. Its performance in a large study of over 1300 adults with hematuria or other symptoms indicative of bladder cancer was evaluated. NMP22 Bladder Chek had an overall sensitivity and specificity of 56% and 85%, respectively, and with sensitivities of 45% to 50% for grade 1 and 2, stage Ta and T1 cancers, but 72% and 80% for high-grade cancers and carcinoma in situ, respectively (Grossman et al, 2005). Impressive was its ability to detect two muscle-invading cancers overlooked on initial cystoscopy and voided cytology (Katz and Messing, 2005). However, sizes of cancers detected or overlooked were not recorded, and it is likely that despite ease of use, this test could not be a successful stand-alone screening tool in high-risk patients.

Telomerase

Telomeres reside at the ends of chromosomes and contain short repetitive DNA sequences that are not completely replicated by DNA polymerase (Rhyu, 1995). Eventually, informative genetic material fails to be duplicated because telomeres shorten with each mitosis. This ultimately leads to cell death after a limited number of cell divisions (Rhyu, 1995). Because a fundamental part of malignant transformation is immortalization of cells, escape from this process is a problem faced by most tumor cells and other rapidly dividing cells. A major mechanism in maintaining telomere length is activity of a ribonucleoprotein with reverse transcriptase activity—telomerase, which uses its RNA component as a template to synthesize the telomere (thus maintaining telomere length) (Harley et al, 1990). By measuring telomerase activity via the telomeric repeat amplification protocol (TRAP) assay (Piatyszek et al, 1995) and/or by examining telomerase's RNA component (Muller et al, 1999), activity of this enzyme or a part of the enzyme itself can be identified in urine. Roughly 80% of patients with bladder tumors have telomerase activity identified in the urine (Landman et al, 1998; Rahat et al, 1999) with nearly equal detection of low-grade and high-grade

tumors. Specificities of approximately 80% have also been reported. However, not all investigators have had similar findings. For instance, in a study of 639 patients being evaluated for hematuria and/or irritable voiding symptoms or bladder cancer surveillance, in whom 95 were found to have bladder cancer by standard clinical means, telomerase activity was reported to have a 21% sensitivity and 92% specificity (Ramakumar et al, 2000). This work points out the difficulties with translating results from studies in which the majority of patients have bladder cancer (Rahat et al, 1999) to ones in which a minority might (Ramakumar et al, 2000). This is even more of a problem in a screening setting where less than 2% will. It is possible that the sensitivity can be improved by detecting telomerase RNA in urine (Muller et al, 1999). Indeed, in a small pilot study with 43 tumor patients, the sensitivity of detecting telomerase RNA by RT-PCR in urine was 95%, and it was 75% for grade 1 tumors (Bowles et al, 2004). Controls in this study were healthy volunteers, and whereas a 94% specificity was reported, the performance of this test if pathologic controls were included is unknown.

Microsatellite Repeat Analyses

Inherent in the propensity for tumor cells to develop genomic instability are errors in replication of DNA. Thus, the repetitive short nucleotide sequences occurring throughout the genome unique to each individual (microsatellites) are also improperly copied. This property can be taken advantage of to detect bladder cancer (Mao et al, 1994). The original assay has gone through numerous modifications (Mao et al, 1994; Hruban et al, 1994; Steiner et al, 1997) to improve its reproducibility, efficiency, and objectivity. **It has nearly a 90% sensitivity for low-grade cancers and more than a 90% sensitivity for high-grade ones and, in small studies, specificities of nearly 90% with several "false-positive" cases subsequently being diagnosed with bladder cancer.** Independent confirmation using similar technologies has been reported (Mourah et al, 1998). This assay is being tested prospectively in patients with hematuria, and thus its performance in this circumstance, let alone in a screening setting, is not known. Intriguingly, different microsatellite deletion patterns have been seen in recurrences of index tumors, and although in some cases this may simply result from additional mutations, in others it may indicate a polyclonal origin to this disease and its recurrences (Sidransky, 2000). Performance of this test using high throughput platforms, including the analysis of single nucleotide polymorphisms (SNPs), is being explored (Hoque et al, 2003).

Survivin

Survivin, an anti-apoptotic protein, is expressed in many cancers. In a pilot study, detection of this protein in urine of patients with bladder cancer using an immunoassay was nearly 100%, with a nearly similar specificity. The only false-positive findings occurred in 3 of 5 subjects with hematuria (Smith et al, 2001). This test also may be useful in predicting which patients will respond (or have responded) to intravesical therapy (see earlier) (Hausladen et al, 2003). However, in a separate study using the same assay, Shariat and coworkers (2004) reported an overall sensitivity of only 63%; whereas this surpassed the sensitivity of either the standard NMP22 assay or urine cytology on the same specimens, it was far less impressive than that found in the initial report. Excellent other performance characteristics, including a specificity and positive predictive value of 93% and 92% were reported. However, survivin was only detected in 71% of stage T2+ cancers and 80% of high-grade cancers. Even more disappointing was that cytology was more sensitive for those "can't miss" lesions (Shariat et al, 2004).

Fluorescence Cytology with DNA and Antigenic Markers

Two fluorescence cytology tests, multiparameter fluorescence in situ hybridization (FISH), using fluorescently labeled centromeric probes to chromosomes 3, 7, and 17 and a separate probe to the 9p21 region of chromosome 9, and the Immuno-Cyt test using fluorescently labeled monoclonal antibodies to three bladder cancer–associated antigens are now commercially available in the United States. Sensitivities of 69% to 89% have been reported using FISH including 85% sensitivity in patients with negative, atypical, or suspicious cytology. Additionally, as with other marker tests, an impressive initial specificity of 90% rose to 97% because FISH diagnosed tumors that would become detectable within 12 months. Other authors, however, have found lower sensitivities, particularly for non–high-grade tumors (Halling et al, 2000; Sarosdy et al, 2002; Friedrich et al, 2003b; Srougi et al, 2004).

In several detection studies, ImmunoCyt when combined with cytology, has had sensitivities that have ranged from 70% to 97% (Pfister et al, 2003; Mian et al, 1999; Fradet and Lockhart, 1997; Hautmann et al, 2004; Messing et al, 2004). Whereas sensitivities for high-grade cancers have approached or matched those of other sensitive markers (85% to 100%), sensitivities for lower-grade tumors were generally better than other commercially available tests (70% to 80%) (Messing et al, 2004; Lodde et al, 2003). Moreover, when looking at tumor size, ImmunoCyt detected 71% of tumors less than 1 cm in diameter. To achieve this, specificities have been in the 70% to 80% range. Follow-ups have not been reported to determine if there were anticipatory false-positive findings or not. Additionally, not all authors have reported as high sensitivities (Bunting et al, 2000).

Combination Marker Studies

A variety of studies have analyzed several marker tests in a single urine specimen to determine if combining several assays can enhance bladder cancer detection (Ramakumar et al, 1999; Bunting et al, 2000). **Evidence indicates that neither alone nor in limited combinations are these tests sufficiently sensitive to replace cystoscopy in the evaluation of hematuria** (Elhilali, 1999; Bunting et al, 2000; Casella et al, 2000a; Ramakumar et al, 2000; Boman et al, 2002a).

Another potential use of diagnostic markers is to replace some surveillance cystoscopic examinations in monitoring superficial bladder cancer for recurrence. Because low malignant potential and low-grade cancers have a small chance of grade progression and even a smaller likelihood of progression to stage T2, even if a cancer is not detected, as long as cystoscopy is performed within several months, the likelihood of

a patient being placed at serious risk is very low. Alternating either BTA stat or the standard NMP22 test with cystoscopy every 3 months has been modeled by Lotan and Roehborn (2002) and found to be cost effective. However, in their study the authors neglected to consider costs of resecting larger cancers if they were missed by the marker test until detected by cystoscopy 3 months later, the risk of grade progression and the possibility of having a more serious disease develop if a tumor is overlooked, and the expense of the more thorough evaluation required if a false-positive marker result occurs (both of the marker tests in the model had roughly a 30% false-positive rate). Other factors likely not calculated were the particularly low sensitivity for small tumors (including even high-grade ones) of these and some other markers (Boman et al, 2002a), and that the greatest likelihood of detecting a recurrence is in the first 3 to 5 months after tumor resection (Holmang and Johansson, 2002), so clearly cystoscopy should be performed near those time points. However, this use of bladder cancer markers holds considerable promise and is being evaluated in several trials.

Also, it is possible that a battery of these tests (yet to be developed) can be used as a second-tier screen in the case of a positive test from the highly sensitive repetitive hematuria reagent strip testing to reduce the number of diagnostic evaluations eventually performed. In this way, a reasonably cost-effective screening paradigm acceptable to subjects, their physicians, and health care payers can be developed that can then be tested in a randomized prospective study to determine the true efficacy of bladder cancer screening.

Screening Populations with Exposures to Putative Carcinogens

Aside from age and sex, potential screening populations at higher risk than those taking part in the Wisconsin and Leeds programs have been studied. These efforts have primarily focused on workers with prolonged exposure to known or possible carcinogens, including 4,4'-methylene-bis-2-chloroaniline (Ward et al, 1990), β-naphthylamine (Marsh et al, 1990), α-naphthylamine, benzidine, auramine, and magenta (Cartwright, 1990; Mason and Vogler, 1990), using cytology, hematuria chemical reagent strips, quantitative fluorescence image analysis, and/or cystoscopy. Studies have been limited, despite considerable efforts by investigators, because of a combination of factors, including incomplete information about previous exposures, changing production standards, and difficulties with compliance and follow-up. **Each study has reported a few patients in whom bladder malignancies have been diagnosed, but the utility of such efforts has not been rigorously assessed. Additionally, the possibility of the chemical exposures themselves causing abnormal test results without leading to diagnosable malignancy is uncertain.**

One of the most impressive industry-based screening programs is one testing younger aluminum workers exposed to benzene-soluble coal-tar-pitch volatiles in Quebec. Researchers have demonstrated that annual urinary cytology examinations have effected a shift of tumors to pre-muscle-invasive stages when compared with historical controls from the 1970s (in the 1970s, 39% non–muscle invading;

in the 1980s, 63% non–muscle invading) without any alteration in tumor grade (roughly 40% to 45% in the 1970s and 1980s groups had high-grade tumors) (Thériault et al, 1990). Because of lead-time issues and because the unscreened control population has been followed longer, it is not surprising that mortality in the screened group (1980s) was significantly less. However, considering that 53% of cases in the unscreened population (who were all younger than 65 years) had already died of bladder cancer at the time of the report, it is likely that further follow-up will give an indication of whether screening actually saves lives. This study, of course, does not replace a randomized, prospective, controlled trial (especially because more modern workers, aware of the seriousness of bladder cancer in the 1970s workers, may have sought medical evaluation much sooner than those in the earlier group did, even if they were not being screened), but it gives an indication that such workers may be appropriate subjects for screening endeavors. A new screening endeavor is underway in this industry that uses ImmunoCyt testing.

Of note is that in a study by Hemstreet and coworkers (1999), in which a large cohort of benzidine-exposed workers' (and nonexposed controls') urine samples were screened using multiparameter image analysis (DNA, GActin/FActin ratio, and M344 expression), the relative risk for subsequently being diagnosed with bladder cancer could be determined. In a follow-up of this study adding the tumor-associated antigen P-300, while only 21% of 1788 Chinese workers exposed to benzidine fit into the high- or moderate-risk group, 87% of all the cancers found were in this cohort and all were organ confined. **A positive biomarker occurred 15 to 33 months before bladder cancer was clinically detected, and time to diagnosis was inversely associated with number of positive biomarkers** (Hemstreet et al, 2001). **Whether this indicates the presence of a premalignant field change that may be reversed by cessation of carcinogen exposure, irreversible changes in the urothelium, or true malignant transformation that was not yet clinically detectable is not clear.** However, by utilizing a variety of markers, along with knowledge of a worker's exposures to environmental carcinogens, and other demographic information, a risk stratification model can be developed in which the intensity and frequency of follow-up can be adjusted to the participant's likelihood of developing bladder cancer. Hemstreet and colleagues are currently testing this hypothesis directly.

Imaging Studies
Computed Tomography

More and more frequently computed tomography (CT) without and with intravenous contrast has replaced excretory urography in the evaluation of hematuria. With computer-assisted reconstruction, longitudinal views of the urinary tract can now be made, although their sensitivity in detecting small or flat tumors of the urothelium is limited. Because these cancers are much more common in the bladder than in upper tracts, cystoscopy is still mandatory in evaluating patients in the bladder cancer age range with hematuria, but ureteroscopy need not be performed unless upper tract abnormalities on CT, or other factors, mandate its performance.

KEY POINTS: EARLY DETECTION AND MARKERS

- Early detection is designed primarily to shift the preponderance of high-grade cancers to superficial stages at diagnosis, where treatments are more effective and less morbid than for muscle-invading or more advanced cancers. Repetitive home hematuria testing with chemical reagent strips appears to accomplish this.

- Several biomarkers detected in urine, when used as a group, can help assign risk for developing bladder cancer in an industrially exposed cohort (e.g., benzidine workers). A positive test precedes the presence of cystoscopically detectable bladder cancer by 15 to 33 months, and the marker "profile" is useful in deciding the intensity and type of follow-up screening to be performed in these workers.

- Of the four marker tests available in the United States, all are more sensitive than cytology in many prospective studies. Two, BTA stat and NMP22 Bladder Chek, are point-of-care tests but have limited sensitivity for small cancers (even high-grade ones). Two, ImmunoCyt and UroVision DNA FISH, use fluorescent cytology requiring a skilled laboratory to perform the assay. ImmunoCyt probably has the greatest sensitivity for small and low-grade cancers, whereas UroVision DNA FISH has the highest specificity. It is not clear that any of these markers, alone or in combination, are satisfactory for screening, but some may be able to replace some surveillance cystoscopies in monitoring patients at low risk for superficial bladder cancer.

- Other promising, but not yet available diagnostic marker tests include microsatellite repeat analyses and assays for survivin, telomerase, BLCA4, and HA/HAase in urine.

Excretory Urography

If CT is not performed, excretory urography is indicated in all patients with signs and symptoms suggestive of bladder cancer. Urography is not a sensitive means of detecting bladder tumors, particularly small ones. However, it is useful in examining the upper urinary tracts for associated urothelial tumors. Large tumors may appear as filling defects in the bladder on the cystogram phase of the urogram. Ureteral obstruction caused by a bladder tumor is usually a sign of muscle-invasive cancer. Additionally, of course, urography can assess other upper tract abnormalities that may affect management decisions.

Cystoscopy

All patients suspected of having bladder cancer should have careful cystoscopy, and if a suspicious lesion is seen, cystoscopy and bimanual examination under anesthesia are mandatory. Abnormal areas should be sampled. Random or selected-site mucosal biopsy specimens may also be obtained (see earlier discussion). Retrograde pyelography should be performed if the upper tracts are not adequately visualized on the excretory urogram or CT. Virtual cystoscopy with CT remains inadequate to detect flat lesions so it cannot currently replace cystoscopy in the initial diagnostic evaluation of bladder cancer. However, if an obvious tumor is seen on CT or excretory urogram, office cystoscopy is probably unnecessary, and cystoscopy and biopsy should be scheduled for the operating room.

Resection of Bladder Tumors

The ideal method for resection of a bladder tumor is to resect first the bulk of the tumor and then the deep portion along with some underlying bladder muscle, sending each specimen separately for histologic examination. This approach usually enables complete removal of the tumor and provides valuable diagnostic information about the grade and depth of infiltration of the tumor. It has been suggested that resecting low-grade superficial tumors into the muscle layer may unnecessarily increase the potential for bladder perforation and also risk muscle-invasive recurrence of tumor implanted in the resected bed. In circumstances in which complete resection is not feasible or is of questionable value, at least taking adequate specimens for accurate histologic diagnosis and staging is mandatory. **With extremely rare exception, fulguration or laser ablation of suspicious lesions without adequate biopsy has no place in the initial evaluation of bladder cancer.** This is so despite experienced urologists being able to predict histologic findings based on cystoscopic appearance alone (Herr et al, 2002b).

Tumors encroaching on the ureteral orifices should be resected without regard for the orifice; however, it is important not to fulgurate the orifice after the tumor has been resected. When the ureteral orifice is resected, a stent may be left in place for several days to prevent obstruction of the orifice by edema.

Tumors on the lateral bladder wall may induce stimulation of the obturator nerve during resection, resulting in violent contraction of the adductor muscle of the thigh. Resections of such tumors should be performed with the patient under general anesthesia, with simultaneous intravenous administration of pancuronium to adequately paralyze the patient to minimize the risk of inadvertent bladder perforation associated with adductor muscle spasm.

Tumors arising in bladder diverticula often should be sampled rather than resected. This is not only because TUR of such tumors is often quite challenging but also because it has a high risk of bladder perforation. Patients with tumors in diverticula are often best treated definitively with either partial or total cystectomy (Faysal and Freiha, 1981; Golijanin et al, 2003).

Finding "Invisible" Tumors

Selected-site mucosal biopsies from areas adjacent to the tumor as well as from the opposite bladder wall, bladder dome, trigone, and prostatic urethra have been recommended at time of resection of the primary tumor. These biopsies provide important prognostic information about the likeli-

hood of tumor recurrence, with 14% to 25% of patients found to have dysplasia or carcinoma in situ on such biopsies (Althausen et al, 1976; Thorstenson et al, 2005). These findings may lead to the institution of intravesical therapy (e.g., BCG), which Thorstenson and colleagues (2005) claim has reduced mortality in these patients. Between 30% and 70% of muscle-invasive bladder cancers are associated with carcinoma in situ elsewhere in the bladder. Mufti and Singh (1992) suggested that abnormalities found on mucosal biopsies in patients with solitary low-grade superficial tumor are particularly predictive of tumor recurrence. In contrast, some investigators believe that selected-site mucosal biopsies are unnecessary (Klemeney et al, 1994) and even potentially hazardous because they denude the urothelium and may create fertile areas for tumor cell implantation (see "Implantation"). Clearly, selected mucosal biopsies run the risk of missing premalignant or malignant areas because of sampling issues, and it has been suggested that taking advantage of the propensity of tumors to retain fluorescent porphyrin derivatives, such as protoporphyrin IX, may be able to reduce this problem. Its precursor, **5-aminolevulinic acid (ALA), when administered intravesically in conjunction with fluorescent cystoscopy using blue light at 375 to 440 nm,** can enable detection of lesions invisible with white light cystoscopy (Kriegmair et al, 1995; Koenig et al, 1998; Filbeck et al, 2000, 2002; Schmidbauer et al, 2004). Although some authors have claimed that this procedure increased sensitivity in detecting small tumors and carcinomas in situ from 77% with white light to nearly 98% with fluorescent cystoscopy, the number of tumors missed is uncertain (Filbeck et al, 2000). Moreover, more than half the regions sampled because of fluorescence were histologically normal or inflamed without neoplasia. Despite this, it is likely that some of the "false-positive" regions contained patches of genetically altered cells destined to become tumors and, more importantly, fluorescence-guided TUR can decrease the likelihood of tumor recurrence (Filbeck et al, 2002). Improvements in the fluorescent solution have now permitted excellent detection with an instillation performed just 1 hour before "blue light" cystoscopy (Schmumbauer et al, 2004). This makes the procedure more practical for patients and busy urologists. Currently, the only cystoscopic lenses available are rigid ones, making this not feasible as a common office-based examination. As of now, this technique is only used in Europe, but it is under active investigation in the United States.

Regardless of the questionable wisdom of obtaining selected-site urothelial biopsies for most bladder tumors, these biopsies are required if partial cystectomy is contemplated or if urinary cytology indicates the presence of high-grade cancer and, cystoscopically, no tumors are seen or all lesions look like low-grade superficial papillary tumors.

STAGING

Because tumor stage is crucial in determining therapy, accurate staging of bladder cancer is desirable. Understaging occurs most frequently in patients with high-grade and intermediate-stage tumors, of whom approximately one third are understaged and 10% are overstaged (Wijkstrom et al, 1984).

Goals of Staging

Superficial versus Infiltrating Tumor

The first treatment decision based on tumor stage is whether the patient has a muscle-invasive tumor. If the tumor is superficial, more elaborate staging techniques such as bone scan, CT (if it was not used in the initial hematuria evaluation), and so forth are not usually indicated. Such techniques are reserved for patients with documented muscle-invasive bladder cancer, because it is so rare for metastases to be associated with superficial disease (Jewett and Strong, 1946; Freeman et al, 1995a).

The primary TUR of the tumor is the most important test for judging its depth of penetration. Maruniak and coworkers (2002) have emphasized the need for careful attention to tissue harvesting and handling to obtain the greatest amount of histologic information.

Variation occurs in the interpretation of histology sections by different pathologists assessing tumor grade and depth of infiltration. **Part of the reason for these discrepancies is related to the smooth muscle fibers of the tunica muscularis mucosa in the lamina propria of the bladder wall, which may be confused with detrusor muscle** (Younes et al, 1990). Additionally, on rare occasions, adipose tissue has been found in the lamina propria, further confusing matters (Bochner et al, 1995). The presence of deep lamina propria involvement probably confers a worse outlook than superficial lamina propria invasion in terms of disease progression and survival; especially for high-grade cancer, when it is treated with local resection alone (Holmang et al, 1997) but not when intravesical BCG is instilled (Kondyles et al, 2000). In those patients in whom the muscularis mucosa is not consistently identified on transurethral biopsies (ranging from 11% [Kondyles et al, 2000] to 46% [Engel et al, 1992] in various reports), defining the extent of invasion below the urothelial surface (above or below 1.5 mm) has correlated well with progression-free 5-year survival (67% for more than 1.5 mm versus 93% for 1.5 mm or less) in a retrospective series of 83 patients (Cheng et al, 2000c).

Bimanual physical examination helps little in distinguishing a tumor confined to the lamina propria from one invading the muscularis propria. However, if the tumor is palpable on bimanual examination before resection, it is usually infiltrating into the deep muscle or perivesical tissues.

Another determination is whether the invasive tumor has penetrated through the bladder wall. In the vast majority of cases, it is unlikely that this can be reliably distinguished through TUR alone. Attempts also have been made to correlate depth of invasion from the epithelial surface with tumor stage, and although tumors invading more than 4 mm on the TUR specimen have a significantly higher likelihood of having extravesical extension at cystectomy than do those with less invasion, more than 40% of patients with extravesical extension still had invasion depths of less than 4 mm. Moreover, depth of invasion did not distinguish superficial from deeper muscle extension or barely extravesical from extensive extravesical extension (Cheng et al, 2000b). Thus, the value of this technique, alone or when analyzed with other features, is unknown. Bimanual examination may be helpful in this circumstance, and particularly if after the resection a mass is still

appreciated, the likelihood that there is extravesical extension is considerable. Body habitus and gender significantly influence the utility of the bimanual examination.

In an intriguing report, Koraitim and colleagues (1995) found that transurethral ultrasonic assessment using 5.5-MHz probes with 60-degree, 90-degree, and 120-degree transducers before and at the end of TUR was helpful in further distinguishing infiltration of superficial versus deep muscle and extravesical spread. One hundred percent sensitivity and more than 98% specificity in distinguishing muscle-invasive from superficial bladder cancers, more than 90% accuracy in distinguishing superficial muscularis invasion from deeper muscle invasion, and 70% positive predictive value in distinguishing vesical-confined from extravesical disease were reported by these authors—certainly far more accurate staging than has been found with other methodologies. Further confirmation of this technique is awaited.

Localized versus Locally Extensive or Metastatic Tumor

The second treatment decision made on the basis of staging is identifying patients with invasive tumors who may benefit from aggressive, potentially curative therapy. For this purpose, CT, ultrasonography, and magnetic resonance imaging (MRI) have been used to evaluate the local extent of bladder tumors. These staging studies may provide valuable information, but, with the possible exception of transurethral ultrasonography (Koraitim et al, 1995), they appear to be inaccurate in determining the presence or absence of microscopic muscle infiltration and minimal extravesical tumor spread (Koss et al, 1981). Moreover, postoperative changes produced by TUR of the primary tumor as well as post-irradiation or post-chemotherapy fibrosis also may cause difficulties in interpreting CT, MRI, and ultrasound scans.

Staging Tests

Computed Tomography

In addition to assessing the extent of the primary tumor, CT also provides information about the presence of pelvic and para-aortic lymphadenopathy and visceral metastases. To accurately assess the depth of penetration, CT should be done before TUR, but this is rarely practical (Husband et al, 1989). Contrast medium–enhanced CT improves the accuracy of staging (Sager et al, 1987). Studies with spiral CT have not yet been fully assessed to determine if they can improve staging further, but at least preliminary information indicates little additional benefit (Paik et al, 2000). CT is limited in accuracy because it can detect only gross extravesical tumor extension, lymph nodes that are quite enlarged, and liver metastases that are larger than 1 cm in diameter (Voges et al, 1989). CT fails to detect nodal metastases in up to 40% to 70% of patients having them (Paik et al, 2000). Although some authors have questioned the practical utility of using CT for local staging of bladder cancer (Nishimura et al, 1988; Paik et al, 2000), the scans are undoubtedly more sensitive than physical examination in evaluating regional and metastatic disease. Also, because of the magnitude of the treatments considered for invasive bladder cancer, it would seem prudent to perform CT before embarking on such therapy (see following discussion).

Magnetic Resonance Imaging

MRI is not much more helpful than CT. With few exceptions (Johnson et al, 1990), the resolution of the pelvic and abdominal anatomy with traditional MRI has not been reported to be as good as that with CT (Buy et al, 1988; Wood et al, 1988; Husband et al, 1989; Tavares et al, 1990). A double-surface coil may permit more accurate MRI staging of bladder cancer than a conventional coil MRI (Barentsz et al, 1988). With MRI, the possibility of multiplane imaging should theoretically provide better visualization of the anatomy. Soft tissue contrast may be enhanced by use of paramagnetic contrast agents, such as gadolinium-diethylenetriamine-penta-acetic· acid complex (Gd-DTPA) and iron-containing materials (Sohn et al, 1990; Barentsz, 1999). Indeed, using these agents, Barentsz (1999) reported a small series in which three-dimensional MRI had a 75% sensitivity and a 96% specificity in detecting nodal metastases in patients with muscle-invasive bladder cancer who eventually underwent surgical staging. Successful percutaneous biopsy of nodes deemed suspicious by this mode of imaging has also been done. Even better performance has been reported for ferromagnetic particles and MRI being able to detect nodal metastases from prostatic cancer, and there is little reason to think that similar performance characteristics will not occur with bladder cancer as well. Better preoperative staging may not only help select patients who unequivocally should be considered for neoadjuvant chemotherapy (Grossman et al, 2003) but also will assist the surgeon in doing as complete a lymphadenectomy as possible. MRI spectroscopy in the future may also have the capacity to provide information about the states of different tissues, but this possibility has not yet been realized for bladder cancer. As might be expected, both CT and MRI are more accurate in very advanced tumors (Vock et al, 1982).

MRI has become particularly useful because it is more sensitive than CT or, for that matter, radionuclide bone scans for determining the presence of bone metastases. Thus, if clinical symptoms, pelvic extension on CT or bimanual examination, or nuclear bone scan indicates suspicious sites of osseous metastases, MRI may be appropriate in such cases.

Ultrasonography

The potential benefit of transurethral ultrasonography has been reported. The findings of Koraitim and colleagues (1995) have been suggested by others (summarized in See and Fuller, 1992). However, this technique has not been adopted for general use. Transabdominal or transrectal sonography has been of minimal value (Yaman et al, 1996).

Positron Emission Tomography

Positron emission tomography (PET) has been useful in assessing masses seen on other imaging studies in the evaluation of metastases—and at times, primary tumors. The current limitation of PET for imaging the bladder is significant because the reagent used, fluorodeoxyglucose (FDG), is excreted in urine, making local tumor diagnoses or assessment almost impossible. But metastatic lesions and those recurring in the bladder bed after cystectomy are another matter. PET with FDG can help in deciding which patient with a questionable mass in a possible metastatic site warrants invasive biopsy procedures. When fused with MRI or CT, PET can also guide biopsies. Attempts to drain the bladder and re-image it in the absence of obscuring urine has been tested, and although it improves PET's imaging capacity, it does not do so sufficiently to consider using it for staging or accurately assessing tumor recurrence.

Using a different isotope not excreted in urine, ^{11}C-choline, as the PET tracer, Treiber and colleagues (2005) reported similar sensitivity to CT in detecting primary invasive bladder tumors, but PET detected metastases in 25% of patients (38% of positive nodes), whereas in this series, CT detected none. However, micrometastases still were not detected well.

Lymphadenectomy

Pelvic lymphadenectomy is the most accurate means of determining regional lymph node involvement. Some patients have only limited nodal metastases below the bifurcation of the common iliac arteries, and without invasion of adjacent organs they may be cured by pelvic lymphadenectomy (Lerner et al, 1993; Poulson et al, 1998; Vieweg et al, 1999a, 1999b). The primary regions of lymphatic drainage of the bladder are the perivesical, hypogastric, obturator, external iliac, and presacral lymph nodes (described earlier). Perivesical nodes tend to be involved less frequently than the others, making it necessary to perform a formal lymphadenectomy if one is to both completely sample and thoroughly remove potentially involved regional nodes. However, Bella and colleagues (2003) have found that involvement of perivesical nodes with or without positive pelvic nodes confers a much worse prognosis than pelvic node involvement alone and that knowledge of their involvement would almost certainly mandate early adjuvant chemotherapy. The common iliac, inguinal, and para-aortic/caval lymph nodes are juxtaregional nodes and serve as secondary landing sites (although there is clearly overlap between medial common iliac and lateral presacral nodes). Fine-needle biopsy of enlarged lymph nodes under CT or MRI guidance may be performed to document lymph node metastases.

The standard staging lymphadenectomy for bladder cancer includes removal of the nodes from slightly above the iliac bifurcations to the femoral canals and from the genitofemoral nerves to the bladder pedicles. Some clinicians have routinely performed more extensive node dissections, including nodes as high as the aortic bifurcation (Poulson et al, 1998), although the benefit of this is uncertain. Recent data indicate that extensive dissections are well tolerated (Brossner et al, 2004). The incidence of lymph node involvement correlates with the stage and grade of the tumor, ranging from 5% to 10% in a highly select group of high-grade, frequently recurrent, lamina propria–invading tumors to 40% in deeply infiltrating tumors. Because some patients with limited nodal metastases can be cured by surgery and because management decisions may be greatly altered if nodes are involved, unless comorbidities contraindicate its performance, *bilateral* thorough node dissection should be done with total or partial cystectomy. Data are increasing to indicate that full or even extended dissections, both alone and with chemotherapy can improve outcome (Quek et al, 2003; Stein et al, 2003; Herr et al, 2002a). Moreover, the concept of lymph node density (number of positive nodes/total number of nodes removed), which in several series predicts outcome (Quek et al, 2003; Stein et al, 2003; Kassouf et al, 2005) would lend further credence to the benefits of performing an extensive and meticulous lymphadenectomy.

Chest Radiograph and Computed Tomography

Metastatic evaluation to rule out distant metastases should be performed before proceeding to pelvic lymphadenectomy. The most sensitive means of detecting pulmonary metastasis is chest CT, but CT frequently detects small, noncalcified pulmonary lesions, most of which are granulomas. There is a direct correlation between the size of a pulmonary lesion and the likelihood of its being a metastasis. Most noncalcified lesions that are 1 cm or larger are metastases (or primary pulmonary neoplasms). **Because standard films do not have resolution sufficient to demonstrate small granulomas but rather detect only lesions larger than 1 cm in diameter, routine chest radiographs, rather than CT scans, are usually relied on to rule out pulmonary metastases in bladder cancer patients.**

Bone Scans

Bone scans seldom reveal metastatic disease in patients with normal liver function tests, especially if the alkaline phosphatase level is normal (Brismar and Gustafson, 1988). However, a bone scan may be useful as a baseline for future reference. Thus, the recommended metastatic evaluation for patients with invasive bladder cancer includes a chest radiograph, abdominal-pelvic CT, bone scan, and liver function tests.

Molecular Staging

While currently beyond standard care, performing molecular techniques to detect a variety of relevant gene products in circulating cells' RNA and protein (Soria et al, 2002; Lu et al, 2000; Gudermann et al, 2000), soluble factors in serum (Matsumoto et al, 2003), and mRNA in lymph nodes (Seraj et al, 2001) has been reported to have promising results in prognosis and staging. The presence of mRNA for uroplakin II (Lu et al, 2000) and cytokeratin 20 (Gudermann et al, 2000) in circulating cells has correlated with tumor stage, while that for telomerase activity was positive in 95% of patients with invasive and regionally metastatic cancer (Soria et al, 2002). Preoperative plasma levels of soluble E-cadherin correlated well with nodal metastases and disease progression, although not with disease-related mortality (Matsumoto et al, 2003). Seraj and colleagues (2001) found mRNA for uroplakin II extracted from pelvic lymph nodes and subjected to RT-PCR assisted in diagnosing metastatic bladder cancer in several cases. Follow-up revealed that of 35 patients with histologically negative nodes, 1 of 22 (5%) who were PCR negative experienced recurrence, whereas 9 of 13 (69%) who were PCR positive recurred (Copp et al, 2005). Similar findings were reported by Kurahashi and associates (2005). Results of further follow-up and expanded studies are awaited.

Staging Systems

The main staging system of bladder cancer, which has been revised, is one developed jointly by the International Union

Table 75-1. 1997 AJCC-UICC, TNM Staging

Ta	Papillary, epithelium confined
Tis	Flat carcinoma in situ
T1	Lamina propria invasion
T2a	Superficial muscularis propria invasion
T2b	Deep muscularis propria invasion
T3a	Microscopic extension into perivesical fat
T3b	Macroscopic extension into perivesical fat
T4a	Cancer invading pelvic viscera (e.g., prostatic stroma, vaginal wall, rectum, uterus)
T4b	Extension to pelvic sidewalls, abdominal walls, or bony pelvis
N0	No histologic pelvic node metastases
N1	Single positive node ≤2 cm in diameter, below common iliacs
N2	Single positive node 2-5 cm in greatest diameter or multiple positive nodes
N3	Positive nodes >5 cm in diameter
Nx	Nodal status unknown
M0	No distant metastases
M1	Distant metastases documented
Mx	Distant metastases status uncertain

Against Cancer (UICC) and the American Joint Committee on Cancer (AJCC) (Sobin and Wittekind, 1997) (Table 75–1). In the 1997 AJCC-UICC system, also termed Tumor-Node-Metastasis (TNM), papillary epithelium–confined tumors are classified as stage Ta, whereas flat in-situ carcinomas are classified as Tis. Tumors that have invaded the lamina propria are classified as stage T1. Muscle-invasive tumors, depending on whether there is superficial or deep muscle invasion, are classified as stage T2a or T2b, respectively. Tumors that have invaded the perivesical fat are classified as stage T3a (microscopic invasion) or T3b (macroscopic invasion). Tumors invading the pelvic viscera, such as the prostatic stroma, rectum, uterus, or vagina, are classified as stage T4a, whereas those extending to the pelvic sidewalls or abdominal wall are stage T4b. In the AJCC-UICC system, the regional lymph nodes from bladder cancer are considered to be the nodes of the true pelvis that lie below the bifurcation of the common iliac arteries. Laterality does not affect the N classification. N1 denotes a single positive node less than or equal to 2 cm in diameter, N2 denotes a single positive node greater than 2 cm but less than 5 cm in diameter or multiple positive nodes less than 5 cm in diameter, and N3 denotes positive nodes greater than 5 cm in diameter. The AJCC-UICC system does not have a particular stage for juxtaregional lymph nodes, but distant metastases are designated as M1, and their absence is designated as M0. In patients in whom the nodal or distant status is uncertain, the classification is Nx or Mx, respectively.

PREVENTION

Because patients with superficial bladder cancer are at such high risk for recurrence, yet in the United States usually are managed by careful surveillance, they present ideal subjects in whom to test new therapeutic or preventive strategies. Presumably, approaches that show efficacy in individuals with very high likelihoods of developing more tumors (secondary prevention) can then be tried in much larger populations who are at some risk for developing, but have never yet had, a bladder tumor (primary prevention). **Additionally, because**

KEY POINTS: RADIOLOGIC, SURGICAL, AND MOLECULAR STAGING

- Radiologic contrast studies of the upper urinary tract collecting systems are needed during the initial evaluation of all patients with cystoscopically evident bladder tumors.

- A deep biopsy and/or TUR is needed to determine the depth of tumor invasion in the bladder.

- The muscularis mucosa is composed of fine smooth muscle fibers in the normal lamina propria, complicating assessment of depth of penetration.

- Fluorescent cystoscopy using intravesically instilled porphyrin precursors such as 5-aminolevulinic acid (ALA) identifies tumors not visualized with white light cystoscopy. Destroying tumors detected with this technique reduces recurrence rates and may prevent disease progression and prolong survival.

- In patients with muscle-invading bladder cancer undergoing total or partial cystectomies, complete bilateral pelvic lymphadenectomies extending above the iliac artery bifurcations and including presacral and hypogastric nodes should be done. These nodal packets must be examined carefully to accurately assess prognosis. Patients with a minimal to moderate burden of nodal metastases may be cured.

- Molecular techniques to detect proteins or mRNA in circulating tumor cells, nodes, and perivesical tissues hold promise in predicting outcomes.

clinical, molecular, and epidemiologic data support the notion that there are likely some common steps shared in the development of both nonaggressive and aggressive urothelial cancers, interventions that inhibit or delay the genesis of indolent tumors may well be effective against the formation of aggressive ones, too. Approaches that have been tried and/or are under evaluation include the use of specific vitamins (alone or in combination), polyamine synthesis inhibitors, cyclooxygenase (COX) inhibitors and other anti-inflammatory medicines, and other more natural approaches, including dietary alterations that affect urinary constituents.

Vitamins

Vitamin A and its analogs have been considered differentiating agents that have been found experimentally to prevent induced bladder cancer in animals (Sporn et al, 1977). Unfortunately, two vitamin A analogs, 13-cis-retinoic acid and tigerson (ethyl-all-trans-9 [4-methoxy-2,3, 6-trimethylphenol]-3,7-dimethyl-2,4,6,8-nonatetraenoate) were found to be ineffective and actually quite toxic (primarily skin and mucous membrane toxicities) in patients with

superficial bladder tumors (Koontz et al, 1981; Pederson et al, 1984).

Building on preliminary evidence of efficacy in preventing bladder tumor recurrences (Alfthan et al, 1983), etretinate, a synthetic retinoid, was studied in 79 patients with stage Ta and T1 bladder cancers after resection in a randomized, prospective, placebo-controlled trial. Although times to first recurrence were identical in the etretinate and placebo study arms, time to subsequent recurrence and total number of TURs were significantly improved in the treated subjects. Side effects such as dryness of mucous membranes were tolerable in treated individuals, but three myocardial infarctions occurred in the etretinate group, making long-term safety and tolerability serious issues with this agent (Studer et al, 1995). However, the design of this study, in which study drug and placebo were continued after the first recurrence under the presumption that those tumors were already present, though undetected at the time of index TUR (so that the drugs were actually treating existing tumors, not preventing new ones) is worth remembering if there are negative results in time-to-first-recurrence after resection (as has been the case in several studies discussed later).

Another vitamin A analog, all-trans-4-hydroxyphenyl retinamide (4-HPR), normalized cytology in patients with histories of prior bladder cancer and abnormal cytology and/or flow cytometry (Decensi et al, 1992). These promising results led to its selection as a test agent in a randomized, prospective, placebo-controlled M. D. Anderson Tumor Institute—National Cancer Institute (NCI) trial, after resection of low-risk superficial bladder cancer. Unfortunately, it does not appear that 4-HPR reduced first recurrences in that group (Lerner et al, 2005).

Vitamins A and E were tested in a well-designed trial in which more than 29,000 50- to 59-year-old Finnish male smokers without known malignancies of any type were randomized to receive α-tocopherol, β-carotene, a combination of both, or placebo. Neither agent alone or in combination had an influence on bladder cancer development (or, for that matter, on lung cancer development or mortality). The study has been criticized despite its enormous size, its double-blind, randomized, prospective design, its excellent compliance, and its extensive follow-up (5 to 7 years) because of questions concerning the specific agents used as representatives of the families of compounds they were to test, their less-than-optimal dosages, and that by starting off with patients with an average 720-pack-per-year history of smoking, the mutagenic events leading to malignancy may have been so far entrenched that even ideal preventive methods were likely to be ineffective (Heinonen et al, 1994).

In a separate study, based on information that vitamin B_6 (pyridoxine) can reduce the level of substituted aminobiphenyls and tryptophan metabolites, which have been found to be carcinogenic in animal bladder cancer (Price and Brown, 1962; Bryan et al, 1964), patients with resected superficial tumors were randomized to receive 20 mg of pyridoxine or placebo daily. No benefit in terms of time-to-recurrence or recurrence rates was seen (Newling et al, 1995). The results of this study are at odds with the results of one previously published in which pyridoxine did reduce the recurrence rate of superficial tumors (Byar and Blackhard, 1977).

Megavitamins

Despite the data just presented on the basis of observations in animal studies and of other human tumors implying that vitamins may be beneficial, Lamm and colleagues (1994) tested high-dose multivitamins (40,000 units vitamin A, 100 mg vitamin B_6, 2000 mg vitamin C, 400 units of vitamin E, and 90 mg zinc) against the recommended daily allowance (RDA) of these vitamins in a high-risk group of patients with superficial bladder cancer who simultaneously received intravesical BCG with or without percutaneous BCG administration. Patients receiving the megadose vitamin regimen did significantly better, with projected 5-year recurrences reduced from 91% in the RDA group to 41% in the megadose group (Lamm et al, 1994). This study has been questioned because of its small numbers (a total of 65 patients), its complex double randomization study design, the relatively poor performance of those in the RDA group, and the highly heterogeneous group of patients studied in terms of histologies and tumor histories. A much larger study testing the value of megadose versus RDA multivitamins in combination with BCG with or without interferon-alfa was started through industry sponsorship but closed because of accrual problems.

A further word of caution about the value of vitamins as bladder cancer preventatives has been offered by Nomura and colleagues (2003), who studied over 9000 Japanese American men in Hawaii who had serum frozen and were followed for development of bladder cancer over 20 years. Sera were analyzed for carotenoids, retinoids, and tocopherol levels by high-pressure liquid chromatography (HPLC). Patients who developed bladder cancer were compared with a matched group of controls who did not. No protective benefit was seen for the tocopherols, but while higher levels of several carotenoids correlated with a lower risk of developing bladder cancer, when adjusted for pack-years of cigarette smoking none of the protective effect remained for any vitamin A analog. Because the incidence of bladder cancer in Japanese American men is only 35% of that of whites in Hawaii, it is possible that had a similar study been performed in whites, other conclusions may have been reached. Appropriate correction for risk factors is critical in any analysis of cancer prevention or risk.

Polyamine Synthesis Inhibitors

Induction of activity of the enzyme ornithine decarboxylase (ODC), which controls the synthesis of the polyamine putrescine and its aminopropyl derivatives, spermidine and spermine, is an integral part of the process of tumor promotion (Boutwell, 1964; Bryan, 1983). In experimental bladder tumors in animals and in human bladder cells in culture, induced ODC activity is greater in malignant than in normal urothelium (reviewed in Loprenzi and Messing, 1992). Additionally, in malignant human urothelial tissues, both ODC activities and putrescine concentrations are higher than in normal urothelium (Messing et al, 1995a). Difluoromethylornithine (DFMO), an irreversible inhibitor of ODC, has been shown to inhibit experimentally induced bladder tumors and other experimental malignancies (reviewed in Loprenzi and Messing, 1992). This agent is actively excreted in urine and is very well tolerated. However, in a randomized trial of DFMO

(1 g/day) versus placebo in 453 patients with totally resected, newly diagnosed, or occasionally recurrent low-grade superficial bladder carcinoma, DFMO was unable to prevent the first bladder tumor recurrence. DFMO was not continued after the first recurrence as had been done in the etretinate study described earlier (Studer et al, 1995).

Dietary Factors

Another therapeutic approach that appears promising is using agents or dietary measures that can influence the urinary milieu. By doing so, urothelial exposure to endogenous and environmental tumor promoters, putative carcinogens, and mitogens may be influenced, perhaps altering susceptibility to developing bladder cancer. Fukushima and colleagues (1988, 1990) noted that saccharine-induced bladder cancer in rats was directly dependent on urinary pH and did not occur in animals with acidic urine. Additionally, the ligand-binding properties of receptors for growth factors like EGF are affected greatly by pH, with reduction in the affinity of the EGF receptor for EGF and TGF-α occurring at pH of 6.5 and lower (Messing, 1990). Patients with active bladder tumors have higher mean, median, minimal, and maximal pHs than do men with benign prostatic hyperplasia (and no urothelial cancer at cystoscopy) (Messing and Resnikoff, 1992). Thus, the potential role for urinary acidification as a preventive approach is theoretically attractive. Indeed, this effect may be responsible in part for any antitumor activity of agents discussed in this section.

High-fat diets and, particularly, diets high in cholesterol intake have been correlated with an increased relative risk of developing bladder cancer in epidemiologic studies (Steinbeck et al, 1990). In animal and human cultured bladder cancer cells and in transplantable bladder tumors in mice, a variety of soy products, including genestein, an inhibitor of growth factor receptor tyrosine kinase activity, inhibited cyclin-dependent kinase-2 activity and induced G2-M cell cycle arrest. Other soy isoflavones induced apoptosis and inhibited neoangiogenesis (Zhou et al, 1998; Su et al, 2000). Genestein's bladder cancer preventive properties are being studied in a phase II NCI-sponsored trial.

Green tea consumption has been reported to reduce the incidence of bladder cancer (Bianchi et al, 2000), perhaps because of the higher concentrations of polyphenolic catechins than in black or oolong tea. Epigallocatechin-3 gallate (EGCG), the most abundant catechin in green tea, has antioxidant and anti-angiogenic properties (Fujiki et al, 1992), and induces apoptosis and cell cycle inhibition for many tumors (Yang et al, 2000). Kemberling and colleagues (2003) showed that intravesical instillations of various concentrations of EGCG prevented tumor implantation and growth of the rat A9 bladder cancer cells in rats. Studies of oral EGCG as a bladder cancer preventative are now going on, and those of intravesical post-TUR instillations are being planned.

Not surprisingly, dilution of carcinogenic agents in the urine by increasing fluid ingestion might protect against bladder cancer—with a relative risk of 0.51 for the highest quartile of chronic fluid ingestion compared with the lowest (Michaud et al, 1999). This must be considered in assessing results of any prevention trial. In this regard, it should be recalled that hydration, to a large degree, raises urinary pH.

This provides a small glimpse of the complexities involved in trying to understand the mechanisms and/or predict the effects of any proposed preventive intervention.

Nonsteroidal Anti-Inflammatory Drugs

Several nonsteroidal anti-inflammatory drugs that primarily inhibit COX-mediated conversion of arachidonic acid to prostaglandins (PGs) have been found to interfere with a variety of cellular processes, including signal transduction pathways, cell proliferation, angiogenesis, adhesion to extracellular matrix molecules, and resistance to apoptosis in a variety of tumor systems (summarized in Taketo, 1998a, 1998b). Data also indicate that the inducible form of COX, COX-2, is preferentially upregulated in tumorous rather than normal epithelial tissues, including urothelium (Liebert et al, 1999). Furthermore, COX-2 is overexpressed in nearly 80% of bladder cancers, with overexpression correlating not only with angiogenesis (Friedrich et al, 2003a), altered expression of a variety of cell cycle regulators and E-cadherin but also with disease progression and cancer-specific mortality (Shahrokh et al, 2003). Additionally, expression of the enzyme that degrades PGs, 15-hydroxyPG dehydrogenase, is downregulated in bladder cancers (Liebert et al, 1999). Studies using low doses of the COX-1 and COX-2 inhibitors sulindac (Rao et al, 1996) and piroxicam alone (Moon et al, 1993; Okajima et al, 1997; Mohammed et al, 2002) or in combination with other chemopreventive agents (Okajima et al, 1997) have shown these agents to be effective in preventing chemically initiated bladder cancer in rodents and naturally occurring bladder cancer in dogs. This and other work (reviewed in Pruthi et al, 2003) has given the impetus for using the COX-2 inhibitor celecoxib, which is associated with less gastrointestinal toxicity than the nonspecific COX inhibitors, as a preventive agent in an ongoing prospective randomized trial in patients with recurrent and/or aggressive superficial bladder cancer who have had complete responses to TUR and an induction course of BCG.

Avoidance Strategies

It must be recognized that in any preventive approach, continued exposure to avoidable putatively carcinogenic agents, such as industrial chemicals or cigarette smoke, should be eliminated. This is the responsibility of counseling physicians, caring family members and friends, and, most importantly, the patients themselves. **In long-term follow-up of patients with superficial tumors who experience late aggressive recurrences, it is frequently patients who continue to smoke who suffer these consequences** (Thompson et al, 1993). Although for some agents the benefits of stopping exposure may take many years to be realized, for others, salutary effects can occur much sooner, which can be assessed by intermediate marker studies. For example, micronuclei are extranuclear fragments of chromosomes lost from the main nucleus at telophase and their quantities accurately measure DNA damage caused by exposure to genotoxic agents. As discussed previously, high arsenic concentrations in drinking water have been associated with bladder cancer in Taiwan, Chile, and Argentina. Moore and coworkers (1997) demonstrated that in individuals with high arsenic exposures, exposure to water with low arsenic levels for only 8 weeks reduced micronuclei excretion by 32% to 58% in all subjects and by 67% in smokers. Removing arsenic from drinking water in Taiwan has successfully reduced the incidence of bladder cancer in the endemic blackfoot disease regions as well.

KEY POINTS: PREVENTION

- Molecular and clinical data strongly imply that the two major forms of urothelial cancer (low grade and high grade) probably share common origins so that prevention of one type of cancer may well prevent the other type also.

- In the future, secondary prevention clinical trials should probably continue the preventive intervention after the first bladder tumor recurrence.

NONUROTHELIAL TUMORS OF THE BLADDER
Small Cell Carcinoma

It is believed that small cell carcinomas of the bladder are derived from neuroendocrine stem cells or dendritic cells. Small cell carcinomas may be mixed with elements of TCCs in the same tumor. They express neuroendocrine markers, such as staining positively for neuron-specific enolase. They are usually biologically aggressive tumors with early vascular and muscle invasion. Patients with small cell carcinoma should be evaluated for primary small cell carcinoma of the lung or the prostate, which may have metastasized or spread to the bladder (Swanson et al, 1988). In general, these are very aggressive malignancies that usually respond to, but are not cured by, cisplatin-containing chemotherapy regimens. Sved and colleagues (2004) recommended that these regimens be given first, even if the cancer can seemingly be removed surgically, and then additional local therapy (cystectomy, partial cystectomy, or radiation therapy) be performed in those who did not progress during chemotherapy. With such an approach, 40% (radiation therapy) to 65% (surgery) of patients can be "cured," while with extensive local therapies alone, only 5% (radiation) to 20% (surgery) of patients are.

Carcinosarcoma

Carcinosarcomas are highly malignant tumors containing malignant mesenchymal and epithelial elements. The mesenchymal elements are usually chondrosarcoma or osteosarcoma (Koss, 1975; Young, 1987). The epithelial elements may be TCC, SCC, or adenocarcinoma. These tumors are rare, usually occurring in middle-aged men. The common presenting symptom is gross, painless hematuria. The prognosis is uniformly poor despite aggressive treatment with cystectomy, radiation, and/or chemotherapy (Schoborg et al, 1980; Uyama and Moriwaki, 1981; Sen et al, 1985; Lopez-Beltram et al, 1998), although recently a favorable response to cisplatin/gemcitabine chemotherapy has been reported (Froehner et al, 2001).

Some urothelial cancers exhibit a prominent spindle cell component and are sometimes referred to as sarcomatoid carcinomas. These are also aggressive tumors with a poor prognosis, but they should not be confused with true carcinosarcoma (Young et al, 1988). Similarly, sarcomatoid inflammatory reactions may sometimes be confused with carcinosarcomas. As mentioned earlier, pseudosarcomatous reactions almost invariably occur in patients who have had bladder surgical procedures or severe infections within the past 6 months.

Metastatic Carcinoma

The bladder may be secondarily involved by cancers from virtually any other primary site. The most common primary sites are prostate, ovary, uterus, colon and rectum, lung, breast, kidney, and stomach; primary melanoma, lymphoma, and leukemia may also involve the bladder (Koss, 1975).

NONEPITHELIAL BLADDER TUMORS

One to 5 percent of all bladder tumors are nonepithelial in origin. The most common nonepithelial bladder tumors are reviewed in the following sections.

Neurofibroma

A neurofibroma is a benign tumor of the nerve sheath resulting from overgrowth of Schwann's cells. Multiple neurofibromas may occur as an inherited autosomal-dominant trait of variable penetrance (neurofibromatosis) (Torres and Bennett, 1966). In the bladder, neurofibromas arise from the ganglia of the bladder wall and usually stain positively for S-100 protein and type IV collagen by immunohistochemistry (Cheng et al, 1999d). Vesical neurofibromatosis often becomes clinically manifest in children or young adults with symptoms of urinary tract obstruction, urinary incontinence, vesical irritability, hematuria, or pelvic mass (Clark et al, 1977; Cheng et al, 1999d). Rarely, bladder neurofibromas may undergo malignant degeneration to form neurofibrosarcoma (Clark et al, 1977).

Pheochromocytoma

Bladder pheochromocytomas account for less than 1% of all bladder tumors and less than 1% of all pheochromocytomas (Albores-Saavedra et al, 1969). They arise from paraganglionic cells within the bladder wall, usually in the region of the trigone (Koss, 1975). There is no sex predilection, and the peak age of incidence is in the second through the fourth decades. About 10% of pheochromocytomas are malignant and have the capacity to metastasize to the regional lymph nodes or to distant sites. Malignancy is determined more by the clinical behavior than by the histologic features of the tumor. Most pheochromocytomas in the bladder are hormonally active, causing paroxysms of hypertension or syncope on filling and/or emptying of the bladder in two-thirds of patients. Hematuria develops in only about half of patients.

On cystoscopic examination, the tumor appears as a submucosal nodule covered by intact urothelium. Histologically, the tumors are composed of nests of polyhedral cells with eosinophilic cytoplasm. Partial cystectomy with complete excision of the tumor is the treatment of choice for patients with bladder pheochromocytomas. TUR is generally contraindicated because it may precipitate a hypertensive crisis. Perioperative management and follow-up are the same as for pheochromocytomas of other sites.

Primary Lymphoma

Primary bladder lymphoma arises in the submucosal lymphoid follicles (Koss, 1975) and is the second most common type of nonepithelial bladder tumor (Binkovitz et al, 1988). The peak age is 40 to 60 years, and women are affected more often than men. All histologic types of malignant lymphomas occur in the bladder, and management is the same as for lymphomas in other sites.

Plasmacytoma, Granular Cell Myoblastoma, Malignant Melanoma, Choriocarcinoma, and Yolk Sac Tumor

These rare primary bladder tumors exhibit the same characteristics as their counterparts in other sites of the body and are managed in a similar fashion.

Sarcoma

Malignant connective tissue tumors containing cell types that are normally present in the bladder include angiosarcoma and leiomyosarcoma.

Angiosarcoma and Hemangioma

Angiosarcomas are extremely rare tumors that arise within the bladder wall. Virtually all patients have macroscopic hematuria that is often massive and even life threatening (Engel et al, 1998). Histologically, they contain dilated vascular channels with prominent papillary endothelial proliferation (Koss, 1975). As many as 20% may arise from preexisting hemangiomas (Engel et al, 1998). These tumors metastasize rapidly to hematogenous sites and less commonly to regional nodes.

Hemangiomas are more common than angiosarcomas but remain quite rare lesions. They are usually diagnosed because they cause macroscopic hematuria. Hemangiomas are often quite small and usually can be managed by complete endoscopic resection. Recurrences and malignant degeneration are rare but can occur (Engel et al, 1998; Cheng et al, 1999b).

Leiomyosarcoma

Leiomyosarcoma is the most common malignant mesenchymal tumor that arises in the bladder of adults. It is twice as common in men as in women. Cystoscopically, it appears as a submucosal nodule or ulcerating mass. Histologically, spindle cells are arranged in parallel bundles. The presence of nuclear abnormalities distinguishes a leiomyosarcoma from a benign leiomyoma. Leiomyosarcomas require aggressive surgical extirpation (Tsukamoto and Lieber, 1991), but with such treatment, 5-year disease-specific survival is 62% (Rosser et al, 2003).

Rhabdomyosarcoma

Rhabdomyosarcomas may occur at any age but are most common in young children. Embryonal rhabdomyosarcomas in children characteristically produce polyploid lesions in the base of the bladder, giving rise to the descriptive term *sarcoma botryoides*. These typically have loss of chromosome 11p (Nigro and MacLennan, 2005). Adult rhabdomyosarcomas include three cell types: spindle cell, alveolar cell, and giant cell. Immunohistochemical stains for myogentin and myo-D1 are usually positive and quite specific for all types of rhabdomyosarcomas (Nigro and MacLennan, 2005). These aggressive tumors respond poorly to radiation therapy or chemotherapy, and, in general, the prognosis is poor (Koss, 1975; Tsukamoto and Lieber, 1991).

Other Sarcomas

The extremely rare liposarcomas, chondrosarcomas, and osteosarcomas of the bladder may occur alone or with malignant epithelial elements as a carcinosarcoma. Aggressive excisional management is usually required.

SUGGESTED READINGS

Boman H, Hedelin H, Jacobsson S, et al: Newly diagnosed bladder cancer: The relationship of initial symptoms, degree of microhematuria and tumor marker status. J Urol 2002;168:1955.
Cheng L, Gee J, Ulbright TM, et al: Precise microdissection of human bladder carcinomas reveals divergent tumor subclones in the same tumor. Cancer 2003;94:104.
Esrig D, Elmajian D, Groshen S, et al: Accumulation of nuclear p53 and tumor progression in bladder cancer. N Engl J Med 1994;331:1259.
Filbeck T, Pichlmeier U, Knuechel R, et al: Clinically relevant improvement of recurrence-free survival with 5-aminolevulinic acid induced fluorescence diagnosis in patients with superficial bladder tumors. J Urol 2002;168:67.
Hayes RB, Friedell GH, Zahm SH, Cole P: Are the known bladder cancer risk-factors associated with more advanced bladder cancer? Cancer Causes Control 1993;4:157.
Jewett HJ, Strong GH: Infiltrating carcinoma of the bladder: Relation of depth of penetration of the bladder wall to incidence of local extension and metastases. J Urol 1946;55:366.
Klemeney LA, Moret NC, Witjes JA, et al: Familial transitional cell carcinoma among the population of Iceland. J Urol 1997;157:1649.
Lynch CF, Cohen MB: Urinary system. Cancer 1995;75(Suppl):316.
Mao L, Lee DJ, Tockman MS, et al: Microsatellite alterations as clonal markers for the detection of human cancer. Proc Natl Acad Sci U S A 1994;91:9871.
Mellon K, Wright C, Kelly P, et al: Long-term outcome related to epidermal growth factor receptor status in bladder cancer. J Urol 1995;153:919.
Messing EM, Young TB, Hunt VB, et al: Comparison of bladder cancer outcome in men undergoing hematuria home screening versus those with standard clinical presentations. Urology 1995;45:387.
Oosterlinck W, Kurth KH, Schroder F, et al: A prospective European Organization for Research and Treatment of Cancer Genitourinary Group randomized trial comparing transurethral resection followed by a single intravesical instillation of epirubicin or water in single Ta, T1 papillary carcinoma of the bladder. J Urol 1993;149:749.
Stein JP, Cai J, Groshen S: Risk factors for patients with pelvic lymph node metastases following radical cystectomy with en bloc pelvic lymphadenectomy: Concept of lymph node density. J Urol 2003;170:35.
Younes M, Sussman J, True L: The usefulness of the level of the muscularis mucosae in the staging of invasive transitional cell carcinoma of the urinary bladder. Cancer 1990;66:543.

76 Non–Muscle-Invasive Bladder Cancer (Ta, T1, and CIS)

J. STEPHEN JONES, MD • STEVEN C. CAMPBELL, MD, PhD

Traditionally known as *superficial bladder cancer,* **malignant urothelial tumors that have not invaded the detrusor are more appropriately termed *non–muscle-invasive tumors*** (Epstein et al, 1998; Smith et al, 1999). The former term suggested that all such tumors shared the relatively benign course of low-grade papillary tumors, giving misleading reassurance to patients with the highly malignant subcategories of carcinoma in situ (CIS) and high-grade Ta and T1 lesions.

The presence of bladder cancer is usually suspected by hematuria. Patients with macroscopic (gross) hematuria have reported rates of bladder cancer of 13% to 34.5% (Lee and Davis, 1953; Varkarakis et al, 1974). Microscopic hematuria is associated with a 0.5% to 10.5% rate of bladder cancer (Golin and Howard, 1980; Mohr et al, 1986; Sultana et al, 1996; Khadra et al, 2000). The **presence of irritative voiding symptoms may double the risk, especially for CIS** (5% vs. 10.5%) (Mohr, 1986). The Mayo Clinic reported that 80% of patients with CIS presented with irritative symptoms (Zincke et al, 1985). In a review of 600 patients diagnosed with interstitial cystitis, 1% of the patients had a missed diagnosis of urothelial carcinoma. Of note, two thirds of these patients did not have hematuria (Tissot et al, 2004). Thus, **cystoscopy and upper tract imaging are indicated in patients with hematuria and/or unexplained irritative symptoms** (Grossfeld et al, 2001).

Approximately 70% of bladder tumors are non–muscle invasive at presentation. Of these, 70% present as stage Ta, **20% as T1, and 10% as CIS** (Fig. 76–1) (Ro et al, 1992). Most reports refer to tumor behavior after initial treatment (Heney et al, 1983a, 1983b; Fitzpatrick et al, 1986) or long-term follow-up after intravesical therapy (Nadler et al, 1994; Cookson et al, 1997).

Recurrence is common in all patients with non–muscle-invasive urothelial cancer but can often be controlled successfully with transurethral surgery, intravesical therapy, or a combination. In contrast, **patients can be divided into low or high risk for progression, which is the true concern. Low-grade Ta lesions are low risk, whereas all high-grade lesions (including CIS) are high risk.** The frequency of progression and death is shown in Table 76–1.

STAGING
Pathologic Grading

Although the World Health Organization (WHO) has determined that **the term *urothelial cancer* (UC) is preferable to the term *transitional cell cancer* (TCC),** the latter remains in widespread use. However, their recommendation to move away from the traditional grading system (1 to 3, from low grade to high grade) is now accepted by many urologists and pathologists. They recommend that **malignant tumors be classified as low grade or high grade, regardless of invasion status.**

In contrast, **papillary tumors with orderly cellular arrangement, minimal architectural abnormalities, and minimal nuclear atypia are distinct from those two grades and are designated papillary urothelial neoplasm of low malignant potential (PUNLMP).** Such tumors would have been labeled either papillomas or grade I TCC in older systems but are now regarded as so unlikely to progress that they are considered benign. However, based on this low risk, the WHO recommends that such pathology reports contain the note, "Patients with these tumors are at risk of developing new bladder tumors ('recurrence') usually of similar histology. However, occasionally these subsequent lesions manifest as UC, such that follow-up of the patient is warranted" (Epstein et al, 1998). Papillomas are truly benign and not associated with risk of progression (Figs. 76–2 to 76–5).

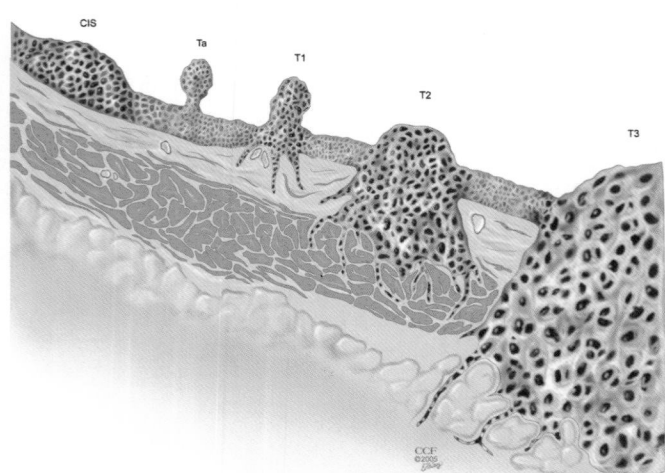

Figure 76–1. CIS is a high-grade, flat malignancy confined to the urothelium. Papillary tumors confined to the urothelium are Ta, whereas papillary tumors invading lamina propria are T1. The T1 tumor here intertwines with the wispy fibers of the muscularis propria but by definition does not invade the smooth muscle fibers of the detrusor. T2 tumors invade the detrusor muscle, and T3 tumors are into extravesical fat as shown.

Table 76–1. Estimates of Disease Progression in Non–Muscle-Invasive Bladder Cancer: WHO/International Society of Urological Pathology Consensus Classification

Tumor Type	% Relative Frequency	% Progression	% Deaths
Noninvasive			
Papilloma	10	0-1	0
PUNLMP	20	3	0-1
Papillary cancer low grade (TaG1)	20	5-10	1-5
Papillary cancer high grade (TaG3)	30	15-40	10-25
Invasive			
Papillary cancer (T1G3)	20	30-50	33
CIS			
Primary	10	>50	—
Secondary	90		

From Donat SM: Evaluation and follow-up strategies for superficial bladder cancer. Urol Clin North Am 2003;30:765-766.

Pathologic Staging

The bladder has three main histologic layers: (1) urothelium, (2) suburothelial loose connective tissue called lamina propria, and (3) detrusor or muscularis propria (which is absent beneath the urothelium of diverticula). Stage Ta denotes a papillary tumor confined to the urothelium. CIS (formally termed Tis) is a flat, high-grade lesion confined to the same layer, and T1 is a tumor invading lamina propria. The TNM grading system for non–muscle-invasive tumors is demonstrated in Figure 76–1.

The demarcation between "superficial" and "invasive" has sometimes been errantly considered between T1 and T2. However, **T1 tumors invade the lamina propria by definition**

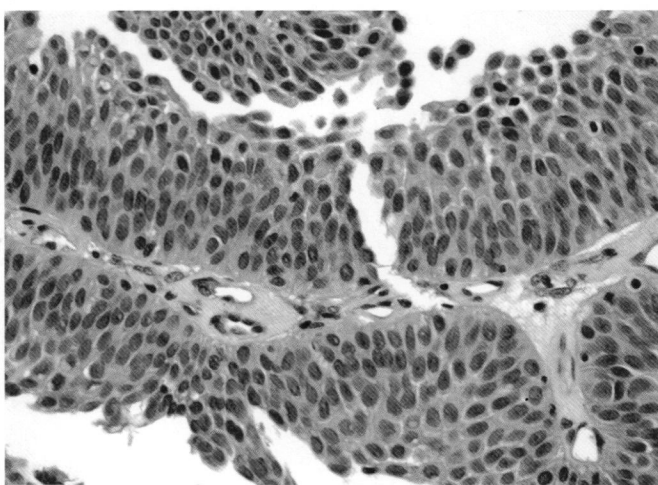

Figure 76–2. The urothelium is thickened, but cells and nuclei are normal in papillary urothelial neoplasm of low malignant potential (×40).

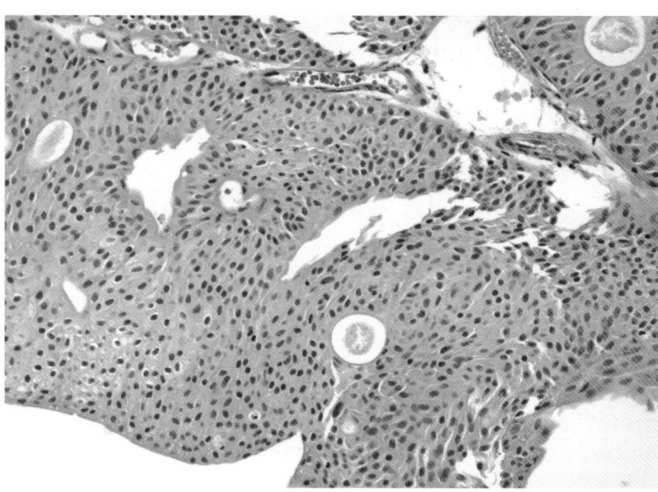

Figure 76–3. Low-grade Ta tumor. Cells are relatively normal but exhibit irregularity and some nuclear differentiation (×40).

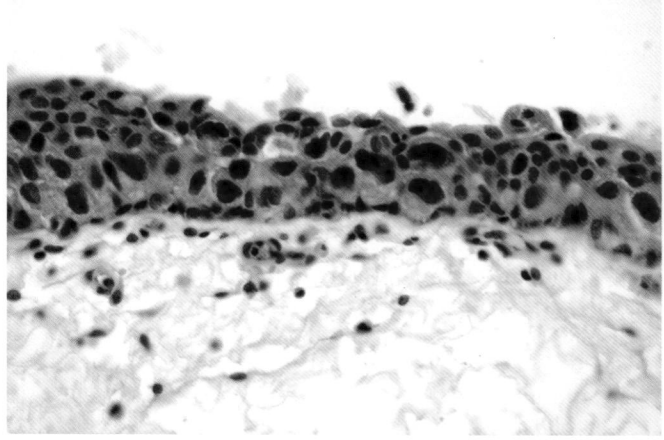

Figure 76–4. CIS exhibits severe irregularity of cellular structure and nuclear pleomorphism, but there is no invasion of lamina propria (×40).

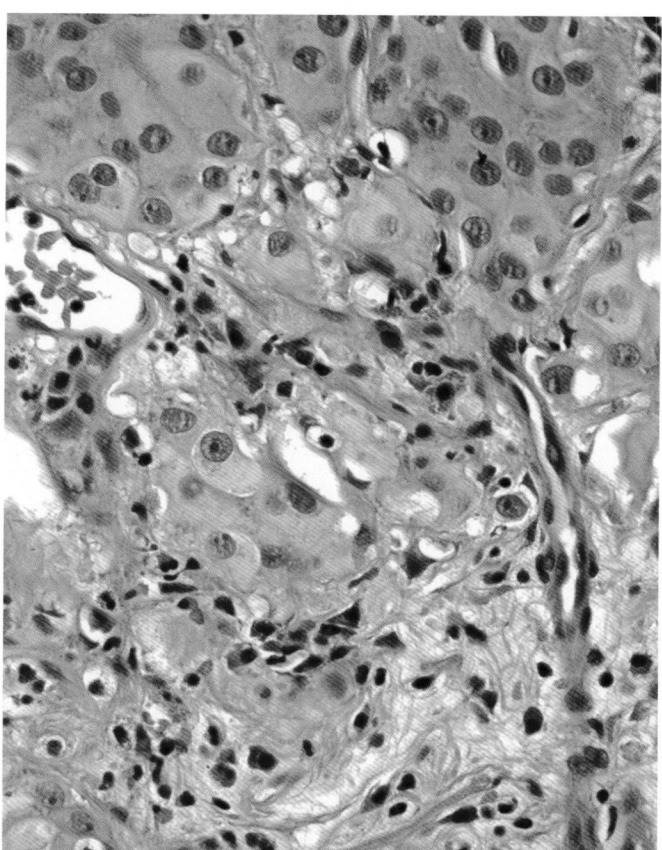

Figure 76–5. High-grade T1 tumor exhibits nesting of abnormal cells and mitotic figures. Tumor cells can be seen invading the lamina propria in the lower one third of the photomicrograph (×40). (All photomicrographs Courtesy of Cristina Magi-Galluzzi, MD, PhD.)

so cannot be accurately characterized as "noninvasive." Unlike the urothelium, which is devoid of vessels or lymphatics, the lamina propria is rich in both, providing opportunity for metastasis. These tumors sometimes invade the wispy and discontinuous muscularis mucosae of the lamina propria, which can be confused for muscularis propria (detrusor) during pathologic interpretation. **Imprecise verbiage on the pathology report can lead the urologist to misinterpret invasion of muscularis mucosae to be "muscle invasive,"** risking overstaging error. Direct communication between urologist and pathologist when this occurs is essential.

Deep lamina propria invasion carries a substantially more serious prognosis in some reports, and some have proposed these be subcategorized as T1b (Younes et al, 1990). However, the value of substaging has not been validated in other studies, so the 1998 Bladder Cancer Consensus Conference Committee rejected the concept (Platz et al, 1996; Epstein et al, 1998).

Tumor Biology

Low-grade tumors rarely invade the lamina propria or detrusor, so invasive tumors may be almost equated with high-grade histology. However, tumors of all grades and degrees of potential aggressiveness can be identified before invasion of the muscularis propria, so no such grading assumption can be made about these lesions.

Low-grade Ta lesions recur at a rate of 50% to 70% and progress in approximately 5% of cases. In contrast, high-grade T1 lesions recur in more than 80% of cases and progress in 50% of patients within 3 years. This behavior is primarily grade, rather than stage, dependent, because patients with high-grade tumors progressed with similar frequency regardless of whether they were invasive (T1) or noninvasive (Ta) (Herr, 2000a). **Prognosis also correlates with tumor size, multiplicity, papillary versus sessile configuration, presence or absence of lymphovascular invasion, and status of the remaining urothelium** (Althausen et al, 1976; Lutzeyer et al, 1982; Heney et al, 1983a, 1983b).

The variance in biologic behavior for low-grade versus high-grade lesions correlates with the known dual molecular lines of genetic development for these two pathways and supports the concept that **high-grade and low-grade cancers may be considered as essentially different diseases** (Hasui et al, 1994; Droller, 2005). **Chromosomal alterations caused by oxidative DNA damage create two separate genetic pathways to the development of UC** (Spruck et al, 1994; Richter et al, 1997; Cote and Chatterjee, 1999). The first and more common (low grade) leads to noninvasive, papillary tumors. These usually follow an indolent course unless they convert to or are associated with a tumor of the second pathway (Kiemeney et al, 1993).

The second pathway leads to the development of high-grade cancer, including CIS, T1, and, ultimately, muscle-invasive carcinoma. Such genetic alterations can be evaluated using karyotyping, microsatellite analysis for allelic imbalance (Mao et al, 1996), comparative genomic hybridization (Kallioniemi et al, 1995), DNA ploidy analysis by flow cytometry (Bittard et al, 1996), and fluorescent in-situ hybridization (FISH) (Degtyar et al, 2004). These evaluations can show that **low-grade papillary tumors tend to exhibit relatively few chromosomal abnormalities, primarily involving loss of all or part of chromosome 9 (particularly the q arm). In contrast, high-grade tumors tend to have numerous and greatly variable chromosomal gains and losses. In addition to their relatively predictable aneuploidy, high-grade tumors can also lose all or part of chromosome 9** (Richter et al, 1997). Although almost any chromosome can be affected, aneuploidy of chromosomes 7, 9, and 17 is associated with especially aggressive tumors (Olumi et al, 1990; Waldman et al, 1991; Degtyar et al, 2004).

Because of these differing genetic imprints, it has been suggested that papillary pTa tumors could almost be considered benign and might be a completely separate disease entity than high-grade tumors (Sauter et al, 1998). Nevertheless, high-grade and low-grade lesions are known to coexist. UC is traditionally considered a field change disease, with tumors arising at different times and sites. Rarely, patients who initially have low-grade tumors will subsequently develop high-grade tumors, often years after the original tumors (Prout et al, 1992).

Pathologic Characteristics by Stage and Implications for Clinical Staging Errors

Stage Ta tumors are usually low grade. Although recurrence is common, especially in the setting of multiplicity, progression is rare. However, **2.9% to 18.0% of Ta tumors are high grade, with an average of 6.9%** (Sylvester et al, 2005). **Their most important risk factor for progression is grade, not stage** (Norming et al, 1992; Millan-Rodriguez et al, 2000). Stein found little difference in survival when comparing noninvasive and muscle-invasive tumors as long as the cancer was confined to an organ (Stein et al, 2001). Because of their high risk of progressing, **high-grade stage Ta tumors should be followed as high risk** (Sylvester et al, 2005).

CIS is occasionally mischaracterized as "premalignant" (Sylvester et al, 2005), **but it is actually a flat, noninvasive UC that is high grade by definition.** Although confined to the urothelium in the same manner as stage Ta, **CIS is regarded as a precursor lesion for the development of invasive high-grade cancer.**

CIS lesions are composed of severely dysplastic urothelium. Microscopically, the slide will demonstrate disorderly histology with nuclear atypia characteristic of high-grade malignancy; denudement of some or all of the mucosa due to loss of cellular cohesion sometimes complicates interpretation. A pathology report read as dysplasia or atypia can create confusion. Most pathologists consider mild versions of these entities to be benign. However, **lesions interpreted as severe dysplasia or severe atypia are regarded as being the same entity as CIS** (Epstein et al, 1998). Again, meticulous communication between pathologist and urologist can minimize the risk for misinterpretation.

Between 40% and 83% of patients with CIS will develop muscle invasion if untreated, especially if associated with papillary tumors (Althausen et al, 1976). Among patients thought to have CIS alone, as many as 20% who are treated with cystectomy are found to contain invasion on final pathology (Farrow et al, 1976). The presence of CIS in cystectomy specimens performed for presumed T1 tumors was associated with upstaging in 55% of patients in a recent series, compared with 6% upstaging in patients without CIS (Masood et al, 2004). **In a series of 1500 patients, CIS was the second most important prognostic factor after grade** (Millan-Rodriguez et al, 2000). Multicentricity presents another ominous characteristic of CIS (Koch et al, 1996). The presence of irritative voiding symptoms has been associated with diffuse disease, invasion, and a compromised prognosis, but there is no consensus on this finding in the literature (Smith et al, 1999; Sylvester et al, 2005).

T1 tumors are usually papillary; a nodular or sessile appearance suggests deeper invasion. Deep penetration into the lamina propria, especially if involving muscularis mucosae, increases the risk of recurrence and progression in some reports. Lymphovascular invasion increases the risk as well (Lotan et al, 2005). **Hydronephrosis usually indicates muscle invasion.**

There is significant potential for understaging in patients with non–muscle-invasive tumors, especially for those that appear to be stage T1. Many tumors are found to be more extensive than the transurethral resection (TUR) specimen indicated when patients undergo cystectomy. **Stein reported that one third of patients believed to have non–muscle-invasive disease at the time of cystectomy were found to actually have muscle invasion, only half of which were organ confined.** Metastases were already present in 8% of these patients (Freeman et al, 1995). His subsequent review noted that

Table 76–2. Risk of Understaging When Cystectomy Is Performed for Presumed Non–Muscle-Invasive Disease

Study	Institution	Risk (%) of Understaging
Ghoneim et al, 1997	Urology and Nephrology Center, Mansoura, Egypt	62
Stein et al, 2001	University of Southern California	39
Dutta et al, 2001	Vanderbilt University	40
Bianco et al, 2004	Wayne State University	27
Bayraktar et al, 2004	Vakif Gureba Hospital Urology Department Aksaray-Istanbul, Turkey	50
Huguet et al, 2005	Servicio de Urologia, Fundacion Puigvert, Barcelona	27
Ficarra et al, 2005	University of Verona, Italy	43

understaging errors from 34% to 62% have been reported (Stein, 2003). Studies from the past decade addressing the risk of understaging of T1 tumors are shown in Table 76–2.

Although it is likely that the patients who underwent cystectomy had more serious risk factors than those who did not, these data offer compelling evidence that the term *superficial* to describe all such lesions is misleading.

KEY POINTS: STAGING

- Malignant tumors are now classified as low grade or high grade, regardless of invasion.

- High-grade and low-grade cancers may be regarded as essentially separate diseases from genetic development, biologic behavior, and management standpoints.

- The most important risk factor for progression is grade, not stage.

- Papillary tumors with orderly cellular arrangement, minimal architectural abnormalities, and minimal nuclear atypia are designated papillary urothelial neoplasm of low malignant potential (PUNLMP).

ENDOSCOPIC SURGICAL MANAGEMENT

When bladder cancer is identified during office-based cystoscopy, the location, number, and nature of tumors is recorded, as is involvement of areas likely to reflect extravesical extension such as the ureteral orifices and bladder neck/prostatic urethra. Urinary cytology is obtained as a baseline and to establish the likelihood of high-grade disease. Positivity will encourage random bladder biopsy at the time of TUR as discussed below.

Upper tract imaging is usually performed both to identify other sources of hematuria and to assess the extravesical urothelium due to the "field change" nature of UC that can affect such cells throughout the urinary tract. **Expert consensus is that patients with solitary or limited low-grade Ta** lesions do not need imaging, owing to the very low risk of extravesical disease (Goessl et al, 1997; Oosterlink et al, 2005).

TUR of bladder tumor (TURBT) under regional or general anesthesia is the initial treatment for visible lesions and is performed both to remove all visible tumors and to provide specimens for pathologic examination to determine stage and grade. Bimanual examination of the bladder should be performed under anesthesia before prepping and draping unless the tumor is clearly small and noninvasive and should be repeated after resection. Fixation or persistence of a palpable mass after resection suggests locally advanced disease. An increase in abdominal girth or fullness after resection indicates intraperitoneal perforation.

Complete visualization to plan the resection is facilitated by either the flexible cystoscope or preferably the 70-degree rod lens, which allows maintenance of the anatomic relationships. Resection is performed using a 30-degree lens placed through a resectoscope sheath, because this deflection allows visualization of the loop placed at this location. **Continuous irrigation with the bladder filled only enough to visualize its contents minimizes bladder wall movement and lessens thinning of the detrusor through overdistention** (Koch and Smith, 1996). **Video TUR allows magnification, facilitates resident teaching, allows documentation of findings, and reduces the risk of body fluid exposure to the surgeon** (Manoharan and Soloway, 2005; Nieder et al, 2005). Resection is performed piecemeal, delaying transection of any stalk until most tumor is resected in order to maintain countertraction. **Friable, low-grade tumors can often be removed without the use of electrical energy,** because the nonpowered cutting loop will break off most segments. This minimizes the chance of bladder perforation. Higher-grade, more solid tumors and the base of all tumors require the use of cutting current; cautery yields hemostasis once all tumor is resected. **Lifting the tumor edge away from detrusor lessens the chance of perforation** (Holzbeierlein and Smith, 2000). Repeated slow fulguration may complicate the ability of the pathologist to determine grade or invasion status.

After all visible tumor is resected, an additional pass of the cutting loop or a cold cup biopsy can be obtained to send to pathology separately to determine the presence of muscle invasion of the tumor base. A chip evacuator gathers the specimen. Final confirmation of hemostasis in the presence of minimal irrigation after all chips are removed through vigorous irrigation is helpful.

Traditionally, TUR has been performed in sterile water, because saline solutions conduct electricity and disperse energy from the monopolar cautery cutting loop. Glycine is more expensive, and there is no evidence of its benefit compared with water (Holzbeierlein and Smith, 2000). Recent introduction of **bipolar electroresection is reported to allow transurethral resection in saline (TURIS) and to minimize the risk of the obturator reflex that can predispose to bladder perforation** (Shiozawa et al, 2002; Miki et al, 2003). **The use of general anesthesia with muscle-paralyzing agents also prevents obturator reflex.** This can also be accomplished by direct injection of 20 to 30 mL of local anesthetic (lidocaine) into the obturator nerve and its canal, but few centers have experience with this.

Resection of diverticular tumors presents significant risk of bladder wall perforation and accurate staging is difficult to achieve in this circumstance because the underlying detrusor is absent. Invasion beyond the lamina propria immediately involves perivesical fat, or stage T3a. Resection in diverticula will almost inevitably lead to perforation. Low-grade tumors are best treated with a combination of resection and fulguration of the base. Conservative resection can be followed with repeat resection if the final pathologic interpretation is high grade. High-grade tumors require adequate sampling of the tumor base, often including perivesical fat, despite the near-certainty of bladder perforation. An indwelling catheter allows healing. **Partial or radical cystectomy should be strongly considered for high-grade diverticular lesions.**

Anterior wall tumors and tumors at the dome in patients with large bladders can be difficult to reach. Minimal bladder filling combined with manual compression of the lower abdominal wall to bring the tumor toward the resectoscope facilitates removal. Modern resectoscopes are long enough to reach the entirety of most bladders; creation of a temporary perineal urethrostomy offers deeper access but is rarely needed except in the obese patient with an inaccessible tumor. Digital manipulation through the rectum or vagina can occasionally facilitate resection.

Care must be taken during resection near the ureteral orifice to prevent obstruction from scarring after fulguration. **Pure cutting current causes minimal scarring and may be safely performed, including direct resection of the orifice if necessary.** Resection of the intramural ureter can lead to complete eradication of the tumor but risks reflux of malignant cells. The clinical implications of this are unclear (Palou et al, 1992).

Alternatively, **small tumors may be resected using the cold cup biopsy forceps** alone. This is especially helpful in the thin-walled bladder of elderly women, who are predisposed to perforation due to their thin-walled bladder. If perforation occurs, the cup causes a smaller hole than does the cutting loop. A Bugbee electrode facilitates hemostasis. **A successful cauterization method involves placing the Bugbee electrode inside the biopsy site with the bladder under minimal distention. Touching the cut surface of the biopsy crater, the electrical energy will cause the mucosa to contract around the electrode unless the bladder is full.** Light irrigation clears the area of blood and vaporization bubbles created during fulguration. **Visualizing a small (1 to 2 mm) ring of white coagulation confirms hemostasis and yields less damage to the bladder than that occurring when the biopsy area is "painted" with cautery.** Removing the electrode from the site before discontinuing the energy current lessens the chance of pulling the fresh clot off as the Bugbee electrode separates from the urothelium.

If a tumor appears to be muscle invasive, biopsies of the borders and base in order to establish invasion may be performed in lieu of complete resection, because cystectomy will likely follow based on confirmatory biopsies. Failure to demonstrate invasion necessitates repeat resection unless the decision is made to proceed to cystectomy-based factors other than muscle invasion.

Complications of TURBT

Minor bleeding and irritative symptoms are common side effects in the immediate postoperative period. The major complications of uncontrolled hematuria and clinical bladder perforation occur in less than 5% of cases, although a majority of patients will exhibit contrast agent extravasation indicative of minor perforation if cystography is performed. The **incidence of perforation can be reduced by attention to technical details, avoiding overdistention of the bladder, and using anesthetic paralysis during the resection of significant lateral wall lesions to lessen an obturator reflex response. Moreover, large, bulky tumors and those that appear to be muscle invasive are often best resected in a staged manner** because it is believed that repeat resection can more safely remove residual tumor if indicated.

The vast majority of perforations are extraperitoneal, but intraperitoneal rupture is possible when resecting tumors at the dome (Collado et al, 2000). The risk of tumor seeding due to perforation is not widely reported but appears to be low (Balbay et al, 2005). Anecdotal reports have identified extravesical recurrences after perforation, theoretically due to seeding (Mydlo et al, 1999). It has been suggested that the risk of tumor seeding is higher in patients who undergo open repair, but this may be related to patient selection because only serious intraperitoneal perforations are likely to be managed in this manner (Mydlo et al, 1999; Skolarikos et al, 2005).

Management of extraperitoneal perforation is usually possible by prolonged urethral catheter drainage. Intraperitoneal perforation is less likely to close spontaneously and often requires open or laparoscopic surgical repair. Decisions for surgical correction should be made on the basis of the extent of the perforation and the clinical status of the patient.

TUR syndrome from fluid absorption is uncommon. As long as resection of the ureteral orifice is done with pure cutting current, scarring is minimal and obstruction unlikely. Cystoscopy to visualize efflux (which is occasionally aided by intravenous administration of indigo carmine or methylene blue, which will color the urine when excreted) or upper tract imaging can determine presence or absence of obstruction. Balloon dilation of the orifice or endoscopic incision can correct the situation, but failure to respond may require reimplantation (Chang et al, 1989).

Repeat TURBT

Complete tumor removal is not always possible, whether due to excessive tumor volume, anatomic inaccessibility, medical instability requiring premature cessation, or risk of perforation. However, even in the absence of these circumstances repeat TUR is often indicated. When repeat TUR is performed within several days to several weeks of the original resection, residual tumor is identified at the site of the initial resection at least 40% of the time (Klan et al, 1991; Mersdorf et al, 1998; Vogeli et al, 1998). In a review, Miladi and associates (2003) found that a second TURBT performed within 6 weeks of the initial resection detected residual tumor in 26% to 83% of cases and corrected clinical staging errors in half of those cases. The potential for understaging high-risk disease ranged from 18% to 37% (Amling et al, 1994).

Repeat TURBT is usually appropriate in the evaluation of T1 tumors, because a repeat TUR can demonstrate worse prognostic findings in up to 25% of specimens (Schwaibold et al, 2000). **This is especially likely if no muscle is identified** on initial pathology, which can occur in almost half of cases. **The Vanderbilt University group reported a 64% risk of understaging T1 lesions when muscle was absent, compared with 30% when muscle was present in the specimen** (Dutta et al, 2001). Herr (1999) reported that a second resection changed treatment in one third of cases. Importantly, survival was 63% in patients who underwent a second TURBT versus 40% for those who did not in a German observational study (Grimm et al, 2003). The efficacy of bacillus Calmette-Guérin (BCG) in preventing progression appears to be higher in patients with high-grade papillary tumors and CIS if a restaging TURBT was performed before instillation of BCG (Herr, 2005).

There appears to be variability in completeness of resection among surgeons. In patients with multiple tumors who had adjuvant treatment, recurrence rates varied between 7.4% and 45.8% depending on the surgeon (Brausi et al, 2002). **Repeat resection is helpful in the setting of a second opinion unless clear evidence of muscle invasion is identified on the initial resection,** or if the outside pathology slides are not available for review.

Consensus is that patients with pT1 and high-grade Ta tumors merit repeat resection. There is no consensus on timing of repeat TURBT, but most authors recommend 1 to 4 weeks after the initial resection (Nieder et al, 2005).

The Role of "Random" or Additional Biopsies

Biopsies of any suspicious areas are an important part of a complete evaluation. Cold-cup biopsies may not provide as much information regarding muscular invasion but provide tissue sampling without cautery artifact that can interfere with pathologic interpretation (Soloway et al, 1978; Smith, 1986).

Based on the understanding that CIS can exist in normal-appearing urothelium, some authors advocate the use of random biopsies to identify CIS in otherwise normal-appearing mucosa. This remains controversial. May and colleagues (2003) performed random biopsies in high-risk patients and found that the results were positive in 12.4% and altered treatment in 7%, including 14 of 1033 patients in whom the only positive tissue was in the random biopsy, not the primary resected tumor. However, even when velvety red patches were sampled, only 11.9% of biopsies were positive in one report (Swinn et al, 2004). A European Organisation for Research and Treatment of Cancer (EORTC) retrospective review found that 10% of random biopsies were positive (3.5% CIS) and concluded such biopsies were not warranted (van der Meijden et al, 1999). Fujimoto and coworkers (2003) prospectively evaluated the role of random biopsies of normal-appearing urothelium and found cancer in only 8 of 100 biopsy samples, 5 of which were CIS. They concluded that random biopsies are indicated only in the setting of multiple tumors or positive cytology. **The current consensus is that random biopsies are not indicated in low-risk patients,** that is, those with low-grade papillary tumors and negative cytology.

Prostatic urethral biopsy using the cutting loop may be performed, especially if neobladder creation is anticipated for high-risk disease, but bleeding may be more common

(Holzbeierlein and Smith, 2000). The additional value of the information obtained from cold cup and urethral biopsies must be weighed against the theoretical risk that biopsies provide an exposed bed to aid tumor implantation (Mufti and Singh, 1992; Kiemeney et al, 1994; Yamada et al, 1996). Traditional teaching is that TUR of the prostate (TURP) and TURBT of a low-grade bladder tumor may be performed at the same setting but that resection of a high-grade bladder tumor should not be resected coincident to TURP to avoid tumor seeding and possible intravasation of tumor cells likely to metastasize. Despite anecdotal reports of low-grade tumors implanting in the prostatic urethra after simultaneous resection, this risk appears to be small; and the literature does not adequately address the risk of metastasis in this setting (Tsivian et al, 2003).

Perioperative Intravesical Therapy to Prevent Tumor Implantation

It is believed that tumor cell implantation immediately after resection is responsible for many early recurrences and this has been used to explain the observation that initial tumors are most commonly found on the floor and lower side walls of the bladder, whereas recurrences are often located near the dome (Heney et al, 1981). Thus, intravesical chemotherapy to kill such cells before implantation has been used (Zincke et al, 1983; Klan et al, 1991).

Mitomycin C (MMC) appears to be the most effective adjuvant intravesical chemotherapeutic agent perioperatively. Consistent with its proposed mechanism of action to prevent tumor cell implantation, a single dose administered within 6 hours lessens recurrence rates, whereas a dose 24 hours later does not (Isaka et al, 1992; Sekine et al, 1994; Solsona et al, 1999; Duque and Loughlin, 2000), **and maintenance therapy does not reduce the risk further** (Bouffioux et al, 1995; Tolley et al, 1996). **Nevertheless, the level 1 data in support of single-dose MMC immediately after resection are compelling** (Table 76–3).

Oosterlinck and colleagues (1993) demonstrated that an immediate 80-mg instillation of epirubicin compared with

---

Table 76–3. Successful Perioperative Administration of Intravesical Chemotherapy

1. Include intent to administer perioperative chemotherapy (and agent) on actual operative schedule.
2. Contact pharmacy prior to case to have medication available. A written prescription may be required.
3. After resection, confirm absence of clinical perforation. Place 3-way catheter into bladder while patient is still in operating room. Attach inflow port to saline infusion bag and clamp inflow.
4. Administer chemotherapeutic agent through catheter outflow port in recovery room within 6 hours of operation and clamp outflow tubing with hemostat to allow retention.
5. Give order for outflow tubing to be opened 1 hour after administration and for irrigation, to be opened to gravity drainage for next 30 to 60 minutes.
6. Remove Foley catheter and discard in biohazard container.
7. Wear gloves.

Modified from O'Donnell MA: Practical applications of intravesical chemotherapy and immunotherapy in high-risk patients with superficial bladder cancer. Urol Clin North Am 2005;32:121-131.

---

one of saline decreased the recurrence rate by nearly 50%. In a three-arm study of 452 patients that compared TUR alone versus one immediate dose of MMC versus one dose of MMC and five further administrations every 3 months, it was shown that the single immediate dose decreased recurrence rates by approximately 50% and increased the recurrence-free interval. Additional instillations yield minimal benefit (Tolley et al, 1996). A meta-analysis found that low-risk patients at a median follow-up of 3.4 years experience an approximate 39% drop in the odds of recurrence (i.e., from 47% to 36%). Patients with multiple tumors experience a 56% reduction in the odds of recurrence. MMC, epirubicin, and pirarubicin all significantly lessened the recurrence of both single and multiple tumors (thiotepa did not show the same benefit, but data were limited and some studies used dilute strengths) (Sylvester et al, 2004).

Although local irritative symptoms are the most common complications of postoperative instillation, serious sequelae and rare deaths have occurred, especially in patients with perforation during resection (Oddens et al, 2004).

BCG can never be safely administered immediately after, because the risk of bacterial sepsis and death is high. Chemotherapy should be withheld in patients with extensive resection or when there is concern about perforation.

Laser Therapy

Laser coagulation allows minimally invasive ablation of tumors up to 2.5 cm in size. The **neodymium:yttrium-aluminum-garnet (Nd:YAG) laser has the best properties for use in bladder cancer.** Lesions can be coagulated until nonviable through protein denaturation using a straight or 90-degree noncontact "free beam" laser using power output of up to 60 W. Unless higher energy is needed for a very large tumor, **limiting energy to 35 W precludes exceeding 60°C on the outer bladder wall, minimizing the risk of perforation** (Hofstetter et al, 1994). **The most efficient delivery appears to be an end-fire noncontact fiber with a 5- to 15-degree angle of divergence, which allows variable penetration depth of up to 5 mm** (Smith et al, 1989; Holzbeierlein et al, 2000).

Laser therapy can be more expensive than resection due to the cost of laser fibers, but bleeding is negligible and there is no risk of obturator reflex. Small lesions can be treated easily using intravesical anesthesia. Because there is no tissue available for pathologic inspection, the optimal candidate for laser therapy is the patient with recurrent, low-grade lesions whose biology is already known. Additional information regarding tumor grade may be obtained with a cold cup biopsy if needed. Some reports suggest lower recurrence rates using laser compared with TURBT, but this remains inconclusive (Smith et al, 1983; Malloy et al, 1984; Beisland and Seland, 1986; Smith, 1986; Beer et al, 1989).

Holmium:yttrium-aluminum-garnet (YAG), argon, and potassium titanyl phosphate (KTP) lasers ablate tissues by cutting (vaporization) and thus have limited applicability due to lack of deep coagulation (Johnson et al, 1991; Benson, 1992; Holzbeierlein and Smith, 2000). The carbon dioxide laser is completely absorbed by fluid so is not appropriate for use in the treatment of bladder cancer (Benson, 1992).

The most significant complication of laser therapy is forward scatter of laser energy to adjacent structures, resulting in perforation of a hollow, viscous organ such as overlying bowel. This is rare but most commonly occurs with the neodymium:YAG laser because of its deeper tissue penetration than with holmium:YAG and KTP lasers (Smith, 1986).

Office-Based Endoscopic Management

Many patients with small (<0.5 mL) low-grade recurrences can be managed safely in the office setting using diathermy or laser ablation under intravesical local anesthetic (Donat et al, 2004). Instillation of viscous or injectable 1% to 2% lidocaine through a catheter and a dwelling time of 15 to 30 minutes yields satisfactory mucosal analgesia. Pain with fulguration of 1- to 2-mm tumors is often acceptable with no analgesia. A tissue diagnosis and a negative cytology for the initial tumor occurrence is mandatory to determine whether the tumor is of high or low grade.

Additionally, many small, low-grade tumors can be safely observed until they exhibit significant growth due to the minimal risk of progression (Soloway et al, 2003; Soloway, 2006). These conservative approaches can obviate the need for anesthesia and use of hospital-based resources for small, low-grade recurrences.

Fluorescent Cystoscopy

Endoscopically, urologists can suspect malignancy based only on the presence of visible changes such as tumors or "red spots." As noted, random biopsy of normal-appearing areas sometimes detects unsuspected malignancy, usually CIS. Moreover, a multicenter study found that 37% of the biopsies performed based on suspicious endoscopic findings resulted in false-negative biopsy (Riedl et al, 2001; Sarosdy et al, 2002). The imperfect sensitivity of cystoscopy potentially explains the high rate of cancer recurrence soon after complete removal of all visible tumors (tumor cell implantation also contributing as described earlier). It is likely that cancer was already present but not visible at the time of resection and simply became visible in follow-up when it became morphologically abnormal enough to differentiate from adjacent normal urothelium. Thus, the false-positive and false-negative rates for cystoscopy are notable.

Photoactive porphyrins accumulate preferentially in neoplastic tissue. Under blue light they emit red fluorescence, which can help in the diagnosis of indiscernible malignant lesions. Hematoporphyrin derivatives must be administered systemically and can cause lengthy, residual cutaneous photosensitization. Intravesical application of 5-aminolevulinic acid (5-ALA), a precursor of photoactive porphyrin, avoids residual systemic photosensitization and has improved the detection of bladder tumors. Modifications of 5-ALA may allow deeper tissue penetration and improved accumulation in neoplastic cells (Lange et al, 1999). A more lipophilic ester, hexaminolevulinate (HAL), is the most studied agent.

When using this technology, both small papillary tumors and almost one third more cases of CIS overlooked by cystoscopy are identified (Jichlinski et al, 2003; Schmidbauer et al, 2004). Of all tumors, 96% were detected with HAL imaging compared with 77% using standard cystoscopy. Detection was

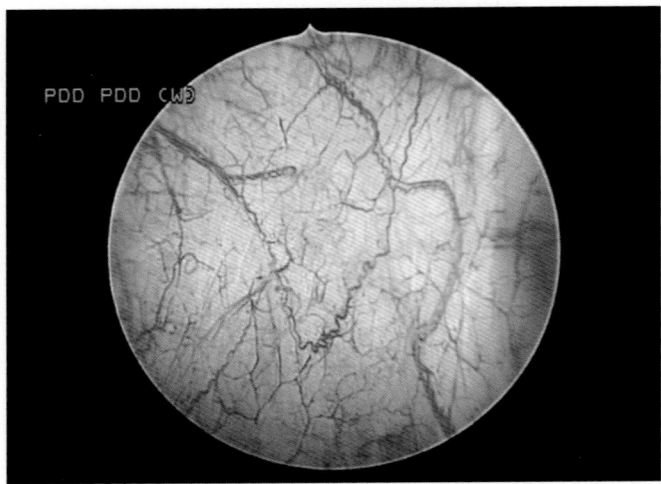

Figure 76–6. White light microscopy reveals normal-appearing mucosa. (Courtesy of H. Barton Grossman, MD.)

improved for dysplasia (93% vs. 48%), CIS (95% vs. 68%), and papillary tumors (96% vs. 85%) (Jocham et al, 2005). The clinical impact of improved tumor detection seems obvious, although there is limited prospective evidence to date that this decreases recurrence rates in patients who undergo HAL fluorescent cystoscopy compared with controls (Filbeck et al, 2003).

Intravesical HAL for use with fluorescent cystoscopy received approval for use in Europe in 2004. A multinational study is underway to determine the actual impact on recurrence rates prior to approval in North America (Figs. 76–6 and 76–7).

KEY POINTS: ENDOSCOPIC SURGICAL THERAPY

- TURBT is performed both to remove all visible tumors and to provide specimens for pathologic examination to determine stage and grade.

- Repeat resection is often indicated in patients with high-grade disease and will be positive for residual cancer in many cases, especially if no muscle was present in the initial TURBT.

- Single-dose intravesical chemotherapy administered within 6 hours of resection reduces recurrence rates by up to 50%.

- All suspicious lesions should be sampled, but "random" biopsies are not required in low-risk patients.

- Office-based fulguration and observation may be applied to certain low-risk patients.

- Fluorescent cystoscopy with 5-ALA derivatives improves the ability to visualize inconspicuous tumors.

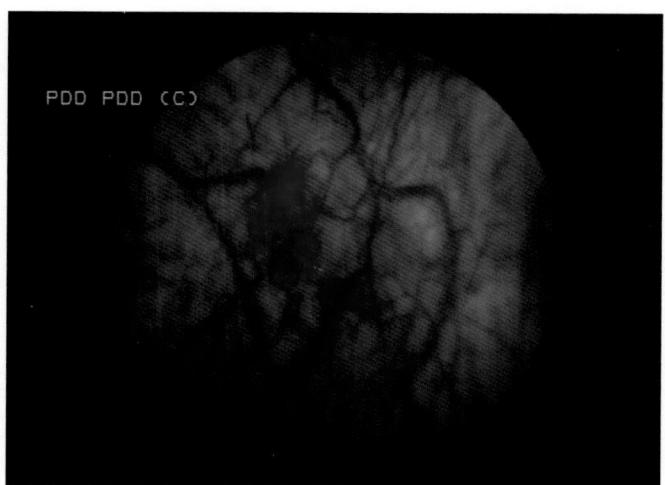

Figure 76–7. Blue light microscopy of the same site shown in Figure 76–6 reveals accumulation of hexaminolevulinate in an area proven subsequently to contain a small focus of CIS. (Courtesy of H. Barton Grossman, MD.)

IMMUNOTHERAPY

Intravesical immunotherapy results in a massive local immune response characterized by induced expression of cytokines in the urine and bladder wall and by an influx of granulocytes and mononuclear cells. The mechanism of action has been intensively investigated. **The initial step appears to be direct binding to fibronectin** within the bladder wall, subsequently leading to direct stimulation of cell-based immunologic response. Numerous cytokines involved in the initiation or maintenance of inflammatory processes, including tumor necrosis factor-α, granulocyte-macrophage colony-stimulating factor, interferon (IFN)-γ, and interleukin (IL)-1, IL-2, IL-5, IL-6, IL-8, IL-10, IL-12, and IL-18, have been detected in the urine of patients treated with intravesical BCG. **The observed pattern of cytokine induction with preferential upregulation of interferon-γ and IL-2 reflects induction of a Th1 response.** This immunologic response activates cell-mediated cytotoxic mechanisms that are believed to underlie the efficacy of BCG in the prevention of recurrence and progression (Bohle and Brandau, 2003).

Bacillus Calmette-Guérin

BCG is an attenuated mycobacterium developed as a vaccine for tuberculosis that has demonstrated antitumor activity in several different cancers, including UC (Morales et al, 1976). The original regimen described by Morales and colleagues included a percutaneous dose, which was discontinued after success using a similar intravesical regimen by Brosman (1982).

BCG is stored in refrigeration and reconstituted from a lyophilized powder. Connaught, Tice, Armand Frappier, Pasteur, Tokyo, and RIVM strains all arise from a common original strain developed at the Pasteur Institute. The vaccine is **reconstituted with 50 mL of saline and should be administered through a urethral catheter under gravity drainage soon thereafter because aggregation occurs** (Ratliff et al, 1994b). **Treatments are generally begun 2 to 4 weeks after**

tumor resection, allowing time for reepithelialization to minimize the potential for intravasation of live bacteria (Lamm, 1992b). **In the event of a traumatic catheterization, the treatment should be delayed for several days. After instillation, the patient should retain the solution for 2 hours.** Some clinicians have advocated the patient turn from side to side to bathe the entire urothelium, but there is no scientific support for this practice. Fluid, diuretic, and caffeine restriction has been recommended to limit dilution of the agent and to facilitate retention of the agent for 2 hours. Oral desmopressin, 200 μg, given 1 hour before administration has also been suggested (Cliff et al, 2000). Patients are instructed to clean the toilet with bleach, although there is no demonstrable risk of close contact infection.

BCG Treatment of Carcinoma in Situ (CIS)

American urologists use BCG by a 2:1 margin compared with intravesical chemotherapy, whereas European urologists favor chemotherapy. BCG is approved for this indication by the U.S. Food and Drug Administration (FDA). **The initial tumor-free response rate is as high as 80%** (Brosman, 1982; DeJager et al, 1991; Lamm 1992a, 1992b; Hudson and Herr, 1995). **Approximately 50% of patients experience a durable response for a median period of 4 years. Over a 10-year period, approximately 30% of patients remain free of tumor progression or recurrence, so close follow-up is mandatory. The majority of these occur within the first 5 years** (Herr et al, 1992). **Herr (1989) reported progression in 19% of initial responders at 5 years but found the rate to be 95% in non-responders—findings confirmed by other investigators** (Coplen et al, 1990; Harland et al, 1992). **The American Urological Association (AUA) Guidelines Panel supported BCG as the preferred initial treatment option for CIS** (Smith et al, 1999).

BCG has gained a preeminent role in North America based on higher efficacy reports compared with intravesical chemotherapy. In over 600 patients, there was a 68% complete response rate to BCG and a 49% complete response rate to chemotherapy. In responders, 68% of patients treated with BCG remained disease-free as compared with 47% of patients receiving chemotherapy, based on a median follow-up of 3.75 years. The overall disease-free rates were 51% and 27%, respectively (Sylvester et al, 2005).

BCG Treatment of Residual Tumor

Intravesical **BCG can effectively treat residual papillary lesions but should not be used as a substitute for surgical resection.** Investigators have demonstrated a nearly 60% response by residual tumor with intravesical BCG alone (Brosman, 1982; Schellhammer et al, 1986; Coplen et al, 1990).

Carcinoma of the mucosa or the superficial ducts of the prostate can be adequately treated by BCG with a 50% tumor-free rate. A limited TURP can be effective in decreasing tumor burden and facilitating exposure of the prostate surface to BCG administration. Tumor-free rates of 50% can be attained (Bretton et al, 1990).

BCG Prophylaxis to Prevent Recurrence

Early single-center studies demonstrated an advantage in decreased tumor recurrence of approximately 30% when a 6-week course of BCG was administered after recovery from TURBT (Brosman, 1982; Morales et al, 1992). In several larger series, tumor recurrence after TURBT was reduced by 20% to 65%, for an average of approximately 40% (Pagano et al, 1991a, 1991b; Herr et al, 1992; Melekos et al, 1993; Krege et al, 1996).

The efficacy of BCG after TURBT for high-risk papillary disease has been demonstrated in several series of T1 lesions, with recurrence rates of 16% to 40% and progression rates of 4.4% to 40%, a substantial improvement compared with TUR alone (Cookson and Sarosdy, 1992; Pansadoro et al, 1995; Herr, 1997; Jimenez-Cruz et al, 1997; Gohji et al, 1999; Hurle et al, 1999a, 1999b). Tumor multiplicity and associated CIS were associated with increased risk of progression. Substaging lesions based on the presence or absence of muscularis mucosae invasion in a series of 49 patients did not improve prediction of recurrence (69% vs. 65%) or progression (22% vs. 29%) after BCG therapy (Kondylis et al, 2000).

Impact of BCG on Progression

Although reports of the impact of BCG on tumor recurrence are important and compelling, the greater need from a survival standpoint is the potential for impact on progression in these patients. In 403 patients with CIS, BCG reduced the risk of progression by 35% compared with intravesical chemotherapy (Sylvester et al, 2002).

In a randomized trial of 86 patients with high-risk superficial disease, **Herr and coworkers** (1988) **demonstrated a greater delay in interval progression for BCG patients versus TUR controls.** Additionally, the cystectomy rate was significantly decreased for CIS patients treated with BCG (11% vs. 55% for controls), as was the time to cystectomy. However, only 27% of patients were alive with an intact functioning bladder after follow-up over 10 to 15 years, so this apparent advantage is temporary in many cases (Cookson et al, 1997). Available data suggest that BCG can delay progression of high-risk bladder cancer, yet the long-term advantage of this therapy cannot be adequately assessed.

Two separate meta-analyses have reached the conclusion that BCG reduces the risk of progression. Progression at 2.5 years' median follow-up was reduced by 27% (9.8% for BCG vs. 13.8% for non-BCG) in one analysis (Sylvester et al, 2002) and by 23% (7.7% for BCG vs. 9.4% for MMC) at 26-month median follow-up in another study (Bohle and Bock, 2004). In both cases the **superior results with BCG were only seen in trials using BCG maintenance therapy. In contrast, no chemotherapy trials have achieved a significant reduction in progression.** Nevertheless, proof of a survival advantage associated with BCG remains hypothetical.

Nuclear P53 overexpression before BCG therapy has not been shown to predict response to therapy, but post-therapy P53 overexpression is an independent marker of disease progression (Lacome et al, 1996; Lebret et al, 1998).

Determining Optimum BCG Treatment Schedule

The optimal treatment schedule and dose for BCG have not been established. Morales wrote in the reply to an editorial comment to his landmark article (see box), "This regimen is arbitrary, and may be modified in the future as additional data become available" (Morales et al, 1976). In reality, **several studies suggest that a 6-week induction course alone is insufficient to obtain an optimal response in many patients.**

One of the enduring urban myths in urology is the story of Dr. Alvaro Morales' initial work with BCG. Although the rumor is usually stated that he chose the dosing regimen based on the fact the drug is shipped in a "6-pack," he relates that there is more to the story:

"A contemporary abstract had indicated that BCG was ineffective for bladder cancer. However, from our experience and that of others, we knew that at least a 3-week period of immunizations was needed for mounting a delayed hypersensitivity reaction. The intradermal administration provided not only assurance of an enhanced systemic recognition, but also an inexpensive and readily available marker of immune competence. To this day, I remain convinced that eliminating the simultaneous transdermal administration is very convenient for patients and physicians, but is not as effective. It was our impression that the skin reactions reached by weeks 4-5 were not further enhanced by more BCG. The Frappier labs provided us with boxes of 6 vials. We thus—for better or worse—decided to stop treatment at 6 weeks assuming that what was seen on the skin was occurring on the bladder mucosa. Fortunately, that turned out to be true. Bohle and others reported years later that 6 weeks were ideal for maximum response to BCG, although we now know that maintenance dosing enhances response even further."

The average additional response to a second induction course is 25% in those patients treated for prophylaxis and 30% in CIS patients (Haaff et al, 1986a, 1986b; Kavoussi et al, 1988; Bretton et al, 1990; Coplen et al, 1990; Sylvester et al, 2002; Bohle and Bock, 2004). However, **additional courses of BCG to treat refractory patients after a second 6-week course are accompanied by a significant risk of tumor progression in 20% to 50% of patients** (Nadler et al, 1994). Catalona and colleagues (1987) reported roughly a 7% actuarial risk of progression with every additional course of BCG therapy. Response to BCG at 6 months can be used as a predictor of prognosis, with the number of patients developing progressive disease being significantly higher among nonresponders (Orsola et al, 1998).

The Southwest Oncology Group (SWOG) reported the most significant impact of maintenance therapy. Patients received a 6-week induction course followed by three weekly instillations at 3 and 6 months and every 6 months there-

after for 3 years. **Estimated median recurrence-free survival was 76.8 months in the maintenance arm and 35.7 months in the control arm ($P = .0001$).** Average recurrence-free survival was 111.5 months in the control arm and not able to be estimated in the maintenance arm ($P = .04$). Overall 5-year survival was 78% in the control arm and 83% in the maintenance arm. No toxicities above grade 3 were observed, yet only **16% of patients tolerated the full dose-schedule regimen. Two thirds of the patients who stopped BCG due to side effects did so in the first 6 months, suggesting that the side effects do not increase appreciably with additional time on therapy.** An interpretation that the intended full course of maintenance therapy cannot be accomplished in most patients due to side effects misses the bigger point. Because the treatment group fared better despite most patients failing to complete the full course of therapy, the maximum benefit may have been achieved earlier, and shorter maintenance schedules may accomplish the same results with less toxicity (Lamm et al, 2000b).

Although some older studies failed to identify a benefit to maintenance therapy (Badalament et al, 1987), most authorities believe that at least 1 year of maintenance therapy is appropriate. The determination of whether the optimal treatment schedule should be as described in the SWOG study or monthly remains unclear (Lamm et al, 2000; O'Donnell, 2005).

Several investigators have evaluated the potential for BCG dose reduction (Morales et al, 1992; Melekos et al, 1993; Martinez-Pineiro et al, 1995; Pagano et al, 1995). **In general, a decrease in toxicity with no statistical difference in efficacy has been noted in small series** (Pagano et al, 1991b; Mack and Frick, 1995; Hurle et al, 1996), although multifocal and **high-grade tumors may respond better to full dosing** (Martinez-Pineiro et al, 2002). Lengthening of the instillation interval may decrease side effects without loss of efficacy (Bassi et al, 2000). European studies, where BCG inoculation for tuberculosis is more common than in North America, suggest the dose may be safely reduced by half (Martinez-Pineiro et al, 2002). The difference in response to doing so in immunologically naive North Americans is unknown, but Morales and associates (1992) found a significant decrease in response rates (67% vs. 37%) especially for patients with CIS in combination with papillary tumors treated with the reduced dose.

Antibiotic therapy may have a beneficial effect in treating or preventing systemic side effects of BCG therapy, yet it may also inhibit the effectiveness of BCG therapy if it is given routinely for urinary tract prophylaxis during a course of BCG therapy (Durek et al, 1999a, 1999b). **Quinolones in particular may affect the viability of BCG and should be avoided if possible during the course of BCG treatments.** In contrast, in vitro data suggest that quinolone antibiotic therapy may augment intravesical chemotherapy with agents such as doxorubicin because both agents affect topoisomerase II inhibitors (Kamat et al, 1999) (Tables 76–4 and 76–5).

Interferon

Interferons are glycoproteins produced in response to antigenic stimuli. Interferons have multiple antitumor activities, including inhibition of nucleotide synthesis; upregulation of tumor antigens, antiangiogenic properties; and stimulation of

Table 76-4. **Contraindications to BCG Therapy**

Absolute Contraindications

Immunosuppressed and immunocompromised patients
Immediately after transurethral resection based on the risk of intravasation and septic death
Personal history of bacillus Calmette-Guérin (BCG) sepsis
Gross hematuria (intravasation risk)
Traumatic catheterization (intravasation risk)
Total incontinence (patient will not retain agent)

Relative Contraindications

Urinary tract infection (intravasation risk)
Liver disease (precludes treatment with isoniazid if sepsis occurs)
Personal history of tuberculosis
Poor overall performance status
Advanced age

No or Insufficient Data on Potential Need for Contraindications

Patients with prosthetic materials
Ureteral reflux
Anti-tumor necrosis factor medications (theoretically predispose to BCG sepsis) (Ehlers, 2005)

cytokine release with enhanced T and B cell activation, as well as enhanced natural killer cell activity (Naitoh et al, 1999). Among several subtypes, interferon-α has been the most extensively studied. It is most active in doses of at least 100 million units, although optimal dose and administration schedule have yet to be determined (Belldegrun et al, 1998; Torti et al, 1988).

Interferon as a solitary agent is more expensive and less effective than BCG or intravesical chemotherapy in eradicating residual disease, preventing recurrence of papillary disease, and treating CIS (20% to 43% complete response). Its long-term efficacy for CIS is less than 15% (Belldegrun et al, 1998). A multicenter randomized trial demonstrated CIS responses from 5% at low doses (10 million units) to as high as 43% at high doses (100 million units) (Torti et al, 1988). As a prophylactic agent, interferon alone demonstrated recurrence rates that were generally inferior to those of BCG alone (from 60% to 16%) (Glashan, 1990; Kalble et al, 1994). It has demonstrated limited activity against T1 tumors (Malmstrom, 2001). However, it can occasionally be effective in patients who have failed BCG (15% to 20% complete response (see later).

Interferon-α has also been studied in a combination treatment regimen with either chemotherapy or BCG (Bercovich et al, 1995; Stricker et al, 1996). There appeared to be additive effects with either epirubicin or MMC. **Several trials investigated the combination of BCG and interferon and suggested the potential superiority of the combination or the possibility of decreasing the dosage of BCG, which may reduce side effects.** However, there are no data to demonstrate equivalent efficacy of BCG with interferon compared with BCG alone as initial treatment, and BCG remains standard therapy for frontline management of high-risk disease.

Investigational Immunotherapeutic Agents

Keyhole-limpet hemocyanin (KLH) is a copper-containing, antigenic protein from the hemolymph of the mollusk

Table 76–5. Cleveland Clinic Approach to Management of BCG Toxicity

Grade 1: Moderate symptoms < 48 hr

Mild/moderate irritative voiding symptoms, mild hematuria, fever <
38.5°C

Assessment

Possible urine culture to rule out bacterial urinary tract infection

Symptom Management

Anticholinergics, topical antispasmodics (phenazopyridine), analgesics,
nonsteroidal anti-inflammatory drugs

Grade 2: Severe symptoms and/or > 48 hr

Severe irritative voiding symptoms, hematuria, or symptoms lasting >
48 hr
All maneuvers for grade 1, plus:

Assessment

Urine culture, chest radiograph, liver function tests

Management

Timely infectious disease consultation with physician experienced in
management of mycobacterial infections/complications
Consider dose reduction to one half to one third of dose when
instillations resume.
Treat culture results as appropriate.

Antimicrobial Agents

Isoniazid and rifampins, 300 mg/day and 600 mg/day, orally until
symptom resolution
Monotherapy not recommended
Observe for rifampin drug-drug interactions (e.g., warfarin, many
others).

*Grade 3: Serious complications (hemodynamic changes, persistent
high-grade fever)*

Allergic Reactions (joint pain, rash)

Perform all maneuvers described for grades 1 and 2, plus:
Isoniazid, 300 mg/day, and rifampin, 600 mg/day, for 3 to 6 months
depending on response

*Solid Organ Involvement (epididymitis, liver, lung, kidney, osteomyelitis,
prostate)*

Isoniazid, 300 mg/day, rifampin, 600 mg/day, ethambutol, 15
mg/kg/day single daily dose for 3 to 6 months
Cycloserine often causes severe psychiatric symptoms and is to be
strongly discouraged.
BCG is almost uniformly resistant to pyrazinamide, so this drug has no
role.
Consider prednisone, 40 mg/day, when response is inadequate or for
septic shock (*never* given without effective antibacterial therapy).

Megathura crenulata. It is a nonspecific immune stimulant whose potential effectiveness in UC was identified serendipitously by Olsson and associates (1974), and Jurincic and colleagues (1989) reported it may be more effective than MMC in small series. Although it is less effective than BCG, KLH is significantly less toxic and may have a role as an alternative biologic response modifier. In a recent multicenter study, response was seen in 50% of patients with CIS, 20% of patients with residual papillary disease, and 33% of patients with both CIS and residual Ta and T1 tumors (Lamm et al, 2003).

Bropirimine is an oral arylpyridinone that is excreted in urine. It is an inducer of host interferon and induces natural killer cell and tumor necrosis factor. It demonstrated a 23% to 55% complete response in patients with CIS, but a SWOG

study failed to show enhancement of BCG efficacy (Sarosdy et al, 1992, 1996, 1998, 2005).

Mycobacterial cell wall DNA extract contains a mixture of immunostimulatory DNA attached to antigenic cell wall. Phase 2 trial results indicate success rates less than that achieved with BCG, but with good tolerability and safety to allow potential administration in the setting of a disrupted urothelium (Morales et al, 2001).

Thiosulfinate extracts of garlic were demonstrated to inhibit tumor growth in older studies and may have an immunostimulatory role (Riggs et al, 1997; Lamm and Riggs, 2001). Interleukin-12 is highly expressed after BCG stimulation and is a key component of the Th1 immune response. Preclinical data suggest a potential benefit and little toxicity (Horinaga et al, 2005). Several recent reports have suggested immunostimulatory activity of mistletoe extract (Elsasser-Biele et al, 2005).

KEY POINTS: IMMUNOTHERAPY

■ Intravesical BCG has higher efficacy against CIS and disease recurrence than intravesical chemotherapy, but more frequent and potentially more serious side effects must be considered.

■ Most evidence suggests that BCG is also superior for initial management of high-grade Ta and T1 disease.

■ BCG is not recommended for patients with low-risk disease because of concern about side effects.

■ BCG is the only agent shown to delay or reduce high-grade tumor progression.

■ The optimum dosage and the treatment schedule for BCG are undetermined, but results are better with at least 1 year of maintenance therapy if tolerated.

■ BCG is contraindicated in the setting of a disrupted urothelium because of the risk of intravasation and septic death.

■ Interferon-α has not been shown to have benefit compared with BCG for primary treatment but appears to work well in combination with BCG, especially for salvage.

INTRAVESICAL CHEMOTHERAPY

Induction therapy using chemotherapeutic agents instilled within 6 hours of TURBT has demonstrated a clear impact on recurrence rates, as described earlier. However, the role of chemotherapy in the adjuvant setting is less clear. Multiple reports show reduction of recurrent tumors and response to CIS, but **a SWOG comparison of doxorubicin and BCG showed a 15% progression rate in BCG patients compared with a 37% progression rate in chemotherapy patients** (Lamm et al, 1991). Nevertheless, the risk of BCG infectious complications is nonexistent with chemotherapy, leading many in the European community to favor this approach.

BCG is relatively inexpensive in most countries, whereas MMC is usually very expensive. However, local manufacture of MMC in Taiwan and some other countries allows this agent

Table 76–6.   Comparisons between Intravesical Agents

Agent	MW	Peri-op Use	Risk Group	Cystitis (%)	Other Toxicity	Dropout (%)	Concentration/ Dosage	Cost*
Doxorubicin (Adriamycin)	580	Yes	Low-Intermediate	20-40	Fever, allergy, contracted bladder, 5%	2-16	50 mg/50 mL	$36
Epirubicin	580	Yes	Low-Intermediate	10-30	Contracted bladder rare	3-6	50 mg/50 mL	$595
Thiotepa	189	Yes	Low-Intermediate	10-30	Myelosuppression 8%-19%	2-11	30 mg/30 mL	$80
Mitomycin	334	Yes	Low-Intermediate	30-40	Rash 8%-19%, contracted bladder 5%	2-14	40 mg/20-40 mL	$130
BCG	N/A	No	Intermediate-High	60-80%	Serious infection, 5%	5-10	1 vial/50 mL	$150
Interferon	23,000	No	Salvage	<5%	Flu-like symptoms 20%	Rare	50-100 MU/50 mL	$670-$1340
Gemcitabine	300	Yes	Salvage	Mild	Occasional nausea	<10	1-2 g/50-100 mL	$540-$1080

Based on 2005 discount acquisition costs from oncology supply distributors.
Adapted from O'Donnell MA: Practical applications of intravesical chemotherapy and immunotherapy in high-risk patients with superficial bladder cancer. Urol Clin North Am 2005;32:121-131.

to be provided at 11.6% to 35.8% the cost of imported BCG (Tang and Chang, 2006).

The agents are summarized in Table 76–6.

Mitomycin C

Mitomycin C is a 334-kD alkylating agent that inhibits DNA synthesis. The drug is usually instilled weekly for 6 to 8 weeks at dose ranges from 20 to 60 mg. A meta-analysis of nine clinical trials compared its efficacy on progression with that of BCG. Within median follow-up of 26 months, **7.67% of the patients in the BCG group and 9.44% of the patients in the MMC group developed tumor progression** (Bohle 2004). **Another review found a 38% reduction in tumor recurrence with MMC. This was not as effective as BCG but was considered in most studies to make MMC a viable option in light of its lesser side effects, particularly the low but real risk of sepsis** (Huncharek et al, 2001).

Optimization of MMC delivery can result in halving of the recurrence rate in some studies. This can be achieved by eliminating residual urine volume, overnight fasting, using sodium bicarbonate to reduce drug degradation, and increasing concentration to 40 mg in 20 mL (Au et al, 2001). The use of local microwave therapy in conjunction with MMC, 20 mg/50 mL, reduced recurrence rates from 57.5% to 17.1% in a multicenter trial. A trial using microwave with higher doses of 40 to 80 mg for 6 to 8 weeks in high-grade bladder cancer found a recurrence-free rate of 75% at 2 years (Gofrit et al, 2004; van der Heijden et al, 2004).

Electromotive intravesical MMC appears to improve drug delivery into bladder tissue. Di Stasi and associates (2003) reported reduction in recurrence rates from 58% to 31%, whereas patients in the BCG arm had a 64% recurrence rate. Peak plasma MMC was significantly higher in the electromotive group, supporting its reputed mechanism of action.

Doxorubicin and Its Derivatives

Doxorubicin (Adriamycin) is a 580-kD anthracycline antibiotic that acts by binding DNA base pairs, inhibiting topoisomerase II, and inhibiting protein synthesis. In a review, **doxorubicin demonstrated a 13% to 17% improvement over TUR in preventing recurrence but no advantage in prevent-**

ing tumor progression (15.2% vs. 12.6%) (Kurth et al, 1997). The principal side effect of intravesical doxorubicin is chemical cystitis, which can occur in up to half of patients. Reduced bladder capacity has been reported in several series (Thrasher and Crawford, 1992).

The **doxorubicin derivative epirubicin decreases recurrence compared with TUR alone by 12% to 15%** (Oosterlinck et al, 1993). This has been demonstrated when epirubicin is given in a single, immediate, perioperative dose as well as in full 8-week courses of intravesical therapy. Epirubicin is available for UC in Europe and FDA approved but is unavailable for treatment of UC in the United States.

Valrubicin is a semisynthetic analog of doxorubicin that has been approved by the FDA for treatment of BCG refractory CIS in patients who cannot tolerate cystectomy, but the drug is not currently available in the United States (Sweatman et al, 1991; Greenberg et al, 1997). In a cohort of 90 patients with BCG-refractory CIS, 21% (19 of 90) demonstrated a complete response (Steinberg et al, 2000).

Thiotepa

Thiotepa (triethylenethiophosphoramide) is the only chemotherapeutic agent approved by the FDA specifically for the intravesical treatment of papillary bladder cancer. It is an alkylating agent and is not cell cycle specific. In controlled clinical trials (N = 950 patients), it has been shown to significantly **decrease tumor recurrence in 6 of 11 studies by up to 41% (mean decrease, 16%).** Systemic side effects can be seen owing to its low molecular weight of 189 kD, resulting in up to half of administered doses being absorbed (Thrasher and Crawford, 1992).

Novel Agents

Gemcitabine and the taxanes paclitaxel and docetaxel have demonstrated activity against metastatic bladder cancer (Calabro et al, 2002). Intravesical gemcitabine can be safely administered either weekly or twice weekly for six to eight treatments. Minimal systemic absorption occurs through the bladder. Several small phase I and phase II studies have demonstrated reduction of recurrence of 39% to 70%, including modest efficacy in heavily pretreated BCG-refractory patients (Maymi et al, 2004; O'Donnell, 2005). Taxanes have been formulated into an active intravesical treatment, but current published data are limited to preclinical studies (Le Visage et al, 2004).

Most gene therapy studies are preclinical or early phase I investigations (Siemens et al, 2000). Replacement strategies for P53 and RB are areas of interest. Novel vectors such as poxvirus and suicide gene strategies are also under investigation (Gomella et al, 1997; Sutton et al, 1997). Antisense technology has shown promise in vitro and in animal studies (So et al, 2005). Additionally, research has been directed toward the genetic modification of therapeutic agents such as BCG.

Combination Therapy

Combining mechanisms of different agents is a logical and often successful approach to improve response rates for systemic therapy. However, studies have not identified clear benefit to doing so in intravesical therapy. For instance, in the study by Fukui and coworkers (1992), MMC (20 mg) was administered on day 1 and doxorubicin (40 mg) on day 2 once a week for 5 weeks in 101 patients. Fifty-one patients demonstrated a complete response and were further randomized to maintenance or no maintenance. Local side effects were significant in 50% of patients. Patients with CIS had fewer recurrences with maintenance therapy. Other studies demonstrated similar outcomes, with a **general theme of increased local side effects with modest outcome** improvement (Isaka et al, 1992; Sekine et al, 1994).

Combination chemotherapy and BCG was evaluated in prospective trials by several investigators. The EORTC reported a 46% complete response rate when a solitary marker tumor was intentionally not resected and patients were subsequently given sequential MMC and BCG (van der Meijden et al, 1996). In a study of 188 patients with Ta and T1 lesions, no difference was seen with regard to recurrence, progression, or side effects in those patients treated with BCG and MMC compared with those treated with MMC alone. There was actually a significantly longer disease-free interval in the BCG monotherapy arm (55%) compared with the same combination arm (45%) in another study of 314 patients (Solsona et al, 2002; Malmstrom et al, 1999). Thus, **no clear advantage is obtained with sequential therapy, combination chemotherapy or chemotherapy and BCG regimens using any of the combinations explored to date** (Rintala et al, 1995, 1996; Witjes et al, 1998a; Nieder et al, 2005).

MANAGEMENT OF REFRACTORY DISEASE
Salvage Intravesical Therapy

Recurrent or persistent disease after an initial 6-week course of BCG has been traditionally referred to as BCG failure, although this term has been poorly defined in the past. Current consensus is that **persistent disease after BCG therapy can be categorized as BCG-refractory (nonimproving or worsening disease despite BCG), BCG-resistant (recurrence or persistence of lesser degree, stage, or grade after an initial course, which then resolves with further BCG), or BCG-relapsing (recurrence after initial resolution**

with BCG). BCG-refractory patients in particular are an **especially high-risk group and should be strongly considered for immediate cystectomy if young and in generally good health** (Herr et al, 2003).

The necessity of biopsy to determine BCG response is unclear, although it should be strongly considered in high-risk patients to determine disease status at this key point in time. Urine cytology can be useful in this setting. Dalbagni reported minimal utility in routine biopsy after BCG if cystoscopy and urinary cytology were both negative. Whereas 5 of 11 patients with erythematous bladder mucosa and positive cytology had positive bladder biopsies, none of 37 with erythematous lesions and negative cytology was positive, and only 1 in 13 patients with a normal mucosa had positive biopsies (Dalbagni et al, 1999). Other studies have suggested that the value of routine post-BCG biopsy is limited (Highsaw et al, 2001). UroVysion FISH (Abbott Molecular, Chicago IL) conversion from positive to negative has been shown to correlate with BCG response in a single-center study (Kipp et al, 2005).

Declaring failure may take up to 6 months, because the response rate for patients with high-grade bladder cancer treated with BCG rose from 57% to 80% between 3 and 6 months after therapy. Clearly, the tumoricidal activity continued for some period after cessation of therapy. This has obvious implications not only for declaring BCG failure and the need for subsequent therapy but also for interpretation of success rates of salvage protocols if administered soon after therapy (Herr et al, 2003).

Whereas most urologists will administer an initial 6-week course of intravesical therapy for high-risk patients (most likely involving BCG in North America and chemotherapy in Europe), **management of patients with persistent disease after the first course is more complex. Such patients are at increased risk of progression, which is particularly likely in the event of early recurrence, progression while on therapy, or multiple recurrences.**

If the initial treatment was chemotherapy, a course of BCG should be undertaken. BCG has demonstrated superiority to chemotherapy in this setting, as the latter will lead to approximately 20% disease-free survival (Malmstrom et al, 1999; Steinberg et al, 2000). For patients who have failed BCG, a second course still gives a 30% to 50% response (Pansadoro et al, 1987; Brake et al, 2000). Patients who cannot tolerate BCG for any reason may be considered for salvage chemotherapy, but the risk of failure and progression is high.

Further courses of BCG or chemotherapy beyond two are not recommended routinely, as they will fail 80% of the time. Rapid disease progression is common in such patients, so salvage chemotherapy, investigational protocols, and interferons alone or in combination with reduced doses of BCG may only be appropriate for patients who are unwilling or unable to undergo surgery even after being informed of their risks (Catalona et al, 1987).

The combination of IFN-α with BCG is very expensive and has not been shown superior to BCG alone in primary therapy, so has been used mostly for BCG failures. Results have been encouraging. Small single-institution studies using low-dose BCG (typically one-third dose) plus 50 to 100 million units of IFN-α have demonstrated 1- to 2-year success rates of 50% to 60%, with better results with a second re-induction option and three sets of 3-week miniseries maintenance treatments 3, 9, and 15 months later (O'Donnell et al, 2001; Lamm et al, 2003; Punnen et al, 2003). A large national multicenter phase II trial of combination BCG plus IFN-α in BCG-naive and BCG-failure patients revealed similar findings (O'Donnell et al, 2004). Estimates for freedom from disease at 2 years were 57% for BCG-naive patients and 42% for BCG-failure patients. Progression was seen in only 8% of patients in each group, suggesting this combination has a potential role regardless of prior BCG response.

The Role of "Early" Cystectomy

Despite local therapy, **many cases of high-grade non–muscle-invasive bladder cancer will progress to invasion and risk of cancer death. Although the initial response rate to BCG therapy in CIS patients can be above 80%, those patients who fail have a 50% chance of disease progression and potential for disease-specific mortality** (Catalona et al, 1987; Nadler et al, 1994). **Early (3-month) failure for T1 tumors after BCG is associated with an 82% progression rate, compared with a 25% progression rate in patients who do not fail at 3 months** (Herr, 1997; 2000b). **Up to 20% of patients with CIS will die of UC within 10 years** (Herr, 1989). **Each occurrence of T1 tumors is associated with a 5% to 10% chance of metastasis** (Herr and Sogani, 2001). **These data offer compelling evidence of the potential to underestimate disease status in high-risk patients.**

Cookson and colleagues (1997) reported that 27% of high-risk patients treated initially with aggressive intravesical therapy did well and died of other causes, and the same low number survived with an intact, functioning bladder 15 years after diagnosis. However, over half of patients experienced progression, and one third died of their disease. In contrast, **patients who undergo immediate cystectomy for pathologic T1 tumors have accurate pathologic staging in addition to a 10-year disease-free survival of 92%, compared with 64% with those with clinical T1 tumors that were found to**

actually have muscle invasion at the time of cystectomy (Bianco et al, 2004).

Despite the benign connotation of the term *superficial* formerly applied, up to 50% of patients with presumed non–muscle-invasive disease who undergo cystectomy will be found actually to have muscle invasive disease. Such procedures have traditionally been termed *early cystectomy* based on the fact that they are performed before the traditional surgical indication of documented muscle invasion. Considering that up to 15% will already have micrometastases (Chang et al, 2005), and that a delay in cystectomy of even 12 weeks is associated with poorer survival, some of these procedures do not seem to be "early" enough (Sanchez-Ortiz et al, 2003).

The risk of progression must be weighed against the risk, morbidity, and impact on quality of life for cystectomy. Thus, **a reasonable goal might be, as termed by Chang and Cookson** (2005), **"timely" cystectomy for patients at risk.**

Ten-year survival after cystectomy for non–muscle-invasive cancer can range from 67% to 92% (Amling et al, 1994; Freeman et al, 1995). However, despite the bias that substantial progression can be averted with the benefit of early detection and close surveillance in patients whose tumors are identified prior to muscle invasion, it appears that such patients who progress to muscle invasion have a poorer prognosis than do those who initially present with muscle-invasive disease (Schrier et al, 2004). Thus, overconfidence in disease control status with high-risk patients on surveillance creates a false sense of security.

The AUA Guidelines Panel listed cystectomy as the first option for patients with refractory disease after an initial course of intravesical therapy (see later). Nevertheless, **less than one in five American urologists surveyed stated that they would recommend cystectomy for their patients with CIS refractory to two courses of intravesical BCG, a group with an 80% risk of failure or progression** (Joudi et al, 2003). **Cystectomy in that setting, or for persistent high-grade papillary disease after two courses of intravesical therapy, is the standard of care and should not be considered "early."**

Retrospective data in most series suggest that tumor markers such as P53 and RB may be useful for stratifying high-risk patients in the future. High-risk P53 lesions have a 75% progression rate, compared with 25% in P53-negative lesions. Survival is 60% at 10 years in patients with P53-positive lesions, whereas it is 88% in patients with P53-negative lesions (Sarkis et al, 1993). Grossman found that for T1 lesions evaluated for P53 and RB, progression at 5 years was 30% if either marker was positive and 47% if both markers were positive. No progression was noted in lesions that were wild type for both markers (Grossman et al, 1998). Although P53 positivity did not predict response for BCG-treated patients in another study, post-BCG P53-positive expression was a marker of tumor progression (P53 positive, 82% progression and 41% mortality; P53 negative, 13% progression and 7% mortality) (Lacome et al, 1996). Other studies have refuted these findings, so **the role of P53 for the prediction of tumor behavior and response to therapy remains unclear** (Peyromaure et al, 2002).

The role of surgical approaches involving potential oncologic concessions such as seminal and nerve-sparing cystectomy in such patients theoretically at lower risk of recurrence compared with patients with muscle invasion remains unknown (Hautmann and Stein, 2005). The availability of neobladder for less disfiguring urinary diversion has been reported to decrease the delay in treatment of such patients, potentially leading to significantly improved disease-free survival (Hautmann et al, 1998).

The role of partial cystectomy has not been widely evaluated, although the practice is common (up to 20% of patients treated with extirpative therapy in the United States) in patients with muscle invasion (Hollenbeck et al, 2005). Holzbeierlein and colleagues (2004) reported that 6.9% of the patients presenting to Memorial Sloan-Kettering Cancer Center for surgical management of bladder cancer underwent partial cystectomy, 29% of whom did so for clinical non–muscle-invasive disease). Five-year survival was 69%, and two thirds of patients were alive with an intact, functioning bladder. CIS was the most significant predictor of progression.

Partial cystectomy provides more accurate pathologic staging than does TURBT and allows lymphadenectomy. Appropriate candidates with non–muscle-invasive tumors would logically be the same as those for invasive cancer—those with solitary nonrecurring tumors at the dome or well away from the trigone and no CIS.

Cystectomy should also be considered in patients whose cancer cannot be reasonably controlled through resection: bulky tumors, inaccessible due to a large bladder or urethral stricture disease, or otherwise not amenable to safe removal endoscopically.

In summary, **radical cystectomy offers the most accurate pathologic staging option and should be strongly considered for patients with non–muscle invasive bladder cancers that are high grade and invading deeply into lamina propria, exhibit lymphovascular invasion, are associated with diffuse CIS, are in diverticula, substantially involve the distal ureters or prostatic urethra, are refractory to initial therapy, and are too large or anatomically inaccessible to remove in their entirety endoscopically. It also can be used in patients who understand the risks and benefits of bladder preservation versus cystectomy and request definitive therapy** (Stein, 2003). Partial cystectomy suffers from limited data but might be a promising bladder preservation option situated between the extremes of TURBT combined with intravesical therapy and radical cystectomy.

Role of Alternative Options for Refractory Disease

Photodynamic therapy (PDT) is performed by administering a photosensitizing agent such as porfimer sodium (Photofrin) systemically or hexaminolevulinate (HAL) intravesically. Two to 3 days after the substance has cleared from the normal tissue (for Photofrin), the patient is given an intravesical treatment with red laser light (630 nm) for 12 to 20 minutes. Intravesical Intralipid allows for more uniform distribution of laser light (Manyak et al, 1990). After excitation by light the photosensitizer reacts with molecular oxygen to form free radicals and reactive singlet oxygen, which are cytotoxic.

The response rate in CIS patients from combined series is 66%, with a duration of 37 to 84 months (Jocham et al, 1989;

Nseyo et al, 1997, 1998; Walther, 2000). For patients with papillary disease, an overall response rate of 51% has been achieved with a median time to recurrence of 24 to 48 months (Naito et al, 1991; Nseyo et al, 1997, 1998; Walther, 2000). PDT has been limited by significant side effects such as bladder contracture or irritability (50%) and dermal sensitivity (19%) (Naito et al, 1991; Uchibayashi et al, 1995; Nseyo et al, 1997, 1998).

Research efforts have been directed at development of improved photosensitizers and modifications in laser dosimetry (Kriegmair et al, 1996a; Nseyo et al, 1997, 1998). A leading candidate for photosensitization is HAL, a more lipophilic ester of 5-ALA, which generates a sensitizer called protoporphyrin IX that appears more tumor specific, although clinical data are limited (Datta et al, 1998; Berger et al, 2003; Waidelich et al, 2003). Preclinical studies using hypericin show promise (Kamuhabwa et al, 2004).

Radiation therapy in the treatment of non–muscle-invasive bladder cancer is generally restricted to those individuals who refuse cystectomy after the failure of intravesical therapy or who are unsuitable for major surgery (van der Werf-Messin, 1984). A complete response to radiation therapy and TUR is attainable in 50% to 75% of patients, but the additional benefit of radiation to TUR remains unclear (DeNeve et al, 1992; Rozan et al, 1992; Jansson et al, 1998). Five-year response rates are 44% to 60%. There is no significant effect on CIS. **Due to reports that up to 50% of patients will develop progression and a high likelihood of death** (Dunst et al, 1994; Rodel et al, 2001), **there is a minimal role for radiation therapy other than for palliative purposes in this population.**

KEY POINTS: MANAGEMENT OF REFRACTORY DISEASE

- Patients who fail to respond to an initial course of intravesical therapy after TURBT are at high risk of recurrence or progression.

- Failure after initial chemotherapy or BCG is most appropriately treated with a subsequent course of BCG, as its efficacy in this setting is significantly greater than that of chemotherapy.

- Patients at high risk for progression should be considered for cystectomy after initial TURBT. Failure to respond to an initial course of intravesical therapy is occasion to reconsider cystectomy. Failure to respond to a second course is an indication for immediate cystectomy unless contraindicated or the patient chooses to pursue clinical trials.

SURVEILLANCE

Although bladder cancer is less common than prostate cancer, expenditures are almost twice as high for bladder cancer due to its chronic nature and the need for long-term surveillance. According to the Agency for Health Care Policy and Research, annual expenditures are $2.2 billion for bladder cancer versus $1.4 billion for prostate cancer (Donat, 2003). A significant portion of this cost is due to surveillance (Hedelin et al, 2002).

Surveillance strategies for UC recurrence have historically relied on the diagnostic combination of cystoscopy and urinary cytology. In clinical practice, only 40% of patients actually comply with a standard surveillance protocol (Schrag, 2003). Most protocols include this combination every 3 months for 18 to 24 months after the initial diagnosis, then every 6 months for the following 2 years, and then annually, resetting the clock with each newly identified tumor (Fitzpatrick, 1993). Although the accuracy of both tests relies on subjective and operator-dependent interpretation of visible findings, their traditional presumed status as the "gold standard" has been widely accepted (Brown, 2000).

Cystoscopic Surveillance

Office-based cystoscopy offers rapid, relatively painless visual access to the urothelium. Papillary tumors are readily identified arising from the smooth bladder surface. CIS is classically described as a velvety red mucosal patch, although the reliability of such findings has been called into question.

The role of cystoscopy as a "gold standard" in cancer detection has come under scrutiny with the emergence of tumor markers and the development of newer endoscopic technology, including fluorescent cystoscopy as described previously (Kriegmair et al, 1996a; 1996b, 1999; Filbeck et al, 1999). Nevertheless, for office-based diagnosis it allows identification of the site and characteristics of most tumors. **There is a high positive predictive value with cystoscopy, because most lesions believed to be malignant are proven so pathologically. The endoscopic appearance cannot reliably predict tumor stage or grade, although sessile morphology and/or the presence of necrosis suggest high-grade disease likely to be invasive** (Cina et al, 2001; Mitropoulos et al, 2005).

Cystoscopy is usually performed in the outpatient setting. Rigid rod lens systems offer accurate visualization of the bladder. Flexible fiberoptic cystoscopes are almost as sensitive and are markedly more comfortable for men (Meyoff et al, 1988; Walker et al, 1993), although there is no clear advantage to their use in women because of the short, straight female urethra. Newer digital chip cystoscopes offer similar tolerability but better visualization due to clarity and magnification on video monitors. Complete visualization of the bladder mucosa is possible in a matter of seconds in most patients. Their high-resolution imaging obviates the only potential advantage of rigid cystoscopy (slightly better optics than fiberoptic flexible scopes). Thus, **flexible cystoscopy has essentially replaced rigid cystoscopy for surveillance in men in North America and may do so in women.**

Using the same technology for flexible cystoscopy as described above for HAL fluorescent rigid cystoscopy, phase II studies have had mixed results but suggest that office-based fluorescent cystoscopy can improve the detection of CIS and papillary tumors (Witjes et al, 2004; Loidl et al, 2005).

The vast majority of both men and women tolerate office-based cystoscopy with minimal discomfort. **Intraurethral injection of local anesthetics is almost universal among urologists despite a paucity of data to support the practice. Most studies have failed to identify benefit** (Palit et al, 2003; Rodriguez-Rubio et al, 2004), and two recent studies actually found that pain experience was higher with the use of local anesthetics than in patients cystoscoped using aqueous lubricant alone (Chen et al, 2003; Ho et al, 2003; Chen et al, 2005). **Considering the fact that anesthetic agents can partially cloud visualization, this ubiquitous practice should be reconsidered.** Use of a video monitor allows the patient to see and understand the findings, theoretically distracting them from any discomfort. Men who are able to do so tolerate the procedure with approximately 50% less pain (VAS 2.21 vs. 1.31, $P < .01$) than those who cannot see their findings on the monitor. This has not been found to be of significant benefit in women for unclear reasons (Jones et al, 2006).

The **bladder should be evacuated before cystoscopy. This removes concentrated amorphous detritus and radiographic contrast** if studies were performed earlier in the day. Aspiration is occasionally needed during the procedure using a 60-mL syringe attached to the irrigant port. This can further lessen clouding. A systematic approach is mandatory to ensure all urothelium is visualized.

Attempts to modify the above surveillance schedule have been made using decision analysis tools (Kent et al, 1989; Abel, 1993). Several authors recommend termination of surveillance at 5 or more years for low risk patients (Haukaas et al, 1999). However, the actual cost of surveillance cystoscopy is responsible for only 13% of the expenditures for bladder cancer care in one study, so the financial opportunity may be limited for such efforts (Hedelin et al, 2002; Schoenberg et al, 2000). In addition, the risk of recurrence and potential for progression exists beyond this period. Reports of late recurrences of high-grade cancer years after the original tumor temper some authors' enthusiasm with terminating surveillance at any point (Thompson et al, 1993; Morris et al, 1995; LeBlanc et al, 1999; Zieger et al, 2000). Thus, there is no consensus on such programs.

Other investigators have examined the predictive impact of early or multiple recurrences and how this might affect surveillance (Parmar et al, 1989; Holmang et al, 1995; Reading et al, 1995). **Tumor recurrence on initial 3-month cystoscopy and number of tumors on initial resection (single or multiple) provide the most predictive information with regard to recurrence in several studies. Absence of recurrence on the 3-month surveillance cystoscopy in patients with TaG1 tumors is associated with recurrence rates so low that annual cystoscopy appears safe even at that point (beginning 12 months after the initial resection** (Fitzpatrick et al, 1986; Olsen et al, 1995; Frydenberg et al, 2005). Finally, patients with a negative cystoscopy and a negative UroVysion assay (see later) are at very low risk of recurrence in the following 6 months, creating opportunity to individualize the surveillance schedule (Sarosdy et al, 2002).

Urine Cytology

Cytology involves microscopic evaluation of stained cellular smears from the urine. Unlike tumor markers, **urinary cytology is not a laboratory test—it is a pathologist's interpretation of the morphologic features of shed urothelial cells. Poor cellular cohesion in high-grade tumors, especially CIS, enhances the yield of cytology.**

Its very high specificity is the most important feature of cytology, because a **positive reading regardless of cystoscopic** or radiographic findings suggests the existence of malignancy in the vast majority of patients. Even in the setting of UC patients with a negative workup (cystoscopy and upper tract imaging) with a persistently positive cytology, 40% were found to have genitourinary cancer within 24 months, with a mean time to diagnosis of 5.6 months (Nabi et al, 2004).

Bladder irrigation or barbotage increases the cellularity available for evaluation compared with voided urine. Nevertheless, Murphy and coworkers (1981) showed that urine collected cystoscopically before obtaining a bladder wash provided additional diagnostic information in their study of 313 patients. Bladder washings had a higher yield, but 13.1% of cancers would have been missed in bladder washings alone. Moreover, mechanical trauma has the potential to create cellular alterations that might interfere with interpretation. Radiographic contrast media have also been implicated in creating cellular shrinkage, nuclear pyknosis, fragmentation, and cytoplasmic vacuolization that might lead to a false-positive reading, especially when injected for retrograde pyelography (McClennan et al, 1978). This may not be a concern when low osmolar, ionic and nonionic, contrast media are used (Andriole et al, 1989).

Although cytology has traditionally been believed to have high sensitivity for high-grade cancer, recent studies do not support this. When the Mayo Clinic recently reviewed findings from its laboratory, they observed that only 58% of bladder tumors were identified using cytology. Its sensitivity was not limited to low-grade tumors, because only 71% of high-grade cancers were identified. Because this was lower than expected, they subsequently reviewed the literature and found that **cumulative data from series published after 1990 reported that cytology actually identified (using the older grading system) 11% of grade 1, 31% of grade 2, and only 60% of grade 3 tumors** (Halling et al, 2000). In contrast, they observed that these recent findings were well below those reported before 1990, when the sensitivity of cytology was 94% for grade 3 tumors, but could find no explanation for this deterioration. A change in the stringency of cytologic criteria for determining a case positive was ruled out, because the very high specificity for studies before and after 1990 was not significantly different and was consistent with specificity in their own laboratory. These findings are supported by numerous other studies and emphasized by a recent multicenter study involving several institutions noted for bladder cancer expertise that found cytology had an overall sensitivity of 15.8% (Grossman et al, 2005).

Thus, cytology has very high specificity but has low sensitivity for both high-grade and low-grade tumors, including CIS in recently published reports.

Tumor Markers

Many attempts have been made to develop a UC biomarker test to complement or replace urinary cytology (Table 76–7). Most of these have had adequate sensitivity but poor specificity, resulting in substantial false-positive readings, creating the need for further diagnostic testing. Current urinary markers have been developed to detect tumor-associated antigens, blood group antigens, growth factors, cell cycle/apoptosis, and extracellular matrix proteins. **The most significant issue limiting widespread adoption of tumor markers is the lack of prospective data to support their impact on prognosis or disease management** (Lokeshwar et al, 2005). They are considered alphabetically below.

The qualitative point-of-care test BTA stat (Polymedco, Inc., Cortlandt Manor, NY) and the quantitative BTA TRAK (Polymedco) assays detect human complement factor H–related protein. The overall sensitivity of these tests ranges from 50% to 80%, whereas the specificity is between 50% and 75%. These tests are more sensitive than cytology but can be falsely positive in patients with inflammation, infection, or hematuria (Irani et al, 1999; Liou, 2006).

ImmunoCyt (DiagnoCure, Inc., Saint Foy, Canada) is a hybrid of cytology and an immunofluorescent assay. Three fluorescent-labeled monoclonal antibodies are targeted at a UC variant of carcinoembryonic antigen and two bladder mucins. Sensitivity and specificity are reported to be 86% and 79%, respectively. It has not been shown to be affected by benign conditions, but interpretation is complex and operator dependent (Toma et al, 2004; Tetu et al, 2005).

The NMP22 BladderChek Test (Matritech, Inc., Newton, MA) is based on the detection of nuclear matrix protein 22, part of the mitotic apparatus released from urothelial nuclei upon cellular apoptosis. The protein is elevated in UC, but it is also released from dead and dying urothelial cells. Benign conditions of the urinary tract such as stones, infection, inflammation, hematuria, and cystoscopy can cause a false-positive reading. Both a laboratory-based, quantitative

Table 76–7. **Commercially Available Markers**						
			Sensitivity		**Specificity**	
Commercially Available Marker	*Reagent Cost**	*Reimbursement*	*Mean (%)*	*Range (%)*	*Mean (%)*	*Range (%)*
Cytology	$2.00	$25.00	48	16-89	96	81-100
Hematuria dipstick	$0.60	$3.00	68	40-93	68	51-97
NMP22	$25.00	$35.00	75	32-92	75	51-94
NMP22 BladderChek	$25.00	$35.00	55.7		85.7	
BTA stat	$14.00	$24.00	68	53-89	74	54-93
BTA TRAK	$7.00	$24.00	61	17-78	71	51-89
ImmunoCyt	$80.00	$109.00-$230.00	74	39-100	80	73-84
UroVysion	$102.47	$407.00	77	73-81	98	96-100

*Reagent only; labor costs vary.
Data from Andriole et al (2005) and Liou (2006).

immunoassay and a qualitative point-of-care test are available. The sensitivities and specificities range from 68.5% to 88.5% for sensitivity and from 65.2% to 91.3% for specificity. (Liou, 2006). A multi-institutional trial involving 1331 patients showed that, overall, the NMP22 was more sensitive than cytology but less specific. Sensitivities were 50% and 90% for noninvasive and invasive cancer, respectively, with an overall sensitivity of 55.7%. Overall specificity was higher for cytology at 99.2% compared with NMP22 at 85.7%. The sensitivity of cystoscopy in this study was 88.6%, but when combined with NMP22 this increased to 93.7% (Grossman et al, 2005).

UroVysion (Abbott Molecular, Chicago, IL) is a cytology-based test that uses FISH of DNA probes or "labels" specifically chosen to identify certain chromosomal foci. Probes to identify aneuploidy of chromosomes 3, 7, and 17 are combined with a probe to the 9p21 locus. The probes can be developed to identify essentially any locus, but this combination has been shown to have the best sensitivity and specificity (Halling et al, 2000). Cumulative data from comparative studies show sensitivity for cytology compared with FISH of 19% versus 58% for grade 1, 50% versus 77% for grade 2, and 71% versus 96% for grade 3. Similar findings occurred by stage where cytology compared with FISH sensitivity was 35% versus 64% for Ta, 66% versus 83% for T1, and 76% versus 94% for muscle invasive carcinoma (Jones, 2006).

Notably, cytology detected only 67% of cases with CIS versus 100% detection by FISH in comparative studies. UroVysion was the only marker whose specificity approaches that of cytology. It will, however, detect chromosomal changes before the development of phenotypic expression of malignancy, so leads to an "anticipatory positive" reading in some patients. Such readings are often not false positives and will lead to identification of clinical tumors within 3 to 15 months in the majority of cases (Sarosdy et al, 2002). This may allow identification of patients at risk of recurrence versus those unlikely to recur in order to individualize surveillance protocols if confirmed.

UroVysion has also been shown to clarify equivocal findings in patients with atypical or negative cytology (Skacel et al, 2003). It is not affected by hematuria, inflammation, or other factors that can cause false-positive readings with some tumor markers, so it appears to be useful as a marker of BCG response (Kipp et al, 2005).

Determining the utility of tumor markers and the choice of which one to use is not clear at this point in time. For example, if indication for biopsy in the operating room is the endpoint, then high specificity is desired to limit the number of negative biopsies. On the other hand, if increasing the interval of cystoscopic surveillance is the endpoint, then high sensitivity, particularly for high-grade tumors, is desired. Defining that a patient has a low likelihood of recurrence within the following year can allow individualization of surveillance protocols (Fig. 76–8) (Grossman, 2006).

Investigational Markers

The foundation for the Accu-Dx (Intracel Corp, Rockville, MD) point-of-care immunoassay is the higher level of vascular endothelial growth factor in UC that increases the permeability of the blood vessels to serum proteins, including plasminogen, fibrinogen, and the members of the clotting

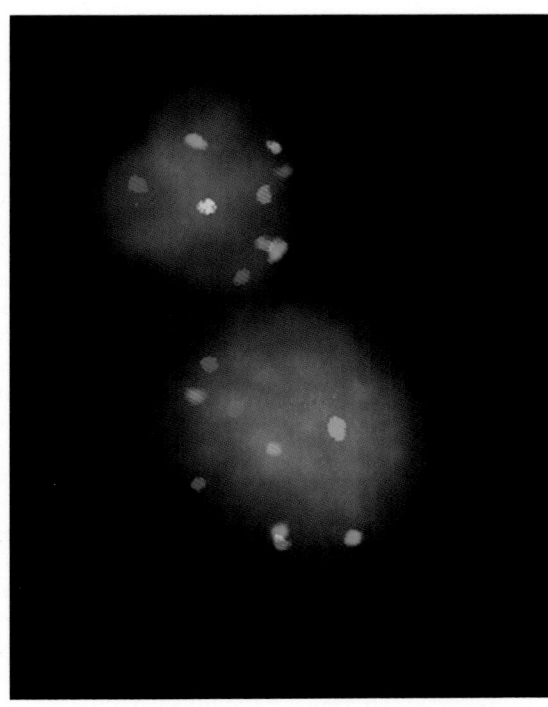

Figure 76–8. An abnormal enlarged cell *(lower right)* demonstrates three copies of chromosome 3 *(red)*, chromosome 7 *(green)*, and chromosome 17 *(aqua)* using fluorescent in situ hybridization (FISH). Homozygous deletion of band 9p21 locus *(yellow)* is also present. (Courtesy of Raymond Tubbs, DO, Department of Laboratory Pathology, Cleveland Clinic Foundation.)

cascade. This test detects fibrin and its degradation products. Its sensitivity and specificity is 68% and 86%, respectively, but it can also be falsely positive in patients with hematuria (Ewing et al, 1987; Lokeshwar et al, 2001). The FDA has approved this test, but it is currently not commercially available.

Telomerase is a protein/RNA complex involved in extension of telomeres during cell cycle DNA replication, so it is elevated in malignant cells. The assay has shown high specificity but suboptimal sensitivity. The stability of telomerase RNA is variable, yielding reports with varying reproducibility (de Kok et al, 2000; Dettlaff-Pokora et al, 2005).

Hyaluronic acid is a nonsulfated glycosaminoglycan in the basement membrane that is degraded by hyaluronidase. The sensitivity and specificity for this test is between 80% and 85%, respectively. Cytokeratins 18, 19, and 20 are highly expressed in bladder cancer. However, all three are also induced with infections. The test for cytokeratin 8 and 18 is the UBC II enzyme-linked immunosorbent assay (Liou, 2006).

Miscellaneous proteins with promise are BLCA4, a nuclear matrix bladder cancer protein; mucin 7, a glycoprotein that is mainly found in invasive and CIS bladder cancer; survivin, an anti-apoptotic protein; Lewis X, found mainly in low-grade cancer; and CD44, a metastatic/invasive protein marker (Liou, 2006).

Extravesical Surveillance

The proportion of patients developing upper tract UC after the diagnosis and treatment of non–muscle-invasive disease has been reported as 0.002% to 2.4% over surveillance intervals of 5 to 13 years (Shinka et al, 1988; Oldbring et al, 1989; Holmang et al, 1995; Sadek et al, 1999), although the risk increases substantially over time to as high as 18% in very high risk populations (Herr, 1997). Synchronous tumors were detected in none of 78 patients (0%) with grade 1 (using the prior grading system) tumors, 4 of 361 (1.1%) with grade 2, and 5 of 360 (1.3%) with grade 3, as well as 0% for low-grade Ta and 7% for T1 (Herranz-Amo et al, 1999). Most patients will require upper tract imaging specifically for the indication of hematuria. **Most reviews have concluded that patients without such indications who have high-grade or multiple tumors should undergo upper tract imaging based on the risk of upper tract disease, but those with low-grade tumors probably do not benefit from imaging at the time of bladder cancer diagnosis.**

The **role of annual imaging surveillance is controversial but usually indicated with high-risk disease.** In a review of 591 patients with a median follow-up of 86 months, upper tract recurrence was 0.9% in low-risk patients (solitary, low-grade, low-stage Ta/T1), 2.2% in patients at intermediate risk (recurrent or multifocal disease), and 9.8% in high-risk patients, including intravesical chemotherapy failures (Hurle et al, 1998).

The proper study to evaluate the upper tract is debatable. Excretory urography is the traditional choice but gives limited information about renal parenchyma and can miss small tumors. Retrograde pyelography requires instrumentation, but this is often not a problem because these patients require removal of the primary tumor. CT urography is a promising technology for the evaluation of hematuria, but its role in the evaluation of patients with non–muscle-invasive bladder cancer has not been reported (Herts, 2003).

Although infrequent, the appearance of upper tract disease is associated with mortality rates of 40% to 70%. Patients with high-risk disease treated with BCG experience upper tract recurrence risk of 13% to 18% (Miller et al, 1993; Herr et al, 1997). The risk for recurrence in this population appears greatest over the first 5 years after treatment (median time to detection, 56 months) yet persists at least 15 years. The cumulative risk of upper tract recurrence is 13% within 5 years, 28% at 5 to 10 years, and 38% at 15 years (Herr et al,

1988), with mortality of approximately one third (Herr et al, 1997).

Selective cytology of the upper tract may increase the yield of upper tract lesions detected, but, in the presence of a bladder tumor, selective upper tract cytology may be falsely positive and is not recommended for most patients (Zincke et al, 1983; Sadek et al, 1999).

Secondary tumor involvement of the prostatic urethra and ducts by UC may be detected in 10% to 15% of patients with high-risk non–muscle-invasive disease within 5 years and in 20% to 40% within 10 years (Donat, 2003). Patients who have refractory disease are at risk for extravesical recurrence in the prostatic fossa in approximately one third of cases, 44% of which are fatal (Herr et al, 1988).

In summary, surveillance strategies should be individualized based on the risk of recurrence in the bladder as well as in extravesical sites (Table 76–8).

Secondary Prevention Strategies

Both lifestyle changes and chemoprevention could potentially reduce the risk of recurrence and should be considered in the comprehensive management of patients with non–muscle-invasive disease. **Unlike primary prevention, secondary prevention seeks to prevent recurrent tumors in patients who already carry a diagnosis of a specific cancer.** Although this also may involve minimizing exposure to carcinogens, it relies more heavily on optimizing host responses and creating an environment that can retard tumor growth.

Lifestyle changes are particularly important because UC is directly linked to environmental factors in the majority of cases. **Smoking cessation, increased fluid intake, and a low-fat diet may all reduce the risk of recurrence,** with the former being of paramount importance. **Increased hydration reduces the concentration and dwell time of carcinogens** and thereby reduces the risk of malignant transformation within the urothelium. The Physician Health Study showed an inverse correlation between fluid intake and the incidence of UC on longitudinal follow-up, but this simple measure may also be of benefit for secondary prevention for patients that already have a history of UC (Michaud et al, 1999). **High fat and cholesterol intake are now firmly established as risk**

Table 76–8.	**Surveillance Strategies**		
Risk	**Tumor Status**	**Cystoscopy Schedule**	**Upper Tract Imaging**
Low	Solitary TaG1	3 mo after initial resection Annually beginning 9 mo after initial surveillance if no recurrence Consider cessation at 5 or more yr. Consider cytology or tumor markers.	Not necessary unless hematuria present
Intermediate	Multiple TaG1 Large tumor Recurrence at 3 mo	Every 3 mo for 1-2 yr Semiannual or annual after 2 yr Consider cytology or tumor markers. Restart clock with each recurrence.	Consider imaging, especially for recurrence. Imaging for hematuria
High	Any high grade (incl. CIS)	Every 3 mo for 2 yr Semiannual for 2 yr Annually for lifetime Cytology at same schedule Consider tumor markers. Restart clock with each recurrence.	Imaging annually for 2 yr; then consider lengthening interval.

factors for many cancers and UC is no exception, although the mechanisms are not as well defined as for other malignancies (Steineck et al, 1990).

A variety of agents have been investigated for chemoprevention strategies for patients with UC and, while not clinically fruitful to date, this remains an active area of investigation. **Retinoids, including vitamin A and its analogs, have been studied most intensively. These agents enhance differentiation of normal and neoplastic cells and appear to have antioxidant and immunostimulatory properties. Whereas animal studies for preventing UC were promising, studies looking at primary prevention in humans were conflicting, and the side effects of these agents were problematic** in this long-term prophylactic setting (Sporn et al, 1977; Becci et al, 1978; Mathews-Roth et al, 1991; Eichholzer et al, 1996; Steinmaus et al, 2000). Synthetic retinoids with the potential for reduced toxicity have been tested in patients with known UC. However, fenretinide failed to reduce recurrence rates when compared with placebo, and 3 patients (12%) in the etretinate arm of another randomized study were found to have myocardial infarctions, although this may have been coincidental (Studer et al, 1995; Decensi et al, 2000; Lerner et al, 2005). Etretinate delayed the time to second recurrence but had no effect on time to first recurrence and potential cardiac risk was of concern.

Pyridoxine (vitamin B_6) breaks down tryptophan metabolites in the urine that may induce UC, but clinical studies have been conflicting (Byar and Blackard, 1977; Newling et al, 1995). Difluoromethylornithine (DFMO), which inhibits the enzyme ornithine decarboxylase that contributes to malignant transformation, was also studied recently in patients with non–muscle-invasive UC (Messing et al, 2005). However, recurrence rates for this agent were not reduced when compared with placebo and enthusiasm has thus waned.

The most promising data for secondary chemoprevention of UC relate to the use of high doses of multivitamins. One small but important study randomized 65 patients with noninvasive UC to either a recommended daily allowance (RDA) multivitamin or megadose vitamins with augmented levels of vitamins A, B_6, C, and E (Lamm et al, 1994). Comparison of the two regimens revealed no difference in recurrence rates in the first year; however, there was a statistically significant advantage for the megadose group when the 5-year recurrence rates were calculated. At this point, 80% of patients in the RDA group had experienced recurrence compared with only 40% in the megadose group. These findings suggest that the beneficial effect of megadose vitamins is related to its suppressive effect on partially transformed cells within the urothelium rather than inhibiting early recurrences, which are typically caused by tumor cell implantation or incomplete resection. Confirmation of these findings by larger prospective trials is needed.

Ongoing phase III trials for patients with noninvasive UC are evaluating the potential chemopreventive roles of celecoxib (a cyclooxygenase-2 inhibitor), erlotonib (an epidermal growth factor receptor inhibitor), and green tea extracts.

KEY POINTS: SURVEILLANCE

- Cystoscopy is the hallmark of surveillance. The optimum schedule is controversial but may be individualized based on risk.

- Patients with solitary low-grade Ta lesions whose initial 3-month surveillance cystoscopy is normal and who have negative cytology can have surveillance on a less aggressive schedule. Annual cystoscopy is probably reasonable, and cessation may be considered in 5 years.

- Patients with high-grade tumors (including CIS) warrant quarterly cystoscopy for 1 to 2 years, semiannual cystoscopy for 1 to 2 years, and annual cystoscopic evaluation for life.

- Upper tract imaging is not necessary for low-grade tumors but should be performed at diagnosis and every 1 to 2 years for high-grade tumors.

- Cytology is usually performed at the time of each cystoscopy. Its specificity is very high, but its sensitivity is suboptimal and a negative cytology does not assure the absence of any grade bladder cancer.

- A number of tumor markers have shown the ability to improve upon the sensitivity of cytology, but specificity is lower for most.

- Increased fluids, smoking cessation, and a low-fat diet are recommended.

SUGGESTED READINGS

Chang SS, Cookson MS: Radical cystectomy for bladder cancer: The case for early intervention. Urol Clin North Am 2005;32:147-155.

Epstein JI, Amin MB, Reuter VR, Mostofi FK: The World Health Organization/International Society of Urological Pathology consensus classification of urothelial (transitional cell) neoplasms of the urinary bladder. Bladder Consensus Conference Committee. Am J Surg Pathol 1998;22:1435-1448.

Koch MO, Smith JA Jr: Natural history and surgical management of superficial bladder cancer (stages Ta/T1/Tis). In Vogelzang N, Miles BJ (eds): Comprehensive Textbook of Genitourinary Oncology. Baltimore, Williams & Wilkins, 1996, pp 405-415.

Lamm DL, Blumenstein BA, Crissman JD, et al: Maintenance bacillus Calmette-Guérin immunotherapy for recurrent Ta,T1 and carcinoma in situ TCC of the bladder: A randomized SWOG study. J Urol 2000;163:1124-1129.

O'Donnell MA: Practical applications of intravesical chemotherapy and immunotherapy in high-risk patients with superficial bladder cancer. Urol Clin North Am 2005;32:121-131.

Smith JA Jr, Labasky RF, Cockett AT, et al: Bladder cancer clinical guidelines panel summary report on the management of non–muscle invasive bladder cancer (stages Ta, T1 and TIS). The American Urological Association. J Urol 1999;162:1697-1701.

Soloway MS: Introduction (and entire supplement). Urology 2005;66(6S1).

Sylvester RJ, Oosterlinck W, van der Meijden AP: A single immediate postoperative instillation of chemotherapy decreases the risk of recurrence in patients with stage Ta, T1 bladder cancer: A meta-analysis of published results of randomized clinical trials. J Urol 2004;171:2186-2190.

77 Management of Invasive and Metastatic Bladder Cancer

MARK P. SCHOENBERG, MD • MARK L. GONZALGO, MD, PhD

Invasive and metastatic bladder cancer remains a persistent clinical and scientific challenge for urologists and their colleagues. The capricious clinical behavior of bladder cancer, the occult nature of its progression, the relative inadequacy of clinical staging techniques, the magnitude of the therapeutic interventions employed, and the sobering absence of reliably curative therapy for many patients draw attention to this complex clinical problem. In this chapter, the treatment of invasive and metastatic bladder cancer is reviewed. Adjuncts to standard therapy are discussed, and alternatives to "gold standard" measures are described.

CLINICAL PRESENTATION, DIAGNOSIS, AND EVALUATION
Presentation

Patients who develop invasive bladder cancer present to their physicians with many of the same symptoms commonly associated with superficial forms of urothelial malignant disease. **Hematuria, either gross or microscopic, is the most common and familiar presenting symptom and affects as many as 80% of patients with bladder cancer.** Irritative voiding symptoms are relatively common among patients with bladder cancer and should not be ascribed to recurrent infection or nonspecific causes unless a thorough search, including a series of well-recognized diagnostic evaluations (urine culture and analysis, cytology, cystoscopy, and upper tract imaging), has been accomplished and a diagnosis of cancer has been excluded. Constitutional symptoms should suggest advanced disease.

Transurethral Resection

Transurethral resection (TUR) of a bladder lesion provides essential information to identify invasive carcinoma. Definitive detrusor invasion is required and is easily appreciated on a TUR specimen. Once a histologic diagnosis of invasion is made, noninvasive imaging may provide valuable insight into the extent of the tumor diathesis. **For patients in whom an invasive lesion is suspected before TUR, axial staging should be accomplished before biopsy or transurethral manipulation of the lesion because of the confounding artifact produced by endoscopic surgery on postoperative studies.**

Bimanual Examination

Bimanual examination is a sensitive and inexpensive method for obtaining evidence of extravesical extension of bladder cancer (Fossa and Berner, 1991). Usually performed at the time of TUR under anesthesia, bimanual palpation of the bladder before and after tumor resection has been correlated with the stage of the lesion. **Wijkstrom and colleagues** (1998) **suggested that the presence of a palpable mass after TUR correlates significantly with stage T3 cancer and prognosis after treatment.**

Restaging Transurethral Resection

Restaging TUR is recommended by some investigators to assess the degree of tumor burden in the bladder after the

significance of prostatic stromal invasion, citing increased likelihood of anterior urethral recurrence (64%) in patients with stromal invasion compared with those with involvement of the prostatic urethral urothelium (0%) or the prostatic ducts (25%) (Hardeman and Soloway, 1990; Levinson et al, 1990). Freeman and colleagues (1994) reported no recurrences in the anterior urethra in patients with prostatic urethral tumor involvement undergoing orthotopic reconstruction, compared with those with similar disease treated by continent cutaneous diversion (24% risk of urethral recurrence). These findings have been reviewed by Stein and colleagues (2005). The significance of this observation remains to be elucidated.

On the basis of contemporary observations, male patients undergoing cutaneous diversion should be encouraged to undergo simultaneous or delayed urethrectomy if carcinoma in situ or gross tumor involves the prostatic urethra. Patients considered candidates for orthotopic reconstruction should be cautioned that the final commitment to use of the residual urethra cannot be made until frozen-section analysis demonstrates a tumor-free distal urethral margin (Lebret et al, 1998). Some have advised preoperative evaluation of the prostatourethral junction in men and the urethrovesical junction in women before cystectomy to identify patients at high risk for recurrence (Wood et al, 1989). Monitoring the retained urethra in patients with cutaneous or orthotopic reconstruction has historically included periodic urethral cytology and, when indicated, biopsy. Studies by Dalbagni and coworkers (2004) suggest that this practice may not be uniformly required or useful. Nonetheless, a positive cytology result or abnormal biopsy finding should prompt immediate urethrectomy (Ahlering et al, 1984; Hickey et al, 1986; Freeman et al, 1994).

Female Urethra

Urethrectomy in the female patient was considered a standard component of anterior exenteration until efforts at orthotopic reconstruction for women focused attention on urethral preservation. Two factors contributed to this practice historically. Studies performed in the first half of the 20th century suggested that the incidence of adjacent structure involvement by cancer (vagina, cervix, uterus) was relatively high, demanding wide excision for the purpose of obtaining a negative surgical margin. Preservation of the urethra was not a priority because orthotopic reconstruction was not thought to be an option in female patients. **Mapping studies have demonstrated that 2% to 12% of female patients undergoing cystectomy for cure of bladder cancer have urethral involvement by tumor** (De Paepe et al, 1990). The presence of carcinoma at the bladder neck is highly correlated with the presence of carcinoma of the urethra in female patients, and most authors emphasize the need for careful intraoperative frozen-section analysis of the urethral margin at the time of cystectomy to ensure that the residual urethra is tumor free (Stenzl et al, 1995; Stein et al, 1998). Female patients with overt cancer at the bladder neck and urethra, diffuse carcinoma in situ, or a positive margin at surgery are poor candidates for orthotopic reconstruction and should be treated by immediate en bloc urethrectomy as part of the radical cystectomy.

Ureteral Frozen-Section Analysis

Analysis of the ureteral margin at the time of cystectomy before urinary tract reconstruction is standard practice. The rationale for this procedure is that carcinoma, and particularly carcinoma in situ, can involve the distal ureteral margin. Urologists have historically resected positive margins to effect clearance of all documented cancer, assuming that this would provide better long-term local disease control. Retrospective studies have, in fact, failed to demonstrate that clearing the ureteral margins at the time of cystectomy provides any long-term benefit (Linker and Whitmore, 1975; Johnson and Bracken, 1977; Schoenberg et al, 1996b). These studies are generally small, single-institution retrospective experiences. Nevertheless, these observations call into question the common-sense practice of immediate frozen-section analysis of the ureteral margins.

Efficacy of Cystectomy

The success of radical cystectomy with pelvic lymphadenectomy in the management of patients with muscle-invasive, clinically organ-confined bladder cancer has been reviewed in the contemporary literature (Mathur et al, 1981; Montie et al, 1984; Skinner and Lieskovsky, 1984; Giuliani et al, 1985; Malkowicz et al, 1990; Wishnow et al, 1992; Waehre et al, 1993; Schoenberg et al, 1996a, 1996b; Ghoneim et al, 1997; Skinner et al, 1998; Bassi et al, 1999). **Numerous series have demonstrated that with improvements in preoperative and postoperative care, refinements in surgical technique, and better appreciation of the long-term metabolic consequences of urinary tract reconstruction, patients with organ-confined disease can anticipate long-term disease-specific survival. Results from international series reveal similar outcomes for surgically treated patients.** Long-term survival is uniformly better for patients with pathologically organ-confined disease (Table 77–2). Although the results of radical cystectomy for patients with clinically organ-confined disease appear unimpeachable, radical cystectomy performed in the context of locoregional disease or malignant pelvic adenopathy is more controversial.

Table 77–2. Percentage Disease-Specific Survival by Pathologic Stage after Radical Cystectomy with and without Pelvic Lymph Node Metastasis: Selected Series (1980-1999)

Selected Series	No. of Patients	P2	P3	P4a	N+
Mathur	58	72	40	29	NA
Montie	99	62	57	75	NA
Giuliani	202	75	19	0	NA
Skinner	197	64	44	36	44
Malkowicz	160	76	NA	NA	NA
Wishnow	71	~80	NA	NA	NA
Waehre	227	79	36	29	22
Schoenberg	101	84	56	NA	48
Ghoneim	1026	66	31	19	23
Bassi	369	63	33	28	15

NA, not available.

Role of Lymphadenectomy

Pelvic lymphadenectomy remains an integral part of the management of patients with invasive bladder carcinoma for two reasons. **Pelvic lymphadenectomy provides insight into the local extent of disease. In addition, patients with limited nodal burden experience unexpectedly high rates of long-term survival in the absence of additional interventions** (Skinner, 1982; Skinner and Lieskovsky, 1984; Lerner et al, 1993; Vieweg et al, 1994, 1999; Schoenberg et al, 1996a, 1996b). The risk of pelvic lymph node metastases increases with tumor stage; patients with stage pT2 disease have a 10% to 30% risk of positive lymph nodes at the time of surgery, whereas patients with disease higher than stage pT3 have a 30% to 65% risk. Smith (1981) observed that in patients undergoing radical cystectomy, the obturator and external iliac lymph nodes are most commonly involved by metastatic cancer. Common iliac lymph nodes and presacral nodes are less frequently involved. In patients considered candidates for curative exenterative surgery based on clinical staging, metastasis above the common iliac arteries is rare. Extended lymph node dissection has been advocated by some authors, but long-term survival in patients to whom this would be applicable is uncommon.

An extended lymph node dissection should include the distal para-aortic and paracaval lymph nodes as well as the presacral nodes (Stein and Skinner, 2005). An extended pelvic lymph node dissection may yield a greater number of positive and total number of lymph nodes compared with standard pelvic lymph node dissection. However, the percentage of patients with node-positive disease who are identified is similar between these two groups (Bochner et al, 2004).

Among patients with lymph node–positive disease, the total number of lymph nodes removed at the time of surgery has been shown to be of prognostic value (Stein et al, 2003). Patients with 15 or fewer lymph nodes removed had 25% 10-year recurrence-free survival compared with 36% when more than 15 lymph nodes were removed. Recurrence-free survival at 10 years for patients with 8 or fewer positive lymph nodes was significantly higher than for those with more than 8 positive lymph nodes (40% versus 10%) (Stein et al, 2003). **The concept of ratio-based lymph node staging or lymph node density (total number of positive lymph nodes divided by total number of extracted lymph nodes) has also been shown to be a significant prognostic factor** (Herr, 2003; Stein et al, 2003). Patients with a lymph node density of 20% or less had 43% 10-year recurrence-free survival compared with 17% survival at 10 years when lymph node density was greater than 20% (Stein et al, 2003).

Complications of Radical Cystectomy

The potential complications of radical cystectomy include mortality as well as major and minor morbidity (Skinner and Kaufman, 1980). The mortality rate for radical cystectomy is 1% to 2%. The overall complication rate for contemporary series is 25%. **The morbidity associated with this surgical procedure falls into three general categories: (1) complications associated with preexisting or comorbid conditions, (2) complications stemming from removal of the bladder** and adjacent structures, and **(3) complications resulting from use of segments of the gastrointestinal tract for the purpose of urinary tract reconstruction or diversion after radical cystectomy.** Cardiopulmonary disease is relatively common in patients who develop invasive bladder cancer. Death from perioperative cardiac arrest is infrequent, but a thorough preoperative evaluation is mandatory in patients with signs, symptoms, or history of significant cardiac disease before surgery. Postoperative pulmonary embolism is rare (2%). Early mobilization and, when appropriate, judicious use of perioperative anticoagulation can minimize the risk of a fatal event. Catastrophic hemorrhage is rare but can occur during cystectomy. Modern blood banking and screening for bloodborne pathogens have made transfusion safe for most patients, even in the absence of preoperative autologous donation. Rectal injury occurs in no more than 1% of patients undergoing cystoprostatectomy. Major vascular injury is also rare. Bowel obstruction is a potential risk of urinary tract diversion or reconstruction when small or large intestine is used. Four percent to 10% of patients experience bowel obstruction postoperatively, although less than 10% require operative intervention to correct this problem.

Ureteral-enteral anastomotic strictures are rare (3%) in refluxing systems but are more common when a nonrefluxing anastomosis is performed. Metabolic disorders, vitamin deficiencies, chronic urinary tract infection, and renal calculous disease occur in varying degrees, depending on the form of reconstruction performed after removal of the lower urinary tract (Sullivan and Whitmore, 1980; Bracken and Johnson, 1981; Frazier and Paulson, 1992; Matveev et al, 1993; Mansson et al, 1998; Turk and Albala, 1999; Cummings, 2000; Rosario and Anderson, 2000).

Depression is common among patients undergoing major surgery, and the cystectomy population is no exception. Signs of this should be actively sought and appropriate intervention provided. The preoperative prevalence of psychological distress in patients diagnosed with bladder cancer is approximately 45% (Palapattu et al, 2004). Pathologic stage is significantly associated with postcystectomy anxiety and general distress.

Follow-up after Radical Cystectomy

After exenterative surgery and reconstruction, patients require long-term surveillance for two specific problems: (1) tumor recurrence and (2) complications related to the interposition of bowel in the urinary tract. Tumor recurrence is most easily assayed by periodic axial imaging. The frequency with which this examination must be performed is controversial. Slaton and colleagues (1999) performed a retrospective review of their experience. They recommended **annual screening with physical examination, serum chemistries, and chest radiograph for patients with pT1 disease; semiannual evaluation for patients with pT2 disease; and quarterly evaluation for patients with pT3 disease. For the last group, semiannual CT scan was also recommended.** With use of this schedule, the authors predicted no decrease in their ability to detect disease recurrence in a timely manner. Upper tract imaging after cystectomy is also useful to exclude the occurrence of ureteral stenosis or upper tract tumor. Upper tract tumors have been found infrequently after cystectomy, but when they are found, they are often advanced lesions requiring operative intervention (Balaji et al, 1999).

ADJUNCTS TO STANDARD SURGICAL THERAPY

Many patients treated by cystectomy, particularly those with tumors higher than stage T3, succumb to the effects of metastatic disease. Efforts to augment the impact of local therapy and, particularly, radical cystectomy have used a variety of strategies, most relying on either radiation or chemotherapy singly or in combination as either preemptive (neoadjuvant) or adjuvant therapy.

Preoperative Radiation Therapy

The role of preoperative radiotherapy has been examined by many investigators and has been reviewed (Thurman and DeWeese, 2000). Routinely performed until the 1980s, preoperative radiation therapy was thought to treat local micrometastases, potentially downstage otherwise unresectable tumors, and improve local control after cystectomy. **Available randomized data suggest that for patients with locoregionally advanced (T3) disease, local control may be improved by preoperative radiotherapy, but the survival advantage resulting from this intervention has been difficult to demonstrate** (Blackard, 1972; Slack and Prout, 1977; Awwad et al, 1979; Anderstrom et al, 1983; Ghoneim et al, 1985; Parsons, 1988; Smith et al, 1997). Nonrandomized trials have tended to support the general impression that preoperative radiation therapy does not significantly improve disease-specific survival (Cole et al, 1995; Pollack et al, 1997). One of the important confounding variables in published studies on this subject is the concomitant use of chemotherapy in the groups studied.

Neoadjuvant Chemotherapy

Chemotherapy given before definitive local treatment is called preemptive or neoadjuvant chemotherapy. **The rationale for this approach is that it allows a demonstration of tumor chemosensitivity and the potential downstaging of otherwise inoperable lesions. Treatment of micrometastases at a time when the patient is not debilitated by a surgical procedure also makes this sequence of chemotherapy administration attractive from a general medical perspective.** The potential disadvantages of this approach include error resulting from a primary reliance on clinical as opposed to pathologic staging and delay in the delivery of definitive local therapy.

Multiple centers have performed randomized trials of neoadjuvant chemotherapy for urothelial carcinoma of the bladder, the results of which appear in Table 77–3 (Wallace et al, 1991; Martinez-Pineiro et al, 1995; Malmstrom et al, 1996, 1999; Bassi et al, 1998; Grossman et al, 2003). There is increasing evidence to support the role of neoadjuvant chemotherapy for the treatment of locally advanced bladder cancer. The Nordic Cystectomy I trial used neoadjuvant combination chemotherapy followed by low-dose irradiation and cystectomy (Malmstrom et al, 1996). The overall 5-year survival rate was 59% in the chemotherapy group and 51% in the control group ($P = .1$). No difference was observed for stage T1 and stage T2 disease; however, there was a 15% improvement in overall survival for patients with stage T3 to stage T4a disease who received neoadjuvant therapy ($P = .03$). The United States Intergroup-0080 trial demonstrated an improvement of approximately 2.5 years in overall median survival among patients with locally advanced disease who received neoadjuvant MVAC therapy compared with cystectomy alone (Grossman et al, 2003). Two comprehensive meta-analyses of randomized controlled trials have also concluded that neoadjuvant cisplatin-based combination chemotherapy may offer a modest improvement in overall survival of 5% to 6% among patients with locally advanced disease (Advanced Bladder Cancer Meta-analysis Collaboration, 2003; Winquist et al, 2004).

Perioperative Chemotherapy

In a variation on the theme of neoadjuvant chemotherapy, several groups have used a perioperative chemotherapy strategy. The investigators at M. D. Anderson Hospital evaluated 100 patients randomized either to two cycles of methotrexate, vinblastine, doxorubicin (Adriamycin), and cisplatin (MVAC) before and three cycles after cystectomy or to five cycles after cystectomy. At 32 months of follow-up, **no difference in survival was identified between the two study groups, although a trend toward downstaging of larger lesions was noted in the group receiving the perioperative regimen** (Logothetis et al, 1996). Similar results were reported by others.

Table 77–3. Select Randomized Neoadjuvant Chemotherapy Trials for Bladder Cancer				
Trial	*No. of Patients*	*Chemotherapy*	*Local Therapy*	*Outcome*
CUETO, Spain	122	Cisplatin	Cystectomy	No difference
WMURG, United Kingdom	159	Cisplatin	XRT	No difference
ABSCG, Australia	96	Cisplatin	XRT	No difference
GUONE, Italy	206	MVAC	Cystectomy	No difference
Nordic I	325	Cisplatin, doxorubicin	XRT + cystectomy	Improved survival (T3/T4a)
Nordic II	316	Cisplatin, methotrexate	Cystectomy	No difference
MRC/EORTC	976	Cisplatin, methotrexate, vinblastine	XRT or cystectomy	Improved survival
Intergroup-0080, United States	317	MVAC	Cystectomy	Improved survival
Egypt	196	Carboplatin, methotrexate, vinblastine	Cystectomy	Improved survival

MVAC, methotrexate, vinblastine, doxorubicin (Adriamycin), and cisplatin; XRT, external-beam radiation therapy.
Modified from Winquist E, Kirchner TS, Segal R, et al: Neoadjuvant chemotherapy for transitional cell carcinoma of the bladder: A systematic review and meta-analysis. J Urol 2004;171:561-569.

Table 77–4. Results of Select Adjuvant Chemotherapy Trials after Cystectomy

Trial	No. of Patients	Chemotherapy	Survival Benefit	P Value
Skinner et al	87	CISCA	Median 4.3 vs 2.4 yr	0.006
			Overall 5-yr 44% vs 39%	Not significant
Studer et al	77	Cisplatin	Overall 5-yr 54% vs 57%	Not significant
Freiha and Torti	50	CMV	Overall 5-yr 54% vs 34%	Not significant
Stockle et al	49 randomized, 117 nonrandomized	MVAC/MVEC	5-yr disease free 50% vs 22%	0.002

CISCA, cisplatin, cyclophosphamide, and Adriamycin (doxorubicin); CMV, cisplatin, methotrexate, and vinblastine; MVAC/MVEC, methotrexate, vinblastine, doxorubicin/epirubicin, and cisplatin.
Modified from Rosenberg JE, Carroll PR, Small EJ: Update on chemotherapy for advanced bladder cancer. J Urol 2005;174:14-20.

Adjuvant Chemotherapy

The rationale for adjuvant chemotherapy is that patients with pathologically staged tumors with evidence of metastatic disease may benefit from systemic therapy that could reduce the likelihood of local recurrence or distant metastatic relapse. The disadvantages of the adjuvant setting include delay in administration of systemic therapy to patients with proven metastatic disease, difficulty of assessing tumor response to therapy in the absence of radiographically demonstrable residual disease, interference of postoperative complications with completion of the adjuvant protocol, and reduced willingness of the patient to participate in adjuvant therapy programs after major surgery.

Four randomized trials of adjuvant chemotherapy after cystectomy have been completed, and the results appear in Table 77–4 (Skinner et al, 1991; Stockle et al, 1992, 1995; Studer et al, 1994; Freiha and Torti, 1996). **The aggregate experience underscores the difficulty in performing single-institution trials on a disease of low prevalence such as invasive bladder cancer. Small numbers, subsequent difficulties imposed on subgroup analysis by low total accrual of patients, termination before complete accrual, and failure to complete the stated chemotherapy program represent only some of the major obstacles encountered in performing this type of research.** Despite these difficulties, the reports suggest that for patients with locoregional disease and pelvic lymph node involvement, cisplatin-based adjuvant therapy may provide a survival advantage worth discussing with appropriately selected patients (Dimopoulos, 1998). There is no evidence to suggest that the administration of adjuvant chemotherapy to patients with organ-confined bladder cancer (stage T1-T2) provides either a survival advantage or an improvement in local control after cystectomy. Consequently, this should not be considered outside a research protocol.

The first meta-analysis of adjuvant chemotherapy trials for bladder cancer based on individual patient data suggested a 9% improvement in survival at 3 years for patients who received chemotherapy compared with controls (Advanced Bladder Cancer Meta-analysis Collaboration, 2005). The impact of this study, however, was limited and insufficient to support the routine use of adjuvant cisplatin-based chemotherapy primarily because too few patients were collectively studied. Accrual of patients in sufficient numbers to demonstrate small survival advantages has been a considerable stumbling block for many centers (see Table 77–4).

ALTERNATIVES TO STANDARD THERAPY

In selected patients with invasive carcinoma, standard therapy may not provide optimal or acceptable management. Intercurrent illnesses that militate against the use of radical cystectomy as well as the patient's preferences in an era of increasing interest in conservative surgical intervention and organ preservation programs have driven the search for alternative methods of treating muscle-invasive carcinoma. These approaches range from TUR to the development of complex bladder preservation regimens employing endoscopic surgery, systemic chemotherapy, and radiation therapy.

Radiation Therapy

No randomized trials have been performed comparing radiation therapy alone with radical cystectomy. Conventional external-beam radiation therapy controls locally invasive tumor in 30% to 50% of patients (Wallace and Bloom, 1976; Jenkins et al, 1988; Gospodarowicz et al, 1989; Mameghan et al, 1992; Fossa et al, 1993; Hayter et al, 1999). Attempts to improve on this rate of success have used hyperfractionation schedules (several low doses of radiation therapy given each day during the treatment period, in contrast to one higher dose each day with standard radiation therapy) (Cole et al, 1992). Randomized trials of hyperfractionation suggest that this approach may be useful in the future, but larger controlled trials comparing this technique with standard conformal radiation therapy are required (Stuschke, 1997).

Transurethral Resection and Partial Cystectomy

Well-defined, small, superficially invasive bladder cancers have been managed by TUR or partial cystectomy for many years. The results of these experiences suggest that in highly selected patients with small, low-stage (T2) lesions, conservative surgical monotherapy can provide excellent local and distant control (Barnes et al, 1967; Herr, 1987; Henry et al, 1988; Solsona et al, 1998; Roosen et al, 1997). **Solsona and colleagues (1998) described a large group of patients with negative tumor bed and normal peripheral biopsy findings after complete, "radical" TUR. These authors cited 5-year disease-specific survival statistics impressively similar to those reported for radical cystectomy.** This study is flawed by its nonrandomized design, but the results still underscore the potential utility of this approach in appropriately selected patients.

Transurethral Resection and Partial Cystectomy with Chemotherapy

One objection to the treatment of patients with invasive bladder cancer by local excision alone is that studies examining the thoroughness of TUR in particular suggest that complete TUR of moderate to large T2 lesions is unlikely (Kolozsy, 1991). Higher stage lesions are, at least theoretically, even less likely to be controlled, leaving the patient treated in this manner with unappreciated residual tumor that may, in time, produce local and distant failure. To augment conservative surgical intervention, investigators have examined the combination of limited surgery and systemic chemotherapy (Socquet, 1981; Herr, 1994; Herr and Scher, 1998; Sternberg et al, 1999). Hall and colleagues (1984) described 61 patients treated with TUR and systemic chemotherapy for T2 bladder cancer. Of these patients, 48 retained the bladder and were free of locally invasive disease. In those patients who were free of muscle-invasive disease at the first surveillance cystoscopy after initial complete TUR, the 5-year disease-specific survival rate was 75% compared with 25% for those with residual or recurrent disease. Other contemporary series have corroborated the observations of these investigators. Chemotherapy has been shown to result in good long-term survival particularly in patients downstaged to p0 at the time of surgery (Herr, 1994). Prospective randomized studies comparing this approach with standard surgical intervention are required to formally evaluate its equivalence to radical cystectomy.

Bladder Preservation Protocols

Combined-modality bladder preservation protocols have been proposed as an alternative to radical cystectomy, motivated by a rationale with two components:
1. Many patients with invasive bladder cancer have micrometastatic disease at the time of presentation. These patients, when asymptomatic, may not derive significant benefit from local intervention without concomitant systemic therapy.

2. Removal of the bladder in the asymptomatic patient with metastatic disease is not necessary, does not enhance quality of life, and delays the delivery of potentially valuable systemic therapy.

These lines of reasoning are countered by arguments suggesting that (1) preservation protocols rely on clinical and not pathologic staging and are thus prone to error with regard to overtreatment and undertreatment, (2) local recurrence and complications ensuing from local relapse or failure to control the local lesion cause significant morbidity and mortality, and (3) orthotopic bladder reconstruction is now widely available for both men and women and provides excellent quality of life for patients interested in retaining the ability to void through the urethra. These issues have been reviewed (Montie, 1999; Shipley et al, 1999; Feneley and Schoenberg, 2000), and many reports examine the role of this strategy in the management of patients with invasive bladder cancer (Kaufman et al, 1993; Tester et al, 1993, 1996; Vogelzang et al, 1993; Letocha et al, 1994).

The North American approach to organ conservation is characterized by its selective nature and identification of patients who are likely to do well with trimodality therapy. General criteria for selective bladder sparing includes presence of muscle-invasive disease, absence of hydronephrosis, normal renal function, normal complete blood count, suitable candidate for cystectomy, and absence of metastatic disease on imaging studies. Only patients who are complete responders are advanced to full-dose regimens. It is believed that this treatment algorithm permits salvage cystectomy to be performed sooner for patients who are incomplete responders and before they have received full-dose radiation (Shipley et al, 2005).

Although no available prospective randomized data exist comparing radical cystectomy with contemporary bladder-sparing protocols, data from single and multi-institutional trials of bladder preservation have been published (Housset et al, 1993; Dunst et al, 1994; Fellin et al, 1997; Vikram et al, 1998) (Table 77–5). Kaufman and colleagues (1993) treated 106 patients with stage T2-T4 NX M0 bladder cancer by TUR, neoadjuvant chemotherapy (MCV), and subsequent radiation therapy. Patients not responding were treated by radical cystectomy. These authors reported a 52% overall survival. Of the patients completing the full course of therapy, 75% retained

Table 77–5. Results of Other Selected Bladder Preservation Studies

Trial	No. of Patients	Stage	Treatment	Survival with Intact Bladder
Housset et al	40	T2-T4	TURBT + chemo + XRT	81% 3-yr overall survival
Vikram et al	21	T2-T3	TURBT + chemo + XRT	37% 5-yr overall survival
Kachnic et al	76	T2-T4a	TURBT + chemo + XRT	43% 5-yr overall survival
Fellin et al	56	T2-T4	TURBT + chemo + XRT	59% 5-yr disease-specific survival
Chauvet et al	109	T2-T4	TURBT + chemo + XRT	42% 4-yr overall survival
Dunst et al	245	T1-T4	TURBT + chemo + XRT	39% 5-yr overall survival
Shipley et al	190	T2-T4a	TURBT + chemo + XRT	45% 10-yr disease-specific survival
Rodel et al	415	T1-T4	TURBT + chemo + XRT	42% 5-yr overall survival
Housset et al	54	T2-T4	TURBT + chemo + XRT	62% 3-yr disease-specific survival
Sternberg et al	104	T2-T4	Neoadjuvant MVAC + TURBT	44% 5-yr overall survival
Herr	99	T2	TURBT alone	57% 10-yr disease-specific survival

TURBT, transurethral resection of bladder tumor; XRT, external-beam radiation therapy; MVAC, methotrexate, vinblastine, doxorubicin (Adriamycin), and cisplatin.
Modified from Torres-Roca JF: Bladder preservation protocols in the treatment of muscle-invasive bladder cancer. Cancer Control 2004;11:358-363.

bladders free of disease with a median follow-up of 64 months. These authors observed that smaller tumors, those not associated with hydronephrosis, and those amenable to complete TUR were the most likely to achieve a favorable outcome by this strategy. Subsequent studies by other investigators using similar chemotherapy regimens and various schedules for the delivery of radiation therapy have lent support to these conclusions (Table 77–6). **The toxicities associated with preservation regimens are those associated with the use of radiation and systemic chemotherapy: nausea, vomiting, fatigue, neutropenia, and diarrhea in 40% to 70% of patients. The treatment-related mortality rate is approximately 1% in reported studies, resulting primarily from neutropenic sepsis. Radiation-induced bladder dysfunction is rare (1%), and sexual dysfunction (particularly impotence in male patients) occurs in approximately 25% of cases. Structural and histologic features that argue against the use of bladder preservation are the presence of hydronephrosis; carcinoma in situ, which responds poorly to multimodality therapy; and a tumor that cannot be completely resected transurethrally.** An algorithm for the use of bladder-sparing strategies has been proposed (Feneley and Schoenberg, 2000) (Fig. 77–2).

Interstitial Radiation Therapy

The use of radiation sources in the management of invasive bladder cancer includes interstitial radiation therapy, although this technique is employed at only a few centers internationally (Grossman and Prez-Tamayo, 1993; Wijnmaalen et al, 1997). Results of this approach, which uses preoperative external-beam radiation therapy, partial cystectomy, or TUR and subsequent placement of iridium 192 wires, are impressive in nonrandomized series. **Overall survival rates for low-stage tumors (T1-T2) of 60% to 80% have been reported. Wijnmaalen and associates (1997) reported relapse-free survival rates of 88% with a 98% probability of bladder preservation in surviving patients.** Complications of interstitial therapy include delayed wound healing, fistula formation, hematuria, and chronic cystitis. As many as 25% of patients have acute local side effects. These experiences suggest that in selected cases, this approach may provide an acceptable alternative bladder preservation strategy.

Intra-arterial Chemotherapy

Intra-arterial chemotherapy for invasive and locally advanced bladder cancer has been evaluated at many centers with variable results (Stewart et al, 1987; Galetti et al, 1989; Jacobs et al, 1989; Mokarim et al, 1997). The rationale for intra-arterial infusion of chemotherapeutic agents is increased dose delivered to the tumor with reduced toxicity. Intra-arterial chemotherapy has been combined with radical cystectomy and definitive radiation therapy. Reduction in local disease burden has been reported, but larger studies are required.

Hyperthermia and Chemotherapy

The use of hyperthermia to improve the antineoplastic activity of chemotherapy or radiation therapy has become a focus of interest as the demand for more effective bladder-sparing and salvage regimens has grown (Cockett et al, 1967). Although positive preliminary studies have appeared in the literature, a randomized prospective study of patients with pelvic malignant neoplasms (including stage T2-T4 N0 MX bladder cancer) treated by radiation or radiation plus hyperthermia was published by a multicenter Dutch collaborative group and failed to show any long-term benefit in the bladder cancer subgroup (van der Zee et al, 2000). The role of this novel adjunct requires further examination.

MANAGEMENT OF METASTATIC BLADDER CANCER
Systemic Chemotherapy

Patients with metastatic bladder cancer are routinely treated with systemic chemotherapy, particularly in the setting of unresectable, diffusely metastatic, measurable disease. Multi-agent chemotherapeutic regimens have greater activity than single-agent protocols (Loehrer et al, 1992; Saxman et al, 1997). The most commonly employed agents are methotrexate, vinblastine, doxorubicin, and cisplatin (Harker et al, 1985; Sternberg et al, 1989). Regimens containing these drugs produce complete response in approximately 20% of patients, although long-term disease-free survival is rare. MVAC, although superior to single-agent therapy, is associated with significant toxicity (more than 20% experience neutropenic fever). Death from sepsis has been reported in 3% to 4% of patients receiving MVAC. Dose escalation with bone marrow–supportive agents, such as granulocyte-macrophage colony-stimulating factor, has resulted in decreased toxicity without significant increase in response rates (Logothetis et al, 1990; Loehrer et al, 1992, 1994). These disappointing results have prompted a search for additional agents and multidrug

Table 77–6.	Results of Selected Bladder Preservation Studies: Radiation Therapy Oncology Group (RTOG)			
Trial	No. of Patients	Radiation Therapy	Radiosensitizing Chemotherapy	5-Year Survival (%)
RTOG 85-12	42	Daily (64.8 Gy)	Cisplatin	52
RTOG 88-02	91	Daily (64.8 Gy)	Cisplatin	51
RTOG 89-03	123	Daily (64.8 Gy)	Cisplatin	49
RTOG 95-06	34	Hyperfractionated	Cisplatin + 5-fluorouracil	N/A
RTOG 97-06	52	Hyperfractionated	Cisplatin	N/A
RTOG 99-06	84	Hyperfractionated	Cisplatin + paclitaxel	N/A

Modified from Shipley WU, Zietman AL, Kaufman DS, et al: Selective bladder preservation by trimodality therapy for patients with muscularis propria–invasive bladder cancer and who are cystectomy candidates—the Massachusetts General Hospital and Radiation Therapy Oncology Group experiences. Semin Radiat Oncol 2005;15:36-41.
NA, not available.

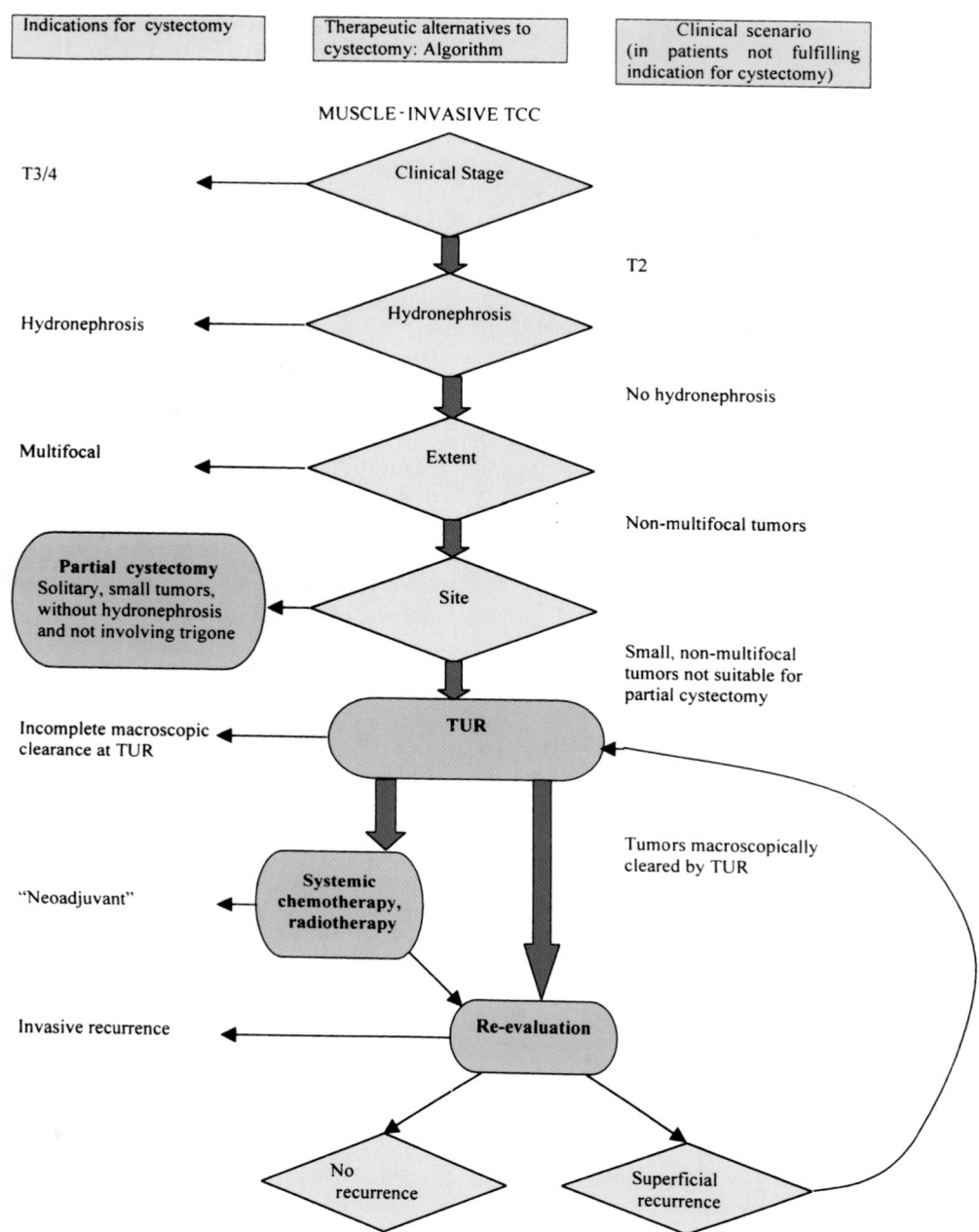

Figure 77–2. Algorithm for use of bladder preservation strategies. TCC, transitional cell carcinoma; TUR, transurethral resection. (From Feneley MR, Schoenberg MP: Bladder-sparing strategies for transitional cell carcinoma. Urology 2000;56:549-560.)

combinations with activity equivalent or superior to the older combinations.

Newer Agents

Gemcitabine (Gemzar) is an antimetabolite chemotherapeutic agent that is an analog of cytosine arabinoside (ara-C). Gemcitabine has been used as a single agent (higher than 25% complete response) and in combination with cisplatin (40% partial response and complete response) with encouraging results in patients with metastatic disease (Stadler et al, 1997; Lorusso et al, 1998; Moore et al, 1999). The combination of

gemcitabine and cisplatin (GC) has demonstrated similar survival outcomes with less toxicity compared with MVAC in patients with metastatic disease (von der Maase et al, 2000). In this study, a total of 405 patients with locally advanced or metastatic urothelial carcinoma were randomized to receive either GC or MVAC combination chemotherapy. Overall survival, time to disease progression, time to treatment failure, and response rate were similar for both groups. **The combination of GC provided a survival advantage similar to that of MVAC with a better safety profile and tolerability. The most significant toxic effects associated with GC combination chemotherapy are thrombocytopenia and neutropenia,** which can occur in up to 50% of patients (Droz et al, 2002; Meliani et al, 2003). The improved risk/benefit ratio has changed the standard of care for patients with locally advanced and metastatic disease from MVAC to GC (Aparicio et al, 2005).

Taxoids are microtubule disassembly inhibitors and represent a new class of agents for use in cancer chemotherapy. Paclitaxel (Taxol) and docetaxel (Taxotere), a semisynthetic taxane, have been used in clinical trials of patients with advanced bladder cancer, with response rates ranging from 25% to 83% in combination regimens (Roth et al, 1994; Tu et al, 1995; de Wit et al, 1998; Dimopoulos et al, 1998; Redman et al, 1998; Sengelov et al, 1998; Vaughn et al, 1998; Zielinski et al, 1998; Pycha et al, 1999).

Gallium nitrate is a naturally occurring metal with antineoplastic activity. In phase II trials, response rates ranging from 10% to 50% have been reported (Einhorn et al, 1994; Dreicer et al, 1997). Toxicity with this agent is significant and limits its general utility.

Trimetrexate is an antifolate that has been studied in patients who previously received and progressed during methotrexate therapy. This drug may be useful in patients resistant to the methotrexate used in certain multidrug regimens (Witte et al, 1994).

In addition to drug combinations such as paclitaxel and cisplatin, **investigators are examining three drug schedules including taxoids** (Bajorin et al, 2000; Dodd et al, 2000). Randomized data are forthcoming.

LOCAL SALVAGE AND PALLIATIVE THERAPY
Salvage Cystectomy

Patients choosing conservative or primarily nonsurgical forms of therapy for invasive or locoregionally advanced bladder cancer may require subsequent definitive surgical intervention when conservative treatment has produced a partial response and residual disease remains clinically confined to the bladder. Several groups have retrospectively reviewed their experiences (Johnson and Bracken, 1977; Blandy et al, 1980; Crawford and Skinner, 1980; Smith, 1981; Osborn et al, 1982; Jenkins et al, 1988; Nurmi et al, 1989; Abratt et al, 1993). Donat and associates (1996) reviewed a series of patients with locoregional disease treated with systemic therapy and subsequent salvage surgery and reported 22% survival among patients with a complete or nearly complete response to systemic therapy. Similar results were reported by Dodd and colleagues (1999). Bochner and coworkers (1998) found that orthotopic reconstruction is safe and effective in selected patients undergoing salvage surgery. Resection appears to help patients who had a complete response to systemic therapy, but surgery for residual extravesical disease confers no long-term survival advantage and should generally be discouraged.

MOLECULAR MARKERS AND INVASIVE AND ADVANCED BLADDER CANCER

The role of molecular markers in the management of invasive and metastatic bladder cancer has been reviewed. Although multiple potential markers of prognosis have been identified, none has been definitively studied in a randomized prospective manner. Some markers, such as the *p53* tumor suppressor gene, are under examination in multi-institutional trials. The results of these and similar studies are awaited with anticipation.

SUMMARY

Invasive and metastatic bladder cancer remains a difficult management problem for physicians and patients. To change the fate of many patients with bladder cancer, further study of diagnostic and staging techniques, development of useful prognostic markers, and, most important, development of effective systemic therapy for advanced disease are required. These goals will be accomplished only through prospective, multi-institutional trials that require the support of the entire urologic community.

KEY POINTS

- Understand staging of urothelial cancer of the urinary bladder
- Indications for partial versus radical cystectomy
- Indications for neoadjuvant chemotherapy
- Limitations of pelvic lymphadenectomy
- Role of bladder-preserving strategies in patients with invasive bladder cancer
- Role for systemic therapy in the management of patients with advanced disease
- Indications for salvage

SUGGESTED READINGS

Fossa SD, Berner A: Clinical significance of the "palpable mass" in patients with muscle-infiltrating bladder cancer undergoing cystectomy after preoperative radiotherapy. Br J Urol 1991;67:54-60.

Ghoneim MA, et-Mekresh MM, el-Baz MA, et al: Radical cystectomy for carcinoma of the bladder: Critical evaluation of the results in 1,026 cases. J Urol 1997;158:393-399.

Gill IS, Fergany A, Klein EA, et al: Laparoscopic radical cystoprostatectomy with ileal conduit performed completely intracorporeally: The initial 2 cases. Urology 2000;56:26-29; discussion 29-30.

Grossman H, Natale R, Tangen C, et al: Neoadjuvant chemotherapy plus cystectomy compared to cystectomy alone for locally advanced bladder cancer. N Engl J Med 2003;349:859-866.

Schlegel PN, Walsh PC: Neuroanatomical approach to radical cystoprostatectomy with preservation of sexual function. J Urol 1987;138:1402-1406.

Skinner DG: Management of invasive bladder cancer: A meticulous pelvic node dissection can make a difference. J Urol 1982;128:34-36.

Stein JP, Lieskovsky G, Cote R, et al: Radical cystectomy in the treatment of invasive bladder cancer: Long-term results in 1,054 patients. J Clin Oncol 2001;19:666-675.

Surgery of Bladder Cancer

PETER T. NIEH, MD • FRAY F. MARSHALL, MD

There have been many technical advances in the surgery of bladder cancer. Survival rates for patients with bladder cancer have improved as a result of better surgical techniques, improved intensive care monitoring, and adjuvant therapy. Contributing to these treatment successes has been the impact of the role of primary surgical therapy on the natural history of this disease. Application of prognostic variables allows use of adjuvant chemotherapy with advanced local disease in patients who are at high risk for systemic disease.

The first cystectomy was performed in the late 1800s; but in 1926, Young and Davis indicated that a high mortality rate and poor success made cystectomy unjustifiable. In 1939, a mortality rate of 34.5% was reported in Hinman's large series of 250 cystectomies (Hinman, 1939). Early series also demonstrated high incidence of local invasion, prompting aggressive surgical therapy in those patients who underwent cystectomy. Anterior exenteration with vaginectomy and salpingo-oophorectomy was common. Improvements in surgical anesthetic techniques as well as perioperative care have reduced the mortality rate of radical cystectomy to 1% to 3% in most contemporary series (Bracken et al, 1981; Stein, 2001).

Patients now often present with less invasive disease, and the large, bulky tumors that were common in early series are less frequently encountered today. These changes have brought about many exciting developments in the field of surgery for bladder cancer. Transurethral resection techniques are often curative in low-stage, noninvasive tumors. Organ-sparing treatments are receiving more attention for the treatment of low-stage disease.

Radical cystectomy is still the mainstay of treatment for muscle-invasive disease of the bladder. However, improvements in bladder substitution techniques now make it possible for a significant percentage of patients treated with radical cystectomy to have orthotopic bladder substitutions or continent diversions. Nerve-sparing radical cystectomy and vagina-sparing techniques continue to improve. Preservation of sexual function and volitional voiding are often achievable goals in both sexes, but about 20% of patients will need to self-catheterize because of incomplete emptying of the neobladder.

Preoperative radiation therapy was promoted as an adjunctive treatment to improve survival in the 1970s. Although the perioperative complications were not increased by such irradiation, there was also no increased survival advantage (Thrasher and Crawford, 1993; Skinner et al, 1998). Combination chemotherapy trials have demonstrated increased efficacy in the treatment of metastatic transitional cell carcinoma in the bladder, and the role of adjuvant or neoadjuvant chemotherapy in high-risk patients with locally advanced disease remains promising. As with many other malignant neoplasms, bladder cancer treatment for high-risk patients has evolved to a combination of less radical extirpative surgery with more effective, better tolerated, adjunctive therapies.

TRANSURETHRAL RESECTION OF BLADDER TUMORS

Transurethral resection (TUR) of bladder tumors is both a diagnostic and a therapeutic procedure. **Diagnostically, the goal of TUR is procurement of tissue for histologic examination to determine type and extent of disease. Therapeutically, the goal of TUR is definitive treatment of all macroscopic noninvasive tumors.** TUR may also be applicable to the management of superficially invasive transitional cell tumors as well as to the treatment of deeply invasive tumors in high-risk patients who are not suitable candidates for conventional radical cystectomy.

Indications

Patients with bladder cancer often present with painless hematuria, either gross or microscopic. Irritative voiding symptoms, such as frequency, urgency, and dysuria, can also be initial symptoms associated with bladder cancer, especially carcinoma in situ (CIS). Flank pain due to obstruction of the ureteral orifice from a bladder tumor can be an unusual presenting symptom. Hydronephrosis from tumor obstruction involving the ureteral orifice is often silent and an indicator of advanced disease. On occasion, a bladder tumor may be found incidentally in a patient undergoing TUR of the prostate or on intravenous pyelography for suspected ureteral calculus. Secondary bladder tumors may develop after radiation therapy for prostate cancer (Neugut et al, 1997) or gynecologic malignant disease (Maier et al, 1997).

Preoperative Evaluation

A thorough history and physical examination should be performed for any patient thought to have a bladder tumor. History includes past or current tobacco use, occupational chemical exposure, prior cyclophosphamide exposure, and prior pelvic radiation therapy. A bimanual examination should be performed preoperatively and postoperatively to help determine extent of disease. If there is significant perioperative perivesical fluid extravasation, any residual mass might be obscured. One should note whether there is a palpable mass and whether the mass is mobile or feels fixed to the pelvic sidewall. Urine cytologic studies may also be performed.

Upper tract imaging is performed to rule out ureteral or renal pelvic filling defects. This can be done with intravenous pyelography or computed tomography (CT) scan, which has replaced intravenous pyelography in most centers. CT scan has the advantage of determining size of the bladder tumor and, to some extent, presence of local invasion or regional lymphadenopathy. In patients with contrast dye allergies or impaired renal function, retrograde pyelography with oblique films can also delineate an upper tract lesion.

Surgical Technique

Before resection, sterile urine is documented with a urine culture. Routine laboratory testing is performed for complete blood count, serum electrolyte determinations including creatinine, and clotting parameters. Any electrolyte or clotting abnormalities should be corrected preoperatively.

The patient is placed in the dorsal lithotomy position, with care taken to protect the popliteal fossa from undue pressure. Prophylactic intravenous antibiotics are administered. For most tumors on the bladder floor or dome, there is no special anesthesic requirement. In dealing with tumors on the lateral bladder wall, however, electrosurgical resection is more likely to stimulate the adjacent obturator nerve, leading to inadvertent bladder perforation. **General anesthesia with paralytic agents is preferred in these situations, but obturator nerve block may also be employed with spinal anesthesia to minimize adductor muscle spasm** (Augspurger and Donohue, 1980).

Panendoscopy is performed to identify the location and number of tumors and the location of and efflux from both ureteral orifices. Water can be used as the bladder irrigant during the procedure because of its cytolytic effects. However, if a lengthy resection is anticipated, a more isotonic solution, such as glycine, sorbitol, or mannitol, is used to reduce the risk of hemolysis if there is bladder perforation or fluid absorption.

If the bladder lesion is small, it may be amenable to cold-cup biopsy and fulguration. This eliminates the cauterization artifact seen with resectoscope specimens. In patients suited for endoscopic treatment of the bladder tumor, biopsy specimens should be obtained from areas of normal-appearing

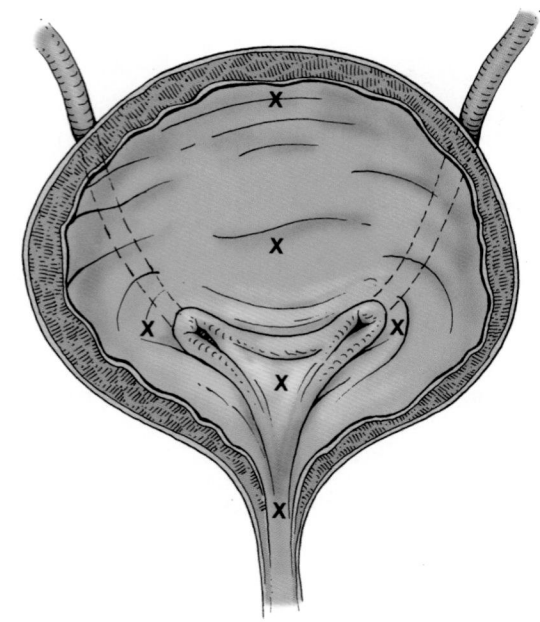

Figure 78–1. Bladder map for recording location, size, and characteristics of bladder tumors. The sites recommended for selected-site mucosal biopsies are represented by X. (From Hudson MA: Transurethral resection of bladder tumors. In Marshall FF, ed: Textbook of Operative Urology. Philadelphia, WB Saunders, 1996.)

bladder as well as the prostatic urethra (Fig. 78–1). This mapping of the bladder aids in determining the presence of CIS or other factors important to the patient's eventual treatment.

Three types of electrical current are used in TUR: cutting, coagulation, and blended. The best current for cutting is the undamped current generated by a **tube oscillator circuit.** Coagulation is accomplished with a highly damped spark-gap current generated from a spark-gap oscillator circuit (Hudson, 1996). A blended current is an adjustable combination of cutting and coagulation currents; it is useful in improving hemostasis when vascular tissues are resected by adding the coagulating effect of a spark-gap current to the tube oscillator cutting current. The current density varies with the surface area of the loop. Finer diameter loops project a more concentrated current and therefore cut more easily; the larger diameter loops produce better hemostasis. The zone of tissue destruction with a cutting current is negligible (Hudson, 1996).

The proper positioning for a spring-loaded resectoscope is demonstrated in Figure 78–2. The bladder should be sufficiently distended so that it does not fold up on itself, but overdistention should be avoided. Continuous flow irrigation maintains a more constant bladder volume so that the targeted tumors remain relatively fixed in space, and more important, the bladder wall thickness is not changing during the resection, decreasing the risk of perforation. It is usually best to begin resection of the most exophytic region of the tumor first, beginning at the most anterior or superior portion. If it is necessary to decrease bleeding and improve visibility, the tumor vessels feeding the lesion can be coagulated before resection. The resection should proceed in an orderly fashion

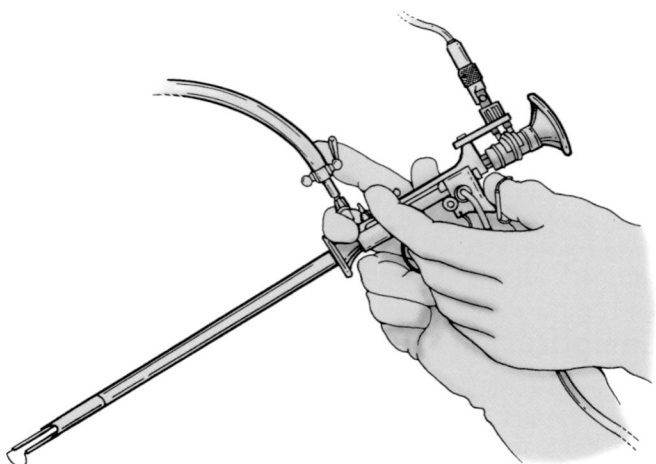

Figure 78–2. Proper positioning of the hands when a spring-loaded resectoscope is used. (From Hudson MA: Transurethral resection of bladder tumors. In Marshall FF, ed: Textbook of Operative Urology. Philadelphia, WB Saunders, 1996.)

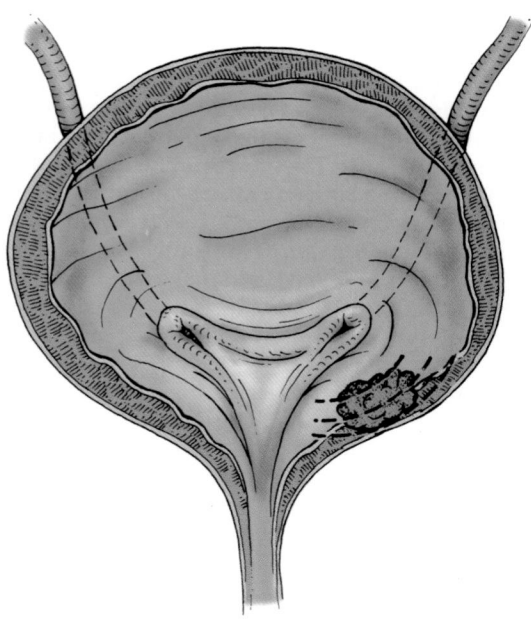

Figure 78–3. Resection of an exophytic lesion in an orderly fashion from one end to the other. The base of the lesion is then resected into the muscularis propria and sent as a separate specimen. The resection should be performed in a manner that follows the contour of the bladder wall. (From Hudson MA: Transurethral resection of bladder tumors. In Marshall FF, ed: Textbook of Operative Urology. Philadelphia, WB Saunders, 1996.)

from one side of the tumor to the other, taking full-length swaths through the tumor and avoiding short, irregular depth divots (Fig. 78–3). Bladder tumors tend to adhere to the loop, so the larger resected specimens will dislodge from the loop more readily. Tumor fragments can be collected with an Ellik-type evacuator. Additional resection of the base of the tumor can then provide a separate specimen to aid in determining depth of invasion. The muscle fibers of the detrusor should be readily visible in place of the granular appearance of tumor at the completion of the resection.

Multiple papillary lesions, if small, may be managed with fulguration. Certainly, if it is the patient's first tumor resection, it is advisable to resect each tumor, if possible; however, repetitive resection of multiple superficial tumors may lead to fibrosis and noncompliance of the bladder. For smaller lesions, fulguration alone may be preferable. Fulguration can be performed with local anesthesia as an outpatient procedure. If larger lesions are present, it may be advisable to begin resection at the dome of the bladder first and then to proceed more posteriorly. This is helpful because of the relative inaccessibility of the dome of the anterior bladder. If these lesions are not resected initially, later visualization can be compromised by excessive bleeding. Resection at the dome of the bladder can be facilitated by suprapubic pressure and avoidance of overdistention of the bladder. Bleeding should be controlled at each site of tumor resection before moving to another lesion to ensure adequate visibility.

Sessile lesions, rather than papillary lesions, are more likely to be high grade and invasive. The role of TUR in the setting of muscle-invasive disease is controversial, but it is clear that **TUR alone is inadequate for the definitive treatment of most muscle-invasive bladder cancers.** No randomized studies have compared TUR alone with cystectomy; however, some studies have suggested that TUR may play a role if careful selection of patients is performed. Up to 10% of patients who undergo radical cystectomy have no residual tumor on pathologic examination of the bladder after the initial endoscopic resection (Herr, 1992), and those **patients**

who are rendered pT0 after resection will have better prognosis than those with incomplete resection (Lee et al, 2004). Solsona and associates (1992) looked at the question of TUR alone for the management of selective cases of muscle-invasive bladder cancer. In a prospective study, 59 of 308 patients with muscle-invasive disease were found to have no evidence of residual disease on repeated TUR. Patients were selected for TUR alone if the initial resection of the tumor was visibly and palpably complete and if normal biopsy findings were obtained from the base of the tumor at the end of the TUR. Fifty-three percent of the patients remained tumor free, with a mean follow-up of 55 months, and an 83% 5-year survival was reported. Overall, 43 of the 59 patients remained free of invasive recurrence with their bladders intact. Herr (1987) reported prospectively on 45 patients suitable for TUR alone from a group of 217 consecutive patients referred for muscle-invasive bladder cancer. These 45 patients were selected because of negative results of urine cytology after resection and either no residual tumor on repeated TUR or only superficial residual recurrences. At 5 years, 30 of the 45 patients (65%) were alive with their bladders intact. There was a 70% survival for stage T2 and a 57% survival for stage T3a. Eleven patients went on to require cystectomy, and 21 of the 30 required additional resections with or without intravesical chemotherapy for superficial recurrences.

Five-year survival rates after TUR for stage B (T2-T3a) bladder cancer in series have ranged from 31% to 83% (Given and Wajsman, 1997). **No randomized studies have compared TUR alone with cystectomy. However, there is probably a small subset of patients with stage T2 transitional cell carcinoma who may be candidates for resection therapy alone. These are likely to be patients with small, solitary, papillary,** moderately differentiated, stage T2 or minimal stage T3a lesions smaller than 2 cm in diameter at the tumor base. Most important, the lesion must be completely resectable transurethrally. Radical cystectomy probably has the best survival rate overall for medically fit patients, but in selected patients with these criteria who are not medically fit for cystectomy, TUR alone may be a reasonable option.

A second endoscopic resection is important in evaluating the true stage of bladder cancer invasion because a high percentage of patients may have residual cancer identified on repeated TUR (Herr, 1999). Follow-up cystoscopy and deep TUR biopsy at 4 to 6 weeks should be performed along with bimanual examination and urine cytology for any patient in whom TUR alone is considered a treatment option (Given and Wajsman, 1997). If the results of any of these follow-up studies are positive, other treatment options should be sought.

The **neodymium:yttrium-aluminum-garnet (Nd:YAG) laser** has also been used in the management of both noninvasive and invasive bladder tumors. Laser therapy has potential advantages because it can be used with local anesthesia with minimal bleeding or obturator nerve stimulation. One of the main disadvantages is that it does not allow significant tissue procurement for pathologic examination. The Nd:YAG laser has been reported to have good local tumor control with superficial bladder tumors. It has also been used with variable success in invasive bladder cancers for patients who are not suitable surgical candidates. Beisland and Sander (1990) treated 15 patients with solitary stage T2 tumors with a combination of TUR and Nd:YAG laser ablation of the tumor bed. Two thirds of the patients were alive at 10 years without evidence of disease, although three had superficial recurrences. Bowel perforations have also been reported.

There has been interest in **photodynamic therapy** for the treatment of superficial transitional cell carcinoma of the bladder. This therapy combines a photosensitizer, such as porfimer sodium (Photofrin), with red laser light (630 nm) to destroy cancer cells. Studies have demonstrated this therapy to be a safe and effective treatment of recurrent, superficial bladder cancer. Nseyo and colleagues (1998) looked at photodynamic therapy as an alternative to cystectomy in patients in whom topical chemotherapy for refractory CIS of the bladder had failed. At a mean follow-up of 12 months, the overall durable response rate was only 31%, with 14 of 36 patients undergoing cystectomy for persistent CIS or recurrence. Clinical trials continue in this area of investigation.

Postoperative Management

All bleeding should be controlled at the time of surgery. Resection of smaller bladder tumors with minimal bleeding may not require postoperative catheterization; however, for most endoscopic resections, a short period of bladder catheterization with a Foley catheter is indicated. The catheter can be removed when the hematuria has resolved, usually the morning after surgery. Catheterization helps monitor both urine output and degree of hematuria. Limiting bladder distention with a catheter may reduce the amount of postoperative bleeding, but sometimes the catheter tip may abrade a midline resection site and promote bleeding. Catheter drainage may be indicated for longer periods if perforation has occurred or is suspected with deep tumor resection.

For patients with single or multiple superficial Ta or T1 tumors, **immediate or early postoperative intravesical instillation of chemotherapy, such as mitomycin C (40 mg in 40 mL of normal saline for 1 hour), has demonstrated more than 50% reduction in tumor recurrences** (Sylvester et al, 2004).

Antibiotics are not required postoperatively; however, many urologists prescribe prophylactic oral antibiotics for a period of 3 to 5 days. Oral analgesics are often prescribed, and antispasmodics can be helpful for bladder spasms.

Complications

Bladder perforation usually occurs when the cutting loop resects through the wall of the bladder. This can happen if the bladder becomes overdistended or if the resectoscope or loop is extended in a manner that does not follow the contour of the bladder surface (Fig. 78–4). Obturator nerve stimulation during resection of an inferior lateral tumor can also increase the likelihood of perforation. Perforation can occur either extraperitoneally or intraperitoneally, where there is potential risk of injury to the bowel. If a bladder perforation is suspected, an intraoperative cystogram can be obtained along with a postdrainage film to delineate the extent of the leak. **Small perforations are of no clinical significance and can be managed with catheter drainage and postoperative antibiotics. Large extraperitoneal perforations often resolve with catheter drainage alone, but some may require placement of a percutaneous drain. Intraperitoneal perforations may also do well with catheter drainage. Open exploration and repair are recommended if there are concerns about bowel injury or if there are ongoing signs of peritoneal irritation despite catheter drainage.** More recently, percutaneous peritoneal drainage (Manikandan et al, 2003) and laparoscopic repair (Golab et al, 2003) have been successfully employed. **The risk of tumor seeding after bladder perforation is low** (Mydlo et al, 1999).

Ongoing bleeding and clot retention are possible postoperative complications, although these are unusual if proper

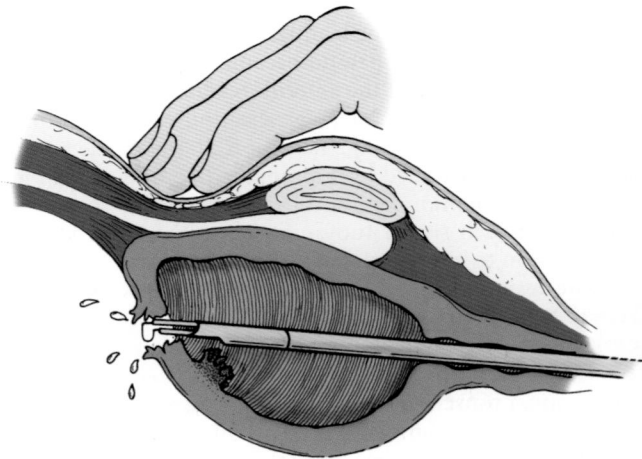

Figure 78–4. Perforation of the bladder with the resectoscope occurs when the bladder is overdistended or when the loop is extended and used in a manner that does not follow the bladder contour. (From Hudson MA: Transurethral resection of bladder tumors. In Marshall FF, ed: Textbook of Operative Urology. Philadelphia, WB Saunders, 1996.)

control is obtained during the operation. These patients should have coagulation parameters checked and, if necessary, appropriate blood products replaced. If hand irrigation fails to clear the clot retention, it is advisable to return to the cystoscopy suite. After an anesthetic has been administered, the clots can be evacuated through a resectoscope sheath and bleeding points coagulated.

During a lengthy resection, it is possible to have absorption of excess irrigation fluid through open veins. This can lead to volume overload, electrolyte imbalances, and intravascular hemolysis, causing acute renal failure. Treatment involves early recognition and administration of diuretics. Fluid restriction as well as supplemental oxygen should be instituted.

Obstruction of a ureteral orifice secondary to resection can occur, but it is unlikely if only cutting current is used across the orifice. Urethral strictures can also occur, as with TUR of the prostate. These tend to occur at the fossa navicularis of the meatus or the bulbomembranous junction.

KEY POINTS: TRANSURETHRAL RESECTION OF BLADDER TUMORS

- It is important to perform complete mapping of the bladder, including normal-appearing bladder, prostatic urethra, and bladder neck, with deep biopsy of sessile or solid tumors to assess for muscle invasion.
- Staged resection may be required to determine muscle invasion.
- Immediate postoperative instillation of intravesical chemotherapy, such as mitomycin C, decreases tumor recurrences.

SURGICAL APPROACHES

The bladder is approached surgically through either transverse or vertical incisions below the umbilicus. Transverse incisions are Pfannenstiel and Cherney. The Pfannenstiel incision is a transverse curvilinear incision made 1 to 2 cm above the pubis. The anterior rectus fascia is divided transversely, the upper and lower fascia flaps are dissected off the rectus muscle, and the rectus muscles are separated in the midline. The Cherney incision is similar to the Pfannenstiel but separates the rectus muscles transversely from the pubis. Transverse incisions are more cosmetic and have been considered to heal more securely, but there may be an increased inguinal hernia risk with extended incisions. Vertical incisions may be midline or paramedian. Vertical midline incisions are easier to perform and can be extended superiorly, if necessary, to gain access to para-aortic nodes. Small midline incisions such as the minilaparotomy can be used for small operations on the bladder or for pelvic lymphadenectomy (Steiner and Marshall, 1993). Operative exposure is facilitated by the use of small fixed ring retractors that provide superficial and deep retraction through these small incisions.

The urinary bladder is highly vascular with a rich blood supply from the superior and inferior vesical branches arising from the anterior division of the internal iliac (hypogastric) artery and also from smaller branches of the obturator and inferior gluteal arteries. As a result, the bladder can tolerate extensive mobilization for partial bladder resections or for ureteral reimplants for distal ureteral disease (psoas hitch). Thus, hemostasis becomes an important surgical issue when operations for bladder cancer are considered. The high compliance of the bladder may result in significant bleeding with little tamponade. Patients should always have blood typed, screened, and crossmatched for the major bladder cancer operations.

Absorbable sutures are always used because of the risks of calculus formation and infections with staples or nonabsorbable suture material in the urinary tract.

RADICAL CYSTECTOMY IN THE MALE

As recently as the early 1990s, most patients who underwent radical cystoprostatectomy experienced erectile dysfunction postoperatively. By employment of **the same techniques to preserve the neurovascular bundles during a radical cystoprostatectomy as described for radical prostatectomy** (Schlegel and Walsh, 1987; Marshall, 1991) and with use of a continent urinary reservoir with a urethral anastomosis (orthotopic neobladder), the patient may remain potent and retain the ability to void with complete control.

Indications

Radical cystectomy is performed for patients with muscle-invasive carcinoma of the bladder and for some patients with recurrent T1 disease or CIS that has been unresponsive to intravesical chemotherapy. The goal of radical cystectomy is to achieve a surgical cure. On occasion, however, the procedure may be performed as a palliative procedure when the symptoms of the disease are severe. For example, local symptoms such as severe hematuria or frequency often necessitate cystectomy and urinary diversion along with adjunctive chemotherapy.

Preoperative Evaluation and Management

The preoperative evaluation is most important, both medically and urologically. Medical problems that may affect surgery necessitate a careful medical evaluation to minimize comorbidities before surgery. **Patients should stop taking aspirin 2 weeks before surgery. Cigarette smoking should be strongly advised against** to maximize pulmonary function during recovery.

The patient is staged urologically with TUR of the bladder tumor and multiple bladder and urethral biopsies. If any transitional cell carcinoma is found in the prostate or the prostatic urethra, a urethrectomy should be considered as well.

A complete and thorough history and physical examination should be performed. Careful palpation of the abdomen may detect large masses. Rectal examination along with bimanual examination may give valuable information as to mobility and stage of the tumor.

Radiologic evaluation includes CT evaluation of the pelvis and abdomen. CT scan of the chest is also recommended, but a normal posteroanterior and lateral chest film may suffice. CT staging of the tumor may be more valuable if it is performed before TUR of the bladder tumor, especially if the bladder tumor is large. Laboratory evaluation includes complete blood count, serum electrolyte determinations, and liver function tests. If the alkaline phosphatase value is normal and there are no symptoms, a bone scan is not necessary because the likelihood of bone metastatic disease is low. A complete gastrointestinal workup, including barium enema study or colonoscopy, is recommended for patients who have preexisting gastrointestinal disease because this may affect the type of urinary diversion that is selected. If the preoperative bladder biopsies have revealed adenocarcinoma, an extravesical site such as the colon should also be considered. Primary vesical adenocarcinoma occurs in the dome and arises from the urachus.

Patients may donate a few units of autologous blood, but this often results in significantly lower preoperative hematocrits. Ferrous gluconate, 300 mg orally three times a day, is prescribed preoperatively. **The risk of deep venous thrombosis and pulmonary emboli always exists.** Some have recommended warfarin (Coumadin) or subcutaneous heparin perioperatively, but there is an associated increased risk of postoperative lymphocele as well as a potential for serious bleeding complications. For this reason, we instead use perioperative external compression boots, aggressive early ambulation, and avoidance of sitting to help reduce the risk of deep venous thrombosis. Patients who have had a previous pulmonary embolus or have a significant history of previous phlebitis are considered high risk and typically receive anticoagulation postoperatively. If there are problems with postoperative bleeding, an inferior vena cava filter may be placed percutaneously in the radiology department or at the bedside with ultrasound or C-arm monitoring.

Bowel preparation is exceedingly important, particularly if continent diversion with an extensive length of bowel is used. Clear liquids are recommended for the 2 days before surgery. Polyethylene glycol–electrolyte solution (GoLYTELY) is given on the day before surgery, and oral antibiotics are administered. The traditional combination of neomycin and erythromycin base, 1 g each, in three doses on the day before surgery, has been modified in many centers to either neomycin or erythromycin, with the addition of metronidazole for anaerobic coverage. **Although most patients are now brought into the hospital the day of surgery, adequate bowel preparation remains important, especially for continent diversions employing large bowel.** In some older patients, dehydration can become a serious issue. For this reason, it may still be necessary to admit the patient on the day before surgery to give intravenous fluids concomitantly with bowel preparation. Patients with impaired bowel motility, such as after spinal cord injury, may require inpatient bowel lavage with cleansing enemas.

Surgical Technique

The patient is positioned with the table flexed, which opens the area between the umbilicus and the pubis (Fig. 78–5A). A 22 French urethral catheter with a 30-mL balloon is placed into the bladder, and at least 50 mL of sterile water is instilled into the balloon. A lower abdominal Pfannenstiel or midline

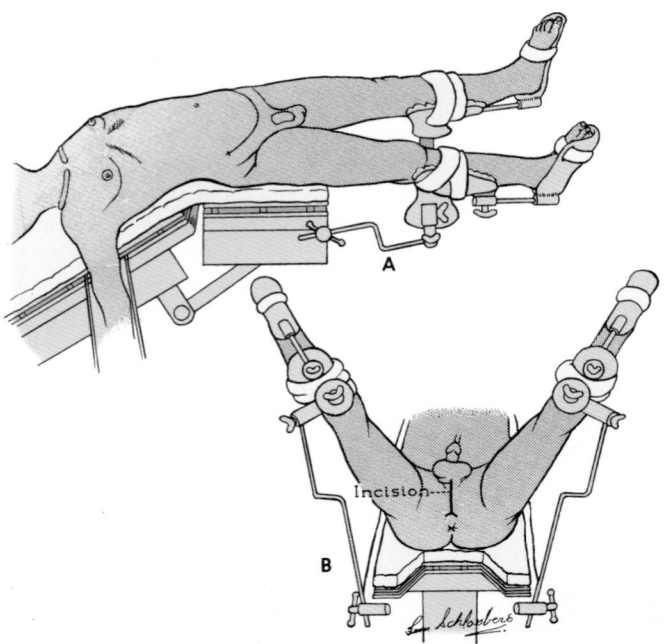

Figure 78–5. **A,** Position of the patient for radical cystoprostatectomy. The umbilicus is placed over the break of the table, and the table is fully flexed and tilted into the Trendelenburg position until the legs are parallel to the floor. **B,** Position of the patient for urethrectomy. The leg braces are elevated until the hips are flexed 60 degrees and the knees are fully extended.

incision is made. If additional length is required with the midline incision, it is extended around the left side of the umbilicus. If patients have had a previous partial cystectomy or suprapubic tube, this track is generally excised with the incision. After the rectus muscles are divided in the midline, Retzius' space is developed. The peritoneal cavity is entered and systematically explored for any possible metastatic disease. The position of the nasogastric tube is verified, and any other obvious abnormalities are duly noted. The urachus (median umbilical ligament) is identified and ligated below the umbilicus. The peritoneum is incised along each side of the bladder. The vasa deferentia are identified lateral to the bladder and are ligated and divided. The descending colon usually has a few adhesions that need to be dissected free on the left side. A moist pack and an additional moist towel are then placed with the ends in each colonic gutter so that the bowel can be placed in the upper abdomen away from the operative field. A self-retaining retractor, such as an Omni-Tract retractor or Bookwalter retractor, helps with exposure. A blade is placed on each side of the abdomen so that the ascending and descending colon and the small bowel contents remain packed in the upper abdomen.

Pelvic Lymphadenectomy

A bilateral pelvic lymphadenectomy is performed next or after the cystectomy (Figs. 78–6 and 78–7). The **"standard" dissection** is initiated medial to the genitofemoral nerve, which is the **lateral limit** of the node dissection. The entire external iliac artery and vein are dissected **up to the bifurcation of the common iliac artery,** which is the cephalad limit of the

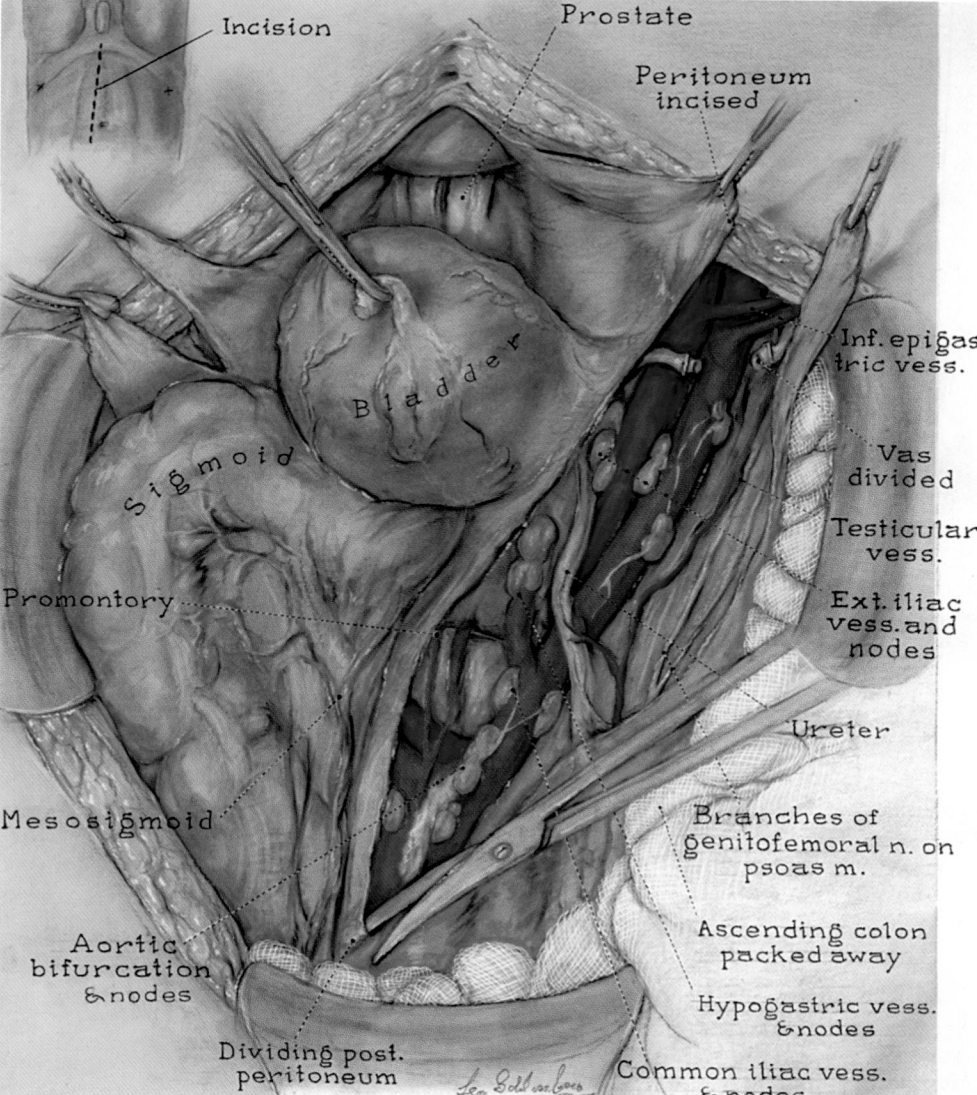

Figure 78–6. Exposure of the right iliac vessels and pelvic lymph nodes after incision of the peritoneal reflection. (From Walsh PC, Schlegel PN: Radical cystectomy. In Marshall FF, ed: Textbook of Operative Urology. Philadelphia, WB Saunders, 1996.)

dissection. The caudal limit of the dissection is the endopelvic fascia. The lymphatic package is then dissected free of the iliac vessels and extended medially into the obturator fossa (Fig. 78–8). The medial limit of the dissection is the bladder, which is retracted medially by a Harrington blade. Care is taken to avoid tearing an accessory obturator vein, which is present frequently. The obturator nerve is visualized. The node of Cloquet is mobilized at the junction of the femoral canal, and a clip is applied to the lymphatic package in this area before lymphatics are divided (Fig. 78–9). The nodes are then dissected from the hypogastric artery and vein.

The "extended" lymphadenectomy includes the tissue along the common iliacs up to the aortic bifurcation, but some would also include the presacral nodes or carry the dissection up to the inferior mesenteric artery. **The extended lymphadenectomy has been shown to improve survival in patients with both lymph node–negative and limited lymph node metastatic disease** (Herr et al, 2002). The lymph node yield is increased more than threefold by dissecting and sub-

mitting separate lymph node packets compared with an en bloc resection (Bochner et al, 2001).

Pelvic Dissection

At the time of the dissection of the hypogastric vessels, the obliterated umbilical and superior vesical arteries are divided. **Branches of the hypogastric artery are divided,** but the hypogastric artery is not ligated to avoid potential compromise of blood flow to the internal pudendal artery and possible vasculogenic impotence (Fig. 78–10).

The ureters are then identified, mobilized with care to preserve periureteral blood supply, and divided close to the bladder. The distal segments of the ureters are sent to the pathology laboratory for frozen-section analysis of the proximal margins. On occasion, CIS necessitates multiple resections of the ureter. The retrovesical cul-de-sac is exposed, and the posterior peritoneum is incised (Fig. 78–11). A plane between the bladder and the rectum is then developed (Fig.

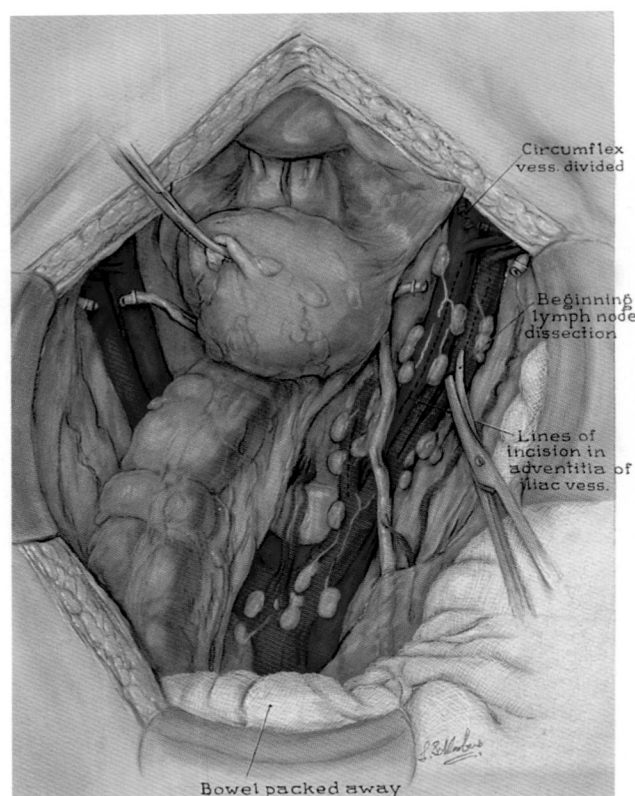

Circumflex vess. divided

Beginning lymph node dissection

Lines of incision in adventitia of iliac vess.

Bowel packed away

Figure 78–7. Position of incisions made along iliac vessels at the commencement of right pelvic and iliac lymph node dissections. (From Walsh PC, Schlegel PN: Radical cystectomy. In Marshall FF, ed: Textbook of Operative Urology. Philadelphia, WB Saunders, 1996.)

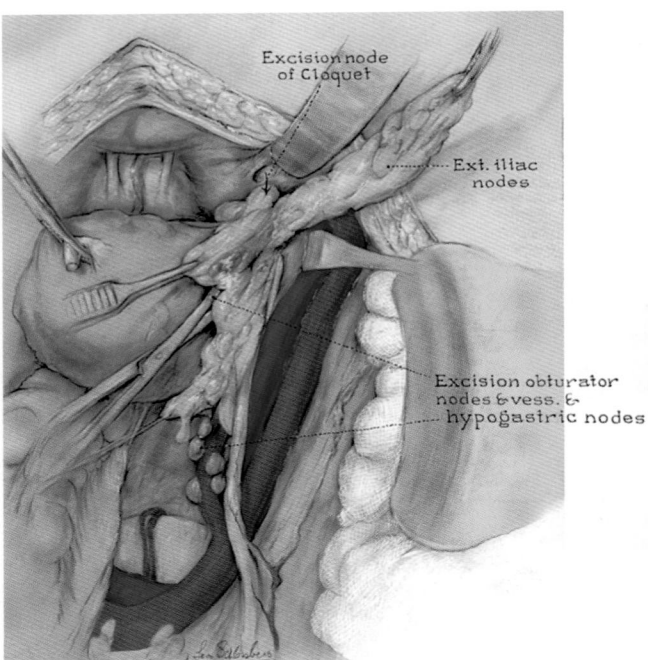

Excision node of Cloquet

Ext. iliac nodes

Excision obturator nodes & vess. & hypogastric nodes

Figure 78–9. Right pelvic lymph node dissection after isolation of the external iliac vessels and excision of the node of Cloquet from the femoral canal. (From Walsh PC, Schlegel PN: Radical cystectomy. In Marshall FF, ed: Textbook of Operative Urology. Philadelphia, WB Saunders, 1996.)

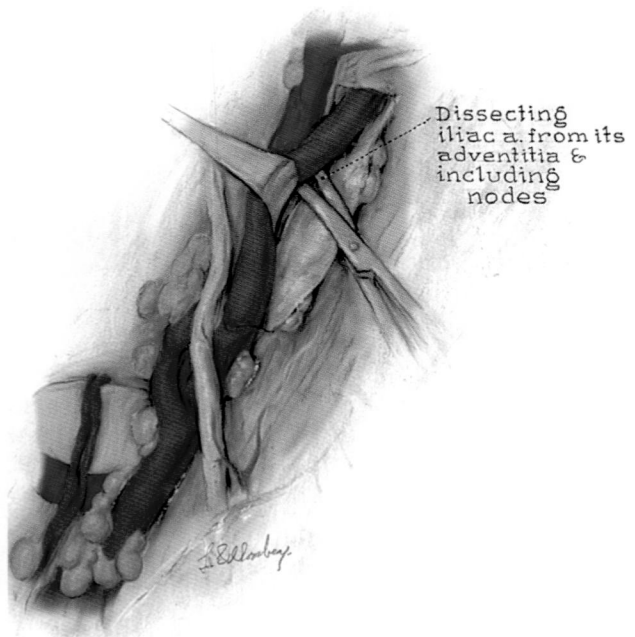

Dissecting iliac a. from its adventitia & including nodes

Figure 78–8. Dissection of the right external iliac lymph nodes away from the isolated external iliac artery. (From Walsh PC, Schlegel PN: Radical cystectomy. In Marshall FF, ed: Textbook of Operative Urology. Philadelphia, WB Saunders, 1996.)

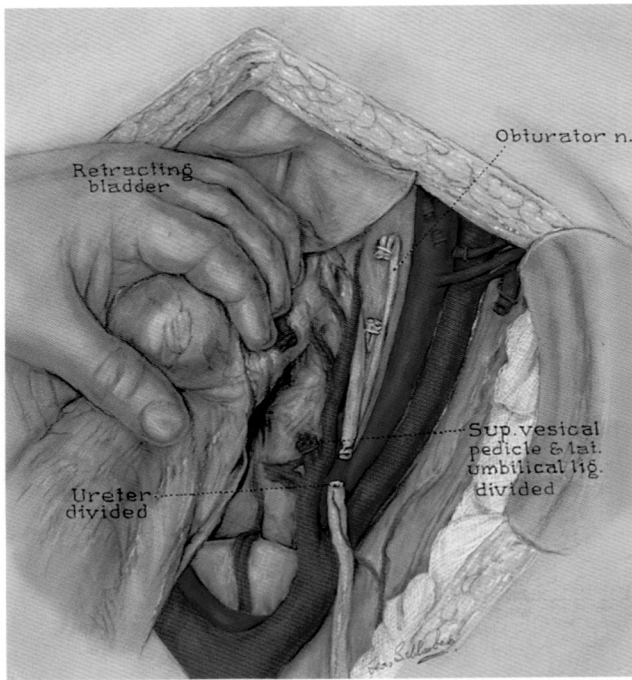

Obturator n.

Retracting bladder

Sup. vesical pedicle & lat. umbilical lig. divided

Ureter divided

Figure 78–10. Dissection of the right lateral pedicle of the bladder after division of the right ureter, the superior vesical pedicle, and the lateral umbilical ligament (umbilical artery). (From Walsh PC, Schlegel PN: Radical cystectomy. In Marshall FF, ed: Textbook of Operative Urology. Philadelphia, WB Saunders, 1996.)

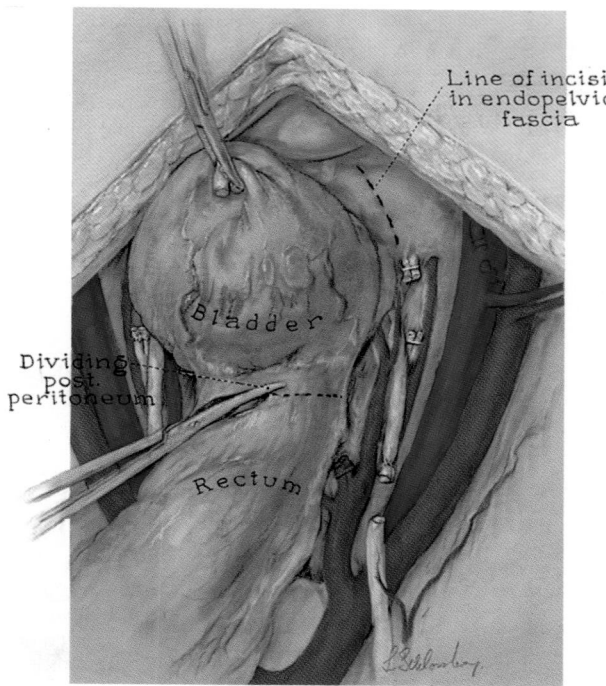

Figure 78–11. Incision of the posterior peritoneum in the rectovesical cul-de-sac. The site of incision of the endopelvic fascia lateral to the prostate is also demonstrated. (From Walsh PC, Schlegel PN: Radical cystectomy. In Marshall FF, ed: Textbook of Operative Urology. Philadelphia, WB Saunders, 1996.)

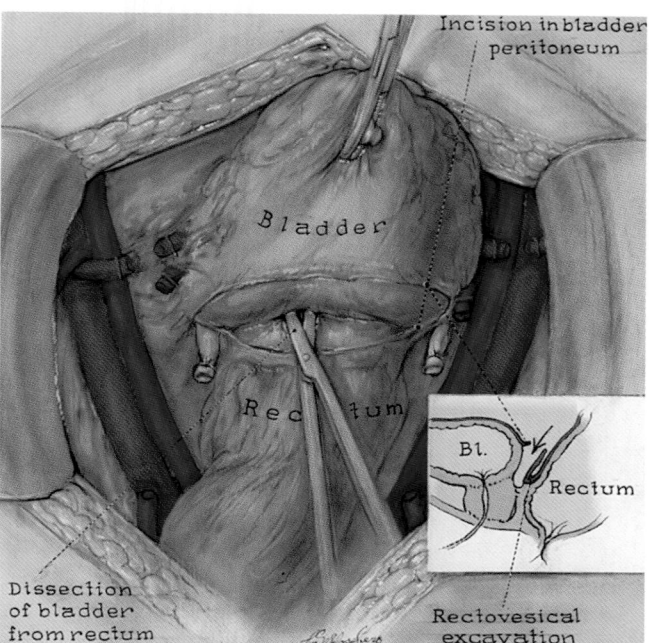

Figure 78–12. Initial dissection of the bladder specimen off the rectum and site of entry into the rectovesical cul-de-sac. (From Walsh PC, Schlegel PN: Radical cystectomy. In Marshall FF, ed: Textbook of Operative Urology. Philadelphia, WB Saunders, 1996.)

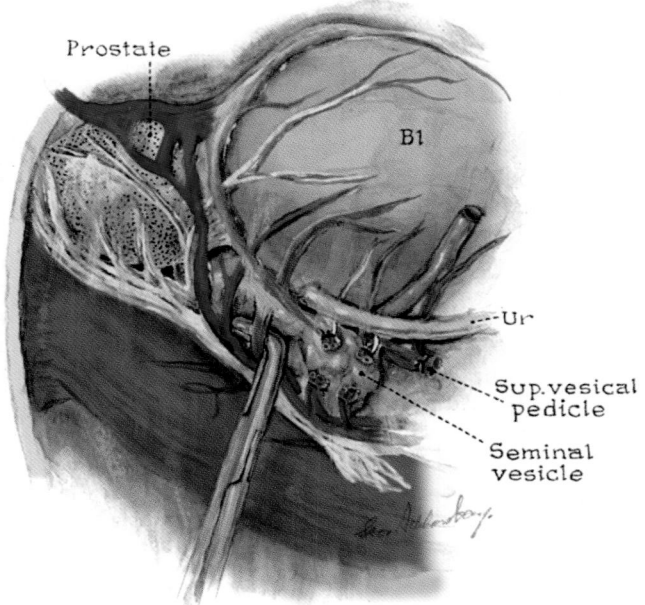

Figure 78–13. Schematic illustration of division of the left posterior pedicle to the bladder, containing branches of the inferior vesical artery and vein. Note the preservation of autonomic innervation to the corpora cavernosa, posterior to the seminal vesicle. (From Walsh PC, Schlegel PN: Radical cystectomy. In Marshall FF, ed: Textbook of Operative Urology. Philadelphia, WB Saunders, 1996.)

78–12). This dissection can usually proceed under direct vision, and the bladder and prostate can be separated from the rectum. The seminal vesicles can then be visualized posteriorly.

If the patient is a candidate for nerve-sparing radical cystoprostatectomy, a retrograde dissection can be initiated now in a fashion similar to that for nerve-sparing radical prostatectomy. Unless the primary bladder cancer is extensive, the neurovascular bundles are rarely infiltrated by disease. It is reasonable, therefore, to attempt nerve-sparing radical cystoprostatectomy, particularly if a continent orthotopic bladder substitution is to be used. If there is any question, wide excision of the neurovascular bundle on the ipsilateral side of the tumor is indicated (Figs. 78–13 and 78–14).

Nerve-Sparing Approach

It is usually feasible to preserve the neurovascular bundles during a cystectomy because the transitional cell carcinoma does not frequently extend beyond the prostate. Some authors have advocated preliminary ligation of vascular pedicles, including the dorsal vein complex, before posterior dissection of the bladder (Fukui et al, 1997). It is sometimes difficult in an obese man to continue the dissection in an antegrade manner, although this can be done in a slender man. Once a retrograde dissection is initiated, the endopelvic fascia is incised, and the puboprostatic ligaments are divided. The dorsal vein complex is divided and oversewn. The urethra is then divided. If a urethrectomy is to be performed, the urethra is dissected under the symphysis so that the perineal dissec-

tion is facilitated. **If a continent urinary diversion is being considered, frozen-section analysis of the prostatic urethra and the apex of the prostate is performed to verify that there is no carcinoma at the urethral margin.** If these frozen sections are positive, alternative diversion should be considered.

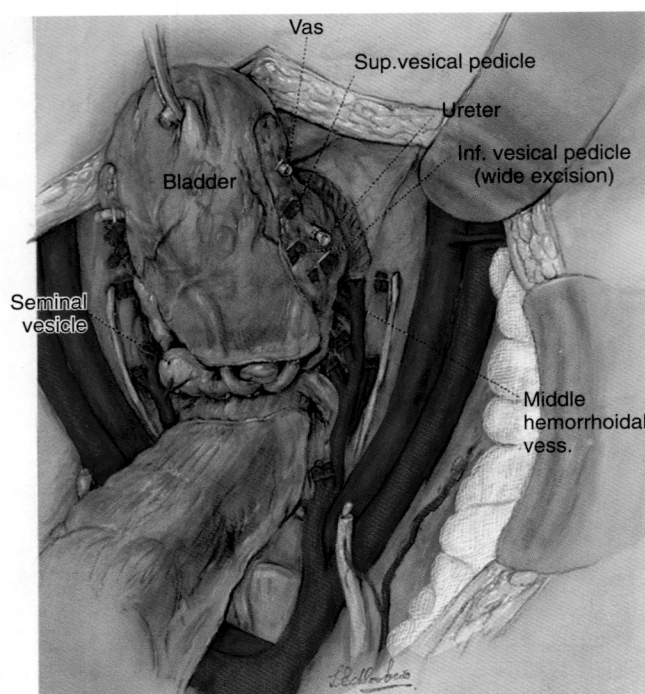

Figure 78–14. The bladder specimen after wide excision of the right posterior pedicle of the bladder, with sacrifice of the right neurovascular bundle. (From Walsh PC, Schlegel PN: Radical cystectomy. In Marshall FF, ed: Textbook of Operative Urology. Philadelphia, WB Saunders, 1996.)

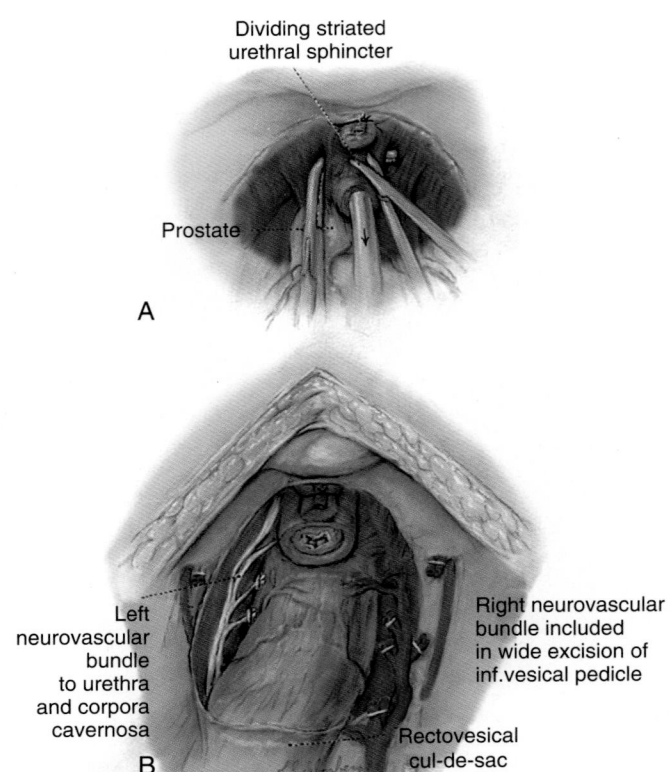

Figure 78–15. **A,** The prostate is retracted superiorly by gentle traction on the urethral catheter. The attachment of the striated urethral sphincter to the prostate is isolated with a right-angled clamp and divided sharply. **B,** The pelvic fossa after removal of the radical cystectomy specimen. The neurovascular structures on the left side have been preserved. Wide excision of the right posterior pedicle, including the neurovascular bundle, has been performed, with preservation of only the middle hemorrhoidal vessels and internal pudendal vessels. (From Walsh PC, Schlegel PN: Radical cystectomy. In Marshall FF, ed: Textbook of Operative Urology. Philadelphia, WB Saunders, 1996.)

The external striated urethral sphincter is divided (Fig. 78–15A). The neurovascular bundle is dissected off the prostate, and the remainder of the pedicles are ligated and divided. We have been using an endoscopic roticulating stapling device with 3.0-mm or larger staples (vascular loads) to facilitate the pedicle division in the deep pelvis (Fig. 78–16) (Hanash et al, 2000). A heavy ligature tied around the urethra at the level of the apex of the prostate may prevent leakage of urine after division of the urethra. The specimen is then removed. If a urethrectomy is to be performed, it may be reasonable to divide the striated muscle of the urethra and mobilize the posterior lateral neurovascular bundles off the urethra distally.

Once the specimen has been removed, the appearance of the pelvis should include the rectum, the urethral stump, the dorsal vein complex, and the preserved neurovascular bundles (Fig. 78–15B).

Postoperative Management and Complications

Operative mortality for radical cystectomy has been shown to be between 1% and 3% in most modern series. However, the overall complication rate after radical cystectomy and urinary diversion may be as high as 25% to 35%. Atelectasis and pulmonary complications are common and require aggressive respiratory therapy in all patients. Early mobilization is important, not only for recovery of pulmonary function but also for prevention of deep venous thrombosis. Early

removal of the nasogastric tube also reduces pulmonary complications (Donat et al, 1999).

Wound infections may occur, especially in obese patients. Extensive use of electrocautery predisposes to infection. Intraoperative wound irrigation with warm genitourinary irrigant, along with meticulous hemostasis and closure of subcutaneous dead space, helps reduce the risk of fluid collections and subsequent infection.

Gastrointestinal complications can occur and include intestinal obstruction, fistula, and rectal injury. Early removal of the nasogastric tube within 24 hours combined with intravenous metoclopramide resulted in earlier return of bowel function and oral feedings after radical cystectomy (Donat et al, 1999). If a rectal injury occurs, it should be repaired with at least a two-layer closure, provided the tissue appears healthy and is not irradiated. If there has been prior irradiation, a colostomy is indicated.

Erectile dysfunction is another recognized complication, but potency can be maintained in the majority of patients with careful dissection of the neurovascular bundle (Schlegel and Walsh, 1987). Age is an important prognostic factor. Patients older than 70 years are at much higher risk for erectile dysfunction. Patients younger than 60 years without

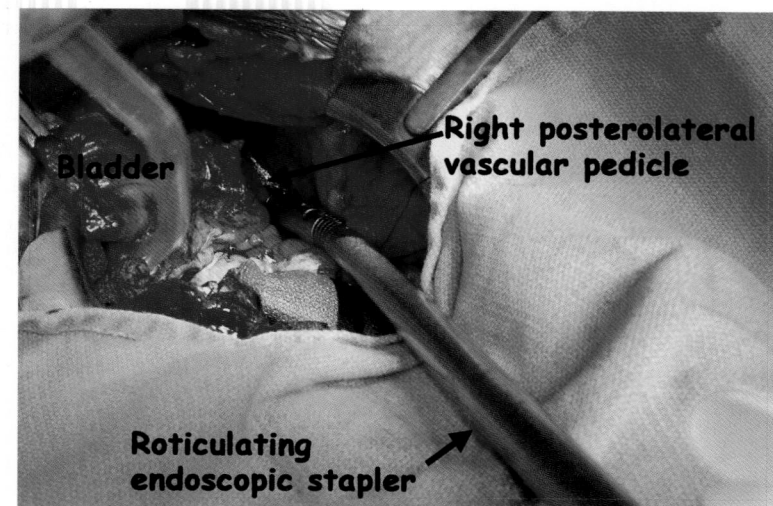

Figure 78–16. A reloadable endoscopic roticulating stapling device is used on the right vascular pedicle as the bladder is retracted medially.

large tumor burdens tend to recover more favorably in terms of potency preservation (Marshall et al, 1991). Thus, it is possible to perform radical surgery to cure a patient with invasive bladder cancer and still maintain continence and sexual function.

KEY POINTS: RADICAL CYSTECTOMY IN THE MALE

- Radical cystectomy is indicated for muscle-invasive carcinoma, recurrent T1 disease, or CIS unresponsive to intravesical chemotherapy or immunotherapy.

- Extended pelvic lymphadenectomy above the iliac bifurcation improves survival for lymph node–negative as well as for limited lymph node metastatic disease.

- A nerve-sparing technique similar to radical prostatectomy is usually able to be employed during cystectomy as transitional cell carcinoma does not usually extend beyond the prostate.

- Operative mortality for radical cystectomy and urinary diversion is only 1% to 3%, but the overall complication rate is 25% to 35%.

URETHRECTOMY

The incidence of urethral recurrence has been documented in prior studies as between 4% and 18% (Darson et al, 2000). Skinner and colleagues (1998) reported an overall incidence of urethral recurrence in the retained male urethra of 7.9%. This was highest for patients with prostatic stromal invasion (21%) or prostatic urethral or ductal involvement (15%).

The cavernosal nerves course posterolaterally along the bladder and prostate to the membranous urethra as they go through the urogenital diaphragm (Schlegel and Walsh, 1987). The most likely cause of erectile dysfunction appears to be neurovascular injury when mobilization is carried out

in the area of the membranous urethra. With careful dissection, it is possible to preserve potency through a retropubic approach (Brendler et al, 1990). By dissection of this membranous urethra during the abdominal approach of the cystoprostatectomy, the subsequent perineal dissection is greatly facilitated.

Indications

The indications for urethrectomy include carcinomatous involvement of the urethra, typically the prostatic urethra. The prognosis is even more serious when the transitional cell carcinoma involves the prostatic stroma. The overall 5-year survival for patients with prostatic stromal invasion is 35.8% (Skinner et al, 1998). However, despite early concerns about prostatic urethral or stromal involvement, **there is a significantly lower urethral recurrence rate with orthotopic neobladder than with cutaneous diversion** (Hassan et al, 2004; Stein et al, 2005).

If there is a solitary tumor at the bladder neck or even multifocal disease, urethrectomy may be required in only 4% of patients (Levinson et al, 1990). Stein and colleagues (2005) reported no increased risk of urethral recurrence with CIS or tumor multifocality in 768 men undergoing orthotopic neobladder. If the urethra is observed closely with urethral washings, most men may be candidates for orthotopic urinary diversion.

Surgical Technique

The urethrectomy from the perineal approach is most easily performed in the exaggerated lithotomy position by raising the leg braces until the hips are flexed 60 degrees (see Fig. 78–5B). It is somewhat more difficult to perform this procedure in a lower lithotomy position, but it can be done and depends partly on body habitus.

If a concomitant radical cystoprostatectomy is being performed, the initial dissection involves dividing the dorsal venous plexus and suturing with a 3-0 absorbable suture. A ligature is passed around the urethra to prevent spillage of potential tumor cells from the bladder (Fig. 78–17A). With a

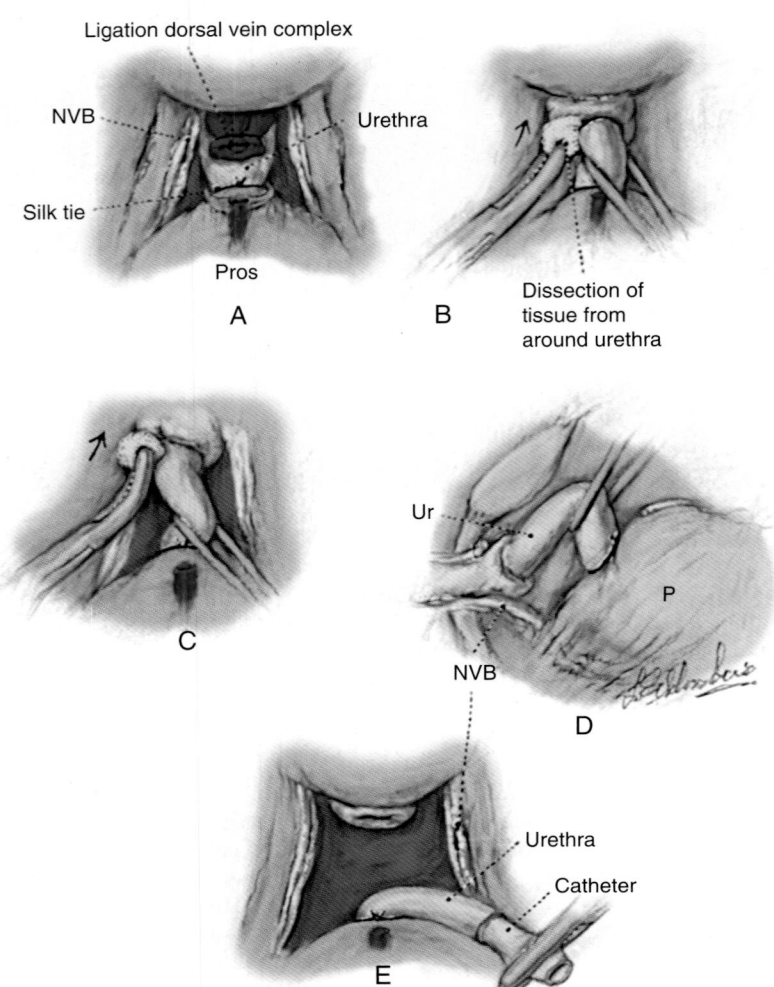

Figure 78–17.   **A,** The urethra is ligated with 1-0 silk suture to prevent spillage of urine around the catheter. NVB, neurovascular bundle; Pros, prostate. **B,** Mobilization of the membranous urethra from the urogenital diaphragm with Kittner dissector. **C,** Further mobilization of the membranous urethra. **D,** Lateral view shows the membranous urethra (Ur) fully mobilized, with neurovascular bundles displaced posterolaterally. **E,** The urethra is transected, and the catheter is drawn cephalad into the wound. Neurovascular bundles are seen intact, lateral to the urethra.

Kittner dissector, the urethra can be dissected from the urogenital diaphragm (Fig. 78–17*B*). The neurovascular bundles can then be dissected away from the membranous urethra gently (Fig. 78–17*C* and *D*). The urethra can then be dissected into the urogenital diaphragm and ultimately transected (Fig. 78–17*E*). This dissection facilitates preservation of the neurovascular bundle as well as subsequent perineal dissection. The remainder of the cystoprostatectomy is then performed, and the specimen is removed. **Frozen-section analysis of the prostatic apex–membranous urethra is obtained.** Depending on the progress of the cystoprostatectomy, a simultaneous urethrectomy can be performed, especially if the frozen-section findings are positive. Urethrectomy is best accomplished at the time of radical cystoprostatectomy. Later, the procedure may be more difficult owing to significant fibrosis involving the deep perineal urethra.

If urethrectomy is to be performed, a 26 French Van Buren sound can be passed through the urethra to the level of the urogenital diaphragm. A vertical incision is made, but if additional exposure is needed, it can be obtained with an inverted Y incision extending from the base of the scrotum toward the anus (Fig. 78–18). After the initial incision has been made

through the subcutaneous tissue, a ring retractor such as a Turner-Warwick, Brantley-Scott, or Jordan retractor can be helpful with this surgery. The bulbocavernosus muscle is divided in the midline to the central perineal tendon. The urethra can then be dissected fairly easily, with the larger sound in place. After initial dissection, a Penrose drain can be placed around the urethra to facilitate retraction. A larger catheter can also be placed in the urethra to the level of the urogenital diaphragm to allow easy movement of the urethra during dissection. The urethra is then dissected anteriorly toward the glans penis by sharp incision of Buck's fascia. The urethra can then be dissected from each adjacent corpus cavernosum (Fig. 78–19).

The penis can easily be inverted, and the urethral dissection can be continued to the glans penis. A T-shaped incision can be made on the ventral surface of the corona of the glans, which effectively splits the glans. However, as transitional cell epithelium does not typically extend to the meatus, it is not always necessary to perform this dissection.

The dissection is carried into the glans, and the urethra is divided from the inside. If there is significant bleeding, a tourniquet around the base of the penis can aid in hemosta-

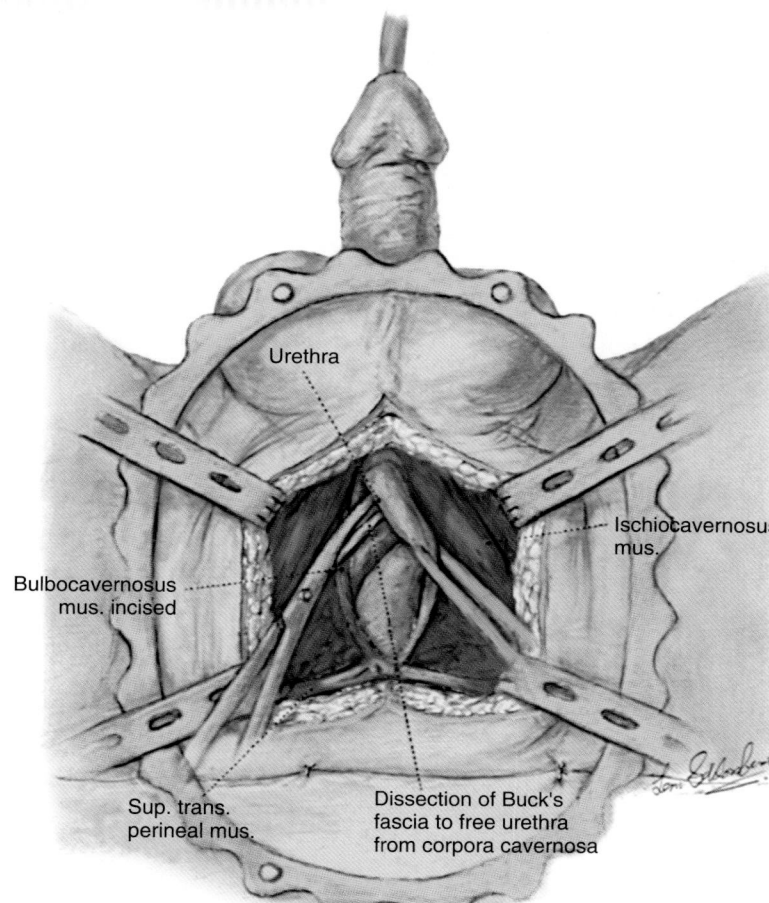

Figure 78–18. Turner-Warwick ring retractor positioned and bulbocavernosus muscle incised to expose bulbar urethra.

Urethra

Ischiocavernosus mus.

Bulbocavernosus mus. incised

Sup. trans. perineal mus.

Dissection of Buck's fascia to free urethra from corpora cavernosa

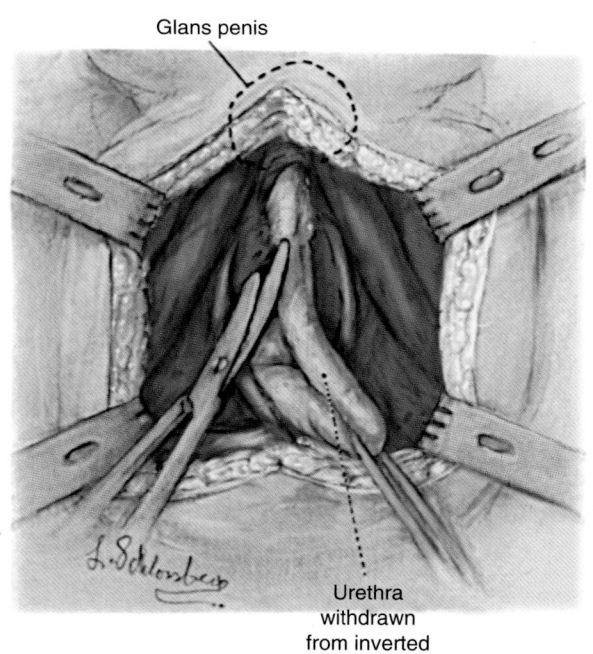

Glans penis

Urethra withdrawn from inverted penis

Figure 78–19. Incision in Buck's fascia to liberate urethra from corpora cavernosa.

sis. Once the urethra is divided distally, it becomes easier to dissect the bulbar urethra. The urethra can be dissected anteriorly under the symphysis (Fig. 78–20). **Careful dissection should be carried out in the areas posterior and lateral to the bulb to identify, expose, and ligate the bulbar urethral arteries** (Fig. 78–21). Inadvertent avulsion of these arteries may cause troublesome bleeding if the ends of the vessels retract into the deep wound. Extensive fulguration in this area may cause injury to the internal pudendal arteries, which supply the corpora cavernosa (Fig. 78–21*C*).

The remainder of the dissection will be greatly facilitated if there has been prior dissection through or into the urogenital diaphragm from the previous retropubic approach (Fig. 78–22). Extensive irrigation with antibiotic solution is given throughout the procedure to help reduce the incidence of wound infection. The urethrectomy specimen can then be removed.

After the urethra has been removed, good hemostasis is required. A small drain, typically a Jackson-Pratt or Penrose drain, is placed in the bed of the urethra and brought out through a stab wound lateral to the incision. The bulbocavernosus muscles are reapproximated with absorbable suture. An additional subcutaneous layer can be closed, and a subcuticular skin closure is performed with a 4-0 absorbable suture. A T binder with fluff gauze is used as a dressing.

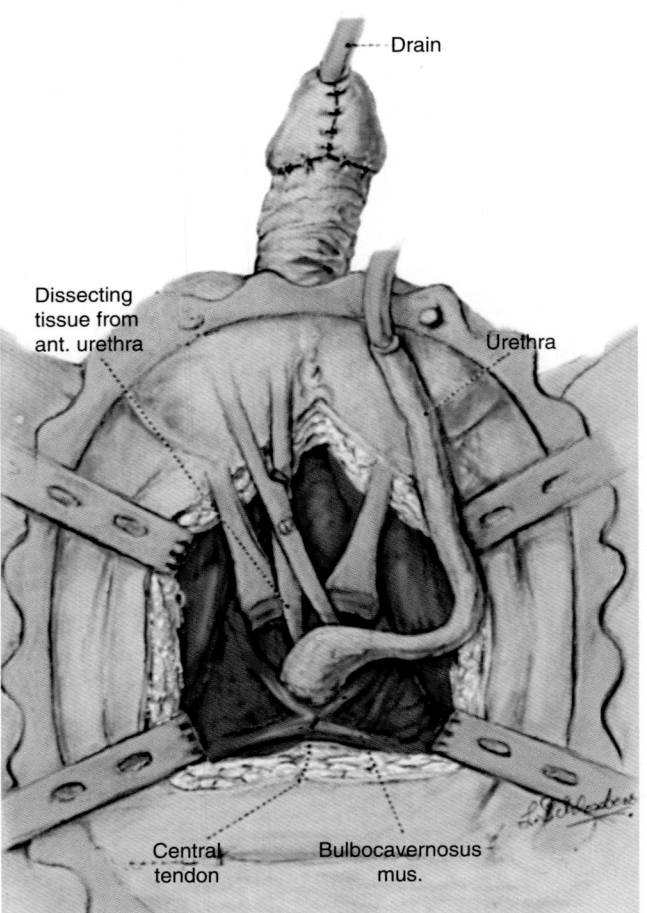

Drain

Dissecting
tissue from
ant. urethra

Urethra

Central
tendon

Bulbocavernosus
mus.

Figure 78–20. Initial dissection of tissue anterior to bulbar urethra to facilitate subsequent exposure and control of posterolateral bulbar urethral arteries.

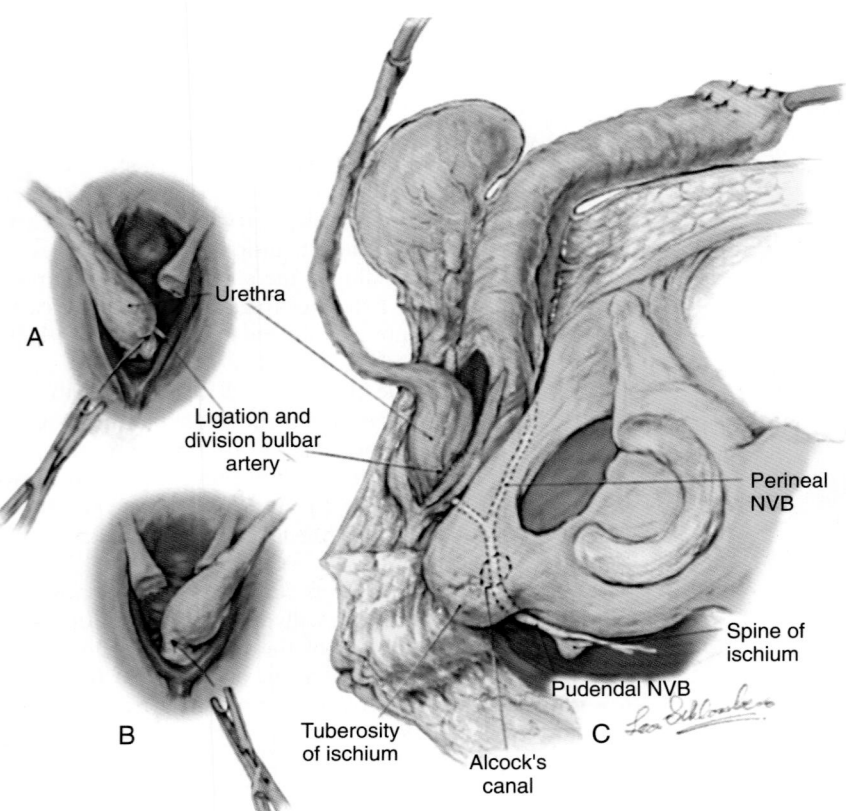

Urethra

A

Ligation and
division bulbar
artery

B

Tuberosity
of ischium

Alcock's
canal

C

Perineal
NVB

Spine of
ischium

Pudendal NVB

Figure 78–21. **A** and **B,** Ligation of the bulbar urethral arteries with hemoclips. **C,** Lateral view shows the relationship between the internal pudendal and bulbar arteries and the ischium and inferior ramus of the pubis. The bulbar arteries should not be fulgurated to prevent injury to the internal pudendal arteries, from which they arise and which provide arterial supply to the corpora cavernosa. NVB, neurovascular bundle.

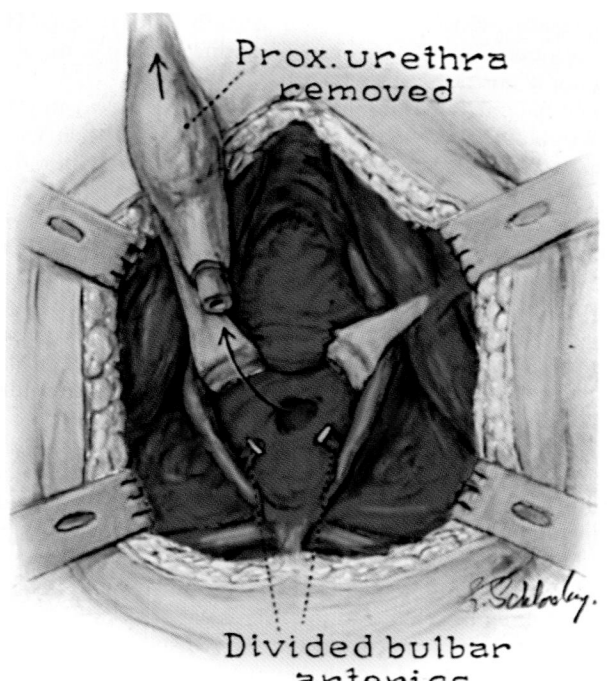

Figure 78–22. Completed urethrectomy. Dissection of bulbar urethra is completed without difficulty because the membranous urethra has previously been mobilized through the pelvis.

Postoperative Management and Complications

Most significant drainage usually stops after 1 to 2 days, and the drains can be removed. Postoperative swelling and ecchymoses are common and generally resolve within 1 to 2 weeks. Wound infections can occur, but the incidence is greatly reduced if care is given to meticulous hemostasis and intraoperative irrigation with antibiotic solution. Patients are encouraged to ambulate the day after surgery. If a concomitant cystectomy has been performed, management relates primarily to the cystectomy.

KEY POINTS: URETHRECTOMY

■ Urethral recurrence after cystectomy is between 4% and 18%.

■ Indications for urethrectomy include prostatic urethral or stromal involvement.

■ There is a significantly lower urethral recurrence rate with orthotopic neobladder than with cutaneous diversion.

RADICAL CYSTECTOMY IN THE FEMALE

Advances in surgical technique have made it possible to consider urethra- and vagina-sparing procedures in the approach to females with muscle-invasive bladder cancer. Earlier studies implied that anterior exenteration with

removal of the vagina and urethra was required in transitional cell carcinoma in the female. This extensive operation was typically required because most invasive tumors involved the posterior bladder wall, there was more invasive local disease at that time, and the female urethra was considered unsuitable for continent orthotopic neobladders.

Now patients may often present with invasive but less extensive disease. For this reason, it is feasible to preserve both the urethra and a portion of the vagina in radical cystectomy. Studies have demonstrated that quality of life goals, such as volitional voiding and preservation of sexual function, can be obtained with orthotopic bladder substitutions in the female (Stein et al, 1994; Schoenberg et al, 1999). However, neobladders require a much more extensive operation, the potential for complications is greater, and the recovery phase is more prolonged as the reconfigured reservoir takes several weeks to months to achieve reasonable capacity. In patients with multiple medical problems, a shorter operation such as an ileal conduit diversion may frequently be the wisest choice of urinary diversion.

Since orthotopic bladder substitution in male patients with bladder cancer has become more prevalent, interest in preservation of the urethra in the female has also increased. In a study of 293 patients, the incidence of urethral involvement of tumor found on cystoscopy in female patients with bladder cancer was 1.4% (Ashworth, 1956). Stenzl and colleagues (1995) found a 2% incidence of urethral tumor involvement in 7 of 356 patients, all at initial presentation. Comparison of defined tumor locations in the study revealed that bladder neck and trigone were significantly more involved in the urethral tumor group. This study concluded that a portion of the urethra can be spared to enable lower urinary tract reconstruction without a significantly increased risk of urethral tumor involvement, provided frozen sections of the proximal urethra are negative and the primary tumor is not located at the bladder neck.

Stein and colleagues (1998) performed a prospective pathologic evaluation of 71 consecutive female cystectomy specimens removed for primary transitional cell carcinoma of the bladder. Tumors at the bladder neck and proximal urethra were seen in 19% and 7% of cystectomy specimens, respectively. **Bladder neck tumor involvement was found to be the most significant risk factor for tumor involvement of the urethra.** All patients with urethral tumors were noted to have concomitant bladder neck involvement; however, more than 60% of patients with bladder neck tumors had a tumor-free proximal urethra. Involvement of tumor at the bladder neck is a sensitive and specific measure of urethral involvement and could have a significant impact on the decision to perform orthotopic reconstruction in women. **An intraoperative frozen-section analysis of the proximal urethra should be considered the best way to determine whether a female patient is a suitable candidate for orthotopic reconstruction** (Darson et al, 2000).

In the past, both ovaries and much of the vagina were often excised so that there was no potential for sexual activity in these patients. In younger patients undergoing anterior exenteration, it is possible to leave one ovary and to reconstruct the vagina. Sexual function can then be maintained. **In the majority of surgical candidates, urethral, vaginal, and cervical involvement is unusual except in patients with risk** factors such as extremely large tumors, tumors involving the bladder neck, diffuse CIS, and locally or regionally advanced tumors (Schoenberg et al, 1999).

Indications

Radical cystectomy in the female is typically performed for invasive transitional cell carcinoma. A vaginal approach has been described for this operation (Marshall and Schnittman, 1947; San Felippo and Kessler, 1978), but an anterior approach is typically preferred (Marshall and Treiger, 1991). **The anterior approach has advantages in that it allows simultaneous pelvic lymphadenectomy, cystectomy, urethrectomy, hysterectomy, salpingo-oophorectomy, and partial vaginectomy if clinically indicated for extensive carcinomatous involvement.** In addition, it allows accurate staging of the tumor. In some instances, adjuvant chemotherapy may be recommended in high-risk patients, particularly ones with positive nodes.

Preoperative Evaluation

All patients undergo a careful medical evaluation and assessment of comorbidities before the operation to ascertain their anesthetic risk. Transitional cell carcinoma typically occurs in an older population. There is often an antecedent history of tobacco use. Prior chemical exposures to known carcinogens can also be inquired about. Physical examination should include careful bimanual examination to help determine the gross extent of the tumor, especially if the pelvic sidewall or rectum is involved. A laboratory evaluation should include hematologic and chemistry studies and liver function tests. A cystoscopic evaluation with bladder mapping should have been performed at the time of bladder tumor resection. Radiographic imaging is typically performed with CT evaluation of the chest, abdomen, and pelvis. A bone scan is not typically performed, provided the patient has a normal alkaline phosphatase value, a smaller lesion, and no other symptoms to suggest bone metastases.

An extensive bowel preparation is given with GoLYTELY. Erythromycin or neomycin and metronidazole are given orally, and patients maintain clear liquids the day before surgery. Intravenous fluids may be administered on the night before surgery, particularly to older patients, in whom significant dehydration can occur. Appropriate attention to the details of proper bowel preparation and preoperative hydration can reduce perioperative morbidity.

If an external stoma is considered for urinary diversion, consultation with enterostomal nursing may be valuable. Marking of a potential stoma site should take into account the patient's abdominal habitus, both sitting and standing. The umbilicus can also be used as a potential stoma site.

Surgical Technique

Positioning of the patient is an important aspect of the operation. All pressure points should be padded. **We use a split-leg fluoroscopy or orthopedic table rather than stirrups. This reduces the risk of peroneal nerve palsy or anterior compartment syndrome in the lower extremities.** The split-leg table allows most of the dissection to be done with the legs

left together. Once the vaginal dissection is approached later in the operation, the legs can be abducted into a modified lithotomy position.

The patient is positioned on the table, flexed to improve abdominal and pelvic exposure. The patient is then widely prepared and draped, and the vagina is prepared with iodine. A Foley catheter is inserted. If a urethrectomy is planned, the meatus and distal urethra may be circumscribed and mobilized at this time while an assistant is proceeding with the abdominal exposure. A midline or Pfannenstiel incision is then made. It may not be necessary to extend a midline incision above the umbilicus unless mobilization of the hepatic flexure is required for continent urinary diversion. **A midline incision is made only to the umbilicus if an ileal conduit is to be performed.**

The retroperitoneal space is entered, and the peritoneum is mobilized off the transversalis fascia. Next, the urachus and umbilical ligaments are ligated and divided. The peritoneum is opened, and any adhesions in the peritoneal cavity are taken down. Palpation is performed to exclude occult metastatic disease in the abdomen and pelvis. The entire intraperitoneal contents are inspected, and the liver is carefully evaluated for metastases. The periaortic area is also palpated to ensure that there is no significant lymphadenopathy.

The peritoneum lateral to the bladder is incised, and the round ligament is ligated and divided. The ovarian vessels in the infundibulopelvic ligament are identified, ligated, and divided. These maneuvers allow the peritoneal contents to be packed away from the pelvis (Fig. 78–23). A moist pack and

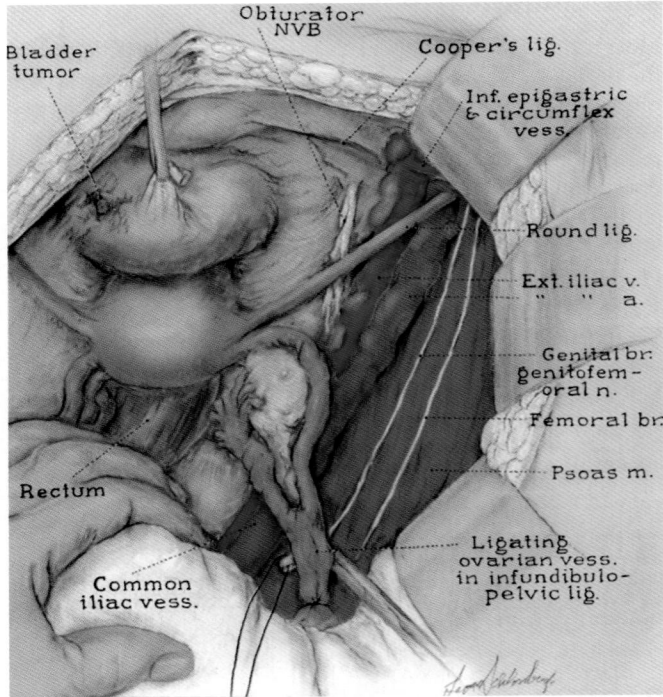

Figure 78–23. General exposure after initial division of the umbilical ligaments and peritoneum. The sigmoid colon has also been dissected free. A moist towel has been placed up each colic gutter to provide exposure. Initial ligation and division of the ovarian vessels are performed. NVB, neurovascular bundle. (From Marshall FF, Treiger BF: Radical cystectomy [anterior exenteration] in the female patient. Urol Clin North Am 1991;18:765-775.)

rolled towel combined with a ring retractor or Omni-Tract retractor provide excellent superficial and deep exposure. Exposure in the female pelvis is somewhat easier than that in the male pelvis because of its broader expanse.

Pelvic Lymphadenectomy

A staging lymphadenectomy is performed above and lateral to the external iliac vessels. It is started with an incision lateral to the external iliac artery. **The genitofemoral nerve should be identified and preserved as it is coursing on the psoas muscle** (Fig. 78–24). The nodal package over the external iliac artery and vein is divided, beginning at the junction of the hypogastric artery and the external iliac artery. The dissection is then carried down the pelvic sidewall behind the vessels to the level of the obturator neurovascular bundle. The lymphatic package is then mobilized as it coalesces in the angle between Cooper's ligament and the inferior aspect of the iliac vein (Fig. 78–25). A large clip is applied here to reduce the occurrence of a lymphocele. The lymphatic package is then mobilized off the obturator neurovascular bundle (Fig. 78–26). A clip can then be placed on the lymphatic package at its point of division along the hypogastric vessels (Fig. 78–26*B*). Dissecting the lymphatic package from lateral to medial facilitates the maneuver and allows an avascular plane of dissection. An anterior dissection of the obturator neurovascular bundle is sometimes more disruptive, with more bleeding.

An **extended pelvic lymphadenectomy,** including the common iliac nodal tissue to the aortic bifurcation, has been demonstrated to offer therapeutic advantage in patients with lymph node metastases (Herr et al, 2002).

Pelvic Dissection

In conjunction with the pelvic lymphadenectomy, dissection is usually carried down the hypogastric artery. Each branch of the hypogastric artery to the pelvic viscera is individually dissected, ligated, and divided with 2-0 absorbable ties (Fig.

78–27). Surgical clips can also be used. We no longer use silk because it is more reactive. **The initial anterior arterial branch is generally the superior vesical artery.** Middle and inferior vesical arteries are also ligated and divided.

The ureters are ligated at the ureterovesical hiatuses and divided. The proximal ureters are gently packed out of the operative fields. Frozen sections of the proximal margins of each ureter can be obtained at this time. **A specimen for frozen-section analysis is obtained to verify that there is no CIS in the distal ureter that would necessitate additional ureteral resection.** If continent diversion is being considered,

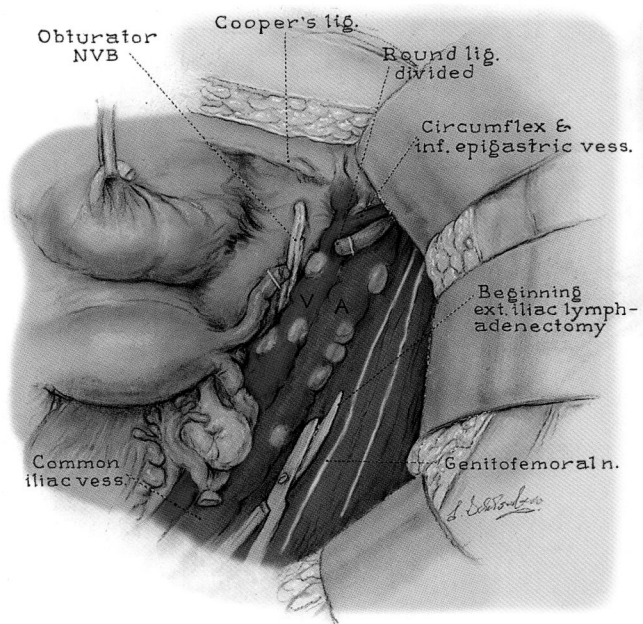

Figure 78–24. Pelvic lymphadenectomy. The dissection is initiated lateral to the external iliac artery. The genitofemoral nerve is avoided. NVB, neurovascular bundle. (From Marshall FF, Treiger BF: Radical cystectomy [anterior exenteration] in the female patient. Urol Clin North Am 1991;18:765-775.)

Figure 78–25. The lymphatic tissue is dissected from the iliac artery and vein. A clip is placed on the coalescence of the lymphatic package in the angle between the iliac vein and Cooper's ligament. NVB, neurovascular bundle. (From Marshall FF, Treiger BF: Radical cystectomy [anterior exenteration] in the female patient. Urol Clin North Am 1991;18:765-775.)

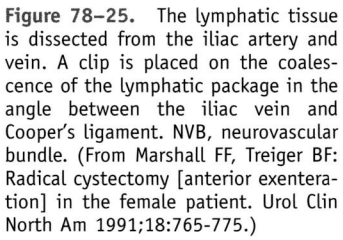
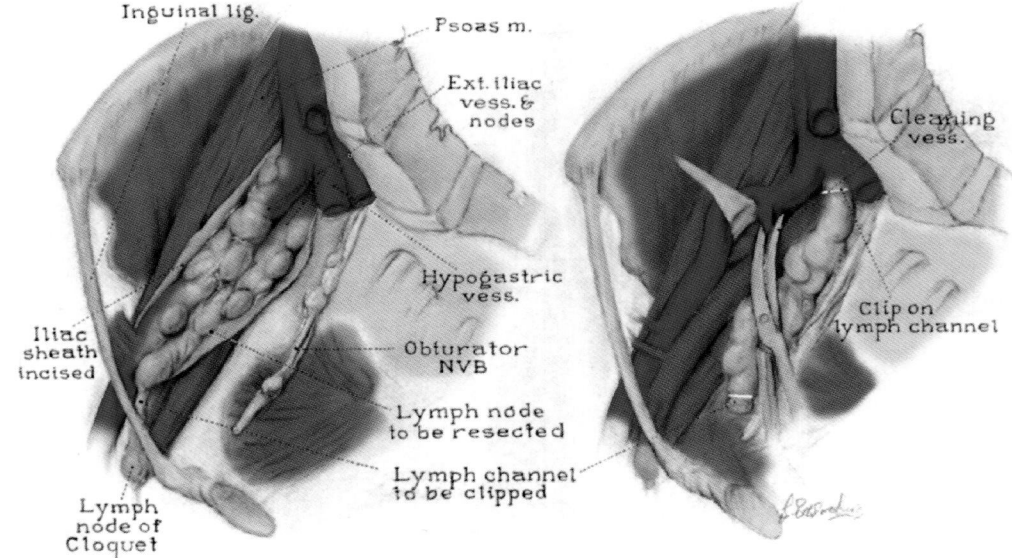

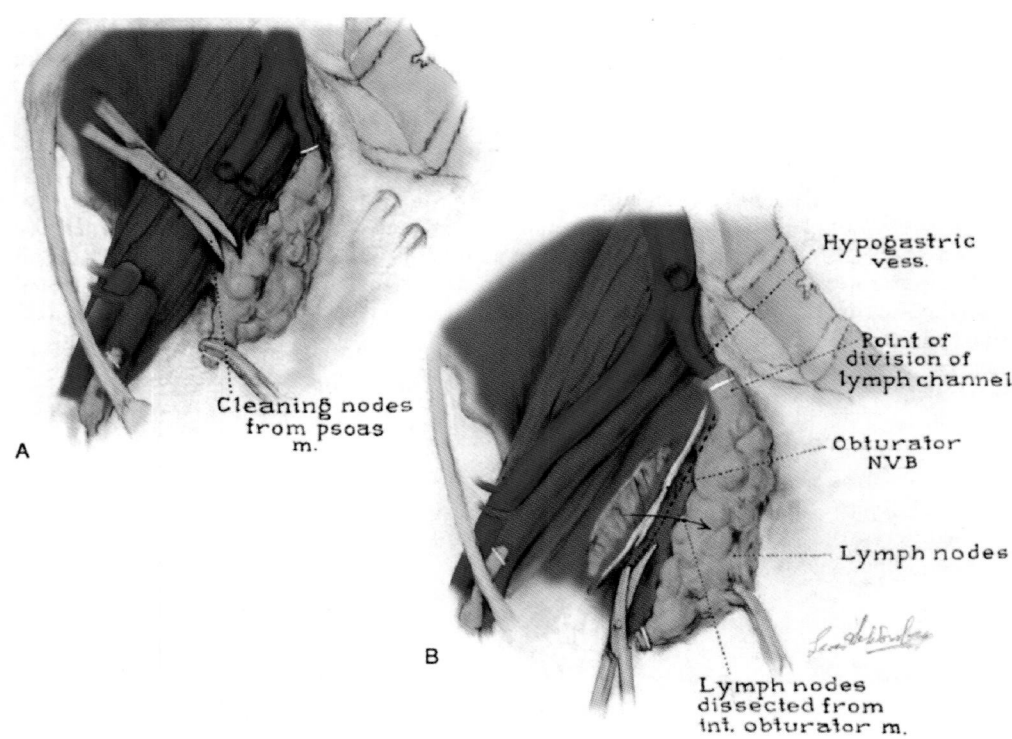

Figure 78–26. Pelvic lymphadenectomy. **A,** The lymphatic package is dissected from underneath the iliac vessels. **B,** The package is rotated medially. The obturator neurovascular bundle can easily be dissected superiorly, where the lymphatics are again clipped. NVB, neurovascular bundle. (From Marshall FF, Treiger BF: Radical cystectomy [anterior exenteration] in the female patient. Urol Clin North Am 1991;18:765-775.)

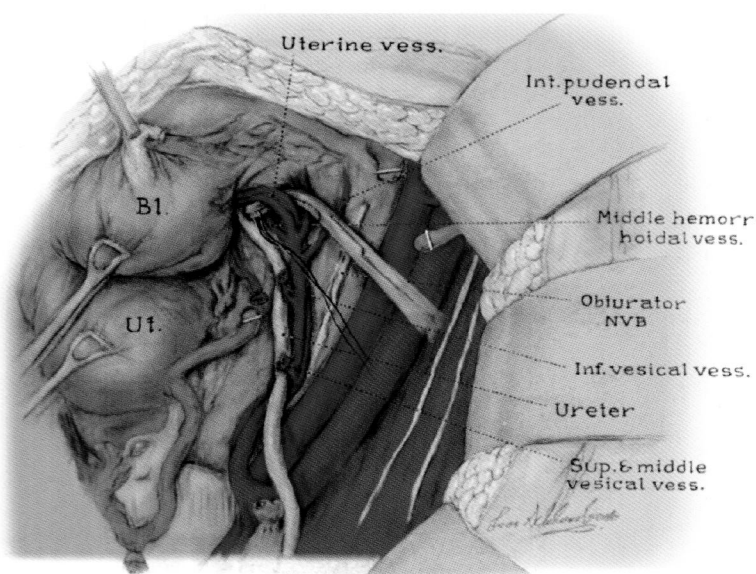

Figure 78–27. Dissection of the hypogastric artery. Superior and inferior divisions of the vesical artery are ligated with individual ties. Bl, bladder; NVB, neurovascular bundle; Ut, uterus. (From Marshall FF, Treiger BF: Radical cystectomy [anterior exenteration] in the female patient. Urol Clin North Am 1991;18:765-775.)

good ureteral length is often helpful in performing the ureterointestinal anastomosis. The ureter is then spatulated at the 12-o'clock position, and a feeding tube is sutured in place to allow gentle, atraumatic manipulation of the ureter during surgery (Fig. 78–28).

Anterior Exenteration with Urethrectomy

Traction can be placed on the uterus anteriorly, with concomitant posterior and superior retraction on the rectosig-

moid. This provides good exposure for incision of the cul-de-sac, and the vaginal wall is mobilized off the rectosigmoid colon (Fig. 78–29). The legs are abducted at this time, and a povidone-iodine–soaked sponge stick is placed in the vagina. This maneuver facilitates identification of the cervix in the posterior vagina. The cervix can usually be palpated easily, so that an incision can be made into the vagina below the cervix. If necessary, a small portion of the cardinal ligament can be ligated and divided to facilitate this exposure (Fig. 78–30).

Cautery can be used to incise the vagina under the cervix (Fig. 78–31). Stay sutures are placed in the thick vaginal wall to help provide hemostasis and traction. Previous external

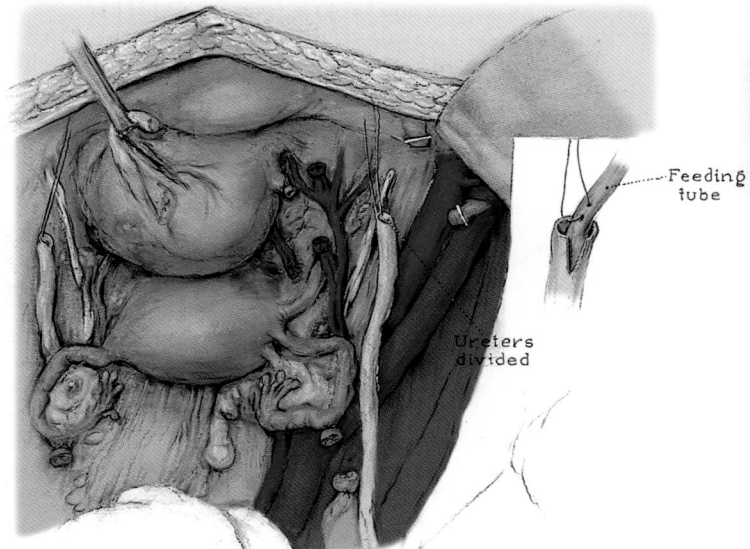

Figure 78–28. The ureters are divided. After a specimen for frozen-section analysis is obtained, a feeding tube is sutured in place after the ureter is spatulated. This maneuver allows easy atraumatic manipulation of the ureter. (From Marshall FF, Treiger BF: Radical cystectomy [anterior exenteration] in the female patient. Urol Clin North Am 1991;18:765-775.)

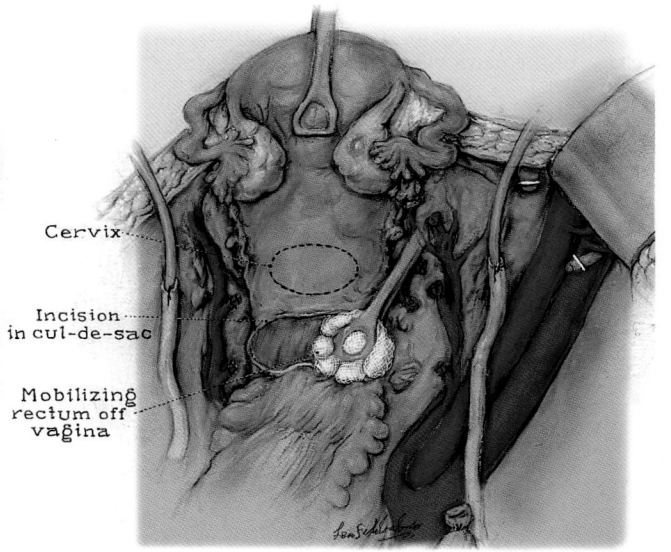

Figure 78–29. Dissection of the cul-de-sac. Traction is maintained superiorly on both the uterus and the rectosigmoid to allow easy identification of the cul-de-sac and palpation of the cervix. (From Marshall FF, Treiger BF: Radical cystectomy [anterior exenteration] in the female patient. Urol Clin North Am 1991;18:765-775.)

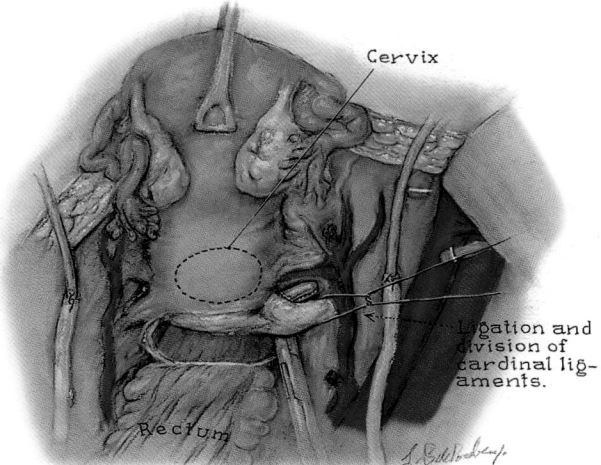

Figure 78–30. The vasculature within the cardinal ligament is ligated and divided to allow exposure of the vagina after the vagina has been mobilized off the rectosigmoid. (From Marshall FF, Treiger BF: Radical cystectomy [anterior exenteration] in the female patient. Urol Clin North Am 1991;18:765-775.)

mobilization of the vagina allows preservation of it for subsequent vaginal reconstruction. It is easy to excise large segments of the vagina inadvertently. **If the primary tumor is small, resection of a large segment of the vagina should be avoided because of the adjacent pelvic plexus and some of the autonomic innervation that runs along its lateral aspect. The pelvic plexus provides some of the autonomic innervation to the smooth muscle of the female urethra. The pudendal nerve provides the innervation to the rhabdosphincter.**

The specimen is now left with only its anterior attachments of the urethra, anterior fascia, and small portion of the vagina. When the posterior dissection is almost complete, the anterior

dissection is begun, and it is analogous to the anterior dissection in the male cystectomy. The endopelvic fascia is divided (Fig. 78–32).

If a urethrectomy is to be performed, the pubourethral suspensory ligaments, which are analogous to the puboprostatic ligaments in the male, are identified and divided; this allows the urethra and bladder to drop inferiorly. The dorsal vein complex can be identified and ligated (see Fig. 78–32). The urethra is then dissected from under the dorsal vein complex so the only remaining attachments of the specimen are the urethral meatus and a small portion of the vagina. At this time, a total radical cystectomy is completed (anterior exenteration). The ovaries, fallopian tubes, uterus, anterior vagina, and cervix are left attached by only a small portion of the anterior vagina and urethra (Fig. 78–33). The remaining vagina can be incised. If the urethra was not removed, a Gelpi retractor can be used to spread the labia, and the urethral meatus is then circumscribed to complete the urethrectomy (Fig. 78–34).

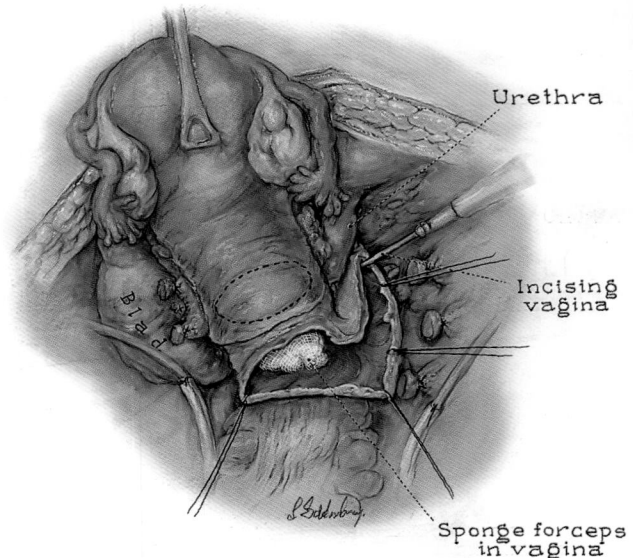

Figure 78–31. A sponge stick is placed in the vagina, and the cautery is used to incise the vagina directly. Stay sutures facilitate the dissection and improve hemostasis. (From Marshall FF, Treiger BF: Radical cystectomy [anterior exenteration] in the female patient. Urol Clin North Am 1991;18:765-775.)

If the patient is sexually active and the tumor is not large, the vagina can be reconstructed. The vaginal flap can be closed in either a posteroanterior or a vertical plane, depending on the amount of vagina left. Later, vaginal reconstruction can be accomplished by skin grafts, various muscle flaps, and bowel segments. Colonic segments appear to be preferable to small bowel segments. It is preferable to defer vaginal reconstruction, if necessary, to a later date when there is no evidence of tumor recurrence or need for chemotherapy.

Urethra-Sparing, Vagina-Preserving Approach

If a continent orthotopic diversion is being considered, the pubourethral ligaments are not divided, and only the bladder neck and the initial 1 cm of urethra are removed. Careful avoidance of a more extensive dissection provides for better preservation of the muscularity and innervation of the urethral sphincter.

The autonomic innervation of the corpora cavernosa clitoris can be identified as it arises lateral to the cervix and passes on the lateral aspect of the vagina and the anterior vaginal vault (Fig. 78–35). The lateral pedicles of the bladder are divided ventral to the vesicovaginal junction, allowing release of the neurovascular bundles. The dorsal vein complex is divided as in retropubic prostatectomy (Fig. 78–36A). The pubourethral ligaments are left intact as they preserve the neobladder–urethral angle for postoperative continence. The vesicourethral junction is dissected circumferentially and ligated with heavy silk ligature to limit tumor spillage around the urethral catheter. The urethra is divided, minimizing the distal dissection, which may disrupt the vaginal support of the

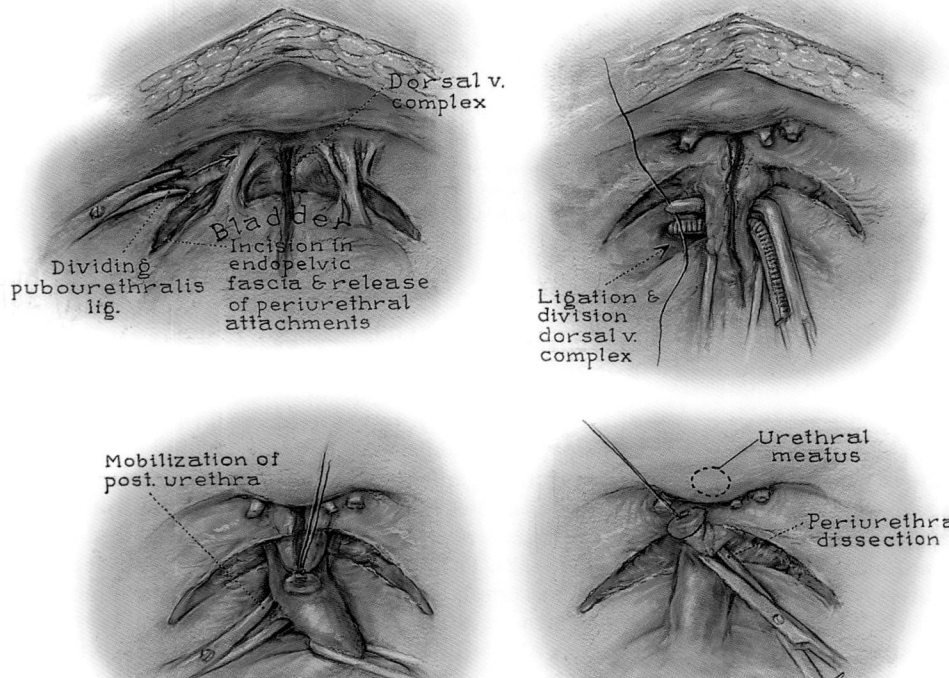

Figure 78–32. Anterior dissection. The suspensory ligaments of the urethra are identified and divided, and the endopelvic fascia is incised. This allows inferior displacement of the urethra. The dorsal vein of the clitoris is ligated and divided, and the urethra is then mobilized. Dissection can be carried out underneath the dorsal vein complex toward the urethral meatus. (From Marshall FF, Treiger BF: Radical cystectomy [anterior exenteration] in the female patient. Urol Clin North Am 1991;18:765-775.)

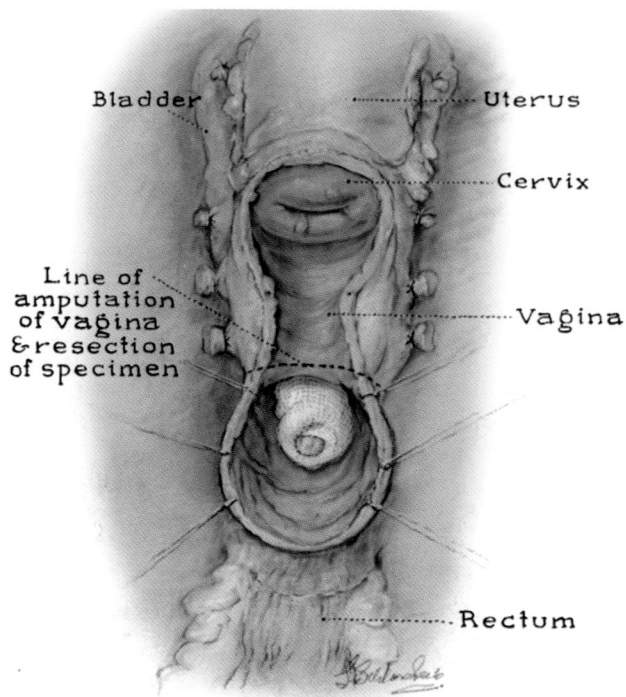

Figure 78–33. Only the vaginal wall and the urethra remain. The vagina is amputated. (From Marshall FF, Treiger BF: Radical cystectomy [anterior exenteration] in the female patient. Urol Clin North Am 1991;18:765-775.)

distal two thirds of the urethra where the rhabdosphincter resides (Fig. 78–36B). The anastomotic sutures may be placed into the urethral stump. The vesicovaginal space is developed in a retrograde direction to the cardinal ligaments and vesicocervical junction. The cardinal ligaments are divided (Fig. 78–37). The vaginal apex is opened just below the cervix (Fig. 78–38), and the specimen is removed. The vagina is closed with running, locked 2-0 absorbable suture.

Completion of Operation

After vaginal closure, a povidone-iodine pack is left in place. Urinary diversion is performed, and if orthotopic reconstruction is performed, the neobladder is anastomosed to the distal urethra. Closed-drain systems are placed on each side. The midline or transverse incision can be closed with either heavy monofilament absorbable suture or heavy nylon suture.

Postoperative Management and Complications

The vaginal povidone-iodine pack is usually removed after 2 days. Closed-system drains are removed after the urinary tract is verified radiographically to be intact. Postoperative complications can vary according to the intestinal segment chosen for reconstruction and the type of pouch preferred by the surgeon. Delayed complication rates for neobladders may be somewhat higher than those for the more straightforward ileal conduit.

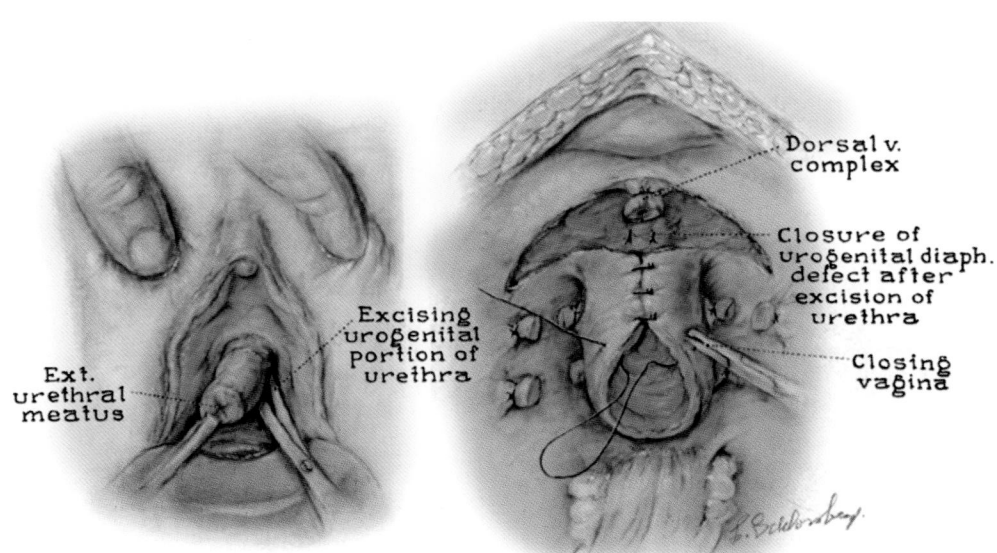

Figure 78–34. The vaginal dissection completes the operation with a circumscribed incision around the urethral meatus. The specimen can then be removed. The vagina is reconstructed. (From Marshall FF, Treiger BF: Radical cystectomy [anterior exenteration] in the female patient. Urol Clin North Am 1991;18: 765-775.)

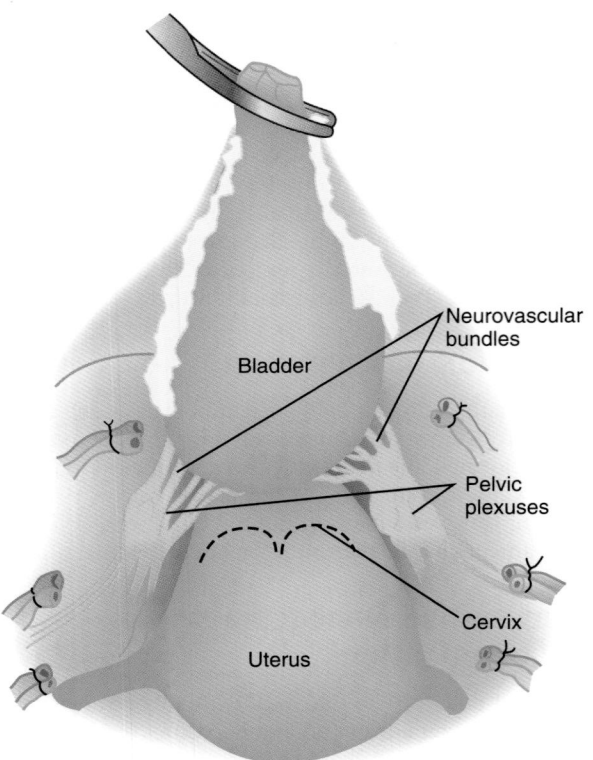

Figure 78–35. The autonomic innervation of the corpora cavernosa clitoris can be identified as it arises lateral to the cervix and courses onto the lateral aspect of the vagina and the anterior vaginal vault. (From Schoenberg M, Hortopan S, Schlossberg L, Marshall FF: Anatomical anterior exenteration with urethral and vaginal preservation: Illustrated surgical method. J Urol 1999;161:569-572.)

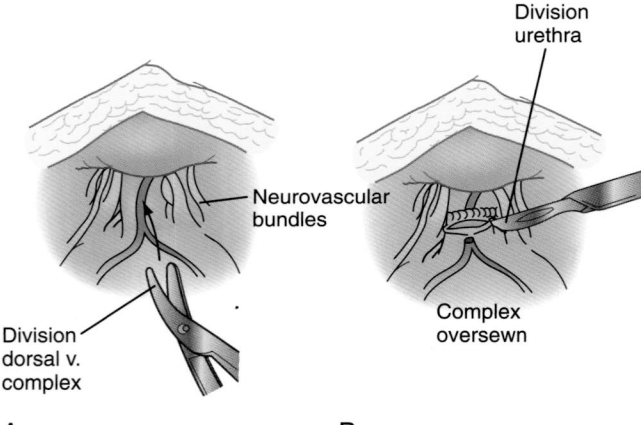

A   B

Figure 78–36. **A,** After lateral pedicles of the bladder are divided ventral to the vesicovaginal junction, the dorsal vein complex is divided and over-sewn distally and proximally as in retropubic prostatectomy. The pubourethral ligaments are left intact. **B,** The urethra is divided, minimizing the distal dissection dorsal to the urethra, which may disrupt the vaginal support of the distal two thirds of the urethra. (From Schoenberg M, Hortopan S, Schlossberg L, Marshall FF: Anatomical anterior exenteration with urethral and vaginal preservation: Illustrated surgical method. J Urol 1999;161:569-572.)

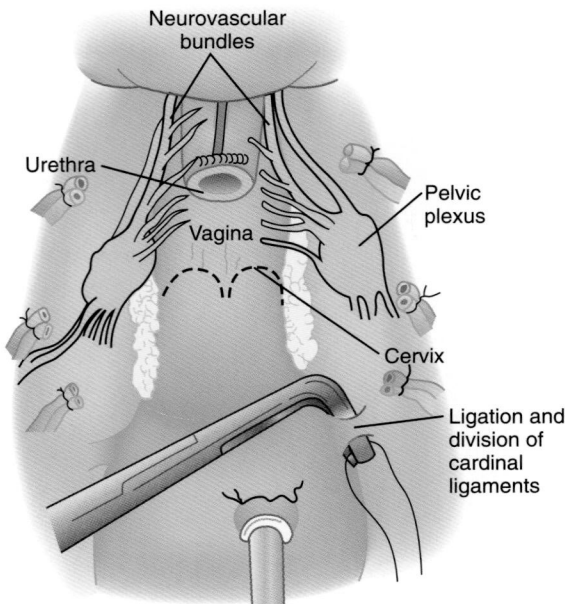

Figure 78–37. The vesicovaginal space is developed in a retrograde direction along the anterior vagina to the cardinal ligaments and vesicocervical junction. The cardinal ligaments are divided. (From Schoenberg M, Hortopan S, Schlossberg L, Marshall FF: Anatomical anterior exenteration with urethral and vaginal preservation: Illustrated surgical method. J Urol 1999;161:569-572.)

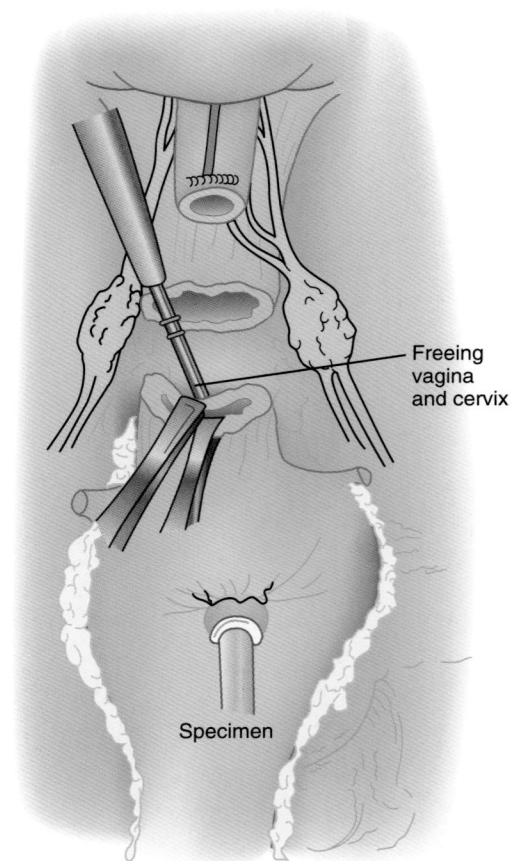

Figure 78–38. The vagina has been opened just below the cervix, and remaining vaginocervical attachments are divided with electrocautery. (From Schoenberg M, Hortopan S, Schlossberg L, Marshall FF: Anatomical anterior exenteration with urethral and vaginal preservation: Illustrated surgical method. J Urol 1999;161:569-572.)

Postoperative complications include infection, pulmonary atelectasis, deep venous thrombosis, and wound problems. Because of the potential for contamination with a vaginal dissection, extensive intraoperative irrigation with antibiotic solution is recommended to decrease infection risk.

Summary

Radical cystectomy in the female can be performed with a precise anatomic approach. Bilateral extended pelvic lymphadenectomy provides for accurate staging and improved survival. Excision of the uterus and a portion of the vagina and the urethra reduces the potential for pelvic recurrence, but urethral preservation can also provide for continent urinary diversion in the female. Vaginal reconstruction and continent urinary diversion improve quality of life. Both sexual function and volitional voiding can be preserved in select female patients undergoing radical cystectomy (Coloby et al, 1994).

KEY POINTS: RADICAL CYSTECTOMY IN THE FEMALE

■ Urethra- and vagina-sparing procedures improve quality of life and have become popular.

■ Extended pelvic lymphadenectomy improves staging accuracy and survival.

■ Orthotopic neobladder has excellent continence rates with preservation of the distal urethra, taking only the proximal 1 cm of urethra and preserving the pubourethral ligaments.

SIMPLE CYSTECTOMY

Simple cystectomy is defined as the removal of the bladder without the removal of adjacent structures. This procedure is performed infrequently today. In the female, the bladder is removed while the urethra, uterus, and vagina are spared. In the male, the bladder is removed while the prostate, urethra, and seminal vesicles are spared. In the male, this has the potential advantage of conserving potency.

Indications

Various benign conditions may warrant simple cystectomy, including pyocystis, neurogenic bladder, severe urinary incontinence, severe urethral trauma, large vesical fistula, cyclophosphamide cystitis, and radiation cystitis after treatment of other pelvic malignant neoplasms.

Patients can experience complications from their retained bladders after supravesical urinary diversions without simple cystectomy. These can include hemorrhage, sepsis, pain, feelings of incomplete emptying, fistulas, pyocystis, and development of cancer. These complication rates from retained bladders can be as high as 80%, and the rate of secondary cystectomy can approach 20% in some series (Eigner and Freiha, 1990). For this reason, some authors recommend simple cystectomy for any patient who is to undergo irreversible urinary diversion.

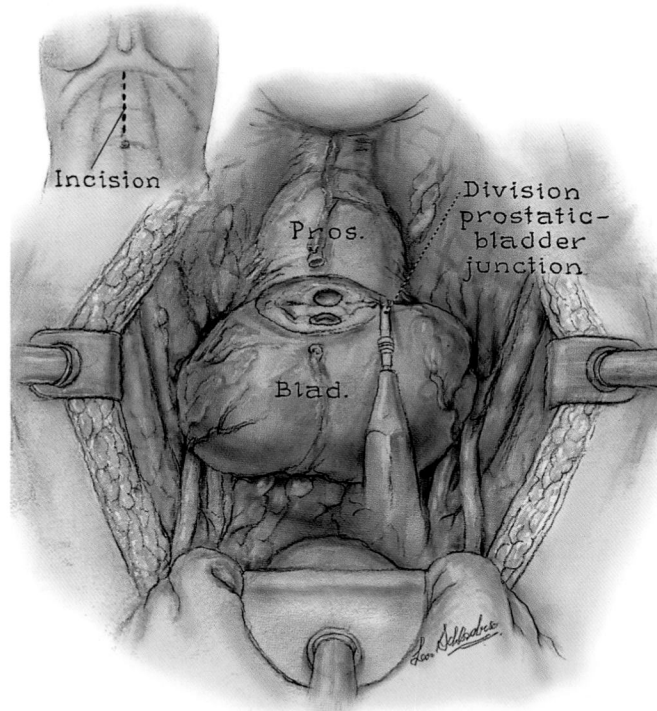

Figure 78–39. The cautery is used to divide the bladder neck.

Surgical Technique

The positioning of the patient and the technique of simple cystectomy can be similar to those described earlier for radical cystectomy. This retrograde approach may be attractive, as the operation can be performed extraperitoneally if prior supravesical diversion has been completed. A low midline incision can be used to enter Retzius' space. The retropubic space is developed with both blunt and sharp dissection. The bladder is partially distended after a catheter has been placed to facilitate dissection. The peritoneum can be swept cephalad. The veins on the surface of the prostate coursing over to the bladder at the 12-o'clock position can be ligated and divided. Cautery is then used to divide the bladder neck (Fig. 78–39). If necessary, individual bleeding points can be sutured or ligated. The bladder neck is divided entirely, and the ureteral orifices are visualized.

The incision is then carried posteriorly through the bladder neck to the area of the seminal vesicles. The dissection proceeds posteriorly, and the bladder is mobilized off the ampulla of vas deferens and seminal vesicles. The prostate is then oversewn in two layers with running absorbable suture (Fig. 78–40). Allis clamps can be placed on the bladder and the dissection continued along the rectum (Fig. 78–41). This plane can often be continued to the peritoneal reflection.

The remaining peritoneum is dissected off the superior aspect of the bladder. The superior and middle vesical branches are individually ligated and divided (Fig. 78–42), and the specimen is then removed.

Alternatively, the bladder can be removed through an antegrade approach. The bladder is partially distended with sterile

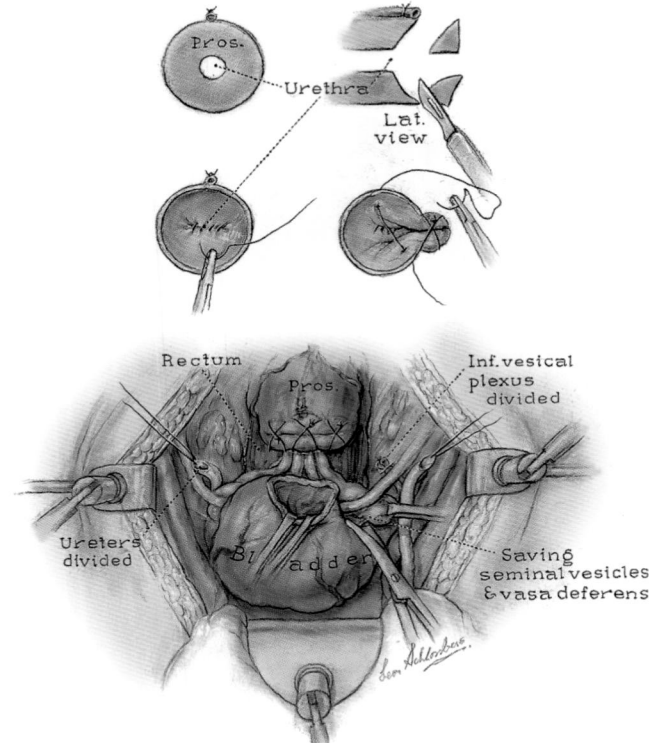

Figure 78-40. The bladder neck is divided, and the prostate is incised so that it can be closed in two layers.

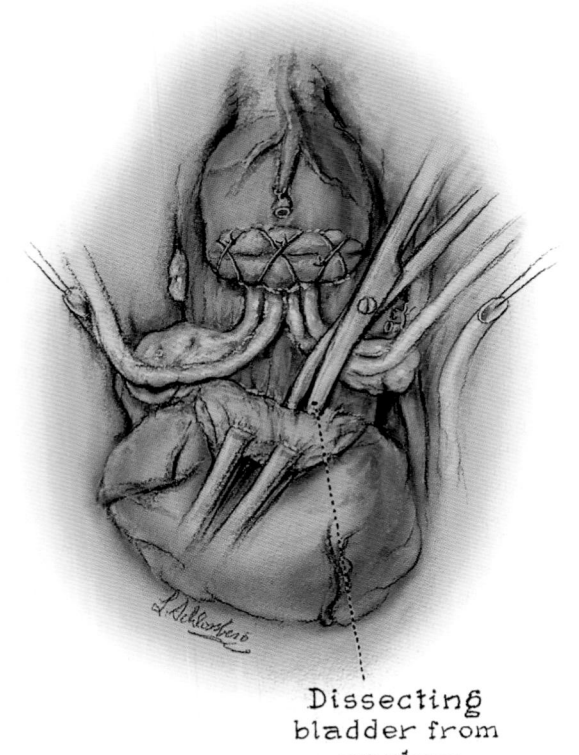

Figure 78-41. The bladder is dissected off the rectosigmoid colon.

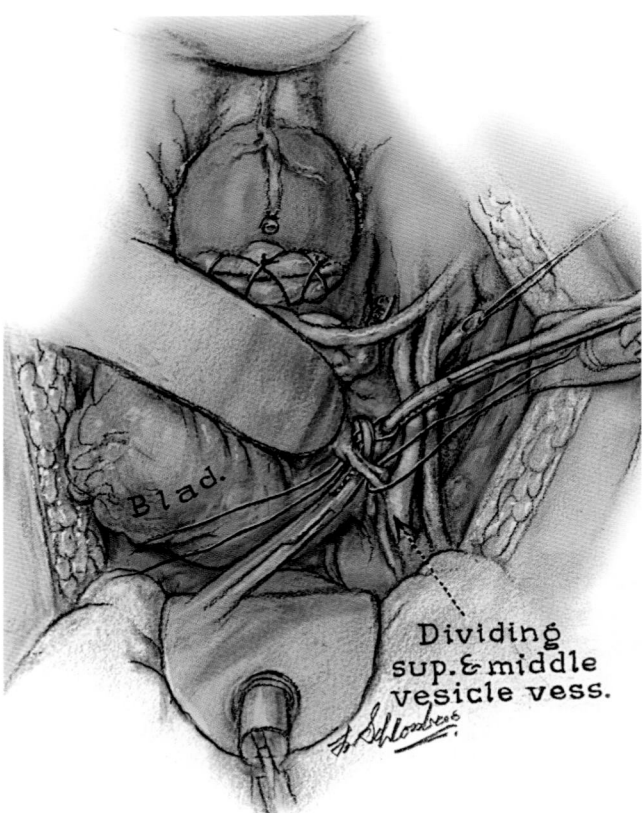

Figure 78-42. The superior and middle vesical branches are individually ligated and divided.

water. Dissection can be initially carried down the hypogastric vessels with ligation of the superior vesical and middle vesical arteries. Early ligation of vessels may facilitate the cystectomy. The ureters are identified where they enter the bladder. In patients who are to undergo a urinary diversion, the ureters can then be divided close to the bladder. In patients who have previously undergone a urinary diversion, the entire segment of the distal ureter is excised along with the bladder specimen. The peritoneum can be dissected off the dome, and the plane behind the bladder to the level of the prostate can be dissected bluntly. The seminal vesicles and ampulla of vas deferens can sometimes be identified if the patient is not too obese or the pelvis is not too deep.

The remainder of the vesical pedicles can be ligated and divided, and the cautery can be used to divide the bladder neck. The prostate is oversewn as previously indicated. The wound is irrigated, and a drain is typically left for no more than 1 or 2 days.

Postoperative Management and Complications

Duration of postoperative stay may be related to the complexity of the urinary diversion performed. Serum electrolyte values are periodically checked. Routine postsurgical care is performed as with radical cystectomy.

Immediate complications relating to simple cystectomy include potential for vascular injury, infection, rectal injury, and injury to adjacent visceral structures. Complications of simple cystectomy often relate to the indication for the cystectomy. For example, there may be a higher risk of complications associated with simple cystectomy performed for pyocystis.

KEY POINT: SIMPLE CYSTECTOMY

■ Simple cystectomy is indicated for a variety of benign but debilitating conditions, including pyocystis, neurogenic bladder, severe urinary incontinence, severe urethral trauma, large vesical fistula, cyclophosphamide cystitis, and radiation cystitis.

PARTIAL CYSTECTOMY

Partial or segmental cystectomy is a bladder-preserving treatment that involves full-thickness surgical excision of the bladder tumor and surrounding bladder wall. It has been performed since the 19th century but became more popular in the 1950s when it was thought that many patients with bladder cancer would be ideal candidates. The advent of TUR made it possible to initially resect most tumors. However, many patients were found to have widespread transitional cell carcinoma, and this led to high rates of recurrent bladder cancer. The rates of local recurrence range from 40% to 78% (Lindahl et al, 1984; Given and Wajsman, 1997).

The benefits of partial cystectomy include complete pathologic staging of the tumor and pelvic lymph nodes as well as preservation of both bladder and sexual function. However, few patients are candidates for partial cystectomy.

Indications

Partial cystectomy still has a defined although infrequent role in the treatment of muscle-invasive bladder cancer. **Appropriate selection of candidates is crucial for the best possible survival rates. One review of the literature concluded that only 5.8% to 18.9% of patients with muscle-invasive bladder cancer would be suitable candidates for partial cystectomy** (Sweeny et al, 1992). Survival rates are adversely affected by higher grade tumors. Retrospective series of partial cystectomy patients have demonstrated survival rates ranging from approximately 25% to 55% overall (Given and Wajsman, 1997). In well-selected patients, partial cystectomy can yield favorable results (Brannan et al, 1978) with a survival rate of 58%. **An ideal patient for partial cystectomy is one who has a normally functioning bladder with good capacity, a first-time tumor recurrence with a solitary tumor, and a tumor location in an area that allows a 1- to 2-cm margin of resection, such as at the dome.** A urachal adenocarcinoma that occurs at the dome of the bladder and may extend up the urachus and toward the umbilicus is another indication for partial cystectomy (Burnett et al, 1991). With use of similar criteria, only 6% of the patients at the Mayo Clinic within a 20-year period were considered candidates for partial cystectomy (Stackl et al, 1998). Partial cystectomy remains a surgical option for a variety of less common malignant lesions of the bladder, such as primary pheochromocytoma and osteosarcoma of the bladder (Kato et al, 2000).

A tumor within a bladder diverticulum is also an indication for partial cystectomy. These patients often do poorly because of a higher risk for metastatic disease. As there is no underlying musculature, invasive tumors will progress directly from T1 (lamina propria) to T3 (perivesical fat) disease. However, partial cystectomy in these patients does not appear to decrease their survival compared with radical cystectomy. Given and Wajsman (1997) reported a 66% invasive disease–free survival rate at 4 years for patients treated with a multimodal approach, combining adjuvant or neoadjuvant chemotherapy, and possibly radiotherapy, with diverticulectomy. The place of radiotherapy in bladder cancer remains uncertain.

Absolute contraindications to partial cystectomy include CIS elsewhere in the bladder and multifocal tumors. Relative contraindications to partial cystectomy include high-grade tumors, tumors located at the trigone or the bladder neck, and tumors that would require ureteral reimplantation. Some authors have reported excision of tumors in the area of the trigone with subsequent ureteral reimplantations (Brannan et al, 1978; Kaneti, 1986), but it is not a sound oncologic approach to this urothelial disease.

Preoperative Considerations

During physical evaluation, a bimanual examination may be helpful in determining the extent and mobility of the tumor. A CT scan should be performed to rule out any metastatic disease in the pelvis, abdomen, or chest. Cystoscopy and multiple mapping bladder biopsies should be performed to rule out multifocality of tumor or presence of widespread CIS. **In high-risk patients, such as those with tumors within diverticula, some authors have recommended a multimodal approach, which includes combined preoperative chemotherapy and possible radiotherapy** (Socquet, 1981; Given and Wajsman, 1997). Tumor cells are easily seeded in the operative field and may implant during partial cystectomy. This has been noted to occur in as many as 10% of patients undergoing partial cystectomy. Some authors have advocated use of preoperative irrigations of intravesical chemotherapy, such as mitomycin C, to reduce the occurrence of tumor implantation (Haddad, 1991).

Surgical Technique

The patient is placed flat on the table with the umbilicus over the break in the table, and the table is flexed to open the pelvis. Typically, a vertical midline incision is made extending from above the symphysis to below the umbilicus. The retroperitoneal space is entered. Cystoscopy may aid in intraoperative delineation of tumor location to achieve an adequate margin of resection. The urachus and obliterated umbilical arteries are identified near the umbilicus and then resected down toward the bladder (Fig. 78–43). The peritoneum is dissected off the bladder laterally, but a portion of the peritoneum may be taken if there is any adherence in the area of the tumor. The bladder should be carefully mobilized so that abundant bladder wall is available beyond any palpable tumor. The initial dissection can be facilitated by filling the bladder with

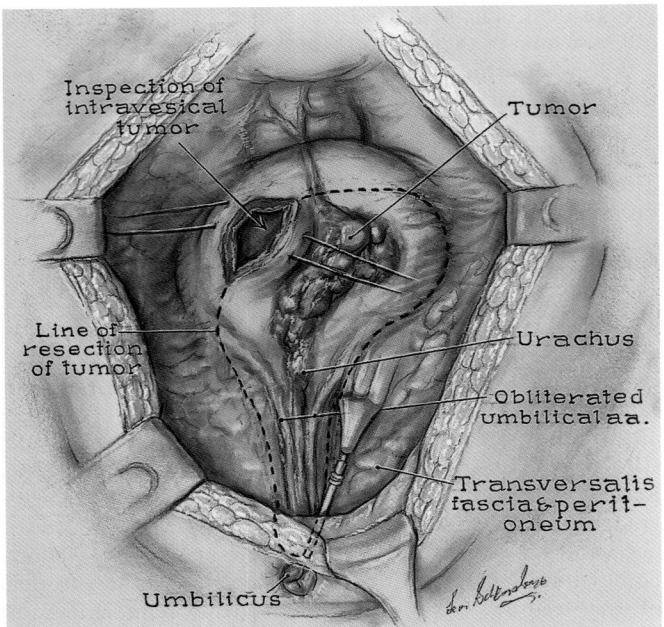

Figure 78–43. The urachus and obliterated umbilical vessels are included en bloc with the partial cystectomy specimen. A small cystotomy is made to inspect the tumor.

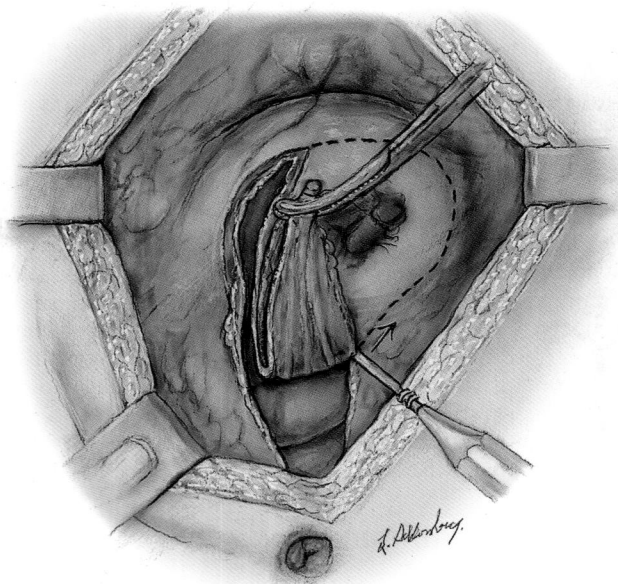

Figure 78–44. A 1- to 2-cm margin is included around the gross tumor.

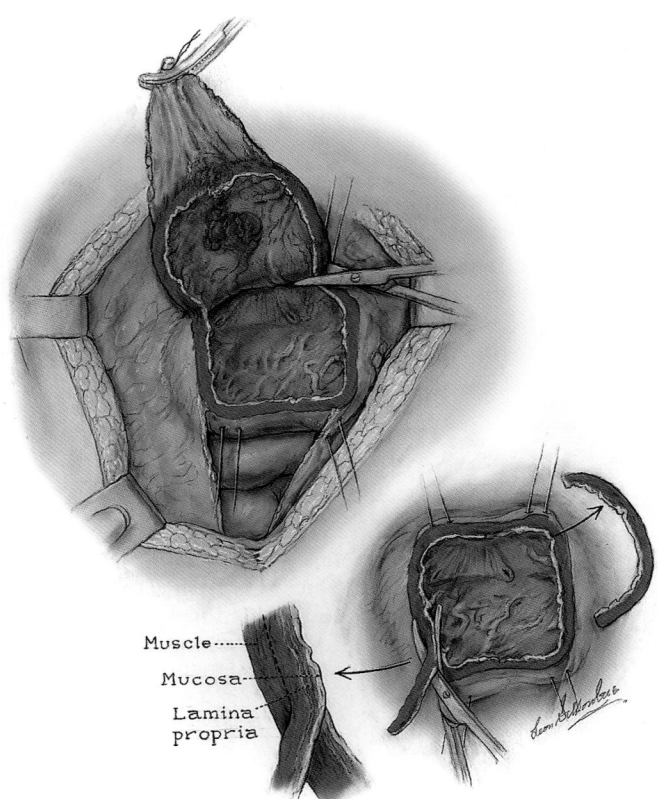

Figure 78–45. A wide margin is excised, and an extensive, long segment of remaining bladder is excised for frozen microscopic pathologic evaluation.

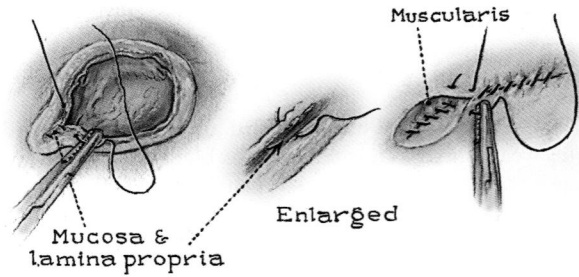

Figure 78–46. The bladder is closed in two layers.

sterile water so that the dissection around the lateral aspect of the bladder is easier. The lateral wall of the bladder is dissected. A small cystotomy is made so that the tumor can be carefully inspected (see Fig. 78–43). All the other tissue in the pelvis is carefully packed off so that there is no obvious spillage. Ligation of the superior vesical artery on the ipsilateral side of the tumor is often necessary for adequate mobilization. Cautery is then used to dissect around the tumor mass with at least a 2-cm margin of tissue in apparently normal bladder (Fig. 78–44).

Stay sutures are then placed in the margin of the resection, which often facilitates the dissection. Cautery or scissors can be used to excise remaining bladder wall with a wide margin of apparently normal tissue (Fig. 78–45). On completion of the tumor resection, a frozen-section margin is obtained from both lateral aspects of the remaining bladder wall. Each side is sent separately (see Fig. 78–45). Assuming the frozen sections are negative and no other lesions are seen, the bladder is then closed in two layers. This is performed with a running suture for the mucosal-submucosal layer. A second layer of running absorbable suture is then used in the muscularis layer (Fig. 78–46). A catheter is left in the bladder, and the bladder is filled with saline to check for a watertight closure.

A drain is brought out through a separate stab wound lateral to the incision. The fascia is usually closed with a No.

1 polydioxanone suture. A urethral catheter is preferred to a suprapubic tube because of the possibility that tumor cells may implant along the suprapubic drainage track.

Postoperative Management and Complications

The urethral catheter is removed on the fifth or sixth postoperative day after the integrity of the bladder closure is assessed with a cystogram. The wound drain is removed on the following day.

Urinary leakage from the bladder closure is the primary postoperative complication and is usually managed by prolonged catheter drainage. Voiding disturbances are also a possibility if a large portion of the bladder has been removed or if the preoperative capacity was small. Good technique reduces wound infection and development of a hernia. Recurrent urothelial tumors and extravesical recurrences are late sources of morbidity. Tumor recurrence has been reported in 38% of partial cystectomy patients (Kaneti, 1986). Dandekar and colleagues (1995) reviewed 32 patients who underwent planned partial cystectomy for muscle-invasive bladder cancer. They found a mean 5-year survival rate after partial cystectomy of 80% for T2-T3b tumors. However, nearly half the patients experienced recurrences, with five superficial tumors, seven muscle-invasive tumors, and two distant metastases. All relapses were associated with stage T3a or higher disease.

Follow-up

Patients who have undergone partial cystectomy should have cystoscopy and urinary cytologic examination every 3 months for at least 2 years. Regular CT scans of the pelvis and abdomen are recommended, particularly in the first several years of follow-up.

KEY POINTS: PARTIAL CYSTECTOMY

■ Only 5.8% to 18.9% of patients with muscle-invasive bladder cancer are suitable candidates for partial cystectomy.

■ Partial cystectomy is indicated in the patient with normally functioning bladder with good capacity and a solitary tumor located where a 1- to 2-cm resection margin is possible.

■ For high-risk tumor in a bladder diverticulum, a multimodal approach with preoperative chemotherapy and possible radiotherapy may be needed.

■ Absolute contraindications include CIS elsewhere in the bladder and multifocal tumors.

■ Ongoing surveillance with cystoscopy and cytology is important because the local recurrence rate is high (40% to 78%).

SUGGESTED READINGS

Bracken RB, McDonald MW, Johnson DE: Complications of single stage radical cystectomy and ileal conduit. Urology 1981;27:141-146.

Given RW, Wajsman Z: Bladder sparing treatments for muscle-invasive transitional cell carcinoma of the bladder. AUA Update Series 1997;16:41-48.

Herr HW, Bochner BH, Dalbagni G, et al: Impact of the number of lymph nodes retrieved on outcome in patients with muscle invasive bladder cancer. J Urol 2002;167:1295-1298.

Hinman F: The technique and late results of ureterointestinal implantation and cystectomy for cancer of the bladder. Int Soc Urol Rep 1939;7:464-524.

Schlegel PN, Walsh PC: Neuroanatomical approach to radical cystoprostatectomy with preservation of sexual function. J Urol 1987;138:1402-1406.

Skinner DG, Stein JP, Lieskovsky G, et al: 25-year experience in the management of invasive bladder cancer by radical cystectomy. Eur Urol 1998;33(suppl 4):25-26.

Stein JP, Esrig D, Freeman JA, et al: Prospective pathologic analysis of female cystectomy specimens: Risk factors for orthotopic diversion in women. Urology 1998;51:951-955.

Stein JP, Lieskovsky G, Cote R, et al: Radical cystectomy in the treatment of invasive bladder cancer: Long-term results in 1,054 patients. J Clin Oncol 2001;19:666-675.

Thrasher JB, Crawford ED: Current management of invasive and metastatic transitional cell carcinoma of the bladder. J Urol 1993;149:957-972.

Young HH, Davis DM: Young's Practice of Urology, vol 12. Philadelphia, WB Saunders, 1926.

79 Laparoscopic Surgery of the Urinary Bladder

INDERBIR S. GILL, MD, MCH

Minimally invasive techniques are currently being applied for the treatment of various benign and malignant conditions of the urinary bladder (Table 79–1). This is primarily because the readily accessible location of the bladder in the midpelvis lends itself nicely to laparoscopic manipulation, both extirpative and reconstructive. With gathering experience, it can be anticipated that laparoscopic surgery of the urinary bladder is likely to increase significantly in scope and application.

LAPAROSCOPIC URETERAL REIMPLANTATION

Laparoscopic ureteroneocystostomy can be performed by either the extravesical or the intravesical technique. The extravesical Lich-Gregoir technique of laparoscopic ureteral reimplantation was initially investigated in the laboratory in the early 1990s (Atala et al, 1993; Schimberg et al, 1994).

Technique

Extravesical

The ureter is dissected distally toward the bladder, and the bladder is mobilized at this location. The detrusor muscle is incised longitudinally along the axis of the ureter, thereby making a 3-cm trough for the ureter (Fig. 79–1). The bladder lumen is not entered during this procedure. **The intact ureter is placed within the trough, and the detrusor muscle fibers are reapproximated superficial to the ureter with three or four interrupted 3-0 Vicryl sutures to complete the non-refluxing submucosal tunnel** (Reddy and Evans, 1994).

Intravesical

Intravesical ureteroneocystostomy involves suprapubic insertion of two 5-mm balloon-tip ports into the bladder under cystoscopic guidance (Gill et al, 2001). With use of a transurethral resectoscope fitted with a Collins knife, the proposed site of a 4- to 5-cm cross-trigonal submucosal tunnel is scored on the bladder base mucosa with electrocautery, extending from the refluxing ureteral orifice, across the trigone, to the contralateral side of the bladder (Fig. 79–2). With a 5-mm endoshears inserted through a suprapubic trocar, mucosal flaps of the proposed submucosal tunnel are developed under cystoscopic visualization, thereby making the bed of the cross-trigonal tunnel. With the transurethral Collins knife, the refluxing ureteral orifice and intramural ureter are detached circumferentially from the full-thickness bladder wall and mobilized extravesically for 2 or 3 cm into the pelvic extraperitoneal space. The mobilized ureter is advanced transtrigonally, and the ureteral neomeatus is anchored to the detrusor muscle at the apex of the trough with three deep interrupted stitches by freehand laparoscopic technique. The elevated mucosal flaps are suture approximated over the ureter with three or four interrupted stitches, thus completing the antireflux submucosal tunnel. **It is vital to maintain both the suprapubic trocars to continuous wall suction, thus minimizing irrigant extravasation intraoperatively.**

This report was the first demonstration of intracavitary freehand laparoscopic suturing and reconstruction within the lumen of the bladder (Gill et al, 2001).

Results

Extravesical

Initial clinical reports of the laparoscopic extravesical Lich-Gregoir technique appeared in the mid-1990s (Ehrlich et al, 1994; Reddy and Evans, 1994; Janetschek et al, 1995). Subsequently, Lakshmanan and Fung (2000) reported 71 extravesical ureteral reimplantations, including 23 unilateral and 24 bilateral cases. Although detailed data were not provided, the authors reported no instance of persistent reflux or obstruction postoperatively.

Shu and colleagues (2004) described six female patients with vesicoureteral reflux (six bilateral, one unilateral) with a mean age of 18.7 years. Mean operative time was 1.8 hours for the unilateral and 3.8 hours for the bilateral procedure. Average hospital stay was 36 hours; five patients were discharged home within 24 hours postoperatively. Convalescence averaged 8 days. At a follow-up of 11.4 months, all six patients had resolution of vesicoureteral reflux.

Case reports of extravesical reimplantation of an obstructed ureter (Fugita and Kavoussi, 2001) and a transected ureter with robotic assistance (Dinlenc et al, 2004) or pure laparoscopic techniques (Andou et al, 2003) have been published.

Intravesical

Gill and colleagues published the initial report of intravesical ureteroneocystostomy in 2001. Three patients with sympto-

matic unilateral vesicoureteral reflux underwent laparoscopic cross-trigonal (Cohen) ureteral reimplantation. Operative time ranged from 2.5 to 4.5 hours, blood loss was 10 to 50 mL, and hospital stay ranged from 1 to 2 days. The Foley catheter was removed at 1 to 3 weeks, and a double-J ureteral stent was left in place for 4 and 6 weeks in two patients. At 6 months of follow-up, complete resolution of reflux was noted in two patients and a persistent grade 2 reflux improved from grade 4 preoperatively in one patient. All three patients were infection free without antibiotics at that follow-up.

Robotic-assisted intravesical cross-trigonal reimplantation has been performed (C. A. Peters, personal communication, 2005).

Conclusion

Laparoscopic ureteroneocystostomy is feasible by either the extravesical or the intravesical technique. Clinical experience available to date is limited.

SEMINAL VESICLE CYSTS

Seminal vesicle cysts are extremely rare, occurring in 0.005% of men. On occasion, seminal vesical cyst disease is associated with ipsilateral renal agenesis or dysgenesis. A literature review identified 79 males, aged 5 months to 63 years (mean age, 27.9 years), who underwent surgical management for this entity (Cherullo et al, 2002). Usually small and asymptomatic, seminal vesicle cysts may become enlarged and inflamed, causing irritation of adjacent organs. Symptoms include bladder irritation, perineal or suprapubic pain, hematospermia, postcoital discomfort, infertility, epididymitis, and prostatitis. Evaluation involves physical examination including digital rectal examination, transrectal (Fig. 79–3A) or transabdominal ultrasonography, computed tomography (Fig. 79–3B), and cystoscopy; magnetic resonance imaging and seminal vesiculography (Fig. 79–3C) are reserved for select cases.

Treatment options include transrectal needle aspiration; cystoscopic aspiration or transurethral deroofing of the

Table 79–1. **Laparoscopic Procedures on the Urinary Bladder**
Ureteral reimplantation
Seminal vesicle disease
Boari flap
Bladder diverticulectomy
Vesicovaginal fistula
Enterocystoplasty
Partial cystectomy
Radical cystectomy
Male
Cystoprostatectomy
Prostate sparing
Female
Anterior exenteration
Uterus, fallopian tube, vagina sparing
Extended pelvic lymphadenectomy
Urinary diversion
Ileal conduit
Mainz pouch
Orthotopic neobladder

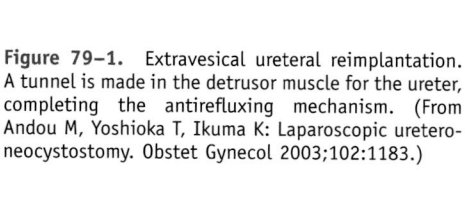

Figure 79–1. Extravesical ureteral reimplantation. A tunnel is made in the detrusor muscle for the ureter, completing the antirefluxing mechanism. (From Andou M, Yoshioka T, Ikuma K: Laparoscopic ureteroneocystostomy. Obstet Gynecol 2003;102:1183.)

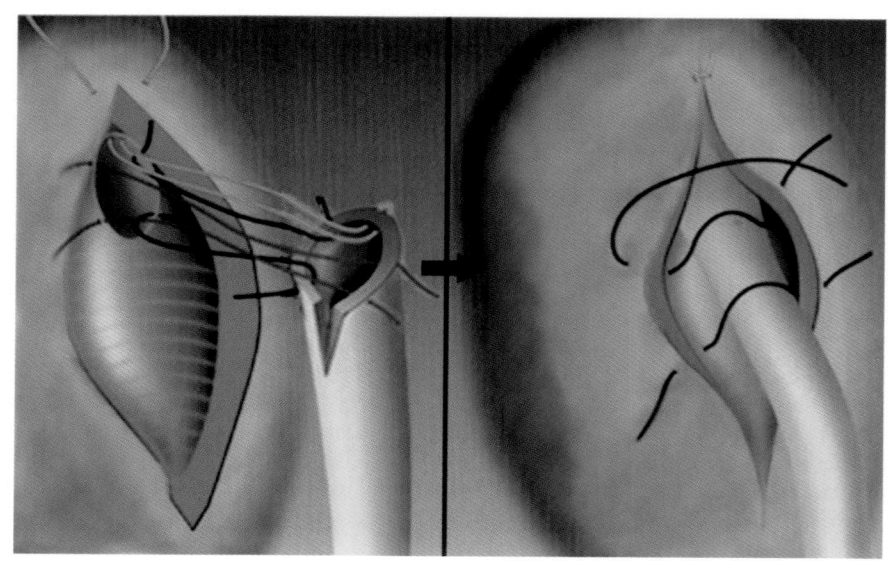

SECTION XV

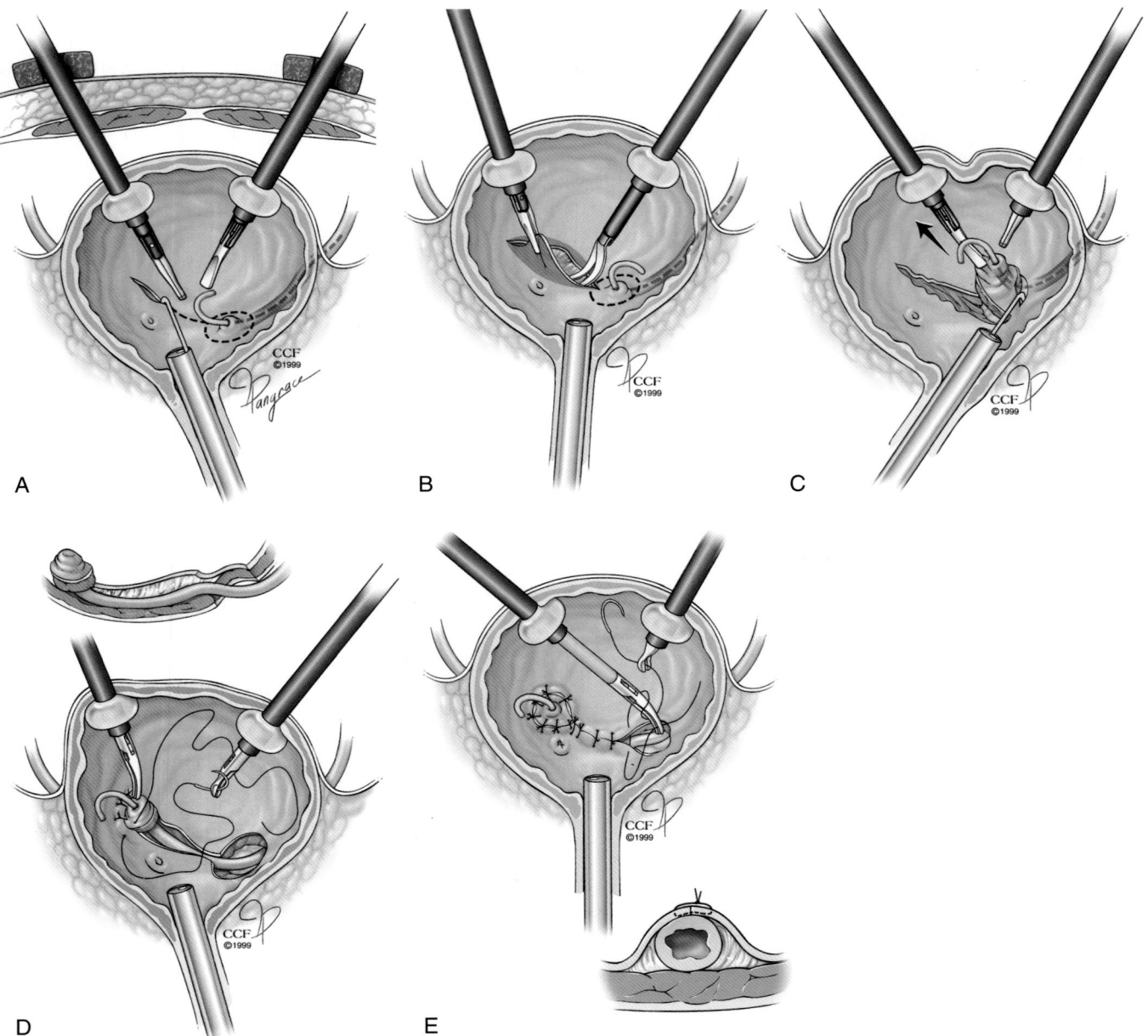

Figure 79–2. Laparoscopic intravesical cross-trigonal (Cohen) reimplantation. **A,** Under cystoscopic visualization, a 4- to 5-cm cross-trigonal tunnel is scored in the bladder base mucosa. **B,** Mucosal flaps are developed cephalad and caudal from the scored line with use of 5-mm instruments inserted through the suprapubic ports. **C,** Mucosal flaps are raised, and the bed of the submucosal tunnel is developed. The ureteral orifice is detached full thickness from the bladder wall, and the intact ureter is mobilized extravesically for 2 to 3 cm. **D,** Transtrigonal advancement of the ureter and anchoring of the new ureteral orifice to the detrusor muscle and mucosa. **E,** The antireflux tunnel is made by approximation of mucosal flaps over the ureter. (Reproduced with permission from The Cleveland Clinic Foundation.)

ejaculatory duct; and open surgical excision, which can be performed by the retroperitoneal, transvesical, transperineal, or posterior transcoccygeal approach. Open surgical access typically involves a large incision and extensive bladder mobilization or a cystotomy. **Laparoscopic techniques efficaciously achieve the goal of surgery, which is en bloc excision of the ipsilateral seminal vesicle cyst and any ectopic ureter with dysplastic renal tissue, if it is present, without compromise of bladder or rectal integrity.**

Technique

Cystoscopic injection of indigo carmine dye into the ejaculatory duct may facilitate laparoscopic identification of the now blue-colored seminal vesicle or cyst (McDougall et al, 2001). A Foley catheter is inserted per urethra, and a four-port transperitoneal laparoscopic approach is employed. The retrovesical peritoneum is incised transversely directly over the readily apparent seminal cystic mass. In case of doubt,

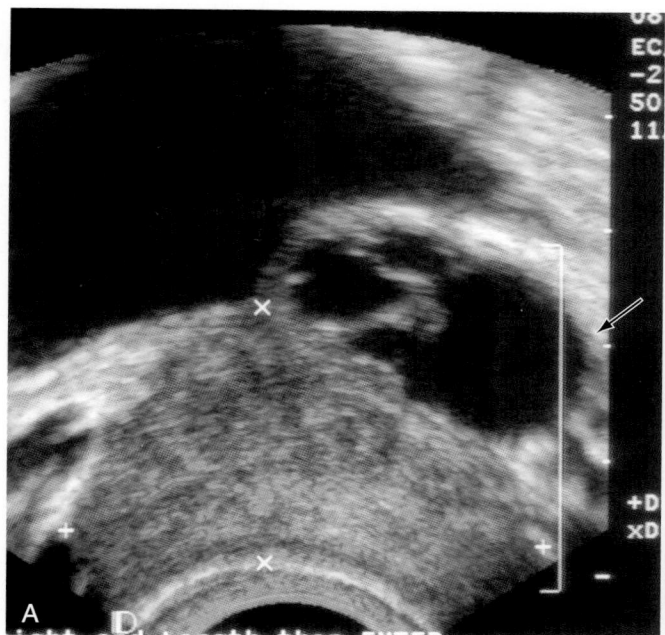

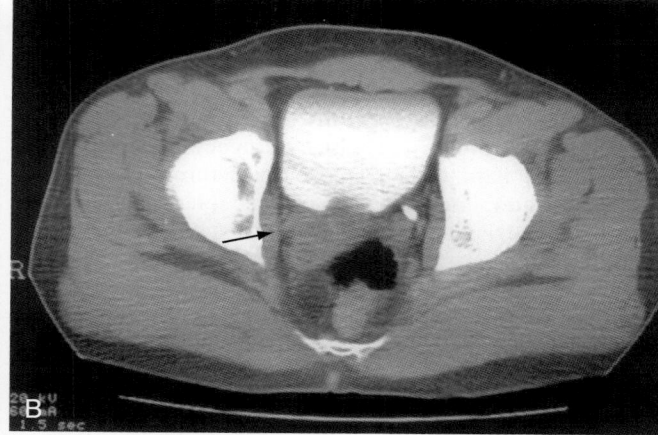

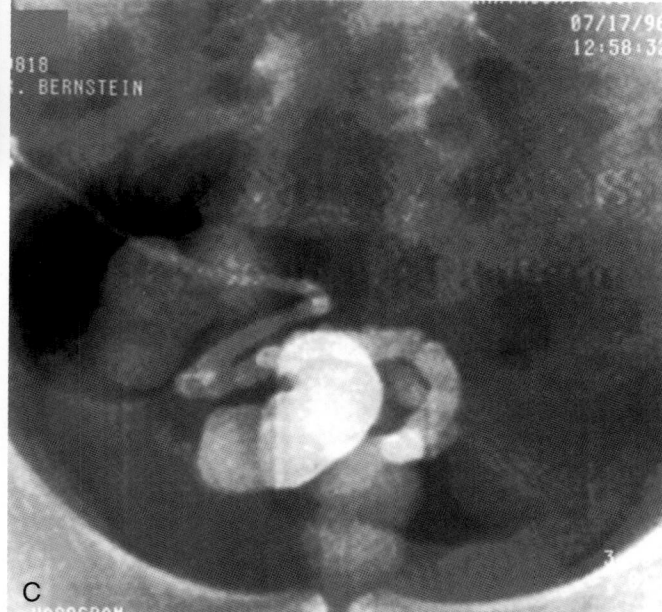

Figure 79–3. **A,** Transrectal ultrasonography demonstrates large right cystic seminal vesicle. **B,** Computed tomographic scan demonstrates dilated right seminal vesicle *(arrow)* compressing the bladder and the rectum. Left ureter is visualized and right ureter is absent. **C,** Vasovesiculography outlines cystic, obstructed right seminal vesicle. (From Cherullo EE, Meraney AM, Bernstein LH, et al: Laparoscopic management of congenital seminal vesicle cysts associated with ipsilateral renal agenesis. J Urol 2002;167:1263.)

intraoperative laparoscopic ultrasonography can be employed. The cystic, dilated seminal vesicle is dissected distally toward its junction with the prostate gland, where it is clipped and divided along with the vas deferens. Any dilated tubular ureteral stump extending proximally from the seminal vesicle is dissected toward the iliac vessels, where it may terminate blindly or be associated with a small dysplastic kidney, which is also excised. On occasion, dissection of this ureteral stump requires mobilization of the cecum and colon, allowing the entire specimen to be removed en bloc (Cherullo et al, 2002).

Results

Nine patients, aged 10 months to 48 years, have undergone laparoscopic excision of seminal vesicle cysts. Operative time has ranged from 1.5 to 6 hours; blood loss, 10 to 350 mL; and hospital stay, 1 to 3 days. During a follow-up ranging from 2 months to 6 years, no significant complications have been reported (Carmignani et al, 1995; Ikari et al, 1999; McDougall

et al, 2001; Nadler and Rubenstein, 2001; Cherullo et al, 2002; Liatsikos et al, 2004).

Conclusion

Laparoscopy is an optimal technique for surgical management of seminal vesicle disease; it allows straightforward access to and excellent visualization of this deep, retrovesically located structure. The seminal vesicles can be cleanly dissected free from the bladder, prostate, ureters, and overlying peritoneum with minimal morbidity and gratifying symptom relief. Because of its excellence of access, laparoscopy appears to be the technique of choice for seminal vesicle disease (Kavoussi et al, 1993).

BOARI FLAP

Distal ureteral loss or disease can occur in a variety of conditions, such as iatrogenic or traumatic disruption; malignant disease; pelvic mass or inflammatory conditions, such as endometriosis, severe stricture disease, tuberculosis, or bilharziasis; and transplant ureteral necrosis. Excision of the diseased ureteral segment followed by reconstruction is often necessary. **Depending on the length of the ureteral defect, various reconstructive options are available, including ureteroureterostomy, direct ureteroneocystostomy, psoas hitch, Boari flap, transureteroureterostomy, renal autotransplantation, and ileal replacement** (Hensle et al, 1987; Gill et al, 2000). First described in 1894, the Boari flap is a consistently reliable and versatile technique to bridge defects of the distal third of the ureter and has occasionally been employed for even mid or proximal ureteral replacement. Laparoscopic Boari flap has been reported.

Technique

The ureter is identified at its crossing over the common iliac artery at the pelvic brim and mobilized distally toward the bladder. After transection at the appropriate location, the ureteral margin is sent for frozen-section analysis. The healthy proximal cut end of the ureter is freshened and spatulated. The urachus is divided, and an inverted U-shaped anterior peritoneotomy is made along the undersurface of the abdominal wall to mobilize the anterior and anterolateral aspects of the bladder within the retropubic space. The bladder is distended with 200 to 300 mL of saline through the urethral Foley catheter. If additional bladder mobilization is deemed necessary, the contralateral superior or mid vesical pedicle can be transected with an endoscopic stapler.

An anterolateral bladder flap based on the ipsilateral vesical pedicle is developed. A flap somewhat longer and wider than anticipated should be developed to ensure a tension-free anastomosis; flap length-to-breadth ratio of 3:1 ensures good vascularity of its apex. If it is deemed necessary, the bladder dome is fixed to the ipsilateral psoas muscle with absorbable 2-0 suture. With 4-0 polyglactin suture on an RB-1 needle, the spatulated cut end of the ureter is affixed to the bladder flap with three or four stitches. A double-J stent is inserted laparoscopically into the ureter in a retrograde manner over a superstiff guide wire. After adequate positioning, the guide wire is removed, and the distal curl of the stent is inserted into the bladder. Mucosa-to-mucosa ureter-to-flap anastomosis is completed with interrupted sutures, tubularizing the apex of the flap as the anastomosis takes shape. Although a refluxing anastomosis is typically performed, a nonrefluxing ureteroneocystostomy can be done by fashioning a submucosal tunnel of adequate length along the luminal surface of the bladder flap. Subsequently, the remainder of the cystotomy incision is closed longitudinally in two layers for a watertight repair. A perivesical drain is placed and laparoscopic exit completed (Nezhat et al, 1999; Fergany et al, 2001; Fugita et al, 2001; Castillo et al, 2005).

Results

In an initial six-animal study, Fergany and colleagues (2001) developed the technique of laparoscopic Boari flap with refluxing (n = 3) and nonrefluxing (n = 3) ureteroneocystostomy. Average length of the Boari flap was 9.5 cm (8.5 to 10 cm), and average length of the submucosal tunnel in the nonrefluxing anastomoses was 4 cm. There were no intraoperative complications, and there was no evidence of obstruction in the animals undergoing nonrefluxing ureteral reimplantation into the Boari flap (Fig. 79–4).

Fugita and colleagues (2001) reported the initial clinical experience with laparoscopic Boari flap in three patients. The length of the distal ureteral defect ranged from 6 to 8 cm, operative time ranged from 2 to 5.5 hours, estimated blood loss was 400 to 600 mL, hospital stay was 3 to 13 days, and convalescence averaged 4 weeks. During a 6- to 14-month follow-up, all three patients had relief of obstruction and were asymptomatic.

Castillo and colleagues (2005) reported laparoscopic Boari flap in eight patients with a distal ureteral stricture and one patient with distal ureteral transitional cell carcinoma. Mean ureteral stricture length was 5.5 cm (range, 4 to 7 cm), mean operative time was 2.6 hours (range, 2 to 4 hours), mean blood loss was 124 mL (range, 20 to 200 mL), mean hospital stay was 3 days (range, 2 to 4 days), and convalescence averaged 3 weeks (range, 2 to 6 weeks). Complications occurred in two patients, including pulmonary embolism (one) and anastomotic urine leakage repaired laparoscopically (one). During a mean follow-up of 17.6 months, all patients were symptom free with unobstructed drainage on intravenous pyelography.

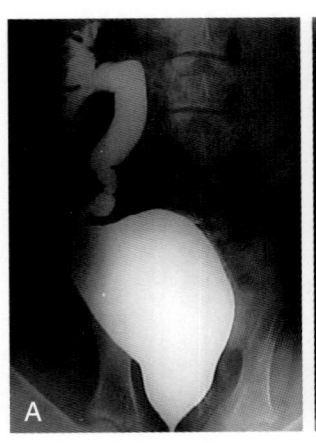
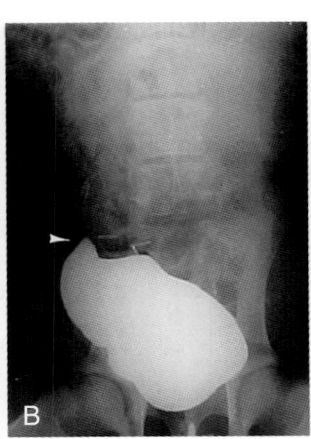
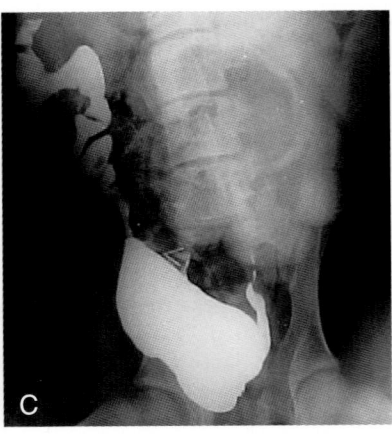

Figure 79–4. **A,** Cystogram after direct refluxing Boari flap reimplantation. **B,** Cystogram after nonrefluxing Boari flap reimplantation (*arrowhead*). **C,** Antegrade pyelography demonstrates free drainage with no evidence of obstruction. (From Fergany A, Gill IS, Abdel-Samee A, et al: Laparoscopic bladder flap ureteral reimplantation: Survival porcine study. J Urol 2001;166:1920.)

Conclusion

Although rarely indicated, laparoscopic Boari flap can be performed efficiently with outcomes comparable to those of open surgery.

LAPAROSCOPIC BLADDER DIVERTICULECTOMY

Bladder diverticulum is a herniation of bladder mucosa through the detrusor muscle fibers, often associated with chronic bladder outlet obstruction due to prostatomegaly. **Whereas small, self-draining, asymptomatic diverticula typically do not require treatment, intervention is indicated when the diverticulum is large and symptomatic; associated with lithiasis, cancer, recurrent infections, or inadequate voiding; or causing ureteral reflux or obstruction.** Selection of surgical approach is determined by the size, number, and location of the diverticula and the need for and timing of concomitant surgery for prostate obstruction or ureteral reimplantation. Typically, a small diverticulum can be fulgurated cystoscopically with concomitant transurethral resection or incision of the prostate (Orandi, 1977; Vitale and Woodside, 1979). Larger diverticula are excised open surgically by an extravesical, intravesical, or combination approach (Clayman et al, 1984).

Laparoscopic bladder diverticulectomy can be performed either transperitoneally or extraperitoneally, by either the extravesical or intravesical technique (Das, 1992; Parra et al, 1992; Nadler et al, 1995). **Goals of surgery include complete mobilization of the diverticular sac and neck; excision of the diverticulum; and precise double-layered bladder closure, with avoidance of injury to the ureters or adjacent structures. Transurethral resection or incision of the prostate and bladder neck can be performed as indicated, either immediately before or after diverticulectomy** (Iselin et al, 1996).

Technique

Specific, individual catheterization of the ureters, diverticulum, and bladder is performed cystoscopically to allow differential filling and distention, which facilitates intraoperative identification (Khonsari et al, 2004) (Fig. 79–5). After ureteral catheterization, a Councill-tip catheter is inserted over a superstiff Amplatz guide wire directly into the diverticulum and its balloon inflated, thereby securing the catheter tip within the diverticulum. Finally, a bladder catheter is inserted, either suprapubically or per urethra.

A four- or five-port transperitoneal laparoscopic approach is employed typically. With the bladder deflated and the diverticulum sac distended by the Councill catheter, the peritoneum overlying the diverticulum is incised directly. Peridiverticular adhesions are dissected; the ureters are carefully identified and preserved. The neck of the diverticulum is circumscribed, entered, and excised at its ostium, completely freeing the diverticulum. The presence of the Councill catheter through the diverticulum neck facilitates its identification. The bladder is suture repaired in two layers, a 4-0 polyglactin suture for the urothelium and a 2-0 polyglactin suture for the detrusor. Alternatively, an endoscopic stapler

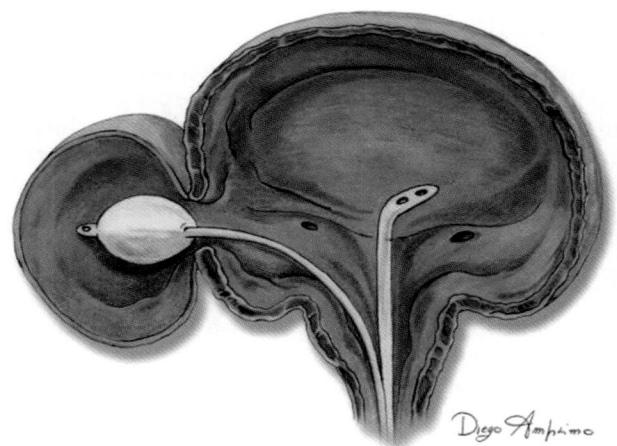

Figure 79–5. Specific, directed catheterization of the diverticulum (Foley catheter with the inflated balloon) and urinary bladder (Tiemann catheter). Unilateral or bilateral ureteral catheterization can also be performed if necessary. (From Porpiglia F, Tarabuzzi R, Cossu M, et al: Is laparoscopic bladder diverticulectomy after transurethral resection of the prostate safe and effective? Comparison with open surgery. J Endourol 2004;18:73.)

has been employed to excise and close the diverticulum neck, although concerns about staple migration and encrustation exist. Watertightness of the bladder closure is confirmed by distending the bladder. Transurethral resection or incision of the prostate or bladder neck is completed as indicated. If it is performed after the diverticulectomy, a suprapubic catheter is advantageous in maintaining low intravesical pressures. A perivesical drain and a bladder catheter are placed, and laparoscopic exit is completed.

Alternatively, an intravesical approach to bladder diverticulectomy has been described. It employs techniques based on the intravesical ureteral reimplantation procedure described before (Pansodoro, personal communication).

Results

Since the initial description of laparoscopic bladder diverticulectomy in 1992 (Parra et al, 1992), additional reports have been published (Rozenberg et al, 1994; Jarrett et al, 1995; Champault et al, 1997; Faramarzi-Roques et al, 2004). Porpiglia and colleagues (2004) compared laparoscopic and open bladder diverticulectomy in 12 and 13 patients, respectively. The laparoscopic group had a longer mean operative time (4 versus 2.3 hours; $P < .0001$), decreased analgesia requirements ($P = .02$), and shorter hospital stay (3.2 versus 9.6 days); there were no complications in either group. The bladder catheter was removed 1 week postoperatively in either group. In this study, transurethral prostatectomy was performed before laparoscopic diverticulectomy. Four patients underwent laparoscopic diverticulectomy for two diverticula, and no patient required ureteral reimplantation. Khonsari and colleagues (2004) reported laparoscopic excision of a giant (>1000 mL) bladder diverticulum by the transperitoneal approach. Intraoperative ureteral injury was repaired laparoscopically without sequelae.

Conclusion

Laparoscopic diverticulectomy and sequential transurethral resection or incision of the prostate can be performed safely and efficaciously with adherence to open surgical principles. Careful preoperative planning and precise intraoperative laparoscopic technique allow results comparable to those of open surgery.

VESICOVAGINAL FISTULA

In developed countries, vesicovaginal fistula (VVF) is most commonly due to iatrogenic trauma during gynecologic surgical procedures. Abdominal hysterectomy is the most common cause, with 1 of every 1800 hysterectomies reportedly resulting in VVF as a complication. Other causes include radiation therapy for urogynecologic cancers and complications of obstructed labor (Miller and Webster, 2001). The exact pathogenesis of posthysterectomy VVF is uncertain and appears to be multifactorial, including iatrogenic electrosurgical injury and suboptimal healing in the presence of chronic vaginal infection and small abscesses (Cogan et al, 2002).

Technique

Confirmatory diagnosis of VVF is beyond the scope of this chapter. Care should be taken to exclude ureterovaginal fistula, urethrovaginal fistula, and nonfistulous urinary incontinence by a judicious combination of various tests (Miller and Webster, 2001) including intravenous urography, digital rectovaginal examination, vaginal swab test, cystography, intravenous indigo carmine test, combined vaginoscopy-cystoscopy (Andreoni et al, 2003), and ureteroscopy, if necessary.

A variety of surgical approaches (transvaginal, transurethral [McKay et al, 2004], transabdominal, combined) can be employed, depending on the cause, location, number, and size of VVF. Generally speaking, an abdominal approach is preferred for VVF in the upper aspect of a narrow vagina, VVF in proximity to the ureteral meatus, larger or multiple VVFs, or associated disease. **Laparoscopy provides an effective alternative to open abdominal surgery, respecting the basic principles of VVF repair: clear exposure of the fistula track, circumferential excision of fibrous and scar tissue from the fistula edge, individual tension-free suture repair of the freshened fistula edges in the vagina and the bladder, interposition of a peritoneal or omental flap, and adequate bladder drainage** (Sotelo et al, 2005a). Timing of VVF surgical repair, early versus delayed, has been debated; recent opinion favors early repair in select cases (Blandy et al, 1991; Blaivas et al, 1995; Langkilde et al, 1999).

Cystoscopy is performed to precisely evaluate the location of the VVF and to insert a ureteral catheter into each ureter; a ureteric or urethral catheter is inserted through the VVF into the vagina to facilitate intraoperative identification. In the preferred technique, an incision into the posterior bladder wall is made vertically in the vicinity of the VVF and extended distally, such that the VVF is entered (Fig. 79–6) (Sotelo et al, 2005a). Alternatively, dissection may be performed between the vagina and the bladder toward the VVF. The vagina and

bladder are entered cephalad to the fistula. The fistula edge is grasped with a laparoscopic Allis clamp, and en bloc excision of the bladder cuff, fistulous track, and vaginal cuff is performed, keeping bilateral ureteric orifices in constant view. **Only the fibrotic VVF track and edges are excised; wide excision is unnecessary. Adequate mobilization of the posterior bladder wall and anterior vaginal wall is necessary to achieve a tension-free repair.** The small vaginal entry is suture repaired vertically with polyglactin suture. The bladder defect is repaired in one and preferably two layers in a transverse manner, with care taken not to compromise the ureteral orifices. Hemostasis is confirmed in the vesicovaginal space, and a formal peritoneal or omental flap is developed, mobilized, introduced between the bladder and vagina, and secured to the anterior vaginal wall with one or two interrupted Vicryl sutures. The bladder is distended with saline through the Foley catheter to confirm watertight repair. A suprapubic cystostomy tube may be inserted at the surgeon's discretion. A pelvic drain is placed, and the ureteral catheters can be maintained for 48 hours in an attempt to provide a relatively dry field for suture healing. The Foley catheter is removed at 10 days to 2 weeks postoperatively after a cystogram confirms complete healing.

Results

First reported by Nezhat in 1994, laparoscopic VVF repair has been reported in 23 patients in the literature to date (Phipps, 1996; von Theobald et al, 1998; Miklos, 1999; Nabi and Hemal, 2001; Ou et al, 2004; Sotelo et al, 2005a). Although varying laparoscopic techniques were employed, a successful outcome was achieved in 22 cases during a follow-up ranging from 3 to 60 months. **Sotelo and colleagues (2005a) reported the largest experience in 15 patients, with a mean operative time of 2.8 hours and hospital stay of 3 days (range 2 to 5 days). During a mean follow-up of 26.2 months (range 3 to 60 months), laparoscopic VVF repair was successful in 14 cases (93%).** Successful laparoscopic repairs of a rectourethral fistula after radical prostatectomy (Sotelo et al, 2005b) and a postcesarean cervicovesical fistula (Hemal et al, 2001) have been reported.

Conclusion

The laparoscopic approach to VVF repair is an efficacious alternative to open abdominal surgery. Surgical principles of wide exposure, excision of fibrous tissue, tension-free repair, and efficient postoperative bladder drainage can be duplicated laparoscopically.

LAPAROSCOPIC ENTEROCYSTOPLASTY

Patients with symptomatic, functionally reduced bladder capacity and compliance in whom conservative management has failed are candidates for surgical augmentation of bladder capacity. Enterocystoplasty is the most widely accepted augmentation technique in clinical practice currently. Alternative techniques, such as laparoscopic autoaugmentation and experimental use of small intestinal submucosa, have yielded suboptimal results (Landman et al, 2004). **By anastomosis of an adequate-sized, well-vascularized, pedicled, detubularized segment of bowel (ileum, ileocecum, right colon, or**

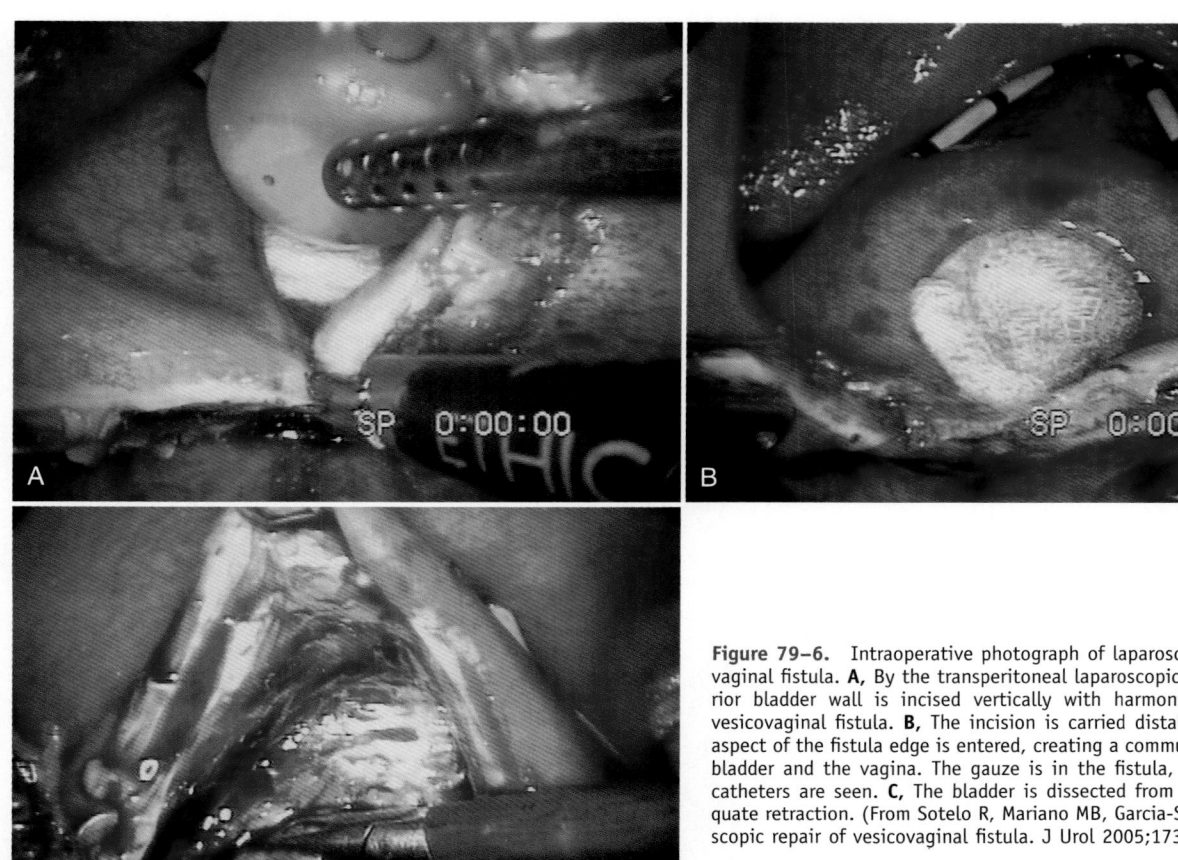

Figure 79–6. Intraoperative photograph of laparoscopic repair of vesicovaginal fistula. **A,** By the transperitoneal laparoscopic approach, the posterior bladder wall is incised vertically with harmonic shears toward the vesicovaginal fistula. **B,** The incision is carried distally until the posterior aspect of the fistula edge is entered, creating a communication between the bladder and the vagina. The gauze is in the fistula, and bilateral ureteral catheters are seen. **C,** The bladder is dissected from the vagina with adequate retraction. (From Sotelo R, Mariano MB, Garcia-Segui A, et al: Laparoscopic repair of vesicovaginal fistula. J Urol 2005;173:1615.)

sigmoid) **with the mobilized, bivalved urinary bladder, enterocystoplasty significantly and durably increases bladder capacity and compliance.** Contraindications to laparoscopic enterocystoplasty, similar to the contraindications to open surgery, include compromised renal function, renal tubular acidosis, inflammatory bowel disease, short gut syndrome, liver failure, and noncompliance with or inability to perform intermittent catheterization reliably. The presence of bowel disease such as diverticulitis, ulcerative colitis, or prior abdominal irradiation should prompt use of alternative bowel segments (Elliott et al, 2002).

Technique

Single-J ileoureteral stents (7 French, 90 cm) are inserted into each kidney cystoscopically and secured to a urethral Foley catheter. A four- or five-port transperitoneal laparoscopic technique is employed, and the bladder is mobilized substantially without compromise of its vascular pedicles (Gill et al, 2000). Depending on preoperative selection of a specific bowel segment, an appropriate 15-cm length of bowel with a well-defined mesenteric arterial arcade is identified that can readily reach the area of the bladder neck without tension. The

selected bowel segment and its mesenteric pedicle are carefully isolated with endoscopic staplers, bowel continuity is reestablished, and the mesenteric window is closed.

The isolated bowel segment is cleaned by irrigation and detubularized along its antimesenteric border with J-hook electrocautery or harmonic scalpel. A U-shaped plate of bowel (typically ileum) is made by side-to-side anastomosis with continuous absorbable (2-0 Vicryl) suture. **This bowel work can be performed either intracorporeally by pure laparoscopic techniques or extracorporeally by open techniques** (Fig. 79–7). When the cecum and proximal ascending colon are selected, the bowel is typically exteriorized through an extended umbilical port site incision. By open techniques, the colocecal segment is detubularized, appendectomy completed, terminal ileum narrowed over an 18 French catheter to construct a catheterizable stoma, ileocecal junction imbricated and intussuscepted to enhance the continence mechanism of the ileocecal valve, and bowel continuity restored. The prepared bowel segment is returned to the abdomen, the skin incision is closed around the reinserted umbilical port, and pneumoperitoneum is reestablished.

A generous (15-cm) anteroposterior cystotomy incision is made laparoscopically. **The bowel segment is oriented**

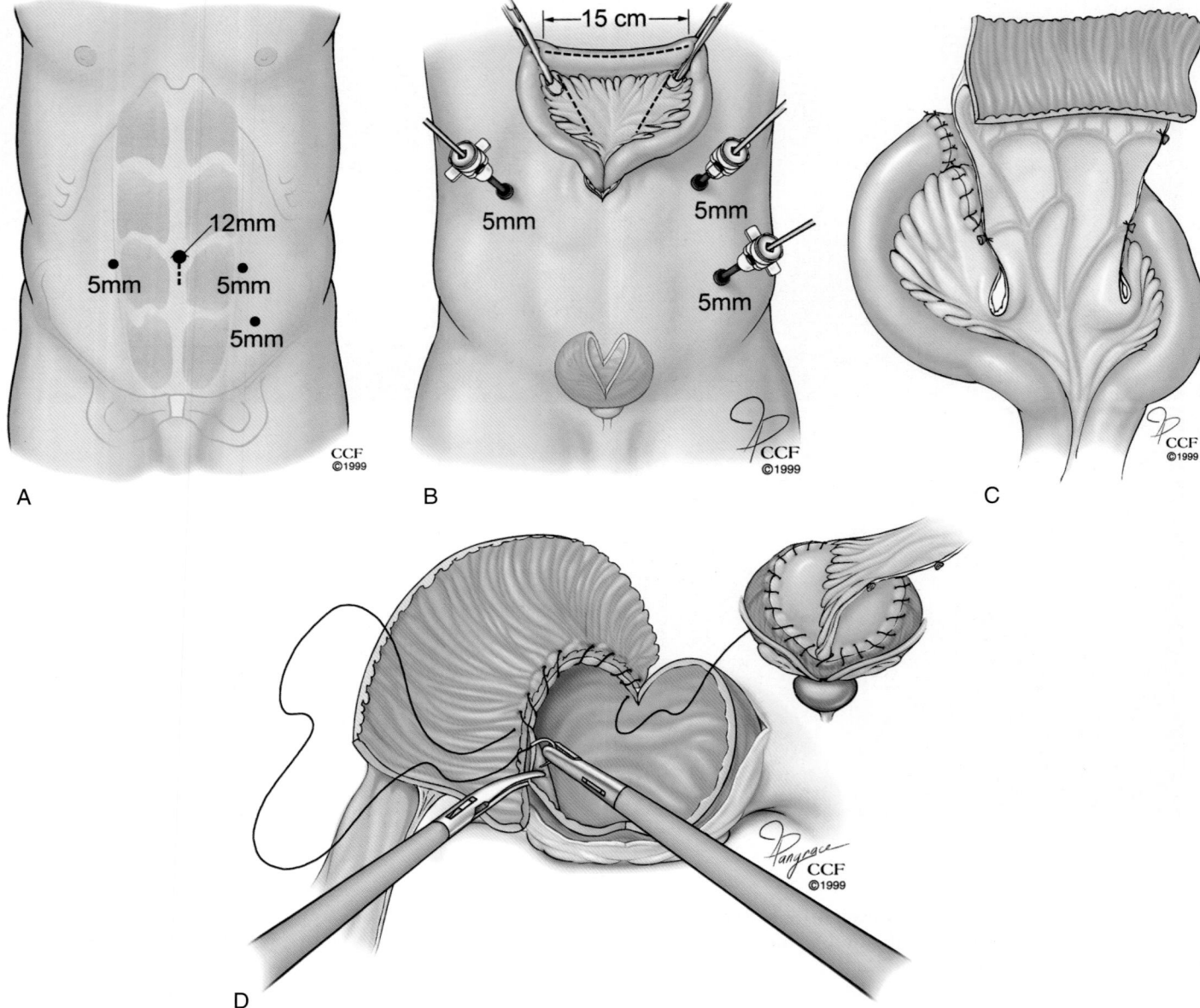

Figure 79–7. **A,** Port placement for laparoscopic enterocystoplasty. Four-port transperitoneal technique is employed, including an umbilical port, one port at each lateral border of the rectus muscle at the level of the umbilicus, and a port in the iliac fossa at the level of the anterior superior iliac spine. **B,** The selected bowel segment (15 cm) is exteriorized through an extension of the umbilical port incision. Alternatively, the bowel work can be performed intracorporeally. The anteroposteriorly bivalved bladder is shown. **C,** Ileoileal reanastomosis is performed cephalad (anterior) to the isolated bowel segment, which is then detubularized and cleaned. Proper orientation of bowel mesentery must be maintained. **D,** Ileovesical anastomosis is performed in a circumferential manner with continuous, full-thickness, freehand laparoscopic suturing with 2-0 Vicryl suture on a CT-1 needle. The completed augmentation ileocystoplasty is shown in the *inset*. (Reprinted with permission from The Cleveland Clinic Foundation. From Gill IS, Rackley RR, Meraney AM, et al: Laparoscopic enterocystoplasty. Urology 2000;55:178.)

properly, **without any torsion of its mesenteric pedicle. Circumferential, continuous, full-thickness, single-layer, mucosa-to-mucosa anastomosis of the bowel and bladder wall is performed with freehand laparoscopic suturing (2-0 Vicryl on a CT-1 needle).** It is efficacious to perform the anastomosis from a posterior to an anterior direction. After watertight anastomosis is confirmed, two perivesical drains are inserted and the laparoscopic exit is completed.

Results

In 1995, Docimo and colleagues first reported laparoscopic gastrocystoplasty in a 17-year-old girl by a five-port transperitoneal technique. A wedge of the greater curvature of the stomach based on the right gastroepiploic pedicle was isolated with an endoscopic gastrointestinal stapler, delivered into the pelvis, and sutured to the bladder.

Operative time was 10 hours and 55 minutes, and hospital stay was 13 days.

Hedican and colleagues (1999) reported laparoscopic-assisted enterocystoplasty in eight patients. The laparoscopic work was limited to bowel mobilization and appendiceal separation from the cecum with a stapler in preparation for an appendiceal Mitrofanoff procedure in two patients; the remainder of the procedure, including the enterovesical anastomosis, was performed open surgically.

In 2000, Gill and colleagues reported laparoscopic enterocystoplasty in three patients with a neurogenic bladder. Ileocystoplasty, sigmoidocystoplasty, and cystoplasty with cecum and proximal ascending colon and a continent, catheterizable ileal conduit with an umbilical stoma were performed in one patient each. Bowel exclusion and reanastomosis were performed extracorporeally, and the enterovesical anastomosis was performed laparoscopically. Operative times were 5.3, 8, and 7 hours, with minimal blood loss and watertight anastomoses. Hospital stays were 7, 5, and 4 days (Gill et al, 2000; Rackley et al, 2005).

Meng and colleagues (2002) reported pure laparoscopic ileocystoplasty in one patient with good long-term outcomes. Laparoscopic ileocystoplasty and continent ileovesicostomy were reported by Siqueira and coworkers (2003) in the porcine model.

Conclusion

Laparoscopic techniques capably duplicate open surgical principles of enterocystoplasty: generous bladder mobilization with an adequate-sized cystotomy or subtotal cystectomy, as necessary; selection of an optimal segment of bowel based on a broad, well-vascularized mesenteric pedicle; isolation of the bowel segment; reestablishment of bowel continuity and closure of the mesenteric window; detubularization and appropriate fashioning of the bowel segment without peritoneal soiling from bowel contents; performance of a tension-free, watertight, full-thickness, circumferential, mucosa-to-mucosa anastomosis of the tailored bowel segment to the bladder; and establishment of adequate urinary drainage. As such, although widespread clinical experience is lacking, at centers of expertise, laparoscopic enterocystoplasty is now a reliable alternative to open surgery.

LAPAROSCOPIC PARTIAL CYSTECTOMY

Laparoscopic partial cystectomy has been performed in a few selected cases for isolated disease of the bladder, such as bladder endometriosis, pheochromocytoma, leiomyoma, and transitional cell carcinoma. **Laparoscopic partial cystectomy, similar to its open counterpart, is indicated for patients with tumor in a bladder diverticulum or a solitary invasive bladder tumor distant from the bladder neck, the ureteral orifices, and the trigone (to allow a resection margin of 1 to 2 cm), with no history or current evidence of multiple tumors or carcinoma in situ and with good bladder capacity.** Contraindications to partial cystectomy include multiple bladder tumors, concomitant carcinoma in situ, and tumors involving the bladder neck or posterior urethra (Brannan et al, 1977; Sweeney et al, 1992).

Technique

A five-port transperitoneal approach, similar to that for laparoscopic radical prostatectomy, is employed (Mariano and Tefilli, 2004). Pelvic lymphadenectomy is performed, and the empty catheterized bladder is completely mobilized posteriorly in the rectovesical pouch as well as anteriorly in the retropubic space. Such mobilization facilitates tension-free closure after partial cystectomy. A small cystotomy is performed on the bladder dome with the aim of inspecting the tumor area inside the bladder. With the urethral Foley catheter clamped, the bladder rapidly distends with carbon dioxide, facilitating intravesical inspection. With either the J-hook electrocautery or ultrasonic scalpel, the tumor is excised with a safety margin of 1.5 to 2 cm of apparently normal bladder mucosa. The excised tumor is immediately entrapped in an impermeable sac and extracted for frozen-section evaluation of the margins. Additional frozen-section biopsy specimens can be obtained from the margin of resection. Bladder closure is performed in two layers, an inner mucosal layer and an outer detrusor layer, achieving a watertight repair. Adequate drainage is achieved with a perivesical drain and a bladder Foley catheter.

Results

Nezhat and coworkers (2002) reported laparoscopic partial cystectomy for invasive bladder endometriosis in 15 patients. Lesions were in the bladder dome in eight patients and in the posterior wall above the trigone in seven patients. Final pathologic examination revealed deeply infiltrating endometriosis in 14 patients and endometrioid adenosarcoma in 1 patient. Chapron and Dubuisson (1999) reported laparoscopic partial cystectomy for infiltrating bladder endometriosis in eight patients. Mean tumor volume of the endometriotic bladder nodules was 9.5 cm³ (range, 3 to 17 cm³). There were no intraoperative or postoperative complications. During a mean follow-up of 31.6 months (range, 6 to 61 months), patients experienced complete recovery. Cystoscopy-assisted laparoscopic resection of extramucosal bladder endometriosis was reported in one patient (Seracchioli et al, 2002). Jeschke and colleagues (2002) reported laparoscopic partial cystectomy for a 3-cm solid leiomyoma in the dome of the bladder with negative margins and no complications (Fig. 79–8). Kozlowski and colleagues (2001) reported laparoscopic partial cystectomy in a patient with a 3.3 × 3.1-cm pheochromocytoma in the left anterolateral aspect of the urinary bladder. After adequate preoperative medical preparation, a transurethral resectoscope with Collins knife was employed to circumferentially score the lesion with a 2-cm margin. The tumor was excised with laparoscopic harmonic shears. Operative time was 300 minutes, blood loss was 200 mL, and hospital stay was 4 days. All antihypertensive medications were discontinued postoperatively, and there were no complications. Pathologic examination confirmed pheochromocytoma of the bladder with negative margins.

Laparoscopic partial cystectomy for bladder transitional cell carcinoma has been reported (Mariano and Tefilli, 2004). **Six carefully selected patients (aged 38 to 76 years) with a solitary, high-grade, invasive, organ-confined bladder tumor underwent the procedure. Mean operative time was 3.4 hours (range, 2.5 to 4.3 hours), and mean blood loss was**

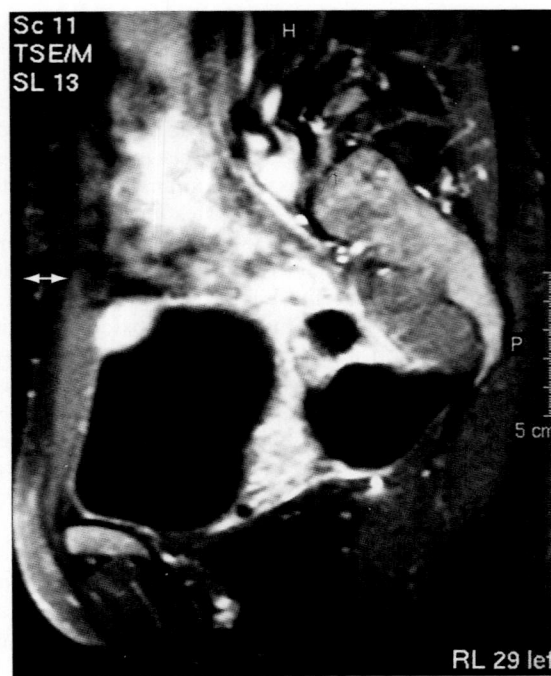

Figure 79–8. Magnetic resonance imaging demonstrates tumor on anterior aspect of the bladder dome. Laparoscopic partial cystectomy was performed, and pathologic examination confirmed leiomyoma. (From Jeschke K, Wakonig J, Winzely M, Henning K: Laparoscopic partial cystectomy for leiomyoma of the bladder wall. J Urol 2002;168:2115.)

200 mL (range, 80 to 300 mL). Postoperatively, two patients developed localized urine extravasation of less than 50 mL, with spontaneous resolution. Mean hospital stay was 4 days (range, 2 to 6 days). Histopathologic examination revealed transitional cell carcinoma stage pT1G3 in bladder diverticulum in one case, pT2aG2 in two cases, pT2bG2 in one case, and pT3aG3 in one case. **All surgical margins and lymph nodes were free of cancer. During a mean follow-up of 30 months (range, 12 to 50 months), no local, intravesical, or systemic recurrences were noted in five patients. The sixth patient with pT3aG3N0 cancer developed locoregional disease and systemic metastases (bone, liver) 9 months postoperatively and was treated with salvage chemotherapy.**

Gerber and colleagues (1995) reported combined cystoscopy-laparoscopy in five patients with noninvasive bladder transitional cell carcinoma who were candidates for radical cystectomy. Therapy was primarily delivered by cystoscopic laser application; in two cases, the bladder serosal surface was also treated laparoscopically with laser. Laparoscopy was used to retract bowel loops away from the bladder and to monitor intravesical laser application. Outcomes were suboptimal; four of five patients developed systemic disease within 9 months postoperatively.

Conclusion

Less than 10% of patients in large series with bladder cancer are candidates for partial cystectomy. In open partial cystectomy series, 5-year survival rates range from 50% to 70% in properly selected patients. Although laparoscopic partial cystectomy has been explored in only a limited number of

carefully selected patients with reasonable results, **extreme care must be taken to minimize chances of local spillage and port site recurrence, which is a serious concern** (Andersen and Steven, 1995; Tsivian and Sidi, 2003). **Suture repair of the cystotomy site must be efficient and watertight to minimize chances of neoplastic cellular implantation due to urine spillage.**

KEY POINTS: LAPAROSCOPIC BLADDER SURGERY

- Because laparoscopy offers excellent access to and visualization of the seminal vesicles, it is considered the surgical approach of choice for seminal vesicle disease.

- Various options for reconstruction of ureteral defects, such as ureteroureterostomy, direct ureteroneocystostomy, psoas hitch, Boari flap, and ileal ureter, can be efficiently and confidently performed laparoscopically with outcomes comparable to those of open surgery.

- Although clinical experience is limited to date, it appears that vesicovaginal fistulas can be definitively repaired by laparoscopic techniques with good success.

- At the author's institution and many others, laparoscopic surgery is now the technique of choice for performing enterocystoplasty. As in open surgery, various bowel segments (ileum, ileocecum, colon) can be employed as necessary in the individual patient. Either a laparoscopic or a laparoscopic-assisted strategy can be employed.

- Laparoscopic partial cystectomy for cancer may be performed only with great caution in the highly selected patient with favorable anatomic location and pathologic attributes.

LAPAROSCOPIC RADICAL CYSTECTOMY AND URINARY DIVERSION

Radical cystectomy is the most effective treatment of patients with organ-confined, muscle-invasive, or recurrent high-grade bladder cancer; recent data suggest that in the appropriately selected patient, early cystectomy is associated with superior oncologic outcomes (Sanchez-Ortiz et al, 2003). With broader acceptance of laparoscopic approaches for treatment of renal and upper tract cancer and more recently for radical prostatectomy for cancer, application of laparoscopic techniques to the only remaining intra-abdominal urologic organ, the urinary bladder, is a logical progression. At this writing, laparoscopic radical cystectomy for cancer is an evolving procedure. **However, interest is rapidly increasing, with multiple centers worldwide reporting their initial experiences with this procedure** (Table 79–2) (Moinzadeh and Gill, 2004). This section describes the technical steps of laparo-

Table 79-2. **World Experience with Laparoscopic Radical Cystectomy and Urinary Diversion**

Technique	Lead Author	Institution Location	n	Comment on Abstract-Manuscript or Technique
Purely laparoscopic	Gill, I.S.	Cleveland, Ohio, USA	30	Purely laparoscopic reconstruction of the urinary diversion
	Tuerk, I.	Massachusetts, USA, and Berlin, Germany	15	Mainz II continent sigmoid-rectal pouch
Laparoscopic assisted	Van Velthoven, R.	Brussels, Belgium	22	Extracorporeal reconstruction, variety of diversions
	Basillote, J.B.	Irvine, California, USA	13	Comparison between LC and open radical cystectomy; extracorporeal reconstruction
	Hemal, A.K.	New Delhi, India	11	Emphasis on complications of the initial experience with LC; extracorporeal ileal conduit
	Simonato, A.	Milan, Italy	10	Detailed steps of LC with illustrations; a variety of diversions including intracorporeal and extracorporeal reconstruction
	Denewer, A.	Mansoura, Egypt	10	Salvage cystectomy after radical radiotherapy; a modified ureterosigmoidostomy diversion through a minilaparotomy (8 cm)
	Abdel-Hakim, A.M.	Cairo, Egypt	9	Extracorporeal reconstruction of ileal neobladder
	Castillo, O.	Santiago, Chile	7	Extracorporeal reconstruction, Studer neobladder
	Paz, A.	Ashkelon, Israel	7	Comparison between LC and open radical cystectomy; extracorporeal reconstruction
	Popken, G.	Berlin, Germany	7	Extra/intracorporeal reconstruction with a variety of diversions
	Puppo, P.	Pietra Ligure, Italy	5	First transvaginal and laparoscopic approach for bladder cancer; ileal conduit was accomplished through a minilaparotomy at the stoma site
	Xiao, L.C.	Guangzhou, China	5	Extracorporeal reconstruction, Indiana pouch
	Huan, S.K.	Chi Mei, Taiwan	4	Extracorporeal reconstruction, Indiana pouch
	Sung, G.T.	Pusan, Korea	4	Extracorporeal ileal conduit
	Guazzoni, G.	Milan, Italy	3	Nerve-sparing LC with extracorporeal W-shaped neobladder
	Pedraza, R.	New York, USA	2	Patients underwent LC with total ureterectomy and construction of pyelocutaneous ileal conduit intracorporeally
Hand assisted	McGinnis, D.E.	Bryn Mawr, Pennsylvania, USA	7	Hand-assisted LC with extracorporeal ileal conduit
	Fan, E.W.	Chi Mei, Taiwan	6	Hand-assisted laparoscopic bilateral nephroureterectomy with radical cystectomy (end-stage renal disease)
	Peterson, A.C.	Tacoma, Washington, USA	1	First reported case of hand-assisted LC with extracorporeal ileal conduit
Robotic assisted	Menon, M.	Detroit, Michigan, USA	14	Nerve-sparing robotic-assisted LC
	Balaji, K.C.	Omaha, Nebraska, USA	3	LC with robotic assistance for intracorporeal suturing of the ureter–ileal conduit anastomosis (2 patients with interstitial cystitis)
	Beecken, W.D.	Frankfurt, Germany	1	First reported case of robotic-assisted LC with intracorporeal orthotopic neobladder
Other	Goharderakhshan, R.	Harbor City, California, USA	25	Series focusing on complications associated with LC; reconstructive technique not detailed
	Vallancien, G.	Paris, France	20	Prostate-sparing cystectomy; reconstructive technique not detailed

LC, laprascopic cystectomy.
Modified from Moinzadeh A, Gill IS: Review of laparoscopic radical cystectomy. Cancer 2004; in press.

scopic radical cystectomy in the male and female; extended pelvic lymphadenectomy; and urinary diversion, including ileal conduit, Mainz pouch, and orthotopic neobladder. Emerging worldwide outcomes data are presented.

Historical Background

In 1992, Parra and colleagues initially described laparoscopic simple cystectomy for pyocystis of an abandoned neurogenic bladder in a female patient who had previously undergone open surgical cutaneous urinary diversion. Also in 1992, the first laparoscopic-assisted ileal conduit was reported; after laparoscopic mobilization of the ureters, the bowel and ureteroileal anastomoses were accomplished extracorporeally through extended port sites (Kozminski and Partamian, 1992). In 1993, the initial laparoscopic-assisted radical cystectomy with extracorporeally constructed ileal conduit in a 64-year-old woman was published (Sanchez et al, 1993). In the same year, laparoscopic-assisted transvaginal radical cystec-

tomy with the ileal conduit constructed through a minilaparotomy incision was reported in five female patients (Puppo et al, 1995). In 1999, laparoscopic salvage cystectomy was reported in 10 patients, demonstrating that prior radiotherapy did not preclude subsequent laparoscopic radical cystectomy (Denewer et al, 1999). In this series, a modified ureterosigmoidostomy diversion was performed through a minilaparotomy incision. Intracorporeal ileal conduit without concomitant laparoscopic cystectomy was reported with normal renal function at 5 years of follow-up in one patient (Potter et al, 2000).

It was not until 2000 that the entire procedure of laparoscopic radical cystectomy with ileal conduit urinary diversion was first performed completely intracorporeally by Gill and colleagues (Gill et al, 2000). Tuerk and colleagues (2001) reported the initial series of laparoscopic radical cystectomy with intracorporeal Mainz II (rectosigmoid pouch) urinary diversion in five patients. In 2002, Gill and colleagues were the first to report laparoscopic radical cystectomy and orthotopic ileal neobladder, the entire procedure performed purely laparoscopically with intracorporeal suturing techniques.

Laboratory Data

The feasibility of laparoscopic-assisted Mainz II pouch was evaluated in nine pigs by Anderson and colleagues (1995). The ureter and large bowel were dissected laparoscopically; the Mainz II pouch was constructed extracorporeally by open techniques. Interestingly, 44% of the animals developed stones across staple lines used to make the pouch.

Fergany and colleagues (2001) performed laparoscopic radical cystectomy with intracorporeal ileal conduit in 10 survival pigs by suturing techniques. Simultaneously, Kaouk and colleagues (2001) were the first to demonstrate the technical feasibility of laparoscopic orthotopic ileal neobladder in 12 survival pigs. In this landmark study, the entire procedure was performed completely laparoscopically with intracorporeal suturing, duplicating all the steps of its open counterpart, with excellent outcomes during a 3-month follow-up. These two studies from the Cleveland Clinic group were instrumental in paving the way for subsequent clinical applications.

Indications and Contraindications

Proper selection of patients is crucial during the early experience to optimize technical efficiency and to minimize complications. **During the initial part of the learning curve, laparoscopic radical cystectomy should be reserved for nonobese patients with organ-confined, nonbulky bladder malignant disease without concomitant pelvic lymphadenopathy as determined by preoperative radiographic and clinical findings** (Gill et al, 2000). Morbid obesity and history of prior radiotherapy or open pelvic surgery constitute relative contraindications because of the likely increase in

laparoscopic technical complexity. In obese patients, difficulty can be expected during retraction of the bulkier bladder specimen, performance of the cephalad extent of the extended lymphadenectomy, handling and mobilization of bowel, and exteriorization of a loop of ileum through the obese abdominal wall. Laparoscopic radical cystectomy in the setting of a history of neoadjuvant chemotherapy has not been reported.

Technique

Laparoscopic Radical Cystectomy

General Considerations. Detailed informed consent is obtained, including discussion of the surgeon's laparoscopic experience with this technique, the possibility of alternative urinary diversion options, and open conversion. A stoma site is premarked in all patients by an enterostomal nurse. Mechanical bowel preparation consists of 4 liters of polyethylglycol the day before surgery; a rectal enema is administered the evening before surgery. Broad-spectrum antibiotics and bilateral sequential compression stockings are routine. After general anesthesia, the patient is placed in low modified lithotomy position with both arms adducted and padded (Fig. 79–9A). A Foley catheter is placed sterilely from the operative field after the patient is prepared and draped.

With the patient in a 20- to 30-degree Trendelenburg incline, a five-port transperitoneal approach is employed (Fig. 79–9B). Ports are placed in a semicircular fan array, similar to laparoscopic radical prostatectomy. A 0-degree laparoscope is employed.

Radical Cystectomy in the Male (Fig. 79–9C to F). **The general operative plan is to perform radical cystectomy initially, followed by bilateral extended pelvic lymphadenectomy** (Table 79–3). The procedure begins with a transverse peritoneotomy deep in the rectovesical cul-de-sac at the

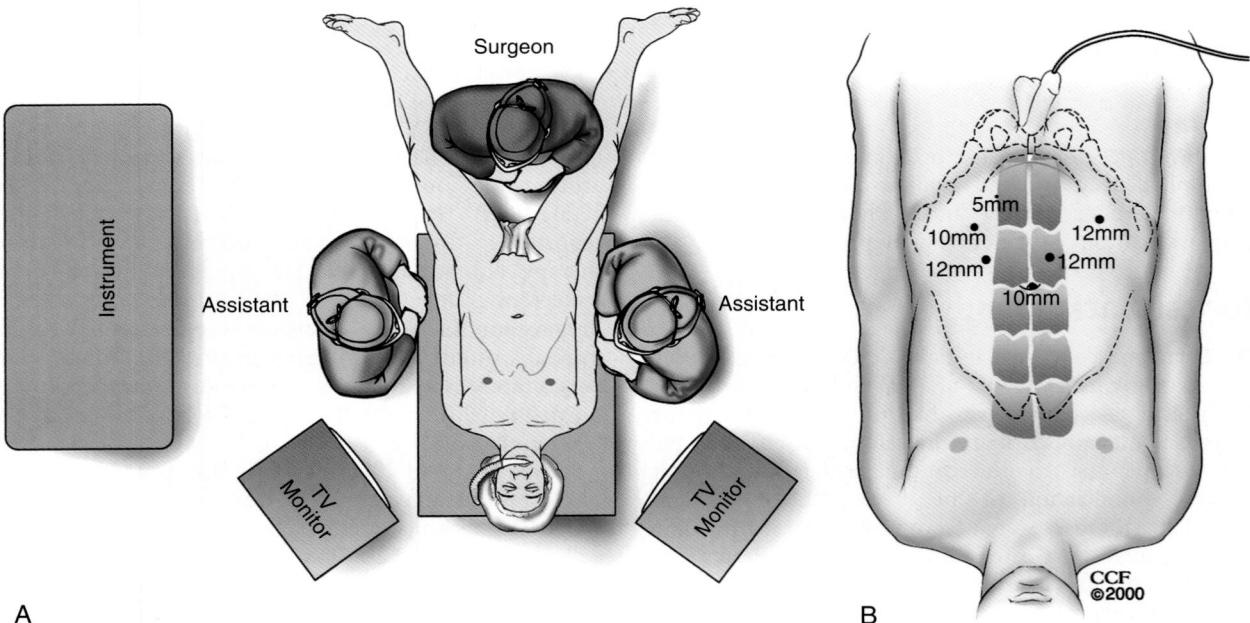

Figure 79–9. **A,** Operative room setup for laparoscopic radical cystectomy. **B,** Port placement for laparoscopic radical cystoprostatectomy with intracorporeal ileal loop urinary diversion.

Continued

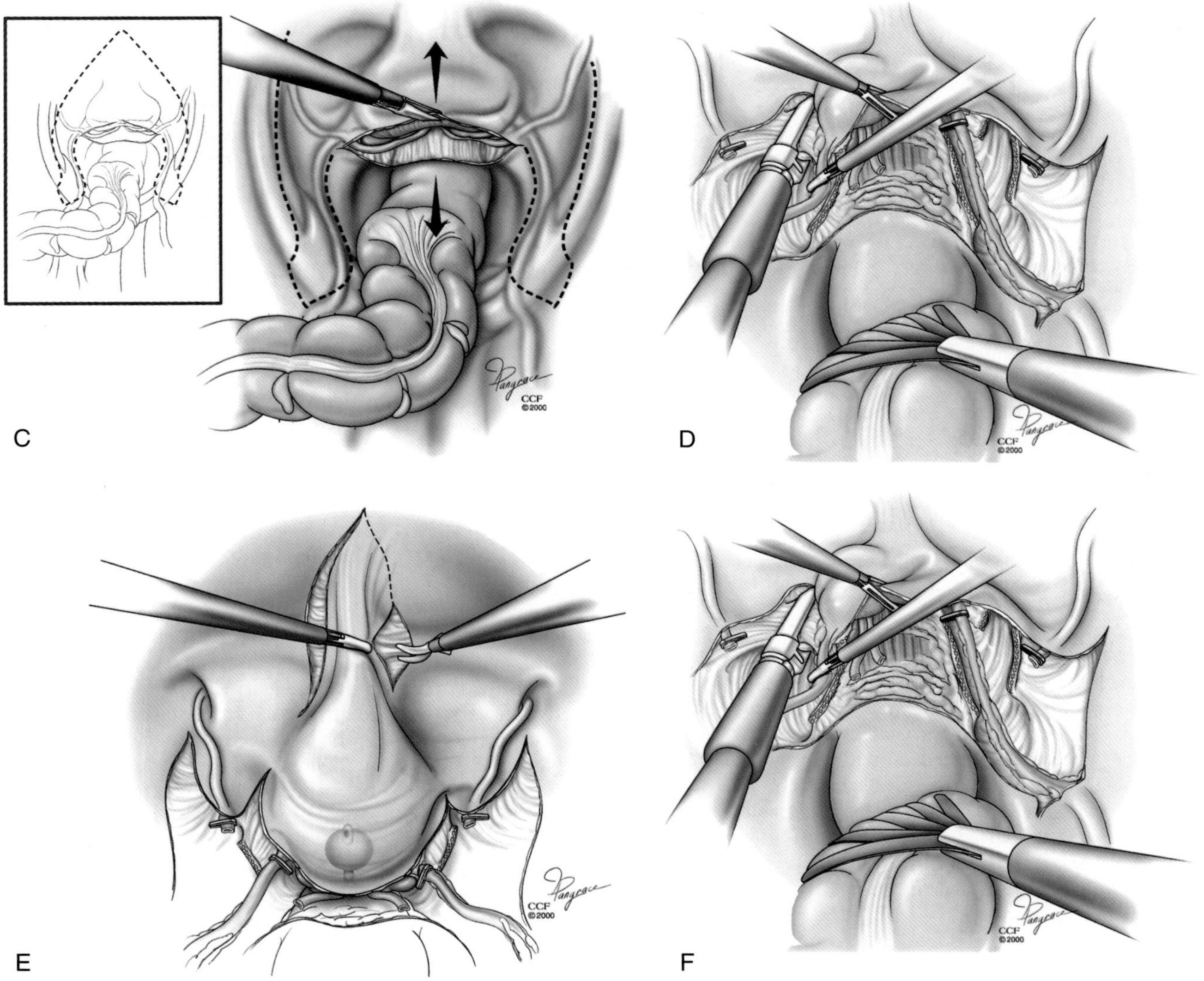

C

D

E

F

Figure 79–9, cont'd. C, Incision of the pelvic peritoneum. Inset outlines the proposed peritoneal incision at the start of the procedure. Initially, the incision is begun in the midline in the rectovesical cul-de-sac, where dissection is carried past Denonvilliers' fascia in the plane between the rectum and the prostate. After the ureters are mobilized, the inverted U peritoneotomy along the undersurface of the anterior abdominal wall is performed, gaining entry into the space of Retzius. Finally, the anterior and posterior peritoneotomies are joined on either side, bringing the vesical vascular pedicles into view. *Arrows* indicate the direction of traction of the bladder and the sigmoid colon. **D,** Completion of the posterior dissection. The bladder and the prostate are mobilized from the anterior surface of the rectum. **E,** The anterior inverted U peritoneotomy incision is made, gaining access into the space of Retzius, incising the endopelvic fascia, and defining the lateral vesical pedicles. (**B** to **E,** reproduced with permission from The Cleveland Clinic Foundation.) **F,** Securing the right vascular pedicle of the bladder with an endo-GIA stapler. Mobilization and division of the ureter at the bladder base facilitate clear visualization of the lateral pedicle. (Reprinted with permission from The Cleveland Clinic Foundation. From Gill IS, Fergany A, Klein EA, et al: Laparoscopic radical cystoprostatectomy with ileal conduit performed completely intracorporeally: The initial 2 cases. Urology 2000;56:26.) **G,** Prostate-sparing radical cystectomy. The *curved transverse line* indicates the level at which the base of the prostate is transected, which is approximately 5 mm to 1 cm distal to the bladder neck. This allows the prostate, seminal vesicles, and vas deferens to be spared. Laparoscopic simple prostatectomy is then performed to excise the adenomatous prostate gland while sparing the prostate capsule. (From Cathelineau X, Arroyo C, Rozet F, et al: Laparoscopic assisted radical cystectomy: The Montsouris experience after 84 cases. Eur Urol 2005;47:780.)

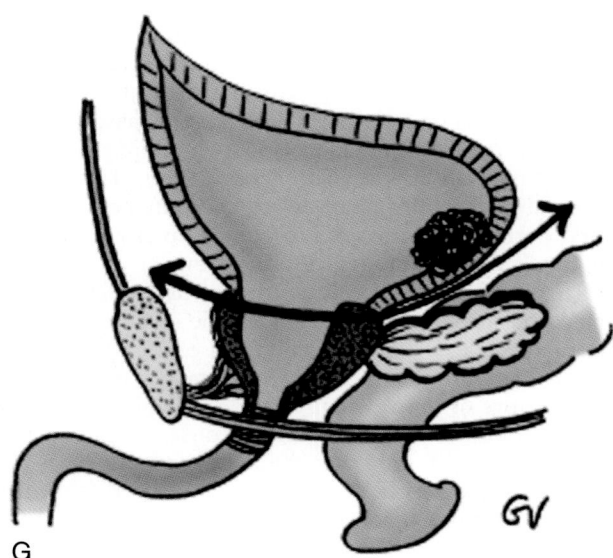

G

Table 79–3. Operative Steps in Laparoscopic Radical Cystectomy in the Male

Step	Procedure
1	Placement of five or six transperitoneal ports similar to standard laparoscopic prostatectomy (fan shape)
2	Transverse peritoneotomy in the rectovesical cul-de-sac with dissection of both the vas deferens and seminal vesicles. These structures are not dissected individually but kept en bloc with the bladder.
3	Incision of Denonvilliers' fascia, thereby developing the plane between the rectum and the posterior aspect of the prostate
4	Identification and dissection of the distal ureter; clip ligation/division of the ureter. Send distal margin for frozen-section analysis.
5	Control and ligation of lateral and posterior pedicles of the bladder and prostate
6	Dissection of the prevesical and retropubic space of Retzius
7	Incision of the endopelvic fascia
8	Placement of dorsal vein stitch
9	Division of the urethra, thereby completely separating the specimen
10	Bilateral extended lymph node dissection (may also be performed before cystectomy)
11	Construction of urinary conduit or neobladder (performed completely intracorporeally at the author's institution)

second (distal) peritoneal fold. Dissection is performed along the posterior aspect of the bilateral vasa and seminal vesicles; unlike in laparoscopic radical prostatectomy, the vasa and seminal vesicles are not mobilized individually but are maintained en bloc along with the bladder specimen. This retrovesical dissection is carried distally toward the prostate, where Denonvilliers' fascia is incised horizontally to enter the prerectal plane. Dissection is bluntly performed between the prostate and the rectum toward the prostate apex, with care taken to avoid rectal injury.

The right ureter is mobilized from the common iliac artery down toward the bladder. The juxtavesical ureter is clipped distally and proximally and transected; margins are sent for frozen-section analysis. Similarly, the left ureter is mobilized and transected. Both vasa deferentia are divided.

An inverted U peritoneotomy is performed along the undersurface of the abdominal wall, dividing the urachus high near the umbilicus and extending caudad widely, lateral to the right and left medial umbilical ligaments, respectively. The anterior surface of the bladder is mobilized, maintaining all prevesical fat with the bladder specimen. The endopelvic fascia is incised bilaterally. **The anterior inverted U and the posterior transverse peritoneotomies are now joined on either side, bringing the lateral vesical pedicles into view.**

The bladder specimen is tautly retracted anterolaterally to the left, placing the right lateral pedicle on stretch. The right lateral pedicle is defatted and transected with sequential firings of the articulating endoscopic stapler. Typically, two or three firings of the vascular cartridge are necessary to completely transect the right lateral pedicle up to the incised endopelvic fascia. Similarly, the left lateral vesical pedicle is controlled. The dorsal vein complex is secured with either a stitch or an endoscopic stapler; the urethra and rectourethralis muscle are divided sharply with cold endoshears, completely freeing the specimen. To prevent local urine spillage, the tran-

sected prostate apex is closed with a stitch. The specimen is immediately entrapped in an Endocatch-II bag. A full-thickness circumferential biopsy specimen of the urethral stump is obtained for frozen-section analysis. The entrapped specimen may be extracted vaginally in women and the defect closed subsequently; alternatively, it may be left in situ and recovered through an extended port site at the end of the operation.

Prostate-Sparing Radical Cystectomy (Fig. 79–9G). **Prostate- and seminal vesicle–sparing laparoscopic radical cystectomy can be considered in the carefully selected potent and continent young man with low-volume, organ-confined (pTa, pT1, pT2) transitional cell carcinoma of the bladder at some distance (at least 1 cm) proximal to the bladder neck without concomitant prostate or urethral disease. Patients with abnormal findings on digital rectal examination, prostate-specific antigen concentration above 3 ng/mL, low percentage of free prostate-specific antigen (<12%), or hypoechoic nodule on transrectal ultrasonography must undergo thorough evaluation to exclude concomitant prostate cancer** (Cathelineau et al, 2005). The seminal vesicles are completely dissected free from the bladder and the anterior aspect of Denonvilliers' fascia, allowing their adequate preservation. To preserve the neurovascular bundles, the lateral vesical pedicles are sectioned close to the bladder. Cathelineau and colleagues do not incise the endopelvic fascia, believing that an intact endopelvic fascia is more likely to preserve neurovascular bundle integrity. The prostate is transected transversely approximately 1 cm distal to the bladder neck, completely excising the bladder specimen (Fig. 79–9G). The bladder neck is sutured shut, and the specimen is immediately entrapped in an impermeable bag to avoid local spillage. **Laparoscopic simple prostatectomy is performed; the adenomatous prostate gland is removed, and the prostate capsule and prostatic urethra are left intact.**

During simple prostatectomy, care is taken to ensure that incision of the prostatic urethra does not extend beyond the verumontanum, thus avoiding damage to the external sphincter. After intracorporeal or extracorporeal construction of the ileal orthotopic neobladder, a prostatoileal anastomosis is performed between the most dependent part of the neobladder and the circumference of the prostate capsule by intracorporeal laparoscopic suturing techniques. An alternative to laparoscopic simple prostatectomy is transurethral prostatectomy, performed either at the beginning of the operation or 1 week preoperatively. From the bladder neck up to the verumontanum is resected in preparation for subsequent prostate-sparing cystectomy. **Cathelineau and colleagues (2005) believe that a more complete excision of the prostate adenoma and urothelium is achieved by laparoscopic simple prostatectomy as opposed to transurethral prostatectomy.**

Cystectomy in the Female (Fig. 79–10). The technique of laparoscopic anterior pelvic exenteration is described herein, with focus on the primary technical differences from cystectomy in the male. Intraoperative manipulation of the uterus is achieved by insertion of a Hulka clamp into the cervix and a sponge stick into the posterior vaginal cul-de-sac or by the RUMI uterine manipulator with KOH colpotomizer system.*

---

*CooperSurgical, Trumbull, Conn.

After both ureters are mobilized and transected, the infundibulopelvic suspensory ligaments containing the ovarian vessels are divided. With the adnexa retracted anteriorly, the peritoneum overlying the apex of the posterior vaginal fornix is scored transversely with J-hook electrocautery. The bladder is filled with 200 mL of saline, the uterus is retroverted, the inverted U-shaped wide peritoneotomy is made, and the space of Retzius is developed. Bilateral vesical pedicles are secured and transected. Endopelvic fascia is incised, and the dorsal vein complex is secured with a stitch. Attention is now returned to the posterior dissection. With the uterus anteverted, the full-thickness transverse incision of the posterior vaginal fornix apex is completed at the previously scored site. The vaginal incision is carried distally on each side of the urethra, with excision of a narrow central strip of vagina en bloc with the bladder specimen. By a transvaginal approach, the external urethral meatus and distal urethra are circumferentially cored out with an electrocautery knife. The anterior vaginal wall is dissected free, and the entire en bloc specimen is retrieved per vagina. A neovagina is fashioned by laparoscopic suturing before proceeding with pelvic lymphadenectomy and urinary diversion.

Uterus-, Fallopian Tube-, and Ovary-Sparing Cystectomy. In the selected, sexually active, younger woman with low-volume organ-confined disease without perivesical extension, the nerve-sparing technique of laparoscopic radical cystectomy with preservation of fallopian tubes, ovaries, uterus, and vagina can be employed. With the uterus retroverted and the bladder precisely identified, the peritoneum over the anterior surface of the uterus is incised transversely. **Careful dissection is performed along the anterior surface of the uterus (not along the posterior surface of the bladder); this avascular plane is developed toward the cervix, with care taken not to thin either the anterior vaginal wall or the bladder.** Next, dissection is performed anteriorly, and the

space of Retzius is prepared, the lateral vesical pedicles are transected, and the urethral preparation is completed as described before. The excised specimen is entrapped for later extraction. The vagina is carefully inspected to ensure its integrity.

Extended Pelvic Lymph Node Dissection (Fig. 79–11). **Anatomic boundaries of the extended dissection include the genitofemoral nerve laterally, the obturator nerve posteriorly, the bladder medially, the internal inguinal ring distally, and the area of the aortic bifurcation proximally.** Right lymphadenectomy is performed first with the patient tilted 30 degrees right side up.

The lateral border of dissection is developed along the genitofemoral nerve by dividing the lymphaticofatty tissue and exposing the iliopsoas muscle. This lymphatic tissue packet is completely lifted en bloc off the psoas and swept medially. The tissue anterior to the external iliac artery and vein is individually split longitudinally by J-hook electrocautery, skeletonizing the two vessels circumferentially (Fig. 79–11A).

Distally, the packet is transected near the internal inguinal ring. Lymphaticofatty tissue is dissected along the anterior and medial aspects of the common iliac artery toward the aortic bifurcation. The hypogastric artery is carefully mobilized, with care taken not to injure the internal iliac vein. The released packet is rolled medially posterior to the mobilized external iliac artery and vein, delivering it into the pelvis. The obturator nerve is identified. Medially, it is important to dissect the perivesical area in the pelvis. **To guard against local seeding, care must be taken to avoid iatrogenic entry into any enlarged lymph node. The entire nodal packet is immediately placed in an Endocatch bag to minimize contact of the specimen with adjacent tissues.**

Left extended lymphadenectomy is performed in similar fashion (Fig. 79–11B).

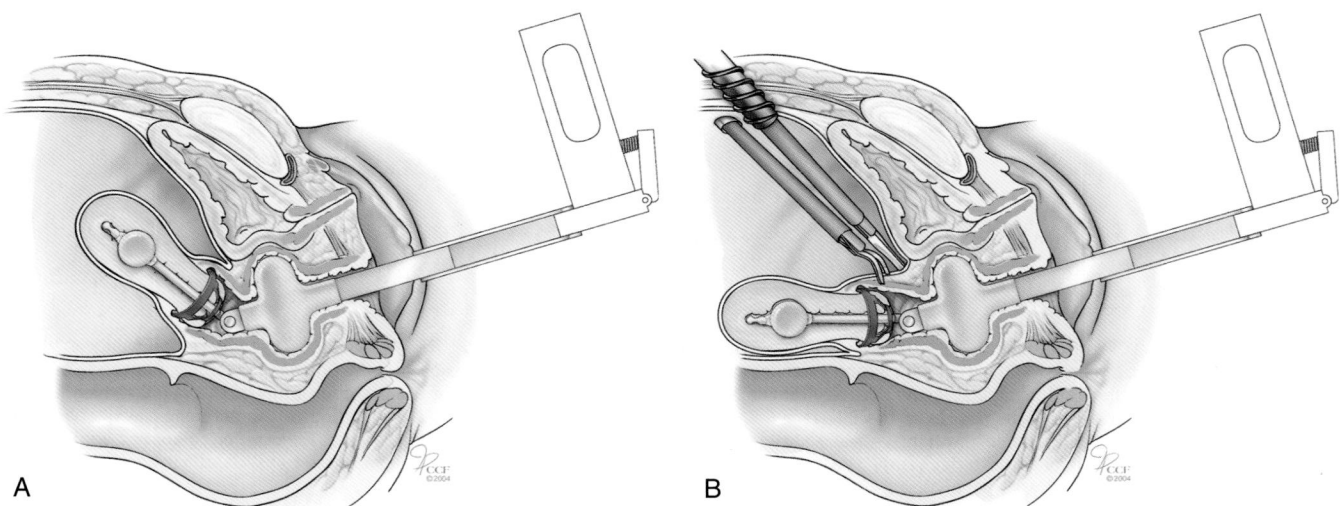

Figure 79–10. Laparoscopic radical cystectomy in the female. **A** and **B,** Assembled RUMI manipulator and KOH colpotomizer system composed of a uterine stylet with inflatable balloon positioned within the uterus, a KOH circular cup placed around the cervix, and a vaginal occluding balloon that prevents carbon dioxide leakage after the vagina is entered laparoscopically. The connecting handle allows four-directional transvaginal manipulation of the uterus during the procedure. (Reprinted with permission from The Cleveland Clinic Foundation. From Moinzadeh A, Gill IS, Desai M, et al: Laparoscopic radical cystectomy in the female. J Urol 2005;173.)

Continued

SECTION XV

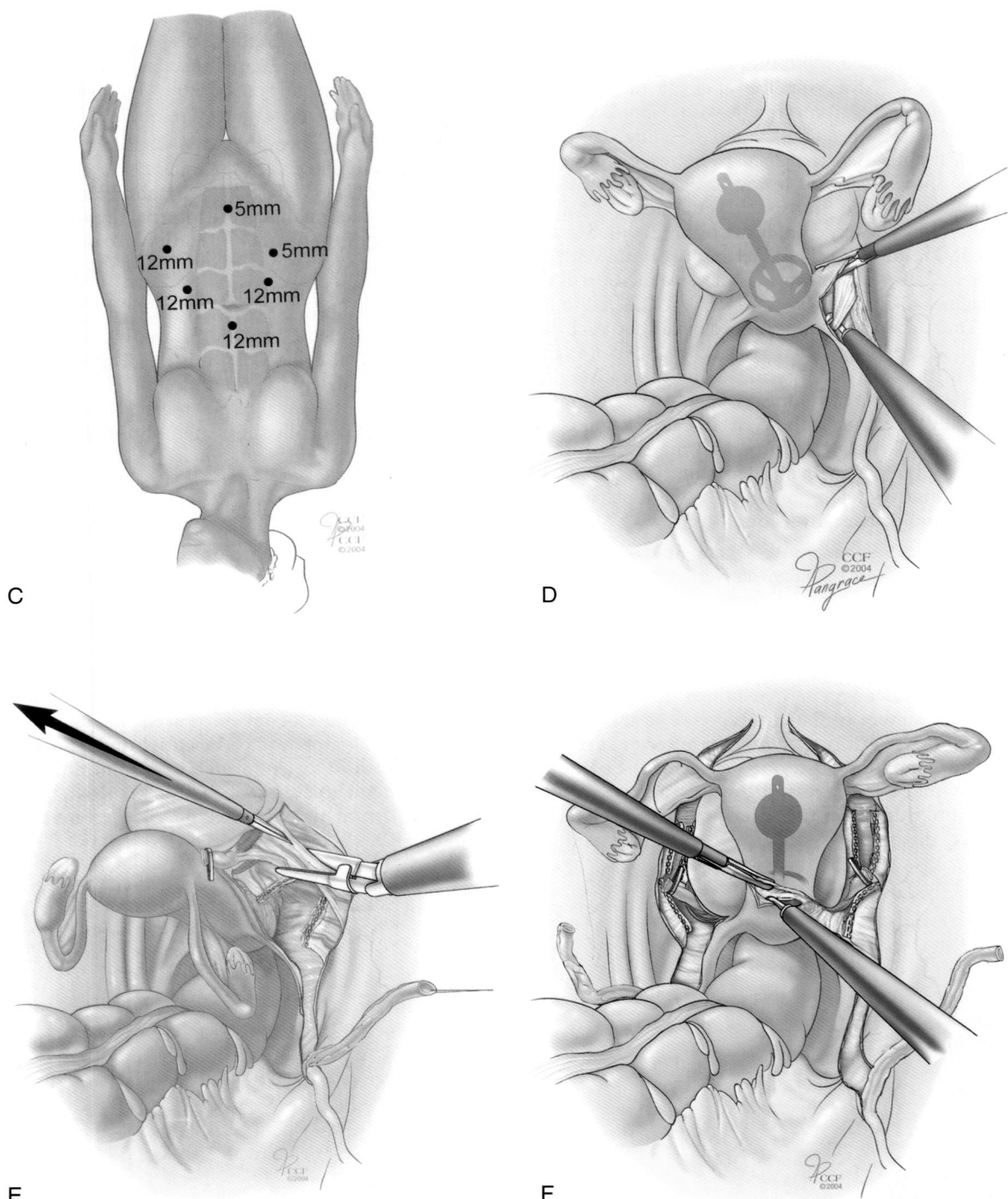

C

D

E

F

Figure 79–10, cont'd. **C,** Port placement. Note that the 12-mm midline port is placed approximately two fingerbreadths cephalad to the umbilicus to allow improved visualization of the aortic bifurcation area during extended pelvic lymphadenectomy. **D,** Incision of right side of the rectouterine cul-de-sac. With the uterus anteverted by the RUMI manipulator, the KOH cervical cup aids in identification of the apex of the posterior fornix of the vagina, which is scored transversely. **E,** Transection of the right pedicle of the bladder with endoscopic stapler. *Arrow* indicates the direction of the anteromedial traction of the bladder to the left side, thereby defining the right vesical pedicle for precise application of the endoscopic stapler. **F,** Posterior colpotomy with KOH cup now visualized end-on in the opened posterior vagina. Note: the uterus is anteverted to facilitate this full-thickness transverse incision of the posterior vaginal fornix. (**C** to **F**, reproduced with permission from The Cleveland Clinic Foundation.)

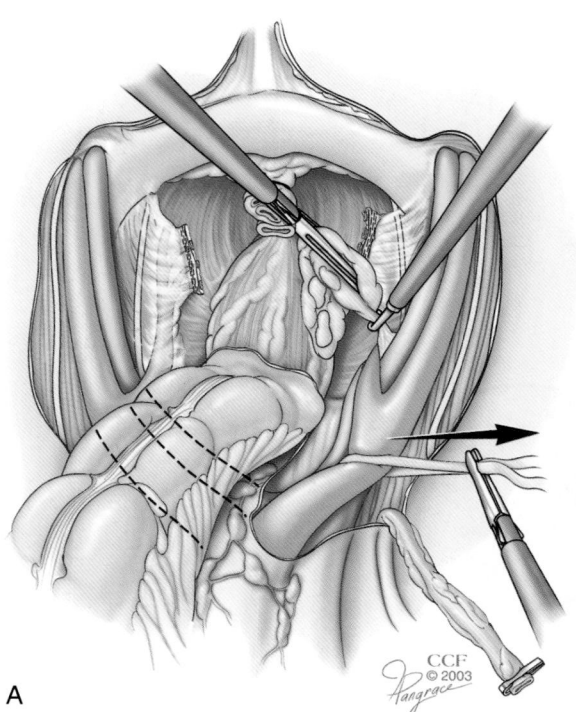
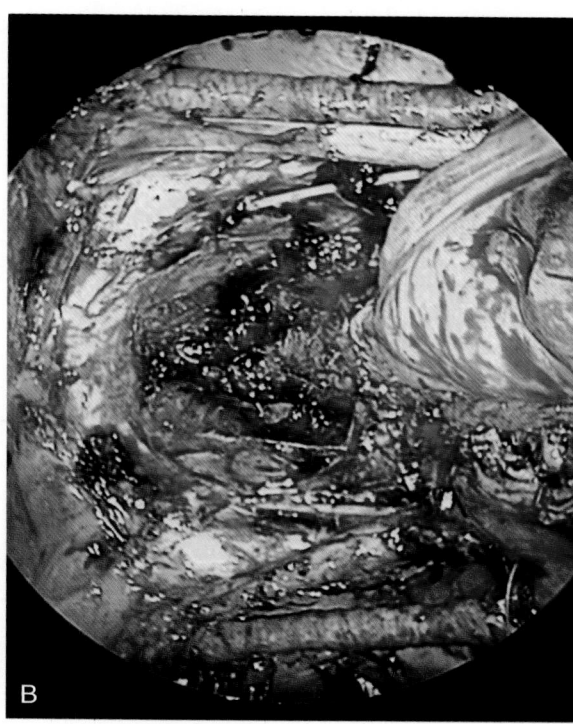

A

B

Figure 79–11. Laparoscopic extended pelvic lymph node dissection. **A,** Tissues anterior to the external iliac artery and vein are split longitudinally with J-hook electrocautery in preparation for split-and-roll technique. The external iliac vessels and common iliac artery are skeletonized. Vessel loop is used to retract (arrow) the iliac artery to facilitate proximal dissection. (Reproduced with permission from The Cleveland Clinic Foundation.) **B,** Intraoperative photograph demonstrating skeletonized bilateral external arteries and veins, obturator nerves, and pubic bone. The skeletonized common iliac arteries are not seen in this laparoscopic view. (From Finelli A, Gill IS, Desai MM, et al: Laparoscopic extended pelvic lymphadenectomy for bladder cancer: Technique and initial outcomes. J Urol 2004;172:1809.)

Laparoscopic-Assisted Urinary Diversion

In the laparoscopic-assisted techniques, an appropriate 5- to 6-cm midline infraumbilical skin incision is made. Per the planned urinary diversion, continent or incontinent, the appropriate bowel segment is exteriorized. By conventional open surgical techniques, the bowel reservoir is constructed, ureteroenteric anastomoses are performed, and bowel continuity is restored. **In cases of orthotopic diversion, the anastomosis of the urethra to the neobladder is performed laparoscopically after the constructed bowel segment has been returned to the abdomen and pneumoperitoneum reestablished.**

Ileal Conduit. Before the bowel segment is selected, the left ureter is transferred to the right side retroperitoneally, posterior to the descending colon. The left ureter is mobilized cephalad toward the kidney, maintaining generous periureteral fat (Fig. 79–12A). An adequate opening is made in the base of the descending mesocolon, in the general area of the sacral promontory. The left ureter is delivered through this mesocolic window toward the right side with gentle traction (Fig. 79–12B).

The technique of pure intracorporeal ileal conduit is described herein (Fig. 79–13). If it has not already been placed, a 5-mm port is inserted midway between the symphysis pubis and umbilicus. A 30-degree laparoscope is inserted in the left lateral port, such that the surgeon is now working toward the

liver, facing the ileocecum. A 15-cm segment of ileum is selected at least 15 to 20 cm proximal to the ileocecal junction. Bowel length is measured by insertion of a malleable plastic ruler through a 12-mm port. The distal end of the selected ileal segment is transected with endoscopic stapler (3.5-mm blue [tissue] cartridge). The ileal mesentery is divided at this location by two sequential stapler firings (2.5-mm gray [vascular] cartridge). The proximal end of the ileal segment is similarly transected; mesenteric division at this location is performed with only one stapler firing. The excluded ileal segment is dropped posteriorly, and side-to-side ileoileal continuity is reestablished with two sequential firings of the endoscopic stapler along the respective antimesenteric borders of the two adjacent loops of ileum. Transverse firing of the stapler secures the open ileal ends, thereby completing the side-to-side anastomosis. For added security, the end of the anastomosis is buttressed with a running 2-0 synthetic absorbable suture. The ileal mesenteric window is closed with two or three separate stitches.

The distal end of the conduit is exteriorized through the previously marked stoma site. An end stoma is created at the skin level by conventional open techniques. A 5-mm laparoscopic right-angled clamp, which grasps the tip of a 90-cm single-J ileoureteral stent, is inserted through the cutaneous stoma into the ileal conduit. A small ileotomy is made laparoscopically on the conduit at the appropriate site selected for ureteroileal anastomosis. The stent is advanced into the peri-

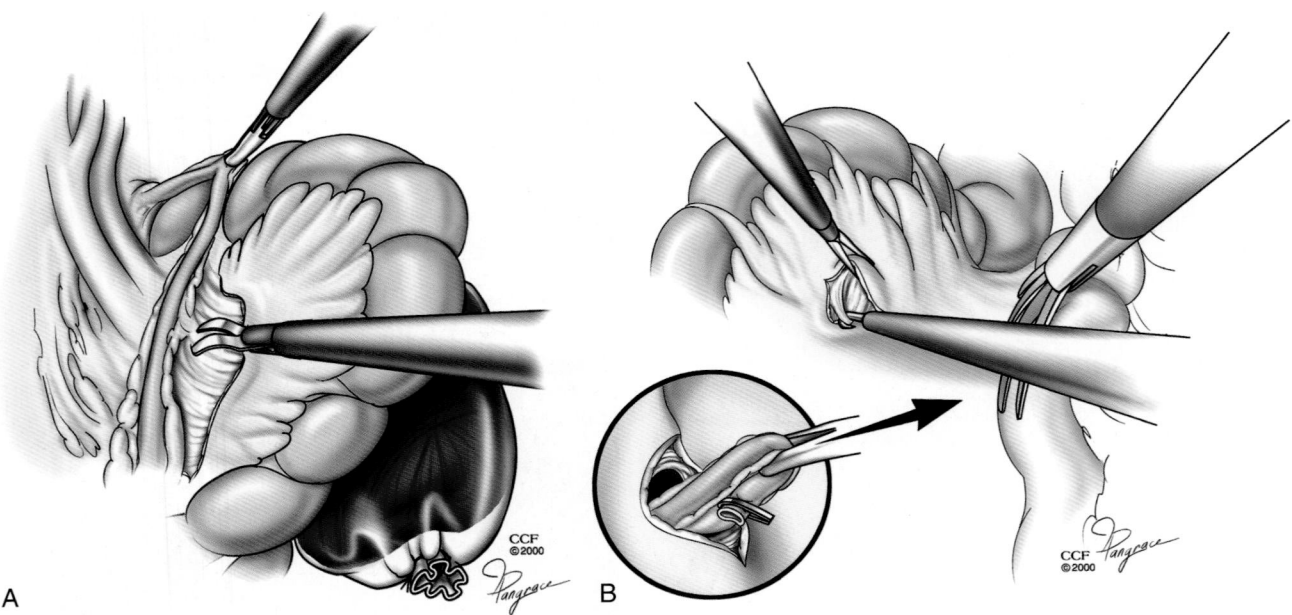

Figure 79–12. Left ureter transfer to the right side. **A,** After proximal mobilization of the left ureter, a window is made in the sigmoid mesentery. **B,** A similar incision is made along the base of the sigmoid mesocolon, and the ureter is transferred to the right side *(inset)*. (Reproduced with permission from The Cleveland Clinic Foundation. From Matin SF, Gill IS: Laparoscopic radical cystectomy with urinary diversion: Completely intracorporeal technique. J Endourol 2002;16:335.)

toneal cavity through the ileotomy incision. Mucosa-to-mucosa ureteroileal anastomosis is performed in continuous fashion with two separate 3-0 Vicryl sutures on an RB-1 needle, one for the anterior and the other for the posterior wall. In similar fashion, the second ureteroileal anastomosis is completed. Both stents are secured to the ileal stoma at the skin level (see Fig. 79–13).

Ileal Orthotopic Neobladder (Fig. 79–14). A 55- to 65-cm segment of ileum is selected and isolated as described previously. Bowel continuity is restored with ileoileal anastomosis. The excluded ileal segment is irrigated with the suction-irrigator cannula through a small ileotomy incision. The proximal 10 cm of the ileal segment is maintained intact for the isoperistaltic Studer limb. The remaining distal 45-cm ileal segment is detubularized along its antimesenteric border with endoshears or harmonic scalpel.

The posterior plate of the neobladder is constructed initially by continuous intracorporeal suturing of the corresponding edges of the detubularized ileum with 2-0 Vicryl on a CT-1 needle. **The reconstructed ileal plate is delivered into the pelvis toward the urethral stump, where an appropriate location at the apex of the ileal plate is selected for a tension-free anastomosis.** Urethroileal anastomosis is performed with a running circumferential 2-0 Vicryl stitch on a UR-6 needle, similar to laparoscopic radical prostatectomy. A 22 French Foley catheter on a curved insertion mandarin is inserted per urethra into the neobladder before completion of the anterior aspect of the left and right urethroileal anastomosis. Two 90-cm single-J stents are delivered through the neobladder into the Studer limb, from which they are retrieved at the two proposed sites of ureteroileal anastomoses. Suturing of the anterior wall of the neobladder is completed to achieve a spherical

neobladder. Ureteroileal anastomoses are completed as described before. Before the anastomosis is completed, the single-J stent is advanced into the renal pelvis. The neobladder is irrigated through the urethral Foley catheter, and any sites of leakage are specifically suture repaired. A suprapubic catheter is inserted into the neobladder through the midline port site incision. The J stents are exteriorized through a 5-mm port site. Two Jackson-Pratt drains are inserted into the pelvis, one through each lateral port site.

Mainz II Pouch (Rectosigmoid Pouch). The sigmoid colon is mobilized along the paracolic gutter to allow adequate manipulation. At the selected site, the sigmoid colon is incised longitudinally along its antimesenteric border. The distal extent of the detubularizing incision is dependent on individual anatomic variations; care is taken to ensure that the length of the distal incision will correspond to the proximal incision once the pouch is completed. The entrapped radical cystectomy specimen is removed transanally, through the sigmoid opening. The corresponding edges of the posterior walls of the sigmoid colon are anastomosed intracorporeally with continuous 3-0 Vicryl suture, making the posterior plate of the pouch. Fixation of the sigmoid facilitates intracorporeal suturing. Two incisions are made along the posterior wall of the sigmoid, one each for the left and right ureter. The incisions are made such that approximately 3 cm of each ureter will lie within the pouch for construction of the submucosal tunnel. Submucosal tunnel flaps are raised sharply. Each ureter is advanced, and the spatulated neo-orifice is secured to the apex of its tunnel with interrupted 4-0 Vicryl sutures. A single-J stent is inserted into each ureter and externalized through the anus. Sigmoid mucosa is reapproximated over the intraluminal extent of the ureter with 4-0 Vicryl suture, thus

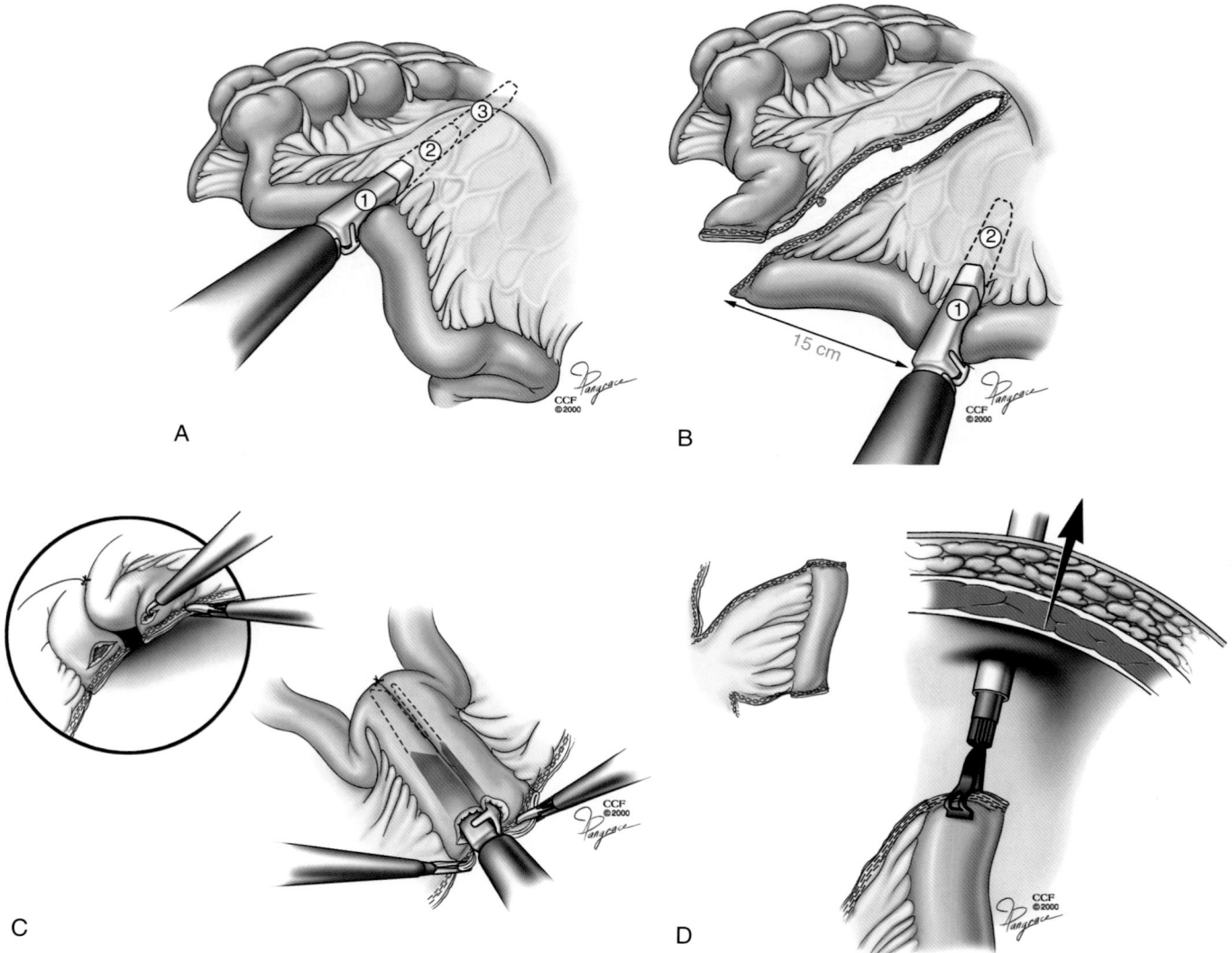

Figure 79–13.   Isolation and division of ileal segment. **A,** Endoscopic stapler (with bowel cartridge) is used to transect the ileum 15 cm from the ileocecal junction. After bowel transection, two additional firings of the endoscopic stapler (vascular cartridge) are used to transect the mesentery. **B,** Proximal transection of the ileum is performed in similar fashion, thereby isolating the 15-cm segment for the ileal conduit. At this proximal location, only one firing of the endoscopic stapler (vascular cartridge) is used to transect the mesentery. This helps in maintaining the arterial arcade that provides vascular supply to the excluded loop of ileum. The ileum loop segment is dropped posteriorly, and bowel continuity is restored anteriorly. **C,** Restoration of bowel continuity. Two sequential firings of the endoscopic stapler (bowel cartridge) are performed to achieve an adequate side-to-side ileoileal anastomosis. The open ends of the two ileal segments are closed transversely with the endoscopic stapler. The transverse staple line is reinforced with simple running absorbable suture. The mesenteric window is closed. **D,** The ileal loop is exteriorized at the preselected stoma site in the belly of the right rectus muscle. The distal end of the isolated ileal loop is grasped with a laparoscopic Allis or Babcock clamp. An end ileal stoma is made in standard fashion.   *Continued*

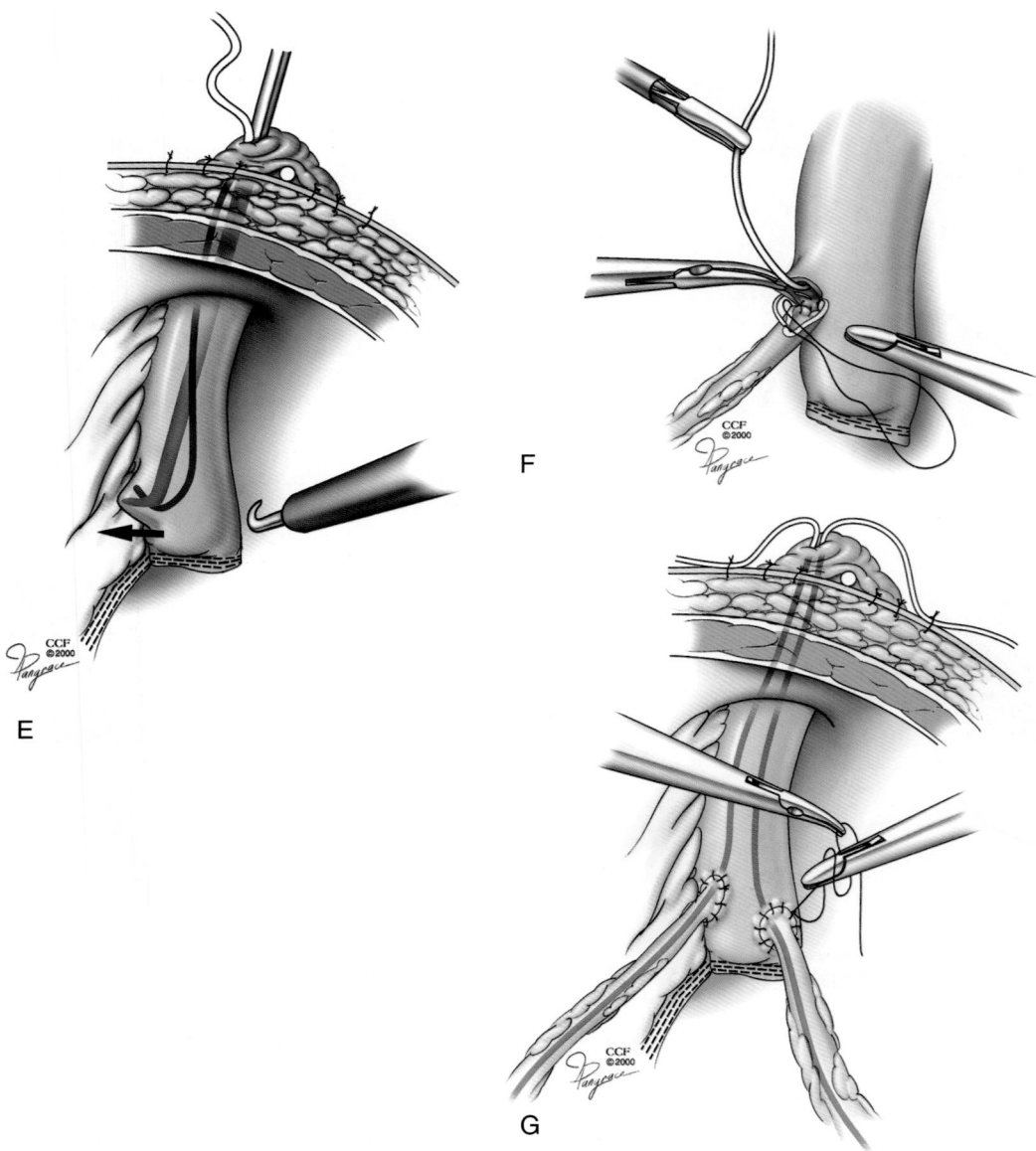

E

F

G

Figure 79–13, cont'd. E, A 19-cm single-J stent, grasped by a 5-mm right-angled laparoscopic clamp, is inserted through the stoma into the proximal portion of the ileal loop. Under laparoscopic visualization, the appropriate location for the ureteroileal anastomosis is selected and a small ileotomy made. The stent is delivered through the ileotomy into the peritoneal cavity. **F,** Ureteroileal anastomosis is performed with precise mucosa-to-mucosa suturing with 4-0 Vicryl suture. The J stent is advanced up to the kidney, and the anastomosis is completed. **G,** The completed ileal loop reconstruction: stented, bilateral ureteroileal anastomosis and ileal conduit diversion are shown. (Reproduced with permission from The Cleveland Clinic Foundation. From Gill IS, Fergany A, Klein EA, et al: Laparoscopic radical cystoprostatectomy with ileal conduit performed completely intracorporeally: The initial 2 cases. Urology 2000;56:26.)

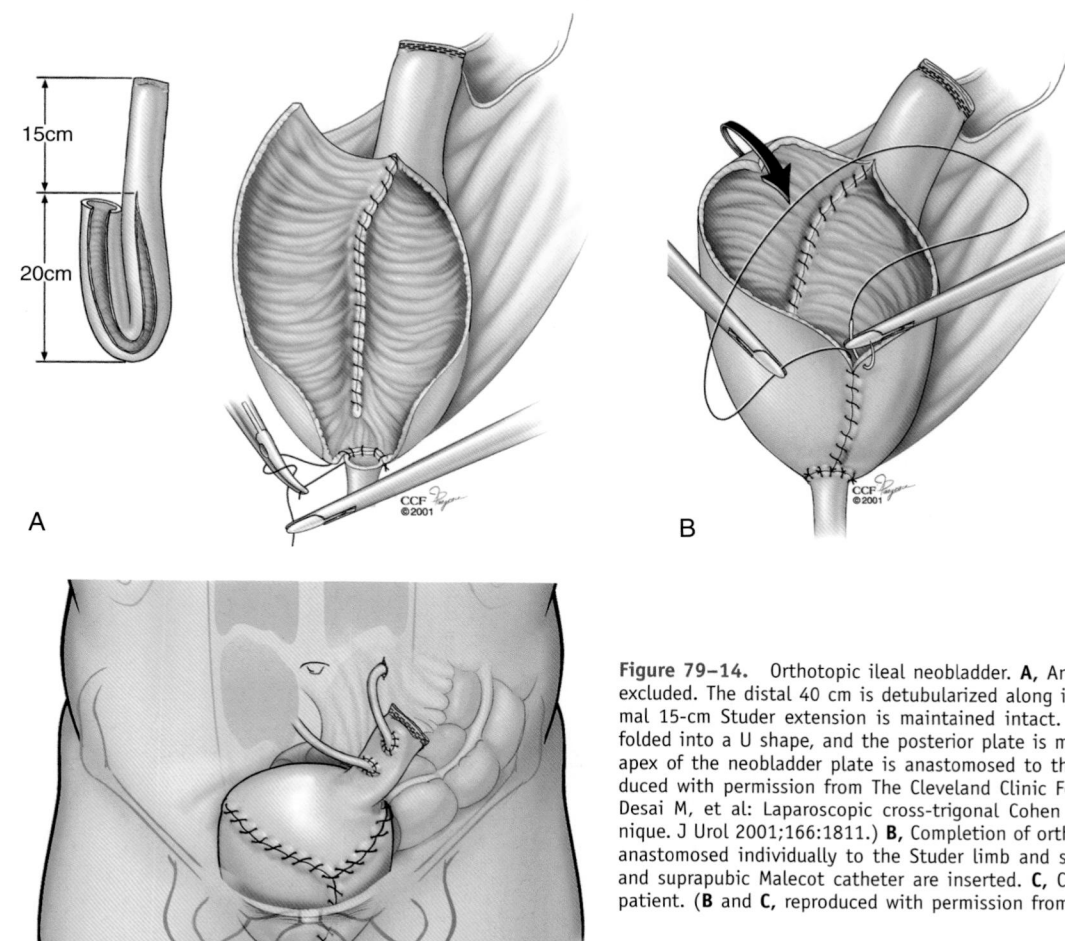

Figure 79–14. Orthotopic ileal neobladder. **A,** An ileal segment, 55 cm in length, is excluded. The distal 40 cm is detubularized along its antimesenteric border; the proximal 15-cm Studer extension is maintained intact. The detubularized ileal segment is folded into a U shape, and the posterior plate is made by intracorporeal suturing. The apex of the neobladder plate is anastomosed to the urethra circumferentially. (Reproduced with permission from The Cleveland Clinic Foundation. From Gill IS, Ponsky LE, Desai M, et al: Laparoscopic cross-trigonal Cohen ureteroneocystostomy: Novel technique. J Urol 2001;166:1811.) **B,** Completion of orthotopic neobladder. Both ureters are anastomosed individually to the Studer limb and stented. The urethral Foley catheter and suprapubic Malecot catheter are inserted. **C,** Completed neobladder in the female patient. (**B** and **C,** reproduced with permission from The Cleveland Clinic Foundation.)

constructing the antirefluxing submucosal tunnel. The anterior wall of the sigmoid pouch is closed with running suture, thus making the rectosigmoid pouch. A 26 French rectal tube is inserted per anum and 250 mL of sterile saline is injected to check for suture line integrity. A single Jackson-Pratt drain is placed into the pelvis.

Clinical Outcomes Data

Initial small series of laparoscopic radical cystectomy have been reported in the literature (Table 79–4). **Tuerk and colleagues (2001) reported laparoscopic rectosigmoid pouch performed completely intracorporeally in five patients. A six-port transperitoneal technique was employed with an overall mean operative time of 7.4 hours (range, 6.9 to 7.9 hours) and mean estimated blood loss of 245 mL (range, 190 to 300 mL).** The authors did not mention whether a lymphadenectomy was performed. Oral fluids were resumed on day 3, and hospital stay averaged 10 days. All patients were discharged without any intraoperative or postoperative complication, with reported good continence per the anal sphincter, normal renal function, and mild hyperchloremic acidosis. All five patients had negative surgical margins; follow-up information was not presented. The group from Cleveland Clinic performed laparoscopic radical cystectomy in 22 patients, with urinary diversion by intracorporeal ileal conduit in 14 patients, intracorporeal orthotopic neobladder in 6 patients, and extracorporeally constructed Indiana pouch in 2 patients. Extended lymphadenectomy required 1.5 hours of operating time, resulting in an overall operative time of 8.6 hours with a mean blood loss of 490 mL. **Negative surgical margins were obtained in 21 of 22 patients; 6 patients (27%) had pathologically confirmed metastatic lymph node involvement.** During a mean follow-up of 11 months (range, 2 to 43 months), three patients died of metastatic disease. Complications included bowel obstruction (three), bowel perforation (one), urethrovaginal fistula (one), deep venous thrombosis (two), and prolonged ileus (six).

Urinary diversion is currently performed by the extracorporeal technique at most centers performing laparoscopic radical cystectomy (Table 79–5). Simonato described 10 patients with extracorporeally constructed urinary diversion including orthotopic neobladder in 6 patients, ureterosigmoidostomy in 2 patients, and cutaneous ureterostomy in 2 patients. Laparoscopic radical cystectomy was performed through a five-port transperitoneal technique, with the

Table 79–4. Operative Outcomes

Lead author (year)	Puppo (1995)	Denewer (1999)	Tuerk (2001)	Abdel-Hakim (2002)	Simonato (2003)	Menon (2003)	Hemal (2004)	Basillote (2004)	Gill (2004)
N	5	10	5	9	10	17	11	13	22
Technique (reconstruction)	Transvaginal and laparoscopic-assisted (extra)	Laparoscopic-assisted (extra)	Purely intracorporeal laparoscopic	Laparoscopic-assisted (extra)	Laparoscopic-assisted (extra)	Robot-assisted (extra)	Laparoscopic-assisted (extra)	Laparoscopic-assisted (extra)	Purely intracorporeal laparoscopic
Urinary diversion	Ileal conduit, 4 Cutaneous, 1	Sigmoid pouch, 10 (extra)	Rectal-sigmoid pouch, 5 (purely intra)	Orthotopic, 9 (extra)	Orthotopic, 6 Sigmoid, 2 Cutaneous, 2 (extra)	Orthotopic, 14 Ileal conduit, 3 (extra)	Ileal conduit, 11 (extra)	Orthotopic, 13 (extra)	Ileal conduit, 14 Orthotopic, 6 (intra) Indiana, 2 (extra)
Mean (range) operative duration, hr	7.2 (6-9)	3.6 (3.3-4.1)	7.4 (6.9-7.9)	8.3 (6.5-12)	Orthotopic, 7.1 Sigmoid, 5.8 Cutaneous, 4.7	Orthotopic, 5.1 Ileal conduit, 4.3	6.1 (4.3-8)	8.0 hr (±77 min)	8.6
Blood loss, mL (transfusion)	(3 transfused 2-6 units)	(mean, 2.2 units; range, 2-3)	245 (190-300)	150-500	310 (220-440)	<150	530 (300-900)	1000 ± 414	490
Ileus, days	2.6 (2-4)	Not stated	Not stated	Not stated	3.3 (1-5)	Not stated	Not stated	Not stated	6 prolonged ileus 3 bowel obstruction
Length of stay, days	10.6 (7-18)	10-13	10 (in all 5)	Not stated	Orthotopic, 8.1 Sigmoid, 8 Cutaneous, 5	Not stated	10.5	5.1 ± 1.2	Not stated
Time to oral intake, days	2-4	Not stated	Liquid 3	3	3-6	Not stated	Not stated	Liquid 2.8 Solid 4.1	8
Time to return to work, days	Not stated	Not stated	Not stated	Not stated	Not stated	Not stated	26	11.0 ± 1.9	Not stated
Follow-up, months	11 (6-16)	Not stated	Not stated	Not stated	12.3 (5-18)	Not stated	18.4 (1-48)	Not stated	11 (2-43)
Functional outcomes	4 of 5 discharged with no postoperative complications 1 discharged after 18 days because of obesity and diabetic problems	All continent 1 ureterosigmoid urine leak 1 pyelonephritis	All 5 continent and no obstruction of upper urinary tract in urogram on postoperative day 10	No complications in pouchgram on postoperative day 10	2 bilateral hydronephrosis and metabolic acidosis 1 monolateral hydronephrosis	13 bilharziasis with periureteric, perivesicular, and pervesical scarring	All had normal renal function and preserved upper urinary tracts	1 ureteral obstruction 1 bladder neck contracture 1 obturator nerve paresis	1 ureteroileal leak 1 urethrovaginal fistula

Modified from Hrouda D, Adeyoju AA, Gill IS: Laparoscopic radical cystectomy and urinary diversion: Fad or future? BJU Int 2004;94:501-505.

Table 79-5. Comparing Technique Characteristics Between Intracorporeal and Extracorporeal

	Intracorporeal Reconstruction			Extracorporeal Reconstruction	
Lead author	Gill	Tuerk	Van Velthoven	Simonato	Basillote
N	22	5	22	10	13
Urinary diversion, N	Ileal conduit, 14 (intracorporeal) Orthotopic, 6 (intracorporeal) Indiana pouch, 2 (extracorporeal)	Rectal-sigmoid pouch, all 5 purely intracorporeal	Orthotopic, 11 Ileal conduit, 6 Mainz II, 2 Kock pouch, 2	Orthotopic, 6 Sigmoid ureterostomy, 2 Cutaneous ureterostomy, 2	Orthotopic, all 13
Skin incision	6 port site only for ileal conduit and orthotopic (20-mm extension of umbilical port incision for Indiana)	6 port site only	5 port plus additional skin incision	5 port and 50-mm midline skin incision above umbilicus	5 port and low abdominal Pfannenstiel incision (150 mm)
Overall operative time (range), hr	8.6	7.4 (6.9-7.9)	7.4	7.1 for orthotopic 5.8 for sigmoid ureterectomy 4.7 for cutaneous ureterectomy	8.0 (8.0 hr ± 77 min)
Cystectomy + lymphadenectomy (LA) time	Extended LA (n = 11) added 1.5 hr	Not stated	Not stated	166 min (150-180) (with limited LA)	Not stated
Blood loss (range), mL	490	245 (190-300)	840 (210-400)	310 (220-440)	1000 (1000 ± 414)
Hospital stay, days	Not stated	10	Not stated	8.1 for orthotopic 8 for sigmoid ureterectomy 5 for cutaneous ureterectomy	5.1 (5.1 ± 1.2)
Days for oral intake	8	Liquid 3	Not stated	3-6	Liquid 2.8 (2.8 ± 1.4) Solid 4.1 (4.1 ± 1.2)
Complications	6 prolonged ileus 3 bowel obstruction 2 deep venous thrombosis 1 bowel perforation 1 ureteroileal leak 1 urethrovaginal fistula 1 postoperative bleed 1 deep pelvic vein injury	All discharged with no intraoperative or postoperative complications (continent, normal renal function, mild hyperchloremic acidosis)	1 rectal injury (other was not detailed)	1 grade 3 bilateral hydronephrosis 1 grade 2 bilateral hydronephrosis 1 monolateral hydronephrosis 2 metabolic acidosis	1 ureteral obstruction 1 bladder neck contracture 1 epididymal abscess 1 wound dehiscence 1 obturator nerve paresis 1 pyelonephritis 1 pouchitis
Note for oncologic outcomes	21/22 negative margin 6/22 (27%) had positive lymph nodes 3/22 died of metastasis	5/5 negative margin	Not stated	10/10 negative margin 2 had diffuse metastasis after 6 months	12/13 negative margin 1 had prostate cancer with a positive apical margin
Mean follow-up, months (range)	11 (2-43)	Not stated	Not stated	12.3 (5-18)	Not stated

urinary diversion completed through a 5-cm supraumbilical skin incision. The mean operative time for radical cystectomy and limited lymphadenectomy was 166 minutes (range, 150 to 180 minutes). Mean blood loss was 310 mL (range, 220 to 440 mL). Overall operative time and hospital stay varied according to the urinary diversion performed: 4.7 hours and 5 days for cutaneous ureterostomy, 5.8 hours and 8 days for ureterosigmoidostomy, and 7.1 hours and 8.1 days for orthotopic neobladder, respectively. Oral intake was resumed within 3 to 6 days after surgery. Complications included bilateral hydronephrosis in two patients, unilateral hydronephrosis in one patient, and metabolic acidosis in two patients. All 10 patients had negative surgical margins. During a mean follow-up of 12.3 months (range, 5 to 18 months), two patients developed diffuse metastatic disease 6 months postoperatively. **Basillote and colleagues (2004) retrospectively compared 11 men undergoing open radical cystectomy with 13 men undergoing laparoscopic-assisted radical cystectomy with orthotopic neobladder.** In the laparoscopic-assisted group, mean blood loss was 1000 mL, and mean total operative time was 8 hours. Complications in the laparoscopic group included ureteral obstruction (one), bladder neck contracture (one), epididymal abscess (one), wound dehiscence (one), obturator nerve paresis (one), pyelonephritis (one), and pouchitis (one) (Table 79–6). Negative surgical margins were obtained in 12 of 13 patients; 1 patient with prostate cancer

had a positive apical margin. Follow-up data were not presented. On comparison of the open and laparoscopic-assisted approaches, the laparoscopic approach was associated with decreased analgesic requirements (61 mg versus 144 mg of morphine sulfate equivalent; $P = .04$), quicker resumption of oral intake (2.8 versus 5 days; $P = .004$), shorter hospital stay (5.1 versus 8.4 days; $P = .0004$), and earlier resumption of light work (11 versus 19 days; $P = .0001$). Operative time and complication rates were comparable between the laparoscopic-assisted and open techniques. **Paz and colleagues (2003) performed a small prospective study comparing 14 patients randomly assigned to either laparoscopic (n = 7) or open (n = 7) radical cystectomy and urinary diversion. The laparoscopic group experienced a significantly quicker resumption of bowel activity (0.7 versus 2.2 days), shorter hospital stay (6.7 versus 13.2 days), and decreased narcotic analgesic requirements.**

Oncologic outcomes data are limited at this writing, given that the early papers focused largely on operative technique and perioperative outcomes (Table 79–7). Hrouda and colleagues (2004) reviewed 54 patients from 8 series of laparoscopic radical cystectomy; no patient had a positive surgical margin. **Gupta and colleagues (2002) reported good outcomes at 2-year follow-up of Gill's initial five patients undergoing laparoscopic radical cystectomy with ileal loop diversion. At 2 years, two patients died of unrelated causes,**

Table 79–6.   Complications in the Papers with Complication Descriptions (n = 10 or more)

Lead Author (year)	N	No. of Complications	Description of Complications (→treatment and event)
Basillote (2004)	13	8 4 major (31%)	1 ureteral obstruction (→percutaneous nephrostomy) 1 bladder neck contracture (→reoperation) 1 epididymal abscess (→orchiectomy) 1 wound dehiscence (→reoperation) 1 obturator nerve paresis (→physical therapy) 1 pyelonephritis (→intravenous antibiotics) 1 pouchitis (intravenous antibiotics) 1 positive margin at prostate apex (prostate cancer)
Simonato (2003)	10	5	2 metabolic acidosis (→sodium bicarbonate administration) 1 grade 3 bilateral hydronephrosis 1 grade 2 bilateral hydronephrosis 1 grade 2 monolateral hydronephrosis
Denewer (1999)	10	6	1 external iliac artery clipped (→vascular resection anastomosis from open part), leading to 1 postoperative deep venous thrombus (→thrombolytics) 1 reactionary hemorrhage (→reexploration) (→delayed death) 1 urine leak (→conservative drainage) 1 pelvic collection (→ultrasound-guided drainage) and 1 pyelonephritis (→parenteral antibiotics) in diabetes patient
Menon (2003)	17	15	13 bilharziasis with periureteric, perivesicular, and perivesical scarring 1 bleeding (→reexploration) 1 for a malfunction of lens (→open conversion)
Hemal (2004)	11	6 3 major (27%)	2 small rectal tear (→laparoscopic suturing) 1 external iliac vein injury (→laparoscopic suturing) 1 subcutaneous emphysema (→resolved in 4 days) 1 hypercapnia (→delayed death, 4 weeks after surgery) 1 positive margin (→cisplatin-based chemotherapy)
Gill (2004)	22	16 6 major (27%)	6 prolonged ileus (→conservative management) 3 bowel obstruction (→open conversion) 2 deep venous thrombosis (→thrombolytics) 1 urethrovaginal fistula (→open conversion) 1 bowel perforation (→open conversion) (→delayed death) 1 ureteroileal leak (→open conversion) 1 postoperative bleed (→laparoscopic suturing) 1 deep pelvic vein injury (→laparoscopic suturing)

Table 79–7. Oncologic Outcomes

Lead Author (year)	N	Technique (reconstruction)	Margins	Lymphadenectomy (n node, range)	Follow-up, mean (range) months	Overall Survival, N
Puppo (1995)	5	Laparoscopic (extracorporeal)	Not stated	Limited (not stated)	10.8 (6-18)	5
Denewer (1999)	10	Laparoscopic (extracorporeal)	Not stated	Limited (not stated)	Not stated	9
Tuerk (2001)	5	Laparoscopic (purely intracorporeol)	5/5 negative	Limited (not stated)	Not stated	5
Abdel-Hakim (2002)	9	Laparoscopic (extracorporeal)	9/9 negative	Limited (n = 2-4)	Not stated	9
Simonato (2003)	10	Laparoscopic (extracorporeal)	10/10 negative	Limited (not stated)	12.3 (5-18)	10
Menon (2003)	17	Robot (extracorporeal)	17/17 negative	Limited (n = 4-27)	Not stated (2-11)	17
Hemal (2004)	11	Laparoscopic (extracorporeal)	10/11 negative	Limited (not stated)	18.4 (1-48)	10
Basillote (2004)	13	Laparoscopic (extracorporeal)	12/13 negative	Limited (not stated)	Not stated	13
Gill (2004)	22	Laparoscopic (purely intracorporeol)	21/22 negative	11/22 extended (n = 21, 6-30)	11 (2-43)	18

Modified from Hrouda D, Adeyoju AAB, Gill IS: Laparoscopic radical cystectomy and urinary diversion: Fad or future? BJU Int 2004;94:501-505.

myocardial infarction (one) and septicemia from pulmonary infection (one). **The three surviving patients were asymptomatic, with normal upper tracts and no evidence of local recurrence or metastatic disease.** DeGer and colleagues (2004) described 12 patients undergoing laparoscopic radical cystectomy with intracorporeal rectosigmoid (Mainz II) urinary diversion with a follow-up of 2 years or more (13 to 42 months; median, 33 months). Median operative time was 8 hours (range, 6 to 14 hours); blood loss, 200 mL (range, 190 to 800 mL); and hospital stay, 15 days (range, 11 to 30 days). Two patients required reoperation because of urine leak and rectovaginal fistula, respectively. **All patients had negative surgical margins, with an average of 10 lymph nodes (range, 5 to 16) retrieved. During a 2-year follow-up, three (25%) developed metastatic disease, with two cancer-related deaths. No patient developed local recurrence, and all patients had diurnal continence.**

Laparoscopic extended pelvic lymphadenectomy for bladder cancer was described by Finelli and colleagues (2004). Of 22 patients undergoing laparoscopic radical cystectomy, the initial 11 underwent a limited dissection and the subsequent 11 underwent an extended lymphadenectomy. **Extended lymphadenectomy added 1.5 hours of operative time. The median number of lymph nodes retrieved was 3 and 21 in the limited and extended groups, respectively ($P = .001$). Three patients in each group were found to have positive nodal disease.** Complications included injury to a deep pelvic vein in one patient in the extended pelvic lymphadenectomy group, which was managed by intracorporeal suturing, with a blood loss of 200 mL. At a mean follow-up of 11 months (range, 2 to 43 months), there were no port site recurrences.

Prostate-Sparing Radical Cystectomy

Occult, unsuspected adenocarcinoma of the prostate has been detected pathologically in 38% of cystoprostatectomy specimens, although only 1.9% of these tumors have a volume in excess of 0.1 mL (Kabalin et al, 1989). Matzkin and colleagues (1991) reported a 25% incidence of prostate transitional cell carcinoma in 86 patients undergoing radical cystoprostatectomy for bladder cancer. In most such patients, transitional cell carcinoma occurs in the prostatic urethra (Wood, 1989). Prostatic stromal invasion by bladder cancer was reported in 15.6% of patients, with an increased risk in the presence of

carcinoma in situ or multifocality (>30%) and a decreased risk when these two factors were not present (4.5%).

Guazzoni and colleagues (2003) reported the initial three cases of laparoscopic nerve- and seminal vesicle–sparing cystectomy with extracorporeally constructed orthotopic ileal neobladder. Operative time was 410 to 480 minutes, blood loss was 150 to 300 mL, and hospital stay was 8 to 9 days. All three patients were fully continent with normal potency 3 months postoperatively. **Cathelineau and colleagues reported the largest experience with laparoscopic radical cystectomy in 84 patients, including cystoprostatectomy in 31 and prostate-sparing cystectomy in 40.** Urinary diversion was performed extracorporeally with orthotopic bladder in 51 and ileal conduit in 33 patients. Thirty-two patients had a history of significant prior open or laparoscopic abdominal-pelvic surgery, and 25 had recurrent bladder tumor after intravesical chemoimmunotherapy. Median operating time was 4.3 hours, with a median blood loss of 550 mL and transfusion rate of 5%. Median hospital stay was 12 days; only 58% of patients required parenteral narcotics (morphine) for 24 hours postoperatively. Postoperative complications occurred in 15 patients, usually minor in nature: urinary tract infection (8), pelvic hematoma (3), urinary fistula (2), pulmonary embolism (1), pyelonephritis (1). All patients had negative surgical margins. Pathologic staging for these tumors comprised pTa-pT1 (13), pT2 (59), pT3 (11), and pT4 (1). Tumor grade included grade 1 (1), grade 2 (13), and grade 3 (17). Positive lymph nodes were identified in seven patients; the number of retrieved nodes was not mentioned. **At an average follow-up of 18 months (range, 1 to 44 months), 83% were disease free, 8 had developed metastatic disease, and 5 had developed recurrence, 3 with concomitant metastatic disease. All 84 patients were alive at last follow-up, without any evidence of trocar or extraction site seeding** (Cathelineau et al, 2005). Five-year global survival in 132 patients undergoing open or laparoscopic prostate-sparing cystectomy reported by Vallancien and colleagues (2002) was similar to that of 507 patients undergoing radical cystoprostatectomy without any adjuvant or neoadjuvant treatment reported by Madersbacher and coworkers in 2003.

Robot-Assisted Laparoscopic Radical Cystectomy

Beecken and colleagues (2003) first reported da Vinci robot–assisted cystectomy with intracorporeal ileal neobladder with an operative time of 8.5 hours. Balaji and colleagues (2004) reported robot-assisted laparoscopic radical cystectomy with intracorporeal ileal conduit in two men and one woman with a mean operative time of more than 10 hours, blood loss of 250 mL, and hospital stay of 7.3 days. Menon and colleagues (2003) performed da Vinci–assisted cystectomy with extracorporeal urinary diversion in 17 patients. Mean blood loss was less than 150 mL; operative times for radical cystectomy, extracorporeal ileal conduit construction, and extracorporeal orthotopic neobladder were 140, 120, and 168 minutes, respectively. Functional and oncologic data were not reported.

Hand-Assisted Radical Cystectomy

Peterson and colleagues reported hand-assisted laparoscopic radical cystectomy with ileal conduit in 2002. Operative time was 7 hours, and blood loss was 750 mL. McGinnis and colleagues (2004) described seven patients undergoing hand-assisted laparoscopic radical cystectomy and ileal conduit with a mean operative time of 7.6 hours, blood loss of 420 mL, and hospital stay of 4.6 days. Taylor and colleagues (2004) performed a nonrandomized comparison of hand-assisted and open radical cystectomy in eight patients each. Similar outcomes were noted with regard to operative time (6.8 versus 7 hours), blood loss (637 versus 957 mL; $P = .2$), and hospital stay (6.4 versus 9.8 days; $P = .06$). The hand-assisted group had earlier resumption of regular diet (4.5 versus 7.9 days; $P = .05$) and required decreased parenteral analgesia (31 mg versus 149 mg of morphine sulfate equivalent; $P = .01$).

Future Directions

Laparoscopic radical cystectomy is now being performed at an increasing number of centers worldwide, particularly those with significant experience with laparoscopic urologic surgery in general and laparoscopic radical prostatectomy in particular. **Since the most technically challenging aspect of laparoscopic radical cystectomy is the reconstructive portion of the procedure, the majority of centers perform the urinary diversion extracorporeally through a minilaparotomy incision. A perusal of published literature suggests that perioperative outcomes of extracorporeal and intracorporeal urinary diversion are similar, albeit with shorter operative times and decreased requirement of advanced laparoscopic skills in the extracorporeal technique. As such, it appears likely that laparoscopic radical cystectomy in the future will evolve into a technically optimal combination, with intracorporeal performance of the radical cystectomy, including extended pelvic lymphadenectomy, ureteral mobilization, and selection of the appropriate bowel segment. The majority of the bowel work, construction of the bowel reservoir, and ureterointestinal anastomoses are likely to be performed extracorporeally through a minilaparotomy incision. In patients undergoing orthotopic reconstruction, the urethroenteric anastomosis will then be completed intracorporeally.**

The majority of patient morbidity and complications of radical cystectomy stem from the use of bowel. In addition, use of intestinal segments in urinary tract reconstruction confers its inherent disadvantages of metabolic alterations,

mucus production, and potential for tumor formation. These disadvantages may be exaggerated in patients with compromised baseline renal function. In the future, it is likely that novel bladder substitutes fashioned from tissue engineering techniques or by chronic ureteral tissue expansion may eliminate the need for bowel (Desai et al, 2003; Atala, 2004). These advances are likely to decrease the degree of technical difficulty associated with laparoscopic reconstruction. Until then, the search for the perfect urinary bladder substitute continues.

KEY POINTS: LAPAROSCOPIC RADICAL CYSTECTOMY

- Various types of radical cystectomy for cancer can be performed laparoscopically: radical cystoprostatectomy, prostate-sparing cystectomy, anterior pelvic exenteration, female reproductive organ–sparing cystectomy, nerve-sparing cystectomy.
- Various types of urinary diversion can be performed laparoscopically: ileal conduit, orthotopic neobladder, Mainz pouch, continent cutaneous diversion. Either the pure laparoscopic or the laparoscopic-assisted technique can be employed; increasingly, the laparoscopic-assisted technique is becoming the preferred approach.
- More attention is being focused on performing the laparoscopic pelvic lymphadenectomy according to the extended template; a current series documented a mean of 21 lymph nodes retrieved.
- Laparoscopic radical cystectomy is advantageous in regard to decreased blood loss and quicker recovery.

In conclusion, minimally invasive surgery for bladder malignant disease and urinary diversion is increasingly gaining acceptance at select institutions across the world. Refinements in technique and instrumentation will only provide impetus for continued improvement. **Careful prospective and long-term evaluation of oncologic and functional outcomes will be necessary to define the role of laparoscopic radical cystectomy vis-à-vis open surgery. An international registry of laparoscopic radical cystectomy has been established by the author to facilitate development of this emerging field in a cohesive manner by optimizing operative techniques, establishing standardized critical care postoperative pathways, and prospectively collecting oncologic, functional, and quality of life outcomes data.**

Acknowledgment

Jose Roberto Colombo Jr., MD, performed literature search and assisted with manuscript preparation.

SUGGESTED READINGS

Basillote JB, Abdelshehid C, Ahlering TE, Shanberg AM: Laparoscopic assisted radical cystectomy with ileal neobladder: A comparison with the open approach. J Urol 2004;172:489.

CHAPTER 79

Castillo OA, Litvak JP, Kerkebe M, et al: Early experience with the laparoscopic Boari flap at a single institution. J Urol 2005;173:862.

Cathelineau X, Arroyo C, Rozet F, et al: Laparoscopic assisted radical cystectomy: The Montsouris experience after 84 cases. Eur Urol 2005;47:780.

Cherullo EE, Meraney AM, Bernstein LH, et al: Laparoscopic management of congenital seminal vesicle cysts associated with ipsilateral renal agenesis. J Urol 2002;167:1263.

Elliott SP, Meng MV, Anwar HP, Stoller ML: Complete laparoscopic ileal cystoplasty. Urology 2002;59:939.

Gill IS, Ponsky LE, Desai M, et al: Laparoscopic cross-trigonal Cohen ureteroneocystostomy: Novel technique. J Urol 2001;166:1811.

Gill IS, Kaouk JH, Meraney AM, et al: Laparoscopic radical cystectomy and continent orthotopic ileal neobladder performed completely intracorporeally: The initial experience. J Urol 2002;168:13.

Kavoussi LR, Schuessler WW, Vancaillie TG, Clayman RV: Laparoscopic approach to the seminal vesicles. J Urol 1993;150:417.

Khonsari S, Lee DI, Basillote JB, et al: Intraoperative catheter management during laparoscopic excision of a giant bladder diverticulum. J Laparoendosc Adv Surg Tech A 2004;14:47.

Mariano MB, Tefilli MV: Laparoscopic partial cystectomy in bladder cancer—initial experience. Int Braz J Urol 2004;30:192.

Reddy PK, Evans RM: Laparoscopic ureteroneocystostomy. J Urol 1994;152:2057.

Simonato A, Gregori A, Lissiani A, et al: Laparoscopic radical cystoprostatectomy: A technique illustrated step by step. Eur Urol 2003;44:132.

Sotelo R, Mariano MB, Garcia-Segui A, et al: Laparoscopic repair of vesicovaginal fistula. J Urol 2005;173:1615.

80 Use of Intestinal Segments in Urinary Diversion

DOUGLAS M. DAHL, MD • W. SCOTT McDOUGAL, MD

Bowel is frequently used in reconstructive urologic surgery for ureteral substitutes, bladder augmentation, and bladder replacement. Less commonly, it may be employed as a urethral or vaginal substitute. The stomach, jejunum, ileum, and colon have been used in these various procedures. The appropriate use of these intestinal segments requires a thorough knowledge of their surgical anatomy, the methods of preparing the intestine for an operative event, the techniques of isolating segments of intestine and reconstituting continuity of the enteric tract, the problems and techniques of anastomosing the urinary tract to the intestine, and the complications that occur with use of the intestine. With this knowledge, reconstruction of the urinary tract may be performed with the proper segment of intestine in the least morbid way. This chapter reviews the technical aspects involved in the use of intestinal segments in urologic surgery that are germane to all types of reconstructive procedures, the difficulties and complications encountered with their use, and the problems that may arise both acutely and during the long term after their placement in the urinary tract. With these fundamental concepts in mind, the construction of various types of conduit urinary diversions and their advantages, disadvantages, and complications are addressed.

SURGICAL ANATOMY

The segments of bowel with which urologists frequently deal include the ileum, the colon, and the rectum. Less commonly, the jejunum and stomach may be used for reconstructive procedures. A thorough knowledge of the surgical anatomy of these structures is necessary to mobilize them and to fashion them properly according to the requirements of the often complex reconstructive procedure being performed.

Stomach

The stomach is a vascular organ that receives its blood supply primarily from the celiac axis (Fig. 80–1). **There are three branches of the celiac axis that give rise to the majority of the arterial supply of the stomach.**

1. The **left gastric (coronary) artery** arises directly from the celiac axis and supplies the lesser curvature.
2. The **hepatic artery,** after arising from the celiac axis, **gives off the right gastric artery,** which also supplies the lesser curve of the stomach, and the **gastroduodenal artery,** which supplies the antrum and duodenum before giving off the **right gastroepiploic artery.**
3. The **splenic artery** originates from the celiac axis and gives off the **vasa brevia (short gastric),** which supply the fundus and cardia, and the **left gastroepiploic artery.**

The right gastroepiploic artery anastomoses with the left gastroepiploic artery, and both supply the greater curve of the stomach. **By use of the gastroepiploic vessels, a pedicle of stomach may be mobilized to the pelvis.** The pedicle may consist of the entire antrum pylori or a wedge of the fundus.

The blood supply for these segments is based on either the left or right gastroepiploic artery, depending on the portion of stomach employed. On occasion, the left gastroepiploic artery is atretic at some point in its course and does not provide an adequate blood supply. Under these circumstances, the right gastroepiploic artery must be employed. **When a wedge of fundus is employed, it should not include a significant portion of the antrum and should never extend to the pylorus or all the way to the lesser curve of the stomach.** When the blood supply is based on the left gastroepiploic artery, the short gastric vessels that course from the gastroepiploic artery to the stomach are ligated along the greater curve proximal to the pedicle to the origin of the gastro-

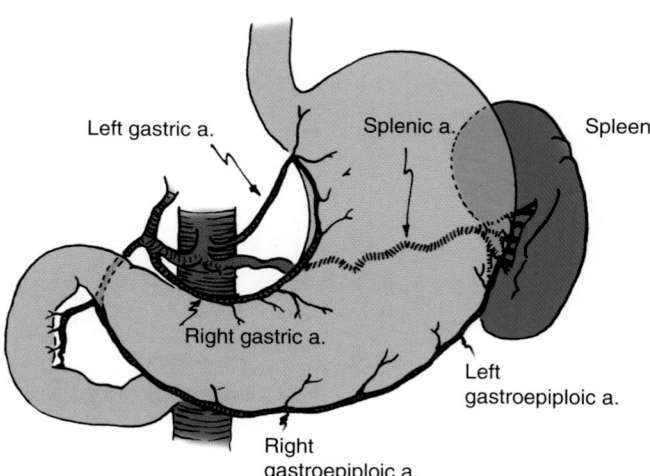

Left gastric a.

Splenic a.

Spleen

Right gastric a.

Left gastroepiploic a.

Right gastroepiploic a.

Figure 80–1. Arterial supply of the stomach.

epiploic artery. The omentum is left attached to the gastroepiploic vessels and helps secure and support them. It may be necessary for proper pedicle mobility to detach the omentum from the colon along the avascular plane located at the point of its attachment to the transverse colon. If an antrectomy is performed, a Billroth I anastomosis reconstitutes gastrointestinal continuity. **The stomach has a thick seromuscular layer that can easily be separated from the mucosa should a submucosal ureteral reimplantation be necessary.**

Small Bowel

The small bowel is about 22 feet long; however, it may vary from 15 to 30 feet in length. Its largest diameter is in the duodenum; the lumen becomes smaller in the more distal portions, reaching its smallest diameter in the ileum, approximately 12 inches from the ileocecal valve. **About two fifths of the small bowel is jejunum, whereas the distal three fifths is ileum.** There is no definite demarcation between the two; however, each possesses several unique properties that allow the surgeon to distinguish one from the other intraoperatively. **The ileum, being more distal in location, has a smaller diameter. It has multiple arterial arcades, and the vessels in the arcades are smaller than those in the jejunum. The ileal mesentery is also thicker than the jejunal mesentery. In contrast, the jejunal diameter is larger, the arterial arcades are usually single, and the vessels composing them are larger in diameter.** The arcades anastomose one with another and give off straight vessels, which enter the bowel and form an anastomotic network within the bowel wall. **It has been shown experimentally that up to 15 cm of small bowel can survive lateral to a straight vessel.** Thus, theoretically, the mesentery could be cleaned from the small bowel for a length of 15 cm without necrosis of the end. In general, however, it is unwise to assume that more than 8 cm of small bowel will survive away from a straight vessel. The arcades receive their blood from the superior mesenteric artery. When segments of jejunum or ileum are isolated, the mesentery should be transected in such a way that the isolated intestinal segment receives its blood supply from an arcade supplied by a palpa-

ble artery of substance that courses through the base of the mesenteric pedicle.

There are **two portions of the small bowel that may lie within the confines of the pelvis** and as such may be exposed to pelvic irradiation and pelvic disease: **the last 2 inches of the terminal ileum,** which is often fixed in the pelvis by ligamentous attachments; **and 5 feet of small bowel beginning approximately 6 feet from the ligament of Treitz,** the mesentery of which is the longest of the entire small bowel, and as such, this portion of the small bowel can descend into the pelvis. **In a postirradiated patient, one should try to avoid use of these two segments of the small intestine in any reconstructive procedure.**

Colon

The large bowel is divided into the cecum, ascending colon, transverse colon, left colon, sigmoid colon, and rectum. Portions of the large bowel are fixed or retroperitoneal, and other segments lie free within the peritoneal cavity. The cecum, on rare occasion, may lie free within the abdominal cavity and as such may have great mobility. In general, however, it is fixed in the right lower quadrant. There are two accessory peritoneal bands that bind the cecum and distal ileum to the retroperitoneum and lateral abdominal wall. One band arises from the distal ileum, attaches to the cecum, and is fixed to the retroperitoneum. A second band arises from the cecum and fixes the cecum to the posterior abdominal wall laterally. The remainder of the ascending colon is fixed to the right posterior abdominal wall to the level of the hepatic flexure, at which point the hepatocolic ligament secures this portion of the colon to the liver. The transverse colon lies free within the abdominal cavity and is fixed in the left upper quadrant at the splenic flexure by the phrenocolic ligament. The transverse colon is attached to the stomach by the gastrocolic omentum. The descending colon is fixed to the lateral abdominal wall; however, the sigmoid colon may or may not lie free within the abdominal cavity. The rectosigmoid colon's most cephalad portion is intraperitoneal, and as its distal, more caudad portions are approached, it becomes retroperitoneal and finally subperitoneal.

The colon receives its blood supply from the superior mesenteric artery, the inferior mesenteric artery, and the internal iliac arteries (Fig. 80–2). **The major arteries supplying the colon and rectum include the ileocolic, right colic, middle colic, left colic, sigmoid, superior hemorrhoidal, middle hemorrhoidal, and inferior hemorrhoidal arteries.** These arteries anastomose one with the other to form the arc of Drummond and allow considerable leeway in mobilizing the colon. The middle colic artery arises from the first portion of the superior mesenteric artery and generally ascends the transverse mesocolon to the right of midline. The right colic artery usually arises just below the middle colic artery from the superior mesenteric artery and courses to the right colon. It may arise, however, from the ileocolic or directly from the middle colic artery. If it arises from the ileocolic artery, mobilization of the distal ascending colon is facilitated so that this portion of the colon can easily be brought into the deep pelvis. On occasion, however, it is necessary to sever the right colic artery at its origin to mobilize the distal portion of the ascending colon to the pelvis. This is particularly true if the right

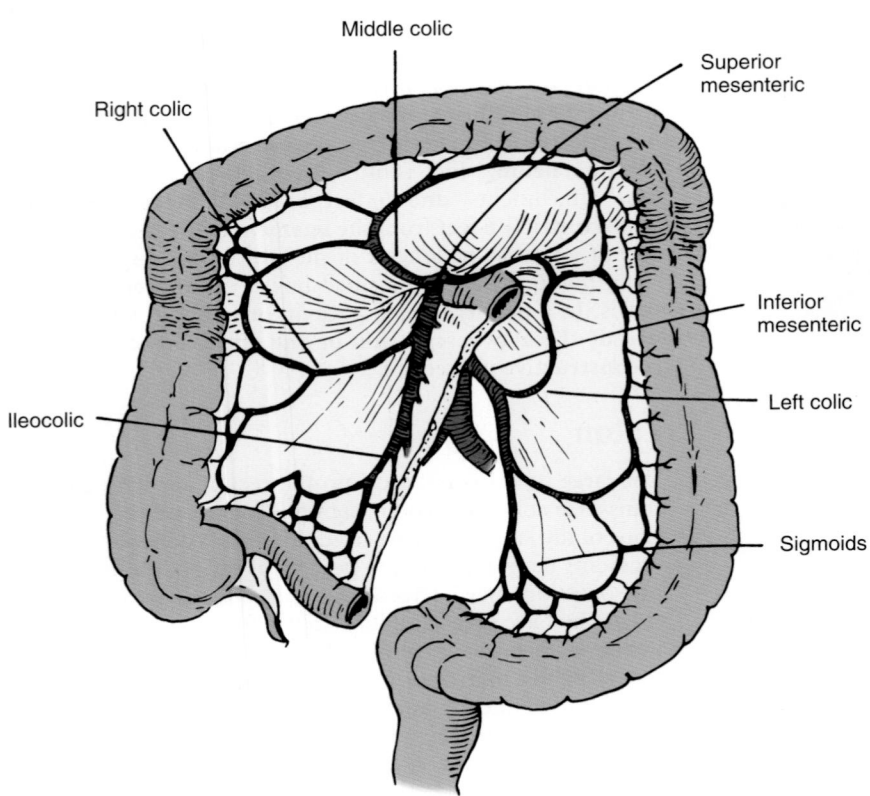

Right colic
Middle colic
Superior mesenteric
Ileocolic
Inferior mesenteric
Left colic
Sigmoids

Figure 80–2. The arterial supply to the small bowel and colon.

colic artery originates from the middle colic artery. The ileocolic artery is the terminal portion of the superior mesenteric artery and supplies the last 6 inches of ileum and ascending colon. The left colic artery arises from the inferior mesenteric artery, and then the inferior mesenteric artery gives off four to six sigmoid branches, the last of which becomes the superior hemorrhoidal artery. This anastomoses with the middle hemorrhoidal artery, a branch of the internal iliac artery, which in turn anastomoses with the inferior hemorrhoidal artery, the terminal branch of the internal pudendal artery. The middle sacral artery, which originates directly from the aorta, may supply the posterior aspect of the rectum.

Three weak points involving the vascular supply to the colon have been described. **Sudeck's critical point,** which is located between the junction of the **sigmoid and superior hemorrhoidal arteries,** was thought to be a particularly tenuous anastomotic area such that if the colon were transected in this region, the anastomosis would heal with difficulty because the blood supply might be compromised. Similarly, the **midpoints between the middle colic and right colic arteries and between the middle colic and left colic arteries also have somewhat tenuous anastomotic communications.** Although anastomoses in these areas generally heal well, provided the principles of proper technique are adhered to, it is usually wise to select an area for the anastomosis to one side of these points.

The ascending colon is mobilized first by transecting the cecal and distal ileal fibrous attachments to the lateral abdominal wall and retroperitoneum described previously and then by detaching it from the lateral abdominal wall along the avascular line of Toldt. This is a bloodless plane, provided the colonic mesentery is not violated. The transverse colon is mobilized by detaching the gastrocolic omentum along the avascular plane of its attachment to the colon; the hepatocolic ligament, which may have some small vessels coursing through it; and the phrenocolic ligament. The descending colon is mobilized much like the right colon by incising the avascular line of Toldt lateral to the colon. When these attachments are taken down, considerable mobility of the colon is achieved. Further mobility is gained by isolating a pedicle of intestine, which should be based on one of the major arterial vessels described earlier.

SELECTING THE SEGMENT OF INTESTINE

The stomach, jejunum, ileum, and colon have unique properties, each of which has special advantages and disadvantages. The selection of the proper intestinal segment should be based on the patient's condition, renal function, history of previous abdominal procedures, and type of diversion or substitution required. The stomach has been employed as a replacement for bladder, for augmentation cystoplasty, as a conduit, and for continent diversions (Leong, 1978; Adams et al, 1988; Bihrle et al, 1989). **The advantage of stomach over other intestinal segments for urinary intestinal diversion is that it is less permeable to urinary solutes, it has a net excretion of chloride and protons rather than a net absorption of them, and it produces less mucus.** Urodynamically, it behaves like other intestinal segments. When it is used in urinary reconstruction, electrolyte imbalance rarely ensues in patients with normal renal function, although a hypochloremic metabolic alkalosis has been described. The incidence of bacteriuria has been reported to be as low as 25%, much less than the 60% to 80% incidence reported for ileal and colon segments. However, more recent data from our institution suggest that there is no difference in bacteriuria among any of the segments. The urine, which usually has a pH of 6 to 7, does not generally result in an increased incidence of peristomal skin problems. We have also noted that in bladder augmentation patients, there is little difference in urinary pH between gastric and ileal augmentations. Serum gastrin levels are generally normal or minimally elevated, depending on what portion of stomach is used and how much (Leong, 1978; Adams et al, 1988). Although exclusion of the antrum from the gastrointestinal tract has not resulted in elevated serum gastrin levels and an ulcer diathesis clinically (Lim et al, 1983), experimentally, antral exclusion results in elevated circulating gastrin levels, which cause major intestinal ulcerative problems in the postoperative period (Tiffany et al, 1986).

There have been no severe ulcerative complications reported thus far in the series that have employed stomach for urinary reconstruction. When the antral portion of stomach is employed, reconstitution is generally by a Billroth I anastomosis. Complications with Billroth I gastroduodenostomy are well documented. The antrum should not be employed if the fundus is available. Early complications of the use of portions of the stomach for reconstruction include gastric retention due to atony of the stomach or edema of the anastomosis; hemorrhage, most commonly originating from the anastomotic site; hiccups secondary to gastric distention; pancreatitis as a consequence of intraoperative injury; and duodenal leakage. Delayed complications include dumping syndrome, steatorrhea, small stomach syndrome, increased intestinal transit time, bilious vomiting, afferent loop syndrome, hypoproteinemia, and megaloblastic or iron deficiency anemia. Postoperative bowel obstruction occurs with an incidence of 10% (2 of 21 patients) (Leong, 1978). Gastroduodenal and gastroureteral leaks have also been reported, occasionally resulting in a fatal outcome (Leong, 1978).

The use of stomach for urinary intestinal diversion may be considered when the use of other intestinal segments in a patient with a decreased amount of intestine would result in serious nutritional problems. One advantage of stomach in the patient with severe abdominal adhesions is that the area of the stomach is generally adhesion free and easily mobilized. **Complications specific to the use of stomach include the hematuria-dysuria syndrome and severe metabolic alkalosis associated with respiratory distress in some patients** (see "Metabolic Complications").

The jejunum is usually not employed for reconstruction of the urinary system because its use may result in severe electrolyte imbalance. In general, diseases that would make the ileum inappropriate for use also make the jejunum inappropriate for use. Rarely, it is the only segment available. Under these circumstances, as distal a segment of jejunum as possible should be employed to minimize the electrolyte problems.

The ileum and colon are used most often for urinary tract reconstruction and have been employed in all types of reconstructive procedures. The ileum is mobile and of small diameter, has a constant blood supply, and serves well for ureteral replacement and the formation of conduits. **Loss of significant portions of the ileum results in nutritional problems**

because of lack of vitamin B_{12} absorption, diarrhea because of lack of bile salt reabsorption, and fat malabsorption. On occasion, the mesenteric fat is excessive, making mobility and anastomosis difficult. Also, the mesentery may be so short that it is difficult to mobilize the ileum into the deep pelvis. **Postoperative bowel obstruction occurs in about 10% of patients who have segments isolated from the ileum for urinary tract reconstruction.** Half of the obstructions occur in the early postoperative period (Schwarz and Jeffs, 1975).

The colon requires mobilization from its fixed positions to give it the mobility necessary for use in urinary reconstruction. It has a larger diameter than ileum and is usually easily mobilized into any area of the abdomen or pelvis. In patients who have received pelvic irradiation, portions of the right, transverse, and descending colon may be used confidently with the knowledge that they have not been exposed to the radiation therapy. Removal of segments of colon from the enteric tract results in fewer nutritional problems than does removal of segments of ileum, provided the ileocecal valve is not violated. Should the ileocecal valve be used, diarrhea, excessive bacterial colonization of the ileum with malabsorption, and fluid and bicarbonate loss may occur. **The incidence of postoperative bowel obstruction with colon is 4%, less than that occurring with ileum.** Both ileal and colon segments result in the same type of electrolyte imbalance with similar frequencies. **An antireflux ureterointestinal anastomosis by the submucosal tunnel technique is easier to perform with use of colon.** In general, ileum and colon are comparable and have few differences, which does not argue strongly for the selection of one over the other except under special circumstances.

BOWEL PREPARATION

It has been a long-held tenet of elective intestinal surgery that bowel preparation is appropriate. The bacterial population in the stomach is relatively low, but in the remaining segments of the bowel including the jejunum, ileum, and colon, there are high bacterial counts. Early studies had suggested that bowel anastomoses in the patients whose intestinal tract had not been prepared before surgery had increased wound infection rates, increased intraperitoneal abscesses, and an anastomotic dehiscence rate greater than in those patients who have had proper bowel preparation before surgery (Irvin and Goligher, 1973; Dion et al, 1980). Other studies showed that mechanical preparation resulted in collapsed bowel at the time of surgery, which was shown to reduce the incidence of anastomotic leaks (Christensen and Kronborg, 1981). Studies have recently begun to question the widely held belief that bowel preparation is mandatory. In a meta-analysis of randomized clinical trials of anastomotic leakage during colon and rectal surgery, researchers found that there was no support for the conclusion that bowel preparation reduces anastomotic leak rates and other complications (Guenaga et al, 2003). In further work, this group found suggestions in their analysis that mechanical bowel preparation may actually increase the rate of anastomotic leakage and wound complications (Guenaga et al, 2005).

In experimental animals, it has been shown that an anastomosis with vascular compromise at the anastomotic line, which would normally result in perforation, heals if the bowel

Table 80–1. Mechanical Bowel Preparation

Preoperative Day	Conventional		Polyethylene Glycol–Electrolyte Solutions	
	Diet	Cathartic	Diet	Polyethylene Glycol
3	Low residue plus supplements		Regular plus supplements	
2	Low residue plus supplements		Low residue plus supplements	
1	Clear liquids	45 mL Fleet Phospho-Soda at 7 AM and 1 PM	Clear liquids	2 to 4 liters (adults) or 25 mL/kg/hr × 2 (children)

has been properly prepared with antibiotics. Also, solid feces may place strain on the anastomosis in the early phase of healing and result in ischemia with subsequent perforation. **Complications that result from bacterial contamination are a major cause of morbidity and mortality in patients undergoing urologic procedures.** Infectious complications after radical cystectomy that are a direct result of fecal contamination may occur in as many as 18% to 20% of patients who undergo cystectomies and include wound infections, peritonitis, intra-abdominal abscesses, wound dehiscence, anastomotic dehiscence, and systemic sepsis (Bracken et al, 1981). More recent series suggest that current management practices appear to have made a substantial improvement with perioperative infectious complications of 7% (Stein et al, 2004). In another contemporary series of radical cystectomy with continent or ileal loop urinary diversion in 167 patients, there was an infection complication rate of 7.2% (Mansson et al, 2003). A 5.2% rate of infectious complications was reported in another contemporary series (Cookson et al, 2003).

There are two aspects to bowel preparation, mechanical and antibiotic. Both methods attempt to reduce the complication rate from intestinal surgery. **The mechanical preparation reduces the amount of feces, whereas the antibiotic preparation reduces the bacterial count.** The bacterial flora in the bowel consists of aerobic organisms, the most common of which are *Escherichia coli* and *Streptococcus faecalis,* and anaerobic organisms, the most common of which are *Bacteroides* species and *Clostridium* species. **The bacterial concentration ranges from 10 to 10^5 organisms per gram of fecal content in the jejunum, 10^5 to 10^7 in the distal ileum, 10^6 to 10^8 in the ascending colon, and 10^{10} to 10^{12} in the descending colon.**

Mechanical Bowel Preparation

A mechanical bowel preparation reduces the total number of bacteria but not their concentration. Thus, the same number of organisms is present per gram of fecal content (Nichols et al, 1972). Therefore, spilling enteric contents during the procedure may be less likely with the mechanically prepared bowel because there is less of it to spill; however, once spilled, cubic centimeter for cubic centimeter, the inoculum is the same as if the bowel had not been prepared. Recent analysis has suggested, however, that there may in fact be an increase in bacterial contamination in patients who have undergone bowel preparation (Fa-Si-Oen et al, 2005).

Conventional bowel preparations commonly used in the past tended to exhaust the patient and exacerbate nutritional depletion because they generally required a 3-day preparation

period of suboptimal calorie intake (Table 80–1). The use of elemental diets has been advocated to clean the colon of feces while not compromising the nutritional status of the patient. Unfortunately, they have not proved useful because the elemental diets do not empty the colon of feces, and they do not reduce the bacterial flora (Arabi et al, 1978). In an attempt to reduce the time required for intestinal preparation and to obviate low-calorie intakes, whole-gut irrigation has been used. Originally, whole-gut irrigation was performed by placement of a nasogastric tube into the stomach and infusion of 9 to 12 liters of lactated Ringer's solution or normal saline during a several-hour period. These fluids were subsequently replaced with 10% mannitol, which was equally successful in ridding the bowel of its fecal content; however, the mannitol served as a bacterial nutrient and thereby facilitated microbial growth (Hares and Alexander-Williams, 1982). These solutions have largely been replaced by a polyethylene glycol–electrolyte solution. Whole-gut irrigation may be exhausting to the patient and may, in fact, result in a fluid gain, particularly when either saline or mannitol is used. **Whole-gut irrigation is contraindicated in patients with an unstable cardiovascular system, patients with cirrhosis, patients with severe renal disease, patients with congestive heart failure, or those with an obstructed bowel.** Whole-gut irrigation has been found to be no more effective than conventional preparations in reducing wound infections and septic complications (Christensen and Kronborg, 1981), even though there is a reduction of aerobic flora compared with the conventional preparations (van den Bogaard et al, 1981). **The advantages of the whole-gut irrigation are that it gives the patient dietary freedom, there is a short preparation time, and it eliminates the enema. Its disadvantages are that it may result in the patient's exhaustion, it is rather rigorous, and it does result on occasion in fluid overload.**

The polyethylene glycol–electrolyte lavage solution (GoLYTELY or the more palatable NuLytely) is an effective lavage agent in preparing the gut for elective colon and rectal surgery as well as for urologic surgery in which bowel is used. For the adult, 20 to 30 mL/min or approximately 1 to 1.5 L/hr for 3 hours is given either orally or through a small-caliber nasogastric tube placed into the stomach. If it is taken by mouth, it is better tolerated if the solution is chilled. The administration of GoLYTELY is stopped when the rectal effluent is clear and there is no particulate matter in it or when 10 liters of fluid has been given. This preparation in the adult has been as effective as conventional preparations. The septic complications with its use are approximately 4%. An inadequate preparation occurs in 5% of the patients using this modality (Wolff et al, 1988). For children, even those younger than 1 year, GoLYTELY may be used at a rate of 25 mL/kg/hour and given until the rectal effluent is clear and free of particulate matter (Tuggle et al, 1987). Metoclopramide (Reglan), 10 mg, in adults is often given simultaneously to control nausea.

Bowel preparation can increase metabolic complications and cause electrolyte disturbances, which could affect surgical care. Caution must be exercised in elderly and debilitated patients receiving sodium phosphate preparation; the sodium phosphate preparation has been shown to cause significant derangements in potassium, calcium, and phosphorus levels in frail individuals (Beloosesky et al, 2003). The only study in postsurgical complications comparing sodium phosphate with polyethylene glycol found no significant difference in complication rates (Oliveira et al, 1997). One study suggested that polyethylene glycol is better tolerated by elderly patients and causes less disruption in potassium and sodium levels (Seinela et al, 2003). Currently, most surgeons practicing in North America prefer a sodium phosphate bowel preparation to polyethylene glycol (Zmora et al, 2001). This regimen appears to be better tolerated by the patients.

A number of studies have questioned the efficacy of mechanical bowel preparation. Some have suggested that a limited mechanical bowel preparation is all that is necessary; others have questioned even the need for a mechanical bowel preparation. In one study, 2 liters of polyethylene glycol plus metoclopramide was compared with the administration of 4 liters of polyethylene glycol solution. There was no difference in surgical complication rate or the extent to which the bowel was clean (Grundel et al, 1997). In another study, when 4 liters of polyethylene glycol was compared with 90 mL of sodium phosphate, there was no significant difference in surgical complication rate (Oliveira et al, 1997). Two meta-analyses have found that there is an increased anastomotic dehiscence rate with preoperative mechanical bowel preparation (Wille-Jorgensen et al, 2003; Bucher et al, 2005). Polyethylene glycol may be the agent responsible for the increased rate of complications, but other preparation strategies have not been adequately analyzed (Slim et al, 2004). No study has adequately addressed the issue of the need for debulking of the intestine before laparoscopic approaches to intestinal surgery. Prospective studies that confirm the findings of these meta-analyses have been published (Bucher et al, 2005; Ram et al, 2005). It is extremely important to note that in these studies, the administration of antibiotics was crucial in keeping the complication rate low.

We prefer to begin the mechanical bowel preparation before any surgery involving intestinal segments with the patient as an outpatient. Two days before the anticipated date of surgery,

the patient is instructed to take a liquid diet. One day before the surgery, 45 mL of sodium phosphate (Fleet Phospho-Soda) is taken orally at 7 AM and 1 PM. This preparation minimizes the rigor of a mechanical bowel preparation while providing a decompressed bowel at the time of surgery. Contraindications to the use of sodium phosphate pertinent to urologic surgery include renal insufficiency, hyperphosphatemia, and hypocalcemia.

Antibiotic Bowel Preparation

There has been considerable controversy as to whether the addition of antibiotics in elective colon and small bowel surgery reduces mortality and morbidity significantly. The wealth of evidence, however, suggests that **an antimicrobial bowel preparation is advantageous in reducing postoperative complications.** In one study, the septic complication rate was reduced from 68% in the control group to 8% in the antibiotic group (Washington et al, 1974). Most series, however, report a lesser incidence of reduction in wound infection, generally from 35% without antibiotics to 9% with their use (Clarke et al, 1977). Others have suggested that the mortality rate drops from 9% to 3% with the use of antibiotics (Baum et al, 1981). It is clear that the use of antibiotics protects vulnerable bowel in that it may allow the tenuous anastomosis to survive. Other studies, however, have shown that without the use of antibiotics in mechanically prepared bowel in elective surgery, the septic complication rate is 6%—comparable to those studies using antibiotics (Menaker et al, 1981). In the presence of a bowel obstruction, however, oral antibiotics are of little value because they do little good in sterilizing the bowel. **The disadvantages of antibiotics include postoperative increase in the incidence of diarrhea; pseudomembranous enterocolitis; theoretical increased incidence of tumor implantation at the suture line that is not germane to urologic surgery; monilial overgrowth resulting in stomatitis, thrush, and diarrhea; and, with prolonged use, malabsorption of protein, carbohydrate, and fat.** The antibiotics that are most commonly used for bowel preparation include kanamycin, which is the best single agent; neomycin and erythromycin base; and neomycin and metronidazole (Table 80–2). With an appropriate antibiotic preparation, enteric organisms are reduced to 10^2 per gram of feces (Nichols et al, 1972).

The use of perioperative intravenous antibiotics is controversial. **Systemic antibiotics must be given before the operative event if they are to be effective.** Ideally, antibiotics should be given between 1 and 2 hours before the start of surgery (Classen et al, 1992). They appear to be most effective against

Table 80–2.	**Antibiotic Bowel Preparation**		
Preoperative Day	**Kanamycin**	**Neomycin plus Erythromycin Base**	**Neomycin plus Metronidazole**
3	1 g kanamycin orally every 1 hour × 4, then 4 times/day	—	—
2	1 g kanamycin orally 4 times/day	—	1 g neomycin 4 times/day plus 750 mg metronidazole 4 times/day
1	1 g kanamycin orally 4 times/day	1 g erythromycin base plus 1 g neomycin at 1 PM, 2 PM, 11 PM	1 g neomycin 4 times/day plus 750 mg metronidazole 4 times/day

the anaerobic flora and apparently reduce the complications caused by these organisms (Dion et al, 1980). Perioperative systemic antibiotics, when added to the oral regimen, reduced the septic complication rate from 15% to 20% to half that rate in several series (Hares and Alexander-Williams, 1982; Gottrup et al, 1985). Other studies, however, have shown no effect of systemic cephalosporin, for example, in reducing septic complications (Wolff et al, 1988). **If perioperative antibiotics are given, they should be effective against anaerobes because it is complications from these organisms against which perioperative antibiotics appear to be particularly effective.** Third-generation cephalosporins have been advocated as an appropriate systemic antibiotic. Most recent studies support the use of both oral and systemic antibiotic prophylaxis before intestinal surgery (Lewis, 2002).

Diarrhea and Pseudomembranous Enterocolitis

Antibiotic bowel preparations may result in diarrhea and pseudomembranous enterocolitis. Pseudomembranous enterocolitis is the more severe form of a spectrum of diarrhea. Clinically, this occurs after a bowel preparation in the postoperative period and is heralded by abdominal pain and diarrhea usually in the absence of fever or chills. As the symptoms and infection become more severe, systemic toxicity supervenes. **These patients can develop a toxic megacolon, and if this occurs, the mortality may exceed 15% to 20%.** Historically, pseudomembranous enterocolitis was thought to be due to staphylococcus, but there was, in fact, little evidence to support that organism as the etiologic agent. It is now clear that *Clostridium difficile* **plays a significant role in the majority of cases.** *C. difficile* elaborates at least two toxins that cause diarrhea and enterocolitis. *C. difficile* does not invade the bowel, and it is not normally a significant inhabitant of the fecal flora. It is held in check by other bacteria that inhibit its growth. Thus, antibiotics destroy the bacteria that inhibit the growth of *C. difficile* and thereby allow it to flourish. The toxin produces a diffuse inflammatory response with cream-colored plaque formation, erythema, and edema of the bowel wall. On microscopic examination, the villi appear to be intact, and there is a polymorphonuclear leukocyte infiltrate of the submucosa (Bartlett, 2002).

As the disease progresses, large areas of mucosa may slough, and areas of the bowel are denuded of their mucosa. The lesions may involve the colon, in which case it is called pseudomembranous enterocolitis, or the small bowel, in which case it is called pseudomembranous enteritis, or they may involve both. **The diagnosis is suspected by the symptoms or endoscopy and confirmed by culture of the organism or identification of its toxin. Because culture takes a prolonged time, it is more expeditious and therefore clinically useful to confirm the diagnosis by identifying the toxin produced by *C. difficile*.** Once the diagnosis has been made, **treatment involves the administration of vancomycin or metronidazole and discontinuance of the other antibiotics that the patient is receiving.** Vancomycin or metronidazole is effective in most cases. **Rarely, toxic megacolon supervenes, which requires subtotal colectomy as a lifesaving procedure** (Chang, 1985).

INTESTINAL ANASTOMOSES

Regardless of the type of anastomosis or the methods used to perform it, certain fundamental principles must be observed to minimize morbidity and mortality from intestinal surgery. **In urologic procedures in which gut is used, the most common cause of mortality and morbidity within the immediate postoperative period relates to complications involving the bowel,** either with the enteroenterostomy or with the segment interposed in the urinary tract. Therefore, it cannot be overemphasized that great care must be taken and proper techniques used in handling bowel in urologic procedures. Unfortunately, the portion of the procedure that involves mobilization of the intestine and reanastomosis often follows a rather lengthy urologic endeavor and is performed when the surgical team is not fresh. Therefore, the following principles should be so firmly ingrained in the surgeon that they are performed without the need to recall each one specifically.

The first principle of proper technique for intestinal anastomoses is adequate exposure. The intestine should be mobilized sufficiently so that the anastomosis may be performed without struggling for exposure. If possible, it is preferable to mobilize the intestine sufficiently so that the anastomosis can be performed on the anterior abdominal wall. The area of the anastomosis should be walled off from the rest of the abdominal cavity with Mikulicz pads. This is important so that any inadvertent enteric spills are not distributed throughout the abdominal cavity. The mesentery must be cleared from the bowel segments to be anastomosed for a suitable distance (usually 0.5 cm) from the intestinal clamps at the severed ends so that good serosal apposition may be achieved without interposed mesentery. Sufficient serosa must be exposed so that the seromuscular sutures can be placed directly in the serosa without traversing the mesentery.

The second principle of performing a proper anastomosis is to maintain a good blood supply to the severed ends of the bowel. The blood supply may be compromised by construction of an anastomosis under tension, excessive dissection or mobilization of the bowel, excessive use of the electrocautery, and tying of the sutures so tight that the intervening tissue is strangulated. A cut margin of bowel that is pink and bleeds freely suggests that the blood supply has not been compromised; however, hemostasis must be ensured before beginning the anastomosis. The site of transection is selected at a point where the blood supply is adequate to both segments. The mesentery should be transilluminated so that the blood supply may be defined before transection of the bowel segment. In urologic surgery, the location of the transection is elective so that an area may be selected in which excellent arcades supply both sections of the transected segment. The area must be selected with an eye to how deep the mesenteric transection must be for proper segment mobility. After location of the appropriate area where the mesentery is to be transected, it is cleaned from the serosa, severed between mosquito clamps, and tied with 4-0 silk sutures.

The third principle involves prevention of local spillage of enteric contents. The best way of preventing spills is to operate on bowel properly prepared (i.e., devoid of feces and collapsed). By stripping of the enteric contents between the fingers both cephalad and caudad from the proposed transection site and application of a noncrushing occlusive clamp across the bowel, a spill is made even less likely. This clamp should prevent enteric contents from exiting the cut ends of the bowel without interference with the mesenteric blood supply. After linen-shod clamps are applied and the area is walled off, Allen clamps are applied to the bowel and the bowel is transected between the Allen clamps. An anastomotic staple device may be used to transect the bowel at this point in place of Allen clamps (see later). Local spills and local sepsis have an adverse effect on the healing anastomosis, and it is for this reason that noncrushing occlusion clamps, in addition to an adequate bowel preparation, are advisable. If a spill does occur, it should be caught in the Mikulicz pads if the bowel has been properly walled off as described previously. The isolated segment that is to be used in the reconstructive procedure should be irrigated thoroughly with copious amounts of normal saline. The segment should be walled off. The irrigant is placed in one end of the segment and caught in a kidney basin as it exits the other end. This should be continued until the efflux is clear. This procedure prevents local spills during the ureterointestinal anastomosis and other aspects of reconstruction.

The fourth principle, germane to all intestinal anastomoses, is that **there should be an accurate apposition of serosa to serosa of the two segments of bowel to be anastomosed.** The anastomosis should be watertight and performed without tension. The bowel must be handled gently with the use of noncrushing forceps. The anastomotic line should be inverted and not everted. There is considerable controversy about this issue in that an everted anastomosis has been shown to heal with few complications. It is clear that when marginal conditions occur, an inverted anastomosis is more likely to remain intact than is the everted anastomosis.

The fifth principle is not to tie the sutures so tight that the tissue is strangulated. Obviously, the sutures must bring the serosa of the two segments firmly together. Nonabsorbable sutures used for the anastomosis result in a stronger anastomotic line in the early healing phase compared with absorbable sutures, but the difference is minimal and probably not particularly significant.

The final principle involves realignment of the mesentery of the two segments of bowel to be joined. These should be parallel to each other and ensure that there is no twist on completion of the anastomosis.

Factors that significantly contribute to anastomotic breakdown include poor blood supply, local sepsis induced by fecal spillage, drains placed on an intra-abdominal anastomosis, and anastomosis performed in irradiated bowel. Poor blood supply and local sepsis cause ischemia. Drains placed on the anastomosis increase the likelihood of an anastomotic leak, and an anastomosis performed in irradiated bowel is more likely to result in an anastomotic failure than one performed in nonirradiated tissue. The importance of careful technique and adherence to these principles is emphasized by the fact that in one series of urinary intestinal diversion, **75% of the lethal complications that occurred in the postoperative period were related to the bowel. Eighty percent of these patients had received radiation before the intestinal surgery** (Mansson et al, 1979).

Types of Anastomoses

Intestinal anastomoses may be performed with use of sutures or staples. Properly performed, both have similar complication rates. In selected circumstances, however, one method may have advantages over the other. **In general, sutured anastomoses with absorbable suture are preferable for intestinal segments that are exposed to urine** (i.e., suturing intestine to renal pelvis or bladder, closing the proximal end of a conduit [Costello and Johnson, 1984], and forming an intestinal pouch for urine).

Enteroenterostomy by a Two-Layer Suture Anastomosis

A 3-0 silk holding suture is placed on the mesenteric border just beneath the Allen clamps traversing both segments to be anastomosed, and a second suture is placed on the antimesenteric border similarly just beneath the Allen clamps (Fig. 80–3). It is important that the mesentery is cleaned sufficiently so that these sutures are placed in the serosa under direct vision. A row of silk sutures is placed 2 mm apart between the two holding sutures. This is accomplished by rotating the two Allen clamps away from each other, thus apposing the serosal surfaces. Sutures must traverse the muscularis but should not traverse the full thickness of the bowel. After all sutures have been placed, each is tied and the tails of all the sutures are cut, except those at each end; these are used as holding sutures. The Allen clamps are removed, and hemostasis is achieved, if necessary, with the light application of electrocautery. A 3-0 double-ended chromic intestinal suture is placed in the posterior suture line through all layers and tied to itself. Each end of the suture is then run in a locking fashion away from the midpoint until the mesenteric and antimesenteric borders are approached. As the lateral aspects of the bowel are approached, the suture is converted to a Connell suture (Fig. 80–4), which proceeds onto the anterior bowel wall. The sutures meet anteriorly in the midline and are tied together. The anterior serosa is then apposed with interrupted 3-0 silk sutures. The noncrushing occlusive clamps are removed, and the mesentery is closed with interrupted 3-0 silk sutures.

Patency of the anastomosis is ensured by palpating the anastomosis with the thumb and forefinger and feeling an

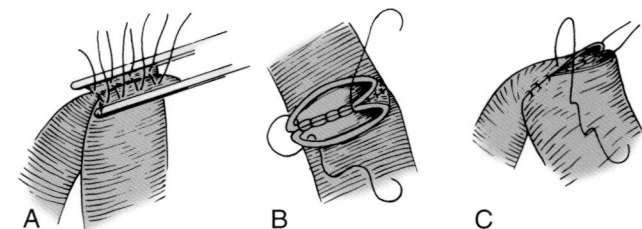

Figure 80–3. Two-layer suture anastomosis. **A,** Two holding sutures of 3-0 silk have been placed at the mesenteric and antimesenteric border, and the posterior wall is approximated with seromuscular sutures of 3-0 silk. **B,** A 3-0 intestinal chromic suture is placed through the full thickness of the bowel posteriorly, tied to itself, and run to the lateral borders with a continuous locking suture. At the lateral borders, it is converted to a Connell suture. **C,** The Connell suture brings the anterior margins together, inverting the suture line. The anastomosis is completed by placement of horizontal mattress seromuscular sutures of 3-0 silk over the anterior suture line (not depicted).

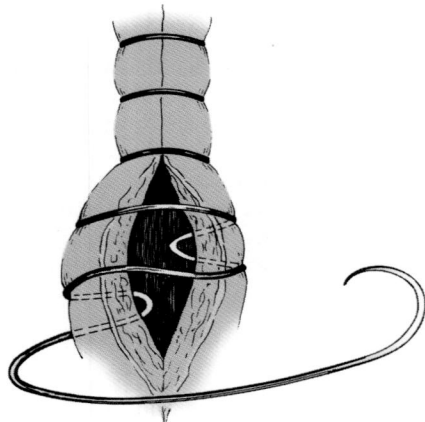

Figure 80–4. Connell suture. The suture traverses the bowel from serosa to mucosa and then from mucosa to serosa on the same side of the anastomosis. The suture is then placed on the opposite side of the anastomosis "outside in–inside out." The sequence is repeated until the two segments are approximated.

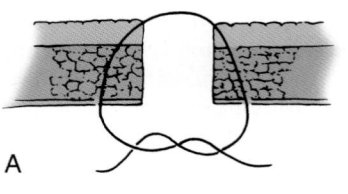

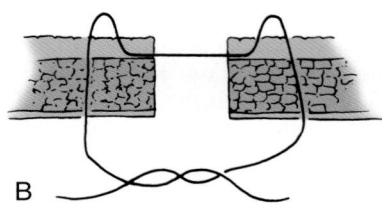

Figure 80–5.   **A,** When it is properly placed, the suture through the intestine should include more serosa than mucosa. **B,** The Gambee stitch. The suture is placed through the full thickness of the bowel, the mucosa is traversed, and then the mirror image procedure is performed on the segment to be anastomosed.

annulus of tissue around the fingers. This anastomotic technique is employed when the antrum pylori is removed and intestinal continuity is restored by a Billroth I procedure. It is also the most secure of all the anastomoses and should be used when one is forced to do an anastomosis under less than ideal circumstances.

Enteroenterostomy by a Single-Layer Suture Anastomosis

The single-layer anastomosis for reapproximating bowel is an excellent technique with a low complication rate, that is, a 0.2% anastomotic leakage rate compared with an 8.4% anastomotic leakage rate for a stapled anastomosis (Leslie and Steele, 2003).

The mesenteries of the two segments of bowel to be anastomosed are aligned, and a 3-0 silk suture is passed through the seromuscular layers of both segments on the mesenteric side; a second suture is similarly placed on the antimesenteric side. The mesenteric suture is tied, and the antimesenteric suture is left untied. The Allen clamps are removed, and hemostasis is achieved with light electrocautery. The critical point of the anastomosis, where most leaks occur, is at the mesenteric border. Leaking generally occurs because the sutures are placed carelessly or the serosa has not been cleaned of mesentery sufficiently so that the sutures are placed through it under direct vision. Because this mesenteric border is the critical area, it is approached first. Two 3-0 silk sutures are placed through the full thickness of the bowel on either side of the mesenteric holding suture. These sutures are placed in such a way as to include more serosa than mucosa, thus causing inversion of the suture line (Fig. 80–5A). Some prefer to use a Gambee stitch at this point, which involves placing the suture through the full thickness of the bowel followed by traversing a small segment of mucosa of each segment of bowel before exiting through the full thickness of the bowel of the other segment (Fig. 80–5B). The two bowel sutures on the mesenteric border are tied, with care taken to invert the suture line, thus apposing serosa. Then 3-0 silk sutures are placed 2 mm apart, both on the anterior and on the posterior

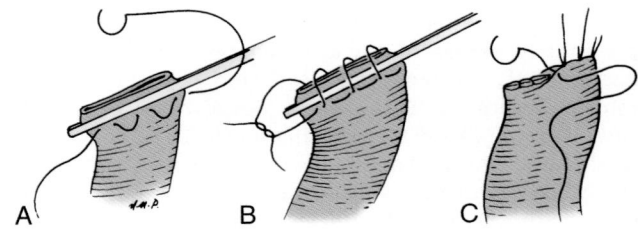

Figure 80–6.   Closure of the proximal end of the intestine. **A,** A 3-0 chromic suture is tied to itself at the antimesenteric border and placed beyond the intestinal clamp in a horizontal mattress fashion until the mesenteric border is reached. The suture is then tied to itself at this point. **B,** The intestinal clamp is removed, and an over-and-over suture through the full thickness of the bowel returns the chromic suture to its point of origin, where it is again tied to itself. **C,** Interrupted horizontal mattress seromuscular sutures of 3-0 silk invert the chromic suture line.

wall, inverting the suture line, thus apposing the serosa of the two bowel segments to each other. On approaching the antimesenteric holding suture, several sutures are placed before all are tied. A patent anastomosis is confirmed by feeling the annulus with the thumb and forefinger as described previously.

End-to-Side Ileocolic Sutured Anastomosis

The transected end of the colon is closed in the following manner (Fig. 80–6). A 3-0 silk suture is placed beneath the Allen clamp on the mesenteric border, and a second suture is placed on the antimesenteric border. These are tied. A 3-0 chromic suture is placed beneath the clamp in a horizontal mattress fashion. Beginning at the mesenteric border, it is tied to itself, and the horizontal mattress suture is placed until the antimesenteric border is reached, at which point the suture is again tied to itself. The clamp is removed, and an over-and-over suture is performed with the same chromic suture throughout the full thickness of the bowel until returning to the point of origin (i.e., the mesenteric border is approached). At this point, the suture is again tied to itself. The suture line

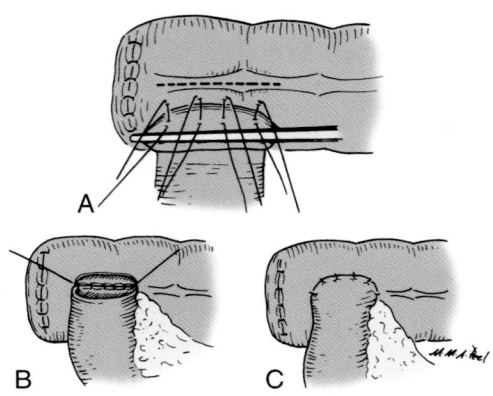

Figure 80-7. End-to-side anastomosis. **A,** The serosa of the ileum is sutured to the serosa of the colon 2 to 3 mm below a taenia. **B,** The taenia is opened for a distance sufficient to accommodate the diameter of the ileum. A 3-0 chromic suture is placed through all layers on the posterior wall, tied to itself, run in a locking fashion to both borders, and converted to a Connell suture laterally, thus completing the inversion anteriorly. **C,** The anterior margin of serosa is reapproximated with interrupted horizontal mattress sutures of 3-0 silk.

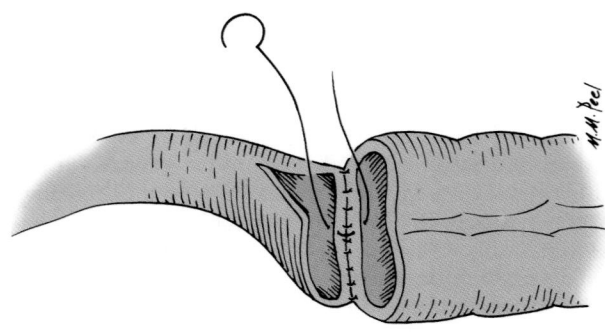

Figure 80-8. Anastomosis of discrepant-sized bowel. A seromuscular suture of 3-0 silk is placed adjacent to each end of the lumen on the mesenteric side. A second 3-0 silk seromuscular suture is placed adjacent to the lumen on the colon and on the antimesenteric border proximal to the cut end of the small bowel at a distance sufficient that when the antimesenteric border is incised, the lumens are the same size. Interrupted seromuscular sutures of 3-0 silk are then placed at 2-mm intervals between the two holding sutures. The small bowel is opened on its antimesenteric border until the opening in the small bowel is the same size as the opening in the colon. A 3-0 chromic suture is placed through all layers, tied to itself, and run laterally in a running locking fashion. At the borders, it is converted to a Connell suture, thus inverting the anterior margin. The anastomosis is completed with interrupted horizontal mattress 3-0 silk sutures that bring the seromuscular layers together anteriorly. This is similar to the closure depicted in Figure 80-3.

is buried by approximating the serosa on each side with interrupted 3-0 silk sutures placed 2 mm apart. Our preference is to close the end of the colon similarly to the way one closes the proximal end of a conduit. After a 3.0 silk suture is placed through the serosa on the antimesenteric and mesenteric sides, the clamp is removed and a 3-0 chromic suture is placed through all layers at the mesenteric and antimesenteric end. A Connell suture is used—the two chromic sutures meet in the middle and are tied together. Seromuscular sutures of 3-0 silk are placed to appose the serosal margins.

The mesenteries are aligned, and the ileal serosa is sutured with interrupted 3-0 silk sutures to the colonic serosa 2 mm below a taenia (Fig. 80-7). The taenia is incised the length of the diameter of the ileum adjacent to it. As described earlier for the two-layer anastomosis, a 3-0 double-ended intestinal chromic suture is placed through all layers of the colon and ileum in the midpoint of the posterior wall and run in a locking fashion laterally to either side of the incision in the taenia. At the most lateral border, the suture is converted to a Connell suture, and the anterior wall is closed. Seromuscular sutures of 3-0 silk placed from ileum to colon bury the anterior suture line. The mesentery is reapproximated.

Ileocolonic End-to-End Sutured Anastomosis with Discrepant Bowel Sizes

A 3-0 silk suture is placed on the mesenteric border of the ileum and colon (Fig. 80-8). A second 3-0 silk suture is placed on the antimesenteric border of the colon immediately beneath the Allen clamp. The other end of the suture is placed on the antimesenteric border of the ileum at a distance proximal to the Allen clamp, such that the serosal lengths between the two sutures of both ileal and colon segments are equal. Thus, an equal amount of ileal serosa is applied to the length of colonic serosa bordering the severed end of bowel. In the seromuscular layers of ileum and colon, 3-0 silk sutures are placed 2 mm apart, thus apposing the serosa of the ileum to the colon. The Allen clamps are removed. Hemostasis is achieved, and the antimesenteric border of the ileum is incised

to the level of the most proximal suture in the ileum. Thus, the bowel lumens now are of identical size. With a 3-0 chromic double-ended intestinal suture, the posterior row is run in a locking fashion, laterally converting to a Connell suture, and the anterior row is completed. Seromuscular sutures of 3-0 silk bury the anterior suture line.

Stapled Anastomoses

The theoretical benefits of a stapled anastomosis are that it provides for a better blood supply to the healing margin, there is reduced tissue manipulation, there is minimal edema with uniformity of suture placement, a wider lumen is constructed, there is greater ease and less time involved in performing the anastomosis, and the length of postoperative paralytic ileus is reduced. When they are placed in intestine through which urine traverses, however, stapled anastomoses employing nonabsorbable staples not infrequently cause stone formation and should be avoided (Bisson et al, 1979; Costello and Johnson, 1984).

The TA stapled anastomosis everts the suture line. Because staples close in a B and do not crush the tissue, theoretically they prevent ischemia at the suture line. This may be obvious when a staple line is used to transect the bowel and bleeding continues to occur. The bleeding points may be lightly electrocoagulated or tied off with fine absorbable suture. Stapled bowel anastomoses have been shown to be as efficacious as hand-sewn anastomoses because both have similar complication rates. **They usually require less time to perform when the techniques are properly learned, but for prolonged procedures, they save little if any time when the length of time for the whole procedure is taken into account.** In a large prospective, randomized trial in which a two-layer closure was compared with a staple closure, it was found that the complication rate was the same, but the time required to complete the stapled anastomosis was 10 minutes less than that for the hand-sewn anastomosis; when the total operative time was compared between the two, it was the same (Didolkar et al, 1986). **A comparison of complications between sutured and stapled anastomoses reveals a leak and fistula rate of 2.8% for stapled and 3.0% for sutured anastomoses** (Chassin et al, 1978). The clinically significant leak rate, however, is only 0.9% (Fazio et al, 1985). A 4.5% incidence of stapled anastomotic leakage has been reported during ileal conduit construction (Costello and Johnson, 1984).

Thus, the use of staples depends on the preference of the surgeon. A stapled anastomosis appears to be superior to a hand-sewn anastomosis in an esophageal-intestinal anastomosis and a low rectal anastomosis. In these two areas, the circular stapler allows a more precise anastomosis than is often possible with hand-sewn techniques. Because these are not problems of urologic surgery, staples are used at the discretion of the surgeon. The one area in urology where the authors believe the stapling device is superior is in the ileocolonic end-to-side anastomosis. With use of the circular stapling device, a widely patent anastomosis can be achieved expeditiously.

There are three staple instruments that are commonly employed in intestinal reconstruction: the linear stapler, the anastomotic stapler, and the circular stapler. The linear stapler places a double or triple row of staggered staples in a straight line. Depending on the cartridge and instrument chosen, various lengths of staple lines and heights of the closed staples may be chosen. The length is selected according to how long one wishes the staple line to be. **The height of staple is selected according to the tissue to be stapled.** Vascular and pulmonary tissues require staples with a closed height of 1 mm (open height of 2.5 mm). Most intestinal anastomoses are performed with medium staples, which have a closed height of approximately 1.5 mm (open height of 3.5 mm). On occasion, for thick tissues, large staples are required that have a closed height of 2 mm (open height of 4.8 mm). If there is any doubt in selecting the staple size, the tissue thickness may be measured with a special instrument used for this purpose. In general, **tissues less than 1 mm or more than 3 mm in thickness are not amenable to the use of staples.**

The anastomotic stapler places two linear double rows of staggered staples. When the knife is advanced, the staple line is divided. The height of the staples is chosen according to the tissue to be transected.

The circular stapler places two concentric, staggered circular staple rows and cuts the tissue within the circle completely from the surrounding tissue. It may be selected in various diameters and with various heights of staples. The diameter and height are selected according to the tissue to be anastomosed. The diameter to be selected is determined by sizing the diameter of the tissue to be stapled. Special sizers are available for this maneuver. In most intestinal anastomoses in urology, the height of the closed staple is 1.5 to 2.0 mm. The following is a description of various types of stapled anastomoses.

Ileocolonic Anastomosis with the Circular Stapling Device

The mesenteric borders are cleared for a distance of 1.5 cm from the cut end of both the colon and the ileum (Fig. 80–9). Holding sutures of 3-0 silk are placed on the mesenteric and

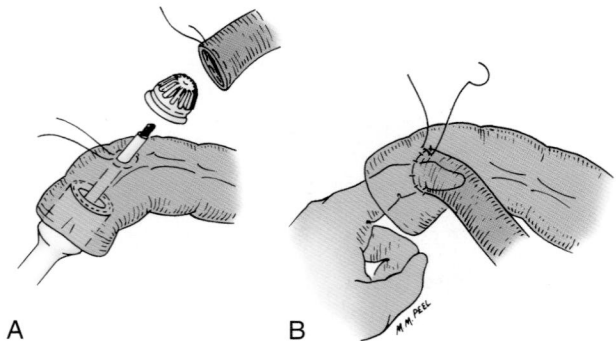

Figure 80–9. Stapled circular anastomosis. **A,** A purse-string suture of 2-0 polypropylene (Prolene) is placed around the circumference of the small bowel, and a second purse-string suture 1 cm in diameter is placed on a medial taenia 5 to 6 cm from the open end of the colon. The anvil is removed. A stab wound is made in the center of the purse-string suture in the colon, and the circular stapler is introduced through the end of the colon, with its post thrust through the stab wound. **B,** The anvil is placed on the post and introduced into the end of the small bowel, the purse-string sutures in the small bowel and colon are tied snugly around the post, and the circular stapler is approximated with a gap of 1.5 to 2 mm, with care taken not to include any mesentery in the gap. The anastomosis is completed by placement of interrupted silk sutures around the circumference of the anastomosis.

antimesenteric border of the colon. Two other holding sutures are placed on the medial and lateral walls of the colon, midway between the mesenteric and antimesenteric sutures. A purse-string suture of 2-0 polypropylene (Prolene) is placed around the ileum no more than 2 mm from the cut end. It is important to take small bites of mucosa to avoid bunching of tissue. Sutures must be placed evenly to avoid a gap. A purse-string instrument is available that can be used for this step, if preferred. The ileal diameter is determined with sizers so that the correct circular stapler diameter instrument may be chosen—usually 25 mm. A purse-string suture is also placed in a circle, 1 cm in diameter, through which a taenia traverses on the medial aspect of the colon. A stab wound is made in the center of the colonic purse-string suture. The distal anvil of the circular stapler is removed, and the instrument is placed through the open end of the colon with its post passed out the stab wound made in the center of the purse-string on the medial wall of the colon. The purse-string is tied tight. The top anvil is then secured to the post, and the ileum is placed over it. The ileal purse-string is tied.

Care must be taken to align the mesenteries at this point. The instrument is approximated with a staple gap of 1.5 to 2.0 mm. Care must be taken not to catch fat or mesentery in the gap. The instrument is fired and removed by rotatory movement from the colon. Two doughnuts of tissue should be identified on the instrument, and they should have their complete circumference intact with no gaps. With a finger in the open end of the colon and through the anastomosis, seromuscular sutures of 3-0 silk are placed 3 to 4 mm apart around the circumference of the anastomotic line.

The transected end of the colon may be closed by the suture technique or by the use of staples. If the end is to be closed with sutures, one 3-0 chromic suture is brought out the mesenteric border and another out the antimesenteric border, and both are tied to themselves with the knots on the inside of the bowel. The two sutures are run to each other by a

Connell suture until they meet, at which point they are tied to each other. The suture line is inverted by placement of a second row of 3-0 silk seromuscular sutures. If staples are preferred, the holding sutures are held up, and a linear stapler is applied across the open end. Excess tissue is trimmed and the stapler removed. By holding the holding sutures up, one is secure in applying the staple line to the serosa and mucosa circumferentially around the bowel. Some invert the staple line with seromuscular sutures of 3-0 silk. This is not necessary, however. The mesentery between the two segments is now approximated with interrupted 3-0 silk sutures.

End-to-End Stapled Anastomosis: Ileal-Ileal or Ileocolonic Anastomosis

The antimesenteric border of the two bowel segments to be joined is approximated with a 3-0 silk suture 5 to 6 cm from the cut ends of the bowel (Fig. 80–10). A holding suture is placed through both segments of bowel at their cut ends at the

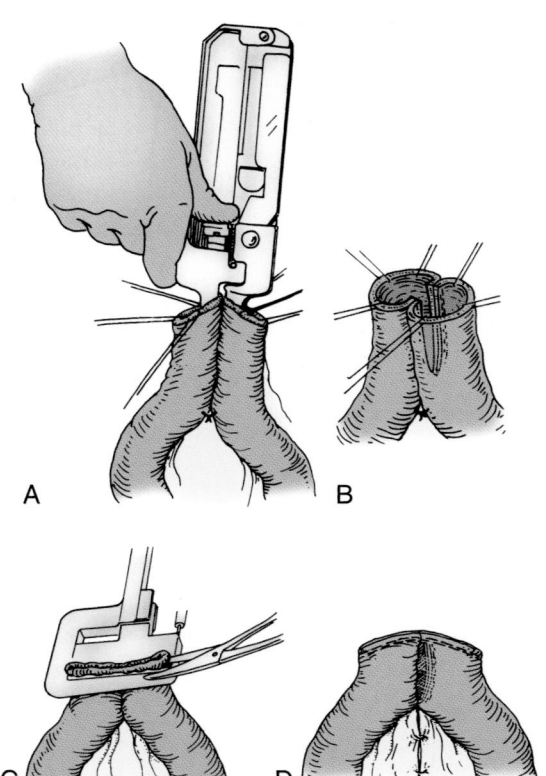

Figure 80–10. Stapled end-to-end anastomosis. **A,** A 3-0 silk suture is placed 5 to 6 cm from the cut ends of the intestine on the antimesenteric borders of both intestinal segments and tied. Holding sutures are placed around the circumference of both intestinal lumens, one suture securing together the antimesenteric borders of both intestinal segments. The linear anastomotic stapler is placed into the lumens, secured and locked in place, and fired, and the knife is advanced. **B,** The appearance of the intestinal anastomosis after firing of the staple device. **C,** The open end of the two intestinal segments is closed with a linear stapler by elevation of the holding sutures while the linear stapler is applied so that the circumferences of the mucosa and serosa are incorporated in the staple margin. **D,** The anastomosis is completed by closure of the mesentery with interrupted 3-0 silk sutures.

midpoint of the antimesenteric borders. Stay sutures are placed at the mesenteric border of each bowel segment, and two other sutures midway between the mesenteric and antimesenteric border on the lateral aspects of the bowel are also placed. The anastomotic stapler is positioned in the lumens of both segments of bowel along the antimesenteric border. The antimesenteric holding suture is pulled up adjacent to the stapler. The anastomotic stapler is locked in place, the staples are fired, and the knife is advanced. The staple lines are inspected for bleeders, which if persistent should be suture ligated with an absorbable suture. It is important for several 3-0 silk sutures to be placed at the apex of the stapled and cut antimesenteric incision. At this point, slight tension on the anastomotic line can place undue stress on the staple margin and cause a leak. The holding sutures are held up, and a linear stapler is placed across the open end of bowel and fired. Care must be taken so that the staples include the serosa in its entire circumference. Excess bowel tissue is excised flush with the instrument before it is disengaged. The mesentery is then reapproximated.

Laparoscopic Anastomoses

Laparoscopic approaches to cystectomy and augmentation cystoplasty have been reported (Gill et al, 2000a, 2002). In these procedures of urinary diversion with continent neobladder or ileal ureter substitution, a purely laparoscopic technique is possible for bowel resection with use of endoscopic stapling devices. Proper placement of the trocars is dependent on the need to mobilize the bowel and the procedure for which the bowel is to be used. Trocar placement for mobilization of the distal ileum is illustrated in Figure 80–11. The technique primarily involves the use of endoscopic linear cutting and stapling devices, which can be used to divide small bowel and its mesentery (Figs. 80–12 and 80–13). Reanastomosis purely intracorporeally can be accomplished with the same endo-GIA stapler to reconstitute bowel continuity with a side-to-side functional end-to-end anastomosis (Gill et al, 2000b; Potter et al, 2000). An endoscopic TA stapler may be used to complete the bowel closure.

Other approaches to laparoscopic intestinal surgery include laparoscopic mobilization of the bowel segment and exteriorization of the segment; the anastomosis is performed in an open fashion through a small laparotomy incision. (Fig. 80–14). This has been a preferred approach for many performing cystoprostatectomy, as a small incision is already required for intact specimen removal. It therefore allows direct tactile assessment of the anastomosis. A laparoscopic ileal conduit can be performed with these techniques. The ureterointestinal anastomosis is performed with freehand laparoscopic suturing. One of the abdominal trocar sites is used to draw the bowel segment through the abdominal wall for stoma construction. Completely laparoscopic orthotopic ileal neobladder has been reported (Gill et al, 2002). The neobladder is constructed by freehand running suture with use of laparoscopic techniques (Fig. 80–15). The results of laparoscopic bowel anastomoses suggest that these anastomoses are safe, but no large series has been published that compares open with laparoscopic approaches for bowel anastomosis (Canin-Endres et al, 1999; Rothenberg, 2002).

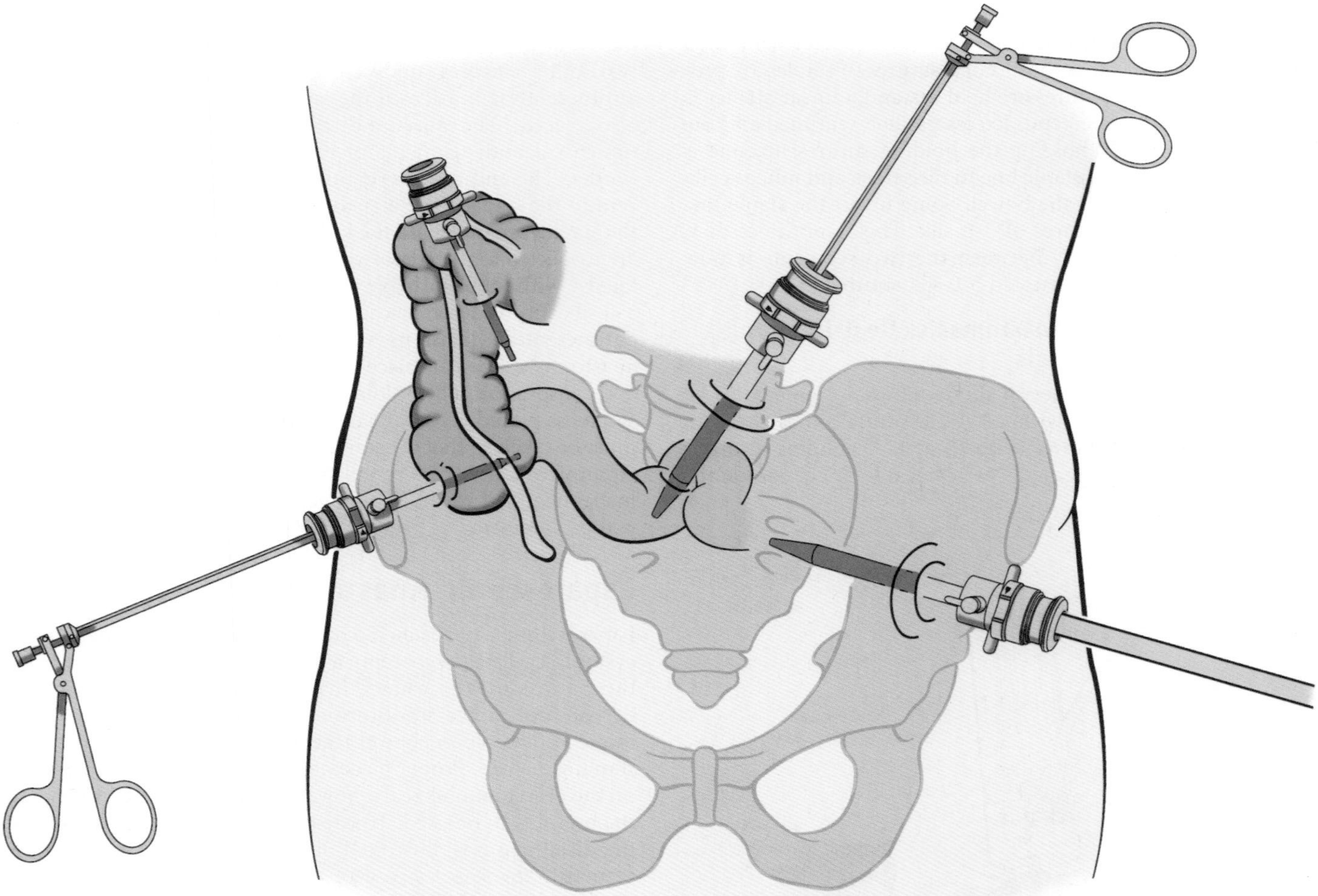

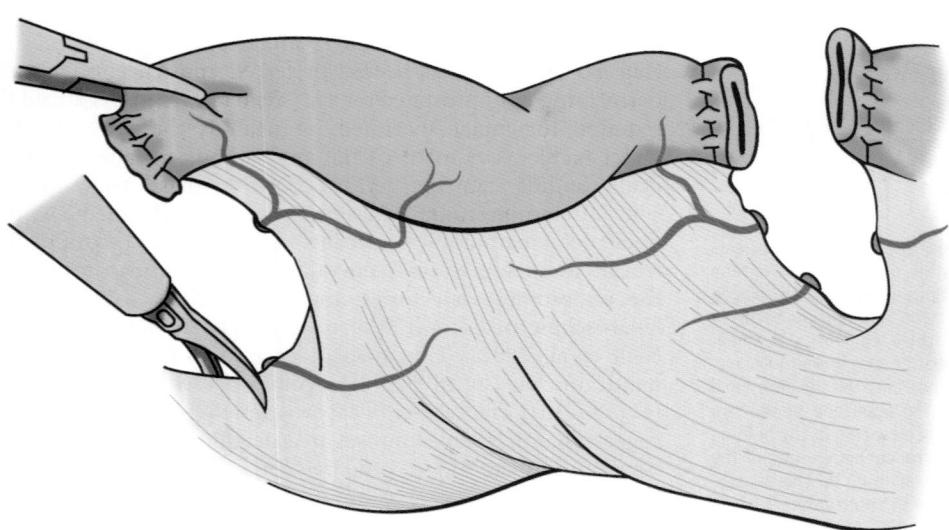

Figure 80–11.   Trocar placement for laparoscopic mobilization of the distal ileum.

Figure 80–12. Laparoscopic mobilization of a small bowel segment for use in reconstruction. The visceral peritoneum is divided sharply; then the mesenteric vessels are ligated and divided. Staplers, ultrasonic shears, or bipolar cautery devices may be used to divide the mesenteric vessels.

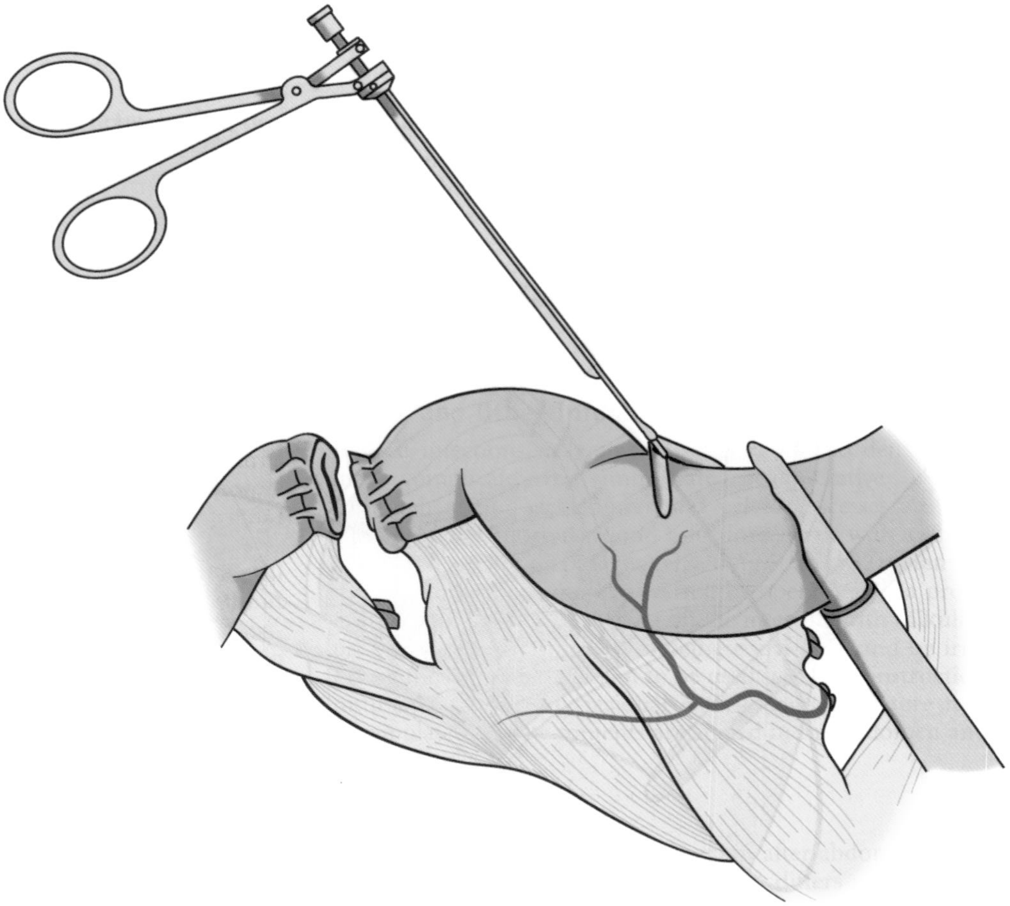

Figure 80–13. The endoscopic gastrointestinal stapler divides the intestinal segment. The staple line must be excised from the segment intended for use in the urinary reconstruction.

Figure 80–14. Many urologic procedures in which intestinal segments are used for reconstruction involve extirpative surgery in which a small laparotomy is employed for specimen removal. In this case, the small laparotomy is used to deliver the bowel segment outside the abdomen. Any form of anastomosis may be employed by this technique, which also reduces the chance of spillage of intestinal contents.

incidence of stomal stenosis with epithelial overgrowth and a better appliance fit with fewer peristomal skin problems. There are two types of protruding stomas: the end stoma and the loop end ileostomy. **Most complications of stomas are the result of technical errors in their construction.** Therefore, to minimize such complications, specific technical points must be rigidly adhered to.

The site of the stoma should be selected preoperatively. This is done by marking the stomal site with the patient in the sitting position as well as in the supine position; care is taken to place it over the rectus muscle at least 5 cm away from the planned incision line. The point chosen should be well away from skin creases, scars, the umbilicus, belt lines, and bone prominences. A site in which radiotherapy has previously injured the area should be avoided. **All stomas should be placed through the belly of the rectus muscle and be located at the peak of the infraumbilical fat roll.** If the stoma is placed lateral to the rectus sheath, a parastomal hernia is likely to occur. The bowel should traverse the abdominal wall perpendicular to the peritoneal lining (i.e., it should come straight out). One should avoid trimming fat or epiploic appendages from around the margin of the stoma, and the appliances should be applied in the operating room.

A circular incision is made at the predetermined site. A perfectly circular opening in the skin may be made by placing the finger hole of a Kelly clamp at the desired point and grasping the skin in the center of the hole with a Kocher clamp. By pulling up on the Kocher and pushing the handle of the Kelly against the abdominal wall, a small button of skin may be removed with a single pass of the knife. This makes a perfectly circular opening in the skin. However, the tendency to remove too much skin is great, resulting in a circular opening that is too large. To avoid this complication, one should not cut the skin flush with the Kelly clamp but rather immediately beneath the Kocher clamp. The subcutaneous tissue is left intact. This is spread, not excising any fat, for the fat falls back adjacent to the bowel and eliminates any dead space. Kocher clamps are placed on the fascia in the incision and pulled medial so that when the fascia and peritoneum are incised, they are incised directly over the skin line and thus do not result in angulation of the gut when the abdominal incision is closed. The fascia is incised in a cruciate manner, and the rectus muscles are spread. The peritoneum is incised. The opening should accommodate two fingers snugly.

Nipple Stoma: "Rosebud"

A Babcock clamp is placed through the opening, and the bowel is grasped and brought out for a distance of 5 to 6 cm to make a nipple of about 2 to 3 cm in length (Fig. 80–18). Two 3-0 chromic sutures are placed through the seromuscular layer of the bowel and the peritoneum on the anterior abdominal wall. Alternatively, the serosa may be sutured to the fascia with two 2-0 chromic sutures. The mesentery is aligned in its normal anatomic direction before the serosa is sutured to the peritoneal wall. The ileum is usually curved concave toward the mesentery. If this is severe, the mesentery may be partially incised 1 cm from the bowel wall (Fig. 80–19). Thus, a portion of mesentery is preserved along the entire length of the bowel. This should straighten the curve in the bowel significantly if not completely. Four 3-0 chromic sutures are placed in quadrants through the full thickness of the bowel

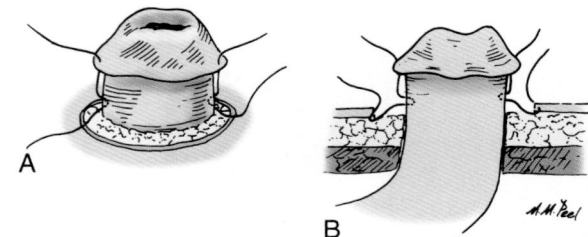

Figure 80–18. **A** and **B,** Nipple stoma. Five to 6 cm of intestine is brought through the abdominal wall. The serosa is scarified, and quadrant 3-0 chromic sutures are placed through the full thickness of the distal end of the intestine. Each suture is placed in the seromuscular layer 3 cm proximal and then secured to the dermis before it is tied.

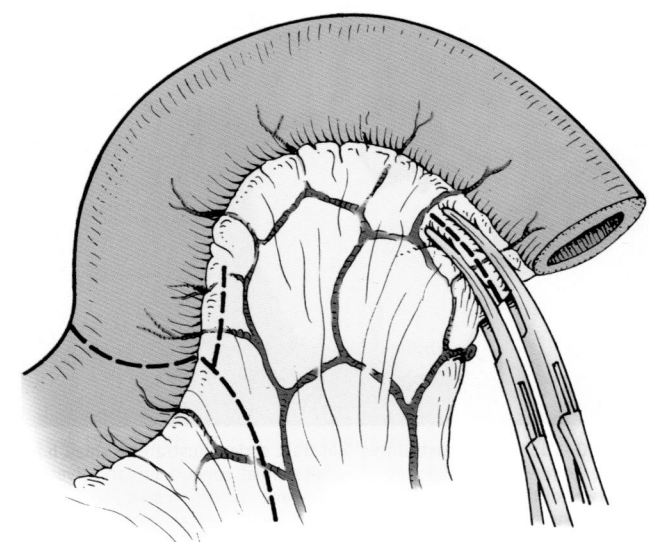

Figure 80–19. If it is tethered by the mesentery, the bowel may be straightened by incising the mesentery several centimeters away from the serosa and parallel to the bowel.

edge and through the seromuscular layer of the bowel 3 to 4 cm from the cut edge and then through the subcuticular skin layer. Sutures should not traverse the full thickness of the skin but should be placed through the subcuticular and subdermal layers only.

When the sutures are tied, the bowel is everted and forms a nipple. A more secure nipple may be made by performing multiple myotomies through the seromuscular layer of the bowel above the skin line before construction of the nipple. The myotomies adhere serosa to serosa and reduce the risk of stomal retraction. This is particularly appropriate for patients who are obese.

Flush Stoma

Quadrant sutures of 3-0 chromic are placed through the full thickness of the bowel and subsequently passed through the subdermal layer of the skin and tied. Several sutures are placed between the quadrant sutures from bowel to subdermal skin. This constructs a flush stoma that has a 1-mm raised margin.

Loop End Ileostomy

Obese patients have a thick abdominal wall and often a thick, short ileal mesentery. This makes construction of an end ileal stoma extremely difficult. **The loop end ileostomy obviates some of these problems and is usually easier to perform than the ileal end stoma in the patient who is obese** (Fig. 80–20). To construct this type of stoma, the distal end of the ileum is closed as described previously for closing the proximal end of an intestinal segment, and a loop is brought up through the belly of the rectus muscle and onto the anterior abdominal wall. This avoids bringing the mesenteric border onto the abdominal wall and prevents one side of the ileostomy from being involved with mesentery. A slightly larger skin opening is required than for the end stoma. A 3-cm disk of skin is removed. The subcutaneous tissue is spread, the fascia incised, the rectus spread, and the peritoneum incised as described earlier. The opening should admit two fingers comfortably. The loop may be pulled through the opening in the abdominal wall by passing an umbilical tape through a small opening in the mesentery at a distance from the distal end that is sufficient to leave that end in the abdomen when the loop has been pulled through the abdominal wall. By gentle traction on the umbilical tape, the loop is brought onto the abdomen.

The distal portion of the bowel is brought through the opening such that the closed end lies cephalad to the body of the segment. When a sufficient amount of loop protrudes beyond the skin edge, a small rod is placed through the hole in the mesentery at the apex of the loop and holds the bowel on the anterior abdominal wall during suturing. If the rent in

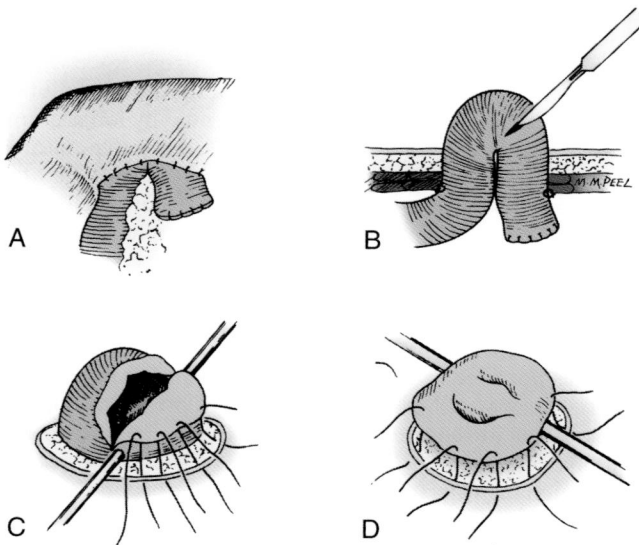

Figure 80–20. Loop end ileostomy. **A,** After the distal end of the loop is closed and the bowel is drawn through the rent in the abdominal wall, the bowel is held in place by a rod passed through the mesentery. The mesentery is realigned, and the peritoneum is sutured to the serosa of the bowel circumferentially. **B,** A transverse incision is made in the bowel four fifths of the loop distance cephalad. **C,** The cephalad portion of the stoma is simply sutured to the dermal layer of skin with interrupted 3-0 chromic sutures. **D,** On the inferior aspect of the incision, 3-0 chromic sutures are placed through the full thickness of the cut edge, then through the seromuscular layer, and then through the dermis. This everts the caudal portion of the stoma.

the rectus muscle is too large, it may be closed with interrupted 0 chromic sutures from within the abdomen. The serosa is sutured to the peritoneum on the anterior abdominal wall. The bowel wall is opened in a transverse direction at a point four fifths of the distance cephalad to the most caudal portion of the loop. With 3-0 chromic sutures, the full thickness of the caudal incision in the bowel is sutured back to itself (serosa) and then to the dermis as in the rosebud technique. The cephalad nonfunctional opening is sutured directly to the dermis. The rod is sutured to the skin and left in place for 7 days.

This type of stoma results in a lesser incidence of stomal stenosis but a higher incidence of parastomal hernias (Emmott et al, 1985). Stomas for the colon may be constructed in much the same way as end stomas for the ileum. Their suturing, however, is usually more flush than everted.

Complications of Intestinal Stomas

Complications of the abdominal stoma are the single most common problem encountered in the postoperative period after urinary intestinal diversion. Early complications of abdominal stomas include bowel necrosis, bleeding, dermatitis, parastomal hernia, prolapse, obstruction, stomal retraction, and stomal stenosis. At some point, virtually every patient has one of these complications. Many of these complications can be reduced by proper construction of the stoma. If periodic visits with the enterostomal therapist are made, products for skin care are appropriately used, nonirritative stomal adhesives are employed, the urine in the collection device is maintained acidic, and properly fitting collection devices are used, most stomal complications can be significantly reduced and many eliminated.

Parastomal skin lesions may be classified as irritative, which are manifested by hypopigmentation, hyperpigmentation, and skin atrophy; erythematous erosive lesions, which appear as macular lesions, scaling of the skin, and loss of the epidermis; and pseudoverrucous, which are wartlike lesions (Borglund et al, 1988).

Stomal stenosis has been reported, on average, in 20% to 24% of patients with ileal conduits and 10% to 20% of patients with colon conduits (see Table 80–3). This incidence has been considerably reduced by better attention to stomal care and better-fitting appliances. Stomal stenosis is less for loop stomas than for end stomas. Parastomal hernias occur rarely (1% to 4%) with end stomas but are more likely to occur with loop stomas, with reported incidences ranging from 4% to 20%. Stenosis of catheterizable stomas is high, reaching to more than 50% in children (Barqawi et al, 2004). Stoma-related complications appear to be more common in an umbilically placed stoma versus one in the abdominal wall (De Ganck et al, 2002). Others have reported excellent long-term results with few complications in the concealed umbilical stoma (Glassman and Docimo, 2001).

Bleeding, stomal stenosis, and dermatitis can be markedly reduced by attention to parastomal skin care and by the use of a properly fitting appliance around a protruding stoma. The other complications are minimized by proper surgical technique.

Parastomal hernia occurs after ileal loop urinary diversion frequently, with an incidence of 2% to 6.6%. It can be effectively treated with open repair (Franks and Hrebinko, 2001; Ho and Fawcett, 2004). Laparoscopic approaches have also been reported with mixed results. One series reported a 56% failure rate within 6 months of laparoscopic parastomal hernia repair with Gore-Tex mesh (Safadi, 2004). This contrasts with the high success rate reported in another small series (Kozlowski et al, 2001).

Massive bleeding from the conduit occasionally occurs, usually as a result of varices. There have been several interesting reports of patients who have developed ileal conduit varices generally as a result of hepatic dysfunction and portal hypertension. Treatment by transhepatic portal-systemic shunt and transhepatic angiography and embolization is a relatively minimally invasive technique that has promise and is worthwhile using in these difficult patients (Lashley et al, 1997; Medina et al, 1998).

URETEROINTESTINAL ANASTOMOSES

The ureter may be anastomosed to the colon or small bowel in such a manner as to produce a refluxing or nonrefluxing anastomosis. There is considerable controversy as to whether a nonrefluxing or refluxing anastomosis is desirable in urinary tract reconstruction. Deterioration of the upper tracts for ileal and colon conduits has been reported in 10% to 60% of the patients (Koch et al, 1992). In one series, 49% of the upper tracts showed changes after conduit diversion, 16% of which had an increase of the blood urea nitrogen of 10 mg/dL or more (Schwarz and Jeffs, 1975). **Deterioration of the upper tracts is usually a consequence of lack of ureteral motility, infection, or stones and less commonly due to obstruction at the ureteral-intestinal anastomosis.** Because bacteriuria occurs in almost all conduits and because the intestine certainly does not inhibit and may, in fact, promote bacterial colonization, many have suggested that a nonrefluxing anastomosis would minimize the incidence of renal deterioration.

The evidence that suggests a nonrefluxing system in urinary intestinal diversions is desirable comes from several observations. **In a group of patients who had nonrefluxing colon conduits constructed, those whose anastomoses remained nonrefluxing had a lesser incidence of renal deterioration than did those in whom the antireflux anastomosis failed.** Follow-up for 9 to 20 years revealed that 79% (22 of 28 patients) of the refluxing renal units deteriorated, whereas only 22% (11 of 51 patients) of the nonrefluxing units deteriorated (Elder et al, 1979; Husmann et al, 1989). Others have reported that in continent diversions, the majority of patients who experience reflux show upper tract dilation and deterioration, whereas few show upper tract deterioration when a nonrefluxing anastomosis is present (Kock et al, 1978). Similar findings have been reported in experimental animals.

If a nonrefluxing ureteral-colonic conduit diversion is constructed, only 7% of the renal units show evidence of pyelonephritic scarring after 3 months; whereas if a refluxing anastomosis is constructed, 83% of the renal units show scarring. Half of the conduits in both groups have significant bacteriuria (Richie and Skinner, 1975). **Others have not found the same high incidence of renal deterioration associated with ureteral-intestinal reflux.** One group of investigators studying colon conduits noted no difference in the incidence of renal deterioration regardless of whether the colon conduit demonstrated reflux; 17% (5 of 29) of nonrefluxing renal units showed deterioration compared with 18% (5 of 27) of refluxing units (Hill and Ransley, 1983). In another series, only 3 of 135 renal units with refluxing ureteral-intestinal anastomoses that were unobstructed showed evidence of renal deterioration (Shapiro et al, 1975). A more recent study compared refluxing and nonrefluxing ureteral-intestinal anastomoses in 58 patients with conduit diversions; 56 renal units were refluxing and 60 renal units were nonrefluxing. There was no difference in renal deterioration or in pyelonephritis between the two groups. Ureteral-intestinal stricture formation occurred in 2% of refluxing units as opposed to 13% of nonrefluxing units (Pantuck et al, 2000).

It does not appear that conduit pressures are transmitted to the renal pelvis. The pressure within the renal pelvis in refluxing conduit diversions is not elevated above normal, and it is not dependent on the segment of bowel used (i.e., ileum or colon) (Magnus, 1977; Kamizaki and Cass, 1978; Hayashi et al, 1986). Peristaltic ureteral contractions apparently dampen pressure transmission from intestine to renal pelvis, attesting to the importance of normal ureters. **When bowel is substituted for the ureter, it does not appear that it makes any difference whether there is reflux at the bladder.** The voiding pressure is blunted by the distensible bowel segment. Indeed, in one study of continent diversions in which a segment of ileum formed the pouch to which the ureters were anastomosed, radionuclide voiding cystography failed to detect reflux to the kidneys (Waidelich et al, 1998). Moreover, there is no difference in ileal and colon conduits between those that experience reflux and those that do not in renal function measured 2 to 5 years postoperatively (Mansson et al, 1984). **Also, the successful construction of an antirefluxing anastomosis does not prevent bacterial colonization of the renal pelvis.** In six of eight patients with nonrefluxing enterocystoplasties and one patient with a nonrefluxing colon conduit in whom the absence of reflux was documented by loopogram, percutaneous renal pelvic aspiration revealed positive cultures (Gonzalez and Reinberg, 1987). **One stated advantage of a refluxing anastomosis in patients who have urothelia that are prone to malignant change is that the upper tracts may be observed by periodic introduction of contrast material into the conduit. From these studies, it appears that reflux associated with impaired ureteral peristalsis in the presence of bacteriuria or obstruction results in renal deterioration, but it has not been established either for conduit or for continent diversions that reflux associated with the normal ureter in the absence of obstruction is detrimental to the adult kidney.**

Although many techniques have been described to make the various types of ureterointestinal anastomoses, certain **basic surgical principles are germane to all the anastomoses** regardless of type. **Only as much ureter as needed should be mobilized** so that there is no redundancy or tension on the anastomosis. **Mobilization should not strip the ureter of its periadventitial tissue** because it is in this tissue that the ureter's blood supply courses. The ureter should be cleaned of its adventitial tissue only for 2 to 3 mm at its most distal portion where the ureter–intestinal mucosa anastomosis is to be performed. **The ureterointestinal anastomosis must be performed with fine absorbable sutures, which are placed so** that a watertight mucosa-to-mucosa apposition is constructed. **The bowel should be brought to the ureter and not vice versa** (i.e., the ureter should not be extensively mobilized so that it can be brought into the wound to the bowel lying on the anterior abdominal wall). **At the completion of the anastomosis, the bowel should be fixed to the abdominal cavity, preferably adjacent to the site of the ureterointestinal anastomosis.** If possible, **the anastomosis should be retroperitonealized,** or a pedicle flap of peritoneum should be placed over the anastomosis.

In those diversions in which the intestinal stoma is brought to the abdomen and the proximal end of the bowel fixed to the retroperitoneum, there are two places where the bowel may be conveniently fixed to the retroperitoneum without jeopardizing mesenteric blood supply. The most convenient point of fixation is below the root of the small bowel mesentery at the level of the pelvic brim. The ureterointestinal anastomosis may be retroperitonealized at the level of the pelvic brim, thus fixing the bowel segment to the posterior body wall. In those situations in which the ureters are short, a more cephalad fixation to the posterior peritoneum may be accomplished by placing the proximal end in the right upper quadrant cephalad to the takeoff of the right colic artery and immediately below the duodenum. This is a relatively avascular area and places the intestine fairly close to the right and left kidneys, thus reducing the length of ureter required to reach the intestinal segment.

Perhaps one of the most difficult complications of ureterointestinal anastomoses to manage is a **stricture. Strictures are generally caused by ischemia, a urine leak, radiation, or infection.** The incidence of urine leak for all types of ureterointestinal anastomoses is 3% to 5% (see Table 80–3). **This incidence of leak can be reduced nearly to zero if soft Silastic stents are used.** In one series of ureterointestinal anastomoses done at the same institution, the nonstented group had a 2% anastomotic leak and a 4% stricture rate. When non-Silastic rigid stents were used, there was a 10% incidence of stricture. When a soft Silastic stent was used, however, there were no strictures or leaks (Regan and Barrett, 1985). In a similar series in which colon conduits were constructed after gynecologic exenterative operations, the nonstented group had an 18% leak rate and an 18% stricture rate, whereas those who had been stented had a 3% leak rate and an 8% stricture rate (Beddoe et al, 1987). Thus, the evidence indicates that modern soft Silastic stents are effective in reducing the leak rate and subsequent stricture formation. Better technique and better suture materials have also reduced the incidence of stricture in nonrefluxing anastomoses. A series of nonrefluxing ureter-colon anastomoses reported an 8% incidence of stricture formation (Stein et al, 1996).

In constructing a submucosal tunnel in those procedures in which a nonrefluxing anastomosis is made, it is often helpful to inject saline with a 25-gauge needle submucosally to raise the mucosa away from the seromuscular layer. This makes dissection considerably easier (Menon et al, 1982).

These principles of surgical technique are common to all ureterointestinal anastomoses. Each type of ureterointestinal anastomosis, however, has specific technical points unique to its construction. Techniques involving ureter-colon anastomoses are discussed first, followed by ureter–small bowel anastomoses.

Ureterocolonic Anastomoses
Combined Technique of Leadbetter and Clarke

This method establishes a nonrefluxing ureterocolonic anastomosis by employing a submucosal tunnel. The technique combines the ureterocolonic anastomosis of Nesbit, which is a refluxing elliptical anastomosis to the intestine, with the tunneled technique of Coffey (Fig. 80–21) (Leadbetter and Clarke, 1954).

The anterior taenia is incised obliquely for 2.5 to 3 cm as close to the mesenteric border as possible. The mucosa is dissected off the muscularis for the entire length of the incision. At the distal end of the incision in the taenia, the mucosa is picked up with a fine Adson forceps, and a small button is excised. The ureter is spatulated for 5 to 7 mm such that an elliptical anastomosis may be made. The ureter is sewn mucosa to mucosa with 5-0 PDS either by interrupted sutures with the knots tied on the outside or by a running suture. If the suture line is to be run, it is well to begin the anastomosis at the apex of the ureter. This suture is tied, and the posterior row is run to the most distal portion of the ureter, which is subsequently tied. A second running suture completes the anterior aspect. The seromuscular layer is then reapproximated loosely over the ureter in such a way as to allow "the ureter [to] lie in the bowel as a hammock without being compressed" (Leadbetter and Clarke, 1954). The bowel should be fixed to the peritoneum so that there is no tension on the ureters.

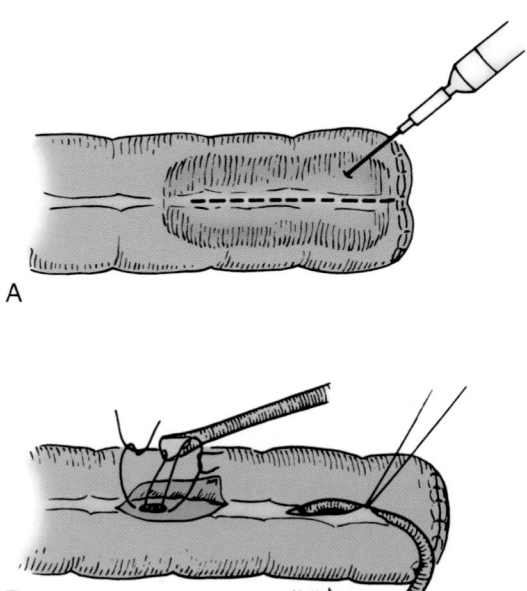

Figure 80–21. Leadbetter-Clarke ureterointestinal anastomosis. **A,** Injection of the submucosal tissues with saline facilitates the dissection. **B,** A linear incision is made in the taenia, the taenia is raised, and the mucosa is identified. A small button of mucosa is removed, and the ureter is spatulated and then sutured to the mucosa with 5-0 PDS. The seromuscular layer is sutured over the ureter, with care taken not to compromise or occlude the ureter.

Table 80–4. Complications of Ureterointestinal Anastomoses

Procedure	No. of Patients	Stricture (%)	Leakage (%)	Reflux (%)
Colon				
Leadbetter-Clark[1-4]	127	14	3	4
Strickler[5]	28	14	—	—
Pagano[6]	63	7	—	6
Small Bowel				
Bricker[7,8]	1809	7	4	—
Wallace-Y[9-11,17]	129	3	2	—
Nipple[8]	37	8	—	17
Serosal tunnel[12]	10	10	—	0
Le Duc[13-17]	82	18	2	13

Literature cited: [1]Hagen-Cook and Althausen, 1979; [2]Leadbetter and Clarke, 1954; [3]Hill and Ransley, 1983; [4]King, 1987; [5]Jacobs and Young, 1980; [6]Pagano et al, 1984; [7]Clark, 1979; [8]Patil et al, 1976; [9]Clark, 1979; [10]Beckley et al, 1982; [11]Wendel et al, 1969; [12]Starr et al, 1975; [13]Hautmann et al, 1988; [14]Le Duc et al, 1987; [15]Klein et al, 1986; [16]Lockhart and Bejany, 1987; [17]Palascak et al, 2001.

The complications reported with this procedure include a leak rate of 2.5%; deterioration of the upper tracts, which varies between 4.3% and 25%; and a stricture rate that varies between 8% and 14% (Table 80–4).

Transcolonic Technique of Goodwin

This method establishes a nonrefluxing ureterocolonic anastomosis by construction of a submucosal tunnel (Fig. 80–22). By this technique, the anastomosis is performed from within the bowel (Goodwin et al, 1953). If it is performed in bowel in continuity with the gastrointestinal tract, a noncrushing occlusive clamp is applied across the bowel cephalad to the desired point of the ureterointestinal anastomosis. This clamp is placed loosely about the bowel and in such a way as not to occlude the arterial supply in the mesentery.

A vertical incision is made in the bowel anteriorly, and the desired point of entrance of the ureter into the bowel is identified. A 0.5-cm incision is made in the posterior mucosa, and with use of a curved hemostat, the mucosa is dissected from the submucosal layer in an oblique fashion coursing from medial to lateral. The hemostat is passed beneath the mucosa for a distance of approximately 3 to 4 cm and then brought through the serosa. A traction suture that has been placed on the ureter is then grasped with the hemostat and the ureter brought into the colon. Both ureters should be brought into the bowel before they are sutured to the mucosa. The ureters should lie without tension or angulation. A No. 5 feeding tube is passed through the ureter to be sure that there is no kinking as it passes through the bowel wall. The redundant ureter is excised, and its end is spatulated and sewn with interrupted 5-0 PDS to the mucosa, with care taken to include with the mucosa some muscularis so that the ureter is securely fixed in place. A Silastic stent is placed up both ureters. As the ureters come through the serosa from without the bowel, the adventitia of the ureter is sutured to the serosa of the colon with two 4-0 PDS sutures. The anterior bowel wall is closed in two layers.

The reported results with this technique appear to be satisfactory. However, specific reliable data on the complication rate are not available.

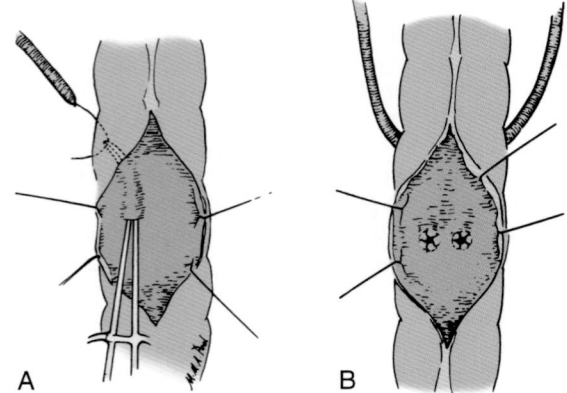

Figure 80–22. Transcolonic technique of Goodwin. **A,** The bowel is opened on its anterior surface; a small rent in the mucosa is made; and with a mosquito hemostat, the mucosa is raised from the submucosa extending laterally. A 3- to 4-cm tunnel is made before the clamp exits the serosal wall. The ureter is grasped and pulled into the submucosal tunnel. **B,** Both ureters have been drawn into the bowel through their submucosal tunnels before each is spatulated and circumferentially sutured to the mucosa. These sutures should also incorporate a portion of the muscularis for security. Where the ureter enters the colonic sidewall adjacent to the mesentery, the adventitia of the ureter is secured to the colonic serosa with interrupted 5-0 PDS sutures.

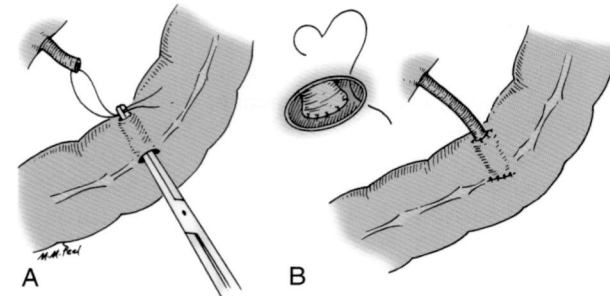

Figure 80–23. Strickler ureterointestinal anastomosis. **A,** A small linear incision is made in the taenia, and the submucosa is dissected from the mucosa laterally. After a distance of 3 to 4 cm is achieved, a small hole is made in the serosa and the ureter is drawn through. **B,** A button of mucosa is excised, and the ureter is spatulated and sutured to the mucosa with 5-0 PDS. The rent in the taenia is closed with interrupted sutures, and an adventitial suture at the ureter's entrance point into the colon secures it to the serosa of the colon.

Strickler Technique

This method establishes a nonrefluxing ureterocolonic anastomosis by construction of a submucosal tunnel (Fig. 80–23) (Strickler, 1965; Jacobs and Young, 1980). A 1-cm incision is made on the margin of the taenia. The technique originally described removal of a 2-mm button of seromuscular tissue. A 2-cm tunnel is formed laterally beneath the seromuscular layer with a hemostat. The seromuscular layer is incised, with care taken not to tent up the mucosa and inadvertently incise it. The holding suture in the ureter is grasped and drawn throughout the submucosal tunnel. The ureter is spatulated for 0.5 cm. A button of mucosa is removed, and the full thickness of the ureter is sewn to the mucosa of the bowel with either interrupted or running 5-0 PDS. The serosa is reapproximated over the ureter with 4-0 silk sutures. The serosal suture line is perpendicular to the course of the ureter. Where the ureters enter the serosa, they are also fixed with interrupted 4-0 PDS sutures. A lateral peritoneal flap is placed over the anastomosis.

The advantage of this anastomosis is that because the taeniae do not need to be aligned, one can form the tunnel according to the normal course of the ureter and avoid angulation. This technique reliably prevents reflux but results in a stricture rate of approximately 14% (see Table 80–4).

Pagano Technique

This method establishes a nonrefluxing ureterointestinal anastomosis by construction of a submucosal tunnel (Fig. 80–24) (Pagano, 1980). The taenia is incised for a length of 4 to 5 cm and the seromuscular layer separated from the mucosa on both sides of the taenia laterally as far as the mesenteric border. The ureter is brought in one end (i.e., the distal end) laterally and laid in the 4- to 5-cm tunnel paralleling the mesenteric border. A button of mucosa is excised, and the ureters are spatulated and sutured to the mucosa with either interrupted or running 5-0 PDS. The seromuscular layer is then closed loosely with silk sutures in the midline. Each suture includes the seromuscular layer of the taenia and the mucosa in the midline.

This technique has a reported low complication rate. The leakage rate is approximately 3%, the stricture rate is 6%, and the reflux rate is approximately 6% (see Table 80–4) (Pagano et al, 1984).

Cordonnier and Nesbit Technique

These techniques use no tunnel and are direct refluxing anastomoses of the ureter to the colon (Nesbit, 1949; Cordonnier, 1950). They are not desirable for ureterosigmoidostomies. They are performed in much the same way a Bricker anastomosis would be performed for the small bowel (see later).

Small Bowel Anastomoses

There are a number of ureter–small bowel anastomoses, which are of two basic types: end-to-side or end-to-end. The end-to-side anastomoses may be constructed in a refluxing or nonrefluxing manner.

Bricker Anastomosis

The Bricker anastomosis is a refluxing end-to-side ureter–small bowel anastomosis that is simple to perform and has a low complication rate (Fig. 80–25) (Bricker, 1950). Although originally described for the small bowel, it may be employed in any suitable intestinal segment.

In the original description, the adventitia of the ureter was sutured with interrupted silk sutures to the serosa of the bowel. The mucosa and serosa were incised; a small mucosa plug was removed; and with fine absorbable chromic sutures, the full thickness of the ureter was sewn to the mucosa of the bowel. The anterior layer of ureteral adventitia was then sewn with interrupted silk sutures to the serosa of the bowel. A less cumbersome method of performing this anastomosis is to excise a small button of seromuscular tissue and mucosa, spatulate the ureter for 0.5 cm, and suture the full thickness of the ureter to the full thickness of the bowel (i.e., mucosa and seromuscular layer to ureteral wall) with either interrupted or running 5-0 PDS. The anastomosis is stented with a soft Silastic catheter.

The stricture rate for this anastomosis varies between 4% and 22% (average of 6%). The leak rate is approximately 3% in the absence of stents (see Table 80–4).

Wallace Technique

A frequently employed anastomotic technique is that of Wallace, in which the end of the intestine is sutured to the end of the ureter (Fig. 80–26) (Wallace, 1970; Albert and Persky, 1971). This is a refluxing anastomosis. The intestinal segment employed may be either small bowel or colon. There are three basic types of anastomoses:

1. the end of one ureter is sutured to the end of the other ureter, and this composite anastomosis is sutured to the end of the bowel;
2. a Y anastomosis of the ureters is constructed, which is sutured to the end of the bowel; or

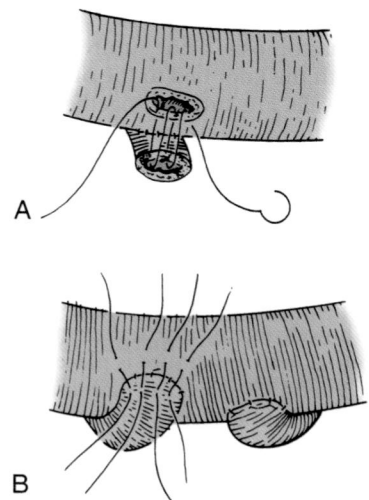

Figure 80–25. Bricker ureterointestinal anastomosis. **A,** The adventitia of the ureter is sutured to the serosa of the bowel. A small full-thickness serosal and mucosal plug is removed. Interrupted 5-0 PDS suture approximates the ureter to the full thickness of the mucosa and serosa. **B,** The anterior layer is completed by interrupted sutures placed through the adventitia of the ureter and the serosa of the small bowel.

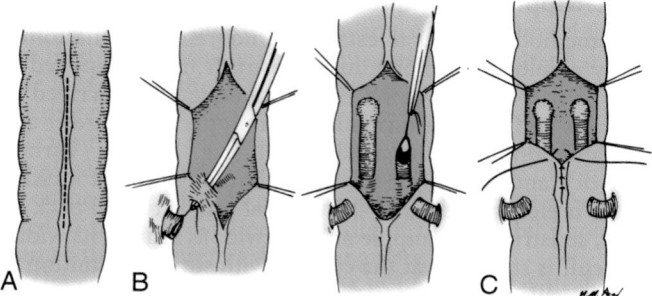

Figure 80–24. Pagano ureterointestinal anastomosis. **A,** A linear incision is made in the taenia between 4 and 5 cm in length. **B,** The submucosa is dissected from the mucosa laterally on both sides to the level of the mesentery. The ureters are drawn into the submucosal tunnel distally and sutured to the mucosa with 5-0 PDS suture proximally. **C,** The serosa is reapproximated, with incorporation of the mucosa in the midline.

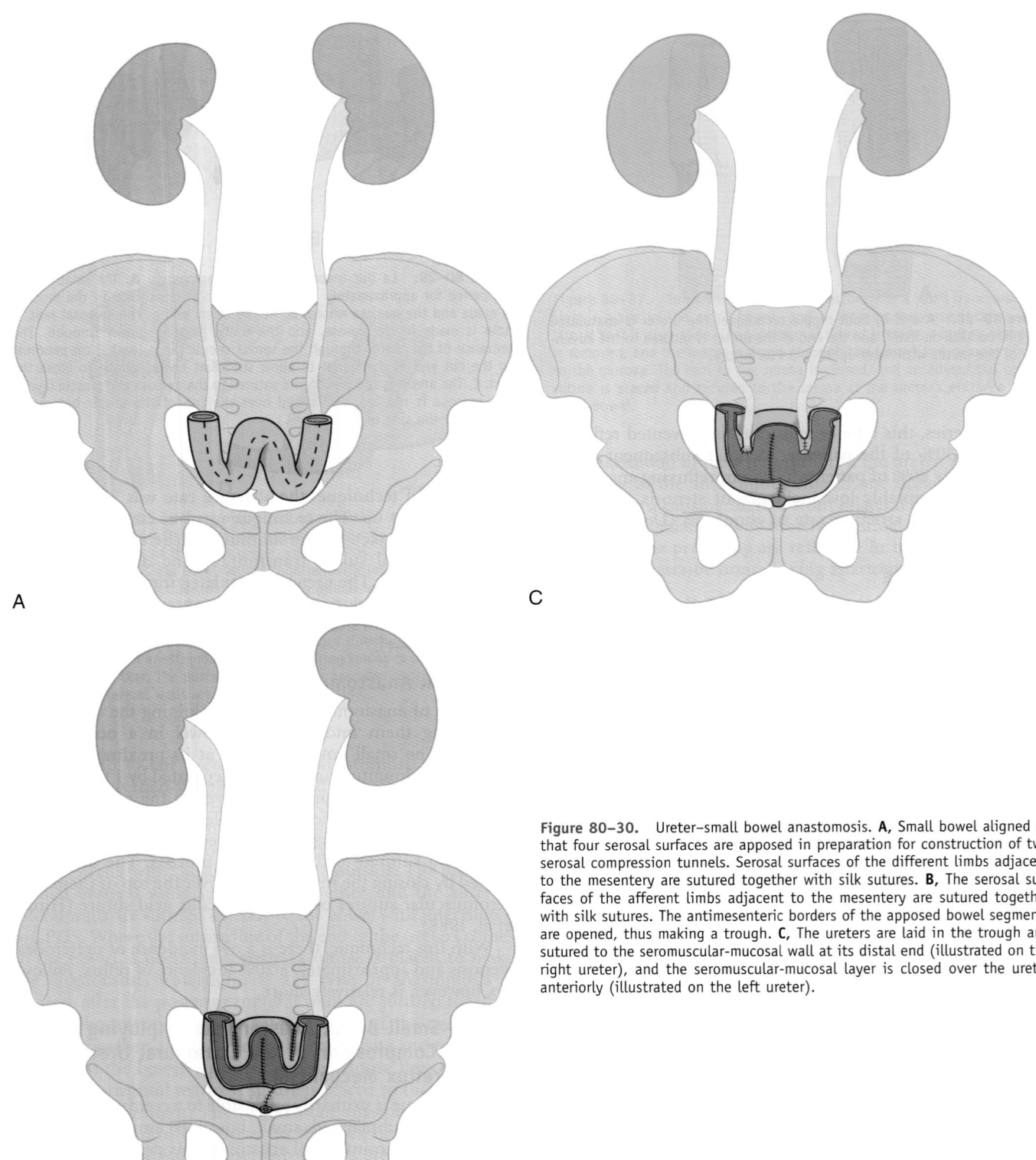

A

B

C

Figure 80–30. Ureter–small bowel anastomosis. **A,** Small bowel aligned so that four serosal surfaces are apposed in preparation for construction of two serosal compression tunnels. Serosal surfaces of the different limbs adjacent to the mesentery are sutured together with silk sutures. **B,** The serosal surfaces of the afferent limbs adjacent to the mesentery are sutured together with silk sutures. The antimesenteric borders of the apposed bowel segments are opened, thus making a trough. **C,** The ureters are laid in the trough and sutured to the seromuscular-mucosal wall at its distal end (illustrated on the right ureter), and the seromuscular-mucosal layer is closed over the ureter anteriorly (illustrated on the left ureter).

spatulated and sutured to the mucosal-seromuscular layer with 5-0 absorbable sutures. The edges of the opened small bowel are then reapproximated over the anterior ureter with absorbable sutures (Fig. 80–30C), thus making a serosal tunnel of 4 cm in length. When the bowel is distended, it then applies pressure to the extramural ureter, thus preventing reflux (Abol-Enein and Ghoneim, 1994).

With an average of 3 years of follow-up, the anastomotic stricture rate is 4% and the failure of the antireflux mechanism is 3% (Abol-Enein and Ghoneim, 2001; Turkolmez et al, 2004).

Intestinal Antireflux Valves

Another technique of preventing reflux into the ureter involves construction of an antireflux mechanism with bowel distal to the ureterointestinal anastomosis. The ureter is sutured by the technique of either Bricker or Wallace (as described earlier) to the end of the bowel, and the bowel is used to make a one-way valve. Unlike with individual ureterointestinal antirefluxing anastomosis, when these valves fail or stenose, both kidneys are affected. Three basic types of antireflux mechanisms commonly employed with use of the bowel are ileocecal intussusception, ileoileal intussusception, and ileal nipple valve placed into colon.

Intussuscepted Ileocecal Valve

The mesentery is cleaned from the ileum for a length of 8 cm beginning at the cecum and coursing proximal (Fig. 80–31).

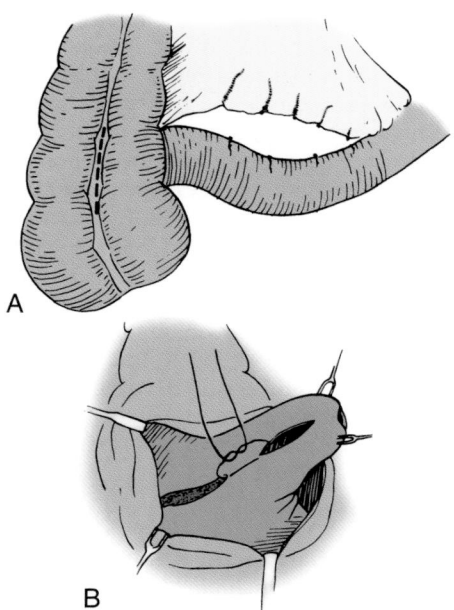

A

B

Figure 80–31. Ileocecal intussusception. **A,** An 8-cm segment of ileal mesentery is cleaned from the serosa beginning at the ileocecal junction. At least 5 cm of mesentery remains attached to the proximal ileum. An incision is made along a taenia at the level of the ileocecal valve. **B,** The ileum is intussuscepted over a No. 22 French catheter into the cecum under direct vision. The mucosa of the intussuscepted segment is incised, and the mucosa of the cecum adjacent to it is also incised. The muscle coats of both segments are sutured together. The serosa of the ileum is secured to the serosa of the cecum with interrupted 3-0 silk sutures placed circumferentially (not depicted).

At least 5 cm of ileum proximal to the detached mesentery must be intact to ensure intestinal viability. Thus, the ileum should not be transected less than 13 cm from the ileocecal junction. A No. 22 catheter is placed through the ileum into the cecum. The ileal serosa is scarified either by multiple cross-incisions with a knife or with the electrocautery unit. The 8-cm segment is intussuscepted over the catheter into the cecum. The intussuscepted ileum is secured to the cecal wall with 3-0 silk sutures placed circumferentially 2 mm apart.

The valve has a moderate tendency to fail because the intussusception has a significant chance of reduction. In one series, the antireflux mechanism remained intact in 55% of the patients during the long term (Hensle and Burbige, 1985). The intussusception may be made more secure by employing a modification described by King. The mesentery is cleaned as described before. The cecum is opened along a taenia, and the ileum is intussuscepted over the catheter under direct vision. Where the intussusception lies adjacent to the cecal wall, mucosa of the intussuscepted ileum and the cecal mucosa adjacent to it are incised down to muscle. The muscles are sewn each to the other with interrupted 3-0 chromic suture. Long-term follow-up in eight patients reveals maintenance of the antireflux valve in seven with the modified technique (King, 1987; Friedman et al, 1992).

Intussuscepted Ileal Valve

The mesentery is cleaned from an 8-cm segment of ileal serosa (Fig. 80–32). There must be 5 cm of ileal mesentery proximal and distal to the cleared segment to ensure proper blood supply. The ureters are sewn to the proximal end of ileum. The distal end of ileum is opened along its antimesenteric border to within 2 to 3 cm of the cleared mesentery to provide adequate exposure and direct visualization of the intussuscepted segment. A Babcock clamp is placed into the lumen of the bowel, and a portion of bowel wall is grasped by invaginating it into the clamp with a finger. The ileal segment is intus-

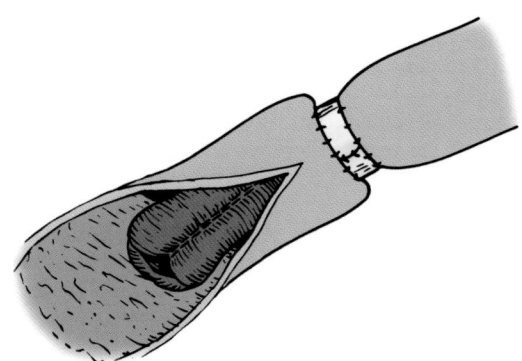

Figure 80–32. Intussuscepted ileal nipple valve. Eight centimeters of ileal mesentery is cleaned from the serosa. The ileum distally is opened within 2 to 3 cm of the rent in the mesentery. Five centimeters of ileum is intussuscepted, and it is secured by placement of staples in quadrants. The ileal mucosa is incised adjacent to an incision in the intussuscepted segment, and the two muscle coats are sutured together with interrupted 3-0 chromic suture. The serosa of the intussuscepted segment is sutured circumferentially to the base of the ileum, into which the proximal segment is intussuscepted with interrupted silk suture.

suscepted by pulling on the Babcock clamp with gentle constant traction. If there is resistance, the mesentery is generally too bulky, and it must be defatted carefully before trying again to intussuscept the segment. A 5-cm intussuscepted segment should protrude. The gastrointestinal stapler without the knife or the linear stapler, from which the distal five to eight staples have been removed, is used to secure the intussusception in place; three rows with the gastrointestinal stapler or four rows with the linear stapler are placed in quadrants. The staple size should be 4.8 mm. The proximal staples are important in securing the intussusception and preventing its reduction, whereas the distal staples are less effective and more likely to be exposed to urine and thus facilitate stone formation. It is for this reason that the distal staples are removed from the staple cartridge before it is placed in the stapler and before the intussusception is stapled. With the cautery unit, the mucosa of the intussusception is incised along its length. Adjacent to this incision, another is made in the mucosa of the ileum. The muscularis of both is exposed and sewn together with interrupted 3-0 chromic suture. The distal serosa is then sutured proximally to the serosa of the intussuscepted segment circumferentially with 3-0 nonabsorbable sutures. This is meant to secure the intussusception and to prevent its reduction with failure of the antireflux mechanism. The valve is successful in preventing reflux 90% of the time (Kock et al, 1982; Skinner et al, 1989).

Because the intussuscepted nipple valve as an antireflux mechanism has resulted in a 10% complication rate (5% stone formation on the exposed staples, 4% stenosis, and 1% prolapse [Stein et al, 1996]), modifications have been developed in an attempt to reduce these untoward outcomes. One such modification has been described by the University of Southern California group. An 8- to 10-cm isolated segment of ileum is tapered distally and laid between two segments of small bowel in which their serosal walls adjacent to the mesentery are sutured together. This serves as the posterior support for the isolated segment. The apposed bowel is opened along its antimesenteric border; lateral flaps are constructed adjacent to the segment and closed over its anterior aspect, thus making a serosal trough in which 4 cm of the segment of tapered ileum is positioned (Stein and Skinner, 2003). When the pouch is closed, a nipple valve is constructed. The concept is that as pressure in the pouch increases, the walls of the tapered nipple valve are compressed, thus preventing reflux. The authors call their modification a T pouch. At the time of this writing, long-term outcomes are not available.

Nipple Valve

The simplest intestinal antireflux valve to make is the nipple valve with use of ileum (Fig. 80–33). The mesentery is cleared from the last 8 cm of the cut end of the ileum. The distal 6 cm of serosa is scarified by multiple cross-striations and then turned back on itself to form a nipple. The nipple should be at least 4 to 4.5 cm in length. The end of the inverted ileum is then sutured to itself with interrupted 4-0 PDS. An incision on the taenia large enough to accommodate the segment is made. A No. 22 catheter is placed through the segment, and its serosa is sutured to the colon serosa circumferentially with interrupted 3-0 silk sutures placed 2 mm apart. The long-term success rate for this type of valve is unknown but would appear to be less than with the other two methods.

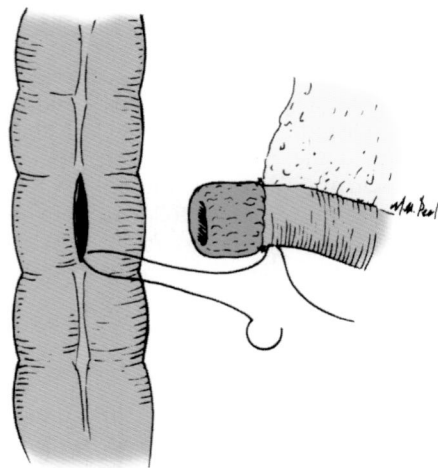

Figure 80–33. Nipple valve. Approximately 8 cm of mesentery is cleaned from the distal end of the ileum, and the serosa is scarified and then turned back on itself to form a nipple of approximately 4 cm in length. The end of the ileum is sutured to itself with interrupted 4-0 PDS. A rent is made in the colon through a taenia, and the nipple valve is placed through the rent and secured with circumferential interrupted 4-0 PDS through the full thickness of the colon and the seromuscular layer of the ileum.

Complications of Ureterointestinal Anastomoses

The complications that occur with ureterointestinal anastomoses include leakage, stricture, reflux in those anastomoses that were performed to prevent reflux, and pyelonephritis. In review of the various types of procedures, it appears that of the colonic antirefluxing procedures, the Pagano technique offers the lowest incidence of stricture with an acceptable incidence of reflux. With respect to small bowel antireflux procedures, the Le Duc procedure and the ureterointestinal serosal apposition procedure seem to offer the lowest incidence of stricture with the highest success rates in preventing reflux. With respect to stricture formation and leakage, it appears the Wallace technique has the best results. In a comparison of the Bricker, the Wallace, and the nipple valve, however, in one series there was no difference in complication rate among any of the procedures. All had an incidence of approximately 29% of some form of obstruction in the long term (Mansson et al, 1979). In a more recent study, there appeared to be no difference between rate of reflux and stricture when a Bricker anastomosis was compared with a split-cuff nipple. The incidence of stricture was 7% for both types (De Carli et al, 1997).

Urinary Fistula

Urinary fistulas invariably occur within the first 7 to 10 days postoperatively with an incidence of 3% to 9% (see Table 80–4) (Beckley et al, 1982; Loening et al, 1982). **The incidence of urinary intestinal leak is markedly reduced by the use of soft Silastic stents** (see earlier). A urinary intestinal leak may cause periureteral fibrosis and scarring with subsequent stricture formation.

Stricture

In general, **the antirefluxing techniques have a higher incidence of stricture.** Patients are at risk for ureterointestinal strictures for the life of the anastomosis and must be observed on a scheduled periodic basis. A stricture has been reported to develop 13 years after the procedure (Shapiro et al, 1975). **Ureteral strictures also occur away from the ureterointestinal anastomosis. This stricture is most common in the left ureter and is usually found as the ureter crosses over the aorta beneath the inferior mesenteric artery.** It has been suggested that this is due to too-aggressive stripping of adventitia and angulation of the ureter at the inferior mesenteric artery.

Once a stricture has developed, various techniques may be used to rectify the situation. The most successful is reexploration, with removal of the stenotic segment and reanastomosis of the ureter to the bowel by one of the aforementioned techniques. A number of studies have compared open surgical correction of ureterointestinal anastomotic strictures with endourologic methods. In general, **open repair has a success rate of approximately 75% at 3 years versus 15% for balloon dilation** with similar follow-up (DiMarco et al, 2001). Open surgical methods may be morbid and difficult procedures. Endourologic procedures employing balloon dilation have not proved to be durable, and therefore many have employed either cold knife incisions or laser incisions. **When several series employing endourologic methods are combined, there is a 50% to 60% success rate** with 2 years of follow-up. Strictures occurring in less than 1 year from the original procedure, strictures 1.5 cm or longer, and left-sided strictures have less favorable outcomes from endourologic methods (Kramolowsky et al, 1987, 1988; Cornud et al, 1996; Laven et al, 2001; Poulakis et al, 2003). These data must be viewed with caution since longer follow-up generally results in additional recurrences. In selected cases, metallic stents have been employed, which might be a reasonable approach in a patient with a limited life expectancy, thus avoiding a major open operation (Barbalias et al, 1998). A more recent study in which nonmalignant ureterointestinal strictures were stented reported that all patients were successfully treated with 2 years of follow-up; one patient developed a stone on the stent (Palascak et al, 2001).

Pyelonephritis

Acute pyelonephritis occurs both in the early postoperative period and during the long term. Its incidence is approximately 10% to 20% in patients diverted with ileal conduits and 9% in those diverted with antirefluxing colon conduits (see Table 80–3). **These complications cause considerable morbidity and in fact are associated with significant mortality.** In one series of intestinal segments in the urinary tract, 8 of 178 patients died of sepsis (Schmidt et al, 1973). **That these complications may result in delayed mortality is indicated by the fact that 2 of 115 children and 3 of 127 adults died of septic complications 5 to 14 years after intestinal diversion** (Pitts and Muecke, 1979). **When sepsis is associated with decreasing renal function and uremia, the morbidity and mortality are markedly increased.**

Table 80–4 summarizes the complications and success rates for the various types of anastomoses. The table is derived from composite reports in the literature in which specific anastomoses were described and from which the data could be accurately analyzed. Because of these two requirements, it is not possible to comment, for example, on the incidences of reflux or leakage among various anastomotic types inclusively. These complications can be minimized by adherence to the principles of ureterointestinal surgery discussed earlier.

RENAL DETERIORATION

The incidence of renal deterioration after conduit urinary intestinal diversion has varied from 10% to 60% (Koch et al, 1992; Madersbacher et al, 2003). This variance is perhaps due to the fact that many reports include both renal units that were abnormal and those that were normal before diversion. **In analyzing abnormal renal units before diversion and documenting progressive disease, it is difficult to be sure whether the urinary diversion caused the progression or whether progression is due to the intrinsic abnormality for which the diversion was constructed. When the incidence of renal deterioration is determined by comparing renal units that were normal before diversion and then deteriorated postoperatively, 18% of patients who have ileal conduits show progressive deterioration versus 13% who have nonrefluxing colon conduits** (see Table 80–3). Twenty percent of patients with nonrefluxing continent ileocecal bladders show some evidence of deterioration of the upper tracts when they are observed during the long term (Benchekroun, 1987). This deterioration leads to a 10% incidence of azotemia in children with ileal conduits (Schwarz and Jeffs, 1975) and a 12% (5 of 41 patients) incidence of renal failure in patients with colon conduits constructed for benign disease (Elder et al, 1979).

The incidence of both sepsis and renal failure is greater in patients with ureterosigmoidostomy than in those with conduits. Sepsis and renal failure may occur either in the immediate postoperative period or many years later. **The most common cause of death in patients who have had a ureterosigmoidostomy for more than 15 years is acquired renal disease (i.e., sepsis or renal failure).** In this group of patients, approximately 10% to 22% die of these disorders (Zabbo and Kay, 1986), some as late as 27 years after diversion (Mesrobian et al, 1988). **In patients with ileal conduits, about 6% ultimately die of renal failure** (Richie, 1974).

Renal Function Necessary for Urinary Intestinal Diversion

The amount of renal function required to effectively blunt the reabsorption of urinary solutes by the intestinal segment and to prevent serious metabolic side effects depends on the type of urinary intestinal diversion constructed (i.e., the amount of bowel to be used and the length of time the urine is exposed to the intestinal mucosa). Thus, **a greater degree of renal function is necessary for retentive (continent) diversions than for short conduit diversions.** Patients who have a glomerular filtration rate (GFR) on average above 40 mL/min generally tolerate a continent diversion reasonably well. Indeed, in one study, two groups of patients were analyzed: those with GFRs around 100 mL/min (range, 91 to 112) and those with GFRs around 55 mL/min (range, 36 to 69). Both seemed to tolerate the metabolic load well with a minimal development of metabolic acidosis. There was a slightly increased incidence of metabolic acidosis in the group with low GFR, as would be expected; however, in this group, distal tubule function was excellently maintained as demonstrated by ammonium chloride loading. This observation points out that GFR is not the sole determining factor that allows the body to manage intestinal diversion. Indeed, GFR is but one factor. Just as important is distal tubule function. This article confirms that when distal tubule function is normal and the GFR is above 40 mL/min, patients do extremely well (Kristjansson et al, 1997).

There are five components of renal function: renal blood flow, glomerular filtration, tubule transport, concentration and dilution, and glomerular permeability. Aspects of renal function that must be specifically addressed are GFR, best measured by inulin clearance; ability of the tubule to acidify, determined by ammonium chloride loading; concentrating ability, determined by water deprivation; and glomerular permeability, reflected by urine protein concentrations. **In general, patients with normal urine protein content who have a serum creatinine concentration below 2.0 mg/dL do well with intestine interposed in the urinary tract.** Serum cytostatin C is a promising serum protein that reflects GFR more accurately than creatinine; however, its usefulness in urinary intestinal diversion has not yet been determined (Herget-Rosenthal et al, 2004). At a level of serum creatinine below 2.0 mg/dL, renal blood flow, GFR, tubule transport, and concentrating and diluting ability are relatively well preserved. **In patients whose serum creatinine concentration exceeds 2.0 mg/dL and who are being considered for retentive diversion or in whom long segments of intestine will be used, a more detailed analysis of renal function is necessary. If the patient is able to achieve a urine pH of 5.8 or less after an ammonium chloride load, has a urine osmolality of 600 mOsm/kg or greater in response to water deprivation, has a GFR that exceeds 35 mL/min, and has minimal protein in the urine, the patient may be considered for a retentive diversion.**

URINARY DIVERSION

This section deals with specific types of conduit urinary diversion. Fundamentally, there are two types of conduits: those using the small bowel, which includes the jejunum or ileum; and those in which a portion of large bowel is used. Conduits made of stomach have been described but are rarely indicated and may carry with them difficult problems of stomal maintenance. Their construction is not discussed here. Each type of conduit has specific indications and advantages, and for each there are specific complications. Some complications, however, are similar among all types. **The indications for a conduit are the need for urinary diversion: after a cystectomy; because of a diseased bladder; before transplantation in a patient who has a bladder that cannot adequately receive the transplant ureter; and for dysfunctional bladders that result in persistent bleeding, obstructed ureters, poor compliance with upper tract deterioration, and inadequate storage with total urinary incontinence.**

Preparation

Regardless of whether small or large bowel is used for the conduit, **all patients require a bowel preparation** as outlined earlier. The specific types of ureterointestinal anastomosis and

stomal construction and their complications are also described in previous sections. This section describes features that are unique to the construction of the conduit. The complications cited for each conduit also depend on the length of follow-up and the concomitant procedure performed.

Ileal Conduit

In this procedure, a portion of distal ileum is chosen. **It is the simplest type of conduit diversion to perform and is associated with the fewest intraoperative and immediate postoperative complications. It is not advisable to use ileum for a conduit in patients with a short bowel syndrome, in patients with inflammatory small bowel disease, and in those whose ileum has received extensive irradiation, often as a consequence of prior radiation therapy for a pelvic malignant neoplasm.**

Procedure

A segment 10 to 15 cm in length is selected 10 to 15 cm from the ileocecal valve. The cecum and ileal appendage (i.e., that portion of the distal ileum fixed to the retroperitoneum) are mobilized. The ileal mesentery is transilluminated and a major arcade identified to the segment selected. With a mosquito clamp, the mesentery immediately beneath the bowel is penetrated, and the bowel is encircled with a vessel loop. An area at the base of the mesentery is selected that is to one side of the feeding vessel, and a second vessel loop is placed through the mesentery. At this juncture, the peritoneum overlying both sides of the mesentery is incised from bowel vessel loop to the base of mesentery vessel loop. With mosquito clamps, the tissue is clamped, severed, and tied with 4-0 silk. A portion of mesentery 2 cm in length is cleaned away from the bowel beneath the mesenteric incision. This procedure is repeated at the other end of the selected segment. The base of the mesentery should be as wide as possible and the mesenteric windows not excessive (generally about 5 cm in length) to prevent ischemia of the segment. Allen clamps are placed across the bowel in an angled fashion such that the antimesenteric portion is shorter than the mesenteric portion. (Some prefer to transect the bowel with staples, that is, anastomotic stapler.) Thus, a triangular piece of bowel is removed and discarded.

The isolated ileal segment is placed caudad, and an ileoileostomy is performed as described earlier (Fig. 80–34). The mesenteric window of the ileoileostomy is closed with interrupted 3-0 silk sutures. The isolated segment is then flushed with copious amounts of saline until the irrigant is clear, at which point the ureters are brought out the retroperitoneum in the right lower quadrant. To accomplish this, the left ureter must be brought over the great vessels and posterior to the sigmoid mesentery to the rent in the posterior peritoneum. This may be done by mobilizing the cecum cephalad to identify the right ureter. The left ureter may be identified by incising the line of Toldt of the left descending colon (Fig. 80–35). This dissection allows anastomosis of the ileal segment as proximal as is necessary to the ureter. Indeed, the ileum may be anastomosed directly to the renal pelvis on both sides if need be (Fig. 80–35C). After a cystectomy, the ureters are identified caudad to the iliac vessels and may be conveniently traced cephalad similar to the previous description.

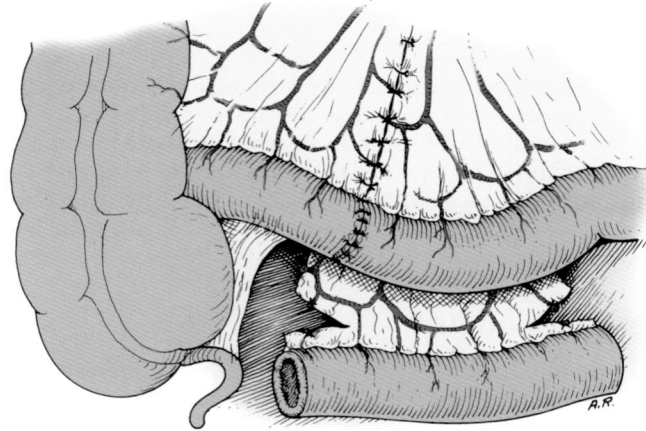

Figure 80–34. The isolated segment of ileum is placed caudal to the ileoileostomy. An incision on the mesentery of the isolated segment 1 cm from the bowel wall straightens the end. This is generally not necessary unless the mesentery is excessively bulky.

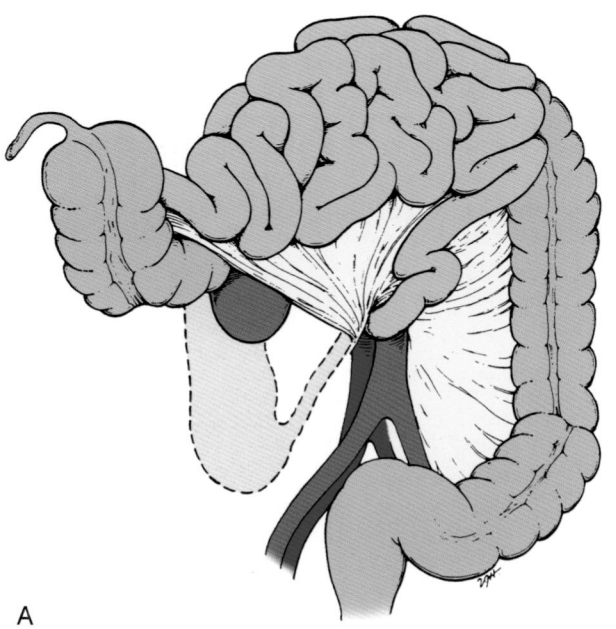

A

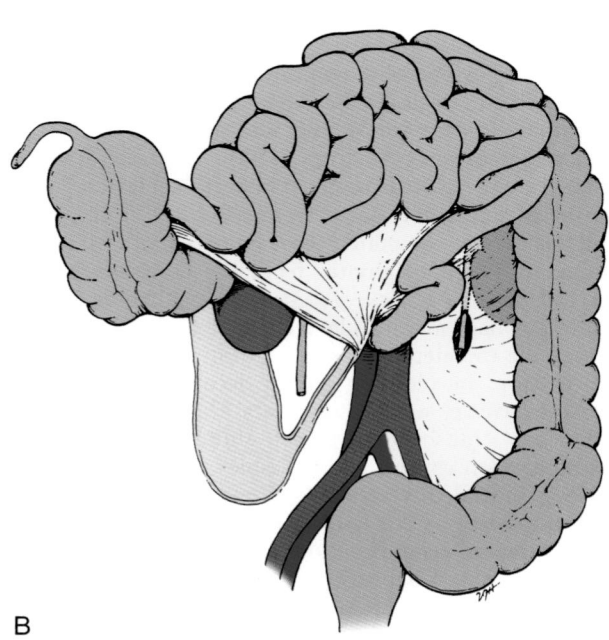

B

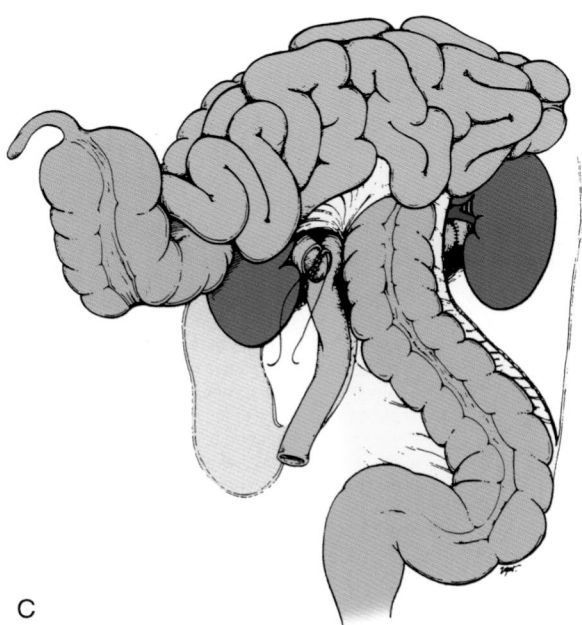

C

Figure 80–35. **A,** The cecum and root of the mesentery are incised. By blunt dissection, the cecum, ascending colon, and small bowel are mobilized cephalad. **B,** The right and left ureters are identified. The left ureter is more easily identified by mobilizing the left colon. **C,** The left colon is mobilized by incising the line of Toldt. This degree of mobilization allows anastomosis of the ileal segment to as proximal a position to the ureter as necessary. This figure depicts a left renal pelvic and right ureterointestinal anastomosis.

The ureteral-ileal anastomoses are performed as described previously. These anastomoses are stented.

A convenient method of introducing the stent through the loop to the opening in the bowel is illustrated in Figure 80–36. The base of the conduit is fixed to the retroperitoneum in the right lower quadrant by suturing the posterior peritoneum to the conduit, thus effectively retroperitonealizing the ureterointestinal anastomosis. The stoma is made as described previously. The authors prefer to suture the loop segment to the lateral peritoneal wall, thus obviating any chance of herniating small bowel lateral to the conduit. Many prefer to bring the segment directly to the anterior abdominal wall, however, thus allowing bowel to descend caudad on either side of the loop.

Complications

Early and late postoperative complications are listed in Table 80–5. It is difficult to clearly ascribe these complications solely to construction of the conduit because many are reported in patients undergoing a cystectomy as well. These incidences in Table 80–5 are therefore expected to reflect the high end of the spectrum. **Bleeding may occur from either the stoma or the conduit itself. Approximately 10% of patients have stomal bleeding. In 4%, it originates from the loop beneath the fascia** (Delgado and Muecke, 1973). Bleeding that is extremely difficult to manage may be due to cirrhosis and varices. In this situation, life-threatening bleeding from the conduit may occur. To stop the bleeding, portal decompression may be required (Chavez et al, 1994). A less morbid method involves percutaneous transhepatic portal shunt or transhepatic angiography with embolization (Lashley et al, 1997; Medina et al, 1998). Indeed, this has been successful in several reported cases. **Complications not listed include hypertension, renal failure, decreased renal function, and death.** These complications in large part depend on the concomitant procedure performed, the length of follow-up, and the status of the kidneys before diversion. **During the long term (20 years), 7% of patients have renal failure requiring dialysis, and 60% show deterioration of the upper tracts** (Koch et al, 1992). **After salvage cystectomy, complications are increased so that approximately one third of patients have one of the early complications** (Abratt et al, 1993). Also, the complication rate is increased in patients in whom an intestinal segment is used in those requiring renal transplantation (Nguyen et al, 1990).

One should be cautious in identifying duplex ureters. A failure to identify a second ureter on one side results in intraperitoneal urine leak and can cause excessive morbidity (Evans et al, 1994). The duplex ureters may be dealt with by implanting them separately if they are of sufficient caliber, or they may be spatulated, sewn together, and then implanted into the ileal conduit as a single unit (Fig. 80–37).

Jejunal Conduit

The jejunum has the largest diameter of the small bowel and the longest mesentery. Jejunal conduits generally have not had a high rate of acceptance because of perceived electrolyte abnormalities. A more recent report of patients, most of whom have been observed for more than 5 years, has shown that the bulk of electrolyte problems are minor—only about 4% in this series had severe hyponatremic metabolic acidosis. Renal calculi (12%), parastomal hernia (6%), and pyelonephritis (4%) constituted the majority of the remaining complications (Fontaine et al, 1997). The advantage of

Table 80–5.	Complications: Ileal Conduit*	
	Early	*Late*
Urine leak	2% (9/356)	
Bowel leak		
Sepsis	3% (7/230)	3% (4/142)
Acute pyelonephritis	3% (21/700)	18% (133/726)
Wound infection	7% (17/230)	2% (4/178)
Wound dehiscence	3% (11/326)	
Gastrointestinal bleed	2% (2/90)	
Abscess	2% (3/168)	
Prolonged ileus	6% (14/230)	
Conduit bleed	2% (3/178)	10% (18/178)
Intestinal obstruction	3% (18/610)	5% (42/878)
Ureteral obstruction	2% (14/610)	6% (56/878)
Parastomal hernia		2% (9/454)
Stomal stenosis		3% (143/486)
Stone formation		7% (59/822)
Excessive conduit length		9% (26/276)
Metabolic acidosis		13% (27/206)
Conduit infarction		2% (2/90)
Volvulus		7% (2/268)
Conduit stenosis		3% (11/320)
Conduit-enteric fistula		<1%

*Incidence as a percentage of the total number of reported cases from the literature. Numbers in parentheses are number of cases from which percentage is derived.

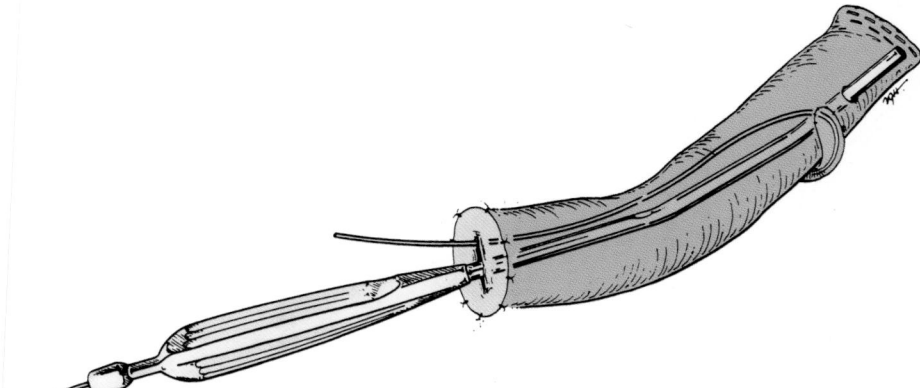

Figure 80–36. The ureterointestinal anastomoses should be stented with soft Silastic stents. These stents may be conveniently introduced with a Yankauer suction instrument from which the tip has been removed. The suction instrument is introduced by way of the distal end of the segment to the desired location of the ureteral anastomosis. When one cuts down on the Yankauer tip, its end protrudes through the bowel at the desired site. The stent is threaded through the suction instrument and the instrument removed.

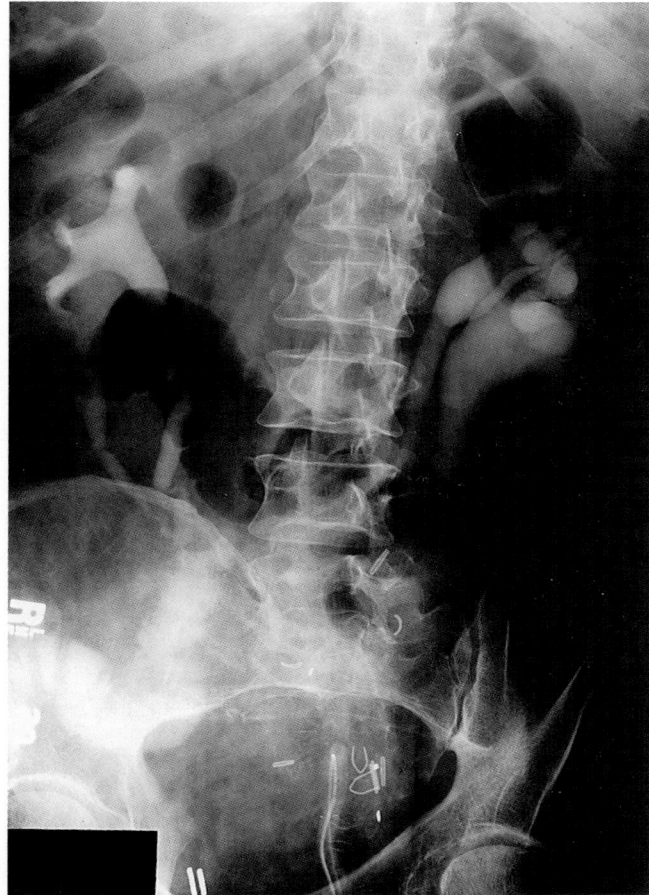

Figure 80–37. Intravenous urogram 6 days postoperatively in a patient who had bilateral duplex ureters. The ureters on each side were spatulated, sewn together, and anastomosed to the ileum.

Table 80–6.	**Complications: Jejunal Conduit***	
	Early	**Late**
Urine leak	14% (3/21)	
Wound dehiscence	5% (1/21)	
Acute pyelonephritis		10% (2/21)
Gastrointestinal bleed	4% (1/27)	
Electrolyte abnormalities		27% (17/62)
Stomal stenosis		7% (2/27)
Bowel obstruction		7% (2/27)
Ureteral stricture		12% (5/41)
Enteric fistula	2% (4/140)	

*Incidence as a percentage of the total number of reported cases from the literature. Numbers in parentheses are number of cases from which percentage is derived.

using the jejunum is that it avoids irradiated bowel and ureter. It is difficult to make a case for the jejunal conduit except in circumstances in which it is inadvisable to use either colon or ileum. However, this series does point out that when necessary, one can successfully use jejunum as a conduit. This might occur in patients who have extensive irradiation that involves the ileum, those with severe adhesions of the ileum and absence of the large bowel, and those who have an absent colon with inflammatory disease of the distal small bowel. **The contraindications to its use are severe bowel nutritional disorders and the presence of another acceptable segment.**

Procedure

The procedure is similar to that for an ileal conduit. A 10- to 15-cm segment of jejunum is isolated 15 to 25 cm from the ligament of Treitz as described for the ileal conduit. One should plan for the stoma to be in the upper quadrant, generally the left upper quadrant. The remainder of the technique is as described for the ileal conduit.

Complications

The early and long-term complications are similar to those listed for ileal conduit except that the electrolyte abnormality is a hyperkalemic, hyponatremic metabolic acidosis instead of the hyperchloremic metabolic acidosis of ileal diversion (Table 80–6). The treatment of the jejunal syndrome consists of administration of sodium chloride and sodium bicarbonate. Thiazides may also be used and are helpful in allaying the hyperkalemia (Hasan et al, 1994).

Colon Conduit

Three types of colon conduits are commonly used: transverse, sigmoid, and ileocecal. Each has specific indications with advantages and disadvantages.

The transverse colon is used when one wants to be sure that the segment of conduit employed has not been irradiated in individuals who have received extensive pelvic irradiation. It is also an excellent segment when an intestinal pyelostomy needs to be performed. The sigmoid conduit is a good choice in patients undergoing a pelvic exenteration who will have a colostomy. Thus, no bowel anastomosis needs to be made. It also allows nonrefluxing submucosal reimplantation and provides for an easily placed left-sided stoma when that is desirable.

The use of sigmoid colon is contraindicated with disease of this segment or when the hypogastric arteries have been ligated and the rectum has been left in situ. The latter circumstance may result in sloughing of the rectum or its mucosa because its blood supply of necessity is interrupted. **It is also unwise to use this segment in individuals with extensive pelvic irradiation** because it has probably been included in the radiation fields.

An ileocecal conduit has the advantage of providing a long segment of ileum when long segments of ureter need replacement as well as the advantage of providing colon for the stoma. It is also used in situations in which free reflux of urine from the conduit to the upper tracts is thought to be undesirable. **Contraindications to the use of transverse, sigmoid, and ileocecal conduits include the presence of inflammatory large bowel disease and severe chronic diarrhea.**

Procedure

Transverse Colon. The segment may be isolated on the right or middle colic arteries, most commonly the latter (Fig. 80–38). The gastrocolic ligament is taken down and the omentum dissected from the portion of colon that is to be isolated. The splenic and hepatic flexures should be mobilized

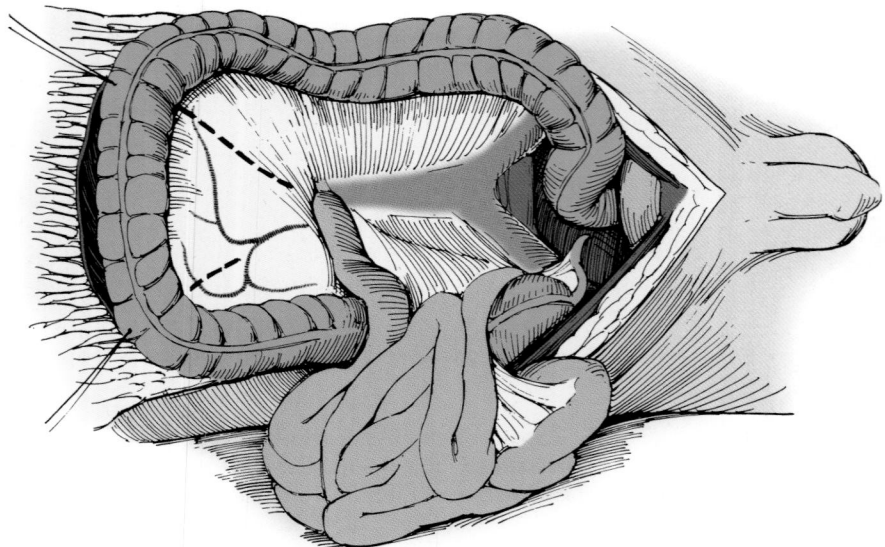

Figure 80–38. Transverse colon conduit may be based on right colic or middle colic arteries (depicted). (From Hinman F Jr: Atlas of Urologic Surgery. Philadelphia, WB Saunders, 1989.)

next. The proper length of segment is determined by taking into consideration the desired location of the stoma and the length of available ureters. In general, a length of 15 cm is sufficient. It is important not to isolate a segment that is too short and therefore incapable of reaching the retroperitoneum in such a position that a tension-free ureterocolonic anastomosis may be performed and retroperitonealized. The segment is isolated between bowel clamps, and a two-layer colocolostomy or stapled anastomosis is performed as outlined earlier. The segment is placed caudad to the anastomosis. If a colopyelostomy is to be performed, the segment should be placed cephalad to the bowel anastomosis. The isolated segment is irrigated with copious amounts of saline until the effluent is clear. The proximal end is closed with a running Connell suture of 3-0 chromic and a second layer of Lembert sutures of 3-0 silk. The ureterocolic anastomoses are then performed (see earlier), and the end is anchored to the retroperitoneum close to the midline. The stoma is usually placed in the right upper quadrant but may be placed anywhere in the abdomen if indicated.

Sigmoid Colon. The sigmoid colon is mobilized by incising its peritoneal attachments and the line of Toldt along the descending colon. The segment is isolated on the sigmoid vessels and placed lateral to the sigmoid colon (Fig. 80–39). The anastomosis of the sigmoid colon and ureterocolic anastomosis are as described for the transverse colon.

Ileocecal Conduit. The ileocecal conduit is based on the terminal branches of the superior mesenteric artery (i.e., ileocecal artery). The segment is placed caudad, and an ileum–ascending colon anastomosis is performed as described previously. The stoma is placed in the right lower quadrant. The ileocecal valve may be reinforced to ensure prevention of reflux. This is described earlier (see Fig. 80–31). For the ureterointestinal anastomoses, see previously as well.

Complications

Early and late complications after a transverse colon (Beckley et al, 1982; Ravi et al, 1994; Schmidt et al, 1985), sigmoid, or ileocecal conduit are listed in Tables 80–7 to 80-9. As is true

Table 80–7. Complications: Transverse Colon Conduit*	Early	Late
Urine leak	8% (11/137)	8% (2/25)
Acute pyelonephritis		11% (8/75)
Wound infection	5% (5/92)	
Wound dehiscence	7% (8/109)	
Abscess		5% (3/62)
Prolonged ileus	6% (2/30)	
Ureteral stricture	6% (5/84)	17% (37/215)
Bowel obstruction	3% (1/30)	2% (2/109)
Parastomal hernia		4% (5/114)
Stones		11% (11/98)
Enterocutaneous fistula		2% (1/62)
Stomal stenosis		2% (1/62)
Stomal prolapse		11% (6/56)
Metabolic acidosis		12% (3/26)

*Incidence as a percentage of the total number of reported cases from the literature. Numbers in parentheses are number of cases from which percentage is derived.

Table 80–8. Complications: Sigmoid Conduit*	Early	Late
Urine leak	1% (1/70)	
Wound infection	1% (1/70)	
Wound dehiscence	1% (1/70)	
Acute pyelonephritis		7% (5/70)
Bowel obstruction		6% (4/70)
Ureteral stricture		9% (6/70)
Stones		4% (3/70)
Parastomal hernia		3% (2/70)
Stomal stenosis		3% (2/70)

*Incidence as a percentage of the total number of reported cases from the literature. Numbers in parentheses are number of cases from which percentage is derived.

for the small bowel, complications not listed, including death, renal failure, and renal deterioration, depend on the concomitant procedure performed and the length of follow-up. Interestingly, early reports suggested a lower incidence of renal deterioration with colon conduits, but some recent series suggest that the incidence of these complications is about the

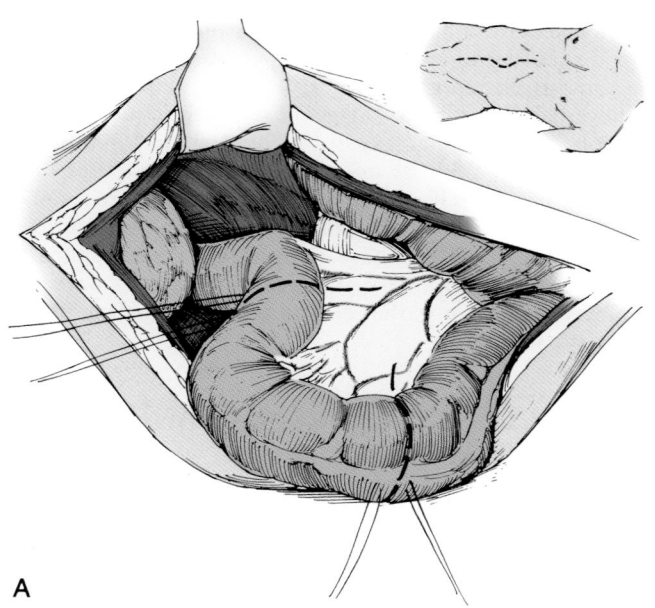

A

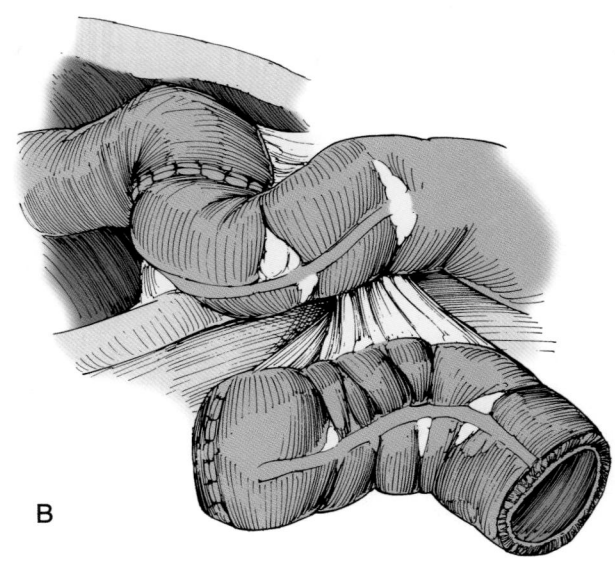

B

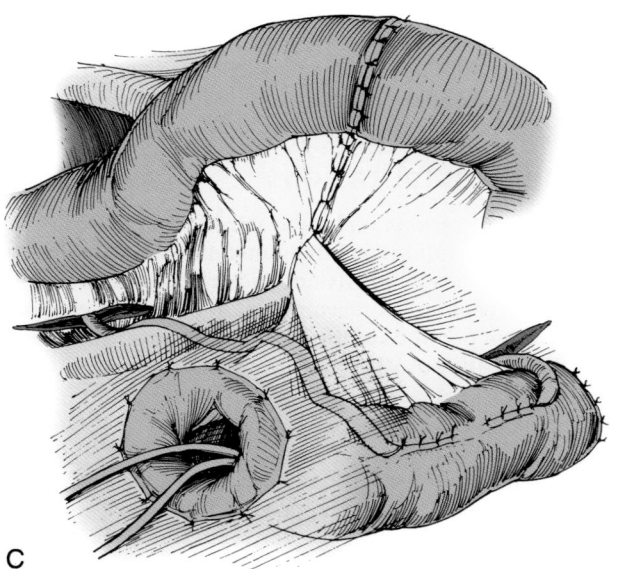

C

Figure 80–39. **A,** The sigmoid colon is freed of any peritoneal attachments. **B,** The segment is isolated and placed laterally. Bowel continuity is restored and the mesenteric window closed. **C,** The ureters are anastomosed to the colon and stented. (**A** to **C,** from Hinman F Jr: Atlas of Urologic Surgery. Philadelphia, WB Saunders, 1989.)

same. However, there continue to be proponents of the colon conduit in that during the long term, there appears to be a 7.6% incidence of pyelonephritis and a 78% incidence of preservation of the upper tracts (Stein et al, 1996).

Complications of the ileocecal conduit in one reported series occurred in 21% of patients (Matsuura et al, 1991). In this series, complications of the ileal conduit were compared with those of the ileocecal conduit, and there appeared to be no difference in the frequency of early and late postoperative complications. Early complications included urinary leakage, bowel obstruction, fecal leakage, acute renal failure, fulminant

hepatitis, pneumonia, gastrointestinal bleeding, hemorrhage, perforation of ileum, heart failure, and wound dehiscence. Late complications included stomal prolapse, acute pyelonephritis, bowel obstruction, urinary stones, parastomal hernia, incisional hernia, stomal stenosis, and fecal leakage. There was no difference in the incidence of deterioration of the upper tracts with either form of diversion. Of some note is that at high pressures, a large portion of the ileocecal conduits experienced reflux. At low pressures, however, there was minimal or no reflux. Whenever a portion of colon is used for a conduit, chronic diarrhea may be a consequence.

Table 80–9. Complications: Ileocecal Conduit*

	Early	Late
Urine leak	6% (9/147)	
Bowel leak	3% (5/147)	
Gastrointestinal bleed	1% (1/147)	
Wound dehiscence	7% (11/147)	
Acute pyelonephritis		14% (20/147)
Bowel obstruction	3% (5/147)	10% (14/147)
Stomal prolapse		16% (24/147)
Parastomal hernia		5% (7/147)
Stomal stenosis		2% (3/147)
Stones		5% (8/147)
Fecal fistula		2% (3/147)

*Incidence as a percentage of the total number of reported cases from the literature. Numbers in parentheses are number of cases from which percentage is derived.

Ileal Vesicostomy

An ileal vesicostomy uses spatulated ileum and a generous transverse cystotomy to decompress the bladder and to allow an appliance to be used on the abdomen. This procedure is particularly well suited to spinal cord injury patients or those with significant neurologic disease. The concept is that patients with a neurogenic bladder have an easier job of caring for themselves with an abdominal stoma. Patients who are particularly good candidates are those with significant detrusor–external sphincter dyssynergia. Those who have detrusor hyperreflexia, particularly women, may have an increased incidence of incontinence. The complications of the procedure include urethral incontinence requiring closure of the urethra in 20% of patients, stomal stenosis, and bladder and renal calculi.

The procedure is performed by spatulating an ileal segment and performing a generous transverse cystotomy. The spatulated ileum is sutured to the bladder with absorbable suture, and the distal segment is brought to the abdominal wall by fashioning a rosebud stoma. This results theoretically in a low-pressure reservoir. Its appeal is that if indicated at a later date, the patient's anatomy can be converted back to normal (Mutchnik et al, 1997; Atan et al, 1999).

Management Common to All Conduits

All anastomoses are stented with Silastic disposable stents. A convenient method for introducing the stents through the conduit and into the ureter is illustrated in Figure 80–36. They are removed individually on the fourth to sixth postoperative days. If there is no increase in drainage, the Jackson-Pratt closed-suction drain is removed. **All conduits are retroperitonealized,** with the ureterointestinal anastomosis being placed in the retroperitoneum. This may be accomplished by suturing the posterior peritoneum to the serosa of the conduit above the ureterointestinal anastomosis. A drain may then be laid into the retroperitoneum. The authors prefer to drain the ureterointestinal anastomosis with a Jackson-Pratt closed-suction drain laid in the retroperitoneum 3 to 4 cm away from the anastomosis. The peritoneal cavity should not be drained.

All patients are given nothing by mouth until bowel function returns. A progressive diet is instituted after confirmation

of bowel activity. It has been the authors' practice to use nasogastric tube decompression in all patients having a bowel anastomosis. In reported surgical series, it is clear that there are advantages and disadvantages of nasogastric tube decompression after intestinal surgery. Without its use, vomiting is more common. With its use, pulmonary complications are more of a problem. For those individuals with severe respiratory disease, consideration should be given to performing a gastrostomy. All patients have compression boots applied as prophylaxis for pulmonary embolus. The authors have not employed heparin or warfarin (Coumadin) prophylaxis in this group of patients.

METABOLIC AND NEUROMECHANICAL PROBLEMS OF URINARY INTESTINAL DIVERSION

Problems that result from interposition of intestine in the urinary tract may be conveniently divided into three areas for the purposes of discussion: metabolic, neuromechanical, and technical-surgical. Metabolic complications are the result of altered solute reabsorption by the intestine of the urine that it contains. Neuromechanical aspects involve the configuration of the gut, which affects storage volume and contraction of the intestine that may lead to difficulties in storage. Finally, technical-surgical complications involve aspects of the procedure that result in surgical morbidity; these have been discussed after each section on the technical aspects of urinary intestinal diversion. The following is a discussion of metabolic and neuromechanical problems.

Metabolic Complications

Metabolic complications include electrolyte abnormalities, altered sensorium, abnormal drug metabolism, osteomalacia, growth retardation, persistent and recurrent infections, formation of renal and reservoir calculi, problems ensuing from removal of portions of the gut from the intestinal tract, and development of urothelial or intestinal cancer. Many of these complications are a consequence of altered solute absorption across the intestinal segment. **The factors that influence the amount of solute and type of absorption are the segment of bowel used, the surface area of the bowel, the amount of time the urine is exposed to the bowel, the concentration of solutes in the urine, the renal function, and the pH of the fluid.**

Electrolyte Abnormalities

Serum electrolyte complications and the type of electrolyte abnormalities that occur are different, depending on the segment of bowel used. If stomach is employed, a hypochloremic metabolic alkalosis may occur. If jejunum is the segment used, hyponatremia, hyperkalemia, and metabolic acidosis occur. If the ileum or colon is used, a hyperchloremic metabolic acidosis ensues. Other electrolyte abnormalities that have been described include hypokalemia, hypomagnesemia, hypocalcemia, hyperammonemia, and elevated blood urea nitrogen and creatinine. Specific abnormalities for each segment of intestine are detailed.

Table 80–10. **Syndromes of Electrolyte Disturbances in Patients in Whom Bowel Is Interposed in the Urinary Tract**

Syndrome	Segment	Symptoms	Associated Abnormalities
Syndrome of severe metabolic alkalosis	Stomach	Lethargy, muscle weakness, respiratory insufficiency, seizures, ventricular arrhythmia	Elevated aldosterone, hypochloremia, hypokalemia
Syndrome of hyperkalemia, hypochloremia, metabolic acidosis	Jejunum	Lethargy, nausea, vomiting, dehydration, muscle weakness	Elevated renin, angiotensin
Syndrome of hyperchloremia, metabolic acidosis	Ileum, colon	Fatigue, anorexia, lethargy, weakness	Total-body potassium depletion, hypocalcemia

When stomach is used, a hypochloremic, hypokalemic metabolic alkalosis may ensue. This is generally not a significant problem unless the patient has concomitant renal failure, in which case there is a significant impairment of bicarbonate excretion or the patient is significantly dehydrated (Kurzrock et al, 1998). The metabolic alkalosis on occasion can be severe and life-threatening (syndrome of severe metabolic alkalosis) (Table 80–10). This syndrome has been reported in patients with normal renal function. When it is fully manifested, lethargy, respiratory insufficiency, seizures, and ventricular arrhythmias may occur (Gosalbez et al, 1993). These symptoms are usually preceded by vomiting resulting in dehydration. A pronounced hypochloremic, hypokalemic metabolic alkalosis ensues. Patients are generally successfully treated with an H2 blocker to reduce proton secretion by the gastric segment and rehydration. In life-threatening circumstances, arginine hydrochloride infusion has been employed to rapidly restore acid-base balance. On occasion, when the H2 blockers are ineffective, the proton pump blocker omeprazole has been successfully employed. Rarely, omeprazole is ineffective, and if the life-threatening metabolic alkalosis persists, the gastric segment must be removed (Gosalbez et al, 1993).

The role the serum concentration of gastrin plays appears pivotal in the syndrome. In the severe cases that have been reported, there is generally an elevated serum gastrin level. We have shown that **serum gastrin levels are significantly correlated with systemic bicarbonate concentration in gastrocystoplasty patients;** the greater the gastrin level, the more severe the metabolic alkalosis (Tanrikut and McDougal, 2004). When volume depletion, hypochloremia, and hypokalemia result from vomiting in those who normally have elevated circulating gastrin levels and a persisting long-standing metabolic alkalosis, the patient is at greater risk for development of the syndrome of severe metabolic alkalosis and manifestation of the symptoms outlined before. Thus, persistent loss of protons from the gastric-augmented bladder with net addition of bicarbonate to the systemic circulation, alteration of normal homeostatic mechanisms for acute changes in acid-base balance, and impaired ability of even a normal kidney to excrete bicarbonate in the face of hypochloremia, hypokalemia, and increased circulating aldosterone levels (due to the dehydration) create a vicious circle in which normal homeostatic mechanisms are circumvented. Indeed, elevated aldosterone levels have been reported in this syndrome (Gosalbez et al, 1993). Hypokalemia, hypochloremia, and increased aldosterone levels impair the kidney's ability to excrete excess bicarbonate. These perturbations coupled with a continued addition of bicarbonate from

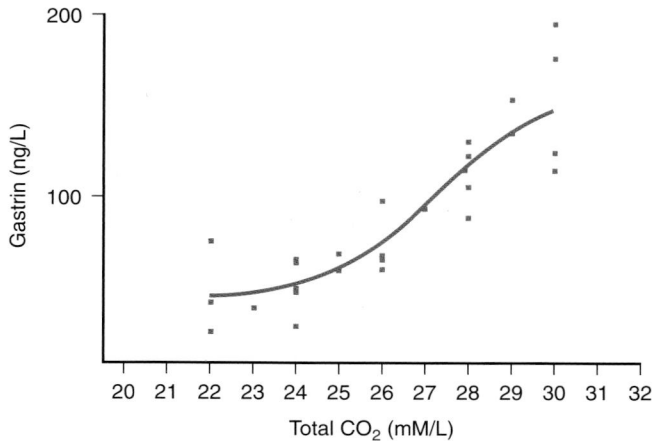

Figure 80–40. Sigmoid relationship of serum gastrin level to serum bicarbonate. Notice that over the physiologic range of normal gastrin levels, 10 to 120 ng/L, there is little change in serum bicarbonate. However, at levels of serum gastrin in excess of 120 ng/L, small changes in serum gastrin levels result in large changes in serum bicarbonate.

the gastric segment produces the extreme electrolyte abnormalities noted in the patients described. In view of the **sigmoid correlation of serum bicarbonate to gastrin levels in patients with gastric segments in the urinary tract, patients at most risk for development of the syndrome of severe metabolic alkalosis are those whose serum gastrin concentrations exceed 120 ng/L, since on this portion of the curve, small additional increments in gastrin concentration result in large increases in serum bicarbonate** (Fig. 80–40). On the other hand, patients with serum gastrin concentrations below 100 ng/L can have significant increases in gastrin levels with little change in serum bicarbonate. **Failure to properly empty the diversion with overdistention of the gastric segment would be expected to increase the serum gastrin level as stretch is a stimulus for gastrin release. For those who have either an elevated resting gastrin level in excess of 120 ng/L or impaired renal function, both patient and physician should be made aware of the consequences of dehydration and distention of the segment.**

Electrolyte disorders that occur when jejunum is used for urinary intestinal diversion, particularly when proximal jejunum is used, **include hyponatremia, hypochloremia, hyperkalemia, azotemia, and acidosis** (see Table 80–10). These disorders result from an increased secretion of sodium and chloride with an increased reabsorption of potassium and hydrogen ions. This excessive loss of sodium chloride carries with it water, and thus the patient becomes dehydrated. The dehydration results in hypovolemia, which increases renin secretion and thereby aldosterone production (Golimbu and Morales, 1975). Aldosterone production may also be stimulated by hyperkalemia. The high levels of renin-aldosterone facilitate sodium reabsorption by the kidney and potassium loss, which produces a urine low in sodium content and high in potassium. This, when presented to the jejunum, results in a favorable concentration gradient for loss of sodium by the jejunum and increased reabsorption of potassium, thus perpetuating the abnormalities.

These electrolyte abnormalities result in lethargy, nausea, vomiting, dehydration, muscle weakness, and elevated temperature. If the abnormalities are allowed to persist, the patient may become moribund and finally die. **This syndrome may be exacerbated by administration of hyperalimentation solutions.** The mechanism by which hyperalimentation solutions exacerbate this syndrome in patients with jejunal intestine interposed in the urinary tract is unclear (Bonnheim et al, 1984). **The severity of the syndrome depends on the location of the segment of jejunum that is used. The more proximal the segment, the more likely the syndrome is to develop.** Its incidence varies from a low of 25% (Klein et al, 1986) to the majority of patients demonstrating significant abnormalities. Severe abnormalities may occur in as few as 4% when short segments are employed (Fontaine et al, 1997). Treatment of the disorder is rehydration with sodium chloride and correction of the acidosis with sodium bicarbonate. Provided that renal function is normal, the hyperkalemia is corrected by renal secretion. On occasion, a diuretic may be helpful to correct the hyperkalemia. After restoration of normal electrolyte balance, long-term therapy involves oral supplements with sodium chloride. A thiazide diuretic has also been useful in selected cases to control hyperkalemia during the long term (Hasan et al, 1994).

The electrolyte abnormality that occurs with the ileum and colon is hyperchloremic metabolic acidosis (see Table 80–10). This acidosis occurs to some degree in most patients who have ileum or colon interposed in the urinary tract but is generally of a minor degree. Its clinical significance when it is of a minor degree at this time is unknown. Hyperchloremic acidosis has been reported with a frequency of 68% of patients (19 of 28 patients; 10 of the 19 cases were severe enough to require treatment) with ileal conduits (Castro and Ram, 1970). In another study, 70% of patients with ileal conduits observed for 4 years or more had a decreased serum bicarbonate concentration (Malek et al, 1971). Severe electrolyte disturbances occur to a much lesser degree. It has been reported to be a major problem in 18% of patients (8 of 45) with intestinal cystoplasties (Whitmore and Gittes, 1983), in 10% of patients (17 of 178) with ileal conduits (Schmidt et al, 1973), and in 80% of patients (112 of 141) with ureterosigmoidostomies (Ferris and Odel, 1950). In continent diversions involving either ileum and cecum or cecum alone, the majority of patients have an elevated serum chloride and depressed serum bicarbonate (Ashken, 1987; McDougal et al, 1989). Sixty-five percent of patients with Mainz pouches require alkali therapy to maintain a normal acid-base balance (Thuroff et al, 1987). Early reports of patients with continent diversions made of ileum have a much lower incidence of electrolyte problems, in the range of 10% to 15% (see Table 80–3) (Allen et al, 1985; Boyd et al, 1989). **Symptoms in those in whom the syndrome**

is severe include **easy fatigability, anorexia, weight loss, polydipsia, and lethargy.** Those with ureterosigmoidostomies also have an exacerbation of diarrhea.

These electrolyte abnormalities, if significant and allowed to persist, result in major metabolic abnormalities, to be discussed subsequently. In and of themselves, however, they may be lethal as severe electrolyte abnormalities have contributed to death of patients (Heidler et al, 1979).

The mechanism of hyperchloremic metabolic acidosis is due to the ionized transport of ammonium. Ammonium substitutes for sodium in the Na^+-H^+ antiport. The exchange of the weak acid NH_4 for a proton is coupled with the exchange of bicarbonate for chloride. **Thus, ammonium chloride is absorbed across the lumen into the blood in exchange for carbonic acid (i.e., CO_2 and water).** Ammonium may also gain entry to the blood from bowel lumen through potassium channels (McDougal et al, 1995).

The treatment of hyperchloremic metabolic acidosis involves administration of alkalizing agents or blockers of chloride transport. Alkalinization with oral sodium bicarbonate is effective in restoring normal acid-base balance. Oral administration of bicarbonate may not be tolerated particularly well, however, because it can produce considerable intestinal gas. An effective alternative is sodium citrate and citric acid solution (Bicitra or Shohl's solution) used together; however, many patients do not care for the taste. Potassium citrate, sodium citrate, and citric acid solution (Polycitra) may be used instead if excessive sodium administration is a problem because of cardiac or renal disease and if potassium supplementation is desirable or at least not harmful. In those patients in whom persistent hyperchloremic metabolic acidosis occurs and in whom excessive sodium loads are undesirable, chlorpromazine or nicotinic acid may be used to limit the degree of the acidosis. These agents used alone do not correct the acidosis in humans, but they limit its development and thus reduce the need for alkalinizing agents. Chlorpromazine and nicotinic acid inhibit cyclic adenosine monophosphate and thereby impede chloride transport. Chlorpromazine may be given in a dose of 25 mg three times a day. On occasion, as much as 50 mg three times a day may be necessary, but at such doses, side effects are not uncommon. Chlorpromazine should be used with care in adults because there are many untoward side effects, including tardive dyskinesia. Nicotinic acid may be given in a dose of 400 mg three or four times a day. The drug should not be used in patients with peptic ulcer disease or significant hepatic insufficiency. Side effects that may be observed include exacerbation of liver dysfunction, exacerbation of peptic ulcer disease, headaches, and double vision. Flushing and dermatitis are not uncommon and generally disappear as the patient becomes adapted to the drug.

Hypokalemia and total-body depletion of potassium may occur in patients with urinary intestinal diversion. This is more common in patients with ureterosigmoidostomies than it is in patients who have other types of urinary intestinal diversion (Geist and Ansell, 1961). In one study, patients with ureterocolonic diversions had a 30% reduction in total-body potassium, whereas those with ileal conduits had, as a group, no significant alteration in total-body potassium; individually, however, some had as much as a 14% reduction in total-body potassium (Williams et al, 1967). Patients with continent diversions have also been noted to have a decrease in total-body potassium. The patients most susceptible to total-body potassium depletion are those with long-standing uncorrected metabolic acidosis (Stein et al, 1998). **The potassium depletion is probably due to renal potassium wasting as a consequence of renal damage, osmotic diuresis, and gut loss through intestinal secretion.** The last-mentioned (probably quantitatively) plays a relatively minor role. Indeed, it has been shown that ileal segments exposed to high concentrations of potassium in the urine reabsorb some of the potassium, whereas colon is less likely to do so (Koch et al, 1990). Thus, **those with ileum interposed in the urinary tract likely blunt the potassium loss by the kidney, whereas those with colon do not, thus explaining why patients with ureterosigmoidostomies and ureterocolonic diversions are more likely to have total-body potassium depletion.** When the depletion is severe, the patient may develop a flaccid paralysis. **In treating these patients, one must remember that if the hypokalemia is associated with severe hyperchloremic metabolic acidosis, treatment must involve both replacement of potassium and correction of the acidosis with bicarbonate.** If the acidosis is corrected without attention to potassium replacement, severe hypokalemia may occur, marked flaccid paralysis may develop, and significant morbidity may ensue (Koff, 1975).

Because the bowel transports solutes and because its membrane is not particularly watertight, osmolality generally re-equilibrates across the bowel wall. Thus, **attempts to deprive a patient of water and determine osmolality as a reflection of renal function are inappropriate because the bowel alters the osmotic content. The bowel also makes the contents more alkaline, and therefore it is impossible to determine the ability of the kidney to acidify simply by measuring urinary pH in patients with urinary intestinal diversion. Finally, because urea and creatinine are reabsorbed by both the ileum and the colon, serum concentrations of urea and creatinine do not necessarily accurately reflect renal function** (Koch and McDougal, 1985b; McDougal and Koch, 1986).

Histologic alterations of the intestine may occur over time when urine is chronically exposed to the mucosa. Villous atrophy and the formation of pseudocrypts may occur, particularly in ileum. These changes are patchy because there is normal ileal mucosa interspersed between these abnormalities. Submucosal inflammatory infiltrates may also be observed. There appear to be fewer changes in the colonic mucosa during the long term. In the colon, a decrease in the size of goblet cells has been described. In time, some transport processes may be altered, with some solutes less actively transported, whereas other processes of solute transport remain active (Philipson et al, 1983). **The ability to establish a hyperchloremic metabolic acidosis, however, appears to be retained by most segments of ileum and colon over time.** In an experimental study, chronic exposure of intestine to urine resulted in a decreased number of transporters, but those that remained were perfectly functional (Grocela and McDougal, 1999).

Altered Sensorium

Alteration of the sensorium may occur as a consequence of magnesium deficiency, drug intoxication, or abnormalities in ammonia metabolism. Patients who develop magnesium deficiency do so either secondary to nutritional depletion or in relation to magnesium wasting by the kidney in much the same way that calcium wasting occurs (see later). Alterations in the sensorium have also occurred because of diabetic hyperglycemia; however, this is not a consequence of the intestinal diversion. In such patients, reabsorption of urinary glucose can result in hyperglycemia without demonstrable glucosuria (Onwubalili, 1982). Perhaps the more common cause of an altered sensorium is a consequence of altered ammonia metabolism. **Ammoniagenic coma in patients with urinary intestinal diversion has been reported in those with cirrhosis** (Silberman, 1958), **those with altered liver function without underlying chronic liver disease** (McDermott, 1957), and those with normal hepatic function as determined by serum enzyme activities (Mounger and Branson, 1972; Kaufman, 1984). The syndrome is most commonly associated with decreased liver function, however, and even in those cases in which normal liver function has been reported, the crude methods by which it was assessed in these reports have been unable to confirm the absence of subtle alterations in liver function. The syndrome is most commonly found in patients with ureterosigmoidostomies but has been reported for those with ileal conduits as well (McDermott, 1957).

The treatment of ammoniagenic coma involves draining the urinary intestinal diversion, either with a rectal tube in the case of ureterosigmoidostomy or with a Foley catheter in those with a continent diversion, so that the urine does not remain exposed to the intestine for extended periods. **Neomycin is administered orally to reduce the ammonia load from the enteric tract, and protein consumption is curtailed,** thus limiting the nitrogen load to the patient until serum ammonium levels return to normal. In severe circumstances, arginine glutamate, 50 g in 1000 mL of 5% dextrose in water, may be given intravenously. This complexes the ammonia by providing substrate for the formation of glutamine (Silberman, 1958). Lactulose may be given orally or by rectum (Edwards, 1984) and complexes the ammonia in the gut and prevents its absorption.

Abnormal Drug Absorption

Drug intoxication has been reported in patients with urinary intestinal diversion. **Drugs more likely to be a problem are those that are absorbed by the gastrointestinal tract and excreted unchanged by the kidney.** Thus, the excreted drug is re-exposed to the intestinal segment, which then reabsorbs it, and toxic serum levels develop. This has been reported for phenytoin (Dilantin) (Savarirayan and Dixey, 1969) and has been seen for certain antibiotics that are excreted unchanged. Although chemotherapy is generally well tolerated by patients with conduits, methotrexate toxicity has been documented in a patient with an ileal conduit (Bowyer and Davies, 1986).

A more recent study suggests that in patients with normal renal function, both those with and without continent diversions tolerate chemotherapy well. The authors studied 23 patients with continent diversions and 19 with ileal conduits who received cisplatin, methotrexate, and vinblastine. The authors concluded that there was no difference in toxicity in patients without diversions, those with ileal conduits, and those with continent diversions. Indeed, the patients with continent diversions did not have a Foley catheter placed during the chemotherapy infusion. However, if one looks carefully at the data, it is clear that there is in fact an increased toxicity in the continent diversion group, although it did not achieve statistical significance (Srinivas et al, 1998). In those patients receiving antimetabolites, it is prudent to carefully monitor the patient for toxic products that are excreted in the urine and capable of intestinal absorption lest lethal toxic serum levels develop. Moreover, **in patients with continent diversions who are receiving chemotherapy, consideration should be given to draining the pouch during the time the toxic drugs are being administered.**

Osteomalacia

Osteomalacia or renal rickets occurs when mineralized bone is reduced and the osteoid component becomes excessive. Osteomalacia has been reported in patients with colocystoplasty (Hassain, 1970), ileal ureters (Salahudeen et al, 1984), colon and ileal conduits, and, most commonly, ureterosigmoidostomies (Harrison, 1958; Specht, 1967). **The cause of osteomalacia may be multifactorial but commonly involves acidosis.** With persistent acidosis, the excess protons are buffered by the bone with release of bone calcium. With its release, it is excreted by the kidney. Support for the theory that chronic acidosis is causative in osteomalacia comes from those patients in whom correction of the acidosis results in remineralization of the bone (Richards et al, 1972; Siklos et al, 1980). It has also been shown, however, that major alterations in serum bicarbonate are not necessary for the development of the syndrome (Koch and McDougal, 1988; McDougal et al, 1988). Moreover, some patients with osteomalacia secondary to urinary intestinal diversion do not have bone demineralization corrected with restoration of normal acid-base balance. **These patients have been found to manifest vitamin D resistance that is independent of the acidosis.** It is likely that this resistance is of renal origin. Resistance can be overcome by supplying 1α-hydroxycholciferol, a vitamin D metabolite that is much more potent than vitamin D$_2$. By providing this substrate in excess amount, remineralization of bone occurs (Perry et al, 1977). Also, it has been shown that reabsorption of urinary solutes may play a role in increasing calcium excretion by the kidney. Sulfate filtered by the kidney inhibits calcium reabsorption and results in both calcium and magnesium loss by the kidney. Thus, if the gut increases its sulfate reabsorption and requires the kidney to increase sulfate excretion, this results in hypercalciuria and hypermagnesuria (McDougal and Koch, 1989). Finally, there is some evidence to indicate that the calcium-to-parathormone ratio is altered, suggesting that a resistance to parathormones develops during the long term (Tanrikut and McDougal, 2004). **Osteomalacia in urinary intestinal diversion may be due to persistent acidosis, vitamin D resistance, and excessive calcium loss by the kidney. It appears that the degree to which each of these contributes to the syndrome may vary from patient to patient.**

It is clear that a number of metabolic problems have been obviated when meticulous attention is paid to correction of the abnormalities prospectively. If a base deficit of more than 2.5 mEq/L is corrected, some investigators have found no evidence of bone mineral density abnormalities (Stein et al, 1998). Indeed, the type of diversion does not seem to make a difference when the acidosis is taken into account and corrected (Kawakita et al, 1996). Others suggest that there is no

difference in continent diversions and ileal conduits (Campanello et al, 1996); however, in such selected series, the distribution of acidosis across both groups is generally identical. It is clear that if the groups are large enough and not preselected, there is an increased incidence of acidosis in continent diversion patients. The take-home message is that if one pays meticulous attention to correction of the acidosis, bone mineral density abnormalities will probably not become a problem.

Patients who develop osteomalacia generally complain of lethargy; joint pain, especially in the weight-bearing joints; and proximal myopathy. Analysis of serum chemistries reveals that the calcium concentration is either low or normal. The alkaline phosphatase level is elevated, and the phosphate level is low or normal (Harrison, 1958). The treatment as indicated earlier involves correction of the acidosis and dietary supplementation of calcium. If this does not result in remineralization of the bone, the active form of vitamin D may be administered. If this is not successful, the more active metabolite of vitamin D$_3$, 1α-hydroxycholciferol, should be administered.

Growth and Development

There is considerable evidence to suggest that urinary intestinal diversion has a detrimental effect on growth and development. In a study of 93 myelodysplasia patients observed for 17 to 23 years, significant aberrations in growth were noted when morphometric parameters were analyzed. Anthropometric measurements in those with urinary intestinal diversion showed a decrease in linear growth in all indices measured, with a statistically significant decrease in biacromial span and elbow-hand length (Koch et al, 1992).

Patients with long-term urinary diversions are more susceptible to fractures and to complications after orthopedic procedures. When myelodysplastic patients with ileal conduits were compared with a similar group of patients who retained their bladder and were on intermittent catheterization, the patients with an ileal conduit had an increased number of fractures as well as malunions and nonunions after orthopedic procedures (Koch et al, 1992). It was found that more patients with urinary intestinal diversion fell below the tenth percentile than did patients who were treated with intermittent catheterization. There was, in fact, no difference in height and weight between the two groups studied (Koch et al, 1992; McDougal, 1992).

There is also experimental evidence for impaired linear growth in urinary intestinal diversion. Rats with unilateral ureterosigmoidostomies observed long term demonstrated significantly decreased femoral bone length compared with nondiverted controls (Koch and McDougal, 1988). Thus, it appears clear that although obvious alterations in growth and development do not occur, when carefully studied, patients who have urinary intestinal diversions constructed in childhood and who maintain these diversions for more than 10 years have significant changes in linear growth.

Infection

An increased incidence of bacteriuria, bacteremia, and septic episodes occurs in patients with bowel interposition. A significant number of patients with intestinal cystoplasty develop pyelonephritis, and 13% have septic and major infectious complications (Kuss et al, 1970). The episodes are more frequent after colocystoplasty than ileocystoplasty (Kuss et al, 1970). Acute pyelonephritis occurs in 10% to 17% of patients with colon and ileal conduits (Schmidt et al, 1973; Schwarz and Jeffs, 1975; Hagen-Cook and Althausen, 1979). Approximately 4% of patients (8 of 178) with ileal conduits die of sepsis (Schmidt et al, 1973).

Patients with conduits have a high incidence of bacteriuria. Indeed, **approximately three quarters of ileal conduit urine specimens are infected** (Guinan et al, 1972; Middleton and Hendren, 1976; Elder et al, 1979). It is clear that some patients are merely colonized at the distal end of the conduit because the incidence of positive cultures can be markedly diminished by culture of the proximal portion of the loop by a double-catheter technique (Smith, 1972). Many of these patients, however, show no untoward effects and seem to do well with chronic bacteriuria. **Deterioration of the upper tracts is more likely when the culture becomes dominant for *Proteus* or *Pseudomonas*. Thus, patients with relatively pure cultures of *Proteus* or *Pseudomonas* should be treated, whereas those with mixed cultures may generally be observed, provided they are not symptomatic. Patients with continent diversions also have a significant incidence of bacteriuria and septic episodes** (McDougal, 1986). Indeed, two thirds of patients with Kock continent diversions have positive cultures (Kock, 1987). The reasons for the increased incidence of bacteriuria and sepsis are unclear, but it is likely that the intestine is incapable of inhibiting bacterial proliferation, in contrast to the urothelium. Thus, intestine that normally lives symbiotically with bacteria when interposed in the urinary tract serves as a source for ascending infection and septic complications. Moreover, the intestine may make the urine less bacteriostatic and thereby promote the growth of bacteria. Distention of the intestinal segment may aid in translocation of bacteria across the intestine and into the blood. Studies have shown some changes in intestinal mucosal immunologic bacterial defense mechanisms; however, for the most part, they seem to be preserved (Wullt et al, 2004).

Stones

One of the consequences of persistent infection is the development of magnesium ammonium phosphate stones. Indeed, **the great majority of stones formed in patients with urinary intestinal diversions are composed of calcium, magnesium, and ammonium phosphate. Those most susceptible to development of renal calculi are patients who have hyperchloremic metabolic acidosis, preexisting pyelonephritis, and urinary tract infection with a urea-splitting organism** (Dretler, 1973). The incidence of renal stones is 3% to 4% in patients with colon conduits (Althausen et al, 1978; Hagen-Cook and Althausen, 1979) and 10% to 12% in those with ileal conduits (Schmidt et al, 1973). In those with continent cecal reservoirs, there is a 20% incidence of calculi within the reservoir (Ashken, 1987). The stones may be due to persistent infection with alkalinization of the urine, persistent hypercalciuria for reasons described previously, and alterations of urinary excretion products by the intestine. A major cause of calculus formation in conduits and pouches is a foreign body, such as staples or nonabsorbable sutures, on which concretions form. In intestinal reservoirs, alterations in bowel mucosa may also serve as a nidus for stone formation. Finally,

alterations in intestinal mucus, particularly in the presence of infection or obstruction, may serve as a nidus or more importantly may interfere with emptying and thereby exacerbate infection and stone formation (N'Dow et al, 2004).

Intestinal Motility, Short Bowel, and Nutritional Problems

Many nutritional problems may occur from the loss of significant intestinal absorptive surface resulting from removal of substantial portions of the gut for construction of a urinary intestinal diversion. **In patients with a significant loss of ileum, vitamin B_{12} malabsorption has been reported and results in anemia and neurologic abnormalities.** Vitamin B_{12} deficiency has been shown to occur in 10 of 41 patients who received preoperative radiotherapy before radical cystectomy and ileal ureterostomy (Kinn and Lantz, 1984). **Loss of significant portions of ileum also results in malabsorption of bile salts.** Because the ileum is the major site of bile salt reabsorption, the lack of reabsorption allows bile salts entry into the colon, which causes mucosal irritation and diarrhea. Also, loss of the ileum results in the loss of the "ileal break." The ileal break is a mechanism whereby gut motility is reduced when lipids come in contact with the ileal mucosa so that increased absorption can occur. With the loss of ileum, the lipid does not result in decreased motility and is presented unmetabolized to the colon, which may result in fatty diarrhea.

Loss of the ileocecal valve may have a number of untoward effects. Because of the loss of the valve, reflux of large concentrations of bacteria into the ileum may occur, which results in small intestinal bacterial overgrowth. This may result in nutritional abnormalities that involve interference with fatty acid reabsorption and bile salt interaction. With the lack of absorption of fats and bile salts, these are presented to the colon and result in diarrhea. Moreover, reflux of bacteria into the small bowel may result in bile salt deficiency. Also, the lack of fat absorption may result in deficiencies of the fat-soluble vitamin A, osteomalacia due to lack of vitamin D, and complexing of calcium with the fats to form soaps and thus lack of its absorption. The ileocecal valve also serves as a break, and an intact valve prolongs transit time of the small bowel and enhances absorption. Thus, its loss may contribute to nutritional abnormalities. Some have advocated reconstruction of the valve mechanism between ileum and colon when the ileocecal segment is used for reconstruction.

Loss of a significant portion of jejunum may result in malabsorption of fat, calcium, and folic acid; however, significant portions of jejunum are rarely used for urologic reconstructive procedures. Loss of the colon may result in diarrhea because of lack of fluid and electrolyte absorption, loss of bicarbonate because of its increased secretion in the ileum and lack of reabsorption, and dehydration because of the loss of fluids.

Of concern when intestinal segments are used in urinary reconstruction is the effect removal of a segment of intestine from the alimentary tract might have on intrinsic bowel function. Indeed, removal of major segments from the alimentary tract may cause nocturnal bowel movements, fecal urgency, fecal incontinence, and diarrhea as well as nutritional deficiencies (Riddick et al, 2004). A study compared patients with ileal conduits with those who had segments used for clam cystoplasty and not surprisingly found that those with clam cystoplasty had a 40% incidence of significant bowel problems. It is known that there is an association between detrusor instability and irritable bowel, perhaps accounting for the incidence of untoward disorders of bowel function in this series (N'Dow et al, 1998). Thus, there is a need for heightened awareness of bowel dysfunction in patients with detrusor instability in whom bowel segments are to be used. Also one should warn patients who will have major portions of the intestinal tract used in the reconstruction that bowel problems may ensue.

Cancer

The incidence of cancer development in patients with ureterosigmoidostomy varies between 6% and 29%, with a mean of 11% (Schipper and Decter, 1981; Stewart et al, 1982; Zabbo and Kay, 1986). There is generally a 10- to 20-year delay before the cancer becomes manifest. **On histologic examination, the tumors include adenocarcinoma, adenomatous polyps, sarcomas, and transitional cell carcinoma.** Case reports of tumors developing in patients with ileal conduits, colon conduits, bladder augmentations, rectal bladder, neobladders, and ileal ureters have been described (Austen and Kalble, 2004). Anaplastic carcinomas and adenomatous polyps have been reported in patients with ileal conduits. Adenocarcinoma has developed in patients with colon conduits; adenocarcinoma, undifferentiated carcinoma, sarcomas, and transitional cell carcinomas have developed in patients with bladder augmentations with both ileum and colon (Filmer, 1986).

The etiologic mechanism of the development of the carcinoma is not understood. Whether the tumor arises from transitional epithelium or colonic epithelium is unclear. Because most of the tumors are adenocarcinomas, it has been assumed that the tumor arises from the intestinal epithelium. Adenocarcinomas have been shown to arise from transitional cell epithelium exposed to the fecal stream in experimental animals (Aaronson et al, 1989). Furthermore, studies show that the ureters in ureterosigmoidostomy patients have an exceedingly high incidence of dysplasia (Aaronson and Sinclair-Smith, 1984). Moreover, if the transitional epithelium is removed from the enteric tract, adenocarcinomas do not develop. **If the urothelium is left in contact with the intestinal mucosa, however, even though the diversion is defunctionalized and the area is not bathed in urine, adenocarcinoma may still develop.** This is illustrated by a case report in which a patient who had a ureterosigmoidostomy that was defunctionalized with a conduit subsequently developed cancer 9 months later. The distal ureters at the sigmoid were left in situ. Twenty-two years later, the patient developed a cancer at the site of the ureterointestinal anastomosis (Schipper and Decter, 1981). This suggests that **when ureterointestinal anastomoses are defunctionalized, they should be excised rather than merely ligated and left in situ.** Other evidence including cell staining techniques suggests that the colon is the primary organ of origin (Mundy, 1991, personal communication). Whether the urothelium or intestine is the primary site of origin, it seems likely that tumors can arise from both tissues.

The highest incidence of cancer occurs when the transitional epithelium is juxtaposed to the colonic epithelium and both are bathed by feces (Shands et al, 1989). Nitrosamines, known mutagens, are produced in rats with ureterosigmoidostomy (Cohen et al, 1987), but there appears at least at this juncture no convincing evidence to support a primary role for them in the genesis of the tumor. An abnormal pattern of colonic mucin secretion has been demonstrated in patients with ureterosigmoidostomy, but its significance is unclear (Iannoni et al, 1986). Induction of specific enzymes associated with carcinoma has also been demonstrated. Ornithine decarboxylase, an enzyme that has been found to be elevated in malignant colonic mucosa, is also elevated in experimental animals with vesicosigmoidostomy (Weber et al, 1988). The role of epidermal growth factor and other growth factors is currently being investigated. There is some evidence that these may at least play a role in development if not in induction. At this time, the cause of the genesis of cancer in urinary intestinal diversion is not known. **Because its incidence is significant in patients with ureterosigmoidostomies, they should have routine colonoscopies on a scheduled periodic basis.**

Neuromechanical Aspects of Intestinal Segments

Both small bowel and colon contract to propel luminal contents in an aboral direction. The ability to propel luminal contents is a consequence of muscle activity as well as coordinated nerve activity. Both the small bowel and the colon have an outer longitudinal layer of muscle and an inner circular layer. There is also a muscularis mucosa, which is immediately beneath the mucosa and may extend into the villi. The outer and inner layers of muscle, however, play the major role in peristalsis. In the colon, the outer longitudinal layer of muscle condenses to form three taeniae coli. The bowel receives its parasympathetic innervation from the vagus. It is also innervated by the sympathetic nervous system. The nerves lie between the circular and longitudinal layers of muscle. The enteral nervous system operates autonomously, and therefore one can denervate the intestine and not affect the coordinated contractions. These contractions are termed activity fronts and may be stimulated by feeding, or they may be inhibited by exposure of the lumen to various substances (i.e., lipid in the ileum decreases ileal motility). There are two aspects of neuromechanical properties that are particularly germane to urinary intestinal diversion: volume-pressure relationships and motor activity.

Volume-Pressure Considerations

The volume-pressure relationships depend on the configuration of the bowel. If one splits the bowel segment and turns it back on itself, the volume may be doubled if the ends are not closed (Fig. 80–41). In reconstruction of intestinal segments for the urinary tract, however, one must close the ends. Thus, the limit of doubling the volume is never quite reached. Indeed, **the greater the ratio of length to diameter, the greater the volume change when the ends are closed. If the ends are closed when a ratio of 1:3.5 diameter to length is reached, splitting the segment no longer increases the volume. By splitting most segments, one is, in fact, increasing the volume by about 50%. The goal in reconfiguring the**

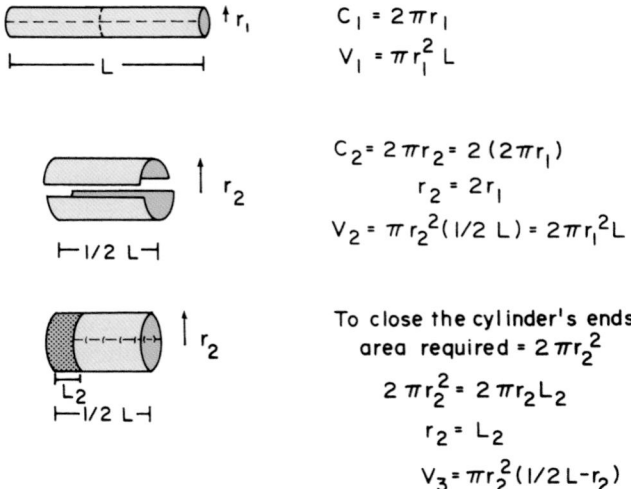

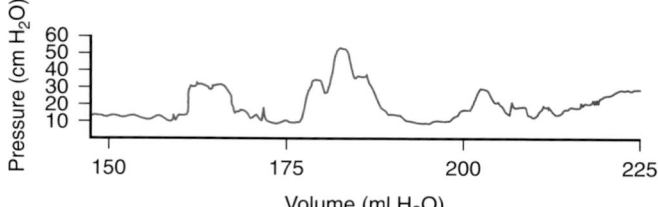

Figure 80–42. Pressure waves recorded 1 year postoperatively in a patient with a continent diversion constructed from detubularized ileum and right colon. Notice that the coordinated pressure waves are of magnitude and frequency similar to those found in a normal colonic or ileal segment.

Figure 80–41. Effect of "detubularization." The bowel is split on its antimesenteric border and divided in two. When the two segments are placed together, the circumference is doubled, thus doubling the volume. Closing the ends of the cylinder requires a reduction in its length equal to the radius of the end. This limits the increase in volume that occurs by reconfiguration.

bowel is to achieve a spherical storage vessel. **This configuration has the most volume for the least surface area.** By increasing the volume, it has been suggested that pressure relationships within the confines of the intestine are reduced. This is based on Laplace's law, which states that for a sphere, the tension of its wall is proportional to the product of the radius and pressure. Thus, theoretically, for a given wall tension, the greater the radius, the smaller the generated pressure. This is desirable in an attempt to prevent deterioration of the upper tracts or incontinence. **This relationship (Laplace's law), however, may not be accurately reflected for intestinal segments because they are not perfectly spherical, and the intestinal wall does not conform to Hooke's law but rather demonstrates viscoelastic properties, which tend to distort the relationship between pressure applied at the wall and tension generated in it.** In any event, it does seem desirable to make an attempt to construct as spherical a container as possible if one is attempting to make a reservoir.

Over time, the volume capacity of segments increases. This occurs only if they are frequently filled. Their volume decreases with time if they are nonfunctional (Kock et al, 1978). Over time, it can be demonstrated that there is a marked accommodation in volume of pouches made from intestine. For ileal pouches, it has been shown that the capacity increases sevenfold after 1 year (Berglund et al, 1987). As the reservoirs increase in volume, there is a significant increase in smooth muscle thickness of the bowel wall (Philipson et al, 1983).

Motor Activity

It has been suggested that splitting the bowel on its antimesenteric border discoordinates motor activity and thereby causes a lesser intraluminal pressure. Clearly, the ideal situation is to provide the patient with a spherical vessel that has few or ineffective contractions of its walls. It can be demonstrated in experimental animals that by **splitting the bowel**

wall on its antimesenteric border and reconfiguring it, acutely there is a marked interruption of coordinated activity fronts, which during a period of 3 months return to their normal coordinated state (Concepcion et al, 1988). This has also been demonstrated clinically as initially after reconfiguration of the bowel (detubularization), coordinated activity fronts have been shown to decrease. During extended periods, however, many of the peristaltic waves (activity fronts) reappear and can be readily demonstrated (Fig. 80–42).

The literature is contradictory with respect to the effect of detubularization on segments of ileum and colon used to construct storage vessels for continent diversions. Pressure within the lumen of bowel that has both ends closed may be increased by adding volume or by reducing the size of the bowel through contractions of its wall. Because the bowel wall is freely permeable to water, the higher osmotic content of urine obligates movement of water into the bowel lumen. Most patients with continent diversions excrete 2 to 4 L/day (McDougal, 1986). In evaluating whether motor activity is the primary determinant of intravesical pressure, one must be cognizant of fluid volume changes. Also, as indicated previously, early reports of detubularized segments would be expected to differ from later reports when coordinated activity fronts in these segments return.

These facts are often forgotten, and because pressure measurements are used to infer motor activity, rather than its direct measurement as reflected by changes in bowel wall tension, it is not difficult to understand why there are so many contradictions reported in the literature. Detubularization of ileal segments has been reported by some to decrease motor activity at a year compared with immediately postoperatively (Berglund et al, 1987), whereas others have noted increased motor activity at 1 year. Involuntary pressure waves occur in 25% of patients with Kock pouches. Maximum intravesical pressures average 41 cm H_2O in these pouches (Chen et al, 1989). Ileum has also been shown to have fewer activity fronts per unit of time than cecum (Berglund et al, 1986). Cecum has been observed to have the same number of activity fronts 1 year postoperatively, but the amplitude of the pressure waves has been observed to decrease over time (Hedlund et al, 1984). Maximum pressures in normal cecum have been shown to range from 18 to 100 cm H_2O (Jakobsen et al, 1987), whereas detubularized cecum has been shown to have pressures that range between 5 and 25 cm H_2O 1 year postoperatively (Hedlund et al, 1984). Others, comparing ileum to cecum, find no difference in pressure generated after a year (Hedlund et al, 1984). The Mainz pouch, which employs both ileum and cecum, has an average pressure at capacity of 39 cm H_2O with a maximum pressure of 63 cm H_2O (Thuroff et al, 1987). **Thus, reconfiguring bowel usually increases the volume, but its long-term effect on motor activity and wall tension is unclear at this time.**

KEY POINTS: URINARY INTESTINAL DIVERSION

- Although 15 cm of small bowel can survive beyond the last vessel, it is unwise to assume that more than 8 cm of small bowel will survive beyond a straight vessel.

- The bacterial concentration ranges from 10 to 10^5 in the jejunum, 10^5 to 10^7 in the distal ileum, 10^6 to 10^8 in the ascending colon, and 10^{10} to 10^{12} in the descending colon.

- A mechanical bowel preparation reduces the total number of bacteria, not their concentration.

- The guiding principles of a proper intestinal anastomosis include adequate exposure, good blood supply, prevention of spillage of enteric contents, accurate apposition of the serosa of the two segments of bowel, proper tension of the sutures, and realignment of the mesentery of the two segments.

- After a ureteral anastomosis, deterioration of the upper tracts during the long term is usually due to a lack of ureteral motility, infection, or stones and less commonly due to a stricture at the anastomotic site.

- Antirefluxing ureteral-intestinal anastomoses have a higher rate of stricture than refluxing anastomoses.

- Limited segments of bowel should be used in patients who have an inability to acidify the urine to less than 5.8, an inability to concentrate greater than 600 mOsm/kg, or a GFR less than 35 mL/min.

- Metabolic complications of intestine interposed in the urinary tract include electrolyte abnormalities, altered sensorium, abnormal drug metabolism, osteomalacia, growth retardation, persistent and recurrent urinary tract infection, formation of calculi, short gut, and development of urothelial or intestinal cancers.

- Those gastrocystoplasty patients most at risk for the development of the syndrome of severe metabolic alkalosis are those with high resting levels of serum gastrin who overdistend their pouches and are dehydrated.

- The electrolyte abnormality that occurs with ileum and colon is a hyperchloremic metabolic acidosis.

- Patients receiving chemotherapy who have intestine interposed in the urinary tract have increased toxic effects of chemotherapeutic agents compared with patients with normal urinary tracts.

SUMMARY

This chapter has addressed complications both independent of and dependent on the specific type of urinary intestinal diversion. Each unique type of diversion has its own set of individual complications. Moreover, the procedure preceding the urinary intestinal diversion also has a set of complications that must be added to those described previously. It is clear that with current modalities of urinary intestinal diversion, long-term complications significantly contribute to mortality and morbidity. Many patients who have intestinal diversion after an extirpative procedure for cancer, however, die of the cancer rather than of these long-term complications. Those for whom a urinary intestinal diversion has been constructed for benign disease and those who are cured of cancer are most likely to experience long-term morbid complications. The knowledge of the frequency of these complications and the correct performance of preoperative preparation, surgical technique, and postoperative care, as outlined in this chapter, should provide the best chance for the least mortality and morbidity in patients undergoing urinary intestinal diversion.

SUGGESTED READINGS

Guenaga K, Matos D, Castro A, et al: Mechanical bowel preparation for elective colorectal surgery. Cochrane Database Syst Rev 2005;CD001544.

Koch MO, McDougal WS, Hall MC, et al: Long-term effects of urinary diversion: A comparison of myelomeningocele patients managed by clean, intermittent catheterization and urinary diversion. J Urol 1992;147:1343-1347.

Kristjansson A, Davidsson T, Mansson W: Metabolic alterations at different levels of renal function following continent urinary diversion through colonic segments. J Urol 1997;157:2099-2103.

McDougal WS: Metabolic complications of urinary intestinal diversion. J Urol 1992;147:1199-1208.

Nelson R, Edwards S, Tse B: Prophylactic nasogastric decompression after abdominal surgery. Cochrane Database Syst Rev 2005;CD004929.

Nichols RL, Condon RE, Gorback SL, Nyhus LM: Efficacy of preoperative antimicrobial preparation of the bowel. Ann Surg 1972;176:227-232.

Ram E, Sherman Y, Weil R, et al: Is mechanical bowel preparation mandatory for elective colon surgery? A prospective randomized study. Arch Surg 2005;140:285-288.

Tanrikut C, McDougal WS: Acid-base and electrolyte disorders after urinary diversion. World J Urol 2004;22:168-171.

81 Cutaneous Continent Urinary Diversion

MITCHELL C. BENSON, MD • JAMES M. McKIERNAN, MD • CARL A. OLSSON, MD

GENERAL CONSIDERATIONS

Continent urinary diversion is widely accepted by both the urologist and the patient as an acceptable form of urinary reconstruction after cystectomy. Orthotopic urethral anastomotic procedures and continent catheterizable stomal reservoirs have stood the test of time, and both procedures should be considered for all appropriate patients. Orthotopic continent diversion and the metabolic consequences of continent urinary diversion are covered in separate chapters. In this chapter the focus is on the continent catheterizable stoma procedures associated with the highest success rates. Over the past 20 years, the design of the reservoir has not substantially changed. What has occurred is an evolution in the techniques utilized to create an effective antireflux mechanism and an effective and reliable continence mechanism. In addition, focus will be given to the long-term quality-of-life outcomes of continent cutaneous reservoirs and the laparoscopic approaches to create such reservoirs.

Despite the considerable enthusiasm for continent urinary diversion operations, those procedures requiring the use of external urinary collecting appliances remain common. Although continent urinary diversion is certainly appropriate in selected patients, the procedures are technically more challenging and are associated with higher short-term and long-term complication rates than those operations that utilize external collecting devices. However, the operating time associated with these more complex procedures has been significantly reduced by the widespread use of absorbable and metal staples in the construction of the reservoirs and limbs. These techniques are discussed in detail. Also, as experience with continent urinary diversion grows, the complication rates have decreased dramatically. As a result, in some centers, continent diversion is now more common than conduit diversion.

Patient Selection

Because the ability to self-catheterize is essential to the patient undergoing continent diversion, the patient must be assessed for the ability to care for himself or herself. The interaction of an enterostomal therapist with the patient and the urologist is extremely helpful in this regard. Often, the patient may be more at ease with the therapist and may be more willing to express any concerns with him or her. Certain patients may not be able to comprehend the regimens that must be followed after continent urinary diversion or they may lack the motor skills to independently perform self-care. **Patients with multiple sclerosis, quadriplegic individuals, and very frail or mentally impaired patients will at some point in their lives require the care of members of the family or visiting nurses, and we view such patients as poor candidates for any form of continent diversion.** Indeed, these patients may also require assistance with external appliances but such assistance is much less burdensome on the patient and society. On the contrary, continent catheterizable diversion requires round-the-clock attention and may limit patient and family options when determining long-term care needs.

Patient Preparation

We prepare all patients undergoing anticipated continent urinary diversion for the possibility that a traditional ileal conduit might be performed. Although it is rare to abandon a continent diversion owing to unanticipated problems, this remains a possible outcome. Therefore, before the operation, the site for an external stoma should be selected with extreme care. In general, the location must be free from fat creases in both the standing and sitting position and it should not be close to prior abdominal scars that might interfere with proper adherence of an external appliance. Here, again, the aid of an enterostomal therapist is extremely helpful. In general, the stoma should be brought through the right (or left) lower quadrant of the abdomen on a line extending between the umbilicus and the anterior superior iliac spine. The stoma should be as far lateral from the midline as possible, but the site should always be selected to require the bowel segment comprising the stoma to traverse the rectus muscle. Failure to adhere to this feature promotes the incidence of parastomal hernias. The selected site for the stoma should be marked with an X scratched on the anterior abdominal wall. Marking the stoma site with ink should be avoided, because the ink may be washed away during the antiseptic preparation of the skin.

The surgeon undertaking continent urinary diversion should be familiar with more than one type of continent diversion procedure. Although it is uncommon to have to abandon a given bowel segment for the reservoir, it is not uncommon to have to modify the antireflux or continence mechanism. In these circumstances, it is prudent that the surgeon be able to elect an alternate form of continent diversion from that originally intended.

Renal and hepatic function must be reviewed carefully in the patient selected for continent diversion (Mills and Studer, 1999). The reabsorption and recirculation of urinary constituents and other metabolites require that liver function be normal and that serum creatinine levels are in the normal range or certainly below the level of 1.8 mg/dL. In cases in which renal function is borderline, creatinine clearance should be measured. A minimal level of creatinine clearance of 60 mL/min should be documented before deeming the patient an appropriate candidate for continent diversion. In patients with bilateral hydronephrosis, in whom renal functional improvement might be anticipated on relief of the ureteral obstruction, the urologist should drain the upper tract, by percutaneous nephrostomy(ies), if needed, with reevaluation of renal function thereafter before opting for a continent diversion.

Procedures that require the use of a large intestinal segment should always be preceded by a colonoscopic assessment of the entire large intestine. Sigmoidoscopy only for a sigmoid colon procedure is insufficient because more proximal disease may leave the patient with a short colon syndrome. We do not routinely perform colon evaluation if small intestine is utilized.

Healthy patients undergoing radical cystectomy can be admitted to the hospital on the day of surgery. A mechanical bowel preparation is administered after a liquid dinner on the night before surgery. The patient is instructed to drink copious amounts of water, and at 8 PM and 10 PM, the patient is administered oral metronidazole, 500 mg. The patient receives cefoxitin, 1 g, intravenously 1 hour before the skin incision.

Cystectomy

All operations described require a midline incision, skirting the umbilicus to the side opposite the selected stoma site. The incision for a right colon pouch usually extends from the pubis to a point midway between the umbilicus and the xiphoid. The cranial extent of the incision is governed by the hepatic flexure, which must be divided to obtain sufficient colonic length and to allow for the right colon to easily fold on itself. On some occasions, the incision will be extended to the xiphoid. The incision for those procedures utilizing ileum only can often stop just above the umbilicus. The cystectomy procedure is covered elsewhere in this text, and only those points germane to continent diversion are covered here.

After abdominal exploration, urinary diversion operations proceed by the isolation, transection, and transposition of the ureters to an appropriate place for subsequent diversion. The right retroperitoneum is opened over the iliac artery to expose the right ureter. In the typical circumstance of conduit diversion, the right ureter is transected below the common iliac artery. For all continent diversions, both the right and left ureters are transected as low as possible and shortened to the appropriate length once the final anatomy is determined. The sigmoid colon is freed from its lateral peritoneal attachments by incising along the line of Toldt. A wide tunnel is created by blunt finger dissection ventral to the aorta and common iliac arteries and caudal to the inferior mesenteric artery. This affords left ureteral access to the previously exposed right retroperitoneum. In cases of uroepithelial malignancy, it is our practice to send a small portion of the most distal ureter on each side for frozen section analysis to ensure proximal ureteral margins free from carcinoma in situ.

All sutures utilized in the urinary tract should be absorbable. The individual surgeon's preference will dictate the caliber and type of suture material utilized. In general, when carrying out bowel surgery for those urinary diversions we prefer a stapled bowel segment division as well as stapled reconstruction of bowel continuity. This shortens operative times greatly and affords safe and reliable bowel anastomoses. Suturing techniques are not necessary except to place two silk Lembert sutures at the apex of side-to-side stapled bowel anastomoses to prevent tension on the staple line. To avoid stone formation on the stapled proximal bowel segments, oversewing the stapled end of the conduit with absorbable material isolates the metal staple line from urinary contact.

In constructing a nonappendiceal continent urinary diversion stoma, a skin button matching the diameter of the structure to be utilized in the diversion is circumcised. Cutaneous tissues are separated down to the level of the anterior rectus fascia and a similar diameter circle excised from this fascia, or the fascia is opened in cruciate fashion. In carrying out this maneuver, the surgeon should take care that the fascia and skin are properly aligned, so that angulation does not occur. Rectus muscle fibers are separated bluntly and an instrument passed through to the posterior peritoneum (and fascia). For appendiceal stomas, we prefer to perform a Y-shaped cutaneous incision that allows for a YV-type plasty incision between the appendiceal limb and the skin (Fig. 81–1). It has been our experience that this will decrease the likelihood of subsequent stomal stenosis. Alternatively, the appendix lends itself to an umbilical stoma (Bissada, 1993; Gerharz et al, 1997). Bissada, in 1998, reported favorable results with this appendiceal YV plasty technique to the umbilical site.

It is our preference to utilize long end-hole single J-type diverting stents in all cases of urinary diversion. The stents drain urine externally, ensuring that urine is safely diverted beyond any anastomotic site during the early healing interval. These stents allow for manipulation or exchange if necessary. The end hole allows for the passage of a straight wire through the stent before removal, which decreases the likelihood of anastomotic trauma at the time of stent removal.

The authors advocate the use of closed suction drains in all cases of urinary diversion. Soft silicone Jackson-Pratt closed suction drains are preferred because they have less potential for tissue damage or migration into pouches.

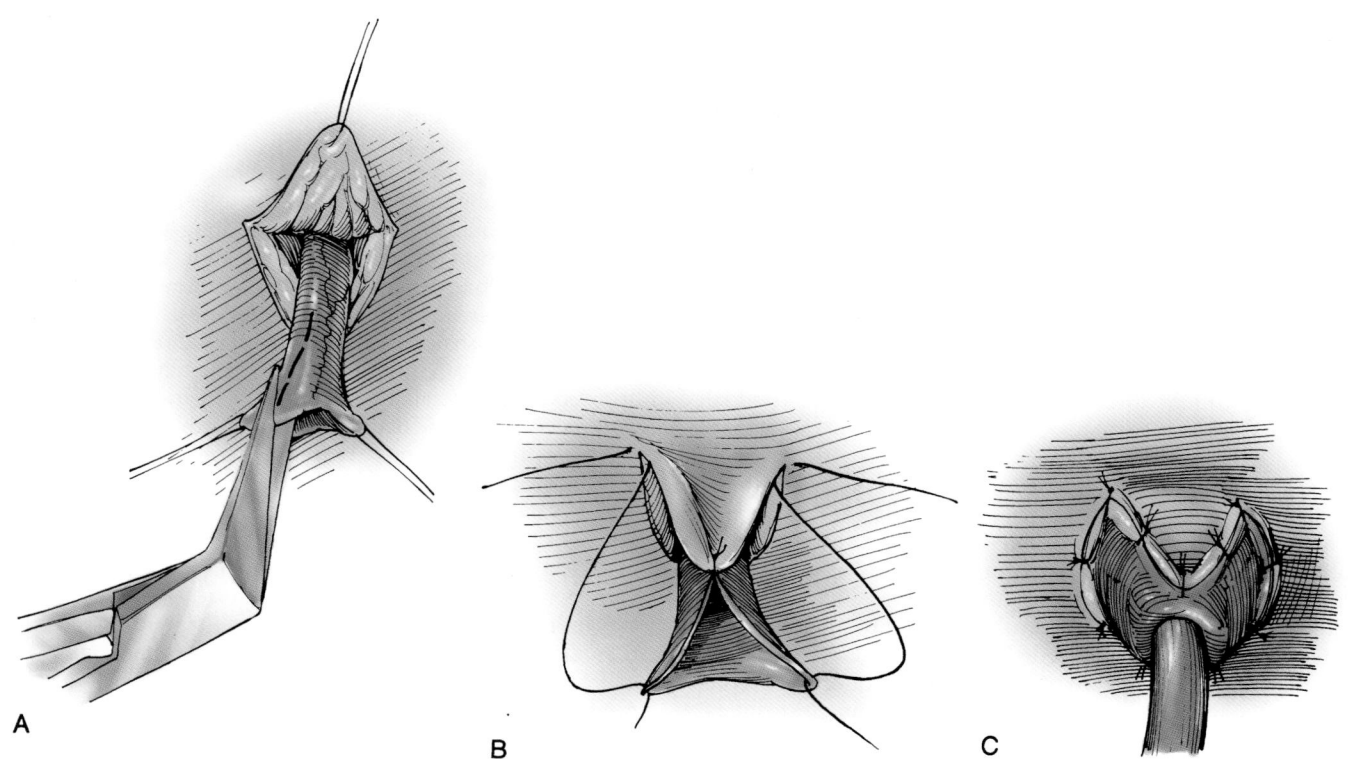

Figure 81–1. **A** to **C,** A V-flap is incised in the skin and a similar length incision made on the adjacent appendiceal surface. This is similar to the technique utilized to mature a cutaneous ureterostomy. For an appendiceal stoma, no eversion is required. (From Hinman F Jr: Atlas of Urologic Surgery. Philadelphia, WB Saunders, 1989.)

Abdominal closure is performed according to the surgeon's preference. It is our prejudice that a single-layer closure, utilizing No. 2 nylon, Surgilene, or Prolene taken through all layers of fascia and muscle provides a rapid and secure abdominal closure in the majority of patients. In obese patients, those with tissues of poor quality, or nutritionally depleted patients, through-and-through stay sutures are also used. Ureteral stents are always brought through separate abdominal stab wounds, sutured to the anterior abdominal wall, and directed into separate drainage bags to monitor urine output. It is important to be certain that there is adequate drainage of the reservoir for safety against pouch rupture, should the ureteral stents become dislodged. Therefore, in the case of limited pouch access, such as with an appendiceal stoma, a Malecot tube is always placed directly into the reservoir and secured to the skin. The reservoir is sutured to the abdominal wall to prevent urine leakage into the peritoneal cavity after tube removal. This maneuver also prevents reservoir migration, which can affect the continence mechanism, either creating incontinence or catheterization difficulties secondary to angulation.

Postoperative Care and Comments

Paralytic ileus is often experienced after urinary diversion procedures. Therefore, gastric decompression can be achieved by means of either nasogastric intubation or else the provision of a gastrostomy at the time of the operation. Gastric decompression is maintained until extubation. Nasogastric tubes

suffice in the majority of patients. However, certain patients may best be managed by formal gastrostomy decompression. These include individuals in whom multiple prior abdominal procedures have been performed and prolonged ileus may be anticipated. If the duration of paralytic ileus is projected to be in excess of 4 to 5 days, intravenous hyperalimentation is initiated on the second postoperative day. **If the patient is nutritionally depleted preoperatively, hyperalimentation has been suggested to be of value if initiated during the preoperative interval** (Hensle, 1983; Askanazi et al, 1985).

Ureteral stents are generally removed 1 week after surgery. Before any manipulation, a urine culture from each stent should be sent for culture and sensitivity. Before stent removal, radiographs of the pouch are obtained to ensure that the pouch is intact. Radiologic contrast studies are performed to ensure against ureteral anastomotic leakage. Each stent is injected with contrast agent in a search for extravasation; if none is seen, guide wires are advanced to each kidney and the stents are removed over the wires. If there is any question of extravasation, stents can be advanced over the wires, positioned fluoroscopically, and left in situ for reevaluation after additional healing has taken place.

Late malignancy has been reported in all bowel segments exposed to the urinary stream, whether or not there is a commingling with feces (Filmer and Spencer, 1990; Shokeir et al, 1995). A study by Gitlin and colleagues (1999) suggests that the malignancy may develop from the urothelial component and not as a result of urine affecting intestinal mucosa. **As a result, urinary cytology should be performed in all**

patients undergoing a continent urinary diversion whether or not the diversion was performed secondary to a urothelial malignancy. When the ureters are directed into the fecal stream, routine colonoscopy should also be performed. There have been isolated reports of malignancy developing earlier, and all patients developing gross or microscopic hematuria should be fully evaluated (Golomb et al, 1989). If an anastomotic transitional cell cancer is discovered, the patient should be fully evaluated with upper tract imaging and ureteroscopy if possible. Antegrade ureteropyeloscopy can be employed if necessary. For an isolated anastomotic recurrence, distal ureterectomy and reimplant is appropriate. If nephroureterectomy is necessary, some patients may require removal of their continent diversion, owing to inadequate residual renal function.

CONTINENT URINARY DIVERSION

Continent, nonorthotopic urinary diversion can be divided into two major categories. First, the variations of ureterosigmoidostomy such as ileocecal sigmoidostomy, rectal bladder, and sigmoid hemi-Kock operation with proximal colonic intussusception are discussed. These techniques allow for excretion of urine by means of evacuation. Second, there is the large category of continent diversions requiring clean intermittent catheterization for emptying urine at intervals from the constructed pouch.

The concept of refashioning bowel so that it serves as a urinary reservoir rather than a conduit has become universally accepted. This concept is based on original pioneering observations by Goodwin and others in the development of the cystoplasty augmentation procedure (Goodwin et al, 1958). The destruction of peristaltic integrity and refashioning of bowel has led to the development of many innovative urinary reservoirs constructed from bowel, utilizing antireflux procedures to avoid upper tract urinary damage by sepsis or reflux and additional surgical techniques to achieve urinary continence.

Because there are numerous variants of continent urinary diversion utilized worldwide, a complete review of all operative techniques is beyond the scope of this or any chapter. However, many of the procedures are simple modifications of parent procedures; in this chapter we address each parent operation as well as major modifications in detail. The very fact that there are as many continent urinary diversion procedures described reveals an obvious corresponding fact: the "best" continent diversion has yet to be devised. There is, to date, no unanimity of opinion that would indicate that one continent diversion is superior to another, but it is becoming apparent that certain procedures are associated with lower early and late complication rates. Points of controversy include which bowel segment is most appropriate for fashioning into a urinary reservoir, the best techniques to utilize for achieving urinary continence, and the best technique for prevention of reflux of urine into the upper urinary tract. There are now various continence mechanisms that appear reliable. In our experience, procedures utilizing a right colon reservoir with some form of appendiceal continence mechanism are the fastest and easiest to perform.

It should be reemphasized that all continent diversions will allow for substantial reabsorption of urinary constituents that will place an increased workload on the kidneys (Mills and Studer, 1999). No patient with substantial renal impairment should be considered for these procedures.

The long-term sequelae of conduit urinary diversion are well understood and, unfortunately, involve a considerable degree of damage to renal units. Although it has been suggested that the absence of reflux to the upper urinary tract in catheterizing pouches may reduce the long-term impact of continent diversion procedures on renal function, it should be cautioned that long-term 15-year data are now available and, in some instances, antireflux procedures are associated with a higher risk of obstruction (Kristjansson et al, 1995).

Many studies from throughout the world have suggested an improved psychosocial adjustment of the patient undergoing continent urinary and fecal diversion compared with those patients with diversions requiring collecting appliances (Gerber, 1980; McLeod and Fazio, 1984; Boyd et al, 1987; Salter, 1992a, 1992b; Bjerre et al, 1995; Filipas et al, 1997; Hart et al, 1999; McGuire et al, 2000). Although this is indeed true and is best exemplified by the individual with a conduit who desires conversion to a continent procedure, it is also true that many individuals seem to adjust easily to the wearing of external appliances. The sense of body image is a remarkably personal and subjective parameter that varies from patient to patient. In fact, most patients are quite content with their choice of urinary diversion be it continent or not.

The process of patient counseling that we employ always refers to ileal conduit diversion as the gold standard against which the newer operations must be compared. The patient is well advised that continent diversion, in general, is associated with a longer hospital stay, higher complication rate, and greater potential for need of reoperative surgery, all other considerations being equal. However, it should be noted that an extensive review from our institution has demonstrated no statistically significant difference in reoperations, mortality, or hospital stay in patients undergoing continent diversion versus conduit diversion by the same three surgeons over a 3-year period (Benson et al, 1992). Analysis of the two patient groups, on the other hand, showed that, in general, those selected for continent diversion were 12 years younger and four times less likely to have significant intercurrent illness. What this review suggests is that, with proper patient selection, continent diversion operations can be safely conducted. To determine if continent diversion could be safely performed in selected elderly patients, Navon and colleagues (1995) analyzed the clinical course of 25 patients older than the age of 75 undergoing a modified Indiana reservoir and compared their outcome to a cohort of 25 randomly selected patients younger than 75. The mean age of the former group was 78.5 years, and the mean age of the latter group was 59.3 years. The complication rates between the two groups were acceptably low and surprisingly similar. Navon and colleagues concluded that age alone should not be a contraindication to continent diversion and that the Indiana reservoir can be successfully performed with an acceptable morbidity.

Rectal Bladder Urinary Diversion

Various innovative surgical techniques have been advocated for separating the fecal and urinary streams, yet still employing ureterosigmoidostomy principles. These operations can generally be discussed together as rectal bladder urinary diversions. In each of these operations, ureters are transplanted to the rectal stump and the proximal sigmoid colon is managed by terminal sigmoid colostomy or, more commonly, by bringing the sigmoid to the perineum, utilizing the anal sphincter in an effort to achieve both bowel and urinary control. Although these operations continue to enjoy some popularity, they have never been well accepted in the United States. The principal reason is the calamitous complication of combined urinary and fecal incontinence, presumably occurring as a consequence of damage to the anal sphincter mechanism during the dissection processes (Culp, 1984).

If the urologist selects one of these procedures, the preoperative evaluation should include all of the caveats of ureterosigmoidostomy. Dilated ureters are not acceptable. The patient with extensive pelvic irradiation is not a candidate. Existing renal insufficiency disqualifies a patient from candidacy. Anal sphincteric tone must be judged competent before electing these operations. **Our preference has been to utilize a 400- to 500-mL thin mixture of oatmeal and water that the patient is asked to retain for 1 hour in the upright position** (Spirnak and Caldamone, 1986). **Finally colonoscopy must be carried out before the procedure to ensure against pre-existing colorectal disease as well as after the procedure to guard against the potential development of colonic cancer after surgery.** The procedures that separated the fecal and urinary streams but brought both out through the rectal sphincter will not be described in this text. Those wishing a detailed description of these procedures can find this in prior editions of this chapter. In this text, we briefly describe the more modern surgical procedures, which utilize the intact anal sphincter for urinary and fecal continence. However, the surgical techniques for these procedures will likewise not be discussed in this edition.

Folded Rectosigmoid Bladder

A modification of the ureterointestinal anastomosis was described by the group from Mansoura, Egypt (Hafez et al, 1995; El-Mekresh et al, 1997). This procedure creates a folded rectosigmoid bladder with the ureters being anastomosed into serosal troughs rather than into the taenia. This procedure has the advantage of a larger sigmoid reservoir and the use of the serous-lined tunnel or trough to prevent reflux. This reimplantation technique was first described by Abol-Enein and Ghoneim (1993) and appears to have a lower complication rate than direct taenial implantation (Hafez et al, 1995).

Postoperative Care and Comments. Patients undergoing this procedure must be closely monitored for the development of hyperchloremic acidosis. This will occur in the majority of instances, and it is wise to initiate a bicarbonate replacement program at the outset. Because hypokalemia is also a feature of ureterosigmoidostomy, replacement of base along with potassium may be achieved with potassium citrate medication. Routine nightly insertion of a rectal tube is advocated in the long-term care of the patient. However, many patients will reject this practice as uncomfortable and unappealing. Nighttime urinary drainage must be mandated, on the other hand, in any patient who cannot maintain electrolyte homeostasis with oral medication. Bissada and associates (1995) reported that 30 of 61 patients were able to stay dry during the night

without awakening. The other 31 required two or more awakenings to remain dry overnight. Hyperchloremic acidosis was reported in 4 of 61 noncompliant patients.

In 1997, El-Mekresh and associates (1997) reported on 64 patients (32 women, 20 men, and 12 children) who had undergone their rectosigmoid bladder procedure from 1992 to 1995. Follow-up ranged from 6 to 36 months. Functional results were assessable in 57 patients; 1 died of a postoperative pulmonary embolism and 6 of their disease. All patients were continent during the day with two to four emptyings. All but 4 of the patients were dry at night with none to two emptyings. Four children experienced enuresis that responded to 25 mg of imipramine at bedtime. Importantly, upper urinary tract function was maintained or improved in 95% of patients. However, six renal units (5.3%) developed obstructive hydronephrosis secondary to ureterocolic anastomotic strictures. Two were remedied by antegrade dilation, one was repaired by open revision, and one nonfunctioning renal unit was removed. The fate of the remaining two units was not specified. No patient in this series developed a postoperative metabolic acidosis. However, all patients were maintained on prophylactic oral alkalinization.

Obviously, all patients have exposure of the urinary tract to fecal flora. Most authors would advocate chronic antibacterial agent administration in all patients (Duckett and Gazak, 1983; Spirnak and Caldamone, 1986). Ureteral strictures require reoperative surgery and are experienced in 26% to 35% of cases over time (Williams et al, 1969; Duckett and Gazak, 1983).

Because of the definite concern for the occurrence of rectal cancer some 5 to 50 years (average 21 years) after ureterosigmoidostomy (Ambrose, 1983), it is suggested that patients with long-term ureterosigmoidostomy be subjected to annual colonic investigation by means of colonoscopy (Filmer and Spencer, 1990). Barium enemas are relatively contraindicated, because reflux of this material into the kidneys (if the antireflux procedure fails) can result in dire consequences (Williams, 1984). A further suggestion that might be utilized in monitoring for colon carcinoma is the monitoring for blood in the stool and the attempted cytologic examination of the mixed urine and feces specimen (Filmer and Spencer, 1990).

Augmented Valved Rectum

Kock developed this technique to be utilized in locales where stoma appliances were not readily available (Kock et al, 1988). This operation is similar to standard ureterosigmoidostomy except that a proximal intussusception of the sigmoid colon confines the urine to a smaller surface area, thus minimizing the problems of electrolyte imbalance. Additionally the rectum was patched with ileum to improve the urodynamic properties of the rectum as a urinary reservoir. Preoperative evaluation is similar to that used in ureterosigmoidostomy. The large bowel must be studied for preexisting disease, and anal sphincteric integrity must be tested before surgery.

Hemi-Kock and T-Pouch Procedures with Valved Rectum

In his description of the augmented valved rectum procedure, Kock described the use of a foreshortened hemi-Kock pouch to be utilized as a rectal patch when the ureters were too

ureterosigmoidostomy who were incontinent. They reported excellent continence, with 14 of 15 of the primary patients achieving documented day- and night-time urinary control and the remaining patient refusing follow-up but reporting continence. The 4 patients undergoing a salvage procedure fared less well. Only 2 became continent. However, the other 2 were found to be in chronic retention and their failure to become continent appeared to be secondary to inadequate emptying. Similar excellent results have been achieved by Venn and Mundy (1999). They reported full day- and night-time urinary continence in 14 of 14 patients and no major postoperative complications.

Bastian and coworkers (2004) have reported on the health-related quality of life in 83 patients undergoing Mainz II urinary diversion. They found that quality of life was similar to that of age-matched controls except for diarrhea symptoms, with 100% daytime continence.

The frequent need for oral alkalinization in this operation is not dissimilar to standard ureterosigmoidostomy so that there is no metabolic advantage to this procedure. In fact, the only difference between this operation and standard ureterosigmoidostomy is the partial reconfiguration of the rectosigmoid junction. It does appear that the reduced intracolonic pressures that result from the partial reconfiguration increases the sigmoid capacity and results in better day- and night-time continence. Whether the increased capacity and lower pressure will decrease the incidence of upper tract problems remains to be determined by longer follow-up.

Continent Catheterizing Pouches

Numerous operative techniques have been developed for continent diversion wherein urine is emptied at intervals by patient self-catheterization, conducted in a clean fashion. Many of these operations are described in this chapter, although certain pioneering procedures such as those of Gilchrist and associates (1950), Ashken (1987), Mansson and colleagues (1984, 1987), Benchekroun (1987), and others are not described because intact bowel was utilized. This is not to discredit the pioneers in the field but simply to allow the chapter to focus on those pouches that incorporate modern principles attempting to achieve a spherical configuration and disruption of peristaltic integrity.

In continent urinary diversion, the two favorite sites for stomal location are at the umbilicus and in the lower quadrant of the abdomen, through the rectus bulge and below the "bikini" line. This location is often preferred because it affords both men and women the opportunity to conceal the stoma. The umbilicus is a preferred location for the individual confined to a wheelchair and has been reported to have a lower incidence of stomal stenosis, especially when fashioning an appendiceal stoma. The umbilical location is also far easier for the paraplegic individual to catheterize without the need for chair transfer and disrobing. In individuals with a recessed umbilicus, the umbilical location of a stoma is barely perceptible from a normal umbilical dimple. Generally, the stoma site is covered with a gauze pad or square bandage to avoid mucous soiling of clothing. Patients undergoing continent urinary diversion to an umbilical location should be advised to wear a medical alert bracelet that informs the examiner of the umbilical stoma.

Before the adaptation of orthotopic neobladder construction to women, there was some enthusiasm for the orthotopic location of a catheterizing portal. This procedure has been carried out in certain female patients with success. The construction of a neourethra to the introitus is attractive, provided there is no substantial difficulty in the catheterizing process. Because it can be so difficult to direct a catheter through the "chimney" of an intussuscepted nipple valve, those continent diversions employing nipple valves are not particularly adaptable to orthotopic location, although they have been performed with success in a small number of patients (Olsson, 1987). In contrast, the imbricated and tapered ileal segment leading to an Indiana pouch is relatively easier to catheterize and can be utilized for orthotopic catheterizing diversion (Rowland et al, 1987). However, it may be difficult to obtain sufficient mesenteric length in some patients. The appendix has been utilized as a neourethra; and, in this instance, mesenteric length should be less of a problem (Hubner and Pfluger, 1995).

Four general techniques have been employed to create a dependable, catheterizable continence zone. For right colon pouches, appendiceal techniques, pseudoappendiceal tubes fashioned from ileum or right colon, and the ileocecal valve plication are adaptable. Appendiceal tunneling techniques are the simplest of all to perform in that they utilize established surgical techniques that are already in the urologic armamentarium. In these procedures, the in-situ or transposed appendix is tunneled into the cecal taenia in a fashion similar to ureterocolonic anastomosis. Appendiceal continence mechanisms have been criticized for three general reasons. First, the appendix may be unavailable in some patients because of prior appendectomy. For those individuals, techniques have been developed that allow for the construction of a similar tube fashioned from ileum (Woodhouse and MacNeily, 1994) or from the wall of the right colon (Lampel et al, 1995a). Second, the appendiceal stump may be too short to reach the anterior abdominal wall or umbilicus while still maintaining sufficient length for tunneling. This criticism has been addressed by an operative variation described by Mitchell, in which the appendiceal stump can be lengthened by the inclusion of a tubular portion of proximal cecum (Burns and Mitchell, 1990) (Fig. 81–3). This lengthening procedure has the added advantage of allowing for a slightly larger stoma made of cecum that is less prone to stomal stenosis. Appendiceal continence mechanisms share the feature of allowing for only small-diameter catheters to be utilized for intermittent catheterization. The large amount of mucus produced by an intestinal reservoir is more easily emptied or irrigated by using a 20- to 22-Fr catheter rather than the typical catheter that would be admitted through an appendiceal stump (14 to 16 Fr). We believe that these criticisms are more theoretical than real and the appendiceal or pseudoappendiceal continence mechanism remains a very attractive and reliable continence mechanism.

The second major type of continence mechanism used in right colon pouches is the tapered and/or imbricated terminal ileum and ileocecal valve. Here again, the technology is rather simple with imbrication or plication of the ileocecal valve region along with tapering of the more proximal ileum in the fashion of a neourethra (Rowland et al, 1985; Lockhart,

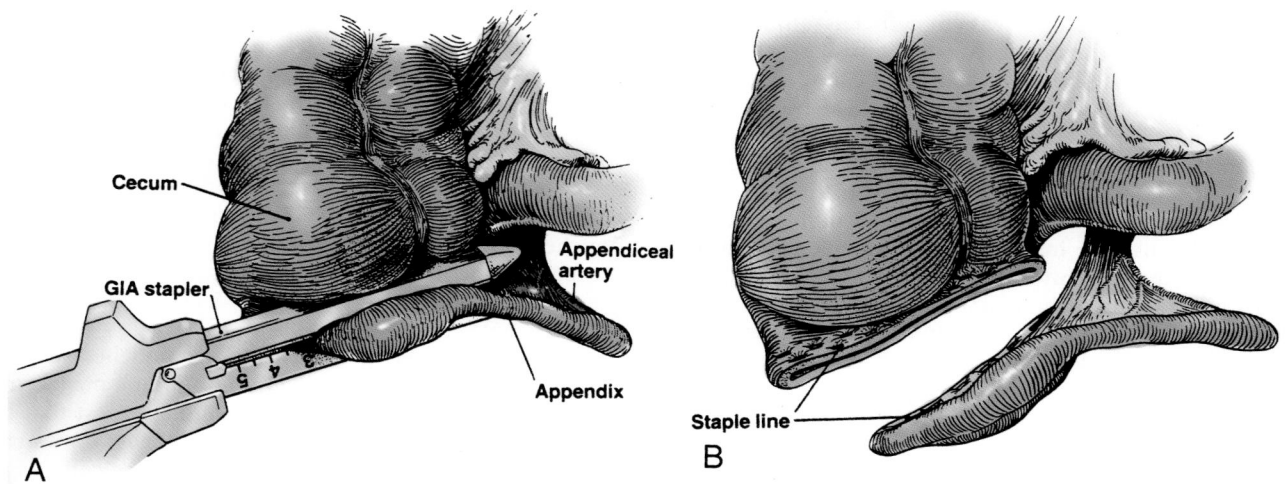

Figure 81–3. **A,** The appendiceal stump is lengthened by the inclusion of a tubular portion of proximal cecum by the application of the GIA stapler to the terminal cecum. A window is made in the mesoappendix and the blade of the GIA stapler advanced through the window. This maneuver ensures that the blood supply is not inadvertently damaged. **B,** The added length is demonstrated. The appendix is rotated and implanted into the taenia; the cecal tube serves as the stoma. (From Burns MW, Mitchell ME: Tips on constructing the Mitrofanoff appendiceal stoma. Contemp Urol, May 1990, pp 10-12.)

1987; Bejany and Politano, 1988). These techniques afford a reliable continence mechanism.

One feature of right colon pouches that has been criticized is the loss of the ileocecal valve. Although this does result in frequent bowel movements for some patients, at least in the short term, the majority will experience bowel regularity either through intestinal adaptation or with the use of pharmacologic therapy. However, some patients have developed rather striking diarrhea/steatorrhea after the loss of the ileocecal valve. This may be particularly true in the pediatric patient in whom there is neurogenic bowel dysfunction (myelomeningocele patient).

The third surgical principle utilized in constructing the continence mechanism is the use of the intussuscepted nipple valve or, more recently, the flap valve, which avoids the need for intussusception. The creation of nipple valves is by far the most technologically demanding of all the continence mechanisms, and it is associated with the highest complication and reoperation rates. Before the surgeon achieves reproducible and dependable results, a significant learning curve must be overcome. For this reason, nipple valve construction should probably not be chosen by the surgeon carrying out occasional construction of continent pouches. Furthermore, it should be noted that in the past 2 decades we have seen the introduction of numerous modifications of the original technique of Kock for construction of a stable nipple valve. The singular reason for all of these modifications is the rather disappointing long-term stability of the nipple valve in some patients. As a result, the group at the University of Southern California has developed a new procedure, the T-pouch, which utilizes a flap valve (Stein et al, 1998). This procedure, which appears much simpler than the intussuscepted nipple valve, has been utilized to create both a continence mechanism and an antireflux mechanism. Nipple valve failure from slippage or valve effacement can be anticipated in 10% to 15% of cases even in the hands of the very best and experienced surgeons. In addition to slippage, nipple valves are

subject to ischemic atrophy. When this occurs, a new nipple valve must be fashioned from a new bowel segment.

A final feature of stapled nipple valves is the potential for stone formation on exposed staples. This has been greatly lessened by the omission of staples at the tip of the intussuscepted nipple valve, as suggested by Skinner and associates (1984). However, more proximal staples occasionally erode into the pouch and serve as a nidus for stone formation. These stones are usually manageable endoscopically with forceps extraction of the stone and staple or else with electrohydraulic or ultrasonic disintegration of the stone with subsequent forceps staple extraction. Although exposed staples may serve as a nidus for stone formation, continent urinary diversion in and of itself results in more urinary excretion of calcium, magnesium, and phosphate as compared with ileal conduit diversion (Terai et al, 1995). Thus, all patients undergoing continent diversion are at an increased risk for the formation of reservoir stones.

The fourth major technique of continence mechanism construction is the provision of a hydraulic valve, as in the Benchekroun nipple (1987). In this procedure, a small bowel segment is isolated and a reversed intussusception is carried out, apposing the mucosal surfaces of the small bowel. Tacking sutures are taken to a portion of the circumference of the intussusception to stabilize the nipple valve while allowing urine to flow freely between the leaves of apposed ileal mucosa. As the pouch fills, hydraulic pressure closes the leaves, ensuring continence. The premise was that as the reservoir filled, the pressure within the valve would also increase, thereby creating continence. Concerns regarding stomal stenosis, especially in children, and nipple destabilization have resulted in this procedure being largely abandoned, and, as a result, it will not be discussed in this chapter (Sanda et al, 1996).

General Procedural Methodology

During construction of the pouch, intraoperative testing for pouch integrity is always performed. The continence

mechanism is also tested for ease of catheterization as well as continence after the pouch construction has been completed. The pouch is filled with saline, the continence mechanism catheter is removed, and the pouch can be compressed slightly to look for points of leakage as well as to test the continence mechanism for its ability to contain urine. **Thereafter, the continence mechanism is catheterized to ensure ease of catheter passage. This is an extremely important and crucial maneuver because the inability to catheterize is a serious complication that will often result in the need for reoperation.** In general, all redundancy should be removed from the continence mechanism. It is often useful to secure the reservoir to the anterior abdominal wall in a manner that prevents the reservoir from migrating. This can prevent the development of a false passage or a kink and thereby ease catheterization.

Postoperatively, the larger-bore catheter utilized for drainage of the pouch should be irrigated at frequent intervals to ensure against mucous obstruction. This can be performed at 4-hour intervals by simple irrigation with 45 to 50 mL of saline. Less frequent intervals of irrigation can be employed when the urine is totally diverted from the kidneys by means of long indwelling stents. As soon as possible, the patient is instructed in conducting his or her own irrigation program. This is performed to familiarize the patients with the catheterization process, to reduce the work burden on the nursing staff, and to allow for earlier discharge.

At the seventh postoperative day, a contrast study is performed to ensure pouch integrity. Thereafter, ureteral stents may be removed if no leaks are demonstrated by imaging studies. When it has been ascertained that the ureteral anastomoses and pouch are intact, the suction drain is removed. The suprapubic tube (if employed) can also be removed at this time, or it can be left in place until the patient is confident of the catheterization technique. The patient is taught to irrigate the tube traversing the continence mechanism at 4-hour intervals and instructed to irrigate whenever any episode of intra-abdominal pressure or discomfort is experienced. Once these procedures are mastered and the patient is tolerating a regular diet, the patient can be discharged. This usually occurs between hospital days 6 and 8.

The following represents a summary of common patient questions and everyday solutions:

- "What kind of catheter do I use?": for nipple valves, a straight-ended 22- to 24-Fr tube; for ileocecal plication, a 20- to 22-Fr coudé tip catheter; and for appendiceal sphincters, a 14- to 16-Fr coudé tip catheter.
- "How do I carry my catheter?": in a zipper-locked bag that can be placed in a women's purse or a man's coat pocket.
- "How do I clean the stoma before catheterizing in a public facility?": with a benzalkonium chloride wipe, which can be purchased in individual foil-wrapped packets.
- "How do I lubricate the catheter?": by tearing off the end of an individual use foil pack of water-soluble lubricant and inserting the tip of the catheter into the pack.
- "What do I do with the stoma after catheterizing?": cover it with a bandage.
- "How do I clean my catheter after draining my pouch?": by rinsing ordinary tap water through the inside channel

and over outside surface before replacing it in its zipper-locked bag.

In the case of ileal pouches, pouch capacity will initially be low (150 mL). Therefore, the frequency of catheterization will have to be significantly different in these individuals compared with those with right colon pouches in which initial comfortable capacities well in excess of 300 mL are experienced. To ensure restful sleeping hours, the smaller capacity pouches may best be managed by indwelling catheterization during sleeping hours.

General Care

Because all patients with catheterized pouches will have chronic bacteriuria, the problem of antibiotic management should be discussed. **Most authors would suggest that bacteriuria in the absence of symptomatology does not warrant antibiotic treatment** (Skinner et al, 1987). The construction of an effective antireflux mechanism in all of these pouches may ensure against clinical episodes of pyelonephritis, in contrast to patients with diversion by means of free refluxing conduits. Obviously, if clinical pyelonephritis does occur, antibiotic treatment should be instituted. Episodes of recurrent pyelonephritis should be evaluated by radiography of the pouch in a search for a failure of the antireflux mechanism or upper tract stones.

A condition has been described that is manifested by pain in the region of the pouch along with increased pouch contractility ("pouchitis"). It should be mentioned that this condition, although infrequent, may result in temporary failure of the continence mechanism because of the hypercontractility of the bowel segment employed for construction of the pouch. The patient typically presents with a history of sudden explosive discharge of urine through the continence mechanism (rather than dribbling incontinence), along with discomfort in the region of the pouch. Appropriate antibiotic therapy will usually result in resolution of these symptoms. It has been our experience that short courses of antibiotics are not usually successful when treating pouch infections. Perhaps this is due to the larger amount of foreign material (mucus and sediment) within intestinal pouches as opposed to the bladder. Intestinal crypts may also serve as bacterial sanctuaries. Therefore, whenever a pouch infection is treated, a minimal course of antibiotic therapy is 10 days. Pyelonephritis will, of course, require longer courses of therapy.

Urinary retention is an infrequent but serious occurrence in catheterizable pouches. It is most commonly seen with pouches whose continence mechanism consists of a nipple valve. In these circumstances, if the chimney of the nipple valve is not near the abdominal surface, the catheter can be directed into folds of bowel rather than into the nipple valve proper such that urinary retention results. **Pouch urinary retention represents a true emergency and the patient must seek immediate attention so that catheterization and drainage by experienced personnel can be achieved promptly.** Sometimes the use of a coudé tipped catheter is helpful in this regard. Rarely, a flexible cystoscope will be necessary. After the immediate problem has been resolved by emptying the pouch, a catheter should be left indwelling for 3 to 5 days to allow the edema and trauma to the catheterization portal to resolve. Subsequently, the patient should be observed for ability to successfully catheterize on a number of occasions. The appropriate angle of entry can be taught to the patient until he is comfortable with the use of the new catheter. In fact, we prefer to routinely utilize coudé catheters with non–nipple valve pouches.

Intraperitoneal rupture of catheterizable pouches has been reported (Kristiansen et al, 1991; Thompson and Kursh, 1992; Watanabe et al, 1994). In general, these episodes are more common in the neurologic patient when sensation of pouch fullness may be less distinct (Hensle, personal communication; Mitchell, personal communication). Often there is associated mild abdominal trauma, such as a fall, that is antecedent to the rupture. In general, these patients require immediate pouch decompression and radiographic pouch studies. For patients with large defects, surgical exploration and pouch repair is required. If the amount of urinary extravasation is small, and the patient does not have evidence of peritonitis, catheter drainage and antibiotic administration may suffice in treating intraperitoneal rupture of a pouch. Patients managed with this conservative approach require careful monitoring. If there is any sign of progressive peritonitis, surgical exploration and repair is imperative. We have successfully employed this nonoperative approach on patients with ruptured right colon pouches.

Continent Ileal Reservoir (Kock Pouch)

This operation was first reported for use in urinary diversion by Kock and associates in 1982. It was this report that was singularly responsible for the reawakened interest in continent diversion procedures. An outgrowth of the Kock procedure for continent ileostomy (Kock, 1971), the Kock pouch combined reasonably dependable techniques for securing continence of urine and preventing reflux to the upper urinary tracts (nipple valves) along with carefully refashioned bowel that provided a low-pressure urinary reservoir. This procedure and the similarly constructed T-pouch are the only catheterizable continent diversions that preserve the ileocecal valve. **Skinner and his coworkers** (1989, 1992) **have carefully studied and improved the technique over the years, while amassing a prodigious experience with the operation and its variants. The high complication rate and the technical difficulties involved with constructing this reservoir have resulted in the procedure being abandoned by most individuals.** As a result, the procedure is not discussed in this edition. Those interested in a detailed description of this operation are referred to our chapter in previous editions of this text. The construction of a Kock limb remains an important procedure for use in repairing failed continence or reflux mechanisms and is described. It is Skinner's operative description that will be followed closely in this chapter.

Procedure. A 15- to 20-cm length of ileum is selected for creating the intussuscepted nipple valve. The proximal 10 cm serves as the valve, and the distal 5 to 10 cm serves as the patch (Fig. 81–4A). The distal length is chosen based on the volume lost when resecting the failed mechanism. Only 5 cm is necessary for the patch, but on some occasions the reservoir requires augmentation. The middle 6 to 8 cm of the 10-cm segment is denuded of mesentery by electrocoagulation. An Allis or Babcock clamp is advanced into the ileal terminus, grasping the full thickness of the intussusceptum and inverting the ileum into the pouch (see Fig. 81–4B). With the TA-55 stapler, three rows of 4.8-mm staples are applied to the intussuscepted nipple valve (see Fig. 81–4C). The distal six

staples from each cartridge are removed before staple application to ensure that the tip of the valve is free of the staples. Most authors suggest that the pin of the stapling instrument should always be kept in place so that staple misalignment does not occur. This will result in a pinhole puncture site at the base of the nipple valve, and this pinhole should be oversewn with absorbable suture material to prevent fistula formation after staple application is complete. The nipple valve is then fixed by one of two stapling techniques to the back wall of the patch (Skinner et al, 1984). A small buttonhole may be made in the back wall of the ileal plate so that the anvil of the stapler can be passed through the buttonhole and advanced into the nipple valve before application of the fourth row of staples (see Fig. 81–4D). If this is carried out, the buttonhole is oversewn afterward with absorbable material. Alternatively, the anvil of the stapler can be directed between the two leaves of the intussuscipiens and the fourth row of staples utilized to fix the inner leaf of the nipple valve to the pouch wall (see Fig. 81–4E).

Some authors, including Skinner and coworkers (1989), suggest the use of absorbable mesh collar to anchor the base of the nipple valve. If a collar is utilized, a 2.5-cm wide strip of absorbable mesh is placed through an additional window of Deaver at the base of the nipple valve. The mesh strip is fashioned into a collar and sewn both to the base of the patch with seromuscular sutures of absorbable material (see Figs. 81-4F and G). The patch is then sewn to the reservoir.

Double T-Pouch

As indicated earlier, many have abandoned the Kock pouch, owing to the technical difficulty of pouch construction, especially the continence and antireflux mechanisms, and the high complication rates associated with these mechanisms. This should not be viewed as a condemnation of the pioneering work of Kock and his associates. Without their initial efforts, many of the procedures described in this chapter would never have come into being. Rather, this represents the natural evolution of surgical techniques.

The group at the University of Southern California modified a technique described by Abol-Enein and Ghoneim (1993, 1994) to devise a novel continence mechanism created entirely from ileum (Bochner et al, 1988). Abol-Einein and Ghoneim described a technique that created an extramural serosal tunnel into which the ureters were implanted. This extramural trough created a pseudotunnel that prevents reflux but in theory is associated with a lower risk of obstruction than either the Goodwin (1958), Leadbetter, or LeDuc and colleagues' (1987) techniques of direct transmural ureteral implantation. Stein and colleagues (1998) first reported on the use of a tapered ileal segment implanted into a serosal trough as the antireflux mechanism for neobladder in 1998. In 1999 they reported on their adaptation of the technique to the ileal-anal reservoir, and in 1999 they presented their early experience with a double T-pouch as a replacement for the Kock pouch at the meeting of the American Urologists Association (Stein et al, 1999a). It is their technique that is presented in this section.

Procedure. A 70-cm segment of terminal ileum is isolated 15 to 20 cm from the ileocecal valve at the line of Treves. The proximal isoperistaltic 10- to 12-cm segment is isolated and

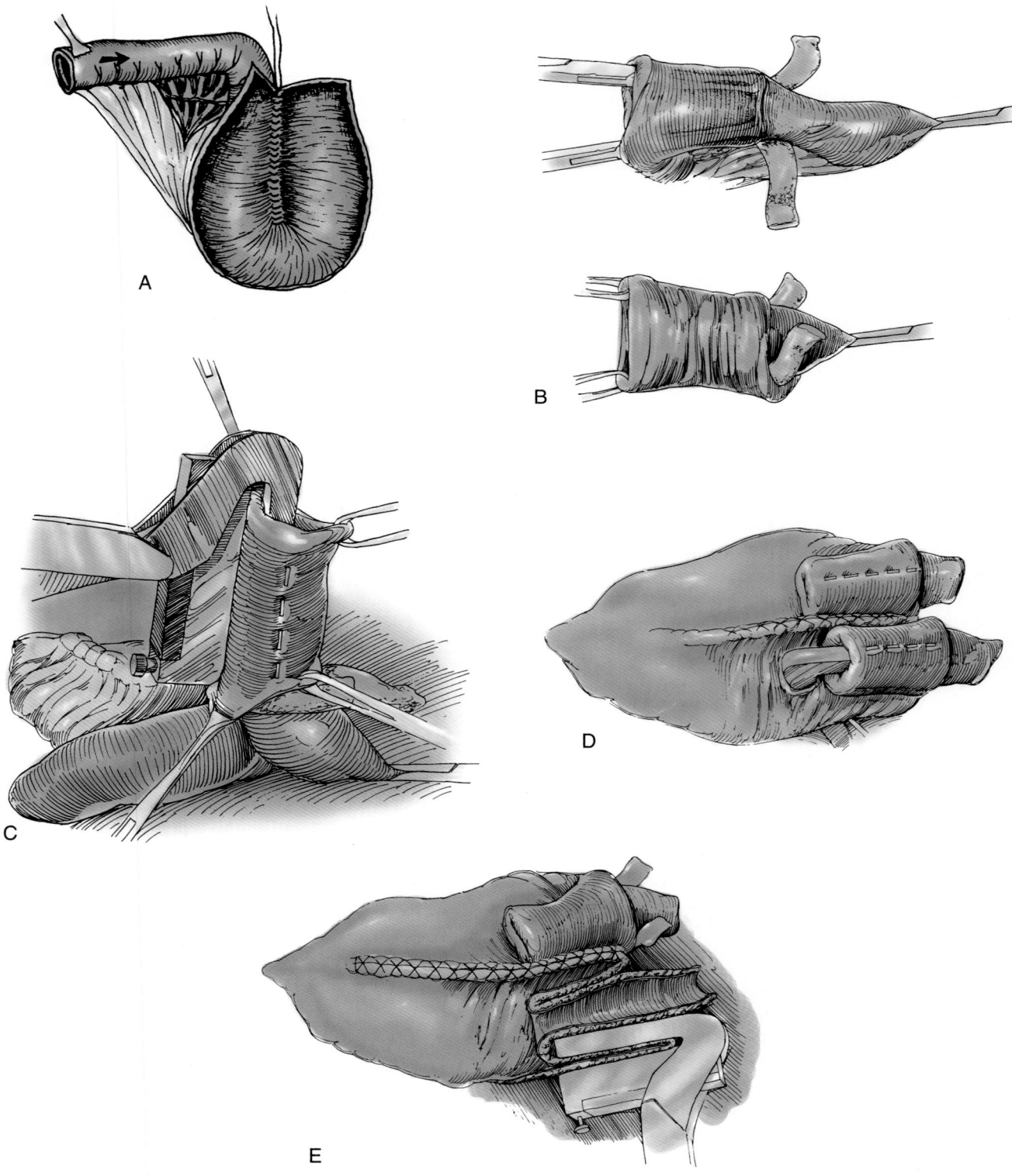

Figure 81–4. **A,** A 15-cm segment of terminal ileum is isolated and opened along its antimesenteric wall. The proximal 10 cm will serve as the continent intussusception and the distal 5 to 10 cm, the patch. The size of the patch will vary according to the size of the excised segment. **B,** An Allis or Babcock clamp is advanced into the ileal terminus, the full thickness of the intussuscipiens is grasped, and it is prolapsed into the pouch. **C,** Three rows of 4.8-mm staples are applied to the intussuscepted nipple valve using the TA55 stapler. **D,** A small buttonhole is made in the back wall of the ileal plate to allow the anvil of the TA55 stapler to be passed through and advanced into the nipple valve. A fourth row of staples is applied. The figure shows two valve mechanisms, but in this instance there would be only one. **E,** The anvil of the stapler can be directed between the two leaves of the intussuscipiens and the fourth row of staples applied in this manner. Two valve mechanisms are shown but in this instance there would be only one. *Continued*

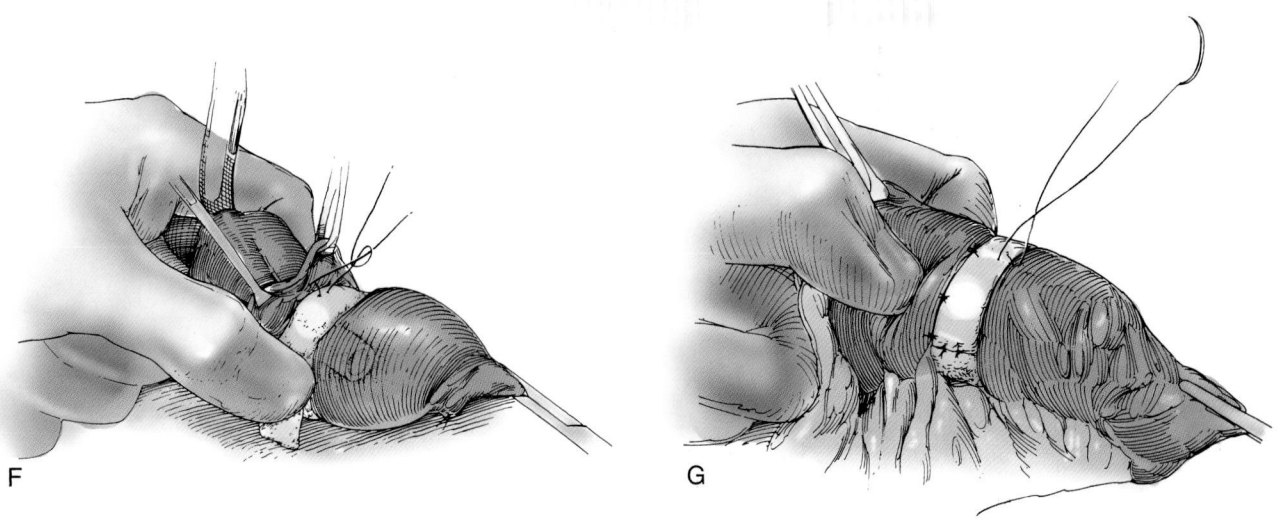

F

G

Figure 81–4, cont'd. **F,** A 2.5-cm wide strip of absorbable mesh is placed through additional windows of Deaver at the base of each nipple valve. The mesh strips are fashioned into collars. **G,** The collars are sewn to the base of the pouch as well as to the ileal terminus with seromuscular sutures. (**A** from Ghoneim MA, Lock NG, Lycke G, El-Din AB: An appliance-free, sphincter-controlled bladder substitute. J Urol 1987;138:1150-1154; **B** to **G** from Hinman F Jr: Atlas of Urologic Surgery. Philadelphia, WB Saunders, 1989.)

will serve as the antireflux mechanism. The distal 12- to 15-cm segment is isolated and rotated in an antiperistaltic fashion and will create the cutaneous continence mechanism (Fig. 81–5A and B). A short 2- to 3-cm mesenteric incision is made to isolate the proximal limb and a 4-cm incision is made for the distal limb, thereby preserving the major vascular arches. The proximal and distal segments can vary in length, depending on ureteral length and the thickness of the anterior abdominal wall. The middle 44 cm of ileum is folded in a W with each limb measuring 11 cm.

The afferent antireflux mechanism is created by opening the windows of Deaver between the vascular arcades along the distal 3 to 4 cm. The efferent continence mechanism is created by opening the proximal 7 to 8 cm of vascular arcades (antiperistaltic) (see Fig. 81–5C). One-fourth-inch Penrose drains are then placed in each window of Deaver to facilitate the passage of the 3-0 silk horizontal mattress sutures that are utilized to approximate the serosa of the corresponding 11-cm limbs of the W (see Fig. 81–5D). The 3- to 4-cm anchored portion of the proximal limb is then tapered over a 30-Fr catheter, and the 7- to 8-cm anchored portion of the efferent limb is tapered over a 16-Fr catheter. In both instances, tapering is performed with a GIA stapler (the staples will not be in contact with urine). Care must be taken in the efferent limb to create a gradual taper so that the catheter does not hit a false cul-de-sac (see Fig. 81–5E). The portions of the 11-cm W limbs not forming the troughs are then sutured together with a running suture of 3-0 polyglycolic acid (PGA). The bowel is now incised along its antimesenteric border in the portion where the serosal trough exists and in close proximity to the medial PGA suture lines when beyond the two limbs (see Fig. 81–5F). The incised mucosa is then closed in two layers with a running suture of 3-0 PGA. The incised intestinal flaps (antimesenteric incision) are then sutured to each ostium with interrupted sutures of 3-0 PGA, and the two ileal flaps are sutured over each segment with a running suture of 3-0 PGA (see Fig. 81–5G). The reservoir is then closed side-to-side in

two layers with 3-0 PGA, completing its construction (see Fig. 81–5H and I). The ureters are anastomosed end-to-side over stents to the proximal limb, which has been closed with a running absorbable Parker-Kerr suture. The efferent limb is then brought to the abdominal wall stoma site, and redundant ileum is resected. The stoma is matured. The reservoir lies immediately adjacent to the anterior abdominal wall.

Postoperative Care and Comments. Postoperative care is similar to that for any continent reservoir. We initially reported on nine patients, seven of whom could be evaluated for continence and long-term complications and two of whom died of disease during follow-up (Stein et al, 1999b). The seven patients achieved immediate continence on catheter removal, but two developed incontinence with time and one has undergone surgical revision. None of the nine patients experienced an early postoperative complication. One patient developed a reservoir stone 9 months after surgery that was removed endoscopically without sequelae. Pouch capacity was excellent: 400 to 700 mL (average: 500 mL). There was no radiographic evidence of reflux in any patient, and there was no upper tract deterioration. This operative procedure appears to have many advantages over the Kock pouch, and long-term continence has been reported. Marino and colleagues (2002) reported on 18 patients with 1-year follow-up with 100% day and night continence and no delayed complications.

Mainz Pouch I

The catheterizable Mainz pouch has undergone considerable modification over the years (Thuroff et al, 1985; Stein et al, 1995; Lampel et al, 1996; Gerharz et al, 1997). **Problems with the nipple valve represented the primary reason for modifications to be carried out.** The operative technique has now been modified to utilize the intact ileocecal valve as a means of further stabilizing the intussusception (Thuroff et al, 1988). This procedure is described here without further reference to earlier prototypes.

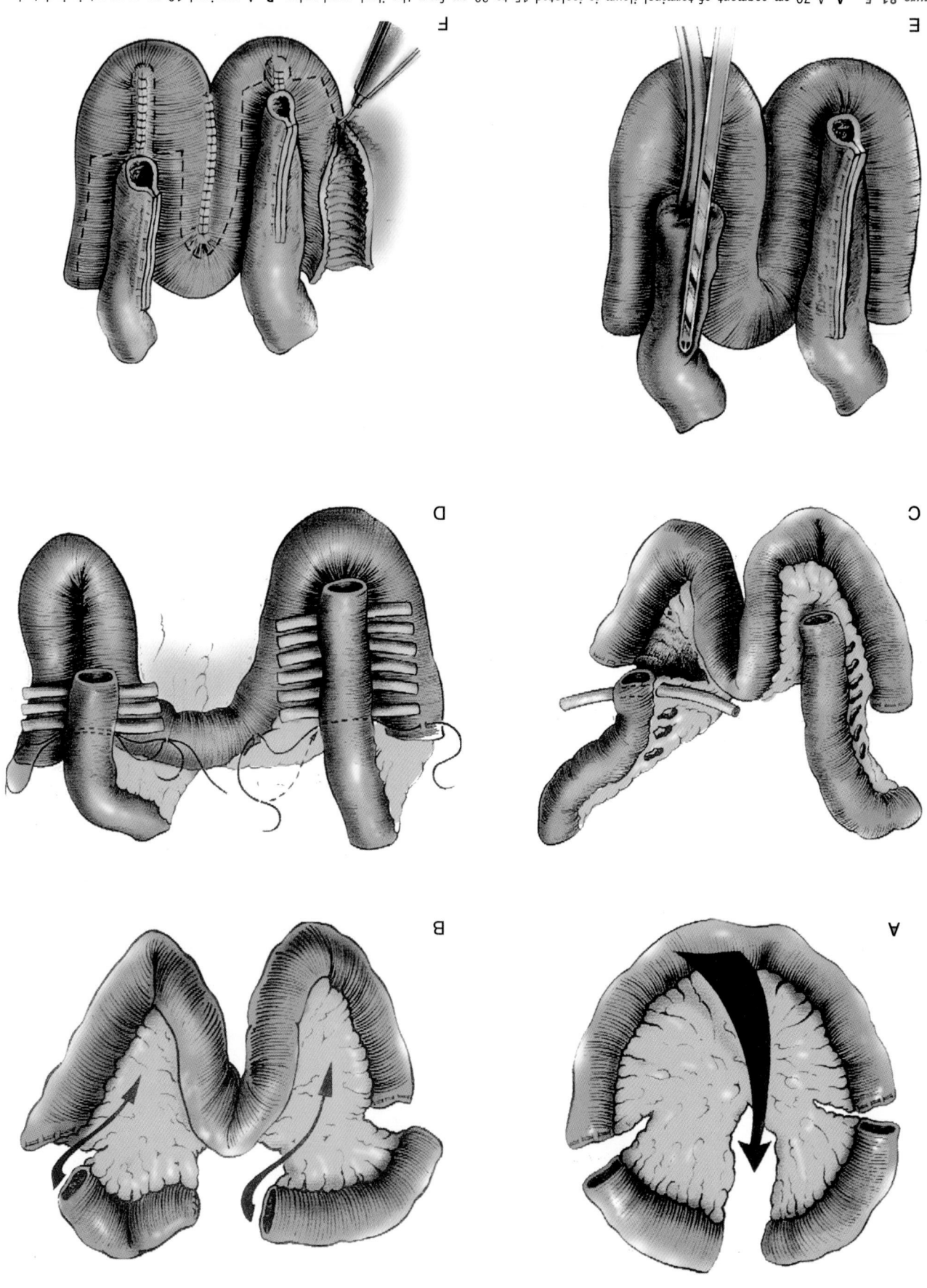

Figure 81–5. A, A 70-cm segment of terminal ileum is isolated 15 to 20 cm from the ileal cecal valve. **B,** A proximal 10-cm segment is isolated and rotated toward what will become the reservoir in an isoperistaltic direction. The distal 12 to 15 cm is rotated toward the reservoir in an antiperistaltic direction. **C,** The windows of Deaver are opened to allow the walls of the W reservoir to be apposed behind the valve mechanisms. Penrose drains are passed to guide suture passage. **D,** Horizontal mattress sutures of 3-0 silk are passed through each window. The distal continence mechanism is longer than the proximal antireflux mechanism. **E,** The proximal and distal mechanisms are tapered with a metal GIA stapler. **F,** The bowel is incised along its antimesenteric border where it will overly the 2 Ts. Distal to the Ts, the bowel is incised close to the approximated limbs of the reservoir.

Continued

staples are applied on the intussusceptum itself (see Fig. 81-6C). Thereafter, the intussusceptum is led through the intact ileocecal valve and a third row of staples is applied to stabilize the nipple valve to the ileocecal valve (see Fig. 81-6D). Finally, a fourth row of staples is applied inferiorly, securing the inner leaf of the intussusception to the ileal wall (see Fig. 81-6E).

Ureterocolonic anastomoses are created at the apex of the reservoir, which is then folded upon itself in a side-to-side fashion to complete the pouch construction. The entire pouch is rotated cephalad so as to bring the ileal terminus to the region of the umbilicus. A small button of skin is removed from the depth of the umbilical funnel, and the ileal terminus

Procedure. The catheterizable Mainz pouch varies somewhat from the orthotopic voiding Mainz pouch. First, a longer segment of bowel is utilized. A 10- to 15-cm portion of cecum and ascending colon is isolated along with two separate equal-sized limbs of distal ileum and an additional portion of ileum measuring 20 cm (Fig. 81-6A). The entire colon and distal segments of ileum are spatulated, taking care to preserve the ileocecal valve. These three bowel segments are folded in the form of an incomplete W and their posterior aspects sutured to one another to form a broad posterior plate (see Fig. 81-6B). A portion of the intact proximal ileal terminus is freed of its mesentery for a distance of 6 to 8 cm, and intussusception of the segment is achieved. Two rows of

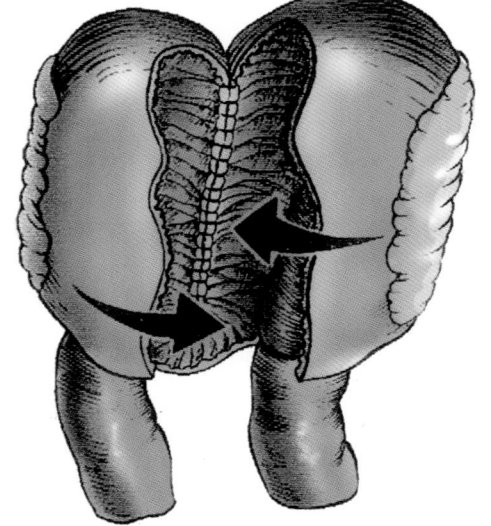

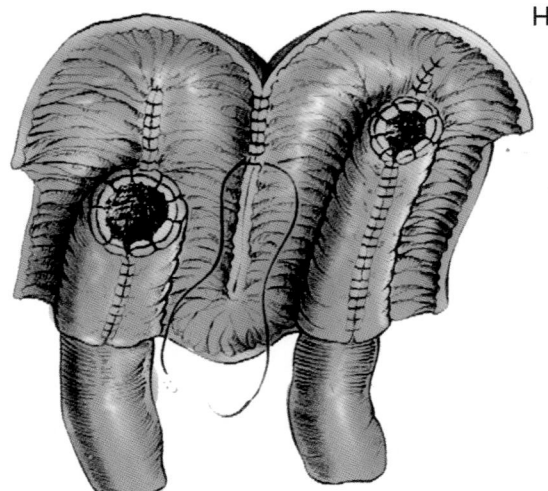

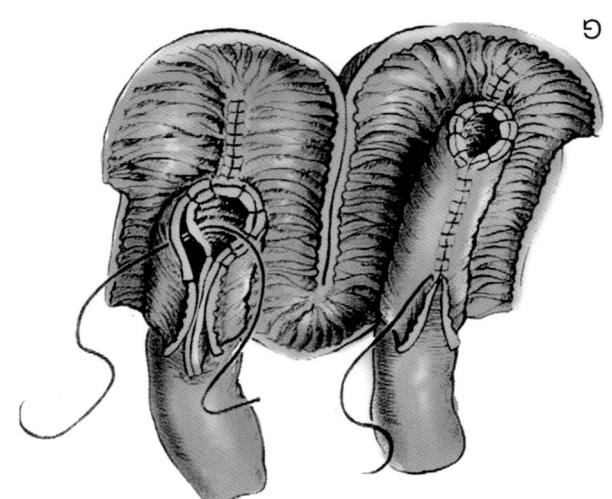

Figure 81-5, cont'd. G, The ostia of the valves are secured to the bowel wall with interrupted absorbable sutures. The two flaps of ileum are closed over the Ts with running absorbable sutures. **H,** The back wall of the reservoir is closed with running absorbable sutures. **I,** The lateral walls are folded medially and the construction completed with running absorbable sutures. (From Stein JP, Buscarini M, DeFilippo M, Skinner RE, Skinner DG: Application of the T pouch as an ileo-anal reservoir. J Urol 1999;162:2052-2053.)

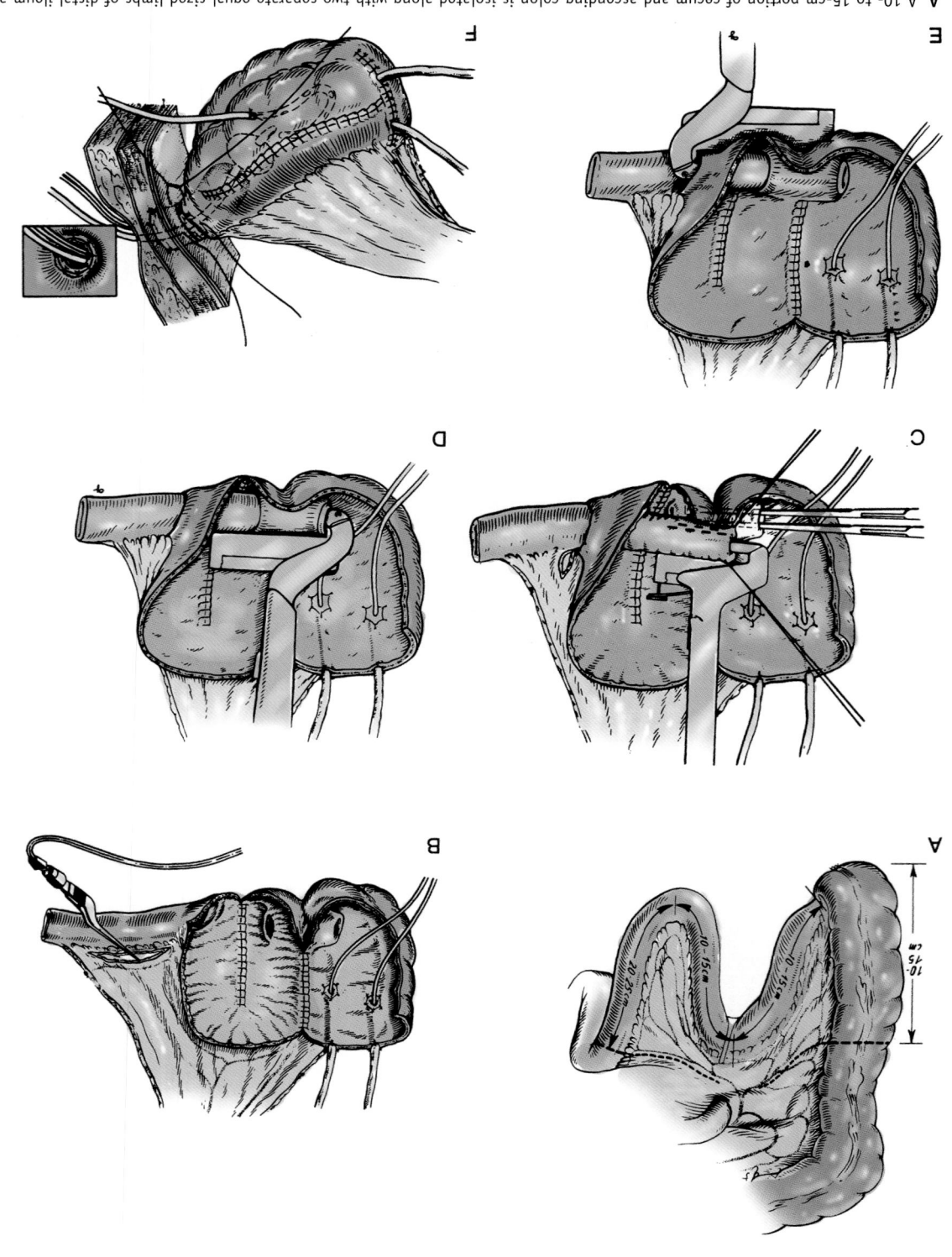

Figure 81–6. **A**, A 10- to 15-cm portion of cecum and ascending colon is isolated along with two separate equal-sized limbs of distal ileum and an additional portion of ileum 20 cm. **B**, A portion of the intact proximal ileal terminus is freed of its mesentery for a distance of 6 to 8 cm. **C**, The intact ileum is intussuscepted, and two rows of staples are taken on the intussuscipiens itself. **D**, The intussuscipiens is led through the intact ileocecal valve, and a third row of staples is taken to stabilize the nipple valve to the ileocecal valve. **E**, A fourth row of staples is taken inferiorly, securing the inner leaf of the intussusception to the ileal wall. **F**, A button of skin is removed from the depth of the umbilical funnel and the ileal terminus is directed through this buttonhole. Excess ileal length is resected and ileum is sutured at the depth of the umbilical funnel. (**A** from Thuroff JW, Alken P, Hohenfellner R: The MAINZ pouch [mixed augmentation with ileum 'n' cecum] for bladder augmentation and continent diversion. In King LR, Stone AR, Webster GD [eds]: Bladder Reconstruction and Continent Urinary Diversion. Chicago, Year Book Medical Publishers, 1987, p 252; **B** to **F** from Thuroff JW, Alken P, Riedmiller H, et al: 100 cases of MAINZ pouch: Continuing experience and evolution. J Urol 1988;140:283-288.)

is directed through this buttonhole (see Fig. 81–6F). The pouch is secured to the posterior fascia with interrupted absorbable sutures, and the ileal terminus is sewn similarly to anterior fascia. Excess ileal length is resected, and ileum is sutured at the depth of the umbilical funnel with interrupted absorbable sutures.

Postoperative Care and Comments. No specific differences in postoperative care or complications associated with the Mainz pouch need be addressed. Initial pouch capacities are higher than in the Kock or T-pouch. Final mean capacity averaging over 600 mL has been reported. Pouch pressures are 23 cm H_2O at half capacity and 31 cm H_2O when the pouch is full. Contraction waves beginning at 50% pouch fullness seems to produce a reasonably low-pressure urinary reservoir, although the pressures are not as low as that achieved with the use of small bowel alone.

Recently, the 10- and 12-year experiences with the Mainz pouch and the variations created by its developers were presented (Stein et al, 1995; Lampel et al, 1996). Between 1983 and July, 1994, 440 patients underwent a Mainz I operation in two urology departments, Mainz and Wuppertal. In 146 the appendix was utilized as the continence mechanism, 270 patients had the intussuscepted nipple used as the continent stoma, in 14 patients a submucosal seromuscular bowel flap was used, and 10 patients underwent a submucosal full-thickness bowel flap (appendiceal) continence mechanisms will be described later in the chapter). The early complication rate was 12% and included mechanical ileus requiring open revision in 9 patients (1.6%), pouch leakage requiring open revision in 5 patients (0.9%), wound dehiscence in 4 patients (0.7%), and fatal pulmonary emboli in 4 patients (0.7%).

The late complication rate was 37% and was predominantly attributable to the pouch. Stomal failure requiring open revision occurred in 45 patients (8%) and was directly related to the continence mechanism. Only 2 of 146 patients (1.4%) with an appendiceal continence mechanism were incontinent, but stomal stenosis occurred in 21%. The developers of this procedure were very innovative in their attempts to bring the incontinence rate down to an acceptable level. To this end they tried alloplastic stoma (4/4 incontinent), sutured intussusception (8/8 incontinent), stapled intussusception (5/22, 23% incontinent), and stapled ileocecal intussusception (10/204, 4.9% incontinent). The stapled ileocecal intussusception described previously is the current recommendation, and the long-term incontinence rate among the patients undergoing the stapled nipple valves was reduced to 10%. Other late complications include ureteral reimplants in 28 patients (4.9%), stomal stenosis in 29 patients with an ileal nipple (11.7%), and 17 patients with an appendiceal stoma (14.7%). Calculus formation in the pouch occurred in 38 patients (6.8%), who underwent 36 percutaneous procedures. Despite the loss of the terminal ileum, we have not seen a significant drop in serum vitamin B_{12} levels and no patient has developed a macrocytic anemia or neurologic symptoms. However, 25% of patients are on oral alkalinization to avoid metabolic acidosis.

The overall complication rate for this procedure since its inception was high (31%). However, Stein and associates (1995) pointed out that 50% of the complications were manageable with percutaneous techniques. Additionally, since 1988 the incontinence rate has only been 3.2% and less than 2% of the patients with an appendiceal continence mechanism have been incontinent.

Gerharz and associates (1997) from Marburg, Germany, reported a single institutional experience with the Mainz I ileocecal pouch. From 1990 to 1996, 202 consecutive patients underwent continent diversion, 96 with a submucosally embedded in-situ appendix and 106 with an intussuscepted ileal nipple. All patients had an umbilical stoma. In 172 of 200 patients (85%), no stomal complications occurred. In 17 of 96 patients (18%) with an appendiceal stoma, 23 revisions were performed for stomal stenosis. In contrast, only 13 of 106 patients (12%) with an intussuscepted ileal nipple developed a stomal problem. However, these patients required more invasive, major procedures for correction and those with an appendiceal stenosis could usually be repaired with a minor procedure. Three patients with an ileal nipple (3%) developed pouch calculi, whereas none of the patients with an appendiceal continence mechanism developed stones. As a result, the authors concluded that the appendix, when available, should be the intestinal continence mechanism of choice.

We share the enthusiasm for the use of the appendix as a continence mechanism. In our experience it has also been a reliable technique that is easy to perform. It has been our prejudice in constructing right colon pouches employing an appendiceal continence mechanism to utilize the entire right colon inclusive of the hepatic flexure to form the reservoir, thereby preserving more terminal ileum. This has the theoretical advantage of fewer metabolic complications, but the Mainz group has not experienced significant metabolic problems.

The introduction of the more reliable appendiceal continence mechanism has greatly increased the acceptance of the Mainz I procedure. The Mainz group has also developed two new techniques for construction of a Mitrofanoff (appendiceal)-type tube for use in patients whose appendix is either unsuitable or absent (Lampel et al, 1995a, 1995b; Lampel and Thüroff, 1998). Both techniques utilize a small-caliber conduit fashioned from the large intestine in the region of the cecum. One technique utilizes a full-thickness tube lined by mucosa (Fig. 81–7) and the other a seromuscular tube lined by serosa (Fig. 81–8). Both techniques appear to be successful, although the full-thickness tube was associated with a lower complication rate and a higher success rate in their initial report (Lampel et al, 1995b). With longer follow-up, the authors have observed a similar success rates with both tubes; 93% of the patients (25 of 27) with a seromuscular tube and 92% of the patients (22 of 24) with a bowel wall tube were continent day and night (Lampel and Thüroff, 1998). The authors believed that either tube was reliable and that each had its own unique advantages and disadvantages. In general, the full-thickness bowel wall tube was more adaptable, owing to the ability to create a longer tube. However, this came with the expense of a more tenuous blood supply. The decreased distal blood supply might be improved by creating a wider base on the tube. This could, however, make taenial implantation more difficult. The seromuscular tube was equally reliable but could only be anastomosed to the umbilicus, owing to the short adit tube. Either tube was believed to be indicated as a continence mechanism in the Mainz I pouch when the appendix was not available or as a continence mechanism for reservoirs created from other large intestinal segments. Either technique could be utilized as a salvage procedure when another primary continence mechanism had failed.

Another novel Mitrofanoff continence mechanism was described by Monti (1997), who conceived of a procedure in which a 2- to 3-cm segment of terminal ileum is isolated on its blood supply (Fig. 81-9A). The width of the segment was chosen to correspond to the circumference of the tube to be created. Once isolated, the segment is opened near one of its mesenteric junctions to create a longitudinal reconfiguration (see Fig. 81-9B and C). The tube is then closed with a running 3-0 absorbable suture (see Fig. 81-9D). It can now be utilized for a Mitrofanoff implant. When longer tubes are necessary, two adjacent segments can be isolated, reconfigured, and joined together (see Fig. 81-9E and F). Although originally described in dogs, the authors have utilized this technique in humans without complication. Monti (1997) reported on a high rate of stomal stenosis in dogs, but this may have been secondary to the infrequent catheterizations. Stomal stenosis has not occurred in our limited series of patients.

Other groups have used tapered ileum to create a tunneled access into the right colon (Fig. 81-10) (Woodhouse and Mac-Neily, 1994; Hampel et al, 1995). Using tapered ileum for this purpose has the advantage of a blood supply independent of the reservoir and no length restrictions while having the disadvantage of further limiting intestinal absorptive surface.

Right Colon Pouches with Intussuscepted Terminal Ileum

Additional pouches utilizing nipple valve technology for the continence mechanism include those right colon pouches in which intussusception of the terminal ileum and ileal cecal valve is employed. As such, they are variations on the continent cecal reservoir initially described by Mansson (1987) employing an intact cecal segment. These three pouches are the UCLA pouch (Raz, personal communication, 1989), the Duke pouch (Webster and King, 1987), and Le Bag (Light and

Scardino, 1986). These operations differ from one another by only a few features, predominantly related to the technique employed for stabilizing the nipple valve. In all instances, unless the appendix is being utilized as a continence mechanism, appendectomy must be performed because the in-situ appendix would serve as a nidus for infection and abscess formation.

These operations were reported on in detail in the prior edition of this text. Since that edition, no new reports or modifications of these procedures have appeared and these procedures will not be described in this edition. The reader is referred to the prior edition of this text for an in-depth description of these operations.

Indiana Pouch

The concept of using the buttressed ileocecal valve as a dependable continence mechanism that can withstand the trauma of intermittent catheterization was first reported from Indiana University by Rowland and colleagues (1987). This operation involving partial spatulation of the cecal segment and attachment of an ileal patch represented major contributions to the original ileocecal reservoir described by Gilchrist and associates (1950) in which the intact bowel reservoir was employed and no attempt was made to strengthen the ileocecal valve. Originally, strengthening the ileocecal valve consisted of a double row of imbricating sutures taken to the entire ileal segment (Rowland et al, 1985, 1987). It soon became apparent that this was necessary only in the region of the ileocecal valve. "Neourethral" pressure profiles showed that the continence zone was confined to the region of the reconfigured ileocecal valve (Bejany and Politano, 1988). The remaining "neourethra" could be tapered and brought through an abdominal or perineal stoma. At Indiana University as well as other institutions it became clear that the concept of marsupializing only a portion of the ascending colon segment left sufficient peristaltic integrity in the cecal region to generate pressures sufficiently high to overcome the continence mechanism in some patients. A number of groups

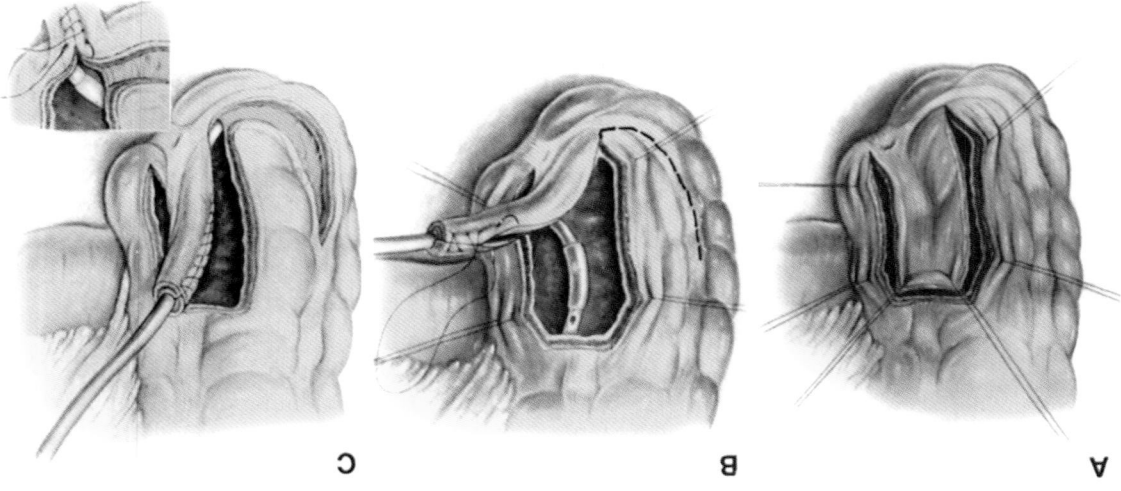

A **B** **C**

Figure 81-7. A to C, A full-thickness tube lined by mucosa is fashioned over an 18-Fr Foley catheter for tunneled reimplantation. The tube is closed with a running 3-0 absorbable suture. For longer tubes, we would advise a wider base to prevent distal ischemia. The continence mechanism is created by placing the tube into the adjacent taenial trough. (From Lampel A, Hohenfellner M, Schultz-Lampel D, Thuroff JW: In-situ tunneled bowel flap tubes: 2 new techniques of a continent outlet for Mainz pouch cutaneous diversion. J Urol 1995;153:308-315.)

contributed to the concept of utilizing the entire right colon or more, marsupializing the entire structure and refashioning it in a Heineke-Mikulicz configuration (Lockhart, 1987; Bejany and Politano, 1988; Benson et al, 1988; Rowland, personal communication, 1989). These variations have been entitled the Florida pouch (Lockhart, 1987) and the University of Miami pouch (Bejany and Politano, 1988). However, they represent relatively minor variations on the theme of the Indiana pouch.

Procedure. The Indiana pouch, in its present form, involves isolating a segment of terminal ileum approximately 10 cm in length along with the entire right colon to the junction of the

right and middle colic artery blood supplies (Fig. 81–11A). After bowel continuity is reestablished, appendectomy is performed and the appendiceal fat pad obscuring the inferior margin of the ileocecal junction is removed by cautery (see Fig. 81–11B). The entire right colon is opened along its antimesenteric border, and ureteral-taenial implants are fashioned (see Fig. 81–11C). The ileocecal junction is buttressed according to different techniques depending on the author. Interrupted Lembert sutures are taken over a short distance (3 to 4 cm) in two rows for the double imbrication of the ileocecal valve as described at Indiana University (see Fig. 81–11D). Nonabsorbable material is utilized for this, and the second row of sutures should attempt to bring the opposite

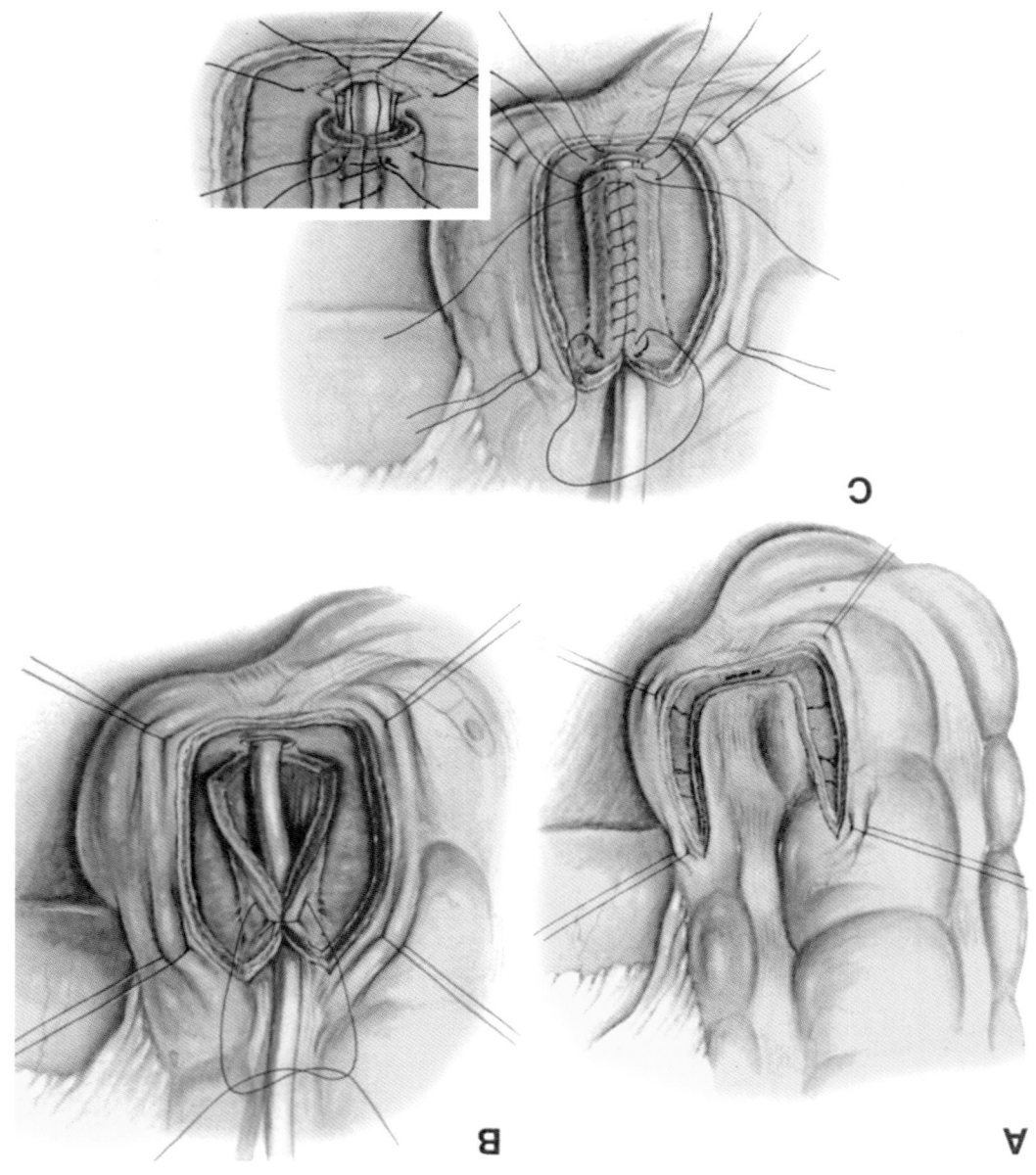

Figure 81–8. *A* to *C*, A 3- to 5-cm seromuscular tube denuded of mucosa and lined by serosa is fashioned for tunneled reimplantation. The tube is rolled over an 18-Fr Foley catheter. A mucosal window is opened at the base of the U and the tube sutured to the mucosa with interrupted sutures. (From Lampel A, Hohenfellner M, Schultz-Lampel D, Thuroff JW: In situ tunneled bowel flap tubes: 2 new techniques of a continent outlet for Mainz pouch cutaneous diversion. J Urol 1995;153:308-315.)

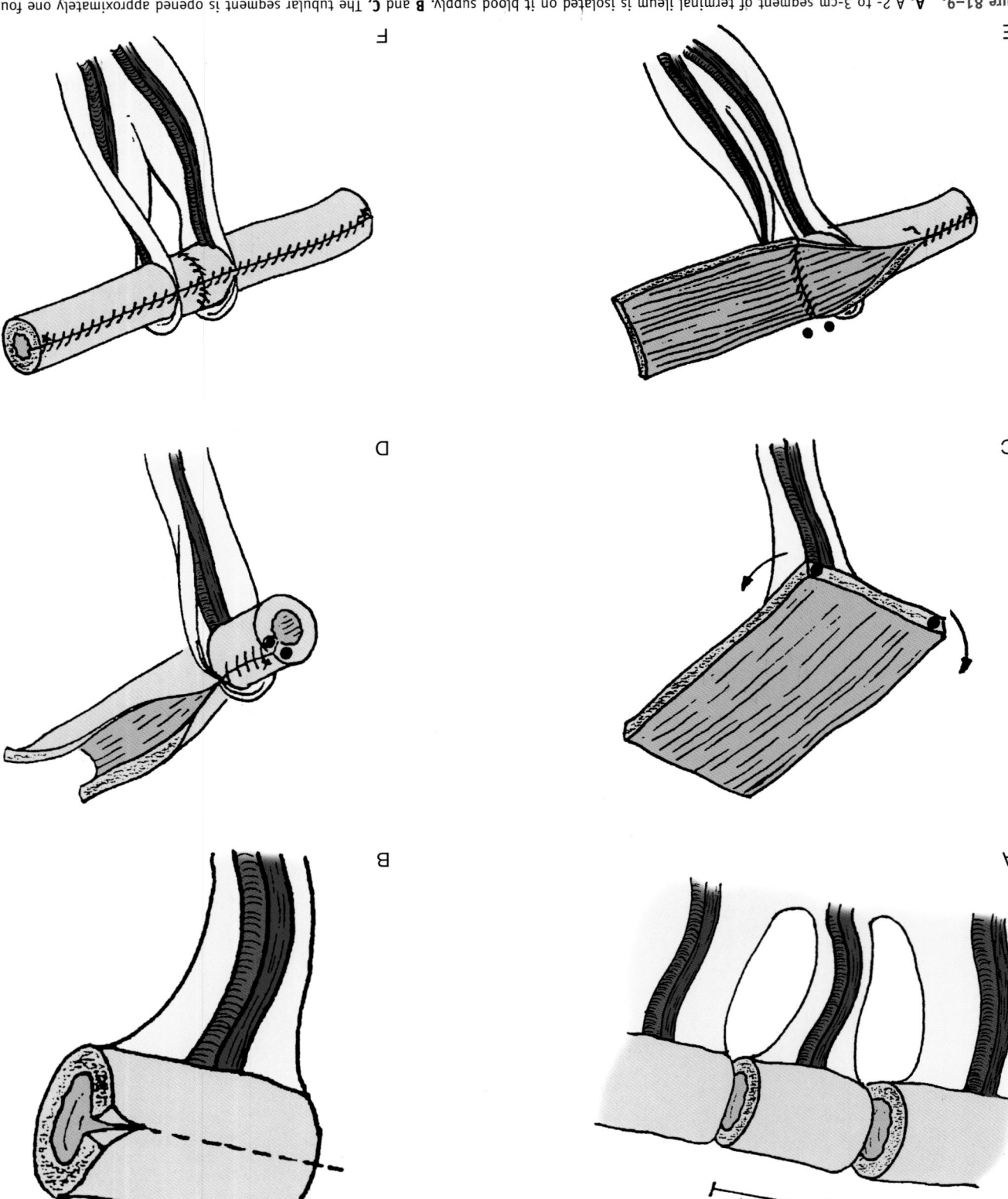

Figure 81-9. *A,* A 2- to 3-cm segment of terminal ileum is isolated on it blood supply. *B* and *C,* The tubular segment is opened approximately one fourth of the way up one side. This results in a well-vascularized rectangular plate. *D,* The rectangular tube is now closed over a catheter with a running absorbable suture. *E* and *F,* Two adjacent segments can be joined together to create one long tube. (From Monti PR, Lara RC, Dutra MA, et al: New techniques for construction of efferent conduits based on the Mitrofanoff principle. Urology 1997;49:112-115.)

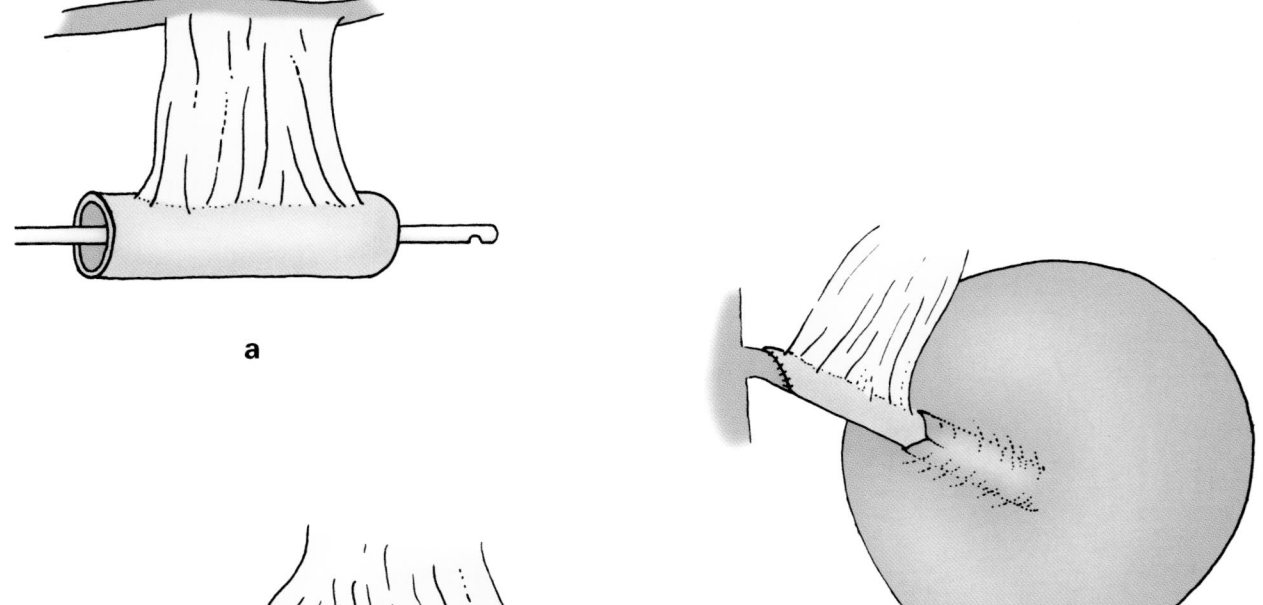

Figure 81–10. Woodhouse tapered ileum. (From Woodhouse CR, MacNeily AE: The Mitrofanoff principle: Expanding upon a versatile technique. Br J Urol 1994;74:447-453.)

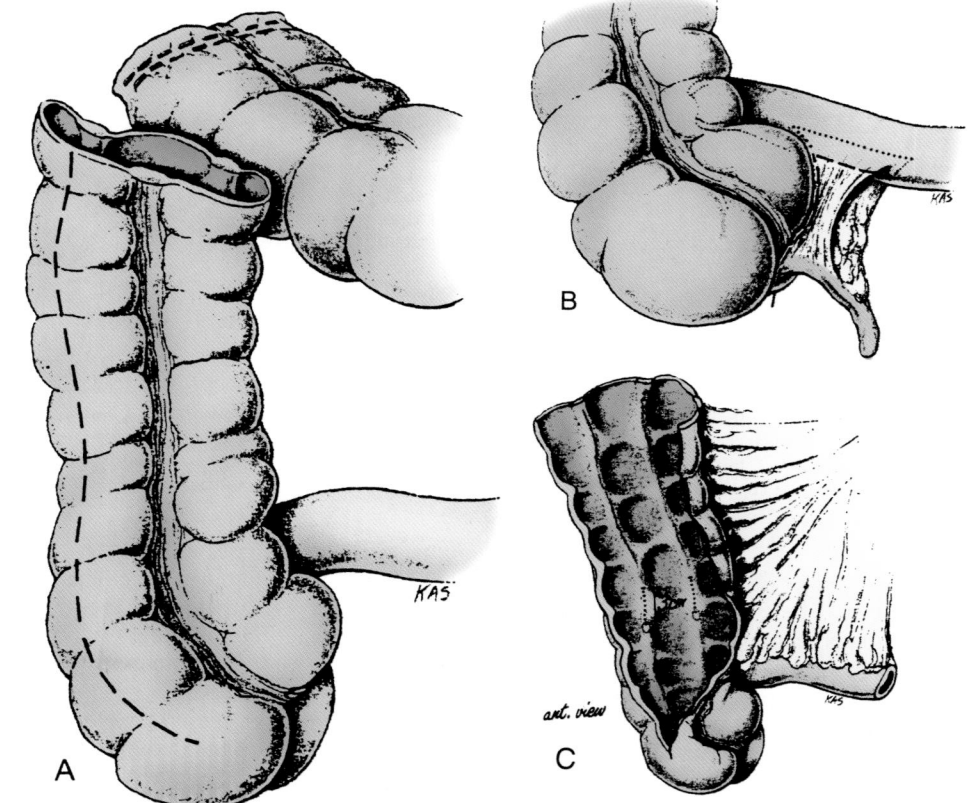

Figure 81–11. **A,** A segment of terminal ileum approximately 10 cm in length along with the entire right colon is isolated. **B,** Appendectomy is performed and the appendiceal fat pad obscuring the inferior margin of the ileocecal junction is removed by cautery. **C,** The entire right colon is opened along its antimesenteric border.

Continued

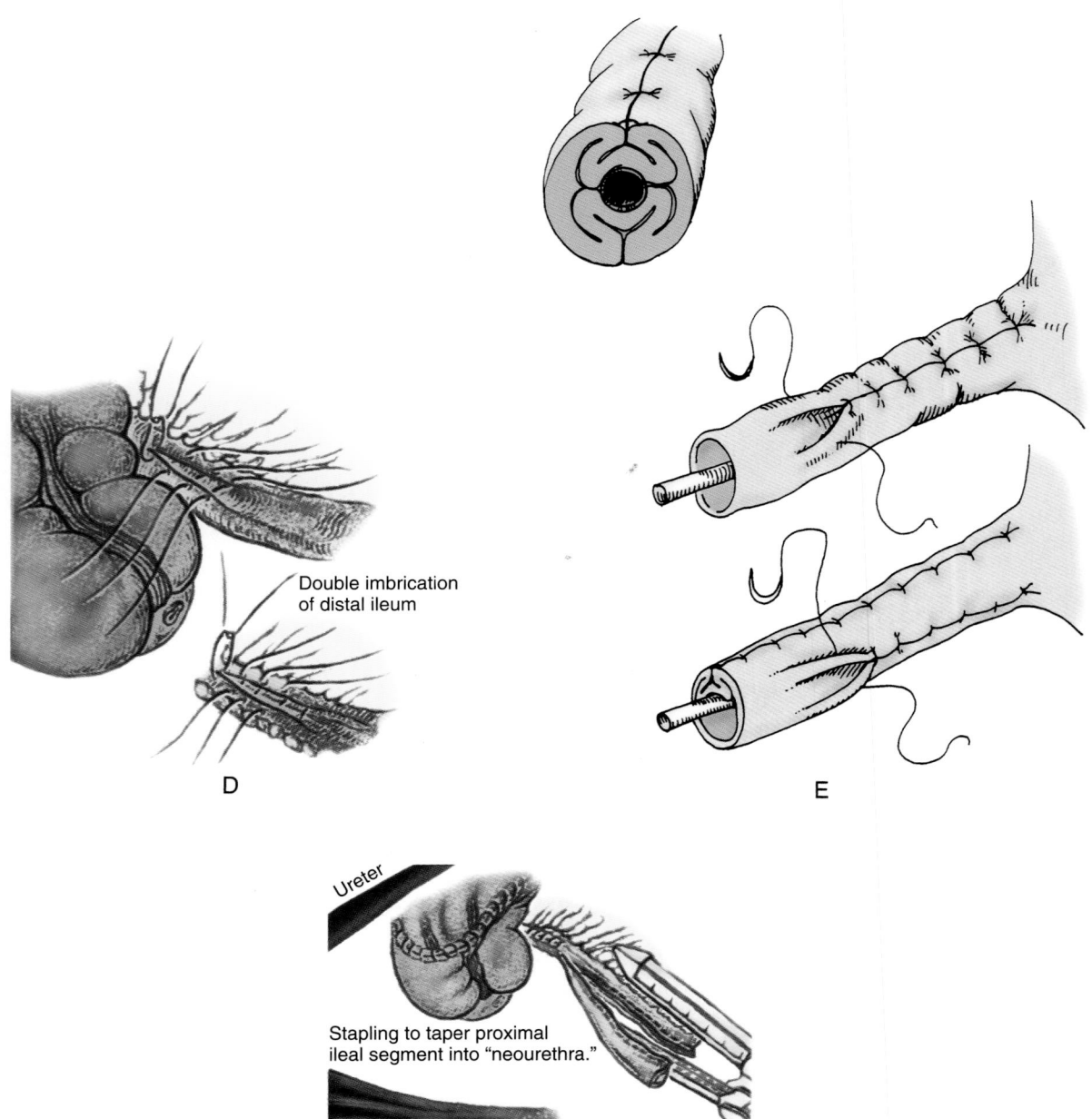

Double imbrication
of distal ileum

D

E

Ureter

Stapling to taper proximal
ileal segment into "neourethra."

F

Figure 81–11, cont'd.   D, Interrupted Lembert sutures are taken over a short distance (3 to 4 cm) in two rows for the double imbrication of the ileoce-cal valve as described at Indiana. **E,** Application of opposing Lembert sutures on each side of the terminal ileum. **F,** Excess ileum can be tapered by sta-pling technique. (**A** to **C** from Benson MC, Sawczuk IS, Hensle TW, et al: Modified Indiana University continent diversion. Curr Surg Tech Urol 1988;1:1-8; **D** and **F,** from Olsson CA: Contemp Urol 62-68, September 1989; **E** from Lockhart J: Remodeled right colon: An alternative urinary reservoir. J Urol 1987;138:730-734.)

mesenteric edges of ileum together, usually over a 12- to 14-Fr catheter. These two rows of sutures should be placed approximately 8 mm from one another, and the initial suture in each row may be taken in a purse-string fashion around the cecal margin as well. Alternatively, the University of Miami group suggests purse-string sutures being taken in the ileum in the same region (Bejany and Politano, 1988). Finally, the Tampa group suggests the application of apposing Lembert sutures being taken on each side of the terminal ileum (see

Fig. 81–11E). The remaining ileum can be tapered over the catheter and excess ileum removed by stapling technique (see Fig. 81–11F).

It is important to carry out the imbrication while the cecal reservoir is still open (Rowland, 1996). In this fashion, one can easily observe the gradual closure of the ileocecal valve. The pouch is then closed in a Heineke-Mikulicz configuration with running absorbable suture material. Ureteral stents and a suprapubic tube are taken through a stab wound in the pouch and led through the right lower abdominal quadrant. The pouch is rotated so as to bring the ileal neourethra as close as possible to the selected stoma site. A fingerbreadth-width skin button is transected along with a similar button from the anterior and posterior fascia. The ileal neourethra is advanced between bundles of the rectus muscle through the stoma and excess ileum is transected. The ileal edges are sewn to skin with interrupted sutures so as to create a flush stoma.

In addition to the differences in the technique of ileocecal valve imbrication, both the University of Miami and the Florida pouches differ in the amount of colon utilized. The entire ascending colon and the right third or half of the transverse colon is isolated along with 10 to 12 cm of ileum. The entire upper extremity of the large bowel is mobilized laterally in the fashion of an inverted U (Fig. 81–12A). The medial limbs of the U are sutured to one another after the bowel is spatulated (see Fig. 81–12B). The bowel plate is then closed side to side (see Fig. 81–12C). This inverted-U closure, however, is exactly the same as a Heineke-Mikulicz reconfiguration.

There have been recent modifications to the Indiana reservoir that allow for more rapid construction and a lower complication rate (Rowland, 1996). The modifications incorporate the use of metal staples to create the efferent limb and absorbable staples to fashion the reservoir. The concept of using a metal GIA stapler to fashion the efferent limb was first introduced by Bejany and Politano (1988). Carroll and Presti (1992) reported on the urodynamic features of the

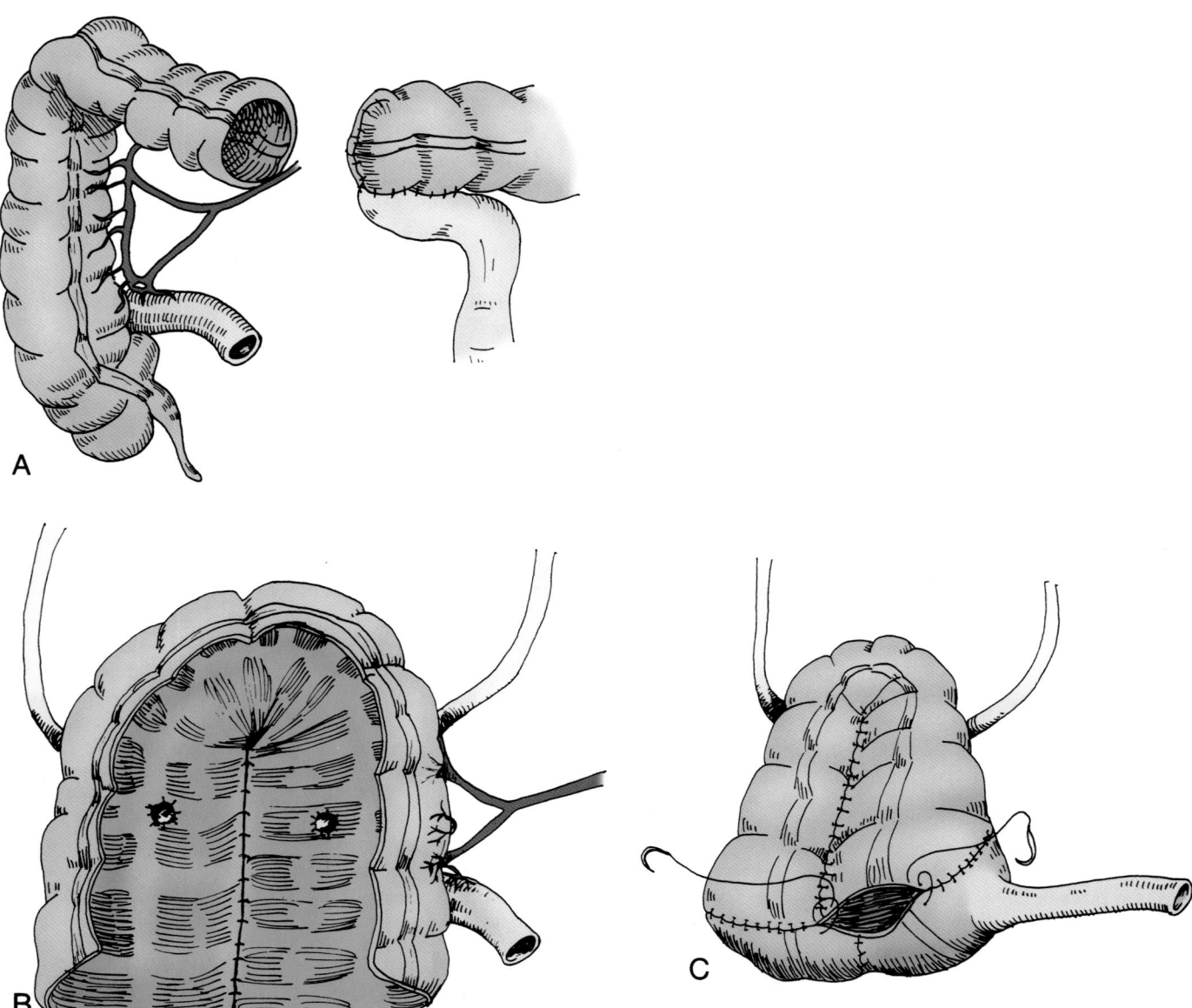

Figure 81–12. **A,** The entire ascending colon and the right third or half of the transverse colon is isolated along with 10 to 12 cm of ileum. **B,** The entire upper extremity of the large bowel is mobilized laterally in the fashion of an inverted U. The medial limbs of the U are sutured after the bowel is spatulated. **C,** The bowel plate is then closed side to side. (From Lockhart J: Remodeled right colon: An alternative urinary reservoir. J Urol 1987;138:730-734.)

stapled and plicated terminal ileum and found that the stapled limb performed equally well and was easier to construct. The use of absorbable staples to create this and other types of reservoirs is described later in the chapter.

Postoperative Care and Comments. The postoperative care of the patient with an Indiana pouch or its variants is not substantially different from that used in patients with other right colon catheterizable diversions. In early reports, Rowland recommended discharging the patient with the suprapubic tube in place until readmission to the hospital 3 weeks later for tube removal and instruction in self-catheterization. In the current medical climate, which places a premium on outpatient procedures, tube removal and catheterization instruction is now an ambulatory procedure at most institutions, including Indiana University (Birhle, 1997).

Average pouch capacities of 400 to 500 mL have been reported by the Indiana group (Rowland et al, 1987). Combining the partially and totally spatulated bowel procedures, this group reports a reoperation rate of 26%. Overall continence rates of 93% were achieved. Very elegant urodynamic studies were conducted in Indiana pouch variants by Carroll and colleagues (1989). They found only 86% of patients totally continent in a small series. However, their pouch capacities exceeded 650 mL. Peak contractions of 47 cm H_2O were recorded at capacity.

The last 81 patients operated on by Rowland underwent construction of a stapled efferent limb; and, in the last 20, the reservoir was created with absorbable staples (Rowland, 1996). **The results in this group of patients were extremely favorable. Early pouch-related complications occurred in only 3 patients (3.7%).** Two patients experienced a pouch leak that was managed conservatively, and 1 patient required open revision of the efferent limb owing to difficulty with catheterization. Early complications not directly attributable to the pouch occurred in 7 patients (8.6%). Transient small bowel obstruction was the most common complication, occurring in 4 patients (4.9%). One patient developed a superficial wound infection, and 1 patient developed an abdominal abscess requiring surgery (1.2%). Late complications related to the reservoir occurred in 23 patients (28.4%). Incontinence occurred in 6 patients (7.4%). The incontinence was secondary to high pouch pressures in 5 patients and secondary to failure of the efferent limb in 1 patient. One of the former and the latter patient underwent reoperation. Three patients (3.7%) developed stomal stenosis, and 3 had parastomal hernias; all 6 underwent surgery. Pouch stones occurred in 3 patients; 1 underwent open removal, and 2 had endoscopic extraction. Acute pyelonephritis was seen in 4 patients (4.9%). The most common late complication not related to the pouch was small bowel obstruction; this was seen in 6 patients and was managed conservatively in 5. In summary, the early reoperation rate was 2.5% and the late reoperation rate 14.8%. **At 1 year, day- and night-time dry intervals of 4 hours or greater were achieved in 98% of patients.** Eighty-four percent of patients stated they slept through the night without the need to awake for catheterization. Similar excellent results in the last 150 patients, 50 with at least 2^1/$_2$-year follow-up, were reported by Birhle (1997).

The Florida pouch has been performed in over 190 patients (Helal et al, 1993). In 165 patients involving 326 ureters no

attempt was made to create a tunneled reimplantation. This approach was adopted owing to the high incidence of ureteral obstruction encountered in the first 30 ureters that were tunneled into a Florida pouch (4 of 30 [13.3%]). In the latter 165 patients, 16/326 ureters (4.9%) developed primary obstruction and were treated by percutaneous balloon dilation, nephrectomy, or observation. Although no attempt is made to create an antirefluxing anastomosis, only 7.1% of the ureters implanted demonstrated reflux. All are being followed conservatively, and no renal deterioration has been demonstrated. In the initial 100 patients, a 7.2% reoperation rate was reported (Lockhart, 1987). Although hyperchloremia was noted in 70% of patients, only 4 patients (including those who had preexisting renal disease) required treatment. Reservoir capacities ranged from 400 to 1200 mL, and maximal reservoir pressures at capacity ranged from 18 to 55 cm H_2O (Lockhart, 1987). The reason why these authors experienced such a high incidence of ureteral obstruction with both nontunneled and tunneled ureteral colonic anastomoses is not clear. It is also surprising that only 23 of 326 ureters that were anastomosed end to side had reflux.

The University of Miami group has reported on its results in 75 patients. Early complications occurred in 19 patients (25%). Sixteen patients experienced late complications (21%). The success rate of the ureterocolonic anastomosis was 90%. Total continence occurred in 98.6%. Average pouch capacities were 750 mL or higher. End filling pressures of 20 cm H_2O were reported. No patient required alkali therapy.

The Indiana pouch remains one of the most reliable of all catheterizable reservoirs. It is among the easiest to construct, and it has very low short-term and long-term complications.

Penn Pouch

The Penn pouch was the first continent diversion employing the Mitrofanoff (1980) principle in which the appendix served as the continence mechanism. As mentioned earlier, this operation enjoys the singular feature of affording a catheterizable continent diversion that can be performed utilizing techniques already in the urologic armamentarium.

Procedure. Two techniques of appendiceal continence mechanisms have been reported. Mitrofanoff reported excising the appendix with a button of cecum and reversing it upon itself before tunneled reimplant (Mitrofanoff, 1980; Duckett and Snyder, 1986). Alternatively, Riedmiller and coworkers (1990) have left the appendix attached to the cecum and buried it into the adjacent taenia by rolling it back onto itself. A wide tunnel is created in the taenia extending 5 to 6 cm from the base of the appendix (Fig. 81–13). Windows are created in the mesoappendix between blood vessels. The appendix is folded cephalad into the tunnel, and seromuscular sutures are placed through the mesoappendix windows to complete the tunneling. The tip of the appendix is amputated and brought to the selected stoma site.

As described by Duckett and Snyder (1986), an ileocecal pouch is created by isolating a segment of cecum up to the junction of the ileocolic and middle colic blood supplies along with a similar length of terminal ileum. These two structures are marsupialized on the antimesenteric borders and sutured

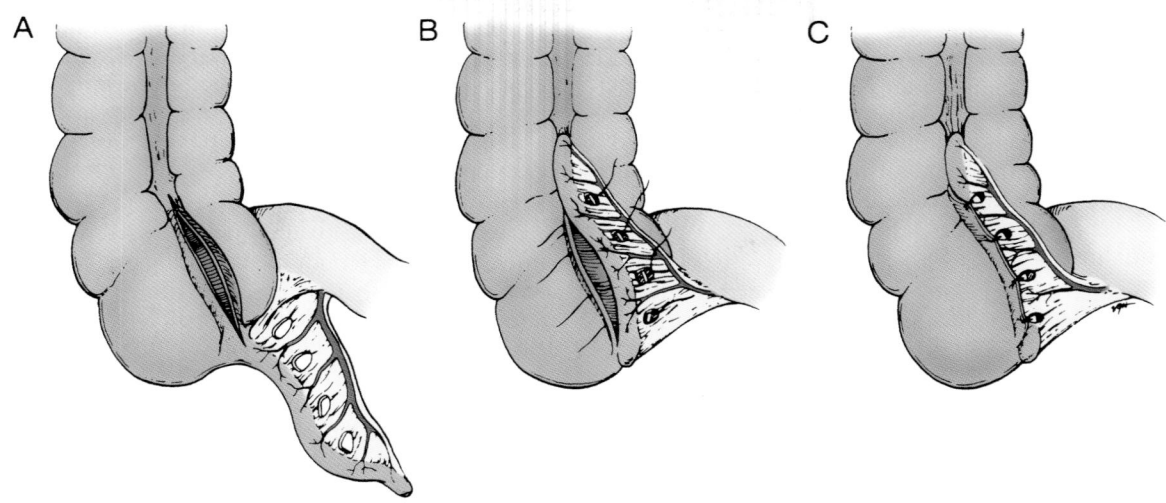

Figure 81–13. **A** to **C,** The appendix is left attached to the cecum and buried into the adjacent cecal taenia by rolling it back onto itself. A wide tunnel is created that extends 5 to 6 cm from the base of the appendix. Windows are created in the mesoappendix between blood vessels. The appendix is folded cephalad into the tunnel, and seromuscular sutures are placed through the mesoappendix.

to one another in the form of a neotubularized pouch. The superior margin of the pouch is sutured in a transverse fashion (all sutures being of absorbable material). A button of cecum surrounding the origin of the appendix is circumcised, and the resulting cecal aperture is closed with running absorbable suture. The mesentery of the appendix is dissected carefully from the base of the cecum, preserving its blood supply. The appendix is then reversed upon itself, so that the cecal button can reach the anterior abdominal wall and the tail of the appendix can be directed to the taenia of the colon (Fig. 81–14). The appendiceal tip is obliquely transected and may be spatulated. A tunneled appendiceal-taenial implantation is carried out. If additional appendiceal length is required the variation proposed by Burns and Mitchell (1990), creating a tube of the base of the cecum, may be employed (see Fig. 81–3). Instead of simply removing the appendix with a button of cecum before preparing it for tunneling, the entire base of the cecum leading to the appendix can be resected in continuity with the appendix by the application of the GIA stapler. The authors have found that spatulating the distal tip of the appendix until a catheter at least 12 to 14 Fr in size can be passed is helpful.

Postoperative Care and Comments. Although not shown in Duckett's surgical drawings, the authors would suggest that a large-bore suprapubic tube be utilized to drain the pouch in the early postoperative interval. The size of the catheter admitted by the appendiceal stump is insufficient to allow for the passage of ureteral stents along with the 12- to 14-Fr catheter. In addition, safe irrigation of mucous debris is best managed by a larger-bore catheter.

Many groups have utilized the Mitrofanoff principle owing to the simplicity and reliability of the continence mechanism (Burger et al, 1992; Bissada, 1993; Sumfest et al, 1993; Woodhouse and MacNeily, 1994; Hampel et al, 1995). Woodhouse and MacNeily (1994) reported on a series of 100 patients operated on from 1985 to 1993. They employed the seven different catheterizable Mitrofanoff principle tubes into six different types of reservoirs. Although they found the

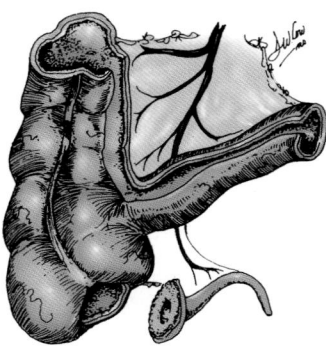

Figure 81–14. A segment of cecum up to the junction of the ileocolic and middle colic blood supplies along with a similar length of terminal ileum is isolated and marsupialized on the antimesenteric borders. A button of cecum surrounding the origin of the appendix is circumcised. The mesentery of the appendix is dissected carefully from the base of the cecum, preserving its blood supply. (From Duckett JW, Snyder HM III: The Mitrofanoff principle in continent urinary reservoirs. Semin Urol 1987;5:55-62.)

Mitrofanoff principle to be versatile and associated with a high success rate (91% continence rate), the reoperation rate for tube complications was 33%. Sumfest and associates (1993) affirmed the use of the appendix as the Mitrofanoff segment of choice. They reported a continence rate of 96%. In their hands, late complications included difficulty with catheterization in 10.6% and stomal stenosis in 19.1%. Urodynamic properties and pouch capacities will be a function of the reservoir constructed. Most often, the appendix is utilized in situ (Burger et al, 1992) and the right colon either alone or with associated terminal ileum (Mainz) serves as the reservoir. We have utilized the in-situ appendix with a detubularized right colon reservoir and the native ileocecal valve as an antireflux mechanism (refluxing ureters implanted end-to-side into terminal ileum). In our hands this has resulted in an excellent success rate with no upper tract problems. The adequacy of the ileocecal valve as an antireflux mechanism was also reported by Alcini and associates (1994). In their series, however, the reservoir was not always detubularized and, as expected, upper tract complications ensued owing to high reservoir pressures. This procedure is uniquely capable of affording continent cutaneous diversion to the patient with short ureters because the terminal ileum can be left long enough to reach high into the retroperitoneum.

Gastric Pouches

Pioneering animal experimentation demonstrated the feasibility of employing stomach as a bladder patch or urinary reservoir (Sinaiko, 1956; Rudick et al, 1977; Leong, 1978). **The use of the stomach to create a urinary reservoir has theoretical and real advantages** (Adams et al, 1988). **First, electrolyte reabsorption would be greatly diminished by utilizing this bowel segment in the reservoir. This would potentially make the stomach the selected reservoir for individuals with preexisting metabolic acidosis or renal insufficiency. Hyperchloremic acidosis would not be an anticipated problem; in fact, in addition to presenting a barrier against the absorption of chloride and ammonium, the gastric mucosa secretes chloride ions** (Piser et al, 1987). **Furthermore, in patients in whom shortening of the bowel may be expected to lead to degrees of malabsorption, the use of stomach is an attractive alternative. The acid pH of the urine may also reduce the risk of bacterial colonization. Finally, when the entire lower bowel has been irradiated,** **stomach tissue may provide healthy nonirradiated tissue to use in performing continent diversion.** Given these theoretical advantages, a number of groups have initiated trials with gastric pouches and composite reservoirs in both pediatric (Adams et al, 1988) and adult populations (Lockhart et al, 1993; Austin et al, 1997).

Procedure. A wedge-shaped segment of stomach whose greatest width is 7 to 10 cm is fashioned from the greater curvature. Care is taken not to extend the wedge through to the lesser curvature to preserve vagal innervation and normal gastric emptying. The left gastroepiploic artery is preferentially utilized as the blood supply for the isolated gastric wedge, dividing the short gastric vessels from the more proximal artery up to the gastric fundus. Alternatively, if there is a problem with the left artery, the right gastroepiploic vessel may be employed, dividing the short gastric vessels to the level of the pylorus (Fig. 81–15A and B). The stomach is then closed according to the surgeon's preference. Neither gastroduodenostomy nor gastrojejunostomy is mandatory unless the antrum of the stomach has been used. The isolated wedge is refashioned into nearly a sphere by folding it back upon itself and suturing the edges together with running absorbable material. Before pouch closure, one ureter is tunneled into the reservoir according to the surgeon's preferred antireflux technique. Contralaterally, proximal transureteroureterostomy is performed. The contralateral distal ureter is utilized to create the continence mechanism. The distal ureter is tunneled into

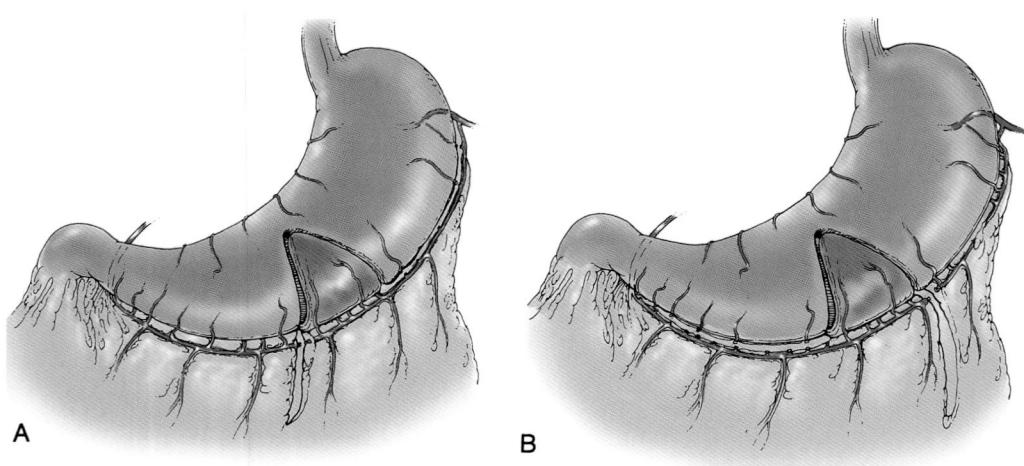

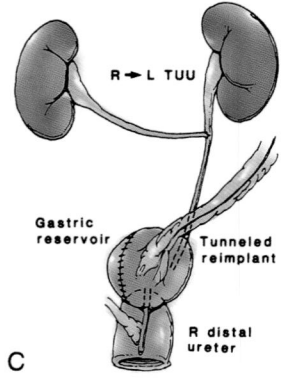

Figure 81–15. **A** and **B**, A wedge-shaped segment of stomach whose greatest width is 7 to 10 cm is fashioned from the greater curvature. The left gastroepiploic artery is preferentially utilized as the blood supply for the isolated gastric wedge, by dividing the short gastric vessels up to the gastric fundus. Alternatively, if there is a problem with the left artery, the right gastroepiploic vessel may be employed. **C,** The isolated wedge is refashioned into nearly a sphere by folding it back upon itself and suturing the edges together with running absorbable material. One ureter is tunneled into the reservoir. A proximal transureteroureterostomy is performed. The ipsilateral distal ureter is tunneled into the reservoir with its distal extent brought to the introitus to serve as a catheterization portal. (From Adams MC, Mitchell ME, Rink RC: Gastrocystoplasty: An alternative solution to the problem of urological reconstruction in the severely compromised patient. J Urol 1988;140:1152-1156.)

the reservoir in a fashion similar to an appendiceal implant. The free portion of the ureter can then be brought to the skin or to the introitus (or urethral stump in males) to serve as a catheterization portal (see Fig. 81–15C). Alternatively, the wedge of stomach can be incorporated into a reservoir composed of detubularized ileum (Lockhart et al, 1993). In this procedure, an 11-cm long segment of stomach is isolated on the right gastroepiploic blood supply (Fig. 81–16A). A 22-cm segment of ileum is then isolated, opened along its antimesenteric border, and refashioned in a U shape (see Fig. 81–16B). The edges of the stomach are then sutured to edges of the ileum with a running absorbable suture of 2-0 PGA.

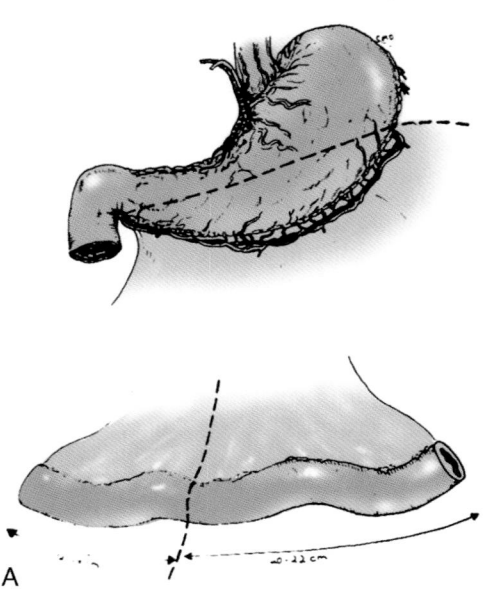

A

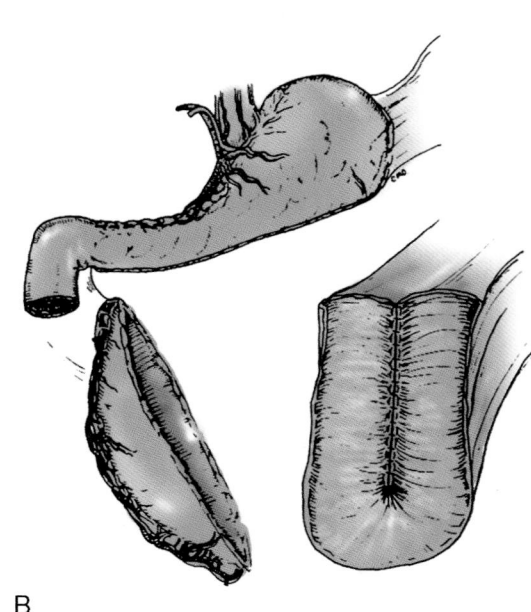

B

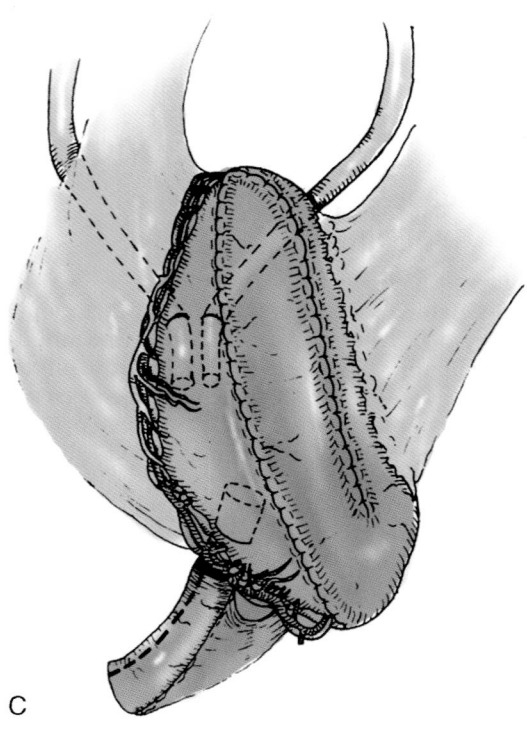

C

Figure 81–16. **A,** An 11-cm long segment of stomach is isolated on the right gastroepiploic blood supply using a GIA-90 stapler. Usually, two staplers are required. **B,** A 22-cm segment of ileum is then isolated, opened along its antimesenteric border, and refashioned in a U shape. **C,** The edges of the stomach are then sutured to edges of the ileum with a running absorbable suture of 2-0 PGA. This completes the reservoir. The ureters are tunneled into the stomach, and a Mitrofanoff continence mechanism is created with a tapered segment of ileum. (From Lockhart JL, Davies R, Cox C, et al: The gastroileal pouch: An alternative continent urinary reservoir for patients with short bowel, acidosis and/or extensive pelvic radiation. J Urol 1993;150:46-51.)

This completes the reservoir. The ureters are tunneled into the stomach, and a Mitrofanoff continence mechanism is created according to the preference of the surgeon; the group from the University of South Florida employed a tapered segment of ileum (see Fig. 81–16C).

Postoperative Care and Comments. Adams and associates (1988) report mean pouch capacities of 245 mL and end filling pressures averaging 35 cm H_2O in a small patient sample. Combining their experience of gastric continent diversion and gastrocystoplasty, they report minimal mucus production; only 3 of 13 patients required any irrigations, and the majority maintained sterile urine. Urine pHs have ranged from 4 to 7, but no introital ulceration from acid urine was reported. Three patients had minor elevations of serum gastrin, and none of the continent divisions required reoperation. Leong (1978) has utilized similar concepts in gastric pouch construction and has alluded to the creation of a voiding pouch created from stomach as well.

The construction of reservoirs entirely from stomach has not seen widespread acceptance. Rather, there has been greater use of stomach segments either for bladder augmentation or as a portion of a reservoir (composite) either alone or with an in-situ catheterizable tube fashioned from a portion of the stomach (Gosalbez et al, 1994; Carr and Mitchell, 1996).

Goslabez and colleagues (1994) reported on 15 patients who received a gastric tube as part of a composite gastric patch. Complications associated with the gastric patch and in-situ tube included one each of early traumatic perforation of the tube, distal tube stenosis, and mucosal redundancy. Two of these patients required reoperation. Peristomal skin irritation from acid secretion occurred in 2 patients but was not considered severe. This is a more frequent complication in other reports and has resulted in skin breakdown in some instances.

Over a 10-year period from January, 1985, to June, 1995, Carr and Mitchell (1996) reported on the use of stomach in 12 patients. Seven had urinary reservoirs totally constructed from stomach, whereas 5 had composite reservoirs. They report continence in all patients but that the continence mechanisms have often required revision. Average bladder capacity was 309 mL, and average compliance was 12.9 mL/cm H_2O. When stomach is used as a bladder augment or as a portion of a neobladder, a dysuria and hematuria syndrome has been reported (Nguyen et al, 1993).

Austin and associates (1997) reported on 9 adult patients with a mean follow-up of 54 months who underwent construction of a continent composite reservoir that was gastroileal in 7 and gastrocolonic in 2. All 9 patients had either preexisting metabolic acidosis or a short bowel syndrome. All 9 patients achieved electrolyte neutrality, and postoperative serum pH was significantly improved ($P < .01$). Three patients had a short-term serum gastrin elevation, which returned to normal during follow-up. One patient developed skin ulceration at the stoma site.

The use of stomach has particular appeal in the pediatric population in which the stomach's unique acid-base properties can be utilized not only to reconstruct but also to help correct the metabolic problems that are often associated with the need for pediatric urinary reconstruction (Carr and Mitchell, 1996). **Although experience with use of the stomach remains small, its various unique intrinsic properties as a reservoir suggest that its use will continue in selected clinical situations.**

QUALITY OF LIFE ASSESSMENTS

Extraordinarily few well designed prospectively conducted studies using validated instruments exist to assess quality of life after continent cutaneous urinary diversion. In fact, no randomized prospective trial has ever been conducted to compare the quality of life after continent cutaneous diversion with either orthotopic continent diversion or incontinent urostomy urinary diversion. In general, most quality of life studies show similar overall quality of life in patients undergoing both ileal conduit and cutaneous continent diversion, with the latter being associated with improvements in stomal and urinary quality of life scores. In one of the few prospective studies to compare quality of life after continent cutaneous diversion with ileal conduit urinary diversion, Hardt and coworkers (2000) followed patients from the preoperative setting until 1 year after surgery. Using validated instruments tested for reliability they found life satisfaction improved over time in patients with continent cutaneous diversion while it worsened during the first year after ileal conduit construction. Using the Beck Depression Inventory and Profile of Mood States in adults, Boyd and colleagues (1987) found that patients choosing ileal conduit diversion had the lowest expectations of their quality of life. Interestingly, they found the highest overall satisfaction among patients undergoing conversion from ileal conduit to Kock cutaneous pouch diversion.

Mansson and associates (2002) found no difference in overall quality of life in men undergoing continent cutaneous diversion when compared with orthotopic neobladder using the FACT-BL and Hospital Anxiety and Depression Scale. In specific questions concerning intestinal, urinary, and sexual function, patients with cutaneous reservoirs experienced less difficulty with incontinence and emptied less frequently. Sexual function appeared better in patients undergoing orthotopic bladder substitution, likely due to urethral preservation.

VARIATIONS IN OPERATIVE TECHNIQUE
Minimally Invasive Continent Cutaneous Diversion

With recent improvement in both laparoscopic as well as robotic assisted laparoscopic techniques, radical cystectomy can now be performed in selected centers using these minimally invasive techniques. Turk has reported on an initial series of five patients who have undergone radical cystectomy with bilateral pelvic lymphadenectomy and continent urinary diversion using a rectosigmoid pouch performed with an intracorporeal laparoscopic technique. A bilateral stented antireflux ureteral reimplantation was utilized, and laparotomy was not performed. Operative time was 7.4 hours with minimal blood loss and a mean hospital stay of 10 days. No intraoperative or postoperative complications were encountered.

The complex nature of minimally invasive reconstructive surgery necessary in continent cutaneous diversion has limited these procedures to select centers. In addition, because of the prolonged time for return of postoperative bowel function, the benefits in hospital stay routinely encountered after laparoscopic nephrectomy do not seem to exist when urinary diversion is performed.

Conduit Conversion to a Continent Reservoir

The major indication for conversion of a functioning conduit to a continent urinary reservoir is the patient's desire for improved quality of life. Pow-Sang and coworkers (1992) reported on conversion in 20 patients. Fifteen were converted from an ileal conduit, and 1 each were converted from a cecal conduit, ureterosigmoidostomy, cutaneous ureterostomy, sigmoid conduit, and a suprapubic tube. In 14 of the 20 patients the conduit was discarded or used only as a patch to a colonic reservoir. It was observed that renal units that were obstructed preoperatively were associated with a 71% failure rate. Metabolic acidosis was seen in 15 (75%) but was believed to be mild. Pouch-related complications are, in general, a function of the reconstruction selected and need not be higher in this setting. However, patient selection is very important in determining appropriate candidates for conversion.

We prefer to use the conduit in some form whenever possible. This strategy was supported in a report on two patients by Oesterling and Gearhart (1990). The use of an existing bowel segment has the potential to diminish metabolic sequelae and may result in a lower complication rate. The form of continent reconstruction chosen will have to depend on intraoperative findings, and no one procedure is more amenable than another. Before undertaking conversion, the patient should be fully evaluated for disease recurrence, renal functional status, urinary anatomy, hydronephrosis, intestinal length, and intestinal health.

Pahernik and colleagues (2004) have described the long-term outcomes of conversion of 39 patients from conduit diversion to Mainz I pouch diversion. With a mean follow-up of 102 months the most common complications were stomal stenosis and pouch calculi. Long-term continence was achieved in 95% of patients.

Absorbable Stapling Techniques in Continent Urinary Diversion

The principle of bowel detubularization to increase reservoir capacity and diminish the effects of peristalsis is a fundamental principle of all contemporary continent urinary diversions. The process of detubularization and refashioning of the spatulated bowel segment approximates at least 1 hour of operating time and is by far the most time-consuming and tedious aspect of pouch construction. **The use of absorbable staplers has substantially reduced the time required to fashion bowel reservoirs and has demonstrated short-term and long-term reliability with respect to reservoir integrity and volume.**

Bonney and Robinson (1990) first demonstrated the potential use of absorbable staplers to substitute for conventional suturing of bowel reservoirs. These authors used a bulky absorbable stapler (Polysorb staples in a TA Premium 55 stapler [U.S. Surgical Corp., Norwalk, CT]) to construct an S-

pouch configuration in a canine ileal urinary pouch model. Although the same stapler was used in humans by the authors in 1992 and by Cummings in 1995, its clinical use was never widely adopted because the bulky staple configuration destroyed a significant portion of the bowel diameter, particularly when applied to the small intestine. The fact that up to 20 costly staple cartridges were required to complete the closure of a bowel reservoir further reduced the potential benefits of absorbable pouch construction.

A 75-mm GIA instrument (PolyGIA [U.S. Surgical Corp., Norwalk, CT]) incorporating substantially smaller absorbable staples was made available for clinical use in 1992. The stapler delivers four rows of polylactic acid and PGA blend copolymer (absorbable) staples, which divides the bowel between the second and third rows. Thus, each staple line of the pouch has a double, staggered, stapled closure. This device has enabled both the refashioning and closure of bowel pouches to be performed with fewer staple applications and is strong and water-tight. Finally, the width of bowel sacrificed with the new instrument is appreciably less than that with the older staple device. Several investigators have subsequently utilized the new "absorbable" GIA stapler to construct catheterizable pouches and neobladders (Olsson et al, 1993, Montie et al, 1994, 1995, Olsson and Kirsch, 1995). **However, it is very important to note that the absorbable PolyGIA staples must not overlap because this will result in the failure of the staples to lock together. This is in direct contrast to metal staples, which are meant to overlap to create anastomotic integrity.** As a result of the inability to overlap absorbable staples, the reservoir construction procedures must be varied, as described next.

Surgical Techniques

Right Colon Pouch

In 1993, the authors described a technique using the absorbable GIA staplers to fully detubularize and refashion large bowel (Olsson et al, 1993). The technique of colon pouch construction described here incorporates the principles of bowel detubularization and refashioning using absorbable staplers in a simple "one-step" process.

The right colon and 10 cm of terminal ileum are mobilized by incising the peritoneum along the white line of Toldt and along the base of the mesentery and are isolated using metal GIA staplers (Fig. 81–17A). After bowel continuity is restored with standard metal GIA and TA staplers, the distal staple line of the right colon is excised and the bowel lumen is irrigated to remove residual enteric contents. Using electrocautery, a small opening (2 cm) is created on the antimesenteric border of the cecum to fit the absorbable stapler. The distal open end of the colon is aligned with the cecostomy by folding the right colon on itself, as depicted in Figure 81–17B. The limbs of the absorbable GIA stapler are inserted into the distal open end and into the cecostomy, and the stapler is fired along the antimesenteric line of the apposed folded bowel (see Fig. 81–17C). It is necessary to evert the bowel to continue subsequent staple applications. This may be achieved by placing Babcock clamps on each side of the distal staple line (Fig. 81–17D). A small incision at the junction of each staple line is made to prevent overlap of the absorbable staple rows and

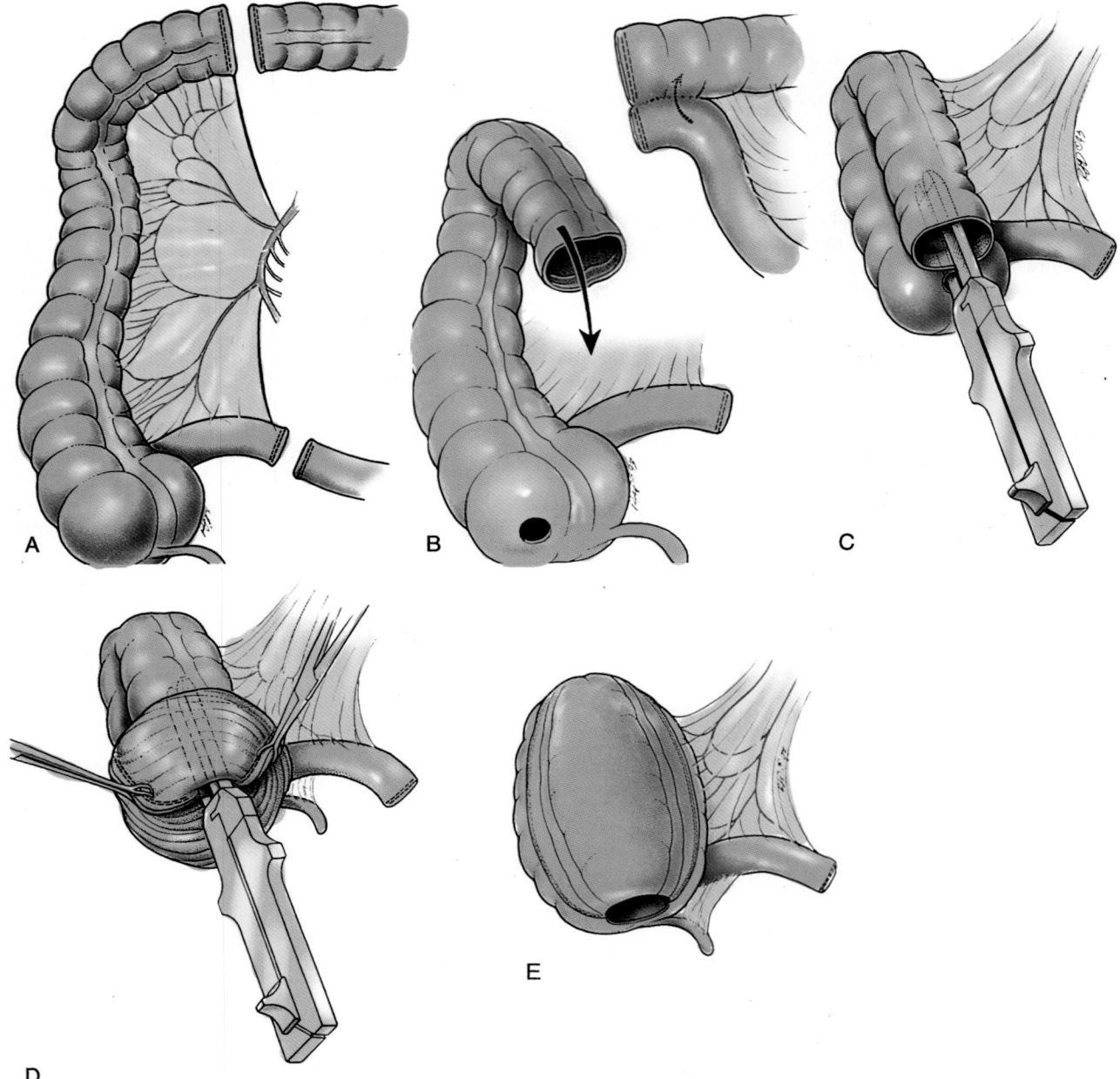

Figure 81–17. **A,** Isolation of colon and blood supply using metal GIA staplers. **B,** Opening created in cecum and open end of colon to fit absorbable stapler. Bowel continuity restored between colon and ileum. **C,** Stapler activated along antimesenteric line and folded bowel. **D,** Inversion of bowel required to continue staple applications. **E,** Pouch inversion is complete. (From Olsson CA, Kirsch AJ, Whang MI-S: Rapid construction of right colon pouch. Curr Surg Tech Urol 1993;6:1-8.)

allow for the next staple application. Because of this incision, there is often a short unstapled area at the junction between each application of the stapler; one or two simple figure-of-eight sutures of 2-0 absorbable material are applied to each of these points. The last staple application traverses the apex of the fold of bowel. In adults, three to four applications of the stapling device have been required to construct the right colon pouch, whereas in children two to three staples suffice. The appearance of the nearly completed pouch is illustrated in Figure 81–17E.

Once the generic right pouch has been fashioned, several options exist for ureteral anastomosis and formation of a sphincter mechanism. These maneuvers may be approached through the coalesced distal colon opening and cecostomy, which accesses the pouch interior (see Fig. 81–17E). The opening permits appropriate stent placement or inspection of a buttressed ileocecal valve. Any of the Mitrofanoff techniques described in conjunction with the Mainz I procedure can be employed. Likewise, the terminal ileum can be either stapled or plicated to create a continence mechanism. Once construction of a continence mechanism and ureteral anastomoses have been performed, the opening can be closed with a running 2-0 absorbable suture or the application of an absorbable TA stapler of appropriate length.

Continent diversion procedures commonly employ the right colon or the cecum and terminal ileum. The array of right colon pouches that can be facilitated by this technique include all of the reservoirs described previously. Reservoirs using terminal ileum and cecum such as the Penn Pouch and the Mainz Pouch can also be fashioned in this manner.

Stapled Sigmoid Reservoir

The same stapling maneuvers can be applied to create a reservoir constructed from the sigmoid colon (Olsson and Kirsch, 1995). A portion of the sigmoid and descending colon measuring approximately 35 cm is mobilized by incising the peritoneum along the white line of Toldt. Once mesenteric windows have been created, the segment of colon is isolated using metal GIA staplers (Fig. 81–18A). Restoration of bowel continuity is achieved with either GIA, TA, or EEA staple devices.

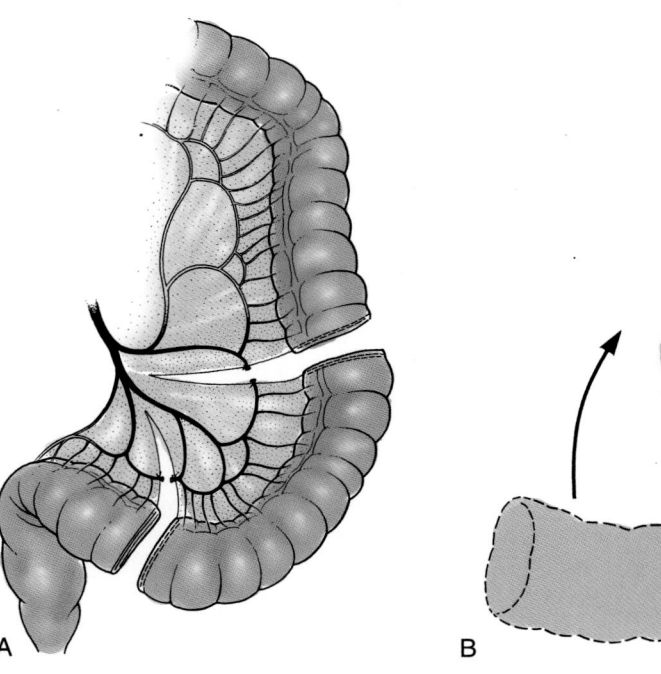
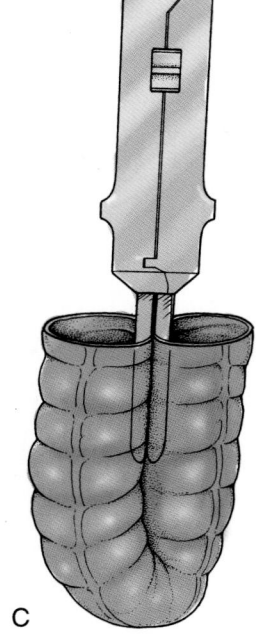
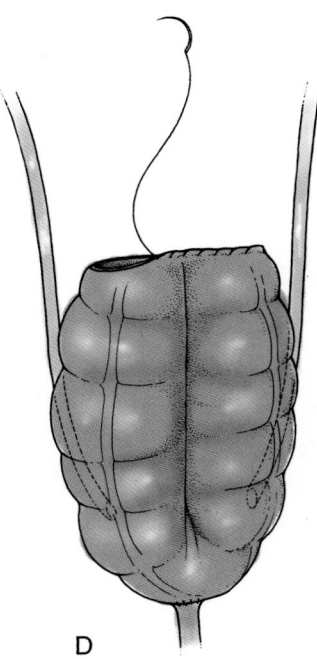

Figure 81–18. **A,** Isolation of colon and blood supply using metal GIA staplers. **B,** Sigmoid bowel folded in U shape. **C,** Stapler fired along antimesenteric border of folded sigmoid. **D,** Oversewing of superior open end completes pouch construction. (From Olsson CA, Kirsch AJ, Whang MI-S: Rapid construction of right colon pouch. Curr Surg Tech Urol 1993;6:1-8.)

Each of the metal stapled ends of the isolated colon are excised, and the bowel lumen is irrigated. The isolated sigmoid is folded on itself in a U configuration, aligning both open ends (see Fig. 81–18B). The absorbable GIA stapler is inserted into the open bowel ends and fired along the antimesenteric line of the folded bowel (see Fig. 81–18C). Following the procedure for bowel eversion described earlier completes the reservoir. Again, usually two or three applications of the stapler are required to complete the pouch, cutting each staple line tip to avoid staple overlap.

After bowel reinversion, ureteral implants into tinea can be carried out, using the residual colon opening to facilitate stent passage. These stents and a suprapubic tube are led through a separate stab wound in the pouch and brought through a lower abdominal wall stab incision. A continence mechanism employing one of the Mitrofanoff variations is then performed.

W-Stapled Reservoir

Montie and coworkers (1994) utilized the absorbable GIA stapler to construct ileal neobladders in patients undergoing cystoprostatectomy. A segment of ileum measuring 50 cm is divided with a standard metal GIA stapler 20 cm from the ileocecal valve. The terminal ends of each limb of the isolated ileal segment are closed with an absorbable TA-55 stapler, and the metal staple line is resected. The bowel is aligned in a W configuration, and an enterotomy is made 10 cm from each end (Fig. 81–19A). To facilitate closure of the enterotomy with a TA instrument (see Fig. 81–19, inset), the enterotomy must be made midway between the mesentery and antimesenteric border. The absorbable GIA device is inserted through the enterotomy and is activated. This maneuver adjoins the two adjacent bowel segments. The enterotomy may be closed with the absorbable TA-55 instrument or running absorbable suture, completing the distal segment of the W. The middle and proximal segments are constructed similarly (see Fig.

81–19B). Montie stresses that the segments of the W must be offset to avoid staple lines that overlap each other. Exceeding a 3 to 6 cm overlap may result in bowel ischemia.

Postoperative Care and Comments

In the first 50 adult patients to undergo our absorbable stapling technique in right colon pouch construction, with at least 7 years of follow-up, there have been no complications attributed to absorbable staples. Similar results have been reported by Rowland (1996). In the pediatric population, we have applied the absorbable stapler to continent urinary diversion, as well as bladder augmentation (Hensle et al, 1995). In the first 18 children observed for up to 3 years, there have been no instances of pouch perforation or inadequate pouch capacity and, to date, only one of the patients developed a reservoir calculus.

Montie and colleagues (1994) used absorbable staplers to create W-stapled ileal neobladders in 25 patients. Ileal pouch construction was performed in approximately 20 minutes, and functional aspects were comparable to bowel reservoirs constructed by conventional suturing. Urodynamic evaluation at 6 months, however, documented a small-capacity reservoir requiring augmentation enterocystoplasty in 3 of 25 patients (12%). Montie and colleagues attributed this complication to either the size of the staples or reservoir fibrosis secondary to foreign body reaction. It is conceivable that a similar situation would arise when constructing a W-stapled T-pouch.

We have used the absorbable stapler to construct both large and small bowel reservoirs. In our experience, colonic pouches appear better suited for construction with the absorbable stapler because of their relatively larger lumen. **The introduction of stapling devices delivering still smaller staples and automatic staple line sealing devices may prevent the problems presently seen when ileal pouches are constructed with current technology.**

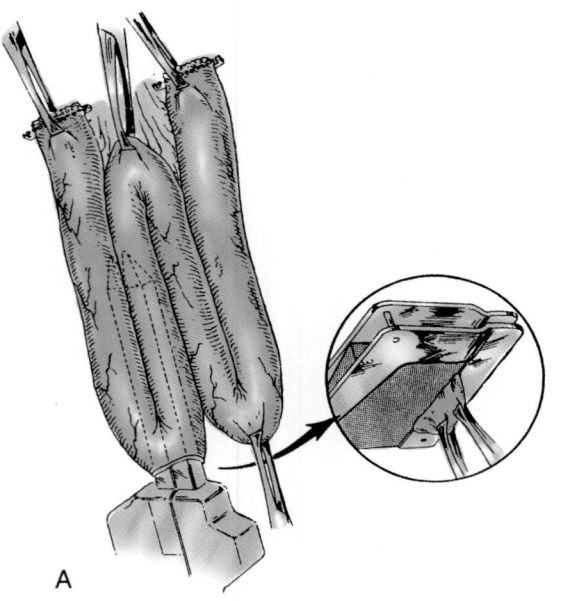

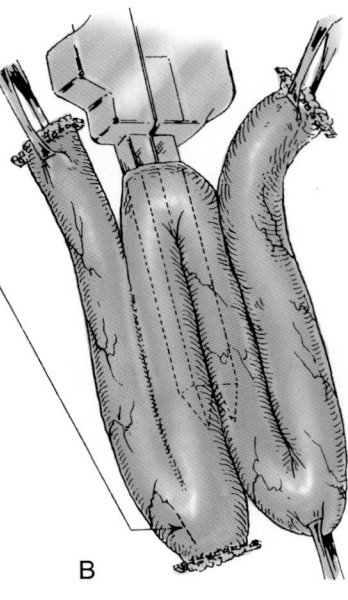

Figure 81–19. **A,** After closure of butt ends of reservoir with TA-55 stapler, enterotomy is made in dependent portion of first limb of W. Absorbable stapler is inserted through enterotomy and fired creating common lumen between two adjacent limbs. *Arrow* indicates close-up of closure of enterotomy with TA-55 stapler. **B,** In middle limb of W, stapler is placed through enterotomy at apex and again common lumen is created. Staple lines are not directly opposing for their entire distance to avoid ischemia between adjacent staple lines. *Arrow* indicates site of enterotomy where urethro-ileal anastomosis will be performed. (From Pontes JE: Genitourinary Oncologic Pelvic Surgery. New York, John Wiley & Sons, 1993.)

A

B

SUMMARY

In summary, continent urinary diversion is now an accepted part of the urologic surgical armamentarium. It is anticipated that in the near future, technologic advances in minimally invasive surgery will allow for the laparoscopic (robotic) construction of these reservoirs. These technologic advances will likely include automated suturing devices and biosealants. We look forward to the introduction of these breakthroughs with great anticipation.

KEY POINTS: CUTANEOUS CONTINENT URINARY DIVERSION

- Because the ability to self-catheterize is essential to the patient undergoing continent diversion, the patient must be assessed for the ability to care for himself or herself.

- Patients with multiple sclerosis, quadriplegic individuals, and the very frail or mentally impaired patient will at some point in their lives require the care of members of the family or a visiting nurse, and such patients are viewed as poor candidates for any form of continent diversion.

- Renal and hepatic function must be reviewed carefully in the patient selected for continent diversion. The reabsorption and recirculation of urinary constituents and other metabolites require that liver function be normal and that serum creatinine levels are in the normal range, certainly below the level of 1.8 mg/dL.

- When the ureters are directed into the fecal stream, routine colonoscopy should also be performed. There have been isolated reports of malignancy developing earlier, and all patients developing gross or microscopic hematuria should be fully evaluated.

- Many studies from throughout the world have suggested an improved psychosocial adjustment of the patient undergoing continent urinary and fecal diversion compared with those patients with diversions requiring collecting appliances.

- Four general techniques have been employed to create a dependable, catheterizable continence zone. For right colon pouches, appendiceal techniques, pseudoappendiceal tubes fashioned from ileum or right colon, and the ileocecal valve plication are adaptable. Appendiceal tunneling techniques are the simplest of all to perform in that they utilize established surgical techniques that are already in the urologic armamentarium.

- The second major type of continence mechanism used in right colon pouches is the tapered and/or imbricated terminal ileum and ileocecal valve. However, some patients have developed rather striking diarrhea/steatorrhea after the loss of the ileocecal valve. This may be particularly true in the pediatric patient.

- The third surgical principle utilized in constructing the continence mechanism is the use of the intussuscepted nipple valve or, more recently, the flap valve, which avoids the need for intussusception. The creation of nipple valves is the most technologically demanding of all the continence mechanisms and is associated with the highest complication rate.

- The fourth major technique of continence mechanism construction is the provision of a hydraulic valve, as in the Benchekroun nipple. In this procedure, a small bowel segment is isolated and a reversed intussusception is used to appose the surfaces of the small bowel.

- Pouch urinary retention represents a true emergency, and the patient must seek immediate attention so that catheterization and drainage by experienced personnel can be achieved promptly.

- Because all patients with catheterized pouches will have chronic bacteriuria, the problem of antibiotic management should be discussed. Most authors would suggest that bacteriuria in the absence of symptomatology does not warrant antibiotic treatment.

- The concept of using the buttressed ileocecal valve as a dependable continence mechanism that can withstand the trauma of intermittent catheterization was first reported from Indiana University by Rowland and Mitchell (1987).

- The Indiana pouch remains one of the most reliable of all catheterizable reservoirs. It is among the easiest to construct, and it has very low short-term and long-term complications.

- The use of absorbable staplers has substantially reduced the time required to fashion bowel reservoirs and has demonstrated short-term and long-term reliability with respect to reservoir integrity and volume.

- It is anticipated that in the near future technologic advances in minimally invasive surgery will allow for the laparoscopic (robotic) construction of these reservoirs. These technologic advances will likely include automated suturing devices and biosealants.

SUGGESTED READINGS

Benson MC, Slawin KM, Wechsler MH, Olsson CA: Analysis of continent versus standard urinary diversion. Br J Urol 1992;69:156-162.
Bonney WW, Robinson RA: Absorbable staples in continent ileal urinary pouch. Urology 1990;3:57-62.
Boyd SD, Feinberg SM, Skinner DG, et al: Quality of life survey of urinary diversion patients: Comparison of ileal conduits versus continent Kock ileal reservoirs. J Urol 1987;138:1386-1389.

SECTION XV

Gerharz EW, Kohl U, Weingartner K, et al: Complications related to different continence mechanisms in ileocecal reservoirs. J Urol 1997;158:1709-1713.

Goodwin WE, Turner RD, Winter CC: Results of ileocystoplasty. J Urol 1958;80:461-466.

Hardt J, Filipas D, Hohenfellner R, Egle UT: Quality of life in patients with bladder carcinoma after cystectomy: First results of a prospective study. Qual Life Res 2000;9:1-12.

McGuire MS, Rimaldi G, Grotas J, Russo P: The type of urinary diversion after radical cystectomy significantly impacts on the patient's quality of life. Ann Surg Oncol 2000;7:4-8.

Olsson CA, Kirsch AJ, Whang M: Rapid construction of right colon pouch. Curr Surg Tech Urol 1993;6:1-8.

Rowland RG, Mitchell ME, Bihrle R, et al: Indiana continent urinary reservoir. J Urol 1987;137:1136-1139.

Stein JP, Lieskovsky G, Ginsberg DA, et al: The T pouch: An orthotopic ileal neobladder incorporating a serosal lined ileal antireflux technique. J Urol 1998;159:1836-1842.

Stein R, Matani Y, Doi Y, et al: Continent urinary diversion using the Mainz Pouch I technique—ten years later. J Urol 1995;153:251A.

Sumfest JM, Burns MW, Mitchell ME: The Mitrofanoff principle in urinary reconstruction. J Urol 1993;150:1875-1878.

Thuroff JW, Alken P, Riedmiller H, et al: 100 cases of MAINZ pouch: Continuing experience and evolution. J Urol 1988;140:283-288.

82 Orthotopic Urinary Diversion

JOHN P. STEIN, MD · DONALD G. SKINNER, MD

EVOLUTION OF URINARY DIVERSION

Since the early 1900s, innovative surgeons have investigated how best to replace the original bladder removed for either benign or malignant disease. In the new millennium, the goals of lower urinary tract reconstruction are evolving from more than simply a means to divert urine and protect the upper urinary tract. Contemporary objectives of lower urinary tract reconstruction should consider quality of life issues, eliminating the need for a cutaneous urostomy stoma, a urostomy appliance, and intermittent catheterization while maintaining a more natural voiding pattern that allows volitional micturition through the intact native urethra. These advances in urinary diversion have been made in an effort to provide patients a more normal lifestyle and improved quality of life and self-image after removal of the bladder. If continued progress is to be made in the field of urinary diversion, a thorough understanding and appreciation of previous techniques and accomplishments must be achieved.

The first reported urinary diversion into a segment of bowel was by Simon in 1852. He attempted a so-called ureterosigmoidostomy in an exstrophy patient by drawing the ureters, with the use of needles and large suture-created fistulas, into the rectum. Although the patient died of sepsis 12 months later, this marked the first reported attempt at some form of urinary diversion. Shortly thereafter, Lloyd (1851) attempted a similar technique in an exstrophy patient; the subject died of peritonitis 7 days postoperatively. The following 100 years in the evolution of urinary diversion were subsequently marked by a continued search for better methods and techniques to reconstruct the lower urinary tract.

Ureterosigmoidostomy is the oldest form of clinically applied urinary diversion. Early experience with this urinary diversion was marked by significant postoperative mortality and complications. These issues led to a number of technical modifications, particularly related to the ureteral implantation technique (Hinman and Weyrauch, 1936). The rates of obstruction and ascending pyelonephritis in patients with ureterosigmoidostomy were significantly reduced after a direct anastomosis of the ureter into the sigmoid colon, incorporating an antireflux submucosal tunnel (Leadbetter, 1951; Goodwin et al, 1953). Ureterosigmoidostomy remained the diversion of choice until the late 1950s, when electrolyte imbalances, renal problems, and secondary malignant neoplasms arising at the ureteral implantation site were described (Leadbetter and Clarke, 1954; Clarke and Leadbetter, 1955; Ridlon, 1963; Wear and Barquin, 1973). These significant complications directed reconstruction efforts to different, better forms of urinary diversion.

Since the 1950s, the evolution of lower urinary tract reconstruction has developed along three distinct paths: (1) a noncontinent cutaneous form of urinary diversion (ileal or colon conduit); (2) a continent cutaneous form of urinary diversion to the skin (continent cutaneous); and, most recently, (3) an orthotopic form of diversion to the native, intact urethra (neobladder).

In 1911, Zaayer reported the results of ileal conduits in two patients, both of whom died within 2 weeks after surgery. It was not until 1950 that Bricker refined and popularized this form of urinary diversion. The ileal conduit is a technically simple urinary diversion. This form of reconstruction became an established and reliable type of urinary diversion and even through the 1990s remained the "gold standard" with which other types of urinary diversion were compared. Concurrent with Bricker's introduction of the ileal conduit, Gilchrist and colleagues (1950) independently reported on the novel concept of a continent cutaneous urinary diversion. This form of urinary reconstruction incorporated the ileocecal valve as the continence mechanism and the distal ileum as a catheterizable stoma. Unfortunately, Gilchrist and colleagues' ingenious continent ileocecal reservoir garnered little support, whereas the Bricker ileal conduit became the simpler urinary diversion technique of choice for the next several decades.

Initial short-term follow-up in patients with the ileal conduit appeared impressive; hyperchloremic metabolic acidosis and pyelonephritis were substantially less problematic than in those patients with ureterosigmoidostomy. **However, with longer follow-up, it became clear that there were also significant problems associated with ileal conduit diversion** (Butcher et al, 1962; Shapiro et al, 1975; Middleton and Hendren, 1976; Johnson and Lamy, 1977; Pitts and Muecke, 1979; Sullivan et al, 1980). **Issues with stomal stenosis, pyelonephritis, calculus formation, ureteral obstruction, and renal deterioration became more apparent with longer follow-up** (Table 82–1). These clinical sequelae were thought to be related to the reflux of infected urinary constituents or obstruction of the upper urinary tract. It was postulated that the addition of an antireflux technique to a conduit form of diversion (adopted from the technical developments during the ureterosigmoidostomy era) could help diminish the problems of reflux and renal deterioration in these patients. In fact, well-performed laboratory experiments provided evidence to support the advantage of nonrefluxing colonic conduits over ileal conduits (Richie et al, 1974; Richie and Skinner, 1975; Claesson et al, 1985). Unfortunately, with longer follow-up, similar complications with colon conduits developed, including upper urinary tract damage, again dampening enthusiasm for this form of urinary diversion (Table 82–2) (Morales and Golimbu, 1975; Althausen et al, 1978).

The concept of a continent cutaneous diversion, introduced by Gilchrist, was subsequently reintroduced in 1982 by Kock and associates. It reformed lower urinary tract reconstruction and directed clinical efforts toward a continent cutaneous type of diversion. Although this form of urinary diversion required catheterization of an abdominal stoma, it eliminated the need for and the associated problems with an external urostomy appliance. Many continent cutaneous urinary diversions have subsequently been described with use of different portions of small and large bowel and incorporation of various antireflux and continent catheterizable mechanisms. **The one constant, and arguably the "Achilles' heel" of these continent cutaneous reservoirs, is providing an adequate, durable, efferent continence mechanism.** The need to provide a reliable continence mechanism while eliminating a cutaneous stoma or the need for intermittent catheterization led to the development of and transition to an orthotopic form of urinary diversion.

Tizzoni and Poggi (1888) were the first to experiment and transplant ureters into an isolated loop of ileum interposed between the ureters and the urethra. This procedure was a two-stage technique using small intestine in a canine. The dog was reportedly continent and subsequently underwent three successful pregnancies before expiring 30 months postoperatively. Lemoine (1913) is credited with performing the first orthotopic reconstruction in a human subject. This patient initially underwent a cystectomy with ureteral reimplantation into the rectum. Complications related to recurrent pyelonephritis led to undiversion in this patient; the rectal segment was isolated, transected, and anastomosed to the urethra, and the sigmoid colon was brought down and anastomosed to the anus.

In 1979, Camey and Le Duc reported their pioneering and extensive clinical experience with orthotopic substitution to the native urethra. This was a substantial accomplishment that demonstrated the feasibility of lower urinary tract reconstruction to the native urethra. **Arguably, the orthotopic bladder substitute has evolved into the most ideal form of urinary diversion available today and should be considered the true gold standard with which other forms of diversion are compared.** In fact, in 1993, at the Fourth International Consensus Conference on Bladder Cancer in Antwerp, Belgium, consensus opinion was that in the properly selected

Table 82–1. Long-term Complications with the Ileal Conduit Diversion

Reference	No. of Patients	Pyelonephritis	Ureteroileal Stenosis	Stones	Stomal Stenosis
Butcher (1962)	307	42 (13%)	7 (2%)	10 (3%)	20 (6%)
Johnson (1977)	214	33 (15%)	39 (18%)	5 (2%)	11 (5%)
Sullivan (1980)	336	65 (19%)	49 (14%)	13 (4%)	17 (5%)
Middleton (1976)	90	18 (20%)	9 (10%)	8 (9%)	17 (5%)
Shapiro (1975)	90	15 (16%)	20 (22%)	8 (9%)	38 (42%)
Pitts (1979)	242	26 (10%)	10 (4%)	14 (5%)	34 (14%)
Total	1279	199 (16%)	134 (10%)	58 (4.5%)	137 (11%)

Table 82–2. Long-term Complications with the Colon Conduit Diversion

Reference	No. of Patients	Pyelonephritis	Ureterocolonic Stenosis	Stones	Stomal Stenosis
Morales (1975)	46	8 (17%)	6 (13%)	2 (4%)	6 (13%)
Althausen (1978)	70	5 (7%)	6 (8%)	3 (4%)	2 (2%)
Total	116	13 (11%)	12 (10%)	5 (4%)	8 (7%)

male bladder cancer patient, urinary reconstruction to the urethra is the procedure of choice in most centers worldwide (Skinner et al, 1995).

The encouraging results initially seen in male patients undergoing orthotopic diversion stimulated a similar interest in applying this diversion to women. However, before 1990, orthotopic reconstruction was reserved for male patients and considered contraindicated in the female subject. Reasons included the fact that the entire urethra was routinely removed during cystectomy in women because it was thought necessary to provide an adequate surgical cancer margin. It was also believed that the female patient would be unable to maintain an appropriate continence mechanism if orthotopic diversion was performed after cystectomy. However, on the basis of a growing body of pathologic evidence, it has been shown that the urethra can be safely preserved in the majority of women undergoing cystectomy for bladder cancer without compromising a proper cancer operation (Stein et al, 1995, 1998a; Stenzl et al, 1995b; Maralani et al, 1997). In addition, anatomic dissections of the female pelvis provided a better understanding of the continence mechanism in women and suggested that women could maintain a continent outlet after orthotopic substitution (Borirakchanyavat et al, 1997; Colleselli et al, 1998). These important discoveries provided a foundation on which to offer women lower urinary tract reconstruction to the urethra. The initial clinical experience in women demonstrated the feasibility of orthotopic reconstruction with outstanding functional results (Stein et al, 1995). This achievement marked another significant step forward in the evolution of lower urinary tract reconstruction.

Although the ideal bladder substitute remains to be developed, the orthotopic neobladder most closely resembles the original bladder in both location and function. The orthotopic neobladder is a natural extension of the continent cutaneous diversion anastomosed directly to the native intact urethra. The orthotopic neobladder eliminates the need for a cutaneous stoma and a cutaneous collection device. This form of lower urinary tract reconstruction subsequently relies on the intact rhabdosphincter continence mechanism, eliminating the need for intermittent catheterization and the often-plagued efferent continence mechanism of most continent cutaneous reservoirs. Voiding is accomplished by concomitantly increasing intra-abdominal pressure (Valsalva maneuver) with relaxation of the pelvic floor musculature. The majority of patients undergoing orthotopic reconstruction are continent and void to completion without the need for intermittent catheterization. The pioneering work of Camey and Le Duc (1979) with orthotopic reconstruction in carefully selected male patients has subsequently evolved into a common form of lower urinary tract reconstruction in all patients requiring urinary diversion.

In many institutional centers worldwide, orthotopic reconstruction has replaced the ileal conduit as the standard form of reconstruction. The experience of urinary diversion at the University of Southern California exemplifies this evolution (Fig. 82–1). Beginning in 1986, the number of orthotopic bladder substitutes performed dramatically increased while the number of conduits dramatically declined. It is hoped that this trend will continue into the general community. It is, however, incumbent on the surgeon who is actively involved

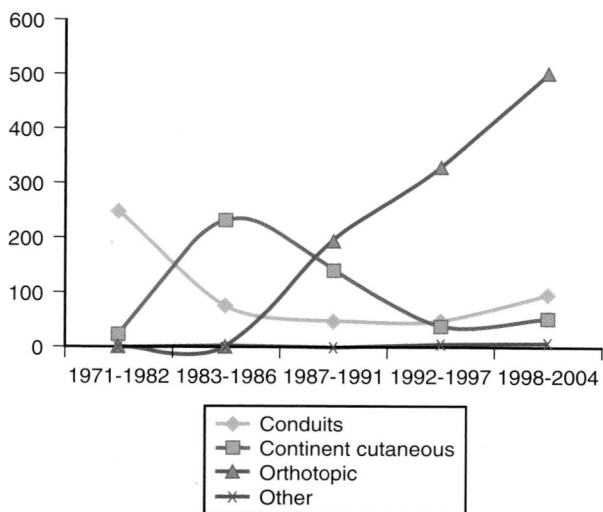

Figure 82–1. Evolution of urinary diversion at the University of Southern California from 1971 to 2004. Orthotopic reconstruction was first applied to men in 1986 and to women in 1990, with a steady increase in the number of bladder substitutes since that time. Note a decline in the number of conduit forms of diversion during the same period.

in lower urinary tract reconstruction to understand the indications for and contraindications to orthotopic diversion as well as to be familiar with the various reconstructive options. This will help ensure optimal clinical outcomes and guarantee satisfaction of patients.

KEY POINTS: EVOLUTION OF URINARY DIVERSION

■ Urinary diversion has developed along three paths: a conduit form of diversion, continent cutaneous diversions, and most recently orthotopic diversion.

■ Long-term complications of the ileal conduit include stomal stenosis, pyelonephritis, calculus formation, ureteral obstruction, and renal deterioration.

■ The major long-term problem with continent cutaneous diversion is providing a durable efferent continence mechanism.

■ The orthotopic neobladder relies on the rhabdosphincter for continence; most patients are continent and able to void to completion without the need for intermittent catheterization.

PRINCIPLES OF CONTINENT URINARY DIVERSION

In general, patients considered appropriate surgical candidates for cystectomy should also be potential candidates for lower urinary tract reconstruction. **Relative contraindications include mental or physical impairments that would preclude the ability to or the understanding of how to and when to self-catheterize, should it be necessary.** The need for intermittent catheterization is not uncommon in patients undergoing orthotopic diversion. If patients are observed closely for a long period, at least 43% of men at 5 years in one study (Steven and Poulsen, 2000) and up to 40% of women in other studies (Stein et al, 1997; Stein et al, 2004) reportedly required some need for intermittent catheterization to completely empty the neobladder. It is therefore important that all patients possess the necessary motor hand and intellectual skills and be instructed in how to properly catheterize per urethra, should it be necessary after orthotopic diversion.

A critical evaluation of renal function is mandatory in all patients considering lower urinary tract reconstruction (McDougal and Koch, 1986; Koch et al, 1991). Complications associated with the incorporation of ileum or colon include metabolic disturbances secondary to hyperchloremic metabolic acidosis (Koch and McDougal, 1985). This is particularly important in patients with compromised renal function and prolonged contact of the urine with the bowel mucosa. Permanently compromised renal function (serum creatinine level above 2 ng/dL) should be considered a contraindication to continent urinary diversion. In patients with borderline renal function, creatinine clearance should be evaluated. A minimum creatinine clearance of 60 mL/min should be documented before a continent form of urinary diversion is undertaken. Patients with elevated serum creatinine secondary to ureteral obstruction should undergo upper urinary tract decompression (by percutaneous nephrostomy), allowing recovery and redetermination of true baseline renal function before it is decided to perform the particular urinary diversion.

A gastric form of neobladder may be more appropriate for patients with borderline renal function who otherwise would be candidates for lower urinary tract reconstruction. This evolution to orthotopic reconstruction with a gastric segment of bowel is based on increasing long-term experience with gastric segments employed in the pediatric population as gastrocystoplasty (Nguyen, 1991). The stomach has been used as an alternative to the intestine because it may offer several advantages in certain clinical situations. There is excretion of chloride and hydrogen ions, which is beneficial in patients with renal failure or compromised renal function. Metabolic disturbances with gastric segments are therefore theoretically less severe and do not result in a hyperchloremic metabolic acidosis. However, other electrolyte abnormalities may occur. A clinically significant hyponatremic, hypochloremic alkalosis has been reported in patients with renal insufficiency undergoing an orthotopic gastric substitute (Adams et al, 1988).

Other reported advantages of a gastric segment include less mucus production, which may reduce the need for neobladder catheterization and irrigation. The acid secretion may also reduce the potential for urinary tract infections (Adams et al, 1988; Lockhart et al, 1994). Gastric neobladders may be an ideal form of diversion in patients with short bowel syndrome. Last, the gastric tissue has an excellent muscle backing that provides for the application of an antirefluxing ureteral anastomosis. Despite these advantages of gastric neobladders, there are clearly some significant disadvantages, including a hematuria and dysuria syndrome that occurs (infrequently) in patients with intact urethral sensation as a result of urine acidity. Attempts to treat this with H_2 blockers can be made.

The results of orthotopic gastric neobladders have been reported in several series (Hauri, 1998; Shamsa, 1998; Lin et al, 2000). Lin and associates (2000) reported their clinical experience and urodynamic findings for eight male patients undergoing gastric neobladders (average follow-up, 43 months) and compared these results with those of a similar group of patients who underwent neobladder construction from either small bowel or an ileocecal segment. They found that the gastric neobladder group had a significantly reduced mean bladder capacity, a reduction in compliance, and higher incontinence rates compared with other forms of neobladder. They concluded that gastric neobladders are associated with poor urodynamic parameters and that the routine use of this orthotopic diversion is not recommended. Gastric segments in orthotopic diversion may, however, be appropriate as composites (in combination with another portion of the bowel) in carefully selected patients with renal failure or inadequate bowel length (Lockhart et al, 1993).

Although it is controversial, we believe that the age of the patient alone should not necessarily be a contraindication to orthotopic diversion. It is generally believed that better continence rates are seen in patients younger than 70 years undergoing orthotopic diversion; however, physiologic age may ultimately be more important than chronologic age with regard to continence. Therefore, a differentiation between physiologic age and chronologic age should be made. It is clear that some elderly patients 80 years or older may do well clinically with an orthotopic form of urinary diversion if they are healthy and motivated enough. In a review of 295 male patients undergoing orthotopic diversion, the overall percentage of patients with good or satisfactory continence was statistically similar when patients older than 70 years were compared with younger age groups (Elmajian et al, 1996). Similar results were reported by Steven and Poulsen (2000), who found no significant difference in day or night continence in men older than 70 years undergoing orthotopic diversion. Advanced age should not, therefore, necessarily be a contraindication to continent diversion.

Obesity is another factor that should not preclude patients from orthotopic diversion. In fact, in obese individuals, an orthotopic diversion may be preferred. The potential difficulty of maintaining a urostomy appliance as well as the difficulty of negotiating a thick abdominal wall while self-catheterizing a continent cutaneous reservoir in these individuals can be challenging. It is not uncommon to have thick and bulky mesenteric attachments in obese individuals that may limit mobility and the ability to manipulate the bowel. In obese patients, it has been the authors' preference to use a portion of the terminal small bowel (ileum) for orthotopic reconstruction, which, if properly done, should reach the urethra in all instances. We have also found that "defatting" the mesentery in obese individuals provides additional mobility to the reservoir, allows easier detubularization and folding of the neobladder, and should help provide a tension-free urethroenteric anastomosis.

Life expectancy is another important factor in determining the form of lower urinary tract reconstruction. The primary goal of cystectomy should be cancer control after exenteration. Complex reconstructive procedures may not be appropriate in patients whose life expectancy may be limited. It is emphasized that patients whose bladder cancer demonstrates extravesical extension and lymph node–positive disease should, however, not necessarily be excluded from orthotopic reconstruction. **If it is properly performed, a significant number of these patients will have durable life expectancies** with a low incidence of a local recurrence (Stein et al, 2001a). Patients with a limited life expectancy may want to consider a more simple and expedient form of diversion that would not need extensive rehabilitation and training requirements, which may detract from their remaining life.

Critical to the success of any continent urinary diversion is the construction of a reservoir that can accommodate a large volume of urine, under low pressure, without the reflux or absorption of urinary constituents. Important principles of reservoir construction include configuration, which determines geometric capacity (volume = height × radius^2); accommodation, which relates pressure and volume to mural tension (Laplace's law, T = P × radius^3); and compliance, which concerns the physical characteristics of the bowel wall (Goodwin et al, 1959). Furthermore, the concept of detubularization and folding of the bowel, described by Goodwin and colleagues in 1959, was critical in the development of spherical reservoirs with a larger diameter (radius) and greater capacity (volume), resulting in significantly lower internal reservoir pressures during filling without coordinated wall contractions (Hinman, 1988). The increase in volume capacity achieved in the intestinal segment depends on the shape; volume is almost double in a U-shaped pouch and is still greater in an S- or W-shaped pouch, or Kock pouch, which most closely resembles an ellipsoid or spherical configuration. Lower intraluminal pressures within the reservoir should therefore allow a better degree of resistance across the continent zone, thus resulting in improved continence.

Much of the literature concerns which bowel segment or reservoir is optimal for construction of a continent reservoir (Skinner et al, 1995). The small intestine, terminal ileum and cecum, large intestine, and a combination of these bowel segments have been used to construct a urinary reservoir. The authors believe that the small bowel (ileal reservoir) provides some distinct advantages over other portions of the bowel. The ileum appears to have less contractility and greater compliance, which may provide improved continence rates compared with large bowel neobladders. Evidence suggests that the muscle-walled colon and cecum are less compliant than the ileum and store urine at higher pressures (Berglund et al, 1987; Hinman, 1988; Steers, 2000; Schrier et al, 2005). In addition, several clinical studies have demonstrated that the urodynamic characteristics of the ileum appear to be superior to those of the colon. Berglund and associates (1987) showed the advantage of ileal versus cecal reservoirs. Lytton and Green (1989) demonstrated that ileal reservoirs appear to accommodate larger volumes at lower pressures than right colon reservoirs do. Davidsson and associates (1992) evaluated the urodynamic profiles of neobladders constructed from the ileum and the right colon and found that although the volume capacity was similar, the pressure at maximum capacity was much lower with the ileal reservoir. Most recently, Schrier and colleagues (2005) compared the urodynamic parameters of an orthotopic ileal and sigmoid neobladder and clearly demonstrated favorable characteristics with ileum, including larger capacity, lower filling pressures, lower maximum capacity pressures, and better compliance.

Further evidence to support the application of ileum as the preferred segment of bowel for a continent reservoir comes from Hohenfellner and associates (1993). They elegantly evaluated the properties of gut smooth muscle layers (circular and longitudinal) of ileal and cecal segments in a canine model. The circular ileal layers were found to be most distensible, followed by the colonic circular and longitudinal ileal layers. The longitudinal layer of the colonic segment however, was relatively nondistensible (Hohenfellner et al, 1993). More recent urodynamic evidence suggests that ileal reservoirs, with lower storage pressures, may be preferable to large bowel diversions (Santucci et al, 1999). This interesting study evaluated six different forms of continent urinary reservoir and noted significantly different continence rates and urodynamic data. They too suggested that neobladders composed of stomach or sigmoid should be constructed only when absolutely necessary because of high incontinence rates (Santucci et al, 1999). Collectively, these data suggest that reservoirs composed of colonic segments have higher storage pressures than ileal segments do, which may in fact influence continence rates in those with an orthotopic neobladder.

Another issue that may favor an ileal segment for continent urinary diversion is mucosal atrophy. Mucosal atrophy, with less reabsorption of urinary constituents, appears to be more reliable in small bowel than in large bowel reservoirs (Norlen and Trasti, 1978; Mills and Studer, 1999).

For these reasons, in addition to the ease with which the small bowel can be surgically manipulated, the use of the ileum in construction of an orthotopic neobladder may be preferred to use of large bowel segments.

KEY POINTS: PRINCIPLES OF CONTINENT URINARY DIVERSION

- Permanently compromised renal function is a contraindication to continent urinary diversion.

- Age alone is not a contraindication to orthotopic diversion, and a differentiation between physiologic age and chronologic age should be made.

- Important principles to continent urinary reservoir construction include configuration, accommodation, and compliance.

- A spherical urinary reservoir will maintain the largest capacity with the lowest pressure.

SELECTION OF PATIENTS

The type of urinary diversion to be performed depends on a combination of clinical factors and the patient's preference, which must be discussed in detail preoperatively. **An honest, informed discussion, carefully explaining the various options along with the short- and long-term risks and benefits of each form of urinary diversion, must be performed. It may also be helpful to have the patient talk with other patients who have undergone the various forms of urinary reconstruction.** The primary patient factor in selection for an orthotopic diversion is the desire of that individual for a neobladder, and there must be a realistic understanding of the potential limitations (possibly some degree of nocturnal incontinence) of this form of lower urinary tract reconstruction. All the potential forms of urinary diversion, including a noncontinent urinary diversion by means of conduit (colon or ileum), a continent cutaneous diversion requiring the need for intermittent catheterization, a rectal form of urinary diversion, and a lower urinary tract reconstruction by means of an orthotopic neobladder to the urethra, must be offered or at least explained to the patient.

It has been the authors' practice to counsel patients about the importance of the urethral biopsy intraoperatively. **Patients interested in an orthotopic diversion should understand that the ultimate decision, from a cancer perspective, is determined at the time of surgery by intraoperative frozen-section analysis of the distal surgical margin.** If tumor is present at the distal surgical margin, the patient is absolutely an inappropriate candidate for an orthotopic bladder substitute, and diversion by means of a continent cutaneous reservoir or conduit should be performed, depending on the patient's preference as discussed preoperatively. Therefore, all patients must be marked for an appropriate cutaneous stoma site preoperatively by the enterostomal therapy nurse and should be instructed in how to catheterize themselves, should it be necessary postoperatively. Some patients may be better served with a simple and more practical diversion, such as an ileal conduit. This may be the frail and sedentary patient who lacks the motivation for the rehabilitation process required in those undergoing a continent diversion postoperatively. Patients must also understand and accept the potential risks of a recurrence in the retained urethra (discussed later in chapter).

Radiographic evaluation or colonoscopic assessment of the entire large bowel should be considered when a portion of the colon is to be employed in the construction of the neobladder. This may be particularly important when the sigmoid colon is to be incorporated in the reconstruction. In general, radiographic assessment is not necessary if only the small intestine is to be used for the construction of the neobladder. Furthermore, unsuspected intraoperative pathologic findings of various portions of the bowel may require a different portion of the intestine to be used. It is therefore imperative that the reconstructive surgeon have the capability to use large, small, or a combination of bowel segments in constructing a continent reservoir.

Two important criteria must be maintained in considering patients for orthotopic urinary diversion. First, the rhabdosphincter mechanism must remain intact to provide a continent means of storing urine. Second, under no circumstance should the cancer operation be compromised by reconstruction at the urethroenteric anastomosis, retained urethra, or surgical margins. Preoperatively, if these criteria can be safely maintained, the patient may be considered an appropriate candidate for orthotopic urinary diversion. On the basis of sound clinical and pathologic data, we and others (Hautmann, 2003; Stein et al, 2005) continue to recommend the intraoperative frozen-section analysis of the proximal urethral margin (in all patients) as an appropriate mechanism to determine who is an appropriate candidate for orthotopic diversion from a cancer perspective.

CONTINENCE MECHANISM IN PATIENTS UNDERGOING ORTHOTOPIC DIVERSION

The preservation of satisfactory urinary continence is critical to the clinical outcomes and the improved quality of life of a patient with an orthotopic bladder substitute. Precise neuroanatomic and histologic dissections of the human pelvis and urethra have provided a better understanding of the rhabdosphincter mechanism and a rational basis for continence in patients after radical pelvic surgery (Borirakchanyavat et al, 1997; Colleselli et al, 1998; Strasser and Bartsch, 2000). Proper knowledge and a fundamental understanding of how to preserve the anatomic configuration of the rhabdosphincter complex, along with the corresponding pudendal nerve supply, during surgery should optimize the continence mechanism and allow volitional voiding postoperatively (Borirakchanyavat et al, 1997; Strasser and Bartsch, 2000; Stein et al, 2001b).

Much of what has been learned of the rhabdosphincter complex comes from elegant neuroanatomic studies of the female urethra. Colleselli and associates (1998) performed extensive microneuroanatomic dissections, histologic examination, and three-dimensional reconstructive imaging to better define the urethral sphincteric and rhabdosphincteric anatomy in women. Although these dissections were performed on female cadavers, the observations and findings have been similarly described in men (Strasser and Bartsch, 2000). Collectively, these findings have allowed a more precise and anatomic approach to maintain the continence mechanism in all patients undergoing cystectomy and orthotopic substitution.

The female urethral sphincter system consists of smooth muscle innervated by the autonomic nervous system and striated muscle supplied by somatic nerves. **There is general agreement that the autonomic nerves that serve the smooth muscle sphincter originate in the pelvic plexus** (Colleselli et al, 1998). **Innervation of the voluntary urinary sphincter system, however, is a matter of some controversy. Most interested investigators agree that the rhabdosphincter is probably supplied primarily by the branches of the pudendal nerve** (Borirakchanyavat et al, 1997; Stenzl et al, 1997; Colleselli et al, 1998).

In an attempt to better define the innervation of the rhabdosphincteric complex, Colleselli and associates (1998) performed neuroanatomic dissections on female fetal specimens and female adult cadavers. The focus of the dissections was to reassess the anatomy and topography of the female urethral sphincter system and its innervation with regard to urethra-sparing anterior exenteration and other radical pelvic surgical procedures. With the aid of three-dimensional computed tomography reconstruction of histologic sections, **Colleselli and associates (1998) demonstrated that the autonomic fibers from the pelvic plexus innervate the bladder neck. These autonomic fibers that supply the pelvic visceral organs emerge from the pelvic plexuses and course along the lateral aspect of the rectum and vagina. These nerve fibers course caudally down toward the bladder neck and very proximal urethra. Some of these fibers branch off from a thick fiber at the lower margin of the lateral vaginal wall and enter the bladder neck and cranial portion of the urethra from the dorsolateral aspect. These autonomic nerves do not appear to play a significant role in the innervation of the rhabdosphincter or the continence mechanism and are essentially sacrificed during the exenterative portion of the operation without compromising continence.**

In the same study, Colleselli and associates (1998) found that the major portion of the striated muscle that corresponds to the striated rhabdosphincter is located on the ventral and lateral aspects (omega shaped) of the urethra. No clear, defined line could be identified between the transverse smooth muscle cranially and the striated muscle caudally. Rather, a gradual transition was noted in the middle third of the urethra, with intermingling fibers of both types of muscle. This area has been found to correspond to the area of continence region on fluorourodynamic studies performed on women who had undergone orthotopic reconstruction after cystectomy (Grossfeld et al, 1996).

Importantly, the innervation of the striated urethral rhabdosphincter was shown to arise from the pudendal nerve (Colleselli et al, 1998). Branches off the pudendal nerve coursing beneath the levator muscle can be traced to rhabdosphincter. Delicate fibers from the perineal portion of the pudendal nerve course underneath the urogenital diaphragm, entering the caudal portion of the urethra laterally. Therefore, any pelvic surgery dedicated to maintaining the rhabdosphincter innervation and ultimate function should avoid excessive dissection along the pelvic floor, where the branches of the pudendal nerve course to the sphincteric complex. The surgical approach has been described and the outcomes have been supported clinically (Stein et al, 2001b). Increasing clinical experience in women undergoing cystectomy with removal of the bladder neck and proximal portion of the urethra has demonstrated excellent continence results when minimal dissection is performed anteriorly along the pelvic floor and if the urethral sphincter system and corresponding innervation can be maintained (Stein et al, 1997; Stenzl et al, 1997).

In a neuroanatomic study performed in male human cadaveric pelves, similar anatomic findings and innervation were described. **Strasser and Bartsch (2000) described the male rhabdosphincter as an independent muscle unit that is not in direct contact with the fibers of the levator ani muscle.** These dissections demonstrated that the male sphincter does not form a horizontal muscular ring around the membranous urethra. Rather, the male rhabdosphincter is a muscular coat situated ventral and lateral to the membranous urethra and prostate, the core of which is an omega-shaped loop that surrounds the membranous urethra. The innervation of the male rhabdosphincter was also found to originate from fine branches that arise off the pudendal nerve. These authors correctly suggested that injury to either the rhabdosphincter or the pudendal innervation impairs the sphincter mechanism in men (Strasser and Bartsch, 2000).

The complex musculofascial urethral support system also plays an important role in the overall continence mechanism in patients undergoing orthotopic substitution. A well-performed cystectomy should pay specific attention to the pudendal innervation, pelvic floor, and musculofascial support system to the proximal urethra. Additional studies are needed to further define and explain the complex rhabdosphincter continence mechanism, to guide the surgical approach, and to optimize the results in patients undergoing orthotopic reconstruction.

> ### KEY POINTS: CONTINENCE MECHANISM IN ORTHOTOPIC DIVERSION
>
> - The innervation of the striated urethral rhabdosphincter arises from the branches of the pudendal nerve and is most important to maintain continence in patients with an orthotopic neobladder.
>
> - Any pelvic surgery intended to maintain the rhabdosphincter function and innervation should avoid excessive dissection along the pelvic floor where the branches of the pudendal nerve course to innervate the sphincter complex.

CONTINENCE PRESERVATION

With the advent of orthotopic urinary diversion, preservation of the rhabdosphincteric continence mechanism has become an important functional goal in the surgical management of the patient undergoing cystectomy, second only to the complete extirpation of the malignant neoplasm. Continence after orthotopic reconstruction is influenced by a combination of the characteristics of the reservoir (large capacity, low pressure) as well as by the outlet (continence) mechanism. **It is generally believed that radical cystectomy abolishes the normal reflex rise in urethral pressure during reservoir filling** (Tanagho et al, 1966). This loss of afferent input from the detrusor to the central nervous system is thought to account, in part, for the worse continence at night in patients with an orthotopic substitute. This phenomenon is less commonly observed in those patients undergoing radical prostatectomy. Therefore, the rhabdosphincteric complex must be maximally preserved to provide a functional continence mechanism.

On the basis of neuroanatomic studies (Schlegel and Walsh, 1987; Brendler et al, 1990) and through steady refinement in the surgical techniques applied to radical retropubic prostatectomy, the importance of the external striated urethral sphincteric complex in maintaining continence has become increasingly evident in patients undergoing orthotopic reconstruction after radical cystectomy. It has also been suggested that in addition to preservation of the rhabdosphincter and its pudendal innervation, preservation of the autonomic supply to the corpora cavernosa (pelvic nerve and inferior hypogastric plexus) may improve or help maintain innervation to the membranous urethra and therefore enhance urinary continence in candidates for orthotopic diversion (Schlegel and Walsh, 1987; Turner et al, 1997; Kessler et al, 2004).

Turner and associates (1997) initially examined the effect of a nerve-sparing cystectomy technique on continence in 165 men who underwent cystectomy and construction of an ileal neobladder. Nerve sparing was attempted bilaterally in 20 men, unilaterally in 96 men, and not at all in 49 patients. The functional outcomes of attempted nerve sparing and of age on continence were then examined. Median times to continence during the day and at night for all men were 3 and 9 months, respectively. Significantly improved continence was reported in patients with attempted nerve-sparing procedures, compared with those without a nerve-sparing surgery, and in men younger than 65 years, compared with those older than 65 years. In this study, nerve-sparing cystectomy was also significantly associated with improved continence (day and night) in a multivariate analysis. The same group subsequently updated their clinical experience of 331 male patients undergoing an attempted nerve-sparing radical cystectomy and concluded similar results—nerve sparing had the greatest impact on daytime continence, whereas age had the greatest impact on nighttime continence (Kessler et al, 2004). **The authors suggested that attempted nerve sparing may be associated with improved urinary continence after orthotopic bladder substitution. However, the authors correctly commented that an attempted nerve-sparing technique may simply indicate a more careful and meticulous dissection around the prostatic apex, with subsequent reduced damage to the external sphincteric mechanism.**

The issue of nerve-sparing cystectomy in women is debatable. Some authors have suggested that a sympathetic nerve-sparing cystectomy may be important in maintaining continence in women undergoing orthotopic diversion (Stenzl et al, 1995a; Hautmann, 1997). Others have routinely sacrificed the autonomic nerves coursing along the lateral aspect of the uterus and vagina and have successfully relied on the pudendal innervation of the rhabdosphincter complex for continence (Stein et al, 1997; Stein et al, 2001b; Ali-El-Dein et al, 2002). In fact, the authors have observed good continence results in women undergoing complete bowel and urinary tract reconstruction after total pelvic exenteration with removal of all pelvic autonomic innervation. This, again, supports the concept that autonomic innervation is not critical to the continence mechanism. Although not well understood, it is possible that preservation of the sympathetic nerves may contribute to the high incidence of so-called hypercontinence and urinary retention in women requiring continuous intermittent catheterization as reported by Hautmann (1997).

In evaluating the continence results and clinical outcomes of various series of cystectomy and orthotopic neobladders, several considerations must be kept in mind. The prevalence and severity of urinary incontinence may be confounded by many variables, including the endpoints, definitions, length and diligence of follow-up, age of the patient, sex, surgical indication, and technique (which collectively includes the type, length, and configuration of bowel incorporated into the reservoir). The postoperative period influences continence results as reservoir capacity generally increases during the first 12 months. Time to maximal reservoir capacity may be slightly longer in patients with refluxing afferent limbs (Studer type) compared with those neobladders incorporating nonrefluxing afferent limbs. Furthermore, the mechanism employed to evaluate lower urinary tract symptoms, incontinence, and voiding pattern must be considered; this may include physician or chart documentation, a third-party review, or less commonly (but more appropriately) a validated outcome instrument. Despite these limitations, some general observations can be made that appear to be consistent in most orthotopic neobladder series.

The clinical goal of most neobladders is to allow volitional voiding four to six times daily (every 3 to 4 hours) with a capacity range of 400 to 500 mL of urine at low pressures (<15 cm H_2O). Despite a technically sound operation, nocturnal incontinence is more commonly observed than daytime incontinence and may be seen in approximately 28% of patients (Steers, 2000). In a pooled analysis of 2238 patients with various forms of an orthotopic neobladder, daytime incontinence was reported in 13% of patients. **Risk factors in this study for daytime incontinence included advanced age of the patient (>65 years), use of colonic segments, and in some series lack of nerve-sparing techniques** (Steers, 2000).

Kessler and associates (2004) assessed various factors influencing urinary continence after radical cystectomy and ileal orthotopic bladder substitution in 331 male patients. In a multivariate analysis, the rate of daytime continence was significantly higher in patients with attempted nerve-sparing techniques and in those patients younger than 65 years. As expected, daytime continence was also significantly better and achieved more quickly than nighttime continence. The time to achieve daytime continence was shorter in patients with attempted nerve-sparing surgery (Kessler et al, 2004). These findings strengthen the relationship of nerve-sparing techniques and continence in these cystectomy patients with an orthotopic substitute. It is the authors' conviction that nerve-sparing techniques for patients with high-grade, invasive bladder cancer should be performed only if the radical tumor resection is not compromised, which truly reflects only a small portion of well-selected patients.

Nighttime incontinence remains one of the most bothersome sequelae of neobladders, seen in approximately 28% of patients (Steers, 2000). Nocturnal incontinence after orthotopic reconstruction results in part from the absence of neurologic feedback and sphincter detrusor reflex as well as decreased sphincter tonus at night. Similar to daytime incontinence, nighttime incontinence generally resolves or improves as functional capacity increases. In general, patients fail to awaken in time during the night to empty the neobladder, allowing increased volumes to overcome the urethral closure mechanism. Note, in elderly patients, this incontinence may worsen with a physiologic diuresis associated with increasing age. Instructing the patient to completely empty immediately before bedtime and to awaken two or three times with the assistance of an alarm clock may help reduce some of the issues of nighttime incontinence.

In general, daytime continence rates after an orthotopic substitute are good (Steers, 2000). However, the development of daytime incontinence has been reported to gradually occur 4 to 5 years after orthotopic reconstruction (Madersbacher et al, 2002). One contributing factor is thought to be worsening urethral sphincter function with age. The importance of age and incontinence in patients with an orthotopic reservoir is underscored by the trend seen in elderly individuals; 10% to 15% of even healthy patients will report urinary incontinence (Temml et al, 2000). Furthermore, decreased urethral sensitivity has been proposed as a potential factor contributing to urinary incontinence after radical cystectomy and orthotopic diversion (Hugonnet et al, 1999). It has been suggested that conscious or unconscious sensation of urine leakage in the membranous urethra may produce either a reflex or voluntary contraction or increased tone of the external urethra, which may be impaired in some patients with an orthotopic diversion. This reflex may also diminish with age and contribute to gradually decreasing continence in some individuals after orthotopic reconstruction.

The evaluation and management of urinary incontinence after orthotopic diversion should be delayed until the neobladder has had time to enlarge. This may take 6 months to a year after surgery. If daytime urinary incontinence continues to be a problem, urodynamic investigation may be indicated to ensure adequate capacity, without pressure waves. If reduction in maximal urethral closure or low Valsalva leak pressure is demonstrated, transurethral injection of bulking agents may be considered, with marginal results. **Alternatively, in men, an artificial urinary sphincter can be considered and may provide a more definitive treatment.** In women, although injection of urethral bulking agents provides a minimally invasive approach with some positive results (Tchetgen et al, 2000), it is best employed for women with minimal symptoms of incontinence, with overall success rates below 50% and with less than optimal durable responses (Wilson et al, 2004). **Pubovaginal sling procedures for incontinence may be favored in women with incontinence after orthotopic reconstruction** (Quek et al, 2004). These female patients, however, must be informed of the likelihood of hypercontinence (urinary retention) and the need to perform intermittent catheterization after treatment. Importantly, it has been our experience that a sling procedure in women with urinary incontinence after orthotopic reconstruction, with use of infrapubic bone anchors, may provide the best surgical approach because it avoids the need to violate the pelvis that was previously operated on and the potential complications associated with a more invasive technique (Quek et al, 2004).

Failure to empty or urinary retention has been reported in 4% to 25% of patients undergoing orthotopic reconstruction and appears to be more common in women undergoing this form of urinary diversion. Risk factors for urinary retention in patients with an orthotopic reservoir include the use of excessive intestinal length (>60 cm of ileum), following nerve-sparing surgical procedures, and increasing length of follow-up (Steven and Poulsen, 2000; Steers, 2000; Stein et al, 2004). **Urinary retention is best managed by intermittent self-catheterization** (Steers, 2000). Pharmacologic intervention (tricyclic antidepressants, anticholinergics, DDAVP) for patients with urinary retention does not appear to be an effective measure to improve this voiding

dysfunction. Furthermore, a significant number of patients with orthotopic reservoirs will develop abdominal wall or incisional hernias postoperatively. These fascial defects will reduce the efficiency in completely evacuating the neobladder by reducing the ability to effectively increase intra-abdominal Valsalva pressure. These hernias should be identified and surgically repaired. All patients must understand the principle of first lowering outlet resistance (rhabdosphincter) and subsequently increasing intra-abdominal pressure, which is the key to proper voiding and to help prevent overdistention. Regular follow-up should be reinforced in all patients undergoing this form of diversion.

A unique voiding dysfunction is hypercontinence in women undergoing orthotopic reconstruction. A growing body of evidence suggests that urinary retention is more commonly seen in women after this diversion (Ali-El-Dein et al, 2002; Stenzl and Holtl, 2003; Lee et al, 2004; Stein et al, 2004). Stein and associates (2004) reported a 25% overall incidence in 209 patients for the need of some form of intermittent catheterization to empty the neobladder, including 20% of men and 43% of women. Ali-El-Dein and associates (2002) elegantly studied the possible causes of chronic retention after radical cystectomy and orthotopic bladder substitution in women. A total of 136 women underwent a standard radical cystectomy and orthotopic substitution, with 100 patients evaluable at a mean follow-up of 36 months. Overall, 95% of the women were continent in the day, 86% were continent at night, 2 were completely incontinent, and 16% were in chronic retention. **Videourodynamics showed that retention appeared to be mechanical in nature due to the pouch's falling back in the wide pelvic cavity, resulting in acute angulation of the posterior pouch–urethral junction.** In addition, herniation of the pouch wall through the prolapsed vaginal stump was observed in most cases. Pelvic floor electromyography demonstrated complete pelvic floor silence during voiding, suggesting that urinary retention was not related to a neurogenic cause. The authors suggested that omental packing behind the reservoir, suturing of the peritoneum on the rectal wall to the vaginal stump, suspension of the vaginal stump by the preserved round ligaments, and suspension of the pouch near the dome to the back of the rectus muscle at cystectomy will help reduce the incidence of chronic retention. These authors also provide sound evidence that chronic urinary retention after orthotopic substitution in women is due to anatomic rather than to functional or neurogenic reasons (Ali-El-Dein et al, 2002). The proposed technical modifications to increase back support of the pouch with ventral suspension near its dome and support of the vaginal stump should help reduce the incidence of urinary retention in these patients.

Surgical Technique for Continence Preservation

Attention to anatomic and surgical detail is important to optimize functional and clinical outcomes in patients undergoing orthotopic diversion after radical pelvic surgery. **Minimal manipulation of the muscle fibers of the rhabdosphincter, the fascial attachments, and the corresponding innervation is essential in providing optimal urinary continence** (Stein

KEY POINTS: CONTINENCE PRESERVATION

- The clinical goal of most orthotopic neobladders is to allow volitional voiding every 3 to 4 hours with a capacity range of 400 to 500 mL.

- Nocturnal incontinence is observed in approximately 28% of patients undergoing orthotopic diversion.

- Factors influencing continence rates include age, intestinal segment used, and possibly the application of a nerve-sparing technique.

- Failure to empty or urinary retention has been reported in 4% to 25% of patients undergoing orthotopic reconstruction and is more common in women.

et al, 1997, 2001b; Colleselli et al, 1998; Stenzl et al, 1998; Strasser and Bartsch, 2000). The pudendal nerve provides somatic innervation to the rhabdosphincter and enters this muscle in the perineum via the perineal nerve and from the pelvis by way of the intrapelvic branch of the pudendal nerve. Branches of the pudendal nerve that run along the pelvic floor below the endopelvic fascia ultimately innervate the rhabdosphincter. Therefore, minimal dissection should be performed during any pelvic surgery along the pelvic floor levator musculature to avoid injury to the rhabdosphincter innervation.

Anterior Apical Dissection in the Male Patient

The technique of an extended bilateral pelvic lymphadenectomy with radical cystoprostatectomy is well established (Stein and Skinner, 2004). Urethral preparation with preservation of the continence mechanism is critical when orthotopic diversion is anticipated. **The continence mechanism in men may be maximized if dissection in the region of the pelvic floor and anterior urethra is minimized.** Attention to surgical technique is important and is described in detail elsewhere (Stein et al, 2001b). Several fundamental key surgical issues in the preparation of the urethra in patients undergoing orthotopic diversion deserve special mention.

Only after the cystectomy specimen is completely freed and mobile posteriorly is attention then directed anteriorly to the urethra. Posterior dissection should not extend distal to the apex of the prostate. All fibroareolar connections among the anterior bladder wall, prostate, and undersurface of the pubic symphysis are divided. The endopelvic fascia is incised adjacent to the prostate, and the levator muscles are carefully swept off the lateral and apical portions of the prostate. The superficial branch of the deep dorsal vein is identified, ligated, and divided. With tension placed posteriorly on the prostate, the puboprostatic ligaments are identified and slightly divided just beneath the pubis and lateral to the deep dorsal venous complex that courses between these ligaments. **Care should be taken to avoid any extensive dissection in this region. The puboprostatic ligaments need only be incised enough to allow proper apical dissection of the prostate.** The apex of the prostate and membranous urethra now become palpable.

Several methods can be performed to properly control the dorsal venous plexus (Stein et al, 2001b). One may carefully pass an angled clamp beneath the dorsal venous complex, anterior to the urethra. The venous complex is then ligated with a 2-0 absorbable suture and divided close to the apex of the prostate. Any bleeding from the transected venous complex can be controlled with an absorbable 2-0 polyglycolic acid suture. In a slightly different fashion, the dorsal venous complex may be gathered at the apex of the prostate with a long Allis clamp. A figure-of-eight 2-0 absorbable suture can then be carefully placed under direct vision anterior to the urethra (distal to the apex of the prostate) around the gathered dorsal venous complex. **This suture is best placed with the surgeon facing the head of the table and with the needle holder perpendicular to the patient.** The suture is then tagged with a hemostat. This maneuver avoids the unnecessary passage of any instruments between the dorsal venous complex and the rhabdosphincter, which could injure these structures and compromise the continence mechanism. After the complex has been ligated, it can be sharply divided with excellent exposure to the anterior surface of the urethra. Once the venous complex is severed, the suture can be used to further secure the complex. The suture is then used to suspend the venous complex anteriorly to the periosteum to reestablish anterior fixation of the dorsal venous complex and puboprostatic ligaments, which may enhance continence recovery.

The anterior urethra is now exposed. Regardless of technique, the urethra is incised 270 degrees just beyond the apex of the prostate. Six 2-0 polyglycolic acid sutures are placed in the urethra circumferentially, carefully incorporating only the mucosa and submucosa of the striated urethral sphincter muscle anteriorly. The urethral catheter is clamped and divided distally. Two additional sutures are then placed, incorporating the rectourethral muscle posteriorly or the caudal extent of Denonvilliers' fascia. After this, the posterior urethra is divided and the specimen removed.

Alternatively, the deep dorsal venous complex can be sharply transected distally without securing vascular control. Cephalad traction on the prostate elongates the proximal and membranous urethra and allows the urethra to be skeletonized. The anterior two thirds of the urethra is again divided, exposing the urethral catheter. The anterior six urethral sutures are then placed under direct vision. The dorsal venous complex, the edge of which acts as a hood overlying the rhabdosphincter, is included in these sutures if the dorsal venous complex was sharply incised without vascular control. This maneuver serves to compress the dorsal vein complex against the urethra for hemostatic purposes. The urethral catheter is again drawn through the urethrotomy, clamped on the bladder side, and divided. Cephalad traction on the bladder side with the clamped catheter occludes the bladder neck, prevents tumor spill from the bladder, and provides exposure to the posterior urethra. Two additional sutures are placed in the posterior urethra, incorporating the rectourethral muscle or distal Denonvilliers' fascia. The posterior urethra is then divided, and the specimen is removed. The urethral sutures are appropriately tagged to identify their location and are placed under a towel until the urethroenteric anastomosis is performed. Bleeding from the dorsal vein is usually minimal at this point. If additional hemostasis is required, one or two anterior urethral sutures can be tied to stop the bleeding.

Regardless of the technique, frozen-section analysis of the distal urethral margin (prostatic apex) on the cystectomy specimen is performed to exclude tumor involvement. The decision to perform an orthotopic bladder substitute is ultimately made at this time. If there is no evidence of tumor, orthotopic reconstruction may be performed. It is important that an adequate surgical specimen be taken from the distal margin (urethra) of the cystectomy specimen, which will facilitate histologic evaluation by the pathologist.

Anterior Dissection in the Female

When orthotopic diversion is considered in female patients, several technical issues should be noted to optimize the continence mechanism (Stein et al, 2001b). In developing the posterior pedicles, the posterior vagina is incised at the apex, just distal to the cervix. This incision is carried anteriorly along the lateral and anterior vaginal wall, forming a circumferential division. The anterolateral vaginal wall is then grasped with a curved Kocher clamp. This provides countertraction and facilitates dissection between the anterior vaginal wall and the bladder specimen. Careful dissection of the proper plane prevents entry into the posterior bladder and reduces the amount of bleeding in this vessel-rich area. Development of this posterior plane and vascular pedicle is best performed sharply and carried just distal to the vesicourethral junction. Palpation of the Foley catheter balloon assists in identifying this region. This dissection should effectively maintain a functional anterior vaginal wall that may also help support the proximal urethra through a complex musculofascial support system that extends from the pelvic floor.

Alternatively, in the case of a deeply invasive posterior bladder tumor for which there is concern about preserving an adequate surgical margin, the anterior vaginal wall may be removed en bloc with the cystectomy specimen. Note, this is not an absolute contraindication to orthotopic reconstruction. After the posterior vaginal apex is divided, the lateral vaginal wall serves as the posterior pedicle and is divided distally. This leaves the anterior vaginal wall attached to the posterior bladder specimen. Again, the Foley catheter balloon facilitates identification of the vesicourethral junction. The surgical plane between the vesicourethral junction and the anterior vaginal wall is then developed distally at this location. A 1-cm length of proximal urethra is mobilized while the remaining distal urethra is left intact with the anterior vaginal wall. Vaginal reconstruction by a clamshell (horizontal) or side-to-side (vertical) technique is required. Other means of vaginal reconstruction include rectus myocutaneous flap, detubularized cylinder of ileum, peritoneal flap, and omental flap (Stein et al, 1994b; Esrig et al, 1997).

Once the posterior dissection is completed, a clamp is placed across the bladder neck, which prevents any tumor spill from the bladder when the urethra is transected. With gentle traction, the proximal urethra is completely divided distal to the bladder neck and clamp, and the specimen is removed. The urethra is in a more anterior position in women, which facilitates placement of at least 8 to 10 urethral sutures after the specimen is removed. Frozen-section analysis is performed on the distal surgical margin of the cystectomy specimen to exclude any tumor.

If the anterior vaginal wall has been preserved, the vagina is closed at the apex with absorbable suture and then suspended. One may suspend the vagina to Cooper's ligament to prevent postoperative vaginal prolapse or development of an enterocele. Alternatively, one may perform a colposacropexy incorporating Marlex mesh, which fixates the vagina without angulation or undue tension (authors' preference). Regardless of the form of vaginal reconstruction, a well-vascularized omental pedicle graft must be placed between the reconstructed vagina and the neobladder and properly secured to the levator ani muscles to separate the suture lines and prevent fistulization between the vaginal and urethroenteric anastomosis or neobladder. Furthermore, the omental pedicle will fill the pelvis and help prevent the neobladder from falling back posteriorly, which may result in hypercontinence.

URETHRAL AND PELVIC RECURRENCE IN PATIENTS WITH BLADDER CANCER AFTER CYSTECTOMY

Appropriate selection of patients from a cancer perspective is critical to reduce the incidence and associated morbidity and mortality of urethral or pelvic recurrence of bladder cancer after radical cystectomy. These are separate oncologic issues as they relate to orthotopic diversion that must be addressed. Importantly, because orthotopic lower urinary tract reconstruction was first applied to male patients, there is a greater body of experience and data with longer follow-up for men than for women undergoing this same form of urinary diversion. Regardless, orthotopic diversion should never be performed if a significant potential for tumor recurrence exists in the retained urethra or in the pelvis, which could potentially affect the functional characteristics of the neobladder. Therefore, a clear understanding of the various risk factors for urethral recurrence and of the potential impact of local pelvic recurrence on an orthotopic bladder substitute in men and women is important. These risk factors should then direct clinical decisions toward performing the most appropriate form of urinary diversion and should help reduce the sequelae related to urethral and pelvic recurrence.

Urethral Recurrence

Primary transitional cell carcinoma of the urethral mucosa is rare. More common is the development of a transitional cell tumor of the urethra, appearing in patients with a history of bladder cancer. The finding of urethral involvement by transitional cell carcinoma after radical cystectomy could arguably be due to either synchronous or metachronous disease. Urethral involvement after cystectomy could be due to unrecognized transitional cell carcinoma in the urethra at the time of cystectomy, growth of transitional cell carcinoma from a positive margin after cystectomy, recurrence from tumor spillage or implantation, or de novo transitional cell carcinoma that arises from the so-called field change throughout the urothelium of patients with bladder cancer.

It is difficult to absolutely assign each episode of a urethral "recurrence" after cystectomy to one of these categories, but it is generally believed that urethral tumors in patients with a history of bladder cancer represent a second manifestation of the multicentric defect of the primary transitional cell mucosa that led to the original bladder tumor. The term *urethral recurrence* is therefore somewhat misleading as it suggests failure of definitive treatment of the bladder cancer as the cause of the urethral lesion. Rather, most urethral tumors probably represent simply another occurrence of the transitional cell carcinoma in the remaining urothelium. As radical cystectomy has emerged as an effective therapy for invasive bladder cancer (Stein et al, 2001a), and as orthotopic diversion to the native intact urethra has increasingly been performed in both men and women, the fate of the retained urethra has become an increasingly important issue.

Urethral Recurrence in Men

An early analysis of pooled data from cystectomy series before 1994 estimated that the overall risk of a urethral recurrence of transitional cell carcinoma after cystectomy is approximately 10% in men (Freeman et al, 1994). More recently, a meta-analysis collectively evaluated the results from this initial study along with five additional series and concluded the overall incidence of a urethral recurrence after cystectomy to be similarly 8.1% (Stenzl et al, 2002). There are clearly differences among various reported series that may account for variations, including heterogeneous populations of patients, differences in follow-up, differences in pathologic stages, patients undergoing cystectomy only, and men with various forms and incidences of prostatic urethral involvement. Furthermore, some series removed the high-risk patients from the at-risk pool and analysis by prophylactic urethrectomy. In the large, comprehensive, pooled analysis of 25 series, Stenzl and colleagues (2002) reported a total of 256 anterior urethral tumor recurrences in 3165 patients (8.1%) undergoing cystectomy for bladder cancer. This figure provides a good estimate of the overall risk for development of a urethral recurrence after cystectomy for transitional cell carcinoma of the bladder in men. This incidence is remarkably similar to the 9% probability of a urethral recurrence at 10 years after radical cystectomy reported by Stein and associates (2005) in 768 male patients.

Specific characteristics of the primary bladder cancer have been analyzed to determine if any particular histopathologic parameters may predict or identify patients at risk for urethral recurrence after cystectomy. Various pathologic risk factors have been implicated, including papillary tumors, tumor multifocality, trigone or bladder neck tumor involvement, associated carcinoma in situ of the upper urinary tract, carcinoma in situ of the bladder, and various involvements of the prostate (urethra, ducts, or invasion of the stroma) (Freeman et al, 1994). Furthermore, there are some data to support that the specific form of urinary diversion performed may also play a role in or influence the incidence of a urethral tumor recurrence; a significantly lower incidence of urethral tumor recurrence was demonstrated in those undergoing an orthotopic diversion (5%) compared with a cutaneous form of diversion (9%) (Stein et al, 2005). This finding has been reported by others as well (Nieder et al, 2004; Hassan et al, 2005).

A growing body of data indicate that by far, the most ominous criterion for urethral tumor recurrence is prostatic urethral involvement. In 1956, Ashworth first reported that patients with prostatic urethral involvement are at increased risk for urethral tumor involvement after cystectomy. Prostatic urethral tumor involvement was found in five of seven patients (71%) who later developed anterior urethral tumors. Other series have subsequently confirmed this finding (Raz et al, 1978; Faysal, 1980; Hardeman and Soloway, 1990; Levinson et al, 1990; Tobisu et al, 1991). Freeman and colleagues (1994) reported on six studies, in which 31 of 122 patients (25%) with some form of prostatic urethral involvement developed an anterior urethral tumor after radical cystectomy for bladder cancer. These findings have subsequently been confirmed in a large cystectomy series in which the incidence of urethral recurrence was only 5% at 5 years in 639 patients without any prostate tumor involvement compared with 11% at 5 years for 129 patients with any prostate involvement (superficial or invasive) (Stein et al, 2005).

The degree of prostatic tumor involvement also appears to confer a variable risk for subsequent urethral recurrence. Hardeman and Soloway (1990) found anterior urethral recurrence in 11 of 30 patients (37%) with prostatic urethral tumors. No patient in this study with only prostatic urethral mucosa tumor developed a recurrence, whereas 25% of men with prostatic ductal involvement and 64% of men with prostatic stromal involvement in this report developed urethral recurrence. In the same series, only 2 of 56 patients (4%) whose tumors did not involve the prostatic urethra suffered urethral recurrence (Hardeman and Soloway, 1990). In another study, Levinson and colleagues (1990) found 67% of urethral recurrences to be associated with prostatic urethral involvement; no patient whose tumor was confined to the prostatic urethral mucosa, 10% of patients with prostatic ductal involvement, and 30% of patients with prostatic stromal involvement developed a urethral recurrence.

In the largest reported series of 768 male patients undergoing radical cystectomy with long-term follow-up (median 13 years) for bladder cancer, Stein and associates (2005) confirmed that the extent of prostatic tumor involvement was a significant predictor for an anterior urethral tumor recurrence. Overall, a total of 45 anterior urethral recurrences were identified at a median of 2.0 years after cystectomy. The overall probability of urethral recurrence for all 768 patients in this study was estimated to be approximately 7% at 5 years and 9% at 10 years. **Those patients with tumor involving any portion of the prostate (who did not undergo prophylactic urethrectomy after cutaneous diversion or who were followed up after orthotopic diversion) had a significantly greater risk of urethral recurrence. This risk was most magnified when the stroma of the prostate was invaded by tumor.** Of the 129 patients with pathologic transitional cell carcinoma involving the prostate identified after cystectomy, 14 (11%) developed urethral recurrence. The 5-year probability of urethral recurrence for superficial (mucosa and ductal, without stroma) involvement was 12%, compared with 18% with stroma-invasive tumors of the prostate. Patients without any prostatic urethral involvement demonstrated only a 6% probability of urethral recurrence, significantly lower than that of those patients with prostatic involvement (Stein et al, 2005). **Collectively, these studies confirm that prostatic stromal invasion is the single strongest pathologic predictor of subsequent recurrence in the anterior urethra after cystectomy for bladder cancer.** In fact, in a multivariate analysis, any prostate tumor involvement (superficial or invasive) remained an independent and significant predictor of a urethral tumor recurrence (Stein et al, 2005).

Understanding that prostatic tumor involvement increases the risk of urethral tumor recurrence after cystectomy, it would therefore seem logical to identify these patients preoperatively. It has been suggested that deep transurethral resection biopsies of the prostate, preferably at the 5- and 7-o'clock positions at the level of the verumontanum, may help identify those with prostatic tumor involvement (Wood et al, 1989; Sakamoto et al, 1993). The ability to diagnose patients reliably with prostatic tumor involvement before cystectomy would then identify patients at high risk for urethral recurrence who may benefit from prophylactic urethrectomy. However, the reliability of preoperative transurethral prostatic biopsies has been appropriately challenged by others (Lebret et al, 1998; Donat et al, 2001). In a prospective series of 118 patients, Lebret and associates (1998) examined the utility of preoperative prostatic biopsies and compared it to intraoperative frozen-section analysis of the prostatic urethral margin at the time of cystectomy in predicting urethral recurrence. They found that intraoperative frozen-section analysis was more accurate than any preoperative parameter, including preoperative prostate biopsies, in predicting urethral recurrence. In another large series of 246 men who underwent preoperative transurethral loop biopsy of the prostate, Donat and associates (2001) reported that this preoperative pathologic evaluation did not accurately determine prostatic tumor involvement. These reports, coupled with the fact that investigators have shown a significantly lower incidence of urethral recurrence after orthotopic diversion (even with prostatic tumor involvement) if the intraoperative frozen-section specimen of the proximal urethra is without evidence of tumor, suggest that preoperative prostate biopsies may not be necessary (Freeman et al, 1996; Iselin et al, 1997; Stein et al, 2005). As a result, it has become the routine practice of the authors and others (Hautmann, 2003) to base a patient's eligibility for orthotopic diversion, at least with respect to his risk of urethral transitional cell carcinoma, on intraoperative frozen-section analysis of the distal urethral margin at the time of radical cystectomy.

Other previously described risk factors appear to be less important in predicting urethral recurrence in men. Several investigators have evaluated the presence of carcinoma in situ in the bladder as a risk factor for urethral recurrence. Tobisu and associates (1991) found anterior urethral recurrence in only 1 of 14 patients (7%) with pathologic stage carcinoma in situ. Levinson and coworkers (1990) found 1 (3%) urethral malignant neoplasm in 37 patients with carcinoma in situ or multifocal tumors of the bladder undergoing simultaneous urethrectomy and cystectomy. Hardeman and Soloway (1990) followed up 22 patients with carcinoma in situ or multifocal tumors after cystectomy (not involving the prostatic urethra), and only 1 patient (5%) developed a recurrence. Finally, Stein and associates (2005) evaluated the pathologic characteristics of the bladder specimen and found that carcinoma in situ and multifocal tumors were not individually associated with a significant risk for anterior urethral recurrence in a large group of patients. **The presence of carcinoma in situ or tumor multifocality, therefore, should not preclude orthotopic diversion if the intraoperative frozen-section analysis of**

the distal urethral margin demonstrates no evidence of malignancy.

It appears that manifestations of multifocal disease, such as carcinoma in situ and upper tract tumors, do not independently confer a significant risk for a urethral recurrence when other risk factors, such as prostatic urethral involvement and possibly even the form of urinary diversion, are controlled for (Stein et al, 2005). However, these risk factors may be more significant when they are considered collectively. Tobisu and associates (1991) showed in a multivariate analysis that the risk of urethral recurrence more than doubled each time the number of risk factors was increased by one. The conclusion that risk factors may be additive may be a useful clinical tool. These factors may provide risk assessment; however, they should not necessarily exclude patients from orthotopic diversion. Rather, they may provide a useful guide to aid in the follow-up of patients who have undergone orthotopic diversion, or they may recommend prophylactic urethrectomy after cystectomy if a cutaneous form of diversion has been performed.

In view of these data, we have advocated and continue to advocate that prostatic tumor involvement should not necessarily preclude orthotopic reconstruction as long as the tumor does not involve the apical prostatic urethral margin as determined by intraoperative frozen-section analysis at the time of surgery (Stein et al, 2005). **Furthermore, we have provided prospective data in women to support the idea that intraoperative frozen-section analysis of the distal surgical margin can be an accurate means to histologically evaluate the urethra at the time of surgery** (Stein et al, 1998a). With an experienced pathologist, the histologic findings at the time of surgery in this study were confirmed postoperatively on routine pathologic analysis. Thus, it appears that the urethra may be appropriately evaluated from a histologic perspective at the time of surgery.

Other centers have adopted a similar philosophy with comparable clinical outcomes. Iselin and associates (1997) evaluated 70 patients undergoing cystectomy for transitional cell carcinoma to determine if urethral preservation and orthotopic replacement in patients with prostatic urethral or stromal involvement placed them at risk for urethral recurrence or death from recurrence. Of the 70 patients, 14 had concomitant tumor of the prostate, including 10 with carcinoma in situ, 1 with ductal tumor involvement, and 3 with stromal tumor involvement. The overall urethral recurrence rate in the entire group of patients at 35 months of follow-up was 3%, compared with 7% for those patients with any prostate tumor involvement. Overall, of the 14 patients who had prostatic transitional cell carcinoma, only 1 (7%) developed urethral recurrence, and this recurrence did not present as the cause of death in this individual. These authors suggested that the guidelines for urethral resection may be relaxed, which would thus increase the opportunities for orthotopic reconstruction without placing patients at increased risk for death from transitional cell carcinoma (Iselin et al, 1997).

Monitoring the retained urethra for all patients after radical cystectomy for bladder cancer is intuitive and particularly important in patients undergoing an orthotopic form of urinary diversion. At a minimum, this should include annual voided cytology and full evaluation, including urethroscopy, in patients who develop symptoms related to the urethra or a change in voiding pattern or continence. A study examined the diagnosis and management of urethral transitional cell carcinoma among 47 men after radical cystectomy (Clark et al, 2004). Although this study was not specific for orthotopic diversion, the majority of patients were symptomatic on presentation for a urethral tumor recurrence. Among the 37 patients in whom urethral tumor recurrence was detected during the long-term follow-up period, cytologic screening alone diagnosed 13 of 37 patients (35%). Among the patients with cytology data available in this study, 94% had a positive cytology result. Symptomatic patients with a urethral tumor recurrence usually present with bloody urethral discharge or gross hematuria. However, 4 of the 14 patients with an orthotopic neobladder who developed a urethral recurrence presented with a change in voiding habits, which in one case was the patient's only complaint (Clark et al, 2004). **It is therefore important to consider a urethral recurrence in the differential diagnosis whenever a patient who has undergone lower urinary tract reconstruction with an orthotopic neobladder presents with any change in voiding habits.**

Urethral Recurrence in Women

Although the incidence, clinical significance, and risk factors of urethral recurrence in men with transitional cell carcinoma of the bladder are understood, little was known about urethral tumor involvement in women before the era of orthotopic diversion. Several factors contributed to this lack of information. First, women clearly have a lower incidence of transitional cell carcinoma than men do. Second, total urethrectomy was routinely performed in women undergoing radical cystectomy, and before the advent of orthotopic lower urinary tract reconstruction, an analysis of the female urethra would not necessarily have provided any additional clinical or pathologic information because its removal was routine. Third, from a cancer perspective, the urethra in women is shorter and close to the bladder and, potentially, to tumor. Therefore, proceeding with orthotopic diversion in women, without an understanding of the potential for urethral tumor involvement and a clear definition of the risk factors, may jeopardize the success of the cancer surgery, possibly resulting in an unacceptable urethral, vaginal, or pelvic recurrence rate. With an increasing interest in orthotopic diversion in women after cystectomy for bladder cancer, it is only logical that identification of the incidence and risk factors of urethral tumor involvement in women is essential.

Ashworth (1956) was one of the first investigators to specifically report on urethral tumor involvement in both male and female patients with bladder cancer. In a large cystoscopic study of 293 patients, urethral tumor involvement was found in 1.4% of female patients compared with 4.1% of male patients presenting with bladder cancer. This important study represents one of the few reports that evaluated urethral tumor involvement in an unselected group of patients presenting with bladder cancer.

Before 1990, sparse literature existed regarding the pathologic features of the urethra in cystectomy specimens in women with transitional cell carcinoma. De Paepe and associates (1990) retrospectively reported the pathologic findings of 22 cystectomy specimens removed from women with bladder cancer during a 15-year period. Of the 22 specimens,

8 (36%) demonstrated some urethral tumor involvement. The authors suggested that this finding supported the continued and routine performance of urethrectomy in conjunction with cystectomy in women. However, they did not specifically distinguish the bladder neck from the proximal urethra or comment on the fact that the majority of cystectomy specimens (64%) had no evidence of urethral involvement. In addition, this study failed to provide details about the total number of women treated for bladder cancer during this period or the number or form of any treatments before cystectomy.

Stenzl and associates (1995b) studied the risk of synchronous or secondary urethral tumors with long-term follow-up in women with bladder cancer. The charts of women treated for various stages of bladder cancer during a 19-year period were reviewed. They evaluated 356 women with a mean follow-up of 5.5 years. Overall, 7 of 356 patients (2%) had a urethral tumor at presentation; a similar incidence was reported by Ashworth (1956) in his earlier endoscopic analysis. **Statistical evaluation of specifically defined bladder tumor localizations revealed that bladder neck involvement was most significantly associated with secondary urethral tumor in these women** (Stenzl et al, 1995b). **Furthermore, no patient in this analysis had an isolated urethral tumor without concomitant bladder neck tumor involvement.** The authors suggested that the apparent lower incidence of urethral tumors in women (compared with men) may be related to the fact that transitional cell mucosa in women covers a smaller urethral segment, with the remainder being normal or metaplastic squamous cell mucosa. The area at risk in the female urethra is therefore smaller and probably diminishes with increasing age as the demarcation line between squamous and transitional cell mucosa migrates cranially during menopause (Peckhman, 1971). Thus, in the sixth and seventh decades of life, when most bladder tumors occur, metaplastic squamous cell mucosa may cover the entire urethra, the bladder neck, and even a portion of the trigone (Peckhman, 1971). Stenzl and colleagues (1995b) also reported that of the women with clinical stages T2 to T3b, N0, M0 (potential candidates for radical cystectomy with preservation of the urethra), only 1% had urethral tumor. The authors emphasized that the only consistent risk factor for urethral tumor involvement was concurrent tumor at the bladder neck. No correlation between urethral tumors and other pathologic factors was found. They concluded that the urethra can be safely preserved in selected cystectomy patients, provided neither preoperative biopsy specimens of the bladder neck nor intraoperative frozen-section specimens of the proximal urethra at the level of dissection demonstrate any tumor or atypia.

In an attempt to identify women who may be appropriate candidates for orthotopic lower urinary tract reconstruction, Stein and associates (1995) retrospectively evaluated a large series of archival cystectomy specimens from female patients undergoing cystectomy for bladder cancer. To better define the incidence of carcinoma of the bladder neck and urethra, 67 consecutive female cystectomy specimens removed for biopsy-proven transitional cell carcinoma of the bladder were pathologically evaluated. **Histologic evidence of tumor involving the urethra was found in 9 women (13%), whereas 17 patients (25%) demonstrated bladder neck tumors. All** female patients with an uninvolved bladder neck also had an uninvolved urethra (no skip lesions), whereas approximately 50% of patients with a bladder neck tumor had concomitant urethral tumor involvement. In this study, the association of bladder neck and urethral tumor involvement was most significant.

Although risk factors for bladder neck involvement in this study included increased grade, stage, and lymph node involvement, no statistically significant relationship could be identified between carcinoma in situ and bladder neck or urethral tumor involvement (Stein et al, 1995). **All female patients with urethral involvement also had concomitant bladder neck involvement regardless of the presence or absence of carcinoma in situ.** Similar to data in men, these data suggest that multifocal carcinoma in situ should not be considered a contraindication to orthotopic urinary diversion in women without evidence of bladder neck tumor.

In addition to bladder neck involvement, Stein and colleagues (1995) **also identified anterior vaginal wall tumor involvement (P4) as a major risk factor for simultaneous urethral tumor.** Although anterior vaginal wall tumor involvement is relatively rare (1%), all women in this study with tumor extending into the vaginal wall had tumor at the bladder neck; 50% of these patients also demonstrated urethral tumors. This pathologic finding was confirmed by Maralani and associates (1997), who retrospectively evaluated 43 female cystectomy specimens removed for bladder cancer. They reported a 16% incidence of urethral tumor involvement, and vaginal involvement in this study was the most significant risk factor for urethral tumor involvement. Similarly, Chen and associates (1997) retrospectively reviewed the risk of secondary urethral, vaginal, and cervical involvement by transitional cell carcinoma in women undergoing radical cystectomy. They found an overall 8% incidence of tumor of the urethra, and approximately 50% of patients with vaginal or cervical invasion also demonstrated urethral tumor involvement. They similarly confirmed previous reports that the most significant risk factor for urethral tumor involvement is tumor at the bladder neck.

From a growing body of pathologic evidence, it has became clear that tumor involving the bladder neck is an important risk factor for urethral tumor involvement in women. Although bladder neck involvement is a significant risk factor for urethral tumors, not all women with tumor involving the bladder neck have urethral tumors. This is an important issue. Approximately 50% of women with tumor at the bladder neck have a urethra free of tumor (Stein et al, 1995, 1998a). In this situation, the female patient may potentially be considered an appropriate candidate for orthotopic diversion.

Stein and associates (1998a) subsequently embarked on a prospective study to evaluate and to confirm the previously established pathologic risk factors in women undergoing cystectomy for bladder cancer to determine if these criteria safely identify appropriate female candidates for orthotopic diversion. Prospective pathologic evaluation was performed on 71 consecutive female cystectomy specimens removed for primary transitional cell carcinoma of the bladder. The histologic grade, pathologic stage, presence of carcinoma in situ, and number and location of all bladder tumors were determined. In addition, final pathologic analysis of the

bladder neck and proximal urethra was performed and compared with the intraoperative frozen-section analysis of the distal surgical margin (proximal urethra). These authors reported tumor involvement at the bladder neck and proximal urethra in 14 (19%) and 5 (7%) cystectomy specimens, respectively. **Bladder neck tumor involvement was again found to be the most significant risk factor for tumor involving the urethra, confirming the findings from retrospective series** (Stein et al, 1995). Similarly, all patients with urethral tumors also demonstrated concomitant bladder neck tumors. However, approximately 50% of patients with bladder neck tumors had a normal (tumor-free) proximal urethra. Furthermore, no patient with a normal bladder neck demonstrated tumor involvement of the urethra. These results were virtually identical to the results from the authors' previous retrospective study (Stein et al, 1995). Interestingly, when one combines these two series of female cystectomy specimens, 31 of 138 (22%) demonstrated bladder neck tumors and 14 (10%) demonstrated urethral tumors (Stein et al, 1995, 1998a), a percentage similar to that seen in men (Freeman et al, 1994; Stenzl et al, 2002). These data suggest that a significant number of women with bladder neck tumors have a normal urethra and may potentially undergo orthotopic diversion safely.

In this same prospective series, intraoperative frozen-section analysis of the distal surgical margin was performed on a total of 47 women, 45 without evidence of tumor and 2 with urethral tumor involvement (Stein et al, 1998a). In all cases, intraoperative frozen-section analysis of the proximal urethra correlated with and was correctly confirmed by final permanent section. **These data suggest that intraoperative frozen-section analysis of the distal surgical margin may provide an accurate and reliable means to evaluate the proximal urethra and should determine which female patients are appropriate candidates for orthotopic diversion** (Stein et al, 1998a).

The authors strengthened their argument and provided clinical follow-up data of the first 88 women undergoing orthotopic diversion after cystectomy for bladder cancer, 71 (80%) with transitional cell carcinoma of the bladder (Stein et al, 2002). No urethral recurrences were observed with a median follow-up of 30 months in this group. These results appear encouraging because urethral recurrence in male patients at the same institution (undergoing orthotopic diversion for primary transitional cell carcinoma) usually occurs within the first 24 months postoperatively (Clark et al, 2004; Stein et al, 2005).

Although most studies confirm that all female patients with urethral tumors also had bladder neck tumor involvement (Coloby et al, 1994; Stein et al, 1995, 1998a; Stenzl et al, 1995b), the potential for so-called skip lesions has been reported (Chen et al, 1997; Maralani et al, 1997). In a pathologic series of cystectomy specimens, Maralani and associates (1997) confirmed the low incidence of urethral involvement in women. Unlike in previous studies, however, bladder mapping in 43 female cystectomy specimens failed to demonstrate a statistically significant relationship between location of tumor (e.g., bladder neck), presence of carcinoma in situ, or tumor multifocality and the risk of a urethral tumor. Only vaginal tumor involvement was associated with the presence of tumor in the urethra. Interestingly, this group also reported a high incidence (five of seven specimens) of periurethral tumor involvement without concomitant mucosal tumor involvement. The authors suggested that preoperative cystoscopy alone would not have accurately evaluated the urethra. Rather, full-thickness urethral biopsies intraoperatively may be necessary to identify suitable female candidates for orthotopic diversion.

Chen and associates (1997) reported on 115 female cystectomy specimens, with 9 patients (8%) demonstrating urethral tumor involvement, 2 of these without bladder neck involvement. **The potential issue of a skip lesion or tumor to the urethra with a normal bladder neck, although rare, again argues for the need to perform intraoperative frozen-section analysis of the urethra before orthotopic diversion in women. As in men, in the hands of an experienced pathologist, intraoperative frozen-section analysis of the distal cystectomy margin (proximal urethra) should provide an accurate and reliable method to prospectively evaluate the proximal urethra for tumor involvement.** Furthermore, concern about the potential risk of injury to the continence mechanism with deep preoperative biopsies of the bladder neck and urethra, coupled with a reliable method to evaluate the proximal urethra intraoperatively, suggests that it is now appropriate to rely primarily on intraoperative frozen-section analysis of the proximal urethra for proper selection of women considering orthotopic substitution.

Urethral tumor recurrence after radical cystectomy and orthotopic reconstruction in women appears to be rare, but it can occur (Jones et al, 2000; Ali-El-Dein et al, 2004). In a large series of 145 women undergoing cystectomy for bladder cancer, with good follow-up (median 56 months), an isolated urethral tumor recurrence was reported in 2 women (1.4%) (Ali-El-Dein et al, 2004). Both patients in this series presented with complaints of bleeding through the urethra, and the tumor recurrence was seen by transvaginal ultrasonography. Jones and associates (2000) described one woman who developed a urethral tumor recurrence after cystectomy and orthotopic diversion for transitional cell carcinoma. This patient presented with symptoms of obstructive voiding. As in men with an orthotopic neobladder, blood per urethra or a voiding change in women with this diversion may be the presenting complaint of the patient and should stimulate a urethral evaluation.

To summarize, intraoperative frozen-section analysis of the distal surgical margin in both men (apical prostatic urethra) and women (proximal urethra) provides an accurate assessment of the urethra and may appropriately determine candidacy for orthotopic diversion. Indications for urethrectomy (contraindication to orthotopic diversion) in male and female patients include carcinoma in situ and overt carcinoma of the urethral margin detected on intraoperative frozen-section analysis. En bloc urethrectomy may be performed at the time of cystectomy in men with known (preoperative) tumor involving the urethra. In male patients who have undergone a cutaneous form of urinary diversion, a delayed urethrectomy can be performed with prostatic stromal tumor involvement demonstrated on final pathologic examination of the cystectomy specimen. Patients with prostatic stromal involvement of tumor demonstrated in the cystectomy specimen who underwent an orthotopic diversion must be closely monitored postoperatively for signs and symptoms with urethral wash cytology for recurrence purposes.

Pelvic Recurrence

Radical cystectomy remains the primary form of therapy at most institutions for high-grade, invasive bladder cancer (Stein et al, 2001a). An important issue in patients undergoing cystectomy and orthotopic diversion for bladder cancer is the potential for pelvic recurrence and the consequences that a pelvic recurrence could have on the form of urinary diversion, particularly an orthotopic form, and the ability to deliver adjuvant therapies to these patients.

Radical cystectomy with bilateral pelvic iliac lymphadenectomy provides excellent local (pelvic) control for the treatment of invasive bladder cancer. Stein and associates (2001a) reported their outcomes in 1054 patients who underwent radical cystectomy for bladder cancer with a median follow-up of more than 10 years. **In this large cystectomy series, an overall local pelvic recurrence rate of 7% was observed for the entire group of patients. The incidence of local recurrences could be further stratified by pathologic subgroups. Patients with organ-confined, lymph node–negative tumors demonstrated only a 6% local recurrence rate, compared with a 13% local recurrence rate in those with non–organ-confined, lymph node–negative tumors. Even those at highest risk for local recurrence (lymph node–positive disease) had only a 13% local recurrence rate after cystectomy. These data suggest that local recurrences after a radical cystectomy and an appropriate lymphadenectomy, even for patients demonstrating locally advanced or lymph node–positive disease, are relatively infrequent and should not necessarily preclude an orthotopic form of urinary diversion. Furthermore, there is a growing body of evidence to suggest that a significant number of patients with even locally advanced or even lymph node–positive bladder cancer after cystectomy and an extended lymph node dissection demonstrate good long-term survival** (Stein, 2004) **and may therefore benefit from the clinical advantages of an orthotopic form of diversion.** Overall, nearly 60% of patients with extravesical tumor extension and one third of patients with lymph node–positive disease are alive without evidence of disease at 10 years after cystectomy (Stein et al, 2001a).

As the application of an orthotopic bladder substitute has become a more standard procedure in patients undergoing cystectomy for invasive bladder cancer, Hautmann and Simon (1999) evaluated the impact of local recurrence on neobladder function and survival in 357 men who underwent radical cystectomy and ileal neobladder substitution at their institution. Local recurrence was reported in 43 of the 357 (12%). Of the 43 patients with a local recurrence, 36 had locally advanced disease on final pathologic evaluation (stage pT3a or higher, or node positive). A total of 17 patients (43%) had concomitant distant metastasis. Of the 43 patients, 40 (93%) maintained good neobladder function. Local recurrence interfered with the upper urinary tract in 24 cases, the neobladder in 10, and the intestinal tract in 7; only one patient required removal of the neobladder because of an intestinal fistula. **The authors concluded that most patients can anticipate normal neobladder function even in the presence of**

recurrent disease or until death. Thus, orthotopic diversion after cystectomy in patients with locally advanced bladder cancer, including macroscopically or microscopically positive lymph nodes, appears to be safe and appropriate. Similar results have been reported by others (Ward et al, 1998; Tefilli et al, 1999).

Tefilli and associates (1999) retrospectively evaluated the impact of urinary diversion on disease status, complications, and subsequent treatment in patients with pelvic tumor recurrence after 201 consecutive cases of radical cystectomy for bladder cancer. A total of 33 patients (16%) demonstrated disease recurrence in the pelvis, with or without systemic metastasis. The form of urinary diversion in patients with a pelvic tumor recurrence was an ileal conduit, continent cutaneous diversion, or orthotopic neobladder in 19, 3, and 11 patients, respectively. In 21 of 33 patients (64%), pelvic recurrence and systemic metastasis were present simultaneously. Although disease recurrence was associated with poor outcome, there was no difference in overall survival or type of therapy delivered, once disease recurrence was diagnosed, between patients with an orthotopic neobladder and those with a cutaneous (continent or incontinent) urinary diversion. The only diversion-related complication resulting from pelvic recurrence was a single case of tumor invasion into an orthotopic neobladder, requiring conversion to an ileal conduit. **The authors concluded that the type of urinary diversion did not affect a patient's risk of complications, ability to receive salvage treatment, or overall survival once a pelvic recurrence is diagnosed** (Tefilli et al, 1999).

To evaluate the impact of orthotopic diversion on the quality of the cystectomy and ensuring appropriate cancer control, Yossepowitch and associates (2003) retrospectively evaluated 214 patients who underwent radical cystectomy and orthotopic reconstruction and compared them with 269 patients similarly treated with an ileal conduit diversion. Adjusting for pathologic stage, there was no cancer-specific survival difference between the two diversion groups. Patterns of relapse in 62 of the 214 patients (29%) with an orthotopic neobladder included local recurrence in 11%, distant recurrence in 9%, and combined local and distant recurrence in 18%. Only 1 patient in this series required the neobladder to be converted to an ileal conduit secondary to a relapse at the ureteroenteric anastomosis and expanding into the pouch. The authors concluded that this cohort of patients undergoing cystectomy and neobladder reconstruction had an overall favorable prognosis that did not appear to have a high risk of local recurrence, suggesting that the quality of the preceding cystectomy was not compromised (Yossepowitch et al, 2003).

Collectively, these data support the notion that even high-risk patients with bladder cancer with locally advanced pathologic stages should not be excluded from undergoing orthotopic urinary diversion as there is long-term survival in a significant portion of these patients even with advanced disease. Local recurrence rates after a properly performed cystectomy should be low. Recurrence seldom affects the function of the neobladder and does not appear to compromise the ability to deliver adjuvant therapies. Furthermore, most patients who develop a local recurrence generally die of systemic disease without local involvement or consequence of the neobladder.

KEY POINTS: URETHRAL AND PELVIC RECURRENCE IN PATIENTS WITH BLADDER CANCER AFTER CYSTECTOMY

- The overall risk of a urethral recurrence of transitional cell carcinoma after cystectomy is approximately 10% in men.
- The two most important risk factors for a urethral tumor recurrence in men are invasive prostatic tumor involvement and the form of urinary diversion.
- The two most important risk factors in women for urethral tumor recurrence are bladder neck involvement and anterior vaginal wall involvement with tumor.
- Intraoperative frozen-section analysis of the distal surgical margin in men (apical prostatic urethra) and women (proximal urethra) provides an accurate assessment of the urethra and appropriately determines candidacy for orthotopic diversion.
- A local pelvic recurrence rate of approximately 10% is seen in patients undergoing radical cystectomy for bladder cancer and rarely interferes with the function of the neobladder.

PREVIOUS PELVIC RADIOTHERAPY

Although radical cystectomy has become the primary form of treatment for high-grade, invasive bladder cancer (Ghoneim et al, 1997; Stein et al, 2001a), radical radiotherapy has gained some popularity in the United Kingdom and some other European countries. In addition, a growing number of patients have been treated with definitive radiotherapy for prostate cancer and have developed locally recurrent disease, nonfunctional bladder ("bladder cripple"), refractory hematuria, or possible involvement of the bladder neck with or without an associated bladder tumor. Management of these patients may be difficult and controversial, but they are best treated with salvage cystectomy. Radiation-induced vasculitis, fibrosis of the ureters and bowel, and ischemic changes that delay and sometimes prevent proper tissue healing have been legitimate concerns that have dampened the enthusiasm for exenterative and reconstructive salvage procedures in patients who have received definitive radiation therapy.

Early reported experience with salvage cystectomy after definitive pelvic radiation therapy for bladder cancer was disappointing and associated with significant morbidity and mortality (Edsmyr et al, 1971). Poor outcomes led many to question the wisdom of surgery in patients after pelvic irradiation. More recent experience with salvage procedures for recurrent bladder cancer or prostate cancer has been much more favorable, with some results reportedly similar to those of nonirradiated patients. Ahlering and associates (1988) found no significant difference between irradiated and non-irradiated patients undergoing continent cutaneous urinary diversion with respect to operative time, blood loss, and transfusion requirements. In this study, prolonged hospitalizations were due to diarrhea and urine leakage; however, no correlation was found between the amount of radiation received and the formation of urine leakage (Ahlering et al, 1988). Although this series represented a preorthotopic group of patients, it suggested that a continent form of urinary diversion could be performed safely in patients after definitive radiation therapy.

Gheiler and associates (1997) evaluated their clinical outcomes in a small group of patients undergoing orthotopic substitution after cystoprostatectomy for radiorecurrent prostate cancer. Of the eight patients, five underwent an ileal conduit diversion and three underwent orthotopic reconstruction. There were no intraoperative complications or perioperative mortalities. In the orthotopic neobladder group, postoperative complications included pyelonephritis in one patient and prolonged ileus in another. All patients with an orthotopic neobladder were continent during the day; one patient required a single pad at night. **This group concluded from their small series that orthotopic urinary diversion is a valid option for well-selected patients with radiorecurrent prostate cancer who require salvage cystoprostatectomy and that it can be performed with minimal complications, resulting in good continence and quality of life** (Gheiler et al, 1997).

Bochner and associates (1998) described their experience with salvage surgery and orthotopic bladder substitution after failed radical radiation therapy. A total of 18 patients who had failed definitive radiation therapy (total minimum dose, 60 Gy or greater) for bladder or prostate cancer and had undergone a salvage procedure with construction of an orthotopic neobladder were evaluated. Operative characteristics, postoperative outcomes, and complications (related or unrelated to the urinary diversion) were found to be similar in irradiated and nonirradiated patients. Good day and nighttime continence after surgery was reported by 67% and 56% of irradiated patients, respectively. Patients with poor postoperative continence (22%) were successfully treated with the placement of an artificial urinary sphincter. **These authors concluded that salvage surgery and orthotopic urinary reconstruction appear to be safe, effective procedures that provide a functional lower urinary tract in patients in whom definitive pelvic radiation therapy has failed** (Bochner et al, 1998).

Schuster and colleagues (2003) described 29 men who received some form of definitive therapy for prostate cancer before cystectomy for bladder cancer; 17 of these patients were treated with previous pelvic radiotherapy. An orthotopic neobladder was constructed in two of these patients without complications. Similarly, Gschwend and associates (1996) determined the risk of postoperative complications in patients receiving high-dose pelvic irradiation before radical cystectomy and orthotopic urinary diversion. Eleven patients were evaluated after salvage cystectomy and orthotopic substitution. The postoperative course in the irradiated group (including duration of hospital stay, perioperative complications, and early functional results) did not differ from that of a control group of nonirradiated patients. These authors concluded that high-dose pelvic irradiation should not be a primary contraindication for orthotopic urinary diversion with segments of small intestine (Gschwend et al, 1996).

It is becoming clear that in carefully selected patients, orthotopic lower urinary tract reconstruction can be performed after definitive, full-dose pelvic irradiation. Even selected women with a history of pelvic irradiation may be appropriate candidates for orthotopic reconstruction with good clinical outcomes (Stein et al, 2002; Lee et al, 2004). However, these are challenging procedures that clearly require technical expertise and keen intraoperative judgment. Astute intraoperative tissue assessment and determination of the condition of the urethra, ureters, and bowel must be done to limit complications and to provide the best possible clinical outcomes. Furthermore, all patients should be informed that incontinence rates after salvage cystectomy and orthotopic diversion are significant and may require artificial urinary sphincter placement in nearly 25% of subjects. If these criteria can be maintained, orthotopic reconstruction may be a viable option in patients previously receiving definitive radiation therapy.

KEY POINTS: PREVIOUS PELVIC RADIOTHERAPY

- Orthotopic lower urinary tract reconstruction can be performed after definitive, full-dose pelvic irradiation in carefully selected male and female patients.

- Incontinence rates after salvage cystectomy and orthotopic reconstruction are higher and may require an artificial urinary sphincter in men or a sling procedure in women.

ORTHOTOPIC DIVERSION AND THE NEED TO PREVENT REFLUX

Controversy exists regarding the need to incorporate an antireflux mechanism in patients undergoing an orthotopic form of urinary diversion. With the increasing popularity and application of the low-pressure orthotopic reservoir, the issue of reflux prevention has regained attention. First, it must be emphasized that only after well-designed, prospective, randomized studies with appropriate numbers of patients and long-term follow-up can a convincing determination be made. Although our institution has embarked on a randomized study comparing the orthotopic T pouch (nonrefluxing) and the isoperistaltic afferent Studor pouch (refluxing) after radical cystectomy, it will be several years before the results will be analyzed. Therefore, as with any debated medical topic, a critical review of the literature, with balanced discussion, should be performed to provide a better understanding of the issues regarding the controversy.

Those against reflux prevention suggest that an antireflux mechanism in an orthotopic bladder substitute is unnecessary on the basis of several critical issues. First, as a result of bowel detubularization and reconfiguration, the neobladder should accommodate a large volume of urine at low intrareservoir pressures. Second is the presumption that the urinary constituents in the orthotopic system are sterile. Granted, reflux prevention is important and not considered

a topic of significant debate in those individuals with a ureterosigmoidostomy, conduit, or continent cutaneous diversion where there is generally colonized bacteriuria. Third is the argument that complete emptying of the neobladder is routinely performed with a Valsalva maneuver (increased abdominal pressure) and simultaneous relaxation of the external sphincter. In this situation, intra-abdominal pressure theoretically affects the neobladder, ureters, and renal pelvis. This concomitantly directed pressure prevents urinary reflux and is thought to protect the upper urinary tract. Fourth, the incorporation of an antirefluxing system is technically more challenging compared with the more simple refluxing systems, which are, in general, less surgically demanding and potentially less time-consuming intraoperatively. Fifth, an antireflux mechanism may be associated with higher complications, particularly obstruction. If so, the complications associated with an antireflux system may thus outweigh the potential benefits of preventing reflux. Sixth, the harmful effects of the urinary constituents (secondary to reflux) have been demonstrated only in animal models. Last, good results have been observed with intermediate follow-up with the isoperistaltic long afferent segment of an ileal neobladder, known as the Studer pouch (Studer et al, 1996b; Thoeny et al, 2002).

The isoperistaltic afferent tubular ileal segment popularized by Studer was based on experimental and clinical observations reported by several innovative investigators (Mann, 1931; Hinman and Oppenheimer, 1958; Sarramon et al, 1971). Proponents of the Studer limb have suggested that reflux prevention in patients undergoing orthotopic low-pressure bladder substitutes with sterile urine is not a major concern. It has also been suggested that the complications of late stenosis from various antireflux techniques outweigh their theoretical advantage of protecting the upper urinary tract. On the basis of a so-called controlled study, Studer and colleagues (1996b) reported that the isoperistaltic, long afferent limb provides better functional results compared with those of an intussuscepted valve. To provide this so-called functional antireflux mechanism with the isoperistaltic afferent limb, the segment should be at least 20 cm long (Sarramon et al, 1971). Therefore, to make the Studer pouch, at least 60 cm of ileum is required, and any compromise in the length of the afferent limb may ultimately place the upper urinary tract at risk. The long-term results with upper tract preservation by this form of orthotopic reconstruction have been positive (Thoeny et al, 2002).

On the contrary, proponents of preventing urinary reflux in an orthotopic system argue that conventional wisdom suggests that preventing urinary reflux is important in protecting the upper urinary tracts in all patients undergoing continent urinary diversion with a reasonable life expectancy. If this were not an important issue, why is it that normal human bladder anatomy has evolved with an effective antireflux mechanism? Should this same argument be applied to those with an orthotopic neobladder? Others also argue that there is significant, indirect, clinical and experimental evidence to support an antireflux mechanism in all forms of lower urinary tract reconstruction. Last, newer and improved antireflux mechanisms have been developed and with good intermediate follow-up are effective in prevent-

ing reflux and protecting the upper tracts; they reportedly have fewer complications and can be incorporated into the orthotopic system (Abol-Enein and Ghoneim, 1994, 2001; Stein et al, 1998b, 2004; Hammouda, 2004).

The importance of preventing the reflux of urinary constituents was seen early in the evolution of urinary diversion. Problems with urinary reflux first became evident in patients undergoing ureterosigmoidostomy (Clarke and Leadbetter, 1955; Wear and Barquin, 1973) and, subsequently, ileal conduit urinary diversion (Middleton and Hendren, 1976; Shapiro and Johnston, 1977). It became apparent that it is important to observe all patients undergoing urinary diversion for a long period. **Upper tract urinary deterioration may not become clinically apparent until as many as 10 to 20 years after urinary diversion. In addition, deterioration of renal function may occur even in the face of normal radiographic studies.** Richie and Skinner (1975) demonstrated in canine experiments that reflux of infected urine could lead to renal impairment and suggested that antireflux techniques be incorporated (Richie et al, 1974).

The application of an antireflux mechanism was also initially supported clinically in patients undergoing colon conduits. However, as in those undergoing an ileal conduit, with longer follow-up, renal deterioration also became a problem in these patients (Morales and Golimbu, 1975; Althausen et al, 1978). **The development of renal insufficiency was thought to be related to a combination of high pressures, obstruction, and chronically infected urine.** In addition, Elder and associates (1979) reported significant renal deterioration radiographically in refluxing renal units compared with those with an antirefluxing anastomosis. In another study, Kristjansson and associates (1995) evaluated renal scarring and bacteriuria in the upper urinary tract of patients undergoing conduit diversion. They found that severe renal scarring and bacteriuria (surrogate markers for renal deterioration) in the upper tract were more common on the side of a refluxing ureteral-intestinal anastomosis.

Experimental evidence to support an antirefluxing system in orthotopic reconstruction has been reported from collaborative efforts by Kristjansson and associates (1996). In a canine experimental model, subtotal cystectomy followed by "cup" ileocystoplasty was performed in 13 dogs, followed by various ureteral reimplantation methods (refluxing, nonrefluxing, and control). This study confirmed that refluxing forms of ureteral reimplantation were associated with bacteriuria in the upper tracts, along with evidence of pyelonephritis. Although these provoking findings in dogs cannot be directly applied to humans, indirect evidence suggests that an antireflux system may be important to protect the upper urinary tract and to prevent renal deterioration over time.

The inclusion of an antireflux mechanism in the chronically infected continent cutaneous reservoir (requiring intermittent catheterization) is important and is not a source of considerable debate. Persistent asymptomatic bacteriuria in those undergoing orthotopic diversion also occurs. Steven and Poulsen (2000) reported 34% 3-year and 24% 5-year prevalence of bacteriuria in 166 men undergoing orthotopic reconstruction. Furthermore, patients may unexpectedly require some form of intermittent catheterization to completely empty the neobladder; this cannot be predicted preoperatively. Patients requiring catheterization will clearly be exposed to colonized bacteriuria. Furthermore, the need for patients to perform intermittent catheterization to completely empty the neobladder appears to increase over time. It has been reported that as many as 40% of women (Stein et al, 1997, 2004) and 44% of men (Steven and Poulsen, 2000) undergoing orthotopic diversion ultimately require some form of intermittent catheterization. **These data suggest that a significant number of patients with an orthotopic bladder substitute will have chronically infected urinary constituents.**

A study by Wood and associates (2003) evaluated 66 patients undergoing an orthotopic neobladder (all with a refluxing ureteral anastomosis) and reported the incidence and significance of urine cultures in this group. Overall, 17% of patients in this study required chronic intermittent catheterization to empty the neobladder. A total of 67% of patients had positive urinalyses, and 39% of individuals had a documented urinary tract infection. They reported an estimated 5-year probability of urinary tract infection and urosepsis for those who void without the need for catheterization of 58% and 18%, respectively (Wood et al, 2003). These data clearly underscore the significant incidence of bacteriuria in patients with an orthotopic substitute, the potential for a urinary tract infection and urosepsis, and a group who may benefit from reflux prevention.

It is generally accepted that intrareservoir pressures with most orthotopic neobladders are low during the storage phase (Kock et al, 1989; Stein et al, 1994b; Studer et al, 1996b; El Bahnasawy et al, 2000; Steven and Poulsen, 2000; Steers, 2000). This, however, may not be true during the evacuation phase. In one study, Gotoh and associates (1995) investigated the urodynamic parameters and pouch-urethral function involved in the storage and evacuation of urine in 18 patients undergoing an orthotopic ileal substitute. They provided urodynamic evidence that voiding is accomplished by increasing intra-abdominal pressure. This Valsalva maneuver, however, significantly increased intrareservoir pressures, with 44% of patients demonstrating considerably higher pressures (80 to 150 cm H_2O) during voiding. Based on Studer's argument to prevent reflux in those patients with an isoperistaltic afferent limb, the intra-abdominal pressure on the ureter and the renal pelvis must be similar to that on the reservoir. Force, however, is a function of pressure applied to the surface area (force = pressure × surface area). Because the force on the neobladder is larger (a result of a larger surface area) than that on either the ureter or the renal pelvis, it is likely that reflux exists during these higher voiding pressure phases and underscores the need for at least 20 cm of interposed intestine to provide any protective effect to the upper tracts.

Because bacteriuria is a frequent finding in patients with orthotopic substitutes and because there is potential for high intrareservoir voiding pressures, several groups continue to support the incorporation of an antireflux mechanism (Abol-Enein and Ghoneim, 1995; Elmajian et al, 1996; Steven and Poulsen, 2000; Stein et al, 2004). Proponents against antireflux techniques argue that the complications associated with them outweigh their potential benefit and that the antirefluxing systems are technically more demanding (Studer et al, 1996b; Pantuck et al, 2000). Complications of non-neoplastic obstruction with the antireflux Camey–Le Duc ureteral implantation technique have been reported to

occur in 7% to 29% (Le Duc et al, 1987; Shaaban et al, 1992; Pitts, 1994; Roth et al, 1997).

Significant complications associated with the antireflux intussuscepted nipple valve have also been reported (Mansson et al, 1986; Stein et al, 1994a, 1996; Studer et al, 1996b). Stein and associates (1996) reported on their extensive experience and on the complications associated with the afferent intussuscepted nipple valve in the Kock ileal reservoir. **An overall complication rate of 10% was observed with the intussuscepted antireflux nipple in more than 800 patients undergoing either a continent cutaneous or an orthotopic Kock ileal reservoir procedure with long-term follow-up (median, 6 years). The three most common complications related to the intussuscepted afferent nipple were the formation of calculi (usually on exposed staples securing the afferent nipple valve) in 5%, afferent nipple stenosis (thought to be caused by ischemic changes resulting from the mesenteric stripping required to maintain the intussuscepted limb) in 4%, and extussusception (prolapse of the afferent limb) in 1%.** Although the majority of these afferent nipple valve complications (60%) can easily be managed with endoscopic techniques, they nonetheless result in some morbidity. In fact, approximately 3% of all patients undergoing a continent Kock ileal reservoir require open surgical revision to repair an afferent nipple complication (Stein et al, 1996).

The need to improve on the intussuscepted nipple valve became obvious. Novel antireflux techniques associated with a low incidence of obstruction and complications that could easily be performed were required. This necessity led to the development and modification of the so-called serous-lined tunnel. This antireflux technique was developed in an animal model by Abol-Enein and colleagues (Abol-Enein and Ghoneim, 1993; Abol-Enein et al, 1993). They reported their first clinical experience in 1994, with excellent results (Abol-Enein and Ghoneim, 1994). **The premise of this technique is based on the construction of a serous-lined trough by adjacent bowel segments that lie side by side. If a tubular structure (ureter, appendix, or intestine) is laid in this trough, the incised intestinal mucosa on either side can be sutured together (covering the tubular structure) and can transform the trough into a serous-lined tunnel—an effective flap-valve technique. Abol-Enein and Ghoneim (2001) subsequently reported their intermediate experience (mean follow-up of 38 months) in 450 patients with this serous-lined extramural technique in an orthotopic neobladder. In this large series, 96% of upper tracts remained unchanged or improved; reflux was observed in only 3% of patients. They did report that an anastomotic ureteral stricture occurred in 3.8% of patients, an incidence similar to that of most refluxing ureteroileal anastomoses** (Pantuck, 2000).

The serous-lined, extramural technique has several distinct advantages compared with other antireflux techniques. A total of 40 cm of ileum is required for the entire reservoir, significantly less bowel than for other methods. This length reduction should help decrease metabolic complications associated with malabsorption or reabsorption. Metallic staples are not required, which should lower complications from the interaction of exposed foreign material and urinary constituents. The ureters can be anastomosed by spatulated, tension-free, mucosa-to-mucosa technique with a low incidence of stricture formation. Furthermore, endoscopic evaluation and manipulation of the ureteroenteric anastomosis is technically easy, and open revision surgery, if necessary, is also feasible. Last, this is a simple technique that is not significantly challenging or time-consuming and can be learned by others.

On the basis of early reports employing the ureteral serous-lined tunnel (Abol-Enein and Ghoneim, 1994, 1995), and with an understanding of the limitations of the intussuscepted antireflux nipple, **Stein and colleagues (1998b) subsequently developed and described a modification of this technique, which has been coined the T mechanism. The flap-valve T mechanism is a versatile technique that can easily be applied as an antireflux mechanism and as a continent cutaneous mechanism. The T mechanism was first successfully incorporated into an afferent antireflux limb of an orthotopic reservoir (T pouch). Advantages of this technique include application even with grossly dilated ureters and in the presence of concomitant disease of the distal ureters that may result in shortened ureteral length. No metallic staples are required, which should reduce the issue of stones as was seen in the Kock ileal reservoir.** In this technique, a separate segment of ileum is tapered and embedded to the serous-lined trough, with the ureters anastomosed to the proximal end of the ileal segment. With intermediate follow-up, this flap-valve T mechanism has eliminated the complications associated with the intussuscepted nipple valve while maintaining an effective antireflux technique (Stein et al, 1998b, 2004). Furthermore, this T mechanism has been successfully applied in a rectal reservoir for antireflux prevention (Stein et al, 1999), as well as in the pediatric (Kurzrock et al, 2003) and adult populations (Stein and Skinner, 2001) for an efferent continent mechanism in a cutaneous catheterizable urinary reservoir, and as a continent ileostomy in patients requiring a total colectomy (Kaiser et al, 2002).

As the overall therapy (medical and surgical) for pelvic malignant neoplasms improves and patients live longer after exenteration and urinary diversion (placing them at further long-term risk for renal deterioration), reflux prevention may become a more important issue even with orthotopic reconstruction. As previously mentioned, several groups have subsequently developed novel antireflux mechanisms intended to improve on existing techniques, eliminating or reducing the complications associated with previous antireflux mechanisms. Longer follow-up is obviously required to accurately evaluate the isoperistaltic Studer limb as well as these more recent antireflux techniques to determine if reflux prevention in patients undergoing orthotopic diversion is truly necessary.

TECHNIQUES OF ORTHOTOPIC BLADDER SUBSTITUTES

Many forms of orthotopic bladder substitutes have been described with use of various portions of bowel. To provide some meaningful comparisons, only published bladder substitutes with significant numbers and adequate follow-up length are presented here. **Differences in populations of patients, selection, techniques, follow-up, and definitions may contribute to some differences in outcome data.** These differences must be kept in mind in evaluating the various forms of orthotopic diversion.

KEY POINTS: ORTHOTOPIC DIVERSION AND THE NEED TO PREVENT REFLUX

- Controversy exists regarding the need to incorporate an antireflux mechanism in patients undergoing an orthotopic form of urinary diversion.

- The inclusion of an antireflux mechanism in the chronically infected continent cutaneous reservoir, requiring intermittent catheterization, is important and is not a source of significant debate.

- Renal deterioration may not become clinically apparent until as many as 10 to 20 years after urinary diversion.

- The development of renal deterioration after urinary diversion is thought to be multifactorial and related to the combination of obstruction and reflux of infected urinary constituents in the upper tracts.

The appropriate use of catheters, stents, and drains is important in all patients undergoing urinary diversion. Judicious use of these surgical tools helps reduce perioperative morbidity. In our experience, a 24 French Simplastic hematuria catheter has been an ideal urethral catheter. This catheter allows excellent irrigation of mucus and blood clots and eliminates the need for a cystostomy tube. Ureteral stents should extend from the ipsilateral renal pelvis across the ureteroenteric anastomosis and may be either externalized to the skin or internalized and anchored to the urethral catheter (our preference). Externalized ureteral stents can be removed 1 to 2 weeks postoperatively. However, stents that are anchored to the urethral catheter are generally removed 3 weeks postoperatively when the urethral catheter is removed. All patients should have a pelvic drain postoperatively. We advocate a 1-inch Penrose drain placed posterior to the bladder substitute and brought out a separate stab wound lateral to the midline incision. This Penrose drain prevents the accumulation of urine and serous fluid and is generally removed after the urethral catheter is removed at 3 weeks postoperatively. A large suction Hemovac drain is placed for the first 24 hours, allowing the evacuation of blood during the acute postoperative period. Last, some authors advocate the placement of a tube gastrostomy that provides a simple means to drain the stomach and obviates the need for an uncomfortable nasogastric tube while the postoperative ileus resolves (Buscarini et al, 2000).

Although no strict guidelines are available regarding optimal timing of reservoir catheter removal, it has been our practice for patients undergoing orthotopic and continent cutaneous forms of diversion to wait until 3 weeks postoperatively. When patients return at the 3-week postoperative mark, if there is minimal drainage from the Penrose drain (less than 100 mL during 24 hours), the catheter is removed, followed by the drain. **Routine pouchograms or radiographic studies of the neobladder are not routinely performed** as suggested by Ankem and associates (2004) unless a significant output from the drain is observed. In this situation, conservative management (advancing the Penrose drain and ensuring adequate reservoir drainage) is generally all that is necessary for the reservoir to heal with time. In rare instances of persistent urinary drainage, proximal diversion of the urinary system with bilateral nephrostomy tubes will help resolve this problem. Open surgical intervention for a persistent urinary leak is indicated only when a foreign body is present or if there is an undrained fluid collection that cannot be managed with computed tomography–directed placement of a drain. Obviously, these are general guidelines on the management of the reservoir drains, and each case must be considered individually to optimize clinical outcomes.

A number of different procedures for orthotopic reconstruction incorporating different segments of bowel have been described. There are clearly some physiologic indications to use various segments of intestine, but the surgeon's preference may be even more influential. It has been suggested that excellent functional and clinical outcomes with voiding can be seen in an orthotopic neobladder when different segments of bowel are employed, as long as the principles of preservation of the periurethral sphincter muscle and construction of an adequate capacity and low-pressure reservoir are maintained (Parekh et al, 2000; Lee et al, 2003). Preservation of the continence mechanism along with these general principles of bowel detubularization and folding must be maintained to achieve good outcomes.

Camey II

The Camey II orthotopic substitute (Camey, 1990) is a modification of the original Camey bladder substitute (Camey I) (Lilien and Camey, 1984). **The modification of the Camey I involves detubularization and folding to eliminate peristaltic activity.** The Camey II has subsequently been modified to provide better functional results (Barre et al, 1996).

A total of 65 cm of ileum is isolated, with an area of the ileum identified to reach to the region of the urethra in a tension-free manner. After the integrity of the bowel is restored, the mesenteric trap is closed, and the isolated portion of ileum is opened along the antimesenteric border for the entire length, except the area previously identified for the urethral anastomosis. In this region, the ileal incision is directed toward the mesenteric border. The ileum is then placed in a transverse U orientation. The medial borders of the U are sutured together with a running absorbable suture. A fingertip opening is made in the preselected area for the ileourethral anastomosis, the entire ileal plate is brought down to the pelvis, and the urethroenteric anastomosis is performed. The ureteroileal anastomosis is then performed by a Le Duc technique (Le Duc et al, 1987). The reservoir is completed by folding the ileal plate and suturing with a running absorbable suture. The ends of the U are anchored to the pelvic floor to reduce tension.

A modification of the Camey II has been described by Barre and colleagues (1996). This places the ileum in a Z configuration and reportedly has the advantages of shorter length requirements, improved reservoir capacity, and improved functional (continence) results (Fig. 82–2).

Vesical Ileal Pouch

A group from Padua, Italy, described an orthotopic ileal substitute called the *vesica ileale Padovana* (VIP) pouch (Pagano et al, 1990). **This technique is a modification of the Camey II that provides for a more spherical reservoir.** Approximately 60 cm of ileum is used, and the ileourethral anastomosis and ureteral implantations are performed in a similar fashion. In the VIP pouch, the spatulated bowel is closed in a jellyroll fashion to produce a posterior plate that is then closed anteriorly.

S Bladder

Schreiter and Noll described the ileal S bladder in 1989. A 75-cm segment of ileum is isolated, arranged in the shape of an S, and opened on the antimesenteric border while the distal

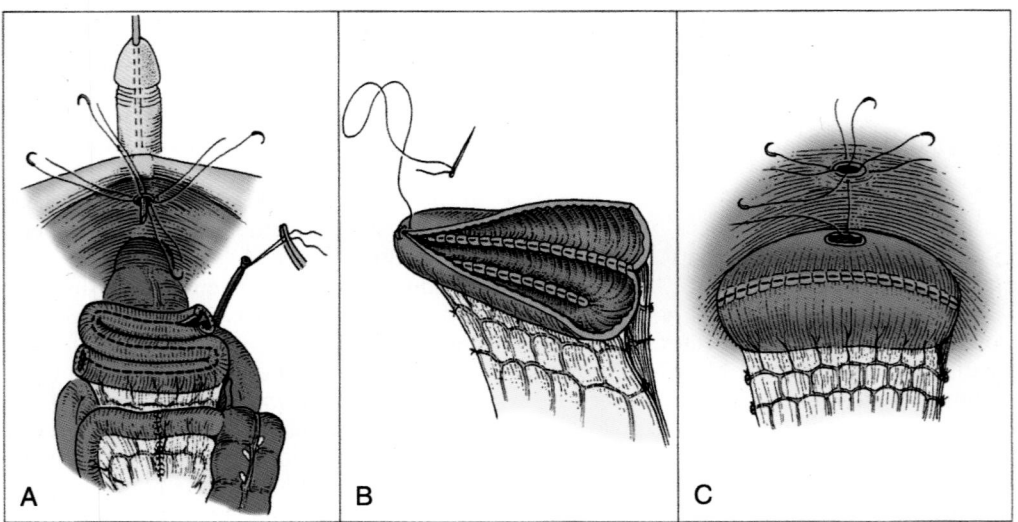

Figure 82–2. Construction of the modified Camey II. **A,** The ileal loop is folded three times (Z shaped) and incised on the antimesenteric border. **B,** The reservoir is closed with a running suture to approximate the incised ileum. **C,** The urethroenteric anastomosis is performed.

5 cm and proximal 15 cm are kept intact. The corresponding antimesenteric borders are sutured together to form an intestinal plate. The proximal 15 cm is transformed into an afferent antireflux Kock nipple as described by Skinner and colleagues (1984). The ureters are spatulated and anastomosed to the proximal portion of the antireflux nipple. The distal ileum is tapered down to the size of the urethra. The bowel plate is then folded and closed along its longitudinal axis, and opposing margins are sutured together. After this, the ileourethral anastomosis is performed. A modification of the S-shaped ileal neobladder has been reported (Deliveliotis et al, 2001).

Ileal Neobladder (Hautmann)

The ileal neobladder was developed at the University of Ulm, Germany, by Hautmann and colleagues (1988). **This neobladder is an intentionally large-capacity, spherical (W configuration) ileal reservoir that is constructed in an attempt to reduce nighttime incontinence** (Fig. 82–3).

A segment of terminal ileum of approximately 70 cm is selected. The bowel is reconstituted, and the mesenteric trap

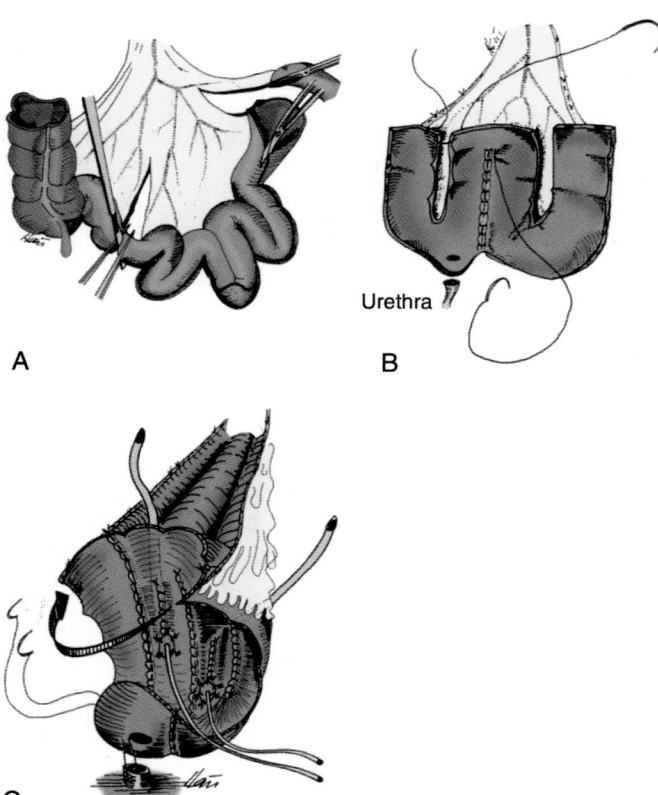

Figure 82–3. Construction of the Hautmann ileal neobladder. **A,** A 70-cm portion of terminal ileum is selected. Note that the isolated segment of ileum is incised on the antimesenteric border. **B,** The ileum is arranged into an M or W configuration with the four limbs sutured to one another. **C,** After a buttonhole of ileum is removed on an antimesenteric portion of the ileum, the urethroenteric anastomosis is performed. The ureteral implants (Le Duc) are performed and stented, and the reservoir is then closed in a side-to-side manner.

is closed. The ileal section that reaches the urethra most easily is identified and marked with a traction suture along the antimesenteric border. The isolated bowel segment is then arranged in either an M or W shape and is incised. The entire segment is opened along the antimesenteric border except for a 5-cm section along the traction suture, where the incision is directed toward the anterior mesenteric border to make a U-shaped flap. This facilitates the anastomosis of the neobladder to the urethra.

The four limbs of the M or W are then sutured to one another with a running absorbable suture. In the center of the previously developed flap, a segment of the ileal wall (approximately the diameter of the small finger) is excised. The ileourethral anastomosis is then performed with the sutures tied from "inside" the neobladder. Once the ileal neobladder is situated in the pelvis and the urethral sutures are tied, the ureters are implanted from inside the neobladder through a small incision in the ileum at a convenient site, similar to that described by Le Duc and coworkers (1987). The remaining portion of the anterior wall is then closed with a running absorbable suture.

Since the original description of this reservoir, Hautmann believed that ureteral obstruction from anastomotic strictures represented a greater potential of short-term and long-term morbidity than reflux. **Subsequently, beginning in 1996, the author modified this technique and now employs a freely refluxing, open end-to-side anastomosis.** This has resulted in a significantly lower incidence of stenosis seen in only 1% of the refluxing ureters compared with a 9.5% stenosis rate of the Le Duc procedure that was initially performed (Hautmann, 2001).

Others have reported a modified Hautmann ileal neobladder using only 40 cm of ileum to reduce the potential issues of metabolic dysfunction, with acceptable clinical outcomes (Sevin et al, 2004).

Studer Ileal Bladder Substitute

The ileal bladder substitute with a long, afferent, isoperistaltic, tubular ileal segment, described by Studer and colleagues (1989), has become a popular orthotopic form of diversion (Fig. 82–4).

A portion of terminal ileum 54 to 60 cm long is isolated approximately 25 cm proximal to the ileocecal valve. Bowel continuity is restored, and the ends of the isolated segment are closed with a running absorbable suture. The distal 40-cm segment of ileum is placed in a U shape and opened along the antimesenteric border. The ureters are split and anastomosed in an end-to-side fashion to the proximal (nonincised) afferent tubular portion of ileum. The two medial borders of the U-shaped ileum are then oversewn with a running absorbable suture. The bottom of the U is folded over between the two ends of the U. After the lower half of the anterior wall and part of the upper half are closed, a finger is introduced through the remaining reservoir opening to determine the most caudal part of the neobladder. A hole is cut out in this dependent portion of ileum, away from the suture line, which allows urethral anastomosis. The urethroenteric anastomosis is performed, and the remaining portion of the reservoir is then closed.

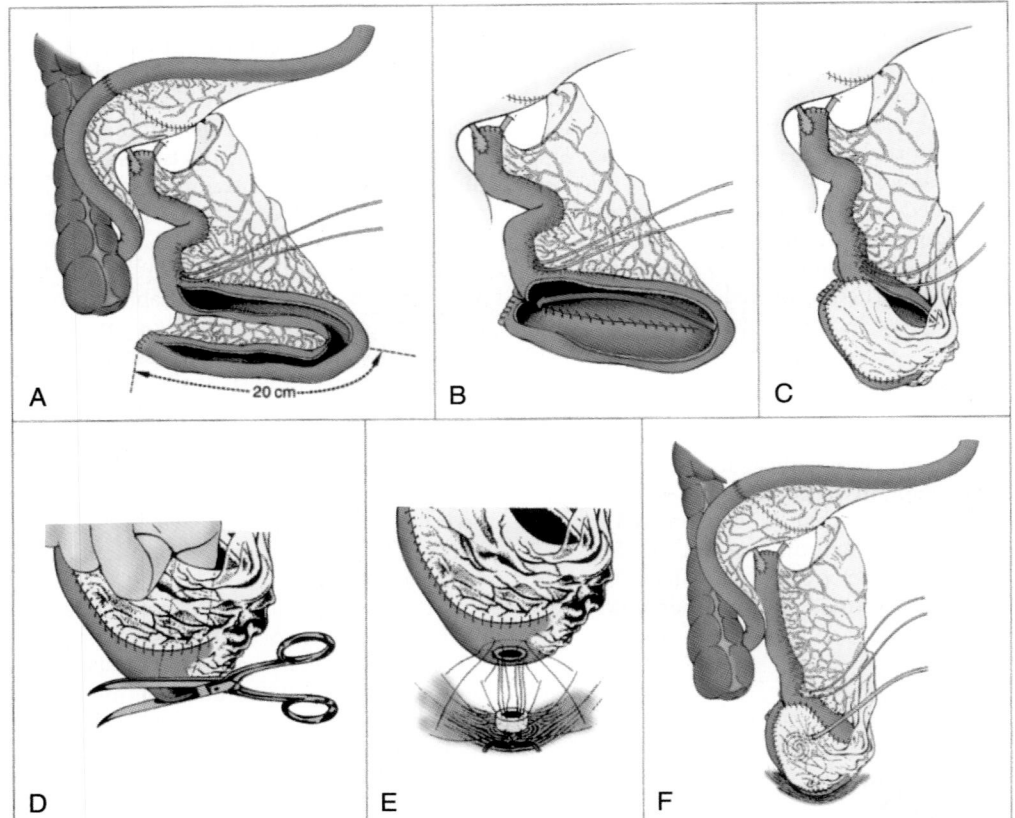

Figure 82–4. Construction of the ileal neobladder (Studer pouch) with an isoperistaltic afferent ileal limb. **A,** A 60- to 65-cm distal ileal segment is isolated (approximately 25 cm proximal to the ileocecal valve) and folded into a U configuration. Note that the distal 40 cm of ileum constitutes the U shape and is opened on the antimesenteric border; the more proximal 20 to 25 cm of ileum remains intact (afferent limb). **B,** The posterior plate of the reservoir is formed by joining the medial borders of the limbs with a continuous running suture. The ureteroileal anastomoses are performed in a standard end-to-side technique to the proximal portion (afferent limb) of the ileum. Ureteral stents are used and brought out anteriorly through separate stab wounds. **C,** The reservoir is folded and oversewn (anterior wall). **D,** Before complete closure, a buttonhole opening is made in the most dependent (caudal) portion of the reservoir. **E,** The urethroenteric anastomosis is performed. **F,** A cystostomy tube is placed, and the reservoir is closed completely.

Orthotopic Kock Ileal Reservoir

The Kock ileal reservoir was first employed as a continent cutaneous ileal reservoir incorporating intussuscepted nipple valves for both the afferent (antireflux) and efferent (continence) limbs (Kock et al, 1982; Skinner et al, 1984) (Fig. 82–5). This subsequently evolved into an orthotopic form of diversion in which the afferent intussuscepted limb was maintained to prevent urinary reflux (Ghoneim et al, 1987; Skinner et al, 1991).

Despite the excellent functional results seen in these patients, complications associated with the afferent intussuscepted antireflux nipple remain problematic in a minority of patients (Stein et al, 1996; Stein and Skinner, 2005). The primary late complications include stone formation on exposed staples (5%), stenosis of the afferent nipple ostium thought to be secondary to a compromised blood supply (4%), and extussusception or prolapse of the afferent limb (1%). With a belief that prevention of urinary reflux is important in patients undergoing orthotopic urinary diversion, several groups have been persistent in developing antireflux mechanisms that reduce or eliminate the late complications observed with the intussuscepted nipple (Stein et al, 1998b;

Abol-Enein and Ghoneim, 1999). These novel techniques are based on the concept of developing a serous-lined extramural tunnel that forms an effective flap-valve and antireflux mechanism. **The technical difficulty of the intussuscepted nipple valve and the associated complications, along with newer and effective antireflux techniques, have made the afferent intussuscepted nipple valve more of historic interest only and well described elsewhere** (Stein and Skinner, 2005).

Serous-Lined Extramural Tunnel

On the basis of experimental studies, Abol-Enein and Ghoneim (1993) demonstrated that an effective reflux mechanism could be made by bringing the ureters into a reservoir through extramural serous-lined tunnels (Fig. 82–6). The authors believed that the construction of an extramural serous-lined tunnel provides several advantages. **Metallic staples or synthetic materials are not required. The serous-lined tunnel protects the implanted portion of the ureter from exposure to urine so that sound healing without scarring is ensured. Moreover, an extralong segment of bowel is not required, and the procedure is versatile and not**

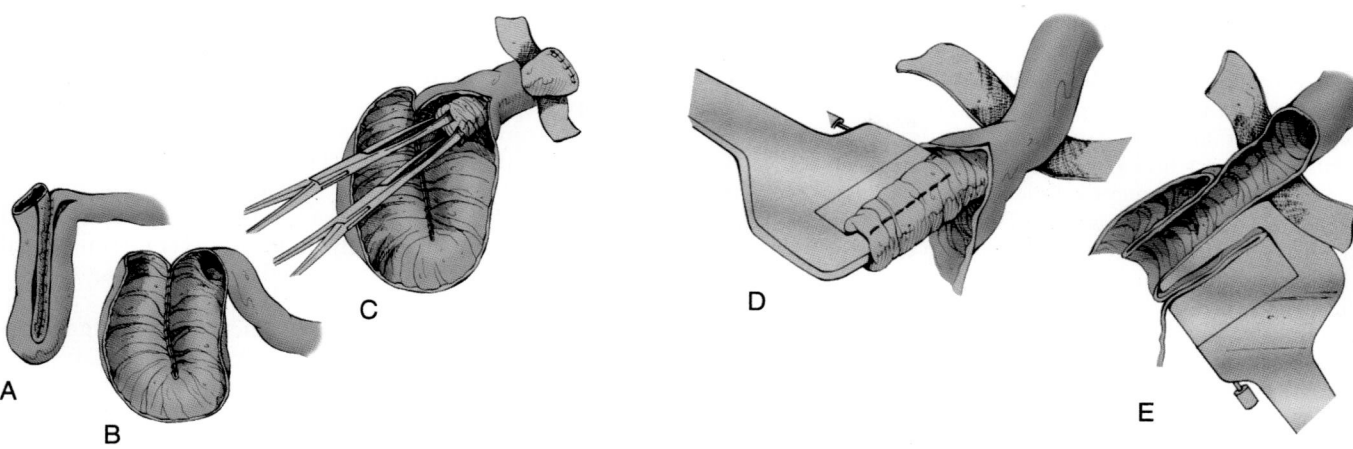

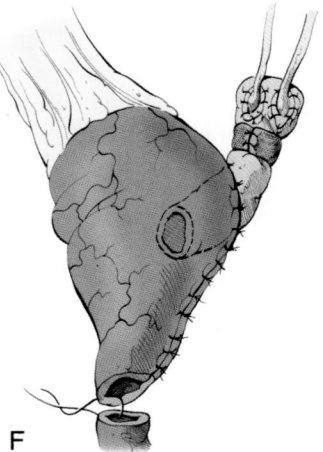

Figure 82–5. Construction of the Kock ileal reservoir. **A,** A total of 61 cm of terminal ileum is isolated. Two 22-cm segments are placed in a U configuration and opened adjacent to the mesentery. Note that the more proximal 17-cm segment of ileum will be used to make the afferent intussuscepted nipple valve. **B,** The posterior wall of the reservoir is then formed by joining the medial portions of the U with a continuous running suture. **C,** A 5- to 7-cm antireflux valve is made by intussusception of the afferent limb with the use of Allis forceps clamps. **D,** The afferent limb is fixed with two rows of staples placed within the leaves of the valve. **E,** The valve is fixed to the back wall from outside the reservoir. **F,** After completion of the afferent limb, the reservoir is completed by folding the ileum on itself and closing it (anterior wall). Note that the most dependent portion of the reservoir becomes the neourethra. The ureteroileal anastomosis is performed first, and the urethroenteric anastomosis is completed in a tension-free, mucosa-to-mucosa fashion.

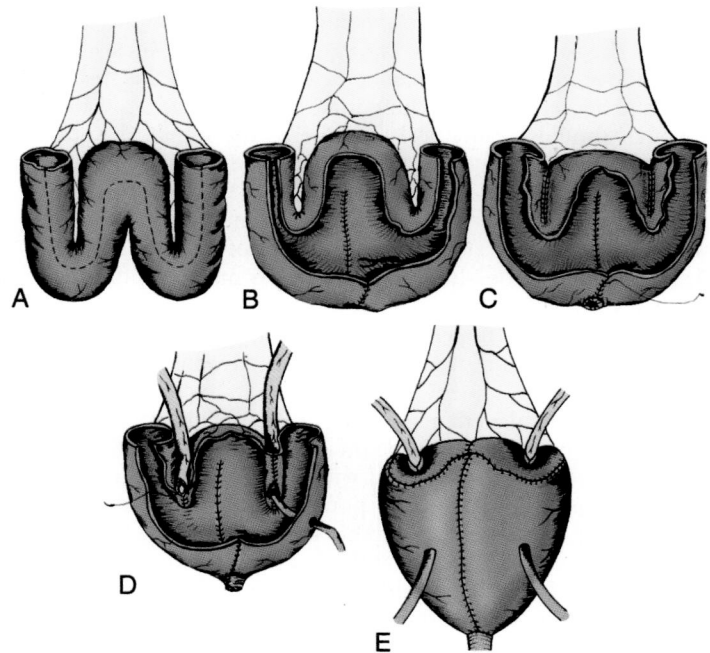

Figure 82–6. Construction of the serous-lined, extramural ileal neobladder. **A,** A 40-cm segment of ileum is isolated and fashioned into a W configuration. **B,** The ileum is opened along the antimesenteric border for the entire length. **C,** The incised mucosa is joined in the middle with a running suture. The two lateral ileal flaps are joined by a seromuscular continuous suture to make the serous-lined intestinal troughs. **D,** The spatulated ureters are laid into each trough, anastomosed to the intestinal mucosa, and stented. The tunnel is closed over the implanted ureter. **E,** The anterior wall of the reservoir is formed by folding the ileum side to side. The reservoir is then anastomosed to the urethra.

technically difficult (Abol-Enein and Ghoneim, 1994). The authors updated their excellent results in 450 patients with this technique and demonstrated that the serous-lined extramural tunnel is an effective and durable antireflux technique, with more than 93% of patients with unidirectional, unobstructed urinary flow (Abol-Enein and Ghoneim, 2001).

A 40-cm ileal segment is isolated from the distal ileum and arranged in a W configuration. The antimesenteric border of the isolated intestine is opened, and the edges of the medial flaps are joined with a running absorbable suture. On either side, the two lateral flaps are joined by a seromuscular continuous suture of silk (3-0). This forms two serous-lined intestinal troughs. Each ureter is laid down in its corresponding trough. A mucosa-to-mucosa anastomosis is performed with the spatulated ureter and the intestinal mucosa at the distal end of the trough. The mucosal edges on each side are then approximated over the reimplanted ureter. The anterior wall of the pouch is then closed in a side-to-side fashion. The suture line of the most dependent portion of the pouch close to the urethral stump is reopened to make a hole that will be anastomosed to the urethra.

Good results with this technique have been reported by others (Papadopoulos and Jacobsen, 2001). A modification of this orthotopic substitute with a serous-lined extramural ureteral reimplantation technique has also been reported by Kato and associates (2001) with good results.

T Pouch Ileal Neobladder

On the basis of reports using a ureteral serous-lined tunnel (Abol-Enein and Ghoneim, 1994), it became apparent that an afferent ileal segment could be incorporated within a serous-lined tunnel in similar fashion. Stein and coworkers (1998b) reported this novel ileal neobladder substitute, called the T pouch, and updated their results with intermediate follow-up of 209 patients (Fig. 82–7) (Stein et al, 2004). The evolution of this technique is detailed elsewhere (Stein and Skinner, 2005).

The orthotopic T pouch ileal neobladder maintains exactly the same geometric configuration as the Kock ileal neobladder, the only difference being the antireflux technique. Theoretically, the functional characteristics of the T pouch should be identical to those of the standard Kock ileal reservoir—a large-capacity, low-pressure urinary reservoir. The unique aspect of the T pouch is the maintenance of the vascular arcades by opening the windows of Deaver, which then allows permanent fixation of a segment of ileum within a serous-lined ileal trough to make an effective flap-valve.

The orthotopic T pouch provides several important advantages over the Kock ileal neobladder. One advantage is that it requires a smaller segment of proximal ileum to construct the antireflux mechanism than the Kock ileal neobladder requires. Only 8 to 10 cm of proximal ileum is required for the afferent limb of the T pouch, compared with 17 cm for an intussuscepted afferent nipple. In the T pouch, only about 3 to 4 cm of the most distal portion of this afferent ileal segment is required to form an effective antireflux mechanism.

It is believed that the intraluminal serous-lined ileal antireflux mechanism will eliminate the observed complications associated with the intussuscepted nipple valve technique.

Because no exposed staples exist within the reservoir, pouch stones typically associated with exposed metallic staples used to maintain the intussuscepted nipple should not develop. In addition, this serous-lined antireflux technique maintains complete preservation of the blood supply to the entire afferent ileal segment. This should prevent problems with afferent nipple stenosis (attributed to the mesenteric stripping and ischemia) seen with the intussuscepted nipple. The serous-lined tunnel also protects the implanted portion of the ileum from exposed urine, allowing healing without scar formation.

Another advantage of this serous-lined ileal antireflux technique is observed when ureteral length is an issue. Considerably greater lengths of pelvic ureter are required in the serous-lined ureteral tunnel technique as described by Abol-Enein and Ghoneim (1994), which, as they acknowledge, is a limitation of their technique. When ureteral length is compromised by pelvic irradiation or by tumor involvement, or when the anastomosis must be performed to the renal pelvis, a longer proximal afferent segment may be harvested to bridge the defect and maintain a tension-free ureteroileal anastomosis. In addition, the T pouch antireflux technique can be performed with large-caliber or dilated ureters, which may also be a problem with the technique proposed by Abol-Enein and Ghoneim (1994).

The T pouch is constructed from 44 cm of distal ileum placed in an inverted V configuration; each limb of the V measures 22 cm, and a proximal 8- to 10-cm segment of ileum (afferent limb) is used to form the afferent antireflux mechanism. If ureteral length is short or compromised, a longer afferent ileal segment (proximal ileum) may be employed. The ileum is divided between the proximal afferent ileal segment and the 44-cm segment that will form the reservoir. The proximal end of the isolated afferent ileal segment is closed with a running absorbable suture.

The isolated 44-cm ileal segment is laid in an inverted V configuration, with the apex of the V lying caudally and a suture marking a point between the two 22-cm adjacent segments of ileum. The opened end of the V is directed cephalad.

The antireflux mechanism is then made by anchoring the distal 3 to 4 cm of the afferent ileal segment into the serous-lined ileal trough formed by the base of the two adjacent 22-cm ileal segments. Mesenteric windows of Deaver are opened between the vascular arcades 3 to 4 cm proximal to the most distal portion of the isolated afferent ileal segment. Preserving these arcades maintains a vascularized afferent limb and allows permanent fixation of this limb into a serous-lined ileal trough with complete preservation of the mesentery and blood supply.

A series of 3-0 silk sutures are then used to approximate the serosa of the two adjacent 22-cm ileal segments at the base of the V, with the sutures passed through the previously opened windows of Deaver. This process is repeated through each individual window of Deaver until the distal 3 to 4 cm of the afferent segment is permanently fixed in the serous-lined ileal trough.

If the portion of the afferent limb (previously anchored in the serous-lined trough) is bulky, this can easily be tapered on the antimesenteric (anterior) border over a 30 French catheter. Tapering this portion of the afferent ileal segment simply reduces the bulk of the afferent limb and facilitates later

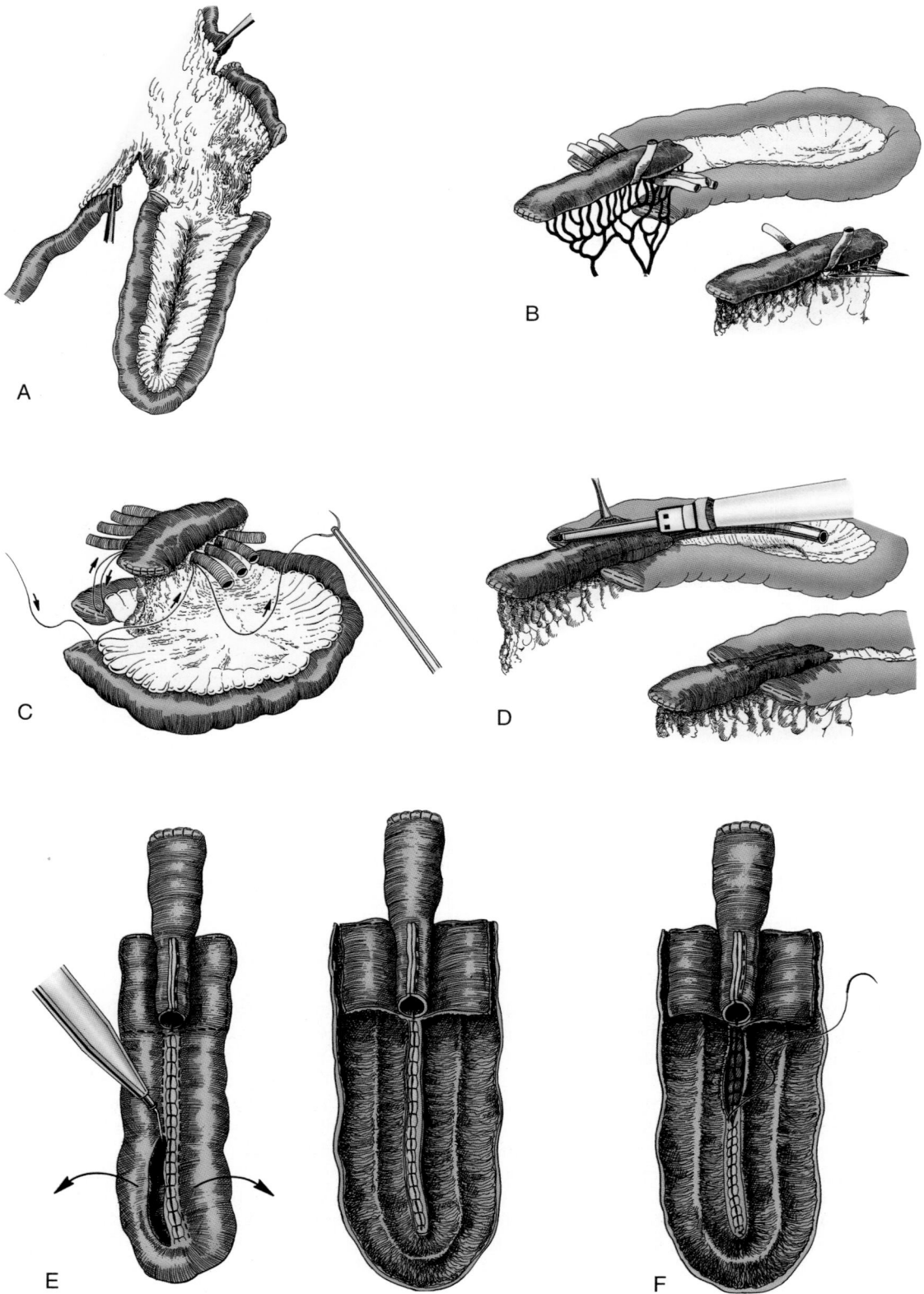

Figure 82–7. Construction of the T pouch orthotopic ileal neobladder. **A,** The T pouch is constructed from a 44-cm segment of terminal ileum placed in a V formation with a more proximal 8- to 10-cm segment of ileum used to form the antireflux limb. Note that the entire mesentery remains intact to provide excellent viability. **B,** The antireflux mechanism is constructed. Windows of Deaver are opened (with Penrose drains placed into each window) in the distal 3 to 4 cm of the isolated afferent limb. Note that blood supply remains intact to this afferent ileal segment. **C,** A series of interrupted silk sutures are used to approximate the serosa of the adjacent 22-cm limbs (cephalad portion), with the passage of sutures through the corresponding window of Deaver. Note that after the silk suture is passed through the window of Deaver, it is placed at a corresponding site on the adjacent 22-cm segment and then brought back through the same window of Deaver and tied down. **D,** The anchored portion of afferent limb is tapered on the antimesenteric border. **E,** The ileal segments are opened adjacent to the mesentery beginning at the apex and carried upward to the ostium of the afferent limb. Note that once the incision reaches the ostium of the afferent limb, it is directed to the antimesenteric border and then carried upward. This provides excellent ileal flaps to cover the tapered afferent ileal segment that is anchored into the serous trough. **F,** The incised ileal mucosa is oversewn.

Continued

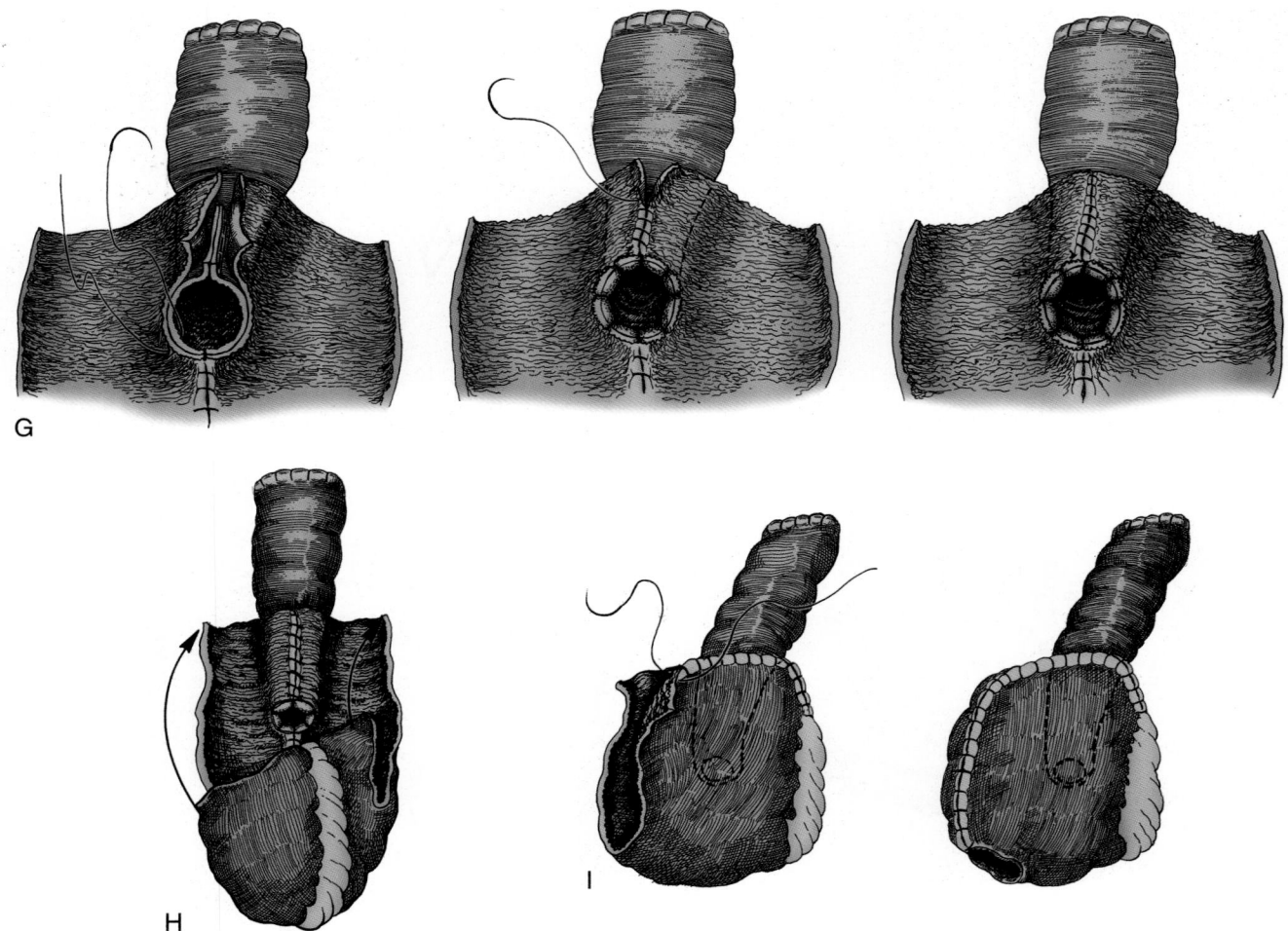

Figure 82–7, cont'd. **G,** The ostium of the afferent segment is sutured to the ileal flaps. The ileal flaps are then brought over and oversewn to cover the tapered afferent ileal segment. This completes the posterior wall of the reservoir and forms the antireflux flap-valve mechanism. **H,** The reservoir is folded and closed in the opposite direction from which it was opened. Note that the ureteroileal anastomosis is performed to the proximal portion of the afferent ileal segment. **I,** The anterior suture line is stopped just short of the right side. This represents the most mobile and dependent portion of the reservoir, which will be anastomosed to the urethra.

coverage of the anchored afferent limb with ileal flaps. In addition, this tapering of the afferent limb will increase the tunnel length–to–lumen diameter ratio, providing a more effective flap-valve mechanism.

After the distal 3 to 4 cm of the afferent ileal segment has been tapered, the remaining portion of the adjacent 22-cm ileal segments is approximated with an absorbable suture. Starting at the apex of the V, the bowel is opened immediately adjacent to the serosal suture line and carried upward to the afferent limb. Once this incision reaches the level of the afferent ostium, it is extended directly lateral to the antimesenteric border of the ileum and carried upward (cephalad) to the base of the ileal segment. This incision provides wide flaps of ileum that will ultimately be brought over the tapered afferent ileal segment to make the antireflux mechanism in a flap-valve technique.

The previously incised ileal mucosa is then oversewn with a running absorbable suture starting at the apex and running upward to the afferent limb. Once the ostium of the afferent limb is reached, an interrupted mucosa-to-mucosa anasto-

mosis is performed between the ostium of the afferent ileal limb and the incised intestinal ileal flaps with absorbable sutures. The mucosal edges of the ileal flaps are then approximated over the anchored portion of the afferent ileal limb (3 to 4 cm) with a running suture. This suture line completes the posterior wall of the reservoir and forms the serous-lined ileal antireflux mechanism.

The reservoir is then closed by folding the ileum in half in the opposite direction to which it was opened, similar to standard Kock pouch construction. The anterior wall is closed. This anterior suture line is stopped before the end of the right side to allow insertion of an index finger. This is the most mobile and dependent portion of the reservoir and will be anastomosed to the urethra. Once the pouch has been closed, each ureter is spatulated, and a standard bilateral end-to-side ureteroileal anastomosis is performed to the proximal afferent ileal segment.

A modification of the T pouch with good results was reported by Hammouda in 2004 with 42 patients in which bowel was placed in an M configuration.

Orthotopic Mainz Pouch

The Mainz (mixed augmentation ileum and cecum) pouch was initially described as a continent catheterizable reservoir that was subsequently modified into an orthotopic neobladder (Thuroff et al, 1986) (Fig. 82–8).

A 10- to 15-cm segment of cecum, in continuity with a 20- to 30-cm segment of ileum, is isolated. An ascending ileocolostomy is performed. The entire segment of bowel is opened along the antimesenteric border, sacrificing the ileocecal valve. The bowel is placed in a W configuration, with the first limb of the W represented by cecum and the middle two limbs represented by ileum. The adjacent three limbs are sutured together with an absorbable suture, forming the posterior plate of the reservoir.

At the cephalad portion of the cecum, tunneled ureterocolonic anastomosis is performed. A buttonhole incision is made in the cecum at the base of the reservoir, and a ureterocolonic anastomosis is performed. After this, the reservoir is closed side to side with absorbable suture.

Ileocolonic (Le Bag) Pouch

The Le Bag ileocolonic bladder substitute was initially described by Light and Engelmann in 1986 (Fig. 82–9). A 20-cm segment of ascending colon and a corresponding length of terminal ileum are isolated, and bowel continuity is restored. The antimesenteric border is incised for the entire length of the colon and ileum to make two flat sheets (one small and one large bowel). These sheets are then sewn to one another

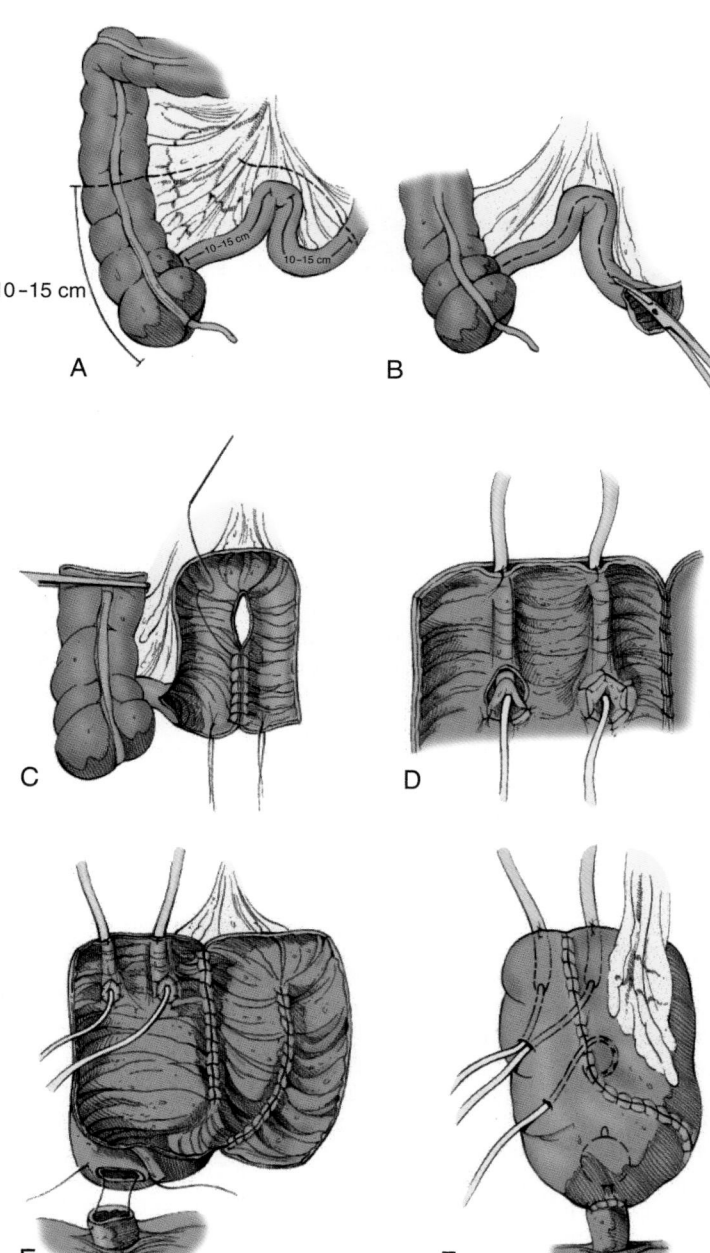

Figure 82–8. Construction of the Mainz ileocolonic orthotopic reservoir. **A,** An isolated 10 to 15 cm of cecum in continuity with 20 to 30 cm of ileum is isolated. **B,** The entire bowel segment is opened along the antimesenteric border. Note that an appendectomy is performed. **C,** The posterior plate of the reservoir is constructed by joining the opposing three limbs together with a continuous running suture. **D,** An antireflux implantation of the ureters through a submucosal tunnel is performed and stented. **E,** A buttonhole incision in the dependent portion of the cecum is made that provides for the urethroenteric anastomosis. Note that the ureterocolonic anastomoses are performed before closure of the reservoir. **F,** The reservoir is closed side to side with a cystostomy tube and the stents exiting.

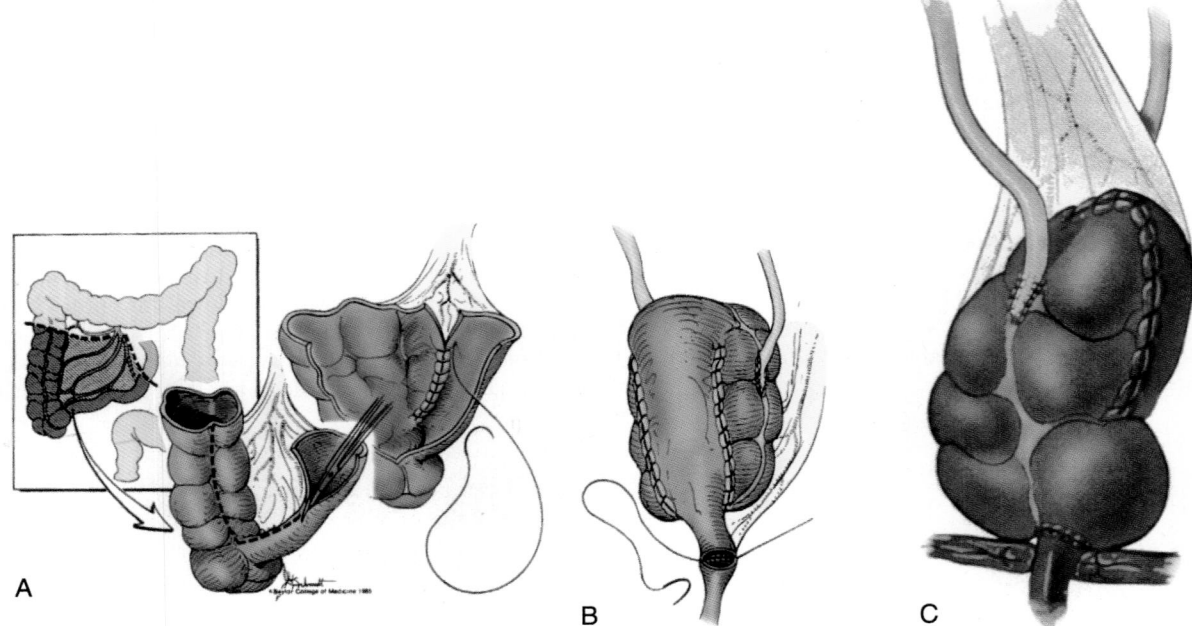

Figure 82–9. Construction of Le Bag (ileocolonic) orthotopic reservoir. **A,** A total of 20 cm of ascending cecum and colon, with a corresponding length of adjacent terminal ileum, is isolated. The bowel is opened along the entire antimesenteric border, and the two incised segments are then sewn to one another. This forms the posterior plate of the reservoir. **B,** This reservoir is folded and rotated 180 degrees into the pelvis with the most proximal portion of the ileum (2 cm non-detubularized) anastomosed to the urethra. **C,** Modification is performed with complete detubularization of the bowel segment, which is then anastomosed to the urethra.

to form the posterior plate. Initially, in the early experience with this neobladder, the incision in the small bowel commenced 2 inches from the cut end so that this intact tube of ileum could be anastomosed end to end to the urethra. This technique was subsequently modified because the small peristaltic ileal segment (intact) was thought to promote urinary incontinence. After this, the entire length of small bowel was incised (Light and Marks, 1990), and the urethra was anastomosed, end to side, to the cecum. The ureters are then brought into the colonic segment and implanted within the reservoir, and the neobladder is closed anteriorly.

A modified version of the Le Bag ileocolonic neobladder has been reported by Baniel and Tal (2004) in which a Studer-like ileal chimney is incorporated as the afferent limb.

Right Colon Pouch

An orthotopic substitute employing the right colon has been reported (Goldwasser et al, 1986; Mansson and Colleen, 1990; Goldwasser, 1995; Mansson et al, 2003). The entire right colon and cecum are isolated, and a transverse ileocolonic anastomosis is performed to provide bowel continuity. The ileal stump at the ileocecal valve is closed with a running absorbable suture. The colonic segment is then opened along the anterior taenia, leaving the proximal 2 to 3 inches of cecum intact. An appendectomy is performed, and the ureters are implanted in an antireflux fashion within the reservoir. The colon is then folded in a Heineke-Mikulicz manner and closed with a running absorbable suture. The ureterocolonic anastomosis is then performed.

Sigmoid Pouch

The use of the sigmoid in construction of an orthotopic substitute was initially described by Reddy and Lange (1987) (Fig. 82–10). A 35-cm portion of descending colon and sigmoid is isolated and arranged in a U configuration. The medial taenia of the U is incised down to an area just short of the urethral anastomosis. The incised medial limbs of the U are then brought together with an absorbable suture. Ureteral implantation is performed in a tunnel antireflux fashion. A small button of colon is removed from the most dependent portion of the reservoir, and the urethroenteric anastomosis is performed. The reservoir is then closed side to side.

A modification of this technique was reported by DaPozzo and associates (1994) in which the entire bowel is detubularized and then folded in a Heineke-Mikulicz fashion to provide a more spherical reservoir.

RESULTS OF ORTHOTOPIC SUBSTITUTES

A strong argument could be made that the orthotopic bladder substitute offers clear advantages over the ileal conduit form of urinary diversion. **Despite the advantages of a superior cosmetic appearance (without the need for a cutaneous stoma or urostomy appliance) and allowing a more natural voiding pattern per urethra, a perception exists that an orthotopic form of diversion may be far more technically demanding and associated with increased morbidity and mortality.** If this is indeed true, one could argue that the ileal conduit should remain the gold standard of urinary diversion.

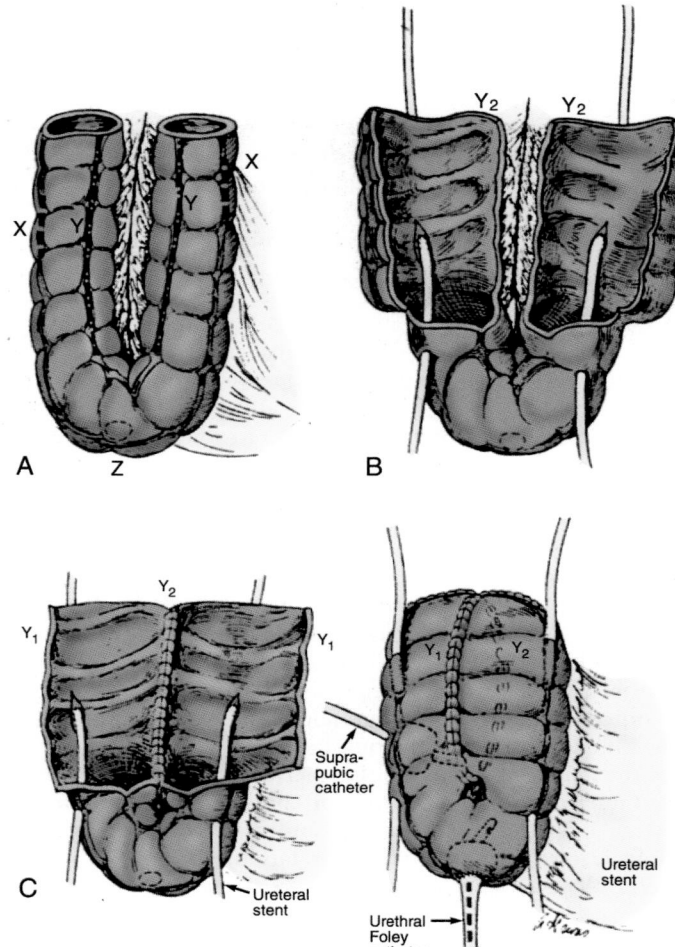

Figure 82–10. Construction of the sigmoid (Reddy) neobladder. **A,** A 35-cm segment of descending and sigmoid colon is isolated and folded into a U shape. **B,** The colon is incised along the medial taenia down to a point a few centimeters short of the entire colon. A buttonhole is made in the caudal portion of the colon that will be the neourethra, which is later anastomosed to the urethra. **C,** The medial portions of the U are sewn together, and a tunneled ureterocolonic anastomosis is performed. **D,** The colonic pouch is closed by folding the reservoir side to side, and it is anastomosed to the urethra.

There is, however, increasing evidence to suggest that the clinical results of orthotopic diversion are not only excellent but also not associated with an obvious increase in perioperative morbidity and mortality compared with the standard ileal conduit.

During a 25-year period, we evaluated our clinical outcomes in 1054 patients who underwent radical cystectomy and some form of urinary diversion for high-grade, invasive bladder cancer (Stein et al, 1998b). The perioperative mortality (any death within 30 days of surgery or before discharge) and early complications (any complication within the first 4 months of surgery) were evaluated and stratified by the form of urinary diversion performed. The form of urinary diversion was reported as either a conduit (ileal or colon) or a continent form of urinary diversion (cutaneous or orthotopic). **There was no significant difference in perioperative mortality and complication rate when these different forms of urinary diversion were compared.** Overall, a 3% perioperative mortality rate was reported (3% of patients undergoing a conduit compared with 2% in the continent diversion group). Similarly, no differences were observed in the early complication rate (30% in the conduit group compared with 27% in the continent cutaneous group). Although not specific for an

orthotopic form of urinary diversion, these data with a large number of patients suggest that a continent form of urinary diversion can be performed with clinical outcomes (perioperative morbidity and mortality) similar to those of a conduit urinary diversion (Stein et al, 1998b).

In another study, Gburek and associates (1998) directly compared the clinical outcomes of an orthotopic ileal substitute (Studer) with those of an ileal conduit form of urinary diversion. In this study, the perioperative and long-term morbidity of patients who had undergone a Studer ileal neobladder was compared with that of a similar cohort of patients who had undergone an ileal conduit urinary diversion during the same period by the same surgeons. An orthotopic ileal neobladder was performed in 62 men and 4 women, and ileal conduit urinary diversion was performed in a total of 66 men. The mean ages of the neobladder and conduit groups were 62 years and 69 years, with mean follow-up of 17 and 20 months, respectively. Although the age was significantly different between the two groups, there was no difference in comorbidity as determined by the Charlson index. The operative time and mean hospital stay (13 days) were identical for each group. Similar perioperative complication and reoperation rates were also reported in these groups. An 18% perioperative complication rate occurred in the neobladder and conduit groups, requiring 5% and 6% reoperation rates in the neobladder and conduit groups, respectively. Of the neobladder cases, 14 patients (21%) sustained 14 late complications with an 11% reoperation rate; 8 conduit patients (12%) developed 9 late complications with an 8% reoperation rate. **These authors concluded that ileal neobladder urinary diversion is a safe procedure with perioperative and long-term morbidity comparable to that of an ileal conduit diversion** (Gburek et al, 1998). These findings were similar to those of a previous study reported by Benson and associates (1992), who found no difference in hospitalization stay, complication rate, and reoperation rate in comparing patients undergoing an ileal conduit with those undergoing various forms of orthotopic diversion.

The clinical results of various forms of orthotopic bladder substitution are presented in Table 82–3 (Thuroff et al, 1986; Barre et al, 1996; Cancrini et al, 1996; Elmajian et al, 1996; Kolettis et al, 1996; Studer et al, 1996a; Hautmann et al, 1999; Hollowell et al, 2000; Steven and Poulsen, 2000; Abol-Enein and Ghoneim, 2001; Mansson et al, 2003; Stein et al, 2004). These results provide a general idea about trends of various orthotopic bladder substitutes, including perioperative morbidity and mortality, daytime and nighttime continence, and need for catheterization. As mentioned earlier, **in interpreting outcomes data from various neobladder series, one must take into consideration the number and age of the patients and the length of follow-up. Furthermore, because there is no standard for the definition of continence and voiding pattern in patients with an orthotopic neobladder, these results also require careful interpretation.**

With the evolution of urinary diversion, several complications specific to the orthotopic neobladder have been observed, including incisional hernias (as a consequence of the Valsalva maneuver required to empty the neobladder) and neobladder-cutaneous fistulas. A unique complication that can be difficult to manage in women undergoing orthotopic reconstruction is a neobladder-vaginal fistula (Rapp et al,

2004). In a report of more than 200 patients undergoing orthotopic reconstruction, Stein and associates (2004) reported on the early (within 3 months of surgery) and late complications and the management (conservative versus reoperation). Early complications specific to the orthotopic urinary diversion were seen in 5% of patients, the most common being urine leakage (all treated conservatively). Late complications specific to the urinary diversion were observed in 18% of patients, the most common being an incisional hernia (50% requiring surgical reoperation). In evaluation of the complications specific to the orthotopic reservoir, standardization of the terminology and assessment of the functional characteristics of the different reservoirs is lacking and may relate to some of the differences in the reporting. Although strides have been made in establishing some uniformity of definitions and outcomes with urinary reservoirs (Thuroff et al, 1996), more work is required in this area.

KEY POINTS: RESULTS OF ORTHOTOPIC SUBSTITUTES

■ There is evidence to suggest that the clinical results of orthotopic diversion are not only excellent but also not associated with an obvious increase in perioperative morbidity and mortality compared with the standard ileal conduit.

■ In interpreting the clinical outcomes from various neobladder series, one must take into consideration the number and age of the patients and the length of follow-up.

■ No standard for the definition of continence and voiding pattern in patients with an orthotopic neobladder exists, and therefore reported results require careful interpretation.

Table 82–3. **Results from Orthotopic Neobladder Series**

| Author | Form | No. of Patients | Follow-up (months) | Mean Age (years) | Mortality (%) | Complications* | | Continence | | IC† (%) | Antireflux Mechanism |
						Early (%)	Late (%)	Day (%)	Night (%)		
Barre (1996)	Camey II, ileum	110	32	62	1	—	—	93	74	1	Le Duc
Elmajian (1996)	Kock, ileum	295	42	66	1	7	12	87	86	8	Nipple valve
Steven (2000)	Kock, ileum	166	32	62	0	12	23	98	80	32	Nipple valve
Hautmann (1999)	W, ileum	363	57	63	3	15	23	96	95	6	Le Duc
Hollowell (2000)	W, ileum	50	20	62	2	10	20	93	86	4	Isoperistaltic "chimney"
Stein (2004)	T pouch, ileum	209	33	69	1.4	5	14	87	72	25	T limb mechanism
Studer (1996a)	Studer, ileum	200	30	64	2	—	—	90	80	0.5	Isoperistaltic limb
Cancrini (1996)	Studer, ileum	96	28	60	6	6	24	98	83	—	Isoperistaltic limb
Thuroff (1986)	Mainz, ileocecal	61	46	—	—	5	18	95	86	13	Submucosal tunnel
Kolettis (1996)	Ileocecal (Le Bag)	38	14	61	0	8	8	91	80	3	Le Duc and Bricker
Abol-Eneim (2001)	Serous-lined extramural, ileum	450	38	47	0.8	9	8	93	80	2	Serous-lined extramural ureter
Mansson (1990)	Right colon	67	70	61	3	4	29	—	—	37	Le Duc

*Complications reported related to urinary diversion.
†IC, some form of intermittent catheterization to empty neobladder.

USE OF ABSORBABLE STAPLING TECHNIQUES IN ORTHOTOPIC SUBSTITUTES

The success of urinary diversion has developed through the concept of bowel detubularization and folding. These principles have allowed the elimination of coordinated peristaltic activity of the bowel, providing a large-capacity spherical reservoir. Although critical, the process of detubularization and refashioning of the bowel is a time-consuming portion of the operation. **To reduce the operative time, the use of absorbable staples has been applied in the construction of the urinary reservoir** (Olsson et al, 1995; Kirsch et al, 1996).

In 1990, the use of absorbable staples in pouch construction in a canine model was first reported by Bonney and Robinson. **The initial application of this technology was hampered by the fact that the stapler was bulky and difficult to manipulate.** Improvements in the staples and the applicators (absorbable staplers) have facilitated the application to continent diversion. A gastrointestinal anastomosis (GIA) instrument* is now available that has a 75-mm GIA configuration, which delivers four rows of absorbable polyglactic acid and polyglycolic acid blend copolymer staples, with a knife mechanism incising the bowel between the second and third rows of staples. This allows a secure, watertight staple line.

The use of absorbable staples has been applied to the construction of various forms of orthotopic reservoirs. This technology has been applied to the sigmoid neobladder (Olsson et al, 1995) as well as to a W-shaped ileal neobladder (Montie et al, 1994) and more recently a Y-shaped ileal neobladder (Fontana et al, 2004). Although the initial results were favorable, Montie and associates (1996) reported on a phase II study comparing hand-sewn orthotopic W-configured ileal reservoirs with reservoirs made by use of absorbable staples, also in a W configuration. They reported that reservoir function appeared to be consistently more favorable in patients with hand-sewn reservoirs using an ileal or ileocolonic segment compared with a stapled construction. Although the authors conceded that the W-stapled ileal reservoir is safe and allows reservoir formation quickly, the inconsistencies of the results discourage the use of absorbable sutures in this particular configuration. The authors suggested that failure of the reservoir to distend could be a function of reservoir design, areas of ischemia in the reservoir, or reactions to staple material. They concluded that the W-configured orthotopic reservoir, constructed with absorbable staples, was inferior to a hand-sewn ileal or ileocolonic neobladder, at least in this study (Montie et al, 1996).

The application of absorbable staples to orthotopic forms of urinary diversion may be easily learned and may decrease operative time. However, only with more experience and longer follow-up will the appropriate application of this technique be better understood.

QUALITY OF LIFE AFTER URINARY DIVERSION

During the past decade, there has been an increasing focus on quality of life issues and outcomes in various urologic diseases. This has been aided by the development of new, health-related quality of life instruments for use specifically in urology. Health-related quality of life instruments are a patient-centered outcome and can be defined as a patient's evaluation of the impact of a health condition and its treatment on relevant aspects of life. As urinary diversion has evolved from an incontinent cutaneous (conduit) form to a continent cutaneous form to, most recently, an orthotopic form, so too has there been an increased interest in studying, evaluating, and assessing quality of life issues and problems that patients face after these various forms of urinary diversion. **Quality of life issues are becoming increasingly important in selection of the type of urinary diversion and are likely to play a larger role in future management of patients undergoing lower urinary tract reconstruction after cystectomy.** The perceived advantage of the various forms of continent urinary diversion (particularly orthotopic diversion) is a presumed improvement in quality of life compared with a conduit form of diversion. However, these more "complicated" forms of urinary diversion may have some disadvantages as well. Continent diversions are technically more challenging and time-consuming. Postoperatively, patients leave the hospital with indwelling catheters and may have a longer convalescence. Once the catheters are removed, patients generally require a period of education in the techniques required to properly care for the reservoir or neobladder. In addition, patients with continent diversions may be at slightly higher risk for bowel dysfunction (diarrhea and vitamin B_{12} malabsorption). However, it is generally believed that the quality of life advantages of continent urinary diversions outweigh the potential disadvantages.

Initial studies by Boyd and coworkers (1987) and Mansson and associates (1988) pioneered comparative evaluation regarding quality of life issues in patients with different forms of urinary diversion after cystectomy. Boyd and associates (1987) compared quality of life in patients with an ileal conduit and in patients with a continent cutaneous Kock ileal reservoir. **They found that all patients surveyed in the study were generally satisfied with their diversion and adapted reasonably well socially, physically, and psychologically. The key to adaptation seemed to be a detailed and realistic preoperative education or discussion about the type of diversion.** Patients with ileal conduit diversions, however, had the lowest expectations of the form of diversion, as defined by preoperative awareness of the need to wear an external ostomy appliance along with the associated inconveniences and changes in external body image. Postoperatively, ileal conduit patients also had the poorest self-images as defined by a decrease in sexual desire and in all forms of physical contact (sexual and nonsexual). Interestingly, a subset of patients who underwent conversion from conduit diversions to continent cutaneous pouches were statistically the most satisfied and the most physically and sexually active. Although not directly related to orthotopic diversion, this early study suggested that from a quality of life perspective, a continent diversion may provide an important alternative to noncontinent forms of urinary diversion (Boyd et al, 1987). Similar results favoring a continent form of urinary diversion over an incontinent diversion have subsequently been reported (Gerharz et al, 1997).

---

*PolyGIA, U.S. Surgical Corp., Norwalk, Conn.

Mansson and associates (1988) also evaluated quality of life issues in patients undergoing cystectomy and urinary diversion. They demonstrated that urinary diversion affects most aspects of life in all patients. Although problems related to the diversion procedure tend to be fewer in patients with continent cutaneous reservoirs than in patients with conduits, both forms of diversion could be associated with serious social, sexual, mental, and emotional problems.

These initial quality of life studies in patients with urinary diversion paved the way to evaluate and compare patients undergoing an orthotopic form of diversion. Bjerre and associates (1995) compared health-related quality of life in patients undergoing an orthotopic neobladder (38 patients) or an ileal conduit (29 patients) form of diversion. Despite higher daytime and nighttime urine leakage in the bladder substitute group, the urine leakage affected conduit patients more severely, and they scored higher on a leakage distress scale. The ileal conduit group was also found not to retain healthy body image as well as patients with a bladder substitute. Although not randomized or prospective, this study showed that health-related quality of life is retained to a higher degree after orthotopic bladder substitution and supported this form of diversion after cystectomy for bladder cancer (Bjerre et al, 1995).

In one of the first studies to compare long-term quality of life outcomes, Hart and associates (1999) reported some interesting findings in patients with advanced bladder cancer undergoing three different forms of urinary diversion. In this study, a total of 224 participating patients completed four self-reporting questionnaires, including a profile of mood states and adapted versions of the sexual history form, body image dissatisfaction scale, and quality of life questionnaire. This study compared self-reports of emotional distress; global quality of life; sexuality; body image dissatisfaction; urinary diversion problems; and problems with social, physical, and functional activities. The diversions included an ileal conduit in 25, a cutaneous Kock pouch in 93, and an orthotopic urethral substitute in 103 patients. Men who had or had not received an inflatable penile prosthesis after cystectomy were also compared with regard to quality of life variables. Regardless of the form of urinary diversion, the majority of patients reported good overall quality of life; little emotional distress; and few problems with social, physical, or functional activities. Problems with urinary diversion and sexual function were identified as most common. After controlling for age, no significant differences in any quality of life area were found among the urinary diversion subgroups. However, controlling for age in men indicated that penile prosthesis placement was significantly associated with better sexual function and satisfaction. Quality of life also appeared good in those patients who were long-term survivors of bladder cancer. The type of urinary diversion, at least in this study, did not appear to be associated with significant differences in quality of life. Furthermore, the authors suggested that the option of erectile aids in men after cystectomy should be considered (Hart et al, 1999).

Weijerman and associates (1998) compared quality of life issues in patients undergoing either an orthotopic or a heterotopic (nonorthotopic) continent urinary diversion. Quality of life assessment in this study revealed only a minor advantage for an orthotopic placement. Importantly, quality of life assessment was found to be favorable for both types of urinary diversion. Similar results have been reported by others (Sullivan et al, 1998).

Most of the studies that evaluated and compared quality of life issues in patients undergoing various forms of urinary diversion have been criticized for methodologic problems that limit their conclusions. Most of these early studies were retrospective and nonrandomized and failed to employ a well-validated measure of assessing quality of life that compared different groups. In one report, McGuire and associates (2000) used a well-validated survey to assess the impact of different forms of urinary diversion on overall quality of life in patients with locoregional bladder cancer after cystectomy. This study evaluated a total of 92 patients (without evidence of disease) undergoing three different forms of urinary diversion who completed (by mail) a validated quality of life survey. Completed surveys were then analyzed into physical and mental components of quality of life and were compared with published age-based norms. A total of 38 men with an orthotopic substitute had a mean physical score of 48.4 and a mean mental score of 51; 16 men and women with an Indiana pouch had a mean physical score of 48.4 and a mean mental score of 55.7. These results were not statistically different from published age-based and sex-based population norms. Thirty-eight men with an ileal conduit diversion had a mean physical score of 41.4 and a mean mental score of 48.2. The physical score was not statistically different from the population-based norm; however, the mental score was significantly decreased from the published norm. These authors concluded that patients with ileal conduits have significantly decreased mental health quality of life, whereas patients with continent urinary diversions do not. Furthermore, they suggested that when it is not medically contraindicated, patients should be offered a continent form of diversion after cystectomy. Although not specific for an orthotopic substitute, these data again provide further support for a continent form of urinary diversion (McGuire et al, 2000).

In a slight variation, Hautmann and Paiss (1998) attempted to determine if the option of a neobladder substitute stimulates the decisions of patient and physician toward an earlier cystectomy in patients with bladder cancer. They reported on a total of 213 men undergoing cystectomy for bladder malignant neoplasm, 135 patients with an ileal neobladder and 78 with an ileal conduit diversion. The interval from the primary diagnosis was 11.8 months in the neobladder and 16.7 months in the conduit group. Five-year survival rate was significantly higher for all disease stages in the neobladder group than in the conduit group. The authors concluded that the availability of ileal neobladder may decrease the physician's reluctance to perform cystectomy early in the disease process, thus increasing the survival rate. They also implied that orthotopic urinary diversion positively influenced patients and physicians to choose radical surgery earlier in the course of disease (Hautmann and Paiss, 1998).

This study further emphasized that the orthotopic neobladder may represent the ideal form of urinary diversion available today. However, despite the advances and advantages of lower urinary tract reconstruction, the ileal conduit remains an often-used option, if not the most common form of urinary diversion performed in nonacademic practices. Reasons for this may include familiarity, simplicity, and the relatively expeditious nature of an ileal conduit. In addition, perioperative management is less demanding and time-consuming. The physician should have a general understanding of the indications and principles of lower urinary tract reconstruction and proper training in the techniques involved. This knowledge will help ensure proper management of patients and allow proper informed consent.

Although these studies support continent urinary diversion with regard to an improved quality of life in patients after cystectomy, it is unclear whether the existing body of literature supports this assumption when validated measures are used in a prospective fashion. Porter and Penson (2005) performed a systematic review to determine if any differences exist in health-related quality of life outcomes among different types of urinary diversion after radical cystectomy. They performed a detailed MEDLINE search of appropriate studies inclusive of the dates 1966 to January 2004. Inclusion criteria included adult patients, patients with bladder cancer, comparative studies, original research, primary study outcome related to quality of life, and use of a quality of life instrument to measure outcomes. Only studies comparing neobladder, continent reservoir, or conduit diversion were included. Of 378 initial articles, only 15 studies met all the inclusion criteria. None of the studies were randomized trials, and only one was prospective. Of 15 studies, 10 (67%) used some type of previously validated health-related quality of life outcomes instrument, 10 (67%) used some form of ad hoc instrument, 11 (73%) used a bladder cancer disease–specific instrument, and 9 (60%) used general instruments. Common limitations included unvalidated health-related quality of life outcomes instruments, use of general health–related quality of life outcomes instruments only, lack of baseline data, cross-sectional analysis, and retrospective study design. The authors found that the current body of published literature is insufficient for it to be concluded that any form of urinary diversion is superior to another on the basis of health-related quality of life outcomes.

Despite the notion that there are insufficient data for a sound conclusion to be made about health-related quality of life outcomes and the various forms of urinary diversion, they do provide some potentially useful information (Porter and Penson, 2005). The authors identified three studies indicating that patients with conduit diversion had more difficulties with urine leakage than did patients with a form of continent diversion. In addition, three studies suggested that patients with neobladder or continent reservoir were more likely to travel than were patients with conduit diversion, and two studies suggested that patients with a continent form of diversion are more likely to score better on social function domains (Porter and Penson, 2005). It is clear that to better understand and evaluate these quality of life issues in patients undergoing various forms of urinary diversion, future studies in this area must incorporate prospective data collection, provide longer term follow-up, and incorporate validated disease-specific health-related quality of life outcomes instruments.

SUMMARY

The development of orthotopic lower urinary tract reconstruction was a significant step in the continued progress of urinary diversion. **Overall, most patients undergoing**

> ### KEY POINTS: QUALITY OF LIFE AFTER URINARY DIVERSION
>
> - Most quality of life studies that evaluated and compared issues in patients undergoing various forms of urinary diversion have been criticized for methodologic problems that limit their conclusions.
>
> - The current body of published literature is insufficient for it to be concluded that any form of urinary diversion is superior to another on the basis of health-related quality of life outcomes.

orthotopic diversion are continent, have the luxury of voiding every 4 to 6 hours with excellent voided volumes, retain a more routine micturition pattern, avoid the need for a cutaneous stoma or external urostomy appliance, and arguably have a more normal lifestyle with an improved self-image. Careful preoperative counseling of patients considering orthotopic lower urinary tract reconstruction should include the possible need for clean intermittent catheterization in the rare patient unable to void with pelvic floor relaxation and Valsalva maneuver. In addition, all patients should understand the potential risk of a urethral recurrence and the need for continued, long-term surveillance of the retained urethra. Meticulous monitoring of the retained urethra should include careful palpation of the urethroenteric anastomosis on vaginal examination in women and on rectal examination in men. In addition, voided urine cytology should be performed on a regular basis in all patients at each follow-up visit.

The orthotopic reservoir should be considered today the gold standard with which other forms of diversion are compared. Orthotopic diversion can be safely offered to both male and female patients undergoing cystectomy. In addition, data suggest that an option of a neobladder diversion may decrease the physician's reluctance to perform cystectomy earlier for bladder cancer at a more curable stage and increase the patient's acceptance (Hautmann and Paiss, 1998). With this form of diversion, we hope that patients with bladder cancer as well as their physicians may be encouraged toward earlier and more aggressive forms of therapy with cystectomy, when cure and ultimately survival are greatest.

The perfect urinary diversion remains to be found. Only the motivated and thoughtful surgeon, improving on existing concepts and techniques, will come closer to the ideal form of lower urinary tract reconstruction.

SUGGESTED READINGS

Abol-Enein H, Ghoneim MA: A novel uretero-ileal reimplantation technique: The serous lined extramural tunnel. A preliminary report. J Urol 1994;151:1193.

Abol-Enein H, Ghoneim MA: Functional results of orthotopic ileal neobladder with serous-lined extramural ureteral reimplantation: Experience with 450 patients. J Urol 2001;165:1427.

Bricker EM: Bladder substitution after pelvic evisceration. Surg Clin North Am 1950;30:1511.

Camey M, Le Duc A: L'enterocystoplastie avec cystoprostatectomie totale pour cancer de la vessie. Ann Urol 1979;13:114.

Colleselli K, Stenzl A, Eder R, et al: The female urethral sphincter: A morphological and topographical study. J Urol 1998;160:49.

Gilchrist RK, Merricks JW, Hamlin HH, Rieger IT: Construction of a substitute bladder and urethra. Surg Gynecol Obstet 1950;9:752.

Hautmann RE, Paiss T: Does the option of the ileal neobladder stimulate patient and physician decision toward earlier cystectomy? J Urol 1998;159:1845.

Hinman F: Selection of intestinal segments for bladder substitution: Physical and physiological characteristics. J Urol 1988;139:519.

Kock NG, Nilson AE, Nilsson LO, et al: Urinary diversion via a continent ileal reservoir: Clinical results in 12 patients. J Urol 1982;128:469.

Le Duc A, Camey M, Teillac P: An original antireflux ureteroileal implantation technique: Long-term followup. J Urol 1987;137:1156.

Porter MP, Penson DF: Health related quality of life after radical cystectomy and urinary diversion for bladder cancer: A systematic review and critical analysis of the literature. J Urol 2005;173:1318.

Skinner DG, Boyd SD, Lieskovsky G: Clinical experience with the Kock continent ileal reservoir for urinary diversion. J Urol 1984;132:1101.

Steers WD: Voiding dysfunction in the orthotopic neobladder. World J Urol 2000;18:330.

Stein JP, Cote RJ, Freeman JA, et al: Indications for lower urinary tract reconstruction in women after cystectomy for bladder cancer: A pathological review of female cystectomy specimens. J Urol 1995;154:1329.

Stein JP, Lieskovsky G, Ginsberg DA, et al: The T pouch: An orthotopic ileal neobladder incorporating a serosal lined ileal antireflux technique. J Urol 1998;159:1836.

Stein JP, Clark P, Miranda G, et al: Urethral tumor recurrence following cystectomy and urinary diversion: Clinical and pathological characteristics in 768 male patients. J Urol 2005;173:1163.

Stenzl A, Draxl H, Posch B, et al: The risk of urethral tumors in female bladder cancer: Can the urethra be used for orthotopic reconstruction of the lower urinary tract? J Urol 1995;153:950.

Studer UE, Ackermann D, Casanova GA, Zingg EJ: Three years' experience with an ileal low pressure bladder substitute. Br J Urol 1989;63:43.

83 | Genital and Lower Urinary Tract Trauma

ALLEN F. MOREY, MD • THOMAS A. ROZANSKI, MD

INJURIES OF THE EXTERNAL GENITALIA

BLADDER INJURIES

URETHRAL INJURIES

INJURIES OF THE EXTERNAL GENITALIA
Penis

Traumatic injuries to the genitalia are uncommon, in part because of the mobility of the penis and scrotum. Blunt phallic traumatic injury is usually of concern only with an erect penis, when fracture of the tunica albuginea may result. In general, prompt surgical reconstruction of most penile injuries usually leads to adequate and acceptable cosmetic and functional results.

Fracture

Etiology. Penile fracture is the disruption of the tunica albuginea with rupture of the corpus cavernosum. Fracture typically occurs during vigorous sexual intercourse, when the rigid penis slips out of the vagina and strikes the perineum or pubic bone (faux pas du coit), sustaining a buckling injury.

The tunica albuginea is a bilaminar structure (inner circular, outer longitudinal) composed of collagen and elastin. The outer layer determines the strength and thickness of the tunica, which varies in different locations along the shaft (Hsu et al, 1994; Brock et al, 1997). The tensile strength of the tunica albuginea is remarkable, resisting rupture until intracavernous pressures rise to more than 1500 mm Hg (Bitsch et al, 1990). When the erect penis bends abnormally, the abrupt increase in intracavernosal pressure exceeds the tensile strength of the tunica albuginea, and a transverse laceration of the proximal shaft usually results.

Whereas penile fracture has been reported most commonly with sexual intercourse, it has also been described with masturbation, rolling over or falling on to the erect penis, and myriad other scenarios. In the Middle East, self-inflicted fractures predominate; the erect penis is forcibly bent during masturbation or as a means to achieve rapid detumescence, the practice of *taghaandan*.

Mydlo (2001) reported that 94% of fractures in Philadelphia, Pennsylvania, were a result of sexual intercourse; Zargooshi (2000) described 69% of fractures in Kermanshah, Iran, as being due to self-manipulation. The tunical tear is usually transverse and 1 to 2 cm in length (Asgari et al, 1996; Mydlo, 2001). The injury is usually unilateral, although tears in both corporal bodies have been reported (Mydlo, 2001; El-Taher et al, 2004). **Although the site of rupture can occur anywhere along the penile shaft, most are distal to the suspensory ligament.**

Diagnosis and Imaging. **The diagnosis of penile fracture is often straightforward and can be made reliably by history and physical examination alone.** Patients usually describe a cracking or popping sound as the tunica tears, followed by pain, rapid detumescence, and discoloration and swelling of the penile shaft. If Buck's fascia remains intact, the penile hematoma remains contained between the skin and tunica, resulting in a typical eggplant deformity (Fig. 83–1). If Buck's fascia is disrupted, hematoma can extend to the scrotum, perineum, and suprapubic regions. The swollen, ecchymotic phallus often deviates to the side opposite the tunical tear because of hematoma and mass effect. The fracture line in the tunica albuginea may be palpable. A blood clot directly against the fracture site can be palpated; the "rolling sign" describes a firm, mobile, discrete, tender swelling over which the penile skin can be rolled (Naraynsingh and Raju, 1985). Because fear and embarrassment are commonly associated, the patient's presentation to the emergency department or clinic is sometimes significantly delayed.

The incidence of urethral injury is significantly higher in the United States and Europe (20%) than in Asia and the Middle East (3%), probably owing to the different etiology—intercourse trauma versus self-inflicted injury (Eke, 2002; Zargooshi, 2002; Jack et al, 2004). Most urethral injuries are associated with gross hematuria, blood at the meatus, or inability to void, although the absence of these findings does not definitively rule out urethral injury (Tsang and Demby, 1992; Mydlo, 2001; Jack et al, 2004). **Given that urethral injury occurs not infrequently and that urethrography is a simple and reliable study, clinicians should have a low threshold for urethral evaluation in all cases of penile fracture.**

The typical history and clinical presentation of fractured penis usually make adjunctive imaging studies unnecessary.

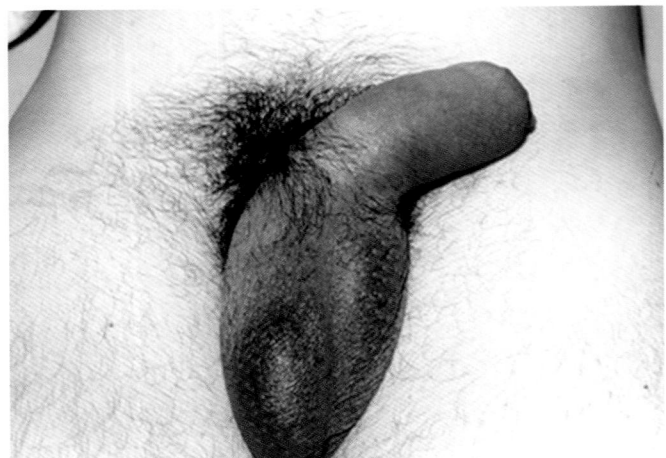

Figure 83–1. "Eggplant deformity," the classic appearance of penile fracture sustained during intercourse.

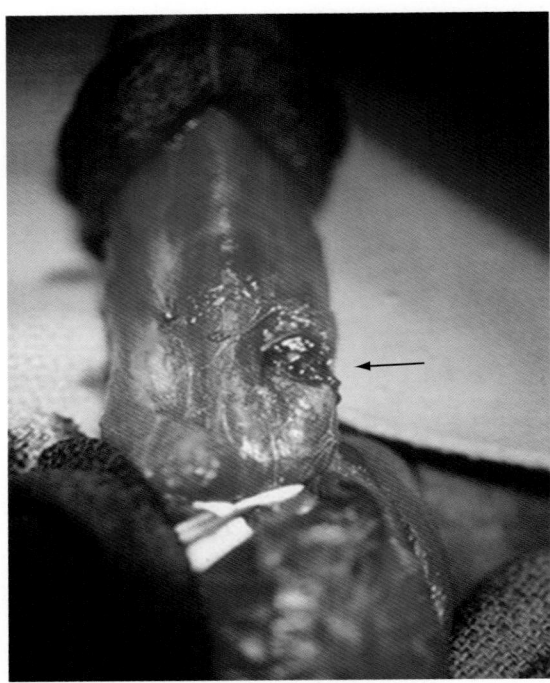

Figure 83–2. Transverse laceration of left corpus cavernosum associated with penile fracture, successfully repaired through a circumcision incision.

Although cavernosography has been advocated to assist in diagnosis, false-negative studies have been reported (Mydlo, 2001); false-positive studies can result from inadequate filling of one corporal body and misinterpretation of complex venous drainage (Pliskow and Ohme, 1979; Beysel et al, 2002). **Cavernosography is discouraged in the evaluation of a suspected penile fracture because it is time-consuming and unfamiliar to most urologists and radiologists** (Morey et al, 2004). Ultrasonography, although noninvasive and easy to perform, has also been associated with significant false-negative studies (Koga et al, 1993; Fedel et al, 1996).

Magnetic resonance imaging is a noninvasive and highly accurate means of demonstrating disruption of the tunica albuginea (Fedel et al, 1996; Uder et al, 2002). Arguments against the routine use of magnetic resonance imaging are the expense, limited availability, and time requirements involved with the study. **Magnetic resonance imaging is reasonable in the evaluation of patients without the typical presentation and physical findings of penile fracture.**

False fracture has been reported in patients who present with penile swelling and ecchymosis, although they do not describe the classic "snap-pop" or rapid detumescence typically associated with fracture. Physical examination may not be adequate for definitive diagnosis of a corporal tear in these circumstances (Shah et al, 2003). Surgical exploration or evaluation with magnetic resonance imaging should be considered. Another condition that may mimic penile fracture is rupture of the dorsal penile artery or vein during sexual intercourse (Nicely et al, 1992; Armenakas et al, 2001).

Management. Multiple contemporary publications indicate that suspected penile fractures should be promptly explored and surgically repaired. A distal circumcising incision (Fig. 83–2) is appropriate in most cases, thus providing exposure to all three penile compartments (Morey et al, 2004). Closure of the tunical defect with interrupted 2-0 or 3-0 absorbable sutures is recommended; deep corporal vascular ligation or excessive débridement of the delicate underlying erectile tissue must be avoided. Partial urethral injuries should be oversewn with fine absorbable suture over

a urethral catheter. Complete urethral injuries should be débrided, mobilized, and repaired in a tension-free fashion over a catheter. Broad-spectrum antibiotics and 1 month of sexual abstinence are recommended.

Outcome and Complications. Immediate surgical reconstruction results in faster recovery, decreased morbidity, lower complication rates, and lower incidence of long-term penile curvature (Nicolaisen et al, 1983; Orvis and McAninch, 1989; Hinev, 2002; El-Taher et al, 2004; Muentener et al, 2004). Conservative management of penile fracture results in penile curvature in more than 10% of patients, abscess or debilitating plaques in 25% to 30%, and significantly longer hospitalization times and recovery (Meares, 1971; Nicolaisen et al, 1983; Kalash and Young, 1984; Orvis and McAninch, 1989). Zargooshi (2002) reported in a personal surgical series of 170 patients that surgical management of penile fractures resulted in erectile function comparable to that of a control population. Timing of surgery may influence long-term success. Among surgically treated patients, those undergoing repair within 8 hours of injury had significantly better long-term results than did those having surgery delayed 36 hours after the fracture occurred (Asgari et al, 1996; Karadeniz et al, 1996).

Gunshots and Penetrating Injuries

Gunshot Wounds. The majority of penetrating wounds to the genitalia are due to gunshots (Mohr et al, 2003), and most require surgical exploration. **Treatment principles include immediate exploration, copious irrigation, excision of foreign matter, antibiotic prophylaxis, and surgical closure.** Gunshot injuries to the phallus are rarely isolated wounds; 77% to 80% of victims have significant associated injuries, including additional genitourinary, abdominal, pelvic, lower extremity, vascular, or inguinal injuries (Goldman et al, 1996; Bandi and Santucci, 2004). Excellent cosmetic and functional outcomes can be expected with immediate reconstruction (Gomez et al, 1993; Goldman et al, 1996).

Urethral injuries have been reported in 15% to 50% of penile gunshot wounds (Miles et al, 1990; Goldman et al, 1996; Mohr et al, 2003). **Retrograde urethrography should be strongly considered in any patient with penetrating injury to the penis, especially with high-velocity missile injuries, blood at the meatus, or difficulty voiding and when bullet trajectory was near the urethra** (Goldman et al, 1996; Mohr et al, 2003; Bandi and Santucci, 2004); alternatively, intraoperative retrograde urethral injection of methylene blue or indigo carmine may identify the site of injury and the adequacy of closure. **Urethral injuries should be closed primarily by use of standard urethroplasty principles;** excellent results have been reported (Miles et al, 1990; Bandi and Santucci, 2004). Patients with urethral injury in the presence of extensive tissue damage and blast effect from high-velocity weapons or close-range shotgun blasts usually require staged repairs and urinary diversion (Bandi and Santucci, 2004).

Animal and Human Bites. The morbidity of animal bites is directly related to the severity of the initial wound. Most victims are boys, and dog bites are the most common injury (Gomes et al, 2001; Van der Horst et al, 2004). Infectious complications are unusual since treatment is sought early. **Initial management of dog bites includes copious irrigation, débridement, and immediate primary closure along with prophylactic broad-spectrum antibiotics** (Cummings and Boullier, 2000). Tetanus and rabies immunizations should be used as appropriate. Because of the risk of polymicrobial infection, empirical treatment with broad-spectrum antibiotics such as cefazolin or cephalexin is recommended. Wolf and colleagues (1993) advised the additional use of penicillin V (500 mg four times daily) to provide coverage against *Pasteurella multocida*, present in 20% to 25% of dog bite wounds. Alternatively, chloramphenicol alone (50 mg/kg daily for 10 days) is a readily available, inexpensive option that has proved effective in developing countries (Gomes et al, 2001).

Human bites produce potentially contaminated wounds that often should not be closed primarily. Most human bite victims seek medical attention after a substantial delay and thus are more likely to present with gross infection. Empirical antibiotic administration is warranted in the same manner as with dog bites, even though the bacteriology of the wounds is not identical.

Amputation

Traumatic amputation of the penis, although rare, is usually the result of genital self-mutilation. Sixty-five percent to 87% of patients performing genital self-mutilation are psychotic (Greilsheimer and Groves, 1979; Aboseif et al, 1993; Romilly and Isaac, 1996). Psychiatric consultation should be sought in all such cases.

Patients should be transferred to a facility with microsurgical capabilities; however, if this is unavailable, macroscopic anastomosis of the urethra and corporal bodies can be performed with good erectile results, albeit with less sensation and greater skin loss. **Reconstruction of the urethra and reanastomosis of the corpora cavernosa with microsurgical repair of penile vessels and nerves achieve remarkably good results.** Every attempt should be made to locate, clean, and preserve the severed portion in a double bag technique. The distal penis should be rinsed in saline solution, wrapped in saline-soaked gauze, and sealed in a sterile plastic bag. The bag should then be placed into an outer bag with ice or slush (Jezior et al, 2001). **Thermal injury to the amputated segment can occur if it is in direct contact with ice for a prolonged period.** Successful reimplantation is possible after 16 hours of cold ischemia time or 6 hours of warm ischemia (Lowe et al, 1991). If the severed part is not available, the penile stump should be formalized by closing the corpora and spatulating the urethral neomeatus, similar to a partial penectomy procedure for malignant disease.

Microvascular reconstruction of the dorsal arteries, vein, and nerves is the preferred method of repair for the amputated penis (see Key Points: Step by Step Approach to Penile Reattachment). Adequate erectile function is possible with both microvascular reanastomosis and macroscopic replantation, with more than 50% of men able to achieve erection with either technique (Bhanganada et al, 1983; Lowe et al, 1991; Aboseif et al, 1993). However, **complications such as urethral strictures, skin loss, and sensory abnormalities are all much higher without microvascular repair.** Normal penile sensation returns in 0% to 10% of patients after macroscopic replantation (Bhanganada et al, 1983; Lowe et al, 1991), whereas sensation is present in more than 80% of microscopic replantations (Jordan and Gilbert, 1989; Lowe et al, 1991; Jezior et al, 2001). Penile skin loss, often complete, is a significant problem after macroscopic repair. One effective strategy is to denude the phallus of all skin and bury it in the scrotum, leaving the glans exposed, with separation of the structures after 2 months (Bhanganada et al, 1983; Jordan and Gilbert, 1989). Mineo and colleagues (2004) reported use of medical leeches on the penis after nonmicroscopic replantation as a means to augment venous outflow and to decrease edema.

KEY POINTS: STEP BY STEP APPROACH TO PENILE REATTACHMENT

- Two-layer urethral closure over a catheter with 5-0 absorbable suture

- Minimal dissection along the neurovascular bundle to identify severed vessels and nerves

- Closure of the tunica albuginea with 3-0 absorbable suture

- Microscopic anastomosis of the dorsal artery with 11-0 nylon

- Microscopic dorsal vein repair with 9-0 nylon

- Microscopic epineural repair of dorsal nerve with 10-0 nylon

- Suprapubic cystostomy

Zipper Injuries

Zipper injuries to the penis usually trap impatient boys or intoxicated adults. Multiple maneuvers are available to free the entrapped skin and to remove the mechanism. After a penile block, the zipper sliding piece and adjacent skin can be lubricated with mineral oil, followed by a single attempt to unzip and untangle (Kanegaye and Schonfeld, 1993; Mydlo, 2000). The cloth material connected to the zipper can be incised with perpendicular cuts in between each tooth to release the lateral support of the zipper, allowing the device to fall apart and release the trapped skin (Oosterlinck, 1981). A bone cutter or similar tool can be used to cut the median bar (diamond-shaped connection) of the slide piece. This maneuver allows separation of the upper and lower shields of the sliding device, and the entire zipper falls apart (Flowerdew et al, 1977; Saraf and Rabinowitz, 1982). Some children may require more than local anesthesia or sedation; circumcision or an elliptical skin excision can be performed in the operating room under anesthesia (Yip et al, 1989; Mydlo, 2000).

Strangulation Injuries

Accidental injuries with thread, hair, or rubber bands occur in children, but child abuse must be considered in such cases. Any child with unexplained penile swelling, erythema, or difficulty voiding should be examined closely for a hidden strangulating hair or string. Adults may place objects around the shaft as a means of sexual pleasure or to prolong an erection. The constricting device can reduce blood flow, cause edema, and induce ischemia; gangrene and urethral injury may develop in delayed presentations. Emergent treatment requires decompression of the constricted penis to allow blood flow and micturition. Depending on the constricting device, significant resourcefulness may be required of the physician.

String, hair, and rubber bands can be incised. Initial attempts to remove a solid constricting device causing penile strangulation involve lubrication of the shaft and foreign body and attempted direct removal. Edema distal to the strangulation often makes removal difficult. A string or latex tourniquet can be wrapped around the distal shaft to decrease swelling and to improve the odds of removing the device with lubrication. If the constricting object cannot be severed or removed, a string technique should be considered (Browning and Reed, 1969; Vahasarja et al, 1993; Noh et al, 2004). A thick silk suture or umbilical tape is passed proximally under the strangulation object and wound tightly around the penis distally toward the glans. The tag of suture or tape proximal to the ring is grasped; unwinding from the proximal end will push the object distally. Glanular puncture with a needle or blade will allow escape of dark trapped blood and improve the odds of removing the object with the string method (Browning and Reed, 1969; Noh et al, 2004).

Plastic constricting devices can be incised with a scalpel or an oscillating cast saw (Pannek and Martin, 2003), but metal objects present a more difficult challenge. Readily available hospital equipment (ring cutters, bolt cutters, dental drills, orthopedic and neurosurgical operative drills) may not be adequate to cut through heavy iron or steel items. The use of industrial drills, steel saws, hacksaws, saber saws, and high-speed electric drills has been reported (Perabo et al, 2002;

Santucci et al, 2004). On occasion, fire department and emergency medical services equipment may be required to cut through iron and steel rings. The phallus should be protected from thermal injury, sparks, and the cutting blade or bits by use of tongue depressors, sponges, or malleable retractors. Such elaborate undertakings are best accomplished in the operating room under anesthesia. If there is any delay in decompression and the patient is unable to void and uncomfortable or distended, a suprapubic bladder catheter should be placed.

Testis

Etiology

Although the testis is relatively protected by the mobility of the scrotum, reflex cremasteric muscle contraction, and its tough fibrous tunica albuginea, blunt injury (usually the result of assault, sports-related events, and motor vehicle accidents) can result in rupture of the tunica albuginea, contusion, hematoma, dislocation, or torsion of the testis. Testis injury results from blunt trauma in about 75% of cases (McAninch et al, 1984; Cass and Luxenberg, 1991). Penetrating injuries due to firearms, explosions, and impalement injuries represent the remainder.

Whereas only 1.5% of blunt testis injury involves both gonads, about 30% of penetrating scrotal trauma results in bilateral injury (Cass and Luxenberg, 1988, 1991). Most penetrating scrotal trauma (72% to 83%) is associated with nongenitourinary injuries including thigh, penis, perineum, urethra, or femoral vessels (Gomez et al, 1993; Cline et al, 1998). In contemporary military conflicts, genital wounds account for a larger percentage of urologic injuries because of the powerful explosive weapons involved and the protective influence of body armor (Thompson et al, 1998).

Diagnosis

Rupture of the testis must be considered in all cases of blunt scrotal trauma. Most patients complain of exquisite scrotal pain and nausea. **Swelling and ecchymosis are variable, and the degree of hematoma does not correlate with the severity of testis injury; absence does not entirely rule out testis rupture, and contusion without fracture can present with significant bleeding.** Scrotal hemorrhage and hematocele along with tenderness to palpation often limit a complete physical examination. Concomitant urethral injury should be suspected and evaluated when examination reveals blood at the meatus or if the mechanism of injury or hematuria suggests the possibility. Penetrating injuries mandate careful examination of surrounding structures, especially the femoral vessels.

Ultrasonography can be helpful to assess the integrity and vascularity of the testis. Ultrasonography is rapid, readily available, and noninvasive. Because sonography may be operator dependent, false-positive and false-negative studies range from 56% to 94% (Fournier et al, 1989; Corrales et al, 1993; Herbener, 1996; Dreitlein et al, 2001). **Ultrasound findings suggestive of testis fracture include inhomogeneity of the testicular parenchymal texture and disruption of the tunica albuginea** (Micallef et al, 2001) (Fig. 83–3). **A normal or equivocal ultrasound study should not delay surgical explo-**

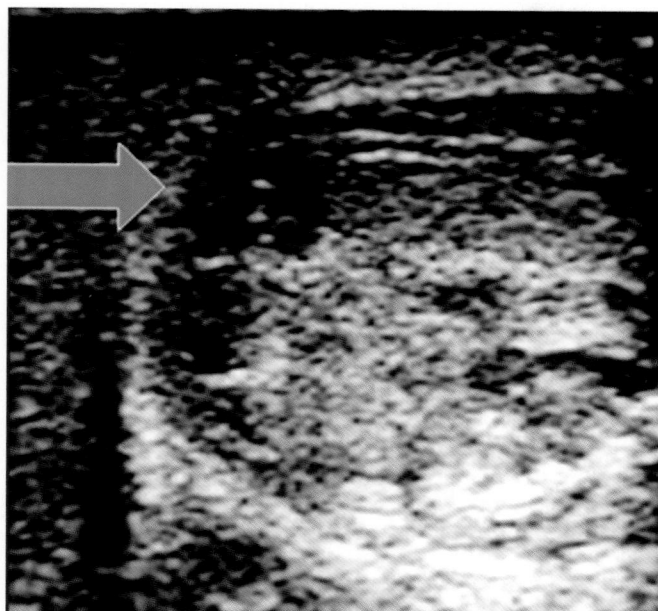

Figure 83–3. Ultrasound examination demonstrates hypoechoic intratesticular areas consistent with testicular rupture sustained by blunt trauma. Scrotal exploration revealed large hematocele and exposed seminiferous tubules.

ration when physical examination findings are suggestive of testicular damage; definitive diagnosis is often made in the operating room. Although magnetic resonance imaging may effectively demonstrate testis integrity, its widespread use is not the norm because of expense, limited availability, and potential delay in definitive surgical care of the patient (Serra et al, 1998; Muglia et al, 2002).

Differential diagnosis of testis fracture includes hematocele without rupture, torsion of the testis or an appendage, reactive hydrocele, hematoma of the epididymis or spermatic cord, and intratesticular hematoma. A nonpalpable testis in a trauma patient should raise the possibility of dislocation outside the scrotum. This entity usually occurs after motorcycle crashes, wherein extreme forces on the scrotum expel the testis into surrounding tissues such as the superficial inguinal pouch (50%) or to a pubic, penile, pelvic, abdominal, or perineal location (Schwartz and Faerber, 1994; Bromberg, 2003). Bilateral dislocation after trauma has been reported (Bromberg et al, 2003; O'Brien et al, 2004). Manual or surgical reduction of the displaced testis is indicated. Finally, approximately 5% of spermatic cord torsions are believed to be precipitated by trauma; torsion should be considered in all cases of significant scrotal pain without signs or symptoms of major scrotal trauma (Elsaharty et al, 1984; Manson, 1989; Lrhorfi et al, 2002).

Management

Early exploration and repair of testis injury is associated with increased testis salvage, reduced convalescence and disability, faster return to normal activities, and preservation of fertility and hormonal function (Kukadia et al, 1996). Minor scrotal injuries without testis damage can be managed

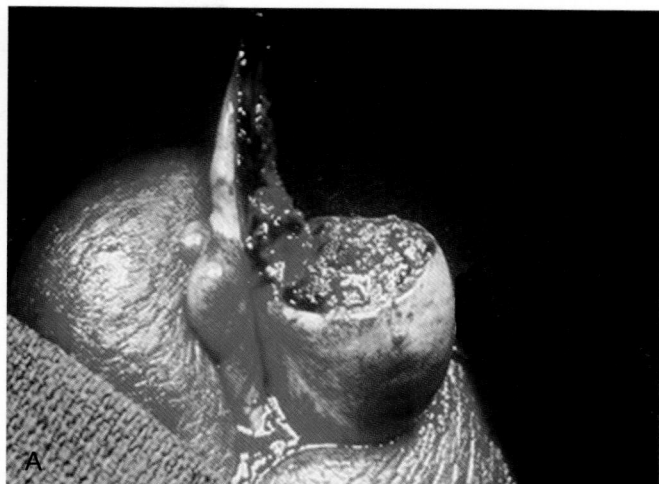

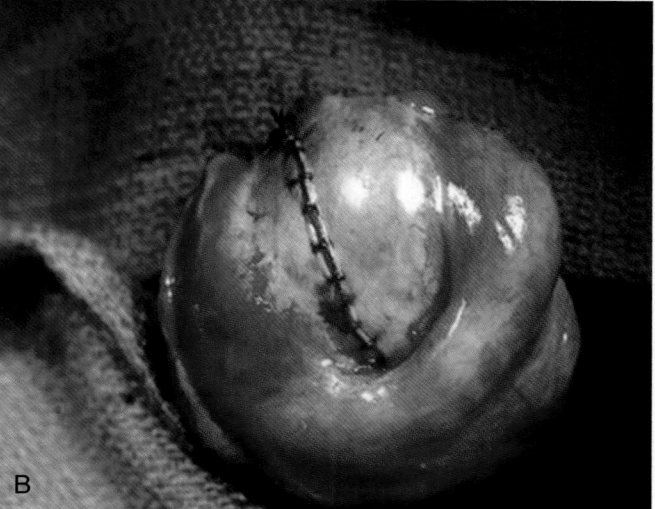

Figure 83–4. A, Seminiferous tubules débrided. **B,** Tunica albuginea reconstructed. (Photo courtesy of Dr. Jack McAninch.)

with ice, elevation, analgesics, and irrigation and closure in some circumstances.

The objectives of surgical exploration and repair are testis salvage, prevention of infection, control of bleeding, and reduced convalescence. Scrotal incision is preferable in most cases. The tunica albuginea should be closed with small absorbable sutures after removal of necrotic and extruded seminiferous tubules. Even small defects in the tunica albuginea should be closed, since progressive swelling and intratesticular pressure can continue to extrude seminiferous tubules. Every attempt to salvage the testis should be performed; loss of capsule tissue may require removal of additional parenchyma to allow closure of the remaining tunica albuginea (Fig. 83–4). Significant intratesticular hematomas should be explored and drained even in the absence of testis rupture to prevent progressive pressure necrosis and atrophy, delayed exploration (40%), and orchiectomy (15%) (Cass and Luxenberg, 1988). Significant hematoceles should also be explored, regardless of imaging studies, since up to 80% are due to testis rupture (Vaccaro et al, 1986).

Penetrating scrotal injuries should be surgically explored to inspect for vascular and vasal injury. The vas deferens is injured in 7% to 9% of scrotal gunshot wounds (Gomez et al, 1993; Brandes et al, 1995). The injured vas should be ligated with nonabsorbable suture and delayed reconstruction performed if necessary. Approximately 30% of gunshot wounds injure both testes; consider exploration of the contralateral testis, depending on physical examination findings and the path of the projectile.

Outcome and Complications

Nonoperative management of testis rupture is frequently complicated by infection, atrophy, necrosis, and delayed orchiectomy. **Testis salvage rates exceed 90% with exploration and repair within 3 days of injury** (Del Villar et al, 1973; Schuster, 1982; Fournier et al, 1989; Cass and Luxenberg, 1991), **versus orchiectomy rates threefold to eightfold higher with conservative management and delayed surgery** (Cass and Luxenberg, 1991). Testis salvage rates with conservative management are as low as 33%, with delayed orchiectomy rates between 21% and 55% (Schuster, 1982; Cass and Luxenberg, 1991; McAleer and Kaplan, 1995). Approximately 45% of patients initially managed conservatively will ultimately undergo surgical exploration for pain, infection, and persistent hematoma (Del Villar et al, 1973; Cass and Luxenberg, 1991). Convalescence and time of return to normal activities are significantly reduced after early surgical repair.

Unlike blunt testis rupture, for which salvage rates are high, penetrating testis trauma is associated with gonad salvage in only 32% to 65% of cases (Bickel et al, 1990; Gomez et al, 1993; Brandes et al, 1995; Cline et al, 1998). Similar nonsalvage and orchiectomy rates have been reported with penetrating injuries in recent military conflict series (Hudolin and Hudolin, 2003). The overwhelming majority of surgical patients have adequate preservation of hormonal and fertility function (Kukadia et al, 1996). Sperm production has been documented in men with appropriately repaired bilateral testis rupture and bilateral penetrating injuries (Pohl et al, 1968; Brandes et al, 1995).

Urologists may be consulted for opinion and guidance with regard to boys with a solitary testis playing a contact sport. Fortunately, testis injuries are exceedingly rare in boys involved in individual or team contact sports and recreational activities (McAleer et al, 2002; Wan 2003a, 2003b). Parents should be appropriately counseled and a protective cup device recommended. The American Academy of Pediatrics Committee on Sports Medicine and Fitness (2001) recommended that many factors be considered regarding whether to allow a child with a solitary testis to play sports; their recommendation was an unqualified yes in this circumstance.

Genital Skin Loss

Etiology

Necrotizing gangrene due to polymicrobial infection in the genital area, or Fournier's gangrene, is the most common cause of extensive genital skin loss (McAninch et al, 1984). Loss is iatrogenic, caused by the necessity for acute débridement of necrotic genital skin when the patient is seen initially.

Penile skin loss can result from traction by mechanical devices, such as farm or industrial machinery, or by suction devices, such as vacuum cleaners. Because the penile tissue is loose areolar tissue, it is often torn free without damage to the underlying structures. Significant scrotal skin loss resulting from penetrating trauma is uncommon.

Penile burns, although rare, are often full thickness because the penile skin is so thin (Horton, 1990). Constricting bands placed on the penis can rarely result in significant skin loss, although a more common injury involves direct pressure necrosis under the band, which usually heals well with device removal alone.

Diagnosis and Initial Management

Although both cellulitis and Fournier's gangrene are commonly associated with significant genital edema and erythema, skin ischemia is the hallmark of Fournier's gangrene. Scrotal ultrasonography (Kane et al, 1996) and computed tomography (CT) may reveal subcutaneous air, a helpful indicator of necrotizing infection (Fig. 83–5).

In cases of Fournier's gangrene, multiple débridements are required during several weeks until active infection is controlled. Significant skin loss must be treated with wet-to-dry dressings until primary coverage is planned. Inspection at least daily by the surgical team is mandatory. **Suprapubic urinary diversion should be strongly considered for extensive injuries to simplify wound care and to prevent urethral complications related to prolonged catheterization.** Hyperbaric oxygen treatment has been advocated as an adjunctive measure to promote wound healing.

Genital burns are largely treated like other burns, with early resection of burn eschar and coverage with split-thickness skin grafts when possible. Partial-thickness skin loss or genital burns may be treated with silver sulfadiazine cream.

Penile Reconstruction

In selected uncircumcised patients, mobilization of redundant foreskin may allow primary closure of middle to distal penile skin loss (Horton, 1990). Scrotal rotation flaps can be used for more proximal defects if skin loss is limited, but the hair-bearing nature of scrotal skin risks an unacceptable cosmetic result. Local flaps, such as from the abdomen and thigh, can also be used but are cosmetically inferior to split-thickness skin grafts. Skin coverage with avulsed skin should be avoided because it often becomes necrotic.

Thick (0.010- to 0.015-inch), nonmeshed, split-thickness skin grafts (McAninch et al, 1984) **are preferred for extensive penile reconstruction.** Meshed grafts can be used but have a tendency toward contracture and are cosmetically less acceptable than unmeshed grafts. Grafts are usually harvested from the anterior thigh with a pneumatic dermatome. **If grafts are to be used, care must be taken to remove any subcoronal skin remaining after débridement. Lymphatic obstruction of this distal foreskin, if it is not excised, will result in circumferential lymphedema.** Skin grafts placed on the penile shaft never regain normal sensation (Horton, 1990), although sexual function is often preserved because of intact sensation in the skin of the glans.

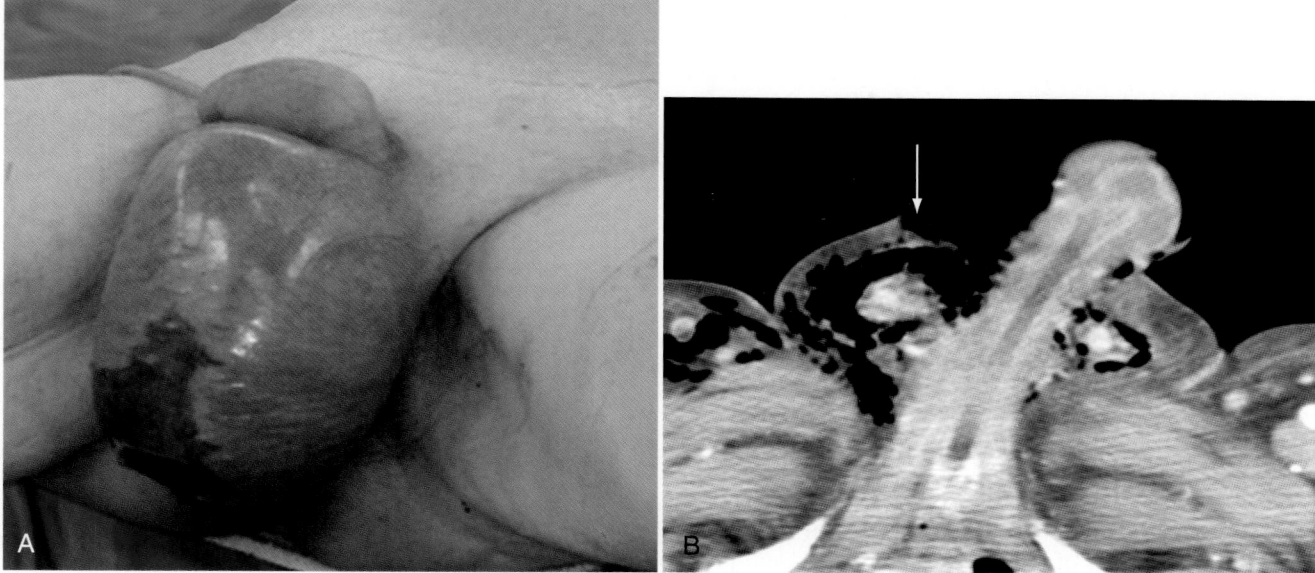

Figure 83–5. **A,** Large erythematous scrotum with central necrosis suggestive of necrotizing infection. **B,** CT reveals subcutaneous air in scrotum secondary to Fournier's gangrene.

Scrotal Reconstruction

Scrotal skin loss defects of up to 50% can often be closed directly. For extensive injuries, the testes may be placed in thigh pouches or treated with wet dressings for up to several weeks until reconstruction (Cummings and Boullier, 2000; Gomes et al, 2001). First, local skin flaps should be used to cover as much of the tissue defect as possible. Meshed split-thickness skin grafts are then employed for scrotal reconstruction. In addition to providing an excellent cosmetic result, meshing allows exudate to escape from the interstices, thus improving graft take. The spermatic cords are sewn together before grafting to prevent a bifid neoscrotum. The neoscrotum may initially appear unnaturally tight, but after 6 to 12 months, the testes serve as natural tissue expanders and eventually occupy a more natural, dependent position. Thigh flaps can be used to reconstruct the scrotum when the testes have been buried in the thighs after traumatic or surgical scrotal removal (Morey and McAninch, 1999). Fibrin sealant has proved useful as a tissue glue to promote healing and to reduce drainage during complex genital reconstruction cases (DeCastro and Morey, 2002).

BLADDER INJURIES
Etiology

The urinary bladder is generally protected from external trauma because of its deep location in the bony pelvis. Most blunt bladder injuries are the result of rapid-deceleration motor vehicle crashes, but they also occur with falls, crush injuries, assault, and blows to the lower abdomen. Whereas disruption of the bony pelvis tends to tear the bladder at its fascial attachments, bone fragments can also directly lacerate the organ. Bladder laceration may also arise from penetrating

trauma or various iatrogenic surgical complications and may occur spontaneously in patients with altered sensorium, such as those who are intoxicated or have neuropathic disease.

Bladder injures that occur with blunt external trauma are rarely isolated injuries; 80% to 94% of patients have significant associated nonurologic injuries (Cass, 1984; Volpe et al, 1999; Hsieh et al, 2002; Parry et al, 2003). Mortality in these multiply injured patients is primarily related to nonurologic injuries and ranges from 8% to 44% (Carroll and McAninch, 1984; Cass and Luxenberg, 1987; Corriere and Sandler, 1989; Volpe et al, 1999; Alli et al, 2003; Parry et al, 2003). **The most common associated injury is pelvic fracture, associated with 83% to 95% of bladder injuries** (Cass, 1989; Corriere and Sandler, 1989; Morey et al, 2001; Parry et al, 2003). Conversely, bladder injury has been reported to occur in only 5% to 10% of pelvic fractures (Cass, 1989; Peters, 1989; Aihara et al, 2002). Sudden force applied to a full bladder may result in a rapid rise in intravesical pressures and lead to rupture without pelvic fracture.

Penetrating bladder trauma is also associated with significant nonurologic injuries and mortality rate. Nearly half of all bladder injuries are iatrogenic (Dobrowolski et al, 2002); **obstetric and gynecologic complications are the most common etiology of bladder injuries during open surgery** (Dobrowolski et al, 2002; Gomez et al, 2004).

Diagnosis

Bladder contusions are due to mucosa or muscularis injury without loss of continuity and are probably underreported in trauma series. Extraperitoneal injury is usually associated with pelvic fracture. Intraperitoneal injuries can be associated with pelvic fracture but are more commonly due to penetrating injuries and burst injuries at the dome by sudden elevated pressures in a full bladder from a direct blow. Appropriate diagnosis and staging are important because of the marked influence on management.

Clinical Signs and Symptoms. **Bladder rupture does not occur as an isolated event in normal individuals. Most conscious patients have pronounced nonspecific symptoms, such as suprapubic or abdominal pain and the inability to void.** Associated abdominal and pelvic injuries may mask or confuse bladder symptoms. Physical signs include suprapubic tenderness, lower abdominal bruising, muscle guarding and rigidity, and diminished bowel sounds. Immediate catheterization should be performed because **the most reliable sign of bladder injury is gross hematuria, which is present in 93% to 100% of cases** (Iverson and Morey, 2001; Hsieh et al, 2002; Parry et al, 2003; Gomez et al, 2004). If blood is noted at the meatus or the catheter does not pass easily, retrograde urethrography should be performed immediately because concomitant bladder and urethra injuries occur in 10% to 29% of patients (Cass, 1989; Dobrowolski et al, 2002).

Radiographic Imaging. Imaging of the bladder should be performed on the basis of suspicion, examination, and presence of hematuria or pelvic fracture. **The absolute indication for immediate cystography after blunt external trauma is gross hematuria associated with pelvic fracture; approximately 29% of patients presenting with this combination of findings have bladder rupture** (Morey et al, 2001). Relative indications for cystography after blunt trauma include gross hematuria without a pelvic fracture, microhematuria with pelvic fracture, and isolated microscopic hematuria (Morey et al, 2001). **The diagnosis of bladder rupture is extremely low in these atypical groups (e.g., 0.6% in patients with pelvic fracture and microhematuria), but the index of suspicion should be raised by associated clinical indicators of bladder injury** (see Key Points: Clinical Indicators of Bladder Injury). **Conversely, penetrating injuries of the buttock, pelvis, or lower abdomen with *any* degree of hematuria warrant cystography.**

tration of the contrast agent, a full bladder anteroposterior film, and a drainage film. Posterior extravasation of contrast material can be missed without a drainage film. Significant bladder distention is required to visualize small tears. False-negative studies have been reported with retrograde instillation of only 250 mL (Peters, 1989; Morey and Carroll, 1997). Although hematuria and mechanism of injury mandate consideration of upper tract imaging studies, upper and lower urinary tract injuries are almost never coincident (0.4%) (Cass and Luxenberg, 1990).

Dense, flame-shaped collection of contrast material in the pelvis is characteristic of extraperitoneal extravasation (Fig. 83–6). Depending on fascial integrity, contrast material may extend beyond the confines of the pelvis and be visualized in the retroperitoneum, scrotum, phallus, thigh, and anterior abdominal wall. The amount of extravasation is not always proportional to the extent of bladder injury. Intraperitoneal extravasation is identified when contrast material outlines loops of bowel.

Since CT is now routinely used to assess trauma patients, CT cystography is now frequently selected as a more efficient means than plain film cystography to assess the bladder. CT cystography is as accurate and reliable as plain film cystography to evaluate suspected bladder injury (Fig. 83–7), as long as the bladder is filled in retrograde fashion with contrast material diluted to 2% to 4% (6:1 with saline) to a volume of 350 to 400 mL (Peng et al, 1999; Hsieh et al, 2002). Drainage films are not required after CT cystography since the retrovesical space can be well visualized (Morey and Carroll, 1997). Dilution of the contrast material is mandatory because undiluted contrast material is so dense that the CT quality is compromised. Clamping the urethral catheter to allow antegrade distention of the bladder is inadequate for diagnosis of bladder rupture. Conventional abdominal CT imaging of the trauma patient may show findings suggestive of bladder injury

KEY POINTS: CLINICAL INDICATORS OF BLADDER INJURY

- Suprapubic pain or tenderness
- Free intraperitoneal fluid on CT or ultrasound examination
- Inability to void or low urine output
- Clots in urine
- Signs of perineal or genital trauma
- Unresponsive, intoxicated, or altered sensorium
- Preexisting bladder disease or urologic surgery
- Abdominal distention or ileus

Retrograde or stress cystography is nearly 100% accurate for bladder injury if it is performed appropriately. The bladder should be filled in cooperative and conscious patients to a sense of discomfort, otherwise to 350 mL. A three-film technique is recommended, including an image before adminis-

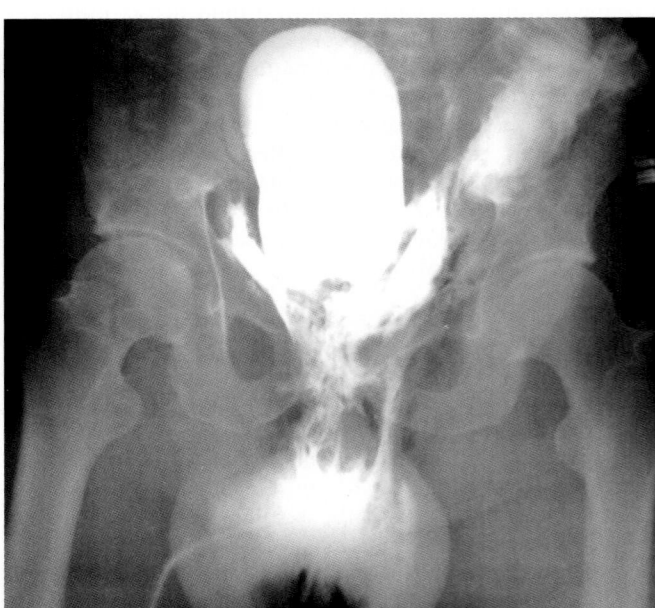

Figure 83–6. Plain film cystogram reveals extraperitoneal bladder rupture with extravasation into scrotum. Surgical exploration revealed anterior bladder neck and prostatic urethral laceration.

but is not considered to be adequate for bladder evaluation alone (Mee et al, 1987; Udekwu et al, 1996; Hsieh et al, 2002).

Management

The usual treatment of uncomplicated extraperitoneal bladder ruptures, when conditions are ideal, is conservative management with urethral catheter drainage alone (Fig. 83–8). A large-bore Foley catheter (22 French) should be used to ensure adequate drainage. Cystography is recommended before catheter removal 14 days after injury. Antimicrobial agents are instituted on the day of injury and continued until 3 days after the urinary catheter is removed.

Several authors (Cass, 1989; Kotkin and Koch, 1995) have reported fewer complications, such as fistula, failure to heal, clot retention, and sepsis, with open repair (5% overall) versus conservative management (12% overall). **For this reason,**

blunt extraperitoneal injuries with any complicating features warrant immediate open repair to prevent complications such as fistula, abscess, and prolonged leak (see Key Points: Indications for Immediate Repair of Bladder Injury). **If a stable patient is undergoing exploratory laparotomy for other associated injuries, it is prudent to repair the extraperitoneal rupture;** the anterior bladder wall is entered, and the tear is closed intravesically with a single layer of absorbable suture. The perivesical pelvic hematoma should not be disturbed. When internal fixation of pelvic fractures is performed, concomitant bladder repair is recommended because urine leakage from the injured bladder onto the orthopedic fixative hardware is prevented, thereby reducing the risk of hardware infection.

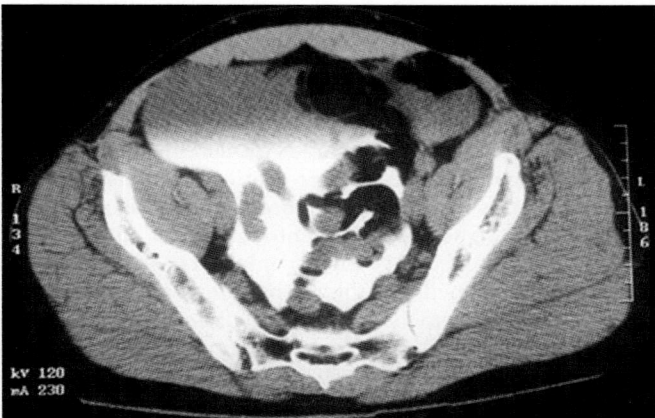

Figure 83–7. CT cystogram demonstrates contrast material surrounding loops of bowel consistent with intraperitoneal bladder rupture.

KEY POINTS: INDICATIONS FOR IMMEDIATE REPAIR OF BLADDER INJURY

- Intraperitoneal injury from external trauma
- Penetrating or iatrogenic nonurologic injury
- Inadequate bladder drainage or clots in urine
- Bladder neck injury
- Rectal or vaginal injury
- Open pelvic fracture
- Pelvic fracture requiring open reduction and internal fixation
- Selected stable patients undergoing laparotomy for other reasons
- Bone fragments projecting into bladder

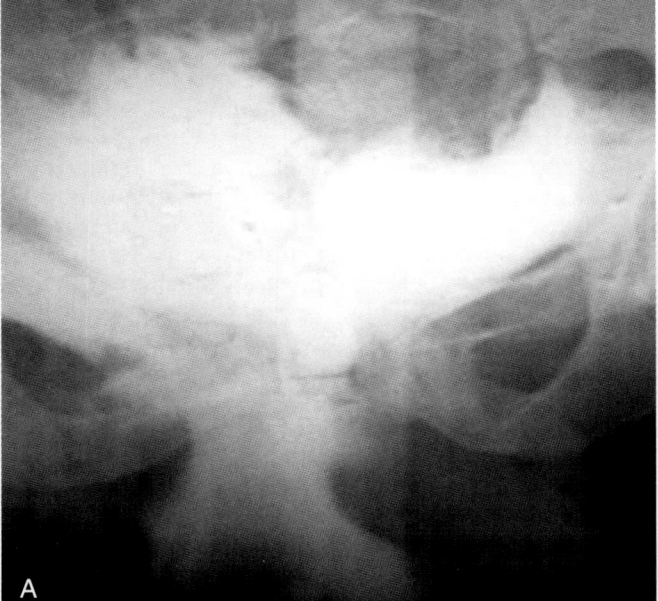

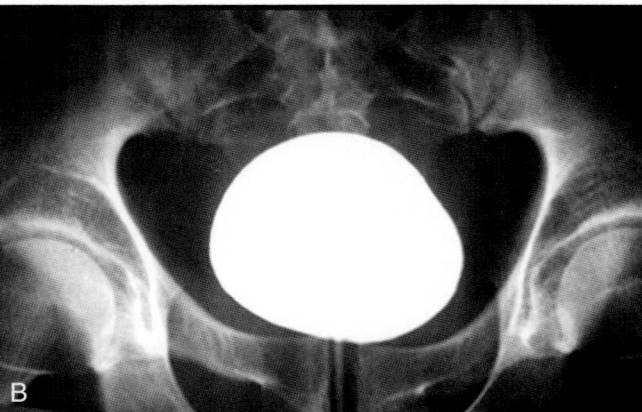

Figure 83–8. **A,** Dense flame-shaped pattern of contrast agent extravasation in pelvis due to extraperitoneal bladder rupture. **B,** Repeated cystogram in same patient after 2 weeks of catheter drainage shows completely healed bladder.

All penetrating or intraperitoneal injuries resulting from external trauma should be managed by immediate operative repair. These injuries are often larger than suggested on cystography and are unlikely to heal spontaneously, and continued leak of urine causes a chemical peritonitis. When bladder injuries are explored, the ureteral orifices should be inspected for clear efflux, or ureteral integrity should be ensured by intravenous administration of indigo carmine or methylene blue or retrograde passage of a ureteral catheter. Any injury close to or involving the ureteral orifice or intramural ureter should be stented or reimplanted. A perivesical drain should be employed. In patients with intraperitoneal rupture, antimicrobials are administered for 3 days, in the perioperative period only. If the bladder has been repaired, a cystogram is obtained 7 to 10 days after surgery (Corriere and Sandler, 1989). **Several studies have now shown that suprapubic tube drainage provides no benefit over urethral catheter drainage alone** (Volpe et al, 1999; Alli et al, 2003; Parry et al, 2003). When concurrent rectal or vaginal injuries exist, the organ walls should be separated, overlapping suture lines avoided, and every attempt made to interpose viable tissue in between the repaired structures. Fibrin sealant injected over the bladder wall closure may help reduce complications when intervening tissue is unavailable (Evans et al, 2003).

Outcomes and Complications

The prompt diagnosis and appropriate management of bladder injuries allow excellent results and minimal morbidity. Serious complications are usually associated with delayed diagnosis or treatment due to misdiagnosis, delayed presentation, or complex injuries resulting from devastating pelvic trauma. Unrecognized bladder injuries may manifest as acidosis, azotemia, fever and sepsis, low urine output, peritonitis, ileus, urinary ascites, or respiratory difficulties. Unrecognized bladder neck, vaginal, and rectal injury associated with the bladder rupture can result in incontinence, fistula, stricture, and difficult delayed major reconstruction. Severe pelvic fractures may cause a transient or permanent neurologic injury and result in voiding difficulties despite an adequate bladder repair.

URETHRAL INJURIES
Posterior Urethra

Etiology

Urethral disruption injuries typically occur in conjunction with multisystem trauma from vehicular accidents, falls, or industrial accidents. Pubic diastasis, localized pubic rami fractures, or more complex pelvic fractures may be associated with urethral disruption. **"Straddle fractures" involving all four pubic rami** (Fig. 83–9), **open fractures, and fractures resulting in both vertical and rotational pelvic instability are associated with the highest risk of urologic injury** (Mundy, 1996; Koraitim, 1999; Brandes and Borelli, 2001). Urethral injury has been reported to occur in approximately 10% of males and up to 6% of females sustaining pelvic fractures (Koraitim et al, 1999). Girls younger than 17 years have a higher risk of urethral injury compared with women, perhaps owing to greater compressibility of the pelvic bones (Hemal, 1999).

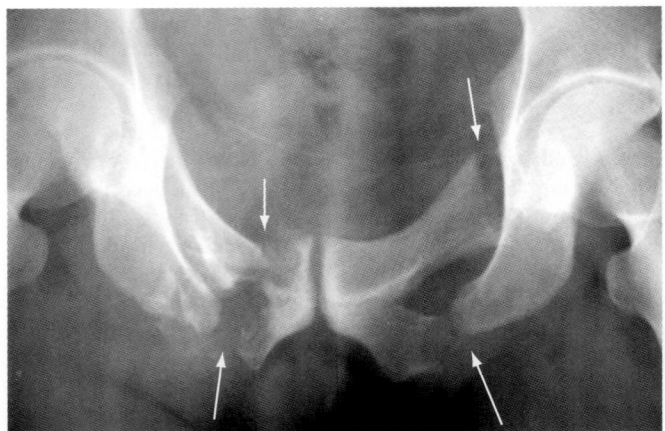

Figure 83–9. Anteroposterior film of the pubis shows a straddle fracture involving all four pubic rami in a patient with a posterior urethral disruption in whom initial perineal posterior urethroplasty failed because of severe bone distortion. Reconstruction was successfully performed by an abdominoperineal technique.

Because the posterior urethra is fixed at both the urogenital diaphragm and the puboprostatic ligaments, the bulbomembranous junction is more vulnerable to injury during pelvic fracture (Colapinto and McCallum, 1977; Brandes and Borelli, 2001). Endoscopic and urodynamic evaluation has confirmed that the membranous urethral sphincter complex tends to be vertically avulsed intact from the underlying bulb and to remain functional (Mundy, 1997; Andrich and Mundy, 2001). In children, injuries are more likely to extend proximally to the bladder neck because of the rudimentary nature of the prostate (Devine et al, 1989; Al-Rifaei et al, 1991; Boone et al, 1992).

Diagnosis

Examination. Urethral disruption is heralded by the triad of blood at the meatus, inability to urinate, and palpably full bladder. Because these and other classic findings such as a "high-riding" prostate or a "butterfly" perineal hematoma may frequently be absent (Sandler and Corriere, 1989), urethral disruption is often first detected when a urethral catheter cannot be placed by the emergency department trauma team or when it is misplaced into pelvic hematoma. Pelvic hematoma often obscures the prostatic contour, resulting in a misdiagnosis of impalpable prostate (Koraitim et al, 1996). Females with urethral injuries present with vulvar edema and blood at the vaginal introitus, thus indicating the need for careful vaginal examination in all female patients with pelvic fracture (Perry and Husmann, 1992).

Urethrography. When blood at the urethral meatus is discovered, an immediate retrograde urethrogram should be performed to rule out urethral injury (Fig. 83–10). A small-bore urethral catheter (16 French) is placed unlubricated 1 cm into the fossa navicularis, and the balloon is filled with 1 cm of water to achieve a snug fit (Sandler and Corriere, 1989). Alternatively, a Brodney clamp or rolled gauze bandage can be used to provide penile traction. Patients should be placed in an oblique or lateral decubitus position, and it is preferable to

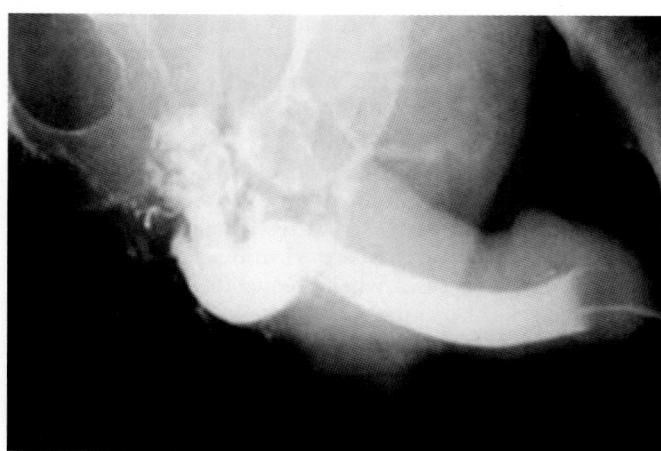

Figure 83–10. Retrograde urethrogram in pelvic fracture patient shows complete disruption of posterior urethra.

perform the study under fluorography when it is available; 25 mL of contrast material is injected gently by a 60-mL catheter-tip syringe, and the film is taken during injection. **Direct inspection by urethroscopy is suggested in lieu of urethrography in females with suspected urethral injury** (Perry and Husmann, 1992; Koraitim, 1999).

Initial Management

Suprapubic Cystostomy. Immediate suprapubic tube placement remains the standard of care. This is best accomplished through a small infraumbilical incision, which allows inspection and repair of the bladder and proper placement of a large-bore catheter at the bladder dome. Trocar suprapubic tube placement is reasonable when the bladder is distended and no other indications for surgery exist. However, during the long term, these smaller "punch" suprapubic tubes are more likely to become obstructed with debris or to fracture, requiring replacement.

Increasingly, patients with pelvic ring fracture undergo early surgical fixation by orthopedists to decrease bleeding, improve healing, and speed ambulation (Connor et al, 2003). **Although orthopedists frequently suggest that a suprapubic tube not be placed if anterior pubic hardware is used in pelvic fracture repair because of concern that the suprapubic tube will lead to hardware infection** (Patterson, 1995), **we and others** (Borelli and Brandes, 2004) **have found that this complication is extremely rare and that cystostomy can be safely used.** However, the catheter should be placed high in the bladder and tunneled through the skin as high as possible on the lower abdominal midline to keep the tube away from the plated symphysis; this will also facilitate prostatic apex identification at the time of reconstruction.

Primary Realignment. An attempt at primary realignment of the distraction with a urethral catheter is reasonable in stable patients (Elliott and Barrett, 1997), either acutely or within several days of injury. We prefer a simple technique consisting of passage of a coudé catheter antegrade through cystostomy, then tying it to another that can be drawn back into the bladder. A variety of more elaborate approaches have

been described (Cohen et al, 1991; Follis et al, 1992; Herschorn et al, 1992; Routt et al, 1996; Elliott and Barrett, 1997; Londergan et al, 1997; Porter et al, 1997; Rehman et al, 1998; Asci et al, 1999; Jepson et al, 1999), although prolonged endoscopic realignment attempts may risk infection of the pelvic hematoma (Morey et al, 1999).

When the urethral catheter is removed after 4 to 6 weeks, it is imperative to retain a suprapubic catheter because most patients will, despite realignment, develop posterior urethral stenosis. If the patient voids satisfactorily through the urethra, the suprapubic catheter can be removed 7 to 14 days later. Placement of a catheter across a urethral disruption injury may rarely allow healing without stricture (Elliott and Barrett, 1997), but in most patients, mild stenosis 1 to 2 cm in length develops (Kotkin and Koch, 1996; Routt et al, 1996; Asci et al, 1999). Those managed with suprapubic tubes alone virtually always (96%) develop complete stenosis requiring posterior urethroplasty (Herschorn et al, 1992; Kotkin and Koch, 1996). Whereas realignment may not prevent symptomatic stenosis, it may ease the difficulty of open posterior urethroplasty by bringing the prostate and urethra closer.

Incomplete urethral tears are best treated by stenting with a urethral catheter. We and others (Al-Ali and Husain, 1983; Mundy, 1991; Herschorn et al, 1992; Kotkin and Koch, 1996) **have not seen any evidence that a gentle attempt to place a urethral catheter can convert an incomplete into a complete transection.** Caution is warranted because misplacement outside the bladder is distinctly possible; assurance of adequate positioning is imperative. In no case is traction used after urethral catheter placement; it is unnecessary and may cause incontinence (Asci et al, 1999).

Complex Injuries

In cases of female urethral disruption related to pelvic fracture, most authorities suggest immediate primary repair, or at least urethral realignment over a catheter, to avoid subsequent urethrovaginal fistulas or urethral obliteration (Koraitim et al, 1996; Dorairajan et al, 2004). **Concomitant vaginal lacerations must also be closed acutely to prevent vaginal stenosis. Delayed reconstruction is problematic because the female urethra is too short (about 4 cm) to be amenable to anastomotic repair when it becomes embedded in scar** (Podesta, 2001).

Some authors advocate open exploration with realignment in cases of high-riding or "pie-in-the-sky" bladder or associated bladder neck tear in males (Webster et al, 1983). Associated rectal injuries require open exploration, repair, irrigation, and placement of drains. Immediate suture reconstruction of posterior urethral disruption injuries is not recommended because of its association with unsatisfactory outcomes, such as impotence and incontinence, stricture formation, and operative blood loss (Webster et al, 1983).

Delayed Reconstruction

In posterior urethral disruption, the rupture defect between the two severed ends fills with scar tissue, resulting in a complete lack of urethral continuity. This separation is not a stricture; it is a true urethral rupture defect filled with fibrosis. **At 3 months, scar tissue at the urethral disruption site is stable enough to allow posterior urethroplasty to be undertaken safely, provided that associated injuries are stabilized and**

the patient is ambulatory. Suprapubic cystostomy drainage should be maintained until the associated injuries have healed and the patient can be appropriately positioned for the reconstructive procedure.

Preoperative Evaluation. Before the reconstructive procedure is planned, imaging studies are necessary to delineate the characteristics of the urethral rupture defect. A cystogram and retrograde urethrogram should be obtained simultaneously (the so-called up-and-down-o-gram, Fig. 83–11). The patient is asked to attempt to void with the bladder filled. Ideally, the prostatic urethra should be visualized as the bladder neck opens, enabling measurement of the distance between the severed urethral ends. Should the bladder neck not open, flexible or rigid endoscopy should be used to supplement radiographic imaging (Mundy, 1997). The appearance of the bladder neck on preoperative imaging, either open or closed, does not correlate well with bladder neck behavior postoperatively (Mundy, 1997), thus making it difficult to predict bladder neck incompetence or obstruction. Magnetic reso-

nance imaging has been used successfully to define defect length and to determine the extent and direction of urethral dislocation (Dixon et al, 1992), and it may provide valuable information about bone anatomy in complex or reoperative cases (Morey et al, 1999).

Endoscopic Treatments. Endoscopic treatments such as direct-vision internal urethrotomy are best reserved for selected short urethral strictures, such as distraction injuries for which early catheterization achieved urethral continuity. In most cases, when preoperative evaluation indicates defects 1 cm or longer, endoscopic procedures such as cutting through the pelvic scar to provide a channel between the two ends of the avulsed urethra ("cut-to-the-light" procedure) are ineffective and have no advantage other than reduced operative time (Levine and Wessels, 2001); moreover, aggressive endoscopic treatments have been associated with complications such as coring of a false passage that inadvertently bypasses the bladder neck (Turner-Warwick, 1989). Cut-to-the-light or similar core-through procedures typically

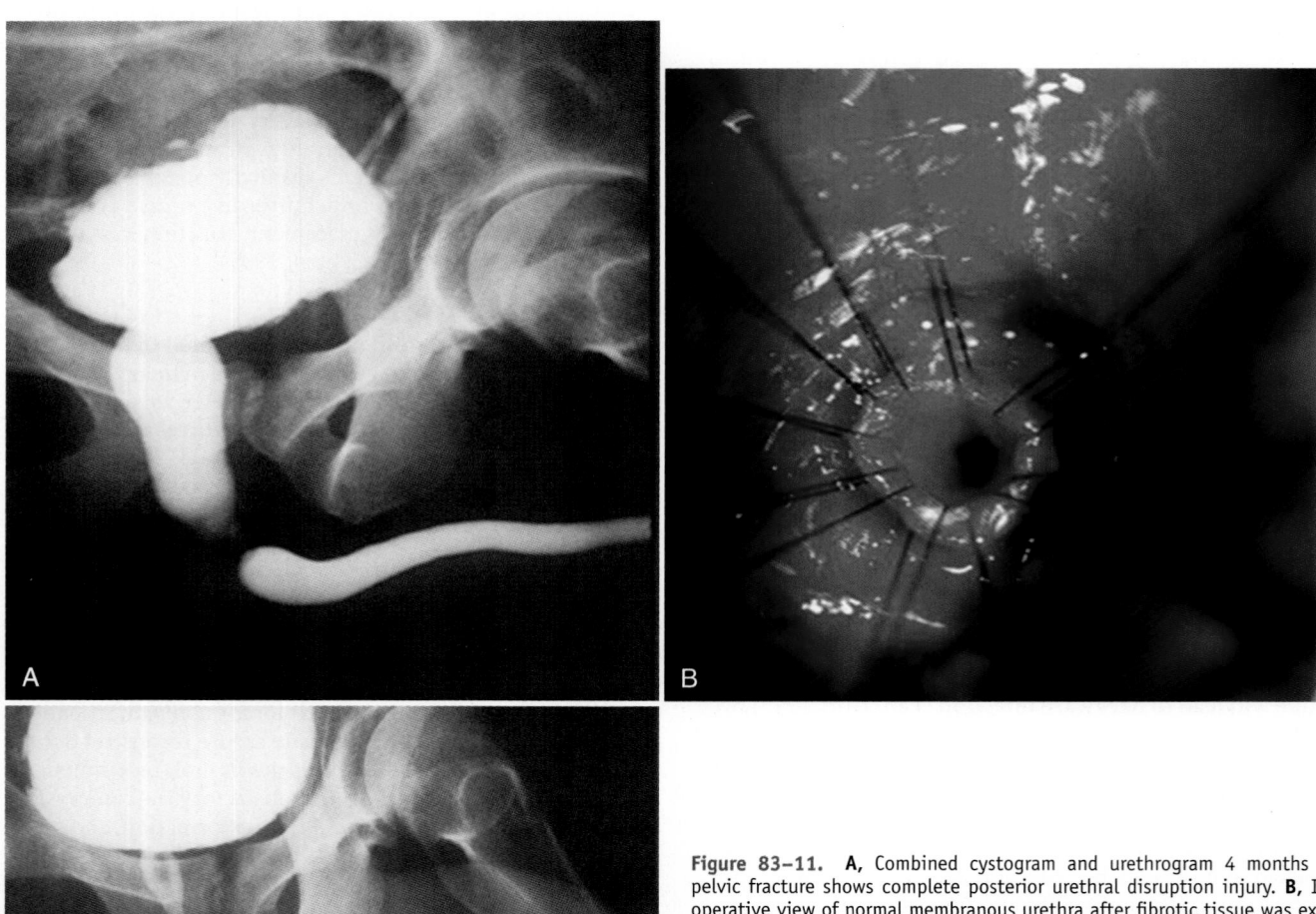

Figure 83–11. A, Combined cystogram and urethrogram 4 months after pelvic fracture shows complete posterior urethral disruption injury. **B,** Intraoperative view of normal membranous urethra after fibrotic tissue was excised during perineal bulbomembranous urethroplasty. **C,** Postoperative appearance reveals normal urethral caliber.

require multiple urethrotomies or long-term dilation by the patient or urologist to keep the channel open.

Surgical Reconstruction. Open posterior urethroplasty through a perineal anastomotic approach is the treatment of choice for most urethral distraction injuries because it definitively cures the patient without the need for multiple procedures. Once preoperative studies have determined that the prostatic urethral apex can be reached by a perineal approach, the patient is placed in the high lithotomy position and a midline or lambda-shaped incision is made. The bulbar urethra is freed and mobilized from the site of urethral rupture to the midscrotum. The scar tissue of the urethral rupture defect is excised, and the prostatic urethra is identified at the apex of the prostate. **Care must be taken to carefully and meticulously excise all fibrotic tissue from the proximal urethral margin until at least a 28 French bougie passes without resistance** (Turner-Warwick, 1989; Morey and McAninch, 1997b). The bulbar urethra is then anastomosed in a tension-free manner to the prostatic urethra.

In 95% of patients, posterior urethral anastomosis will be successfully achieved through a perineal approach alone (Carr and Webster, 1997). Adjunctive maneuvers such as corporal separation, inferior pubectomy, and corporal rerouting have been routinely implemented if direct anastomosis proves difficult (Mundy, 1997; Flynn et al, 2003); others have found these maneuvers to be necessary only rarely (Morey and McAninch, 1997a; Rosenstein and Jordan, 2003; MacDonald and Santucci, 2005).

Total removal of the symphysis pubis, first reported by Pierce in 1962, has been recommended when severe injuries result in complicating features such as fistula or marked displacement or retropubic fixation of the prostate (Netto, 1985; McAninch, 1989; Asci et al, 1999). **Alternatively, a combined abdominoperineal approach (with or without partial pubectomy) has proved helpful in cases of severe fibrosis, previous failed anastomotic urethroplasty, or associated bladder neck injury and in pediatric cases** (Waterhouse, 1976; Al-Rifaei et al, 1991; Koraitim, 2003, 2005). It is important to limit the lithotomy time to 5 hours or less to prevent lower extremity complications (Anema et al, 2000) when any complex urethral reconstruction is undertaken.

Complications

Some degree of impotence is noted in 30% to 60% of patients with pelvic fracture and urethral distraction injury (Corriere et al, 1994; Routt et al, 1996; Elliott and Barrett, 1997; Asci et al, 1999). However, the complications of the original pelvic injury are difficult to differentiate from the complications of attempts to repair urethral and bladder injuries. Several studies have shown that patients treated with primary endoscopic realignment have rates of impotence and incontinence similar to those of patients who have had either no treatment or open reconstruction (Kotkin and Koch, 1996; Asci et al, 1999; Koraitim, 2005). **These studies support the conclusion that these complications are the result of the injury itself and not of the treatment** (Follis et al, 1992; Herschorn et al, 1992; Elliott and Barrett, 1997; Porter et al, 1997; Corriere, 2001). Some patients who become impotent after injury spontaneously recover erectile function

a year or two later (Turner-Warwick, 1989; Morey and McAninch, 1997a).

Most patients who become impotent as a result of pelvic fracture have some degree of arterial insufficiency (Armenakas, 1993; Matthews, 1995). **Because impotent patients may be more vulnerable to restenosis after posterior urethroplasty as a result of bulbar urethral ischemia, some experts have suggested that "at-risk" patients undergo preoperative penile arterial duplex Doppler studies to identify candidates suitable for initial penile revascularization** (Rosenstein and Jordan, 2003; Matthews et al, 1995). Overall rates of incontinence, anejaculation, and areflexic bladder are low (2% to 4%) (Corriere et al, 1994; Elliott and Barrett, 1997; Asci et al, 1999) and also tend to be secondary to the original injury.

After posterior urethroplasty, 12% to 15% of patients have recurrent stenosis at the anastomosis (Mundy, 1996; Morey and McAninch, 1997a). Fortunately, endoscopic treatment (e.g., with direct-vision internal urethrotomy) is often successful in this setting because the majority of fibrotic tissue has been eliminated (Netto et al, 1989).

Anterior Urethra

In contrast to posterior urethral distraction, anterior injuries are most often isolated (Kiracofe et al, 1975). The majority occur after straddle injury and involve the bulbar urethra, which is susceptible to compressive injury because of its fixed location beneath the pubis. A smaller percentage are the result of direct penetrating injury to the penis.

As with posterior urethral injury, a high index of suspicion must be maintained in all patients with blunt or penetrating trauma in the urogenital region, and urethrography should be performed in any case of suspected urethral injury (Husmann et al, 1993). Clinical signs of anterior urethral injuries include blood at the meatus, perineal hematoma, gross hematuria, and urinary retention. In severe trauma, Buck's fascia may be disrupted, resulting in blood and urinary extravasation into the scrotum. **The primary morbidity of straddle injury is urethral stricture, which may become symptomatic up to 10 years later** (Park and McAninch, 2004).

Initial Management

Armenakas and McAninch (1996) proposed a simple, practical classification scheme dividing anterior urethral injuries on the basis of radiographic findings into contusion, incomplete disruption, and complete disruption. Contusions and incomplete injuries can be treated with urethral catheter diversion alone. **Initial suprapubic cystostomy is the treatment of choice for major straddle injuries involving the urethra** (Park and McAninch, 2004).

Primary surgical repair is recommended for low-velocity urethral gunshot injuries; catheter alignment alone is associated with a far worse stricture rate (Husmann et al, 1993). Débridement of the corpus spongiosum after trauma should be limited since corporal blood supply is usually robust, enabling spontaneous healing of most contused areas (Kiracofe et al, 1975; Husmann et al, 1993). Initial suprapubic urinary diversion is recommended after high-velocity gunshot wounds to the urethra, followed by delayed reconstruction.

Delayed Reconstruction

Before any planned procedure, a retrograde urethrogram and voiding cystourethrogram should be obtained to define the site and length of the obliterated urethra clearly. Urethral ultrasound examination may help delineate the length and severity of stricture. Retrograde injection of saline combined with antegrade bladder filling will fill the urethra proximally and distally, and a 10-MHz sonogram will clearly define the nondistensible segment to be excised. Dense fibrous tissue from trauma often results in significant shadowing (Morey and McAninch, 2000).

Anastomotic urethroplasty is the procedure of choice in the totally obliterated bulbar urethra after a straddle injury. The typical scar is 1.5 to 2 cm long and should be completely excised. The proximal and distal urethra can be mobilized for a tension-free, end-to-end anastomosis. This is a highly successful procedure in more than 95% of cases (Santucci et al, 2002).

Endoscopic incision through the scar tissue of an obliterated urethra is a hopeless procedure and uniformly fails. Partial urethral narrowing can initially be treated by endoscopic incision with higher success. It is now recognized that repeated urethrotomy and dilation is neither clinically effective nor cost-effective for the treatment of urethral strictures (Greenwell et al, 2004). Further, patients who have had repeated endoscopic procedures are also more likely to require complex reconstructive procedures such as grafts (Park and McAninch, 2004). Open repair should be delayed at least several weeks after instrumentation to allow the urethra to stabilize. Finally, UroLume stents are contraindicated in the setting of traumatic urethral strictures (Wilson et al, 2002).

SUGGESTED READINGS

Andrich DE, Mundy AR: The nature of urethral injury in cases of pelvic fracture urethral trauma. J Urol 2001;165:1492-1495.

Koraitim MM: Pelvic fracture urethral injuries: The unresolved controversy. J Urol 1999;161:1433-1441.

Morey AF, Iverson AJ, Swan A, et al: Bladder rupture after blunt trauma: Guidelines for diagnostic imaging. J Trauma 2001;51:683-686.

Morey AF, Metro MJ, Carney KJ, et al: Consensus on genitourinary trauma. BJU Int 2004;94:507-515.

84 Lower Urinary Tract Calculi

KHAI-LINH V. HO, MD • JOSEPH W. SEGURA, MD

Urinary tract stones have afflicted mankind for many centuries. One of the earliest examples of a urinary calculus was found in the pelvis of a mummified 16-year-old boy of predynastic (circa 7000-3100 BC) Egypt (Goldman et al, 1990). Although bladder calculi were uncommon at the time, the prevalence increased such that lithotomy was mentioned in the Hippocratic Oath, and by the 19th century, bladder calculi accounted for 80% of urolithiasis in Europe (Streem, 1987). Some historical figures who suffered from vesical calculi include King Leopold I of Belgium, Napoleon Bonaparte, Emperor Napoleon III, Peter the Great, Louis XIV, George IV, Oliver Cromwell, Benjamin Franklin, Chief Justice John Marshall, Sir Francis Bacon, Sir Isaac Newton, the physicians Harvey and Boerhaave, and the anatomist Scarpa.

BLADDER CALCULI

In the lower urinary tract, most calculi occur in the bladder. Vesical calculi can be classified as migrant, primary idiopathic, or secondary calculi, which include calculi related to urinary stasis, infection, and foreign bodies.

Migrant Calculi

Migrant bladder calculi are formed in the upper tracts, pass into the bladder, and are retained there. Most calculi that migrate out of the ureter into the bladder are smaller than 1 cm and, in adults, are easily passed per urethra. Calculi that are retained are associated with a small bladder outlet (children) or bladder outlet obstruction. Retained upper tract stones may grow to a large size in the bladder (Becher et al, 1978). The primary etiology of the calculus is related to the metabolic factors associated with renal calculi formation.

Primary Idiopathic (Endemic) Calculi

Endemic bladder stones form in children in the absence of obstruction, local disease, neurologic lesion, or known primary infection. The incidence has decreased with industrialization and affluence, such that it is rare in developed countries. However, endemic bladder calculi remain common in infants and children of lower socioeconomic background in North Africa and the Middle and Far East (Van Reen, 1976). They are uncommon in Central and South Africa, Central and South America, and the Pacific Islands (Valyasevi and Van Reen, 1968). Similarities are seen in the afflicted children of these areas. Stone formation results from dietary and nutritional deficiencies. **Children in these areas are dependent on a cereal-based diet that is lacking in animal proteins, especially cow's milk** (Anderson, 1962). **Cereals commonly used are whole wheat flour, millet, and rice.** Less than 25% of the total protein intake is of animal origin (Teotia and Teotia, 1977). Compared with cow's milk, human breast milk and foods such as polished rice and cereals are low in phosphorus (Anderson, 1962; Thalut et al, 1976). This dietary phosphate deficiency leads to low urine phosphate excretion and high peaks of ammonia excretion (Brockis et al, 1981). Chronic dehydration, excessive protein or oxalate consumption, high endogenous oxalate production, and deficiencies in vitamins A, B_1, and B_6 and magnesium have been associated with stone formation. These conditions act to decrease urine production, acidify the urine, and increase the concentration of uric acid and calcium oxalate excretion, leading to precipitation of insoluble salts in the urine (Valyasevi and Dhanamitta, 1974; Van Reen, 1980; Brockis et al, 1981; Pak, 1988; Lerner et al, 1989). **Endemic bladder calculi are most commonly composed of ammonium acid urate alone or in combination with calcium oxalate,** but many also contain calcium phosphate (Brockis et al, 1981).

Children younger than 10 years are typically affected, with the peak incidence around 3 years (Teotia and Teotia, 1990). The cloudy, sandy urine produced by children in endemic areas indicates the early stages of stone formation. Girls are able to pass most of the debris through their short, nontortuous urethra, but boys may retain these potential nidi. This accounts for the male-to-female ratio of 10:1 for endemic bladder calculi (Halsted, 1977; Teotia and Teotia, 1990). Common symptoms are vague abdominal pain, hypogastric discomfort, interruption of the urinary stream, and pulling

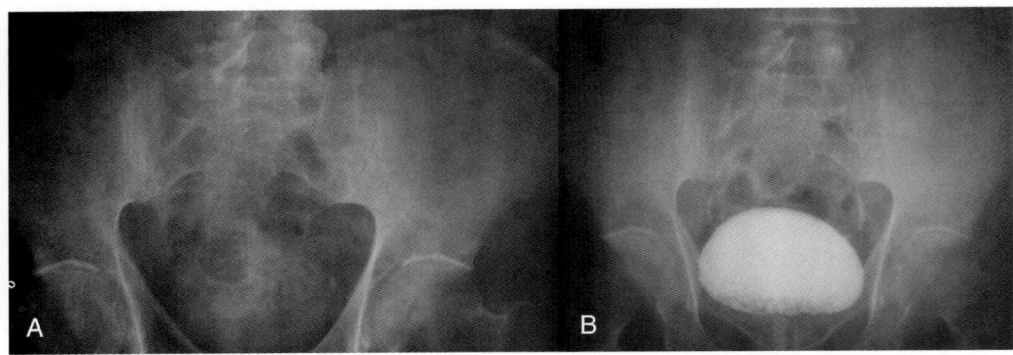

Figure 84–1. Radiographic appearance of uric acid bladder calculi. **A,** Multiple low densities are seen in the pelvis on the scout film. **B,** The filling defects (calculi) settle to the bladder base on the upright excretory urogram.

and rubbing of the penis. Some children complain of dysuria, frequency, suprapubic pain, and dribbling. The sudden onset of symptoms of urinary tract obstruction is rare. Rectal prolapse or conjunctival hemorrhages may be seen in association with straining to void. The duration of symptoms ranges from a few days to several years. Symptoms caused by mechanical obstruction or irritation and cystitis may be mistaken for an infectious or inflammatory process. Small calculi may be passed with hydration, antispasmodics, and analgesics, but most cases will require surgical intervention. **Endemic bladder calculi are usually solitary and rarely recur once removed. A mixed cereal diet with milk supplements reduces the incidence of endemic bladder calculi** (Teotia and Teotia, 1990).

Secondary Bladder Calculi

Progress in nutrition and diet has decreased the incidence of bladder calculi; it is now predominantly a disease of adults and accounts for approximately 5% of urinary calculi in developed countries (Takasaki et al, 1979; Yoshida, 1990). **These secondary bladder calculi are most often related to urinary stasis or recurrent urinary tract infection due to bladder outlet obstruction or neurogenic bladder dysfunction.** Patients with intestinal mucosa or foreign bodies in the urinary tract are also at risk for development of calculi (Abol-Enein, 2001).

Calculi Related to Bladder Outlet Obstruction

Bladder outlet obstruction may be an etiologic factor in more than 75% of bladder calculi cases (Otnes, 1983). Bladder calculi associated with outlet obstruction primarily affect men older than 50 years and are most often related to benign prostatic hyperplasia (Drach, 1992). However, only 1% to 2% of men undergoing surgery for benign prostatic hyperplasia will have bladder calculi (McConnell et al, 1994). **Calculi resulting from obstruction may be composed of uric acid** (Fig. 84–1), **calcium oxalate** (Fig. 84–2), **or magnesium ammonium phosphate** (Fig. 84–3) **if infected.** In a review of 652 cases of vesical calculi, Smith and O'Flynn (1975) reported that 92% occurred in men, and 80% of the cases were found in patients older than 50 years. **Incomplete bladder emptying was identified as the greatest single factor in vesical stone formation, and prostatic hypertrophy was the most frequent condition causing incomplete emptying.** The major components of vesical calculi were phosphate (59.4%), oxalate (25.6%), and uric acid (5.4%). In a more recent review of 100

patients with vesical calculi, Douenias and associates (1991) found that 80% occurred in patients older than 60 years, and all but two patients were male. Eighty-eight cases were attributed to some form of outlet obstruction. Fifty percent of the patients had uric acid calculi; this was attributed to the diet of the mostly Jewish population they served. Other causes of outlet obstruction are urethral stricture, bladder neck contracture, neurogenic bladder dysfunction, and, in women, urogenital prolapse. No definite correlation between stone composition and etiology of obstruction has been identified.

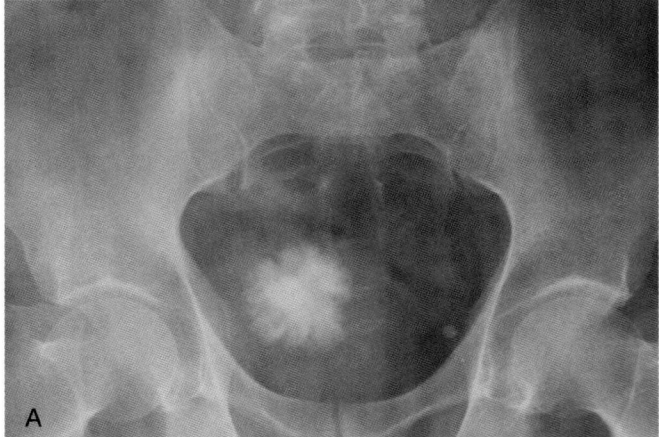

Figure 84–2. Radiographic (**A**) and gross appearance (**B**) of a calcium oxalate monohydrate calculus (jackstone).

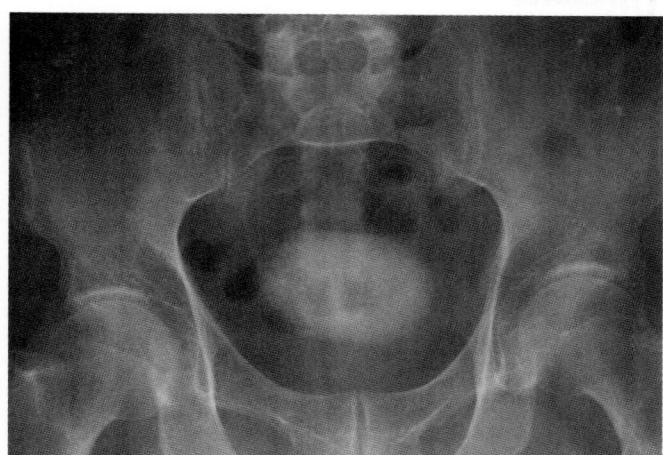

Figure 84–3. Plain radiograph (KUB) of a large laminated bladder calculus composed of magnesium ammonium phosphate.

Single stones are usually encountered in the bladder, but multiple stones are seen in 25% to 30% of cases (Drach, 1992) (Fig. 84–4). Bladder diverticula may predispose to the formation of multiple stones (Fig. 84–5); these may become faceted and vary in size (Sarica et al, 1994).

Bladder calculi may also be observed in post-prostatectomy patients. These calculi are usually associated with obstruction, bladder neck contracture, residual nidus from liberated prostatic calculi, and urinary stasis from neurogenic bladders (Haddad and Chinichian, 1991; Melone et al, 1996). Bladder calculi form in 40% of patients with bilharziasis as a result of outlet obstruction from bladder neck fibrosis (Hanna, 1977). There is often superimposed infection.

Calculi Related to Infection or Catheterization

Although urinary stasis may be the only cause of bladder calculi in some cases, infection is frequently a coexistent lithogenic factor. Residual urine from outlet obstruction predisposes to infection, and combined, these factors may result in stone formation. **Between 22% and 34% of bladder calculi are associated with urinary tract infection, most commonly with *Proteus*.** Organisms such as *Pseudomonas, Ureaplasma urealyticum, Providencia, Klebsiella, Staphylococcus,* and

Mycoplasma are also capable of producing bacterial urease (Otnes, 1983; Naqvi et al, 1984). The urease hydrolyzes urea, forming ammonium and carbon dioxide, which increases urine pH. Alkaline urine promotes supersaturation and precipitation of crystals of magnesium ammonium phosphate and carbonate apatite (Griffith, 1979). Although magnesium ammonium phosphate and carbonate apatite are pathognomonic of infection, calcium oxalate and phosphate calculi may be associated.

Long-term bladder catheterization often places patients at risk for urinary infection and calculus formation. A study identified a prevalence of 0.07% of long-term catheterization (0.5% for patients older than 75 years) in a population of more than 825,000, of which 2.2% were found to have bladder calculi (Kohler-Ockmore and Feneley, 1996). Approximately 50% to 98% of catheter-associated calculi are composed of magnesium ammonium phosphate; the remainder are a combination of calcium oxalate and phosphate or pure calcium phosphate (Otnes, 1983; DeVivo et al, 1984). Patients who are particularly prone to infectious bladder calculi include those with neurogenic bladder from trauma, stroke, or similar conditions or with foreign bodies in the urinary system. Patients with spinal cord injury frequently require catheterization, either continuous or intermittent, for bladder management (DeVivo et al, 1985; Hall et al, 1989). Of 898 patients with spinal cord injury, 261 (29%) were found to have bladder calculi; 62.5% were managed with indwelling catheters, whereas the remainder wore external appliances for urine collection (Hall et al, 1989). Thirty-six percent of patients with spinal cord injury at one institution developed bladder calculi during an 8-year period; patients with spinal cord injury and bladder calculi were more likely to have a neurologically complete lesion, to have urinary tract infection caused by a *Klebsiella* species, and to use chronic indwelling catheterization (DeVivo et al, 1985). In a follow-up study, the initial incidence of bladder stone formation decreased to 15% for patients with spinal cord injury who had contemporary urologic management. **Patients managed with an indwelling urethral or suprapubic catheter had a ninefold increased risk and those using intermittent catheterization or a condom catheter had a fourfold increased risk for development of a bladder stone compared with patients who were catheter free and had continent bladder control** within the first year after injury. The relative risk for initial development

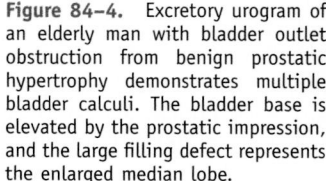

Figure 84–4. Excretory urogram of an elderly man with bladder outlet obstruction from benign prostatic hypertrophy demonstrates multiple bladder calculi. The bladder base is elevated by the prostatic impression, and the large filling defect represents the enlarged median lobe.

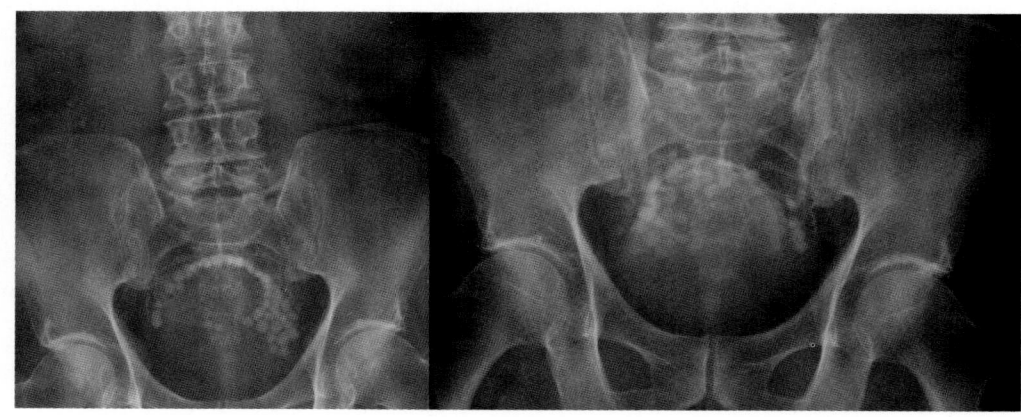

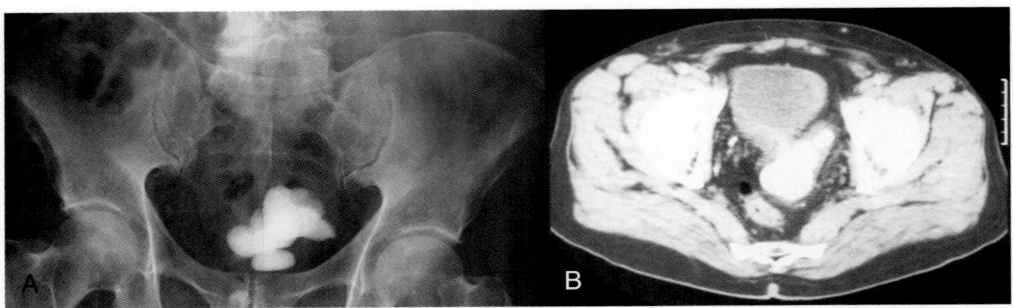

Figure 84–5. A, Plain radiograph shows a large lobulated calcific density in the pelvis. **B,** Computed tomography reveals the density as calculi in a large posterior bladder diverticulum.

of a bladder stone for those with indwelling and intermittent catheterization was stronger in later years after injury (Chen et al, 2001). Another study also found a substantial difference in the risk of bladder stone formation according to the method of bladder management. The risk of stone formation was 0% to 0.5% per year for condom drainage combined with sphincterotomy, 0.2% per year for intermittent catheterization, and 4% per year for indwelling urethral or suprapubic drainage. This increased to a 16% annual risk for patients managed with indwelling catheters who had already developed one bladder stone (Ord et al, 2003). This may represent persistent or recurrent infection.

Foreign Body Nidus Calculi

The urinary tract is the occasional repository for a wide array of foreign objects, and calculi may form around those that find their way into the bladder. **These foreign bodies can be classified as self-induced, iatrogenic, or migrant.** Self-induced insertion may be the result of autoerotic behavior, psychological abnormalities, senility, or inebriation. Dalton and colleagues (1975) reviewed foreign body–induced stone formation in an animal model and noted that (1) calculi may develop on foreign objects in the absence of infection; (2) stone formation is inhibited by dilution, diuresis, and acidification of urine; (3) stone formation is enhanced with infection, especially with urea-splitting organisms; and (4) calculi may form around nearly any type of suture. They also catalogued an extensive list of items involved in bladder stone formation, including a steel washer, chewing gum, fountain pen, knife blade, hairpins, and thermometers. Multiple cases of self-induced bladder calculi have been reported in the literature with infrequent significant morbidity or mortality (Sivaloganathan, 1985; Williams et al, 1985; Basu et al, 1994).

Iatrogenic nidi from urinary tract manipulation and stenting have been widely reported. As mentioned previously, Foley catheters act as foreign bodies; encrustations may form around the tip or the balloon of the catheter. These encrustations may act as nidi for further stone growth. Furthermore, patients on intermittent self-catheterization may introduce pubic hairs into the bladder, which may act as nidi for stone formation (Amendola et al, 1983). Retained ureteral stents may often have encrustations or calculus on the bladder portion. Calculi may form around sutures and staples used in urinary diversions that are exposed to urine (Fig. 84–6).

Bladder calculi from migrant foreign bodies have been reported as complications of urologic and nonurologic surgical procedures. Calculi have been reported around a migrated

titanium prostatic stent (Squires and Gillatt, 1995), a penile prosthesis reservoir (Dupont and Hochman, 1988), and a silk suture initially used to ligate the dorsal vein complex during a radical prostatectomy (Miller et al, 1992). Although there are numerous reports in the literature concerning migration of intrauterine and intravaginal gynecologic devices into the bladder with subsequent calculus formation (Staskin et al, 1985; Ehrenpreis et al, 1986; Robertson and Azmy, 1988; Khan and Wilkinson, 1990; el-Diasty et al, 1993; Mahazan, 1995; Chow et al, 1997; Cumming et al, 1997; Maskey et al, 1997), cholelithiasis (Chia and Ross, 1995), surgical clips used in a laparoscopic hernia repair (Maier and Treu, 1996), vascular graft (Pomerantz, 1989), and methyl methacrylate cement (Radford and Thomson, 1989) have also been reported as nonurologic nidi. Thus, any foreign body placed in proximity to the bladder has calculus potential, and the best treatment of these calculi is prevention.

Calculi in Augmentations and Urinary Diversions

The popularity of lower urinary tract reconstruction with intestinal segments has contributed to an increased frequency of bladder calculi. The incidence of bladder calculi in the pediatric and adult population with bladder augmentation varies between 0% and 53% (Blyth et al, 1992; Kreder and Webster, 1992; Palmer et al, 1993; Fontaine et al, 1997). The incidence of stones in urinary diversions is primarily dependent on the type constructed. Calculi have been reported in 4% to 20% of ileal conduit series (Schmidt et al, 1973; Middleton and Hendren, 1976; Althausen et al, 1978; Hagen-Cook and Althausen, 1979; Brenner and Johnson, 1985; McDougal, 1998), 5% of ileocecal conduits (McDougal, 1998), and 3% to 11% of colon conduits (Althausen et al, 1978; Hagen-Cook and Althausen, 1979; McDougal, 1998). In general, conduits have lower calculi rates than continent diversions do. The Indiana pouch has a stone incidence of 3% to 13% (Arai et al, 1993; Terai et al, 1996; Benson and Olsson, 1998; Turk et al, 1999); the Kock pouch, 4% to 43% (Ginsberg et al, 1991; Arai et al, 1993; Terai et al, 1996; Benson and Olsson, 1998; Turk et al, 1999); the orthotopic hemi-Kock pouch, 3% to 16% (Benson and Olsson, 1998; Shaaban et al, 2003); the Mainz pouch, 8% (Benson and Olsson, 1998); and the cecal reservoir, 20% (Ashken, 1987).

Risk factors associated with calculi formation include urinary stasis, mucus production, urinary infection with a urea-splitting organism, foreign bodies, and metabolic

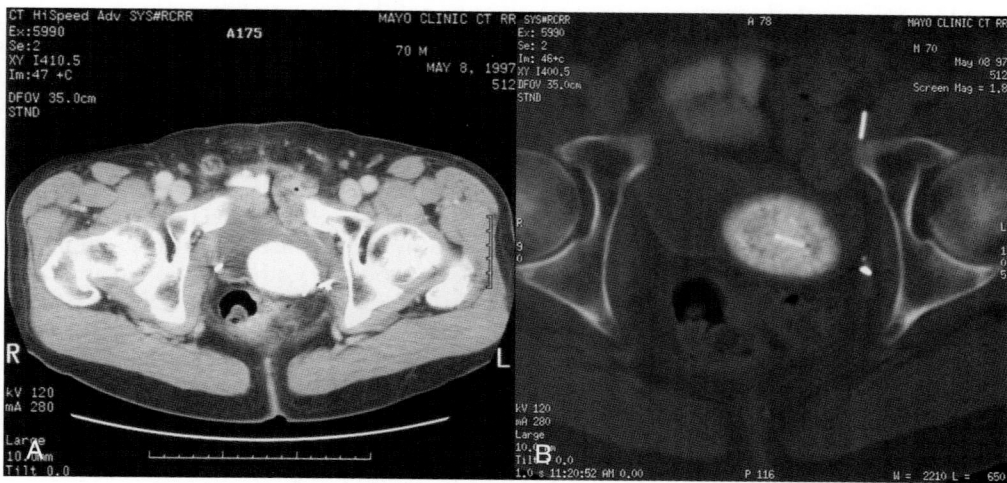

Figure 84–6. Computed tomographic scan of a patient with an orthotopic ileal diversion with complaints of difficulty emptying. A 5-cm calculus is seen in the pouch (**A**), and a surgical clip is seen in the middle of the calculus (**B**).

disturbances (Dretler, 1973; McLean et al, 1990; Blyth et al, 1992; McDougal, 1992; Palmer et al, 1993; Nurse et al, 1996; Kronner et al, 1998; Bertschy et al, 2000). The efficiency of bladder drainage has been implicated as a risk factor for stone formation (Blyth et al, 1992). This is reflected in the finding that continent diversions had a stone rate three times that of orthotopic cystoplasties; those with orthotopic diversions who voided by catheterization urethrally and abdominally had a rate five and ten times, respectively, that of those who voided spontaneously (Nurse et al, 1996). Furthermore, bladder calculi were found in 6% of patients with augmentation only; 14% with augmentation with either a bladder neck procedure or an abdominal stoma; and 21% with augmentation, bladder neck surgery, and stoma creation (Kronner et al, 1998). Mucus may be a factor in stone formation because it could act as a nidus, hinder adequate bladder drainage with voiding or catheterization, and harbor urea-splitting organisms (Khoury et al, 1997; Bertschy et al, 2000).

In some augmentation series, lower stone rates were seen with the regular use of an irrigation protocol to minimize mucus; in others, it made no difference (Wan and Bloom, 1993; Nurse et al, 1996; Brough et al, 1998; Kronner et al, 1998; DeFoor et al, 2004; Hensle et al, 2004). Bowel that normally lives symbiotically with bacteria, when interposed in the urinary tract, may serve as a source for asymptomatic bacteriuria or infection with subsequent calculus formation. **The majority of calculi in augmentations and diversions are composed of magnesium ammonium phosphate or carbonate apatite, signifying that infection with urea-spitting bacteria plays a role in calculi formation** (Ginsberg et al, 1991; Terai et al, 1995; Kaefer et al, 1998). The use of stomach for augmentation significantly lowers the incidence of calculi compared with other intestinal segments (Kaefer et al, 1998; Kronner et al, 1998). Gastric segments produce minimal mucus and secrete acid, thereby lowering urine pH and inhibiting bacterial growth. Bladder calculi that do develop are usually uric acid or are seen in conjunction with the use of histamine blockade medications (Palmer et al, 1998; Kaefer et al, 1998). **Contemporary series reporting the results of interposing intestinal mucosa into the urinary tract report lower rates of bladder calculi** (Arif et al, 1999; Turk et al, 1999; Abol-Enein and Ghoneim, 2001; Deliveliotis et al, 2001). This is believed to be due to the recognition of the lithogenic potential of nonabsorbable material and its avoidance in lower tract reconstruction (Arai et al, 1993; Terai et al, 1996). The predominant location of calculi in the Kock pouch is along staple lines of the afferent nipple valve. Substituting polyglycolic mesh for Marlex mesh in collar construction and limiting the number of staples reduced the incidence of pouch calculi from 28% to 10% in one study (Ginsberg et al, 1991). Arif and colleagues (1999) reported a sixfold reduction in stone formation with absorbable compared with nonabsorbable staples in the construction of hemi-Kock pouches.

Patients with augmentations and diversions often have reabsorption of urinary solutes, especially sulfate and ammonium, through the intestinal segment with resultant metabolic disturbances. Chronic hyperchloremic metabolic acidosis may develop, which in turn can result in hypercalciuria, hyperphosphaturia, hypermagnesuria, and hypocitraturia, predisposing the patient to urinary tract calculi (McDougal and Koch, 1989; Palmer et al, 1993; Terai et al, 1995; Khoury et al, 1997; Beiko and Razvi, 2002).

Symptoms and Diagnosis

Most bladder or urinary diversion calculi are asymptomatic and are found incidentally. Patients with significant bladder outlet obstruction may initially present with lower urinary tract symptoms or recurrent (persistent) urinary tract infections, especially with a urea-splitting organism. The typical presentation in patients with symptomatic bladder calculi includes intermittent, painful voiding and hematuria. The pain may be of varying quality and may be exacerbated by exercise and sudden movement. The pain is usually located in the lower abdomen but may be referred to the tip of the penis, the scrotum, or the perineum and on occasion to the back or the hip. The urinary stream may be interrupted intermittently, with the accompanying increase in terminal dysuria caused by lodging of the calculus at the bladder neck. Assuming a recumbent position may alleviate the symptoms. Whereas smaller bladder calculi may spontaneously pass, larger calculi may cause acute urinary retention.

Patients with urinary diversions and calculi may present with gross hematuria, pressure sensations in the diversion, difficultly with catheterization or emptying, mild incontinence, lower abdominal discomfort, or recurrent urinary tract infections (Ginsberg et al, 1991). Calculi in diversions may also impair drainage and lead to renal insufficiency.

Although bladder calculi can be visualized on plain radiographs, a significant number may be missed because of overlying bowel gas, soft tissue shadowing, and the radiolucent quality of some calculi. Ultrasonography can be used to detect radiolucent calculi but may be limited by bowel gas in the setting of urinary diversion. Computed tomography is superior to ultrasonography in detection of calculi in cases of lower tract reconstruction (Myers et al, 2001). Radiolucent calculi may be identified as filling defects in the partially filled bladder or diversion on excretory urogram, pouchogram, or loopogram. **Cystoscopy is the single most accurate examination to document the presence of a bladder calculus.** Cystoscopy assists in surgical planning by identifying prostatic enlargement, bladder diverticulum, or urethral stricture that may need correction before or in conjunction with the treatment of the stone.

Management of Bladder Calculi

The majority of bladder calculi are treated endoscopically, but treatment strategies may range from chemolysis to open surgery. Bladder calculi may be surgically treated by shockwave lithotripsy; cystolitholapaxy; cystolithotripsy with mechanical, electrohydraulic, ultrasonic, or laser energy sources; percutaneous cystolithotomy; and open cystolithotomy. The approach is influenced by the patient's anatomy and comorbidities; stone size, location, and composition; previous stone treatment; and risks and complications. In addition to removal of the calculi, treatment should address predisposing factors such as bladder outlet obstruction, urinary stasis, infection, and foreign bodies to minimize recurrence.

Chemolysis

Suby solution G or hemiacidrin has been used in the past to dissolve magnesium ammonium phosphate calculi. The calculi are dissolved because of the acidity (pH 4), and the magnesium salts formed are more soluble than calcium salts (Sant et al, 1983; Dretler and Pfister, 1984). Uric acid calculi may be amenable to dissolution with oral sodium or potassium citrate. In refractory cases, direct irrigation of the calculus with sodium bicarbonate may be successful (Rodman et al, 1984). Dissolution for primary treatment of bladder calculi can be protracted and is now rarely employed. Hemiacidrin may be used as an adjunct to surgical treatment (Heimbach et al, 2004) or prophylactically to prevent encrustation of indwelling catheters. Similarly, irrigations with 0.25% or 0.5% acetic acid solution or use of medications that inhibit urease may prevent recurrent magnesium ammonium phosphate calculi on chronic indwelling catheters (Burns and Gauthier, 1984).

Shockwave Lithotripsy

Shockwave lithotripsy (SWL) has been used successfully in the treatment of bladder calculi (Vandeursen and Baert, 1990; Bosco and Nieh, 1991; Delakas et al, 1998; Frabboni et al, 1998). A three-way Foley catheter is placed, and the patient is placed in the prone position on the cushion. The prone position avoids the dampening effects of air interfaces from the rectum and gluteal crease and the interference from the projection of the coccyx over a portion of the focusing ellipsoid (Bosco and Nieh, 1991). The bladder is filled with 100 to 150 mL of normal saline through the catheter to improve visualization. After the calculus has been localized, the bladder is drained, which minimizes stone migration. Intermittent saline irrigation through the catheter is used to create an expansion chamber for better fragmentation (Bhatia and Biyani, 1994). Catheterization may also introduce air and obscure stone localization. Obstructed patients with high postvoid residuals and patients with larger calculi have lower success rates of SWL and higher rates of ancillary procedures (Bhatia and Biyani, 1994; Frabboni et al, 1998). Multiple treatments of bladder calculi with SWL may be required to achieve stone-free status (Delakas et al, 1998; Frabboni et al, 1998; Kojima et al, 1998). Poor results with SWL have been reported with use of a piezoelectric lithotriptor (Vallancien et al, 1988). SWL may be considered for those who are unfit for surgery because of comorbid medical conditions or who refuse surgery. Stone recurrence may be high because SWL fails to address the etiology of bladder calculi.

Cystolitholapaxy

Cystolitholapaxy is the crushing of the calculus with irrigation of the fragments from the bladder in a single operation. Introduced by Bigelow, this procedure has been accomplished with either a tactile or optical lithotrite since the late 1800s. Contraindications include small-capacity bladders, multiple stones or calculi larger than 2 cm that cannot be engaged, hard stones, bladder calculi in children, and small-caliber urethras (Bhatia and Biyani, 1994; Mebust, 1998). During the procedure, the bladder should be filled with about 200 mL of irrigant. When the stone is grasped, bladder mucosa should be excluded from the instrument. The stone is then crushed manually, and the procedure is repeated several times until fragments can no longer be caught. Cystolitholapaxy has a high success rate in experienced hands (Razvi et al, 1996). However, it can be technically difficult and is associated with a complication rate of between 9% and 25% (Smith and O'Flynn, 1977; Bhatia and Biyani, 1994; Asci et al, 1999). Amplatz sheath use after initial urethral dilation may help reduce urethral trauma and operative time during cystolitholapaxy (Maheshwari et al, 1999). Complication rates when cystolitholapaxy and transurethral prostatectomy are combined have varied widely (Nseyo et al, 1987; Razvi et al, 1996; Asci et al, 1999). Transurethral prostatectomy may be performed after cystolitholapaxy if the bladder is in adequate condition. Cystolitholapaxy with mechanical crushing of the calculus has been eschewed for endourologic techniques with energy sources that are safer and more effective.

Pneumatic lithotripsy uses mechanical energy for fragmentation. It is almost always successful at fragmentation and produces multiple small fragments (Denstedt et al, 1992; Schulze et al, 1993). **Pneumatic lithotripsy was found to be more efficient than ultrasonic lithotripsy or electrohydraulic lithotripsy for large or particularly hard calculi** (Razvi et al, 1996). The device is compact, the cost is relatively inexpensive, and the probes are reusable and may be used through a standard cystoscope. A combination of pneumatic lithotripsy and transurethral prostatectomy has been found to be safe and effective with minimal increases in overall operative times (Sinik et al, 1998).

Electrohydraulic lithotripsy can efficiently fragment most bladder calculi. A success rate of 92% in 302 patients treated with electrohydraulic lithotripsy with a mean operative time of 26 minutes has been reported (Bulow and Frohmuller, 1981). Bladder rupture occurred in 1.9% of all cases; only one patient required laparotomy for an intraperitoneal perforation. The electrohydraulic lithotripsy probes are flexible and are able to be passed through standard cystoscopic equipment, but the probe must be kept away from the mucosa and the lens to prevent injury or damage. Stone and fragment propulsion may be problematic during use; the ideal setting is the lowest that will fragment the stone without excessive movement. Hard or large calculi may require prolonged procedure times, consume multiple probes, and result in incomplete fragmentation (Razvi et al, 1996).

Ultrasonic lithotripsy is effective in the treatment of bladder calculi (Razvi et al, 1996). An 88% stone-free rate was reported in patients with stones of 12 to 50 mm (average, 29 mm) with a mean anesthesia time of 56 minutes. Two cases were converted to open cystolithotomy because of stone hardness. Ultrasonic energy has no significant adverse effects on bladder mucosa other than a local edematous reaction; it is able to clear large stone burdens with simultaneous stone evacuation and relatively low cost. The rigid lithotrite must be passed through a cystoscope with an offset lens and can perforate the bladder. Operative times may be prolonged with calcium oxalate monohydrate and calcium phosphate calculi larger than 3 cm; uric acid calculi are resistant to ultrasonic fragmentation (Streem, 1987).

Use of the holmium:YAG laser for lithotripsy of large bladder calculi is safe, effective, and facile (Teichman et al, 1997; Gould, 1998). A side- or end-firing laser fiber can be used to contact and ablate the stone. To prevent mucosal injury, the fiber is kept a minimum of 0.5 mm from the urothelium. A stone-free rate of 100% was reported in 14 patients with bladder calculi larger than 4 cm treated with the holmium:YAG laser and either a 365-μm end-firing fiber or a 550-μm side-firing fiber in a mean anesthetic time of 57 minutes. Migration of fragments was minimal, and the 550-μm side-firing fiber was found to be almost twice as fast at stone vaporization as the 365-μm end-firing fiber (Teichman et al, 1997). The authors have had satisfying results with the 1000-μm end-firing fiber for lithotripsy of bladder calculi.

Percutaneous Cystolithotomy

Percutaneous cystolithotomy is indicated in pediatric patients with narrow urethras and in patients with large stone burdens or multiple calculi with anticipated prolonged operative times. Contraindications include a history of bladder malignant disease, prior abdominal or pelvic surgeries, prior pelvic radiotherapy, active urinary or abdominal wall infection, and pelvic prosthetic devices (Badlani et al, 1990). The percutaneous puncture is positioned above the symphysis or at a prior suprapubic tube site to avoid inadvertent bowel or vascular injury. Cystoscopic guidance through either the urethra or the cutaneous stoma can facilitate access and track dilation when Amplatz fascial dilators are used. Amplatz sheaths (26 to 36 French) allow the use of large instruments for rapid lithotripsy or removal of large intact fragments. Success rates for percutaneous cystolithotomy range from 85% to 100% with various energy sources (Ikari et al, 1993; Agrawal et al, 1999; Franzoni and Decter, 1999; Maheshwari et al, 1999). One report suggested that this approach be used for all children with vesical calculi and for adults with stones larger than 4 cm or more than three calculi (Maheshwari et al, 1999).

Cystolithotomy

Although rarely used today, open cystolithotomy for the treatment of bladder calculi is associated with a high success rate (Bhatia and Biyani, 1994). For very large stone burdens or hard stones, cystolithotomy is certainly the most expeditious. Other indications are abnormal anatomy precluding safe access, failure of an endoscopic approach, and concomitant open prostatectomy or diverticulectomy (Bulow and Frohmuller, 1981; Bhatia and Biyani, 1994).

Management of Calculi in Augmentations and Urinary Diversions

Most treatment options available for bladder calculi are applicable to calculi in augmentations and diversions. Surgical management of calculi in augmentations and urinary diversions is dependent on the anatomy and the stone burden.

Stones in conduit diversions often pass spontaneously, and intervention may not be required (Shapiro et al, 1975; Middleton and Hendren, 1976; Brenner and Johnson, 1985; Ginsberg et al, 1991).

Endoscopic lithotripsy or stone extraction is best suited for the adult with a simple augmentation and normal urethra and bladder neck. Prudent use of any of the energy sources will provide effective stone clearance. In adult patients with reconstructed bladder necks or urethras, gentle dilation to 21 French, use of safety guide wires, and peel-away sheaths allow safe access for multiple passes of the cystoscope without any apparent detriment to urinary continence (Palmer et al, 1994). Patients with an orthotopic diversion and a low stone burden may also be rendered stone free with transurethral lithotripsy and any of the energy sources. Endoscopic removal of multiple small fragments lodged within the mucosal folds of capacious diversions may be difficult. Prolonged operative times may increase the risk of bladder neck contracture or sphincter damage in orthotopic diversions (Patel and Bellman, 1995). Patients with continent cutaneous diversions and low stone burdens may also be treated trans-stomally through intussuscepted nipple valves of adequate caliber. There are multiple reports of successful treatment with a rigid nephroscope passed under direct vision into the efferent nipple without dilation of the valve and without apparent detrimental effect on the continence mechanism in Kock and Indiana pouches (Ginsberg et al, 1991; Huffman, 1992; Terai et al, 1996). Flexible pouchoscopy may be used in cases of minimal stone burden. Despite the reported high success rate of transstomal and transurethral therapy, lithotripsy through the efferent limb or urethra can be difficult because of location, size, and composition of the stone or the efficiency of the small-diameter instruments that are used (Thomas et al, 1993).

The percutaneous approach is ideally suited for patients with impassable or obliterated bladder necks or urethras, small-caliber stomas such as the Mitrofanoff valve, Monte procedure or tapered imbricated terminal ileum, or large stone burdens. Passage of large instruments through an abdominal stoma may cause disruption of the continence mechanism or postoperative stenosis (Roth et al, 1994; Patel and Bellman, 1995). In this setting, percutaneous treatment of augmented bladder and pouch calculi with dilation of tracks for working ports and trocars has been rewarding (Hollensbe et al, 1993; Thomas et al, 1993; Roth et al, 1994; Seaman et al, 1994; Ramin et al, 1997; Docimo et al, 1998; Franco and Levitt, 1998). Access to the augmented bladder is carried out two to four fingerbreadths above the pubic symphysis or at a previous suprapubic tube site. Amplatz sheaths or laparoscopic trocars can be placed with computed tomographic guidance, or preoperative computed tomography and intraoperative ultrasonography may guide pouch access to avoid injury to the mesenteric blood supply of the reservoir or adjacent bowel (Roth et al, 1994; Franco and Levitt, 1998). Stone removal is carried out in a fashion similar to percutaneous nephrolithotomy. Additional ports may be placed if needed. To help avoid residual fragments, stones can be placed in a laparoscopic entrapment sac; a small incision can be made to deliver the bag intact, or lithotripsy can be carried out within the sac (Jarrett et al, 1999; Miller and Park, 2003).

If the augmented bladder is not well fixed to the anterior abdominal wall, extravasation of the irrigating fluid could lead to peritonitis. A minilap cystolithotomy (Franco and Levitt, 1998) is a safer alternative in such cases. A 2- to 3-cm incision is made near the previous suprapubic tube site and a purse-string suture is placed in the augmented bladder. The Amplatz sheath is placed through a cystotomy, and the bladder is inspected with cystoscopy. Smaller calculi are removed intact; larger stones are removed either by fragmenting them or by expanding the incision and removing them intact. Any extruded staples or nonabsorbable sutures are removed, the cystotomy is closed in layers with a large-bore catheter left through the catheterizable stoma, and a drain is placed for 48 hours.

Open surgical removal is considered in augmentations and diversions when endoscopic techniques cannot be accomplished safely or expeditiously because of stone location, excessive burden or number (Fig. 84–7), or abnormal anatomy or when open surgery is planned on the diversion.

SWL is best suited for small solitary calculi of augmented bladders in male children and adults (Franco and Levitt, 1998). Although it has been used with success in the Kock and Indiana pouches, SWL in diversions can result in multiple small fragments that may lead to stone recurrence in the face of impaired clearance from the diversion, and endoscopic removal is often required to achieve a stone-free state (Boyd et al, 1988; Weinerth and Webster, 1990; Cohen and Streem, 1994).

The recurrence rate in this population of patients is estimated to be 65% during 5 years (Cohen et al, 1996). Thus, prophylactic measures, such as adequate oral fluid intake, ensuring complete regular evacuation of the reservoir, daily irrigation of the pouch with saline or tap water to remove mucus and crystals, and eradication of urea-splitting organisms, should be instituted (Palmer et al, 1993; Kronner et al,

1998). Routine endoscopic surveillance, particularly in an active stone former, may be warranted (Seaman et al, 1994; Terai et al, 1996; Turk et al, 1999).

CALCULI OF PROSTATIC AND SEMINAL VESICLES

Prostatic calculi are depositions of calcified material on corpora amylacea. The corpora amylacea have a laminated structure composed of a lecithin that is formed around sloughed epithelial cells. Prostatic calculi are primarily composed of calcium phosphate trihydrate and carbonate (Sutor and Wooley, 1974). Huggins and Bear (1944) observed that the proteins cholesterol and citrate compose about 20% of the calculus.

The incidence of prostatic calculi is unknown. They are noted incidentally during routine radiographic or ultrasonic evaluation of the prostate. They occur in approximately 5% of men (Joly, 1931) and are most often seen in evaluation of benign prostatic hyperplasia. On ultrasound examination, they appear highly echogenic with shadowing (Resnick et al, 1977; Jones et al, 1989). Calculi in the seminal vesicles are extremely rare (White, 1928); the nucleus is composed of epithelial cells, and the mucoid substance is covered with lime salts.

Prostatic calculi are most commonly seen in men older than 50 years. It is believed that infection contributes to the formation of some prostatic calculi (Sutor and Wooley, 1974). They are not believed to cause the infection. Ochronosis, which has been associated with alkaptonuria and precipitation of homogentisic acid, has also been implicated in the formation of prostatic calculi (Douenias et al, 1991). Prostatic calculi can also form secondary to radiation therapy (Jones et al, 1979), transurethral surgery of the prostate (Koh, 1995; Benjamin et al, 1997; Aus et al, 1997), and placement of a prostatic stent (Chiu et al, 1991; Chiou et al, 1996).

Prostatic calculi are usually asymptomatic. However, when symptoms do occur, they are secondary to an underlying disease, such as prostatitis or benign prostatic hypertrophy. Terminal hematuria can be a presenting sign along with hematospermia or perineal discomfort with ejaculation (Drach, 1975).

Cystoscopy is usually unremarkable. Digital rectal examinations will rarely detect induration. On occasion, stones can be visualized eroding into the urethra. The stones are usually an incidental finding on ultrasonography. Diffuse calcifications can occasionally be seen in the prostate as a result of chronic inflammatory disease, such as tuberculosis.

No treatment is indicated for asymptomatic prostatic stones. In those who are symptomatic, transurethral resection can unroof and remove the calculus. Rarely, surgical prostatectomy may be indicated in patients with intractable infection (Drach, 1992).

URETHRAL CALCULI

Urethral calculi represent less than 2% of all urinary stone disease in the Western world (Koga et al, 1990). However, in developing nations, particularly in the Middle and Far East, the incidence is higher because of the increased incidence of

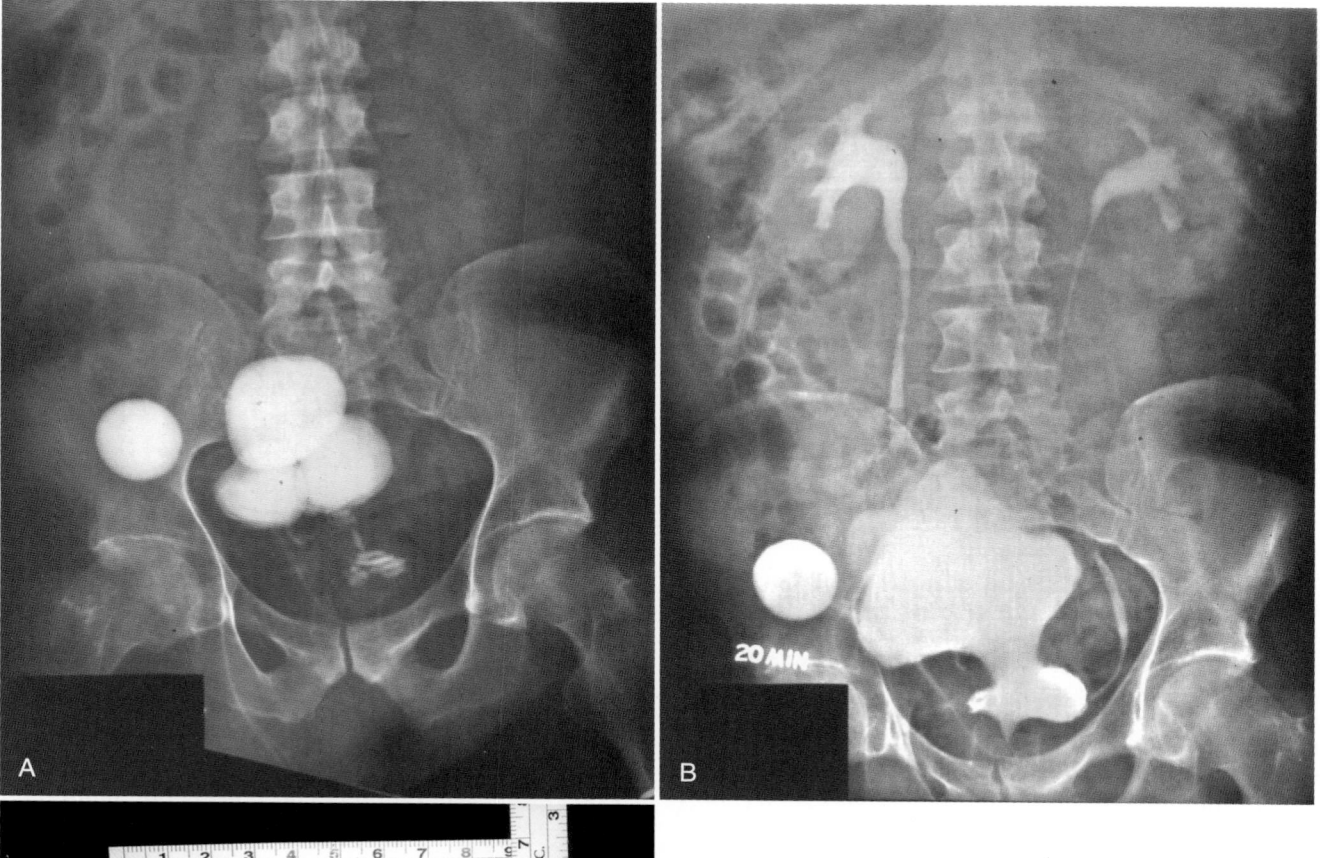

Figure 84–7. Plain radiograph (**A**) and excretory urogram (**B**) of a patient with a bladder augmentation and bladder stones. This patient was managed with a cystolithotomy because of his excessive stone burden (**C**). The spherical density overlying the right ilium of the pelvis is the reservoir to an artificial urinary sphincter filled with contrast material.

bladder stones (Amin, 1983). Urethral calculi in women are exceptionally rare because of low rates of bladder calculi and a short urethra that permits passage of many smaller calculi.

Urethral calculi can be classified as either native or migrant. Native urethral calculi form de novo in association with abnormalities that predispose to urinary stasis and infection. Calculi may form proximal to strictures, in congenital or acquired diverticula, with chronic infection (especially with urea-splitting organisms), with foreign bodies, in schistosomiasis, and with use of hair-bearing skin for urethroplasty. These calculi are frequently composed of struvite, calcium phosphate, or calcium carbonate. Calculi in the female urethra are typically associated with urethral diverticulum or urethrocele (Fig. 84–8). The majority of urethral calculi in men are migrant, formed in the urinary bladder or upper tract, whose passage has been impeded in the urethra (Englisch, 1904; Paulk et al, 1976). Hence their composition, usually calcium oxalate and phosphate, relates to their underlying cause. Although stones smaller than 10 mm should pass through the normal urethra, areas of possible stone impaction are the prostatic urethra, the bulb, the proximal penile urethra, the fossa navicularis, and the external meatus. A migrant stone may become impacted at the site of a urethral stricture. In a review of 361 cases, Englisch (1904) observed that in 41.2%, the stones were in the posterior urethra; Amin (1973) reported 86 cases and noted that 63% presented with stones in the anterior urethra. In both studies, approximately 10% of stones were lodged in the fossa navicularis.

Native urethral stones generally do not cause acute symptoms because of their slow development and growth.

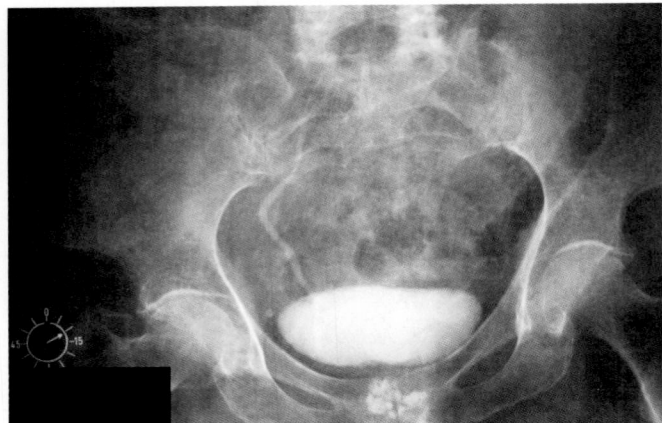

Figure 84–8. Excretory urogram of an elderly woman with lower urinary tract infections. Calculi are seen in a large urethral diverticulum.

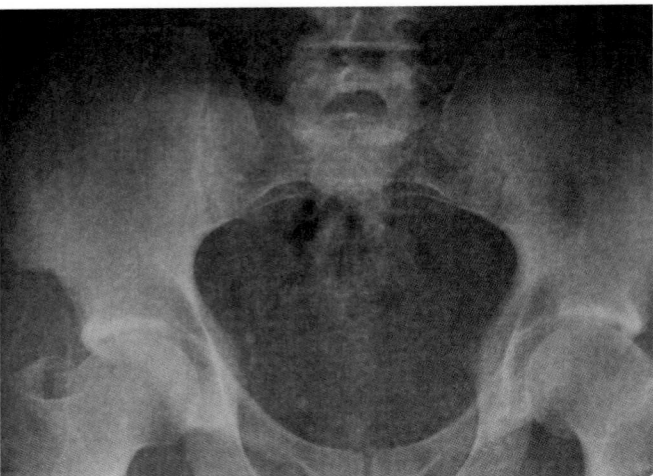

Figure 84–9. Plain radiograph (KUB) of a man presenting with acute urinary retention. The calcification was a calculus lodged in the prostatic urethra.

Patients may present with a mass that has gradually increased in size and hardness on the undersurface of the penis or anterior wall of the vagina, urethral discharge, dyspareunia, irritative voiding symptoms, and hematuria. Migrant calculi, however, may achieve sizable dimensions before descending into the urethra and often cause acute symptoms (Fig. 84–9). Adult men with urethral calculi may present with acute retention or complaints of frequency, dysuria, poor or interrupted urinary stream, incomplete emptying, and dribbling or incontinence. Pain caused by the stone may be severe. When the calculus is lodged in the posterior urethra, the pain is referred to the perineum or the rectum. When the calculus is lodged in the anterior urethra, the pain may be localized at the site of the impaction. A careful history is suggestive of a urethral calculus, and external palpation will reveal the stone if it is situated in the penile or bulbous urethra. Rectal examination may detect stones in the posterior urethra. Radiography can be helpful but requires proper positioning of the patient as urethral calculi are frequently overlooked on plain films and intravenous urograms. **In a Mayo Clinic series, only 42% of urethral calculi were detected at urography** (Paulk et al, 1976). Endoscopy is diagnostic.

Treatment is contingent on the size and location of the calculus and condition of the urethra. The objective of treatment is relief of obstruction and foreign body removal without damaging the urethra and periurethral tissues. Patients with acute retention may be best managed by suprapubic catheterization, which allows appropriate planning for definitive care. Urethroscopic lithotripsy and removal of stone fragments is useful in almost any situation. Meatotomy may be used if the stone is lodged in the fossa navicularis or the external meatus. A stone in the anterior urethra may be treated with the judicial use of forceps. Pressure is exerted simultaneously on the urethra proximal to the calculus so it is not pushed retrograde. On occasion, a small stone may sometimes be gently massaged or milked outward, so that it can be expelled. el-Sherif and el-Hafi (1991) reported spontaneous expulsion of impacted urethral stones in 14 of 18 patients treated with intraurethral instillation of 2% lidocaine jelly. When a stricture obstructs passage of a stone, dilatation or internal urethrotomy may be necessary before the manipulation. External urethrotomy,

with a two-layer closure, may be required in cases of chronic impaction. Calculi in the posterior urethra can be treated in situ or pushed back into the bladder and treated as vesical calculi. When the calculus occupies a urethral diverticulum, diverticulectomy and repair should be performed. Associated urinary calculi may be found in a significant number of patients with urethral calculi (Koga et al, 1990).

PREPUTIAL CALCULI

Preputial calculi occur most commonly in underdeveloped countries. Their incidence is inversely related to living standards and the amount of industrialization, such that they are exceedingly rare in the Western world. Preputial calculi primarily occur in adults and are associated with phimosis, poor genital hygiene, and low socioeconomic status (Ellis et al, 1986).

The key factors for preputial stone formation include obstruction with stasis, infection with alkalization, and presence of a foreign body. Smegma (Greek, soap) is an accumulation of cellular debris in the subpreputial space that can act as a lithogenic nidus and as an irritant, inducing inflammation, adhesions, and stenosis (Parkash et al, 1973). In the presence of phimosis, the subpreputial space acts as a reservoir that promotes urinary stasis, infection, and mineral crystallization (Williamson, 1932). Urinary infection can induce stone formation through urea degradation with subsequent alkalization and precipitation of struvite crystals. Preputial calculi can be classified according to their pathogenesis. Stones formed from inspissated smegma that becomes impregnated with urinary salts are usually brown, are soft in consistency, and can be single or multiple. Stones formed secondary to infection or stagnant urine are composed of struvite or calcium phosphate and can be single or multiple, round or faceted. Calculi that are formed in the proximal urinary tract that are trapped during migration or by ulceration through the fossa navicularis are often composed of calcium oxalate and calcium phosphate (Drach, 1992).

The symptoms and physical findings in patients with preputial calculi often are secondary to severe phimosis and balanoposthitis. A foul-smelling, blood-stained discharge, edema, pain and distention of the preputial sac with voiding, or ulceration in chronic cases may be found. Superficial inguinal adenopathy may result from reaction to the inflammatory process, but carcinoma must also be suspected when the calculus has been present for a long time (Mohapatra and Kumar, 1989). Obstruction may manifest with strangury, decreased force and caliber of the urinary stream, and prolonged voiding time. This may be compounded further by a ball-valve effect created by an entrapped calculus. The patient may learn to facilitate passage of urine by manipulation of the calculus (Williamson, 1932). Palpation of the penis may not easily differentiate calculus from the glans, although diagnosis is by palpation of the stone.

The treatment of preputial calculi is removal of the offending calculus and elimination of the predisposing conditions. **If untreated, preputial calculi may result in significant morbidity with chronic inflammation and urinary fistula formation.** An acute infection is temporized with a dorsal preputial slit to establish drainage. The definitive treatment is circumcision.

KEY POINTS: BLADDER CALCULI

- In industrialized societies, bladder calculi are most often related to bladder outlet obstruction, most frequently from benign prostatic hypertrophy.

- Urinary tract infection is associated with approximately one third of bladder calculi, most frequently with the *Proteus* species.

- Patients with intestinal mucosa or foreign bodies in the urinary tract are also at risk for development of calculi.

- The majority of bladder calculi are treated endoscopically.

SUGGESTED READINGS

Dalton DL, Hughes J, Glenn JF: Foreign bodies and urinary stones. Urology 1975;6:1-5.
Van Reen R, ed: Idiopathic Urinary Bladder Stone Disease, vol 37. Washington, DC, U.S. Government Printing Office, 1977.

SECTION XVI

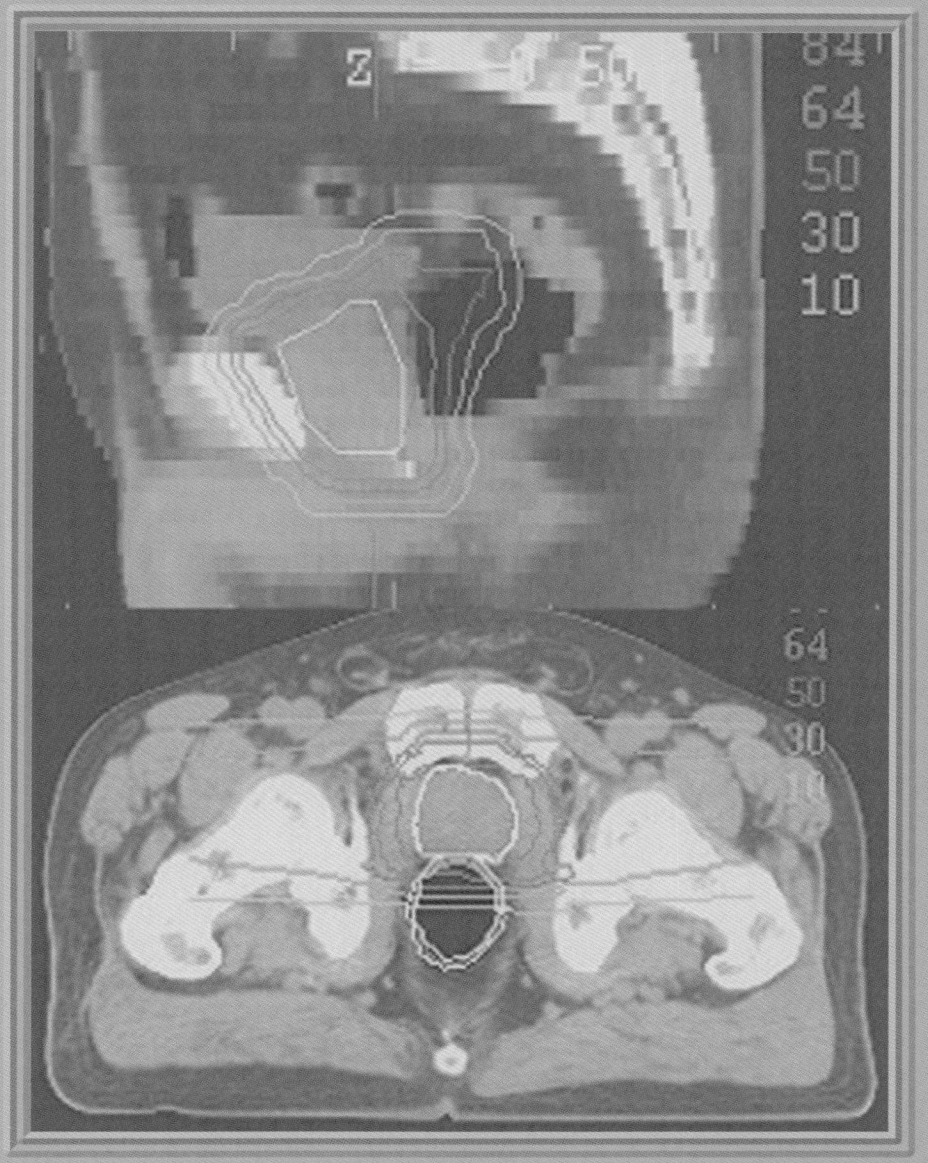

PROSTATE

85 Molecular Biology, Endocrinology, and Physiology of the Prostate and Seminal Vesicles

ROBERT VELTRI, PhD • RONALD RODRIGUEZ, MD, PhD

Sex accessory tissues include the prostate, seminal vesicles, ampullary glands, and bulbourethral glands, and they are believed to play a major but unknown role in the reproductive process. The presence of the prostate is *universal* in mammals. However, it is marked by considerable variation in anatomy, biochemistry, and pathology. This species variation is reflected in the comparative volumes of the ejaculate, that is, 250 mL in the boar, 70 mL in the stallion, 9 mL in the dog, 4 mL in the bull, 3 mL in the human, and only 1 mL in the ram. In addition, the human ejaculate forms a clot and subsequently lyses, whereas in the rodent, a solid copulatory plug is formed. Furthermore, in the human ejaculate, the major anion is citrate; in the dog seminal plasma, it is chloride ion.

In the human, the sex accessory tissues produce extremely high concentrations of many important and potent biologic substances that appear in the seminal plasma, such as fructose (2 mg/mL), citric acid (4 mg/mL), spermine (3 mg/mL), prostaglandins (200 μg/mL), zinc (150 μg/mL), proteins (40 mg/mL) that include immunoglobulins, human kallekriens, semenogelins, and so forth, and specific enzymes such as proteases, esterases, and phosphatases. At present, there is only limited knowledge of the physiologic function of any of these potent secretory products in the seminal plasma, with the exception of specific enzyme activities in the clotting and lysing process occurring with seminal plasma proteins that have unknown physiologic functions. Although the seminal plasma may not contain factors that are absolutely essential for fertilization, the secretions nevertheless may optimize conditions for fertilization by providing a buffered effect, by increasing sperm motility or survival, or by enhancing sperm transport in both the male and female reproductive tracts. The seminal plasma may extend viability of the sperm and decrease environmental shock. The role of sex accessory secretions in male infertility has long been suspected, but no single factor has ever been clearly implicated. These sex accessory glands are well positioned to block or to intercept the entrance of pathogens by secreting potent biologic protective substances, such as high concentrations of metal ions like zinc or highly charged organic molecules like spermine, as well as potent proteases. The mechanical washing of the urethra by these secretions as well as the establishment of a hostile milieu to invading pathogens may be one of the primary functions of the sex accessory tissues and may account for why these glands show such a large variability in structure and composition between species. In this chapter, we review the normal physiologic processes of the prostate and seminal vesicles with particular attention to recent advances in our understanding of the molecular biology and endocrinology of these sex accessory organs.

DEVELOPMENT AND CELL BIOLOGY
Embryonic Development

The sex accessory glands differ in their embryonic origin and the type of steroids that induce their developmental growth. Aumuller (1983) provided an early detailed classic review of the embryology, histology, and endocrinologic aspects of the development of the prostate and seminal vesicles (other reviews include Cunha et al, 1992; Bonkhoff et al, 1993; Randall, 1994; Small, 1995); however, since that time, concepts regarding the presence of prostate epithelial stem cell populations and intermediate cells have largely evolved. A more detailed discussion of these newer concepts is presented here.

The wolffian ducts develop into the seminal vesicles, epididymis, vas deferens, ampulla, and ejaculatory duct, and the developmental growth of this group of glands is stimulated by fetal testosterone and not dihydrotestosterone (DHT). The developmental growth of the wolffian-derived sex accessory glands is completed by the 13th week. In contrast, the prostate first appears and starts its development from the urogenital sinus during the third month of fetal growth, and development is directed primarily by DHT and not testosterone. DHT is produced from the metabolic conversion of fetal testosterone through the action of the enzyme 5α-reductase, which is located within the urogenital sinus. **Five epithelial buds form in a paired manner on the posterior side of the urogenital sinus on both sides of the verumontanum, and they then invade the mesenchyme to form the prostate.** The top pairs of buds form the inner zone of the prostate and appear to be of mesodermal origin; the lower buds form the outer zone of the prostate and appear to be of endodermal origin. This is of potential importance since the inner zone gives rise to benign prostatic hyperplasia (BPH) tissue, whereas the outer zone contains the primary origin of cancer. These two zones of the prostate develop as concentric circles around the urethra. The long branched ducts along the outside of this zone form the thick outer layer of the true prostate gland. The center portion of the prostate contains the mucosal and submucosal gland and the ejaculatory ducts as well as the small remnants of the müllerian duct—the utriculus prostaticus, which forms the small prostatic utricle. The prostate is well differentiated by the fourth month of fetal development.

There has been much debate and divergent views on the development of the zones of the prostate. For instance, there are some data to suggest that the central zone of the prostate may be derived from the wolffian duct; unilateral complete wolffian agenesis was found in a prostatectomy specimen lacking the ipsilateral prostatic central zone (Argani et al, 1998). However, such evidence does not necessarily exclude the possibility that the wolffian duct provides a trophic or supportive role for central zone development without directly contributing cell mass. Zonal anatomy has been exhaustively reviewed by McNeal (1980, 1981). The full embryology of the prostate in relation to its zones still requires modern histologic, morphologic, biologic, and molecular techniques for a precise definition (Cunha et al, 1992; Podlasek et al, 1999a, 1999b).

The prostate forms acini and collecting ducts by arborization into the urethra; the growth occurs primarily on the tips, as the ducts extend and branch during development. This concept that dynamic growth processes occur along a budding and branching system was developed from studies on the mouse and rat prostate (Sugimura et al, 1986; Banerjee et al, 1993a, 1993b; Cunha, 1994). Studies indicate that several homeobox proteins are centrally involved in this process (Sciavolino and Abate-Shen, 1998), including the sonic hedgehog protein (shh), the forkhead box A1 gene (*Foxa1*), and its downstream regulated target *NKX3.1*. Homeobox proteins derive their name from a shared DNA motif (box) discovered in the early 1980s in *Drosophila* genes encoding a functional DNA-binding domain (homeodomain) shared among multiple genes involved in homeotic regulation (i.e., fruit fly body segment development). Although these genes were initially discovered to be centrally involved in fruit fly anterior-posterior segmental development, homologues have since been discovered to be involved in a wide range of developmental processes for many multicellular organisms (Hombria and Lovegrove, 2003). Interestingly, homeobox genes are often clustered together chromosomally (e.g., *HOX* genes). Hence, it appears that the prostate gland has retained much of this evolutionary segmental patterning through the use of androgen-dependent induction of certain homeobox genes. For instance, the sonic hedgehog protein is expressed in the urogenital sinus contemporaneously with the timing for the first induction of prostatic buds. This induction of sonic hedgehog is androgen dependent, and inhibition of this pathway results in abrogation of prostatic duct formation (Podlasek et al, 1999a). Transgenic experiments have also revealed requirements for the *Foxa1* and *NKX3.1* homeobox protein genes. In the mouse, the *Foxa1*-deficient mouse prostate shows a severely altered ductal pattern (Hsing et al, 2000); an *NKX3.1*-deficient mouse revealed a loss of ductal morphogenesis, restricted to the prostate and palatine glands, but interestingly, the animals were still fertile (Poukka et al, 2000).

At $3^1/_2$ months of fetal development (14 weeks), the prostate has developed a ratio of approximately 70 ductal structures surrounded by stromal components that arise from the mesonephric and paramesonephric mesenchyme. At 5 months of development, an extensive squamous cell metaplasia begins to appear that reaches a peak at 36 weeks and then starts to subside. The decrease in the squamous cell metaplasia, and of the resultant secretions after birth, results in a diminution in the size of the fetal prostate at 3 months of life. During in utero development, the fetus is dependent on the androgens formed from the fetal testes by the Leydig cells that are activated during the second month of gestation and reach a peak at the fourth month.

During the development of the prostate from the urogenital sinus, there is a close reciprocal interaction between the stromal and epithelial tissue components (Verhoeven et al, 1992; Cunha, 1994). DHT is produced from testosterone by both the epithelium and the mesenchyme; however, the epithelium appears to make much larger amounts of DHT (Randall, 1994). In contrast, Cunha has clearly demonstrated by elegant tissue recombination experiments that it is the androgen receptors in the mesenchyme (not the epithelium) that are required for proper prostate development (Cunha et al, 1983a, 1983b). It has been suggested that a reciprocal action occurs in that DHT is formed in the epithelial cells and diffuses to the androgen receptor in the stromal nuclei of the mesenchymal cells, which then produce an unknown inductive factor that drives the morphogenesis of the epithelial cells. This is thought to be accomplished in part by the DHT induction of specific soluble growth factors, such as epidermal growth factor, keratinocyte growth factor (FGF-7), insulin-like growth factors, fibroblast growth factor (FGF-10) (Thompson and Chung, 1986), and transforming growth factors (TGF-β and TGF-α), in addition to alterations in the insoluble extracellular matrix components interfacing the stromal and epithelial cells. Resolving the exact growth factors and extracellular matrix changes related to these temporal development events will be an important basic research frontier in andrology and urology.

In the development of other organs, it is apparent that growth factors are of a multifunctional nature and can be either stimulators or inhibitors of growth, depending on their dose combinations and sequence of presentation to target cells. For example, the interaction and combination of epidermal growth factor with TGF-β and insulin-like growth factor as well as gonadotropins have been shown to affect the differentiation of other types of reproductive cells, and it is expected that similar roles will be further elucidated for prostate cells as well (Bendell and Dorrington, 1990; Cohen et al, 1991; Martinoli and Pelletier, 1991; Yan et al, 1992; Cohen, 1993; Steiner, 1993). **Growth factors are discussed later, but it is important to note that the müllerian-inhibiting substance (MIS) that is expressed early in gonadal differentiation in the male causes the regression of the müllerian duct as a prerequisite for virilization in the male.** MIS, also called anti-müllerian hormone, is produced by the Sertoli cells of the testes during development of the male, and high local concentration of MIS must be present to bring about ipsilateral regression of each müllerian duct. The requirement for MIS in human male development is well established; the human gene has been isolated, the primary amino acid sequence of MIS has been determined, and it now appears that it is closely related to a family of proteins that include TGF-β, which is a potent inhibitor of normal epithelial growth and functions in a wide variety of cell types (Lane and Donahoe, 1998; Swain and Lovell-Badge, 1999; Hiort and Holterhus, 2000).

The temporal events in the development of the male reproductive tract and the involvement of both steroids and growth hormones are of fundamental importance in developmental biology but also may be of great interest to pathology of the prostate. McNeal (1984) proposed that BPH may be caused by an adult reawakening of dormant embryonic growth potential of the adult stroma and that the proliferation of the stromal elements in the periurethral region of the human prostate can stimulate the ingrowth of epithelial cells to produce a benign growth.

Postnatal Development and Hormone Imprinting of Growth

At birth, the majority of the prostatic acini are lined with epithelia characterized by extensive squamous metaplasia (Andrews, 1951; Aumuller, 1979). **The stimulation of postnatal development is believed to be under the control of residual maternal steroids such as estrogens, and there is a**

> ### KEY POINTS: EMBRYONIC DEVELOPMENT
>
> - The wolffian ducts develop into the seminal vesicles, epididymis, vas deferens, ampulla, and ejaculatory duct. The developmental growth of this group of glands is stimulated by fetal testosterone and not dihydrotestosterone.
>
> - Through tissue recombination experiments in mice and rats, the developing mesenchyme and epithelium have been shown to be reciprocal. That is, the development, growth, and function of the male and female urogenital tract require stromal-epithelial interaction and action of steroid sex hormones.

postnatal prostatic involutional phase that occurs during the first 5 months after birth. Large transient surges of serum androgen, estrogen, and progesterone normally occur very early in postnatal life in both rats and humans. **In the human male, neonatal surges in testosterone are observed to peak between 2 and 3 months of age. During this period, serum testosterone levels rise to 60 times normal prepubertal levels and often reach the adult serum testosterone range of about 400 ng/dL** (Forest, 1979; Pang et al, 1979). Serum estradiol levels are high at birth in both humans and rats but quickly fall to nearly undetectable levels in the first few days after birth. There is a subsequent transient prepubertal surge in serum estradiol levels in the rat but not in the human. Human progesterone levels are high at birth and are believed to be elevated from placental progesterone production. There is a second transient progesterone surge that occurs in humans at approximately 2 months of age (Forest, 1979).

Rodent studies have shown that neonatal estrogens are of critical importance in initiating the long-term growth potential of the prostate, in a process referred to as imprinting (Kincl et al, 1963; Swanson and van der Werff Ten Bosch, 1963; Morrison and Johnson, 1966; Bronson et al, 1972; Rajfer and Coffey, 1978, 1979; Chung and MacFadden, 1980; Naslund and Coffey, 1986, 1987; Prins and Birch, 1995). Imprinting specifically refers to permanent differential gene expression in somatic cells through epigenetic processes, such as DNA methylation (Higgins et al, 1982). High doses of neonatal estrogens result in prostatic imprinting, leading to significant increases in subsequent prostatic hyperplasia and dysplasia as well as net decreases in androgen receptor expression (Prins, 1992; Risbridger et al, 2005). The estrogen receptors (ER) are differentially expressed in prostate. ER-α is expressed early (1 week) in the stroma of the ventral prostate morphogenesis but by 2 weeks is preferentially expressed in the epithelia, and ER-α is absent altogether in the ventral prostate by 4 weeks. By contrast, ER-β exists in the epithelial compartment as the dominant estrogen receptor by the fourth week. High-dose neonatal estrogen imprinting does not occur in ER-α knockout mice, whereas it does occur in ER-β knockout mice, suggesting that the stromal compartment plays a major role in regulating prostatic imprinting (Prins et al, 2001). Thus, it appears that both the androgen and estrogen receptors in the stromal compartment play a dominant role in prostate imprinting and ductal morphogenesis.

Whereas the ability of neonatal and prepubertal steroids to imprint the prostate has been established as a critical factor in these animal studies, these findings have not been fully defined for the human prostate, although it does seem likely that similar processes may be involved in the development of BPH (Naslund and Coffey, 1986, 1987).

KEY POINT: HORMONE IMPRINTING OF GROWTH

■ For hormone imprinting of the prostate to be complete, in addition to the testosterone surge, there is also the need for neonatal estrogens.

Prostate Cell Types

The prostatic epithelium in the human is composed of two major cell types, epithelial cells and stromal cells (Table 85–1). The prostate epithelial compartment consists of stem cells, basal epithelial cells, transit-amplifying cells, neuroendocrine cells, and terminally differentiated luminal secretory epithelial cells (De Marzo et al, 1998a). The stromal compartment architecturally serves as structural support (De Marzo et al, 1998a, 1998b) and consists predominantly of connective tissue, smooth muscle cells, and fibroblasts. Most of these prostate cell types have been at least partially characterized in vitro (Peehl, 2005).

In most glands with renewing cell populations, there is a steady-state flow of cells from quiescent stem cells to a more rapidly dividing pool of transient proliferating cells. This proliferating population finally reaches terminal differentiation, characterized by metabolically active secretory epithelium. Cells that have reached their limit of replication are said to be senescent if they are still metabolically active or apoptotic if they have initiated the irreversible process of programmed cell death (Kyprianou and Isaacs, 1988; Tenniswood et al, 1992; Isaacs, 1993; De Marzo et al, 1998a, 1998b). Senescence, apoptosis, and cellular replication are all normal physiologic processes whose dysregulation may lead to hyperplasia or neoplasia (Isaacs, 1993).

Epithelial Cells

In the prostate, the most common, tall (10 to 20 μm) columnar secretory epithelial cells are terminally differentiated and have a low proliferative index (De Marzo et al, 1998b; Uzgare et al, 2004); they are easily distinguished by their morphologic features and abundant secretory granules and enzymes. Secretory cells stain abundantly with prostate-specific antigen (PSA), acid phosphatase, androgen receptor, leucine amino peptidase, and 15-lipoxygenase 2 (Shappell et al, 1999, 2001; Bhatia et al, 2003), and they are also rich in keratins (subtypes 8 and 19) (Brawer et al, 1985; Goossens et al, 2002; van Leenders and Schalken, 2003; Peehl, 2005). These tall, columnar secretory cells appear like rows of a picket fence resting next to each other connected by cell adhesion molecules; the apical aspect of these cells projects into the lumen, with the

---

Table 85–1. Summary of the Anatomy and Cell Biology of the Prostate Gland

Components	Properties
Development	
Seminal vesicles	From wolffian ducts through testosterone stimulation
Prostate	From urogenital sinus through dihydrotestosterone stimulation
Prostate zones	
Anterior fibromuscular	30% of prostate mass, no glandular elements, smooth muscle
Peripheral	Largest zone, 75% of prostate glandular elements, site of carcinomas
Central	25% of prostate glandular elements, surrounds ejaculatory ducts, may be of wolffian duct origin, seminal vesicle–like
Preprostatic transition	
	Smallest, surrounds upper urethra complex, sphincter
	5% of prostate glandular elements, site of benign prostatic hyperplasia
	15% to 30% of prostate volume
Epithelial cells	
Basal	Small undifferentiated, keratin-rich (types 4, 5, 6) pluripotent cells; less than 10% of epithelial cell number
Transient proliferating	Incorporate thymidine
Columnar secretory	Terminal differentiated, nondividing, rich in acid phosphatase and prostate-specific antigen; 20 μm tall, most abundant cell; keratin types 8, 18, 19
Neuroendocrine	Serotonin rich, APUD type
Stroma cells	
Smooth muscle	Actin-rich, myosin
Fibroblast	Vimentin rich and associated with fibronectin
Endothelial	Associated with fibronectin, alkaline phosphatase positive
Tissue matrix	
Extracellular matrix	
Basement membrane	Type IV collagen meshwork, laminin rich, fibronectin
Connective tissue	Type I and type III fibrillar collagen, elastin
Glycosaminoglycans	Sulfates of dermatan, chondroitin, and heparin; hyaluronic acid
Cytomatrix	Tubulin, actin, and intermediate filaments of keratin
Nuclear matrix	DNA tight-binding proteins, RNA and residual nuclear proteins

base attached to a basement membrane through integrin receptors (De Marzo et al, 1998a). The nucleus is at the base just below a clear zone (2 to 8 μm) of abundant Golgi apparatus, and the upper cellular periphery is rich in secretory granules and enzymes. The apical plasma membrane facing the lumen possesses microvilli, and secretions move into the open collecting spaces of the acinus. These epithelial cells ring the periphery of the acinus and produce secretions into the acini that drain into ducts connected to the urethra. With androgen ablation, the typical secretory cells decrease by 90% in number, become cuboidal, and shrink by 80% in volume and 60% in height (DeKlerk et al, 1976; De Marzo et al, 1998a; Uzgare et al, 2004). Interspaced among these secretory epithelial cells are two important classes of cells, the **neuroendocrine cells** and the **transit-amplifying cells.**

Neuroendocrine Cells

The neuroendocrine cells are intraglandular and intraductal hybrid epithelial cells that reside among the more abundant secretory epithelium in the normal prostate gland (diSant-Agnese 1984, 1985; Bonkhoff and Remberger, 1996; Xue et al, 1997, 2000; Huss et al, 2004). These cells are found in the epithelium of the acini and in ducts of all parts of the gland as well as in the urothelium of the prostatic urethral mucosa (diSant-Agnese, 1984; Abrahamsson et al, 1987; Abrahamsson and Lilja, 1989; Abrahamsson, 1999; Sadar et al, 1999). Neuroendocrine cells are scattered throughout the glands but are most often found in the periurethral ducts and verumontanum. **There are two types of neuroendocrine cells: the first is open and possesses specialized microvilli that protrude into the lumen; the second is closed with long dendrite-like processes that extend to nearby epithelial cells and basal cells close to afferent and efferent nerves** (diSant-Agnese, 1984, 1985; Abrahamsson, 1999; Vashchenko and Abrahamsson, 2005). Neuroendocrine cells are terminally differentiated (i.e., nonproliferating) and are negative for expression of androgen receptor, PSA, and Bcl-2. They may typically express chromogranin-A, neuron-specific enolase, serotonin (5-hydroxytryptamine), and synaptophysin (Abrahamsson and Lilja, 1989; Abrahamsson, 1999; Vashchenko and Abrahamsson, 2005). Xue and colleagues (1997, 2000) reported the cell kinetics of the prostate exocrine and neuroendocrine epithelium in the human and suggested a link between early development of the prostate and this system. Later, Aumuller and associates (1999) demonstrated for the first time that neuroendocrine cells within the prostate may represent a distinct cell lineage of their own, different from other prostatic cells that derive from the urogenital sinus. Current evidence suggests that neuroendocrine cells regulate the growth, differentiation, and secretory activity of the prostate epithelium through paracrine and autocrine control (Abrahamsson, 1999; Vashchenko and Abrahamsson, 2005). Neuroendocrine cells bring about their regulatory activity by the secretion of hormonal polypeptides or biogenic amines such as serotonin, which is a common marker for these cells. High-pressure liquid chromatography measurements have shown that normal human prostate tissue contains approximately 1400 ng of serotonin per gram of tissue, and this would certainly emphasize the importance of these cells (Davis, 1987). Higgins and Gosling (1989) have studied the structure and intrinsic

innervation of the normal human prostate and have observed acetylcholinesterase-containing nerves associated with smooth muscle in both the peripheral and the central parts of the prostate. In addition, they have shown that the majority of the acini in the peripheral and central regions possess a rich plexus of autonomic nerves and that vasoactive intestinal peptide–positive nerve fibers are found in relation to the epithelial lining acini in the central and peripheral regions of the gland. Lepor and Kuhar (1984) characterized and studied the location of the muscarinic cholinergic receptor in human prostate tissue and localized it to the epithelial cells. This is consistent with the neuropharmacology of muscarinic cholinergic agonist, which has a marked effect on increasing prostatic secretion. However, the α_1-adrenergic receptor has its effect in the human prostatic stromal compartment. This is of great clinical importance because of the use of selective α_1-adrenergic antagonists to alleviate bladder outlet obstruction secondary to BPH (Lepor and Shapiro, 1984; Lepor et al, 1988; Lepor, 1990, 1993, 1995). **Recent work has demonstrated three subtypes of the α_1-adrenergic receptor (α_{1A}, α_{1B}, and α_{1D}).** Of these, the α_{1A} receptor appears to be linked to smooth muscle contraction of the prostate. The "uroselectivity" and the clinical use of various pharmacologic agents are discussed in Chapter 87.

There are in fact numerous bioactive macromolecules (serotonin, bombesin, neuron-specific enolase, calcitonin gene family members, thyroid-stimulating hormone–like peptide, somatostatin, synaptophysin, and parathyroid hormone–like peptide) and numerous receptors for these molecules that are produced by neuroendocrine cells, which are likely to influence the growth, differentiation, and secretion of epithelium of the prostate in both normal and malignant conditions (Long et al, 2005; Vashchenko and Abrahamsson, 2005).

Transit-Amplifying Cells

Isaacs and Coffey (1989) **reported the concept of transit-amplifying cells, which are located in the basal layer of the epithelial compartment** (Bonkhoff, 1998a, 1998b), **as intermediate cell types between undifferentiated stem cells and the nonproliferating basal layer.** Several investigators have characterized the pluripotential prostate phenotype of the transit-amplifying cells. This indicates that they have an intermediate keratin biomarker profile that includes keratin 5/14 basal cell and keratin 8/18 secretory cell characteristics and numerous other stem-like cells or progenitors of this cell (De Marzo et al, 1998a, 1998b; Schalken and van Leenders, 2003; Huss et al, 2004; Uzgare et al, 2004). Uzgare and colleagues (2004) characterized select phenotypic and protein biomarker expression of basal and luminal compartments of the prostate in terms of stem cells, transit-amplifying cells, and intermediate cells on the basis of their limited life span (7 to 10 passages) but high proliferative activity (~65%) as assessed by the Ki67 biomarker (Fig. 85–1). The transit-amplifying cells tend to be androgen receptor negative and also possess high-molecular-weight keratins 5 and 14 as well as 8 and 18, which are secretory biomarkers for differentiated secretory epithelial cells. In addition, these transit-amplifying cells produce p53-related p63 mRNA, c-Met, plasma receptor for hepatocyte growth factor, and Bcl-2 (a pro-survival protein) (Bonkhoff

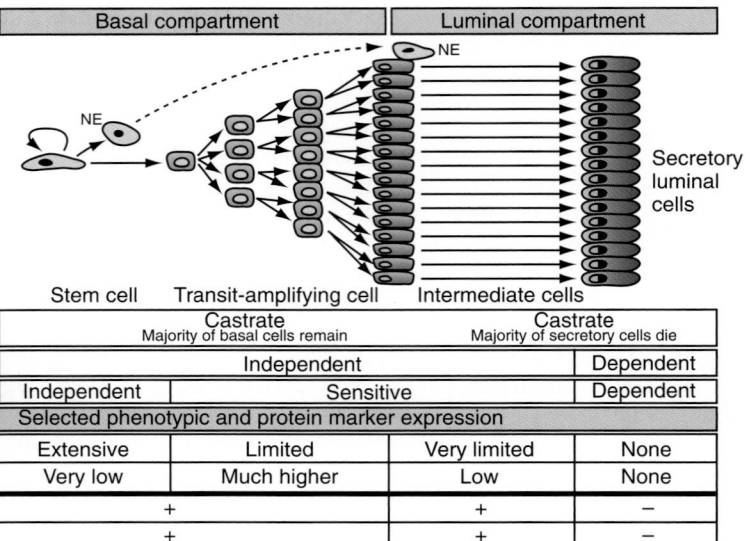

	Basal compartment		Luminal compartment	

	Stem cell	Transit-amplifying cell	Intermediate cells	
		Castrate Majority of basal cells remain	Castrate Majority of secretory cells die	
Androgen response		Independent		Dependent
Andromedin response	Independent	Sensitive		Dependent
Selected phenotypic and protein marker expression				
Self-renewal capacity	Extensive	Limited	Very limited	None
Proliferative index	Very low	Much higher	Low	None
Keratin 5		+	+	−
Keratin 14		+	+	−
p63		+	−	−
Bcl-2		+	+	−
P-cadherin		+	?	+
GST-pi		+	+/−	−
c-Met		+/−	+/−	−
p27^{Kip1}	+	−	−/+	+
Keratins 8 and 18		−	+	+
NKX3.1		−	−/+	+
PSA		−	−/+	+
PSAP		−	−/+	+
AR		−	−/+	+

Figure 85–1. Stem cell model of prostatic epithelial cell compartmentalization. Prostate gland consists of a number of stem cell units that arise from one stem cell. Such a stem cell is located in the basal epithelial layer of the prostate and on division gives rise to a population of transit-amplifying cells. The transit-amplifying cells divide in the basal layer, and a fraction of them differentiate and move into the secretory luminal epithelial layer. As transit-amplifying cells differentiate and move into a secretory luminal layer from the basal layer, they acquire expression of a number of genetic markers, as indicated. AR, androgen receptor; NE, neuroendocrine cells; PSA, prostate-specific antigen; PSAP, prostate-specific acid phosphatase; + denotes expression of marker; − denotes lack of detectable expression of marker.

et al, 1993; Bonkhoff and Remberger, 1996; van Leenders and Schalken, 2003; Uzgare et al, 2004). Survival of terminally differentiated secretory luminal cells and proliferation of transit-amplifying cells require androgens presumably through the secretion of androgen-regulated growth factors referred to as andromedins (Planz et al, 1999; Hayward, 2002; Uzgare et al, 2004; Long et al, 2005).

Basal/Stem Cells

In comparison to the secretory epithelial cells, the basal cells are much smaller, have a low mitotic index, and are less abundant, accounting for less than 10% of the total cell number. Basal cells express a distinct keratin subtype profile (subtypes 5, 14, and 15) compared with the columnar epithelial cells (subtypes 8 and 18) (O'Bryan et al, 1990; Hudson, 2004). Basal cells are small and flattened with relatively little cytoplasm and condensed chromatin or large, cuboidal cells with increased cytoplasm and less condensed chromatin (De Marzo et al, 1998b). Basal cells rest on the basement membrane wedged between the bases of adjacent, tall, columnar epithelial cells (Bonkhoff and Remberger, 1996; De Marzo et al, 1998a, 1998b). Understanding the biology of basal cells is important because there is growing evidence that many neoplasms may represent stem cell diseases (Isaacs and Coffey, 1989; Bonkhoff and Remberger, 1996). The basal cell compartment is the likely source of the epithelial stem cells of the prostate (Robinson et al, 1998; Uzgare et al, 2004) as they are relatively undifferentiated with a low proliferative index (~1%) and almost devoid

of secretory products, such as PSA and prostatic acid phosphatase (De Marzo et al, 1998a) (also see Fig. 85–1).

Androgen deprivation does not affect stem cells but rather enriches for them, as the more terminally differentiated cells initiate apoptosis. After castration, testosterone supplementation can restore prostate growth by stimulating stem cell proliferation. When mice are castrated after implantation with human prostate primary xenografts and then restimulated with testosterone, the basal cell population is highly overrepresented, consistent with the concept that the basal compartment contains prostate epithelial stem cells (Huss et al, 2004). The phenotypic plasticity of human prostate stem cells is clearly exemplified in this model as evidenced by the multiple lineages produced in response to several microenvironmental signals when the tissue architecture is fully maintained, a phenomenon also duplicated by other in vivo and in vitro models (Liu et al, 1997b; Tsujimura et al, 2002; Hudson and Masters, 2003; van Leenders and Schalken, 2003; Hudson, 2004; Peehl, 2005).

Advances have been made in the molecular identification of the prostate stem cells and transient proliferating cells. Previously, lectins were used as cell markers to identify some types of basal and secretory cells (Sinowatz et al, 1990). Merk and coworkers (1986) reported that atrophic canine prostatic epithelial cells have a pluripotentiality of response and can change their keratin pattern, secretory granules, and phenotype on the basis of treatment with estrogens or androgens. More recently, Bonkhoff (Bonkhoff and Remberger, 1996) studied the immunoprofile of three well-characterized prolif-erating antigens (Ki-67, PCNA, and MIB-1), in normal and hyperplastic prostate, and demonstrated that basal cells may serve a proliferative role in epithelial cell renewal within the prostate. Finally, Walensky (Walensky et al, 1993) reported on a novel 32-kD (pp32) nuclear phosphoprotein selectively expressed by prostate cells that were competent for self-renewal ("stem cells"). This protein, as well as the mRNA for this protein, was present in the "stem cell" population within the rat prostate; the mRNA and not the protein was present within the amplifying population of cells, and neither the message nor the product of pp32 was present in the terminally differentiated "transit" population of cells. Several investiga-tors have better defined the molecular signatures of the basal stem-like cells in both normal and disease states (Hudson, 2004; Huss et al, 2004). Multiple studies have catalogued candidate prostate-specific stem cell biomarkers, including prostate stem cell antigen (PSCA), stem cell antigen 1 (Sca-1), α_6 integrin, $\alpha_2\beta_1$ integrin, $p27^{Kip1}$, keratins 5/14, telomerase, pp32, p63, glutathione S-transferase pi (GSTpi), cluster deter-minant (CD133), and Bcl-2 (Liu et al, 1997b; De Marzo et al, 1998a, 1998b; Collins et al, 2001; van Leenders and Schalken, 2003; Richardson et al, 2004; Uzgare et al, 2004; Burger et al, 2005; Long et al, 2005).

KEY POINTS: PROSTATE CELL TYPES

■ The prostatic epithelium in the human is composed of two major cell types, epithelial cells and stromal cells.

■ The epithelium cell types include mature secretory and terminally differentiated cells, neuroendocrine cells, transit-amplifying cells, and basal/stem cells.

The Stroma and Tissue Matrix

The noncellular stroma and connective tissue of the prostate make up what is termed the ground substance and the extra-cellular matrix in what was first suggested by Arcadi (1954) to play an important role in prostate function and disease. The extracellular matrix has long been recognized as one of the important inductive components during normal development of many different types of cells (Cunha, 1976; Hay, 1981; Bissell et al, 1982; Getzenberg et al, 1990; Risbridger et al, 2005). Classic tissue recombination experiments by Cunha and colleagues (Chung and Cunha, 1983; Cunha et al, 1983a, 1983b, 2003, 2004; Cunha, 1994) have clearly shown the direct importance of the isolated embryonic mesenchyme to the induction of differentiation of normal prostatic epithelial cells (see discussion in earlier section). McNeal proposed that in BPH, the stroma may be reactivated in adult life to return to an embryonic state, thus stimulating abnormal growth; this concept has generated a great deal of interest and effort to understand these tissue components of the prostate. To test whether adult prostate cells could be stimulated by embryonic factors, Chung and colleagues (1984a, 1984b) transplanted a fetal urogenital sinus into an adult rat prostate and induced a large hyperplastic overgrowth of adult prostatic tissue stimu-lated by the presence of the factors from the fetal tissue. It is unknown whether direct contact with an insoluble embryonic extracellular matrix or soluble diffusible growth factors and steroids are responsible for these observations (Chung et al, 1992; Stewart et al, 2004). Figure 85–2 is a schematic of path-ways of coupling stromal-epithelial interactions involving both soluble (growth factors and steroids) and insoluble (extracellular matrix, cell-cell, and integrin) interactions.

The epithelial cells rest on the basement lamina or membrane, which is a complex structure containing, in part, collagen types IV and V, glycosaminoglycans, complex polysaccharides, and glycolipids. This layer forms an interface to the stromal compartment that provides structural support

Figure 85–2. The tissue matrix system, a superstructure scaffold network that connects the extracellular matrix components to the cell through interactions with cell adhesion mole-cules (e.g., integrins). Cell adhesion molecules extend through the plasma membrane and connect directly or indirectly to the cytomatrix structures. The cytomatrix directly couples to the nuclear matrix, which attaches and organ-izes the cellular DNA. Cell adhesion molecules and desmosomes connect neighboring cells. (From Getzenberg RH, Pienta KJ, Coffey DS: The tissue matrix: Cell dynamics and hormone action. Endocr Rev 1990;11:399-416.)

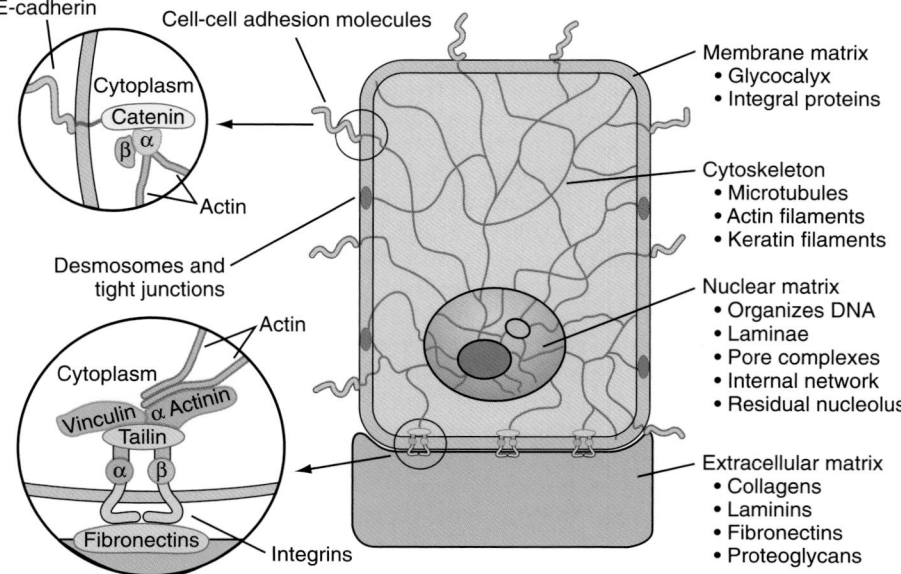

for the basal cells, stem cells, transit-amplifying cells, and secretory epithelium. It consists of an extracellular matrix, ground substance, and a variety of stromal cells, including the fibroblasts, capillary and lymphatic endothelial cells, smooth muscle cells, neuroendocrine cells, and axons (Aumuller, 1983; Mawhinney, 1989; Hayward, 2002; Brar et al, 2003; Saito and Munakata, 2004; Laczko et al, 2005; Long et al, 2005).

In contrast to the extracellular matrix, all mammalian cells are composed of an intracellular cytomatrix or cytoskeleton that is formed from a network of microtubules of 20-nm diameter (tubulins), microfilaments of 6-nm diameter (actins), and intermediate filaments of 10-nm diameter (keratin, desmin, vimentin) (Brar et al, 2003; Etienne-Manneville, 2004; Saito and Munakata, 2004; Lexander et al, 2005). For example, desmin is a central component of all muscle cells, whereas vimentin is found in all fibroblasts. Tubulin is ubiquitous in cells as a microtubular structure that appears to anchor many cellular structures and is a critical factor in determining the shape of the cell. The microfilaments are composed primarily of actin, one of the major proteins in all cells. Actin has the ability to rapidly polymerize and depolymerize and, as such, produces an important structural chemomechanical system when it interacts with myosin within the cell (Etienne-Manneville, 2004). The cytomatrix is centrally involved in the transport of particles as well as in locomotion. The primary intermediate filaments in epithelial cells are the keratins, for which there may be as many as 20 different molecular types and whose expression pattern varies widely among the different epithelial population (e.g., stratified squamous, secretory, basal cell, transit-amplifying cells, stem cells) (Isaacs et al, 1981; Ellis et al, 1984; Purnell et al, 1984; Achtstatter et al, 1985; Brawer et al, 1985; Merk et al, 1986; De Marzo et al, 1998a, 1998b; Schalken and van Leenders, 2003). In contrast, there is usually just one type of vimentin and desmin in fibroblast or muscle cells.

The **cytomatrix** (cytoplasmic skeleton) terminates in the center of the cell by direct attachment to the **nuclear matrix** (see Fig. 85–2). The prostatic epithelial cell therefore has direct structural linkage via the matrix system from the DNA to the plasma membrane. The cytomatrix then makes direct contact with the basement membrane, extracellular matrix, and ground substance of the stroma. This entire interlocking tissue scaffolding or superstructure is termed the **tissue matrix** and may have dynamic properties in ordering and controlling biologic processes as well as in the transport of secretions from the sex accessory tissues (Getzenberg et al, 1990; Konety and Getzenberg, 1999; Etienne-Manneville, 2004; Miner and Yurchenco, 2004; Hallmann et al, 2005).

Understanding the biologic components of the tissue matrix system within sex accessory tissues is of paramount importance to understanding its physiology. The laminin proteins are glycoproteins of the extracellular matrix that mediate attachment of cells to the type IV collagen of the basement membrane (Miner and Yurchenco, 2004; Yurchenco et al, 2004; Hallmann et al, 2005). Laminin is produced by epithelial cells but not by fibroblasts; it is a large molecule with molecular domains that interact with the type IV collagen of the basement membrane and integrin-type receptors within the cell surface glycocalyx of the epithelial cell (Aumailley et al, 2005). Laminins are the major anchor filaments in the basement membranes of epithelial cells that stabilize attachment

of hemidesmosomes via $\alpha_6\beta_4$ integrin (Brar et al, 2003; Miner and Yurchenco, 2004). **The key functional properties of the laminins are cell adhesion, proliferation, differentiation, growth, and migration.** Laminin surrounds the basement membrane of prostate acinar epithelial cells, capillaries, smooth muscle, and nerve fibers but not lymphatics, lymphocytes, or fibroblasts; the laminin structure and its distribution are disrupted in BPH and higher grade prostatic interepithelial neoplasia and higher grade prostate neoplasms (Sinha et al, 1989; Brar et al, 2003; Miner and Yurchenco, 2004; Yu et al, 2004).

In summary, the development and maintenance of the normal zonal anatomy of the prostate (Laczko et al, 2005) **occur through androgen-dependent and highly regulated tissue morphogenesis in processes involving epithelial cell differentiation, proliferation, and apoptosis** (Cunha et al, 2003, 2004; Risbridger et al, 2005). **Communication through numerous extracellular interactions is directed to the intracellular cytoskeleton and then to the nuclear matrix, which ultimately regulates a variety of transcriptional cell functions that control cell size and shape, cell motility, epithelial cell turnover, and proliferation as well as differentiation** (Getzenberg et al, 1990; Pienta, 1993a; Sommerfeld et al, 1996; Miner and Yurchenco 2004). The anatomy and cell biology of the prostate gland are summarized in Table 85–1.

KEY POINTS: LAMININ PROTEINS

■ Laminin surrounds the basement membrane of prostate acinar epithelial cells, capillaries, smooth muscle, and nerve fibers but not lymphatics, lymphocytes, or fibroblasts.

■ The laminin structure and its distribution are disrupted in BPH and higher grade prostatic interepithelial neoplasia and higher grade prostate neoplasms.

■ The key functional properties of the laminins are cell adhesion, proliferation, differentiation, growth, and migration.

ENDOCRINE CONTROL OF PROSTATE GROWTH
Endocrine Overview

The prostate, like other sex accessory tissues, is stimulated in its growth, maintenance, and secretory function by the continued presence of certain hormones and growth factors. Foremost among these is testosterone, which is converted within the prostate into the more active androgen dihydrotestosterone (DHT). Testosterone is synthesized in the Leydig cells of the testes from pregnenolone by a series of reversible reactions. However, once testosterone is converted by 5α-reductase into DHT or converted by aromatase into estrogens, the process is irreversible; **testosterone can be converted to DHT or estrogens, but estrogens and DHT cannot be converted to testosterone.** Androgens, estrogens, and adrenal steroids are believed to have strong effects on different cells and tissues in the body that can vary with development and age. This varies from embryonic development and differentiation into neonatal genomic imprinting, through to puberty, and on into adult maintenance and later senescence. Therefore, androgen ablation or androgen treatments have a wide variety of physiologic effects that must be taken into consideration.

The generalized endocrine physiology of the prostate is depicted in Figure 85–3. The hypothalamus releases a small 10-residue polypeptide (decapeptide) referred to as luteinizing hormone–releasing hormone, also called gonadotropin-releasing hormone. Under the stimulation of luteinizing hormone–releasing hormone, the pituitary releases luteinizing hormone that is transported to the testes and acts directly on the Leydig cells to stimulate de novo steroid synthesis and release of testosterone, the major serum androgen of the body. Most of the estrogen in the male is derived from peripheral conversion of androgens to estrogens through aromatization. Exogenous estrogens, such as diethylstilbestrol, block androgen action not primarily by direct effects on the prostate but indirectly through blocking pituitary function. The estrogen causes a negative feedback on luteinizing hormone release that reduces the serum signal for testicular testosterone production; therefore, estrogen acts as an effective "chemical castration."

In addition to testosterone, the adrenal secretes a weak androgen, androstenedione; however, this is not a major pathway since, in both animals and humans, castration leads to almost complete involution of the prostate, meaning that insufficient adrenal androgens are present to stimulate any meaningful growth of the normal prostate. Similar to serum testosterone, androstenedione can undergo aromatization to estrone. Overproduction of androstenedione, such as occurs in certain forms of congenital adrenal hyperplasia, may stimulate prostate growth; however, again, the role of adrenal androgens in regulating prostate growth is minor. The presence of a nontesticular minor androgen source has led to the concept of total androgen blockade for the treatment of advanced prostate cancer, whereby both a luteinizing hormone–releasing hormone agonist and a nonsteroidal autoantigen are combined to eliminate testosterone production and block any residual androgen stimulation of the prostate from the adrenal gland. This strategy remains controversial and is discussed at length elsewhere.

Androgen Production by the Testes

Since the testes produce the major serum androgen supporting prostate and sex accessory tissue growth, it is important to briefly review this function. In the normal human male, the major circulating serum androgen is testosterone, which is almost exclusively (>95%) of testicular origin. **Under normal physiologic conditions, the Leydig cells of the testis are the major source of the testicular androgens.** The Leydig cells are stimulated by the gonadotropins (primarily the luteinizing hormone) to synthesize testosterone from acetate and cholesterol. The spermatic vein concentration of testosterone is 40 to 50 µg/100 mL, approximately 75 times more concentrated than the level detected in the peripheral venous serum (Hammond, 1978), which is approximately 600 ng of testosterone per 100 mL. Other androgens also leave the testes by the spermatic vein, and these include androstanediol, androstenedione (3 µg/100 mL), dehydroepiandrosterone (7 µg/100 mL), and DHT (0.4 µg/100 mL). The concentra-

Figure 85–3. Simplified endocrinology of the prostate. Luteinizing hormone–releasing hormone (LHRH), also termed gonadotropin-releasing hormone (GnRH), stimulates the pituitary to release the gonadotropins luteinizing hormone (LH) and follicle-stimulating hormone (FSH), which stimulate the Leydig cells of the testes to synthesize testosterone. Testosterone is the major serum androgen stimulating prostate growth. Peripheral conversion of testosterone by aromatization forms the estrogens in the male. The adrenal gland is under stimulation by adrenocorticotropic hormone (ACTH) and releases the minor androgens, such as androstenedione, which is also converted peripherally to estrogens. Prolactin has also been shown to have a minor effect in stimulating androgen-induced prostate growth. The prostate can produce its own growth factors (autocrine or paracrine) or respond to circulating growth factors.

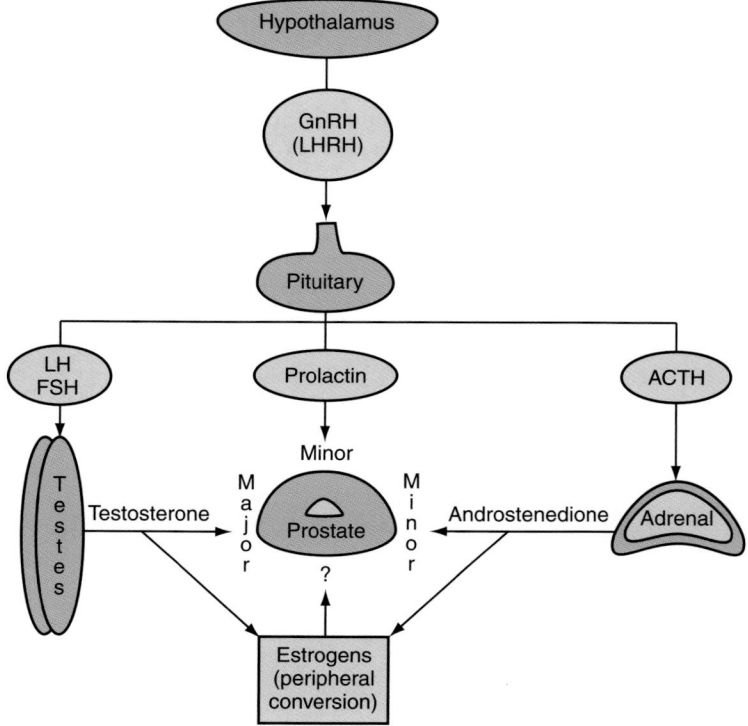

tions of these androgens are much lower in the spermatic vein than the concentration of testosterone, with all being less than 15% of the concentration of testosterone.

The total testosterone that enters the plasma is referred to as the testosterone blood production rate and is 6 to 7 mg/day in the human. Although other steroids, such as androstenedione from the adrenals, can be converted by peripheral metabolism to testosterone, they probably account for less than 5% of the overall production of plasma testosterone. The plasma half-life of testosterone is only 10 to 20 minutes, which means that a man undergoing bilateral simple orchiectomy is functionally castrate within 1 to 2 hours of surgery.

The average testosterone concentration in the adult human male plasma is approximately 611 ng/100 mL ± 186 with a normal range of 300 to 1000 that is equal to 10.4 to 34.7 nmol/L in SI units (Table 85–2). Serum testosterone level is not remarkably related to age between 25 and 70 years, although it does decline gradually to approximately 500 ng/100 mL after 70 years of age. It is recognized that plasma concentrations of testosterone can vary widely in an individual on any one day and may reflect both episodic and diurnal variations in the production rate.

Only 2% of the total serum testosterone is unbound (free testosterone) in the plasma, corresponding to a concentration of approximately 15 ng/100 mL or less than 1 nM. It is only this free testosterone that is available for prostate uptake for metabolism to DHT or for uptake by the liver and intestines primarily to form 17-ketosteroids. Metabolic androgens such as 17-ketosteroids are then secreted into the urine as water-soluble glucuronide or sulfate conjugates. The total 17-ketosteroid level in the urine in adult men is 4 to 25 mg/24 hours and is not an accurate index of testosterone production, since other steroids from the adrenals as well as nonandrogenic steroids can be metabolized to 17-ketosteroids. Only small (25 to 160 µg/day) amounts of testosterone enter the urine without metabolism, and this urinary testosterone represents less than 2% of the daily testosterone production.

Although testosterone is the primary plasma androgen inducing growth of the prostate gland and other sex accessory tissues, it appears to function as a prohormone in that the most active form of the androgen in the prostate is not testosterone but rather DHT (Farnsworth and Brown, 1963; Shimazaki et al, 1965a, 1965b; Anderson and Liao, 1968; Bruchovsky and Wilson, 1968a, 1968b) (Fig. 85–4). The formation of DHT involves the reduction of the double bond in the A ring of testosterone through the enzymatic action of the enzyme 5α-reductase (Fig. 85–5). There are at least two isoforms of this enzyme (type I and type II). Type II 5α-reductase expression predominates in human accessory sex tissues and is localized to the fibromuscular stromal compartment (Silver et al, 1994). The type I isoform predominates in skin, in prostatic epithelia, and to a lesser extent in prostatic fibromuscular stroma. Inhibition of 5α-reductase by finasteride appears to be largely selective for the type II isoform (Iehle et al, 1995; Habib et al, 1997); the newer agent dutasteride inhibits both type I and type II 5α-reductase. Both drugs appear to exert similar effects in terms of reduction in prostatic volume and serum PSA concentration, suggesting that the type II isoform is the only clinically significant isoform present in the prostate. **DHT concentration in the plasma of normal men is low, 56 ± 20 ng/100 mL, in comparison to testosterone,** which is 11-fold higher at approximately 611 ng/100 mL (see Table 85–2). In summary, although DHT is a potent androgen (1.5 to 2.5 times as potent as testosterone in most bioassay systems), its low plasma concentration and tight binding to plasma proteins diminishes its direct importance as a circulating androgen affecting prostate and seminal vesicle growth. In contrast, DHT is of paramount importance within the prostate, where it is formed from testosterone. **DHT is the major form of androgen found within the prostate gland (5 ng/g tissue wet weight) and is fivefold higher than testosterone.** In the prostate, DHT binds to androgen receptors and activates the receptors to regulate a variety of cellular processes. In summary, DHT becomes the major androgen regulating the cellular events of growth, differentiation, and function in the prostate.

The normal adult male plasma levels of some important steroids are summarized in Table 85–2. These values are derived as averages from numerous studies. Individual values can fluctuate with age, time of day, medications, stress, hospitalization, and environmental changes.

Table 85–2. Average Plasma Levels of Sex Steroids in Healthy Human Males

Steroid (common name)	Plasma Concentration (ng/100 mL)	Relative Molarity	Daily Blood Production Rate (mg/day)	Relative Androgenicity (rat VP assay)
Testosterone	611 ± 186	100	6.6 ± 0.5	100
Dihydrotestosterone	56 ± 20	9	0.3 ± 0.06	181
5α-Androstane-3α, 17β-diol (3α-androstanediol)	14 ± 4	2	0.2 ± 0.03	126
5α-Androstane-3β, 17β-diol (3β-androstanediol)		<2	<0.3	18
Androstenediol	161 ± 52	26		0.21
Androsterone	54 ± 32	9	0.28	53
Androstenedione	150 ± 54	25	1.4	39
Dehydroepiandrosterone	501 ± 98	81	29	15
Dehydroepiandrosterone sulfate	135,925 ±48,000	17,619		<1
Progesterone		30	4.5	
17β-Estradiol	2.5 ± 0.08		0.4	0.75
Estrone		4.6	0.8	0.045

VP, ventral prostate.

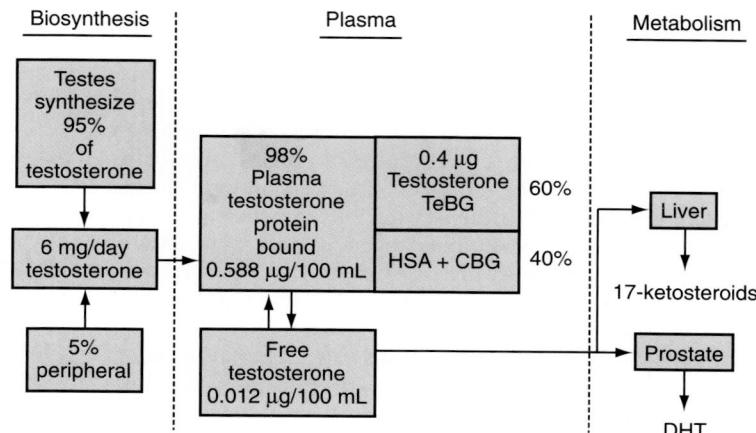

Figure 85-4. Quantitative assessment of the testicular biosynthesis, plasma transport, and metabolism of testosterone. Plasma testosterone is bound to testosterone-binding globulin (TeBG), human serum albumin (HSA), and cortisol-binding globulin (CBG). All numbers are average values for the normal adult male. DHT, dihydrotestosterone.

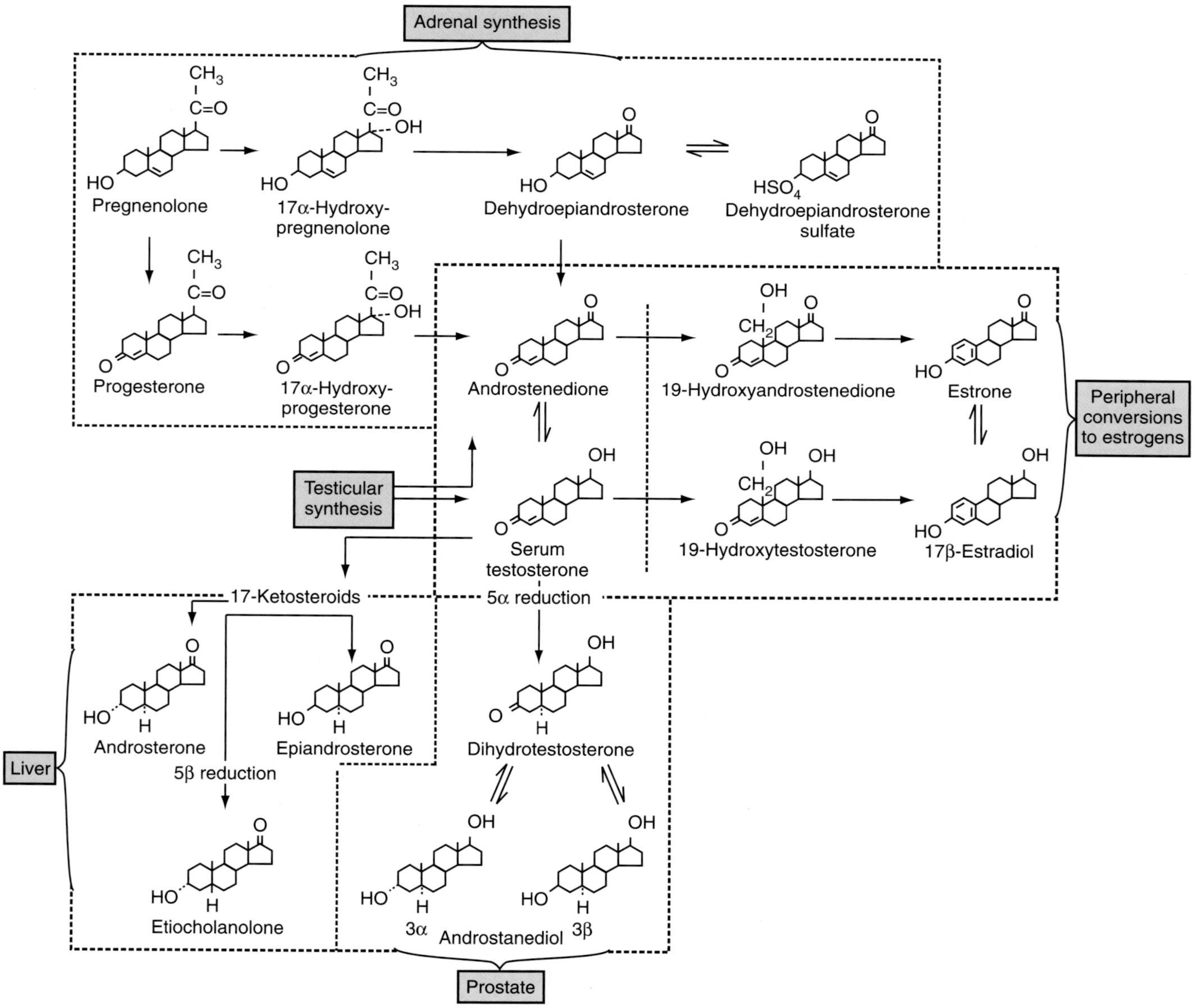

Figure 85-5. Overview of the synthesis and metabolism of testosterone in four main body compartments: adrenal synthesis of androstenedione; peripheral conversion of androgens (androstenedione and testosterone) to estrogens; formation of active androgen (DHT) within the prostate; inactivation in the liver of testosterone to three types of 17-ketosteroids.

Adrenal Androgens

There is evidence that overproduction of adrenal steroids can stimulate growth of the prostate gland. For example, in humans, abnormal virilism has been observed in immature males with a hyperfunctioning adrenal cortex. In rodents, overstimulation of the adrenals can also induce limited prostate growth even in the absence of testicular androgens. For example, administration of exogenous ACTH to castrated animals does significantly increase the growth of sex accessory tissue (Tullner, 1963; Tisell, 1970; Walsh and Gittes, 1970). However, the effect of normal levels of adrenal androgens on the prostate in non-castrated humans and adult male rats does not appear to be significant since adrenalectomy has little effect on prostate size, DNA, or morphologic characteristics of the sex accessory tissue (Mobbs et al, 1973; Oesterling et al, 1986). Furthermore, after castration in animals, with the adrenals intact, the prostate will finally diminish to a very small size (90% reduction in total cell mass). Finally, the small involuted ventral prostate in the castrated rat cannot be significantly reduced further by additional adrenalectomy or hypophysectomy (Kyprianou and Isaacs, 1987). In castrated rats, the DHT level in the prostatic tissue is approximately 20% of that in normal intact animals. Adrenalectomy lowers the DHT to nondetectable levels without further diminution in prostate growth. This indicates that a threshold level of DHT is required in the prostate to stimulate growth and the castrate level is below this threshold. It has also been concluded similarly that the prostate of man does not restore itself after castration, indicating that adrenal androgens are insufficient to compensate for the loss of testicular function. Quantitative morphometry of the human prostate (Oesterling et al, 1986) also confirms that the adrenal gland has little effect on the normal prostate epithelial cell size.

The adrenal steroids dehydroepiandrosterone and the conjugate dehydroepiandrosterone sulfate as well as androstenedione are androgens synthesized from acetate and cholesterol (Fig. 85–5) that are secreted by the normal human adrenal glands. Essentially all of the dehydroepiandrosterone in the male plasma is of adrenal cortex origin, and the production rate in man is 10 to 30 mg/day. **Less than 1% of the total testosterone in the plasma is derived from dehydroepiandrosterone** (Horton, 1976; MacDonald, 1976). The prostate and seminal vesicles of the rat and the human prostate can slowly hydrolyze dehydroepiandrosterone sulfate to free steroids through a prostate sulfatase enzymatic activity, but the degree of conversion is low; hence, dehydroepiandrosterone sulfate is not a potent androgen.

A second adrenal androgen is androstenedione, and the plasma concentration in adult men is approximately 150 ± 54 ng/100 mL (see Table 85–2). The blood production rate of androstenedione in human males is about 2 to 6 mg/day, with approximately 20% of the androstenedione being generated by peripheral metabolism of other steroids. **Androstenedione cannot be converted directly to DHT.** An important role for androstenedione in the male may be its peripheral conversion to estrogens through the aromatase reaction (see Fig. 85–5).

The adrenal gland also produces C21 steroids (e.g., progesterone). The plasma production rate at 0.75 mg/day is low, producing a low plasma progesterone concentration of 30 ng/100 mL. Although progesterone is weakly androgenic, it does not exert a significant effect on the prostate at the low concentrations present in normal male plasma. **In summary, under normal conditions, the adrenals do not support significant growth of prostatic tissue.**

Estrogens in the Male

Only small amounts of estrogen are produced directly by the testes. Approximately 75% to 90% of the estrogens in the plasma of young healthy human males are derived from the peripheral conversion of androstenedione and testosterone to estrone and estradiol through the aromatase reaction (see Fig. 85–5) (Horton, 1976; MacDonald, 1976). The androgenic C19 steroids (testosterone and androstenedione) are converted to the estrogenic C18 steroids first by removal of the 19-methyl group followed by the formation of an aromatic or phenolic steroid A ring (aromatase reaction), present in both estradiol and estrone. Estradiol is formed from testosterone and estrone from androstenedione; these two estrogens are interconvertible. **The daily production of estradiol in the human male is about 40 to 50 μg, and only 5 to 10 μg (10% to 25%) can be accounted for by direct testicular secretion** (see Table 85–2).

Estrogen synthesis in human males has been carefully studied by Siiteri and MacDonald (1973), who showed that of the 7.0 mg of testosterone produced in man each day, only 0.35% is converted directly to estradiol, forming 24 μg/day. Of the 2.5 mg of androstenedione produced per day, 1.7% is converted to estrone, producing 42 μg/day. The interconversion of estrone and estradiol yielded a final total peripheral production of approximately 40 μg of estradiol per day. The exact location in the periphery where estrogen production occurs has not been elucidated on a quantitative basis, but it is believed that most of the daily production may involve adipose tissue. The small amount of estrogens secreted directly from the testes may originate in part from the Sertoli cells, since in culture these cells respond to follicle-stimulating hormone stimulation by producing small amounts of estradiol (Dorrington and Armstrong, 1975); in the adult rat, the Leydig cell may be the source of estradiol.

Men older than 50 years may have an increase in total plasma estradiol levels of approximately 50%, with minimal change (<10%) in the free estradiol levels because of increases in binding of the estradiol by elevated serum sex hormone–binding globulin (SHBG, also known as TeBG) levels, which are age related (Vermeulen, 1976). The result of an age-related decrease in the plasma free testosterone level while the free estradiol level is maintained produces a 40% increase in the ratio of free estradiol/free testosterone (Vermeulen et al, 1969; Vermeulen, 1976). It is apparent that the availability of estrogens and androgens in the serum is regulated not only by their total level but also by the free level (i.e., unbound). Since the steroid-binding proteins in the serum can regulate the free levels, it is important to understand how they function.

Androgen-Binding Proteins in the Plasma

Less than 2% of the total testosterone in human plasma is free or unbound; the remaining 98% is bound to several different types of plasma proteins (see Fig. 85–4). The plasma proteins that bind steroids include human serum albumin, testosterone-estrogen–binding globulin (denoted TeBG or SHBG, sex hormone–binding globulin), corticosteroid-binding globulin (also termed transcortin), progesterone-binding globulin, and, to a lesser extent, α-acid glycoprotein. Under normal conditions, the total amount of testosterone bound to progesterone-binding globulin and α-acid glycoprotein is nominal and is usually ignored.

The regulation of the amount of androgen that is free is an important physiologic variable and varies in different species. **The total amount of steroid bound depends on two factors: (1) the *affinity* of the steroid to bind to a specific protein and (2) the *capacity*, which is the maximal potential binding when all of a binding protein is saturated with bound steroid; the capacity is governed by the amount of binding protein in the plasma.** Serum albumin has a relatively low affinity for testosterone, but given its abundance, it has a high capacity. In contrast, SHBG (TeBG) has a high affinity for binding steroids, but the protein is present in relatively low concentrations; however, the plasma molarity of each binding protein exceeds the plasma molarity for total testosterone concentration. The majority of testosterone bound to plasma protein is associated with SHBG (TeBG). For example, Vermeulen (1973) has calculated that in the normal human male, 57% of testosterone in the plasma is bound to SHBG (TeBG) and 40% is bound to human serum albumin. Less than 1% is bound to corticosteroid-binding globulin, and only 2% of the total testosterone is free (see Fig. 85–4). The normal plasma free testosterone level is therefore 12.1 ± 3.7 ng/100 mL or 0.42 nM; this non–protein bound "free testosterone" is bioavailable to diffuse into the sex accessory tissue and into liver cells for metabolism. In addition, a large percentage of the SHBG (TeBG) is saturated, whereas only a small fraction of the total capacity of corticosteroid-binding globulin and albumin is used under normal conditions. As testosterone levels increase in the plasma, the order of increasing saturation of the plasma proteins proceeds from TeBG to corticosteroid-binding globulin to albumin. Therefore, the binding of androgen is a dynamic equilibrium between various serum proteins.

The total plasma levels of SHBG (TeBG) can be altered by hormone therapy. **Administration of testosterone decreases SHBG (TeBG) levels in the plasma, whereas estrogen therapy stimulates SHBG (TeBG) levels** (Forest et al, 1968; Vermeulen et al, 1969; Burton and Westphal, 1972). Estrogen also competes with testosterone for binding to SHBG (TeBG), but estrogen has only one third the binding affinity of testosterone. **Therefore, administration of small amounts of estrogen increases the total concentration of TeBG, and this effectively increases the binding of testosterone and thus lowers the free testosterone plasma concentration.**

Since only free testosterone is bioavailable, the binding of testosterone to plasma proteins inhibits net testosterone uptake into the prostate (Lasnitzki and Franklin, 1972). It is apparent that androgenic activity is regulated in part by the extent of binding of an androgen to the steroid-binding proteins in the plasma.

Prolactin

Prolactin, a 22.5-kD somatomammotropin, is secreted by the estrogen-sensitive lactotrophs of the peripheral and lateral anterior pituitary. Exogenous androgens can restore 80% of the normal adult prostate size in hypophysectomized rats, but the addition of prolactin is required to achieve full restoration (Grayhack et al, 1955). This permissive effect on the growth of the lateral prostate of the rat may be associated with increased nuclear androgen levels (Manandhar and Thomas, 1976; Assimos et al, 1984). Prolactin receptors have been identified in prostatic tissue (Aragona and Friesen, 1975; Witorsch and Smith, 1977). In addition, the direct action of prolactin on prostate epithelial cells has also been suggested through tissue and organ culture experiments (McKeehan et al, 1984). Prolactin-deficient mice have grossly normal prostates with only minor differences in epithelial content (Robertson et al, 2003) and preserved fertility (Binart et al, 2003). However, ectopic prolactin expression in the prostate in a transgenic mouse leads to significant hyperplasia (Kindblom et al, 2003).

It is currently thought that in the normal prostate, prolactin plays a supportive role in the regulation of zinc (Moger and Geschwind, 1972) and androgen uptake and metabolism (Lloyd et al, 1973) as well as in the regulation of citrate and fructose. Like estrogens in combination with androgens, this peptide hormone has often been postulated to enhance androgen-induced growth; however, several decades of study have failed to indicate the mechanism of this action. It does not appear at present to be a major means of regulating *normal* prostatic growth as it is not required for prostatic development. However, given that local expression of prolactin in a transgenic model is sufficient for induction of prostatic hyperplasia, it may well have a significant role in the development of human BPH (Kindblom et al, 2003). Of note, estrogens combined with androgens are potent stimulants of prostatic hyperplasia. Since prolactin expression is induced by estrogens, it is conceivable that the potency of this combination may be due in part to the prolactin effect on prostatic growth; however, any role for prolactin in the pathophysiology of clinically significant BPH is still speculative at this point.

> ## KEY POINTS: ENDOCRINE CONTROL OF PROSTATE GROWTH
>
> ■ Free testosterone in the plasma is converted in the prostate by 5α-reductase type II into dihydrotestosterone, which is 1.5 to 2.5 times more active than testosterone.
>
> ■ Dihydrotestosterone, testosterone, and estrogens are responsible for multiple metabolic actions in the prostate (growth, differentiation, and biologic functions). Free testosterone can be converted to estrogens, but estrogens cannot be converted to testosterone.

REGULATION OF PROSTATE GROWTH BY STEROIDS AND PROTEIN GROWTH FACTORS

There are multiple levels of prostate growth regulation that include steroid hormone action, growth factors, and direct cell-cell communication and interactions with the extracellular matrix. These interactive types of growth control are accomplished by several generalized systems, as depicted in the schematic in Figure 85–6. They include the following:

- *endocrine factors* or long-range signals arriving at the prostate by serum transport of hormone originating from the secretions of distant organs; this includes serum steroid hormones such as testosterone and estrogens and serum peptide hormones like prolactin and gonadotropins;
- *neuroendocrine signals* originating from neural stimulation, such as 5-hydroxytryptamine (serotonin), acetylcholine, and norepinephrine;
- *paracrine factors* or soluble tissue growth factors that stimulate or inhibit growth, which are elaborated over short ranges between neighboring cells within the prostate tissue compartment (basic fibroblast growth factor, epidermal growth factor);
- *autocrine factors* that are produced and released by a cell and then fed back on the same cell's external membrane receptors to regulate its own growth or function, such as autocrine motility factor;
- *intracrine factors*, which function like autocrine factors but work inside the cell;
- *extracellular matrix factors* that are insoluble tissue matrix systems and make direct and coupled contact by being attached through integrins and adhesion molecules of the basal membrane and couple cytoskeleton organization with the extracellular matrix components that include the

glycosaminoglycans, such as heparan sulfate (Getzenberg et al, 1990);
- *cell-cell interactions* of the epithelial or stromal cells occurring through tight membrane junctions on intramembrane proteins such as the cell adhesion molecules, like E-cadherin, that couple neighboring cells.

Of these seven growth control systems, the first extensively studied on the prostate was the endocrine effect of androgenic steroids, such as testosterone, in the regulation of prostate growth through changes in serum testosterone levels and conversion to DHT. However, androgens alone are not sufficient for full prostate growth. In the last two decades, extensive progress has been made in the understanding of the other systems, particularly the interactive role of growth factors and their receptors. At present, the roles of these receptors in cell signaling to the nucleus and of the structural elements in cellular control involving the tissue matrix are being developed. We review these mechanisms starting with androgen action at the cell level beginning with the arrival of testosterone in the serum.

Androgen Action at the Cellular Level

Testosterone in the serum arrives at the prostate bound to albumin and to the steroid-binding globulins as depicted in Figure 85–7. Free testosterone enters the prostate cell by diffusion, where it is then subjected to a variety of steroid metabolic steps that appear to regulate the activity of the steroid hormone and its downstream effectors. A simplified schematic of the temporal sequence of intracellular events is depicted in Figure 85–7 and includes

- cellular uptake of testosterone;
- testosterone conversion to DHT by metabolism of 5α-reductase;
- DHT or testosterone binding to specific androgen receptors in the cytoplasm;
- dimerization and activation of the steroid receptor by a variety of post-translational steps, including, for instance, phosphorylation;
- active nuclear transportation of the activated androgen receptor in an ATP-dependent fashion;
- chromatin remodeling through interaction with coregulatory molecules;
- transactivation or transrepression, through interactions with other co-activators or co-repressors, in a histone acetyltransferase–dependent process;
- binding of the activated receptor–co-activator complex to androgen response elements, which are short specific sequences of DNA recognized specifically by androgen receptor dimers;
- gene regulation. The receptor acts as a transcription factor, and when it is bound to the DNA and matrix in proximity to androgen target genes, it increases the RNA polymerase II transcription of the DNA into mRNA. The transcribed message (mRNA) is large and contains introns, exons, and a poly-A tail. The intron portion is excised from the initial RNA species, so that only the exon portion is retained in the final message. The trimming and processing of the mRNA are accomplished on the nuclear matrix as it is transported through the nucleus and out through the nuclear pore complex. The

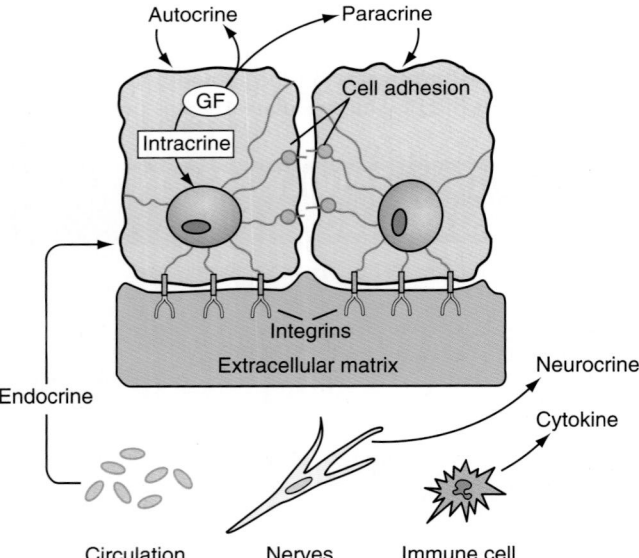

Figure 85–6. Types of growth control. Endocrine signals are carried through the circulation from distant organs. Paracrine signals are produced in proximity by neighboring cells. Autocrine signals feed back on the same cells from which they are produced. Intracrine signals are a special subset of autocrine signals that never leave the cell but rather act locally within that cell. Cytokines are paracrine-like factors (typically) that are made by immune cells. Neurocrine factors are released by nerves. Cell adhesion molecules directly link neighboring cells, often through association with cognate adhesion molecules. Cells are also bound to the extracellular matrix through interactions with other cell adhesion molecules (e.g., integrins). GF, growth factor.

Figure 85–7. Simplified schematic of the effects of testosterone in inducing growth in an epithelial cell. In the plasma, testosterone (T) is bound to serum-binding globulins (SBG), such as testosterone-binding globulin and albumin. Unbound testosterone is transported by passive diffusion into the prostate, where it is enzymatically converted to dihydrotestosterone (DHT) by 5α-reductase (type II) and further metabolized to diols (3α or 3β) and irreversibly metabolized into the more water-soluble triols (6α or 7α). DHT binds to a cytoplasmic receptor (androgen receptor) that is activated and translocated to the nucleus. There the androgen receptor localizes in matrix acceptor sites and subsequently activates or represses certain target genes by regulating production of their mRNA. The RNA is then transported to the cytoplasm, where it is translated into a variety of proteins (e.g., secretory proteins such as PSA).

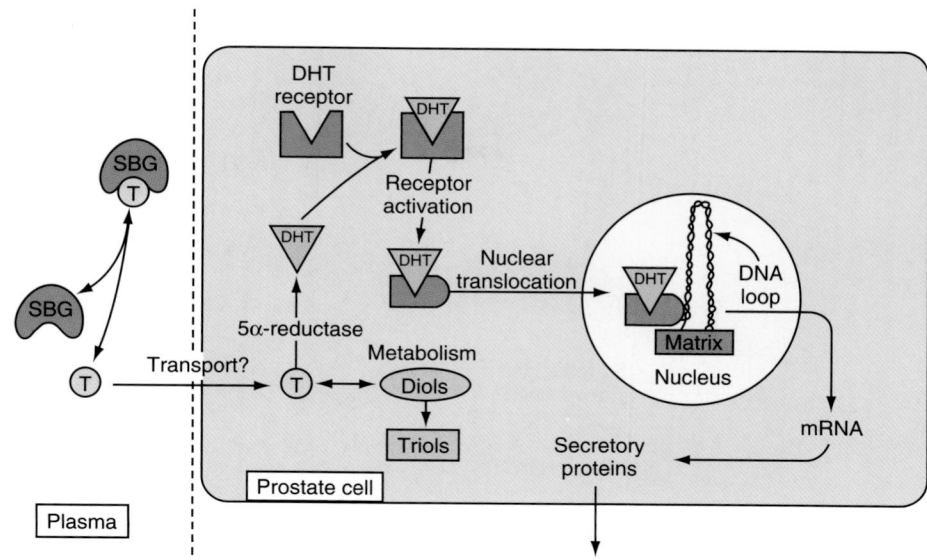

stabilized mRNA is transported into the cytoplasmic compartment to be translated at the ribosome into protein, which is then transported to specific cellular sites. Depending on the target gene, some proteins will undergo storage in secretory granules poised for secretion into the lumen on command during the physiologic process of ejaculation.

The epithelial cell is the primary unit in secretion, but specific genes are also activated in the stromal cells, and these events are also regulated by testosterone, estrogens, and growth factors in a similar chain of events. However, not all cells respond the same to androgens or estrogens. For simplicity, these steps are discussed in relation to the epithelial cells. Androgens and estrogens, both together and separately, can affect prostate cells through interaction with receptors, and it appears that estrogens might have their primary effect on the stromal cells.

5α-Reductase and Androgen Metabolism Within the Prostate

After the free testosterone in the plasma has entered the prostatic cells through diffusion, it is rapidly metabolized to other steroids by a series of prostatic enzymes (Isaacs et al, 1981; Isaacs and Coffey, 1981; Isaacs, 1983a, 1983b; Bruchovsky and Dunstan-Adams, 1985). More than 90% of testosterone is *irreversibly* converted to the main prostatic androgen DHT (Fig. 85–8) through the action of NADPH and the enzyme 5α-reductase located on the endoplasmic reticulum and on the nuclear membrane. The enzyme 5α-reductase reduces the unsaturated bond in testosterone between the 4 and 5 positions to form the 5α-reduced product DHT. The K_m for testosterone is 8.3 nM, and the serum level of testosterone is only in the range of 0.5 to 3.0 nM, indicating that the enzyme cannot be saturated since the testosterone substrate would be less than the K_m value. Bruchovsky and Dunstan-Adams (1985) reported a 10-fold increase in the maximal velocity in the stromal tissue compared with the epithelium. They

observed 262 pmol of DHT formed in 30 minutes per milligram of protein from testosterone measured in the stroma and less than 10% of that amount with a maximal velocity of 19 for the epithelium. The stromal K_m was 76 nM and the epithelial 13 nM; it is intriguing that there may be alterations occurring in the enzyme or in its regulatory mechanism or different isoforms.

In the human, rat, and monkey, there are two isozymes of 5α-reductase (Table 85–3). The human and rat 5α-reductase isozymes are composed of 254 to 260 amino acids with a molecular weight of 28,000 to 29,000. These enzymes are N- and O-glycosylated and have a high percentage of hydrophobic amino acids that are distributed throughout the enzyme.

Table 85–3. Properties and Distribution of 5α-Reductase Types I and II

	Type I	Type II
Human		
Chromosome	5p15	2p23
Molecular weight	29,000	28,000
Amino acids	259	254
Exons	4	4
Introns	5	5
Homology	49%	49%
pH optima	Alkaline (6-8.5)	Acidic (5.0)
K_m testosterone (μM)	1.5	0.1-1.0
K_i finasteride (nM)	325	12
Half-life, hour	20-30	20-30
5α-Reductase deficiency	Normal	Mutated
Prostate cells		
Epithelial	–	–
Basal	–	–
Stromal	–	+
Skin	+	–
Rat		
Prostate cells		
Epithelial	–	–
Basal	+	–
Stromal	–	–

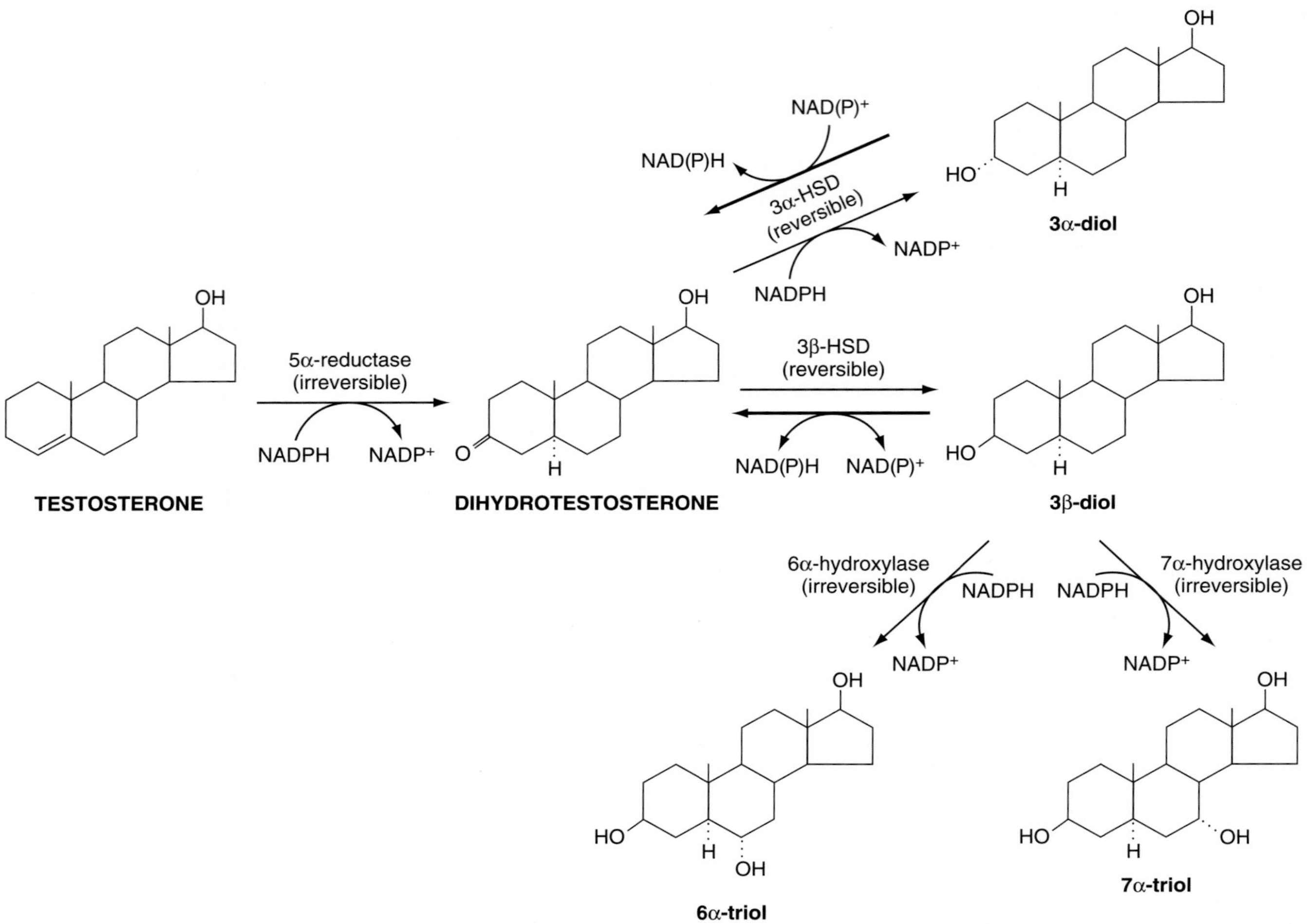

Figure 85–8. Metabolic pathways for testosterone within the prostate. Testosterone is irreversibly metabolized by 5α-reductase to dihydrotestosterone (DHT), which is then reversibly converted into 3α-diol and 3β-diol. The 3β-diol is irreversibly inactivated to the more soluble 6α-triol and 7α-triol. 3α-HSD, 3α-hydroxysteroid dehydrogenase.

The chromosomal localization of the human 5α-reductase isozyme genes has been reported; the type I enzyme is at the extreme tip of the short arm of chromosome 5, and the human type II gene is on the short arm of chromosome 2. There is a 49% homology between type I and II enzymes in the human. The properties of these enzymes have been reviewed in detail by David Russell and Jean Wilson (Russell and Wilson, 1994) and for the effects on prostate growth by John McConnell (McConnell, 1995). The effect of finasteride on 5α-reductase activity has been reviewed by Roger Rittmaster (Rittmaster, 1994). The type I enzyme is in the skin and in the adult scalp and is believed to be involved in hair formation. It is present to lesser degrees in the prostate epithelium and stroma. This isoform is found in normal levels in men with congenital 5α-reductase deficiency. **The type II enzyme is mutated in 5α-reductase deficiency and is the dominant isoform present in the prostate gland.** The type II enzyme appears in the basal cells of the epithelium and in the stromal cells but is absent in the secretory epithelial cells. This has raised the possibility that DHT stimulation of epithelial cells is derived from DHT converted within the stromal or basal cells. Silver and coworkers (1994) have studied the cell type–specific expression of these reductases as well as their regulation. It appears that the 5α-reductase type II in the prostate does not change dramatically in individuals undergoing short-term androgen ablation.

Berman and associates (1995) have studied the distribution of the two 5α-reductase isozymes in the urogenital tract of the fetal rat. At 17 to 21 days of development, the expression of type I gene predominated in the epithelial cells; the type II gene was limited to the mesenchymal cells. This is true in both the testosterone-dependent and DHT-dependent anlagen of the urogenital tract. They observed that androgens could stimulate the expression of the type II gene in the urogenital tract but not of the type I gene. They suggested that the type II 5α-reductase gene exhibits positive feedback control in that the product of the enzyme, DHT, can stimulate expression of the gene; however, no evidence for such regulation of either 5α-reductase gene was detected in the fetus.

In summary, 5α-reductase is of great importance because the product DHT is important in the differentiation of the prostate during fetal development, and mutations in 5α-reductase give rise to a rare form of pseudohermaphroditism. In prostate physiology, expression of the

5α-reductase gene is regulated by androgens in both the prostate and liver. It is also believed that the 5α-reductase is involved in male pattern baldness, acne, and hirsutism as well as in BPH. The 5α-reductase inhibitors finasteride (type II inhibitor) and dutasteride (type I and II inhibitor) are clinically useful drugs in the treatment of BPH and male pattern baldness when they are given to appropriate populations of patients.

After DHT is formed from testosterone in the prostate, it is then subjected to a series of reversible metabolic reactions to form 3α-diol (5α-androstane-3α,17β-diol) and 3β-diol (5α-androstane-3β,17β-diol) (Fig. 85-8). The enzymes that perform this transformation of DHT are 3α- or 3β-hydroxysteroid oxidoreductases. These enzymes use NADP as a cofactor, but in contrast to 5α-reductase, they can also use NAD. The equilibrium for the metabolism of DHT favors the formation of DHT, that is, the 3-hydroxy group of 3α-diol and 3β-diol is oxidized to the 3-ketone that is present in DHT. It is known that administration of 3α-diol to an animal is a strong androgen through its rapid conversion to the effective DHT. On the other hand, 3β-diol is not effective as an androgen because it is rapidly and irreversibly converted to the triol form by hydroxylation in the 6α or 7α position (see Fig. 85-8). The triols are dead-end products of testosterone metabolism but are water soluble and inactive as androgens they cannot reform DHT. Steroids also can form glucuronide or sulfate conjugates and be secreted in a more soluble form. **In summary, testosterone is irreversibly metabolized to DHT that is in equilibrium with other reduced steroids primarily through oxidation and reduction at the 3 position. The steroids are inactivated by being irreversibly hydroxylated to the inactive triols.**

Estrogens and Estrogen-Androgen Synergism

Physiologic levels of estrogens do not block androgen-induced growth of the prostate cell but rather synergize androgen effects. This has been well documented in the canine prostate in a classic study first published by Walsh and Wilson (1976) and subsequently confirmed and extended by DeKlerk and colleagues (DeKlerk et al, 1979; Tunn et al, 1979; Juniewicz et al, 1989). In these studies, the simultaneous administration of estradiol to castrate dogs receiving 5α-androstane metabolites such as DHT or 3α-diol produced a twofold to fourfold enhancement in the weight of the prostate that was due to an increase in total cell number and was a true glandular hyperplasia. The mechanism of the androgen-estrogen synergism on prostate growth is not understood; however, it has been shown that estrogens increase the androgen nuclear receptor content in the prostate cell that might be an important factor in this phenomenon (Trachtenberg et al, 1981). Estrogen combined with DHT also induces other changes, such as increase in steroid metabolism toward DHT formation, collagen formation, and alteration in cell death modification. These changes have been summarized by Coffey and Walsh (1990) in relation to BPH.

The synergism of estrogens on androgen-induced growth in the dog prostate is observed only with the 5α-reduced androgens such as DHT or 3α-diol and is not observed when testosterone is administered (Walsh and Wilson, 1976; DeKlerk et al, 1979; Moore et al, 1979). In addition, this synergism with androgens and estrogens in the dog does not occur in the rat prostate (Ehrlichman et al, 1981). Whether this species difference is due to the fact that the rat that does not develop BPH and the dog does is a matter of conjecture.

Estrogens are capable, either directly or indirectly, of stimulating the stromal elements of the prostate. These studies have been carried out in animal models such as the monkey (Habericht and el Etreby, 1988) and the guinea pig (Mawhinney and Neubauer, 1979; Mariotti and Mawhinney, 1983; Goodwin and Cummings, 1984; Neubauer et al, 1989). Young males receiving androgen blockade with antiandrogens combined with estrogen therapy did not have enlarged prostates, but their stromal elements were markedly enhanced while the epithelial component involuted (de Voogt et al, 1987). In human BPH nuclei, total assayed estrogens in stromal nuclei (58 fmol per milligram of DNA) are five times higher than those found in epithelial nuclei (9 fmol per milligram of DNA) (Kozak et al, 1982). It is unknown what this large amount of estrogen is bound to in the nucleus.

The distribution of estrogen receptors (ER) and estrogen binding in the prostate is heterogeneous; ER-α is found predominantly in the stroma and ER-β predominantly in the epithelial compartment (Harkonen and Makela, 2004). It is clear that stroma is a major target for estrogen action (Krieg et al, 1981; Eaton et al, 1985; Schulze and Barrack, 1987; Mobbs et al, 1990). It is still uncertain whether the modest amounts of estrogen receptor in the prostate (Donnelly et al, 1983; Mobbs et al, 1990) can account for any of the pathologic growths that occur in the prostate. It is also unclear whether the prostate can make physiologically significant amounts of estrogens and whether antiestrogens would be an effective treatment of abnormal prostate growth (Stone et al, 1986; Habericht and el Etreby, 1988; Oesterling et al, 1988; Neubauer et al, 1989; Harkonen and Makela, 2004). It is apparent that early estrogen treatments in the neonatal period do imprint on and retard prostate growth, and the role of estrogens in development may be of paramount importance (Naslund and Coffey, 1986, 1987; Prins and Birch, 1995). **Estrogens can cause a florid squamous cell metaplasia in prostate growth that can be offset by androgens** (DeKlerk et al, 1979; Juniewicz et al, 1989). How this is regulated by stem cells is of paramount importance for the role of estrogen in abnormal growth (DeKlerk et al, 1979; Merk et al, 1982). Estrogens may have other actions including effects on prostatic secretion and water and electrolyte transport (Isaacs, 1983) as well as the potential for affecting urethral musculature and its neurologic control (Schreiter et al, 1976).

Androgen Regulation of Stromal-Epithelial Interactions

It is now apparent that there is a dynamic and reciprocal interaction between the functions of epithelial cells and those of stromal cells (Steiner, 1993; Sikes et al, 1995; Cunha et al, 2003, 2004). These crosstalk interactions are mediated through the spatial organization of extracellular matrix elements that form the basement membrane linkage. This linkage presents, filters, and organizes the two-way

paracrine signals and the flow of information between those two cellular compartments. For example, fluids, gases, nutrients, hormones, and many growth factors arriving in the prostate through the circulation must first pass through the stromal ground substance, the extracellular matrix, and the basement membrane before reaching the base of the secretory epithelial cells. Early in development, the functions of the epithelial and mesenchymal (stromal) elements vary as to their cell types, compositions, properties, and interactions. It is the integrated system biology of these two tissue elements as well as their dynamics during aging that plays a vital role in the prostate's functions as a unit and gland. Indeed, it is the breakdown of these tissue interactions that is one of the hallmarks of the abnormal growth of the prostate that starts very early in life and is initiated sometime just after maximum virilization, at approximately 25 years of age. The prostate is extremely susceptible to permanent early alterations in form and structure as a consequence of genetic, environmental, dietary, or metabolic factors with aging (Cunha et al, 2004; Risbridger et al, 2005). In fact, it is essential to establish the link between hormonal (androgens and estrogens) changes that occur during the fetal or neonatal period that *imprint* and hence may result in onset of late-life disease. With aging, during a period of 50 to 60 years, this organ slowly progresses through the transition from normal zonal histologic anatomy and function to the early signs of BPH, to prostatic inflammatory atrophy, to prostatic interepithelial neoplasia, and finally to various types of prostatic adenocarcinoma. This concept has been thoroughly documented in several rodent models (Rajfer and Coffey, 1978, 1979; Naslund and Coffey, 1986, 1987; Prins and Birch, 1995; Singh et al, 1999; Prins et al, 2001; Risbridger et al, 2005).

Normal prostate development requires epithelial-mesenchymal interactions that are highly dependent on hormonal actions of both androgens and estrogens for growth and maturation of this complex tissue matrix (Bonkhoff and Remberger, 1996; Hayward, 2002; Cunha et al, 2003, 2004; Risbridger et al, 2005). Once mature, the stromal compartment consists of fibroblasts, smooth muscle, blood vessels, a variety of immune cells, and nerves, forming a basis for structural support of the basal and epithelial compartments; it also includes the extracellular matrix and its communication with the intracellular network of the cytoskeleton and nuclear

matrix (Getzenberg et al, 1990; Hayward, 2002; Cunha et al, 2003, 2004). The main androgen metabolite in the prostate is 5α-dihydrotestosterone (DHT) that drives production of several key stromal growth factors (andromedins) through the androgen receptors, resulting in the production by androgen-dependent epithelial cells of prostatic secretions such as PSA and prostatic acid phosphatase. The spectrum of stromal andromedins includes numerous tissue remodeling enzymes as well as cytokines and hormones (Cunha et al, 2003) and growth factors (Wong and Wang, 2000) responsible for wound healing and maintaining turnover (proliferation and apoptosis) as well as the differentiation of epithelial cells and their critical secretory functions (Hayward, 2002; Cunha et al, 2003, 2004; Condon, 2005; Laczko et al, 2005). In addition, a prostate-specific transcriptome analysis has identified more than 500 genes each for the basal and epithelial cells and numerous (more than 100) unique expressed sequence tags (Liu et al, 1997a). The transcriptomes identified are involved in specific structural and important functional biochemical pathways that control and sustain balance among several activities that influence normal prostate zonal anatomic tissue organization through hormonally driven processes such as epithelial cell differentiation, proliferation, and apoptosis (Liu et al, 1997a, 2002).

Smooth muscle cells are important to stromal-epithelial interactions. They are clustered around the acinar structure and are thought to be involved in the mechanical expression of ejaculate fluid under neural stimulation. Smooth muscle also plays a role in prostate organogenesis through its differentiation by regulating signaling between mesenchyme and the epithelium (Thomson et al, 2002). In an animal model, these investigators demonstrated that testosterone (androgens) regulates smooth muscle thickness, which in turn controls maturation of the prostate by facilitating mesenchyme-epithelial interactions as evidenced by epithelial embryonal branching morphogenesis.

Cell Adhesion Molecules

Cell-cell and extracellular matrix interactions are becoming major targets for understanding how the phenotype of a cell is regulated. Transmembrane receptors on the cell surface extend out through the plasma membrane and form a bridge directly connecting the cytoskeleton with proteins and recep-

tors located within the extracellular matrix or on neighboring cells. The cell adhesion molecules (CAM) are divided into four major types: (1) integrins, which link the cell to the basement membrane and extracellular matrix components through heterodimer interactions; (2) cadherins, which link the cell to neighboring cells through homotypic polymers; (3) selectins, which link the cell to carbohydrate moieties prima- rily on the vascular system; and (4) immunoglobulin super- family adhesion molecules. The most extensively studied of these cell adhesion molecules in the prostate in order of inter- est have been E-cadherins that bind prostate epithelial cells to each other and CD71 that binds to transferrin, as well as several of the integrin molecules. These bindings have been surveyed in prostate tumor cell lines in vitro (Rokhlin and Cohen, 1995), but more extensive work needs to be carried out in vivo in the normal developing prostate and in prostate cancer.

The integrins are made up of two covalently linked het- erodimers termed α and β subunits. These integrins serve externally to contact the extracellular matrix receptors of fibronectin, fibrinogens, collagen, and laminin as well as gly- cosaminoglycans in the proteoglycans of the extracellular matrix. The integrin receptor domains inside the cell com- partment serve as focal points for determining the structure and organization of the cytoskeleton. Approximately eight subunits of α and β can interact in different heterodimers that are tissue specific and can be of several types even on one cell. These integrins can vary with development of pathologic function, particularly in cancer (Albelda, 1993). Most prostate cancer cell lines express dimers of $\alpha_2\beta_1$, which binds collagen (I, II, III, IV) and laminin; $\alpha_3\beta_1$, which binds collagen, laminin, and fibronectin; and $\alpha_5\beta_1$, which binds invasin and fibronectin (Rokhlin and Cohen, 1995; Miner and Yurchenco et al, 2004; Hallmann et al, 2005). For example, $\alpha_5\beta_1$ binds to laminin, collagen, and fibronectin and does so by recognizing a triplet of amino acids in those proteins made up of arginine, glycine, and aspartic acid.

Other types of transmembrane receptors also extend out of the cell to make direct cell-cell contact with the neighboring cell by recognizing similar receptors and forming homodimer bonds. Homophilic dimers that require calcium for interac- tions to form cell-cell bonds with neighboring cells are termed cadherins. Four of the cadherin types have been cloned. They contain between 723 and 748 amino acids that are composed of a single peptide, an extracellular region with three repeated hydrophobic transmembrane domains, a region, and a long cytoplasmic tail. There is approximately 50% homology across species and between integrins. The cadherins are classified into three subtypes: E-cadherins found in adult epithelial cells (also termed uvomorulin, cell CAM 120/80, ARC-1, or L-CAM); N-cadherins found in neural tissues of muscle (also termed A-CAM); and P- cadherins found primarily in placenta and epithelium (Albelda, 1993). In the prostate cell, for example, E-cadherins extending out of the cell surface membrane make contact with the neighboring cell and form a homodimer, and the E-cadherin extending inside the cell by passing through the membrane would form as an organizing center that binds a complex of three cytoplasmic proteins termed catenins α, β, and γ. This complex is localized to the zonula adherins of the cell and participates in junction formation and stabilization of the cytoskeleton. These interlocking matrix systems interact to form a structural network extending externally from cell-cell contact and the extracellular matrix interactions, then inter- nally to cytoskeleton organization and centrally, terminating by direct contact with the nuclear matrix that forms tissue- specific DNA organization.

The interactions of the nonhistone tissue matrix regulate many aspects of DNA functions involved in growth and differentiation (Getzenberg et al, 1990; Boccardo et al, 2003). The nonhistone proteins such as high-mobility group (HMG) proteins include HMGI/Y (HMGA) that participate in numerous cellular processes, such as regulation of inducible gene transcription, integration of retroviruses into chromo- somes, and induction of malignant transformation (Reeves and Beckerbauer, 2003). Through protein-DNA and protein- protein interactions, the members of the HMGA family can influence growth, cell proliferation, differentiation, and cell death; they influence chromosome dynamics by acting as architectural transcription factors affecting several genes that have an impact on tissue structure and organization. This class of genes is often upregulated in cancer (Reeves and Beckerbauer, 2003). These types of tissue matrix interac- tions are essential to the understanding of stromal-epithelial interactions because they form direct structural linkages and communications between the stroma and the epithelial nuclear DNA. In summary, under the influence of hormones (estrogens and androgens) and diet, it is the regulation of chromatin structure and organization through the histone and nonhistone pathways that replaces and maintains the tissue organization as well as interactions in health and disease.

The cell adhesion molecules have been implicated as having a major role in tumor progression and metastasis (Albelda, 1993). The repertoire of integrins can vary during the neo- plastic process. This has been noted for $\alpha_6\beta_4$ as a differentially expressed antigen that can occur in carcinoma (Van Waes et al, 1995). The $\alpha_6\beta_4$ integrin is expressed in normal epithelial cells at their base in an area that forms the hemidesmosome complex linking it to the basement membrane for its attach- ment to laminin. The $\alpha_6\beta_4$ integrin is absent in LNCaP cells and downregulated in PC-3 and DU-145 cells (Rokhlin and Cohen, 1995). Laminin has been proposed to be an important extracellular matrix protein that changes its isoform during the neoplastic transformation, and this has been studied in prostate carcinoma cell lines (Rabinovitz et al, 1994). In the prostate, there has been differential expression of extracellu- lar matrix molecules in the α_6 integrins in normal and neoplastic human prostates. These integrin expressions and patterns could be an important new frontier in cell adhesion and extracellular matrix changes related to cancer (Bonkhoff et al, 1993; Knox et al, 1994). In addition, it has been reported that C-CAM can act as a tumor suppressor in prostate cancer development, and when C-CAM gene was transfected into the PC-3 prostate tumor cell line, it repressed growth (Kleinerman et al, 1995).

Much interest in cancer of the prostate has been placed in the study of E-cadherin expression, which has been shown to suppress tumor cell invasion and metastasis in experimental tumor models and to be reduced in or absent from high-grade prostate cancers (Umbas et al, 1992;

Bussemakers et al, 1994). In some cases, the reduction and redistribution of the E-cadherin protein on the periphery of the cell is associated with mutations or deletion of the α-catenin gene in human prostate cancer cells (Morton et al, 1993). It has been reported that E-cadherin expression can be silenced or reduced by DNA hypermethylation of the CpG islands in the promoter region of the E-cadherin gene (Graff et al, 1995; Yoshiura et al, 1995).

Elements of the stroma and tissue matrix can be isolated by extensive extraction of tissue, and the insoluble residue is termed a biomatrix; when this is used as a substratum for epithelial growth in tissue culture, it is apparent that it has the ability to regulate the growth and function of the prostate epithelial cells (Isaacs, 1984). Canine prostatic epithelial cells will grow rapidly as primary outgrowth on plastic and do not require stromal elements; however, when these cells are growing on prostatic biomatrix, they reduce their growth, maintain their morphologic appearance and secretory ability, and more closely approximate what is occurring in vivo (Isaacs, 1984). This would indicate that the stromal elements can also act as a braking system for growth and therefore limit proliferation and maintain the state of functional differentiation and secretion. Indeed, in normal prostate and in BPH tissue where there is stromal-epithelial interactions, there is usually little growth and mitotic figures are rare. Removing cells from this normal state and placing them on plastic removes the brake and permits the epithelial cells to grow. The extent of disruption in these braking systems in BPH and cancer is a developing area of tumor biology (Sikes et al, 1995).

Cancer cells can migrate out of the prostate and are capable of growing elsewhere in the body as metastatic lesions and therefore either can use stromal elements from other tissues to support their growth or are free of stromal cell restraints, possibly because of autocrine factors. Chung and colleagues have shown that the development and establishment of transplanted cancer cells are dependent on their transplantation with collagen and either live or dead fibroblasts isolated primarily from the bone (Chung et al, 1989; Sikes et al, 1995).

The discussion, to this point, has concerned primarily insoluble elements in inducing stromal-epithelial interactions, but soluble hormones such as steroids, vitamins, and growth factors are also important (Sikes et al, 1995). The prostatic stromal cells contain steroid receptors and respond to both androgens and estrogens (see earlier discussion), and the stroma has an androgen metabolizing ability to form DHT almost equal to or greater than that of the epithelium. Androgens and estrogens can alter the formation of collagen (Coffey and Walsh, 1990) and other extracellular matrix components, such as glycosaminoglycans, in the prostate (DeKlerk, 1984, 1985; Kofoed et al, 1990; Horsfall, Mayne et al, 1994).

In summary, different components of matrix interactions can have either an inhibitory role in negative regulation of normal prostate growth or a positive role in establishing tumor growth. There have been many hypotheses concerning the mechanism of these epithelial-stromal interactions, but they have yet to be fully resolved (Muntzing, 1980; Tenniswood, 1986; Getzenberg et al, 1990; Chung et al, 1992; Sikes et al, 1995).

KEY POINTS: CELL ADHESION MOLECULES

■ Transmembrane receptors on the cell surface extend out through the plasma membrane and form a bridge directly connecting the cytoskeleton with proteins and receptors located within the extracellular matrix or on neighboring cells.

■ The cell adhesion molecules are divided into four major types: integrins, which link the cell to the basement membrane and extracellular matrix components through heterodimer interactions; cadherins, which link the cell to neighboring cells through homotypic polymers; selectins, which link the cell to carbohydrate moieties primarily on the vascular system; and immunoglobulin superfamily adhesion molecules.

REGULATION OF PROSTATE GROWTH AT THE MOLECULAR LEVEL: STEROID RECEPTORS

In almost all cells in the body, steroids can enter the nucleus, but only a few cells can retain this steroid within the nucleus for any length of time. The cells that retain the steroid have receptors that are steroid specific, which can regulate specific steroid-sensitive genes within the nucleus to alter the expression of certain proteins. The androgen receptor's affinity for the nuclear acceptor site to which it binds in the nucleus is probably a compilation of binding to specific sequences on DNA (androgen response elements) as well as tissue-specific binding to co-regulatory factors. The uptake and binding of the androgen receptor in the nucleus are regulated by the presence of the androgen ligand bound to the receptor, resulting in receptor activation. When androgens are not present, the receptor decreases its affinity for nuclear binding and can easily be removed, and indeed, under castrate conditions, receptors may leak back out into the cytoplasm (Husmann et al, 1990). Immunohistochemical techniques indicate that in the presence of androgen, the androgen receptor localizes primarily to the nucleus.

The prostate and seminal vesicles contain steroid-specific and high-affinity (10^{-9} to 10^{-10} M K_d) saturable (100 to 1000 fmol of receptor per milligram of DNA equivalents of tissue) androgen receptors that were first described by Liao and Fang in 1969. There are 5,000 to 20,000 molecules of these receptors per cell, far more than can bind to the androgen response element sites, which are probably fewer than 400. Classic androgen receptor function has been characterized as a genomic process wherein certain transgenes are regulated by the activated androgen receptor. More recently, however, attention has been focusing on the nongenomic mechanisms of androgen action (Benten et al, 1997; Jones et al, 2004). Nongenomic androgen action is characterized by extremely rapid changes in cellular physiology, typically measured in seconds or minutes, as opposed to the longer times required for target gene regulation to be translated into protein changes. Whether nongenomic androgen action occurs

through the same androgen receptors involved in genomic regulation remains to be determined. The properties and hormonal regulation of androgen receptors as well as their uses have been reviewed in detail (Barrack and Tindall, 1987; Parker, 1991; Luke and Coffey, 1994a, 1994b; Small and Prins, 1995; MacLean et al, 1997; Whitfield et al, 1999; Black and Paschal, 2004).

KEY POINT: ANDROGEN RECEPTORS

■ The androgen receptor, an intracellular steroid-binding protein, is activated by androgens, resulting in both genomic and nongenomic actions, which in turn regulate cellular action. This regulation is central to prostate development, growth, and homeostasis and occurs in both the stromal and epithelial compartments.

Androgen Receptor

The cloning of the human androgen receptor and its expression was a hallmark in the study of the mechanism of androgen action (Chang et al, 1988a, 1988b; Lubahn et al, 1988a, 1988b). This led to the study of the sequence of the gene and its protein product—and how this is altered in inherited androgen insensitivity syndromes—as well as receptor function (Chang et al, 1988; Lubahn et al, 1988; Kuiper et al, 1989; Tilley et al, 1989; Marcelli et al, 1990). This powerful new technique is providing the resolution to many questions of andrology (Brown et al, 1988; Tilley et al, 1990; Luke and Coffey, 1994).

The androgen receptor gene is on the long arm of the X chromosome at position Xq11.2-q12. Since there is only one X chromosome in a male, it is a single copy on only one allele. The coding sequence on this gene is divided into 8 exons that are transcribed and processed into mRNA and then subsequently translated into protein. The total exon and intron DNA makes a large gene for the androgen receptor that spans a minimum of 54 kilobases (Marcelli et al, 1990) but forms a final message of only 9.6 kilobases, that is, only 17% of the total gene. This is similar to the organization of many other steroid receptors that also contain information from 8 exons, such as the progesterone and estrogen receptors. The andro-

gen receptor is a member of the nuclear receptor superfamily, which is a group of ligand-inducible transcription factors. The nuclear receptor superfamily has more than 200 members at present (Escriva et al, 2004). All of these receptors share certain structural features that allow them to regulate gene expression, although the ligands for many of these receptors have yet to be identified (so-called orphan receptors). Such receptors include the glucocorticoid receptor, the retinoic acid receptors (RXR and RAR), the vitamin D receptor, the estrogen and progesterone receptors, the peroxisome proliferator-activated receptor (PPAR-γ), and many orphan receptors. Like other steroid receptors, the androgen receptor is divided into three distinct, modular domains: the amino terminal domain, the DNA-binding domain, and the carboxyl terminal ligand-binding domain. Despite the similarity in structural organization of all of the nuclear receptors, activation of different receptors results in markedly different cellular responses. Mutational analyses of the human androgen receptor have allowed a detailed mapping of a variety of different functions, which are diagrammed schematically in Figure 85–9.

Upstream (5′ direction) of the transcriptional initiation site is the regulatory element of the gene that controls its expression. It is unusual in that it contains the GC box rather than the classic TATA and CCAAT that are commonly found in promoters of polymerase II–dependent genes. Closer to the initiation site located only 70 base pairs upstream is a 50–base pair purine-rich region that is a *cis*-acting element for androgen receptor transcription. There are other *cis*-acting elements, including an AP-1 (which is bound by a heterodimer of c-Fos and c-Jun) and a RARE (retinoic acid response element) as well as a cAMP response element (AR/CRE1). This suggests that the regulation of expression of the androgen receptor gene may involve cAMP, activation of c-Fos/c-Jun, or retinoids (Kuiper et al, 1989; Faber et al, 1993; Mizokami et al, 1994; Young et al, 1994). Activation of the androgen receptor appears to be a function of multiple steps including initial complex formation with certain chaparonins, binding of ligand, post-translational modifications, dimerization, nuclear localization, and binding of the receptor to certain transcriptional co-activator complexes that remodel chromatin, target the initiation site, and stabilize the RNA polymerase II machinery for repeated rounds of transcription. Each of these features is discussed in the context of known structural features of the receptor as diagrammed in Figure 85–10.

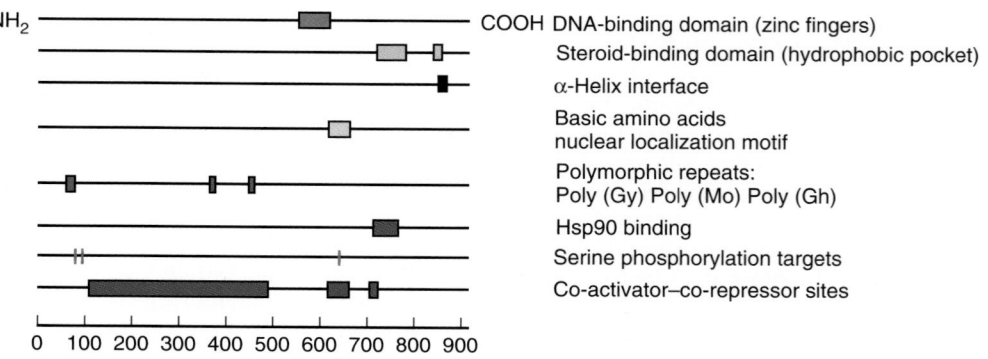

Figure 85–9. Structure of the human androgen receptor protein. The androgen receptor is divided into several functional domains including the DNA-binding domain (consisting of two zinc fingers), a steroid-binding domain (consisting of a hydrophobic pocket), a nuclear localization motif, and several co-activator–co-repressor binding sites. There are three polymorphic repeats of glycine, proline, and glutamine with varying sizes among different populations. The relative positions of the functional elements are shown to scale.

Shown are the coordinates of all known functional elements

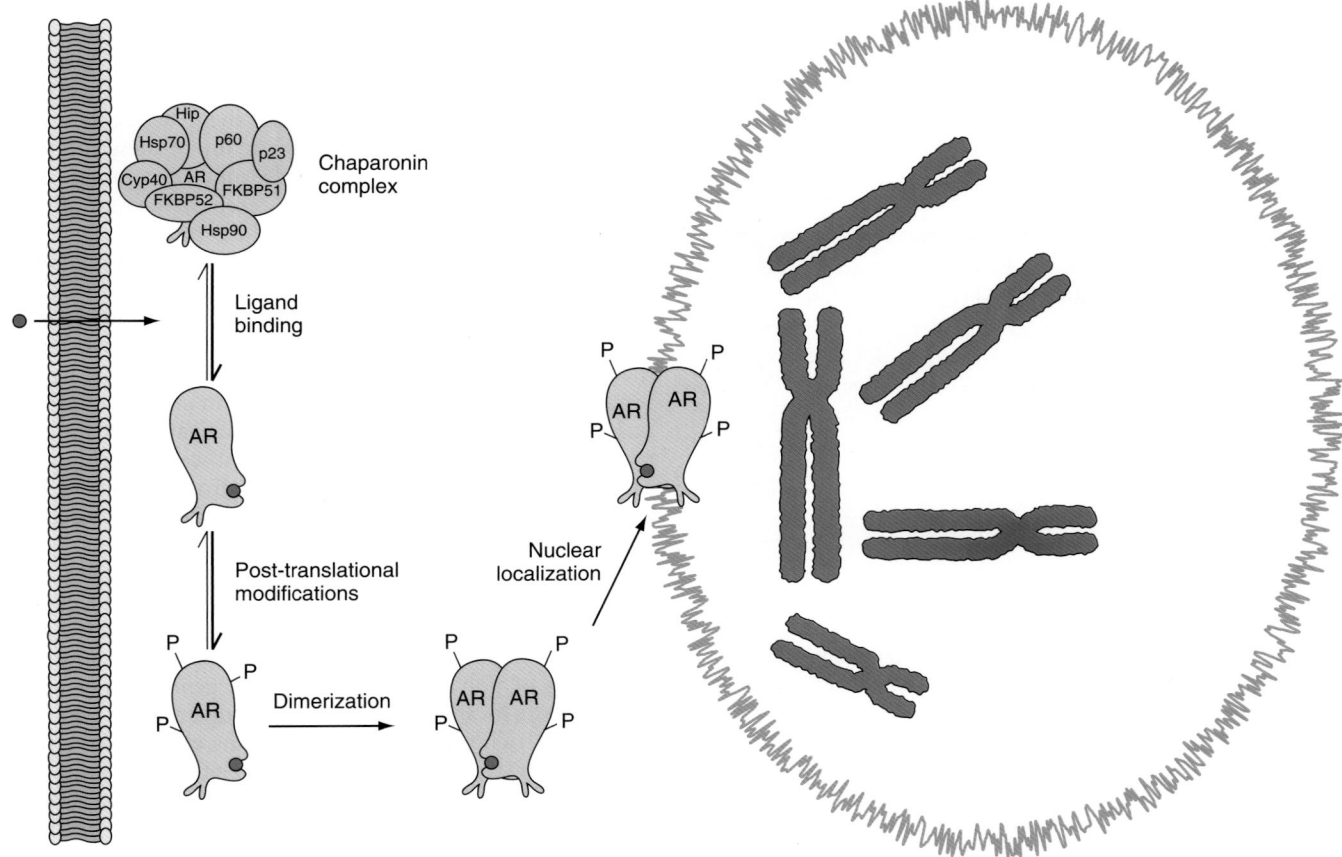

Figure 85–10. Mechanism of androgen receptor (AR) activation by ligand. Androgen enters the cell membrane by passive diffusion and binds the androgen receptor in the cytoplasm. The androgen receptor exists in equilibrium with the chaparonin complex, consisting of at least eight different components including Hsp90, Hsp70, Hip, p60, p23, FKBP51, FKBP52, and Cyp40. Once activated by binding ligand, post-translational modifications occur, such as phosphorylation. Contemporaneously, dimerization occurs, and the activated modified androgen receptor is translocated to the nucleus by active transport.

Chaparonin Binding

Immediately after nascent production of the protein in the ribosome, the receptor forms complexes with several other proteins, referred to as chaparonins. These chaparonins form an aggregate complex, which is known as the 8S complex, in reference to the size of the complex on sucrose gradient sedimentation analysis. This chaparonin complex includes at least eight known components (Hsp90, Hsp70, Hip, p60, p23, FKBP51, FKBP52, and Cyp40), which serve to sequester the receptor into an inactive pool (Fig. 85–10). By analogy to the progesterone receptor, which has had the most detailed scrutiny in regard to the molecular biology of the chaparonin complex (Nair et al, 1996; Smith, 2000), the androgen receptor can dissociate into a monomeric form (4S on sucrose gradient centrifugation) that is in equilibrium with the 8S form, with the preponderant species existing in the chaparonin complex. This larger complex may be particularly favored by virtue of mass action alone, since the heat shock proteins tend to be among the most abundant proteins in the cell. While the androgen receptor is uncomplexed, it is susceptible to various different post-translational processing steps, including phosphorylation or glycosylation. Such interactions may then inhibit reaggregation with the chaparonins, leading to ligand-

dependent activation, ligand-independent activation, or receptor inactivation with proteasome-mediated degradation. Evidence for such a mechanism includes a PEST sequence similar to one in the vitamin D receptor that is present in the hinge region of all known mammalian androgen receptors, suggesting that it may function in proteasome-mediated androgen receptor turnover. Moreover, proteasome inhibition leads to a significant increase in androgen receptor isoforms (Sheflin et al, 2000).

DNA-Binding Domain

Near the end of exon 1 and extending into exon 3 is the coding sequence for the DNA-binding domain. The DNA-binding domain of the androgen receptor consists of 72 amino acids rich in cysteine and encoding two zinc finger motifs, which allows specific recognition of certain DNA sequences referred to as androgen response elements. Such elements typically consist of a palindromic repeat separated by a three-nucleotide spacer, for example, GG(A/T)ACAnnnTGTTCT (Roche et al, 1992). X-ray crystallography of certain steroid receptors (glucocorticoid receptor and progesterone receptor) has shown that the first zinc finger directs sequence specificity of binding by directly contacting the DNA bases in the major

groove; the second zinc finger functions to stabilize the protein-DNA complex by contacting the sugar-phosphate backbone. Although the protein-DNA interaction appears to be largely limited to the zinc finger motifs, sequences in the amino terminus appear to be important in stabilizing these structures as mutations in this region result in a mildly diminished DNA-binding affinity. This DNA-binding domain of the zinc fingers in the steroid receptor molecule is highly conserved. In this region of exon 2-3, there is a 79% homology with the progesterone receptor, 76% with the glucocorticoid receptor, and 56% with the estrogen receptor (Chang et al, 1988). The closest homology of the androgen receptor is with the progesterone receptor (Chang et al, 1988; Lubahn et al, 1988; Marcelli et al, 1990). Mutations of amino acids in this area of the androgen receptor can make the receptor unable to activate androgen-sensitive genes (Govindan, 1990), which is the basis of one of the inherited androgen-insensitive syndromes.

The DNA-binding domain binds to its cognate DNA-regulatory site, referred to as a hormone response element. Hormone response elements can be divided into different groups on the basis of common structural features for which whole groups of receptors are capable of binding. Class I hormone response elements include the glucocorticoid receptor, the progesterone receptor, and the mineralocorticoid receptor and are characterized by a half-site consensus sequence of TGTTCT. Class II hormone response elements include the estrogen receptor, whose prototype half-site sequence is TGACC. The hormone response elements to which androgen receptors have been shown to bind belong to the class I subgroup (Tan et al, 1990). A consensus sequence for the androgen response element has been determined by an RNA-binding site selection assay with an androgen receptor fusion protein to be GG(A/T)ACAnnnTGTTCT (Roche et al, 1992). Such binding sites are characterized by an inverted palindromic repeat with a dyad axis of symmetry, indicating that the receptors are binding in a head to head fashion. Recently, however, the androgen response element of the rat probasin promoter has been found to be a direct repeat, indicating binding in that situation in a head to tail fashion (Schoenmakers et al, 2000). Thus, the receptor may be able to dimerize and regulate genes in more than one configuration. Among the identified androgen response elements, there exists some degree of sequence variation (Luke,1994).

Ligand-Binding Domain

Ligand-dependent activation is characterized by ligand-receptor dimerization, post-translational modifications (e.g., phosphorylation), nuclear translocation, and subsequent target gene activation (or repression). It is believed that binding of *either* DHT or testosterone to the ligand-binding domain can facilitate these processes, although the binding affinity for DHT is significantly higher than for testosterone. Binding of the androgen to the carboxyl terminal ligand-binding domain is required for activation; however, deletion of the ligand-binding domain can lead to a constitutively active androgen receptor. Thus, at least part of the interaction with the chaparonin complex involves the carboxyl portion of the receptor (Marcelli et al, 1990). However, small point mutations in the ligand-binding region can lead to significant changes in the characteristics of androgen receptor action. For

instance, a single point mutation in the ligand-binding domain of the androgen receptor (codon 877, Thr→Ala) identified in the LNCaP cell line of prostate cancer renders it weakly inducible by inappropriate steroids such as progesterone while retaining the ability to be stimulated by androgens. Such mutations are frequently encountered in human clinical specimens of prostate cancer (Gaddipati et al, 1994). Marcelli and coworkers (1990) reported that mutations in the androgen receptor at amino acid 587 or 794 are inactive in the assay for androgen binding and for transcriptional activation. However, the removal of amino acids from 708 to the carboxyl end at 917 (i.e., the entire ligand-binding domain) leads to the synthesis of a receptor protein that does not bind androgens but is still constitutively active in activating transgenes.

Dimerization

The identification of the palindromic structure of certain hormone response elements for all steroid receptors led to the proposal that these transcription factors bind to the DNA as a dimer. Subsequent analysis of the receptor-DNA interactions has confirmed this hypothesis, and dimerization is now thought to represent an important step in the regulation of steroid receptor action. A hydrophobic heptad repeat within the ligand-binding domain at codons 859 to 880 is conserved among all steroid receptors and is thought to be necessary for high-affinity dimerization. Removal of these sequences leads to low-affinity dimerization, presumably through the action of the DNA-binding zinc fingers on the palindromic androgen response elements. Abolishment of the DNA-binding domain does not inhibit the strong affinity dimerization present in the ligand-binding domain. The strong dimerization signal appears to be related to a hydrophobic α helix interface formed by the conserved heptad. Most androgen response elements exist in an inverted repeat structure; however, the recent identification of direct repeat androgen response elements suggests that more than one type of homodimer can exist.

Post-translational Modifications

Once the androgen receptor has been bound to steroid ligand and dissociated from the chaparonin complex, it is susceptible to a variety of post-translational modifications, any one of which may significantly affect the function and turnover of the receptor. For instance, the androgen receptor can be acetylated (Fu et al, 2004) or phosphorylated. In the rat ventral prostate, it has been reported that this occurs through a nuclear cAMP-dependent protein kinase (Goueli et al, 1984; Kemppainen et al, 1992). Receptor phosphorylation may be an important mechanism in the nuclear translocation of steroid receptors as well as in DNA binding and transcriptional regulation. The stimulation for phosphorylation appears to be optimal with the binding of an androgen agonist, as antagonists like flutamide appear to favor the dephosphorylated state, suggesting that the phosphorylation status may be associated with the ultimate activity of the receptor (Wang et al, 1999). Both serine and tyrosine residues have been found to be phosphorylated in other steroid receptors (Landers and Spelsberg, 1992; Sadar et al, 1999). In addition to phosphorylation by protein kinase A, androgen receptors also appear to stimulate mitogen-activated protein kinases, which may provide a different level of regulation of gene activity as such kinases often modulate other transcription factors, such as Elk-1 (Peterziel et al, 1999). The prostate is a rich source of acid phosphatases, and some have suggested that these enzymes may be active in regulating the phosphotyrosyl residues of the androgen receptor, thus playing a role in dephosphorylation and inactivation of androgen receptors (Goldsteyn et al, 1989), although this relationship is certainly not causal.

Nuclear Localization

After activation by the binding of steroid ligand, the androgen receptor is transported to the nucleus across the nuclear pore complex by a process involving at least two nuclear localization signals. Evidence for nuclear localization signal–dependent nuclear translocation is well established and can be found in a variety of nuclear proteins, including the SV40 large T antigen. In most cases, it consists of a stretch of basic amino acids. The prototype nuclear localization signal from the SV40 large T antigen is PKKKRKV, although various other basic sequences have also been implicated in nuclear localization signaling. The nuclear localization of the androgen receptor appears to involve multiple steps, including the binding of the basic amino acid nuclear localization signal to importins α and β, docking of an importin-cargo complex to the nuclear pore, translocation to the nucleus, and Ran-GTP–mediated release of the cargo (Rao et al, 2002). Two regions of steroid receptors have gained most attention as regulators of receptor trafficking. The first region is the second DNA-binding zinc finger region together with the flanking hinge region (NL1) consisting of a bipartite signal including flanking leucines and the core signal ^{628}RKLKKLGN (Kemppainen et al, 1992; Ylikomi et al, 1992; Poukka et al, 2000). However, this one putative nuclear signal peptide is not sufficient by itself for high-efficiency translocation, and by analogy to other steroid receptors, additional nuclear localization signals may exist in the steroid-binding domain (Kemppainen et al, 1992). NL1 acts constitutively and participates in rapid nuclear import that in the case of glucocorticoid receptor is shown to be connected to importin α binding (Savory et al, 1999). A number of co-regulators of steroid receptor–mediated transactivation interact with regions that encompass NL1 (Jackson et al, 1997; Moilanen et al, 1998a, 1998b; Powers et al, 1998; McKenna et al, 1999; Poukka et al, 1999). Some of these proteins, such as SNURF and Ubc9, lose their ability to interact with androgen receptor when the region overlapping with the bipartite NL1 is destroyed (Moilanen et al, 1998b; Poukka et al, 1999, 2000). The second nuclear localization signal (NL2) of glucocorticoid receptor is importin α independent and embedded in the ligand-binding domain (Picard et al, 1990; Savory et al, 1999); but as for estrogen receptor and progesterone receptor (Ylikomi et al, 1992), the exact location of the hormone-inducible NL2 of androgen receptor has not been precisely mapped.

Transcriptional Activation Domains

Once the androgen receptor has achieved translocation into the nucleus, it must coordinate binding to a number of associated factors referred to as co-activators and co-repressors that subsequently regulate gene expression (Fig. 85–11). A list of recently identified co-activators is provided in Table 85–4. Most of these factors interact promiscuously with many steroid receptors, although more androgen receptor–specific

Table 85–4. Abbreviated List of Putative Androgen Receptor Co-Activators

ARA24, ARA54, ARA55, ARA70, ARA160
ART-27, ARIP3
β-Catenin
BRCA1, BRCA2
CARM1, CBP, c-Jun, Cdc25B, cyclin E
FHL2 (specific to androgen receptor)
GT198
HBO1
Ku
MAGE 11
Oct-1
p68 helicase, p160, pp32-Rb
pCAF, p300, PGC-1, PNRC, p54nrb
RAC3
RNF-4
SNURF
SRC1, SRC1a, SRC3, SRCAP
TIF2
Tip60
TRAM-1
TRAP/DRIP/GRIP/NRIP
Ubc9, UBCH7
Zac1

factors are routinely being discovered. As the number of potential co-regulators clearly exceeds the capacity for direct interaction by a single receptor, the most likely mechanism is that transcriptional activation by androgen receptor involves multiple factors that act in both a sequential and combinatorial manner to reorganize chromatin templates (Pollard and Peterson, 1998). The precise timing and sequence of binding of these factors remain to be elucidated; however, one can generally break down the processes empirically into chromatin/nucleosomal remodeling (an energy-dependent process), histone acetyltransferase activity, and subsequent recruitment of TATA-binding protein–associated factors, all of which promote an increased rate of gene transcription by RNA polymerase II. Under certain conditions, such as binding of an androgen receptor antagonist (e.g., flutamide), the histone acetyltransferase activity is actually inhibited and transrepression may occur. Such inhibition of gene expression appears to involve the nuclear co-repressor proteins N-CoR and SMRT (Glass and Rosenfeld, 2000). Other proteins may play a similar role, such as the *HBO1* gene (Sharma et al, 2000). N-terminal deletions in region 46-408 result in dominant negative suppression of hormone-inducible transgene activation, indicating that the co-activator functions require an interaction within that site and that in the absence of this region, the receptor forms dysfunctional complexes in the chromatin (Palvimo et al, 1993).

The transcription domain of the androgen receptor is coded in exon 1, which is the largest of the exons, containing 1607 base pairs. Analysis of this region reveals three homopolymeric repeated regions including a repeat of approximately 20 glutamines, followed by a space containing 8 repetitive prolines and 23 repetitive glycine units (see Fig. 85–11). The glutamine repeats form a β sheet that helps form a polar zipper, which favors certain protein-protein interactions. Fusion of this type of polymeric glutamine repeat with the DNA-binding domain of GAL4 in yeast results in a GAL4-

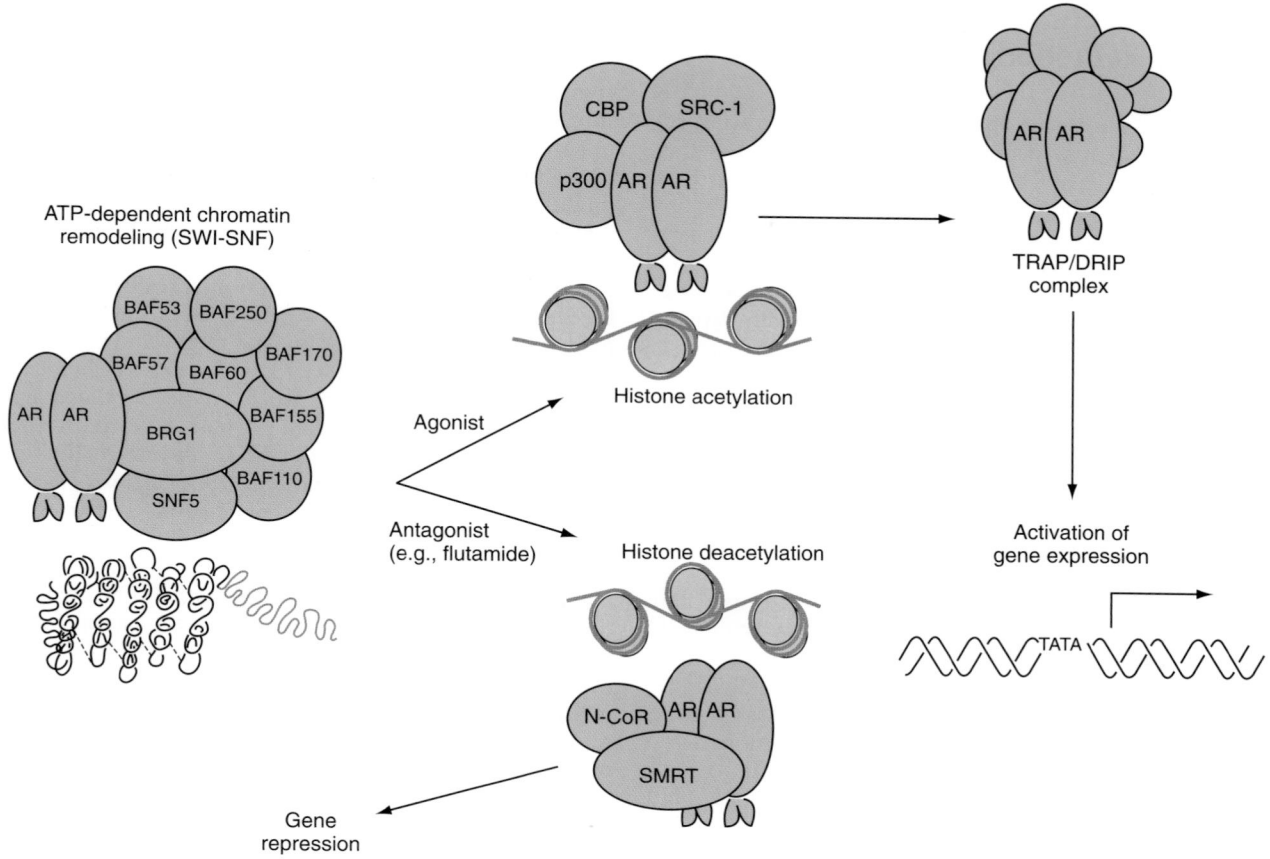

Figure 85–11.   Mechanism of action of the nuclear-activated androgen receptor. Once the androgen receptor has been translocated to the nucleus, it undergoes several steps (many of which may occur contemporaneously), including (1) chromatin remodeling in an ATP-dependent fashion via the SWI-SNF complex. (2) Agonist (i.e., DHT)–mediated histone acetylation in a process involving multiple transmission factors including p300, CBP, and SRC1. In the case of a certain antagonist, histone deacetylation may be favored, and the activated nuclear receptors complex with repressors of gene expression such as N-CoR and SMRT. (3) The activated androgen receptor complexes then associate with other γ-trans-acting factors via the TRAP/DRIP complex at sites typically upstream of the target gene known as androgen response elements. This complex then leads to androgen-regulated activation of gene expression.

directed increase in transcriptional activity, demonstrating the importance of this region in promoting transgene activation (Gerber et al, 1994).

Studies demonstrate that these polyglutamine repeats appear to interact directly with the carboxyl terminus of the transcription factor p160 (Irvine et al, 2000). These glutamine repeats may undergo somatic mutations in prostate cancer (Schoenberg et al, 1994). In the normal population, this repeat varies over a length of 11 to 31 residues, resulting in a true allelic polymorphism. This means that different people have alleles of variant polyglutamine repeat units. This variation is racially defined, and it has been suggested that this may be related to the differences in the incidence rates of prostate cancer in different ethnic groups. The most common CAG repeat length in whites is a modal value of 21; in African Americans, it is shorter at 18; and in Asians, it is longer at a mean of 23. The longer the glutamine repeats, the lower the activity of the androgen receptor in activating target genes. Population-based studies of the Chinese population reveal that the longer polymorphisms seen in this group appear to be directly related to the risk for development of prostate

cancer and serve to confirm the supposition that the polyglutamine polymorphisms may account in part for the difference in the risk of prostate cancer between African Americans and American whites (Hsing et al, 2000). Kantoff and others have demonstrated that patients diagnosed with prostate cancer tend to have a higher grade and stage if their polyglutamine polymorphisms are short (Giovannucci et al, 1997), a finding similar to Barrack's experience with the Hopkins dataset (Hakimi et al, 1997). Patients with X-linked spinal and bulbar muscular atrophy, termed Kennedy's disease, possess a larger glutamine repeat in the range of 40 to 60. The androgen receptors in Kennedy's disease exhibit markedly less transactivation activity (Laspada et al, 1991). Moreover, men with male factor infertility are found to have longer than average polymorphisms of the androgen receptor than in normal controls (Tut et al, 1997). Genetic studies of inherited diseases of androgen insensitivity and overvirilization as well as changes in the androgen receptor mutation associated with prostate cancer and its biologic properties will be of great help in unraveling the role of the human androgen receptor in relation to its structure.

Androgen Receptor–Dependent Chromatin Remodeling

Part of the tissue and gene specificity in the recognition of receptors and DNA may depend on the organization of the DNA within the nucleus (Getzenberg et al, 1990). The steroid-receptor complex can interact only with genes that are in regions that are "open" or in the transcriptionally active form. Studies show that these open regions of chromatin (euchromatin) can extend up to 100,000 base pairs in length, or more than 10-fold the size of a typical gene, which usually ranges from 1,000 to 10,000 base pairs. It is unknown how such a large range of DNA is altered in conformation, but it may be through binding to structures like the nuclear matrix, which can order large loop domains in the region of 60,000 to 120,000 base pairs. Nuclear receptors are thought to interact with chromatin remodeling complexes in an ATP-dependent fashion, and this may be among the earliest steps in the ultimate regulation of certain target genes (Glass and Rosenfeld, 2000).

During cell division, chromosomal organization is spatially regulated at each of the critical phases of mitosis (Williams and Fisher, 2003). Epigenetic regulation of chromosome structure and function is highly ordered during cell division, differentiation, and development (Lam et al, 2005; Margueron et al, 2005). In fact, chromosomal proteins are required to maintain such ordered structure for euchromatin, heterochromatin, and centromeric chromatin to sustain normal cell and tissue functions (Lam et al, 2005). To achieve such coordinate regulation, the protective packaging of DNA is engineered through an elegant system of tightly wound DNA around an eight-component histone core called a nucleosome. This core consists of dimers of H2A, H2B, H3, and H4, whose ability to compact DNA is directly regulated by post-translational modifications. The selective regulation of such post-translational histone modification constitutes a major regulatory mechanism for gene expression and is referred to as the histone code (see Fig. 85–11). Histone modifications include acetylation, phosphorylation, ubiquination, and methylation (Downs and Jackson, 2003; He et al, 2003; Cosgrove and Wolberger, 2005; Lam et al, 2005).

Androgen receptors are known to interact with structural components of the chromatin organizing complexes. Such complexes include the multisubunit human SWI-SNF complex, which has been shown to remodel mononucleosome and polynucleosome templates in an ATP-dependent manner (Peterson and Tamkun, 1995). The isolated hSWI-SNF ATPase subunits BRG1 and hBRM also have these activities (Phelan et al, 2000).

The transcriptional activation of nuclear receptors (neuroendocrine cells) requires multiple factors including SWI-SNF complex, CPB/p300, and SRC family members, which are large and contain numerous subunits, many of which make contact with a variety of nucleosome components and the nuclear matrix (Huang et al, 2003). Such components include BAF53a, BAF57, BAF60, BAF110, BAF155, BAF170, BAF250, BRG1, BRM, and SNF5. Because condensed chromatin renders genes inaccessible for transcription, the combination of a steroid receptor along with the SWI-SNF complex formation appears to be critical for appropriate nucleosomal

remodeling to allow appropriate target genes to be accessible for gene regulation (Sudarsanam and Winston, 2000; Huang et al, 2003; Marshall et al, 2003). Once the receptor SWI-SNF complex, CPB/p300, and other mediators have successfully "opened" the structure of the chromatin to allow transcriptional regulation, the androgen receptor must interact with a distinctly different set of cofactors. Post-translational histone modification clearly appears to be requisite for chromosome remodeling and optimal gene expression (Ewen, 2000; He et al, 2003; Cosgrove and Wolberger, 2005). In most models tested, the rates of gene transcription actually correlate with the degree of modification of histones through acetylation, phosphorylation, ubiquination, and methylation (Downs and Jackson, 2003; He et al, 2003; Cosgrove and Wolberger 2005; Lam et al, 2005). In other words, hyperacetylated histone regions correspond to the highest gene-transcriptional regions, whereas the hypoacetylated histone regions correspond to the lowest gene-transcriptional regions (Pazin and Kadonaga, 1997). A number of histone acetyltransferase complexes have been found to be associated with nuclear receptors, including the androgen receptor. These complexes include p/CAF, a homologue to the yeast GCN5, which participates in the yeast SAGA complex. This complex includes factors that possess HAT activity but also the TATA-binding protein (TBP) and a number of TBP-associated factors. The p/CAF protein has been found to be associated with the retinoic acid receptor and may be involved with multiple nuclear receptors. It is also known to bind to other HAT proteins, including CBP/p300, which is known to acetylate not only histones but other transcription factors as well. The CBP/p300 complex is an essential co-activator for many genes and may actually serve as a molecular scaffold in stimulating gene transcription (McKenna et al, 1999; Huang et al, 2003; Marshall et al, 2003). Such complexes include the SRC1 co-activator, among others. More recently, the modifiers of the histone code have expanded considerably to include sophisticated enzyme-mediated alterations in the histones H2A, H2B, H3, and H4 by phosphorylation, ubiquination, and methylation that open the chromatin, allowing the recruitment of important transcription factors that allow normal cell functions (Lam et al, 2005; Margueron et al, 2005). The list of co-activators associated with nuclear receptors and the androgen receptor in particular is extensive and almost certainly incomplete. A short list of factors found to be associated with the receptor at this level of gene regulation is given in Table 85–4. Among the most important factors is SRC1 (steroid receptor coactivator 1), which has mild HAT activity and seems to be required for optimal stimulation of steroid-dependent transcription. Additional factors include SRA, a structural RNA necessary for the co-activator complex to function optimally (McKenna et al, 1999), and p160 co-activator, which appears to be required for hormone-dependent activation and to directly interact with the polyglutamine repeats found in the amino terminal transactivation domain (Irvine et al, 2000).

Most genes have a regulatory region immediately upstream of the transcriptional start site. The regulatory region is divided into a core *promoter element* that is present in all genes as well as other upstream elements that serve to regulate the overall gene expression pattern. This promoter element specifies the site to which RNA polymerase II will attach to the

DNA and will determine the accuracy point for the initiation of transcription. The RNA polymerase will copy or transcribe the DNA code into mRNA, a process termed transcription. This promoter area starts at −16 nucleotides to −32 upstream from the gene initiation site. This region of −32 to −16 was originally referred to as the Goldberg-Hogness box and has a consensus sequence of TATAAAAG. The RNA polymerase II enzyme binds to this TATA box as one of the initial steps in transcription. Farther upstream from the TATA box is a second gene control element termed generically the *hormone response element*, which has been identified in many genes regulated by steroid hormones and is one of multiple sites where the receptor binds to the DNA. As stated earlier, in androgen-regulated genes, this area is termed the androgen response element; in estrogen, the estrogen response element; and in glucocorticoid, the glucocorticoid response element. This hormone response element area may contain several discrete sequences, but its overall role is to modulate the frequency of transcription initiation vis-à-vis interactions with transcriptional factors. In independent analysis, thyroid hormone receptors were found to be associated with affinity purified proteins, which were found to markedly enhance ligand-dependent cell-free transcription. This complex was referred to as TRAP, for thyroid receptor–associated proteins (Fondell et al, 1996). In a similar set of experiments, the same type of complex was isolated for the vitamin D receptor and was termed DRIP for D receptor–interacting proteins (Rachez et al, 1998). Subsequent analysis revealed that they shared at least nine proteins, and this activator-recruited cofactor complex (TRAP/DRIP/ARC) is part of a large composite co-activator complex used by a variety of transcription factors for the regulation of certain target genes. Such transcription factors include SREBP, NFκB, and VP16 (Sun et al, 1998; Gu et al, 1999; Ito et al, 1999; Naar et al, 1999; Ryu et al, 1999).

In summary, the TATA box tells where RNA polymerase binds and where the initiation of transcription is to start, and the hormone response element regulates how frequently it is to be transcribed when it is bound to a hormone receptor. This is accomplished by the presence of certain cofactors in the TRAP/DRIP complex. Since the hormone response element of DNA sequence has been shown to be independent of its position or its orientation, it resembles what has been called the transcription *enhancer element* that has been found in many other types of genes. The hormone response element section can vary in its location upstream from the initiation of the gene from −20 to −2,600 for various different types of hormones. With the steroid hormones, it appears to reside about −140 nucleotides upstream from the initiation site. For example, in the glucocorticoid receptor recognition element, the site for glucocorticoid receptor recognition is approximately −140 and contains a sequence of nucleotides of AAAATGGAC. Deletion mapping experiments have indicated that the receptor-binding domain located in the hormone response element is indeed required for receptor binding and is necessary for steroid-mediated control of transcription.

Once the DNA is transcribed into mRNA, a series of adenine units are added to the end (called the poly-A tail), and then the mRNA is cut and spliced on small nuclear particles (called splicesomes) located on the nuclear matrix, and this splicing removes the intron portion of the message. The final mRNA is shipped out of the nucleus, believed to occur on the structural components of the nuclear matrix, and passes through the pore complexes of the nucleus and out to the ribosomes where the mRNA is then translated into protein product, a step termed translation. The proteins have specific amino acid sequences that instruct the cell where to ship the protein in relation to secretory granules or to the membrane area. The protein can also be modified after translation by the subsequent addition of carbohydrates to become glycoproteins or to be phosphorylated by kinases. Under appropriate signals, such as neurologic control, secretory proteins can then be excreted into the lumen of the prostate. This is a process that occurs when secretory proteins of the prostate and seminal vesicles are formed into the ejaculate. A schematic example of this process is shown in Figure 85–6, and such a system would include PSA and acid phosphatase as well as many other protein products that are regulated in their synthesis by androgens through receptor interactions.

During embryonic development, the androgen receptor appears first in the mesenchyme of both the rat ventral prostate and seminal vesicle and a few days later in the epithelial cells, but it is unknown what regulates this timing. **In the development of the seminal vesicles and the wolffian duct, testosterone appears to be the primary androgen in glandular development, and in the ventral prostate that forms from the urogenital sinus, the androgen is primarily DHT.** Both testosterone and DHT can bind to the androgen receptor; however, on a molar basis, DHT is 3 to 10 times more potent. This decrease in potency of testosterone is believed to be due to the rapid off rates of the testosterone once it is bound so that equilibrium results in less receptor occupancy compared with DHT at similar tissue levels. A report indicates that in some cases, androgen receptor–mediated transcriptional regulation can occur even in the absence of direct interaction of the androgen receptor with the specific androgen response elements (Kallio et al, 1995). The report stated that the androgen receptors are able to elicit both transrepression and transactivation without interacting directly with the specific DNA elements. This may indicate that the androgen receptor can bind to regulatory units within the transcription factors and thus alter their properties even in the absence of direct DNA binding to an androgen response element.

We now turn our attention to the structure of the nucleus, where the genetic information of the genes, the androgen receptor interactions, and the mRNA processing occur and are integrated. This is within a highly ordered structure of the nucleus that is determined by a residual scaffolding framework, called the nuclear matrix, which provides three-dimensional organization to both the nucleus and the DNA.

Role of the Nuclear Matrix in Androgen Action

The DNA may be identical in every cell of different tissues in the body, but it appears to be organized in a different three-dimensional array in different cell types. This spatial organization of DNA appears to be determined in part by nuclear architecture and structure dictated by the scaffolding element termed the nuclear matrix. Therefore, more may be required than just a steroid receptor and a DNA sequence with an androgen response element to determine the high tissue specificity of androgen hormone action. It may require regulation of DNA conformation and three-dimensional structure. There is strong evidence to support the belief that structural components of the nucleus may organize the DNA into different topologic constraints that permit specific steroid receptor interactions themselves. It is also believed that these structural modifications of DNA topology may be an integral part of differentiation. The nuclear matrix has been proposed to be an important structural element in this type of DNA organization (Getzenberg et al, 1990; Boccardo et al, 2003). The matrix facilitates the location of target genes and their conformation and facilitates their co-interaction with steroid receptors. For this reason, we discuss the properties and structure of the nuclear matrix. For additional details, see the reviews by Luke and Baccardo (Luke, 1994; Luke and Coffey, 1994; Boccardo et al, 2003).

Barrack and Coffey first showed that the nuclear matrix is a major target for androgen and estrogen receptor binding (Barrack and Coffey, 1980, 1982). Because the matrix has been implicated in many important nuclear events, it would provide an ideal target for androgen action. The nuclear matrix has been defined as the dynamic structural subcomponent of the nucleus that directs the functional organization of DNA into loop domains and provides sites for the specific control of nucleic acids (Nelson et al, 1986; Getzenberg et al, 1990). Conceptually, it can be viewed as the nuclear equivalent to the cytomatrix or cytoskeleton. The nuclear matrix contains residual nuclear elements, including the pore complex lamina, the residual nucleolus, and an internal ribonucleoprotein particle network attached to a dynamic fibrous protein mesh (Berezney and Coffey, 1977). The nuclear matrix may be isolated by sequential extractions employing nonionic detergent, brief digestion with DNase I, and a hypertonic salt buffer wash. The residual nuclear matrix structures represent only 15% or less of the original total nuclear mass. More than 98% of the DNA, 70% of the RNA, and 90% of the nuclear proteins have been extracted, and the remaining structure is essentially devoid of histones and lipids.

The nuclear matrix has been implicated as an important structural component in a wide variety of biologic functions. There are approximately 50,000 DNA loop domains in a nucleus, each containing about 60 kilobase pairs of DNA, and these loops are attached at their bases to the nuclear matrix (Pardoll et al, 1980; Vogelstein et al, 1980; Luke, 1994). This loop organization is maintained during interphase and throughout metaphase (Nelson et al, 1986). Topoisomerase II, an enzyme that modulates DNA twisting and topology, is associated with the nuclear matrix and the mitotic chromosome scaffold. Many studies with a wide variety of systems have demonstrated that active genes are associated with the nuclear matrix, whereas transcriptionally inactive genes are not close to the matrix. This location of active genes on the matrix provides evidence that the matrix plays an important organizing role in differentiation, placing genes in different configuration.

Androgens can activate DNA synthesis and cell replication in target tissues. The nuclear matrix also serves an important role in DNA replication. The matrix contains fixed sites for DNA synthesis (Pardoll et al, 1980) located at the base of the

DNA loop. During DNA synthesis, the DNA loop domains are reeled down through the attached replicating complex that is fixed on the matrix. Therefore, the DNA replication fork, DNA polymerase, and newly replicated DNA have been shown to be associated with the nuclear matrix. It is easy to visualize how hormone action and alteration in the nuclear matrix structures could impinge on the androgen regulation of DNA synthesis and growth in a prostate cell.

The nuclear matrix is also associated with mRNA synthesis during transcription. O'Malley and colleagues (Ciejek et al, 1982) observed that more than 95% of the unprocessed mRNA precursor for ovalbumin is associated with nuclear matrix of the chick oviduct. When the intron portions of the RNA were spliced out, the mature mRNA was released from the nuclear matrix. This led them to suggest that the nuclear matrix is involved in RNA processing. Mariman and van Venrooij (1985) have reported that all RNA cleavage products and RNA processing intermediates are firmly bound to nuclear matrix. Once again, alterations in nuclear matrix structures with steroid receptor interactions could alter important steps in transcription and RNA processing. The nuclear matrix contains the attachment sites for the small nuclear ribonucleoprotein particles that are part of the nuclear splicesome system central to the nuclear processing of RNA to the final mRNA, which is transported out to the cytoplasm to be translated.

Khalil Ahmed and his colleagues have carried out an extensive series of studies of the phosphorylation of the nuclear matrix and related proteins in the ventral prostate of the rat after androgen stimulation and withdrawal (Ahmed and Goueli, 1987; Ahmed et al, 1993; Tawfic et al, 1993, 1994). They have shown that the nuclear matrix can be phosphorylated by casein kinase 2 (CK-2). One of the targets of this phosphorylation is nucleolin, which is an abundant nucleolar phosphoprotein involved in the synthesis of ribosomal DNA and exquisitely regulated by androgens (Tawfic et al, 1994). Another important protein in nucleolar function that is required for growth is B23, which is also regulated by CK-2 (Tawfic et al, 1993).

In summary, the nuclear matrix is an important structural modulator of nuclear regulation and is an ideal target for hormonal regulation. Indeed, the nuclear matrix is a major site of steroid hormone receptor binding (Barrack and Coffey, 1982; Donnelly et al, 1983; Wilson and Colvard, 1984; Alexander et al, 1987; Barrack, 1987; Metzger and Korach, 1990; Luke, 1994). In the prostate, more than 60% of all nuclear androgen receptors are associated with the nuclear matrix (Barrack and Coffey, 1982). The matrix is also a target for many other types of regulatory interactions, including the nuclear products of oncogenes and viral proteins that can also induce growth regulation similar to hormone-induced growth. For example, the nuclear matrix is reported to be a cellular target for the retrovirus Myc oncogene protein and the polyoma large T antigen. All of these transformation proteins that bind to the nucleus are believed to be early molecular events in carcinogenesis or transformation. Therefore, the observation that androgen receptors interact with the matrix has precedence with the matrix as a common target in factors that regulate cell structure and function. (For a more detailed review of the matrix in hormone action, see the following reviews: Pienta et al, 1989; Getzenberg et al, 1990; Luke, 1994.)

Role of Vitamins A and D in Normal Prostatic Function

We have previously discussed androgens and estrogens stimulating growth, but vitamins, such as A and D, also affect the prostate, and since they bind to receptors that are similar to the steroid receptors in protein sequence, we discuss them before introducing the growth factors. Considerations of vitamin A and its retinoid derivatives as well as vitamin C, vitamin E, and vitamin D on prostate growth have been reviewed by Kadmon and Thompson (1995).

Vitamin A

It has long been known that vitamin A can protect against development of prostate cancer in carcinogenesis-induced animal models (Lasnitzki, 1955; Lasnitzki and Goodman, 1974; Chopra and Wilkoff, 1979; Pollard et al, 1991). Vitamin A is a retinol; the natural and synthetic analogues are called retinoids, and there are more than six human retinoid receptors RAR (α, β, γ) and RXR (α, β, γ); all six belong to the steroid receptor superfamily. This complex field is exemplified by the fact that the retinoids bind to receptors and can produce a pleiotropic response including proliferation, differentiation, morphogenesis, programmed cell death, and interactions with the extracellular matrix formation and the immune system (Kadmon and Thompson, 1995). Retinoids have the ability to modify growth factor activity, particularly TGF-β, and to induce protein kinase C and other kinase cascades. There is approximately 60 ng/g wet weight of retinoids in the normal prostate, 146 in BPH, and 75 in prostatic carcinoma (Kadmon and Thompson, 1995). At present, chemoprevention in prostate cancer trials has used a compound called fenretinide (4-HPR) and 9-*cis*-retinoic acid.

Retinoids can inhibit the growth of both normal and cancerous prostate cells both in vivo (Pollard et al, 1991) and in vitro (Peehl et al, 1991; Igawa et al, 1994; Young et al, 1994). It was observed that retinoic acids can antagonize the effects of androgens on LNCaP cells, and this was modulated by a decrease in the expression of the androgen receptor in a concomitant downregulation of PSA (Young et al, 1994). In those studies, retinoic acid did not block the binding to the androgen receptor but did affect its expression, and it was postulated that it may also affect other transcription factors (Young et al, 1994). It is of interest that retinoic acid can also affect the expression of other receptors, such as vitamin D_3, progesterone, and estrogen receptors. 4-HPR also inhibits the growth of PC-3 cells, and this was shown to be the result of a block in the cell cycle transition from G_1 to S phase; this inhibition was associated with the suppression of c-*myc* gene expression (Igawa et al, 1994). This results in suppression of growth without cytotoxicity. 4-HPR has been used to effectively treat the Dunning prostatic cancer model (Pienta et al, 1993b).

Vitamin D

Vitamin D was originally classified as a "vitamin" because in the early 1900s, it was determined to be essential for the maintenance of calcium homeostasis and normal skeletal development. On determination of the chemical structure, it became apparent that it is actually not a vitamin but a steroid (Bouillon et al, 1995). Indeed, the receptor for vitamin D has been shown to be a steroid receptor and is present in prostate cells (Miller et al, 1992). Skowronski and others have shown that vitamin D blocks proliferation of LNCaP and PC-3 cells (Skowronski et al, 1993; Feldman et al, 1995; Stewart and Weigel, 2004). It appears that 1,25-hydroxyvitamin D_3 markedly stimulates the levels of insulin growth factor–binding protein 6 in human prostate tumor cells (Drivdahl et al, 1995).

Whereas it is evident that the prostate and other sex accessory tissues are clearly hormonally regulated, the role of vitamin D in the normal prostate is only beginning to be elucidated. Recent investigations have revealed that vitamin D is involved in the differentiation of the normal prostate and has a pronounced effect on the organization of the rat prostate with vitamin D receptors in epithelial and stromal cells. Specifically, vitamin D has been found to induce columnar differentiation resulting in increased secretory capacity in prostate epithelium and to induce stromal atrophy. In castrate animals, vitamin D was shown to significantly enhance the growth and differentiation of the prostate, resulting in a prostate twice the size of the prostate of an animal that did not receive vitamin D (Konety et al, 1996; Getzenberg et al, 1997). Importantly, although changes in the seminal vesicle were noted, they are not of the magnitude of changes seen in the prostate. Overall, these studies suggest the importance of vitamin D in prostate growth and differentiation.

GROWTH FACTORS AND GROWTH SUPPRESSORS

The growth factors common to the prostate and other tissues are summarized in Table 85–5. In addition, other identified growth factors are claimed to originate in the prostate, but as yet there is no proven growth factor that is unique only to the prostate. It is possible that common growth factors may be altered in processing to produce increased specificity for an organ. Because the normal adult prostate is not growing rapidly or increasing in size, one would not anticipate an abundance of active growth factors in the normal prostate. Paradoxically, however, many adult tissues that are not rapidly growing still contain high levels of growth factors. This can be demonstrated by extracting the tissues and showing that they contain soluble factors that can stimulate in vitro fibroblast growth (Chung et al, 1992; Sikes et al, 1995; Hayward, 2002; Cunha et al, 2003, 2004). It has been proposed that many of these prostate growth factors in the normal human prostate may not be active because they are sequestered by binding to components of the extracellular matrix, such as heparin or heparan sulfates that are part of the glycosaminoglycans. Indeed, it is known that heparin binding to growth factors is one of the most efficient ways to remove and purify many growth factors, such as those in the basic fibroblast growth factor family. If the prostate growth factors are sequestered at the extracellular matrix, it would be important to know what mechanisms are involved in their binding and in their release. Therefore, the simple measuring of total growth factor levels in the prostate is, in itself, not sufficient to define their actual biologic activity in the prostate. In all types of growth, it now appears that there is a balance between factors that activate growth and factors that suppress these growth-promoting

Table 85–5. **Properties of Growth Factors**

Abbreviation	Name	Type		
		Size		Comment
bFGF	Basic fibroblast growth factor (prostate growth factor, endothelial growth factor, tumor angiogenesis factor, osteoblastic factor)	155 amino acids 17.6 kD		Present in normal prostate Elevated in benign prostatic hyperplasia In tissues of mesoderm origin, stromal elements
	Related *int*-2 oncogene	27 kD		Overexpression produces prostate epithelial hyperplasia but not glandular hyperplasia in transgenic mice
EGF	Epidermal growth factor; urogastrone	67-kD single chain		Controversial in normal human prostate but elevated in cancer Prevalent in rat ventral prostate
TGF-α	Transforming growth factor α 30% similar to EGF, not related to TGF-β	5.6 kD		Low levels in human prostate Overexpression in transgenic mouse causes epithelial hyperplasia
TGF-β	Transforming growth factor β Two genes (1 + 2), three combinations, TGF-β1, TGF-β2, TGF-β3	25 kD		Inhibitor of epithelial growth Stimulates growth of fibroblast TGF-β2 elevated in benign prostatic hyperplasia Related to MIS and to inhibin and activin
MIS	Müllerian-inhibiting substance	140-kD dimer of 2 identical 70-kD units		Causes repression of müllerian ducts
IGF	Insulin-like growth factor 1 and 2 Somatomedin family	7.5-kD single chain		Related to proinsulin
PDGF	Platelet-derived growth factor	30-kD dimer		Mitogen for connective tissue cells

factors. These inhibitory or braking elements have been termed suppressors. In this regard, the extracellular matrix could be termed a suppressor element because of its ability to sequester growth factors. In addition, extracellular matrix interactions with cells can determine or direct the response of a cell to a mitogen like a growth factor.

In summary, both stromal and epithelial cells can, themselves, synthesize and respond to growth factors in a reciprocal and interactive manner (Fig. 85–12) (Marengo and Chung, 1994; Sikes et al, 1995; Hayward, 2002; Cunha et al, 2003, 2004; Risbridger et al, 2005). **Many of these growth factors appear to be under hormonal regulation, particularly in response to androgens, estrogens, and other endocrine factors.** Androgens and growth factors can also stimulate the synthesis and degradation of extracellular matrix components that can alter a cell's response to steroids and growth factors. Therefore, the interaction of steroids, growth factors, and the extracellular matrix with the cell is reciprocal and dynamic and can have either positive or negative effects in regulating cell growth.

KEY POINTS: GROWTH FACTORS

■ Both stromal and several types of epithelial cells can, themselves, synthesize and respond to growth factors in a reciprocal and interactive manner (see Fig. 85–13).

■ Many of these growth factors appear to be under hormonal regulation (androgens, estrogens). Both positive and negative growth regulation of the prostate can occur in response to production of these macromolecules.

Growth Factor Mechanisms

Growth factors are most commonly peptide hormones that regulate cellular proliferation. Regulation of their synthesis, post-translational modification, transport, presentation, and binding to a specific target cell receptor is a multistep process that can vary with each type of growth factor. The generalized scheme is introduced to provide the reader with a flow diagram to help orient the understanding of these processes (Fig. 85–13). Not all steps are realized with each growth factor, but they are usually modifications of the generalized scheme and pathways and involve four general phases of regulation: synthesis, secretion, target cell interactions, and cellular effects mediated through cell signaling pathways. The cell is signaled to produce synthesis of a growth factor by environmental signals that include cell-cell and cell–extracellular matrix communications and hormone levels. The genes for the growth factors are activated, making mRNAs that can be processed to various forms, which are then translated, usually to an inactive or progrowth factor form. Proteolysis activates the growth factor, which then can work internally in the cell (intracrine) or be secreted extracellularly to serve as a soluble signal to the cell in which it was synthesized (autocrine) or to stimulate a nearby cell (paracrine). Alternatively, the growth factor may function by binding to receptors on cells located distantly and transported by the bloodstream (endocrine). After being secreted, the growth factor can be sequestered by binding to the extracellular matrix, but on release, it is capable of binding to specific growth factor receptors that reside on the plasma membrane of the target cell.

Growth Factor Receptors and Cell Signaling

The growth factors bind specific receptors that are transmembrane proteins, with the intracellular portion of the

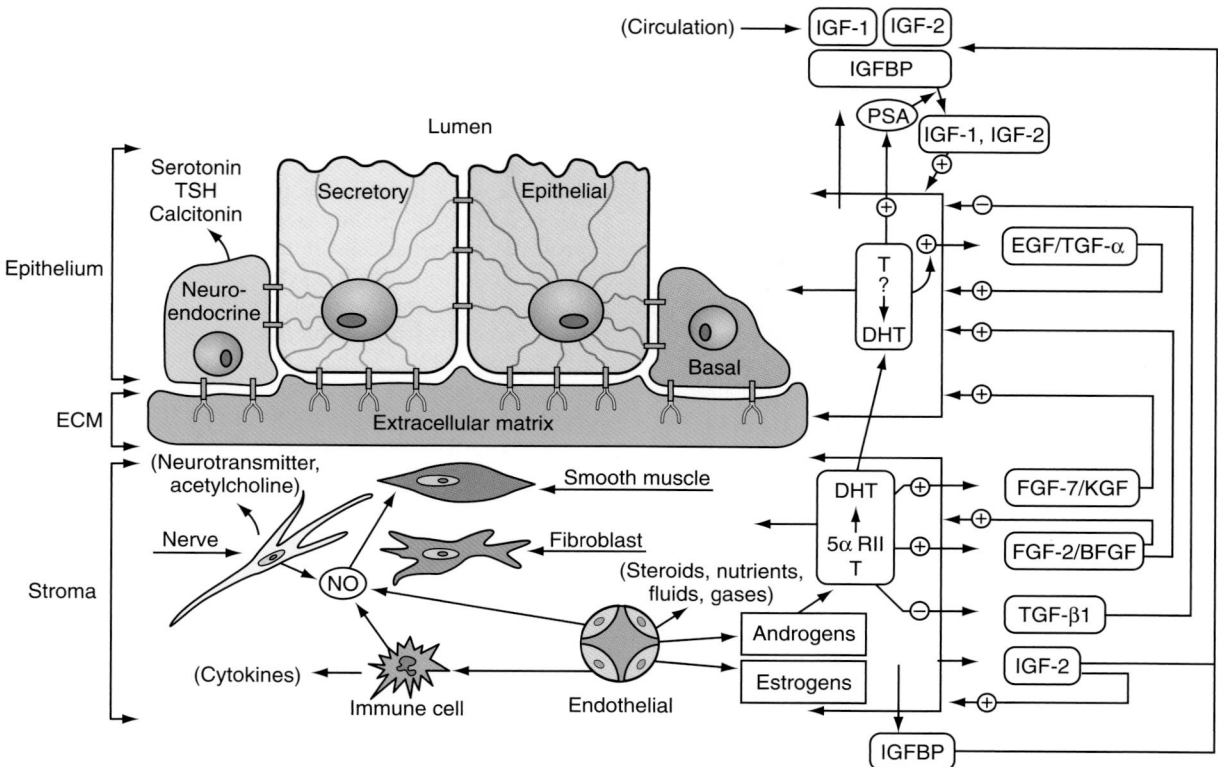

Figure 85–12. Stromal-epithelial interactions. Shown is a schematic of the types of stromal-epithelial interactions in information transfer and regulation within the prostate. Testosterone and growth factors interact on and between stromal and epithelial cells. The production of growth factors is either stimulated or inhibited by androgens. The growth factors can function on the same cell (autocrine) or on distant cells (paracrine). Nitric oxide (NO) is formed from nerve cells, endothelial cells, or macrophages and affects smooth muscle contraction (see text for details). Important features in this schematic are (1) three types of prostate epithelial cells—neuroendocrine, secretory, and basal; (2) five important prostatic stromal cells—smooth muscle, fibroblast, immune cells, endothelial cells, and nerve cells; (3) testosterone converted to dihydrotestosterone (DHT) by 5α-reductase in the stromal compartment; (4) three sources of NO production in the prostate—nerve, immune cells (e.g., macrophages), and endothelial cells; and (5) stromal-epithelial interactions mediated through various growth factors (see text). ECM, extracellular matrix.

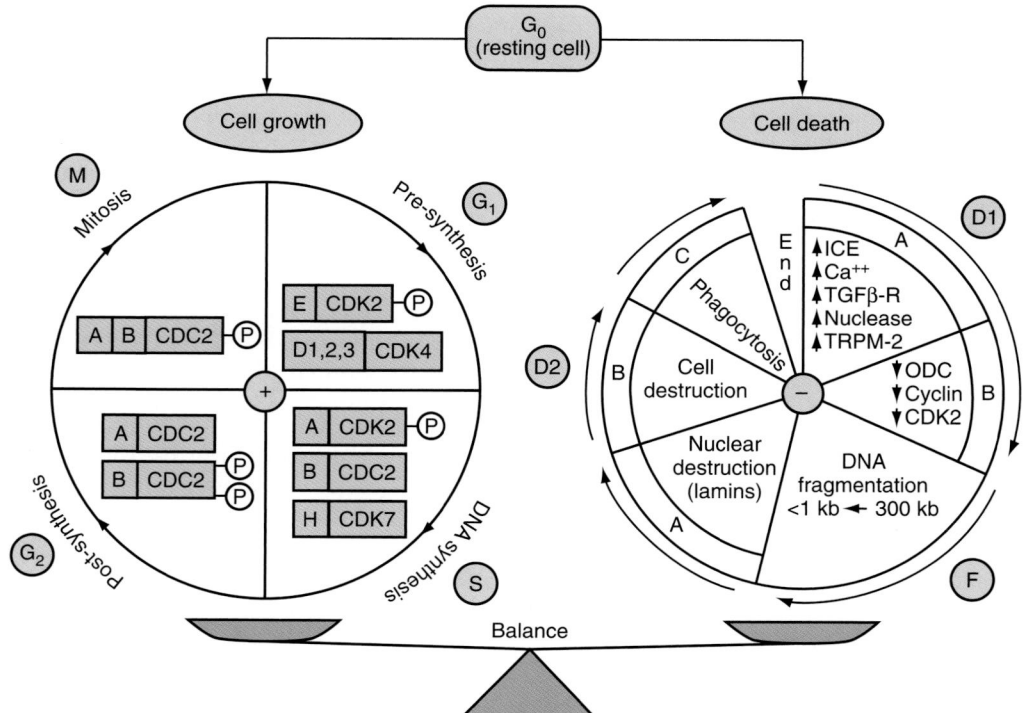

Figure 85–13. Schematic diagram of the balance between cell cycle growth and cell death. On the cell cycle, A, B, C, D, E, and H are the cyclins. CDK and CDC2 are kinases. ODC, ICE, TGFβ-R, and TRPM-2 represent modulators of the cell death cycle (apoptosis).

receptor possessing enzymatic activity that is activated by the receptor binding to the growth factor. Once bound, these growth factors may form dimers or oligomers or otherwise alter their topology in such a way as to stimulate internalization or a series of second-messenger signals that initiate a cascade of downstream effectors. Such signaling includes activation of protein kinases (type A and C), membrane phospholipases (type A, B, or C) that convert lipids into signals, and G protein pathways like Ras, Rho, or Rac.

The early result of binding to the receptor is the activation of one of the many general types of enzymes that phosphorylate proteins called kinases. These dominant kinases phosphorylate either certain target tyrosine or serine/threonine residues. The receptor kinases can themselves activate a cascade of other kinases, such as cAMP-dependent protein kinase A, protein kinase C, mitogen-activated protein (MAP) kinase, or kinases that phosphorylate the MAP kinases, called MAPKK or MAPPKKK. Many of these kinases are either part of the growth factor–receptor complex itself or are located adjacent to the receptor in the plasma membrane. The growth factor–induced activation of these kinases and second messengers produces the cascade of phosphorylation reactions of specific target regulatory proteins and often the subsequent release of calcium ions from the mitochondria and endoplasmic reticulum storages. Usually in concert, this cascade brings about the final signal to the nucleus to turn on the expression of specific growth factor–activated genes or to induce or activate Jun/Myc, Fos, or AP-1 in the nucleus that leads to DNA synthesis and cell replication. Overall growth is always a net balance between the rate of cell replication and the rate of cell death. The growth factors can either stimulate or suppress growth through affecting this balance. See later section on the cell cycle and apoptosis.

Fibroblast Growth Factor

The same growth factors often received a wide variety of names as they were first isolated from different tissues, and this has often caused much confusion. For example, fibroblast growth factor (FGF) is a family of related growth factors. Each time a growth factor was first identified, it was given a specific target name, and it was later proved to be in the family of fibroblast growth factors. These earlier terms include prostate growth factor, osteoblastic growth factor, a form of tumor angiogenesis factor, endothelial growth factor, uterine growth factor, seminiferous growth factor, and keratinocyte growth factor, just to name a few. Fibroblast growth factors can be isolated from many tissues and come from cells of embryonic mesoderm or neuroectoderm origin. They can also be found in a wide variety of tumors and are produced by many cells in culture. In 1979, Jacobs and associates identified a prostatic growth factor that they were able to show is a mitogenic factor present in human prostatic extracts (Jacobs et al, 1979; Jacobs and Lawson, 1980; Lawson et al, 1989). All of these earlier growth factors are now focused down to specific members of the FGF family.

There are now at least 22 members of the FGF family that have been characterized and studied (Ezzat and Asa, 2005). Of these, FGF-1 (aFGF), FGF-2 (bFGF), FGF-3 (int), FGF-5, and FGF-7 (keratinocyte growth factor) have been identified in the prostate (Story et al, 1994; Story, 1995). FGF-1 is the acidic FGF (aFGF) and slightly stimulates prostatic epithelial cells in

culture but has a stronger effect on stromal cells. This growth factor is primarily found in the brain and central nervous system. FGF-2 is the basic fibroblast growth factor (bFGF) and is far more important in the prostate in that it is a potent mitogen for prostatic stromal cells in which it is made, but it is only a weak mitogen for prostatic epithelial cells. FGF-7 is the keratinocyte growth factor and is a potent mitogen for prostatic epithelial cells, but it is not a mitogen for prostatic stromal cells in which it is synthesized. There is growing belief that androgens may work on epithelial cells indirectly through their paracrine stimulation from the stromal cells (Story et al, 1994; Story, 1995; Cunha et al, 2004). FGF-3, FGF-4, and FGF-5 are not detected in normal adult rat prostate but may be related to early embryonic-like effects. They have been found, however, in Dunning tumor epithelial cells (Yan et al, 1992).

Binding of all the FGF family to heparin-like molecules means that they are enriched in the extracellular matrix; this may provide a reservoir for these growth factors and protect them from degradation, preparing them for presentation to the receptors. It is believed that tissue-specific glycosaminoglycans and heparins may serve as a cofactor with the receptors.

The FGF growth factors bind to high-affinity receptors on the cells (K_d = 0.1 nM), and there are more than 10,000 of these binding sites per cell (Story et al, 1994; Story, 1995). There are four genes that encode different types of fibroblast growth factor receptors (FGFRs); these include FGFR-1 (flg), FGFR-2 (bek), FGFR-3, and FGFR-4. These are a highly conserved series of transmembrane receptors and are all intracellular tyrosine kinases that are capable of being autophosphorylated. There is a high degree of cross-reactivity among these receptors, and FGFR-1 and FGFR-2 bind both the acidic FGF-1 and the basic FGF-2 with similar affinities. Much of the tissue diversity of the FGF receptors comes from the fact that they can be alternatively spliced with 15 splice variants that can produce different isoforms. This is particularly the case for FGFR-2; if the exon IIIb is used, the receptor exhibits tight binding to FGF-1 (aFGF) and FGF-7 (keratinocyte growth factor) but does not bind well to FGF-2 (bFGF). If the FGFR-2 uses exon IIIc, this produces a receptor with high affinity for FGF-1 (aFGF) and FGF-2 (bFGF), but it does not bind tightly to FGF-7. At present, FGFR-2–IIIb is the only known high-affinity receptor for FGF-7. The role of alternative splicing in tissue specificity in the normal and malignant prostate has been pioneered by the excellent work of W. L. McKeehen (McKeehan, 1991; Yan et al, 1992).

In summary, FGF-2 (bFGF) is a potent mitogen working on the stromal cells and involved in angiogenesis and cellular chemotaxis, but it is a weak epithelial mitogen. Working in conjunction with TGF-β, FGF-2 can affect the induction and remodeling of the extracellular matrix. FGF-1 and FGF-2 do not have the amino acid sequences thought to be necessary to be activity secreted, so they may also work in the intracrine manner within the cell. The role of FGF-2 and FGF-7 in abnormal growth of the prostate is intriguing as transgenic models with overexpression of the FGF homologue int-2 produced a glandular hyperplasia that is 22-fold higher in the transgenic prostate than in the control mice (Muller et al, 1990). FGF-1 and FGF-7 may have their largest role in the prostate during development, and FGF-2 may have its largest effect in the adult prostate under androgen stimulation, but these roles have not been fully resolved in vivo or in abnormal growth of the prostate, although there is no doubt that these powerful factors need to be considered.

Epidermal Growth Factor

Sherwood and Lee (1995) reviewed the importance of epidermal growth factor (EGF) in normal and abnormal growth of the prostate. **They compared EGF and TGF-α and concluded that EGF appears to be the predominant EGF-related growth factor in the normal prostate and in BPH. They believed that these two growth factors are important for maintaining the structural and functional integrity of BPH.** These growth factors are localized to the secretory epithelium, and their secretion is augmented by the presence of androgens. The receptors for EGF (EGFR) are located in the basal neuroendocrine cells and appear to be androgen independent in the expression of this receptor. They concluded that most studies indicate that EGFR does not play a functional role in androgen-stimulated growth of prostate cells. The early name of this growth factor was urogastrone, a growth factor that is a cleaved polypeptide of 53 amino acids with 3 disulfides that was first found in the urine and is now known to be similar to mouse EGF (MW, 16,000). EGF has been reported to be of high concentration (272 ng/mL) in human ejaculate and is produced in the prostate (Gregory et al, 1986).

High levels of fibroblast growth factor (bFGF) are found in all prostates, but EGF level is usually much lower. This has led Story to conclude that EGF is not the major growth factor in the human prostate (Story et al, 1983); indeed, mRNA for EGF has been difficult to detect in normal or abnormal growth of the human prostate (Mori et al, 1990). In contrast, EGF may be prevalent in the rat ventral prostate. It has been reported that EGF-related mitogen with a slightly higher molecular weight than EGF is present in the dorsal prostate of the rat (Nishi et al, 1988).

There is still much conflict over the role of EGF in the normal human prostate, but prostate cancer cells in culture (LNCaP) do have a significant level of EGF that is 100 times the TGF-α level measured intracellularly (Connolly and Rose, 1990). Morris and Dodd (1990) have measured the level of EGF and EGFR in the human prostate and have shown the highest levels in prostate cancer tissues, thus emphasizing the potential importance of EGF in cancer.

The EGFR extends through the plasma membrane. It has a molecular weight of 170,000, and as for bFGF, the receptor is an enzyme tyrosine kinase. The receptor is capable of being autophosphorylated and when active appears to dimerize with Src homology 2 (SH-2) proteins, particularly phosphoinositide 3-kinase and phospholipase C(γ), which are important in converting lipids into second messages in the cell. These SH-2 proteins are involved in the recruitment of Ras and Raf-1 in the G protein signaling pathway, which results in the MAP kinase cascade of phosphorylation that activates transcription factors in the nucleus (Sherwood and Lee 1995). The c-erb-B2/neu oncoprotein is a 185-kD transmembrane glycoprotein that is closely related to but not identical with EGFR. This protein is located in the cytoplasm and is not amplified in prostate cancer cells as it has been in breast cancer. This oncoprotein receptor has been reviewed in relation to prostate growth by Sikes and colleagues (1995). The c-erb-B2/neu (also known as HER2/neu) oncoprotein has been demonstrated to

be overexpressed in 11 of 16 human prostate cancer specimens and in transfected cells can cause altered growth (Zhau et al, 1992; Giri et al, 1993; Kuhn et al, 1993). It has been demonstrated that EGFR and the neu oncoprotein can heterodimerize to create an active receptor complex that transforms rodent cells and may be involved in the progression of human prostate cancers (Sikes et al, 1995). However, recent clinical evidence has failed to document clinical efficacy in targeting the HER2/neu complex for prostate cancer treatment (Morris et al, 2002).

Other proteins related to the EGF include amphiregulin, heregulin-α (HRG-α), and cripto-1 (CR-1). All are ligands capable of activating the EGFR, but their function in the prostate has not been resolved.

Transforming Growth Factor α

TGF-α is a sister molecule closely related to EGF (Sherwood and Lee 1995; Sikes et al, 1995). The transforming growth factors were first so named because of their ability to promote cell colony formation in suspension cultures; it was therefore an initial operational definition, but now the factors are purified. TGF-α is made as a pre-hormone precursor of 160 amino acids and is then processed by elastase to a smaller 50–amino acid peptide with a molecular weight of 5600. TGF-α is structurally similar to EGF and is believed to bring about most of its effects by interacting with the same EGFR as does EGF. Both EGF and TGF-α can serve as transmembrane proteins, or if truncated, they are excreted into the extracellular space. Both the free and membrane forms can bind to EGFR. TGF-α has been shown to stimulate the growth of human prostate cancers in culture and may be an autocrine factor in androgen-independent growth (Wilding et al, 1989; Sherwood and Lee, 1995; Sikes et al, 1995). TGF-α is present in breast cancer and is thought to be an autocrine growth factor stimulated by estrogen treatment. Transgenic mice that overexpress TGF-α produce both mammary cancers and, in males, an epithelial hyperplasia in the mouse prostate lobe termed the coagulating gland (Jhappan et al, 1990).

Transforming Growth Factor β

TGF-β and its related superfamily in the prostate have been reviewed by Steiner (1993) and Sikes and coworkers (1995). TGF-β, containing five isomers, is not related to TGF-α, and the unfortunate similarity in nomenclature often causes some confusion. There are two genes for TGF-β, termed 1 and 2, and they have a 70% homology. There are three combinations possible between these two genes when a dimer is formed; thus, there is TGF-β1, -β2, and -β3. TGF-β is made as a large precursor of 391 amino acids that is initially in an inactive or latent form; it can be activated by proteolysis, such as by plasminogen activator, or by acid to produce a 25,000 molecular weight growth factor of 1 monomer each with 112 amino acids. Although both TGF-β1 and -β2 are expressed in prostate tissue, TGF-β2 has been shown to be significantly increased in expression in BPH compared with the normal prostate, whereas TGF-β1 was not (Mori et al, 1990). TGF-β is of paramount interest because it may function as a braking system in negatively regulated normal prostate epithelial cell growth while being a positive factor in stimulating normal stromal cell growth. These generalizations may be changed in cancers or BPH tissues, in which the epithelial cells have changed their response to TGF-β and now instead of inhibiting may stimulate growth (Steiner and Barrack, 1992; Steiner, 1993). In normal prostate epithelial cells, TGF-β1 inhibits epithelial cell growth by blocking the cell's entry into S phase (DNA synthesis phase of the cell cycle). With androgen withdrawal, there is an upregulation of the TGF-β1 as well as the TGF-β receptor in the rat normal ventral prostate, and Steiner has suggested that androgens inversely regulate TGF-β1 and TGF-β receptor expression (Kyprianou and Isaacs, 1988; Steiner, 1993; Kyprianou, 1994). In prostate cancer, androgens appear to lose their ability to regulate TGF-β (Steiner and Barrack, 1992). TGF-β2 and TGF-β3 are expressed in human prostate cancer; TGF-β1 is overexpressed and has the ability to suppress the immune system and to promote angiogenesis in the formation of extracellular matrix components as well as to increase cell motility, all of which are factors important in the progression of prostate cancer cells (Steiner, 1993; Sikes et al, 1995). Therefore, the opposite effects of TGF-β on normal prostate epithelial cells versus adenocarcinoma are important but still remain a mystery. This may be mediated by changes in the function of the receptors of TGF-β; at present, three of these receptors have been identified, and they appear to function through G proteins activating cAMP pathways. The downregulation of these receptors could release the brake on epithelial growth. Alternative splicing of the mRNA for TGF-β and its multiple forms due to the combinations of these dimers as well as the multiple receptor actions attest to the complexity of this important growth factor system.

Other growth factors related to the TGF-β family are müllerian-inhibiting substance (MIS), activin, inhibin, and bone morphogenic proteins. MIS is a 140,000 molecular weight protein that causes regression in the müllerian ducts; inhibin is a peptide involved in feedback control of follicle-stimulating hormone. Inhibin has been reported to be present in the human prostate and seminal plasma and is synthesized in the rat ventral prostate under hormonal control (Sheth et al, 1984; Sathe et al, 1986).

Bone Morphogenic Proteins

Prostate cancer cells often metastasize to the bone and produce osteoblastic lesions where new bone elements are laid down. **The growth factors that are capable of inducing bone formation include TGF-β1 and TGF-β3 and members of the bone morphogenic protein (BMP) family.** As mentioned earlier, TGF-β1 is overexpressed in prostate cancer cells (Steiner 1993), and it is now apparent that normal tissue, BPH, and prostate cancer can also form and secrete bone morphogens (Bentley et al, 1992; Harris et al, 1994; Barnes et al, 1995). These bone morphogens are produced in the human and rat prostate as well as in the Dunning tumor model. There are several forms of the bone morphogens; BMPs 2, 3, 4, and 6 are the predominant forms identified in prostatic tissue. The bone morphogens not only have the ability to stimulate the formation of osteoblasts but are also strong growth factors operating in the embryonic period, and they can induce LNCaP cells to form a fibroblast-like appearance (Harris et al, 1994). Bone morphogens as well as TGF-β stimulate the proliferation of fibroblasts and inhibit osteoclasts and through this pathway could produce increased bone formation seen in osteoblastic metastasis. Bentley (Bentley et al, 1992) suggested that there may be a correlation between the presence of BMP-6 in human prostate cancer and the ability of prostate cells to metastasize to the bone. Steiner and coworkers (Barnes et al, 1995) showed that BPM-6 mRNA and protein expression was higher in prostate cancer compared with adjacent normal prostates and elevated in higher Gleason grade tissues and that this morphogen was not under androgen control.

Media taken from Dunning rat tumor cell growth have the ability to induce the growth of osteoblasts. Similarly, Leland Chung and coworkers have studied the ability of human fibroblast, LNCaP, and bone stromal cells to produce factors that induce growth in bone formation both in vitro and in animal models (Chung et al, 1992; Gleave et al, 1992; Thalmann et al, 1994; Wu et al, 1994; Sikes et al, 1995). These investigators have brought attention to the bone-derived growth factor 1 of 70 kD as well as osteopontin and a 157 kD protein (p157) that is related to human complement factor H.

Human bone stromal cells also produce hepatocyte growth factor/scatter factor (HGF/SF), which is also a strong mitogen for inducing prostatic epithelial cell growth. In addition, prostatic fibroblasts can produce this growth factor and should serve as a paracrine signal. The HGF/SF receptor is coded by the c-*met* proto-oncogene, and Pisters and coworkers (1993) have observed the presence of this receptor in basal epithelial layers of normal prostate glands and its absence in luminal cells. HGF was expressed in abundant amounts in prostate cancer cells and in prostate and bone fibroblasts (Pisters et al, 1993; Sikes et al, 1995). **In summary, there is a reciprocal stimulation of prostate cells on the growth of the bone and vice versa.**

Insulin-like Growth Factors 1 and 2 (Somatomedin)

The insulin-like growth factors (IGFs) are two protein growth factors, IGF-1 and IGF-2, related in sequence to insulin. These growth factors interact with two different types of receptors, type 1 and type 2. In addition, this system is involved in a complex equilibrium with six different insulin-like growth factor–binding proteins (IGFBPs) that are present in both the serum and tissues. These IGFBPs can be altered in expression at various times and in various tissue compartments, and they can be processed by a series of proteases to cleave these binding proteins to release the free form of the IGFs (Peehl et al, 1995). There are many of these proteases, one of the most prominent being the serine protease PSA. This attests to the difficulty in analyzing the role of IGFs, binding proteins, and proteases in the regulatory control of both normal and abnormal growth of the prostate. This complex field has been analyzed in a classic review by Peehl and associates (1995). They pointed out that prostate epithelial cells contain type 1 IGF receptor and the prostatic stromal cells synthesize and secrete IGF-2.

Both the prostate stromal and epithelial cells can secrete a number of the IGFBPs; most attention has been placed on IGFBP-3, which is cleaved by PSA. Peehl pointed out that there are aberrations in the IGF associated with BPH, including an increase in transcription of IGF-2, increased levels of the type 1 IGF receptor, and an altered pattern of protease expression in the BPH stromal cells. In prostate cancer, IGFBP-2 increases while IGFBP-3 decreases. These complex equilibria and changes in the IGF system with development, growth, and malignant transformation are of potentially great importance because of the strong mitogenic effect of these proteins on the growth of the prostate.

Platelet-Derived Growth Factor

Platelet-derived growth factor (PDGF) is expressed in many tissues and found in the urine, although it is primarily derived from platelets and a modified form is expressed by the c-*sis* oncogene. PDGF has a strong mitogenic effect on mesenchymal and connective tissue cells and makes cells competent to respond to other growth factors. It has been shown to be expressed in prostate tumor models and cells in culture (Rijnders et al, 1985; Smith and Rinker-Schaeffer, 1995) but has not received as much attention as has bFGF.

There are two genes involved in the formation of PDGF, one making the polypeptide chain A and the other chain B, which are covalently linked to form three different dimers, AA, AB, and BB. There are two receptors for PDGF that are different genes, α and β, with both being expressed on most cells but with the β predominating. It appears that the two receptors give different cellular functions (Sikes et al, 1995).

The interest in PDGF may be as a mediator of the effects of inflammation on prostate growth as first proposed by Gleason and colleagues (1993). Inflammation is tightly associated with BPH (Kohnen and Drach, 1979) and most recently prostate cancer (De Marzo et al, 2004). However, the cause and effect have not been fully resolved. It is intriguing that both activated oxygen and growth factors form by these types of interactions associated with inflammation.

Endothelins

There is increased activity in the study of the biologic properties of the peptide endothelins, of which there are three kinds, ET-1, ET-2, ET-3. These peptides have the most potent activity in constricting blood vessels and elevating blood pressure in mammals, and they may have profound effects on the muscle tone of the prostate as well as on growth. Human seminal fluid contains the highest concentration of endothelins, where it is about five times as high as in plasma (Casey et al, 1992; Nelson et al, 1995). Lepor and colleagues observed that prostate epithelial cells produce ET-1 and that the high-affinity ET-1 receptors are present in the prostate gland, exceeding even the concentration of cholinergic and adrenergic binding sites, and can function in muscle tone (Langenstroer et al, 1993; Kobayashi et al, 1994a, 1994b; Nelson et al, 1995). Nelson and colleagues studied the level of ET-1 and its relation to prostate cancer and metastasis as well as its possibility as a serum marker. They reported that immunoreactive endothelin is significantly elevated in men with metastatic prostate cancer and is present in all cell lines of human prostate cancer tested. Nelson also reported that ET-1 is a prostate cancer mitogen in vitro and elevates alkaline phosphatase activity in new bone formation. He has proposed that this may be a mediator of the osteoblastic response of bone to metastatic prostate cancer. In addition, he has brought attention to the fact that ET-1, ET-2, and ET-3 have sequence homology to snake venom sarafotoxins and this causes painful effects. Nelson proposes that endothelins may be part of the prostate cancer–induced bone pain.

Each of the endothelins has 21 amino acids with 2 disulfide rings that act on G protein–coupled receptors. It is apparent that the endothelins and their receptors will become an important new factor in understanding normal and cancerous prostate growth and its effects on bone metastasis and the morbidity of cancer, particularly pain. Currently, inhibitors of endothelin are in late-stage clinical trials for the treatment of osseous metastasis of prostate cancer (Lassiter and Carducci, 2003).

REGULATION OF PROSTATE GROWTH: BALANCE OF CELL REPLICATION AND CELL DEATH

Throughout life, the prostate responds to endocrine signals as it develops, undergoes a rapid phase of growth at puberty, maintains its size, and then, in some cases, develops an abnormal growth with aging that may result in either benign or malignant disease. The cell kinetics of this process are now being defined in terms of the dynamic interplay of growth-promoting and growth-suppressing factors and how they regulate a cell cycle of DNA synthesis and mitosis as well as balance a cell cycle of replication and cellular death or apoptosis (Denmeade et al, 1996), especially in clinical prostate cancers (Berges et al, 1995). Isaacs has defined the major step in the interaction of the cell cycle between growth and death. This has been reviewed, and the two interlocking cycles are depicted in Figure 85–13 (Denmeade et al, 1996). The net balance between the rate of cell growth and cell death maintains the steady-state size of the prostate; it appears to be under hormonal and growth factor control and is age dependent. Resolving the mechanisms that control this normal growth balance is most crucial to understanding the imbalance that occurs in tumor growth.

DNA Synthesis and Cell Cycle Control

Prostate growth requires cell replication, and cells must first undergo DNA synthesis; this can be determined on human prostatic tissue by the incorporation of precursors into the DNA, such as thymidine (Meyer et al, 1982), iododeoxyuridine (Masters and O'Donoghue, 1983), and bromodeoxyuridine (Nemoto et al, 1990). Other markers include antibodies against specific nuclear proteins associated with proliferation, such as Ki-67, PCNA, histones, and topoisomerase enzymes, or mitotic indices are counted to detect the proliferation of DNA in prostate cells (Berges et al, 1995). These techniques have been helpful in working out the temporal sequence of events that occur in the growth of the prostate under hormonal stimulation in animal models (Coffey et al, 1968; Lesser and Bruchovsky, 1973; Sufrin and Coffey, 1973; DeKlerk et al, 1976; Humphries and Isaacs, 1982; English et al, 1985, 1986, 1987, 1989; Evans and Chandler, 1987). Castration causes a 90% loss in the total number of prostatic epithelial cells and a slower but less complete reduction of approximately 40% in the number of stromal cells (DeKlerk et al, 1976). In castrates treated with androgen restoration, there is an initial delay of 1 day before the onset of DNA synthesis, which then reaches a maximum rate at 2 to 3 days and then subsides to normal levels even in the continued presence of androgen stimulation (Coffey et al, 1968; Sufrin and Coffey, 1973; DeKlerk et al, 1976). It is unknown why the rapid synthesis of DNA stops after the gland is restored to its full size. It is believed that a permissive factor involves the number of stem cells and the amount of extracellular matrix and mesenchyme. In development, the growing epithelial cells have the ability to invaginate into the stroma, folding into three-dimensional tubular glands, budding, and branching into the final architecture that forms the prostate glandular pattern. These permissive factors and limitations must include angiogenesis to support the gland and the stromal-epithelial interactions discussed earlier. They are driven overall by available androgens, growth factors and their corresponding receptors, and intracellular signaling events that initiate the replication and death cell cycle regulations and possible regulation of homeotic genes.

Buttyan and colleagues (Katz et al, 1989) have studied the sequence of events following testosterone repletion in the castrate that precede the onset of DNA synthesis. They demonstrated that the oncogene *c-fos* showed the earliest transient rise, increasing threefold within 1 hour, followed by an increase in *ras* oncogenes with 2 hours, followed by the transient transcription of both *myc* and *myb* within 6 to 8 hours. This is typical of many other tissues that are stimulated to grow where similar transient rises in oncogenes precede the onset of DNA synthesis.

Chromatin Organization and Regulation

The nucleus contains dense patches of chromatin, called **heterochromatin,** as well as a more delicate form of chromatin called **euchromatin.** Heterochromatin usually lines the nuclear envelope and is seen in resting cells and is transcriptionally inactive. Euchromatin is more thread-like and delicate in structure and is most abundant in actively transcribing cells. DNA is packed extremely densely (a 10,000-fold reduction in length of DNA in interphase nuclei) by substructures termed **nucleosomes, which consist of an octamer of histones.** Nucleosomes are responsible for DNA packaging, regulation of gene expression, and regulation of DNA synthesis, replication, and mitosis. At the first level of organization of the euchromatin, one is able to observe uncoiled 20- to 30-nm chromatin fibers when the nucleus is disrupted to release the chromatin from its supercoiled structure. With further unraveling of the DNA and proteins, one can observe a 4-nm DNA filament that is wrapped around a 10-nm nucleosome, which is then wrapped again into 30-nm fibers of DNA and nucleosomes. Each *chromosome* contains one molecule of DNA that is organized to maximize condensation of the DNA and its basic histone protein nucleosome structures, responsible ultimately for transcription of the DNA during the cell cycle for cell proliferation (Bradbury, 2002; Dey, 2005). The positions of the chromosomes in interphase nuclei during the cell cycle occupy specific three-dimensional nonrandom space critical to their position in the daughter cells (Williams and Fisher, 2003). The maintenance of chromatin organization when cells are dividing is extremely critical to homeostasis; loss of this chromosomal balance can create aneuploidy (abnormal chromosome replication) found in cancer cells (Knudson, 2001; Neely and Workman, 2002).

The eukaryotic or mammalian cell cycle consists of a prearranged set of molecular events that culminate in cell growth and division into two daughter cells (mitosis). Before a cell can divide, it has to grow in size, duplicate its chromosomes, and separate the chromosomes and cytoplasm for distribution between the two daughter cells. These different processes are coordinated in the cell cycle (Nurse, 2002). The stages of the cell cycle are the interphase, where the first gap 1 phase (G_1) cell grows; when it has reached its appropriate size, it enters the phase of DNA synthesis (S), where the chromosomes are duplicated. Next in gap (G_2) phase, the cell prepares for division or mitosis (M). During mitosis, the chromosomes separate and assume specific spatial locale (see earlier), and the cell divides into two daughter cells. The M stage, mitosis, is when nuclear and cytoplasmic (cytokinesis) division occurs. Mitosis can be further divided into four additional phases, which include **prophase** (chromosomes are duplicated), **metaphase** (chromosomes are aligned along a central axis or plate), **anaphase** (pairs of duplicated chromosomes separate), and finally **telophase** (separation of nucleus and cytoplasm).

Regulation of the cell cycle requires several hundred genes (termed cell cycle–dependent genes) that are critical to management of the cell through this process (Kel et al, 2001; Oliva et al, 2005). However, to ensure integrity of normal cell cycle progression, there are several **checkpoints** (Zhou and Elledge, 2000; Melo and Toczyski, 2002). These ensure that (1) the cell does not enter mitosis until DNA replication is complete and any DNA damage is repaired, (2) chromosomal segregation occurs along the mitotic spindle and that the spindle is intact, and (3) key processes of metabolism and homeostasis are coordinated within the various stages of the cell cycle (G_1, S, G_2, and M).

In the review by Melo (Melo and Toczyski, 2002), the checkpoint proteins for several eukaryotic organisms are presented. In the mammalian system, there are **sensors,** such as RAD1, Hus1, ATR, ATRIP, and ATM; **adaptors,** such as BRCA1 and claspin; and **effector kinases,** including **Chk2** and **Chk1** that are responsible for DNA repair and ensuring that the cell cycle progresses to generate two daughter cells. A recent and comprehensive model of mammalian DNA damage and replication checkpoints is exemplified by Li and Zou (2005) in which specific genes that regulate signal transduction, mediators, signaling kinases (Chk1, Chk2), and targets/effectors (CDCs, p21, p53, and SMC1) are designated and their positions in the cell cycle illustrated.

Next, a large cascade of genes regulate the cell cycle stages: cyclins in a partnership with cyclin-dependent kinases control cell cycle progression in combination with other important genes and pathways that involve interactions among elongation (transcription) factor (E2F)/retinoblastoma protein (pRb) pathway, p53 pathway, and control of DNA replication (Nurse, 2002; Murray, 2004; Sanchez and Dynlacht, 2005). The cell cycle pathway is aligned with the various cyclins, cyclin-dependent kinases, and other key pathway factors that are involved in progression through G_1, S, G_2, and M. The retinoblastoma gene (Bookstein et al, 1990) was first discovered in retinoblastoma but is now known to be a general controller of the cell cycle in most normal cells, whereas it undergoes aberrations in many types of cancer. When the retinoblastoma gene is hypophosphorylated, it binds to the nuclear matrix and inhibits cell proliferation by acting at the G_1/S checkpoint. When the retinoblastoma protein is phosphorylated, it releases the brake and allows the cell to move through the rest of the cell cycle. These restriction checkpoints in the cell cycle are regulated by a group of gate-keepers termed cyclins, denoted A, B, C, D, or E according to where they monitor throughout the cycle (see Fig. 85–13). The A and B cyclins increase during DNA synthesis (S phase) and during the postreplication (G_2 phase). The result of their action initiates mitosis; therefore, they are called the mitotic cyclins. The cyclins C, D, and E function in the preparatory period that occurs before DNA synthesis starts (G_1); therefore, they are termed the G_1 cyclins.

The cyclins interact by forming direct complexes with a family of kinases that are relatively constant throughout the cell. These cyclin complexes activate the ever-present kinases to phosphorylate specific regulatory proteins. These kinases are called cyclin-dependent kinases (CDKs) and are currently numbered 1 to 7. The cyclin-dependent kinases are serine/threonine kinases. They are highly conserved, sharing between 50% and 70% amino acid homology. As an example, cyclin D can complex with either CDK4 or CDK6, activating the kinase to initiate DNA synthesis by phosphorylating the retinoblastoma protein and releasing the brake at the G_1/S restriction checkpoint. Mitogenic stimulants, such as growth factors, can increase cyclin D levels to form complexes with cyclin-dependent kinase. Alternatively, when the retinoblastoma protein is not phosphorylated, it suppresses cell proliferation and promotes cell differentiation. If, rather than undergoing phosphorylation, the retinoblastoma protein is inactivated by binding to virus proteins, such as the large T antigen of the polyomavirus or the E7 protein of the papillomavirus, it may also activate cell division by removing the retinoblastoma brake through competitive binding to these virus proteins. Indeed, inducing SV40 T antigen activity in a prostate cell will activate abnormal growth when its overexpression serves to complex the retinoblastoma protein and remove the brake, resulting in a prostate tumor. This is the basis of Greenberg's TRAMP model of transgenic prostate cancer (Greenberg et al, 1994), whereby the large T antigen is expressed specifically in prostate cells by virtue of the rat probasin promoter (a prostate-specific gene).

Just as cyclin-dependent kinases can be activated by binding to cyclins to form a complex that phosphorylates regulatory proteins in the nucleus, they can, conversely, be inhibited by binding to a family of cyclin-dependent kinase inhibitors, such as p15, p16, p18, p21, and p27 (see Fig. 85–13). When a cell replicates its DNA during the S period, it must first stop at the G_1/S checkpoint and assess whether its DNA is damaged. If the DNA is damaged, the cell cycle is blocked at this point because p53 is induced, thereby stimulating the cyclin-dependent kinase inhibitors p16 and p21. The cyclin-dependent kinase inhibitor p21 is also called WAF-1 or CIP1 and by convention is now referred to as p21$^{CIP1/WAF1}$. These p53-induced cyclin-dependent kinases are inhibitors that arrest cell division. Thus, dysregulation in either p53, p16, or p21$^{CIP1/WAF1}$ allows the cell cycle to proceed with damaged DNA that can be copied, inducing tumor cell genetic instability (Koh et al, 1995; Waldman et al, 1995). There are a variety of potential stimulants of cyclin-dependent kinase inhibitor activity, including TGF-β, cAMP, contact inhibition, and interactions of the cell with extracellular matrix components. Of note, p21$^{CIP1/WAF1}$ can also affect the ability of the proliferating cell nuclear antigen (PCNA) to activate the replicative DNA polymerase delta, thus blocking cells in the S phase rather than through blocking the cell cycle–dependent kinases.

In summary, the molecular events for cell cycle initiation and progression are well coordinated to control for DNA damage during DNA replication through checkpoints and then subsequent stages of the cell cycle that require the appropriate cyclins, cyclin-dependent kinases, and other pathway effectors. Two normal daughter cells will result.

Cell Aging, Senescence, and Immortality

Initially, diploid cells grown in vitro were noticed to divide only a finite number of times (Hayflick, 2000), resulting in an irreversible loss of replicative capacity referred to as the Hayflick limit or biologic clock. This limit was thought to reflect the physical limitation of asymmetric DNA replication, as the lagging strand of DNA synthesis cannot fully replicate the ends of the DNA (telomeres), and hence DNA information is lost with each round of replication. Today, *telomere* dynamics have been shown to be a critical component of the Hayflick limit, cellular senescence, and the development of cancer both in vitro and in vivo (Cristofalo et al, 2004; Shay and Wright, 2005). Telomeres are nucleoprotein complexes at the end of chromosomes; telomeric DNA contains several kilobases of TTAGGG double-stranded repeats and approximately 400 to 500 bases of TTAGGG repeats in a 3′ single-stranded overhang (Cristofalo et al, 2004). Telomere length dictates cell life span, as each round of DNA replication results in successive telomere shortening until the telomeres become critically shortened, resulting in cellular crisis. Stem cells overcome this Hayflick limit by an enzyme, **telomerase** (a ribonucleoprotein with reverse transcriptase activity), that adds TTAGGG repeats back to the telomere, preventing telomere shortening and subsequent crises. The enzyme is made up of a telomerase RNA component (**TERC**) that provides the template to add the TTAGGG repeats; a second component of the telomerase is telomerase reverse transcriptase (**TERT**). Telomerase is expressed primarily in germ cells, stem cells, and transit-amplifying cells as well as in most cancer cells. At least two barriers appear to exist that may alter replicative senescence for diploid cell types; one is premature telomere shortening, and the other is an accumulation of environmental stress-imposed DNA damage, limiting the number of cell divisions to 10 to 15 instead of 50 or more in vitro (Von Zglinicki, 2003; Cristofalo et al, 2004). Normal telomeres are protectively capped with certain proteins (e.g., DNA-PK), such that any free DNA ends are perceived by the cell as a double-stranded DNA break (i.e., damaged DNA). An excellent review by Campisi (2005) outlines the current understanding of the relationship of cellular senescence, tumor suppression, and organism aging.

In summary, the decision of a cell to replicate, repair its DNA, differentiate, senesce, or initiate apoptosis is dependent on the regulation of the cell cycle, involving activators and inhibitors of a variety of cell cycle–dependent kinases, as well as on the ability of the cell to repair its DNA and undergo successful mitosis. Cellular aging, senescence, and immortality are critical processes in cells that undergo mitosis and hence are capable of renewal, repair, and in some cases regeneration as described before in the prostate. Such cell types are in danger of repeated environmental genotoxic insults resulting in hyperproliferative disease and more seriously cancer by acquiring mutations, deletions, translocations, or epigenetic alterations over time.

KEY POINTS: CELL AGING, SENESCENCE, AND IMMORTALITY

■ Telomere length dictates cell life span (immortality or not). Stem cells overcome this Hayflick limit by an enzyme, telomerase (a ribonucleoprotein with reverse transcriptase activity), which adds TTAGGG repeats back to the telomere, preventing telomere shortening and subsequent crises. Telomerase is expressed primarily in germ cells, stem cells, and transit-amplifying cells as well as in most cancer cells.

■ The interlocking cycles of cell death (apoptosis) and cell replication are paramount events in regulating balance in the prostate. The cell cycle pathway is aligned with the various cyclins, cyclin-dependent kinases, and other key pathway factors (p53, Rb) that are involved in progression through G_1, S, G_2, and M. Apoptosis or programmed cell death acts as a balance to cell replication in maintaining the static size of the prostate.

DNA Damage

DNA can be damaged in somatic cells by a variety of mechanisms, for example, during the cell cycle by telomere loss; by errors in replication that cannot be repaired by mismatched repair enzymes; by failure of the cell cycle to monitor itself and to inhibit damaged DNA from going through the cycle; by aberrations in the suppressor system; by xenophiles and carcinogens in the environment; and by oxidative damage brought about by free radicals such as activated oxygen. Free radicals can be generated in the prostate through oxidative processes, resulting in lipid peroxidation and DNA damage, as well as through the activity of macrophages and lymphocytes that can cause spurious damage. Nitric oxide (NO) is a newly recognized and potent radical-forming agent in the prostate, where Chung and colleagues have shown it to be activated or enriched after castration in the rat lateral prostate and seminal vesicles but not in the ventral prostate or coagulating gland (Chamness et al, 1995). NO is formed by the action of nitric oxide synthase (NOS), which can convert arginine to citrulline, forming NO. NO reduces muscle tone. It is also a producer of free radicals. NOS can be of neural origin (n-NOS), from endothelial cells (e-NOS) that can affect smooth muscle cells, or induced (i-NOS) in macrophages.

The prostate protects itself against electrophilic attacks from carcinogens by inducing a battery of protective enzymes, of which the glutathione-S-transferases are the most prominent. Lee and colleagues (1994) have reported that human prostate basal cells contain high levels of glutathione S-transferase pi (GSTpi) and that, in prostate cancer, this

activity is uniformly absent in cancer lesions removed at the time of radical prostatectomy. They have drawn attention to the importance of these enzymes in protecting stem cells in the prostate from carcinogenic attack and to the fact that these enzymes can be induced by dietary and environmental considerations. This holds promise as an explanation for the tremendous epidemiologic differences seen in different geographic locations. It appears that the gene encoding GSTpi is turned off in prostate cancer by DNA methylation of cytosine residues in the CpG promoter region of the gene.

Apoptosis and Cell Death

Apoptosis is the natural, programmed type of cell death that is a part of the normal process of life. The term is taken from the Greek word meaning "the falling of leaves from a tree." Apoptosis acts as a balance to cell replication in maintaining the static size of the prostate. It is a dynamic system, and there are marked differences between necrosis and apoptosis at the histologic and the biochemical levels. The mechanism of apoptosis, in addition to factors that cause the survival of cells, is one of the most active areas of research in sex accessory tissues. Excellent reviews on prostatic apoptosis and cell death have been made available through the work of John T. Isaacs and colleagues (Isaacs, 1993; Denmeade et al, 1996).

In 1973, Kerr and Searle first drew attention to the fact that histologically, the cells of the prostate appear to undergo apoptosis during castration-induced involution of the rat prostate (Kerr and Searle, 1973). It was long believed that cell death after androgen withdrawal was simply the choking off of an important biologic factor required to maintain the life of the cell. Now we know that this involution process is an induced and active biochemical process rather than merely a passive loss of factors. Lee and associates were the first to report that if protein or RNA synthesis is blocked after castration, the rate of prostate gland involution is markedly reduced (Stanisic et al, 1978; Engels et al, 1980; Lee et al, 1985; Lee and Sensibar, 1987). Kyprianou and Isaacs (1988) have reported that there is an increase in TGF-β receptors during castration and that this may regulate cell death from a growth factor standpoint. Barrack and Berry (Barrack, 1987) have studied DNA synthesis in canine prostates induced to massive growth by the combination of androgens and estrogens and have shown that there is a decrease in the amount of DNA synthesis per unit amount of DNA required to maintain a large gland when 5α-reduced androgens and estrogens are given simultaneously. This has led them to suggest that estrogens decrease the rate of cell death in the prostate in the presence of 5α-reduced androgens, as opposed to increasing proliferation. What determines the set point for the level of cells in the prostate, and their rates of growth and death, is of paramount importance in understanding BPH and prostate cancer. Buttyan and colleagues (1988) have studied the cascade of induction of a series of oncogenes and heat shock proteins that follows castration and precedes cell loss.

Later, it was reported that a temporal series of proteins are induced in the prostate after castration, and the most actively studied was TRPM-2 in the work of Tenniswood and colleagues (Montpetit et al, 1986). This was followed by cloning of the gene (Leger et al, 1987, 1988). This TRPM-2 protein was dramatically increased 48 hours after castration and was associated with epithelial cell involution in the prostate. TRPM-2 now appears to be a secondary marker associated with but not causing involution. TRPM-2 has been shown to be similar to clusterin, a sulfated glycoprotein 2 normally found in Sertoli cells and present in human seminal plasma, and is suggested to be important in fertility (O'Bryan et al, 1990).

Proteolytic enzymes, such as cathepsin D, are activated during castration-induced involution in the rat prostate (Tanabe et al, 1982; Senabaugh et al, 1990). Plasminogen activators are also increased after castration (Rennie et al, 1984), and three forms are increased in prostate epithelial cells after castration (Andreasen et al, 1990).

Several groups have studied the appearance of two-dimensional protein patterns altered by castration or androgen treatment (Anderson et al, 1983; Lee et al, 1985; Chang et al, 1987; Lee and Sensibar, 1987; Saltzman et al, 1987). In studying the effects of castration, it must always be recognized that there is a tremendous decrease in overall ribosomal and messenger RNA. Pool levels of androgen-independent mRNA in the normal would be greatly enriched in the castrate RNA pool. This is also the case for proteins, and the problem is complicated by the fact that after castration, 90% of the epithelial cells involute and are lost, whereas the basal cells remain and become heavily enriched, as do elements of the stroma and extracellular matrix. Therefore, relative enrichments, and even correction for the total amount of DNA, can be misleading, and the data must be expressed either by total amount in the prostate gland or by in situ hybridization in a quantitative manner. This has not been done in many cases, and it has led to great confusion. For a critical discussion of enzymes and factors changing in prostatic cell death, see the definitive review by Denmeade and colleagues (1996). They reviewed data indicating that after castration in the rat, serum testosterone levels fall by 90% within 2 hours and by 98% within 6 hours. Active DHT increases 95% in prostate cells by 12 to 24 hours; and within 12 hours of castration, the androgen receptor is no longer detected in the nucleus. By 24 hours, there is little androgen receptor remaining. After this dramatic decrease in androgens, there is a much slower involution of the cells that may require the loss of survival factors other than DHT. They suggest that keratinocyte growth factor (FGF-7), produced in the stromal cells, secondarily stimulates prostate epithelial cells and may be a prime candidate.

Following is a summary of the review of the temporal events occurring in apoptosis of the prostate as presented by Denmeade and colleagues (Denmeade et al, 1996). The first phase is termed D1a, when after the reduction in androgen, there is a decrease in the secretory proteins, cyclins, CDK2, and ornithine decarboxylase. D1a and D1b are associated with upregulation of TGF-β and its receptor as well as TRPM-2, calmodulin, and calcium-dependent nucleases. There is also a decrease during this period in polyamines as well as changes in chromatin packing. At the end of D1, the reversible cycle is lost. Now the cells are irreversibly damaged as they enter the F period, and DNA fragmentation is initiated in which it is first cut to 50- to 300-kilobase size, then degraded into a ladder of less than 1 kilobase. After a period of complete nuclear fragmentation in which the laminins are degraded and the nucleus is dissolved with the formation of apoptotic bodies, there is a marked stimulation of tissue transglutaminase during what is termed a D2 period. The last phase is D2c,

when there is phagocytosis of the apoptotic bodies and changes in the membrane phospholipids.

It is obvious that the interlocking cycles of cell death and cell replication are paramount events in regulating balance in the prostate. This has been reviewed by Denmeade and colleagues (1996) and Harriss and Saville (1995). It is apparent that *p53* knockout mice are still capable of undergoing prostate involution after castration. It is known, therefore, that *p53* is not required for involution, although it may still alter the pathway in some noncritical manner. Most interestingly, cytokines and extracellular matrix can provide exogenous survival signals, and attention is turned to Bcl-2, a strong survival factor that seems to block cell death. Overexpression of Bcl-2 has been proposed to block cell death and to increase growth in malignant cells. This may be involved with a complex pathway of interaction with c-*myc* and the binding of Bcl-2 to a series of related proteins such as Bax to form active or inactive dimers. Overexpression of Bax, which can form heterodimers with Bcl-2, can actually promote apoptosis; however, this is a complex problem because Bcl-2/Bax heterodimers favor cell survival and prevent apoptosis, whereas a high level of Bax with excess Bax homodimers favors cell death. The level of Bax expression is, therefore, critical.

A series of proteases appear to be involved in controlling the onset of cell death, and some of these are in the family of interleukin-converting enzyme (ICE), a protein of 503–amino acid residues that is homologous to interleukin-1β–converting enzyme. This is a cysteine protease related to CED-3, which is a key factor in cell death in flatworms.

The switching, regulation, and inhibition of apoptosis, starting with p53 pathways, survival factors, and the Fas pathway, are at present being resolved and they involve CED-3/ICE, CED-9/Bcl-2, and CED-4–like proteins that have not all been identified. As each of these families is expanded—Bcl-2 now appears to be a family of proteins, and ICE is likewise a set of proteins—we must await further resolution before we will be able to fully decipher these complex interactions. In the meantime, apoptosis is now being used as a quantitative tool in studying the balance of cell proliferation and cell death in prostate disease (Gaffney, 1994; Montironi et al, 1994; Wheeler et al, 1994).

PROMINENT, NONPEPTIDE COMPONENTS OF PROSTATIC SECRETIONS

The seminal plasma is formed primarily from the secretions of the sex accessory tissues, which include the epididymis, ampullae, seminal vesicles, prostate, Cowper's (bulbourethral) gland, and glands of Littre. **The average volume of the normal human ejaculate is approximately 3 mL, ranging from 2 to 6 mL, and it has two components: spermatozoa and seminal plasma. Spermatozoa, which represent less than 1% of the total ejaculate, are present in the range of 100 million per milliliter. The major contribution to the volume of seminal plasma (average 3 mL) comes from the seminal vesicles (1.5 to 2 mL), from the prostate (0.5 mL), and from Cowper's gland and glands of Littre (0.1 to 0.2 mL).** During ejaculation, the secretions of these glands are released in a sequential manner (Amelar, 1962; Amelar and Hotchkiss, 1965; Tauber et al, 1975, 1976; Tauber and Zaneveld, 1976). The first fraction of the human ejaculate is rich in sperm and prostatic secretions, such as citric acid. Fructose, which represents a major secretory product of the seminal vesicles, is elevated in the later fraction of ejaculate. The overall chemical composition of normal human and rodent prostatic secretions and seminal plasma has been widely studied, and the results have been summarized in excellent reviews (Mann and Mann, 1981; Zaneveld and Tauber, 1981; Aumuller et al, 1990; Daniels and Grayhack, 1990; Chow et al, 1993; Gonzalez, 1993).

In relation to other body fluids, the seminal plasma is unusual because of its high concentrations of potassium, zinc, citric acid, fructose, phosphorylcholine, spermine, free amino acids, prostaglandins, and enzymes (most notably acid phosphatase, diamine oxidase, β-glucuronidase, lactate dehydrogenase, α-amylase, PSA, and seminal proteinase).

Citric Acid

One of the major anions in human seminal plasma is citrate (mean, 376 mg/dL), which is present in the range of 20 mM or 60 mEq/L. This is compared with the chloride ion (155 mg/dL) at 40 mM. Citrate is a potent binder of metal ions, and the seminal plasma concentration of citrate, 20 mM, is comparable to that of the total divalent metals at 13.6 mM (calcium, 7 mM; magnesium, 4.5 mM; zinc, 2.1 mM). Prostatic citrate levels approximate 15.8 mg/mL (Zaneveld 1981), and the values for seminal vesicle citric acid secretions are almost 100-fold less, being only 0.2 mg/mL. Citric acid is formed in the prostate at 100 times higher concentration than is seen in other soft tissues (e.g., prostate tissue, 30,000 nmol/g; other tissues, range of 150 to 450 nmol/g). **The concentration of citrate in the ejaculate is 500 to 1000 times higher than that in the plasma. Prostate secretory epithelial cells form citrate from aspartic acid and glucose. The high concentrations within the prostate result partly from the inability of the prostate cell mitochondria to oxidize citrate readily once it is formed; therefore, the rate of citrate synthesis far exceeds the rate of citrate oxidation** (Costello and Franklin, 1989, 1994). Kavanagh (1994) measured citrate and isocitrate levels, which are catalyzed by aconitase, and demonstrated ratios of 33:1 in the prostate, whereas other tissues demonstrate ratios of 10:1. This decreased activity of aconitase might explain the high levels of citrate within the prostate.

Diamine oxidase, an enzyme that degrades polyamines within the prostate, has been linked to citric acid concentrations and, indirectly, to sperm motility and fertility (Gonzalez, 1994; LeCalve et al, 1995). Yascoe and associates (1991) used magnetic resonance spectroscopy to investigate the relationship between citrate metabolism and prostate cancer and demonstrated small but statistically insignificant differences between normal epithelium and prostate cancer cell lines. The relationship between prostatic inflammatory disease and citric acid has also been investigated (Wolff et al, 1991). In addition, it is now possible to accurately quantify the concentration of citrate within the prostate by proton magnetic resonance spectroscopy (Liney et al, 1996, 1997; Lowry et al, 1996; Lynch and Nicholson, 1997). Most recently, the ratio of citrate to other components of prostatic secretions has been used to diagnose prostate cancer (Costello and Franklin, 1989; Kim et al, 1998; Pucar et al, 2005).

Fructose

The source of fructose in human seminal plasma is the seminal vesicles (Mann and Mann, 1981). Patients with congenital absence of the seminal vesicles also have an associated absence of fructose in their ejaculates (Phadke et al, 1973). The seminal vesicle secretion contains smaller amounts of other free sugars such as glucose, sorbitol, ribose, and fructose, and these sugars usually amount to less than 10 mg/dL. In comparison, the concentration of the reducing sugar fructose is approximately 300 mg/dL in human seminal secretion, and it has a level of 200 mg/dL in seminal plasma.

Fructose levels are under androgenic regulation, but many factors, such as storage, frequency of ejaculation, blood glucose levels, and nutritional status, can also affect seminal plasma concentration (Mann and Mann, 1981); these considerations may account for the wide variations encountered in different semen samples from the same patient. Furthermore, plasma levels of androgens do not always correlate with seminal plasma fructose levels; therefore, these levels are not a reliable index of the androgenic state of the subject. Seminal fructose levels have also been proposed to be under sympathetic control (Lamano-Carvalho et al, 1993; Kempinas et al, 1995). The physiologic role of fructose in seminal vesicle secretion has been indirectly linked to forward sperm motility through prostasome function (Fabiani et al, 1995) and to seminal viscosity (Gonzalez et al, 1993).

The source of fructose in seminal vesicles appears to proceed from glucose by aldose reduction to sorbitol and a subsequent ketone reduction to form fructose. The fructose of the seminal plasma appears to provide an anaerobic and an aerobic source of energy for the spermatozoa (Mann and Mann, 1981). The cervical mucus has high concentrations of glucose and very low levels of fructose, and the sperm are capable of using both types of sugars. In an epidemiologic study conducted among nearly 50,000 participants in the Health Professionals Follow-up Study of Cancer 1986, fructose consumption (70 versus 40 g/day) and high fruit intake were identified as protective against the development of advanced prostate cancer (Giovannucci et al, 1998).

Polyamines

Polyamines are the most basic (positively charged) small organic molecules in nature. They occur ubiquitously in tissues at high concentrations and are believed to be involved in diverse physiologic processes that share a relationship to cell proliferation and growth. Indeed, polyamines can serve as growth factors for cultured mammalian cells and bacteria and as inhibitors of enzymes, including protein kinases.

The exact role of polyamines at the molecular level still eludes science, but they represent important biologic compounds and are found at high levels in the ejaculate. Polyamines may affect the gating and transport of substances through membrane channels. From a clinical perspective, polyamines (spermidine and spermine) have been investigated as markers of androgen deprivation therapy among men with advanced-stage prostate cancer by Cipolla and colleagues (1994). Other researchers (Heston, 1991; Kadmon, 1992; Madhubala and Pegg, 1992; Love et al, 1993) have investigated the role of polyamines in the pathophysiology of prostate cancer. The first and rate-limiting step in polyamine synthesis within the prostate is controlled by the enzyme ornithine decarboxylase (ODC). ODC gene expression has been demonstrated to be increased in BPH tissue (Liu et al, 2002). ODC can be inhibited by difluoromethylornithine (DMFO), which in turn inhibits polyamine synthesis. DMFO has been proposed as an agent for chemoprevention of prostate cancer (Kadmon, 1992).

Spermine levels in normal human seminal plasma range from 50 to 350 mg/dL and originate primarily from the prostate gland, which is the richest source of spermine in the body. Spermine [NH_2-$(CH_2)_3$-NH-$(CH_2)_4$-$(CH_2)_4$-NH-$(CH_2)_3$-NH_2] is a basic aliphatic polyamine and, because of its four positive charges, binds strongly to acidic or negatively charged molecules such as phosphate ions, nucleic acid, and phospholipids. When semen is allowed to stand at room temperature, acid phosphatase enzymatically hydrolyzes seminal phosphorylcholine to form free inorganic phosphate ions, which then interact with the positively charged spermine and precipitate as large, translucent salt crystals of spermine phosphate. Polyamines can also form amide bonds and make their covalent addition to protein carboxylic groups (Williams-Ashman et al, 1975), and this modification may be involved in regulatory function.

There has been much interest in spermine and other related polyamines, such as spermidine and putrescine, because of the rapid and dramatic changes in levels and ratios associated with many types of cells that have been induced into growth. Williams-Ashman and colleagues have investigated in detail the biosynthesis and regulation of polyamines in the male reproductive tract and have characterized the enzymatic reactions that progress from ornithine to putrescine to spermidine to spermine (Williams-Ashman et al, 1969, 1972, 1975). Polyamines are oxidized enzymatically by diamine oxidase (present in the seminal plasma) to form highly reactive aldehyde compounds that can be toxic to both sperm and bacteria (LeCalve et al, 1995). The formation of these aldehyde products produces the characteristic odor of semen. It is also possible that these aldehydes or polyamines may, themselves, protect the genitourinary tract from infective agents. Relationships between spermine levels in seminal plasma and sperm count and motility have also been suggested (Stamey et al, 1968; Fair et al, 1973; Fair and Parrish 1981; LeCalve et al, 1995). Like citrate, spermine can also be quantified within prostate tissue by magnetic resonance spectroscopy (van der Graaf et al, 2000).

KEY POINT: POLYAMINES

■ Polyamines are the most basic (positively charged) small organic molecules in nature. They occur in prostate tissues at high concentrations and are believed to be involved in diverse physiologic processes that share a relationship to cell proliferation and growth. Polyamine and citrate can be quantified in a clinical setting by magnetic resonance spectroscopy.

Phosphorylcholine

Other positively charged amines are at high concentrations in the ejaculate, including choline and phosphorylcholine, which are usually found as components of lipid or as lipotropic factors. The semen of mammals is rich in choline [$(CH_3)_3$-N^+-$(CH2)_2$-OH]. In humans, phosphorylcholine predominates, whereas in most other species, much higher levels of α-glycerylphosphorylcholine are present, often exceeding 1 g/dL of seminal plasma. Seligman and associates (1975) have demonstrated that phosphorylcholine is a highly specific substrate for prostatic acid phosphatase, which is also active in seminal plasma. The result of this enzymatic activity is the rapid formation of free choline in the first ejaculate. In contrast, α-glycerylphosphorylcholine is secreted primarily in the epididymis and is not readily hydrolyzed by acid phosphatase. For these reasons, Mann and Mann (1981) have suggested that the level of α-glycerylphosphorylcholine can be used as an index for assessing the contribution of the epididymal secretion to the ejaculate. The secretion from the epididymis is also under androgenic control. The function of these choline compounds is unknown; it appears that they are not metabolized by spermatozoa, nor do they affect the respiration of the sperm (Dawson et al, 1957).

Prostaglandins

The richest sources of prostaglandins in the human are the seminal vesicles (Pourian et al, 1995). Prostaglandins are present in seminal plasma at a total concentration of 100 to 300 μg/mL. Von Euler (1934) proposed the name prostaglandins for the active components in seminal plasma in the belief that they originated from the prostate gland, but Eliasson (1959) established that the primary source of prostaglandin is the seminal vesicles, not the prostate; however, the original name has survived to date. Prostaglandins have a wide distribution in mammalian tissues but at much lower concentrations than in the seminal vesicles (Vane and Botting, 1995).

There are more than 90 different prostaglandins present in the human, with 15 prostaglandins present in human semen, and they are all 20-carbon hydroxy fatty acids with a cyclopentane ring having two side chains; as such, they are derivatives of prostanoic acid. The 15 types of prostaglandins within the prostate are divided into four major groups, designated A, B, E, and F according to the structure of the five-membered cyclopentane ring. Each of these groups is further subdivided according to the position and number of double bonds in the side chain (therefore, PGE_3 indicates prostaglandins of E type with three double bonds in the side chain). The E group of prostaglandins is the major component in the male reproductive tract, whereas the F group predominates in the female system. Fuchs and Chantharaski (1976) have summarized the reported levels of human seminal plasma prostaglandins and report the following mean values (μg/mL): PGE_1, 20; PGE_2, 15; (PGE_1 + E_2) − 19-OH, 100; PGA_1 + A_2, 9; (PGA_1 + A_2) − 19-OH1, 31; PGB_1 + B_2, 18; (PGB_1 + B_2) − 19-OH, 13; $PGF_{1\alpha}$, 3; and $PGF_{2\alpha}$, 4.

These compounds are potent pharmacologic agents that have been implicated in a wide variety of biologic events in the male, including erection, ejaculation, and sperm motility and transport, as well as in testicular and penile contractions. In addition, prostaglandins from seminal fluid deposited in the vagina have been reported to affect cervical mucus, vaginal secretion, and sperm transport in the female genital tract. Chaudry and colleagues (1994) investigated the relationship between prostaglandin metabolism and both benign prostatic tissue and prostate cancer tissue. Prostaglandin E has been related to the immunosuppressive effects of seminal plasma mediated through the extracellular organelles, or "prostasomes" (Kelly et al, 1991). Finally, Olin and associates (1993) have investigated the effect of prostaglandins on fertility.

Cholesterol and Lipids

Scott (1945) reported that human seminal plasma contains 185 mg/dL of total lipids, 103 mg/dL of cholesterol, and 83 mg/dL of phospholipids (Vignon et al, 1992). In comparison, human prostatic secretion contains the following: total lipids, 186 mg/dL; cholesterol, 80 mg/dL; and phospholipids, 180 mg/dL. The lipids of semen have been further described (White et al, 1976), and the phospholipids of seminal plasma are composed of 44% sphingomyelin, 12.3% ethanolamine plasmalogen, and 11.2% phosphatidylserine (Poulos et al, 1973).

The reported levels of cholesterol in seminal plasma have varied considerably from 11 to 103 mg/dL (Scott, 1945; Eliasson, 1959; Poulos et al, 1973). White (1975) believes that the ratio of cholesterol to phospholipid in seminal plasma stabilizes the sperm against temperature and environmental shock. Thompson and associates (1987), Rohan and coworkers (1995), and Rose and Connolly (1992) have reviewed the role of dietary lipids in the pathogenesis of prostate cancer.

Zinc

The high level of zinc in human seminal plasma (140 μg/mL) appears to originate primarily from secretions of the prostate gland (488 ± 18 μg/mL) (Bedwal and Bahuguna, 1994). The prostate has the highest concentration of zinc (50 mg/100 g dry weight) of any organ. Mackenzie and colleagues (1962) reported that human seminal plasma contained 310 mg of zinc/100 g dry weight and that spermatozoa contained 200 mg/100 g dry weight. In comparison, prostatic secretions from eight normal subjects had 720 mg zinc/100 g dry weight. Byar (1974) has reviewed many of the early experiments and concepts related to zinc in the reproductive tract. Zinc levels are elevated or stable in BPH, whereas there is a marked decrease in zinc content associated with prostatic adenocarcinoma. The localization of zinc 65 in the human prostate by radioautography appears to be within the epithelial cells; however, in the lateral prostate of the rat, large quantities of zinc were also associated with the stroma and particularly with the basal membrane and the elastin protein component (Chandler et al, 1977). Oral intake of zinc does not alter zinc levels in prostatic fluid.

Many physiologic roles have been postulated for zinc since the classic studies of Gunn and associates (Gunn and Gould, 1956; Gunn et al, 1965), who correlated endocrine effects on zinc uptake and concentration in the prostate of the rodent. There are many important zinc-containing metalloenzymes, but the concentration of zinc in the prostate probably exceeds that present in zinc-associated enzymes. Zinc is known to bind many proteins (Sansone et al, 1991). Johnson and associates (1969) characterized zinc-binding proteins in the prostatic secretion of the dog, on hydrolysis, as containing only eight types of amino acids. Heathcote and Washington (1973) described a zinc-binding protein in human BPH that was rich in histidine and alanine. Jonsson and colleagues (2005) suggested that one possible role of zinc in semen may be to regulate the activity of PSA by binding to semenogelins I and II and fragments thereof. There have been other studies on zinc-binding proteins from the prostate (Reed and Stitch, 1973; Fair et al, 1976), and additional information on these interesting proteins is needed.

An important role for zinc in prostatic secretion has been postulated in the studies of Fair and Wehner (Fair et al, 1976), which suggest the direct role of zinc as a prostatic antibacterial factor. In the study of 36 normal men free from bacterial prostatic infections, the mean value of zinc in the prostatic secretion was approximately 350 μg/mL, with a wide range of 150 to 1000 μg/mL. In comparison, the prostatic fluid obtained from 61 specimens collected from 15 patients with documented chronic bacterial prostatitis had a reduction of more than 80% and averaged only 50 μg/mL, with a range of 0 to 139 μg/mL. The authors proposed a lower limit of normal at 150 μg/mL. In addition, in vitro studies of free zinc ions at concentrations normally found in prostatic fluid have confirmed the bactericidal activity of zinc against a variety of gram-positive and gram-negative bacteria. However, a considerable portion of the zinc in the prostate appears to be bound to unique proteins, such as metallothionein, and it is not certain how this might alter the biologic properties of zinc (Suzuki et al, 1994, 1995).

PROSTATIC SECRETORY PROTEINS

The predominant secretory proteins of the sex accessory tissues have been reviewed (Lilja and Abrahamsson, 1988; Aumuller and Seitz, 1990; Aumuller et al, 1990; Lilja, 1993a, 1993b; Rittenhouse et al, 1998; Saedi et al, 2001; Diamandis and Yousef, 2002; Yousef and Diamandis, 2002). High-resolution, two-dimensional electrophoresis profiles of the major secretory protein markers from human ejaculate, seminal plasma, and prostatic secretions have been reported (Edwards et al, 1981; Carter and Resnick, 1982; Rui et al, 1984; Tsai et al, 1984; Dube et al, 1987; Aumuller and Seitz, 1990); however, several are found in abundance and have clinical significance. These include PSA (human kallikrein 3 [hK3, protein; or *KLK3*, gene]); human kallikrein 2 (hK2 or *KLK2*); prostase/*KLK-L1* (Yousef et al, 1999); prostatic acid phosphatase; and prostate-specific protein (PSP-94), also termed β-microseminoprotein or β-MSP. Table 85–6 lists some characteristics of the major secretory proteins in the sex accessory tissues.

Prostate-Specific Antigen

Major changes in the use of PSA have occurred since the 1980s; for a general overview, see the work of Polascik and coworkers (1999). A serine protease, PSA-like molecule was first demonstrated in human prostatic tissue in 1970 (Ablin et al, 1970), found in seminal plasma in 1971 (Hara et al, 1971), purified from prostatic tissue in 1979 (Wang et al, 1979), measured in the serum of men in 1980 (Kuriyama et al, 1980), and widely

Table 85-6.   Major Proteins Secreted by the Sex Accessory Tissue

Protein/Gene Identification	Molecular Weight (kD)	Seminal Plasma (mg/nL)	Activity
Prostate-specific antigen (PSA) (hK3 [protein] or KLK3 [gene])	33-36	0.70	Serine protease; arginine esterase
Human kallikrein 2 (hK2 or KLK2)	28.4	0.012 mg/nL	In vivo activation of proPSA, arginine esterase
Human kallikrein L1 (KLK-L1)	Unknown	Unknown	Serine protease, also in testes, breast, adrenal, uterus, thyroid, and salivary glands
Human kallikrein 11	~40	0.002-0.037	Serine protease, breast, ovary, and prostate
Prostatic acid phosphatase (PAP)	102-106	0.3-1.0	Phosphotyrosyl protein phosphatase
Prostate-specific transglutaminase	17	Unknown	PTGases are involved in the formation of stable, functional peptide-bound glutamine and primary amine groups.
Semenogelins I and II	50, 63	2 mM*	Chymotrypsin-like activity, and it inhibits PSA activity in the semen.
Prostate specific membrane antigen	~120	Unknown	Its structure is identical to glutamate carboxypeptidase II and folate hydrolase I. The PSMA antigen is found in kidney, testis, ovary, brain, salivary gland, small intestine, colon, liver, spleen, breast, and skeletal muscle.
Prostate stem cell antigen	~24	Unknown	A prostate cancer-associated tumor antigen. Northern blot and in situ data show that PSCA is predominantly prostate-specific in normal tissues and is overexpressed in greater than 80% of prostate cancers.
Prostate-specific protein (PSP-94) β-micro-seminoprotein (β-MSP)	10.7-16	0.6-0.9	Also epithelial cells of antrum of stomach
Immunoglobulins	160	0.007-0.022	Human IgG
C3 Complement	~178	0.018	An integral part of the complement cascade (C3 activates alternate pathway).
Transferrin	77	0.18	A plasma protein that transports iron through the blood to the liver, spleen, and bone marrow

*Only given in mM concentrations.

used as a clinical marker of prostate cancer by 1988 (Seamonds et al, 1986; Chan et al, 1987; Stamey et al, 1987; Oesterling et al, 1988). The historical information, molecular characteristics, physiologic properties, and immunoassay for PSA have been reviewed elsewhere (Oesterling, 1991, 1993; Shellhammer and Wright, 1993; Vessella and Lange, 1993; Partin and Oesterling, 1994; McCormack et al, 1995; Polascik et al, 1999).

The discovery of PSA resulted from a search of the ejaculate and prostatic fluid by immunoprecipitation to find specific proteins for forensic use. In 1971, Japanese workers isolated, from the seminal plasma, a protein that was proved to be antigenically specific for semen; they reported its chemical and physical characteristics and termed it γ-seminoprotein (Hara et al, 1971). Several years later, in an attempt to develop this protein further as a forensic marker for semen identification, γ-seminoprotein was purified from human seminal plasma. These seminal proteins, initially called γ-seminoproteins, have now been shown by sequence to be the same as PSA. Lilja and Abrahamsson (1988) reported the same proteolytic activity and site of glycosylation, the same molecular weight protein and gene sequence, and identical immunohistochemical characteristics and serum characteristics in these proteins.

Wang and coworkers (1979) first reported this human PSA that has now proved to be an important marker of the prostate and prostate disease. **PSA is a glycoprotein acting as a serine protease of molecular weight 33,000 that contains 7% carbohydrate** (Watt et al, 1986) and is found almost exclusively in the epithelial cells of the prostate (Armbruster, 1993; Rittenhouse et al, 1998). PSA was measured in the serum and was demonstrated to be a clinically important assay for monitoring prostate cancer (Kuriyama et al, 1980, 1981). For a

detailed description of the use of PSA and its limitations, both clinically and in laboratory medicine analysis, see the work of McCormack and associates (McCormack et al, 1995; Rittenhouse et al, 1998; Polascik et al, 1999).

Watt and coworkers (1986) have studied PSA extensively and were the first to report its complete amino acid sequence. The single polypeptide chain contains 240 amino acids and an O-linked carbohydrate side chain attached to a serine residue. Lundwall and Lilja (1987) cloned the complementary DNA (cDNA) that encodes the PSA gene. Their study indicates that the mRNA of PSA in the prostate is approximately 1.5 kilobases.

PSA acts physiologically like a serine protease and an arginine esterase with both chymotrypsin-like and trypsin-like activity. The sequence of the protein is similar to that of other kallikreins (Rittenhouse et al, 1998) involved in prostatic cell regulatory mechanisms. Lilja (1985) and Watt and coworkers (1986) reported that one of the structural proteins of the seminal fluid, semenogelin, causes the ejaculate to clot. Semenogelin is the predominant seminal vesicle–secreted protein and one of the physiologic substrates for PSA. **One possible biologic role of PSA is to lyse the clot in the ejaculate, but it is at present unknown why this clotting and lysing mechanism is important to reproductive physiology.**

The PSA gene (*hKLK3*) is a member of a human tissue kallikrein gene family that includes *hKLK1, hKLK2, hKLK3*, and *KLK-L1* (Lundwall, 1989; McMullen et al, 1991; Berg et al, 1992; Carbini et al, 1993; Clements, 1994; McCormack et al, 1995; Rittenhouse et al, 1998; Nelson et al, 1999; Yousef and Diamandis, 2003). To date, there are more than 15 different human kallikreins, with expression noted in prostate, breast, ovarian, and testicular cancers (Obiezu and Diamandis, 2005). These genes are all located on chromosome 19 (Reigman et al, 1992; Yousef et al, 1999; Yousef and Diamandis, 2003). The ectopic expression of PSA has been reported in smaller concentrations in the tissue of malignant breast tumors (Yu et al, 1994a, 1994b, 1994c), normal breast tissue, breast milk, female serum, and adrenal and renal carcinomas; however, for practical and clinical purposes, PSA is an organ-specific but not a cancer-specific marker. A limitation of PSA as a tumor marker is demonstrated in the substantial overlap in values between benign and malignant prostate disease (Oesterling et al, 1988; Partin et al, 1990).

Most work regarding the molecular biology and biochemistry of PSA is based on extensive study of purified protein from seminal fluid in which the concentration of PSA is nearly a million-fold higher than that found routinely in serum (McCormack et al, 1995). The concentrations found in seminal plasma range from 0.5 to 5.0 mg/mL, whereas normal serum concentrations in men aged 50 to 80 years without prostatic disease range between 1.0 and 4.0 ng/mL (Catalona et al, 1991). Pre-pro-PSA (261 amino acids) is processed in the endoplasmic reticulum of prostatic epithelial cells, where a 17-peptide pre-region residue is cleaved. Seven more peptides are then cleaved from the pro-peptide to form the active PSA peptide (Rittenhouse et al, 1998). This pro-PSA represents an inactive (zymogen) precursor of PSA and is secreted and cleaved by hK2 (Lilja, 1985; Villoutreix et al, 1994; Rittenhouse et al, 1998).

The most exciting and clinically useful discovery in this area is the demonstration of different molecular forms of PSA (free [unbound] and complexed [bound]) circulating within the blood (Lilja et al, 1991; Stenman et al, 1991; Christensson et al, 1993; Lilja, 1993; McCormack et al, 1995; Partin and Carter, 1996; Polascik et al, 1999). **Complexed PSA is found in the serum irreversibly and covalently bound to α_1-antichymotrypsin** (ACT), an endogenous serine protease inhibitor. This form of complexed PSA (PSA-ACT) is enzymatically inactive yet has immunoreactivity. In addition, an unknown quantity of PSA is also complexed to α_2-macroglobulin (PSA-A2M). Free PSA, found in lower concentrations than complexed PSA (PSA-ACT), is also enzymatically inactive, yet it is also immunoreactive, whereas PSA-A2M is not. Depending on the monoclonal antibodies used to measure serum PSA, various amounts of free and complexed PSA are recognized and contribute to the total (measurable) amount. Development of new monoclonal antibodies specific for free PSA and complexed PSA has allowed accurate measurement of the different molecular forms of PSA and their ratios. This has the potential of increasing the sensitivity and specificity of PSA for diagnosis of prostate cancer (Catalona et al, 1998).

Human Kallikrein 2

Human kallikrein 2 (hK2 [protein] or *KLK2* [gene]) is a prostate-specific serine protease closely related to PSA and has largely been overlooked thus far (Rittenhouse et al, 1998). hK2 was first demonstrated from a low-stringency hybridization screen of a human liver genomic library in 1992, and the amino acid sequence is predicted to have 80% homology with PSA (hK3, *KLK3*) (Young et al, 1992). The striking homology

between these two "prostate-specific" proteins suggested a close physiologic relationship. More recently, recombinant hK2 has been expressed and purified (Kumar et al, 1996; Mikolajczyk et al, 1998). Unlike PSA, hK2 is shown to be trypsin-like with selective cleavage at arginine residues and has a more potent (20,000-fold greater than PSA) protease activity (Mikolajczyk et al, 1998). Monoclonal antibodies to hK2 have been developed and have a low incidence of cross-reacting with PSA (Finlay et al, 1998). An exciting finding has been the independent demonstration that hK2 cleaves pro-PSA to generate the enzymatically active form of PSA (Kumar et al, 1996). Immunohistochemical studies have shown hK2 to be prostate localized and to increase in expression from normal to metastatic, poorly differentiated prostatic epithelium (Darson et al, 1997). Preliminary studies of hK2 in the serum of men with prostate cancer have suggested clinical utility for early detection of prostate cancer (Partin et al, 1999).

Human Kallikrein L1

Attempts to find other novel human kallikrein–like genes on chromosome 19 have identified yet another member of the human kallikrein gene family, *KLK-L1* (Nelson et al, 1999; Yousef et al, 1999; Diamandis, 2000). Nelson and associates (1999) constructed a cDNA library enriched through subtraction with the cDNAs from four other normal tissues to yield an expressed sequence tag identifying a gene that they have called prostase. The sequence of prostase exhibits features similar to the other members of the kallikrein family. Yousef and coworkers (1999) also found *KLK-L1* in breast tissue and demonstrated that it is hormonally regulated. Although the clinical utility of the members of the kallikrein gene family has not yet been determined, it is under investigation.

Human Kallikrein 11

Human kallikrein 11 (hK11) is a serine protease that shares similarities to human kallikrein 3 (hK3) or PSA with significant homologies at the levels of nucleotide and protein structure (Diamandis and Yousef, 2002). Diamandis' laboratory has demonstrated localization immunohistochemically of hK11 in epithelial cells of various organs and further detected hK11 in amniotic fluid, milk of lactating women, cerebrospinal fluid, follicular fluid, and breast cancer cytosols. The highest levels of hK11 were observed in prostatic tissue extracts and seminal plasma, in which it was present at 300-fold lower levels than PSA. Elevated serum levels of hK11 were found in 60% of men with prostate cancer; the ratio of hK11 to total PSA was able to reduce the number of biopsies required, and the data were similar to free PSA assays (Diamandis and Yousef, 2002; Nakamura et al, 2003).

Prostate-Specific Transglutaminases

Human prostate-specific transglutaminase 4 belongs to a family of enzymes that irreversibly cross-link peptide-bound glutamine residues through reactions with either lysines or primary amines such as polyamines (Dubbink et al, 1998). Transglutaminases are located throughout the body, but they are highly tissue specific. Dubbink and coworkers (1998) described a new prostate-specific transglutaminase with 35-kilobase genomic DNA and consisting of 13 exons and 12 introns. The main transcription initiation site is located 52 base pairs upstream of the translational start code. At least one splice variant was described, and a transglutaminase 4 gene (*TGM4*) promoter was analyzed by sequencing and transfection experiments and found at −1276 to −563. Subsequently, an Sp1 binding site (promoter) required for basal activity of *TGM4* was identified (Dubbink et al, 1999). The *TGM4* promoter was characterized by deletion mapping and mutational analysis. Dubbink determined that positions between −113 and −87 were essential for core activity of the promoter. The sequences identified are binding sites for the Sp1 and Sp3 transcription factors; however, their precise role in *TGM4* regulation was not deduced from experiments described (Dubbink et al, 1999). Of importance is the fact that the major gel-forming proteins in semen, semenogelins I and II, are substrates for transglutaminase 4 (Peter et al, 1998). Esposito (Esposito and Caputo, 2005) reviewed the range of substrates for transglutaminases in detail and characterized the molecular basis of transglutaminase-catalyzed reactions and also assessed possible physiologic function and pathophysiologic processes due to such interactions. The transglutaminase for the prostate is transglutaminase 4; it is 77 kD in size, androgen regulated, and found extracellularly. Transglutaminases catalyze the post-translational modification of proteins by formation of polymerized cross-linkages between the γ-carboxamide group of protein-bound glutamine residues and the ε-amino group of protein-bound lysine residues, which results in a stabilized molecular complex. There is evidence to suggest that the biochemical affinity of transglutaminase 4 for acyl-type substrates such as kinesin proteins in protein secretions of the semen may be important for correct extrusion of transglutaminase 4 from the coagulating gland (Esposito and Caputo, 2005).

An and coworkers (1999) also described cloning of *TGM4* (human prostate-specific transglutaminase) and its promoter in the elements of −1 to −500 and also at −520 to −1400. In addition, this group applied Northern blot hybridization and reverse-transcription polymerase chain reaction (RT-PCR) analysis to confirm prostate specificity and Gleason grade–specific expression by RT-PCR and noted significant downregulation in high Gleason grade as well as in metastatic tissue extracts. From a protein perspective, Birckbichler and colleagues (2000) revealed by quantitative immunofluorescence that prostate cancer was significantly decreased compared with normal prostate and prostatitis cases, but this is in contrast with what was observed with RT-PCR results (An et al, 1999), where the higher Gleason grade tumors tended to be significantly decreased. This discrepancy of results needs to be rectified in larger experiments comparing RT-PCR with protein expression to determine whether this is a technical problem or rather one of translation of transglutaminase 4 mRNA versus protein in the malignant disease process.

Semenogelins I and II

Semenogelin I and semenogelin II are dominant proteins in human semen coagulum that are degraded by PSA to form various biologically active peptides, which in combination with fibronectin give rise to the gel-like coagulum of newly ejaculated semen (Lilja, 1985; Malm et al, 1996; de Lamirande et al, 1997). The genes encoding semenogelins I and II are located in separate regions 11.5 kilobase pairs apart on chromosome 20. The major biologic function of semenogelin involves **capacitation,** which is defined as a series of changes in cell membranes, enzyme activities, and ion fluxes that sperm undergo as they traverse the female urogenital tract to reach the zona pellucida and fertilize the egg (de Lamirande et al, 1997). de Lamirande and associates (2001) demonstrated that biologically active peptides from semenogelin I and semenogelin II proteolysis scavenge superoxide anion and may affect sperm oxidase to serve as natural regulators of sperm capacitation. It is of physiologic and possibly pathophysiologic importance that these major gel-forming proteins in semen, semenogelins I and II, are substrates for transglutaminase 4 (Peter et al, 1998). Both of these proteins originate from the glandular epithelium of the seminal vesicles and are produced in high concentrations; however, in the epididymis, only semenogelin I is expressed. There is evidence by immunohistochemistry that other cell types including the vas deferens, prostate, and trachea demonstrate strong signals for semenogelins I and II, and weaker but positive signals were seen in skeletal muscle cells and in the central nervous system (Lundwall et al, 2002).

KEY POINTS: SECRETORY PROTEINS

- Prostate-specific transglutaminases (specifically transglutaminase 4) catalyze the post-translational modification of proteins by formation of polymerized cross-linkages between the γ-carboxamide group of protein-bound glutamine residues and the ε-amino group of protein-bound lysine residues, which results in a stabilized molecular complex.

- The major gel-forming proteins in semen, semenogelins I and II, are substrates for transglutaminase 4. There is evidence to suggest that the biochemical affinity of transglutaminase 4 for acyl-type substrates such as kinesin proteins in protein secretions of the semen may be important for correct extrusion of transglutaminase 4 from the coagulating gland and may be involved in capacitation.

- PSP-94 has as one of its main biologic functions the inhibition of follicle-stimulating hormone.

Prostate-Specific Membrane Antigen

Recent reviews of the biochemistry and biology of the prostate-specific membrane antigen (PSMA) in human tissues and prostate cancer surveys describe the differential regulation of the molecule, its enzymatic functions, and its potential as a biomarker for in vivo imaging and immunotherapy (Elgamal et al, 2000; Ghosh and Heston, 2004). The gene encoding PSMA is located on chromosome 11p11-12 and codes for a type II membrane glycoprotein (M_r ~100,000 daltons) with intracellular (1 to 18 amino acids), transmembrane (19 to 43 amino acids), and large extracellular (44 to 750 amino acids) domains (Israeli et al, 1994; Ghosh and Heston, 2004; Davis et al, 2005). The cDNA (2.65 kb GenBank Accession M99487) encoding PSMA was first reported by Israeli and colleagues in 1993 and its deduced amino acid sequence determined (Israeli et al, 1994). It encodes a 750–amino acid protein with a predicted molecular mass of 84 kD (excluding carbohydrates). The hydrophobic amino acids found on amino acid residues 20 to 43 suggested that this protein is a type II integral membrane protein with a small intracellular domain and a large extracellular domain (Fair et al, 1997). The promoter for PSMA has been cloned (Good et al, 1999), and PSMA has been expressed and purified from a baculovirus expression system (Lodge et al, 1999). A portion of the transmembrane domain of this protein (amino acid residues 1250 to 1700) shares 57% homology with the human transferrin receptor mRNA (Mahadevan and Saldanha, 1999). Alternative splicing variants of PSMA (PSM′–PSA′ extracellular domain protein) are at present under investigation to better understand the clinical significance of this important membrane protein found within the prostate (Liu et al, 1997; Grauer et al, 1998; Murphy et al, 1998; Ghosh and Heston, 2004; Rajasekaran et al, 2005). PSMA has been crystallized and its structure deduced at 3.5-Å resolution. These analyses reveal a homodimer with structural similarity to the transferrin receptor, a receptor for iron-loaded transferrin that lacks protease activity (Davis et al, 2005). However, unlike the transferrin receptor, the protease domain of PSMA (glutamate carboxypeptidase II) contains a binuclear zinc site, catalytic residues, and a proposed substrate-binding arginine patch.

PSMA in the central nervous system metabolizes the brain neurotransmitter N-acetyl-aspartyl-glutamate or NAAG (named NAALADase). In the intestine, PSMA is found in the proximal small intestine, where it removes γ-linked glutamates from poly-γ-glutamated folate (folate hydrolase 1), or as a carboxypeptidase, glutamate carboxypeptidase II. Another interesting potential targeting feature of PSMA expression in the prostate is that it is overexpressed in neovasculature of other tumors (Silver et al, 1997; Chang et al, 1999a, 2001). A PSM-like molecule has been located at 11q14.3, but only PSMA is overexpressed in prostate cancer. In the prostate, there are three alternatively spliced variants of PSMA. However, only one of these isoforms (PSM′ located at the 5′ end of PSMA cDNA) is known to be differentially expressed in normal tissue, BPH, and prostate cancer (Elgamal et al, 2000; Rajasekaran et al, 2005). PSMA mRNA expression within prostate cancers is highest in the hormone-deprived state, contrary to PSA mRNA, which often demonstrates lower, even absent expression in the hormone-deprived state (Henttu et al, 1992; Israeli et al, 1994; Wright et al, 1995; Rajasekaran et al, 2005).

PSMA is hormonally controlled by steroids similar to PSA (Israeli et al, 1994; Elgamal et al, 2000). A study by Su and colleagues (1995) using RT-PCR on peripheral blood demonstrated that the PSMA:PSM′ ratio is threefold to sixfold upregulated in prostate cancer compared with BPH (0.76 to 1.6) and normal (0.075 to 0.45). Also, Elgamal and associates (2000) assessed the overall RT-PCR assay results described for six separate RT-PCR peripheral blood studies; the data yielded a pooled sensitivity of 66% for RT-PCR PSMA versus 62% for RT-PCR PSA, suggesting inadequate sensitivity for routine clinical use.

Today, only a few studies have investigated PSMA protein levels in the blood of patients with prostate disease in spite of numerous publications regarding the production of numerous new monoclonal antibodies made to PSMA (Chang et al, 1999b; Tino et al, 2000). The existing assays can be characterized as research assays only, and the clinical data represent preliminary testing and not validation for a new clinical assay for assessment of diagnostic clinical performance. Reports to date used Western slot blot, a competitive enzyme-linked immunosorbent assay (ELISA), and more Immuno-SELDI. A competitive ELISA developed by Horoszewicz and colleagues (1987) using 9h10-A4 and 7E11-C5 monoclonal antibodies found an increased PSMA level in 47% of patients (20 of 43) with prostate cancer versus only 5% of patients (3 of 66) without prostate cancer, and the result was negative in 30 normal blood donors. In addition, PSMA expression within cancerous lesions appears to correlate directly with the degree of differentiation and not with tumor stage (Wright et al, 1995). Other investigators had employed a competitive ELISA and Western blotting and confirmed increasing expression with higher grade and stage, thus implicating PSMA in recurrence and progression (Rochon et al, 1994; Douglas et al, 1997; Murphy et al, 1997). A significant effort has been made to demonstrate tissue expression by quantitative immunoassays in the LNCaP cell line, human prostate cancer, and normal or BPH tissues as well as in metastatic tissue, seminal fluid, and urine (Su et al, 1995; Troyer et al, 1995; Sokoloff et al, 2000; Ross et al, 2003), but none of these assays were developed into serum immunoassays. However, Xiao and colleagues (2001) reported the use of an Immuno-SELDI assay for PSMA. The Immuno-SELDI assay used the 7E11-C5 immunoglobulin G1 monoclonal antibody developed by Horoszewicz and colleagues (1987) and employed in the clinically available ProstaScint scans. In that study, the ProteinChip Array was coated with 1 μg of G protein, and then residual active sites were blocked with 1M ethanolamine, washed, and treated with 1.5 μg 7E11-C5 monoclonal antibody (Xiao et al, 2001). The assay was formatted to create a 96-well array, and the same exact clinical samples were processed that were run with Western blotting (Beckett et al, 1999; Elgamal et al, 2000). The results of the Immuno-SELDI assay clearly revealed that serum PSMA with the 7E11-C5 antibody differentiated prostate cancer (623.1 ng/mL; n = 17) from BPH (117.1 ng/mL; n = 10, P < .001). The authors showed considerable age-related overlap in serum activity in normal subjects and patients with BPH older than 50 years.

Finally, a current review of the multifunctional potential of the PSMA molecule by Rajasekaran and colleagues (2005) indicates that **PSMA dimerization is similar to transferrin receptor and may function as a receptor for internalizing a putative ligand. PSMA enzyme activities (NAALADase and folate reductase) are consistent with a role in nutrient uptake. The PSMA peptidase activity may be involved in signal transduction in prostate epithelial cells and may activate cascades that result in cell survival, cell proliferation, and cell migration functions. This multifunctional molecule not only has numerous physiologic benefits but also has several diagnostic and therapeutic potential benefits to manage prostate cancer as well.**

Prostate Stem Cell Antigen

Reiter and coworkers (1998) identified prostate stem cell antigen (PSCA), a cell surface antigen that is expressed in the prostate (among other tissues including bladder). The PSCA gene encodes a 123–amino acid glycoprotein, with 30% homology to stem cell antigen 2 (Sca-2). Like Sca-2, PSCA is a member of the Thy-1/Ly-6 family and is anchored by a gly-cosylphosphatidylinositol linkage. **By use of mRNA in situ hybridization, PSCA expression was localized in normal prostate to the _basal cell epithelium_, the putative stem cell compartment of prostatic epithelium; hence, PSCA may be a marker of prostate stem/progenitor cells.** Hara and associates (2002) performed an analysis of PSA, PSMA, and PSCA mRNA level on peripheral blood by RT-PCR in 58 cases of prostate cancer and 71 cases of nonmalignant disorders. The results were 7 of 58 (12.1%) for PSA, 12 of 58 (20.7%) for PSMA, and 8 of 58 (13.8%) for PSCA; zero samples were positive for nonmalignant diseases. A summary of prognostic value for the three biomarkers was a hierarchy of PSCA > PSA > PSMA for RT-PCR of the 58 patients with prostate cancer. Note that in this group of patients, when the RT-PCR result was positive for PSCA, the patients had a lower disease progression–free survival than with the other two biomarkers. The PSCA expression increased with higher Gleason score and cancer stage as well as with progression to metastasis and may be a useful biomarker for staging of prostate cancer (Hara et al, 2002). Han and associates (2004) performed immunohistochemistry analysis of PSCA by a 246-patient tissue microarray; the results revealed that a PSCA staining intensity of 3.0 correlated with adverse prognostic features including Gleason score of 7.0 ($P = .001$), seminal vesicle invasion ($P = .005$), and capsular involvement ($P = .033$). However, following multivariate analysis, PSCA did not hold up as an independent predictor of PSA recurrence. Zhigang and Wenlv (2004) studied BPH, low-grade prostatic interepithelial neoplasia (LGPIN), high-grade prostatic interepithelial neoplasia (HGPIN), and prostate cancer at the tissue level by immunohistochemistry and at the mRNA level by in situ hybridization. In BPH and LGPIN, the staining of PSCA protein and mRNA was weak or negative and less intense and uniform than in HGPIN and prostate cancer. There was moderate to strong PSCA protein as well as mRNA expression in 8 of 11 (72.7%) HGPIN and in 40 of 48 (83.4%) prostate cancer specimens that were examined by immunohistochemistry and in situ hybridization analyses. When the prostate cancer specimens examined by immunohistochemistry and in situ hybridization analyses were compared with BPH (20%) and LGPIN (22.2%) samples, the results were statistically significant ($P < .05$, respectively). The expression level of PSCA increased with high Gleason grade, advanced stage, and progression to androgen independence ($P < .05$, respectively). In addition, in this study, protein immunostaining and in situ hybridization mRNA stain showed a high degree of correlation between PSCA protein and mRNA overexpression in prostate cancer, supporting the potential of PSCA as a prognostic biomarker. Clearly, the value of this protein to the biology of prostate epithelial tissue morphogenesis and also as a new biomarker for diagnosis and treatment of prostate cancer is yet to be realized.

Prostatic Acid Phosphatase

Acid phosphatase activity is more than 200 times more abundant in prostate tissue than in any other tissue and is the source of the high levels of acid phosphatase in ejaculate. Phosphatase enzymes hydrolyze many types of organic monophosphate esters to yield inorganic phosphate and alcohol. Many phosphatase enzymes exhibit optimal activity in vitro in the acid (pH 4 to 6) or alkaline (pH 8 to 11) ranges and are thus classified broadly as either acid or alkaline phosphatase.

Acid phosphatase activity may be further defined by factors that inhibit its enzymatic activity. For example, erythrocyte acid phosphatase is particularly sensitive to inhibition by 0.5% formaldehyde or copper ions (0.2 mM), whereas prostatic acid phosphatase (PAP) activity is far more sensitive to inhibition by fluoride ions (1 mM) or L-tartrate (1 mM).

Osteoclasts are also a rich source of tartrate-insensitive acid phosphatase. Minor elevations in serum acid phosphatase levels can accompany Paget's disease, osteoporosis, nonprostatic bone metastasis, and other conditions of increased bone resorption as well as metastatic prostate cancer. All acid phosphatases hydrolyze a wide range of natural and synthetic phosphomonoesters, and this has provided a wide variety of assay systems and the expression of different units of activity, depending on the assay. These synthetic substrates include, in part, phenylphosphate (Gutman and Gutman, 1938); phenolphthalein phosphate; paranitrophenyl phosphate, also called Sigma 104; and thymolphthalein phosphate (Roy et al, 1971). The specificity of these substrates varies with the type and source of acid phosphatase; it appears that thymolphthalein phosphate may be the most specific substrate for assaying serum levels of prostate-specific acid phosphatase, but specific antibodies are now available for immunoassays. Interest in acid phosphatase assays in serum as a measure of prostatic cancer metastasis before definitive therapy has decreased with the availability of the more sensitive and specific PSA assay (Burnett et al, 1992).

The natural substrate for PAP may be phosphorylcholine phosphate, which is rapidly hydrolyzed in the semen (Seligman et al, 1951). The biologic functions of this enzyme and its reactions are not known, but it is of interest that PAP can hydrolyze protein tyrosine phosphate esters, natural products of many oncogene protein tyrosine kinases (Li et al, 1984; Lin and Clinton, 1986). By magnetic resonance spectroscopic techniques, it has been shown that the ratio of intracellular choline to citrate levels within the prostate can help differentiate normal from cancerous prostate tissue (Scheidler et al, 1999). Further clinical testing is required before this finding will influence clinical practice. It is unknown whether acid phosphatase is a regulatory factor in the tyrosyl protein kinase systems so essential as signaling mechanisms in growth factor function.

Human PAP is a glycoprotein dimer of molecular weight 102,000 and contains about 7% carbohydrate by weight, composed of 15 residues per mole of neutral sugars (fructose, galactose, and mannose), 6 residues per mole of sialic acid, and 13 residues of _N_-acetylglucosamine (Chu et al, 1977). The protein can be dissociated into two subunits of molecular weight 50,000. The activity of the purified human enzyme is 723 U/mg with α-naphthyl phosphate, and the

SECTION XVI

seminal plasma contains 0.3 to 1 g/L or 177 to 760 U/mL. The high enzymatic activity of PAP is not characteristic of accessory tissues in many other species; the level is 1000 times higher per gram of tissue in the human prostate than in the rat prostate. The clinical aspects of PAP were reviewed by Romas and Kwan (Lowe and Trauzzi, 1993; Romas and Kwan, 1993).

Prostate-Specific Protein 94, β-Microseminoprotein, and β-Inhibin

A major, cysteine rich, nonglycosylated 16-kD protein that contains 94 amino acids has been found in prostatic secretions and termed prostate-specific protein 94 (PSP-94); it is one of the three predominant proteins secreted in the prostate glands and found in seminal fluids along with PSA and PAP. This protein had previously been designated β-inhibin and also β-microseminoprotein (Dube et al, 1987; Ulvsback et al, 1989). Transcripts of mRNA for this protein have also been identified in nongenital tissues (Ulvsback et al, 1989). **One of the main biologic functions of PSP-94 is the inhibition of follicle-stimulating hormone** (Garde et al, 1999). Whereas follicle-stimulating hormone is made by the pituitary gland, the prostate has been shown to be an extrapituitary source of follicle-stimulating hormone. There are follicle-stimulating hormone receptors in the prostate, and it appears that an autocrine or paracrine regulation of this hormone influences prostate epithelial proliferation (Ben-Josef et al, 1999; Porter et al, 2001). Also, Chan and colleagues (Partin et al, 1999) used in situ hybridization to study expression of PSP-94 in human prostates. They found that fetal prostate at 6 to 7 months synthesizes PSA and PAP but not PSP-94, and this observation appears to relate to the development of the prostate gland. Zonal anatomic distribution of PSP-94 in the adult prostate demonstrated that the protein is expressed mostly in the acini of the peripheral zone rather than the central or transitional zones. Also, the authors found in this study that PSP-94 is markedly downregulated with increasing Gleason grade of prostate cancer.

Shukeir and coworkers (2003) demonstrated a significant decrease in growth of the Dunning R3327 subline MatLyLu rat prostate metastatic model transfected with parathyroid hormone–related protein by treatment with varying doses of commercial PSP-94 purified from human seminal plasma (0, 0.1, 1.0, and 10 μg/kg per day). Serum levels of parathyroid hormone–related protein and calcium were used to monitor the efficacy of treatment with PSP-94. **Hence, PSP-94 is an effective inhibitor of hormone-independent, late-stage prostate cancer in this Dunning MatLyLu animal model.** The PSP-94 molecule has not yet been crystallized; however, Joshi and Jyothi (2002), in a computer-simulated molecular model, have predicted its structure and calculated its binding activity and related biologic activity (follicle-stimulating hormone inhibition) and immunogenic properties.

Leucine Aminopeptidase

Aminopeptidases hydrolyze the N-terminal amino acid from small polypeptides. Leucine aminopeptidases are particularly active against the substrate L-leucyl-glycine, and some of these enzymes are referred to as arylamidases because the optimal substrate is L-leucyl-β-naphthylamine. The human prostate is rich in the arylamidase type of leucine aminopeptidase, with a presence in prostatic fluid of 30,000 units/mL.

Leucine aminopeptidase is a product of the epithelial cells of the prostate (Niemi et al, 1963) and is secreted into the lumen of the acini (Kirchheim et al, 1964; Vafa et al, 1993). Rackley and associates (1991) demonstrated that extracts from prostatic carcinoma contained less leucine aminopeptidase activity than did tissue obtained from BPH.

Lactate Dehydrogenase

The isoenzyme ratios of lactate dehydrogenase (LDH) in human semen may be altered in a patient with prostate cancer (Oliver et al, 1970; Grayhack et al, 1977). LDH (MW, 150,000) is composed of four subunits (each of MW 35,000) of only two different types of proteins, denoted M and H. The LDH of muscle has four M units, and that of heart has four H units. Five isoenzymes of LDH can be found in tissues with a four-subunit composition as follows: LDH I, MMMM; LDH II, MMMH; LDH III, MMHH; LDH IV, MHHH; and LDH V, HHHH. The M and H subunits appear to be the same in all tissues, but the amounts of LDH I to V can vary. Denis and Prout (1963) observed increased levels of LDH IV and V in prostatic cancer tissue. Several investigators have observed elevated ratios of LDH V/LDH I in human prostatic cancer (Elhilali, 1968; Oliver et al, 1970; Flocks and Schmidt, 1972).

Immunoglobulins, C3 Complement, and Transferrin

There are many reports establishing the presence of immunoglobulins in human seminal plasma (Liang et al, 1991; Gahankari and Golhar, 1993). It is possible to measure levels of immunoglobulin G from 7 to 22 mg/dL and of immunoglobulin A from 0 to 6 mg/dL; however, immunoglobulin M is at low, often undetectable levels (Friberg and Tilly-Friberg, 1976). The complete source of these antibodies is not known, although they are found in expressed prostatic fluid (Grayhack et al, 1979) and may be related to infections (Fowler et al, 1982). They are usually found at lower levels in seminal plasma than in blood, but the possibility of diffusion across the "blood–seminal plasma barrier" has not been eliminated (see discussion by Friberg and Tilly-Friberg, 1976).

Expressed prostatic fluid contains considerable amounts of the C3 component of complement, present at 1.82 mg/dL, and this increases nearly 10-fold in fluid collected from patients with prostatic adenocarcinoma to levels of 16.9 mg/dL (Grayhack and Lee, 1981). Prostatitis has also been shown to be related to C3 among men with chronic prostatitis (Blenk and Hofstetter, 1991). Prostatitis and BPH increase the level only approximately twofold. In the same manner, transferrin, an iron-carrying protein, is increased, going from levels of 5.3 mg/dL in normal prostatic fluid to 42.4 mg/dL in prostatic carcinoma (Grayhack and Lee, 1981).

John and colleagues (2003) conducted a prospective study of the ejaculate of 88 patients with chronic prostatitis by surveying immunoglobulins G, A, and M and interleukin-1α, soluble interleukin-2 receptor, and interleukin-6. The control group consisted of 96 normal ejaculates according to the World Health Organization criteria. Ejaculates of patients with chronic prostatitis increased during symptoms and subsided when clinical symptoms decreased. The authors observed that a combination of the humoral immune (immunoglobulin A and interleukin-6) changes and T-cell rich infiltrates is suggestive of an autoimmune component of the disease. Alexander and coworkers (2004) are studying a group of patients with chronic granulomatous prostatitis consisting of histologically diffuse nonspecific inflammatory changes that include epithelioid histiocytes and occasional multinucleate giant cells admixed with lymphocytes and plasma cells. Alexander has identified an association between the major histocompatibility locus HLA-DRB2*1501 and granulomatous prostatitis and has suggested the possibility that it may be an autoimmune disease.

Seminal Vesicle Secretory Proteins

Williams-Ashman (1983) presented a classic review on regulatory features of development and function of the seminal vesicles. The secretory proteins of the seminal vesicles are major proteins and enzymes involved in the rapid clotting of the ejaculate (Cunha et al, 1992). The major clotting protein has been termed semenogelin (Lilja and Abrahamsson, 1988). It has been shown to be the seminal vesicle–specific antigen. These clotted proteins from the seminal vesicle serve as substrates for PSA that enzymatically lyse the clot through their protease activity (Lilja, 1985; Aumuller and Seitz, 1990). Beyond the coagulation reaction, we are not certain what role these seminal vesicle proteins play, but their effects on fertility and uterine sperm motility have been studied in the mouse (Peitz and Olds-Clarke, 1986). Many of the proteins secreted by the seminal vesicle are under androgen regulation (Higgins and Hemingway, 1991; Hagstrom et al, 1992). More recent work (Harvey et al, 1995) has identified an androgen-regulated protease with elastase-like activity within seminal vesicle secretions.

COAGULATION AND LIQUEFACTION OF SEMEN

Within 5 minutes after ejaculation, human semen coagulates into a semisolid gel. On further standing for a 5- to 20-minute period, the clot spontaneously liquefies to form a viscous liquid (Huggins and Neal, 1942; Tauber and Zaneveld, 1976; Mann and Mann, 1981). Calcium-binding substances, such as sodium citrate and heparin, do not inhibit the coagulation process, nor are prothrombin, fibrinogen, or factor XII required because they are absent in seminal plasma (Mann and Mann, 1981). The seminal clot is formed of fibers 0.15 to 10 nm in width, and its morphologic appearance differs from that of a blood fibrin clot (Huggins and Neal, 1942; Tauber et al, 1976; Mann and Mann, 1981). Factors affecting blood coagulation do not regulate semen viscosity (Amelar, 1962). From these observations and others, it appears that the coagulation of human semen is different from that of blood.

Examination of split human ejaculates indicates that the first fraction, originating primarily from Cowper's gland and the prostate, contains the liquefaction factors. The final fraction of the ejaculate, enriched in seminal vesicle secretions, is responsible for the coagulation of the ejaculate (Lilja et al, 1987).

It has long been known that prostatic fluid has a dramatic, fibrinolytic-like activity and that 2 mL of this secretion can liquefy 100 mL of clotted blood in 18 hours at 37°C (Huggins and Neal, 1942; Mann and Mann, 1981). The factors involved in such proteolytic activity in semen have been resolved (Huggins and Neal, 1942; Syner et al, 1975; Tauber et al, 1975, 1976; Mann and Mann, 1981; Zaneveld and Chatterton, 1982; Lilja et al, 1987). Two types of seminal plasma proteolytic enzymes appear to be major factors in the liquefaction process: plasminogen activators and PSA. Two plasminogen activators have been isolated from seminal plasma; they have molecular weights of 70,000 and 74,000 and appear to be related to urokinase (Propping et al, 1974). It is believed that the plasminogen activators originate from the prostatic secretions.

The seminal plasma contains a variety of other proteolytic enzymes, including pepsinogen, lysozyme, α-amylase, and hyaluronidase. In addition, human semen inhibits the activity of the proteolytic enzyme trypsin, and this is the result of the presence in the seminal plasma of such proteinase inhibitors as α_1-antitrypsin and α_1-antichymotrypsin. Coagulation and liquefaction vary in different species. For example, the semen of the bull or dog does not coagulate, whereas rodents, such as the rat and guinea pig, ejaculate a firm pellet that does not appear to liquefy (Tauber et al, 1975, 1976). In rodents, the plugs form through the action of an enzyme called vesiculase, which comes from the anterior lobe of the prostate and reacts with seminal vesicle secretions. Because of this action, the anterior lobe of the rodent prostate is also called the coagulating gland. Vesiculase is not identical to thrombin because it does not coagulate fibrinogen, nor does thrombin clot the secretions of the seminal vesicles. Williams-Ashman and associates (1977) have established that vesiculase has transamidase activity, catalyzing the formation of γ-glutamyl-ε-lysine cross-links in a clottable protein derived from the seminal vesicles. This seminal vesicle protein, which serves as a substrate for vesiculase, is a basic substance with a molecular weight of 17,900; it has been characterized as to its physical properties.

In summary, it appears that seminal plasma coagulation and liquefaction are under enzymatic control, but the biologic purpose of this process has not been resolved. Enzymes and proteins of the seminal vesicles and prostate gland are involved in this system. There have been reports that some infertile men may have impairment of the liquefaction process (Bunge and Sherman, 1954; Bunge, 1970; Eliasson, 1973; Amelar et al, 1977).

KEY POINT: COAGULATION AND LIQUEFACTION OF SEMEN

■ PSA is one of several serine proteases secreted by the prostate in high concentrations into the ejaculate. Although its main function may relate to regulation of semen coagulation, it has proved to be a valuable marker of prostate disease states.

PROSTATIC SECRETIONS AND DRUG TRANSPORT

Aumuller and Seitz (1990) have reviewed the secretory mechanism for the sex accessory tissues. Isaacs and associates (1983) have also reviewed the concepts related to the fluid and drug transport properties of the prostate and seminal vesicles. Isaacs has compared the composition and volume of prostatic secretion under basal stimulation and under neurologic stimulation during ejaculation or pilocarpine stimulation. Isaacs calculated that under neurologic stimulation, there is a 205-fold increase in the total potassium, chloride, and sodium output over the basal secretory rate, and he has shown that the prostate is capable of secreting five times its total content of sodium and chloride during this active secretion. These findings show the tremendous transport powers of this system. Smith and Hagopian (1981) have studied the transepithelial voltage changes during prostatic secretion in the dog and have concluded that although sodium may move passively through the plasma in the prostatic fluid during ejaculation, the movements of potassium and chloride ions involve active transcellular transport. Isaacs and associates (1983) have shown that the androgen-induced secretions can be blocked in the presence of estrogen, although the growth properties and biologic properties of the androgen on the prostate are not markedly altered. This would suggest a direct effect of estrogen in blocking a major transport system in the prostate.

Only a few compounds, including ethanol, iodine, and a few antibiotics, are capable of entering the semen by simple diffusion (Reeves, 1982). Drugs entering prostatic secretions have been of interest because of the prevalence of prostatitis and the need for new modalities of chemotherapy. Earlier, Stamey and colleagues had made extensive studies of the ability of chemotherapeutic agents to concentrate in the prostatic fluid of humans and dogs (Hessl and Stamey, 1971; Stamey et al, 1973), and many other investigators have also contributed to this knowledge (Madsen et al, 1968, 1976, 1978; Fowler et al, 1982). Few drugs reach concentrations in the prostatic secretion that approach or surpass their concentrations in blood, but some exceptions are the basic macrolides erythromycin and oleandomycin, sulfonamides, chloramphenicol, tetracycline, clindamycin, trimethoprim, and fluoroquinolones (Reeves, 1982).

In general, these drugs are assumed to pass across the membrane by nonionic diffusion, possibly by lipid solubility, through the membrane; when they reach the more acidic prostatic fluid, they are protonated and acquire a more positive charge. Thus, the charged drugs become relatively trapped within the prostatic secretions. Several factors are critical, including the pK_a of the drug and the pH of the prostatic secretions, as well as the drug binding to proteins in each compartment. Basic drugs would be more positively charged in acidic prostatic fluid than in blood. Slight changes in pH can have large effects on this nonionic diffusion. Samples of prostatic secretions from humans varied widely in pH from 6 to 8, with a mean value of 6.6; however, with prostatic inflammation, the pH tended to be 7 or higher (White, 1975). Although prostatic secretions are slightly acidic, the pH of freshly ejaculated human semen is slightly alkaline (pH 7.3 to 7.7); on standing, semen first becomes more alkaline with the loss of carbon dioxide and then later acidic owing to accumulation of lactic acid. Drugs may be developed in the future that are transported into the prostate as therapeutic agents, as chemoprotectors, or as a route to the semen to regulate fertility; however, more must be learned about the fundamental transport system in and out of the male reproductive tract before such an approach is feasible.

SUGGESTED READINGS

Berezney R, Coffey DS: Nuclear matrix. Isolation and characterization of a framework structure from rat liver nuclei. J Cell Biol 1977;73:616-637.

Bonkhoff H: Analytical molecular pathology of epithelial-stromal interactions in the normal and neoplastic prostate. Anal Quant Cytol Histol 1998;20:437-442.

Campisi J: Senescent cells, tumor suppression, and organismal aging: Good citizens, bad neighbors. Cell 2005;120:513-522.

Cunha GR, Fujii H, Neubauer BL, et al: Epithelial-mesenchymal interactions in prostatic development. I. Morphological observations of prostatic induction by urogenital sinus mesenchyme in epithelium of the adult rodent urinary bladder. J Cell Biol 1983;96:1662-1670.

Cunha GR, Ricke W, Thomson A, et al: Hormonal, cellular, and molecular regulation of normal and neoplastic prostatic development. J Steroid Biochem Mol Biol 2004;92:221-236.

De Marzo AM, Nelson WG, Meeker AK, Coffey DS: Stem cell features of benign and malignant prostate epithelial cells. J Urol 1998;160:2381-2392.

Diamandis EP, Yousef GM: Human tissue kallikreins: A family of new cancer biomarkers. Clin Chem 2002;48:1198-1205.

Ewen ME: Where the cell cycle and histones meet. Genes Dev 2000;14:2265-2270.

Hayward SW: Approaches to modeling stromal-epithelial interactions. J Urol 2002;168:1165-1172.

Hudson DL: Epithelial stem cells in human prostate growth and disease. Prostate Cancer Prostatic Dis 2004;7:188-194.

Laczko I, Hudson DL, Freeman A, et al: Comparison of the zones of the human prostate with the seminal vesicle: Morphology, immunohistochemistry, and cell kinetics. Prostate 2005;62:260-266.

Li L, Zou L: Sensing, signaling, and responding to DNA damage: Organization of the checkpoint pathways in mammalian cells. J Cell Biochem 2005;94:298-306.

Luke MC, Coffey DS: The male sex accessory tissues: Structure, androgen action and physiology. In Knobil E, Neill JD, eds: The Physiology of Reproduction, 2nd ed. New York, Raven Press, 1994:1435-1487.

Nurse P: Cyclin dependent kinases and cell cycle control [Nobel Lecture]. Chembiochem 2002;3:596-603.

Podlasek CA, Barnett DH, Clemens JQ, et al: Prostate development requires Sonic hedgehog expressed by the urogenital sinus epithelium. Dev Biol 1999;209:28-39.

Pollard KJ, Peterson CL: Chromatin remodeling: A marriage between two families? Bioessays 1998;20:771-780.

Shay JW, Wright WE: Senescence and immortalization: Role of telomeres and telomerase. Carcinogenesis 2005;26:867-874.

Thomson AA, Timms BG, Barton L, et al: The role of smooth muscle in regulating prostatic induction. Development 2002;129:1905-1912.

Uzgare AR, Xu Y, Isaacs JT: In vitro culturing and characteristics of transit amplifying epithelial cells from human prostate tissue. J Cell Biochem 2004;91:196-205.

Williams RR, Fisher AG: Chromosomes, positions please! Nat Cell Biol 2003;5:388-390.

KEY POINT: PROSTATIC SECRETIONS AND DRUG TRANSPORT

- Only a few compounds, including ethanol, iodine, and a few antibiotics, are capable of entering the semen by simple diffusion. A few exceptions for drugs are the basic macrolides erythromycin and oleandomycin, sulfonamides, chloramphenicol, tetracycline, clindamycin, trimethoprim, and fluoroquinolones. Perhaps these molecules, because of their lipid solubility, are transported by nonionic diffusion.

Benign Prostatic Hyperplasia: Etiology, Pathophysiology, Epidemiology, and Natural History

CLAUS G. ROEHRBORN, MD • JOHN D. MCCONNELL, MD

ETIOLOGY AND PATHOPHYSIOLOGY

EPIDEMIOLOGY AND NATURAL HISTORY

ETIOLOGY AND PATHOPHYSIOLOGY

Benign prostatic hyperplasia (BPH) is a pathologic process that contributes to, but is not the sole cause of, lower urinary tract symptoms (LUTS) in aging men. Despite intense research efforts in the past five decades to elucidate the underlying etiology of prostatic growth in older men, cause-and-effect relationships have not been established. For example, androgens are a necessary but not a clearly causative aspect of BPH. **Previously held notions that the clinical symptoms of BPH (prostatism) are due simply to a mass-related increase in urethral resistance are too simplistic.** It is now clear that **a significant portion of LUTS is due to age-related detrusor dysfunction.** Bladder outlet obstruction itself may induce a variety of neural alterations in the bladder, which contribute to symptomatology. Moreover, bothersome LUTS may be seen in men with polyuria, sleep disorders, and a variety of systemic medical conditions unrelated to the prostate-bladder unit. Undoubtedly, the constellation of cellular pathologies that give rise to the symptoms of LUTS is far more complex than we currently realize. Only by unraveling these complexities, however, will we be able to design alternative strategies to treat successfully and possibly prevent the adverse impact of BPH on lower urinary tract function.

The nomenclature of voiding dysfunction in aging men is confusing and often inaccurate (Thomas and Abrams, 2000). The term BPH should be used with reference to the histologic process of hyperplasia, which can be demonstrated microscopically. Men with benign prostatic enlargement (BPE) presumably have an increase in total prostate volume because of BPH. BPE may or may not produce clinically significant LUTS and may or may not produce urodynamically proven bladder outlet obstruction. In the ensuing discussion of BPH etiology, we refer to the pathologic process of benign prostatic growth and enlargement.

Etiology of Benign Prostatic Hyperplasia

BPH is but one cause of the LUTS in aging men commonly, and probably incorrectly, referred to as prostatism. Histopathologically, BPH is characterized by an increased number of epithelial and stromal cells in the periurethral area of the prostate. The observation of new epithelial gland formation is normally seen only in fetal development and gives rise to the concept of embryonic reawakening of the stroma cell's inductive potential (Cunha, 1983). The precise molecular etiology of this hyperplastic process is uncertain. **The observed increase in cell number may be due to epithelial and stromal proliferation or to impaired programmed cell death leading to cellular accumulation.** Androgens, estrogens, stromal-epithelial interactions, growth factors, and neurotransmitters may play a role, either singly or in combination, in the etiology of the hyperplastic process.

Hyperplasia

In a given organ, the number of cells, and thus the volume of the organ, is dependent upon the equilibrium between cell proliferation and cell death (Isaacs and Coffey, 1987). An organ can enlarge not only by an increase in cell proliferation but also by a decrease in cell death. **Although androgens and** growth factors stimulate cell proliferation in experimental models, **the relative role of cell proliferation in human BPH is questioned because there is no clear evidence of an active proliferative process.** Although it is possible that the early phases of BPH are associated with a rapid proliferation of cells, the established disease appears to be maintained in the presence of an equal or reduced rate of cell replication. Increased expression of antiapoptotic pathway genes (e.g., *bcl-2*) supports this hypothesis (Kyprianou et al, 1996; Colombel et al, 1998). **Androgens not only are required for normal cell proliferation and differentiation in the prostate but also actively inhibit cell death** (Isaacs, 1984). In the dog, experimental BPH can be produced by androgens combined with estradiol (Walsh and Wilson, 1976; DeKlerk et al, 1979; Berry et al, 1986a; Juniewicz et al, 1994). Despite a significant increase in gland size, there is actually a reduction in the rate of DNA synthesis compared with untreated controls (Barrack and Berry, 1987), indicating that androgens and estrogens both inhibit the rate of cell death. Neural signaling pathways, especially α-adrenergic pathways, may also play a role in balancing cell death and cell proliferation (Anglin et al, 2002; Partin et al, 2003).

The hyperplasia results in a remodeling of the normal prostatic architecture (Untergasser et al, 2005). Epithelial budding from preexisting ducts and the appearance of mesenchymal nodules characterize the early stages of the process, but the tissue phenotype of patients with established disease is highly variable.

BPH may be viewed as a stem cell disease (Barrack and Berry, 1987). Presumably, dormant stem cells in the normal prostate rarely divide, but when they do, they give rise to a second type of transiently proliferating cell capable of undergoing DNA synthesis and proliferation, thus maintaining the number of cells in the prostate. When the proliferating cells mature through a process of terminal differentiation, they have a finite life span before undergoing programmed cell death. In this paradigm, **the aging process induces a block in this maturation process so that the progression to terminally differentiated cells is reduced, reducing the overall rate of cell death.** Indirect evidence for this hypothesis comes from the observation that secretion, one parameter of epithelial cell differentiation, decreases with age, suggesting that the number of differentiated cells capable of secretory activity may be decreasing (Isaacs and Coffey, 1987). A survey of human BPH specimens for a marker of cellular senescence (senescence-associated β-galactosidase [SA-beta-gal]) demonstrated a higher portion of senescent epithelial cells in men with large prostates, suggesting that an accumulation of those cells may play a role in the development of prostate enlargement (Choi et al, 2000). More recent studies support the hypothesis that impaired cell senescence may play a significant role in the etiology of BPH (Castro et al, 2003).

Hormones may exert their influence over the stem cell population not only with advancing age but also during embryonic and neonatal development (Naslund and Coffey, 1986). The size of the prostate may be defined by the absolute number of potential stem cells present in the gland, which in turn may be dictated at the time of embryonic development. Studies in animal models have suggested that **early imprinting of prostatic tissue by postnatal androgen surges is critical to subsequent hormonally induced prostatic growth** (Naslund and Coffey, 1986; Juniewicz et al, 1994). As with the hormonal regulation of adult prostatic tissues, sex steroid hormones may exert their imprinting effect directly or indirectly through a complex series of signaling pathways (Lee and Peehl, 2004).

The Role of Androgens

Although androgens do not cause BPH, the development of BPH requires the presence of testicular androgens during prostate development, puberty, and aging (McConnell, 1995; Marcelli and Cunningham, 1999). Patients castrated prior to puberty or who are affected by a variety of genetic diseases that impair androgen action or production do not develop BPH. It is also known that prostatic levels of dihydrotestosterone (DHT) as well as the androgen receptor (AR) remain high with aging despite the fact that peripheral levels of testosterone are decreasing. Moreover, androgen withdrawal leads to partial involution of established BPH (Peters and Walsh, 1987; McConnell et al, 1994).

Assuming normal ranges, there is no clear relationship between the concentration of circulating androgens and prostate size in aging men. In the Olmsted County cohort (median age 60.9) serum bioavailable testosterone levels were found to decline with increasing age, while the estradiol/bioavailable testosterone ratio increased (Roberts et al, 2004). Bioavailable testosterone correlated negatively and estradiol/bioavailable testosterone ratio positively with prostate volume, but this associated was much less apparent after age adjustment. A much smaller study from Turkey also failed to show a clear relationship between serum androgen levels and prostate size (Tan et al, 2003).

In the brain, skeletal muscle, and seminiferous epithelium, testosterone directly stimulates androgen-dependent processes. **In the prostate, however, the nuclear membrane bound enzyme steroid 5α-reductase converts the hormone testosterone into DHT, the principal androgen in this tissue** (Fig. 86–1) (McConnell, 1995). Ninety percent of total prostatic androgen is in the form of DHT, principally derived from testicular androgens. Adrenal androgens may constitute 10% of total prostatic androgen, although the importance of this stored hormone source in the etiology of BPH is negligible. Inside the cell, both testosterone and DHT bind to the same high-affinity androgen receptor protein (Chatterjee, 2003). DHT is a more potent androgen than testosterone because of its higher affinity for the AR. Moreover, the DHT-receptor complex may be more stable than the testosterone-receptor complex. The hormone receptor then binds to specific DNA binding sites in the nucleus, which results in increased transcription of androgen-dependent genes and ultimately stimulation of protein synthesis. Conversely, androgen withdrawal from androgen-sensitive tissue results in a decrease in protein synthesis and tissue involution. **Besides inactivation of key androgen-dependent genes (e.g., prostate-specific antigen), androgen withdrawal leads to the activation of specific genes involved in programmed cell death** (Kyprianou and Issacs, 1989; Martikainen et al, 1990). Despite the importance of androgens in normal prostatic development and secretory physiology, there is no evidence that either testosterone or DHT serves as the direct mitogen for growth of the prostate in older men. Indeed, neither hormone is mitogenic to cultured prostatic epithelial cells

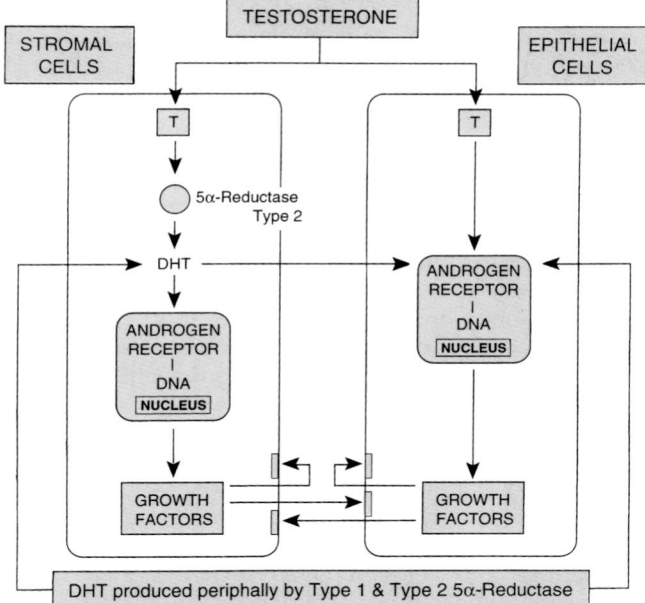

Figure 86–1. Testosterone (T) diffuses into the prostate epithelial and stromal cell. T can interact directly with the androgen (steroid) receptors bound to the promoter region of androgen-regulated genes. In the stromal cell a majority of T is converted into dihydrotestosterone (DHT)—a much more potent androgen—which can act in an autocrine fashion in the stromal cell or in a paracrine fashion by diffusing into epithelial cells in close proximity. DHT produced peripherally, primarily in the skin and liver, can diffuse into the prostate from the circulation and act in a true endocrine fashion. In some cases, the basal cell in the prostate may serve as a DHT production site, similar to the stromal cell. Autocrine and paracrine growth factors may also be involved in androgen-dependent processes within the prostate.

(McKeehan et al, 1984). In the rat ventral prostate, differential gene expression experiments failed to demonstrate direct activation of mitogenic pathways (Wang et al, 1997). However, many growth factors and their receptors are regulated by androgens (see later). Thus, the action of testosterone and DHT in the prostate is mediated indirectly through autocrine and paracrine pathways.

Androgen Receptors.   The prostate, unlike other androgen-dependent organs, maintains its ability to respond to androgens throughout life. In the penis, AR expression decreases to negligible rates at the completion of puberty (Roehrborn et al, 1987; Takane et al, 1991). Thus, despite high circulating levels of androgen, the adult penis loses its ability for androgen-dependent growth. If the penis maintained high levels of AR throughout life, presumably the organ would grow until the time of death. In contrast, AR levels in the prostate remain high throughout aging (Barrack et al, 1983; Rennie et al, 1988). In fact, there is evidence to suggest that nuclear AR levels may be higher in hyperplastic tissue than in normal controls (Barrack et al, 1983). Age-related increases in estrogen, as well as other factors, may increase AR expression in the aging prostate, leading to further growth (or to a decrease in cell death), despite decreasing levels of androgen in the peripheral circulation and "normal" levels of DHT in the prostate.

The potential role of AR mutations, polymorphisms, or other alterations in the pathogenesis of BPH is unclear (Chatterjee, 2003). A polymorphism in the number of CAG repeats (short versus control) in the AR gene has been associated with larger prostate size (Giovannucci et al, 1999a) and an increased risk of surgery (Giovannucci et al, 1999b). However, another study from the Netherlands showed no relationship between the number of CAG repeats and BPH (Bousema et al, 2000). The later study also found no relationship between BPH and vitamin D receptor polymorphisms, although one Japanese study suggested an association (Habuchi et al, 2000b). A more recent study of U.S. men showed a positive correlation between short CAG repeats and prostate volume (Roberts et al, 2004a), but a study of Finnish men found that short CAG repeats were significantly less common in men with BPH compared with control subjects (Mononen et al, 2002). Given the significant variation in reported findings, if short CAG repeats play a role in BPH pathogenesis, it is likely to be minor.

Dihydrotestosterone and Steroid 5α-Reductase. Intraprostatic DHT concentrations are maintained but not elevated in BPH. Initial studies of resected prostatic tissue suggested that prostatic DHT levels were higher in the hyperplastic gland than in normal control tissues. However, the controls used for these early studies were largely accident victims. Ongoing metabolism of DHT after death lowers the level of this androgen in cadaveric tissues. This was clearly shown in a study by Walsh and colleagues (1983) in which prostatic surgical specimens from men without BPH were used as the control. These investigators demonstrated that DHT levels are the same in hyperplastic glands as in normal glands. However, the aging prostate maintains a high level of DHT as well as a high level of AR; thus, the mechanism for androgen-dependent cell growth is maintained. There is little question that androgens have at least a permissive role in the development of the disease process.

Two steroid 5α-reductase enzymes have been discovered, each encoded by a separate gene (Russell and Wilson, 1994). Type 1 5α-reductase, the predominant enzyme in extraprostatic tissues, such as skin and liver, is normally expressed in the 5α-reductase deficiency syndrome and is inhibited by dutasteride but not substantially by finasteride. Type 2 5α-reductase is the predominant prostatic 5α-reductase, although it is also expressed in extraprostatic tissues. Mutations in the type 2 enzyme are responsible for the clinical phenotype observed in the 5α-reductase deficiency syndrome. It is exquisitely sensitive to inhibition by finasteride and dutasteride (Carson and Rittmaster, 2003). Clearly, **the type 2 enzyme is critical to normal development of the prostate and hyperplastic growth later in life.** The role of type 1 5α-reductase in normal and abnormal prostate growth remains to be defined. Given that finasteride produces prostate size reduction identical to that with dual type1/type 2 inhibitors and roughly equivalent to that with castration, it is unlikely that type 1–derived DHT is critical to hyperplastic growth.

Immunohistochemical studies with type 2 5α-reductase specific antibodies show primarily stromal cell localization of the enzyme (Silver et al, 1994b). Epithelial cells uniformly lack type 2 protein, and some basal epithelial cells stain positively. Type 1 5α-reductase protein could not be detected in BPH or prostate cancer using initially available antibodies (Silver et al, 1994a), although trace levels of type 1 messenger RNA (mRNA) have been seen in normal prostates, BPH, and cancer (Shirakawa et al, 2004). A study with a selective type 1 antibody demonstrated positive staining in only 7% of BPH cases (Thomas et al, 2003). In the same study, type 1 enzymatic activity was found in only 2 of 29 BPH specimens.

These data demonstrate that the **stromal cell plays a central role in androgen-dependent prostatic growth and that the type 2 5α-reductase enzyme within the stromal cell is the key androgenic amplification step.** Thus, a paracrine model for androgen action in the gland (see Fig. 86–1) is evident. In addition, it is possible that **circulating DHT produced in the skin and liver may act on prostate epithelial cells in a true endocrine fashion** (McConnell, 1995). If dual type 1/type 2 5α-reductase inhibition has clinical utility over selective type 2 inhibitors, it is likely to be due to inhibition of peripherally produced DHT.

Polymorphisms in the type 2 5α-reductase enzyme (SRD5A2) have been reported, but their linkage to BPH is uncertain. The SRD5A2 gene on chromosome 2p23 frequently encompasses A49T and V89L substitutions and a TA dinucleotide repeat polymorphism. The 89L allele has been associated with lower enzyme activity, whereas the 49T allele has been associated with higher activity. Longer TA repeats are associated with mRNA instability and thus decreased enzyme activity. The number of L alleles, but not testosterone alleles or TA repeats, in one study correlated significantly with the presence of BPH (Salam et al, 2005). In the Olmsted County population, consistent associations between SRD5A2 genotypes and BPH were not demonstrated, although there was a weak correlation between V89L polymorphisms and prostate volume (Roberts et al, 2005).

Androgen withdrawal may partially exert its effect on the prostate through vascular effects (Buttyan et al, 2000; Ghafar et al, 2002b). Castration induces acute and drastic vasoconstriction of blood vessels in the rat prostate (Hayek et al, 1999; Shabisgh et al, 1999). This effect does not appear to be mediated through vascular endothelial growth factor (Burchardt et al, 2000). There is indirect evidence to suggest that abnormalities in the prostatic vascular system produced by other disease states (e.g., diabetes) may be a risk factor of BPH (Berger et al, 2005).

The Role of Estrogens

There is animal model evidence to suggest that estrogens play a role in the pathogenesis of BPH; the role of estrogens in the development of human BPH, however, is less clear. In the dog, where estrogens act synergistically with androgens to produce experimental BPH, estrogen appears to be involved in induction of the AR (Moore et al, 1979). Estrogen may, in fact, "sensitize" the aging dog prostate to the effects of androgen (Barrack and Berry, 1987). The canine prostate contains an abundance of high-affinity estrogen receptor. In the dog, estrogen treatment stimulates the stroma, causing an increase in the total amount of collagen (Berry et al, 1986a, 1986b). There are at least two forms of the estrogen receptor. Estrogen receptor α is expressed by prostate stromal cells, and estrogen receptor β is expressed by prostate epithelial cells (Prins et al, 1998). The estrogenic response of the prostate is determined by the type of estrogen receptor present within the prostatic cells. Experiments in knock-out mice suggest a "constraining influence" of estrogens on the prostate (Krege et al, 1998). In vitro studies suggest that upregulation of estrogen receptor α in cultured prostate stromal cells is also associate with upregulation of fibroblast growth factor 2 (FGF-2), FGF-7, and other growth factors; the addition of androgens downregulated the estrogen receptor and various stroma-derived growth factors (Smith et al, 2000, 2002, 2004).

Serum estrogen levels increase in men with age, absolutely or relative to testosterone levels. There is also suggestive evidence that intraprostatic levels of estrogen are increased in men with BPH. Patients with larger volumes of BPH tend to have higher levels of estradiol in the peripheral circulation (Partin et al, 1991). In the Olmsted County cohort, in men with above median levels of bioavailable testosterone, the serum estradiol level correlated positively with prostate volume, even after adjusting for age (Roberts et al, 2004b). Data on obesity, serum testosterone, estradiol, and prostate volume are conflicting (Zucchetto et al, 2005) Although there are relatively low concentrations of classical high-affinity estrogen receptors in human BPH (Farnsworth, 1999; Sciarra and Toscano, 2000), there may be a sufficient amount for biologic activity.

From experimental studies with aromatase inhibitors it appears that decreases in intraprostatic estrogen in animal models may lead to reduction in drug-induced stromal hyperplasia (Farnsworth, 1999). At present, however, the role of estrogens in human BPH is not as firmly established as the role of androgens. Species variation and cause-effect relationships are problematic.

There are high levels of progesterone receptor in the normal and hyperplastic prostate. However, the role of the progesterone receptor in normal prostatic physiology as well as in BPH remains to be defined.

Regulation of Programmed Cell Death

Programmed cell death (apoptosis) is a physiologic mechanism crucial to the maintenance of normal glandular homeostasis (Kerr and Searle, 1973). Cellular condensation and fragmentation precede phagocytosis and degradation, during which the apoptotic cell is phagocytosed by neighboring cells and degraded by lysosomal enzymes. Apoptosis occurs without activation of the immune system but requires both RNA and protein synthesis (Lee, 1981). In the rat prostate, active cell death occurs naturally in the proximal segment of the prostatic ductal system in the presence of normal concentrations of plasma testosterone (Lee et al, 1990). Androgens (presumably testosterone and DHT) appear to suppress programmed cell death elsewhere in the gland. **Following castration, active cell death is increased in the luminal epithelial population as well as in the distal region of each duct.** Tenniswood (1992) suggested that there is regional control over androgen action and epithelial response, with androgens providing a modulating influence over the local production of growth regulatory factors that varies in different parts of the gland. Members of the transforming growth factor β (TGF-β) family are likely candidates for this regulatory step (Martikainen et al, 1990).

In the rat prostate, at least 25 different genes are induced following castration (Montpetit et al, 1986). Normal glandular homeostasis requires a balance between growth inhibitors and mitogens, which respectively restrain or induce cell proliferation but also prevent or modulate cell death. Abnormal hyperplastic growth patterns, such as BPH, might be induced by local growth factor or growth factor receptor abnormalities, leading to increased proliferation or decreased levels of programmed cell death.

Stromal-Epithelial Interaction

There is abundant experimental evidence to demonstrate that **prostatic stromal and epithelial cells maintain a sophisticated paracrine type of communication.** The growth of canine prostate epithelium can be regulated by cellular interaction with the basement membrane and stromal cells. Isaacs, using a marker of canine prostatic epithelial cell function, demonstrated that epithelial cells grown on plastic quickly lose their ability to secrete this protein (Isaacs and Coffey, 1987). In addition, the cells begin to grow rapidly and change their cytoskeletal staining pattern. In contrast, if the cells are grown on prostatic collagen, they maintain their normal secretory capacity and cytoskeletal staining pattern and do not grow rapidly. This is strong evidence that **one class of stromal cell excretory protein (i.e., extracellular matrix) partially regulates epithelial cell differentiation. Thus, BPH may be due to a defect in a stromal component that normally inhibits cell proliferation, resulting in loss of a normal "braking" mechanism for proliferation.** This abnormality could act in an autocrine fashion to lead to proliferation of stromal cells as well.

Further evidence of the importance of stromal-epithelial interactions in the prostate comes from the elegant developmental studies of Cunha, which demonstrate the importance of embryonic prostatic mesenchyme in dictating differentiation of the urogenital sinus epithelium (Cunha et al, 1983). **The process of new gland formation in the hyperplastic prostate suggests a "reawakening" of embryonic processes in which the underlying prostatic stroma induces epithelial cell development** (Cunha et al, 1983; McNeal, 1990). Many of the prostatic stromal-epithelial interactions observed during normal development and in BPH may be mediated by soluble growth factors or by the extracellular matrix (ECM), which itself has growth factor–like properties. This model is even more intriguing, given the cellular localization of 5α-reductase (and thus DHT production) in the prostate stromal cell (Silver et al, 1994b).

The complexity of the stromal-ECM-epithelial relationship is revealed in studies of the ECM signaling protein CYR61. CRY61 (an early immediate response gene) is an ECM-associated protein that promotes adhesion, migration, and proliferation of epithelial and stromal cells. A variety of growth factors increase the expression of CYR61 in both cell types, and the suppression of CYR61 expression by an antisense oligonucleotide significantly affects normal cell morphology (Sakamoto et al, 2004). CRY61 expression is significantly increased in human BPH tissues and is induced by lysophosphatidic acid (an endogenous lipid growth factor) (Sakamoto et al, 2003, 2004).

As our understanding of stromal-epithelial cell relationships in the prostate increases, it is possible that therapies may be designed to induce regression of established BPH by modulating these autocrine/paracrine mechanisms.

Growth Factors

Growth factors are small peptide molecules that stimulate, or in some cases inhibit, cell division and differentiation processes (Steiner, 1995; Lee and Peehl, 2004). Cells that respond to growth factors have on their surface receptors specific for that growth factor that in turn are linked to a variety of transmembrane and intracellular signaling mechanisms. **Interactions between growth factors and steroid hormones may alter the balance of cell proliferation versus cell death to produce BPH** (Fig. 86–2). Lawson's group was the first to demonstrate that extracts of BPH stimulate cellular growth. This putative prostatic growth factor was subsequently found on sequence analysis to be basic fibroblastic growth factor (bFGF) (Story et al, 1989). Subsequently, a variety of growth factors have been characterized in normal, hyperplastic, and neoplastic prostatic tissue. In addition to bFGF (FGF-2), acidic FGF (FGF-1), Int-2 (FGF-3), keratinocyte growth factor (KGF, FGF-7), transforming growth factors (TGF-β), and epidermal growth factor (EGF) have been implicated in prostate growth. TGF-β is a potent inhibitor of proliferation in normal epithelial cells in a variety of tissues. In models of prostatic cancer, there is evidence that malignant cells have escaped the growth inhibitory effect of TGF-β (McKeehan and Adams, 1988). Similar mechanisms may be operational in BPH (Salm et al, 2000), leading to the accumulation of epithelial cells (Kundu et al, 2000). Growth factors may also be important in modulating the phenotype of the prostate smooth muscle cell (Peehl and Sellers, 1998).

There is mounting evidence of interdependence between growth factors, growth factor receptors, and the steroid hormone milieu of the prostate (Rennie et al, 1988; Lee and Peehl, 2004). Although data on the absolute level of growth factor and growth factor receptors in hyperplastic as opposed to normal tissue are conflicting, it is likely that growth factors play some role in the pathogenesis of BPH. However, further research is necessary to establish the role of growth factors in a disease process in which cellular proliferation is not obvious.

If cellular proliferation is a component of the BPH process, it appears that growth stimulatory factors such as the FGF-1, -2, -7, and -17 families; vascular endothelial growth factor (VEGF); and insulin-like growth factor (IGF)

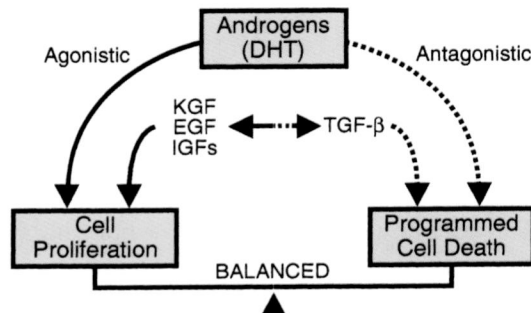

Figure 86–2. Prostate hyperplasia is probably due to an imbalance between cell proliferation and cell death. Androgens play a necessary—but probably permissive—role. Growth factors are more likely to be sites of primary defects. DHT, dihydrotestosterone; EGF, epidermal growth factor; IGF, insulin-like growth factor; KGF, keratinocyte growth factor; TGF, transforming growth factor.

may play a role, with DHT augmenting or modulating the growth factor effects. In contrast, TGF-β, which is known to inhibit epithelial cell proliferation, may normally exert a restraining influence over epithelial proliferation that is lost or downregulated in BPH (Wilding et al, 1989; Sporn and Roberts, 1990, 1991; Peehl et al, 1995; Cohen et al, 2000; Walsh et al, 2002; Lee and Peehl, 2004) . TGF-β1 is a potent mitogen for fibroblasts and other mesenchymal cells but is also an important inhibitor of epithelial cell proliferation (Roberts and Sporn, 1993). TGF-β1 also regulates ECM synthesis and degradation and can induce cells to undergo apoptosis. In addition, TGF-β upregulates the production of basic fibroblast growth factor (bFGF-2), which is known to be an autocrine growth factor for prostate stromal cells (Story et al, 1993), and at least on one prostate smooth muscle cell line (PSMC1), TGF functions as an autocrine mitogen (Salm et al, 2000). Thus, upregulation of TGF-β1 (which is expressed in prostate stromal cells) during BPH would favor expansion of the stromal compartment.

Indirect evidence to support this view comes from studies of reconstituted mouse prostate (Yang et al, 1997). Interestingly, the observation that TGF-β1 may regulate smooth muscle contractile protein expression suggests that TGF-β isoforms may be physiologic regulators of prostatic smooth muscle function (Orlandi et al, 1994). Cohen and colleagues (2000) found that stromal cells isolated from BPH specimens exhibited a blunted TGF-β growth inhibition relative to normal stromal cells and that the blunted response appeared to be due to a reduction in TGF-mediated increase in IGF binding protein 3 (IGFBP-3) expression. TGF-β may stimulate the overexpression of versican (chondroitin sulfate proteoglycan 2) in the ECM through inhibition of key metalloproteases (ADAMTS lineage) that normally degrade versican, leading to accumulation in the ECM (Cross et al, 2005). An increased risk for BPH was described in patients with a codon 10 polymorphism in TGF-β (Li et al, 2004).

The first evidence of increased FGF-2 levels in BPH came from the studies of Begun and coworkers (1995), who demonstrated a two- to threefold elevation of FGF-2 in BPH compared with histologically normal glands. Further studies have demonstrated that both FGF-2 and FGF-7 are overexpressed in BPH tissues (Ropiquet et al, 1999). The major target of FGF-2 is thought to be the stroma itself (autocrine), although transgenic mice overexpressing FGF-2 develop glandular epithelial hyperplasia (Konno-Takahashi et al, 2004). KGF, a member of the FGF family (FGF-7), is produced in prostatic stromal cells (Yan et al, 1992). However, cell surface receptors for stroma-derived KGF are expressed exclusively in epithelial cells. As a result, **FGF-7 (or a homolog) is the leading candidate for the factor mediating the stromal cell–based hormonal regulation of the prostatic epithelium.** There is direct evidence that FGF-7 plays this role in the androgen-dependent mesenchymal-epithelial interactions involved in development of the seminal vesicle (Alarid et al, 1994). Abnormalities in stromal FGF-7 production or epithelial FGF-7 receptor could promote epithelial cell proliferation. Indirect evidence supporting this hypothesis comes from a study of transgenic mice overexpressing FGF-7 that develop atypical prostatic hyperplasia (Kitsberg and Leder, 1996). McKeehan's laboratory demonstrated that FGF-10, a homolog of FGF-7, is expressed at high levels in the rat prostate, specifically in

stromal cells of smooth muscle origin (Lu et al, 1999; Nakano et al, 1999). FGF-10 expression is increased by androgens and may have a mitogenic effect on prostate epithelium. Others studies suggest that cells expressing FGF-7 are localized in the stroma immediately adjacent to the epithelium, suggesting that the epithelial cells may induce FGF-7 expression (Giri and Ittmann, 2000). The paracrine factor most likely responsible for this effect is cytokine interleukin (IL)-1a (Giri and Ittmann, 2000; Lee and Peehl, 2004).

Some investigators have speculated that local hypoxia in the prostate (perhaps from atherosclerosis or other vascular events) is the initial event that induces FGF production (Lee and Peehl, 2004). Further growth of BPH nodules could impede blood flow, leading to further hypoxia (Berger et al, 2003). Hypoxia leads to upregulation of hypoxia inducible factor 1, which in turn increases the secretion of FGF-2 and FGF-7 from stromal cells.

Other growth factors implicated in BPH include FGF-17 (Polnaszek et al, 2004), FGF-10, and VEGF (Walsh et al, 2002). It remains difficult to ascertain which of the growth factors and growth factor receptors are key mediators of the BPH disease process and which are bystanders.

A unique animal model provides additional evidence that FGF-like factors may be involved in the etiology of BPH. **A transgenic mouse line expressing the Int-2/FGF-3 growth factor demonstrated androgen-sensitive epithelial hyperplasia in the male mouse prostate histologically similar to human and canine BPH** (Tutrone et al, 1993).

Insulin-like growth factors, binding proteins, and receptors also appear to be important modulators of prostatic growth, at least as it relates to cell growth in culture (Peehl et al, 1995; Lee and Peehl, 2004). A transgenic mouse model with overexpression of IGF-1 demonstrated prostate gland enlargement (Konno-Takahashi et al, 2003). Studies of BPH tissue demonstrate a higher concentration of IGF-2 in the periurethral area than in the peripheral zone (Monti et al, 2001). A study of Chinese men demonstrated a significant correlation between circulating IGF-1 and IGFBP-3 level and BPH (Chokkalingam et al, 2002), but a study of the Olmsted County cohort failed to demonstrate any relationship between serum IGF-1 and prostate volume (Roberts et al, 2003).

Other Signaling Pathways

Sympathetic signaling pathways are important in the pathophysiology of LUTS, as reviewed subsequently. In addition, there is increasing evidence that sympathetic pathways may be important in the pathogenesis of the hyperplastic growth process. Alpha blockade, in some model systems, can induce apoptosis (Anglin et al, 2002; Partin et al, 2003). α-Adrenergic pathways can also modulate the smooth muscle cell phenotype in the prostate (Lin et al, 2001). All the components of the renin-angiotensin system (RAS) are present in prostatic tissue and may be activated in BPH (Dinh et al, 2001a, 2001b, 2002; Fabiani et al, 2001, 2003; Nassis et al, 2001). Either with or without sympathetic modulation, local RAS pathways may contribute to cell proliferation and smooth muscle contraction.

The early growth response gene 1 (EGR-1) transcription regulation pathway was found to active in a BPH cell line (Mora et al, 2005). Also of interest is the finding that α2-macroglobulin, a large protein that binds prostate-specific antigen (PSA) and many growth factors, is very highly expressed in human prostate and is upregulated in BPH (Lin et al, 2005). Trapping and inactivation of inhibitory molecules could promote growth pathways.

The Potential Role of Inflammatory Pathways and Cytokines in Benign Prostatic Hyperplasia

An additional source of growth factors in human BPH tissue may be the inflammatory cell infiltrates seen in many men with BPH. In the 1990s, descriptive studies suggested a link between inflammation and BPH-related growth. Theyer and associates (1992) reported extensive infiltration of human BPH tissues by activated T cells. Peripheral blood and tumor infiltrating T cells are known to express VEGF, a potent epithelial mitogen (Blotnik et al, 1994; Freeman et al, 1995). T cells are known to produce and secrete a variety of other growth factors, including HB-EGF and bFGF/FGF-2 (Blotnik et al, 1994). Thus, T cells present in the local prostate environment were thought to be capable of secreting potent epithelial and stromal mitogens that promote stromal and glandular hyperplasia.

In the last 5 years, specific inflammatory mediator pathways have been studied in detail to elucidate the potential role of these pathways in BPH pathogenesis. A large number of cytokines and their receptors are seen in BPH tissue (Konig et al, 2004). Specifically, significant levels of IL-2, IL-4, IL-7, IL-17, interferon γ (IFN-γ), and their relevant receptors are found in BPH tissue (Kramer et al, 2002; Steiner et al, 2003a, 2003b). IL-2, IL-7, and IFN-γ stimulate the proliferation of prostatic stromal cells in vitro (Kramer et al, 2002). Prostatic epithelial cell senescence results in increased expression of IL-8, which can promote proliferation of nonsenescent epithelial and stromal cells (Castro et al, 2004). Macrophage inhibitory cytokine 1 is expressed in normal prostate tissue but significantly downregulated in BPH (Kakehi et al, 2004; Taoka et al, 2004). Chronic inflammation in BPH is also associated with focal upregulation of cyclooxygenase 2 (COX-2) in the glandular epithelium (Wang et al, 2004). To date, however, no firm cause-and-effect relationships have been established between prostatic inflammation and related cytokine pathways and stromal-epithelial hyperplasia.

Genetic and Familial Factors

There is substantial evidence that **BPH has an inheritable genetic component.** Sanda and colleagues (1994) conducted a retrospective case-control analysis of surgically treated BPH patients and control subjects at Johns Hopkins. The BPH patients were men whose resected prostate weights were in the highest quartile (greater than 37 g) and whose age at prostatectomy was in the lowest quartile. **The hazard-function ratio for surgically treated BPH among first-degree male relatives of the BPH cases compared with the first-degree male relatives of the controls was 4.2 (95% confidence interval [CI], 1.7 to 10.2), demonstrating a very strong relationship** (Table 86-1). The results did not appear to be due to differences in health-seeking behavior between the two groups. A segregation analysis showed that the results were most consistent with an **autosomal dominant inheritance pattern.** Utilizing this model, **approximately 50% of men undergoing prostatectomy for BPH at less than 60 years of age could be attributable to inheritable form of disease.** In contrast, **only about 9% of men undergoing prostatectomy for BPH at more than 60 years of age would be predicted to have a familial risk.** In addition, monozygotic twins demonstrate a higher concordance rate of BPH than dizygotic twins (Partin et al, 1994).

In a community-based cohort study of more than 2000 men, Roberts and colleagues (1997) found an elevated risk of moderate to severe urologic symptoms in men with a family history of an enlarged prostate and a family history of BPH compared with those with no history. Analysis of the subjects who participated in the U.S. finasteride clinical trial identified 69 men who had three or more family members with BPH, including the proband (Sanda et al, 1996). Regression analysis demonstrated that **familial BPH was characterized by large prostate size, with a mean prostate volume of 82.7 mL in men with hereditary BPH compared with 55.5 mL in men with sporadic BPH.** Serum androgen levels and the response to 5α-reductase inhibition were similar in familial and sporadic BPH. A more recent familial aggregation study in the finasteride database confirmed that a strong family history of early onset and large prostate volume is more likely to be associated with inheritance of risk than symptom severity or other factors (Pearson et al, 2003).

These studies clearly demonstrate the presence of a familial form of BPH and suggest the presence of a gene contributing to the pathogenesis of the disease. The studies of Miekle and coworkers (1997, 1999) also support a genetic basis for BPH. Preliminary studies demonstrate evidence of DNA mutations (White et al, 1990), DNA hypomethylation

Table 86-1.   Family History of Early-Onset Benign Prostatic Hyperplasia (BPH) Increases Risk of Clinical Significant BPH

BPH (%) * Relatives	Frequency of Clinical		Age-Adjusted		Significance‡	
	Case Relatives	Control Relatives	Odds Ratio (unadjusted)†	Relative Risk of Clinical BPH‡	Chi-Square	P Value
All first-degree male relatives	28.3	8.6	4.2 (1.7-10.2)	4.4 (1.9-9.9)	13.36	0.0003
Fathers of proband	33.3	13.2	3.3 (1.1-10.2)	3.5 (1.3-9.5)	5.94	0.0148
Brothers of proband	24.2	3.9	8.0 (1.6-40.5)	6.1 (1.3-29.7)	6.85	0.0089

*Percent of informative male relatives with history of prostatectomy (open or transurethral) for BPH (60 case relatives and 105 control relatives).
†Chi-square analysis of proportions; Taylor 95% confidence intervals in parentheses.
‡Cox proportional hazards survival model. Censored outcome—prostatectomy. Time variable—age at death or current age. Values in parentheses indicate 95% confidence intervals.
From Sanda MG, Beaty TH, Stutzman RE, et al: Genetic susceptibility of benign prostatic hyperplasia. J Urol 1994;152:115-119.

(Bedford and van Helded, 1987), and abnormalities of nuclear matrix protein expression (Partin et al, 1993), miscellaneous genetic polymorphisms (Werely et al, 1996; Konishi et al, 1997; Habuchi et al, 2000a), and abnormal expression of the Wilms' tumor gene (WT-1) (Dong et al, 1997) in human BPH. However, the specific gene or genes involved in familial BPH or that contribute to the risk of significant prostatic enlargement in sporadic disease remain to be elucidated.

Other Etiologic Factors

Androgens and soluble growth factors are clearly not the only important factors for the development of BPH. All mammalian prostates studied have testosterone, DHT, and AR as well as most of the known growth factor signaling pathways; however, only dog and man develop BPH. Interestingly, another glandular organ that remains androgen responsive throughout life, the seminal vesicle, does not develop hyperplasia. Obviously, other mechanisms or cofactors must be present in these two unique species making them susceptible to the disease. Nonandrogenic substances from the testis, perhaps transmitted through the vas deferens or deferential blood vessels, for example, may play some role (Darras et al, 1979; Dalton et al, 1990). Rats with intact testes treated with exogenous androgen demonstrate a greater degree of prostatic growth than castrated rats treated with androgen. Sutkowski and coauthors (1993) have demonstrated that human spermatocele fluid is mitogenic to both human prostatic epithelial and stromal cells in culture. Similar results have been seen in castrated versus testes-intact dogs treated with exogenous androgen and exogenous testosterone and estradiol combination (Juniewicz et al, 1994). In addition to increases in prostate weight, the incidence of histologic BPH was significantly higher in the dogs with intact testes. Grayhack and colleagues (1998) have identified a putative substance that may be a candidate for such a factor.

Prolactin has long been speculated to play a role in BPH because of the known effects of this hormone on prostate cells in vitro. Transgenic mice overexpressing the prolactin gene develop significant enlargement of the prostate (Wennbo et al, 1997). However, despite the documented presence of prolactin receptors in the human prostate and low circulating levels of the hormone, the role of prolactin in human prostate disease is unclear.

Molecular profiling, fingerprinting, microarrays, and high-throughput screening tools have uncovered new genes, as well as known genes not previously associated with BPH. Preliminary findings from the Getzenberg laboratory (Prakash et al, 2002; Shah and Getzenberg, 2004) and other groups (Fromont et al, 2004; Dhanasekaran et al, 2005) suggest that new markers for BPH and new therapeutic targets will be forthcoming in the next few years.

Pathophysiology

The pathophysiology of BPH is complex (Fig. 86–3). **Prostatic hyperplasia increases urethral resistance, resulting in compensatory changes in bladder function.** However, the elevated detrusor pressure required to maintain urinary flow in the presence of increased outflow resistance occurs at the expense of normal bladder storage function. **Obstruction-induced changes in detrusor function, compounded by**

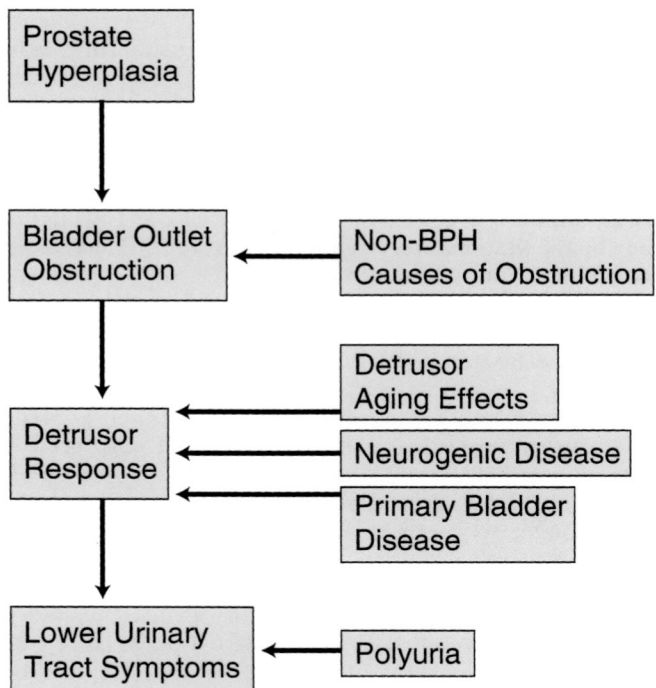

Figure 86–3. The pathophysiology of benign prostatic hyperplasia (BPH) involves complex interactions between urethral obstruction, detrusor function, and urine production.

age-related changes in both bladder and nervous system function, lead to urinary frequency, urgency, and nocturia, the most bothersome BPH-related complaints. Thus, an understanding of BPH pathophysiology requires detailed insight into obstruction-induced bladder dysfunction.

Pathology

Anatomic Features. McNeal (1978) demonstrated that **BPH first develops in the periurethral *transition zone* of the prostate.** The transition zone consists of two separate glands immediately external to the preprostatic sphincter. The main ducts of the transition zone arise on the lateral aspects of the urethral wall at the point of urethral angulation near the verumontanum. Proximal to the origin of the transition zone ducts are the glands of the *periurethral zone* that are confined within the preprostatic sphincter and course parallel to the axis of the urethra. All BPH nodules develop either in the transition zone or in the periurethral region (McNeal, 1978, 1990). Although early transition zone nodules appear to occur either within or immediately adjacent to the preprostatic sphincter, as the disease progresses and the number of small nodules increases, they can be found in almost any portion of the transition or periurethral zone. However, **the transition zone also enlarges with age, unrelated to the development of nodules** (McNeal, 1990).

One of the unique features of the human prostate is **the presence of the prostatic capsule, which plays an important role in the development of LUTS** (Caine and Schuger, 1987). In the dog, the only other species known to develop naturally occurring BPH, symptoms of bladder outlet obstruction and urinary symptoms rarely develop because the canine prostate lacks a capsule. Presumably the capsule transmits the "pressure" of tissue expansion to the urethra and leads to an increase in urethral resistance. Thus, the clinical symptoms of BPH in man may be due not only to age-related increases in prostatic size but also to the unique anatomic structure of the human gland. **Clinical evidence of the importance of the capsule can be found in series that clearly document that incision of the prostatic capsule (transurethral incision of the prostate) results in a significant improvement in outflow obstruction, despite the fact that the volume of the prostate remains the same.**

The size of the prostate does not correlate with the degree of obstruction. Thus, other factors such as dynamic urethral resistance, the prostatic capsule, and anatomic pleomorphism are more important in the production of clinical symptoms than the absolute size of the gland. In some cases, predominant growth of periurethral nodules at the bladder neck gives rise to the "middle lobe" (Fig. 86–4). The middle lobe must be of periurethral origin because there is no transition zone tissue in this area. It is not clear whether middle lobe

growth occurs at random in men with BPH or whether there is an underlying genetic susceptibility to this pattern of enlargement.

Histologic Features. BPH is a true **hyperplastic** process. Histologic studies document an increase in the cell number (McNeal, 1990). In addition, thymidine uptake studies in the dog clearly indicate an increase in DNA synthesis in experimentally induced BPH (Barrack and Berry, 1987). The term benign prostatic **hypertrophy** is pathologically incorrect.

McNeal's studies demonstrate that the majority of **early periurethral nodules are purely stromal in character** (McNeal, 1990). These small stromal nodules resemble embryonic mesenchyme with an abundance of pale ground substance and minimal collagen. It is unclear whether these early stromal nodules contain mainly fibroblast-like cells or whether differentiation toward a smooth muscle cell type is occurring. In contrast, **the earliest transition zone nodules represent proliferation of glandular tissue** that may be associated with an actual reduction in the relative amount of stroma (Fig. 86–5). The minimal stroma seen initially consists

Figure 86–4. Gross appearance of hyperplastic prostatic tissue obstructing the prostatic urethra forming "lobes." **A,** Isolated middle lobe enlargement. **B,** Isolated lateral lobe enlargement. **C,** Lateral and middle lobe enlargement. **D,** Posterior commissural hyperplasia (median bar). (From Randall A: Surgical Pathology of Prostatic Obstruction. Baltimore, Williams & Wilkins, 1931.)

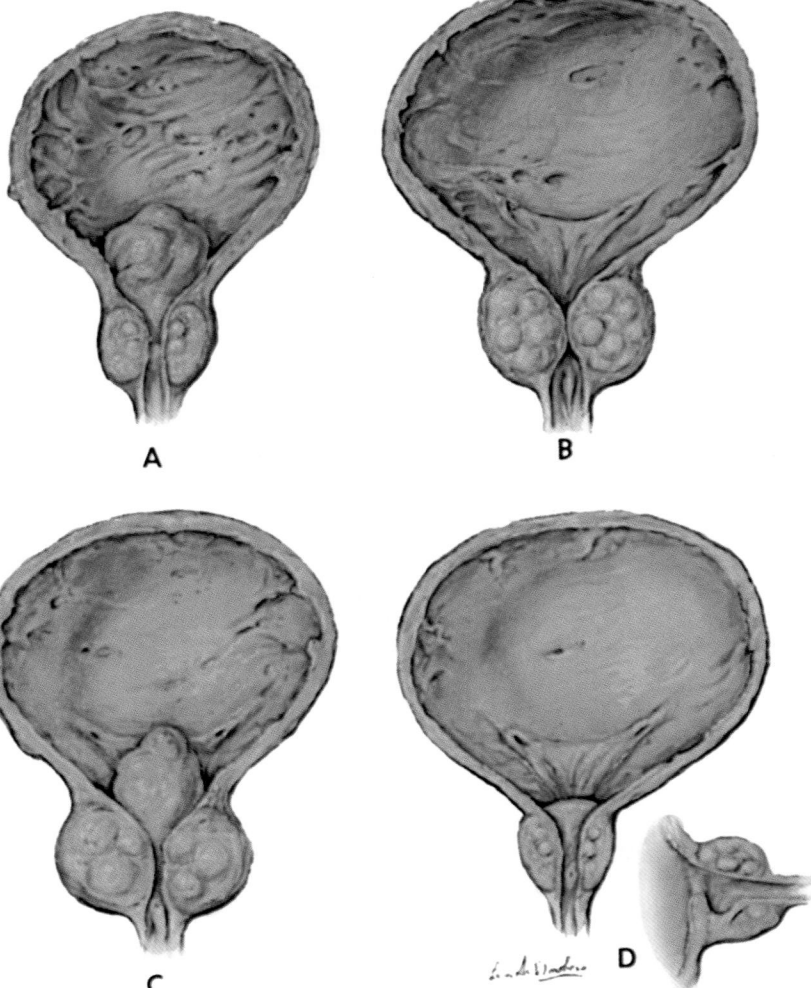

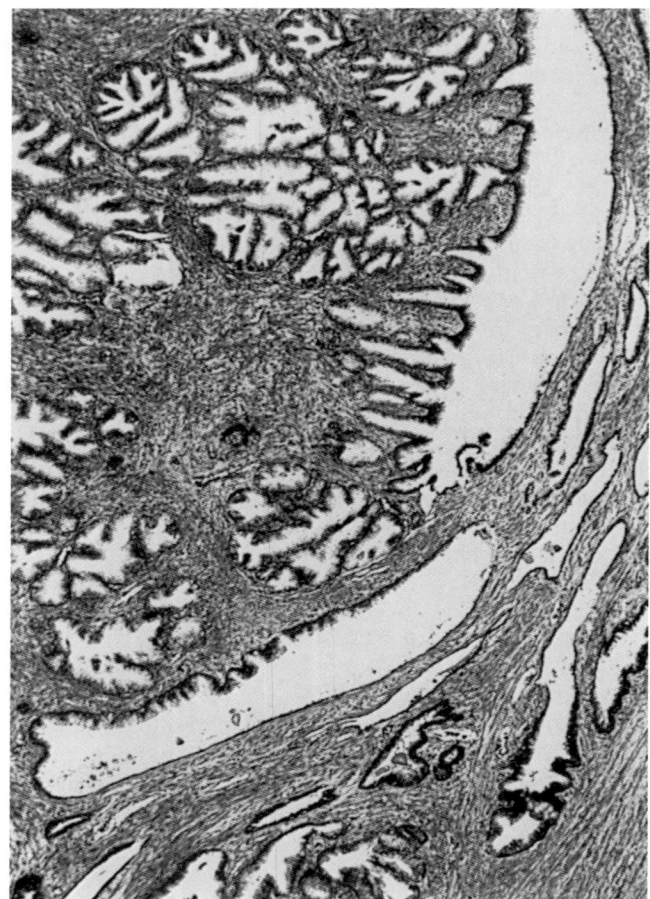

Figure 86–5. Larger glandular nodule (upper left) with focus of stromal hyperplasia. Tangent ducts bordering nodule show epithelial hypertrophy and formation of new gland branches, which are seen exclusively on wall of duct that faces nodule. Hematoxylin and eosin, ×70. (From Bostwick DG: Pathology of the Prostate. New York, Churchill Livingstone, 1990.)

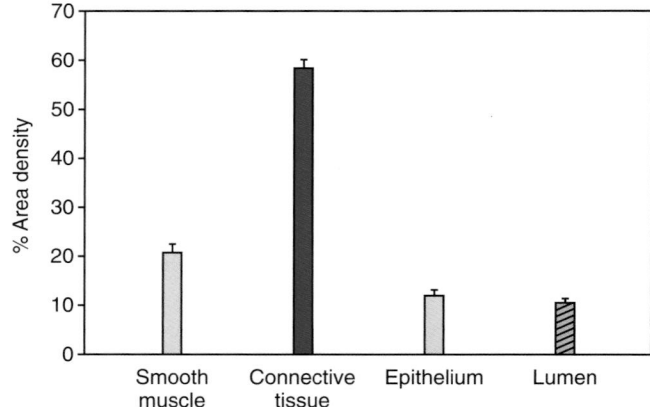

Figure 86–6. Prostate sections obtained from men with symptomatic benign prostatic hyperplasia were analyzed by double immunoenzymatic staining and quantitative image analysis. The percent area density of smooth muscle and connective tissue is significantly greater than glandular epithelium and glandular lumen area density (mean ± SEM). (From Shapiro E, Hartanto V, Lepor H: Anti-desmin vs. anti-actin for quantifying the area density of prostate smooth muscle. Prostate 1992;20:259.)

There is significant pleomorphism in stromal-epithelial ratios in resected tissue specimens. Studies from primarily **small resected glands demonstrate a predominance of fibromuscular stroma** (Shapiro et al, 1992b). Larger glands, predominantly those removed by enucleation, demonstrate primarily epithelial nodules (Franks, 1976). However, an increase in stromal-epithelial ratios does not necessarily indicate that this is a "stromal disease"; stromal proliferation may well be due to "epithelial disease."

Importance of Prostatic Smooth Muscle

Regardless of the exact proportion of epithelial to stromal cells in the hyperplastic prostate, there is no question that **prostatic smooth muscle represents a significant volume of the gland** (Shapiro et al, 1992a) (Fig. 86–6). Although the smooth muscle cells in the prostate have not been extensively characterized, presumably their contractile properties are similar to those seen in other smooth muscle organs. The spatial arrangement of smooth muscle cells in the prostate is not optimal for force generation; however, there is no question that **both passive and active forces in prostatic tissue play a major role in the pathophysiology of BPH** (Shapiro et al, 1992a). The factors that determine passive tone in the prostate remain to be elucidated. The series elastic elements in the stromal and epithelial cells and (most important) the ECM contribute to passive tissue force, independent of active smooth muscle contraction. However, **stimulation of the adrenergic nervous system clearly results in a dynamic increase in prostatic urethral resistance. Blockade of this stimulation by α-receptor blockers clearly diminishes this response.** However, α-blockade does not decrease passive tension in the prostate, which may be an equal determinant of urethral resistance.

Several additional observations on the prostatic stromal/smooth muscle cell are important. It is generally assumed that the stromal cells are resistant to the effects of androgen withdrawal. In short-term studies, androgen ablation appears to affect primarily the epithelial cell population.

primarily of mature smooth muscle, not unlike that of the uninvolved transition zone tissue. These **glandular nodules are apparently derived from newly formed small duct branches** that bud off from existing ducts, leading to a totally new ductal system within the nodule. This type of **new gland formation is quite rare** outside embryonic development. This proliferative process leads to a tight packing of glands within a given area as well as an increase in the height of the lining epithelium. There appears to be hypertrophy of individual epithelial cells as well. Again, the observed increase in transition zone volume with age appears to be related not only to an increased number of nodules but also to an increase in the overall size of the zone.

During the first 20 years of BPH development, the disease may be predominantly characterized by an increased number of nodules, and the subsequent growth of each new nodule is generally slow (McNeal, 1990). Then a second phase of evolution occurs in which there is a significant increase in large nodules. In the first phase, the glandular nodules tend to be larger than the stromal nodules. In the second phase, when the size of individual nodules is increasing, the size of glandular nodules clearly predominates.

In general, however, stromal cells have much slower turnover rates than epithelial cells. If the effect of androgen ablation is primarily to increase cell death rates, a decrease in stromal cell numbers may not be appreciated until a year or more of therapy. Thus, further study is required to determine whether the stromal cell is really resistant to androgen withdrawal. Likewise, it cannot be assumed that hormonal therapy has no effect on the stroma even if stromal cell volumes are not decreased. In a variety of smooth muscle cell systems (e.g., vascular and myometrial), contractile proteins, neuroreceptors, and ECM proteins are regulated by a variety of hormones and growth factors. In vitro, androgens have been shown to modulate the effects of α agonists on prostate smooth muscle cells (Smith et al, 2000). Thus, a given therapy may affect stromal cell function without decreasing the absolute number or volume of cells.

Studies of human tissue samples by Lin and colleagues (2000) have clearly shown that the smooth muscle cells from men with BPH have a significant downregulation of smooth muscle myosin heavy chain and a significant upregulation of nonmuscle myosin heavy chain. This myosin expression pattern is typical of dedifferentiated smooth muscle and indicates either proliferation or loss of normal modulation pathways.

Active smooth muscle tone in the human prostate is regulated by the adrenergic nervous system (Schwinn, 1994; Roehrborn and Schwinn, 2004). The α_1-adrenoreceptor nomenclature has been standardized (Hieble et al, 1995) to reconcile differences in nomenclature based on pharmacologic and molecular studies. **Receptor binding studies clearly demonstrate that the α1A is the most abundant adrenoreceptor subtype present in the human prostate** (Lepor et al, 1993a, 1993b; Price et al, 1993; Roehrborn and Schwinn, 2004). **Moreover, the α1A receptor clearly mediates active tension in human prostatic smooth muscle** (Lepor et al, 1993a). It is still unclear whether other factors may regulate smooth muscle contraction. Endothelin and endothelin receptors (Kobayashi et al, 1994a, 1994b; Imajo et al, 1997; Walden et al, 1998) have been reported in human prostate. However, the physiologic role of this potent contractile agent in prostate smooth muscle function remains to be defined. Various components of the kallikrein-kinin system (e.g., bradykinin) may play a role in the regulation of both smooth muscle proliferation and contraction in the prostate (Walden et al, 1999; Srinivasan et al, 2004). The presence of type 4 and type 5 phosphodiesterase isoenzymes in the prostate implies that phosphodiesterase inhibitors may be appropriate candidate therapies for BPH-related LUTS (Uckert et al, 2001).

The role of adrenergic stimulation in the prostate may exceed simple smooth muscle contraction. Adrenergic neurotransmitters are known to regulate expression of contractile protein genes in cardiac myocytes (Kariya et al, 1993) and to be involved in the development of cardiac hypertrophy (Matsui et al, 1994). Interestingly, evidence suggests that testosterone may regulate the expression of adrenergic receptors, at least in the kidney (Gong et al, 1995). It is possible that adrenergic neurotransmitters may play a role in prostatic smooth muscle cell *regulation* as well as contraction (Smith et al, 2000). α-Adrenergic blockade in patients with documented BPH leads to a significant downregulation of normal contractile protein gene expression, specifically smooth muscle myosin heavy chain (Lin et al, 2001).

Autonomic nervous system overactivity may contribute to LUTS in men with BPH. McVary and coworkers (2005) demonstrated that autonomic nervous system activity, as measured by a standard set of physiologic tests, plasma, and urinary catecholamines, correlates positively with symptom score and other BPH measures. Serum norepinephrine increase after tilt predicted prostate size (transition zone).

The Bladder's Response to Obstruction

Current evidence suggests that the bladder's response to obstruction is largely an adaptive one. However, it is also clear that many lower tract symptoms in men with BPH or prostate enlargement are related to obstruction-induced changes in bladder function rather than to outflow obstruction directly. Approximately one third of men continue to have significant voiding dysfunction after surgical relief of obstruction (Abrams et al, 1979). Obstruction-induced changes in the bladder are of two basic types. First, the **changes that lead to detrusor instability or decreased *compliance* are clinically associated with symptoms of frequency and urgency** (Andersson, 2003). Second, the **changes associated with decreased *detrusor contractility* are associated with further deterioration in the force of the urinary stream, hesitancy, intermittency, increased residual urine,** and (in a minority of cases) detrusor failure. Acute urinary retention should not be viewed as inevitable result of this process. Many patients presenting with acute urinary retention have more than adequate detrusor function, with evidence of a precipitating event leading to the obstruction.

Much of our knowledge of the detrusor's response to obstruction is based upon experimental animal studies. Limited information is available on the natural history of the human bladder's response to obstruction. Gosling has demonstrated that **the major endoscopic detrusor change, trabeculation, is due to an increase in detrusor collagen** (Gosling and Dixon, 1980; Gosling et al, 1986). Severe trabeculation is associated with significant residual urine (Barry et al, 1993), suggesting that incomplete emptying may be due to increased collagen rather than impaired muscle function. Severe trabeculation, however, is seen in fairly advanced disease. In experimental animal models, **the initial response of the detrusor to obstruction is the development of smooth muscle hypertrophy** (Levin et al, 1995, 2000). It is likely that this **increase in muscle mass, although an adaptive response to increased intravesical pressure and maintained flow, is associated with significant intra- and extracellular changes in the smooth muscle cell that lead to detrusor instability and in some cases impaired contractility.** Obstruction also induces changes in smooth muscle cell contractile protein expression, impaired energy production (mitochondrial dysfunction), calcium signaling abnormalities, and impaired cell-to-cell communication (Levin et al, 1995, 2000).

There is considerable evidence that the response of the detrusor smooth muscle cell to stress (increased load related to outlet obstruction) is not as adaptive as the response of skeletal muscle to stress. In the latter case, a relatively normal repertoire of contractile protein genes are upregulated and an increased number of normally organized contractile units assemble in the muscle cell. In the detrusor smooth muscle

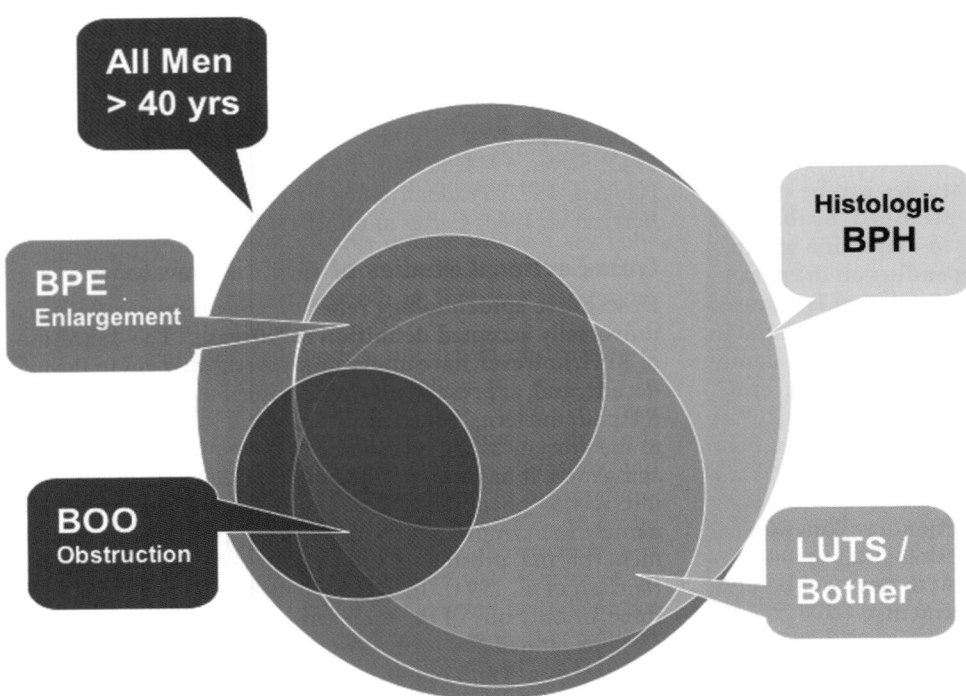

Figure 86–8. Diagram showing the relationship between histologic benign prostatic hyperplasia (BPH), lower urinary tract symptoms (LUTS), benign prostatic enlargement (BPE), and bladder outlet obstruction (BOO). The sizes of the circles do not represent actually proportions but rather illustrate the partial overlap between the different disease definitions.

points have been established that allow differentiation between disease absent or present states (e.g., one might argue that a prostate volume over 30 mL constitutes clinical BPH, but others might argue for a higher or lower cutoff point; similar observations apply for symptoms and degrees of obstruction). **Thus, rather than describing truly the prevalence of a disease in populations, one can describe the distribution of certain attributes of such disease in different populations stratified by age.** Figure 86–9 illustrates the different estimates of prevalence of disease when different definitions are applied ranging from autopsy prevalence to a combination of clinical threshold parameters and insurance examination data (Berry et al, 1984; Garraway et al, 1991; Chute et al, 1993; Gu et al, 1994; Jolleys et al, 1994; Bosch et al, 1995a; Guess, 1995; Moon et al, 1995; Overland et al, 2001).

Symptom Severity and Frequency

From a pragmatic point of view, studies of symptom severity and frequency are of greatest importance in a disease that is rarely fatal and is characterized by its effect on the quality of life. The development, validation, and translation with cultural and linguistic validation of the standardized, self-administered seven-item American Urological Association (AUA) symptom index (also known as the International Prostate Symptom Score [I-PSS]) has been a pivotal event in the clinical research on LUTS and BPH (Barry et al, 1992a, 1992b, 1992c; O'Leary et al, 1992). With the total score running from 0 to 35 points, patients scoring 0 to 7 points are classified as mildly symptomatic, those scoring from 8 to 19 points as moderately symptomatic, and those scoring 20 to 35 points as severely symptomatic. The instrument is an integral part of virtually every epidemiologic study as well as treatment studies in the field, and the availability of validated transla-

tions in many common languages allows cross-cultural comparisons of unprecedented scope. Socioeconomic factors do not seem to influence responses to the questionnaire (Moon et al, 1994), and fundamentally similar responses are obtained when the questionnaire is self-administered, read to the patient, mailed in, or administered in some other way (Barry et al, 1995a, 1995b). However, there is no question that subtle differences in comprehension of the translated questionnaire as well as different perception of the symptoms, willingness to admit to the symptoms, and other factors are the cause for cross-cultural differences in symptom severity reported in the literature. Figure 86–10 shows the prevalence of at least moderate to severe symptoms stratified by decade of life as reported in 11 cross-sectional population-based studies from around the world (Garraway et al, 1991; Chute et al, 1993; Hunter et al, 1994, 1996; Norman et al, 1994; Bosch et al, 1995a; Moon et al, 1995; Tsukamoto et al, 1995; Sagnier et al, 1996; Overland et al, 2001).

A very large international investigation of LUTS in Asian men was undertaken by Homma and colleagues (1997) in which 7588 men from Japan, China, Taiwan, Korea, the Philippines, Thailand, Singapore, Pakistan, India, and Australia were queried. The finding of 18%, 29%, 40%, and 56% of men in their 40s, 50s, 60s, and 70s having moderate to severe symptoms is in line with the other studies reported both from Asia and from Europe and North America. In addition to the major community-based studies listed, other studies have been published with similar findings but often done under less stringent conditions (Nacey et al, 1995; Tay et al, 1996). **Despite the significantly different proportion of men admitting to moderate to severe symptoms, a clear trend toward an increase in symptom scores with advancing age is noticeable in all reported studies.**

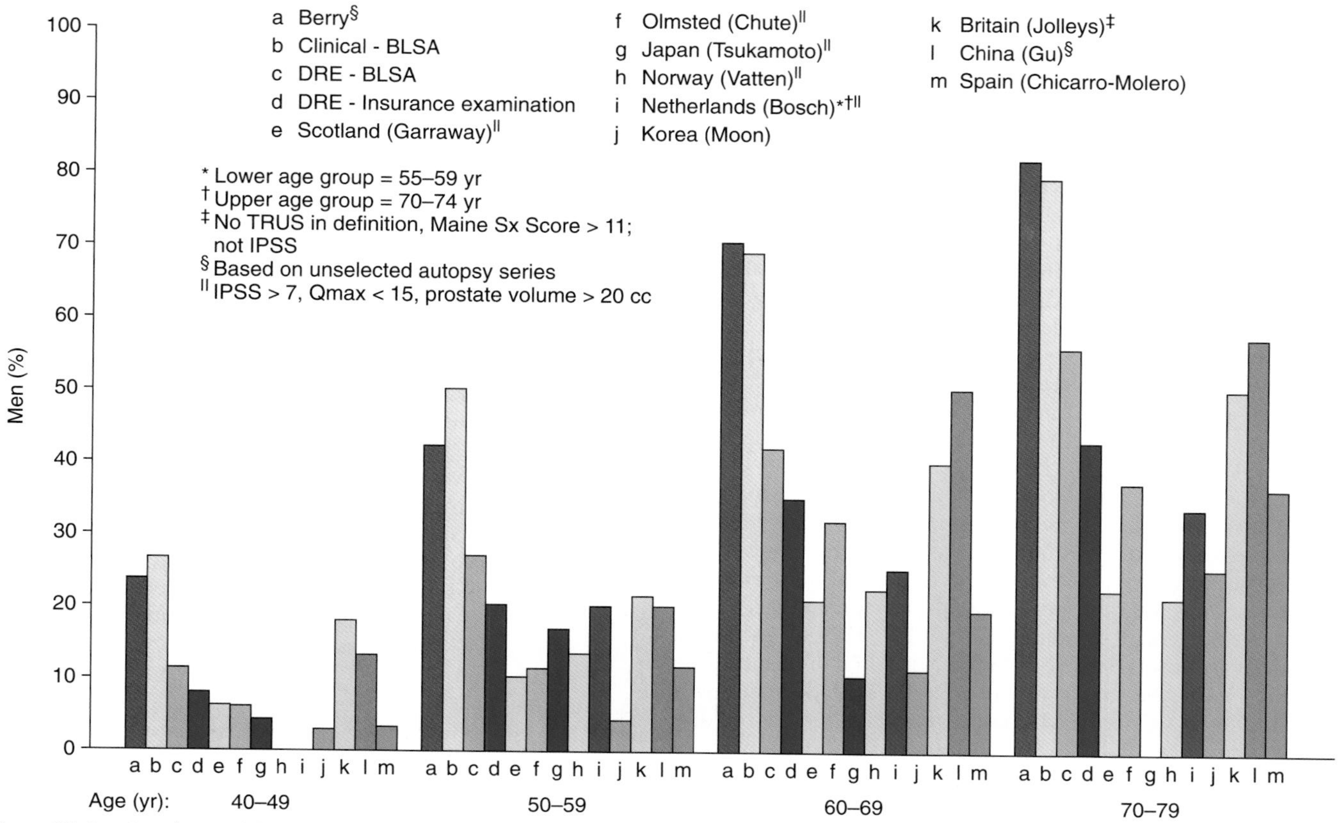

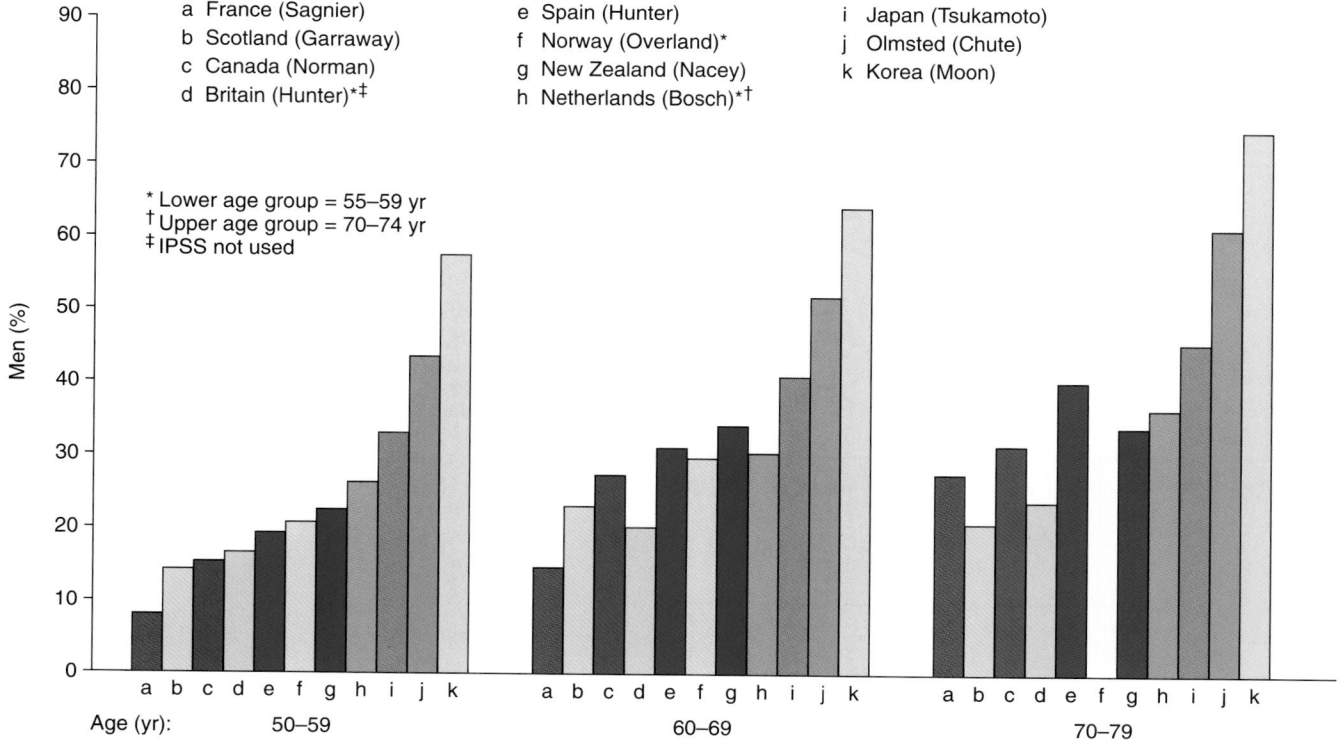

Figure 86–9. Prevalence of disease using autopsy series, clinical diagnosis, low maximum flow rate, palpable prostatic enlargement by DRE, and community-based studies. BLSA, Baltimore Longitudinal Study of Aging; DRE, digital rectal examination; IPSS, International Prostate Symptom Score ; TRUS, transrectal ultrasonography. (Data from Berry et al, 1984; Garraway et al, 1991; Chute, Panser et al, 1993; Gu et al, 1994; Jolleys et al, 1994; Bosch et al, 1995a; Guess, 1995; Moon et al, 1995; Overland et al, 2001.)

Figure 86–10. Prevalence of at least moderate to severe symptoms stratified by decade of life as reported in cross-sectional population-based studies from around the world (Garraway et al, 1991; Chute et al, 1993; Hunter et al, 1994; Norman et al, 1994; Bosch et al, 1995a; Moon et al, 1995; Tsukamoto et al, 1995; Hunter et al, 1996; Sagnier et al, 1996; Homma et al, 1997; Overland et al, 2001).

Bother, Interference, and Health-Related Quality of Life

Bother and interference with activities of daily living related to LUTS are equally if not more important than the enumeration of symptom frequency and severity alone (Garraway et al, 1993; Tsang and Garraway, 1993; Roberts et al, 1994b). Embarrassment related to symptoms has been found to be an important determinant in seeking medical care (Roberts et al, 1994b). LUTS and clinical BPH affect overall quality of life as measured, for example, with the Medical Outcomes Trust Short Form 36 (SF-36) only marginally (Hunter et al, 1995). Accordingly, several instruments were developed and validated to assess bother, interference, and the disease-specific quality of life and sexual function (Epstein et al, 1992; Barry et al, 1995; Hansen et al, 1995; Lukacs et al, 1995; O'Leary et al, 1995; Donovan et al, 1996). These instruments have not been as widely applied to cross-sectional descriptive epidemiologic studies as the I-PSS score. However, as observed for symptom severity and frequency, both bother and interference scores increase with advancing age, and disease-specific health-related quality of life (HRQOL) measures are significantly worse in men with higher symptom frequency and severity ratings in population-based studies done in Olmsted County, Minnesota; Forth Valley, Scotland; France; and a small fishing village in Japan (Shimamaki-mura) (Girman et al, 1998).

Prostate Size

Prostate size can be estimated by DRE, although the reliability across observers is in general considered poor (Roehrborn et al, 1997). In addition, DRE tends to underestimate true prostate size as determined by TRUS or other imaging modalities. The magnitude of the underestimation increases with increasing prostate size from 25% up to 50% or more (Roehrborn et al, 1997). For the purpose of epidemiologic studies, TRUS and MRI measurements are preferred, although MRI measurements are somewhat expensive when attempting cross-sectional examinations of populations. **TRUS volume measurements using the prolate ellipsoid volume formula are the most widely accepted measure of prostate volume with reasonable statistical performance characteristics, particularly when performed by a single or several well-trained examiners** (Sech et al, 2001).

In general, in all cross-sectional studies prostate volume as assessed by TRUS has been found to increase slowly but steadily with advancing age. The slight differences in the absolute volume measures and the different slopes of increase with advancing age may be caused by differences in the population examined as follows (Fig. 86–11).

A cohort of 344 men between 40 and 60 years old with no evidence of BPH enrolled in an alopecia study had baseline endorectal coil MRI measurements (Roehrborn et al, 2000b). Mean total prostate volume (TPV) increased from 31.3 to 33.7, 36.1, and 43.1 mL in increment of 5 years. MRI tends to yield prostate volume measurements approximately 10% larger compared with TRUS. A series of 100 men aged 40 to 80 years without BPH or LUTS underwent TRUS measurements of TPV and transition zone volume (TZV). TPV increased from 22.1 to 29.1, 41.5, and 43.2 mL by decade and TZV from 7.2 to 9.9, 19.0, and 19.6 mL . A cross-sectional study of 611 Norwegian men from 55 to 70 years of age exhibited increases in

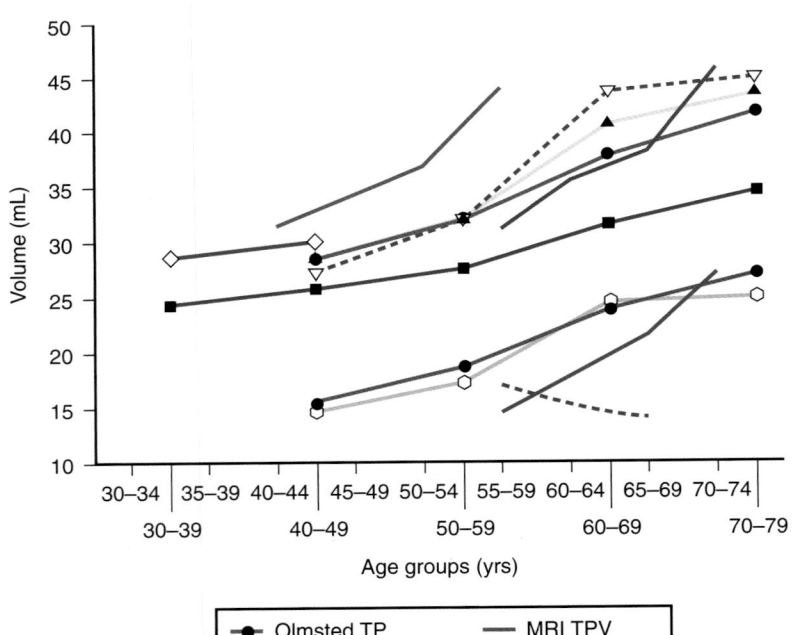

Figure 86–11. Mean estimates for total prostate volume (TPV) and transitional zone volume (TZV) of the prostate based on one autopsy series (Berry et al, 1984), one series of baseline magnetic resonance imaging (MRI) measurements in men with alopecia (Roehrborn et al, 2000b), and cross-sectional population-based studies (Torp-Pedersen et al, 1988; Oesterling et al, 1993; Bosch et al, 1994; Benaim et al, 1998; Chicharro-Molero et al, 1998; Overland et al, 2001).

TPV from 26.5 to 31.0 and 32.0 mL in increments of 5 years (Overland et al, 2001), and Jakobsen and colleagues (1988) examined patients between 30 and 50 years by TRUS, the mean TPV being 23.9 and 25.7 mL per decade of life. TPV and TZV were assessed in 1104 men older than 40 years in a Spanish cross-sectional study, yielding increases from 23.4 to 41.9 mL for TPV and from 7.9 to 21.9 mL for TZV (Chicharro-Molero et al, 1998). Finally, the Olmsted County Study of Urinary Symptoms in Men provided baseline data on men from 40 to 79 years of age (Oesterling et al, 1993).

Overall, TPV increased in these cross-sectional studies from approximately 25 mL for men in their 30s to 35 to 45 mL for men in their 70s, and TZV increased from 15 to 25 mL for similarly aged men. In fact, the similarities between the TZV measurements done in Spain, Dallas, and the Netherlands are striking (see Fig. 86–11).

Measures of Obstruction

Subvesical obstruction can be measured only by invasive pressure-flow studies; nonintubated free flow rates provide at best an indirect measure for the probability of obstruction being present (Abrams, 1995). **Unfortunately, no large-scale cross-sectional studies have been done employing pressure-flow tests because of the invasive and costly nature of the test, and it is unlikely that significant data sets will ever become available.**

It is commonly accepted that a maximum flow rate of less than 10 mL/sec indicates a high probability of obstruction and a flow rate of greater than 15 mL/sec indicates a low probability, with 10 to 15 mL/sec presenting an intermediate range. The utility of this categorization is reduced by several observations. First, the maximum flow rate is somewhat dependent on the voided volume (Girman et al, 1993). This has prompted some to propose a nomogram to correct for this phenomenon; however, at present no single nomogram is accepted universally (Garrelts, 1956, 1957, 1958; Scott and McIlhaney, 1961; Beck and Gaudin, 1969; Susset et al, 1973; Siroky et al, 1979, 1980; Drach and Steinbronn, 1986; Haylen et al, 1989). A high degree of diurnal variability (Golomb et al, 1992) and within-subject day-to-day variability (Barry et al, 1995c) further reduces the utility of flow rate recording in defining disease.

Aging men and women experience a decrease in the maximum urinary flow rate, which is nearly linear in nature. In the Olmsted County study the median flow rate decreased from 20.3 mL/sec for men 40 to 44 years old to 11.3 mL/sec for men 75 to 79 years old (Girma et al, 1993), and similar declines have been reported from other cross-sectional studies. When applying combined thresholds such as at least moderate symptoms of greater than 7 points on the I-PSS score and a maximum flow rate of less than 15 mL/sec, in the Olmsted County study 17% of men in their 50s, 27% of men in their 60s, and 35% of men in their 70s would fall into such category (Jacobsen et al, 1995a, 1995b), versus 14.4%, 28.6%, and 38.7% of men in the respective age groups in the Spanish population-based study (Chicharro-Molero et al, 1998).

Analytic Epidemiologic Studies

Analytic epidemiologic studies address the search for determinants of a disease. Inasmuch as a clear disease definition is lacking, such a search could attempt to find determinants for LUTS, prostate growth, or bladder outlet obstruction, consistent with the previously outlined concepts. The presence of functioning testes at the time of puberty (hormonal factor) as a required permissive element has long been established and accepted (McConnell, 1991), and age has been shown to be the most critical determinant of all aspects of this complex entity. Numerous other demographic and environmental factors have been suggested as risk factors or contributors to the disease process. When evaluating the associations identified, one has to ask critically whether or not other factors could contribute to the association without there being a cause-effect relationship. For example, it seems intuitive that the husbands and family members of nurses are more likely to seek medical care and practice preventive medicine. Therefore, the detection rates of prostate cancer in a cohort of nurses' husbands might be higher not because of a truly higher incidence rate of cancer but because of an increased rate of seeking medical attention and an increase in the number of *diagnosed* cancers. Such pitfalls are abundant in epidemiologic studies and have to be suspected and carefully ruled out.

Religion

The case-control study by Morrison (1978), the cohort study by Lytton and coworkers (1968), and the Normative Aging Study (Glynn et al, 1985a, 1985b) all revealed Jewish religion to be associated with a higher prostatectomy rate (2.2- to 2.6-fold increase). The fact, however, that Jewish religion is not associated with an increase in the *diagnosis* of BPH allows the speculation that Jewish patients are more likely to see a physician or to be offered surgical therapy.

Socioeconomic Factors

Araki and coauthors (1983) found higher rates of BPH in higher income groups, whereas Glynn and associates (1985) reported higher rates of surgery in lower income groups. One could argue that higher income groups might have better access to health care and lower income groups might submit more readily to the suggestion of a surgical procedure. Education and socioeconomic status do not influence responses to the I-PSS (Moon et al, 1994; Badia et al, 2001), but they do appear to influence both expectations from treatment for BPH and perception of improvement, with patients in higher income strata requiring a larger drop in symptom scores following treatment to perceive subjectively similar levels of improvement (Padley et al, 1997). This finding suggests at least some impact of socioeconomic factors if not in the growth of the prostate or measures of obstruction but probably in the perception of symptoms. Data from the Olmsted County study suggest a relationship between care-seeking behavior and physician visit and retirement status. Bivariate analysis suggested significant associations between a propensity to seek care for physical reasons and retirement (odds ratio [OR] 2.0; 95% CI, 1.1 to 2.6), age of 65 years or older (OR, 1.9; 95% CI, 1.5 to .4), incomplete high school education (OR, 1.6; 95% CI, 1.1 to 2.2), and an annual income of less than \$25,000 (OR, 1.4; 95% CI, 1.1 to 1.9). Multivariable logistic regression analysis demonstrated that retired men were more likely to have a high propensity to seek care (OR, 1.7; 95% CI, 1.2 to 2.4), with the other variables no longer being significant (Roberts et al, 1997a).

Sexual Activity and Vasectomy

Ekman (1989) suggested that the increase in the fibromuscular stroma is a result of sexual activity, and many authors since then have attempted to find relevant associations. Morrison (1992) reported a 49% reduction in risk for prostatectomy in widowed versus single men. A similar association could not be verified by other authors. Cross-sectional data from the Olmsted County study suggest that the frequency of ejaculation has no effect on LUTS, peak urinary flow rates, or prostate volume; the apparent protective association appears to be an artifact caused by the confounding effects of age (Jacobsen et al, 2003). The decrease in sexual ability and frequency of sexual activity with advancing age, exactly when the prevalence of BPH increases, in fact might suggest a reverse relationship, namely a causative effect of BPH on sexual function (Altwein and Keuler, 1992).

There is evidence suggesting a strong correlation between the severity of LUTS and impairment of sexual function, that is, erectile dysfunction (ED), as well as ejaculatory distur-

bances (Boyle et al, 2003; Chung et al, 2003; Rosen et al, 2003). Cross-sectional questionnaire-based data from various countries suggest that ED and ejaculatory disturbances increase with advancing age but also within each decade of life with increasing LUTS symptom severity (Fig. 86–12). Although these correlations do not necessarily imply a causative mechanism, it is possible that similar pathophysiologic events underlie the development of both problems in the aging male, the most obvious being ischemia in both the genital and lower urinary tract organs (McVary, 2005).

Sidney (1987) analyzed the Kaiser Permanente database and initially found a risk ratio (RR) of 1.2 for the diagnosis of BPH among men who had a vasectomy. However, after 5 years of follow-up, the RR was 0.97 and not significant. There does not appear to be a relationship between vasectomy and BPH development or prostate size (Jakobsen et al, 1988), and in the Massachusetts Male Aging Study, Meigs and colleagues (2001) did not find that vasectomy increased the risk of being diagnosed with BPH.

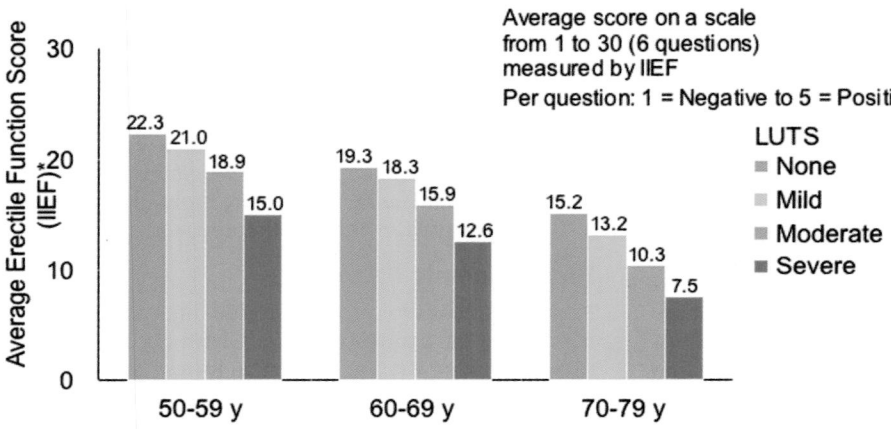

Base: Men sexually active/sexual intercourse during past 4 weeks, *as measured by IIEF.

A

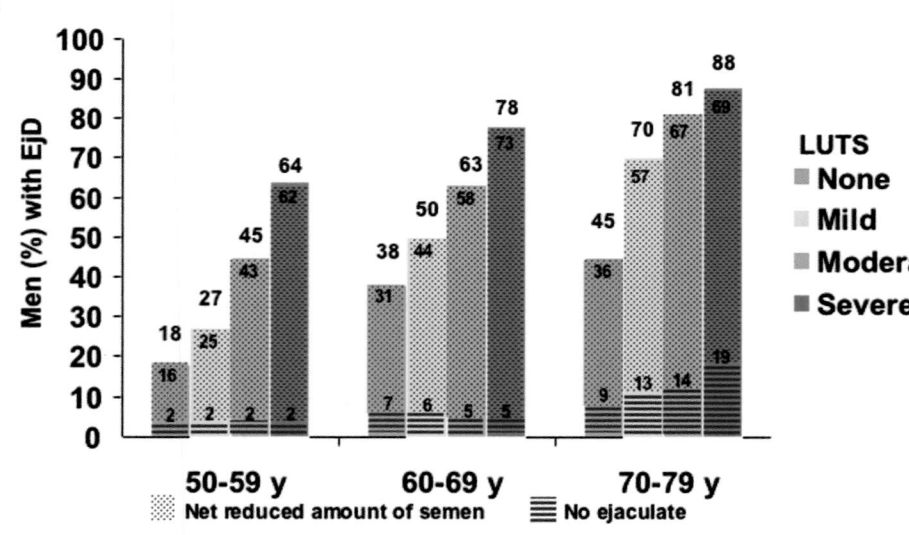

Base: Men who have erections, *As measured by DAN-PSS *sex*.

B

Figure 86–12. Erectile function (**A**) decreases and ejaculatory disturbances (EjD) (**B**) increase with advancing age, but within each decade of life they also decrease and increase, respectively, with increasing severity of lower urinary tract symptoms (LUTS). IIEF, International Index of Erectile Function; DAN-PSS, Danish Prostatic Symptom Score. (From Rosen R, Altwein J, Boyle P, et al: Lower urinary tract symptoms and male sexual dysfunction: The multinational survey of the aging male [MSAM-7]. Eur Urol 2003;44:637-649.)

Alcohol and Liver Cirrhosis

Alcohol may decrease plasma testosterone levels and production and increase clearance of testosterone (Chopra et al, 1973). **Despite of this hypothetical reason for a lower incidence of BPH, inverse relationships have been described.** Both Morrison (1992) and Sidney and colleagues (1991a, 1991b) reported a multivariate adjusted RR of 0.49 and age-adjusted RR of 0.75, respectively, for the risk of having surgery for BPH when consuming more than three glasses of alcohol per day. However, one might argue that the poorer health in heavy drinkers might bias physicians against surgery. Glynn and coauthors (1985a, 1985b), in fact, found no increased risk for either the clinical diagnosis or surgical rates.

Of five studies examining the relationship between liver cirrhosis and BPH based on autopsy material, four found a lower prevalence of BPH in men with cirrhosis (Bennett et al, 1950; Stumpf and Wilens, 1953; Robson, 1966; Frea et al, 1987); one study—admittedly with some design flaws—found a higher prevalence (Wu, 1942). Because most cirrhosis cases are alcohol induced, separation of the effects of alcohol versus cirrhosis is virtually impossible.

Hypertension

The sympathetic nervous system, through α-adrenergic fibers and receptors, plays an important role in both hypertension and the symptoms of BPH. However, because both hypertension and LUTS/BPH increase with advancing age, it is difficult to prove a causal relationship between these two conditions (Boyle and Napalkov, 1995). The previously cited studies by Glynn (Glynn et al, 1985a, 1985b) and Sidney (Sidney et al, 1991a, 1991b) did not find an association. In a small clinic cohort study with methodologic flaws, Pressler and associates (1997) reported an increase in the incidence of hypertension from 15% to 18% and 31% for men with mild, moderate, and severe symptoms. Autonomic hyperactivity has been implicated in the development of both LUTS and ED in the aging male, but conclusive clinical data are lacking (McVary, 2005). Further studies are needed to validate some form of a cause-and-effect relationship.

Smoking

Smoking cigarettes appears to increase both testosterone and estrogen levels because of the nicotine level and thus should have a positive and inductive effect on the development of BPH. However, severe smoking causes other health problems, and surgery rates are probably a poor indicator of a possible correlation as physicians are biased against surgery in heavy smokers. Seitter and Barrett-Connor (1992) indeed found no correlation between smoking and prostatectomy rates, and Glynn and colleagues (1985a, 1985b) failed to identify a correlation between smoking and the clinical diagnosis of BPH. Sidney and associates (1991) observed 16,000 men over 15 years and found a negative correlation between being a smoker at baseline and subsequent risk of prostatectomy. Daniell (1993) examined the records of 345 patients who underwent prostatectomy and found smaller gland volumes in smokers and a lower age-adjusted prevalence of ever-smokers compared with a control group. Roberts and others examined this issue in the Olmsted County study (Roberts et al, 1994a) and later in a Japanese population (Roberts et al, 1997b). In Olmsted County, only 16% of the over 2000 men were current smokers, which appears low but understandable considering the population mix in Rochester, Minnesota. A biphasic association was found, with light to moderate smokers being less likely to have moderate to severe LUTS and heavy smokers at least the same risk as never smokers.

An update from the Olmsted County study suggests that smoking is associated with decreased urinary flow rates and moderate to severe symptoms but not with enlarged prostate volume or increasing serum PSA (Rule et al, 2005). This is in contrast to earlier studies suggesting a relationship between smoking and prostate size (Kupeli et al, 1997). **Any relationships between current or past smoking and LUTS/BPH are likely to be weak and of limited clinical significance.**

Diet, Obesity, and Body Mass Index

Chyou and colleagues (1993) examined 33 food items in relationship to prostatectomy rates and found only beef intake significantly associated. Araki and associates (1983) reported an increased clinical diagnosis of BPH in men with higher milk consumption and lower consumption of green and yellow vegetables. **Overall, there is no convincing evidence that any dietary factors play a major role in the development of LUTS/BPH.**

Many investigators evaluated the relationship between body habitus, body mass index (BMI), and obesity and LUTS/BPH. **There are plausible biologic considerations: adipose tissue is the main source of aromatization of testosterone to estrogen, and men with lower BMI have higher serum testosterone levels** (Eldrup et al, 1987). Several caveats must be mentioned: DRE is less likely to yield a diagnosis of BPH and prostate enlargement in very obese patients because of anatomic obstacles, and patients with high BMI may be biased against surgical interventions.

BMI was negatively associated with surgically treated BPH in the Kaiser Permanente cohort study (Sidney et al, 1991) and with a clinical diagnosis of BPH in the normative aging study (Glynn et al, 1985a, 1985b). In contrast, in a study of 68 men the average prostate weight increased both with age and with increasing obesity together with an increase in serum estradiol levels (Soygur et al, 1996). Daniell (1993) also found larger adenomas in more obese men undergoing prostatectomy. Both latter studies reported a positive correlation between obesity and prostate size but none between obesity and symptom severity.

Men aged 40 to 75 years who were participants in the Health Professionals Follow-up Study and who were without a prior diagnosis of cancer or prostatectomy provided data on weight, height, and waist and hip circumferences. After adjustment for age, smoking, and BMI, abdominal obesity was related to prostatectomy (OR = 2.38) and frequent urinary symptoms among those without prostatectomy (OR = 2.00). BMI, hip circumference, and waist-to-hip ratio were not associated with BPH independently of waist circumference. **These results suggest that abdominal obesity in men may increase the frequency and severity of urinary obstructive symptoms and may increase the likelihood that such obese men will undergo a prostatectomy** (Giovanucci et al, 1994).

Hammarsten and Hogstedt (1999) examined 250 patients with LUTS and found non–insulin-dependent diabetes mellitus, hypertension, tallness, obesity, high insulin, and low high-density lipoprotein cholesterol levels to be risk factors for the development of BPH. They suggested a causal relationship between high insulin levels and the development of BPH and hypothesized increased sympathetic nerve activity in men with BPH. In a hospital-based case-control study overweight was modestly inversely related to BPH. The hypothesis of reduced testosterone levels in obese individuals may explain the different BPH risk and need to be tested (Zucchetto et al, 2005).

The evidence at present suggests a positive relationship between obesity and prostate volume and LUTS, and the risk of prostatectomy has been reported to be either lower or higher with increasing BMI.

Medications

Very limited information is available. **Cold medications containing α-sympathomimetic drugs exacerbate LUTS by the expected effect on the smooth muscles of the bladder outlet. A careful analysis of the data from the Olmsted County study demonstrated that daily use of antidepressants, antihistamines, or bronchodilators is associated with a 2- to 3-point increase in the I-PSS compared with age-matched nonusers and daily use of antidepressants with a decrease in the age-adjusted flow rate** (Su et al, 1996).

Correlations between Parameters

As noted, all relevant parameters such as symptom severity and frequency, bother, interference, disease-specific health-related quality of life (HRQOL), maximum flow rate, and prostate volume tend to worsen with advancing age. However, reported correlations between these parameters as well as urodynamic pressure-flow studies are in general weak with some exceptions. Strong correlations exists between measures of symptom severity and frequency (I-PSS score), bother, disease-specific HRQOL, and interference scores (Barry et al, 1995a, 1995b; Girman et al, 1999) (Fig. 86–13).

Weak numerical correlations can arise artifactually, regardless of whether true physiologic relationships exist (Girman, 1998). Correlations are further affected by intraindividual variability of measured parameters, day-to-day variability, measurement errors associated with the technique or equipment, or the natural history of the condition itself (Bruskewitz et al, 1982; Diokno et al, 1992; Golomb et al, 1992; Barry et al, 1995c; Sagnier et al, 1996).

It is furthermore crucial to consider the population utilized to evaluate correlations. A correlation is easier identified if patients exhibiting the full spectrum of the parameters of interest are included. In most LUTS/BPH studies, however,

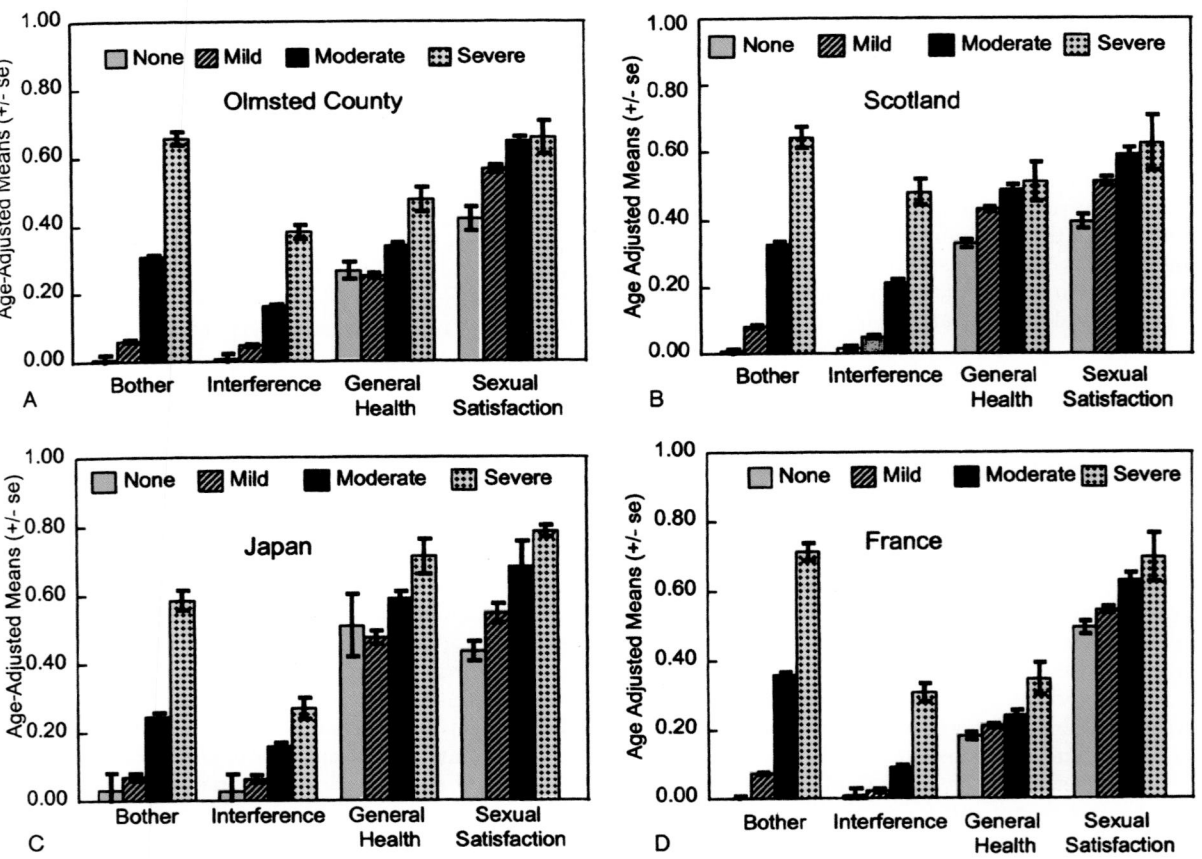

Figure 86–13. Age-adjusted means of disease-specific health-related quality of life (HRQOL) measures after transformation to a 0 to 1 scale stratified by levels of symptom severity and frequency (International Prostate Symptom Score). (From Girman CJ, Jacobsen SJ, Tsukamoto T, et al: Health-related quality of life associated with lower urinary tract symptoms in four countries. Urology 1998;51:428-436.)

patients are excluded on the basis of thresholds imposed, making it more difficult for a significant correlation to emerge. There are many examples in clinical medicine where weak numerical correlations exist but strong clinical relationships are well accepted (Wilson and Cleary, 1995).

The absence of meaningful baseline correlations for symptoms, flow rate, and prostate volume in a tightly controlled population of men with LUTS and BPH enrolled in a BPH treatment study is shown in Table 86–2.

An example of how restriction of the full range of parameters affects correlations is shown in Figure 86–14. Volunteers without known prostatic diseases were asked to have an AUS score and flow rate determined. When all data are considered,

a clear relationship exists with the maximum flow rate decreasing with increasing symptom severity (r = 0.4; P < .05). However, when only the patients typically seen in a BPH study are considered, namely those with a score above 10 points and a maximum flow rate between 5 and 15 mL/sec, the correlation of that limited cohort is very weak (r = 0.08; not significant) because of the limited range of observation permitted on both scales, and the regression line becomes flat.

The correlations observed between symptoms, flow rate, and prostate volume in true community-based population studies without artificially imposed entry criteria are consequently somewhat higher than those seen in BPH clinic or trial populations. In the Olmsted County study, after adjusting for age, the odds of moderate to severe symptoms were 3.5 times greater for men with prostatic enlargement (more than 50 mL) than for men with smaller prostates, and the odds were similarly increased (2.4-fold) for men not achieving a peak urinary flow rate of 10 mL/sec (Girman et al, 1995). Men with enlarged prostates were about twice as likely to have bother related to symptoms (OR 2.4) or activity interference (OR 1.8) as men with smaller prostates (Girman et al, 1999). In a similar study from the Netherlands, Bosch and colleagues (1995a) reported numerically weak but statistically significant correlations between the I-PSS and TPV (r = 0.19, P < .001), peak flow rate (r = −0.18, P < .001) and postvoid residual urine volume (r = 0.25, P < .001).

Although weak correlations between prostate volume and symptoms as well as flow rate have been accepted, more recently attention focused on correlations between the transition zone of the prostate and physiologic measures. A stronger correlation between transition zone and symptoms (r = 0.48, P = .03) and peak urine flow (r = −0.34, P = .05) was reported first by Kaplan and coauthors (1995), who also showed a significant correlation between transition zone index (TZV/TPV) and symptoms (r = 0.75), peak urine flow (r =

Table 86–2. **Correlation Table between Baseline Parameters in a Benign Prostatic Hyperplasia Treatment Study of 2800 Men Older than 50 years, an I-PSS Score >12, Qmax <15 mL/sec, Serum PSA between 1.5 and 10 ng/mL, and Total Prostate Volume (TPV) >30 mL (Transition Zone Volume [TZV] Not Specified)**

	PSA	Qmax	I-PSS	TPV	TZV
Age	0.092	−0.078	−0.069	0.152	0.154
	<0.0001	<0.0001	<0.0001	<0.0001	<0.0001
PSA		−0.031	−0.016	0.384	0.352
		0.111	0.423	<0.0001	<0.0001
Qmax			−0.117	−0.059	−0.047
			<0.0001	<0.001	<0.05
IPSS				0.020	0.005
				0.293	0.761
TPV					0.775
					<0.0001

Note the lack of strong correlations except for age and serum PSA versus volume between parameters.
I-PSS, International Prostate Symptom Score; PSA, prostate-specific antigen.

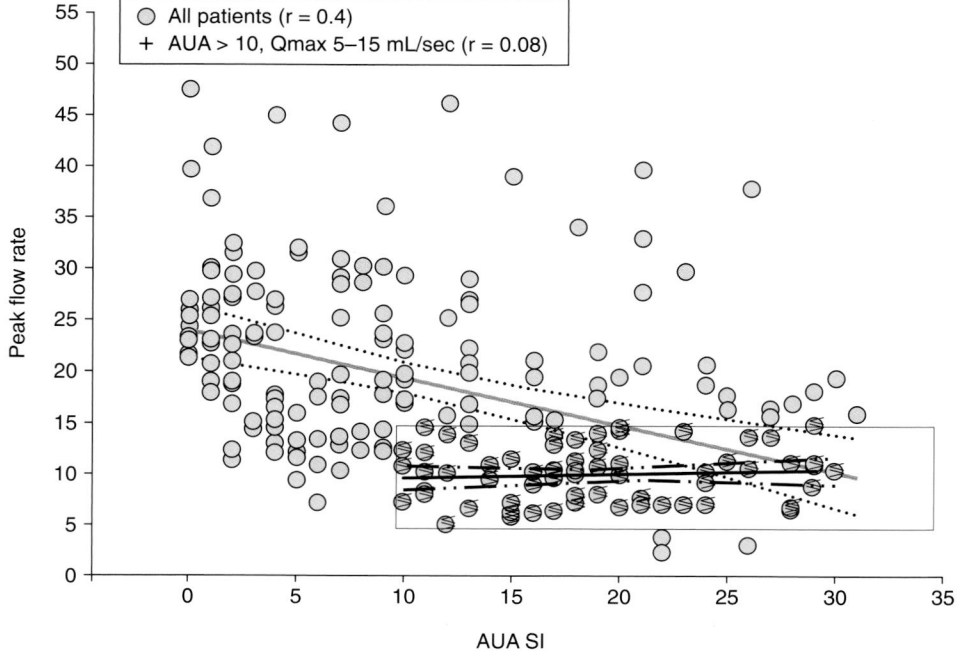

Figure 86–14. Correlation and regression (95% confidence interval) between symptom score and maximum flow rate in volunteers (r = 0.4; P < .05). When only the volunteers with a symptom score above 10 points and a flow rate between 5 and 15 mL/sec (+) are considered, the correlation is virtually absent (r = 0.08; not significant) as indicated by a flat regression line *(black)*. AUA, American Urological Association.

○ All patients (r = 0.4)
+ AUA > 10, Qmax 5–15 mL/sec (r = 0.08)

Peak flow rate

AUA SI

−0.71), and, somewhat unexpectedly, detrusor pressure at peak urine flow (r = 0.43). These data were generated from a relatively small cohort of 61 men with BPH. Invasive pressure-flow studies are not performed in community-based studies, and thus comparative data from population-based studies cannot be reviewed. However, the finding of a relationship between measures of obstruction and prostate volume is rare, with most authors denying such a relationship in series of BPH clinic or trial patients (Bosch et al, 1995; Yalla et al, 1995; Ezz el Din et al, 1996; Witjes et al, 1997; d'Ancona et al, 1998; Homma et al, 1998; Kuo, 1999; Steele et al, 2000).

Data from the Olmsted County study suggest no stronger correlation between symptoms and peak flow rates with TZV (r = 0.17, P = .001 and r = −0.20, P < .001, respectively) than with total volume (r = 0.16, P < .001 and r = −0.16, P < .001, respectively). The transition zone index weakly correlated with AUA symptom index (r = 0.08, P = .103) and peak urinary flow rate (r = −0.08, P = .0823) (Corica et al, 1999). In a large BPH treatment trial, the TZV also did not correlate more strongly with other measures than the TPV (see Table 86–1).

The correlation between serum PSA and prostate volume, both total and transition zone, has been described in greater detail (Roehrborn et al, 1999a, 1999b) (Fig. 86–15A). Although the variability is significant, precluding the accurate prediction of prostate volume by serum PSA in individual patients, there is a strong log linear relationship between these parameters that can be shown in both population-based and clinical studies (Hochberg et al, 2000; Morote et al, 2000; Hedelin et al, 2005). The relationship is further influenced by patients' age, with older patients having a greater increase in prostate volume per unit of serum PSA (Roehrborn et al, 1999a, 1999b) (see Fig. 86–15). In Asian men, similar relationships exist; however, in general, prostate volume and serum PSA tend to be smaller and lower (Fig. 86–15B) (Gupta et al, 2005). Relationships between other PSA-derived parameters have been examined, and certain subforms of PSA

("benign" PSA [BPSA]) have been shown to be more strongly related to BPH than total serum PSA (Canto et al, 2004).

With the exception of age, correlations between various measures of LUTS and BPH are modest in community-based population studies and weak in BPH clinic and trial populations, not precluding, however, a clinical meaningful relationship. The relationship between serum PSA and prostate volume is moderate and dependent on age and racial and ethnic origin. Neither symptoms nor flow rate nor prostate volume measures can predict presence and degree of obstruction reliably.

Natural History of Untreated Benign Prostatic Hyperplasia

The natural history of a disease process refers to the prognosis of the disease over time. In other words, the measurement of changes in parameters of interest and the incidence rates of significant outcomes constitute what is commonly referred to as the natural history of a disease. It is important for clinicians to gain as good an understanding as possible of the natural history of any illness because the benefits and risks of any therapeutic interventions should always be balanced with the risks involved in just watching the disease (i.e., the natural history). In fact, the degree to which natural history must be studied depends on the seriousness of the disease as well as the risks involved with the therapeutic intervention. For example, it is crucial to understand the natural history of abdominal aortic aneurysms and how their prognosis is determined by their size to counsel patients adequately regarding surgical interventions, which have considerable risks in themselves.

Clinical Parameters and Outcomes of Interest

Table 86–3 lists the beneficial and harmful changes in measurable parameters and outcomes that are of interest in both

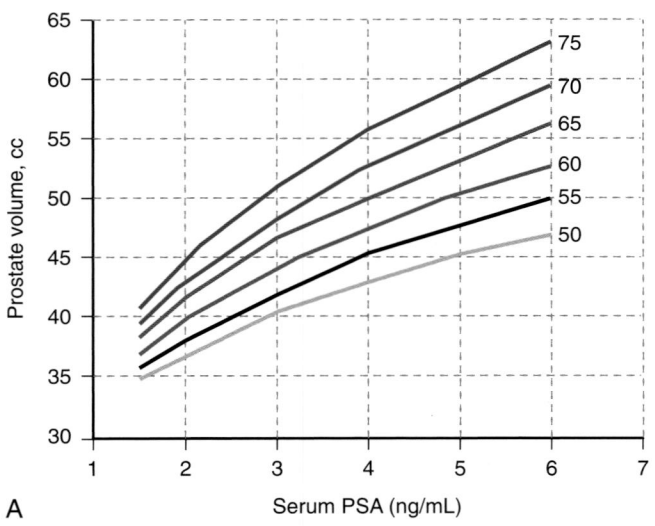

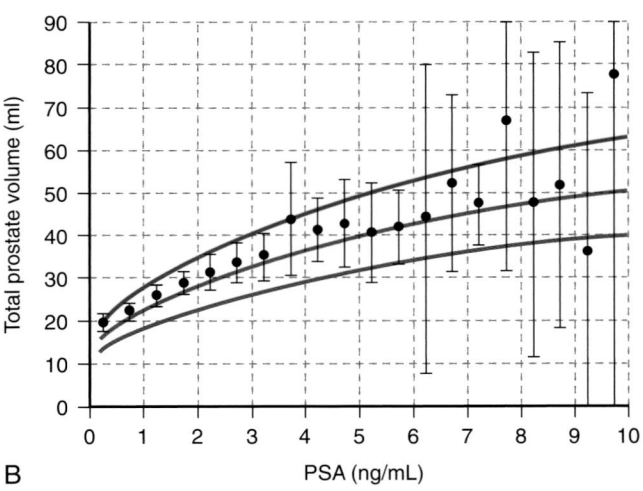

Figure 86–15. Prediction of prostate volume based on serum prostate-specific antigen (PSA) stratified by age in white men (**A**) and in Japanese men (**B**). (**A**, From Roehrborn CG, Boyle P, Gould AL, Waldstreicher J: Serum prostate-specific antigen as a predictor of prostate volume in men with benign prostatic hyperplasia. Urology 1999;53:581-589; **B**, from Gupta A, Aragaki C, Gotoh M, et al: Relationship between prostate specific antigen and indexes of prostate volume in Japanese men. J Urol 2005;173:503-506.)

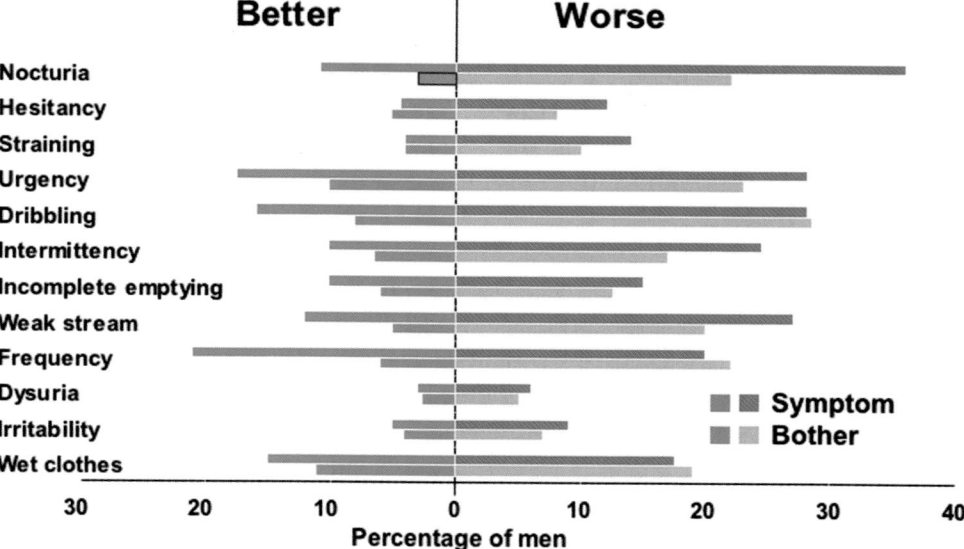

Figure 86–19. Changes in urinary symptoms and bothersomeness status between baseline and 3 years in a Scottish population-based study. (From Lee AJ, Russell EB, Garraway WM, Prescott RJ: Three-year follow-up of a community-based cohort of men with untreated benign prostatic hyperplasia. Eur Urol 1996;30:11-17.)

age at baseline from a mean of 0.05 ± 1.06 (standard deviation) per year among men in the 40s to 0.44 ± 1.35 per year for men in the 60s and decreased to 0.14 ± 1.42 per year for men in the 70s (Jacobsen et al, 1996). More recently, 92-month data showed an annual change of 0.34 points per year, with 31% of all men reporting at least a three-point increase. The greatest annualized increase was observed in men in their 60s with 0.6 points per year (Rhodes et al, 2000).

In addition, 6-year follow-up data on peak flow rate measurements in a subset of about 500 men showed a median peak urinary flow rate slope decrease of −2.1% per year (25th percentile −4.0, 75th percentile −0.6). Peak urinary flow rate declined more rapidly with decreasing baseline rate and increasing baseline age, prostate volume, and symptom severity (all $P = .001$). When the variables were simultaneously adjusted for each other, a rapid decline (negative slope 4.5% or greater per year) was more likely in men 70 years old or older and those with a rate less than 10 mL/sec at baseline compared with those 40 to 49 years old and those with a rate of 15 mL/sec or greater, respectively. Prostate volume and symptom severity were not statistically significant predictors of a rapid decline in peak urinary flow rate when variables were considered simultaneously (Roberts et al, 2000).

On the basis of TRUS, the growth of the prostate in the men 40 to 79 years old was estimated to be about 0.6 mL per year or 6 mL per decade of life. However, prostate growth followed an exponential growth pattern with a slope estimate of 0.4 mL per year for men aged 40 to 59 years at baseline and of 1.2 mL per year for those 60 to 79 years at baseline (Rhodes et al, 1995). An updated analysis revealed a median growth rate of about 1.9% per year independent of age and symptoms. However, a higher baseline serum PSA and larger prostate volume predicted greater annualized volume increases (Rhodes et al, 1999).

Complications of Benign Prostatic Hyperplasia

Many of the complications of progressive BPH are rare, and much of the knowledge comes from studies of men presenting with such complications for treatment (i.e., cases) rather than observations of cohorts of men for the development of complications.

Mortality

Between 1950 and 1954, 17 of 24 countries reported mortality rates of greater than 10 per 100,000, and between 1985 and 1989, data were available for 61 countries, only one reporting a mortality rate greater than 10 per 100,000 (Boyle et al, 1996). If the mortality rates from 1950 were applied to 1990, 13,681 fewer deaths occurred in the United States alone than expected, a major but unheralded health care achievement.

Bladder Stones

In a large autopsy study the prevalence of bladder stones was eight times higher in men with a histologic diagnosis of BPH (3.4%) than in control subjects (0.4%), but no increased incidence of ureteral or kidney stones was found (Grosse, 1990). In a study comparing watchful waiting and TURP in men with moderate symptoms, only 1 of 276 patients assigned to watchful waiting developed a bladder stone in 3 years of follow-up (Wasson et al, 1995). The self-reported rate of a bladder stone in a cross-sectional study in 2002 Spanish men was 0.7% (Hunter et al, 1996).

In clinical practice, the risk of bladder stone development is small and screening is indicated only if clinical circumstances warrant it (e.g., hematuria, stuttering of urination).

Urinary Tract Infections

In older surgical series, urinary tract infections (UTIs) constitute the main indication for surgical intervention in about

12% (Holtgrewe et al, 1989; Mebust et al, 1989). **Although one might intuitively assume that increased amounts of residual urine would predispose to the development of UTIs, clear evidence is lacking.** Hunter and colleagues (1996) cited a rate of 5.2% self-reported episodes of UTI in a cross-sectional survey of 2002 men in Madrid, Spain. The best data to date come from the MTOPS study, where the incidence of UTIs in the placebo-treated patients was only 0.1 per 100 patient-years (McConnell et al, 2003) (see Table 86–8).

Bladder Decompensation

Urologists search for a progression from a normal mucosa to advancing trabeculation, development of cellules, and diverticula with ultimate detrusor muscle failure in mind when evaluating the bladder in men with BPH endoscopically. However, when the process starts, whether it really is related to BPH and obstruction, and when an intervention is necessary to prevent decompensation with resultant inability to void are unclear.

Biopsy specimens from trabeculated, obstructed bladders show dense connective tissue deposition, a finding similar to that seen in animals experimentally obstructed (Gosling and Dixon 1980; Levin et al, 1990; Chapple et al, 1991; Gosling, 1997; Levin et al, 2000). However, bladder fibrosis is seen in both sexes with advancing age and may be a normal consequence of aging (Lepor et al, 1992a).

The critical question is whether or not delayed intervention might lead to progressive irreversible loss of bladder function and miss a window for cure. There is no direct evidence for this from longitudinal population or clinic patient studies. However, in the Veterans Affairs (VA) cooperative study comparing watchful waiting with TURP, the patients who crossed over from the conservative arm to TURP later in the trial had not as significant an improvement in symptoms and flow rate as those who underwent TURP at the beginning after randomization (Flanigan et al, 1998).

Urinary Incontinence

Incontinence is one of the most feared complications from surgical intervention for BPH (McConnell et al, 1994a, 1994b). Although it may be the result of BPH secondary to overdistention of the bladder (overflow incontinence) or to detrusor instability, estimated to affect up to one half or more of all obstructed patients (urge incontinence) (McConnell et al, 1994a, 1994b), it is also associated with aging, and in a community study an incidence of incontinence of 24% and 49% in men and women older than 50 years was reported (Roberts et al, 1998). In the VA cooperative study, a 4% incidence of incontinence in both the surgical and conservative treatment arms was reported (Wasson et al, 1995). The self-reported rate of incontinence in a cross-sectional study in 2002 Spanish men was 6.1% (Hunter et al, 1996). In MTOPS the rate of socially unacceptable incontinence was 0.3 per 100 patient-years (McConnell et al, 2003) (see Table 86–8).

Upper Urinary Tract Deterioration and Azotemia

The Agency for Health Care Policy and Research (AHCPR) BPH guidelines reported a mean of 13.6% (range from 0.3% to 30%) of patients presenting for TURP with evidence of renal failure based on predominantly older studies (McConnell et al, 1994a, 1994b). Patients in renal failure have an increased risk for complications following TURP compared with patients with normal renal function (25% versus 17%) (Holtgrewe et al, 1989; Mebust et al, 1989) and the mortality increases up to sixfold (Holtgrewe and Valk, 1962; Melchior et al, 1974). In the large database of patients who had upper tract imaging prior to surgery, 7.6% of 6102 patients in 25 series had evidence of hydronephrosis, of whom one third had renal insufficiency (McConnell et al, 1994a, 1994b).

The term silent obstruction or silent prostatism has been used to describe the constellation of asymptomatic patients who eventually develop renal failure resulting from bladder outlet obstruction, a case both rare and important (Mukamel et al, 1979). In the VA cooperative study, only 3 of 280 surgically treated patients and 1 of 276 patients in the watchful waiting arm developed renal azotemia, defined as a doubling of serum creatinine from baseline (Wasson et al, 1995). In none of the cohort or population-based studies have cases of renal failure clearly attributable to BPH been reported. However, the self-reported rate of an episode of renal failure in a cross-sectional study in 2002 Spanish men was 2.4% (Hunter et al, 1996).

In MTOPS, there was not a single case of renal insufficiency related to BPH in over 3000 men observed for over 4 years (McConnell et al, 2003). One has to be careful, however, not to overinterpret these findings. Participants in MTOPS were screened at baseline, and one might argue that some at higher risk for developing renal failure were excluded from participation.

Hematuria

It has always been recognized that patients with BPH might develop gross hematuria and form clots with no other cause being identifiable. Evidence suggests that in the patients predisposed to hematuria the microvessel density is higher than in controls (Awad et al, 2000). Some renewed interest in the issue of BPH-related hematuria stems from the observation that finasteride appears to be a reasonable first-line therapy apparently influencing the expression of VEGF (DiPaola et al, 2001). The self-reported rate of hematuria in a cross-sectional study in 2002 Spanish men was 2.5% (Hunter et al, 1996). Precise population estimates and incidence rates are not available, and the clinical management is dictated by the circumstances.

Acute Urinary Retention

Acute urinary retention (AUR) is one of the most significant complications or long-term outcomes resulting from BPH for a variety of reasons. It has in the past represented an immediate indication for surgery. Between 25% and 30% of men who underwent TURP had AUR as their main indication in older series (Holtgrewe et al, 1989), **and today most patients failing to void after an attempt of catheter removal still undergo surgery. For this reason alone, AUR is an important and feared event from an economic viewpoint as well as from the viewpoint of the patient.** For the patient it arises as the inability to urinate with increasing pain, eventually a visit to the emergency room, catheterization, follow-up visits to physicians, an attempt at catheter removal, and eventually recovery or surgery, a painful and time-consuming process. In older literature the risk of recurrent AUR was cited as 56% to 64% within 1 week of the first episode and 76% to

83% in men with diagnosed BPH (Breum et al, 1982; Klarskov et al, 1987; Hastie et al, 1990).

The etiology of AUR is poorly understood. Prostate infection, bladder overdistention (Powell et al, 1980), **excessive fluid intake, alcohol consumption, sexual activity, debility, and bed rest have all been mentioned** (Stimson and Fihn, 1990). **Prostatic infarction has been suggested as an underlying event causing AUR** (Graversen et al, 1989). Spiro and colleagues (1974) found evidence for infarction in 85% of prostates removed for AUR versus 3% of prostates of men having surgery for symptoms only. In contrast, there was no evidence of infarction in six prostatectomy specimens removed from men who had surgery for AUR (Jacobsen et al, 1997). Anjum and coworkers (1998) found fundamentally similar rates of infarction in 35 men each in AUR versus no AUR (1.9% versus 3.0%).

From a clinical and prognostic point of view, spontaneous AUR should be separated from precipitated AUR, although this is by no means consistently done in the literature. Precipitated AUR refers to the inability to urinate following a triggering event such as non–prostate-related surgery, catheterization, anesthesia, or ingestion of medications with sympathomimetic or anticholinergic effects or antihistamines. All other AUR episodes are classified as spontaneous (Roehrborn et al, 2000a). The importance of differentiating the two types of AUR becomes clear when evaluating the ultimate outcomes of patients. Following spontaneous AUR, 15% of patients had another episode of spontaneous AUR and a total of 75% underwent surgery, whereas after precipitated AUR only 9% had an episode of spontaneous AUR and 26% underwent surgery (Roehrborn et al, 2000a).

Descriptive Epidemiology (Table 86–10)

Older estimates of occurrence of AUR range from 4 to 15 to as high as 130 per 1000 person-years (calculated by Jacobsen et al, 1997, based on studies by Clarke, 1919; Craigen et al, 1969; Birkhoff et al, 1976; Ball et al, 1981; Kadow et al, 1988), which leads to 10-year cumulative incidence rates ranging from 4% to 73%. The self-reported rate of AUR in a cross-sectional study in 2002 Spanish men was 5.1% (Hunter et al, 1996).

Data from carefully controlled studies in better defined population shed additional light on the incidence rates in community-dwelling men and clinical BPH populations. AUR occurred in the VA cooperative study over 3 years in one man after TURP and in 8 of 276 men in the watchful waiting arm for an incidence rate of 9.6 per 1000 person-years (Wasson et al, 1995). Barry and coauthors (1997) reported outcomes of 500 men diagnosed by urologists with BPH who were candidates for prostatectomy by established criteria but elected to be observed conservatively. In 1574 person-years 40 episodes of AUR occurred at a constant rate throughout the 4 years of follow-up for an incidence rate of 25 per 1000 person-years.

During 15,851 person-years of follow-up in the Physicians Health Study, 82 men reported an episode of AUR for an incidence rate of 4.5 per 1000 person-years (95% CI 3.1 to 6.2) (Meigs et al, 1999). Of the 2115 men aged 40 to 79 years in the Olmsted County study, 57 had a first episode of AUR during 8344 person-years of follow-up (incidence 6.8 per 1000 person-years, 95% CI 5.2, 8.9) (Jacobsen et al, 1997). **The first excellent data from men diagnosed with BPH stem from the PLESS study** (McConnell et al, 1998). **In PLESS, 1376 placebo-treated men with enlarged prostates and moderate symptoms had complete follow-up over 4 years; 99 of the men experienced an episode of AUR for a calculated incidence rate of 1.8 per 100 person-years. The placebo treatment groups from three 2-year studies with a similar population of patients were meta-analyzed by Boyle and colleagues** (Andersen et al, 1997). **Of 2109 patients, 57 experienced AUR over the 2 years with a constant hazard for an incidence rate of 14 per 1000 person-years (see Table 86–10). In the MTOPS placebo group the incidence rate was 0.6 per 100 patient-years for a cumulative incidence of 2%** (see Table 86–8).

Analytic Epidemiology

Several well-controlled studies provided considerable insights into the risk factors for AUR. In the Physicians

Table 86–10. Descriptive Studies on the Incidence of Acute Urinary Retention (References in Text)

Author/Source	Description of Cohort	Cases	Cohort	Years of Follow-Up	Percent Overall	Percent per Year	IR/1000 Patient-Years	95% CI
Ball, 1981	Watchful waiting study	2	107	5	1.9	0.37	3.7	
Craigen, 1969	Watchful waiting study						15.0	
Birkhoff, 1976	Watchful waiting study	10	26	3	39	13	130	
Wasson, 1995	TURP versus watchful waiting VA cooperative	8	276	3	2.8	0.9	9.6	
Hunter, 1997	Self-reported prior events in Spanish men	102	2002	?	5.1		50.9	
Barry, 1997	Prostatectomy candidates	40	500	4	8	2.5	25	
Meigs, 1999	Physicians Health Study, self-reported	82	6,100	3	1.3		4.5	3.1;6.2
Olmsted, 1997	Community cohort 40-49 years old	57	2,115	4			6.8	5.2;8.9
McConnell, 1998	Placebo group of PLESS study	99	1,376	4	7.2	1.8	18	
Andersen, 1997	Placebo groups of 2-year BPH studies	57	2,109	2	2.7	1.35	13.5	

BPH, benign prostatic hyperplasia; PLESS, Proscar Long-Term Efficacy and Safety Study; TURP, transurethral resection of the prostate; VA, Veterans Affairs.

Health Study, **rates increased with age and baseline symptom severity** (Meigs et al, 1999). In men with mild symptoms the incidence of AUR increased from 0.4 per 1000 person-years for those 45 to 49 years old to 7.9 per 1000 person-years for those 70 to 83 years old. In men with symptom score 8 to 35, rates increased from 3.3 per 1000 person-years for those 45 to 49 years old to 11.3 per 1000 person-years for those 70 to 83 years old. Men with a clinical diagnosis of BPH and a symptom score of 8 or greater had the highest rates (age-adjusted incidence 13.7 per 1000 person-years). All seven lower urinary tract symptoms constituting the AUA symptom index individually predicted AUR. The sensation of incomplete bladder emptying, having to void again after less than 2 hours, and a weak urinary stream were the best independent symptom predictors. Use of medications with adrenergic or anticholinergic side effects also predicted AUR.

The Olmsted County study analyses focused on age, symptom severity, maximum flow rate, and prostate volume (Jacobsen et al, 1997) (see Figs. 86–14 and 86–15). **Incidence rates per 1000 person-years increased from 2.6 to 9.3 for men in their 40s to their 70s if they had mild symptoms and from 3.0 to 34.7 if they had more than mild symptoms** (Fig. 86–20). **The relative risk increased for older men, men with moderate to severe symptoms (3.2-fold), those with a flow rate under 12 mL/sec (3.9-fold), and those with a prostate volume greater than 30 mL by TRUS (3.0-fold), all compared with a baseline risk of 1.0-fold for the corresponding groups** (Fig. 86–21). The highest relative risk by proportional hazard models exists for 60- to 69-year-old men with more than mild symptoms and a flow rate of less than 12 mL/sec (10.3-fold), and for 70- to 79-year-old men except if they had mild symptoms and a flow rate over 12 mL/sec. All other stratification of men older than 70 years had a relative risk ranging from 12.9- to 14.8-fold (all compared with men 40 to 49 years old with mild symptoms and a flow rate over 12 mL/sec, for whom the base risk is 1.0-fold).

Although age is an important risk factor in community-dwelling men, in a BPH trial population of men who are already diagnosed with BPH, other factors can be analyzed. In the placebo groups of three 2-year studies (Marberger et al, 2000) and a 4-year study (PLESS) (McConnell et al, 1998; Kaplan et al, 2000; Roehrborn et al, 2000a), prostate volume, serum PSA, and symptom severity were all predictors of AUR episodes. **The incidence increased from 5.6% to 7.7% in men with a serum PSA less than 1.4 ng/mL from mild to severe symptoms and from 7.8% to 10.2% for those with a serum PSA over 1.4 ng/mL over 4 years.** In the 2-year studies the rate of AUR was eightfold higher in those with a serum PSA over 1.4 ng/mL (0.4% versus 3.9%) and threefold higher if the prostate volume was over 40 mL (1.6% versus 4.2%) (Marberger et al, 2000). **A detailed analysis showed a near-linear increase in risk for AUR with increasing thresholds of serum PSA (Fig. 86–22) in PLESS, an observation that applies to both spontaneous and precipitated AUR** (Roehrborn et al, 1999c). **The risk for both types of AUR increases with increasing serum PSA as well as prostate volume stratified by tertiles** (Fig. 86–23). Similar observations were made in MTOPS, where the risk for AUR increased with increasing prostate volume as well as increasing baseline serum PSA (Fig. 86–24), **and in the 2-year phase III studies comparing dutasteride with placebo** (Roehrborn et al, 2002). **An analysis of over 100 possible outcome predictors alone or in combination revealed a combination of serum PSA, urinating more than every 2 hours, symptom problem index, maximum urinary flow rate, and hesitancy as being only slightly superior to PSA alone in predicting AUR episodes** (Roehrborn et al, 2001).

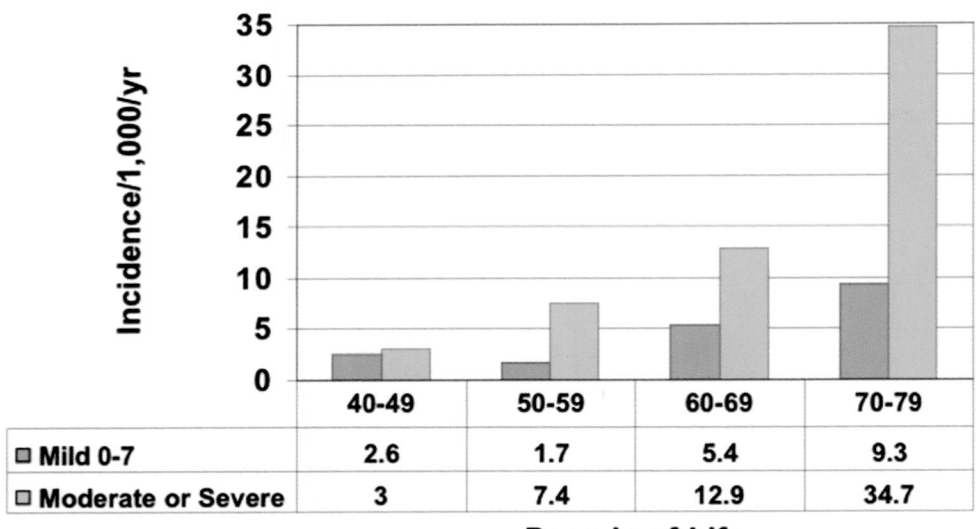

Figure 86–20. Incidence rates of acute urinary retention in Olmsted County study by age and symptom severity. (Data from Jacobsen SJ, Jacobson DJ, Girman CJ, et al: Natural history of prostatism: Risk factors for acute urinary retention. J Urol 1997;158:481-487.)

Decade of Life	40-49	50-59	60-69	70-79
Mild 0-7	2.6	1.7	5.4	9.3
Moderate or Severe	3	7.4	12.9	34.7

□ Mild 0-7 □ Moderate or Severe

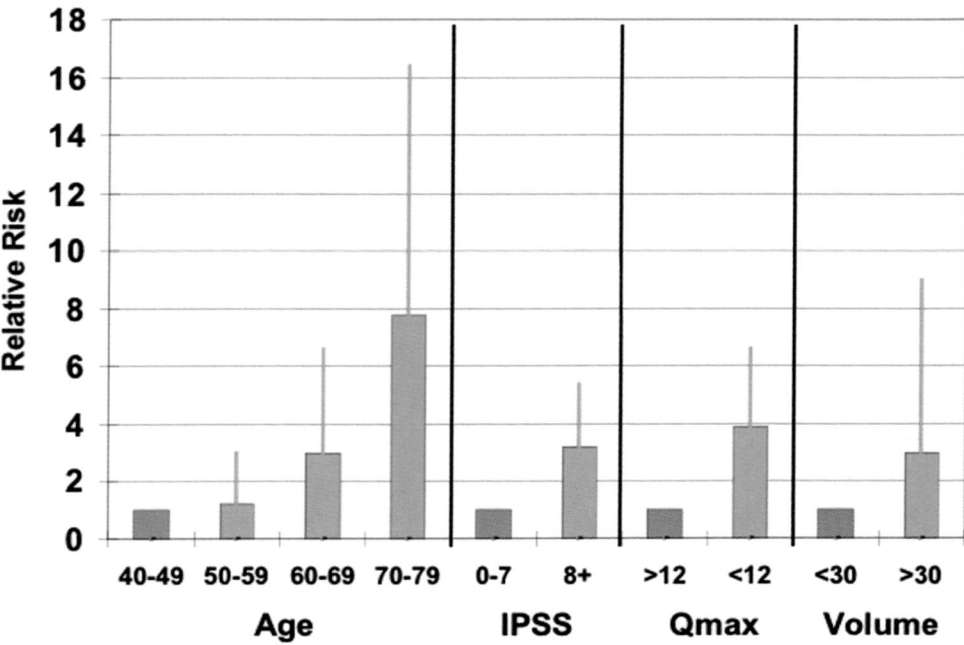

Figure 86-21. Relative risk of acute urinary retention in Olmsted County study by age, symptom severity, peak flow rate, and prostate volume; the dotted column represents the baseline and a relative risk of 1.0; the vertical line represents the 95% confidence interval. IPSS, International Prostate Symptom Score. (Data from Jacobsen SJ, Jacobson DJ, Girman CJ, et al: Natural history of prostatism: Risk factors for acute urinary retention. J Urol 1997;158:481-487.)

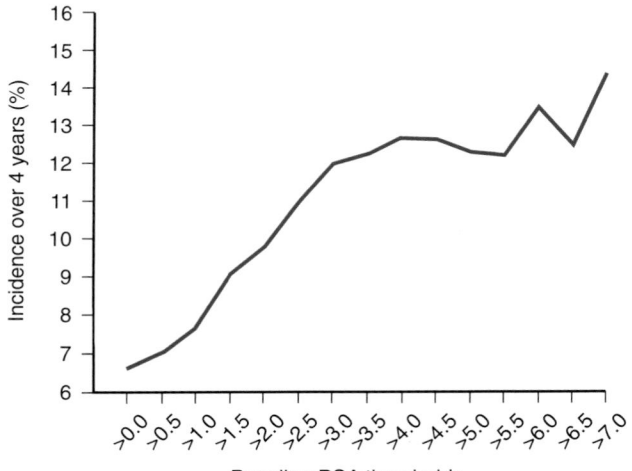

Figure 86-22. Incidence of spontaneous or precipitated acute urinary retention in the Proscar Long-Term Efficacy and Safety Study over 4 years stratified by increasing thresholds of serum prostate-specific antigen (PSA) at baseline. (From Roehrborn CG, McConnell JD, Lieber M, et al: Serum prostate specific antigen concentration is a powerful predictor of acute urinary retention and need for surgery in men with clinical benign prostatic hyperplasia. Urology 1999;53:473-480.)

Surgery for Benign Prostatic Hyperplasia

Both surgery and AUR represent endpoints in the disease progression of BPH. There are, however, distinct differences. AUR is an outcome mandating management, and surgery is on of the commonly employed management styles. AUR is probably one of the clearer indications for surgery, leaving the treating physician little choice in a patient who failed a trial without catheter. However, most patients undergo surgery not for AUR but for symptoms (Holtgrewe et al, 1989). Depending on local practice patterns, AUR accounts for 5% to over 30% of the indications for surgery. AUR can be compared with a fracture. It is impossible for the physician in his or her interaction with the patient to increase or decrease the probability for that outcome to occur. Furthermore, once it has occurred, no interaction or consultation can undo it. In contrast, it is easy to see that patients can be influenced in their decision to undergo surgery by the consultation with the physician. The interaction style, the cited probabilities of beneficial and harmful outcomes to occur, and many other factors cause considerable variability in the incidence rates of prostate-related surgery, an observation that caused the AHCPR to develop guidelines for the treatment of BPH (Wennberg et al, 1988). This situation is similar to that of myocardial infarction (MI) and coronary artery bypass graft (CABG) surgery. The analytic epidemiology of MIs is well understood, and risk factors are characterized. Not all MIs result in CABGs, and in fact CABGs are frequently performed for indications other than a recent MI. Consequently, there is abundant literature focusing on the geographic variation in the usage of CABG. From this brief discussion it becomes clear that surgery for BPH is a softer endpoint from an epidemiologic point of view than AUR, and data on rates of prostatectomy need to be interpreted in light of variation in its use, from provider to provider, region to region, health care plan to health care plan, and over time.

Of all prostate surgeries, TURP is clearly the most common procedure and the best studied one. Cross-sectional descriptive data on incidence rates are available from the Medicare database. Whereas in 1962 TURP constituted over 50% of all major surgeries performed by American urologists, this number had dropped to 38% by 1986 (Holtgrewe et al, 1989). Although the number of TURPs performed on Medicare

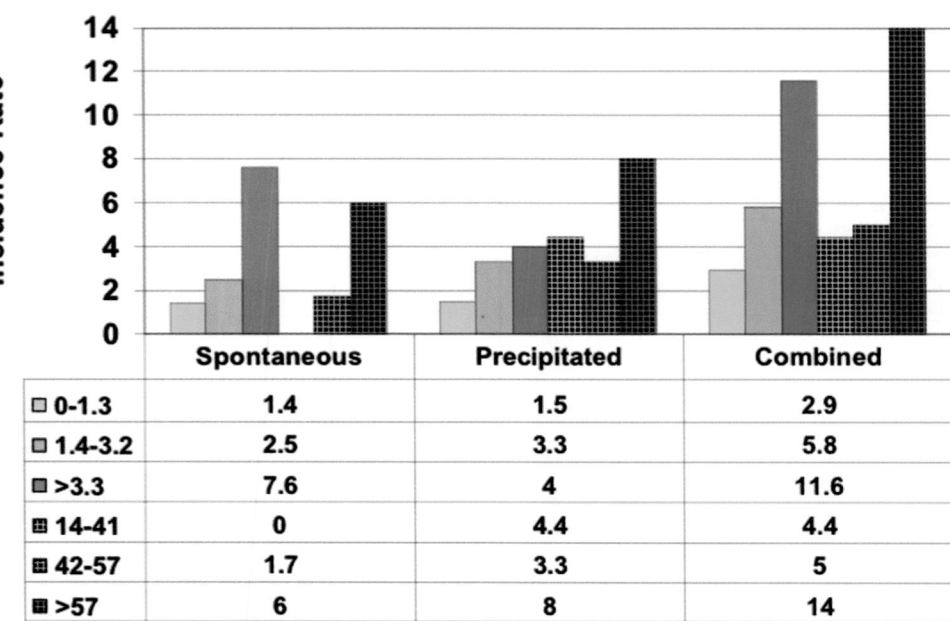

	Spontaneous	Precipitated	Combined
☐ 0-1.3	1.4	1.5	2.9
☐ 1.4-3.2	2.5	3.3	5.8
☐ >3.3	7.6	4	11.6
⊞ 14-41	0	4.4	4.4
⊞ 42-57	1.7	3.3	5
■ >57	6	8	14

☐ 0-1.3 ☐ 1.4-3.2 ■ >3.3 ⊞ 14-41 ⊞ 42-57 ■ >57

Figure 86–23. Spontaneous, precipitated, or combined acute urinary retention incidence over 4 years in the Proscar Long-Term Efficacy and Safety Study stratified by tertiles of serum prostate-specific antigen or prostate volume at baseline. (From Roehrborn CG, McConnell JD, Lieber M, et al: Serum prostate specific antigen concentration is a powerful predictor of acute urinary retention and need for surgery in men with clinical benign prostatic hyperplasia. Urology 1999c;53:473-480.)

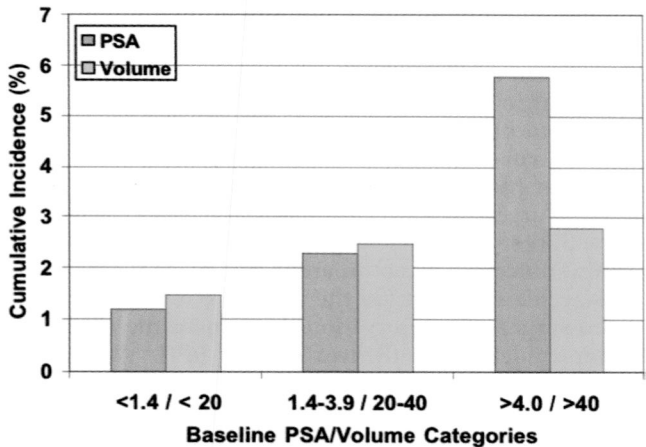

Figure 86–24. Cumulative incidence of acute urinary retention in placebo-treated patients in the Medical Therapy of Prostatic Symptoms study stratified by baseline prostate volume *(yellow)* and baseline serum prostate-specific antigen (PSA) *(orange)*. (From McConnell J, Roehrborn CG, Bautista OM, et al: The long-term effects of doxazosin, finasteride and the combination on the clinical progression of benign prostatic hyperplasia. N Engl J Med 2003;349:2385-2396.)

patients declined from an all time peak of 258,000 in 1987 to 168,000 in 1993—a reduction by 34%—it remains second only to cataract surgery on the list of Medicare's most costly surgical procedures. A 20% sample of Medicare beneficiaries was examined to specify rates of TURP in the United States. In 1990, the rates of TURP (including all indications) were approximately 25, 19, and 13 per 1000 for men older than 75, 70 to 74, and 65 to 69, respectively. The 30-day mortality

following TURP for the treatment of BPH decreased from 1.20% in 1984 to 0.77% in 1990 (Lu-Yao et al, 1994). **Compared with 1984 to 1990, age-adjusted rates of transurethral resection for BPH during 1991 to 1997 declined further by approximately 50% for white (14.6 to 6.72/1000) and 40% for black (11.8 to 6.58/1000) men** (Wasson et al, 2000). Medicare databases are relevant only to men older than 65 years enrolled in Medicare and therefore are less interesting from a longitudinal epidemiologic point of view.

Older series of the natural history of BPH such as the one reported by Craigen and colleagues (1969) projected somewhat unrealistic estimates of a 35% incidence of prostatectomy at 1 year and 45% at 7 years. Diokno and coworkers (1992) reported an annual incidence rate of 2.6% and 3.3% for years 1 and 2 in their cohort of men followed longitudinally. Frequency, hesitancy, straining, and an interrupted stream were all associated with an increased risk.

The first study of substantial quality reporting on incidence rates and risk factors of prostate surgery was the Baltimore Longitudinal Study of Aging (BLSA) (Arrighi et al, 1990, 1991). More than 1000 men were observed for 30 years with yearly symptom assessments, questionnaires, and examinations. **Age, incomplete emptying, change in size, and force of stream were all independently associated with the risk of prostate surgery, as was a reportedly enlarged prostate by DRE.** Of 464 men without risk factors, only 3% required surgery during follow-up. For men with one risk factor the cumulative incidence was 9%, with two risk factors 16%, and with three risk factors 37%. In a similar study, the VA Normative Aging Study, nocturia and hesitancy emerged as independent predictors of surgery in 1868 men aged 49 to 68 observed for over 20 years (Hindley et al, 2001). Age and five LUTS (dysuria, incontinence, trouble initiating flow, nocturia, and slow stream) were associated with the risk of surgery in 16,219 men older than 40 years enrolled in the Kaiser Permanente Health Plan in California, of whom 1027 men underwent prostatectomy over 12 years of follow-up (Sidney et al, 1991a, 1991b).

In the VA cooperative trial comparing surgery with watchful waiting, 65 of 276 (24%) patients assigned to watchful waiting crossed over to surgery within 3 years of follow-up, of whom 20 met predefined endpoints (azotemia, high residuals, incontinence, or high symptom scores). High baseline bother score was a strong predictor of requiring surgery (Wasson et al, 1995).

The probability of undergoing surgery over 4 years increased from 10% in the men diagnosed with BPH who had mild symptoms to 24% in those with moderate symptoms and 39% in those with severe symptoms at baseline as reported in a natural history and observation study by Barry and associates (1997).

The Olmsted County study and the placebo-treated patients from the PLESS study provide additional insights into the risk factors for undergoing prostate surgery in either community-dwelling men or men enrolled in a BPH treatment trial.

In the Olmsted County study during more than 10,000 person-years of follow-up 167 men were treated, yielding an overall incidence of 16.0 per 1000 person-years. There was a strong age-related increase in risk of any treatment from 3.3 per 1000 person-years for men 40 to 49 years old to more than 30 per 1000 person-years for those 70 years old or older. Men with moderate to severe symptoms, depressed peak urinary flow rates (less than 12 mL/sec), enlarged prostate (greater than 30 mL), or elevated serum PSA (1.4 ng/mL or greater) had about four times the risk of BPH treatment of those who did not. After adjustment for all measures simultaneously, an enlarged prostate (hazard ratio 2.3, 95% CI 1.1, 4.7), depressed peak flow rate (hazard ratio 2.7, 95% CI 1.4, 5.3), and moderate to severe symptoms (hazard ratio 5.3, 95% CI 2.5, 11.1) at baseline each independently predicted subsequent treatment. Overall, nearly one in four men received treatment in the eighth decade of life. **These data suggest that men with moderate to severe LUTS, impaired flow rates, or enlarged prostates are more likely to undergo treatment, with increases in risk of similar magnitude to those associated with adverse outcomes, such as AUR** (Jacobsen et al, 1999).

Over 1500 patients with moderate LUTS and enlarged prostate glands were followed up in the PLESS study on placebo for 4 years. Of these, 10% or 2.5% per year underwent surgery for BPH (McConnell et al, 1998). Although the hazard of undergoing surgery was linear (i.e., it remained constant throughout the duration of the study), it was different when patients were stratified by either prostate volume or serum PSA in tertiles at the beginning of the study (Fig. 86–25). **Similar to the incidence of AUR, the rates of surgery increased from 6.2% to 14.6% for patients in the lowest to the highest PSA tertile and from 6.7% to 14.0% from the lowest to the highest prostate volume tertile.**

In MTOPS the incidence of invasive therapy for BPH in the placebo group increased equally nearly linearly when stratifying by baseline serum PSA or prostate volume (Fig. 86–26) (McConnell et al, 2003).

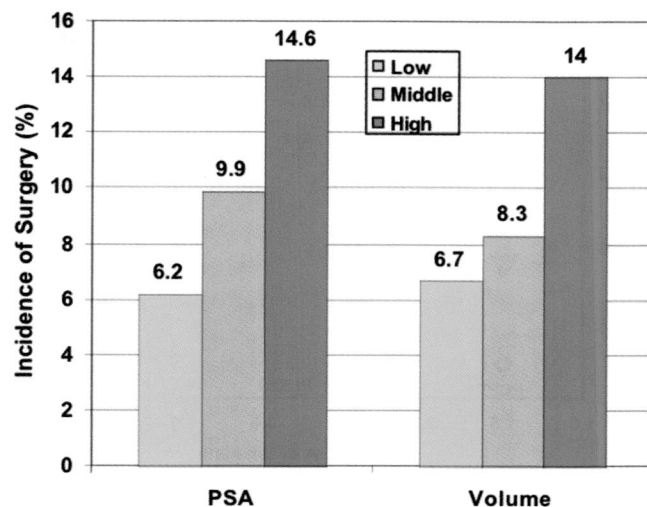

Figure 86–25. Incidence of surgery stratified by tertiles of serum prostate-specific antigen (PSA) and prostate volume in placebo-treated patients in the Proscar Long-Term Efficacy and Safety Study. (From Roehrborn CG, McConnell JD, Lieber M, et al: Serum prostate specific antigen concentration is a powerful predictor of acute urinary retention and need for surgery in men with clinical benign prostatic hyperplasia. Urology 1999c;53:473-480.)

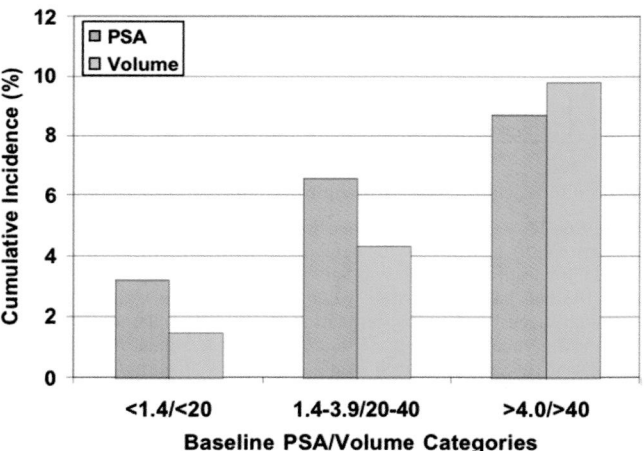

Figure 86–26. Cumulative incidence of invasive therapy (surgery) for benign prostatic hyperplasia in placebo-treated patients in the Medical Therapy of Prostatic Symptoms study stratified by baseline prostate volume *(yellow)* and baseline serum prostate-specific antigen (PSA) *(orange)*. (From McConnell J, Roehrborn CG, Bautista OM, et al: The long-term effects of doxazosin, finasteride and the combination on the clinical progression of benign prostatic hyperplasia. N Engl J Med 2003;349:2385-2396.)

There are four placebo groups available from large controlled trials in whom the annual incidence rates of AUR or surgery can be estimated, namely the PLESS, MTOPS, PCPT, and dutasteride phase III studies (McConnell et al, 1998, 2003; Roehrborn et al, 2002; Thompson et al, 2003). When plotting the studies along the x-axis by increasing mean baseline serum PSA or prostate volume and showing the annualized incidence rates of AUR or surgery on the y-axis, it becomes evident that the mean baseline PSA and volume are strongly predictive of the annualized rates of AUR or surgery (Fig. 86–27).

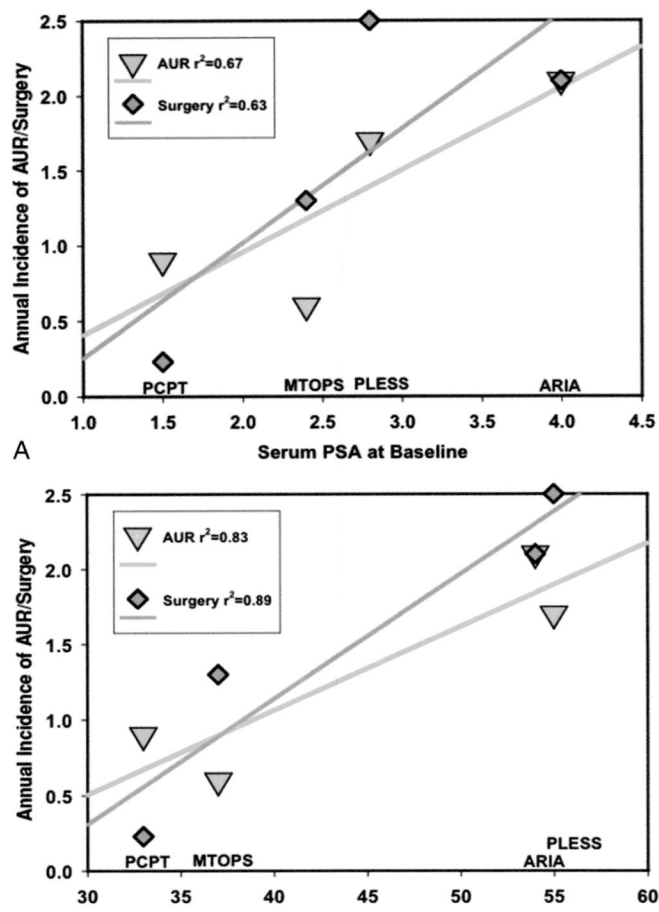

Figure 86–27. Comparison of annualized incidence rates of acute urinary retention (AUR) and surgery for benign prostatic hyperplasia in four large placebo groups of controlled trials sorted by serum prostate-specific antigen (PSA) (**A**) and baseline prostate volume (**B**) along the x-axis with linear regression suggesting a strong correlation between mean baseline serum PSA and prostate volume in the placebo groups and the annual incidence rates of AUR and surgery. (McConnell et al, 1998, 2003; Roehrborn et al, 2002; Thompson et al, 2003). ARIA, Dutasteride Phase III Trial "A"; MTOPS, Medical Therapy of Prostatic Symptoms; PLESS, Proscar Long-Term Efficacy and Safety Study; PCPT, Prostate Cancer Prevention Trial.

KEY POINTS: EPIDEMIOLOGY AND NATURAL HISTORY

- There is no globally accepted epidemiologic definition of BPH, and, thus, prevalence and incidence rates must be viewed in the context of the definitions chosen by the investigator reporting the data.

- Despite the significantly different proportion of men admitting to moderate to severe symptoms, a clear trend toward an increase in symptom scores with advancing age is noticeable in all reported studies.

- In general, in all cross-sectional studies prostate volume as assessed by TRUS has been found to increase slowly but steadily with advancing age.

- Analytic epidemiologic data suggest a limited role of classical determinants of the disease such as religion, socioeconomic factors, sexual activity, alcohol intake, hypertension, dietary factors, and others. There is conflicting evidence regarding smoking and some evidence suggesting dietary factors, obesity, and increased BMI as determinants of disease severity.

- As noted, all relevant parameters such as symptom severity and frequency, bother, interference, disease-specific HRQOL, maximum flow rate, and prostate volume tend to worsen with advancing age. However, reported correlations between these parameters as well as urodynamic pressure-flow studies are in general weak with some exceptions. Strong correlations exist between measures of symptom severity and frequency (I-PSS score), bother, disease-specific HRQOL, and interference scores.

- The natural history of the disease has been studied in many longitudinal population-based studies as well as in placebo and sham control groups of treatment trials of men diagnosed with the condition. These studies suggest in general a worsening of the signs and symptoms of LUTS and BPH with time. There are several key baseline parameters allowing a stratification of patients according to the risk of progression. Age, symptom severity, flow rate, prostate size, and serum PSA are useful predictors of the risk of progression.

- Complications of LUTS and BPH such as mortality, urinary tract infections, bladder decompensation, bladder stones, hematuria, urinary incontinence, upper urinary tract deterioration with renal insufficiency, and others are in general rare in properly supervised patients.

- The two most significant progression events are acute urinary retention and the need for BPH-related surgery. Although not exceedingly common, there is a significant baseline incidence rate and the risk is cumulative; that is, with increasing time of observation the incidence rate increases linearly.

- The risk of AUR and need for surgery is to some degree predictable from baseline parameters with advancing age, increased prostate size, and higher serum PSA levels representing the most significant risk factors.

SUGGESTED READINGS

Arrighi HM, Metter EJ, Guess HA, Fozzard JL: Natural history of benign prostatic hyperplasia and risk of prostatectomy. Urology 1991;38:4-8.

Barrack E, Berry S: DNA synthesis in the canine prostate: Effects of androgen induction and estrogen treatment. Prostate 1987;10:45-56.

Barry MJ, Fowler FJ Jr, Bin L, et al: The natural history of patients with benign prostatic hyperplasia as diagnosed by North American urologists. J Urol 1997;157:10-15.

Barry MJ, Fowler FJ Jr, O'Leary MP, et al: The American Urological Association's symptom index for benign prostatic hyperplasia. J Urol 1992;148:1549-1557.

Barry MJ, Williford WO, Chang Y, et al: Benign prostatic hyperplasia specific health status measures in clinical research: How much change in the American Urological Association symptom index and the benign prostatic hyperplasia impact index is perceptible to patients? J Urol 1995;154:1770-1774.

Berry S, Coffey D, Ewing LL: Effects of aging on prostate growth in beagles. Am J Physiol 1986;250:R1039-R1046.

Berry S, Coffey D, Strandberg JD, Ewing LL: Effect of age, castration, and testosterone replacement on the development and restoration of canine benign prostatic hyperplasia. Prostate 1986;9:295-302.

Berry SJ, Coffey DS, Walsh PC, Ewing LL: The development of human benign prostatic hyperplasia with age. J Urol 1984;132:474-479.

Boyle P, Maisonneuve P, Steg A: Decrease in mortality from benign prostatic hyperplasia: A major unheralded health triumph. J Urol 1996;155:176-180.

Boyle P, Robertson C, Mazzetta C, et al: The association between lower urinary tract symptoms and erectile dysfunction in four centres: The UrEpik study. BJU Int 2003;92:719-725.

Castro P, Giri D, Lamb D, Ittmann M: Cellular senescence in the pathogenesis of benign prostatic hyperplasia. Prostate 2003;55:30-38.

Cohen P, Nunn S, Peehl DM: Transforming growth factor-beta induces growth inhibition and IGF-binding protein-3 production in prostatic stromal cells: Abnormalities in cells cultured from benign prostatic hyperplasia tissues. J Endocrinol 2000;164:215-223.

Cunha C, Chung L, Shannon JM, et al: Hormone-induced morphogenesis and growth: Role of mesenchymal-epithelial interactions. Recent Prog Horm Res 1983;39:559-598.

DeKlerk D, Coffey D, Ewing LL, et al: Comparison of spontaneous and experimentally induced canine prostatic hyperplasia. J Clin Invest 1979;64:842-849.

Girman CJ: Natural history and epidemiology of benign prostatic hyperplasia: Relationship between urologic measures. Urology 1998;51(4A Suppl):8-12.

Gosling J, Dixon J: Structure of trabeculated detrusor smooth muscle in cases of prostatic hypertrophy. Urol Int 1980;35:3351-3372.

Isaacs J, Coffey D: Etiology and disease process of benign prostatic hyperplasia. Prostate 1987;2(Suppl):33-50.

Kitsberg D, Leder P: Keratinocyte growth factor induces mammary and prostatic hyperplasia and mammary adenocarcinoma in transgenic mice. Oncogene 1996;13:2507-2515.

Kyprianou N, Issacs J: Expression of transforming growth factor-beta in the rat ventral prostate during castration-induced programmed cell death. Mol Endocrinol 1989;3:1515.

Lee C, Sensibar J, Dudek SM, et al: Prostatic ductal system in rats: Regional variation in morphological and functional activities. Biol Reprod 1990;43:1079-1086.

McConnell JD: The pathophysiology of benign prostatic hyperplasia. J Androl 1991;12:356-363.

McConnell JD, Barry M, Bruskewitz R, et al: Benign prostatic hyperplasia: diagnosis and treatment. Clinical Practice Guideline, Number 8. Rockville, Md: Agency for Health Care Policy and Research, Public Health Service, U.S. Department of Health and Human Services, 1994.

McConnell JD, Bruskewitz R, Walsh P, et al: The effect of finasteride on the risk of acute urinary retention and the need for surgical treatment among men with benign prostatic hyperplasia. Finasteride Long-Term Efficacy and Safety Study Group. N Engl J Med 1998;338:557-563.

McConnell J, Roehrborn CG, Bautista OM, et al: The long-term effects of doxazosin, finasteride and the combination on the clinical progression of benign prostatic hyperplasia. N Engl J Med 2003;349:2385-2396.

McConnell JD, Barry M, Bruskewitz R, et al: Benign prostatic hyperplasia: Diagnosis and treatment. Quick Reference Guide for Clinicians. AHCPR Publication No. 95-0583. Rockville, Md, Agency for Health Care Policy and Research, Public Health Service, U.S. Department of Health and Human Services, 1994.

McNeal JE: Origin and evolution of benign prostatic enlargement. Invest Urol 1978;15:340.

Meigs JB, Barry MJ, Giovannucci G, et al: Incidence rates and risk factors for acute urinary retention: The health professionals followup study. J Urol 1999;162:376-382.

Naslund J, Coffey D: The differential effects of neonatal androgen, estrogen, and progesterone on adult prostate growth. J Urol 1986;136:1136-1140.

Roehrborn CG, Boyle P, Bergner D, et al: Serum prostate-specific antigen and prostate volume predict long-term changes in symptoms and flow rate: Results of a four-year, randomized trial comparing finasteride versus placebo. PLESS Study Group. Urology 1999;54:662-669.

Roehrborn CG, Boyle P, Gould AL, Waldstreicher J: Serum prostate-specific antigen as a predictor of prostate volume in men with benign prostatic hyperplasia. Urology 1999;53:581-589.

Roehrborn CG, Bruskewitz R, Nickel GC, et al: Urinary retention in patients with BPH treated with finasteride or placebo over 4 years. Characterization of patients and ultimate outcomes. The PLESS Study Group. Eur Urol 2000;37:528-536.

Roehrborn CG, McConnell JD, Lieber M, et al: Serum prostate specific antigen concentration is a powerful predictor of acute urinary retention and need for surgery in men with clinical benign prostatic hyperplasia. Urology 1999;53:473-480.

Rosen R, Altwein J, Boyle P, et al: Lower urinary tract symptoms and male sexual dysfunction: The multinational survey of the aging male (MSAM-7). Eur Urol 2003;44:637-649.

Russell D, Wilson J: Steroid 5alpha-reductase: Two genes/two enzymes. Annu Rev Biochem 1994;63: 25.

Sanda M, Beaty T, Stutzman RE, et al: Genetic susceptibility of benign prostatic hyperplasia. J Urol 1994;152:115-119.

Shapiro E, Hartanto V, Lepor H: Quantifying the smooth muscle content of the prostate using double-immuno-enzymatic staining and color assisted image analysis. J Urol 1992;147:1167-1170.

Walsh P, Hutchins G, Ewing LL: Tissue content of dihydrotestosterone in human prostatic hyperplasia is not supernormal. J Clin Invest 1983;72:1772-1777.

87 Evaluation and Nonsurgical Management of Benign Prostatic Hyperplasia

ROGER KIRBY, MD • HERBERT LEPOR, MD

The term *benign prostatic hyperplasia* (BPH) has very different connotations to the pathologist, radiologist, urodynamicist, practicing urologist, and patient. BPH to the pathologist is a microscopic diagnosis characterized by cellular proliferation of the stromal and epithelial elements of the prostate (Strandberg, 2000). The radiologist makes the diagnosis of BPH on the basis of an enlarged prostate either on ultrasound or with three-dimensional diagnostic imaging studies of the male pelvis (Haas and Resnick, 2000). The hallmark of BPH to the urodynamicist is the synchronous observation of elevated voiding pressure and a low urinary flow rate in the absence of other disease processes that cause bladder outlet obstruction (BOO) (Nitti, 2000). BPH to the practicing urologist represents a constellation of signs and lower urinary

tract symptoms (LUTS) that develop in the male population in association with aging and prostatic enlargement presumably caused by BOO (Shapiro and Lepor, 1995), together with ultrasound imaging. The patient is typically concerned about the impact of BPH on quality of life rather than the presence of cellular proliferation, prostatic enlargement, or elevated voiding pressures.

Because of the diverse connotations of the term, it is necessary to define BPH as microscopic BPH, macroscopic BPH, or clinical BPH. **Microscopic BPH** represents histologic evidence of cellular proliferation of the prostate. Macroscopic BPH refers to enlargement of the prostate resulting from microscopic BPH. Clinical BPH represents the LUTS, bladder dysfunction, hematuria, and urinary tract infection (UTI) resulting from macroscopic BPH. Abrams (1994) has suggested using the more clinically descriptive terms benign prostatic enlargement (BPE), BOO, and LUTS to replace BPH.

Microscopic BPH describes a proliferative process of the stromal and epithelial elements of the prostate (Bartsch et al, 1979). The proliferative process originates in the transition zone and the periurethral glands (McNeal, 1983). It is rarely identified in males younger than 40 years of age (Berry et al, 1984). The autopsy incidence of BPH is age dependent, the proliferative process being present in approximately 70% and 90% of males in their seventh and ninth decades of life, respectively. The development of microscopic BPH requires aging and testes as the source of androgens (Walsh, 1986). Androgens play a passive role in the proliferative process. The specific biochemical event that initiates and promotes microscopic BPH has yet to be identified and characterized. Growth factors (e.g., epidermal growth factor [EGF]) are involved through autocrine and paracrine stromal epithelial interactions (Steiner, 2000).

Macroscopic BPH describes an "enlarged" prostate. Digital rectal examination (DRE) provides a relatively crude estimate of prostate size when compared with measurements using transrectal ultrasonography or magnetic resonance imaging (MRI) (Roehrborn et al, 1997). Knowledge of prostate size may be clinically relevant in some cases, in terms of selecting appropriate medical or surgical therapy. A strong correlation exists between serum prostate-specific antigen (PSA) levels and prostate volume (Roehrborn et al, 1999); and, as a consequence, in the absence of adenocarcinoma, the PSA value may be used as a surrogate for prostate volume (Roehrborn et al, 2001). The transition zone (inner gland) accounts for the majority of BPH tissue. The transition zone volume can be quantified using transrectal ultrasonography (Lepor et al, 1994) or MRI (Tempany et al, 1993). There is no consensus regarding the extent of enlargement required to establish the diagnosis of macroscopic BPH; however, prostate volume between 20 and 30 mL may be regarded as normal .

The clinical manifestations of BPH include LUTS, poor bladder emptying, urinary retention, an overactive bladder, UTI, hematuria, and rarely now renal insufficiency (Jepsen and Bruskewitz, 2000). Historically, the pathophysiology of clinical BPH was attributed to BOO secondary to macroscopic enlargement of the prostate gland (Lepor, 2000). This hypothesis was supported by epidemiologic data suggesting that the prevalence of microscopic BPH, macroscopic BPH, and clinical BPH is age dependent and, therefore, causally related (Isaacs and Coffey, 1989). This rather simplistic concept of the pathophysiology of BPH has been challenged by more recent studies that demonstrated only weak relationships between prostate size, severity of BOO, and severity of symptoms (Barry et al, 1993; Bosch et al, 1995; Girman et al, 1995; Yalla et al, 1995). However, there are numerous epidemiologic data to confirm that BPH is a slowly progressive disease and that men with a larger prostate (or higher PSA) are at significantly greater risk of LUTS, impaired quality of life, and complications such as acute urinary retention (AUR) (Roehrborn et al, 2001).

DIAGNOSIS

The complex of symptoms now commonly referred to as LUTS is not specific for BPH. Aging men with a variety of lower urinary tract pathologic processes may exhibit similar, if not identical, symptoms. The initial diagnostic challenge in these patients is to establish that the symptoms are, in fact, a result of BPH. This is the primary focus of initial evaluation and diagnostic testing. Fortunately, nonprostatic causes of symptoms can be excluded in a significant majority of patients on the basis of history, physical examination, and urinalysis. Additional diagnostic testing is necessary in patients in whom the diagnosis is still unclear after initial evaluation. These tests may also have a modest (but still unproven) value in predicting the response to treatment. The following recommendations reflect the consensus opinion for several independent groups who have developed practice guidelines (McConnell et al, 1994; Denis et al, 1998). The recent American Urological Association (AUA) BPH Guidelines Committee also addresses many of the issues surrounding the initial evaluation of men presenting with LUTS (AUA Practice Guidelines Committee, 2003).

Initial Evaluation

Medical History

A detailed medical history should be taken to identify other causes of voiding dysfunction or cormorbidities that may **complicate treatment** (McConnell et al, 1994; Denis et al, 1998). **Other validated symptom assessment instruments are supplementary to the AUA (IPSS) Symptom Score.** Specific additional areas to discuss when taking the history of a man with BPH symptoms include a history of hematuria, UTI, diabetes, nervous system disease (e.g., Parkinson's disease or stroke), urethral stricture disease, urinary retention, and aggravation of symptoms by cold or sinus medication. Current prescription and over-the-counter medications should be discussed to determine whether the patient is taking drugs that impair bladder contractility (anticholinergics) or that increase outflow resistance (α sympathomimetics). A history of prior lower urinary tract surgery raises the possibility of urethral stricture or bladder neck contracture. Use of a voiding diary (recording times and volume) may help identify patients with polyuria or other nonprostatic disorders.

Physical Examination

A DRE and a focused neurologic examination should usually be performed (McConnell et al, 1994; Denis et al, 1998). In addition, examination of the external genitalia is indicated to exclude meatal stenosis or a palpable urethral mass, and an abdominal examination is necessary to exclude an overdistended, palpable bladder. The DRE and focused neurologic examination are done to detect prostate or rectal malignancy, to evaluate anal sphincter tone, and to rule out any neurologic problems that may cause the presenting symptoms. The presence of induration is as important a finding as the presence of a nodule and should be correlated with a serum PSA value so that the need for prostatic biopsy can be assessed.

DRE establishes the approximate size of the prostate gland. In patients who choose or require either medical or invasive therapy, estimation of prostate size is important to select the most appropriate pharmacologic or technical approach. DRE provides a sufficiently accurate measurement in most cases. However, the size of the prostate is not critical in deciding whether active treatment is required. Prostate size does not correlate precisely with symptom severity, degree of urodynamic obstruction, or treatment outcomes (Bissada et al, 1976; Meyhoff et al, 1981; Roehrborn et al, 1986; Simonsen et al, 1987). If a more accurate measurement of prostate volume is needed to determine whether to perform open prostatectomy rather than transurethral resection of the prostate (TURP), ultrasound (transabdominal or transrectal) is more accurate than cystourethroscopy. It is now established that a larger gland is associated with a greater risk of disease progression (Roehrborn et al, 2001) and AUR.

Urinalysis

A urinalysis should be done either by using a dipstick test or microscopic examination of the spun sediment to rule out UTI and hematuria, either of which strongly suggest a non-BPH pathologic process as a cause of symptoms (McConnell et al, 1994; Denis et al, 1998).

There is insufficient evidence that urinalysis is an effective screening procedure for asymptomatic men (Preventative Services Task Force, 1989). Because serious urinary tract disorders are relatively uncommon, the positive predictive value of screening for them is low and the effectiveness of early detection and intervention is unproved. **However, in older men** with BPH and a higher prevalence of these disorders, the benefits of an innocuous test such as urinalysis clearly outweigh the harms involved. The test permits the selective use of renal imaging and endoscopy for those patients with the greatest chance of benefiting from them. More important, urinalysis assists in distinguishing UTIs and bladder cancer from BPH. These conditions may produce urinary tract symptoms (e.g., frequency and urgency) that mimic BPH. If a dipstick approach is used, a test that includes leukocyte esterase and nitrite tests for the detection of pyuria and bacteriuria should be used.

The positive predictive value of urinalysis for cancer or other urologic diseases is 4% to 26%, depending on the patients screened and the rigor of follow-up studies (Mohr et al, 1986a, 1986b, 1987; Messing et al, 1987). **Urine cytology should always be considered in men with severe irritable symptoms and dysuria, especially if they have a smoking history.** Carcinoma in-situ of the bladder is a diagnosis that may have serious consequences if overlooked.

Serum Creatinine Measurement

Although the measurement of serum creatinine has been recommended to be performed in the initial evaluation of all patients with symptoms of LUTS to exclude renal insufficiency caused by the presence of obstructive uropathy (McConnell et al, 1994; Denis et al, 1998), at the Fifth International Consultation on BPH it was suggested that serum creatinine determination should be optional or secondary. **The recently published AUA guidelines on BPH no longer recommend routine creatinine measurement in the standard patient.** However, it is well established that BPH patients with renal insufficiency have increased risk for postoperative complications. The risk is 25% for patients with renal insufficiency, compared with 17% for patients without the condition (Mebust et al, 1989). Moreover, the mortality increases up to sixfold for BPH patients treated surgically if they have renal insufficiency (Holtgrewe and Valk, 1962; Melchior et al, 1974). Of 6102 patients evaluated in 25 studies by intravenous urography (IVU) before prostate surgery, 7.6% had evidence of hydronephrosis (McConnell et al, 1994). Of these patients, 33.6% had associated renal insufficiency.

Elevated serum creatinine in a patient with BPH is an indication for imaging studies (ultrasound) to evaluate the upper urinary tract. In a retrospective analysis of 345 patients who had undergone prostatectomy, 1.7% (N = 6) had occult and progressive renal damage (Mukamel et al, 1979). These patients had minimal or no urinary symptoms and presumably fit the category of patients with "silent prostatism." Measurement of serum creatinine is one modality to identify such patients.

Serum Prostate-Specific Antigen

Prostate cancer can lead to LUTS by producing bladder outflow obstruction similar to BPH. Moreover, prostate cancer commonly coexists with BPH. In most men with a 10-year or greater life expectancy, the knowledge of concomitant prostate cancer may well alter management of the BPH component. The detection of a large nodular prostate cancer on DRE would no doubt alter therapy; however, the "early detection" of small volume prostate cancer in an 80-year-old man is unlikely to increase life expectancy. A PSA test and DRE increase the detection rate of prostate cancer over DRE alone. **Therefore, measurement of the serum PSA value should be performed in patients in whom the identification of cancer would clearly alter BPH management** (McConnell et al, 1994; Denis et al, 1998). There is significant overlap between the serum PSA values of men with BPH and men with clinically localized prostate cancer. Twenty-eight percent of men with histologically proven BPH have a serum PSA greater than 4.0 ng/mL (McConnell et al, 1994). Serum PSA trends over time (PSA velocity), measurement of free versus complexed PSA, and PSA density may help to improve the specificity of PSA in men with BPH.

In the absence of prostate cancer the PSA value can provide a guide to prostate volume and also provide an indication of the likelihood of response to pharmacotherapy with a 5α-reductase inhibitor. A special concern relates to men with BPH already treated with a 5α-reductase inhibitor (e.g., finasteride or dutasteride). Serum PSA is reduced 40% to 50% after 3 to 6 months of treatment. Failure to establish a baseline (pretreatment) PSA level complicates interpretation of future PSA values. Men who are taking these agents should have their PSA value doubled to correctly assess their risk of harboring a prostatic adenocarcinoma.

Symptom Assessment

The International Prostate Symptom Score (IPSS), which is identical to the AUA Symptom Index, is recommended as the symptom scoring instrument to be used for the baseline assessment of symptom severity in men presenting with LUTS (McConnell et al, 1994; Denis et al, 1998). When the IPSS system is used, symptoms can be classified as mild (0 to 7), moderate (8 to 19), or severe (20 to 35). The symptom score should also be the primary determinant of treatment response or disease progression in the follow-up period. Although other symptom score questionnaires are used, the IPSS is now utilized in the United States and is regarded as the international standard.

However, the IPSS cannot be used to establish the diagnosis of BPH. Men (and women) with a variety of lower urinary tract disorders (e.g., infection, tumor, neurogenic bladder disease) will have a high IPSS. Nonetheless, the IPSS is the ideal instrument to grade baseline symptom severity, assess the response to therapy, and detect symptom progression in those men managed by watchful waiting. Optimal treatment decisions in individual patients will also need to take into account how a given level of symptoms affects each man's quality of life (degree of bothersomeness).

Most patients seeking treatment of BPH do so because of bothersome symptoms that affect the quality of their lives. Questionnaires that quantify those symptoms are important to assess the patient's symptoms, to determine the severity of the disease, to determine the progression of the disease over time, and to help identify the points of necessary intervention, as well as to document response to therapy. Such assessment methodologies also allow comparison of the effectiveness of various interventions. To the patient, of course, relief of symptoms is the single most important outcome, rather than his flow rate, detrusor pressure, or complex urethral resistance factors.

The IPSS was developed by the Measurement Committee of the AUA (Barry et al, 1992a, 1992b). Each question on the IPSS can yield 0 to 5 points, producing a total symptom score that can range from 0 to 35. This seven-question set is internally consistent (Cronbach's alpha, 0.85) and reliable (test-retest correlation, 0.93). The index correlates strongly with patients' global ratings of their urinary difficulties (r = 0.78) and is sensitive to treatment response.

The AUA score can be divided into "mild," "moderate," and "severe" symptom categories (Barry et al, 1992a). Only 1 of 120 men with scores from 0 to 7 was bothered more than a little by his symptoms; these men can be considered the mild symptom group. The majority of the 108 men with symptom scores from 8 to 19 were still bothered "not at all" or "a little." Only 4 of the 108 men were bothered "a lot." These men can be labeled as having moderate symptoms. Most men with scores from 20 to 35 were bothered by their condition "some" or "a lot" and can be considered to have severe symptoms.

Clearly, symptom scores alone do not capture the complete picture of a prostate problem as perceived by the individual patient. Symptom impact on a patient's lifestyle must be considered as well. An intervention may make more sense for a moderately symptomatic patient who finds his symptoms very bothersome than for a severely symptomatic patient who finds his symptoms tolerable. Although the IPSS correlates well with quality of life measures (Sagnier et al, 1995), there is still a need for sensitive BPH-specific quality of life instruments.

Additional Diagnostic Tests

Additional testing should be considered after the initial evaluation if there is a significant chance the patient's LUTS may not be due to BPH.

In the Agency for Health Care Policy and Research's (AHCPR) BPH Guidelines, patients with a normal initial evaluation and only mild symptomatology on the IPSS (scores 0 to 7) do not need additional diagnostic evaluation (McConnell et al, 1994). These patients should be considered for an active surveillance program and observed. Men who have developed serious complications of BPH should be treated surgically in most cases. Urinary flow rate, postvoid residual (PVR) urine, and pressure-flow urodynamic studies are appropriate tests to consider in the evaluation of men with moderate to severe symptoms (IPSS $\geq$ 8). The value of pressure-flow studies is debated, especially in men who elect watchful waiting or medical therapy as their management option. **Cystoscopy should not be done routinely** but is optional during later evaluation if invasive treatment is strongly considered (McConnell et al, 1994). In the International Consensus recommendations, urinary flow rate and PVR are recommended tests (Cockett et al, 1993; Denis et al, 1998).

It may be appropriate for the clinician to offer treatment alternatives to the patient without performing any further diagnostic tests. Especially if the patient chooses watchful waiting or noninvasive therapy, invasive diagnostic tests may not be necessary. Conversely, even if additional diagnostic tests were not performed initially and if the patient elects an invasive treatment option, it may be appropriate for the physician to consider further evaluation.

Diagnostic Tests in Men Who Require Surgery for Benign Prostatic Hyperplasia

Both AHCPR and International Consensus Guidelines recommend surgery if the patient has refractory urinary retention (failing at least one attempt of catheter removal) or any of the following conditions clearly secondary to BPH: recurrent UTI, recurrent gross hematuria, bladder stones, renal insufficiency, or large bladder diverticula (McConnell et al, 1994; Denis et al, 1998).

In this situation, the performance of further diagnostic testing is not necessary unless there is reason to suspect that the patient's retention may be due to detrusor hypocontractility. In that case, urodynamic studies (e.g., filling cystometry) may be helpful. Pressure-flow urodynamic studies are not informative if the patient cannot urinate. Cystoscopy is appropriate to consider before the operative procedure to help plan the most prudent approach. The presence of infection and hematuria in patients should prompt appropriate evaluation and therapy for these conditions before treatment of BPH.

Uroflowmetry

Uroflowmetry involves the electronic recording of the urinary flow rate throughout the course of micturition. It is a common, noninvasive urodynamic test used in the diagnostic evaluation of patients presenting with symptoms of BOO. The results of uroflowmetry are nonspecific for causes of the symptoms. For example, an abnormally low flow rate may be caused by an obstruction (e.g., hyperplastic prostate, urethral stricture, meatal stenosis) or by detrusor hypocontractility. **The AHCPR Guideline Panel reached the following conclusions regarding uroflowmetry** (McConnell et al, 1994):

- **Flow rate measurements are inaccurate if the voided volume is less than 125 to 150 mL.**
- **Flow rate recording is the single best noninvasive urodynamic test to detect lower urinary tract obstruction. Current evidence, however, is insufficient to recommend a given "cutoff" value to document the appropriateness of therapy.**
- **The peak flow rate (PFR; Qmax) more specifically identifies patients with BPH than does the average flow rate (Qave).**
- **Although Qmax decreases with advancing age and decreasing voided volume, no age or volume correction is currently recommended for clinical practice.**
- **Although considerable uncertainty exists, patients with a Qmax greater than 15 mL/s appear to have somewhat poorer treatment outcomes after prostatectomy than patients with a Qmax of less than 15 mL/s.**
- **A Qmax of less than 15 mL/s does not differentiate between obstruction and bladder decompensation.**

The Fourth International Consultation on BPH concluded that flow rate measurement represents a reproducible way to quantify the strength of the urinary stream and, when used in combination with symptom scores for a small subset of patients (20%), has a high probability of correctly characterizing whether there is BOO (Denis et al, 1998).

Despite its limitations, flow rate recording has demonstrated some sensitivity in diagnosing BOO due to BPH. Scott found that in about half the cases the patients with LUTS could be correctly classified as obstructed or nonobstructed by Qmax alone but that the addition of the detrusor pressure at Qmax allowed correct classification in two thirds of the group. The remaining one third of the patients were assessed by pressure-flow plot. In many of these patients, both pressure and Qmax were low, indicating a decompensating detrusor muscle as the source for the low Qmax.

Pressure-flow studies provide much more specific insight into detrusor function and the etiology of voiding dysfunction than do flow rate measurements. However, a number of outcome-based investigations demonstrate a modest additional value of pressure-flow studies over symptom and flow rate evaluation. **Detailed discussion of treatment options with the patient is recommended before pressure-flow testing is organized.**

Filling Cystometry (Cystometrography)

Filling cystometry adds limited information to the evaluation of most men with LUTS and is not recommended in routine cases (Cockett et al, 1993; McConnell et al, 1994). The test may have value in the evaluation of patients with known or suspected neurologic lesions and LUTS, but pressure-flow studies provide more specific information. In patients with suspected primary bladder or neurologic lesions and who cannot urinate (retention), filling cystometry may be useful.

Filling cystometry, an invasive urodynamic study, provides information on bladder capacity, the presence and threshold of overactive bladder contractions and bladder compliance. **Overactive bladder (OAB) contractions are present in about 60% of men with LUTS and correlate strongly with irritative voiding symptoms** (McConnell et al, 1994). However, overactive bladder contractions resolve in most patients after surgery. Only about one fourth of patients who have an overactive bladder before treatment retain the problem afterward. Patients whose symptoms do not improve after surgery are more likely to have a persistently overactive bladder, but preoperative cystometrography does not reliably identify those patients.

Although filling cystometry may demonstrate a poorly contractile detrusor in men with primary bladder dysfunction, pressure-flow studies provide much more insight into the interaction between bladder contraction and urethral resistance. Filling cystometry may be considered for men in urinary retention who are unable to urinate for a pressure-flow study but are seldom clinically helpful.

Urethrocystoscopy

Urethrocystoscopy is not recommended to determine the need for treatment (Cockett et al, 1993; McConnell et al, 1994). The test is recommended for men with LUTS who have a history of microscopic or gross hematuria, urethral stricture disease (or risk factors such as history of urethritis or urethral injury), bladder cancer or suspicion of carcinoma-in-situ, or prior lower urinary tract surgery (especially prior TURP). Urethrocystoscopy may be considered in men with moderate to severe symptoms who have chosen (or require) surgical or other invasive therapy to help the surgeon determine the most appropriate technical approach.

Urethrocystoscopy provides visual documentation of the appearance of the prostatic urethra and bladder in men with BPH. Historically, many urologists believed that the visual appearance of the lower urinary tract defines the severity of disease or predicts the outcome of treatment. However, this common urologic procedure has been poorly evaluated. No data are available on the sensitivity, specificity, or predictive value of the test. Potential benefits of urethrocystoscopy include the ability to demonstrate prostatic enlargement and visual obstruction of the urethra and the bladder neck; identification of specific anatomic abnormalities that alter clinical decision making; identification of bladder stones, trabeculation, and diverticula; measurement of PVR; and the ruling out of unrelated bladder and urethral pathologic processes. Potential adverse problems include patient discomfort, anesthetic or sedative risk, UTI, bleeding, and urinary retention. However, the probability of any of these problems occurring is uncertain. Except for discomfort, their occurrence is likely to be infrequent.

The endoscopic appearance of the bladder and prostate is often believed to be helpful in the decision to treat. **Although the linkage between the endoscopic appearance of the lower urinary tract and the treatment outcome is poorly documented, available information suggests that the relationship is minimal.** The endoscopic demonstration of obstruction (e.g., "kissing" lateral lobes) is of little or no predictive value. Bladder trabeculation may predict a slightly higher failure rate in patients managed by watchful waiting but does not predict the success or failure of surgery. Urethroscopy may, nevertheless, be useful in determining the technical feasibility of specific invasive therapies. For example, if urethrocystoscopy reveals a large middle lobe, transurethral incision of the prostate (TUIP) is unlikely to be successful. The decision to perform an open prostatectomy or laser vaporization may be appropriately influenced by the shape of the gland, as well as its size. In all of these cases, however, the patient and his physician have already selected invasive therapy. Urethroscopy is therefore performed to select (or rule out) specific techniques, not to determine the need for treatment.

Imaging of the Urinary Tract

Upper urinary tract imaging is not recommended in the routine evaluation of men with LUTS unless they also have one or more of the following: hematuria, UTI, renal insufficiency (ultrasound recommended), history of urolithiasis, or history of urinary tract surgery (McConnell et al, 1994; Denis et al, 1998).

IVU, to image the urinary tract of men with BPH before treatment, was performed by 73.4% of urologists in the United States in the late 1980s (Holtgrewe et al, 1989). The number of urologists using ultrasonography to image the urinary tract is unknown but likely to be considerable. IVU is associated with a 0.1% incidence of significant adverse events. There are no direct adverse events known to be associated with ultrasonography.

Of all renal imaging studies performed in men with BPH, 70% to 75% are entirely normal (McConnell et al, 1994; Denis et al, 1998). Only a small fraction of the 25% to 30% of abnormal findings mandate changes in the management of the patient. The incidence of any significant findings is no higher in the urinary tract of men with PBH, compared with age- and sex-matched controls, except for bladder stones, diverticula, and trabeculation indicating the presence of BOO.

Bundrick and Katz (1986) reported a change in management in 2.2% (4 of 180) of patients, based on findings obtained on IVU in a population preselected by excluding men with hematuria, infections, and a history of bladder tumors. Pinck and coworkers (1980) deferred TURP in favor of a more urgent intervention in 2.5% (14 of 557). These data indicate that a change in management would result in about 10% of the 25% of patients in whom the imaging study is "abnormal."

The presence or history of hematuria, renal insufficiency, UTI, and/or history of stones or prior urinary tract surgery increases the likelihood that IVU or ultrasonography will demonstrate clinically significant findings (Andersen et al, 1977; Bauer et al, 1980; Morrison, 1980; Christofferson and Moller, 1981; Wasserman et al, 1987; Juul et al, 1989). Donker and Kakiailatu (1978) reported that by screening those men with UTIs, gross hematuria, and renal insufficiency, they would have diagnosed almost all of the abnormal findings in their population of 307 men with BPH. Although there are no conclusive data on the combined incidence of the important clinical predictors just listed, approximately one third of all men with BPH have one or another indication for urinary tract imaging.

Assuming that an indication for renal imaging exists, a number of investigators strongly recommend, instead of IVU, ultrasonography combined with a kidney-ureter-bladder (KUB) radiograph and a determination of the renal function by measurement of the serum creatinine value (Matthews et al, 1982; Lilienfeld et al, 1985; Cascione et al, 1987; Hendrikx et al, 1988; Solomon and Van Niekerk, 1988).

ASSESSING THE EFFECTIVENESS AND SAFETY OF MEDICAL THERAPY FOR BENIGN PROSTATIC HYPERPLASIA

The role of treatment for any disease process depends on the magnitude of the clinical effect and the incidence and severity of treatment-related morbidity. Assessing the effectiveness of medical therapies for BPH requires defining clinically relevant endpoints, identifying quantitative and reliable clinical outcome measures, eliminating investigator and patient bias, accounting for the placebo response, and enrolling the proper number of subjects so that only clinically significant changes are statistically significant. Assessing the safety of medical therapies requires a rigorous effort to identify all treatment-related clinical, biochemical, teratogenic, and mutagenic adverse effects associated with drug treatment.

Clinical Endpoints

The clinical consequences of BPH include LUTS and associated reduction of quality of life, detrusor dysfunction characterized by detrusor acontractility, detrusor instability, and detrusor fibrosis; incomplete bladder emptying; acute and chronic urinary retention; UTI; renal insufficiency; and hematuria (Shapiro and Lepor, 1995). **The goals of treatment for BPH include relieving LUTS, decreasing BOO, improving bladder emptying, ameliorating overactive bladder activity, reversing renal insufficiency, and preventing disease progression, which may include a deterioration of symptoms,** **future episodes of gross hematuria, UTI, AUR, or the need for surgical intervention.**

Quantitative Outcome Measures

Symptoms

The primary objective of the AUA Symptom Index was to provide a universally accepted instrument to quantify the impact of BPH therapies on LUTS (Cockett et al, 1992). There is no standardized format for reporting changes in the AUA symptom score or other quantitative indices of symptom severity after treatment. Symptom response has been reported as a percentage of patients achieving a threshold response or as group mean changes in a symptom score. The literature typically reports the percentage of men achieving between a 30% and a 50% reduction in the symptom score. Expressing the symptom response as a single threshold response does not discriminate the overall magnitude of the clinical effect. When the baseline symptom scores are mild to moderate, small and clinically insignificant changes correspond to large percentage changes. When baseline symptom scores are severe, relatively large absolute changes may not be clinically significant. Symptom outcome should be expressed both as a percentage of patients achieving a threshold reduction response and as group mean changes in the symptom score.

The clinical significance of changes in the AUA Symptom Index has been reported by Barry and colleagues (1995). There were 1165 subjects who participated in a randomized double-blind placebo-controlled study of medical therapy and completed the AUA Symptom Index at baseline and after 3 months of treatment. The absolute and percentage changes in AUA Symptom Index and BPH Impact Index were correlated with five global ratings of symptom improvement (Fig. 87–1). The group mean changes in AUA Symptom Index for subjects rating their improvement as markedly, moderately, or slightly improved, unchanged, or worse were −8.8, −5.1, −3.0, −0.7, and +2.7, respectively. The relationship between the patients' global ratings of improvement and the AUA Symptom Index and BPH Impact Index changes were dependent on the baseline AUA Symptom Index. This important study provides the data required to determine sample sizes and interpret the clinical significance of symptom improvement in BPH clinical trials.

Bladder Outlet Obstruction

Experimental animal models of BOO have demonstrated profound changes in bladder ultrastructure, cellular composition, metabolism, and function resulting from BOO (Levin et al, 2000). These experimental observations must be cautiously extrapolated to man, because the response to BOO depends on the species and the severity and duration of obstruction (Levin et al, 1995). Animal studies demonstrate that under experimental conditions, BOO causes alterations likely to adversely affect bladder function. The justification for measuring and treating BOO in males with BPH is to reverse or prevent these deleterious consequences of BOO.

The primary limitation of urodynamic measurements of BOO is their lack of proven clinical relevance. The degree of BOO is not related to the severity of symptoms. Nitti and associates (1994) have shown that patients with BPH classi-

Table 87–1. Classification of α-Adrenergic Blockers and Recommended Doses

Class of α Blocker	Dose
Nonselective	
Phenoxybenzamine	10 mg bid
α₁	
Prazosin	2 mg bid
IR Alfuzosin	2.5 mg tid
Indoramin	20 mg bid
Long-Acting α₁	
Terazosin	5 or 10 mg qd
Doxazosin	4 or 8 mg qd
Alfuzosin SR	10 mg qd
Subtype Selective	
Tamsulosin	0.4 mg qd

noxybenzamine and prazosin are comparable; however, prazosin is better tolerated, implying that efficacy and toxicity are mediated primarily by the α_1 AR and α_2 AR, respectively (Lepor, 1989). Prazosin and other α_1 antagonists, including intermediate-release (IR) alfuzosin (Jardin et al, 1991) and indoramin (Ramsay et al, 1985), require at least twice-daily dosing, owing to the relatively short serum elimination half-lives.

The next advance in the development of α-adrenergic blockers was the development of pharmacologic agents with serum elimination half-lives that allowed for once-a-day dosing. Terazosin (Lepor et al, 1992) and doxazosin (Gillenwater et al, 1995) are long-acting α blockers that have been shown to be safe and effective for the treatment of BPH.

Molecular cloning studies have identified three subtypes of the α_1 AR (Andersson et al, 1997). Price and coworkers (1993) reported that the mRNA encoding the α_{1a} AR is predominant in the human prostate. The fact that the α_{1a} mRNA is translated does not mean the encoded protein is translated. Lepor and associates reported that, using autoradiographic (Kobayashi et al, 1993) and immunohistochemical (Walden et al, 1997) techniques, the α_{1a} AR and α_{1b} AR are predominant in the human stroma and epithelium, respectively. Prostate smooth muscle tension has been shown to be mediated by the α_{1a} AR (Forray et al, 1994a, 1994b). This observation is consistent with the localization of the α_1L AR to prostatic stroma. Muramatsu and colleagues (1994) subsequently reported that the α_1L AR was present in the prostate and mediated prostate smooth muscle contraction. The overwhelming evidence to date suggests that the α_1L AR binding site is a conformational state of the α_{1a} AR (Andersson et al, 1997).

Tamsulosin is a once-daily administered α_1 antagonist that exhibits some modest degree of selectivity for the α_{1a} versus the α_{1b} AR and no selectivity for the α_{1a} versus the α_{1d} AR (Foglar et al, 1995). The pharmaceutical industry has developed α_1 antagonists that are 1000-fold selective for the α_{1a} AR versus α_{1b}/α_{1d} (Forray et al, 1994b). Because the α_1 AR subtypes mediating efficacy and adverse effects are unknown, the optimal specific α_1 AR subtype antagonist for the treatment of BPH cannot be predicted (Lepor, 1996). **The clinical utility of these highly selective α_1 AR antagonists have not been confirmed by randomized controlled trials.**

Interpreting the α-Adrenergic Blocker Literature

The α blocker literature has recently been reviewed (Chapple, 1998; Djavan and Marberger, 1999; Lowe, 1999; Lepor, 2000). **Meta-analyses derived from the α blocker literature are often misleading because all of the data for a given drug are combined independent of dose and study design.**

Study Designs

Four study designs have been used to investigate α blockers for BPH: titration to fixed dose, titration to response, randomized dose withdrawal, and titration to maximal dose.

Subjects enrolled in **titration to fixed dose** studies receive one of several predetermined final doses independent of clinical response unless significant adverse effects are encountered. An advantage of this study design is that dose-dependent efficacy and safety of different doses are determined. A disadvantage is the requirement for a large sample size to identify statistically significant differences between placebo and all of the treatment groups.

Titration to response design allows the investigators to titrate the dose to a threshold response or maximal dose. An advantage of this design is a smaller sample size because all subjects receiving active treatment are analyzed as a composite group independent of final dose. A disadvantage of this design is that the maximal therapeutic effect may be underestimated if the titration is not to maximal response. The data are also misleading if expressed in terms of group mean changes according to final dose because all nonresponders are titrated to the maximal dose in the absence of toxicity.

A **randomized dose withdrawal** design begins with an open-label dose titration. All responders are randomized to active drug or placebo. An advantage of this design is the enrichment of responders. A disadvantage is that the results are not generalizable to untreated patients.

A **titration to maximal dose** design, like titration to response, requires a relatively small sample size because there is only one active treatment group. This study design defines maximal clinical response achievable in practice, providing the maximal dose is also the most efficacious tolerable dose.

Dose Response

Multicenter, randomized, placebo-controlled studies have consistently shown that symptom and flow improvement is dependent on the dose of the α_1 blockers. **The differences between the effectiveness of different doses were often not statistically significant because these dose-ranging studies were not adequately powered to show significant differences between dose groups.** MacDiarmid and coworkers (1999) have provided the most compelling evidence for a positive correlation relationship between dose and effectiveness of α_1 blockers in the treatment of BPH. Responders to 4 mg of doxazosin were randomized in a double-blind manner to receive 4 mg or 8 mg of doxazosin. The improvement observed in the 8-mg group was 3.7 symptom units greater than in the 4-mg group ($P = .03$). In phase III trials, the impact of dose observed in the responders is diluted by the lack of effect in the nonresponders. In clinical practice, nonresponders are withdrawn from treatment.

Review of the Literature

Several reviews have summarized the extensive clinical experiences with α blockade in BPH (Chapple, 1998; Djavan and Marberger, 1999; Lowe, 1999; Lepor, 2000; Roehrborn, 2004). Nonselective and short-acting $α_1$ antagonists are used less commonly in clinical practice, owing to tolerance and the requirement for multiple daily dose. Randomized, double-blind, placebo-controlled studies have reported the safety and efficacy of phenoxybenzamine (Caine et al, 1978; Abrams et al, 1982), prazosin (Hedlund et al, 1983; Martorana et al, 1984; Kirby et al, 1987; LeDuc et al, 1990; Ruutu et al, 1991; Chapple et al, 1992), indoramin (Iacovou and Dunn, 1987; Chow et al, 1990; Scott and Abrams, 1991), and IR alfuzosin (Ramsay et al, 1985; Carbin et al, 1991; Jardin et al, 1991; Hansen et al, 1994). With the exception of alfuzosin, these studies typically enrolled relatively small numbers of subjects into short-term single-dose studies without quantitative assessment of symptom improvement.

Multicenter, randomized, double-blind, placebo-controlled studies have examined the safety and efficacy of the long-acting α blockers terazosin, doxazosin, tamsulosin, and slow-release (SR) alfuzosin. Subjects enrolled in these studies generally presented with moderate/severe symptoms, PVR less than 300 mL, and no absolute indications for surgical intervention. Representative studies are reviewed to illustrate the safety, efficacy, and most effective use of α blockers in BPH. The reader is referred to the original articles for more comprehensive outcome assessments.

Terazosin

Terazosin is one of the most extensively investigated $α_1$ blockers for BPH. Randomized, double-blind, multicenter, placebo-controlled studies have consistently demonstrated the efficacy and safety of terazosin for BPH (DiSilverio, 1992; Lepor et al, 1992; Lloyd et al, 1992; Brawer et al, 1993; Elhilali et al, 1996; Lepor et al, 1996; Roehrborn et al, 1996) (Table 87–2). **The multicenter, double-blind, parallel-group, randomized, placebo-controlled study of once-a-day administration of terazosin to patients with symptomatic BPH reported by Lepor and associates (1992) is representative of the expectations of terazosin therapy.** Two hundred eighty-five patients entered the double-blind treatment receiving either placebo or 2, 5, or 10 mg of terazosin once daily.

Statistically significant decreases from baseline obstructive, irritative, and total symptom scores were observed for all terazosin treatment groups. The level of improvements in the symptom scores were dose dependent. The 10-mg terazosin treatment group exhibited significantly greater decreases in mean irritative and total symptom scores relative to the placebo group. The 5- and 10-mg terazosin treatment groups exhibited a significantly greater mean decrease in obstructive scores relative to the placebo group. The percentages of patients experiencing a greater than 30% improvement in the total symptom scores for the placebo, 2-, 5-, and 10-mg treatment groups were 40%, 51%, 57%, and 69%, respectively (Fig. 87–3). The percentage of patients experiencing greater than

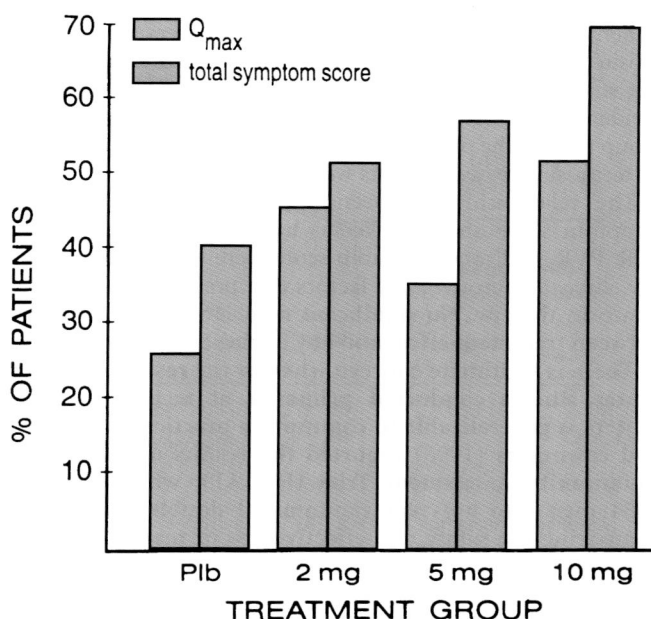

Figure 87–3. Two hundred eighty-five patients were enrolled in a randomized double-blind study comparing placebo and 2 mg, 5 mg, and 10 mg terazosin once daily. Percentages of patients experiencing greater than 30% improvement in total symptom scores and peak urinary flow rates are shown. (From Lepor H: Medical therapy for benign prostatic hyperplasia. Urology 1993;42:483-501.)

Table 87–2. Efficacy of Terazosin in Benign Prostatic Hyperplasia

Study	Enrolled (N)	Randomized Treatment (mo)	Dose(mg)	Group Mean Difference from Placebo	
				PFR (mL/s)	Symptom Score
Lepor et al, 1992	285	3	2	+1.1	−1.0
			5	+0.6	−1.3*
			10	+1.9†	−2.3‡
Brawer et al, 1993	160	6	Titration to response§	+1.4*	−3.5*
Roehrborn et al, 1996	2084	12	Titration to response§	+1.4*	−4.0‡
Elhilali et al, 1996	224	6	Titration to response§	+1.3	−1.8

*$P < .05$.
†$P < .01$.
‡$P < .001$.
§Maximal dose 10 mg.
PFR, peak flow rate.

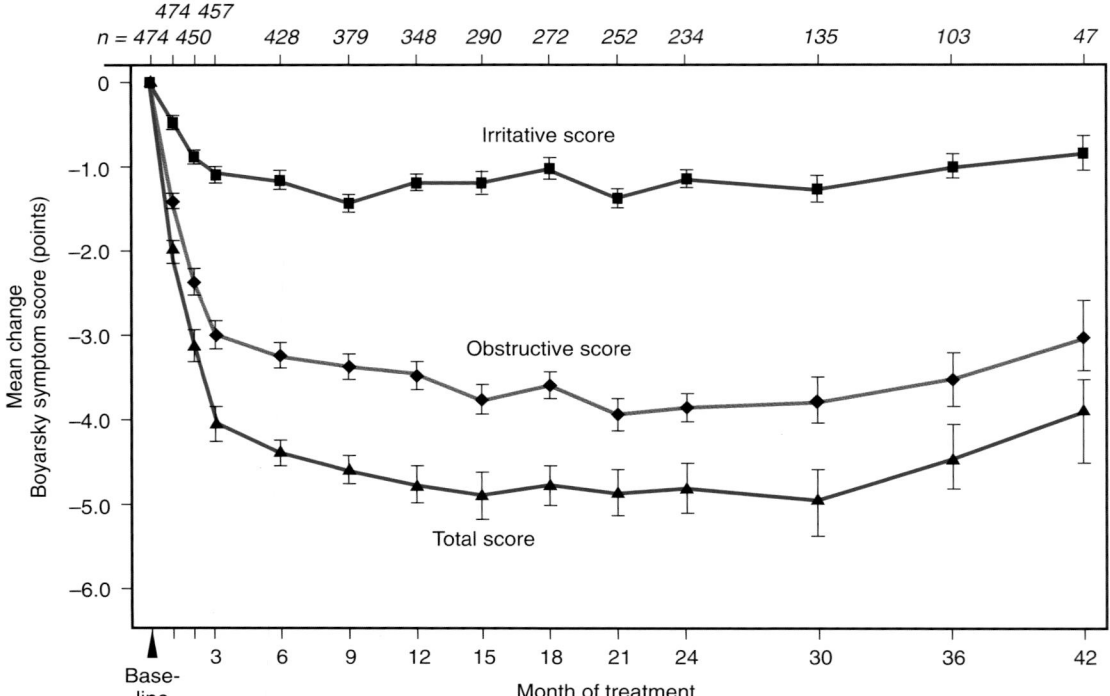

Figure 87–6. Mean change in Boyarsky symptom scores from baseline to 42 months. Baseline scores were 10.5 for total score, 6.2 for obstructive scores, and 4.3 for irritative scores. The numbers across the top of the graph indicate number of patients available at each time interval. All changes were significant at the $P \leq .05$ level. (From Lepor H and the Multicenter Study Group: Long-term efficacy and safety of terazosin in patients with benign prostatic hyperplasia. Urology 1995;45:406-413.)

Table 87–4. **Efficacy of Doxazosin in Benign Prostatic Hyperplasia**

Study	Enrolled (N)	Randomized Treatment (mo)	Dose (mg)	Group Mean Difference from Placebo	
				PFR (mL/s)	Symptom Score
Chapple et al, 1994	135	3	4	+1.5	NR
Fawzy et al, 1995	100	4	Titration 2-8 mg	+2.2*	−3.2†
Gillenwater et al, 1995	248	3.5	2	+1.4	−2.5
			4	+2.2‡	−4.7*
			8	+3.2*	−3.9†
			12	+3.5*	−2.1

*$P < .01$.
†$P < .001$.
‡$P < .05$.
NR, not reported; PFR, peak flow rate.

event were 14% and 2.1% in the doxazosin and placebo groups, respectively. The treatment-related incidence of adverse clinical events in this doxazosin study appears slightly higher than that of terazosin and may be a result of its greater effect on blood pressure.

Gillenwater and coworkers (1995) **reported a multicenter, randomized, double-blind, placebo-controlled titration to fixed dose study comparing placebo versus 2, 4, 8 and 12 mg of doxazosin** in 248 men with mild to moderate essential hypertension. The group mean changes in PFR and Boyarsky symptom score are summarized in Table 87–4 according to treatment groups. Because relatively small numbers of subjects were randomized into the individual treatment groups, the failure to demonstrate statistical significance between placebo and some of the active treatment groups reflects the small sample size. The group mean improvement in PFR was dose dependent and statistically significant relative to placebo for all active treatment groups. The mean improvements in symptom scores relative to placebo were statistically significant for the 4- and 8-mg doxazosin groups. Statistically and clinically significant changes in systolic blood pressure were observed between the placebo and the 4-, 8-, and 12-mg doxazosin groups. Lowering of blood pressure was a desirable outcome in these hypertensive patients. The overall treatment-related incidence of dizziness and fatigue was 15% and 10%, respectively. The percentages of subjects withdrawing because of an adverse event in the doxazosin versus placebo groups were 11.1% and 4.1%, respectively.

Statistically significant changes in symptom scores and PFR relative to baseline have been reported in a long-term open-label doxazosin extension study (Lepor, 1995). **The initial improvements in symptom scores and PFR in 450 subjects were maintained for up to 42 months.**

Kirby (1995) summarized the effects of doxazosin on blood pressure in normotensive and hypertensive men enrolled into two double-blind, placebo-controlled trials (Fawzy et al, 1995; Gillenwater et al, 1995). The treatment-related mean reductions in sitting systolic blood pressure in the normotensive and hypertensive subjects were 3 and 17 mm Hg, respectively. The treatment-related mean reductions in sitting diastolic blood pressure in the normotensive and hypertensive subjects were 4 and 3 mm Hg, respectively.

With the standard preparation of doxazosin, multiple titration steps are used to obtain optimal therapeutic response. Often, doxazosin standard is started at 1 mg/day and titrated through 2 and 4 mg/day to 8 mg/day to obtain the optimal response. The controlled release GITS formulation of doxazosin reduces the plasma peak-to-trough ratio to minimize the need for titration.

To compare the two formulations in 795 men with BPH, doxazosin standard was initiated at 1 mg/day, titrated to 2 mg/day after 1 week, to 4 mg/day at 3 weeks and 8 mg/day at 7 weeks if indicated. This regimen was compared with doxazosin GITS initiated at 4 mg/day and titrated to 8 mg/day after 7 weeks if indicated, and to a placebo group over 13 weeks. The symptoms of BPH were measured on the International Prostate Symptom Score (IPSS), which has seven questions (covering frequency, nocturia, weak urinary stream, hesitancy, intermittence, incomplete emptying, and urgency) scored 0 (absent) to 5 (severe). On the IPPS there was an improvement of −8.4 and −8.0 with doxazosin standard and GITS, respectively, compared with −6.0 in the placebo group. Doxazosin standard and GITS produced clinically comparable increases in mean peak urinary flow rate, compared with placebo, with a greater improvement observed earlier after treatment with doxazosin GITS than with doxazosin standard. A similar number of patients in both doxazosin groups were titrated to the maximal dose of 8 mg for both formulations. The incidence of adverse effects was slightly higher with doxazosin standard than doxazosin GITS and placebo, which caused a similar incidence.

The above study and another with 680 men were combined to further analyze the comparison between doxazosin standard and GITS (Kirby et al, 2003). In addition to confirming the results just given, a subgroup reporting sexual dysfunction at baseline had a modest clinical improvement in sexual function with both preparations of doxazosin. Treatment-related adverse events occurred in 16.1% of patients on doxazosin GITS, 25.3% of patients on doxazosin standard, and 7.7% of patients on placebo. Headache and dizziness occurred in 6.0% and 5.3% of doxazosin GITS patients, compared with 5.1% and 9.1% of doxazosin standard patients, respectively (placebo, 4.5% and 1.9%, respectively). Fewer patients on doxazosin GITS (5.7%) or placebo (2.6%) discontinued treatment because of adverse events than on doxazosin standard (7.2%). The reduction in blood pressure was not clinically significant in the normotensive patients, but there were clinically significant reductions in blood pressure with both preparations of

doxazosin (placebo, 3.9/5.0; doxazosin standard, 7.4/6.1; doxazosin GITS, 9.4/6.8).

A comparison of the nonconcurrent multicenter, randomized, double-blind, placebo-controlled studies of terazosin (see Table 87–2) and doxazosin (see Table 87–4) shows similar efficacy. Studies of doxazosin versus tamsulosin (Kirby et al, 2004) and doxazosin versus alfuzosin (De Reijke et al, 2004) revealed only minor, clinically insignificant, differences in safety and efficacy.

α-Adrenergic blockers such as doxazosin may possibly influence smooth muscle growth in the prostate. In BPH patients treated with α_1-adrenoceptor antagonists, there is a decreased expression of myosin heavy chain mRNA, a functional marker for the smooth muscle phenotype (Lin et al, 2002).

Biopsy and prostatectomy specimens from untreated and doxazosin-treated BPH patients suggest that doxazosin may induce apoptosis in both the epithelial and stromal cells with little effect on cell proliferation (Chon et al, 1999). The apoptosis was associated with a decrease in smooth muscle α-actin expression and stromal regression (Chon et al, 1999). Another study showed that the mean pretreatment baseline apoptosis was 1.9% and 1.0% for the epithelial and stromal prostate components (Kyprianou et al, 1999). The mean apoptotic indexes increased after 3 months of doxazosin treatment for BPH to 6% in the glandular epithelial and 12% in the smooth muscle cells (Kyprianou et al, 1999). By 12 months after treatment, epithelial apoptosis had decreased to constitutive levels, whereas the apoptotic index of prostatic stromal cells remained high (Kyprianou et al, 1999).

In primary cultures of human prostate stroma cells, doxazosin increased apoptosis and decreased cell numbers (Ilio et al, 2001). Transforming growth factor (TGF)-β_1 also decreases cell numbers, and because doxazosin increased the levels of TGF-β_1 in the cells, it was suggested that the effect of doxazosin may be mediated through TGF-β_1 (Ilio et al, 2001).

The ability of doxazosin to induce apoptosis may be shared with the other quinazoline-based α_1-adrenoceptor antagonists terazosin and prazosin, although it seems unlikely that this effect is α_1-adrenoceptor mediated (Gonzalez-Juanatey et al, 2003). The apoptotic effects of the quinazoline-based α_1-adrenoceptor antagonists may be linked to their ability to inhibit HERG potassium channels, which has been demonstrated using cloned channels expressed in *Xenopus* oocytes (Thomas et al, 2004).

Recent data also suggest that doxazosin may have a mildly beneficial impact on sexual function in men suffering from BPH (Kirby et al, 2005). The mechanism for this effect is still uncertain but may be the result of a vasodilatory action within the corpora cavernosa.

Tamsulosin

Tamsulosin is the most potent available α_1 antagonist indicated for the treatment of BPH (Foglar et al, 1995). One of the unique features of tamsulosin is that it exhibits some degree of specificity for the α_{1a} AR (Foglar et al, 1995). The efficacy and safety of tamsulosin has been investigated in four multicenter, randomized, double-blind, placebo-controlled studies (Kawabe et al, 1990; Abrams et al, 1995; Lepor et al, 1998; Narayan et al, 1998) (Table 87–5).

Table 87–5. **Efficacy of Tamsulosin for Benign Prostatic Hyperplasia**

Study	Enrolled (N)	Randomized Treatment (mo)	Dose (mg)	Group Mean Difference from Placebo	
				PFR (mL/s)	Symptom Score
Kawabe et al, 1990	270	1	0.1	+0.3	NR
			0.2	+2.6	NR
			0.4	+2.1	NR
Abrams et al, 1995	313	2¼*	0.4	+1.7*	−1.3†
Lepor et al, 1998	756	3	0.4	+1.3†	−2.8‡
			0.8	+1.7‡	−3.2‡
Narayan et al, 1998	735	3	0.4	+0.6	−1.5†
			0.8	+0.9†	−2.2†

*$P < .05$.
†$P < .01$.
‡$P < .001$.
NR, not reported; PFR, peak flow rate.

Lepor and coworkers (1998) reported a multicenter, randomized, double-blind, placebo-controlled study of 756 American men with clinical BPH randomized to receive placebo or 0.4 or 0.8 mg of tamsulosin for 13 weeks. The mean changes in AUA symptom score, PFR, and adverse events are summarized in Table 87–5. The symptom score improvements were significantly greater in the 0.8-mg tamsulosin group compared with the 0.4-mg group. The treatment-related incidences of dizziness, asthenia, rhinitis, and abnormal ejaculation in the 4-mg group were 5%, 3%, 3%, and 6%, respectively and, in the 0.8-mg group, they were 6%, 3%, 9%, and 18%, respectively. The mean changes in systolic and diastolic blood pressure in the placebo and tamsulosin groups were not significantly different for both hypertensive and normotensive subjects. In the subjects who were hypertensive and uncontrolled, the systolic blood pressure changes in the placebo, 0.4-mg, and 0.8-mg groups were −8.4, −7.2, and −10.2 mm Hg, respectively. The advantage of not lowering blood pressure in men who are hypertensive at baseline is controversial.

Of the 618 subjects who completed the 13-week randomized study reported by Lepor and coworkers (1998), 418 (68%) continued into the 40-week extension study on the same double-blind medication and dose. **The symptom and flow rate improvements observed at the end of the 13-week study were maintained throughout the 40-week extension study.**

Narayan and associates (1998) reported the results of a randomized, double-blind, placebo-controlled trial comparing the safety and effectiveness of 0.4 and 0.8 mg of tamsulosin versus placebo. Seven hundred thirty-five men were randomized in the study. The active treatment was 13 weeks. The treatment-related improvements in the AUA symptom score and PFR were comparable with those reported by Lepor and coworkers (1998). The differences between 0.4 mg and 0.8 mg were not statistically significant; however, the study lacked statistical power to show clinically significant differences between the active treatment groups. The treatment-related incidences of asthenia, dizziness, rhinitis, and abnormal ejaculation observed for the 0.4-mg tamsulosin group were 2%, 5%, 3%, and 11%, respectively; and for the 0.8-mg tamsulosin group they were 3%, 8%, 9%, and 18%, respectively. The incidences of retrograde ejaculation and rhinitis were significantly greater in the 0.8-mg group compared with the 0.4-mg group. No statistically or clinically significant differences were observed for systolic blood pressure between any of the treatment groups.

A systematic review of tamsulosin therapy for BPH has been published (Wilt et al, 2002). This included 14 studies with a total of 4122 patients. The mean change in symptom score was 12% for the 0.4-mg dosage and 16% with the 0.8-mg dose. Improvements in flow rate were 1.1 mL/s for both dosages. Adverse events were generally mild and included dizziness, rhinitis, and abnormal ejaculation. These increased in a dose-dependent manner with discontinuations due to such effects similar to placebo at 0.2 mg, but increasing to 16% with the 0.8-mg/day dosage.

Alfuzosin

Alfuzosin is another α-adrenergic blocking agent that has been extensively utilized in BPH pharmacotherapy. **Jardin and colleagues (1991) reported the first large-scale, multicenter, randomized, placebo-controlled trial demonstrating that alfuzosin was safe and effective for the treatment of BPH** (Table 87–6). A long-term open-label extension study showed that the effectiveness of alfuzosin was durable up to 30 months (Jardin et al, 1994). The primary limitation of alfuzosin was a requirement for multiple daily doses (2.5 mg three times a day or 5 mg twice a day). In the absence of any demonstrable advantage over the once-a-day drugs like terazosin, doxazosin, and tamsulosin there was no compelling reason to prescribe alfuzosin.

SR alfuzosin is a new formulation that allows for a once-daily dosing regimen without dose titration. Buzelin and coworkers (1997) reported the first randomized, multicenter, placebo-controlled trial evaluating the safety and effectiveness of SR alfuzosin for the treatment of BPH. Three hundred and ninety subjects were randomized to once-daily 5 mg alfuzosin versus placebo for 12 weeks. The treatment-related improvements in the IPSS and PFR were −1.6 symptom unit and 1.3 mL/s, respectively. The incidence of dropouts because of adverse events was 4.6% and 7.1% in the SR alfuzosin and placebo groups, respectively. The 2-mm Hg change in systolic and diastolic blood pressure was not significantly different from that in the placebo group. The incidences of dizziness and asthenia were similar in the SR alfuzosin and placebo groups.

Table 87-6. Efficacy of Alfuzosin in Benign Prostatic Hyperplasia

Study	Enrolled (N)	Randomized Treatment (mo)	Dose (mg)	Group Mean Difference for Placebo	
				PFR (mL/s)	Symptom Score
Jardin et al (1994)	518	6	7.5–10	1.5*	−1.0[†]
Buzelin et al (1997)	390	3	5 mg bid	1.3[†]	−1.6[‡]
Kerrenbroeck et al (2000)	447	3	10 qd	0.9*	−2.0[‡]
			2.5 tid	1.8[†]	−1.5[‡]

*$P < .05$.
[†]$P < .001$.
[‡]$P < .01$.
PFR, peak flow rate.

SR alfuzosin (10 mg/day) has been compared with IR alfuzosin (2.5 mg three times daily) and placebo (van Kerrenbroeck et al, 2000). After a 1-month placebo lead-in, 447 patients were randomly assigned in equal proportions to the three treatment groups for 3 months. The improvement in the IPSS was 6.9, 6.4, and 4.9 in the alfuzosin 10 mg/day, alfuzosin 2.5 mg three times a day, and placebo groups, respectively. The symptom improvement observed in both active treatment groups was significantly greater than that in the placebo group. The improvements in the filling and voiding subscores and quality of life index were also significantly greater in the active treatment group relative to the placebo group. The improvement in the PFR was 2.3 mL/s, 3.2 mL/s, and 1.4 mL/s in the SR alfuzosin, IR alfuzosin, and placebo groups, respectively. The modest improvements in the PFR were significantly greater in both active treatment groups compared with placebo. The incidences of dizziness were 2.1%, 4.7%, and 1.3%; and those for asthenia were 3.5%, 0.7%, and 2.6% in the SR alfuzosin, IR alfuzosin, and placebo groups, respectively. No sexual dysfunction was reported in the 10-mg/day alfuzosin group. There were no statistically or clinically significant treatment-related effects on blood pressure in normotensive or hypertensive subjects. Of those men who were hypertensive at baseline, the mean reductions in the standing blood pressure were 8.1, 8.6, and 5.8 mm Hg, respectively, in the SR alfuzosin, IR alfuzosin, and placebo groups.

Alfuzosin has been shown to have a beneficial effect on the quality of life of men suffering from BPH. In the ALFUS study (Roehrborn, 2001) the quality of life index improved by 18% in both active groups compared with 8% in the placebo arm ($P = .002$). In an open extension of the ALFORTI trial there was a 35% improvement from baseline of quality of life (van Kerrebroeck et al, 2002). Some part of this effect may be the result of a mildly beneficial impact on sexual function (Van Moorselarr et al, 2005).

Because of the lack of adverse effects and blood pressure changes, alfuzosin has been described as a uroselective drug (Kirby, 1998a). SR alfuzosin exhibits no pharmacologic uroselectivity for any of the α_1 subtypes (Andersson et al, 1997). In vivo studies in the conscious rat have shown that alfuzosin reduces urethral pressure without significantly altering blood pressure (Martin et al, 1995). This experimental observation does not prove clinical uroselectivity because terazosin and doxazosin do not alter blood pressure in normotensive subjects. Another explanation for the lack of adverse events has been the low penetration of alfuzosin into the brain (Rouguier et al, 1994). It is also important to consider that the better tol-

erance may simply be related to a lower level of α_1-adrenergic blockade because the treatment-related improvement of the 10 mg of alfuzosin appears to be less than that achieved with 10 mg of terazosin and 8 mg of doxazosin.

The long-term effectiveness of IR alfuzosin 2.5 mg three times a day is supported by an open-label prospective 3-year trial involving 3228 men with clinical BPH (Lukacs et al, 2000). The improvements in symptom score in BPH-specific health-related quality of life index observed at the 3-month visit were maintained throughout the 36 months of follow-up. A total of 20.1% of the men withdrew from the study. Only 4.2% of the men discontinued therapy because of an adverse event. The other reasons for withdrawal were death, 7.6%; loss of follow-up, 1.7%; lack of efficacy, 1.8%; study withdrawal owing to personal reasons, 0.8%; concomitant disease, 0.7%; and other reasons, 3.3%. Only 0.3% of men experienced AUR.

Effects of α-Adrenergic Blockers on Bladder Outlet Obstruction

The primary objective of medical therapy is to improve urinary symptoms. The relevance of urodynamic studies for assessing the clinical use of medical therapy for BPH is controversial. A drug that improves urodynamic parameters of BOO without relieving LUTS would be of limited clinical utility. Conversely, a drug that relieves LUTS without improving urodynamic parameters of BOO would be of great clinical importance. There are relatively few randomized, placebo-controlled studies examining the effects of α-adrenergic blockers on pressure-flow parameters. One of the limitations to designing these urodynamic studies is the definition of a clinically significant outcome.

Martorana and colleagues (1997) reported a randomized, double-blind, placebo-controlled study examining the effect of 1 month of alfuzosin, 2.5 mg three times a day, on pressure-flow urodynamic parameters. The changes in detrusor pressure at maximal flow, detrusor opening pressure, and maximal detrusor pressure were significantly greater in the alfuzosin-treatment group compared with the placebo group. There were no significant differences between the effects of alfuzosin and those of placebo on PFR.

Acute Urinary Retention

It is reasonable to speculate that urinary retention is caused in part by dynamic factors because a significant proportion of men void spontaneously after catheter placement (Taube and Gajraj, 1989). If urinary retention is caused by increased sympathetic activity at the level of the prostatic smooth muscle, an α-adrenergic blocker should increase the likelihood of spontaneous voiding after catheter removal. McNeill and coworkers (1999) examined the effects of SR alfuzosin, 5 mg twice a day, versus placebo in men presenting with AUR. The indwelling urinary catheter was removed 24 hours after initiation of treatment. Men were excluded if the bladder volume at the time of catheter drainage was greater than 1.5 liters. Fifty-five percent and 29% of men randomized to the SR alfuzosin and placebo groups voided spontaneously after catheter removal, respectively. The clinical effect was greatest in younger men. Of the men who successfully completed the voiding trial, 32% ultimately experienced a second episode of AUR or underwent prostatectomy.

The advantage of SR alfuzosin, tamsulosin, and doxazosin XL over terazosin in the management of AUR is that a therapeutic dose can be administered at the onset of treatment, thereby decreasing the time for attempting catheter removal.

A large-scale, randomized, double-blind, placebo-controlled trial of long-term duration is required to determine whether a medical therapy prevents AUR. In the MTOPS trial finasteride or combination therapy of finasteride with doxazosin, but not doxazosin alone, reduced the incidence of AUR (McConnell et al, 2003) . Because men with large prostates have on average a threefold greater chance of developing urinary retention (Jacobsen et al, 1997), enrolling men with large prostates would enhance the probability of observing an effect on AUR. **The 3-year open-label prospective study of alfuzosin supported a 0.3% risk of retention** (Lukacs et al, 2000). This is significantly lower than the predicted risk of developing urinary retention in an age-matched cohort of men (Jacobsen et al, 1997).

α-Adrenergic Blockers in the Elderly

The adverse events associated with terazosin and doxazosin that may be particularly problematic in the elderly are dizziness and orthostatic hypertension. Kaplan and colleagues (1997) reviewed a personal series of 36 men with BPH older than 80 years treated with terazosin or doxazosin. α-Adrenergic blockers were well tolerated, and no serious adverse events were observed. This experience was not of adequate size to address the incidence of falls. Pooled analysis of multicenter, randomized, placebo-controlled studies of terazosin (Zhang and Manski, 1998), doxazosin (Kaplan and D'Alisera, 1998), and tamsulosin (Chapple et al, 1997) have reported that the incidences of adverse events are not age dependent. It is important to emphasize that men enrolled into these studies were highly selected and so the tolerability and safety is not generalizable to all elderly men.

α-Adrenergic Blockers and the Treatment of Benign Prostatic Hyperplasia and Coexisting Hypertension

The α-adrenergic blockers terazosin and doxazosin are established agents for the treatment of hypertension (Joint National Committee on Prevention, Detection, Evaluation and Treatment of High Blood Pressure, 1997). The overwhelming clinical evidence demonstrates that terazosin and doxazosin lower blood pressure primarily in hypertensive men and that the blood pressure lowering is clinically significant (Fawzy et al, 1995; Gillenwater et al, 1995; Lepor et al, 1997; Kirby, 1995, 1998a; Lowe et al, 1999). **Approximately 30% of men treated for BPH have coexisting hypertension** (Boyle and Napalkov, 1995). It is reasonable to advocate the use of α-adrenergic blockers as the treatment of choice for men with hypertension and BPH.

A recent interim analysis of the Anti-Hypertensive and Lipid Lowering Treatment to Prevent Heart Attack Trial (ALLHAT) questions the use of doxazosin in men at risk for developing congestive heart failure (ALLHAT Collaborative Research Group, 2000). In this study of 24,335 subjects with hypertension and at least one other coronary risk factor, men were randomized to chlorthalidone, doxazosin, amlodipine, or lisinopril. A significant increased risk of congestive heart failure in the doxazosin group relative to the chlorthalidone group was the basis for the decision to discontinue the doxazosin arm of the antihypertensive trial. There was no significant increase in congestive heart failure between doxazosin and the other antihypertensive agents. It is interesting that comparable levels of blood pressure reduction were achieved by both drugs. **The ALLHAT study questions the role of doxazosin as first-line therapy for the treatment of hypertension. The study does not assess the relative risks and benefits of doxazosin in men with BPH and hypertension, nor does it have any bearing on the use of doxazosin in combination with other antihypertensive agents.** Doxazosin remains an acceptable agent to treat BPH that coexists with hypertension. It should be the discretion of the physician managing the hypertension to add additional agents for treating the hypertension.

Mechanism of Adverse Events Associated with α-Adrenergic Blockade

Dizziness and asthenia are the adverse events most commonly associated with α-adrenergic blocker therapy. Elucidating the mechanism of action for these adverse events is essential for α_1 subtype drug development programs. It has been assumed that dizziness and possibly asthenia were caused by cardiovascular effects. Lepor and colleagues (2000) correlated the incidence of adverse events associated with terazosin relative to blood pressure changes. Men experiencing dizziness and asthenia did not exhibit greater changes in blood pressure while on terazosin therapy. Only postural hypotension was associated with greater changes in blood pressure. α_1-Adrenergic-mediated dizziness and asthenia are likely due to effects at the level of the central nervous system. Therefore, it cannot be assumed that developing an α blocker that eliminates effects on blood pressure will necessarily improve the tolerability of α blockers.

Comparison of α-Adrenergic Blockers

Because the therapeutic effect and adverse events associated with α blockers are both dose dependent, the effectiveness

and tolerability of two different α blockers can be determined only in a randomized, double-blind, placebo-controlled trial. It is imperative that these studies be appropriately powered to show statistically significant effects for effectiveness and tolerability.

Buzelin and coworkers (1997a) reported a randomized, placebo-controlled study comparing α blockers (IR alfuzosin, 2.5 mg three times a day, versus tamsulosin, 0.4 mg/day). The improvements in Boyarsky symptom score and PFR and the incidences of dizziness and asthenia were not significantly different between the two treatment groups. The effects of alfuzosin and tamsulosin on systolic and diastolic supine or standing blood pressures in the hypertensive patients were also not significantly different. This study suggests that IR alfuzosin and tamsulosin have equivalent effectiveness and tolerability. The obvious benefit of tamsulosin is that the dose does not have to be titrated.

The recommended daily doses of terazosin, doxazosin, tamsulosin, and SR alfuzosin are 10 mg, 8 mg, 0.4 mg, and 10 mg, respectively. The clinical data suggest that terazosin, 10 mg, and doxazosin, 8 mg, are more effective than tamsulosin, 0.4 mg, and alfuzosin, 10 mg (see Tables 87–2 and 87–4 to 87–6). The incidences of asthenia and dizziness appear to be higher for terazosin and doxazosin. **The apparent better tolerability of tamsulosin and SR alfuzosin may simply be because of degree of α_1 blockade and not uroselectivity.** Assessing the relative efficacy and tolerability of daily terazosin, 10 mg, or doxazosin, 8 mg, versus tamsulosin, 0.4 mg, or SR alfuzosin, 10 mg, would address this issue. In the absence of these studies, nonconcurrent studies can be compared, recognizing the potential impact of differences in study design, patient selection, recording of adverse events, and dosing.

Terazosin and doxazosin exhibit very similar pharmacologic and pharmacokinetic properties. It is, therefore, not surprising that the effectiveness and tolerability of these two agents are also comparable. The effectiveness of terazosin and doxazosin are both dose dependent, with the greatest recorded improvements in symptom scores observed at the 10-mg and 8-mg daily doses, respectively. These doses have both been shown to be significantly more effective than lower doses. Although the incidence of adverse events is dose dependent, the 10-mg and 8-mg doses of terazosin and doxazosin are generally well tolerated.

Terazosin is unit priced so that there is no financial disincentive to titrate up to the 10-mg dose. There is no significant cost advantage between 10 mg of terazosin and 8 mg of doxazosin. **Thus, until data from randomized, double-blind comparative trials demonstrate the contrary, 10 mg of terazosin and 8 mg of doxazosin should be considered equivalent.** Although the price of doxazosin therapy can be reduced by dividing the 8-mg tablet, this comes at the expense of significant loss of effectiveness.

Tamsulosin and SR alfuzosin have been positioned as uroselective α_1 blockers. Randomized studies have shown that 0.8 mg of tamsulosin is significantly more effective at relieving symptoms than the 0.4-mg dose (Lepor et al, 1998). No dose-ranging studies have been performed with SR alfuzosin. Unfortunately, an 0.8-mg tamsulosin dose has not been manufactured. The cost of 0.8-mg tamsulosin is twice that of 10-mg terazosin and 8-mg doxazosin. The 0.8-mg dose is therefore cost prohibitive, especially because there is no greater efficacy over the 10 mg of terazosin or 8 mg of doxazosin. One of the assumed advantages of a uroselective α_1 blocker is better tolerance. Whereas the 0.8-mg tamsulosin dose appears to cause less asthenia than terazosin and doxazosin, the incidence of dizziness is comparable and rhinitis and abnormal ejaculation are markedly greater. **Tamsulosin, 0.4 mg, is the most appropriate dose, owing to the cost and adverse events associated with the 0.8-mg dose.** The available clinical data suggest that 0.4 mg of tamsulosin is less effective than 10 mg of terazosin and 8 mg of doxazosin and exhibits no better tolerance. The advantage of 0.4 mg of tamsulosin is that this clinically effective dose can be administered without dose titration. For those prescribers who routinely do not offer the higher doses of terazosin (10 mg) and doxazosin (8 mg), 0.4 mg of tamsulosin is a reasonable and even preferred alternative.

The major advantage of 0.4 mg of tamsulosin and SR alfuzosin is the lack of requirement for dose titration. For men presenting in urinary retention, tamsulosin and SR alfuzosin will likely decrease the time to voiding trial because of the lack of titration to an effective dose. The data suggest that tamsulosin and SR alfuzosin exhibit less effect on blood pressure in hypertensive men compared with terazosin and doxazosin. The fact that terazosin and doxazosin lower blood pressure in men who are hypertensive may in some circumstances be an advantage, especially because 30% of men with BPH have hypertension.

The Future of α-Adrenergic Blocker Therapy

Several major pharmaceutical companies have active drug development programs for prostate selective α_1 antagonists. **The advantages of the α_1 AR subtype-selective antagonists will depend on the α_1 AR subtype that mediates efficacy, vascular effects, toxicity, and some of the desirable nonprostate effects such as alterations of serum lipids** (Lepor, 1996). Although the α_{1a} AR mediates prostate smooth muscle, it is conceivable that efficacy is also mediated by nonprostate smooth muscle mechanisms. The advantages of α_1 AR subtype—selective antagonists cannot be reliably predicted from animal models and therefore will await properly designed clinical trials.

Summary

Multicenter, randomized, double-blind, placebo-controlled studies have unequivocally demonstrated the safety and efficacy of α-adrenergic blockers for the treatment of BPH. The clinical response is rapid and dose dependent. Long-term open-label studies have demonstrated that the clinical response is durable. The long-acting α_1 blockers are well tolerated. The α_1 blockers are safe in the elderly, diminish BOO, and reduce the risk of urinary retention. Terazosin and doxazosin significantly lower blood pressure only in hypertensive subjects, allowing treatment of coexisting BPH and hypertension. Direct comparison studies of the α blockers are sparse and involve small numbers of patients; therefore, any claims of superiority cannot be justified.

ANDROGEN SUPPRESSION AS A TREATMENT OPTION

Rationale for Androgen Suppression

The rationale for androgen suppression is based on the **observation that the embryonic development of the prostate is dependent on the androgen dihydrotestosterone (DHT)** (Shapiro, 1990). Testosterone is converted to DHT by the enzyme 5α-reductase. The genetic deficiency of 5α-reductase in males results in a rudimentary prostate and in feminized external genitalia (Walsh et al, 1974). The development of BPH is also an androgen-dependent process (Coffey and Walsh, 1990). Castration and pharmacologic agents suppressing testosterone and DHT synthesis or action have been shown to reduce prostate volume in men with established BPH (McConnell, 1990). Peters and Walsh (1987) demonstrated that androgen suppression causes regression primarily of the epithelial elements of the prostate. Reducing prostate volume is thought to decrease the static component of BOO resulting from BPH. The primary limitations of the androgen suppression hypothesis are that the pathophysiology of clinical BPH is not dependent on prostate size.

Classification of Pharmacologic Agents

Surgical castration was reported to be an effective treatment for enlarged prostates in the 1890s (White, 1895; Cabot, 1896). Scott and Wade (1969) reported the first study investigating androgen suppression (medical castration) for BPH. Cyproterone acetate, an antiandrogen, was reported to decrease symptoms and increase PFR in the majority of treated subjects. The pharmacologic strategies of androgen suppression that have been investigated for BPH over the past 3 decades are summarized in Table 87–7.

Caveats Related to Interpreting Androgen Suppression Studies

The efficacy of androgen suppression in BPH is presumed to be mediated by reduction of prostate volume. **Maximal reduction of prostate volume after initiation of androgen suppression is achieved within 6 months** (Peters and Walsh, 1987; Gormley et al, 1992). Therefore, randomized treatment must be at least 6 months to capture maximal therapeutic effect.

Because the mechanism of action is by means of reduction of prostate volume, it is reasonable to assume that subjects with larger prostates achieve the greatest therapeutic benefit. **The majority of randomized, double-blind, placebo-controlled clinical trials evaluating androgen suppression enrolled subjects with larger prostates** (Gormley et al, 1992; Eri and Tveter, 1993a, 1993b; Finasteride Study Group, 1993; McConnell et al, 1998). The results of studies enrolling a disproportionate number of men with large prostates may not be generalizable to the "typical" patient with clinical BPH.

Review of the Literature

Several excellent reviews of androgen suppression for BPH have been published (Vaughan and Lepor, 1996; McConnell,

Table 87–7. Androgen Suppression: Classification of Pharmacologic Agents and Dosages

Drugs	Dose	Reference
GnRH Analogs		
Leuprolide	3.75 mg IM qd mo	Schroeder et al, 1986
		Keane et al, 1988
		Eri and Tveter, 1993
Nafarelin acetate	400 mg SQ qd	Peters and Walsh, 1987
Cetrorelix	1 mg SQ qd ± loading dose	Lepor et al, 1997
Progestational Agents		
17α-Hydroxycortisone	200 mg IM weekly	Meiraz et al, 1977
Megestrol	250 mg PO tid	Donkervoort et al, 1975
	40 mg PO tid	Geller et al, 1979
Antiandrogens		
Flutamide	100 mg tid	Caine et al, 1975
	250 mg tid	Stone, 1989
Oxandolone	200 mg IM weekly	Ostri et al, 1989
Bicalutamide (Casodex)	50 mg qd	Eri and Tveter, 1993
Zanoterone	100-800 mg qd	Berger et al, 1995
5a-Reductase Inhibitors		
Finasteride	5 mg PO qd	Gormley et al, 1992
	5 mg PO qd	Finasteride Study Group, 1993
	5 mg PO qd	Andersen et al, 1995
	5 mg PO qd	Marberger et al, 1998
	5 mg PO qd	McConnell et al, 1998

2000). The overwhelming majority of pharmacologic studies evaluating androgen suppression were not randomized, enrolled small numbers of subjects, and utilized qualitative outcome measures. This section reviews only multicenter, randomized, double-blind, placebo-controlled trials. **Finasteride, a type 2 5α-reductase inhibitor, and dutasteride, a dual inhibitor of both type 1 and type 2 5α-reductase inhibitor, together represent the paradigm for androgen suppression and are emphasized in this section.**

Finasteride

Finasteride is a competitive inhibitor of the enzyme 5α-reductase (Vermeulen et al, 1989). Finasteride lowers serum and intraprostatic DHT levels. At least two isozymes (types 1 and 2) of 5α-reductase exist (Jenkins et al, 1992). Finasteride is a selective inhibitor of the type 2 isozyme. Finasteride does not reduce DHT levels to castrate levels because circulating testosterone is converted to DHT by type I isozymes that exist in skin and liver (Thigpen et al, 1993).

Gormley and coworkers (1992) reported the first multicenter, randomized, double-blind, placebo-controlled trial investigating the safety and efficacy of finasteride in 895

men with BPH. The subjects were randomized to receive placebo or 1 or 5 mg of finasteride for 1 year. This study is often referred to as the North American Finasteride Trial. The mean baseline prostate volumes in the placebo and 1- and 5-mg finasteride groups were 61, 61, and 59 cm³, respectively. The primary outcome measures were group mean changes in a modified Boyarsky symptom score (maximal score, 36) and PFR (Figs. 87–7 and 87–8). The group mean changes in symptom score, PFR, and prostate volume are shown in Table 87–8. The group mean percentage changes in symptom score at 12 months in the placebo and 1- and 5-mg finasteride groups were −2%, 9%, and 21%, respectively. The mean percentage changes in PFR were 8%, 23%, and 22% in the placebo and 1- and 5-mg finasteride groups, respectively. The group mean percentage changes in prostate volume were −3%,

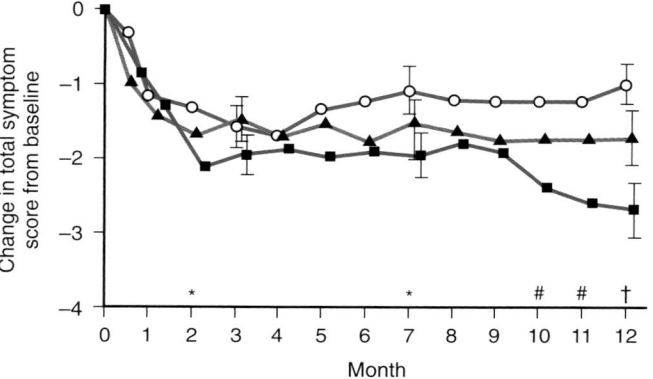

Figure 87–7. Mean (±SE) change in the total symptom score in men with BPH during treatment with placebo *(circles)*, 1 mg of finasteride *(triangles)*, or 5 mg of finasteride *(squares)*. The *asterisks* (P ≤ .05), the *pound* symbols (P < .01), and the *dagger* (P < .001) indicate significant differences between the finasteride-treated groups and the placebo group. Month 0 represents the baseline. (From Gormley GJ, Stoner E, Brusekewitz RC, et al: The effect of finasteride in men with benign prostatic hyperplasia. N Engl J Med 1992;327:1185-1191. Copyright © 1992 Massachusetts Medical Society.)

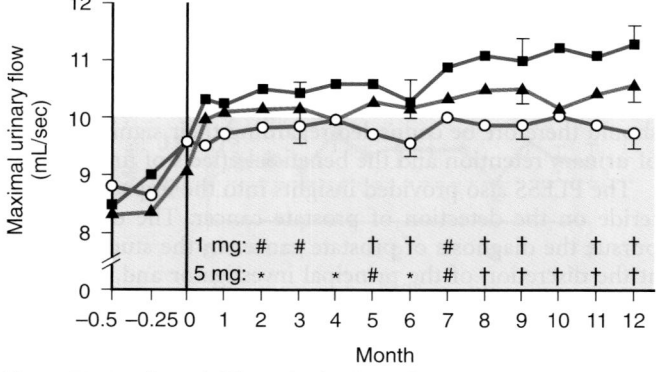

Figure 87–8. Mean (±SE) maximal urinary flow rates in men with BPH during treatment with placebo *(circles)*, 1 mg of finasteride *(triangles)*, or 5 mg of finasteride *(squares)*. The *blue area* indicates the range in which urinary flow was considered to be obstructed. Month 0 represents the baseline. Values before month 0 were obtained during the 2-week placebo run-in period. The *asterisks* (P < .05), *pound* symbols (P < .001), and *daggers* (P < .01) indicate significant differences between the finasteride-treated groups and the placebo group. (From Gormley GJ, Stoner E, Brusekewitz RC, et al: The effect of finasteride in men with benign prostatic hyperplasia. N Engl J Med 1992;327:1185-1191. Copyright © 1992 Massachusetts Medical Society.)

−18%, and −19% in the placebo and 1- and 5-mg finasteride groups, respectively. The difference between the group mean changes in PFR and prostate volume was statistically significant for both the 1- and the 5-mg finasteride groups versus the placebo group. The difference between the group mean changes in symptom scores was statistically significant only for placebo versus 5 mg of finasteride. The dose-dependent symptom response was not associated with a dose-dependent prostate volume or PFR response. The changes in prostate volume were not directly related to the magnitude of the clinical response to finasteride. These observations suggest that the efficacy of finasteride may not be mediated exclusively by reduction of prostate volume. The incidences of decreased libido, ejaculatory disorder, and impotence were significantly greater in the finasteride groups compared with the placebo group. The treatment-related incidences of decreased libido, ejaculatory disorder, and impotence in the 1- and 5-mg treatment groups were 4.7%, 2.7%, and 3.7%, respectively, and 3.4%, 2.7%, and 1.7%, respectively. The percentage of subjects withdrawing because of an adverse clinical event were equivalent in the three treatment groups. Prostate volume regression was maximal at 6 months. The greatest change in symptom scores and PFR occurred within the first 2 months of initiating active treatment.

The Finasteride Study Group (1993) **reported another multicenter, randomized, double-blind, placebo-controlled clinical trial that is referred to as the International Finasteride Study. The effect of finasteride on symptom scores, PFR, and prostate volume are in agreement with the North American Finasteride Trial.**

Andersen and associates (1995) reported the results of a multicenter, randomized, double-blind, placebo-controlled study investigating the safety and efficiency of finasteride in 707 Scandinavian subjects maintained on randomized treatment for 2 years. The mean baseline prostate volumes in the placebo and finasteride groups were 41.7 and 40.6 cm³, respectively. A selection bias for enrolling large prostates did not exist in this study. A modified Boyarsky symptom score was used to capture changes in symptom score. The differences in the group mean changes in the symptom score and PFR between finasteride and placebo after 12 and 24 months on active treatment are summarized in Table 87–8. **The difference between the group mean changes in symptom scores and PFR after 1 year of randomized treatment is slightly less than that in the North American Finasteride Study. This may be attributed to the smaller baseline prostate volumes.** Although the proportion of subjects experiencing any adverse clinical event and the number of withdrawals from adverse clinical events were similar to those in the finasteride and placebo groups, there were more patients with sexual dysfunction in the finasteride versus placebo groups (19% vs. 10%). The time-dependent symptom score changes demonstrate that the placebo response returns to baseline between 1 to 2 years, whereas the finasteride response remains stable. The authors interpret this to show that finasteride halts or alters the natural history of the disease. The mean differences between the symptom scores at 12 and 24 months in the finasteride and placebo groups were only −0.3 and 0.6 symptom unit, respectively.

Marberger and coworkers (1998) **reported the results of a 2-year randomized, placebo-controlled trial of 3270 men**

severe obstruction. The mean changes in detrusor pressure at maximal flow were +3 and −39 cm H_2O in the placebo and finasteride groups, respectively. Although the difference between placebo and finasteride was highly statistically significant, the overwhelming majority of the finasteride-treated subjects remained obstructed after treatment. The marked treatment-related changes in detrusor pressure were not associated with statistically significant changes in symptom scores. The authors did not comment on whether the changes in detrusor pressures correlated with changes in prostate volume. Of the subjects participating in the randomized, double-blind study, 27 completed a 4-year open-label extension study (Tammela and Kontturi, 1995). The detrusor pressure at maximal flow showed further improvements over time.

PSA has become widely accepted as a screening instrument for prostate cancer (Tchetgen and Oesterling, 1995). An elevated or significantly rising PSA value is often an indication for prostatic biopsy. Finasteride reduces group mean serum PSA levels approximately 50% (Guess et al, 1993). The effect of finasteride on individual serum PSA levels is highly variable. **Because of the variable effect on PSA, men who are candidates for early detection of prostate cancer should have their PSA level determined before beginning finasteride therapy.** A biopsy should be performed if the PSA level is elevated. A repeat biopsy should be performed for progressively rising PSA levels after initiation of therapy.

Gross hematuria is a relatively rare, yet troublesome, manifestation of BPH. Puchner and Miller (1995) reported an uncontrolled personal experience of 18 BPH patients treated with finasteride for refractory gross hematuria secondary to BPH. Of the 18 reported cases, 12 had undergone a prior prostatectomy. Finasteride was very effective in relieving the post-prostatectomy gross hematuria. Miller and Puchner (1998) reported a follow-up series that demonstrated the long-term effectiveness of finasteride for the treatment of hematuria from BPH. Carlin and coworkers (1997) reported resolution of gross hematuria in 12 of 12 men treated with finasteride. **These preliminary observations have been confirmed by a randomized, double-blind, placebo-controlled study by Foley and associates** (2000) **demonstrating that finasteride prevents recurrent gross hematuria secondary to BPH.** Gross refractory hematuria recurred within 1 year for 63% and 14% of men randomized to placebo and finasteride, respectively.

Dutasteride

Dutasteride is a dual inhibitor of 5α-reductase and, therefore, has a greater impact on inhibiting serum DHT levels (Clark et al, 1999). In a randomized controlled trial of 4325 men (2951 completed) Roehrborn and coworkers (2002) reported that serum dihydrotestosterone was reduced by 90.2%. The symptom score was improved by 4.5 points (21.4%) ($P <$ .001), and the maximal flow rate improved significantly by 2.2 mL/s ($P <$ .001) at 24 months. The risk reduction of AUR was 57%, and the risk reduction of BPH-related surgery was 48% compared with placebo. Debruyne and associates (2004) reported the pooled results of a 2-year open-label extension study in which both dutasteride- and placebo-treated groups received dutasteride 0.5 mg/day. Significant improvements in symptom scores and maximal flow rates were observed in both study groups. It was concluded that long-term treatment

with dutasteride results in continuing improvements in both symptoms and urinary flow and that the risk reduction of AUR and BPH-related surgery was durable over 4 years. Similar to finasteride, the principal side effects were loss of libido and erectile dysfunction, but these were most frequently seen at the start of therapy and declined over time with treatment. Roehrborn and coworkers (2004) reported similar results and confirmed 93% suppression of DHT at 4 years.

Zanoterone

Zanoterone is a steroidal competitive AR antagonist (Juniewicz et al, 1990). Berger and coworkers (1995) reported a multicenter, randomized, double-blind, placebo-controlled study in 463 subjects receiving placebo and 100, 200, 400, or 800 mg of zanoterone for 6 months. The group mean changes in AUA symptom score were not reported; however, the differences between placebo and all of the zanoterone groups were not statistically significant. The mean baseline prostate volumes ranged between 37.7 and 42.2 cm^3 in the five treatment groups. The differences between the percent group mean changes in prostate volume in the placebo (−6%) and active treatment groups (−4% to −8%) were not significantly different. Interestingly, the differences between the percent group mean changes in serum PSA in all of the active treatment groups were significantly greater than those in the placebo group, despite the lack of an apparent drug effect on prostate volume. The difference between the group mean changes in PFR for placebo and the 200-mg dose was 0.7 mL/s. Fifty-six percent and 22% of all zanoterone subjects reported breast pain and gynecomastia, respectively. The incidence and severity of adverse clinical events and the equivocal efficacy precluded further development of this drug for BPH.

Flutamide

Flutamide is an orally administered nonsteroidal antiandrogen that inhibits the binding of androgen to its receptor (Sufrin and Coffey, 1973). The first reported randomized, double-blind, placebo-controlled trial in BPH examined the safety and efficacy of flutamide in 31 males with symptomatic BPH (Caine et al, 1975). Statistically significant differences were not observed between placebo and 300 mg of flutamide for symptoms, prostate size, PVR, and PFR.

Stone (1989) **reported a multicenter, randomized, double-blind study comparing flutamide and placebo in men with BPH.** Eighty-four patients were randomized to receive 24 weeks of either flutamide, 250 mg three times a day, or placebo. Of the 84 patients, 58 (69%) and 12 (14%) were evaluable 12 and 24 weeks on double-blind treatment. The small sample size at 24 weeks precludes any meaningful conclusions. The between-group comparisons of group mean changes from baseline for placebo versus flutamide were not statistically significant at any time point. The incidences of breast tenderness and diarrhea in the flutamide group were 53% and 11%, respectively. Although the interim analysis was reported in 1989, a subsequent report of the multicenter study has not been published.

Cetrorelix

Cetrorelix is the only gonadotropin-releasing hormone antagonist that has been investigated for BPH. **A potential advantage of a gonadotropin-releasing hormone antagonist over** the luteinizing hormone–releasing hormone agonists in the treatment of BPH is the ability to titrate the level of androgen suppression. This would be clinically relevant if different levels of androgen suppression mediate prostate size reduction and adverse events (hot flashes, decreased libido, erectile dysfunction). An open-label study of 11 men demonstrated that cetrorelix reduced prostate volume and improved LUTS without significant adverse events (Barona et al, 1994). Lepor and coworkers (1997) reported a proof of concept randomized, double-blind, placebo-controlled study of cetrorelix in men with BPH. After an 8-day placebo lead-in, men received daily subcutaneous injections of placebo or 1 mg of cetrorelix (C_{01}) for 27 days. One group received loading doses of 10 mg of cetrorelix on the first 4 days of active treatment (C_{10}). Maximal lowering of testosterone was observed within 24 hours. The testosterone level was reduced to castrate levels in the C_{10} group and to intermediate testosterone suppression level in the non–loading-dose group (C_{10}) ($\approx$ 20 ng/dL). Men exhibiting a clinical effect were followed for 1 year. In the C_{10} and C_{01} groups, the treatment-related improvement in AUA symptom score was 3.0 and 2.0 symptom units, respectively. In both the C_{10} and the C_{01} groups, the treatment-related improvement in PFR was 2.0 mL/s. The treatment-related reductions of prostate volume were 5.5 and 3.0 cm³, respectively. The treatment-related incidence of hot flashes and sexual dysfunction in the C_{01} group was negligible. During the open-label extension, prostate volume did not return to baseline, suggesting a prolonged effect on the disease. Because of problems with the drug formulation, phase III studies with cetrorelix were not pursued.

The primary disadvantage of cetrorelix and other gonadotropin-releasing hormone antagonists will be the requirement for an injection and the cost. If single-injection therapy provides desirable clinical response with minimal adverse events and the mechanism of action is unique to that of 5α-reductase inhibitors, there may exist a role for these antagonists in the treatment of BPH.

Androgen Suppression in Clinical Practice

Finasteride and dutasteride are the only drugs available that achieve reliable androgen suppression with acceptable tolerance. Both symptoms and flow rates are improved, especially in men with larger glands. Impotence and decreased ejaculatory volume are the primary treatment-related adverse experiences. The literature also suggests finasteride may be offered to men with hematuria secondary to friable prostatic tissue and in those men with LUTS and enlarged prostates who elect to reduce their risk of developing urinary retention.

Summary

Finasteride represents the androgen suppression drug that has been most extensively characterized in BPH. Multicenter, randomized, double-blind, placebo-controlled studies support its role in the treatment of BPH. Finasteride reduces prostate volume approximately 20%. The overall treatment-related improvements in symptom score ($\approx$1.0 symptom unit) and PFR ($\approx$1.5 mL/s) relative to placebo are modest.

The long-term safety and durability of efficacy has been demonstrated for finasteride and dutasteride. The adverse clinical events associated with both agents are minimal and are related primarily to sexual function. Finasteride alters the natural history of urinary retention in men with LUTS and enlarged prostates. Finasteride is effective in the management of gross hematuria associated with BPH, especially in the presence of friable prostate tissue. Antiandrogens have also been investigated for BPH. These studies failed to demonstrate statistically significant treatment-related efficacy. The equivocal efficacy and problematic toxicity of antiandrogens limited the enthusiasm for marketing these drugs for the treatment of BPH. The role of gonadotropin-releasing hormone antagonists requires further study.

COMBINATION THERAPY
Veterans Affairs Cooperative Study No. 359

Lepor and coworkers (1996) reported the first multicenter, randomized, double-blind trial comparing placebo, finasteride, terazosin, and combination therapy (finasteride + terazosin) in 1229 U.S. veterans with clinical BPH. All subjects randomized to finasteride received a daily dose of 5 mg. The dose of terazosin was titrated in all patients up to 10 mg, providing adverse clinical events were not encountered. The dose of terazosin was reduced at the discretion of the investigators to 5 mg for adverse events. Of the 1229 subjects randomized, 1007 (81.9%) completed the 1-year randomized treatment on assigned study medication.

The AUA symptom score (Fig. 87–11) and PFRs (Fig. 87–12) are shown for the four treatment groups throughout the study. The group mean changes between baseline and final study visit for the relevant primary and secondary outcome measures are summarized in Table 87–9. The mean group differences between finasteride and placebo were not statistically significant for AUA Symptom Index, Symptom Problem Index, BPH Impact Index, and PFR. The mean group differences between terazosin versus placebo and terazosin versus finasteride for all of the outcome measures

Table 87–9. Comparison of Placebo, Finasteride, Doxazosin, and Combination Therapy: Veterans

Outcome Measures	Difference between Final and Baseline Study Visits			
	Placebo	Finasteride	Doxazosin	Combination Therapy
AUA Symptom Index	−2.6	−3.2	−6.6*	−6.2*
Symptom Problem Index	−1.4	−1.7	−3.9†	−4.2†
BPH Impact Index	−0.5	−0.5	−1.2†	−1.7†
Prostate volume (cm³)	+0.5	6.1*	+0.5	+7.2*
PFR (mL/s)	+1.4	+1.6	+2.7*	+3.2*

*$P < .001$ relative to placebo.
†$P < .01$ relative to placebo.
PFR, peak flow rate.

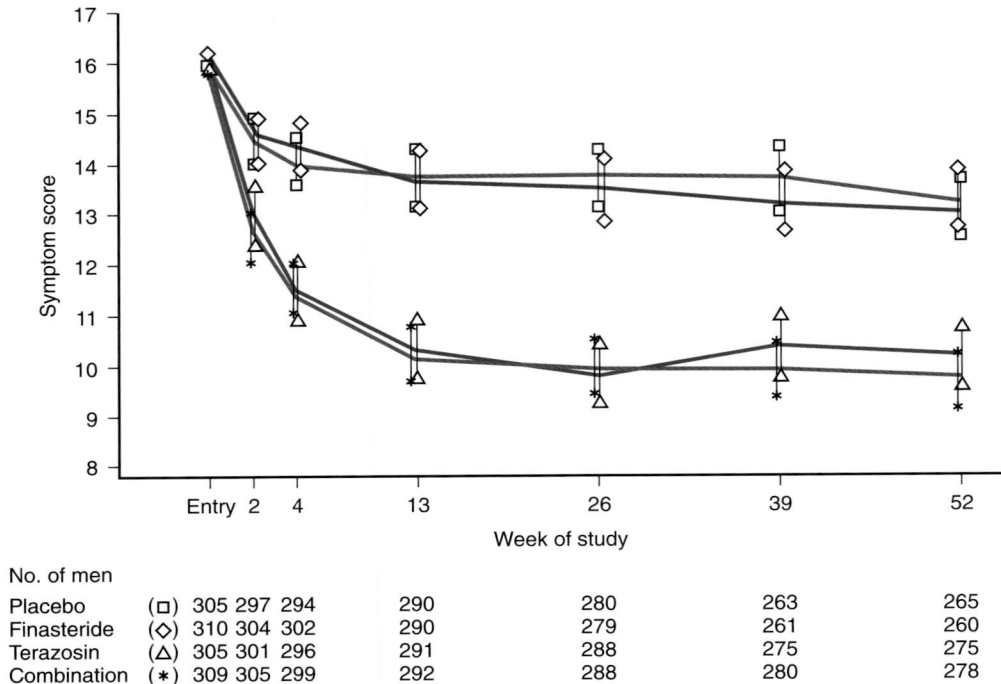

No. of men

		Entry	2	4	13	26	39	52
Placebo	(□)	305	297	294	290	280	263	265
Finasteride	(◇)	310	304	302	290	279	261	260
Terazosin	(△)	305	301	296	291	288	275	275
Combination	(∗)	309	305	299	292	288	280	278

Figure 87–11. AUA symptom scores in men with BPH, according to treatment group. Scores are expressed as adjusted means and 95% confidence intervals. The results of primary pairwise comparisons (with Bonferroni's adjustment) are as follows: finasteride and terazosin, $P < .001$; finasteride and combination therapy, $P < .001$; and terazosin and combination therapy, $P = 1.00$. The results of secondary pairwise treatment comparisons are as follows: finasteride and placebo, $P = .63$; terazosin and placebo, $P < .001$; and combination therapy and placebo, $P < .001$. (From Lepor H, Williford WO, Barry MJ, et al: The efficacy of terazosin, finasteride or both in benign prostatic hypertrophy. N Engl J Med 1996;335:533-539. Copyright © 1996 Massachusetts Medical Society.)

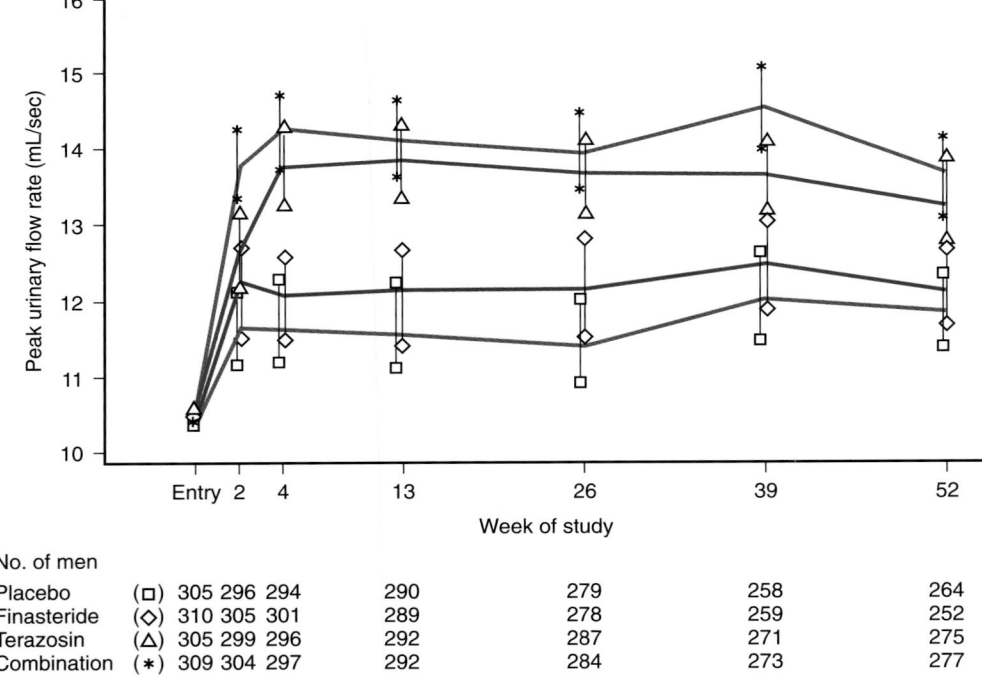

No. of men

		Entry	2	4	13	26	39	52
Placebo	(□)	305	296	294	290	279	258	264
Finasteride	(◇)	310	305	301	289	278	259	252
Terazosin	(△)	305	299	296	292	287	271	275
Combination	(∗)	309	304	297	292	284	273	277

Figure 87–12. Peak urinary flow rates in men with BPH, according to treatment group. Rates are expressed as adjusted means and 95% confidence intervals. The results of primary pairwise comparisons (with Bonferroni's adjustment) are as follows: finasteride and terazosin, $P < .001$; finasteride and combination therapy, $P < .001$; and terazosin and combination therapy, $P = .15$. The results of secondary pairwise treatment comparisons are as follows: finasteride and placebo, $P = .07$; terazosin and placebo, $P < .001$; and combination therapy and placebo, $P < .001$. (From Lepor H, Williford WO, Barry MJ, et al: The efficacy of terazosin, finasteride or both in benign prostatic hypertrophy. N Engl J Med 1996;335:533-539. Copyright © 1996 Massachusetts Medical Society.)

other than prostate volume were highly statistically significant. The group mean differences between combination therapy and terazosin for all of the outcome measures other than prostate volume were not statistically significant, owing to the lack of treatment-related efficacy of finasteride. The VA study unequivocally demonstrated the superiority of α-adrenergic blockade over androgen suppression for the treatment of clinical BPH over a 1-year interval. Prostate volume decreased approximately 20% in the finasteride and combination groups. The numbers of subjects withdrawing from the study because of adverse clinical events in the finasteride, terazosin, and combination groups were similar.

The efficacy of terazosin observed in the VA study is in agreement with the literature, whereas the efficacy of finasteride is less than previously reported in the studies comparing finasteride versus placebo. The most likely explanations are differences in the symptom score instrument and baseline prostate volumes in the finasteride studies. The average prostate volume in the VA study treatment groups ranged between 36.2 and 38.4 cm^3. These volumes are comparable with those of finasteride studies reported by Andersen and associates (1995) and Marberger and colleagues (1998) and clinical investigations of other α-adrenergic blockers, antiandrogens, and minimally invasive therapies. A subset analysis of the VA study demonstrated that the group mean changes in AUA symptom scores for placebo and finasteride in men with baseline prostate volumes over 50 cm^3 were −2.0 and −2.9, respectively (Lepor et al, 1998). The mean changes in PFR for placebo and finasteride in men with prostate volumes over 50 cm^3 were +0.4 and +2.5 mL/s, respectively. These differences between placebo and finasteride are in agreement with the results of the North American and International Finasteride Trials that enrolled a disproportionate number of men with large prostates. In the group of men with prostate volumes greater than 50 cm^3, the mean changes in AUA symptom score and PFR in the terazosin group were −5.8 and 3.9 mL/s, respectively. Terazosin is more effective than finasteride in those subjects with large prostates.

A multicenter, randomized, double-blind, placebo-controlled study comparing placebo, doxazosin, finasteride, and combination therapy confirmed the findings of the VA Cooperative Study (Kirby et al, 2003). In the Prospective European Doxazosin and Combination Therapy Trial (PREDICT), 1089 men were randomized in equal proportions to one of the just discussed four treatment groups for 1 year. The daily dose of doxazosin was titrated up to 8 mg. The baseline prostate volume was approximately 36 cm^3. The group mean improvement of AUA symptom score and PFR and change in prostate volume between baseline and final study visit are shown in Table 87–10.

A multicenter, double-blind study compared SR alfuzosin (5 mg), finasteride (5 mg), and combination therapy in 1051 men receiving active treatment for 6 months (Debruyne et al, 1998). The improvement in IPSS was not significantly different in the alfuzosin versus combination groups, questioning once again the lack of effectiveness of finasteride in the short term. At 6 months, there were no significant differences between PFR among any of the treatment groups (Fig. 87–13).

Table 87–10. Comparison of Placebo, Finasteride, Doxazosin, and Combination Therapy in the PREDICT Study

Outcome Measures	Differences between Final and Baseline Study Visits			
	Placebo	Finasteride	Doxazosin	Combination Therapy
International Prostate Symptom Score	−5.7	−6.6	−8.3*	−8.5*
Peak flow rate (Qmax)	1.4	1.8	3.6*	3.8*
Acute urinary retention	1.5	1.1	0	0.0

*$P < 0.05$ relative to placebo.
PREDICT, Prospective European Doxazasin and Combination Therapy Trial.

MTOPS

The results of all three large-scale studies just described appear to suggest that the role of 5α-reductase inhibitors as generalized monotherapy for LUTS may be somewhat limited, a finding at variance with some of the original studies on finasteride. An additional, longer-term trial, which has been progressing in parallel to these studies, has generated important new information on both the clinical potential of 5α-reductase inhibitors as monotherapy and the potential of drug combinations.

The Medical Therapy of Prostatic Symptoms (MTOPS) trial, a prospective, randomized, double-blind, multicenter, placebo-controlled trial, was established to determine whether medical therapy can prevent or delay the progression of BPH in the long term. Further elucidation of the natural history of BPH, determining baseline factors associated with more rapid disease progression, was a secondary aim of the study.

In 18 academic centers across the United States a total of 3047 patients were recruited and randomized to receive doxazosin, finasteride, a combination of both, or placebo. Mean age of participants was 62.6 years, most were white (82.6%), with 8.8% black and 7.2% Hispanic participants. The inclusion/exclusion criteria allowed men with all prostate sizes to be enrolled, as long as the serum PSA was less than 10 ng/mL. This resulted in a wide distribution of prostate sizes and serum PSA values, allowing for stratified analyses of subsets based on these criteria.

Disease progression was defined as a worsening of BPH symptoms according to the AUA symptom index (AUASI). Progression was deemed to have occurred in the case of one of the following: a 4-point rise in AUASI, confirmed by a second visit within 4 weeks; a 50% increase in creatinine relative to baseline levels; AUR; two or more UTIs within 1 year or a single episode of urosepsis due to BOO; and socially unacceptable incontinence. The first occurrence of any of these events indicated BPH progression. Progression as an endpoint represented a novel concept at the time of the initiation of the MTOPS study, although the PLESS study as well as the dutasteride studies later on utilized AUR and surgery as endpoints in their study design (McConnell et al, 1998; Roehrborn et al, 2002). Entirely novel was the concept of utilizing a threshold to define symptom progression. Based on data from the VA Cooperative Study, in which men perceived general improvement in their symptom status once the AUASI improved by more than 3 points, a threshold of 4 points was chosen—to be confirmed within 4 weeks—to indicate global subjective worsening of symptom status.

To assess the natural history of BPH, Qmax, prostate volume, sexual function, and quality of life were regularly recorded with respect to BPH symptoms. Transrectal ultrasound and DRE were used to evaluate prostate volume, the Sexual Function Inventory Questionnaire evaluated sexuality, and the Short Form-36 Health Survey instrument recorded quality of life scores. Prostatic biopsies were obtained at baseline and at 5 years (or at primary endpoint) in 37% of study participants who volunteered to take part in a biopsy substudy. Patients were randomized to receive 5 mg finasteride and doxazosin placebo, 5 mg finasteride and doxazosin titrated to up to 8 mg, titrated doxazosin and finasteride placebo, or two placebo drugs.

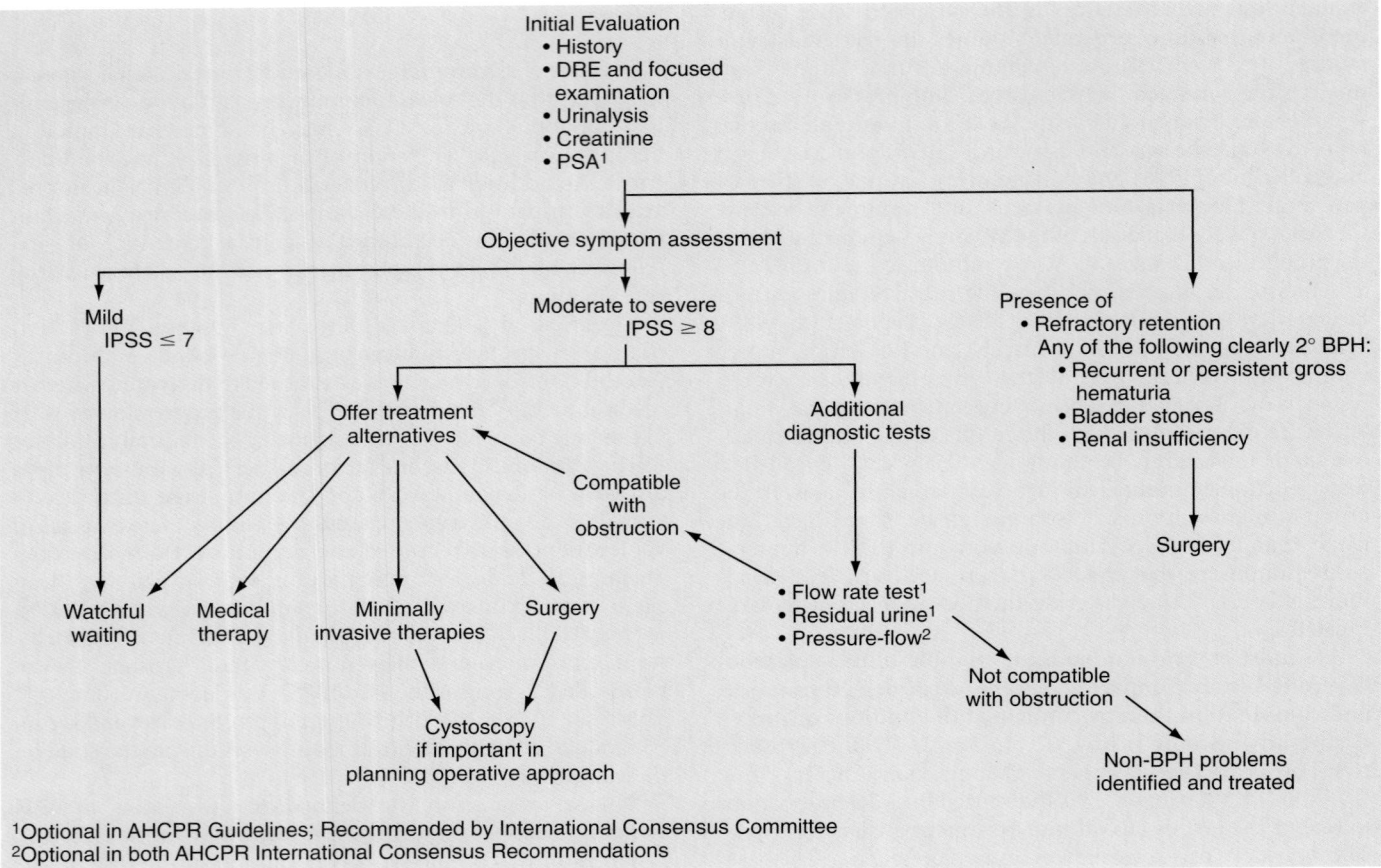

Figure 87–13. Algorithm for medical management of BPH. AHCPR, Agency for Health Care Policy and Research; DRE, digital rectal examination; IPSS, International Prostate Symptom Score; PSA, prostate-specific antigen.

The results of the trial suggest that the combination of doxazosin and finasteride exerts a clinically relevant, positive effect on rates of disease progression (McConnell et al, 2003). Men who received combination therapy were significantly less likely to experience BPH progression than those receiving either monotherapy or placebo, with risk reduction rates of 39% for doxazosin, 34% for finasteride, and 67% for combination therapy compared with placebo.

Invasive therapy and AUR risk were significantly reduced by finasteride and combination therapy (by 69% and 64%, and by 79% and 67%, respectively), whereas all treatment regimens (placebo, doxazosin, finasteride, and combination) brought about a significant improvement in AUA symptom score (4.0, 6.0, 5.0, and 7.0, respectively) and Qmax (1.4, 2.5, 2.2, and 3.7 mL/s, respectively) at 4 years.

AUA symptom score and Qmax improved significantly more in the combination therapy group compared with the monotherapy groups, whereas adverse events were similar to previously reported studies.

In addition to indicating the potential benefits of combination therapy, MTOPS provided important data regarding the natural history of untreated BPH and the prediction of BPH patients who will respond most effectively to medical treatment. Although the patients receiving finasteride alone or in combination experienced the expected decrease in prostate volume, patients on placebo or doxazosin alone experienced an increase in prostate volume from a baseline of 34.0 mL by 9.3 (30.3%) (placebo) and from 36.4 mL by 9.9 (31.4%) (doxazosin), respectively

Stratified by PSA quartiles, total prostate volume in both placebo and doxazosin-treated patients increased from 4.9 mL (24.9%) to 16.2 mL (34.5%) from the lowest to the highest quartile for an annualized growth of 1.1 to 3.6 mL/yr. These findings suggest that doxazosin, despite its apoptotic effect (Glassman et al, 2001), does not interfere with the natural growth tendency of the prostate gland and that baseline PSA is a useful predictor of future prostate growth in men with LUTS and BPH.

Examination of baseline measures and the disease outcomes of 737 patients treated with placebo revealed that PSA, Qmax, PVR, and prostate volume at baseline correlated with clinical progression of the disease and the need for BPH-related surgery ($P = .03$ to $< .001$). Age was linked to clinical progression ($P < .001$) and AUA symptom score correlated with need for surgery (p = .002). Baseline PSA and prostate volume correlated with risk of AUR ($P = .03-.003$). Risk of progression, BPH-related surgery, and AUR increased alongside levels of serum PSA.

In medically treated patients, however, baseline values were variably predictive of BPH outcome. In doxazosin-treated patients, for example, PSA, Qmax, and prostate volume were predictive of outcome; however, this was not true of patients treated with finasteride alone or combined therapy.

The number needed to treat (NNT) to prevent a case of BPH progression as defined in MTOPS in the overall population was 8.4 for the combination therapy group and 13.7 and 15.0, respectively, for the doxazosin- and finasteride-treated patients. For those men treated with combination therapy who had a baseline PSA of more than 4.0 ng/mL, however, the NNT was 4.7, and for those with a prostate volume over 40 mL it was 4.9, suggesting that, in fact, combination therapy becomes economically a viable option in patients at higher risk for progression.

The link between sexual dysfunction and severity of LUTS was also confirmed by the MTOPS data. A correlation was observed between LUTS and five domains of sexual dysfunction (libido, sexual function, ejaculatory function, the patient's assessment of his sexual problems, and overall satisfaction). In addition, men with larger prostates were more likely to have low libido, low overall sexual functioning, reduced ejaculatory function, and greater sexual problems.

Another study of combination therapy in BPH employing dutasteride and tamsulosin has been reported by Barkin and colleagues (2003). Three hundred twenty-seven patients were treated with both drugs for 24 weeks and then the α-adrenergic blocker was withdrawn for a further 12 weeks; of those patients with an IPSS less than 20, 84% continued without noticeable deterioration of their symptoms. In contrast, in the 27% of patients with more severe symptoms (IPSS > 20), 42.7% reported a worsening of their symptoms compared with 14% of those who remained on combination therapy. It was concluded that a 5α-reductase inhibitor can be used in combination with an α-adrenergic blocker to receive rapid onset of symptom relief in patients at risk of underlying disease progression and the α-adrenergic blocker can then be discontinued. In patients with severe symptoms, combination therapy should be continued for a longer term.

AROMATASE INHIBITORS
Rationale for Aromatase Inhibitors for Benign Prostatic Hyperplasia

The rationale for aromatase inhibition is that estrogens may be involved in the pathogenesis of BPH. The estrogenic effect most likely mediates stromal-epithelial interactions that regulate the proliferative activity of the prostate. Several observations support the role of stroma in the development of BPH and the influence of estrogens on prostatic stroma. The inductive potential of prostatic mesenchyme (stroma) is supported by the observation of Cunha and colleagues (1980) in a mouse embryonic animal model. Coffey and Walsh (1990) reported that estrogen treatment of castrated beagles produced a threefold to fourfold increase in the total amount of prostatic stroma. Estrogens also greatly enhanced the ability of androgens to induce BPH in a canine model (Walsh and Wilson, 1976; DeKlerk et al, 1979). This synergistic effect may be mediated by the ability of estrogens to upregulate prostatic AR content. Stromal hyperplasia can be induced in the prostates of dogs and monkeys treated with aromatizable androgens

and prevented by aromatase inhibitors such as atamestane (Habenicht et al, 1987; Habenicht and El Etreby, 1989).

Review of the Literature

Atamestane is a highly selective aromatase inhibitor that lowers both serum and intraprostatic levels of estradiol and estrone (El Etreby et al, 1991). **Gingell and coworkers (1995) reported a multicenter, randomized, double-blind, placebo-controlled study comparing placebo and 400 mg of atamestane** in 160 subjects with clinical BPH. Atamestane resulted in a statistically significant decrease in serum estradiol and estrone levels and a statistically significant increase in serum testosterone. No statistically significant group mean differences were observed for changes in Boyarsky symptom score, PFR, or prostate volume between the atamestane and the placebo groups. One of the explanations contributing to the failure of atamestane to achieve clinical efficacy was the increase in testosterone. The development of atamestane for BPH was suspended because of these negative clinical findings. The failure to demonstrate that atamestane causes regression of established BPH or clinical improvement does not negate the influence of estrogens in the pathogenesis of BPH.

PHYTOTHERAPY

Phytotherapeutic agents for LUTS/BPH have gained widespread usage since about 1990 (Lowe and Fagelman, 1999). Previously, these agents were popular in Europe, particularly in France and Germany where they are often prescribed and their costs reimbursed (Dreikorn et al, 1998). However, usage in the United States and throughout the world has escalated. It has been estimated that over $1 billion was spent in the United States alone for these products (Lowe and Fagelman, 1999). A U.S. survey conducted by National Family Opinion, Inc., determined that the widespread use of these agents was due to philosophic congruence with peoples' own values, beliefs, and orientation toward health and life (Astin, 1998). These agents have been marketed to "promote prostatic health," and, therefore, it is not surprising that many men try them. Additional factors that contribute to their widespread use include being "natural" products (not medications), presumed safety, ease of accessibility (no prescription necessary), avoidance of prostate surgery, and prevention of prostate cancer (falsely assumed). The widespread availability of these products in health food stores, vitamin shops, traditional pharmacies, and supermarkets, as well as at numerous web sites on the Internet, has contributed to their use and reflects the demand for these phytotherapeutic agents.

Origin of Phytotherapaeutic Agents

Phytotherapeutic products are not the actual plant but are extracts derived from either the roots, the seeds, the bark, or the fruits of the various plants used (Table 87–11). Although monopreparations (single plant only) are available, many companies manufacture combination products (two or more plant extracts) in an attempt to provide "enhanced" efficacy (never proven), to improve marketability, and to provide their own "unique" product that can be registered because there is

SECTION XVI

Table 87–11.	**Origin of Plant Extracts**
Species	**Common Name**
Serenoa repens, Sabal serrulata	Saw palmetto berry/American dwarf palm
Hypoxis rooperi	South African star grass
Pygeum africanum	African plum tree
Urtica dioica	Stinging nettle
Secale cereale	Rye pollen
Cucurbita pepo	Pumpkin seed
Opuntia	Cactus flower
Pinus	Pine flower
Picea	Spruce

Table 87–12.	**Components of Plant Extracts**	
Phytosterols	**Phytoestrogens**	**Terpenoids**
β-Sitosterol	Coumestrol	Lectins
Δ-5-Sterol	Genistein (isoflavone)	Polysaccharides
Δ-7-Sterol	Flavonoids	Aliphatic alcohols
Stigmasterol	Fatty acids	Plant oils
Campesterol	Free	
	Esterified	

Table 87–13.	**Suggested Mechanisms of Action of Plant Extracts**

Inhibition of 5α-reductase
Anti-inflammatory
Interference with growth factors
Antiandrogenic
Estrogenic
Inhibition of aromatase
Decrease of sex hormone-binding globulin
Alteration of cholesterol metabolism
Action on α-adrenergic receptors
Free radical scavenger
Alteration of lipid peroxidation
Modulation of prolactin-induced prostatic growth
Protection of bladder and detrusor function
Placebo effect

no patent protection for these products. However, to determine mechanisms of action and efficacy, only the monopreparations are evaluated and reviewed here.

Composition of the Phytotherapy Extracts

The composition of plant extracts is very complex. They contain a wide variety of chemical compounds, which include phytosterols, plant oils, fatty acids, and phytoestrogens (Table 87–12). Which of these is the exact "active" component is not definitely known. Both the free fatty acids and the sitosterols have been thought to be the active components.

Most of the plant extracts are unique. First, the plants are not identical, owing to natural variability. Second, the extraction processes used by the various manufacturers are frequently different and use various substrates for the process. Thus, even if the phytotherapeutic compounds produced by two different companies contain the same plant, the exact composition of the final products is probably different and the content of the "active" component in each preparation may also be different. For example, analysis by the National Consumer Lab (2000) of free fatty acid content in 27 different saw palmetto products showed variability from 0% to 95%, with only 17 containing more than the presumed standard amount of 85%.

Mechanism of Action

The mechanisms of action of the phytotherapeutic agents are generally unknown (Dreikorn et al, 1998). Many in-vitro experimental studies have been undertaken to elucidate this; thus, there are numerous proposed mechanisms of action (Table 87–13). Almost all these studies use supraphysiologic doses that are many times higher than the standard doses used clinically. The biologic effects are typically examined in tissue

culture, which might not be an accurate reflection of in vivo effects (Lowe and Ku, 1996). The three mechanisms of action that have received the greatest attention are anti-inflammatory effects, 5α-reductase inhibition, and growth factor alteration.

The anti-inflammatory effects are modulated by effects on prostaglandin synthesis. Plant flavonoids are inhibitors of both cyclooxygenase and lipoxygenase enzymes (Bach, 1982; Buck, 1996). Flavone, a phytoestrogen commonly found in plants and herbs, has been shown to be a strong inhibitor of cyclooxygenase (Mower et al, 1984; Alcaraz and Ferrandiz, 1987). *Serenoa repens* (Permixon) has been shown to inhibit phospholipase A_2 activity, thereby decreasing arachidonic acid metabolites and prostaglandin E_2 synthesis (Ragab et al, 1988; Plosker and Brogden, 1996). Additionally, in two different studies, Paubert-Braquet and colleagues (1994a, 1997) demonstrated inhibition of the production of lipoxygenase metabolites and leukotrienes by neutrophils by *S. repens* and *Pygeum africanum* (Tadenan).

The most widely suggested mechanism of action of *S. repens* is as a 5α-reductase inhibitor (Plosker and Brogden, 1996). The human prostate contains both type I and predominantly type 2 isoforms of the 5α-reductase enzyme, which catalyzes the conversion of testosterone to DHT (Rhodes et al, 1993; Span et al, 1999). DHT is important for the development of BPH. Decreasing DHT with the use of a 5α-reductase inhibitor, such as finasteride, leads to reduction of prostate volume (Gormley et al, 1992).

Although inhibition of 5α-reductase activity by *S. repens* was found in experimental models using foreskin fibroblasts (Sultan et al, 1984), transfected Sf9 insect cells (Iehle et al, 1995), DU145 cancer cell line (Delos et al, 1994), primary cultures of human BPH and adenocarcinoma epithelial and fibroblast cells (Delos et al, 1995), and cocultures of human epithelial and fibroblast cells (Bayne et al, 1999), other in-vitro and in-vivo data have not confirmed this effect (Rhodes et al, 1993; Weisser et al, 1996).

Two ex-vivo experiments have demonstrated conflicting results. Pretreatment with *S. repens* for 3 months before suprapubic prostatectomy demonstrated a decrease in prostatic DHT and an increase in prostatic testosterone concentrations compared with controls, which suggests inhibition of 5α-reductase activity (DiSilverio et al, 1998). In a similar pretreatment study using *Sabal serrulata* (IDS-89) for 3 months, prostate tissue levels of 5α-reductase, 3α-hydroxysteroid, and 3β-hydroxysteroid oxidoreductase were not different compared with placebo (Weisser et al, 1996). An in-vivo experiment of healthy male volunteers demonstrated a reduction of serum DHT levels with finasteride but not with *S. repens* (Strauch et al, 1994). Clinically, in a large multicenter trial comparing *S. repens* with finasteride, no effect on PSA levels and only 6% reduction in prostate volume were noted for *S. repens*–treated patients, whereas the finasteride-treated patients had reduction of PSA levels by 41% and prostate volume by 18% (Carraro et al, 1996).

It has been subsequently postulated that *S. repens* inhibits intracellular 5α-reductase while having little or no effect on other androgen-dependent processes (e.g., PSA production) that rely on binding of androgens to their receptor. *S. repens* causes disruption of nuclear membrane in cell culture but has no effect on the integrity of the cell membrane (Bayne et al, 1999); therefore, the intracellular theory has been promulgated. Whether this supraphysiologic cell culture experiment actually reflects what is happening in vivo is uncertain and unproved.

Plant extracts are also thought to act by altering growth factor–induced growth and proliferation. In-vitro studies with *P. africanum* demonstrated an inhibitory effect on both basic fibroblastic growth factor (bFGF)– and epidermal growth factor (EGF)–induced human and rat prostate fibroblast proliferation (Paubert-Braquet et al, 1994b; Yablonsky et al, 1997). Subsequent experiments with *S. repens* have also shown inhibition of bFGF- and EFG-induced proliferation of human BPH prostate cells from biopsy specimens (Paubert-Braquet et al, 1998). Additionally, an ex-vivo experiment in men treated with *S. repens* before prostatectomy demonstrated reduced levels of tissue EGF, particularly in periurethral tissue (DiSilverio et al, 1998). **Although experimental data have suggested numerous possible mechanisms of actions for the phytotherapeutic agents** (see Table 87–13), it is uncertain which, if any, of these proposed mechanisms is responsible for the clinical responses.

Serenoa repens (Saw Palmetto Berry)

Although numerous clinical trials with saw palmetto berry extracts have been published, many were uncontrolled open-label studies, which provides little useful information in determining the efficacy of these phytotherapies. However, in an open-label study of 50 patients treated with *S. repens* (Nutraceutical Corporation) for 6 months, symptomatic improvement was observed without significant improvement in PFR, PVR, detrusor pressure at peak flow, and Abrams-Griffiths number (Gerber et al, 1998).

Even though many placebo-controlled studies have been published (Table 87–14), most of them are flawed and none of them would meet the generally accepted criteria developed by the International Consultation on BPH for assessing treatment results in men with LUTS (Roehrborn, 1998). The studies are of limited value because of their small numbers of patients, short duration (only 1 to 3 months), and lack of use of standardized symptoms scores.

For example, nocturia was the only symptom available for analysis in all the studies reviewed in two meta-analyses (Wilt et al, 1998; Boyle et al, 2000). In the Wilt and colleagues (1998) meta-analysis of 18 trials involving 2939 patients using various *S. repens* monotherapy and combination preparations, the mean weighted difference for nocturia between patients and subjects taking a placebo was −0.76 times per evening (−1.22 to −0.32) for 10 trials. In the Boyle and coworkers (2000) meta-analysis of 13 trials involving 2859 patients using only the Permixon brand of *S. repens,* the attributable reduction of nocturnal urinations was 0.50 (±0.01) times per night.

In terms of other objective criteria, PFRs were also evaluated in the meta-analyses. Wilt and colleagues (1998) determined that saw palmetto extracts improved peak urinary flow over placebo by a mean weighted difference of 1.93 mL/s (0.72 to 3.14 mL/s) for 8 studies. Boyle and coworkers (2000) showed that the attributable effect of Permixon over placebo was an additional improvement of 2.20 mL/s (±0.51) for 10 studies.

Despite inherent weaknesses in meta-analyses (Table 87–15), these analyses attempt to maximize the information available from clinical trials using *S. repens* in the treatment of symptomatic BPH/LUTS and to provide the best information available until the appropriate placebo-controlled, randomized clinical studies are conducted. However, approximately 35% of the prior meta-analyses performed are not accurately predicted by the subsequent randomized controlled trials (LeLorier et al, 1997). **Therefore, the safety and efficacy of *S. repens* has yet to be determined.**

Pygeum africanum (African Plum)

In addition to the proposed mechanisms of actions previously discussed, *P. africanum* has been postulated to have additional beneficial effects on LUTS by having a protective effect on the obstructed bladder. Using a rabbit model with partial BOO, Levin and associates (1996) demonstrated that changes in bladder mass, decrease in compliance, and alterations in contractile response to various forms of stimulation could be tempered by pretreatment with *P. africanum.*

Table 87–14. Placebo-Controlled Trials of *Serenoa repens* (Permixon)

Trial	Patients Randomized (N)	Duration (mo)	Significant Improvement in Symptoms vs. Placebo	Significant Improvement in Peak Urinary Flow Rate
Descotes (1996)	176	1	Yes	$P < 0.05$
Cukier (1985)	146	2-3	Yes	Not available
Champault (1984)	88	1	Yes	$P < 0.001$
Reece Smith (1986)	70	3	No	No
Emili (1983)	30	1	No	No
Tasca (1985)	27	2	No	No
Boccafoschi (1983)	22	2	Yes	$P < 0.05$

Table 87–15.	Inherent Weaknesses of Meta-Analyses

Pooled results incorporate biases of individual studies
New sources of biases created
    Selection of studies
    Publication bias (only positive trials usually published)
    Language bias
Heterogeneity of the studies
    Inclusion/exclusion criteria
    Study designs
    Assessments of efficacy
    Variable placebo response rates
    Study duration

A review of the published experience with *P. africanum* (Tadenan) identified 2262 patients treated with this extract: 1810 in open-label studies and 452 in comparative trials (Andro and Riffaud, 1995). Twelve double-blind, placebo-controlled studies were completed between 1972 and 1990. Only one study enrolled more than 100 subjects, and none was longer than 12 weeks or used standardized symptom scores. Thus, none of those trials meets the guidelines recommended by the International Consultation Conferences on BPH. Therefore, **the data concerning the efficacy of *P. africanum* are not conclusive.** One placebo-controlled trial has been completed; however, the data are not yet available (Lowe and Fagelman, 1999).

The only recently published clinical trials were a 2-month open-label study (Breza et al, 1998) and a 2-month comparison trial of 50 mg twice daily versus 100 mg daily (Chatelain et al, 1999). Both trials demonstrated a reduction in IPSS score of approximately 40% (5.7 and 6.4 units) and an improvement in PFRs of approximately 18% (2.1 and 1.7 mL/s) over baseline. However, without a placebo arm, the actual magnitude of drug effect cannot be determined. Thus, without at least the data from the Tadenan-IPSS study, the efficacy of *P. africanum* cannot be determined. Additionally, there are few other significant data available with regard to any of the other *P. africanum* extracts (Table 87–16).

Hypoxis rooperi (South African Star Grass)

Hypoxis rooperi (Harzol) has been studied in both a 6-month double-blind, placebo-controlled trial of 200 patients (Berges et al, 1995) and, subsequently, an open-label follow-up (Berges et al, 2000). In the initial study, statistically significant improvements were documented for symptom scores (IPSS), quality of life, PFRs, and PVRs (Berges et al, 1995). The placebo group showed appropriate mild improvement in these parameters. The IPSS improved by 7.4 units for β-sitosterol patients and 2.3 units for placebo. Similarly, peak urinary flow rates improved by 5.2 mL/s for treated patients compared with 1.1 mL/s for placebo. **This magnitude of improvement had not been observed with any other medical therapy previously evaluated for BPH and needs verification.**

During the follow-up study, patients were able to remain on or switch over to Harzol therapy. For those 38 patients who continued Harzol therapy, IPSS improvements were maintained. The 27 patients who received placebo initially and were then treated with Harzol demonstrated similar levels of improvement in IPSS scores and PFRs. Surprisingly, the 14 patients who stopped therapy still maintained similar levels of improvement over the next 12 months. This suggests that intermittent therapy could be an option.

Table 87–16.	Dosages of Common Phytotherapeutic Preparations	
Agent		**Dose**
Serenoa repens (Permixon)		160 mg bid
Pygeum africanum (Tadenan)		50 mg bid
Secale cereale (Cernilton)		6 capsules
β-Sitosterol (Harzol)		20 mg tid
β-Sitosterol (Azuprostat)		65 mg tid

Another product (Azuprostat) contains primarily β-sitosterols from *H. rooperi* as well as from *Pinus* (pine) and *Picea* (spruce). Although this is a combination preparation of extracts, its proposed active ingredient β-sitosterol is common to all three. Azuprostat was evaluated in a 6-month randomized, placebo-controlled trial with 177 patients (Klippel et al, 1997). Significant improvements in IPSS scores, PFRs, and PVRs were found. IPSS scores improved by 8.2 units for treated patients and 2.8 units for patients on placebo. PFRs improved by 8.9 mL/s for treated patients and 4.4 mL/s for placebo. This magnitude of improvement has not been reported for any type of medical therapy for BPH. It is hard to believe these results, in which the mean post-treatment PFRs are 19.4 mL/s, which is a normal value for younger men and not for the typical age of men in the study. If these results are reproducible, they would rival surgical intervention.

Wilt and associates (1999) produced a meta-analysis for β-sitosterol products. It included four trials (two mentioned earlier and two earlier suboptimal ones) encompassing three different products: Harzol, Azuprostat, and WA184, all of which have different amounts of β-sitosterol. WA184 did not improve PFRs (Kadow et al, 1986). Again, this meta-analysis is tempered by the same factors mentioned previously. **Their conclusion was that β-sitosterol does improve urologic symptoms and urinary flow rates, but its long-term effectiveness, safety, and ability to prevent the complications of BPH are unknown** (Wilt et al, 1999).

Other Extracts

The other extracts listed in Table 87–11, *Urtica dioica, Cucurbita pepo, Secale cereale,* and *Opuntia* have even fewer relevant clinical studies published than the aforementioned ones. Of these extracts, *Secale cereale* (Cernittan) had two placebo-controlled trials published over a decade ago that did not have standardized scores, used different dosages of the preparation, lasted 12 and 24 weeks, and enrolled only 103 and 60 subjects (Buck et al, 1990; Becker and Ebeling, 1998). Wilt and associates in a systematic review and meta-analysis of Cernitton concluded that it modestly improves overall urologic symptoms including nocturia, but additional trials are needed to evaluate clinical effectiveness (MacDonald et al, 1999).

Summary

Most phytotherapeutic preparations are plant extracts with different components manufactured by different extraction procedures, which prevents comparison of the preparations. Although numerous in-vitro experiments have been conducted to determine their possible mechanisms of

pharmaceutical action, it is uncertain which of the actions demonstrated in vitro might be responsible for clinical responses in vivo. Appropriate randomized placebo-controlled clinical trials monitored by an outside agency are needed to ascertain and to confirm the efficacy of these products.

FUTURE STRATEGIES FOR DRUG DEVELOPMENT IN BENIGN PROSTATIC HYPERPLASIA

Medical therapies provide symptom relief for a significant proportion of men with BPH. The therapeutic response to medical therapy is less than that of prostatectomy. Therefore, opportunities exist to develop novel strategies that may be more effective than existing therapies. Developing different classes of drugs to relax smooth muscle and targeting nonprostatic factors are potential opportunities.

New Strategies for Altering Dynamic and Static Obstruction

Endothelins are potent vasoconstrictors. Langenstroer and associates (1993) reported that human prostate contains endogenous endothelin and that **endothelin elicits a very potent contraction in the human prostate.** The contractile response elicited by endothelin in the human prostate is not abolished by pretreatment with selective α_1 blockers. These observations suggest that relaxation of prostatic smooth muscle in BPH may also be achieved by endothelin antagonists. The pharmaceutical industry is actively engaged in efforts to synthesize selective endothelin antagonists. Kobayashi and colleagues (1994) have characterized the binding properties of endothelin receptor subtypes in the human prostate. Both ETA and ETB receptors are present in the human prostate. The ETA and ETB receptors are localized primarily in the stroma and glandular epithelium, respectively. Preliminary studies suggest that both ETA and ETB receptors mediate the tension of prostate smooth muscle. Endothelin antagonists may emerge as another treatment for BPH.

    Nitric oxide is a nonadrenergic noncholinergic mediator of smooth muscle activity. Nitric oxide has been shown to mediate cavernosal smooth muscle activity. Burnett and coworkers (1995) have reported nitric oxide synthase activity in the prostate using immunohistochemical and biochemical investigations. Takeda and associates (1995) have shown that prostate smooth muscle tension is mediated by nitric oxide. These preliminary studies suggest that nitric oxide inhibitors may also play a future role in treating BPH.

Development of Therapy Directed toward Unrecognized Factors Resulting in Clinical Benign Prostatic Hyperplasia

It is generally assumed that the clinical manifestations of BPH are the result of BOO. Therefore, pharmacologic strategies have been directed toward reducing BOO. **Several observa-**

tions suggest that nonprostatic factors may also contribute to clinical BPH. The severity of clinical prostatism as captured by symptom scores is poorly correlated with measure of BOO. In addition, the changes in symptom scores after therapy for BPH are poorly correlated with changes in PFR and obstruction grade. The discordance between symptom severity and measures of obstruction suggests that nonprostatic factors may be contributing to clinical BPH. The authors believe that several factors such as aging, the hormonal milieu, nonurologic diseases, and prostatic growth affect bladder morphometry, neurologic innervation, BOO, and renal function, and that these factors collectively contribute to clinical BPH. Our present understanding of the pathophysiology of clinical BPH is rudimentary. It is, therefore, imperative to develop a more comprehensive understanding of the pathophysiology of symptoms. This knowledge will result in more effective use of existing therapies and will provide the rationale for the next generation of therapeutic modalities.

KEY POINTS: EVALUATION AND NONSURGICAL MANAGEMENT OF BENIGN PROSTATIC HYPERPLASIA

■ Benign prostatic hyperplasia is the most common cause of lower urinary tract symptoms in men older than middle age.

■ Evaluation requires a history and symptom score and a careful physical examination including a digital rectal examination.

■ Uroflowmetry and ultrasound estimation of postvoid residual urine volume are often helpful; a prostate-specific antigen determination is requested when a diagnosis of prostate cancer would alter the management of the individual patient.

■ Medical therapy is now the usual first-line management of uncomplicated BPH with either an α-adrenergic blocker of (if the prostate is large) a 5α-reductase inhibitor. Combination therapy with both an α-adrenergic blocker and a 5α-reductase inhibitor has been demonstrated to be the most effective means of preventing disease progression.

SUGGESTED READINGS

AUA Practice Guidelines Committee: AUA guideline on the management of benign prostatic hyperplasia: Diagnosis and treatment recommendations. J Urol 2003;170:530-547.

Girman CJ, Jacobsen SJ, Guess HA, et al: Natural history of prostatism: Relationship among symptoms, prostate volume and peak urinary flow rate. J Urol 1995;153:1510-1515.

Kirby RS, O'Leary MP, Carson C: Efficacy of extended-release doxazosin and doxazosin standard in patients with concomitant benign prostatic hyperplasia and sexual dysfunction. BJU Int 2005;95:103-109.

Kirby RS, McConnell J, Roehrborn C, et al: Textbook of Benign Prostatic Hyperplasia, 2nd ed. London, Taylor & Francis, 2002.

McConnell JD, Bruskewitz R, Walsh P, et al: The effect of finasteride on the risk of acute urinary retention and the need for surgical treatment among men with benign prostatic hyperplasia. N Engl J Med 1998;338:557-563.

McConnell JD, Roehrborn CG, Bautista OM, et al: The long-term effect of doxazosin, finasteride, and combination therapy on the clinical progression of benign prostatic hyperplasia. N Engl J Med 2003;349:2387-2398.

Roehrborn CG, Boyle P, Gould AL, et al: Serum prostate-specific antigen as a predictor of prostate volume in men with benign prostatic hyperplasia. Urology 1999;53:581-589.

Roehrborn CG, Malice M-P, Cook TJ, Girman CJ: Clinical predictors of spontaneous acute urinary retention in men with LUTS and clinical BPH: A comprehensive analysis of the pooled placebo groups of several large studies. Urology 2001;58:210-216.

Roehrborn CG, Boyle P, Nickel JC, et al: Efficacy and safety of a dual inhibitor of 5 alpha-reductase types 1 and 2 (dutasteride) in men with benign prostatic hyperplasia. Urology 2002;60:434-441.

Roehrborn CG, Schwinn DA: Alpha1-adrenergic receptors and their inhibitors in lower urinary tract symptoms and benign prostatic hyperplasia. J Urol 2004;171:1029-1035.

88 Minimally Invasive and Endoscopic Management of Benign Prostatic Hyperplasia

JOHN M. FITZPATRICK, MCh, FRCSI, FRCS(Glas), FRCS

The prostate continues to be central to urologic practice in terms of the volume of cases that arise having a disorder of that organ, be it benign, malignant, or inflammatory. Because of this, the amount of money available from grant-giving authorities for research into prostatic diseases is probably the highest for any research on the genitourinary tract, and so inevitably our interest in and understanding of the pathogenesis of problems relating to prostatic conditions have increased greatly. This has led to increasingly effective therapies for some prostatic abnormalities, but after the initial advances in the management of benign prostatic hyperplasia (BPH) of 10 to 12 years ago, how far have things moved forward? And, although groups of patients are continually being identified who would benefit from individual or combined medical treatments, can we say that the same has been happening in our development of minimally invasive therapies?

One thing that is certain is that in our investigation of medical therapy of BPH, the identification of groups of patients who would best respond to different drugs has taken many large trials with long-term follow-up and careful statistical powering to demonstrate equivalence or a predefined difference. One always has the feeling that drug trials keep moving forward, leading to a greater understanding of the condition itself and of the ideal treatment for BPH. It can be said with some degree of confidence that the advent of medical management has reduced greatly the indications for and the number of patients undergoing transurethral resection of the prostate (TURP) and has also strongly influenced the wish of patients to have a TURP, in that they would now prefer to try most other types of treatment before agreeing to undergo a TURP.

As the pharmacologic management of BPH was flourishing, many new minimally invasive therapies were being introduced. The huge success that greeted the development of technological innovations in the management of renal calculus disease with percutaneous nephrolithotomy and extracorporeal shockwave lithotripsy prompted most of us to believe that the same could be achieved with BPH.

The yardstick against which the new minimally invasive therapies were measured was, of course, TURP. This was a very significant technological innovation when it was introduced, and it went through a considerable amount of evolution before it reached the high levels of excellence that it has reached today. We know that it does not seem to produce as good results as the open prostatectomy, but it is not far behind. This statement is made without there having been a randomized trial between the two, and comments on the safety and efficacy of one against the other are not evidence based. However, TURP can be viewed as a highly effective treatment with an acceptable complication rate, so much so that it is now accepted as the "gold standard," that is, the standard against which other minimally invasive therapies must be measured and the standard that it is hoped they can achieve.

One of the slightly disappointing things is that although many of these therapies have been introduced, in spite of the fact that they were originally welcomed as a significant advance in the treatment of BPH, in the longer term they have not turned out to be so. In many cases, the conclusion that they were of value was based on a series of poorly constructed short-term trials in which intention-to-treat analysis of the results may not have been rigidly adhered to. However, the demise of some of the earlier technologies has led to strengthening and evolution of the newer ones, all of which has been beneficial for patients with BPH.

It should also be remembered why it is that the new minimally invasive techniques have been introduced. Ideally, they have been popularized and developed in the hope that they will have less complications than TURP, less requirement for anesthesia, and a shorter hospital stay and if possible will be cheaper. If the treatment is as effective as TURP, it should be ahead on one of these counts, and if it is not as efficacious, a rationale for its use should be devised, in addition to attempts at the identification of the patients most likely to benefit from it. Its exact therapeutic positioning in the management of BPH should be found.

The template of the chapter on the same topic in the eighth edition of *Campbell's Urology* has been used by me once more. The reader will be updated with the current approach to the minimally invasive and endoscopic management of BPH. The literature has once again been critically and fairly reviewed, and the information outlined has relied heavily on evidence-based principles. Where level I evidence is available, such as a meta-analysis or systematic literature review, the reader's attention will be drawn to it. The purpose of all of this is to present the data so that readers will be able to make a valued judgment on the various treatment options, thus helping in their urologic practice.

INTRAPROSTATIC STENTS

One of the earliest attempts to find less traumatic methods of treating symptomatic BPH was the introduction of either temporary or permanent intraprostatic stents, and, to a degree, they are still being used. They were first introduced as a method of treating certain cardiovascular conditions; and since the work of Dotter (1969), they have also been part of the treatment for peripheral vascular disease. They have since been used to treat stenosis of the coronary, femoral, and renal arteries (Maass et al, 1982; Dotter et al, 1983; Wright et al, 1985; Palmaz et al, 1987). Other types of obstruction have also been treated by the placement of stents: vena caval obstruction (Furui et al, 1990), bronchial obstruction (Mair et al, 1990), and tracheal stenosis (Skapshay et al, 1989). Even cervical stenosis (Luesley et al, 1990) and lacrimal duct obstruction (Hurwitz, 1989) have been treated in this manner. It is clear that stents have a role to play in treating obstruction in different parts of the body, but the exact role needs to be defined accurately. In the case of coronary artery disease, for example, a trial comparing stents with coronary artery bypass grafting is still awaited. In the case of the prostate, it took some time before it was realized that the role of stents was rather a limited one and that they would not replace TURP in every patient.

There has been very little new in this section since the last edition. One of the few innovations has been the introduction of a new temporary prostatic stent, which is based on a modification of the Foley catheter. This is described in detail in the appropriate section.

The idea of using stents for splinting the lobes of the prostate was derived from their original use in the cardiovascular system, where they are used to prevent arterial restenosis after angioplasty. Fabian (1980) first described the use of stents in urology when he suggested their usefulness in the treatment of outlet obstruction secondary to enlargement of the prostate. At some time after this, the use of stents was advocated in the treatment of urethral strictures, and, subsequent to this, the use of prostatic stents became widespread, with the introduction of many different types: stents are now available in different lengths, diameters, materials, and designs.

As mentioned earlier, when stents were introduced as a treatment for symptomatic BPH, their exact role was uncertain and tended to be overstated as perhaps something that could be used in virtually every case. **Eventually, it became clear that their major role was likely to be found in the management of patients who were unfit for surgery, in either the short or the long term, where the alternative would have been months or, indeed, a lifetime of indwelling urethral catheterization.**

Along with these changes in the indications for their use have emerged two basic types of stent: that which is put in for a short time and can be removed with ease and that which is placed as a permanent type of treatment and can be removed only with much greater difficulty.

Temporary Stents

Temporary stents are tubular devices that are made of either **a nonabsorbable or a biodegradable material.** They remain in the prostatic urethra for a limited period of time; they neither become covered by the urethral epithelium nor become incorporated into the urethral wall. The nonabsorbable stents need to be removed every 6 to 36 months, depending on which type of material is used. They can usually be removed, and, if necessary, replaced, without difficulty with the patient under topical anesthesia with sedation.

They are designed for short-term use, to relieve bladder outlet obstruction, and to act as an alternative to an indwelling urethral or suprapubic catheter in high-risk patients considered unfit for surgery. In such patients, these temporary stents permit normal micturition with an acceptable side effect profile. Success rates have been reported as lying in the range of 50% to 90%. They are easy to reposition or replace, but catheterization or cystoscopy cannot be performed while the stent is in place. Complications such as encrustation, migration, breakage, stress incontinence, and bacteriuria have been reported in varying degrees of frequency.

Spiral Stents

First-Generation Stents. The Urospiral (Porges) and the Prosta Kath (Pharma-Plast) are examples of spiral stents. The former is made of stainless steel with a caliber of No. 21

Fr and a length varying between 40 and 80 mm. The latter is also made of stainless steel and also has a caliber of No. 21 Fr but is gold plated in an attempt to prevent encrustation. It has a length varying between 35 and 95 mm. Neither stent should remain in the prostatic urethra for longer than 12 months.

The spiral stents should be inserted with a No. 21 Fr panendoscope using either a 30-degree or a 0-degree lens under direct vision and with the aid of a grasping forceps. It may also be inserted over a catheter guide under ultrasound visualization (Nordling et al, 1989).

In the original series reported by Nordling and colleagues (1989), the Prosta Kath was inserted under topical anesthesia in 45 patients with acute or chronic retention. Ultrasound was used in 35 patients and endoscopy in 6 to facilitate stent placement. **Retention was relieved in 41 of the 45 patients, leading the authors to advocate its use in high-risk patients.**

Ozgur and coworkers (1993) reported reestablishment of voiding with the Urospiral with good results after 4 months of follow-up in 31 patients who were unfit for surgery. The Urospiral was also used in 10 patients with advanced prostate cancer (Anson et al, 1993). All had retention or severe obstruction. The patients were started on antiandrogens after stent insertion. The stent was removed 3 months later, and all patients were reported as voiding satisfactorily, although one patient subsequently required a limited TURP. In another report, 18 high-risk patients with BPH had a Urospiral inserted (Karaoglau et al, 1992). **All voided without difficulty and with complete bladder emptying. However, the complications were rather high: hematuria in 2, migration in 1, and infection in 8.**

In 87 patients declared unfit for TURP, Thomas and colleagues (1993) reported an experience extending over 4 years using the Prosta Kath. Sixty-four patients presented with acute urinary retention, and, after treatment, 57 voided successfully whereas 7 failed to void. A further 14 patients presented with chronic urinary retention; 5 of these voided satisfactorily, but 9 required alternative therapy. **Complications included hematuria with clot retention (5%), stent migration (15%), recurrent urinary tract infections (10%), and encrustation (4%).** These findings of relatively high complications are also reported by other authors (Nordling et al, 1989; Harrison and De Souza, 1990). Braf and coworkers (1996) followed up 55 men for between 12 and 16 months, 32 of whom were treated with the Prosta Kath and 23 with the Urospiral. Ten patients failed in the Prosta Kath group, and eight patients failed in the Urospiral group. Complications in both groups include encrustation, urinary tract infection, migration, stricture formation, and failure to void. In the largest number of patients reported from one center, Nordling reported on the use of the Prosta Kath in 318 patients. He divided the complications into none, moderate, and severe. In the patients who were described as having severe complications, stress or urge incontinence occurred in 63, emptying problems in 8, and frequency or nocturia (more than three) or both in 57.

Second-Generation Stents. Other spiral stents have been developed as second-generation models in an attempt to overcome the problems of the first-generation stents just described while maintaining the efficacy and ease of insertion. These are the Memokath and the Prosta Coil.

The Memokath (Engineers and Doctors A/S, Copenhagen, Denmark) is made of nitinol, a nickel-titanium alloy, which has the property of shape memory. It is malleable and heat expandable at a temperature of 45° to 50° C. Like other temporary stents, it is easy to insert and maintains its expanded position in the prostatic urethra. With the earlier model of the Memokath, epithelial hyperplasia at the apex of the prostate was reported in some cases, but modifications have since been made. The later model ensured close contact of the wires even in the expanded position, thus reducing the possibility of hyperplastic growth of the urethral epithelium through the gaps in the expanded spiral. The Memokath is soft and malleable when cooled, returning to its original shape when heated to the preceding temperatures. It has a caliber of No. 22 Fr and a length of 35 to 95 mm. It permits the passage of a flexible cystoscope and may be left in place for up to 36 months.

The Prosta Coil is a self-expanding and self-retaining stent made of a nickel-titanium alloy (Instent, Minneapolis, Minn). It is inserted by being mounted on a delivery catheter of No. 17 Fr under fluoroscopy; once released from the mounting, it takes the form of a wave-shaped tube whose diameter varies from No. 24 to 30 Fr. Its length is from 40 to 80 mm, and it can be left in position for up to 36 months.

The Memokath was reported as being used in **30 patients who were unfit for surgery or who refused it; the success rate was 80%. Normal voiding is described as having occurred in all patients.** The peak urinary flow rate reached a mean of 16 mL/sec immediately after insertion (Poulsen et al, 1993). However, there was a wide range of flow rates, from 4 to 25 mL/sec. Unfortunately, three patients later developed urinary retention at 5 days, 2.5 months, and 5 months, respectively, after insertion. Two more stents needed to be removed because of hyperplastic growth of the epithelium. A total of 24 stents were still in place at 3 months. Nordling (1996) updated these authors' experience after inserting 64 of the modified Memokath stents. Similar successful voiding was reported. The complications that patients described as severe were few, with urge incontinence being the most common (10 patients). However, moderate symptoms were relatively more common.

Results are available from a long-term study conducted in the United Kingdom. The Memokath was inserted in men who were either permanently or temporarily unfit for TURP, in most cases because of severe respiratory or cardiovascular disease. **In this study, 211 men had 217 stents inserted over an 8-year period. In the same time frame, 1511 TURPs were performed. The mean age of patients having stents was 80.2 years and in the TURP group 70.2 years. The patients who had stents fitted experienced an improvement in the mean International Prostate Symptom Score (I-PSS) from 20.3 to 8.2 in just 3 months, with results being maintained for 7 years. However, these results must be viewed in the light of the fact that 38% died with stents in place, 34% remain alive with their stents, and 23% had stent removal because of failure. Migration occurred in 13%, and 16% required repositioning. This study suggests that long-term success can be achievable using the Memokath, but failure can also be anticipated in a significant minority** (Perry et al, 2002).

The Prosta Coil has been used in a small series of patients with short follow-up (Yachia et al, 1994). The mean follow-up was 14 months, with a range of 2 to 28 months. There were initial irritative urinary symptoms that were reported as having disappeared within 1 month. **The mean peak urinary flow rate at the most recent follow-up was 21.3 mL/sec (with a range of 15 to 36 mL/sec) and the mean I-PSS was 9 (with a range of 6 to 12).**

Thus, spiral stents were among the earliest type of temporary stents to be introduced, and they have developed to a large degree from the original designs. New models have reduced such complications as encrustation and urothelial hyperplasia, but stress incontinence and urge incontinence still occur, as does displacement of the stent. However, they are easy to insert and do not require general anesthesia. Although the follow-up is relatively short term, in most of the reported series, good success rates are reported. The place of spiral stents is clearly that of a nontraumatic therapy for urinary retention in patients unfit for surgery, and they have a reasonable chance of a successful outcome.

It is hard to predict whether further design changes will take place. The earlier type of spiral stents had the advantage of being less expensive. The newer models are made of compounds aimed to reduce complications or prevent stent migration but are all more expensive than the earlier models. With a limited market and with a restricted acceptability, further developments in this type of stent are unlikely.

Polyurethane Stents

Polyurethane stents are also known as intraurethral catheters. There are three types: the intraurethral catheter (Angiomed, Germany), the Barnes stent (Bard, Inc., Covington, GA), and the trestle stent (Boston Scientific Microvasive).

Intraurethral Catheter. The intraurethral catheter, the first to be introduced, was reported initially by Nissenkorn (1991). It is made of a type of polyurethane known as Puroflex and has a fixed caliber of No. 16 Fr. Its length varies from 40 to 60 mm, and it can be left in place for up to 6 months. It has a double device at its proximal end shaped like the head of a de Pezzer or Malecot catheter. It has a nylon string at its distal end and a flared split end proximally, which sits in the bladder. It is inserted under topical anesthesia using a No. 22 Fr cystoscope. The nylon string is cut after placement, and any positional adjustment required can be performed by the use of a grasping forceps. **Eighty-five devices were inserted into 73 patients, and, of these, 60 patients had an indwelling catheter for 1 week to 3 years before insertion.** Nissenkorn (1991) described a successful outcome in 63 patients who believed that their quality of life was considerably better than it had been when they had an indwelling catheter. He therefore believed that this was suitable for use in such patients, with a high likelihood of success.

A later study reported the use of the Nissenkorn intraurethral catheter in 43 patients (Sassine and Schulman, 1994). Once again, the patients treated had developed urinary retention and were unfit for surgery but also had a short life expectancy. Thirty-six of the 43 patients were able to void satisfactorily after stent insertion. The intraurethral catheter should not be inserted in the presence of bladder stones or anything else likely to block or have a ball-valve effect on the device.

One of the potential uses of temporary prostatic stents is as an expedient to overcome the early retentive effects of heat treatment to the prostate. Clearly, an objection to this might be that such a therapeutic strategy effectively doubles the cost of the treatment and so makes it less attractive. However, it is an attractive way of overcoming an early complication of heat treatment, which might have been seen by some as a significant limitation of heat treatment. The Barnes stent and the Trestle stent may have such an application.

Barnes Stent. What has been called the Barnes stent is made of polyurethane, has a caliber of No. 16 Fr, and is of a single length. It also has a de Pezzer end proximally, but this time a single one. It is thus a modification of the original intraurethral catheter. It was used in 25 patients who underwent endoscopic laser ablation of the prostate (ELAP). Twenty-two of the 25 voided immediately. Early stent migration occurred in one patient, but late migration did not occur. The stent was inserted with ease, could be removed with ease at 12 weeks, and was inexpensive. Peak urinary flow rates improved from 8 mL/sec before ELAP to 16.5 mL/sec at 6 weeks with the stent in place (Barnes et al, 1996). The Nissenkorn catheter has also been used safely and with equal success after laser therapy (Nissenkorn et al, 1996).

Trestle Stent. The trestle stent or prostatic bridge catheter has been described and consists of two tubes and an interconnecting thread. The tube that lies in the prostate has a diameter of No. 22 Fr and has a 30-degree angulation. The length is 75 mm, and it has a smooth tip: It is to be used in prostates with a volume of less than 80 mL. The connecting thread is 25 mm, which passes through the distal sphincteric mechanism. The second tube lies in the bulbar urethra and is 35 mm long. It is inserted with the patient under topical anesthesia using a delivery system comprising a positioning stylet, an inflatable balloon with injection cannula, and an outer pusher tube. The technique is described in detail by Djavan and colleagues (1999).

In a report from Devonec and Dahlstrand (1998), the results of its use **in 52 patients after high-energy transurethral microwave therapy were described. Tolerance was good in 32 patients, acceptable in 13, and poor in 6. Retrograde ejaculation occurred in eight. Flow rates reached 14.6 mL/sec on the day of removal of the device. The device was left in place for 1 month, but the improvement in flow rate was maintained at 1 year.** Djavan and colleagues (1999) also described its use in 54 patients who had received high-energy transurethral microwave thermotherapy. The device was left in place for up to 1 month, and it was found that the incidence of post-treatment retention was prevented, with concurrent early but significantly improved symptom scores and peak urinary flow rates. Toleration was high, with 48 of 54 devices remaining in place for 1 month. Early removal was required because of urinary retention in three and migration in three.

The intraurethral catheter or its more recent variations are being used in a rather different context than the spiral stents. They have been used successfully, albeit in a small number of nonrandomized short-term studies, with few problems related to tolerance. A further cost-efficacy evaluation is required, in addition to larger multicenter randomized controlled comparative trials.

The Spanner. This has a design very similar to the proximal 4 to 6 cm of a Foley catheter. It includes a balloon to prevent displacement, a port for urine drainage that lies proximal to the balloon, and a reinforced stent that spans most of the prostatic urethra, of varying length (Fig. 88–1).

In the first study using this device, the stent was inserted under topical anaesthesia in 30 patients (Corica et al, 2004), of whom 5 had been in urinary retention. The stents remained in place for a mean of 57 days. The mean Qmax improved by 42% from 8.2 to 11.6 mL/sec. The overall mean I-PSS decreased from 22.3 to 7.1, a 68% difference. The adverse events were few, and the device was found to be stable and patent at the end of the study.

This article describes an early open study designed to test the efficacy, safety, and stability of the device. It could be criticized in that it was composed of a group of patients whose characteristics were not adequately described, with no entry criteria defined. It is, however, an interesting new device that may well be important for many patients as a temporary method of bypassing prostatic obstruction.

Biodegradable Stents

The concept of stents that can be put in place after a procedure that has a high incidence of secondary and temporary obstruction has been mentioned earlier in the context of stents being inserted after laser or high-energy transurethral microwave therapy. These stents are removed some weeks later. With the biodegradable stent, the concept is brought one step further; the stents do not need to be removed, and eventually they disappear by biodegrading. This interesting idea was first introduced in urology when Kemppainen and colleagues (1993) used a biodegradable stent in rabbits after urethrotomy. The idea has now been extended to the ureter (Schlick and Planz, 1998; Lumiaho et al, 1999; Clayman, 2000), after endoscopic urethroplasty (Oosterlinck and Talja, 2000), and in coronary artery disease (Tamai et al, 2000).

Figure 88–1. The transurethral needle ablation of the prostate (TUNA) device, PROVu. (Courtesy of Neo Vitalis Limited, Southport, UK.)

Further experimental studies have shown that biodegradable stents can potentially be used as a bridge across the prostate after minimally invasive procedures, without the necessity of having to remove them later (Petas et al, 1997a, 1998; Laaksovirta et al, 2002; Vaajanen et al, 2003).

In addition, clinical studies have been performed that examine the use of biodegradable stents after various procedures (Talja et al, 1995; Dahlstrand et al, 1997; Petas et al, 1997b). The benefit is that these stents prevent the development of obstruction that can occur after laser procedures; however, the use of the second procedure in association with, for example, laser prostatectomy takes away a great deal from the value of the first procedure, not least in terms of cost-effectiveness. There are three types of biodegradable stent.

A randomized study (Petas et al, 1997b) **compared self-reinforced polyglycolic acid biodegradable spiral stents (group 1), no device (group 2), or an indwelling catheter (group 3) after visual laser ablation of the prostate. The procedure was performed on 72 men, and 27 were in group 1, 23 in group 2, and 22 in group 3. Voiding began at a median of 1 day in group 1 and a median of 6 days in group 2; the indwelling catheter was required for an average of 6.5 days in group 3, and voiding commenced a median of 6 days after this.** The authors found, as they had in previous in vitro studies, that the stent degraded into small fragments of polymer debris that were passed out in the urine. They commented that voiding became more obstructed at 3 to 4 weeks postoperatively, presumably from degradation and sloughing of the stent, but they found that this was only a transient effect.

In another study, Dahlstrand and colleagues (1997) evaluated the same polyglycolic acid stent after high-energy transurethral microwave therapy with the Prostasoft 2.5. They compared the use of the stent in 15 patients against a further 15 patients in whom a standard No. 16-Fr urethral catheter was inserted. The mean duration of catheterization was 14.1 days, with a standard deviation of 4.1 days; this was obviously prevented by the stent, which did not cause problems, even when it was degrading.

In a rather innovative way, Knutson and colleagues (2003) described the use of a biodegradable polyglycolic acid stent to assess the risk of post-TURP incontinence in patients with combined bladder outlet obstruction and overactive bladder. In 37 patients with severe overactive bladder and moderate to severe bladder outlet obstruction, this biodegradable stent was inserted into the prostatic urethra; 25 noticed either no leakage or minor leakage and 19 have had TURP with good results. Twelve of the 37 had a major problem with incontinence after the insertion of the stent. There was a small complication rate related to stent insertion.

These stents are definitely of interest for the future, but their exact place in the treatment of BPH needs to be established, with larger and longer term studies. In addition, the problem related to the overall cost must be defined accurately; otherwise, the value of the primary procedure will be questioned.

Permanent Stents

With permanent stenting of the prostate, the urologist is attempting to treat definitively and permanently patients who present with symptomatic BPH. To be of proven value, this type of treatment, like any other, must be shown to be at least comparable to TURP. The initial enthusiasm for permanent stents has been replaced by relative silence in the literature at present. Permanent stents were initially introduced as treatment for recurrent urethral strictures and were subsequently used in patients with lower urinary tract symptoms. In urologic terms, permanent stents are being used preferentially for the treatment of detrusor-sphincter dyssynergia (Chancellor et al, 1999; Chartier-Kastler et al, 2000; Gajewski et al, 2000), postbrachytherapy bladder outlet obstruction (Konety et al, 2000), anastomotic strictures and urinary incontinence after radical prostatectomy (Meulen et al, 1991), and complex urethral strictures (Tillem et al, 1997). There have been no reports in the recent literature that relate to the long-term follow-up of the patients originally treated with permanent stents, and there has been no indication of new interest in their use.

UroLume

The UroLume endourethral prosthesis (American Medical Systems, Minnetonka, Minn.) is a woven tubular mesh that maintains its position in the urethra by outward external pressure, thus maintaining the patency of the prostatic urethra. The original device had a caliber of No. 42 Fr and was made of metal superalloy; it varied in length from 1.5 to 4.0 cm. It is inserted with a special deployment tool of No. 21 Fr using a 0-degree panendoscope. Gradually, epithelialization occurs, ideally in a smooth manner, covering the individual wires of the mesh. The stent can be removed by securing about 5 mm of the distal aspect in the jaws of a grasping forceps and then pulling the distal end inside a resectoscope sheath to minimize any possibility of urethral trauma while removing it.

The original stent tended to shorten while it expanded outward, leading to its replacement by a stent less likely to do so. However, this stent tended to migrate more easily, and a further modification was required. In addition to these changes, the delivery tool was modified, leading to the present, more satisfactory model.

Chapple and colleagues (1990) reported on the initial experience with the UroLume. **Twelve patients who were considered to be a poor risk for surgery presented with lower urinary tract symptoms; 9 of the 12 patients presented with urinary retention. The results were encouraging, with 11 of 12 voiding satisfactorily for a mean follow-up of 8.2 months. The mean peak urinary flow rate after the procedure was 13.6 mL/sec.** Further encouragement came from the low complication rate, consisting mainly of short-term irritative voiding symptoms, with only 1 of the 12 being dissatisfied because of severe urgency and frequency (the patient was subsequently found to have detrusor instability). A further study in a similar group of unfit patients was performed by McLoughlin and colleagues (1990). All 19 patients in their study group presented in urinary retention, and all voided satisfactorily after the stent was inserted under local anesthesia.

In a larger, multicenter open trial from the United States, Oesterling and colleagues (1994) reported on 126 men who presented either with moderate or severe lower urinary tract symptoms (95 men) or with urinary retention (31 men). There were strict inclusion and exclusion criteria in the trial design, but fitness for surgery was not among them. **In the nonretention group, 80 of 95 were evaluable at 12 months and 52 at 24 months; the Madsen symptom score decreased from 14.0 to 5.9 and 5.4, respectively. In the retention group,** the 24 of the 31 patients evaluable at 12 months had a mean symptom score of 6.1. In the nonretention group, the peak urinary flow rate increased from 9.1 to 13.0 and 13.1 mL/sec, respectively, with the retention group having a mean flow rate of 11.7 mL/sec at 12 months.** Difficulties with insertion were experienced in 16% of cases. Irritative voiding symptoms occurred in 10%.

Guazzoni and coworkers (1994) described a European study using the modified UroLume stent (the so-called less shortening variety described earlier). Once again, the strict inclusion and exclusion criteria did not refer to fitness for surgery, and at this time the stent was being presented as a proposed therapy for prostatic obstruction, not necessarily only for unfit patients. In this multicenter study, 135 healthy patients (91 with lower urinary tract symptoms, 44 with urinary retention) were treated. In the nonretention group, 74 of 91 patients were evaluable at 12 months. The mean Madsen-Iversen symptom score had decreased from 14.1 to 6.4, but the tight standard deviations of the mean observed in the U.S. study (0.4) were not seen in this study (5.1); the peak urinary flow rate improved from 9.3 to 15.7 mL/sec at 12 months (with a very wide standard deviation of 6.5, unlike that in the U.S. study). In the retention group, 34 of 44 were evaluable at 12 months; the mean symptom score was 4.5 and the mean flow rate was 13.1 mL/sec. The complications were well described but were found to be significant in the long term.

In a British study (Bajoria et al, 1995), 44 men fit for TURP accepted as an alternative a second-generation UroLume stent. The stent was inserted in 44 patients, who either were in urinary retention or had urodynamically proven outflow obstruction. The results achieved were similar to those reported by Guazzoni and colleagues (1994), but there was also a relatively high complication rate. Both sets of authors noted **epithelial hyperplasia and migration of the stent in addition to irritative urinary symptoms and painful ejaculation. The second-generation less shortening stent was not recommended for general use,** and a third-generation stent was then produced. However, Bajoria and colleagues (1995) strongly suggested that permanent stents should still be considered as being under evaluation rather than for general use.

In a multicenter study of 96 men who were unfit for prostatic surgery, 73 presented in acute urinary retention and 11 in chronic retention. **All but six were able to void immediately after stent insertion; two required a second stent, and four required a period of suprapubic catheter drainage. At 12 months, the peak flow rate was 15 mL/sec in the retention group and 18.1 in the nonretention group. Severe irritative symptoms were seen in the majority of patients for up to 3 months, and encrustation was encountered in 15 of 27 patients who underwent cystoscopy** (Williams et al, 1993).

The results of a long-term analysis of the UroLume wallstent have been published by Masood and coworkers (2004). The stent was inserted in 62 patients with moderate or severe lower urinary tract symptoms secondary to BPH. The 5- and 12-year follow-up was completed by 22 and 11 patients, respectively. Death occurred in 21 patients (34%), and the stent was removed in 29 patients (47%), the vast majority of these removals occurring in the first 2 years. The authors concluded that this is a safe treatment but that cases must be carefully selected and that it should be performed only by experienced hands.

The use of the UroLume stent can be seen to have some application in patients with prostatic obstruction, particularly if they are unfit. However, interest in this type of stent seems to have waned somewhat because of the use of other types of less invasive treatments, which appear more satisfactory to patient and urologist alike.

Memotherm

The Memotherm (Angiomed, Germany) is a heat-expandable stent of nickel-titanium alloy with a caliber of No. 42 Fr after expansion. When it is cooled, it can easily be compressed and distorted, but, when warmed to body temperature, it expands to a flexible cylinder and does not shorten. It is made from a woven single wire, which makes it easy to remove; traction unravels the wire. It is manufactured in lengths varying between 1.5 and 8.0 cm and is available in a prepacked sterile delivery service. It is inserted under direct vision with a 0-degree telescope.

Williams and White (1995) reported on 48 men with lower urinary tract symptoms and urodynamic findings suggestive of bladder outflow obstruction. The results were disappointing. **Only 37 patients were able to void immediately after stent insertion, the others requiring a suprapubic catheter for up to 8 weeks. Symptomatic improvement occurred in many, but complications, including stent migration, were relatively high. Thirteen of the 48 patients required removal of their stents.** These authors suggested that the results were not appropriate to encourage marketing of the device.

Gesenberg and Sintermann (1998) used the Memotherm in 123 patients considered to be at high risk for prostatic surgery; 46 of these presented in urinary retention. Of the 123 patients, only 52 were evaluable at 12 months. The mean peak urinary flow rate increased from 7.4 to 13.0 mL/sec (with a standard deviation of 6.2) and the I-PSS improved from 24.0 to 8.8 (standard deviation 6.2). **The authors noted a considerable improvement in quality of life. However, the complication rate was relatively high, with recurrent infections and urge symptoms in 56%, urothelial hyperplasia in 34%, and urethral stricture in 10%. There was a high number of retreatments,** and the authors suggested that there may be an additional role for medical treatment in some of these patients.

These results have not appeared to be convincing large numbers of urologists to use these stents on patients with symptomatic BPH, but modifications may occur. Heat-expandable stents are widely used in cardiovascular conditions and in biliary stenosis.

Other Permanent Stents

The ASI stent (Advanced Surgical Instruments) was evaluated in several centers (Kirby et al, 1992; Kaplan et al, 1995). It was introduced on a balloon, which was then inflated, thus expanding the stent. The early results suggested an improvement in symptom score (44%) and peak urinary flow rate (22%), but complications also occurred that made it less attractive for general use. It has since been withdrawn from production.

The Ultraflex stent (Boston Scientific Instruments) is made of nickel-titanium alloy that also has a capacity to expand to

a caliber of No. 42 Fr when exposed to body heat. It is available in lengths varying from 2 to 6 cm. There have been reports of its use in patients with prostatic obstruction, but it has been studied in a group of patients with detrusor-sphincter dyssynergia (Chartier-Kastler et al, 2000), and the incidence of epithelial hyperplasia and migration was encouragingly low.

Conclusion

Originally, permanent prostatic stents were introduced as a definitive treatment for prostatic obstruction, particularly (but not in every study) for patients unfit for prostatic surgery who presented with urinary retention. Patients were able to void satisfactorily in most cases, but complications were relatively high. One stent has been removed from the market, one has not yet been reported on as a treatment for prostatic problems, variable results have been reported on another, and the most frequently investigated, the UroLume, has not received recent attention in the literature as a specific treatment for BPH.

Temporary stents are receiving widespread attention, but the original idea that they should be used as a temporary expedient to overcome outflow problems in the medically unfit is being modified. The newer stents, whether biodegradable or not, are being viewed as possible methods of overcoming the temporary retention that can occur secondary to treatments such as laser therapy or high-energy transurethral microwave therapy.

TRANSURETHRAL NEEDLE ABLATION OF THE PROSTATE

Heat treatment of whatever kind to the prostate is intended to reduce outflow resistance and the volume of the obstruction by increasing the temperature within the prostate and inducing necrosis of prostatic tissue. The aim is to increase prostatic temperature to in excess of 60° C. Transurethral needle ablation of the prostate (TUNA) uses low-level radiofrequency (RF) energy that is delivered by needles into the prostate and that produces localized necrotic lesions in the hyperplastic tissue. It has previously been used to ablate cardiac nerve bundles in the Wolff-Parkinson-White syndrome (Calkins et al, 1992) and to destroy malignant tissue (Rossi et al, 1995; Zlotta et al, 1995). It has also been used to treat chronic cervical zygapophyseal joint pain (Lord et al, 1996). The advantage of TUNA is that it can be delivered under topical anesthesia to patients with symptomatic BPH, causing very precise and reproducible lesions within the prostate.

Delivery of Radiofrequency Energy

The TUNA system (Medtronic Inc, Minneapolis, Minn) consists of a special catheter attached to a generator. At the end of the catheter are two adjustable needles that are withdrawn into two adjustable shields made from Teflon. The needles are advanced into the prostatic tissue and can be placed accurately into the required position.

The generator produces a monopolar RF signal of 490 kHz, which allows excellent penetration and uniform tissue distribution. The patient has a grounding pad placed over the sacrum, and the current passes toward this through the prostatic tissue. In other words, tissue heating is created because of tissue resistance to the current as it flows from the active to the return electrode. The active electrode has a small surface area, with the RF current being concentrated in an area immediately surrounding it. The return electrode is large, and so the diffusion of the RF current is greater. This arrangement allows heat to be concentrated near the active electrode early, thus accurately controlling the tissue effect. The size of the lesion caused by RF relates to the position and depth of insertion of the electrode as well as the power used and the duration of the treatment.

RF produces molecular or ionic agitation with collision of particles that relates to the frequency of the energy, and this results in a central hot core inside the prostate and away from the urethra (Schulman et al, 1993). The limited distance dissipation reinforces the safety of the procedure because RF can be applied to tissue only by direct contact, with heat being generated proportional to one over the fourth power of the radius. If the power generated is too high, the prostate rapidly desiccates with a rise in tissue impedance, preventing the desired heating effect. Therefore, the appropriate energy level required to produce the localized necrotic lesion must be found, preventing the increase in tissue impedance resulting in prostatic charring around the needle caused by excessive generation of energy (Schulman et al, 1993). Interestingly, heat is lost by convection, and so increased vascularity can have an effect on the degree of localization of the lesion. RF is very much affected by blood flow and has almost no effect on vessels larger than 2 to 3 mm in diameter (Organ, 1976).

There is a difference in the method of tissue heating brought about by RF and, for example, microwave application. Microwaves treat a broad area and can penetrate tissue more deeply than RF. The central temperature is therefore lower than with RF in order to maintain safe heat levels at the treatment rim. Therefore, treatment with microwaves takes longer than RF to produce coagulative necrosis. RF, however, has a much hotter central area with a very quick decline in temperature as the distance increases from the treatment needle. This results in faster generation of the necrotic lesion but of a smaller area (Perlmutter et al, 1993).

Experimental Studies

In a series of preliminary studies on animals and ex vivo human prostates, it has been shown that the TUNA system can create 1-cm necrotic lesions without difficulty in the prostate with no damage to rectum, bladder base, or distal prostatic urethra (Goldwasser et al, 1993; Ramon et al, 1993). Other studies showed that the lesions are accurate with sharp delineation from the untreated areas (Schulman et al, 1993). These authors also showed that the lesion appeared first as a hemorrhagic lesion along the needle path, with slight discoloration in the surrounding area. Necrosis was maximal at 7 days, with fibrosis having developed by 15 days.

In an elegant neurohistochemical study, Zlotta and colleagues (1997) removed prostates from patients scheduled for prostatectomy 1 to 46 days after TUNA. Immunohistochemistry was used with anti-S100 protein and neuron-specific enolase for nerve staining and anti–prostate-specific antigen and antidesmin for glandular and muscle cells. They showed that the maximal lesion size ranged from 10×7 to 20×10 mm^2 and that there was destruction of all tissue components. The lesions were accurately positioned 0.3 to 1.0 cm from the urethra, which remained undamaged. In the treated area, there was an absence of staining for prostate-specific antigen, smooth muscle actin, and α-adrenergic neural tissue. Even in specimens removed 24 hours after TUNA, no positively staining nerve cells were seen in the treated areas.

It has also been shown (Issa et al, 1996) that there may be sequential damage to different types of nerve endings. Nitric oxide synthase receptors were found to be most vulnerable to thermal damage, which occurred earliest, with damage to the α-adrenergic receptors maximal at 1 to 2 weeks.

The temperatures achieved in the largest area have been studied by Rasor and coworkers (1993) using an infrared temperature monitor in an ex vivo animal model. They showed that the central core of the lesion around the tip of the lesion reached 90° to 100° C. Treatment times of 5 to 7 minutes were required to produce coagulation necrosis in the treatment zone. Dosimetry studies have shown that the temperatures at the edge of the zone were 50° C.

Instruments

The generator produces low-level monopolar RF waves of about 490 kHz, which produce temperatures of about 100° C in the target area. The RF generator is connected to the TUNA catheter, which has changed somewhat in design since it was first manufactured.

The TUNA catheter is, in fact, a specifically designed endoscopic instrument. This has evolved from what was a device through which a panendoscope lens could be inserted. A number of other changes have also been made. The most up-to-date version of the TUNA catheter is called the Pro Vu system, and part of this device is reusable, unlike previous models (Fig. 88–2; see Fig. 88–1). The new system also contains a markedly improved optical system. Previously, the needles were introduced either blindly or under transrectal ultrasound guidance, which had the advantage in the latter case of seeing how close to the surrounding tissues the needles lay. However, an adequate visualization of the needle entering the prostate tissue gives the urologist a better idea of the treatment area. The final change concerns the angle between the catheter and the needles, which is at present not fixed. This means that a high bladder neck that is hypertrophied or a genuine median lobe enlargement can now be treated easily by this technique.

The configuration of the needles within their protective sheath ensures that the treatment area is deep inside the prostatic lobes, and this ensures that the prostatic urethra is spared. Because there is a limited number of nerve endings in the prostatic glandular tissue and because the higher concentration of nerve endings immediately underlying the urethral epithelium remains undisturbed, topical anesthesia can be used with the patient experiencing only moderate discomfort. In addition, postprocedural irritative urinary symptoms are kept to a minimum.

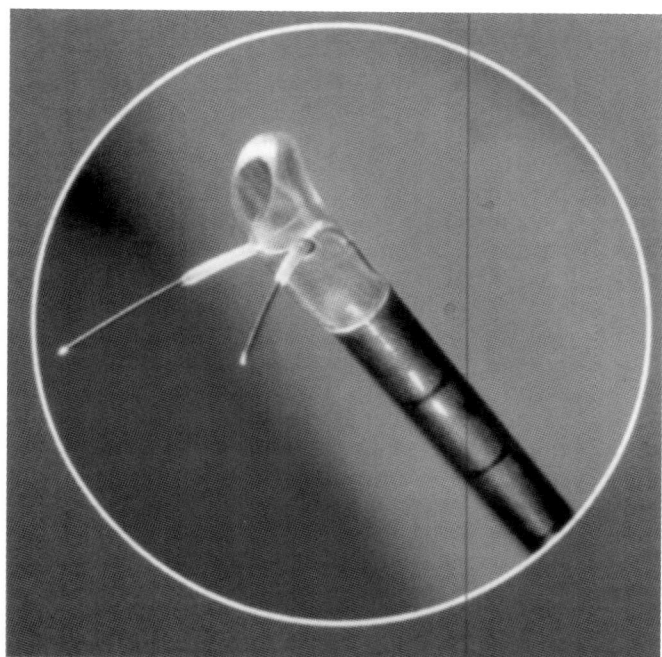

Figure 88–2. The transurethral needle ablation of the prostate (TUNA) radiofrequency needles deployed. (Courtesy of Neo Vitalis Limited, Southport, UK.)

Table 88–1. Studies Using Transurethral Needle Ablation with 12-Month Follow-Up

Reference	Patients (N)	Symptom Score Preop.	Symptom Score Postop.	Peak Urinary Flow Preop.	Peak Urinary Flow Postop.
Roehrborn et al (1998)	130	23.7	11.9	7.8	14.6
Bruskewitz et al (1998)	65	24.7	11.1	8.7	15.0
Schulman et al (1993)	36	21.6	7.8	9.9	16.8
Campo et al (1997)	72	20.8	6.2	8.2	15.9
Ramon et al (1997)	68	22.0	10.0	8.8	11.5
Rosario et al (1997)	58	22.0	10.0	8.8	11.5
Steele and Sleep (1997)	41	22.4	7.0	6.6	10.2
Millard et al (1996)	20	19.0	8.2	3.0	11.4

Treatment

The patient is placed in the lithotomy position and topical anesthesia with 2% intraurethral lidocaine (Xylocaine) is achieved. The best result is attained by applying a penile clamp for 10 minutes and by giving intravenous (IV) sedation if required. There is a variation from institution to institution as to the optimum form of anesthesia; for many, what is described previously is satisfactory, but some prefer spinal or even general anesthesia, particularly for their initial experience with the technique. In other cases, a local prostatic block, either transperineally or transrectally, may be the method of choice.

With the new modifications, **the TUNA catheter is advanced under vision with the 0-degree fiberoptic telescope, which also allows the urologist to see the needles being advanced accurately into the prostate. The exact position within the prostate of the needle tip can be visualized by transrectal ultrasonography.** Preprocedural assessment of the size of the prostate by this method allows calculation of the length of deployment of the needle within the prostate; this can also be done at the beginning of the procedure, as described earlier, with the ultrasound showing the exact position of the needle tip. It is important to remember that the thermal lesion may extend for up to 5 to 6 mm beyond the position of needle deployment with lesions measuring up to 20 × 10 mm. When the position is deemed satisfactory, the Teflon shield on the proximal part of the needle is advanced to protect the urethral epithelium and the underlying tissue. Therefore, the tip of the needle should not lie within 5 to 6 mm of the outer rim of the prostate, and the urethra is protected by the shields that extend from 5 to 6 mm from the TUNA catheter itself.

The number of lesions depends on the size of the prostate, but because there are two needles, each time power is switched on in the generator, two lesions are produced. It is usually advised that one pair of lesions should be used to treat 20 g of prostate tissue; it can also be expressed in terms of length, with one pair of lesions, or treatment plane, being used for less than 3 cm of prostatic urethral length, two planes for 3 to 4 cm, and one extra plane of treatment for every extra centimeter of urethral length. The procedure is then repeated in the opposite lobe.

The RF power that is delivered is 2 to 15 W for 5 minutes per lesion. In earlier models, the treatment was begun at a low power, but now the whole thermal process is automated, with temperature levels at treatment areas preset. The temperature at the tip of the needle varies from 80° to 100° C. The urethral temperature is kept below 46° C, and the temperature in the lesion is sustained for the treatment period.

At the end of the procedure, some urologists like to leave a urethral catheter in overnight; others do not put in a catheter and allow the patients to go home after they have voided and feel that they are emptying their bladder.

Clinical Results

Table 88–1 shows the results of the total world experience in the use of TUNA. There is a wide variety in the number of patients in each series and in the length of follow-up. Of note is that most are open series, with a minority of randomized studies (Issa and Oesterling, 2000). Although the inclusion and exclusion criteria are the same in most series, they are not exactly the same and are not as strict as those in studies testing α-adrenergic blockers and 5α-reductase inhibitors. The size of the studies varies from 12 to 130 patients, and, in many cases, the number of patients followed up for the longest period of time consists of less than 50% of the original sample, which makes it difficult to draw definite conclusions. However, when looking at them all together, a number of points can be considered.

A total of 546 patients has been followed up for 12 months, with an increase in the mean peak urinary flow rate by an average of 6 mL/sec, representing an average improvement of 77%. The mean symptom score decreased by an average of 13.1 symptom units, which is an average improvement of 58%. Although there was consistency of the general improvements, there was a range. The greatest improvement in the mean peak flow rate was 9.2 mL/sec (Giannakopoulos et al, 1996), and in the mean symptom score, it was 15.4 symptom units (Steele and Sleep, 1997). The least improvement in mean peak flow was 2.7 mL/sec (Rosario et al, 1997) and in symptom score was 10.8 (Millard et al, 1996). Although the numbers followed up for longer are less (176 for 24 months and 88 for 36 months), the mean improvements appear to be maintained (Issa and Oesterling, 2000).

In the U.S. randomized trial comparing TUNA with TURP, 65 patients were treated by TUNA and 56 by TURP (Bruskewitz et al, 1998). At 1 year, 59 of the TUNA group (90%) and 47 of the TURP group (84%) were available for evaluation. **In the TUNA group, the symptom score improved from 24.7 to 11.1 (13.6 symptom units) and the peak urinary flow rate from 8.7 to 15.0 mL/sec (6.3 mL/sec). In the TURP group, the symptom score improved from 23.3 to 8.3 (15.0 symptom units) and the peak urinary flow rate improved from 8.4 to 20.8 mL/sec (12.4 mL/sec).** The reasons for patients being lost to follow-up are clearly stated, but it was because of ineffectiveness in only two patients (3.1%) of the TUNA group and none of the patients treated by TURP. The treatment was found to be effective and safe. The complication rate of TUNA was low, in both the short and the long term; the most commonly reported adverse events were bleeding (32.3%), urinary tract infection (7.7%), and urethral stricture (1.5%). There was no adverse effect of any kind on sexual function in patients treated by TUNA.

There are some additional long-term studies that are of interest. Zlotta and coworkers (2003) entered 188 consecutive patients into a study; there were 5-year data on 121 of these. At the 5-year assessment, 41 of the 176 patients who were evaluable (2 dead, 10 lost to follow-up) required additional treatment after TUNA (23.3%). Although there were 5-year data on 121 patients, and this was defined as a 5-year follow-up, the 10 patients on whom there were only 4-year data were also included, giving a total of 131 patients. **The mean I-PSS decreased from 20.9 to 8.7, with tight standard deviations, but a range at long-term follow-up of 2 to 20. The Qmax improved from 8.6 to 12.1 with a range at long-term follow-up of 6.5 to 19.2, once again giving the impression of quite a wide scatter of results. Although the drop in the mean I-PSS is 12.2, which is an impressive decrease, the improvement in Qmax is a less impressive decrease, being 3.5 mL/sec and comparable to that achieved by medical management at the same time point.**

In another study from the United States (Hill et al, 2004), 121 men were enrolled in a prospective, randomized, multicenter clinical trial; 65 (54%) were randomly selected to receive TUNA and 56 (46%) were selected to receive TURP. It was reported that 9 of the 65 men (14%) required further intervention in the TUNA cohort, compared with 1 of the 56 men (2%) in the TURP cohort. The requirement for additional medical management in the TUNA cohort was not stated, presumably explaining the difference observed between

this study and that described in the previous paragraph. Although this was reported as a 5-year study, only 18 of the 65 men in the TUNA group (28%) and 22 of the 56 (39%) in the TURP were evaluable at 5 years. This makes the 5-year data difficult to interpret despite the highly significant statistical differences described by the authors. At 3 years, the mean I-PSS had decreased from 24.0 to 15.2 in the TUNA group and from 24.1 to 10.1 in the TURP group. The mean Qmax had improved from 8.8 to 13.0 in the TUNA group and from 8.8 to 19.1 in the TURP group.

A cost comparison of medical management and TUNA for treating BPH over a 5-year period was performed by Naslund and colleagues (2005). They constructed a cost analysis model using published costs for tamsulosin, finasteride, TUNA, and TURP. They found that over the 5 years tamsulosin was less expensive than TUNA and that finasteride cost the same as TUNA. Combination therapy was more expensive, reaching a break-even point at 2 years and 7 months of treatment. The authors also calculated that TURP is more expensive than TUNA for achieving improvements in I-PSS but less expensive for improving Qmax.

A meta-analysis of trials of TUNA for treating symptomatic BPH has been reported (Boyle et al, 2004). Meta-analyses are dependent on the data that are put into them. In the case of TUNA, the trials analyzed were often poorly constructed, with inadequate numbers, and not randomized. **In fact, there were 2 randomized trials, 2 nonrandomized observational protocols, and 10 single-aim observational studies. One thing that was consistent, however, was that in all studies, the patients had severe lower urinary tract symptoms, the mean I-PSS at entry being greater than 20. The effect of TUNA was to halve the mean I-PSS at 1 year. The shortage of long-term studies makes it difficult to draw specific conclusions, but although there was a tendency for the I-PSS to increase in the long term the 50% decrease was maintained. The Qmax increased by about 70% from baseline to 1 year. The Qmax tended to decline over time, but a 50% or greater improvement was maintained.** One question has not been answered: although the mechanism of action of TUNA is an adequate explanation for the early improvements, how can it explain any positive long-term effect?

Pressure-Flow Studies

There have been six studies that examined relief of urodynamically proven obstruction as an endpoint, and these are summarized in Table 88–2. The number of patients in each group varies considerably (from 12 to 108), as does the length of follow-up. The largest number of patients are evaluable at 3 months (253), with smaller numbers having been followed

Table 88–2. Pressure-Flow Studies after Transurethral Needle Ablation with 12-Month Follow-Up

Reference	Patients (N)	Detrusor Pressure at Maximum Flow	
		Preop.	Postop.
Campo et al (1997)	72	85.3	63.7
Steele and Sleep (1997)	29	92.4	72.9
Rosario et al (1997)	39	97.0	84.0
Millard et al (1996)	20	70.7	59.9

out to 12 months (140) or even longer. All patients had pressure-flow studies performed before and after treatment by TUNA.

At 3 months, the average maximal detrusor pressure at peak urinary flow was 85.4 cm H_2O, which 3 months after treatment had decreased to an average of 64.8 cm H_2O (average decrease of 20%). The range at 3 months was 53.2 to 79.0 cm H_2O. It is difficult to draw too many conclusions from these average figures because of the variability in each series, but they do point to the fact that there is a decrease in the Pdet Qmax in most series, if not quite relieving obstruction reliably in every case. At 12 months, the average Pdet Qmax was 91.6 before treatment and 73.5 after treatment. In each series, there was a small decrease in the difference that had been observed at 3 months.

In another urodynamic study (Minardi et al, 2001), a small number of patients (24) was observed out to 24 months. The authors showed that there was initially no change in the prostatic volume or the prostate-specific antigen levels and that pressure-flow studies showed a reduction in the mean opening pressure and detrusor pressure at maximum flow. **This led them to speculate that the ideal patient for TUNA was a man younger than 70 years with a prostatic volume of less than 6 mL, with a pretreatment detrusor pressure at maximum flow of less than 60 cm H_2O and residual volume of less than 100 mL.**

Adverse Effects

The adverse effects that occurred in the U.S. randomized study (Bruskewitz et al, 1998) have been alluded to earlier. **By far the most common complication reported, however, is post-treatment urinary retention, occurring at a rate between 13.3% and 41.6%.** It can be expected that within the first 24 hours, about 40% of patients experience urinary retention. The second most common adverse event reported is that of irritative voiding symptoms, occurring in about 40% of patients in the early period after treatment. Given the mechanism of the TUNA treatment, this high rate is surprising, but the symptoms are usually mild, lasting between 1 and 7 days.

Urinary tract infection was not commented on in every series, but it was reported in up to 3.1% of patients. It is advisable to give a prophylactic antibiotic to cover the treatment, using whatever regimen the particular urologic department uses for other endoscopic procedures. In this way, symptomatic infections leading to epididymo-orchitis or significant sepsis can be completely prevented. Urethral strictures are uncommon, with the highest rate reported as being 1.5%. Hematuria occurs in a large number of treated patients but is almost always mild and short lasting. Patients who are taking aspirin, in whatever dosage, should be advised to refrain from taking it for 7 days before the procedure.

Sexual dysfunction is rare after TUNA. Urinary incontinence has not been reported in any series.

Reoperation

The reoperation rate must be compared with that of TURP. **Although a 14% requirement for reoperation because of lack of efficacy of the primary treatment with TUNA may seem low, it occurred in less than 2 years** (Schulman and Zlotta, 1995). In addition, the 12.7% incidence reported by Steele and Sleep (1997) occurred inside a 2-year period. In the multicenter study reported by Ramon and colleagues (1997), 9 of 76 patients were deemed to have failed because of an absence of improvement in peak urinary flow rate. Eight of these patients had no symptomatic improvement, but five had an improvement in quality of life.

Indications

The patient most likely to benefit from TUNA would be one who had lateral lobe enlargement and a prostate of 60 g or less (Naslund, 1997). Larger glands can be treated, but more time has to be spent treating each 1-cm segment. Patients with larger prostates, purely bladder neck hypertrophy, or median lobe enlargement are not ideal patients to be treated in this way, but they can be treated; for example, median lobe enlargement can be treated by rotating the TUNA catheter so that the needles point posteriorly, with special care being taken in assessing the depth of their penetration into the prostate.

Conclusions

The TUNA procedure is simple to perform, and the technology is improving all the time. As long as it is performed carefully, with special emphasis on placement of needles and awareness of the depth of their penetration, complications can be kept to a minimum. With the combination of improved endoscopic visualization of the needles and placement using transrectal ultrasonography, efficacy can be high, with **an average improvement in the mean symptom score of 13.1 symptom units and in the mean peak urinary flow rate of 6 mL/sec to be expected at 12 months. A treatment by some other modality can be expected in 12.7% to 14% of patients within 2 years. TUNA can be given with the patient under topical anesthesia or local prostatic or perineal block, and so it is useful in poor-risk cases also. About 40% of patients have retention within the first 24 hours. The long-term efficacy of the treatment has not been clearly evaluated, with no large series of patients having long-term follow-up.**

TRANSURETHRAL MICROWAVE THERAPY

Transurethral microwave therapy (TUMT) has been much evaluated in the past decade and has been widely used. Many urologists have a high regard for its usefulness in treating patients with lower urinary tract symptoms, but, for many others, it has no place in the therapeutic line-up. It has been examined clinically in many centers throughout the world, although the very large number of patients who have been entered into open noncomparative studies may surprise some urologists. The rationale for its effect on symptoms has also been studied carefully by authors from different centers, which is unlike that of many of the other so-called minimally invasive treatment modalities. In addition, there has been an evolution in the technology of TUMT (Figs. 88–3 and 88–4), from low-energy to high-energy application, perhaps indicating that this technique has a future in the treatment of lower urinary tract symptoms.

The current transurethral method has developed from the early transrectal devices that supplied heat ranging from 42° to 44° C. The results with this early form of treatment were rather disappointing, and transurethral catheters were developed that would allow higher temperatures to be used

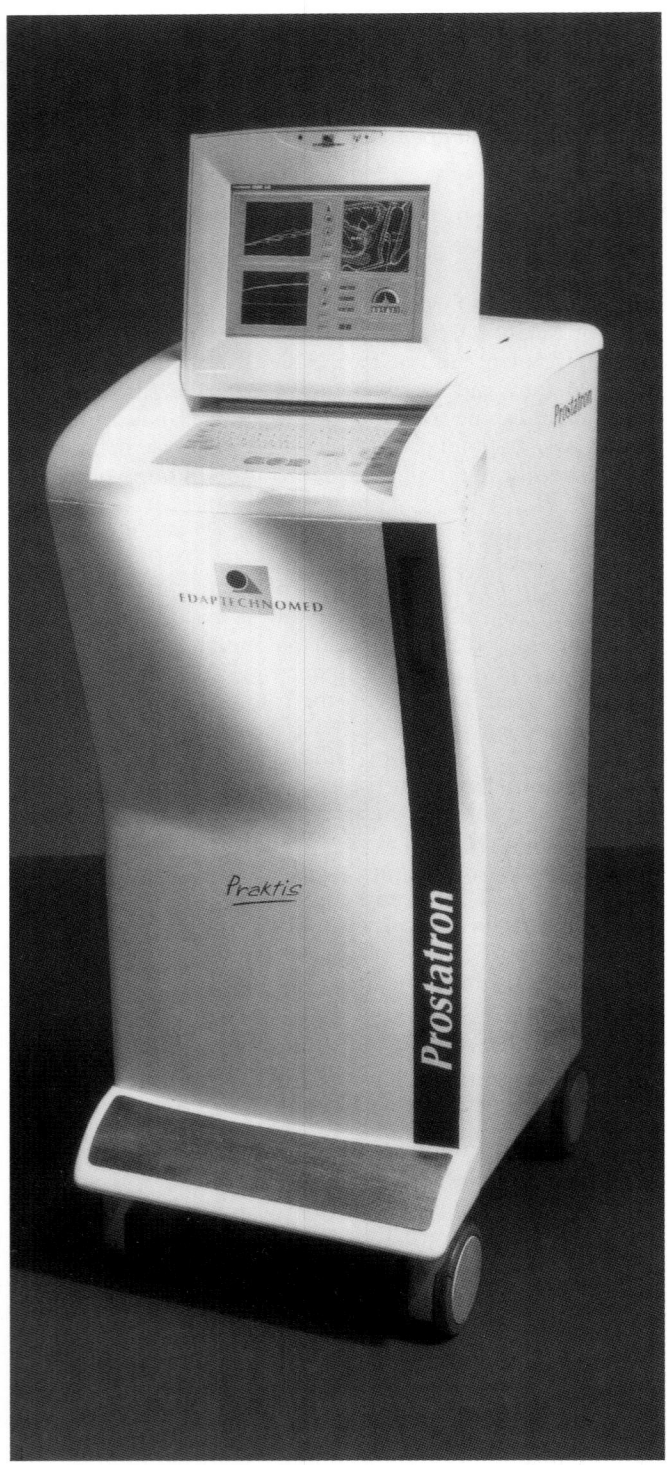

Figure 88–3. The Prostatron device. (Courtesy of Urologix, Inc, Minneapolis, Minn.)

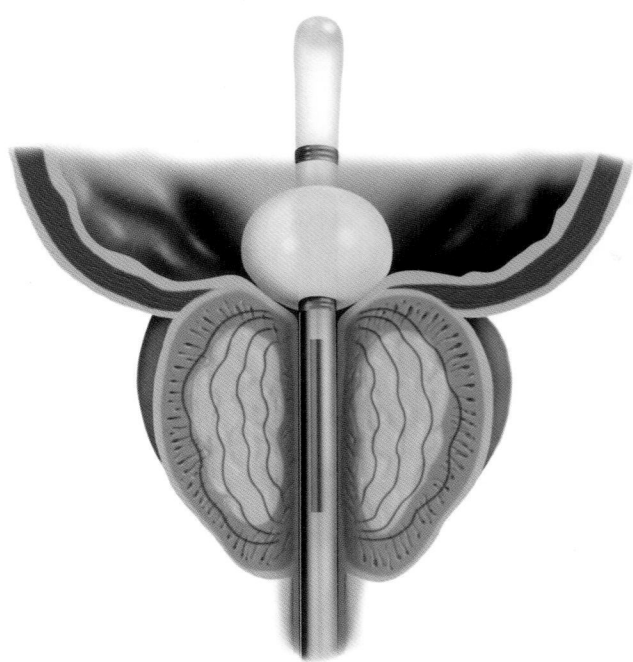

Figure 88–4. The Prostatron antenna, treating the prostatic transition zone. (Courtesy of Urologix, Inc, Minneapolis, Minn.)

et al, 1985; Leib et al, 1986) showed that microwave energy could create high temperatures in the prostate of laboratory animals without damaging the surrounding structures.

Early clinical results using transrectal probes suggested some efficacy (Yerushalmi et al, 1985; Servadio et al, 1987), but overall results were disappointing when tested against sham controls and did not demonstrate that further use of this type of treatment would be beneficial to patients (Zerbib et al, 1992). Later changes resulted in the transurethral method of applying microwave treatment, and this has been further developed, leading ultimately to the sophisticated machines that are being used today. The two most commonly used are the Prostatron and the Targis, but there are several others all producing similar effects. The Prostatron has three different types of software programs, ranging from relatively low to higher energy: the Prostasoft 2.0, 2.5, and, more recently, 3.5.

Method of Action

The effect of TUMT on prostatic tissue has been studied widely, and a number of different theories, none mutually exclusive, have been presented. These cover heat changes and differential blood flow in the prostate, damage to the sympathetic nerve endings, and induction of apoptosis.

Temperature and Blood Flow

Several studies have been performed that described the interstitial thermal mapping in canine and human subjects (Astrahan et al, 1991; Kaplan et al, 1992; Roehrborn et al, 1992; Devonec et al, 1993). These have all shown that **the temperature varies in the prostatic adenoma, with the area around the urethra being relatively spared from high temperatures and with surrounding tissues such as the rectum also being**

while cooling the urethral mucosa. In one of these devices currently used, the Prostatron, the cooling fluid in the catheter maintains the urethral temperature at about 44° C or lower while producing temperatures within the prostate of up to 70° C. The early experimental studies (Magin et al, 1980; Harada

unaffected. Some of these studies involved a limited number of measurement sites, the use of periodic rather than continuous temperature monitoring, and difficulties with positioning of the temperature probes.

In an extensive study involving careful and accurate placement of probes, Larson and Collins (1995a) measured temperature gradients within the prostate. Their interstitial thermal mapping method involved the placement of thermosensors using a biplane ultrasound imaging system; this allowed accurate needle placement in both the anteroposterior and the longitudinal dimensions. In their study, they increased the microwave power by 5 W, reaching a maximum of 36 W in 11 minutes and then maintaining an average power of 31.4 W. **In one representative patient, urethral temperature reached a nadir of 21.7° C,** then rose progressively to 40.1° C, and remained between 38.7° and 41.1° C for the duration of the treatment. Rectal temperature did not show an initial decline but remained at 37.7° to 39.1° C throughout. Prostatic temperature at a distance of 5 mm radially from the urethra reached 62.4° C about 7 minutes after the initial power maximum and remained between 60.9° and 68.7° C. At 10 mm radially from the urethra, the average temperature was 50.5° C, whereas at 15 mm it was indistinguishable from urethral or rectal temperature (Larson and Collins, 1995a; Larson et al, 1998a).

Osman and colleagues (2000) performed a study in 13 patients in which they recorded maximum mean peak temperatures of 66.8° ± 13° C at 4 mm from the urethra using the Targis device. No temperature higher than 45° C was recorded beyond 15 mm on either side of the urethra anteroposteriorly or beyond 16 mm on either side of the urethra transversely. **Using gadolinium-enhanced magnetic resonance imaging (MRI), they found postprocedural perfusion defects with means of 28.1% ± 2.1% of the total gland and 63.6% ± 34% of the transition zone volume.**

Histopathologic changes were found to be related to the temperature rises in different parts of the prostate (Larson et al, 1996). **They showed that tissue exposed to a minimum of 45° C for about 60 minutes suffered hemorrhagic necrosis with uniform extirpation of tissue.** The border between viable and necrotic tissue was sharply defined. The histologic changes were related to temperature rises within the prostate, and it was also believed that differences in the thermal sensitivity between stromal and epithelial elements appeared unlikely to account for differences in treatment outcomes. However, there has been some disagreement about these findings. In an evaluation with MRI, Nordenstam and coworkers (1996) did not find that there was significant necrosis in the prostate. Similarly, D'Ancona and colleagues (1999), using the high-energy Prostasoft hardware (Larson and colleagues used the Targis T3), found that histologic parameters were moderately predictive of response; large prostates and prostates with a high epithelium to stroma ratio responded better to high-energy TUMT.

With the use of color Doppler ultrasonography, blood flow changes were estimated during microwave treatment in two patients with BPH (Larson and Collins, 1995b). At rest, a comparatively low level of blood flow was seen. **As heat energy was delivered, the blood flow rose in a marked and sustained manner. This increase was seen in the posterior half of the prostate, including the peripheral zone and the posterior**

half of the transition zone. Marked recruitment of posterior and periurethral vessels was noted. It was also believed that peripheral resistance within the prostatic vessels was reduced. Therefore, these authors in a series of studies linked temperature changes to histologic and blood flow findings. However, the blood flow alterations were performed in only two patients, and experimental confirmation with more accurate methods of blood flow estimation is required.

In another study, Larson and coworkers (1998b) showed that in terms of heating patterns, the Targis antenna (operating at a frequency of 902 to 1928 MHz) gave a more efficient delivery of thermal energy than the Prostatron antenna (operating at a frequency of 1296 MHz).

Sympathetic Nerve Degeneration

In a histologic study, 10 patients underwent TUMT and some days later had an open prostatectomy (Perachino et al, 1993). Multiple prostatic samples were taken for examination from the periurethral prostatic tissue to a depth of 2.5 cm. The samples were stained with hematoxylin and eosin and with S100, neuron-specific enolase, and vimentin. The authors found microabscesses, epithelial necrosis, and vasculitis in the prostate. **Compared with controls, it was found that nerve fibers were disrupted, with axons rarely being seen. This study suggested that thermal damage to the adrenergic fibers was behind the improvement in symptoms after TUMT.** The authors did not attempt to quantify their findings. They also believed that the variable response sometimes noted was due to the variable numbers of nerve endings seen in different parts of the prostate.

Support for this theory came from an investigation into human prostatic α_1-adrenoreceptor density after TUMT. Radioligand-binding assays using ^{3}H-prazosin were performed on prostatic tissue from 25 patients, 10 of whom had received TUMT. Binding was saturable, and a single class of high-affinity binding sites was identified in all cases. **In the controls (untreated by TUMT), the mean α_1-adrenoreceptor density** was 96.4 fmol/mg as against 71.3 fmol/mg in those who had undergone TUMT, a statistically significant difference. The mean dissociation constants were 0.56 in both groups (Bdesha et al, 1996). These results suggested that there was a significant reduction in prostatic α_1-adrenoreceptor density in the region of the prostate that had been subjected to maximal heating.

Another study has been performed to test this hypothesis, but using a different methodology. Ten patients had TUMT 1 week before scheduled TURP. Biopsy samples were taken, 5 to 6 mm deep, and stained with hematoxylin and eosin and with anti-PGP 9.5; this is a nonspecific neural marker gene product that is immunoreactive to all neurons. With this method, nerve fibers were found in the urethral epithelial layer, lamina propria, and smooth muscle layer of controls. **Almost all of the TUMT biopsy samples had nerve fibers in the epithelial layer and the lamina propria, but there were no nerve fibers in the smooth muscle layer in virtually all of the specimens** (Brehmer et al, 2000).

Induction of Apoptosis

Seven patients, all with glands weighing more than 100 g, were selected for open prostatectomy, and all had TUMT with the

ECP (Comair, Sweden) 915-MHz equipment 2 hours to 1 week before surgery. Specimens were stained with hematoxylin and eosin, and apoptosis was verified by the terminal deoxynucleotidyl nick-end labeling (TUNEL) technique in sections showing histologic changes suggestive of apoptosis, such as pyknotic nuclei and chromatin segregation. Necrotic areas were frequently seen in the prostate to a depth of 4 to 5 cm. Outside these necrotic areas, normal and apoptotic areas were interspersed, the latter confirmed by TUNEL. The author found that **the area of tissue damage seen after TUMT was relatively small compared with the volume of the prostate** (Brehmer, 1997). The heat was implicated as the cause of the apoptosis, but there was no speculation about the exact mechanism whereby it brought this about.

In another study, Brehmer and Svensson (2000) performed culture of prostatic stromal cells from patients undergoing TURP. These were then stained for several cytoskeletal proteins and assessed for apoptosis by light microscopy of cells stained with the Giemsa nuclear stain, by transmission electron microscopy, and by measurement of caspase-3–like activity, the latter being one of the main effects of apoptosis. The cell cultures were exposed to moderate hyperthermia (47° C). **Twenty-four hours after heat exposure, 76% of the cells were apoptotic, with only 14% of the cells being necrotic.** The caspase activity (indicating increased apoptosis) had increased to about sixfold by 24 hours after heat treatment. The application of moderate heat for a longer period was found to be the most effective way of inducing apoptosis. Higher temperatures for shorter times resulted in a greater degree of necrosis. It was believed that, in vivo, other factors might modify the apoptotic result, such as stromal-epithelial interactions or heat dissipation by increased blood flow.

Thus, these studies have shown that there may be several factors involved in the mode of action of TUMT. High temperatures cause necrosis of prostatic cells, whereas lower temperatures for longer periods of application induce programmed cell death or apoptosis. It is possible that the greater prostatic blood flow that has been found during treatment may be an attempt to dissipate the heat and that this may modify the induction of apoptosis. There is also evidence that TUMT causes disruption of α_1-adrenoreceptor nerves in the smooth muscle of the prostate, another possible cause of the beneficial effect of TUMT, but this effect depends on the number of nerve endings in the treated area of the prostate. A further study investigating the combination of these findings and assessing the relative contribution of many of them was reported by Bolmsjo and coworkers (1996).

Clinical Results

The literature on TUMT is characterized by a large number of open studies, much more than any other technology-based treatment for BPH. In addition, many of them are short-term studies; some of those that purport to be longer term have in fact only a small percentage of patients who have reached what might be called long-term follow-up. However, there are also many carefully carried out comparative studies, both against sham treatment and against TURP. The lesson that can be learned from these studies about TUMT is that machines delivering higher power yield better results than those delivering lower power. At the same time, it might be said that this use of

higher energy makes the procedure more complicated in that there is a greater requirement for sedation or analgesia.

Two of the earliest reports investigated, in a small number of patients, the use of the lower energy Prostatron device. In the first of these, **37 patients were treated and at 3 months had an improvement in Boyarsky symptom score from 12 to 8 and an increase in the peak urinary flow rate from 8.4 to 10.8 mL/sec** (Devonec et al, 1991). These results were statistically significant if perhaps not quite so clinically impressive. In another study, 19 patients with lower urinary tract symptoms who were not in retention were treated (Carter et al, 1991), but, at 12 weeks, only 9 of these patients were evaluable. The mean symptom score had improved from 12.0 to 2.8 and the mean peak flow rate from 8.2 to 14.3 mL/sec. However, this study could be criticized for the fact that fewer than half of the patients were evaluable at 12 weeks and that the standard deviations of the mean flow rates were very large. The results were elegantly presented in terms of histopathology and technique and spurred many urologists to assess the TUMT in their own departments.

At this stage in the development of the technique, the concept was specifically that heat treatment even with lower energy caused necrosis of prostatic tissue. The other ideas about sympathetic nerve damage and apoptosis were introduced later.

Open Studies

In an attempt to find medium- to long-term efficacy results, only studies with a follow-up of 1 year or greater are reviewed. A study performed with the Prostatron 2.0 software (Blute et al, 1993) evaluated 150 patients; 44% of these required oral or IV sedation. There were 150 patients, and results were presented from 118 who had Madsen symptom scores before treatment and at 12 months and from 104 who had peak urinary flow rates. **The symptom score improved from a mean of 13.7 to 5.4 and the peak flow rate improved from 8.5 to 11.3 mL/sec. A total of 43 patients (36%) required catheterization for urinary retention; 63% required catheterization for 1 week or less, but it was necessary for more than 30 days in 4 patients.** In another study with the same device, 30 patients were treated and 20 of these were evaluable at 1 year. The mean symptom score improvement was from 16.5 to 6.9, and the peak flow improved from 7.2 to 10.7 mL/sec (Homma and Aso, 1993). The study reported in 1996 by Baba and coworkers entered 135 patients into treatment with the same device, and although they refer to "durability of response," it can be seen that less than 20% of the total are followed to 2 years and less than 50% for 12 months. They noted that by 2 years 61 patients had been lost to follow-up. The same 3 mL/sec improvement as just mentioned was noted in those evaluable at 1 year.

A 4-year open study observed 187 patients treated with the Prostatron software 2.0 (Hallin and Berlin, 1998). At the end of the 4-year period, 56 were evaluable, although only 9 were truly lost to follow-up because the fate of all the rest was known. A total of 97 patients had needed further treatment for their lower urinary tract symptoms. The satisfaction rate was 62% at 1 year, 34% at 2 years, and 23% at 4 years, with 66% having required further treatment and 11% being dissatisfied at the same time point. The authors believed that the patients who would respond best to this treatment were those with a peak flow rate of 10 mL/sec or more or those with an initial irritative score in the lower range. The fact that many patients do not respond to TUMT treatment but that some do for long periods of time was commented on. The patterns of treatment after the introduction of TUMT in Sweden were reported on by Blomqvist and coworkers (1997). They found that the number of TUMT procedures performed in Sweden increased rapidly after the technique was introduced but then decreased equally rapidly. Three years after the introduction of drugs for BPH, the number of men receiving drug treatment was greater than the number of men having both TURP and TUMT annually.

Pressure-flow analysis has also been performed on patients being treated by the lower energy TUMT (De la Rosette et al, 1995; Tubaro et al, 1995). These authors found that **there was no noticeable change in the detrusor pressure at maximal flow at 6 months but that there was a marginally greater improvement (although not statistically better) in those with constrictive obstruction as opposed to those with compressive obstruction.** Finally, a series of patients being treated with the Prostatron 2.0 was followed out to 5 years (Keijzers et al, 1998). Of the 231 patients treated, only 89 patients reached 5 years without requiring further treatment for BPH. The total number of patients treated in six European centers was 1092. Overall, the improvement in flow rate was between 2 and 3 mL/sec and the retreatment rate relatively high (Francisca et al, 1999).

It was thought that by increasing the energy the results achieved with TUMT could be improved. Of 85 patients treated with the Prostasoft 2.5 protocol, 74 were evaluable at 1 year (De Wildt et al, 1996b). **The mean Madsen symptom score improved from 13.9 to 5.8, and the mean peak flow rate increased from 9.4 to 14.9 mL/sec. The detrusor pressure at maximal flow improved from a mean of 63.6 to a mean of 38.9 cm H_2O at 26 weeks.** A further study of 116 patients using the same protocol was reported by a European group (De la Rosette et al, 1996), with 67 patients having reached 52 weeks of follow-up. The Madsen score improved from 13.6 to 4.9 and the peak urinary flow from 9.6 to 14.5 mL/sec. More recently, the Prostasoft 3.5 protocol has been introduced and has been found to be well tolerated (Francisca et al, 2000a). Early results of its use in a small number of patients in urinary retention have indicated some value (Floratos et al, 2000).

A large open study was performed into the use of the 30-minute algorithm for high-energy TUMT with the Prostasoft 3.5 protocol (De La Rosette et al, 2000). Of 108 men treated, 86 were evaluable at 6 months (with only 41 at 1 year). At 6 months, the I-PSS had improved from 20.0 to 9.3 and the peak urinary flow rate improved from 9.5 to 14.6 mL/sec. The detrusor pressure at maximal urinary flow decreased from 58.7 cm H_2O at baseline to 46.9 cm H_2O at 6 months. As reflected on the Abrams-Griffiths nomogram, this represented a shift from the obstructed to the equivocal zone for most patients. The mean duration of catheterization after treatment was 17.9 days, with a range of 6 to 62 days. The authors commented that at 3 months, all treatment-related complications had disappeared. It was noted that the faster treatment was an improvement on previous methods from the viewpoint of tolerability to patients but had the same subjective and objective improvement as the Prostasoft 2.5 protocol.

In a study using the high-energy T3 Urologix device, it was found that at 1 year, there was a 63% improvement in symptom score and a 64% improvement in peak flow rate. Urodynamic analysis showed that there was a better improvement in patients with marginal obstruction rather than unequivocal obstruction (Javlé et al, 1996).

A full urodynamic evaluation of the Prostalund Compact Device was carried out by Alivizatos and coworkers (2005). **In this study 38 patients were evaluated, 19 of whom had an indwelling catheter. The treatment lasted a mean of 43.1 minutes, and the maximum intraprostatic temperature achieved was 58.7° C; a mean of 18.4 ± 14.3 g of prostatic tissue was destroyed. All of the urodynamic parameters improved in the patients without a pretreatment catheter. The mean changes were: I-PSS from 21.5 to 6.5, Qmax from 7.2 to 18.1 mL/sec, pdet Qmax from 87.5 to 48.4 cm H_2O. In those who had a pretreatment catheter, the Qmax at 3 months was 13.2 mL/sec. This is a small series, but the results are encouraging.**

To complete the equipment types, the Core Therm–monitored feedback TUMT was used in 102 patients, but only early results were presented, and, of note, the median catheter time was 8.5 days (David et al, 2004). The results of the Cooled Thermo Cath (Urologix) have been published in abstract form (Roehrborn et al, 2004), and again in a small relatively short-term study it is hard to draw too many conclusions, although at 6 months the symptom score improved from a mean of 21.0 to 8.3, with a less encouraging improvement in Qmax, from 7.8 to 12.5 mL/sec.

In a prospective cohort study, 31 patients with acute urinary retention were treated with the Targis machine (Djavan et al, 1999a). **By 4 weeks, 29 of the 31 were able to void, with a median time to spontaneous voiding being 3.0 weeks. The flow rate gradually improved to a maximum at 12 weeks.** The authors suggested that this type of treatment is helpful in patients who present with acute urinary retention but are unsuitable for surgical treatment.

A further study attempted to determine the efficacy of high-energy TUMT in treating patients with medically refractory urinary retention secondary to BPH (Kellner et al, 2004). This was a relatively small series of 39 patients, all of whom received treatment. The mean prostate volume was quite large (75.2 mL), but the standard deviation was 57.6. The treatment was unsuccessful in 18%. **Of the 32 patients (82%) in whom success was achieved, there was a mean of 1.6 voiding trials, and these patients required a catheter for a mean period of 4.1 weeks after treatment. Only six patients (15%) were able to stop their medication for BPH. The follow-up for this study was relatively short, 18 ± 10.2 months.**

Berger and colleagues (2003) evaluated the use of TUMT in a similar but larger group of patients. A total of 78 patients in poor general health presented with acute urinary retention secondary to BPH with a mean prostatic volume of 53.9 mL. The mean follow-up was 34 months (range 6 to 42 months), with 38.5% lost to follow-up (30 patients), but early results in these were evaluable. Three months after the procedure, 68 (87.1%) were able to urinate spontaneously. Of the 68, 5 (7.3%) developed a further episode of retention within 2 years. The catheter was in place for a mean of 21 days, with six patients requiring prolonged catheterization. **It can be seen, therefore, that treating patients in acute urinary**

retention with TUMT is a possibility, but the requirement for maintaining medical therapy is a cost burden that may limit its acceptability.

Long-term results are becoming available. Trock and colleagues (2004) reported the long-term pooled analysis of results using the Targis cooled thermotherapy system. Although the article is entitled results of 3 months to 4 years, only 171 of 540 patients had symptoms evaluable at 4 years and only 67 of 524 had a Qmax result. In fact, there is no parallel between the number of patients who had a symptom score result or a Qmax result at any given time point with a significant drop-off in the number of flow rate results occurring at 2 years. The 4-year results must be viewed with some caution; the mean symptom score fell from 20.91 to 11.54, and the mean Qmax rose from 7.91 to 10.94. It was not possible to conclude how many patients dropped out of the study because of lack of efficacy or how many required alternative treatment. In another study using the same technology, Miller and colleagues (2003) reported on 5-year data. Of note was that they previously reported on their 1-year and 3-year results in separate publications, but even in this report only 132 of 150 were evaluable at 1 year, 90 of 150 at 3 years, and 59 of 150 at 5 years. The results are similar to those of the multicenter trial mentioned earlier in this paragraph. Other long-term results have been published by Ohigashi and colleagues (2002), showing that in their experience using the Prostatron the durability of successful results was limited.

In another 2-year study (Thalmann et al, 2002), 200 patients with urodynamically proven outflow obstruction were found to have derived benefit from TUMT. However, as observed clearly by the authors, 13 (6.5%) were lost to follow-up, 15 (7.5%) had died, and 43 (21.5%) required a second or third treatment (TUMT or TURP). Of the 10 patients who required a repeated TUMT, only 4 voided successfully without obstruction and without requiring another intervention.

TUMT versus Sham Procedure

A short-term, 3-month study compared TUMT (21 patients) with the Prostasoft 2.0 to a sham procedure (19 patients) (Ogden et al, 1993). The mean Madsen score changed from 14.2 to 12.8 in the sham group and 14.5 to 4.3 in the TUMT group. The peak urinary flow rate changed from 8.6 to 9.2 mL/sec in the sham group and from 8.5 to 13.0 in the TUMT group. A further study was performed in which 50 patients were randomly assigned to TUMT or sham treatment (De la Rosette et al, 1994). Twenty-four of the 25 patients in each group were evaluable at 12 weeks. In the sham group, the mean Madsen score had changed from 12.1 to 8.2 and in the TUMT group from 13.2 to 5.9. The peak urinary flow rate had changed from 9.7 to 9.5 mL/sec in the sham group and from 9.6 to 13.0 mL/sec in the TUMT group. **In a U.S. study, 110 patients were randomly assigned to sham treatment (35 patients) or TUMT (75 patients)** (Blute et al, 1996). At 3 months, the sham-treated patients had changed their symptom score from 14.9 to 10.8 and the TUMT patients had changed from 13.9 to 6.3. The peak flow rate had changed in the sham group from 7.4 to 9.4 mL/sec and in the TUMT group from 7.2 to 11.5 mL/sec.

A randomized controlled trial compared TUMT with the Prostatron 2.0 to a sham procedure (Nawrocki et al, 1997).

There were three groups: group 1 received standard TUMT; group 2, a sham treatment; and group 3, no treatment. Patients were followed up for 6 months after treatment. In group 1, the American Urological Association (AUA) symptom score improved from 19 to 9.5, in group 2 from 17.5 to 9.5, and in group 3 from 18 to 17. The peak urinary flow rate changed from 8.83 to 9.94 mL/sec in group 1, from 9.44 to 9.49 in group 2, and from 8.79 to 8.47 mL/sec in group 3. That is, there was no difference in the degree of improvement in peak flow rate whether the patient had the machine switched on or off or had no treatment. However, the symptomatic improvement was greater than with no treatment, but once again it did not matter whether the machine was on or off.

In a further study, using the Dornier microwave, 147 patients received TUMT and 73 received a sham procedure (Roehrborn et al, 1998). Symptom score changed from 23.9 to 18.0 in the sham group and from 23.6 to 12.7 in the TUMT group. Peak flow changed from 8.1 to 9.8 in the sham group and from 7.7 to 10.7 mL/sec in the TUMT group, all observations being made at 6 months. Using the T3 Targis, 125 were treated with TUMT and 44 with a sham procedure and reviewed at 6 months (Larson et al, 1998a). **The sham group showed a symptom score improvement from 21.3 to 14.3 and the TUMT group from 20.8 to 10.5. The peak flow increased from 7.8 mL/sec to 9.8 in the sham group and to 11.8 in the TUMT group.**

A further sham-controlled study was performed using the ECP system (Brehmer et al, 1999). In this study, patients were reviewed at 1 year, and a peak flow improvement of 3.6 mL/sec was noted in the TUMT group, with a change of 0.4 mL/sec in the sham group. The changes in symptom score were similar in that there was a relatively smaller improvement in the sham group.

Finally, in this section, it is appropriate to include the results of a study in which α-adrenergic blockers were given either adjuvantly or neoadjuvantly in addition to TUMT with the Targis machine. It was found that the use of this treatment improved the early results achieved in the treatment of lower urinary tract symptoms (Djavan et al, 1999b).

Sham-controlled studies are helpful in assessing whether the improvement noted after a specific treatment is merely a placebo effect. They are sometimes difficult to justify in that they involve a nontreatment arm, but several have been performed in the treatment of lower urinary tract symptoms. In one, patients were reviewed at 3 months; and those who had had a sham treatment and were not improved were given definitive TUMT (De Wildt et al, 1996a). Virtually all of the sham-controlled studies showed a greater improvement in the TUMT group except one (Nawrocki et al, 1997), where the results suggested a placebo improvement only. In a further study, where TUMT was compared with urethral catheterization, the changes in symptom score and peak flow rate were no different at 3 months (Mulvin et al, 1994).

TUMT versus TURP

Comparative studies between TUMT and TURP can help to define the exact place TUMT occupies in the management of BPH. For example, the weight of evidence was that it had a therapeutic benefit when compared with sham treatment or when viewed singly. However, it was unlikely that it would compete realistically with TURP in terms of symptomatic or flow rate improvement, and a more valuable approach might have been to concede the battle in terms of efficacy and concentrate almost entirely on post-treatment morbidity.

The earliest comparative trial against TURP randomly assigned 39 patients to TUMT and 40 patients to TURP (Dahlstrand et al, 1993). **One-year follow-up was possible in 25 and 22 patients, respectively. The mean Madsen symptom score improved from 11.2 to 2.7 in the TUMT group and from 13.3 to 0.9 in the TURP group. The peak urinary flow rate improved from 8.0 to 12.3 mL/sec in the TUMT group and from 7.9 to 17.7 mL/sec in the TURP group.** Both of these differences are statistically significant in favor of TURP-treated patients. Retrograde ejaculation occurred in 25% of the sexually active patients treated by TURP and in none of those treated by TUMT. In addition, the urethral stricture rate was 7.5% in the TURP group but zero in the TUMT group. The authors concluded that the improvements were not as great as with TURP but that the complication rate was much lower, although a detailed evaluation of all the complications would have been interesting.

In a follow-up study, the results achieved by these treatments in 69 patients were evaluated at 2 years (Dahlstrand et al, 1997). There were 31 patients treated by TUMT and 30 treated by TURP who had reached 2 years of follow-up. In the TUMT group, the Madsen-Iversen score had improved from 12.1 to 2.3 and in the TURP group from 13.6 to 1.2. The peak urinary flow rate increased from 8.6 to 12.3 mL/sec in the TUMT group and from 8.6 to 17.6 mL/sec in the TURP group. The authors carried out pressure-flow studies 6 months after treatment and found that the decrease in infravesical outflow resistance was greater after TURP than after TUMT. However, they also found that when the obstruction was calculated in terms of urethral resistance, there was a statistically significant decrease in both groups. This is in keeping with other observations on pressure-flow and urethral resistance changes after TUMT, where previous studies had suggested that TUMT induced a change from constrictive to compressive obstruction, with an increased elasticity in the prostatic urethra (Höfner et al, 1993). The long-term complications were not discussed.

The higher energy Prostatron 2.5 was also evaluated against TURP in a 6-month study (Ahmed et al, 1997). After TUMT, the AUA symptom score changed from 18.5 to 5.3, and, after TURP, it changed from 18.4 to 5.2. The peak urinary flow rate actually worsened slightly from 10.1 to 9.1 mL/sec after TUMT and improved from 9.5 to 14.6 mL/sec after TURP. Pressure-flow studies showed a change from 98.5 to 105.6 cm H_2O in the TUMT group and from 96.7 to 48.8 mL/sec in the TURP group. Obviously, in this study not only did TUMT not relieve obstruction but it was also associated with a marginal worsening of flow rate. However, in spite of this, the improvement in symptom score was exactly comparable to the symptom score of TURP at 6 months. **Complications were higher in the TURP group, but prolonged catheter time (either clean intermittent or indwelling) was more marked in the TUMT group.**

A further comparative study was performed using the Prostatron 2.5 device and comparing results with those of TURP in a prospective randomized trial (D'Ancona et al,

1997). A total of 31 patients underwent TUMT and 21 underwent TURP, of whom 26 and 18, respectively, were evaluable at 12 months. **The Madsen symptom score improved from 13.3 to 4.2 in the TUMT group and from 13.8 to 2.8 in the TURP group. The peak urinary flow rate improved from 10.0 to 16.9 mL/sec in the TUMT group and from 9.3 to 18.6 mL/sec in the TURP group. Pressure-flow studies showed that whereas 62% of the TUMT group and 76% of the TURP group were obstructed before their respective treatments, at 6 months 40% and 15%, respectively, were still considered to be obstructed.** All of the TUMT procedures were done as day cases, and the average number of days in hospital for patients having TURP was 4.1. The length of catheterization was 4.1 days for TURP with a range of 4 to 5 days and was 12.7 days for TUMT with a range of 6 to 35 days. The incidence of urinary tract infections was 4% and 16%, respectively. Irritative voiding symptoms were present in 19% of those who underwent TURP and 29% of those who were treated by TUMT.

Later evaluation of these results took place at a mean of 2.4 years, although 17 of 31 patients who had TUMT and 12 of 21 who had TURP were all who remained in the study. Eight of the original 31 TUMT patients and 1 of the 21 who had TURP required alternative treatment. The Madsen score improved from 13.3 to 5.8 in the TUMT group and from 13.8 to 3.6 in the TURP group. The peak urinary flow rate increased from 9.3 to 15.1 mL/sec in the TUMT group and from 9.3 to 19.1 mL/sec in the TURP group (D'Ancona et al, 1998).

A full quality of life study was performed on 147 patients randomly assigned to either TUMT with the Prostasoft 2.5 protocol or TURP. It was found that both treatments had a positive effect on various aspects of quality of life. The areas of perception of urinary difficulties and daily activities particularly were improved. However, TURP caused a greater improvement on both quality of life and clinical outcome, with neither treatment influencing sexual function (Francisca et al, 2000b).

Overall, the main complication, particularly with the higher energy TUMT, was prolonged catheterization and, with it, urinary infection. It would seem that sexual side effects such as erectile dysfunction and retrograde ejaculation were significantly less common than after TURP.

There have been two systematic reviews of the literature, which give level I evidence concerning the value of this technique. It must be remembered that these reviews are only as good as they are allowed to be by the data put into them. One of the issues characterizing the entire technology in BPH literature is the large number of poorly constructed trials that have been carried out.

The first of these systematic reviews came from an Australian group attached to the Royal Australian College of Surgeons (Wheelahan et al, 2000) and covers trials performed up to 1999. **It found that TUMT offered less morbidity that TURP but was not as effective as TURP in improving symptoms or reducing bladder outlet obstruction. TUMT was associated with a lengthy period of catheterization after treatment, thus causing the higher rates of urinary tract infection and urinary retention. The durability of TUMT, which showed that 23% of patients remained satisfied with a single such treatment after 4 years, was not particularly** convincing. The authors concluded that it was not possible to determine the safety and efficacy of TUMT because of the poor-quality evidence base.

The second systematic review came from the United States and included all the trials from the previous review up to 1999 but added four other papers up to 2002 (Hoffman et al, 2004). The authors were specific in including only randomized trials of TUMT and TURP and found that this meant only 6 of 26 possible trials could be reviewed, with 540 participants (322 TUMT, 218 TURP). Without being directly critical of the standard of these trials, the authors outlined clearly the shortcomings of each of them, showing a lack of uniformity that makes it difficult to draw definite conclusions. **The pooled mean Qmax increased from 7.9 to 13.5 mL/sec after TUMT and from 8.6 to 18.7 mL/sec after TURP. Only two studies reported a mean Qmax after TUMT that had reached 15 mL/sec or greater.** The authors were unable to find statistically significant differences between low-energy and high-energy systems. Only four studies provided a follow-up of 12 months or greater with 85% to 93% of patients available for follow-up. There was an absence of comprehensive reporting of adverse perioperative events in most of the trials, but the findings of previous systematic reviews in this regard appeared to remain the same. **The very definite conclusion once again was that TURP produced greater improvement in symptom scores and Qmax and that fewer men required retreatment for BPH than with TUMT. The recommendation was that further research was required to evaluate the long-term efficacy and safety of TUMT.**

Conclusions

TUMT is not as effective as TURP in improving the objective signs of outflow obstruction, in terms of either peak urinary flow rate or detrusor pressure at maximal flow. However, it does seem to have a measurable effect on the prostate because the elasticity of the urethra is increased after treatment.

The symptomatic improvement that occurs after TUMT seems to be energy related. However, the surprising finding is that even when no objective signs of improvement are seen in comparative trials, the improvement in symptom score caused by TUMT can be considerable. Whether this is a placebo effect or not is unclear because in the two trials in which it occurred, the results are given only from the 6-month time point, at which the placebo effect would be at its maximum. Long-term results from these two trials are needed.

Complications are less than with TURP, with prolonged catheterization and infection being the most common. However, the fact that the procedure can be performed as a day case with the patient under mild sedation is an important positive side of the procedure. **The success associated with this treatment cannot be guaranteed in every patient, as can be seen from the relatively high number of nonresponders in many series.** Why this should be is unclear, but several possible explanations have been given and were outlined earlier.

It would seem that the higher energy devices will be used preferentially to those producing lower energy, but long-term studies, particularly multicenter studies, would be particularly helpful in our being able to assess them fully. Because it is clear that TUMT does not outperform TURP, it is to be hoped that trials will be aimed specifically at assessing the exact place of TUMT in the treatment of symptomatic BPH and that the standard of trials will improve.

LASERS

The introduction of the laser as a treatment option for BPH was greeted by urologists and patients with a high degree of expectancy. However, as with other types of minimally invasive therapy, an initial excess of optimism gave way to realism, with the development of a clearer view of the indications for this type of treatment and, indeed, of its limitations. Newer modifications have taken place, allowing even an endoscopic "enucleation" to be performed. When the original laser techniques were introduced, it was hard to predict this being possible, and so it is reasonable to suggest that with technologic advances happening at an increasingly fast rate, the laser may well play a greater role in the management of BPH in the future. However, although TURP is now recognized as the gold standard, it was not always the case; in fact, it took TURP several decades to achieve this exalted status. It may be that the absence of randomized clinical trials delayed the ultimate recognition of TURP as the treatment against which all others must be compared. For this reason, large multicenter randomized clinical trials comparing the laser with other modalities are needed for this technology to achieve widespread acceptance; these must be adequately statistically powered and have a sufficiently long follow-up time. In addition, it would probably be a more satisfactory approach if the authors of these trials tried to find the exact role of the laser in the treatment of BPH8 rather than suggesting that it is a method that will supplant TURP. It is likely that both methods of treatment will have a role to play, but that of the laser still needs to be accurately defined (Fitzpatrick, 1998, 2000).

The volume of papers in the literature on lasers has increased beyond all expectations since the chapter on this topic that appeared in the eighth edition of *Campbell's Urology* was written. This reflects a continuing interest in the technology and a belief on the part of urologists that the laser will be the way that symptomatic BPH should be treated. Many of the older technologies are now of no interest to urologists, but it is to be hoped that the somewhat uncritical approach that was taken toward the earlier lasers will not be taken toward the new favorites, the holmium laser and the photoselective KTP laser.

Types of Laser

As is well known, laser stands for light amplification by the stimulated emission of radiation. The mechanism of the operating principle of lasers is a process known as stimulated emission of radiation (Nau et al, 2000). In the laser, a flashlamp gives out high-intensity light, which then bombards a resonator cavity with photons. These excite electrons in the resonator cavity to higher energy status. Most of the photons that come from the flashlamp to the resonator cavity are wasted in the form of heat, with less than 5% being absorbed. For this reason, lasers used in the treatment of BPH require rather elaborate cooling devices.

The electrons in the resonator cavity, which are excited by the bombardment of photons, are caused to jump to higher or "excited state" orbitals. Because of the instability of these excited state orbitals, there is a very rapid decay of the electrons, which emit a photon. This process is known as spontaneous emission of radiation. However, the emitted photon has the energy required to interact with other excited state atoms. If this interaction happens, further electron orbital decay and photon emission are induced. This photon has the same characteristics and travels in the same direction as the incident photon. This is known as stimulated emission of radiation and, as stated earlier, is the operating principle of lasers. These photons leave the resonator cavity as a coherent laser beam.

There are four types of laser that can be used to treat the prostate.

Neodymium:Yttrium-Aluminum-Garnet Laser

The neodymium:yttrium-aluminum-garnet (Nd:YAG) laser emits light at a wavelength of 1064 nm, and its active medium consists of neodymium atoms in an yttrium-aluminum-garnet rod. Because this light is poorly absorbed by water and body pigments, it can penetrate tissues relatively deeply. This poor absorption in a fluid medium causes thermal coagulation of the surface tissue and of areas just under the surface. The tissue that has been coagulated becomes white, and hemostasis is total. Subsequently, the coagulated tissue sloughs, and this may occur over a period of some weeks. It may take up to 3 months to achieve complete healing.

One of the more recent modifications of laser application is the process of tissue vaporization and desiccation, and this can be achieved with the Nd:YAG laser. This technique requires a higher energy density for a longer period of time, and surface carbonization occurs, leading to increased laser light absorption superficially and a limitation of the depth of penetration, further increasing the energy density.

Potassium Titanyl Phosphate Laser

The potassium titanyl phosphate (KTP) laser uses a KTP crystal to double the frequency of an Nd:YAG laser and produces a 532-nm wavelength. This provides an intermediate level of coagulation and vaporization. Only half the depth of tissue penetration is reached compared with that of the Nd:YAG laser. However, the consequent higher energy per unit tissue volume produced may increase tissue vaporization and desiccation. This may be used as an advantage in that the prostate and bladder neck may be incised with the KTP laser.

Holmium:Yttrium-Aluminum-Garnet Laser

The holmium:yttrium-aluminum-garnet (Ho:YAG) laser emits light at a frequency of 2100 nm. The energy is emitted in a series of rapid pulses over a few milliseconds, the Q-switched laser. This is unlike the continuous wave of the Nd:YAG or KTP lasers. Whereas the same type of standard optical fiber can be used for the Nd:YAG or the KTP laser, a different flexible optical fiber is required for the Ho:YAG laser. Because it produces a cutting effect by vaporization of the tissue water, its hemostatic properties are less than those of the continuous wave lasers.

Diode Laser

With conventional lasers, less than 5% of the electrical input is converted into laser light, and this inefficiency means that conventional lasers require high-energy cooling devices and radiators, thus increasing the size of the machine. The high gain of the diode laser allows the more efficient use of the photons that are generated. Thus, the available diode lasers used for medical purposes are small and portable, and special connections are not required.

Methods of Delivery

The energy from lasers can be delivered as either:
  End firing
  • Bare tip
  • Sculptured tip
  • Sapphire tip
  Side firing
  • Metal or glass reflector
  • Prismatic internal reflector
  Interstitial
  • Bare tip
  • Diffuser tip
  • Diffuser tip with temperature transducer

Energy levels can be varied, depending on the type of laser, to allow coagulation or evaporation to occur, as alluded to earlier. As with any form of heat treatment, an increase in the temperature of the tissue being treated has different effects, and it is important to be able to control and localize this temperature rise. When the temperature is between 45° and 50° C, desiccation of tissue occurs, and then, as the temperature increases from 50° to 100° C, coagulation begins and becomes irreversible. When the temperature exceeds 100° C, the tissue boils and there is resultant carbonization and vaporization.

Coagulation alone may make the procedure imprecise, with danger to neighboring tissue such as the distal sphincter mechanism. During the process of vaporization, tissue water is converted to steam, and miniexplosions occur within tissues, increasing the mechanical rupture. The vaporization is determined by the intensity of laser application to tissue rather than its duration. Once the cells become coagulated, laser energy penetrates through them less well, halting the forward process of ablation and increasing backscatter and surrounding coagulation (Stein and Narayan, 2000).

Delivery Systems and Laser Techniques

The laser experience has shown that it is possible to adapt a technique and then evolve it almost completely into something new while still using the same basic form of energy. For example, the evolution from the transurethral ultrasound-guided laser-induced prostatectomy (TULIP) device (Intrasonic, Burlington, Mass) to the currently used interstitial and contact devices has been relatively quick but demonstrates clearly the wish on the part of investigators to remove imperfections and to improve results. The aim to find a truly minimally invasive technique is encapsulated in this evolution.

There are two ways in which lasers can have an effect on the prostate, either by coagulation or by vaporization. In the first of these, coagulation is achieved at temperatures of 70° to 90° C. The Nd:YAG laser supplies a wide scatter of power over a relatively large surface area with deep penetration. The second way is by vaporization, which raises the temperature to several hundred degrees Celsius. The power density is high, delivered by a narrow beam. Vaporization can be achieved by using a laser tip that increases the absorption of power by the prostate. **Therefore, the factors determining whether coagulation or vaporization occurs are essentially the power density of the laser beam itself, the total energy delivered, and the time for which it is applied.**

The TULIP device was one of the earliest laser systems and consisted of a characteristic balloon, which maintained the distance between the laser beam and the prostate. Also contained in the tip was a 7.5-MHz ultrasonic transducer and an Nd:YAG laser. The probe was moved from the bladder neck to the verumontanum and was then moved to another position, so that, in this longitudinal manner, the entire circumference of the prostate could be treated. The TULIP device has not withstood the test of time in spite of many improvements made to the original model. It is likely that the reason is that urologists prefer being able to visualize a technique directly rather than indirectly by ultrasonography.

Side-Firing Laser

Probably the first study of the side-firing laser was performed by Costello and colleagues (1992). This was carried out using a canine model. **The energy used was 60 W for a duration of 60 seconds in four quadrants of the prostate, and this caused coagulative necrosis.** The canine prostate is different from the human, but it served as an indicator to how the procedure could be performed in humans. Considerable improvements have been made since that time in terms of the laser fibers, the formula for dosimetry, and the technique used.

A large volume of work has been performed on the side-firing laser systems, and this has up to now dominated the literature. **The fiber bends the laser beam at various angles, and this is accomplished by reflection or refraction, depending on the fiber used.**

Reflective systems use a gold-plated mirror or solid gold tip to deflect the beam. The angle of reflection varies from 45 to 105 degrees, with 90 degrees being the most common. There is a further divergence depending on the design of the reflector mechanism that also is variable. This is important because it determines the power density by establishing the size of the laser spot on the prostate. Reflective systems tend to absorb more energy than refractive systems. At present, this type of system is more suited to tissue coagulation. Refractive systems either are glass capped or use a quartz tip to deflect the beam. The angle of divergence is narrow, allowing either coagulation or vaporization.

The most popular method using the side-firing laser is that of coagulation. Some surface vaporization occurs, but most of the tissue is coagulated, followed later by sloughing, which lasts for some weeks. The power settings have been recommended as 40 to 60 W for 60 seconds or even 90 W for 60 seconds. This latter higher power may cause mainly vaporization. In this situation, the lack of coagulative necrosis means an absence of tissue sloughing. A hybrid procedure has also been described that combines coagulation of the prostate with contact incision through the prostate.

The technique has also varied in description. One method is the use of a quadrant spot application, or even a sextant approach for larger glands, extending every 1 to 2 cm along the prostate from bladder neck to verumontanum (Kabalin, 1993; Norris et al, 1993; Kabalin et al, 1995). The beam is applied until the treated area becomes white. It is then moved onto a normally colored area, which is then treated until the entire surface of the prostate gland has been rendered white. After an initial increase in prostate size from edema, sloughing of the tissue takes place, with the tissue being passed urethrally.

Another technique has been described (Nau et al, 2000). The treatment begins proximal or distal to the bladder neck, dependent on whether retrograde ejaculation is a factor of importance. If the procedure is begun 1 cm distal to the bladder neck, it can reduce the incidence of this complication from up to 15% to zero, according to these authors. They scan the laser beam either longitudinally or radially. That is, from the beginning of their treatment in the region of the bladder neck, the fiber is scanned distally at a rate of 1 mm/sec to the level of the verumontanum; it is then returned to the starting point and rotated slightly so that the next line of tissue that is coagulated is immediately beside the previously treated line. This is continued until the entire prostate appears white.

Alternatively, a radial scanning technique can be used. With this method, the probe is rotated through 360 degrees at a speed of 1 mm/sec, starting in the region of the bladder neck. The fiber is then withdrawn 5 mm distally and the circumferential treatment continued. This is repeated at 5-mm distances until the level of the verumontanum is reached.

Contact Laser

Although the technique of the side-firing laser is well described and the results are well known, a number of possible criticisms have led to further evolution of the laser technique. For example, there is difficulty in controlling the distribution of energy and predicting the eventual result; the side effects of post-treatment retention and urethral discomfort with irritable bladder symptoms have also deterred many urologists from using it. These criticisms have led to the evolution of other methods, one of which is the use of the contact laser, which removes some tissue immediately, thereby decreasing post-treatment voiding difficulties (McNicholas and Singh, 2000).

Contact laser tips are made of synthetic sapphire and can be made in different shapes, either conventionally round or in the shape of a wedge. Initially, the size of the tips was 1.5 mm (Watson et al, 1994). The success of these led to the introduction of tips of 5 mm (Bartsch et al, 1994) and most recently to tips of 10 mm (McNicholas and Hines, 2000). A removable side-firing contact probe has been introduced. This allows the surgeon to remove the contact tip and replace it with a side-firing free-beam device.

Because the size of the contact tip exceeds the size of the instrument channel of the cystoscope, it is usual to advance the fiber until it protrudes through the end of the instrument and then to attach the contact tip. It is then advanced along the length of the urethra. Special instruments to facilitate the passage of this type of laser have been designed (Press and Smith, 1995).

Once in position, the contact tip should be placed just above the verumontanum and 20 W power applied at this level. After allowing this power to raise the temperature at the treatment position and visually obvious tissue contraction to occur, the tip is advanced proximally in the curve of the prostate to the bladder neck, taking care not to undermine it. This procedure is then repeated, from verumontanum to bladder neck, by rotating the instrument so that a further channel can be cut adjacent to the previous one. At the end of the procedure, a bladder neck incision can be performed if required (McNicholas and Hines, 2000).

Interstitial Laser

The purpose of this method of applying laser energy is to reduce post-treatment voiding difficulty and urethral obstruction because the integrity of the prostatic urethra can be preserved. A small fiber is introduced into the prostate, usually transurethrally, and energy from either the Nd:YAG or the diode laser at low power heats the prostate and induces coagulative necrosis. **The necrotic tissue is removed by the process of tissue repair and is not sloughed off and passed urethrally as with other methods.**

The laser energy is applied to the prostate by one of three possible fibers: (1) a bare fiber, (2) a bare fiber within a cannula with saline solution irrigation, and (3) a fiber with a distal diffusor tip.

In a study by McNicholas and colleagues (1993), **it was shown that the size of the intraprostatic lesion is dependent on the power applied, the duration of treatment, and the vascularity of the tissue.** In addition, the ratio of fibrovascular to epithelial tissue is important. The aim of interstitial treatment is to create spherical lesions of 1 to 2 cm diameter within the prostate. The prostate should be heated slowly to avoid carbonization, which limits the effect of the treatment and prevents further coagulative necrosis.

Two types of laser generators are used for interstitial laser therapy. The Dornier ITT system (Dornier, Germering, Germany, and Kennesaw, Ga) uses the Nd:YAG laser to generate 1064-nm energy with a power range of 2 to 100 W. The other generator is the Indigo LASEROPTIC system (Indigo Medical, Johnson and Johnson, Cincinnati, Ohio). This generator is portable, weighing about one eighth as much as the Dornier system. It is a diode laser generator, which uses a diode pump source and gallium-aluminum-arsenide to generate a 830-nm wavelength with a power range of 2 to 20 W.

The laser fiber is inserted through a standard cystoscope and is passed transurethrally into the prostatic adenoma. Using the Nd:YAG interstitial laser, it is left in each position for 10 minutes at 5 to 7 W. The diode laser requires a 3-minute treatment session at each location. The length of the procedure depends on the size of the gland and the type of laser system being used.

The position of the laser tip within the prostate can be visualized by the use of transrectal ultrasonography. It is possible that conventionally positioning the fiber under vision will place it too close to the prostatic urethra, risking urethral damage and edema with resultant post-treatment voiding problems. Issa and colleagues (1998) have modified this using the Indigo laser so that the fiber can enter the prostate at a greater angle, thus keeping it away from the prostatic urethra.

There is no definite agreement about how much tissue should be ablated, with some investigators using a lower number of treatment sites, paying particular attention to the position of the tip of the fiber. Others suggest a more aggressive approach, such as one lesion per 5 to 7 mm^3 (Arai et al, 1996).

Prostatectomy with Holmium Laser

The vaporization techniques described earlier using the Nd:YAG laser with high-energy-density beams at high power (60 to 100 W) at a wavelength of 1064 nm have been effective in removing small amounts of tissue immediately during the procedure. However, it is a relatively inefficient way to do this because of the high power required. The Ho:YAG laser beam is absorbed by water (unlike the Nd:YAG beam) at a wavelength of 2140 nm and causes considerable tissue vaporization.

It was first evaluated in canine experiments in 1992 (Johnson et al, 1992) and subsequently with improved technology in 1996 by Kabalin. In the latter study, the mean transverse diameter of the defect was almost 2 cm. A surrounding rim of 2 mm of tissue coagulation was also produced.

The methods of using the Ho:YAG laser have evolved because of several modifications in both the technology and the methodology (Webb et al, 1993; Dennstedt et al, 1995; Gilling et al, 1995, 1996, 1999). The technique has passed through simple vaporization to combined endoscopic laser ablation of the prostate (CELAP) and is now used to resect large pieces of prostatic tissue.

The dual-wavelength Versa Pulse Select laser (Coherent Inc, USA) was used, and a maximal power of 60 W in a pulsed mode was used to resect tissue. A No. 26 Fr continuous flow resectoscope was modified, and an end-firing bare fiber was passed through it; its position was stabilized by passing it through a No. 6 Fr ureteral catheter. **The median lobe was first resected by initial bilateral bladder neck incisions and then with a transverse incision just proximal to the verumontanum. The median lobe was then undermined to the bladder neck and detached back into the bladder. The lateral lobes were removed by making incisions at 1 and 5 o'clock and then at 7 and 11 o'clock and then commencing distally and undermining proximally by detaching them backward into the bladder.** If the lobes were large, they could be cut into smaller pieces. They were retrieved from the bladder with a modified grasping forceps, or more recently using a morcellator, and by irrigation (Fig. 88–5).

Clinical Results

Part of the difficulty with trials using surgical instruments such as the laser is that a placebo-based randomized controlled trial cannot be performed. This effectively means that to test efficacy, the laser must be compared against what is accepted as the best method to treat lower urinary tract symptoms endoscopically, which is recognized as TURP. Unfortunately, and particularly with the laser (whose name implies modernity and success in the public's mind), this does not exclude a preexisting bias that might be present toward the laser. In addition, and this is similar to the other technologies for treating BPH, none of the comparative trials is as carefully statistically powered as those testing medical management of BPH. It might be said that a large number of the open studies are too large and that a comparative study should have been introduced at an earlier stage. However, there have been many trials, both open and comparative, and a large amount of relevant information is available.

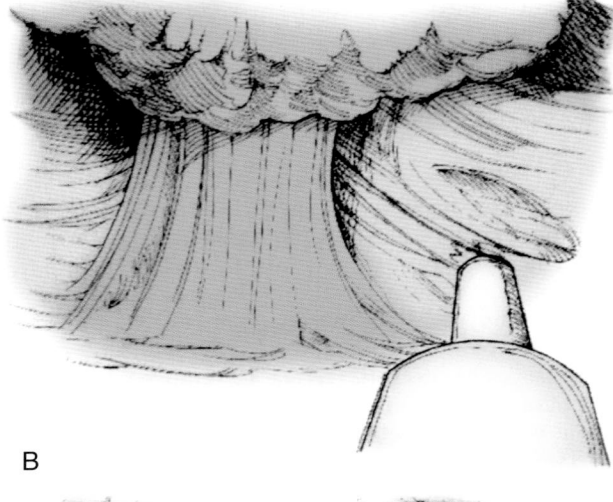

A

B

C

Figure 88–5. **A,** Bilateral bladder neck incisions with the holmium laser. **B,** Undermining the median lobe with the holmium laser. **C,** Releasing the median lobe with the holmium laser. (**A** to **C,** courtesy of Peter Gilling, Tauranga, New Zealand.)

Transurethral Ultrasound-Guided Laser-Induced Prostatectomy

TULIP has ceased to be used by urologists, but because it was the first to be introduced and is currently out of favor because it has been surpassed by instruments that are easier to use rather than because of its lack of efficacy, it is worth looking briefly at the results achieved with its use.

The initial results came from the TULIP National Human Cooperative Study Group (McCullough et al, 1993; McCullough, 1994). These showed that in a small subset followed up for 6 months only (68 of 242 patients), there was a 78% improvement in peak urinary flow (6.7 to 11.8 mL/sec), although, as can be seen, the final mean flow rate is still rather low, in spite of treatment. There was also a 68% improvement in symptom score. However, 4% of the patients underwent a TURP, and irritative symptoms and urgency lasted for 2 to 3 months in a high percentage of patients. When patients were observed up to 1 year, it could be seen that the incidence of post-treatment retention was 22%, with a stricture rate of 5% and bladder neck contractures in 1%.

Schulze and coworkers (1995) carried out the procedure in 89 patients who were followed up for a maximum of 1 year. **The mean peak urinary flow rate increased from 7 to**

15 mL/sec but was reported as exceeding 20 mL/sec in about half. The modified Boyarsky symptom score decreased from 17 to 5 at 1 year. Although it was efficacious in this group, the patients were chosen only as candidates for TURP rather than having strict inclusion and exclusion criteria.

Chatzopoulos and colleagues (1996) evaluated 38 patients with a maximal follow-up of 30 months after the TULIP procedure. **The authors pointed out that the mean symptom score decreased by 54% and the peak urinary flow increased by 112%. However, an improvement in symptom score was seen in 43.6% and in the flow rate in 41%, but in only 28.2% was there an improvement in both.** In addition, reoperation was required in 16% and the incidence of complications was considered high.

In a further study (Horninger et al, 1997), it was found that the efficacy of TULIP, contact laser, and interstitial laser was similar. However, because simpler machines were becoming available, interest waned in the TULIP and techniques with an improved side effect profile were sought.

Side-Firing Laser

The side-firing laser has several advantages over the TULIP technique, related to the ease with which it can be used. The fact that it can be passed through an endoscope and the effect that the procedure is having can be visualized (at least on the urethral surface) make it especially attractive to the urologist. When viewing the results achieved with this technology, the reader must remember that ultimately it should be compared with TURP in terms of efficacy and side effects, to say nothing of cost effectiveness.

The initial study (Costello et al, 1992), looking at 6-week results in 17 patients, found an increase in the peak urinary flow rate from 5 to 9 mL/sec and an improvement in the Madsen-Iversen symptom score from 15 to 4. Costello and coworkers (1994) reported on 33 patients followed up for 3 months. They showed that the flow rate increased from 8.5 to 15.2 mL/sec and that the AUA symptom score improved from 21.5 to 9.5. That the short-term results were encouraging was also supported by a further study (Norris et al, 1993). One hundred eight patients were followed up for a maximum of 6 months; the peak urinary flow rate increased from 7.6 to 12 mL/sec, and the AUA symptom score improved from 22.3 to 9.2. These studies were noncomparative and were performed essentially to find out whether the technique might be submitted to trials against TURP. It can be seen that there is a variation to the peak flow rate improvement in the important series just cited.

However, the longer term study of Kabalin (1996) suggested that the results could be maintained. **In 227 patients, the peak flow rate was 7.3 mL/sec before treatment and the improvement to 15.2 at 3 months was still attained through 1 year (17 mL/sec), 2 years (18.3 mL/sec), and 3 years (18.5 mL/sec). The AUA symptom score decreased from 20.3 to 10 at 3 months and to 5.7 in those who had been followed up to 3 years.** Therefore, although a symptom score of 10 after treatment might have appeared disappointing because it is still in the moderately symptomatic range, the fact that it had further decreased to 8 at 1 year and 8.6 at 2 years, with a further drop to 5.7 at 3 years, showed the benefit of long-term follow-up.

The efficacy of visual laser ablation of the prostate (VLAP) has been subjected to urodynamic analysis. James and colleagues (1995) reported on 79 patients waiting for TURP who were treated by VLAP as an alternative treatment. They had preoperative symptom scores and urodynamic evaluation, and these were repeated 3 months after treatment. The AUA symptom score decreased from 21.4 to 9.4, and the peak urinary flow rate increased from 6.5 to 10.6 mL/sec. **The detrusor pressure at maximal flow decreased from 74 to 54.2 cm H$_2$O.** In another carefully performed urodynamic study (Te Slaa et al, 1995), results were assessed preoperatively and at 6 months follow-up. The I-PSS decreased from 21.3 to 5.3, and the peak urinary flow rate increased from 7.9 to 17.8 mL/sec. The percentage of patients demonstrating urodynamically proven obstruction decreased from 80% before treatment to 5% at 6 months after treatment.

All of these were, of course, open studies, but they did lead to a number of comparative studies, in each case against TURP. In 60 patients observed for 6 months, it was found that VLAP gave a significantly better result in terms of symptom score than TURP but that TURP gave a significantly greater improvement in peak urinary flow rate (Sengor et al, 1996). However, in a multicenter trial in the United States at six investigational sites, a longer follow-up took place (Cowles et al, 1995). In this study, 115 men who were not in retention

were randomly assigned to TURP (59 patients) or VLAP (56 patients); initially, all of these were observed for 1 year after treatment. The authors showed that VLAP required less operating time (23.4 against 45.2 minutes) and a shorter hospitalization (1.8 against 3.1 days). The AUA symptom score improved by 13.3 in the TURP group and by 9.0 in the VLAP group, and the peak urinary flow rate improved by 7.0 mL/sec in the TURP group and by 5.3 mL/sec in the VLAP group. The I-PSS improvement was statistically significantly better in the patients who had TURP. The authors noted a quality of life improvement in 93.0% of the patients who had TURP and in 78.2% of those who had VLAP.

A further comparative study showed 1-year results in 151 patients (Anson et al, 1995). In this trial, **75 patients were randomly assigned to TURP and 76 to VLAP. In 1 year, the AUA symptom score had improved from 18.2 to 5.1 in the TURP group and from 18.1 to 7.7 in the VLAP group; the peak urinary flow rate increased from 10.0 to 21.8 mL/sec (improvement of 11.8) in the TURP group and from 9.5 to 15.4 mL/sec (improvement of 5.9) in the VLAP group.** These authors and those of the previously mentioned trials concluded on the evidence described that VLAP was a safe and viable or useful alternative therapy to TURP.

However, the last-mentioned study has been reevaluated at 5 years (McAllister et al, 2000). **Of the original 151 patients, 109 could be traced; of these, 69 patients had not required further treatment.** In those in whom further treatment was not required and who had not been lost to follow-up, VLAP had produced results comparable with those of TURP. Unfortunately, because this was less than 50% of the original sample, it is difficult to be absolutely certain which patients respond better than others to VLAP. Of the original group treated, 26 patients had required further surgical treatment: 8 of 51 (16%) TURP patients and 18 of 47 (38%) VLAP patients. These authors then admitted that the figures did not support their original conclusion that VLAP could be offered to every patient with BPH.

A urodynamic study was performed on 90 patients having VLAP and 43 having TURP (Jung et al, 1996). This suggested that TURP eliminated obstruction in all patients but that the grade of obstruction was lowered to normal in those treated by VLAP having prostate sizes of 50 mL or less.

The complication rates vary from center to center. The figures related to blood loss and blood transfusion are absolutely clear. Neither the U.K. study (Anson et al, 1995) nor the U.S. study (Cowles et al, 1995) had any patient treated with VLAP requiring a blood transfusion. In fact, two studies have shown that **VLAP can be performed on patients either on full anticoagulation therapy or having abnormal coagulation indices because of hematologic disorders** (Costello and Crowe, 1994; Kingston et al, 1995). It is also certain that VLAP causes neither "TURP syndrome" nor any particular effect on serum sodium levels (Cummings et al, 1995).

The retrograde ejaculation rate varies from 27% to 33%, urethral stricture rate from 0% to 1.8%, and bladder neck contracture occurs in 4.4% (Anson et al, 1995; Cowles et al, 1995). The U.K. study showed a higher incidence of post-treatment dysuria (15% at 3 months) and bacteriuria (28 of 76 patients). The development of post-treatment urinary retention was 30.4% in the patients treated by VLAP by Cowles and colleagues (1995). This has led them and other

technique, with an operative time of 94.7 minutes, a range of 27 to 263 minutes for enucleation, and a further mean of 33.4 minutes for morcellation. If the long operating time was a negative, the fact that the mean postoperative catheterization was 15.1 hours and the mean length of hospitalization was 26.0 hours was a strong positive.

A number of randomized trials comparing HoLEP with TURP have been performed. The statistical powering of these studies was not commented upon in many cases, leading the reader to question the outcomes of the studies. However, the comments of the authors were all clearly in favor of the value of HoLEP to patients with lower urinary tract symptoms. Tan and colleagues (2003b) found that HoLEP was superior to TURP in terms of time of catheterization, hospital stay, and amount of tissue removed, but it took almost twice as long as a TURP to perform. It was also superior to TURP in relieving urodynamically proven obstruction at 6 months, but there was no significant difference in the improvement in symptom score and Qmax. Exactly the same findings were produced in other randomized trials (Kuntz et al, 2004a, 2004b; Montorsi et al, 2004). The most recent holmium laser technology, holmium laser resection of the prostate (HoLRP), was subjected to a randomized trial against TURP (Westenberg et al, 2004). There were 120 patients, of whom 73 completed a 48-month assessment. The authors found no difference between the two techniques in terms of urodynamic indices, potency, continence, and symptom scores. As in the other studies, HoLRP took much longer to perform than TURP but was associated with less perioperative morbidity, catheter time, and hospital stay.

There have been three systematic literature reviews, one specifically of holmium laser prostatectomy (Tooher et al, 2004) and two of laser prostatectomy in general (Wheelahan et al, 2000; Hoffman et al, 2004). These reviews showed that there were three randomized controlled trials comparing HoLRP and TURP and two comparing HoLEP and TURP. As with the other minimally invasive procedures, the majority of the studies were nonrandomized comparative studies or case series. The quality of the available evidence was found to be poor in most cases; most studies were lacking information on statistical powering, methods of randomization, allocation concealment, and blinding; had short follow-up periods; and had significant losses to follow-up. All three studies suggested that it was impossible to draw any long-term conclusions but that the laser techniques offered an option other than TURP for treating symptomatic BPH. However, the report of Wheelahan and colleagues (2000), which did not look at holmium, photoselective vaporization of the prostate, or interstitial lasers, said that it could not determine safety or efficacy because of an incomplete and poor evidence base.

Photoselective KTP Laser

Photoselective vaporization of the prostate (PVP) using a high-power 80 W KTP laser (Greenlight PV Laser System, Laserscope, San Jose, Calif) has produced an alternative laser technology seen by many as an exciting new advance. KTP/532 laser energy is delivered by a side-firing glass fiber through a 27F continuous flow resectoscope. Sterile water irrigation is used, and the procedure is performed under spinal anaesthe-

sia. The endpoint of the procedure is the production of a TURP-like cavity that has resulted from complete vaporization of the prostatic adenoma.

The only comparative trial thus far reported is an experimental one using a porcine kidney model, where ex vivo blood-perfused kidneys were used to verify the hemostatic effect of KTP laser vaporization against TURP-like tissue resection. The laser technique was associated with highly significantly decreased bleeding with larger coagulation zones (Reich et al, 2004).

The remainder of the reported literature indicates a low level of evidence on which to base clinical decision-making. Kumar (2005) treated 18 patients and found a mean 51% reduction in prostate volume, but the follow-up was only 2.8 months. Sulser and coworkers (2004) described their early experience with PVP in 65 patients. The mean operating time was 57 minutes and the mean prostatic volume before treatment was 49 mL. All patients were catheter free by 1 month, but this was only a short-term 3-month observational study. Qmax increased from a mean of 7.7 to 18.2 mL/sec, and I-PSS decreased from 18.5 to 7.2. There were no major complications. Hai and Malek (2003) reported on only 10 patients who had a mean prostate volume decrease of 27%. There was a significant improvement in Qmax and symptom score.

There has been a prospective clinical trial from six American medical centers on 139 men with symptomatic bladder outlet obstruction related to BPH, and the 1-year efficacy and safety data have been reported (Te et al, 2004). The mean symptom score had decreased at 1 year from 23.9 to 4.3 and the mean Qmax increased from 7.8 to 22.6 mL/sec. No significant complications were noted. The authors conceded that although the results were encouraging, long-term follow-up data were required.

PVP has been performed in 64 men with symptomatic BPH who had large-volume prostates (greater than 60 mL). The mean operative time was over 2 hours (123 minutes), and 62 of the 64 patients were discharged within 23 hours. At 12 months, the mean I-PSS had decreased from 18.4 to 6.7 and the mean Qmax had improved from 7.9 to 18.9 mL/sec (Sandhu et al, 2004). There has also been a report of PVP being performed in 66 high-risk patients, who had an American Society of Anesthesiologists score of 3 or greater; 29 patients were treated with ongoing oral anticoagulants or had severe bleeding disorders (Reich et al, 2005). No major complications occurred, nor was blood transfusion required. The average catheterization time was 1.8 days. The mean I-PSS improved from 20.2 to 6.5 at 1 year, and the mean Qmax improved from 6.7 to 21.6 mL/sec at 1 year.

Conclusions

The use of the laser to treat symptomatic BPH has evolved from the relatively cumbersome TULIP technique to other methods that require smaller pieces of equipment or that can treat a wider range of prostates. The difficulties in treating large prostates have been overcome using the newer technology. The minimal invasiveness of the laser has been improved, and the complications, particularly prolonged catheterization, bacteriuria, and urethral strictures, have been lowered very considerably. Cost effectiveness still remains a question in urologists' minds, but it would appear that quality of life improvement is as good as that achieved with TURP (Arai et al, 2000). Further long-term results from comparative studies are required from multicenter groups, which it is hoped would also answer the question of a higher reoperation rate seen in some long-term laser studies.

TRANSURETHRAL RESECTION OF THE PROSTATE

History

TURP, as we know it today, was developed in the United States in the 1920s and 1930s. Nesbit (1975) pointed out that there were several significant factors important in its development: (1) the invention of the incandescent lamp by Edison in 1879; (2) the cystoscope, developed independently by Nitze and Lieter in 1887; and (3) the development of the fenestrated tube by Hugh Hampton-Young, which allowed the obstructing tissue to be sheared off blindly. Other important factors were the invention of the vacuum tube in 1908 by De Forest, which allowed the constant production of high-frequency electrical current that could be used in resecting tissue. In 1926, Bumpus combined the cystoscope and the tubular punch. Also, at that time, Stearns developed the tungsten loop that could be used for the resection. This was put together by McCarthy in 1932, using a foroblique lens so that he could resect the tissue under direct vision using a wire loop.

In the 1970s, the development of the fiberoptic lighting system, together with the Hopkins (1976) rod lens wide-angle system, significantly improved visualization for endoscopic surgery. Previously, the optical system was a series of small lenses placed in a rigid tube. In the Hopkins rod lens wide-angle system, the air spaces were replaced by solid glass rods. The spacer tubes were shorter, resulting in minimal obstruction and increased admission of light.

Over the years, TURP, as a treatment modality for obstructing BPH, gained popularity throughout the world. It is now considered the gold standard for the surgical management of BPH. In the 1986 National Health Survey, 96% of patients had a TURP when they had surgery done for BPH. It was estimated that 350,000 Medicare patients had a TURP that year. However, today there are many medical and surgical alternatives to transurethral prostatectomy, and the number of TURPs has fallen to less than 200,000 per year in the Medicare age group.

Another factor that may have influenced the incidence of transurethral prostatectomy was the formal development of care guidelines for patients with BPH (McConnell et al, 1994). In 1989, the Omnibus Budget Reconciliation Act created the Federal Agency for Health Care Policy and Research (AHCPR). Patient care guidelines were demanded by Congress, and two of the first selected were the diagnosis and management of BPH. **It was the BPH Guideline Panel's recommendation that patients with minimal symptoms should undergo watchful waiting and that if intervention was to be considered in patients who were more symptomatic, the patient should be informed of the harms and benefits of each therapeutic modality and participate actively in making the decision, not only whether to intervene but which treatment modality would be his choice.** Many

patients opted for a less invasive procedure, although less effective than TURP.

Indications

In 1968, Lytton and coworkers (1968) estimated that the chance of a 40-year-old man having a prostatectomy in his lifetime was approximately 10%. However, Glynn and colleagues in 1985 raised the estimate to 29%. Arrighi and associates (1991), in reviewing the Baltimore Longitudinal Study on Aging (BLSA), believed that men older than 60 years had a 39% risk of requiring surgery in the next 20 years; men 50 to 59 years of age, a 24% chance; and men 40 to 49 years of age, a 13% chance.

There are very few studies of the natural history of patients who are seen initially because of modest symptoms of prostatism without an absolute indication for intervention (i.e., acute refractory urinary retention, recurrent infections). Ball and coworkers (1981) observed 97 patients for 5 years and found that the patients' symptoms were essentially the same in 52% and worse in only 16.5%. The urodynamic studies revealed little change in that group, and only 1.6% of the patients developed retention. Conversely, Birkhoff and associates (1976) observed 26 patients for 3 years and found a 50% to 70% worsening of the patients' subjective symptoms and 71% deterioration in objective criteria. Furthermore, acute retention was unpredictable.

The most common reasons for recommending intervention in a patient with symptoms of bladder outlet obstruction and irritability are that the symptoms are moderate to severe, bothersome, and interfere with the patient's quality of life. Mebust and colleagues (1989) noted that 90% of patients undergoing a TURP had symptoms of prostatism, but 70% had another indication as well (e.g., acute urinary retention, occurring in 27%).

In 1989, the AUA initiated the Guideline Panel for Diagnosis and Management of Benign Prostatic Hyperplasia. Recognizing the significance of assessing the patients' symptoms, a system score was developed by the AUA's Measurement Committee, Winston Mebust, Chairman. Barry (1992) was the senior author of this questionnaire, which came to be known as the AUA-7 Symptom Index (Table 88–3). Other scoring systems have been developed, such as the Madsen and Iversen (1983), Boyarsky and associates (1977), and the International Continence Society Study on BPH. However, the AUA-7 was validated as to its clarity, test-retest reliability, internal consistency, and criteria validity. The AHCPR took over the AUA BPH Guideline Panel in 1990. The guideline panel subsequently recommended a formal assessment of the patients' symptoms, using any scoring system but preferring the AUA-7. Patients with mild symptoms (having a score of 0 to 7) were assigned to watchful waiting; those with moderate (8 to 19) or severe (20 to 35) symptoms would undergo further testing or treatment, or both. **The AUA-7 Symptom Index is not disease specific.** The questionnaire has been given to older women, who obviously do not have a prostate but may have bladder dysfunction, resulting in a significant score in the Symptom Index. The Symptom Score was considered to be part of the patient's initial evaluation but did not make the diagnosis of BPH.

Table 88–3. AUA-7 Symptom Index for Benign Prostatic Hyperplasia

	Not at All	Less Than 1 Time in 5	Less Than Half the Time	About Half the Time	More Than Half the Time	Almost Always
1. Over the past month, how often have you had a sensation of not emptying your bladder completely after you finished urinating?	0	1	2	3	4	5
2. Over the past month, how often have you had to urinate again less than 2 hours after you finished urinating?	0	1	2	3	4	5
3. Over the past month, how often have you found you stopped and started again several times when you urinated?	0	1	2	3	4	5
4. Over the past month, how often have you found it difficult to postpone urination?	0	1	2	3	4	5
5. Over the past month, how often have you had a weak urinary stream?	0	1	2	3	4	5
6. Over the past month, how often have you had to push or strain to begin urination?	0	1	2	3	4	5
7. Over the past month, how many times did you most typically get up to urinate from the time you went to bed at night until the time you got up in the morning?	None	1 time	2 times	3 times	4 times	5 or more times

AUA Symptom Score = sum of questions A1 – A7 = _____

Modified from McConnell JD, Barry D, Bruskewitz RC, et al: Benign prostatic hyperplasia: Diagnosis and treatment. Clinical practice guideline. Agency for Health Care and Policy Research, Publication No. 94-0582, Feb 1994.

Table 88–4. Benign Prostatic Hyperplasia Impact Index

1. Over the past month, now much physical discomfort did any urinary problems cause you?	None	Only a little	Some	A lot
2. Over the past month, how much did you worry about your health because of urinary problems?	None	Only a little	Some	A lot
3. Overall, how bothersome has any trouble with urination been during the past month?	Not at all bothersome	Bothers me a little	Bothers me some	Bothers me a lot
4. Over the past month, low much of the time has any urinary problem kept you from doing the kinds of things you would usually do?	None of the time	A little of the time	Most of the time	All of the time

BPH Impact Index = sum of questions B1 – B4 = _____

BPH, benign prostatic hyperplasia.
From Barry MJ, Fowler FJ Jr, O'Leary MP, et al: Measuring disease-specific health slatus in men with benign prostatic hyperplasia. Med Care 1995;33(Suppl):AS145-AS155.

The AUA-7 Symptom Index was adopted at the World Health Organization Consultation on BPH in Paris in 1991 (Mebust et al, 1991). In addition to the AUA-7 Symptom Index, one global quality of life question was added—"If you were to spend the rest of your life with your urinary condition, just the way it is now, how would you feel about it?" Responses ranged from "delighted" to "terrible." Therefore, not only should the patient's severity of symptoms be considered in deciding whether intervention is warranted but also how much the patient is being bothered by his symptoms and how they affect his overall quality of life. It should be pointed out that patients having symptoms secondary to an obstructing prostate may have a variation in their symptoms over time. Ball and Smith (1982) noted that 31% of the patients they were following up had improvements in their symptoms. More recently, there have been efforts to develop a concise questionnaire to evaluate further the degree to which the condition is bothersome or the impact on quality of life of patients with symptoms from BPH (Barry et al, 1995). Such an example is the BPH Impact Index developed by Barry and associates (1995) (Table 88–4).

Although symptoms constitute the primary reason for recommending intervention, in patients with an obstructing prostate there are some absolute indications. These are acute urinary retention, recurrent infection, recurrent hematuria, and azotemia. A postvoid residual urine has been used by some urologists as an indication, but, as pointed out by Bruskewitz and coworkers (1982), there can be extreme variability within a given patient as to the amount of postvoid residual when this factor is assessed repetitively over a period of time. Furthermore, there is no information on the amount of postvoid residual urine that represents the point "that if nothing is done, irreparable damage to the bladder will occur." It was believed by the AHCPR BPH Panel (McConnell et al, 1994) that it might be of some use in following patients who are assigned to watchful waiting. In the AHCPR BPH Guideline, the patient's history is taken with focus on the urinary tract. Many of these patients have other comorbidity problems, and Mebust and colleagues (1989) noted that only 23% did not have a significant medical problem before surgery. The most common were pulmonary (14.5%), gastrointestinal (13.2%), myocardial infarction (12.5%), arrhythmia (12.4%), and renal insufficiency (4.5%). Therefore, a general medical evaluation is warranted.

A urinalysis is also recommended to be sure that the patient's symptoms are not related to infection. A digital rectal examination should be done, taking into consideration the consistency of the prostate, to help the urologist in determining whether the patient has cancer or not and also for an estimate of size. The size of the prostate might be important in selecting what type of surgical therapy would be warranted (e.g., transurethral incision of the prostate or, in the very large prostate, an open prostatectomy). A serum creatinine value is also to be obtained. It was noted by Mebust and colleagues (1989) that patients with a serum creatinine level greater than 1.5% had a 25% incidence of postoperative complications versus 17% in those who had a normal creatinine level.

A number of tests are considered to be optional for the urologist in evaluating the patient with moderate to severe symptoms from BPH. Many consider uroflowmetry to be the single best noninvasive urodynamic test to detect lower tract obstruction. However, it should be pointed out that the patient's obstructive symptoms, when evaluated with a formal questionnaire, correlate poorly with uroflowmetry measurements. Furthermore, there is no specific cutoff point at which one can state that the patient is definitely obstructed. **A Qmax less than 15 mL/sec does not differentiate between outflow obstruction and detrusor impairment.** Pressure-flow studies are recommended as an optional test. This is one of the best ways to evaluate a patient's degree of obstruction and detrusor function, particularly when the diagnosis is unclear. However, it is invasive, is uncomfortable for the patient, requires expensive equipment, and requires considerable experience in performing so that the results are reproducible.

A number of tests are not recommended, such as a filling cystometrogram. Although this test can demonstrate uninhibited bladder contractions, it is invasive and does not give much more information than can be obtained from the patient's history of bladder irritability symptoms. **Cystoscopy, done routinely in the physician's office as a diagnostic procedure, is not recommended.** The only reason for performing cystoscopy in the urologist's office is if the urologist needs to know the size of the prostate and its configuration in making a recommendation about the type of therapy that would be useful for the patient (e.g., transurethral incision if a small prostate or an open prostatectomy if a very large prostate). If it is critical for the urologist to know the exact size when deciding whether the patient should have an open prostatectomy, transrectal ultrasonography is more precise than cystoscopy. Upper tract imaging is also not recommended to be performed routinely. Rather, it should be reserved for patients with hematuria or renal insufficiency or for those with a history of urinary infection, urinary tract surgery, or stones.

Anesthesia

Transurethral surgery of the prostate is usually performed with the use of a general or spinal anesthetic. However, Sinha and associates (1986) have reported doing a TURP with the patient under local anesthesia. Birch and colleagues (1991) have recommended performing a TURP using sedation and local anesthesia. However, they pointed out that the gland size

should be less than 40 g. Nielsen and associates (1981) noted no difference in blood loss when the surgery was done with either an epidural or a general anesthetic. McGowan and Smith (1980) evaluated spinal anesthesia versus general anesthesia and found no difference in blood loss, postoperative morbidity, or mortality.

We believe that a patient's anesthetic should be tailored to the particular patient. During the procedure, the anesthetist should monitor the patient's tissue oxygen saturation, electrocardiogram, and, if warranted, a serum sodium level, in addition to the usual parameters.

Perioperative Antibiotics

Urinary tract infections can be found in 8% to 24% of BPH patients preoperatively. The infection should be treated before surgery. The use of prophylactic antibiotics is somewhat controversial. Gibbons and colleagues (1978) found that prophylactic antibiotics did not reduce postoperative infection, but Nielsen and coworkers (1981), Leroy and associates (1992), Viitanen and colleagues (1993), and Prescott and associates (1990) have found them useful. In the AUA study (Mebust et al, 1989), over 60% of the patients were given prophylactic antibiotics. **It is our recommendation that the patients be given systemic antibiotics before the initiation of surgery, and we usually recommend a first-generation cephalosporin or a combination of this with gentamicin. It is valuable to maintain the patient on oral antibiotics until the catheter is removed.**

Surgical Technique

Because Creevy and Webb (1947) pointed out the danger of water causing hemolysis, the emphasis has been on using nonhemolytic fluids for irrigation during transurethral prostatectomy. Although water is less expensive and a TURP can be performed safely using it, probably the majority of urologists today use a nonhemolytic solution. A variety of fluids are available today (e.g., 1.5% glycine, cytol—a combination of sorbitol and mannitol, and mannitol). These are not isotonic fluids but rather nonhemolytic (e.g., 1.5% glycine and have an osmolarity of approximately 200 mOsm/L).

The patient is placed in the lithotomy position with the buttocks just off the end of the table. We prefer Alcock leg holders over knee crutches for leg support. The perineum is not shaved but scrubbed for 5 minutes with a germicidal soap. An O'Connor rectal shield is inserted for manipulation of the gland during surgery.

At the time of surgery, the urethra is calibrated with bougie à boule. The majority of patients calibrate at No. 28 Fr or greater, but a significant number are less, as pointed out by Emmett and coworkers (1963). If the distal urethra is inadequate to accommodate the more commonly selected No. 28 Fr resectoscope, a smaller size should be used. For several years, we have successfully used a No. 24 Fr resectoscope sheath, even in patients with very large glands. However, if the distal urethra is inadequate, a perineal urethrostomy may be performed by inserting the resectoscope through the more commodious bulbar urethra. The technique of perineal urethrostomy has been described elsewhere (Melchior et al, 1974b). Alternatively, an internal urethrotomy can be performed as advocated by Emmett and colleagues (1963) and Bailey and Shearer (1979). The common area of narrowing is at the postnavicular region, and, in this instance, we would perform a dorsal internal urethrotomy using a curved No. 12 scalpel blade. A generous ventral meatotomy often leads to a splattering or an errant direction of the urinary stream and is to be avoided.

Various surgical techniques have been espoused by urologists for removing the prostate adenoma. **However, every surgical technique basically employs the principle that the resection should be performed in a routine, step-by-step manner.** The resection technique may vary according to the size or configuration of the prostate but should be based on an orderly plan. All of the techniques use the general principle of resecting ventrally first so that the adenomatous tissue drops down, allowing the surgeon to resect from the top downward rather than from the floor upward. However, some surgeons have suggested resecting the floor of the median lobe to improve water flow during the resection.

In our teaching technique, we often resect one lobe of the prostate and the residents resect the other. Today, we use the video camera in almost all transurethral prostatectomies. We find that this helps in teaching residents, but it also reduces the back strain encountered by the surgeon bending over the resectoscope.

Our standard technique was described by Nesbit (1943) over 50 years ago. The Nesbit technique is divided into three stages.

First Stage

After the preliminary endoscopy and urethral calibration, the bladder is filled with approximately 150 mL of a nonhemolytic irrigation solution (e.g., 1.5% glycine) (Fig. 88–6). The resection begins at the bladder neck, starting at the 12 o'clock position and carried down to the 9 o'clock position in a stepwise

fashion. The adenoma is resected down to the level where the apparent circular fibers of the bladder neck become visible. Over-resection of the entire neck, or excessive cauterization, may lead to vesical neck contracture. The anterior quadrant, from 12 to 3 o'clock, is now resected. The posterior quadrants are then individually resected, down to the 6 o'clock position. **If, at the completion of the entire resection, the bladder neck appears to be partially obstructing, which is particularly true of glands weighing less than 20 g, we advise incising the bladder neck with a Collings knife at the 6 o'clock position.** This step is recommended by Kulb and associates (1987) to reduce the incidence of postoperative vesical neck contracture.

Second Stage

The adenoma is resected in quadrants (Figs. 88–7 to 88–9). The resectoscope is placed in front of the verumontanum. The resection begins at 12 o'clock, so that the lateral lobe tissue falls into the midfossa. The resection is carried down to the prostatic capsule, which is recognized as a rather fibrous structure compared with the granular appearance of the prostatic adenoma. The right lateral lobe and then the left lateral lobe are resected so that the tissue now falls to the floor. With the right lateral lobe on the floor of the prostatic fossa, resection of this fallen lobe is started at approximately the 3 o'clock position. The posterior portion on the floor of the prostatic fossa is resected. Care must be taken not to resect too deeply in the region of the posterior aspect of the vesical neck to prevent undermining of the trigone. The resection is carried to the right side of the verumontanum. A similar procedure is started at approximately 9 o'clock. The posterior portion of the lobe is resected to the left side of the verumontanum. The apical portion of the lobe remains. At this stage, therefore, the posterior portions of the lateral lobe, including the floor tissue, have been resected to the verumontanum. As one resects the lower two quadrants in the floor of the prostate,

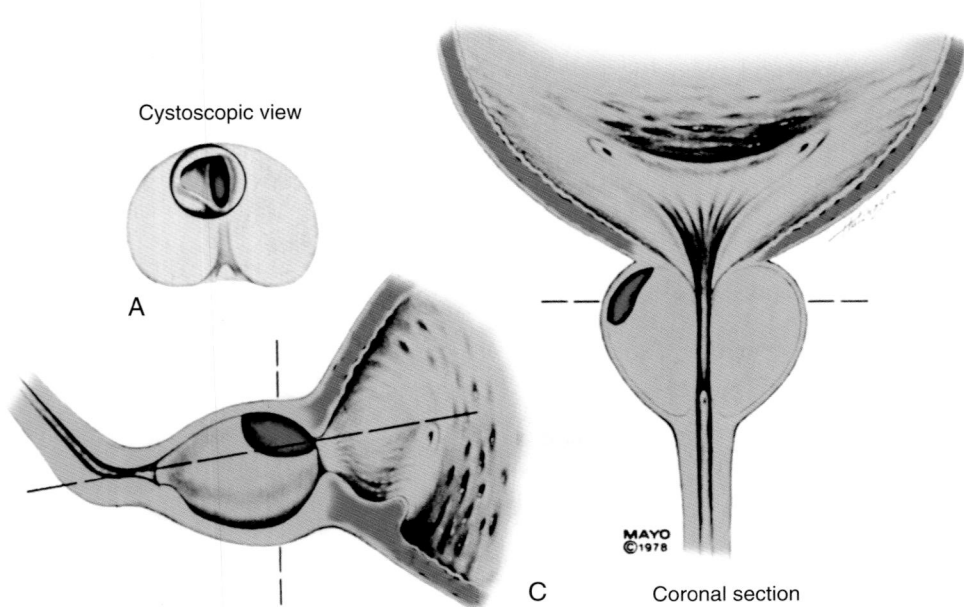

Cystoscopic view

A

B

Right sagittal section

C

Coronal section

MAYO
©1978

Figure 88–6. A to **C,** First stage of resection of the prostate. The resection is begun at the 12 o'clock position, and the tissue at the bladder neck and the adjacent adenoma are resected in quadrants. (**A** to **C,** From the Mayo Foundation.)

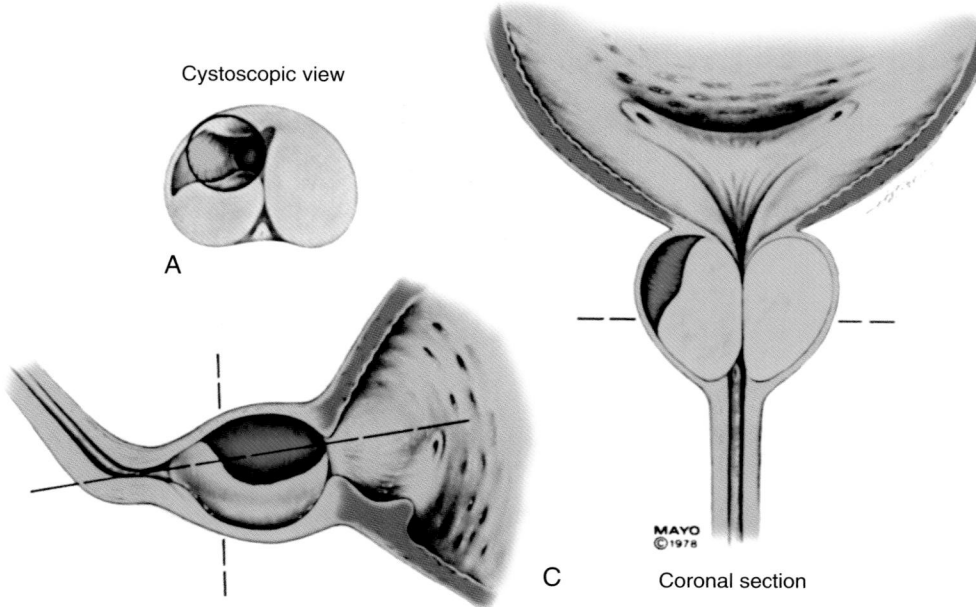

Cystoscopic view

A

B   Right sagittal section

C   Coronal section

Figure 88–7. **A,** The midportion of the gland is resected starting at the 12 o'clock position and carrying it down to the 9 o'clock position. **B** and **C,** The sagittal and coronal section views are noted. (**A** to **C,** From the Mayo Foundation.)

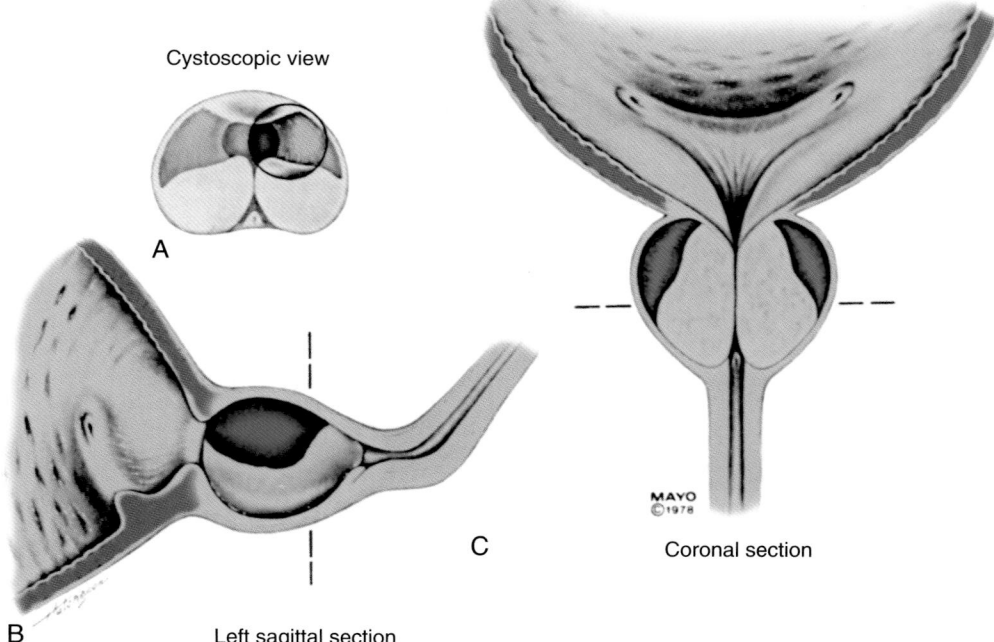

Cystoscopic view

A

B   Left sagittal section

C   Coronal section

Figure 88–8. **A,** The resection is now begun at the 12 o'clock position, and the left side of the patient's gland in the midfossa is resected down to the 3 o'clock position. **B** and **C,** Sagittal and coronal sections. (**A** to **C,** From the Mayo Foundation.)

the capsule fibers become less distinct. The resection is performed with an O'Connor rectal shield in place. We employ the Iglesias modification of the Nesbit scope so that one hand is free to palpate the depth of resection as the floor tissue is removed.

Third Stage

The adenoma is removed immediately proximal to the external sphincter mechanism, preserving the verumontanum

(Figs. 88–10 to 88–12). The prostatic apex is concave. A sweeping motion is used so that the loop is moved from a lateral to a medial direction as it approaches the sphincter mechanism. However, Shah and coworkers (1979) observed that 10% to 20% of the prostate projects below the verumontanum. Therefore, it may be necessary to leave a small rim of the adenoma to avoid sphincter injury.

Turner-Warwick (1983) has divided the sphincter mechanism into three areas: (1) immediately adjacent to the veru-

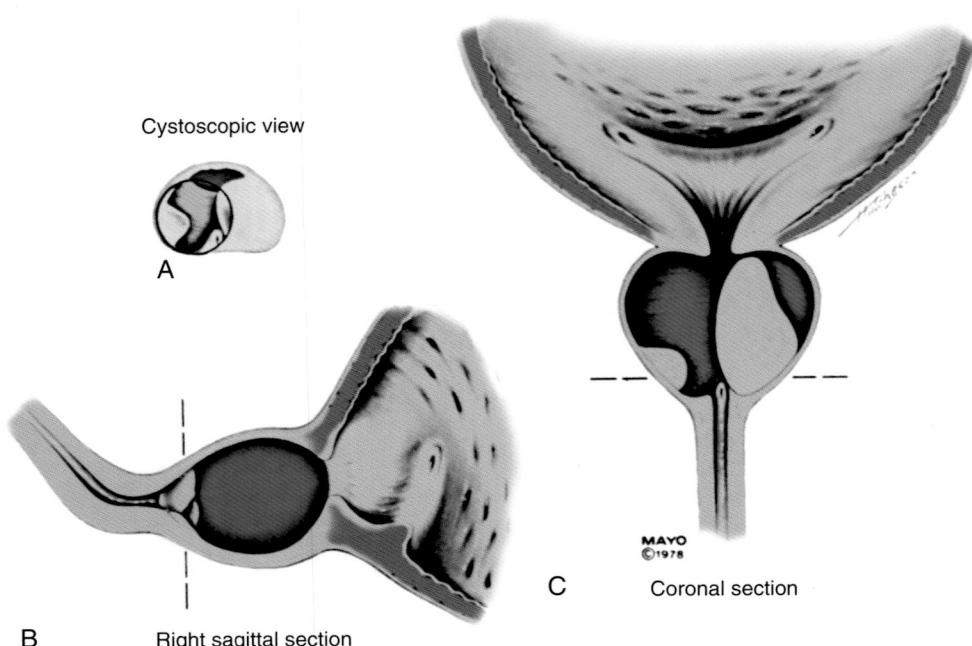

Cystoscopic view

A

B   Right sagittal section

C   Coronal section

Figure 88-9. **A,** The midportion of the gland is resected farther down from the 9 o'clock position to the 6 o'clock position. **B** and **C,** Sagittal views. (**A** to **C,** From the Mayo Foundation.)

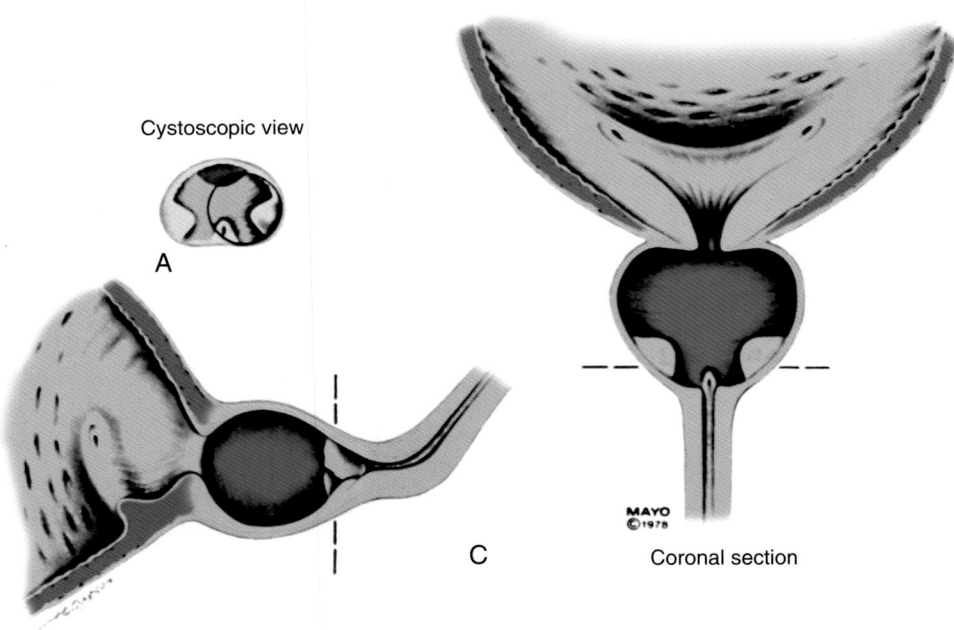

Cystoscopic view

A

B   Left sagittal section

C   Coronal section

Figure 88-10. The tissue remaining at the apex is now resected. It is begun by initiating the resection next to the verumontanum and carrying it toward the 12 o'clock position. **A** to **C,** Small amounts of residual tissue at the apex. (**A** to **C,** From the Mayo Foundation.)

montanum, (2) from the verumontanum to the capsule, and (3) beyond the capsule of the prostate. Injury to the second or third portion of the sphincter mechanism can result in significant urinary incontinence. Therefore, we begin our resection by placing the resectoscope next to the verumontanum. We continue the resection up to the 12 o'clock position, rather than starting at the 12 o'clock position as in the previous two steps.

With the patient in the lithotomy position, the distal portion of the prostate is not always parallel to the surgical table but is tilting slightly toward the cephalad end. The most common area of damage to the external sphincter is at the 12 o'clock position. Thus, care must be taken as one approaches the 12 o'clock position.

When the resection is completed, the surgeon should pull the resectoscope into the urethra, just distal to the verumontanum, and note that there is no falling and obstructing tissue. Some small wings of adenoma may be attached to the sphincter area. These can be judiciously trimmed. Care must be taken not to cut too deeply and thus damage the sphincter

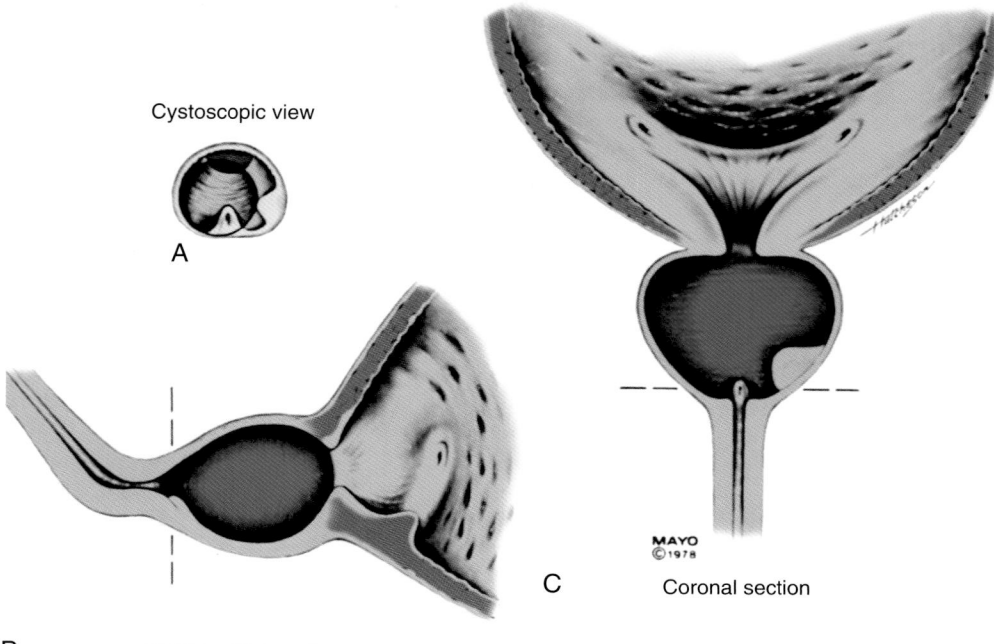

Cystoscopic view

A

Coronal section

B   Right sagittal section

C

Figure 88–11. A to **C,** Residual tissue is carefully cleared on the patient's right side. (**A** to **C,** From the Mayo Foundation.)

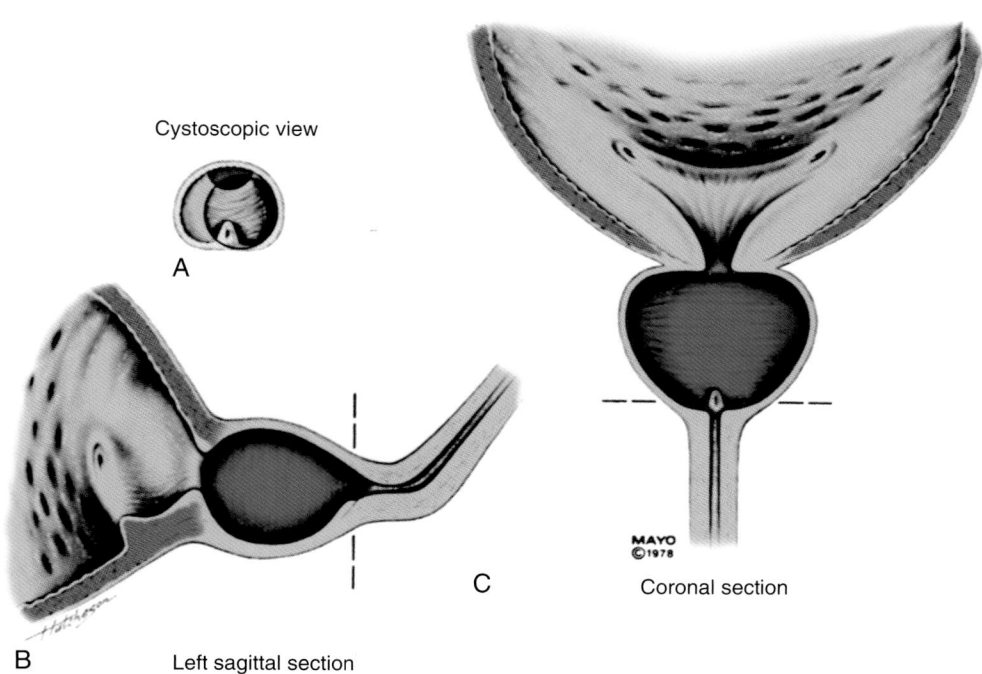

Cystoscopic view

A

Coronal section

B   Left sagittal section

C

Figure 88–12. A to **C,** The remaining residual tissue is cleared from the patient's left side, leaving an unobstructed view from the verumontanum through the bladder neck into the bladder. (**A** to **C,** From the Mayo Foundation.)

mechanism. Occasionally, there is tissue that is nothing more than mucosal tags, which are unimportant. They slough and do not cause obstruction. When significant tissue droops into the prostatic fossa, with the scope in the distal urethra, it is usually the tissue that remains at the roof of the midfossa area. The surgeon should replace the scope in the midfossa and resect the adenoma down to the fibrous capsule.

Management of Intraoperative Problems

Hemostasis

The amount of intraoperative bleeding depends on the size of the prostate, the length of time required to resect the adenoma, and, to a degree, the surgeon's skill. Arterial bleeding is controlled by electrocoagulation. This should be done as one completes each stage of the resection, before moving on to the next stage. **After the catheter is inserted, at the end of the surgical procedure, the irrigation fluid should be light pink.** If the irrigation fluid has a continued red color, one should suspect arterial bleeding. The surgeon should reinsert the resectoscope and coagulate the arterial bleeding. Venous bleeding is apparent at the end of the procedure, when on irrigating the catheter the return is initially clear but then dark blood later oozes from the catheter. Venous bleeding can be controlled by filling the bladder with 100 mL of irrigating fluid and placing the catheter on traction for 7 minutes at the operating table. The balloon of the catheter is overinflated to 50 mL of fluid.

Extravasation, or perforation of the prostatic capsule, occurs in about 2% of patients. The symptoms of extravasation are restlessness, nausea, vomiting, and abdominal pain, despite spinal anesthesia. Pain is usually localized to the lower abdomen and back. If extravasation is suspected, the operation should be terminated as rapidly as possible, but hemostasis must be secured. Bleeding must be controlled, even as the extravasation is increased, because simultaneous postoperative management of extravasation and hemorrhage is difficult. Cystography may provide information about the diagnosis and, to some degree, the extent of the extravasation. Over 90% of these patients can be managed simply by urethral catheter drainage and cessation of the operative procedure. If there is extensive extravasation and concern about infecting the perivesical tissue, suprapubic drainage should be instituted.

Transurethral Resection Syndrome

In the AUA cooperative study (Mebust et al, 1989), transurethral resection (TUR) syndrome occurred in 2% of the patients. The syndrome was characterized by mental confusion, nausea, vomiting, hypertension, bradycardia, and visual disturbance. Usually, the patients do not become symptomatic until the serum sodium concentration reaches 125 mEq/dL. The risk is increased if the gland is larger than 45 g and the resection time is longer than 90 minutes.

In 1950, several studies were undertaken to determine the amount of fluid absorbed during TURP. Hagstrom (1955) weighed patients preoperatively and postoperatively and calculated that approximately 20 mL/min of fluid was absorbed by the patient. However, there was significant variation in patients. Oester and Madsen (1969), using a double-isotope technique, demonstrated that the average amount of fluid absorbed by the patient was 1000 mL and that one third of this fluid was absorbed intravenously. Madsen and Naber (1973) demonstrated that pressure in the prostatic fossa and the amount of fluid absorbed were dependent on the height of the fluid by the patient. They noted that when the height of the fluid was changed from 60 to 70 cm, fluid absorption was greater than twofold. They also reported that approximately 300 mL/min of fluid was needed for a good vision field. This could not be achieved when the fluid level was below 60 cm H_2O. Harrison and colleagues (1956) believed that the TUR syndrome was related to dilutional hyponatremia. Certainly, the syndrome can be reduced by the administration of 3% saline solution. However, other factors have been suggested as a possible cause. Glycine is metabolized to glycolic acid and ammonium. Ammonium intoxication has been suggested as a possible cause of the TUR syndrome or direct toxic effect of the glycine. **Nevertheless, it is our belief that the TUR syndrome is secondary to dilutional hyponatremia.** This can be corrected by giving the patient 200 mL of 3% saline solution very slowly over a period of time.

Conversely, one can attempt to calculate the amount of water overload by determining the serum sodium preoperatively and postoperatively, knowing the patient's weight, and determining the amount of extracellular fluid. Stalberg and coworkers (1992), in patients undergoing a TURP with general anesthesia, tagged the irrigating fluid with 1% ethanol and measured the amount of ethanol excreted in the breath. This is believed to be a very effective and quick way of determining which patients are becoming overloaded with fluid. In patients who have a large gland or when the operating time is being prolonged, we obtain a serum sodium value routinely, although the patient is still undergoing surgery. When patients demonstrate a drop in serum sodium level, we treat with diuretics (e.g., furosemide [Lasix]). The serum sodium concentration is measured in the postoperative recovery room, and, if need be, further diuretics are used.

Intraoperative Priapism

During the surgical procedure, a penile erection may occur, which may obviate the surgery unless a penile urethrostomy is performed. This has usually been managed by injecting an α-adrenergic agent directly into the corpora cavernosa. We would usually dilute the solution of ephedrine or phenylephrine (e.g., 0.3 mL 1% phenylephrine diluted to 3 mL with normal saline solution for 100 μg/1 mL) (Lee et al, 1995).

Outcomes

Patients' Symptoms

In developing the guideline for the diagnosis and management of BPH, the AHCPR panel (McConnell et al, 1994) asked patients what was the most significant factor they considered in deciding what type of therapy should be used in treating their bladder outlet obstruction secondary to BPH. The foremost factor was relief of symptoms.

In reviewing the literature, the AHCPR Guideline Panel used meta-analysis to combine the various clinical studies. They noted that the chance of improvement of patients' symptoms after a TURP was 70% to 96% confidence interval (CI), with a mean of 88%. The magnitude of reduction in symptom score was 85%. **This was significantly better than with less invasive procedures.**

Mortality

Over the past 50 to 60 years, there has been a gradual reduction in the immediate postoperative mortality rate associated with TURP. Perrin and colleagues (1976) found a mortality rate of 5%, reported in the 1930s. Holtgrewe and Valk (1962) reported 2.5%; Melchior and associates (1974b), 1.3%; and Mebust and coworkers (1989), 0.2%. This was the mortality rate noted at 30 days. The number of patients noted in each of these three studies was well over 2000.

Roos and colleagues (1989), using insurance claim data from England, Denmark, and Manitoba, Canada, noted that the death rate at 90 days was significantly higher compared with an open prostatectomy. They noted an early postoperative death rate of 2.9% in a study involving almost 40,000 patients. A meta-analysis of other series showed a mortality rate of 1.18%. However, including the study by Roos and colleagues with other reports, the mean estimate was 1.5% (90% CI, 0.5% to 0.3%).

In more recent studies, Ala-Opas and colleagues (1993) found no immediate mortality in a series of over 400 patients undergoing a TURP. Chute and associates (1991), in an epidemiologic study, compared patients who had a TURP with those who did not have a TURP and found that the mortality rate over time was identical. Montorsi and coworkers (1993) compared a group of patients who underwent either TURP or open prostatectomy and found the mortality rate in each group was identical. Concato and colleagues (1992) compared a group of patients retrospectively, undergoing a TURP or prostatectomy, and, when corrected for comorbidity, the mortality rate was the same for both groups. However, a chart review had been conducted by Malenka and associates (1990), looking at comorbidity factors in the Canadian population. They could not identify comorbidity factors to account for the apparent difference in mortality rate between TURP and open prostatectomy.

Fuglsig and coworkers (1994) age matched a group of patients who had undergone a TURP with those who had not, and the mortality rate for the two groups was identical. The mortality rate could not be influenced by many factors, such as the type of hospital where the surgery was performed, the skill of the surgeon, the size of the gland, the operating time, or, again, comorbidity factors.

In reviewing the cause of death in the Canadian series, it was secondary to cardiac disease. In the patients who were studied in Denmark, the cause of death was pulmonary complications. **This suggests that the observation by Roos and associates** (1989) **was truly related to comorbidity being significant in those undergoing TURP as opposed to those who underwent an open prostatectomy.**

The immediate morbidity rate after TURP was reported by Mebust and coworkers (1989) as 18%. This was similar to the rates reported by Holtgrewe and Valk (1962) and Melchior and associates (1974b). Although the incidence was unchanged, in the Mebust report the incidence of significant complications (e.g., acute pyelonephritis) was not as high as that noted in the previous studies. The most common

complications in the immediate postoperative period were failing to void (6.5%), bleeding requiring transfusion (3.9%), and clot retention (3.3%). The AHCPR BPH Guideline Panel (McConnell et al, 1994) found a mean immediate postoperative complication rate of 14.95% with a 90% CI of 5.2% to 30.7%. In more recent studies, the immediate postoperative complication rate has been noted by Plentka and associates (1991) (3.1%), Estey and colleagues (1993) (7.8%), and Chute and coworkers (1991) (4.2%). However, these are all retrospective studies.

Wasson and associates (1995) reported on a prospective randomized study in which patients were assigned to either watchful waiting or a TURP. **Ninety-one percent of the men had no complication during the first 30 days after surgery. Specifically, there was no difference between either group in the incidence of urinary incontinence or impotence.** The most frequent complications noted were a need for replacement of urinary catheter (4%), perforation of the prostatic capsule (2%), and hemorrhage requiring transfusion (1%). At the end of 3 years of follow-up, the mortality rate was the same for each group. Twenty-three patients in the treatment group were considered treatment failures, and 47 patients were in the watchful waiting group. The failure rate in the watchful waiting group was 6.1 per 100 person-years of follow-up compared with 3 per 100 person-years of follow-up in the surgery group ($P = 0.002$). The higher rate in the watchful waiting group was largely attributed to a higher incidence of three outcomes: (1) intractable urinary retention (2.9% versus 0.9%), (2) a high volume of residual urine (5% versus 1.1%), and (3) a high urinary symptom score (4.3% versus 0.4%). In those undergoing surgery, there was improvement in peak flow rate, reduction in the severity of symptoms, and reduction in the degree to which the symptoms bothered the patient. The authors noted that the outcomes of surgery were best for the men who were most bothered by urinary symptoms at baseline. This study refutes the uncontrolled observations in prior retrospective series that TUR frequently leads to incontinence and impotence, and it confirms that the incidence of short-term complications and retreatment after surgery is low.

There are few data on the long-term outcomes of patients undergoing TURP. In the study conducted by Wasson and colleagues of 280 men undergoing surgery, at 3 years follow-up, 9 men had vesical neck contracture requiring endoscopic surgery; 9 had a urethral stricture that required dilatation; and 8 underwent a second TUR, 4 because of adenocarcinoma. Bruskewitz and coworkers (1986), in observing a series of patients over 3 years, noted that at 1 year most patients' symptoms improved (84%) and 10% remained approximately the same. At 3 years, 75% had improved and 13% remained the same. The change in symptomatology was the development of urge incontinence occurring in those patients several years after surgery. Only 1 of the 84 patients required a repeated resection, resulting in an incidence of 2%. However, 10% of the patients developed a vesical neck contracture.

Meyhoff and Nordling (1986) noted that 90% of their patients were considered to have satisfactory results at 5 years after TURP. Flow rates were improved from preoperative values, although there had been a slight decline in flow rates over the 5-year period. They did note an 8% re-resection rate, but all patients were noted to have especially small glands, suggesting that these might have been postoperative vesical neck contractures, as had been noted in the prior studies.

Ala-Opas and associates (1993) found that 92% of the patients were satisfied with the results of their surgery 6.5 years after the procedure had been done. Montorsi and associates (1993), in a group of patients observed for 5 years, found that 95% of the patients were unobstructed and subjectively satisfied about their urinary status.

In a large U.K. study, entitled The National Prostatectomy Audit (Emberton et al, 1995, 1996; Neal, 1997), 5361 patients who had undergone prostatectomy were reviewed by questionnaire. The findings were significant because of the large number of patients who responded, representing 89% of all those who had undergone the operation in four health regions of the United Kingdom. It was found that patients who were most bothered by their symptoms had the best response to surgery. The degree of preoperative evaluation varied greatly from urologist to urologist. Men who waited longer for surgery had worse symptoms by the time of their operation. Older men and those of a higher social class were more likely to undergo prostatectomy with fewer symptoms. Twelve percent of men throughout the study were undergoing surgery for the second time, and the clinical course of men having a second operation differed considerably from that of men having a first procedure.

A large study from Australia assessed the mortality and prostate cancer risk in 19,598 men after surgery for BPH. This was a population-based cohort of men in Western Australia operated on over a 17-year period (Holman et al, 1999). It was found that at 10 years the relative survival was 116.5% in patients who had a TURP and 123.5% in patients after open prostatectomy. However, the rate ratio (RR) of 1.20 fell to 1.10 (0.99 to 1.23) after adjustment for comorbidity. It was concluded that any excess mortality risk from TURP was small and clinically unimportant.

Another study found that just looking at mortality after TURP without attention to other issues could be misleading (Hargreave et al, 1996). A total of 81,997 men underwent prostatectomy in Scotland between 1968 and 1989. Although the study confirmed the increased risk of late mortality after TURP compared with open prostatectomy, it was found that limitations in the coding of the comorbidities and the absence of coding of more subtle aspects of the condition of the patient that may influence the choice between different types of prostatectomy mean that the differential mortality after the two procedures could reflect preoperative selection rather than the effects of the procedure itself.

Finally, in a review of 166 patients older than 80 years who had undergone TURP, with a mean follow-up of 60 months, it was found that 88.5% had an American Society of Anesthesiologists operative risk classification of III or IV, indicating a poor risk. All patients had at least one serious associated medical disease. Early complications occurred in 25.9%, late complications in 13.2%, and reoperation in 4.2%. The mortality rate within 30 days of operation was 1.2%, and 43 patients died during the follow-up period. The authors compared the Kaplan-Meier survival curves of the group under review with the expected survival rate of the age-matched population and found no statistical difference (Matani et al, 1996).

Bipolar Transurethral Resection

The standard monopolar TURP is now being challenged by the use of bipolar resection (Gyrus PlasmaKinetic System, Gyrus Medical, Maple Grove, Md). The rationale for the introduction of this system is that the complications of standard monopolar TURP need to be reduced to improve acceptability by patients. There has been a series of studies with the Gyrus system (Botto et al, 2001; Dunsmuir et al, 2003) and with the Vista CTR system (ACMI Corp.) (Singh et al, 2005). In a small retrospective study, 18 patients had conventional monopolar TURP, and 26 had bipolar TURP. The point was made by the authors that there have been few innovations in TURP technique in recent years and that this latest change has allowed earlier removal of the catheter and earlier discharge from hospital. The fact that all of these studies are short-term, nonrandomized, and in some cases retrospective means that the observations on relative complication rates must be taken with some caution. However, this new technology may have something to offer. The Gyrus bipolar system consists of a generator with 200 W capability, a radiofrequency range of 320 to 450 kHz, and a voltage range of 254 to 350 V. There is a plasmakinetic resectoscope with a TUR loop of 80/20 platinum/iridium alloy electrode with the active and return electrode on the same axis (axipolar) separated by a ceramic insulator (Botto et al, 2001; Patel and Adshead, 2004).

Conclusions

TURP was introduced as a method of treatment that was less invasive than open prostatectomy. Although evidence-based medicine now considers it imperative that a new treatment should be compared in a randomized fashion against a known standard, this did not happen with TURP. Hence, it took at least 50 years for it to be accepted as the established treatment and it took even longer for its exact role in the therapeutic armamentarium to be found. Although comparative trials evaluating minimally invasive treatments against TURP in terms of efficacy have lost that particular battle in the majority of cases, the complication rate after TURP has not been thus compared. When looked at without the benefit of comparison in a randomized trial, TURP is still an incomparable treatment for BPH, particularly if the patient has a high "bother" score, has recurrent urinary tract infections caused by incomplete bladder emptying, or has outflow obstruction when measured by pressure-flow urodynamic studies.

TRANSURETHRAL VAPORIZATION OF THE PROSTATE

Whereas TURP removes tissue by resection of prostatic tissue and causes hemostasis by fulguration, transurethral vaporization of the prostate (TUVP) is brought about by combining the concepts of vaporization and desiccation. Desiccation is the drawing out of water from tissue, by drying out, rather than vaporizing the cells. This concept was introduced by Mebust and coworkers (1972, 1977) using a transurethral probe with direct-vision capabilities to heat and desiccate the prostate. TUVP was first described by Kaplan and Te (1995a, 1995b).

Mechanism of Action

With TUVP, two electrosurgical effects are combined: vaporization and desiccation. Vaporization steams tissue away using high heat, and coagulation uses lower heat to dry out tissue. Other factors are also involved that modify the delivery of electrical energy. These include the voltage production by the generator, the current density of the surface area of contact of the electrode, and the electrical resistance of the tissue being treated (Kaplan et al, 1998).

In the case of TUVP, the electrode's leading edge is the point at which maximal efficiency for vaporization occurs, as well as that of current density delivery. At the point of the trailing edge of the electrode, there is a decrease in the delivery of current, lowering the power and permitting tissue desiccation to occur. Therefore, vaporization occurs at the leading edge and desiccation occurs at the trailing edge (Kaplan et al, 1998).

The power of the generator determines whether vaporization occurs at the leading edge of the electrode. The electricity that is transmitted to the cell is converted to heat, resulting in the cell exploding or drying out. This is dependent on the conduction of electricity by the cell or the tissue resistance encountered by the current. In simple terms, the well-hydrated cell conducts electricity well, whereas the dryer the tissue, the greater the electrical resistance. Clearly, a higher power is required to overcome this resistance, which may lead to poor vaporization if the power cannot be varied.

The type of generator used is also important in deciding the effectiveness of the vaporization. Older machines do not have a method of modulating delivery of power to the tissues depending on the degree of resistance encountered. Usually, therefore, the power is switched high to overcome this problem. The balance then is in some cases controlled by the limitation of the amount of current required to maintain a constant power. This safety feature prevents the delivery of an ever-increasing voltage that would compensate for the increase in resistance associated with the drying out of tissue that would occur with vaporization. This could potentially lead to unwanted damage both to the local tissues and to other areas such as the urethra. For this reason, modern generators specifically designed for TUVP can vary the delivery of power by reading tissue resistance. In addition, the safety feature described earlier whereby power can be limited is set at a higher level, thus making TUVP more efficient.

For TUVP, the cutting current power should be set to a maximum of 75% higher power than for a standard TURP, but the power used need not always be as high as this. In fact, it has been estimated that a minimal power delivery of 150 W is required for TUVP (van Swol et al, 1999).

Electrode Design

The *rollerball,* which is traditionally used for fulgurating the base of superficial bladder tumors, can be used for TUVP. However, it should not be used for prostates that are particularly large. In the study by Juma (1996), it was most effective in patients with glands whose mean volume as estimated by transrectal ultrasonography was 31.9 mL. The effectiveness in larger glands is probably limited by the shape of the rollerball,

where the most satisfactory vaporization takes place at the middle part of the leading edge, assuming an equal distribution of contact pressure.

A *grooved rollerbar* has been widely used and consists of a bar that is 3 mm wide and 3 mm in diameter, which is composed of nickel-silver and insulated with Teflon (Vapor Trode, Circon-ACMI, Stamford, Conn). The design is superior to the standard rollerball because the grooved design increases the number of leading edges at which electrovaporization takes place, and this allows increased efficiency of vaporization to a wide contact area and thus to a larger volume of tissue (Narayan et al, 1996; Reis et al, 1999). A similar grooved electrode has also been produced (Richard Wolf, Germany), known as the EVAP.

New second-generation vaporizing electrodes have been manufactured and evaluated. They have the aim of both vaporizing and resecting prostatic tissue simultaneously and have been termed "vaporizing loops" by some. The technique has been given several possible names in the literature, all amounting to the same thing: e.g., transurethral vaporization-resection of the prostate (TUVRP), thick-loop TURP, vapor-cut, electrovaporization-resection (Cabelin et al, 2000).

Some examples of these are testament to the inventiveness of many of the instrument companies in relation to design. The Vapor Tome (Circon-ACMI, Stamford, Conn) is a thick loop with grooves, giving a thin leading edge for vaporization and a thick trailing edge for desiccation. The Wedge (Microvasive, Natick, Mass) is a smooth loop with the same edge configuration, made of stainless steel, tungsten, and chromium. The Wing EVAP (Richard Wolf, Germany) is a semicircular gold-plated wide loop that is wider and thicker than the standard TURP loop (Cabelin et al, 2000). Other modifications are under investigation, in which not only new electrodes but also specific electrosurgical generators are being developed, the aim of which is to reduce side effects while maintaining efficacy and also decreasing the potential risks of high-voltage power to the tissues surrounding the prostate.

Clinical Experience with Electrovaporization

The first report of TUVP was from Kaplan and Te (1995a), using the Vapor Trode. They reported on 25 men with moderate lower urinary tract symptoms with a mean prostatic size of 57.6 mL. **There was an improvement in symptom score from 17.8 to 4.2 at 3 months and in Qmax from 7.4 to 17.3 mL/sec at the same time.** The most encouraging findings were that all of the patients had their catheters removed within 24 hours (mean, 14.6), but by 3 months one patient had developed a distal urethral stricture. In the study by Juma (1996) using the standard rollerball in a study of 20 men for 3 months, the results were similar, although one patient developed a bladder neck stenosis and one required a repeated TURP.

Other pilot studies also suggested that a comparative trial would be appropriate because of the efficacy and safety that had been demonstrated. Galluci and his colleagues (1996) treated 35 patients with the Vapor Trode and found that improvements at 28 days were as encouraging as those at 3 months in other studies (Qmax, 9.8 to 20.74; symptom score,

statistically significant difference between the two treatments. The only apparent difference was the higher incidence of bladder neck contraction after TURP.

Miller and associates (1992) reported on 108 patients who underwent a bladder neck incision and compared them with a similar group undergoing TURP. They believed that bladder neck incision was better than TURP in terms of a shorter operative time and shorter duration of catheterization. No other perioperative differences were found. For the 10-year follow-up, there was no difference in reoperation rates between the two groups, with an equally high approval by patients after both procedures. In another comparative study, Soonawalla and Pardanini (1992) found that the peak urinary flow rates increased from 8 to 19 mL/sec after TUIP and from 8 to 21 mL/sec after TURP.

Dorflinger and coworkers (1992) randomly assigned 60 patients to either TURP or TUIP. They found that both operations significantly improved symptom score and maximal flow rates, but the improvement in flow rate was better for the TURP group. Neither operation caused any significant change in sexual activity or erectile function postoperatively. Retrograde ejaculation was a more common occurrence in patients treated by TURP. Riehmann and colleagues (1995) randomly assigned 56 patients to TURP and 61 to TUIP, and there was a mean follow-up of 34 months. Differences in peak urinary flow improvement were significant statistically at 3 months and 24 months only and not at any other time. Retrograde ejaculation was twice as common in the TURP group. Reoperation was required in slightly more patients in the TUIP group, but the difference was not statistically significant. The AHCPR BPH Guideline Panel (McConnell et al, 1994) carried out a meta-analysis of the various studies, and the results are noted in Table 88–5. There is a slightly better chance of improvement of symptoms of patients treated by TURP, as there is in the degree of that improvement.

Conclusion

TUIP is effective in treating patients with lower urinary tract symptoms caused by bladder outlet obstruction. It has been shown to have an important role in the management of younger patients, especially if the prostate is smaller than 30 g. The efficacy is comparable in such patients with TURP, and the results are maintained in the long term. The technique is simple, and the morbidity is low.

OTHER TECHNOLOGIES

There are some other approaches that have not been previously mentioned in this chapter, but they are included only to complete the picture. There is no significant evidence available to support any of these as having a future in the treatment of symptomatic BPH. The literature mainly consists of open studies, which in many cases would correspond to phase I trials or very small phase II trials.

Water-Induced Thermotherapy

Water-induced thermotherapy is another treatment introduced to treat lower urinary tract symptoms and to reduce bladder outlet obstruction secondary to BPH. An early paper (Corica et al, 2000) assessed its effect on prostatic tissue, using it in both benign and malignant prostates, in 27 patients. The patients were awake, with local anesthetic gel inserted urethrally. The discomfort experienced by patients was recorded as mild. On pathologic examination of the removed prostate, periurethral hemorrhagic necrosis, extending up to 11 mm from the urethra; focal or extensive urothelial denudation; and mild inflammation were found. These changes were consistently seen.

The same group of authors subsequently developed a novel rapid high-temperature, liquid-filled, flexible balloon thermotherapy system (Corica et al, 2003). The same anesthesia as previously was used in 17 patients, and a full histologic study was carried out. Again, consistent findings were recorded, including periurethral hemorrhagic necrosis, extensive denudation, and varying degrees of inflammation. The mean depth of necrosis was 0.9 cm, involving a mean of 16% of the prostatic adenoma. In the prostates examined later, the necrotic tissue had been replaced by scar tissue (fibrosis and hyalinization) with a mean depth of 0.13 cm.

In a small open study, two slightly different temperatures were used in two groups of patients (Breda and Isgro, 2002). Because of the small numbers, the results are somewhat difficult in that the temperature did not matter and that previously catheter-dependent patients were able to void with a Qmax of 10.7 to 11.5 mL/sec in 73% to 88% of patients.

There has been a prospective multicenter trial performed involving 125 patients (Muschter et al, 2000). Improvement was noted at 3 months, extending to 12 months. The I-PSS at 12 months had improved by a median of 12.5 symptom units, the Qmax by 6.4 mL/sec over baseline. This was not a comparative study. Side effects were minimal. The authors concluded that the treatment held promise as a useful and cost-effective option for management of BPH. In a later review of the topic, the failure rate and rate of subsequent TURP were reported as 5.6% after 12 months, 9.6% after 24 months and 11.2% after 36 months (Muschter, 2003).

Table 88–5. **Treatment Outcomes Balance Sheet**		
	TUIP	*TURP*
Chance of symptom improvement	78-83% (80)	75-96% (88)
Degree of symptom improvement	73%	85%
Morbidity (20% significant)	2.2-33% (14)	5.2-30.7% (16)
Mortality (30-90 days)	0.2-1.5%	0.53-3.31%
Incontinence—total	0.061–1.1%	0.68-1.4%
Operative treatment for surgical complications	1.34-2.65%	0.68-10%
Impotence	3.9-24.5%	3.3-34.8%
Retrograde ejaculation	6-55%	25-99%

TUIP, Transurethral incision of the prostate; TURP, transurethral resection of the prostate.
From Barry MJ, Fowler FJ Jr, O'Leary MP, et al: The American Urological Association's symptom index for benign prostatic hyperplasia. J Urol 1992;148:1549-1557. Copyright © 1992, Lea & Febiger.

Transurethral Ethanol Ablation of the Prostate

This technique has not been subjected to a great deal of in-depth study. It was initially introduced as a transperineal injection, with phenol being the agent injected (Talwar and Pande, 1966; Angell, 1969). There was clear evidence from several early studies that the agent injected leaked extraprostatically, with consequently a relatively high incidence of significant adverse events. The development of a transurethral method of injecting ethanol has been seen as a safer approach (Goya et al, 1999; Ditrolio et al, 2002). A detailed description of the injection technique is to be found in these articles and in the study presented by Plante and colleagues (2003), who also describe the histologic findings observed in the canine prostate. They found a considerable lobular volume of necrosis (mean of 42.6%), and although the findings were not absolutely consistent, they found that the prostate capsule always acted as a relative barrier to ethanol diffusion after transurethral injection.

A European multicenter study has been performed in 115 symptomatic BPH patients using transurethral ethanol ablation of the prostate (Grise et al, 2004), and 94 of these patients were followed up for 12 months. An average reduction in prostate volume of 16% was found, with a small adverse event rate and a requirement for TURP in 7% of patients in that time period. Relatively modest improvements in I-PSS and Qmax were reported, with 98% of patients voiding spontaneously 4 days after treatment.

Rotoresection of the Prostate

This technique has not been widely reported, but early studies, both experimental and clinical, have been published. It has been designed for conventional transurethral application, with an axially adjustable actively rotating crank with a milling-head spiked electrode fitting into a specifically designed working element instead of a loop electrode. It is driven by a micromotor, which transmits rotation to the electrode by an angled drill handle. The first use of this system was reported by Michel and coworkers in 1996. In an experimental porcine model, they found a rate of time ablation comparable to that of a standard resection loop (5.5 to 6.0 g/min) and more than twice that of electrovaporization (1.7 to 2.0 g/min). The rate of bleeding was significantly better than for either, and the depth of tissue coagulation was 1.5 mm, compared with 0.4 mm with TURP.

There have been three clinical studies. Michel and coworkers (2003) used the rotoresect system in 84 patients and evaluated them for up to 4 years. They found no change in hemoglobin or serum sodium. The mean duration of catheterization was 1.4 days. There was an early significant improvement in I-PSS and Qmax, which lasted to the 4-year evaluation.

A prospective study was carried out, and results at 12 months (Wadie et al, 2003) **and 24 months** (Wadie et al, 2005) **have been published. In the latter report, the results of 23 of the original 24 patients have been evaluable. The AUA symptom score decreased from 20.5 ± 3.8 to 1.12 ± 1.56, and** the Qmax rose from 8.7 ± 2.1 to 21.8 ± 8.5 mL/sec, results comparable to those reported earlier. Again, the complication rate was found to be low.

SUMMARY

I have carefully reviewed the literature on minimally invasive therapies and endoscopic management of BPH since writing the chapter in the last edition of *Campbell's Urology*. It must be said that there is very little new apart from the explosion of interest in the newer types of laser therapy. Many of the recent papers on thermotherapy describe newer techniques but once again fail to get to the meat of the subject, which is to answer the question as to the exact position of thermotherapy in the management of BPH. Even in the case of the laser therapies, the authors do not tell the reader if they consider that they will actually overtake TURP and supplant it in the future. In addition, the standard of trials has not improved greatly, with many still being open label studies with no comparator group; some of the comparative studies have group sizes that do not give the impression of having been powered statistically to show either equivalence or a specifically stated difference. There have been several new meta-analyses or systematic literature reviews, which may help the reader to make a more balanced, evidence-based decision.

There has been much discussion of which of these therapies is better than TURP. At present, it would seem that TURP is either equivalent to the best of the minimally invasive therapies or better than most in terms of improvement of subjective and objective indices. As was stated in the introduction, however, it is not only the efficacy of the treatment that must be compared with TURP. The adverse event profile, the requirement for IV sedation, length of hospitalization, and cost are all very important also.

The vast majority of trials that have been reported compare a treatment with TURP only against efficacy, whereas it would be of benefit to the urologist if trials could view the comparison of the other factors in a prospective way, perhaps even excluding efficacy. This has been done by some authors, but a major multicenter approach would give the best information. In this way, it would be clear which is the best way to treat BPH.

However, the view could be taken that it is not necessary to find a minimally invasive treatment that is better than TURP. For example, none of the drug treatments have even come close to the efficacy of TURP, but they have been demonstrated to be of lasting value in management and have found a very specific place in the treatment armamentarium of BPH. In that case, the questions just posed would need to be answered very carefully.

It might be considered controversial to state that perhaps patients should be allowed to have sequential treatments. It is known that some patients do not respond well to specific minimally invasive treatments, so perhaps they might have a second treatment with the same modality, even a relatively short time after the first. There may be cost implications that would have the hospital managers shaking their heads, but it would certainly lower hospital bed requirements if it proved successful. In the same way, if a treatment proved efficacious for a 3-year period and then the symptoms returned, it is conceivable that a further treatment might return the patient to symptomatic well-being, even if a further full evaluation was required.

What is definitely necessary is that the exact place for each treatment modality should be found. Some may well have a small but well-defined role in the management of BPH, and, in the case of others, this role may be larger. One of the problems with extracorporeal shock wave lithotripsy was that it took a long time to find exactly how it should be used to treat, for example, staghorn renal calculi; no comparative trial was performed. In the same way, TURP was introduced without a comparative trial; and although it is recognized now as the gold standard, it took several decades before this happened. Minimally invasive treatments are in most cases pitted against TURP, but with many of them this has been a wasted exercise because in the preliminary open studies they could have clearly been seen not to be as efficacious. Commercial necessity requires comparison against a recognized treatment, but often this is not in the patients' best interests. It may be that the treatment has a lesser, but equally important, role to play.

At the International Consultation on BPH, held in July 2000, the committee that discussed "International Therapy for Benign Prostatic Hyperplasia" prepared a report (Debruyne et al, 2001). In it, they outline final recommendations on the use of such treatments and define them as acceptable, acceptable with restriction, investigational, or unacceptable. This decision was based on several meetings between the members of the panel and is rather a suggestion than an instruction to urologists.

The panel found that a number of treatments for BPH were unacceptable: balloon dilatation, hyperthermia, and high-intensity focused ultrasound. It is widely accepted that this is so, and these treatments have not been dealt with in this chapter because it is unlikely that they will have a role in the future in their present form. Prostatic stents are deemed acceptable with restriction, which once again is not controversial because that restriction has been clearly described in the large number of original and review articles related to them.

Rather more interesting is the list of treatments described as being acceptable, presumably without restriction in the minds of the panel: TUMT, transurethral needle ablation, interstitial laser coagulation, laser-vaporization, and transurethral electrovaporization (naturally, TURP and open prostatectomy are also included). It may be that these newer treatments are acceptable, but it is absolutely necessary to define in what way and to remember that, in most of these treatments, the results are short term. In some cases, they may be considered as possible replacements for TURP, but, in that case, a large amount of further information is required related to the points previously discussed and to long-term efficacy. In the case of those being considered as alternative treatments for BPH not necessarily as good as TURP, their exact role needs to be defined.

It is very likely that some day TURP will be replaced as the ideal interventional treatment for BPH. It took a considerable amount of time for TURP to achieve its exalted position, but it could happen soon that some other treatment will occupy that position.

KEY POINTS

- Intraprostatic stents are confined to alternative therapy for BPH for patients unfit for TURP.

- Transurethral needle ablation has been modified several times and has a significant beneficial effect on Qmax and I-PSS. Not enough long-term studies are available.

- The literature base for transurethral microwave therapy is inconsistent, and it is not possible to draw conclusions on long-term efficacy. It also improves Qmax and I-PSS.

- The holmium laser and the high-power PVP laser are the most popular instruments in this technology section and are efficacious in improving Qmax and I-PSS, probably in a way that is comparable to TURP. Long-term studies are required.

- TUVP and TUIP are also effective, particularly for small prostates, but have not overtaken TURP as the chosen method to treat obstructive BPH.

- In well-trained hands, TURP is a safe and effective way of treating BPH, with an acceptable side effect profile.

- Other means of prostatic resection, such as rotoresection of the prostate, are under evaluation, without long-term multicenter trials as yet. The efficacy of water-induced thermotherapy and ethanol injection of the prostate remains unproved.

SUGGESTED READINGS

Boyle P, Robertson C, Vaughan ED, Fitzpatrick JM: A meta-analysis of trials of transurethral needle ablation for treating symptomatic benign prostatic hyperplasia. BJU Int 2004;94:83-88.

Emberton M, Neal DE, Black N, et al: The National Prostatectomy Audit: The clinical management of patients during hospital admission. Br J Urol 1995;75:301-316.

Hoffman RM, MacDonald R, Wilt TJ: Laser prostatectomy for benign prostatic obstruction. Cochrane Database Syst Rev 2004;(1):CD001987.

McAllister WJ, Absalom MJ, Mir K, et al: Does endoscopic laser ablation of the prostate stand the test of time? Five-year results from a multicentre randomised controlled trial of endoscopic laser ablation against transurethral resection of the prostate. BJU Int 2000;85:437-439.

Mebust WK, Holtgrewe HL, Cockett ATK, et al: Transurethral prostatectomy: Immediate and postoperative complications. A cooperative study of thirteen participating institutions evaluating 3,885 patients. J Urol 1989;141: 243-247.

Roehrborn CG, Preminger G, Newhall P, et al: Microwave thermotherapy for benign prostatic hyperplasia with the Dormier Urowave: Results of a randomized, double blind, multicenter, sham-controlled study. Urology 1998;51:19-28.

Tan AH, Gilling PJ, Kennett KM, et al: Long-term results of high-power holmium laser vaporization (ablations) of the prostate. BJU Int 2003; 92:707-709.

Te AE, Malloy TR, Stein BS, et al: Photoselective vaporization of the prostate for the treatment of benign prostatic hyperplasia: 12-month results from the first United States multicentre prospective trial. J Urol 2004;172:1404-1408.

Wheelahan J, Scott NA, Cartmill R, et al: Minimally invasive non-laser thermal techniques for prostatectomy: A systematic review. BJU Int 2000;86:977-988.

89 Retropubic and Suprapubic Open Prostatectomy

MISOP HAN, MD, MS • ALAN W. PARTIN, MD, PhD

OVERVIEW

The treatment options for bladder outlet obstruction caused by benign prostatic hyperplasia (BPH) have been expanded dramatically over the past two decades with the development of medical and minimally invasive therapies. The current medical therapies for lower urinary tract symptoms include selective long-acting α_1-adrenergic antagonists, such as terazosin (Hytrin) (Lepor et al, 1992; Roehrborn et al, 1996), doxazosin (Cardura) (Gillenwater et al, 1995), and tamsulosin (Flomax) (Abrams et al, 1995), and the 5α-reductase blockers, such as finasteride (Proscar) (Gormley et al, 1992; Andersen et al, 1995; Lepor et al, 1996) and dutasteride (Avodart) (Roehrborn et al, 2002, 2004). Minimally invasive procedures include visual laser ablation of the prostate (Cowles et al, 1995), transurethral electrovaporization of the prostate (Kaplan et al, 1996), transurethral needle ablation (Schulman et al, 1993; Campo et al, 1997), transurethral microwave thermotherapy (Ogden et al, 1993; Javle et al, 1996), interstitial laser coagulation (Muschter and Hofstetter, 1995) and transurethral incision of the prostate (Cornford et al, 1997). However, these approaches are usually reserved for men with moderate symptoms and a small to medium-sized prostate gland.

For patients with acute urinary retention, persistent or recurrent urinary tract infections, severe hemorrhage from the prostate, bladder calculi, severe symptoms unresponsive to medical therapy, or renal insufficiency as a result of chronic bladder outlet obstruction, transurethral resection of the prostate (TURP) or open prostatectomy is indicated. **When compared with TURP, open prostatectomy offers the advantages of a lower retreatment rate and more complete removal of the prostatic adenoma under direct vision and avoids the risk of dilutional hyponatremia (the TURP syndrome), which occurs in approximately 2% of patients undergoing TURP** (Mebust et al, 1989). Several contemporary series have demonstrated objective improvement in urinary symptoms following open prostatectomy (Tubaro et al, 2001; Gacci et al, 2003; Varkarakis et al, 2004). **The disadvantages of open prostatectomy compared with TURP include the need for a lower midline incision and a resultant longer hospitalization and convalescence period. In addition, there may be an increased potential for perioperative hemorrhage** (Serretta et al, 2002).

Open prostatectomy can be performed by either the retropubic or suprapubic approach. **In retropubic prostatectomy, the enucleation of the hyperplastic prostatic adenoma is achieved through a direct incision of the anterior prostatic capsule.** This approach to open prostatectomy was popularized by Terrence Millin, who reported the results of the procedure in 20 patients in *Lancet* in 1945 (Millin, 1945). **The advantages of this procedure over the suprapubic approach are (1) excellent anatomic exposure of the prostate, (2) direct visualization of the prostatic adenoma during enucleation to ensure complete removal, (3) precise transection of the urethra distally to preserve urinary continence, (4) clear and immediate visualization of the prostatic fossa after enucleation to control bleeding, and (5) minimal to no surgical trauma to the urinary bladder. The disadvantage of the retropubic approach, compared with the suprapubic prostatectomy, is that direct access to the bladder is not achieved.** This may be important when one considers excising a concomitant bladder diverticulum or removing bladder calculi. The suprapubic approach may also be the preferred method when the obstructive prostatic enlargement includes a large intravesical median lobe.

Suprapubic prostatectomy, or transvesical prostatectomy, consists of the enucleation of the hyperplastic prostatic adenoma through an extraperitoneal incision of the lower anterior bladder wall. This approach to open prostatectomy was first carried out by Eugene Fuller in New York in 1894; it was later popularized by Peter Freyer in London, who

2845

described the procedure in 1900 and later reported the results of his first 1000 patients in 1912 (Freyer, 1912). The major advantage of this suprapubic procedure over the retropubic approach is that it allows direct visualization of the bladder neck and bladder mucosa. As a result, *this operation is ideally suited for patients with (1) a large median lobe protruding into the bladder, (2) a clinically significant bladder diverticulum, or (3) large bladder calculi.* It may also be preferable for obese men, in whom it is difficult to gain direct access to the prostatic capsule and dorsal vein complex (Culp, 1975). The disadvantage, compared with the retropubic approach, is that direct visualization of the apical prostatic adenoma is reduced. As a result, the apical enucleation is less precise, and this factor may affect postoperative urinary continence. Furthermore, hemostasis may be more difficult because of inadequate visualization of the entire prostatic fossa after enucleation.

INDICATIONS FOR OPEN PROSTATECTOMY

The indications for prostatectomy, by either open approach or transurethral resection, include (1) acute urinary retention; (2) recurrent or persistent urinary tract infections; (3) significant symptoms from bladder outlet obstruction not responsive to medical therapy; (4) recurrent gross hematuria of prostatic origin; (5) pathophysiologic changes of the kidneys, ureters, or bladder secondary to prostatic obstruction; and (6) bladder calculi secondary to obstruction. Currently, transurethral resection accounts for over 90% of prostatectomies performed for BPH.

Open prostatectomy should be considered when the obstructive tissue is estimated to weigh more than 75 g. If sizable bladder diverticula justify removal, suprapubic prostatectomy and diverticulectomy should be performed concurrently. If the prostatectomy is performed without the diverticulectomy, incomplete emptying of the bladder diverticulum and subsequent persistent infection may occur. Large bladder calculi that are not amenable to easy transurethral fragmentation may also be removed during the open procedure. Open prostatectomy should also be considered when a man presents with ankylosis of the hip or other orthopedic conditions, preventing proper positioning for transurethral resection. Also, it may be wise to perform an open prostatectomy in men with recurrent or complex urethral conditions, such as urethral stricture or previous hypospadias repair, to avoid the urethral trauma associated with transurethral resection. Finally, the association of an inguinal hernia with an enlarged prostate suggests an open procedure, as the hernia may be repaired through the same lower abdominal incision (Schlegel and Walsh, 1987).

Contraindications to open prostatectomy include a small fibrous gland, the presence of prostate cancer, and previous prostatectomy or pelvic surgery that may obliterate access to the prostate gland.

PREOPERATIVE EVALUATION

In deciding whether to perform an open prostatectomy for symptomatic obstruction related to BPH, it may be necessary to consider the upper and lower urinary tracts. Usually the patient has already completed the International Prostate Symptom Score (I-PSS) questionnaire and had a peak urinary flow rate determination. The postvoid residual urine volume may also have been verified with an abdominal ultrasound examination. A cystoscopic examination is not indicated in the routine evaluation of a patient with obstructive voiding symptoms (McConnell et al, 1994). However, cystoscopy should be performed in men with hematuria, suspected urethral stricture, bladder calculus, or diverticulum. It can also be helpful in confirming the presence of a large median lobe or in assessing the length of the prostatic urethra. For this indication, it is ideal to perform the cystoscopic examination under anesthesia just prior to surgery, when the pelvic floor musculature is relaxed.

Before performing an open prostatectomy, the presence of prostate cancer should be excluded. All men should undergo a digital rectal examination and have a serum prostate-specific antigen determination. If the digital rectal examination detects induration or nodularity or the serum prostate-specific antigen level is elevated, a transrectal ultrasound-guided biopsy of the prostate gland should be performed. Transrectal ultrasonography, by itself, is not indicated as a first-line diagnostic test for evaluating the prostate gland to detect early, curable prostate cancer. However, it can be useful in determining prostate size.

The upper urinary tracts should be evaluated preoperatively in men with known renal disease, abnormal renal function, recurrent urinary tract infection, or hematuria. This can be accomplished by an intravenous pyelogram with a postvoid drainage film or computed tomography in patients with normal renal function or by renal sonography in men with compromised renal function. Magnetic resonance imaging scan is not commonly indicated.

Prior to surgery, the patient should undergo a complete medical evaluation consisting of a detailed history, thorough physical examination, and an appropriate laboratory assessment. Most patients are of an age with an increased risk for cardiovascular and pulmonary disease, hypertension, diabetes mellitus, and other medical conditions. All abnormalities uncovered in this evaluation should be addressed. The patient's medications should be reviewed and attention should be given to the agents such as aspirin and nonsteroidal anti-inflammatory agents that can contribute to perioperative bleeding. These medications should be discontinued and therapeutic anticoagulation reversed before surgery. In addition, a chest radiograph, electrocardiogram, routine electrolytes, coagulation studies, and a complete blood count are usually required for these patients before surgery.

Men with urinary retention should have evaluation of renal function. If serum creatinine is elevated, surgery should be delayed until this parameter stabilizes. Urinalysis is performed to rule out a urinary tract infection, and if infection is suspected, a urine specimen should be sent for culture and sensitivity. If an infection is present, appropriate antimicrobial therapy must be instituted prior to surgery to prevent urinary sepsis (Serretta et al, 2002).

Historically, 5% to 10% of men undergoing an open prostatectomy require one or more units of blood in the perioperative period (Serretta et al, 2002; Varkarakis et al, 2004). Thus, it may be prudent to have one or two units of blood available intraoperatively. Patients who are concerned about infectious processes associated with blood transfusion can donate one to two units of their own blood prior to surgery so that it is available at the time of the procedure. The preferred autologous donation schedule is one unit per week, with the last donation being 2 weeks prior to surgery. During this process, the patient should receive an oral iron supplement (ferrous sulfate or ferrous gluconate).

Lastly, the patient must be informed of the benefits and risks associated with open prostatectomy and written informed consent should be obtained. Clearly, the benefit to be achieved is improved urination. **Potential risks include urinary incontinence, erectile dysfunction, retrograde ejaculation, urinary tract infection, bladder neck contracture, urethral stricture, and the need for a blood transfusion. Other potential untoward effects include deep vein thrombosis and pulmonary embolus.**

OPERATING DAY PREPARATION

The patient is kept without oral intake after midnight and self-administers a Fleet enema the morning of surgery. The type of the anesthesia to be used and the risks associated with it are discussed and finalized with the patient and his family in conjunction with the anesthesiologist. One dose of a first- or second-generation cephalosporin is administered before making the incision.

SURGICAL TECHNIQUE
Anesthesia

The preferred anesthesia is spinal or epidural. Regional anesthesia may reduce intraoperative blood loss and the frequency of postoperative deep vein thrombosis and pulmonary embolus (Peters and Walsh, 1985). **General anesthesia is utilized when there is a medical or anatomic contraindication to regional anesthesia or when the patient simply prefers general anesthesia.**

Retropubic Prostatectomy
Proper Positioning of the Patient

When anesthesia has been induced, the patient is positioned on the operating table in a supine position. If a cystoscopic examination is to be performed, the patient is prepared and draped in the usual manner for a transurethral diagnostic procedure. Flexible cystoscopy, in this situation, obviates major repositioning of the patient. Following the cystoscopy, the table is placed in a mild Trendelenburg position without extension of the table.

Incision and Exposure of the Prostate

The suprapubic area is shaved, prepared, and draped in the usual sterile manner. A No. 22 Fr urethral catheter with a 30-mL balloon is passed into the bladder and connected to a sterile closed-drainage system and the balloon is inflated with 30 mL of saline. A lower midline incision from the umbilicus to the pubic symphysis is made. It is deepened through the subcutaneous tissue. **The linea alba is incised, allowing the rectus abdominis muscles to be separated in the midline.**

The transversalis fascia is incised sharply *to expose the space of Retzius.* At the superior aspect of the wound, the posterior rectus abdominis fascia is incised above the semicircular line to the level of the umbilicus. The peritoneum is mobilized cephalad starting at the pubic symphysis and swept anterolaterally. The pelvis is inspected for any abnormalities and the inguinal area examined for hernias. If such a hernia is identified, it can be repaired using the preperitoneal approach described by Schlegel and Walsh (1987). A self-retaining Balfour retractor is placed in the incision and widened. A well-padded, malleable blade is connected to the retractor and used to displace the bladder posteriorly and superiorly. Unlike the procedure in an anatomic radical retropubic prostatectomy, the balloon of the catheter is not positioned beneath the malleable blade. Instead, it is allowed to rest at the level of the bladder neck and aids in identifying the prostatovesical junction later in the operation. The anterior surfaces of the bladder and prostate are exposed. Using DeBakey forceps and Metzenbaum scissors, the preprostatic adipose tissue is gently removed to expose the superficial branch of the dorsal vein complex and the puboprostatic ligaments (Fig. 89–1).

Hemostatic Maneuvers

Before proceeding with enucleation of the prostatic adenoma, it is important to achieve complete control of the dorsal vein complex as well as the lateral pedicles at the bladder neck (the main arterial blood supply to the prostate gland) (Walsh and Oesterling, 1990). To accomplish this task, the endopelvic fascia is incised laterally and the puboprostatic ligaments are partially transected, similar to the maneuver in an anatomic radical retropubic prostatectomy (Reiner and Walsh, 1979). In patients with marked prostatic enlargement, this maneuver can be easier because the enlarged prostate gland protrudes out from beneath the pubic symphysis. A 3-0 monocryl suture on a 5/8 circle-tapered needle is passed

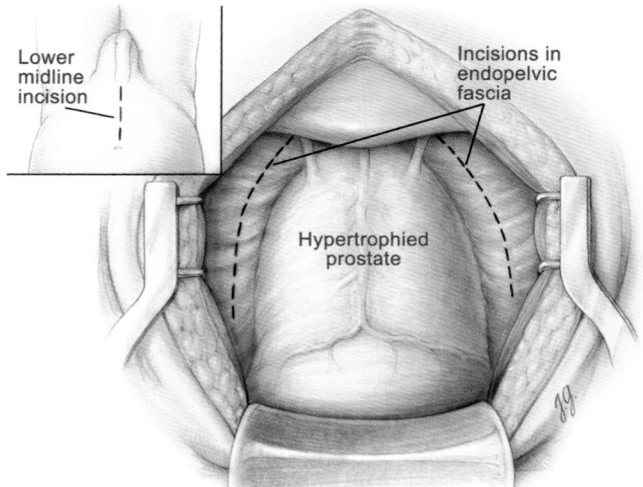

Figure 89–1. Retropubic prostatectomy. The space of Retzius has been opened and the periprostatic adipose tissue has been dissected free from the superficial branch of the dorsal vein complex. The endopelvic fascia is incised bilaterally *(dashed lines)*, and the puboprostatic ligaments are transected bilaterally. (Courtesy of Juan R. Garcia, The Johns Hopkins University, Baltimore, Maryland.)

in the avascular plane between the urethra and the dorsal vein complex at the apex of the prostate and tied (Fig. 89–2A). The superficial branch of the dorsal vein at the bladder should be coagulated or ligated.

At this point, attention is focused on securing the lateral pedicles at the prostatovesical junction. The 30-mL balloon of the catheter is used to identify the junction between the bladder and the prostate. The balloon is then deflated and a chromic suture on a large CTX needle is used to place a figure-of-eight stitch deep into the prostatovesical junction at the level where the seminal vesicles approach the prostate gland bilaterally (Fig. 89–2B). With this maneuver, the main arterial blood supply to the prostate adenoma is controlled. Having secured the dorsal vein complex earlier, the major sources of hemorrhage for this operation have been eliminated.

Enucleation of the Adenoma

With a sponge stick on the bladder neck to depress the bladder posteriorly, a No. 15 blade on a long handle is used to make a transverse capsulotomy in the prostate approximately 1.5 to 2.0 cm distal to the bladder neck (Fig. 89–3). The superficial branch of the dorsal vein complex is transected as the transverse capsulotomy is made. It does not bleed because the dorsal vein complex has previously been controlled both proximally and distally. The incision is deepened to the level of the adenoma and extended sufficiently laterally in each direction to permit complete enucleation. A pair of Metzenbaum scissors is used to dissect the overlying prostatic capsule from the underlying prostatic adenoma. Once a well-defined plane is sufficiently developed, the index finger can be

inserted between the prostatic adenoma and the capsule to develop the plane further laterally and posteriorly (Fig. 89–4). A pair of Metzenbaum scissors is then used to incise the anterior commissure from the bladder neck to the apex, separating the lateral lobes of the prostate anteriorly. The posterior prostatic urethra is exposed and the index finger is inserted down to the verumontanum. The mucosa of the urethra over-

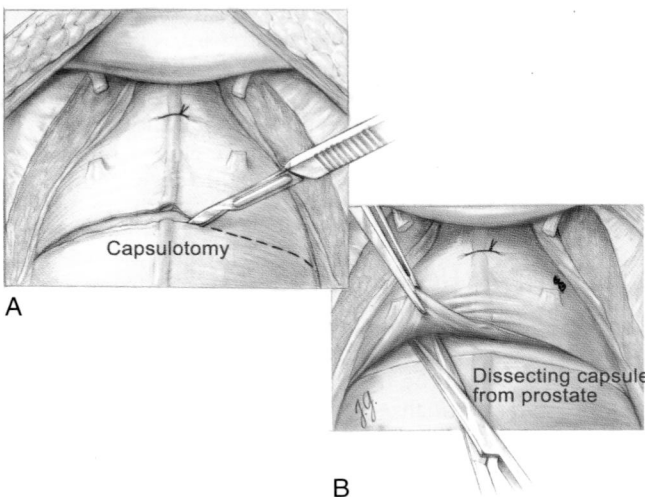

Figure 89–3. Retropubic prostatectomy. **A,** With the superficial branch of the dorsal vein complex secured proximally and distally, a No. 15 blade on a long handle is used to make the transverse capsulotomy. **B,** Metzenbaum scissors are used to develop the plane anteriorly between the prostatic adenoma and the prostatic capsule. (Courtesy of Juan R. Garcia, The Johns Hopkins University, Baltimore, Maryland.)

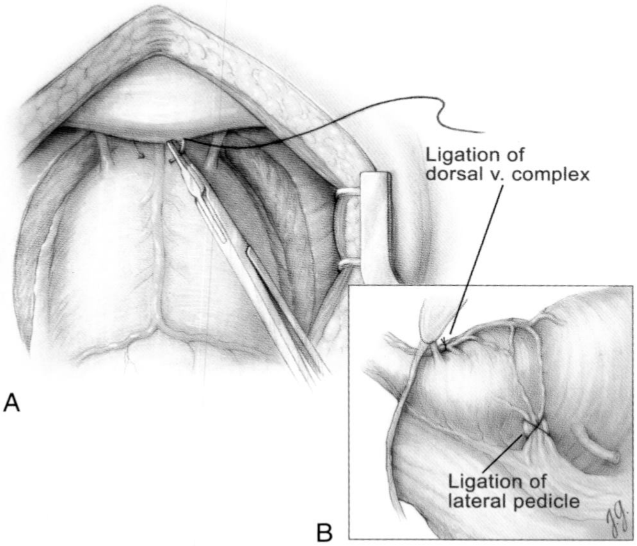

Figure 89–2. Retropubic prostatectomy. **A,** A 2-0 chromic suture on a 5/8 circle-tapered needle is passed in the avascular plane between the urethra and the dorsal vein complex at the apex of the prostate. A tie is grasped and tied around the dorsal vein complex. **B,** Using a 2-0 chromic suture on a CTX needle, a figure-of-eight stitch is placed through the prostatovesical junction just above the level of the seminal vesicles to control the main arterial blood supply to the prostate gland. When placing this stitch, care must be taken to avoid entrapment of the neurovascular bundles located posteriorly and slightly laterally. (Courtesy of Juan R. Garcia, The Johns Hopkins University, Baltimore, Maryland.)

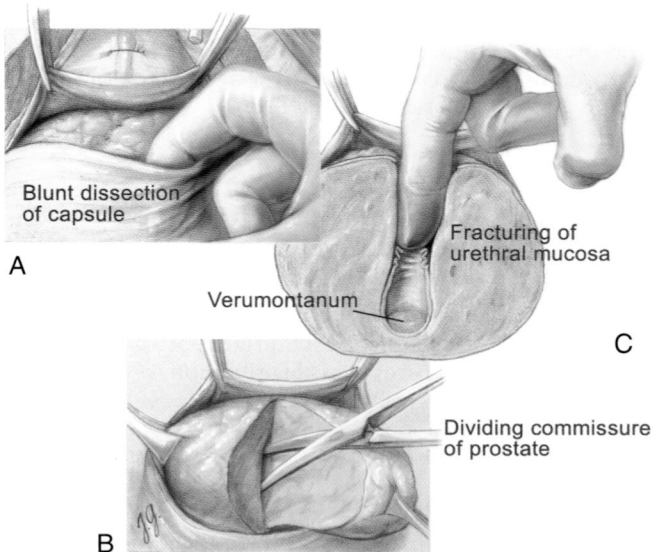

Figure 89–4. Retropubic prostatectomy. **A,** Using blunt dissection with the index finger, the prostatic adenoma is dissected free laterally and posteriorly. **B,** Metzenbaum scissors are used to divide the anterior commissure in order to visualize the posterior urethra and verumontanum. **C,** The index finger is then used to fracture the urethral mucosa at the level of the verumontanum. With the latter maneuver, extreme care is taken not to injure the external sphincteric mechanism. (Courtesy of Juan R. Garcia, The Johns Hopkins University, Baltimore, Maryland.)

lying the left lateral lobe is divided sharply at the level of the apex under direct vision without injury to the external urinary sphincter. With the aid of a Babcock clamp, the left lateral lobe is removed safely. This maneuver is then repeated for the right lateral lobe. If a median lobe is present, the overlying mucosa is incised at the level of the bladder neck, and this lobe is removed (Fig. 89–5). In this manner, the entire prostatic adenoma is removed with preservation of a strip of posterior prostatic urethra. **Because the capsulotomy is a transverse rather than longitudinal incision, there is little risk that the incision will be inadvertently extended into the sphincteric mechanism during the enucleation process, which would compromise subsequent urinary continence.**

The prostatic fossa is now carefully inspected to ensure that all of the adenoma has been removed and that hemostasis is complete. **If hemorrhage is persistent, a 4-0 chromic suture can be used to place a figure-of-eight stitch in the bladder neck at the 5 and 7 o'clock positions. When placing these stitches, it is necessary to visualize the ureteral orifices so that they are not incorporated into the stitches.** Indigo carmine dye may be given intravenously to aid in the visualization of the ureteral orifices if necessary. If the bladder neck appears obstructive at the completion of the operation, it may be appropriate to perform a wedge resection at the 6 o'clock position and advance the bladder mucosa into the prostatic fossa. This maneuver helps prevent the development of a bladder neck contracture.

Closure

After inspecting the bladder for a complete adenoma removal and hemostasis, a No. 22 Fr, three-way Foley catheter with a 30-mL balloon is inserted through the anterior urethra and prostatic fossa into the bladder. With the urethral catheter in place, the prostatic capsule is closed (Fig. 89–6). A 2-0 chromic suture on a 5/8 circle-tapered needle is used to create two running stitches. These stitches begin laterally and meet in the midline; they are first tied separately and then together to create a watertight closure. Fifty milliliters of water is then placed in the balloon to ensure that the catheter balloon remains in the bladder and does not retract into the prostatic

fossa. The bladder is then irrigated with saline to ensure continued hemostasis and to test the capsular closure for leakage. A small, closed-suction drain is placed through a separate stab incision lateral to the prostate and bladder on one side to prevent hematoma and urinoma formation. The pelvis is irrigated with copious amounts of normal saline solution, and the rectus fascia is reapproximated with a No. 1 polydioxanone suture (PDS) on a TP-1 needle in a running fashion. The skin is closed with skin staples. The drain is secured to the abdominal wall, and the urethral catheter is secured to the lower extremity.

Suprapubic Prostatectomy

Proper Positioning of the Patient

After anesthesia has been induced, the patient is positioned on the operating table in a supine position. Cystoscopy, if clinically indicated, is performed as previously described. **The table is placed in a mild Trendelenburg position without extension.** The suprapubic area is shaved. **After the lower abdomen and external genital area are prepared and draped in the usual sterile manner, a No. 22 Fr catheter is inserted into the bladder. After residual urine is drained, 250 mL of saline is instilled into the bladder and the catheter is clamped.**

Incision and Exposure of the Prostate

A lower midline incision is made from the umbilicus to the pubic symphysis (Fig. 89–7). It is deepened through the subcutaneous tissue. The linea alba is incised, allowing the rectus abdominis muscles to be separated in the midline. The transversalis fascia is incised sharply to expose the space of Retzius. At the superior aspect of the wound the posterior rectus

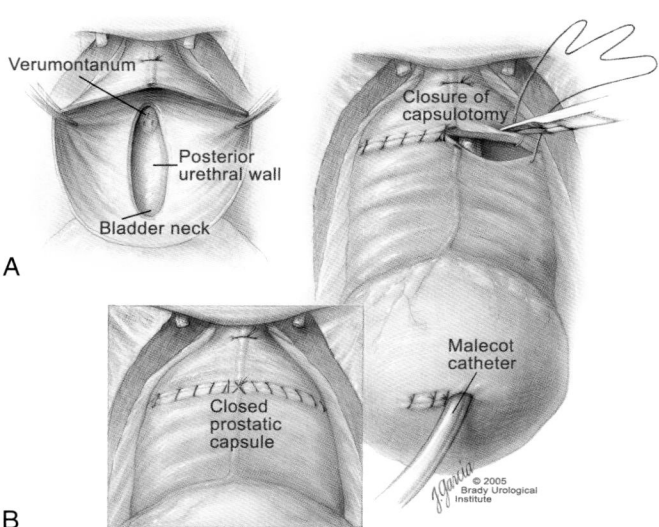

Figure 89–6. Retropubic prostatectomy. **A,** View of the prostatic fossa and posterior urethra after enucleation of all the prostatic adenoma. Note that the verumontanum and a strip of posterior urethra remain intact. **B,** After placement of a urethral catheter and, if needed, a Malecot suprapubic tube, the transverse capsulotomy is closed with two running 2-0 chromic stitches. The two stitches are tied first to themselves and then to each other across the midline to create a watertight closure of the prostatic capsule. (Courtesy of Juan R. Garcia, The Johns Hopkins University, Baltimore, Maryland.)

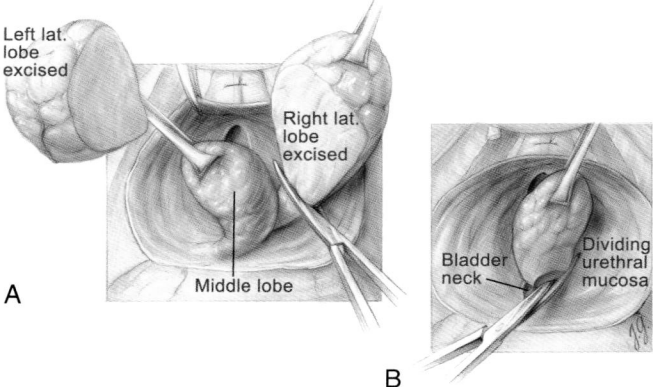

Figure 89–5. Retropubic prostatectomy. **A,** After removal of the left lateral lobe of the prostate, the right lateral lobe is excised with the aid of a tenaculum and Metzenbaum scissors. **B,** Lastly, the median lobe is removed under direct vision. (Courtesy of Juan R. Garcia, The Johns Hopkins University, Baltimore, Maryland.)

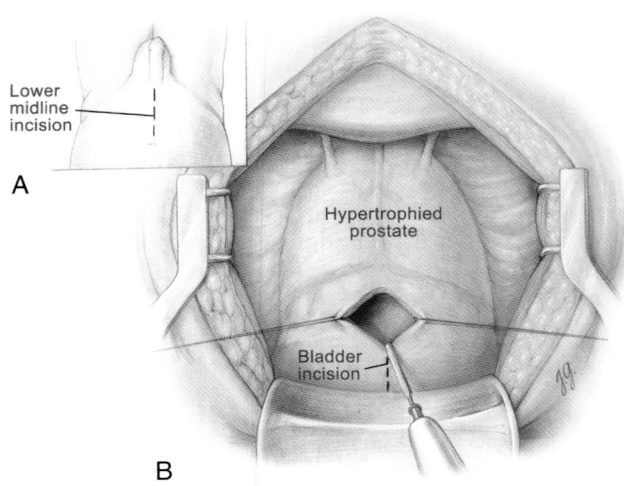

Figure 89–7. Suprapubic prostatectomy. **A,** A lower midline incision is made from the umbilicus to the pubic symphysis. **B,** After developing the prevesical space, a small, longitudinal cystotomy is made with an electrocautery. (Courtesy of Juan R. Garcia, The Johns Hopkins University, Baltimore, Maryland.)

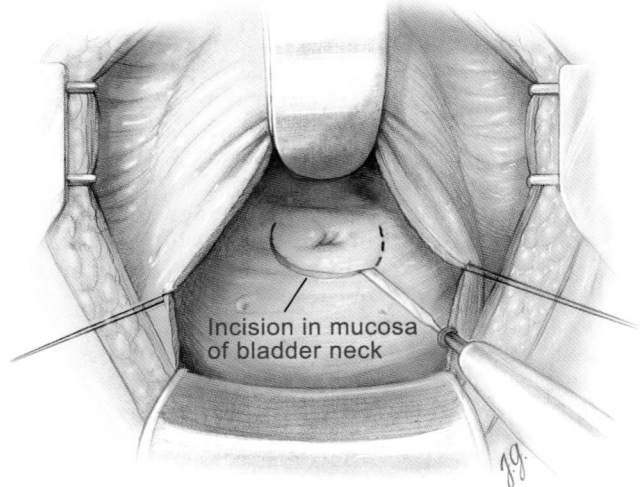

Figure 89–8. Suprapubic prostatectomy. With adequate exposure of the bladder neck, a circular incision in the bladder mucosa is made distal to the trigone, using an electrocautery. (Courtesy of Juan R. Garcia, The Johns Hopkins University, Baltimore, Maryland.)

abdominis fascia is incised above the semicircular line to the level of the umbilicus and the peritoneum is then swept cephalad to develop the prevesical space. A self-retaining Balfour retractor is placed in the incision to retract the rectus muscles laterally. The anterior bladder wall is identified, and two 3-0 Vicryl stitches are placed on each side of the midline below the peritoneal reflection. **A vertical cystotomy is made with an electrocautery. Using a pair of Metzenbaum scissors, a cystotomy is then extended cephalad and caudally to within 1 cm of the bladder neck (Fig. 89–8). Several pairs of stay stitches are placed using 3-0 Vicryl sutures on each side of the midline to facilitate exposure. A figure-of-eight stitch using a 3-0 Vicryl suture is placed and tied at the most caudal position of the cystotomy to prevent further extension of the cystotomy incision during blunt finger dissection of the adenoma.** Alternatively, a transverse bladder incision can be utilized. After inspecting the bladder, a well-padded, malleable blade is placed in the bladder, connected to the Balfour retractor, and used to retract the bladder cephalad. The bladder neck and prostate gland can now be visualized. A narrow Deaver retractor can be placed over the bladder neck and used to expose the trigone further. **Indigo carmine dye may be given intravenously to aid in the visualization of the ureteral orifices if it should be necessary.**

Enucleation of the Adenoma

An electrocautery is used to create a circular incision in the bladder mucosa distal to the trigone (see Fig. 89–8). Care is taken not to injure the ureteral orifices. Using a pair of Metzenbaum scissors, the plane between the prostatic adenoma and prostatic capsule is developed at the 6 o'clock position (Fig. 89–9). Once a well-established plane is created posteriorly, the prostatic adenoma is dissected circumferentially and inferiorly toward the apex, using blunt dissection (Fig. 89–10). At the apex, the prostatic urethra is transected using a pinch action of two fingertips, avoiding excessive traction so as not to avulse the urethra and injure the sphincteric mechanism.

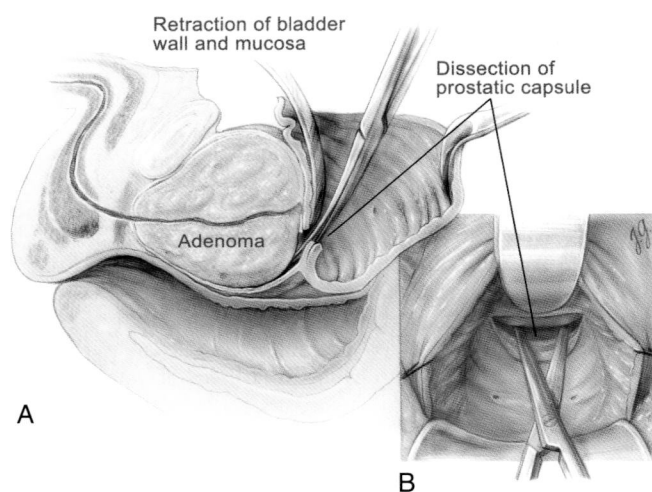

Figure 89–9. Suprapubic prostatectomy. **A,** Starting at the bladder neck posteriorly, Metzenbaum scissors are used to develop the plane between the prostatic adenoma and the prostatic capsule (lateral view). **B,** Anterior view of the same maneuver. (Courtesy of Juan R. Garcia, The Johns Hopkins University, Baltimore, Maryland.)

At this point the prostatic adenoma, as either one unit or separate lobes, can be removed from the prostatic fossa.

Hemostatic Maneuvers

Following enucleation of the adenoma, the prostatic fossa is inspected for residual tissue. If found, these nodules are removed by sharp or blunt dissection. **The prostatic fossa must also be examined for discrete bleeding sites, which can frequently be controlled with an electrocautery or 4-0 chromic suture ligatures. In addition, a 0-chromic suture is used to place two figure-of-eight stitches to advance the bladder mucosa into the prostatic fossa at the 5 o'clock and 7 o'clock positions at the prostatovesical junction to ensure**

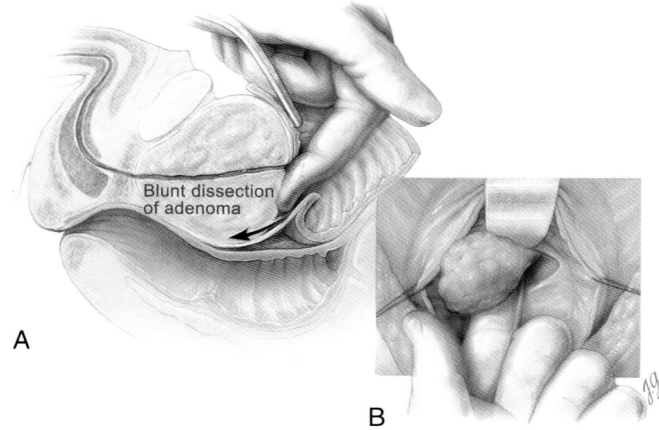

Figure 89–10. Suprapubic prostatectomy. **A,** Using the index finger, the prostatic adenoma is enucleated from the prostatic fossa (lateral view). **B,** Anterior view of the same maneuver. With extreme large prostate glands, the left, right, and median lobes should be removed separately. (Courtesy of Juan R. Garcia, The Johns Hopkins University, Baltimore, Maryland.)

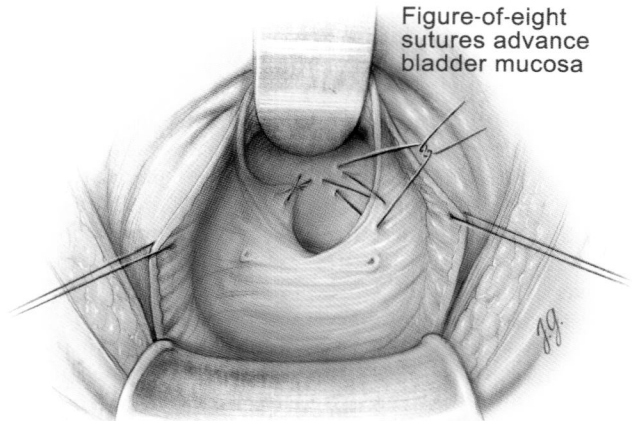

Figure 89–11. Suprapubic prostatectomy. After enucleation of the entire prostatic adenoma, a 0-chromic suture is used to place two figure-of-eight stitches to advance bladder mucosa into the prostatic fossa at the 5 and 7 o'clock positions at the prostatovesical junction to ensure control of the main arterial blood supply to the prostate. (Courtesy of Juan R. Garcia, The Johns Hopkins University, Baltimore, Maryland.)

control of the main arterial blood supply to the prostate (Fig. 89–11). With this maneuver, hemostasis is usually complete.

If hemorrhage remains pronounced despite the hemostatic stitches, a No. 2 nylon purse-string suture can be placed around the vesical neck, brought out through the skin, and tied firmly, as described by Malament (1965). This maneuver closes the bladder neck and tamponades the prostatic fossa. The nylon suture is removed by cutting it at the skin and applying gentle traction on postoperative day 2 or 3. Plicating sutures can be placed transversely in the posterior prostatic capsule to prevent further bleeding, as described by O'Conor (1982).

Closure

A No. 22 Fr urethral catheter with a 30-mL balloon is passed through the urethra into the bladder. In addition, a No. 20 to 24 Fr Malecot suprapubic tube is placed into the dome of the bladder and secured with a 4-0 chromic purse-string stitch. The suprapubic tube exits the bladder through a separate stab incision at the lateral aspect of the dome, avoiding the peritoneal cavity (Fig. 89–12). Next, **the cystotomy incision is closed in two layers.** The first layer of closure is performed using a 2-0 Vicryl suture to create two running stitches. Care is taken to get a small amount of bladder mucosa in the stitch. The two stitches begin cephalad and caudally and meet in the midbladder, where they are first tied separately and then together. Previously placed 3-0 Vicryl stay sutures are tied over the first layer of closure to complete the two-layer closure. With this approach, the bladder closure is watertight and completed in a timely manner. Fifty milliliters of saline is placed in the balloon to ensure that the catheter balloon remains in the bladder and does not retract into the prostatic fossa. The urethral catheter and suprapubic tube are irrigated to confirm a watertight closure and to verify that hemorrhage is minimal. A small, closed-suction drain is placed through a separate stab incision lateral to the bladder. The drain exits the skin on the opposite side of the suprapubic tube. The pelvis is irrigated with copious amounts of normal saline solution, and the

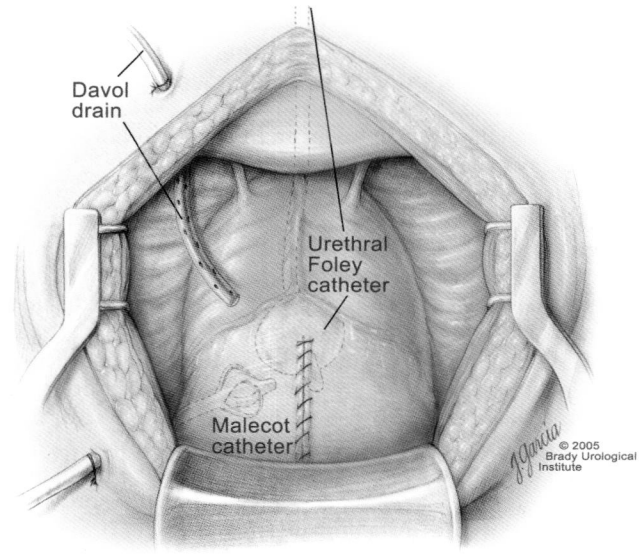

Figure 89–12. Suprapubic prostatectomy. After placing a urethral catheter and a Malecot suprapubic tube, the cystotomy is closed in two layers using a running 2-0 Vicryl suture, enforced by tying of multiple interrupted 3-0 Vicryl stay sutures. A closed, Davol suction drain is placed on one side of the bladder and exits through a separate stab incision. (Courtesy of Juan R. Garcia, The Johns Hopkins University, Baltimore, Maryland.)

rectus fascia is closed with a No. 1 PDS suture on a TP-1 needle in a running fashion. The skin is closed with skin staples. Next, the suprapubic tube and drain are secured to the abdominal wall, and the urethral catheter is anchored to the lower extremity.

POSTOPERATIVE MANAGEMENT

In the recovery room, the outputs from the pelvic drain, suprapubic tube, and urethral catheter are monitored. In addition, it is routine to verify the hematocrit. **If significant hemorrhage is noted, the urethral catheter may be placed on traction so that the balloon containing 50 mL of saline can compress the bladder neck and prostatic fossa. Constant and reliable traction can be maintained by securing the catheter to the abdomen. In addition, continuous bladder irrigation should be initiated to prevent clot formation. For maximal effect, the inflow should be through the urethral catheter and the outflow through the suprapubic tube.** For most patients these measures are adequate and effective. **However, if excessive bleeding persists after these measures, the urethral catheter can be removed in the operating suite and a cystoscopic inspection of the prostatic fossa and bladder neck can be performed to identify and fulgurate discrete bleeding sites. If marked hemorrhage continues to persist, open reexploration should be strongly considered.**

On the evening of the day of surgery, the patient is asked to perform the dorsiflexion and plantarflexion exercises 100 times per hour while awake and to perform pulmonary exercises. Effective pain management consists of intravenous morphine sulfate on an as-needed basis through a patient-controlled analgesic pump.

On the first postoperative day, the patient is started on a clear liquid diet and asked to ambulate four times per day. Pulmonary exercises are continued. **If the hematuria is resolved, continuous bladder irrigation can be discontinued with both urethral catheter and suprapubic tube placed to gravity drainage. Also, the balloon in the urethral catheter is partially deflated to 30 mL of saline and residual clots are removed by irrigation.**

On the second postoperative day, if urine is clear, the urethral catheter may be removed and the suprapubic tube is clamped to allow a voiding trial. The patient is encouraged to ambulate and continue pulmonary exercises. **When the patient tolerates a regular diet, oral analgesics can be given and parenteral narcotics discontinued.** Appropriate discharge instructions are reviewed with the patient at this time in preparation for discharge on the third day following surgery. **On the third postoperative day, the pelvic drain is removed if the drainage is less than 75 mL per 24-hour period.** The skin staples are removed and replaced with Steri-Strips in nonobese men. A pathologic examination of the enucleated prostatic adenoma should be performed to confirm the absence of adenocarcinoma of the prostate.

On discharge from the hospital, the patient is encouraged to increase his activity gradually. If the patient voids well with a minimal postvoid residual urine volume, the suprapubic tube is removed in the clinic on the fifth day following surgery. He should be able to resume full activity 4 to 6 weeks postoperatively with outpatient visits at 6 weeks and 3 months.

COMPLICATIONS

The overall rate of morbidity and mortality associated with open prostatectomy is extremely low. Historically, excessive hemorrhage had been a major concern. With modern surgical techniques, blood loss is now minimal and the need for a blood transfusion is uncommon. In retropubic open prostatectomy, controlling the dorsal vein complex distal to the apex of the prostate and ligating the lateral pedicles to the prostate at the prostatovesical junction markedly reduce venous and arterial bleeding, respectively. Nevertheless, it may still be prudent to have one to two units of autologous blood available at the time of open prostatectomy.

Urinary extravasation can also be of concern in the immediate postoperative period; this most likely results from an incomplete closure of the prostatic capsulotomy in retropubic prostatectomy or the cystotomy in suprapubic prostatectomy. It usually resolves spontaneously with continued catheter drainage. The drain should be left in place until urinary extravasation ceases.

Following an open prostatectomy, urgency and urge incontinence may be present for several weeks to several months, depending on the preoperative bladder status. If the condition is severe, the patient may be given an anticholinergic agent such as oxybutynin (Ditropan). Stress incontinence and total incontinence are rare. With a precise enucleation of the prostatic adenoma, risk of injury to the external sphincter mechanism is minimal. If stress incontinence does result after the procedure, the patient may benefit from transurethral collagen injections for a mild condition or an artificial urinary external sphincter when the situation is more severe.

Late urologic complications are not common. Acute cystitis rarely occurs as long as the patient voids to completion. Acute epididymitis can occur occasionally if infected urine refluxes into the ejaculatory ducts.

Erectile dysfunction occurs in approximately 3% to 5% of patients undergoing an open prostatectomy; it is more common in older men than in younger men. *Retrograde ejaculation occurs in approximately 80% to 90% of patients following surgery.* The risk of this adverse effect is reduced if the bladder neck is preserved at the time of surgery. Also, approximately 2% to 5% of patients develop a bladder neck contracture 6 to 12 weeks after an open prostatectomy (Tubaro et al, 2001; Varkarakis et al, 2004). This commonly occurs in men who have a relatively small opening at the bladder neck at the end of the operation. As stated earlier, for these men, it may be appropriate to perform a wedge resection at the 6 o'clock position and advance the bladder mucosa into the prostatic fossa in the retropubic prostatectomy. However, if a bladder neck contracture does develop, the initial management should be dilatation with urethral sounds or a direct vision incision of the bladder neck using a Collings knife to create a No. 22 Fr opening in diameter.

The most common nonurologic adverse effects include deep vein thrombosis, pulmonary embolus, myocardial infarction, and a cerebral vascular event. The incidence of any one of these complications is less than 1%, and the overall mortality rate associated with this operation should approach zero (Varkarakis et al, 2004).

SUMMARY

Open prostatectomy, whether performed by a retropubic approach or a suprapubic approach, is an excellent treatment option for (1) men with symptomatic bladder outlet obstruction related to benign prostatic hyperplasia causing a markedly enlarged prostate gland, (2) individuals with a concomitant bladder condition such as a bladder diverticulum or large bladder calculi, and (3) patients who cannot be placed in the dorsal lithotomy position for a transurethral

resection of the prostate gland. With improved surgical technique, these procedures can be routinely performed in a precise manner with minimal hemorrhage. Efficacy, in terms of durable improvement in symptom score and peak urinary flow rate, is superior to that of other treatment options available for the obstructing prostate gland, including TURP. Meanwhile, complications are minimal and the length of hospitalization has been markedly reduced. For most patients, the length of hospital stay is 3 days or less. Thus, for the properly selected individual, an open prostatectomy is a highly effective and well-tolerated operation.

KEY POINTS

- Open prostatectomy should be considered when the obstructive tissue is estimated to weigh more than 75 g or sizable bladder diverticula or calculi exist.

- Before performing an open prostatectomy, the presence of prostate cancer should be excluded.

- Potential risks of open prostatectomy include urinary incontinence, erectile dysfunction, retrograde ejaculation, urinary tract infection, bladder neck contracture, urethral stricture, deep vein thrombosis, pulmonary embolus, and the need for blood transfusion.

- Advantages of open prostatectomy over TURP are a lower retreatment rate, more complete removal of the prostatic adenoma under direct vision, and no risk of TURP syndrome.

- Disadvantages of open prostatectomy over TURP are a lower midline incision, longer hospitalization, and increased potential for perioperative hemorrhage.

- Two approaches to open prostatectomy are retropubic and suprapubic

- Suprapubic prostatectomy is ideal for men with a large median lobe, clinically significant bladder diverticulum, or large bladder calculi.

SUGGESTED READINGS

Gacci M, Bartoletti R, Figlioli S, et al: Urinary symptoms, quality of life and sexual function in patients with benign prostatic hypertrophy before and after prostatectomy: A prospective study. BJU Int 2003;91:196-200.

Malament M: Maximal hemostasis in suprapubic prostatectomy. Surg Gynecol Obstet 1965;120:1307.

Millin R: Retropubic prostatectomy: New extravesical technique: Report on 20 cases. Lancet 1945;2:693.

O'Conor VJ Jr: An aid for hemostasis in open prostatectomy: Capsular plication. J Urol 1982;127:448.

Serretta V, Morgia G, Fondacaro L, et al: Open prostatectomy for benign prostatic enlargement in southern Europe in the late 1990s: A contemporary series of 1800 interventions. Urology 2002;60:623-627.

Tubaro A, Carter S, Hind A, et al: A prospective study of the safety and efficacy of suprapubic transvesical prostatectomy in patients with benign prostatic hyperplasia. J Urol 2001;166:172-176.

Varkarakis I, Kyriakakis Z, Delis A, et al: Long-term results of open transvesical prostatectomy from a contemporary series of patients. Urology 2004;64:306-310.

Walsh PC, Oesterling JE: Improved hemostasis during simple retropubic prostatectomy. J Urol 1990;143:1203-1204.

90 Epidemiology, Etiology, and Prevention of Prostate Cancer

ERIC A. KLEIN, MD • ELIZABETH A. PLATZ, SCD, MPH • IAN M. THOMPSON, MD

EPIDEMIOLOGY
Incidence and Mortality Trends

Incidence

Prostate cancer has been the most common visceral malignant neoplasm in U.S. men since 1984, now accounting for one third of all such cancers (Jemal et al, 2004). The estimated lifetime risk of disease is 17.6% for whites and 20.6% for African Americans, with a lifetime risk of death of 2.8% and 4.7%, respectively (Table 90–1). The incidence of prostate cancer peaked in 1992, approximately 5 years after introduction of prostate-specific antigen (PSA) as a screening test; it fell precipitously until 1995 and has been rising slowly since, at a slope similar to that observed before the PSA era (Fig. 90–1). The fall in incidence between 1992 and 1995 has been attributed to the "cull effect" of identifying previously unknown cancers in the population by the use of PSA, followed by a return to baseline, when fewer cases were detected in previously screened individuals (Stephenson et al, 1996). For 2005, the American Cancer Society estimates 232,090 new cases of prostate cancer in the United States (American Cancer Society, 2005).

Mortality

Prostate cancer mortality rates in the United States rose slowly between 1973 and 1990 (Fig. 90–2). This may have resulted from a gradual increase in the number of biologically lethal cancers or a decreasing use or effectiveness of therapy during this interval. In the early 1990s, an abrupt rise in mortality was observed. This increase may have been caused by an increase in attribution bias occurring when the National Center for Health Statistics made a change from manual to automated methods for assignment of cause of death (Feuer et al, 1999). **Subsequent to 1991, the peak mortality year, steady declines in prostate cancer mortality were reported for the next decade. The magnitude of this decline is nearly 2.5 times larger than the increase in mortality seen as a result of attribution bias, so it seems likely that the declines in prostate cancer mortality in the United States since 1991 are real and clinically significant** (Stephenson, 2004). In 2005, the American Cancer Society estimates 30,350 prostate cancer–related deaths in the United States, for an approximate annual rate of 30 per 100,000 population, representing a 25% decrease from the peak in 1991 (American Cancer Society, 2005). **Furthermore, the mortality rate for prostate cancer in white men in the United States has declined to a level lower than that observed before the introduction of PSA-based screening in 1987** (Tarone et al, 2000).

The observed decline in mortality since 1991 is temporally related to increased diagnostic and treatment activity in both the pre-PSA and PSA eras. Rates of both radical prostatectomy and radiation therapy rose steadily through the 1980s (pre-PSA era), whereas hormone therapy and no-treatment rates remained stable (Stephenson, 2004). Outcomes for patients treated in the 1980s should be reflected in the mortality data of the 1990s, whereas outcomes for patients treated in the PSA era (the 1990s) have had less time to affect recent mortality data. **Given the long natural history of low-stage cancers detected in the PSA era, their treatment would not be expected to have a substantial effect on mortality statistics for 10 to 15 years. Additional observation time is necessary to determine if screening, PSA-induced stage migration, and more aggressive use of therapy have contributed to declining mortality.**

Racial Differences

Whereas anthropologists accept that there are subtle biologic differences between populations, commonly used categories such as African American, white, and Hispanic are social and cultural descriptors that have no defined biologic basis. **Observed disease-related differences between groups defined in this fashion may therefore be reflective of common environmental exposure, diet, lifestyle, and attitudes toward health care more than of differences in genetic structure or function. Recognizing these caveats, it is noteworthy that African American men have the highest reported incidence of prostate cancer in the world, with a relative incidence of 1.6 compared with white men in the United States** (American Cancer Society, 2005). **Furthermore, age-adjusted prostate cancer–related mortality is 2.4 times higher for African Americans than for whites.** Recent Medicare data quantify this difference, demonstrating a 1.8-year shorter survival for African Americans with localized disease treated by radical prostatectomy, 0.7 year shorter after radiation therapy, and 1 year shorter in those choosing watchful waiting, findings that persist after adjustment for other covariates including education and income levels (Godley et al, 2003).

Many biologic, environmental, and social hypotheses have been advanced to explain these differences: postulated differences in genetic predisposition; differences in mechanisms of tumor initiation, promotion, or progression; higher fat diets, higher serum testosterone levels, or higher body mass index; structural, financial, and cultural barriers to screening, early detection, and aggressive therapy; and physician bias. Differences in screening rates between whites and African Americans may play a role in explaining the differences in mortality, since a more completely screened population will have better apparent survival because of the inclusion of more individuals with nonlethal cancers. **Currently, there are no data to clearly indicate that any of these hypotheses is the determining factor in explaining the observed differences in incidence or mortality, and it seems likely that the source of the disparity is multifactorial.** Recent observations suggest that the incidence of organ-confined disease at diagnosis among African Americans is increasing, that the disparity in mortality is lessening in the PSA era, and that those with organ-confined disease can be cured at a high rate regardless of race (Powell et al, 2004; American Cancer Society, 2005-2006).

The incidence of prostate cancer in other ethnic groups is lower than that in whites and African Americans. Comparative data for prostate cancer–related mortality are not available for these groups.

Worldwide Incidence and Mortality

Prostate cancer is the fourth most common male malignant neoplasm worldwide. Its incidence varies widely between countries and ethnic populations, and disease rates differ by more than 100-fold between populations. The lowest yearly incidence rates occur in Asia (1.9 cases per 100,000 in Tianjin, China) and the highest in North America and Scandinavia, especially in African Americans (272 cases per 100,000) (Quinn and Babb, 2002). As in the United States, prostate cancer incidence has increased in many countries since the early 1990s. Although much of the increase can be correlated with the introduction of PSA screening, some of the increase predates screening (Gronberg, 2003). **Mortality also varies widely among countries, being highest in Sweden (23 per 100,000 per year) and lowest in Asia (<5 per 100,000 per**

Table 90–1. The Burden of Prostate Cancer in the United States

	Whites	African Americans	Total
Incidence*	164.3	272.1	170.1
Mortality*	30.2	73.0	32.9
New cases in 2005	201,320	30,770	232,090
Mortality in 2005	25,300	5,050	30,350
Lifetime risk of disease	17.6%	20.6%	NA
Lifetime risk of death from disease	2.8%	4.7%	NA

*Age standardized per 100,000 population, 1996-2000.
Data from Ries et al, 2004; Jemal et al, 2004; and American Cancer Society, 2005.

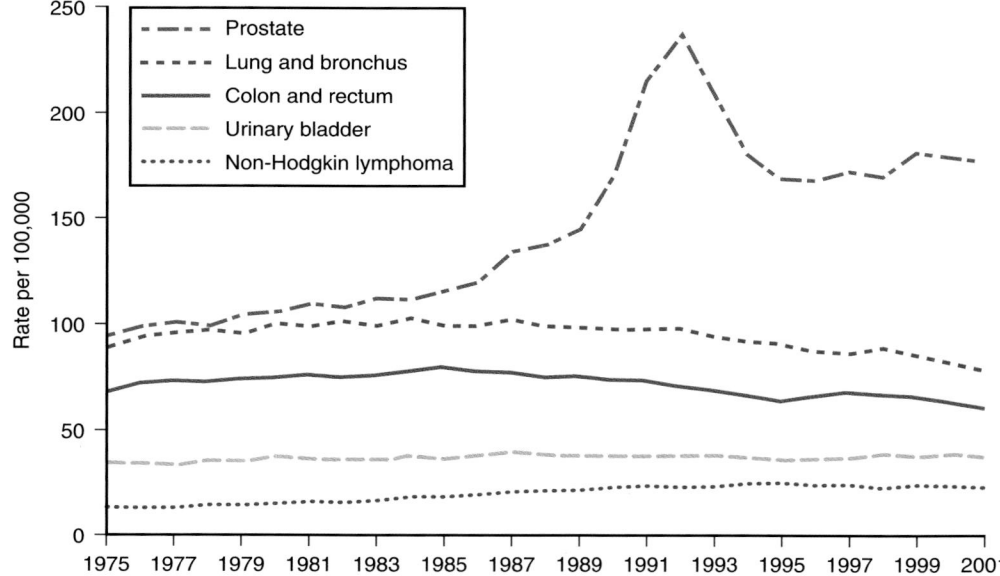

Figure 90–1. Cancer incidence rates for men, United States, 1975-2001, age adjusted to the 2000 U.S. standard population. (Source: Surveillance, Epidemiology, and End Results Program, 1975-2001, Division of Cancer Control and Population Sciences, National Cancer Institute, 2004.)

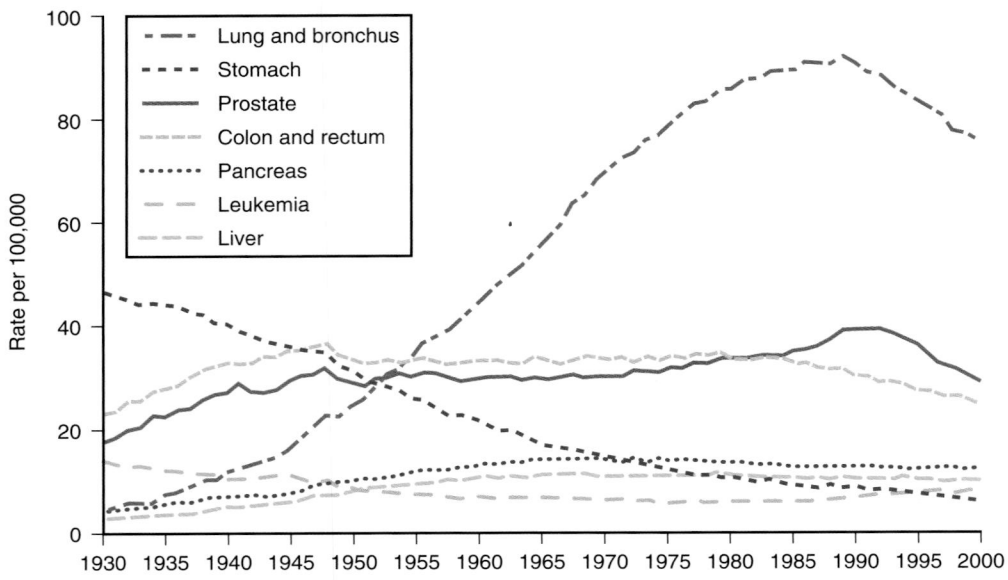

Figure 90–2. Cancer death rates for men, United States, 1930-2000, age adjusted to the 2000 U.S. standard population. (Source: Surveillance, Epidemiology, and End Results Program, 1975-2001, Division of Cancer Control and Population Sciences, National Cancer Institute, 2004.)

year in Singapore, Japan, and China) (Quinn and Babb, 2002). Mortality rates increased slowly for most countries between 1985 and 1995 (Quinn and Babb, 2002).

There are multiple complex causes for the worldwide and ethnic variations in prostate cancer incidence. Access to and quality of health care, accuracy of cancer registries, and penetrance of PSA screening affect how rates of disease are reported. Before reliable data were available from African countries, rates of prostate cancer in Africa were thought to be much the same as those in Asia. However, in Uganda and Nigeria, prostate cancer is common, and it is the most common cancer in men in Nigeria (Gronberg, 2003).

Environment also plays an important role in modulating prostate cancer risk around the world. Japanese and Chinese men in the United States have a higher risk for development of prostate cancer and dying of it than do their relatives in Japan and China (Muir et al, 1991; Shimizu et al, 1991). Likewise, prostate cancer incidence and mortality have increased in Japan as the country has become more westernized (Landis et al, 1999). However, Asian Americans have a lower prostate cancer incidence than white or African American men do, indicating that genetics still plays a role in determining prostate cancer predisposition.

Age at Diagnosis

Prostate cancer is rarely diagnosed in men younger than 50 years, accounting for less than 0.1% of all patients. Peak incidence occurs between the ages of 70 and 74 years, with 85% diagnosed after the age of 65 years (Ries et al, 2004). At 85 years of age, the cumulative risk of clinically diagnosed prostate cancer ranges from 0.5% to 20% worldwide, despite autopsy evidence of microscopic lesions in approximately 30% of men in the fourth decade, 50% of men in the sixth decade, and more than 75% of men older than 85 years (Sakr et al, 1993; Gronberg, 2003). PSA-based screening has induced an important age migration effect; the incidence of prostate cancer in men 50 to 59 years has increased by 50% between

1989 and 1992 (Hankey et al, 1999), with important implications for deciding on the need for, type of, and complications after therapy.

Stage at Diagnosis

In addition to changes in prostate cancer incidence and mortality during the past several decades, there has been a substantial shift to more favorable stage at presentation in men with newly diagnosed disease. **This clinical stage migration is largely if not exclusively accounted for by PSA screening** (Mettlin et al, 1993). **Since the introduction of PSA testing, the incidence of local-regional disease has increased, whereas the incidence of metastatic disease has decreased** (Newcomer et al, 1997). Diagnosis of local-regional disease increased 18.7% annually in white men between 1988 and 1992 and then decreased, on average, 9.8% annually through 1995 (Hankey et al, 1999). In contrast, the incidence of metastatic disease decreased 1.3% annually from 1988 to 1992 and then 17.9% annually through 1995. **Nonpalpable cancers (AJCC clinical stage T1c) now account for 75% of newly diagnosed disease** (Derweesh et al, 2004). Concomitant with these changes, the percentage of men treated for clinically localized disease with radical prostatectomy increased substantially (Hankey et al, 1999). **Clinical stage migration has also been associated with improvements in 5- and 10-year survival rates, which for all stages combined now are 100% and 92%, respectively** (American Cancer Society, 2005).

The use of PSA has also resulted in a substantial downward pathologic stage migration as evidenced by an increasing incidence of organ-confined disease at radical prostatectomy (Fig. 90–3) (Jhaveri et al, 1999; Derweesh et al, 2004). **The improvement in pathologic stage has been seen for tumors of clinical stages T1 to T3 and for all tumor grades and has resulted in improved cancer-specific survival after external radiation or surgery for patients treated late in the PSA era** (Fig. 90–4) (Jhaveri et al, 1999, Derweesh et al, 2004; Kupelian et al, 2005).

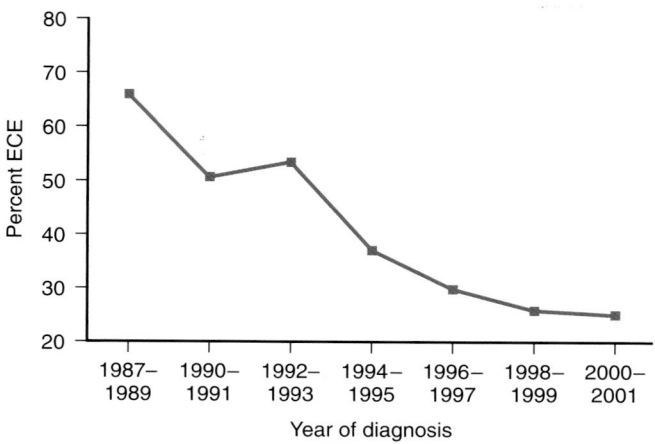

Figure 90-3. Declining rate of extracapsular extension (resulting in increased rate of organ-confined disease) on radical prostatectomy specimens at the Cleveland Clinic, 1987-2001. Since 2001, rates of extracapsular extension (ECE) have remained stable at about 25%.

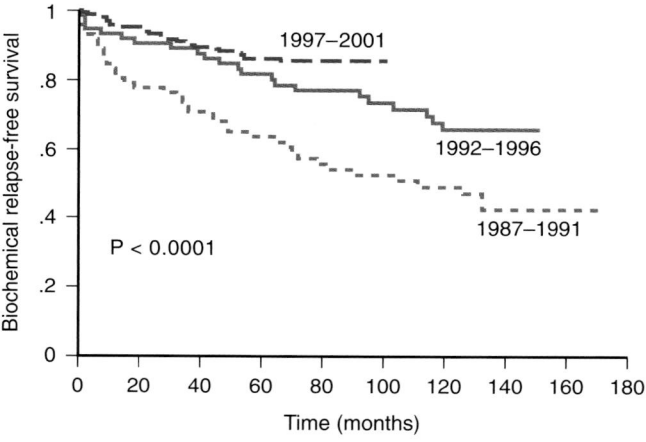

Figure 90-4. Biochemical relapse-free survival after radical prostatectomy at the Cleveland Clinic in the PSA era.

Effect of Screening on Mortality

Screening for prostate cancer remains controversial because of the lack of randomized controlled trials demonstrating a reduction in mortality in screened populations. However, the observed trends in PSA-induced clinical and pathologic stage migration and declining mortality where screening is common provide inferential evidence that screening is beneficial (Horninger at al, 2005). Opponents of screening contend that there is no proof that earlier detection has led to the observed declines in prostate cancer mortality, that increased treatment of screen-detected cancers does more harm than good, and that the long natural history of prostate cancer means that any beneficial effects of screening are not yet evident in mortality statistics (Etzioni et al, 1999). The debate over the effect of screening on mortality is unlikely to be settled until the results of two large, randomized trials in the United States and Europe (the Prostate, Lung, Colorectal, and Ovarian Cancer Screening Trial and the European Randomized Study of Screening for Prostate Cancer) are reported.

Table 90-2. Family History and Risk of Prostate Cancer		
Family History	Relative Risk	Absolute Risk (%)
None	1	8
Father or brother	2	15
Father or brother affected < 60 years	3	20
Father and brother	4	30
Hereditary prostate cancer	5	35-45

From Bratt O: Hereditary prostate cancer: Clinical aspects. J Urol 2002;168:906-913.

RISK FACTORS

Although the specific causes of prostate cancer initiation and progression are not yet known, considerable evidence suggests that **both genetics and environment play a role in the origin and evolution of this disease.** Classic and molecular epidemiology have identified a number of potential risk factors associated with the development of prostate cancer.

Familial and Genetic Influences

Ample epidemiologic evidence suggests that prostate cancer has both a familial and genetic component. The first reports of a familial clustering were published in the mid-20th century and suggested that the risk for development of prostate cancer was higher in those with an affected first-degree relative (Woolf, 1960). Subsequent case-control and cohort studies have confirmed this observation (Eeles et al, 1997). Twin studies have also suggested a genetic component, with higher rates of concordance for monozygotic than for dizygotic brothers (Ahlbom et al, 1994; Gronberg et al, 1994; Page et al, 1997). **Relative risk increases according to the number of affected family members, their degree of relatedness, and the age at which they were affected** (Table 90-2) (Bratt, 2002).

For investigative purposes, prostate cancer may be conveniently divided into three phenotypes: sporadic, familial, and hereditary. Sporadic cancers occur in individuals with a negative family history. Familial prostate cancer is defined as cancer in a man with one or more affected relatives. Hereditary prostate cancer is a subset of the familial form and has been operationally defined as nuclear families with three or more affected members, prostate cancer in three successive generations, or two affected individuals diagnosed with cancer before the age of 55 years (Carter et al, 1993). **Whereas most prostate cancer is likely to be polygenic in origin, the existence of true hereditary prostate cancer is suggested by three epidemiologic observations: (1) relatives of patients younger than 55 years are at higher risk for prostate cancer than are those with older affected relatives; (2) there is stronger familial clustering in families with early-onset prostate cancer; and (3) the number of affected family members and their age at onset are the most important determinants of risk among relatives.** Sporadic cancers account for about 85% of all prostate cancers, and about 15% are familial or hereditary. Hereditary prostate cancer accounts for 43% of early-onset disease (55 years of age or younger) but only 9% of all cancers occurring by the age of 85 years (Carter et al, 1992).

Evidence for major prostate cancer susceptibility genes that segregate in families has been obtained from several complex segregation analyses, with the majority supporting a dominant and the remainder supporting a recessive or X-linked mode of inheritance (Gillanders et al, 2004). **At least eight candidate prostate cancer susceptibility genes have been reported,** including RNase L/*HPC1* (Carpten et al, 2002), *ELAC2/HPC2* (Tavtigian et al, 2001), SR-A/*MSR1* (Xu et al, 2002a), *CHEK2* (Dong et al, 2003a), *BRCA2* (Edwards et al, 2003), *PON1* (Marchesani et al, 2003), *OGG1* (Xu et al, 2002b), and *MIC1* (Lindmark et al, 2004) (Table 90–3). **Individually, these genes are likely to account for only a small fraction of the observed genetic predisposition to prostate cancer.** Other segregation studies have suggested the existence of other prostate cancer susceptibility loci on chromosomes 1q42.2-43 (named *PCAP*) (Berthon et al, 1998), 1p36 (named *CAPB*, also linked to brain tumors) (Gibbs et al, 1999), and Xq27-28 (Xu et al, 1998), but the gene or genes linked to these regions have not been identified. More recent genome-wide scans in larger cohorts of hereditary prostate cancer families have identified additional chromosomal loci linked to prostate cancer, and it is likely that the number of known susceptibility genes will increase (Gillanders et al, 2004).

Of the known susceptibility genes, *HPC1* is the best characterized. The existence of *HPC1* was suggested by a genome-wide scan of families with hereditary prostate cancer (Smith et al, 1996) and later confirmed by linkage studies (Cooney et al, 1997; Eeles et al, 1998). **A subsequent report putatively identified the gene encoding the antiviral and proapoptotic enzyme RNase L as *HPC1*** (Carpten et al, 2002). RNase L is the terminal enzyme of the 2-5A system, an RNA degradation pathway that plays an important role in mediating the biologic effects of interferons, especially in response to viral infection. Type I interferons induce a family of 2-5A synthetases that are activated by double-stranded RNA, resulting in the conversion of ATP to a series of short 2′- to 5′-linked oligoadenylates (2-5A). **2-5A binds with high affinity to RNase L, converting it from its inactive form as a monomer to a potent dimer that degrades single-stranded RNA, preventing viral replication, interfering with protein synthesis, and causing caspase-mediated apoptosis** (Fig. 90–5) (Silverman, 2003). RNase L knockout mice are more susceptible to viral infections (Silverman, 2003). A variety of inactivating and missense mutations of RNase L have been identified in families with hereditary prostate cancer (Xiang et al, 2003). **Of these, the single nucleotide polymorphism R462Q, resulting from an arginine to glutamine substitution, has been shown to be associated with an increased risk of prostate cancer** (Casey et al, 2002); **men and cell lines with this allelic variant have been shown to have reduced RNase L activity leading to deficient apoptosis** (Carpten et al, 2002; Xiang et al, 2003; Malathi et al, 2004), **presumed to lead to an accumulation of genetic defects and to result in cancer.**

The epidemiologic data suggest that *HPC1* is a rare autosomal dominant gene that has high penetrance, meaning that although it does not account for many prostate cancers, an individual carrier is highly likely to be affected by prostate cancer. Cancers linked to *HPC1* have been reported to present with higher grade and more advanced stages, although there are no reported histologic differences with sporadic cancers (Gronberg et al, 1997; Goode et al, 2001). The known molecular pathway of RNase L activation and its downstream targets should allow delineation of molecular strategies aimed at overcoming the enzymatic defect in affected men for both prevention and therapy.

The biologic functions of the other known susceptibility genes fall into several classes. **SR-A/*MSR* and MIC-1 are mediators of inflammation.** SR-A/*MSR1* modulates macrophage–host cell interactions, macrophage adhesion, phagocytosis of apoptotic cells and microbes, and clearance and detoxification of microbial products (Platt and Gordon, 2001). Mice deficient in SR-A/*MSR1* are more susceptible to bacterial infections (Thomas et al, 2000). *MIC1* is a member of the transforming growth factor-β superfamily and regulates macrophage activity (Lindmark et al, 2004). ***PON1* encodes paraoxonases, which bind to high-density lipoprotein in the serum and contribute to the detoxification of organophosphorus compounds and carcinogenic lipid-soluble free radicals from lipid peroxidation** (Marchesani et al, 2003). Both SR-A/*MSR1* and *PON1* have been suggested to play a role in mediating inflammation integral to atherosclerosis (Shih et al, 1998; De Winther et al, 2000). ***CHEK2, BRCA2,* and *OGG1* are important in DNA repair.** *CHEK2* is activated by damaged DNA and acts to prevent it from being replicated by coordination of DNA repair, cell cycle progression, and apoptosis (Dong et al, 2003a). *BRCA2* promotes repair of double-stranded DNA breaks by promotion of homologous recombination. *OGG1* is a DNA glycosylase–AP lyase that repairs oxidative damage to DNA (Boiteux and Radicella, 2000). The function of *ELAC2/HPC2* is unknown, but it is highly expressed in the primate testis and has been linked to germline proliferation (Smith and Levitan, 2004), tRNA 3′ processing endoribonuclease activity (Takaku et al, 2003), and interactions with the γ-tubulin complex of mitotic spindles (Korver et al, 2003).

Table 90–3.	**Prostate Cancer Susceptibility Genes**		
Gene	**Chromosome Location***	**Year Identified**	**Function**
ELAC2/HPC2	17p11	2001	Unknown
RNase L/*HPC1*	1q24-25	2002	Apoptosis and susceptibility to infection
SR-A/*MSR1*	8p22-23	2002	Inflammation and susceptibility to infection
OGG1	3p26.2	2002	DNA repair of oxidative damage
CHEK2	22q12.1	2003	DNA damage signaling and cell cycle control
BRCA2	13q12.3	2003	DNA repair
PON1	7q21.3	2003	Antioxidant, free radical scavenger
MIC1	19p13	2004	Inflammation

*From Online Mendelian Inheritance in Man. Available at: http://www.ncbi.nlm.nih.gov.

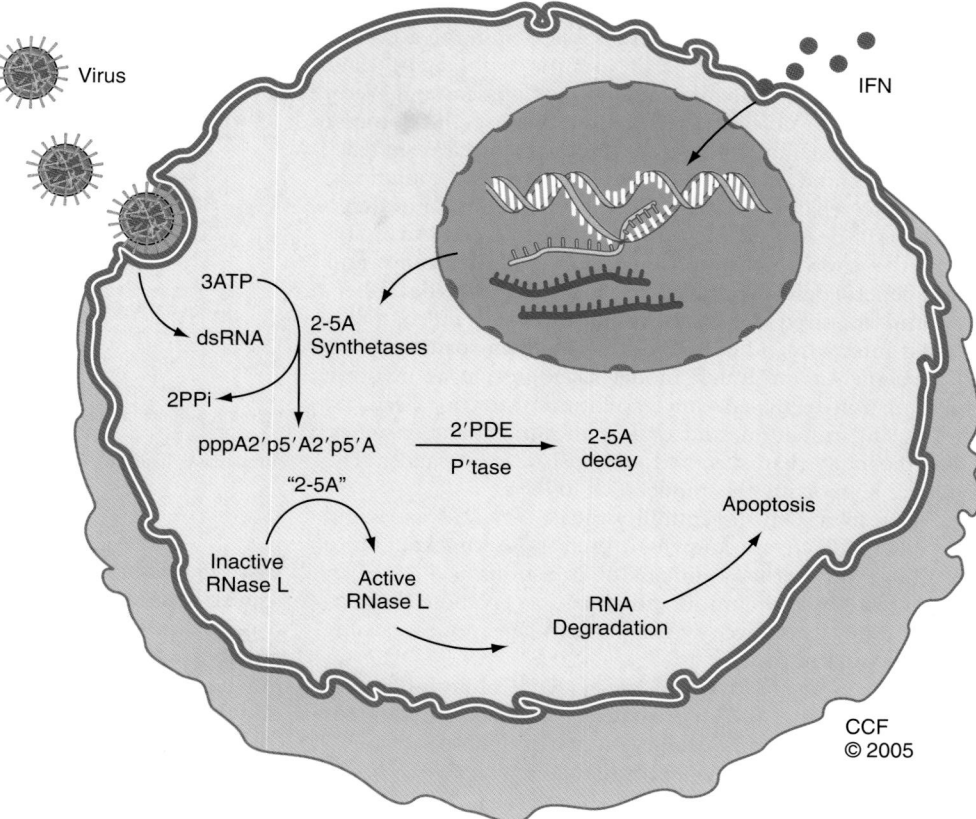

Figure 90–5. Cellular effects of RNase L. In response to interferon (IFN) and viral infection, a family of oligoadenylate synthetases are activated, resulting in the conversion of ATP to a series of short 2′- to 5′-linked oligoadenylates (2-5A). 2-5A binds with high affinity to RNase L, converting it from its inactive form as a monomer to a potent dimer that degrades single-stranded RNA and causes caspase-mediated apoptosis of the host cell. Prostate cancer cells deficient in RNase L are resistant to apoptosis. (Courtesy of R. Silverman, Cleveland Clinic.)

Inflammation, Infection, and Genetic Susceptibility

Chronic inflammation leading to cellular hyperproliferation to replace damaged tissue contributes to the development of infection-associated cancers of the colon, esophagus, stomach, bladder, and liver (Coussens and Werb, 2002; Platz and De Marzo, 2004). Accumulating epidemiologic, histologic, and genetic evidence suggests that a similar process may underlie the development of prostate cancer.

Accumulating evidence suggests that prostate cancer may have an infectious etiology. Two meta-analyses examining 34 case-control studies reported statistically significant associations of prostate cancer with a history of sexually transmitted infection (relative risk = 1.4) or prostatitis (odds ratio = 1.57) (Dennis and Dawson, 2002; Dennis et al, 2002b). Supportive evidence is provided by studies demonstrating positive associations of antibodies against syphilis, human papillomavirus, and human herpesvirus 8 with prostate cancer (Platz and De Marzo, 2004). Case-only or case-control studies have also reported higher plasma concentrations of acute-phase reactants and proinflammatory cytokines in men with prostate cancer (Platz and De Marzo, 2004). Two studies have demonstrated evidence of viral pathogens in human prostate tissue, including polyomavirus, human papillomavirus, and cytomegalovirus (Zambrano et al, 2002; Samanta et al, 2003). **Inflammatory infiltrates and a histologic lesion called proliferative inflammatory atrophy are frequent in clinical** prostate specimens (De Marzo et al, 1999). **Proliferative inflammatory atrophy is a spectrum of lesions characterized by epithelial atrophy, low apoptotic index, and increased proliferative index, usually associated with inflammatory infiltrates** (Putzi and De Marzo, 2000). Inflammation in proliferative inflammatory atrophy may include mononuclear infiltrates in the stroma and macrophages or neutrophils in the glandular lumen or epithelium. Macrophages activated by interferon-γ secrete proinflammatory cytokines and reactive nitrogen species (e.g., nitric oxide). Inducible nitric oxide synthase, which catalyzes the generation of nitric oxide, is overexpressed in macrophages in proliferative inflammatory atrophy but not in normal epithelium (Nelson et al, 2003). It seems that proliferative inflammatory atrophy is a regenerative lesion appearing as a consequence of infection or cell trauma resulting from oxidant damage, hypoxia, infection, or autoimmunity and that its hyperproliferative state leads to cancer. Proliferative inflammatory atrophy is often found adjacent to high-grade prostatic intraepithelial neoplasia or early cancer (Putzi and De Marzo, 2000), and there is an identifiable genetic pathway between proliferative inflammatory atrophy, high-grade prostatic intraepithelial neoplasia, and cancer (Shah et al, 2001; Nakayama et al, 2003; Nelson et al, 2003).

The previously described genetic and histologic observations in prostate cancer strongly suggest that compromised cellular defenses against inflammatory oxidants may initiate and perpetuate prostatic carcinogenesis. Oxidative stress is mediated by reactive oxygen and nitrogen species that bind

DNA and cause mutations, and oxidant stresses from exogenous and endogenous sources are implicated in the accumulation of DNA damage that occurs with aging and subsequently leads to malignant change (Coussens and Werb, 2002). Cellular defense mechanisms against this process include frontline antioxidant enzymes, which scavenge reactive oxygen and nitrogen species and prevent mutations; enzymes to repair mutated DNA; and the ability to undergo apoptosis if the DNA damage is too severe to repair. **An analysis of the known prostate cancer susceptibility genes and other genetic defects in prostate cancer suggests that inherited and acquired defects in cellular defense mechanisms against infection and oxidative stress allow prostate cancer to develop.** An integrated model suggests that as in other inflammation-mediated cancers, chronic infection leads to chronic inflammation, and defects in antioxidant enzymes, DNA repair mechanisms, and apoptosis lead to cancer. The evidence supporting this model is as follows:

1. Defects in two susceptibility genes, *HPC1*/RNase L and SR-A/*MSR1*, are known to predispose knockout mice (and thus perhaps humans) to infections.
2. Infections and chronic inflammation promote the generation of reactive oxygen and nitrogen species, causing oxidative stress.
3. There is abundant histologic evidence of an inflammatory response in the prostate, evidenced by inflammatory infiltrates and proliferative inflammatory atrophy.
4. Defects in frontline antioxidant enzymes *PON1* and *GSTP1* permit oxidative DNA damage.
5. Defects in SR-A/*MSR1* and *MIC1* allow an unrestrained inflammatory response.
6. Defects in RNase L allow mutated cells to escape apoptosis and result in the establishment of clonal expansion of malignant cells.

Subsequent expression by tumor cells of α-methylacyl-CoA racemase (Kumar-Sinha et al, 2004), an enzyme that oxidizes branched-chain fatty acids from dietary sources, results in generation of hydrogen peroxide, which may contribute to continued oxidative stress and tumor growth. This model is illustrated in Figure 90–6. **In addition to providing a framework for further experimental study, this model gives strong theoretical rationale for the use of antioxidants as chemopreventive agents** (see later).

Molecular Epidemiology

In molecular epidemiologic studies of prostate cancer, the association of biomarkers of exposure measured in blood or other tissues is evaluated in relation to incidence or mortality. These biomarkers capture aspects of diet, environmental contaminants, and factors for which concentrations are partly inherently determined. A brief survey of major molecular epidemiologic studies relating to prostate cancer is presented here.

Androgens

Androgens influence the development, maturation, and maintenance of the prostate, affecting both proliferation and differentiation of the luminal epithelium. There is little doubt that a lifetime of variable exposure of the prostate to androgens plays an important role in prostate carcinogene-

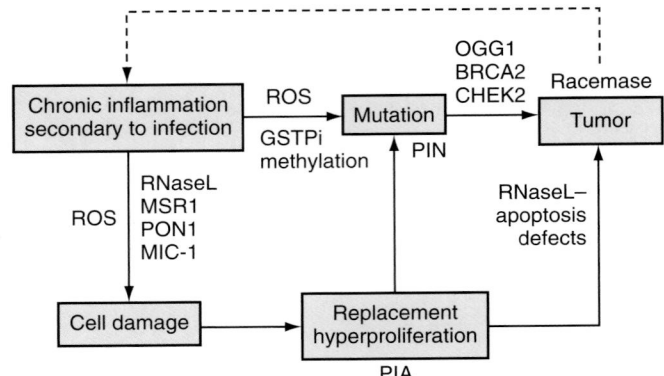

Figure 90–6. Model of prostate cancer pathogenesis related to infection, chronic inflammation, and defects in cellular defense against oxidative stress. See text for details. PIN, prostatic intraepithelial neoplasia; PIA, proliferative inflammatory atrophy; ROS, reactive oxygen species.

sis. One hypothesis is that the higher incidence of prostate cancer observed in African Americans may be related to elevated levels of circulating androgen, as suggested by a study demonstrating that young African American men have a 15% higher total circulating testosterone level than whites do and higher levels of androgen metabolites that reflect levels of 5α-reductase conversion of testosterone to dihydrotestosterone than Japanese men do (Ross et al, 1986, 1992, 1998). **Long-term absence of androgen exposure to the prostate appears to protect against the development of cancer, but a dose-response relationship between androgen levels and cancer risk has not been established. In particular, whether normal-range androgen concentrations are associated with risk of prostate cancer remains unclear** (Hsing, 2001; Chen et al, 2003; Parsons et al, 2004; Platz et al, 2005). A meta-analysis of prospective studies did not find case-control differences in serum androgen concentrations (Eaton et al, 1999), whereas a PSA-era prospective study showed that men with higher plasma total and free testosterone levels had a lower risk of high-grade prostate cancer (Platz et al, 2005).

Androgen receptor mediates testosterone and dihydrotestosterone activity by initiating transcription of androgen-responsive genes. Numerous studies have identified a shortened CAG trinucleotide repeat length in exon 1 to be associated with increased risk as well as advanced, hormone-refractory disease (Balic et al, 2002; Taplin et al, 2003). In vitro studies suggest that long CAG repeat lengths are associated with decreased transactivation of testosterone once it is bound to the androgen receptor (Tut et al, 1997), potentially defining a protective effect against cancer by decreasing epithelial proliferation in response to androgens.

The type II isozyme of steroid 5α-reductase, which converts testosterone to dihydrotestosterone, is encoded by the *SRD5A2* gene. **Polymorphisms of *SRD5A2* have functional consequences in vitro and in humans** (Makridakis and Reichardt, 2004). **Substitution for alanine by threonine at codon 49 confers a fivefold greater enzymatic activity and has been associated with poor prognosis, particularly in Hispanic and African American men** (Makridakis et al, 1999; Jaffe et al, 2000). **Studies to determine if polymorphisms in *SRD5A2* can predict the protective effect of finasteride seen in the Prostate Cancer Prevention Trial** (see later) **are currently under way.**

Genes involved in biosynthesis of testosterone have also been implicated in prostate carcinogenesis. Cytochrome P450c17, encoded by the *CYP17* gene, catalyzes two important steps in the synthesis of testosterone in both the testis and adrenal gland. Some reports have linked a T to C polymorphism in the 5′ untranslated region with an increased risk of prostate cancer in white men, others in hereditary cancer; others have found no association with prostate cancer risk (Nam et al, 2003; Cicek et al, 2004; Loukola et al, 2004). Two homologous and closely linked genes, *HSD3B1* and *HSD3B2*, code for 3β-hydroxysteroid dehydrogenase, an enzyme that catalyzes reductive reactions that inactivate dihydrotestosterone. This enzyme is thought to play an important role in regulating intraprostatic androgen levels. **Case-control studies of *HSD3B2* genetic polymorphisms have identified a complex series of $(TG)_n (TA)_n (CA)_n$ repeats to have substantial differences among different populations at risk for prostate cancer** (Devgan et al, 1997; Chang et al, 2002). Another enzyme, **CYP3A4, is involved in the oxidative degradation of testosterone.** A polymorphism of *CYP3A4* has been associated with locally advanced and poorly differentiated tumors and is found more commonly in African Americans (Ando et al, 1999; Paris et al, 1999; Rebbeck, 2000).

Estrogens

Estrogens have been postulated to protect against prostate cancer by inhibition of prostate epithelial cell growth but alternatively to increase risk by eliciting inflammation in concert with androgens (Naslund et al, 1988) **or by the production of mutagenic metabolites** (Yager, 2000). Estradiol promotes prostate epithelial cell growth through binding of estrogen receptor-α and inhibits growth by effects mediated through estrogen receptor-β (Harkonen and Makela, 2004). **Estrogen receptor-β may play an important role in initiation of prostate cancer.** In estrogen receptor-β knockout mice, there is prostatic epithelial cell hyperplasia characterized by arrested cellular differentiation, an ideal milieu for the development of an epithelium-derived cancer (Imamov et al, 2004). Furthermore, estrogen receptor-β expression is silenced by methylation in human prostate cancer (Horvath et al, 2001; Sasaki et al, 2002; Zhu et al, 2004). **Age-related prostatic disease parallels increases in serum estrogen levels, and there is a low incidence of prostate cancer in cultures with diets rich in phytoestrogens** (Denis et al, 1999). However, the data on serum estrogen levels and prostate cancer risk are mixed (Barrett-Connor et al, 1990; Gann et al, 1996a; Chen et al, 2003). Complicating interpretation of serum measurements is the fact that estradiol can be produced from testosterone by intraprostatic aromatase (Risbridger et al, 2003).

Insulin-like Growth Factor Axis

Insulin-like growth factor 1 (IGF-1) is a peptide hormone that promotes growth in adolescence and childhood and is correlated with adult lean body mass (Severson et al, 1988). IGF-1 promotes proliferation and inhibits apoptosis in normal prostate and tumor cells in vitro (Cohen et al, 1991, 1994).

IGF-1 circulates bound to binding proteins, the most prevalent of which is insulin-like growth factor binding protein 3 (IGFBP-3). In the prostate, IGFBP-3 promotes apoptosis and may mediate growth inhibition by 1,25-dihydroxyvitamin D (Boyle et al, 2001). IGFBP-3 can be cleaved by PSA, reducing its proapoptotic activity (Koistinen et al, 2002).

A positive association between plasma IGF-1 level and prostate cancer is supported by several studies (Mantzoros et al, 1997; Chan et al, 1998; Wolk et al, 1998; Harman et al, 2000; Stattin et al, 2000; Chokkalingam et al, 2001; Khosravi et al, 2001; Stattin et al, 2004a), with a summary adjusted odds ratio of 1.49 (95% confidence interval, 1.14 to 1.95) comparing high and low IGF-1 concentrations in a meta-analysis (Renehan et al, 2004). The findings for IGFBP-3 and prostate cancer risk have been inconsistent (Chan et al, 1998; Harman et al, 2000; Stattin et al, 2000; Chokkalingam et al, 2001; Chan et al, 2002; Renehan et al, 2004; Stattin et al, 2004a).

Leptin

Leptin, a peptide hormone produced by adipocytes, contributes to the control of body weight by modulating energy use and is found at higher levels in obese individuals (Friedman, 2002). Obese men become leptin resistant and exhibit elevated plasma leptin (Chu et al, 2001). **Leptin has been shown to stimulate proliferation of the androgen-independent prostate cancer cell lines DU145 and PC-3** (Onuma et al, 2003; Somasundar et al, 2004). **In addition, leptin appears to induce expression of vascular endothelial growth factor and basic fibroblast growth factor and to stimulate cell migration** (Frankenberry et al, 2004). Associations between circulating leptin concentrations and prostate cancer risk have not been consistent (Lagiou et al, 1998; Chang et al, 2001; Hsing et al, 2001; Stattin et al, 2001, 2003), although one case-control study found that prostate cancer patients were almost five times more likely to carry a polymorphism that results in increased leptin expression compared with controls (Ribeiro et al, 2004). Energy imbalance, perhaps mediated by leptin, is emerging as a possible contributor to the progression of prostate cancer to metastasis and death (Calle et al, 2003; Platz et al, 2003).

Vitamin D, Vitamin D Receptor, and Calcium

Vitamin D (1,25-dihydroxyvitamin D_3) is an essential vitamin that is a part of the steroid hormone superfamily. Human sources are dietary intake and through sunlight exposure, which converts inactive to active vitamin D in the skin. **Interest in vitamin D as a determinant of prostate cancer risk comes from several epidemiologic observations** (Peehl et al, 2003):

1. **Men living in northern latitudes with less sunlight-derived ultraviolet exposure have a higher mortality rate from prostate cancer.**
2. **Prostate cancer occurs more frequently in older men, in whom vitamin D deficiency is more common because of both less ultraviolet exposure and age-related declines in the hydroxylases responsible for synthesis of active vitamin D.**
3. **African Americans, whose skin melanin blocks ultraviolet radiation and inhibits activation of vitamin D, have the highest worldwide incidence and mortality rates for prostate cancer.**

4. **Dietary intake of dairy products rich in calcium, which depresses serum levels of vitamin D, are associated with a higher risk of prostate cancer.**
5. **Native Japanese, whose diet is rich in vitamin D derived from fish, have a low incidence of prostate cancer.**

In addition, prostate cancer cells express vitamin D receptor, and several studies have demonstrated an antiproliferative effect of vitamin D on prostate cancer cell lines by inducing cell cycle arrest (Krishnan et al, 2003).

Many studies show no or weak association between vitamin D levels and prostate cancer risk (Gann et al, 1996b; Chan et al, 2001; Freedman et al, 2002; Platz et al, 2004). The Cancer Prevention Study II Nutrition Cohort, a prospective cohort of 65,321 men, demonstrated a modestly increased relative risk of 1.2 for total calcium intake (dietary and by supplements) and 1.6 for high dietary calcium intake alone ($\geq$2000 versus <700 mg/day) but not for dairy intake (Rodriguez et al, 2003). The results suggest that very high calcium intake above daily recommendation may modestly increase risk. **These conflicting results regarding vitamin D, calcium, and prostate cancer risk may be explained by variants in the vitamin D receptor. Polymorphisms resulting in vitamin D receptor with lower activity have been associated with increased risk for prostate cancer as well as with increased risk of biochemical recurrence after radical prostatectomy** (Mederios et al, 2002; Oakley-Girvan et al, 2004; Williams et al, 2004).

Other Influences

Sexual Activity

Sexual activity has been hypothesized to expose the prostate to infectious agents, which may increase the risk of prostate cancer, akin to the causal relationship between human papillomavirus and cervical cancer in women. Some studies have found a link among early sexual intercourse, number of sexual partners, and prostate cancer (Honda et al, 1988), although not consistently (Ewings and Bowie, 1996; Giles et al, 2003; Fernandez et al, 2005). Two studies have reported a protective effect against prostate cancer for frequent ejaculation with relative risk ranging from 0.66 to 0.89 (Giles et al, 2003; Leitzmann et al, 2004). In the Giles study, the protective effect was seen in men who reported more than five ejaculations per week in their 20s; the large prospective cohort study by Leitzmann demonstrated a protective effect for men reporting 21 or more ejaculations per month in their 20s and 40s, in the previous year, and as a lifetime average. The biologic basis for this effect is not known.

Vasectomy

A relationship between vasectomy and prostate cancer risk was initially suggested in 1993 with a relative risk of 1.6 based on two large cohort studies (Giovannucci et al, 1993a, 1993b). Risk increased with time, so that men who underwent vasectomy at an early age had a higher risk. A recent meta-analysis reported a pooled risk of 1.37, with a linear trend suggesting a 10% increase for each additional 10 years since vasectomy (Dennis et al, 2002a). The biologic mechanism by which vasectomy might predispose to cancer is unknown, although presence of antisperm antibodies and decreased seminal androgen concentrations or secretory activity have been proposed. The magnitude of the relative risk is small enough to potentially be explained by ascertainment bias because men who have undergone vasectomy may be more likely to seek follow-up with a urologist.

Smoking

Cigarette smoke may be a risk factor for prostate cancer because it is a source of cadmium exposure, increases circulating androgen levels, and causes significant cellular oxidative stress. Both case-control and cohort studies have produced conflicting results, and none has demonstrated a clear dose-response relationship, although some studies have suggested an association with more advanced stage at diagnosis and increased prostate cancer–related mortality (Bostwick et al, 2004).

Diet

Descriptive epidemiologic studies of migrants, geographic variations, and temporal studies suggest that dietary factors may contribute to prostate cancer development (Bostwick et al, 2004). The incidence of latent prostate cancers is similar around the world, but the incidence of clinically manifest cancers differs, with Asians having the lowest rates of clinical prostate cancer. Thus, the most convincing evidence for the role of the diet and other environmental factors in modulating prostate cancer risk comes from migration studies showing an increased incidence of prostate cancer in first-generation immigrants to the United States from Japan and China (Muir et al, 1991; Shimizu et al, 1991). These observations suggest that diet may play a role in converting latent tumors into clinically manifest ones. **A strong positive correlation exists between prostate cancer incidence and the corresponding rates of several other diet-related cancers, including breast and colon cancers** (Bostwick et al, 2004).

Dietary Fat

Prostate cancer incidence and mortality rates around the world correlate highly with the average level of fat consumption, especially for polyunsaturated fats (Bostwick, 2003). Potential mechanisms of action include fat-induced changes in the hormonal milieu and induction of oxidative stress. **High levels of dietary fat stimulate proliferation of prostate cancer cells both in vitro and in vivo, and animal models have shown that a fat-free diet can reduce the growth of androgen-dependent tumors in the Dunning model** (Clinton et al, 1988; Wang et al, 1995; Aronson et al, 1999).

Epidemiologic studies on polyunsaturated fat intake and prostate cancer are mixed. Two nested case-control studies suggest a positive association between plasma α-linolenic acid concentration and prostate cancer risk (Gann et al, 1994; Harvei et al, 1997), although another did not (Mannisto et al, 2003). In a small case-control study, men in the top three quartiles of α-linolenic acid consumption had a nonstatistically significant higher prostate cancer risk (Godley et al, 1996). Serum linoleic acid has not been associated with an increased risk of prostate cancer, and some studies are compatible with an inverse association. **Observations on the association of dietary fat and risk may have alternative explanations. Diets high in meat that are sources of fat are also usually low in vegetables, which contain nutrients that** may protect against prostate cancer. Furthermore, meats and dairy products contain other constituents, such as zinc and calcium, that may affect prostate cancer risk.

Obesity

Obesity as measured by body mass index (BMI) has been suggested to be a risk factor for prostate cancer because of their common occurrence in middle-aged men and clear links to colon and breast cancer risk (Giovannucci, 1995; Madigan et al, 1998). White fat in mammals serves not only as an important energy reservoir but also as an endocrine organ, with secretion of cytokines and agents with cytokine-like activity (tumor necrosis factor-α; interleukins 1β, 6, 8, and 10; transforming growth factor-β) as well as their soluble receptors (Trayhurn and Wood, 2004). Several studies have shown that BMI and waist circumference show significant positive correlation with markers of oxidative stress (Keaney et al, 2003; Furukawa et al, 2004). **Treatment of obesity through reduction in fat intake and increased exercise has been shown to reduce oxidative stress, suggesting that lifestyle modification could be important in reducing the risk of prostate cancer** (Roberts et al, 2002).

Cohort studies have examined the relationship between anthropometric variables and prostate cancer risk with conflicting results (Andersson et al, 1997; Giovannucci et al, 1997; Schuurman et al, 2000), although two studies have suggested a protective effect for higher BMI in men 60 years and younger (Giovannucci et al, 2003; Porter and Stanford, 2005). **There is an inverse relationship between circulating androgen levels and measures of obesity** (Svartberg et al, 2004). **This observation may explain why higher BMI is associated with lower serum PSA concentration** (Baillargeon et al, 2005), **which in obese men could lead to ascertainment bias against biopsy, perhaps explaining the previously noted protective effect of obesity on prostate cancer risk.** One study has suggested that severe obesity (BMI ≥ 35) was associated with higher grade tumors and higher rates of biochemical failure after radical prostatectomy in a cohort of men with favorable pathologic findings (Freedland et al, 2004).

Alcohol Consumption

Alcohol consumption is of interest for risk of prostate cancer because of its association with other cancers, its effect on estrogen and testosterone, and the high content of polyphenolic compounds with antioxidant activity in red wine. A review of relevant epidemiologic studies showed no increased risk for prostate cancer among light to moderate drinkers (Breslow and Weed, 1998). A later prospective cohort study found a dose-dependent increase in prostate cancer risk highest in those imbibing more than three hard liquor drinks per day (relative risk, 1.85) during a period of 11 years (Sesso et al, 2001). There was no association with wine or beer consumption and prostate cancer risk, although the wine consumption was not separated into red or white varieties. Another study concluded that prostate cancer risk was unassociated with total alcohol consumption but that consumption of one to three glasses of red wine per week had a protective effect (relative risk, 0.82), even when adjusted for age, PSA screening, total lifetime number of female sexual partners, and smoking (Marieke Schoonen et al, 2005).

ETIOLOGY AND MOLECULAR GENETICS

Prostate cancer is unique among solid tumors in that it exists in two forms: a histologic or latent form, which can be identified in approximately 30% of men older than 50 years and 60% to 70% of men older than 80 years; and a clinically evident form, which affects approximately 1 in 6 U.S. men. Latent prostate cancer is believed to have a similar prevalence worldwide and among all ethnicities, whereas the incidence of clinical prostate cancer varies dramatically between and within different countries. For this reason, an understanding of prostate cancer etiology must encompass the steps leading to both the *initiation* of histologic cancer and the *progression* to clinically evident disease. **The exact molecular relationship between latent and clinical cancers is not known, and it is likely that the progression from latent to clinically evident cancer is a biologic continuum with overlap in the associated molecular events.** Mutations, downregulation by promoter methylation and other mechanisms, and protein modification have been implicated in progression of prostate cancer (Fig. 90–7).

The Influence of Androgens

As previously discussed, androgens play an important role in prostate carcinogenesis. **The primary androgen of the prostate is dihydrotestosterone, irreversibly catalyzed from testosterone by 5α-reductase. Dihydrotestosterone binds to intracytoplasmic androgen receptor with much greater affinity than testosterone does, and binding of dihydrotestosterone to the androgen receptor enhances translocation of the steroid-receptor complex into the nucleus and activation of androgen response elements** (Steers, 2001). There are two isoenzymes of 5α-reductase, the products of two separate genes. **Type 1 5α-reductase is expressed primarily in the skin and liver and to lesser extent in prostate; the type 2 enzyme is expressed predominantly in prostate epithelium and other genital tissues** (Andriole et al, 2004d).

Functional type 2 5α-reductase is a prerequisite for normal development of the prostate and external genitalia in males, and insufficient exposure of the prostate to dihydrotestosterone appears to protect against the development of prostate cancer. Transrectal ultrasonography in males with inherited 5α-reductase deficiency demonstrates minuscule prostatic tissue, and biopsies demonstrate stroma but no epithelium (Imperato-McGinley et al, 1992). **In addition to the lack of enzyme activity, a lack of testosterone may also protect against the development of prostate cancer, as evidenced by the atrophic prostates seen in men after surgical castration** (Wilson et al, 1999).

Additional evidence for the role of dihydrotestosterone in prostatic carcinogenesis comes from population-based studies that demonstrate an association between benign prostatic hyperplasia and prostate cancer with levels of testosterone and dihydrotestosterone. **Wu and colleagues found that total and bioavailable testosterone levels are highest in Asian Americans, intermediate in African Americans, and lowest in whites** (Wu et al, 1995). **These investigators also demonstrated that the dihydrotestosterone-to-testosterone ratio was highest in African Americans, intermediate in whites, and lowest in Asian Americans. This distribution of dihy-**

2000). Loss of either one or both *NKX3-1* alleles becomes increasingly common in prostate lesions as they progress from prostatic intraepithelial neoplasia to local, metastatic, and androgen-independent tumors (Bowen et al, 2000).

PTEN

PTEN on chromosome 10q23 is another tumor suppressor gene that may play a role in both initiation and progression of prostate cancer (De Marzo et al, 2003a). *PTEN* inactivates second messengers (including Akt), which are phosphorylated in response to growth factors, including IGF-1. Loss of *PTEN* results in increased phosphorylation of Akt, downregulation of apoptosis, and increased cellular proliferation. Loss of *PTEN* function is seen in prostatic intraepithelial neoplasia and is associated with high Gleason score and advanced stage (Rubin et al, 2000).

Classical Oncogenes

Genetic alterations in the tumor suppressor genes *RB1* and *TP53* are commonly present in metastatic or hormone-refractory disease, suggesting a role in tumor progression. Alterations in *MYC*, *ERBB2*, and *BCL2* have also been observed in advanced and hormone-refractory prostate cancer but not commonly in lower stage and grade cancers, suggesting that mutations of proto-oncogenes usually occur as secondary events associated with tumor progression (Gurumurthy et al, 2001; Fossa et al, 2002; Qian et al, 2002).

Telomerase

Eukaryotic chromosomes have telomeres on their ends that consist of repeating units of six base pairs (TTAGGG), which protect the chromosome ends from inappropriate recombination. **Normal cellular aging is characterized by the progressive loss of these repeated elements, and consequently telomere length decreases successively with every cell replication.** After 50 to 100 doublings, telomeres reach a critically short length, at which point cells undergo senescence and are arrested from further division. Critical telomere shortening leads to chromosomal instability, leading to an increased incidence of cancers due to chromosomal fusions, breakage, and rearrangements (Blasco et al, 1997). Telomerase, a ribonucleo-protein enzyme, acts as a reverse transcriptase to maintain or to increase telomere length. The precise role of telomere length and telomerase expression in prostate cancer is unknown, but changes appear to occur early in tumor development (Sakr and Partin, 2001). Studies have identified both increased telomerase expression and (paradoxically) shortened telomere length in high-grade prostatic intraepithelial neoplasia and invasive cancers (De Marzo et al, 2003b).

Glutathione S-Transferase

Reactive oxygen species are inactivated by a host of protective enzymes, including glutathione S-transferase (GST), glutathione peroxidase, and superoxide dismutase. The expression of one of these enzymes, GSTP1, is absent in about 70% of prostatic intraepithelial neoplasia and virtually all cases of prostate cancer (Nelson et al, 2003). This loss of expression results from hypermethylation of CpG islands in the *GSTP1* promoter and causes a defect in cellular defense against oxidant stress, leading to a higher mutation rate. In addition, *GSTP1* hypermethylation has been identified in prostate biopsy specimens with histologic findings of proliferative inflammatory atrophy (Nakayama et al, 2004). Germline polymorphisms of the GST gene family may have functional consequences that modify cancer risk, but case-control studies of GST polymorphisms have failed to establish a clear association (Kidd et al, 2003; Nakazato et al, 2003; Aktas et al, 2004; Medeiros et al, 2004; Ning et al, 2004).

p27

p27 belongs to the Cip/Kip family of cyclin-dependent kinase inhibitors and regulates progression of the cell cycle from G_1 to S phase. Loss of p27 may accelerate tumorigenesis by enabling cells to progress unregulated through the cell cycle. **Mice deficient in p27 develop prostate hyperplasia, and mice deficient in both p27 and *Pten* have a high incidence of prostate cancer** (Cordon-Cardo et al, 1998; Pandolfi et al, 2001). Studies in humans have found loss of heterozygosity for p27 in 50% of patients with metastatic prostate cancer (Kibel et al, 2000). Studies of patients undergoing radical prostatectomy have found an association between loss of p27 expression and increased risk of biochemical recurrence (Guo et al, 1997; Cordon-Cardo et al, 1998).

Vascular Endothelial Growth Factor

Vascular endothelial growth factor, which is an important mediator of tumor angiogenesis, is expressed in a majority of prostate cancers, and increased expression may correlate with clinical aggressiveness (Latil et al, 2000). Vascular endothelial growth factor is regulated by androgen, suggesting a potential pathway by which androgen regulates prostate cancer growth (Joseph and Isaacs, 1997). Vascular endothelial growth factor has been shown to mediate the bone tropism of metastatic prostate cancer through activation of integrins on tumor cells (De et al, 2003).

E-Cadherin

The cadherins are a family of molecules responsible for cell-cell adhesion through connection to the cytoskeleton. Dysfunction of the cadherins results in loss of adhesion and is involved in cancer invasion and progression. **E-cadherin expression is reduced in a significant percentage of prostate cancers, particularly in poorly differentiated tumors, and E-cadherin expression in prostate cancer correlates inversely with grade, stage, metastasis, recurrence, and survival** (Umbas et al, 1992; Bostwick et al, 2004). Loss of expression of E-cadherin can be caused by loss of heterozygosity or hypermethylation of its promoter, and the severity of methylation of E-cadherin correlates with cancer progression (Li et al, 2001).

α-Methylacyl-CoA Racemase

α-Methylacyl-CoA racemase catalyzes the conversion of *R*- to *S*-stereoisomers of branched-chain fatty acids to permit metabolism through β-oxidation and is upregulated in virtually all prostate cancer (Gonzalgo and Isaacs, 2003). Because epidemiologic studies have suggested that the consumption of dairy products and beef (the main dietary sources of branched-chain fatty acids) is associated with an increased risk of prostate cancer, it has been suggested that α-methylacyl-CoA racemase overexpression is related to tumor progression. One unconfirmed study has linked germline variants of this gene to the risk for development of prostate cancer (Zheng et al, 2002).

Prostate-Specific Membrane Antigen

Prostate-specific membrane antigen (PSMA) is a transmembrane glycoprotein that is expressed by prostate cancer epithelium and on the neovasculature of other solid tumors (Ghosh et al, 2005). **Overexpression of PSMA is observed after androgen withdrawal and in hormone-refractory disease, and it is the basis of clinical imaging studies using anti-PSMA monoclonal antibodies.** Surprisingly, PSMA overexpression inhibits tumor invasiveness in cell culture (Ghosh et al, 2005). Because of its restricted tissue expression, PSMA is being actively investigated as an immunotherapeutic target (Schulke et al, 2003).

Epidermal Growth Factor and Epidermal Growth Factor Receptor

There is substantial evidence that epidermal growth factor (EGF) signaling through the epidermal growth factor receptor (EGFR) is important in prostate cancer, including observations that prostate cancer produces EGF; prostate cancers express EGFR; addition of EGF stimulates prostate cancer cell line growth, which is blocked by anti-EGFR antibodies; levels of EGFR are higher in prostate cancer than in benign prostate tissue; and EGF stimulates vascular endothelial growth factor gene expression, which enhances angiogenesis and vascular permeability (Bostwick et al, 2004). Members of the EGFR family of related oncogenes *HER2/neu, HER3,* and *HER4* also are expressed differentially in the prostate and may also be important in tumor progression.

EZH2

EZH2 is a histone lysine methyltransferase with activity dependent on its association with other components of the polycomb repressive complexes 2 and 3 (PRC2/3). EZH2 levels are increasingly elevated during prostate cancer progression. Overexpression of EZH2 in tissue culture promotes formation of the PRC4 complex that contains a histone deacetylase, suggesting an epigenetic role in prostate cancer by resetting patterns of gene expression through regulation of chromatin structure (Kuzmichev et al, 2005). EZH2 expression is modulated by the transcription factor E2F3, which has been shown to be differentially expressed in prostate cancer compared with benign epithelium (Foster et al, 2004). E2F3 expression levels predict survival after radical prostatectomy (Foster et al, 2004), and elevated levels of EZH2 and E-cadherin predict the likelihood of biochemical failure after radical prostatectomy (Rhodes et al, 2003).

CHEMOPREVENTION
Rationale

Prevention is so much better than cure, because it saves the labor of being sick.

Thomas Adams, 1618

Prostate carcinogenesis is a multistep molecular process induced by genetic and epigenetic changes that disrupt pathways controlling, and the balance between, cell proliferation, apoptosis, differentiation, and senescence. **The presence of precursor lesions that represent intermediate stages between normal and malignant cells as long as 20 years before the appearance of cancer coupled with the age-dependent incidence of most cancers suggests that carcinogenesis occurs slowly during a protracted interval. In theory, this provides the opportunity to intervene before a malignant neoplasm is established, with lifestyle changes (dietary alterations, smoking cessation, exercise) or by chemoprevention, defined as the use of natural or synthetic agents that reverse, inhibit, or prevent the development of cancer. The goal of primary chemoprevention is to decrease the incidence of a given cancer, simultaneously reducing both treatment-related side effects and mortality. Effective chemoprevention requires the use of nontoxic agents that inhibit specific molecular steps in the carcinogenic pathway.**

Prostate cancer is an attractive and appropriate target for primary prevention because of its incidence, prevalence, and disease-related mortality (see Table 90–1). The burden of prostate cancer can also be measured in other terms. A study of complications after surgical therapy for localized disease in an unselected population-based cohort reported that at more than 18 months after radical prostatectomy, 8.4% of men were incontinent and 41.9% reported that their sexual performance was a moderate to large problem (Stanford et al, 2000). In a prospective cohort study comparing outcomes 5 years after radiation or surgery to age-matched controls, the authors concluded that "declines in urinary and sexual function domains after diagnosis and treatment of localized cancer far exceeded any effects from aging" (Hoffman et al, 2004). Although many single-institution studies have reported better results in highly selected cohorts of treated patients, it is clear that the majority of men treated for localized disease in the community pay a substantial price to be cured, and fear of cancer recurrence remains substantial for as long as 2 years after treatment (Mehta et al, 2003). It seems self-evident that an effective prevention strategy would spare many men this burden of diagnosis and cure.

The molecular pathogenesis of prostate cancer also lends itself to a primary prevention strategy. Histologic lesions including atypical small acinar proliferation, proliferative inflammatory atrophy, and prostatic intraepithelial neoplasia contain both genetic and epigenetic changes intermediate between normal prostatic epithelium and prostate cancer. Clinically evident prostate cancer is rare in men younger than 50 years, whereas prostatic intraepithelial neoplasia is apparent at autopsy in men younger than 30 years. Furthermore, the prevalence of prostatic intraepithelial neoplasia is similar in populations at much different risks for development of clinically evident cancer, suggesting that external environmental influences are important and potentially modifiable.

Clinical Trial Design

Target populations appropriate for primary prevention studies can be subdivided into those with low, intermediate, and high risk for development of prostate cancer based on current epidemiologic evidence (Klein and Meyskens, 2001). Each group has its own clinical characteristics that lend advantages and disadvantages for trial design, endpoints, and statis-

events that ultimately are manifested through the diagnosis of prostate cancer. Complicating the understanding of this process are the various confounds associated with the diagnosis of the disease in clinical trials, in general populations, and in epidemiologic studies. In addition, the current inability to distinguish biologically significant from biologically insignificant disease complicates full understanding of the interaction of these factors.

Prostate cancer is an attractive target for chemoprevention because of its ubiquity, treatment-related morbidity, long latency between premalignant lesions and clinically evident cancer, and defined molecular pathogenesis. The PCPT is the first firm evidence that this cancer can be prevented by a relatively nontoxic oral agent. Additional agents, many of which are antioxidants with antiandrogenic effects, are currently being tested or are about to be tested in large-scale human clinical trials. The current body of evidence is insufficient to make a routine recommendation of any dietary or nutritional supplement for the prevention of prostate cancer.

KEY POINTS: PROSTATE CANCER

Epidemiology

- In the United States, prostate cancer is the most common visceral malignant neoplasm in men and the second leading cause of cancer-related deaths.

- Incidence peaked in 1992 approximately 5 years after the introduction of PSA as a screening test, declined until 1995, and is now increasing at a rate similar to that observed in the pre-PSA era.

- Mortality has declined since 1991 and for white men is now lower than before PSA was introduced.

- Worldwide, prostate cancer incidence and mortality rates vary significantly between countries and regions and are highest in African American men.

- PSA testing has induced a significant downward migration in age and stage (both clinical and pathologic) at diagnosis.

- A beneficial effect of PSA screening on mortality has been suggested but not proved.

Risk Factors

- Both genetics and environment are important in the origin and evolution of prostate cancer.

- Most prostate cancer is polygenic, but some hereditary forms may be determined by variants in a single gene or relatively few genes.

- *HPC1* is an autosomal dominant gene with high penetrance.

- *HPC1* encodes the enzyme RNase L, which has both antiviral and proapoptotic activity.

- Commonly observed variants in RNase L result in reduced enzymatic activity and have been associated with an increased risk of prostate cancer.

- Other prostate cancer susceptibility genes are mediators of inflammation, DNA repair, and defenses against oxidative stress.

Inflammation, Infection, and Genetic Susceptibility

- Chronic inflammation leading to cellular hyperproliferation to replace damaged tissue contributes to the development of infection-associated cancers, possibly including prostate cancer.

- Epidemiologic data suggest that a history of sexually transmitted infection or prostatitis is associated with a higher risk of prostate cancer.

- Histologic evidence of inflammation, as manifested by proliferative inflammatory atrophy, is common in prostate cancer and may represent a key pathobiologic process in its development.

- Both genetic and histologic observations suggest that compromised cellular defenses against inflammatory oxidants are important in prostate cancer initiation and promotion.

Molecular Epidemiology

- Androgen exposure of the prostate plays an important but incompletely defined role in prostate carcinogenesis.

- Long-term absence of androgen exposure to the prostate appears to protect against the development of cancer, but a dose-response relationship between androgen levels and cancer risk has not been established.

- Polymorphisms in genes encoding the androgen receptor and various enzymes related to androgen metabolism may be important determinants of prostate cancer risk.

- Estrogen is also important in prostate cancer development and may have varying effects, depending on local tissue activity of estrogen receptor-α and estrogen receptor-β.

- Elevated serum levels of IGF-1 have been associated with prostate cancer risk.

- Dietary factors, including saturated fat consumption, are also important in prostate cancer risk.

Etiology and Molecular Genetics

- The primary androgen of the prostate is dihydrotestosterone, formed by the action of 5α-reductase on testosterone.

- Epigenetic regulation of gene expression by promoter methylation and histone acetylation has been implicated in the progression of prostate cancer.

- The inducible proinflammatory enzyme COX-2 has been implicated in prostate cancer progression, and the use of anti–COX-2 agents such as NSAIDs may have a protective effect.

Continued

- Somatic mutations in a variety of genes with diverse biologic functions have been implicated in prostate cancer development and progression.

Chemoprevention

- The goal of primary chemoprevention is to decrease the incidence of a given cancer, simultaneously reducing both treatment-related side effects and mortality.

- Effective chemoprevention requires the use of nontoxic agents that inhibit specific molecular steps in the carcinogenic pathway.

- Prostate cancer is an attractive and appropriate target for primary prevention because of its incidence, prevalence, and disease-related mortality.

- Target populations appropriate for primary prevention studies can be subdivided into those with low, intermediate, and high risk for development of prostate cancer. The molecular mechanisms that underlie disease progression are likely to be different for each target population, and the results from a particular trial may not be generalizable to other clinical scenarios.

- The Prostate Cancer Prevention Trial demonstrated that finasteride reduces the period prevalence of prostate cancer by 25%, albeit with a slightly higher risk of high-grade disease. Whether the risk of higher grade disease is real or an artifact of the study design is currently under study.

- Other 5α-reductase inhibitors, the antioxidants selenium and vitamin E, and other agents are currently under study as potential chemopreventive agents.

SUGGESTED READINGS

Bostwick DG, Burke HB, Djakiew D, et al: Human prostate cancer risk factors. Cancer 2004;101:2371-2490.

Bratt O: Hereditary prostate cancer: Clinical aspects. J Urol 2002;168:906-913.

De Marzo AM, Marchi VL, Epstein JI, Nelson WG: Proliferative inflammatory atrophy of the prostate: Implications for prostatic carcinogenesis. Am J Pathol 1999;155:1985-1992.

Gonzalgo ML, Isaacs WB: Molecular pathways to prostate cancer. J Urol 2003;170:2444-2452.

Jhaveri FM, Klein EA, Kupelian PA, et al: Declining rates of extracapsular extension after radical prostatectomy: Evidence for continued stage migration. J Clin Oncol 1999;17:3167-3172.

Silverman RH: Implications for RNase L in prostate cancer biology. Biochemistry 2003;42:1805-1812.

Tarone RE, Chu KC, Brawley OW: Implications of stage-specific survival rates in assessing recent declines in prostate cancer mortality rates. Epidemiology 2000;11:167-170.

Thompson IM, Goodman PJ, Tangen CM, et al: The influence of finasteride on the development of prostate cancer. N Engl J Med 2003;349:215-224.

Pathology of Prostatic Neoplasia

JONATHAN I. EPSTEIN, MD

PROSTATIC INTRAEPITHELIAL NEOPLASIA

ADENOCARCINOMA

SUBTYPES OF PROSTATE ADENOCARCINOMA

This chapter covers the pathology of adenocarcinoma of the prostate from its precursor lesions to invasive carcinomas, from needle biopsies to radical prostatectomies. Other tumors involving the prostate are also discussed. In particular, practical points of pathology that are critical for urologists to know for the management of their patients are emphasized.

PROSTATIC INTRAEPITHELIAL NEOPLASIA

Prostatic intraepithelial neoplasia (PIN) consists of architecturally benign prostatic acini or ducts lined by cytologically atypical cells and is classified into low grade and high grade (McNeal and Bostwick, 1986) (Fig. 91–1). **Low-grade PIN should not be commented on in diagnostic reports.** First, pathologists cannot reproducibly distinguish between low-grade PIN and benign prostate tissue (Epstein et al, 1995). Second, when low-grade PIN is diagnosed on needle biopsy, these patients are at no greater risk of having carcinoma on repeated biopsy than are men with a benign biopsy finding (Epstein, 2006). Evidence that high-grade PIN is a precursor to some prostate carcinomas includes the following: there is an increase in the size and number of high-grade PIN foci in prostates with cancer compared with prostates without carcinoma; with increasing amounts of high-grade PIN, there are a greater number of multifocal carcinomas; both high-grade PIN and carcinoma preferentially involve the peripheral zone; and biomarkers and molecular changes show similarity between high-grade PIN and carcinoma (Bostwick et al, 1996; Haggman et al, 1997).

The incidence of high-grade PIN on biopsy averages 7.6% among 38 studies with a median of 5.2%. There is a tremendous variation in the numbers reported, ranging from 0% to 25%, with no apparent correlation to number of cores sampled or whether the study was from an academic or community hospital setting (Epstein, 2006). The most likely explanation to account for this variation is interobserver threshold. The distinction between low-grade and high-grade PIN is based on the prominence of the nucleoli. This is a subjective exercise, and those pathologists with a lower threshold as to what defines prominent nucleoli will have a higher incidence of high-grade PIN. **The largest studies reported a 16% to 44.6% risk of cancer on subsequent biopsy. Of the 11 studies with at least 50 cases of high-grade PIN on needle biopsy with follow-up, the mean risk of cancer is 26.4%** (Epstein, 2006). **In the majority of studies, serum prostate-specific antigen (PSA) levels, results of digital rectal examination, and transrectal ultrasound findings do not enhance the prediction of who is more likely to have carcinoma on repeat biopsy.** PIN by itself does not give rise to elevated serum PSA values (Ronnett et al, 1993). Of eight studies in which the risk of cancer after a needle biopsy diagnosis of high-grade PIN was compared with the risk of cancer after a benign biopsy finding, six showed no difference between the groups (Epstein, 2006). **For patients diagnosed with high-grade PIN on extended initial core sampling, a repeat biopsy within the first year is unnecessary in the absence of other clinical indicators of cancer.** Lefkowitz and colleagues (2002) described 31 men who had an initial diagnosis of high-grade PIN on 12-core biopsy with an interval to follow-up prostate biopsy of 3 years. The rate of cancer on repeat 12-core biopsy was 25.8% compared with an earlier study of theirs in which rebiopsy within 1 year of a diagnosis of high-grade PIN yielded cancer in only 2.3%. They hypothesized that the 3-year interval allowed unsampled small cancers that were associated with the high-grade PIN at the time of initial biopsy to grow to a size at which repeat biopsy could detect them, or alternatively, some of the high-grade PIN lesions progressed to cancer during the 3-year interval. **Further studies are needed to confirm whether routine biopsy should be repeated several years after a diagnosis of high-grade PIN, and if so, how often and when. If a repeat prostate needle biopsy is performed, it should sample the entire prostate and not just the initial sextant site where the high-grade PIN was found** (Langer et al, 1996; Shepherd et al, 1996).

The finding of high-grade PIN on transurethral prostatectomy also appears to place men at higher risk of harboring cancer, although there are fewer studies on this topic (Gaudin et al, 1997; Pacelli and Bostwick, 1997). It is reasonable to perform needle biopsies on patients who have high-grade PIN on transurethral prostatectomy, especially younger men.

The one piece of evidence we have for premalignant lesions in other organs that is lacking in the prostate is the natural

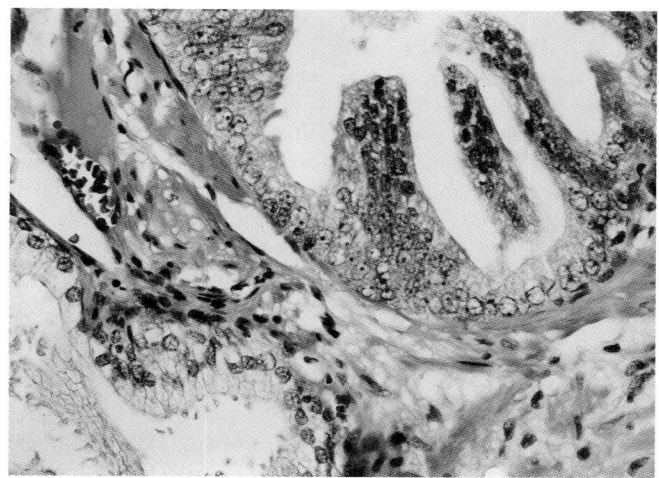

Figure 91–1. High-grade prostatic intraepithelial neoplasia. Note cytologically atypical cells with prominent nucleoli in an architecturally benign gland, contrasted with a benign gland *(lower left)*.

history of high-grade PIN. With the prostate, there is no capability to monitor a PIN focus to determine whether there is not already infiltrating carcinoma at that site or infiltrating carcinoma has evolved in the immediate vicinity of the PIN focus. Because we do not know what percentage of patients develop infiltrating carcinoma during a given follow-up interval when high-grade PIN is found on biopsy material, most authorities do not use the term *carcinoma in situ of the prostate.* **It appears that high-grade PIN is a precursor lesion to many peripheral intermediate- to high-grade adenocarcinomas of the prostate. However, PIN need not be present for carcinoma to arise.** Low-grade carcinomas, especially those present within the transition zone, are not closely related to high-grade PIN.

ADENOCARCINOMA
Location

In clinical stage T2 carcinomas and in 85% of nonpalpable tumors diagnosed on needle biopsy (stage T1c), the major tumor mass is peripheral in location (McNeal, 1969; Byar et al, 1972; Epstein et al, 1994). In the remaining cases, tumors are predominantly located in the transition zone (i.e., periurethrally or anteriorly). Tumors that appear to be unilateral on rectal examination are bilateral in approximately 70% of cases when they are examined pathologically. Adenocarcinoma of the prostate is multifocal in more than 85% of cases (Byar et al, 1972). In many of these cases of bilateral or multifocal tumor, the other tumors are small, low grade, and clinically insignificant. Consequently, the distinction between pathologic stages T2a and T2b is meaningless (Freedland et al, 2004).

Spread of Tumor

Because the prostate lacks a discrete histologic capsule, *extraprostatic extension* is preferable to "capsular penetra-

tion" as the term to describe tumor that has extended out of the prostate into periprostatic soft tissue (Ayala et al, 1989). Some authors use the term *capsular invasion* when they believe that the "capsule" is infiltrated by tumor but the tumor does not extend out of the prostate. Because there is no such entity as the prostatic capsule, "capsular invasion" makes no sense. Peripherally located adenocarcinomas of the prostate tend to extend out of the prostate through perineural space invasion (Villers et al, 1989). Perineural invasion by itself in radical prostatectomy specimens does not worsen prognosis because perineural invasion merely represents extension of tumor along a plane of decreased resistance and not invasion into lymphatics (Hassan and Maksem, 1980; Ng et al, 2004). In contrast, vascular invasion increases the risk of recurrence after radical prostatectomy (Ferrari et al, 2004). Extraprostatic extension preferentially occurs posteriorly and posterolaterally, paralleling the location of most adenocarcinomas.

Further local spread of tumor may lead to seminal vesicle invasion, which is diagnosed when tumor extends into the muscle wall of the seminal vesicle. The most common route of seminal vesicle invasion is by tumor penetration out of the prostate at the base of the gland, with growth and extension into the peri–seminal vesicle soft tissue and eventually into the seminal vesicles. Less commonly, there may be direct extension through the ejaculatory ducts into the seminal vesicles or direct extension from the base of the prostate into the wall of the seminal vesicles. Least commonly, there may be discrete metastases to the seminal vesicle (Ohori et al, 1993). Local spread of prostate cancer may also rarely involve the rectum, where it may be difficult to distinguish from a rectal primary (Fry et al, 1979).

The most frequent sites of metastatic prostate carcinoma are lymph node and bone. Prostate cancer may present with metastases to the left supradiaphragmatic lymph nodes. Lung metastases from prostate carcinoma are extremely common at autopsy, and almost all cases have bone involvement as well (Varkarakis et al, 1974). Metastatic lesions usually take the form of multiple small nodules or diffuse lymphatic spread rather than large metastatic deposits. Clinically, prostate carcinoma metastatic to the lung is usually asymptomatic. Following in frequency after lymph nodes, bones, and lung, the next most common regions of spread of prostate cancer at autopsy are bladder, liver, and adrenal gland (Saitoh et al, 1984).

Tumor Volume

In general, the size of a prostate cancer correlates with its stage. Extraprostatic extension is uncommon in tumors of less than 0.5 cm^3, and tumors that are less than 4 cm^3 uncommonly reveal lymph node metastases or seminal vesicle invasion (McNeal, 1992). Tumor volume is also proportional to grade (see following discussion). The location and grade of the tumor also modulate the effect of tumor volume (Christensen et al, 1990; Greene et al, 1991; McNeal, 1992). For example, **transition zone tumors extend out of the prostate at larger volumes than do peripheral zone tumors as a result of their lower grade and greater distance from the edge of the gland.**

Grade

Although numerous grading systems exist for the evaluation of prostatic adenocarcinoma, the Gleason grading system is the most widely accepted (Gleason et al, 1974). **The Gleason system is based on the glandular pattern of the tumor as identified at relatively low magnification** (Fig. 91–2). **Cytologic features play no role in the grade of the tumor. Both the primary (predominant) and the secondary (second most prevalent) architectural patterns are identified and assigned a grade from 1 to 5, with 1 being the most differentiated and 5 being the least differentiated.** Because both the primary and the secondary patterns are influential in predicting prognosis, there resulted a Gleason sum or score obtained by the addition of the primary and secondary grades. If a tumor has only one histologic pattern, then for uniformity, the primary and secondary patterns are given the same grade. Gleason scores range from 2 (1 + 1 = 2), which represents tumors uniformly composed of Gleason pattern 1 tumor, to 10 (5 + 5 = 10), which represents totally undifferentiated tumors. This author prefers to assign both a primary and a secondary pattern even when presented with limited cancer so as to not give rise to any confusion. For example, cases that the pathologist signs out as only "Gleason grade 4" could be interpreted to mean Gleason pattern 4 (high-grade cancer) or Gleason score 4 (low-grade cancer). In radical prostatectomy specimens, it has been demonstrated that tertiary (third most common pattern) high-grade components adversely affect biologic behavior, yet not always equivalent to the sum of the primary pattern and highest grade pattern. **It is recommended that in radical prostatectomy specimens, the routine Gleason score, consisting of the most prevalent and the second most prevalent architectural patterns, be recorded along with a note stating that there is a tertiary high-grade pattern** (Pan et al, 2000). For needle biopsy specimens in which the typical scenario includes tumors with patterns 3, 4, and 5 in various proportions, both the primary pattern and the highest grade should be added to derive the Gleason score. Any amount of high-grade tumor sampled on needle biopsy most likely indicates a more significant amount of high-grade tumor within the prostate because of the correlation of grade and volume and the problems inherent with needle biopsy sampling.

Gleason pattern 1 and pattern 2 tumors are composed of relatively circumscribed nodules of uniform, single, separate, closely packed, medium-sized glands (see Fig. 91–2B and C). Gleason pattern 3 tumor infiltrates the non-neoplastic prostate, and the glands have marked variation in size and shape, with smaller glands than in Gleason pattern 1 or pattern 2 (see Fig. 91–2D). Gleason pattern 4 glands are no longer single and separate as in patterns 1 to 3. In Gleason pattern 4, one may also see large, irregular, cribriform glands as opposed to the smoothly circumscribed smaller nodules of cribriform Gleason pattern 3 (see Fig. 91–2E). **It is important to recognize Gleason pattern 4 tumor because tumors with this pattern have a significantly worse prognosis than those with pure Gleason pattern 3** (McNeal et al, 1990; Epstein et al, 1993). It has also been demonstrated in radical prostatectomy specimens that tumors with Gleason score 4 + 3 = 7 have a worse prognosis than those with Gleason score 3

+ 4 = 7 (Chan et al, 2000). Gleason pattern 5 tumor shows no glandular differentiation and is composed of solid sheets, cords, single cells, or tumor with central comedonecrosis (see Fig. 91–2F).

There is fairly good interobserver reproducibility of the Gleason system among uropathology experts and poorer reproducibility among practicing pathologists (Allsbrook et al, 1999). It has been demonstrated that although current use of the Gleason grading system is not optimal, significant improvements can be made after participation in relatively brief educational programs, such as those on Web sites (e.g., www.pathology.jhu.edu/prostate) (Kronz et al, 2000).

The Gleason grade on biopsy material has also been shown to correlate fairly well with that of the subsequent prostatectomy specimen (Bostwick, 1994; Spires et al, 1994; Steinberg et al, 1997). One of the most frequent causes of discordant grading is grading of tumors that straddle two grades. Undergrading of needle biopsy specimens is more of a problem than overgrading and is unavoidable to some extent owing to sampling error. **One way the practice of Gleason scoring can be improved is by virtually never assigning Gleason score 2 to 4 for adenocarcinoma of the prostate on needle biopsy.** The reasons for doing this are as follows: (1) most tumors graded as Gleason score 2 to 4 on needle biopsy are graded as Gleason score 5 to 6 or higher when reviewed by experts in urologic pathology (Steinberg et al, 1997); (2) there is poor reproducibility in the diagnosis of Gleason score 2 to 4 on needle biopsy even among urologic pathology experts (Allsbrook et al, 1999); and (3) most important, assigning Gleason score 2 to 4 to adenocarcinoma on needle biopsy can adversely affect the patient's care because clinicians may incorrectly assume that all low-grade cancers on needle biopsy do not need definitive therapy. Although low volume, Gleason score 2 to 4 adenocarcinoma of the prostate on transurethral prostatectomy has a relatively indolent course; low-grade cancer on needle biopsy does not.

The ultimate value of any grading system is its prognostic ability. Both Gleason's data with 2911 patients and subsequent studies with long-term follow-up have demonstrated a good correlation between Gleason sum and prognosis (Mellinger, 1977; Sogani et al, 1985). When stage of disease is factored in with grade, prognostication is enhanced (Mellinger, 1977).

Some men with low-grade cancers develop high-grade tumor after several years (Brawn, 1983). It is unclear whether the residual low-grade cancer progressed or whether there was subsequent development of multifocal, more aggressive tumor. Although, in general, larger tumors are high grade and small tumors are low grade, exceptions occur (Epstein et al, 1994). There is a tendency to hypothesize that tumors begin as low-grade tumors and, on reaching a certain size, dedifferentiate into higher grade lesions, accounting for the relationship between size and grade. Alternatively, high-grade tumors may be high grade at their inception but are detected at an advanced size because of their rapid growth. Similarly, low-grade tumors may evolve so slowly that they tend to be detected at lower volumes. During a 1.5- to 2-year period after biopsy, there is no evidence that prostate cancer grades worsen significantly (Epstein et al, 2001).

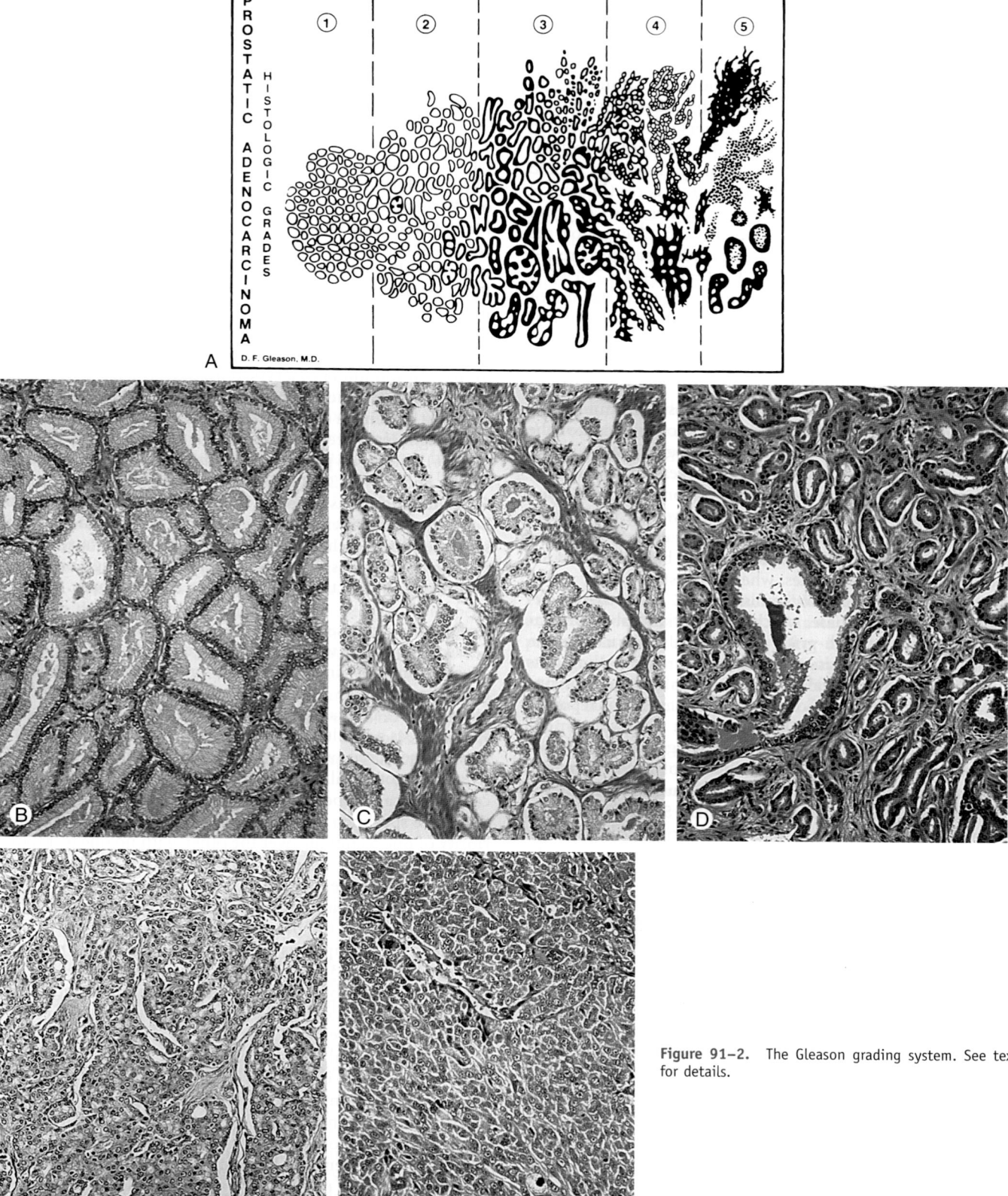

Figure 91–2. The Gleason grading system. See text for details.

in which margins histologically appear to be positive, additional tissue removed from the site does not always show tumor (Epstein, 1990). It has also been demonstrated that tumor close to the margins does not result in a higher risk of recurrence (Epstein and Sauvageot, 1997). Artifactually positive margins relate to the scant tissue surrounding the prostate, which may easily be disrupted during surgery or pathologic evaluation of the gland.

In a multivariate analysis, Gleason grade, extraprostatic extension, and margins of resection are strong independent predictors of progression (i.e., elevated postoperative serum PSA level). A more refined prognostication is not needed for men with Gleason scores of 2 to 4 because these men are almost all invariably cured by surgery. Men with Gleason scores of 8 to 10 have a poor prognosis after prostatectomy, with nodal metastases as the major prognostic determinant (Partin et al, 1994). Of cases with negative seminal vesicles and lymph nodes, Gleason scores of 5 to 7 account for 88% of tumors removed by radical prostatectomy and have a prognosis that can be stratified by various clinical and pathologic parameters (Epstein et al, 1993b, 1998; Kattan et al, 1999).

Tumor volume correlates well with pathologic stage and Gleason grade in clinical stage T2 cancers (McNeal et al, 1990). **However, most studies have found that tumor volume does not independently predict post–radical prostatectomy progression once grade, pathologic stage, and margins are accounted for** (Epstein et al, 1993a; Salomon et al, 2003b; Kikuchi et al, 2004). Consequently, it is not currently recommended that tumor volume be calculated for clinical purposes in radical prostatectomy specimens. Rather, there should be some overall subjective indication of tumor volume to identify those cases with minute amount of tumor and an excellent prognosis and those cases with extensive tumor and a worse prognosis.

The evaluation of ploidy on radical prostatectomy specimens is controversial (Shankey et al, 1993; Adolfsson, 1994). The strongest data to support the prognostic importance of ploidy are in patients undergoing radical prostatectomy with pelvic node metastases (Seay et al, 1998). This author does not recommend that ploidy be routinely evaluated on radical prostatectomy specimens.

Adenocarcinoma with Treatment Effect

The major effect of combination endocrine therapy on benign prostate tissue is the presence of atrophic changes with immature squamous metaplasia (Vaillancourt et al, 1996). On histologic examination, the changes seen in adenocarcinoma are more problematic, and for pathologists who have not seen a lot of these specimens, it may be difficult to recognize treated cancer (Armas et al, 1994; Vaillancourt et al, 1996). One of the problems with evaluating carcinomas that have been treated with hormone therapy is that the grade often appears artifactually higher (Smith and Murphy, 1994). **Pathologists should not assign a Gleason score to carcinomas with treatment effect.** However, if other areas of the tumor do not show a pronounced hormone effect, these areas can be Gleason graded.

Radiation changes in the prostate are usually seen in patients who have been irradiated for adenocarcinoma of the prostate. When carcinoma is present in a biopsy specimen

obtained 12 to 18 months after radiotherapy, it is a powerful predictor of either local or distant postirradiation failure (Scardino et al, 1986). Some studies have demonstrated that the morphologic appearance of the cancer (whether or not the cancer appears altered by the radiation) correlates with prognosis (Crook et al, 1997). Radiation alters the histologic features of benign prostate tissue so that it may mimic prostate cancer (Bostwick et al, 1982). Radiation atypia in benign prostate glands may persist for a long time (up to 72 months) after the initial treatment, resulting in a significant pitfall in evaluating prostate biopsy specimens (Magi-Galluzzi et al, 2003). If clinicians are aware of such treatment, this information should be provided to the pathologist.

SUBTYPES OF PROSTATE ADENOCARCINOMA

Mucinous adenocarcinoma of the prostate gland is one of the least common morphologic variants of prostatic carcinoma (Epstein and Lieberman, 1985; Ro et al, 1990). It has an aggressive biologic behavior and, like nonmucinous prostate carcinoma, has a propensity to develop bone metastases and increased serum acid phosphatase and PSA levels with advanced disease.

Even in ordinary adenocarcinomas of the prostate without light microscopic evidence of neuroendocrine differentiation, almost half show neuroendocrine differentiation on evaluation with immunohistochemistry for multiple neuroendocrine markers (di Sant'Agnese, 1992). Most of these neuroendocrine cells contain serotonin and, less frequently, calcitonin, somatostatin, or human chorionic gonadotropin. Most of these cases have no evidence of ectopic hormonal secretion clinically. Most studies do not demonstrate a convincing relation between the extent of neuroendocrine differentiation in ordinary prostate cancer and prognosis. Small cell carcinomas of the prostate are identical to small cell carcinomas of the lung (Tetu et al, 1987). In approximately 50% of the cases, the tumors are mixed small cell carcinoma and adenocarcinoma of the prostate. Although most small cell tumors of the prostate lack clinically evident hormone production, they account for the majority of prostatic tumors with clinically evident adrenocorticotropic hormone or antidiuretic hormone production. **The average survival of patients with small cell carcinoma of the prostate is less than a year.** There is no difference in prognosis between patients with pure small cell carcinoma and those with mixed glandular and small cell carcinomas.

Between 0.4% and 0.8% of prostatic adenocarcinomas arise from prostatic ducts (Epstein and Woodruff, 1986; Christensen et al, 1991). When prostatic duct adenocarcinomas arise in the large primary periurethral prostatic ducts, they may grow as an exophytic lesion into the urethra, most commonly in and around the verumontanum, and give rise to either obstructive symptoms or hematuria. Tumors arising in the more peripheral prostatic ducts may present like ordinary (acinar) adenocarcinoma of the prostate and may be diagnosed on needle biopsy (Brinker et al, 1999). Tumors are often underestimated clinically because rectal examination findings and serum PSA levels may be normal. **Most prostatic duct adenocarcinomas are advanced stage at presentation and** have an aggressive course; they should be regarded as Gleason score 4 + 4 = 8 because of their shared cribriform morphologic features with acinar adenocarcinoma Gleason score 8 and similar prognosis (Brinker et al, 1999). **Pure primary squamous carcinoma of the prostate is rare and is associated with poor survival** (Parwani et al, 2004). These tumors develop osteolytic metastases, do not respond to estrogen therapy, and do not develop elevated serum acid phosphatase levels with metastatic disease. More commonly, squamous differentiation occurs in the primary and metastatic deposits of adenocarcinomas that have been treated with estrogen therapy.

Mesenchymal Tumors

Sarcomas of the prostate account for 0.1% to 0.2% of all malignant prostatic tumors (Sexton et al, 2001). Rhabdomyosarcoma is the most frequent mesenchymal tumor within the prostate and is seen almost exclusively in childhood (see Chapter 130). Leiomyosarcomas are the most common sarcomas involving the prostate in adults (Cheville et al, 1995). There are two benign reactive spindle cell lesions that may simulate a leiomyosarcoma. Inflammatory myofibroblastic tumors may occur soon after TUR or without a history of TUR (Proppe et al, 1984; Sahin et al, 1991). There are also mesenchymal tumors of the prostate arising from the unique prostatic specialized stroma. These lesions range from prostatic stromal tumors of uncertain malignant potential to prostatic sarcomas. On histologic examination, these lesions are variable; one subtype resembles a tumor seen in the breast and is termed phyllodes tumor of the prostate (Gaudin et al, 1998, Bostwick et al, 2004). Carcinosarcomas (sarcomatoid carcinoma) have also been reported within the prostate and have a dismal prognosis (Lauwers et al, 1993).

Transitional Cell Carcinoma

Primary transitional cell carcinoma of the prostate without bladder involvement accounts for 1% to 4% of all prostate carcinomas (Sawczuk et al, 1985). In cases of primary transitional cell carcinoma of the prostate, stromal invasion is almost always identified (Greene et al, 1976). Primary transitional cell carcinomas of the prostate show a propensity to infiltrate the bladder neck and the surrounding soft tissue such that more than 50% of the patients present with stage T3 or T4 tumors. Twenty percent of the patients present with distant metastases, with bone, lung, and liver being the most common sites. In contrast to adenocarcinoma of the prostate, bone metastases tend to be osteolytic. Treatment of stage T3 disease with radiation results in a 5-year survival of approximately 34%. In the minority of cases with tumor localized to the prostate (T2), radical surgery has resulted in long-term disease-free survival in several patients.

More commonly, transitional cell carcinoma involves prostatic ducts and acini in patients with a history of flat transitional cell carcinoma in situ of the bladder who have been treated for a period of months to years with intravesical topical chemotherapy (Schellhammer et al, 1977; Mahadevia et al, 1986; Wood et al, 1989; Matzkin et al, 1991; Njinou Ngninkeu et al, 2003). Between 35% and 45% of cystoprosta-

tectomies performed for transitional cell carcinoma contain prostatic involvement. However, this number is dependent on the amount of histologic sampling of the prostate tissue and may be much higher in completely mapped specimens (Sakamoto et al, 1993). If cystoprostatectomy is performed and only intraductal transitional cell carcinoma is present, the prostatic involvement does not worsen the prognosis, which is determined by the stage of the bladder tumor (Esrig et al, 1996). Intraductal transitional cell carcinoma of the prostate appears to involve the prostate by direct extension from the overlying urethra, which is usually involved by carcinoma in situ. Intraductal and infiltrating transitional cell carcinoma involving the prostate tends to be seen in higher stage bladder tumors, in which the patients have a poor prognosis attributable to either advanced bladder or prostatic disease. A minority of these cases will have low-stage bladder tumor and a poorer prognosis, demonstrating the adverse effect of prostatic stromal infiltration (Esrig et al, 1996). It is therefore prognostically important to identify prostatic stromal invasion in cases of intraductal transitional cell carcinoma, especially in patients with low-stage bladder tumor. Extensive sampling of the periurethral area in cystoprostatectomy specimens performed for transitional cell carcinoma is necessary to identify and to evaluate the prostate for transitional cell carcinoma.

Finally, one may find direct invasion from bladder transitional cell carcinoma into the stroma of the prostate. The distinction between poorly differentiated transitional cell carcinoma and poorly differentiated adenocarcinoma of the prostate can be difficult. There are numerous studies demonstrating that even for high-grade adenocarcinomas of the prostate, immunohistochemical stains for PSA and prostate-specific acid phosphatase are usually positive (Epstein, 1993). With only a few exceptions, immunoperoxidase staining for PSA and prostate-specific acid phosphatase is specific for prostatic tissue (Epstein, 1993). However, in a small fraction of cases, which may vary according to the amount of tumor available for examination, stains may be negative for both antigens and still represent prostate adenocarcinoma. More recently, several studies have explored the use of other markers that may be expressed preferentially in transitional cell carcinoma. The most specific is high-molecular-weight cytokeratin (34βE12), which is negative in prostate adenocarcinoma. Transitional cell carcinomas express this antigen in 57% to 70% of cases (Genega et al, 2000). The other two markers sometimes used are cytokeratins 7 and 20 (CK7 and CK20). CK7 and CK20 positivity in transitional cell carcinoma is 70% to 100% and 15% to 71%, respectively. The problem with these markers is that they are not specific. CK20 is seen in 2% to 72% and CK7 is seen in 19% to 35% of prostate adenocarcinomas (Genega et al, 2000; Mhawech et al, 2002). Newer markers that also help differentiate transitional cell carcinoma from adenocarcinoma of the prostate are uroplakin and thrombomodulin, which in this differential diagnosis are specific yet not that sensitive (Genega et al, 2000; Mhawech et al, 2002).

Miscellaneous Malignant Tumors

Primary prostatic lymphoma without lymph node involvement appears to be much less common than secondary infiltration of the prostate (Bostwick and Mann, 1985). The most common form of leukemic involvement of the prostate is that of chronic lymphocytic leukemia, although monocytic, granulocytic, and lymphoblastic leukemias have also been found in the prostate (Dajai and Burke, 1976).

KEY POINTS: PATHOLOGY

- Low-grade PIN should not be commented on in diagnostic reports because the diagnosis is not reproducible among pathologists and lacks clinical significance.

- For patients diagnosed with high-grade PIN on extended initial core sampling, repeat biopsy within the first year is unnecessary in the absence of other clinical indicators of cancer, as the risk of cancer on rebiopsy is similar to the risk associated with repeat biopsy after a benign diagnosis. Further studies are needed to determine whether biopsy should be routinely repeated several years after a high-grade PIN diagnosis, and if so, how often and when.

- Regardless of the serum PSA level, all patients with an initial atypical diagnosis on needle biopsy should undergo repeat biopsy; the risk of cancer is approximately 40%, and clinical findings are not helpful in predicting who is more likely to have cancer.

- Cases diagnosed as atypical have the highest likelihood of being changed on expert review. Urologists should consider sending such cases for consultation to attempt to resolve the diagnosis as either definitively benign or malignant before subjecting the patient to repeat biopsy.

- Tumor volume measured in the radical prostatectomy specimen does not independently predict postsurgical progression once grade, pathologic stage, and margins are accounted for and should not be required for routine pathologic analysis.

- Gleason grade, whether it is assessed on needle biopsy, transurethral resection, or radical prostatectomy specimens, remains one of the most influential prognostic factors.

SUGGESTED READINGS

Eble JN, Sauter G, Epstein JI, Sesterhenn IA: Pathology and Genetics: Tumours of the Urinary System and Male Genital Organs. Lyon, France, IARC Press, 2004.

Epstein JI, Yang XJ: Prostate Biopsy Interpretation. Philadelphia, Lippincott Williams & Wilkins, 2002.

Humphrey PA: Prostate Pathology. Chicago, ASCP Press, 2003.

92 Ultrasonography and Biopsy of the Prostate

JOHN R. RAMEY, MD • ETHAN J. HALPERN, MD •
LEONARD G. GOMELLA, MD

ULTRASONOGRAPHIC ANATOMY OF THE PROSTATE

GRAY-SCALE TRANSRECTAL ULTRASONOGRAPHY (TRUS)

PROSTATE BIOPSY TECHNIQUES AND OUTCOMES

ADVANCED ULTRASONOGRAPHIC TECHNIQUES FOR PROSTATE IMAGING

Deaths due to prostate cancer in the United States approach 30,000/year, representing a 25% decrease in the mortality rate compared with a decade ago (Jemal et al, 2005). Although the reasons for this improvement are often debated, early prostate cancer detection programs have likely played a role. Early detection has benefited greatly from prostate-specific antigen (PSA) screening efforts, the introduction and refinement of systematic transrectal ultrasound (TRUS)-guided prostate biopsy techniques, and increased public awareness about prostate cancer.

TRUS of the prostate, first described by Wantanabe and colleagues (1968), expanded to routine clinical use with improvements in ultrasound technology and the introduction of the TRUS-guided systematic sextant biopsy protocol by Hodge and associates (1989a, 1989b). Concurrent with improved biopsy techniques, the use of PSA screening increased the number of men undergoing early prostate cancer screening and prostate biopsy, with estimates as high as 800,000 biopsies annually in the United States alone (Halpern and Strup, 2000). Given the prevalence of prostate cancer and the frequency with which TRUS-guided prostate biopsies are performed, significant efforts have been focused on determining the appropriate indications for biopsy and the ideal technique by which to image and biopsy the prostate.

TRUS technology has become a mainstay of many image-guided prostate interventions, including prostate biopsy, brachytherapy, cryotherapy, and high-intensity focused ultrasound (HIFU), as well as being used in the evaluation of appropriate patients for treatment of benign prostatic hyperplasia (BPH) (Beerlage, 2003). Fiducial gold seeds are being placed under ultrasound guidance to verify and correct the position of the prostate during megavoltage irradiation (Dehnad et al, 2003). In this chapter our focus primarily is on the use of TRUS and biopsy techniques for the diagnosis of prostate cancer.

ULTRASONOGRAPHIC ANATOMY OF THE PROSTATE

The prostate lies between the bladder neck and the urogenital diaphragm, just anterior to the rectum, an ideal position to be imaged via TRUS. The prostate gland is traditionally described based on a pathologic zonal architecture. These divisions consist of the anterior fibromuscular stroma (AFS) that is devoid of glandular tissue, transition zone (TZ), central zone (CZ), periurethral zone, and peripheral zone (PZ). Unfortunately, these regions are not visible sonographically as distinct entities (Fig. 92–1).

However, the TZ may often be discernible from the PZ and CZ, particularly in glands with significant BPH. Located posteriorly, the normal CZ and PZ, from which a majority of adenocarcinomas arise, have a homogeneous echogenic appearance whereas the anteriorly situated TZ is more heterogeneous. **Frequently, calcifications along the surgical capsule known as "corpora amylacea" highlight the plane between the PZ and TZ (Halpern, 2002). Small, multiple diffuse calcifications are a normal, often incidental ultrasonographic finding in the prostate and represent a result of age rather than a pathologic entity.** Larger prostatic calculi associated with symptoms may be related to underlying inflammation and require further evaluation and, possibly, treatment (Geramoutsos et al, 2004).

The prostatic urethra traverses the length of the gland in the midline and thus must be imaged in the sagittal plane to be simultaneously viewed along the entirety of its course (Fig. 92–2A and B). The distended urethral lumen has a hypoechoic appearance whereas periurethral calcifications may produce a thin echogenic outline. The smooth muscle of the internal sphincter extends from the bladder neck, encircling the urethra to the level of the verumontanum. These muscle fibers may be visualized sonographically as a hypoechoic ring around the upper prostatic urethra, giving it a funneled appearance proximally as it arises from the bladder neck. On

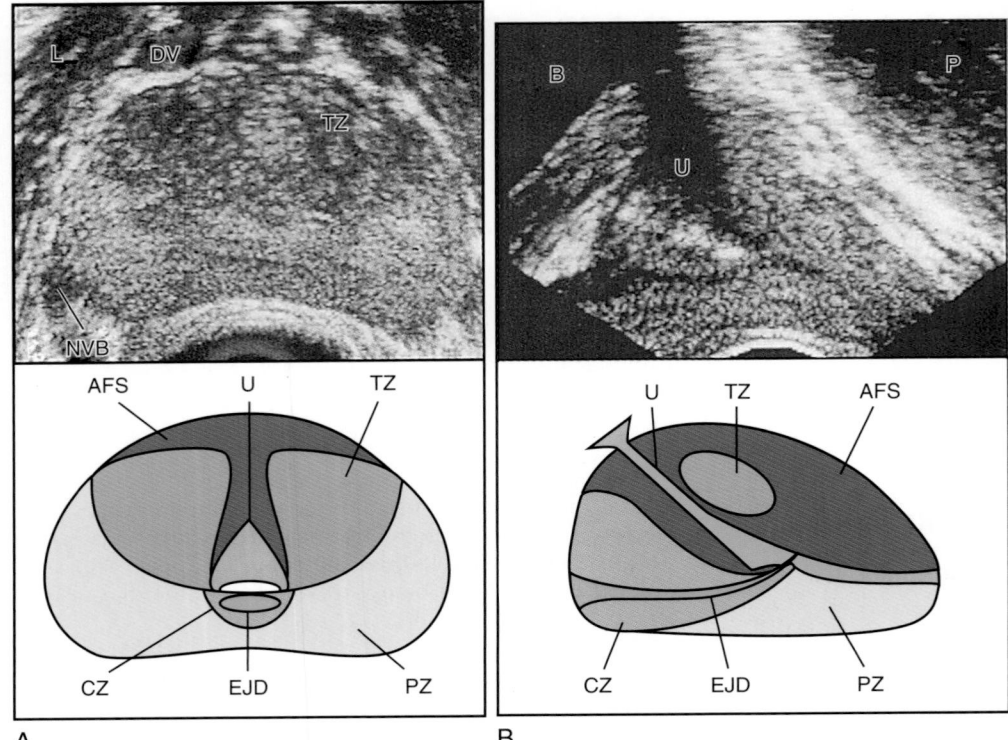

Figure 92–1. Normal prostate ultrasound images *(top)* with diagrams *(bottom)* at approximately the level of the verumontanum demonstrating zonal anatomy. **A,** Transverse view. **B,** Sagittal view. AFS, anterior fibromuscular stroma; CZ, central zone; DV, dorsal vein complex; EJD, ejaculatory ducts; NVB, neurovascular bundle; L, levator muscles; PZ, peripheral zone; TZ, transition zone; U, urethra.

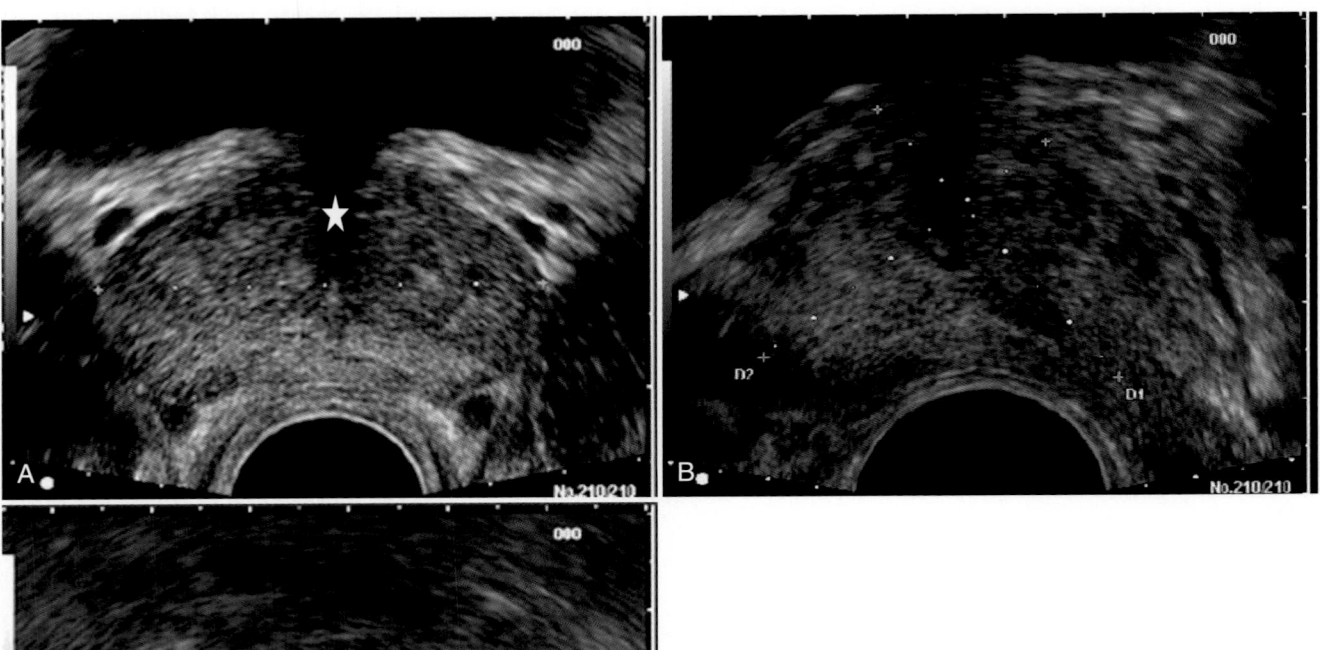

Figure 92–2. Classic gray-scale TRUS imaging of the prostate. **A,** In the transverse plane with the hypoechoic urethra centrally located *(star)* and *dotted line* representing transverse measurement. **B,** Midline sagittal view with the hypoechoic urethra running the length of the gland, D1 represents longitudinal and D2 anteroposterior measurement. **C,** Seminal vesicles *(large arrow)* and vasa deferentia *(small arrow)* in the transverse plane.

reaching the verumontanum the urethra angles anteriorly and runs through the remainder of the gland to exit at the apex of the prostate. This angle gives the prostatic urethra an anteriorly concave appearance when viewed along its entire course in the sagittal plane.

The paired seminal vesicles (SVs) are positioned posteriorly at the base of the prostate (see Fig. 92–2C). **They have a smooth, saccular appearance and should be symmetrical. The normal SV measures 4.5 to 5.5 cm in length and 2 cm in width.** A cystic SV mass is presumptively benign, whereas a solid lesion has a small probability of being malignant, especially if the patient has a primary neoplasm elsewhere. Schistosomiasis should be considered when making a differential diagnosis in patients who live in areas where infestation is endemic with a solid SV mass (Al-Saeed et al, 2003). In the transverse plane, the vasa deferentia course just above their ipsilateral SV before diving caudally toward the prostate near the midline. Here they lie just medial to the tapering ipsilateral SV before the two structures fuse to form an ejaculatory duct. The ejaculatory ducts (occasionally seen as a hypoechoic structure) enter the gland posteriorly and empty into the urethra at the verumontanum (see Fig. 92–2C). Their course parallels that of the prostatic urethra distal to the verumontanum.

GRAY-SCALE TRANSRECTAL ULTRASONOGRAPHY (TRUS)

Gray-scale TRUS has become the most common imaging modality for the prostate. Most commonly used for prostate cancer detection, TRUS may also be used in the evaluation of other conditions such as infertility (see Chapter 19, "Male Infertility"). Although the role of TRUS is expanding in directing the biopsy of prostate cancer, the role of staging localized prostate cancer using TRUS is very limited (Onur et al, 2004).

Commercially available endorectal probes come in both side- and end-fire models and transmit frequencies of 6 to 10 MHz. Most modern ultrasound machines have optimized self-programming for TRUS and biopsy. Some newer biplane probes provide simultaneous sagittal and transverse imaging modes. Probes provide a scanning angle approaching 180 degrees to allow simultaneous visualization of the entire gland in both the transverse and sagittal planes. Increasing frequency yields increased resolution. As the frequency of the probe is increased, the portion of the image that is in focus (*focal range*) is closer to the transducer (Kossoff, 2000). The commonly used 7-MHz transducer produces a high-resolution image with a focal range from 1 to 4 cm from the transducer (best for PZ where most cancers arise). Lower-frequency transducers (e.g., older 4-MHz transducers) have a focal range from 2 to 8 cm but at lower resolution. Lower-frequency transducers improve anterior delineation of large glands, increasing the accuracy of volume measurements, but provide poor internal architecture visualization. **Acoustic properties of soft tissue are similar to those of water, but clinically useful ultrasound energy does not propagate through air. For this reason, a water-density substance, termed a *coupling medium*, is used.** The coupling medium, usually sonographic jelly or lubricant, is placed between the probe and the rectal surface. If the probe is covered with a protective condom, the coupling medium is placed between the probe and the condom, as well as between the condom and the rectal surface.

Techniques

The complete TRUS evaluation of the prostate includes scanning in both the sagittal and transverse planes to obtain a volume calculation. The CZ and PZ are inspected for hypoechoic lesions and contour abnormalities, and the SVs and vasa deferentia are fully visualized.

Machine Settings

The image magnification is adjusted so that most of the prostate is visible without the image being too small to allow detection of abnormalities. In general, the magnification is low during prostate measurements so that the entire gland is seen. During biopsies, magnification is maximal for visualization of needle passage. The ultrasonographer can manually alter the brightness (or gain) slightly with each new patient and occasionally during imaging of different areas within the same prostate. **The optimal brightness setting results in a medium-gray image of the normal PZ. This gray tone serves as the reference point for judging lesions as hypoechoic (darker than the normal PZ), isoechoic (similar to the normal PZ), hyperechoic (lighter than the normal PZ), or anechoic (completely black).**

Probe Manipulation

Patients are typically scanned in the left lateral decubitus position (see "Patient Positioning" later). **TRUS should be performed in both the transverse and the sagittal planes.** There are two approaches to probe manipulation for transverse imaging (see Fig. 92–2A). With radial and some biplane probes, advancing the probe cephalad into the rectum images the prostate base, the SVs, and the bladder neck. Pulling the probe caudally toward the anal sphincter images the prostatic apex and proximal urethra. Transverse imaging with end-fire, side-fire, and some biplane probes is accomplished by angling the handle of the probe right or left using the anal sphincter as a fulcrum (see Fig. 92–2B). Angling the probe toward the scrotum produces more cephalad images, and angling the probe toward the sacrum produces more caudal images. There are also two approaches to probe manipulation for sagittal imaging. One method is rotation of the probe. Clockwise rotation yields images of the left side of the prostate, and counterclockwise rotation yields images of the right side. Alternatively, sagittal imaging can be accomplished by angling the probe up or down using the anal sphincter as a fulcrum. In the left lateral decubitus position, angling the handle of the probe down (toward the floor) images the right side of the prostate and angling the handle of the probe up (toward the ceiling) images the left side. Urologists often prefer angling the probe because this method is similar to manipulation of a cystoscope and is less uncomfortable for the patient.

Volume Calculations

Prostate volume can be calculated through a variety of formulas. Volume calculation requires measurement of up to three prostate dimensions. In the axial plane, the transverse and anteroposterior (AP) dimensions are measured at the point of widest transverse diameter (see Fig. 92–2A and B). The longitudinal dimension is measured in the sagittal plane just off the midline because the bladder neck may obscure the cephalad extent of the gland (see Fig. 92–2B). Most formulas assume that the gland conforms to an ideal geometric shape: either an ellipse ($\pi/6 \times$ transverse diameter $\times$ AP diameter $\times$ longitudinal diameter), sphere ($\pi/6 \times$ transverse diameter^3), or a prolate (egg shaped) spheroid ($\pi/6 \times$ transverse diameter$^2 \times$ AP diameter). Despite the inherent inaccuracies that arise from these geometric assumptions, all formulas reliably estimate gland volume and weight, with correlation coefficients greater than 0.90 with radical prostatectomy specimen weights, since 1 cm^3 equals approximately 1 g of prostate tissue (Terris and Stamey, 1991). **The mature average prostate is between 20 and 25 g and remains relatively constant until about age 50, when the gland enlarges in many men** (Griffiths, 1996).

When a more accurate determination of gland volume is required, such as during brachytherapy, planimetry may be employed. With the patient in the lithotomy position, the probe is mounted to a stepping device and serial transverse images are obtained at set intervals (e.g., 3 to 5 mm) through the entire length of the gland. The surface area of each serial image is determined, and the sum of these measurements is then multiplied by total gland length to yield the prostate volume.

Once gland volume has been obtained, one can calculate derivatives such as the PSA density (PSAD = serum PSA/gland volume). An elevated PSAD of the entire gland has been shown to have a sensitivity and specificity of 75% and 44%, respectively, for predicting a positive cancer diagnosis on repeat biopsy (Djavan et al, 2000). Unfortunately, there is high inter-operator and intra-operator variability in PSAD determinations and similar predictive information can now be obtained using serum free:total PSA (Djavan et al, 2003).

Cystic Lesions of the Prostate

Cystic prostatic structures are common on TRUS. Simple cysts have the same sonographic appearance as in any other part of the body: they are thin walled, are anechoic, and show acoustic enhancement posterior to the cyst. Prostatic cysts may be congenital or acquired but are rarely clinically significant regardless of etiology.

Congenital prostatic cystic lesions may arise from either müllerian (müllerian duct cysts and prostatic utricles) or wolffian (ejaculatory duct and seminal vesicle cysts) structures. An enlarged prostatic utricle represents a diverticular projection from the posterior urethra at the level of the verumontanum (Cochlin, 2002) and appears as a midline anechoic structure. These are associated with genital anomalies including hypospadias (most common), ambiguous genitalia, undescended testes, and congenital urethral polyps (Greg and Sty, 1989). Müllerian duct cysts also appear as midline anechoic lesions that result from failure of the müllerian ducts to fuse with the urethra. They are generally ovoid to pear shaped with the cyst neck oriented toward the verumontanum. When müllerian duct cysts are present, men should be evaluated for unilateral renal agenesis (McDermott et al, 1993).

Lateral paraprostatic cystic structures include seminal vesicle and vas deferens cysts (wolffian in origin). Ejaculatory duct cysts are typically small, lie off of the midline, and may accompany ejaculatory duct obstruction/obliteration with azoospermia (Fig. 92–3A and B). Seminal vesicle cysts can be caused by congenital or acquired obstruction of the ejaculatory duct and are associated with cystic renal disease; up to two thirds of men with seminal vesicle cysts may also have renal agenesis (King et al, 1991). Acquired cysts of the TZ result from hemorrhagic degeneration of BPH nodules (Hamper et al, 1990), whereas those of the outer gland have no proven etiology.

Prostate Cancer Imaging on TRUS

All hypoechoic lesions within the PZ should by noted and included in the biopsy material (Fig. 92–4). The lack of a distinct hypoechoic focus does not preclude proceeding with biopsy because 39% of all cancers are isoechoic and up to 1% of tumors may be hyperechoic on conventional gray-scale TRUS (Shinohara et al, 1989). Despite the higher prevalence of cancers discovered in prostates with hypoechoic areas, the hypoechoic lesion itself was not associated with increased

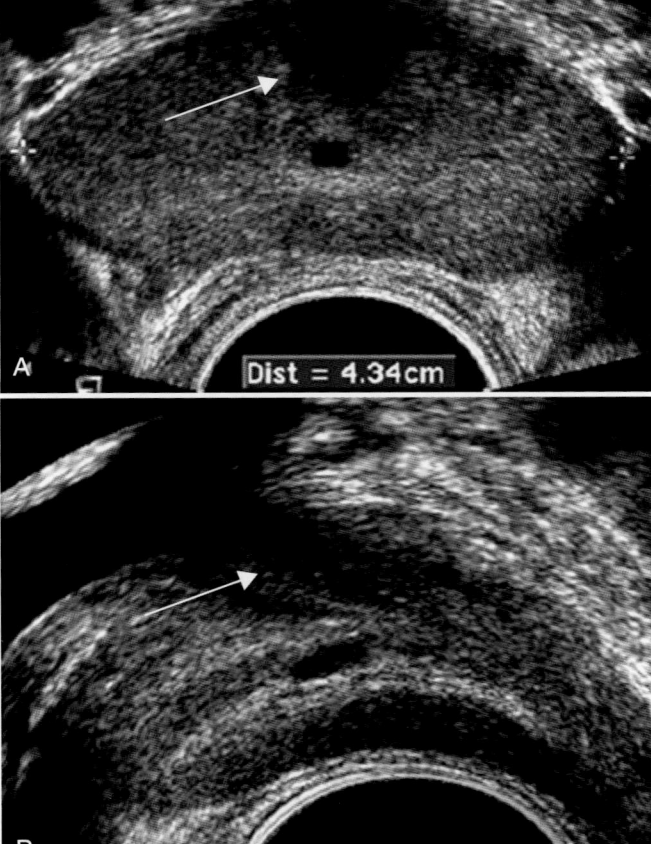

Figure 92–3. A hypoechoic midline cystic structure *(arrow)* arising from the ejaculatory duct is shown in the transverse (**A**) and sagittal (**B**) planes and demonstrates through-transmission classic for simple cysts.

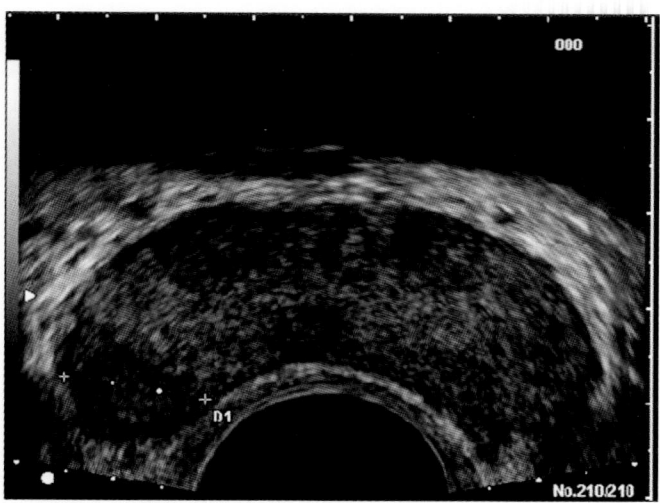

Figure 92–4. Classic hypoechoic peripheral zone (PZ) lesion *(dotted line)* in the right mid gland that TRUS-guided biopsy proved to be a Gleason 3+3=6 adenocarcinoma.

cancer prevalence compared with biopsy cores from isoechoic areas in a contemporary series of almost 4000 patients (Onur et al, 2004). Furthermore, other disease processes such as granulomatous prostatitis (Terris et al, 1997b), prostatic infarct (Purohit et al, 2003), and lymphoma (Varghese and Grossfeld, 2000) may all produce hypoechoic lesions. TZ BPH nodules are typically hypoechoic but may contain isoechoic or even hyperechoic foci. A hypoechoic lesion is malignant in 17% to 57% of cases (Frauscher et al, 2002a), highlighting the need to biopsy these lesions but recognizing they are not pathognomonic for cancer as once thought.

Any focal contour abnormalities along the outer edge of the gland and any asymmetries in echotexture from the PZ of one lobe to that of the other are noted. **Extracapsular extension of prostate cancer, although not well visualized if present as a microfocus, is suggested by a focal loss of the typically bright white periprostatic fat.**

TRUS Appearance after Treatment

External-beam radiation therapy typically decreases volume by 6 months after treatment. Irradiated prostates are diffusely hypoechoic, with poorly defined anatomy. Large hypoechoic tumors, particularly those not responding to therapy, show little change in echogenicity once irradiated, but smaller foci responding well to therapy tend to become isoechoic (Egawa et al, 1991). In general, TRUS findings correlate poorly with pathologic findings and outcomes in irradiated prostates.

With interstitial brachytherapy there is initial post-implantation edema followed by long-term changes as with external-beam radiation therapy (Whittington et al, 1999). With an ideal permanent implant, seeds should be distributed evenly throughout the gland. These seeds are hyperechoic and demonstrate posterior shadowing.

Androgen ablation with luteinizing hormone–releasing hormone (LHRH) analogs will cause an average 30% volume decrease with androgen deprivation in prostates with and without cancer (Whittington et al, 1999). The decrease ranges

up to 60% in large glands and as little as 10% in small glands. Volume decreases by approximately 21% at 6 months using agents such as finasteride (Marks et al, 1997)

Post–radical prostatectomy TRUS is considered normal if there is smooth tapering of the bladder neck to the urethra (Kapoor et al, 1993). Many patients demonstrate a nodule of tissue anterior to the anastomosis, representing the ligated dorsal vein complex (Goldenberg et al, 1992). Any other hyperechoic or hypoechoic lesions or interruptions of the retroanastomotic fat plane are considered suspicious (Kapoor et al, 1993). Hypoechoic lesions have been reported in 75% to 95% of patients with locally recurrent cancer, and color Doppler has been used to improve cancer detection in the prostatic fossa (Sudakoff et al, 1996). Patients with detectable PSA who are candidates for salvage radiation therapy were once considered for routine biopsy of the anastomotic area. **Recent data suggest that biopsy of the anastomotic region with PSA recurrence and in the absence of palpable nodule is not usually informative** (Scattoni et al, 2004).

TRUS and Other Malignancies

Prostatic involvement with transitional cell carcinoma (TCC) from the bladder is generally not detectable by TRUS, but 71% of prostatic stromal TCC lesions are hypoechoic. Prostatic TCC detected by TRUS must be confirmed by biopsy because granulomas resulting from instillation of bacille Calmette-Guérin are common in TCC patients and are also hypoechoic (Terris et al, 1997b).

Extension to the prostate from the bladder, or urethral squamous cell carcinoma (SCC), is much more common than is primary prostatic SCC. Prostatic SCC appears as an irregular, anterior mass demonstrating relative hyperechogenicity (Terris, 1999).

Adenoid cystic/basal cell carcinoma of the prostate is rare but potentially fatal. Histologically, cribriform or adenoid cystic patterns predominate. Numerous cystic glands give this tumor an unusual appearance on TRUS, characterized by multiple, evenly distributed, small, anechoic cysts (Iczkowski et al, 2003).

Prostatic sarcoma is a rare complication of prostatic irradiation, and the TRUS appearance is typified by an irregular, hypoechoic mass with an anechoic area consistent with necrosis (Terris, 1998). Unlike radiation-induced sarcoma, the echogenicity of rhabdomyosarcoma is similar to that of normal prostate tissue.

Hematologic and lymphoid malignancies involving the prostate are generally not visualized with TRUS (Terris and Freiha, 1998). Biopsies may demonstrate a lymphocytic infiltrate, but this is often attributed to chronic inflammation if no suspicion of nonprostate malignancy exists.

PROSTATE BIOPSY TECHNIQUES AND OUTCOMES
Indications for Prostate Biopsy

Before TRUS improvements and serum PSA testing became widespread, clinicians relied mainly on digital rectal examination to establish a suspicion of prostate cancer and performed

KEY POINTS: GRAY-SCALE TRANSRECTAL ULTRASONOGRAPHY (TRUS)

■ TRUS technology has become a mainstay of many image-guided prostate interventions, including prostate biopsy, brachytherapy, cryotherapy, and high-intensity focused ultrasound (HIFU).

■ The classic zonal anatomy of the prostate is not evident on TRUS, but the peripheral zone (PZ) may typically be distinguished from the transition zone (TZ), allowing biopsies to be reliably aimed toward the more commonly cancer-bearing PZ.

■ Typically, benign cystic lesions of the prostate demonstrate thin-walled architecture with sonographic through-transmission and may become symptomatic if infected.

■ Several formulas exist for determining prostate volume on TRUS. For highly accurate volume determinations such as for brachytherapy, planimetry is required.

■ Hypoechoic foci seen on gray-scale TRUS should be considered suggestive of adenocarcinoma of the prostate and included in the biopsy specimen. However, up to 39% of cancers are not visible on routine gray-scale ultrasound imaging.

Table 92–1. Commonly Cited Recommendations for Transrectal Ultrasonography (TRUS) and/or Biopsy

TRUS without Biopsy

- Treatment planning volume measurements: brachytherapy, cryotherapy, benign prostatic hyperplasia therapy (e.g., transurethral microwave thermotherapy, radiofrequency ablation)
- Volume measurement during hormonal downsizing for external-beam radiation therapy or brachytherapy
- Placement of fiducial markers for external-beam radiation therapy
- Evaluation of azoospermia: ejaculatory duct cysts, seminal vesicle cysts, etc.
- Therapeutic aspiration or unroofing of prostatic cysts; drainage of prostatic abscess

TRUS-Directed Biopsy

- Diagnosis of suspected symptomatic prostate cancer (i.e., bone metastasis, cord compression)
- Screening for prostate cancer in asymptomatic patient > age 50 with > a 10-year life expectancy (if strong family history or if African American, consider screening at age 45)
  Prostate nodule or significant prostate asymmetry regardless of PSA level
  PSA > 4.0 ng/dL regardless of age
  In men < age 60-65 years, consider biopsy if PSA > 2.5 ng/dL
  If PSA > 0.6 ng/dL at age 40
  Increased PSA velocity (>0.75-1.0 ng/dL/yr)
  Free PSA in considering initial biopsy with PSA < 10 ng/mL: >25% no biopsy; >10% and <15%, consider biopsy; <10%, biopsy
- Prior to intervention in symptomatic benign prostatic hyperplasia (e.g., surgical therapy or initiation of 5α-reductase inhibitors)
- Prior to cystoprostatectomy or orthotopic urinary diversion
- To diagnose failed radiation therapy before use of second-line therapy
- Follow-up biopsy (3-6 mo) after diagnosis of high-grade PIN or ASAP

PSA, prostate-specific antigen; PIN, prostatic intraepithelial neoplasia; ASAP, atypical small acinar proliferation.
Data from AUA (2000), Derweesh et al (2004), and NCCN (2005).

digitally directed lesional biopsies. **Today, PSA-based screening of asymptomatic men has resulted in the adaptation of TRUS biopsy as the standard of care for routine prostate biopsy.** The presence of focal nodules on digital rectal examination still will prompt a biopsy using the TRUS technique regardless of PSA levels. **TRUS-directed prostate needle biopsy remains the gold standard for diagnosis of prostate cancer.**

Early prostate cancer detection has been markedly improved by PSA-based screening programs. These initiatives have been shown to significantly increase the rate of organ-confined, and potentially curable, disease (Catalona et al, 1993). **Currently, most clinicians recommend biopsy once a patient's serum PSA rises above 4.0 ng/mL, although significant research efforts are ongoing to identify the optimal PSA threshold to recommend prostate biopsy in the asymptomatic patient.** Evidence for lowering the PSA threshold from work by Catalona's group showed higher rates of organ-confined disease at the time of radical retropubic prostatectomy in men sampled with PSAs in the 2.6- to 4.0-ng/mL range (Krumholtz et al, 2002). **These findings have led many urologists to now recommend prostate biopsy to men younger than 60 years of age once their PSA level rises above 2.5 ng/mL.** Despite this downward shift in the PSA cutoff for younger men, there remains a general trend toward allowing older men (70 years or older) to have slightly higher "normal" PSAs, in the range of 5.5 to 6.5 ng/mL, although this is not universally accepted (AUA, 2000; Derweesh et al, 2004; NCCN, 2005).

Adjuncts to serum PSA testing include measuring the free:total PSA, PSA velocity, PSA density (PSAD), and PSAD of the transition zone (PSAD-TZ) (Derweesh et al, 2004). For patients with a serum PSA value between 4.0 and 10.0 ng/mL, using a percentage of free PSA threshold of less than 25% detected 95% of cancers while eliminating 20% unnecessary biopsies, and within this group the risk of prostate cancer increased dramatically as the percentage of free PSA level declined (Catalona et al, 1998).

Regardless of initial PSA value, a PSA velocity greater than 0.75 to 1.0 ng/mL per year is frequently associated with prostate cancer and warrants biopsy (Derweesh et al, 2004), whereas an elevated PSAD and PSAD-TZ have both been shown to increase the likelihood of diagnosing prostate cancer on repeat biopsy (Djavan et al, 2000). The indications for TRUS and prostate biopsy are rapidly evolving and being continually refined (Table 92–1). Details concerning screening for prostate cancer and the role of prostate biopsy are discussed in Chapter 94, "Diagnosis and Staging of Prostate Cancer."

Prostate biopsy may also be indicated on the basis of the pathologic analysis of previous biopsy specimens. In men who have undergone prostate biopsy and are found to have only high-grade prostatic intraepithelial neoplasia (HGPIN) or atypical small acinar proliferation (ASAP) a follow-up biopsy should be performed. HGPIN represents a premalignant lesion and carries a 23% to 35% risk of diagnosing prostate cancer on subsequent biopsy (Davidson et al, 1995; O'Dowd et al, 1999; Kronz et al, 2001). The natural history of ASAP is less well defined than that of HGPIN, but if ASAP is present in the initial biopsy specimen the risk of diagnosing prostate cancer on subsequent biopsy is significantly increased (Iczkowski et al, 1998; Ouyang et al, 2001). **Thus, irrespective of follow-up PSA values, current recommendations are to resample all patients with either HGPIN or ASAP in their initial biopsy specimen within 3 to 6 months.**

Contraindications to Prostate Biopsy

Significant coagulopathy, painful anorectal conditions, severe immunosuppression, and acute prostatitis are all contraindications to prostate biopsy.

Preparing Patients for Biopsy

Patients should be informed of the risks and benefits of the procedure and provide informed consent. All anticoagulant therapy (warfarin, clopidogrel, aspirin/NSAIDs, herbal supplements) should be stopped 7 to 10 days before prostate biopsy. For those patients with underlying coagulopathy or on warfarin, prostatic biopsy should not be performed until the International Normalized Ratio has been corrected below 1.5. A small amount of urine in the bladder can facilitate the examination.

Antibiotic Prophylaxis

A wide variety of prophylactic regimens have been studied using both oral and intravenous antibiotics, with widely varying opinions of the use of antibiotics and the choice of agents. **Our current practice is to give patients a dose of an oral fluoroquinolone 30 to 60 minutes before biopsy and continue therapy for 2 to 3 days. By using similar protocols, recent large studies have reported minimal infectious complications, although bacteremia/sepsis still occurs in 0.1% to 0.5% of patients** (Djavan et al, 2001b; Raaijmakers et al, 2002). The postbiopsy duration of antibiotics also remains controversial even in those who agree the antibiotics are indicated; single-dose oral fluoroquinolone prophylactic regimens demonstrated equivalent efficacy to 3-day regimens in preventing infections (Kapoor et al, 1998; Sabbagh et al, 2004). For those patients at risk of developing endocarditis or infection of prosthetics, pacemakers, and automated implanted cardiac defibrillators, prophylaxis should consist of intravenous ampicillin (vancomycin, if penicillin allergic) and gentamicin preoperatively, followed by 2 to 3 days of an oral fluoroquinolone. The AUA and American College of Orthopedic Surgeons (2005) have released specific recommendations for joint prosthesis prophylaxis.

Cleansing Enema

We routinely have patients self-administer a cleansing enema at home before biopsy. **This practice decreases the amount of feces in the rectum, thereby producing a superior acoustic window for prostate imaging.** However, many clinicians may elect not to use an enema because this may allow more spontaneous performance of a prostate biopsy. The enema's effect on reducing infections is debatable, but it seems logical that a cleansing enema and empty rectal vault may reduce bacterial seeding of the prostate.

Analgesia

Comments on periprocedural pain control utilizing topical lidocaine jelly have been published (Issa et al, 2000; Obek et al, 2004); in our experience and in the literature this provides only suboptimal analgesia. **Data now suggest that infiltration anesthesia around the nerve bundles with local anesthetic may provide excellent pain control, which is increasingly important using extended biopsy techniques** (Trucchi et al, 2005). A local prostatic block is achieved using 2% lidocaine, a long spinal needle (7-inch, 22-gauge), and TRUS guidance along the biopsy channel of the transducer. Multiple variations exist for the infiltration of local anesthetic for transrectal biopsy (Nash et al, 1996; Soloway and Obek, 2000). We have found that injecting 5 mL of lidocaine at the level of the seminal vesicles near the bladder base at the hyperechoic fat pad that demarcates the junction of the seminal vesicles and the prostate bilaterally produces an excellent block. Other approaches include infiltration of 10 mL starting at the junction of the seminal vesicles and infiltrating along the lateral aspect of the prostate from base to apex (Derweesh et al, 2004). **Direct infiltration into the prostate produces an inferior block and should be avoided because of the risk of systemic lidocaine absorption.** Local anesthesia for transperineal biopsies should include infiltration of the skin and subcutaneous tissues of the perineum initially. Ultrasound guidance may then be employed to aid infiltration of deeper tissues along the anticipated tracts of the biopsy needle. Postbiopsy analgesic regimens, if used, should avoid aspirin and NSAIDs because of increased risk of bleeding.

Patient Positioning

Patients are usually placed in the left lateral decubitus position with knees and hips flexed 90 degrees. An armboard attached parallel to the table and a pillow between the knees helps maintain this position. The buttocks should be flush with the end of the table to allow manipulation of the probe and biopsy gun without obstruction. If necessary, the right lateral decubitus or lithotomy position can be used. **The lithotomy position is used by some clinicians and is preferred for transperineal biopsies, brachytherapy treatment planning, or placement of fiducial gold markers for external-beam therapy** (Dehnad et al, 2003). Because the distribution of color Doppler flow within the prostate is dependent on patient position, the lithotomy position is preferred when color Doppler imaging is used to identify areas of hyperemia for targeted biopsy of the prostate (Halpern et al, 2002a).

Transrectal Prostate Biopsy Techniques

The prostate volume is assessed, and imaging of the prostate in both the transverse and sagittal planes is begun. The examination usually starts at the base of the gland and extends to the apex. Most modern ultrasound units are automatically set for optimal prostate viewing, and the TRUS gray-scale exam of the prostate is conducted as previously described, noting the location and characteristics of any lesions (i.e., hypoechoic, hyperechoic, calcifications, contour abnormalities, cystic structures).

identification of transition zone cancers not detected by previous transrectal prostate biopsy in high-risk patients (Pinkstaff et al, 2005).

Transurethral Prostate Biopsy

Transuretheral resection biopsies were once advocated for the diagnosis of TZ cancers or after negative TRUS sampling. In contemporary series, TZ cancers are estimated to be less than 5% (Mazhar and Waxman, 2002). **With improved TRUS techniques including local anesthesia, the TZ can now be adequately sampled and the need for transurethral biopsy is usually not necessary** (Derweesh et al, 2004).

Risks and Complications of Prostate Biopsy

Post-Biopsy Infections

Most infectious complications after TRUS biopsy are limited to symptomatic urinary tract infection and low-grade febrile illness, which can be readily treated with oral or intravenous antibiotics; however, rare case reports of fatal septicemia after prostate biopsy have been published (Breslin et al, 1978; Brewster et al, 1993; Bates et al, 1999; DaSilva et al, 1999). Historical series prior to the routine use of antibiotic prophylaxis found bacteriuria in 32% to 36% of patients and bacteremia/febrile illness in 48% to 69% of patients undergoing TRUS biopsy (Brown et al, 1981; Crawford et al, 1982). **Recent studies show that 2% of patients will go on to develop a febrile urinary tract infection, bacteremia, or acute prostatitis and require hospitalization for intravenous antibiotics** (Kapoor et al, 1998; Lindert et al, 2000). Additional infections such as epididymitis have been reported infrequently (Donzella et al, 2004).

Bleeding

Even with normal coagulation parameters, bleeding is the most common complication seen after prostate biopsy. As noted, any potential medications that can alter coagulation parameters, including herbal remedies, should be held for 5 to 7 days before biopsy and those on warfarin managed as noted. Two large European screening programs noted hematuria in 23% to 63% of men after sextant biopsy, with clot retention developing in 0.7% (Djavan et al, 2001b; Raaijmakers et al, 2002). Rectal bleeding is common and seen in 2.1% to 21.7% of patients (Enlund and Varenhorst, 1997; Djavan et al, 2001b). **Rectal bleeding is typically minor and readily controlled with direct pressure by the ultrasound probe or digitally; persistent brisk hematochezia may require anoscopic intervention for control. Hematospermia, commonly seen post biopsy, is of minimal clinical importance but can be cause for significant concern on the part of the patient if not discussed at the time of biopsy; 9.8% to 50.4% of men experience some blood in their ejaculate** (Djavan et al, 2001b; Raaijmakers et al, 2002), which may persist for 4 to 6 weeks after prostate biopsy.

Other Complications

Excessive anxiety and discomfort from the endorectal probe may produce a moderate or severe vasovagal response in 1.4% to 5.3% of patients (Rodriguez and Terris, 1998; Djavan et al, 2001b) and may require termination of the procedure. Placing the patient in the Trendelenburg position and use of intravenous hydration usually resolve these symptoms, with further intervention as clinically indicated.

Acute urinary retention requiring temporary catheterization develops in 0.2% to 0.4% of patients after TRUS biopsy (Enlund and Varenhorst, 1997; Raaijmakers et al, 2002). Men with significantly enlarged glands and those with significant lower urinary tract symptoms (e.g., high International Prostate Symptoms Score), are more prone to develop retention (Rodriguez and Terris, 1998; Raaijmakers et al, 2002).

ADVANCED ULTRASONOGRAPHIC TECHNIQUES FOR PROSTATE IMAGING
Color and Power Doppler TRUS

Color Doppler imaging is based on the frequency shift in the reflected sound waves from the frequency of insonation and thus depicts the velocity of blood flow in a directionally dependent manner (Fig. 92–6A). **Color assignment is based on the direction of blood flow related to the orientation of the transducer receiving the signal; flow toward the transducer is depicted in shades of red and flow away in shades of blue; the color is not specific for arterial or venous flow.** Power Doppler imaging (also known as enhanced color Doppler, color amplitude imaging [CAI], or color angiography) utilizes amplitude shift to detect flow in a velocity and directionally independent manner (Bude and Rubin, 1996) (see Fig. 92–6B). The advantages of power Doppler imaging are its ability to detect slower flow and to have less reliance on the Doppler angle, making it more suitable for detection of prostate cancer neovascularity. Although power Doppler imaging offers improved sensitivity to small amounts of flow, neither modality has yet proved itself superior to the other for cancer detection. In 251 patients, Halpern and Strup (2000) found color Doppler sensitivity and specificity of 14.6% and 93.9%, respectively, to identify cancer. Whereas Doppler modes showed an improved diagnosis versus gray-scale TRUS, 45% of cancers still went unidentified by any sonographic modality. Others have shown increased cancer detection rates using Doppler-targeted biopsy strategies (Kelly et al, 1993; Rifkin et al, 1993; Newman et al, 1995; Sakarya et al, 1998; Cornud et al, 2000; Okihara et al, 2000; Shigeno et al, 2000), but none is sufficiently accurate to replace systematic biopsy (Halpern et al, 2002b). Enhancements in the technical aspects of color Doppler TRUS, including the use of contrast agents (see later), may provide the necessary improvements to specifically identify cancer sites in the future.

Multiple studies have shown that angioneogenesis and the resultant increase in microvessel density that occurs within foci of prostatic adenocarcinoma correlates with the presence of metastases (Weidner et al, 1993), stage of disease (Fregene et al, 1993; Brawer et al, 1994; Bostwick et al, 1996), and disease-specific survival (Lissbrant et al, 1997; Borre et al, 1998). Interest in using color and power Doppler TRUS to aid in prostate cancer detection stems from studies of radical

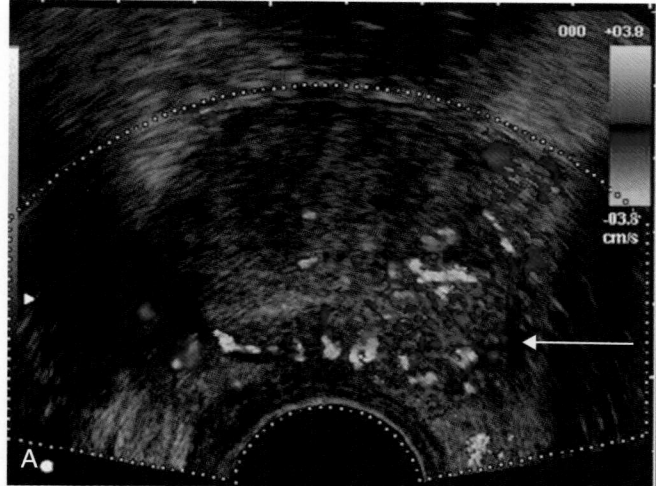
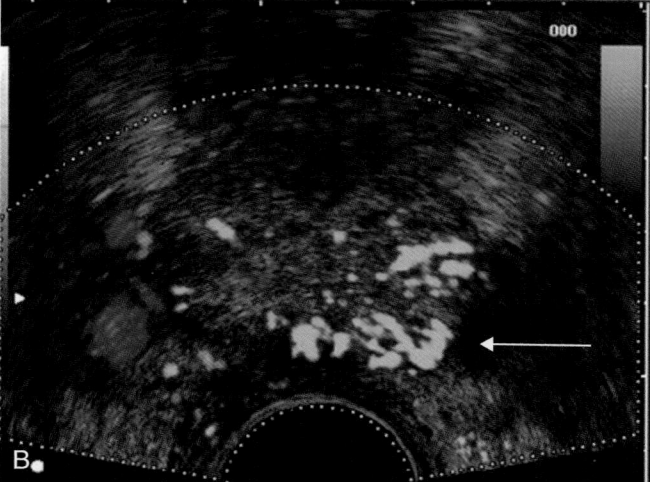

Figure 92-6. Color Doppler (**A**) TRUS and power Doppler (**B**) TRUS identify a Gleason 4 + 4 = 8 adenocarcinoma in the left mid gland.

prostatectomy specimens demonstrating that foci of adenocarcinoma possess an increased density of microvessels compared with surrounding normal parenchyma (Bigler et al, 1993).

Patients with detectable color Doppler flow within their dominant tumor at the time of TRUS-guided biopsy are at a 10-fold increased risk for PSA recurrence after radical retropubic prostatectomy (Ismail et al, 1997). The presence of increased flow was also associated with higher Gleason grade, increased incidence of SV invasion, and a lower biochemical disease-free (bNED) survival rate versus subjects without increased flow on preoperative TRUS (50% vs. 96% bNED at 31 months) (Ismail, 1997). Other investigators have also shown the association of power Doppler flow signals as an indicator of microvessel density with higher Gleason score and have suggested a correlation with outcome (Wilson, 2004).

Current Doppler modalities are not able to identify the microvessels of prostate cancer, which are typically 10 to 15 μm in diameter. The flow signals associated with malignant foci detected by unenhanced color and power Doppler imaging are due to detection of larger feeding vessels (Ismail

and Gomella, 2001). Intravenous microbubble ultrasound contrast agents, similar to those currently approved and used in echocardiography, have been infused systemically during gray-scale and TRUS Doppler imaging to amplify flow signals within the microvasculature of prostate tumors, allowing selective visualization of malignant foci in clinical trials (Halpern et al, 2000; Ismail and Gomella, 2001). **These intravenous "bubble" contrast agents are constructed with air or higher-molecular-weight gas agents encapsulated (albumin or polymer hard shell, lipid or surfactant coated) for longevity and are generally 1 to 10 μm.**

Using CE-TRUS for prospective prostate cancer detection, Halpern and associates (2001) demonstrated an increase in sensitivity from 38% to 65% versus baseline unenhanced imaging, without significantly altering specificity. Subsequent studies by our group and others have improved sonographic detection of malignant foci utilizing CE-TRUS and targeted biopsy of enhancing lesions (Frauscher et al, 2001, 2002b; Halpern et al, 2002b, 2005a; Roy et al, 2003). Imaging using microbubble contrast agents combined with three-dimensional image reconstruction of enhanced power Doppler images also demonstrated increased diagnostic accuracy (Unal et al, 2000) (Fig. 92–7). Future developments in these and other imaging modalities that can selectively visualize prostate cancers based on the presence of angioneogenesis may ultimately allow more accurate localization of the sites of cancer.

Other Investigational Techniques

Artificial neural networks are another potential way to enhance TRUS images and identify malignant foci. Investigational automated image analysis, including pattern recognition and artificial neural networks applied to TRUS images, may successfully identify lesions that cannot be seen by the human eye (Loch et al, 1999).

A new sonographic technique known as elastography may prove to be superior to color Doppler imaging in the identification of malignant areas in the prostate (Klauser et al, 2003; Ives et al, 2005). This technique employs real-time sonographic imaging of the prostate at baseline and under varying degrees of compression (Fig. 92–8). Through computerized calculations, differences in displacement between ultrasonic images from baseline and during compression may be visualized and regions with decreased tissue elasticity may be tagged as suggestive of malignancy. In a preliminary study of 404 cases with 151 cases positive for prostate cancer, the malignancy was found in 127 patients (84.1%) with real-time elastography directing the biopsy (Konig et al, 2005).

Endorectal magnetic resonance imaging (MRI) and MR spectroscopy as combined modalities might be able to guide and therefore limit the number of iterative biopsies and cores for patients (Amsellem-Ouazana et al, 2005). Utilization of MRI will require modifications in instrumentation and the technique of biopsy (Beyersdorff and Hamm, 2005). These MRI-directed biopsy techniques require expensive equipment that is not widely available for biopsy procedures.

New Doppler, contrast medium–enhanced, and other developing techniques have the potential to allow accurate localization and diagnosis of prostate cancer and minimize or eliminate the need for multiple biopsy sites to diagnose

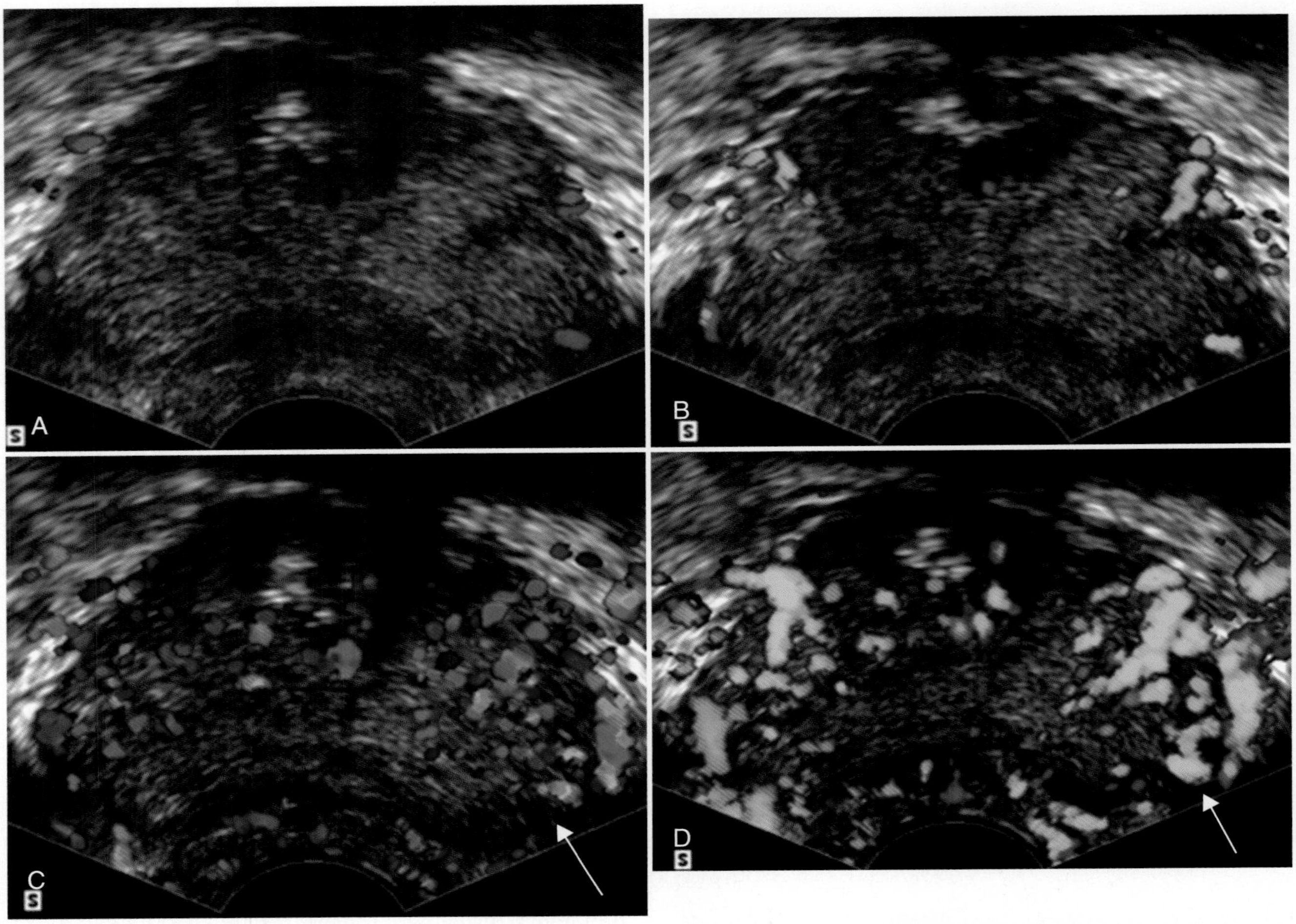

Figure 92–7. Unenhanced color (**A**) TRUS and power Doppler (**B**) TRUS fail to detect evidence of an underlying malignancy. After infusion of a microbubble contrast agent, color (**C**) TRUS and power Doppler (**D**) TRUS demonstrate an area of increased flow in the left mid gland that proved to be a Gleason 3+4=7 adenocarcinoma on targeted biopsy *(arrows)*.

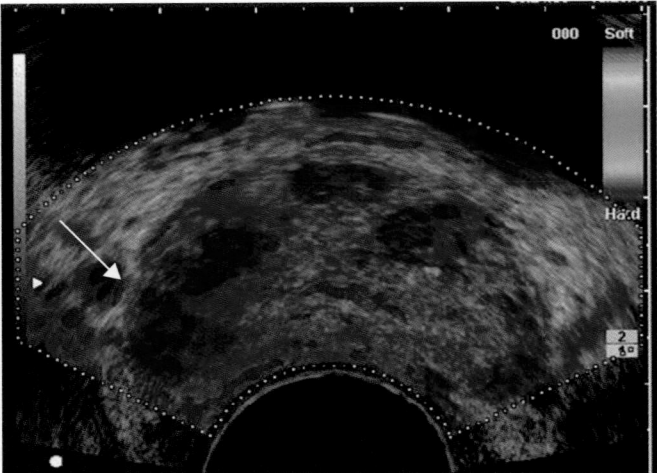

Figure 92–8. Elastography demonstrates an area of decreased compliance in the right base consistent with an underlying malignancy *(blue near arrow)*. Note color scale in upper right corner indicating relative tissue "firmness." Targeted biopsy of this region revealed a Gleason 4+4=8 adenocarcinoma.

prostate cancer in the future. However, until these techniques are proved superior in the localization of prostate cancer, systemic TRUS gray-scale core needle biopsy will continue to be regarded as the "gold standard" for the diagnosis of prostate cancer.

KEY POINTS: ADVANCED ULTRASONOGRAPHIC TECHNIQUES FOR PROSTATE IMAGING

- TRUS alone cannot diagnose prostate cancer without a tissue biopsy.

- Local prostate anesthesia is becoming commonplace and most useful when using extended core biopsy schemes.

- Patients undergoing TRUS-guided prostate biopsy require oral antibiotic prophylaxis for at least 24 hours perioperatively.

- Sextant biopsy of the prostate for prostate cancer detection is inadequate, and systematic biopsy procedures should include a minimal 8 to 13 cores.

- Investigational imaging modalities such as contrast medium–enhanced TRUS and elastography may allow more precise targeted biopsy protocols to replace extended core schemes by improved localization of malignant foci within the prostate in the future.

- Color and power Doppler imaging modes improve cancer detection but do not reliably identify all malignant foci and thus cannot obviate the need for systematic biopsy at the present time.

SUGGESTED READINGS

Djavan B, Waldert M, Zlotta A, et al: Safety and morbidity of first and repeat transrectal ultrasound-guided prostate needle biopsies: Results of a prospective European prostate cancer detection study. J Urol 2001a;166: 856-860.

Hodge KK, McNeal JE, Terris MK, Stamey TA: Random systematic versus directed ultrasound guided transrectal core biopsies of the prostate. J Urol 1989b;142:71-75.

Ismail M, Gomella LG: Ultrasound and enhanced ultrasound in the management of prostate cancer. Curr Opin Urol 2001;11:471-477.

Presti JC, Chang JJ, Bhargava V, Shinohara K: The optimal systematic prostate biopsy scheme should include 8 rather than 6 biopsies: Results of a prospective clinical trial. J Urol 2000;163:163-167.

Trucchi A, De Nunzio C, Mariani S, et al: Local anesthesia reduces pain associated with transrectal prostatic biopsy: A prospective randomized study. Urol Int 2005;74:209-213.

93 Prostate Cancer Tumor Markers

MATTHEW B. GRETZER, MD • ALAN W. PARTIN, MD, PhD

KALLIKREIN TUMOR MARKERS

PROSTATE-SPECIFIC MEMBRANE ANTIGEN

MOLECULAR BIOLOGY AND DISCOVERY OF SERUM
BIOMARKERS FOR PROSTATE CANCER

SUMMARY

The discovery and utilization of tumor markers have positively affected early detection, diagnosis, and staging for many malignancies. By improving early detection, tumor markers contribute to improved curative success rates. Optimal treatment and cure depend not only on accurate and early diagnosis but also on reliable follow-up for efficient detection of clinical recurrence. The identification of new markers and the development of sensitive tools to measure them will contribute to improved cure rates.

Among urologic malignancies, prostate cancer has greatly benefited from the discovery and application of tumor markers. **Since its discovery in 1979 to clinical application in the late 1980s through 1990s, prostate-specific antigen (PSA) has evolved into an invaluable tool for the detection, staging, and monitoring of men diagnosed with prostate cancer** (Sensabaugh et al, 1978; Wang et al, 1979, 1981; Papsidero et al, 1980; Kuriyama et al, 1981). The widespread use of PSA screening has generated greater awareness about prostate cancer. During the PSA era, identification of cancers while confined to the prostate has improved curability with either radical prostatectomy or radiation therapy. **Whereas the majority of prostate cancers in the 1980s and early 1990s commonly arose with an abnormal digital rectal examination (DRE) or elevated PSA, or both, today most prostate cancer arises as clinically nonpalpable (stage T1c) disease with PSA between 2.5 and 10 ng/mL. The evolving demographics and natural history of prostate cancer have resulted in a stage migration to nonpalpable, clinically localized (stage T1c) disease and a parallel reduction in mortality** (Pound et al, 1997, 1999; Stephenson et al, 1997; Polascik et al, 1999). However, these PSA-detected T1c cancers are not homogeneous. Although PSA screening has improved survival, outcomes are not the same for all T1c detected disease as some of these cancers may not pose a threat to survival (Gretzer et al, 2002). Methods for improved detection of clinically significant prostate cancer are needed.

Despite routine application of PSA assays, limitations of specificity for this marker remain. Although PSA is widely accepted as a prostate cancer tumor marker, it is organ specific and not disease specific. **Unfortunately, there is an overlap in the serum PSA levels among men with cancer and those with benign disease. Thus, elevated serum PSA levels may reflect alterations within the prostate secondary to tissue architectural changes such as cancer, inflammation, or benign prostatic hyperplasia (BPH).** Currently, serum PSA levels as low as 2.6 ng/mL are used as a threshold to perform transrectal ultrasound-guided biopsy. **Although up to 30% of men presenting with an elevated PSA may be diagnosed following this invasive procedure, as many as 75% to 80% are not found to have cancer.** In some instances the biopsy needle may fail to sample representative areas, thus failing to detect present cancer. To this end, application of PSA derivatives such as PSA density, PSA velocity, age-adjusted values, and, more recently, molecular derivatives have attempted to improve the performance of PSA (Christensson et al, 1990; Benson et al, 1992a, 1992b; Carter et al, 1992a, 1992b; Oesterling et al, 1993a, 1993b, 1993c; Riehmann et al, 1993; Seaman et al, 1993; Bazinet et al, 1994; Rommel et al, 1994; Lilja, 1997; McCormack et al, 1995; Morgan et al, 1996). Although these alterations to PSA attempt to improve specificity, the dichotomous relationship of this value will undoubtedly affect its counterpart and thus impair sensitivity.

We are in a midst of a PSA biomarker crisis as the specificities of PSA and its derivatives require supplementation in order to improve specificity and to differentiate cancer from benign diseases of the prostate. Research into the biochemistry of PSA is yielding advances that have the potential to contribute to the detection and management of prostate cancer. New understanding of the molecular biology of carcinogenesis and prostate cancer is beginning to yield a new era in prostate cancer tumor research. Exploiting the knowledge of molecular oncology and application of novel techniques have provided innovative tools for the discovery of new biomarkers. Application of these promising diagnostic tests may be instrumental not only for detection but also to aid in discrimination between aggressive and indolent cancers. This chapter reviews our currently used markers and describes some promising markers that have evolved from our improved knowledge and methods used to evaluate genomic alterations, epigenetic modifications, and protein expression.

KALLIKREIN TUMOR MARKERS

A source of prostate cancer markers has been identified among the protein products of the human kallikrein gene family (Fig. 93–1). Originally, only three genes of this family of genes were identified: the pancreatic/renal kallikrein (hKLK1), the human kallikrein 2 (hKLK2), and PSA (hKLK3) (McCormack, 1995; Rittenhouse et al, 1998; Diamandis et al, 2000; Lilja, 1997). Since the identification of 12 other kallikrein genes, this family of proteases now consists of 15 members and is described with a distinct nomenclature (Diamandis et al, 2000; Yousef and Diamandis, 2001). Located on the long arm of chromosome 19 within the region spanning q13.2-q13.4, these genes share similar structural similarities. The serine proteases encoded by the three originally described genes have been identified as KLK1 (hk1 or hPRK), KLK2 (hK2 or hGK-1), and KLK3 (hK3 or PSA). The amino acid sequence has been demonstrated to be similar among these serine proteases, with hK1 expressing 60% and hK2 expressing 78% homology with PSA (Schedlich et al, 1987; Clements, 1989). Both hK2 and hK3 are released in zymogen form from the prostatic epithelium and are found in seminal fluid as well as serum. As they share structural homology, they can both form complexes with endogenous protease inhibitors such as α_2-macroglobulin and α_1-antichymotrypsin (ACT) (Young et al, 1995; Lilja, 1997; Rittenhouse et al, 1998).

Although hK1 has been identified in tissues other than prostate (kidney, pancreas, salivary gland), hK2 and hK3 are released almost exclusively from the prostate (Morris, 1989). The expression of hK2 within the prostate is lower than that of PSA (Chapdelaine et al, 1988; Henttu et al, 1990; Young et al, 1992). The PSA/hK2 ratio in male sera has been found to be 0.1 to 34 and in seminal plasma 100 to 500 (Black et al, 1999). **Furthermore hK2 has been shown to regulate PSA activity by cleaving a leader amino acid sequence from PSA (proPSA), thus activating PSA** (Kumar et al, 1997; Lovgren et al, 1997; Takayama et al, 1997). **Although PSA is less expressed in prostate cancer tissue, hK2 levels have been shown to be elevated in poorly differentiated prostate cancer** (Darson et al, 1997; Tremblay et al, 1997). Like PSA, hK2 has been shown to aid in the detection of prostate cancer (Kwiatkowski et al, 1998; Partin et al, 1999; Nam et al, 2000). It is likely that several other members of the kallikrein family of serine proteases will become useful tumor markers. Both hK6 and hK10 have been described as potential serum biomarkers for nonprostatic diseases, especially ovarian cancer (Luo et al, 2001; Yousef, 2001).

Prostate-Specific Antigen (PSA or hK3)

The most notable marker in the kallikrein family is hK3, also known as PSA. It was first identified and purified in the late 1970s, but widespread use in clinical urology did not occur for another decade (Ablin et al, 1970; Sensabaugh, 1978; Wang et al, 1979; Papsidero et al, 1980; Kuriyama et al, 1980, 1981; Wang et al, 1981; Seamonds et al, 1986; Chan et al, 1987; Stamey et al, 1987; Oesterling et al, 1988). PSA is a 33-kD glycoprotein that acts as a serine protease. The ectopic expression of PSA has been reported in smaller concentrations in the tissue of malignant breast tumors (Yu et al, 1994a, 1994b, 1994c), normal breast tissue (Monne et al, 1994; Yu et al, 1995), breast milk (Yu et al, 1995b), female serum (Yu et al, 1995), and adrenal and renal carcinomas (Levesque et al, 1995a); however, for practical and clinical purposes PSA is organ specific, primarily produced by the prostatic luminal epithelial cells (Yu et al, 1994, 1995; Levesque et al, 1995; Diamandis et al, 2000, 2001). Although it is organ specific, PSA is not cancer specific, as demonstrated by the substantial overlap in values between men with benign versus malignant prostate disease (Oesterling et al, 1988; Partin et al, 1990).

The function of this androgen-regulated protease is to liquefy semen through its action on the gel-forming proteins semenogelin and fibronectin within the semen following ejaculation (Lilja and Laurell, 1984; Lilja, 1985; Lilja et al, 1987; McGee and Herr, 1988; Christensson et al, 1990). **PSA is normally found in low concentration in sera (ng/mL). Within sera, PSA circulates in both bound and unbound forms** (Fig. 93–2). **Most PSA in sera is bound or complexed to the antiproteases ACT and macroglobulin (MG)** (Christensson et al, 1990; Lilja et al, 1991; Stenman et al, 1991). Binding of free PSA to ACT inactivates the protease, but the complex PSA-ACT remains immunodetectable by current assays (Partin et al, 2003). Binding of PSA to MG still allows some proteolytic activity but renders the PSA-MG complex undetectable by most current assays (Christensson et al, 1990). **Free PSA without proteolytic activity is probably rendered inactive within the prostatic epithelial cell before release into the sera. This free inactive PSA does not form complexes with antiproteases, circulates unbound in sera, and is immunodetectable by current assays** (Lilja et al, 1991). The primary

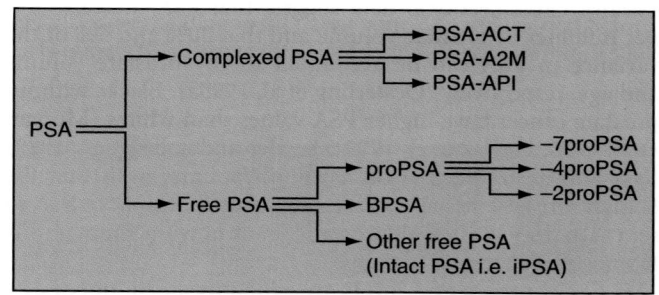

Figure 93–2. Molecular forms of prostate-specific antigen (PSA). Molecular derivatives of PSA include free PSA, such as proPSA (and the various clipped forms), BPSA (benign PSA), and other free PSA forms such as intact, inactivated PSA. Complexed PSA includes free PSA that is bound to proteases such as ACT (α_1-antichymotrypsin), API (α_1-protease inhibitor), and A2M (α_2-macroglobulin).

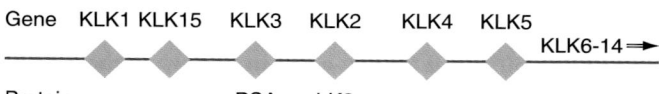

Figure 93–1. Human kallikrein gene map. Map of the human kallikrein locus and corresponding proteins as described by Yousef and Diamandis (2001).

Table 93–1.	**Prostate-Specific Antigen Derivatives**	
PSA Derivative	**Definition**	**Limitations**
PSA density	Serum PSA/prostate volume ≥0.15 associated with the presence of prostate cancer	Variations in prostate size, shape, ratio of stromal to epithelial tissue. Variations in ultrasound measurement.
PSA velocity	Rate of change of PSA >0.75ng/mL per year	Variations in assay, lack of previous results. Need for extended wait to make clinical recommendations.
Age-specific PSA	Age-specific normalized PSA values	Risk missing significant cancer in older men, overdetection in younger men.

PSA, prostate-specific antigen.

this diagnostic gray zone include PSA density, PSA velocity, and age-specific PSA (Table 93–1). Although the ability of these PSA derivatives to improve the specificity of total PSA remains debatable among many investigators, these values have become additional tools to help measure prostate cancer risk during consultation in clinical practice.

PSA Density. The majority of men with PSA elevations greater than 80% have serum levels in the range of 4 to 10 ng/mL (Catalona et al, 1994). In these men, the most likely reason for the PSA elevation is prostate enlargement, not prostate cancer, because of the high prevalence of BPH in this population. Benson and colleagues (1992a, 1992b) introduced a method to correlate more directly the degree to which cancer contributes to the serum PSA and to compensate for BPH and prostate size as determined from transrectal ultrasonography. **A direct relationship between PSA density (PSAD) and the likelihood of cancer has been documented** (Seaman et al, 1993; Bazinet et al, 1994; Rommel et al, 1994). **For men with a PSA between 4.0 and 10.0 ng/mL and a normal digital rectal examination, a PSAD greater than 0.15 has been suggested as discriminatory for the presence of cancer** (Seaman et al, 1993; Bazinet et al, 1994).

The usefulness of PSAD in prostate cancer detection has not been confirmed in all studies. Catalona and colleagues (1994) found that PSAD failed to detect up to 50% of cancers in men with PSA values within the diagnostic gray zone of 4 to 10 ng/mL. Brawer and associates (1993) found that PSAD did not enhance the ability of PSA level alone to predict the presence of cancer in men with PSA values of 4 to 10 ng/mL and normal DRE. Higher PSA densities may be found among groups of men with positive biopsies compared with men with negative biopsies because prostate cancers are more likely to be found when a constant number of biopsies are obtained in men with smaller prostate volumes than in men with larger prostate volumes (Uzzo et al, 1995).

The conflicting results with PSAD have been addressed by Cooner (1994). There is variation in the amount of epithelium (source of PSA) between prostates of similar size, but there is no noninvasive method for determining how much epithelium is contributing to overall PSA. In addition, variability in prostate shape limits the use of a common volume equation for calculating prostate size. Although imperfect,

PSAD has remained a useful adjunct in cancer risk assessment for counseling patients.

The major determinant of serum PSA in men without prostate cancer is the transition zone epithelium, not the epithelium of the peripheral zone of the prostate (Lepor et al, 1994). Because BPH represents an enlargement of the transition zone—and serum PSA levels are primarily a reflection of transition zone histology in men with BPH—adjusting PSA for transition zone volume may help distinguish between BPH and prostate cancer (Kalish et al, 1994). Djavan and colleagues (1999b) found that PSA/transition zone volume was the parameter with the highest overall validity (sensitivity and specificity) for prostate cancer among 974 men with PSA levels between 4 and 10 ng/mL. Although application of this value has resulted in improved sensitivity, it has yet to gain widespread application because of variability with ultrasound measurement of this region within the prostate.

PSA Velocity. Substantial changes or variability in serum PSA can occur between measurements in the presence or absence of prostate cancer (Carter et al, 1992a, 1992b, 1995; Riehmann et al, 1993; Prestigiacomo and Stamey, 1996). The short-term changes in PSA between repeated measures are primarily due to physiologic variation (Prestigiacomo and Stamey, 1996). The changes in serum PSA can be adjusted (corrected) for the elapsed time between the measurements, a concept known as PSA velocity or rate of change of PSA (Carter et al, 1992b). Using frozen sera to measure PSA years before the diagnosis of prostate cancer in men with prostate cancer, Carter and colleagues (1992b) showed **that a rate of change in serum PSA more than 0.75 ng/mL per year was a specific marker for the presence of prostate cancer and that men with cancer had significantly more rapid rates of rise in PSA than men without prostate cancer at a time (5 years before diagnosis) when PSA levels were not elevated.** In that study, 72% of men with cancer and 5% of men without cancer had a PSA velocity of more than 0.75 ng/mL per year. Specificity of PSA velocity using a cut point of 0.75 per year remained high in this study (over 90%) when PSA levels were between 4 and 10 ng/mL or below 4 ng/mL, but sensitivity for cancer detection was 11% at levels below 4 ng/mL compared with 79% for levels between 4 and 10 ng/mL. PSA velocity cutoffs have not been determined for men with PSA values below 4 ng/mL.

Other studies have demonstrated that men with prostate cancer have more rapid rises in PSA than men without prostate cancer. In a large prospective screening study, the cancer detection rate was 47% among men with a PSA velocity of more than 0.75 ng/mL per year compared with 11% among men with a PSA velocity of less than 0.75 ng/mL per year (Smith and Catalona, 1994). In addition, less than 5% of men without a history of prostate cancer have a PSA velocity of more than 0.75 ng/mL per year (95th percentile for PSA velocity), supporting the specificity of rate of change in PSA as a marker for the presence of cancer (Carter et al, 1995; Kadmon et al, 1996; Lujan et al, 1999). **The minimal follow-up time over which changes in PSA should be adjusted for PSA velocity to be useful in cancer detection has been calculated in separate studies to be 18 months** (Smith and Catalona, 1994; Carter et al, 1995; Kadmon et al, 1996). **Furthermore, evaluation of three repeated PSA measurements, to determine an average rate of change in PSA, would** appear to optimize the accuracy of PSA velocity for cancer detection (Carter et al, 1992a, 1992b, 1995).

Age-Specific Serum PSA Levels. The 95th percentile of PSA among "healthy" populations of men carefully screened to exclude prostate cancer (95% specificity) has been used to establish age- and race-specific PSA ranges (Oesterling et al, 1993; Morgan et al, 1996). PSA thresholds based solely on the expected ranges for men without prostate cancer may lead to underdiagnosis of significant cancers among those with the disease (low sensitivity) (Catalona et al, 1994; Morgan et al, 1996). Morgan and colleagues (1996) defined by age the PSA thresholds that would result in detection of 95% of prostate cancers among whites and blacks with the disease (95% sensitivity). The identified thresholds for detecting 95% of prostate cancers among men 40 to 50 years old are lower than 4 ng/mL, but for men 50 to 69 years old (the primary target group for early detection efforts at present), the thresholds are very close to 4 ng/mL for white males (3.5 ng/mL) and for black males (4 to 4.5 ng/mL). This method was introduced as method to improve the sensitivity of PSA in younger men as well as enhance the specificity in older men in order to detect more cancers in the younger men and decrease overdiagnosis of clinically insignificant tumors in older men. However, application of age-specific ranges remains controversial as review of some series suggests that this method may result in missing an unacceptable number of clinically significant cancers in older men (Crawford et al, 1999; Catalona et al, 2000b).

Molecular Derivatives of Prostate-Specific Antigen

One of the most exciting and clinically useful discoveries since the introduction of PSA has been the demonstration of different molecular forms of PSA within serum (Christensson et al, 1990, 1993, 1994; Lilja et al, 1991; Stenman et al, 1991; McCormack et al, 1995; Lilja, 1997; Polascik et al, 1999). Measurable PSA found circulating within the blood exists either complexed (bound, cPSA) to proteins or as a free (unbound) form (fPSA) (see Fig. 93–2). **Three proteins that are recognized to bind to PSA within the blood are ACT, α₂-macroglobulin (A2M), and α₁-protease inhibitor (API)** (Christensson et al, 1990, 1993, 1994; Lilja et al, 1991; McCormack et al, 1995; Tewari et al, 1996; Lilja, 1997). Figure 93–4 illustrates the molecular model of PSA and its epitope sites. **The majority of PSA that enters the serum is bound (70%) to these proteins.** When bound to A2M, all PSA epitope sites become masked, making this complex difficult to measure (Fig. 93–5). **Of the complexed PSA derivatives found in serum, PSA bound to ACT (PSA-ACT) is immunoreactive and found in the greatest concentration.** Although representing a lower proportion of total PSA in the blood, fPSA is also immunoreactive and therefore measurable. Development of new monoclonal antibodies specific for fPSA and cPSA has allowed more accurate measurement of the different molecular forms of PSA and their ratios in serum (Table 93–2) (Lilja et al, 1991; Stenman et al, 1991).

Free PSA and the Percent Free PSA. Although the majority of serum PSA is found complexed to these proteases (most to ACT), 5% to 35% of PSA exists as fPSA (McCormack et al, 1995; Tewari et al, 1996; Woodrum et al, 1998). **Although prostate cancer cells do not produce more PSA than benign prostate epithelium, the PSA produced from malignant cells appears to escape proteolytic processing. Thus, men with prostate cancer have a greater fraction of serum PSA complexed to ACT and a lower percentage of total PSA that is free compared with men without prostate cancer**

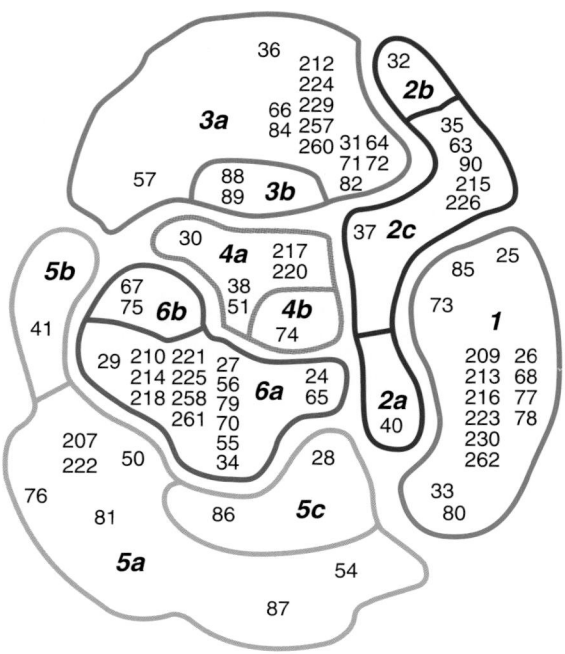

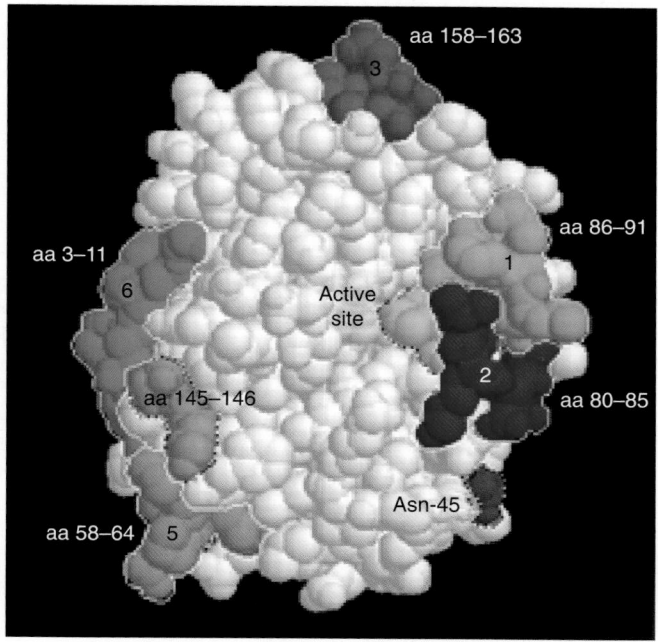

A   B

Figure 93–4. Molecular model of prostate-specific antigen demonstrating the available epitopes.

(Christensson et al, 1993; Leinonen et al, 1993; Lilja, 1993a; Stenman et al, 1994). Utilizing this important observation led to the measurement of the percentage of the ratio of free to total PSA (%fPSA) and has since provided an additional degree of specificity for prostate cancer detection (Catalona et al, 1998; Partin et al, 1998). The difference in the ratio of free to total PSA (percentage of free PSA or %fPSA) is greatest when comparing men without prostate cancer who have prostate enlargement (BPH) with those with prostate cancer and no prostate enlargement. This difference may be due to differential expression of PSA isoforms by transition zone (zone of origin of BPH) tissue compared with peripheral zone

(zone of most prostate cancer) tissue (Chen et al, 1997; Mikolajczyk et al, 2000). **The role for %fPSA is more applicable to PSA levels less than 10 ng/mL as the positive predictive rate of total PSA above 10 to 20 ng/mL has been demonstrated to be as high as 80%. Currently, %fPSA is approved by the Food and Drug Administration (FDA) for use to aid PSA testing in men with benign DRE and minimal PSA elevations, within the diagnostic gray zone of 4 to 10 ng/mL.** More recent data have demonstrated utility of %fPSA for PSA levels less than 4.0 ng/mL to aid in decision-making about whether a patient requires an initial or repeat biopsy.

Christensson and coworkers (1993) measured free and total PSA fractions in men with and without prostate cancer and found that a free/total PSA cutoff of 0.18 (18% free/total PSA) significantly improved the ability to distinguish between subjects with and without cancer compared with use of total PSA alone. Other %fPSA cutoff values have also been identified to improve risk stratification. Catalona and colleagues (1995) have found that %fPSA provided independent predictive information regarding the presence or absence of cancer above that provided by other clinical indices including age, total PSA, DRE results, and prostate size. To date, there remain many cutoff thresholds for %fPSA, depending on the assay used and the targeted sensitivity and specificity (Table 93–3). As many as 20% to 65% of unnecessary biopsies may be avoided when using %fPSA cutoff values ranging between 14% and 28% while maintaining sensitivity rates from 70% to 95% within the tPSA range of 4 to 10 ng/mL (Catalona et al, 1998; Partin et al, 1998; Veltri and Miller, 1999; Vessella et al, 2000; Stephan et al, 2002). In a prospective, multi-institutional study of men 50 to 75 years old with PSA levels between 4 and 10 ng/mL and palpably benign prostate glands, a %fPSA cutoff of 25% (biopsy less than 25%) detected 95% of cancers while avoiding 20% of unnecessary biopsies (Catalona et al, 1998). **These data confirm that the application of %fPSA can help counsel men with PSA elevation between 4 and 10 ng/mL regarding their risk of cancer and the need for further evaluation to rule out the disease** (Fig. 93–6).

A number of other studies have demonstrated the usefulness of %fPSA in prostate cancer detection (for reviews see Polascik et al, 1999; Karazanashvili et al, 2003). Increased use of PSA as a screening tool has led to increased interest in the evaluation of PSA levels below 4.0 ng/mL. Examination of

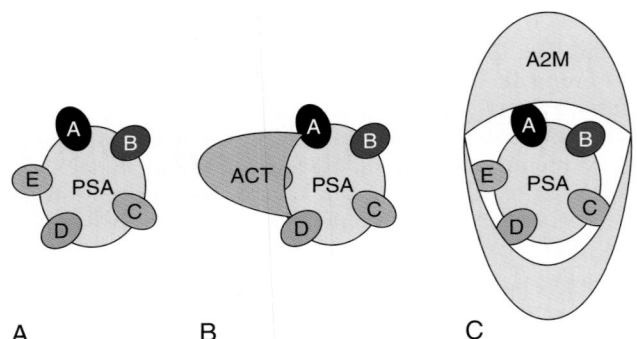

Figure 93–5. Prostate-specific antigen (PSA)-binding proteases. **A,** Free PSA with A to E representing immunoreactive epitopes of free PSA. **B,** α_1-Antichymotrypsin (ACT) blocks the E epitope during binding. **C,** α_2-Macroglobulin (A2M) blocks all immunoreactive sites on PSA, making this derivative difficult to measure in serum.

Table 93–2. Molecular Derivatives of Prostate-Specific Antigen

PSA Type	% in Serum
Complexed PSA	60–95
PSA-ACT	60–90
PSA-API	1–5
PSA-A2M	10–20
Free PSA	5–40

ACT, α_1-antichymotrypsin; API, α_1-protease inhibitor; A2M, α_2-macroglobulin; PSA, prostate-specific antigen.

Table 93–3. Cutoff Thresholds for Percent Free Prostate-Specific Antigen

Author (yr), Assay	N	tPSA Range (ng/mL)	ROC PSA	ROC %fPSA	%fPSA Cutoff	Sensitivity (%)	Specificity (%)
Partin et al (1998), Hybritech	219	4–10	—	0.612	0.25	95	20
Catalona (2000a), Hybritech	773	4–10	0.540	0.720	0.25	95	20
Horninger (2000), Delphia	308	2.5–10	—	—	0.20	100	55
Vessella et al (2000), AxSYM	297	4–10	0.476	0.762	0.10	25	95
					0.11	35	90
					0.24	90	40
					0.26	96	27
Basso (2000), Immulite	330	—	—	—	0.22	58	95
Veltri and Miller (1999), Tosoh	531	2–20	0.579	0.727	0.21–0.25	89	30
					0.31–0.35	98	10
Kuriyama et al (1998), Immulize HS	121	4–10	0.598	0.745	0.23	90	19
					0.16	85	57

PSA, prostate-specific antigen; tPSA, total PSA; ROC, receiver operating characteristic; %fPSA, percentage of free PSA.

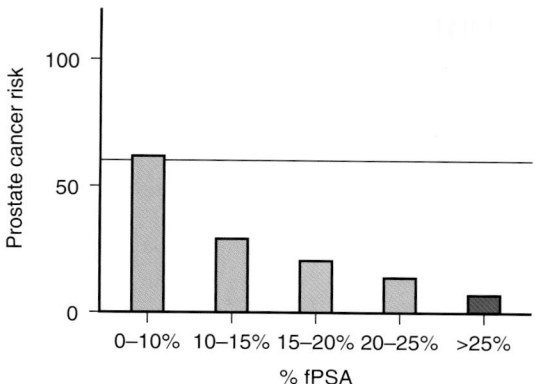

Figure 93–6. Prostate cancer risk stratification for men with prostate-specific antigen (PSA) values between 4 and 10 ng/mL (the diagnostic gray zone) based on percent free PSA (%fPSA). (From Catalona WJ, Partin AW, Slawin KM, et al: Percentage of free PSA in black versus white men for detection and staging of prostate cancer: A prospective multicenter clinical trial. Urology 2000a;55:372-376.)

cancers detected within the PSA range 2.5 to 4.0 ng/mL has shown numbers of cancers similar to those detected in the 4 to 10 ng/mL range and also that these cancers are clinically significant and may exhibit aggressive pathologic potential (Colberg et al, 1993; Smith et al, 1998; Schroder et al, 2000; Recker et al, 2001). Djavan and colleagues (1999) demonstrated that for men with PSA levels less than 4 ng/mL a %fPSA cutoff value of 27% could detect up to 90% of cancers while preventing 18% of unnecessary biopsies. Furthermore, comparison against PSA derivatives such as PSAD, PSA velocity, and transition zone density favored %fPSA. Haese and coworkers (1997) demonstrated that %fPSA in the total PSA range of 2 to 4.0 ng/mL does not substantially increase the number of biopsies needed to detect clinically significant prostate cancer compared with that in the 4 to 10 ng/mL range. In this study, a %fPSA cutoff value of 18% to 20% detected almost half of cancers while sparing 73% of men from undergoing biopsy, with a biopsy-to-cancer ratio of 3:1 to 4:1.

One study has demonstrated that a %fPSA cutoff of 25% would lead to detection of 95% of prostate cancers in both white and black men (Catalona et al, 2000a), suggesting that race may not be important when using %fPSA in cancer detection. **Free PSA and total PSA both decrease in men receiving finasteride. As both decline, the percentage of fPSA is not altered significantly by this medication** (Keetch et al, 1997; Pannek et al, 1998).

In addition to contributing to detection, %fPSA has been shown to provide prognostic information. Serial measurement of %fPSA within archival serum demonstrated early marked and sustained differences in aggressive and nonaggressive prostate cancers (Carter et al, 1997). This group identified a statistically significant difference in %fPSA in men with and without metastatic disease up to 10 years prior to the development of prostate cancer. For the same cohort of men, total PSA levels failed to differentiate aggressive from nonaggressive prostate cancer 10 years prior to diagnosis. This study suggests that the longitudinal measurement of %fPSA changes may aid in detection and contribute information regarding

disease behavior, thus providing useful information for therapeutic decision-making.

Despite these encouraging results, several important factors should be kept in mind with regard to interpretation of %fPSA in clinical practice for cancer detection (Meyer et al, 1997). Such factors include prostatic manipulation, specimen handling, and assay variation (Partin et al, 1996a, 1996b; Stephan et al, 1997; Roth et al, 1998; Woodrum et al, 1998). Prostatic manipulation and urethral instrumentation have been shown to affect the interpretation of the ratio of fPSA to total PSA. Although there may be marginal changes in total PSA, fPSA levels may fluctuate, affecting the %fPSA calculation. Furthermore, because fPSA is cleared more rapidly from serum than complexed PSA forms (i.e., total PSA), the resulting calculated %fPSA is directly affected. Thus, it is recommended that PSA determinations be avoided for several weeks following prostatic manipulation (surgery, biopsy, cystoscopy) (Partin et al, 1996; Lein et al, 1997; Bjork et al, 1998).

Prostate volume has also been shown to influence the serum ratio of free to total PSA (Catalona et al, 1995; Partin et al, 1996; Haese et al, 1997; Stephan et al, 1997; Woodrum et al, 1998). The cutoff for %fPSA that optimizes sensitivity and specificity for cancer detection depends on prostate size because overlap in %fPSA is greatest among men without cancer who have enlarged prostates and men with cancer in the setting of prostate enlargement (Catalona et al, 1995). This group demonstrated that using a %fPSA cut point of 23% in men with PSA levels between 4 and 10 ng/mL and a prostate volume of less than 40 cm^3 could yield 90% sensitivity. However, for men with larger prostates, the %fPSA cut point dropped to 14% in order to maintain this degree of sensitivity.

Stability and storage conditions have been shown to affect the accuracy of PSA measurements (Woodrum et al, 1998). Free PSA is less stable than bound forms of PSA. Specific handling requirements have been recommended in order to avoid sample degradation. Once procured, samples should be processed and serum separated from blood within 2 hours. To avoid further degradation, serum to be stored longer than 24 hours should be maintained at −70° C to prevent further specimen disruption.

Given the lack of standardization, results from the various PSA assays are not uniform in their measurement of fPSA and total PSA, with a resulting pronounced impact on the interpretation of %fPSA (Roth et al, 1998; Brawer, 1999). When analytes from different assays are used, the variation among these assays becomes compounded, which affects the calculated ratio of free to total PSA. This has resulted in different cutoff values for %fPSA in order to achieve 95% sensitivity among the different assays. This observation suggests that each laboratory should be responsible for determining the appropriate PSA cutoff value according to the assay used. Accurate application of this ratio to cancer risk assessment requires information regarding the origin of the total and fPSA values.

The recommended and FDA-approved use for %fPSA remains for men with PSA levels within the diagnostic gray zone of 4 to 10 ng/mL. However, many clinicians use this ratio to aid in the decision-making process regarding repeat biopsy (Stephan et al, 1997; Hayek et al, 1999; Djavan et al, 2000). For an initial biopsy, %fPSA ranges of 18% to 25% are commonly suggested; however, a widely accepted cutoff value has yet to be determined. For a repeat biopsy, Stephan and colleagues (1997) reported a 5% cancer miss rate when using a %fPSA value of 21% to trigger rebiopsy. A study by Hayek and coworkers (1999) illustrated a 16% positive rebiopsy rate regardless of %fPSA and concluded that this derivative was unable to provide further risk stratification for men in their population. Djavan and colleagues concluded that %fPSA is an accurate predictor of prostate cancer at rebiopsy. This group identified a %fPSA of 30% as the most accurate predictor of cancer in repeat biopsy specimens. However, until more series mature, the aggressiveness of this application in screening and follow-up biopsies should be tailored on a case-by-case basis (Luderer et al, 1995; Catalona, 1996; Partin et al, 1996b; Stephan et al, 1997; Catalona et al, 1998; Hayek et al, 1999; Djavan et al, 2000).

Serum Isoforms of Free PSA. PSA originates with a 17-amino-acid chain that is cleaved to yield a precursor inactive form of PSA termed proPSA (pPSA) (Zhang et al, 1995; Kumar et al, 1997, 2000; Mikolajczyk et al, 1997, 2001, 2002; Peter et al, 2001). As depicted in Figure 93–7, **the precursor form of PSA contains a 7-amino-acid proleader peptide, in addition to the 237 constituent amino acids of mature PSA, and is termed [−7]pPSA.** Once released, the proleader amino

acid chain is cleaved at the amino terminus by hK2, converting pPSA to its active 33-kD PSA form. In addition to hK2, pPSA may be activated to PSA by other prostate kallikreins, including hK4 (Takayama et al, 1997). Incomplete removal of the 7-amino-acid leader chain has led to the identification of various other truncated or clipped forms of pPSA. These include pPSAs with 2, 4, and 5 leader amino acids ([−2]pPSA, [−4]pPSA, and [−5]pPSA) (Zhang et al, 1995; Kumar et al, 1997, 2000; Mikolajczyk et al, 1997, 2001, 2002; Peter et al, 2001). **With cellular disruption, these inactive forms circulate as free PSA and may constitute the majority of the circulating free PSA in patients with prostate cancer** (Mikolajczyk et al, 1997) (Fig. 93–8).

Reports by Mikolajczyk and colleagues (2000,2001) have revealed significantly elevated levels of these truncated forms of pPSA in prostate cancer tissue. Incomplete cleavage and processing of pPSA may contribute to the relative increase of these PSA isoforms identified in prostate cancer tissue. One of these clipped forms that is cleaved between leucine 5 and serine 6 of the propeptide has been termed [−2]pPSA. The decreased PSA processing in prostate cancer may result in a relative increase in pPSA and its cleaved forms, in particular [−2]pPSA. Immunohistochemical studies by Mikolajczyk and colleagues (2001) have demonstrated increased binding of monoclonal antibodies recognizing [−2]pPSA in prostate

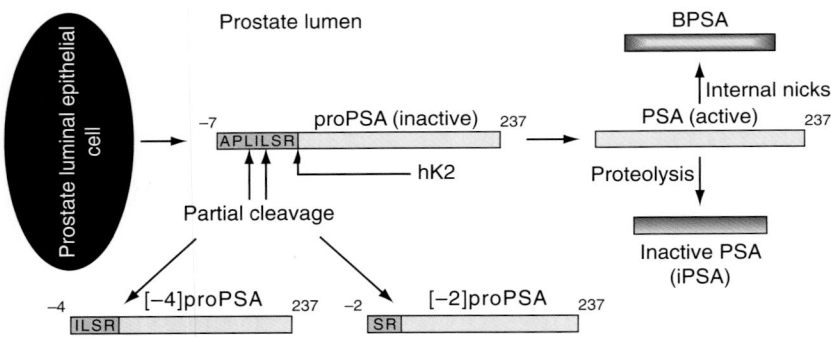

Figure 93–7. Differential cleavage and activation of pro-prostate-specific antigen (PSA). ProPSA is released from the prostate epithelial cell with a 7-amino-acid leader sequence. hK2 cleaves the amino acid leader to activate PSA. Active PSA undergoes proteolysis to yield inactive PSA (iPSA) and may also undergo internal degradation to form benign PSA (BPSA). Partial cleavage of the 7-amino-acid leader sequence yields inactive forms of proPSA (i.e., [−2]pPSA or [−4] pPSA).

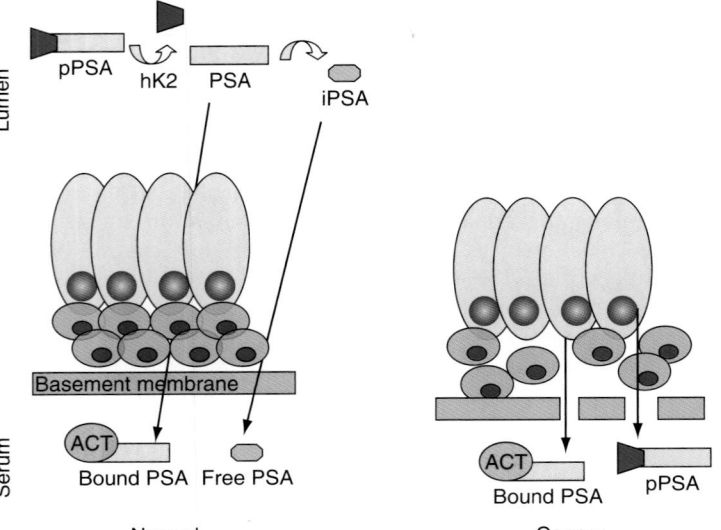

Figure 93–8. Prostate-specific antigen (PSA) synthesis in normal versus cancer tissue. ProPSA is secreted into the lumen, where the 7-amino-acid leader sequence is cleaved by hK2 to yield active PSA. Some of the active PSA diffuses into the serum, where it is bound to proteases such as α_1-antichymotrypsin (ACT). The luminal active PSA undergoes proteolysis, and the resulting inactive PSA (iPSA) may also enter the circulation to circulate in the unbound or free state. In prostate cancer, loss of the tissue architecture may permit a relative increase in bound PSA and proPSA in serum.

cancer tissue. Measuring the ratio of this clipped form of PSA to total PSA may serve as a strong discriminator between men with and without prostate cancer. These truncated forms in serum are being studied as potential prostate cancer markers.

Two studies (Khon et al, 2003; Sokoll et al, 2003) support these findings, demonstrating a positive diagnostic impact of pPSA in the early detection of prostate cancer in men with total PSA levels between 2.5 and 4 ng/mL and between 4 and 10 ng/mL. In the study by Sokoll and colleagues (2003), %pPSA detected up to 75% of cancers and avoided 59% of unnecessary biopsies (compared with 33% when %fPSA was applied) in men presenting with PSA levels between 2.5 and 4 ng/mL.

Another form of fPSA, referred to as benign PSA or BPSA, represents a cleaved form of PSA that has been identified in tissue from the nodular BPH transition zone tissue (Chen et al, 1997; Mikolajczyk et al, 2000; Wang et al, 2000). In a study by Marks and colleagues (2001), BPSA discriminated men with symptomatic BPH from men without BPH. Although serum BPSA alone is unlikely to differentiate between hyperplasia and cancer, in combination with assays for pPSA it may allow additional discrimination. Studies are under way to evaluate this important question further.

In addition to BPSA and pPSA, other isoforms of PSA have been identified in serum and have demonstrated promise as additional tools to aid in clinical detection of prostate cancer (Mikolajczyk et al, 2001, 2002; Peter et al, 2001). An additional form of pPSA that is found intact and inactive and that does not form a complex with ACT has been identified. This form of pPSA has been termed intact PSA and has been identified in human prostate cancer cells (Nurmikko et al, 2000, 2001; Steuber et al, 2002). It is likely that pPSA exists in various forms within tissue and serum from men with and without prostate cancer. Preliminary studies have demonstrated that the ratio of intact to free PSA may improve the accuracy of prostate cancer detection (Nurmikko et al, 2000, 2001; Steuber et al, 2002). Although encouraging, these studies using subfractions of fPSA await further scrutiny.

The introduction of assays measuring free, noncomplexed PSA, such as pPSA, introduces the potential for improved specificity for early prostate cancer detection. The relationship of pPSA, a form of fPSA, to prostate cancer is of particular interest because previous observations have noted an elevation in fPSA levels with benign disease. The answer to this dilemma may rest with the fact that pPSA forms, in fact, refine the loss of specificity in the %fPSA range of 10% to 25% (Mikolajczyk et al, 2001, 2002). Sokoll and colleagues (2003) have demonstrated that pPSA testing offers increased cancer detection rates compared with %fPSA, especially within the range 2.5 to 4.0 ng/mL. With a cancer incidence of 20% to 25% in the 2.5 to 4 ng/mL range, pPSA testing has the potential to contribute to the early diagnosis of these cancers.

Complexed PSA. As noted earlier, serum PSA exists both in a free form and complexed to serine protease inhibitors. **The current clinically relevant immunodetectable complexed forms of PSA are bound to ACT and, to a lesser extent, to API (Brawer, 1999). The sum of these and other presently unknown PSA complexes is represented by the term complexed PSA (cPSA).** The major form of cPSA in serum, PSA bound to ACT, is found in greater serum concen-

trations in men with cancer than in men with benign disease. Nonspecific binding hampered initial assays directed at measuring cPSA (Chan et al, 1996; Kuriyama et al, 1998). As a result, the corollary, fPSA, has become a surrogate approximation of the desired cPSA. Advances in immunoassay technology have resulted in a novel serum measurement for cPSA (Allard et al, 1998; Morris et al, 1998; Wu et al, 1998; Jung et al, 1999). This assay, the Bayer Immuno 1 cPSA (cPSA-BI) (Bayer Healthcare, Tarrytown, NY), is based on using a "cold antibody" to the E epitope (see Figs. 93–4 and 93–5) to clear all forms of fPSA from the sera to allow measurement of only cPSA (Morris et al, 1998). Preincubation with high concentrations of this cold anti–E epitope monoclonal antibody minimizes nonspecific binding and essentially makes this assay specific for all cPSA.

Since the introduction of this cPSA assay, numerous studies have demonstrated its equivalence to the enhancement of test specificity previously afforded by assays measuring %fPSA and its suitability for early detection of prostate cancer (Brawer et al, 1998, 2000; Sokoll, 1998; Croal et al, 1999; Maeda et al, 1999). In a retrospective analysis comparing the cPSA-BI assay with Hybritech total and Hybritech free-to-total assays (Beckman Coulter Inc, Fullerton, CA), Brawer and colleagues (1998) demonstrated enhanced specificity with the cPSA relative to total PSA at similar sensitivities. These authors also demonstrated specificities of 21.8% and 26.7% for tPSA and cPSA, respectively, for cutoff values to achieve 95% sensitivity. Follow-up studies by Sokoll (1998) and Brawer (2000) confirmed these earlier findings, as shown by improved receiver operator characteristic (ROC) analysis that favored cPSA over tPSA that was similar to results using the ratio of free to total PSA. Although similar sensitivities were demonstrated using a cPSA cutoff value of 3.75 ng/mL and a tPSA cutoff value of 4.0 ng/mL, cPSA increased specificity by as much as 13%.

Djavan and coworkers (2002) have evaluated the validity and performance of the cPSA and cPSA parameters (ratio of cPSA to tPSA, complexed PSA density [cPSAD], and cPSAD of the transition zone) versus earlier established markers (total PSA, fPSA/tPSA, PSAD, PSAD of transition zone). Studying tPSA in the range of 2.5 to 10 ng/mL, these investigators reported that although cPSA/tPSA offered minimal enhancement over fPSA/tPSA, cPSA volume-based parameters offered superior performance.

A multicenter study has also demonstrated superior performance of cPSA (Partin et al, 2003). This study compared the clinical performance of cPSA with that of tPSA (and %fPSA and %cPSA) as a first-line test for prostate cancer detection. To achieve sensitivity in the range of 80% to 95%, cPSA cutoff values ranging between 1.5 and 8.3 ng/mL provided up to 8% improvement in specificity over tPSA. Using a cutoff value of 2.5 ng/mL for tPSA and 2.2 ng/mL for cPSA provided specificity of 21.2% and 35%, respectively, with a sensitivity of 85%. The use of PSA ratios such as %fPSA and %cPSA provided no additional improvement in specificity over tPSA.

Recognizing the reported 25% incidence of prostate cancer in men with tPSA levels in the 2.5 to 4 ng/mL range, Horninger and colleagues (2002) sought to assess the clinical value of cPSA in comparison with tPSA as well as %fPSA and %cPSA for men with PSA levels in this range. Although earlier studies suggested decreased performance for fPSA in this low range, cPSA maintained its performance with improved specificity and sensitivity versus fPSA. A cutoff value of 2.5 ng/mL for tPSA and 2.1 ng/mL for cPSA provided specificities of 20.3% and 34%, respectively, with a sensitivity of 86%. For cutoff values of 25% fPSA and 74% cPSA, specificities of 11% and 21.5%, respectively, were obtained at sensitivity levels of 97%. More than 92% of these cancers were found to be organ confined, with Gleason scores ranging from 5 to 9. This study illustrated that this single test for cPSA improved detection as well as supporting earlier reports regarding the existence of clinically significant cancers in men with PSA levels less than 4 ng/mL.

In addition to cancer detection, cPSA may provide information regarding prostate cancer staging (Sokoll et al, 2002; Taneja et al, 2002). In the study by Taneja and colleagues (2002), cPSA levels were shown to correlate with the likelihood of extracapsular extension in prostate specimens following radical prostatectomy. Comparing cPSA with other parameters such as tPSA, fPSA/tPSA, and PSAD, this study demonstrated that regardless of PSA parameter, cPSA could perform at levels equal to those of tPSA, and that although cPSA appears to have an overall sensitivity similar to that of tPSA, this derivative is capable of maintaining higher specificity at higher cutoff points. Sokoll and colleagues (2002) have also demonstrated the utility of cPSA levels to provide prognostic staging information in a contemporary series of patients undergoing radical prostatectomy. Multivariate analysis using Gleason score, clinical stage, and cPSA provided an area under the ROC curve (AUC-ROC) of 0.69. Replacing cPSA with tPSA in this model provided similar information because these two variables were highly correlated. This implies that cPSA levels can provide staging information.

In the age of cost containment, it seems logical to streamline laboratory testing. Ellison and coworkers (2002) employed statistical modeling to determine the PSA derivative with the most appropriate cost-to-benefit ratio for prostate cancer screening. Comparing five screening strategies (tPSA 4 ng/mL, fPSA/tPSA, and three cutoff values for cPSA: 3.8, 3.4, 3 ng/mL), these authors noted that given the lack of an established sensitivity, at values for 92% sensitivity, a cPSA level of 3 ng/mL identified a similar number of cancers with fewer biopsies. Although this level demonstrated a marginal increased cost compared with tPSA, the reduced biopsy rate and overall cost of screening that would result positively affected overall expenditures.

Human Kallikrein 2 (hK2)

The human kallikrein hK2 has been found to share many important properties with PSA and has demonstrated potential as another prostate cancer tumor marker (Young et al, 1992; Darson et al, 1997; Kumar et al, 1997; Rittenhouse et al, 1998; Lovgren et al, 1999; Becker et al, 2000; Yousef et al, 2001a). **Among many similarities, hK2 and PSA share 80% amino acid homology** (see Fig. 93–1), **exhibit similar specificity for prostate tissue, and are both hormonally regulated by androgens.** The exact function of hK2 remains under further study, but this protease has been shown to perform enzymatic activities, one of which is to activate the zymogen (pPSA) to the active PSA through cleavage of the amino acid presequence (see Fig. 93–7) (Young et al, 1992; Kumar et al, 1997; Yousef et al, 2001a).

The concentration of hK2 in samples of prostatic tissue, seminal fluid, and serum is many times lower than that of PSA (Young et al, 1992; Darson et al, 1997; Lovgren et al, 1999). In prostatic tissue, the hK2 mRNA concentration represents only 10% to 50% of PSA mRNA concentrations, and in semen and serum samples, the concentration of hK2 is 1% to 3% that of PSA (Young et al, 1992; Darson et al, 1997; Lovgren et al, 1999). Together with specificity issues, cross-reactivity with PSA and the detection limits of the available assays for these low hK2 concentrations challenged earlier analytic experiments. However, the development of hK2 purification techniques and more specific monoclonal antibodies has resulted in more reliable assays and thus increased study in the clinical setting (Piironen et al, 1996; Finlay et al, 1998; Klee et al, 1999; Becker et al, 2000).

Immunohistochemical studies revealed different tissue expression patterns for hK2 and PSA. In benign epithelium, PSA is intensely expressed compared with the minimal immunoreactivity of hK2 (Tremblay et al, 1997; Darson et al, 1999). **In contrast, in cancerous tissue more intense expression of hK2 is seen.** Furthermore, hK2 immunohistochemically stains the different Gleason grades of prostate cancer differently than PSA. This inverse staining relationship of hK2 is seen as intense staining in high-grade (Gleason primary grade 4 or 5) cancers and lymph node metastasis compared with minimal staining in low-grade (Gleason primary grade 1 to 3) cancers and even weaker association in benign tissue, in which PSA exhibits intense staining (Darson et al, 1997, 1999; Tremblay et al, 1997; Kwiatkowski et al, 1998).

The development of improved monoclonal antibodies for hK2 has minimized the previous cross-reactivity with PSA and permitted more accurate measurement of hK2 in serum samples (Finlay et al, 1998; Klee et al, 1999; Becker et al, 2000). Since the introduction of these assays, many researchers have demonstrated elevated levels of hK2 in men with prostate cancer compared with men without cancer (Becker et al, 2000). Furthermore, men with low-grade disease have lower concentrations of serum hK2 than men with more aggressive cancer (Darson et al, 1999; Becker et al, 2000). Application of the ratio of hK2 to free PSA (hK2/fPSA) allows discrimination between benign tissue and cancer (Kwiatkowski et al, 1998). For men with tPSA in the 4 to 10 ng/mL range, hK2/fPSA significantly differentiated prostate cancer from BPH, whereas hK2/tPSA did not (Becker et al, 2000). Data from a multicenter study demonstrated a statistically significant difference between men with biopsies positive for cancer, looking at hK2 alone and in combination with fPSA/tPSA (Kwiatkowski et al, 1998). Combining %fPSA and hK2/fPSA, Partin and associates (1999) demonstrated an increased cancer detection rate within the tPSA range of 2 to 10 ng/mL. Furthermore, this group was able to identify up to 40% of men with cancer in the 2 to 4 ng/mL range measuring hK2/fPSA.

Additional reports have demonstrated the ability of hK2 levels to predict pathologic outcome and to aid in repeat prostate biopsy decision-making (Haese et al, 2000, 2003; Nam et al, 2001). Haese and colleagues (2000, 2003) evaluated the ability of hK2 levels to distinguish between pathologic organ-confined and non–organ-confined prostate cancer. In univariate ROC and multivariate logistic regression analyses, hK2 optimally predicted organ-confined disease. Nam and coworkers (2001) showed that men found to have cancer upon repeat biopsy had higher hK2 and hK2/fPSA levels than men with a negative biopsy, suggesting that hK2 may be helpful in improving the selection criteria for repeat biopsy. Although these results are encouraging, further evaluation is under way before recommendation and widespread application of hK2 to the clinical armamentarium of tumor markers.

Additional Kallikrein Tumor Markers

In addition to PSA (hK3) and hK2, 15 other kallikrein genes have been identified. The expression products of these genes have demonstrated diagnostic potential as prostate cancer tumor markers. Many of these proteases have a highly conserved structural organization and have been shown to contribute to biologic events such as angiogenesis and growth factor release (Diamandis and Yousef, 2001). Study of these proteins suggests interaction among the kallikreins in pathways that affect normal physiologic and pathologic processes (Yousef et al, 2002b). Among these genes, the studies have evaluated some of the potential of the expression products of KLK4, KLK11, KLK14, and KLK15 as biomarkers for prostate cancer.

KLK4

The gene KLK4 encodes hK4 and is predominantly expressed in basal cells of the normal prostate (Xi et al, 2004). Although its function and structure continue to evaluated, current studies suggest that this peptide is not targeted for secretion and is predominantly localized to the nucleus (Xi et al, 2004). It was originally demonstrated to be unique to prostatic expression, but improved reverse transcription polymerase chain reaction (PCR) techniques have identified KLK4 mRNA expression in the testis, adrenal, uterus, and thyroid (Nelson et al, 1999). Although hK4 expression has been shown to occur in both normal and cancerous prostate tissue, KLK4 mRNA was found to be expressed at higher levels in the majority of prostate cancer tissues compared with matched normal prostate tissues (Obiezu et al, 2002; Xi et al, 2004). In ovarian cancer, hK4 has demonstrated an association with advanced disease. Further evaluation is under way to explore the value of this kallikrein as a biomarker for prostate cancer.

KLK11

The gene KLK11 encodes hK11, formally referred to as hippostasin or PRSS20 (Diamandis et al, 2002). It was initially found to be present in the serum of cancer patients, but further studies have demonstrated that this protease may aid in discrimination from men with BPH, as immunofluorometric assays have displayed lower hK11 values in prostate cancer patients compared with men with BPH (Nakamura et al, 2003). Applying the ratio of hK11 to total PSA resulted in a further reduction in unnecessary biopsies. Nakamura and colleagues (2003) have demonstrated that at 90% sensitivity, the ratio of hK11 to total PSA has a specificity of 51.5%. Confirmatory studies are under way for this promising new biomarker.

KLK14

Yousef and coworkers (2001b) have identified KLK14 of the kallikrein gene family. Expression of this gene has been demonstrated to occur in brain, spinal cord, prostate, thyroid, and testis. The expression of hK14 is similar to that of hK2 and PSA and has been noted in the secretory epithelial cells of the prostate (Hooper et al, 2001). Elevated levels of this protein have been demonstrated in prostate cancer tissues compared with normal prostate tissues. Although it is still early in development, this marker may aid in prognosis as this protease appears to correlate with aggressiveness of disease (Yousef et al, 2003).

KLK15

The gene KLK15 encodes hK15. Although it is most notably expressed in the thyroid, lower levels of hK15 expression have also been measured from the prostate, salivary gland, adrenal, colon, testis, and kidney (Yousef et al, 2001). Using a human prostate cancer cell line, KLK15 expression was found to be upregulated compared with normal prostate tissues (Yousef et al, 2001). As with hK14, hK15 has shown association with tumor aggressiveness and has potential as a diagnostic and prognostic prostate cancer biomarker (Stephan et al, 2003).

PROSTATE-SPECIFIC MEMBRANE ANTIGEN

The glycoprotein prostate-specific membrane antigen (PSMA) is a folate hydrolase and is found embedded within the cell membrane of prostatic epithelial cells. The hydrophobic amino acids found on amino acid residues 20 to 43 suggest that this protein is a type II integral membrane protein with a small intracellular domain and a large extracellular domain (Israeli et al, 1997; Fair et al, 1997). PSMA has been identified in central nervous system, intestine, and prostate. In the brain, PSMA functions to metabolize the neurotransmitter N-acetyl-aspartyl-glutamate. In the intestine, PSMA has been localized to the proximal small bowel, where it works as a carboxypepsidase. Although isolated in these other tissues, PSMA is predominantly expressed in the prostate gland.

Of interest for diagnosis and imaging is the discovery of elevated expression of this protein in tissue from prostate cancer compared with normal prostate tissue (Silver et al, 1997; Chang et al, 1999; Elgamal et al, 2000). Furthermore, PSMA mRNA expression within prostate cancers is highest in the hormone-deprived state (Henttu et al, 1992; Israeli et al, 1994). **During cancer progression, differentially expressed variants of PSMA have been identified. Of three alternatively spliced variants of PSMA, one, known as PSM′, is differentially expressed in normal tissue, BPH, and prostate cancer.** Su and colleagues (1995) demonstrated that the PSMA/PSM′ ratio is up-regulated three- to sixfold in prostate cancer compared with BPH (0.76 to 1.6) and normal (0.075 to 0.45) tissue. Further reports to date have demonstrated the production of antibodies to PSMA. Horoszewicz and coworkers (1987) have found increased PSMA levels in 47% of prostate cancer patients (20 of 43) versus only 5% of noncancer patients (3 of 66) and negative results in 30 normal blood donors. Utilizing the antibody produced by Horoszewicz and coworkers, Xiao and colleagues (2001) reported use of an Immuno-SELDI assay for PSMA. Applying the antibody to PSMA on a ProteinChip array, these authors were able to differentiate cases of prostate cancer from BPH. The clinical usefulness of PSMA for diagnosis, monitoring, and imaging is promising and remains under investigation.

MOLECULAR BIOLOGY AND DISCOVERY OF SERUM BIOMARKERS FOR PROSTATE CANCER

New understanding of the molecular biology of carcinogenesis and prostate cancer is beginning to yield a new era in prostate cancer tumor research. Applications of sensitive tools are providing clinicians with improved methods for diagnosis and management of disease. These advances in molecular oncology have vastly improved our current understanding of prostate cancer etiology and molecular pathogenesis and have identified the importance of genomic alterations, epigenetic modifications, and gene-protein expression that contribute to the development and progression of prostate cancer.

Genomic Alterations and Susceptibility in Prostate Cancer

The presence of a positive family history has been known to be a risk factor for the development of prostate cancer. Through studies of affected families with prostate cancer, a number of susceptibility loci probably involved in the risk of development of cancer have been identified (Lichtenstein et al, 2000). Prostate cancer susceptibility genes have been located on chromosome 1q24-25 (*HPC1*), 1q42-2-q43 (*PCaP*), 1p36 (*CAPB*), 16q23.2, 17p11(*ELAC2* or *HPC2*), 20q13 (*HPC20*), and Xq27-28 (*HPCX*) (Monroe et al, 1995; Lichtenstein et al, 2000; Nam et al, 2003; Simard et al, 2003). Key susceptibility genes that have been proposed to be involved in the inflammatory response are *MSR1* and *RNAEL* (DeMarzo et al, 2003).

Within these families, genetic polymorphisms are likely to occur at higher frequency and contribute to the increased risk of prostate cancer. **Polymorphic variants in genes encoding androgen receptor (AR), CYP17, and 5α-reductase type II (SRD5A2) have been evaluated and suggest a role of infection and inflammation in the development of prostate cancer** (DeMarzo et al, 2003). Other polymorphic variants in genes encoding CYP3A, vitamin D receptor, PSA, GST-T1, GST-M1, GST-P1, IGF-1, and IGF-binding protein 3 have also been studied. Among these, GST-P1 and IGF have shown correlation with the presence of cancer on biopsy in men with elevated PSA levels (Nam et al, 2003).

Although this information has aided and continues to contribute to the study of prostate cancer, familial susceptibility genes and polymorphisms are unlikely to account completely for the development of prostate cancer. Development of a large-scale test for these genes as a screening modality in the male population would probably not be very effective. Other factors such as diet, lifestyle, and chronic inflammation have also been implicated in the cause and progression of prostate cancer (Nelson et al, 2002; Foley et al, 2004b; Montironi et al, 2004).

Epigenetic Modifications

Changes in gene expression may occur as a result of alterations in DNA. Alterations known as epigenetic modifications include changes in DNA methylation and histone acetylation status. **Segments within the gene promoter that are composed of GC-rich regions are termed CpG islands. Alterations in the methylation status of these regions may affect gene expression and have been shown to play a role in carcinogenesis** (Jones and Baylin, 2002). **Furthermore, cumulative effects of environmental exposures such as diet and stress throughout life may affect DNA methylation status and thus contribute to the risk of cancer development** (Li et al, 2004). Assays for detection of CpG island hypermethylation include Southern blot, restriction endonuclease PCR (RE-PCR), bisulfite genomic sequencing (BCR), and methylation-specific PCR (MSP). Although each assay is sensitive, technical limitations exist. Currently, MSP is most commonly employed for the detection of methylated CpG islands. **The products of two hypermethylated genes that have been evaluated in prostate cancer development are glutathione S-transferase P1 (GSTP1) and ras association domain family protein isoform A (RASSF1A).**

GSTP1 belongs to a family of detoxifying enzymes that are involved in metabolic reduction of electrophilic carcinogens. These enzymes have been suggested to be involved in the development of prostate cancer. Elevated levels of GSTP1 CpG hypermethylation have been detected in tissues from precancerous lesions (atypia and prostatic intraepithelial neoplasia [PIN]) and within ejaculates, urine, and plasma from men with prostate cancer (Nakayama et al, 2003). To date, many studies have evaluated these hypermethylated CpG islands as a prostate cancer tumor marker (Cairns et al, 2001; Goessl et al, 2001a, 2001b; Gonzalgo et al, 2003; Bastion et al, 2004). Cairns and coworkers (2001) have demonstrated the presence of elevated GSTP1 hypermethylation in up to 79% of prostate cancer specimens. Utilizing urine specimens obtained after prostate massage, Goessl and colleagues (2001a, 2001b) found elevated levels of this marker in 68% of men with organ-confined disease, 78% of men with locally advanced or metastatic disease, 29% of men with PIN, and 2% of men with BPH.

Gonzalgo and coworkers (2003) demonstrated elevated GSTP1 hypermethylation in up to 50% of urine sediments taken from men immediately after transrectal prostate biopsy. Hypermethylation was also detected in 33% of men with negative biopsies and up to 67% of men found to have PIN or atypia, suggesting that these patients may harbor occult prostate cancer and require more rigid follow-up with a low threshold for repeat biopsy. The use of MSP to measure GSTP1 hypermethylation in body fluids represents an emerging tool that is feasible and has demonstrated reproducible results, and it is likely to become a valued screening modality for prostate cancer detection.

In addition to GSTP1, hypermethylation of RASSF1A has been noted to occur in up to 70% of prostate cancers (Kuzmin et al, 2002; Liu et al, 2002). Early findings have noted an association of this marker with more aggressive tumors, and it may aid in distinguishing between these cancers and more indolent cancers. Although early, this work is promising, and the subject remains under investigation.

Gene Expression and Proteomics in Tumor Marker Discovery

Application of sensitive tools in the study of molecular biology is becoming essential for the discovery of novel tumor markers. Identifying unique genetic expression in cancer states compared with normal tissues will provide not only insight into the molecular etiology of disease but also novel methods for detection. In addition to identifying genes that are either on or off, identification of post-translational events that are unique to disease states will undoubtedly become invaluable in the discovery of cancer biomarkers. The identification of biomarkers from human serum and body fluids has been assessed by a variety of proteomic technologies. Advances in proteomic technologies such as surface-enhanced laser desorption-ionization time-of-flight (SELDI-TOF) mass spectroscopy offer the potential to identify the presence of disease from human serum and other body fluids and may also provide new targets for diagnosis and therapy.

α-Methylacyl Coenzyme A Racemase

The α-methylacyl coenzyme A racemase (AMACR) gene, located on chromosome 5, has been found to be upregulated in prostate cancer tissues (Luo et al, 2002; Rubin et al, 2002). AMACR functions as an enzyme responsible for the beta-oxidation of branched-chain fatty acids obtained in diets consisting of beef and dairy products. Upregulated AMACR mRNA levels have been identified using immunohistochemical analysis and Western blot assays in clinical prostate cancer tissue. Luo and colleagues (2002) demonstrated that 88% of prostate cancer cases and both untreated metastasis and hormone-refractory prostate cancers were strongly positive for AMACR. Rogers and colleagues (2004) measured AMACR levels in the voided urine from 26 men following transrectal prostate biopsy. Elevated AMACR levels were detected in 18 of 26 (69%) of the men and provided 100% sensitivity (12 of 12 positive biopsies) and 58% specificity. Immunohistochemical studies by Rubin and coworkers (2002) have shown that AMACR expression in biopsy tissue may provide 97% sensitivity and 100% specificity for prostate cancer detection. Furthermore, through combination with other markers such as p63 that aid in identifying basal cells absent in prostate cancer, AMACR has potential for the development of molecular probes to aid in the detection of prostate cancer.

Prostate Breast Overexpressed Gene1 (PBOV1) or *UROC28*

An and colleagues (2000) have cloned and characterized a novel gene *UROC28* found to be overexpressed in prostate, breast, and bladder carcinomas. This gene is on chromosome 6q23-24, and the expression product protein is measurable in serum. Early immunohistochemical studies have demonstrated differential expression and characterization between normal and cancerous tissues. This group has also identified and measured the protein UC28 in serum. Application of the antibody to a ProteinChip and SELDI analysis has provided encouraging results correctly distinguishing cancer specimens from normal and BPH specimens. This preliminary work remains under investigation.

Hepsin

Complementary DNA (cDNA) microarray analysis has demonstrated overexpression of hepsin in prostate cancer compared with normal prostate and BPH tissues (Luo et al, 2001; Magee et al, 2001; Stamey et al, 2001). Hepsin is a type II transmembrane serine protease and was originally found as a cDNA clone in a human liver cDNA library (Leytus et al, 1988). Immunohistochemical studies have shown abundant staining of hepsin in tumor cell membranes. Stephan and coworkers (2004) have shown hepsin staining in 90% of all cases of prostate cancer. Furthermore, these authors demonstrated that in 53% of cases hepsin overexpression was more than 10-fold in cancerous tissue. In addition to providing a method for cancer detection, hepsin expression may provide prognostic information that may be used to assess prostate cancer aggressiveness.

DD3^{PCA3}

Utilizing differential display and Northern blot analysis to compare normal and prostate cancer tissue, Bussemakers and colleagues (1999) identified the DD3 prostate-specific gene on chromosome 9q21-22. Study of this gene has determined that it may function as noncoding RNA as it has been found to be alternatively spliced, contains a high density of stop codons, and lacks an open reading frame. **Expression of the DD3^{PCA3} protein has been localized to prostatic tissue and has been found in 95% of prostate cancer and prostate metastasis specimens.** de Kok and colleagues (2002) have developed a real-time quantitative reverse transcriptase PCR (QRT-PCR) assay for DD3 and showed **66-fold upregulation of this protein in cancerous tissues compared with normal control tissues. Furthermore, DD3 was detected from specimens containing as little as 10% cancer, indicating that this test was capable of finding cancer within a large background of normal cells.** Utilizing this discovery, Hessels and coworkers (2003) developed a test to detect DD3 in urine specimens from men following prostate massage and biopsy. Using QRT-PCR to analyze the urine from these men undergoing biopsy for serum PSA greater than 3 ng/mL, the test demonstrated 67% sensitivity and 83% specificity for men diagnosed with cancer after confirmatory biopsy. As also reported, a negative predictive value of 90% supports the potential of the test as a modality to reduce the number of invasive diagnostic procedures such as TRUS biopsy. Developments of clinical assays are currently under way for DD3.

NMP 48 (50.8 kD)

Utilizing proteomic patterns based on SELDI-TOF mass spectroscopy, Hlavaty and colleagues (2003) discovered a unique 50.8-kD protein. This protein was subsequently characterized as vitamin D binding protein using peptide mass fingerprinting. Utilizing preprocessed serum samples from men with prostate cancer, BPH, and no cancer, this group was able to identify correctly vitamin D binding protein in the samples from men with cancer. SELDI-TOF identified the protein in 50 of 52 (96%) cancer cases, 5 of 20 (25%) biopsy-confirmed benign cases, 3 of 10 (30%) BPH cases, and 2 of 50 (4%) normal controls. Validation studies are under way for this potential prostate cancer tumor marker.

SUMMARY

Early detection when cancer remains confined to the prostate will not only improve cure rates but also decrease mortality from this disease. Although the discovery and application of PSA have revolutionized current prostate cancer detection and management, stage migration and changes in the natural history of this cancer have outrun the currently maximized application of this tumor marker. Application of various PSA derivatives, although improving sensitivity, risks impairing specificity. Discovery of molecular derivatives of PSA and new kallikrein markers has also improved prostate cancer detection.

Innovations and new understanding in the field of molecular oncology have provided a host of potential prostate cancer tumor markers. As prostate cancer has been shown to be a heterogeneous disease, application of a panel of markers will probably ultimately provide added sensitivity and specificity for detection of disease. Identification of hypermethylated regions such as GSTP1 and overexpressed proteins such as DD3 and NMP48 provides greater diagnostic and prognostic potential to improve detection of prostate cancer. As these discoveries mature, development of these markers from research into clinically applicable tools will improve detection and management of prostate cancer.

KEY POINTS: PROSTATE CANCER TUMOR MARKERS

- Today, most prostate cancer arises as clinically nonpalpable (stage T1c) disease with PSA between 2.5 and 10 ng/mL. The evolving demographics and natural history of prostate cancer have resulted in stage migration to nonpalpable, clinically localized (stage T1c) disease and a parallel reduction in mortality.

- Although PSA is widely accepted as a prostate cancer tumor marker, it is organ specific and not disease specific.

- PSA is normally found in low concentration in serum (ng/mL). In serum, PSA circulates in both bound and unbound forms. Three proteins that are recognized to bind to PSA within the blood are α_1-antichymotrypsin (ACT), α_2-macroglobulin (A2M), and α_1-protease inhibitor (API).

- Although prostate cancer cells do not produce more PSA than benign prostate epithelium, the PSA produced from malignant cells appears to escape proteolytic processing. Thus, men with prostate cancer have a greater fraction of serum PSA complexed to ACT and a lower percentage of total PSA that is free compared with men without prostate cancer.

- The serum half-life of PSA, calculated after removal of all prostate tissue, is 2 to 3 days.

- Uncomplexed PSA is cleared from the serum within 2 to 3 hours.

- Finasteride (5 mg) and other 5α-reductase inhibitors for treatment of BPH have been shown to lower PSA levels by an average of 50%.

- Although saw palmetto has not been shown to affect PSA levels, possible contaminants of these unregulated supplements may include compounds that can alter PSA levels (i.e., PC-SPES, now off the market). Interpretation of PSA values should always take into account the presence of prostate disease, previous diagnostic procedures, and prostate-directed treatments.

- The role for %fPSA is more applicable to PSA levels less than 10 ng/mL as the positive predictive rate of total PSA above 10 to 20 ng/mL has been demonstrated to be as high as 80%.

- PSA originates with a 17-amino-acid chain that is cleaved to yield a precursor inactive form of PSA termed proPSA (pPSA)

- The current clinically relevant immunodetectable complexed forms of PSA are bound to ACT and, to a lesser extent, to API. The sum of these and other presently unknown PSA complexes is represented by the term complexed PSA (cPSA).

- Immunohistochemical studies reveal different tissue expression patterns for hK2 and PSA. In benign epithelium, PSA is intensely expressed compared with the minimal immunoreactivity of hK2. In contrast, in cancerous tissue more intense expression of hK2 is seen.

- Polymorphic variants in genes encoding androgen receptor (AR), CYP17, and 5α-reductase type II (SRD5A2) have been evaluated and suggest a role of infection and inflammation in the development of prostate cancer.

- Segments within the gene promoter that are composed of GC-rich regions are termed CpG islands. Alterations in the methylation status of these regions may affect gene expression and have been shown to play a role in carcinogenesis.

- The products of two hypermethylated genes that have been evaluated in prostate cancer development are glutathione S-transferase P1 (GSTP1) and ras association domain family protein isoform A (RASSF1A).

- The AMACR gene, located on chromosome 5, has been found to be upregulated in prostate cancer tissues.

- Expression of the DD3[PCA3] protein has been localized to prostatic tissue and has been found in 95% of prostate cancer and prostate metastasis specimens.

SUGGESTED READINGS

Bastian PJ, Nakayama M, De Marzo AM, Nelson WG: GSTP1 CpG island hypermethylation as a molecular marker of prostate cancer. Urologe A 2004;43:573-579.

Becker C, Noldus J, Diamandis E, Lilja H: The role of molecular forms of prostate-specific antigen (PSA or hK3) and of human glandular kallikrein 2 (hK2) in the diagnosis and monitoring of prostate cancer and in extraprostatic disease. Crit Rev Clin Lab Sci 2001;38:357-399.

Catalona WJ, Partin AW, Slawin KM, et al: Use of the percentage of free prostate-specific antigen to enhance differentiation of prostate cancer from benign prostatic disease: A prospective multicenter clinical trial. JAMA 1998;279:1542-1547.

Christensson A, Laurell CB, Lilja H: Enzymatic activity of prostate-specific antigen and its reactions with extracellular serine proteinase inhibitors. Eur J Biochem 1990;194:755-763.

DeMarzo AM, Nelson WG, Isaacs WB, Epstein JI: Pathological and molecular aspects of prostate cancer. Lancet 2003;361:955-964.

Diamandis EP, Yousef GM: Human tissue kallikrein gene family: A rich source of novel disease biomarkers. Expert Rev Mol Diagn 2001;1:182-190.

Li LC, Okino ST, Dahiya R: DNA methylation in prostate cancer. Biochim Biophys Acta 2004;1704:87-102.

Lilja H: Prostate-specific antigen: Molecular forms and the human kallikrein gene family. Br J Urol 1997;79(Suppl 1):44-48.

Mikolajczyk SD, Marks LS, Partin AW, Rittenhouse HG: Free prostate-specific antigen in serum is becoming more complex. Urology 2002;59:797-802.

Polascik TJ, Oesterling JE, Partin AW: Prostate specific antigen: A decade of discovery—What we have learned and where we are going. J Urol 1999;162:293-306.

Rittenhouse HG, Finlay JA, Mikolajczyk SD, Partin AW: Human kallikrein 2 (hK2) and prostate-specific antigen (PSA): Two closely related, but distinct, kallikreins in the prostate. Crit Rev Clin Lab Sci 1998;35:275-368.

Stephan C, Jung K, Diamandis EP, et al: Prostate-specific antigen, its molecular forms, and other kallikrein markers for detection of prostate cancer. Urology 2002;59:2-8.

Diagnosis and Staging of Prostate Cancer

H. BALLENTINE CARTER, MD • MOHAMAD E. ALLAF, MD • ALAN W. PARTIN, MD, PHD

DETECTION OF PROSTATE CANCER

DIAGNOSTIC MODALITIES

GUIDELINES FOR EARLY DETECTION OF PROSTATE CANCER

STAGING OF PROSTATE CANCER

The histologic diagnosis of prostate cancer is made, in the majority of cases, by prostate needle biopsy. Prostate cancer rarely causes symptoms until it is advanced. Thus, suspicion of prostate cancer resulting in a recommendation for prostatic biopsy is most often raised by abnormalities found on digital rectal examination (DRE) or by serum prostate-specific antigen (PSA) elevations. Although there is controversy regarding the benefits of early diagnosis, it has been demonstrated that an early diagnosis of prostate cancer is best achieved using a combination of DRE and PSA. Transrectal ultrasound (TRUS)-guided, systematic needle biopsy is the most reliable method, at present, to ensure accurate sampling of prostatic tissue in men considered at high risk for harboring prostatic cancer on the basis of DRE and PSA findings.

The goal of cancer staging is to determine the extent of disease as precisely as possible to assess prognosis and guide management recommendations. The local extent of disease determined by DRE (tumor [T] stage), serum PSA level before prostatic biopsy, and tumor grade correlates directly with pathologic extent of disease and is useful in the staging evaluation of men with adenocarcinoma of the prostate. Magnetic resonance imaging (MRI) and nuclear medicine imaging have been investigated as modalities to identify lymphatic spread of cancer. There are no available imaging studies capable of reliably identifying early local extraprostatic spread of disease. Although not routinely utilized, less invasive methods of lymph node sampling (laparoscopic lymphadenectomy) have been used to detect metastatic disease in men judged to be at high risk for harboring lymph node metastases on the basis of preliminary evaluation with DRE, serum PSA level, and tumor grade.

DETECTION OF PROSTATE CANCER

Prostate cancer rarely causes symptoms early in the course of the disease because the majority of adenocarcinomas arise in the periphery of the gland distant from the urethra. The presence of systemic symptoms (e.g., bone pain, renal failure, anemia) as a result of prostate cancer suggests locally advanced or widely metastatic disease. Growth of prostate cancer into the urethra or bladder neck can result in obstructive (e.g., hesitancy, decreased force of stream, intermittency) and irritative (e.g., frequency, nocturia, urgency, urge incontinence) voiding symptoms. Local invasion of prostate cancer can involve the trigone of the bladder and lead to ureteral obstruction that, if bilateral, can cause renal failure. Local progression of disease and obstruction of the ejaculatory ducts can result in hematospermia and the finding of decreased ejaculate volume. Although rare in the PSA era, impotence can be a manifestation of prostate cancer that has spread outside the prostatic capsule to involve the branches of the pelvic plexus (neurovascular bundle) responsible for innervation of the corpora cavernosa.

Metastatic disease involving the axial or appendicular skeleton can cause bone pain or anemia from replacement of the bone marrow or microfractures. Lower extremity edema can result from cancerous involvement of the pelvic lymph nodes and compression of the iliac veins or lymphatics. Less common findings from metastatic disease include malignant retroperitoneal fibrosis from dissemination of cancer cells along the periureteral lymphatics, paraneoplastic syndromes from ectopic hormone production, and disseminated intravascular coagulation (DIC).

Although the patient with prostate cancer may present with voiding symptoms suggestive of prostate disease and signs and symptoms related to metastatic disease, the vast majority (over 80%) of men diagnosed today with prostate cancer are initially suspected of disease on the basis of DRE abnormalities or serum PSA elevations. Changes in prostate cancer screening or early detection—primarily owing to the widespread use of PSA testing in the late 1980s—have reduced the proportion of patients with prostate cancer detected because of symptoms suggestive of advanced disease. The 50% to 70% decline in the incidence of distant stage disease between 1986 and 1999 among men age 50 years or older (Chu et al, 2003) is a direct result of PSA screening and early detection efforts.

Detection Issues

The routine use of DRE and PSA testing in asymptomatic men as a means of reducing prostate cancer mortality by earlier detection and treatment remains controversial (Coley et al, 1997; Houston et al, 1998; Denis et al, 2000; Thompson et al, 2000). Screening efforts in the past decade have resulted in a marked downward stage migration, and the resultant increase in the incidence of early stage prostate cancer could have contributed to a decline in prostate cancer mortality. Nevertheless, there are legitimate concerns about population screening of asymptomatic men using PSA and DRE (Barry, 1998).

First, the lifetime risk (from age 0 to 90 years) of death from prostate cancer is 3% and the lifetime risk of a diagnosis of prostate cancer is 17% (Surveillance, Epidemiology, and End Results [SEER] Program). Thus, in the absence of markers that accurately identify men who have life-threatening cancers, screening will result in overdiagnosis (i.e., detection of a cancer through screening that would have otherwise remained clinically silent) and overtreatment of some men. It has been estimated that overdiagnosis rates with screening are in the range of 30% to 50% and increase directly with age (Etzioni et al, 2002; Draisma et al, 2003). Furthermore, the prevalence of PSA screening among older men is higher than among younger men. A telephone survey found that the prevalence of PSA screening within the last year was 48% among men age 50 to 59 years and 56% among those 80 years and older (Sirovich et al, 2003). Information from a population-based health survey suggested that PSA screening occurred in one in three men age 75 years or older versus 18% of men age 45 to 54 years (Lu-Yao et al, 2003). This suggests that a substantial proportion of the men undergoing screening and treatment of prostate cancer will undergo a treatment unlikely to extend life (Wasson et al, 2002).

Second, screening for prostate cancer in asymptomatic men results in false-positive screens prompting unnecessary prostate biopsies, and treatment of prostate cancer regardless of the management option chosen can result in unwanted side effects—a poor tradeoff if the treatment resulted in no benefit in terms of years of life saved.

Third, the costs of screening may not be justified if the societal harm of diagnosis and treatment is far greater than any health benefits obtained. All of these as yet incompletely addressed issues are considerations of any screening program and not unique to prostate cancer screening.

Specialty Group and Task Force Recommendations for Screening

The U.S. Preventive Services Task Force (2002) concluded that the evidence is insufficient to recommend for or against routine screening for prostate cancer using PSA testing or DRE. This conclusion was based on good evidence that PSA testing can lead to the detection of prostate cancer at an early stage but inconclusive evidence that early detection improves health outcomes. A 1995 report by the Office of Technology Assessment concluded that research to date has not determined whether systematic early screening for prostate cancer with PSA or DRE would save lives and that the choice to have screening or forgo it depends on patients' values (U.S. Congress, Office of Technology Assessment, 1995). The American Cancer Society (Smith et al, 2002) and the American Urological Association (Thompson et al, 2000) recommended that prostate cancer screening with PSA and DRE be offered to all men older than 50 years and that the risks and benefits of screening be discussed with the patient. **Although the value of PSA screening remains controversial, men who present for periodic health examinations should be made aware of the availability of the PSA test so that they can make an informed decision about the need for routine screening.** The enthusiasm for screening in general in the United States suggests that most men will decide to be tested (Schwartz et al, 2004).

Simulations and Population-Based Observations of Screening

In the absence of randomized trials, some investigators have used computer simulations that model the natural history of prostate cancer to address the potential benefits of prostate cancer screening (Krahn et al, 1994; Barry et al, 1995). Results from these models suggest minimal benefit in terms of lives saved, especially when adjusted for quality of life. However, the outcomes can be questioned based on (1) the use of unrealistically low progression rates to model the natural history of the disease, (2) the assumption that a single screen would lower cancer mortality, or (3) the assignment of similar utility weights (for calculation of quality-adjusted life years) for development of metastatic disease, for which there is no treatment, and incontinence after radical prostatectomy, for which there is effective treatment. More recent simulations have estimated that 16 (range 13 to 22) of every 100 patients between ages 50 and 70 years with screen-detected cancer could have their life extended with surgical treatment (McGregor et al, 1998) and that approximately 100 screen-detected prostate cancers would have to be treated per 17 lives saved at age 65 years (Ross et al, 2005).

Population-based observations before and after the onset of widespread PSA-based screening can provide clues regarding the benefits of screening (Gann, 1997). Since 1995 to 1997, the age-adjusted prostate cancer mortality rates for black and white men age 50 to 84 years in the United States dropped below the rate in 1986, a year in which PSA testing was rarely performed (Tarone et al, 2000; Chu et al, 2003). Between 1991 and 2001, the mortality rate from prostate cancer declined by 27% (SEER Program). This decrease in mortality could be due to the earlier detection and treatment of prostate cancer in the PSA era compared with the era before PSA testing began. In fact, Chu and colleagues (2003) have shown that the decrease in distant disease mortality was due to a decline in distant disease incidence, not to improved survival of patients with distant disease. This suggests that earlier detection and treatment of prostate cancer before it becomes metastatic, rather than improvements in the treatment of advanced disease, probably had the greatest impact on the observed mortality declines.

Changes in prostate cancer mortality comparing different countries are shown in Table 94–1. A downturn in prostate cancer mortality in countries where there was a decline could have occurred in countries where PSA uptake and treatment

Table 94-1. Percent Change in Mortality by Country and Time Period for All Ages

Country	Percent Change in Mortality	
	1990-1995	1995-1999
United States*	−3.4	−15.3
Austria	6.2	−11.2
Bulgaria	−0.1	−2.2
Croatia	12.3	61.1
Czech Republic	6.6	−3.4
Denmark	13.3	−6.7
Finland	−7.4	9.1
France	−11.4	3.6
Germany	0.8	−12.8
Greece	5.4	−9.2
Hungary	13.2	−2.4
Ireland	5.6	−15.7
Italy	−16.1	−3.2
Netherlands	−3.6	−2.5
Norway	1.5	4.4
Poland	13.9	−2.4
Portugal	17.4	−2.2
Romania	3.5	−2.8
Russian Federation	17.8	8.6
Slovakia		22.1
Slovenia	18.0	14.1
Spain	−5.6	−12.1
Sweden	6.6	−10.0
Switzerland	−10.0	−6.0
United Kingdom	−3.2	−12.7
European Union	−5.1	−9.1

*Data from Surveillance, Epidemiology, and End Results (SEER) Program (www.seer.cancer.gov) SEER*Stat Database.
Adapted from Levi F, Lucchini F, Negri E, et al: Leveling of prostate cancer mortality in Western Europe. Prostate 2004;60:46.

of prostate cancer were greatest (Oliver et al, 2001; Levi et al, 2004). A change in classification of cause of death is believed to have contributed to changes in prostate cancer mortality in the United Kingdom (Oliver et al, 2000).

Between- and within-country comparisons have not shown consistent associations between screening intensity and mortality reductions (Shibata et al, 1998; Bartsch et al, 2001; Crocetti et al, 2001; Oliver et al, 2001; Lu-Yao et al, 2002; Perron et al, 2002), but that does not mean that none exists. For example, Shaw and coauthors (2004) urge caution in interpreting the effectiveness of PSA testing using ecologic studies, the results of which can be confounded by changing treatment patterns occurring concurrently with PSA uptake, the choice of methods for assessing changes in disease-specific mortality, and the calendar period over which the study was conducted because a mortality assessment too soon after introduction of PSA testing may fail to show screening efficacy when it exists.

One clear change in treatment pattern in the United States was the increasing rate of surgical treatment for non–screen-detected prostate cancer that began in the decade prior to the onset of widespread PSA testing (Mettlin et al, 1994) because of improved quality of life outcomes associated with an anatomic approach to radical prostatectomy (Walsh et al, 1983). Because surgical treatment of non–screen-detected prostate cancer has been proved to reduce deaths from prostate cancer when compared with no treatment (Holmberg et al, 2002), the decline in prostate cancer mortality that began in the United States in 1991 could have been due in part to

the increased application of an effective treatment (surgery) for prostate cancer that began 8 years earlier. This same phenomenon could also explain the mortality reductions that occurred in Tyrol, Austria (Bartsch et al, 2001), where surgery rates for prostate cancer were increasing in the decade prior to initiation of a mass screening program (Carter, 2001).

Alternative explanations for the observed mortality reductions including changing risk factors, attribution bias, and greater use of hormonal therapy cannot be excluded at this time (Etzioni et al, 1999a; Feuer et al, 1999; Albertsen, 2003). Randomized trials comparing the disease-specific outcomes of men who are screened and those who are not represent the highest level of evidence of screening efficacy.

Randomized Trials

The 1988 Quebec prospective randomized controlled trial was updated after 11 years. The endpoint in this trial was prostate cancer–specific mortality among 46,486 men aged 45 to 80 years who were invited or not invited for screening at a ratio of 2:1 in favor of screening (Labrie et al, 2004). In the screened arm of the trial, a PSA cut point of 3.0 ng/mL and an abnormal DRE (used only at first visit) were the indications for a prostate biopsy. The authors reported a 62% reduction in cause-specific mortality in the screened arm compared with those not screened and suggested that this reduction is in line with population trends in North America after the onset of widespread PSA-based screening. However, many experts would not consider this a "true" randomized trial with the power to address the benefits of prostate cancer screening because the study design compared men who were invited and then volunteered for screening (24% of the invited group were actually screened) with those who were not invited and did not undertake screening on their own initiative (Elwood, 2004; Pinsky, 2004). An intention to treat analysis of those randomly assigned to screening or not showed a statistically insignificant relative risk of 1.08 associated with screening (Labrie et al, 2004).

The Prostate, Lung, Colorectal, and Ovary (PLCO) cancer trial of the National Cancer Institute (NCI) and the European Randomized Screening for Prostate Cancer (ERSPC) trial are two large-scale randomized trials that are designed to evaluate the effectiveness of screening for prostate cancer by comparing individuals assigned to a screened arm with those in a control arm who are not screened (Auvinen et al, 1996; International Prostate Screening Trial Evaluation Group, 1999; de Koning et al, 2002; Schroder, 2003; Andriole et al, 2004). Both the PLCO and ERSPC have a common endpoint—prostate cancer–specific mortality—for assessing the effectiveness of screening.

The PLCO trial has multiple U.S. sites that all use the same screening protocols for detection of the four different cancers being evaluated, whereas the ERSPC centers (multiple European countries) are using different criteria for trial recruitment and screening. PSA and DRE are the primary prostate screening tests in these randomized trials, with some variation in PSA cut points and the absence of DRE among some ERSPC centers. The age of participants in both trials is from 50 to 74 years with a target age group of 55 to 69 years. The ERSPC has a 4-year rescreening interval in most centers compared with yearly screening in the PLCO trial.

Randomization to the PLCO began in 1993 and ended in 2001 (Andriole et al, 2004, 2005). There are 38,350 males in the intervention arm and 38,355 males in the control arm (Andriole et al, 2005). For the prostate portion of the trial, the intervention is a PSA performed at entry and then annually for 5 years and DRE at trial entry and then annually for 3 years. Participants will be observed for at least 13 years from randomization.

The PLCO trial was designed to address whether or not screening reduced prostate cancer mortality given the practices of diagnosis and treatment in the community. Follow-up biopsies for a positive screen and specific treatments for prostate cancer are not mandated in this trial. Pinsky et al (2005) reported low follow-up biopsy rates after a positive screen in the PLCO trial, and whether this will compromise the ability of the trial to demonstrate a screening effect is controversial (Pinsky, 2005; Walsh, 2005). The PLCO has a calculated power of 90% to show a mortality reduction of 20% in the screened population if the compliance rate is 90% and the contamination rate is 20% (Schroder, 2003).

In the ERSPC, recruitment of 165,000 men to the core age group of 55 to 69 years will have a power of 86% to show a 20% to 25% mortality reduction in 2008 if the contamination rate is 20% (Schroder, 2003a). A combined analysis of the PLCO and ERSPC trials is planned (Auvinen et al, 1996), and this could improve the power of these trials to demonstrate any benefit of screening if it exists.

In summary, PSA-based prostate cancer screening over the past 10 to 15 years has reduced the incidence of advanced prostate cancer and may have contributed to the decline in prostate cancer mortality that began in the early 1990s in the United States. Randomized trials designed to address the benefits of screening are ongoing in the United States and in Europe.

DIAGNOSTIC MODALITIES

The triad of DRE, serum PSA, and TRUS-directed prostatic biopsy is used in the early detection of prostate cancer. **The combination of DRE and serum PSA is the most useful first-line test for assessing the risk of prostate cancer being present in an individual** (Catalona et al, 1994b; Littrup et al, 1994; Stone et al, 1994; Bangma et al, 1995; Van Der Cruijsen-Koeter et al, 2001). TRUS is not recommended as a first-line screening test because of its low predictive value for early prostate cancer (Carter et al, 1989; Ellis et al, 1994; Flanigan et al, 1994; Van Der Cruijsen-Koeter et al, 2001) and high cost of examination.

Prostate-Specific Antigen

PSA is a member of the human kallikrein gene family, which includes other related proteins (see Chapter 93, "Prostate Cancer Tumor Markers," for details). PSA is secreted in high concentrations (mg/mL) into seminal fluid, where it is involved in liquefaction of the seminal coagulum (Lilja, 1985; McGee and Herr, 1988), and it is normally found in low concentration in serum (ng/mL). PSA in serum circulates in both bound (complexed) and unbound (free) forms that can be measured using assays approved by the U.S. Food and Drug Administration (FDA). Most detectable PSA in serum (65%

to 90%) is bound to α_1-antichymotrypsin (ACT), whereas 10% to 35% of detectable PSA is unbound or free (Lilja et al, 1991; Stenman et al, 1991).

Factors to Be Considered When Using PSA for the Diagnosis of Prostate Cancer

PSA expression is strongly influenced by androgens (Young et al, 1991; Henttu et al, 1992). Serum PSA becomes detectable at puberty with increases in luteinizing hormone and testosterone (Vieira et al, 1994). In hypogonadal men with low testosterone levels, serum PSA may be low because of decreased expression and may not reflect the presence of prostate disease such as cancer (Morgentaler et al, 1996). Data suggest that obese men have lower PSA levels than nonobese men and that this could mask the presence of a significant cancer (Baillargeon et al, 2005). In the absence of prostate cancer, serum PSA levels vary with age, race, and prostate volume.

In men without benign prostatic hyperplasia (BPH), the rate of change in PSA is 0.04 ng/mL per year (Carter et al, 1992b; Oesterling et al, 1993), compared with 0.07 to 0.27 ng/mL per year in men with BPH who are between ages 60 and 85 years (Carter et al, 1992b). Cross-sectional data suggest that PSA increases 4% per milliliter of prostate volume and that 30% and 5% of the variance in PSA can be accounted for by prostate volume and age, respectively (Oesterling et al, 1993). Blacks without prostate cancer have higher PSA values than whites (Morgan et al, 1996; Fowler et al, 1999). Fowler and colleagues (1999) have demonstrated that on a volume/volume basis, the benign prostatic tissue of black men contributes more PSA to serum than does the benign prostatic tissue of white men—a difference that increases with age.

The presence of prostate disease (prostate cancer, BPH, and prostatitis) is the most important factor affecting serum levels of PSA (Wang et al, 1981; Ercole et al, 1987; Robles et al, 1988). **PSA elevations may indicate the presence of prostate disease, but not all men with prostate disease have elevated PSA levels. Furthermore, PSA elevations are not specific for cancer.**

Serum PSA elevations may occur as a result of disruption of the normal prostatic architecture that allows PSA to diffuse into the prostatic tissue and gain access to the circulation. This can occur in the setting of prostate disease (BPH, prostatitis, prostate cancer) and with prostate manipulation (e.g., prostate massage, prostate biopsy, transurethral resection) (see Klein and Lowe, 1997 for review). Prostatic inflammation (acute and chronic) and urinary retention can cause PSA elevations to variable degrees (Armitage et al, 1988; Dalton, 1989; Nadler et al, 1995). PSA elevations may not be related to the histologic finding of inflammation in men without clinical prostatitis (Morote et al, 2000). Prostatic trauma such as occurs after prostatic biopsy can result in a "leak" of PSA into the circulation that may require more than 4 weeks for return to baseline values (Yuan et al, 1992). DRE as performed in an outpatient setting can lead to slight increases in serum PSA. However, the change in PSA after DRE would not appear to be clinically significant because the change is within the error of the assay and rarely causes false-positive tests (Chybowski et al, 1992; Crawford et al, 1992).

Prostate-directed treatment (for both BPH and cancer) can lower serum PSA by decreasing the volume of prostatic epithelium available for PSA production and by decreasing the amount of PSA produced per cell. Manipulation of the hormonal environment for treatment of cancer and BPH with orchiectomy, luteinizing hormone–releasing hormone analogs, and 5α-reductase inhibitors; radiotherapy for cancer; and surgical ablation of prostate tissue for BPH or cancer can all lead to reductions in serum PSA.

5α-Reductase inhibitors that are used for treatment of BPH have been shown to lower PSA levels by about 50% after 12 months of treatment. Both type 2 isoenzyme inhibitors (finasteride) and dual type 1 and 2 isoenzyme inhibitors (dutasteride) lower PSA to the same extent (Guess et al, 1993; Roehrborn et al, 2002). Multiplying the PSA level by two to obtain the "true" PSA level of a patient who has been taking a 5α-reductase inhibitor for 12 months or more preserves the usefulness of PSA in the detection of prostate cancer (Andriole et al, 1998).

Men who are to be treated with a 5α-reductase inhibitor should have a baseline PSA measurement before initiation of treatment and should be followed up with serial PSA measurements. If PSA does not decrease by 50% or if there is a rise in PSA when the patient is taking the inhibitor, these men should be suspected of having an occult prostate cancer. Finasteride 1 mg (trade name Propecia) is marketed for the treatment of male pattern hair loss (androgenetic alopecia), and the 1-mg dosage results in the same decline in serum PSA levels as the 5-mg dosage (Gormley et al, 1992).

Studies examining the effect of ejaculation on serum PSA have shown both no significant change in PSA (Kirkali et al, 1995; Yavascaoglu et al, 1998) after ejaculation and a significant decrease in serum PSA after ejaculation (Simak et al, 1993; Westphal et al, 1995) in men age 30 to 40 years or younger. However, in the age group in which PSA testing is primarily used for early detection of prostate cancer (50 years and older), ejaculation can lead to an increase in PSA that could result in a false-positive elevation (Tchetgen et al, 1996; Herschman et al, 1997). In a screened population of men age 60 years, Stenner and coworkers (1998) found no significant change in PSA after ejaculation but did find that men with higher baseline PSA levels had the greatest change in PSA after ejaculation. After 48 hours, the PSA would be expected to return to baseline levels in most men (Tchetgen et al, 1996; Stenner et al, 1998). A history of sexual activity and a repeated PSA after 48 hours of sexual abstinence may be helpful in the interpretation of serum PSA levels that are minimally elevated.

Interpretation of PSA values should always take into account the presence of prostate disease, previous diagnostic procedures, and prostate-directed treatments.

Clinical Use of Prostate-Specific Antigen

The initial assays for PSA that were approved by the FDA in 1994 for early detection of prostate cancer detected both free PSA and PSA complexed to ACT. Thus, measurement of free PSA and complexed PSA by these assays is generally referred to as the serum PSA level. The distribution of PSA levels in men age 50 years and older in an invitational screening study is shown in Table 94–2 (Smith et al, 1996). Specific assays that detect free PSA alone and PSA complexed to ACT alone have been evaluated and approved for prostate cancer detection (see later).

The effectiveness of PSA as a screening method for prostate cancer is debated (see earlier). **However, it has been proved that use of PSA increases detection rates of prostate cancer and leads to the detection of prostate cancers that are more likely to be confined when compared with detection without the use of PSA.** This has been documented in population-based data, observational studies, and randomized screening trials.

After the onset of widespread PSA testing began in the late 1980s, the incidence of prostate cancer increased in the U.S. population as PSA elevations became the primary indication for a prostate biopsy, and PSA-diagnosed cancers surpassed the cancers detected by DRE and those detected at the time of simple prostatectomy for BPH (Fig. 94–1). The annual percent change (APC) in prostate cancer incidence for whites increased from around 2.4 between 1975 and 1985 to 6.9 in 1985 and to 18.4 in 1989, after which incidence began to decline for whites after 1992 (Hankey et al, 1999). The age-adjusted incidence in 2001 was 49% higher than the incidence in 1986, when PSA testing was uncommon (SEER Program).

After 1991 the incidence of distant stage disease began decreasing at an annual rate of 17.9% (Hankey et al, 1999) while the APC in the incidence of localized/regional disease increased by 19% (Hankey et al, 1999). These population changes have been directly attributed to the removal of larger prevalent cancers from the population after the onset of PSA testing with a stage shift toward a higher prevalence of lower stage disease with continued PSA use (Hankey et al, 1999; Chu et al, 2003). Furthermore, these changes reflect what has been described in observational studies and randomized screening trials evaluating the use of PSA for prostate cancer detection.

When DRE and PSA are used as screening tests for prostate cancer detection, detection rates are higher with PSA than with DRE and highest with a combination of the two tests (Catalona et al, 1994b; Littrup et al, 1994; Stone et al, 1994; Schroder et al, 1998). Results from a randomized trial of prostate cancer screening demonstrated that DRE alone resulted in detection of 56% of 473 cancers, and 17% of the 473 cancers would have been missed by PSA-based screening

Table 94–2. Distribution (%) of Prostate-Specific Antigen (PSA) Levels among 10,248 Men by Age

PSA Level (ng/mL)	Age 50-59 Years; n = 3652	Age 60-69 Years; n = 5041	Age 70 Years or Older; n = 1555	Total n = 10,248
≤2.5	88	75	61	78
2.6-4.0	8	14	18	12
4.1-9.9	3	9	16	8
≥10	1	2	5	2

From Smith DS, Catalona WJ, Herschman JD: Longitudinal screening for prostate cancer with prostate-specific antigen. JAMA 1996;276:1309.

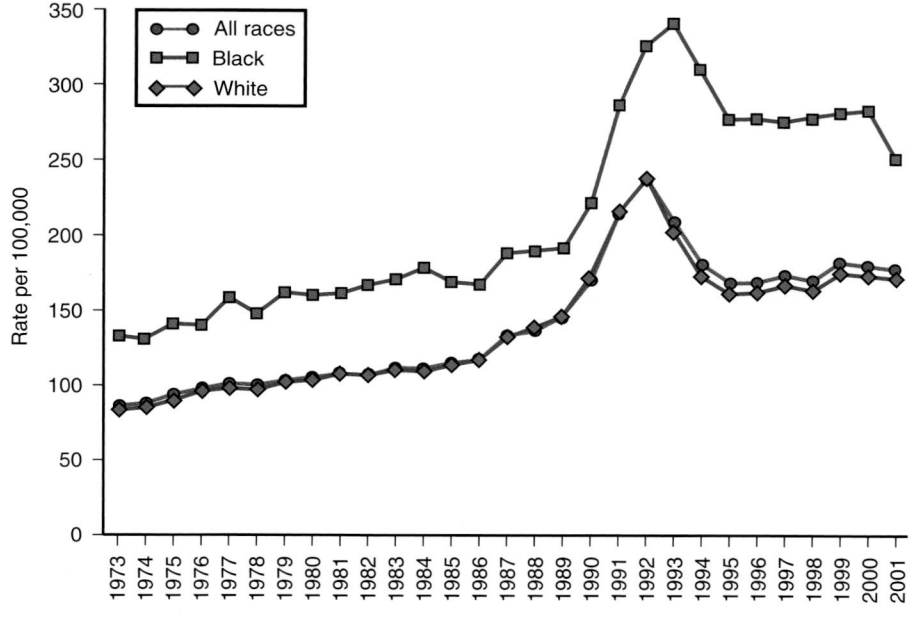

Figure 94–1. Age-adjusted incidence of prostate cancer (rate per 100,000) by year of diagnosis (all ages) for all races (red), black males (blue), and white males (green). Data from Surveillance, Epidemiology, and End Results (SEER) Program (www.seer.cancer.gov) SEER*Stat Database.

alone (Schroder et al, 1998). Of the 264 men with cancers detectable by DRE, 31%, 18%, and 13% had PSA levels below 4.0, 3.0, and 2.0 ng/mL, respectively. Thus, these cancers would have been missed if PSA without DRE had been used to recommend biopsy at these lower PSA levels. In addition, when PSA levels are similar, DRE-detected cancers are more likely to be high grade and thus life threatening when compared with PSA-detected cancers (Table 94–3). **Because DRE and PSA do not always detect the same cancers, the tests are complementary and are recommended in combi-**nation as methods of assessing the risk that prostate cancer is present.

The pathologic features of prostate cancers detected with PSA testing are more favorable than those of cancers detected without PSA testing. In a PSA-based prostate cancer screening study, 57% of men who were referred primarily for evaluation of DRE abnormalities (nonscreened) had clinically or pathologically advanced disease, compared with 37% and 29% of men with prostate cancer discovered by initial or serial PSA-based screening, respectively (Catalona et al, 1993).

Table 94–3. Prostate Cancer Detection as a Function of Serum Prostate-Specific Antigen (PSA) Level and Digital Rectal Examination (DRE) Findings in Contemporary Series

PSA Level (ng/mL)	DRE Findings*	Cancer Detection Rate (%)†	Cancer Yield on Biopsy (%)‡	Rate of High-Grade Cancer on Biopsy (%)§
0-1	−		8.8	0.9
1-2	−		17.0	2.0
0-2	−		12	1.4
		0.7	8	
2-4	−		15-25	5.2
		2	21	
4-10	+	11	17-32	4.1
		11-27	45-51	11.7
>10	−	41	43-65	19.4
	+	31-76	70-90	50.5
<4	−		15	2.3
	+	1-3	13-17	
>4	−	14	23-38	5.8
	+	14-38	55-63	20.6

*DRE nonsuspicious for cancer (−); DRE suspicious for cancer (+).
†Cancer detection rate is the number of cancers found in those screened (total number of detected cancers divided by the total number of men screened).
‡Cancer yield is the total number of cancers detected divided by the total number of men undergoing a biopsy. For DRE (−) this indicates the positive predictive value of PSA at a specified level when the DRE is not suspicious for cancer; for DRE (+) it is the positive predictive value of a suspicious DRE when the PSA is at a specified level.
§Gleason score of 7 or more.
Data in table extracted from the results of contemporary series (Andriole et al, 2005; Catalona et al, 1998; Crawford et al, 1996; Schroder et al, 1998; Thompson et al, 2004).

When a PSA cutoff of 4 ng/mL and an abnormal DRE were used together as screening criteria for prostate cancer, pathologically organ-confined disease was found in 71% of men who underwent surgery for prostate cancer (Catalona et al, 1994b). With serial PSA-based screening, there is an increase in the rate of smaller, organ-confined prostate cancers (Rietbergen et al, 1999; Hoedemaeker et al, 2000), and by comparison when DRE is used alone to screen for prostate cancer, organ-confined disease is found in less than 50% of men undergoing surgery (Thompson et al, 1987; Mueller et al, 1988; Chodak et al, 1989). **Thus, the addition of PSA testing to DRE leads to detection of a greater proportion of pathologically confined cancers compared with cancer detection by DRE alone. With the widespread use of PSA, a stage shift favoring localized disease occurred because PSA increases the lead time for prostate cancer detection** (Carter et al, 1992a; Helzlsouer et al, 1992; Stenman et al, 1994; Gann et al, 1995, Tibblin et al, 1995).

Lead time is the time by which the diagnosis of prostate cancer is advanced by screening. Early studies suggested lead times in the range of 5 years using frozen serum samples to measure PSA prior to diagnosis (Gann et al, 1995; Carter and Pearson, 1997). Data from the Baltimore Longitudinal Study of Aging (BLSA) (Shock et al, 1984) using multiple frozen serum samples have allowed comparison of serial PSA measurements in men ultimately diagnosed with prostate cancer and in men without the disease (Carter et al, 1992b). These data reveal that men with prostate cancer have higher PSA levels than men without prostate cancer years before conventional diagnosis with DRE (Fig. 94–2). Because lead time is probably shorter for more advanced cancers than early stage cancers, this could explain more recent estimates of lead time based on screened populations that are in the range of 10 years (Draisma et al, 2003; Tornblom et al, 2004).

An increase in detection lead time for a disease with a long natural history can increase the probability of detecting cancers with more favorable biology and those that are unlikely to pose a threat during the host's remaining life (Gosselaar et al, 2005). The extent to which PSA uncovers cancers that would have remained clinically quiescent is currently unknown. However, there are legitimate concerns and controversy about the serendipitous detection of prostate cancers among men with PSA elevations not influenced by cancer (McNaughton Collins et al, 1997; Carter 2004; Catalona 2004; Stamey, 2004; Stamey et al, 2004).

It was initially believed that PSA would not be useful as a marker for prostate cancer detection because of overlap in serum levels between men with BPH and men with cancer (Stamey et al, 1987). Earlier studies suggested that 21% to 86% of men with BPH had PSA elevations (Stamey et al, 1987; Oesterling et al, 1988; Hudson et al, 1989). However, if serum PSA is elevated, a greater proportion of men actually have cancer found at biopsy when compared with an abnormality on DRE or TRUS (Catalona et al, 1994b; Van Der Cruijsen-Koeter et al, 2001). **Thus, an elevated PSA level has the highest positive predictive value for prostate cancer.** In addition, whereas DRE and TRUS are dependent on the examiner, PSA is an objective measure of prostate cancer risk.

The future risk of prostate cancer detection and the chance of finding cancer on a prostate biopsy increase incrementally with the serum PSA level (Table 94–4; see Table 94–3)—a finding that has been demonstrated in cohort studies using frozen serum samples that predate a cancer diagnosis, observational studies, and randomized screening trials (Catalona et al, 1991, 1993, 1994b; Brawer et al, 1992; Labrie et al, 1992; Littrup et al, 1994; Stone et al, 1994; Gann et al, 1995; Schroder et al, 1998; Fang et al, 2001; Hakama et al, 2001; Antenor et al, 2004; Thompson et al, 2004; Andriole et al, 2005).

In a longitudinal case-control study by Gann and associates (1995), the ability of a single PSA measurement made on a frozen serum sample at baseline to predict prostate cancer over the subsequent 10 years was evaluated for 366 cancer cases with a mean age of 63 years at PSA measurement. Cancers were detected primarily by DRE (nonscreened) after baseline blood sampling in an era prior to the availability of PSA testing. Seventy-five percent of the 366 men with prostate cancer in this study eventually died of prostate cancer. Thus, these data show the ability of PSA to predict the presence of

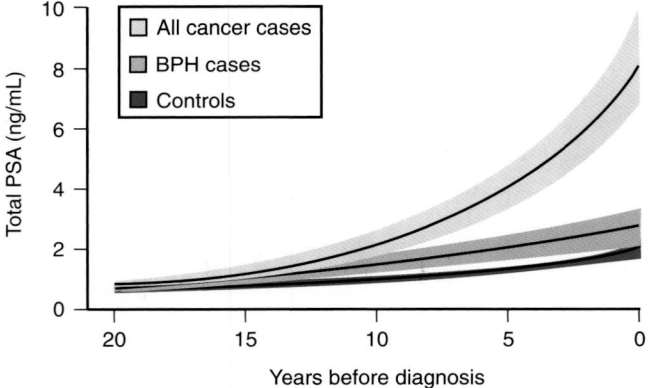

Figure 94–2. Average curves (+95th percentile confidence intervals) of prostate-specific antigen (PSA) levels (ng/mL) as a function of years before diagnosis for 48 men with prostate cancer, 39 men with histologically diagnosed benign prostatic hyperplasia (BPH), and 243 men with no history of prostate disease. All subjects had at least three repeated measurements within 10 years of diagnosis or exclusion of disease. Average number of repeated PSA measurements: cancer subjects, 7; BPH subjects, 6; subjects without prostate disease, 5.

Table 94–4. Relative Risk of Subsequent Prostate Cancer Diagnosis after an Initial Baseline Prostate-Specific Antigen (PSA)

Baseline PSA (ng/mL)	Relative Risk of Cancer (95% Confidence Interval)	
	Gann et al, 1995	**Antenor et al, 2004**
0.0-1.0	1.0	1.0
1.0-1.5	2.2 (1.3-3.6)	4.3 (3.0-5.3)
1.5-2.0	3.4 (1.9-5.9)	8.8 (7.0-10.8)
2.0-3.0	5.5 (3.3-9.2)	14.9 (12.3-18.0)
3.0-4.0	8.6 (4.7-15.6)	23.3 (19.0-28.7)
4.0-10.0	22.2 (12.9-38.2)	38.7 (32.2-46.7)
More than 10.0	145.3 (59.1-357.0)	104.2 (80.0-135.7)

From Antenor JA, Han M, Roehl KA, et al: Relationship between initial prostate specific antigen level and subsequent prostate cancer detection in a longitudinal screening study. J Urol 2004;172:90.

life-threatening cancers (see Table 94-4). Antenor and associates (2004) evaluated the relationship between an initial PSA measurement and the subsequent risk of prostate cancer in a longitudinal screening study of 26,111 community male volunteers with a mean age of 59 years observed for a mean of 51 months (see Table 94-4). The higher relative risks of cancer found by Antenor and associates (2004) compared with Gann and colleagues (1995) might be explained by differences in study design (case-control versus longitudinal cohort) and differences in the significance of the cancer cases in the two studies. However, both studies show that a baseline PSA provides information on the future risk of prostate cancer—information that might be useful in designing detection programs (see later).

Contemporary studies evaluating the use of PSA and DRE for cancer detection have shown that the probability of detecting a prostate cancer increases directly with PSA among men with a normal DRE, and that the predictive value of a suspicious DRE increases directly with the PSA level (see Table 94-3) (Crawford et al, 1996; Catalona et al, 1998; Schroder et al, 1998; Thompson et al, 2004; Andriole et al, 2005).

In summary, both PSA and DRE are used to assess the risk that prostate cancer is present. The addition of PSA to DRE increases both the detection rate of prostate cancer and the detection of cancers with a more favorable prognosis.

Approaches for Improving Prostate-Specific Antigen Test Performance

Because PSA elevations are associated with both false-negative and false-positive results, a great deal of effort has been devoted to improving the performance characteristics of the test. The use of different PSA thresholds depending on age and ethnicity and lowering thresholds to improve sensitivity (Oesterling et al, 1993; Catalona et al, 1994a; Morgan et al, 1996; Abdalla et al, 1998; Gelmann et al, 2001; Ku et al, 2002; Punglia et al, 2003; He et al, 2004), the adjustment of the PSA level for total prostate volume (PSA density) (Babaian et al, 1990; Littrup et al, 1991; Benson et al, 1992a, 1992b; Bazinet et al, 1994; Rommel et al, 1994; Catalona et al, 2000b; Fowler et al, 2000; Djavan et al, 2002; Egawa et al, 2002; Naya et al, 2002; Gjengsto et al, 2005) and for PSA transition zone volume (Djavan et al, 1999a; 1999b; Taneja et al, 2001; Singh et al, 2004; Gjengsto et al, 2005), and the evaluation of rate of change in PSA (PSA velocity) (Carter et al, 1992a; Smith and Catalona, 1994; Carter et al, 1995; Fowler et al, 2000; Fang et al, 2002; Riffenburgh and Amling, 2003; Ciatto et al, 2004; Raaijmakers et al, 2004b; Roobol et al, 2004a,b; Thompson et al, 2004) have all been evaluated. In addition, the discovery that PSA exists in bound (complexed) and unbound (free) molecular forms within serum and the development of specific assays to measure molecular forms of PSA have resulted in investigation of their use for prostate cancer detection (McCormack et al, 1995; Lilja, 1997, 2003; Polascik et al, 1999a; Lilja et al, 2000; Gretzer and Partin, 2003).

Prostate-Specific Antigen Thresholds

The choice of a PSA threshold or cut point above which one would recommend further evaluation to rule out prostate

cancer (prostate biopsy) is controversial (Carter, 2000, 2004; Catalona et al, 2000a). **The PSA threshold that most efficiently leads to the detection of life-threatening cancers while avoiding unnecessary testing (PSA measurements and biopsies) and overdiagnosis is not known.** The controversy stems from the following: the use of higher PSA thresholds risks missing an important cancer until it is too late for a cure, whereas the use of lower PSA thresholds increases not only unnecessary biopsies but also the proportion of biopsies that identify clinically insignificant disease (disease that would not have been detected in the absence of screening). The use of a PSA threshold of 4.0 ng/mL for men older than 50 years has been accepted by most clinicians as striking a reasonable balance between these tradeoffs.

Age- and ethnic/race-specific PSA ranges have been established among "healthy" populations of men and in general are higher for blacks compared with Hispanics and whites and lowest for men of Asian descent (Oesterling et al, 1993; Morgan et al, 1996; Abdalla et al, 1998; Gelmann et al, 2001; Ku et al, 2002; He et al, 2004). However, PSA thresholds based solely on the expected ranges for men without prostate cancer (age-specific ranges) may lead to underdiagnosis of significant cancers among those with the disease (low sensitivity) (Catalona et al, 1994a; Morgan et al, 1996). In a multi-institutional prospective study of men age 50 to 75 years, age-specific PSA cutoffs missed 20% to 60% of cancers in men older than 60 years (Catalona et al, 2000b).

Gann and coauthors (1995) found that a cutoff value of 3.3 ng/mL resulted in optimal sensitivity and specificity for the detection of life-threatening cancer among men at a mean age of 63 years, but the gain was minimal compared with that afforded by a cutoff value of 4.0 ng/mL. In addition, Morgan and colleagues (1996) have shown that the PSA cutoff value that results in 95% sensitivity (the detection of 95% of cancers) is close to 4.0 ng/mL for men between the ages of 50 and 70 years (the target population for screening at present) and 2.5 ng/mL *for men age 40 to 50 years*. Because most of the variability in PSA levels is due to benign prostate enlargement that occurs with age and men younger than 50 years are unlikely to have such enlargement, a threshold of 2.5 ng/mL seems reasonable for men younger than 50 years.

Gann and coauthors (1995) pointed out that the "dichotomization of PSA results into normal and abnormal obscures important information contained in levels below the usual cutoff." Because low PSA levels (below the thresholds of 2.5 to 4.0 ng/mL) are predictive of the future risk of prostate cancer (Gann et al, 1995; Fang et al, 2001; Hakama et al, 2001; Antenor et al, 2004) (see Table 94-4), lower levels of PSA should prompt careful consideration of the likelihood of cancer in men at particularly high risk, such as those with a strong family history of the disease, younger men with lower PSA levels, and those with a rising PSA (see later). **Regardless of the threshold chosen, an isolated PSA elevation should be remeasured before performing a prostate biopsy because of fluctuations in PSA that could represent a false-positive elevation in the test** (Eastham et al, 2003).

Recognizing that prostate cancers are prevalent at PSA levels below 4.0 ng/mL (Thompson et al, 2004) (see Table 94-3), some investigators suggest the use of PSA thresholds below 4.0 ng/mL to improve test sensitivity (correct classification of men who have the disease) and avoid missing potentially important cancers (Catalona et al, 1997; Raaijmakers et al, 2004a). Improvements in test sensitivity are associated with the tradeoff of reduced specificity (correct exclusion of cancer in men who do not have the disease) and lead to an increase in the numbers of unnecessary biopsies.

Punglia and coworkers (2003) argued that sensitivity and specificity have been biased because of the inability to verify the disease status of individuals correctly. After using a mathematical method to correct for verification bias, they demonstrated that without this correction, the sensitivity of the PSA test has been overestimated and the specificity underestimated in prior analyses. Thus, a substantial proportion of cancers are missed when prostate biopsies are recommended at PSA levels above 4.0 ng/mL. They argue that these findings, together with the finding that men who have lower PSA levels at diagnosis have more favorable disease than those with higher PSA values at diagnosis (Krumholtz et al, 2002), support the routine use of a PSA threshold of 2.6 ng/mL.

Adoption of lower PSA thresholds as a policy for all men regardless of age raises the following concerns. First, prostate cancers detected at lower PSA levels are more likely to be small volume and low grade and are thus more likely to represent clinically insignificant disease (Carter et al, 1997; Gosselaar et al, 2005) for which treatment not only may be unnecessary but also may fail to improve survival (Vis et al, 2002). Second, detection of prostate cancer at a PSA threshold lower than 4.0 ng/mL has not been shown to improve the disease-free outcome with contemporary therapy. Thus, any approach to prostate cancer detection that finds more cancers without quantifying the clinical significance of the detected disease will only increase overdiagnosis and overtreatment. In the absence of proof that PSA screening saves lives, lowering PSA thresholds for all men as a policy seems premature (Carter, 2000; Schroder and Kranse, 2003b; Carter, 2004).

Volume Based Prostate-Specific Antigen Parameters

PSA elevations below 10 ng/mL (see Table 94–3) in men with a DRE that is not suspicious for prostate cancer are more likely the result of prostatic enlargement (BPH) and represent "false" elevations. **Distinguishing between men who have PSA elevations driven by BPH or cancer is difficult because PSA is not specific for cancer and the prevalence of BPH in the population is high compared with prostate cancer.** Volume-based PSA parameters (with prostate volume determined by ultrasonography) including PSA density (PSA divided by prostate volume), complexed PSA density (complexed PSA divided by prostate volume), and PSA transition zone (PSA divided by transition zone volume) have been evaluated as methods for excluding men with PSA elevations related to BPH.

Benson and coworkers (1992a, 1992b) suggested that adjusting PSA for ultrasound-determined prostate size—by calculating the quotient of PSA and ultrasound-determined prostate volume—could help distinguish between PSA elevations caused by BPH and those caused by prostate cancer. A direct relationship between PSA density and the chance of cancer has been documented (Seaman et al, 1993; Bazinet et al, 1994; Rommel et al, 1994), and a PSA density of 0.15

or greater was proposed as a threshold for recommending prostate biopsy in men with PSA levels between 4 and 10 ng/mL and no suspicion of cancer on DRE or TRUS (Seaman et al, 1993; Bazinet et al, 1994). Naya and associates (2002) have suggested that complexed PSA density may enhance the performance of complexed PSA.

The usefulness of PSA density in prostate cancer detection has not been confirmed in all studies. Catalona and colleagues (1994b) found that half the cancers detected in men with PSA levels between 4 and 10 ng/mL would have been missed using a PSA density greater than 0.15 as a threshold for biopsy, and Lujan and coauthors (2001) reported that 31% of cancers would be missed using the same cutoff. The finding of higher PSA densities among groups of men with positive biopsies—compared with men with negative biopsies—may occur because prostate cancers are more likely to be found when a constant number of biopsies are obtained in men with smaller prostate volumes compared with men with larger prostate volumes (Uzzo et al, 1995). In fact, with repeated screening of almost 1000 men 1 year after an initial negative prostate biopsy, the most important factor responsible for failure to diagnose cancer at the initial screen was a significantly greater prostate volume among men whose cancers were missed compared with those whose cancers were not missed (Rietbergen et al, 1998).

The conflicting results with PSA density to predict the presence of cancer may be attributed to variations in the amount of epithelium (source of PSA) between prostates of similar size, variability in prostate shape that limits the use of a common volume equation for calculating prostate size, and the application of published PSA density cutoffs to populations with different prostate volumes (Cooner, 1994; Taneja et al, 2001). Although PSA density is an imperfect predictor of cancer, it is an additional method of risk assessment with potential usefulness for counseling men with intermediate PSA levels (4 to 10 ng/mL) regarding the need for prostate biopsy (Benson, 1994) or repeat biopsy if PSA is persistently elevated (Keetch et al, 1996). Catalona and colleagues (2000b) have suggested that the percentage of free PSA can be used as a surrogate for PSA density (see later).

The major determinant of serum PSA in men without prostate cancer is the transition zone epithelium, not the epithelium of the peripheral zone of the prostate (Lepor et al, 1994). Because BPH represents an enlargement of the transition zone—and serum PSA levels are primarily a reflection of transition zone histology in men with BPH—adjusting PSA for transition zone volume has been evaluated as a method to help distinguish between BPH and prostate cancer (Kalish et al, 1994). Djavan and associates (1999b) found that PSA transition zone volume was the parameter with the highest overall validity (sensitivity and specificity) for prostate cancer among 974 men with PSA levels between 4 to 10 ng/mL. They recommended cutoffs of 0.23 ng/mL/cm³ when transition zone volume was above 20 cm³ and 0.38 ng/mL/cm³ when transition zone volume was below 20 cm³ as a threshold above which prostate cancer was more likely. In men undergoing a repeat prostate biopsy after an initial negative biopsy, a PSA transition zone above 0.2 ng/mL/cm³ was associated with a threefold greater risk of a missed prostate cancer when compared with a PSA transition zone below 0.2 ng/mL/cm³ (Singh et al, 2004).

Prostate-Specific Antigen Velocity

Substantial changes or variability in serum PSA can occur between measurements in the presence or absence of prostate cancer (Carter et al, 1992a, Riehmann et al, 1993; Carter et al, 1995; Prestigiacomo et al, 1996; Eastham et al, 2003). The short-term changes in PSA between repeated measures are primarily due to physiologic variation (Prestigiacomo and Stamey, 1996). The changes in serum PSA can be adjusted (corrected) for the elapsed time between the measurements, a concept known as PSA velocity or rate of change in PSA (Carter et al, 1992b).

Using frozen sera to measure PSA years before the diagnosis of prostate disease in men with and without prostate cancer, Carter and colleagues (1992b) showed that a rate of change in PSA more than 0.75 ng/mL per year was a specific marker for the presence of prostate cancer and that men with cancer had significantly more rapid rates of rise in PSA than men without prostate cancer at a time (5 years before diagnosis) when PSA levels were not elevated. In that study, 72% of men with cancer and 5% of men without cancer had a PSA velocity of more than 0.75 ng/mL per year. Specificity of PSA velocity using a cut point of 0.75 ng/mL per year remained high in this study (over 90%) when PSA levels were between 4 and 10 ng/mL or below 4 ng/mL, but sensitivity for cancer detection was 11% at levels below 4 ng/mL, compared with 79% for levels between 4 and 10 ng/mL (see Fig. 94–2).

More recently, it has been shown that PSA velocity might be useful for prostate cancer detection among men with PSA levels below 4.0 ng/mL. In a longitudinal aging study, the cumulative probability of freedom from prostate cancer at 10 years after a baseline PSA between 2 and 4 ng/mL was 97.1% (range 91.4% to 100%) and 35.2% (range 14.0% to 56.4%) when the PSA velocity was less than and greater than 0.1 ng/mL per year, respectively (Fang et al, 2002). Roobol and coworkers (2004b) did not find that PSA velocity was an independent predictor of a prostate cancer diagnosis at the second screening round of a randomized screening trial when PSA was less than 4.0 ng/mL. However, Thompson and colleagues (2004) found that among men with PSA values below 4.0 ng/mL and a nonsuspicious DRE, the annualized rate of change in PSA was positively associated with the risk of prostate cancer over a 7-year period ($P < .001$).

Other studies have demonstrated that men with prostate cancer have more rapid rises in PSA than men without prostate cancer (Smith and Catalona, 1994; Raaijmakers et al, 2004b; Thompson et al, 2004). In addition, less than 5% of men without a history of prostate cancer have a PSA velocity of more than 0.75 ng/mL per year (95th percentile for PSA velocity), supporting the specificity of rate of change in PSA as a marker for the presence of cancer (Carter et al, 1995; Kadmon et al, 1996; Lujan et al, 1999).

The minimal length of follow-up—time over which changes in PSA should be adjusted—for PSA velocity to be useful in cancer detection has been calculated in separate studies to be 18 months (Smith and Catalona, 1994; Carter et al, 1995; Kadmon et al, 1996). Furthermore, evaluation of three repeated PSA measurements, to determine an average rate of change in PSA, would appear to optimize the accuracy of PSA velocity for cancer detection (Carter et al, 1992a, 1992b, 1995).

Free Prostate-Specific Antigen

It has been shown that **men with prostate cancer have a greater fraction of serum PSA that is complexed to protease inhibitors—lower percentage of total PSA that is free—than men without prostate cancer** (Christensson et al, 1993; Leinonen et al, 1993; Lilja, 1993; Stenman et al, 1994). The difference in the ratio of free to total PSA (percentage of free PSA) is greatest when comparing men without prostate cancer who have prostatic enlargement (BPH) with those with prostate cancer and no prostatic enlargement. This difference is thought to be due to differential expression of PSA isoforms by transition zone (zone of origin of BPH) tissue compared with peripheral zone (zone where most prostate cancers arise) tissue (Chen et al, 1997; Mikolajczyk et al, 1997; 2000a; 2000b).

Free PSA levels vary directly with age and prostate volume and indirectly with total PSA level. Thus, recommended percentage of free PSA cutoffs varies among studies because of differences in study populations with respect to these variables (Woodrum et al, 1998). In addition, because assays differ in their ability to determine both free and total PSA, results may differ depending on the assay or combination of assays used (Woodrum et al, 1998). Race does not appear to be important when using percentage of free PSA in cancer detection (Catalona et al, 2000c). Free PSA and total PSA both decrease in men taking 5α-reductase inhibitors, and therefore the percentage of free PSA is not altered significantly in men taking these medications (Keetch et al, 1997; Pannek et al, 1998).

Christensson and coworkers (1993) measured free and total PSA fractions in men with and without prostate cancer and found that a free/total PSA cutoff of 0.18 (18% free/total PSA) significantly improved the ability to distinguish between cancer and noncancer subjects as compared with use of total PSA alone. In the intermediate PSA range between 4 and 10 ng/mL, Catalona and colleagues (1995) found that the percentage of free PSA provided independent predictive information regarding the presence or absence of cancer above that provided by other clinical indices, including age, total PSA, DRE results, and prostate size. The cutoff for percentage of free PSA that optimizes sensitivity and specificity for cancer detection depends on prostate size because overlap in the percentage of free PSA is greatest among men without cancer who have enlarged prostates and men with cancer in the setting of prostate enlargement (Catalona et al, 1995). Maintaining a sensitivity for cancer detection of 90% among men with PSA levels between 4 and 10 ng/mL and nonsuspicious DREs, Catalona and associates (1995) found that a free PSA cutoff of 23% (biopsy only if 23% or less) would have eliminated 31% of unnecessary biopsies in men with prostate glands larger than 40 cm^3, whereas a free PSA cutoff of 14% would have eliminated 76% of unnecessary biopsies in men with prostate glands smaller than 40 cm^3.

Percentage of free PSA appears to be most useful in distinguishing between those with and without prostate cancer when total PSA levels fall in the range 4 to 10 ng/mL. In a prospective multi-institutional study of men age 50 to 75 years with PSA levels of 4 to 10 ng/mL and palpably benign prostate glands, a percentage of free PSA cutoff of 25% detected 95% of cancers while avoiding 20% of unnecessary biopsies (Catalona et al, 1998). In this study, the risk of cancer was stratified by levels of percentage of free PSA and ranged from 8% when the percentage of free PSA was more than 25% to 56% when the percentage of free PSA was 0% to 10%.

Percentage of free PSA (at a cutoff of 25%) and PSA density (using a threshold of 0.078) have been shown to have comparable specificity (at a sensitivity of 95%), and Catalona and colleagues (2000b) suggested that the percentage of free PSA be used in place of PSA density for biopsy decisions because the former does not require ultrasonography. Thus, percentage of free PSA can be used to counsel men with PSA elevations in the range 4 to 10 ng/mL regarding their risk of cancer and the need for further evaluation to rule out the disease.

The percentage of free PSA has also been evaluated for prostate cancer diagnosis among men with PSA values below 4.0 ng/mL (Gann et al, 2002; Roehl et al, 2002a; Hugosson et al, 2003a; Raaijmakers et al, 2004a). Gann and associates (2002) measured total and free PSA using banked plasma in a case-control study of 430 men who were diagnosed with prostate cancer during 12 years of observation following blood donation. They found that a free PSA cutoff of 20% when PSA was 3 to 10 ng/mL detected 10% more cancers, with 13% fewer false-positive tests when compared with the conventional approach of a PSA threshold of 4.0 ng/mL. However, Roehl (2002a) and Raaijmakers (2004a) and their colleagues found that the percentage of free PSA had only moderate value in avoiding unnecessary biopsies at lower PSA values in the range of 2 to 4 ng/mL when the sensitivity was over 90%.

Complexed Prostate-Specific Antigen

Because men with prostate cancer have a greater fraction of total PSA that is complexed to protease inhibitors than men without prostate cancer, measurement of complexed PSA (cPSA) has been studied as a marker for detection (Brawer, 2002). Brawer and coauthors (2000) demonstrated that when total PSA levels were between 4 and 10 ng/mL, cPSA provided improved specificity when compared with total PSA and similar specificity when compared with the percentage of free PSA at a sensitivity of 95%—findings that were confirmed by Okegawa and others (2000). In the 2.6 to 4.0 ng/mL range of total PSA, cPSA as a single test provides improved specificity over total PSA but comparable specificity to the percentage of free PSA for detecting prostate cancer (Parsons et al, 2004). **There is general agreement that at high sensitivity, cPSA provides higher specificity compared with total PSA and comparable specificity to the percentage of free PSA in prostate cancer detection.** The potential advantage of cPSA as a screening modality is the requirement for one assay.

Investigational Markers

PSA is secreted from the prostatic luminal epithelium in a precursor or zymogen form (pPSA or proPSA) with a 7-amino-acid leader sequence and then either cleaved by hK2 (a closely related serine protease in the PSA/kallikrein gene family) to active free PSA or partially cleaved into isoforms of free PSA with 2- or 4-amino-acid leader sequences (see Chapter 93, "Prostate Cancer Tumor Markers") (Gretzer and Partin, 2003; Lilja, 2003). Active free PSA can be further cleaved to BPSA (a cleaved form of PSA found in the transition zone of the prostate) or intact PSA (iPSA) that is inactive and not complexed. Research assays have been developed for measuring hK2, BPSA, iPSA, and pPSA (both native and truncated

forms), and these assays have allowed evaluation of new markers for prostate cancer detection.

Expression of hK2 is higher in more poorly differentiated cancer tissues than in normal and benign tissues (Darson et al, 1997; Tremblay et al, 1997). Preliminary evidence suggested that the ratio of hK2 and free PSA might improve the ability of PSA to identify men with prostate cancer (Kwiatkowski et al, 1998; Partin et al, 1999; Becker et al, 2000), but more recent analyses have not convincingly demonstrated the value of hK2 in diagnosis (Becker et al, 2003; Bangma et al, 2004). hK2 does appear to correlate directly with grade and cancer volume and could be helpful in assessment of patients after diagnosis (Haese et al, 2003; Steuber et al, 2005).

BPSA, a nicked form of free PSA, is found preferentially in nodular BPH tissue from the transition zone of the prostate (Mikolajczyk et al, 200b) and can be considered a marker for BPH (Canto et al, 2004). When it was used in conjunction with proPSA, Khan and colleagues (2004) showed that BPSA statistically significantly improved cancer detection among men with lower percentages of free PSA.

The native form of pPSA and the truncated or clipped forms of pPSA are elevated in the tissue and blood of patients with prostate cancer compared with those without the disease (Mikolajczyk et al, 1997, 2000a, 2001; Peter et al, 2001). Evaluations of these pPSA isoforms of free PSA for prostate cancer detection among men with PSA levels of 2 to 4 ng/mL (Catalona et al, 2003, 2004), 4 to 10 ng/mL (Mikolajczyk et al, 2004), and 2 to 10 ng/mL (Catalona et al, 2003) suggest that these novel markers have the potential to improve the accurate identification of men with cancer and the identification of those with more aggressive disease (Catalona et al, 2004).

In the future, it is likely that panels of biomarkers (Etzioni et al, 2003) will be used in combination with other measures of risk (age, family history, race) to identify more selectively men who should undergo further evaluation for the presence of prostate cancer.

Digital Rectal Examination

Before the availability of PSA testing, physicians relied solely on DRE for early detection of prostate cancer. **DRE is a test with only fair reproducibility in the hands of experienced examiners** (Smith and Catalona, 1995) that misses a substantial proportion of cancers and detects most cancers at a more advanced pathologic stage, when treatment is less likely to be effective. In both screened and nonscreened populations, DRE misses 23% to 45% of the cancers that are subsequently found with prostatic biopsies done for serum PSA elevations (Cooner et al, 1990; Catalona et al, 1994b; Ellis et al, 1994). Results from a randomized trial of prostate cancer screening demonstrated that DRE alone resulted in detection of 56% of 473 cancers, and 17% of the 473 cancers would have been missed by PSA-based screening alone (Schroder et al, 1998).

PSA improves the positive predictive value (i.e., the proportion of men with a positive test who actually have disease) **of DRE for cancer** (see Table 94–3). The positive predictive value of DRE in contemporary series increases directly with the PSA level (see Table 94–3). The positive predictive value of DRE also depends on age and race (Schroder et al, 1998; Carvalhal et al, 1999). In a screened population of men with suspicious DREs and PSA levels less than 4 ng/mL, Carvalhal and colleagues (1999) found that black race and older age were associated with higher cancer detection rates. Schroder and associates (1998) evaluated a screened population and found that the positive predictive value of DRE ranged from 4% to 11% in men with PSA levels of 0 to 2.9 ng/mL and from 33% to 83% in men with PSA levels of 3 to 9.9 ng/mL or more. In that study, 82 (17.3%) of the 473 cancers would have remained undetected by PSA-based screening alone.

Some investigators (Schroder et al, 1998; Vis et al, 2001) have suggested that the value of DRE for screening at PSA levels below 3.0 ng/mL is limited. However, **because of the risk of prostate cancer among men with abnormalities on DRE and the simplicity of the examination, most urologists use PSA and DRE together for prostate cancer detection.**

Transrectal Ultrasound-Directed Prostate Biopsy

Enthusiasm for using TRUS to identify early prostate cancers by detection of hypoechoic lesions has not been justified with longer follow-up (see Chapter 92, "Ultrasonography and Biopsy of the Prostate"). A number of studies have confirmed the inability of TRUS to localize early prostate cancer (Rifkin et al, 1990; Ellis et al, 1994; Flanigan et al, 1994). Rifkin and colleagues (1990) found that only 60% of prostate cancers measuring more than 5 mm on pathologic examination were identified by MRI and that ultrasonography identified only 59% of these cancers. Flanigan and associates (1994) found that only 18% of 855 sonographically suspicious quadrants actually contained cancer on biopsy, whereas 65% of quadrants containing cancer were not sonographically suspicious. In another study, analysis of 6006 sectors biopsied revealed that 17% of hypoechoic sectors contained cancer, whereas 37% of sectors containing cancer were not suspicious by ultrasonography (Ellis et al, 1994). **The limitations of TRUS in prostate cancer detection are that most hypoechoic lesions found on TRUS are not cancer and that 50% of nonpalpable cancers more than 1 cm in greatest dimension are not visualized by ultrasonography** (Carter et al, 1989). Although hypoechoic areas on TRUS are more than twice as likely to contain cancer as isoechoic areas (Ellis et al, 1994; Hammerer and Huland, 1994), 25% to 50% of cancers would be missed if only hypoechoic areas were biopsied. **Therefore, any patient with a DRE suspicious for cancer or a PSA elevation should undergo prostate biopsy regardless of TRUS findings if an early diagnosis of cancer would result in a recommendation for treatment.**

Because TRUS is not an accurate method for localizing early prostate cancer, it is not recommended as a first-line screening tool. The primary role of TRUS in the detection of prostate cancer was originally outlined by Cooner and coworkers (1990). **The major role of TRUS is to ensure accurate wide-area sampling of prostate tissue in men at higher risk for harboring prostate cancer on the basis of DRE and PSA.** This is best accomplished by targeted biopsy of TRUS-suspicious lesions and systematic biopsy of areas without hypoechoic lesions (Hodge et al, 1989; Littrup and Bailey, 2000). The optimal biopsy technique in terms of the number of biopsies and the needle placement for tissue procurement that minimizes the chance of missing a relevant cancer is controversial (Babaian, 2000; Terris, 2000). There is evidence that more

laterally placed biopsies within the peripheral zone of the prostate are important to exclude prostate cancer in men with PSA elevations only (see Chapter 92, "Ultrasonography and Biopsy of the Prostate").

Advances in ultrasound imaging are being studied as methods for improving prostate cancer detection (Purohit et al, 2003). Color Doppler ultrasonography and power Doppler to evaluate the blood flow within prostate vessels and three-dimensional Doppler with use of contrast agents could improve the visualization of more subtle tissue alterations caused by cancer.

GUIDELINES FOR EARLY DETECTION OF PROSTATE CANCER

Detection guidelines determine the burden of screening of the population in terms of unnecessary tests, false-positive tests, and downstream effects of false-positive testing and are thus an important aspect of a successful screening program. If prostate cancer screening is proved to be an effective method for reducing deaths from prostate cancer in ongoing randomized trials, careful evaluation of cost-effective screening strategies will be a high priority. The age at which screening should begin, rescreening intervals, and the age at which screening should be discontinued are important in designing a cost-effective screening strategy.

Timing of Early Detection Measures

Age to Begin Screening

The optimum age at which to begin prostate cancer screening has not been determined. The American Cancer Society (Smith et al, 2002) and the American Urological Association (Thompson et al, 2000) recommend that prostate cancer screening be offered annually beginning at age 50 years and perhaps earlier for those at higher risk (family history of disease, black). Although only 8% of black men and men with a family history of prostate cancer who are age 40 to 50 years have positive screening tests, 55% of those with positive tests have prostate cancer (Catalona et al, 2002)—a finding that supports the recommendation for early screening of high-risk individuals. The National Comprehensive Cancer Network (NCCN) has recommended that all men be offered baseline PSA screening at age 40 years and that the frequency of follow-up testing should depend on PSA test results (National Comprehensive Cancer Network, 2004).

The incidence and mortality of prostate cancer increase directly with age. For men age 40 to 49 years the incidence and mortality are 25 and 0.6 per 100,000 men, respectively; compared with 237 and 6.1 for men age 50 to 59 years (Surveillance, Epidemiology, and End Results Program, 2003). Thus, early detection efforts in men younger than 50 years could potentially require more testing per cancer detected compared with men older than 50 years. However, there are reasons to believe that less frequent testing that begins at an early age (younger than 50 years) could be a rational and cost-effective approach to screening.

First, a substantial number of men whose prostate cancers go undetected prior to age 50 years die of prostate cancer in the next one to two decades. Approximately 54 per 100,000 men age 50 to 64 years die of prostate cancer yearly (Surveillance, Epidemiology, and End Results Program, 2003). Most men with an early prostate cancer that progresses to death die of the disease 15 to 20 years after diagnosis (Horan et al, 2000; Johansson et al, 2004), and thus it is likely that most of the prostate cancer deaths occurring in men age 50 to 64 years could have been prevented by detection and treatment when these men were age 40 to 50 years. Second, younger men are more likely to have curable disease than older men and may have improved disease-free outcomes (Alexander et al, 1989; Carter et al, 1999a; Stamey et al, 2000; Smith et al, 2000). Third, PSA is a more specific test in younger men, who are less likely to have prostate enlargement as a cause of false-positive elevations than older men (Morgan et al, 1996). Fourth, because prostate cancers progress slowly (Johansson et al, 2004), it may not be necessary to screen younger men frequently. The screening frequency among younger men could be based on a baseline PSA, the results of which have been shown to predict the risk of a prostate cancer diagnosis over the next 25 years (Fang et al, 2001).

In the absence of long-term screening data, computer simulations have been used to explore the effectiveness of different screening strategies (Etzioni et al, 1999b; Ross et al, 2000), and these suggest that the current standard of yearly screening starting at age 50 years may not be a cost-effective approach to early detection of prostate cancer.

Using a Markov model of the natural history of prostate cancer, Ross and colleagues (2000) evaluated the numbers of biopsies and PSA tests per life saved with different screening strategies. They found that a strategy of PSA testing at age 40 years, age 45 years, and biennially (every other year) after age 50 years with a PSA threshold of 4 ng/mL used fewer resources and saved more lives than a strategy that tested annually starting at age 50 years. Because the PLCO and ERSPC randomized screening studies are evaluating the effectiveness of screening in men age 50 years and older, evidence-based recommendations for screening men younger than 50 years will not be available from randomized trials.

Rescreening Intervals

Rescreening intervals can influence the effectiveness of a screening program; long rescreening intervals could miss detecting curable disease for those with fast-growing cancers, and short intervals could lead to unnecessary testing, overdiagnosis, and overtreatment with no impact on disease mortality for those with slowly growing cancers. Annual screening is recommended for all men older than 50 years—regardless of risk—by the American Cancer Society (Smith et al, 2002), the American Urological Association (Thompson et al, 2000), and the NCCN (National Comprehensive Cancer Network, 2004).

Carter and coauthors (1997) suggested that a screening interval of 2 years for men with PSA levels of 2 ng/mL or less was not likely to miss a curable cancer. On the basis of longitudinal data, the authors observed that among cancer cases, conversion to a PSA of 4.1 to 5.0 ng/mL was rare 2 years after a baseline PSA level that was below 2 ng/mL but common 2 years after a baseline PSA level of 2 to 3 ng/mL or 3 to 4 ng/mL. The authors recommended biennial screening for men with PSA levels below 2 ng/mL and annual screening for those with PSA levels of 2 ng/mL or above. This concept of using a baseline PSA to determine the rescreening interval is supported by longitudinal studies using frozen plasma samples that show that future prostate cancer risk can be stratified by a baseline PSA measurement (see Table 94–4). Furthermore, analyses from sections of the ERSPC suggest that annual screening is not necessary to maintain the detection of curable disease in most men.

Hugosson and associates (2003b) reported on the results of biennial screening from the Swedish section of the ERSPC and found that rescreening 2 years after a baseline screen was sufficient to detect prostate cancers at a curable stage for men with PSA levels below 2 ng/mL at the initial screen. The authors recommended more frequent screening for those with baseline PSA levels above 2 ng/mL. Investigators from the Rotterdam section of the ERSPC (van der Cruijsen-Koeter et al, 2003) have reported on interval cancers detected during 4 years after randomization in the screened arm outside the screening protocol—an indicator of the sensitivity of screening and safety of a rescreening interval of 4 years. Among men who complied with biopsy recommendations at the initial screen, only 18 interval cancers were detected and all were considered low-risk disease with a favorable prognosis as defined by D'Amico and coauthors (1998). The rate of interval cancers compared with the number in the control arm was 13% and the sensitivity of the screening protocol was 86%, suggesting that a rescreening interval of 4 years may even be reasonable.

Evaluation of intermediate pathologic endpoints in the ERSPC suggests that most cancers detected at 2 to 4 years after the prevalent screen (first round) will be curable (Hoedemaeker et al, 2001; Hugosson et al, 2004; Postma et al, 2004). Because of the long natural history of prostate cancer and the ability of PSA screening to uncover advanced life-threatening cancer at the prevalent screen, frequent screening may be unnecessary for most men. Data on interval cancers and intermediate endpoints among screened and control arms of the PLCO trial (annual rescreening interval) and sections of the ERSPC trial (2- and 4-year rescreening intervals) should provide guidance regarding appropriate rescreening intervals in the near future.

Age to Discontinue Screening

The upper age limit for enrollment in current randomized screening trials of prostate cancer is 74 years. Organizations that have endorsed screening have generally recommended screening for men with a life expectancy of 10 years or more. But the benefits of screening decline rapidly with age. Using a Markov model, Ross and colleagues (2005) found that compared with screening to age 65 years, screening to age 75 years and 80 years required twice and three times, respectively, the number of treatments per person-year of life saved.

There is reason to believe that a substantial proportion of men with a life expectancy longer than 10 years may not benefit from screening. A prevalent screen detects most advanced cases (Hoedemaeker et al, 2001) and rescreening detects disease at an early curable stage in most men (Hoedemaeker et al, 2001; Hugosson et al, 2004; Postma et al, 2004) with a lead time of 10 years or more (Draisma et al, 2003; Tornblom et al, 2004). Because men who have non–screen-detected cancers rarely die of disease before 15 years without treatment (Johansson et al, 2004), it may be that screening could be discontinued earlier in life (before age 70 years) for most men who have taken part in a screening program and have maintained PSA levels consistent with a low risk of later prostate cancer development. For example, in a prospective cohort study, Carter and colleagues (1999b) showed that if PSA testing were discontinued in men age 65 years with PSA levels below 0.5 to 1.0 ng/mL, it would be unlikely that a prostate cancer would be missed later on in life.

Prostate Biopsy Recommendations

TRUS-guided prostate biopsies are recommended for men who have a DRE that is suspicious for cancer of the prostate or an elevated or rising PSA level suggesting the presence of prostate cancer, or both (NCCN, 2004) (see sections on "Prostate-Specific Antigen Thresholds" and "Prostate-Specific Antigen Velocity"). For men who have a prostate biopsy that shows only benign tissue but for whom there is continued suspicion of prostate cancer on the basis of DRE findings, repeated PSA measurements, or other PSA derivatives (percentage of free PSA, cPSA, PSA density, PSA velocity), a repeat prostate biopsy should be considered (NCCN, 2004). However, more than 90% of prostate cancers are detected by the performance of two sextant biopsies (Roehl et al, 2002b), and therefore with the biopsy approaches preferred today it is unlikely that two extended biopsies would miss a life-threatening cancer. Biopsy of the transition zone of the prostate, although not recommended at initial biopsy, should be considered for men undergoing a repeat biopsy for whom a suspicion of a missed cancer anteriorly is high (NCCN, 2004).

For men who have high-grade prostatic intraepithelial neoplasia (PIN) found at the time of an extended prostate biopsy, the risk of cancer on a repeat biopsy is similar to the risk of cancer on repeat biopsy if the initial biopsy is negative (O'dowd et al, 2000; Lefkowitz et al, 2001). Thus, a repeat biopsy is not indicated for men with high-grade PIN if the original biopsy technique was adequate (NCCN, 2004). *Whether these men will need repeat biopsies further out and, if so, when and how often are unknown.* A prostate biopsy that reveals atypical glands that are suspicious but not diagnostic of cancer should be repeated because the chance of finding prostate cancer on a repeat biopsy is 40% to 50% (Iczkowski et al, 1998; Chan et al, 1999; NCCN, 2004). A biopsy approach for men with atypical findings has been recommended (Allen et al, 1998).

STAGING OF PROSTATE CANCER

Clinical staging of prostate cancer aims to utilize pretreatment parameters to predict the true extent of disease. The goals of cancer staging are to allow the assessment of prognosis and facilitate educated decision-making regarding available treatment options. An accurate assessment of disease extent is critical for men with newly diagnosed prostate cancer because pathologic stage is the most reliable means of predicting the outcome of definitive treatment in men with clinically localized cancer (Pound et al, 1997). Available pretreatment modalities that can help predict true disease extent in men with prostate cancer include DRE, serum PSA, tumor grade, radiologic imaging, and pelvic lymphadenectomy. The local extent of disease can be predicted by a combination of

DRE, serum tumor markers such as PSA, and tumor grade. Although in unique circumstances imaging modalities may assist in the detection of extraprostatic spread of cancer, in the vast majority of cases these tests are not yet reliable. Pelvic lymphadenectomy remains the "gold standard" for the detection of lymph node spread in men at high risk for harboring occult lymph node metastases. Ultimately, clinical staging may provide the patient and urologist with valuable information regarding whether newly diagnosed prostate cancer is localized, locally advanced, or metastatic. This information helps guide management decisions.

Staging: Clinical versus Pathologic

Clinical staging is an assessment of the extent of disease using pretreatment parameters such as DRE, PSA, needle biopsy findings, and radiologic imaging. Pathologic stage, on the other hand, is determined after prostate removal and involves careful histologic analysis of the prostate, seminal vesicles, and pelvic lymph nodes if a lymphadenectomy is performed. Thus, pathologic staging represents a more accurate estimate of the true disease burden and is more useful in the prediction of prognosis. Tumor volume and grade, extracapsular extension, and surgical margins are all accurately determined by pathologic staging. The importance of pathologic stage is underscored by the fact that biochemical recurrence-free survival and cancer-specific survival are both inversely related to the pathologic stage of disease (Fig. 94–3). The most important pathologic criteria that predict prognosis after radical prostatectomy are tumor grade, surgical margin status, presence of extracapsular disease, seminal vesicle invasion, and pelvic lymph node involvement (Jewett, 1975; Epstein, 1990; Epstein et al, 1993a, 1993b; Partin et al, 1993a; Pound et al, 1997; Walsh and Jewett, 1980).

Clinical Staging Classification Systems

Two main classification systems for clinical staging exist today: the Whitmore-Jewett and the tumor, node, metastases (TNM) classification systems. Whitmore introduced the first clinical staging classification system for prostate cancer in 1956 and Jewett later modified it in 1975 (Jewett, 1956; Whitmore, 1956). The TNM system was first adopted in 1975 by the American Joint Committee for Cancer Staging and End Results Reporting (AJCC) (Wallace et al, 1975). A new TNM classification system was adopted in 1992 by the AJCC and International Union Against Cancer (UICC), and this system was then modified in 1997 to reduce the subdivision of T2 disease from three categories (T2a, T2b and T2c) to two substages by combining single-lobe disease (T2a and T2b) into a single stage (T2) (Schroder et al, 1992; Flemming et al, 1997). Several authors have questioned the 1997 modification, arguing that the prior distinction between stages T2a and T2b is clinically important (Iyer et al, 1999; Han et al, 2000). Table 94–5 summarizes and compares the Whitmore-Jewett and TNM staging schemes.

Interestingly, a nonpalpable lesion identified by imaging in the prostate is considered a T2 lesion by the current TNM clinical staging system. This is controversial in light of several studies documenting that TRUS findings do not predict tumor extent in PSA-detected nonpalpable lesions (Epstein et

Table 94-6. Combination of Prostate-Specific Antigen, Clinical Stage, and Gleason Score to Predict Pathologic Stage of Localized Prostate Cancer (Partin Tables)

PSA Range (ng/mL)	Pathologic Stage	Gleason Score				
		2-4	5-6	3 + 4 = 7	4 + 3 = 7	8-10
Clinical Stage T1c (Nonpalpable, PSA Elevated)						
0-2.5	Organ confined	95 (89-99)	90 (88-93)	79 (74-85)	71 (62-79)	66 (54-76)
	Capsular penetration	5 (1-11)	9 (7-12)	17 (13-23)	25 (18-34)	28 (20-38)
	Seminal vesicle (+)	—	0 (0-1)	2 (1-5)	2 (1-5)	4 (1-10)
	Lymph node (+)	—	—	1 (0-2)	1 (0-4)	1 (0-4)
2.6-4.0	Organ confined	92 (82-98)	84 (81-86)	68 (62-74)	58 (48-67)	52 (41-63)
	Capsular penetration	8 (2-18)	15 (13-18)	27 (22-33)	37 (29-46)	40 (31-50)
	Seminal vesicle (+)	—	1 (0-1)	4 (2-7)	4 (1-7)	6 (3-12)
	Lymph node (+)	—	—	1 (0-2)	1 (0-3)	1 (0-4)
4.1-6.0	Organ confined	90 (78-98)	80 (78-83)	63 (58-68)	52 (43-60)	46 (36-56)
	Capsular penetration	10 (2-22)	19 (16-21)	32 (27-36)	42 (35-50)	45 (36-54)
	Seminal vesicle (+)	—	1 (0-1)	3 (2-5)	3 (1-6)	5 (3-9)
	Lymph node (+)	—	0 (0-1)	2 (1-3)	3 (1-5)	3 (1-6)
6.1-10.0	Organ confined	87 (73-97)	75 (72-77)	54 (49-59)	43 (35-51)	37 (28-46)
	Capsular penetration	13 (3-27)	23 (21-25)	36 (32-40)	47 (40-54)	48 (39-57)
	Seminal vesicle (+)	—	2 (2-3)	8 (6-11)	8 (4-12)	13 (8-19)
	Lymph node (+)	—	0 (0-1)	2 (1-3)	2 (1-4)	3 (1-5)
>10.0	Organ confined	80 (61-95)	62 (58-64)	37 (32-42)	27 (21-34)	22 (16-30)
	Capsular penetration	20 (5-39)	33 (30-36)	43 (38-48)	51 (44-59)	50 (42-59)
	Seminal vesicle (+)	—	4 (3-5)	12 (9-17)	11 (6-17)	17 (10-25)
	Lymph node (+)	—	2 (1-3)	8 (5-11)	10 (5-17)	11 (5-18)
Clinical Stage T2a (Palpable < Half of One Lobe)						
0-2.5	Organ confined	91 (79-98)	81 (77-85)	64 (56-71)	53 (43-63)	47 (35-59)
	Capsular penetration	9 (2-21)	17 (13-21)	29 (23-36)	40 (30-49)	42 (32-53)
	Seminal vesicle (+)	—	1 (0-2)	5 (1-9)	4 (1-9)	7 (2-16)
	Lymph node (+)	—	0 (0-1)	2 (0-5)	3 (0-8)	3 (0-9)
2.6-4.0	Organ confined	85 (69-96)	71 (66-75)	50 (43-57)	39 (30-48)	33 (24-44)
	Capsular penetration	15 (4-31)	27 (23-31)	41 (35-48)	52 (43-61)	53 (44-63)
	Seminal vesicle (+)	—	2 (1-3)	7 (3-12)	6 (2-12)	10 (4-18)
	Lymph node (+)	—	0 (0-1)	2 (0-4)	2 (0-6)	3 (0-8)
4.1-6.0	Organ confined	81 (63-95)	66 (62-70)	44 (39-50)	33 (25-41)	28 (20-37)
	Capsular penetration	19 (5-37)	32 (28-36)	46 (40-52)	56 (48-64)	58 (49-66)
	Seminal vesicle (+)	—	1 (1-2)	5 (3-8)	5 (2-8)	8 (4-13)
	Lymph Node (+)	—	1 (0-2)	4 (2-7)	6 (3-11)	6 (2-12)
6.1-10.0	Organ confined	76 (56-94)	58 (54-61)	35 (30-40)	25 (19-32)	21 (15-28)
	Capsular penetration	24 (6-44)	37 (34-41)	49 (43-54)	58 (51-66)	57 (48-65)
	Seminal vesicle (+)	—	4 (3-5)	13 (9-18)	11 (6-17)	17 (11-26)
	Lymph node (+)	—	1 (0-2)	3 (2-6)	5 (2-8)	5 (2-10)
>10.0	Organ confined	65 (43-89)	42 (38-46)	20 (17-24)	14 (10-18)	11 (7-15)
	Capsular penetration	35 (11-57)	47 (43-52)	49 (43-55)	55 (46-64)	52 (41-62)
	Seminal vesicle (+)	—	6 (4-8)	16 (11-22)	13 (7-20)	19 (12-29)
	Lymph node (+)	—	4 (3-7)	14 (9-21)	18 (10-27)	17 (9-29)
Clinical Stage T2b (Palpable > Half of One Lobe, Not on Both Lobes)						
0-2.5	Organ confined	88 (73-97)	75 (69-81)	54 (46-63)	43 (33-54)	37 (26-49)
	Capsular penetration	12 (3-27)	22 (17-28)	35 (28-43)	45 (35-56)	46 (35-58)
	Seminal vesicle (+)	—	2 (0-3)	6 (2-12)	5 (1-11)	9 (2-20)
	Lymph node (+)	—	1 (0-2)	4 (0-10)	6 (0-14)	6 (0-16)
2.6-4.0	Organ confined	80 (61-95)	63 (57-59)	41 (33-48)	30 (22-39)	25 (17-34)
	Capsular penetration	20 (5-39)	34 (28-40)	47 (40-55)	57 (47-67)	57 (46-68)
	Seminal vesicle (+)	—	2 (1-4)	9 (4-15)	7 (3-14)	12 (5-22)
	Lymph node (+)	—	1 (0-2)	3 (0-8)	4 (0-12)	5 (0-14)
4.1-6.0	Organ confined	75 (55-93)	57 (52-63)	35 (29-40)	25 (18-32)	21 (14-29)
	Capsular penetration	25 (7-45)	39 (33-44)	51 (44-57)	60 (50-68)	59 (49-69)
	Seminal vesicle (+)	—	2 (1-3)	7 (4-11)	5 (3-9)	9 (4-16)
	Lymph node (+)	—	2 (1-3)	7 (4-13)	10 (5-18)	10 (4-20)
6.1-10.0	Organ confined	69 (47-91)	49 (43-54)	26 (22-31)	19 (14-25)	15 (10-21)
	Capsular penetration	31 (9-53)	44 (39-49)	52 (46-58)	60 (52-68)	57 (48-67)
	Seminal vesicle (+)	—	5 (3-8)	16 (10-22)	13 (7-20)	19 (11-29)
	Lymph node (+)	—	2 (1-3)	6 (4-10)	8 (5-14)	8 (4-16)
>10.0	Organ confined	57 (35-86)	33 (28-38)	14 (11-17)	9 (6-13)	7 (4-10)
	Capsular penetration	43 (14-65)	52 (46-56)	47 (40-53)	50 (40-60)	46 (36-59)
	Seminal vesicle (+)	—	8 (5-11)	17 (12-24)	13 (8-21)	19 (12-29)
	Lymph node (+)	—	8 (5-12)	22 (15-30)	27 (16-39)	27 (14-40)

Continued

Table 94-6. Combination of Prostate-Specific Antigen, Clinical Stage, and Gleason Score to Predict Pathologic Stage of Localized Prostate Cancer (Partin Tables)—cont'd

		Gleason Score				
PSA Range (ng/mL)	Pathologic Stage	2-4	5-6	3 + 4 = 7	4 + 3 = 7	8-10
Clinical Stage T2c (Palpable on Both Lobes)						
0-2.5	Organ Confined	86 (71-97)	73 (63-81)	51 (38-63)	39 (26-54)	34 (21-48)
	Capsular penetration	14 (3-29)	24 (17-33)	36 (26-48)	45 (32-59)	47 (33-61)
	Seminal vesicle (+)	—	1 (0-4)	5 (1-13)	5 (1-12)	8 (2-19)
	Lymph node (+)	—	1 (0-4)	6 (0-18)	9 (0-26)	10 (0-27)
2.6-4.0	Organ confined	78 (58-94)	61 (50-70)	38 (27-50)	27 (18-40)	23 (14-34)
	Capsular penetration	22 (6-42)	36 (27-45)	48 (37-59)	57 (44-70)	57 (44-70)
	Seminal vesicle (+)	—	2 (1-5)	8 (2-17)	6 (2-16)	10 (3-22)
	Lymph node (+)	—	1 (0-4)	5 (0-15)	7 (0-21)	8 (0-22)
4.1-6.0	Organ confined	73 (52-93)	55 (44-64)	31 (23-41)	21 (14-31)	18 (11-28)
	Capsular penetration	27 (7-48)	40 (32-50)	50 (40-60)	57 (43-68)	57 (43-70)
	Seminal vesicle (+)	—	2 (1-4)	6 (2-11)	4 (1-10)	7 (2-15)
	Lymph node (+)	—	3 (1-7)	12 (5-23)	16 (6-32)	16 (6-33)
6.1-10.0	Organ confined	67 (45-91)	46 (36-56)	24 (17-32)	16 (10-24)	13 (8-20)
	Capsular penetration	33 (9-55)	46 (37-55)	52 (42-61)	58 (46-69)	56 (43-69)
	Seminal vesicle (+)	—	5 (2-9)	13 (6-23)	11 (4-21)	16 (6-29)
	Lymph node (+)	—	3 (1-6)	10 (5-18)	13 (6-25)	13 (5-26)
>10.0	Organ confined	54 (32-85)	30 (21-38)	11 (7-17)	7 (4-12)	6 (3-10)
	Capsular penetration	46 (15-68)	51 (42-60)	42 (30-55)	43 (29-59)	41 (27-57)
	Seminal vesicle (+)	—	6 (2-12)	13 (6-24)	10 (3-20)	15 (5-28)
	Lymph node (+)	—	13 (6-22)	33 (18-49)	38 (20-58)	38 (20-59)

Prostate-Specific Antigen

PSA is a member of the human kallikrein gene family of serine proteases located on chromosome 19. It is the most important tumor marker available today for the diagnosis, staging, and monitoring of prostate cancer (Polascik et al, 1999). Serum PSA has been shown to correlate directly with pathologic stage and tumor volume (Stamey et al, 1987; Stamey et al, 1989; Noldus et al, 1998). Because PSA can be influenced by BPH and tumor grade and PSA levels overlap between stages, it cannot be used alone to predict accurately the extent of disease for an individual patient. Men with more advanced prostate cancer have higher grade and higher volume tumors that produce less PSA per gram of tumor (Partin et al, 1990). In addition, the contribution of BPH to overall serum PSA has been estimated to be 0.15 ng/mL of PSA per gram of BPH tissue (Benson et al, 1992a, 1992b). Despite these confounding factors, 80% of men with PSA less than 4.0 ng/mL have pathologically proven organ-confined disease, 66% of men with PSA levels between 4.0 and 10.0 ng/mL have organ-confined disease, and more than 50% of men with PSA greater than 10.0 ng/mL have extraprostatic disease (Catalona et al, 1997; Rietbergen et al, 1999). Also, 20% of men with PSA greater than 20 ng/mL and 75% of those with PSA greater than 50 ng/mL are found to have pelvic lymph node involvement (Partin et al, 1990, 1993b).

ProPSA is released from cells with a 7-amino-acid leader sequence that is cleaved by human kallikrein 2 (hK2) to produce active PSA. In addition to its potential role in cancer detection, some studies suggest that hK2 may be a useful predictor of pathologically proven organ-confined disease (Haese et al, 2003). The role of proPSA and other PSA isoforms in prostate cancer staging remain unclear (Gretzer and Partin, 2003). Multiple studies have found an association between percentage of free PSA and more extensive pathologic disease (Carter et al, 1997; Southwick et al, 1999). Most recently, a

study found that men whose PSA level increases by more than 2.0 ng/mL/year before the diagnosis of prostate cancer have an increased risk for death from prostate cancer despite undergoing radical prostatectomy (D'Amico et al, 2004). The role of molecular forms of PSA and PSA kinetics in staging requires further clarification before wide clinical use.

Although prostatic acid phosphatase (PAP) elevations are directly related to the pathologic stage of prostate cancer, the closer relationship between PSA and disease extent has virtually eliminated the use of this parameter in clinical practice (Heller, 1987). PAP rarely adds additional information in men who are considered to have clinically localized prostate cancer based on the results of DRE, PSA, and Gleason grade (Burnett et al, 1992). Nevertheless, two studies demonstrated that preoperative PAP levels may provide independent prognostic information with respect to predicting progression following radical prostatectomy (Moul et al, 1998; Han et al, 2001).

Digital Rectal Examination

DRE determines whether a lesion is palpable and thus is a surrogate for the local extent of disease (clinical T stage). Because of its poor sensitivity and lack of reproducibility, DRE can both overestimate and underestimate the extent of disease. Studies from the 1970s demonstrated that of men predicted to have extracapsular disease by DRE, only 25% were confirmed to have that finding on pathologic examination (Turner and Belt, 1957; Byar and Mostofi, 1972). Subsequent studies in presumed organ-confined cases revealed a pattern of understaging or false-negative prediction of organ-confined status by DRE (Walsh and Jewett, 1980). The sensitivity and specificity of DRE in determining organ-confined status were evaluated in a large series in which all DREs and radical prostatectomies were performed by one urologist with pathologic evaluations by a single pathologist (Partin et al,

1993b). In this series of 565 men in whom the DRE suggested organ-confined disease (T2), 52% actually had organ-confined disease, 31% had capsular penetration, and the remaining 17% exhibited either seminal vesicle or lymph node involvement. In the same series, of 36 men in whom extraprostatic disease was suspected on DRE (T3a), 19% were organ confined, 36% had capsular penetration, and 45% had involvement of the seminal vesicles or lymph nodes. This represents a sensitivity of 52% and a specificity of 81% for prediction of organ-confined disease by DRE alone. When combined with other parameters, as mentioned earlier, DRE can assist in the precise prediction of overall tumor extent.

Imaging

A variety of imaging modalities have been evaluated for staging prostate cancer. None of these techniques are sensitive enough to detect reliably the extraprostatic spread of prostate cancer. The inability to image microscopic disease limits the accuracy of current imaging modalities.

Radionuclide bone scan (bone scintigraphy) is the most sensitive modality for the detection of skeletal metastases (Schaffer and Pendergrass, 1976; Gerber and Chodak, 1991; Terris et al, 1991). This is in contrast to bone survey films (skeletal radiography), which require more than 50% of the bone density to be replaced with tumor before they can identify distant spread (Lachman, 1955; Lentle et al, 1974). Today, skeletal radiography is obtained only to confirm a positive bone scan in men at low risk for bone metastases. Radionuclide bone scan can also screen for upper urinary tract obstruction and thus can obviate the need for further evaluation of the urinary tract in men with prostate cancer (Narayan et al, 1988). Because bone metastases at diagnosis are rare in men without bone pain in the PSA screening era, the routine use of bone scans in this population may not be useful and can create needless stress by detecting benign conditions that require further tests to rule out occult malignant disease. In addition, a strategy of using bone scintigraphy in the staging evaluation of all PSA-screened men may not be cost-effective (Chybowski et al, 1991). Bone scans are not routinely obtained for patients with PSA levels less than 10 ng/mL and no bone pain. When a bone scan is performed, however, it provides a baseline evaluation for comparison in men who later may complain of bone pain.

The use of computed tomography (CT) and MRI to evaluate the local extent of disease and the possibility of nodal involvement is not routinely recommended because of the low sensitivity of these modalities (Rifkin et al, 1990; Tempany et al; 1994, Wolf et al, 1995). Such tests may be appropriately reserved for high-risk patients such as those with locally advanced disease by DRE, a PSA greater than 20 ng/mL, or men with poorly differentiated cancer on needle biopsy. Furthermore, the cost effectiveness of these tests in populations with probabilities of lymph node involvement less than 30% has been questioned (Rifkin et al, 1990; Tempany et al, 1994; Wolf et al, 1995). Given the rarity of lymph node involvement in screened populations, it appears that these imaging modalities are being overused in the staging of prostate cancer (Kindrick et al, 1998).

Combined MRI and MRI spectroscopy (MRIS) are being evaluated for staging prostate cancer, but there is no evidence that these methods will overcome the current limitation of the inability to image microscopic disease (Yu et al, 1999; Kurhanewicz et al, 2000). Specialized techniques such as high-resolution MRI used in tandem with the intravenous administration of lymphotropic superparamagnetic nanoparticles may allow the detection of small and otherwise undetectable lymph node metastases in patients with prostate cancer (Harisinghani et al, 2003). These techniques, however, require further clinical evaluation before widespread use.

TRUS is an insensitive method for detecting local extension of tumor, but some experts still believe that TRUS can add staging information over that gained with DRE (Rifkin et al, 1990). Intravenous urography is rarely obtained to stage prostate cancer but can evaluate the upper urinary tract in cases of hematuria or suspected obstruction. A chest radiograph is generally a low-yield examination in the staging of prostate cancer because lung metastases are exceedingly rare in the absence of widespread metastatic disease.

Radioimmunoscintigraphy

Monoclonal antibody radioimmunoscintigraphy (radiolabeled monoclonal antibody scan) is an approach used for the identification of microscopic cancer deposits in regional and distant sites. The ProstaScint scan (Cytogen Corporation, Princeton, NJ) utilizes this technology but has had limited accuracy in the detection of lymph node metastases because the antibody targets an intracellular epitope that is exposed in dying or dead cells only (Troyer et al, 1997; Chang et al, 1999). Future generations of this technology that circumvent this limitation are being developed.

Molecular Staging

Molecular staging has focused on the detection of circulating prostate cancer cells either directly through centrifugation/immunostaining methods or indirectly by identifying the genetic message (messenger RNA [mRNA]) for prostate-specific biomarkers such as PSA or prostate surface membrane antigen (PSMA) from circulating prostate cells (Moreno et al, 1992; Ts'o et al, 1997). The latter technique, referred to as RT-PCR, involves reverse transcription of circulating mRNA to complementary DNA and amplification of the DNA coding for the biomarker by polymerase chain reaction (RT-PCR). Although studies have shown that these PCR assays are strong predictors of pathologic stage, their sensitivity for detecting circulating cancer cells has been variable among different investigators (Cama et al, 1995; Israeli et al, 1995; de la Taille et al, 1999). In addition, 25% of 65 men found to have organ-confined disease at prostatectomy in one study had a positive PCR-PSA assay (Katz et al, 1994). These men would have been denied surgery if one equated the PCR test results with incurable disease. Thus, until the significance of a positive PCR assay is known with long-term follow-up, men with clinically localized disease should not be denied curative treatment on the basis of these tests.

Pelvic Lymphadenectomy

The presence of lymph node metastasis in men diagnosed with clinically localized prostate cancer portends a poor prognosis. Accurate identification of these men allows more precise prognostication and may have important implications for the initiation of adjuvant therapy. Although the prevalence of pelvic lymph node metastases correlates directly with T stage, serum PSA level, and biopsy grade, pelvic lymphadenectomy remains the most accurate staging modality for the detection of occult nodal involvement (Parker et al, 1999). The advent of PSA screening has resulted in a steady decline in the incidence of lymph node metastasis from rates of 20%

to 40% in the 1970s and 1980s to less than 6% today (Partin et al, 1997; Parker et al, 1999). As a result of this stage shift, lymphadenectomy is often omitted before various curative treatment approaches (radical retropubic prostatectomy, perineal prostatectomy, and radiation therapy) (Bishoff et al, 1995). The criteria for laparoscopic pelvic lymphadenectomy prior to treatment are controversial, and this procedure is often reserved for patients with Gleason score greater than 8, extraprostatic extension on DRE, PSA greater than 20 ng/mL, or when there is suspicion of enlarged lymph nodes on radiologic evaluation.

Given the individual variation in prostatic lymphatic drainage patterns, some investigators have favored an extended pelvic lymphadenectomy in lieu of a limited dissection. A retrospective study demonstrated that an extended pelvic lymphadenectomy may maximize the detection rate of lymph node–positive disease compared with a limited lymph node dissection in a contemporary series of PSA-screened men with clinically localized prostate cancer undergoing radical prostatectomy (Allaf et al, 2004). Information regarding the therapeutic value of such a strategy is confounded by the issue of stage migration and is difficult to evaluate in the absence of prospective trials.

KEY POINTS: DIAGNOSIS AND STAGING OF PROSTATE CANCER

- Although the value of PSA screening remains controversial, men who present for periodic health examinations should be made aware of the availability of the PSA test so that they can make an informed decision about the need for routine screening.

- The combination of DRE and serum PSA is the most useful first-line test for assessing the risk of prostate cancer being present in an individual.

- The presence of prostate disease (prostate cancer, BPH, and prostatitis) is the most important factor affecting serum levels of PSA.

- However, it has been proved that use of PSA increases detection rates of prostate cancer and leads to the detection of prostate cancers that are more likely to be confined when compared with detection without the use of PSA.

- The future risk of prostate cancer detection and the chance of finding cancer on a prostate biopsy increase incrementally with the serum PSA level.

- Biochemical recurrence-free survival and cancer-specific survival are both inversely related to the pathologic stage of disease.

- The most important pathologic criteria that predict prognosis after radical prostatectomy are tumor grade, surgical margin status, presence of extracapsular disease, seminal vesicle invasion, and pelvic lymph node involvement.

- The Gleason grading system is the most commonly used classification scheme for the histologic grading of prostate cancer.

SUGGESTED READINGS

Catalona WJ, Partin AW, Slawin KM, et al: Use of the percentage of free prostate-specific antigen to enhance differentiation of prostate cancer from benign prostatic disease: A prospective multicenter clinical trial. JAMA 1998;279:1542.

Catalona WJ, Smith DS, Ratliff TL, Basler JW: Detection of organ-confined prostate cancer is increased through prostate-specific antigen based screening. JAMA 1993;270:948.

Catalona WJ, Smith DS, Wolfert RL, et al: Evaluation of percentage of free serum prostate-specific antigen to improve specificity of prostate cancer screening. JAMA 1995;274:1214.

Chu KC, Tarone RE, Freeman HP: Trends in prostate cancer mortality among black men and white men in the United States. Cancer 2003;97:1507.

D'Amico AV, Chen MH, Roehl KA, et al: Preoperative PSA velocity and the risk of death from prostate cancer after radical prostatectomy. N Engl J Med 2004;351:125.

Draisma G, Boer R, Otto SJ, et al: Lead times and overdetection due to prostate-specific antigen screening: estimates from the European Randomized Study of Screening for Prostate Cancer. J Natl Cancer Inst 2003;95:868.

Fang J, Metter EJ, Landis P, et al: Low levels of prostate specific antigen predict long term risk of prostate cancer: Results from the Baltimore Longitudinal Study of Aging. Urology 2001;58:411-416.

Gann PH, Hennekens CH, Stampfer MJ: A prospective evaluation of plasma prostate-specific antigen for detection of prostatic cancer. JAMA 1995;273:289.

Partin AW, Kattan MW, Subong EN, et al: Combination of prostate-specific antigen, clinical stage, and Gleason score to predict pathological stage of localized prostate cancer. A multi-institutional update. JAMA 1997;277:1445.

Thompson IM, Pauler DK, Goodman PJ, et al: Prevalence of prostate cancer among men with a prostate-specific antigen level < or =4.0 ng per milliliter. N Engl J Med 2004;350:2239.

95 Definitive Therapy for Localized Prostate Cancer—An Overview

WILLIAM J. CATALONA, MD • MISOP HAN, MD

The purpose of this chapter is to provide an overview of the definitive treatment of clinically localized prostate cancer. In reporting differences in treatments, we have attempted to be objective but have included our editorial perspective. We have grouped treatments into *established treatments,* such as radical prostatectomy and radiotherapy, for which abundant published information is available; and *other treatments,* including active monitoring, primary hormone therapy, cryoablation, radiofrequency ablation, and high-intensity focused ultrasound, for which data are more limited for localized disease.

BACKGROUND

Prostate cancer is the most common noncutaneous cancer and the second-leading cause of death from cancer in men in the United States (Jemal et al, 2006). In 2006, it is estimated that more than 234,000 men were diagnosed with prostate cancer; in more than 27,000, it is the cause of death (Jemal et al, 2006). Because prostate cancer is prevalent in many countries and exhibits a wide spectrum of aggressiveness, different methods of treatment have been developed, and the preferred methods for detection and treatment are controversial. The prevalence of prostate cancer increases strikingly with age (Jemal et al, 2006). Autopsy studies have documented microscopic foci of prostate cancer in about one fourth to one third of men in the

fourth and fifth decades of life and in more than three fourths in the ninth decade (Sakr et al, 1993). Yet, a disproportionately lower but still substantial number of men (about one in six) are diagnosed with prostate cancer during their lifetime (Jemal et al, 2006). **Because of effective treatment of some prostate cancers and the biologic indolence relative to life expectancy of others, only about 16% of men diagnosed with prostate cancer ultimately die of it. Prostate cancer is the cause of death in about 3% of the U.S. male population** (Jemal et al, 2006). An additional (unquantified) proportion suffers from prostate cancer but dies of other causes.

The marked disparity between prevalence and incidence rates of prostate cancer on one hand and morbidity and mortality rates on the other has led some to conclude that many prostate cancers are harmless and perhaps would better be left undetected. Nevertheless, if the present trends of increasing life expectancy continue, given the current age-specific incidence, morbidity, and mortality rates of prostate cancer, this disease will become a far greater public health problem in the future.

Since the 1980s, the methods of diagnosis of clinically localized prostate cancer have changed. Widespread screening with serum prostate-specific antigen (PSA) and digital rectal examination (DRE) has allowed earlier detection (Catalona et al, 1991, 1993). Furthermore, with a remarkable stage migration, approximately 90% of cases are being detected in a clinically localized stage, whereas metastatic disease at the time of diagnosis is now rare in the United States (Han et al, 2001a; Jemal et al, 2006).

The natural history of prostate cancer varies from indolent disease that might not cause symptoms during a patient's lifetime to highly aggressive cancer that metastasizes quickly and causes terrible suffering and untimely death. The challenge for the physician who treats patients with prostate cancer is to advise effective treatment in those for whom treatment is necessary. Selection of the appropriate treatment requires assessment of the tumor's potential aggressiveness and the general health, life expectancy, and quality of life preferences of the patient.

Patients whose tumor has a low malignant potential are predetermined to fare better with most treatments.

Therefore, the treatment outcomes in any patient series may be influenced by the malignant potential of the tumors as well as by the treatment used. Accordingly, it is difficult to compare the results of different reports because the populations of patients are usually not strictly comparable. Furthermore, outcome measurements are not necessarily comparable between different forms of therapy (e.g., different definitions of biochemical progression for surgery and radiotherapy), complicating comparisons between them.

Characterization of the Primary Tumor

DRE and prostate ultrasound findings usually provide some information about the extent of the primary tumor. The serum PSA data, including the total PSA level, the rate of change of PSA (PSA velocity and doubling time), the PSA density (serum PSA divided by prostate volume), and the percentage of PSA in the free or complexed isoforms, are significantly associated with prostate cancer aggressiveness (Benson et al, 1992; Carter et al, 1997; Catalona et al, 1998; D'Amico et al, 2004a; Thompson et al, 2004). The biopsy findings (Gleason score; the number of cores containing cancer; the distribution and volume of cancer in the cores; the presence of perineural space invasion, lymphovascular invasion, or ductal or neuroendocrine differentiation) also correlate with cancer aggressiveness and the likelihood of the cancer's being organ confined. Nomograms, prediction tables, and algorithms have been developed to assist in this assessment (Partin et al, 1997, 2001). However, such statistical aids are more useful in *groups* than in individual patients, and wide confidence intervals surrounding estimates of outcomes sometimes limit the usefulness of risk assessment for an individual patient. In this regard, it has been claimed that the simultaneous assessment of multiple variables in nomograms provides more accurate predictions than tables do for individual patients (Kattan, 2003).

Evaluation of the Patient

There is no general agreement about how extensive the initial staging workup should be. Some physicians believe that a radionuclide bone scan, abdominal-pelvic computed tomography (CT) scan, and magnetic resonance imaging (MRI) scan are not indicated if the tumor has a Gleason sum of less than 7, the serum PSA level is less than 10 ng/mL, and the biopsy findings do not reveal an extensive or highly aggressive cancer because the likelihood of finding metastases is very low.

In patients contemplating surgical treatment, a more complete workup should be considered, including coagulation studies, baseline bone scan for future reference with confirmatory imaging studies, if necessary, and CT or MRI scan of the abdomen and pelvis to evaluate the primary tumor and regional lymph nodes and to rule out other possibly important pathologic conditions that might need to be addressed at the time of surgery. However, tumor-selective imaging tests such as monoclonal antibody scans, positron emission tomographic scans, magnetic resonance spectroscopy, and lymphotrophic MRI are not widely used, although they might prove more useful in the future.

CONSERVATIVE MANAGEMENT
Active Monitoring or Watchful Waiting

Active monitoring and *watchful waiting* are almost unique to prostate cancer. There are different concepts of deferred treatment of prostate cancer. Watchful waiting is monitoring the patient until he develops metastatic disease that requires palliative treatment. Active monitoring allows delayed primary treatment if there is evidence of cancer progression. Active monitoring is less established in patients with a long life expectancy because criteria for selecting candidates and trigger points for instituting treatment have yet to be defined and validated. Currently, treatment is frequently initiated because of the patient's anxiety from living with untreated cancer combined with a rising PSA level or biopsy findings that suggest an increase in the volume or Gleason grade of the cancer. Findings on DRE or transrectal ultrasonography are seldom the sole indications for intervention.

Traditionally, deferred treatment has been reserved for men with a life expectancy of less than 10 years and a low-grade (Gleason score 2 to 5) prostate cancer. However, active monitoring is now being studied in younger patients with low-volume, low- or intermediate-grade tumors to avoid or to delay treatment that might not be immediately necessary.

Models have been generated in an attempt to predict which tumors can be observed without aggressive treatment. For example, Epstein and associates (1994, 1998) proposed a model involving preoperative clinical and pathologic features that would predict "insignificant tumors" (tumor volume less than 0.2 mL, Gleason score below 6, and organ confined). The preoperative features used in the model include no Gleason pattern 4 or 5 in the biopsy specimen, PSA density of 0.1 ng/mL per gram or less, fewer than three biopsy cores involved (minimum of six total cores), and no core with more than 50% involvement or PSA density of 0.15 ng/mL per gram or less and cancer smaller than 3 mm on only one prostate biopsy sample. This model was reported to have a positive predictive value of 95% for predicting "insignificant" cancer but a negative predictive value of only 66% (Epstein et al, 1994). Approximately 16% of the men in this series met criteria for insignificant tumors (Epstein et al, 1994). Subsequently, Epstein and colleagues (1998) updated the model to include a free/total PSA ratio (≥0.15) and favorable needle biopsy findings (fewer than three cores involved, no core with more than 50% tumor, and Gleason score of 6 or lower). Recent data from ex vivo biopsies suggest that an 18-core saturation biopsy could provide an even more accurate prediction of clinically insignificant prostate cancer (Epstein et al, 2005). However, this model needs to be validated with in vivo biopsies and in other populations of patients.

Kattan and associates (2003) proposed another statistical model to predict small, moderately differentiated, organ-confined cancer on the basis of PSA, clinical stage, biopsy Gleason score, ultrasound-determined prostate volume, and variables derived from systematic biopsies. They defined indolent cancer as being organ confined, less than 0.5 mL tumor volume, without poorly differentiated elements. Approximately 20% of their patients treated with radical prostatectomy met the criteria for indolent tumors according to their prediction model.

Some authors have claimed that even patients who do not fulfill such criteria may be legitimate candidates for active monitoring (Eastham, 2005). **A potential untoward consequence of recommending active monitoring for all men without obviously aggressive, clinically localized disease is that largely men with clearly aggressive and often incurable disease would be treated immediately, whereas a substantial proportion of those with curable disease destined to progress would be monitored, often with multiple extended biopsy procedures that could complicate subsequent attempts at nerve-sparing surgery or delay treatment until the window of opportunity for cure is closed.**

All prostate cancer patients are at risk for progression. In reports of deferred therapy for prostate cancer, patients are usually observed with semiannual PSA determinations and DRE and annual biopsies (Zietman et al, 2001; Carter et al, 2002; Choo et al, 2002; el-Geneidy et al, 2004; Klotz, 2004; Patel et al, 2004). Intervention is recommended if Gleason pattern 4 or 5 is present, more than two biopsy cores are involved, or more than 50% of a biopsy core is involved. Progression is more likely in patients who have cancer present on every biopsy procedure. Lack of cancer on repeated biopsy significantly decreases the likelihood of progression (Carter et al, 2002). In this regard, biopsy criteria have been reported to be more accurate than PSA criteria in predicting progression. No study has found DRE or imaging studies to independently predict progression.

The percentage of patients with curable cancer at the time of progression has been reported to vary from 33% to 92%. In most studies of active monitoring, approximately 25% to 50% of patients, depending on their individual risk factors, develop objective evidence of tumor progression within 5 years (Neulander et al, 2000; Patel et al, 2004). Although some studies suggest that patients with Gleason score 2 to 4 tumors do not suffer or die of prostate cancer with conservative management, those with higher Gleason score tumors have a substantial risk for morbidity and mortality (Albertsen et al, 1995; Johansson et al, 2004). **A prospective, randomized clinical trial from Scandinavia reported that patients with clinically localized prostate cancer managed with watchful waiting have significantly higher rates of local cancer progression, metastases, and death from prostate cancer and a shorter cancer-specific and overall survival (lower death rate from prostate cancer) than those treated initially with radical prostatectomy** (Bill-Axelson et al, 2005).

One rationale for active monitoring is the belief that there is substantial overdiagnosis of prostate cancer as a result of widespread PSA screening coupled with aggressive biopsy regimens. *Overdiagnosis* refers to a cancer detected by screening that would not be detected during the patient's lifetime without screening or would never cause disability or death. Some reports have estimated that 30% to 50% or more of cases in older men are overdiagnosed (Etzioni et al, 2002; Draisma et al, 2003). However, estimates of overdiagnosis derived from older men should not be generalized to younger men. Prostate cancers diagnosed in younger men are less likely to be harmless in the long term, and it is uncertain whether all cases labeled as overdiagnosed are clinically insignificant.

Contrary evidence suggests that screening with low PSA thresholds for biopsy in young patients detects tumors that fulfill the criteria for insignificant cancer in only 12% of

patients (Krumholtz et al, 2002). Even among those that do, some tumors are multifocal or do not have a diploid complement of chromosomes. Presently, no tumor marker can identify indolent tumors with certainty.

The physician confronting the patient with newly diagnosed prostate cancer must decide on management based on the PSA level, the estimated tumor volume, and the Gleason score (up to one third of patients are upgraded on the basis of the radical prostatectomy specimen) to select patients for immediate treatment or active monitoring. Repeated biopsies are always subject to sampling errors and may induce changes in and around the prostate gland that could compromise subsequent nerve-sparing surgery as well as trigger inflammation leading to PSA fluctuations that are difficult to interpret.

Treatment is more likely to be successful if it is given earlier while the tumor is smaller and the prospects for potency-sparing surgery are greater. Deferred treatment is more appropriate for older patients with a limited life expectancy or comorbidities. Additional clinical research and laboratory research are needed to define the parameters for safe use of active monitoring in younger men, including the appropriate selection criteria, follow-up procedures, and trigger points for intervention (Carter et al, 2003; Allaf and Carter, 2004). It will also be necessary to determine the proportion of patients that would still have curable disease when they are treated at the time of objective disease progression. In many instances, active monitoring delays the treatment by only a few years.

For the present, patients who opt for active monitoring should be evaluated with DRE and PSA testing quarterly or semiannually and consider having repeated prostate biopsy procedures yearly or biennially. Although it is assumed that quality of life should be largely preserved with active monitoring, studies have demonstrated significant decrements in quality of life with time, including waning erectile function, diminished urinary continence, and adverse psychological effects from living with untreated cancer (Penson et al, 2005). **If the PSA level is rising, the DRE suggests tumor growth, or biopsy specimens show evidence of increased involvement by cancer, treatment should be instituted. Patients may change their mind about remaining on a watchful waiting protocol; therefore, the physician should review management options on follow-up visits.**

In patients with a long life expectancy, there is a certain risk associated with active monitoring. Clearly, it can avoid or delay treatment for some patients, but there will inevitably be those who will miss their opportunity for cure and, tragically, ultimately progress to metastases and death from prostate cancer. More clinical research is required to evaluate these tradeoffs.

RADICAL PROSTATECTOMY

Radical prostatectomy was the first treatment used for prostate cancer and has been performed for more than 100 years (Kuchler, 1866; Young, 1905). It is a technically formidable operation, and as a result, simpler treatments have been sought for the treatment of early-stage disease. However, **no treatment has supplanted radical prostatectomy, and it still remains the "gold standard" because of the realization that hormone therapy and chemotherapy are never curative, and**

KEY POINTS: CONSERVATIVE MANAGEMENT

- The prostate cancer treatment outcomes may be influenced by the malignant potential of the tumors as well as by the treatment used. Furthermore, outcome measurements are not necessarily comparable between different forms of therapy, complicating comparisons between them.

- Traditionally, deferred treatment has been reserved for men with a life expectancy of less than 10 years and a low-grade prostate cancer. Additional clinical research and laboratory research are needed to define the parameters for safe use of active monitoring in younger men, including the appropriate selection criteria, follow-up procedures, and trigger points for intervention.

- A prospective, randomized clinical trial reported that patients with clinically localized prostate cancer managed with watchful waiting have significantly higher rates of local cancer progression, metastases, and death from prostate cancer than do those treated initially with radical prostatectomy.

not all cancer cells can be eradicated consistently by radiation or other physical forms of energy, even if the tumor is contained within the prostate gland.

Recent innovations have led to the wider use of radical prostatectomy:

1. the development of the anatomic radical retropubic prostatectomy, which allows the dissection to be performed with good visualization and preservation of the cavernosal nerves responsible for erectile function and **preservation of the external sphincter muscle that yields urinary continence rates in excess of 90%** (Walsh and Donker, 1982);
2. the development of extended ultrasound-guided biopsy regimens, performed under local anesthesia as an office procedure (Arnold et al, 2001); and
3. the widespread use of PSA testing, which has led to the majority of patients being diagnosed with clinically localized disease.

In recent years, the laparoscopic approach has been developed as another approach to performing the operation.

The main advantage of radical prostatectomy is that if it is skillfully performed, it offers the possibility of cure with minimal collateral damage to surrounding tissues (Han et al, 2001b; Hull et al, 2002). Further, it provides more accurate tumor staging by pathologic examination of the surgical specimen. Also, treatment failure is more readily identified, and the postoperative course is much smoother than in the past. Few patients require nonautologous blood transfusions. The hospital stay is usually 1 to 3 days, and operative mortality is rare in the modern era. Moreover, radical prostatectomy significantly reduces local progression and distant metastases and improves cancer-specific and overall survival rates compared with watchful waiting (Bill-Axelson et al, 2005). Some patients with tumor recurrence after radical prostatectomy

can be salvaged with potentially curative postoperative radiotherapy (Stephenson et al, 2004b).

The potential disadvantages of radical prostatectomy are the necessary hospitalization and recovery period; a possibility of incomplete resection of the tumor, if the operation is not performed properly or if the tumor is not contained within the prostate gland; and a risk for erectile dysfunction and urinary incontinence. However, erectile dysfunction and rectal complications are less likely with nerve-sparing surgery than with radiotherapy, and good treatment options are available for both urinary incontinence and erectile dysfunction.

Surgical Approaches to Radical Prostatectomy

Perineal. The perineal approach is an acceptable surgical treatment when it is performed by a surgeon familiar with this approach (Scolieri and Resnick, 2001). It is usually associated with **less blood loss and a shorter operative time than the retropubic approach. The disadvantages are that it does not provide access for a pelvic lymph node dissection, there is a higher rate of rectal injury, and there is occasional postoperative fecal incontinence that does not occur commonly with other approaches** (Bishoff et al, 1998). It is more difficult to spare the cavernous nerves through the perineal approach.

Retropubic. The open retropubic approach is **preferred by most urologists because of their familiarity with the surgical anatomy; the lower risk for rectal injury and postoperative fecal incontinence; the wide exposure and ready access provided for pelvic lymphadenectomy and prostate excision with preservation of the neurovascular bundles; and the lower risk for positive surgical margins.**

Laparoscopic. The laparoscopic approach is by far the most daunting approach to radical prostatectomy. It has been suggested that laparoscopic prostatectomy **may be associated with less bleeding, better visualization, less postoperative pain, and shorter convalescence than the standard open approach. However, these outcomes are usually less important to the patient than the cure of his cancer, the preservation of his potency, and the avoidance of other more serious complications. Laparoscopic prostatectomy can be performed through a transperitoneal or extraperitoneal approach.** The transperitoneal approach facilitates the lymphadenectomy but carries a higher risk of intestinal and vascular injury, urinary ascites, and postoperative intestinal obstruction.

Furthermore, laparoscopic prostatectomy is associated with a higher risk for severe complications. Hemostasis in the neurovascular bundles is difficult to achieve safely because of the relative difficulty in rapidly placing hemostatic sutures or applying hemostatic clips laparoscopically. Heat from a harmonic scalpel or electrocautery can irreversibly damage the cavernous nerves. Although intraoperative blood loss is less with laparoscopic surgery, postoperative bleeding may occur after the release of positive pressure in the operative field. Rectal, ureteral, and vascular injuries and anastomotic leaks have also been more common with laparoscopic prostatectomy (Rassweiler et al, 2003).

When laparoscopic prostatectomy is performed by a skilled laparoscopic surgeon, reported incontinence and anastomotic stricture rates are comparable to those achieved with open surgery. It has been claimed that nerve sparing is equivalent or even better with laparoscopic surgery, but direct comparisons and validated results are lacking (Menon and Tewari, 2003). The reported rates of positive surgical margins have been higher with laparoscopic prostatectomy, and the adequacy of cancer control is as yet uncertain because of lack of long-term results.

Robotic. Remotely controlled laparoscopic surgery has recently been popularized because of its **greater technical ease for the surgeon, especially for tying sutures and performing the vesicourethral anastomosis.** It has been marketed as a less invasive, technologically more advanced method of performing the operation with less pain and a quicker recovery. **The availability of three-dimensional visualization is an advantage over standard laparoscopic techniques.** Early reported results are favorable but have not been validated (Menon et al, 2002; Menon and Tewari, 2003). It is uncertain whether the results of laparoscopic prostatectomy are as good as those achieved with open prostatectomy (Smith, 2004; Webster et al, 2005).

Salvage Radical Prostatectomy

Radical prostatectomy can be performed in patients whose other local treatments have failed (Pontes et al, 1993; Chen et al, 2003). However, the rate of complications is far higher, and the complications are more serious and much more difficult to manage (Stephenson et al, 2004a). Moreover, the prospects for long-term disease-free survival are more limited for salvage prostatectomy than for primary radical prostatectomy.

Most of the reported experience with salvage radical prostatectomy is from the pre-PSA era. Contemporary series of patients selected because of biochemical recurrence have lower morbidity and better cancer control rates (Stephenson et al, 2004a; Ward et al, 2005). Nevertheless, postoperative incontinence rates are as high as 44% and bladder neck contracture rates as high as 22% (Ward et al, 2005). The incontinence rate is even higher after brachytherapy, presumably because of the higher dose of radiation administered. Long-term progression-free survival rates after salvage prostatectomy in the absence of hormone therapy have not been well documented.

Selection of Patients for Radical Prostatectomy

An ideal candidate for radical prostatectomy is healthy and free of comorbidities that might make the operation unacceptably risky. He would have a life expectancy of at least 10 years, and his tumor would be deemed to be biologically significant and completely resectable. The generally accepted upper age limit for radical prostatectomy is about 75 years.

Because imaging studies are not accurate for staging prostate cancer, **preoperative clinical and pathologic parameters are often used to predict the pathologic stage and thus identify patients most likely to benefit from the operation** (Partin et al, 1997, 2001). These parameters are frequently used in tables and nomograms designed to predict pathologic tumor stage or post-treatment recurrence-free survival probabilities (Kattan et al, 1998, 2000; Ross et al, 2001; Han et al, 2003).

Patients with a low probability of resectable disease or a short life expectancy should not be advised to have surgery. Neoadjuvant hormone therapy does not enhance the resectability of prostate cancer and often increases the difficulty of performing nerve-sparing surgery.

The surgeon should realistically counsel the patient on the nerve-sparing aspects of the operation. Nerve-sparing prostatectomy does not materially compromise cancer control in appropriately selected patients; however, it is inappropriate in men with advanced disease. The feasibility of performing nerve-sparing surgery is questionable when there is extensive cancer in the biopsy specimens, palpable extraprostatic tumor extension, serum PSA level above 10 ng/mL, biopsy Gleason score higher than 7, poor-quality erections preoperatively, current and future lack of a sexual relationship, or other medical conditions that may adversely affect erections (e.g., diabetes mellitus, hypertension, psychiatric diseases, neurologic diseases, or medications that produce erectile dysfunction).

Postoperative treatment of erectile dysfunction also should be discussed, including information on phosphodiesterase type 5 (PDE-5) inhibitors, intraurethral and intracorporal administration of vasodilators, vacuum erection devices, venous flow constrictors, and implantable penile prostheses. The discussion also should include the timing of the return of erections. The patient should be warned about the risk for development of Peyronie's disease from injury to the penis during sexual activity without a rigid erection (Ciancio and Kim, 2000). If erectile function is a high priority for the patient, he should be reassured that erections almost always can be restored, regardless of whether nerve-sparing surgery could be performed.

The preoperative evaluation should consider the likelihood of success in achieving all goals of surgery and in determining whether nerves can safely be spared. The surgeon should also discuss the possibility of performing cutaneous nerve graft interposition if one or both cavernous nerves must be resected (Quinlan et al, 1991; Kim et al, 1999, 2001). There are limited data concerning the effectiveness of such grafts. In most patients with a tumor so advanced that one or both nerves must be resected, postoperative radiotherapy or hormone therapy is likely to be required, which could nullify the potential benefits of nerve grafting.

The surgeon should also discuss the possible need for and potential side effects of adjuvant postoperative radiotherapy and/or hormone therapy, if the final pathology specimen reveals adverse prognostic features.

Surgical Technique

Radical prostatectomy involves complete removal of the prostate gland and seminal vesicles and usually includes a modified pelvic lymph node dissection as well. The key steps in performing anatomic nerve-sparing radical prostatectomy are as follows:

1. pelvic lymphadenectomy;
2. opening of the endopelvic fascia and limited incision of the puboprostatic ligaments;
3. suture ligation and transection of Santorini's dorsal venous complex;
4. dissection of the urethra at the apex of the prostate and transection of the urethra (sometimes the anastomotic sutures are placed at this point in the operation);
5. dissection of the prostate from the neurovascular bundles;
6. securing and transection of the prostatic pedicles;
7. transection and reconstruction of the bladder neck;
8. dissection of the seminal vesicles and ampullary portions of the vasa deferentia; and
9. performance of the vesicourethral anastomosis.

The surgeon should strive for complete apposition of the bladder neck and the urethra, with a watertight, tension-free closure.

Pelvic lymphadenectomy is optional in patients at low risk for lymph node metastases. Patients who elect to undergo lymphadenectomy should decide in advance whether they wish to proceed with the prostatectomy if there are nodal metastases. If they do not wish to proceed, the excised lymph nodes are sent for frozen-section examination during the operation. Otherwise, intraoperative frozen-section analysis of pelvic lymph nodes is unnecessary. Some have argued that a more extensive pelvic lymphadenectomy yields better outcomes, but compelling evidence for this is lacking, and more extensive lymphadenectomy carries a greater risk for postoperative genital and lower extremity lymphedema and lymphocele (Bader et al, 2002; Allaf et al, 2004).

The key to preserving urinary continence is to perform a meticulous dissection, avoiding injury to the external urinary sphincter. Preservation of the bladder neck is unnecessary to achieve good urinary continence. In patients with high-volume or high-grade tumors involving the base of the prostate, preservation of the bladder neck may risk positive surgical margins.

Meticulous dissection is required to preserve the neurovascular bundles. In performing nerve-sparing surgery, the neurovascular bundles are identified at the apex of the prostate (the dissection can also be performed in an antegrade fashion beginning at the base), and the bundles are dissected free of the posterolateral surface of the prostate gland. Hemostatic sutures or clips may be used to control bleeding from the neurovascular bundles. Use of electrocautery or a harmonic scalpel risks irreversible thermal injury to the neurovascular bundles.

If the neurovascular bundles must be resected, a cutaneous nerve graft can be removed from the leg or forearm or a segment of the genitofemoral nerve can be harvested and interposed between the transected ends of the cavernous nerves. Nerve grafting should be performed by a surgeon who has training and expertise in microsurgical nerve grafting techniques.

The prostatic pedicles are suture ligated or hemoclipped and divided close to the gland, avoiding incision into the prostatic capsule. In performing the seminal vesicle dissection, care must be taken to avoid injury to the neurovascular bundles situated immediately lateral and posterior to them.

Postoperative Care

Patients should ambulate with assistance beginning on the afternoon or evening of surgery. **The catheter may be removed 3 to 21 days after surgery, depending on how watertight the vesicourethral anastomosis is and the amount of tension on the vesicourethral anastomosis. Removal of the catheter before 7 days is associated with a 15% to 20% risk of urinary retention.**

After the catheter has been removed, Kegel exercises should be initiated. A protective pad is used until complete urinary control is achieved. The postoperative serum PSA level should be undetectable by 1 month after the operation.

Cancer Control

The principal objective of radical prostatectomy is to completely excise the cancer. Important cancer control endpoints are pathologically organ-confined disease with clear surgical margins, biochemical recurrence (detectable serum PSA), local progression, metastases, cancer-specific survival, and overall survival. **Depending on the Gleason score and the PSA doubling time, biochemical (PSA) evidence of recurrence usually precedes clinical metastases by a mean of about 8 years and cancer-specific mortality by about 13 years** (Pound et al, 1999b).

Nonprogression rates vary with clinical and pathologic risk factors. Independent clinical prognostic factors are tumor stage, Gleason score, preoperative PSA level, and calendar year of diagnosis and treatment. Adverse prognostic features include non–organ-confined disease, perineural or lymphovascular space invasion, extracapsular tumor extension, positive surgical margins, seminal vesicle invasion, and lymph node metastases (Grossfeld et al, 2000; Shariat et al, 2004). **In the PSA era, there has been a dramatic stage migration and improvement in prognostic features and treatment outcomes** (Han et al, 2001a; Moul et al, 2002).

A rising serum PSA level is usually the earliest evidence of tumor recurrence after radical prostatectomy (Pound et al, 1999b). **Biochemical recurrence is frequently used as an intermediate endpoint for treatment outcomes; however, not all patients with biochemical recurrence ultimately develop metastases or die of prostate cancer. In rare instances with high-grade or neuroendocrine tumors that do not produce much PSA, there can be palpable evidence of recurrence despite an undetectable PSA level, indicating a role for DRE in monitoring of patients.**

In the first author's personal series, including more than 4400 open anatomic radical retropubic prostatectomies dating to 1983, the actuarial 10-year cancer progression-free survival probability was approximately 85% for patients with organ-confined disease, 65% for men with extracapsular tumor extension without cancerous surgical margins, 55% for men with extracapsular tumor extension and cancerous surgical margins, 25% for patients with seminal vesicle invasion, and 10% for patients with lymph node metastases. Patients treated in the PSA era have approximately 5 percentage points more favorable results within each pathologic category. Within these pathologic tumor stages, cancer progression rates also were strongly associated with other parameters. Case selection and the duration and frequency of follow-up monitoring are also important determinants of postoperative outcomes.

Urinary Continence

Urinary continence after radical retropubic prostatectomy is generally good and varies according to the experience and skill of the surgeon. For high-volume radical prostatectomy surgeons, more than 90% of men recover complete urinary continence. **The return of urinary continence is associated with the patient's age:** more than 95% of men younger than 50 years are continent after surgery; 85% of men older than 70 years regain continence. Few require implantation of an artificial urinary sphincter or a sling procedure for stress urinary incontinence.

Erectile Function

Potency after radical prostatectomy is usually defined as the ability to maintain erections sufficiently rigid for penetration and sexual intercourse with or without the help of a PDE-5 inhibitor. Most patients with intact libido and erections wish to maintain these functions. Others with poor-quality erections would wish to have erections that at least offer some rigidity to provide sensory satisfaction for both sexual partners. **The return of erectile function after radical retropubic prostatectomy correlates with the age of the patient, preoperative potency status, extent of nerve-sparing surgery, and era of surgery.** In the most favorable candidates in whom preoperative potency is normal and bilateral nerve-sparing surgery can be performed, up to 95% in their 40s, 85% in their 50s, 75% in their 60s, and 50% in their 70s can recover erections sufficient for penetration and intercourse.

In most patients, erections usually begin to return as partial erections 3 to 6 months after surgery and may continue to improve for up to 3 years or more (Burnett, 2005). **Patients should be encouraged to use erectile aids postoperatively, including PDE-5 inhibitors, intraurethral suppositories, intracavernosal injections, or vacuum erection devices. Erection rehabilitation programs using intracavernosal injection therapy or PDE-5 inhibitors might hasten the return of erections and increase the proportion of men who recover erections** (Montorsi et al, 1997).

Complications

Anatomic nerve-sparing radical prostatectomy provides excellent cancer control with an acceptable complication rate in appropriately selected patients. The overall early complication rate after radical prostatectomy is less than 10% in experienced hands (Kundu et al, 2004). With a careful selection of patients and performance of necessary preoperative cardiovascular evaluation, perioperative mortality has been largely avoided (Mettlin et al, 1997).

Early Complications

Early complications include hemorrhage; rectal, vascular, ureteral, or nerve injury; urinary leak or fistula; thromboembolic and cardiovascular events; urinary tract infection; lymphocele; and wound problems. It is advisable routinely to use support stockings and to ensure early ambulation.

Prophylactic anticoagulation and sequential compression devices are advisable in patients at high risk for thromboembolic complications.

Inadvertent injury to the obturator nerve can occur during the pelvic lymphadenectomy. When a tension-free primary nerve repair is not feasible, nerve grafting can be performed by a cutaneous or genitofemoral nerve graft. However, even without a nerve repair, conservative management with physical therapy can compensate for the deficit, and therefore many patients do not have a significant thigh adductor deficit after the injury (Kirdi et al, 2000).

Ureteral injury is a rare complication. A minor injury or ligation can be managed with removal of the ligature and ureteral stenting. Mobilization of the distal ureter and ureteroneocystostomy should be performed for more severe injuries.

Although uncommon, a rectal injury can occur and be repaired primarily by a multiple-layer closure (Lepor et al, 2001). However, a diverting colostomy should be considered in men with a large rectal defect, a history of pelvic radiotherapy, or long-term preoperative glucocorticoid therapy.

Late Complications

The most common late complications of radical prostatectomy are erectile dysfunction, urinary incontinence, inguinal hernia, and urethral stricture. Early rehabilitation measures, including Kegel exercises to increase the strength and the bulk of the external sphincter muscle and the use of PDE-5 inhibitors, vacuum erection devices, and intraurethral or intracavernosal vasodilators, appear to be helpful. Anastomotic or other urethral strictures should be managed initially with dilation, but internal incision and endoscopic injection of glucocorticoids may often be required. For a long or persistent anastomotic stricture, a transurethral resection of the scar tissue cephalad to the external sphincter may be necessary. After the resection, an interval of catheter self-dilation of the anastomosis is usually necessary. Continued self-dilation or intermittent dilation by the urologist is required in difficult, persistent cases. Urethroplasty is rarely required.

RADIATION THERAPY
External Beam Radiotherapy (Three-Dimensional Conformal Radiotherapy)

External beam radiotherapy involves the use of beams of gamma radiation (usually photons) directed at the prostate and surrounding tissues through multiple fields. To minimize radiation injury to the bladder and the rectum, three-dimensional conformal radiotherapy (3D-CRT), in which a computer alters the radiation beams to focus the radiation dose to the region of the prostate gland, has been developed (Fraass, 1995). **The most sophisticated form of 3D-CRT, called intensity-modulated radiation therapy (IMRT), can provide localization of the radiation dose to geometrically complex fields** (Burren et al, 1999). Heavy particle therapy that uses beams of high-energy protons (Shipley et al, 1995; Rossi, 1999) or neutrons (Lawton et al, 1991; Russell et al, 1994) has also been used to treat patients with prostate cancer. Heavy particle therapy is also a form of 3D-CRT in which the radiation beam can be virtually "stopped" within the tissue,

KEY POINTS: RADICAL PROSTATECTOMY

- Radical prostatectomy was the first treatment used for prostate cancer, and it still remains the gold standard. An ideal candidate for radical prostatectomy is a healthy man with a life expectancy of at least 10 years. Preoperative clinical and pathologic parameters are often used to predict the pathologic stage and thus to identify patients most likely to benefit from the operation.

- A rising serum PSA level is usually the earliest evidence of tumor recurrence after radical prostatectomy and is frequently an intermediate endpoint for treatment outcomes. However, not all patients with biochemical recurrence ultimately develop metastases or die of prostate cancer.

- The most common late complications of radical prostatectomy are erectile dysfunction, urinary incontinence, inguinal hernia, and urethral stricture. The return of erectile function after surgery correlates with age of the patient, preoperative potency status, extent of nerve-sparing surgery, and era of surgery; the return of urinary continence is associated with the patient's age.

allowing high doses of radiation to be delivered to a localized region.

A possible disadvantage of extreme conformal therapy with IMRT and heavy particles is that they can be too narrowly targeted, so that movement of the prostate caused by differences in rectal or bladder filling could result in geographic miss of the tumor, especially in the important posterior peripheral region of the prostate.

Radiation therapy has been extensively studied for localized prostate cancer. **The outcomes of radiation therapy corrected for anatomic disease extent and other prognostic factors have been reported to be roughly comparable to those of radical prostatectomy; however, this is misleading because the endpoints for determining treatment success or failure are different for radiotherapy and surgery** (Gretzer et al, 2002).

Radiation Dose and Field of Treatment

There is evidence from prospective, randomized trials that **dose escalation and three-dimensional definition improve results considerably** (Pollack et al, 2002). Currently, doses of 76 to 80 Gy or more have been shown to improve cancer control (Pollack et al, 2000). Low-risk patients are now frequently treated with 70 to 72 Gy, intermediate-risk patients with 75 to 76 Gy, and high-risk patients with 80 Gy or more.

Although the prostate itself can tolerate high doses of radiation, the rectal toxicity limits the dose that can be given in brachytherapy. Image guidance for better target definition is crucial for dose escalation, and high radiation doses require protection of normal tissues. IMRT produces steep dose

gradients where the gradient between 100% and 50% of dose can be as little as 1 to 1.5 cm. Radiation dose escalation requires precision in target definition and a high degree of accuracy in the daily placement of the radiation dose.

CT imaging is considered the standard imaging modality for 3D-CRT and 3D-IMRT, but CT is less precise than MRI. Therefore, larger margins are required to accurately ensure that the entire prostate gland received the daily radiation dose. When CT imaging uses only the bone landmarks to localize the prostate gland, the daily radiation treatments might be directed inconsistently, and the rectum might receive increased doses of radiation. New technologies are being developed to accurately place the radiation beam before every treatment (Cheng et al, 2003).

Radiation Side Effects

The main adverse side effects of radiation therapy are related to injury to the microvasculature of the bladder, rectum, striated sphincter muscle, and urethra. However, urinary incontinence or radiation-induced complications requiring surgical correction are uncommon. **Approximately one third of patients experience acute symptoms of proctitis or cystitis during the course of radiotherapy, usually after the dose exceeds 50 Gy. In the great majority, symptoms subside after the completion of therapy. About 5% to 10% have permanent symptoms (irritable bowel syndrome and intermittent rectal bleeding or bladder irritability and intermittent gross hematuria).** Some patients require laser cauterization of radiation-induced telangiectasia for bleeding from the bladder or the rectum. External beam radiotherapy causes more rectal toxicity and less urinary toxicity than brachytherapy does.

A prior transurethral resection of the prostate is a relative contraindication to brachytherapy and external beam radiation therapy because the prostate does not hold the seeds well, and radiation after transurethral resection of the prostate is associated with an increased risk for urethral stricture. The presence of severe obstructive urinary symptoms is also a relative contraindication because of the risk for acute urinary retention. Another relative contraindication is inflammatory bowel disease.

Approximately half of patients develop erectile dysfunction after radiotherapy for prostate cancer. This is caused by injury to the vasculature of the cavernous nerves and to the corpora cavernosa of the penis, usually beginning about 1 year after the completion of treatment. Younger patients with good baseline erectile function are more likely to retain adequate erections. PDE-5 inhibitors are useful in ameliorating the erectile dysfunction associated with radiotherapy (Merrick et al, 1999; Valicenti et al, 2001). Lower doses of radiation to the penile bulb have been investigated as a means of minimizing radiation-induced erectile dysfunction (Roach et al, 2004).

Combined External Beam Radiation Therapy and Hormone Therapy for Locally Advanced Prostate Cancer

Randomized clinical trials have demonstrated that **patients with high PSA value, high Gleason score, or large-volume tumor benefit from androgen deprivation therapy in** conjunction with radiotherapy, whereas those with lower risk tumors do not. For example, Bolla and colleagues (1997, 2002) demonstrated that a 3-year adjuvant hormone therapy started concurrently with external beam radiation improved local control and survival in patients with locally advanced prostate cancer. Hanks and associates (2003) explored the optimal duration of hormone therapy after radiation therapy. They showed that 28 months of hormone therapy before, during, and after radiation therapy, compared with 4 months of hormone therapy before and during the radiation therapy, provides significant improvement in all clinical endpoints, except for overall survival (Hanks et al, 2003). However, **the overall survival benefit of a longer hormone therapy was observed in patients with Gleason grade 8 to 10 disease.**

Radiation Therapy for Localized Prostate Cancer

High-Risk Localized Prostate Cancer (PSA > 20 ng/mL or Gleason score 8 to 10). No randomized trial has exclusively studied the additional benefit of hormone therapy in the high-risk patients receiving radiotherapy for localized prostate cancer. However, on the basis of the aforementioned randomized trials involving locally advanced disease, long-term concurrent hormone therapy is advocated in radiation therapy for the high-risk patients with localized prostate cancer.

Intermediate-Risk Localized Prostate Cancer (PSA between 10 and 20 ng/mL, Gleason score 7, or clinical stage T2b). In a retrospective cohort study, D'Amico and coworkers (2000) demonstrated that 6 months of androgen deprivation therapy (beginning 2 months before and continuing during and after radiation therapy) improved the PSA outcomes in intermediate- and high-risk patients but not in low-risk patients. In a subsequent randomized trial, D'Amico and colleagues (2004b) confirmed that **6 months of hormone therapy improves outcomes, mostly in intermediate-risk patients.**

On the basis of these studies, long-term hormone therapy is usually recommended along with external beam radiotherapy in patients with locally advanced disease or localized, high-risk disease. In patients with intermediate-risk, localized disease, short-term (6-month) hormone therapy is usually recommended.

Endpoints for Treatment Success or Failure

Evaluation of the outcomes of radiotherapy is complicated because cancer cells are not killed immediately after radiation. Rather, they sustain lethal DNA damage but do not die until they next attempt to enter into cell division. Thus, **the PSA level gradually decreases for up to 2 to 3 years after the completion of radiotherapy.** Accordingly, the PSA level is usually monitored at 6-month intervals until it reaches a nadir. In patients treated with external beam radiotherapy, the prostate gland is not completely ablated, and the remaining prostatic epithelium continues to produce PSA. Also, **inflammation in the prostate gland can produce transient PSA elevations, called a PSA "bounce"** (Critz et al, 2000). **PSA bounce usually occurs during the first 2 years after treatment and is less common with external beam therapy than with brachytherapy.**

The biochemical endpoint used to determine treatment success after external beam radiation therapy is controversial. Currently, the most frequently used definition is the American Society of Therapeutic Radiology and Oncology (ASTRO) definition (Cox, 1997). **It requires three consecutive PSA increases measured 6 months apart and back-dates the time of cancer progression to halfway between the PSA nadir and the first rising PSA level. Thus, it usually takes years to determine whether progression has occurred after radiotherapy.** Without long-term follow-up, the ASTRO definition yields progression-free survival estimates that appear 10% to 20% better than they actually are because it takes time for the PSA level to reach a nadir and even more time for three consecutive rises to occur. Moreover, back-dating of the time of failure moves the time of recurrence to a point in the patient series where the denominator is larger and thus minimizes the impact of the recurrence on the survival curve.

Recently, the so-called Phoenix definition was proposed to replace the ASTRO definition. It eliminates back-dating but requires the PSA level to rise by 2 ng/mL before treatment failure is declared. Thus, the time to recurrence is further prolonged after the PSA level begins to rise, and often it takes a considerably longer time for the PSA level to increase by 2 ng/mL. In practice, the Phoenix definition can yield results that are even more favorable than those obtained with the ASTRO definition. Accordingly, it is not possible to make fair comparisons between radical prostatectomy and radiotherapy by use of these outcome measurements.

Treatment Results of External Beam Radiotherapy

With conventional external beam radiotherapy, the 10-year cancer cure rates for patients with clinically localized prostate cancer are approximately 50% (Zietman et al, 2004). However, **better results may be achieved with 3D-CRT and dose escalation. High-risk patients are frequently treated with 2 to 3 years of androgen deprivation after radiotherapy** (Bolla et al, 1997; Pilepich et al, 1997). With this regimen, the 5-year progression-free probabilities have been reported to be 70% to 85% (Bolla et al, 1997). There are limited data concerning the durable and favorable responses to radiation therapy, especially in young patients. A substantial proportion of patients who are unsuccessfully treated with radiotherapy have tumor recurrences within the radiation fields, usually in the central part of the tumor.

High-dose proton or neutron beam therapy has been advocated as a more effective method of conformal radiotherapy, but there is no convincing evidence that treatment results are superior to those achieved with photons. Moreover, because the radiation beam passes through the urethra, there may be a higher rate of urethral strictures with heavy particle radiation.

In high-risk patients, external beam radiotherapy has also been combined with brachytherapy. The brachytherapy is usually given first, so that the external beam therapy can be discontinued if the patient begins to experience toxicity (Ragde et al, 1997, 1998; Critz et al, 1998).

Current research involves the use of magnetic resonance spectroscopy to guide radiation administration by directing higher doses to the metabolically active areas of the tumor.

Similarly, imaging of hypoxic areas of the tumor with positron emission tomography is being evaluated to direct higher doses of radiation to hypoxic regions of the tumor.

Brachytherapy

With brachytherapy, radioactive sources (seeds or needles) are implanted directly into the prostate gland, and sometimes into the surrounding tissues, to deliver a high dose of radiation to the tumor while sparing, to the extent possible, the bladder and the rectum. Modern brachytherapy for prostate cancer was originally unsuccessful because freehand implantation of the seeds provided a poor dose distribution; however, newer external template-based techniques provide more uniform implantation patterns.

Brachytherapy is relatively easy to perform and therefore has become popular for treatment of patients with clinically localized prostate cancer. It can be performed under general or regional anesthesia. The most commonly used permanent implants are iodine-125 or palladium-103 seeds. Theoretically, palladium offers a higher radiation dose rate that would be expected to be advantageous for treatment of poorly differentiated tumors that have a shorter cell cycle. However, in practice, **no significant advantage has been demonstrated for the use of palladium.** Although high–dose rate temporary implantation with iridium-192 wires has been used for more aggressive tumors, logistical considerations make it time-consuming, inconvenient, and impractical in many clinical settings.

Radiation Dose and Fields

After the implant has been completed, a post-treatment CT scan is routinely obtained to check the post-implant dosimetry. Dosimetry can be adversely affected by poor implantation or migration of the seeds after implantation. The radiation doses delivered to the prostate are approximately 145 Gy for iodine and 125 Gy for palladium, which are substantially higher than those with external beam radiotherapy. However, direct comparisons of radiation doses between external beam radiotherapy and brachytherapy are not valid. Because of the much higher doses of radiation delivered, brachytherapy causes more ablation of the prostate gland than external beam radiotherapy does. In many patients treated with brachytherapy, post-treatment PSA levels decrease into the undetectable range. Despite this, **brachytherapy is seldom used for the treatment of high-volume, high-risk prostate cancers, as 3D-CRT is the preferred method for treatment of aggressive tumors.**

In patients who have an enlarged prostate gland, it can be technically challenging to implant the entire prostate volume, especially anteriorly. Accordingly, patients are often treated with androgen deprivation therapy to shrink the prostate before brachytherapy is performed. Long-term androgen deprivation therapy confounds assessment of the response to brachytherapy because it delays PSA rises signaling tumor persistence or recurrence.

At present, transrectal ultrasound-guided brachytherapy is the standard approach. MRI is currently being investigated for use in pre-planning and post-planning dosimetry with urethral sparing. MR-CT fusion scans have also been used for this purpose. Magnetic resonance spectroscopy–optimized

implants are also under study to give higher doses to metabolically active regions of the tumor.

Results of Brachytherapy

Excellent short-term cancer control rates have been reported with brachytherapy. With the ASTRO failure criteria, 5- and 7-year progression-free survival estimates of 85% and 80%, respectively, have been reported (Ragde et al, 2001).

Side Effects of Brachytherapy

Urinary symptoms are more common after brachytherapy than after external beam radiotherapy, especially in patients with prostatic hyperplasia. To avoid these problems, α blockers and hormone therapy are usually administered before treatment. Urinary retention occurs in up to 22% of patients. Approximately 10% of patients require transurethral resection of the prostate after brachytherapy. If an aggressive transurethral resection of the prostate is performed, there is a high rate of incontinence, occurring in 20% to 40% of patients. However, a more conservative, "channel" transurethral resection or laser prostatectomy can usually restore voiding function while preserving continence. Preservation of erectile function has been reported in 62% to 86% of patients treated with brachytherapy alone. Impotence rates are higher when brachytherapy is combined with external beam radiotherapy. Furthermore, neoadjuvant hormone therapy frequently used before brachytherapy adversely affects postoperative erectile function. PDE-5 inhibitors may be helpful in restoring erections.

Proctitis and rectal injury are less common with brachytherapy than with external beam therapy, whereas erectile dysfunction occurs more commonly with brachytherapy than with external beam radiation. Other complications associated with brachytherapy include seed migration and rectourethral fistula (Theodorescu et al, 2000; Di Muzio et al, 2003).

Adjuvant Radiotherapy after Radical Prostatectomy

Patients with adverse findings in the radical prostatectomy specimen may benefit from adjuvant radiotherapy; however, no improvement in long-term survival has yet been demonstrated for adjuvant radiotherapy. Adjuvant radiotherapy is usually administered to the bed of the prostate gland in doses of 60 to 64 Gy. **It is advisable to wait at least 3 to 4 months after surgery to allow complete wound healing and return of urinary continence.** Radiation to the whole pelvis is usually discouraged because of the higher risk for bowel complications. Depending on the risk for recurrence, some patients do not opt for adjuvant radiotherapy but rather choose to monitor their PSA levels and avoid further treatment unless there is convincing biochemical (PSA) evidence of tumor progression.

Retrospective cohort studies have shown that postoperative radiotherapy reduces recurrence rates in patients with pathologic stage T3 disease and positive margins (Leibovich et al, 2000). Recently, **randomized prospective trials demonstrated the benefit of postoperative radiotherapy compared with observation** (Bolla et al, 2005; Thompson et al, 2005).

However, there has not been a randomized trial that compared adjuvant postoperative radiotherapy with early salvage radiotherapy. A European Organization for Research and Treatment of Cancer trial showed benefit not only in patients with positive surgical margins but also in those with extracapsular tumor extension and seminal vesicle invasion (Bolla et al, 2005). A Southwest Oncology Group trial revealed benefits in reducing recurrence and PSA progression at 10 years with an overall survival advantage that was not statistically significant, perhaps due in part to the small size of the trial (Thompson et al, 2005).

Adjuvant radiotherapy is most likely to benefit patients with positive surgical margins or extracapsular tumor extension without seminal vesicle invasion or lymph node involvement. However, not all patients with extracapsular tumor extension or positive margins have tumor recurrence without radiotherapy, and most patients with highly adverse findings have treatment failure with distant metastases despite adjuvant radiotherapy. Nevertheless, it is possible that a small proportion of patients with seminal vesicle invasion or lymph node metastases might benefit from adjuvant radiotherapy (Cozzarini et al, 2004).

Side Effects of Adjuvant Radiotherapy

Side effects of adjuvant radiotherapy also include a 5% to 10% risk of radiation proctitis and a 50% probability that return of erectile function will be materially compromised. Radiotherapy also can compromise borderline postoperative urinary continence, but radiation-induced incontinence is relatively uncommon.

Patients with highly unfavorable prognostic parameters who are more likely to fail with distant metastases are more likely to benefit from postoperative androgen deprivation therapy.

Adjuvant Hormone Therapy

In high-risk patients who opt for postoperative radiotherapy, it is uncertain whether they also should receive adjuvant hormone therapy. Clinical trials are under way to answer this question. The only disadvantages of adding hormone therapy in this setting are the expense and associated side effects of the hormone therapy. In patients with lymph node metastases, a prospective, randomized trial has demonstrated significantly improved survival in those treated with early androgen deprivation therapy (Messing et al, 1999).

Future Research

Future research will address issues about whether adjuvant radiotherapy offers an advantage over early salvage radiotherapy. Another issue being addressed in research is the definition of optimal target volume and mapping of postoperative recurrence patterns to ensure that the radiation addresses the right areas.

Comparison of Radiotherapy with Radical Prostatectomy

An important limitation of radiotherapy as a curative modality is tumor heterogeneity with respect to radiation sensitivity. Tumor persistence within the fields of radiation occurs in one third to one half of patients with clinically localized prostate cancer treated with radiation therapy. Thus, in many patients, there are some tumor cells that are not eradicated by therapeutic doses of radiation. Accordingly, even if the tumor is confined to the prostate, radiotherapy might not cure it. Despite high-dose (>75 Gy) 3D-CRT, nearly half of patients had cancerous biopsy findings more than 2.5 years after treatment (Zelefsky et al, 1998). In addition, cancerous biopsy findings after treatment are usually associated with a poor prognosis (Scardino and Wheeler, 1985). The patterns of failure after surgery are different from those after radiotherapy. No modality affords 100% local control. Surgery is more likely to fail at the margins, and radiation therapy is more likely to fail in the center of the tumor. The strategies of dose escalation and better dose placement are designed to improve the central local control.

A study with a minimum follow-up of 23 years of men treated with radiotherapy for stage T1 to T3 prostate cancer revealed that more than two thirds developed recurrence, and more than half died of prostate cancer. Half of the recurrences occurred after 10 years, and some recurrences developed after 20 years; however, late recurrences might represent a new primary tumor (Swanson et al, 2004).

A systematic overview of radiotherapy for prostate cancer, involving more than 150,000 patients, reported that there are no randomized studies to compare the outcomes of radiotherapy with radical prostatectomy for patients with low-risk disease. Risk group comparisons of T stage, Gleason score, and PSA value have reported similar results between radiotherapy and surgery; however, different endpoints were used for treatment failure (Nilsson et al, 2004).

It is impossible to compare the results of surgery with those of radiotherapy because of the difference in the endpoints used for treatment failure, that is, undetectable PSA for surgery versus the ASTRO criteria for radiotherapy. For instance, applying the ASTRO criteria to patients treated with radical prostatectomy, the respective 5-, 10-, and 15-year progression-free rates improved from 85%, 77%, and 68% to 90%, 90%, and 90%, respectively (Gretzer et al, 2002).

In a study of conventional external beam radiotherapy in men with clinical stage T1-2 disease treated from 1991 to 1993, freedom from progression by use of the ASTRO criteria was 49% with back-dating the time of recurrence and 42% without back-dating (Zietman et al, 2004).

The use of PSA nadir of 0.2 ng/mL for patients treated with combined external beam therapy and brachytherapy has been recommended. Failure to achieve this nadir by 60 months almost always is associated with persistent disease (Critz, 2002). However, because external beam radiotherapy is more organ sparing than brachytherapy is, post-treatment PSA levels usually are higher in patients treated with external beam radiotherapy only and thus might not easily achieve a nadir of 0.2 ng/mL.

Valid comparisons of radiotherapy with current treatment methods are lacking. However, the available evidence suggests that radical prostatectomy is more effective in achieving long-term progression-free survival in patients with clinically localized prostate cancer. In a population-based study of long-term survival in nearly 60,000 patients with clinically localized prostate cancer from the U.S. Surveillance, Epidemiology, and End Results (SEER) cancer registry, radical prostatectomy yielded better results than radiotherapy (Lu-Yao and Yao, 1997). However, better results from both treatments would be expected in the PSA era and with recent technical advances.

Management of Postoperative Biochemical Recurrence

Patients with detectable PSA (>0.1 ng/mL) after radical prostatectomy usually have persistent cancer, although some have only retained benign prostatic tissue causing the PSA elevation. In the latter case, the serum PSA level increases slowly. Of patients destined to have biochemical recurrence after radical prostatectomy, approximately 50% of recurrences appear within 3 years, 80% within 5 years, and 99% within 10 years. Rarely, recurrences appear more than 15 years after radical prostatectomy.

The PSA velocity or doubling time, the interval from surgery to biochemical recurrence, and the Gleason score usually reflect how rapidly the tumor is likely to progress (Freedland et al, 2005). In many patients, progression occurs relatively slowly, and only about one third actually develop metastases (Pound et al, 1999b; Ward et al, 2003). Numerous studies have demonstrated that patients with a rapidly rising PSA level after biochemical recurrence have a high risk of progression to metastases and prostate cancer–specific mortality (D'Amico et al, 2003; Albertsen et al, 2004). In a study of men with a rising PSA level after radical prostatectomy who did not receive immediate radiation therapy, the median actuarial time to metastases was 8 years after PSA elevation, and only 34% of men developed clinically apparent metastases (Pound et al, 1999b).

If salvage radiotherapy is planned, it should be initiated before the PSA level rises much above 0.5 ng/mL (Cox et al, 1999). Patients most likely to have favorable responses to salvage radiotherapy are those with PSA recurrence long after surgery, slowly rising PSA level, low-grade tumor, and no seminal vesicle invasion or lymph node metastases. There is conflicting evidence concerning whether cancer at the surgical margins is a favorable or unfavorable parameter for predicting response to postoperative radiation therapy, although reports suggest that patients with positive margins have a more favorable response rate. In one study, a multivariate analysis revealed that PSA doubling time, pathologic grade, and PSA level at the time of salvage radiotherapy were independent predictors of clinical recurrence, whereas the interval from prostatectomy did not add independent predictive information (Ward et al, 2004). A multi-institutional retrospective analysis reported that 50% of patients had disease progression at a median follow-up of 45 months after radiation therapy, 10% developed metastases, and 4% died of prostate cancer (Stephenson et al, 2004b). The actuarial 4-year progression-free probability was about 45%. In this series, predictors of progression were Gleason grade of 8 or higher, pre-radiation PSA level above 2 ng/mL, negative surgical margins, and PSA doubling time of 10 months or less.

As with adjuvant radiotherapy, the beneficial effects of salvage radiotherapy are controversial. Some patients fare well without it, whereas others will fail with distant metastases despite it.

Some patients with PSA recurrence are better managed with hormone therapy than with salvage radiotherapy. Although many men with biochemical failure are treated with hormone therapy, there are no data from prospective trials to address a possible progression-free or overall survival benefit. **The most appropriate PSA level at which to institute hormone therapy is unknown. Because of the substantial side effects associated with long-term, continuous hormone therapy (decreased libido, impotence, hot flashes, osteopenia with increased fracture risk, metabolic alterations, and changes in cognition and mood), delayed or intermittent hormone therapy is frequently used in patients who have biochemical recurrence, especially those with a slowly rising PSA level** (Sharifi et al, 2005).

The Veterans Administration Cooperative Urological Research Group trials conducted in the 1960s did not show a survival benefit in patients with metastatic disease treated with early hormone therapy (Walsh et al, 2001). However, since then, other prospective, randomized clinical trials suggest that early hormone therapy is more effective than delayed hormone therapy in patients with pelvic lymph node metastases (Messing et al, 1999) or those with locally advanced or asymptomatic metastatic disease (The Medical Research Council, 1997). Nevertheless, it is uncertain whether these studies can be extrapolated to patients who have biochemical recurrence after primary treatment. A retrospective study reported no difference in early clinical outcome between early and delayed hormone therapy in men with biochemical recurrence after radical prostatectomy (Moul et al, 2004). However, in high-risk patients, early hormone therapy delayed the time to bone metastases.

High-dose bicalutamide administration has been reported to delay disease progression and yield overall survival results equivalent to those of treatment with orchiectomy among patients with PSA recurrence (Wirth et al, 2004). A possible advantage of this form of early hormone therapy is that it is associated with less risk for sexual dysfunction and osteoporosis than other forms of androgen deprivation therapy are. A disadvantage is a possible increased risk for cardiovascular complications and death associated with high-dose bicalutamide therapy.

Intermittent hormone therapy is a reasonable alternative of providing early androgen deprivation therapy while limiting the adverse side effects and expense of continuous hormone therapy. There is accumulating evidence from prospective randomized trials that intermittent androgen deprivation is safe and has survival outcomes comparable to those of continuous hormone therapy (Lane et al, 2004; Da Silva et al, 2005a, 2005b).

OTHER TREATMENTS
Primary Hormone Therapy

Primary androgen deprivation therapy may be appropriate for older men, those with significant medical comorbidities precluding the use of curative therapy, or those who do not

KEY POINTS: RADIATION THERAPY

- External beam radiotherapy uses gamma radiation beams directed at the prostate and surrounding tissues through multiple fields. To minimize radiation injury to the bladder and the rectum, three-dimensional conformal radiotherapy and intensity-modulated radiation therapy have been developed. Patients with a high PSA level, high Gleason score, or large-volume tumor benefit from androgen deprivation therapy in conjunction with radiotherapy.

- Currently, the most frequently used definition to determine treatment success after radiation therapy is the American Society of Therapeutic Radiology and Oncology definition, which requires three consecutive PSA increases measured 6 months apart and back-dates the time of cancer progression to half-way between the PSA nadir and the first rising PSA level.

- With brachytherapy, radioactive seeds or needles are implanted directly into the prostate gland to deliver a high dose of radiation to the tumor while possibly sparing the bladder and the rectum. Brachytherapy is relatively easy to perform and therefore has become popular for treatment of patients with clinically localized prostate cancer, but it is seldom used for the treatment of high-volume, high-risk prostate cancers. Urinary symptoms are more common after brachytherapy than after external beam radiotherapy, especially in patients with prostatic hyperplasia.

- Adjuvant radiotherapy shortly after surgery is most likely to benefit patients with positive surgical margins or extracapsular tumor extension without seminal vesicle invasion or lymph node involvement. Patients most likely to have favorable responses to salvage radiotherapy are those with PSA recurrence long after surgery, slowly rising PSA level, low-grade tumor, and no seminal vesicle invasion or lymph node metastases.

KEY POINTS: PRIMARY HORMONE THERAPY

- Primary androgen deprivation therapy may be appropriate for older men, those with significant medical comorbidities precluding the use of curative therapy, and those who do not wish to undergo curative therapy.

- Hormone therapy is never curative; nevertheless, many patients experience long-term remissions.

wish to undergo curative therapy. There are limited published contemporary data of men treated with primary hormone therapy for clinically localized prostate cancer.

Hormone therapy is never curative; nevertheless, many patients experience long-term remissions. Bilateral orchiectomy and estrogen administration have largely been replaced by luteinizing hormone–releasing hormone analogs. Antiandrogens produce less sexual dysfunction and osteoporosis but have a greater risk for adverse cardiovascular complications.

Cryoablation

Cryoablation destroys prostate tissue through freezing. **Current technology uses argon gas circulating through hollow needles to freeze the prostate and helium gas to warm the urethra.** Cryoablation has been used as primary treatment for salvage after radical prostatectomy or radiotherapy. The initial results were poor with incomplete eradication of the tumor and high complication rates, including urinary retention, incontinence, urinary-intestinal fistula, stricture, chronic rectal or perineal pain, and nearly uniform loss of erections (Porter et al, 1997; Perrotte et al, 1999; Long et al, 2001). With technical modifications, the complication rates have decreased, cancer control has improved, and the procedure is better tolerated (Chang et al, 1994; De La Taille et al, 2000; Long et al, 2001; Onik, 2001; Cytron et al, 2003).

Although a multicenter cryotherapy study of more than 900 patients has been published, recurrence-free outcomes are difficult to interpret because no clear definition of recurrence after cryotherapy has been established (Long et al, 2001). In addition, many patients in the study received neoadjuvant hormone ablation.

Cryotherapy has also been evaluated as a possible salvage therapy for men who have failed radiotherapy, but limited long-term data are available. One study reported undetectable PSA in 74% with 2 years of follow-up (Pisters et al, 1999). However, complications associated with salvage cryoablation were much more frequent than for primary treatment (Bales et al, 1995; Perrotte et al, 1999; Pisters et al, 1999).

Potential advantages of cryoablation are that it is minimally invasive, it does not involve radiation exposure or surgical risk, repeated treatments are possible, and preservation of potency is possible with cavernous nerve warming. However, these advantages have yet to be documented or validated. In addition, **long-term biochemical control and quality of life outcomes data for cryoablation are not yet available.**

Radiofrequency Interstitial Tumor Ablation

Heating prostate tissue to high temperatures destroys it nonselectively, whereas *hyperthermia* at less elevated temperatures is claimed to kill cancer cells selectively. Radiofrequency interstitial tumor ablation–induced hyperthermia has been investigated as a treatment of the primary tumor, in combination with radiotherapy, and for salvage after radiotherapy failure (Prionas et al, 1994; Zlotta et al, 1998; Shariat et al, 2005).

Like cryoablation, this office-based treatment can be repeated. Careful and constant monitoring is critical to limit the risk of damage to normal tissue (Shariat et al, 2005). Advantages claimed for hyperthermia are that it can be

Table 95–1. The Definition of Risk Group

Risk Group	Clinical Stage	PSA (ng/mL)	Gleason Score	Biopsy Criteria
Low	T1a or T1c	<10	2-5	Unilateral or <50% of core involved
Intermediate	T1b or T2a	<10	6 or 3 + 4 = 7	Bilateral
High	T2b or T3	10-20	4 + 3 = 7	>50% of core involved or perineural invasion or ductal differentiation
Very high	T4	>20	8-10	Lymphovascular invasion or neuroendocrine differentiation

repeated and does not preclude the use of other therapies. However, **long-term data on complications and cancer control are not available** (Beerlage et al, 2000).

High-Intensity Focused Ultrasound

Acoustic energy can be used with ultrasound focusing to generate heat within the prostate gland, thus ablating focal lesions or the entire gland. Transrectally applied high-intensity focused ultrasound (HIFU) can elevate the tissue temperature of the prostate up to 100°C (Madersbacher et al, 1995). Within several seconds, a lesion develops with a sharp and predictable volume, leaving the surrounding tissue intact. Mechanisms of action of HIFU involve mechanical interaction of ultrasound waves with tissue, producing coagulating heat, high pressure, cavitation bubbles, and chemically active free radicals that ultimately induce tissue destruction by coagulation necrosis (Chapelon et al, 1999). **Days to months are required for necrosis and cavitation to occur.** Because HIFU energy is nonionizing, treatment can be repeated.

Treatment is performed under general or spinal anesthesia and takes 1 to 4 hours, depending on the prostate volume, which should not exceed 40 mL. The rectal mucosa is cooled (Blana et al, 2004), and a limited transurethral resection of the prostate or a bladder neck incision is often performed at the beginning of the procedure to reduce the risk of postoperative urinary retention (Chaussy and Thuroff, 2003). Most patients require a urethral or suprapubic catheter for several days.

One commercially available apparatus for HIFU has been tested in a multicenter trial and is available in Europe (Thuroff et al, 2003). Another is investigational with multicenter phase III trials under way (Uchida, 2005).

The procedure is usually well tolerated; the most common side effect is acute urinary retention, occurring in about 20% of patients. **Other potential complications are urinary fistula, incontinence, urethral stricture, and perineal pain** (Blana et al, 2004). **Erectile dysfunction** has been reported in 27% to 61% (Blana et al, 2004; Pickles et al, 2005).

The initial results report a 70% progression-free survival rate with a mean follow-up of 23 months. The progression criteria used were any cancerous biopsy finding or a PSA rise of more than 0.4 ng/mL, but the durability of responses has not been documented (Blana et al, 2004). HIFU has also been used to treat radiation failures, but limited results have been reported (Gelet et al, 2004). Early outcomes reflect the risk characteristics of the tumors before radiation therapy. Adverse effects associated with salvage HIFU include rectourethral fistula in 6%, severe incontinence in 7%, and bladder neck stenosis in 17% (Gelet et al, 2004). Overall, **there is insufficient information to recommend HIFU as a standard therapy.**

Table 95–2. Recommended Treatment

Risk Group	Life Expectancy (years)	Recommended Treatment
Low	0-5	AM, HT
	5-10	AM, RT, HT, O
	>10	RP, RT, AM, O
Intermediate*	0-5	AM, HT, RT, O
	5-10	RT, HT, RP, O
	>10	RP, RT, O, HT
High*	0-5	AM, RT, O
	5-10	RT, HT, RP, O
	>10	RT, RP + RT + HT, HT
Very high*	0-5	AM, RT, O
	5-10	H, RT + HT, ST
	>10	RT + HT, RP + RT + HT, HT, ST, IT

AM, active monitoring; HT, hormone therapy; RT, radiation therapy; O, others; RP, radical prostatectomy; ST, systemic therapy; IT, investigational multimodal therapy.

*If there is more than a 20% probability of positive lymph nodes, AM, HT, ST + HT.

RECOMMENDATIONS FOR TREATMENT BY PATIENT RISK GROUPS

The tumor is staged at the time of diagnosis and the patient evaluated for comorbidities. The legitimate treatment options and their associated risks and potential benefits are discussed (Tables 95–1 and 95–2). Choice of therapy for an individual patient depends on the availability of high-quality delivery.

SUGGESTED READINGS

Allaf ME, Carter HB: Update on watchful waiting for prostate cancer. Curr Opin Urol 2004;14:171-175.

Bagnall S, Klotz L: Conservative versus radical therapy of prostate cancer: How have recent advances in molecular markers and imaging enhanced our ability to prognosticate risk? Semin Oncol 2003;30:587-595.

Blana A, Walter B, Rogenhofer S, Wieland WF: High-intensity focused ultrasound for the treatment of localized prostate cancer: 5-year experience. Urology 2004;63:297-300.

Blasko JC, Mate T, Sylvester JE, et al: Brachytherapy for carcinoma of the prostate: Techniques, patient selection, and clinical outcomes. Semin Radiat Oncol 2002;12:81-94.

Bolla M, Gonzalez D, Warde P, et al: Improved survival in patients with locally advanced prostate cancer treated with radiotherapy and goserelin. N Engl J Med 1997;337:295-300.

Guillonneau B, el-Fettouh H, Baumert H, et al: Laparoscopic radical prostatectomy: Oncological evaluation after 1,000 cases at Montsouris Institute. J Urol 2003;169:1261-1266.

Han M, Partin AW, Pound CR, et al: Long-term biochemical disease-free and cancer-specific survival following anatomic radical retropubic prostatectomy. The 15-year Johns Hopkins experience. Urol Clin North Am 2001;28:555-565.

Menon M, Tewari A, Baize B, et al: Prospective comparison of radical retropubic prostatectomy and robot-assisted anatomic prostatectomy: The Vattikuti Urology Institute experience. Urology 2002;60:864-868.

Rebillard X, Gelet A, Davin JL, et al: Transrectal high-intensity focused ultrasound in the treatment of localized prostate cancer. J Endourol 2005;19:693-701.

Sharifi N, Gulley JL, Dahut WL: Androgen deprivation therapy for prostate cancer. JAMA 2005;294:238-244.

Walsh PC, Donker PJ: Impotence following radical prostatectomy: Insight into etiology and prevention. J Urol 1982;128:492-497.

Zelefsky MJ, Leibel SA, Gaudin PB, et al: Dose escalation with three-dimensional conformal radiation therapy affects the outcome in prostate cancer. Int J Radiat Oncol Biol Phys 1998;41:491-500.

96 Expectant Management of Prostate Cancer

JAMES A. EASTHAM, MD • PETER T. SCARDINO, MD

"WATCHFUL WAITING" VERSUS ACTIVE
SURVEILLANCE WITH SELECTIVE DELAYED
DEFINITIVE THERAPY

WATCHFUL WAITING

WATCHFUL WAITING VERSUS TREATMENT

IDENTIFYING MEN WITH "LOW-RISK" PROSTATE
CANCER

ACTIVE SURVEILLANCE WITH SELECTIVE DELAYED
DEFINITIVE THERAPY

SUMMARY

The clinical course of newly diagnosed prostate cancer is difficult to predict. Men with similar clinical stage, serum prostate-specific antigen (PSA) level, and biopsy Gleason sum can have markedly different outcomes. Whereas prostate cancer is unequivocally lethal in some patients, most men do indeed die with rather than of their cancer. The ratio of approximately six newly diagnosed cases for every one death from cancer each year—relatively constant during the past 30 years—results from the protracted natural history of the disease in most patients. Further highlighting the remarkable variation in behavior of this disease, **histologically apparent cancer can be found in the prostates of approximately 42% of men older than 50 years who die of other causes; the lifetime risk that an American man will be diagnosed with prostate cancer is estimated to be about 17% and the risk of dying of this disease only 3.6%** (Scardino et al, 1992; Sakr et al, 1993; Landis et al, 1999; Stanford et al, 1999) (Table 96–1). The challenge to physicians today is to identify the minority of men with an aggressive, localized prostate cancer with a natural history that can be altered by definitive local therapy while sparing the remainder the morbidity of unnecessary treatment.

Epidemiologic data demonstrate a marked increase in the number of men diagnosed with prostate cancer and a profound migration toward earlier stage disease at the time of diagnosis. Implementation of large-scale serum PSA screening programs and more extensive biopsy strategies are largely responsible for the increase in diagnosis. An analysis of the control group in the Prostate Cancer Prevention Trial illustrates the potential for extensive biopsy to result in overdiagnosis of prostate cancer (Thompson et al, 2004). Among 2950 men with normal findings on digital rectal examination (DRE) and PSA levels less than 4.0 ng/mL, 15.2% harbored prostate cancer by biopsy, as did 6.2% of men with PSA levels of 0.5 ng/mL or less. In an era of increasing prostate cancer incidence and stage migration toward earlier disease, appropriate management of the disease requires assessment of risk: How likely is a given man's cancer to progress or to metastasize during his remaining lifetime? What is the probability of success with treatment? What are the risks of side effects and complications with each treatment?

Prostate cancer is relatively slow growing, with doubling times for local tumors estimated at 2 to 4 years. **Some prostate cancers prove to be so small, low grade, and noninvasive that they appear to pose little risk to the life or health of the host.** Recent patient series suggest that 20% to 30% of men undergoing radical prostatectomy have pathologic features in the radical prostatectomy specimen consistent with an insignificant or "indolent" cancer that posed little threat to life or health (organ-confined cancer less than 0.5 mL, no Gleason grade 4 or 5 component). However, **the biologic potential of histologically detectable cancers is difficult to characterize with certainty,** and biopsy may underestimate the extent of cancer in the prostate. Consequently, most physicians recommend aggressive treatment even for small biopsy-detected cancers. Nevertheless, **conservative management, that is, deferring definitive therapy until evidence that the cancer is sufficiently aggressive to warrant therapy, may be appropriate for many patients with a favorable (low-risk) cancer, and identification of such cancers before treatment would be a significant benefit to these patients.**

"WATCHFUL WAITING" VERSUS ACTIVE SURVEILLANCE WITH SELECTIVE DELAYED DEFINITIVE THERAPY

Traditionally, watchful waiting has meant no active treatment until a patient develops evidence of symptomatic disease progression, at which time androgen deprivation therapy is initiated. The goal of this non-interventionalist

approach is to limit morbidity from the disease and therapy, not to administer potentially curative treatment (Table 96–2). The assumption is that definitive local therapy provides little or no benefit to the majority of patients. A more recent concept is to delay curative local therapy until the natural history and threat posed by the cancer can be more accurately characterized. **Active surveillance with selective delayed definitive therapy attempts to distinguish clinically insignificant cancers from life-threatening cancers while they are still localized to the prostate.** This approach assumes that the risk posed by a given cancer can be assessed with some degree of certainty and that delayed treatment will be as curative as immediate treatment. **With active surveillance, we attempt to avoid overtreatment in the majority of patients but also to administer curative therapy to selected cases** (see Table 96–2).

WATCHFUL WAITING

Because prostate cancer is often diagnosed in older men with competing comorbidities, many clinicians recommend watchful waiting: observation until disease progression, followed by hormone therapy. Several investigators have attempted to document the long-term risk for development of metastases and of death from prostate cancer in men with clinically localized cancers treated conservatively (Adolfsson et al, 1994; Chodak et al, 1994; Albertsen et al, 1995, 1998; Johansson et al, 1997, 2004). The impact of this slow-growing cancer depends on the life expectancy (age and comorbidities) of the patient (Table 96–3). **For those expected to live less than 5 years, most prostate cancers will grow locally, and some patients will develop metastases, but few will die of the disease.**

The risk of metastases and of death from clinical stage T1 to T2 cancer with conservative management was estimated in a meta-analysis of six watchful waiting series (Chodak et al, 1994). **The risk of metastasis at 10 years was 19% for well-differentiated cancers, 42% for moderately differentiated cancers, and 74% for poorly differentiated cancers.** Note that if the primary tumor was not controlled, the risk for development of metastases persisted, even accelerated, after 10 years. These findings were confirmed by Johansson and colleagues (2004), who reported their long-term results among men with early-stage prostate cancer (T0-T2, NX, M0) managed without initial therapy. They observed a consecutive sample of 223 men for a mean period of 21 years. Most cancers had an indolent course during the first 10 to 15 years. However, further follow-up from 15 to 20 years revealed a substantial decrease in cumulative progression-free survival (from 45% at 15 years to 36% at 20 years), survival without metastases (from 77% to 51%), and prostate cancer–specific survival (from 79% to 54%) (Fig. 96–1). The authors concluded that **although most prostate cancers diagnosed at an early stage have an indolent course, local tumor progression and aggressive metastatic disease may develop in the long term, and early radical treatment should be considered for men with a life expectancy exceeding 15 years.**

The impact on mortality was documented in a large, population-based study (Albertsen et al, 2005). The probability of death from prostate cancer within 15 to 20 years of diagnosis depended on the Gleason sum of the cancer and the age of the patient at diagnosis (Table 96–4). **Patients with a well-differentiated cancer (Gleason sum 2 to 4) had a low probability of death from cancer within 20 years; higher grade cancers took a substantial toll even among older men.**

We reviewed United Kingdom cancer registry data to determine predictors of long-term outcomes for men with clinically localized prostate cancer managed without curative intent (Kattan et al, 2005). Chart reviews were conducted to identify men who at the time of diagnosis were aged 30 to 75 years (inclusive), had a baseline serum PSA level (measured within 6 months of their diagnosis) of 100 ng/mL of less, were not treated with curative intent, did not have evidence of metastatic disease, and were alive for at least 6 months after their diagnosis. For the time frame of this study (cancer diagnosis between January 1990 and December 1996), 2446 men were eligible for evaluation. Diagnosis was by transurethral resection of the prostate in 1358 (56%) and needle biopsy in 1088 (44%). The description of the DRE was used to assign a

Table 96–1. Lifetime Risk for Development of or Dying of Prostate Cancer for a 50-Year-Old Man in the United States

Lifetime Risk for	Risk (%)	Risk Ratio	Proportional Risk
Development of incidental cancer	42	11.7	100
Development of clinical cancer	16.7	4.4	38
Dying of prostate cancer	3.6	1	8.6

Modified from Scardino, 1989; Scardino et al, 1992; Greenlee et al, 2000.

Table 96–2. Contrasts Between Active Surveillance and Watchful Waiting (Parker, 2004)

	Active Surveillance	Watchful Waiting
Aim	To individualize treatment	To avoid treatment
Patient characteristics	Fit for radical treatment	Age > 70 yr or life expectancy < 15 yr
	Age 50-80 yr	
Tumor characteristics	T1-T2, GS ≤ 7, initial PSA < 15 ng/mL	Any T stage, GS ≤ 7, any PSA
Monitoring	Frequent PSA testing	PSA testing unimportant
	Repeated biopsies	No repeated biopsies
Indications for treatment	Short PSADT	Symptomatic progression
	Higher grade or more extensive cancer on biopsy	
Treatment timing	Early	Delayed
Treatment intent	Radical	Palliative

GS, Gleason sum; PSADT, PSA doubling time.

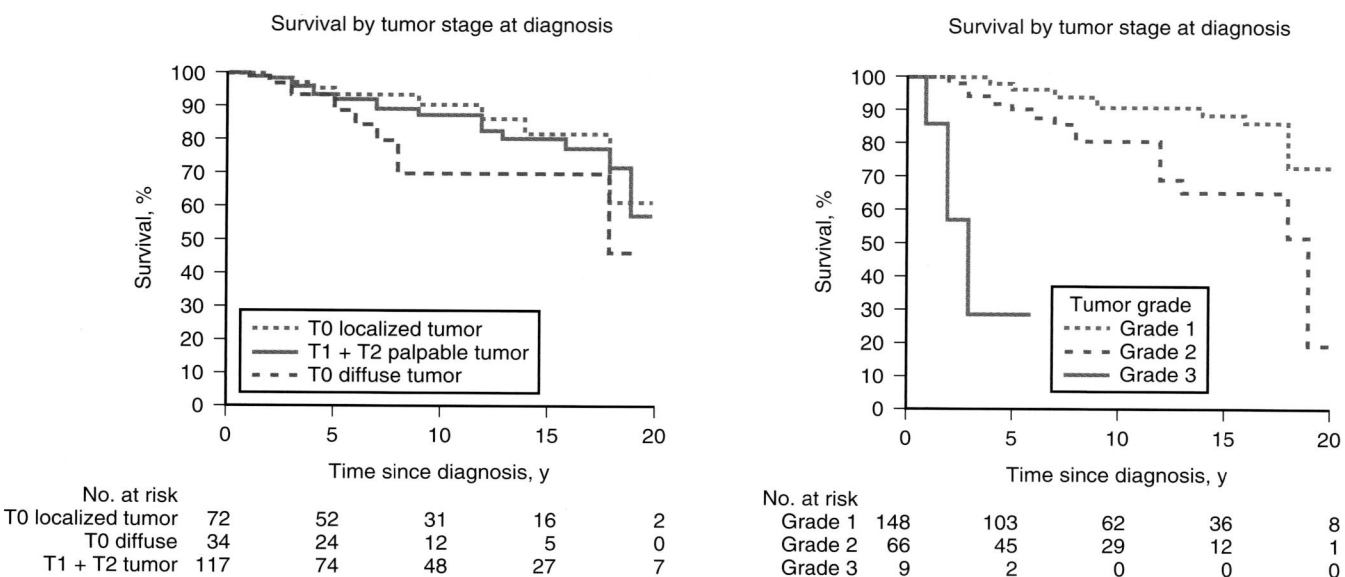

Figure 96–1. Cause-specific survival of men with prostate cancer managed conservatively, by stage of disease and tumor grade at diagnosis. Disease stages were T0 localized, T0 diffuse, and T1-T2. Grades were as follows: grade 1, highly differentiated; grade 2, moderately differentiated; and grade 3, poorly differentiated. (From Johansson JE, Andren O, Andersson SO, et al: Natural history of early, localized prostate cancer. JAMA 2004;291:2713-2719.)

Table 96–3. Life Expectancy of Men (All Races) in the United States by Age in 5-Year Increments

Age	Life Expectancy (years), 1998
50	27.6
55	23.5
60	19.6
65	16.0
70	12.8
75	10.0
80	7.5
85	5.5

Modified from Martin JA, Smith BL, Mathews TJ, Ventura SJ: Births and deaths: Preliminary data for 1998. Natl Vital Stat Rep 1999;47:1-45.

Table 96–4. Rates of Cancer-Specific Mortality (Probability of Dying of Prostate Cancer) within 15 Years of Diagnosis in Men with Clinically Localized Prostate Cancer Treated Conservatively

Gleason Sum	Age (years)			
	50-59	60-64	65-69	70-74
2-4	4%	5%	6%	7%
5	6%	8%	10%	11%
6	18%	23%	27%	30%
7	70%	62%	53%	42%
8-10	87%	81%	72%	60%

Modified from Albertsen PC, Hanley JA, Gleason DF, Barry MJ: Competing risk analysis of men aged 55 to 74 years at diagnosis managed conservatively for clinically localized prostate cancer. JAMA 1998;280:975-980.

clinical stage, and pathologic materials from the diagnostic procedure (biopsy or transurethral resection of the prostate) were centrally reviewed to confirm the diagnosis and to assign a Gleason sum. Outcomes were determined through medical records, cancer registry data, and death certificates. We then analyzed which factors were associated with the development of metastatic disease and death from prostate cancer. Most men were managed without initial treatment, with 30% treated with hormone therapy within 6 months of their diagnosis. The median follow-up was 88.9 months (interquartile range, 60 to 107). In a competing risks analysis, 30% of the patients have died of prostate cancer and 30% of other causes within 12 years. For men who did not die of another cause, the probability of metastases, death from prostate cancer, or additional therapy within 12 years was 90%. This is the largest cohort of conservatively managed patients to date that included baseline PSA determination and reviewed Gleason grade. Our results suggest that clinically localized prostate cancer managed with watchful waiting results in a high rate of progression or secondary treatment within 12 years. **Whereas age and baseline clinical features can identify men at increased risk for the development of metastatic disease and death from prostate cancer, not all men with "adverse" features do poorly.** Additional clinical and pathologic parameters are needed to improve our ability to predict outcomes for an individual patient.

WATCHFUL WAITING VERSUS TREATMENT

Perhaps the most compelling evidence that selected patients with prostate cancer benefit from active treatment compared with watchful waiting comes from the recently completed Scandinavian Trial, which randomized 695 men with clinically localized prostate cancer to either radical prostatectomy or watchful waiting with systemic treatment deferred until the development of symptomatic progression (Bill-Axelson et al,

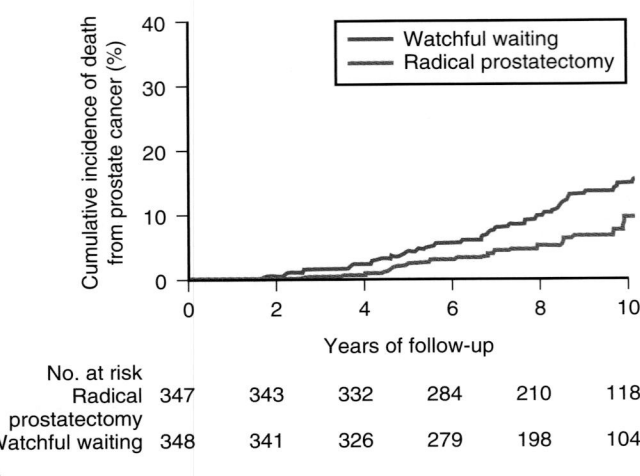

No. at risk

Radical prostatectomy	347	343	332	284	210	118
Watchful waiting	348	341	326	279	198	104

A

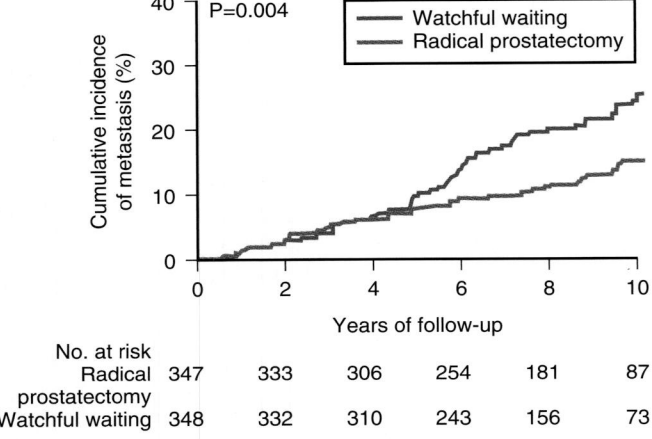

No. at risk

Radical prostatectomy	347	333	306	254	181	87
Watchful waiting	348	332	310	243	156	73

B

Figure 96–2. Swedish randomized trial comparing radical prostatectomy and watchful waiting. Surgical excision alters the natural history of prostate cancer, reducing cancer-specific mortality (**A**) and metastases (**B**) at 10 years. (From Bill-Axelson A, Holmberg L, Ruutu M, et al: Radical prostatectomy versus watchful waiting in early prostate cancer. N Engl J Med 2005;352:1977-1984.)

Table 96–5. Comparison of Urinary Quality of Life (Function) Between Radical Prostatectomy and Watchful Waiting Patients from the Scandinavian Prostatic Cancer Group

Function	RP	WW	Relative Risk (95% CI)
Leak once per week or more often	49%	21%	2.3 (1.6-3.2)
Distress from leakage	29%	9%	3.0 (1.8-5.2)
Urinary obstruction	28%	44%	0.6 (0.5-0.9)
Low/moderate urinary quality of life	40%	45%	0.9 (0.7-1.2)

RP, radical prostatectomy; WW, watchful waiting.
From Steineck G, Helgesen F, Adolfsson J, et al: Quality of life after radical prostatectomy or watchful waiting. N Engl J Med 2002;347:790-796.

Although the development of metastatic disease and death from prostate cancer are important outcomes, local progression can also have significant impact on quality of life. For example, the Scandinavian Prostate Cancer Group evaluated quality of life in their study comparing surgery to watchful waiting in men with localized prostate cancer (Steineck et al, 2002). **Whereas erectile dysfunction and incontinence were higher in men treated with radical prostatectomy, men on watchful waiting experienced significantly more obstructive voiding complaints and bowel problems, resulting in similar levels of treatment-related distress** (Table 96–5). In addition, Aus and colleagues (1995) performed a retrospective analysis of 514 prostate cancer patients who died between 1988 and 1990. Of patients who died of prostate cancer, 61% had required one or more palliative treatments (transurethral resection of the prostate, radiation treatment, or upper urinary tract diversion). Considering any individual factor in isolation would not reflect global aspects of urinary or overall quality of life, and patients must be aware of potential side effects if watchful waiting is selected.

These studies provide strong evidence for the varied natural history of clinically localized prostate cancer. Some prostate cancers progress slowly and present little risk to the overall health of the patient. Watchful waiting may be a reasonable option in these patients, especially those with a life expectancy of less than 10 years. Other prostate cancers, however, can cause morbidity and mortality. The current difficulty is deciding which patients require aggressive therapy and which patients are best managed expectantly.

IDENTIFYING MEN WITH "LOW-RISK" PROSTATE CANCER

Because of the risk of overtreatment, many physicians and patients consider conservative management for selected low-risk prostate cancers. The difficulty in this approach is an appropriate definition for "low risk." Currently available clinical staging tools have limited potential for accurately characterizing localized prostate cancers, although systematic needle biopsies, serial PSA determinations, and modern imaging are promising tools for more accurate assessment of the extent of local tumor.

2005). The primary endpoint of this study was death from prostate cancer. During a median follow-up of 8.2 years, **50 of 348 of those assigned to watchful waiting died of prostate cancer, compared with 30 of 347 of those assigned to radical prostatectomy** (relative hazard, 0.56; 95% confidence interval, 0.36 to 0.88; P = .01) (Fig. 96–2A). **The men assigned to surgery had a lower relative risk of distant metastases than did the men assigned to watchful waiting** (relative hazard, 0.60; 95% confidence interval, 0.42 to 0.86) (Fig. 96–2B). For men who were managed conservatively, the cumulative probability for development of metastatic disease 10 years after diagnosis was 25% and the cancer-specific mortality rate was 15%. This elegant study firmly documents the overall benefit of radical prostatectomy in patients with clinically localized prostate cancer diagnosed in the absence of systematic screening of the population. The relevance of this study to cancers detected by screening, which may be much earlier in their natural history, is uncertain.

Systematic Biopsy Results

In an attempt to identify patients who have low-risk tumors, Epstein and associates (1994) examined preoperative clinical and pathologic features in 157 men with clinical stage T1c prostate cancer who underwent radical prostatectomy to find features that could predict "insignificant" tumors (organ-confined tumors less than 0.2 mL, pathologic Gleason sum 6 or lower). Their model for predicting an insignificant tumor was no Gleason grade of 4 or 5 in the biopsy specimen and either (1) PSA density of 0.1 ng/mL per gram or less, fewer than three biopsy cores involved with cancer (minimum of six cores obtained), and no core with more than 50% involvement or (2) PSA density of 0.15 ng/mL per gram or less and cancer smaller than 3 mm on only one prostate biopsy sample (minimum of six cores). As a test for significant disease, this model had a positive predictive value of 95% and a negative predictive value of 66% in their own dataset. These investigators predicted that 73% of their cases were insignificant tumors.

Similarly, Goto and associates (1996) evaluated 170 patients who had six or more systematic needle biopsies and determined that a PSA density of less than 0.1, no Gleason grade 4 or 5 in the prostate biopsy specimen, and cancer smaller than 2 mm in a single biopsy core predicted a 75% probability of an unimportant or "indolent" cancer (<0.5 mL, confined, no Gleason grade 4 or 5). Last, Epstein and colleagues (1998) evaluated 163 radical prostatectomy specimens of clinical stage T1c prostate cancer to determine whether free/total serum PSA ratios, which reflect prostate volume indirectly, combined with needle biopsy results would be more accurate. Using the same definition of indolent cancer as that of Goto and associates, they determined that the best model to predict insignificant tumor is a free/total serum PSA ratio of 0.15 or greater and favorable needle biopsy findings (fewer than three cores involved, none of the cores with more than 50% tumor involvement, and Gleason sum below 6). This model had a 94% positive predictive value for insignificant cancer. None of these models have been validated prospectively or on a separate cohort.

Indolent Cancer Nomogram

To better counsel men diagnosed with prostate cancer, we developed a statistical model to predict the presence of an indolent cancer (as defined before) from standard clinical variables (serum PSA concentration, prostate volume determined by ultrasound examination, clinical stage, prostate biopsy Gleason grade, and systematic biopsy findings) (Kattan et al, 2003). The biopsy features included number and percentage of biopsy cores involved with cancer, total length of cancer in all cores, and total length of noncancerous tissue.

The analysis included more than 400 patients diagnosed by systematic needle biopsy who had features of a low-risk cancer (clinical stage T1c or T2a, biopsy Gleason patterns 2 or 3, PSA less than 20 ng/mL). By analysis of the radical prostatectomy specimen, 80 patients (20%) had an indolent cancer. Logistic regression was used to construct prediction models of increasing complexity, from a base model that included only stage, grade, and PSA to a full model that added prostate volume and length of cancer and of noncancerous tissue in the cores. The

nomograms predicted the presence of an indolent cancer with discrimination (area under the receiver operating characteristics curve) that increased from 0.64 for the base model to 0.79 for the full model (Fig. 96–3).

Using such prognostic information, physicians can identify, with reasonable accuracy, patients with low tumor burden for whom aggressive management may not be indicated initially, especially in men who are older or with significant comorbidity.

ACTIVE SURVEILLANCE WITH SELECTIVE DELAYED DEFINITIVE THERAPY

Active surveillance (AS), like watchful waiting, has the goal of avoiding unnecessary treatment of men with low-risk cancers, those that would seem to pose little risk to life or health during the next 5 to 10 years (Patel et al, 2004). To recommend AS for a healthy man with a life expectancy longer than 10 years risks permitting a curable cancer to become metastatic, either because the initial evaluation seriously underestimates the grade and extent of the present cancer or because a small, indolent cancer grows undetected and becomes metastatic before it is treated. The initial evaluation of a candidate for AS aims to reduce the chance that a large, aggressive cancer has been missed. Subsequent evaluations aim to detect progression before the cancer metastasizes. Watchful waiting studies (Chodak et al, 1994; Johansson et al, 2004) suggest that the risk of progression *accelerates* over time, a pattern different from the risk of progression or recurrence after definitive therapy, which diminishes over time. Hence, AS patients must accept frequent, regular detailed evaluations of the status of their cancer for as long as they are healthy and young enough to be a candidate for definitive therapy.

For AS candidates who have been diagnosed with what appears to be a low-risk cancer, we recommend a complete reevaluation at baseline, including DRE, free and total PSA determinations, imaging study of the prostate (we prefer endorectal magnetic resonance imaging with spectroscopy), and ultrasound-guided systematic needle biopsy. If these studies confirm a low-risk cancer and the patient chooses AS, we recommend a check-up every 6 months with DRE and PSA determinations indefinitely, with repeated imaging and biopsy 12 to 18 months after the baseline evaluation, then every 2 to 3 years. The goal is to detect progression of the cancer while cure is still possible.

Outcomes of Active Surveillance

There are, as yet, few reports of outcomes of deferred definitive therapy for localized prostate cancer (Zietman et al, 2001; Carter et al, 2002; Choo et al, 2002; el-Geneidy et al, 2004; Klotz, 2004; Patel et al, 2004). Carter and associates (2002) observed a cohort of 81 men (median age, 65 years) with stage T1c prostate cancer who were thought to have small-volume prostate cancer on the basis of needle biopsy findings and PSA density (by the Epstein criteria noted earlier). Patients were observed for more than 1 year (median, 23 months) with semiannual PSA determinations and DRE and annual prostate

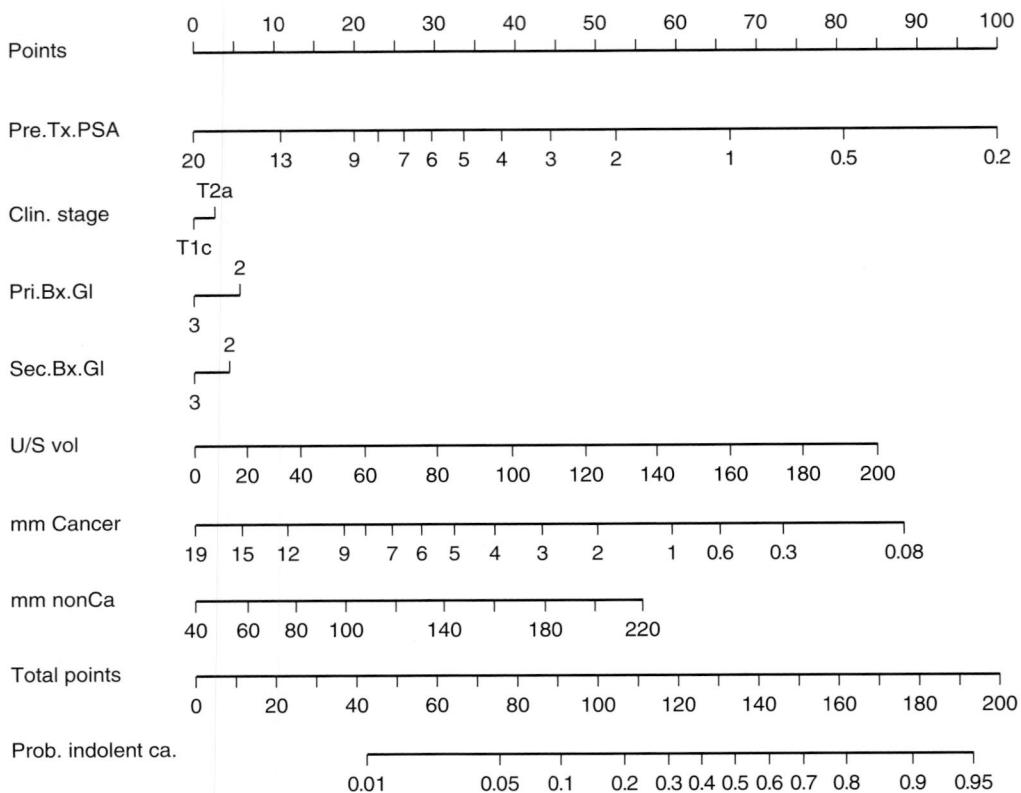

Figure 96–3. Nomogram for predicting an "indolent" prostate cancer (see text for definition) from clinical data and systematic biopsy results (full model). Pre.Tx., pretreatment; Clin., clinical; Pri.Bx.Gl, primary biopsy Gleason grade; Sec.Bx.Gl, secondary biopsy Gleason grade; U/S, ultrasound; Ca, cancer; Prob., probability. (From Kattan MW, Eastham JA, Wheeler TM, et al: Counseling men with prostate cancer: A nomogram for predicting the presence of small, moderately differentiated, confined tumors. J Urol 2003;170:1792-1797.)

Instructions for Physician: Locate the patient's PSA on the **PreTX PSA** axis. Draw a line straight upwards to the **Points** axis to determine how many points towards having an indolent cancer the patient receives for his PSA. Repeat this process for the remaining axes, each time drawing straight upward to the **Points** axis. Sum the points achieved for each predictor and locate this sum on the **Total Points** axis. Draw a line straight down to find the patient's probability of having indolent cancer.

Instruction to Patient: "Mr. X, if we had 100 men exactly like you, we would expect < predicted probability from nomogram * 100 > to have indolent cancer."

biopsies. Treatment was recommended if disease progression was indicated by unfavorable follow-up needle biopsy findings (Gleason grade 4 or 5, more than two biopsy cores with cancer, more than 50% involvement of any core with cancer). Of the 81 men managed with AS, 25 (31%) had progression of disease during follow-up. PSA density was higher ($P = .01$) and the percentage of free PSA lower ($P = .04$) in men with disease progression compared with those without disease progression. Although PSA criteria were significant predictors of cancer progression, there was extensive overlap in PSA density and percentage free PSA values in men with and without progression, suggesting that accurate prediction of progression would be difficult by these criteria. Of 39 men in whom every follow-up biopsy specimen showed cancer, 22 (56%) had disease progression, compared with 3 of 42 men (7%) with normal findings on one or more follow-up biopsies ($P < .001$). The investigators suggested that annual surveillance biopsies are necessary for men on AS, since **PSA criteria are not likely to reveal disease progression accurately.**

Our group has studied outcomes for patients with low-risk cancer who were eligible for definitive therapy but chose AS (Patel et al, 2004). This prospective study enrolled 88 patients with clinical stages T1-2, N0 or NX, M0 prostate cancer, mean age of 65.3 years, and mean initial PSA value of 5.9 ng/mL who were observed for a median of 44 months (range, 7 to 172). Follow-up involved office evaluations (DRE and serum PSA levels) every 3 months for year 1 and every 6 months thereafter. Repeated ultrasound-guided needle biopsy was recommended at baseline, 1 year later, and then every 2 to 3 years or sooner if DRE, transrectal ultrasonography (endorectal magnetic resonance imaging was not available during this study), or PSA level indicated progression. Since DRE and transrectal ultrasonography are subjective, and PSA and systematic biopsy results are inherently variable, there was no objective definition of progression during the study. We retrospectively reviewed the data to develop criteria for "objective progression" in AS patients so we could estimate the probability of progression as opposed to the likelihood that a patient would change from surveillance to active treatment because of the physician's or patient's preference. Points were assigned for changes in Gleason score, PSA level, DRE/transrectal ultrasonography, and biopsy results (Table 96–6); patients with 3 or more points were classified as having objective progression. During a median follow-up of 44 months, 22 patients met the criteria for progression. The actuarial probability of progression was 36% at 5 years and 45% at 10 years

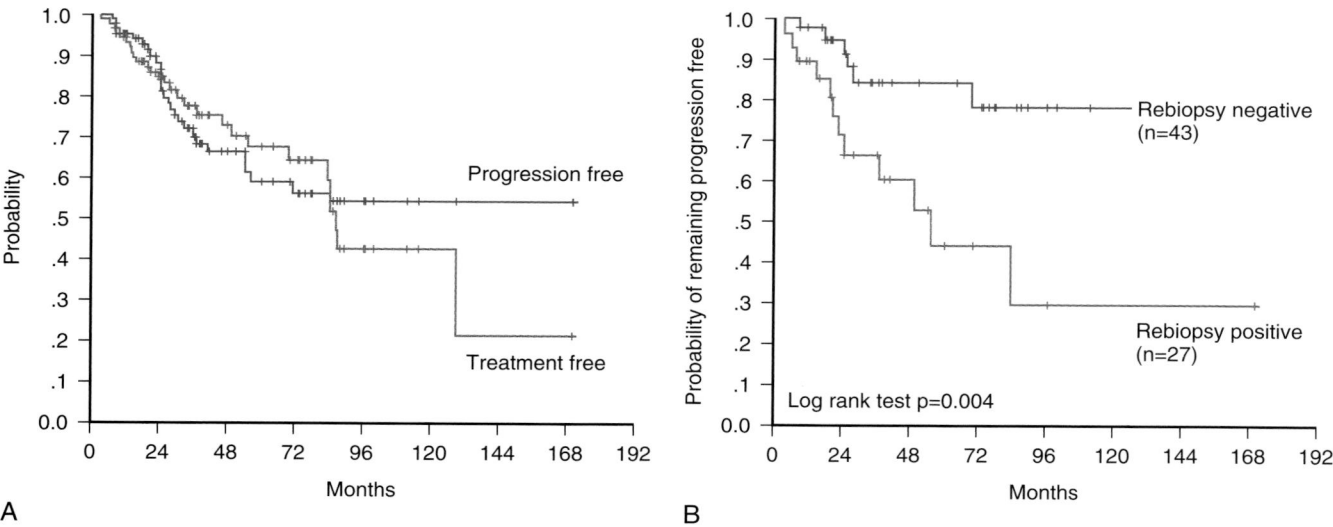

Figure 96–4. **A,** Probability of remaining progression free and treatment free for patients on active surveillance. **B,** Probability of remaining progression free stratified by first repeated biopsy results. (From Patel MI, DeConcini DT, Lopez-Corona E, et al: An analysis of men with clinically localized prostate cancer who deferred definitive therapy. J Urol 2004;171:1520-1524.)

Table 96–6.   Point System for Evaluating Progression in Patients Treated with Deferred Therapy (Patel et al, 2004)

	1 Point	*2 Points*	*3 Points*
Gleason score increase	1	>1	Any new Gleason pattern 4 or 5
PSA velocity (ng/mL/yr)		>0.75 during 12 months	>0.75/yr during 24 months
DRE/transrectal ultrasonography	Increasing old lesion*	New lesion not biopsy proven†	New biopsy-proven lesion†
Biopsy specimens		Bilateral or multifocal cancer	>4 cores with cancer

*More than 25% increase in cross-sectional area ($\pi/4 \times$ length $\times$ perpendicular width).
†New nodule on DRE or hypoechoic lesion on transrectal ultrasonography separate from any previously recorded lesion.
From Patel MI, DeConcini DT, Lopez-Corona E, et al: An analysis of men with clinically localized prostate cancer who deferred definitive therapy. J Urol 2004;171:1520-1524.

(Fig. 96–4*A*). Factors that predicted progression in univariate analysis were initial repeated biopsy showing cancer (*P* = .004) and initial PSA level (*P* = .014). Changes in PSA level were not indicative of progression; nearly half of the patients had a lower PSA level at last evaluation than at baseline. Of the 88 patients, 70 had a repeated biopsy within 6 months of diagnosis, and 47% of these showed no cancer. In multivariable analysis, the result of this repeated biopsy was the most important predictor of progression (Fig. 96–4*B*). Whereas only 36% of the patients showed objective progression within 5 years, 44% were treated, the difference being those treated because of the patient's preference. Of the 31 patients treated, 17 had radical prostatectomy, 13 radiation therapy, and one androgen ablation. Seven men without objective progression were treated. Only one patient, who was treated with radiation therapy, had biochemical recurrence. **We concluded that AS may be a feasible alternative to initial curative treatment in select patients with favorable, localized prostate cancer. About half of these patients remain free of progression at 10 years, and definitive treatment appeared effective in those with progression.** Consistent with the study by Carter and associates (2002), we found that **absence of cancer on repeated needle biopsy early after initial diagnosis identified cases unlikely to progress during 10 years.**

The University of Toronto conducted a prospective phase II study of AS (Klotz, 2004). The cohort consisted of 299 patients with good-risk prostate cancer or intermediate-risk prostate cancer in men older than 70 years. Baseline PSA level was less than 15 ng/mL, Gleason sum 7 or lower, and clinical stage T2b or lower. Patients were observed until they met specific criteria defining rapid or clinically significant progression. These criteria were as follows:

1. PSA progression, defined by all of three conditions: PSA doubling time (PSADT) of 2 years or less, final PSA level of more than 8 ng/mL, and *P* < .05 from a regression analysis of ln(PSA) on time;
2. clinical progression, defined by meeting any of four conditions: more than a doubling of the product of the maximum perpendicular diameters of the primary lesion as measured by DRE, local progression of prostate cancer requiring transurethral resection of the prostate, development of ureteral obstruction, and radiologic or clinical evidence of distant metastasis; and
3. histologic progression, namely, Gleason sum 8 or higher on repeated biopsy of the prostate at 12 to 18 months.

Patients who had progression were offered radical intervention; those without progression were closely monitored. Median PSADT was 7.0 years, and 35% of the men had a

PSADT of more than 10 years. **At a median follow-up of 55 months, 60% of patients remained on AS;** 12% came off surveillance because of rapid biochemical progression, 8% because of clinical progression, 4% because of histologic progression, and 16% because of the patient's preference. **At 8 years, overall actuarial survival was 85%, and disease-specific survival was 99%.** The two patients who died of prostate cancer did so 5 years or longer after diagnosis. Of the 299 men in this study, 24 were treated with radical prostatectomy for a PSADT of 2 years or less. Final pathologic examination demonstrated pT2 cancer in 10 (42%), pT3a-c in 14 (58%), and node-positive disease in 2 (8%). The investigators concluded that most men with favorable-risk prostate cancer will die of unrelated causes. They suggested that an approach of AS based on PSADT represents a practical compromise between radical therapy in all, which results in overtreatment in patients with indolent disease, and watchful waiting with palliative therapy only, which results in undertreatment in those with aggressive disease.

For Men on Active Surveillance, What Are the Factors Predicting Progression?

An assumption of AS is that signs of progression can be identified while the cancer is still curable. A variety of clinical criteria have been investigated in an attempt to define those patients requiring treatment and those still suitable for AS. Serial serum PSA testing, including free and total levels, has been examined by a number of investigators (Gerber et al, 1998; Choo et al, 2001, 2002; Do et al, 2002; Stephenson et al, 2002; de Vries et al, 2004; Klotz, 2004; Panagiotou et al, 2004). Gerber and associates (1998) examined changes in serum PSA levels with time in 49 men (mean age, 72 years) with untreated clinically localized prostate cancer. All patients had at least three PSA levels measured at intervals of at least 6 months. **The investigators found significant variability in the rate of change of PSA with time.** They concluded that changes in PSA level may not be helpful in determining the need for therapy in men on AS.

Numerous studies have examined the role of PSADT as a prognostic factor in men on AS, with the majority identifying PSADT as a predictor of progression. Choo and associates (2002) observed 206 men with clinically localized prostate cancer managed with AS for a median of 29 months. PSADT was estimated from a linear regression of ln(PSA) on time, assuming a single exponential growth model. The median PSADT was 6.68 years, with 42% of patients having a PSADT of 10 years or longer. These investigators suggest that the definition of progression for men on AS include a PSADT of less than 2 years on the basis of at least three separate measurements during a minimum of 6 months. This PSADT may, however, be too short, as six of nine men who underwent radical prostatectomy had extraprostatic disease. Further concern about PSADT as a predictor of progression for men on AS comes from a study that examined PSADT before radical prostatectomy (Egawa et al, 2000). In this study, men with a PSADT of 3 years or less were more likely to have stage pT3 cancer at surgery, and 3 of 19 men with a PSADT longer

than 6 years had pT3 cancer, two of them with positive nodes. These studies suggest that **although PSADT is a predictor of cancer progression for men on AS, the exact trigger point at which to recommend treatment requires further investigation.**

Other PSA values, including free/total PSA ratio, PSA density, and PSA velocity, have been investigated for their potential to characterize disease progression (Do et al, 2002; Khan et al, 2003). None has yet demonstrated benefit in routine practice, although investigators are examining whether the rate of change in these variables can improve their predictive accuracy.

Although all AS studies have included periodic DRE as part of routine follow-up, none has found this to be an independent predictor of cancer progression. DRE is therefore unlikely to provide prognostic benefit if serial PSA measurements and prostate biopsy specimens are taken. In addition, DRE is subjective, and there is significant inter-examiner variation. **It remains important, however, as an indicator that a repeated prostate biopsy is warranted during AS** and in clinical staging and the prediction of outcome if active treatment is recommended.

Serial imaging studies have also proved to be of limited value in the AS population. The value of serial 6-monthly transrectal ultrasonography was examined in 174 men in a prospective study of AS (Hruby et al, 2001). Findings on transrectal ultrasonography were scored as consistent with clinical progression if they demonstrated a new or enlarging hypoechoic peripheral zone lesion or a 30% or greater increase in overall prostate volume at the time of progression. The group of 28 men who progressed to require radical intervention underwent 83 transrectal ultrasound examinations (median, three per patient). Of these 28 men, only 7 had changes on transrectal ultrasonography that were regarded as consistent with progression; in all 7, the change was the growth of an existing nodule or the appearance of a new nodule. In only one case was this accompanied by an increase of 30% or more in gland volume. In the 136 men who underwent two or more serial transrectal ultrasound examinations, there was no correlation between changes in either gland volume or the number of peripheral zone hypoechoic lesions and the rate of change of PSA. The investigators concluded that serial transrectal ultrasonography is of limited value as a determinant of disease progression in men with known but untreated prostate cancer.

The role of serial pelvic imaging with either computed tomography or endorectal magnetic resonance imaging has not been investigated but is likely to be limited. These men are at low risk for macroscopic extraprostatic disease, so interval changes in any of these examinations are unlikely. Improvement in imaging tools to better characterize intraprostatic disease is needed before serial imaging can be routinely recommended for men on AS.

Yap and coworkers (2003) assessed the role of serial bone scans in the AS population at the University of Toronto. This aspect of their AS study included 244 eligible patients. Bone scintigraphy was repeated annually for the first 2 years, then every 2 years thereafter if the patient remained on AS. If the follow-up PSA level was above 15 ng/mL, the patient underwent bone scintigraphy annually. During follow-up (median, 30 months), 299 bone scans were taken. All 299 were negative for bone metastasis. The probability of a normal bone scan was estimated to be 88% to 100% (95% confidence interval) when PSA level is below 15 ng/mL. The investigators concluded that bone scans are unnecessary for men on AS. The role of serial bone scintigraphy remains undefined even for men with a PSA level above 15 ng/mL.

Repeated prostate biopsies are considered an important aspect of continued evaluation of men managed with AS, not only to identify men with cancer progression but also to identify men unlikely to progress. In our cohort of 88 men on AS, an abnormal finding on second biopsy was the most significant prognostic factor for progression (Patel et al, 2004) (Fig. 96–4*B*). Progression occurred in 5 of the 43 men (11%) who had a first repeated biopsy that was negative for cancer, compared with 12 of 27 (40%) with an abnormal finding on first repeated biopsy (*P* = .004). **Actuarial progression-free probability at 5 years was 83% in patients with normal findings on repeated biopsy compared with 43% in those with abnormal findings on repeated biopsy.** An increase in Gleason sum was noted in 59% of patients with any cancer on repeated biopsy. Increases in Gleason sum, the number of positive cores, or areas containing cancer could be due to cancer growth or sampling error on previous biopsy (Epstein et al, 2001). Of 17 patients undergoing radical prostatectomy, 15 had higher Gleason sums in the prostatectomy specimen than in the initial biopsy specimen.

SUMMARY

Patients with a life expectancy (based on age and comorbidities) of less than 10 years and cancer with Gleason score of 6 or lower may be suitable for watchful waiting, especially if clinical stage and PSA values are favorable. Cancer progression and prostate cancer death are unlikely in this group of patients (see Table 96–4). Routine PSA testing is less important in the management of these patients, and follow-up radiographic studies or biopsies are not performed according to any predetermined schedule. Intervention is palliative and delayed until symptoms develop.

AS appears to be feasible in many men diagnosed with prostate cancer. Studies suggest that **AS may be a safe alternative to immediate treatment in compliant men with a low risk of cancer progression.** Fewer than half of such patients have progression on long-term follow-up, and treatment appears to be effective in those whose cancers do progress. More detailed recommendations cannot be given at this point because of our current inability to predict the course of the disease with certainty. Major areas of future study include identification of appropriate baseline clinical parameters to select men for AS, such as the nomogram shown in Figure 96–3, as well as appropriate follow-up regimens and definitions of progression. PSADT and repeated prostate biopsy appear to be critical to defining progression. With appropriate selection of patients, close follow-up, and selective use of local therapies in those with local cancer progression, AS is an acceptable choice for the management of selected patients with low-risk, early-stage prostate cancer.

KEY POINTS: EXPECTANT MANAGEMENT OF PROSTATE CANCER

- Many prostate cancers pose little risk to life or health.

- Low-risk prostate cancer can be identified, with high probability, by any of several models based on various combinations of biopsy Gleason grade, amount of cancer in biopsy cores, and PSA level, PSA density, or ratio of free to total PSA.

- The goal of watchful waiting is to allow men with low-risk cancer to avoid radical treatment and the associated morbidity. Palliative treatment is offered on the development of symptoms.

- For patients with early-stage prostate cancer managed by watchful waiting, the probability of death from cancer is low for the first 10 years from diagnosis but rises rapidly during the next 10 years.

- Watchful waiting is a reasonable option in patients with a life expectancy of less than 10 years and clinically localized, well-differentiated or moderately well differentiated prostate cancer.

- Active surveillance with selective delayed definitive therapy (AS) involves careful monitoring of men with prostate cancer. Definitive therapy is recommended to men who show signs of rapid cancer progression.

- Men on AS should be monitored by periodic PSA measurements, DRE, and prostate biopsy.

- Decreased PSA doubling time and increased Gleason sum or amount of cancer on repeated biopsy indicate that definitive therapy may be warranted. Absence of cancer on repeated biopsy is a strong indicator that the cancer is unlikely to progress.

- Long-term outcomes for patients on AS are not yet available, but the majority of patients remain on AS and free of progression at 4 years after diagnosis. Definitive therapy appears to be effective in the majority of patients who have progression.

SUGGESTED READINGS

Albertsen PC, Hanley JA, Gleason DF, Barry MJ: Competing risk analysis of men aged 55 to 74 years at diagnosis managed conservatively for clinically localized prostate cancer. JAMA 1998;280:975-980.

Albertsen PC, Hanley JA, Fine J: 20-year outcomes following conservative management of clinically localized prostate cancer. JAMA 2005;293:2095-2101.

Klotz L: Active surveillance with selective delayed intervention: Using natural history to guide treatment in good risk prostate cancer. J Urol 2004;172:S48-S50; discussion S50-S41.

Patel MI, DeConcini DT, Lopez-Corona E, et al: An analysis of men with clinically localized prostate cancer who deferred definitive therapy. J Urol 2004;171:1520-1524.

Anatomic Radical Retropubic Prostatectomy

PATRICK C. WALSH, MD • ALAN W. PARTIN, MD, PHD

There is no better way to cure cancer that is confined to the prostate than total surgical removal. Radical prostatectomy is the only form of treatment for localized prostate cancer that has been shown in a randomized controlled trial to reduce progression to metastases and death from the disease (Holmberg et al, 2002). Furthermore, on the basis of improved understanding of the periprostatic anatomy, today there is less bleeding and improved rates of postoperative continence and potency (Walsh, 1998, 2000).

The open surgical approach to radical prostatectomy has recently been challenged by advocates of laparoscopic and robotic techniques. It is our opinion that the open procedure is still the "gold standard" providing the best outcomes in terms of cancer control and quality of life.

Technically, radical retropubic prostatectomy is one of the most difficult operations in the field of urology. **The three goals of the surgeon, in order of importance, are cancer control, preservation of urinary control, and preservation of sexual function.** Great skill and experience in the selection of surgical candidates and operative technique are necessary to achieve all three. This chapter summarizes our 30-year experience with the hope that it will shorten the reader's learning curve. A video demonstrating a detailed description of the surgical technique is available (Walsh and Garcia, 2004).

SURGICAL ANATOMY
Venous and Arterial Anatomy

The veins of the prostate drain into Santorini's plexus. It is necessary to have a complete understanding of these veins to avoid excessive bleeding and to ensure a bloodless field in exposing the membranous urethra and the apex of the prostate. **The deep dorsal vein leaves the penis under Buck's fascia between the corpora cavernosa and penetrates the urogenital diaphragm, dividing into three major branches: the superficial branch and the right and left lateral venous plexuses** (Reiner and Walsh, 1979) (Fig. 97–1). The superficial branch, which travels between the puboprostatic ligaments, is the centrally located vein overlying the bladder neck and prostate. This vein is easily visualized early in retropubic operations and has communicating branches over the bladder itself and into the endopelvic fascia. The superficial branch lies outside the anterior prostatic fascia.

The common trunk and lateral venous plexuses are covered and concealed by the prostatic and endopelvic fascia. The lateral venous plexuses traverse posterolaterally and communicate freely with the pudendal, obturator, and vesical plexuses. Near the puboprostatic ligaments, small branches from the lateral plexus often penetrate the pelvic sidewall musculature and communicate with the internal pudendal vein. The lateral plexus interconnects with other venous systems to form the inferior vesical vein, which empties into the internal iliac vein. With the complex of veins and plexuses anastomosing freely, any laceration of these friable structures can lead to considerable blood loss.

The prostate receives arterial blood supply from the inferior vesical artery. According to Flocks (1937), after the inferior vesical artery provides small branches to the seminal vesicle and the base of the bladder and prostate, the artery terminates in two large groups of prostatic vessels: the urethral and capsular groups (Fig. 97–2). The urethral vessels enter the prostate at the posterolateral vesicoprostatic junction and supply the vesical neck and periurethral portion of the gland. The capsular branches run along the pelvic sidewall in the lateral pelvic fascia posterolateral to the prostate, providing branches that course ventrally and dorsally to supply the outer portion of the prostate. The capsular vessels terminate as a small cluster of vessels that supply the pelvic floor. On histologic examination, the capsular arteries and veins are

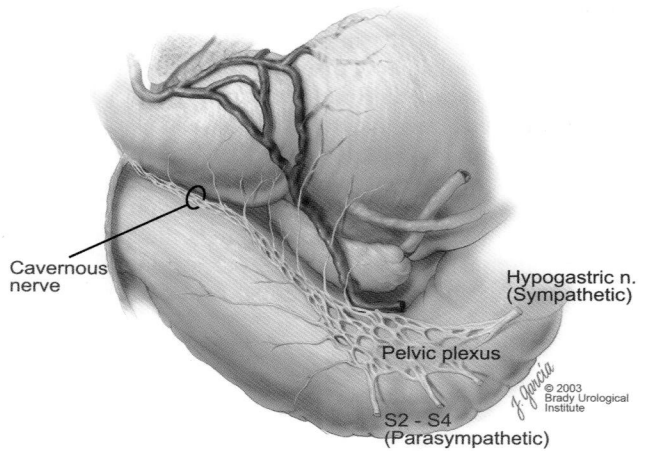

Figure 97–1. Location of the superficial and deep branches of the dorsal vein as they travel over the anterior and anterolateral surfaces of the prostate. Note the common trunk located immediately over the urethra. This is the site where the dorsal vein is transected. The pelvic plexus: The autonomic innervation of the pelvic organs arises from the pelvic plexus, which is formed by parasympathetic fibers that arise from the sacral center (S2 to S4) and sympathetic fibers via the hypogastric nerve from the thoracolumbar center. The pelvic plexus provides visceral branches that innervate the bladder, ureter, seminal vesicles, prostate, rectum, membranous urethra, and corpora cavernosa. The branches that innervate the corpora cavernosa enter in a spray-like distribution 20 to 30 mm distal to the junction of the prostate and bladder, where they continue distally posterolateral to the prostate.

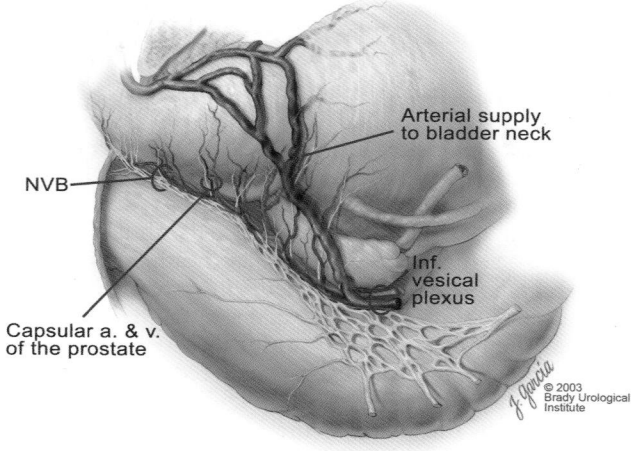

Figure 97–2. Arterial supply to the prostate. The inferior vesical artery terminates in two large groups of vessels. One group, called the urethral vessels, enters the prostate at the posterolateral vesicoprostatic junction to supply the bladder neck and periurethral portions of the gland. The second group, the capsular branches, runs along the pelvic sidewall in the lateral pelvic fascia posterolateral to the prostate, providing branches that course ventrally and dorsally to supply the outer portion of the prostate. These capsular arteries and veins are intimately associated with the branches of the pelvic plexus forming the neurovascular bundle (NVB) that is used as the macroscopic landmark to aid in the identification of the microscopic branches of these nerves. Note at the apex that small branches of the nerves travel anteriorly away from the vessels.

surrounded by an extensive network of nerves (Walsh and Donker, 1982; Walsh et al, 1983; Lue et al, 1984; Lepor et al, 1985). These capsular vessels provide the macroscopic landmark to aid in the identification of the microscopic branches of the pelvic plexus that innervate the corpora cavernosa.

The major arterial supply to the corpora cavernosa is derived from the internal pudendal artery. However, **pudendal arteries can arise from the obturator, inferior vesical, and superior vesical arteries. Because these aberrant branches travel along the lower part of the bladder and anterolateral surface of the prostate, they are divided during radical prostatectomy.** This may compromise arterial supply to the penis, especially in older patients with borderline penile blood flow (Breza et al, 1989; Polascik and Walsh, 1995; Rogers et al, 2004).

Pelvic Plexus

The autonomic innervation of the pelvic organs and external genitalia arises from the pelvic plexus, which is formed by parasympathetic, visceral, efferent, preganglionic fibers that arise from the sacral center (S2 to S4) and sympathetic fibers via the hypogastric nerve from the thoracolumbar center (Walsh and Donker, 1982; Lue et al, 1984; Lepor et al, 1985; Schlegel and Walsh, 1987) (see Fig. 97–1). The pelvic plexus in men is located retroperitoneally beside the rectum 5 to 11 cm from the anal verge and forms a fenestrated rectangular plate that is in the sagittal plane with its midpoint at the level of the tip of the seminal vesicle.

The branches of the inferior vesical artery and vein that supply the bladder and prostate perforate the pelvic plexus. For this reason, ligation of the so-called lateral pedicle in its

midportion not only interrupts the vessels but also transects the nerve supply to the prostate, urethra, and corpora cavernosa. The pelvic plexus provides visceral branches that innervate the bladder, ureter, seminal vesicles, prostate, rectum, membranous urethra, and corpora cavernosa. In addition, branches that contain somatic motor axons travel through the pelvic plexus to supply the levator ani, coccygeus, and striated urethral musculature. **The nerves innervating the prostate travel outside the capsule of the prostate and Denonvilliers' fascia until they perforate the capsule where they enter the prostate.**

The branches to the membranous urethra and corpora cavernosa also travel outside the prostatic capsule in the lateral pelvic fascia dorsolaterally between the prostate and rectum (see Fig. 97–1). Although these nerves are microscopic, their anatomic location can be estimated intraoperatively by use of the capsular vessels as a landmark. This structure, which is referred to here as the neurovascular bundle, has been termed the *neurovascular bundle of Walsh* (Stedman's Medical Dictionary, 2000) (see Fig. 97–2). As emphasized by Takenaka and colleagues (2004) and Costello and associates (2004), the cavernous branches join the capsular arteries and veins in a spray-like distribution to form the neurovascular bundle 20 to 30 mm distal to the junction of the bladder and prostate (see Fig. 97–2). The neurovascular bundles are located in the lateral pelvic fascia *between* the prostatic fascia and the levator fascia. At the apex of the prostate, the branches of the nerves to the cavernous bodies and striated sphincter also have a spray-like distribution both anteriorly and posteriorly with wide variation (Costello et al, 2004; Takenaka et al, 2005a). After piercing the urogenital diaphragm, they pass behind the dorsal penile artery and dorsal penile nerve before entering the corpora cavernosa (Walsh and Donker, 1982).

Striated Urethral Sphincter

The external sphincter, at the level of the membranous urethra, is often depicted as a "sandwich" of muscles in the horizontal plane. However, Oelrich (1980) demonstrated clearly that the striated urethral sphincter with its surrounding fascia is a vertically oriented tubular sheath that surrounds the membranous urethra. In utero, this sphincter extends without interruption from the bladder to the perineal membrane. As the prostate develops from the urethra, it invades and thins the sphincter muscle, causing a reduction or atrophy of some of the muscle (Fig. 97–3).

In the adult, the fibers at the apex of the prostate are horseshoe shaped and form a tubular, striated sphincter surrounding the membranous urethra. Near the apex of the prostate, the edges fuse in the midline posteriorly (Fig. 97–4A). Thus, as Myers (1987) has shown, the prostate does not rest on a flat, transverse urogenital diaphragm like an apple on a shelf, with no striated muscle proximal to the apex. Rather, the external striated sphincter is more tubular and has broad attachments over the fascia of the prostate near the apex. This has important implications in the apical dissection and reconstruction of the urethra for preservation of urinary control postoperatively (Walsh et al, 1990).

The striated sphincter contains fatigue-resistant, slow-twitch fibers that are responsible for passive urinary control. Active continence is achieved by voluntary contraction of the levator ani musculature, which surrounds the apex of the prostate and membranous urethra. Some fibers of the levator ani (levator urethrae, pubourethralis) surround the

proximal urethra and the apex of the prostate and insert into the perineal body in the midline posteriorly (Myers, 1991, 1994). **The pudendal nerve provides the major nerve supply to the striated sphincter and levator ani.** When patients are instructed to perform sphincter exercises postoperatively, they are actually contracting the levator ani musculature. However, because the striated urethral sphincter has similar innervation, patients are exercising this important muscle as well. Somatic motor nerves traveling through the pelvic plexus provide additional innervation to the pelvic floor musculature (Zvara et al, 1994; Costello et al, 2004, Takenaka et al, 2005a).

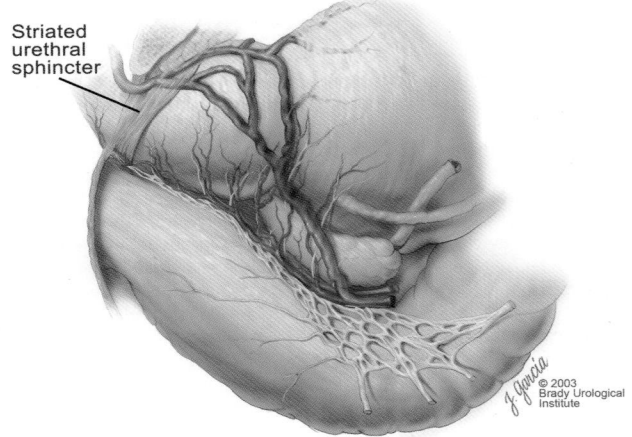

Figure 97–3. The striated urethral sphincter with its surrounding fascia is a vertically oriented tubular sheath that surrounds the membranous urethra. The dorsal vein complex travels through the sphincteric complex.

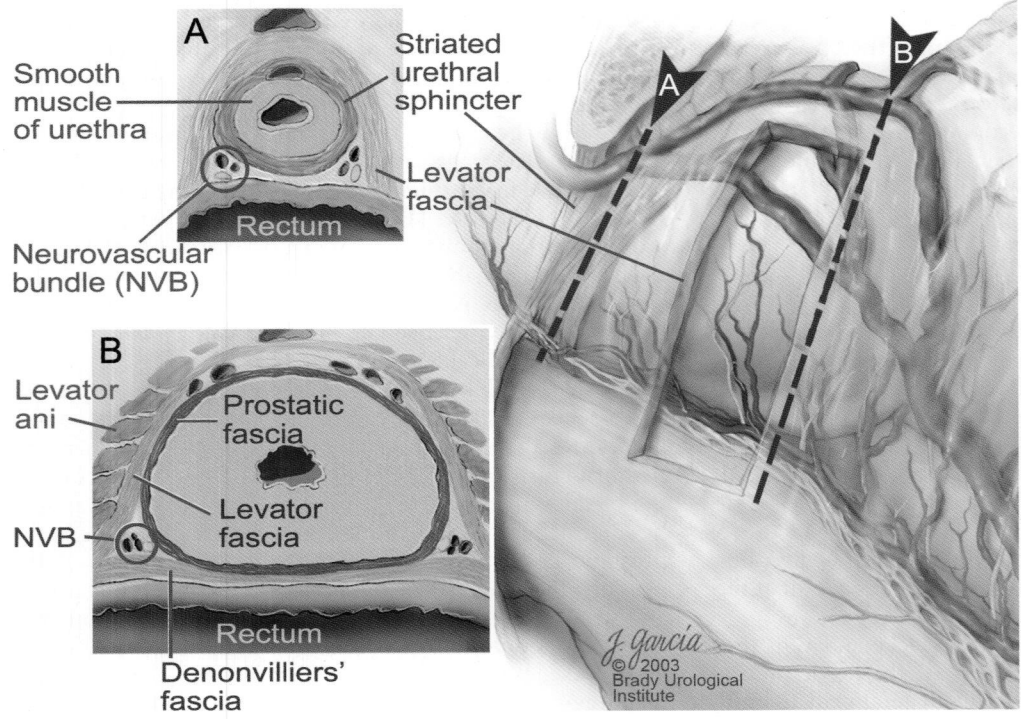

Figure 97–4. A, A cross section through the apex of the prostate demonstrating the relationship between the fascia surrounding the striated sphincter, the striated sphincter, and the smooth muscle of the urethra. Note that at this level, the striated sphincter circumferentially surrounds the urethra. Note that the neurovascular bundles are posterolateral to the circumferential striated sphincter. **B,** A cross section through the midportion of the prostate demonstrating the relationship between the levator fascia, Denonvilliers' fascia, and prostatic fascia. Note that the neurovascular bundles are located between the layers of the levator fascia and prostatic fascia. In performing a proper nerve-sparing operation, the prostatic fascia must remain on the prostate.

Pelvic Fascia

The prostate is covered with three distinct and separate fascial layers: Denonvilliers' fascia, the prostatic fascia, and the levator fascia. Denonvilliers' fascia is a filmy, delicate layer of connective tissue located between the anterior walls of the rectum and prostate (Fig. 97–4B). This fascial layer extends cranially to cover the posterior surface of the seminal vesicles and lies snugly against the posterior prostatic capsule. This fascia is most prominent and dense near the base of the prostate and the seminal vesicles and thins dramatically as it extends caudally to its termination at the striated urethral sphincter. On microscopic examination, it is impossible to discern "posterior" and "anterior" layers of this fascia (Jewett et al, 1972). For this reason, one must excise this fascia completely to obtain an adequate surgical margin.

In addition to Denonvilliers' fascia, the prostate is also invested with the prostatic fascia and levator fascia. Anteriorly and anterolaterally, the prostatic fascia is in direct continuity with the true capsule of the prostate. The major tributaries of the dorsal vein of the penis and Santorini's plexus travel within the anterior prostatic fascia. Laterally, the prostatic fascia fuses with the levator fascia, which covers the pelvic musculature, to form the lateral pelvic fascia (Fig. 90–5) (Myers, 1991, 1994). Posterolaterally, the levator fascia separates from the prostate to travel immediately adjacent to the pelvic musculature surrounding the rectum. **The prostate receives its blood supply and autonomic innervation between the layers of the levator fascia and prostatic fascia** (see Figs. 97–4B and 97–5).

In an effort to avoid injury to the dorsal vein of the penis and Santorini's plexus during radical perineal prostatectomy, the lateral and anterior pelvic fasciae are reflected off the prostate. This accounts for the reduced blood loss associated with radical perineal prostatectomy. In performing radical retropubic prostatectomy, the prostate is approached from outside these fascial investments. For this reason, the dorsal vein complex must be ligated and the lateral pelvic fascia must be divided (Walsh et al, 1983).

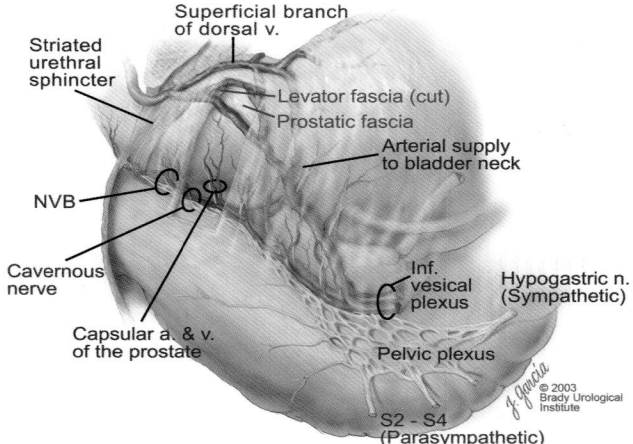

Figure 97–5. A lateral view illustrating that the prostate receives its blood supply and autonomic innervation between the layers of the levator fascia and prostatic fascia. NVB, neurovascular bundle.

SURGICAL TECHNIQUE
Preoperative Preparation

Surgery is deferred for 6 to 8 weeks after needle biopsy of the prostate and 12 weeks after transurethral resection of the prostate. This delay enables inflammatory adhesions or hematomas to resolve so that the anatomic relationships between the prostate and the surrounding structures return to a nearly normal state before surgery. This is especially important if one hopes to preserve the neurovascular bundles intraoperatively and avoid rectal injury.

During this delay, patients may be offered the opportunity to donate autologous blood. While donating blood and immediately before surgery, patients should avoid taking high doses of vitamin E, aspirin, or nonsteroidal anti-inflammatory agents that interfere with platelet function. Patients are prescribed a clear liquid diet on the day before surgery, are requested to drink half a bottle of magnesium citrate in the evening, and have an enema on the morning of surgery. They are admitted to the hospital on that day. One dose of a first-generation cephalosporin is administered before the incision is made.

Special Instruments

Unlike radical perineal prostatectomy, radical retropubic prostatectomy requires few special instruments. A fiberoptic headlight is most useful because much of the procedure is performed beneath the pubis in an area where visualization can be difficult. A standard Balfour retractor with both narrow and wide malleable blades is useful during lymph node dissection and is necessary during radical prostatectomy to provide cranial and posterior retraction on the peritoneum and bladder. Coagulating forceps, small fine and regular right-angled clamps, Metzenbaum and Jamison scissors, and 2.5- to 4.5-power loupes are the only other specialized instruments that should be available.

Anesthesia, Incision, and Lymphadenectomy

A spinal or epidural anesthetic is preferable for this procedure. **Regional anesthesia is associated with less blood loss and a lower frequency of pulmonary emboli** (Peters and Walsh, 1985; Shir et al, 1995). The anesthesiologist is encouraged to maintain relative hypotension with systolic blood pressure of no more than 100 mm Hg and to limit the replacement of crystalloid to 1500 mL until the prostate is removed (Davies et al, 2004). The patient is placed in the supine position. We no longer routinely break the table. Exposure is more than adequate with the patient lying flat, and there appears to be less tension on the rectus muscles and peritoneum, resulting in a more rapid postoperative recovery with less pain and ileus.

The skin is prepared and draped in the usual way. A No. 16 Silastic Foley catheter is passed into the bladder, inflated with 20 mL of saline, and connected to sterile, closed, continuous drainage. The use of a 16 French catheter facilitates placement of sutures in the mucosa of the urethra. A right-handed surgeon always stands on the left side of the patient.

A midline, extraperitoneal, lower abdominal incision is made extending from the pubis to halfway to the umbilicus. This short incision (8 cm) provides excellent exposure because the rectus muscles are separated maximally by the retractor at the pubis. There are only two circumstances in which the incision is inadequate: to palpate the lateral surface of the prostate, it is often necessary to remove the Balfour retractor temporarily; if the prostate is very large, it may be necessary to remove the malleable blade while excising the seminal vesicles. The anterior fascia is incised down to the pubis, but the posterior fascia is left intact. The rectus muscles are separated in the midline, and the transversalis fascia is opened sharply to expose Retzius' space. Laterally, the peritoneum is mobilized off the external iliac vessels to the bifurcation of the common iliac artery. **Care is taken to preserve the soft tissue covering the external iliac artery that contains the lymphatics draining the lower extremity. Interruption of these lymphatics may lead to lower extremity edema and lymphocele formation.** This maneuver is accomplished without dividing the vas deferens. Next, a self-retaining Balfour retractor is placed. Exposure for the lymph node dissection is facilitated by placement of a narrow, malleable blade attached to the Balfour retractor beneath the mobilized vas deferens to displace the peritoneum superiorly and a deep Deaver retractor to retract the bladder medially. Previously, when the vas deferens was routinely divided, some patients complained of persistent testicular pain that we attributed to excessive traction on the spermatic cord during this maneuver. However, if the vas deferens is not divided, the traction on the spermatic cord is absorbed by the vas deferens, and persistent testalgia is rare.

The pelvic lymph node dissection is performed before the radical prostatectomy. The dissection is initiated on the ipsilateral side of the major tumor in the prostate by dividing the adventitia over the external iliac vein (Fig. 97–6). The lymphatics overlying the external iliac artery are preserved. The dissection proceeds beneath the external iliac vein out to the pelvic sidewall and then inferiorly to the femoral canal, where the lymphatic channels are ligated at a convenient point. There is no need to remove Cloquet's node. The dissection then proceeds superiorly along the pelvic sidewall to the bifurcation of the common iliac artery, where the lymph nodes in the angle between the external iliac and hypogastric arteries are removed. Next, the obturator lymph nodes are removed with care to avoid injury to the obturator nerve. The obturator artery and vein are skeletonized but are usually left undisturbed and are not ligated unless excessive bleeding occurs. The dissection then continues down to the pelvic floor, exposing the hypogastric veins. This extended dissection removes more lymph nodes than in a more limited dissection, improving staging and providing potential therapeutic benefit in some patients (Allaf et al, 2004; Palapattu et al, 2004). A similar procedure is performed on the opposite side. **If the patient has a well-differentiated to moderately well-differentiated tumor (Gleason grade below 8) and the lymph nodes are normal to palpation, frozen-section analysis is not performed** (Sgrignoli et al, 1994; Cadeddu et al, 1997).

Exposure

To expose the anterior surface of the prostate, it is necessary to displace the peritoneum superiorly. **We no longer place the balloon on the Foley catheter in the dome of the bladder beneath the malleable blade because we believe that excessive traction on the bladder may damage the detrusor musculature and thereby delay recovery of urinary continence.** Also, the short incision limits the amount of traction. A malleable blade is used to retract the peritoneum superiorly and to gently displace the bladder posteriorly.

Incision in Endopelvic Fascia

The fibroadipose tissue covering the prostate is carefully dissected away to expose the pelvic fascia, puboprostatic ligaments, and superficial branch of the dorsal vein.

The endopelvic fascia is entered where it reflects over the pelvic sidewall, well away from its attachments to the bladder and prostate (Fig. 97–7). The point of incision is where the fascia is transparent, revealing the underlying levator ani musculature. After the fascia has been opened, one can usually visualize the bulging lateral venous plexus of Santorini, which is located medially. Therefore, **an incision in the endopelvic fascia too close to the bladder or the prostate risks laceration of these veins, with potential severe blood loss.** Beneath this venous complex lie the prostatic arteries and the branches of the pelvic plexus that course toward the prostate, urethra, and corpora cavernosa.

The incision in the endopelvic fascia is then carefully extended in an anteromedial direction toward the puboprostatic ligaments. This allows the surgeon to palpate the lateral surface of the prostate. **At this point, one often encounters small arterial and venous branches from the pudendal vessels that perforate the pelvic musculature to supply the prostate. These vessels should be ligated with clips to avoid coagulation injury to the pudendal artery and nerve, which are located just deep to this muscle as they travel along the pubic ramus.** By finger dissection, the fibers of the levator ani

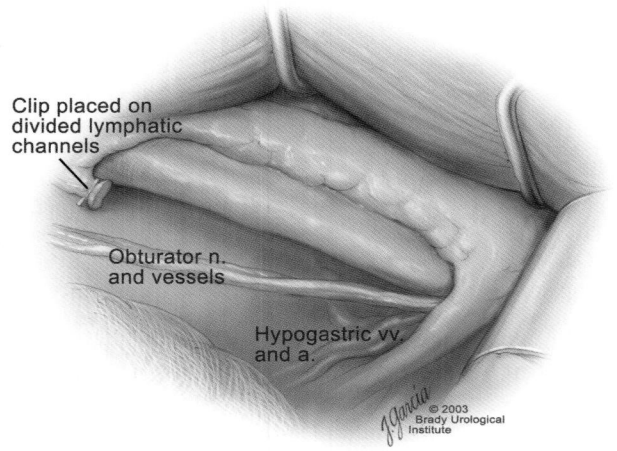

Clip placed on
divided lymphatic
channels

Obturator n.
and vessels

Hypogastric vv.
and a.

© 2003
Brady Urological
Institute

Figure 97–6. View of the right pelvis after completion of the staging pelvic lymph node dissection. Note that the fibroadipose tissue overlying the external iliac artery has not been disturbed and that the obturator nerve, obturator vessels, and hypogastric veins over the pelvic floor have been skeletonized.

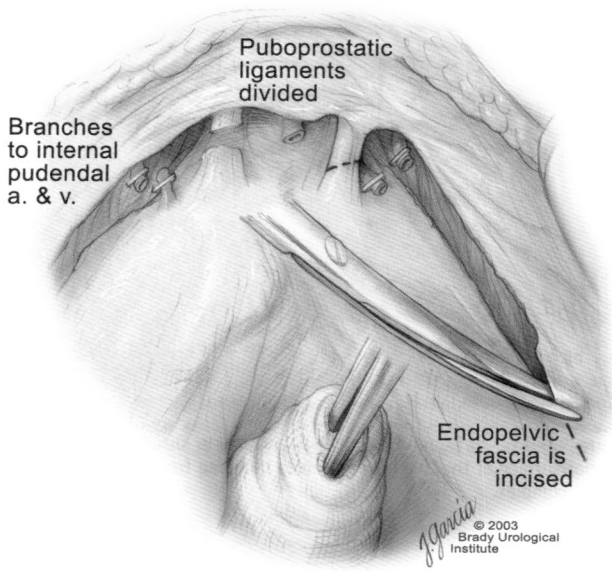

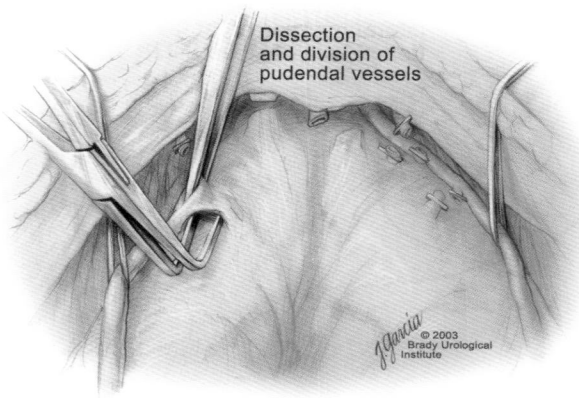

Figure 97–8. Preservation of bilateral large accessory pudendal arteries. The anterior prostatic fascia is elevated with a right-angled clamp to facilitate release of the accessory pudendal vessels.

Figure 97–7. Incision in the endopelvic fascia and division of the puboprostatic ligaments. The incision in the endopelvic fascia is made at the juncture with the pelvic sidewall well away from the prostate and bladder. Anteriorly, near the puboprostatic ligaments, small arterial and venous branches from the internal pudendal vessels have been clipped and divided. The puboprostatic ligaments are divided superficially far enough down to expose the juncture between the apex of the prostate and the anterior surface of the dorsal vein complex. However, the pubourethral component of the complex is intact to preserve anterior fixation of the striated sphincter to the pubis.

musculature are released from the lateral surface of the prostate down to the apex of the prostate.

Division of the Puboprostatic Ligaments

The fibrofatty tissue covering the superficial branch of the dorsal vein and puboprostatic ligaments is gently teased away to prepare for division of the ligaments without injury to the superficial branch of the dorsal vein. After the superficial branch has been dissected away from the medial edge of the ligaments, it is coagulated and divided. After all fibrofatty tissue has been removed, a sponge stick is used to displace the prostate posteriorly, and scissors are used to divide each ligament (see Fig. 97–7).

The dissection should continue down far enough to expose the juncture between the apex of the prostate and the anterior surface of the dorsal vein complex at the point where it will be divided. The pubourethral component of the complex must remain intact to preserve the anterior fixation of the striated urethral sphincter to the pubis (Burnett and Mostwin, 1998).

Preservation of Accessory Pudendal Arteries

Arterial insufficiency is a factor contributing to erectile dysfunction in patients after nerve-sparing radical retropubic

prostatectomy. One source for this insufficiency may arise from accessory pudendal arteries that travel over the anterolateral surface of the prostate. These arteries have been found in 70% of cadaveric dissections and in 7% of patients by selective internal pudendal angiography. In our experience, large visible accessory pudendal arteries are present in 4% of men (Rogers et al, 2004).

Because release of accessory arteries may be associated with significant blood loss necessitating prompt ligation and division of the dorsal vein complex, it is useful to have the contralateral dissection completed before accessory vessels are released. For this reason, when these vessels appear to be prominent and are present unilaterally, the endopelvic fascia and puboprostatic ligament on the contralateral side should be divided first. The surgical technique for preservation of the arteries begins with division of the endopelvic fascia lateral to the vessels and division of the puboprostatic ligament (the vessels are beneath the puboprostatic ligament). Next, a vessel loop is used to elevate the artery, and then with sharp dissection and a right-angled clamp, the accessory artery is released from its investing fascia (Fig. 97–8). As the dissection proceeds, venous tributaries are divided. At times, there may be substantial blood loss from the venous complex over the prostate; hemostasis, however, is usually easily obtained with a 2-0 running absorbable suture. The dissection must extend caudally beyond the site at which the dorsal vein complex will be divided.

Ligation of the Dorsal Vein Complex

The goal is to divide the complex with minimal blood loss while avoiding damage to the striated sphincter and inadvertent entry into the anterior apex of the prostate. With use of the sponge stick to push the prostate posteriorly, a 3-0 Monocryl suture is passed superficially through the dorsal vein complex just distal to the apex of the prostate (Fig. 97–9). In placing this stitch, the surgeon should face the head of the table, holding the needle driver against the pubis perpendicular to the patient. Next, the needle is reversed in the needle holder and the same suture is placed through the perichondrium of the pubic symphysis (Fig. 97–10). Once this

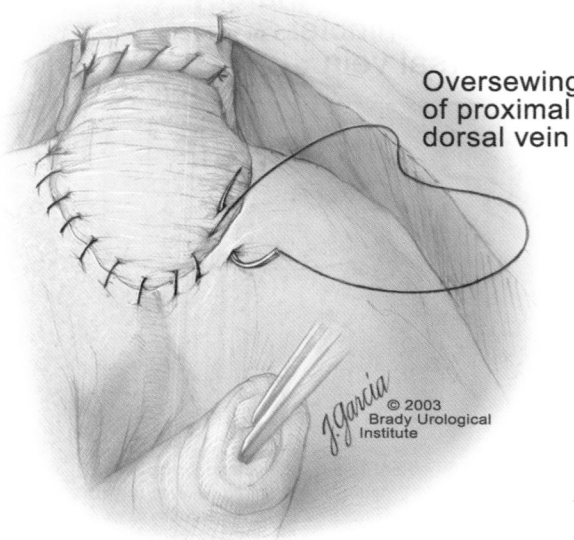

Figure 97–15. The dorsal vein complex over the anterior surface of the prostate is oversewn in the shape of a V with a running 2-0 absorbable suture.

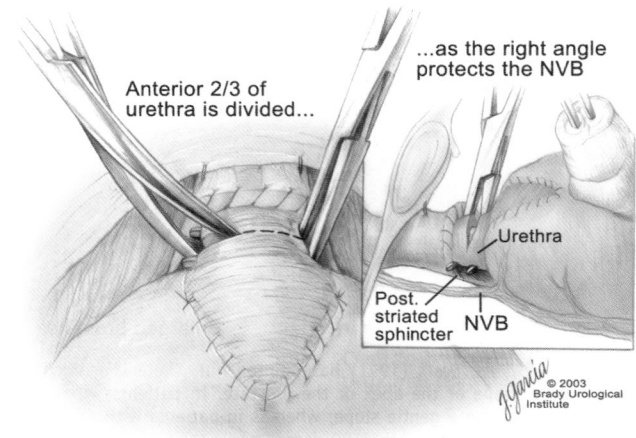

Figure 97–16. A right-angled clamp is placed around the smooth muscle of the urethra close to the apex of the prostate. Note in the inset that the neurovascular bundles (NVB) are protected from injury by the posterior component of the striated sphincter, which is still intact. Also see Figure 97–5.

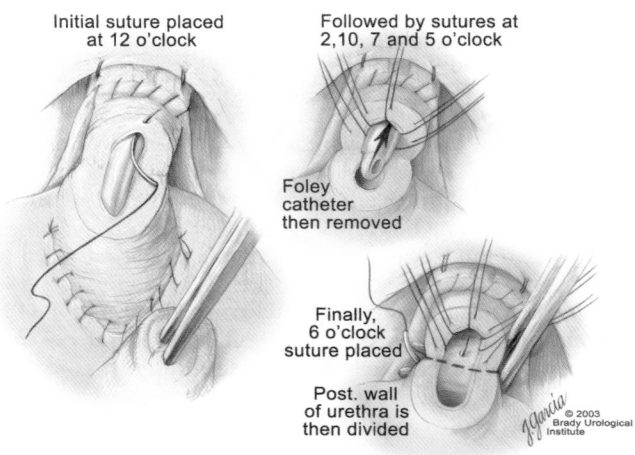

Figure 97–17. The 3-0 Monocryl sutures are placed in the distal urethral mucosa and submucosa at the 12-, 2-, 10-, 7-, and 5-o'clock positions. The Foley catheter is then removed, the 6-o'clock suture is placed, and the posterior wall of the urethra is divided.

up as much of the urethra as possible. A right-angled clamp is then passed around the smooth musculature of the urethra near the apex of the prostate to ensure that the urethra is transected as close to the apex as possible (Fig. 97–16). With scissors, the anterior two thirds of the urethra is divided with care to avoid damage to the Foley catheter. This provides excellent exposure for placement of five sutures in the distal urethral segment at the 12-, 2-, 5-, 7-, and 10-o'clock positions. With 3-0 Monocryl on a ⅝-circle tapered needle, **the needle should incorporate just the urethral mucosa and submucosa but not the smooth muscle** (Fig. 97–17). As stated previously, the surgeon should face the head of the table to place these sutures and should hold the needle driver against the pubis perpendicular to the patient. The first suture is placed in the mucosa and submucosa of the urethra at the 12-o'clock position. By use of a 16 French catheter, the mucosa is easily identified. The smooth muscle should not be incorporated in this stitch because stitches in the smooth muscle delay the recovery of urinary control. If the urethral tissue appears flimsy, this suture should then be placed through the dorsal vein complex to improve tensile strength. Once the mucosa and submucosa have been elevated by the 12-o'clock stitch, the remaining sutures are more easily placed. For a right-handed surgeon, it is easiest to place the 7- and 10-o'clock sutures from the outside of the lumen to the inside. The other three sutures are more easily placed beginning on the luminal surface and then proceeding outside. In performing the final anastomosis, a French eye needle can be used to place these three sutures through the lumen of the bladder. The sutures are covered with towels to avoid inadvertent traction or displacement.

After the sutures are placed, the catheter is removed. The 6-o'clock suture is placed through the mucosa of the urethra, from the outside to the inside. The posterior band of urethra is now divided to expose the posterior portion of the striated urethral sphincter complex (see Fig. 97–17). The posterior wall of the striated sphincter complex is composed of skeletal muscle and fibrous tissue. **Identification and precise division of this complex are important in (1) obtaining adequate margins of resection for apical lesions, (2) identifying the correct plane on the anterior wall of the rectum to ensure that all layers of Denonvilliers' fascia are excised, (3) avoiding blunt trauma to the neurovascular bundles that are located immediately posteriorly, and (4) preserving urinary continence.**

To divide the posterior portion of the sphincter safely, a right-angled clamp is passed immediately beneath the left edge of this complex (Fig. 97–18). The clamp should pass midway between the apex of the prostate and the urethra. If it is passed too close to the apex of the prostate, it may damage the neurovascular bundle. However, midway, the neurovascu-

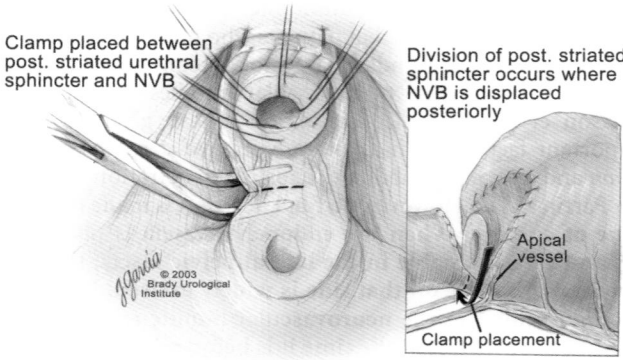

Figure 97–18. Division of the posterior component of the striated sphincter. A right-angled clamp is passed beneath the left edge of the striated sphincter midway between the apex of the prostate and urethra, at a site where the neurovascular bundles (NVB) have fallen posteriorly. After the left edge of the complex is divided, a right-angled clamp is then passed along the right edge and the maneuver is repeated.

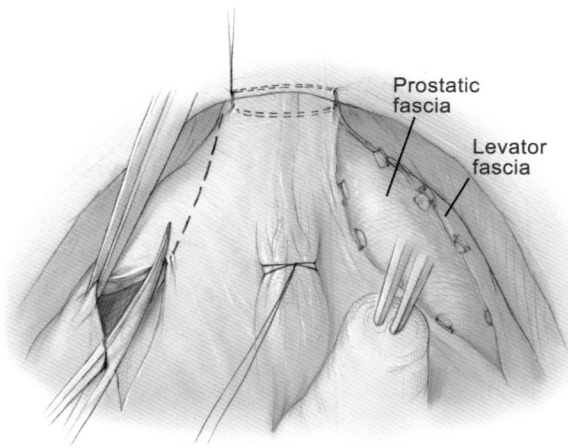

Figure 97–19. High anterior release of the levator fascia. The levator fascia over the anterior apex of the prostate is incised along the lateral edge of the dorsal vein complex, preserving the underlying prostatic fascia. The dissection extends distally beyond where the dorsal vein was ligated. Venous tributaries are controlled with clips. The dissection on the right side has been completed.

lar bundle is located more posteriorly and is beneath the right-angled clamp (Walsh et al, 2000b) (see Fig. 97–5).

The left border of the complex is then divided with scissors. Next, the right-angled clamp is placed beneath the right edge of the complex, and the complex is divided. It is necessary to divide the complex from each side because if one tries to divide the entire complex from one side, the contralateral neurovascular bundle may be damaged. Finally, the central component of the complex is divided.

High Anterior Release of the Neurovascular Bundles at the Apex before Division of the Dorsal Vein Complex. The purpose of this approach is to speed up the recovery of sexual function and continence by reducing traction on the branches of the nerves to the cavernous bodies and striated sphincter or avoiding inadvertent transection of the small branches that travel anteriorly (Costello et al, 2004; Takenaka et al, 2004, 2005a; Horninger et al, 2005; Menon et al, 2005; Montorsi et al, 2005). **However, because there is less soft tissue at the apex, the risk of positive surgical margins may be increased by this approach. Until this possibility has been fully evaluated, this approach should be used only in men who are likely to have organ-confined disease and who are candidates for bilateral nerve sparing (see later).**

The procedure begins after the dorsal vein has been ligated distally with 3-0 Monocryl but not divided and the proximal vessels oversewn with a 2-0 absorbable suture; these sutures should not be cut because they will be used later for hemostasis. The levator fascia over the anterior apex of the prostate is incised, as suggested by Takenaka (2005b), and the incision is extended distally along the lateral edge of the dorsal vein complex on the anterolateral surface of the prostate, preserving the underlying prostatic fascia (Fig. 97–19). **To identify the correct plane and to avoid inadvertent incision into the prostate, it is essential to have excellent visualization and magnification (4.5-power loupes).** In many patients, there will be venous tributaries that must be divided and controlled. Cautery should not be used. Instead, hemostasis should be achieved by use of small hemoclips. As the dissection proceeds distally, the levator fascia should be released from the lateral

shoulders of the prostate, with care taken not to enter the underlying prostatic fascia. Once the dissection has extended distally beyond where the dorsal vein was ligated, the dorsal vein is again ligated distally as far as possible with the 3-0 Monocryl suture, and the proximal dorsal vein is oversewn with the 2-0 chromic. With downward displacement of the prostate by the sponge stick, the dorsal vein complex is divided between the two ties down to the urethra as described previously. Because the levator fascia has previously been released, prominent neurovascular bundles can usually be visualized lateral to the urethra. Bleeding from the distal dorsal vein complex is controlled with the 3-0 Monocryl suture. Residual back-bleeding from the proximal dorsal vein on the anterior surface of the prostate is controlled with the 2-0 chromic suture. Because less of the striated sphincter is excised by this technique, the bleeding edges can usually be brought together in the midline. Next the urethra is transected, the urethral sutures are placed, and the posterior component of the striated sphincter is transected. At this point, any residual fragments of Denonvilliers' fascia should be released (Fig. 97–20). This approach avoids traction on the neurovascular bundles as they are released at the apex and makes the subsequent steps in preservation of the neurovascular bundles much easier.

Identification and Preservation or Wide Excision of the Neurovascular Bundles

Today, in most men who are candidates for surgery, it is safe to preserve both neurovascular bundles and rarely necessary to excise both of them (Walsh, 2001). With improved surgical techniques and the availability of phosphodiesterase type 5 inhibitors, most healthy potent men younger than 65 years should be potent after surgery. As discussed before, **the neurovascular bundle is outside the prostate between layers of lateral pelvic fascia (the levator fascia and prostatic fascia). If nerve sparing is performed correctly, the prostatic fascia must remain on the prostate. Furthermore, when cancer extends through the capsule, it rarely penetrates**

vesicle in its entirety when the dissection is difficult. This might eliminate the potentially damaging dissection near other important anatomic structures.

In a follow-up study, Theodorescu and colleagues (1998) looked at the importance of complete seminal vesicle excision by comparing radical retropubic prostatectomy with radical perineal prostatectomy. In two similar groups (stage, race, age, PSA level, and grade), 64% underwent radical retropubic prostatectomy and 36% underwent radical perineal prostatectomy (seminal vesicles are not routinely removed). In the follow-up period, 45% of the men in the perineal prostatectomy group demonstrated biochemical (PSA) elevation (>0.2 ng/mL) compared with only 18% in the retropubic prostatectomy group. When they broke down the perineal prostatectomy group on the basis of no seminal vesicle excision or seminal vesicle excision, the PSA recurrence rate was 69% versus 20%, respectively. The authors concluded that complete excision of the seminal vesicle during radical prostatectomy is essential for cancer control.

John and Hauri (2000) investigated the influence of seminal vesicle preservation during radical retropubic prostatectomy on urinary continence. They observed 54 men, of whom 34 underwent radical retropubic prostatectomy with seminal vesicle removal and 20 with seminal vesicle preservation. A modified pad test at 6 weeks and 6 months postoperatively demonstrated continence rates of 60% at 6 weeks and 95% at 6 months for the seminal vesicle preservation group compared with 18% at 6 weeks and 82% at 6 months for the seminal vesicle resected group. They concluded that seminal vesicle preservation may preclude damage to the pelvic nerves and maintain urinary continence during radical retropubic prostatectomy. Clearly, a double-blinded (patient and third-party reviewer) randomized trial of this method must be performed to fully understand these results.

The authors of this chapter do not perform seminal vesicle–sparing surgery.

Interposition Nerve Grafting

Although wide resection of both neurovascular bundles is rarely indicated when curative intent is the desired effect for anatomic radical prostatectomy (Walsh and Worthington, 2001a), investigators have suggested interposition sural nerve grafts after unilateral and bilateral neurovascular bundle resection during radical retropubic prostatectomy (Kim et al, 1999, 2001a, 2001b, 2001c; Scardino and Kim, 2001; Walsh, 2001b; Singh et al, 2004). Early studies in the rat (Quinlan et al, 1991a; Ball et al, 1992a, 1992b; Burgers et al, 1991) provided experimental evidence documenting the beneficial effect of interposition nerve grafting after unilateral or bilateral cavernous nerve damage or resection. However, in man, as opposed to the rat, the cavernous nerves are composed of many fibers that are separated by as much as 3 cm (Costello et al, 2004; Takenaka et al, 2004). This raises the legitimate question of whether it is possible to perform a classic end-to-end nerve graft. The precise pathophysiologic mechanism of cavernous nerve regeneration has yet to be fully understood; however, basic science studies and human clinical testing have suggested that return of parasympathetic function can be demonstrated after interposition grafting of the brachial plexus, facial nerves, and peripheral nerves.

It is universally accepted that preservation of erectile function after radical prostatectomy is quantitatively related to preservation of the autonomic innervation and that, with resection of both neurovascular bundles, recovery of erectile function satisfactory for spontaneous erection and intercourse is limited (Quinlan, 1991b). To this end, Kim and colleagues (1999) first suggested interposition sural nerve grafting at the time of anatomic radical prostatectomy to replace resected cavernous nerves. In this initial report, they described the first unilateral and bilateral grafting (Kim et al, 1999a). The same group, later that same year (Kim et al, 1999b), described nine sexually active men with locally extensive disease who underwent bilateral nerve-excising radical retropubic prostatectomy with bilateral sural nerve grafting. They demonstrated nocturnal penile tumescence with the RigiScan device at 4 to 6 months in two patients and sufficient erectile function return ("an erection of substance") in one man 14 months after surgery to allow him to have unassisted intercourse. In a later follow-up study, the same group (Kim et al, 2001a) demonstrated on 28 men with bilateral non–nerve-sparing radical prostatectomy who underwent bilateral sural nerve grafts with 12-month follow-up that 26% had unassisted erections sufficient for intercourse, 26% had partial erections, and 43% had erections sufficient for intercourse with the aid of sildenafil citrate. Sexual function returned 5 months after grafting at the earliest time. The control group, all of whom did not have nerve grafts, had no return of erectile function.

Typically, most urologists performing radical retropubic prostatectomy and neurovascular bundle excision or preservation require the participation of a plastic surgeon to perform the harvest and implantation of the nerve graft material. A difficulty of this combined approach is the need for finding common operative time and the need for precise timing of the procedures, which require careful scheduling of two surgeons. Kim and associates (2001b) suggested that with enough training and experience, the urologic oncologist performing the radical retropubic prostatectomy should feel comfortable with harvest of the nerve and placement of the graft. Their technique was demonstrated (Kim et al, 2001b) and increased operative time by only 15 minutes on average and added only 5 mL of blood loss. No wound infection (graft site) or significant sensory or affective changes to the graft site (leg) were noted.

Another group (Singh et al, 2004) investigated the return of urinary control with respect to sural nerve grafting. They reported a series of 111 men with purposeful unilateral nerve excision, 53 of whom underwent unilateral sural nerve graft after the prostatectomy. The median follow-up of this group was 26 and 12 months for the nongrafted and grafted groups, respectively, and a mailed questionnaire was used to ascertain erectile function. At 12 months, 95% of the grafted group reported "complete" urinary control (leakage of only a few drops) compared with only 53% of the nongrafted group ($P = .012$). The authors suggested that the cavernous nerves may play a role in return of continence. These findings have yet to be validated and should be viewed cautiously until a randomized study can be conducted.

Technically, the sural nerve (width of 1.5 to 3 mm, ovoid) graft is harvested with iris scissors through a 3-cm incision that is placed 1 cm inferior to the lateral malleolus. The saphenous vein will be encountered. Dissection should be carried out with loupe magnification. The nerve is divided at the distal end and the foot-side end fulgurated. A tendon stripper (6 mm in diameter) is used to strip the nerve proximally for about 20 cm toward the back of the calf, and a 1-cm incision is used to retrieve the proximal end. Fulguration of the proximal (leg) side of the nerve is also required. The graft is placed in cooled saline. The skin is closed, and compression stockings ensure decreased hematoma formation (Kim et al, 2001b). The average length of nerve needed per side is 5 to 6.5 cm; however, 40-cm segments can be isolated for bilateral procedures with minimal sensory deficit (Kim et al, 2001b). **The nerve graft is reversed, and the distal nerve is attached to the proximal cavernous nerve endings under magnification; similarly, the proximal nerve end is attached to the distal cavernous nerve endings.** The nerve endings can be identified at the time of resection and marked with a stitch through the use of the CaverMap nerve stimulator (Canto et al, 2001). The nerves are attached to the nerve endings with 7-0 polypropylene sutures secured with microclips. After the procedure, suction drains are placed and directed away from the graft site.

Although many questions remain with respect to the need for nerve grafting following wide excision of the neurovascular bundle after radical retropubic prostatectomy (Walsh, 2001a), the techniques have been demonstrated and the early results suggest that this is a safe and feasible method with adequate proof-of-principle for preservation of erectile function after wide excision (Scardino and Kim, 2001). The beneficial effect of bilateral nerve grafting has been demonstrated, yet we await the long-term cancer control data from this group. The true benefit of unilateral nerve grafting will require a randomized sham-controlled trial.

The authors of this chapter do not perform nerve-grafting surgery.

SALVAGE RADICAL PROSTATECTOMY

The goal of primary external beam radiation therapy (intensity modified or three-dimensional conformal) or primary brachytherapy in the treatment of clinically localized prostate cancer is to eradicate all tumor. Failure to achieve this goal leads to local progression, distant metastasis, and potentially death. The recognition of local recurrence after definitive radiation therapy is complex (American Society of Therapeutic Radiology and Oncology criteria, PSA nadir, PSA bump), yet all would agree that it portends a poor outcome with few options for salvage. This poor prognosis has led to development of several options to salvage cure: cryosurgery (Chapter 101), watchful waiting (Chapter 96), androgen deprivation (Chapter 104), and salvage prostatectomy. **Salvage radical prostatectomy has been used successfully to eradicate locally recurrent cancer after definitive radiotherapy, but complications are common** (Rogers et al, 1995; Cheng et al, 1998; Garzotto and Wajsman, 1998; Gheiler et al, 1998; Tefilli et al, 1998a, 1998b; reviewed by Chen and Wood, 2003; Stephenson et al, 2004; Ward et al, 2005). From the literature, several generalizations can be made:

- The procedure (salvage prostatectomy) is reserved for patients with excellent health and with a life expectancy of more than 15 years.
- Patients must have no evidence of metastatic disease.

- Salvage surgery should be offered only to men who at initial presentation had unequivocally clinically localized prostate cancer.
- Prostate biopsy, histologic grade, clinical examination findings, and serum PSA levels must continue to suggest localized disease.

In summary, candidates for salvage surgery should be unrecognizable from the candidates we would choose for initial therapy with radical retropubic prostatectomy and be highly motivated individuals who understand and accept the potentially higher morbidity associated with salvage surgery.

Scardino and associates (Rogers et al, 1995) have reported a large series (N = 80) with long-term outcome data for salvage radical prostatectomy. Early in their series, the estimated blood loss, transfusion requirements, and average length of stay in the hospital were greater than with standard classic radical prostatectomy. Since the mid-1990s, they have reported major improvements in the morbidity associated with this operation. **Whereas rectal injuries occurred in 15% of the first 39 cases, this morbidity is now rare** (Chen and Wood, 2003). **With complete bowel preparation (mechanical and intraluminal antimicrobial) before the operation, rectal injuries, if encountered, can be primarily repaired without altering postoperative recovery. Urinary incontinence rates remain high. Scardino and associates reported an estimated 58% with persistent leakage requiring two or more pads per day, and 20% required placement of an artificial urinary sphincter; 27% developed an anastomotic stricture** (Rogers et al, 1995). A summary of the published literature (1985-2000) regarding salvage prostatectomy (Chen and Wood, 2003) demonstrates that the length of hospital stay has dropped from 13 days to 3.2 days, mean estimated blood loss has remained stable around 1000 mL, overall incontinence (stress, total) rates have remained stable at nearly 50% and total incontinence rates have remained stable at 20% to 30%, rectal injury has decreased from 30% to nearly 6%, and bladder neck contracture has remained constant at 20% to 30%. Erectile dysfunction is nearly universal; however, sural nerve grafting (Kim et al, 2001a-c) has been suggested to improve potency after salvage surgery.

Another review of a salvage prostatectomy experience by Stephenson and colleagues (2004) recounted a series of nearly 100 men treated between 1984 and 2003 with either external beam (N = 58) or interstitial (N = 42) radiotherapy. The authors saw a decrease in complication rates (overall from 33% to 13%, rectal injuries from 15% to 2%). They also reported urinary continence rates of 39% totally dry and 86% with one or less pad per day. Potency rates for this group (previously potent men) were 28% with unilateral nerve sparing and 45% with bilateral nerve sparing. Nearly 20% required an artificial sphincter. The most recent report (Ward et al, 2005) recounted a 30-year experience with salvage retropubic prostatectomy and cystoprostatectomy for radioresistant adenocarcinoma of the prostate. From 1967 to 2003, they found sufficient data to comment on 199 men; 138 were treated with retropubic prostatectomy and 61 with cystoprostatectomy. Average follow-up was 7 years. Rectal injury occurred in 5% of radical retropubic prostatectomies and 10% of cystoprostatectomies. Incontinence was "zero pads" in 43% of the more contemporary cohort. Cancer-specific survival was 65% at 10 years.

contraindication to positioning. Some patients, such as those having renal transplantation or those with severe inflammation secondary to placement of synthetic mesh for repair of a hernia or the morbidly obese, who may not be amenable to RRP, typically may undergo prostatectomy by the perineal approach (Yiou et al, 1999; Boczko and Melman, 2003).

PREOPERATIVE CARE

A full bowel preparation is administered on the day before surgery on the basis of the surgeon's preference; the patient is instructed either to consume polyethylene glycol or to administer a Fleet Phospho-Soda enema in the afternoon before surgery. Also, 1.0 g of neomycin is administered orally at 12:00, 2:00, 4:00, 6:00, 8:00, and 10:00 PM. This bowel preparation allows primary closure of any inadvertent rectal injury at the time of surgery without problem. A sample for blood type and antibody screen is obtained from all patients in the days or hours before surgery, but because blood loss is minimal and transfusion rarely required, a crossmatch is unnecessary; preoperative donation and storage of blood by the patient is not required either.

In the preoperative holding area, antithromboembolic surgical stockings are positioned, and the patient is administered a second-generation cephalosporin intravenously. Patients with cephalosporin allergy are administered intravenous gentamicin at a dose of 2 to 5 mg/kg body weight and 1 gm of vancomycin. Although perineal prostatectomy lends itself to regional anesthetics such as spinal or epidural anesthesia, most patients receive a general anesthetic. The only specialized instruments needed are curved and straight Lowsley tractors, a self-retaining retractor such as the mini-crescent or Thompson, and a headlight.

POSITION

After the induction of anesthesia, the patient is positioned supine so that when the leg portion of the operating table is lowered, the buttocks are extended beyond the table edge. Allen stirrups are stationed 2 inches cranially on the rail so that there is ample room for the attachment of the self-retaining retractor. The patient is then placed in an exaggerated lithotomy position with the perineum almost parallel to the floor or in a modified exaggerated lithotomy position (preferred by the authors) with the perineum only slightly elevated (Fig. 98–1). The perineum, anus, and scrotum are shaved, and the abdomen inferior to the umbilicus, penis, scrotum, perineum, anus, and both thighs are painted with povidone-iodine in the standard sterile fashion. After gowning, a sterile towel is sewn from the 9-o'clock to the 3-o'clock position around the anus at the mucocutaneous pigmentation line with silk suture, maintaining a sterile environment. Leg and perineal drapes are placed. The upright of the self-retaining retractor is secured to the table rail on the patient's left while the sterility of the upright is maintained.

EXPOSURE OF THE PROSTATE

A curved Lowsley tractor is placed transurethrally into the bladder and its wings opened. A curvilinear incision is made from a position just medial to the right ischial tuberosity to a

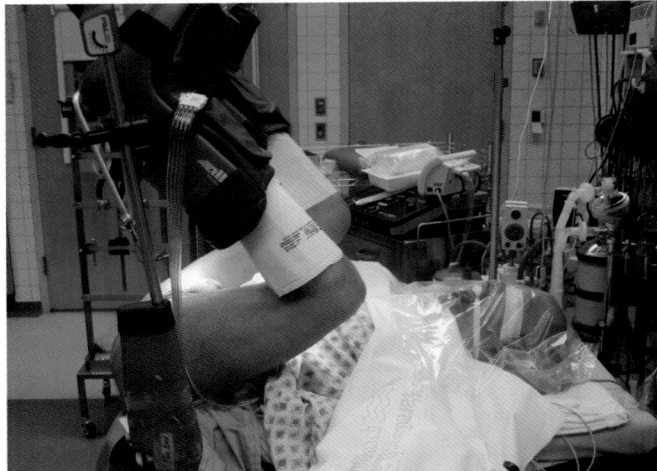

Figure 98–1. The modified exaggerated lithotomy position. The perineum is only slightly elevated and almost at a 90-degree angle with the floor. The legs are positioned at nearly a 75-degree angle with the floor.

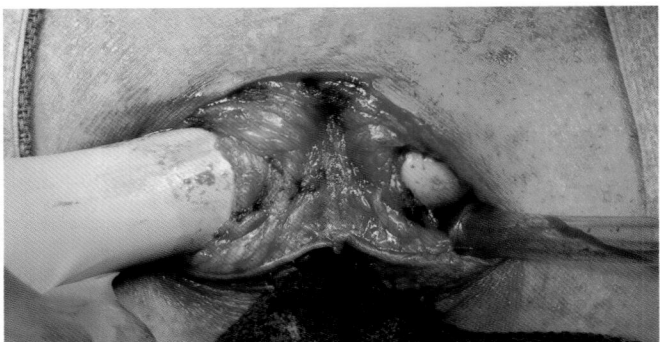

Figure 98–2. Each ischiorectal fossa is dissected bilaterally, and the finger is bluntly brought beneath the central tendon. The central tendon will be divided with electrocautery as traction is maintained with the finger.

position just medial to the left ischial tuberosity. The incision should not extend posteriorly beyond the 3- and 9-o'clock positions relative to the anus. Blunt dissection is employed to open and develop each ischiorectal fossa lateral to the central tendon, and the central tendon is then divided by electrocautery (Fig. 98–2). In the original description by Young, the dissection is carried anteriorly along the external anal sphincter until arriving at the rectourethralis muscle (1905). However, with the Belt approach preferred by the authors, the fibers of the external anal sphincter are dissected and retracted anteriorly with an appendiceal retractor; these fibers are not incised (1939). The longitudinal muscle fibers of the rectum are identified, and gentle traction is placed dorsally on the rectum by a dampened sponge. The plane is developed leading to the rectourethralis muscle, which is formed by fascicles of the rectal muscle, connecting the rectum to the perineal body. It appears as a strap of muscle tenting the rectum ventrally. **Without any traction on the Lowsley tractor, the rectourethralis muscle is divided close to the apex of the prostate with vertically oriented scissors, allowing the rectum to fall dorsally; caution must be exercised to prevent rectal injury at this point of the procedure.** Gentle pressure is then applied on the Lowsley tractor toward the anterior abdominal wall. This maneuver delivers the prostate well into the field of view and allows the blunt, digital dissection of the prostate from the rectum in a cephalad direction until the base of the prostate is identified at the vesicoprostatic junction (Fig. 98–3). Classically, the proper plane is between the anterior and posterior leafs of Denonvilliers' fascia.

NERVE-SPARING DISSECTION

Resumed traction on the Lowsley tractor toward the anterior abdominal wall again brings the prostate into the incision. If preservation of the neurovascular bundles is intended, the exposed anterior layer of Denonvilliers' fascia is incised vertically in the midline from the vesicoprostatic junction to the apex of the prostate with a No. 15 blade scalpel. **Avoiding use of electrocautery, careful lateral dissection with gentle lateral traction preserves the neurovascular bundles as they course between the layers of Denonvilliers' fascia at the posterolateral edge of the prostate. The fascia and enclosed nerves must be sufficiently mobilized to allow eventual extraction of the prostate without stretching or damage of the bundles.**

Attention is then directed toward the prostatic apex and urethra. The Lowsley tractor can be palpated within the urethra, and a right-angled clamp is placed with the open points facing cephalad on either side of the urethra to dissect the neurovascular bundles away from the urethra as they course distally. The No. 15 blade scalpel is again used to incise the posterior aspect of the urethra over the Lowsley tractor (Fig. 98–4). The curved Lowsley tractor is then replaced by a straight Lowsley, and the wings are opened in a vertical fashion. With moderate traction on the Lowsley tractor, the remaining intact anterior aspect of the membranous urethra is sharply transected from the prostatic apex, and the anterior prostate is freed to the bladder neck by sharp and blunt dissection.

The self-retaining retractor is attached to the previously placed upright, and blades are placed in the 3-, 9-, and 12-

o'clock positions. Dissection is then directed over the anterior prostate from the apex toward the bladder neck. Traction on the Lowsley tractor aids in this portion by bringing the prostate into the incision. **The surgeon must be mindful not to dissect too far ventrally and to touch on the dorsal venous complex.** To sufficiently expose the anterior prostate, the puboprostatic ligaments are encountered and divided with scissors (Fig. 98–5).

The junction of the bladder neck and prostate base is then identified by palpating the wings of the Lowsley tractor. This junction is then further developed with blunt and sharp dissections, preserving the bladder neck. The bladder is entered anteriorly with a scalpel, the Lowsley tractor is removed from the urethra, and a long right-angled clamp is passed retrograde through the prostatic urethra and bladder neck. A 14 French red rubber catheter is then fed into the open right-angled clamp and pulled through the prostatic urethra; the ends are clamped together with a Kelly clamp, making a loop that may be used for manipulation of the

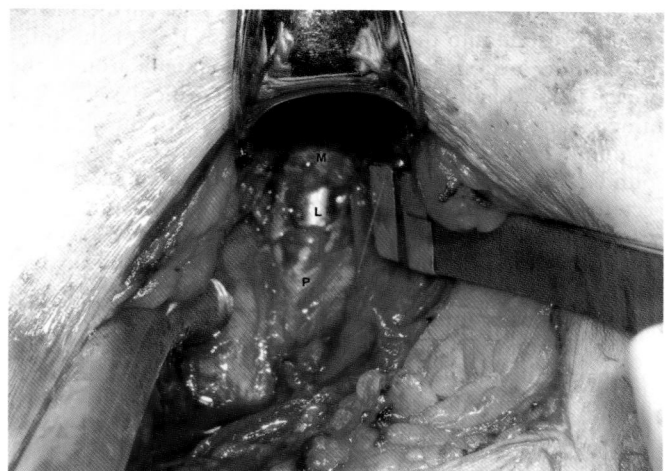

Figure 98–4. The anterior urethra is incised over the curved Lowsley tractor (L) between the membranous urethra (M) and prostate (P).

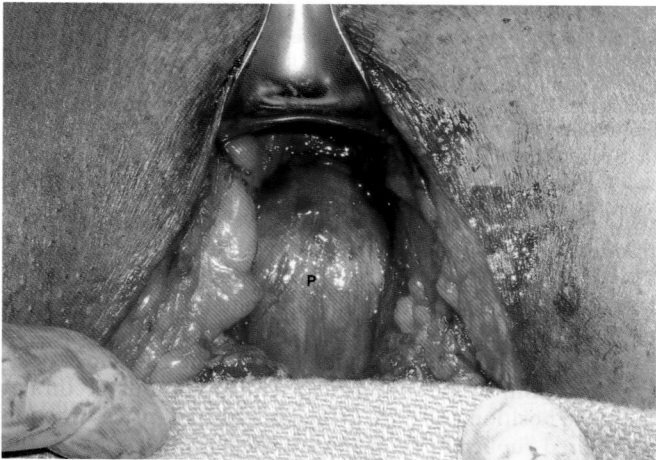

Figure 98–3. The external anal sphincter is retracted anteriorly and the rectourethralis muscle is divided. The prostate (P) is delivered into the field of view.

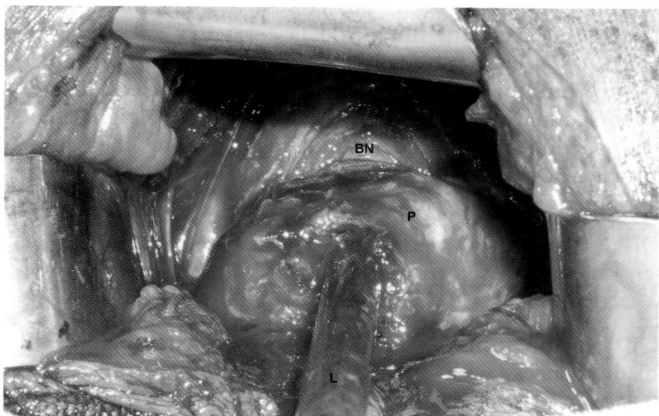

Figure 98–5. The urethra is divided, and the curved Lowsley has been replaced with a straight Lowsley tractor (L). The anterior prostate (P) has been dissected, and the puboprostatic ligaments are divided, exposing the bladder neck (BN).

only 5% in the retropubic group. In a prospective longitudinal assessment by Dahm and colleagues (2003), rectal urgency was the most common complaint and symptoms resolved over time; only 2.9% of patients reported involuntary stool leakage by 12 months after radical perineal prostatectomy.

Urinary Continence

The exposure of the vesicourethral anastomosis generated with the perineal approach results in excellent continence outcomes. In a series of 220 cases, with incontinence defined as daily use of pads, Weldon and coworkers (1997) reported a 95% continence rate within 1 year, with younger age being a significant predictor of improved urinary continence. Yang and associates (2004) confirmed these results in a prospective study. **In studies comparing the outcomes of perineal prostatectomy and RRP, urinary continence was either improved by the perineal approach or not significantly different** (Parra et al, 1994; Bishoff et al, 1998; Gray et al, 1999; Sullivan et al, 2000; Lance et al, 2001). To date, studies comparing laparoscopic radical prostatectomy and perineal prostatectomy are not available.

Potency

Erectile function is negatively affected with all prostate cancer treatment modalities. Rabbani and colleagues (2000) prospectively demonstrated that older age, diminished erections preoperatively, and excision of one or both neurovascular bundles significantly reduced potency after radical prostatectomy. **A review of the literature demonstrates potency in 35% to 70% of patients after nerve-sparing radical perineal prostatectomy** (Lerner et al, 1994; Harris and Thompson, 1996; Weldon et al, 1997; Ruiz-Deya et al, 2001; Harris, 2003). At 24 months of follow-up, Weldon and colleagues (1997) reported 73% potency in 22 patients who had a bilateral nerve-sparing procedure and 63% potency in 28 patients who had a unilateral bundle preserved, although these results were not statistically different. Lerner and colleagues (1994) demonstrated unassisted potency in 22% of nerve-spared patients and an additional 30% who achieved vaginal penetration with pharmacotherapy.

SUMMARY

The resurgence of the radical perineal prostatectomy for the treatment of localized prostate cancer has been facilitated by the current emphasis on reducing medical costs, the identification of prostate cancer at earlier stages, and the selected use of laparoscopic lymph node sampling. This technique offers a small incision and provides cancer control for localized prostate cancer as efficacious as with the radical retropubic prostatectomy in a manner that is cost-effective and with low morbidity.

KEY POINTS: RADICAL PERINEAL PROSTATECTOMY

- There are few contraindications to radical perineal prostatectomy.

- Radical perineal prostatectomy demonstrates the proven long-term cancer control of radical retropubic prostatectomy.

- A nerve-sparing approach may be applied to radical perineal prostatectomy with excellent potency outcomes.

- Radical perineal prostatectomy is renowned for rapid convalescence and overall low morbidity.

SUGGESTED READINGS

Iselin CE, Robertson JE, Paulson DF: Radical perineal prostatectomy: Oncological outcome during a 20-year period. J Urol 1999;161:163-168.

Partin AW, Kattan MW, Subong EN, et al: Combination of prostate-specific antigen, clinical stage, and Gleason score to predict pathological stage of localized prostate cancer. JAMA 1997;277:1445-1451.

Sokoloff MH, Brendler CB: Indications and contraindications for nerve-sparing radical prostatectomy. Urol Clin North Am 2001;28:535-543.

Weldon VE, Tavel FR: Potency-sparing radical perineal prostatectomy: Anatomy, surgical technique and initial results. J Urol 1988;140:559-562.

Weldon VE, Tavel FR, Neuwirth H: Continence, potency and morbidity after radical perineal prostatectomy. J Urol 1997;158:1470-1475.

99 | Laparoscopic and Robotic-Assisted Laparoscopic Radical Prostatectomy and Pelvic Lymphadenectomy

LI-MING SU, MD · JOSEPH A. SMITH JR., MD

LAPAROSCOPIC AND ROBOTIC-ASSISTED LAPAROSCOPIC RADICAL PROSTATECTOMY
Evolution of Minimally Invasive Laparoscopic Prostatectomy

A century has passed since Hugh Hampton Young performed the first open prostatectomy for carcinoma through a perineal approach (Young, 1905). In 1947, Millin reported on the retropubic approach to prostatectomy. Although effective as a technique for curing prostate cancer, radical retropubic prostatectomy (RRP) was fraught with significant morbidity, including excessive blood loss, urinary incontinence, and impotence. In the late 1970s and early 1980s several detailed anatomic studies performed in fetal and adult cadavers provided important insights into the periprostatic anatomy, especially that of the dorsal venous complex (Reiner and Walsh, 1979), neurovascular bundle (Walsh and Donker, 1982), and striated urethral sphincter (Oelrich, 1980). These landmark observations led to an anatomic approach to radical prostatectomy and, more importantly, a significant reduction in operative morbidity. As a result, the anatomic nerve-sparing radical retropubic prostatectomy has remained the cornerstone of surgical treatment for clinically localized prostate cancer.

In an effort to further decrease the morbidity of open prostatectomy, a minimally invasive surgical approach to treating prostate cancer was described by Schuessler and colleagues in 1997, who performed the first successful laparoscopic radical prostatectomy (LRP). Based on a series of 9 patients (Schuessler et al, 1997), they found that operative times for LRP were long (range: 8 to 11 hours) as was the average length of hospital stay of 7.3 days (range: 1 to 22 days). Although cancer cure with LRP was deemed comparable to open surgery, the authors concluded that LRP offered no significant advantage over open surgery. As such, LRP was not widely adopted into the field of urology.

By the 20th century, advances in task-specific surgical instrumentation, optics, digital video equipment, as well as computer and robotic technology opened a new frontier for minimally invasive laparoscopic prostatectomy. These advances led urologists to revisit LRP, spearheaded by two centers in France who reported on their techniques and early results in 2000 (Guillonneau and Vallancien, 2000a; Abbou et al, 2000). Their stepwise approach to LRP proved to be both reproducible and teachable, although the learning curve remained steep. Operative times were reported in the 4- to 5-hour range with a positive margin rate of 15% to 28%. Both groups reported excellent continence rates (Guillonneau and Vallancien: 72%; Abbou et al: 84%) and potency was maintained in 45% of men who were potent preoperatively in the series by Guillonneau and Vallancien (2000b). As a consequence of their pioneering work, these two French centers rekindled worldwide interest in LRP.

The recent introduction of advanced robotic devices such as the daVinci Surgical System (Intuitive Surgical, Inc., Sunnyvale, CA) to the field of urologic surgery has added new hopes of reducing operative times and the learning curve for minimally invasive prostatectomy (Menon et al, 2002). By incorporating sophisticated wristed technology at the terminal ends of the robotic instruments, a surgeon is able to operate, suture, and dissect with the facility of a human wrist. In addition, the superior three-dimensional view offered by this robotic system provides the surgeon with an unprecedented view of the periprostatic anatomy. In this chapter we highlight the advances in both laparoscopic and robotic-assisted laparoscopic radical prostatectomy (RALP) and present the currently available data on oncologic as well as functional outcomes with these techniques.

Patient Selection

Indications and Contraindications

The indications for LRP and RALP are identical to that for open surgery, that is, patients with clinical stage T2 or less with no evidence of metastasis either clinically or radiographically (computed tomography [CT] and bone scan). Contraindications to minimally invasive laparoscopic prostatectomy include uncorrectable bleeding diatheses or the inability to undergo general anesthesia due to severe cardiopulmonary compromise. Patients with a history of prior complex lower abdominal/pelvic surgery, morbid obesity, large prostate size (e.g., >100 g), prior pelvic irradiation, neoadjuvant hormonal therapy, or prior prostate surgery (e.g., transurethral resection of the prostate) are more challenging, but these features are not by themselves contraindications for laparoscopic or robotic prostatectomy (Brown et al, 2005a; Erdogru et al, 2005; Singh et al, 2005; Stolzenburg et al, 2005a).

Preoperative Preparation

Bowel Preparation

As with open surgery, a preoperative mechanical bowel preparation is used. Most commonly, an oral electrolyte solution is taken on the day before surgery and diet is limited to clear liquids. An enema is recommended by some surgeons. Oral antibiotics (i.e., a Nichols prep) are being replaced in most centers by a broad-spectrum antibiotic administered intravenously 30 minutes before surgery.

Informed Consent

In addition to bleeding, transfusion, and infection, patients undergoing LRP and RALP must be aware of the potential for conversion to open surgery. As with open surgery, patients must be counseled on the risk of impotence, incontinence, incisional hernia, and adjacent organ injury (e.g., ureter, rectum, bladder, small bowel). The risks of general anesthesia must also be presented to the patient.

Operating Room Personnel, Configuration, and Equipment

LRP and RALP require that the surgical team including the scrub technician, circulating nurse, and surgical assistant(s) be fully trained and skilled in these minimally invasive laparoscopic techniques. Only one skilled assistant is generally required for these procedures, but a second assistant may be used if available to provide retraction of tissues. Operating personnel and room setup for LRP is as depicted in Figure 99–1. The scrub technician is an integral part of the operative team and must be versed in the wide array of laparoscopic instruments that may be used to accomplish this procedure. The instrumentation that is generally required to perform LRP and RAP is listed in Table 99–1.

Patient Positioning

After induction of general endotracheal anesthesia, the patient is placed in a supine position in steep Trendelenburg with

Table 99–1. Instrumentation for Laparoscopic and Robotic-Assisted Laparoscopic Radical Prostatectomy

Laparoscopic Radical Prostatectomy

AESOP 3000 Robotic Arm, if available (Intuitive Surgical, Inc., Sunnyvale, CA)
Monopolar electrocautery scissors
Monopolar electrocautery hook device
Bipolar forceps
Ultrasonic shears
Maryland dissector
60-degree and 90-degree fine-tipped (0.8 mm) graspers for cavernous nerve dissection
Laparoscopic needle drivers (2)
Suction-irrigation device
10-mm 0-degree and 30-degree laparoscope lens
Veress needle
5-mm trocars (2)
12-mm trocar
Visiport device (U.S. Surgical, Norwalk, CT)
20-Fr van Buren urethral sound
18-Fr silicone urethral catheter
5-mm and 10-mm Hem-o-lok clips (Teleflex Medical, Research Triangle Park, NC)
2-0 polyglactin suture (GS21) for dorsal venous complex
2-0 polyglactin suture (UR6) for vesicourethral anastomosis

Robotic-Assisted Laparoscopic Radical Prostatectomy

daVinci Surgical System (Intuitive Surgical, Inc., Sunnyvale, CA)
Endowrist Maryland bipolar forceps
Endowrist curved monopolar scissors
Endowrist needle drivers (2)
Endowrist Prograsp forceps
InSite Vision System with 0-degree and 30-degree lens
12-mm trocars (2)
8-mm metal robotic trocars (3 if using a fourth robotic arm)
18-Fr silicone urethral catheter
5-mm and 10-mm Hem-o-lok clips (Teleflex Medical, Research Triangle Park, NC)
2-0 polyglactin suture for dorsal venous complex and anastomosis

arms tucked and padded at the sides (Fig. 99–2). Sequential compression stocking devices are placed on both legs and activated. The patient's legs are spread far apart to allow for access to the rectum and perineum. Alternatively, the patient's legs may be placed in stirrups in the low lithotomy position. The patient is then secured to the table using tape and/or an egg-crate pad. If available, for LRP an AESOP 3000 robotic arm (Intuitive Surgical Inc., Sunnyvale, CA) is attached to the operating table at the level of the patient's right shoulder, is assembled to the laparoscope, and can be controlled either by voice activation or by the assistant using a hand-held remote control device. For RALP, camera movement is controlled by the console surgeon. An orogastric tube and urethral catheter are placed to decompress the stomach and bladder, respectively.

Anesthesia Considerations

Both LRP and RALP require general anesthesia. Because the patient's arms are tucked at the side and difficult to access, establishing accurate pulse oximetry, blood pressure cuff placement, and intravenous access is critical before patient positioning. **The anesthesiologist must be aware of the**

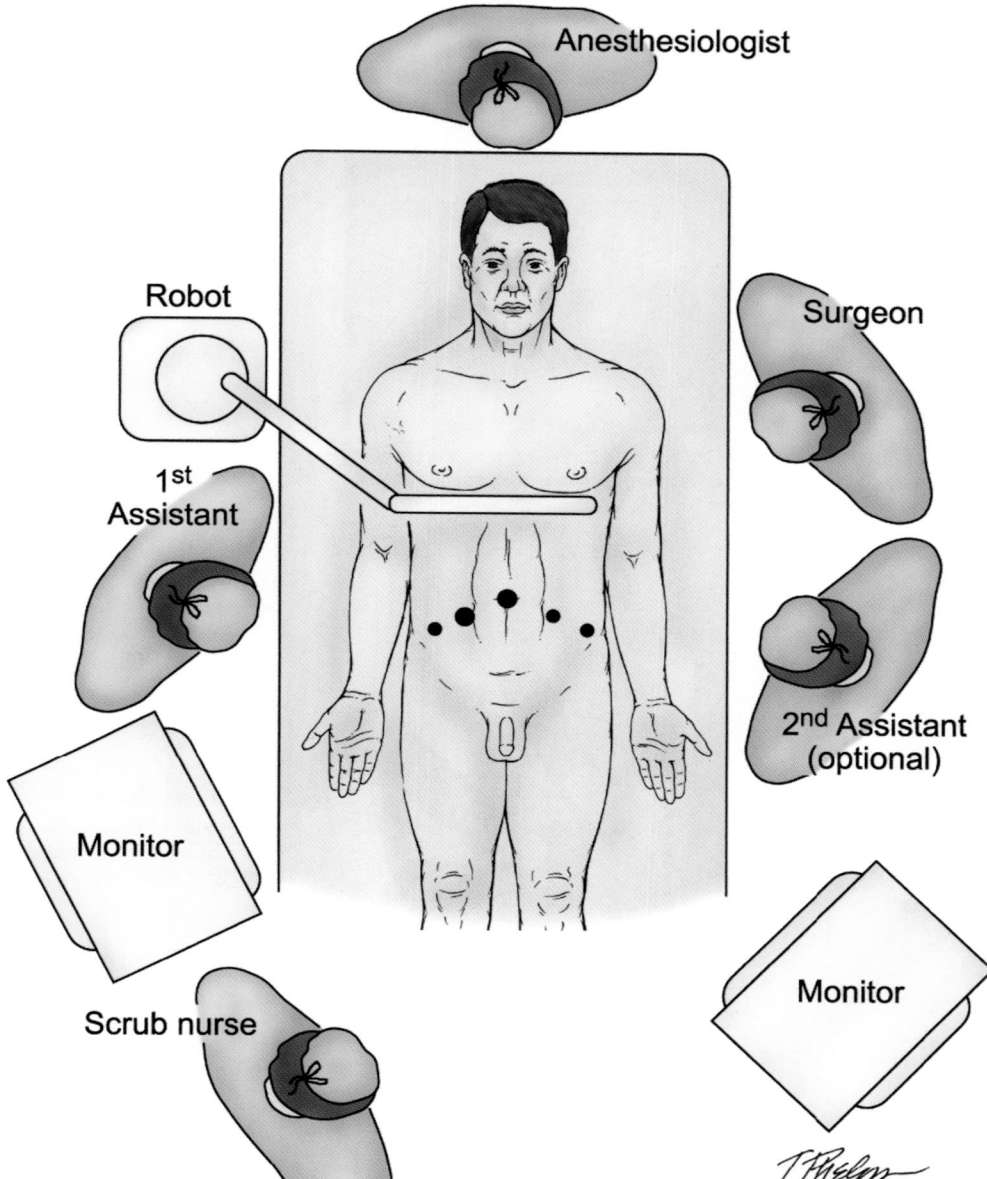

Figure 99–1. Operating room and trocar configuration for laparoscopic radical prostatectomy. (Copyright 2005, Johns Hopkins University.)

potential consequences of CO_2 insufflation and pneumoperitoneum, including oliguria and hypercarbia. Prompt adjustments in minute and tidal volumes may be required by the anesthesiologist in the event of rising end-tidal CO_2 levels and hypercarbia (Meininger et al, 2004). Adjustments in CO_2 insufflation pressures may also be required by the surgeon to reduce the risk of continued hypercarbia. Taken together, maintaining good communication between the surgeon and the anesthesia team is important during these procedures.

Surgical Technique

Most of the principles and considerations for the surgical dissection are similar regardless of whether a pure laparoscopic or robotic-assisted approach is used. For RALP, virtually all reported experiences are with the daVinci Surgical System. This is a master/slave system that consists of a surgical robot with three working arms (Fig. 99–3) and a remote surgeon console (Fig. 99–4). The robot is docked at the foot of the operating table between the patient's legs. The tableside assistant is responsible for docking/undocking the robot, suction-irrigation, passing sutures into the operative field, and robotic instrument changes. The surgeon is seated at the remote console, which provides a superb three-dimensional view and allows for the surgeon to have complete control of all camera movements as well as the three robotic arms. The surgeon's thumb and index fingers are inserted into master controls that allow his natural hand and wrist movements to be precisely replicated by wristed instruments at the terminal ends of the robotic arms in real time.

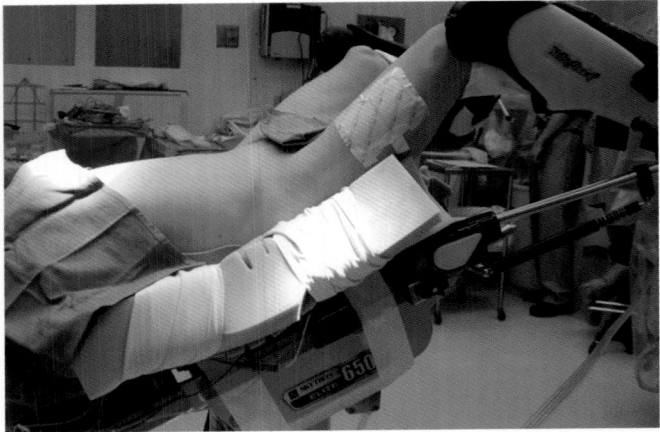

Figure 99–2. Patient positioning for a laparoscopic prostatectomy. Lithotomy position with steep Trendelenburg is shown. The patient's arms are tucked and padded at the sides.

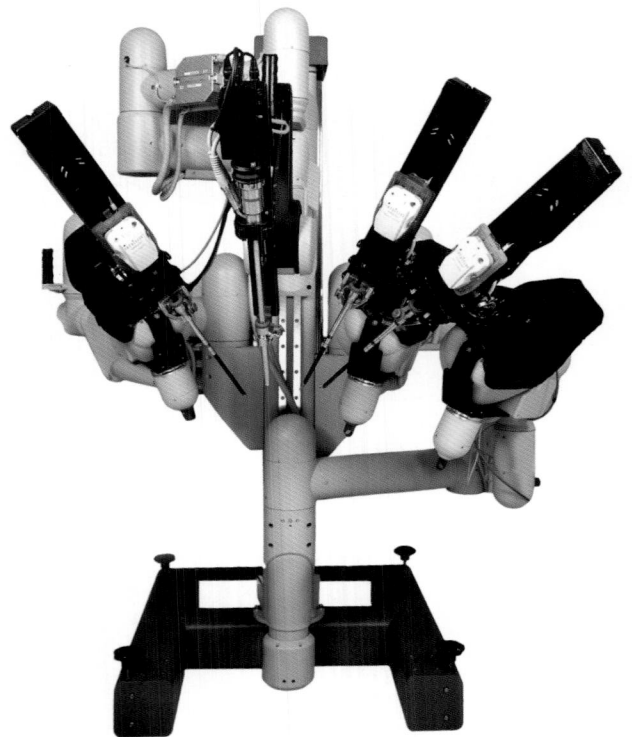

Figure 99–3. The daVinci Surgical System robot. The device includes a camera with three-dimensional view and three working arms. (Courtesy of Intuitive Surgical, Sunnyvale, CA.)

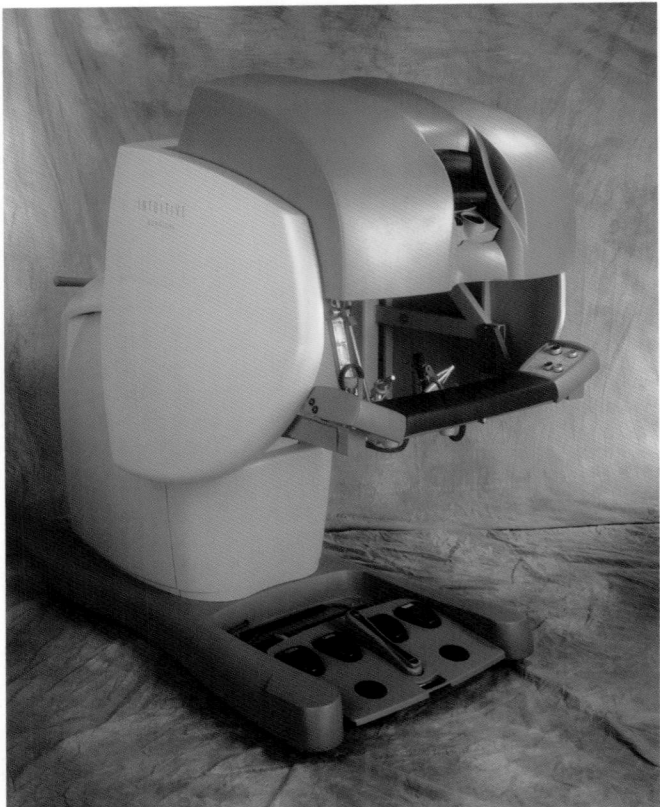

Figure 99–4. The surgeon console for the daVinci Surgical System. The surgeon has operating control of camera movement and three working arms. (Courtesy of Intuitive Surgical, Sunnyvale, CA.)

Highly skilled laparoscopic surgeons may find the robotic technology unnecessary and that they are equally as facile with pure laparoscopic suturing and dissection as with the robot (Guillonneau, 2005). **Most surgeons, however, believe that the robotic technology significantly facilitates suturing (especially for the vesicourethral anastomosis) and other aspects of the surgical dissection** (Dasgupta et al, 2005). Other than setup of the operating room and surgical fields, there is little difference in the surgical technique between

RALP and LRP. In general, the following discussion of technique and the pros and cons of various maneuvers and approaches apply to either approach.

Transperitoneal Approach

Abdominal Access and Trocar Configuration. For a transperitoneal LRP approach, pneumoperitoneum is established using either a Veress needle inserted at the base of the umbilicus or an open trocar placement with a Hasson technique. The insufflation pressure is maintained at 15 mm Hg. Secondary trocars are then placed under laparoscopic view, including a 12-mm right pararectus trocar, 5-mm left pararectus trocar, and two 5-mm trocars placed halfway between the anterior-superior iliac crest and pararectus trocar on the right and left sides (Fig. 99–5). The surgeon operates primarily through the two pararectus trocars and the assistant through the 5-mm trocar in the right lower quadrant. The left lower quadrant 5-mm trocar is used for retraction purposes and can be manipulated by a second assistant or endoscopic instrument holder (Landman et al, 2004).

For RALP, once intraperitoneal access and a pneumoperitoneum are established, the camera is inserted through a trocar immediately above the umbilicus. In a morbidly obese or very tall patient, infraumbilical camera placement may be preferable. The console surgeon controls camera movement by depressing a foot pedal and using brief arm movements to affect camera positioning. Laparoscopes with either angled

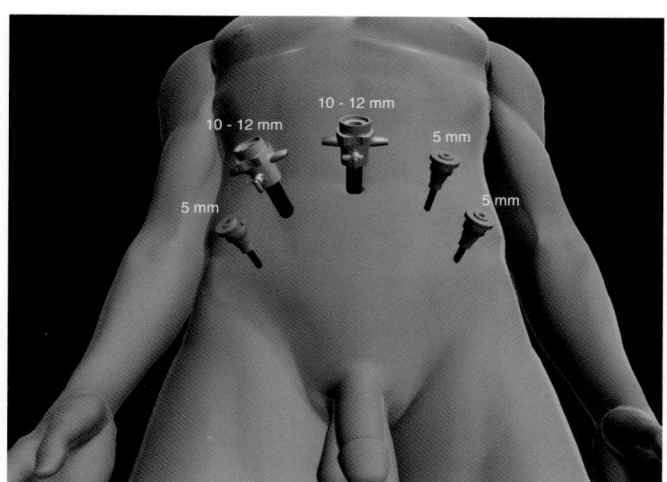

Figure 99–5. Trocar configuration for a laparoscopic radical prostatectomy.

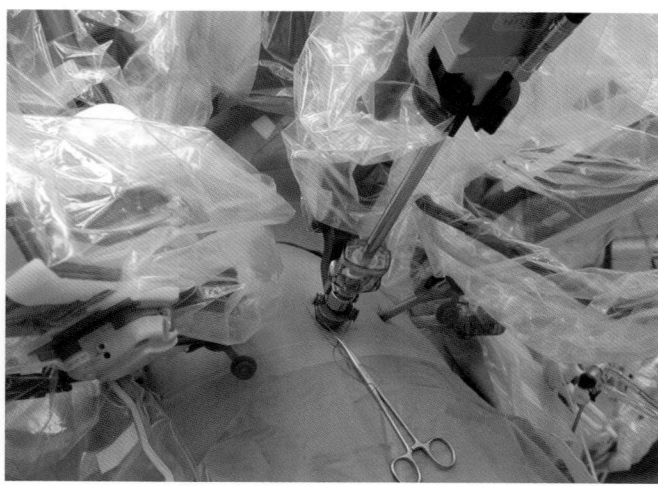

Figure 99–6. Abdominal trocar placement for a robotic-assisted laparoscopic radical prostatectomy. The camera trocar *(center, purple)* is placed just above the umbilicus. Three 8-mm trocars *(green)* are used for the robotic arm, and a 12-mm port in the right lower quadrant is used by the table-side assistant.

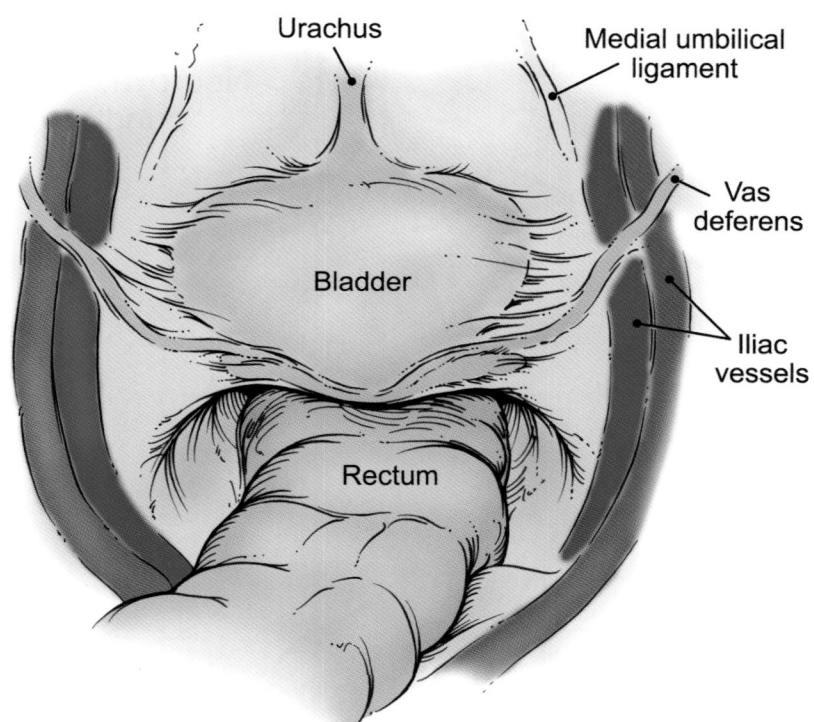

Figure 99–7. Initial intraperitoneal view detailing the relevant landmarks within the male pelvis during transperitoneal laparoscopic radical prostatectomy. (Copyright 2005, Johns Hopkins University.)

(30 degrees) or straight ahead (0 degree) viewing are available and interchangeable at various portions of the procedure.

Typically, four additional trocars are placed. An 8-mm trocar is placed in both the right and the left pararectus sites to accommodate the robotic arms. A "fourth arm" is also available and is usually placed in the left lower quadrant (Sundaram et al, 2005). The fourth arm can replace a table-side assistant, is under the control of the console surgeon, and can be used to grasp and retract tissue. A 12-mm trocar placed in the right lower quadrant is used by the table-side assistant for

suctioning, passage and cutting of suture, and retraction (Fig. 99–6).

Dissection of the Seminal Vesicles and Vasa Deferentia. On initial inspection of the operative field, the relevant landmarks include the bladder, median (urachus) and medial umbilical ligaments, vasa deferentia, iliac vessels, and rectum (Fig. 99–7). During transperitoneal LRP or RALP, two different approaches to dissection of the seminal vesicles have been described. With the Montsouris technique, the initial step is retrovesical dissection of the vasa deferentia and seminal vesicles (Guillonneau and Vallancien, 2000a). The peritoneum overlying the vas deferens is incised sharply. The vasa are divided and traced distally toward the seminal vesicles, which are subsequently identified and dissected. The alternative approach often employed with RALP involves identification and dissection of the seminal vesicles after separation of the prostate from the posterior bladder neck (Menon et al, 2004b). **With both techniques, use of thermal energy should be limited to avoid injury to the cavernous** **nerves, which lie in close proximity to the seminal vesicle** (Fig. 99–8).

Posterior Prostatic Dissection. By lifting both seminal vesicles and vasa anteriorly (Fig. 99–9), a 2- to 3-cm horizontal incision is made through Denonvilliers' fascia approximately 0.5 cm below the base of the seminal vesicles. Blunt dissection is carried out between Denonvilliers' fascia and the rectum, hugging the posterior aspect of the prostate (Fig. 99–10). The presence of perirectal fat confirms the proper plane of dissec-

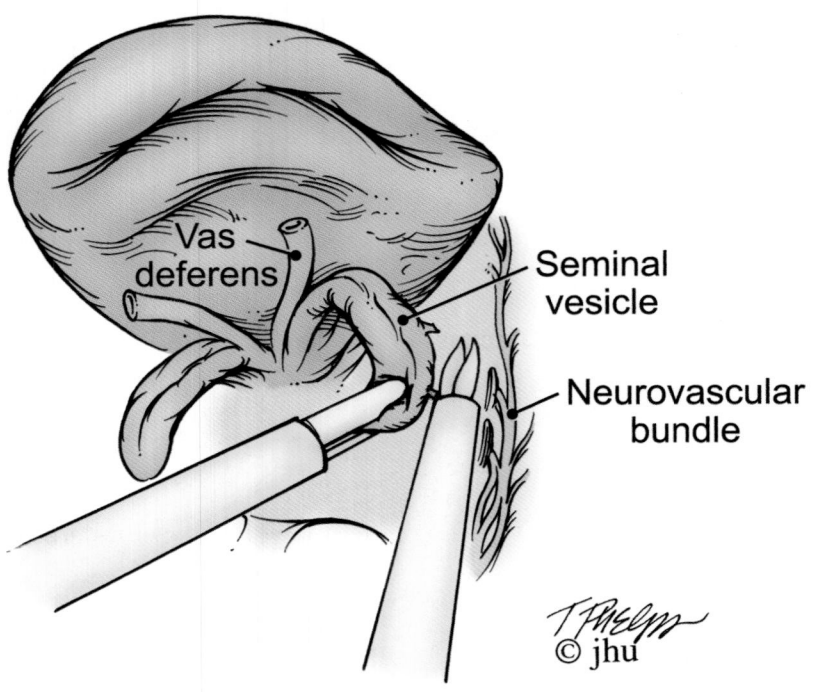

Figure 99–8. Seminal vesicle dissection. In lieu of using electrocautery for hemostasis, hemoclips are applied along the lateral aspect and tip of the seminal vesicle to secure the vascular pedicle and avoid thermal injury to the nearby neurovascular bundle. (Copyright 2005, Johns Hopkins University).

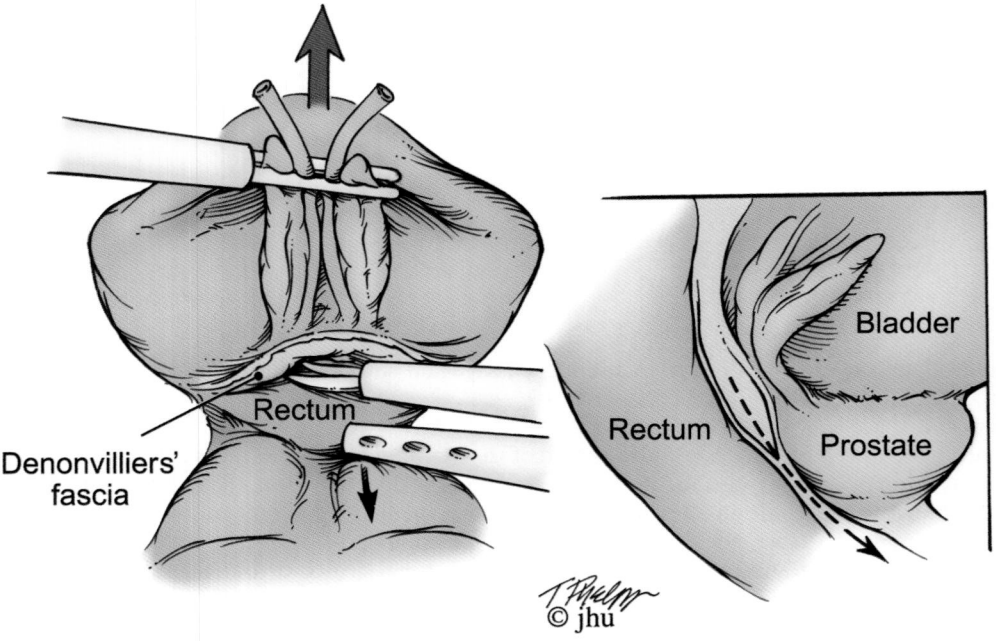

Figure 99–9. Posterior dissection of the prostate. As the assistant applies upward traction on the seminal vesicles and vasa and downward traction on the rectum, a transverse incision is made in Denonvilliers' fascia below the seminal vesicles and blunt dissection is used to develop a plane between Denonvilliers' fascia and the rectum. *Inset* demonstrates the direction of dissection towards the prostatic apex. (Copyright 2005, Johns Hopkins University.)

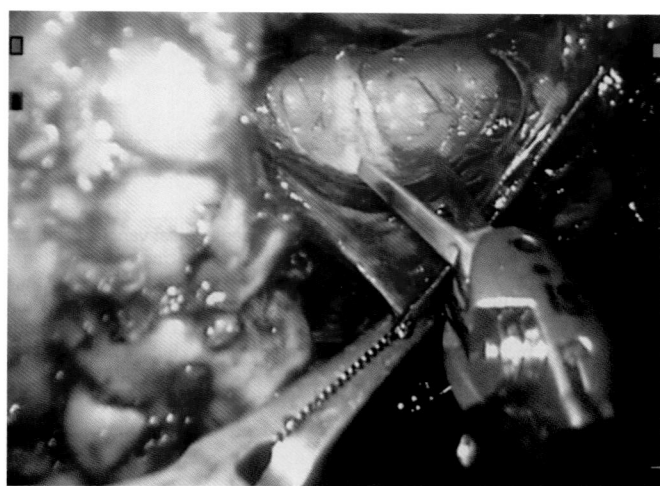

Figure 99-10. Intraoperative view demonstrating the plane between the rectum and prostate during robotic-assisted laparoscopic radical prostatectomy. Denonvilliers' fascia has been incised sharply, exposing perirectal fat immediately beneath the posterior aspect of the prostate *(top of image)*.

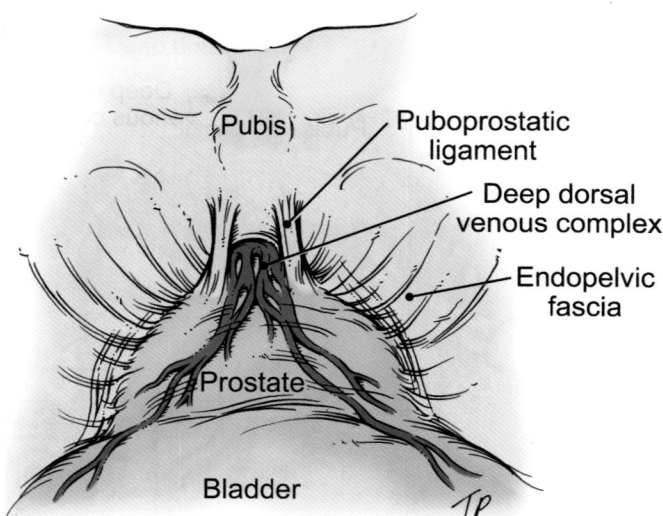

Figure 99-12. Retropubic view of the bladder and prostate following entry into the space of Retzius. The fatty tissue overlying the anterior aspect of the prostate has been removed, exposing the puboprostatic ligaments and endopelvic fascia. (Copyright 2005, Johns Hopkins University.)

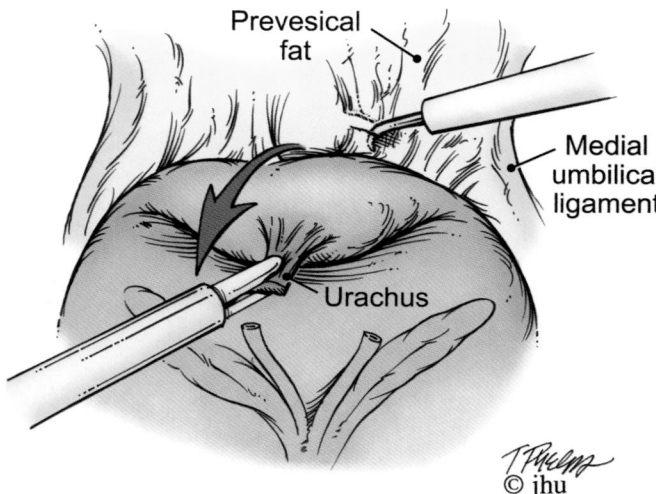

Figure 99-11. Division of urachus and entry into the space of Retzius. Cephalad traction on the urachus helps to identify the fatty alveolar tissue immediately anterior to the bladder, which marks the proper plane of dissection. The medial umbilical ligaments demarcate lateral extent of the bladder dissection. (Copyright 2005, Johns Hopkins University.)

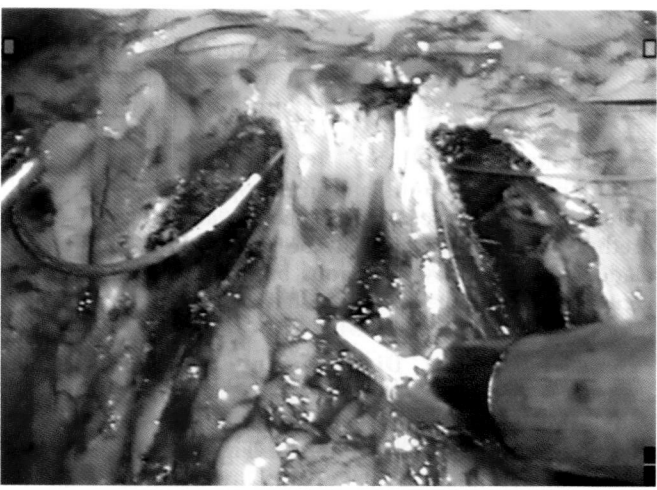

Figure 99-13. Intraoperative view demonstrating passage of a suture incorporating the deep dorsal vein complex during robotic-assisted laparoscopic radical prostatectomy.

tion. Thorough dissection of the rectum off of the posterior prostate is critical to minimize the risk of rectal injury during subsequent steps such as division of the urethra and dissection of the prostatic apex.

Developing the Space of Retzius. With the Montsouris technique, developing the space of Retzius is the next step after dissection of the seminal vesicles. With RALP, this is often the first step in the operation. The bladder is dissected from the anterior abdominal wall by dividing the urachus high above the bladder and incising the peritoneum bilaterally just medial to the medial umbilical ligaments using a hook electrocautery device. The presence of fatty alveolar tissue confirms the proper plane of dissection. Applying posterior traction on the urachus, the prevesical fat is identified and bluntly dissected, exposing the space of Retzius (Fig. 99–11). The fat overlying

the anterior prostate is removed using sharp dissection and electrocautery as needed, and the superficial branches of the dorsal venous complex are coagulated using bipolar electrocautery. Visible landmarks include the anterior aspect of the bladder and prostate, puboprostatic ligaments, endopelvic fascia, and pubis (Fig. 99–12). The endopelvic fascia and puboprostatic ligaments are sharply divided, exposing levator muscle fibers attached to the lateral and apical portions of the prostate. These fibers are meticulously and bluntly dissected from the surface of the prostate exposing the prostatourethral junction.

Ligation of the Deep Dorsal Venous Complex. The deep dorsal venous complex (DVC) is suture ligated using a figure-of-eight 2-0 polyglactin suture (Fig. 99–13). The needle is

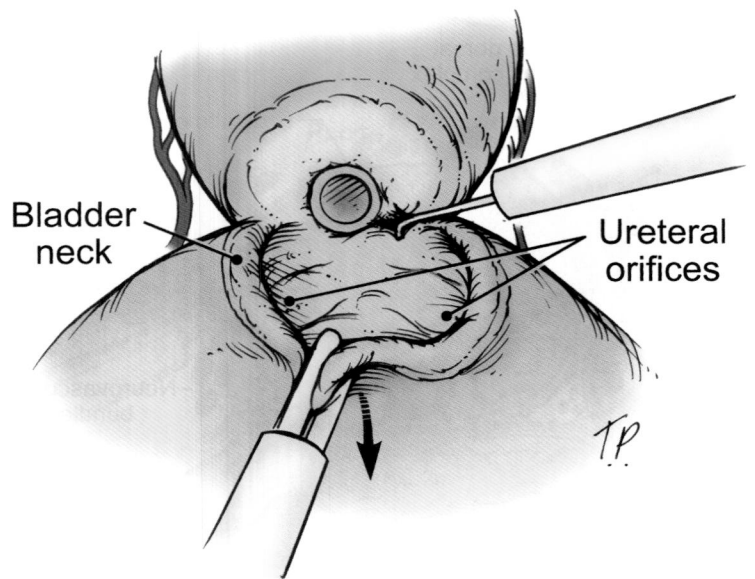

Bladder neck

Ureteral orifices

Figure 99–18. Bladder neck transection using a hook monopolar electrocautery device along the posterior bladder neck. Cephalad traction on the bladder and anterior traction of the prostate with the urethral sound can help expose and delineate the posterior bladder neck margin. (Copyright 2005, Johns Hopkins University.)

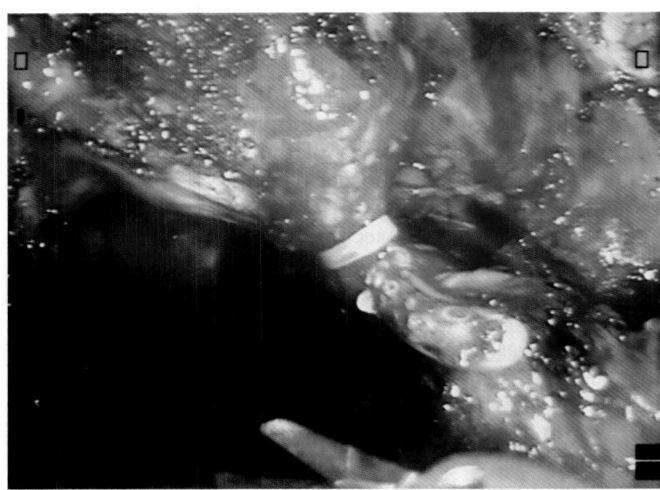

Figure 99–19. Intraoperative view demonstrating Hem-o-lok clips (Teleflex Medical, Research Triangle Park, NC) placed to secure the right prostatic pedicle. The pedicle is sharply divided close to the prostate surface without electrocautery.

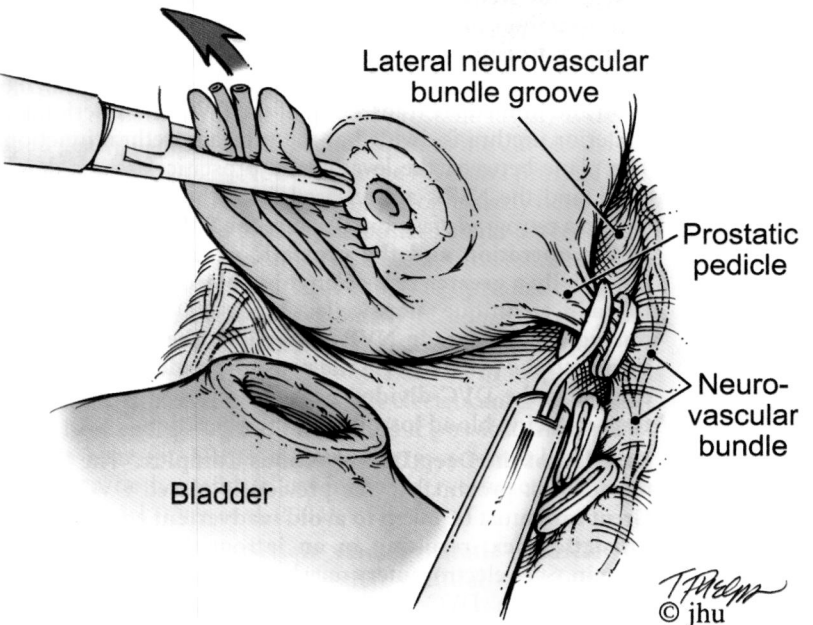

Lateral neurovascular bundle groove

Prostatic pedicle

Neurovascular bundle

Bladder

Figure 99–20. Ligation of the prostatic pedicles and antegrade dissection of the neurovascular bundle. With anterior traction on the seminal vesicles and vasa, the prostatic pedicles are identified, clipped, and divided without electrocautery staying close to the prostate surface. Direction and course of antegrade neurovascular bundle dissection is guided by the previously defined lateral neurovascular bundle groove. (Copyright 2005, Johns Hopkins University.)

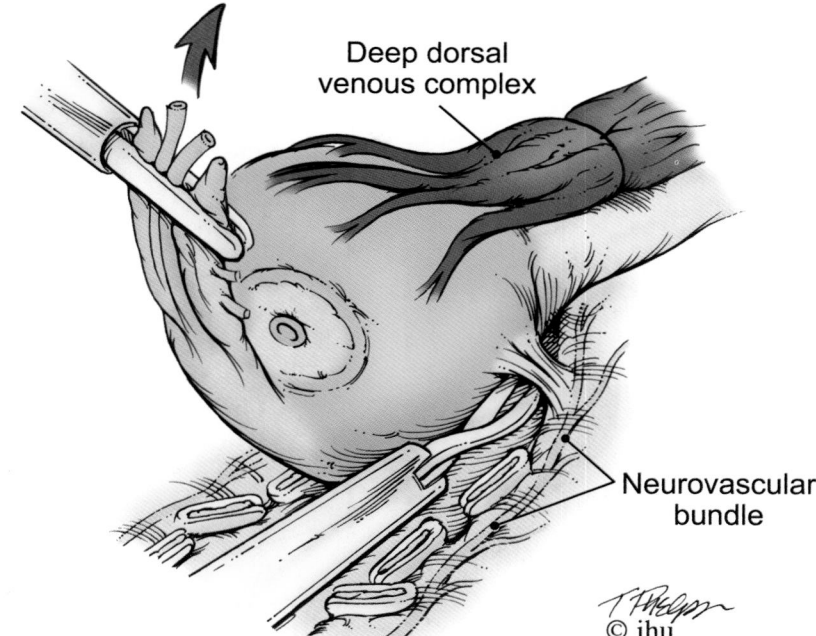

Figure 99–21. Completion of antegrade dissection of the neurovascular bundle. With the use of both blunt and sharp dissection, the remaining attachments between the neurovascular bundle and prostate are gently swept off of the posterolateral surface of the prostate toward the prostatic apex. (Copyright 2005, Johns Hopkins University.)

adjacent to the NVBs. Occasionally, additional DVC sutures may be required if large venous sinuses are encountered that were not adequately secured by the first DVC suture. After complete division of the DVC, the anterior aspect of the prostatourethral junction should be visible.

Prostatic Apical Dissection and Division of Urethra. Because the distal portion of the NVBs lies in intimate association with the lateral aspect of the prostatic apex, the remaining attachments between the NVB and prostatic apex are gently and meticulously dissected free using a fine right-angled dissector and sharp dissection without electrocautery. By withdrawing the urethral sound into the prostatic urethra, the tip of the urethral sound can be useful for defining the precise junction between the prostatic apex and urethra, thus optimizing preservation of urethral length. The anterior urethra is divided sharply, taking care to preserve the NVBs coursing along the posterolateral surface of the urethra (Fig. 99–23). Before division of the posterior urethra, great care must be taken to inspect the contour of the posterior prostatic apex. **In some patients, the posterior prostatic apex can protrude beneath the urethra, resulting in an iatrogenic positive margin if not identified and excised.** Having already completed the posterior prostatic dissection, little additional dissection is often required to free the prostate in its entirety once the posterior urethra and posterior striated urethral sphincter complex is divided. On the other hand, without previously accomplishing complete posterior prostatic dissection, the prostate remains fixed to the rectum after urethral division, increasing the risk of rectal injury while attempting to free the prostate, as the posterior attachments may be difficult to view adequately in this particular situation.

Laparoscopic Inspection and Entrapment of the Prostate Specimen. Once the prostate specimen is released com-

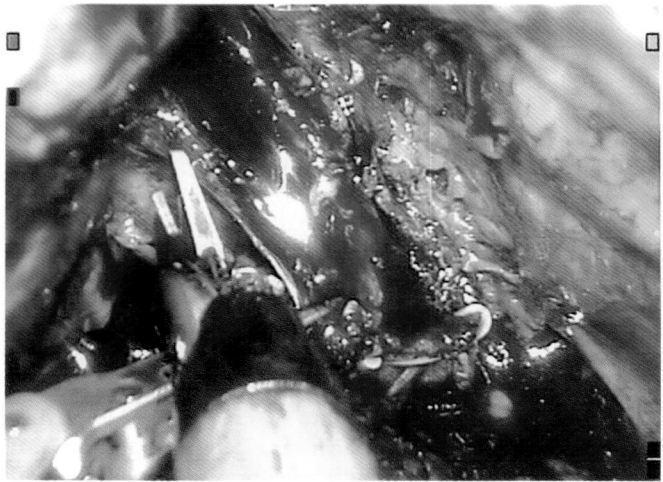

Figure 99–22. Intraoperative view demonstrating sharp release of the right neurovascular bundle from the posterolateral margin of the prostate *(top left)* during robotic-assisted laparoscopic radical prostatectomy.

pletely, the surgical margins are closely inspected laparoscopically. The specimen is placed in an entrapment sac and stored in the right lower quadrant of the abdomen until completion of the operation. If concern of a positive margin exists, further tissue may be excised and sent for frozen section. The rectum should be inspected carefully both visually and digitally (i.e., transrectally) if concern of rectal injury arises. Rectal insufflation with air using a Foley catheter can be useful in identifying smaller injuries if the index of suspicion remains high.

Vesicourethral Anastomosis. A critical first step in accomplishing the vesicourethral anastomosis is the establishment of

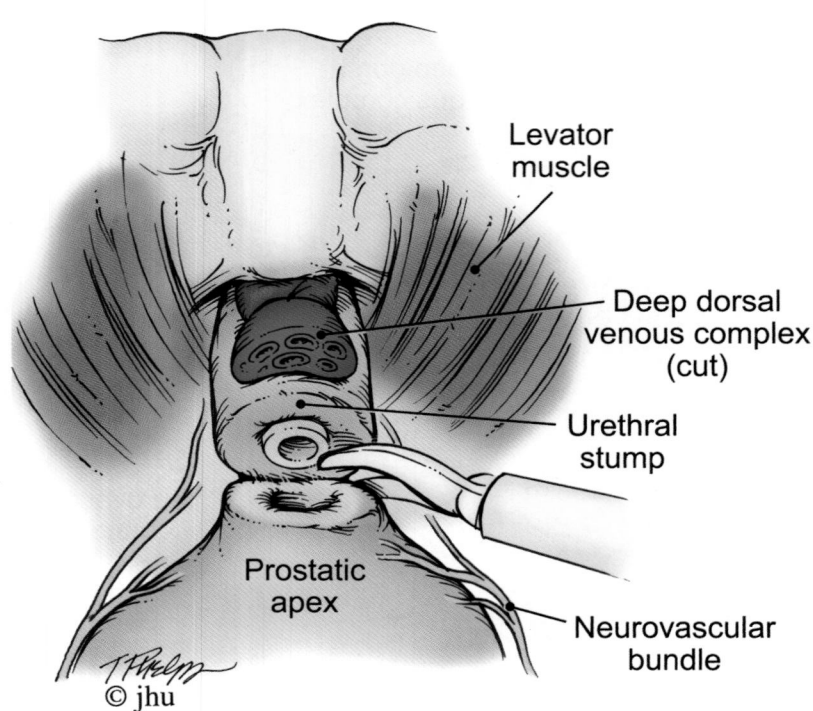

Levator muscle

Deep dorsal venous complex (cut)

Urethral stump

Prostatic apex

Neurovascular bundle

© jhu

Figure 99–23. Division of urethra. After division of the deep dorsal venous complex, the anterior and posterior urethra is divided sharply without electrocautery. A urethral sound can help identify the precise location between the urethra and the prostatic apex. (Copyright 2005, Johns Hopkins University.)

secure posterior tissue approximation. The posterior anastomosis is typically the site of relatively greater tension. It is at risk for disruption and subsequent urinary leakage during passage of the urethral catheter if mucosa-to-mucosa approximation of the posterior anastomosis is not established. To avoid this complication, the assistant can apply pressure to the perineum using a sponge stick to better reveal the posterior urethra. In addition, this maneuver may reduce tension at the posterior anastomosis while the surgeon places and secures the sutures. Although rarely necessary to further reduce tension at the anastomosis, the lateral bladder attachments may be released further from the pelvic sidewall and the operating table may be brought out of the Trendelenburg position.

The vesicourethral anastomosis may be accomplished using either an interrupted closure (Fig. 99–24) or a running continuous suture with a single knot (van Velthoven et al, 2003) (Fig. 99–25). Either an anterior or a posterior tennis racquet closure of the bladder neck may be required if there is significant discrepancy between the bladder neck opening and urethra. A urethral catheter is placed under vision before completion of the anastomosis if interrupted sutures are used or at the completion of the anastomosis with a running suture. The anastomosis is tested by filling the bladder with 100 to 150 mL of saline. Visible leaks at the anastomosis may be repaired with additional sutures as necessary. A closed suction drain is left in the prevesical space.

Delivery of the Prostate Specimen and Exiting the Abdomen. The entrapment sac containing the prostate specimen is delivered via extension of the infraumbilical incision and fascia. The fascia of the infraumbilical and 12-mm trocar site is closed primarily to prevent incisional hernia. The 5- and 8-mm robotic trocars generally do not require fascial closure.

Extraperitoneal Approach

For an extraperitoneal LRP approach, a 1.5-cm incision is made at the base of the umbilicus and dissection is carried out down to the peritoneum. With blunt finger dissection, a space is created anterior to the peritoneum. A trocar-mounted balloon dilator device (PDB Balloon, U.S. Surgical, Norwalk, CT) is inserted into the preperitoneal space and 500 to 700 mL of air is inflated (40 to 50 pumps) to develop the space of Retzius (Fig. 99–26). Secondary trocars are then inserted as described previously under laparoscopic view. The operation proceeds similar to that of the transperitoneal approach with the exception of dissection of the seminal vesicles and vasa deferentia, which are dissected after bladder neck transection.

Pros and Cons of Extraperitoneal versus Transperitoneal LRP Approach

In a retrospective comparison between extraperitoneal LRP versus transperitoneal LRP, Hoznek and colleagues (2003) found that the mean operative time was shorter with the extraperitoneal approach (169.6 vs. 224.2 minutes, $P < .001$), with the greatest time saved during access to the space of Retzius. They suggested that time to full diet was less with the extraperitoneal versus the transperitoneal LRP approach (1.6 vs. 2.6 days, $P = .002$) because the peritoneum had not been violated and postoperative ileus was minimized. Eden and colleagues (2004) found a statistically significant advantage in operative time, hospital stay, and return of early continence favoring patients undergoing extraperitoneal versus transperitoneal LRP, postulating that earlier return to urinary control may be secondary to less bladder dissection and, perhaps, less bladder dysfunction as compared with transperitoneal LRP. **Most studies, however, have found little or no difference in**

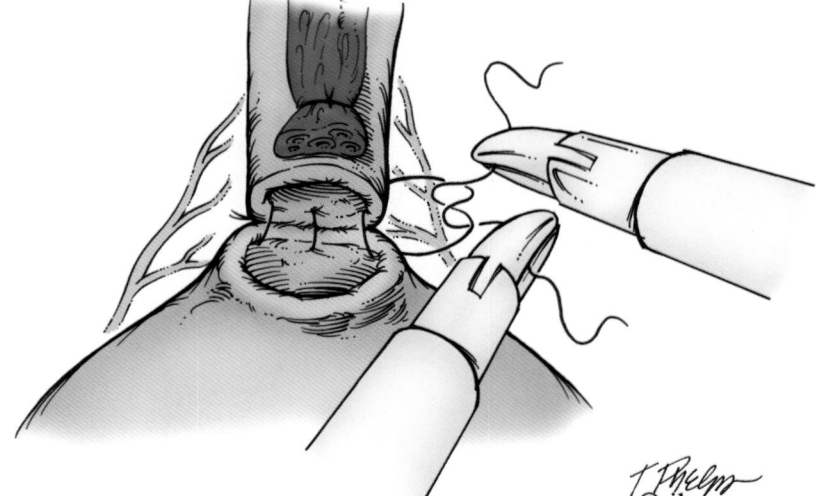

Figure 99–24. Vesicourethral anastomosis using interrupted sutures. Great care must be taken to avoid incorporating the neurovascular bundles when placing and tying the sutures. (Copyright 2005, Johns Hopkins University.)

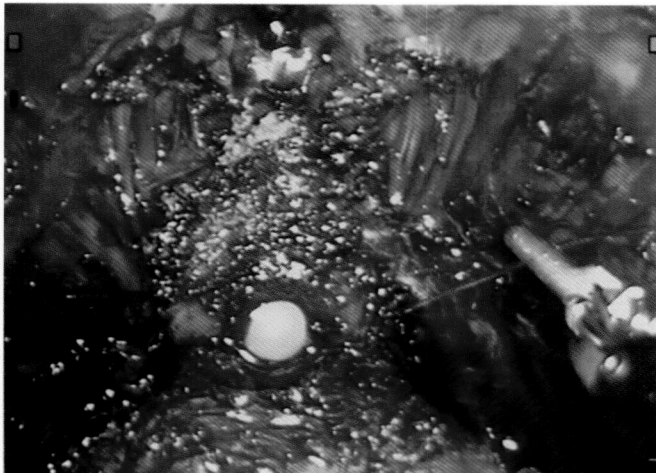

Figure 99–25. Intraoperative view demonstrating the use of a running continuous suture for the vesicourethral anastomosis during robotic-assisted laparoscopic radical prostatectomy. The posterior anastomosis from the 3- to 9-o'clock position is completed in this view with a single knot tied anteriorly after completion of the anastomosis.

operative time and perioperative outcomes between transperitoneal and extraperitoneal approaches (Cathelineau et al, 2004a; Erdogru et al, 2004; Brown et al, 2005b).

With an extraperitoneal approach, the simultaneous laparoscopic management of concurrent inguinal hernias using prosthetic mesh is feasible (Stolzenburg et al, 2003a). Simultaneous inguinal herniorraphy has also been reported during transperitoneal LRP (Allaf et al, 2003); however, proper coverage of the mesh prosthesis is necessary using peritoneal flaps, omentum, or a second absorbable mesh to reduce the risk of adhesions and bowel fistulas. The extraperitoneal technique may be preferable in patients with previous extensive abdominal surgery or morbid obesity (Erdogru et al, 2004). **With the extraperitoneal approach, the peritoneum acts as a natural barrier, minimizing the potential for bowel injury and preventing the bowels from falling into the operative field and obscuring the surgeon's view. Furthermore, this approach helps to confine any urine leak that may occur**

from the vesicourethral anastomosis within the extraperitoneal space.

One limitation with the extraperitoneal approach is the reduced working space as compared with the relatively larger working space of the peritoneal cavity gained with transperitoneal access. This is especially relevant when a well-meaning assistant attempts to clear the operative field of blood or smoke. Suctioning can evacuate CO_2 gas and rapidly collapse the already limited extraperitoneal working space, thus significantly compromising visualization. A second theoretical limitation to the extraperitoneal approach is the potential for increased tension at the vesicourethral anastomosis. The bladder remains fixed by the urachus during extraperitoneal LRP, thus limiting bladder mobility. This may result in increased tension at the vesicourethral anastomosis, especially in a patient with a large prostate where a longer distance must be accounted for when suturing the bladder to the urethra. One group has even described modifications including a racket handle closure at the posterior bladder neck in conjunction with an anterior sagittal cystotomy to achieve a tension-free anastomosis during extraperitoneal LRP (Hoznek et al, 2003). Lastly, higher CO_2 absorption has been reported with extraperitoneal versus transperitoneal insufflation, requiring a higher minute volume to compensate for hypercarbia and associated acidosis (Meininger et al, 2004). **Overall, whether to use an extraperitoneal or transperitoneal approach for LRP or RALP is largely a matter of surgeon preference and experience and there is no consistently demonstrated advantage for either approach.**

Results

Although the use of LRP and, in particular, RALP, is expanding rapidly, there are still a relatively limited number of published large series evaluating surgical results, complications, and long-term patient outcomes (Link et al, 2005). **No randomized trials have been conducted evaluating laparoscopic versus open techniques, and retrospective comparisons are limited by disparities in surgeon experience, the influence of patient selection, and nonstandardized methods of outcome assessment.**

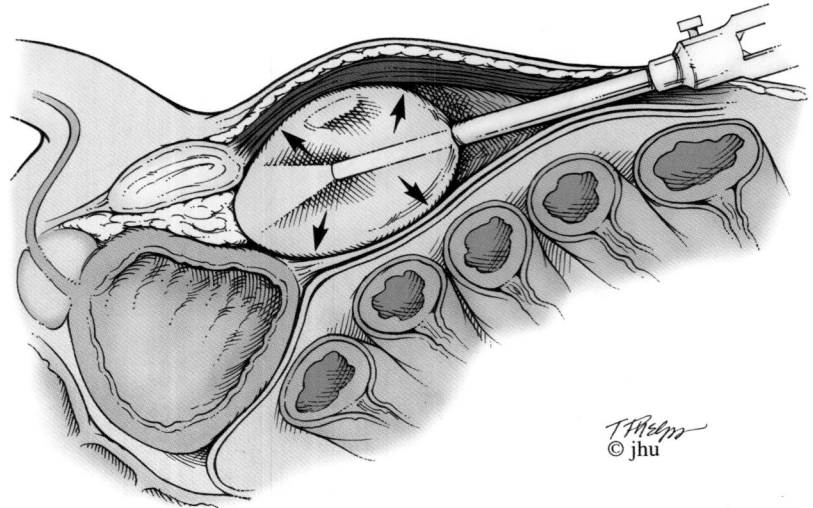

Figure 99–26. Creation of working space for extraperitoneal laparoscopic radical prostatectomy using a trocar-mounted balloon dilator device. (Copyright 2005, Johns Hopkins University.)

KEY POINTS: TECHNIQUE OF LAPAROSCOPIC/ROBOTIC-ASSISTED LAPAROSCOPIC RADICAL PROSTATECTOMY

- An extraperitoneal approach helps confine any urine leak but provides a smaller operative working space.

- The robotic technology facilitates suturing and dissection for surgeons who do not have advanced laparoscopic skills.

- Sharp incision of Denonvilliers' fascia and complete mobilization of the rectum from the prostate is an important step in avoiding rectal injury.

- Use of thermal energy should be minimized during dissection near the neurovascular bundles.

- Either a single knot running suture or an interrupted suture may be used to accomplish the vesicourethral anastomosis.

Perioperative Outcomes

Operative Time. The duration of surgery is typically longer with LRP or RALP compared with open surgery, especially early in the surgeon's experience. In fact, operating times often are used as a surrogate for assessing the "learning curve" with laparoscopic prostatectomy (Herrell and Smith, 2006). As both surgeon and operating team experience is gained, virtually all reported series have documented a substantial decrease in operative times that approach and, in some series, surpass those for open surgical techniques. **Operative times of 5 to 6 hours are reported for LRP in the initial experience at most centers but decrease within 20 or 30 patients to durations of 3 to 4 hours** (Salomon et al, 2004; Guillonneau and Vallancien, 2000b; Bollens et al, 2001; Turk et al, 2001).

Similar findings have been observed with RALP. Inexperience of both the console surgeon as well as the table side operating team can lead to lengthy procedures initially. The table side operating team is responsible not only for trocar placement but also for docking and undocking of the robot and instrument changes throughout the procedure. Lack of familiarity with the robot can lengthen this aspect of the procedure. Once experience is gained, operative times of less than 3 hours have been reported for the total procedure (Tewari et al, 2003; Smith, 2004; Dasgupta et al, 2005; Martina et al, 2005).

Postoperative Pain. One of the distinct advantages of laparoscopy for many surgical procedures is its minimally invasive nature, resulting in less postoperative pain than comparative open approaches. For radical prostatectomy, however, this advantage seems to be less dramatic as radical retropubic prostatectomy is performed through an infraumbilical muscle-splitting incision. In addition, relatively little pain occurs after radical perineal prostatectomy. Some series have shown decreased pain in patients undergoing either LRP or RALP compared with RRP (Menon et al, 2002; Bhayani et al, 2003). Other reports have shown no substantial difference in postoperative narcotic use or in patient-reported pain (Webster et al, 2005). **The lack of a significant advantage for laparoscopic prostatectomy is attributable primarily to low pain scores even in the open surgical group.**

Intraoperative Blood Loss. Because most of the blood loss that occurs during radical prostatectomy is from venous sinuses, the tamponade effect from the pneumoperitoneum helps diminish ongoing blood loss during LRP and RALP. Furthermore, techniques that use antegrade dissection of the prostate divide the dorsal vein complex near the completion of the procedure. Thus, the portion of the procedure with the greatest potential for blood loss is reserved until near the end. Both of these factors, as well as the excellent visualization with laparoscopy, account for the minimal blood loss reported in most series. Estimation of blood loss during LRP or RALP is difficult because blood and urine are mixed in the aspirate and some of the blood may accumulate in the upper portion of the abdomen because of the steep Trendelenburg position.

Nonetheless, blood loss of less than a few hundred milliliters is routinely reported (Guillonneau et al, 2001; Hoznek et al, 2002). A prospective comparison between RRP and RALP showed that median discharge serum hematocrit was higher in the RALP (38%) than after RRP (33%) (Farnham et al, 2006).

Perhaps the most meaningful parameter clinically is the proportion of patients requiring transfusion of homologous blood products. Most studies have shown a significant decrease in transfusion requirement for patients undergoing LRP or RALP compared with RRP (Tewari et al, 2003; Ahlering et al, 2004a). Others have shown no statistically significant difference if the transfusion requirement with open prostatectomy can be limited to only a few percent of patients (Farnham et al, 2006).

Hospital Stay. Over the past decade, hospital stay after radical prostatectomy has diminished remarkably regardless of the surgical approach. Some centers have reported a length of stay as short as 1 or 2 days after either radical perineal or radical retropubic prostatectomy (Holzbeierlein and Smith, 2000). With laparoscopic approaches, a hospital stay of only 1 day has become routine in many centers (Bhayani et al, 2003; Tewari et al, 2003). Ileus or inability to tolerate a regular diet are the most common factors limiting early discharge. Pain control does not typically contribute to prolonged length of stay, because parenteral narcotics are rarely required. **With early discharge programs for radical perineal and retropubic prostatectomy being commonly used, no distinct advantage exists for LRP or RALP, although discharge on the first postoperative day may be more easily accomplished routinely with the minimally invasive laparoscopic approaches.**

Functional Outcomes

The complications of radical prostatectomy with the greatest potential for an adverse effect on quality of life are urinary incontinence and erectile dysfunction. Greater surgical experience with radical prostatectomy and refinements in surgical technique have diminished the frequency with which these problems are observed in most radical prostatectomy series from centers of excellence. However, most large population-based studies show substantial rates of erectile dysfunction and incontinence after both RRP and radical perineal prostatectomy (Fowler et al, 1993). Whether laparoscopic approaches offer improved functional outcomes is still a matter of debate, and comparison of published series is difficult because of differences in patient populations and methods of assessment.

Urinary Incontinence. Urinary incontinence after radical prostatectomy is usually manifested as stress incontinence secondary to intrinsic sphincter deficiency. Although over 90% of patients ultimately regain good urinary control and do not require pads for incontinence in reports from high volume centers (Walsh, 1998; Catalona et al, 1999), other studies have shown that a substantial proportion of patients may be bothered by some degree of stress incontinence (Fowler et al, 1993). The exact physiologic mechanisms that contribute to urinary control after radical prostatectomy are not entirely understood. However, surgical technique is undoubtedly a contributing factor (Smith, 2002).

With laparoscopic approaches, visualization of the prostatic apex typically is superb. The minimal bleeding and magnification of the operative field allow precise dissection of the prostatic apex with limited trauma to the periurethral striated sphincter and genitourinary diaphragm (Menon et al, 2004a). Potentially, earlier return of continence or better long-term results may be achieved with LRP or RALP. **However, none of the currently published studies allows definitive conclusions about whether postoperative continence is improved with laparoscopic radical prostatectomy compared with open surgical approaches** (Guillonneau et al, 2001; Hoznek et al, 2002; Salomon et al, 2004).

The method used to evaluate continence in reported series varies (Table 99–2). Differences exist whether the information

Table 99–2. Reported Continence Rates Following LRP and RALP

Reference	Total Patients	Mean Age (Years)	Method of Assessment	Definition Used	Time of Assessment	Continence Rate
Laparoscopic Radical Prostatectomy Series						
Hoznek et al, 2001	200	64.8	Questionnaire	No pad	12 months	86%
Turk et al, 2001	125	59.9	Physician	0-1 pad	9 months	92%
Olsson et al, 2001	228	65.2	Questionnaire	No pad	12 months	78.4%
Salomon et al, 2002	235	63.8	Questionnaire	No pad	12 months	90%
Eden et al, 2002	100	62.2	Physician	No pad	12 months	90%
Guillonneau et al, 2002b	550	NA	Physician	No pad	12 months	82.3%
Anastasiadis et al, 2003	230	64.1	Questionnaire	No pad	12 months	71.6%
Roumeguere et al, 2003	85	62.5	Questionnaire	No pad	12 months	80.7%
Stolzenburg et al, 2003b	70	63.4	Physician	No pad	6 months	90%
Rassweiler et al, 2004	500	64	Questionnaire	No pad	12 months	83.6%
Rozet et al, 2005	600	NA	Questionnaire	No pad	12 months	84%
Stolzenburg et al, 2005b	700	63.4	Questionnaire	No pad	12 months	92%
Rassweiler et al, 2006	5824	64	Questionnaire	No pad	12 months	84.9%
Goeman et al, 2006	550	62.4	Questionnaire	No pad	12 months	82.9%
Robotic-Assisted Laparoscopic Prostatectomy Series						
Menon et al, 2003	100	60	Physician	0-1 security pad	6 months	92%
Ahlering et al, 2004a	60	62.9	Questionnaire	No pad	3 months	76%
Patel et al, 2005	200	59.5	Questionnaire	No pad	12 months	98%
Joseph et al, 2006	325	60	Unknown	No pad	6 months	96%

is gathered by questionnaire, the physician, or an independent third party. Furthermore, even though validated instruments for assessment of incontinence exist, the manner and location in which the data are collected can affect results. A common observation after radical prostatectomy, regardless of surgical approach, is that urinary incontinence improves substantially within the first 3 to 6 months after surgery and to some extent for another year or more. Therefore, the time points at which data on incontinence are collected are highly influential.

Erectile Dysfunction. Preservation of erectile function after radical prostatectomy depends on precise and adequate separation of the cavernous nerves in the neurovascular bundle from the prostate (Walsh and Donker, 1982). The anatomic course of these nerves has been described but can be variable. Intraoperative localization using nerve stimulation has not been sufficiently accurate for clinical utility (Holzbeierlein et al, 2001). The principles and anatomic dissection for nerve preservation are the same regardless of surgical approach. It is still uncertain whether the magnified image of the operative field afforded by laparoscopy and the precision of the surgical instruments allows more anatomically accurate and less traumatic dissection of the neurovascular bundles, resulting in improved postoperative erectile function. As with incontinence, comparison of the published literature is difficult (Salomon et al, 2004). Differences in the method of assessment, definition of potency (e.g., spontaneous erections vs. intercourse), and patient populations complicate comparisons. In addition, the use of adjunctive therapies such as phosphodiesterase-5 inhibitors or vasoactive injections can substantially influence results. Also, in concordance with other nerve injuries, improvement in erectile function is a prolonged process that is ongoing for years after radical prostatectomy. Good results with erectile function after both LRP and RALP have been reported (Guillonneau et al, 2002b;

Menon et al, 2003; Su et al, 2004) (Table 99–3). **However, there are no published data that allow definitive conclusions about the relative merits of either laparoscopic or robotic-assisted approaches for radical prostatectomy in avoiding erectile dysfunction compared with open surgical approaches.** Nevertheless, the avoidance of hemostatic energy sources during neurovascular bundle preservation and the performance of meticulous interfascial dissection and preservation of the cavernous nerves appears to be critical to optimizing postoperative recovery of potency (Ong et al, 2004; Su et al, 2004).

Anatomic studies indicate that the cavernous nerves in the neurovascular bundle course posterolateral to the prostate and urethra. A technique during robotic prostatectomy for division of the lateral pelvic fascia along the anterior portion of the prostate has been described (Menon et al, 2004a). Although some neural tissue can be shown histologically to be present on the anterior prostate, the significance of any nerves in this location or their contribution to erectile function is uncertain.

Oncologic Outcomes

The goal of radical prostatectomy is complete surgical removal of the entire prostate and its investing fascia as well as the seminal vesicles. Because most adenocarcinomas of the prostate occur in the peripheral zone and approach the capsular margin, surgical technique can influence oncologic outcomes. Proper surgical dissection should allow negative margins with pathologic stage T2 tumors while also permitting complete removal and negative margins for some extracapsular lesions. Efforts to avoid urinary incontinence or erectile dysfunction by dissecting too closely to the prostatic apex or the posterolateral aspect of the prostate can compromise margins, regardless of the surgical approach. Once again, comparison of positive margin rates in reported series is

Table 99–3.	Reported Potency Rates Following Bilateral Nerve-Sparing LRP and RALP							
Reference	Total Patients	Evaluable Patients	Mean Age (Years)	Percent of Patients Receiving BNS*	Method of Assessment	Definition Used	Time of Assessment	Potency Rate
Laparoscopic Radical Prostatectomy Series								
Hoznek et al, 2001	200	82	64.8	32	Questionnaire	Intercourse	1 month	46%
Turk et al, 2001	125	44	59.9	11	Physician	Intercourse	12 months	59%
Salomon et al, 2002	235	43	63.8	39.5	Questionnaire	Intercourse	12 months	58.8%
Eden et al, 2002	100	100	62.2	58	Physician	Erections	12 months	62%
Guillonneau et al, 2002b	550	47	NA	NA	Physician	Intercourse	1.5 months	66%
Katz et al, 2002	232	143	63	44	Questionnaire	Erections	12 months	87.5%
Anastasiadis et al, 2003	230	230	64.1	33.5	Questionnaire	Intercourse	12 months	53%
Stolzenburg et al, 2003b	70	40	63.4	7.5	Physician	Intercourse	2 months	66.7%
Roumeguere et al, 2003	85	85	62.5	30.9	Questionnaire	Intercourse	12 months	65.3%
Su et al, 2004	177	177	57.8	51.4	Questionnaire	Intercourse	12 months	76%
Rassweiler et al, 2004	500	109	67	37.6	Questionnaire	Intercourse	12 months	67%
Rozet et al, 2005	600	231	NA	60.2	Questionnaire	Intercourse	6 months	64%
Stolzenburg et al, 2005b	700	185	63.4	10.1	Questionnaire	Intercourse	6 months	47%
Wagner et al, 2006	220	220	58	66	Questionnaire	Intercourse	12 months	72%
Rassweiler et al, 2006	5824	NA	64	NA	Questionnaire	Intercourse	12 months	52.5%
Goeman et al, 2006	550	NA	62.4	NA	Questionnaire	Intercourse	12 months	56%
Robotic-Assisted Laparoscopic Prostatectomy Series								
Menon et al, 2003	250	200	59.9	NA	Questionnaire	Intercourse	6 months	64%
Joseph et al, 2006	325	150	60	86%	Questionnaire	IEEF-5[†] score of 22-25	6 months	68%

*BNS, bilateral nerve sparing surgery.
[†]IEEF-5, International Index of Erectile Function.

difficult because of patient selection. **Importantly, the method and detail of pathologic analysis of the surgical specimen can be highly influential in assessing surgical margin status.** Some reports have used only biopsies of remaining tissue after removal of the surgical specimen to assess margin status, whereas others rely on step-sectioned whole-mount histology.

In most series of LRP and RALP, positive margin percentages decrease as greater familiarity with the procedure is obtained (Ahlering et al, 2004b; Salomon et al, 2004; Rassweiler et al, 2005). This implies that inexperience with the surgery accounts for positive margins in some cases. Sometimes, this may be from difficulty in identifying the proper anatomic plane of dissection between the bladder neck and the base of the prostate. The most common site of a positive margin, whether the operation is performed via open or laparoscopic approaches, is the prostatic apex (Touijer et al, 2005). Insufficient removal of prostatic tissue at the apex in an effort to avoid incontinence can result in positive margins even with tumors that do not pathologically violate the capsule (stage pT2). Reported rates of positive margins for LRP or RALP are shown in Table 99–4.

The primary factor that determines the positive margin rate in a given series is patient selection. As discussed earlier, the method and detail of pathologic analysis is also influential. Evaluating positive margin rates from one series to another, then, is not necessarily a comparison of surgical technique. A more accurate technical comparison is analysis of the pathologic results in stage T2 tumors wherein a positive margin implies surgical violation of the prostatic capsule. Even in this circumstance, however, the methodology for pathologic analysis is important. Intra-institutional comparisons from some studies have shown a reduced rate of positive margins with laparoscopic approaches compared with radical retropubic prostatectomy. **However, comparison of margin status between high-volume centers with the operations performed by experienced surgeons has shown no definitive advantage for one surgical approach over the other in achieving negative surgical margins** (Brown et al, 2003; Khan and Partin, 2005).

Regarding biochemical recurrence, Guillonneau and colleagues (2003b) reported on their oncologic outcomes with 1000 consecutive LRPs performed over a 4-year period with a median follow-up period of 12 months. Their overall actuarial biochemical progression-free survival rate was 90.5% at 3 years. By pathologic stage, the rates were 92% for pT2a, 88% for pT2b, 77% for pT3a, and 44% for pT3b.

Economic Considerations

Both the duration of surgery and equipment expenses contribute to operating room costs for laparoscopic prostatectomy, which typically are higher than those for open approaches (Lotan et al, 2004; Link et al, 2005). This is particularly true with robotic-assisted surgery. The robotic equipment itself costs in excess of $1 million with charges for the multiple use but disposable robotic instruments of up to $600 per case. **In the study by Link and colleagues (2005), the factors that most influenced overall cost in order of importance included operative time, length of hospital stay, and consumable items (e.g., disposable laparoscopic equipment and trocars).** They found that the calculated cost equivalence between open and laparoscopic prostatectomy could be met if disposable equipment was eliminated by using reusable items and operative times for LRP were reduced to 3.4 hours.

These increased costs may be partially mitigated by shorter hospital stays compared with open procedures. The decrease in expense for hospital stay depends partly on the discharge day for the laparoscopic procedure but also the customary length of stay at a given hospital for open radical prostatectomy. Published reports detailing a length of stay of a week or more for radical retropubic prostatectomy are not in concordance with other contemporary reports wherein patients are discharged on the second or even first postoperative day after radical perineal or radical retropubic prostatectomy (Holzbeierlein and Smith, 2000).

Table 99–4. Positive Margin Rates with LRP and RALP

Author	Number of Patients	Positive Margins (%) pT2	pT3
Laparoscopic Radical Prostatectomy			
Hoznek et al, 2002	250	16.4	39.3
Guillonneau et al, 2003b	1000	15.5	31.1
Roumeguere et al, 2003	85	18.4	45.7
Su et al, 2004	177	4.7	44.8
Rassweiler et al, 2005	500	7.4	31.8
Rozet et al, 2005	600	14.6	26.2
Stolzenburg et al, 2005b	700	10.8	31.2
Rassweiler et al, 2006	5824	10.6	32.7 (pT3a)
			56.2 (pT3b)
Goeman et al, 2006	550	17.9	44.8
Robotic-Assisted Laparoscopic Prostatectomy			
Menon et al, 2003	100	10.6	40
Wolfram et al, 2003	81	12.7	42
Ahlering et al, 2004b	140		
Overall		12.3	48.8
Cases 1–50		27.3	50
Cases 51–140		4.7	44
Cathelineau et al, 2004b	105	11.7	43
Patel et al, 2005	200	5.7	26.3
Joseph et al, 2006	325	9.9	32.7
Atug et al, 2006	140		
Overall		18.1	54
Cases 1–33		38.4	60
Cases 34–66		13.7	66
Cases 67–140		3.6	40

KEY POINTS: RESULTS OF LAPAROSCOPIC/ROBOTIC-ASSISTED LAPAROSCOPIC RADICAL PROSTATECTOMY

- Blood loss is minimal in part owing to the tamponade effect of the pneumoperitoneum.

- Hospital length of stay is often only 1 day.

- Whether continence and/or potency are better with a laparoscopic/robotic-assisted approach compared with open surgery in expert hands is uncertain.

- Surgical margins are comparable to those with open approaches and are partly influenced by surgical technique and experience.

Complications

Overall Complication Rate and Severity of Complications

A comprehensive description of the incidence and types of complications after 567 consecutive LRPs over a 3-year period has been reported by the Montsouris group (Guillonneau et al, 2002a). They reported total, major, and minor complication rates of 17%, 4%, and 14.6%, respectively. The majority of complications were urologic, with the most common being that of anastomotic leak, which occurred in 57 patients (10% rate). Nearly all (95%) resolved with conservative measures and prolonged catheterization. Mean catheterization period was 5.8 days for this study and 4 days in a report by Nadu and colleagues (2001). Early catheter removal was complicated by acute urinary retention in 10% of cases in Nadu and colleagues' study, suggesting that, although feasible, a longer catheterization period (at least 7 days) is probably advisable. Other series have reported complication rates with LRP between 4% and 12% (Salomon et al, 2004).

Gonzalgo and colleagues applied a morbidity grading scheme designed to detail the frequency and severity of complications after general surgical procedures (Dindo et al, 2004; Gonzalgo et al, 2005). A total of 34 (13.8%) morbidities were encountered during 246 LRP cases, the majority (94.1%) of which were self-limited (i.e., grade II to III). There were only 2 (5.9%) grade IV complications (i.e., potentially life threatening requiring intensive care unit management) and no grade V complications (i.e., deaths). Postoperative ileus and bleeding requiring transfusion were the most frequent complications, with incidences of 3.3% and 2.8%, respectively.

Similar complication rates with RALP have been reported with few problems unique to the robot-assisted approach versus pure LRP. Bowel or epigastric injury from trocar insertion has been reported as with most laparoscopic procedures. Conversion to an open operation occurs in fewer than 1% of cases once satisfactory surgical experience is attained.

Rectal Injury

Rectal injuries, although uncommon during LRP and RALP (0.7% to 2.4%), have been reported and repaired successfully by laparoscopic means (Katz et al, 2003; Guillonneau et al, 2003a; Gonzalgo et al, 2005). Rectal injury can occur after transection at the prostatic apex if the posterior dissection is incomplete and the rectum remains fixed to the posterior surface of the prostate. **With LRP and RALP, sharp and complete incision of Denonvilliers' fascia is necessary after seminal vesicle dissection to allow adequate mobilization of the rectum.** Another location for rectal injury is the lateral border of the rectum that is at risk when performing wide resection of the NVBs. Use of a rectal balloon or bougie has been advocated by some authors to help delineate the limits of the rectum and avoid iatrogenic injury (Guillonneau and Vallancien, 2000a; Rassweiler et al, 2001).

If a rectal injury is suspected, the rectum should be inspected digitally as well as by filling the pelvic cavity with saline and insufflating the rectum with air through a transrectally placed Foley catheter. If air bubbles are detected on insufflating the rectum, the site of injury is identified and integrity of the surrounding tissues inspected carefully. The rectal injury is then closed in two layers followed by coverage with either omentum or perirectal fat (Katz et al, 2003). If identified and repaired as described, simultaneous colostomy is generally not required. Because patients undergo a bowel preparation before surgery, gross contamination of the operative field is minimized. The site of repair should be irrigated with copious antibiotic solution, appropriate parenteral antibiotics given to cover gram-negative and anaerobic organisms, and digital dilation of the anus performed at the end of the operation.

Open Conversion and Reoperation

In the Montsouris series, open conversion to RRP occurred in 1.2% of patients and reoperation was required in 3.7% (Guillonneau et al, 2002a). The indications for reoperation included bowel injury, ureteral injury, hemoperitoneum, epigastric artery injury, persistent anastomotic urinary fistula, and wound dehiscence. In a multi-institutional study of open conversions during attempted LRP, a 1.9% incidence of open conversion was observed during 670 LRP procedures. Most reported conversions occurred during the surgeons' early experience and with associated contributing patient factors, including morbid obesity and prior pelvic surgery. The most common cited reason for conversion included failure to progress, injury to adjacent structures, and hypercarbia (Bhayani et al, 2004). Smith (2004) has reported a single conversion to open operation with over 400 RALPs. **The authors recommended careful patient selection in a surgeon's early experience avoiding patients with morbid obesity, prior pelvic surgery, and those at high risk for periprostatic adhesions (e.g., prostatitis, multiple prostate biopsies, prior transurethral resection of the prostate) to minimize the chance of open conversion.**

Anastomotic Strictures

Postoperative anastomotic strictures are uncommon after LRP (0% to 3%) (Rassweiler et al, 2001; Turk et al, 2001; Guillonneau et al, 2002a) in contrast to a 3% to 20% incidence in patients after RRP (Fowler et al, 1993; Geary et al, 1995; Lepor et al, 2001; Kundu et al, 2004). **Mobilization of the bladder during LRP or RALP allows for a tension-free anastomosis. Equally important is the excellent visualization provided by laparoscopy, which optimizes mucosa-to-mucosa approximation between the bladder and urethra.** There is no reported difference in the rate of anastomotic stricture whether a running or interrupted suture is used.

Deep Venous Thrombosis

The occurrence of a clinically significant deep venous thrombosis is an infrequent event after LRP (0.4%) (Guillonneau et al, 2002a) and may be of slightly lower incidence than after RRP (2%) (Catalona et al, 1999). This may be attributable to the Trendelenburg positioning, lack of venous compression as can occur in open surgery when using a fixed retractor system, and a rapid return to ambulation and normal activities in LRP patients.

Other Complications

Ureteral injury and trocar site hernias after LRP are relatively rare but have been reported (Gregori et al, 2003). No deaths attributed to the LRP or RALP technique have been reported in any published study.

LAPAROSCOPIC PELVIC LYMPH NODE DISSECTION

Indications

Currently, pelvic lymph node dissection (PLND) is rarely indicated as an independent staging procedure. In some patients with a significant risk for nodal metastasis, such as those with a high Gleason grade tumor, a large tumor volume, or a markedly elevated prostate specific antigen (PSA) level, PLND may be useful for staging and selection of therapy before external-beam irradiation. Also, staging PLND may have a role in some patients in whom radical perineal prostatectomy is planned. With RRP, LRP, or RALP, it is the usual practice that PLND be performed simultaneously with the radical prostatectomy.

There are some patients in whom PLND may be unnecessary because of a low risk of nodal metastasis. Most studies show histologic evidence of nodal metastasis in fewer than 5% of patients with good risk features (cT1c, PSA < 10 ng/mL, Gleason score 6). If PLND is planned, it can be performed either before or after dissection of the prostate.

Surgical Technique

Laparoscopic PLND can be performed by either the transperitoneal or extraperitoneal approach and using either a pure laparoscopic technique or robotic assistance. Two options for trocar configuration include a four-trocar diamond-shaped configuration or a five-trocar inverted U-shaped configuration as in LRP. When performing a transperitoneal staging lymphadenectomy, the peritoneum is incised longitudinally and immediately lateral to the medial umbilical ligament from the pubis to the bifurcation of the iliac vessels (Fig. 99–27). The course of the ureter is near the proximal extent of the dissection and should be avoided. In contrast, when performing PLND after completion of LRP or RALP, an incision has already been made medial to the median umbilical ligament as a consequence of the lateral bladder dissection.

There is some controversy as to the appropriate extent of PLND in patients with carcinoma of the prostate. Some authors advocate an extended dissection that reaches above the bifurcation of the common iliac artery and includes all external iliac, obturator, and hypogastric lymph nodes (Stone et al, 1997). Others use a more limited dissection that extends to the external iliac artery anteriorly, the obturator nerve posteriorly, the node of Cloquet distally, and the bifurcation of the iliac vessels proximally. Either an extended or more limited node dissection can be performed laparoscopically.

As with an open approach, a key initial step is separation of the nodal packet from the external iliac vein. The lymph node packet is grasped and retracted medially, and a relatively avascular plane between the lymph node packet and lateral pelvic sidewall is identified and dissected bluntly using a suction-irrigation device. Dissection is carried out proximally to the iliac bifurcation and distally to the pubis, thus defining the lateral extent of the lymph node packet. By retracting the lymph node packet medially, the precise course of the obturator nerve and vessels can be identified and protected (Fig. 99–28). After securing the distal extent of the lymph

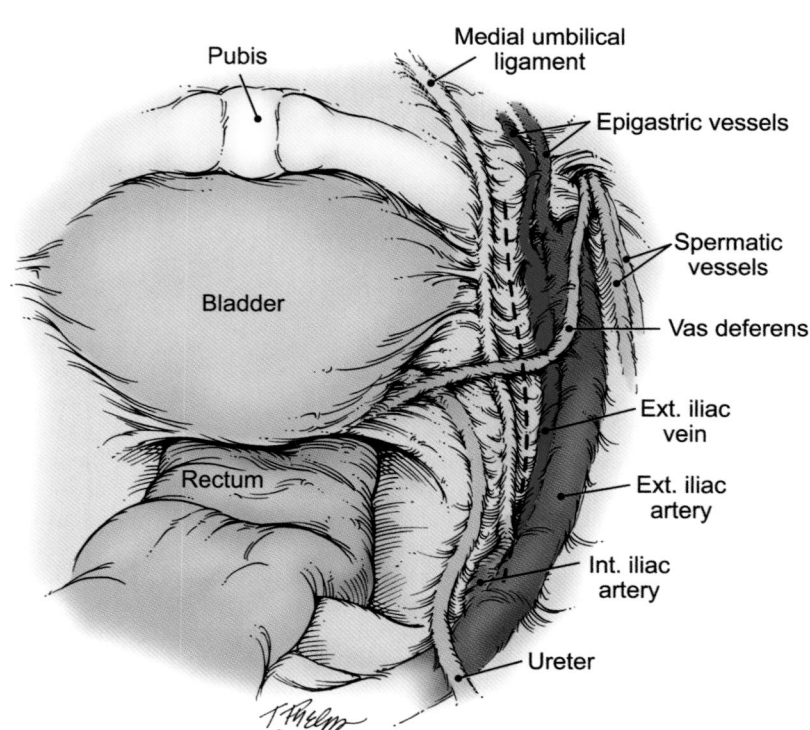

Figure 99–27. Anatomic landmarks for laparoscopic pelvic lymphadenectomy. *Dashed line* indicates the line of incision for exposure of the pelvic lymph nodes. (Copyright 2005, Johns Hopkins University.)

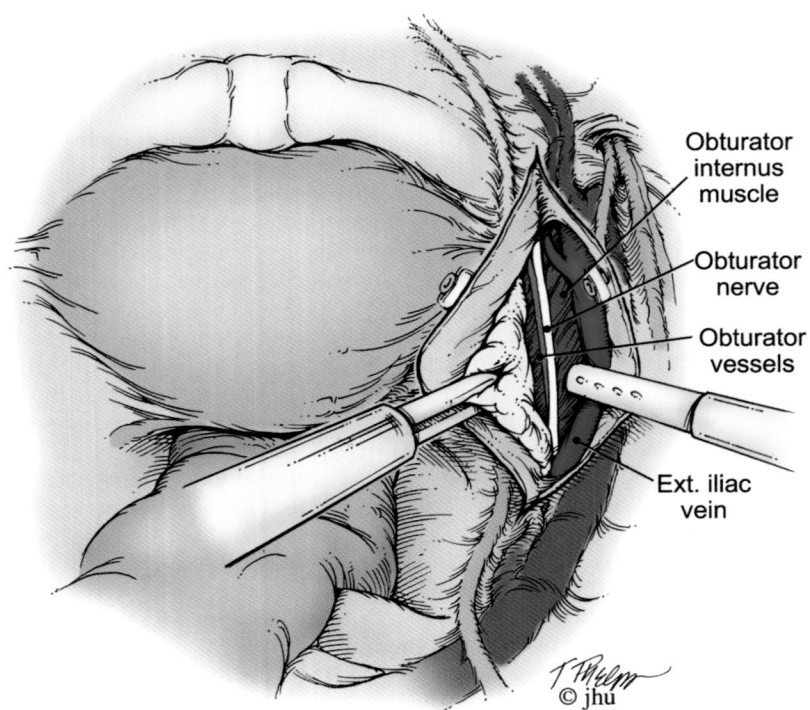

Obturator
internus
muscle

Obturator
nerve

Obturator
vessels

Ext. iliac
vein

Figure 99–28. Initial dissection of the lymph node packet. The vas deferens has been clipped and divided. With medial traction on the lymph node packet, the lateral extent of the dissection is defined using blunt dissection with a suction-irrigator device. (Copyright 2005, Johns Hopkins University.)

node packet, the packet is then retracted cranially to separate it from the obturator vessels and nerves. Hemoclips are used to control lymphatics and vessels at the most proximal and distal extent of the dissection (Fig. 99–29). The lymph nodes can usually be removed as a single packet and extracted either through the 12-mm trocar or by placing them in the entrapment sack along with the prostate specimen.

KEY POINTS: LAPAROSCOPIC PELVIC LYMPH NODE DISSECTION

■ Laparoscopic PLND can be performed by either the transperitoneal or extraperitoneal route.

■ Postoperative lymphoceles are uncommon with transperitoneal laparoscopic PLND due to absorption of lymphatic fluid by the peritoneum.

Complications

Most complications related to pelvic lymph node dissection are either a consequence of trocar placement or vascular injury (Burney et al, 1993; Rukstalis et al, 1994). Often an accessory obturator vein is encountered arising from the distal aspect of the external iliac vein and traveling toward the lymph node packet. This vessel can be a source of bleeding if not anticipated. When present, this vessel may be clipped and divided or avoided if possible when securing the distal extent of the lymph node packet. Bleeding from the obturator vessels can occur when defining the deep extent of the lymph node dissection. Sharp dissection should be avoided when possible

during PLND to avoid iatrogenic injury to the obturator and iliac vessels. Bleeding from the obturator vessels can be managed using a hemoclip or bipolar electrocautery, but bleeding from the iliac vessels can be more difficult to manage laparoscopically. Immediate pressure to an iliac vessel injury should be applied and maintained for several minutes. Bleeding from a tiny venous injury may stop with this maneuver, but for a larger injury an attempt can be made to secure the opening with either hemoclips or sutures. Prompt conversion to open surgery and repair may be required if these attempts are unsuccessful.

Great care must be taken to avoid thermal injury or transection of the obturator nerve resulting in the inability of the patient to adduct the ipsilateral thigh. Defining the precise course of the obturator nerve before application of hemoclips to secure the proximal and distal extent of the lymph node packet is imperative to avoid accidental injury to the obturator nerve.

Postoperative lymphocele and deep venous thrombosis are two major morbidities associated with open pelvic lymph node dissection. **With laparoscopic lymph node dissection, postoperative lymphoceles are less common** (Kavoussi et al, 1993; Kerbl et al, 1993; Chow et al, 1994). **A transperitoneal laparoscopic approach allows continuous egress and absorption of lymphatic fluid by the peritoneum in the event of a lymphatic leak.** However, loculation of lymphatic fluid can occur, even with a transperitoneal approach. Deep venous thrombosis is relatively uncommon after a laparoscopic lymph node dissection owing to the steep Trendelenburg position used and avoidance of venous compression of the iliac veins that can occur when using a fixed retractor system during open surgery. One comparative study found a lower total complication rate with laparoscopic (0%) as compared with open PLND (21%) (Herrell et al, 1997).

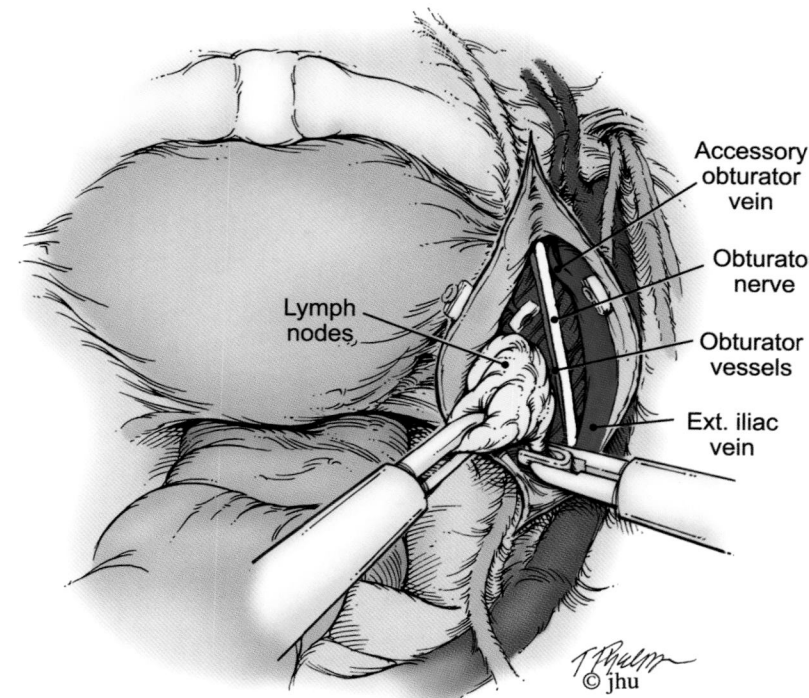

Figure 99–29. Final dissection of the lymph node packet. The proximal and distal extent of the lymph node packet are clipped and divided, taking great care to avoid injury to the obturator nerve and vessels as well as the accessory obturator vein. (Copyright 2005, Johns Hopkins University.)

SUMMARY

In only a few years of worldwide use, minimally invasive laparoscopic prostatectomy has become an accepted surgical approach for the management of patients with localized carcinoma of the prostate. As expertise with the procedure is achieved, operative times diminish and approach those for open radical prostatectomy. Robotic-assisted approaches facilitate suturing and other technical aspects of the operation for surgeons who do not have highly advanced laparoscopic skills.

Comparison of outcomes between reported series is imprecise because of differences in patient selection, methods of collecting and reporting data, and the methodology for pathologic analysis. However, intraoperative blood loss with laparoscopic/robotic prostatectomy has consistently been reported as minimal and transfusion is required in only a small percentage of patients. Postoperative morbidity and return to activity are both improved compared with open surgery in most reports. Good results with postoperative urinary continence and erectile function are reported, although there is still debate about whether these outcomes are superior with laparoscopic/robotic surgery compared with open radical prostatectomy performed by experienced surgeons. Pathologic tumor margin status seems to be comparable between laparoscopic and open series overall.

Improvements in the available instruments are highly likely to advance even further the technologic capabilities of surgeons performing laparoscopic and robotic-assisted laparoscopic radical prostatectomy. Equipment expense remains a significant issue for some hospitals and not all may be able to offer the state of the art technology necessary for minimally invasive laparoscopic radical prostatectomy. Nonetheless, there seems to be little doubt that minimally invasive approaches for radical prostatectomy will in the future assume an even greater and, perhaps, dominant role, in the surgical treatment of localized prostate cancer.

SUGGESTED READINGS

Guillonneau B, Rozet F, Cathelineau X, et al: Perioperative complications of laparoscopic radical prostatectomy: The Montsouris 3-year experience. J Urol 2002;167:51-56.

Menon M, Tewari A, Peabody JO, et al: Vattikuti Institute prostatectomy, a technique of robotic radical prostatectomy for management of localized carcinoma of the prostate: Experience of over 1100 cases. Urol Clin North Am 2004;31:701-717.

Ong AM, Su LM, Varkarakis I, et al: Nerve sparing radical prostatectomy: Effects of hemostatic energy sources on the recovery of cavernous nerve function in a canine model. J Urol 2004;172(4 pt 1): 1318-1322.

Salomon L, Sebe P, De la Taille A, et al: Open versus laparoscopic radical prostatectomy: I and II. BJU Int 2004;94:238-250.

Smith JA Jr: Robotically assisted laparoscopic prostatectomy: An assessment of its contemporary role in the surgical management of localized prostate cancer. Am J Surg 2004;188:63S-67S.

Su LM, Link RE, Bhayani SB, et al: Nerve-sparing laparoscopic radical prostatectomy: Replicating the open surgical technique. Urology 2004; 64:123-127.

100 Radiation Therapy for Prostate Cancer

ANTHONY V. D'AMICO, MD, PhD • JUANITA CROOK, MD •
CLAIR J. BEARD, MD • THEODORE L. DeWEESE, MD, PhD •
MARK HURWITZ, MD • IRVING KAPLAN, MD

HISTORICAL PERSPECTIVE

LOCALIZED DISEASE

TREATMENT: CANCER CONTROL AND
QUALITY OF LIFE

HISTORICAL PERSPECTIVE

Two major advances in the radiotherapeutic management of adenocarcinoma of the prostate have occurred since the early 1980s. The first advance was the generation of linear accelerators and conformal techniques capable of delivering high doses of radiation deep within the pelvis while simultaneously respecting the normal tissue tolerance of the anterior rectal wall, prostatic urethra, femoral heads, and bladder neck. The second advance occurred when image-guided techniques were introduced for use during the insertion of radioactive sources directly into the prostate gland. Eliminating the former freehand technique has vastly improved the physician's ability to deliver high doses of radiation to the prostate gland while sparing interposed and juxtaposed normal structures. These two advances have increased the therapeutic ratio of radiation therapy (RT) in the management of prostate cancer. Specifically, decreased gastrointestinal toxicity has been documented (Dearnaley et al, 1999), and improved cancer control has been suggested (Pollack et al, 1999).

The physical property that permits the photon radiation generated from a linear accelerator to penetrate deeply and spare normal tissue is the high energy of the beam. As the energy of the beam increases, the beam penetrates deeper before exerting its cytocidal effect. Whereas orthovoltage and ^{60}Co units deposited their maximum dose within 1.25 cm below the skin surface, high-energy linear accelerators deliver the maximum dose of radiation at more than 15 cm below the skin surface. In addition, the use of multiple and conformal fields has minimized the amount of rectum receiving the high-dose radiation volume, leading to lower rates of radiation-induced proctitis (Pollack et al, 1999).

With respect to image guidance and brachytherapy, transrectal ultrasonography (TRUS) has provided an improved monitoring system compared with freehand or fluoroscopically guided radioactive source deposition. Using this image guidance system, geometric feedback on source location within the prostate gland intraoperatively has provided the potential for delivering high doses of radiation within the prostate gland while limiting dose to the prostatic urethra and the anterior rectal wall. The theoretical advantage of brachytherapy is the physical property of very rapid dose falloff (a few millimeters) because of the very low energy of the radioactive sources used—only 21 and 28 keV for palladium 103 and iodine 125, respectively. This very rapid falloff, however, also mandates millimeter precision in the placement of these sources to ensure that the tumor-bearing regions within the prostate gland are not underdosed. These issues are discussed in more detail in the brachytherapy sections.

In brief, the close of the 20th century saw the introduction of three-dimensional, conformal-based RT using high-energy radiation beams and image guidance for the placement of permanent radioactive sources into the prostate gland. As discussed in this chapter, these advances in the radiotherapeutic management of adenocarcinoma of the prostate provided the basis for improvement in both quality of life and cancer control.

LOCALIZED DISEASE
Pretreatment Prognostic Factors

Recommendations for the treatment of clinically localized adenocarcinoma of the prostate should be made using the results of evidence-based medicine. The ideal endpoint on which to make therapeutic decisions is cause-specific survival. At present, follow-up is too short to make statistically meaningful statements regarding cause-specific survival for men diagnosed and treated for clinically localized disease in the prostate-specific antigen (PSA) era as a function of pretreatment prognostic factors and treatment modality. However, pretreatment prognostic factors have established roles in predicting recurrence (PSA, clinical) after external-beam RT (Pisansky et al, 1993; Zietman et al, 1994; Hanks et al, 1995b; Lee et al, 1995; Zagars et al, 1995; Pisansky et al, 1997). These pretreatment factors include PSA level, biopsy Gleason grade, and 1992 American Joint Commission on Cancer Staging (AJCC) clinical stage. Combining these three factors has led to a definition of the three risk groups for patients managed with RT who have clinically localized disease. These three risk groups are as follows:

- Low risk: more than 85% 5-year PSA failure-free survival, 1992 AJCC clinical stage T1c-T2a and PSA level of 10 ng/mL or lower, and biopsy Gleason grade of 6 or lower
- Intermediate risk: approximately 50% 5-year PSA failure-free survival, 1992 AJCC clinical stage T2b or PSA higher than 10 but no higher than 20 ng/mL, or biopsy Gleason grade of 7
- High risk: approximately 33% 5-year PSA failure-free survival, 1992 AJCC clinical stage T2c or PSA higher than 20 ng/mL, or biopsy Gleason grade of 8 or more; patients having at least clinical stage T3a disease are grouped with high-risk patients with localized disease

Figure 100–1 shows 5-year actuarial data for 473 patients stratified using the clinical risk groups based on pretreatment PSA, biopsy Gleason grade, and 1992 AJCC clinical stage.

Pretreatment Risk Groups and Prostate Cancer–Specific Mortality

Data (D'Amico et al, 2003) now exist to support the significant association of the pretreatment risk groups and prostate cancer–specific mortality (PCSM) following external-beam radiation as shown in Figure 100–2. Specifically, in a multi-institutional study of 2370 radiation-managed patients, the relative risk of PCSM for patients with high- or intermediate-risk disease compared with low-risk disease was 14.3 (95% confidence interval [CI]: 5.2 to 24.0; $p_{Cox} < .0001$) and 5.6 (95% CI: 2.0 to 9.3; $p_{Cox} = .0012$), respectively. For illustration,

Figure 100–3 contains the relative contribution of PCSM and non-PCSM following treatment to all-cause mortality stratified by the patients' age at the time of RT and the pretreatment risk group.

Percentage of Positive Prostate Biopsies and Intermediate-Risk Patients

The fraction of prostate biopsies found to contain prostate cancer is readily available information for all patients with

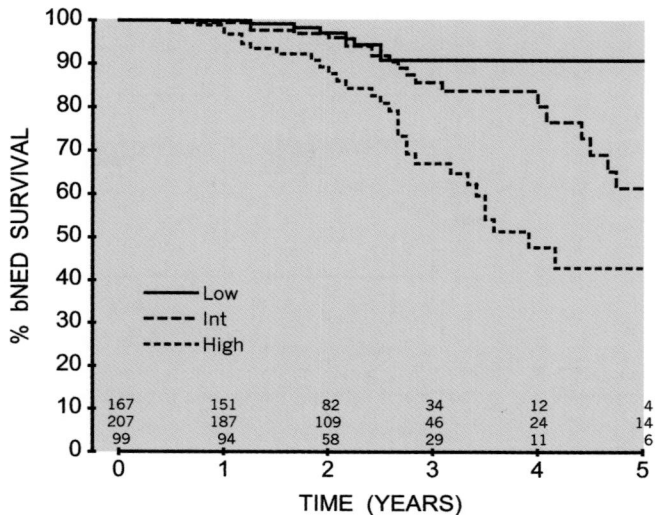

Figure 100–1. Prostate-specific antigen (PSA) failure-free survival stratified by risk group, defined using PSA value, biopsy Gleason grade, and 1992 American Joint Commission on Cancer Staging (AJCC) clinical T stage for 473 patients managed using external-beam radiation therapy. Pairwise, *P* values are as follows: low versus intermediate, *P* = .02; intermediate versus high, *P* = .0004; low versus high, *P* = .0001.

Figure 100–2. Pretreatment risk groups and prostate cancer–specific mortality following external-beam radiation.

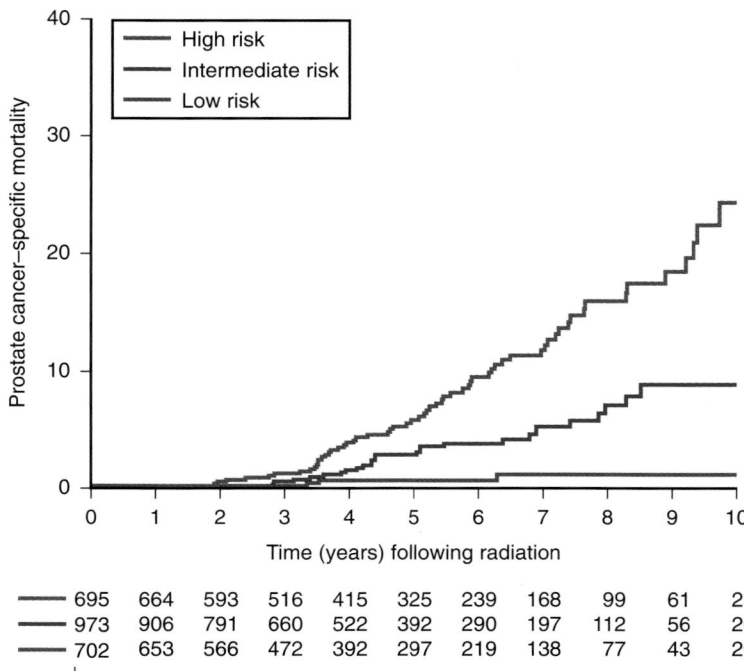

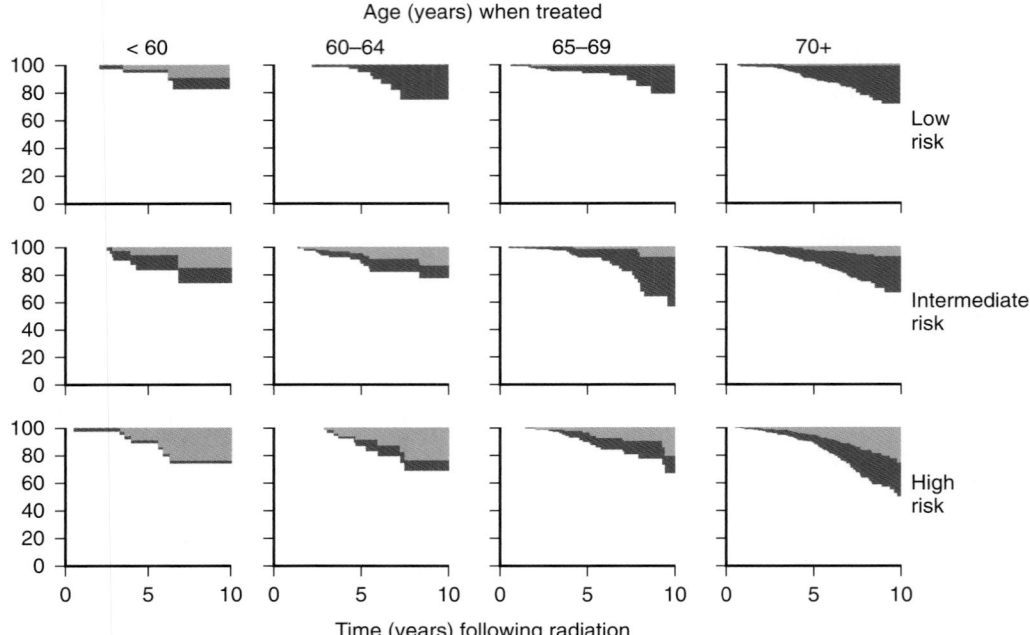

Figure 100–3. Relative contribution of prostate cancer–specific mortality (PCSM) and non-PCSM following treatment to all-cause mortality stratified by the patients' age at the time of radiation therapy and the pretreatment risk group.

PSA-detected or clinically palpable prostate cancer. The fraction of positive biopsies is obtained by dividing the number of positive cores by the number of cores sampled. Studies investigating the ability of the fraction of positive prostate biopsies × 100 (percentage of positive biopsies) to predict pathologic endpoints after RT suggest a role for this clinical factor in predicting tumor volume (Terris et al, 1995), extracapsular extension (Badalment et al, 1996; Borirakchanyavat et al, 1997), seminal vesicle invasion (D'Amico et al, 1996), lymph node involvement (Conrad et al, 1998), and percentage of Gleason grade 4 and 5 disease in the radical prostatectomy specimen (Epstein et al, 1994).

The percentage of positive prostate biopsies has been shown to be an independent predictor of time to postoperative PSA failure after controlling for the established prognostic factors (D'Amico et al, 2000b). The percentage of positive prostate biopsies has also been shown to provide information in addition to the known prognostic factors for predicting PSA control after external-beam RT. Specifically, 473 men treated using three-dimensional conformal external-beam RT at the Joint Center for Radiation Therapy between 1989 and 1998 had detected PSA or clinically palpable prostate cancer. Figure 100–1 illustrates the ability of the previously described risk group system (D'Amico et al, 1998b) that was based on pretreatment PSA level, biopsy Gleason grade, and 1992 AJCC clinical stage to stratify patients according to PSA outcome. Specifically, 5 years after RT, 91%, 62%, and 43% of low-, intermediate-, and high-risk patients, respectively, had not experienced PSA failure as defined by the American Society for Therapeutic Radiology and Oncology (ASTRO) consensus panel (Cox, 1997).

Figure 100–4 illustrates the clinically relevant stratification provided by the percentage of positive biopsies in the

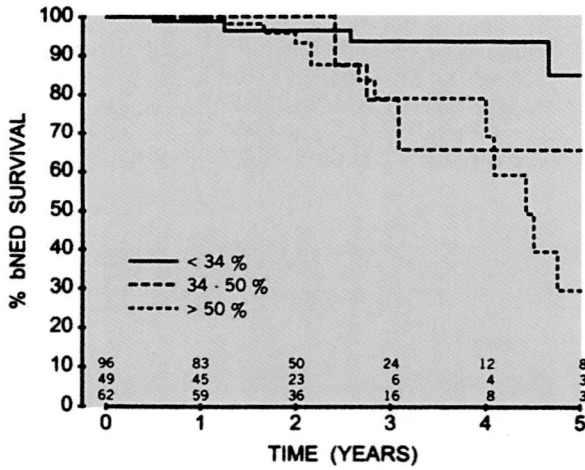

Figure 100–4. Prostate-specific antigen failure-free survival stratified by percentage of positive biopsies for 207 intermediate-risk patients managed using external-beam radiation therapy. Pairwise, *P* values are as follows: 34% versus >34% to 50%, *P* = .02; >34% to 50% versus >50%, *P* = .06; 34% versus >50%, *P* = .002.

previously defined intermediate-risk group based on pretreatment PSA level, biopsy Gleason grade, and the 1992 AJCC clinical stage. Specifically, patients in the intermediate-risk subgroups who also had fewer than 34% of the positive biopsies improved their risk stratification for PSA outcome by one category to low risk. Conversely, patients with more than 50% of the positive biopsies performed less well than expected and were comparable to the high-risk patients.

Of particular importance, however, is that the majority of patients (158 of 207 [76%]) in the intermediate-risk group could be classified into either a 30% or an 85% 5-year PSA control high- or low-risk cohort, respectively, using the preoperative prostate biopsy data. Therefore, of the 473 study patients, all but 49 (10%) were classified into high- or low-risk groups regarding PSA outcome after RT, using the percentage of positive prostate biopsies, the PSA level, the biopsy Gleason grade, and the 1992 AJCC clinical stage.

Percentage of Positive Prostate Biopsies and Prostate Cancer–Specific Mortality in Low-Risk and Favorable Intermediate-Risk Patients

With longer follow-up, the impact of the percentage of prostate positive biopsies (PPBs) on prostate cancer–specific mortality in low-risk and favorable intermediate-risk patients has become available (D'Amico et al, 2004). Specifically, from a series of 421 patients with low-risk (PSA ≤ 10 ng/mL and biopsy Gleason score ≤ 6) or favorable intermediate-risk (PSA > 10 to 15 ng/mL or biopsy Gleason 7 but not both factors) disease who underwent three-dimensional conformal radiation therapy (3DCRT) to a median dose of 70.4 Gy, a significant association between PCSM and the percentage of positive prostate biopsies at diagnosis was documented. In particular, the relative risk of PCSM following 3DCRT for patients with 50% or more as compared with less than 50% PPB was 10.4 (95% CI: 1.2 to 87; p_{Cox} = .03), 6.1 (95% CI: 1.3 to 28.6; p_{Cox} = .02), and 12.5 (95% CI: 1.5 to 107; p_{Cox} = .02) in men with a PSA of 10 or less and Gleason score 6 or less, PSA 10 or less and Gleason score 7 or less, and PSA 15 or less and Gleason score 6 or less, respectively. By 5 years after 3DCRT, up to 10% as compared with 2% or less($p_{log\ rank}$ ≤ .01) of these patients experienced PCSM if they had 50% or more as compared with less than 50% PPB as shown in Figures 100–5, 100–6, and

100–7. For the purpose of illustration, Figure 100–8 contains the relative contributions of PCSM and non-PCSM following treatment to all-cause mortality stratified by the % PPB (<50% versus 50% or more) and the PSA level and biopsy Gleason score at diagnosis.

Therefore, the percentage of positive prostate biopsies should be considered in conjunction with the PSA level, the biopsy Gleason grade, and 1992 AJCC clinical stage at diagnosis when counseling patients with newly diagnosed and clinically localized prostate cancer about both PSA outcome and, more important, the chance of avoiding PCSM after RT.

KEY POINTS

- Prostate cancer–specific mortality can be estimated on the basis of the pretreatment PSA level, biopsy Gleason score, and clinical T category.

- The percentage of positive prostate biopsies provides additional information regarding prostate cancer–specific mortality in men with low-risk or favorable intermediate-risk disease.

Post-Treatment Prognostic Factors

Localized Disease—Evaluating the Response to Radiation

PSA Follow-up—Definition of Failure. Serum PSA has become widely accepted as a surrogate endpoint for monitoring the success of definitive treatment for localized prostate

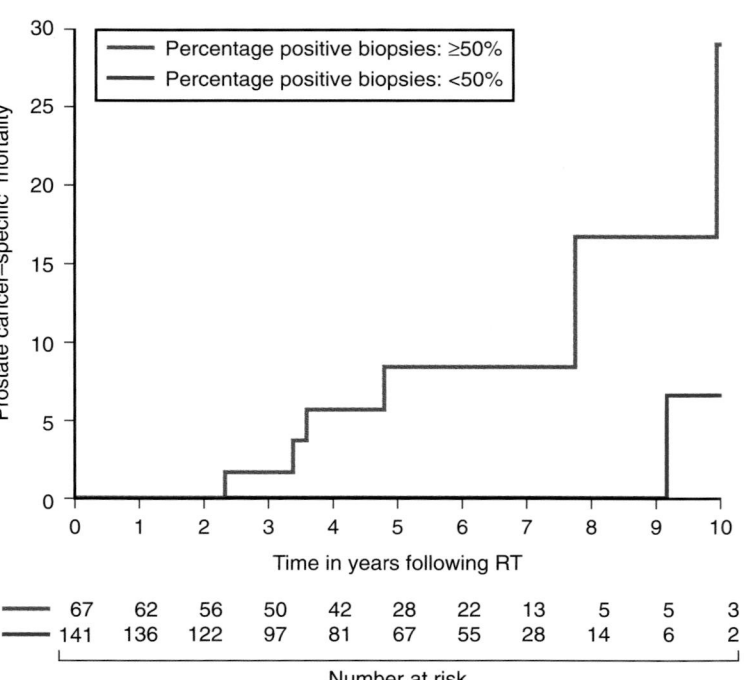

Figure 100–5. Prostate cancer–specific mortality following three-dimensional conformal radiation therapy for patients with 50% or more as compared with less than 50% prostate positive biopsy in men with a prostate-specific antigen (PSA) of 10 or less and Gleason score of 6 or less. RT, radiation therapy.

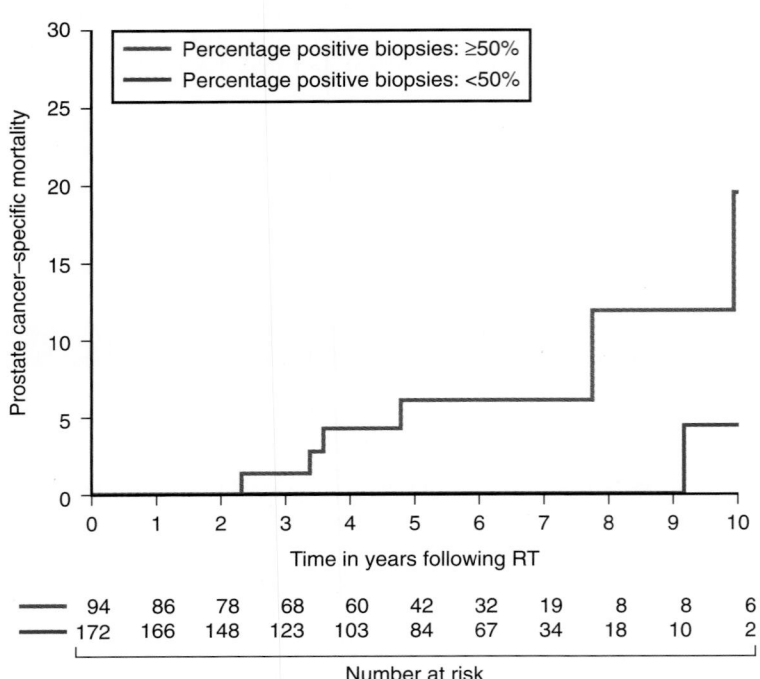

PSA ≤ 15 AND GLEASON ≤ 6

Figure 100–6. Prostate cancer–specific mortality following three-dimensional conformal radiation therapy for patients with 50% or more as compared with less than 50% prostate positive biopsy in men with a prostate-specific antigen (PSA) of 10 or less and Gleason score of 7 or less. RT, radiation therapy.

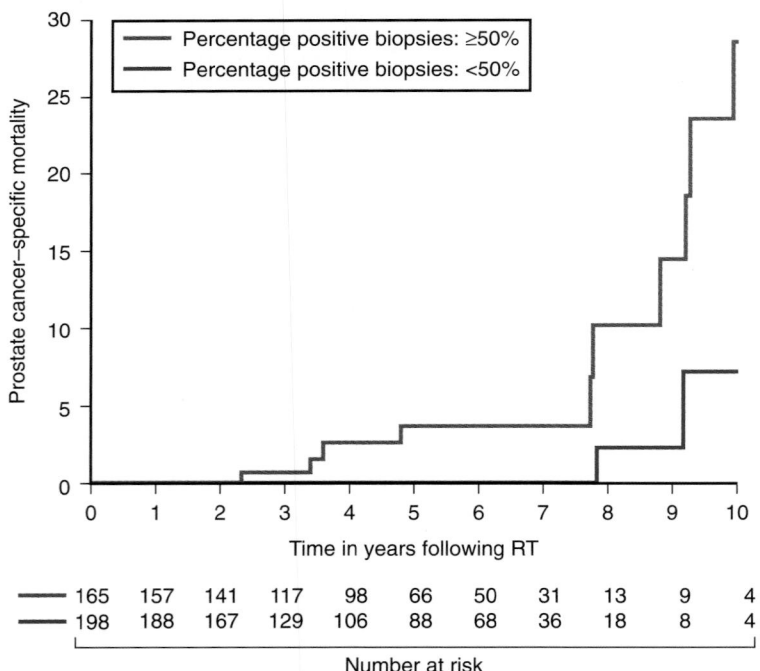

PSA ≤ 10 AND GLEASON ≤ 3 + 4

Figure 100–7. Prostate cancer–specific mortality following three-dimensional conformal radiation therapy for patients with 50% or more as compared with less than 50% prostate positive biopsy and a prostate-specific antigen (PSA) of 15 or less and Gleason score of 6 or less, respectively. RT, radiation therapy.

cancer. However, the definition of biochemical failure after RT remains controversial. Unlike the situation after radical prostatectomy, the patient successfully treated with radiotherapy still has a prostate gland and therefore is not expected to achieve an undetectable PSA reading. However, an "acceptable" PSA level after successful radiotherapy is markedly lower than the range of normal for an age-matched unirradiated population because of marked atrophy and a reduction in the size and number of nonmalignant acini (Grignon and Sakr, 1995).

Ablation of normal prostatic epithelium appears to be dose dependent. In a randomized trial comparing 70 and 78 Gy, Pollock and colleagues (2002b) found that with 78 Gy, 80% of patients achieved a nadir of less than 0.5 ng/mL, compared

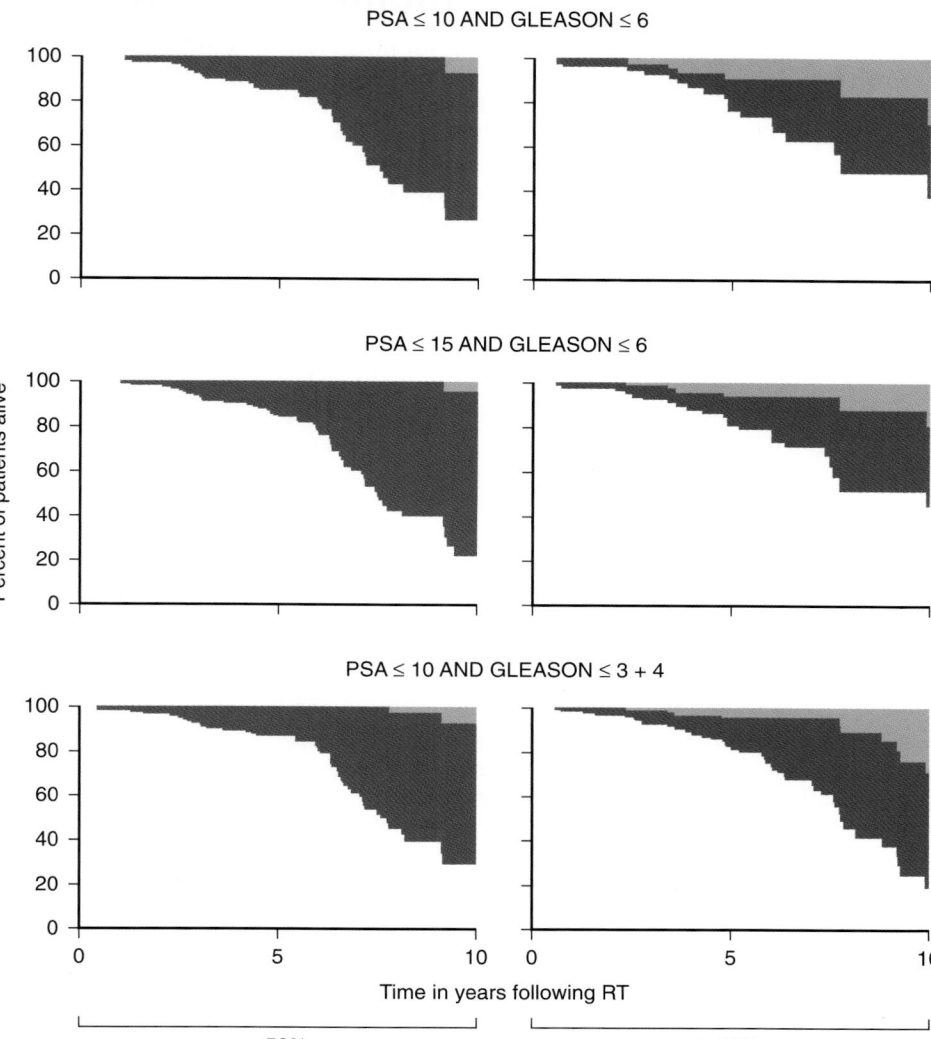

Figure 100-8. Relative contributions of prostate cancer–specific mortality (PCSM) and non-PCSM following treatment to all-cause mortality stratified by the % prostate positive biopsy (less than 50% versus 50% or more) and the prostate-specific antigen (PSA) level and biopsy Gleason score at diagnosis. RT, radiation therapy.

with 67% who received 70 Gy (P = .02). Although higher nadirs are associated with decreased disease-free survival, it is probably not necessary to ablate all the normal epithelium in order to achieve cure. Five-year freedom from biochemical failure is in the range of 80% to 90% for nadirs less than 0.5 ng/mL (Zincke et al, 1994; Lee et al, 1996; Crook et al, 1998; Critz et al, 1999a; Kestin et al, 1999; DeWitt et al, 2003) but drops to 29% to 60% for nadirs of 0.6 to 1.0. However, even for PSA nadirs above 1.0 ng/mL, up to one third of patients remain free of recurrence at 5 years (DeWitt et al, 2003). Nadir PSA is a significant predictor of outcome, but no absolute nadir threshold can or should be used to define cure (DeWitt et al, 2003; Ray et al, 2004).

The 1996 ASTRO Consensus Conference (Consensus Statement, 1997) proposed a standardized definition of biochemical failure after radiotherapy. Although there is no distinct PSA threshold that defines successful treatment, PSA stability following the nadir is important. The panel concluded that three consecutive increases in PSA is a reasonable definition of biochemical failure, recommending that the PSA determi-

nations be 3 to 4 months apart in the first 2 years after radiotherapy and every 6 months thereafter. The requirement for three readings and the temporal spacing between the readings are necessary to avoid overcalling failure on the basis of temporary instability related to biologic noise or fluctuations in PSA of benign etiology (Crook et al, 1997a). It must be emphasized that establishing that a patient meets the criteria for biochemical failure is not justification for intervention. However, for the purposes of clinical trials and the reporting of data, a standard definition of failure is required. For these purposes, the date of failure should be backdated to midway between the PSA nadir and the date of the first increase.

Although the ASTRO definition provided uniformity in reporting of results, it is not a perfect solution to the problem of defining biochemical failure after radiotherapy. Waiting for three rises delays the establishment of failure by 18 months or more (Cherullo et al, 2002). This has no consequences for the individual patient, as no individual requires intervention before the third rise, which defines the change in status. Furthermore, biochemical failure is not equivalent to clinical failure and is not of itself an indication for additional treatment. However, when reporting results, waiting for three rises and then backdating failure to midway between the nadir and the first rise tends to flatten the tail of the survival curve, underestimating late failures (Coen et al, 2003). Long follow-up minimizes this effect and short follow-up overestimates treatment success (Horwitz et al, 2003), as outcome cannot be predicted when the median follow-up is shorter than the median time to failure. One means of overcoming this shortcoming in the ASTRO definition is to backdate the follow-up time for all patients with one or two PSA rises (Coen et al, 2003; Thames et al, 2003). These patients can be censored (as disease free) midway between their nadir and first rise at the same time as they would be censored as a failure should they go on to have a third rise. In this way, the actuarial calculation does not benefit from extended follow-up for these patients whose status is uncertain. An alternative definition of biochemical failure that is particularly useful when few PSA values are available, as occurs when a patient has been lost to follow-up for a period of time or when PSAs are checked only annually, is any PSA value that is more than 2 ng/mL above the nadir (Coen et al, 2003).

Time to Nadir. Serum PSA declines slowly after completion of radiotherapy. The time to nadir has been shown to be inversely proportional to disease-free survival (Ray et al, 2004). The median time to nadir in patients who remain with no evidence of disease (NED) is 22 to 34 months (Hanlon et al, 2002; Pollack et al, 2002a). In a series of 615 men with a median follow-up of 64 months, Hanlon and coauthors (2002) reported that a lower nadir ($P < .0001$) and longer time to nadir are independent predictors of freedom from distant metastases ($P = .0002$). Lee and associates (1996) reported that 75% of men whose PSA reached a nadir in less than 12 months had distant metastases by 5 years as compared with 25% of those whose PSA took more than 12 months to reach a nadir ($P < .001$). Kestin and colleagues (1999) found that 92% of men whose PSA reached a nadir at 36 months or longer remained disease free as compared with 30% of those who reached a nadir in less than 12 months. The slow decline in PSA and the long time to PSA nadir are explained by the fact that, unlike other ablative treatment modalities such as surgery and cryotherapy, radiotherapy does not cause immediate cell death. The double-stranded DNA chromosomal breaks caused by radiotherapy are not immediately fatal but do not permit successful cell reproduction. Postmitotic cell death is not expressed until a cell tries to reproduce. Given the long doubling time of most prostate cancers, a fatally damaged cell may survive 18 to 24 months before unsuccessfully attempting cell division and dying.

Significance of Nadir Value and Doubling Time. The level of PSA nadir achieved to some extent reflects the type of failure (Table 100–1). The median PSA nadir for NED patients in most series treated with external-beam radiotherapy is 0.4 to 0.5 ng/mL (Zietman et al, 1996; Critz et al, 1999a; Crook et al, 2000), whereas for those exhibiting local failure it is often greater than 1.0 ng/mL and for distant failure greater than 2 ng/mL. A study by Hanlon and coworkers (2004) ($n = 615$, follow-up median 64 months) reported that freedom from distant metastases was 96% for a nadir less than 1.0 ng/mL, 89% for nadirs 1.1 to 2.0 ng/mL, and 61% for nadirs greater

Table 100–1. Failure Pattern According to Level of PSA Nadir, Time to Nadir, and PSA Doubling Time

	PSA Nadir (ng/mL)	Time to Nadir (mo)	PSA Doubling Time
NED	0.4-0.5	22-33	NA
Local failure	1.0-2.0	12-18	11-13 mo
Distant failure	>2.0	<12	3-6 mo

NA, not applicable; NED, no evidence of disease; PSA, prostate-specific antigen.

than 2.0 ng/mL. The postnadir doubling time of the PSA also correlates with the type of failure, with distant failures having shorter PSA doubling times of 3 to 6 months (Zagars et al, 1993; Hancock et al, 1995; Lee et al, 1997) and local failures having longer PSA doubling times of 11 to 13 months (Zagars et al, 1993; Hancock et al, 1995). D'Amico and coauthors (2003) reported that a PSA doubling time of less than 3 months is associated with prostate cancer mortality. Kuban and associates (2004) ($n = 4839$) found that PSA doubling time (less than 10 months versus more than 10 months) and time to PSA failure (less than 2 years versus more than 2 years) were the most significant factors in predicting distant metastasis–free survival after PSA failure.

The manner in which PSA nadir and time to nadir reflect the type of failure requires explanation. There are potentially three sources of PSA that contribute to the nadir: residual benign prostatic epithelium, residual local prostate cancer cells, and subclinical disseminated micrometastases. The longer the time to nadir and the lower the absolute nadir, the more likely it is that only benign prostatic epithelium remains, hence the NED status. A higher radiation dose achieves a more complete ablation of normal epithelium and thus a lower nadir. For patients in whom radiotherapy fails to eradicate all the local tumor, the PSA declines progressively until the rate of growth of the surviving prostate cancer cells is greater than the death rate of those fatally damaged by the radiation, at which point the PSA begins to rise. In the third scenario, subclinical micrometastases continue to grow unchecked despite successful treatment of the primary tumor. This growth rate outstrips the rate of decline in the local tumor population relatively early after treatment, leading to a higher and earlier nadir.

In any multivariate analysis of prognostic factors, if PSA nadir is included in the model with pretreatment PSA, Gleason score, and T stage, it becomes the strongest independent predictor of outcome (Ben-Josef et al, 1998; Crook et al, 1998; Preston et al, 1999). This is not surprising considering the close temporal relationship between the PSA nadir and the definition of biochemical recurrence. Although it is common practice to mix pretreatment prognostic factors in the same multivariate model with postradiotherapy PSA nadir, the latter should more correctly be considered a means of evaluating the response to radiotherapy.

Neoadjuvant Hormones and the Definition of Biochemical Failure. When neoadjuvant androgen deprivation is used prior to radiotherapy, patients often start radiotherapy with an already undetectable PSA. If the PSA remains undetectable, it is impossible to determine a true nadir or time to nadir. If hormonal therapy is only neoadjuvant or concurrent, or both, rapid recovery of the serum testosterone may cause a temporary increase in PSA shortly after completion of radiotherapy and cessation of hormonal therapy. Subsequently, as the effect of the radiotherapy is expressed, the PSA declines once again. Although complete data from randomized trials are still pending on this point, this secondary nadir probably has the same prognostic significance as PSA nadir in the absence of neoadjuvant hormonal therapy. Adherence to the ASTRO definition of biochemical failure, requiring three successive PSA increases 3 to 4 months apart, usually allows sufficient time for this phenomenon to pass and to avoid incorrectly labeling the patient as a radiotherapy failure.

The Benign Bounce Phenomenon. In the presence of residual benign epithelium or before the full effect of radiotherapy has been expressed, PSA may fluctuate or show several consecutive increases. A spike or bounce can be defined as a rise greater than 0.2 ng/mL followed by a durable decline (Merrick et al, 2003c). This phenomenon is especially common after brachytherapy, where it is reported to occur in 24% to 35% of men (Critz et al, 2000; Smathers et al, 2001; Merrick et al, 2002a, 2003c; Reed et al, 2003). Spikes have been reported to be more common in younger men and after implantation with ^{125}I rather than ^{103}Pd (33% versus 17%) (Merrick et al, 2003a). Spikes can start any time from 9 to 30 months after brachytherapy (Reed et al, 2003) and may reach a maximum PSA value of up to 10 ng/mL, although the majority show a cumulative rise of not more than 2 to 3 ng/mL. Spikes may last as long as 12 to 18 months and double peaks can be seen. Biopsies performed to investigate the rising PSA may show residual cancer with treatment effect (indeterminate) (Reed et al, 2003). Currently, there is no reliable way to discern whether a rising PSA in the first 3 years after brachytherapy represents treatment failure. Many meet the ASTRO definition of biochemical failure. Only patience and careful follow-up demonstrate the subsequent spontaneous PSA decline to low levels.

Post–Radiation Therapy Biopsy

Although serum PSA nadir has been widely adopted as a surrogate endpoint to determine treatment efficacy, it cannot distinguish between local and systemic failure. Postradiotherapy prostate biopsies would seem to be the logical means of evaluating the local effect of radiotherapy. The major issues involve:

- Timing of the biopsies with respect to completion of radiotherapy
- Interpretation of indeterminate biopsies that show residual tumor with marked radiation effect and uncertain viability
- The usefulness of markers of cellular proliferation
- The uncertainty imposed by sampling error

Timing. In early reports, little was known about the rate of histologic clearance of irradiated tumor and failures were declared as early as 6 months after completion of radiotherapy (Scardino and Wheeler, 1985). It is now recognized that the time for histologic resolution of tumor parallels the time to serum PSA nadir and for the same reasons. Radiation causes postmitotic cell death, and fatally damaged cells may survive a limited number of cell divisions (Mostofi et al, 1992, 1993). Biopsies taken before histologic resolution is complete show a moderate to marked radiation effect (Crook et al,

1997b). Ultimate viability of these cells cannot be predicted. Crook and colleagues (1995) have determined that the optimal time to biopsy is 30 to 36 months after radiotherapy.

Interpretation. Gleason scoring of irradiated prostate cancer should be performed only if the histologic evidence of radiation effect is absent or minimal. Gleason's original work was based on surgically obtained material that had not been exposed to prior radiotherapy or hormonal therapy. It is based on gland architecture, which is known to be markedly altered by radiotherapy. Inappropriate application of the Gleason scoring system to disintegrating malignant glands showing a marked RT effect (Siders and Lee, 1992; Grignon and Sakr, 1995) results in a false-positive biopsy and perhaps unnecessary "salvage" therapy.

Radiation atypia in benign glands can be severe enough to mimic malignancy (Bostwick et al, 1982; Grignon and Sakr, 1995; Cheng et al, 1999). Anticytokeratin monoclonal antibody for high-molecular-weight keratin labels the basal cell layer of benign glands and therefore helps to distinguish radiation atypia in benign glands from residual tumor where the basal cell layer would be absent (Brawer et al, 1989).

Scoring systems for the degree of radiation effect have been proposed (Dhom and Degro, 1982; Bocking and Auffermann, 1987) on the basis of cytoplasmic and nuclear changes (Table 100–2) and can be helpful in interpreting the significance of residual tumor in the biopsy (Crook et al, 1997a). Their importance is to emphasize the need to differentiate between biopsies showing no or minimal radiation effect and those showing marked treatment effect (Zelefsky et al, 2004). Failure to do so dilutes the prognostic significance of biopsy status and may lead to inappropriate salvage therapy.

Markers of Cellular Proliferation. Immunohistochemical stains for markers of cellular proliferation can also be useful in interpretation of the significance of residual tumor. The two nuclear proteins expressed in proliferating cells for which there is the most clinical experience are proliferative cell nuclear antigen or PCNA (Crook et al, 1994) and Ki-67 (Ljung et al, 1996). PCNA is expressed both at DNA replication for cell division and during cellular repair. It is not formalin stable and is unreliable if the duration of formalin fixation is not closely monitored (Wiatrowska et al, 1997). On the other

Table 100–2. **Grading Scheme for Cytoplasmic and Nuclear Radiation Effect**
(The scores for cytoplasmic and nuclear changes are added together. A score of 5-6 represents marked treatment effect, 3-4 is moderate, and 0-2 minimal.)
Cytoplasmic changes   0   No identifiable RT effect
1 Swelling and microvesicular change
2 Extensive vacuolation, macrovesicular change, and voluminous cytoplasm
3 Indistinct or ruptured cytoplasm
Lipofuscin pigment accumulation
Glands dilated or just single cells with no glandular formation
Nuclear changes   0   No identifiable RT effect
Some swelling or smudging of nuclei but nucleoli still visible
Smudged and distorted chromatin
Nucleoli rare or absent
Large bizarre nuclei
Pyknotic small condensed nuclei

RT, radiation therapy.

prospective patient-based assessments yield higher percentages of patients experiencing side effects, irrespective of the type of treatment studied (Beard et al, 1997; Talcott et al, 1998). If there is still some debate about whether complication rates have decreased as a result of conformal treatment, it is probably because clinicians increased their doses as treatment portals became smaller. Also, although normal tissue complication rates have been established to be related to radiation dose and volume, they are also influenced by other dosimetric and clinical factors, such as coexisting disease in individual patients that cannot be fully controlled or described in clinical studies (Pollack et al, 2003).

Several authors (Sandler et al, 1992, 1995; Leibel et al, 1994; Schultheiss et al, 1995, 1997) have compared the complication rates in their own prostate cancer patients receiving conventional versus conformal radiation. Most authors use the Radiation Therapy Oncology Group (RTOG) late-radiation morbidity scales, as shown in Table 100–4.

A prospective randomized trial was performed in the University Hospital of Rotterdam and the Daniel den Hoed Cancer Center of the Netherlands comparing the effect of 66 Gy delivered by either conventional therapy or CRT in a group of 266 patients (Koper et al, 1999). All patients were evaluated for gastrointestinal and genitourinary outcomes. A statistically significant reduction was seen in the proportion of patients experiencing grade 2 rectal toxicity in the conformal arm of the study (19% versus 32%) ($P = .02$). Most of the benefit with conformal RT was due to a very low incidence of anal side effects (8% compared with 16% experienced by the control group). Interestingly, no difference was seen in the percentages of patients who experienced bladder symptoms, which were minimal in both arms of the trial. A second prospective randomized trial comparing conformal and conventional radiation was performed at the Royal Marsden Hospital (Dearnaley et al, 1999). In that trial, 225 men were randomly assigned to receive 64 Gy of one or the other form of radiation. Only 5% of the conformal group developed grade 2 proctitis and bleeding, compared with 15% of the conventional group ($P = .01$). As in the Dutch study, no difference was seen between the groups in the development of grade 1 or 2 bladder symptoms.

Sexual function after conformal RT has been evaluated by several groups. At the Joint Center for Radiation Therapy and the Dana-Farber Cancer Institute (DFCI), patients participating in a prospective multi-institutional outcomes trial were divided into three groups on the basis of their RT treatment technique (Beard et al, 1997). As shown in Table 100–5, fewer patients reported sexual side effects after treatment with

Table 100–4. RTOG Late Gastrointestinal and Genitourinary Morbidity Scales

Grade	Genitourinary	Gastrointestinal
2	Moderate frequency; generalized telangiectasia; intermittent macroscopic hematuria	More than two antidiarrheals per week; regular non-narcotic for pain; occasional blood transfusion; occasional steroids; occasional dilation; intermittent use of pads
3	Severe frequency and dysuria; severe generalized telangiectasia; frequent hematuria; reduction in bladder capacity (<150 mL)	More than two antidiarrheals per day; regular narcotic for pain; frequent blood transfusions; steroid enemas; hyperbaric oxygen for ulceration; regular dilation; daily use of pads
4	Necrosis; contracted bladder (<100 mL); severe hemorrhagic cystitis	Perforation; life-threatening bleeding; surgical repair
5	Fatal toxicity	Fatal toxicity

RTOG, Radiation Therapy Oncology Group.

Table 100–5. Prospective Multi-institutional Outcomes Data on Sexual Symptoms over Time in Patients Treated with Conventional Whole-Pelvis Irradiation, Conventional Small-Field Irradiation, and Conformal Irradiation without Dose Escalation

Variable	Treatment Group	No. of Patients	Pre-XRT	3 Months (%)	12 Months (%)	P value
No erections at all	WP	16	6	25	44	.31
	SF	34	18	24	32	
	C	20	15	5	20	
Erections present but inadequate for intercourse	WP	15	33	60	73	.69
	SF	32	38	56	63	
	C	20	60	55	60	
Difficulty achieving erections	WP	18	56	78	50	.25
	SF	45	56	64	38	
	C	24	50	50	25	
No or infrequent sexual desire	WP	21	19	43	43	.22
	SF	41	49	46	37	
	C	25	40	28	20	
No sexual satisfaction	WP	18	33	50	56	.13
	SF	39	38	49	38	
	C	21	38	33	24	

C, conformal; SF, small field; WP, whole pelvis; XRT, external-beam radiation therapy.
Beard C, Propert K, Rieker P, et al: Complications after treatment with external-beam irradiation in early-stage prostate cancer patients: A prospective multiinstitutional outcomes study. J Clin Oncol 1997;15:223-229.

conformal radiation than with small-field or whole-pelvis treatment. None of the values were statistically significant, but this may have been due in part to the small sample size studied.

New data exist on the relationship between dose and morbidity. For prostate cancer, most of the progress has been made in the area of rectal complications. Predictors of bladder complications have yet to be identified, perhaps because they manifest many years after treatment (Gardner et al, 2002). Most "late" rectal complications, however, are seen within 2 years and almost always within 4 years of treatment (Pollack et al, 2002b) and are more easily evaluated. In the M.D. Anderson Cancer Center trial, the 5-year freedom from a complication above grade 2 was 26% in the 78 Gy arm and 12% for those in the 70 Gy arm, nicely demonstrating the relationship that can exist between dose and complications. When further analysis was performed to identify factors other than total dose that might be used to predict for rectal toxicity, it was shown that the risk of complications increased from 25% to 46% when the rectal volume exposed to 70 Gy increased from less than 25% to greater than 25% (Pollack et al, 2002a). A more detailed analysis followed which showed that it was the proportion of the rectum receiving greater than 70 Gy that was more significant than the absolute rectal volume (Huang et al, 2002b), but the basic premise remained the same.

Unlike that after radical prostatectomy, sexual dysfunction after RT increases slowly with time (Talcott et al, 1998). Zelefsky and associates (1999a) from Memorial Sloan-Kettering Cancer Center reported that 39% of 542 previously potent patients given 64.8 to 81 Gy of conformal radiation became impotent within 5 years of treatment. A retrospective evaluation of 287 men from the University of Chicago yielded similar results, with 53% of previously potent men reporting impotence by 60 months after conformal therapy (Mantz et al, 1999). As with other studies of sexual function after radiation, the men most likely to remain potent after treatment were those with good pretreatment sexual function and little or no comorbid illness and those who did not receive androgen therapy.

KEY POINT

- Randomized control trials show a benefit in PSA control for doses of radiation therapy of 78 to 79 Gy as compared with 70 Gy.

Tumor Control after Conformal Radiation Therapy

Long-term (more than 10 years of follow-up) data after conformal RT are not yet available, but early data have been reported by several centers. Most of these data are measured by freedom from PSA failure.

Zelefsky and colleagues (1998) reported their results for the first 743 men with prostate cancer treated with prospective dose-escalation conformal radiation. Patients were divided into favorable (stage T1 or T2, PSA less than 10 ng/mL, Gleason grade less than 6), intermediate (having one unfavorable feature), and unfavorable (having two unfavorable features) groups. For these three groups, the 5-year PSA freedom-from-relapse rates were 85%, 65%, and 35%, respectively. Almost identical data were obtained by Fukunaga-Johnson and colleagues (1997) at the University of Michigan. In that series, 707 patients received conformal radiation at doses of up to 80 Gy, with most patients receiving more than 69 Gy. Patients with favorable features (defined as stage T1 or T2, Gleason grade 7, and PSA less than 10 ng/mL) enjoyed a 75% 5-year freedom from PSA relapse, compared with a 37% rate in those with unfavorable features (T3 or T4, Gleason grade above 7, or PSA above 10 ng/mL). Researchers at the Fox Chase Cancer Center in Philadelphia modeled the effect of dose levels less than 74 Gy against those greater than 74 Gy using pairs of patients matched by stage, pretreatment PSA level, and Gleason grade (Hanks et al, 1999). When PSA was discounted, delivered dose greater than 74 Gy correlated significantly with freedom from local disease progression, freedom from distant metastases, and increased cause-specific and overall survival. The results were still significant for freedom from disease progression and freedom from distant metastases when PSA was included as an independent variable.

Six hundred eighteen patients who received conformal radiation were divided into groups on the basis of their pretreatment tumor characteristics (Gleason grade, clinical stage, and PSA level) and their total radiation dose (76 Gy versus more than 76 Gy). Six subgroups were created. Patients with favorable tumors (Gleason grade 6, stage T1 or T2a) who also had a PSA less than 10 ng/mL derived no benefit from dose escalation because all patients in this group did well. Patients with unfavorable tumors (Gleason grade 7 to 10, stage T2b or T3) who had a PSA greater than 20 ng/mL also derived no benefit from dose escalation. In this cohort, both arms fared poorly, with freedom-from-relapse rates that were less than 30%. All other patients demonstrated statistically significant improved freedom-from-relapse rates with high-dose conformal treatment, as shown in Figure 100–10.

It has long been understood that increased doses of external RT are associated with better cancer control rates for patients with prostate cancer. For many years, an isocenter dose of 70 Gy was considered the maximum dose that could be safely delivered. With the advent of CRT, several groups looked at higher doses in the setting of a randomized trial. At Massachusetts General Hospital, a trial randomizing between 67.2 Gy (conventional arm) and 75.6 Gy (proton boost arm) was undertaken in patients with locally advanced disease. The study showed a significant increase in local control with the higher dose, with 8-year rates of 19% and 84% ($P = .0014$) for patients in the high- and low-dose arms, respectively (Shipley et al, 1995). Disease-free survival was also better for a subset of patients with Gleason 8 to 10 cancer but no differences in overall or cancer-specific survival were noted.

A number of CRT and intensity-modulated radiotherapy (IMRT) dose escalation trials are under way or have completed accrual (Pollack), but only the M.D. Anderson Cancer Center trial has reached maturity and been published. In this trial, a total of 301 patients were randomized; 150 received the standard CRT dose of 70 Gy at isocenter, and the other 150 received the higher dose of 78 Gy at isocenter (Pollack et al, 2002b). The 6-year rates of freedom from failure were significantly higher for those randomly assigned to the 78-Gy arm (70% versus 64%, $P = .03$). The greatest benefit was observed

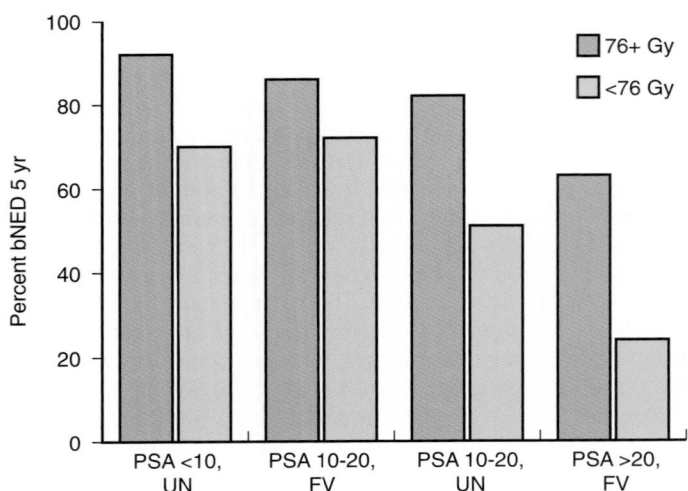

Figure 100–10. The advantage of dose escalation is shown in these dose-response graphs. Patients are divided into groups on the basis of their pretreatment clinical characteristics and the dose of radiation they received. FV, favorable characteristics (Gleason grade 6, stage T1c-T2a); UN, unfavorable characteristics (Gleason grade 7-10, stage T2b-T3). (Modified from Hanks G, Hanlon A, Pinover W, et al: Survival advantage for prostate cancer patients treated with high-dose three-dimensional conformal radiotherapy. Cancer J Sci Am 1999;5:152-158.)

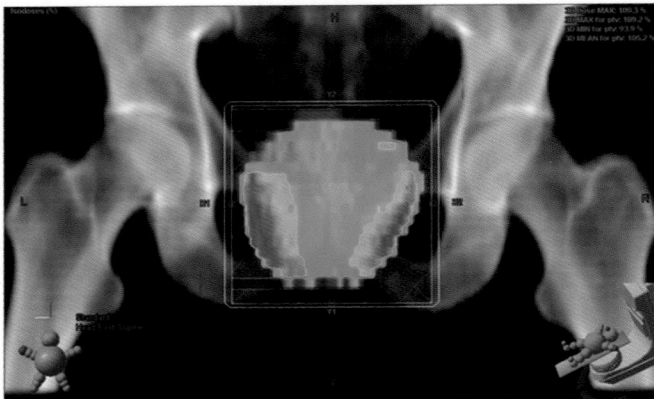

Figure 100–11. Intensity-modulated radiotherapy fluence.

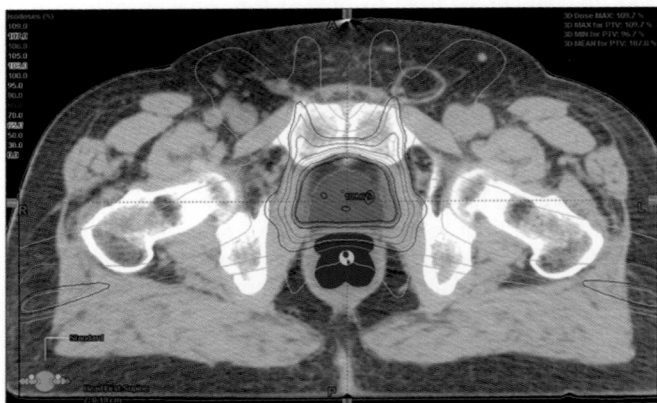

Figure 100–12. New intensity-modulated radiotherapy.

for patients with a pretreatment PSA greater than 10 ng/mL. These intermediate- to high-risk patients had 6-year freedom-from-failure rates of 62% and 43% when treated with 78 and 70 Gy, respectively ($P = .12$). There was also a borderline reduction in distant metastases for patients in this group who received the higher dose (2% versus 12%, $P = .056$).

Patients who receive conformal radiation, as opposed to conventional radiation, may be treated with higher doses safely. They appear to develop fewer complications and to enjoy a decreased risk of tumor recurrence during the first 5 years after treatment. Given the benefit demonstrated by both single-institutional retrospective reviews and prospective randomized trials, conformal radiation has become the standard against which other therapies must be measured. Dose escalation therapy to doses greater than 75 Gy is still experimental, but the early data appear to be highly favorable.

Intensity Modulation

Although CRT was a major technological advance, it represented advancement of treatment planning processes that had been in place since the 1980s. Real progress in the delivery of radiation came with the advent of IMRT. IMRT is an exciting form of conformal RT that uses extremely advanced software, specialized personnel, and hardware adaptations to linear accelerators (Burman et al, 1997). At present, its availability is limited to a small number of radiation centers because of its complexity, but in time it may replace CRT in popularity and availability. The goal of IMRT treatment planning and delivery is to maximize treatment to the target—for example, the prostate—while minimizing treatment to the surrounding tissues to a degree that is not possible with conformal therapy (Oh et al, 1999).

The term IMRT is now applied to a family of methodologies that use different methods of treatment planning and delivery in order to achieve a precise, nonuniform beam fluence (Jani et al, 2003). IMRT uses a new planning approach referred to as inverse treatment planning. This approach gives equal attention to the areas where radiation dose is to be minimized and the areas that are to receive high-dose treatment. Inverse planning uses a mathematical approach to convert a desired dose distribution to the target volume and normal organs into a clinically applicable treatment plan. The planning computer, using a mathematical optimization technique known as simulated annealing, determines the optimized beam arrangement. The second component of IMRT is computer-controlled modulation of the intensity of the radiation beam during treatment. The outcome is a set of radiation beams with changing intensities across the field, as shown in Figure 100–11. With this technology, the prostate can receive a daily dose of 180 cGy, whereas the majority of the adjacent bladder receives less than half of this dose.

An example of an intensity-modulated beam is shown in Figure 100–12. The tight distribution of radiation around the prostate with avoidance of most of the rectum and bladder is seen on inspection of the figure. IMRT for prostate cancer generally utilizes five or seven radiation ports or fields per day, as shown in Figure 100–13. Prostate cancer is currently the single most common tumor site treated with IMRT worldwide (Guerrero Urbano et al, 2004). When IMRT is compared with CRT in the same patient, using the same prescribed dose,

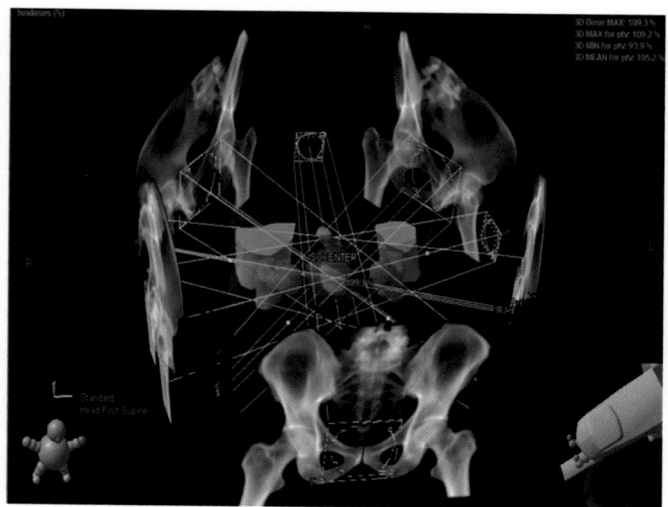

Figure 100–13. Intensity-modulated radiotherapy setup.

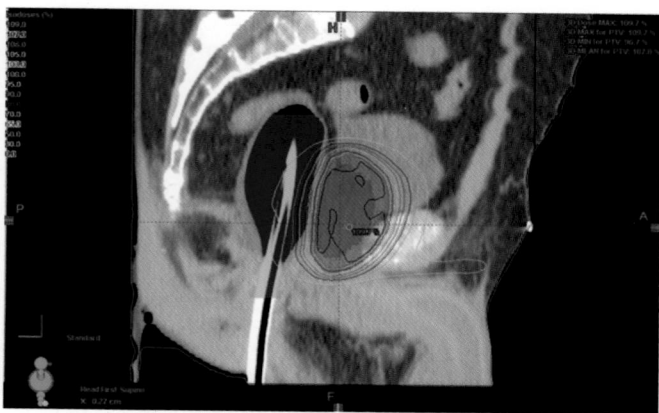

Figure 100–14. Balloon intensity-modulated radiotherapy. (Courtesy of Fred Hacker, PhD, Department of Radiation Oncology, Brigham and Women's Hospital.)

statistically significantly lower doses are delivered to the critical normal tissues: rectum, bladder, and small bowel (Luxton et al, 2004).

As the risk of rectal and bladder complications is believed to be a continuous function of dose, the lower the proportion of these organs that receive high dose, the lower the complication probability, all else being equal. For this reason, radiation oncologists who deliver IMRT choose dose constraints before initiating treatment planning. At the Brigham and Women's Hospital, we limit the volume of rectum that receives more than 65 Gy to 25%. The volume of rectum that receives more than 47 Gy is limited to less than 43%. Although the exact relationship between bladder dose and complication rates has not been established, it is common practice to define constraints for the bladder as well. In general, the goal is to limit less than 25% of the bladder volume to more than 65 Gy and less than 50% of the bladder volume to more than 40 Gy. Each practitioner may have his or her own set of constraints. There is no universally accepted standard.

One of the important considerations for radiation oncologists who treat prostate cancer is the issue of prostate motion. That prostate motion occurs is well documented, both on a day-to-day basis (Ten Haken et al, 1991; Beard et al, 1996) and, to a lesser extent, during the time it takes to deliver a daily radiation treatment (Huang et al, 2002a). Radiation oncologists can either expand the size of the radiation beam to accommodate prostate motion and accept the risk of increased morbidity or, if small fields are to be used, check the location of the prostate each day before delivering radiation. This can be done with a daily ultrasound determination of the prostate location immediately prior to treatment while the patient is on the treatment table, but this approach is highly operator independent and susceptible to error (Lee et al, 2002). Another option is to introduce radiopaque markers into the prostate under ultrasound guidance and to use a commercially available software program to localize the prostate each day prior to treatment while the patient is on the treatment table. Neither approach, however, addresses the issue of intrafraction motion. The solution to this problem

may be prostate immobilization. At Brigham and Women's Hospital, a balloon immobilization device is introduced through the rectum prior to treatment planning and each of the first 15 treatments. The balloon is inflated with 60 to 100 cm³ of air. Inflation of the balloon pins the prostate against the pubic bone. Each day with the patient on the treatment table, positioning films are taken and the fields are set up to the balloon immobilizer. Because the immobilized prostate does not move during treatment, very small posterior margins can be used (Fig. 100–14), thus minimizing dose to the rectum. In the first 28 patients studied with this approach at Brigham and Women's Hospital, the use of the balloon immobilizer decreased the percentage of rectum receiving more than 70 Gy from 36% if no balloon was used to 3.5% with 15 immobilized treatments (Sanghani et al, 2004).

In a retrospective analysis of patients treated in a phase I/II trial, investigators from Memorial Sloan-Kettering Cancer Center reported a reduction in morbidity from 14% at 3 years to 2% after moving from CRT (81 Gy, $n = 189$) to IMRT (81 Gy, $n = 61$) (Zelefsky et al, 2002). Ninety percent of the patients in this study were treated to 81 Gy and 10% to 86.4 Gy, doses never attempted before in prostate cancer patients. After 2 years, only 4.5% of patients had acute grade 2 rectal toxicity and none experienced grade 3 or 4. Late grade 2, 3, and 4 toxicity occurred in 1.5%, 0.1%, and 0% of patients, respectively. One caveat in the interpretation of these data is as follows. Rectal blocks were used and the entire prostate gland with a margin did not receive the prescribed dose. Specifically, prostate tissue in the region of the anterior rectal wall received much lower doses, on the order of 74 to 76 Gy. However, much of the gland was treated to the prescribed dose and the complication rates were very low. In a retrospective analysis of 77 patients treated at Baylor College of Medicine, investigators demonstrated a statistically significant difference for both rectal and bladder toxicity ($P < .001$) between the IMRT and CRT groups. These publications created immediate interest in dose escalation and IMRT for prostate cancer.

Published reports suggest that erectile dysfunction after radiation is caused predominantly by vascular damage. More recent data suggest that it is dose to the penile bulb that correlates best with erectile dysfunction after CRT (Roach et al,

2000; Fisch et al, 2001; Merrick et al, 2001). With the interest in dose escalation, there is some concern that post-therapy potency rates will decline (Kao et al, 2004), and preliminary data from Memorial Sloan-Kettering suggest that this may be true (Zelefsky et al, 1999a). In order to maintain or lower the risk of erectile dysfunction after dose escalation, it is necessary to modify existing techniques with this goal in mind. Researchers at the University of Chicago Medical Center undertook a planning exercise in 10 consecutive patients with prostate cancer. They planned each patient with an optimized CRT technique and then replanned each for IMRT, without adding dose constraints for the erectile tissue. IMRT significantly decreased the percentage of the penile bulb receiving 40 Gy ($P < .001$) and the percentage of volume receiving more than 70 Gy was nearly identical for both CRT and IMRT.

A similar modeling study was undertaken by investigators at Fox Chase Cancer Center (Buyyounouski et al, 2004). In this study, the object was to limit the radiation dose to the penile bulb and corpora without increasing radiation dose to the rectum and bladder. Twenty-three patients were studied. The dose to the erectile tissue was easily decreased by 60% (compared with standard CRT) in all patients. Limiting the dose received by erectile tissue to 15 Gy was easily accomplished in 80% of patients but required significant alteration of field arrangement in the other 20%. These investigations provided interesting dosimetric evidence that IMRT allows an increased therapeutic ratio in prostate cancer. However, long-term clinical data to prove this hypothesis are not yet available.

Only a few groups have used IMRT for enough time to report any efficacy data. The group at Memorial Sloan-Kettering has the most experience in the United States with IMRT. As shown in their outcome data, the PSA-relapse-free survival rates were highest after treatment with IMRT when the dose of radiation delivered was greater than 81 Gy (Leibel et al, 2003). The median time to follow-up for these patients was 50 months but the range was broad (6 to 150 months) and presumably the patients who received the highest doses were also those treated most recently.

KEY POINT

■ Intensity-modulated radiation therapy provides the ability to deliver higher doses of radiation with lower rates of rectal bleeding.

Heavy Particle Beams

Since the 1950s, radiation oncologists have used particle beam therapy for their patients with cancer. The common application of particle therapy is with the electron beam, which is created by all modern linear accelerators. Other particles, such as protons, neutrons, helium ions, heavy ions (neon, argon, carbon), and negative ions, are available as well. These heavy particle beams are difficult to produce and to control but have certain theoretical advantages over conventional x-ray and electron beams. They are more densely destructive in tissue, and the damage they create is less easily repaired by tumor cells. In addition, they travel differently in tissue and exhibit a Bragg peak, which refers to a sharp cutoff in dose at the end

of the particle's range in tissue; see Figure 100–15. Beyond this depth, the tissue receives little or no radiation. Thus, with appropriate focus and application, it can be easier to spare the normal tissues surrounding the cancerous target.

The most commonly used particles are neutrons and protons. The RTOG sponsored a phase III trial in 1977 (Lawton et al, 1991) in which 91 patients with prostate cancer were randomly assigned to receive treatment with neutrons or conventional x-rays. At 10 years, survival was better in the neutron arm (46%) than in the photon arm (26%). However, the patients were not equally divided between the two arms. Poor prognosticators such as stage D1 disease were more common in the photon arm. A survival difference between the two groups may have been due to this aspect more than to any therapeutic benefit of neutrons per se. However, the data were compelling enough to lead the National Cancer Institute to fund the construction of several state-of-the-art neutron beam facilities. Again, trials were undertaken to study the efficacy and morbidity of neutron treatment. Because today's cyclotrons are large and extremely expensive, there are few national facilities using neutron beam treatment for cancer patients. In the mid-1980s, a second prospective randomized trial was undertaken by the RTOG (Russell et al, 1994). One hundred seventy-eight prostate cancer patients were randomly assigned to receive either neutron beam or conventional x-ray treatment (nonconformal). The local control rate was higher for the patients who received neutron therapy than for those who received photons (89% versus 68%), as was the 5-year rate of freedom from PSA failure (83% versus 55%). However, survival rates were the same for both arms. Morbidity was higher in patients who received neutron beam treatment and was described as severe in 11% compared with 3% for those who underwent photon irradiation.

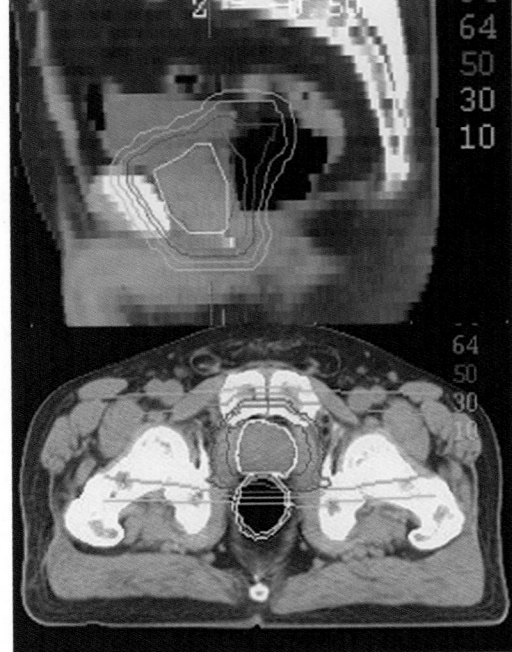

Figure 100–15. Proton beam therapy. (Courtesy of Anthony Zietman, Massachusetts Hospital.)

In general, acceptance of neutron beam therapy by radiation oncologists has been limited because of the perception that complication rates are high without much gain in tumor control as well as because of the limited availability and expense associated with neutron production. Nonetheless, efforts are ongoing in neutron beam facilities to improve outcomes using the same computer-driven technologies used in x-ray treatment. A form of conformal neutron beam therapy is now possible in several centers (Forman et al, 1995). At Wayne State University, 300 patients were entered into a phase III trial and randomly assigned to conformal neutron therapy followed by standard CRT or CRT followed by a neutron therapy boost. A statistically significant difference in 5-year disease-free survival was seen for patients treated with neutrons first (93% compared with 73%, $P = .008$) (Forman et al, 2002). Treatment-related morbidity was the same for both groups in this study. A larger retrospective review from the same group of neutron therapy and standard x-ray CRT revealed a statistically significant improvement in 5-year relapse-free survival for the group that received neutrons as any component of their therapy. The effect was most pronounced for high-risk patients who had a 35% 5-year relapse-free survival rate versus 7% in the photon-only group ($P = .0004$). Although these data are provocative, one criticism is that the relapse-free survival in the photon-only group from Wayne State is much lower than that of other series reporting on the same population of patients.

Despite the data from Wayne State, most radiation oncologists believe that neutron beam therapy causes greater normal tissue damage than x-ray photon beam therapy. Investigators from the Catholic University of Louvain, Belgium, used a mailed questionnaire to assess quality-of-life changes in 262 patients who received mixed neutron-photon irradiation. Twenty-two percent of the 230 patients who replied had four or more bowel movements per day. Retaining stool was a problem in 26% of the patients, and only 38% reported full bowel continence. The patients in this trial received neutron beam therapy using equipment that was not conformal. These data were sufficiently concerning to close their program and demonstrate the importance of up-to-date equipment and technology for the delivery of neutron beam therapy.

Proton beams are also used to treat cancer. These charged particles are generated by a linear accelerator, cyclotron, or synchrotron. Each method of manufacturing has strengths and weaknesses, and, to date, it has been difficult to create a simple, cost-effective, and robust system that can be used for cancer treatment. Most proton facilities are located near nuclear physics laboratories, but a free-standing unit does exist at Loma Linda Medical Center in California. Two others are under development, one in Boston, Massachusetts and the other in Switzerland.

Protons have the same theoretical advantage over conventional x-rays as neutrons (i.e., they are more densely ionizing in tissue and have a sharp dose falloff in tissue; see Fig. 100–14). At Massachusetts General Hospital, clinicians have used a cyclotron housed at Harvard University for the treatment of patients for many years. In the 1980s, a prospective randomized trial was undertaken in men with locally advanced prostate cancer (Shipley et al, 1995). Patients treated with proton beam had a 95% incidence of clinical local control at 5 years, compared with a 64% incidence for those treated

with photons. Although no grade 3 to 5 toxicities were reported in either arm of this trial, grade 1 and 2 rectal bleeding rates were higher in the proton group (32% versus 12%, $P = .002$), as were urethral strictures (19% versus 8%, $P = .07$). When the group with rectal bleeding was carefully analyzed, a relationship between the volume of rectum treated and the dose of protons given was established, and guidelines were developed for future trials (Hartford et al, 1999).

At Loma Linda University Medical Center, 643 patients have received treatment with protons alone or in combination with photons (Rossi, 1999). Eighty-nine percent of early-stage patients (stage T1b or T2b, PSA less than 15 ng/mL) achieved 5-year biochemical disease-free survival, as opposed to 68% of those with more advanced tumors. In this series, 21% of patients developed minimal radiation proctitis, and severe side effects were seen in less than 1%. Similar results were published in 16 patients from Kobe University of Japan, emphasizing how few new data are available on this form of therapy. In this study, none of the patients evidenced PSA failure within the first 12 months.

The same technical advances that allow delivery of improved photon therapy (conformal radiation) must be used by particle beam specialists. In time, it may be possible to deliver particle beams safely and inexpensively. At present, conformal particle beam treatment units are extremely expensive to construct and operate, and this poses a problem for those interested in particle beam therapy, particularly because, to date, the single-institution results in prostate cancer demonstrate disease control rates that are similar to those seen with conformal radiation.

KEY POINT

- Proton radiation therapy also provides the ability to deliver higher doses of radiation therapy while minimizing rectal bleeding.

Brachytherapy

Brachytherapy ("close" therapy) is the placement of radioactive sources into or near tumors for therapeutic purposes. The discovery of x-rays and the purification of radium in the early 20th century paved the way for the development of this form of therapy. Subsequent technical advances and refinements led to the increasingly accurate techniques currently in use, which are associated with lower cost and morbidity rates. Today, the number of patients undergoing brachytherapy for early-stage prostate cancer has increased dramatically. The CaPSURE database reported an increase in the use of brachytherapy from 3.1% to 12.0% in the past decade (Cooperberg et al, 2004).

Pasteau and Degrais described the temporary placement of radium-containing needles into the prostate through the urethra (Pasteau et al, 1913). During the 1920s, Young (1922) at Johns Hopkins performed prostate brachytherapy using intracavitary radium sources in the bladder, rectum, and urethra "cross-firing" into the prostate (Young, 1922). This technique was refined at Memorial Hospital in New York by Benjamin Stockwell Barrington, who pioneered implanting

Table 100–6. Postimplantation Biopsy Results

Author	Isotope	Results
Prestidge et al, 1997	^{125}I and ^{103}Pd	201 postimplantation biopsies—80% negative, 17% indeterminate, 3% positive
Ragde et al, 1997	^{125}I	82% negative 13% indeterminate 5% positive
Stock et al, 1996a	^{125}I and ^{103}Pd	Post-treatment biopsies on patients (T1b-T2c)—26% positive
Stock et al, 2004	9 months hormonal therapy, external beam with ^{103}Pd boost	4% post-treatment biopsies at 2 years in a "high-risk" group
Sharkey et al, 1998	^{103}Pd	11% positive at 2 years after implant
Kuban et al, 1992	^{125}I	Biopsy at least 18 months after implant, negative DRE, 18% positive biopsy
Stone et al, 2004	^{125}I, ^{103}Pd monotherapy or as boost ± hormones	"Low risk" group, 4.1% positive

DRE, digital rectal examination.

Table 100–7. Actuarial Freedom from Biochemical Relapse: Implant Monotherapy and Combined Implant and External Beam

Implant Monotherapy	Author	Number of Patients	Isotope	Freedom from Relapse (%)	Time (yr)
	Zelefsky et al, 2000	146	^{125}I	88	5
	Potters et al, 1999	112	^{125}I	92	5
	Kollmeier et al, 2003	73	^{125}I, ^{103}Pd	88	8
	Brachman et al, 2000	392	^{125}I, ^{103}Pd	82	5
	Grado et al, 1998	62	^{125}I, ^{103}Pd	95	5
	Kwok et al, 2002	41	^{125}I	85	5
	Ellis et al, 2003	67	^{125}I, ^{103}Pd	97	4
	D'Amico et al, 1998b*	32	^{103}Pd	85	5
	Lawton et al, 2004 (RTOG)	97	^{125}I	96.8	3
	Blasko et al, 2000[†]	103	^{103}Pd	94	5
	Grimm et al, 2000[†]	97	^{125}I	87	10
External beam with implant boost	Brachman et al, 2000	465	^{125}I, ^{103}Pd	85	5
	Sylvester et al, 2003[†]	232	^{125}I, ^{103}Pd	85	10
		212		86*	

*Excludes patients with T2b disease.
[†]PSA failure—two consecutive rises in serum PSA.

reported that 11% of patients who experienced a PSA bounce would have met the ASTRO criterion for PSA failure. In addition, Reed (2003) reported eight patients who had a positive post-treatment prostate biopsy during a PSA bounce and subsequently remained free from recurrence. Some investigators have reported improved rates of cancer control in patients who experience a PSA bounce (Das et al, 2002; Patel et al, 2004).

Pretreatment prognostic factors such as pretreatment PSA, clinical examination, Gleason score, and percentage of biopsy cores positive have been used to define risk groups in relation to pathologic findings at surgery and freedom from PSA relapse after RT or radical surgery (D'Amico et al, 1998b, 2002; Partin et al, 2001; Kuban et al, 2003). There is no consensus in the definition of these prognostic groupings. However, there is general agreement that "low risk" (defined as a low risk for extracapsular disease at prostatectomy and a high probability of disease-free survival after treatment) includes patients with clinical T1-T2 disease, a Gleason score less than 6, and a pretreatment PSA less than 10 ng/mL (D'Amico et al, 1998b,

2002; Partin et al, 2001; Kuban et al, 2003). Some investigators exclude T2b from the low-risk group (D'Amico et al, 1998b). There is no consensus in the definition of risk groups with an intermediate risk or high risk of failure after local treatment (D'Amico et al, 1998b; Blasko et al, 2002; Kollmeir et al, 2003). The high-risk grouping typically includes patients with multiple high-risk features, such as Gleason score greater than 7, PSA above 10 ng/mL, or large palpable tumors. The intermediate group is very heterogeneous and includes patients who have features in between low and high risk.

Table 100–7 summarizes the clinical outcomes of permanent implant monotherapy without hormone ablation in several large series using the ASTRO definition for biochemical failure. These studies report on more than 1000 patients treated with permanent implant monotherapy. Although these are retrospective single-institution studies (with the exception of RTOG 98-05), they represent results from a uniform population of patients. These results compare favorably with those of similarly selected patients treated with external-beam irradiation or radical prostatectomy (D'Amico et al, 1998b; Quaranta et al, 2004).

Seed Brachytherapy with External Irradiation

Seed brachytherapy can be used as a boost either before or after external-beam irradiation for prostate cancer. Generally, brachytherapy combined with external-beam irradiation, rather than brachytherapy alone, is used for patients with higher stage disease. External-beam irradiation is employed in these higher stage patients to treat the prostate and periprostatic tissues. Typically, a dose of 4100 to 4500 cGy of external-beam RT is delivered (compared with 7000 to 7600 cGy when external-beam irradiation is used alone). The dose of the implant boost in such combination therapy is generally 60% to 70% of the dose prescribed for patients treated with implant alone. Table 100–8 summarizes the results of several studies employing combined external-beam radiation and implant boost for low-risk-group patients. Potters (1999) and Grado (1998) and their colleagues did not find the addition of external beam to implantation to be statistically significant in a multivariate analysis. The role of external beam with permanent seed brachytherapy versus brachytherapy alone is being investigated in a randomized clinical trial by the RTOG (RTOG trial 02-32).

Assessment of Implant Quality

The goal of prostate brachytherapy is to deliver a homogeneous dose to the prostate while minimizing dose to nearby sensitive normal structures such as the rectum and urethra. Postimplant dosimetry in these dose-limiting regions is important for an assessment of implant quality. The matched peripheral dose is defined as the dose to a volume of an ellipsoid having the calculated volume of the prostate ([height] × [length] × [width] × [pi/6]). However, this dosimetric calculation does not take into account geographic misses and cannot directly calculate point doses to structures such as urethra, rectum, or prostatic apex. To determine the minimum dose within the prostate and to assess the distribution of volume and dose, three-dimensional reconstruction of the prostate and unambiguous determination of seed location within the prostate are needed. These factors can be calculated with postimplantation imaging using either CT or MRI (Moreland et al, 1997; Willins and Wallner, 1997; Amdur et al, 1999). The American Brachytherapy Society (ABS) has proposed the D_{90} (the minimal dose covering 90% of the prostate volume) and the V_{100} and V_{150} (the percent volume of the prostate receiving 100% and 150% of the prescribed dose, respectively) as parameters to assess implant quality (Nag et al, 1999). However, these descriptive parameters may not adequately predict for tumor control, and more sophisticated measures have been proposed.

A significant source of error in these calculations is prostatic edema, which is invariably observed after implantation (Prestidge, 1998; Waterman et al, 1998). Accordingly, Yue and colleagues (1999) suggested that postimplantation scans should be performed 2 weeks after [103]Pd and 6 weeks after [125]I. However, Taussky and associates (2004) analyzed serial postimplantation MRI images and reported that edema effects are minimal and the time to postimplantation scan is not important.

Toxicity

Implant techniques and procedures vary from institution to institution. Variations in these factors are important when assessing rates of treatment toxicity. Implants are currently performed using peripheral loading techniques. With this scheme, there is a greater density of seeds placed in the periphery of the gland than in the center. This ensures a more uniform distribution of dose throughout the gland and minimizes "hot spots" around the urethra. Some investigators completely exclude the transitional zone of the prostate from the treatment volume, significantly reducing the urethral dose (D'Amico et al, 2000a). Other groups intentionally place seeds outside the gland to improve peripheral dose coverage. This increases the dose received by the rectum and the neurovascular bundles. Age, existing comorbid diseases such as peripheral vascular disease or diabetes mellitus, and tobacco use may also predispose to increased toxicity from treatment.

Table 100–8. High-Dose-Rate Boost with External-Beam Irradiation

Martinez phase I prospective trial (Martinez et al, 2002)	58 pts	46 Gy external beam + "Low-dose" HDR (up to 6.5 Gy × 3 applications) "High-dose" HDR (up to 11.5 × 2 applications)	52%	5 yr	Fewer patients with Gleason ≥8 and PSA >20.0 ng/mL in "high-risk" group
	149 pts		87%	5 yr	
Galalae prospective phase II trial (Galalae et al, 2002)	46 pts	50 Gy pelvis, 40 Gy prostate	94.7%	5 yr	WHO grading used
	22 pts	2 HDR applications of 15 Gy	93%	8 yr	
	25 pts	PSA<10 and grade 1-2	67.7	5 yr	
		PSA>20 and grade 1-2	63.9	8 yr	
		PSA>20 and grade 3	38%	5 yr	
			32%	8 yr	
Mate et al, 1998		50.4 Gy external beam			Mean follow-up 46 mo
	54 pts	4 HDR applications of 3-4 Gy	93%		
	29 pts	PSA <10 ng/mL	90%		
	20 pts	PSA 10-20 ng/mL	60%		
		PSA ≥20			
Deger et al, 2002		45 Gy external beam	100%	5 yr	
		Two applications of 9-10 Gy	75%	5 yr	
		T1	60%	5 yr	
		T2			
		T3			

HDR, high dose rate; PSA, prostate-specific antigen; WHO, World Health Organization.

Determining incidence rates and severity of treatment-related morbidity is also dependent on the instrument used and how the information is gathered. The ABS proposed as a minimal set of assessment criteria the International Prostate Symptom Score (I-PSS) for assessing urinary function, the International Index of Erectile Function for erectile function, and RTOG toxicity grading criteria for rectal toxicity.

Urinary Toxicity

Brachytherapy after TURP was initially reported to be associated with a significant rate of serious urethral toxicity. Blasko and associates (1993) reported that 24% of patients who underwent implantation after TURP developed urinary morbidity, compared with 3% of patients who did not undergo this procedure. However, several more recent reports have demonstrated that men who have undergone prior TURP can be implanted as long as there is adequate tissue remaining to accommodate the seed sources. Most patients who have had a TURP can safely be implanted without an increased risk of urinary retention (Stone et al, 2000).

The I-PSS tends to increase significantly immediately after implantation. Subsequently, the score decreases, but it is still significantly elevated at 3 months after treatment (Lee et al, 1999). Gelblum and coworkers (1999) observed that 37% of patients report grade I urinary toxicity (defined as symptoms not requiring medical intervention) within the first 60 days after implantation. Zelefsky and associates (1999a) reported grade II urinary toxicity (symptoms requiring medical intervention) occurring at a mean duration of 19 months after implantation, with a likelihood of resolution of 68% at 36 months. Continued significant urinary obstruction requiring self-catheterization occurs in 1% to 5% of patients (Grado et al, 1998; Gelblum et al, 1999; Peschel et al, 1999). The use of α blockers prior to implantation may decrease the severity and duration of urinary symptoms (Merrick et al, 2002b).

Longitudinal studies are being conducted to assess late urinary morbidity. Merrick and colleagues (2003a) reported the results of a survey of 225 patients who reached an average of 5.5 years after brachytherapy and compared their urinary symptoms with those in a cohort of more recently diagnosed patients. No significant difference was seen between the two groups (Merrick et al, 2003a). Stone and Stock (2003) reported a small but significant long-term increase in urinary frequency and weak stream in their series.

Wallner and colleagues (1995) reported the risk of urinary toxicity to be a function of the length of the urethra receiving a high dose. Grade II-III morbidity was observed when 20.0 mm + 11.0 mm of the urethra received more than 400 Gy with ^{125}I implants. Larger prostatic volumes—specifically, glands greater than 60.0 cm^3—were also associated with higher rates of urinary toxicity (Wallner et al, 1995). Terk and associates (1998) reported on 251 patients using the I-PSS to assess urinary function prior to and after ^{125}I or ^{103}Pd implantation. Patients with a pretreatment I-PSS above 20 demonstrated a 29% risk of developing urinary retention, and a pretreatment score less than 10 was associated with only a 2% risk. Overall, significant postbrachytherapy obstructive symptoms refractory to medical management occur in approximately 2% to 3% of patients. Postbrachytherapy TURP can be performed with a very low rate of post-TURP incontinence if care is taken to preserve the urethral blood supply (Flam et al, 2004).

Rectal Toxicity

Minor rectal symptoms secondary to brachytherapy are usually self-limiting. The usual scale to assess rectal toxicity, the RTOG acute and late toxicity scale, is not a sensitive enough measure to report minor changes in rectal function after treatment. Rectal toxicity—specifically, rectal bleeding secondary to radiation proctitis—can be a minor, self-limiting side effect of radiation or a major toxicity requiring surgical intervention, such as argon plasma coagulation (Smith et al, 2001) or, in the worst cases, diverting colostomy. The rate of minor rectal bleeding after implant therapy has been reported to be approximately 1% to 4% (Zelefsky et al, 1999a). The incidence of significant rectal complications has been reported to be 0% to 1% (Grado et al, 1998; Zelefsky et al, 1999a). A postimplantation colostomy rate of 0.3% was observed in a study of Medicare claims (Benoit et al, 2000a, 2000b). The rate of rectal complications is correlated with the dose and the length of rectum receiving a high dose. For example, rectal complications have been observed when 17.0 mm^2 (±5.0 mm) of the rectal wall received more than 100 Gy (Wallner et al, 1995). Wallner and colleagues (1995) accordingly recommended minimizing the amount of rectum receiving 100 Gy in ^{125}I implants. Merrick and associates (2003a) reported that rectal complications were rarely observed when the rectal wall received 85% of the prescribed dose.

Potency

Impotence is defined by the National Institutes of Health (NIH) consensus on erectile dysfunction (ED) as the "inability to attain and maintain a penile erection sufficient to permit satisfactory sexual intercourse" (NIH Consensus Conference, 1993). The cause of implant-related ED is multifactorial. Factors such as underlying small vessel disease, nerve damage, and dose to specific tissues have been implicated in postimplantation ED.

Di Biase and coworkers (2000) reported that dose to the neurovascular bundle was related to development of postbrachytherapy ED. Merrick and colleagues (2001) reported that dose to the penile bulb correlates with rates of ED, although the penile bulb is composed of corpus spongiosum, not corpus cavernosum (Muhall and Yanover, 2001). In any case, potency preservation rates for patients undergoing implantation are superior to those reported for patients receiving external-beam irradiation or neoadjuvant hormonal therapy, external beam, and brachytherapy boost. Zelefsky (1999c) and Stock (1996b) and their coauthors reported that potency was maintained in 79% of patients undergoing brachytherapy compared with 68% receiving external-beam irradiation. There is continued drop-off in potency with continued follow-up past 3 years (Zeitlin et al, 1998). Merrick and associates (2002a) reported that 50% of men who were fully potent prior to brachytherapy maintained potency at 6 years after treatment.

The potency rate has been reported to be 62% in patients receiving combined external beam with an implant boost (Zeitlin et al, 1998). Potters and coworkers (2001) reported a 5-year potency maintenance rate of 76% with brachytherapy monotherapy, 56% with combined external beam and brachytherapy boost. The addition of hormones to external beam and brachytherapy boosted lower potency rates to 52%. Similarly, Stock and Stone (2002) reported that potency was maintained in 43% at 3 years after combined neoadjuvant hormonal therapy with external beam and brachytherapy boost. Age was a significant prognostic factor in a univariate analysis (Merrick et al, 2002a), and the addition of external beam and a history of diabetes mellitus were significant factors in a multivariate analysis (Robinson et al, 2002). In a meta-analysis, the probability of maintaining potency at 1 year after treatment was 76% (69% to 82%) with brachytherapy monotherapy and 60% (48% to 73%) with external beam with brachytherapy boost (Robinson et al, 2002). When the probability of ED was adjusted for age, the difference between prostate brachytherapy and prostatectomy increased (Robinson et al, 2002). Sildenafil citrate and other phosphodiesterase-5 inhibitors have been reported effective in 74% to 81% of patients who avail themselves of oral therapy for ED (Albert et al, 2003; Merrick et al, 2003a; Raina et al, 2003).

High-Dose-Rate Brachytherapy

HDR brachytherapy afterloading techniques have been developed to treat prostate cancer. This procedure utilizes high-activity ^{192}Ir sources in cables stored in a mobile computer-controlled lead safe. ^{192}Ir emits gamma radiation at 400 keV, which is significantly more penetrating than either ^{125}I or ^{103}Pd. Needles are first implanted transperineally into the prostate under ultrasound guidance. The precise positions of the needles are then determined by CT, and a dosimetric plan is calculated before the radiation is administered. Under computer guidance, the ^{192}Ir sources are transferred to the needles for a predetermined time. A precise dose is administered by varying the dwell times of the source in each needle. Kini and colleagues (1999) reported on 20 HDR treatments delivered in 11 patients. An average of 16 needles was used. Ninety-two percent of the prostatic volume received 100% of the prescribed dose; this is slightly superior to the dosimetry generally achieved during permanent seed implantation (Merrick et al, 1999a).

HDR has been used primarily in combination with external-beam irradiation for patients with intermediate- or high-risk features. It is delivered as a boost in two to four applications, either before or after external-beam irradiation. HDR is a new technology, and there is heterogeneity in dose per fraction delivered and techniques employed. Consequently, the reports with the longest follow-up are from phase I dose escalation studies. Dinges and associates (1998) reported on 82 patients with a mean pretreatment PSA of 14.0 ng/mL. All patients had pathologic node-negative disease as determined by laparoscopic staging. Two HDR treatments calculated to deliver 9 to 10 Gy were followed by 40 to 45 Gy of external-beam irradiation. Seventy-three percent of patients had negative biopsies at 2 years. Local failure (defined as a positive post-treatment biopsy and a PSA above 1.0 ng/mL) was observed in 21.5% of patients. In a multi-institution report in which different dose fractionation schemes and doses of external beam were used, a 5-year biochemical disease-free survival (ASTRO definition) of 96% was observed in patients with low-risk disease, with 87% and 69% for an intermediate- and high-risk group of 137 and 240 hormonally naïve patients, respectively (Galalae et al, 2004). Table 100–8 summarizes results of trials of HDR delivered as

a boost with external-beam irradiation, utilizing the ASTRO definition for biochemical failure.

Early results with HDR used as monotherapy for patients with low-risk prostate cancer have demonstrated acceptable toxicity and early biochemical freedom-from-relapse rates similar to those for permanent seed implants (Grills et al, 2004). Further experience with more patients and longer follow-up is required to assess the efficacy of this approach.

KEY POINT

■ Prostate brachytherapy is best performed using intraoperative real-time dosimetry in order to minimize normal tissue complications and maximize tumor control.

Radiation Therapy and Androgen Suppression Therapy

Locally Advanced Prostate Cancer

Among strategies to improve outcome for patients with locally advanced prostate cancer, hormonal manipulation in combination with RT has consistently demonstrated improvement in treatment outcome as compared with standard-dose radiation alone (Pilepich et al, 1995, 1997; Bolla et al, 1997; Vicini et al, 1999). A meta-analysis of both retrospective and prospective trials of androgen deprivation in combination with RT demonstrated near-universal benefit in regard to local/regional control, disease-free survival, and freedom-from-failure survival. However, the ultimate impact on overall and cause-specific survival remains to be fully defined (Vicini et al, 1999). There are now three published cooperative group phase III trials and a single-institution phase III trial reporting advantage in various outcome parameters with the use of androgen deprivation compared with use of radiation alone.

In RTOG 86-10, 456 patients with large (25 cm^3), stage T2B to T4, Nx tumors randomly assigned to 4 months of total androgen suppression with RT given after the first 2 months had improved local control, disease-free survival, and freedom from metastases compared with patients receiving RT alone. At 8 years significant improvements in rates of local control of 42% versus 30%, distant metastases of 34% versus 45%, disease-free survival of 33% versus 21%, biochemical disease-free survival (PSA less than 1.5 ng/mL) of 24% versus 10%, and cause-specific mortality of 23% versus 31% were noted with versus without addition of this short course of neoadjuvant androgen suppression. Subset analysis indicates that the beneficial effect of short-term androgen ablation appears preferentially in patients with Gleason score 2 to 6. In that population, there is a highly significant improvement in all endpoints, including survival (70% versus 52%, $P = .015$) (Pilepich et al, 1995, 1998, 2001).

In European Organization for Research in the Treatment of Cancer (EORTC) 22863, a phase III trial of androgen suppression, Bolla and associates (1997, 1999) reported an overall survival advantage for patients receiving 3 years of goserelin starting at the initiation of RT. Most of the patients in this study had stage T3 disease, and the remainder were eligible owing to high-grade tumors. With median follow-up of 66 months, 5-year clinical disease-free survival was 40% (95% CI 32 to 48) in the radiotherapy-alone group and 74% (67 to 81) in the combined-treatment group (P = .0001). Five-year overall survival was 62% (52 to 72) and 78% (72 to 84), respectively (P = .0002) and 5-year specific survival 79% (72 to 86) and 94% (90 to 98), supporting the use of androgen suppression (Bolla et al, 2002).

The optimal type, timing, and duration of androgen suppression in combination with RT remain to be defined. In RTOG 92-02, patients with stage T2c-T4, N0-1, M0 disease were randomly assigned to 4 months of total androgen suppression with radiation administered after 2 months or the same regimen followed by an additional 2 years of goserelin. As with RTOG 85-31, subgroup analysis revealed significant improvement in overall survival, 80% versus 69%, and disease-specific survival, 90% versus 78%, in patients with Gleason grade 8 to 10 tumors.

The question of timing of hormonal therapy and impact of radiation field size was addressed by RTOG 94-13, a four-arm study comparing whole-pelvis versus small-field radiation with 4 months of either neoadjuvant or adjuvant total androgen suppression. Eligible patients had adverse risk factors, with estimated risk of positive-node disease of more than 15%. A difference was seen in progression-free survival at 4 years, 54% versus 47% for the whole-pelvis versus prostate-only radiation, respectively (P = .022), but no difference was seen in overall survival. The best outcomes occurred with a combination of neoadjuvant androgen blockade and whole-pelvis radiation with 4-year progression-free survival of 60%.

Additional strategies for high-risk patients under investigation include combinations of radiation and androgen deprivation therapy with chemotherapy, hyperthermia, or radiosensitizers, particle therapy, and dose escalation. These approaches to treatment of patients with localized high-risk disease are discussed elsewhere in this section.

Radiation Therapy for Node-Positive Disease

Optimal management of patients with established lymph node involvement remains to be defined. The findings of survival advantage in a randomized study of immediate versus delayed androgen suppression therapy in patients found to have nodal metastases at the time of lymph node dissection have clarified the importance of hormonal manipulation in this setting (Messing et al, 1999). The benefit of radiation in addition to androgen deprivation has not been addressed in a randomized study, and the degree of benefit may vary depending on whether disease is identified by microscopic assessment after lymph node dissection or by the finding of gross lymphadenopathy. More recently, MR lymphangiography was reported to improve dramatically detection of pelvic metastases in high-risk patients who subsequently underwent lymph node dissection for pathologic correlation followed by radical prostatectomy (Harisinghani et al, 2003). With this technique, ferromagnetic nanoparticles are injected intravenously and taken up in lymph nodes. Thereby, architectural distortions typical of metastatic infiltration, even in normal-sized lymph nodes, can be detected. Should the accuracy of this staging technique be validated in a wider range of prostate cancer patients, the potential for stage migration is significant

as some patients previously designated as clinically node negative are likely to be found to harbor lymphatic metastases. The impact of these findings on treatment approaches would require additional study.

On the basis of currently available staging technology, three single-institution studies indicated benefit with combination of androgen suppression and radiation (Sands et al, 1995; Whittington et al, 1997; Buskirk et al, 2001). At the Mayo Clinic, 60 consecutive patients treated with androgen ablation plus RT for stage IV (T1-4 N1 M0) adenocarcinoma of the prostate were analyzed. With median follow-up of 101 months, biochemical relapse-free, clinical disease-free, overall, and cause-specific survival rates at 5 years were 82%, 84%, 76%, and 80%, respectively (Buskirk et al, 2001). In a follow-up report from M.D. Anderson, 255 men with lymphadenectomy-proven pelvic nodal metastases treated with early androgen ablation alone (N = 183) or with combined ablation and radiation (N = 72) were retrospectively reviewed for disease outcome and survival. With a median follow-up of 9.4 years in patients treated with early androgen ablation alone versus 6.2 years in those receiving combined androgen suppression with radiation, the 10-year freedom-from-relapse or rising PSA rate was 25% versus 80% and overall survival rates were 46% versus 67%, respectively (Zagars et al, 2001). A subgroup analysis of RTOG 85-31 patients with node-positive disease noted 5-year freedom-from-failure survival of 55% with combination therapy as opposed to 11% with RT alone (Lawton et al, 1997). In light of the available data, particularly in the setting of micrometastatic lymph node disease, addition of RT to androgen deprivation is worthy of consideration.

KEY POINTS

- Randomized controlled trials have shown a survival benefit for the addition of androgen suppression therapy to external-beam radiation therapy.

- Six months of hormonal therapy compared with 3 years of hormonal therapy provides a survival benefit for men with localized high-risk versus locally advanced prostate cancer, respectively.

Radiation Therapy for Palliation

Bone Metastases

In genitourinary cancers, bone metastases are a common problem (Abrams et al, 1950; Gilbert and Dagan, 1976). Many therapies are available for bone metastases, including surgery, medical management, and radiation. RT can treat most patients with highly effective symptom relief.

The hallmark of osseous metastases is localized pain, which is frequently continuous and unrelenting regardless of the site. The pain caused by bone metastases is not well understood. Some investigators have hypothesized that irritation of the periosteal membrane or release of biologic mediators is responsible for bone pain. The most serious complication of osseous metastases is spinal cord compression, which is discussed later.

Most bone metastases can be diagnosed by physical examination, plain radiographs, and bone scan. CT and MRI are sometimes required if there is suspicion of bone involvement, but x-ray and bone scans are negative or if there is soft tissue involvement.

With respect to treatment, reviewing the currently available data from prospective studies has shown overall response rates ranging from 85% to 100% using various treatment schedules (Madsen, 1983; Price et al, 1988; Cole, 1989). A single-fraction regimen (800 cGy × 1) appears to be as effective as other, more protracted regimens but is also associated with increased acute morbidity, particularly to the abdominal organs. A frequently used regimen in the United States is 3000 cGy in 10 divided fractions. This dosage is adequate for most osseous metastases.

Metastasis to a weight-bearing region raises many concerns. A pathologic fracture can be painful and disabling, both functionally and psychologically. Radiographic and clinical factors that warrant consideration of prophylactic surgical fixation include:

An intramedullary lytic lesion equal to or greater than 50% of the cross-sectional diameter of the bone

A lytic lesion involving a length of cortex equal to or greater than the cross-sectional diameter of the bone or greater than 2.5 cm in axial length (Lane et al, 1980)

These patients should be evaluated by an orthopedic surgeon. If a pathologic fracture has occurred in a weight-bearing region, surgical fixation is required for pain control and to promote adequate healing. In all situations, postoperative radiation is required. Because prostate cancer produces primarily blastic metastases, pathologic fracture is correspondingly infrequent.

Spinal Cord Compression

Spinal cord compression is a medical emergency. Failure to diagnose and treat promptly can lead to significant morbidity, including paraplegia and autonomic dysfunction. The predominant symptom of cord compression is pain, which occurs in about 95% of patients (Gilbert et al, 1978). Pain usually precedes a diagnosis of spinal cord compression by about 4 months. Symptoms, however, can progress rapidly to neurologic dysfunction in a matter of hours to days. When a patient has progressed to paraplegia, return of function is infrequent. Therefore, early diagnosis and therapy are critical. The diagnostic tool of choice to evaluate spinal cord compression is MRI.

Once the diagnosis of spinal cord compression is made, the physician is left with the dilemma of how to treat. There are a few instances in which surgery should be considered as an option before radiation, including pathologic fracture with spinal instability or compression of the spinal cord by bone, unknown tissue diagnosis, or history of previous radiation to the same area.

When the diagnosis of cord compression is made or even suspected, all patients should receive steroid therapy. Steroids can decrease vasogenic edema and provide striking analgesic benefit. The loading dose of dexamethasone (Decadron) is 4 to 10 mg, followed by a maintenance dosage of 4 to 24 mg every 6 hours.

Table 100–9. Physical Characteristics of Radionuclides Reviewed

Radiounclide	Physical Half-Life	Beta Energy (MeV)	Gamma Energy (keV)	Chelate
^{32}P	14.3 days	1.71	0	Orthophosphate
^{89}Sr	50.6 days	1.46	0	Chloride
^{186}Re	90.6 hours	1.07	137	HEDP
^{153}Sm	46.3 hours	0.84	103	EDTMP

Table 100–10. Clinical Efficacy and Toxicity of Radionuclides Reviewed

Radionuclide	Response Rate (%)	Response Duration (Months)	Toxicity
^{32}P	60–80	~5	++
^{89}Sr	60–90	~6	+
^{186}Re	75–80	1–2	+
^{153}Sm	75–90	2–3	+

Systemic Radionuclide Therapy

The first report on the use of systemic radionuclides for the treatment of bone metastases was published by Pecher in 1942. Tables 100–9 and 100–10 provide a summary of the physical characteristics and the clinical usefulness of the radionuclides discussed.

Clinical Experience with Strontium 89

The efficacy of strontium 89 has been demonstrated in multiple studies (Firusian et al, 1976; Correns et al, 1979; Silberstein and Williams, 1985; Robinson et al, 1987; Tennvall et al, 1988; Montebello and Hartson-Eaton, 1989; Williams and Dillehay, 1989; Laing et al, 1991). Most of these studies involved patients with hormone-refractory prostate cancer. The limited experience in patients with metastatic breast cancer, however, suggests similar efficacy. In one retrospective review, 89% of 28 patients reported moderate or good relief of pain (Robinson et al, 1992).

Toxicity of strontium 89 is mainly hematologic. Platelet depression is dose dependent. Most patients have a 20% to 50% drop in their counts after doses of 3 to 4 mCi (1.5 to 2 MBq/kg).

KEY POINT

- Spinal cord compression, brain metastasis, and pathologic fractures are conditions that require external-beam radiation therapy for palliation.

Gene Therapy for Prostate Cancer

Advances in RT technique have clearly resulted in improved biochemical control of clinically localized prostate cancer (Shipley et al, 1999). Although continued refinement of these techniques will result in further gains, other innovative approaches, such as gene therapy, may enhance or comple-

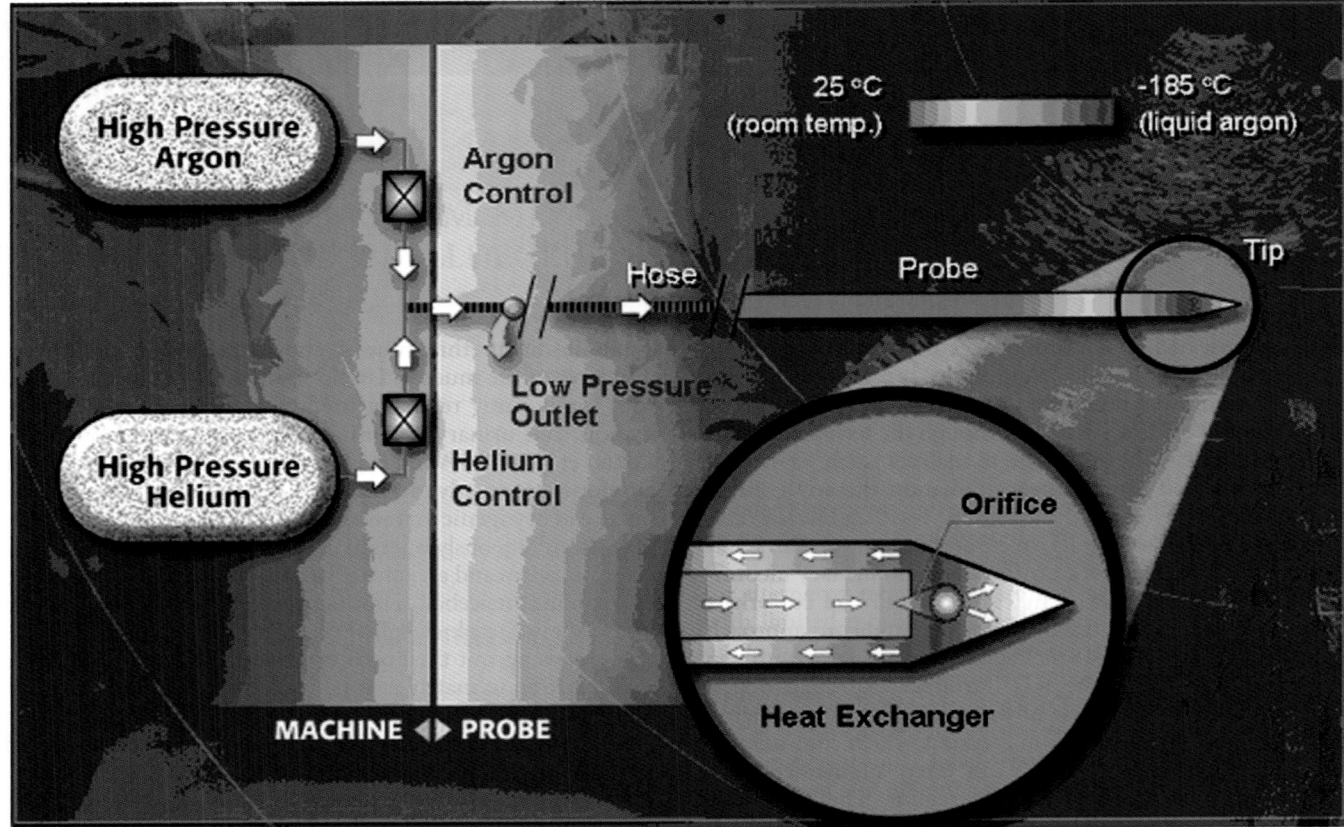

Figure 101–1. Joule-Thompson principle. High-pressure gases enter through the spiraled central port and expand at a narrow terminal port to effect cooling. In accordance with the gas coefficient and the dimension of the nozzle, different gaseous elements generate different thermal exchange events at the area close to the nozzle. Expanded gases return back through the larger, outer lumen and are vented outside the patient into the room. Argon gas is used for cooling (−185.7°C), and helium is used for heating (67°C).

in the second-generation systems, improving the control of iceball formation. It is noteworthy that both argon and helium are inert gases, and therefore safe. However, both will displace oxygen from a room and thus adequate air circulation should be maintained within the cryogenic suite. This transition from liquid to gas allowed for the development of ultra-thin 17-gauge (1.47-mm) cryoprobes, which permitted direct transperineal needle placement through a template without making incisions or using tract dilatation and insertion kits (Fig. 101–2). Another advantage is that gas systems are more compact and easier to use and maneuver within the operating room environment. The introduction of pinpoint thermocouples for systematic temperature monitoring has also substantially contributed to a reduction in cryotherapy-associated morbidity. They are used to ensure both that adequately cold temperatures are reached within the prostate and that sensitive adjacent structures, namely, the rectum and external sphincter, are maintained at temperatures warm enough to ensure maintenance of their structural and functional integrity. In addition, the risk of rectal freezing can be lessened by injection of saline solution into Denonvilliers' fascia, increasing the space between the prostate and the rectum.

CRYOBIOLOGY
Mechanisms of Cell Injury and Death
by Cryotherapy (Table 101–2)

The principles of cryotherapy, including the mechanisms of cell injury and cell death, have been well studied (Gonder et al, 1964; Gage and Baust, 1998). Unlike radiation (mitotic arrest) or androgen deprivation (apoptosis), the main mechanism of cytotoxicity that cryotherapy produces is the induction of targeted areas of coagulative necrosis in the prostate gland. **The key factors involved in freezing injury include direct mechanical shock, osmotic shock, and cellular hypoxia.** Mechanisms of action include protein denaturation via dehydration, transfer of water from the intracellular space to the extracellular space, rupture of cell membranes from ice crystal expansion, toxic concentration of cellular constituents, thermal shock from rapid supercooling, slow thawing, vascular stasis, and increased apoptosis (Cooper and Hirose, 1966).

The extracellular fluid begins to crystallize after reaching a tissue temperature below 0°C. The osmotic pressure of the unfrozen portion of the extracellular fluid compartment

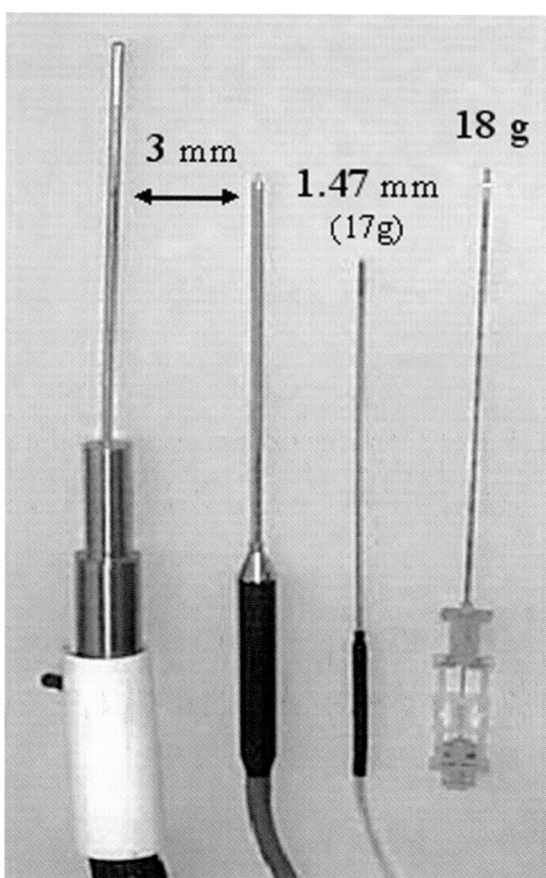

Figure 101-2. Evolution of cryoprobes. Development of third-generation cryotherapy included the transition from liquid nitrogen to gas-driven cryoprobes, which permitted the use of smaller-diameter cryoprobes that allow for direct transperineal probe placement through a brachytherapy-like template, without using tract dilatation and insertion kits.

Table 101-2. Cytotoxic and Antineoplastic Effects of Cryotherapy
Mechanical
Rapid formation of intracellular and extracellular ice crystals exerting mechanical shear forces on cell membranes and organelles
Biochemical
pH change
Osmolarity
Electrolyte concentration
Lipoprotein damage (thermal shock from rapid supercooling)
Ischemic
Microvascular damage: stasis of blood leading to thrombosis
Freeze major blood supply (neurovascular bundle)
Apoptotic
Activation of programmed cell death pathways (only in injury zone)
Immunologic
Freezing may release antigens that stimulate an antitumor immune response.

increases, causing dehydration of cells to occur due to the shift of water from the intracellular to the extracellular space, which also results in an accumulation of toxins within the cell. Changes in cellular pH lead to the denaturing of cellular proteins. At a temperature of −15°C, most of the extracellular environment is frozen, which causes trapping of tissue and shearing forces to disrupt cellular structure (mechanical shock). Further decreases in temperature lead to crystallization of water in the intracellular space that mechanically breaks the cellular membrane.

The delayed or indirect destructive effects of cryotherapy continue primarily because of vasculature disruption, resulting in tissue hypoxia and vascular thrombosis. Zacarian and associates (1970) reported that at temperatures below −20°C, venules were more susceptible to injury than arterioles. Freezing promotes stasis of blood, leading to thrombosis and subsequent coagulative necrosis of tissue. This process includes local edema with activation of the inflammatory cascade. Upon thawing, extracellular fluid shifts back into the intracellular space, leading to lysis of both the intracellular organelles and the cell membrane itself. The blood vessels around the targeted tissue initially dilate after thawing, and hyperpermeability of the vessel wall occurs. After a few hours

of this hyperemic state, microthrombi form on the damaged vessel wall, leading to regional tissue ischemia.

Apoptosis is recognized as a mechanism of cell death that occurs in both normal tissues and various pathologic conditions. Apoptotic cells are characterized by nonrandom DNA cleavage, blebbing of membranes, phospholipid inversion in the membranes, and caspase activation (Kerr et al, 1994). **Apoptotic cells after freezing are found primarily in the peripheral zone of the cryogenic lesion outside the killing zone, where the temperature was not sufficiently cold to kill all the cells** (Hollister et al, 1998). In addition, kinetic studies have shown that cells are susceptible to entering the apoptotic state up to 8 hours after rewarming (Yang et al, 2003). The recent finding of apoptosis in cells in the peripheral zone of the cryogenic injury may one day be exploited therapeutically using other proapoptotic stimuli to extend the zone of cell death.

In-vivo experiments have suggested that cryodestruction of living tissues can elicit an immunologic response by the host that may itself eradicate cancer cells (Ablin, 1972). Experiments with MRMT-1 mammary adenocarcinoma cells and R3327 prostate adenocarcinoma cells in rats have demonstrated the appearance of tumor immunity by 7 to 10 weeks after cryotherapy that was associated with a decrease in growth of metastatic lesions. However, cryotherapy of the Dunning AT-1 cell line, an androgen-insensitive cell line, in Copenhagen rats was associated with a minimal increase in T-cell counts without an effect on the local tumor growth rate (Hoffmann et al, 2001). **Although the potential for a cryoimmunologic effect against residual prostate cancer cells is exciting, cryotherapy must still be considered as a local therapy.**

Tissue Response to Freezing

The response to freezing injury varies from inflammatory to destructive, depending on the severity of freezing (Hoffmann and Bischof, 2002). Minor freezing injury features only inflammatory responses, whereas severe freezing injury destroys cells and tissues, which is the prime requirement for treating tumors. The cryogenic lesion is characterized by a

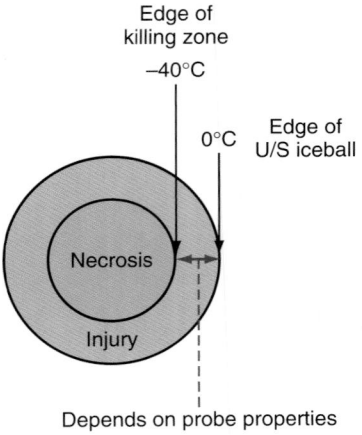

Edge of
killing zone
−40°C

0°C Edge of
U/S iceball

Necrosis

Injury

Depends on probe properties

A

B

Figure 101–3. **A,** The cryogenic lesion is characterized by a central uniform coagulation necrosis surrounded by a peripheral zone. Tissue temperatures range from 0°C to −40°C in the peripheral zone leading to partial cell death and apoptosis. **B,** Complete necrosis within central portion of scar with rim of sublethal injury was seen after cryotherapy. (Hematoxylin and eosin, reduced from ×80.)

Table 101–3. **Factors Affecting Tissue Destruction during Cryotherapy**
Velocity of cooling
Velocity of thawing
Lowest temperature achieved
Duration of freezing
Number of freeze-thaw cycles
Existence of heat sinks

destruction include the cooling rate during freezing, the warming rate during thawing, and the lowest temperature achieved in the tissue. Tatsutani and associates (1996) described these effects in an in-vivo prostate cancer cell experiment. Complete cell death was unlikely to occur at temperatures higher than −20°C, and temperatures lower than −40°C were required to completely destroy cells. A double freeze-thaw cycle significantly increased the extent of cell damage compared with a single freeze-thaw cycle. A faster freezing rate and a slower thawing rate resulted in optimal cellular destruction.

A tissue temperature of −40°C to −50°C, which is lethal for cells, should be produced within the tumor, including a safe distance around the tumor (Bischof et al, 1997; Gage and Baust, 1998; Hoffmann and Bischof, 2002). In addition to the temperature that should be achieved, the duration of freezing has been demonstrated to be an important factor leading to tissue destruction. Once the tissue temperature reaches a certain level, more cellular destruction can be achieved by prolonged freezing at this temperature. The tissue should be held in the frozen state for several minutes to allow time for solute effects, ice crystal formation, and recrystallization effects. When the tissue is held at −15°C to −40°C, biochemical changes and growth of ice crystals are enhanced, increasing the rate of cell death. However, the optimum duration of freezing is not well defined and may be cell/tissue-type specific. Slow thawing of the frozen tissue is a prime destructive factor. The rate of thawing should be as slow as practical. A longer duration of the thaw will cause greater damage to the cells due to solute effects, ice crystal restructuring (recrystallization), prolonged oxidative stress, and growth of ice crystals. The large ice crystals that form during "warming" recrystallization create shearing forces, which disrupt the tissues. Repetition of the freeze-thaw cycle is important. The first freeze-thaw cycle increases the thermal conductivity of the tissue caused by cellular breakdown; the second freeze-thaw subjects the tissue to extended physiochemical changes, while passing through damaging thermal conditions for the second time. With repetition, the second cycle increases the extent of necrosis up to 80% of the previously frozen volume. The second cycle also moves the lethal isotherm close to −20°C, permitting a closer approach to the margins of the prostate without endangering the rectum. The interval between freeze-thaw cycles is also an important factor in tissue injury. A longer thaw time supports complete vasoconstriction of larger blood vessels, continued ice crystal growth, and more extensive osmotic damage. A further delay after thawing, but prior to the second freeze cycle, leaves the tissue in a hypothermic state and allows time for the microcirculation to fail. In combination, these events provide the targeted tissue

central uniform coagulation necrosis surrounded by a peripheral zone, where the tissue temperature was 0°C to −40°C and in which only partial cell death has occurred, which develops several days after freezing (Fig. 101–3). The process of wound repair begins in the peripheral zone in the areas in contact with viable tissue; inflammatory cells infiltrate and new blood vessels may grow into the injured tissue. Over the following weeks or months, the dead tissue is slowly replaced by fibroblasts and new collagen formation. A contracted healed area is the end result.

Factors Affecting Tissue Destruction during Cryotherapy (Table 101–3)

The optimal technique of cryotherapy requires a thorough understanding of the freeze-thaw cycle and its components. **The variables that correlate with the likelihood of cell**

with conditions consistent with severe oxidative stress that may ultimately give rise to additive post-thaw cell death.

In a clinical setting, the number of freezing cycles, the lowest temperature achieved, and the existence of any regional "heat sinks" may be important factors relating to cancer destruction. **Double freeze-thaw cycles during cryotherapy for prostate cancer in humans have been associated with lower positive biopsy rates, as well as improved PSA results, when compared with a single freeze-thaw cycle, without an increase in the development of cryotherapy-related morbidities** (Shinohara et al, 1996; Pisters et al, 1997; Wong et al, 1997). Temperature mapping studies performed in patients with localized prostate cancer, who agreed to undergo focal cryotherapy of the prostate before undergoing radical prostatectomy, have begun to define the mechanics of freezing human prostate tissue more clearly. These studies demonstrated that cryotherapy resulted in a central zone of complete cellular necrosis surrounded by a more peripheral zone of cell damage and that **two consecutive 10-minute freeze cycles produced a larger area of coagulative necrosis than a single 20-minute freeze** (Larson et al, 2000). Furthermore, a **double freeze at temperatures below −40°C resulted in complete necrosis.** This fact has important clinical implications because the hyperechoic edge of the iceball visualized is 0°C to −2°C, and temperatures as low as −20°C to −40°C are inside this edge (see Fig. 101–3). Therefore, the iceball should be extended beyond the edge of the prostate to ensure adequate tissue ablation. Although the available literature supports the use of a minimum of two freeze-thaw cycles, whether there is any additional benefit to more than two cycles is not known. Temperature mapping studies in patients undergoing full-gland cryotherapy demonstrate that the effect of multiple cryoprobe placement produces a larger effective freezing zone due to the additive effect of overlapping cryoprobes. Finally, large blood vessels may act as heat sinks and highly vascular areas may not achieve target temperatures even though they are completely enclosed in the treatment area.

TECHNICAL IMPROVEMENTS IN CRYOTHERAPY EQUIPMENT
Transrectal Ultrasound Systems

One of the most significant advances has been real-time ultrasound-guided placement of the cryoprobes and continuous visualization of freezing. **Biplanar TRUS allows for transverse and longitudinal views of the prostate as well as the frozen area and the views are easily interchangeable during the procedure.** Frozen tissue is significantly different from unfrozen tissue in sound impedance, resulting in strong echo reflection at the interface of frozen and normal tissue. **The leading edge of frozen tissue is seen as a bright line** (Fig. 101–4). The tissue

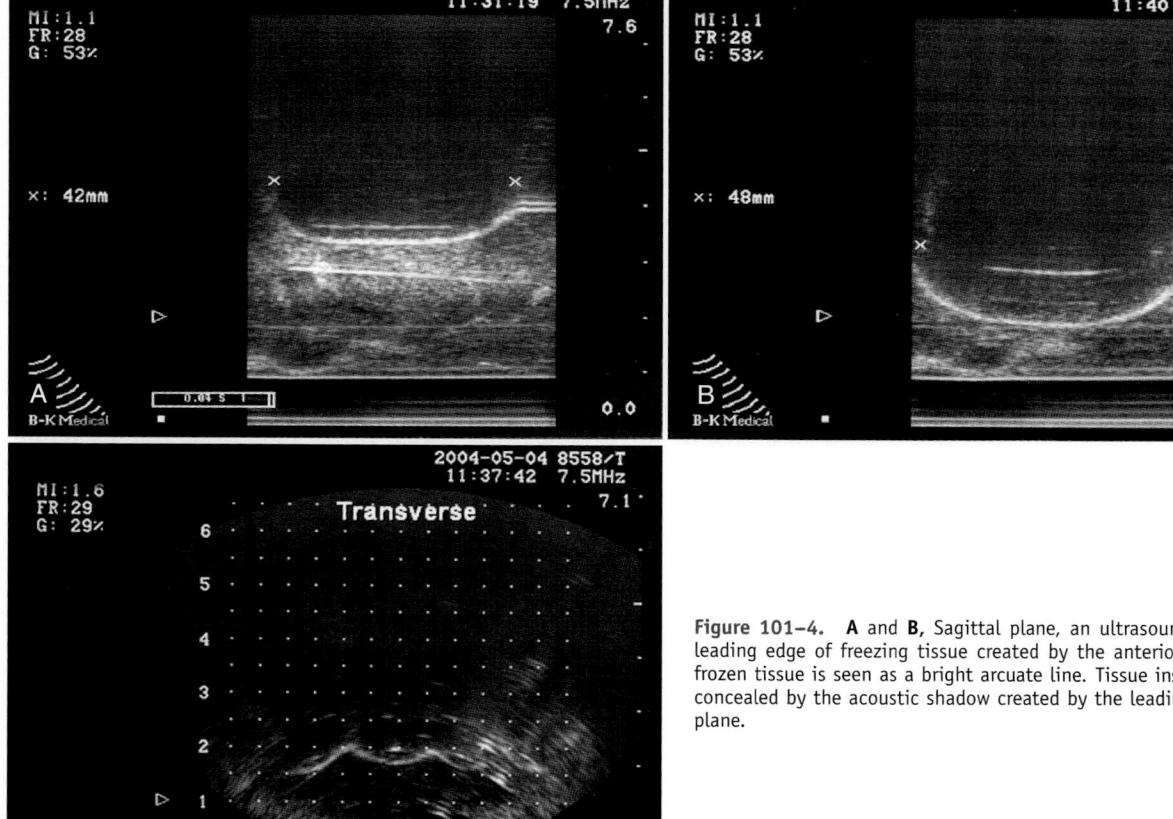

Figure 101–4. A and **B,** Sagittal plane, an ultrasound image showing the leading edge of freezing tissue created by the anterior probes. The edge of frozen tissue is seen as a bright arcuate line. Tissue inside the frozen area is concealed by the acoustic shadow created by the leading edge. **C,** Transverse plane.

inside is concealed in the acoustic shadow created by this boundary so that the anterior boundary of the freezing area cannot be monitored. The refraction and reflection of the sound wave can also overestimate the lateral boundary of the iceball. The use of color Doppler imaging may be helpful for monitoring tissue viability (vascularity) as freezing approaches the rectum. Although not an objective parameter, color Doppler imaging provides some indication about the vascular state between the ice and the rectal mucosa and thus provides some information about the likely speed of freezing in this area. Sonography provides no information about the temperature distribution within the ice nor does it show the extent of freezing at the lateral or anterior aspects of the prostate. Reports of three-dimensional ultrasound during cryosurgery show potential, especially for preoperative planning of a procedure and cryoprobe placement (Chin et al, 1998). In practice, these have been relatively slow and cumbersome to apply, making their clinical implementation difficult. Nonetheless, this technology is progressing rapidly.

Template and Stands

A brachytherapy-like stepper has a holding device adapting cradle to which the multifrequency biplanar TRUS probe is attached. A brachytherapy-like template drilled with a matrix of holes that will accommodate the cryoprobes is attached to the holding device (Fig. 101–5). Systems are available with a floor stand or table-mounted device. The brachytherapy-like grid can be adjusted to ensure accuracy with any ultrasound.

Cryogenic Systems (Third Generation)

Liquid nitrogen (−195.8°C) is the coldest practical cryogenic agent and has the greatest freezing capacity, but it cannot be used in probes of less than 3 mm in diameter. The transition from systems circulating liquid nitrogen to gas-driven probes permits the use of ultra-thin probes. In accordance with the gas coefficient and the dimension of the nozzle, different gaseous elements generate different thermal exchange events

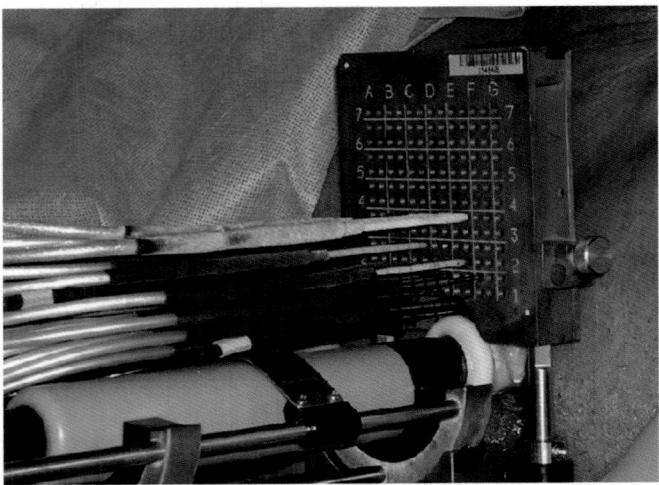

Figure 101–5. Brachytherapy-like template drilled with a matrix of holes to accommodate cryoprobes.

(Joule-Thompson principle) at the area close to the nozzle. **Argon gas is used for cooling, and helium gas is used for heating.** Two cryogenic systems for prostate cancer treatment are currently available in the United States. Third-generation cryotherapy using gas-driven delivery systems and 17-gauge cryoprobes inserted via a direct transperineal route into the prostate without using an insertion kit were first reported in 2000 (Zisman et al, 2000). The SeedNet system (Oncura, Plymouth Meeting, PA) uses pressurized argon gas as the source of freezing, and up to twenty-five 17-gauge (1.47-mm) cryoprobes (CryoNeedle) can be used to create a conformal freezing pattern. The iceball created with the CryoNeedle is approximately 18 mm in diameter and 27 mm in length. The Oncura system also has available the IceRod needles in which the iceball created is approximately 32 mm × 56 mm and allows for the treatment of larger prostates. The CRYOcare system (Endocare Inc., Irvine, CA) also uses pressurized argon gas as a cryogen and can freeze up to eight 2.4-mm vacuum-insulated cryoprobes simultaneously; the iceball created is approximately 33 mm in diameter and 54 mm in length. Future developments include cryoprobes with varying iceball dimensions.

Warming Probes

Warming probes can be used to protect tissues and organs from being inadvertently damaged during cryotherapy. Warming probes actively warm by using helium gas, which warms when it expands through the Joule-Thompson principle. Warming probes can also be used to protect the neurovascular bundles (NVBs) to preserve sexual function.

Thermocouples

Ultrasound alone has been reported to be unreliable to ensure adequate freezing (Steed et al, 1997). In addition, fairly reliable coagulative necrosis could be achieved when temperatures of −40°C to −50°C occurred in the target areas (Gage and Baust, 1998). As a result, some investigators place thermocouples at the margins of the targeted treatment zones to ensure that cytotoxic temperatures are achieved during freezing. Several studies reported improved PSA recurrence-free rates and post-cryotherapy biopsy results with thermocouple monitoring when compared with patients in whom this had not been used (Lee et al, 1997; Wong et al, 1997). Thermocouples are also used to ensure maintenance of nonablative temperatures within Denonvilliers' fascia, the external sphincter, or the neurovascular bundle targeted to be spared.

Urethral Warming Device

The primary objective of the use of the urethral warming device during prostate cryotherapy is to protect the urethra and the external urinary sphincter to minimize urethral sloughing and prevent urinary incontinence. The urethral warmer is a closed double-lumen catheter made of a polyethylene membrane through which saline heated to 43°C is continuously circulated by a water pump at a rate of 350 to 500 mL/min. The first urethral warming system was marketed as a nonsignificant risk device until approximately July 1994. Initial experiences with this system were notable for fairly low rates of urethral sloughing, ranging from 4% to 10% (Onik et al, 1993; Coogan and McKiel, 1995; Wieder et al, 1995). Because of concerns submitted to the U.S. Food and Drug Administration (FDA) surrounding the safety of this particular device, it was taken off the market in mid 1994 for approximately 18 months while it underwent regulatory review. During this time period, numerous investigators reported a sharp increase in post-cryotherapy transurethral resection of the prostate (TURP) and overall urethral sloughing rates due to the use of alternative urethral warmers or warming systems that did not have many of the features of the original one (Cohen et al, 1996; Lee et al, 1997). As expected, the safety of the original warmers was easily confirmed during this period and, since 1996, approved urethral warming devices have been widely available. The precise mechanisms by which adequate urethral warming ensures the most protective heat transfer during cryotherapy are still being evaluated. Studies directed toward improving catheter design and urethral warming efficacy are ongoing, with the hope that slough rates will decline even further as new devices are marketed.

Computerized Planning

Computer-guided systems now provide improved intraoperative treatment planning with a potential for increased tissue destruction. The thermal distribution is predictable around a cryoprobe and can be modeled using computer simulation (Rewcastle et al, 1998, 2001). Similar to the treatment planning strategies used for radiation therapy, it is possible to determine optimal placement of cryoprobes in the prostate to maximize ablation of the prostate while minimizing collateral damage (Sandison, 2002). Research and development are focusing on the incorporation of functional and multimodality imaging data, as well as on the development of accurate mathematical models for in-vivo tissue injury response to thermal history (including cryotherapy-induced ischemia) to optimize treatment planning.

PATIENT SELECTION
Primary Cryotherapy

As with other forms of local therapy for prostate cancer, outcomes after cryotherapy correlate with stage and grade. In general, **primary cryotherapy is suitable for patients with clinical stage T1c-T3 disease of any tumor grade who are not potent or not interested in maintaining their potency** and is regarded mainly as an alternative treatment to radiation therapy. However, extensive disease in a periurethral location is a contraindication to primary cryotherapy, because use of the urethral warming catheter will not allow eradication of disease in these patients. We believe that radical prostatectomy remains the gold standard of treatment for localized prostate cancer and the preferred treatment in younger patients. For clinical stage T3 disease, primary cryotherapy is more appropriate for small volume disease in which the tumor is likely to be encompassed in the freezing process. Because of the minimally invasive nature of cryotherapy, it may have specific advantages in select patients with certain comorbidities including those who are poor candidates for radical prostatectomy (e.g., men with Crohn's disease, ulcerative colitis,

cardiac disease, morbid obesity, and/or body habitus unfavorable for radical prostatectomy). Primary cryotherapy can also be offered to patients who have no evidence of metastatic disease with more than a 10-year life expectancy who, after reviewing available information on prevailing therapeutic options for new diagnoses of prostate cancer, are unsatisfied with or refuse to undergo radical prostatectomy or radiation therapy. In particular, many patients who are candidates for EBRT may wish to consider primary cryotherapy because treatment can be administered in 1 day as opposed to 7 to 9 weeks of treatment.

Patients with a high risk of metastatic disease should undergo imaging, radionuclide bone scan, or cross-sectional imaging of the abdomen and pelvis, based on stage and grade as well as serum PSA concentrations. Patients at high risk for lymph node metastases may undergo regional lymph node dissection if identification of disease would alter treatment choice. Patients with gross extracapsular extension or seminal vesicle invasion are treated with neoadjuvant hormone therapy to reduce the tumor volume and allow for easier inclusion within the iceball. **If the prostate size exceeds 50 cm^3, complete freezing of the prostate may be difficult and neoadjuvant hormone therapy is indicated to reduce the target volume and allow for more effective cryotherapy** (Bales et al, 1995; Miller et al, 1996; Shinohara et al, 1996; Baust et al, 1997; Cespedes et al, 1997; Pisters et al, 1997). The use of androgen deprivation for 3 months before the procedure has been reported to increase the distance between the base of the prostate and the anterior rectal wall (Ghafar et al, 2001).

Salvage Cryotherapy

Nearly one third of men with newly diagnosed prostate cancer are treated with EBRT and/or brachytherapy as primary therapy each year (Mettlin et al, 1998, 1999). Despite modifications in radiation delivery methods to the gland, such as intensity modulated radiation therapy (IMRT), three-dimensional conformal radiation therapy (3DCRT), and computer-guided seed implantation, urologists will see more failures from such therapies. Radioresistant or recurrent prostate cancer is an aggressive form of localized prostate cancer that represents a serious health risk for patients treated with primary radiation therapy for clinically localized prostate cancer. According to the recent literature, the rates of biochemical failures have ranged from 15% to 65% and local failure rates range from 25% to 32% (Touma et al, 2005). The majority of patients exhibit large volume and poorly differentiated disease at the time of diagnosis, which limits the ability of salvage therapy to eradicate the cancer. Early detection with serum PSA monitoring and prostate needle biopsy after primary radiation therapy may identify residual adenocarcinoma at an earlier stage and increase the likelihood of successful salvage therapy. The goal of salvage therapy is to improve local control and possibly affect long-term survival.

Radical prostatectomy, cryotherapy, brachytherapy, and radiation therapy are the options available for salvage treatment of radiorecurrent prostate cancer (Touma et al, 2005). Salvage prostatectomy is associated with significant morbidity, and salvage brachytherapy or radiation therapy has the potential for increased rectal and urinary toxicity to occur in a previously irradiated prostate. As a result, patients are often left with the option of either watchful waiting or temporary palliation with hormone deprivation therapy and its attendant toxicity. Recent modifications in the technique of salvage cryotherapy have led to the ability to eradicate radiorecurrent prostate cancer safely and with decreased morbidity. However, complications associated with salvage cryotherapy are higher than those associated with primary treatment (Bales et al, 1995; Pisters et al, 1997; Long et al, 1998; Perrotte et al, 1999; Han et al, 2003).

Only patients with a rising PSA value after radiation and who have a positive post-radiation biopsy are candidates for salvage cryotherapy. Our practice has been to wait at least 18 to 24 months after radiation therapy and to perform a biopsy of the prostate if the PSA value rises above the nadir level and there are three consecutive rises. Patients with a post-radiation PSA result greater than 10 ng/mL have been shown to be more likely to have unsuccessful salvage cryotherapy. **If a biopsy is undertaken, multiple cores should be obtained and the pathologist needs to be informed that the patient has had previous radiation.** Severe radiation effects with both nuclear and cytoplasmic alterations are seen in many prostatic biopsies and may confound the diagnosis of residual cancer (Cheng et al, 1999). The incidences of positive biopsy results after primary radiation therapy vary widely in the literature but seem to be higher after EBRT than after brachytherapy (Stone et al, 2000).

Once it has been determined that primary therapy has failed, local recurrences must be distinguished from systemic recurrences. Local failure has been defined as histologically proven active adenocarcinoma on repeat prostate biopsy in the absence of radiographic evidence of metastatic disease. Unfortunately, multiple studies have demonstrated the relative lack of sensitivity and specificity of most radiographic tests including computed tomography (CT), magnetic resonance imaging (MRI), bone scan, and, more recently, monoclonal antibody-labeled nuclear scans (ProstaScint, Cytogen Corp, Princeton, NJ) for the diagnosis of systemic disease in biochemically recurrent prostate cancer (Albertsen et al, 2000; Sodee et al, 2000). Despite these shortcomings, these modalities should be applied if recurrence is suspected, because the presence of overt metastatic disease may obviate the patient being exposed to unnecessary local therapies. In this setting, pathologic confirmation via prostate biopsy of locally recurrent disease is warranted before consideration of invasive salvage therapies. **There may be a role in performing an open or laparoscopic biopsy of the pelvic lymph nodes since between 20% and 40% of patients will have lymph node metastases** (Rogers et al, 1995). Caution is advised for novice laparoscopic surgeons, since the dissection of these nodes can be technically challenging owing to potential adherence to the pelvic side wall and external iliac vessels.

Contraindications

Relative contraindications to cryotherapy are similar to those for brachytherapy and include prior TURP with a large tissue defect, significant symptoms of urinary obstruction before treatment, large prostate size, and a history of abdominoperineal resection for rectal cancer, rectal stenosis, or other major rectal pathology. Prior TURP is associated with an increased

risk for sloughing and urinary retention. **Absolute contraindications include fistulas for any reason (including but not limited to inflammatory bowel disease) and previous surgery or trauma to the pelvis (e.g., urethroplasty, open book fracture) that may distort the anatomy of the prostate.** Significant preoperative obstructive symptoms increase the likelihood of postoperative urinary retention. Cryotherapy is not as sensitive to pubic arch interference as brachytherapy, since the iceball migrates away from the cryoprobe. In rare cases, pubic arch interference may preclude adequate placement of cryoneedles. In these cases, the prostate may be cytoreduced with neoadjuvant hormonal ablation.

Combination Treatment

Patients with locally progressive disease despite hormonal manipulation may be treated with cryotherapy to prevent urinary obstruction or bleeding (Cohen et al, 1996; Shinohara et al, 1996). Cryotherapy could also be used in combination with radiation therapy to more effectively manage the primary or dominant cancer lesion. Whether such combination therapy will improve cancer-specific outcomes compared with radiation alone or neoadjuvant androgen deprivation in combination with radiation awaits further study. A study evaluating the feasibility and complications of cryotherapy followed by radical prostatectomy in patients with clinical stage T3 disease demonstrated complete tumor destruction in four of seven patients (Fig. 101–6) (Pisters et al, 1999). However, all seven patients who underwent radical prostatectomy had significant urinary incontinence requiring the use of pads. Cryotherapy has also been used to treat select patients with ultrasonically visible bulky local recurrences after radical prostatectomy.

SURGICAL TECHNIQUE
Patient Preparation

Patients undergo a light bowel preparation consisting of oral magnesium citrate the day before and a Fleet enema the

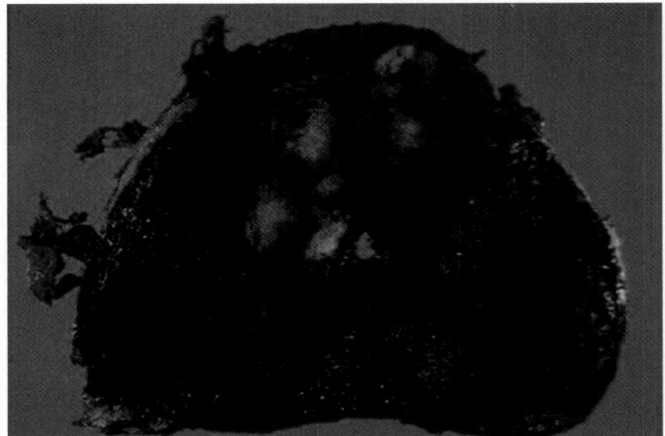

Figure 101–6. Cross section of prostatectomy specimen after two freeze-thaw cycles during cryotherapy of the prostate without the use of a urethral warming catheter. There was no histologic evidence of residual viable prostate cancer (pT0).

morning of the procedure. After induction of regional or general anesthesia, the patient is placed in a dorsal lithotomy position, which can be exaggerated to improve transperitoneal access to the prostate. Sequential compression devices are used preoperatively and during the procedure. A Foley catheter is inserted and clamped to allow the bladder to distend.

Transrectal Ultrasound Evaluation

A multifrequency biplanar TRUS probe is inserted in the rectum and attached into the holding device adapting cradle of a stepper. The prostate is imaged and its dimensions measured. The aiming grid software is activated and projected on the TRUS image. The attached probe is lowered posteriorly until a slight resistance from the posterior rectal wall is felt or the image of the shiny anterior fibromuscular stroma is lost at 5 MHz. This maneuver opens up the distance between the prostate gland and the rectum. This assists in preventing rectal wall ischemia during freezing and therefore increases the safety of the procedure. Once the adjustments are completed, the holding device is fixed in place. A brachytherapy-like template drilled with a matrix of holes to accommodate the cryoprobes is attached to the holding device (see Fig. 101–5) and gently fixed against the perineum and stabilized with a stepper. The holes in the template are 5 mm apart and correspond to the aiming grid projected on the ultrasound image.

Computerized treatment planning systems have been devised that incorporate serial transverse TRUS images of the prostate to render an individualized plan for cryoprobe positioning. Image recognition software is used with the aid of anatomic reference points defined by the user to determine the geometric anatomy of the prostate, urethra, and rectum to specify optimal cryoprobe placement.

Cryoprobe Placement

Cryoprobe placement is dependent on the characteristics of the specific cryoprobe being used. Knowledge of the isotherm profile (temperature range within the iceball) and iceball geometry for a particular cryoprobe is critical to achieve adequate overlap and confluence between adjacent iceballs (Fig. 101–7). Both cryotherapy systems currently on the market allow for direct transperineal placement of cryoprobes using a brachytherapy-like template without the use of insertion or dilation kits. Cryoprobes are inserted under TRUS guidance and positioned in layers so that prostate is adequately covered (Fig. 101–8). Since the iceball progresses longitudinally past the needle tip, the cryoprobes are advanced into the prostate base and positioned just caudal to the bladder neck, depending on the iceball geometry of the cryoprobe. The distance that the most posterior layer is located anterior to the prostate capsule also depends on the iceball geometry of the particular cryoprobe used. Given the propensity of prostate cancer to expand through the capsule in locations pierced by the branches of the NVB, lateral needles are placed to permit extraprostatic freezing and facilitate killing by early shut down of the arterial supply to the gland. The prostatic urethra is identified by TRUS in both the longitudinal and the transverse views, and the distance the cryoprobes are placed away from the urethra is dependent on the geometry of the iceball. The

full technique using the different cryogenic systems has previously been reported (Zisman et al, 2001; Ellis, 2002).

Thermocouple and Urethral Warmer Placement

Depending on the preference and experience of the surgeon, thermocouples may be placed in the mid gland, at the level of the external sphincter, at each NVB, and at Denonvilliers' fascia. Thermocouples placed at the level of the external sphincter and in Denonvilliers' fascia are used to minimize the risk of incontinence or rectourethral fistula, whereas those in the mid gland and NVB ensure that the required temperature of −40°C is reached (Fig. 101–9). It is recommended that the temperature in the sphincter be maintained above 15°C. Some operators place a thermocouple in the distal apex to ensure adequate freezing at the apex and to help determine the need for a pull-back adjustment of the cryoprobes to ensure adequate coverage of the prostate.

After all the probes have been positioned, the Foley catheter is gently removed. Any difficulty may indicate that a probe is wrongly positioned and potentially piercing the urethra. A meticulous 360-degree examination of the urethra is performed using a flexible cystoscope. If a misplaced probe is visualized in the urethra or a wall hematoma is detected, probe repositioning is indicated to avoid the detrimental outcome of direct urethral freezing or freezing the circulating urethral warmer fluid into a standstill position. Once the urethra and the bladder are found to be normal, a soft 10- to 12-Fr suprapubic catheter may be inserted under vision, closed, and secured to the skin. Some surgeons prefer to conclude the procedure with a 16-Fr Foley catheter left indwelling for 24 to 72 hours. A 0.038-inch super-stiff guide wire is inserted through the working channel of the cystoscope, which is then withdrawn, and a heavily lubricated urethral warming catheter is introduced into the bladder over the guide wire. During the procedure, the bladder is kept nearly full to prevent injury from the rigid tip of the warmer device.

Monitoring of Freezing Process

To maintain TRUS visibility, the freezing is started at the anterior probe layer and continued posteriorly. Uncovered areas may be visualized and a correcting maneuver may be used. Two freezing cycles are performed. Between the cycles, the prostate may be allowed to thaw passively (~15 to 20 minutes) or actively (~7 to 8 minutes) using helium. If the apex-to-base measurement of the prostate is greater than the length of the iceball that the cryoprobe produces, pull-back of the cryoprobes is performed to cover the apex that has not been treated and two freeze-thaw cycles are repeated. To ensure adequate cancer treatment, the iceball is often allowed to extend 2 to 4 mm laterally into the periprostatic tissues, beyond the apex, and into the muscularis propria of the rectum posteriorly. In areas of extracapsular cancer extension, greater propagation of the iceball is permitted laterally and, if necessary, an additional cryoprobe may be placed in such areas. When seminal vesicle invasion is present, a cryoprobe may be placed deep into the invaded seminal vesicle. After completion of the last freeze cycle, the urethral warmer

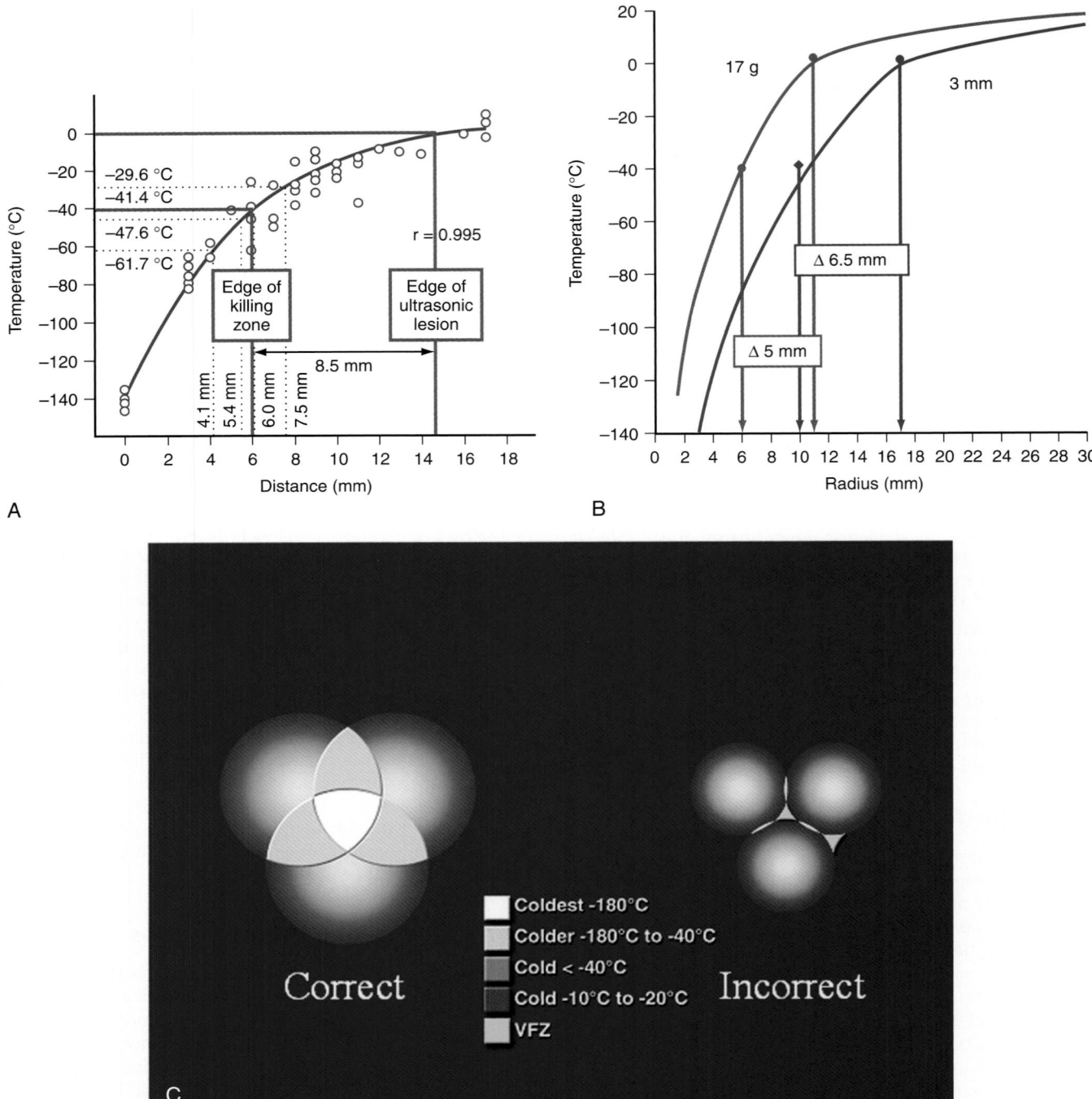

Figure 101–7.   Isotherm curves for cryoprobes. **A,** Temperature and distance from the cryoprobe at the edge of the kill zone and the edge of the ultrasound. **B,** Comparison of isotherm curves for 17-gauge and 3-mm cryoprobes illustrating differences between the edge of the kill zone and the ultrasonic lesion. **C,** Multiple cryoprobe placement produces a larger effective freezing zone due to the additive effect of overlapping cryoprobes. Cryoprobes placed too far apart will result in areas not covered by the freezing zone.

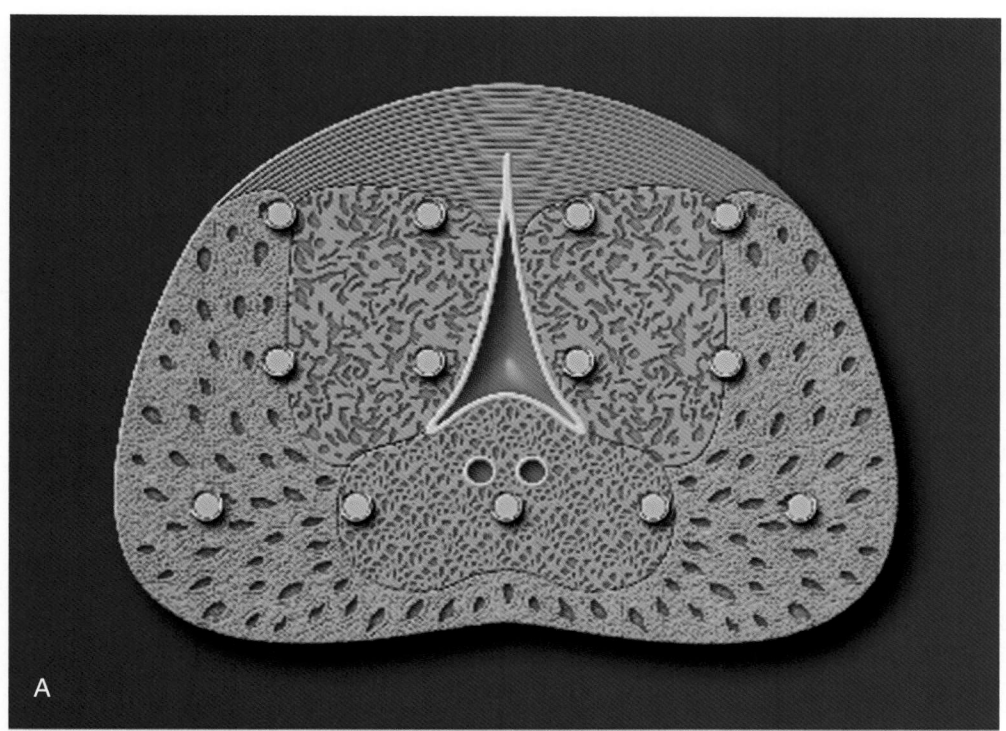

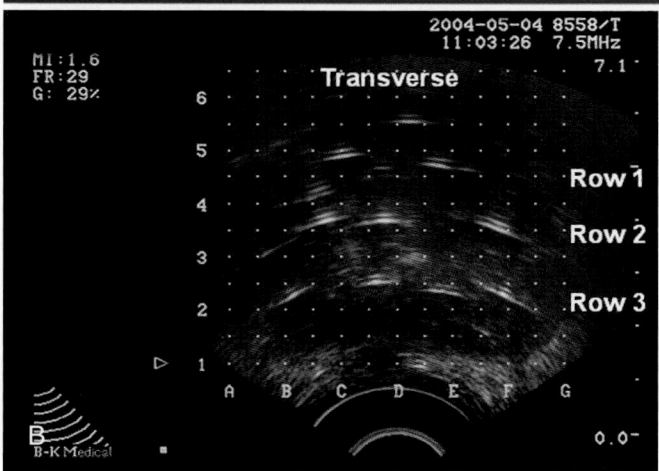

Figure 101–8. **A,** Tranverse template for placement of 17-gauge cryoprobes. **B,** Transverse ultrasound image showing placed cryoprobes in prostate.

Figure 101–9. Sagittal view of placed cryoprobes *(gray)* and thermocouples *(green)* in prostate. Cryoprobes are placed in layers with the tip at the base of the prostate. Thermocouples are placed at the level of the external sphincter and in Denonvilliers' fascia.

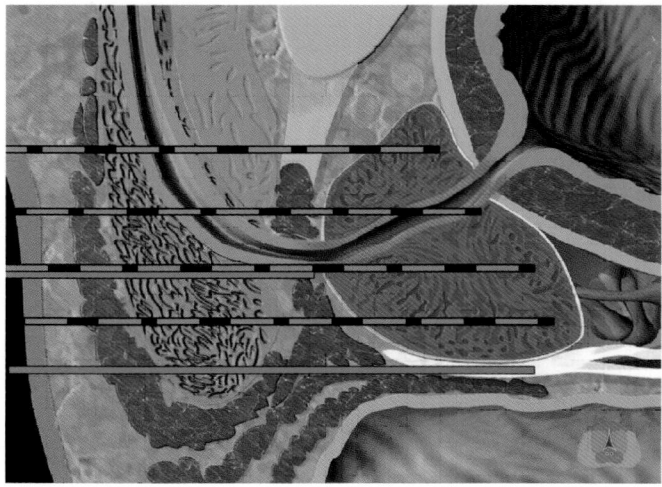

is left in place for up to 10 minutes to minimize the risk of urethral sloughing and subsequent urinary retention and irritative voiding symptoms. At this point, a full TRUS image of the prostate is regained and no iceball is seen. Cryoprobes are removed and pressure is applied to the perineum for 2 to 5 minutes. The urethral warmer is gently removed, and a Foley catheter is inserted afterward or, alternatively, the suprapubic catheter is opened if one was inserted before the procedure.

In patients undergoing salvage cryotherapy, previously placed radioactive seeds may cause some confusion, because their sonographic appearance is similar to that of the tip of the cryoprobes. This can be overcome by utilizing the sagittal view to assist in placing the cryoprobes. In this view, the length of the cryoprobes can be easily followed. Some degree of fibrosis may be encountered during placement in patients undergoing salvage cryotherapy. The gland may be adherent to the anterior rectal wall due to the previous radiation, diminishing the thickness of the Denonvilliers' fascia. If the space between the anterior rectal wall and posterior prostatic capsule is less than 5 mm, it may not be possible to drive the temperature down to −40°C safely, and freezing should be terminated when the leading edge of the iceball has extended just beyond the capsule, even if the target temperature of −40°C is not reached. Injection of saline into the area of Denonvilliers' fascia may help increase the distance between the prostate and anterior rectal wall provided the tissue is not too fibrotic to separate. Urologists learning to perform cryotherapy should be aware of these considerations, as well as maintain a high awareness of the potential increased risk of incontinence in previously irradiated patients.

Nerve-Sparing and Focal Cryotherapy

Prostate cancer poses a particular challenge to focal ablation techniques such as cryotherapy in that it is difficult to reliably define the location or extent of local tumor burden in the prostate. It has been shown that prostate cancers are usually multifocal, typically consisting of two to five tumors per gland (Miller and Cygan, 1994). However, stage migration resulting from widespread PSA screening has led some investigators to question the clinical significance of ancillary multifocal tumors and to ask whether it is possible to predict unifocal cancer, unilateral cancer, or clinically insignificant multifocal prostate cancer preoperatively. Unfortunately, there is still no radiographic modality that can reliably determine the exact location and tumor volume of prostate cancer foci. Thus, **until clinical significant foci of prostate carcinoma can be accurately identified preoperatively, cryotherapy for the treatment of patients with prostate cancer should be directed toward treating the entire prostate gland as the ideal means of eradicating the disease.** We believe that focal cryotherapy should be considered only in the context of an Institutional Review Board-approved research protocol.

The feasibility of nerve-sparing cryotherapy by active warming of the NVB has been evaluated in a canine model (Janzen et al, 2005). Cryotherapy was performed using 17-gauge gas-driven cryoprobes on nine prostate lobes from five dogs. Seven lobes were treated with active warming of the NVB, and two lobes were treated without active warming. All seven prostate lobes treated with active warming demonstrated complete or partial NVB preservation, but four

prostate lobes demonstrated adjacent gland preservation (Fig. 101–10). All prostate lobes treated with a double freeze-thaw cycle demonstrated complete and uniform ablation of prostate tissue, whereas one of three prostate lobes treated with a single freeze-thaw cycle demonstrated incomplete ablation of the prostate tissue. Future studies include the feasibility of injecting antifreeze proteins (Jia and Davies, 2002) or saline to protect or separate the NVB.

Onik and associates (2002) reported on a controversial pilot study of nine patients treated with focal, unilateral nerve-sparing cryotherapy. The focal prostate cryotherapy procedure described was an attempt to exploit the advantages of cryotherapy, particularly with respect to excellent treatment of potential extracapsular extension while minimizing the sexual function morbidity after whole-gland cryotherapy. Focal cryotherapy involves minimal vascular disruption if an NVB is spared and lack of nerve manipulation and associated nerve trauma when a nerve is spared by cryotherapy. At a mean follow-up of 36 months, all nine had stable PSA levels and six patients who subsequently underwent biopsy had negative results. No patients had significant incontinence after the procedure, and potency, defined as erection sufficient to complete intercourse to the satisfaction of the patient, was maintained in seven (77%) of nine patients. Whereas these results are provocative and intriguing, we currently do not recommend nerve-sparing cryotherapy as a mainstream therapy given the current inability to determine the aggressiveness, extent, and

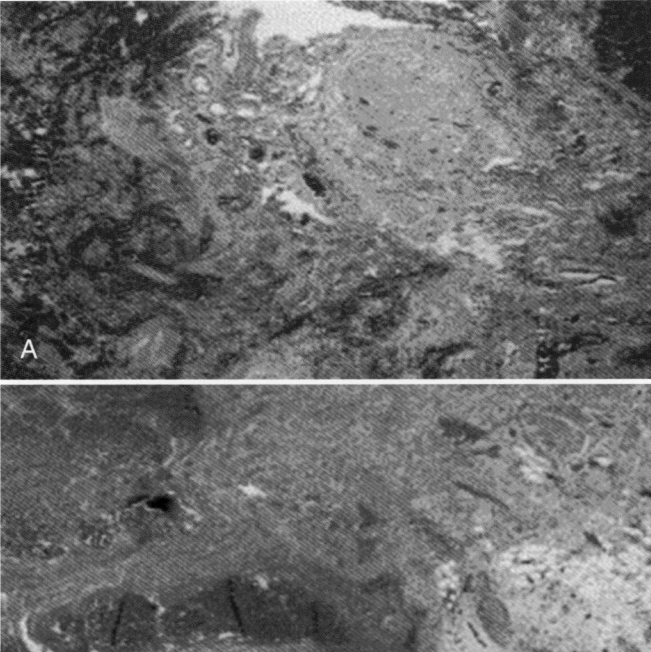

Figure 101–10. Preservation of the neurovascular bundle by active warming. **A,** Preserved nerve adjacent to hemorrhagic necrosis of the prostate. **B,** Presence of viable prostate glands immediately adjacent to a preserved neurovascular bundle.

able to avoid injury to the rectum, ureters, or other surrounding structures. The most significant postoperative complications were temporary incontinence and impotence. Future studies are needed to define cancer control and complications of these various treatment modalities for PSA failure after cryotherapy.

ADJUNCTIVE THERAPY

At the moment, **no therapy has proven beneficial in an adjuvant setting with cryotherapy.** However, several therapies warrant further investigation for possible adjuvant use. Although radiation therapy has been used after cryotherapy has failed, the timing of delivery of radiation is unclear for its use as an adjunctive agent. In-vitro experiments have shown that cooled cells have a greater sensitivity to irradiation (Znati et al, 1998). Nevertheless, this has not yet been investigated in a clinical setting. The most common adjuvant therapy is the use of cytotoxic drugs. Trials of docetaxel in a neoadjuvant setting have shown promise of benefit in prostate cancer (Dreicer et al, 2004). Many cryotherapy treatments for various cancers use adjuvant chemotherapy, but the optimum time and dose for delivery of chemotherapeutic drugs remain uncertain. Drugs that are given during the period of tissue thawing remain concentrated in the frozen tissue for a longer time. Therefore, the appropriate cytotoxic drug should be delivered systemically during the period of thawing and before the microcirculation fails, in about 1 hour. An alternative technique is instillation of the drug locally into the previously frozen tissue, possibly attached to an agent for slow release. As adjunctive therapeutic agents, the role of immunologic enhancers should be considered. Many investigations have been directed at the nature of the immunologic response. Although an immunologic benefit was reported from cryotherapy of animal tumors, clear evidence of benefit in

human tumors is lacking. Drugs have been used to stimulate the immune response and have been considered experimentally and clinically helpful.

COMPLICATIONS (Table 101–6)
Erectile Dysfunction

Erectile dysfunction after cryotherapy of the prostate is common. Although some series have reported rates ranging from 40% to 47% (Bahn et al, 1995), **more contemporary series report rates of more than 80%** (Long et al, 2001; Bahn et al, 2002; Han et al, 2003). This is likely due to the use of multiple freeze-thaw cycles and the extension of the iceball beyond the prostate, into the area of the NVBs. Donnelly and coworkers (2002) have reported that 47% of their patients had return of function at 3-year follow-up. Despite this report, we do not routinely perform cryotherapy in patients interested in maintaining their potency. We currently believe that complete eradication of the NVB is necessary to ensure complete eradication of tissue at the periphery of the prostate gland. Future prospective studies evaluating the role of focal cryotherapy after saturation biopsies may allow for the NVBs to be spared without compromising oncologic efficacy.

Urinary Incontinence

The incidence of incontinence varies among series, probably owing to varying definitions of incontinence, and an effective urethral warming catheter was not available in all patients in some series. Causes of urinary incontinence include sphincter muscle destruction/scarring leading to intrinsic sphincter deficiency, disruption of the pudendal nerve, urethral sloughing, and detrusor factors, such as detrusor instability or overflow incontinence. Han and associates (2003) reported an

Table 101–6. Complication Rates of Localized Prostate Cancer Treatments

| Series, Year | Treatment Period | No. Patients | Erectile Dysfunction | Complication Rates (%) | | | |
				Fistula/Major GI	Incontinence	Sloughing/TURP
Cryotherapy						
Han et al, 2003	2000-2002	122	87	0	4.3	5.8
Ellis, 2002	2000-2001	75	82.4	0	5.5	6.7
Long et al, 2001	1993-1998	975	93	0.5	7.5	13
Bahn et al, 2002	1993-2001	590	94.9	<0.1	4.3	5.5
EBRT						
Lawton et al, 1991; Long et al, 2001; Pollack et al, 1996; Sandler et al, 1995; Schultheiss et al, 1997; Zelefsky et al, 1995, 1997	NA	NA	37-70	1-9	0-13	0-3
Brachytherapy						
Critz et al, 1995; Gelblum and Potters, 2000; Gelblum et al, 1999; Kaye et al, 1995; Long et al, 2001; Merrick et al, 2002; Miller and Cygan, 1994; Potters et al, 2001; Stock et al, 2001; Wallner et al, 1996; Zeitlin et al, 1998	NA	NA	14-66	0-7	0-5	0-4

GI, gastrointestinal; TURP, transurethral resection of the prostate.

incontinence rate of 3%, whereas Cox and Crawford (1995) reported a rate of 27%. Prior TURP increases the risk of urinary incontinence in patients undergoing cryotherapy. Shinohara and colleagues (1996) reported that 12 (48%) of 25 patients who underwent TURP after cryotherapy developed urinary incontinence. The major risk of salvage cryotherapy remains incontinence, but this risk is significantly lower than with salvage radical prostatectomy. Reported post-salvage cryotherapy urinary incontinence rates range from 0% to 83% (Miller et al, 1996; Cespedes et al, 1997; Pisters et al, 1997; Long et al, 2001; Han et al, 2003). However, the use of an external sphincter thermocouple has decreased urinary incontinence rates to less than 5% in recently reported salvage cryosurgery series (Chin et al, 2001; Ghafar et al, 2001; Han and Belldegrun, 2004).

Complications Specific to Cryotherapy

Urethral Sloughing and/or Urethral Stricture

Tissue **sloughing has been reported to occur in 3.8% to 23% of cases** (Coogan and McKiel, 1995; Wieder et al, 1995; Cohen et al, 1996; Shinohara et al, 1996; Long et al, 1998; Han et al, 2003). With the current refinement of the freezing technique, however, symptomatic sloughing is a minor and infrequent event occurring in less than 3% of patients. Treatment consists of antibiotics and adequate drainage of urine. Self-intermittent catheterization may lead to spontaneous tissue dislodgment. However, transurethral resection or removal of the necrotic tissue may be required if the condition persists. Urethral stricture rarely forms after cryotherapy if an effective urethral warming device is used. However, if extensive tissue sloughing occurs, stricture at the bladder neck or the middle of the prostatic urethra can occur. Transurethral incision or balloon dilation is usually successful. Calcification of the stricture may also occur, necessitating transurethral resection. The use of an effective urethral warming catheter is essential to minimize the risk of tissue sloughing.

Pelvic and/or Rectal Pain

Pelvic or rectal pain after the procedure is an event that occurs in 0.4% to 11% of patients (Coogan and McKiel, 1995; Cohen et al, 1996; Shinohara et al, 1996; Long et al, 1998; Han et al, 2003). This complaint has been reported to be more common in older series and especially in previously irradiated patients (Pisters et al, 1997; De La Taille et al, 2000). Periosteum and bone may be frozen by anterior probes placed close to the symphysis pubis, which may lead to osteitis pubis. Seigne and colleagues (1996) reported that 4 (2.7%) of 147 patients undergoing postradiation salvage cryotherapy developed symptomatic osteitis pubis. Although patients undergoing salvage cryotherapy may have been at higher risk for osteitis pubis because of prior radiation therapy, this complication could potentially occur in those undergoing primary cryotherapy. Generally, such patients are best managed with anti-inflammatory agents, once a urinoma or abscess has been excluded by imaging. Han and colleagues (2003) reported that 3% of patients treated with cryotherapy developed transient penile numbness. **Penile numbness is caused by damage to the dorsal nerve of the penis due to close proximity of the cryoprobe.** This complication generally resolves spontaneously.

Rectourethral Fistula

Rectourethral fistula formation has been reported to occur in 0% to 3% of patients who undergo cryotherapy of the prostate (Cox and Crawford, 1995; Izawa et al, 2000; Ghafar et al, 2001; Long et al, 2001; Han et al, 2003). This complication is most commonly seen in those previously treated with radiation. However, owing to the high accuracy of modern-day TRUS combined with temperature monitoring at the anterior rectal wall, the complication is near 0% in contemporary series. **This complication may occur either early after the procedure or several months later. Watery diarrhea, pneumaturia, or fecaluria should alert the clinician to the possibility of fistula formation.** A voiding urethrogram or CT scan will confirm the diagnosis and location of the fistula. Conservative treatment with Foley catheter drainage is sometimes successful and should be tried initially in patients who underwent primary cryotherapy. Conservative measures are unlikely to be successful in patients who underwent postradiation salvage cryotherapy. Early fecal and urinary diversion is an important component of fistula management in these patients. If the fistula tract matures and epithelializes, fulguration may facilitate spontaneous closure. Formal fistula repair should be delayed until the inflammatory process has resolved completely, usually in 4 to 6 months. **A transperineal, posterior, or anterior approach for closure is recommended** (Nyam and Pemberton, 1999; Izawa et al, 2000).

Other Complications

Hydronephrosis is not a common complication. However, extensive freezing of the bladder neck area or placing of a cryoprobe deep into the seminal vesicle may result in freezing of the ureteral orifices or distal ureters (Bales et al, 1995). Small bowel obstruction after cryotherapy of the prostate has been reported (Koppie et al, 1999). This complication may occur if the iceball is allowed to extend into the cul-de-sac of the peritoneal cavity. Distention of the bladder with normal saline during the procedure and placing patients in a Trendelenburg position if the cul-de-sac is anatomically low generally prevents this complication by moving the peritoneal contents away from the freezing process.

QUALITY OF LIFE AFTER CRYOTHERAPY

The importance of assessing quality of life (QoL) in evaluating treatment outcome for prostate cancer is now well established. Robinson and colleagues (1999) assessed 69 patients having cryotherapy for localized prostate cancer. Patients were asked to complete the Functional Assessment of Cancer Treatment-Prostate (FACT-P) and the Sexuality Follow-up Questionnaire (SFQ) before treatment and again at 6 weeks and 3, 6, and 12 months afterward. Total FACT-P scores demonstrated a significant decline from baseline at 6 weeks, with a steady increase over the year of follow-up to scores not significantly different from baseline scores. However, the sexual function scores were significantly below baseline at 1 year. Only 1 of the 46 sexually active participants who were potent before treatment had recovered the ability to have erections sufficient for intercourse at 12 months. Subsequently, the same authors reported 3-year follow-up QoL data from this same group of patients (Robinson et al, 2002). QoL remained stable over the following 2 years; at 3 years, 13% of patients had regained erectile function and an additional 34% of patients were sexually active with the help of aids. All other areas of functioning remained high, and no delayed-onset morbidity was associated with cryotherapy.

With more global measures of QoL, these results compare favorably with those from Litwin and associates (1995), who measured the 5-year QoL outcomes of radical prostatectomy, radiation therapy, and observation, and with those of Krupski and coworkers (2000), who performed a 9-month QoL follow-up study in brachytherapy patients. All authors used the FACT-P questionnaire to measure QoL. **Although there were differences between the studies, QoL scores at 1 year after treatment were equally as high after cryotherapy as after surgery, radiation therapy, or observation, despite the higher incidence of erectile dysfunction in cryotherapy patients.** Compared with patients who underwent cryotherapy, brachytherapy patients manifested significantly worse scores on the "Social/Family Well-Being" scale; cryotherapy patients had higher scores on the "Functional Well-Being" scale than patients who underwent radical surgery and radiation therapy; and cryotherapy patients produced higher scores on the "Relationship with Doctor" scale than patients receiving all other treatments (scores on this scale were unavailable for brachytherapy patients). Thus, QoL among cryotherapy patients was comparable with that of patients receiving surgery, radiation therapy, brachytherapy, or observation and was superior along some QoL outcome dimensions.

Perrotte and coworkers (1999) evaluated QoL after salvage cryotherapy using a modified UCLA Prostate Cancer Index that measures health-related QoL. Treatment without an effective urethral warming catheter was highly associated with urinary incontinence ($P < .003$), perineal pain ($P < .001$), tissue sloughing ($P < .003$), and AUA symptom score greater than 20 ($P < .004$). Erectile dysfunction was higher in the double freeze-thaw cycle group ($P < .05$). However, this study was performed on patients who had undergone cryotherapy with older-generation technology. Anastasiadis and colleagues (2003) compared QoL between 81 patients who underwent primary or salvage cryotherapy. Primary cryotherapy patients fared significantly better regarding physical ($P = .005$) and social ($P = .024$) functioning than did salvage cryotherapy patients. **The most prominent prostate-related symptom in both patient groups was sexual dysfunction, followed by urinary symptoms, which were significantly more severe in the salvage group** ($P = .001$). Incontinence rates were 5.9% and 10% in the primary and salvage groups, respectively. Severe erectile dysfunction was reported in 86% and 90% of the primary and salvage groups, respectively.

COSTS OF CRYOTHERAPY

Costs become a critical factor in healthcare. In the literature, two studies have evaluated the cost of cryotherapy for prostate cancer (Miller et al, 1996; Schmidt et al, 1998). Schmidt and associates (1998) estimated that the typical charge for cryotherapy of the prostate is approximately $13,000, including all professional fees and hospital and technical components. This amount represented half of the usual cost for either radical prostatectomy or radiation therapy at that institution. Benoit and colleagues (1998) reviewed the costs of 114

cryotherapy cases performed in the same period time as 67 radical prostatectomies. Average hospital costs were $4,150 for radical prostatectomy and an additional 34% of cryotherapy and $5,660 for radical prostatectomy (difference ~27%, $P < .0001$). These costs did not include the physician fees. The shorter hospital stay of patients can explain the difference between cryoablation and radical prostatectomy (1.1 days vs. 3.4 days for radical prostatectomy).

FUTURE DIRECTIONS

As with all forms of treatment for clinically localized prostate cancer, cryotherapy is being refined. Clinical experience continues to grow, as does our understanding of cryobiology. Patient selection has been better defined, and complication rates have declined. The development of new imaging systems, such as interventional MRI (Gilbert et al, 1997) and three-dimensional ultrasound units (Chin et al, 1998), may allow more effective freezing. The use of biologic modifiers, such as antifreeze proteins, at the time of the procedure is being investigated and may improve the efficiency of the freezing process (Pham et al, 1999).

A modified technique of active rectal wall protection has been reported to permit deeper freezing of the peripheral zone of the prostate and for longer duration, rendering the procedure safer and more effective (Cytron et al, 2003). Two warming probes are placed in between the prostate and rectal wall to serve as active warming using the thawing mode when temperatures drop to approximately 0°C and as rectal lumen temperatures drop to approximately 0°C and as the temperature drops washing with warm water (40°C) when the temperature drops to −8°C to −10°C. This technique enabled a safe generation of an iceball at the peripheral zone of the prostate, which resulted in no rectal injuries and was effective in ablating the prostate gland.

Imaging techniques used in the definition of the extent of disease and in monitoring the process of tissue freezing have improved substantially over the years, and further advances are expected from CT and MRI in the next decade. Both CT and MRI are able to visualize the complete circumference of frozen tissue as well as demonstrate its internal structure, potentially permitting continuous real-time monitoring of the complete three-dimensional progression of prostate freezing (Rubinsky et al, 1993). CT application is hindered by imaging artifacts created by metal cryoprobes, the physical restriction of the gantry, and the need for continuous radiation for real-time monitoring. CT also cannot directly determine the temperature of completely frozen tissue by objective assessment of tissue density or other parameters (Sandison et al, 1998). In addition to visualizing the entire frozen surface of tissue, MR thermometry can potentially correlate measurable MR signal with the actual temperature of frozen tissue down to the critical level of about −40°C and could assist in objectively monitoring target tissue temperature within the iceball (Daniel et al, 1999; Wansapura et al, 2001). MRI is not ionizing and readily generates three-dimensional imaging. There are also evolving scanner designs that use a relatively "open" magnet that is easily applicable to intraoperative application. Even without thermometry, both MRI and CT lend themselves to computer integration with mathematical models that can generate real-time three-dimensional thermal maps of tissue freezing (Gilbert et al, 1997; Rewcastle et al, 1998; Jankun et al, 1999). These models can potentially integrate the visualized margin of freezing and a finite number of measurable temperature readings into a volumetric thermal model of frozen tissue. These interpolations could then be overlaid as graphical models on real-time images to create a virtual thermal map of the inside of a frozen prostate.

The use of low-dose chemotherapy combined with freezing has been proposed as a means of promoting intercellular signaling to enhance freezing-induced cell death. It has been hypothesized that enhanced cell death is a result of the chemotherapeutic agent initiating mild apoptotic signaling before freezing (Clarke et al, 1999, 2001). PC-3 cells have been studied extensively in an attempt to understand the efficacy of the chemo-cryo combination (Clarke et al, 2001). The response of PC-3 cells exposed to either freezing (−15°C) or freezing (−15°C) in combination with either 5-fluorouracil (5-FU), cisplatin, or folinic acid demonstrated augmentation of cell death with 5-FU or cisplatin but not folinic acid (Baust et al, 2004). Although 5-FU is not an effective agent in the treatment of prostate cancer, the action of 5-FU may have been supplemental to the effect of freezing or cellular sensitivity to freezing may be increased by the exposure to 5-FU. Adjunctive therapy, including anticancer drugs, radiation therapy, or other agents is under investigation (Clarke et al, 2001, 2004; Hanai et al, 2001; Yang et al, 2003) in an attempt to target cells in the periphery of the frozen volume, thereby potentiating the initiation of apoptosis. Inclusion of an apoptotic inhibitor during freezing has also been shown to protect against cell death at temperatures as low as −75°C.

KEY POINTS: CRYOTHERAPY FOR PROSTATE CANCER

- Third-generation cryotherapy includes TRUS guidance, pinpoint thermocouples, and the use of a brachytherapy-like template, with argon gas (freeze) and helium gas (thaw).

- There are two main mechanisms of cytotoxicity: direct cellular toxicity (e.g., ice crystals disrupting cellular membrane) and vascular complications (thrombosis and ischemia).

- A minimum temperature of −40°C must be reached.

- At least two freeze-thaw cycles must be used.

- Long-term PSA follow-up is necessary before cryotherapy can be considered a minimally invasive first-line option, especially in younger men.

- Morbidity is minimal.

- Nerve-sparing cryotherapy is under investigation.

- Salvage cryotherapy is associated with minimal morbidity and is an alternative to salvage radical prostatectomy.

- Cryotherapy may be repeated.

SUGGESTED READINGS

Ellis DS: Cryosurgery as primary treatment for localized prostate cancer: A community hospital experience. Urology 2002;60:34-39.

Ghafar MA, Johnson CW, De La Taille A, et al: Salvage cryotherapy using an argon-based system for locally recurrent prostate cancer after radiation therapy: The Columbia experience. J Urol 2001;166:1333-1338.

Han KR, Cohen JK, Miller RJ, et al: Treatment of organ confined prostate cancer with third generation cryosurgery: Preliminary multicenter experience. J Urol 2003;170:1126-1130.

Izawa JI, Madsen LT, Scott SM, et al: Salvage cryotherapy for recurrent prostate cancer after radiotherapy: Variables affecting patient outcome. J Clin Oncol 2002;20:2664-2671.

Katz AE, Rewcastle JC: The current and potential role of cryoablation as a primary therapy for localized prostate cancer. Curr Oncol Rep 2003;5:231-238.

Larson TR, Robertson DW, Corica A, Bostwick DG: In vivo interstitial temperature mapping of the human prostate during cryosurgery with correlation to histopathologic outcomes. Urology 2000;55:547-552.

Long JP, Bahn D, Lee, F, et al: Five-year retrospective, multi-institutional pooled analysis of cancer-related outcomes after cryosurgical ablation of the prostate. Urology 2001;57:518-523.

Pisters LL, Dinney CP, Pettaway CA, et al: A feasibility study of cryotherapy followed by radical prostatectomy for locally advanced prostate cancer. J Urol 1999;161:509-514.

Pisters LL, Perrotte P, Scott SM, et al: Patient selection for salvage cryotherapy for locally recurrent prostate cancer after radiation therapy. J Clin Oncol 1999;17:2514-2520.

Prepelica KL, Okeke Z, Murphy A, Katz AE: Cryosurgical ablation of the prostate: High-risk patient outcomes. Cancer 2005;103:1625-1630.

Zisman A, Pantuck AJ, Cohen, JK, Belldegrun AS: Prostate cryoablation using direct transperineal placement of ultrathin probes through a 17-gauge brachytherapy template—technique and preliminary results. Urology 2001;58:988-993.

102

Treatment of Locally Advanced Prostate Cancer

MAXWELL V. MENG, MD · PETER R. CARROLL, MD

DEFINITION

TRENDS IN INCIDENCE AND TREATMENT

NATURAL HISTORY

RADICAL PROSTATECTOMY

RADIATION THERAPY

ANDROGEN DEPRIVATION AND ITS TIMING

MANAGEMENT OF DELAYED SEQUELAE

CLINICAL TRIALS

The widespread application of prostate cancer early detection efforts in the United States has resulted in both an increased number of prostate cancers diagnosed and the earlier identification of these tumors. Despite the stage migration associated with prostate-specific antigen (PSA) testing and the growing number of low-stage and organ-confined tumors, at least 10% of men with newly diagnosed prostate cancer have locally advanced disease (T3 NX/+ M0). Although this proportion has declined somewhat, it remains significant and has been relatively constant during the past decade. Those men with locally advanced or metastatic prostate cancer at the time of presentation contribute disproportionately to prostate cancer mortality, and improved treatments in these cohorts could have a significant positive impact on overall morbidity and mortality due to this disease.

Currently, no consensus exists regarding the optimal management of locally advanced prostate cancer. Unlike with clinically localized and low-grade prostate cancer, for which comparable and excellent outcomes may be achieved with a variety of interventions, treatment of disease with local or regional spread by any single modality is associated with significant risk of recurrent disease. Ongoing interest in and study of combination therapy as well as improvements in risk assessment and their use may yield improved cancer outcomes while minimizing treatment-related morbidity and adverse impact on quality of life in these patients.

DEFINITION

Traditionally, the identification of patients with locally advanced disease was based on clinical examination (e.g., digital rectal examination) and clear evidence of spread outside of the prostate capsule (clinical stage T3a), involvement of the seminal vesicles (cT3b), or involvement of adjacent organs (cT4) (Greene et al, 2002). However, the contemporary use of PSA has led to the majority of men diagnosed with prostate cancer initially having nonpalpable cancers (cT1c). **Features other than clinical T stage most often contribute to the identification of men with advanced disease and a concomitant increased risk of failure after primary therapy.** Thus, improved methods of risk assessment have facilitated categorization of men as "high risk" and involve consideration of variables such as serum PSA level and Gleason score in addition to clinical stage. The subsequent discussion focuses on this broader definition of locally advanced disease, with inclusion of those with regional or lymph node involvement without distant metastasis (T3-4 N± M0).

Contemporary Risk Assessment

Multiple methods are currently available to accurately risk stratify men with prostate cancer (Partin et al, 1997; D'Amico et al, 1999; Tewari et al, 2001). The Partin tables were initially constructed in the 1990s and updated in 2001, assisting in the preoperative prediction of final pathologic stage in men with clinically localized prostate cancer undergoing radical prostatectomy (Partin et al, 2001). Although clinical stage, serum PSA level, and Gleason score individually predict pathologic stage and prognosis, the combination of these three variables increases the accuracy of this assessment. These data continue to illustrate that a significant number of men thought to harbor organ-confined tumors have more advanced disease. The ability to assess pathologic stage permits better pretreatment counseling of patients as well as more appropriate selection of therapy and consideration of those with more advanced disease for novel clinical trials. **The most important pathologic criteria predicting prognosis after radical prostatectomy are Gleason score, surgical margin status, and presence of non–organ-confined disease (extracapsular extension, seminal vesicle invasion, lymph node involvement).**

In addition, to help predict pathologic stage, biopsy information has been incorporated into models estimating cancer outcomes, primarily PSA- or biochemical-free survival, after treatment. Whereas biochemical-free survival is a frequent endpoint of current prostate cancer studies, it merely represents a purported intermediate surrogate outcome variable; further trials and studies are necessary to confirm the utility of biochemical recurrence as a marker for reduced prostate cancer–specific survival after treatment. The most widely used nomograms developed by Kattan and colleagues (Kattan, 1998, 2000). In all pretreatment nomograms, clinical stage, biopsy Gleason grade, and pretreatment serum PSA level are incorporated to predict the continuous risk of disease progression after definitive local therapy; models for radiation therapy also include data on use of androgen deprivation therapy (AD), total radiation dose, and combination treatment (AD), total radiation dose, and combination treatment (i.e., external beam and permanent brachytherapy). The radical prostatectomy nomogram was based on nearly 1000 patients with clinically localized disease (T1c-T3a NX M0); thus, this model is not applicable for those men with evidence of seminal vesicle involvement or regional spread.

To simplify risk stratification, men with prostate cancer can be grouped into fewer categories but with maintenance of ability to predict disease behavior and response to intervention. D'Amico and associates (1998) defined patients at low, intermediate, and high risk for biochemical failure, still based on pretreatment disease characteristics (clinical stage, PSA value, Gleason score). Recurrence after treatment may be due to unrecognized micrometastatic disease or persistence of locoregional disease. Other variations of simplified risk stratification have been developed and validated, with inclusion of features such as ethnicity and pathologic findings (Moul et al, 2001; Cooperberg et al, 2005). **Although men with "low-risk" disease generally do well and are unlikely to have biochemical recurrence, men in the intermediate- and high-risk groups may have widely discrepant outcomes. Therefore, men in these groups benefit from more modern and accurate risk prediction models and nomograms** (Mitchell et al, 2005).

Imaging Modalities

Although observations on traditional gray-scale ultrasonography can identify extraprostatic disease, the general ability to improve cancer staging is limited (Figs. 102–1 and 102–2). Directed biopsy of the seminal vesicles or prostate capsule can be obtained to confirm cT3 disease. Smith and coworkers (1997) found that transrectal ultrasonography did not

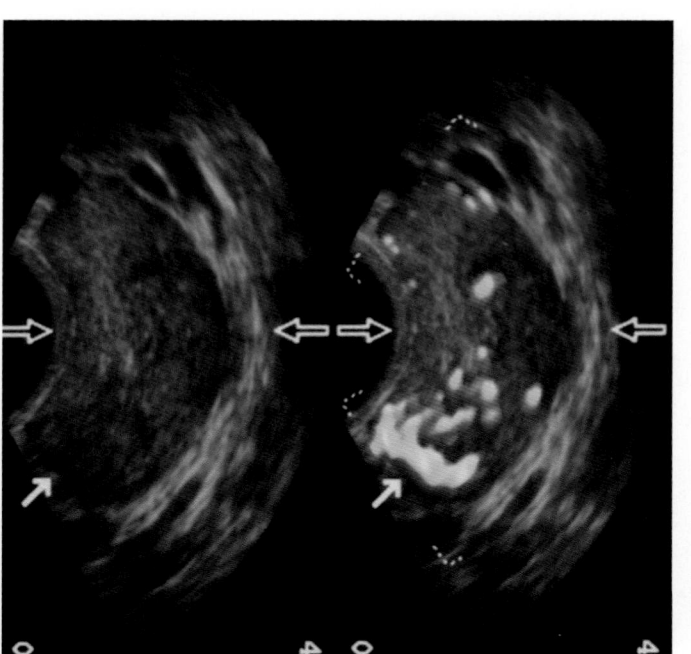

Figure 102–1. Transrectal ultrasound examination demonstrates increased flow on color Doppler study at the left posterior (*upper panel, arrow*) with corresponding hypoechoic area on gray-scale images (*lower panel, arrow*). Note the left lateral distortion and squaring of the capsule, suggesting extracapsular extension. (Image courtesy of Dr. Katsuto Shinohara.)

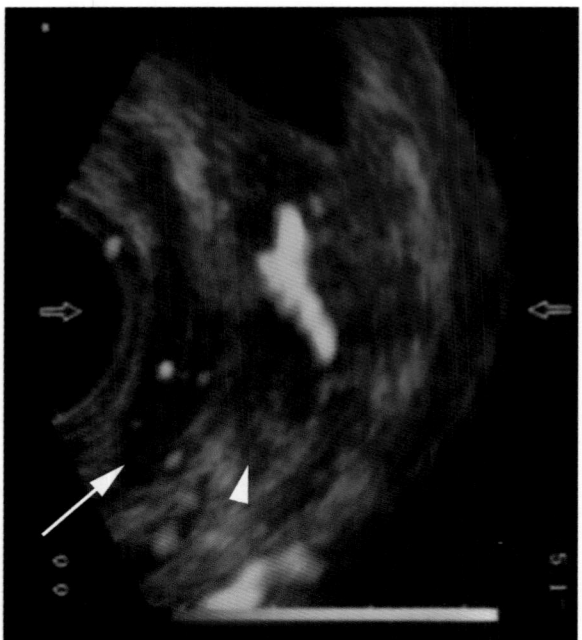

Figure 102–2. Transrectal ultrasound examination demonstrates hypoechoic tumor in the left base (*arrowhead*) with likely extension into the ipsilateral seminal vesicle (*arrow*). (Image courtesy of Dr. Katsuto Shinohara.)

improve the ability to stage prostate cancer; the area under the curve was 0.69 and 0.74 for transrectal ultrasonography in predicting extracapsular extension and seminal vesicle invasion, respectively, compared with 0.72 and 0.69 for digital rectal examination, respectively. Salo and colleagues (1987) reported high sensitivity (86%), specificity (94%), positive predictive value (92%), and negative predictive value (89%)

of ultrasonography in predicting extracapsular extension in patients undergoing radical prostatectomy. However, more contemporary studies suggest otherwise, with lower sensitivities (23% to 66%), specificities (46% to 86%), positive predictive values (50% to 62%), and negative predictive values (49% to 69%). The inaccuracy of ultrasound staging for prostate cancer is likely to be the result of significant interobserver variability, often subtle signs of extraprostatic spread, and lower volume tumors currently diagnosed. In general, transrectal ultrasonography understages rather than overstages prostate cancer. Newer ultrasound techniques, such as color and power Doppler studies, are under investigation to determine if observations of abnormal blood flow can increase the ability to detect and stage prostate tumors.

Endorectal magnetic resonance imaging (MRI) uses a magnetic coil placed in the rectum to achieve better visualization of the zonal anatomy of the prostate and may delineate subtle distinctions between T2a/b disease and T3 disease (Fig. 102–3). However, use of MRI, alone or in combination with magnetic resonance spectroscopy, for tumor staging remains controversial. Variable sensitivities (13% to 91%) and specificities (49% to 97%) have been reported for predicting extracapsular extension, in part attributed to variability in interpreting MRI and lack of uniform diagnostic criteria. In a cohort of 336 men with more than three cores involved with cancer, abnormal findings on digital rectal examination, and PSA level higher than 10 ng/mL undergoing radical prostatectomy, the specificity of MRI in predicting pT3 disease was 95% (Cornud et al, 2002). Thus, the use of MRI may be best limited to those patients with higher risk features.

Novel Markers

It is clear that traditional clinical and pathologic parameters are limited in their ability to accurately predict local extent of

tumor before treatment. Given the importance of assessing true pathologic stage, novel markers of advanced disease are needed. Freeman and associates (2004) reported an interesting relationship between prostatic polyunsaturated fatty acid and risk of locally advanced cancer. In 196 men undergoing radical prostatectomy, the percentage of total polyunsaturated fatty acid in the prostate was inversely correlated with higher pathologic stage ($P = .035$), primarily due to the risk of seminal vesicle invasion (odds ratio, .86; $P = .003$). Chu and colleagues (2003) used comparative genomic hybridization in primary prostate specimens and identified chromosomal regions potentially useful in discriminating between organ-confined and locally advanced tumors (Table 102–1). Prediction of stage by a model incorporating six aberrations in a stepwise fashion was accurate in 91.1% of cases. Further metabolic, genetic, and proteomic signatures will likely better define and discriminate between organ-confined and non–organ-confined prostate cancer (Ashida et al, 2004; Paris et al, 2004).

TRENDS IN INCIDENCE AND TREATMENT

Within the Cancer of the Prostate Strategic Urological Research Endeavor (CaPSURE), **Cooperberg and associates (2003) observed a significant decrease in the fraction of men presenting with high-risk disease characteristics, as defined by D'Amico criteria, from 40.9% in 1989-1990 to 14.8% in 2001-2002.** However, alterations in cancer screening and use of PSA are likely to account for this reduction, with significantly fewer men presenting with elevations in PSA level higher than 20 ng/mL (32.8% to 7.2%); indeed, currently, higher Gleason grade defines a larger number of high-risk patients (61.5%). Overall, **the presence of clinically advanced disease (i.e., T3-4) decreased from 11.8% to 3.5%, with a decline from 32.3% to 21.9% in the high-risk group during the observation period.**

In men undergoing radical prostatectomy, the number of men with clinical evidence of locally advanced disease, as defined by clinical stage (T3), has declined from 25.3% in 1987 to 2.8% in 2001 (Ward and Zincke, 2003). Although the use of PSA screening can account for part of this change, the more

Table 102–1. Chromosome Abnormalities Associated with Pathologic Stage

Chromosome Aberration (independent or in combination)	P Value
−8p	.001
−8p/−10q23 → qter	.002
−10q25 → qter	.029
−6p21	.031
−6q24 → qter	.031
−18cen-q12	.035
−5q31/−10q24 → qter	.04
−5q31 → qter/−8p	.04
−6p21/−10q24 → qter	.04
−6p12 → pter/−6q24 → qter	.04
−6q25 → qter/−11q23 → qter	.04
+7p11/−10q24 → qter	.04
−8p/−15q22	.04
−8p/−11q24 → qter	.42

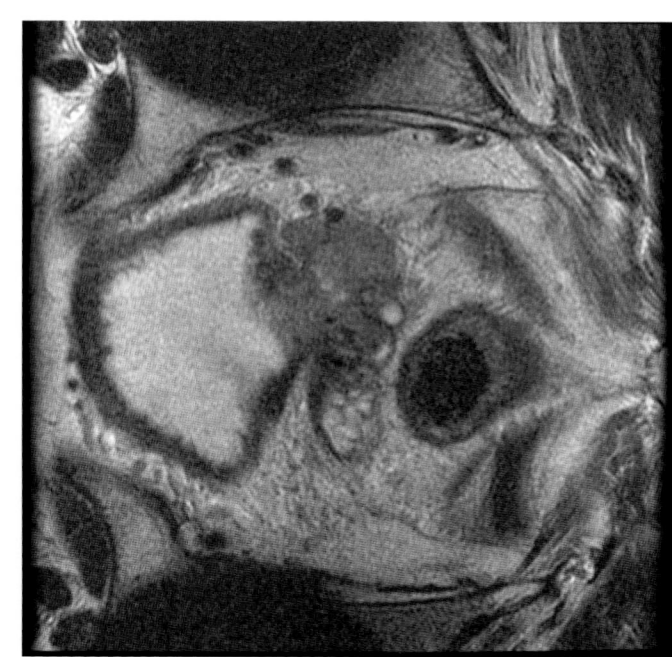

Figure 102–3. Axial T2-weighted MRI shows tumor involving the seminal vesicle and bladder base and extending into the adjacent fat.

Table 102–2. Pathologic Findings in Men Undergoing Radical Prostatectomy

Author (year)	No. of Patients	Era	ECE	Seminal Vesicle/Lymph Node
Stamey (1998)	896	1988	60%	18%/NR
		1996	25%	5%/NR
Quinn (2001)	732	1986-1999	42.8%	13.1%/2.3%
Hull (2002)	1000	1982-1999	25%	8.1%/6.9%
Han (2003)	2091	1987-1998	41%	4%/5%
Derweesh (2004)	1505	2000-2001	66%	NR
Roehl (2004)	3478	1983-1991	25%	14% (combined)
		1992-2003	27%	4% (combined)
Bott (2005)	1001	1988-2001	47%	10%/2%

ECE, extracapsular extension; NR, not reported.

selective application of surgery and improved techniques of radiation therapy are likely to explain the decline in patients with clinical stage T3 disease undergoing prostatectomy. Within reports of men undergoing radical prostatectomy, the fraction of men with pT3 disease has decreased; these are highly selected patients with clinically localized disease at the time of treatment (Table 102–2). Roehl and colleagues (2004) reported that pathologically advanced disease decreased from 39% (1983-1991) to 31% (1992-2003). In men undergoing radical prostatectomy alone at the Cleveland Clinic, the overall rate of extracapsular extension declined from 65.8% (1987-1989) to 25.2% (2000-2001), and this trend was true for all clinical stages of tumor (T1c-T2b/c) as well as for pretreatment variables (PSA value, Gleason score).

KEY POINTS: TRENDS IN INCIDENCE AND TREATMENT

- Fewer men are presenting with locally advanced prostate cancer.
- There has been an increase in organ-confined cancers identified after radical prostatectomy.
- There is an increasing use of treatment modalities other than surgery for high-risk prostate cancers.

The National Comprehensive Cancer Network provides updated decision trees for men with prostate cancer to aid in treatment selection (2004). High risk for recurrence or spread outside the prostate encompasses men with clinically advanced disease, both cT3a and cT3b-T4. In general, radical prostatectomy with pelvic lymphadenectomy is reserved for those high-risk men with smaller tumors that can be completely removed. The alternative treatment strategy for these men with locally advanced disease and higher risk of biochemical failure is AD therapy combined with radiation therapy. The shift in treatment is also reflected within the CaPSURE database (Meng et al, 2005). A total of 6074 men with prostate cancer (clinical stage lower than T3a, N0, M0) were stratified according to risk group, of whom 26% were high risk. Fewer men in this group underwent radical prostatectomy compared with the low-risk cohort, with older age, advanced disease, and increased number of comorbidities significant predictors of treatment (external beam radiation or AD therapy) in multivariate modeling. In addition, more than half of high-risk men receiving radiation therapy also received AD, significantly more than in the low- and intermediate-risk groups (P < .0001).

NATURAL HISTORY

Active surveillance, with deferred treatment when necessary, is becoming a viable treatment alternative in men with prostate cancer. Multiple studies have suggested that cancer-specific mortality is low and primarily associated with higher grade and stage disease. Even in those low-risk cancers, however, an increased and unexpected progression of disease and associated prostate cancer mortality may be seen during an extended period (Johansson et al, 2004). In men with higher risk disease characteristics, it has been recognized that disease progression occurs more rapidly and that some form of intervention is typically warranted in healthy patients.

Few reports address the specific question of outcome in men with locally advanced cancers merely observed for a prolonged period. Older studies, such as that from Nesbit and Plumb (1946), have little relevance to current disease management. Other studies have included only a small number of patients with higher clinical stage. A range of clinical progression (22% to 75%), local progression (22% to 84%), and development of distant metastasis (27% to 56%) has been reported during 5 and 10 years of follow-up. **Overall survival is reported from 10% to 92% at 5 years and 14% to 78% at 10 years for patients who harbor cancers of high grade or stage.** The Veterans Administration Cooperative Urological Research Group (VACURG) study reported a 58% overall 5-year survival in 248 men with clinical stage III disease treated with placebo. Comparable survival outcomes were reported within the Medical Research Council study (Adib et al, 1997) randomizing previously untreated patients with locally advanced, nonmetastatic disease (n = 501) to early or delayed AD therapy (castration or luteinizing hormone-releasing hormone [LHRH] agonist). The median time to clinical progression and death from prostate cancer in the 244 patients receiving delayed treatment was 10 months and 48 months, respectively.

In the analysis from Chodak and associates (1994), grade 3 tumors were significantly associated with disease-specific mortality (risk ratio, 10.04) in men treated conservatively, compared with low-grade (grade 1) cancers. The 10-year disease-specific survival was 87% in men with grade 1 or grade

2 tumor and 34% with grade 3 tumor, with metastasis-free survival of 81% for grade 1, 58% for grade 2, and 25% for grade 3 diseases. Johansson and colleagues (1997) prospectively observed 642 men with prostate cancer diagnosed between 1977 and 1984, with any stage of disease. Of those with clinically localized disease, 11% of men died of prostate cancer with corrected 15-year survival comparable for those who received initial and deferred treatment. Conversely, the corrected 15-year survival was 57% in patients with locally advanced cancer. Approximately half of men had well-differentiated tumors, and only 6% of these men died of prostate cancer. Death from prostate cancer increased with moderately differentiated (17%) and poorly differentiated (56%) disease. These data are summarized in Table 102–3. Albertsen and coworkers (1998) reported the long-term outcomes of watchful waiting in 767 men identified from the Connecticut Tumor Registry with clinically localized prostate cancer (1971-1984). The 15-year cancer-specific mortality in men with Gleason sum 6 was 18% to 30%, compared with the 25% to 59% risk of death from other causes. The chances of death from prostate cancer increased with Gleason score 7 (42% to 70%) and 8 to 10 (60% to 87%). It is likely that a significant proportion of this cohort had non-organ-confined disease since none of the men underwent PSA testing and therefore probably had more advanced stages of disease com-

pared with contemporary cohorts. In contrast to the report from Johansson and associates (2004), the annual mortality rate from low-grade prostate cancer appears to remain stable beyond 15 years after diagnosis (Albertsen et al, 2005) (Fig. 102–4). **Men with high-risk prostate cancer, including those with locally advanced disease, are at significant risk of disease progression and cancer-specific death if left untreated.**

RADICAL PROSTATECTOMY

The use of radical prostatectomy for management of locally advanced prostate cancer has decreased. In part, the shift in paradigm is due to the recognition that prostatectomy alone is often insufficient. In addition, improved risk assessment has permitted better identification of these patients before treatment. Advances in delivery of radiation therapy and recognition of similar outcomes of less invasive but combined modalities (e.g., radiation and AD) have further contributed to the migration away from surgery for high-risk and locally advanced tumors. Nevertheless, radical prostatectomy can cure some men with high-risk disease features.

Surgery for Clinical Stage T3 Prostate Cancer

Several series report outcomes of radical prostatectomy for clinical stage T3 tumors (Table 102–4). In examining all reports, **overall survival ranges from 64% to 96% at 5 years, 12.5% to 72% at 10 years, and 20% to 51% at 15 years after treatment.** Earlier data reflected less accurate risk assessment and potentially greater number of patients with unsuspected lymph node metastases and associated earlier progression and death. Less variability exists in more contemporary cohorts, in which the **cancer-specific survival rates are 85% to 92% and 79% to 82% at 5 and 10 years, respectively, regardless of adjuvant therapy.**

Table 102–3.   **Conservative Management of Patients with Prostate Cancer**

Clinical Stage	No. of Patients	Progression-Free Survival		Disease-Specific Survival	
		%	95% CI (%)	%	95% CI (%)
T1-T2	300	48	37-59	81	74-88
T3-T4	183	47	33-61	57	45-68
M+	159	6	0.8-11	6	–0.1-12

From Johansson et al (1997).

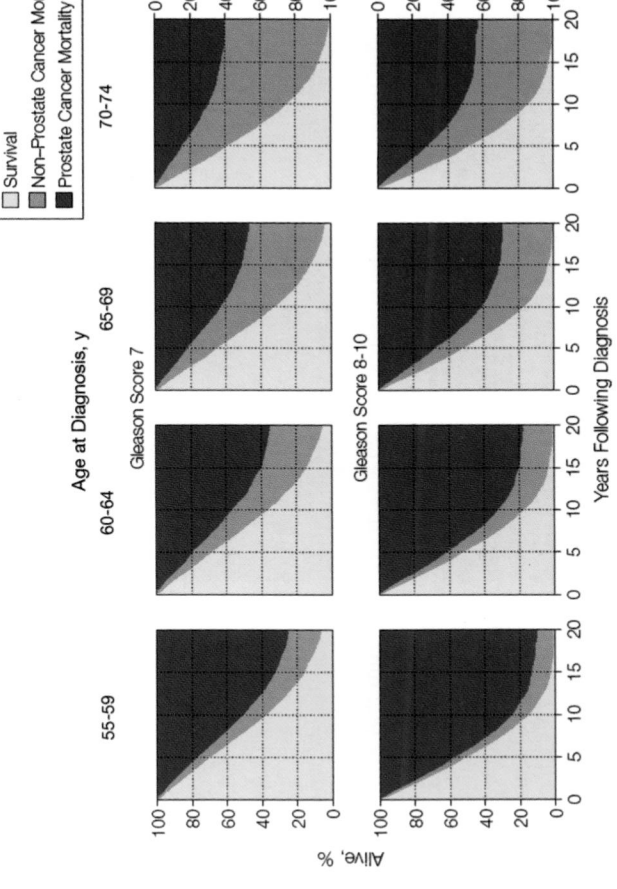
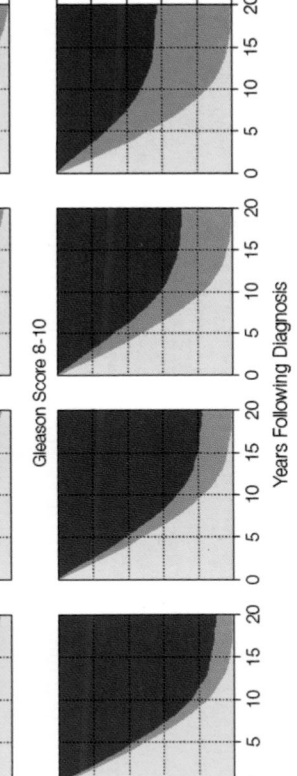

Figure 102–4. Prostate cancer mortality as a factor of Gleason grade and age at diagnosis in men managed conservatively. Brown-shaded areas represent proportion of patients dying of prostate cancer. Light brown-shaded areas represent death from competing causes. Blue areas represent proportion of patients alive. (Modified from Albertsen PC, Hanley JA, Fine J: 20-year outcomes following conservative management of clinically localized prostate cancer. JAMA 2005;293:2095-2101.)

Table 102–4. Radical Prostatectomy for Higher Clinical Stage in Contemporary Series

Author (year)	No. of Patients	Adjuvant Treatment	Overall Survival		Cancer-Specific Survival	
			5-year	10-year	5-year	10-year
Morgan (1991)	232	54%	85%	72%	89%	82%
van den Ouden (1994)	59	83%	83%	90%	90%	—
Lerner (1995)	812	60%	86%	70%	90%	80%
Gerber (1997)	242	NR	—	—	88%	70%
van den Ouden (1998)	83	0%	75%	60%	85%	72%
Pound (1999)*	55	0%	—	—	60%†	49%†
Ward (2005)	842	62%	90%	76%‡	95%	90%‡

*Updated data from Han et al (2001).
†Biochemical-free survival (PSA < 0.2 ng/mL); 15-year actuarial metastasis-free survival of 82% in *entire* cohort.
‡15-year overall and cancer-specific rates of 53% and 79%, respectively.

Pound and coworkers (1999) found that a reasonable outcome was possible after prostatectomy for clinical stage T3a disease, with a 52% 8-year recurrence-free survival. Similarly, Ward and Zincke (2003) reported 5- and 10-year cancer-free survival of 60% and 44%, respectively, without application of adjuvant AD. Freedom from local or systemic disease at 5 and 15 years after surgery was 73% and 67%, respectively (Ward et al, 2005). In the 812 patients from the series of Lerner and associates (1995), 10-year cancer-specific survival was 80%, with only 31% of men with clinical stage T3 disease dying of prostate cancer 15 years after radical prostatectomy. It is unclear, however, whether surgical intervention improves survival compared with alternative treatment strategies. Another interesting observation from the Mayo Clinic was that clinical *over*-staging was identified in 27% of patients, consistent with other reported rates of 7% to 26%, suggesting that uniformly excluding patients from prostatectomy on the basis of clinical staging may not be appropriate (Ward et al, 2005). Gerber and colleagues (1997) reviewed results in 298 men with clinical stage T3 disease undergoing radical prostatectomy and pelvic lymphadenectomy. Although the overall 10-year cancer-specific survival was 57%, an apparent benefit of radical prostatectomy in some men with locally advanced disease was suggested by the increased survival (70%) in those who actually underwent prostatectomy and lymph node dissection. **Many men with clinical stage T3 disease have regional spread and may not benefit from prostatectomy; however, select patients (e.g., lower volume disease) may benefit as local control may be achieved in most, and complete cancer excision is possible in some men.**

Biochemical progression after radical prostatectomy is difficult to assess, given the frequent use of adjuvant therapy (e.g., radiation or AD). Without the use of secondary treatment, 5-year biochemical relapse is higher than 60% (van den Ouden et al, 1998). In other series with variable use of adjuvant therapy, 5- and 10-year biochemical progression was observed in 42% to 49% and 59% to 62%, respectively. The impact of adjuvant therapy may be minimal with respect to clinical progression (i.e., biopsy-proven local recurrence or objective distant metastasis) after radical prostatectomy. Rates of clinical progression at 5, 10, and 15 years are 12% to 39%, and 50% to 71%, respectively.

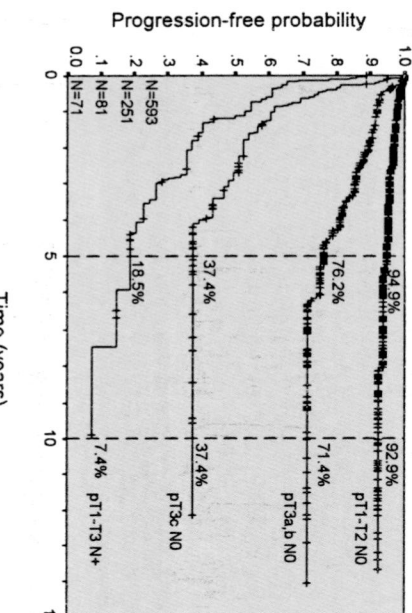

Figure 102–5. Progression-free probability curves based on pathologic stage, whether or not the tumor is organ confined.

Outcomes of Prostatectomy for Pathologically Advanced Disease

A significant minority of patients undergoing radical prostatectomy for clinically organ-confined disease will ultimately be found to have *pathologic* evidence of spread outside the prostate. Although these patients may be expected to have progression and survival rates comparable to those of patients with clinically advanced disease, as defined by grade and serum PSA level, those men who present with clinical stage T3 disease are likely to have greater tumor volume, higher grade, and increased likelihood of regional spread. Currently, the majority of men undergoing prostatectomy for pathologically advanced disease are categorized as high risk on the basis of serum PSA value or biopsy Gleason score. Nevertheless, there is overlap in the groups of men undergoing radical prostatectomy for clinical stage T3 and for pathologic stage T3.

As discussed, pathologic stage after radical prostatectomy provides important prognostic information and is a powerful predictor of outcome, considering all clinical and pathologic factors (Fig. 102–5). **The presence of focal and established extracapsular extension increases the rate of clinical progression from 7% for organ-confined disease to 18% and**

35%, respectively, at 5 years. Patients with evidence of seminal vesicle invasion or lymph node metastasis are highly likely to develop clinical progression (86% and 95%, respectively) after radical prostatectomy. In men undergoing radical prostatectomy for clinically organ-confined disease, Hull and associates (2002) reported 5-year PSA-free survival of 95%, 76%, 37%, and 18% for men with pathologic organ-confined disease, extracapsular extension, seminal vesicle invasion, and positive lymph nodes, respectively. In multivariate analysis, pathologic parameters increasing the relative risk (RR) for progression included extracapsular extension (RR, 2.17 to 2.72), seminal vesicle involvement (RR, 2.61), and lymph node involvement (RR, 3.31). The presence of a positive surgical margin was associated with the greatest relative risk (4.37; range, 2.90 to 6.58). This reinforces the concept that complete surgical removal of all prostatic tissue, regardless of clinical or pathologic stage, should be accomplished when prostatectomy is undertaken.

Biochemical progression after prostatectomy for pathologically advanced tumors depends on the definition applied. Five-year rates of biochemical recurrence have been as high as 65% to 72% when a PSA threshold of 0.2 ng/mL is used; less stringent thresholds may yield recurrence rates of 26% at 5 years and at least 50% at 10 years. Seminal vesicle involvement not only increases the risk of biochemical recurrence but also significantly increases the risk of local recurrence after radical prostatectomy. With prolonged follow-up, Hawkins and coworkers (1995) reported local recurrence in nearly half of patients. This risk appears to be lower in contemporary series of patients because of improved selection of patients for surgery, improved surgical technique, and earlier use of secondary treatment at the time of biochemical relapse.

Predictive models have permitted preoperative estimation of PSA-free survival after prostatectomy. Patients with higher biopsy Gleason score and more elevated serum PSA level are at increased risk of failure after surgery. **Overall, the actuarial PSA-free survival after surgery in high-risk men is approximately 50% at 5 to 7 years.** The validity of the Kattan preoperative nomogram was examined in a community-based cohort of patients undergoing radical prostatectomy (Greene et al, 2004). Interestingly, although the overall concordance index (.68) supported the applicability of the tool to a broad spectrum of patients, the nomogram underestimated recurrence in lower risk men and overestimated recurrence in men at higher calculated risk. Indeed, up to half of men with Gleason sum 8 to 10 or higher PSA level (>20 ng/mL) may achieve prolonged disease-free survival with prostatectomy alone. Further refinements of risk assessment and novel markers will help determine which high-risk men and locally advanced tumors truly benefit from aggressive surgical intervention, either alone or in combination with other therapy.

Neoadjuvant Androgen Deprivation

To improve outcomes of radical prostatectomy in men with locally advanced or high-risk tumors, several investigators have assessed the use of neoadjuvant AD (NAD) before radical prostatectomy. In 1944, Vallet reported performing radical perineal prostatectomy after orchiectomy in a 59-year-old man with prostate cancer. Others reported the use and effi-

cacy of diethylstilbestrol (DES) before surgery. In 1964, Scott evaluated the results of NAD in 31 men who were observed for 10 years. The majority of patients (52%) were alive and free of clinical recurrence. The prospective randomized trials of NAD in patients with stage cT1-T3 prostate cancer before radical prostatectomy are summarized in Table 102–5.

Various measures of outcome have been evaluated in these studies, including changes in digital rectal examination (clinical stage); appearance of tumor on imaging; detection of micrometastatic or circulating cancer cells; and pathologic features, such as T stage, surgical margin and lymph node status, and histopathologic changes. Ultimately, the utility of AD must be assessed by its impact on disease-specific survival or its current surrogate, biochemical-free survival. It is clear that NAD affects tumor behavior and biology, evaluable by changes in metabolic patterns of atrophy on magnetic resonance spectroscopy, lowering of serum PSA level, and histologic atrophy (fibrosis, vacuolization, glandular collapse). Studies have demonstrated that significant reductions in prostate volume (30% to 50%), tumor volume, and PSA level (90%) are consistently noted, with maximal effects occurring during the first 2 months of treatment. However, conflicting results have been reported with respect to pathologic downstaging after NAD in patients with clinical stage T3 cancer. **Overall, only 20% of such patients have organ-confined disease at the time of radical prostatectomy despite clinical**

Table 102–5. **Prospective Randomized Trials of Neoadjuvant Androgen Deprivation in Patients with Prostate Cancer (Stage cT1-T3) before Radical Prostatectomy**

Reference (year)	LHRH Agonist	Antiandrogen	Duration (months)
Labrie (1997)	Leuprolide	Flutamide	3
Witjes (1997)[a]	Goserelin	Flutamide	3
Soloway (1995)[b]	Leuprolide	Flutamide	3
Hugosson (1996)[c]	Triptorelin	Cyproterone	3
Dalkin (1996)	Goserelin		3
Goldenberg (1996)[d]		Cyproterone	3
Van Poppel (1995)	Estramustine		1.5

Follow up reports: [a]Schulman (2000); [b]Soloway (2002); [c]Aus (1998); [d]Klotz (1999).

downstaging in 32% to 90%. Schulman and colleagues (2000) described 402 patients with cT2-T3 N0 M0 tumors randomized to either radical prostatectomy alone or 3 months of total androgen blockade followed by surgery. Pathologic downstaging was seen more frequently in the neoadjuvant group (15%) than in the prostatectomy-alone group (7%; $P < .01$); however, in men with cT3 disease, there was no difference in pathologic downstaging ($P = .36$) and the incidence of lymph node metastases ($P = .18$) in the neoadjuvant and surgery-alone cohorts. Thus, whereas clinical downstaging may occur frequently, **pathologic downstaging is significantly less common after NAD, ranging between 8% and 31%**. Most studies do not show decreased seminal vesicle invasion (Table 102–6). Similarly, rates of lymph node metastases are not altered, with the incidence varying between 3.3% and 16% in both the prostatectomy-alone and neoadjuvant groups.

Klotz and associates (2003) provided long-term follow-up (median, 6 years) of a prospective randomized trial comparing 3 months of NAD before prostatectomy and surgery alone. There was no overall benefit of neoadjuvant therapy as measured by biochemical recurrence (34% to 38%), although in the subgroup of men with PSA level above 20 ng/mL, those receiving NAD had greater PSA-free survival (53%) compared with those undergoing prostatectomy alone (35%; $P = .015$). The Southwest Oncology Group (SWOG) Study 9109 was a phase II feasibility study of 16 weeks of goserelin and flutamide before radical prostatectomy in men with T3-4 N0 M0 prostate cancer (Powell et al, 2002). Of the 55 patients who underwent prostatectomy, 31% had seminal vesicle invasion and 19% had lymph node metastasis. Organ-confined disease was identified in 67% of cases. At median follow-up of 6.1 years, 5-year progression-free and overall survival estimates were 70% and 90%, respectively. The study demonstrated the feasibility of 4 months of AD before surgery, with acceptable morbidity, and outcomes comparable with radiotherapy for this population of patients.

Studies have also examined the incidence of positive surgical margins in those with cT3 disease. Witjes and coworkers (1997) reported similar rates of positive margins in men receiving NAD and those undergoing radical prostatectomy alone (43% and 59%, respectively; $P = .14$). Van Poppel and associates (1995) did not find a statistically significant difference between these groups with respect to positive margins—41.3% in the neoadjuvant cohort and 44% in the surgery-alone group. SWOG 9109 reported positive surgical margins in 30% of patients. In contrast, the randomized and nonrandomized studies of NAD in men with lower clinical stage (cT1-T2) clearly demonstrate a reduction in the rate of positive surgical margins. This advantage has not translated into improved long-term PSA-free survival. **For locally advanced tumors (specifically cT3), current data, both retrospective and prospective, do not support a significant benefit of neoadjuvant androgen deprivation before surgery** (Table 102–7).

The apparent lack of benefit of NAD before radical prostatectomy, in men with both lower stage and locally advanced prostate cancer, may be due to a number of factors. It has been suggested that 3 months of AD may be insufficient to cause an improvement in disease-free survival compared with prostatectomy alone. Meyer and colleagues (1999) followed 680 men treated with radical prostatectomy, of whom 292 received NAD. Although there was no difference in risk of biochemical recurrence between the two groups, patients receiving both LHRH agonist and antiandrogen for more than 3 months had significantly lower risk of PSA failure than did those treated with surgery alone (hazard rate [HR], 0.52; 95% confidence interval [CI], 0.29 to 0.93). Subsequently, the Canadian Urologic Oncology Group (Gleave et al, 2001) randomized patients with clinically localized disease to either 3 or 8 months of NAD before radical prostatectomy. In the 500 patients with pathologic staging, positive surgical margins were identified in 23% of the 3-month group and 12% of the 8-month group ($P = .011$); organ-confined disease was found in 68% and 80% of the 3- and 8-month groups, respectively ($P = .0019$). In addition, the rate of non-specimen-confined or lymph node extension was greater in the 3-month group (25.6%) compared with the 8-month group (12.6%). However, despite evidence of continued biochemical and pathologic regression of the tumor between 3 and 8 months, no significant difference in PSA recurrence rates were observed at 4 years.

Neoadjuvant Chemotherapy and Chemotherapy–Hormone Therapy

The role of chemotherapy in the treatment of prostate cancer has primarily been limited to men with the most advanced disease. Taxanes, alone or in combination with other agents,

Table 102–6.   Pathologic Findings from Studies of Neoadjuvant Androgen Deprivation (NAD) in Patients with cT1-T3 Prostate Cancer before Radical Prostatectomy

Author (year)	No. of Patients	Seminal Vesicle		Lymph Node	
		Control	NAD	Control	NAD
Vaillancourt (1996)	96	6%	0%	NR	NR
Soloway (1995)	282	22%	15%	5.8%	6.3%
Dalkin (1996)	56	14%	18%	NR	NR
Aus (1998)	122	14.5%	21.8%	16%	5.5%
Meyer (1999)	680	16%	17%	16%	14%
Klotz (1999)	213	14%	28%*	6.9%	3.3%
Schulman (2000)	402	23%	20%	23%	15%

NR, not reported.
*$P = .035$.

Table 102–7.   Neoadjuvant Androgen Deprivation (NAD) Therapy for 3 Months before Radical Prostatectomy in Patients with Localized Prostate Cancer: Impact on PSA Recurrence after Surgery

Author (year)	No. of Patients	Control	NAD	Follow-up (months)
Fair (1997)	194	16%	11%	29
Aus (1998)	122	41%	35%	38
Meyer (1999)	680	30%	35%	38
Klotz (1999)	213	30%	40%	36
Schulman (2000)	398	32.5%	26.4%	48
Soloway (2002)	255	32%	35%	60

have proved effective in those with hormone-refractory prostate cancer, with significant PSA declines (>50%) in more than half of patients and measurable disease response in 28% to 75% (Oh, 2004). Mitoxantrone plus low-dose steroids has shown benefit in pain relief compared with steroids alone and is approved for use in hormone-refractory disease (Kantoff et al, 1999; Tannock et al, 1996). On the basis of these observations, interest has increased in earlier use of chemotherapy in high-risk patients or those with locally advanced disease. These studies are summarized in Table 102–8.

Pettaway and colleagues (2000) treated 33 higher risk patients with a 3-month combination regimen consisting of two 6-week cycles of ketoconazole and doxorubicin alternating with vinblastine and estramustine. In addition, concurrent androgen blockade was accomplished with an LHRH agonist and antiandrogen. Lower pathologic stage was found in 18% of patients with cT3 disease, and the overall positive surgical margin rate of only 17% suggests that the regimen may have improved the ability to resect the cancer above that achieved with NAD alone. A second report of combined chemotherapy and hormone therapy before surgery combined 4 to 6 months of NAD with paclitaxel, estramustine, and carboplatin in patients with androgen-dependent, high-risk prostate cancer (Konety et al, 2004). No patients were downstaged to pT0 after neoadjuvant therapy, and organ-confined disease was reported in 36%, with a 22% positive surgical margin rate. Overall, 45% remain without biochemical relapse, defined as PSA level above 0.05 ng/mL on three occasions, at median follow-up of 29 months, and no patient has had documented local recurrence.

Other centers have used chemotherapy without concurrent NAD. At the Cleveland Clinic, 16 patients with locally advanced disease (clinical M0) underwent three cycles of oral estramustine and etoposide and subsequent surgery (Clark et al, 2001). Although grade 3 or grade 4 toxicity was seen in 34% of patients, surgery was not delayed in any individual, and surgical outcomes were comparable to those in series of prostatectomy without neoadjuvant therapy. With a median follow-up of 14 months, 88% were free of disease, and the early PSA failures occurred in the two patients with lymph node metastases.

Single-agent docetaxel is well tolerated before radical prostatectomy, with minimal toxicity (Oh et al, 2001; Dreicer et al, 2004). Again, no cases of complete pathologic response were observed, but no lymph node metastases were identified in one series, whereas the other reported 11% with organ-confined disease. Two thirds and 24% of patients, respectively, experienced a more than 50% reduction in PSA level in response to docetaxel alone. Combination therapy with mitoxantrone or estramustine has been reported in small numbers, and the use of chemotherapy or novel therapy with surgery requires additional study.

Adjuvant Radiation Therapy

Withholding regional or systemic therapy until after the prostate has been removed may (1) prevent delay in time to surgery, (2) reduce operative morbidity, and most important (3) identify those men with adverse pathologic features or evidence of residual disease who truly need additional therapy, thereby avoiding overtreatment in those found to have more favorable disease. The selection of appropriate adjuvant therapy remains difficult because knowledge of the ultimate site of failure (discriminating local-regional from distant recurrence) determines the actual type, timing, and efficacy of such intervention.

Adjuvant radiation therapy (RT) has not clearly been demonstrated to be of benefit after radical prostatectomy; older studies demonstrate no impact on development of distant metastasis or cancer-specific survival, and more recent data show improved biochemical control. Table 102–9 summarizes selected comparative series of adjuvant RT for pathologically advanced disease. In the matched pair analysis of Valicenti and colleagues (1999), early adjuvant RT was administered within 3 to 6 months of surgery with undetectable PSA; control subjects were observed until PSA recurrence. The reduction in risk of PSA relapse was 88% after adjuvant RT with 5-year PSA-free survival of 89%. Anscher and coworkers (1995) provided long-term follow-up (median, 10 years) in 46 patients receiving adjuvant RT after radical prostatectomy for pT3-4. At 10 and 15 years, overall survival and disease-free survival in the RT groups were 62% and 62% and 55% and 48%, respectively; these were not statistically different from the rates in the group not receiving adjuvant RT. In addition, development of distant metastases was comparable in the two cohorts. Nevertheless, local control was better after adjuvant RT (82% at 15 years) compared with surgery alone (53%).

The use of adjuvant RT is associated with a range of biochemical-free survival, from 50% to 88% at 5 years. This appears to be an improvement (30% to 50%) compared with the results of surgery alone in high-risk patients. Nevertheless, the benefit of adjuvant RT needs to be proven in appropriately designed clinical trials. The results of SWOG 8794, which randomized men between surgery alone and surgery followed by adjuvant RT, will be reported shortly. In addition, the decision to administer adjuvant RT is often based on various adverse pathologic features, not all of which carry the same prognosis. Thus, it is difficult to assess the outcomes of adjuvant RT

Table 102–8. Trials of Chemotherapy, Hormone Therapy, and Combined Chemotherapy–Hormone Therapy before Radical Prostatectomy

	Pettaway (2000)	Clark (2001)	Konety (2004)	NAD*
Number of patients	33	16	36	—
Clinical stage T3	55%	13%	47%	100%
Regimen	KAVE	E/VP-16	TEC	—
Androgen deprivation	3 months	—	4–6 months	
Organ confined	33%	31%	36%	21%
Positive margins	17%	13%	22%	37%
Positive lymph nodes	37%	13%	5.5%	21%
Seminal vesicle invasion	85%	—†	56%	39%
Undetectable preoperative PSA	50%	50%	45%	—
pT0	0%	0%	0%	0%–4%

KAVE, ketoconazole + doxorubicin/vinblastine + estramustine; E/VP-16, estramustine + etoposide; TEC, paclitaxel + estramustine + carboplatin.
*Combined results of 23 trials of neoadjuvant hormonal therapy in cT3 disease.
†Grouped together with positive lymph nodes.

Table 102–9. Early Adjuvant Radiation Therapy for Locally Advanced Prostate Cancer (pT3 N0 M0)

Author (year)	No. of Patients	Radiation Dose (Gy)	Progression-Free Survival	P Value	Follow-up (months)
Morgan (1991)	33	60–66	64%	.02	11
Stein (1992)	17	—	94%	—	—
Anscher (1995)	91	55–60	43%	.04	48
	24		75%		
	113	55–65	37%	.16	120
Schild (1998)	46		55%		
	228	57–68	40%	.0003	32
Valicenti (1998a)	60		90%		
	20		48%		
Valicenti (1999)	15	64.8	85%	.01	36
	36		55%		
	36	59–70	88%		
Petrovich (1999)	201		69%	NS	41
	40	48	68%		60
Eggener (2005)	144	NR	53%/37%*	.4/.9*	48
	58		62%/38%*		

*Negative surgical margin/positive surgical margin.

when the populations are composed, variably, of those with positive surgical margins, extracapsular extension, seminal vesicle invasion, or a combination of these features. Those men with positive surgical margin are at an increased risk of biochemical recurrence. A decision analytic model examining this question demonstrated that the benefit may be limited to those with high likelihood of recurrent local, rather than distant, disease; thus, initial RT was recommended for patients with low- to intermediate-grade disease without evidence of seminal vesicle invasion (Grossfeld et al, 2000). This report suggested that adjuvant RT should be considered in those with extensive or multiple positive surgical margins. However, the report from Stephenson and associates (2004) suggests that the application of adjuvant RT in a broader group of men may be beneficial; 501 men received salvage RT for biochemical recurrence after radical prostatectomy, and 50% experienced disease progression after treatment at a median follow-up of 45 months. Although higher Gleason score and seminal vesicle invasion were poor prognostic variables in predicting response to salvage RT, selected patients with high-grade disease or other adverse features (e.g., rapid PSA doubling time) could still achieve a durable response. Indeed, more than half of patients with Gleason sum 8 to 10 and positive surgical margins had a PSA nadir of 0.1 ng/mL or less without subsequent rise above this level. **Thus, early use of secondary therapy, be it RT or AD, may be beneficial in locally advanced tumors as well as at the time of biochemical recurrence in select patients.**

In general, men with seminal vesicle invasion are at significant risk for distant metastasis and may not benefit from local or regional RT; however, some men with pT3c may have only local recurrence alone. Valicenti and coworkers (1998a) identified a group of 53 men undergoing radical prostatectomy with pT3c N0 disease, with 35 achieving undetectable PSA after surgery. The biochemical-free survival (3 years) in the 15 patients receiving adjuvant RT was 86% compared with 48% in the 20 men who were observed ($P = .01$). Prospective randomized studies of this issue have completed accrual, and the forthcoming publication of the results should answer many crucial questions. **On the basis of limited data, it appears that men with seminal vesicle invasion who achieve a low PSA level (<0.3 ng/mL) after prostatectomy may be a more**

favorable group in whom adjuvant RT may be considered. Conversely, those men with more advanced disease never reaching an undetectable PSA level generally constitute a poor prognostic group likely harboring unrecognized lymph node or distant disease.

Traditionally, adjuvant RT has been delivered in lower doses compared with the dose for salvage therapy, with the range from 45 Gy to more than 60 Gy. Most contemporary series of adjuvant RT report doses greater than 60 Gy. Valicenti and coworkers (1998b) evaluated the dose response in a small number of patients (n = 52) receiving adjuvant RT for pT3 N0 disease. The difference in 3-year biochemical-free survival between those treated with less than 61.2 Gy (64%) and more than 61.2 Gy (90%) was statistically significant ($P = .015$), suggesting that higher doses may be necessary. In 27 men with detectable PSA 6 months after prostatectomy, Schild and colleagues (1994) noted that RT doses of 64 Gy or more had improved 30-month freedom from failure (62%) compared with lower RT doses (17%; $P = .03$), supporting the hypothesis of a postoperative RT dose response similar to what has been observed for primary RT in prostate cancer.

KEY POINTS: ADJUVANT RADIATION THERAPY

- Adjuvant radiation therapy improves local control and may reduce biochemical relapse in selected patients after radical prostatectomy.

- Improved outcomes of adjuvant radiation therapy are associated with dose escalation.

Adjuvant Androgen Deprivation

Indirect evidence from the Medical Research Council and VACURG trials suggesting a benefit of early AD compared with delayed AD, in men with various stages of prostate cancer, served as the impetus for studying adjuvant AD after radical prostatectomy. In addition, evidence of a benefit of continued AD after therapeutic RT supports a potential role for combined systemic treatment after local therapy in the form of prostatectomy. However, limited clinical data are currently published on this issue in men with locally advanced tumors (Table 102–10).

Beyer and associates (1993) retrospectively reviewed the outcomes of 86 patients undergoing radical prostatectomy and any form of adjuvant therapy (89% endocrine treatment). In the subset of patients with stage pT3 N0 tumors, adjuvant treatment did not demonstrate an advantage with respect to time to progression or survival. Cheng and associates (1993) reviewed the Mayo Clinic experience with 1035 patients undergoing radical prostatectomy for pathologic stage C prostate cancer; a significant number (n = 103) received adjuvant AD with orchiectomy. Adjuvant therapy of any type (AD or RT) decreased the rate of progression but did not improve cancer-specific or overall survival, with no difference between the two modalities. Prayer-Galetti and colleagues (2000) presented data of 201 men with pT3 disease receiving adjuvant goserelin, demonstrating a 25.4% improvement in disease-free survival at median follow-up of 5 years ($P < .05$).

Recent publications provide some evidence supporting a benefit of early AD after radical prostatectomy in high-risk men with locoregional disease spread. Zincke and coworkers (2001) retrospectively reviewed data of men with stage pT3b cancer and found that early, adjuvant AD positively affected time to progression and cancer-specific survival. These findings were true not only with seminal vesicle invasion but also with limited lymph node disease, with a 10-year cause-specific survival of 94% after prostatectomy and adjuvant AD with a single positive lymph node. Similar findings arose from the Eastern Cooperative Oncology Group (ECOG 7887) study randomizing men with nodal metastases after radical prostatectomy (cT1-T2) to immediate (adjuvant) or delayed AD (Messing et al, 1999). At a median follow-up of 7.1 years,

adjuvant AD decreased recurrence (82% to 23%; $P < .001$) and increased survival (65% to 85%; $P = .02$).

RADIATION THERAPY

The contemporary trend is to treat high-risk or locally advanced prostate tumors with methods other than surgery. Although a plethora of studies describe the results of RT for clinical stage C and T3 disease, many were performed before the widespread use of serum PSA determinations for early detection and modern radiation techniques for treatment, such as three-dimensional conformal RT, intensity-modulated RT, and irradiation of the whole pelvis in addition to the prostate (Kupelian et al, 2003). In addition, contemporary data suggest that the optimal radiation dose is higher than that used in previous reports. In the treatment of men with locally advanced or high-risk prostate tumors, monotherapy with RT or permanent interstitial brachytherapy is likely to be inadequate; yet it must be emphasized that the outcome measures with demonstrated benefit of AD and RT compared with RT alone often do not include overall survival. The focus has shifted to improving outcomes by combining RT with AD, often in conjunction with whole-pelvis irradiation.

Overall survival after RT alone for stage C cancer is approximately 60% to 70% at 5 years and below 50% at 10 years. In high-risk patients, defined by individual parameters alone or in combination, the 5-year progression-free survival rates after RT are typically less than 50%.

Neoadjuvant Androgen Deprivation and Radiation Therapy

The theoretical benefit of AD before RT in men with locally advanced cancers is the ability to reduce target volume as well

Table 102–10. Trials of Androgen Deprivation with External Beam Radiation Therapy

Study (author, year)	No. of Patients	Eligibility	RT Dose (Gy)	Study Arm	Disease-Free Survival	Overall Survival	Median Follow-up
Neoadjuvant							
RTOG 86-10 (Pilepich, 2001)	471	cT2-4, ≥25 cm²	44-46 WP 65-70 p	RT PT + nAD + cAD	21% 33%	44%* 53%*	6.7 years
Canadian trial (Laverdiere, 1997)	120	cT2b-4	64 p	RT RT + nAD RT + n/c/aAD (6 mo)	22% 72% 90%	NR NR NR	24 months
Adjuvant							
RTOG 85-31 (Pilepich, 2003)	977	cT3, pT3 or N1	44-46 WP 65-70 p	RT RT + aAD (∞)	8% 32%	38% 53%	7.3 years
EORTC 22863 (Bolla, 2002)	412	T1-2 + grade 3, T3-4	50 WP 70 p	RT RT + aAD (3 yr)	40% 74%	62%† 78%†	66 months
Swedish trial (Granfors, 1998)	91	T1-4, pN0-3, M0	50 WP 65 P	RT RT + orchiectomy	39% 69%	38%‡ 61%‡	9.3 years
RTOG 92-02 (Hanks, 2003)	1514	T2c-4 + PSA < 150	44-50 WP 65-70 p	RT + n/cAD RT + n/c/aAD (2 yr)	28% 46%	79% 80%	5.8 years
RTOG 94-13 (Roach, 2003)	1292	PSA < 100 + >15% risk of nodes	50.4 WP 70.2 p	n/cAD + WP n/cAD + pRT WP + aAD (4 mo) pRT + aAD (4 mo)	60% 44% 49% 50%	89% 86% 84% 87%	59.5 months

p, prostate; WP, whole pelvis; nAD, neoadjuvant androgen deprivation; cAD, concurrent androgen deprivation; aAD, adjuvant androgen deprivation.
*Different only for Gleason 2 to 6.
†$P = .0002$.
‡$P = .02$.

as the potential cytotoxic synergy of radiation and hormone manipulation. Several Radiation Therapy Oncology Group (RTOG) trials (75-06, 83-07, 85-19) examined the combination of AD and RT in locally advanced disease, suggesting that the regimen was tolerable and improved local tumor control. On the basis of this information, RTOG 86-10 was designed to compare short-term AD combined with RT with RT alone (Pilepich et al, 2001). The phase III trial randomized 471 men with cT2-T4 tumors (surface area of more than 25 cm² on rectal examination) to either goserelin plus flutamide for 2 months before and during external beam RT or RT alone. 4 months of AD was associated with reduction in distant metastases and improvements in local control, disease-free survival, and cancer-specific mortality. At 8 years, the PSA-free survival in the AD plus RT and RT-alone groups was 24% and 10%, respectively (P < .0001). No difference in overall survival between the two groups (51% AD plus RT versus 43% RT) was found, although men with lower Gleason sum (2 to 6) appeared to have a survival benefit from combined AD and RT. In men with Gleason sum 7 to 10, no significant improvement was observed from AD with respect to locoregional control or survival. Subsequent analysis of RTOG 86-10 (Chakravarti et al, 2003) revealed that loss of p16 expression on immunohistochemistry was associated with reduced overall survival (P = .039), disease-specific survival (P = .006), and higher risk of local progression (P = .0007) and distant metastasis (P = .026); overall survival was not significantly associated (P = .07) in multivariate analysis. Other correlative studies of tissue from RTOG 86-10 found that the proliferative marker Ki-67 was significantly associated with distant metastasis and cancer-specific survival but not with overall survival (Li et al, 2004).

Similar observations were made by Laverdiere and associates (1997) in a prospective randomized study of 120 men with cT2b-4 disease. Treatments included (1) external beam RT alone, (2) 3 months of NAD before RT, and (3) 3 months of NAD before RT and 6 months of adjuvant AD. Evidence of residual cancer on prostate biopsy was present in 62%, 30%, and 4% of the treatment arms, respectively, at 12 months and 65%, 28%, and 5% at 24 months. Biochemical-free survival at 12 and 24 months paralleled the biopsy data, with the difference between the neoadjuvant and adjuvant AD groups disappearing at 24 months. These observations not only supported neoadjuvant and concurrent AD with RT but also suggest a benefit of prolonged AD.

Adjuvant Androgen Deprivation and Radiation Therapy

Several prospective studies have assessed the role of adjuvant AD after RT as well as the appropriate duration of such therapy. RTOG 85-31 (Pilepich et al, 1997; Lawton et al, 2001) randomized 977 patients with T3 NX M0 or T1-2 N+ M0 prostate cancer to RT and either goserelin, started during the last week of RT, continued indefinitely, or goserelin at the time of relapse (i.e., early or late AD). The groups were matched with respect to disease risk characteristics, and less than 30% had lymph node involvement. Improved local control and biochemical disease-free and metastases-free survival were noted in the adjuvant AD group at 8 years of follow-up, and this advantage was most prominent with Gleason sum 8 to 10. Overall survival was not statistically different at 5 years (75% versus 72%) and 8 years (49% versus 42%). In those with high-grade tumors, adjuvant AD improved cancer-specific (90% versus 78%) and overall (80% versus 69%) survival at 5 years.

In the European Organization for Research and Treatment of Cancer (EORTC) 22863 study (Bolla et al, 1997), men undergoing external beam RT for clinically localized disease (cT1-2 and grade 3, cT3-4 any grade) were randomized to RT alone or the addition of goserelin starting at the beginning of treatment and continuing for 3 years. This is the only study to demonstrate an overall survival benefit, with 5-year survival of 79% in the adjuvant AD group and 62% in the RT-alone group (P = .001). Disease-free survival was 85% and 48%, respectively, and local control was also improved with AD (97% versus 79%). Of note, the cohort presented with very high-risk disease, with a median PSA level of 30 ng/mL, and this may account for the relatively low overall survival in the RT-alone cohort.

It does not appear that the method of AD affects the outcome of combined treatment with RT. Granfors and associates (1998) randomized men with cT1-4 pN0-3 M0 cancer to either external beam RT alone or combined orchiectomy and RT; men treated with RT alone received AD at clinical disease progression. At median follow-up of 9.3 years, clinical progression in the RT-alone and RT plus AD patients was 61% and 31%, respectively (P = .005). Cancer-specific mortality was not different; overall mortality was 61% and 38%, respectively (P = .02). However, in men with negative lymph nodes, there was no significant difference in survival rates, and the poor survival was primarily due to metastatic disease at the time of initial treatment.

A meta-analysis of 2742 men treated for clinically localized prostate cancer within RTOG trials from 1975 to 1992 supports use of adjuvant AD in subsets of patients (Roach et al, 2000). Patients were stratified into four prognostic risk groups, and those in risk group 2 (cT3 NX, Gleason 2 to 6; cT1-2 NX, Gleason 7; N+, Gleason 2 to 6) appeared to have improved disease-specific survival with addition of short-term (4 months) AD. In further refining the population of patients, limiting the analysis to men with bulky or cT3 disease alone demonstrated a significant survival advantage.

If adjuvant AD is of benefit, the duration of such therapy remains uncertain. RTOG 92-02 supports the use of long-term AD after initial AD with external beam RT (Hanks et al, 2003). Men with locally advanced tumors (cT2c-4

N0-1 M0) received either 4 months of AD (2 months neoadjuvant and 2 months concurrent) with RT or that and 24 additional months of AD. Long-term AD was beneficial in all endpoints evaluated *except* overall survival, with 5-year rates of both approximately 80%. Subset analysis of men with Gleason sum 8 to 10 noted improved overall survival with 24 months of AD (81%) compared with short-term AD (71%; $P = .044$) as well as improved disease-specific survival. More recently, D'Amico and associates (2004) described 206 men with clinically localized but higher risk (PSA $\geq$ 10 ng/mL, Gleason sum $\geq$ 7, cT3) prostate cancer randomized to RT alone (70 Gy) or RT with 6 months of AD. Overall and cancer-specific survival rates were improved with AD compared with RT alone. Actuarial five-year survival and freedom from salvage AD was 88% and 82%, respectively, after early AD and 78% and 57% with RT alone. **Thus, a limited period of AD (2 to 4 months) appears to be appropriate for those men with intermediate-risk cancers; more prolonged AD may be beneficial for those with high-risk disease characteristics, including high-stage cancers or very high pretreatment serum PSA values.**

Other aspects of RT for men with more advanced tumors require clarification, including the dose and extent (i.e., prostate only versus prostate and pelvis) applied. RTOG 94-13 randomized men with an estimated risk of lymph node metastasis of 15% into one of four arms: (1) whole-pelvis RT plus neoadjuvant and concurrent AD, (2) prostate-only RT plus neoadjuvant and concurrent AD, (3) whole-pelvis RT plus adjuvant AD, and (4) prostate-only RT plus adjuvant AD (Roach et al, 2003). Progression-free survival was improved for whole-pelvis compared with prostate-only RT ($P = .022$). No difference was observed for the two types of AD. In comparing the four groups, progression-free survival rates were 60%, 44%, 49%, and 50%, respectively ($P = .008$). The differences in RT dose among the various prior and contemporary studies make comparisons of efficacy difficult, as emerging data support doses greater than 72 Gy as being more effective (Cheung et al, 2005; Jacob et al, 2005). In addition, the role of combined external beam RT and brachytherapy (both permanent and high-dose rate) needs to be better elucidated. Brachytherapy has generally been used to treat patients with lower risk features. Its use in those with high-risk disease characteristics, often in combination with AD as well as external beam RT, has been less well studied. Potters and associates (2005) noted a 63% biochemical-free survival in those treated with permanent prostate brachytherapy. A similar outcome has been noted with the use of high-dose rate intensity-modulated brachytherapy with external beam RT (Demanes et al, 2005). Sylvester and colleagues (2003) treated men with interstitial permanent brachytherapy combined with moderate-dose (45 Gy) neoadjuvant external beam RT. In those with high-risk disease (D'Amico criteria), the 10-year biochemical relapse-free survival was 48%; of note, AD was not used. Stock and coworkers (2004) evaluated a multimodal protocol using neoadjuvant and concomitant AD (9 months total), brachytherapy, and three-dimensional conformal RT in a high-risk cohort. The 5-year biochemical-free survival was 86%, with Gleason sum the only variable associated with PSA failure. Excellent local control was also demonstrated, with no patient harboring cancer on the last post-treatment biopsy.

Radiation Therapy and Chemotherapy

The role of chemotherapy in conjunction with RT is less well studied than that for surgery and chemotherapy. Khil and associates (1997) administered estramustine and vinblastine concurrently with RT (total, 65 to 70 Gy) in men with locally advanced disease. Although clinical control was reasonable at 5 years at 81%, only 48% of patients had a PSA level below 4 ng/mL at this time. Zelefsky and colleagues (2000) enrolled 27 patients with high-risk disease (Gleason sum $\geq$ 8 and PSA >10 ng/mL; Gleason sum 7 and PSA > 20 ng/mL; cT3 N0 M0 and PSA > 20 ng/mL; cT4 N0 M0; cTX N1 M0) in a phase II clinical trial of the same agents, with RT at 75.6 Gy. Only modest increase in grade 2 toxicity was noted, and no late grade 3 or grade 4 toxicities were observed. The 2-year biochemical-free survival was 60%. An update reported median time to PSA relapse of 12 months, with 48% of patients receiving no additional therapy, and median time to metastasis had not been reached (Ryan et al, 2004).

An estramustine-based regimen has also been examined with etoposide before and during definitive RT (Ben-Josef et al, 2001). Actuarial disease-free and overall survival was 73% and 88%, respectively, at 3 years. Local control as determined by biopsy was 71% at 18 months. A phase I study examined concurrent docetaxel and RT (70.2 Gy) in 22 men (Kumar et al, 2004). The maximal tolerated dose was determined to be 20 mg/m^2, with diarrhea and dysuria the primary toxic effects. All patients were alive at last follow-up, and 77% had continued biochemical response. These promising results support further study of the combined use of RT and chemotherapeutic agents.

ANDROGEN DEPRIVATION AND ITS TIMING

The VACURG and Medical Research Council trials suggest a benefit to early application of AD in men with locally advanced prostate cancer. The first VACURG study randomized 1050 patients with stage III disease and 853 patients with stage IV disease to placebo, 5 mg of DES, orchiectomy plus placebo, or orchiectomy plus 5 mg of DES. All three AD arms had significantly less progression than the placebo group had, but this did not translate into an overall survival benefit. The inability to demonstrate a survival benefit cannot be completely attributed to the increased cardiovascular deaths within the DES groups, as survival in the orchiectomy plus placebo group was not significantly different from that in the placebo-alone group. The second VACURG study randomized 1506 men with stage III and stage IV disease to placebo or one of three doses of DES (0.2 mg, 1 mg, 5 mg). DES at 1 mg and 5 mg delayed progression of stage III disease, and patients receiving 1 mg had improved overall survival. However, the 5-mg dose of DES again resulted in increased cardiovascular death. Subsequent analysis suggested that immediate estrogen therapy was most beneficial in patients younger than 75 years with high-grade tumors (Gleason sum 7 to 10). The third VACURG study supported that only a subset of men with prostate cancer benefit from early AD. In men with stage II disease, 5-year survival with placebo and 1 mg of DES was 48% and 75%, respectively. **Taken together, the VACURG data**

provide evidence of benefit for early AD with respect to disease progression and potentially survival only in subsets of men with more aggressive disease. **The studies also clearly show that alternatives to estrogen should be used, given the cardiovascular toxicity associated with higher doses of DES.** The current ability to better monitor disease progression, with use of PSA kinetics and imaging modalities, may improve the outcomes of delayed AD by better determining when institution of AD is necessary.

The Medical Research Council also evaluated the issue of early versus delayed AD (orchiectomy or LHRH agonist) in 938 patients with prostate cancer, of whom 501 had locally advanced disease. The majority of deaths (67%) were attributed to prostate cancer. Cancer-specific mortality was 55% in the early AD group and 43% in the deferred group (P = .001). Overall survival was also improved in the immediate AD arm (P = .02). The reduction in prostate cancer death was primarily due to patients with M0 disease. This study also provides important data for comparison to other forms of treatment. Median time to death due to prostate cancer (cT3 M0) was 90 months, comparing favorably to EORTC 22863, in which median time was not reached after 65.7 months. Similarly, median overall survival in the Medical Research Council study was 64 months but not reached in EORTC 22864 (56.7 months of follow-up). Thus, the apparent beneficial effects of combined AD and RT may be due in part to AD alone with uncertain incremental advantage of RT.

Studer and colleagues (2004) evaluated the timing of AD in a study randomizing 197 asymptomatic men with prostate cancer to either immediate or deferred subcapsular orchiectomy; of note, patients were either unsuitable for or unwilling to undergo surgery or RT. A significant fraction of the cohort had higher risk features, with clinical stage T3 or higher in 67% and median serum PSA level above 46 ng/mL. Of the 92 men in the deferred treatment arm, 42% never required AD; the majority died of causes unrelated to prostate cancer. The median time to deferred AD was 3.2 years, the most common indication being skeletal metastases (45%) and ureteral obstruction (25%). Although overall survival was not different between the immediate and deferred groups (P = .96), a trend toward improved cancer-specific survival was noted in those men receiving immediate AD, with a hazard rate for death from prostate cancer of 0.63 (P = .09).

To minimize adverse impact on quality of life, antiandrogen therapy alone has been proposed as an alternative to orchiectomy or LHRH agonists. Iversen and colleagues (2004) reported on the effects of 150 mg of bicalutamide in men with localized or locally advanced prostate cancer, the majority of whom were untreated initially (81%). At median 5.3 years of follow-up, survival in those with locally advanced disease was improved with bicalutamide compared with placebo (HR, .68). Overall, risk of disease progression was reduced with placebo (HR, .4). The combined analysis of the three Early Prostate Cancer bicalutamide trials (n = 8113) confirmed improved progression-free survival in the bicalutamide group (Wirth et al, 2004a). Overall survival was not different between the treatment and placebo arms in each trial, but men with locally advanced disease receiving bicalutamide alone (i.e., no surgery or RT) appeared to have improved survival. Although apparently

promising in men with high-risk tumors, bicalutamide at 150 mg must be approached cautiously; both in men deferring local therapy and after definitive treatment. In analysis of the Early Prostate Cancer data (median follow-up of 5.4 years), men with localized prostate cancer receiving bicalutamide as primary therapy had an increased risk of death (HR, 1.23; 95% CI, 1.00 to 1.50) compared with surveillance alone. Immediate high-dose bicalutamide is not currently appropriate in men with low risk of disease progression, and potentially adverse effects should be sought in higher risk patients with extended follow-up.

Wirth and colleagues (2004b) tested adjuvant flutamide (750 mg) after radical prostatectomy in men with pT3-4 N0 disease. Recurrence-free survival, defined as a single PSA value above 5 ng/mL or two PSA values above 2 ng/mL, was improved with flutamide (HR, .51) at median follow-up of 6.1 years; however, overall survival was comparable (HR, 1.04). Significant toxicity was associated with flutamide and accounted for nearly half of withdrawals from the treatment arm.

Intermittent Androgen Deprivation

Another approach to minimizing AD-related morbidity is the intermittent application of androgen suppression. Forty-nine patients (28 with cT3-4 N0 M0) were treated with total AD until the PSA level was less than 4.0 ng/mL between 24 and 32 weeks, after which treatment was withheld after 36 weeks (Sato et al, 2004). PSA level was monitored and treatment was recommended when the PSA level reached either pretreatment level (when it was less than 15 ng/mL) or 15 ng/mL (when the initial PSA level was higher than that). During median follow-up of 126.1 weeks, mean time off-treatment during cycles 1, 2, and 3 was 46.1, 36.9, and 23.3 weeks, respectively. No symptomatic or clinical disease was reported in the nonmetastatic subgroup, and PSA failure was observed in 3 (11%) of these patients, with all patients alive at last evaluation. The optimal timing of intermittent AD for reduction of patient morbidity and disease-specific endpoints remains to be determined.

Quality of Life

The early institution of AD in men with prostate cancer, whether it is localized or locally advanced, must be balanced against the known side effects and long-term morbidity. Only recently has the impact of AD been appreciated and reported on bone events, cognitive function, and quality of life. In comparing bicalutamide (150 mg) and castration with locally advanced but nonmetastatic disease, both sexual interest and physical capacity were better with bicalutamide monotherapy

(Iversen et al, 2000). Although hot flashes were more common with castration, a trend toward reduced quality of life was associated with bicalutamide, including higher incidence of gynecomastia, breast pain, and asthenia. In the study of intermittent AD from Sato and colleagues (2004), many quality of life domains were improved during off-treatment cycles, including potency and social and family well-being.

The multimodal approach with AD and RT may increase the relative toxicity compared with each intervention alone. Schultheiss and colleagues (1997) reported that NAD was correlated with later gastrointestinal and genitourinary (grade 2 or higher) morbidity. Another study found that adjuvant AD after RT predicted for late grade 2 to grade 4 rectal toxicity (Sanguineti et al, 2002). Within RTOG 86-10, potency after RT with or without AD was similar at 81% and 74%, respectively. Chen and associates (2001) also found that the addition of AD did not further contribute to decline in sexual function after RT. Zelefsky and associates (1999) evaluated predictors of late toxicity in men treated with three-dimensional conformal radiotherapy. Although the 5-year actuarial likelihood of urinary toxicities was low (<10% overall), use of NAD was an independent predictor ($P = .01$) of post-treatment erectile dysfunction. The incidence of rectal morbidity as well as sexual dysfunction may be related to duration of AD longer than 6 or 9 months.

The benefits of adjuvant AD plus RT for locally advanced prostate cancer, both short and long term, appeared to outweigh the associated side effects in a number-needed-to-treat analysis (Jani et al, 2003). A model was constructed that compared treatment options while incorporating benefit and complications, and data from randomized trials of RT with or without AD for cT2c-4 N0-1 were input into the calculation.

Even considering the increased incidence of side effects of long-term AD, this approach appeared to be better than short-term AD for virtually all endpoints evaluated.

MANAGEMENT OF DELAYED SEQUELAE

The direct comparison of prostatectomy and RT in the treatment of locally advanced prostate cancer is challenging and primarily based on historical studies. Even with the addition of neoadjuvant and adjuvant systemic therapy, leaving the prostate gland in situ poses potential problems. First, effective local control of some high-risk cancers may influence survival. Second, local recurrence may lead to the need for additional treatment of the prostate. At 10 years, local recurrence rates after RT for cT3 or stage C range from 24% to 74%. Holzman and associates (1991) reported that 36% of patients required transurethral resection of the prostate because of urinary obstruction after RT alone, without AD. Other morbidity included hydronephrosis (20%) and incontinence (13%). An older report (Tomlinson et al, 1977) also demonstrated significant local complications of stage C prostate cancer with nonextirpative interventions—infection (80%), bladder outlet obstruction (75%), gross hematuria (45%), and ureteral obstruction (40%). Systemic therapy in the form of AD may not prevent local progression or reduce need for palliative intervention. Despite orchiectomy for bladder outlet obstruction, 31% of men with locally advanced disease required transurethral prostate resection because of persistent voiding dysfunction after 60 days. Similarly, in 277 patients with cT2-4 randomized to orchiectomy, RT, or both, rates of local disease control were comparable (Fellows et al, 1992). Studer and coworkers (2004) demonstrated that AD alone, whether

Table 102–11.   Current Phase III Clinical Trials in Locally Advanced/High-Risk Prostate Cancer

Study	Eligibility Criteria	Treatments
Radical Prostatectomy		
Neoadjuvant		
CALGB 90203	Clinically localized, ≤ 60% 5-year disease free	Surgery alone vs. estramustine and docetaxel
Adjuvant		
SWOG 9921	Gleason 8-10, pT3b-4, N+, Gleason 7 and + margin	AD (2 year) vs. AD + mitoxantrone and prednisone
RTOG 0011	Gleason ≥ 7 and PSA > 10 ng/mL or + margin or pT3b, Gleason < 7 and 2 or 3 (PSA, margin, pT3b)	AD + RT vs. RT vs. AD (63-66 Gy)
SWOG 8794	pT3 N0 M0	Observation vs. RT
EORTC 22911	pT3 N0	Observation vs. RT (60 Gy)
External Beam Radiation Therapy		
Neoadjuvant		
RTOG 9910	Gleason 2-6 and PSA 10-100 ng/mL, Gleason 7 and PSA < 20 ng/mL, cT1 and Gleason 8-10 and PSA < 20	8 weeks NAD vs. 28 weeks NAD
Adjuvant		
RTOG 9902	Gleason ≥ 7 and PSA 20-100 ng/mL, ≥ cT2 and Gleason ≥ 8 and PSA < 100 ng/mL, cT1c-2b N1-2, cT2c-4 N0-2	AD vs. AD + estramustine, etoposide, and paclitaxel
EORTC 22961		6 months AD vs. 3 years AD
Androgen Deprivation		
CAN-NCIC-PR3	cT3-4 N0 M0, cT2 and PSA > 40 ng/mL cT2 and PSA > 20 ng/mL and Gleason ≥ 8	AD alone vs. additional pelvic RT
NCT 55731	Gleason > 7, cT3-4, N1 PSA > 20 ng/mL	AD vs. AD + docetaxel and estramustine

it is instituted early or late, does not prevent local morbidity. More than half of the men in their study required transurethral resection of the prostate. In addition, delayed institution of AD was necessary because of ureteral obstruction (25%), anticipation of local complications (10%), and rectal infiltration (4%).

Quality of life is an increasingly important endpoint for prostate cancer. However, the impact of untreated local tumor progression or the various treatment modalities for locally advanced disease on quality of life outcomes is poorly characterized. Rosenfeld and colleagues (2004) examined the relationship between cancer stage and quality of life in 341 ambulatory men with prostate cancer. Instruments used included the Functional Assessment of Cancer Therapy (FACT), urinary function subscale of the UCLA Prostate Cancer Index, and Hospital Anxiety and Depression Scale (HADS). The stage of prostate cancer was significantly associated with most FACT scales. Increasing stage was negatively correlated with nearly every FACT subscale score and the observation persisted in multivariate models, accounting for covariates such as comorbidity and time since diagnosis. Interestingly, stage was more strongly associated with physical domains of health-related quality of life, and there was no association with psychological symptoms as measured by HADS.

CLINICAL TRIALS

Given that outcomes of therapy are not optimal for those men with high-risk disease features, patients who present with such cancers should be considered for enrollment in novel clinical trials. Table 102–11 summarizes phase III clinical trials for high-risk or locally advanced prostate cancer, some of which have completed accrual; others are ongoing. The resulting data should answer some of the current questions regarding the optimal type and timing of traditional combination treatment as well as the role of chemotherapy in men with locally advanced and high-risk prostate cancer.

SELECTED READING

Albertsen PC, Hanley JA, Fine J: 20-year outcomes following conservative management of clinically localized prostate cancer. JAMA 2005;293:2095-2101.

Bolla M, Collette L, Blank L, et al: Long-term results with immediate androgen suppression and external irradiation in patients with locally advanced prostate cancer (an EORTC study): A phase III randomised trial. Lancet 2002;360:103-106.

Cooperberg MR, Lubeck DP, Mehta SS, Carroll PR: Time trends in clinical risk stratification for prostate cancer: Implications for outcomes (data from CaPSURE). J Urol 2003;170:S21-S27.

Johansson JE, Andren O, Andersson SO, et al: Natural history of early, localized prostate cancer. JAMA 2004;291:2713-2719.

Lerner SE, Blute ML, Zincke H: Extended experience with radical prostatectomy for clinical stage T3 prostate cancer: Outcome and contemporary morbidity. J Urol 1995;154:1447-1452.

Petrovich, Lieskovsky G, Langholz B, et al: Comparison of outcomes of radical prostatectomy with and without adjuvant pelvic irradiation in patients with pathologic stage C (T3N0) adenocarcinoma of the prostate. Am J Clin Oncol 1999;22:323-331.

Pilepich MV, Winter K, John MJ, et al: Phase III radiation therapy oncology group (RTOG) trial 86-10 of androgen deprivation adjuvant to definitive radiotherapy in locally advanced carcinoma of the prostate. Int J Radiat Oncol Biol Phys 2001;50:1243-1252.

Roach M 3rd: Hormonal therapy and radiotherapy for localized prostate cancer: Who, where and how long? J Urol 2003;170:S35-S40.

103

The Clinical State of the Rising PSA Level after Definitive Local Therapy: A Practical Approach

MICHAEL J. MORRIS, MD · HOWARD I. SCHER, MD

No tumor marker has had as great an impact on the diagnosis, management, and treatment of a disease as prostate-specific antigen (PSA) has had on prostate cancer. On an international scale, PSA measurements have been used for screening, early detection, and determination of local disease extent and the probability of durable disease control after surgery or radiation therapy; for more advanced disease, PSA is an indicator of whether a patient is responding to systemic treatments. Perhaps the most controversial aspect of PSA monitoring is that it has created a new "clinical state": patients with a rising PSA level as the sole manifestation of disease recurrence after definitive local therapy. Indeed, for most of these cases, the standard imaging modalities used to detect disease are unrevealing. **On the basis of the estimated probabilities of relapse after surgery or radiation therapy, more than 50,000 American men fall into this category every year**

(Moul, 2000). Unfortunately, the management of these patients remains controversial because the course of the illness going forward is highly variable, and there are no prospective randomized studies that address directly when a systemic approach should be initiated and, perhaps most important, whether an intervention prolongs life.

It follows that within the clinical spectrum of men with a rising PSA level are some who are at high risk for development of symptoms from or dying of their cancers. Such patients may well benefit from the early administration of systemic treatments to prevent metastases, to preserve quality of life by delaying the complications of osseous lesions, and to prolong survival. In other patients, the disease will follow a more indolent clinical course for which observation may be appropriate because the risk for development of metastases or symptoms or dying of the disease may be low during their anticipated life expectancy (Pound et al, 1999). Between these extremes are patients who would benefit from additional therapy directed at the prostate or prostate bed.

Accordingly, management is centered on two key issues. The first is to determine whether the rising PSA level represents disease that is exclusively localized to the prostate or prostate bed that can potentially be eliminated by additional local therapy; whether the rising PSA level represents a systemic recurrence not amenable to cure by local therapy alone; or whether the rising PSA level represents both a local and systemic recurrence. The second is how to distinguish the high-risk and the low-risk patient and to determine the probability that a clinically significant event will occur, such as growth in the primary site that can no longer be eliminated, detectable metastases on scan, or death from disease. In both scenarios, the therapeutic question is how to balance the need for therapy on the basis of what the cancer might do to the patient relative to the anticipated decrement in quality of life associated with therapy. Not to be underestimated in the equation is the anxiety experienced by patients knowing that their cancer is "progressing." Yet, with the ever-decreasing age at which men are being diagnosed and treated for prostate cancer, most men have never experienced symptoms related to cancer, only the therapy. The clinical dilemma facing both the patient and the physician is how to balance the anxiety, knowing that the rising PSA level means the cancer is progressing, with the paucity of objective data regarding who would benefit from treatment, whether that treatment should be local or systemic, and what the tangible benefits are to such interventions. In this discussion, we provide a framework to assess the prognosis of patients in the clinical state of a rising PSA level (Scher and Heller, 2000) so that a rational risk-adapted approach can be implemented. This is done with the recognition that the tools for both prognostication and treatment continue to evolve and at present must be considered works in progress.

WHEN DOES A PATIENT OCCUPY THE CLINICAL STATE OF A RISING PSA LEVEL?

Prostate Cancer: A States-Based Model

Prostate cancer represents a wide clinical spectrum from localized to metastatic, driven by a range of biologic factors that often change as the disease evolves. As shown in Figure 103–1, these variable disease manifestations can be segregated into patient groups, represented as easily recognizable clinical

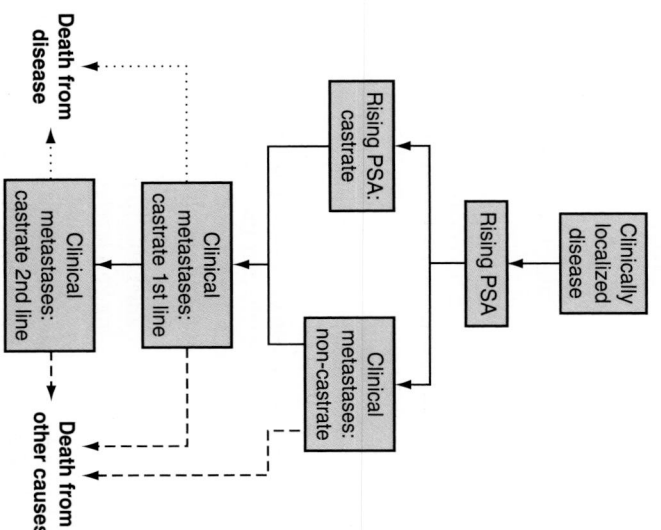

Figure 103–1. Prostate cancer can be considered a series of clinical states. Each state defines a discrete set of patient characteristics, clinical needs, and treatment aims and therefore is a practical means of distinguishing populations of patients and developing clinical trials. Prognostic models are developed on a state-by-state basis to risk stratify patients in each state. (Derived from Scher HI, Heller G: Clinical states in prostate cancer: Towards a dynamic model of disease progression. Urology 2000;55:323-327.)

states that share clinical needs and treatment goals (Scher, 2000). Patients with localized disease have common treatment aims of disease eradication along with the preservation of potency, continence, bladder and rectal integrity, and other measures of quality of life. Patients with newly diagnosed metastatic disease have the treatment goal of maintaining disease control and prolonging hormone sensitivity while minimizing the impact of hormones and other treatment strategies on quality of life and bone integrity. For patients with disease that is progressing despite androgen deprivation, the issues of prolonging life and finding treatment strategies to mitigate the effects of an increasing burden of disease, such as pain, neurologic compromise, fatigue, hematologic disorders, bone fracture, and others, are more acute.

Defining the Clinical State of a Rising PSA Level

When a patient has entered the clinical state of a rising PSA level depends on the primary therapy he has received and the sensitivity of the assay used to measure PSA. By consensus, this clinical state does not include patients with localized disease who are being observed expectantly under a policy of "watchful waiting" or "deferred therapy." Nor does it include patients who are receiving androgen deprivation in lieu of definitive treatment. Like many issues relating to prostate cancer, there is no single uniform definition that can be used to describe when a patient has officially relapsed "biochemically." A patient who has undergone a prostatectomy should have no or minimal remaining normal, viable, PSA-producing nonmalignant prostate tissue. By contrast, patients who have received external beam radiation therapy or brachytherapy, alone or in combination, have an intact although irradiated gland in place that may produce low levels of PSA that are not indicative of a treatment failure. In addition, not all PSA assays have the same level of sensitivity, so a given PSA level may be reported "undetectable" in one laboratory but detectable at another. Another confounder is that PSA production is in part contingent on testosterone levels. Patients who have undergone neoadjuvant or adjuvant hormone strategies in conjunction with their local therapy may have variable rates of treatment failure on the basis of testosterone recovery rates. In general, testosterone levels return to baseline within 3 to 6 months after cessation of short-term gonadotropin-releasing hormone analogue treatment, but the recovery can be prolonged in individual patients (Padula et al, 2002; Gulley et al, 2003). Older age, length of androgen deprivation, and even type of gonadotropin-releasing hormone analog therapy used will have an impact on the rate of biochemical failure (Lukka et al, 2001).

Radical Prostatectomy

As noted, post-prostatectomy patients may have very low levels of PSA that can represent benign glands at the surgical margin, and as a result there is debate as to what precise level of PSA represents treatment failure definitively. Commonly discussed ranges that signify PSA failure are ≥0.2 or ≥0.4 ng/mL (Han et al, 2003), although some authors have recognized that levels as low as 0.01 to 0.07 ng/dL can also

represent failure (Amling et al, 2001; Gretzer et al, 2002; Han et al, 2003). **In point of fact, the argument is moot because a single PSA value that is abnormal does not necessarily indicate that a clinically significant event has occurred.** This is because a rising PSA level alone does not necessarily mean that a patient will develop symptoms or die of his disease. Nevertheless, most clinicians accept that a PSA level of 0.4 ng/mL or higher that is rising represents treatment failure on the basis of follow-up studies showing that PSA values above this level do not plateau (Amling et al, 2000). Therefore, by consensus (Scher et al, 2004), a patient is considered to have progressed after a radical prostatectomy if the PSA level is 0.4 ng/mL or higher 8 weeks or more after the procedure and rises on a subsequent measurement. The 8-week time frame after surgery is ample to allow the PSA to clear, given a half-life of 2 to 3 days (Oesterling, 1991). The date of failure is the date of the first detectable PSA.

Radiation Therapy

Biochemical failure after radiation therapy has been defined by the American Society for Therapeutic Radiology and Oncology (ASTRO) as three consecutive PSA rises, optimally separated by 3 months between measurements, after radiation therapy starting at least 2 years after the start of radiation, with the time of failure as the midpoint between the nadir and the first confirmed rise (1997). Even ASTRO, however, has recognized that such a definition has its shortcomings. Because cell death that follows radiation therapy is a post-mitotic event, some radiation therapists suggest a minimum 18-month period of observation for nadir values to occur (Critz, 2002). In other cases, transient elevations in PSA level are documented that do not represent treatment failures. These so-called bounces have been reported in 12% to 61% of cases as long as 18 to 36 months after treatment (Taplin, 2003), and there are no validated guidelines to differentiate a bounce from recurrent disease (Das et al, 2002). Furthermore, it is unclear whether any three rises, regardless of how low the PSA level is, represent recurrent disease. Values ranging from 0.5 to 1.5 ng/mL have been proposed as thresholds for defining relapse (Critz et al, 1996). In addition, patients who are destined to relapse do not necessarily have three consecutive rises. At the point of this writing, the ASTRO definitions are undergoing revision to address these issues (Kattan et al, 2000). The definitions under consideration include two documented increases of at least 0.5 ng/mL, values above a nadir plus 2 ng/mL, an absolute nadir plus 2 ng/mL, or values at the current nadir plus 2 ng/mL. These are undergoing validation (Ward et al, 2005a, 2005b).

RADIOGRAPHIC AND OTHER TESTS TO DETERMINE WHETHER THE RISING PSA LEVEL SIGNIFIES LOCALIZED DISEASE, METASTATIC DISEASE, OR BOTH

One of the most difficult aspects of formulating a treatment plan for the patient with a rising PSA level is determining whether the rising PSA level represents locally persistent disease, nonlocalized systemic disease, or both. The stakes of such a decision are high. Treating every patient who has undergone a prostatectomy with salvage radiation therapy exposes patients with systemic disease to unnecessary radiation therapy and the risk, albeit low, of proctitis, cystitis, and a reduced likelihood of maintaining or preserving erectile function. On the other hand, with careful selection, salvage radiation therapy offers the potential to eliminate the disease completely. Present methods of detecting disease, whether in the prostatectomy bed, in an irradiated gland, or in metastatic sites such as bone and lymph nodes, are usually of limited value. Moreover, the finding of local disease on an imaging study does not exclude a systemic component, which explains in part why radiation therapy to the prostate bed or salvage surgery after radiation therapy is not curative for the majority of patients (Laufer et al, 2000; Leventis et al, 2001).

By definition, the finding of overt radiographic metastases on an imaging study signifies that a patient is in the state of clinical metastases, non-castrate disease, and no longer in the state of a rising PSA level. Nevertheless, to ensure that patients do indeed have a rising PSA level in the absence of radiographic metastases, a staging evaluation should be undertaken. **However, bone scintigraphy and computed tomography of the abdomen and pelvis, the traditional modalities used, are of limited value because they are insensitive at detecting early metastatic disease.**

Bone scintigraphy will detect only metastatic disease of sufficient size that interferes with normal osteoblast-osteoclast interactions to produce an overall metabolic profile favoring bone deposition. Areas of marrow involvement that do not affect bone metabolism will remain undetected, as will lesions that are smaller than 0.4 cm. Frequently, patients present to the clinician years before bone scintigraphy is likely to detect abnormality, and there is no single PSA value that predicts abnormal scan findings. In most series, PSA levels will be well above 20 to 30 ng/mL before bone scintigraphy reflects metastatic disease (Cher et al, 1998). Even when bone scintigraphy detects an abnormality, tracer uptake in areas of trauma, infection, or inflammation can easily be mistaken for metastatic disease. More recently, a nomogram to predict the likelihood of an abnormal scan was developed. The nomogram included parameters that describe PSA kinetics—the PSA slope (odds ratio [OR], 2.71; $P = .03$) and PSA velocity (OR, 0.93; $P = .003$) as well as the trigger PSA or current PSA value (OR, 1.022; $P < .001$). The concordance index for predicting the bone scan result was 0.93 (Dotan et al, 2005a).

Computed tomographic scanning is also suboptimal for the detection of metastasis because it has a lower limit of detection of 0.5 cm and because it can be difficult to distinguish scar tissue or fibrosis from tumor. The scans are also nonspecific, as some of the abnormalities detected may signify fibrosis or scar rather than tumor (Moul et al, 2001b). An additional factor is that in many cases, soft tissue disease never develops even when advanced osseous disease is present. In an analysis of 134 men registered to contemporary clinical trials for patients with castrate metastatic disease, only 15% of patients had exclusively soft tissue disease, and 45% had disease both in bone and in soft tissue. Only 50% of these patients had soft tissue lesions of sufficient size to be measurable, and the majority of these lesions were small lymph nodes on the order of 2.5 cm. The median number of lesions 2 cm or larger per patient was only two (range, one to six). The distribution of disease was similar to that reported in recently completed multicenter trials (Scher et al, 2005).

Other Imaging Modalities to Distinguish Localized from Distant Recurrence

Other imaging modalities that are under investigation for the detection of early metastatic disease are magnetic resonance imaging, positron emission tomography (PET), and ProstaScint scanning. Magnetic resonance imaging with use of an endorectal coil and a pelvic-specific acquisition methodology can reveal sites of recurrent disease in and around the prostate bed and bladder. This methodology may be able to identify sites of disease that would otherwise not be sampled by routine blind biopsies of the prostate bed and therefore may be useful for identifying areas suggestive of locally recurrent disease or for guiding biopsies (Sella, 2004). Transrectal ultrasonography is being investigated as a means of identifying residual disease in patients who have undergone radiation therapy (Goldenberg et al, 1992; Connolly et al, 1996).

PET is another area of active investigation in identifying occult metastatic or locally recurrent disease. Fluoro-deoxyglucose (FDG) is excreted through the kidneys, so detection of nodal and locally recurrent disease even in highly controlled populations of patients with known progressive metastatic disease is compromised. In one such study in patients with definitively established progressive soft tissue disease, only 39% of lesions were seen by standard imaging modalities and PET. An additional 39% could be detected by standard imaging modalities but were not detected by PET (Morris et al, 2002). On the other hand, FDG-PET may well be able to distinguish progressive disease in bone from non-malignant areas of uptake on bone scintigraphy and may even be able to detect bone metastases before such lesions appear on a bone scan (Morris et al, 2002). These applications are still under study, as are other tracers, some of which may even be prostate specific (Larson et al, 2004). Preliminary data suggest that the probability of an abnormal scan finding correlates with PSA doubling times (Schoder et al, 2005). At this time, however, an abnormal finding on PET scan should not be considered definitive proof that a patient has either metastatic or locally persistent disease.

The ProstaScint scan is the only test approved by the Food and Drug Administration to detect occult metastatic disease in patients with early prostate cancer. However, its role in managing a patient in the state of a rising PSA level is still investigational. The basis of this scan is a murine antibody, 7E11, that targets the internal domain of prostate-specific membrane antigen, a transmembrane type II glycoprotein found on normal prostate tissue and prostate cancers (Israeli et al, 1993, 1994). However, anti–prostate-specific membrane antigen antibodies are also taken up in the gut, liver, kidney, and other normal tissues. ProstaScint scanning is associated with a significant number of false-positive and false-negative results, in part related to these areas of uptake (Sartor and McLeod D, 2001), in part due to inflammation and even vascular sludge (Hinkle et al, 1998). A study suggested that the specificity of the test can be increased if the images obtained are fused with magnetic resonance images

(Schettino et al, 2004). Similar to the situation with PET scanning, the application of ProstaScint scanning to detect occult metastases or locally recurrent disease should be considered investigational.

Biopsies and Clinical Decision-Making

Many clinicians would opt to perform biopsy of palpable abnormalities in the prostate bed in a post-prostatectomy patient. Indeed, even radiographic findings that are suggestive of locally recurrent or locally persistent disease may warrant pathologic confirmation. **Biopsies that reveal locally persistent disease may prompt a decision to opt for salvage radiation therapy or systemic therapy, for at least local control of palpable tumor masses. However, most patients will not have palpable lesions, and most patients will not have evidence of locally recurrent disease. The yield of blind biopsies in the prostate bed is usually low, tends not to affect clinical decision-making, poorly predicts for the efficacy of salvage radiation therapy, and should not be considered a standard of care** (Leventis et al, 2001; Scher et al, 2004).

By contrast, biopsy proof of locally persistent disease in the prostate after external beam radiation therapy is essential before recommending that a patient receive a salvage radical prostatectomy, cryosurgery (Izawa et al, 2002), brachytherapy (Beyer, 1999), or intraprostatic biologic or cytotoxic treatment. The risk of false-positive biopsy findings declines after 2 years from the completion of radiation therapy.

MODELS TO PREDICT LOCAL VERSUS SYSTEMIC RECURRENCE AND TO PREDICT FOR SURVIVAL

The preceding discussion focused on the role of different imaging modalities in distinguishing localized from metastatic disease and whether pathology plays a significant role in determining treatment. **However, for the overwhelming majority of patients, biochemical relapse occurs far earlier than the development of radiographic findings or findings on physical examination or by biopsy. As such, a more critical question is, What is the probability that a patient with systemic disease will develop metastases detectable on imaging studies, at a point in the disease when death from prostate cancer exceeds death from other causes, or that he will develop symptoms and ultimately die of the disease rather than with it? Once this is addressed and the need for treatment is determined, consideration can be given to what options are available and their likelihood of success in controlling the disease or, preferentially, eliminating it completely** (Beekman et al, 2005). This question is distinct from the determination of whether the disease is local, systemic, or both.

Many prognostic and predictive models have been reported. Some use determinants that reflect the disease at the time of initial diagnosis and treatment, others at the time of relapse; others center on PSA kinetics after the patient has definitively relapsed biochemically. **All of the models "work" in defining what they are designed to predict. Indeed, clinicians are often at a loss to decide which of several models to** use in predicting a key clinical event. Multiple models now exist to predict the likelihood of a patient's transition to the clinical state of a rising PSA level (D'Amico et al, 1998; Zelefsky et al, 1998; Moul et al, 2001a), the likelihood that a tumor removed surgically will have a specific pathologic stage by pretreatment clinical features such as PSA value or Gleason score (Partin et al, 1993; Roach, 1993; Roach et al, 1996), and the likelihood that a patient with localized disease will achieve a given median overall survival (Roach et al, 2000; Vollmer and Humphrey, 2001; D'Amico et al, 2003a; Sandler et al, 2003). Nomograms that combine many of these prognostic determinants treat them as continuous variables in multivariate models and allow specific predictions of an outcome for a patient with given clinical features (Kattan et al, 2000).

The models that have specific relevance to patients in the clinical state of a rising PSA level fall into several categories and are summarized in Table 103–1.

Predicting Local Versus Systemic Relapse

The first question the clinician evaluating a patient with a rising PSA level must address is, Where is the disease? **In general, low pretreatment PSA levels, lower grade tumors, low clinical or pathologic staging, late time from definitive local therapy to PSA relapse, and long PSA doubling times generally prognosticate a low likelihood for development of distant, radiographically apparent metastases** (Pound et al, 1999). Such patients can have durable remissions after salvage radiation therapy to the prostate bed (Moul, 2000; Leventis et al, 2001).

Another modeling strategy employed is to examine patients who have been successfully "cured" by salvage radiation therapy and to extrapolate from those data which features predict for exclusively locally recurrent disease. Features such as negative or close margins ($P = .03$), absence of extracapsular extension ($P < .01$), and presence of seminal vesicle invasion ($P < .01$) have been shown to predict for successful salvage radiation therapy (Katz et al, 2003). One multivariate model derived from a retrospective examination of a multi-institutional database of patients who underwent salvage radiation therapy showed that predictors of progression after salvage radiation therapy were Gleason score of 8 to 10 (hazard ratio [HR], 2.6; 95% confidence interval [CI], 1.7 to 4.1; $P < .001$), preradiotherapy PSA level above 2.0 ng/mL (HR, 2.3; 95% CI, 1.7 to 3.2; $P < .001$), negative surgical margins (HR, 1.9; 95% CI, 1.4 to 2.5; $P < .001$), PSA doubling time of 10 months or less (HR, 1.7; 95% CI, 1.2 to 2.2; $P = .001$), and seminal vesicle invasion (HR, 1.4; 95% CI, 1.1 to 1.9; $P = .02$) (Stephenson et al, 2003). In a second model derived from 211 patients, factors predictive of biochemical failure included a PSA doubling time of less than 12 months (HR, 3.88; $P = .032$), seminal vesicle invasion in the surgical specimen (HR, 3.22; $P = .08$), pathologic grade (HR, 1.58; $P = .23$), and PSA value at the time of salvage radiotherapy (HR, 1.29 for a twofold increase; $P = .04$) (Ward et al, 2004). What odds of "predicted" success or failure justifies recommendation of treatment is controversial, with the recognition that external beam radiation therapy is the only proven option that offers a chance for cure.

Risk for Development of Metastatic Disease

A corollary of distinguishing patients who will benefit from salvage radiation therapy from those with micrometastatic disease is modeling the risk for development of radiographic metastases and at what time interval. Pound and colleagues (1999) observed a cohort of men who underwent a radical prostatectomy and relapsed biochemically, followed up without therapy until symptoms or radiographic metastases were found. As one would anticipate, high-grade disease, short interval to biochemical relapse (2 years or less versus longer than 2 years), and PSA doubling time of less than 10 months versus 10 months or longer predicted for a shorter time to radiographic progression. In an updated analysis, time to PSA failure was no longer predictive when PSA doubling time was considered (Eisenberger et al, 2003). **In numerous studies, PSA doubling time is the dominant factor used to assess the risk for development of metastasis-free survival** (Roberts et al, 2001; Kwan et al, 2003; Sandler et al, 2003). In one study, a PSA doubling time of 6 months or less was associated with a 5-year progression-free survival of 64% versus 93% of patients who had a longer PSA doubling time (Roberts et al, 2001). In the Mayo Clinic series, metastases were detected at 5 and 10 years, respectively, in 10% and 29% of patients with a PSA doubling time of 12 months or less versus 0% and 17% for those with a longer PSA doubling time. The estimation was based on a total of 23 metastatic events representing 10% (23 of 211) of the population studied (Ward et al, 2004). In a series of 1650 patients treated with external beam radiation therapy at Memorial Sloan-Kettering Cancer Center, 381 (23%) had a biochemical recurrence, of whom 98 (26%) developed distant metastases at an incidence of 10%, 21%, and 29% at 1, 3, and 5 years, respectively. In a multivariate competing-risk regression model, PSA doubling time ($P < .001$), clinical T stage ($P < .001$), and Gleason score ($P = .007$) from the time of diagnosis were the only independent variables that predicted for distant metastases. At 3 years, patients with a PSA doubling time of 0 to 3, 3 to 6, 6 to 12, and 12 months or more had a frequency of metastasis of 49%, 41%, 20%, and 7%, respectively ($P < .001$), at a relative risk of 7.0, 6.6, and 2.8 times higher than with doubling times longer than 12 months. The median follow-up time was 92 months from the completion of radiotherapy (Zelefsky et al, 2005).

Concerns about the use of PSA doubling time are that at present, there is no consensus regarding the optimal number of PSA values that should be used, the time interval over which they should be determined, whether these values need to be consecutive, and whether these values should be separated by a minimum time. Complicating the issue further is that PSA values can fluctuate independently of treatment. Most calculations are based on a first-order kinetics assumption, where

$$PSA(t) = PSA(0)e^{at}$$

and a is the relative velocity of PSA. Published reports are inconsistent. In our experience, a minimum of three and ideally four or five measurements are required. Given this, more than one third of the PSA profiles in this population of

Table 103–1. Models to Predict Clinically Significant Events in Patients with a Rising PSA Level after Definitive Local Therapy

| Author | N | Type of Model | Event Predicted | PSADT | Prognostic Variables | | | |
					Margin	Gleason	PSA	Other
Leventis et al (2001)	49	Multivariate	Biochemical relapse-free survival after RT	Treated as continuous, HR 0.30 (0.11-0.83); P = .02	NA	NA	Pre-RT PSA treated as continuous, HR 3.22 (1.16-8.93); P = .025	NA
Stephenson et al (2004)	501	Multivariate	PSA progression after salvage RT	≤10 months, HR 1.7 (1.2-2.2; P = .001)	Negative margin, HR 1.9 (1.4-2.5; P < .001)	Gleason 8-10, HR 2.6 (1.7-4.1; P < .001)	Pre-RT PSA > 2, HR 2.3 (1.7-3.2; P < .001)	SVI, HR 1.4 (1.1-1.9; P = .02)
Ward et al (2004)	211	Multivariate	PSA progression after salvage RT	≤12 months, (HR 3.88; P = .032)	SVI (HR 3.22; P = .023)	Pathologic grade (HR 1.58; P = .023)	2-fold increase (HR 1.29; P = .04)	NA
Pound et al (1999)	1997	Multivariate	Metastasis-free survival	≤10 months, poor prognosis (Gleason ≤ 7 only)	NA	Gleason 8-10, poor prognosis	NA	≤2 years to biochemical failure, poor prognosis
Zagars and Pollack (1997)	841	Multivariate	Metastasis-free survival	≤8 months poor prognosis	NA	NA	NA	NA
Roberts et al (2001)	587	Multivariate	Metastasis-free survival	<0.5 year, RR 62; 0.5-0.9 year, RR 9.1; 1-9.9 yr, RR 4.1	NA	NA	NA	NA
Slovin et al (2005c)	148	Multivariate	Metastasis-free	<6 months	NA	NA	NA	Nomogram T stage, PSA, Gleason score
Zelefsky et al (2005)	381 (all patients)	Multivariate	Metastasis-free survival	Continuous, HR 0.59 (0.49-0.71; P = .001)	NA	Gleason 7-10, HR 1.0 (1.2-3.3; P = .007)	NA	NA
Zelefsky et al (2005)	229 (no neoadjuvant ADT)	Multivariate survival	Metastasis-free survival	Continuous, HR .54 (0.41-0.70)	NA	Gleason 7-10, HR 2.7 (1.4-5.2; P = .002)	NA	T3 or T4, HR 2.0 (1.2-3.6; P = .01)
Kwan et al (2003)	1786	Multivariate	Overall survival (disease-specific survival is also included)	NA	NA	Grouped by overall risk category, P < .001	Any evidence of biochemical failure, P < .001 Absolute PSA level, P < .001	T stage, P = .033 PSA
Lee et al (1997)	151	Multivariate	Disease-specific survival and overall survival	NA	NA	P = .004 (disease-specific) or .03 (overall)	P = .168	NA
Sandler et al (2000)	154	Multivariate	Cause-specific survival	Relative PSA rise and log of slope of rise (P < .001 and .007)	NA	NA	NA	NA
D'Amico et al (2002)	94	Multivariate	Cause-specific death and all-cause death	PSADT ≤12 months (P = .03 cause specific; P = .05 all causes)	NA	NA	NA	NA
D'Amico et al (2003)	1451	Multivariate	Cause-specific mortality	<3 months, HR 19.6 (12.5-30.9)	NA	NA	NA	PSADT ≥ 3 months (continuous) HR 0.78 (0.74-0.82)

PSADT, prostate-specific antigen doubling time; HR, hazard ratio; NA, not applicable (either not analyzed or not statistically significant in a multivariate model); RT, radiation therapy; SVI, seminal vesicle invasion; RR, relative risk; ADT, androgen deprivation therapy.

patients follow higher order kinetics, and so the equation does not represent the kinetics for more than 30% of patients (Ballentine Carter et al, 1992; Patel et al, 1997). Higher order mathematical methods may better describe the PSA profiles for these men.

Another confounder in calculating PSA doubling time is the effect of neoadjuvant or adjuvant hormone therapy during radiation therapy. Rapid testosterone recovery may induce a rapid rise in PSA level, which may not reflect disease kinetics. Such a patient may not be at a significant risk for development of metastatic disease despite a seemingly rapid doubling time, because were he observed for a sufficient time for the testosterone level to stabilize, the rate of rise in PSA level may plateau or at least slow. Other confounders include estrogenic herbs or other alternative medicines the patient may be taking and prostatitis in patients after radiation therapy. Even with the caveats, PSA kinetics can and should be used to estimate metastatic risk and high-risk patients considered for early systemic treatment.

Risk of Disease-Specific and All-Cause Risk of Death

Data now exist that demonstrate an association between PSA doubling time and disease-specific survival after radiation therapy (Lee et al, 1997; Zagars and Pollack, 1997; Sandler et al, 2000; D'Amico et al, 2002, 2003b) **and post-treatment PSA doubling time with time to prostate cancer–specific and all-cause mortality (all Cox $P < .001$)** (D'Amico et al, 2004b). These data are illustrated in Figure 103–2. In this last analysis, the hazard ratio for death from prostate cancer for a patient with a PSA doubling time of less

than 3 months was 19.6, with a 95% confidence interval of 12.5 to 30.9 (D'Amico, 2004b). A similar association between a PSA doubling time of less than 3 months and overall survival and disease-specific survival was found in postprostatectomy patients (D'Amico, 2004b). **It is therefore reasonable to incorporate PSA doubling time into the consideration of whether any salvage strategy is worth applying, whether systemic therapy is more appropriate, and whether such systemic options should be applied early or deferred.**

In what is perhaps the largest series, 5000 patients underwent surgery between 1982 and 2000, with a mean and median follow-up of 6 and 5 years, respectively. Of these patients, 979 (19%) had a biochemical recurrence, and 379 (7.6%) were deemed to have systemic as opposed to local progression along with a minimum of two PSA values to estimate the doubling times; 66 patients (1.3% of the entire group) died of disease. Overall, 6% had a doubling time less than 3 months and 15% less than 6 months. Considering the entire cohort, the 5-, 10-, and 15-year cause-specific survival from the time of biochemical recurrence was 93% (95% CI, 90% to 96%), 73% (95% CI, 66% to 79%), and 55% (95% CI, 41% to 67%). Patients were then stratified into high- and low-risk categories by the Gleason score from the radical prostatectomy specimen, time from surgery to PSA relapse, and PSA doubling time. In an example presented, the median survival of the 23 patients with a PSA doubling time of less than 3 months was 6 years; for patients with a PSA doubling time of less than 3 months, biochemical recurrence within 3 years, and pathologic Gleason score of 8 to 10, the median survival was 3 years (N = 15). This contrasted with a 100% 15-year cause-specific survival for those with a PSA doubling time of 15 months or more and a biochemical recurrence more than 3 years after

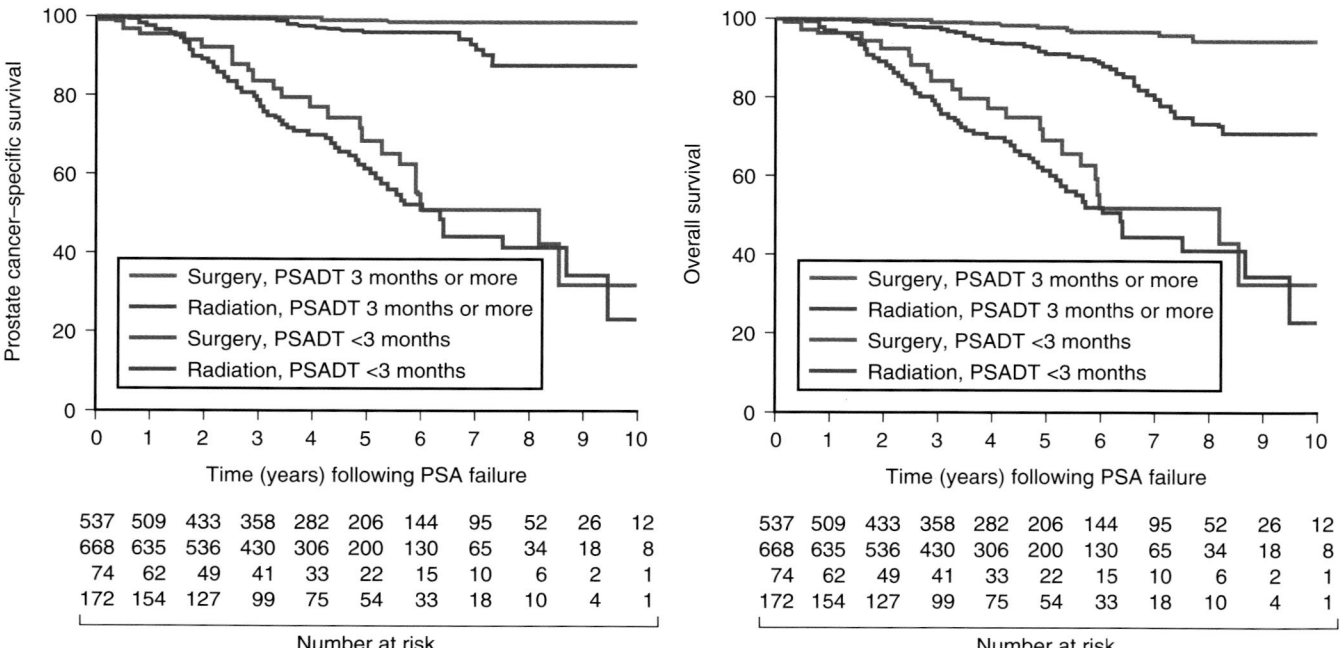

Figure 103–2. PSA doubling time (PSADT) can be used to predict disease-specific *(left)* or all-cause *(right)* mortality for patients who have a rising PSA level. In the model shown, patients are stratified on the basis of primary therapy and PSADT. Such models exist to predict development of radiographic metastases as well and are crucial for rational clinical decision-making and clinical trial design. (From D'Amico AV, Moul JW, Carroll PR, et al: Surrogate end point for prostate cancer–specific mortality after radical prostatectomy or radiation therapy. J Natl Cancer Inst 2003;95:1376-1383.)

surgery. With different combinations of these same variables, cohorts of patients with 15-year survivals ranging from 94% to less than 1% could be derived (Freedland et al, 2005).

A limitation of all of these analyses is that they are retrospective; the imaging modalities used to detect disease were not the same, nor were they performed at fixed intervals; and the number of events on which the models are based is often small. Consequently, the confidence limits around the estimated survival probabilities are large. Despite these limitations, the models and in particular PSA doubling times do provide prognostic information. They do not represent surrogate markers for metastatic progression or survival because they were not derived from prospective randomized comparisons in which a beneficial effect of treatment was shown.

TREATMENT STRATEGIES FOR THE PATIENT WITH A RISING PSA LEVEL
Clinical Considerations for Systemic Treatment

In the past, the treatment aim for patients with a rising PSA level after local therapy was focused on preventing the development of detectable metastases or symptoms of the disease, at a point in the illness when the probability of death from disease exceeds that of other causes. This model is outdated because we now have more effective tools to determine who needs treatment on the basis of the prognosis of the cancer. With the demonstration that chemotherapy can prolong life in patients with castrate metastatic disease, we are now in a position to investigate multimodality approaches in a minimal disease setting with an objective of cure. On the reverse side, it is essential to recognize that treatments given to patients with a low risk of a clinically significant event can be harmful in ways traditionally not assessed in clinical trials. In fact, few studies have systematically and prospectively assessed the compromises in patients' cognitive, functional, and emotional well-being and the overall quality of life, sexual health, or bone integrity. Those studies that have been performed suggest that hormone therapy can be detrimental in all of these areas (Herr and O'Sullivan, 2000; Berruti et al, 2002; Green et al, 2004; Shahinian et al, 2005).

An additional issue that has long been debated is the optimal time at which to begin androgen deprivation therapy as there have been no clinical trials to compare hormones with expectant observation specifically in the population with rising PSA level. Indeed, the American Society of Clinical Oncology Clinical Practice Guidelines argue formally against an "early" treatment policy (Loblaw et al, 2004). In spite of this, **there is a significant body of literature to suggest that early hormone therapy has the potential to confer a survival advantage in selected patients relative to hormones that have been deferred to the point of radiographically evident metastases.** Most are randomized trials of androgen deprivation applied before, during, and after radiation therapy for variable amounts of time from 6 months to continuous, which show improvements in disease-free and overall survival compared with either no hormone therapy or hormone therapy that has been deferred until the time of

metastatic disease (Lawton et al, 2001; Pilepich et al, 2001, 2003; Bolla et al, 2002; D'Amico et al, 2004a). They are summarized in Table 103–2. The caveat is that the patients in the state of localized disease enrolled in these trials may not be directly comparable to those in the clinical state of rising PSA level who have already failed either local or combined modality treatments and are now at risk for development of radiographic metastases as the next point in the natural history.

As a result, **one cannot assume that patients with a rising PSA level will derive the same benefits demonstrated in trials that enrolled patients occupying other clinical states.** Hence, to the strictest and most orthodox adherents of evidence-based medicine, there is only a single true standard of care for these patients: observation. Such practitioners argue that there are no clinical data to demonstrate that hormones applied at biochemical relapse make patients live longer than hormones applied at the time of metastatic disease and that early hormone therapy subjects such patients to a risk of impotence, gynecomastia, depression, weight gain, osteoporosis, fatigue, anemia, and other hormone-related disorders with no proven benefit. This same limitation applies to trials involving non-castrating forms of therapy, such as the Early Prostate Cancer trial. That study enrolled 8113 men with T1-4, M0, any N (though N0 in one study) disease, who were randomized to receive either 150 mg of bicalutamide or placebo in addition to standard care, which was surgery, radiation, or observation. No survival difference between the two arms was seen in the overall population (HR, 1.03; 95% CI, 0.92, 1.15; $P = .582$), although the patients with localized disease on observation appeared to have a survival decrement if they received bicalutamide (HR, 1.23; 95% CI, 1, 1.5; $P = .05$) (Iversen et al, 2004; Wirth et al, 2004). However, the Early Prostate Cancer trial, which was designed to address adjuvant or primary therapy, does not address early treatment of patients who have already biochemically relapsed.

Some practitioners have advocated that androgen deprivation be started at the time of biochemical relapse or at arbitrarily established thresholds, such as when the PSA level reaches a certain point, such as 10 or 20 ng/mL. Such thresholds are based on data indicating that the risk of radiographically evident metastases is higher as the PSA level rises. However, guidelines based on absolute PSA levels do not account for the rate of PSA rise, Gleason score, or pretreatment PSA level, all of which have been shown, as described before, to be important prognosticators of time to metastatic disease, progression-free survival, and overall survival. Indeed, although there are some contemporary models that incorporate the absolute value of the PSA at a given time in predicting metastatic disease (Dotan et al, 2005b) and overall survival (Freedland et al, 2005), many do not. Therefore, contemporary models that help determine an individual patient's risk and timing of metastatic progression and death from disease should be used as the basis of risk assessment in this population. What level of risk in what time frame warrants treatment is a decision to be made after a critical discussion between the patient and his physician.

Once the decision is made to administer treatment, the same controversies relating to hormone therapy in patients with clinical metastases apply. Can intermittent hormones mitigate the side effects of androgen deprivation and improve

Table 103-2. Prospective Randomized Studies of Deferred Versus Early Hormones*

Study	No. of Patients	Clinical Setting	Therapy	Disease-Free Survival, Early vs. Deferred Arms	Survival, Early vs. Deferred Arms
Pilepich, 10-year data updated 2005 (RTOG 85-31) (Pilepich et al, 2005)	977 T1-T3 Some node positive	Adjuvant after RT vs. at relapse	None vs. goserelin indefinitely or to progression of disease	16% vs. 22%; $P = .0052$	49% vs. 39%; $P = .002$
Bolla (EORTC), 5-year data updated 2002 (Bolla et al, 2002)	412 T1-T4	Adjuvant after RT vs. observation	None vs. goserelin adjuvant × 3 yr	40% vs. 74%; $P = .0001$	62% vs. 78%; $P = .0002$
Medical Research Council (1997)	938 T2-T4 or metastasis	Immediate primary therapy vs. deferred	Orchiectomy or LHRH agonist	54% vs. 70% in the M0 arm; $P < .01$	16% vs. 18% in the M0 arm; $P < .001$
Messing et al, 1999, 2003	98 node-positive men after RRP	Early therapy for node-positive disease vs. observation	Goserelin or orchiectomy vs. observation	87.2% vs. 56.9%; $P = .001$	72% vs. 49%; $P = .025$
Early Prostate Cancer Trial, 5.4-year data updated 2004 (Wirth et al, 2004)	8,113 T1-T4, any N (1 trial N0)	Adjuvant therapy after radiation or prostatectomy or observation vs. placebo	Bicalutamide 150 mg	19.7% vs. 21.6% (HR, 0.73; 95% CI, 0.66, 0.80; $P < .0001$)	15.5% vs. 15% (HR, 1.03; 95% CI, 0.92, 1.15; $P = .582$) In one of the three studies: locally advanced disease: HR 0.68 associated with treatment localized disease: HR 1.47 associated with treatment

RT, radiation therapy; RRP, radical retropubic prostatectomy; LHRH, luteinizing hormone–releasing hormone.
*None addresses the population with rising PSA level directly, but use of the results of these trials and the models in Table 103–1 can help the clinician decide whether a given patient would benefit from early hormone therapy.

the period of sensitivity to androgen withdrawal? Is total androgen blockade superior to orchiectomy or gonadotropin-releasing hormone monotherapy? Does high-dose bicalutamide prolong or, as it does in patients with localized disease (Wirth et al, 2004), shorten overall survival? Should bisphosphonates be employed to prevent bone wasting? These questions are presently not answerable and are the source of great discussion and debate.

Clinical Considerations for Local Treatment

Patients who have demonstrable disease in the prostate bed should be considered for salvage radiation therapy or hormone therapy specifically for the purposes of local control, preservation of pelvic functionality, or disease eradication. Whereas there is uncertainty as to when it might occur, patients with local tumor masses are at risk for bowel and urinary obstruction, pain, and bleeding, and the avoidance of this is a critical element of preservation of quality of life. Whether this is achieved best with androgen deprivation alone is uncertain. A consideration is that patients who are anticipated to survive longer than the median duration of androgen deprivation (which generally occurs by 2 years) may fare better with salvage radiation therapy in addition to or instead of hormone therapy. In one analysis of 42 patients with a rising PSA level after prostatectomy with palpable cancer on digital rectal examination, patients who underwent

salvage radiation therapy had a median rate of remaining free of recurrent local disease of 94%, despite the fact that only 27% of patients were free of biochemical progression (MacDonald et al, 2003). In another investigation of 35 patients with clinically evident, locally recurrent disease (by biopsy or physical examination), the 8-year clinical relapse-free survival rate was 80% (vander Kooy et al, 1997). Although patients with clinically evident, locally recurrent disease may have a worse overall prognosis than that of patients with a rising PSA level alone (median survival of 78% versus 96%; $P = .02$ in one study [MacDonald et al, 2004]), salvage radiation therapy may be an important tool in preserving quality of life.

The majority of patients in this clinical state do not have clinically evident disease in conjunction with a rise in PSA level. It is for these patients that the models were developed to help assess the likelihood of durable PSA control after salvage radiation therapy. Although many models have been reported, the recurring factors associated with a favorable outcome are Gleason score of 8 or lower, long PSA doubling time (more than 6 to 12 months, depending on the trial), and positive margin status. An additional factor is the so-called trigger PSA value above which the chance of durable control is reduced. A consensus report from the American Society for Therapeutic Radiology and Oncology recommends a trigger PSA value of 1.5 (Cox, 1999). Other authors have suggested that this threshold is set too high, however. One group found that a PSA level of 1.1 optimally dichotomized patients between responders and nonresponders, with a 3-year progression-free rate of 76% versus 26% (Schild et al, 1994).

proportion of patients who remain in a study without metastatic disease, the proportion who receive a secondary therapy before the endpoint of metastatic disease, and the proportion who develop metastatic disease should be recorded separately. Finally, assessing quality of life in this cohort is essential, particularly when the morbidity of the therapy may outweigh the survival benefit and the therapy is administered early in the disease process. Symptom-induced distress, sense of well-being, and self-assessed quality of life should be evaluated by utilities that yield a quality-adjusted survival time metric or a sensitive measure of symptom frequency, intensity, and duration (Scher et al, 2004).

Phase I/II Versus Phase III Trial Considerations in the Patient with Rising PSA Level

Trials are classified traditionally into one of three phases: phase I trials define a dose and schedule, phase II trials seek evidence of a biologic or antitumor effect, and phase III trials are designed to establish efficacy and safety of the new approach in comparison to an established standard of care or placebo. Trials designed to determine treatment effect are essential to assess whether to commit the human and financial resources necessary to conduct a definitive randomized trial with objective, non–PSA-based, clinical benefit endpoints. The need for informative phase II trials is heightened by an increasing number of agents now available for testing. Eligibility criteria should include patients with a predetermined risk for development of metastatic disease or ideally with the expectation that patients with the same risk profile would be treated in the phase III study (Fazzari et al, 2000).

The evaluation for treatment effects involves three components: (1) defining an intervention-specific post-therapy PSA change could represent a change in the natural history; (2) determining the proportion of treated patients who show the change; and (3) measuring the proportion of patients who do not develop metastatic disease at different fixed time points. Prospective randomized comparisons provide the most definitive evidence of clinical benefit. The "gold standard" endpoint is overall survival. The proportion of patients who are alive at time *x* with no evidence of disease determining disease-free survival is an alternative. Survival-based endpoints are inefficient for patients with a rising PSA level because many patients have long survival times independent of therapy. **A survival-based endpoint is feasible for patients with a high risk of prostate cancer–specific death. As an alternative to survival, the time to the development of objective evidence of disease on an imaging study or on physical examination might be used.** This is because it is the point in the illness where a patient is at risk for development of symptoms and dying of prostate cancer (Pound et al, 1999). Trial design for this population of patients can be exceedingly challenging. A complete discussion of these issues can be found in a consensus report by experts in the field (Scher et al, 2004).

SUMMARY

The widespread implementation of PSA monitoring has created a new disease state that now includes a group of prostate cancer patients second only to those with localized disease. It is unique in that patients are characterized by an absence of symptoms, radiographic findings, or pathologic findings—correlates to determine treatment effects. Whereas there is no definitive standard of care for these patients, risk-stratifying models can be used to distinguish patients who are at high risk for development of metastatic disease or death. PSA doubling time is one of the elements for stratifying patients and may one day be accepted as a true surrogate for survival. These patients should be treated in clinical trials and in the absence of such should be considered for androgen ablative therapies. A wide range of new therapies are available for testing, from traditional cytotoxic drugs to novel agents that target specific pathways. Alternatively, patients whose predicted risk of metastatic disease is low may benefit from local salvage therapies.

KEY POINTS: CLINICAL STATE OF RISING PSA LEVEL

- The clinical state of rising PSA level is the second largest group of prostate cancer patients.

- This clinical state is defined by biochemical failure after definitive local therapy, in the absence of findings of metastatic disease on standard imaging studies.

- The value of the PSA that defines biochemical failure is contingent on the type of primary therapy (surgery versus radiation), the testosterone recovery rate after neoadjuvant or adjuvant hormone therapy, and the sensitivity of the PSA assay used.

- Prognostic models can and should be used to determine the likelihood that a rising PSA level signifies local or systemic recurrence. Therapeutic decision-making should be guided accordingly.

- Prognostic models can and should be used to stratify patients for metastasis-free survival, disease-specific survival, and overall survival. Decisions about the timing and type of systemic therapy applied should be guided accordingly.

- Although there are many different models, most have shown that PSA doubling time and Gleason score are highly prognostic for clinical outcome.

- There is no standard of care for patients who occupy this clinical state. Clinical trials are highly appropriate for these patients and generally use risk-adapted strategies to match patients who face a given clinical risk with treatments of appropriate intensity and mechanism of action. Indirect and highly derivative data suggest that early androgen deprivation may be of benefit to high-risk patients.

- Trial designs for these patients, who have no measurable disease and who face highly variable clinical risks, are unique. Efforts to standardize the elements of these studies are under way and have been published as a consensus report.

SUGGESTED READINGS

Consensus statement: Guidelines for PSA following radiation therapy. Int J Radiat Oncol Biol Phys 1997;37:1035-1041.

D'Amico AV, Moul JW, Carroll PR, et al: Surrogate end point for prostate cancer–specific mortality after radical prostatectomy or radiation therapy. J Natl Cancer Inst 2003;95:1376-1383.

Freedland SJ, Humphreys EB, Mangold LA, et al: Risk of prostate cancer–specific mortality following biochemical recurrence after radical prostatectomy. JAMA 2005;294:433-439.

Scher HI, Eisenberger M, D'Amico AV, et al: Eligibility and outcomes reporting guidelines for clinical trials for patients in the state of a rising PSA: Recommendations from the Prostate-Specific Antigen Working Group. J Clin Oncol 2004;22:537-556.

Hormone Therapy for Prostate Cancer

JOEL B. NELSON, MD

HISTORIC OVERVIEW OF HORMONE THERAPY FOR PROSTATE CANCER

The response of prostate cancer to androgen ablation is among the most reproducible, durable, and profound of any systemic therapy for a solid tumor. The early and frequent descriptions of the immediate relief of bone pain from metastatic prostate cancer after castration do not diminish the marvel of observing this phenomenon firsthand. As is the case with many paradigm-shifting observations, endocrine therapy was based on a simple hypothesis. Described as a "biological syllogism" (Huggins, 1947), the idea had a major premise: *In many instances a malignant prostatic tumor is an overgrowth of adult epithelial cells;* a minor premise: *All known types of adult prostatic epithelium undergo atrophy when androgen hormones are greatly reduced in amount;* and a conclusion: *Therefore, significant improvements should occur in the clinical condition of patients with far advanced prostate cancer subjected to castration.*

It had been known for at least a century that prostatic epithelium undergoes atrophy after castration (Hunter, 1840). The breakthrough in Huggins' hypothesis was the recognition that benign prostatic epithelium and prostate carcinoma are biochemically analogous and respond in a similar fashion to androgen ablation. With emphasis on the importance of basic observations—"The evidence for the facts which represent the premises was obtained entirely in the laboratory" (Huggins, 1944)—studies on acid phosphatase provided the crucial link between benign and malignant prostate cells. Large amounts of acid phosphatase were found in the prostate glands of men and monkeys (Kutscher and Benjamin, 1935), in primary and metastatic prostate cancer (Gutman et al, 1936), and the levels increased with androgen administration (Gutman and Gutman, 1938a). Serum levels of acid phosphatase were increased in men with disseminated prostate cancer (Gutman and Gutman, 1938b; Barringer and Woodard, 1938). With localization of the enzyme to prostatic epithelial cells and primary and metastatic prostatic cancer cells (Gomori, 1939), the stage was set for Charles Huggins, R. E. Stevens, and Clarence V. Hodges to test the hypothesis in men with prostate cancer.

Despite negative results of castration in two men with prostate cancer reported by Young (1936), a series of 21 consecutive patients with locally advanced or metastatic prostate cancer underwent surgical castration at the University of Chicago. "A noticeable improvement occurred in the clinical status of all but three patients," with weight gain, resolution of anemia, and improvement in pain (Huggins et al, 1941). Other reported consequences of castration, a large appetite for food, loss of sexual desire and penile erections, and hot flashes, remain the common side effect profile of androgen ablation therapy today. **Although this report was the first to describe the benefits of androgen ablation in the treatment of prostate cancer, it also created a new disease state, androgen-refractory prostate cancer.**

In considering these "failure cases" (Huggins, 1942), it was found that those with small testes at time of castration had a poor prognosis, the first description of a more ominous prostate cancer arising in the hypogonadal man. After castration, rises in the levels of urinary 17-ketosteroids, a major metabolite of the adrenal gland, led to the hypothesis that adrenal androgens contributed to subsequent disease progression. The first reports of bilateral adrenalectomies for the treatment of hormone-refractory disease (Huggins and Scott, 1945) are described later in a somewhat defensive manner (Scott, 1954), perhaps because of the lack of response and high perioperative mortality. Hypophysectomy and pituitary irradiation (Murphy and Schwippert, 1951) were also investigated. Unfortunately, the benefits of surgical castration were soon equaled by the tenacity and inevitable progression of androgen independence, a state still synonymous with the lethal form of the disease. Even in accepting the Nobel Prize (1966) for this work, Charles Huggins admitted, "Despite regressions of great magnitude, it is obvious that there are many failures of endocrine therapy to control the disease."

Direct ablation of the source of androgen, like surgical castration, is only one of the perturbations of the hypothalamic-pituitary-gonadal axis developed to treat prostate cancer. **The first central inhibition of the axis exploited the potent negative feedback of estrogen on luteinizing hormone (LH) secretion. It is now known that estradiol is a thousand-fold more potent at suppressing LH and follicle-stimulating hormone (FSH) secretion by the pituitary compared with testosterone** (Swerdloff and Walsh, 1973). The effects of estrogen on the male phenotype, namely, regression of androgen-sensitive tissues, have been exploited, historically, to produce the effects of castration without surgical removal of the testes. For example, capons (neutered roosters) were produced by placement of estrogen pellets in the neck of the bird rather than by castration (Scott, 1954). Among the various estrogenic compounds, diethylstilbestrol (DES) has been most widely studied and used. Early studies indicating improved survival in men treated with both surgical castration and continuous DES (Nesbit and Baum, 1951) have not held up under further scrutiny, but the equivalence of DES compared with castration has. Indeed, given the effectiveness of the considerably less expensive estrogenic compounds, it is unfortunate that the associated cardiovascular toxicity has limited their widespread use.

The first isolation of luteinizing hormone–releasing hormone (LHRH) by Andrew Schally and colleagues (1971) required the hypothalami of 165,000 pigs to obtain 800 μg of the 10–amino acid peptide. This Nobel Prize (1977)–winning work led to the development of synthetic LHRH analogs, peptides generated by substituting D–amino acid residues at certain locations in the natural compound, creating both LHRH agonists and LHRH antagonists. **After an initial surge in LH release (and testosterone levels) in response to LHRH agonists, the loss of phasic pituitary stimulation results in plummeting LH levels. In the absence of LH, Leydig cell production of testosterone drops to castrate levels.** Initially, the clinical utility of these agents was hampered by their short half-life, requiring daily injections to maintain suppression of the hypothalamic-pituitary axis. The generation of long-acting depot preparations, lasting several months, has established LHRH agonists as the dominant treatment in hormone therapy for prostate cancer. Recently, direct LHRH antagonists have been developed for clinical use. Lacking agonist action, these agents do not produce the surge in LH and testosterone. It is interesting that both classes of compounds were developed within a few years of the discovery of LHRH, and yet it took decades to develop clinically useful agents.

Moving beyond strategies targeting the hypothalamic-pituitary axis, interruption of ligand-receptor interaction with antiandrogenic compounds is another way to reduce androgen action in prostate cancer. **All antiandrogens inhibit androgen action by binding to the androgen receptor in a** competitive fashion and are classified as steroidal or nonsteroidal. The steroidal antiandrogen cyproterone acetate is a derivative of 17-hydroxyprogesterone and suppresses LH release (and testosterone production) through its central progestational inhibitory effects. Therefore, steroidal antiandrogens block androgen action at the cellular level and also reduce circulating testosterone levels, leading to the classic side effects of hypogonadal state, such as loss of libido and erectile dysfunction. On the other hand, **the nonsteroidal antiandrogens have no antigonadotropic effects and simply block androgen receptors, including those in the hypothalamic-pituitary axis. By blocking the normal inhibiting feedback of testosterone, the antiandrogens produce a paradoxical increase in LH and testosterone.** Although this maintenance of testosterone can preserve potency, the peripheral conversion of this excessive testosterone to estrogen can lead to painful gynecomastia.

MOLECULAR BIOLOGY OF ANDROGEN AXIS

The androgen receptor is a member of the nuclear receptor superfamily that includes the sex steroids (androgen, estrogen, progestin), adrenal steroids (mineralocorticoids, glucocorticoids), thyroid hormones, vitamin D, and retinoids. These receptors act as ligand-inducible transcription factors, meaning they cause transcription of target genes within specific cells after ligands, for example, testosterone, bind to them. **All current forms of androgen deprivation therapy (ADT) function by reducing the ability of androgen to activate the androgen receptor, whether through lowering levels of androgen or by blocking androgen–androgen receptor binding** (Fig. 104–1). Therefore, the androgen receptor is not directly affected by ADT, leading many to hypothesize that hormone-refractory prostate cancer is a result of reactivation of androgen receptor–mediated pathways.

A variety of molecular mechanisms are implicated in this process. First, the promiscuity of the androgen receptor for ligands other than androgen has been widely recognized. Several growth factor peptides, such as epidermal growth factor and insulin-like growth factor 1, can increase androgen receptor transcriptional activity in the absence of androgen (Culig et al, 1994). The cytokine interleukin-6 can activate androgen receptor, as can protein kinases A and C (Nazareth and Weigel, 1996; Lin et al, 2001). If these ligands can reactivate androgen receptor signaling in the absence of androgen, prostate cancer can still progress in the castrate state. Second, the androgen receptor pathway can become hypersensitive through a variety of molecular alterations and be activated by even lower levels of androgen (Linja and Visakorpi, 2004). In androgen-refractory tumors, approximately one third of patients will show evidence of androgen receptor gene amplification, meaning that many more copies of the androgen receptor gene are present (Koivisto et al, 1997; Linja et al, 2001). Mutations of the androgen receptor can also increase receptor activity (Tilley et al, 1996; Gottlieb et al, 1998; Taplin et al, 1999; Marcelli et al, 2000; Balk, 2002). Increased expression of androgen receptor co-regulators, proteins involved in the complex that binds to DNA, has been found in hormone-refractory prostate cancer, suggesting autonomous activation

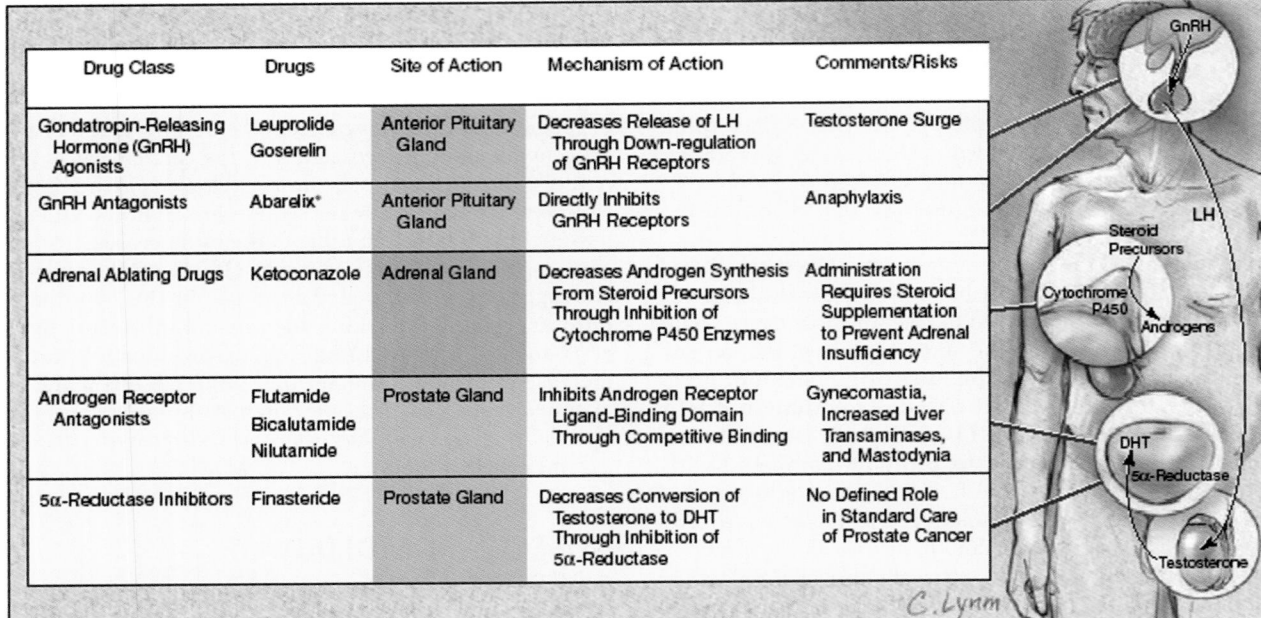

Drug Class	Drugs	Site of Action	Mechanism of Action	Comments/Risks
Gondatropin-Releasing Hormone (GnRH) Agonists	Leuprolide Goserelin	Anterior Pituitary Gland	Decreases Release of LH Through Down-regulation of GnRH Receptors	Testosterone Surge
GnRH Antagonists	Abarelix*	Anterior Pituitary Gland	Directly Inhibits GnRH Receptors	Anaphylaxis
Adrenal Ablating Drugs	Ketoconazole	Adrenal Gland	Decreases Androgen Synthesis From Steroid Precursors Through Inhibition of Cytochrome P450 Enzymes	Administration Requires Steroid Supplementation to Prevent Adrenal Insufficiency
Androgen Receptor Antagonists	Flutamide Bicalutamide Nilutamide	Prostate Gland	Inhibits Androgen Receptor Ligand-Binding Domain Through Competitive Binding	Gynecomastia, Increased Liver Transaminases, and Mastodynia
5α-Reductase Inhibitors	Finasteride	Prostate Gland	Decreases Conversion of Testosterone to DHT Through Inhibition of 5α-Reductase	No Defined Role in Standard Care of Prostate Cancer

Figure 104–1. Hormonal interventions and endocrine axis in prostate cancer. DHT, dihydrotestosterone; LH, luteinizing hormone. *Abarelix is no longer available for new patients in the United States. (From Sharifi N, Gulley JL, Dahut WL: Androgen deprivation therapy for prostate cancer. JAMA 2005;294:238-244.)

of the pathway (Yeh et al, 1999; Fujimoto et al, 2001; Gregory et al, 2001).

Even when prostate cancer progresses despite castrate levels of androgen, it is rarely resistant to androgen action. In 87% of patients with androgen-refractory prostate cancer, the administration of exogenous androgen results in symptomatic tumor flare (Fowler and Whitmore, 1982). Therefore, the term *androgen independent* is not completely precise; such a cancer is no longer dependent on androgen (and thus may be considered independent), but since it remains responsive to androgen, it is not wholly independent of the influence of androgen. The term *androgen refractory* is more precise, indicating a disease state where the cancer is able to progress in the absence of androgen but is definition-neutral about a responsiveness to androgen. Likewise, the word *hormone* is broad and includes the host factors defining the field of endocrinology. Therefore, the term *hormone independent* is vague; as evident from the therapeutic response to secondary hormonal manipulation, estrogens, and glucocorticoids, androgen-refractory prostate cancer is not actually independent of hormone action. The terms *hormone independent* and *hormone refractory* should be reserved for the rare cancers that are completely nonresponsive to any hormone agent (Chang et al, 2005).

SOURCES OF ANDROGEN

Testosterone is the major circulating androgen, with 90% produced by the testes. More than half of testosterone is bound to sex-binding globulin and 40% is bound to albumin. Only 3% of testosterone remains unbound, and this is the functionally active form of the hormone. After passive diffusion through the cell membrane into the cyto-

KEY POINTS: MOLECULAR BIOLOGY OF ANDROGEN AXIS

■ Androgen deprivation is one of the most effective therapies against any solid tumor; unfortunately, with time, almost all prostate cancers will become androgen refractory.

■ All current forms of ADT function by either lowering levels of circulating androgens or blocking the binding of androgen to the androgen receptor.

■ Almost all androgen-refractory prostate cancer remains sensitive to androgen; therefore, ADT should continue in hormone-refractory disease.

plasm, testosterone undergoes conversion to dihydrotestosterone (DHT) through the action of the enzyme 5α-reductase. Although the relative potencies of testosterone and DHT are similar (as defined by the ability to cause half-maximal response in a prostate regrowth model), if the conversion of testosterone to DHT is blocked by the 5α-reductase inhibitor finasteride, 13-fold more testosterone is required for the same effect (Wright et al, 1999). Both testosterone and DHT exert their biologic effects by binding to the androgen receptor in the cytoplasm, promoting the association of androgen receptor co-regulators. The complex then translocates to the nucleus and binds to androgen response elements in the promoter regions of target genes (Heinlein and Chang, 2004).

Androgens produced by the adrenal gland, androstenedione and dehydroepiandrosterone, are stimulated by adrenocorticotropic hormone (ACTH) released by the pituitary gland in

Table 104–1. Major Circulating Androgens

Source	Androgen	Amount Produced per Day (mg)	Relative Potency	Relative Potency/Amount Produced
Testes	Testosterone	6.6	100	15.2
Testes and peripheral tissues	Dihydrotestosterone	0.3	160-190	533-633
Adrenal	Androstenedione	1.4	39	27.9
Adrenal	Dehydroepiandrosterone	29	15	0.5

response to corticotropin-releasing factor. Adrenal androgens do negatively feed back on ACTH secretion; cortisol acts as the feedback signal. **Adrenal androgens are relatively weak compared with testosterone and DHT and are almost entirely bound to albumin** (Table 104–1). Adrenal androgens remain normal in men who have undergone orchiectomy (Walsh and Siiteri, 1975), and adrenal androgens are insufficient to maintain prostatic epithelium in such men.

MECHANISMS OF ANDROGEN AXIS BLOCKADE

There are four therapeutic approaches for androgen axis blockade in current clinical use: ablation of androgen sources, inhibition of androgen synthesis, antiandrogens, and inhibition of LHRH or LH release (Table 104–2).

Ablation of Androgen Sources

Bilateral orchiectomy quickly reduces circulating testosterone levels to less than 50 ng/dL, which, on the basis of this procedure, is considered the castrate range. **Within 24 hours of surgical castration, testosterone levels are reduced by more than 90%** (Maatman et al, 1985). The Veterans Administration Cooperative Urological Research Group (VACURG) conducted a series of large clinical trials, demonstrating the clinical effectiveness of surgical castration in reducing pain and performance status in men with advanced disease (VACURG, 1967a, 1967b; Byar, 1973; Byar and Corle, 1988).

Scrotal (Simple) Orchiectomy

A straightforward outpatient procedure, the simple scrotal orchiectomy can be performed under local anesthesia. At the level of the external ring, each spermatic cord is grasped and infiltrated with 10 mL of 1% lidocaine without epinephrine. This cord block can be performed before the formal skin preparation and draping. After infiltration of the skin overlying the median raphe with 1% lidocaine, a 6- to 8-cm incision is made directly over the median raphe. After the skin incision, electrocautery is used exclusively to transect the other tissue layers, reducing the risk of scrotal hematoma formation. The incision is directed into one hemiscrotum, where the tunica vaginalis is divided and the testicle delivered through the wound. The cord is mobilized above the testicle but below the level of the external ring. The cord structures are divided into two or three equal components, and the cord is ligated with nonabsorbable sutures. I favor double ligation of the proximal cord with two sutures, one of which is a suture ligature. The cord is transected relatively close to the ligatures to limit the amount of nonviable tissue distal to the ligature. Care

Table 104–2. Therapeutic Approaches to Androgen Deprivation Therapy*

Ablation of Androgen Sources	Inhibition of Androgen Synthesis	Antiandrogens	Inhibition of LHRH or LH
Orchiectomy	Aminoglutethimide Ketoconazole	Cyproterone acetate Flutamide Bicalutamide Nilutamide	DES Leuprolide Goserelin Triptorelin Histrelin Cetrorelix Abarelix

DES, diethylstilbestrol; LH, luteinizing hormone; LHRH, luteinizing hormone–releasing hormone.
*Several agents have multiple mechanisms of action.

is taken to examine for any bleeding as a scrotal hematoma after scrotal orchiectomy can be dramatically large. The identical procedure is performed on the contralateral side. The dartos is then reapproximated in the midline, closing each semiscrotal incision at the same time in one layer. The skin is closed with interrupted absorbable sutures. Drains are not used for clean scrotal wounds. Scrotal supports are used for the first several days after surgery, and ice is applied for symptomatic relief.

Subcapsular orchiectomy has been advocated as a technique of ADT that avoids the psychological consequences of an empty scrotum (Desmond et al, 1988). Because this approach relies on the complete removal of all intratesticular tissue and Leydig cells, it is more dependent on technique to achieve ADT than a simple orchiectomy is. In a properly performed operation, however, the hormonal and cancer responses are indistinguishable from those of a simple, complete orchiectomy (Zhang et al, 1996).

Antiandrogens

Cyproterone Acetate

The classic steroidal antiandrogen with direct androgen receptor–blocking effects, cyproterone acetate also rapidly lowers testosterone levels to 70% to 80% through its progestational central inhibition (Jacobi et al, 1980; Goldenberg and Bruchovsky, 1991; Barradell and Faulds, 1994). An oral agent, the recommended dose is 100 mg, two to three times per day. Side effects are consistent with the hypogonadal state and include loss of libido, erectile dysfunction, and lassitude. **Severe cardiovascular complications can occur in up to 10% of patients, limiting the use of cyproterone acetate** (de Voogt et al, 1986). Gynecomastia occurs in less than 20% of men. Rare cases of fulminant hepatotoxicity have been reported

(Parys et al, 1991). It has been used at doses of 50 to 100 mg/day for the treatment of hot flashes (Goldenberg and Bruchovsky, 1991).

Nonsteroidal Antiandrogens

By blocking the testosterone feedback centrally, the nonsteroidal antiandrogens cause LH and testosterone levels to increase. Testosterone levels reach about 1.5 times the normal levels of hormonally intact men (Neri, 1977). This allows antiandrogen activity without inducing hypogonadism; potency, therefore, can be preserved (Brufsky et al, 1997). However, in clinical trials specifically examining erectile functioning and sexual activity in men receiving flutamide monotherapy, long-term preservation of those domains was only 20%, not much different from men undergoing surgical castration (Schröder et al, 2000). The peripheral aromatization of increased testosterone to estradiol has been demonstrated after antiandrogen administration (Knuth et al, 1984), leading to the widely recognized gynecomastia and mastodynia associated with these agents. Gastrointestinal toxicity, most notably diarrhea, is more common with flutamide than with the other nonsteroidal antiandrogens (Han and Nelson, 2000). Liver toxicity, ranging from reversible hepatitis to fulminant hepatic failure, is associated with all nonsteroidal antiandrogens, and periodic monitoring of liver function is required (Lund and Rasmussen, 1988; Wysowski et al, 1993; Dawson et al, 1997; Thole et al, 2004).

Antiandrogen Withdrawal Phenomenon

Patients treated with a combination of an antiandrogen and an LHRH agonist can experience a decline in prostate-specific antigen (PSA) level and even objective responses with the withdrawal of the antiandrogen from the combination. On the basis of this response, it appears that the antiandrogen is actually exerting agonistic activity on prostate cancer cells. This phenomenon, first described with flutamide (Kelly and Scher, 1993), has now been demonstrated with all antiandrogens, including cyproterone acetate as well as DES and progestational agents (Kelly et al, 1997). Declines in PSA level are seen within 4 weeks with flutamide withdrawal and within 6 weeks with bicalutamide and nilutamide withdrawal (Nieh, 1995). **Between 15% and 30% of patients may have declines in PSA level of more than 50% after antiandrogen withdrawal and have a median duration of 3.5 to 5 months** (Scher and Kelly, 1993; Small, 1995). Objective, measurable tumor responses are observed less commonly. Overall survival has not been shown to be increased in those demonstrating the antiandrogen withdrawal phenomenon compared with those who have not (Small, 1995). Clinical trial designs of novel agents must take this phenomenon into consideration, given the possible confounding effects (Scher and Kelly, 1993). Prospective criteria to predict who will demonstrate this response have not been established, but it has been recognized that those with rapid PSA responses after androgen ablation have higher rates of antiandrogen withdrawal phenomenon.

It has been postulated that mutations in the androgen receptor may underlie this phenomenon, allowing the antiandrogen to behave like an activator of the androgen receptor (Taplin et al, 1995). The widely used prostate cancer cell line LNCaP expresses an androgen receptor with a specific point mutation that causes cell proliferation in the presence of hydroxyflutamide; the identical mutation was found in human tumor samples from patients who had remarkable declines in PSA level after antiandrogen withdrawal (Suzuki et al, 1996). Similar point mutations in the androgen receptor have been described for bicalutamide to act as an agonist (Hara et al, 2003); the structural basis of this mutation, resolved by x-ray crystallography, demonstrates the ability of bicalutamide to bind to the mutant androgen receptor in a fashion similar to DHT to the wild-type androgen receptor (Bohl et al, 2005).

Flutamide

A nonsteroidal antiandrogen, flutamide was the first "pure" antiandrogen (Neri et al, 1967). Because of the short half-life (6 hours) of the active metabolite, 2-hydroxyflutamide, this oral agent requires a three-times-a-day dosing schedule, 250 mg per dose. Elimination of hydroxyflutamide is by renal excretion. Unlike with the steroidal antiandrogens, there are no associated side effects of fluid retention or thromboembolism (Delaere and Van Thillo, 1991). In a randomized, double-blind study comparing flutamide with DES (3 mg/day) in metastatic prostate cancer, overall survival was significantly shorter with flutamide (28.5 months) than with DES (43.2 months) (Chang et al, 1996).

Bicalutamide

A nonsteroidal antiandrogen with a long serum half-life (6 days), bicalutamide has a once-per-day dosing schedule and therefore is likely to have better compliance. It is the most potent of the nonsteroidal antiandrogens (Kolvenbag and Nash, 1999) and the best tolerated (Kolvenbag and Blackledge, 1996; Fradet, 2004; Schellhammer and Davis, 2004). The pharmacokinetics of bicalutamide are not affected by age, renal insufficiency, or moderate hepatic impairment (Mahler et al, 1998). The *R* isomer of bicalutamide has about a 30-fold higher binding affinity to the androgen receptor compared with the *S* isomer and functionally processes the antiandrogen activity (Mukherjee et al, 1996). Like the other antiandrogens, bicalutamide is associated with maintenance of serum testosterone levels; in the majority of patients, these remain within the normal range (Denis and Mahler, 1996; Tay et al, 2004).

Bicalutamide as monotherapy has been most extensively studied, and like the inferiority of flutamide monotherapy to DES, bicalutamide monotherapy at a dose of 50 mg/day was inferior to castration in survival of men with metastatic disease (Kaisary et al, 1995; Bales and Chodak, 1996; Kolvenbag and Nash, 1999). **At higher dose of 150 mg/day, however, bicalutamide monotherapy appears to have efficacy equivalent to that of medical or surgical castration** (Tyrrell et al, 1998; Iversen et al, 2000, Anderson, 2003; Iversen, 2004; Wirth et al, 2004, 2005) in men with metastatic or locally advanced disease. In these large phase III studies, bicalutamide monotherapy (150 mg/day) had significantly better quality of life in the domains of sexual interest and physical capacity (Iversen, 2003). There was, however, a high rate of gynecomastia (66.2%) and breast pain (72.8%) (Iversen, 2003). Of more concern, **in men with low-risk, localized prostate cancer, bicalutamide was associated with significantly worse overall survival compared with those on watchful waiting** (see later).

Nilutamide

The plasma half-life of nilutamide is 56 hours, and elimination is by hepatic clearance employing the cytochrome P-450 system. Because steady-state plasma levels are achieved in 14 days on once-per-day dosing (Creaven et al, 1991), dosing recommendations are a single 300-mg daily dose for the first month of treatment followed by a single 150-mg daily dose (Mahler et al, 1998). **About one quarter of men receiving nilutamide therapy will note a delayed adaptation to darkness after exposure to bright illumination** (Creaven et al, 1991). In approximately 1% of patients, nilutamide is also associated with interstitial pneumonitis, which can progress to pulmonary fibrosis (Pfitzenmeyer et al, 1992). The early effects are usually reversible with cessation of nilutamide. In a small study, there was a suggestion of a role for nilutamide as an effective secondary hormonal agent (Desai et al, 2001).

Inhibition of LHRH

LHRH Agonists

The LHRH agonists exploit the desensitization of LHRH receptors in the anterior pituitary after chronic exposure to LHRH, thereby shutting down the production of LH and, ultimately, testosterone. **The clinical utility of the current LHRH agonists is based on the creation of analogs of native LHRH by amino acid substitutions, particularly position 6 in the peptide, increasing their potency and half-lives** (Table 104–3). Pharmacologic depot preparations and osmotic pump devices allow dosing to extend from 28 days to 1 year, respectively (Table 104–4) (Ahmann et al, 1987). **In a review of 24 trials involving more than 6600 patients, survival after therapy with an LHRH agonist was equivalent to that of orchiectomy** (Seidenfeld et al, 2000).

The initial exposure to more potent agonists of LHRH results in a flare of LH and testosterone levels (Waxman et al, 1985). **This phenomenon is seen with all available LHRH preparations and can result in a severe, life-threatening exacerbation of symptoms.** The flare, associated with up to a 10-fold increase in LH, may last 10 to 20 days (Weckerman and Harzmann, 2004). Fortunately, **the co-administration of an antiandrogen functionally blocks the increased levels of testosterone** (Labrie et al, 1987; Kuhn et al, 1989; Schulze and Senge, 1990). Although it had been argued that the administration of the antiandrogen should precede the administration of the LHRH agonist by a week, others have found no differences in PSA levels with the simultaneous administration of both agents (Tsushima et al, 2001). Given the predictable length of the flare phenomenon, co-administration of antiandrogens is required for only 21 to 28 days.

LHRH Antagonists

The LHRH antagonists bind immediately and competitively to the LHRH receptors in the pituitary, reducing LH concentrations by 84% within 24 hours of administration (Weckerman and Harzmann, 2004). **The direct antagonistic activity eliminates the LH and testosterone flare, which is a major therapeutic advantage of these agents; there is no need for antiandrogen co-administration.** Hormonally naive patients with impending spinal cord compression or severe bone pain for whom surgical castration is not appropriate may uniquely benefit from this class of agents; clinical response has been observed with the LHRH antagonist cetrorelix (Gonzalez-Barcena et al, 1995).

In clinical trials of the LHRH antagonist abarelix, testosterone levels dropped quickly, with 34.5%, 60.5%, and 98.1% of men chemically castrate at 2, 4, and 28 days, respectively (Tomera et al, 2001). Compared with an LHRH agonist and an antiandrogen, abarelix monotherapy was equally effective in achieving castrate levels of testosterone (Trachtenberg et al, 2002). Ninety percent of men with symptomatic prostate

Table 104–3. Structure of LHRH and Therapeutic Analogs

Amino acid number	1	2	3	4	5	6	7	8	9	10
Native LHRH	(pyro)Glu-	His-	Trp-	Ser-	Try-	Gly-	Leu-	Arg-	Pro-	Gly-NH$_2$
Leuprolide	(pyro)Glu-	His-	Trp-	Ser-	Try-	D-Leu-	Leu-	Arg-	Pro-	Ethylamide
Goserelin	(pyro)Glu-	His-	Trp-	Ser-	Try-	D-Ser(tBu)-	Leu-	Arg-	Pro-	Gly-NH$_2$
Triptorelin	(pyro)Glu-	His-	Trp-	Ser-	Try-	D-Trp-	Leu-	Arg-	Pro-	Gly-NH$_2$
Histrelin	(pyro)Glu-	His-	Trp-	Ser-	Try-	D-His(Imbzl)-	Leu-	Arg-	Pro-	N-Et-NH$_2$

LHRH, luteinizing hormone–releasing hormone.

Table 104-4. LHRH Agonists Approved for the Treatment of Prostate Cancer

Generic Name	Trade Name	Dosages (mg)	Route of Administration	Dosing Interval (days)
Leuprolide acetate for depot suspension	Lupron Depot	7.5	IM	28
		22.5		84
		30		112
Goserelin acetate implant	Zoladex	3.6	SC	28
		10.8		84
Triptorelin pamoate for injectable suspension	Trelstar Depot	3.75	IM	28
	Trelstar LA	11.25		84
Leuprolide acetate for injectable suspension	Eligard	7.5	SC	28
		22.5		84
		30		112
Leuprolide acetate implant	Viadur	65	SC	365
Histrelin acetate implant	Vantas	50	SC	365

LHRH, luteinizing hormone–releasing hormone.

cancer treated in an open-label fashion had improvements in pain or disease-related problems (Koch et al, 2003).

Many of the first- and second-generation antagonists induced significant histamine-mediated side effects, complications not as often observed in third- and fourth-generation agents (Weckerman and Harzmann, 2004). Nevertheless, **severe allergic reactions can occur, even after previously uneventful treatment** (Koch et al, 2003). Abarelix is approved in the United States for the treatment of advanced prostate cancer in patients who cannot take other hormonal therapies and have refused surgical castration. Given the rare but serious allergic reactions, patients must be monitored for at least 30 minutes after administration.

FSH levels are only partially suppressed by LHRH agonists, and FSH levels are significantly elevated after surgical castration, given the loss of inhibitory feedback. LHRH antagonists reduce both LH and FSH levels. In an androgen-insensitive prostate cancer xenograft model, cetrorelix significantly reduced tumor growth (Lamharzi et al, 1998), suggesting that other factors stimulate tumor growth. In men with disease progression after surgical castration, treatment with abarelix reduced FSH levels by nearly 90% but did not meet criteria for PSA response (Beer et al, 2004a).

Inhibition of Androgen Synthesis

Aminoglutethimide

Aminoglutethimide inhibits the conversion of cholesterol to pregnenolone, an early step in steroidogenesis (Cash et al, 1967; Blankenstein and Bakker, 1985). **Given its inhibition of a very proximal step in adrenal function, aminoglutethimide blocks production of aldosterone and cortisol. As the medical version of a total adrenalectomy, the use of this agent requires replacement of cortisone and fludrocortisone.** Side effects include anorexia, nausea, rash, lethargy, vertigo, hypothyroidism, and nystagmus. Clinical responses have been observed in a subset of patients with androgen-refractory prostate cancer treated with aminoglutethimide plus cortisone (Sanford et al, 1976; Ponder et al, 1984). In the PSA era, 37% of patients had more than a 50% decline in PSA level with treatment by aminoglutethimide (1000 mg/day) and hydrocortisone acetate (40 mg/day), with median response times lasting 9 months (Kruit et al, 2004).

Ketoconazole

An orally active, broad-spectrum azole antifungal agent, ketoconazole interferes with two cytochrome P-450–dependent pathways: inhibition of 14-methylation in the conversion of lanosterol to cholesterol and blockade of 17,20-desmolase, affecting the conversion of C21 to C19 steroids. On the basis of the observation that some patients taking the drug developed gynecomastia, investigations of its effects on steroid synthesis demonstrated loss of adrenal steroid synthesis (Pont et al, 1982b) and testosterone synthesis by Leydig cells (Pont et al, 1982a). The effects were rapid, with testosterone levels dropping to the castrate level within 4 hours of administration in some cases (Trachtenberg et al, 1983); the effects were also immediately reversible, indicating that dosing must be continuous to maintain low testosterone levels (400 mg every 8 hours).

KEY POINTS: MECHANISMS OF ANDROGEN AXIS BLOCKADE

- There are four general forms of ADT: ablation of androgen sources, inhibition of androgen synthesis, antiandrogens, and inhibition of LHRH or LH.

- Bilateral orchiectomy reduces testosterone by 90% within 24 hours of surgery.

- Nonsteroidal antiandrogens cause LH and testosterone levels to increase.

- Serious liver toxicity is a possible side effect of all antiandrogens.

- Antiandrogens can act agonistic on some tumors; antiandrogen withdrawal results in decline of PSA level in 15% to 30% of patients.

- Bicalutamide 150-mg monotherapy appears to have efficacy equivalent to that of medical or surgical castration for locally advanced or metastatic prostate cancer.

- All LHRH agonists induce a testosterone increase on initial exposure. Co-administration of an antiandrogen functionally blocks the effects of testosterone.

Early experience with ketoconazole in the treatment of prostate cancer showed this agent to be tolerable, durable, and effective (Trachtenberg and Pont, 1984) and palliative for those whose first-line androgen ablation therapy had failed (Pont, 1987). **Although it is effective in rapidly bringing testosterone levels into the castrate range, with continuous treatment with ketoconazole in the otherwise hormonally intact individual (no other surgical or chemical ADT), testosterone levels begin to rise and can reach low-normal ranges within 5 months of therapy** (Vanuytsel et al, 1987). Therefore, ketoconazole is currently used for men with androgen-refractory prostate cancer, often as the first or second agent in so-called secondary hormonal manipulation (Small et al, 2004). In addition to gynecomastia (caused by alterations in testosterone-to-estradiol ratios [Pont et al, 1985]), ketoconazole is associated with lethargy, weakness, hepatic dysfunction, visual disturbance, and nausea (Wilkinson and Chodak, 2004; Scholz et al, 2005). Because of the adrenal suppression, ketoconazole is usually given with hydrocortisone (20 mg, twice per day).

RESPONSE TO ANDROGEN BLOCKADE

After the initiation of ADT, most patients with prostate cancer will show some evidence of clinical response; the magnitude and rapidity of that response remain the best predictors of its durability. Assuming that ADT effectively targets the androgen-sensitive population of prostate cancer cells, an incomplete or sluggish response is evidence of a significant androgen-refractory population. Early in the clinical use of PSA as a biomarker of prostate cancer, it was recognized that decline of PSA level could predict response

(Hudson et al, 1989; Aria et al, 1990; Cooper et al, 1990). For example, **patients who had more than an 80% drop of PSA level within 1 month of initiation of ADT had significantly longer disease-free progression rate** (Aria et al, 1990). Likewise, the nadir PSA predicted the progression-free interval (Matzkin et al, 1992; Benaim et al, 2002b), as did pretreatment testosterone levels (Imamoto et al, 2001). **A rise in PSA level, evidence of the emergence of androgen-refractory disease, preceded bone metastatic progression by several months, with a mean lead time of 7.3 months** (Cooper et al, 1990; Miller et al, 1992).

More recent studies of PSA response to ADT have confirmed and amplified those observations. The odds ratio for progression to androgen-refractory disease within 24 months of starting ADT was almost 15 times higher for patients who did not achieve undetectable PSA (Benaim et al, 2002b). For each unit increase in Gleason score, the cumulative hazard of androgen-refractory progression was nearly 70% (Benaim et al, 2002a). In one cohort of Asian men, nadir PSA was the most accurate predictor of disease progression and was independently prognostic of survival; achieving a PSA level of 1.1 ng/mL or less at 6 months after initiation of ADT was the most sensitive and specific predictor of progression at 2 years (Kwak et al, 2002). Considering the kinetics of PSA rise before ADT compared with the rate of PSA decline after ADT also predicted outcome, specifically prostate cancer–specific mortality (D'Amico et al, 2005). If the pre-ADT rise in PSA level was rapid and the decline after ADT was slow, the cancer-specific mortality was significantly worse than for those with slow rises of PSA level before ADT and rapid declines after ADT (D'Amico, 2004b).

Almost without exception, those no longer responding to ADT (androgen refractory) remain on ADT. Therefore, factors influencing survival in that disease state should be considered in this discussion. In most cases, available data are based on pretreatment or post-treatment responses to other systemic treatments (Galsky and Kelly, 2003). Consistently predictive variables (by both univariate and multivariate analysis) of survival in this state include performance status, serum lactate dehydrogenase concentration, serum alkaline phosphatase concentration, hemoglobin level, and PSA response to secondary therapy (Smaletz et al, 2002). The survival of men treated on seven sequential chemotherapy protocols at one institution provided an early experience in developing predictive measures (Kelly et al, 1993). A 50% decline in PSA level in response to chemotherapy was one of the most significant variables predicting survival. A nomogram based on a larger group of patients found the presence of visceral disease, Gleason score, performance status, baseline PSA level, serum lactate dehydrogenase and alkaline phosphatase concentrations, and hemoglobin level useful in modeling prognosis (Smaletz et al, 2002; Halabi et al, 2003).

KEY POINT: RESPONSE TO ANDROGEN BLOCKADE

■ The magnitude and rapidity of the initial response to ADT are strong predictors of the durability of that response.

GENERAL COMPLICATIONS OF ANDROGEN ABLATION
Osteoporosis

The increased number of men being prescribed androgen ablation therapy much earlier in the course of their disease allows the chronic manifestations of the hypogonadal state to emerge. **Widespread androgen ablation therapy applied to an increasingly aging population, already predisposed to loss of bone mineral density, has created an epidemic of osteopenia and osteoporosis.** Fragile bones increase the risk of skeletal fracture. **More than half of men meet the bone mineral density criteria for osteopenia or osteoporosis— defined as more than 2.5 standard deviations below an age-specific reference mean—before the initiation of ADT** (Wei et al, 1999; Conde et al, 2004). The longer a man receives ADT, the greater the risk of fracture (Daniell et al, 2000; Krupski et al, 2004). After 5 years of ADT, 19.4% of men experienced fractures compared with 12.6% of controls (Shahinian et al, 2005); with more than 15 years, cumulative incidence of fractures was 40% compared with 19% of non-castrate controls (Melton et al, 2003a). **It has been estimated that 4 years of ADT will place the average man in the osteopenia range** (Wei et al, 1999). Rarely discussed even 10 years ago, skeletal health is now becoming a major concern of patients and their physicians (Chen et al, 2002).

Treatment of osteoporosis begins with recognition. Bone mineral density of the hip, as measured by dual energy x-ray absorptiometry, should be considered for all men anticipated to be prescribed long-term ADT (Bae and Stein, 2004; Diamond et al, 2004). Smoking cessation, weight-bearing exercise, and vitamin D and calcium can help improve bone mineral density. Prevention of osteoporosis in men receiving ADT has been demonstrated in controlled studies with the bisphosphonate pamidronate (Smith et al, 2001); **bone mineral density actually increased in men receiving ADT with the considerably more potent bisphosphonate zoledronic acid** (Smith et al, 2003a). Bisphosphonate therapy should be considered in any man with evidence of osteopenia or osteoporosis (Bae and Stein, 2004). Transdermal estradiol also increases bone mineral density in men with prostate cancer (Ockrim et al, 2004). Not surprisingly, serum testosterone and estradiol levels were much lower in men receiving LHRH agonists compared with those receiving a nonsteroidal antiandrogen; interestingly, markers of bone turnover were significantly higher in men receiving LHRH agonists compared with those receiving a nonsteroidal antiandrogen, suggesting that nonsteroidal antiandrogens may help maintain bone mineral density (Smith et al, 2003b).

Hot Flashes

For more than 100 years, hot flashes (also called hot flushes, vasomotor symptoms) have been recognized as a side effect of androgen ablation; in 1896, Cabot mentioned "uncomfortable flushes of heat, similar to those experienced by women at the time of menopause" in men undergoing castration for prostatic enlargement (Cabot, 1896; Stearns, 2004). **Described as a subjective feeling of warmth in the upper torso and head followed by objective perspiration, hot flashes are not life-**

threatening but are among the most common side effects of androgen ablation, affecting between half and 80% of patients (Moyad, 2002; Spetz et al, 2003; Nishiyama et al, 2004). Occurring spontaneously and precipitated by changes in body position, ingestion of hot liquids, or changes in environmental temperature, the exact etiology of hot flashes remains undefined. The proposed mechanisms include increases in hypothalamic adrenergic concentrations, alterations in β-endorphins, and involvement of calcitonin gene–related peptides acting on the thermoregulatory center in the hypothalamus (Yuzurihara et al, 2003). Hot flashes generally decrease in both frequency and intensity over time but can persist in some men (Holzbeierlein et al, 2004).

Treatment of hot flashes should be reserved for those who find them bothersome. Just as hot flashes are a consequence of alterations in the hormonal milieu, the mainstay of treatment has been based on efforts to influence that milieu (Kouriefs et al, 2001). In a double-blind, placebo-controlled, cross-over study, the progestational agent megestrol acetate (20 mg, twice per day) significantly reduced the frequency of hot flashes (Loprinzi et al, 1994b). The dose can be reduced to 5 mg twice daily, which may help reduce the appetite-stimulating effect of this agent. The efficacy of cyproterone acetate is based on its progestational effects (Cervenakov et al, 2000). Dosing should start at 50 mg/day and be titrated to 300 mg/day. Estrogenic compounds, such as low-dose DES and transdermal estradiol, appear to be the most effective treatment, with up to 90% partial or complete resolution of symptoms (Miller and Ahmann, 1992; Smith, 1994; Gerber et al, 2000). With estrogen compounds, however, the cure may be worse than the disease; painful gynecomastia and thromboembolic effects have limited the utility of this approach. Clonidine, a centrally acting α agonist that decreases vascular reactivity, has been used with mixed results; in a placebo-controlled study, transdermal clonidine did not significantly decrease hot flashes (Loprinzi et al, 1994a). Antidepressant agents, particularly the selective serotonin reuptake inhibitor venlafaxine (12.5 mg, twice daily), have reduced hot flashes in more than 50% of men (Quella et al, 1999; Loprinzi et al, 2004).

Sexual Dysfunction (Erectile Dysfunction and Loss of Libido)

The effects of ADT on sexual function are profound, as first described by Huggins: "Sexual desire and penile erections were absent in all cases following castration" (Huggins et al, 1941). **Loss of sexual functioning is not inevitable, however; up to 20% of men receiving ADT are able to maintain some sexual activity** (Rousseau et al, 1988; Clark et al, 2001). Specifically, between 10% and 17% of men undergoing ADT can maintain an erection adequate for intercourse (Tomic, 1983; Potosky et al, 2001). **Libido is more severely compromised, with approximately 5% of men maintaining a high level of sexual interest with ADT** (Potosky et al, 2001). Sexual desire is inversely related to the duration of androgen deprivation (Basaria et al, 2002). Loss of penile volume, penile length, nocturnal penile tumescence, and, for those undergoing medical ADT, testicular volume are common (Marumo et al, 1999; Higano, 2003).

Treatment for loss of libido is extremely difficult if not impossible for those receiving ADT. Likewise, medical treatments, such as oral phosphodiesterase type 5 inhibitors, or local treatments, such as intracavernosal injections of alprostadil, can still be effective in selected patients, but patients may decide not to use them during the long term. If there is any fairness in the negative effects of ADT on sexual function, it is the decline in both libido and erectile functioning; despite no erections or desire, the majority of patients have little or no problem with their lack of sexual functioning (Potosky et al, 2001).

Cognitive Function

In both men and women, the hypogonadal state is associated with declines in cognitive functioning (Gouchie, 1991; Sherwin and Tulandi, 1996). Testosterone supplementation improves verbal fluency (Alexander et al, 1998); other controlled studies have found no effect of such supplementation on memory (Sih et al, 1997). In a small study, men with prostate cancer randomized to ADT performed worse in cognitive studies compared with men with prostate cancer under surveillance (Green et al, 2002); the declines were associated with tasks requiring complex information processing (Green et al, 2004). Compared with tests for other cognitive domains, tests for spatial ability uniquely declined in men receiving intermittent hormone therapy (Cherrier et al, 2003). In men receiving neoadjuvant ADT before radiotherapy, cognitive functioning declined (Jenkins et al, 2005). Unfortunately, the studies examining the effects of ADT on cognitive functioning have been small and underpowered.

Not surprisingly, given the many side effects of ADT, quality of life worsens, specifically in men receiving flutamide in addition to castration, compared with placebo, in the domain of emotional functioning (Moinpour et al, 1998). A short course of ADT (36 weeks) increased depression and anxiety scores on formal neuropsychological evaluations (Almeida et al, 2004); major depressive disorder was prevalent in 12.8% of men receiving ADT, 8 times greater than the national rate and 32 times the rate of men older than 65 years (Pirl et al, 2002). Finally, psychological distress accounted for approximately one third of declines in fatigue severity scale in men undergoing ADT (Stone et al, 2000).

Changes in Body Habitus

A loss of muscle mass and increase in percentage of fat body mass are common in men undergoing ADT. After 1 year of ADT, the mean overall weight increases 1.8% to 3.8%, which translates into about 5 pounds for a 200-pound man (Berruti et al, 2002; Smith et al, 2002; Smith, 2004). One study found weight increased a median of 6 kg (13.2 lb), with a range of 3 to 15 kg (6.6 to 33 lb) (Higano et al, 1996). Since lean body mass usually decreases by the same magnitude, the weight gain is largely due to an increase in fat mass. The average increase in fat mass ranges from 9.4% to 23.8% (Berruti, 2002; Smith et al, 2002; Smith, 2004). As noted by Huggins, ADT is associated with an increase in appetite, and low testosterone level is associated with increased insulin level and abdominal girth (Huggins et al, 1941; Seidell et al, 1990).

The Cancer Prevention Studies I and II (1959-1972 and 1982-1996, respectively) were large population-based studies of obesity and the risk of cancer mortality. In both studies, the risk of death from prostate cancer in obese men was 34% (Study I) and 36% (Study II) compared with men of normal weight (Rodriguez et al, 2001; Calle et al, 2003). Furthermore, men older than 65 years who engaged in vigorous exercise more than 3 hours per week had a 70% reduction in prostate cancer–specific death (Giovannucci et al, 2005). The body composition changes associated with ADT may portend a worse prognosis for men with prostate cancer. Regular vigorous exercise may help patients limit the accumulation of fat and even prevent prostate cancer progression.

Gynecomastia

Depending on the agents used in ADT, alterations in breast tissue are common. **Gynecomastia, an increase in breast tissue, and mastodynia, or breast tenderness, may occur together or independently.** Estrogenic compounds, such as DES, induce gynecomastia in 40% of patients (Smith, 1996). Likewise, **the peripheral conversion of testosterone to estradiol associated with the antiandrogens induces gynecomastia at high rates; 66.3% of men taking 150 mg of bicalutamide developed gynecomastia and 72.7% developed mastodynia.**

Prophylactic radiation therapy (10 Gy) has been used to prevent or to reduce painful gynecomastia (Payne et al, 2002) as a result of DES or antiandrogen therapy. Radiation has no benefit once gynecomastia has begun. Liposuction and subcutaneous mastectomy have been used to treat established gynecomastia (Higano, 2003). The selective estrogen receptor modulator tamoxifen has been used to treat mastodynia (Serels and Melmann, 1998).

Anemia

The anemia associated with ADT is normochromic, normocytic, and it is common; 90% of men receiving combined androgen blockade experienced declines in hemoglobin concentration of at least 10% (Strum et al, 1997). Although anemia can be further complicated by tumor growth in the marrow space, compromising hematopoiesis, even men with nonmetastatic prostate cancer experience anemia with ADT (Choo et al, 2005). Unfortunately, anemia (defined as hemoglobin level below 12 g/dL) is associated with a shorter survival in those anemic before initiation of ADT (Beer et al, 2004b). Declines in hemoglobin concentration begin within 1 month of ADT initiation (Strum et al, 1997) and continue for 24 months (Choo et al, 2005). Compensatory mechanisms limit the symptomatic effects of anemia to a small subset (13%) of men (Strum et al, 1997).

The etiology of anemia is thought to be secondary to lack of testosterone stimulation of erythroid precursors and a decrease in erythropoietin production. In an animal model, however, erythropoietin levels increased after ADT (Voegeli et al, 2005). Whatever the etiology, clinically, patients respond to recombinant human erythropoietin. The anemia is reversible after ADT is stopped, but it may take up to a year (Strum et al, 1997).

COMBINATION THERAPY

The advent of nonsurgical, reversible hormone therapy coupled with its profound effects on prostate cancer has led to a broad investigation of the combination of ADT with nearly every other treatment applied to prostate cancer. In some cases, most notably external beam radiotherapy, the combination clearly improves the outcomes; in others, most notably radical prostatectomy, there is no obvious benefit.

With Radical Prostatectomy

In nonrandomized clinical trials of ADT before radical prostatectomy, the effects on the final surgical specimen were dramatic. Positive surgical margin rates fell from nearly 50% in hormonally intact patients to 15% in ADT patients (Lee et al, 1997). Glands with no evidence of malignancy (P0) were not uncommon. There was a nonsignificant trend toward improved biochemical outcome with neoadjuvant ADT. On the basis of these findings and a perception that neoadjuvant ADT reduced blood loss and rendered the procedure easier to perform, randomized prospective studies were performed to compare 3 months of ADT followed by radical retropubic prostatectomy with radical retropubic prostatectomy alone (Witjes et al, 1997; Soloway et al, 2002; Klotz et al, 2003) (Table 104–5). **In both short follow-up (mean, 15 months) and longer follow-up (4 to 7 years), there was no significant difference in PSA progression between the groups** (Fig. 104–2). The lack of improved biochemical recurrence in these three randomized prospective trials with 3 months of neoadjuvant ADT before radical retropubic prostatectomy argues strongly that this combination is not indicated in the treatment of prostate cancer. Studies comparing longer term (8 months) with 3 months of ADT are under way, but at a 3-year interim analysis, there is no difference in biochemical recurrence between the groups (Gleave et al, 2003).

With Radiation Therapy

In contradistinction to the lack of long-term improved cancer-specific progression with the combination of ADT and radical prostatectomy, several phase III clinical trials have shown a benefit with the combination of ADT and external beam radiation in overall survival, cancer-specific survival, and freedom from disease progression. The benefit appears to be in men with locally advanced disease or those with high-grade, high-risk disease.

A phase III study comparing radiation alone with the combination of radiation and orchiectomy in men undergo-

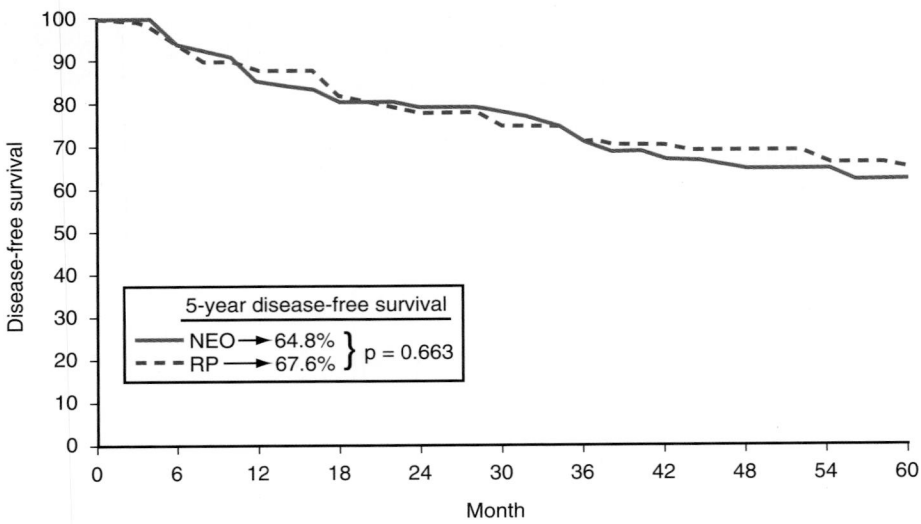

Figure 104–2. Biochemical failure rate in prostatectomy only (RP) and neoadjuvant androgen ablation plus prostatectomy (NEO) groups. (From Soloway MS, Pareek K, Sharifi R, et al: Neoadjuvant androgen ablation before radical prostatectomy in cT2bNxM0 prostate cancer: 5-year results. J Urol 2002;167:112-116.)

Table 104–5. Randomized, Prospective Studies of Neoadjuvant Androgen Deprivation Therapy before Radical Prostatectomy: No Significant Difference in Biochemical (PSA) Progression

Author	Design	N	Follow-up	Biochemical Failure Rate
Schulman et al, 2000	3 months ADT* + RRP	192	4 years	26.4%
	RRP alone	210		32.5%
Soloway et al, 2002	3 months ADT† + RRP	138	5 years	35.2%
	RRP alone	144		32.4%
Aus et al, 2002	3 months ADT‡ + RRP	63	7 years	50.2%
	RRP alone	63		48.5%
Klotz et al, 2003	3 months ADT§ + RRP	112	6 years	37.5%
	RRP alone	101		33.6%

ADT, androgen deprivation therapy; RRP, radical retropubic prostatectomy.
*Goserelin and flutamide.
†Leuprolide and flutamide.
‡Triptorelin.
§Cyproterone acetate.

ing pelvic lymph node dissection was closed because of high frequency of progression in the radiation-only arm (Granfors et al, 1998). A report at 9.3 years of median follow-up, based on 91 patients randomized in this study, demonstrated a significant difference in clinical progression (61% versus 31%), overall mortality (61% versus 38%), and prostate cancer–specific mortality (44% versus 27%) in radiation alone versus radiation and orchiectomy, respectively (Granfors et al, 1998). This observation was supported by another study randomizing men with locally advanced prostate cancer to radiation alone versus radiation combined with goserelin for 3 years (Bolla et al, 1997). The significant disease-free and overall survival advantage of the combination was confirmed at a long-term analysis of the trial (Fig. 104–3) (Bolla et al, 2002). **Clearly, in locally advanced, high-risk disease, the combination of radiation therapy with ADT is certainly better than radiation alone.** A number of trials have been designed to address the timing of ADT (length, neoadjuvant, adjuvant) (Crook et al, 2004); some of the results are summarized in Table 104–6 and in several review articles (D'Amico, 2002; Lawton, 2003). Changes in the dose and field of the external beam radiation therapy make direct study to study comparisons difficult;

unlike the uniformity of radical prostatectomy (complete ablation of the prostate), the optimum radiation technique remains undefined.

Combined Androgen Blockade

Among all the efforts to improve the efficacy of ADT, none has been as widely studied as combinations of the various forms of hormone therapy, particularly if they are mechanistically nonredundant. For example, ablation of the source of androgen (castration) coupled with inhibition of LHRH with DES was one of the first combinations studied clinically to suggest improved survival (Nesbit and Baum, 1951); on closer scrutiny in the first VACURG study, the survival advantage of this combination was lost (Blackard et al, 1973). Likewise, an early experience with an LHRH analogue and an antiandrogen in 30 patients suggested improved outcomes compared with standard treatment (Labrie et al, 1983); **on extensive scrutiny in a meta-analysis of 27 prospective, randomized, international clinical trials of the combination of an antiandrogen with either castration or an LHRH agonist, the collective result was clinically insignificant** (Prostate Cancer Trialists' Collaborative Group, 2000).

Table 104–6. Phase III Randomized, Prospective Trials Comparing Primary Radiation Therapy Alone with a Combination with Androgen Deprivation Therapy

Trial	Treatment Arms	N	5-Year Overall Survival	5-Year Cancer-Specific Survival	5-Year PSA Progression
EORTC 22863 (Bolla et al, 1997, 2002)	Goserelin, 3 years vs.	208	78% vs. 62%	94% vs. 79%	76% vs. 45%
	None	207			
RTOG 85-31 (Pilepich et al, 1997, 2005; Lawton et al, 2001)	Goserelin lifetime adjuvant vs.	477	75% vs. 71%*	91% vs. 87%*	54% vs. 21%
	None until relapse	468			
RTOG 86-10 (Pilepich et al, 2001; Shipley et al, 2002)	Goserelin + flutamide, 4 months (2 months neoadjuvant, 2 months concurrent) vs.	226	72% vs. 68%†	85% vs. 80%	28% vs. 10%
	None	230			
RTOG 92-02 (Hanks et al, 2003)	Goserelin, 2 years adjuvant vs.	761	80% vs. 78.5%‡	91.2% vs. 94.6%	28% vs. 55.5%
	None	753			
DFCI 95096 (D'Amico et al, 2004)	Goserelin or leuprolide + flutamide, 6 months vs.	102	88% vs. 78%		
	None	104			

*The 5-year overall survival and cancer-specific survival differences between the two study arms were not significant. At 10 years of follow-up, however, the combination of adjuvant goserelin and radiation therapy compared with radiation therapy alone was significantly different: for overall survival, 49% versus 39%, respectively; for cancer-specific survival, 84% versus 78%, respectively.
†Difference not significant.
‡Difference not significant.

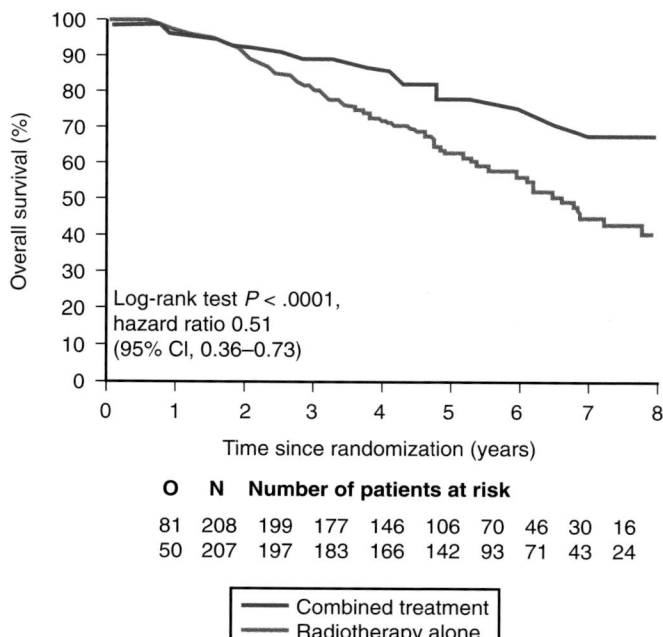

Figure 104–3. Kaplan-Meier estimates of overall survival by treatment group: 3 years of goserelin combined with external beam radiation versus external beam radiotherapy alone for locally advanced prostate cancer. (From Bolla M, Collette L, Blank L, et al: Long-term results with immediate androgen suppression and external irradiation in patients with locally advanced prostate cancer [an EORTC study]: A phase III randomized trial. Lancet 2002;360:103-108.)

The concept of adding an antiandrogen to surgical castration or LHRH agonists is based on the idea that after the elimination of testicular androgens through surgical or medical castration, adrenal androgens still contribute to prostate cancer progression (Labrie et al, 1988; Miyamoto et al, 1998; Miyamoto and Chang, 2000). The fact that serum testosterone concentration does not drop to zero after surgical or medical castration is clear evidence for additional sources of androgen (Geller, 1985; Sandlow et al, 1988). The idea of trying to eliminate all sources of endogenous androgen in treating prostate cancer is not new; bilateral surgical adrenalectomy was performed with failure far outweighing success (Huggins and Scott, 1945). Also referred to, somewhat presumptuously, as total androgen blockade or maximum androgen blockade—as if such a state is actually achieved—combined androgen blockade (CAB) is the more appropriate term. The antiandrogens are nonspecific in blocking the binding of androgens to the androgen receptor: both testicular and adrenal androgens are affected. In concept, the approach is sensible, and some clinical trials showed prolonged survival in patients treated with CAB with advanced prostate cancer compared with standard ADT (Crawford et al, 1989; Dijkman et al, 1997; Denis et al, 1998).

One study showing a survival advantage to CAB compared the antiandrogen flutamide (250 mg, three times per day) in combination with *daily* leuprolide (a formulation not currently used) with placebo plus daily leuprolide in men with metastatic prostate cancer (Crawford et al, 1989). The combination therapy resulted in a significantly longer progression-free survival and longer overall median survival (35.6 months versus 28.3 months) compared with the placebo-treated controls. In a hypothesis-generating subset analysis, the authors found that those with minimal metastatic disease (defined as the absence of metastases in the skull, ribs, long bones, and non-nodal soft tissue) enjoyed the largest survival benefit compared with similarly defined men receiving placebo. Another positive study compared orchiectomy plus the antiandrogen nilutamide with orchiectomy plus placebo (Dijkman et al, 1997); at 8.5 years of follow-up, the CAB group had significantly longer median time to progression (21.2 months versus 14.7 months) and higher overall survival (37 months versus 29.8 months). Finally, a study of depot goserelin combined with flutamide compared with orchiectomy showed increased survival in the CAB group (Denis et al, 1998).

Against the backdrop of these positive studies are a host of randomized trials showing no significant survival advantage for CAB. A landmark randomized clinical trial comparing surgical castration alone with surgical castration combined with flutamide in men with metastatic prostate cancer showed no significant survival advantage for those undergoing CAB (Eisenberger et al, 1998). **Unlike in the previous study, in which an advantage of CAB was suggested for men with minimal metastatic disease, stratification of outcome by disease burden—defined prospectively—was not significant** (Fig. 104–4).

In a clinical trial, when the variability in a possible outcome is large and the effect being studied may be small, confidence in the interpretation of the result is dependent on the size of the study. When several studies testing the same idea in presumably the same population of patients demonstrate both positive and negative results, concerns about the existence of a real treatment effect increase. Such is the case with many of the studies of CAB; in studies consisting of only a few hundred men or based on subset analysis of a larger study, there is a

risk that chance and not an antiandrogen drives the survival outcomes. Those favoring a role of CAB in prostate cancer management point to the selected studies supporting their point of view, only to be met by those against CAB who trot out the negative studies that support their point of view.

KEY POINTS: COMBINATION THERAPY

- There is no evidence that 3 months of neoadjuvant ADT before radical prostatectomy improves biochemical outcomes.

- There is considerable evidence that ADT combined with external beam radiation therapy improves overall survival, cancer-specific survival, and freedom from disease progression. The optimal timing and duration of ADT in this combination remain undefined.

- On the basis of a large meta-analysis of many clinical trials, combined androgen blockade with nonsteroidal antiandrogens provides about a 3% survival benefit at 5 years compared with standard ADT.

Fortunately, the idea of CAB has been extensively studied. Since the early 1980s, 27 randomized studies including 8275 men have been conducted, providing the basis for a meta-analysis comparing CAB with standard ADT (Prostate Cancer Trialists' Collaborative Group, 2000). In these studies, 88% of patients had metastatic disease; the remainder had locally

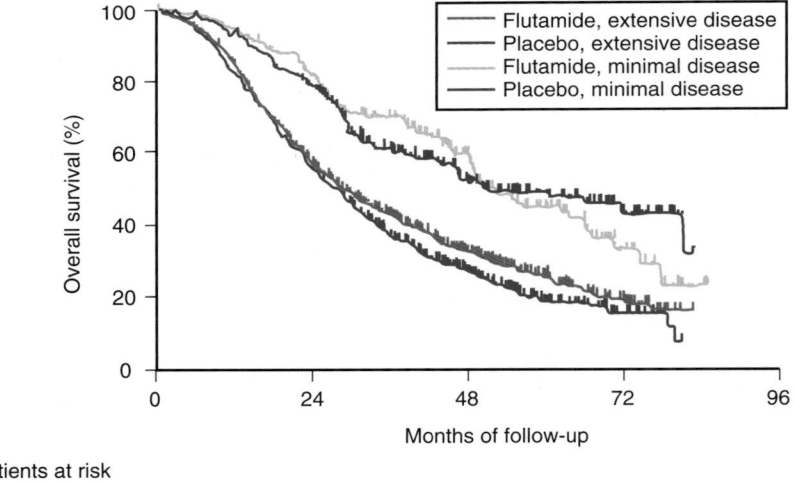

Legend:
- Flutamide, extensive disease
- Placebo, extensive disease
- Flutamide, minimal disease
- Placebo, minimal disease

No. of patients at risk

Flutamide, extensive disease	556	310	120	20	0
Placebo, extensive disease	539	295	101	16	0
Flutamide, minimal disease	141	115	58	13	0
Placebo, minimal disease	146	114	51	16	0

Figure 104–4. Overall survival among eligible patients with follow-up, according to treatment assignment and extent of disease: orchiectomy plus placebo versus orchiectomy plus flutamide. (From Eisenberger MA, Blumenstein BA, Crawford ED, et al: Bilateral orchiectomy with or without flutamide for metastatic prostate cancer. N Engl J Med 1998;339:1036-1042.)

advanced disease. Interestingly, **in studies recording specific cause of death, 20% died of causes other than prostate cancer; not everyone with metastatic prostate cancer died of their disease.** In this meta-analysis, the 5-year survival with CAB was 25.4% compared with 23.4% with standard ADT, a nonsignificant gain in favor of ADT of 1.8% (Fig. 104–5). Studies including the steroidal antiandrogen cyproterone acetate had a slightly worse outcome on the CAB arms (5-year survival, 15.4% versus 18.1% for ADT alone), suggesting increased non–prostate cancer deaths in those receiving cyproterone acetate. **When studies examining the outcomes of the nonsteroidal antiandrogens flutamide and nilutamide were considered independently of those with cyproterone acetate, the 5-year survival improved from 24.7% (standard ADT) to 27.6% for CAB. This 2.9% improvement was significant, but the meta-analysis had a 0% to 5% range of uncertainty about the true size of the benefit.**

TIMING OF THERAPY

The timing of the initiation of ADT, although not as extensively studied as CAB, remains one of the most contested areas of prostate cancer management. The spectrum of opinions ranges from ADT initiation at the first sign of primary prostate cancer failure (early) to ADT initiation only with objective evidence of distant metastatic disease (late) (Reese, 2000; Walsh et al, 2001; Loblaw et al, 2004; Miyamoto et al,

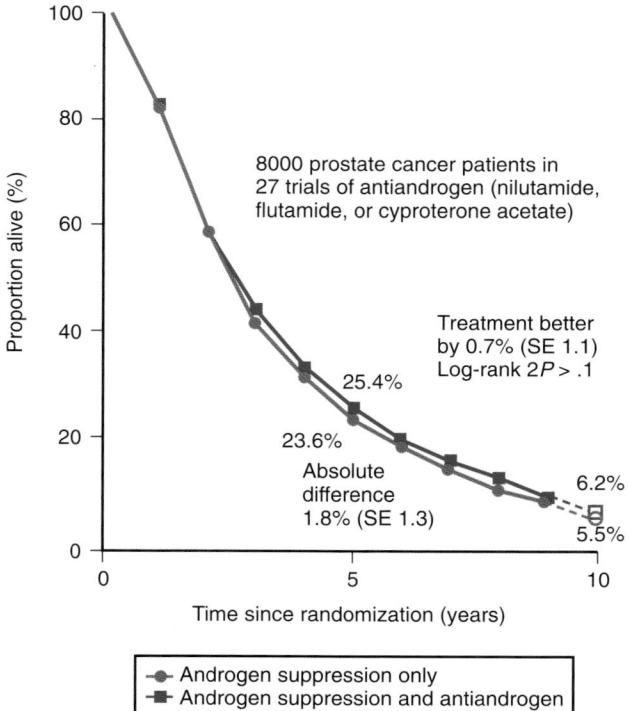

Figure 104–5. Meta-analysis of maximal androgen blockade versus testicular androgen suppression alone in 27 randomized trials and 8275 patients, with an average follow-up of about 5 years. Overall survival curves are for all men irrespective of the antiandrogen used. (From Prostate Cancer Trialists' Collaborative Group: Maximum androgen blockade in advanced prostate cancer: An overview of randomized trials. Lancet 2000;255: 1491-1498.)

2004; Sharifi et al, 2005). Unfortunately, the clinical data to support the various perspectives are limited, and it is not uncommon for proponents of a particular opinion to extrapolate data from one clinical state to another for which data do not exist. **There is no question that early ADT delays biochemical and clinical disease progression, but the effects of early ADT on survival remain unclear.** Likewise, there is no question that ADT is indicated in symptomatic, metastatic disease. For the sake of this discussion, ADT is considered continuous, from initiation until death; intermittent ADT is discussed in a subsequent section. Likewise, this discussion focuses on overall and prostate cancer–specific survival resulting from ADT.

It is useful to consider some facts about ADT and prostate cancer progression. First, the natural history of prostate cancer progression, even in the hormonally intact individual, is protracted. In a cohort of 304 men with a biochemical recurrence after radical prostatectomy, the median time from recurrence to metastasis was 8 years and from metastasis to death, 5 years (Pound et al, 1999). In an update of this study, the median time to prostate cancer–specific mortality had not been reached after 16 years of follow-up (Freedland et al, 2005). Therefore, even in the absence of ADT, men with progressive prostate cancer live for a long time. **Second, despite dramatic clinical responses, men undergoing ADT either will die of a non–prostate cancer cause (estimated at 20% on the basis of the CAB meta-analysis) or will eventually demonstrate evidence of hormone-refractory disease and die of prostate cancer.** In the randomized prospective study of orchiectomy with or without the antiandrogen flutamide, only 7% of men were still alive at 10 years after the initiation of ADT (Tangen et al, 2003). In a study using a 5% national random sample of Medicare beneficiaries undergoing ADT for prostate cancer, the median overall survival after the initiation of ADT was 4.4 years, and after 8 years, only 4.5% of the population was still alive (Krupski et al, 2004). **Third, ADT is not an innocuous therapy. Beyond the quality of life side effects discussed before, in a global sense, men receiving ADT age more rapidly; the natural extension of more rapid aging is earlier death.** Therefore, the long natural history of prostate cancer progression coupled with the inevitability of its progression after ADT initiation in a population with a growing risk of death from all causes should temper enthusiasm to indiscriminately apply this therapy to all men with progressive prostate cancer.

The questions about the timing of ADT are not new. In **1973, the results of a large (more than 1900 men) study performed in the Veterans Administration of early versus late hormone therapy were reported** (Byar, 1973). **In men with metastatic disease, death from prostate cancer occurred in 48% of men treated early versus 47% of men treated late. In men with locally advanced disease, death from prostate cancer occurred in 14% of men treated early versus 17% of patients treated late.** The lack of a survival benefit in men treated early coupled with the known side effects of therapy supports the recommendation for institution of hormone therapy in men with symptomatic disease. Several randomized studies have since applied ADT at different times in the natural history of prostate cancer; the results of those studies must be considered within the context of when ADT is used and the circumstances of the study.

Immediate Versus Delayed ADT in Clinically Localized Disease

In the bicalutamide Early Prostate Cancer program, men were randomized to 150 mg of bicalutamide or placebo in addition to standard for care (See, 2003). Endpoints of these trials included overall survival, progression-free survival, and tolerability. **In the subset of men with clinically localized disease, the overall survival was significantly *worse* in those undergoing ADT with 150 mg of bicalutamide compared with placebo** (Iversen, 2004). No specific cause for this decline in overall survival with ADT was identified, but it appeared to be the result of increased deaths from non–prostate cancer causes for those receiving bicalutamide. It is unlikely that the excessive death rate in the bicalutamide arm in those with clinically localized disease will lose significance with longer follow-up.

This observation is important for several reasons. First, it resoundingly answers the claim that "ADT can't hurt, so why not use it early?" **In this study, men *without* ADT had significantly better survival.** Second, when ADT is applied in situations in which the risk of death from prostate cancer is already low, demonstration of a prostate cancer–specific survival benefit from that therapy will be difficult. If ADT itself increases overall mortality compared with no ADT, a demonstration of a prostate cancer–specific benefit will be nearly impossible. Third, men with localized, low-risk prostate cancer should not be treated with ADT without first being informed of these preliminary results. Avoidance of prostate cancer progression and death may come at the expense of a higher overall death rate. These data support the hypothesis that the more rapid aging associated with ADT will bring men with low-risk prostate cancer more quickly to their deaths.

Immediate Versus Delayed ADT in Lymph Node Metastatic Prostate Cancer

A randomized prospective study of immediate ADT compared with delayed ADT was performed in men with histologic evidence of metastatic prostate cancer in regional lymph nodes after radical prostatectomy by the Eastern Cooperative Oncology Group (ECOG). At the time of the initial report, **at 7.1 years of median follow-up, overall survival significantly (*P* < .02) favored the immediate ADT group compared with the delayed ADT group. In the immediate ADT group, only 3 of the 7 deaths were due to prostate cancer compared with 16 of the 18 cancer-specific deaths in the delayed ADT group** (Messing et al, 1999). In an updated report, median overall survival was significantly longer in the immediate ADT group compared with the delayed ADT group, 13.9 years versus 11.3 years, respectively (Fig. 104–6) (Messing et al, 2003b, 2004). Of 18 men in the immediate ADT group, 8 died of prostate cancer compared with 25 of 28 in the delayed ADT group. Given the previous discussion of the increased non–prostate cancer death rate with bicalutamide 150 mg, it is interesting that there have been proportionally more non–prostate cancer deaths in the immediate ADT group (55%) than in the delayed ADT group (11%). Nevertheless, **on the basis of this randomized, prospective trial, there appears to be a benefit to immediate ADT in those with histologic evidence of lymph node metastases at the time of radical prostatectomy.**

There have been several criticisms of this study (Eisenberger and Walsh, 1999). First, the study was designed to enroll 240 patients, yet only 100 were enrolled. When a large difference in outcome is found in a small study, there is a risk of a type I error (assuming a treatment has an effect when in reality it

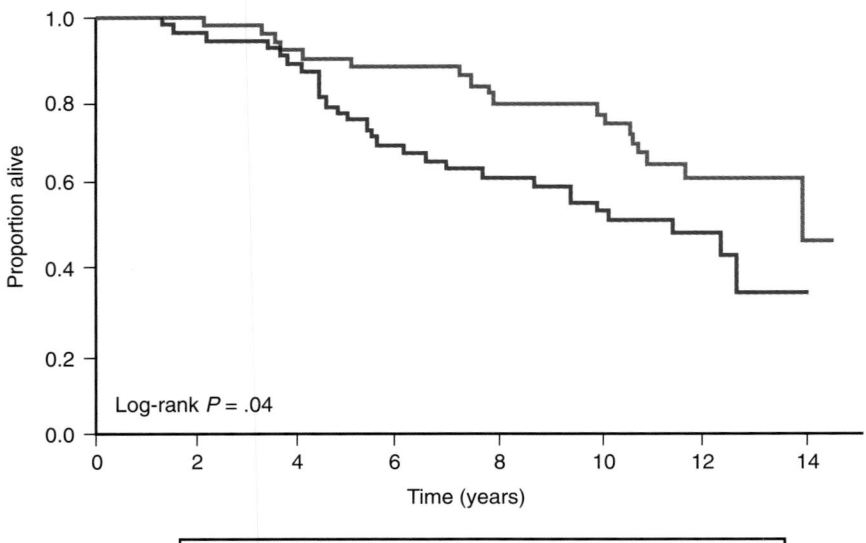

Treatment arm	Total	Dead	Alive	Median
—— Hormone	47	18	29	13.9 yrs
— Observation	51	28	23	11.3 yrs

Figure 104–6. Long-term overall survival of men randomized to immediate hormone therapy compared with observation after radical prostatectomy with pelvic lymphadenectomy in men with node-positive prostate cancer: At median 11.9-year follow-up, overall survival was 64% (30 of 47) in the immediate hormone therapy group compared with 45% (23 of 51) in the observation group (*P* = .04, log-rank). (Messing EM, Manola J, Yao J, et al: Immediate versus deferred androgen deprivation treatment in patients with node-positive prostate cancer after radical prostatectomy and pelvic lymphadenectomy. Lancet Oncol 2006;7: 472-479.)

does not). There was no evidence for an imbalanced randomization, but unrecognized prognostic factors can influence outcomes in smaller studies. Second, Gleason grading was not centralized, and the absence of a correlation between histologic grade and survival suggests that an imbalance may exist. This concern was partially addressed by a central pathologic review in a blinded fashion of a subset (51%) of the initial specimens. On the basis of this reanalysis, there was no significant difference in outcomes from the original report. Third, those receiving delayed ADT experienced disease progression and death from prostate cancer that was much more rapid than would have been expected from contemporary series of N+ patients (Zincke et al, 1992; Cadeddu et al, 1997). **In the absence of an ADT-only arm in this study, the benefits of primary treatment in this study are unknown.**

The magnitude of the difference observed in this study has not been seen in larger similar—but not identical—populations of patients. **A European Organization for the Research and Treatment of Cancer (EORTC) trial of immediate versus delayed ADT in pN1-3, M0 disease without local treatment of the primary tumor was performed in 302 patients, of whom 115 were randomized to delayed ADT and 119 to immediate ADT** (Schröder et al, 2004). **At a median follow-up of 8.7 years, there was no significant difference in overall survival (38.3% versus 39.5%) or prostate cancer–specific death (76.1 % versus 76.2%) between delayed ADT and immediate ADT, respectively.** Median survival was 7.8 years (95% confidence interval [CI], 6.3 to 8.9) for immediate ADT and 6.2 years (95% CI, 5.4 to 7.6) for delayed ADT. Considering the percentage 4-year survival, there was a 23% increase in the hazard ratio (HR) of death in the group randomized to delayed treatment (HR, 1.23; 95% CI, 0.88 to 1.71). As articulated by the authors of this study, "those results remain compatible with a 12% benefit for the deferred treatment and up to a 71% detriment for the same treatment group compared to immediate treatment. Therefore, the results can neither prove a statistically significant difference . . . nor prove inferiority" (Schröder et al, 2004).

There are significant differences between the ECOG and EORTC studies of immediate ADT in N+ disease. In the EORTC study, 66% had T3 disease compared with 95% with T2 disease in the ECOG study. In the ECOG study, the primary tumor was removed, a local treatment that is supported by the benefit observed in the combination of primary radiation therapy and 3 years of ADT (Bolla et al, 2002). In the EORTC study, median difference of time on ADT between the two arms was 2.5 years. In the absence of a significant survival advantage, delayed ADT had a 1.6-year worse median survival yet a 1.8-year benefit of being free of ADT. Perhaps **the best use of these data is to provide patients with the average quantity of life gained by immediate ADT versus the average quality of life gained by delayed ADT.**

Immediate Versus Delayed ADT in Locally Advanced or Asymptomatic Metastatic Disease

A trial of immediate versus delayed ADT in men with locally advanced or asymptomatic prostate cancer was conducted by the Medical Research Council (MRC) Prostate Cancer Working Party Investigators Group (1997). A total of 934 men were included (500 M0, 261 M1, and 173 MX), with 469 randomized to immediate ADT and 465 randomized to delayed ADT. **As originally reported, there was a significant survival advantage in the M0 group; on longer follow-up. the overall survival advantage is not significant** (Fig. 104–7) (Kirk, 2004). Overall, men in the delayed ADT arm died significantly more often from prostate cancer and had significantly more

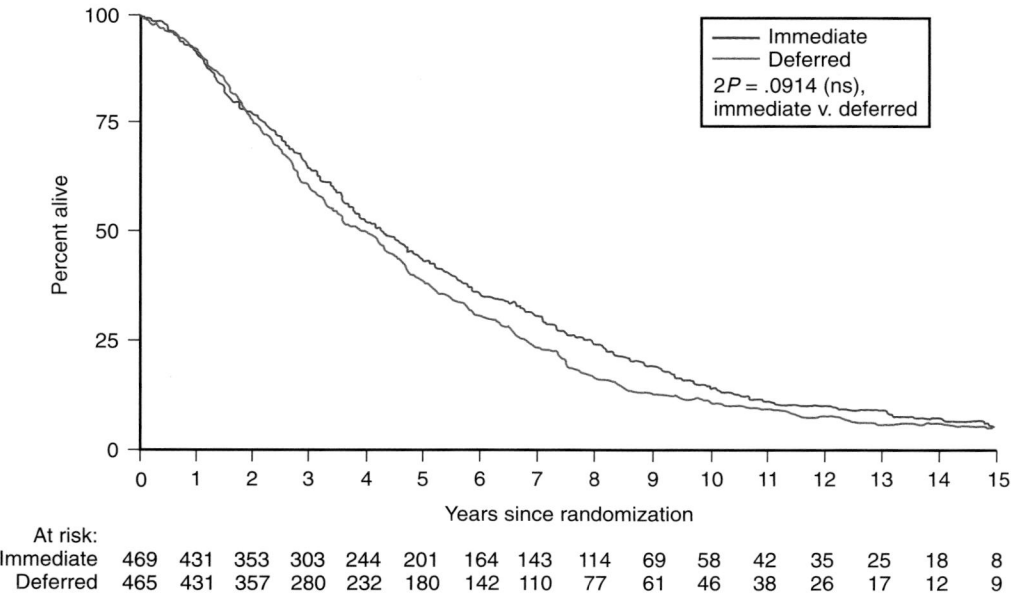

TIME TO DEATH FROM ANY CAUSE: ALL PATIENTS, BY RANDOMIZATION GROUP

Legend:
— Immediate
— Deferred
2P = .0914 (ns), immediate v. deferred

At risk:

	0	1	2	3	4	5	6	7	8	9	10	11	12	13	14	15
Immediate	469	431	353	303	244	201	164	143	114	69	58	42	35	25	18	8
Deferred	465	431	357	280	232	180	142	110	77	61	46	38	26	17	12	9

Figure 104–7. MCR trial of immediate versus deferred hormone treatment: overall survival, not significant. (From Kirk D: Timing and choice of androgen ablation. Prostate Cancer Prostatic Dis 2004;7:217-222.)

symptoms related to disease progression. On the basis of these data, the benefits of immediate ADT would seem to support its use.

There have been many criticisms of the MRC trial. First, 6% of men (29 of 465) in the delayed ADT arm "died from prostate cancer before treatment could be started," meaning they died without ever receiving ADT. Delayed ADT is not the same as no ADT. Second, 173 subjects included in the study were not staged (MX). When nearly one in five men could have been incorrectly randomized, the impact on the study's outcome may be significant. Third, almost 10% of men in the delayed group were treated only when they had developed spinal cord compression or pathologic fractures. The emergency implementation of hormone therapy is a rare event in patients observed closely; it certainly should not occur in 10% of patients. Finally, the lack of a standardized follow-up protocol—"follow-up and management were otherwise according to the participating clinician's normal practice"—may provide meaningful "real-world" results but is likely to introduce major deviations from rigorous clinical trial design.

Since the majority of men in the MRC study have died (92.5% in the immediate ADT group, 93.6% in the delayed ADT group), the data are now mature and unlikely to change significantly in the future (Kirk, 2004). **Time to death from prostate cancer remains significantly in favor of the immediate ADT group ($P = .019$), whereas time to death from any cause is not significantly different between the groups ($P = .0914$).** The total difference in prostate cancer–specific deaths was 46 men: 241 died of prostate cancer in the immediate ADT arm, 287 in the delayed ADT arm (Kirk, 2004); the impact of the 29 men in the delayed ADT arm who never received ADT on this result is unknown but could reasonably be considered significant. Unlike the increased overall mortality for immediate ADT found in the Early Prostate Cancer bicalutamide 150 mg study for localized, low-risk disease, no similar increase was observed in immediate ADT in the MRC study of a higher risk cohort.

Immediate Versus Delayed ADT: Integrating the Data

With the emerging data from ongoing clinical trials and the recently published results of new studies, it is possible to consider the timing of ADT from the perspective of the natural history of the disease.

1. **There is no overall survival benefit to immediate ADT in low-risk, localized prostate cancer.** In fact, from the perspective of overall survival, men treated in this fashion do significantly worse than do those spared ADT in this setting.
2. **In locally advanced, asymptomatic metastatic and clinically present but undefined prostate cancer treated in a community setting with limited follow-up, immediate ADT results in significantly better prostate cancer–specific survival but not better overall survival.**
3. **In N+ disease without primary treatment, there is no significant advantage to immediate ADT, although**

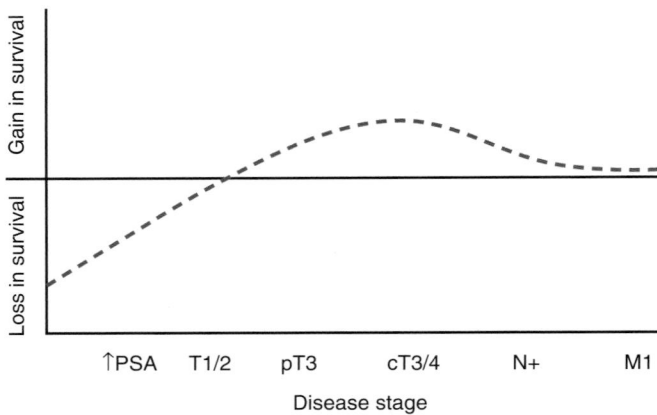

Figure 104–8. On the basis of available clinical trial data, the hypothetical gain or loss in overall survival based on the time in the natural history of the disease that ADT is instituted, as demonstrated by the dotted line. (Concept and figure provided by P. Iversen.)

on balance, there is a 1.6-year median survival advantage. In N+ disease with radical prostatectomy, there is a significant survival advantage favoring immediate ADT, with a 2.6-year difference in median overall survival.

In Figure 104-8, conceived and developed by P. Iversen, one can see the relative gain and loss in survival from adjuvant ADT based on the stage of the disease. In low-risk disease, the toxicity of ADT exceeds any prostate cancer–specific benefit, so there is an overall net loss in overall survival. For locally advanced disease, particularly in combination with local treatment directed at the primary tumor, ADT provides a net gain in survival. As the disease progresses, the inevitability of hormone-refractory progression and prostate cancer–specific death limits the magnitude of the nonetheless real benefit of ADT. **Since life is more than simply survival, discussions about ADT should include the expected impact on quality of life.**

KEY POINTS: TIMING OF THERAPY

- The natural history of prostate cancer progression is protracted. Many men with evidence of disease will never require ADT.

- The use of ADT in low-risk, localized prostate cancer significantly increases overall (non–prostate cancer) mortality.

- In lymph node metastatic prostate cancer, ADT improves overall survival if the primary tumor is removed but has no significant effect if the primary tumor is not removed.

- On long-term follow-up, there was no overall survival advantage associated with early ADT compared with deferred ADT in men with metastatic or locally advanced prostate cancer.

ECONOMIC CONSIDERATIONS

In the United States, the cost of drug therapy for ADT (LHRH agonists) in the Medicare Program was $761,000,000 in 1997 (Holtgrewe et al, 2000). Considering the entire expenditures for all urologic services from the Medicare Program to urologists as $1.1 billion (excluding LHRH agonists), the cost of these agents was 64% of the total costs of all other urologic professional services. This expense is not unique to the United States. In 1997, the annual cost of these agents in Sweden was $17,000,000, and in Germany, the annual cost was $142,000,000. In a study of 96 men undergoing ADT for prostate cancer during a 10-year period, the cost of LHRH agonists ranged from more than 10.7 to 13.5 times the cost of bilateral orchiectomy, and the cost of CAB was 17.3 to 20.9 times greater (Mariani et al, 2001). **Clearly, the cost of ADT, as it is currently being delivered, is extraordinary.**

Although DES is associated with increased cardiovascular toxicity, from a strictly cost point of view, it is the cheapest form of ADT, particularly at the dose of 1 mg/day, with no prophylactic breast irradiation (Mariani et al, 2001). **There is no significant survival advantage of LHRH agonists over orchiectomy, so from an economic perspective, LHRH agonists would be more cost effective than orchiectomy only if a patient lived for a few months after initiation of ADT. The 3-month formulations of leuprolide acetate and goserelin become more expensive than orchiectomy on the administration of a second 3-month depot;** specifically, the break-even rate is 4.2 months for leuprolide acetate and 5.3 months for goserelin compared with orchiectomy (Mariani et al, 2001).

Combined androgen blockade is the most expensive form of ADT. Although there is no significant benefit of CAB over orchiectomy alone (Eisenberger et al, 1998), some patients may experience a large benefit. Assuming a cost-effectiveness threshold of $100,000—meaning the expense of CAB minus the expense of orchiectomy—for each quality of life year, CAB would need to decrease the risk of disease progression by 20% compared with orchiectomy to be considered cost-effective (Seidenfeld et al, 1999). **The earlier that medical ADT is initiated, the more expensive it becomes. In models examining the cost-effectiveness, ADT was most cost-effective if it was initiated after patients became symptomatic from prostate cancer metastases** (Bayoumi et al, 2000). In this model, LHRH agonists, nonsteroidal antiandrogens, and CAB had higher costs and lower quality-adjusted survival than did orchiectomy.

If orchiectomy is just as effective and so much cheaper, why is it not used more widely? In two studies that offered orchiectomy versus medical therapy for ADT, 70% of patients chose medical therapy (Iversen et al, 1998). Clearly, patients (and physicians) choose medical ADT for reasons other than efficacy or expense. Indeed, the use of ADT in all stages of prostate cancer has increased significantly between 1989 and 2001; for example, primary ADT rose from 32.8% to 48.2% in men with high-risk disease (Cooperberg et al, 2003). **Avoidance of the largely psychological quality of life issues unique to orchiectomy (disfigurement, permanence) comes at an expense that would seem disproportionate to the risk, and yet society has chosen to accept the expense.** It is not known how much longer we can afford to ignore the cost of ADT; recent adjustments to the reimbursement from the Medicare Program for the administration of LHRH agonists suggest the scrutiny has begun.

THE FUTURE OF HORMONE THERAPY
Intermittent ADT

The use of intermittent ADT is being studied in large randomized clinical trials, based on two complementary ideas. First, in preclinical animal models (Shionogi breast cancer tumor, LNCaP prostate cancer tumor), exposure to androgen deprivation on an intermittent rather than continuous basis lengthened the time to the emergence of androgen-refractory cancer growth (Akakura et al, 1993; Sato et al, 1996). Since androgen-refractory prostate cancer is synonymous with lethal prostate cancer, any manipulation of the hormonal milieu that can delay progression into this state would be welcomed. Second, many patients (and their physicians) have increasingly questioned the real benefit of continuous ADT, given the profound and often debilitating side effects associated with its use. With readily reversible ADT, recovery of normal testosterone levels should occur when androgen ablation is stopped. In theory, the quality of life side effects of ADT with intermittent treatment should be some fraction of those side effects when ADT is used continuously.

There are several reasons to await the results of the randomized trials of intermittent ADT before it is adopted as a standard treatment of advanced prostate cancer. There is no evidence that cycling androgen levels in men with prostate cancer will delay the emergence of androgen-refractory disease. Indeed, preclinical models using the Shionogi tumor strongly predicted that neoadjuvant ADT would benefit men undergoing radical prostatectomy (Gleave et al, 1997), and yet the clinical trials resoundingly rejected this hypothesis. One could make a compelling argument why return of normal androgen levels associated with intermittent ADT would actually accelerate cancer progression, recalling the 87% tumor flare associated with testosterone administration (Fowler and Whitmore, 1982) or the exacerbations of symptoms with initial use of LHRH agonists (Waxman et al, 1985). Quality of life should improve, but at what cost? The studies of intermittent ADT may bring the balance between quantity and quality of life into fuller view, but not necessarily into clearer focus.

Androgen Receptor Pathway–Focused Therapy

All current forms of ADT target androgen or its interaction with the androgen receptor. There is growing evidence that hormone-refractory prostate cancer is a disease associated with an active androgen receptor pathway (see earlier). Since the attempts to block all androgen, through castration and LHRH agonists coupled with antiandrogens, have met with limited success in increasing survival, it seems unlikely that better ligand-targeted therapies will be an improvement. Targeting the androgen receptor pathway—independent of the activating ligands—is more promising.

SUGGESTED READINGS

Bolla M, Collette L, Blank L, et al: Long-term results with immediate andro-gen suppression and external irradiation in patients with locally advanced prostate cancer (an EORTC study): A phase III randomized trial. Lancet 2002;360:103-108.

Huggins C, Stevens RE, Hodges CV: Studies on prostatic cancer: II. The effects of castration on advanced carcinoma of the prostate gland. Arch Surg 1941;43:209-223.

Messing EM, Manola J, Sarosdy M, et al: Immediate hormonal therapy compared with observation after radical prostatectomy and pelvic lymphadenectomy in men with node-positive prostate cancer. N Engl J Med 1999;341:1781-1788.

Prostate Cancer Trialists' Collaborative Group: Maximum androgen blockade in advanced prostate cancer: An overview of randomized trials. Lancet 2000;255:1491-1498.

Soloway MS, Pareek K, Sharifi R, et al: Neoadjuvant androgen ablation before radical prostatectomy in cT2bNxM0 prostate cancer: 5-year results. J Urol 2002;167:112-116.

105 Treatment of Hormone-Refractory Prostate Cancer

MARIO A. EISENBERGER, MD • MICHAEL CARDUCCI, MD

During the past several decades, endocrine manipulations developed to inhibit hormone-dependent prostate cancer growth and differentiation have constituted the basic strategy for the systemic control of prostate cancer. **Suppression of gonadal testosterone is the central principle of androgen deprivation therapy (ADT), and this represents one of the most effective systemic palliative treatments known for solid tumors. Although it is extremely effective initially, virtually all patients eventually develop clinical evidence of resistance to treatment. The outcomes with endocrine treatment have not changed significantly during the past few decades. Progression-free and overall survival figures of patients with metastatic disease with various methods of ADT have ranged from 12 to 20 months and 24 to 36 months, respectively** (Byar, 1980; Leuprolide Study Group, 1984; Eisenberger et al, 1986, 1998; Turkes et al, 1987; Crawford et al, 1989; Denis et al, 1993; McLeod, 1995). **Whereas somewhat longer survival times are reported in more recent studies, this is most likely due to a "lead time effect" observed in contemporary populations of patients. The development of hormone resistance is virtually a universal issue that affects all patients treated with ADT. Undoubtedly, further improvement in the outcome of patients with metastatic disease rests on the discovery of nonhormonal approaches that can effectively control the growth of the disease.**

During recent years, clinical investigations testing nonhormonal approaches have shown that systemic chemotherapy improves survival and quality of life of patients with hormone-refractory disease. Advances in the understanding of the biology of prostate cancer and characterization of key molecular pathways have added an important new dimension for treatment and the opportunity to design disease-specific targeted treatment approaches. Evolving data suggest that targeted approaches may play an important role in treatment of prostate cancer and other malignant neoplasms that may improve the outcome of our patients.

Progress in cell and molecular biology during the past decades has also enhanced our understanding of the mechanisms involved in the progression of prostate cancer, and this may provide the opportunity for rational planning of the appropriate timing of systemic therapeutic intervention with the objective of preventing or delaying progression of disease to lethal proportions. **Cancer cells demonstrating the androgen-independent phenotype can be identified during early stages of development of prostate cancer. Somatic alterations of the androgen receptor are frequently observed in patients with evidence of disease progression after androgen deprivation. It has been demonstrated that during progression, in the absence of androgens, a molecularly altered androgen receptor can still undergo ligand-dependent activation by other hormones such as estrogens and progestational agents and non–ligand-dependent activation by growth factors and cytokines** (Feldman and Feldman, 2001; Gelmann, 2002; Nelson et al, 2003). **The observation that the androgen receptor can still be activated even after long-term gonadal ablation suggests that it continues to play an important role in prostate cancer growth and may indeed be a reasonable target for treatment in patients with androgen-independent disease.**

In the presence of androgens, prostatic cancer growth is based on a cell proliferation rate that exceeds that of cell death (Isaacs et al, 1992). Androgen ablation affects primarily the cell death rate by inducing a swift apoptotic cascade (Isaacs et al, 1992). **As the tumor progresses, the threshold of apoptosis progressively rises to a point that cell proliferation exceeds cell death** (Berges et al, 1995). This results in the accumulation of endocrine-independent cells that eventually dominate the biologic behavior of prostate cancer in late stages.

Preclinical data suggest that the relatively low growth fraction expressed by adenocarcinoma of the prostate, compared with other common tumor types, may be a determining factor to explain the relative insensitivity to conventional cytotoxic chemotherapy. The proliferation rate of prostate cancer cells, which is directly proportional to its growth fraction (Berges et al, 1995), **appears to increase with tumor progression, especially after androgen ablation.** Cell proliferation antigens, such as Ki-67 expressed by cycling cells (Cattoretti et al, 1992), may have important prognostic and therapeutic implications since most conventional cytotoxic chemotherapeutic agents available are usually more effective in tumors with high proliferative rates, such as lymphomas, small cell lung carcinomas, and germ cell tumors of the testis.

Changes in differentiation pathways in prostate cancer have been increasingly emphasized, particularly in the form of neuroendocrine cells (diSant'Agnese, 1995). Evolving experience with cytotoxic chemotherapy suggests that this aggressive clinical entity may be responsive to treatment regimens frequently employed for comparable tumors at other sites with similar phenotypic characteristics, such as small cell carcinoma of the lung. There is strong evidence to support the relationship between prostate cancer growth and various peptide growth factors (Djakiew et al, 1991; Watts, 1992; Steiner, 1993; Hofer et al, 1995; Story, 1995; Sherwood et al, 1998; Kaplan et al, 1999; Nelson et al, 2003). Peptide growth factors may also exert their effects through the activation of the androgen receptor. Androgens are capable of inducing stromal production of various growth factors that could replace the androgen requirements for cell growth and differentiation (Lee, 1996). In addition, cytokines released primarily by stromal cells, such as interleukin-6, for example (Nelson et al, 2003), may also be important in the pathogenesis of prostate cancer. Indeed, small molecules and other modalities of treatment (monoclonal antibodies) are being actively designed to target intracellular pathways associated with the expression of various growth factors and their receptors. Such strategies have involved inhibition of receptor tyrosine kinase family activity and other intracellular molecular pathways of signal transduction or other critical pathways of cell growth and survival.

CLINICAL CONSIDERATIONS
Disease Assessment and Selection of Treatment

Conventional staging criteria, such as the TNM staging system, do not describe the extent of disease beyond a simple anatomic classification. Treatment practices result in the creation of different disease states as described by Scher and colleagues (2004). **This system allows classification of patients in a more clinically applicable fashion. Figure 105–1 illustrates the natural history of prostate cancer relative to treatment practices and identifies the various paradigms according to the response status to the different treatments applied.** Throughout this chapter, prognostic and therapeutic

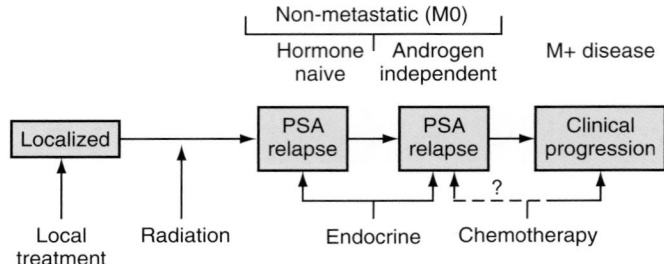

Figure 105–1. Prostate cancer treatment paradigms. PSA, prostate-specific antigen.

Table 105–1. **Metastatic Hormone-Refractory Prostate Cancer: Survival According to Mode of Progression***

Mode of Progression	Minimal Disease, Median Survival	Extensive Disease, Median Survival
PSA only	40 months	18 months
PSA + bone scan	23 months	11 months

*Data presented by one of the authors (M. E.). (Eisenberger M, et al: Proceedings ASCO, 1995.)

considerations are largely based on the concepts advanced by this classification, which is increasingly used throughout the literature. A complete characterization is required to estimate the outcome and to make therapeutic considerations. Critical baseline components include extent of disease; mode and site of progression—rising prostate-specific antigen (PSA) level alone, new bone metastasis, visceral and nodal metastasis, presence or absence of symptoms; and response to prior endocrine treatment. Regular monitoring with serial bone scans and serum PSA levels during hormone treatment provides important information in patients demonstrating evidence of disease progression while they are receiving hormone therapy. Table 105–1 describes the post-progression survival of patients with stage D2 disease who demonstrated progression of disease with hormone therapy in a large prospective trial (Eisenberger et al, 1995). The data shown in Table 105–1 illustrate the broad range in post-progression survival according to the mode of progression (PSA only versus PSA plus bone scan progression) and according to the extent of bone metastasis. This observation highlights the importance of establishing precisely the predominant mode of progression in these patients. It also provides critical information for the interpretation of subsequent phase II trials with regard to time-dependent outcome observations, such as time to disease progression and survival. Usually the first manifestation of disease progression after hormone therapy is a rising serum PSA level. In patients with metastatic disease, a rise in serum PSA level precedes evidence of advancing disease in the bone scan by about 6 months, and during this time, patients may remain relatively asymptomatic (Eisenberger et al, 1995). Routine evaluation of serum testosterone levels may provide important leads for the choice of treatment. This is especially important when there are reasons to suspect treatment compliance or if the choice of prior treatment involved regimens known not to result in a sustained suppression of serum testosterone concentration to the castrate range (such as monotherapy with nonsteroidal antiandrogens, low-dose estrogens, 5α-reductase inhibitors, or a combination thereof).

KEY POINTS: CLINICAL CONSIDERATIONS

■ Evaluate extent of disease and compare with previous workup.

■ Critical issues are extent of disease, clinical versus biochemical relapse, symptoms, and PSA history (PSA doubling time, PSA velocity).

■ Make therapeutic considerations.

For several years, it has been postulated that discontinuation of androgen suppression in non-orchiectomized patients may adversely influence the outcome of disease in terms of progression and survival (Taylor et al, 1993). Similarly, it has been shown that administration of exogenous testosterone and its derivatives may indeed produce a significant clinical flare that results in severe pain and neurologic, urologic, and coagulation complications in a small proportion of patients (Fowler and Whitmore, 1981, 1982; Manni et al, 1988). In a retrospective analysis of 205 patients with hormone-refractory disease treated with chemotherapy, various prognostic variables, including orchiectomy, were evaluated by Hussain and associates (1994). This multivariate analysis failed to indicate a significant correlation between prior orchiectomy and time to disease progression and survival. In Hussain's patients, all medical forms of androgen deprivation were discontinued at least 4 weeks before initiation of chemotherapy, and contrary to that suggested by Taylor and colleagues (1993), discontinuation of treatment did not significantly affect outcome. No data on serum testosterone levels were available in both retrospective evaluations. Until this issue is resolved, we recommend that for all patients, especially those referred for clinical trials with chemotherapy, adequate gonadal androgen suppression should be verified and maintained. If discontinuation of treatment is elected, intermittent monitoring of serum testosterone concentration may provide potentially important information for the management of these patients.

Another important management aspect relates to the antiandrogen withdrawal effects (Scher and Kelly, 1993). **Discontinuation of antiandrogens (both steroidal and nonsteroidal) can result in short-term clinical responses expressed by decreases in PSA levels, symptomatic benefits, and less frequently objective improvements in soft tissue and bone metastasis in a small proportion of these patients.** Because of this, we recommend that in patients treated with antiandrogens in combination with other forms of androgen deprivation, the first step should involve the discontinuation of these agents and careful observation including serial monitoring of PSA levels for a period of 4 to 8 weeks before embarking on the next therapeutic maneuver.

The next step is to determine which modality of treatment should be employed first, either administration of a relatively nontoxic treatment, such as a second-line hormonal manipulation, or cytotoxic chemotherapy. There is an increasing body of data on second-line endocrine approaches that suggests there may be a role for this approach before institution of chemotherapy (Small and Vogelzang, 1997; Small et al, 2004a). Whereas response rates range between 20% and 60%, the median duration of response is short, ranging between 2 and 4 months. Among agents that have been reported to produce some benefit in this setting are diethylstilbestrol (Smith, 1995), the herbal compound PC-SPES (Small et al, 2000) that most likely represents primarily the effects of phytoestrogens contained in the preparation (DiPaola et al, 1998), aminoglutethimide (Sartor and Myers, 1995), ketoconazole (Wilding, 1998), and corticosteroids (Storlie et al, 1995) as well as withdrawal of antiandrogens (Scher and Kelly, 1993; Small and Srinivas, 1995). An interesting observation is that the older reported experience with some agents—amino-

glutethimide (Drago, 1984), ketoconazole (Trump, 1989), and low-dose corticosteroids (Tannock et al, 1989)—was much less encouraging than more contemporary data with the same compounds. It is likely that the explanation for the more positive experience with second-line endocrine approaches in contemporary series relates to better selection of patients and a shift in the timing of initiation of treatment that results from earlier recognition of disease progression with sequential PSA monitoring. **In view of the potential higher toxicity profile associated with cytotoxic chemotherapy, this sequential hormonal approach may be a reasonable alternative for those patients with relatively limited metastatic disease who remain asymptomatic at the time of disease progression (rising serum PSA levels without other clinical manifestations of disease).**

Another important consideration is the initial clinical assessment of the potential biologic behavior of these tumors, which is frequently alluded to as the metastatic clinical phenotype. **Evolving data evaluating the role of PSA dynamics suggest that the PSA doubling time predicts for the rapidity of bone scan progression and survival** (D'Amico et al, 2005). **Patients with PSA doubling time shorter than 3 months have a particularly aggressive clinical course and should be considered for more aggressive management approaches. Poorly differentiated, anaplastic or neuroendocrine tumors usually have a low likelihood of significant and durable responses to androgen deprivation.** Anaplastic and neuroendocrine tumors are less common subtypes that require special therapeutic considerations (see later). It has been suggested (Logothetis et al, 1994) that systematic biopsies of disease sites in patients with clinically aggressive disease and relatively low serum PSA levels may demonstrate evidence of a neuroendocrine component by immunostaining, which may be of prognostic and therapeutic significance (see later). The usefulness of systematic biopsies in all patients with extensive metastasis and relatively low PSA levels, however, needs to be better defined before routine clinical application.

Nonmetastatic, Androgen-Independent, Castrate Disease

The extraordinary stage migration that affected all stages of prostate cancer has profoundly modified the spectrum of clinical presentation of patients with hormone-refractory disease. An increasing number of patients are initiated on androgen deprivation at very early stages of their disease before clinical and radiologic evidence of metastasis is present. As a result of this shift of treatment paradigm, a number of patients demonstrate rising serum PSA levels as the sole evidence of disease progression without other clinical manifestations of disease while they are receiving ADT. This group of patients, termed the androgen-independent, M0 (nonmetastatic), castrate subset, is seen in increasing proportions in the clinic, and given the changes in treatment practices regarding initiation of androgen deprivation, it is conceivable that the numbers will continue to increase. At this time, there are few data on their natural history.

A number of clinical trials employing second-line hormonal manipulations and noncytotoxic chemotherapeutic

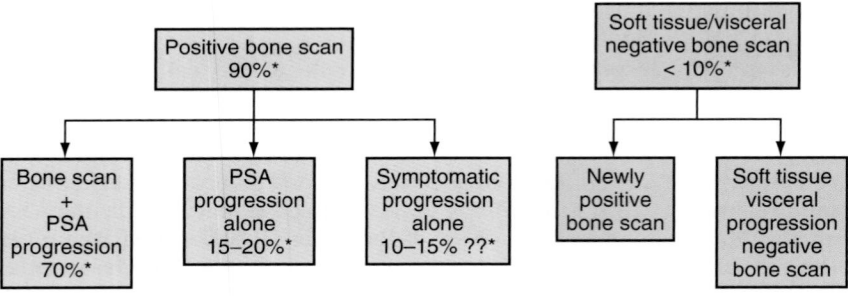

Figure 105–2. Clinical heterogeneity of hormone-refractory prostate cancer. Subpopulations according to their type of progression after androgen deprivation. PSA, prostate-specific antigen. *The percentages illustrated represent an estimation based on the distribution reported in multiple trials reviewed by the authors.

interventions (bone-targeted treatments) focusing on time to development of bone metastasis should provide us with this much needed information. A report of 201 patients studied prospectively in a clinical trial comparing the effects of the bisphosphonate zoledronic acid and placebo in patients with biochemically progressing (M0), castrate prostate cancer suggests that the time to bone scan progression may be very long. At 2 years, only 33% of the patients had evidence of bone metastasis, with a median time to bone metastasis (in this group) of 30 months. The baseline PSA level (>10 ng/mL) and the PSA velocity independently predicted time to bone metastasis and survival (Smith et al, 2005). In a retrospective review of a similar group of patients prescribed ADT before the development of metastatic disease, the median time to clinical metastasis was 9 months. The pretreatment PSA level and PSA nadir on ADT predicted the outcome (Dotan et al, 2005). The wide difference observed with these two reports (30 months versus 9 months for time to bone scan metastasis) underscores the heterogeneity of this group of patients and the need for careful prospective evaluation. Their outcome is dependent on various factors, among which are pre-ADT characteristics (pretreatment PSA level, PSA doubling time, initial stage, Gleason score), as well as response to treatment. The rate of progression may be estimated by PSA constructs such as PSA doubling time and PSA velocity.

At present, there is no consensus on the most appropriate management for these patients, although the sequential endocrine approach is the most commonly employed therapeutic approach. A trial investigating the relative efficacy of a second-line endocrine manipulation versus a docetaxel-based chemotherapy regimen was closed prematurely because of poor accrual. More data are needed to characterize the natural history and to define the best treatment approach of the M0 castrate subset, which represents an important evolving new paradigm.

Metastatic Hormone-Refractory Disease

Patients with metastatic hormone-refractory prostate cancer represent a heterogeneous group with respect to their clinical status at the time of disease progression (Fig. 105–2). **Metastatic adenocarcinoma of the prostate has an overwhelming predilection to involve primarily bone.** Although the explanation for this unique metastatic pattern has not been completely elucidated, it probably reflects the combination of various biologic factors starting at the time of metastatic spread. Circulating prostatic adenocarcinoma cells are arrested in the cortical and medullary bone spaces, where they subsequently adhere to bone surfaces through specific receptors for moieties such as integrins, collagens, laminin, and other bone-derived proteins. Cell growth is subsequently promoted by various factors such as hormones, growth factors, and stromal-epithelial biologic interactions, most of which operate in the bone marrow. Expansion of tumor from the bone may cause pain, compression, or pathologic fractures, and extensive bone marrow replacement may cause a major impairment in hematologic function.

Clinical involvement of visceral sites is relatively uncommon even in patients with widespread hormone-resistant disease. Table 105–2 illustrates the distribution of metastatic sites reported in different series included in selected chemotherapy phase II and phase III trials. These figures suggest that clinical evidence of visceral metastasis is observed in less than 10% of patients, whereas about 20% have demonstrable soft tissue nodal disease. Since the majority of tumor burden in metastatic prostate cancer is localized in bone, responses to treatment (tumor shrinkage) in soft tissue sites alone (such as nodal or visceral) may not reflect a major treatment benefit because it represents only a small proportion of the overall burden of disease.

Table 105–2. Typical Distribution of Metastatic Sites in Patients with Hormone-Resistant Prostate Cancer Entered in Clinical Trials

Investigator	Total No. of Patients	Bone	Lung	Liver	Soft Tissue–Nodal
Pienta (1994)	42	42 (100%)	3 (7%)	5	13
Sella (1994)	39	36 (92%)	3 (8%)	3	9
Moore (1994)	27	22 (81%)	2 (9%)	2	10
Eisenberger (1995)	109	108 (99%)	6 (5.5%)	4	15
Hudes (1992)	36	36 (100%)	0	2	7
Tannock (2004)	1006	915 (91%)			
Petrylak (2004)	674	579 (86%)	67 (10%)	57 (8.5%)	168 (25%)

Patients with hormone-refractory prostate cancer may present with a range of hematologic problems caused primarily by the disease or secondary to treatment. Anemia is the most common hematologic abnormality, which can be explained by a variety of factors, such as anemia of chronic disease (Waterbury, 1979), bone marrow invasion (Berlin, 1974), blood loss, and rarely secondary to a picture of microangiopathic hemolytic anemia that is usually associated with a consumption coagulopathy (disseminated intravascular coagulation) (Antman et al, 1979; Coleman et al, 1979). **A decrease in the red blood cell count of patients with advanced hormone-resistant prostate cancer commonly results from a combination of factors, such as prior treatment with local irradiation of bone marrow harboring sites, systemic use of radiopharmaceuticals, long-term androgen deprivation, and systemic chemotherapy, as well as from extensive bone marrow invasion by tumor resulting in substantial decrease in the bone marrow reserve. The use of erythropoietin can be effective, especially in patients with a history of long-term androgen suppression, and repeated administration may require the use of iron preparations.** Iron preparations alone and vitamin supplementation usually provide unsatisfactory results. **Granulocytopenia and thrombocytopenia are most commonly a complication of extensive radiation therapy or systemic chemotherapy.** Rarely, rapidly growing tumors with bone marrow involvement result in pancytopenia. Thrombocytosis is also a nonspecific manifestation associated with various neoplastic conditions including prostate cancer (Williams, 1977). Thrombotic complications associated with thrombocytosis are rarely seen in patients with prostate cancer, and treatment is not necessary.

Among the most important urologic complications in patients with advanced prostate cancer is the development of obstructive uropathy. This complication, related to the primary disease, can be devastating from the quality of life point of view and even have major therapeutic implications. Besides an increased incidence of infection and pain, obstructed kidneys may critically impair renal function to a point where various chemotherapeutic agents, which depend largely on renal mechanisms for their clearance, cannot be safely employed. In general, patients who are otherwise candidates for treatment with cytotoxic drugs are best managed by relief of obstruction either with placement of internal stents or by percutaneous nephrostomies.

One of the most important complications in oncology is the development of epidural cord compression (Sorensen et al, 1990). Because of the frequent involvement of vertebral bodies by prostate cancer, the incidence of cord compression is particularly prominent (see later).

EXPERIENCE WITH CYTOTOXIC CHEMOTHERAPY
Evaluation of Treatment Efficacy

The evaluation of chemotherapy based on uncontrolled clinical trials in patients with metastatic prostate cancer is usually confounded by significant methodologic challenges. The most common metastatic site is bone, manifested by diffuse osteoblastic lesions that cannot be measured reliably, by

---

KEY POINTS: CYTOTOXIC CHEMOTHERAPY

■ Docetaxel is the standard treatment for hormone-refractory prostate cancer. It prolongs progression-free and overall survival, improves pain, and improves quality of life.

■ Toxicity of docetaxel includes myelosuppression, fatigue, edema, moderate to modest neurotoxicity, and changes in liver function (seldom dose limiting).

■ Several contemporary regimens consistently demonstrate a benefit.

■ Chemotherapy should be discussed and offered to all patients with hormone-refractory prostate cancer.

---

current methods, to allow assessments of therapeutic benefits. Soft tissue or visceral metastatic sites (bidimensionally measurable disease) that allow serial measurements are uncommon (Table 105–2) and represent only a small fraction of the total burden of the disease (Yagoda, 1984). Selection of bidimensionally measurable disease sites to assess therapeutic efficacy with serial "tumor measurements" has been the subject of significant criticism. Patients with soft tissue metastasis (especially visceral disease) are considered by many a subgroup with biologic and clinical features distinct from those of the usual patient with prostate cancer who presents with bone metastasis only. A number of prognostic models evaluating baseline and post-treatment characteristics have been developed (Smaletz et al, 2002; Halabi et al, 2003). Among various clinical and laboratory parameters with consistent prognostic significance by most reports are baseline functional status (performance status), presence of pain, and pretreatment hemoglobin levels (cutoffs have ranged from 10 to 12 g/dL). Other possible parameters are the baseline PSA level, extent of bone scan involvement (number of lesions or pattern of distribution of bone involvement), and presence of visceral disease. Semiquantitative methods to evaluate PSA message in circulating cells (reverse transcription–polymerase chain reaction for PSA) and various PSA constructs, such as PSA doubling time and PSA velocity, are among post-treatment parameters likely to be of prognostic significance (Kantoff et al, 2004; Scher et al, 2004).

Preclinical observations have suggested that several drugs may reduce PSA secretion without concomitant changes in tumor growth (Larocca, 1991; Steiner et al, 1995; Eisenberger and Nelson, 1996). Whereas these laboratory observations are likely to be clinically relevant, assays employed to evaluate a separate drug effect on PSA secretion still require careful clinical validation. A PSA consensus meeting developed by several leading investigators in the field generated initial guidelines with regard to the use of the PSA test for clinical trials in patients with androgen-independent prostate cancer (Bubley et al, 1999). The use of serum acid phosphatase (by any method of measurement) and alkaline phosphatase has not been proved beneficial (Yagoda, 1984). Undoubtedly, new biomarkers are needed to enhance our ability to rapidly identify active treatments for this disease. The evolving new types of nonclassic cytotoxic compounds may require a new set of endpoints and identification of drug-specific intermediate markers that reflect mechanism-specific biologic activity.

Clinical Trials

Most of the single chemotherapeutic agents available in practice have been employed in patients with hormone-resistant prostate cancer (Eisenberger et al, 1985; Eisenberger, 1988) (Table 105–3). Evolving data with chemotherapy during this decade suggest that the survival of patients with hormone-resistant prostate cancer is most likely between 16 and 18 months (Eisenberger et al, 1995; Petrylak et al, 2004; Tannock et al, 2004) as opposed to 6 to 12 months as previously described (Eisenberger et al, 1985; Eisenberger, 1988).

The data shown in Table 105–4 describe the long-term experience with various drug regimens. Earlier studies suggested a modest single-agent activity with the bifunctional alkylating drug cyclophosphamide, which, however, has shown modest antitumor effects in only about 10% to 20% on the basis of the older literature. Interestingly, in contemporary trials, cyclophosphamide given in standard oral doses or high intravenous doses with hematopoietic growth factor support has been reported to have a higher order of activity (Smith et al, 1992; von Roemeling et al, 1992; Abell et al, 1995). Doxorubicin, 5-fluorouracil, and cisplatin, agents with signif-

icant activity in various tumor types, have demonstrated only modest single-agent benefits in patients with hormone-resistant prostate cancer. Mitoxantrone, a semisynthetic anthracenedione derivative, has shown modest subjective benefits with otherwise minimal evidence of objective antitumor activity (Osborne et al, 1983; Raghavan et al, 1986; Rearden et al, 1995). This agent was evaluated in combination with low-dose prednisone (10 mg/day orally), which resulted in significant palliative benefits (Moore et al, 1994). In two prospective randomized trials of mitoxantrone plus prednisone versus prednisone alone (Tannock et al, 1996) or mitoxantrone plus hydrocortisone versus hydrocortisone alone (Kantoff et al, 1999), the combination resulted in significant improvements of various quality of life parameters including pain, but survival was not significantly different between the treatment arms in both studies (Table 105–5). These studies provided the justification for the Food and Drug Administration's approval of the combination of mitoxantrone and prednisone for *symptomatic* metastatic prostate cancer in 1997.

Estramustine phosphate, a nitrogen mustard derivative of estradiol 17β-phosphate, has demonstrated limited single-agent activity in this disease. In a prospective randomized study in patients with hormone-refractory disease, estramustine phosphate given in a dose of 560 mg/day orally was not shown to be superior to a placebo in terms of both

Table 105–3. Single-Agent Experience in Patients with Hormone-Refractory Prostate Cancer

Drug	Reference	Dose and Schedule	Overall Response	Common Toxicities	Response Criteria
Cyclophosphamide	von Roemeling (1992)	75-150 mg/day PO	4/13 (30%)	Nausea, heme	Primarily ≤50% PSA decline, but measurable responses also seen
	Abell (1995)	100 mg/m²/day PO × 14 days every 2 weeks × 3 cycles	6/20 (30%)	Nausea, heme	
	Smith (1992)	1.5-4.5 g/m² + GM-CSF + mesna	6/10	Nausea, heme	
Taxol	Roth (1992)	135-170 mg/m² IV in 24 hr	1/23	Heme Cardiovascular, anaphylaxis	Measurable criteria and PSA responses (≤50%)
	Ahmed (1997)	150 mg/m² IV in 1 hr weekly × 6 weeks repeated every 8 weeks	6/12 2/4	Neurotoxicity and myelosuppression	50% decline in PSA measurable responses
Mitoxantrone	Rearden (1995)	3-4 mg/m² IV weekly	0/14	Heme	1 measurable response, 3 subjective improvements; 0/14 ≤50% decline in PSA
Taxotere	Picus (1999)	75 mg/m² every 3 weeks	16/35 (45%) 4/25 (28%)	Fatigue, stomatitis, myelosuppression, edema	50% decline in PSA measurable responses
	Friedland (1999)	75 mg/m² every 3 weeks	5/12 1	Stomatitis, edema, myelosuppression	50% decline in PSA
	Beer (2000)	36 mg/m² every 3 weeks × 6 weeks followed by 2 weeks of rest	9/19 (47%)	Leukopenia (9%)	50% decline in PSA
Navelbine	Oudard (1999)	25 mg/m²/wk	19/47 (40%)	Modest neutropenia	50% decline in PSA
Estramustine phosphate	Yagoda (1991)	14 mg/kg/day PO, 3× daily	9/42 (21%)	Nausea, heme, thromboembolic, gynecomastia	≥50% decline in PSA
5-Fluorouracil	Kuzel (1993)	1000 mg/m²/day × 5 days by continuous IV infusion every 28 days	0/18	Heme, mucositis	No objective measurable responses or ≥50% PSA decline
Etoposide	Hussain (1994)	50 mg/m²/day PO × for 21 days, monthly	2/24 (8%)	Heme	One patient had ≥50% decline in PSA and one had a measurable response
Carboplatin	Canobbio (1993)	150 mg/m² IV weekly	3 (2)/25 (12%)	Heme	3 had ≥50% PSA declines; 2 had measurable responses

Table 105–4. Selected Experience with Multidrug Regimens

Regimen	Reference	Responses ≥50% Decline in PSA	Measurable Responses	Toxicity	Comments
Estramustine phosphate, 10 mg/kg/day PO in 3 divided doses × 6-7 weeks + Vinblastine, 4 mg/m² IV weekly	Seidman (1992) Hudes (1992)	13/24 22/36	2/5 1/7	Heme, nausea and vomiting, gynecomastia, thromboembolism	No information on prior flutamide treatment
Estramustine phosphate, 15 mg/kg/day PO × 3 weeks + Etoposide, 50 mg/m²/day PO × 3 weeks	Pienta (1994)	29/42 (69%)	9/18 (50%)	As above; however, 25% had severe heme	Prior flutamide treatment effects unclear; responses seen in patients with no prior antiandrogen treatment
Estramustine phosphate, 600 mg/m²/day PO + Paclitaxel, 120-140 mg/m² by 96-hr infusion	Hudes (1995)	10/17 (59%)	3/6	Heme, mucositis, nausea and vomiting, edema, deep venous thrombosis	All patients with prior flutamide treatment had objective progression before study entry
Estramustine phosphate, 280 mg PO 3× day, days 1-5 + Docetaxel, 70 mg/m², day 2 (every 3 weeks)	Petrylak (2000)	23/35 (74%)	4/7	Heme, edema, fatigue, deep venous thrombosis	As above; encouraging survival data (77% at 1 year)
Estramustine phosphate, 280 mg PO every 6 hr × 5 doses + Docetaxel, 70 mg/m², day (every 3 weeks)	Sinibaldi (2000)	13/29 (45%)	3/13	Neutropenia, fatigue	Total 1 day of estramustine, no thrombotic complications
Estramustine phosphate, 420 mg PO 3× day for 4 doses, then 280 mg × 5 doses, weekly + Docetaxel, 35 mg/m², day 2 (weekly)	Copur (2000)	13/18 (72%)	4/8	Modest neutropenia, edema, diarrhea	12 patients had prior estramustine + vinblastine
Estramustine phosphate, 280 mg PO 3× day × 14 days + Etoposide, 100 mg/day × 14 days + Paclitaxel, 135 mg/m² during 1 hr on day 2 (every 21 days)	Smith (1999)	26/40 (65%)	10/22	Heme, deep venous thrombosis	Poor-risk patients Majority received prior chemotherapy, and 9 had liver metastases
Estramustine phosphate, 280 mg 3× day, days 1-3 + Vinorelbine, 15-20 mg/m² on day 2 (weekly × 8 weeks, then every other week up to 26 weeks)	Sweeny (2000)	15/21 (71%)	1/8	Modest heme, edema, 17% deep venous thrombosis	Cardiovascular toxicity with estramustine was significant
Doxorubicin, 40 mg/m² IV + Cyclophosphamide, 800-2000 mg/m² + G-CSF 5 mg/kg/day	Small (1995)	12/29	4/12	Heme, nausea and vomiting	As above
Suramin, various doses and schedules + Hydrocortisone, 30-40 mg/day PO	Review by Eisenberger (1995); 9 studies	128/338 (38%)	25/85 (29.5)	Malaise, anorexia, renal, neurologic, adrenal insufficiency	This is a review of 9 studies. Individual responses have ranged from 20% to 65%.
Mitoxantrone, 12 mg/m² IV every 3 weeks + Prednisone, 10 mg PO daily	Moore (1994)	5/23 (21.5%)	1/7	Heme	9 of 25 were reported to have good palliative responses
Ketoconazole, 1200 mg PO daily + Doxorubicin, 20 mg/m² by 24-hr infusion weekly + Hydrocortisone, 30 mg/day (to most patients)	Sella (1994)	21/39 (55%)	7/12	Heme, mucositis, adrenal insufficiency	Flutamide withdrawal possible in some, but responses seen in patients with no prior antiandrogen treatment

Table 105-5. Survival Comparisons in Prospective Randomized Trials*

Drug/Regimen	Median Survival (weeks, unless otherwise specified)	Comments
Cyclophosphamide	47	More patients on the chemotherapy arms had stable disease
5-Fluorouracil	44	Difference in survival not significant statistically
No chemotherapy[†]	38	
Estramustine phosphate	26	More patients on the chemotherapy arms had stable disease
Streptozotocin	25	Difference in survival not significant statistically
No chemotherapy[†]	24	
Cyclophosphamide	27	Survival difference not significant
Dacarbazine	40	
Procarbazine	31	
Estramustine + prednimustine	37	Difference in survival not significant statistically
Prednimustine	36	
Cyclophosphamide	41	High inevaluability rate
Semustine	22	Survival differences are not statistically significant
Hydroxyurea	19	
Estramustine (E)	26	Difference in survival not significant statistically
Vincristine (V)	27	
E + V	32	
Estramustine	43	Difference in survival not significant statistically
Methotrexate	37	
Cisplatin	33	
Mitoxantrone + prednisone	9-10 months	Improved control of pain and prolongation of time to
Prednisone (Tannock, 1996)	No difference	symptomatic progression in favor of the combination PSA
Mitoxantrone + hydrocortisone	12.3 months	38% vs. 22% PSA response. Quality of life not significantly
Hydrocortisone (Kantoff, 1999)	12.6 months	different and pain better controlled
Suramin + hydrocortisone	9-10 months	33% vs.16% PSA response. Pain control and time to pain
Placebo + hydrocortisone (Small, 2000)	No difference	progression significantly better with suramin. Toxicity was modest
Estramustine + vinblastine	11.9 months	PSA response 25% vs. 3%
Vinblastine (Hudes, 1999)	9.2 months	
Estramustine (E)	38	Difference in survival not significant statistically
Cisplatin (C)	28	
E + C	40	
Doxorubicin	29	Survival differences are not statistically significant
5-Fluorouracil	24	
CAF	25	Survival differences are not statistically significant
5-Fluorouracil	34	
CA	27	Difference in survival not significant statistically
Hydroxyurea	28	
Estramustine (Iversen, 1995)	34	Survival differences are not statistically significant
Placebo	24	
Docetaxel every 3 weeks + prednisone	18.9	Difference between the every-3-weeks docetaxel schedule and
Docetaxel weekly + prednisone	17.3	mitoxantrone + prednisone is significant with a HR = 0.76;
Mitoxantrone + prednisone (Tannock, 2004)	16.4	two-sided $P = .009$
Estramustine + docetaxel	18	Difference is significant
Mitoxantrone + prednisone (Petrylak, 2004)	16	HR = 0.8; two-sided $P = .01$
Docetaxel + high-dose calcitriol (DN-01)	23.5	Unadjusted HR = 0.7; $P = .07$
Docetaxel (Beer, 2005)	16.4	Multivariate HR = 0.67; $P = .035$

CAF, cyclophosphamide, doxorubicin (Adriamycin), and fluorouracil; CA, cyclophosphamide and doxorubicin (Adriamycin).
*Modified from Eisenberger, 1985. This table includes only trials with at least 20 evaluable patients per treatment arm.
[†]No chemotherapy; palliative treatment with radiation, corticosteroids, and other hormones or analgesics only.

palliative effects and survival (Iversen and Rasmussen, 1995) (see Table 105–5). Preclinical data indicate that estramustine exerts its cytotoxic activity through microtubular inhibition (Hudes et al, 1992) and binding to nuclear matrix (Hartley-Asp and Kruse, 1986), and therefore it was commonly combined with other drugs that also exert their cytotoxic effects at the level of the microtubule, such as vinblastine, docetaxel (Taxotere), and paclitaxel (Taxol).

Docetaxel is a cytotoxic agent and member of the taxoid family. It induces apoptosis in cancer cells through p53-independent mechanisms that are thought to be due to its inhibition of microtubule depolymerization and inhibition

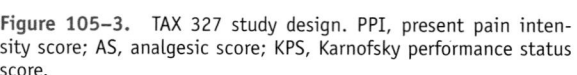
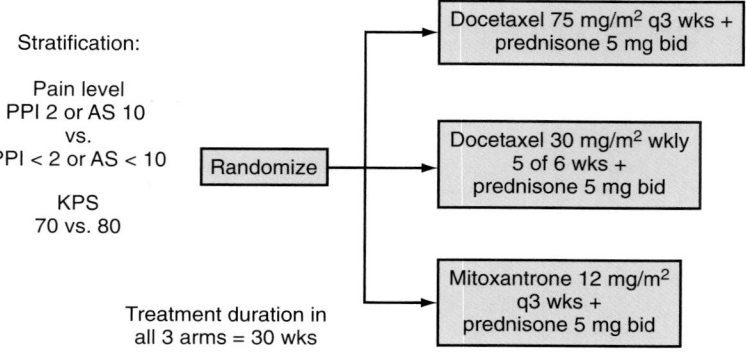

Stratification:

Pain level
PPI 2 or AS 10
vs.
PPI < 2 or AS < 10

KPS
70 vs. 80

Treatment duration in
all 3 arms = 30 wks

Figure 105–3. TAX 327 study design. PPI, present pain intensity score; AS, analgesic score; KPS, Karnofsky performance status score.

of anti-apoptotic signaling. The induction of microtubule stabilization intracellularly through β-tubulin interactions causes GTP-independent polymerization and cell cycle arrest at G_2/M, and some have reported a twofold greater microtubule affinity compared with paclitaxel. In addition, docetaxel has been found to induce Bcl-2 phosphorylation in vitro, a process that has been correlated with caspase activation and loss of its normal anti-apoptotic activity. Unable to inhibit the pro-apoptotic molecule Bax, phosphorylated Bcl-2 may also induce apoptosis through this independent mechanism. However, additional mechanisms may be important, such as p27[Kip1] induction and repression of Bcl-xL. Data with single-agent docetaxel suggested that this compound has significant activity as a single agent (Friedland et al, 1999; Picus and Schultz, 1999; Beer, 2004) (see Table 105–3).

Docetaxel has become the agent of choice as of 2004 on the basis of a large phase III randomized trial, TAX 327 (Figs. 105–3 to 105–5 and Tables 105–6 to 105–8), **which demonstrated its superiority to the past standard, mitoxantrone and prednisone** (Tannock et al, 2004). TAX 327 enrolled 1006

patients with no prior chemotherapy and stable pain scores to one of three arms, all with concomitant prednisone at 5 mg orally twice a day: mitoxantrone, 12 mg/m² intravenously every 21 days; docetaxel, 75 mg/m² intravenously every 21 days; and docetaxel, 30 mg/m² intravenously weekly. Patients remained on gonadal suppression but had all other hormonal agents discontinued within 4 to 6 weeks. Treatment duration was 30 weeks in all arms, or a maximum of 10 cycles in the every-3-week arms, with more patients completing treatment in the every-3-week docetaxel arm than in the mitoxantrone arm, mostly because of differences in disease progression (46% versus 25%). **After a median 20.7 months of follow-up, overall survival in the every-3-week docetaxel arm was 18.9 months with a pain response rate of 35% and a PSA response of 45%, contrasted with weekly docetaxel at 17.3 months, 31% and 48%, respectively. This translated into a 24% relative risk reduction in death (95% confidence interval, 6% to 48%; $P = .0005$) with every-3-week docetaxel** (see Fig. 105–4). **Patients on the mitoxantrone arm had a median survival of 16.4 months, a pain response of 22%, and a PSA response of 32%.**

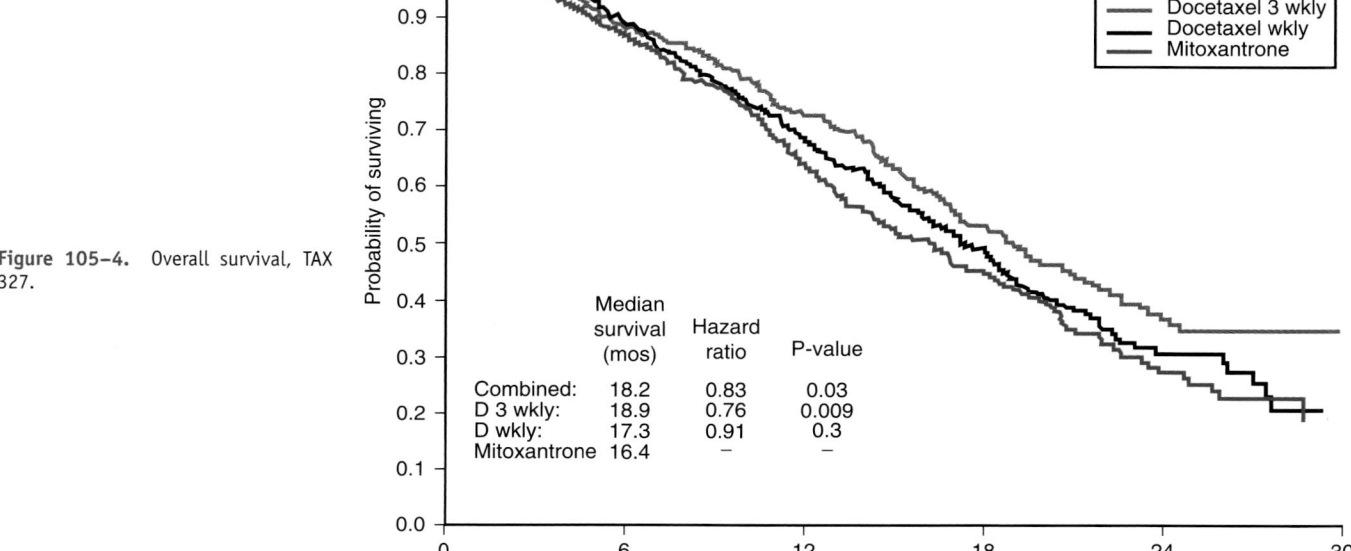

Figure 105–4. Overall survival, TAX 327.

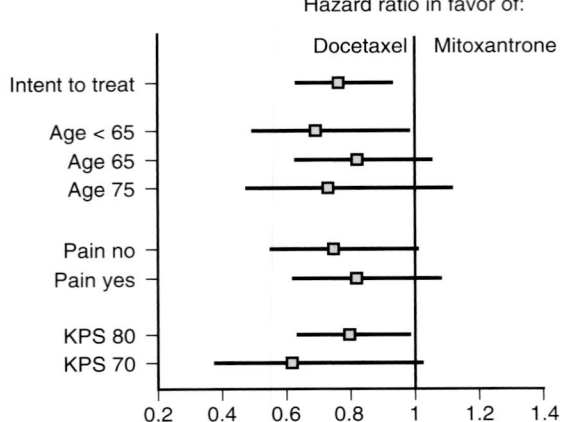

Hazard ratio in favor of:

Figure 105–5. Survival in subgroups, docetaxel every 3 weeks versus mitoxantrone. KPS, Karnofsky performance status score.

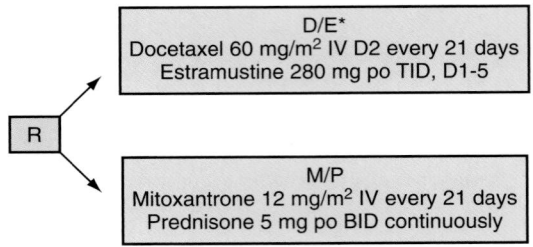

* Coumadin 2 mg PO daily + ASA 325 mg PO daily was added Docetaxel and mitoxantrone doses could be increased to 70 mg/m² and 14 mg/m², respectively, if no grade 3 or 4 toxicities were seen in cycle 1

Figure 105–6. SWOG 9916 study design. D/E, docetaxel plus estramustine; M + P, mitoxantrone plus prednisone.

Table 105–6. TAX 327: Secondary Objectives Response Rates

	Docetaxel 3-weekly	Docetaxel weekly	Mitoxantrone
*Pain response rate**			
n, evaluable	153	154	157
PSA response rate (%)	35	31	22
P value (vs. mitoxantrone)	.01	.07	—
*PSA response rate**			
n, evaluable	291	282	300
Response rate (%)	45	48	32
P value (vs. mitoxantrone)	.0005	<.0001	—
*Tumor response rate**			
n, evaluable	141	134	137
Response rate (%)	12	8	7
P value (vs. mitoxantrone)	.1	.5	—

*Determined only for patients with pain or PSA ≥ 20 ng/mL or measurable disease at baseline, respectively.

Table 105–7. TAX 327: Quality of Life Response >16 Points FACT-P Score Compared with Baseline

	Docetaxel 3-weekly	Docetaxel weekly	Mitoxantrone
Evaluable patients	278	270	267
Response (%)	22	23	13
(95% CI)	(17-27)	(18-28)	(9-18)
P value*	.009	.005	

*Compared with mitoxantrone.

Toxicity in the every-3-week versus weekly docetaxel arms was notable for more hematologic toxicity in the every-3-week arm (3% neutropenic fever versus 0%, and 32% grade 3-4 neutropenia versus 1.5%) (see Table 105–8) but slightly lower rates of nausea and vomiting, fatigue, nail changes, hyperlacrimation, and diarrhea. Neuropathy was slightly more common in the every-3-week arm (grade 3-4 in 1.8% versus 0.9%). Quality of life responses as measured by the FACT-P scores did not differ significantly among the

Table 105–8. TAX 327: Grade 3-4 Hematologic Toxicity (%)

	Docetaxel 3-weekly	Docetaxel weekly	Mitoxantrone
Treated (N)	332	330	335
Anemia	5.0	5.0	2.0
Neutropenia	32.0	1.5	22.0
Neutropenic infection	3.0	0.0	0.9
Febrile neutropenia	2.7	0.0	1.8
Septic death	0.0	0.3	0.3

docetaxel schedules but were more favorable than in the mitoxantrone arm.

The Southwest Oncology Group (SWOG) 9916 study was the second largest phase III trial (see Figs. 105–6 to 105–8) (Petrylak et al, 2004) in which 770 patients with progressive hormone-refractory prostate cancer were randomly assigned to oral estramustine (280 mg orally three times a day) with docetaxel (60 mg/m² every 21 days) or mitoxantrone (12 mg/m² every 21 days) with prednisone. Because of a high rate of cardiovascular thromboembolic events, prophylactic low-dose warfarin (Coumadin) and aspirin were added to the estramustine arm, which did not reduce the incidence of thromboembolism. Similarly, 20% and 15%, respectively, of patients in the estramustine plus docetaxel arm had grade 3 and grade 4 gastrointestinal and cardiovascular toxicities. Although comparisons between the docetaxel arms across trials may not be appropriate because of differences in schedule, populations of patients, and docetaxel dosing (60 mg/m² in SWOG 9916 and 75 mg/m² in TAX 327), it may be concluded that it is unlikely that estramustine contributes significantly to the activity observed with single-agent docetaxel. Figure 105–9 illustrates the overall landscape of metastatic prostate cancer at present. Table 105–5 illustrates additional phase III trials reported in patients with hormone-resistant disease.

The Neuroendocrine Subtype

Laboratory and clinical evidence indicates that alterations in the differentiation pathway (neuroendocrine transformation) of prostate cancer can be seen in a variable proportion of

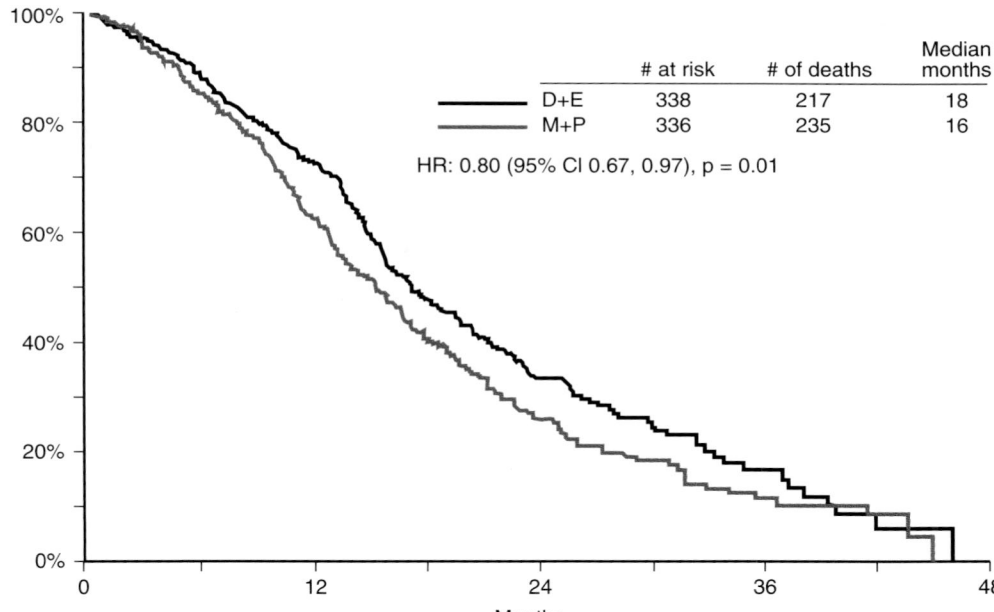

	# at risk	# of deaths	Median months
D+E	338	217	18
M+P	336	235	16

HR: 0.80 (95% CI 0.67, 0.97), p = 0.01

Figure 105–7. Overall survival, SWOG 9916. D + E, docetaxel plus estramustine; M + P, mitoxantrone plus prednisone.

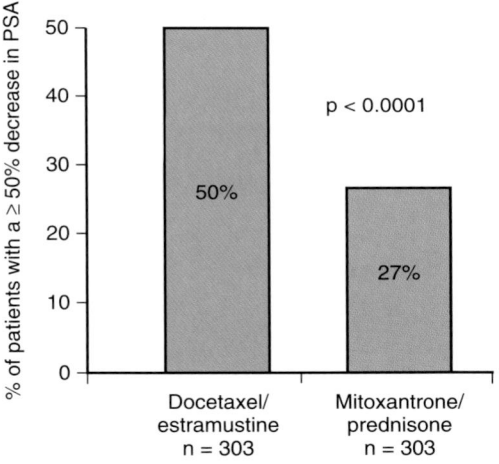

Figure 105–8. SWOG 9916 PSA response rate.

KEY POINTS: THE NEUROENDOCRINE SUBTYPE

■ Rapidly growing disease with the following clinical characteristics should be evaluated for the neuroendocrine phenotype: pelvic masses, visceral involvement, lytic bone metastasis with hypercalcemia (associated with high serum levels of parathyroid hormone–related protein), and brain metastasis.

■ PSA is most commonly undetectable (or levels are low or declining despite categorical evidence of rapid disease progression).

■ These tumors are highly radiosensitive and responsive to platinum and etoposide combination chemotherapy.

■ These tumors are invariably unresponsive to hormonal manipulations.

patients with primarily advanced disease (Logothetis et al, 1994; diSant'Agnese, 1995). The therapeutic implications of this finding are of significance because tumors demonstrating the neuroendocrine phenotype usually represent an inherently endocrine-resistant disease, and in view of their different clinical and biologic properties compared with the usual adenocarcinoma of the prostate phenotype, these tumors usually require separate therapeutic considerations.

These tumors express a number of biologic characteristics unique to neuroendocrine tumors that can also arise from other organs, most commonly the lung. Among these are the expression of receptors to various neuroendocrine peptide growth factors, such as bombesin/gastrin-releasing peptide antagonist, somatostatin, chromogranin A, and serotonin, as well as parathyroid hormone–related protein and *p53* mutations. These tumors have an uncharacteristic clinical behavior (compared with the usual metastatic

prostate cancer) reflected by frequent visceral involvement and rapidly growing soft tissue metastasis. Clinical manifestations are suggestive of the clinical entity. These patients frequently present with subacute, rather dramatic changes in their disease pattern characterized primarily by a rapidly growing soft tissue mass (frequently involving the primary site but also with retroperitoneal masses), rapid development of visceral (lung and liver) involvement, lytic bone metastasis (as opposed to the usual blastic pattern), and a high incidence of brain involvement (see Fig. 105–9). Histologic evaluation of the site demonstrating rapid clinical changes is strongly encouraged. This frequently culminates with demonstration of a small cell variant or a poorly differentiated neoplasm with tissue demonstration of neuro-

Clinical Characteristics :
- Rapidly growing soft tissue metastasis (visceral and pelvic masses)
- Relatively low or undetectable serum PSA
- Lytic bone metastasis
- Frequent brain metastasis
- Elevated plasma chromogranin levels
- Hypercalcemia

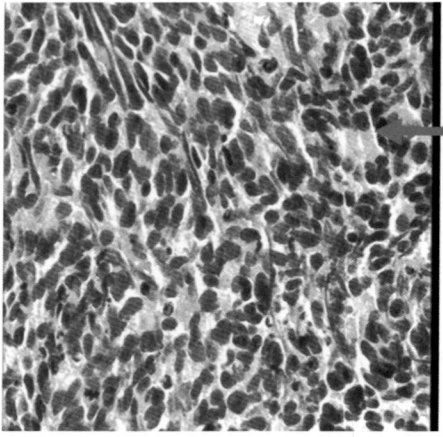

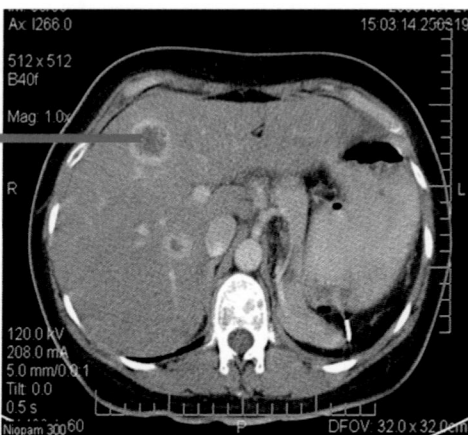

Figure 105–9. Small cell undifferentiated carcinoma of the prostate.

endocrine markers by immunostaining (diSant'Agnese, 1995). Typically, patients either stop expressing PSA in the face of major tumor progression or, more frequently, have undetectable levels at the time of this transformation.

Treatment is usually similar to that of patients with other neuroendocrine tumors (e.g., small cell carcinoma of the lung) and includes combinations of cisplatin or carboplatin and etoposide (Frank, 1995), paclitaxel or docetaxel, and topotecan. Doxorubicin-containing combinations have been reported to be moderately effective by one group (Logothetis et al, 1994). Radiation therapy is effective and should be considered in cases with bulky disease and brain metastasis and when local disease control in critical areas will have a positive impact on quality of life (pain, potential pathologic fractures, and bladder outlet obstruction). A combined chemotherapy and radiation therapy approach is frequently necessary to accomplish maximal control of disease. Despite high response rates with chemotherapy and radiation treatment, the prognosis of these patients remains poor and is dependent on various factors including extent of disease at the time of presentation.

PALLIATIVE MANAGEMENT OF PATIENTS WITH HORMONE-REFRACTORY PROSTATE CANCER
Pain and Epidural Cord Compression

As in other disseminated malignant neoplasms, palliation of symptoms and maintenance of adequate levels of quality of life represent the most important objectives in the management of advanced prostate cancer.

KEY POINTS: PALLIATIVE MANAGEMENT

- Patients with back pain and a history of bone metastasis should be aggressively evaluated for epidural cord compression. The clinical syndrome has at least one of the following signs and symptoms: back pain, focal neurologic findings (leg weakness, sensory levels), changes in bladder or bowel control.

- Management includes immediate magnetic resonance imaging of the spine (or the next appropriate imaging modality to rule out cord compression) and high-dose intravenous corticosteroids.

- Evaluate local decompressive treatment with surgery, radiation, or both.

Cancer-related pain is undoubtedly the most debilitating symptom associated with metastatic prostatic carcinoma. **Prompt recognition of the various pain syndromes associated with this disease is critical to accomplish effective control of this devastating symptom.** Table 105–9 describes the most common pain syndromes and their respective therapeutic considerations.

Focal bone pain in patients with hormone-refractory disease can be well controlled by external localized radiotherapy. In general, we also recommend that painful areas known to be abnormal on bone scan should be evaluated with plain radiographs to exclude the presence of lytic lesions or

Table 105–9. Common Pain Syndromes in Metastatic Hormone-Refractory Prostate Cancer

Pain Syndrome	Initial Management	Other Therapeutic Alternatives
Localized bone pain	Pharmacologic pain management Localized radiotherapy (special attention to weight-bearing areas, lytic metastasis, and extremities)	Surgical stabilization of pathologic fractures or extensive bone erosions Epidural metastasis and cord compression should be evaluated in patients with focal back pain Radiopharmaceuticals should be considered if local radiation therapy fails
Diffuse bone pain	Pharmacologic pain management "Multi-spot" or wide-field radiotherapy Radiopharmaceuticals	Corticosteroids Bisphosphonates Calcitonin Chemotherapy
Epidural metastasis and cord compression	High-dose corticosteroids Radiotherapy Surgical decompression and stabilization should be indicated in high-grade epidural blocks, extensive bone involvement, or recurrence after irradiation	Pharmacologic pain management
Plexopathies caused by direct tumor extension or prior therapy (rare)	Pharmacologic pain management Radiation therapy (if not previously employed) Neurolytic procedures (nerve blocks)	Tricyclics (amitriptyline) Anticonvulsants
Miscellaneous neurogenic causes: post-herpetic neuralgia, peripheral neuropathies	Careful neurologic evaluation Pharmacologic pain management Discontinuation of neurotoxic drugs: paclitaxel, docetaxel, vinca alkaloids, platinum compounds, suramin	Tricyclics (amitriptyline) Anticonvulsants
Other uncommon pain syndromes: extensive skull metastasis with cranial nerve involvement, extensive painful liver metastasis or pelvic masses	Radiotherapy Pharmacologic pain management Corticosteroids (cranial nerve involvement)	Chemotherapy Intrathecal chemotherapy may ameliorate symptoms of meningeal involvement; regional infusions may be considered

[1]Recommended reference U.S. DHHS, 1994.

pathologic fractures. Such considerations become even more important when the painful areas affect extremities and weight-bearing sites.

Epidural metastasis is a common and potentially devastating complication of systemic cancer. In view of the propensity of prostate cancer to metastasize to the vertebrae and paravertebral region, the incidence of epidural cord compression is particularly high. Early diagnosis and treatment of epidural metastasis are critical in preserving ambulation and bowel and bladder function and aid in the management of back pain (Rodichok et al, 1981, 1986; Grossman and Lossignol, 1990). Epidural cord compressions arising from vertebral bodies account for the majority of spinal cord compression; only less frequently is it associated with soft tissue masses involving the paravertebral region. Most patients have abnormalities on bone scans and abnormal findings on radiography at the time of diagnosis; however, an abnormality on neurologic examination may be the only finding in patients who have soft tissue epidural metastasis in the paravertebral region (Wright, 1963).

Spinal magnetic resonance imaging is routinely used to exclude the possibility of significant epidural disease, and it has almost entirely replaced other methods, such as computed tomographic myelography and conventional myelography. The first therapeutic intervention should include the administration of high doses of intravenous glucocorticoids. **Dexamethasone at doses ranging from 16 to 100 mg daily is most commonly employed. Most frequently, patients are given an intravenous "loading dose" of 10 mg of dexamethasone followed by 4 mg every 6 hours; the optimal dose remains relatively undefined.** On improvement of symptoms, which can be accomplished promptly with steroids, the treatment dose may be tapered during a 2- to 3-week period (Greenberg et al, 1980).

Radiation therapy is often the main modality of treatment; however, recent reports suggest that surgery followed by radiation therapy is superior to radiation therapy alone. Surgery should be considered in patients who present with evidence of progression of signs and symptoms during radiotherapy, develop or present with unstable pathologic fractures, or have recurrence after radiotherapy. Clearly, the overall prognosis of the underlying disease should be taken into consideration during treatment selection. Chemotherapy is rarely used to treat epidural cord compressions.

Bone-Targeted Approaches

The pathogenesis of bone metastases in prostate cancer remains a subject of major study (Coleman, 1997). Alterations in the normal process of bone absorption and formation, which usually follows an orderly and sequential basis, appear to be a key determining factor (Galasko, 1986) in the development of bone metastasis associated with most malignant neoplasms. Under normal physiologic conditions, the process of bone remodeling is initiated by an increase in osteoclastic activity followed by an increase in osteoblastic differentiation and maturation, which will result in the formation of new bone and repair of the initial absorption caused by osteoblasts. Bone loss associated with prostate cancer can result from an enhanced osteoclastic activity associated with long-term androgen suppression, which in turn will cause excessive resorption of bone mineral and organic matrix. Tumor cells may also cause mineral release and matrix resorption in the areas involved by metastatic disease (Galasko, 1986). In addition to various cytokines, growth factors, tumor necrosis factors, and bone morphogenic proteins have been shown in preclinical studies to play a major role in the induction of both osteoclastic and osteoblastic activity (Galasko, 1986; Reddi and Cunningham, 1990). In prostate cancer, bone metastases are predominantly blastic, which reflects a predominance of osteoblastic activity in the process of bone remodeling (Coleman, 1997). This phenomenon may be due to specific growth factor secretion that is responsible for the induction of osteoblastic activity (Jacobs et al, 1979). Hypercalcemia is rare in metastatic prostate cancer; in fact, significantly elevated serum calcium concentration is most frequently (although the actual incidence is rare) due to the neuroendocrine prostate cancer phenotype discussed before (diSant'Agnese, 1995).

Bisphosphonates have become an integral part in the management of metastatic prostate cancer to the bones. These compounds reduce bone resorption by inhibiting osteoclastic activity and proliferation. Zoledronic acid is a potent intravenous bisphosphonate approved for the treatment of hypercalcemia (Green and Rogers, 2002) and the treatment of decreased bone mineral density in postmenopausal women (Green and Rogers, 2002). In patients with progressive hormone-refractory disease with bone metastasis, zoledronic acid was shown to reduce the incidence of skeletal events compared with placebo in a prospective randomized trial. In addition, it has also been shown to increase mineral bone density in patients with prostate cancer receiving long-term androgen deprivation (Saad et al, 2002, 2004; Smith et al, 2003). At present, this compound is indicated for the treatment of patients with progressive prostate cancer with evidence of bone metastasis at doses of 4 mg given by short intravenous infusion repeated at intervals of 3 to 4 weeks for several months. Side effects include fatigue, myalgias, fever, anemia, and mild elevations of serum creatinine concentration. Hypocalcemia has been described, and concomitant use of oral calcium supplements (1500 mg/day) and vitamin D (400 units/day) is recommended. **An unusual complication is the development of severe jaw pain associated with osteonecrosis of the mandibular bone.** The etiology of this complication is not well understood; however, it is most frequently seen in patients undergoing dental work or those with a history of poor dentition and chronic dental disease. The drug should not be administered to patients with these problems. Other bisphosphonates evaluated in prostate cancer are pamidronate, alendronate, and clodronate; however, their benefit has not been established in prospective randomized clinical trials (Saad, 2002, 2004).

Interaction between tumor cells and the bone marrow microenvironment has been postulated as an important mechanism in the pathogenesis of bone metastasis. Tumor-associated cytokines have been shown to induce the expression of the receptor activator of nuclear factor κB ligand (RANKL), which will bind and activate RANK, which is found in osteoclasts. Inhibition of the RANKL system has been the focus of research and represents an evolving bone-targeted strategy. Among the approaches are monoclonal antibodies to RANKL and the use of recombinant osteoprotegerin, which significantly inhibited osteoclastic function in vitro and in vivo (Brown et al, 2001).

The introduction of "bone-seeking" radiopharmaceuticals has provided a useful resource for the management of diffuse bone pain. Among the most commonly used compounds are strontium 89 (Porter et al, 1993; Porter and Davis, 1994) and samarium 153–lexidronam (Sartor et al, 2004). Initial studies with ^{89}Sr have shown palliation of pain to various degrees in 25% to 65% of patients with hormone-refractory disease with diffuse pain (Porter et al, 1993; Porter and Davis, 1994); in one clinical trial, it resulted in more durable pain control in combination with local external beam radiotherapy for localized bone pain (Porter and Davis, 1994). The pharmacokinetics of ^{89}Sr vary considerably according to the extent of bone involvement. The retention of the isotope is significantly longer in patients with diffuse osteoblastic metastasis compared with those with relatively limited bone involvement (Robinson, 1989). It is important to recognize this factor because it will undoubtedly affect the degree and duration of myelotoxicity associated with this radioactive compound. **The clinical experience with [153]Sm suggests that this isotope is associated with a lower incidence of severe myelotoxicity, probably because of its shorter half-life.** Encouraging results were reported by Sartor and colleagues (2004) in a phase III trial comparing radioactive ([153]Sm) and nonradioactive ([152]Sm) lexidronam complexes, indicating that the dose of [153]Sm of 1 mCi/kg is both safe and effective palliation for patients with hormone-refractory disease and severe bone pain. A study reported encouraging synergism with ^{89}Sr and doxorubicin, a known and well-studied radiosensitizer (Tu et al, 2001). Randomized studies evaluating the synergism of various chemotherapeutic agents, including taxanes and radiopharmaceuticals, are under way.

NOVEL APPROACHES
Rational Target Overview

An understanding of basic biology steps involved in the pathogenesis of prostate cancer provides the opportunity to identify potential targets that predict the clinical outcome of the disease. The first is the demonstration of a mutation or functional dysregulation of the target. Simply targeting overexpressed proteins has been less efficient than the specific targeting of novel mutations that drive the bulk of the tumor growth. The second is target causality, indicating the importance of the target alone or in combination with other mutations in reproducing the phenotypic findings of prostate cancer. Finally, there should be evidence from preclinical models that inhibition of the target leads to tumor regression or quiescence. In prostate cancer, the androgen receptor is one potential target. Various molecular changes in the androgen receptor have been shown to parallel disease progression in castrate patients and in some situations may provide the explanation for the responses associated with some therapeutic maneuvers (antiandrogen withdrawal syndrome, responses to secondary endocrine manipulations with compounds designed to bind to the receptor). Despite this, a precise role of the androgen receptor in the pathogenesis of disease progression remains to be better eluci-

dated. Given the molecular complexity of the prostate cancer cell pathways and relatively poor understanding of the role of individual pathways in the process of disease-specific progression, the inhibition of multiple pathways remains a common strategy to induce sustained and clinically meaningful responses in prostate cancer and other common malignant neoplasms.

The major biologic processes under therapeutic investigation in prostate cancer involve growth and survival, chemotherapy and hormone therapy resistance, angiogenesis, immune surveillance and escape, and stem cell renewal. This section provides an overview of these pathways as they pertain to prostate cancer specifically as rational targets and the approaches that are currently developed for therapeutic purposes.

Growth and Survival Pathways

Although a prostate cancer stem cell has yet to be conclusively demonstrated, prostate cancer clearly progresses from an androgen-dependent tumor with features similar to the luminal differentiated glands of the prostate to a hormone-refractory tumor that has features of adult stem cells, including anti-apoptotic mechanisms, chemotherapy resistance, and reliance on nonhormonal signaling pathways. **Candidate pathways currently evaluated include hedgehog signaling, phosphatidylinositol 3-kinase (PI3-kinase)/Akt signaling, MAP kinase signaling, or a combination of these.** Activation of the hedgehog developmental pathway has been demonstrated in prostate cancer metastases and in preclinical models, and inhibition of this pathway has led to antitumor effects and significant inhibition of prostatic epithelial regeneration after androgen withdrawal. Inhibitors of this pathway, such as cyclopamine analogues, are in preclinical development.

PI3-Kinase/Akt Pathway

In advanced prostate cancer, loss of the tumor suppressor *PTEN* **(phosphatase and tensin homologue deleted on chromosome 10) occurs in more than 50% of metastatic lesions and in approximately 20% of locally advanced lesions** (McMenamin et al, 1999; Graff, 2002). **Loss of** *PTEN* **correlates with advanced Gleason sum, stage, chemotherapy resistance, and other features of advanced prostate cancers** (McMenamin et al, 1999). *PTEN* **is a negative regulator of the PI3-kinase/Akt survival pathway, and advanced prostate cancers frequently have elevated levels of phosphorylated (activated) Akt** (Gera, 2004). The Akt pathway is involved in signal transduction from multiple cell surface receptors, including the insulin receptor, epidermal growth factor receptor, insulin-like growth factor receptor, platelet-derived growth factor receptor, and interleukin-6 receptor, and it is likely to function as a cellular sensor for nutrient and growth signals (Vivanco, 2002). In addition to promoting cell survival through the inhibition of apoptosis, the Akt pathway regulates cell growth, proliferation, and angiogenesis through the mTOR (mammalian target of rapamycin) pathway and the facilitated translation of signals such as c-Myc, cyclin D, and vascular endothelial growth factor (Gera, 2004). Restoration of functional *PTEN* activity or inhibition of mTOR activity can block the growth of $PTEN^{-/-}$ prostate cancer xenografts

and restore chemotherapy and possibly hormonal sensitivity (Neshat, 2001; Podsypanina, 2001; Grunwald, 2002).

Rapamycin is a natural compound isolated by Sehgal on Easter Island and is derived from soil samples containing the bacterium *Streptomyces hygroscopicus*. It was initially discarded as an antifungal agent because of its immunosuppressive properties but later revived as a potent immunosuppressive agent for use in solid organ transplantation. Its antiproliferative properties and antitumor activity in NCI cell lines led to its clinical development in cardiology as a means of preventing stent restenosis and in oncology, in which a wide variety of tumors were found to exhibit sensitivity to this agent and its analogue, CCI-779 (Hidalgo, 2000). Toxicities with rapamycin and rapamycin analogues have been predictable and often not dose related; they include maculopapular rash, hypertriglyceridemia, allergic reactions, mucositis, and thrombocytopenia (Atkins, 2004; Raymond, 2004; Hidalgo, 2000). The combination of these agents with docetaxel is attractive, given their ability to induce apoptosis when they are given in combination with chemotherapy in patients who have demonstrable activation of the Akt pathway as a result of *PTEN* mutation or loss or other genetic alterations.

Epidermal Growth Factor Receptor and Platelet-Derived Growth Factor Receptor Pathways

The rapid development in the last several years of small molecules that inhibit tyrosine kinase has yielded encouraging results in a host of cancers, including bronchoalveolar-type non–small cell lung cancer, chronic myelogenous leukemia, and gastrointestinal stromal tumors. Demonstration of response in these tumors has usually correlated with mutation in the target tyrosine kinase, such as epidermal growth factor receptor (EGFR), BCR-ABL, and c-Kit, respectively. In these cases, the target mutation has played a central role in the pathogenesis of these tumors. In prostate cancer, however, no such mutation has been identified, and indeed, early trials of tyrosine kinase inhibitors in prostate cancer have been disappointing.

EGFR is overexpressed in 40% to 80% of prostate cancer cells, and overexpression may be more common in African American men with prostate cancer (Shuch, 2005). Furthermore, preclinical data suggested a correlation of EGFR expression with Gleason sum and androgen independence (Syed, 2003). In a phase II study of approximately 100 patients with hormone-refractory disease evaluating the EGFR tyrosine kinase inhibitor gefitinib, minimal activity and no PSA responses were reported (Schroder, 2004; Moore, 2002). Gefitinib resistance may be related to overactivity of the PI3-kinase/Akt pathway in prostate cancer, and thus combinations of agents that target multiple pathways may be more beneficial (She, 2003). Further trials of combination EGFR or dual kinase inhibitors with chemotherapy or other novel agents are in development.

Prostate cancer cells express high levels of platelet-derived growth factor receptor, and this signaling pathway uses the PI3-kinase/Akt pathway, which has been implicated in prostate cancer progression. Single-agent activity with imatinib has been disappointing; however, encouraging results in combination with weekly docetaxel have been reported. A randomized trial of this combination compared with docetaxel alone is in progress.

Vitamin D Analogues

Vitamin D analogues may have differentiation, antiproliferation, and chemosensitizing properties. A phase II trial of weekly docetaxel and high-dose calcitriol demonstrated PSA responses in 30 of 37 patients (80%) and measurable responses in 8 of 15 (53%), with a median time to progression of 11.4 months and median survival of 19.4 months (Beer et al, 2005). **A randomized study with a total of 250 patients (125 per arm) comparing the combination with docetaxel alone resulted in more than 50% decline of PSA level in 63% of the patients receiving the combination compared with 52% with docetaxel alone ($P = .07$, not significant); however, interestingly, the authors reported a survival difference in favor of the combination (23.4 months versus 16.4 months; adjusted P value of 0.03).** These results should be considered preliminary since the study was not specifically designed to evaluate survival as the primary endpoint. A phase III study designed to evaluate survival as the main study endpoint is necessary for more definitive conclusions regarding the relative efficacy of this interesting therapeutic regimen compared with docetaxel alone.

Endothelin-1 Axis

Preclinical studies suggest that endothelin A receptors are overexpressed in prostate cancer, and higher plasma endothelin levels in patients with prostate cancer have been shown to correlate with tumor stage, grade, and metastases. Endothelin-1 is a potent vasoconstrictor, and antagonists have been developed for the treatment of pulmonary hypertension. In oncology, endothelin is likely to be involved in the paracrine signals between osteoblasts and prostate cancer cells that regulate the development of bone metastases and have been shown to influence cell growth and proliferation, regulate osteoblast activity, and inhibit apoptosis. These preclinical observations suggest that this pathway may be a rational target for the interference of tumor-stromal interactions (Nelson et al, 2003; Carducci, 2002; Yin, 2003).

Atrasentan has been developed as a highly selective endothelin A receptor antagonist and has been extensively tested in prostate cancer. In preliminary phase II trials, a 10-mg dose of atrasentan was found to prolong time to progression compared with placebo in men with metastatic hormone-refractory prostate cancer (196 versus 129 days, respectively; $P = .021$) (Carducci, 2002). Adverse events with atrasentan were mild and related to vasomotor reactions, including headache, rhinitis, flushing, and peripheral edema. Favorable effects were seen in markers of bone deposition and resorption, which led to its further clinical development.

In a placebo-controlled, double-blinded, phase III trial involving 809 patients with metastatic hormone-refractory prostate cancer, oral atrasentan (10 mg/day) prolonged time to progression, although the difference was not found to be statistically significant. Several secondary endpoints, including improvements in quality of life scores and pain scores and reductions in the rise of laboratory markers including alkaline phosphatase and PSA, favored atrasentan (Nelson et al, 2003). These results point to biologic activity of the endothelin axis in modulating osteoblastic metastases and suggest that continuing evaluation is clearly warranted.

Proteasome Inhibitors

The ubiquitin-proteasome degradation pathway is an essential component of normal cellular machinery for the processing and recycling of proteins, including those active in cell cycle progression, checkpoint regulation, and cell death (Mitchell, 2003; Papandreou, 2004; Richardson, 2003).

Bortezomib, a boronic acid derivative, was the first proteasome inhibitor to be tested and approved for use in humans, specifically in multiple myeloma. Its use in solid tumors, including prostate cancer, is being actively developed either as a single agent or in combination with docetaxel (Dreicer et al, 2004; Papandreou, 2004).

Immunotherapy

Active immunotherapy with vaccination against tumor antigens has been pursued in many different cancer models. A variety of approaches have been employed, including dendritic cell–based therapies; novel adjuvants, such as bacille Calmette-Guérin, granulocyte-monocyte colony-stimulating factor (GM-CSF), and viral carriers; single-antigen or whole cell vaccines; and genetically modified tumors. More recently, combination therapies using co-stimulatory molecules, CTLA-4 blockade, toll-like receptor agonism, and intracellular viral or bacterial mediators have been developed (Pardoll, 1992; Fuchs, Mapara, Blattman).

In prostate cancer, several vaccine strategies have been under active clinical development. These include the Provenge autologous prostatic acid phosphatase (PAP)–loaded dendritic cell vaccine, the GVAX allogeneic recombinant whole cell vaccine, the Prostvac-VF recombinant pox viral PSA vaccine, and the BLP25 MUC1 liposomal vaccine. Each of these vaccines is designed to stimulate the immune system to recognize a previously toleragenic tumor in a cancer-specific way.

Provenge is a vaccine derived from CD54+ dendritic cells, the major antigen-presenting cells, which are pheresed from individuals and processed with the recombinant fusion protein PAP and GM-CSF. PAP was chosen on the basis of its prostate cell membrane localization and the success of preclinical models using it to generate prostate-specific immune responses and autoimmune prostatitis. Modest activity was reported in phase II trials in patients with hormone-refractory disease. In a subsequent randomized trial comparing Provenge against placebo in 127 asymptomatic men with metastatic hormone-refractory prostate cancer (PAP positive), the investigators reported no significant differences in time to disease and pain progression, which corresponded to the main study endpoint. Patients randomized to placebo were crossed over to receive the active vaccine at the time of progression, whereas those initially randomized to receive the active vaccine were treated at their physician's discretion at the time of progression. This post-progression management period was not part of the study and not prospectively controlled. Whereas the study as designed was negative, a 3-year update suggested a statistically significant improvement in survival for those randomly assigned to receive the active vaccine initially. It is highly probable that survival differences were due to post-vaccine treatments. A prospectively randomized phase III study is necessary to adequately evaluate survival. Post hoc analyses also suggested that the benefits of Provenge may be limited to the subgroup of men with tumor Gleason sums of 7 or lower. At present, a randomized placebo-controlled study prospectively evaluating the benefits of Provenge in patients with Gleason sums of 7 or lower is in progress. Although preparation and production of large-scale quantities of individually tailored vaccine may be difficult, this vaccine was well tolerated, with minimal infusion-related fever and rigors being the predominant adverse event.

Prostate GVAX is based on the demonstration in mouse melanoma models of improved tumor rejection when the irradiated tumor vaccine expressed the cytokine GM-CSF compared with other cytokine adjuvants (Dranoff, 1993, 2003). Given that GM-CSF probably leads to the maturation and activation of dendrite cells, further work extrapolated these findings in mouse models of prostate cancer, with results showing prolonged survival and tumor regression. Clinical trials with GVAX in patients with hormone-refractory disease are in progress.

Angiogenesis Targets

Tumor angiogenesis is likely to be an important biologic component of prostate cancer metastasis, and elevated levels of the potent angiogenic molecule vascular endothelial growth factor (VEGF) have been shown to correlate with advanced clinical stage and survival (George, 2002; Duque, 1999).

In a retrospective study of archived serum samples from CALGB 9480, VEGF levels were independently associated with survival from prostate cancer (George, 2002). Similarly, antibodies to VEGF have slowed prostate xenograft growth rates, especially in combination with chemotherapy (Fox, 2002; Sweeney, 2002). This led to the phase II CALGB 90006, which added bevacizumab to docetaxel and estramustine in men with metastatic hormone-refractory prostate cancer. Bevacizumab was given at 15 mg/m^2 on day 2, estramustine at 280 mg orally three times daily on days 1 to 5, and docetaxel at 70 mg/m^2 on day 2 every 3 weeks. Prophylactic dexamethasone and low-dose warfarin were also given. Among 79 treated patients, a decline of more than 50% in PSA level was seen in 81%, median time to progression was 9.7 months, and overall median survival was 21 months. These favorable results have led to the design of a phase III trial of bevacizumab with single-agent docetaxel in hormone-refractory prostate cancer.

Thalidomide was originally developed in the 1960s for treatment of morning sickness and subsequently linked to teratogenic effects resulting in dysmelia, or limb shortening. Whereas the exact mechanism of teratogenesis is unproven, the metabolites of thalidomide have been shown to inhibit angiogenesis through multiple potential mechanisms, including inhibition of pro-angiogenic signals such as VEGF, basic fibroblast growth factor, interleukin-6, and tumor necrosis factor-α (Franks, 2004; Bartlett, 2004). Preclinical studies suggest that thalidomide has T-cell co-stimulatory activity and immunomodulatory properties. Phase I/II studies with high doses of thalidomide as a single agent have yielded low response rates on the order of 18% for PSA declines (Figg, 2001; Franks, 2004). In a randomized phase II trial of weekly docetaxel and low-dose thalidomide and docetaxel alone, response and survival data appeared to be more favorable with the combination (Dahut, 2004). Whereas this trial was underpowered to detect a difference from the standard arm, the clinical activity and manageable toxicity led to the development of more potent thalidomide analogues for combination therapy, currently undergoing clinical evaluation.

Toxicities with thalidomide include deep venous thrombosis, sedation, neuropathy, constipation, and fatigue. Newer thalidomide analogues with immunomodulatory features have been developed that lack the neurotoxicity of thalidomide but retain many of the T-cell modulatory functions, anti-angiogenic properties, and even direct pro-apoptotic functions (Bartlett, 2004). CC-5013 (Revlimid) and CC-4047 (Actimid) are second-generation compounds with much more potent tumor necrosis factor-α inhibition than the parent compound, and clinical testing with these agents in phase II trials has begun.

SUGGESTED READINGS

Eisenberger M, Nelson WG: How much can we rely on PSA as an endpoint for clinical trials in prostate cancer? A word of caution. J Natl Cancer Inst 1996;88:779-780.

Eisenberger MA, Simon R, O'Dwyer PJ, et al: A reevaluation of nonhormonal cytotoxic chemotherapy in the treatment of prostatic carcinoma. J Clin Oncol 1985;3:827-841.

Halabi S, Small EJ, Kantoff PW, et al: Prognostic model for predicting survival in men with hormone refractory metastatic prostate cancer. J Clin Oncol 2003;22:1232-1237.

Petrylak DP, Tangen CM, Hussain MH, et al: Docetaxel and estramustine compared with mitoxantrone and prednisone for advanced refractory prostate cancer. N Engl J Med 2004;351:1513-1520.

Scher H, Kelly KW: Flutamide withdrawal syndrome: Its impact on clinical trials in hormone refractory prostate cancer. J Clin Oncol 1993;11:1566-1572.

Smaletz O, Scher H, Small EJ, et al: Nomogram for survival of patients with progressive metastatic prostate cancer after castration. J Clin Oncol 2002;20:3972-3982.

Tannock I, Osoba D, Stockler MR, et al: Chemotherapy with mitoxantrone plus prednisone or prednisone alone for symptomatic hormone-resistant prostate cancer: A Canadian randomized trial with palliative endpoints. J Clin Oncol 1996;14:1753-1755.

Tannock I, DeWit R, Berry W, et al: Docetaxel plus prednisone or mitoxantrone plus prednisone for advanced prostate cancer. N Engl J Med 2004;351:1502-1512.

INDEX

Angiotensin-converting enzyme (ACE) gene
    polymorphisms, implication of, in renal
    scarring, 3238
Angiotensin-converting enzyme (ACE)
    inhibitors
    abnormal renal structure and function due to,
        3135
    causing geriatric incontinence, 2308t, 2309
    erectile dysfunction caused by, 743, 744t
    for glomerulopathy, after partial nephrectomy,
        1613-1614
    renal protection with, 1350
Angiotensinogen, in renin-angiotensin-
    aldosterone system, 1161
Animal bites, to penis, 2650
    in children, 3945
Animal models, painful bladder
    syndrome/interstitial cystitis in, 337-338,
    338f
Anion(s), transport of, effect of ureteral
    obstruction on, 1202-1203
Anion gap
    definition of, 1153, 3154
        normal, 1153t
    urinary, 3155
Anogenital cancer, HPV-related, in AIDS
    patients, 399
Anorchia, bilateral (vanishing testis syndrome),
    640
Anorectal malformations
    in bladder exstrophy, 3503
    Wingspread classification of, 3647t
Anorgasmia, 87
Antegrade Continence Enema (ACE) procedure,
    for fecal continence, in myelomeningocele,
    3640
Antegrade continence enemas, in children,
    3700-3701, 3700f
Antegrade pyelography. See Pyelography,
    antegrade.
Anthracyclines, causing congestive heart failure,
    in children, 3898
Antiandrogen(s)
    androgen blockade with, 3085-3087, 3085t
    erectile dysfunction caused by, 745
    for priapism, 846t
    nonsteroidal, 3086
Antiandrogen withdrawal phenomenon, 3086
Antiangiogenic agents, for renal cell carcinoma,
    1590
Antibiotics
    as inhibitors of angiogenesis, 543
    causing interstitial cystitis, 338-339
    effect of, on ureteral function, 1920
    for acute pyelonephritis, 269-270, 270t
    for bacteriuria, in pregnancy, 292-293, 292t
    for cystitis, 256-257, 256t
    for human and animal bite wounds, 2651
    for prostatitis, 318-321
        clinical trial data in, 318-320, 320t
        dosage of, 325t
        pharmacology and pharmacokinetics in, 318
        rationale in, 318
    for renal abscess, 276
    for urinary tract infections
        bacterial resistance to, 244-245
        choice of, 249
        duration of therapy and, 249
        formulary of, 245-249, 245t, 246t-247t
        in children, 3247-3249, 3248t
            dosages of, 3248t
            prophylactic, 3249-3252, 3250t
            selection of, 3249
        mechanism of action of, 245t

Antibiotics (Continued)
    principles of, 243-249, 244t
    prophylactic
        cystoscopy and, 252
        endocarditis risk and, 253-254, 254t
        endoscopic procedures and, 253
        indwelling orthopedic hardware and,
            254, 254t
        low-dose, 262-265, 262t
        open and laparoscopic surgery and, 253,
            253t
        post-intercourse, 265
        principles of, 250, 250t, 251t
        shockwave lithotripsy and, 252
        transrectal prostate biopsy and, 251-252,
            2889
        transurethral procedures and, 252
        ureteroscopy and, 1514-1515
        urethral catheterization and, 250
        urodynamics and, 251
        urologic procedures and, 250-254, 251t
    for urodynamic studies, 1987
        prophylactic, 251
    in bowel preparation
        disadvantages of, 2539
        for urinary tract reconstruction, 2538-2539,
            2538t
    intravenous, in hypospadias repair, 3718-3719
    low-dose prophylactic, for recurrent urinary
        tract infections, 262-265, 262t
        biologic basis in, 262-263
        efficacy of, 264
    perioperative
        for transurethral resection of prostate, 2831
        in vesicovaginal fistula repair, 2332
    post-intercourse prophylactic, for recurrent
        urinary tract infections, 265
    prophylactic, 225
        for bacteremia, 1515
        for bacterial endocarditis, 1515
        for pediatric urinary tract infections, 3249-
            3252, 3250t
        for percutaneous nephrolithotomy, 1485-
            1486
        for ureteroscopy, 253, 1514-1515
        for urodynamic studies, 251
        for vesicoureteral reflux, 4348, 4349t, 4350
    resistance of, to urinary tract infections, 3266-
        3267
    suppressive, 225
Antibody(ies). See also Immunoglobulin entries.
    antisperm. See Antisperm antibodies.
    monoclonal
        in tumor immunology, 500
        synthesis of, 478
    production of, 478
    structure and binding of, 478, 478f
Antibody assay(s), for HSV infection, 373-374
Anticholinergics
    affecting lower urinary tract function, 3628t
    causing geriatric incontinence, 2308, 2308t
    for painful bladder syndrome/interstitial
        cystitis, 360t, 361
    uropharmacology of, 1950, 1950t
Anticholinesterase, effect of, on ureteral
    function, 1905
Antidepressants
    effect of, on ureteral function, 1920
    erectile dysfunction caused by, 745
    for incontinence, in elderly, 2317t
    for overactive bladder/detrusor overactivity,
        2093t, 2104-2105
    for painful bladder syndrome/interstitial
        cystitis, 359-360, 360t

Antidepressants (Continued)
    for premature ejaculation
        on-demand, 786
        serotonergic, 785-786
    for stress incontinence, 2111-2112
    tricyclic
        erectile dysfunction caused by, 744
        for urethral sphincter dysfunction, in
            children, 3620
    uropharmacology of, 1962
Antidiuretic hormone (ADH)
    actions of, 1137, 1138f
    and renal development, 3159
    in renal hemodynamics, 1134
    release of, factors affecting, 1137-1138, 1137t
Antifungals, 468-469
    cost of, 464t
    dosage of, 461t
    topical
        for seborrheic dermatitis, 415
        for vulvovaginal candidiasis, 385
Antigen(s), 478. See also specific antigen.
    impaired presentation of, mechanism of
        tumor escape in, 497
    presentation of, in immune response, 480-
        481, 480f
    tumor-associated, 495-496, 496t
    in cancer vaccines, 499-500
Antigen detection kits, for HSV infection,
    374
Antigenic markers, in bladder cancer, 2436
Antigen-presenting cell(s), 477
Antihistamines, for painful bladder
    syndrome/interstitial cystitis, 360, 360t
Antihypertensive agents, erectile dysfunction
    caused by, 743, 744t
Antilymphocyte antibodies, in
    immunosuppressive regimens, 1316-1317
Antimuscarinic agents
    for incontinence, 2071-2072, 2072t
    for overactive bladder/detrusor overactivity,
        2093-2099, 2093t
    for urethral sphincter dysfunction, in
        children, 3620
    quaternary compounds, 2094
    selectivity of, 1951
    tertiary compounds, 2094
    uropharmacology of, 1950, 1950t
Antimuscarinic Clinical Effectiveness Trial
    (ACET), 2096
Antioxidants, for prostate cancer,
    chemopreventive, 2870-2871
Antiproliferative factor, in painful bladder
    syndrome/interstitial cystitis, 347-348, 347t,
    348f, 353
Antipsychotics, erectile dysfunction caused by,
    744
Antireflux mechanism
    functional anatomy of, 4327-4328, 4327f,
        4328t
    incorporation of, in orthotopic urinary
        diversion, 2630-2633
Antireflux surgery, 4350-4360
    Cohen-Anderson technique of, 4356-4357,
        4357f
    complications of
        early, 4360-4361
        long-term, 4361-4362
    cystoscopy in, 4351
    endoscopic, 4362-4366
        follow-up of, 4363-4364
        materials used in, 4364-4365, 4364t
        recurrence of reflux after, 4365-4366
        STING technique of, 4362-4363, 4363f

Antireflux surgery *(Continued)*
  extravesical procedures in, 4357, 4358f, 4359-4360
  Gil-Vernet procedure in, 4366
  Glenn-Anderson technique of, 4356, 4356f
  in children, 3661-3663
    peritoneoscopic, 3926-3927, 3927f
    single ureteral reimplantation as, 3661-3662
    transureteroureterostomy as, 3661-3662, 3661f
    with intestinal segments, 3662
    with psoas hitch, 3662, 3663f
  in exstrophy repair, 3524, 3525f-3526f, 3526
    postoperative care after, 3526
  incision in, 4351
  intravesical procedures in, 4352
  laparoscopic, 4366-4367
  Paquin technique of, 4352, 4356
  patient positioning for, 4351
  Politano-Leadbetter technique of, 4352, 4353f-4355f
  postoperative evaluation in, 4360
  principles of correction in, 4350-4351
Antireflux valves, in ureterointestinal anastomosis, 2561-2562, 2561f, 2562f
Antiretroviral therapy
  and genital secretions, 388
  for HIV infection, 401-403, 402f
Antispasmodics, for painful bladder syndrome/interstitial cystitis, 360t, 361
Antisperm antibodies
  assays for, 624t
  detection of, 624-625
  development of, risk factors for, 623-624
  effect of, on sperm function, 624
  in male infertility, analysis of, 623-625
Antituberculous drugs, for genitourinary tuberculosis, 443-444, 445t
Antrum technique, of gastrocystoplasty, in children, 3678
Anus. *See* Anal; Ano- *entries.*
  imperforate, 3647, 3647t
    associated findings in, 3647-3648
    evaluation of, 3648, 3649f
    in neonate, 3195
    in unilateral renal agenesis, 3275, 3275f
Anxiolytics, erectile dysfunction caused by, 745
Aorta, abdominal, 6f, 9, 13
  aneurysm of
    as contraindication to laparoscopy, 175
    ureteral obstruction due to, 1221, 1222f
  branches of, 9, 11f, 13, 13t
  complications of, after renal bypass surgery, 1752
Aortic syndrome, middle, 1191, 1191f
Aortorenal bypass, 1734-1737, 1735f-1738f
  thoracic, 1742-1743, 1742f, 1743f
APC gene, 516
  in colorectal cancer, 516
Aphallia, 3756-3757, 3757f
Aphthous ulcers, of male genitalia, 417-418, 418f
Apical support defects, in vaginal wall prolapse, surgical management of
  abdominal approach to, 2224
  abdominal sacral colpopexy in, 2228, 2229f
  iliococcygeus ligament suspension in, 2227-2228, 2228t
  laparoscopic, 2229-2230, 2230t
  sacrospinous ligament fixation in, 2225-2226, 2226f
  uterosacral ligament suspension in, 2226-2227, 2227f
  vaginal approach to, 2223-2224, 2224f, 2225f

Apnea, sleep, testosterone therapy causing, 859
Apomorphine
  for erectile dysfunction, 782
  in male sexual function, 729
Apoptosis, 488-490, 529-533
  bcl-2 family member-mediated, 530-531, 532
  caspase-mediated, prostate cancer cells and, 2858, 2859f
  cell death and, 531
  cell survival and, 530-531
  death receptor pathway in, 488-489, 489f
  death receptor–dependent receptors in, 530
  death receptor–induced, 529-530, 530f
  global defects in, 532
  in genitourinary malignancies, 531-532
    alternative regulators of, 532-533
  induction of, in transurethral microwave therapy, 2815-2816
  initiation of, caspases in, 531
  ligand-dependent receptors in, 530
  markers of, 2430
  mechanisms of, in cryotherapy, 3035, 3035t
  mitochondrial pathway in, 489-490
  NFκB regulation of, 490
  regulation of, 2730-2731
    in kidney development, 3167, 3167f
    in prostate growth, 2714-2715
  renal damage due to, 1342-1343
  TP53-induced, 530, 531f, 532
  tumor-induced, in T cells, 498-499
Appendicovesicostomy, for continent urinary diversion, 3694-3695, 3694f
  results of, 3696-3697
Appendix
  in antegrade continence enemas, for continent urinary diversion, 3700, 3700f
  in ileocecocystoplasty, 3675
Appendix epididymis, 3137, 3792
Appendix testis, 3792
Arcus tendineus fasciae pelvis, 2195, 2196f
Arcus tendineus levator ani, 2195
Areflexia
  definition of, 1981
  of detrusor muscle. *See* Detrusor muscle, areflexia of.
L-Arginine, for painful bladder syndrome/interstitial cystitis, 360t, 361
Argon beam coagulator, in laparoscopy, 192-193
Aristolochia fangchi herb, bladder cancer associated with, 2416
Aromatase inhibitors, for benign prostatic hyperplasia, 2797
Arrhythmias
  anesthesia-related, in laparoscopy, 210-211
  pneumoperitoneum and, 200
Arterial embolization, for nonischemic priapism, 848
Arteriography. *See* Angiography.
Arteriovenous fistula
  delayed bleeding due to, following percutaneous procedures, 1546, 1546f
  renal, 1189-1190, 1189f, 3297
    acquired, 1189, 1189f
    congenital, 1189
    idiopathic, 1189
Arteritis, Takayasu's, in children, 1184
Artery(ies). *See also specific artery, e.g.,* Aorta.
  dilation of, penile blood flow and, 758-759, 759f
  kinking of, after renal transplantation, 1318
Artificial sweeteners, bladder cancer associated with, 2415
Artificial urinary bladder. *See also* Bladder.
  for filling/storage disorders, 2297-2298

Artificial urinary sphincter
  evolution of, 2398f
  for bladder filling/storage disorders, 2294
  for bladder neck reconstruction, in children
    results of, 3667-3668
    technique of, 3666-3667, 3667f
  for male incontinence, 2077, 2396-2403
    complications of, 2399-2401
    history and development of, 2396-2397, 2398f
    implantation technique of, 2397, 2399f
    in special circumstances, 2401-2403
    indications for, 2391-2392
    results of, 2397
  for stress incontinence, in females, 2076-2077
  incompetence of
    in children, 2402
    in females, 2401-2402
  mechanical failure of, 2401
ARTs. *See* Assisted reproductive techniques (ARTs).
Ascites
  as complication of post-chemotherapy surgery, 956
  as contraindication to laparoscopy, 175
  chylous, after laparoscopy, 219
  urinary
    in neonate, 3196
    posterior urethral valves causing, 3586t, 3588
ASI stent, 2809
Ask-Upmark kidney, 1191
  clinical features of, 3311
  histopathology of, 3311
  treatment of, 3312
Aspergillosis, 464-465, 465f
Aspergillus, 464
Aspiration
  fine-needle. *See* Fine-needle aspiration biopsy.
  in laparoscopy, 196
  of gastric contents, 211
  in radical laparoscopic nephrectomy, hand-assisted, 1797-1798
  of bladder, suprapubic, 238-239
  of renal cysts, 1551, 3347
  of seminal vesicles, in assessment of ejaculatory duct obstruction, 710, 712f
  of sperm
    from epididymis
      microsurgical technique of, 652, 700, 703f-704f
      percutaneous technique of, 652, 700, 702f-703f
    from vas deferens, 700
Aspirin, associated with Reye's syndrome, 3206
Asplenism, risk of priapism with, 840
Assisted reproductive techniques (ARTs), 650-653, 651t
  in vitro fertilization with, 652
  intrauterine insemination with, 651-652
  semen processing in, 651
  sperm retrieval in, 652-653
  success of, 609
Asthenospermia, evaluation of, 622-623, 622f
Ataxia, cerebellar, voiding dysfunction with, 2017
Atelectasis
  after radical nephrectomy, 1720
  as complication of post-chemotherapy surgery, 956
Atheroembolism, ischemic nephropathy due to, 1166

Bladder (*Continued*)
  in exstrophy patient. *See also* Bladder exstrophy.
    bladder neck repair in
      failed, 3536-3537
      results of, 3533-3534, 3533t
    closure of, 3510, 3511f-3512f, 3513
      combined with epispadias repair, 3517-3518, 3526, 3527f-3530f, 3530
        results of, 3531-3533, 3535
      failed, 3535-3536, 3536f
      results of, 3531, 3531t
    defects of, 3505-3507, 3506f, 3507f
    small, unsuitable for closure, management of, 3516-3517
  in prune-belly syndrome, 3484, 3484f
  in utero decompression of, indications for, 3187-3188, 3187t
  infections of, 254-265. *See also* Urinary tract infection; *specific infection.*
  inflammation of. *See* Cystitis.
  injury to. *See* Bladder injury.
  innervation of, 60, 3605, 3606f
    afferent pathways in, 1938-1939, 1938f, 1939t
    interruption of, 2289-2291
    parasympathetic pathways in, 1938
    peripheral, 1937-1939, 1938f
    somatic pathways in, 1938
    sympathetic pathways in, 1938
  internal surface of, 57-58
  lymphatic drainage of, 60
  magnetic resonance imaging of, 135, 137f
  male, dissection of, 58f
  manual compression of, for emptying disorders, 2298
  mechanical compression of, for filling/storage disorders, 2291-2292
  mucosa of, free graft, for neourethral formation in hypospadias repair, 3734, 3736-3728, 3738f
  muscles. *See* Smooth muscle, bladder.
  myoplasty of, to facilitate emptying, 2299-2300
  native, management of, in augmentation cystoplasty, 3672-3673, 3673f
  natural defenses of, 235-236
  neck of. *See* Bladder neck.
  neurogenic. *See* Neurogenic bladder.
  outlet obstruction of. *See* Bladder outlet, obstruction of.
  overactivity of. *See* Overactive bladder.
  overdistention of, therapeutic, 2288
  pain in. *See also* Painful bladder syndrome/interstitial cystitis.
    related to filling, 2084
  paralytic, 1982
  perforation of. *See also* Bladder injury.
    delayed
      after augmentation cystoplasty, 3684-3686, 3685f
      etiology of, 3685
      incidence of, 3685-3686
      treatment of, 3686
    resectoscope causing, 2482, 2482f
  reconstruction of, sling procedures associated with, 2249
  reflexes of. *See under* Reflex(es).
  regeneration of
    in children, 3690-3691
    matrices for, 559-560
  relationship between brain dysfunctions and, in nocturnal enuresis, 3624

Bladder (*Continued*)
  replacement of
    for painful bladder syndrome/interstitial cystitis, 367
    tissue engineering in, 561-562, 562f, 563f
  retrograde flow of urine from. *See* Vesicoureteral reflux.
  sensory aspects of, 1976
  sensory input to, therapeutic inhibition of, 2106-2109
  sphincter of. *See* Urethral sphincter.
    artificial. *See* Artificial urinary sphincter.
  storage function of, 1976
    cystometrographic studies of, 1993, 1993f, 1995, 1995f
    failure in, 1976-1977
      electrical stimulation for, 2151-2163. *See also* Electrical stimulation, of bladder.
      functional classification of, 1978-1979, 1978t, 1979t
        expanded, 1980t
      phases in, 1939-1941, 1940t, 1942f, 1943f
      reflexes promoting, 2149, 2149f
      therapy to facilitate, 1979t, 2091-2114, 2288-2298. *See also specific therapy.*
  structure of, 57-58, 58f, 59f
  suprapubic aspiration of, in urinary tract infection, 238-239
  surgical approaches to, 2483
    laparoscopic, 2506-2532, 2507t. *See also specific procedure.*
  surgical compression of, for filling/storage disorders, 2293-2294
  tissue engineering of, 558-562, 559f
    artificial replacement by, 561-562, 562f, 563f
    matrices for, 559-560
    tissue expansion for bladder augmentation in, 558-559, 559f
    with cell transplantation, 561, 561f
  transection of, 2290-2291
  trigone of, 59f, 60, 60f
    embryology of, 3132-3133, 3134f
  tuberculosis of, 438, 439f
  tumors of. *See* Bladder cancer.
  ulcers of, schistosomal, 453
  ultrasonography of, 122, 124, 125f
  underactivity of, 1978
  unstable (overactive). *See also* Overactive bladder.
    definition of, 2079
  urachal anchoring of, 57
  ureterovesical junction of, 58-59, 60f
  urothelial layer of, 1932-1935, 1933f. *See also* Urothelium.
  viscoelastic properties of, 1974
Bladder augmentation
  calculi in, 2666-2667
    management of, 2669-2670, 2671f
  for incontinence, 2074
  for urethral sphincter dysfunction, in children, 3620
  laparoscopic technique of, 560
  overactivity in, drug treatment for, 2108-2109
  tissue expansion for, 558-559, 559f
Bladder autoaugmentation, in children, 3688-3690, 3689f
  laparoscopic, 3925
Bladder calculi, 1427, 2663-2670
  after augmentation cystoplasty, 3684
  diagnosis of, 2668

Bladder calculi (*Continued*)
  in augmentations and urinary diversions, 2666-2667
    management of, 2669-2670, 2671f
  management of, 1428, 2668-2670
    chemolysis in, 2668
    cystolitholapexy in, 2668-2669
    cystolithotomy in, 2669
    endoscopic lithotripsy in, 2669-2670
    shockwave lithotripsy in, 2668
    surgical approach to, 2670, 2671f
  migrant, 2663
  primary idiopathic (endemic), 2663-2664
  secondary, 2664-2666
    foreign body nidus, 2666, 2667f
    related to bladder outlet syndrome, 2664-2665, 2664f-2666f
    related to infection or catheterization, 2665-2666
  symptoms of, 2667-2668
  with benign prostatic hyperplasia, 2757
Bladder cancer, 2407-2446
  adenocarcinoma as, 2422
  age associated with, 2409
  analgesic abuse as, 2415
  apoptosis in, 532
  autopsy data and, 2409
  biology of, 2407
  cystectomy for. *See* Cystectomy.
  diagnosis of, 2430-2432
    flow cytometry in, 2431
    image analysis in, 2432
    microscopic cytology in, 2431
    signs and symptoms in, 2430-2431
    specimen interpretation in, 2432
  early detection of, 2432-2438
    antigenic markers in, 2436
    biases and pitfalls in, 2432-2433
    combination markers studies in, 2436
    CT imaging in, 2437
    cystoscopy in, 2437-2438
    excretory urography in, 2437
    fluorescence cytology tests in, 2436
    microsatellite repeat analyses in, 2435
    nuclear matrix proteins in, 2434-2435
    rationale for, 2432
    reported studies in, 2433-2434
    screening for, 2432-2434
      carcinogen exposure and, 2436-2437
    site-selected biopsies in, 2438
    survivin in, 2435-2436
    telomerase in, 2435
    tumor resection in, 2438
  enterocystoplasty as risk factor for, 1324
  etiology of, 2410-2413
    amplification and overexpression in, 2412-2413
    basic biology in, 2410
    CDKN2A gene in, 523
    oncogenes in, 2410
    retinoblastoma gene and regulators in, 2411-2412
    TP53 gene in, 2411, 2414
    tumor suppressor genes in, 2410-2411
  in renal transplant recipients, 1324, 2416
  in situ carcinoma as, 2418-2419, 2418f
  incidence of, 2407-2408
    regional and national differences in, 2409
  interstitial cystitis and, 335
  invasive, 2468-2476
    bimanual examination of, 2468
    bladder preservation protocols for, 2475-2476, 2476t, 2477f
    chemotherapy for

Children (*Continued*)
undescended testes in. *See* Cryptorchidism.
ureteropelvic junction obstruction in, 3359-
3382. *See also* Ureteropelvic junction
obstruction, in children.
ureteroscopy in, 1520
ureters in, length and diameter of, 4328t
urethral duplication in, 3601, 3602f, 3603
urethral polyps in, 3601, 3601f
urethral prolapse in, 3210
urethral stricture in, 3600, 3601f
urethral valve anomalies in. *See* Urethral
valves, posterior.
urgent evaluations of, 3199t, 3203
urinary tract infection in, 3232-3268. *See also*
Urinary tract infection, in children.
urinary tract reconstruction in, 3656-3702.
See also Urinary tract reconstruction, in
children; *specific procedure.*
urologic office visit for, 3204-3215
hematuria in, 3212
history in, 3205
laboratory examination in, 3211-3212
outpatient procedures in, 3214-3215
physical examination in, 3205-3210, 3206t,
3207t, 3208f, 3209f, 3211f, 3211t
radiologic examination in, 3212-3214,
3214f
surgical procedures performed in, 3215,
3215f
voiding history in, 3205
vaginal bleeding in, 3209
tumors and, 3210
vaginal discharge in, 3209
vesicoureteral reflux in, 4323-4367. *See also*
Vesicoureteral reflux.
voiding dysfunction in
neuropathic, 3625-3653
central nervous system insults and, 3648-
3653
neurospinal dysraphisms and, 3628-3648
urodynamic evaluation of, 3625-3628
non-neuropathic. *See also* Urethral
sphincter, dysfunction of.
classification of, 3609-3611, 3610f
epidemiology of, 3609
evaluation of, 3614-3618
management of, 3618-3620
prevalence of, 3609
sacral neuromodulation for, 2157-2158
urinary tract infections and, 3262
Children's Oncology Group Staging System, for
testicular germ cell tumors, 3903t
Chills, patient history of, 88
Chlamydia, in urinary tract infections, 229
Chlamydia pneumoniae, in painful bladder
syndrome/interstitial cystitis, 339
Chlamydia trachomatis
in lymphogranuloma venereum, 377
in proctitis, 371
in prostatitis, 306-307
infection with
diagnosis of, 378
testing for, 627
treatment of, 378-379
prevalence of, 372
Chloramphenicol, for *Pasteurella multocida*
infection, 2651
Chloride, renal reabsorption of
in cortical collecting tubules, 1144-1145
in distal tubules, 1144
in loop of Henle, 1142
Chloroquine derivatives, for painful bladder
syndrome/interstitial cystitis, 360t, 361

Chlorothiazide, for renal tubular acidosis, in
infant and child, 3155
Chlorthalidone
for absorptive hypercalcemia, 1418
for renal hypercalciuria, 1419, 1421t
Cholesterol, in prostatic secretions, 2718
Cholesterol embolism, of renal artery, 1166
Cholinergic agonists, role of, in ureteral
function, 1904
Cholinergic receptors
in pontine micturition center, 1965
muscarinic, 1949-1951, 1949f, 1950t
drug selectivity for, 1951
Cholinesterase inhibitors, causing geriatric
incontinence, 2308t, 2309
Chondrocyte injections
autologous, for incontinence, 2286
for vesicoureteral reflux, 568, 568f
Chondrocytes, for endoscopic correction of
reflux, 4364t, 4365
Chondroitin sulfate, for painful bladder
syndrome/interstitial cystitis, 362t, 364
Chordee, 1087. *See also* Penile curvature.
correction of, 1048-1049, 1048f, 1049f
etiology of, 3707-3708
release of, in exstrophy patient, 3519-3520
without hypospadias, 1088-1089, 3756, 3756f
Choriocarcinoma
of bladder, 2445
testicular, 895
incidence, pathology, and presentation of,
898t
Chromaffin cells, 1828, 1829f
Chromatin
abnormal, risk factors for, 626
integrity testing of, in male infertility, 626-627
organization and regulation of, in prostate
growth, 2712-2713
Chromophilic renal cell carcinoma, 1592t, 1593-
1594, 1594f
cytogenetic abnormalities associated with,
1594-1595
Chromophobic renal cell carcinoma, 1592t,
1595, 1595f
Chromosomal abnormalities
in bladder cancer, 2429-2430
in locally advanced prostate cancer, 3055t
in neuroblastoma, 3870
in urothelial tumors, 1639-1640
in Wilms' tumor, 3887-3888, 3892
Chromosomal rearrangement, in proto-
oncogene conversion to oncogene, 514
Chromosomal resistance, of bacteria, to
antibiotics, 244
Chromosomal sex, 3799-3801, 3800f-3802f
Chromosomal syndromes, associated with
genitourinary anomalies, 3201t
Chromosomal translocations, male infertility
and, 640
Chromosome 8p, loss of heterozygosity on, in
prostate cancer, 536
Chromosome 9 deletions, in bladder cancer,
2412, 2429
Chromosome 10q, loss of heterozygosity on, in
prostate cancer, 535
Chromosome 13q deletions, in bladder cancer,
2412, 2429
Chromosome 17p deletions, in bladder cancer,
2429
Chronic obstructive pulmonary disease,
incontinence and, 2190
Chronic pelvic pain syndrome
clinical presentation of, 311-312
cytokine levels in, 317-318

Chronic pelvic pain syndrome (*Continued*)
diagnostic algorithm for, 318, 318f
evaluation of, 318, 319t
sacral neuromodulation for, 2157
symptom assessment in, 312, 313f
therapeutic algorithm for, 326f
zinc levels in, 318
Chylous ascites, after laparoscopy, 219
Chyluria, 96-97
in filariasis, 457
Cigarette smoking. *See* Smoking.
Ciliary dyskinesia, primary, 611, 623
Cimetidine, for painful bladder
syndrome/interstitial cystitis, 360, 360t
Cip/cik, G_1S checkpoint and, 523-524
Ciprofloxacin
for chancroid, 375
in HIV patients, 395-396
for gonorrhea, 379
for pediatric urinary tract infections, 3248t
for prostatitis, 320t, 321, 327t
Circadian rhythm, in cortisol secretion, 1826,
1826f
Circle loop nephrostomy, 1560, 1561f
Circular stapling device, ileocolonic stapled
intestinal anastomosis with, 2543-2544,
2543f
Circulation, to pelvis, 46, 50f, 51-52, 51f
Circumcaval ureter. *See* Ureter(s), circumcaval
(retrocaval).
Circumcision, 1045-1046, 1046f, 3747-3750
and limited excision, for penile cancer, 973
anesthesia for, 3747
complications of, 1045, 3748-3750, 3750f
contraindications to, 3747-3748, 3749f
controversies surrounding, 1045
decreased risk of urinary tract infection with,
3232, 3239
female, 3839-3840, 3841f
Gomco clamp for, 1045
HIV and STDs and, 388
in adults, 1046
in pediatric office, 3215
incision in, for corpus cavernosum laceration,
2650, 2650f
meatal stenosis following, 1044-1045, 1045f
neonatal
advantages and benefits of, 3747
prophylactic effect of, on penile cancer, 965,
966
urethral injury after, 3941
Circumferential compression mechanism, of
stone fragmentation, 1475
Circumflex artery, 72, 72f, 721f, 1034, 1035f
Circumflex vein, 72, 72f, 722f, 723f, 1031,
1034f
Cisapride, to facilitate bladder emptying, 2116
Cisplatin
for seminomas, stage IIC and stage III, 912
gemcitabine with, for bladder cancer,
metastatic, 2477
toxicity of, 924
Cisterna chyli, 14
Citrate, as inhibitor of stone formation, 1370
Citric acid, in prostatic secretions, 2716
Citrus juices, increased intake of, for
nephrolithiasis, 1412
C-kit, in cell migration and proliferation, 1896
Clamp(s)
Gomco, 1045
vas deferens fixation, ring-tipped, 1099f
CLCN5 gene, DNA screening for, 1375
Clean intermittent catheterization. *See*
Catheterization, clean intermittent.

Clear cell carcinoma, genetics of, 1584t, 1585-1587, 1585t, 1586f

Clear cell sarcoma, of kidney, in children, 3898

Clenbuterol, for overactive bladder/detrusor overactivity, 2104

Clindamycin, for bacterial vaginosis, 384

Clinical preservation, of kidney, for transplantation, 1306-1308

Clinical Symptom Scales, in painful bladder syndrome/interstitial cystitis, 354-355, 354t, 355t, 357t

Clipping devices, in laparoscopy, 194f, 195

Clitoris
  atrophy of, 871f
  bifid, in exstrophy patient, 3505, 3505f, 3524
  development of, 3142f, 3143
  dorsal vein of, 51
  glans of, absent, 869f
  hypertrophy of, 3855f
    high vaginal confluence with, management of, 3858-3859, 3859f-3861f
    low vaginal confluence with, management of, 3856-3858, 3858f
    management of, 3858-3859, 3859f-3861f
  nerves of, stimulation of, 2159
  phimosis of, 866, 868f, 869f
  physical examination of, 866, 867f
  sexual pain disorders involving, 883
  suspensory ligament of, 67

Clitoromegaly, in 46,XY complete gonadal dysgenesis, 3813, 3813f

Clitoroplasty, for intersex conditions
  results of, 3863-3864
  simultaneous vaginoplasty and labioplasty with, 3854
  technique of, 3854-3855

Cloaca
  anatomy of, spectrum of, 3853, 3853f
  embryology of, 3831

Cloacal anomaly(ies)
  evaluation of, 3848
  history and physical examination of, 3848-3849, 3850f
  radiographic and endoscopic evaluation of, 3852-3853, 3852f, 3853f
  surgical resection of, 3865-3869
    definitive repair of, 3866-3868
    gastrointestinal decompression in, 3865
    genitourinary decompression in, 3865-3866, 3866f
    initial timing, management, and principles of, 3865
    obstructive urinary pathology repair in, 3866
    operative technique in, 3866-3868, 3867f
    results of, 3868-3869, 3868t

Cloacal exstrophy, 3538-3544
  anatomic considerations in, 3538-3541
  antenatal detection of, 3575
  at birth, evaluation and management of, 3541-3542, 3541t. See also Cloacal exstrophy, reconstruction for.
  cardiopulmonary abnormalities with, 3540
  coding grid for, 3541f
  embryology of, 3499-3500, 3499f
  emergent evaluation of, 3199
  gastrointestinal abnormalities with, 3540
  genitourinary abnormalities with, 3540
  neurospinal abnormalities with, 3538-3539, 3539f
  prenatal diagnosis of, 3540-3541

Cloacal exstrophy (Continued)
  reconstruction for, 3541-3544
    complete primary exstrophy repair in, 3564, 3567-3569, 3567f-3570f
    results of, 3571
    continence after, 3543-3544
    gender assignment in, 3542, 3542f
    immediate, 3542
    long-term issues in, 3544
    modern staged functional, 3541t
    urinary reconstruction in
      modern staged, 3542-3543
      osteotomy in, 3543, 3543f
      single-staged, 3543
  skeletal abnormalities with, 3539-3540

Cloacal fold, development of, 3141, 3141f, 3142f

Clomiphene citrate, for male infertility, 646

Clomipramine, for premature ejaculation, 785, 786, 786t

Clonal anergy, in lymphocyte tolerance, 491

Clonidine suppression test, for pheochromocytoma, 1862

Clorpactin WCS-90, for painful bladder syndrome/interstitial cystitis, 362-363, 362t

Clots, blood. See Blood clots.

Cluster of differentiation (CD) markers, 475-477, 476t. See also CD entries.

Clusterin, in regulation of apoptosis, 532

CMV. See Cytomegalovirus (CMV).

Coagulation
  interstitial laser ablative, of renal tumors, 1817
  of semen, 2725

Coagulopathy, uncorrected, affecting renal calculi surgery, 1448

Coaptite, for endoscopic correction of reflux, 4365

Cobra catheter, 1541

Cocaine, effect of, on ureteral function, 1906

Coccidioidomycosis, 467

Coccygeus muscle, 44, 46f, 2191, 2191f, 2192

Cockcroft-Gault formula, for creatinine clearance, 1133, 1325

Coffee consumption
  bladder cancer associated with, 2415
  urothelial tumors associated with, 1639

Cognitive dysfunction, androgen deprivation therapy causing, 3090

Cohen cross-trigonal technique, of antireflux surgery, 4356-4357, 4357f

Colchicine, for Peyronie's disease, 827

Cold storage, of kidney for transplantation, 1306

Colic artery(ies), 2535, 2535f

Collagen
  cross-linked bovine, for endoscopic correction of reflux, 4364, 4364t
  for tissue engineering, 555, 556f
  of bladder wall, 1931

Collagenase, for Peyronie's disease, 828

Collecting devices, external, for bladder filling/storage disorders, 2298

Collecting duct (Bellini's duct) renal cell carcinoma, 1592t, 1596

Collecting system, renal. See Renal collecting system.

Colles' fascia, 40, 40f, 68, 1031, 1032f, 1036, 1037f

Colon. See also Bowel entries.
  anatomy of, 19, 20f, 2534-2535, 2535f
  injury to, percutaneous nephrolithotomy causing, 1500-1501
  malposition of, in renal ectopia, 3281
  reflection of, in laparoscopic nephrectomy, 1762-1763, 1766f
    hand-assisted, 1791, 1796, 1797f
    transperitoneal approach to, 1781

Colon (Continued)
  selection of, for urinary diversion, 2536
  sigmoid
    harvesting of, for neovagina, 3836, 3836f, 3837f
    in cystoplasty, 3677, 3677f

Colon conduit, in conduit urinary diversion
  complications of, 2568-2569, 2568t
    long-term, 2614t
  preparation for, 2564
  procedure in, 2567-2568, 2568f, 2569f

Colon pouch, right
  for continent urinary diversion, 2607-2609, 2608f
    with intussuscepted terminal ileum, 2596
  for orthotopic urinary diversion, 2642

Colonization, of bacteria, in pediatric urinary tract infections, 3238-3239

Color, of urine, 96, 96t

Colorectal cancer, hereditary nonpolyposis, 515t
  genetic mutations in, 517
  inherited susceptibility to cancer in, 519

Colorectal surgery, ureteral injury caused by, 1283

Colostomy, for cloacal anomalies, 3865

Colpocleisis, for apical vaginal prolapse repair, 2230

Colpopexy, sacral, in apical vaginal prolapse repair, 2228, 2229f
  laparoscopic, 2229-2230, 2230t
  vs. sacrospinous ligament fixation, 2229

Colporrhaphy
  anterior
    for central defect, 2217-2218, 2217f
    with needle bladder neck suspension, 2220t, 2221-2222, 2221f
    with sling procedures, 2220t, 2222
  posterior, and perineorrhaphy, 2230-2232, 2231f

Colposuspension
  Burch, 2170, 2171f
    results of, 2181, 2253t
    technique of, 2176, 2178, 2178f-2180f
  laparoscopic, 2170
  open retropubic, 2170
  vs. tension-free vaginal tape procedure, 2188

Columns of Bertin, 25

Coma, ammoniagenic, conduit urinary diversion causing, 2573

Combination therapy, for benign prostatic hyperplasia, 2793-2797
  Medical Therapy of Prostatic Symptoms Study of, 2795-2797
  Veterans Affairs Cooperative Study of, 2793, 2793t, 2794f, 2795, 2795t, 2796f

Combined Intracavernous Injection and Stimulation (CIS) test, in erectile dysfunction, 757-758

Communicating hydrocele, 3788-3789

Complement component C3, 474, 474f
  in seminal plasma, 2724

Complement component C5, 474, 474f

Complement system
  activation of, 474
  classical and alternate pathways of, 474, 474f

Complete primary exstrophy repair, 3554-3571
  background of, 3554-3555
  disassembly technique of, 3555-3557
    anatomic considerations in, 3555-3556, 3556f, 3557f
    complications of, 3571
  for bladder exstrophy
    complete, 3559, 3560f

Contusion, ureteral, management of, 1286, 1286f
Conus medullaris, 2031
Conventional fill urodynamic studies, of urethral sphincter dysfunction, in children, 3617
Cooper's ligament, 38
Cordonnier and Nesbit technique, of ureterocolonic anastomosis, 2557
Core biopsy, extended, TRUS-guided, of prostate, 2890, 2890f, 2890t
Corporotomy incision, in penile prosthesis placement, 790-791, 791f
Corpus amylacea, prostatic secretions causing, 306
Corpus cavernosum
  anatomy of, 69, 69f, 70f, 1028, 1029f
    functional, 720-721
  atrophy of, after complete primary exstrophy repair, 3571
  autonomic innervation of, in exstrophy patient, 3504-3505
  decompression of, in priapism, 845
  electromyography of, in erectile dysfunction, 767
  endothelium of, erectile dysfunction and, 742
  in penile erection, hemodynamics of, 723-724, 723f, 724f
  laceration of, 2650, 2650f
  smooth muscle of, reconstruction of, 564-565, 564f
  venous drainage of, 722-723, 722f
Corpus epididymis, 598. See also Epididymis.
Corpus spongiosum
  anatomy of, 69f, 70f, 71, 1028, 1029f
    functional, 721
  in hypospadias repair, 3716, 3718
  in penile erection, hemodynamics of, 724
  venous drainage of, 722-723, 722f
Corrective gene therapy, for prostate cancer, 3030
Cortical microcystic disease, 3329
Corticosteroids
  for cutaneous diseases, of external genitalia, 406-407, 407f
  for immunologically mediated infertility, 649
  for lichen planus, 412-413
  for painful bladder syndrome/interstitial cystitis, 360t, 361
  for retroperitoneal fibrosis, 1217
  immunosuppression with, in renal transplant recipients, 1317
  release of, regulation of, 1825-1826, 1826f
  synthesis of, 1825, 1825f
  topical, for atopic dermatitis, 408
Corticotropin-releasing hormone (CRH), synthesis of, 1826
Cortisol metabolites, in primary hyperaldosteronism, 1853
Corynebacterium
  in prostatitis, 306
  in trichomycosis, 423, 423f
Corynebacterium minutissimum, in erythrasma, 424
Cosmesis, hypospadias repair and, 3742
Cost(s), of health care, 144-147
Cost-benefit analysis, of health care, 145
Cost-effective analysis, of health care, 145
Coudé catheters, 162, 162f
Coudé-tipped catheter, 1541
Councill catheter, 164, 164f
  in percutaneous nephrostomy, 1545, 1545f, 1558f, 1559-1560
Cowden's disease, 516t
Cowper's glands. See Bulbourethral glands.

COX inhibitors. *See* Cyclooxygenase (COX) inhibitors.
Crab louse, 383-384, 425, 425f
C-reactive protein, elevated, in urinary tract infection, 3245
Creatinine
  plasma levels of
    in benign prostatic hyperplasia, 2768
    in glomerular filtration rate, 1133, 1133f
  urinary excretion of, 3219
Creatinine clearance
  Cockcroft-Gault formula for, 1133, 1325
  estimation of glomerular filtration rate by, 3230t
  in children, estimation of, 1134
  in estimation of glomerular filtration rate, 1132-1133
Credé maneuver, 2298, 3630, 3636, 3637f
Cremasteric reflex, absence of, 3790
CRH (corticotropin-releasing hormone), synthesis of, 1826
Criterion validity, of HRQOL instruments, 154, 154t
Crohn's disease, rectourethral fistula due to, 2354, 2354f
Cromakalim, effect of, on ureteral function, 1920
Cross-linked bovine collagen
  for bladder neck reconstruction, in children, 3666
  for endoscopic correction of reflux, 4364, 4364t
Crural vein, 1034, 1034f
Cryogenic systems, third generation, 3038
Cryopreservation, of sperm, at time of vasovasostomy, 678
Cryoprobe(s)
  evolution of, 3034, 3035f
  isotherm curves for, 3042f
  placement of, 3041, 3043f
Cryotherapy
  computerized planning in, 3039
  contraindications to, 3040
  cryogeneration systems in, 3038
  cytotoxic and antineoplastic effects of, 3035t
  equipment for, technical improvements in, 3037-3039, 3037f, 3038f
  for adrenal lesions, 1887
  for genital warts, 381
  for localized renal cell carcinoma, 1616-1618, 1617t
  for prostate cancer, 2944, 3032-3052
    adjunctive therapy with, 3049
    biochemical disease-free survival after, 3045, 3046t, 3047, 3047t
    combination therapy with, 3040, 3040t
    complications of, 3049-3050, 3049t
    costs of, 3051
    cryoprobe placement in, 3041, 3042f, 3043f
    evolution of, 3033t
    focal, 3044-3045
    future directions of, 3051-3052
    generations of, 3032-3034, 3033t, 3038
    local recurrence after, 3048-3049
    monitoring of freezing process in, 3041, 3044
    nerve-sparing, 3044, 3044f
    patient follow-up after, 3045
    patient preparation and, 3040-3041
    patient selection for, 3039-3040
    positive biopsy rate after, 3045, 3047
    postoperative care after, 3045
    primary, 3039
    quality of life after, 3050-3051

Cryotherapy (Continued)
    repetition of, 3048
    salvage, 3039-3040
    surgical technique of, 3040-3045
    thermocouple and urethral warmer placement in, 3041, 3043f
    transrectal ultrasound evaluation in, 3041
    vs. other minimally invasive options, 3045-3047
    vs. salvage radical prostatectomy, 3047-3048
  for renal tumors, 1811-1814
  history of, 3032-3034, 3033t, 3034f, 3035f
  laparoscopic, 1804-1805, 1812, 1812t, 1813f
    complications of, 1806-1807
    results of, 1805-1806
  mechanisms of cell injury and death by, 3034-3035, 3035t
  mode of action of, 1811-1812
  open surgical, 1812
  percutaneous, 1813-1814
  primary, 3039
    outcomes after, 3045-3047, 3046t
  rectourethral fistula repair after, 2357
  salvage, 3039-3040
    outcomes after, 3047-3048, 3047t
  templates and stands for, 3038, 3038f
  thermocouples for, 3038
  tissue destruction during, factors affecting, 3036-3037, 3036t
  tissue response to, 3035-3036, 3036f
  transrectal ultrasound systems in, 3037-3038, 3037f
  urethral warming device for, 3038-3039
  warming probes for, 3038
Cryptococcosis, 465-466, 466f
Cryptococcus neoformas, 465
Cryptorchidism, 3763-3787
  associated with hypospadias, 3709
  bilateral, 610
  carcinoma in situ associated with, 3773, 3902
  classification of, 3764-3765
  consequences of, 3771-3773
  definition of, 3763
  epidemiology of, 3764
  evaluation of, 3204, 3208
  germ cell tumors associated with, 900-901
  hernia due to, 3773
  histopathology of, 3712-3713
  incidence of, 3763-3764
  infertility due to, 640-641, 3771-3772
  maldescent in, 3766-3770
    calcitonin gene–related peptide in, 3769
    endocrine factors in, 3766-3768
    epididymis related to, 3769-3770
    genitofemoral nerve in, 3769
    gubernaculum in, 3768-3769
    intra-abdominal pressure and, 3770
    theories of, 3766
  management of, 3775-3787
    hormonal therapy in, 3775-3776
    laparoscopic, 3781-3787
      assessment in, 3782-3784, 3783f
      diagnostic, 3782
      technique of, 3782
      vs. surgical exploration, 3784-3785
    laparoscopic orchidopexy in, 3785-3786
      Fowler-Stephens, 3786
    microvascular autotransplantation in, 3787
    orchidopexy in
      complications of, 3787
      for high undescended testes, 3779, 3781
      Fowler-Stephens, 3781
        laparoscopic, 3786
      laparoscopic, 3785-3786

Dutasteride
  for benign prostatic hyperplasia, 2792
  for prostate cancer, prophylactic, 2870
Dye test, for incontinence, 2063
Dynamic fracture mechanism, of stone fragmentation, 1476-1477, 1476f
Dysfunctional elimination syndrome, of childhood, 3611, 3613
Dysgenetic male pseudohermaphroditism (partial gonadal dysgenesis), 3812-3813
Dyspareunia, in females, 864
  causes of, 885
Dysplasia, urothelial, 1642
Dysraphism, neurospinal, voiding dysfunction in, 2029-2030
Dyssynergia, sphincter. See also Detrusor-sphincter dyssynergia.
  definition of, 1981
  proximal, 2038
  smooth, 2038
Dystrophy. See specific type, e.g., Reflex sympathetic dystrophy.
Dysuria, 84

E

EBV. See Epstein-Barr virus (EBV).
E-cadherin, 540, 2695
  in prostate cancer, 2866
Ecchymosis, abdominal and scrotal, after laparoscopic surgery, 217
Echinococcosis, 458-459, 459f
  renal, 285-286, 286f
Economic considerations
  in androgen deprivation therapy, 3099
  in robotic-assisted laparoscopic radical prostatectomy, 3000-3001
Ecthyma gangrenosum, of male genitalia, 424, 424f
Eczema (atopic dermatitis), 407-408, 407f
Edema
  in infants, 3207
  penile, after penile revascularization, 810
  scrotal
    miscellaneous causes of, 3793
    testicular torsion causing, 3792
Eggplant deformity, of penis, 2649, 2650f
Ehlers-Danlos syndrome, voiding dysfunction in, 2042
Ehrlich technique, in management of prune-belly syndrome, 3493
Ejaculate
  biochemical properties of, 605-606
  coagulation of, 605
  failure of, 87
  low-volume
    evaluation of, 619, 620f, 620t, 621
    history of, 611
  premature, 87
Ejaculation
  absent, 619, 620f, 621
    history of, 611
  antegrade, preservation of, retroperitoneal lymph node dissection and, 940, 941, 945
  dysfunction of
    in sperm delivery, 648-649
    in spinal cord injury, 619, 649
    management of, 649
  premature, 784-787
    classification of, 784
    definition of, 784
    diagnosis of, components in, 784
    etiology of, 784-785, 784t
    exclusionary factors in, 784

Ejaculation (Continued)
    office management of, 786, 787t
    treatment of
      pharmacologic, 785-786, 786t
      psychological/behavioral, 785
  retrograde, 648-649
    after laparoscopic retroperitoneal lymph node dissection, 947
    definition of, 715
    management of, 715
    medical therapy for, 648
Ejaculatory duct(s)
  function of, pelvic and retroperitoneal surgery affecting, 610-611
  obstruction of, 619, 621
    detection of, 627-628, 628f
    diagnosis of, 707-708, 708f
    surgical management of, 707-714
      complications of, 708
      outcomes of, 708-710, 709t
      seminal vesical aspiration in, 710, 712f
      seminal vesiculography in, 710, 711f
      transrectal ultrasonography in, 707, 708f
      transurethral balloon dilatation in, 708
      transurethral resection in, 708, 709f
    vasography of, 707-708
      complications of, 714
      technique of, 710-711, 713f, 714, 714f
ELAC2 gene, in hereditary prostate cancer, 518
Elastin, of bladder wall, 1932
Elderly. See Geriatric patient.
Electrical activity
  of bladder smooth muscle, 1927-1928
    propagation of, 1929
  of ureteral smooth muscle, 1892-1897
    propagation of, 1897
Electrical responses, in bladder smooth muscle, propagation of, 1929
Electrical stimulation. See also Transcutaneous electrical nerve stimulation (TENS).
  applications of, for voiding dysfunctions, 2148t
  for incontinence, 2071, 2135
  for stress incontinence, 2074
  future research in, 2167
  history of, 2147-2148, 2148t
  of bladder
    for emptying disorders, 2163-2167
      direct, 2163-2164
      neurophysiology of, 2148-2150, 2149f-2151f
      sacral neuromodulation in, 2166-2167
      to nerve roots, 2164-2165, 2164f
      transurethral, 2165-2166
    for storage disorders, 2151-2163
      bilateral, 2158
      complications of, 2160-2163
      contraindications to, 2152
      criteria for patient selection in, 2151-2152
      efficacy and safety of, 2160-2162, 2161f, 2162f
      neurophysiology of, 2148-2150, 2149f-2151f
      sacral neuromodulation in, 2153-2158
        outcome of, 2155
        special populations and, 2155-2158
        technique of, 2153-2155, 2153f-2155f
      sacral rhizotomy in, 2152-2153
      selective nerve stimulation in, 2158-2160
      transurethral, 2152
      troubleshooting algorithm for, 2162-2163, 2163f

Electrical stimulation (Continued)
  of sacral nerve
    for painful bladder syndrome/interstitial cystitis, 365
    responses to, 2148t
Electrocautery, for genital warts, 382
Electrode(s)
  design of, in transurethral vaporization of prostate, 2839
  electromyographic, types of, 1989-1990
  in urodynamic studies, 1989-1990
Electroejaculation
  for anejaculation, 715-716, 716f
  for spinal cord-injured men, 649
Electrohydraulic (spark gap) generator, for shockwave lithotripsy, 1465, 1465f, 1466t, 1470t
Electrohydraulic lithotripsy, 1458-1460, 1459f, 1513-1514
  advantages and disadvantages of, 1459-1460
  technique of, 1460
Electrolyte(s)
  abnormalities of, conduit urinary diversion causing, 2570-2573, 2571f, 2571t
  management of
    in neonate, 3156, 3157f
    postoperative, in renal transplant recipient, 1312-1313
Electromagnetic generator
  for shockwave lithotripsy, 1465, 1467t, 1468, 1468f
  imaging and financial aspects of, 1470t-1471t
Electromagnetic therapy, for incontinence, 2136
Electromyography
  corpus cavernosum, in erectile dysfunction, 767
  equipment for, 1989-1990
  in urodynamic studies, 2002
  of urethral sphincter, 3626-3627, 3628f
  sphincter, 2068
Electronic dip stick flowmeter, 1989
Electronic spread, of current, 1897
Electrosurgical devices, bipolar, in laparoscopy, 192
Elephantitis
  penile, 457
  scrotal, 456, 456f, 457
    Onchocerca volvulus causing, 455
    treatment of, 458
El-Ghorab shunt, for priapism, 847f, 848
Elimination syndrome, dysfunctional, of childhood, 3611, 3613
ELISA (enzyme-linked immunosorbent assay)
  for antisperm antibodies, 624t
  for HIV infection, 393
Elsberg syndrome, 2033
Embolization
  arterial, for nonischemic priapism, 848
  of pseudoaneurysm, 1546-1547, 1547f
  percutaneous, in varicocele repair, 662-663
Embolus (embolism)
  carbon dioxide, pediatric laparoscopy and, 3917
  gas, with pneumoperitoneum, 205
  pulmonary, due to radical retropubic prostatectomy, 2973
  renal artery, 1190, 1190t
    cholesterol, 1166
Embryonal carcinoma, testicular, 895
  incidence, pathology, and presentation of, 897t
Embryonal rhabdomyosarcoma, 3879
Emissary vein(s), 723, 723f

Emphysema
  insufflation-related, laparoscopic renal surgery
      causing, 1807
  subcutaneous, with pneumoperitoneum,
      205-206
Encephalomyelitis, acute disseminated, voiding
    dysfunction in, 2036
Encephalopathy, Wernicke's, voiding dysfunction
    in, 2042
Endemic bladder calculi, 2663-2664
Endocarditis. *See* Bacterial endocarditis.
  in pediatric genitourinary procedures,
      3242t
Endocrine signals, in prostate, 2690, 2690f
Endocrine system
  effect of
    on male infertility, 635-638
    on prostate growth, 2684-2689
  in testicular descent, 3766-3768
Endocrine/paraendocrine mechanisms, in
    renin-angiotensin-aldosterone system,
    1162
Endogenous inhibitors, of angiogenesis, 544
Endometriosis
  definition of, 1220
  painful bladder syndrome/interstitial cystitis
      and, 351
  ureteral obstruction due to, 1220-1221
  within urethral diverticula, 2389
Endometrium, biopsy of, in evaluation of
    fertility, 612
Endopelvic fascia, 2194-2195
  incision of, in radical retropubic
      prostatectomy, 2960-2961, 2961f
Endopyelotomy
  antegrade, for ureteropelvic junction
      obstruction
    complications of, 1236-1237
    in children, 3374-3375, 3375f
    indications for and contraindications to,
        1233, 1233f
    patient preparation in, 1233
    postoperative care following, 1234, 1236
    results of, 1236
    simultaneous nephrolithotomy with, 1234
    technique of, 1233-1234, 1235f, 1236f
  cautery wire balloon, for ureteropelvic
      junction obstruction
    complications of, 1238-1239
    indications for and contraindications to,
        1237, 1237f
    postoperative care following, 1237
    results of, 1237-1238
    technique of, 1237, 1238f
  in children
    access for, 3913
    incision for, 3913
    indications for, 3912-3913
    results of, 3913
  ureteroscopic, for ureteropelvic junction
      obstruction
    complications of, 1241
    indications for and contraindications to,
        1239
    results of, 1241
    success of, 1522
    technique of, 1239, 1240f, 1241
Endoscope(s), pediatric application of, 3908t
Endoscopic lithotripsy, for bladder calculi, 2669-
    2670
Endoscopic resection, of urothelial tumors,
    1647-1648
  percutaneous approach to, 1648
    results of, 1648, 1648t

Endoscopy
  antegrade, of urothelial tumors, 1645
  antibiotic prophylaxis for
    of lower urinary tract, 252
    of upper urinary tract, 253
  in bladder cancer, non–muscle-invasive
      office-based, 2454
    therapeutic, 2450-2454
  in incontinent patient, 2069-2070
  in laparoscopy, 177
  in prostatitis, 316
  in surgical approach, to seminal vesicles, 1125
  in vesicoureteral reflux, 4362-4366
    emerging role of, 4348
    follow-up of, 4363-4364
    materials for, 4364-4365, 4364t
    reflux recurrence after, 4365-4366
    STING technique of, 4362-4363, 4363f
  of bladder diverticula, 2365, 2366f
  of cloacal anomalies, 3852
  of ureterocele, 3406
  of ureteropelvic junction obstruction, in
      children, 3374-3375, 3375f
  of urethral strictures, 2660
  of urogenital sinus anomalies, 3851, 3852f
  of urothelial tumors, 1672-1680
    basic attributes of, 1672, 1673f, 1674f
    biopsy and definitive treatment in, 1675,
        1676f, 1677f
    collection of urine in, 1674-1675
    percutaneous approach to, 1677-1680
      biopsy and definitive treatment in, 1678,
          1679f, 1680f
      establishment of nephrostomy tract in,
          1677-1678, 1677f, 1678f
      results of, 1679-1680
      second-look nephroscopy in, 1679
    results of, 1675, 1677
    steps in, 1674-1675, 1676f, 1677f
    technique and instrumentation in, 1673-
        1674, 1674f
  ureteral injury due to, in children, 3937
Endothelial barrier, traversing, 493-494
Endothelial cell(s)
  adhesion molecule expression on, 493
  T cell interaction with, 493, 493f
  vascular, 477
Endothelial growth factor, in urothelial tumors,
    2425
Endothelin(s), 2711
  effect of, on ureteral function, 1920
  in male sexual function, 728
  in renal hemodynamics, 1134
  uropharmacology of, 1956
Endothelin-1, 537-538, 2711
  in hormone-refractory prostate cancer, 3116
Endothelium, of corpus cavernosum, erectile
    dysfunction and, 742
Endothelium-dependent vasodilation, impaired,
    in erectile dysfunction, 741-742
Endoureterotomy, for ureteral stricture, 1257-
    1259
  antegrade approach to, 1258
  cautery wire balloon incision in, 1257-1258
  combined approaches to, 1259
  retrograde approach to, 1257, 1257f
Endourologic procedures
  for ureteroenteric anastomotic stricture, 1269
  for ureteropelvic junction obstruction, 1232-
      1241
    complications of, 1236-1237, 1238-1239,
        1241
    indications for and contraindications to,
        1232, 1233f, 1237, 1237f, 1239

Endourologic procedures *(Continued)*
    patient preparation in, 1232
    postoperative care following, 1234, 1236,
        1237
    results of, 1236, 1237-1238, 1241
    technique of, 1232-1234, 1235f, 1236f,
        1237, 1238f, 1239, 1240f, 1241
  in children, 3907-3914
  prior to laparoscopy, 176
Endovascular stenting. *See* Stent (stenting).
End-stage renal disease
  acquired renal cystic disease in, 3351
  causes of, 1345
    in worldwide renal registries, 1354t
  drug dosing in, 1352
  family history of, 1344-1345
  hospitalization for, 1357-1359, 1358t
  impotence in, 1301
  in children, 1296, 3229-3230, 3230t
    renal transplantation for, 1296
    urinary tract infection and, 3261
  incidence of, 1295, 1345t
  long-term survival with, 1355, 1356t
  Medicare co-insurance for, 1297
  preoperative evaluation of, 1350-1352
  prevalence of, 1295, 1345t
  renal cell carcinoma in, 3352
  renal transplantation for
    in children, 1296
    results of, 1296, 1296t
  treatment options for, 1295-1296, 1354-1357,
      1356t, 1357f, 1357t
End-to-end ileocolonic sutured anastomosis,
    2542, 2542f
End-to-end stapled anastomosis, ileal-ileal or
    ileocolonic, 2544, 2544f
End-to-side ileocolonic sutured anastomosis,
    2541-2542, 2541f, 2542f
Enemas
  antegrade continence, in children, 3700-3701,
      3700f
  cleansing, for TRUS-guided prostate biopsy,
      2889
Enteric hyperoxaluria, 1378, 1378f, 1403
Enterobiasis, 458
Enterocele(s)
  repair of
    abdominal approach to, 2224
    vaginal approach to, 2223-2224, 2224f, 2225f
  types of, 2200, 2200t, 2201f
Enterococcus faecalis, endocarditis due to,
    antibiotic prophylaxis for, 254, 254t
Enterocolitis, pseudomembranous, antibiotic
    bowel preparation causing, 2539
Enterocystoplasty
  as risk factor for bladder cancer, 1324
  laparoscopic, 2512-2515
    in children, 3925
    results of, 2514-2515
    technique of, 2513-2514, 2514f
Enteroenterostomy
  by single-layer sutured anastomosis, 2541,
      2541f
  by two-layer sutured anastomosis, 2540-2541,
      2540f
Enteroplasty, seromuscular, in children, 3690,
      3691f
Enucleation
  in partial nephrectomy, 1728
  of adenoma
    in retropubic prostatectomy, 2848-2849,
        2848f, 2849f
    in suprapubic prostatectomy, 2850, 2850f,
        2851f

Excitation, vanilloid-induced, 1959

Excitation-contraction coupling
in bladder smooth muscle, 1928-1929, 1928t, 1929f
in ureteral smooth muscle, 1899-1900

Excretory urography. *See* Urography, excretory.

Exenteration, anterior, urethrectomy with, in female radical cystectomy, 2496-2498, 2497f-2499f

Exercise(s)
incontinence associated with, 2190
pelvic floor, for erectile dysfunction, 770

Exercise-induced hematuria, 100

Exstrophy
bladder. *See* Bladder exstrophy.
cloacal. *See* Cloacal exstrophy.
in female patient
obstetric implications of, 3552-3553
sexual function and fertility issues in, 3552
in male patient, sexual function and fertility issues in, 3550-3552
repaired, residual genital defect with, 1047-1049
chordee as, 1042f, 1048-1049, 1048f
reconstruction goals in, 1047-1048, 1048f
urethral construction for, 1049

Exstrophy-epispadias complex, 3497-3500, 4323-4326
causes of, 4326
embryology of, 3499-3500, 3499f
etiologies of, 3498
historical aspects of, 3497
incidence of, 3497
inheritance of, 3497-3499
omphaloceles in, 3503
one-stage reconstruction of, 3554-3571
background in, 3554-3555
Mitchell technique in. *See* Complete primary exstrophy repair.
variants of, 3548, 3550, 3551f, 3552f

Extended core biopsy, TRUS-guided, of prostate, 2890, 2890f, 2890t

Extracellular matrix
components of, in bladder cancer, 2428
imbalance of, renal disease associated with, 1344
in renal cell carcinoma, 1591
prostatic, 2690, 2690f

Extra-chromosomal resistance, of bacteria, to antibiotics, 244-245

Extracorporeal shockwave lithotripsy. *See* Shockwave lithotripsy.

Extragonadal germ cell tumor(s), 924-925

Extramural tunnel, serous-lined, for orthotopic urinary diversion, 2636, 2637f, 2638

Extraperitoneal space, development of, in laparoscopic surgery, 181-189. *See also* Laparoscopic surgery, development of extraperitoneal space in.

Extraperitoneoscopy, 182
open and closed technique in, 184

Extrarenal calyces, 3301, 3301f

Extrarenal pelvis, 3303

Extrarenal tissues, damage to, shockwave lithotripsy causing, 1477

Extraurethral incontinence, 2047. *See also* Incontinence.

Extravasation, retroperitoneal, percutaneous nephrolithotomy causing, 1500

Extravesical procedures, in antireflux surgery, 4357, 4358f, 4359-4360

EYA1 gene, in BOR syndrome, 3135

Eyeball urodynamic monitoring, of incontinent patient, 2064, 2064f

Eyelashes, pediculosis of, 384

EZH2 lysine methyltransferase, in prostate cancer, 2867

F

Facial appearance, characteristic, in bilateral renal agenesis, 3270-3271, 3271f, 3272

Factitial dermatitis, of male genitalia, 419

Failure to thrive, 3205-3206
approach to, 3206t
definition of, 3205
organic causes of, 3206t
psychosocial, 3205

Fallopian tubes
evaluation of, in female fertility, 612
sparing of, in laparoscopic radical cystectomy, 2521

Famciclovir, for herpes simplex virus infection, 374t
in HIV patients, 394t

Familial adenomatous polyposis, 516t

Familial aspects, of hypospadias, 3708-3709

Familial benign prostatic hyperplasia, 2733-2734, 2733t

Familial hypoplastic glomerulocystic kidney disease, 3329
characteristics of, 3314t

Familial papillary renal cell carcinoma, 1584t, 1587

Familial pheochromocytoma, 1860, 1861t

Familial prevalence, of hypospadias, 3708-3709

Familial prostate cancer, 2857-2858, 2857t
definition of, 2857

Familial renal cell carcinoma
molecular genetics and, 1584-1585, 1585t
von Hippel–Lindau disease in, 1584t, 1585-1587, 1585t, 1586f

Family history, 88

Family members, examination of, for autosomal dominant polycystic kidney disease, 3325

Fanconi syndrome, in children, 3228, 3228t

Fas ligand, in cytolysis of target cell, 488

Fas-associated death domain, in apoptosis, 489

Fascia. *See also* named fascia.
abdominal wall, subcutaneous, 38, 40, 40f, 41f
endopelvic, 2194-2195
lumbodorsal, 3, 6f, 7f, 8
pelvic, 44-46
components of, 45-46, 48f, 49f
surgical anatomy of, 2959, 2959f
perineal, 46, 49f, 73, 73f
spermatic, 73

Fascia lata, for sling procedures
autologous, 2247
indications for, 2236-2237
outcome of, 2247
cadaveric, 2238
outcome of, 2247
harvesting of, 2237-2238

Fascial dehiscence, after complete primary exstrophy repair, 3571

Fascial dilators, 1542

Fascial sling, for bladder neck reconstruction, in children, 3665

Fasciitis, necrotizing. *See* Fournier's gangrene.

Fasciocutaneous (tissue) flap. *See also* Flap(s).
in hypospadias repair, 3716-3717

Fas/Fas-L-mediated induction, of apoptosis, 488-489, 489f

Fast and calcium load test, 1398-1399

Fast-twitch muscle fibers, of urethra, 1936-1937

Fat, dietary, prostate cancer and, 2862-2872

Fat injections, autologous, for incontinence, 2275
efficacy of, 2281
safety of, 2285

Febrile illness, impaired spermatogenesis due to, 611

Fecal colonization, in pediatric urinary tract infection, 3239

Fecal continence
after cloacal surgery, 3868-3869
after radical perineal prostatectomy, 2983-2984

Fecal impaction, in geriatric incontinence, 2307t, 2309

Fecal incontinence
epidemiology of, 2188
in exstrophy patient, 3503
in pelvic organ prolapse, 2204
myelodysplasia and, management of, 3640
sacral neuromodulation for, 2158

Feet, soles of, secondary syphilis affecting, 376f

Feline interstitial cystitis, 337-338

Female eunuch syndrome, infertility and, 636

Female-to-male transsexualism, reassignment surgery in, 1096-1097

Femoral artery, 46, 1031, 1033f

Femoral cutaneous nerve
lateral, 18, 18f
posterior, 53, 53t

Femoral nerve, 18-19, 18f, 53, 53f, 53t
palsy of, 53, 53f
after osteotomy, in exstrophy patient, 3516

Femoral vein, 46, 51

FemSoft urethral insert, 2140, 2140f

Fenoldopam, for acute renal failure, 1336-1337

Fertility
after hypospadias repair, 3742
female
after renal transplantation, 1323
evaluation of, 611-613
fallopian tubes in, 612
ovulation and luteal phase in, 612
peritoneal cavity in, 612-613
uterus in, 612
in exstrophy patient, 3552
in advanced testicular germ cell tumors, 957
in low-stage testicular germ cell tumors, 949
male. *See also* Infertility, male.
in exstrophy patient, 3550-3552
sperm maturation and, 602-603
potential for, in true hermaphrodites, 3816

Fetal tissue, engineering of, 566-567, 567f

Fetus
bladder anomalies in, prenatal detection of, 3574-3575, 3575f
bladder in, antenatal sonographic findings of, 3573
female, differentiation of, 3805, 3807f
glomerular filtration rate in, 3149-3150
kidney in
development of
anatomic stages in, 3149, 3150f
functional, 3149-3150
function of, evaluation of, 3150-3151, 3151f
male, masculinization of, 3805, 3807f
plasma renin activity in, 3157
sex of, determination of, 3573
sexual differentiation in. *See* Sexual differentiation.
urologic anomalies in, antenatal diagnosis and management of, 3598, 3598f
uropathy in. *See also specific pathology, e.g.,* Hydronephrosis, fetal.
appearance of, 3180-3185, 3181f-3184f

Fetus (Continued)
    diagnostic findings in, 3176-3178, 3177f,
        3177t, 3179f, 3180f
    incidence of, 3186
    interventions for, 3187-3189, 3187t, 3188f
    management of, 3186-3189
    pathophysiology of, 3185-3186
    postnatal evaluation and management of,
        3189-3194, 3190f
    vesicoureteral reflux in, 4324
Fever
    filarial, 456
    in children
        bacterial infections and, 3206, 3206t
        management of, 3206
        urinary tract infection and, 3198, 3203
            management of, 3261
    in early graft dysfunction, 1318, 1319t
    in urinary tract infection, 240-241
    patient history of, 88
Fexofenadine, for Peyronie's disease, 827
Fibrin glue, in laparoscopy, 193
Fibroblast growth factor, 2708-2709
    in activation of angiogenesis, 542
    in benign prostatic hyperplasia, 2731-2732,
        2731f
    properties of, 2706t
Fibroepithelial polyps, 431, 433
    in children, 3900
    of upper urinary tract, abnormal urothelium
        in, 1643
    percutaneous treatment of, 1556-1557
Fibroid. See Leiomyoma.
Fibroma
    ovarian, ureteral obstruction due to, 1221
    renal medullary, 1582
Fibromuscular hyperplasia, of renal artery,
    1157t, 1161
Fibromyalgia, painful bladder
    syndrome/interstitial cystitis and, 336
Fibroplasia, of renal artery
    intimal, 1157t, 1159, 1159f, 1160f
    medial, 1157t, 1159-1160, 1160f
    perimedial, 1157t, 1160-1161, 1160f, 1161f
Fibrosis
    associated with intracavernous injection
        therapy, 781
    cavernosal, penile prosthesis for, 798-800,
        799f, 800f
    in urinary tract obstruction
        cellular and molecular changes leading to,
            1204
        congenital, 3169-3171, 3170f
        initiation of, angiotensin II in, 1204
    pelvic, as contraindication to laparoscopy,
        174-175
    renal, experimental treatment approaches to,
        1205-1206
    retroperitoneal. See Retroperitoneal fibrosis.
Fibrous dysplasia, percutaneous transluminal
    angioplasty for, 1181-1182, 1181t, 1182f
Fibular osteocutaneous flap. See also Flap(s).
    in penile reconstruction, 1093
Field theory, of epithelial spread, of urothelial
    tumors, 1641
Filariasis, lymphatic, 455-458
    clinical manifestations of, 456-457
    diagnosis of, 457
    early infection in, 456
    late infection in, 456, 456f
    pathogenesis of, 455-456
    pathology of, 455-456
    prevention of, 458
    treatment of, 457-458

Filiform catheter, 163, 165f
Filmy penile adhesions, after circumcision, 3748
Filtration fraction, in renal blood flow, 1131
Finasteride
    erectile dysfunction caused by, 745
    for benign prostatic hyperplasia, 2788-2792,
        2789f, 2791f
        dosage of, 2788t
        efficacy of, 2790t
        vs. combination therapy, 2793, 2795t
    for lowering PSA levels, 2916
    for prostate cancer, prophylactic, 2869-2870,
        2870t
    for prostatitis, clinical trial data on, 322-323,
        327t
Finasteride Study Group, 741
Fine-needle aspiration biopsy
    of inguinal lymph nodes, in penile cancer, 980
    of prostate, 2891
    of renal cell carcinoma, disease staging with,
        1603
    of renal cysts, 1772
    of renal tumors, 1571-1572
    of testicular sperm, 658
    of testis, sperm retrieval through, 701, 703,
        705-706, 705f-707f
FISH (fluorescent in situ hybridization), in
    diagnosis of oncology, 548
Fistula(s)
    arteriovenous
        delayed bleeding due to, following
            percutaneous procedures, 1546, 1546f
        renal, 1189-1190, 1189f, 3297
    complex, of posterior urethra, reconstructive
        surgery for, 1086-1087, 1086f
    due to intestinal anastomosis, 2549
    due to ureterointestinal anastomosis, 2556t,
        2562
    pancreatic, after radical nephrectomy, 1719
    pyeloenteric, 2353
    pyelovascular, 2357
    rectourethral, after cryotherapy, 3050
    renovascular, 2357
    ureteroenteric, 2353
    ureterovaginal, 2341-2345
        diagnosis of, 2341-2343, 2342f-2344f
        etiology and presentation of, 2341, 2342t
        management of, 2343-2345
    ureterovascular, 2357-2359, 2358t
    urethral, congenital, 3757-3758
    urethrocutaneous, 1042-1043, 1043f
        after hypospadias repair, 3739
    urethrorectal (rectourethral), 2353-2357
        etiology and presentation of, 2354-2355,
            2354f, 2355f
        management of, 2355-2357, 2356f
    urethrovaginal, 2347-2351
        diagnosis of, 2348, 2348f, 2349f
        etiology and presentation of, 2347-2348,
            2347f, 2348f
        management of, 2348-2351, 2350f
    urinary tract, 2322-2359
        after partial nephrectomy, 1730
        cutaneous, 2359
        general considerations in, 2322-2323
        repair of, 2322-2323, 2323t
            urethrocutaneous, 2359
    uroenteric, 2351-2357
    urogynecologic, 2323-2351
    urovascular, 2357-2359
    vesicoenteric, 2351-2353
        diagnosis of, 2352
        etiology and presentation of, 2351, 2351t
        management of, 2352-2353

Fistula(s) (Continued)
    vesicouterine, 2345-2347
        diagnosis of, 2345-2346, 2345f-2346f
        etiology and presentation of, 2345
        management of, 2346-2347
    vesicovaginal, 2323-2340, 2323f. See also
        Vesicovaginal fistula.
Fixed particle growth theory, of crystal
    formation, 1367-1368
Flank incisions, in renal surgery, 1691-1694,
    1691f-1695f
Flank muscles, lateral, 8-9, 9t, 10f
Flank pain
    in urinary tract infection, 240-241
    ureteropelvic junction obstruction and, in
        children, 3363, 3364f
Flap(s)
    axial, 1026, 1027f
    Boari. See Boari flap.
    in correction of Peyronie's disease, H-shaped,
        833, 835f, 836, 836f
    in hypospadias repair, 3725, 3726f-3727f
        onlay island, 3725-3726, 3728, 3728f-
            3729f
            one-stage, 3729, 3731
            split prepuce in-situ technique of, 3725,
                3728, 3730f-3731f, 3743
        reoperative, 3740-3741
        subcutaneous (dartos), 3716, 3716f
        tissue (fasciocutaneous), 3716-3717
        transverse preputial island, 3731-3732,
            3732f-3733f, 3734
    in penile reconstruction
        bipedicled, 1095-1096
        fibular osteocutaneous, 1093
        forearm, 1092-1093
            disadvantages of, 1093
            modifications of, 1093, 1094f, 1095f
        upper arm, 1094-1095
    in pyeloplasty techniques, 1243-1245, 1245f
    in reconstructive surgery, 1026, 1026f, 1027f,
        1028
    in urethral diverticula repair, 2387f, 2388
    in urethral stricture repair, 1067, 1067f-1073f,
        1073
    in urethrovaginal fistula repair, 2349, 2351
    in vesicovaginal fistula repair, 2332, 2340
        splitting of, 2333-2335, 2334f, 2335f
    island, 1026, 1027f, 1028
    musculocutaneous, 1026, 1027f
    onlay island, in hypospadias repair, 3725-
        3726, 3728, 3728f-3729f
        one-stage, 3729, 3731
        split prepuce in-situ technique of, 3725,
            3728, 3730f-3731f, 3742
    peninsular, 1026, 1027f
    random, 1026, 1026f
    skin island, 1028
        in urethral stricture repair, 1072f-1074f,
            1073-1075
    skin paddle, 1028
    subcutaneous (dartos), in hypospadias repair,
        3716, 3716f
    tissue (fasciocutaneous)
        in hypospadias repair, 3716-3717
        in reoperative hypospadias repair, 3740-
            3741
    transverse preputial island, in hypospadias
        repair, 3731-3732, 3732f-3733f, 3734
Flavoxate
    for incontinence, in elderly, 2317t
    for overactive bladder/detrusor overactivity,
        2093t, 2103
Floating ball electrode, in laparoscopy, 191-192

Flow cytometry
  of bladder cancer, 2431
  of urothelial tumors, 1644
Flowmeters, in urodynamic studies, 1989, 1989t
Fluconazole, 469
  cost of, 464t
  dosage of, 461t
  for funguria, 300
  for pediatric fungal infections, of urinary tract, 3265
  for urinary tract infection, candidal, 463
  for vulvovaginal candidiasis, 385
Flucytosine, 469
  for funguria, 300
Fluid(s)
  absorption of, percutaneous nephrostomy causing, 1547
  collection of, after renal transplantation, 1319-1320, 1320t
  for acute renal failure, 1337-1338
  for nephrolithiasis, 1411-1412
  in renal transplant recipient, postoperative management of, 1312-1313
  intake of, renal stones associated with, 1365
  management of, in neonate, 3156, 3157f
  restriction of, in behavioral therapy for incontinence, 2128-2129
  retention of, testosterone therapy causing, 859
Fluorescent in situ hybridization (FISH), in diagnosis of oncology, 548
Fluoroquinolones
  for acute pyelonephritis, 270, 270t
  for cystitis, 256t, 257
  for prostatitis, 320-321, 320t
  for urinary tract infections, 245t, 246t, 247t, 248-249
Fluoroscopy
  in nephrostomy procedures, 1531-1532, 1531f, 1531t
  in shockwave lithotripsy, 1469
    ultrasonography with, 1469, 1470t-1471t
5-Fluorouracil
  for hormone-refractory prostate cancer, 3105t
  for penile cancer, 987
Fluoxetine, for premature ejaculation, 785, 786t
Flush stoma, 2552
Flutamide
  androgen blockade with, 3085t, 3086
  for benign prostatic hyperplasia, 2792
    dosage of, 2788t
  for priapism, 846t
Foam cells, in glomerulus, 1344
Foley catheter, 162, 162f
  for percutaneous nephrostomy, 1559-1560
  in urethral diverticula repair, 2387f, 2388
Foley Y-V plasty technique, for ureteropelvic junction obstruction, 1243-1245, 1245f
  in children, 3370, 3370f
Follicle-stimulating hormone (FSH)
  deficiency of, in male, 636
  for male infertility, 636
  in evaluation of fertility, 612
  in evaluation of infertility, 618-619, 618t
  in male reproductive axis, 577, 578f
  increased levels of, following varicocele repair, 664
  role of, in spermatogenesis, 596
  secretion of, 578
  Sertoli cell stimulation by, 579-580
Folliculitis, of male genitalia, 421, 422f

Foods
  avoidance of, ICA recommendations for, in painful bladder syndrome/interstitial cystitis, 359t
  oxalate-rich, 1378, 1403t
Force-length relations, of ureteral smooth muscle, 1902-1903, 1902f, 1903f
Force-velocity relations, of ureteral smooth muscle, 1903, 1903f
Forearm flap. See also Flap(s).
  in penile reconstruction, 1092-1093
    disadvantages of, 1093
    modifications of, 1093, 1094f, 1095f
Forebrain, involved in sexual function, 726t
Foreign body(ies), bladder calculi related to, 2666, 2667f
Foreskin, neonatal bacterial colonization of, 3238
Fosfomycin, for pediatric urinary tract infections, 3248t
Fossa navicularis, urethral, 1029, 1030f
Four-corner bladder neck suspension, for vaginal wall prolapse, 2219-2221, 2220t, 2221f
Fournier's gangrene, 301-302
  genital skin loss due to, 2654
  in AIDS patients, 397
  of male genitalia, 421, 421f
Fowler syndrome, voiding dysfunction in, 2040
Fowler-Stephens orchidopexy, 3781
  for prune-belly syndrome, 3492-3493
  laparoscopic, 3786
Fowler-Stephens test, 3781
Fractional excretion of sodium
  gestational age and, 3150
  in infant and child, 3154
  in preterm and term neonates, 3151, 3153f
Fracture(s)
  pelvic
    associated with posterior urethral injury, in children, 3940
    urethral disruption related to, 2659
  penile, 2649-2650, 2650f
  straddle, of pubic rami, 2658, 2658f
Frank technique, in creation of neovagina, modification of, 3835
Free graft. See also Graft(s).
  in hypospadias repair, 3716
    neourethral formation and, 3734, 3736-3738, 3738f
    reoperative, 3741
Freeze-thaw cycle, in cryotherapy, 3036-3037
Freezing process, in cryotherapy. See also Cryotherapy.
  monitoring of, 3041, 3044
  tissue response to, 3035-3036, 3035f
Frenulae, sexual pain disorders involving, 883
Frequency, 84
  causes of, 370t
  definition of, 331, 2079
  in elderly, 2311
  measurement of, 2084
  nocturnal, 84
Fructose, in prostatic secretions, 2716
FSH. See Follicle-stimulating hormone (FSH).
Fuhrman's classification, of renal cell carcinoma, 1591, 1591f
Fulguration, of urothelial tumors, 1647-1648
Fumagillin, as inhibitor of angiogenesis, 543
Fungal bezoar(s)
  Aspergillus, 465f
  Candida, 460, 460f, 463, 463f
  in children, 3265
  percutaneous treatment of, 1556

Fungal infection(s), of genitourinary tract, 459-469. See also specific infection, e.g., Candidiasis.
  pediatric, 3265
Funguria, 299-301
  clinical presentation of, 299
  diagnosis of, 299
  in pediatric urinary tract infections, 3265
  management of, 299-301, 300f
Funiculoepididymitis, 456-457
Furunculosis, of male genitalia, 422, 422f
Fusiform aneurysm, of renal artery, 1187, 1188f
Fusion anomaly(ies). See also specific anomaly.
  of female genitalia
    lateral, 3839, 3839f, 3840f
    vertical, 3832-3839, 3833f-3839f

G

G protein, muscarinic receptor-coupling to, 2092
G protein–coupled ligand, cancer and, 537-538
G protein–coupled receptor(s), 539
G_1S checkpoint, in cell cycle, 521-524
  cip/cik function and, 523-524
  cyclin-dependent kinase complexes and, 523-524
  INK4 function and, 523
  retinoblastoma protein and, 524
  TP53 in urologic malignancies and, 522-523
  TP53 regulator of, 521-522, 522f
G_2M checkpoint, in cell cycle, 525, 525f
Gabapentin, effect of, on detrusor overactivity, 2108
Gallium nitrate, for bladder cancer, metastatic, 2478
Gamma-aminobutyric acid
  in male sexual function, 730
  uropharmacology of, 1962, 1965, 2120-2121
Gamma-glutamyl transpeptidase, in testicular tumors, 907
Ganglioneuroma, 3871, 3871f
Gangliosides, in suppression of tumor immunity, 497
Gangrene
  Fournier's. See Fournier's gangrene.
  necrotizing, genital skin loss due to, 2654, 2655f
Gap junctions
  in penile function, 742
  in ureteral function, 1897
Gardnerella vaginalis, in painful bladder syndrome/interstitial cystitis, 339
Gartner's duct, abnormalities of, vs. urethral diverticula, 2383, 2383f
Gartner's duct cyst, 3843, 3843f
Gas embolism
  insufflation-related, laparoscopic renal surgery causing, 1807
  with pneumoperitoneum, 205
Gasless technique, for pneumoperitoneum, 181
Gastric artery, 2533, 2534f
Gastric contents, aspiration of, in laparoscopy, 211
Gastric pouches, for continent urinary diversion, 2604-2606
  postoperative care of, 2606
  procedure in, 2604-2606, 2604f, 2605f
Gastrocystoplasty, in children
  antrum technique of, 3678
  body technique of, 3678-3679, 3678f
Gastroepiploic artery, 2533, 2534f
Gastrointestinal tract. See also specific part.
  anomalies of
    in cloacal exstrophy, 3540
    in prune-belly syndrome, 3485t, 3487

Gastrointestinal tract (Continued)
  decompression of, for cloacal anomalies, 3865
  disorders of
    radiation-induced, 3016t
    renal pain associated with, 82
  effects of augmentation cystoplasty on, 3680
  hemorrhage in, as complication of post-
    chemotherapy surgery, 956
  injury to
    laparoscopic, trocar placement causing,
      206-207
    radical nephrectomy causing, 1718-1719
Gastroparesis, voiding dysfunction in, 2041
Gastrostomy decompression, after intestinal
  anastomosis, 2548-2549
Gelatin agglutination test, for antisperm
  antibodies, 624t
Gelport device, hand-assist, 186, 186f
Gemcitabine, for bladder cancer
  metastatic, 2477
  non–muscle-invasive, 2459
Gender
  assignment of, 3829
    in cloacal exstrophy reconstruction, 3542,
      3542f
    in true hermaphroditism, 3816
  pediatric urinary tract infections and, 3237
  reassignment of, micropenis and, 3753
  renal stones and, 1363
  vesicoureteral reflux and, 4324
Gender identity, 3805, 3808
  issues of, in hypospadias, 3742
Gender orientation, 3808
Gene(s). See also specific gene.
  cancer. See Oncogene(s); specific oncogene.
  hereditary tumor
    identification of, 517, 517f
    inactivation of, 516
    role of, in malignancies, 516-517
  hormone response element in, 2703
  involved in kidney development, 3134-3135
  involved in sexual differentiation, 3802-3803,
    3802f
  involved in vesicoureteral reflux, 4326
  promotor element in, 2702-2703
  protein products of, 3306
  susceptibility, in prostate cancer, 2858,
    2858t
  tumor suppressor. See Tumor suppressor
    gene(s).
Gene amplification, in proto-oncogene
  conversion to oncogene, 514
Gene chip, 503
Gene expression
  analysis of, in penile cancer, 979
  in tumor marker discovery, 2909
  of retroviruses, 389
  profile of
    in transplantation, 503, 504f
    in urologic oncology, 503
Gene map, for kallikrein tumor marker, 2897,
  2897f
Gene mutations, in hypogonadotropic
  hypogonadism, 3767
Gene therapy, 551
  for prostate cancer, 3029-3031
    corrective, 3030
    cytolytic/proapoptotic, 3030
    enzyme/prodrug, 3030
General population, prevalence of hypospadias
  in, 3708
Genetic counseling, in autosomal dominant
  polycystic kidney disease, 3325
Genetic engineering, advances in, 546

Genetic factors
  in autosomal dominant polycystic kidney
    disease, 3320
  in autosomal recessive polycystic kidney
    disease, 3315
  in benign prostatic hyperplasia, 2733
  in bladder cancer, 2429-2430
  in chronic renal failure, 1344-1345
  in clear cell carcinoma, 1584t, 1585-1587,
    1585t, 1586f
  in germ cell tumors, 900
  in hypospadias, 3709
  in juvenile nephronophthisis, 3326, 3326t
  in medullary cystic disease, 3326, 3326t
  in neuroblastoma, 3870
  in papillary renal cell carcinoma, 1584-1585,
    1584t, 1587
  in pediatric urinary tract infections, 3236-
    3237
  in pelvic organ prolapse, 2190
  in prostate cancer, 2858, 2858t, 2859f
  in prune-belly syndrome, 3482
  in rhabdomyosarcoma, 3878-3879
  in tuberous sclerosis, 3330-3331
  in vesicoureteral reflux, 4325-4326
  in von Hippel–Lindau disease, 3332-3333
Genetic imprinting, in autosomal dominant
  polycystic kidney disease, 3320
Genetic testing, in male infertility work-up, 632-
  633
Genital burns, 2654
Genital nerve, dorsal, stimulation of, 2159
Genital ridges, formation of, 3136, 3136f-3138f
Genital secretions, antiretroviral therapy and,
  388
Genital squamous cancers, in AIDS patients,
  399
Genital tissue, engineering of, 563-566
  in females, 565-566
  in males, corporal tissues reconstruction for,
    564-565, 564f, 565f
Genital tubercle, development of, 3141, 3141f,
  3142f
Genital ulcer, 372, 373t
Genital warts, 420f
  diagnosis of, 380-381, 380f, 381f
  treatment of, 381-382
Genitalia. See also specific part.
  ambiguous. See also Hermaphroditism;
    Pseudohermaphroditism.
    evaluation and management of, 3827-3829,
      3828f
  defects of, bladder exstrophy and, failed repair
    of, 3537
  female
    anomalies of. See also specific anomaly.
      in bladder exstrophy, 3505, 3505f, 3524
      in renal ectopia, 3279-3280
      in unilateral renal agenesis, 3274, 3274f
      lateral fusion, 3839, 3839f, 3840f
      nonobstructive, 3840-3846, 3841f-3846,
        3842f-3846f
      obstructive, 3832-3840
        acquired, 3839-3840, 3841f
        vertical fusion, 3832-3839, 3833f-3839f
    candidiasis of, 460
    development of, 3139-3140, 3140f
      molecular mechanism in, 3146f, 3147-
        3148
    embryology of, 3123f, 3136-3148
    external
      characterization of, in fetus, 3178
      development of, 3140-3141, 3141f-3143f,
        3143

Genitalia (Continued)
  fetal
    abnormalities of, prenatal diagnosis of,
      3184-3185
    external
      characterization of, 3178
      development of, differentiation in, 3762-
        3763
  male, 3745-3760
    allergic dermatitis of, 407-410, 407f, 407t,
      409f, 410f
    anomalies of, 3746-3760. See also specific
      anomaly.
      miscellaneous, 3760
      penile, 3746-3758
      scrotal, 3758-3759, 3758f, 3759f
      vascular, 3759-3760
    candidiasis of, 460
    cutaneous diseases of, 407-435. See also
      specific disease.
      benign, 430-431, 432f
      examination of, 405, 406t
      malignant, 426-430, 427f-431f
      miscellaneous, 431, 433, 434f, 435f
      treatment of, 406-407, 407f
    defects of, in bladder exstrophy, 3503-3505,
      3504f, 3505f
    development of, 3136-3137
      molecular mechanism in, 3146-3147,
        3146f
    examination of, 613-614, 613t
    external, development of, 3141, 3141f,
      3142f
    infections of, 419-425, 420f-425f
    infestations involving, 425, 425f, 426f
    injuries to, 2649-2655
      penile, 2649-2652
      skin loss in, 2654-2655, 2655f
      testicular, 2652-2654, 2653f
    noninfectious ulcers of, 417-419, 417t, 418f,
      419f
    normal, and association with other
      abnormalities, 3745-3746, 3746t
    papulosquamous disorders of, 410-415,
      410t, 411f-414f
    secondary syphilis affecting, 376f
    vesicobullous disorders of, 415-417, 415t,
      416f, 417f
Genitocerebral evoked potential studies, in
  erectile dysfunction, 766
Genitofemoral nerve, 18, 18f, 73
  in testicular descent, 3769
  transection of, cryptorchidism and, 3145
Genitography
  of cloacal anomalies, 3852
  of urogenital sinus anomalies, 3849, 3851,
    3851f
Genitoplasty, feminizing, for congenital adrenal
  hyperplasia, 3820
Genitourinary tract
  anomalies of
    chromosomal syndromes associated with,
      3201t
    in bladder exstrophy, failed reconstruction
      of, 3537
    in cloacal exstrophy, 3540
    in prune-belly syndrome, 3483-3485,
      3483f-3485f
  decompression of, for cloacal anomalies,
    3865-3866, 3866f
  infections of. See also Urinary tract infection;
    specific infection.
    fungal, 459-469
    HIV-related, 396-397

Genitourinary tract (*Continued*)
  parasitic, 448-459
  pediatric, 3232-3268
  tuberculous, 436-447. *See also* Tuberculosis.
  injury to, in children, 3929-3945. *See also*
      specific anatomic site; specific injury.
    assessment and treatment of, 3930-3932
    grading of, 3931t
    imaging of, indications for, 3930
    vs. adult injury, 3929-3930
  pediatric urinary tract infections and, 3240-
      3241. *See also* Urinary tract infection, in
      children.
    recurrent, 3261-3262
  radiation-induced, 3016t
Gentamicin
  for pediatric urinary tract infections, 3248t
    intravenous, 3249
  prophylactic, prior to pediatric genitourinary
      procedures, 3242t
Geriatric patient
  bacteriuria in, 293-296, 295f, 1138f
  benign prostatic hyperplasia in, α-adrenergic
      blockers for, 2786
  detrusor hyperactivity with impaired
      contractility in, 2310
  frequency in, 2311
  incontinence in, 2306-2309
    cause(s) of
      detrusor overactivity as, 2309-2310
      detrusor underactivity as, 2310
      DIAPERS mnemonic for, 2306, 2307t
      established, 2309-2311
      functional, 2310-2311
      lower urinary tract, 2309-2310
      outlet obstruction as, 2310
      pathologic, 2306-2308, 2307t
      pharmaceutical, 2308-2309, 2308t
    diagnostic categorization of, empirical,
        2313-2314
    diagnostic evaluation of, 2059-2070, 2311-
        2313
    functional, 2310-2311
    history-taking in, 2311-2312, 2312t
    laboratory investigation of, 2313
    physical examination for, 2312-2313
    stress, 2310
    stress testing in, 2313
    transient, causes of, 2059t, 2306-2309,
        2307t, 2308t
    treatment of, 2314-2320, 2314f
      adjunctive measures in, 2317-2318
      behavioral therapy in, 2314-2316
      stepwise approach to, 2315t
    urodynamic testing in, 2314
    voiding diary in, 2312, 2312f
  nocturia in, 2311-2312, 2312t
  tension-free vaginal tape procedure in, 2254
Germ cell(s)
  aplasia of, infertility and, 634
  primordial, migration of, 579, 3803, 3803f
  Sertoli cells associated with, 588, 589f, 591-
      592, 591f
  transformation of, 3803-3804
Germ cell tumor(s), testicular, 893-925. *See also*
    specific type.
  acquired causes of, 901
  clinical manifestations of, 902-903
  clinical staging of, 903-904, 904t, 905t, 938
  congenital causes of, 900-901
  diagnosis of, delay in
  differential diagnosis of, 903
  epidemiology of, 899-900
  etiology of, 900-901

Germ cell tumor(s), testicular (*Continued*)
  high-stage
    fertility in, 957
    post-chemotherapy pathologic findings in,
        951t
    surgery for
      complications of, 955-956
      high-risk post-chemotherapy patients
          and, 953-954
      histologic findings and controversies in,
          950-951
      late-relapse and, 953
      lung resection as, 955
      mediastinal resection as, 955
      neck resection as, 955
      nonseminomatous tumors and, 950-956
      post-chemotherapy RPLND as, 954-955
      predicting necrosis in, 952-953
      preoperative preparation for, 950
      reoperative retroperitoneal, 954-955
      teratomas and, 951-952
      timing of, 950
  histologic classification of, 893-895, 894t
  imaging of, 905
  in children, 3902-3904, 3903t
  incidence of, 899
  intratubular, 896-897, 899, 899t
  low-stage
    fertility in, 949
    treatment options for, 948-949
  natural history of, 901, 938
  nongonadal, 924-925
  nonseminomatous, 895-896. *See also*
      Nonseminomatous germ cell tumor(s).
  pathogenesis of, 901
  patterns of spread of, 901-902, 939
  scrotal ultrasonography of, 903
  seminomatous, 894-895. *See also*
      Seminoma(s).
  signs and symptoms of, 903
  treatment of, 936-950. *See also* Orchiectomy;
      Retroperitoneal lymph node dissection
      (RPLND).
    anatomic considerations in, 939, 939f
    for nonseminomatous tumors, 913-924,
        950-956
      options in, 948-949
    for seminomas, 909-913, 956-957
    organ-preserving surgery in, 908-909
    principles of, 908-924
  tumor markers for, 893, 906-908
Gerota's fascia, 26, 27f, 28
Gestational age
  fractional excretion of sodium and, 3150
  glomerular filtration rate and, 3151
  maximal renal calyceal diameter according to,
      1220t
GH (growth hormone), affected by aging, 856t,
    857
Gibson incision, in renal transplantation,
    1310
Giggle incontinence, in children, 3612
Gil-Vernet procedure, in antireflux surgery,
    4366
Ginkgo biloba, for erectile dysfunction, 770t
Ginseng, for erectile dysfunction, 770t
Girlie disease, 1160. *See also* Perimedial
    fibrodysplasia.
Gishiri cutting, vesicovaginal fistula following,
    2325
Gitelman's syndrome, in children, 3229
Gittes bladder neck suspension, for stress
    incontinence, 2212-2213
Glands of Littre. *See* Periurethral glands.

Glans penis. *See also* Penis.
  anatomy of, functional, 721
  cutaneous lesions of, 960
  in erection, hemodynamics of, 724
  lymphatic drainage of, 1035
  partial removal of, with Mogen clamp, 3748
  poor support of, in penile prosthesis
      implantation, 797, 798f
  squamous cell carcinoma of, 1012, 1012f
Glansectomy, partial, for squamous cell
    carcinoma, 1012-1013, 1013f
Glanuloplasty. *See also* Meatoplasty and
    glanuloplasty (MAGPI) technique.
  in hypospadias repair, 3718
Gleason grading
  of adenocarcinoma of prostate, 2876, 2877f
  of prostate cancer, 2926, 2928t-2929t
Glenn-Anderson technique, of antireflux
    surgery, 4356, 4356f
Glial cell line–derived neurotrophic factor
  in ureteral development, 1891
  in ureteric bud outgrowth, 3129, 3129f
Global Response Assessment, of painful bladder
    syndrome/interstitial cystitis, 355, 356t
Globulin, sex hormone–binding, 767
  assessment of, in females, 872
Glomerular circulation, effect of angiotensin II
    on, 1163
Glomerular filtration rate
  autoregulation of, 1132
  clinical assessment of, 1132-1133
  determinants of, 1131-1132, 1326
  estimation of
    by creatinine clearance, 3230t
    mathematical formulas in, 1133
  factors influencing, 1195
  in acute renal failure, 1325-1326
  in chronic renal failure, 1341-1342, 1342t
  in fetus, 3149-3150
  in infant and child, 3153
  in neonate, 3151-3152, 3152f, 3153f
    regulation of, 3158, 3158f
  oncotic pressure in, 1132
  permeability in, 1132
  plasma markers in, 1133, 1133f
  regulation of, 1132
  renal clearance in, 1132-1133
  renal plasma flow and, 1132
  transglomerular (hydraulic) pressure in, 1131-
      1132
  tubuloglomerular feedback in, 1132
  urinary tract obstruction and, 1195-1196
Glomerulations, in painful bladder
    syndrome/interstitial cystitis, 352-353,
    352f
Glomerulocystic kidney disease
  familial hypoplastic, 3329
    characteristics of, 3314t
  sporadic, 3350-3351
    characteristics of, 3314t
    conditions associated with, 3350t
Glomerulonephritis
  acute, 1327-1328, 1328t
  focal. *See* IgA nephropathy (Berger's disease).
  membranoproliferative, in chronic renal
      failure, 1345-1346
  membranous, retroperitoneal fibrosis
      associated with, 1270-1271
  postinfectious, in children, 3226
  rapidly progressive, differential diagnosis of,
      1328t
Glomerulosclerosis
  focal segmental, in children, 3225-3226
  in renal transplant recipient, 1297-1298

Herbal supplements, for erectile dysfunction, 770, 770t

Hereditary hypophosphatemic rickets, in hypercalciuria, 1375

Hereditary leiomyomatosis and renal cell carcinoma (HLRCC) syndrome, 1584t, 1587-1588

Hereditary nonpolyposis colorectal cancer. *See* Colorectal cancer, hereditary nonpolyposis.

Hereditary papillary renal cell carcinoma, 515t, 518, 1584t, 1587

Hereditary spastic paraplegia, voiding dysfunction in, 2035

Heredity
   of bladder cancer, 2416-2417
   of urothelial tumors, 1639

Hermaphroditism, true, 3815-3816, 3815f

Hernia(s)
   cryptorchidism and, 3773
   diaphragmatic, as contraindication to laparoscopy, 175
   differential diagnosis of, 3787
   incisional
     after laparoscopy, 217-218
     after radical nephrectomy causing, 1720
     laparoscopic renal surgery causing, 1807
   inguinal
     associated with hypospadias, 3709
     examination for, 92-93, 92f
     in children, 3203
     in exstrophy patient, 3503
   laparoscopic examination of, in children, 3915-3916, 3915f
   parastomal, after ileal loop urinary diversion, 2553-2554
   repair of
     orchialgia after, 1108
     vasal obstruction after, 676-678, 676f-677f
   umbilical, as contraindication to laparoscopy, 175
   ureteral, 3420-3421, 3421f

Hernia uteri inguinale, 3826-3827

Herpes simplex virus (HSV), serologic testing for, prior to renal transplantation, 1298

Herpes simplex virus (HSV) infection
   anogenital, urinary retention associated with, 2033
   genital, 420f
     diagnosis of, 373, 374f, 400f
     treatment of, 374, 374t
     in HIV patients, 394-395, 394t

Herpes zoster virus (HZV), infection with, voiding dysfunction caused by, 2033

Herpesvirus types 1 and 2, in erythema multiforme, 409

Herpesvirus type 8, in Kaposi's sarcoma, 398

Heterochromatin, 2712

Heterozygosity, loss of, in urothelial tumors, 1644

Hidden penis, 3749f, 3751, 3751f

Hidradenitis suppurativa, of male genitalia, 422-423, 422f

High-dose-rate brachytherapy, for prostate cancer, 3027

High-intensity focused ultrasonography
   extracorporeal, 1817-1818
   for prostate cancer, 2945
   mode of action of, 1817

Highly active antiretroviral therapy (HAART)
   for HIV infection, 401
     immune-based strategies with, 403-404
   for HIVAN, 398

Hinman syndrome, 2038, 3612-3613

Hirsutism, in 46,XY complete gonadal dysgenesis, 3813

Histamine, effect of, on ureteral function, 1918

Histamine H_2 receptor antagonists, erectile dysfunction caused by, 746

Histocompatibility, in renal transplant rejection, 1314-1315, 1315f, 1315t

Histologic classification, of renal cell carcinoma, 1592-1593, 1592t

Histoplasmosis, 468

HIV. *See* Human immunodeficiency virus (HIV) *entries.*

HIV-associated neuropathy (HIVAN), 397-398

hK2 tumor marker, of prostate cancer, 2906-2907

hK3 tumor marker, of prostate cancer, 2897-2906. *See also* Prostate-specific antigen (PSA).

HLAs (human leukocyte antigens), in allograft rejection, 1314-1315, 1315f, 1315t

HLXB9 gene, in sacral agenesis, 3644

HMB-45 immunoreactivity, in renal angiomyolipoma, 1579

HMOs (health maintenance organizations), care provided by, 146

Holmium laser resection, for benign prostatic hyperplasia, 2823, 2824f
   clinical results of, 2827-2828

Holmium:yttrium-aluminum-garnet (Ho:YAG) laser
   for benign prostatic hyperplasia, 2821
   for bladder cancer, non–muscle-invasive, 2453
   in lithotripsy, 1460-1462, 1461t, 1462t, 1513-1514
   in children, 3908

Homing, of immune cells, 475

Hormonal control, of renal function, during development, 3157-3159, 3158f

Hormonal imprinting, of prostate, 2679-2680

Hormonal manipulation, before hypospadias repair, 3711
   timing of, 3712

Hormone(s). *See also specific hormone.*
   affected by aging, 856-857, 856t
     historical perspective on, 850-851
   controlling male sexual differentiation, 3761
   effect of, in laparoscopic surgery, 202
   evaluation of
     in erectile dysfunction, 767-768
     in male infertility, 618-619, 618t
   in regulation of renal functional development, 3172
   in regulation of spermatogenesis, 595-596
   in renal physiology, 1133-1138, 1134f, 1134t, 1136f, 1137t, 1138f
   neural, in male sexual function, 729-730
   role of, in painful bladder syndrome/interstitial cystitis, 349
   uropharmacology of, 1956

Hormone response element, in genes, 2703

Hormone therapy. *See also specific hormone.*
   chemotherapy with, for locally advanced cancer, before radical prostatectomy, 3061, 3061f
   for cryptorchidism, 3775-3776
   for erectile dysfunction, 771-773, 771t
   for metastatic renal cell carcinoma, 1625-1626
   for painful bladder syndrome/interstitial cystitis, 360t, 361
   for prostate cancer, 3082-3099
     adjuvant, 2942
     combined androgen blockade in, 3092-3095, 3094f, 3095f
     economic considerations of, 3099

Hormone therapy (*Continued*)
     complications of, 3089-3091
     economic considerations in, 3099
     future of, 3099
     historic overview of, 3082-3083
     immediate vs. delayed
       in clinically localized disease, 3096
       in locally advanced or asymptomatic metastatic disease, 3097-3098, 3097f
       in lymph node metastatic disease, 3096-3097, 3096f
       integration of data in, 3098, 3098f
     molecular biology of, 3083-3084, 3084f
     primary, 2943-2944
     response to, 3088-3089
     timing of, 3095-3098
     with radiation therapy, 3091-3092, 3093f, 3093t
     with radical prostatectomy, 3091, 3092f, 3092t
   for prostatitis, 322-323, 325t, 327t
   for sexual health problems
     in perimenopausal women, 878-881, 879f
     in premenopausal women, 875-878
   postmenopausal, incontinence and, 2108
   replacement, testicular, 569, 569f

Horseshoe kidney, 3287-3291
   associated anomalies with, 3289
   blood supply to, 3288, 3289f
   diagnosis of, 3290, 3290f
   embryology of, 3287-3288, 3288f
   features of, 3288
   in Turner's syndrome, 3811
   incidence of, 3287
   isthmusectomy for, 1755-1756
   multicystic dysplastic kidney in, 3336, 3336f
   percutaneous access to, 1540, 1540f
   percutaneous nephrolithotomy into, 1497-1498
   prognosis for, 3290-3291
   renal cell carcinoma in, 3290
   stone formation in, 1390
     surgical management of, 1443
   symptoms of, 3289-3290
   ureteropelvic junction obstruction and, in children, 3362, 3363f
   Wilms' tumor in, 3290-3291

Hospitalization, risk of, for chronic renal failure, 1357-1359, 1358t

Host defense, altered
   in prostatitis, 308
   in urinary tract infections, 236

Hot flashes
   androgen deprivation therapy causing, 3089-3090
   treatment of, 3090

Ho:YAG laser. *See* Holmium:yttrium-aluminum-garnet (Ho:YAG) laser.

HPV. *See* Human papillomavirus (HPV).

HRQOL. *See* Health-related quality of life (HRQOL).

H-shaped incisions, in Peyronie's disease surgery, 833, 833f, 834f

HSP27, in regulation of apoptosis, 532-533

HSV. *See* Herpes simplex virus (HSV) *entries.*

Human bites, to penis, 2651

Human chorionic gonadotropin (hCG)
   for cryptorchidism, 3775
   for erectile dysfunction, 772
   in penile development, 3752
   in testicular tumors, 906

Human immunodeficiency virus (HIV)
   detection of, 391-392
   drug-resistant, assays for, 394

Immunity (*Continued*)
    phagocytosis in, 474
        role of, 496
    passive, 502
    primary, 478
    secondary, 478
    T-cell receptor in, 479-480
    to infections, 500-502, 502t
    to uropathogens, 235-236
Immunobead test, for antisperm antibodies,
    624t
Immunobiology, of renal cell carcinoma,
    1588-1589
Immunoglobulin(s). *See also* Antibody(ies).
    classes of, 478
    in seminal plasma, 2724
Immunoglobulin A, secretion of, 475
Immunohistochemistry, in diagnosis of
    oncology, 547-548
Immunologic infertility, in males, 649-650
Immunology, molecular, 502-503, 504f
Immunosuppressants
    in renal transplantation, 1316-1317
        infection and peptic ulcer prophylaxis and,
            1317, 1318t
        mechanism of action of, 1316t
        potential drug interactions among, 1317,
            1317t
        protocol for, 1317, 1317f
        sites of action of, 1316f
        toxicity of, organ targets for, 1317,
            1318t
    pregnancy safety and, 1323t
    secretion of, as mechanism of tumor escape,
        497-498, 498f
Immunotherapy
    for bladder cancer, non–muscle-invasive,
        2455-2458
        bacille Calmette-Guérin in, 2455-2457,
            2457t, 2458t
            chemotherapy with, 2460
        interferon in, 2457
        investigational agents in, 2457-2458
    for painful bladder syndrome/interstitial
        cystitis, 360t, 361
    for prostate cancer, 3030
        hormone-refractory, 3116-3117
    for renal cell carcinoma, 1588-1589
        metastatic, 1629
    for retroperitoneal fibrosis, 1217, 1272
    for tumors, 499-500
    for urothelial tumors, 1651, 1651t
Imperforate anus, 3647, 3647t
    associated findings in, 3647-3648
    evaluation of, 3648, 3649f
    in neonate, 3195
    in unilateral renal agenesis, 3275, 3275f
Imperforate hymen, 3843-3844, 3844f
    with hydrocolpos, 3194
Imperforate vagina, cervix and uterine
    duplication with, 3839, 3839f, 3840f
Impetigo, in HIV patients, 396-397
Implant, penile. *See* Penile prosthesis.
Implantable microballoons
    for bladder filling/storage disorders, 2292
    for incontinence, 2286-2287
Impotence, 86. *See also* Erectile dysfunction;
    Penile detumescence; Priapism.
    after urethral distraction injuries, 2661
    arteriogenic, 740-742
    hormonal, 740
    in end-stage renal disease, 1301
    neurogenic, 739-740
    patient history of, 87

Impotence (*Continued*)
    psychogenic, 739
    venogenic, 742
In vitro fertilization. *See also* Assisted
    reproductive techniques (ARTs).
    with intracytoplasmic sperm injection, 650,
        651, 652, 717-718, 718f
Incision(s). *See also specific incision.*
    electrosurgical, 191
    in adrenal surgery
        flank, 1871-1873, 1872f, 1873f
        lumbodorsal, 1873, 1874f
        subcostal, 1874, 1875f
        thoracoabdominal, 1875-1876, 1876f
    in antireflux surgery, 4351
    in radical nephrectomy, thoracoabdominal,
        1709-1710, 1711f, 1712f
    in radical retropubic prostatectomy, 2959-
        2960
        endopelvic fascia, 2960-2961, 2961f
    in renal surgery
        abdominal, 1695-1698, 1697f-1701f
        dorsal lumbotomy, 1695, 1696f
        flank, 1691-1694, 1691f-1695f
        thoracoabdominal, 1698, 1701f-1702f,
            1703
    in simple nephrectomy
        flank, 1703, 1703f-1705f
        transperitoneal, 1703, 1707, 1707f
    sites of, in varicocele repair, 659, 660f
Incisional hernia
    after laparoscopy, 217-218
    after radical nephrectomy, 1720
Inconspicuous penis, 3749f, 3751, 3751f
Incontinence, 2046-2077. *See also* Fecal
    incontinence; Voiding dysfunction.
    after cryotherapy, 3049-3050
    after robotic-assisted laparoscopic radical
        prostatectomy, 2999, 2999t
    after urethral injury, 3944
    age-related changes and, 2189, 2305-2306,
        2306f
    assessment of, initial, 2059
    bladder abnormalities in, 2053-2056, 3658-
        3659
        conditions causing, 2054-2056, 2055t,
            2056f-2058f, 2056t
        urodynamic observation of, 2053-2054,
            2053f, 2054f
    causes of, 2049t
        established, 2309-2311
        functional, 2310-2311
        lower urinary tract, 2309-2310
    classification of, 2046-2047
    clinical evaluation of, 2202-2203, 2202t
        self-administered questionnaire in, 2203t
        self-administered short forms in, 2203t
    continuous, 86, 2047
    definition of, 2187
        International Continence Society, 2046,
            2082
    detrusor overactivity causing. *See also*
        Overactive bladder.
        medical treatment of, 2071-2073
        surgical treatment of, 2073-2074
    diagnostic evaluation of, 2059-2070, 2311-
        2313
        empirical categorization in, 2313-2314
        history in, 2311-2312, 2312t
        laboratory examination in, 2313
        physical examination in, 2312-2313
        stress testing in, 2313
        urodynamic testing in, 2314
        voiding diary in, 2312, 2312f

Incontinence (*Continued*)
    during abdominal pressure increase, 1975-
        1976
    dye testing for, 2063
    effect of, on quality of life, 2062, 2062t
    endoscopy in, 2069-2070
    epidemiology of, 2047-2049, 2187-2190
    etiology of, 2053-2059
    extraurethral, 2047
    eyeball urodynamics in, 2064, 2064f
    female, 1936, 2047-2048, 2048f
        physical examination for, 2059-2060
        retropubic suspension surgery for, 2168-
            2185. *See also* Retropubic suspension
            surgery, for female incontinence.
        sphincter abnormalities and, 2058-2059
    geriatric. *See* Geriatric patient, incontinence
        in.
    history of, 2059-2060, 2060t
    impact of, 2124-2125, 2125t
        on sexual function, 2204-2205
    in children, 3612
        giggle, 3612
        injection therapy for, 2273
            intraurethral technique of, 2280
        urinary tract infection associated with,
            3263
    in schizophrenia, 2041
    in stroke patients, 2014-2015
    in ureterovaginal fistula, 2341
    in urethrovaginal fistula, 2347-2348
    in valve patients, 3597
    incidence of, 2187, 2188, 2188t
    laboratory investigation in, 2313
    leak point pressures in
        abdominal, 2066, 2066f
        detrusor, 2067, 2067f
    low bladder compliance causing, treatment of,
        2071-2074
    male, 2048-2049
        physical examination for, 2060
        prosthesis for, history and development of,
            2392-2393
        sphincter abnormalities and, 2059
        surgical treatment of, 2391-2403. *See also*
            Artificial urinary sphincter; Perineal
            sling.
            contraindications to, 2392
            indications for, 2391-2392
    micturition diary in, 2062
    mixed, 2046, 2084, 2084f, 2202
        management of, 2145
        tension-free vaginal taping for, 2256-2257
    multichannel videourodynamic monitoring
        of, 2068-2069, 2069f
    myelodysplasia and, management of, 3636-
        3639, 3638f
    neurologic examination in, 2060
    overflow, 86, 2047
    pad testing for, 2063
    pathophysiology of, 2053-2059
    patient history of, 86
    pelvic examination in, 2060
    physical examination in, 2060-2061, 2312-
        2313
    postvoid residual volume in, 2060
    pressure-flow relation in, 2068
    prevalence of, 2187, 2188, 2188t
    radical retropubic prostatectomy causing,
        2974
    recurrent
        artificial sphincter placement–induced,
            2400-2401
        perineal sling procedure causing, 2396

Laparoscopic radical prostatectomy (Continued)
antegrade neurovascular bundle
preservation in, 2993, 2994f, 2995f
bladder neck transection in, 2992,
2994f
delivery of prostate specimen in, 2996
developing space of Retzius in, 2991,
2991f
dorsal vein complex division in, 2993,
2995
dorsal vein complex ligation in, 2991-
2992, 2991f, 2992f
exiting abdomen in, 2996
inspection and entrapment of prostate
specimen in, 2995
interfascial dissection of neurovascular
bundles in, 2992, 2993f
posterior prostatic dissection in, 2990-
2991, 2990f, 2991f
prostatic apical dissection in, 2995
prostatic pedicle ligation in, 2992-2993,
2994f
retrograde neurovascular bundle
preservation in, 2993
seminal vesical and vas deferens
dissection in, 2989-2990, 2989f,
2990f
urethral division in, 2995, 2996f
vesicourethral anastomosis in, 2995-
2996, 2997f
vs. extraperitoneal approach to, 2996-
2997
Laparoscopic renal biopsy, 1770-1772, 1770f,
1771f
Laparoscopic retroperitoneal lymph node
dissection, for testicular cancer, 945-948
bilateral, 947
complications of, 947
left-sided, 946-947
nerve-sparing techniques in, 947
patient positioning for, 945-946
patient preparation for, 945
results and current status of, 947-948
right-sided, 946
transperitoneal approach to, 946
Laparoscopic retropubic suspension surgery, for
female incontinence, 2180, 2182
Laparoscopic sacral colpopexy, for apical vaginal
prolapse repair, 2229-2230, 2230t
Laparoscopic stone surgery, 1506-1507
Laparoscopic surgery, 171-220
antibiotic prophylaxis for, 253, 253t
blood product preparation for, 175
bowel preparation for, 175
complication(s) of, 203-219, 203t
exiting abdomen as, 216
intraoperative, 211-216
bowel injury as, 211-213, 212f
nerve injury as, 215-216
pancreatic injury as, 215
splenic injury as, 215
urinary tract injury as, 214-215
vascular injury as, 213-214
minimizing incidence of, 203
postoperative, 216-218
deep venous thrombosis as, 218
hydrocele as, 216-217
incisional hernia as, 217-218
late, 218-219
pain as, 217
rhabdomyolysis as, 218
scrotal and abdominal ecchymosis as,
217
wound infection as, 218

Laparoscopic surgery (Continued)
procedural, 203-219
related to anesthesia, 210-211
related to pneumoperitoneum, 204-209. See
also Pneumoperitoneum,
complication(s) related to.
secondary trocar placement and, 209-210,
209f, 210f
contraindications to, 174-175
development of extraperitoneal space in
balloon dilatation in, 181-182, 182f
extraperitoneoscopy in, 184
gasless peritoneal laparoscopy in, 182
instrumentation for, 181-189
retroperitoneoscopy in, 183, 183f, 184f
trocar placement in, 185, 185f, 186f, 188f,
189f
diagnostic, in children, 3914-3916
indications for, 3914
of hernia, 3915-3916, 3915f
of intersex conditions, 3914-3915, 3914t
of testis, 3914
endourologic procedures prior to, 176
exiting abdomen in
complications of, 216
port removal in, 197-198
port site closure in, 198, 198f
skin closure in, 198
extraperitoneal approach to, 173
for cryptorchidism, 3781-3787
assessment in, 3782-3784, 3783f
diagnostic, 3782
technique of, 3782
vs. inguinal exploration, 3784-3785
for ureteral stricture
Boari flap in, 1264
ileal ureteral substitution in, 1266-1267
psoas hitch in, 1261
for urinary diversion, 2523-2527, 2524f-2526f
for vesicovaginal fistula, 2512, 2513f
hand-assist devices in, 171-173, 186-187, 186f
historical aspects of, 171-174
in children, 3914-3928
anesthetic issues in, 3917-3918
antireflux, 3926-3927
complications of
operative, 3919
related to access, 3918-3919
for bladder reconstruction, 3924-3926,
3925f
indications for, 3916
instruments for, 3916-3917
perivesical, 3927
renal, 3919-3924. See also Renal surgery,
laparoscopic, in children.
robotic-assisted, 3927-3928, 3928f
vaginoplasty as, 3927
informed consent for, 175
initial incision in, procedures prior to, 178
instrumentation in, 189-197
for aspiration and irrigation, 196
for grasping and blunt dissection, 190-191,
191f
for incising and hemostasis, 191-193
for morcellation, 195-196
for retraction, 196-197, 197f
for specimen entrapment, 195, 196f
for stapling and clipping, 194-195, 194f
for suturing and tissue anastomosis, 193-
194
for visualization, 189-190
pediatric, 3916-3917
of seminal vesicles, 1120, 1122-1125
patient preparation for, 1120

Laparoscopic surgery (Continued)
potential complications of, 1124-1125
retroperitoneal approach to, 1124
robotic approach to, 1124
transperitoneal approach to, 1120, 1122-
1124, 1124f
operating room setup for, 176, 176t
patient draping for, 176
patient positioning for, 176
patient selection for, 174-175
physiologic consideration(s) in, 199-203
acid-base metabolic effects of
pneumoperitoneum as, 201-202
cardiovascular effects of
pneumoperitoneum as, 200, 200t
choice of insufflant as, 199-200
choice of pneumoperitoneum pressure as,
200, 200t
hemodynamic effects as, 202
hormonal effects as, 202
immunologic effects as, 202-203
metabolic effects as, 202
renal effects of pneumoperitoneum as,
201
respiratory effects of pneumoperitoneum
as, 200-201
postoperative management in, 198-199
preoperative management in, 174-176
procedures in, 178-198
radiologic procedures prior to, 176
retroperitoneal approach to, 173
robotic-assisted, 173-174
skin closure in, 198
standard, 171-173
strategic placement of team and equipment
for, 177-178, 177f
transperitoneal, 171-173
vs. extraperitoneal pelvic surgery, 220
vs. retroperitoneoscopy, 219
transperitoneal access in, 178-181
troubleshooting in, 203-219, 203t
ureteral injuries due to, 1283-1284
in children, 3937
Laparoscopic ureteral reimplantation, 2506-
2507, 2507f, 2508f
Laparoscopic ureterocalicostomy, for
ureteropelvic junction obstruction, 1253
Laparoscopic ureterolithotomy, for ureteral
calculi, 1455
Laparoscopic ureterolysis, for retroperitoneal
fibrosis, 1273
Laparoscopic ureteroneocystostomy, for ureteral
stricture, 1261
Laparoscopic ureteronephrectomy, proximal,
1665-1666, 1666f
Laparoscopic ureteroureterostomy, for ureteral
stricture, 1261
Laparoscopic varicocelectomy, 659-661, 661f,
1125-1126
indications for, 1125
results of, 1126
technique of, 1125-1126, 1126f
Lapdisc device, hand-assist, 186-187, 186f
Lapides classification, of voiding dysfunction,
1982-1983, 1982t
Laplace equation, 1908, 1912, 1924, 1924f
Laser(s). See also specific laser.
in laparoscopy, 192
in treatment of benign prostatic hyperplasia,
2820-2821
Laser lithotripsy, 1460-1462, 1513-1514
advantages and disadvantages of, 1461,
1461t
technique of, 1461-1462, 1462t

Magnesium oxide, for hypomagnesiuric calcium nephrolithiasis, 1423-1424
Magnetic resonance angiography (MRA), 139-138
    of penis, 763
    of renovascular hypertension, 1171-1172
Magnetic resonance imaging (MRI), 135-139
    in percutaneous procedures, 1532-1533
    of adrenal carcinoma, 1835-1836, 1836f
    of adrenals, 135, 137f
    of autosomal dominant polycystic kidney disease, 3323, 3324f
    of autosomal recessive polycystic kidney disease, 3318f
    of bladder, 135, 137f
    of bladder cancer, 2440
        invasive, 2469
    of brain
        during sexual arousal, 726-727
        for female sexual health problems, 874
    of ectopic ureter, 3392-3393
    of genitourinary tuberculosis, 443
    of germ cell tumors, 905
    of kidneys, 135, 136f
    of lipomeningocele, 3643, 3644f
    of myelomeningocele, 3634, 3635f
    of neuroblastoma, 3872, 3872f, 3873f
    of pelvic organ prolapse, 2210-2211, 2211f
    of penile cancer, 970
    of pheochromocytoma, 1860f, 1863, 1864f, 1865f
    of prostate, 135, 138, 138f, 139f
    of prostate cancer
        localized vs. metastatic, 3072
        locally advanced, 3055, 3055f
    of renal cell carcinoma, 1602
    of renal cysts, 3345, 3347f
    of renal tumors, 1571, 1573f
    of retroperitoneal fibrosis, 1216, 1217f
    of sacral agenesis, 3645, 3646f
    of seminal vesicles, 1112-1113, 1113f
    of tumor involvement of inferior vena cava, 1620, 1620f
    of ureteropelvic junction obstruction, in children, 3367-3368, 3368f, 3369f
    of urethra, 138
    of urethral diverticula, 2381-2382, 2381f, 2382f
    of urinary tract infections, 243
        in children, 3256
    of Wilms' tumor, 3891, 3891f, 3895f
Magnetic resonance urography (MRU), 138, 139f
    of megaureter, 4374, 4374f
    of pediatric patient, 3214, 3214f
    of ureteral obstruction, 1211
Magnetic stimulation
    for incontinence, 2136
    noninvasive, 2160
Mainz ileocecocystoplasty, in children, 3675, 3676f
Mainz pouch, for orthotopic urinary diversion, 2641, 2641f
Mainz pouch I, for continent urinary diversion, 2591, 2593, 2595-2596
    postoperative care in, 2595-2596, 2596f-2599f
    procedure in, 2593, 2594f, 2595
Mainz pouch II
    for continent urinary diversion, with augmented valved rectum, 2584, 2586
    in laparoscopic-assisted urinary diversion, 2524, 2527

Major histocompatibility complex (MHC)
    in allograft rejection, 1314-1315, 1315f, 1315t
    in allorecognition, 481
    in immune response, 479, 479f
Malacoplakia
    clinical presentation of, 284-285
    differential diagnosis of, 285
    management of, 285
    pathogenesis of, 283-284
    pathology of, 284, 284f
    radiologic findings in, 285
Malassezia furfur, autoimmune response to, seborrheic dermatitis and, 415
Male Sexual Function Scale, 752, 754f-755f
Malecot catheter, 162, 162f
Malecot tubes, for percutaneous nephrostomy, 1558
Malignancy. See Cancer; specific neoplasm.
Malignant melanoma, of bladder, 2445
Malleable dilators, 1542, 1542f
Malnutrition
    due to conduit urinary diversion, 2575
    in acute renal failure, 1337-1338
    in chronic renal failure, 1353
Malposition, of colon, in renal ectopia, 3281
Malrotation, of kidney, 3291-3292, 3292f, 3293f
Mannitol, for acute renal failure, 1336
Manual compression, for bladder emptying disorders, 2298
MAO (monoamine oxidase) inhibitors, erectile dysfunction caused by, 744
Marsden symptoms scores, 2816, 2819
Marsden-Iversen score, 2819
Marshall test, for stress incontinence, 2206, 2313
Marshall-Marchetti-Krantz procedure
    for female incontinence, 2170, 2171f
        results of, 2175
        technique of, 2174-2175, 2176f
    vs. Burch colposuspension and paravaginal repair, 2184-2185
Martius flap. See also Flap(s).
    in urethrovaginal fistula repair, 2349, 2350f
    in vesicovaginal fistula repair, 2338-2339, 2338f
Massachusetts Male Aging Study (MMAS)
    of erectile dysfunction, 738, 765
    of late-onset hypogonadism, 854
Massage therapy, for prostatitis, 323-324
Mast cells, involvement of, in painful bladder syndrome/interstitial cystitis, 341-343, 342f
Maternal anemia, bacteriuria and, 291-292
Mathieu hypospadias repair, 3725, 3726f-3727f
Matrix (matrices)
    extracellular. See Extracellular matrix.
    for bladder regeneration, 559-560
    nonfibrillar, of bladder wall, 1932
    nuclear, 511
    of urinary stones, 1371
Matrix calculi, 1388
Matrix metalloproteinases
    in Peyronie's disease, 821-822
    in ureteral obstruction, 1204
    in urothelial tumors, 2424-2425
Mayer-Rokitansky-Küster-Hauser syndrome
    atypical form of, 3834
    genital anomalies associated with, 3833-3834
    typical form of, 3834
McIndoe technique, in creation of neovagina, 3835-3836, 3835f
MCKD1 gene, in medullary cystic disease, 3326
MCKD2 gene, in medullary cystic disease, 3326
Meares-Stamey four-hour glass test, for prostatitis, 314, 314f

Meatal stenosis
    after circumcision, 3215, 3749-3750
    after hypospadias repair, 3739
Meatoplasty
    for meatal stenosis, after circumcision, 3749-3750
    in hypospadias repair, 3718
Meatoplasty and glanuloplasty (MAGPI)
    technique, of hypospadias repair, 3722, 3723f
Meatotomy, as outpatient procedure, 3215
Mechanical compression, nonsurgical, for bladder filling/storage disorders, 2291-2292
Mechanical failure
    of artificial sphincter, 2401
    rates of, for penile prosthesis, 800, 800t
Mechanical preparation, of bowel, for urinary tract reconstruction, 2537-2538, 2537t
Mechanical properties, of ureteral smooth muscle, 1902-1903
    force-length relations in, 1902-1903, 1902f, 1903f
    force-velocity relations in, 1903, 1903f
    pressure-length-diameter relations in, 1903
Meconium, passage of, 3210
Medial fibroplasia, of renal artery, 1157t, 1159-1160, 1160f
Mediastinal resection, postchemotherapy, testicular tumors and, 955
Medical history, of erectile dysfunction, 752, 755, 755t
Medical Therapy of Prostatic Symptoms (MTOPS), 2754
Medical Therapy of Prostatic Symptoms (MOPS) study, of combination therapy for benign prostatic hyperplasia, 2795-2797
Medication regimen change, for erectile dysfunction, 769-770
Medullary carcinoma, renal, 1596
Medullary cystic disease, 3326-3328, 3327f, 3328f. See also Juvenile nephronophthisis/medullary cystic disease complex.
    genetics of, 3326, 3326t
    in chronic renal failure, 1346
Medullary fibroma, renal, 1582
Medullary sponge kidney, 3348-3350
    asymptomatic, 3349
    characteristics of, 3314t
    clinical features of, 3349
    diagnosis of, 3350
    histopathology of, 3349-3350
    imaging of, 3349f, 3350
    stone formation associated with, 1390-1391, 3349
    treatment and prognosis of, 3350
Megacalycosis, 3299-3301, 3300f
    definition of, 3299
    of renal calyces, 3299-3301, 3300f
Megacystis-megaureter association
    postnatal evaluation and management of, 3191
    vesicoureteral reflux in, 4344
Megacystitis, congenital, antenatal detection of, 3574, 3575f
Megalourethra, in prune-belly syndrome, 3485, 3485f
    surgical repair of, 3491, 3492f
Megameatus intact prepuce (MIP) variant, in hypospadias, 3703, 3704f
    repair of, 3725
Megaprepuce, 3749f, 3756
Megathura crenulata, for bladder cancer, non–muscle-invasive, 2458

Patient history *(Continued)*
  urine turbidity in, 96-97
  urobilinogen in, 104
  vesical pain in, 82-83
Patient-partner counseling, preoperative, in penile prosthesis placement, 788-790
Patient-partner satisfaction, with penile prosthesis, 800-801
PAX2 gene
  in renal-coloboma syndrome, 3134-3135
  in vesicoureteral reflux, 4326
PBOV1 gene, in prostate cancer, 2909
PCA3, in diagnosis of oncology, 549
Peak systolic velocity
  in penile blood flow, arterial dilation and, 758-759, 759f
  in renal artery, 1170
Pearly penile papules, 431, 432f
Pedicles
  in radical retropubic prostatectomy, dissection and division of, 2968-2969, 2969f
  in robotic-assisted laparoscopic radical prostatectomy, ligation of, 2992-2993, 2994f
Pediculosis pubis, 425, 425f
  diagnosis of, 383-384
  treatment of, 384
PEER retractors, in laparoscopy, 196, 197f
Pelvic artery(ies), 46, 48t, 50f, 51
Pelvic diaphragm, 2191-2192, 2191f, 2192f
Pelvic dissection, in radical cystectomy
  in females, 2495-2496, 2496f, 2497f
  in males, 2485, 2486f-2488f, 2487
Pelvic fibrosis, as contraindication to laparoscopy, 174-175
Pelvic floor
  abnormal musculature of, in prostatitis, 309
  anatomy of, 2190-2198
  defects of, in bladder exstrophy, 3502f, 4328-4329
  dysfunction of
    in painful bladder syndrome/interstitial cystitis, 349
    sexual pain associated with, 885-886
    vaginal delivery and, 2189
  hyperactivity of, 2002
  massage of, for prostatitis, 323-324
  support structures of
    bony, 2190-2191, 2191f
    connective tissue, 2194-2198
      anterior supports, 2195, 2196f, 2197f
      middle supports, 2195, 2197, 2198f
      posterior supports, 2197-2198, 2198f
    muscular, 2191-2194, 2191f-2194f
Pelvic floor exercises
  for erectile dysfunction, 770
  for geriatric incontinence, 2318
  Kegel, 2130
Pelvic floor muscle training
  definition of, 2130
  for incontinence, 2071, 2130-2132
    effectiveness of, 2131
    vs. other conservative modalities, 2132
  for stress incontinence, 2074, 2142
  implementation of, in clinical practice, 2131-2132
  in childbearing women, 2131
  vs. exercises, 2130
Pelvic floor rehabilitation
  for incontinence, 2130-2136
    biofeedback techniques in, 2133, 2133f-2135f
    electrical stimulation in, 2135

Pelvic floor rehabilitation *(Continued)*
    magnetic stimulation in, 2136
    muscle training in, 2130-2132
      implementation of, 2131-2132
      vs. other conservative modalities, 2132
      tools for, 2133, 2134f-2135f
  for urethral sphincter dysfunction, in children, 3618, 3619f, 3620f
Pelvic fracture
  associated with posterior urethral injury, in children, 3940
  urethral disruption related to, 2659
Pelvic inflammatory disease, tubo-ovarian abscess in, 1220
Pelvic kidney, percutaneous access to, 1540-1541
Pelvic lipomatosis, ureteral obstruction due to, 1218-1219, 1218f, 1219f
Pelvic lymph node dissection. *See* Pelvic lymphadenectomy.
Pelvic lymphadenectomy
  for penile cancer, 982
  in radical retropubic prostatectomy, 2960, 2960f
  in staging of prostate cancer, 2930-2931
  laparoscopic
    complications of, 3003-3004
    indications for, 3002
    port site seeding after, 1779
    technique of, 3002-3003, 3002f-3004f
    with radical cystectomy, 2521, 2523f
  with radical cystectomy
    in females, 2495, 2495f, 2496f
    in males, 2484-2485, 2485f, 2486f
Pelvic musculature education, in behavioral therapy for incontinence, 2127
Pelvic organ prolapse, 2198-2211
  anatomic classification of, 2200, 2200t, 2201f
  clinical classification of, 2207, 2208f, 2209, 2209f
  clinical evaluation of, 2202-2207, 2202t
  cystoscopy in, 2209-2210
  definition of, 2188-2189
  genetic factors in, 2190
  in anterior compartment, 2200, 2200t
  in middle compartment, 2200, 2200t, 2201f
  in posterior compartment, 2200, 2200t, 2201f
  incidence of, 2189
  magnetic resonance imaging of, 2210-2211, 2211f
  parity and, 2189
  pathophysiology of, 2198-2199, 2199t
  pelvic examination in, 2205-2207, 2206f
    instrumentation for, 2205
  physical examination in, 2205
  risk factors for, 2189-2190, 2199t
  signs and symptoms of
    bowel, 2204
    local, 2205
    lower urinary tract, 2202-2204, 2203t
    sexual, 2204-2205, 2204t
  sling procedures for, 2249
  stages in, 2207, 2209
  surgical management of
    goals in, 2215t
    vaginal approach to, 2199-2200, 2199f
    tension-free vaginal taping for, 2255-2256
  ultrasonography of, 2210
  urodynamic testing in, 2209, 2210f
  vaginal pessaries for, 2137-2138, 2138f, 2139f, 2215
  voiding dysfunction in, 2204
Pelvic organ prolapse quantification (POPQ) classification system, 2207, 2208f
Pelvic pain, after cryotherapy, 3050

Pelvic Pain and Urgency/Frequency Patient System Scale, for painful bladder syndrome/interstitial cystitis, 355, 356t
Pelvic pain syndrome, chronic. *See* Chronic pelvic pain syndrome.
Pelvic plexus
  stimulation of, 724-725
  surgical anatomy of, 2957, 2957f
  transvesical infiltration of, 2291
Pelvic radiation therapy, previous, orthotopic urinary diversion with, 2629-2630
Pelvic surgery
  erectile dysfunction associated with, 739-740
  extensive, as contraindication to laparoscopy, 174
  glossary of terms for, 2215t
  incontinence associated with, 2189-2190
  pelvic organ prolapse associated with, 2190
  radical, voiding dysfunction after, 2012t, 2032
  ureteral injury caused by, 1283
Pelvic vein(s), 51-52, 51f
Pelvis
  arterial supply to, 46, 48t, 50f, 51
  benign anomalies of, ureteral obstruction due to, 1220-1221
  bifid, 3303
  bladder cancer recurrence in, after cystectomy, 2628-2629
  bony, 38, 39f, 2190-2191, 2191f
    abnormalities of, in exstrophy patient, 3500-3501, 3500f
  examination of
    in incontinence, 2060
    in organ prolapse, 2205-2207, 2206f
    landmarks for, 2207, 2208f
  extrarenal, 3303
  fascia of, 44-46
    components in, 45-46, 48f, 49f
  female, 2190-2191, 2191f
    physical examination of, 95
    support in, 67-68
    viscera in, 65, 65f-67f, 67
  innervation of, 52-55, 53f-55f, 53t
  irradiation of, bladder cancer associated with, 2416
  lymphatics of, 52, 52f
  muscles of, 43-44, 46f, 47f
  soft tissues of, 43-46
  venous supply to, 51-52, 51f
  viscera of, 56-68. *See also specific organs.*
Pemphigoid, bullous, of male genitalia, 415-416, 416f
Pemphigus vulgaris, of male genitalia, 415, 416f
Pendulous penis, 723
Penectomy, for penile cancer
  local recurrence after, 998
  partial, 973-974, 996, 997f, 998, 998f
  radical, 998, 1001f, 1002, 1002f
  total, 973-974, 998, 999f-1001f
Penetrating injury
  to kidney, 1274
    hematuria with, 1276
  to penis, 1049-1054
  to ureters, 1282-1283
ᴅ-Penicillamine, for cystinuria, 1424
Penicillin(s)
  for pediatric urinary tract infections, 3248t
  Jarisch-Herxheimer reaction to, 377
Penicillin G, for syphilis, 377
  in HIV patients, 395
Penicillin V, for *Pasteurella multocida* infection, 2651
Penile adhesions, filmy, after circumcision, 3748

Penile reconstruction (Continued)
total, 1092-1096
bipedicled flap in, 1095-1096
fibular osteocutaneous flap in, 1093
forearm flaps in, 1092-1093
disadvantages of, 1093
modifications of, 1093, 1094f, 1095f
principles of, 1092
rigidity for intercourse with, 1096
saphenous interposition graft in, 1095
upper arm flap, 1094-1095
Penile shaft
anatomy of, 1028-1031, 1029f-1030f, 1032f-1035f
coverage of, in hypospadias repair, 3718
length of, 719t
rotational defect of, 3754, 3754f
skin of, 71
Penile sinusoids, loss of compliance of, erectile dysfunction associated with, 742
Penile skin bridges, after circumcision, 3748-3749, 3750f
Penile thermal sensory testing, in erectile dysfunction, 767
Penile torsion, 3754, 3754f
Penile tumescence, nocturnal, monitoring of, 763-764, 764f
Penile tumor(s), 959-991
benign
cutaneous, 960
noncutaneous, 959-960
Buschke-Löwenstein, 963-964
malignant. See Penile cancer.
premalignant
cutaneous horn as, 960
keratotic balanitis as, 960
leukoplakia as, 961
lichen sclerosus as, 960
pseudoepitheliomatous micaceous growths as, 960
viral-related, 961-963
bowenoid papulosis as, 962
Kaposi's sarcoma as, 962-963
malignant transformation of, 961-962
Penile (pendulous) urethra, 1029, 1030f
carcinoma of, 1012-1013, 1012f, 1013f
Penile vascular surgery
arterial, 803-812
complications of, 810-811
dorsal artery dissection in, 806-807, 808f
inferior epigastric artery harvesting in, 807-809, 808f
microvascular anastomosis in, 809-810, 809f, 810f
disruption following, 810-811
penile edema following, 810
penile numbness following, 810
penile shortening following, 810
results of, 811-812, 811t
selection criteria for, 803-805, 803t, 804f, 805f
technique of, 806-810, 806f, 806t, 807t
venous, 812-816
complications of, 815-816
results of, 816, 816t
selection criteria for, 812, 813f-814f
technique of, 812, 815, 815f
Penile vibratory stimulation
for anejaculation, 715-716, 716f
for spinal cord–injured men, 649
Penile warts, human papillomavirus causing, 380, 381f

Penis. See also Micropenis.
anatomy of, 69, 70f-72f, 71-72, 1028-1031, 1029f-1035f
functional, 719-723, 719t
of arterial system, 1034-1035, 1035f
of lymphatics, 1035
of nerve supply, 1035
of venous drainage, 1031, 1034, 1034f
anomalies of, 3746-3758. See also specific anomaly.
arterial supply to, 721-722, 721f, 1031, 1033f
anatomy of, 1034-1035, 1035f
cancer of. See Penile cancer.
corpus cavernosum of, 69, 69f, 70f. See also Corpus cavernosum.
corpus spongiosum of, 69f, 70f, 71. See also Corpus spongiosum.
duplication of, 3757
edema of, after penile revascularization, 810
elongation of, 3141, 3142f, 3143
erectile tissue of, 1028-1029, 1030f. See also Penile erection.
examination of, 91-92
flaccid
length of, 719t
neurotransmitters in, 728
smooth muscle contraction in, 723
hidden, 3749f, 3751, 3751f
hilum of, 69
HSV infection of, 374f
hypersensitivity of, in premature ejaculation, 784-785
in exstrophy patient, functional and cosmetically pleasing, 3503-3504, 3519
inconspicuous, 3749f, 3751, 3751f
infrapubic, 722f, 723
injury to. See Penile injury.
innervation of, 724-725, 725f, 726t
anatomy of, 1035
lymphatics of, anatomy of, 1035
molluscum contagiosum affecting, 382f
neonatal, evaluation of, 3209
normal, 3745
numbness of, after penile revascularization, 810
pendulous, 723
prosthetic. See Penile prosthesis.
reconstruction of. See Penile reconstruction.
scabies affecting, 383f
shortening of
after penile revascularization, 810
in bladder exstrophy, 3501
strangulation of, 2652
tissue engineering of, corporal tissues reconstruction in, 564-565, 564f, 565f
trapped, 3751
resulting from circumcision, 3750f
tuberculosis of, 440
tunica albuginea of, 70f, 72f. See also Tunica albuginea.
vasculature of, 51, 51f, 71-72, 72f
venous drainage of, 722-723, 722f, 813f
anatomy of, 1031, 1034, 1034f
webbed, 3749f, 3751
Penn pouch, for continent urinary diversion, 2602-2604
postoperative care of, 2603-2604
procedure in, 2602-2603, 2603f
Penography, radionuclide, 762-763
Penoscrotal transposition, 3758-3759, 3758f
PENS. See Posterior tibial nerve stimulation (PENS).

Pentosan polysulfate
for painful bladder syndrome/interstitial cystitis, 360-361, 360t, 362t, 363-364
for prostatitis, clinical trial data on, 322, 327t
Peptic ulcer, postoperative, prophylactic management of, 1317, 1318t
Peptide(s), excretion of, effect of ureteral obstruction on, 1203
Peptidergic agents, effect of, on ureteral function, 1906
Percussion, of bladder, 90
Percutaneous antegrade endopyelotomy, for ureteropelvic junction obstruction, 1233-1237. See also Endopyelotomy, percutaneous antegrade.
Percutaneous epididymal sperm aspiration (PESA), 652, 700, 702f-703f
Percutaneous nephrolithotomy. See Nephrolithotomy, percutaneous.
Percutaneous nephrostomy. See Nephrostomy, percutaneous.
Percutaneous procedures. See also specific procedure.
antibiotic prophylaxis for, 253
Percutaneous transluminal angioplasty (PTA)
complications of, 1181
for atherosclerotic renal artery stenosis, 1182, 1183f, 1183t, 1184, 1184t
for fibrous dysplasia, 1181-1182, 1181t, 1182f
for inflammatory renal artery stenosis, 1184
for renovascular hypertension, 1180-1184
in children, 1184
mechanism of, 1181
technique of, 1180-1181
with endovascular stenting, 1185-1186, 1185t
Percutaneous vasectomy, 1101. See also Vasectomy.
Pereyra technique, modified, for stress incontinence, 2212
Perforation. See at anatomic site.
Perfusion studies, of ureteral obstruction, 1913-1914, 1914f
Perimedial fibroplasia, of renal artery, 1157t, 1160-1161, 1160f, 1161f
Perimenopausal women, hormonal therapy for, sexual health problems and, 878-881, 879f
Perineal body, 1036, 1037f, 1039, 2194, 2194f
defects of, 2200
examination of, 2207
fascia of, 46, 49f
Perineal mass, in female neonate, 3194-3195
Perineal membrane, 2193
Perineal pain, in children, 3207
Perineal sling, for male incontinence, 2077, 2393-2396
complications of, 2395-2396
implantation technique of, 2393, 2394f
indications for, 2391-2392
results of, 2393-2395, 2395t
special circumstances and, 2396
Perineal space
deep, 1038f, 1039
superficial, 1036, 1037f
Perineorrhaphy, posterior colporrhaphy and, 2230-2232, 2231f
Perinephric abscess, 276-278
after injury, 1282
Candida causing, 462
clinical presentation of, 277
in children, diagnosis of, 3246
management of, 278
radiologic findings in, 277-278, 277f, 278f
vs. acute pyelonephritis, 278

Primary ciliary dyskinesia, 611, 623
PRL. *See* Prolactin (PRL).
Proapoptotic gene therapy, for prostate cancer, 3030
Probiotic therapy, prophylactic, for pediatric urinary tract infections, 3252
Processus vaginalis
  ligation of, in orchiopexy, 3777, 3778f
  patent
    in undescended testis, 3773
    laparoscopic examination of, 3915f
    separation and ligation of, in orchiopexy, 3777, 3777f, 3778f
Proctitis, 371
Prodrug gene therapy, for prostate cancer, 3030
Progesterone
  and female sexual function, 875
  for sexual dysfunction
    in perimenopausal and postmenopausal women, 880
    in premenopausal women, 875-876
  for vaginal atrophy, 880
  midluteal phase, in evaluation of fertility, 612
Progestin, maternal administration of, 3820-3821
Programmed cell death. *See* Apoptosis.
Prolactin (PRL)
  effects of, on prostate, 2689
  excess of, in males, 637
  in male sexual function, 730
  secretion of, 578
Prolapse. *See at specific anatomic site.*
Promoter element, in genes, 2702-2703
Pronephros, 3121, 3124f, 3149, 3150f
Propanolamine, for retrograde ejaculation, 648
Propantheline, for overactive bladder/detrusor overactivity, 2093t, 2094-2095
Prophase, in mitosis, 2712
Propiverine, for overactive bladder/detrusor overactivity, 2093t, 2102-2103
Proscar Long Term Efficacy and Safety Study (PLESS), 2753, 2754, 2790, 2791f
Prosta Coil stent, 2805
Prosta Kath stent, 2804-2805
Prostaglandin(s)
  and renal development, 3159
  in male sexual function, 732-734
  in prostatic secretions, 2717-2718
  in ureteral function, 1919-1920
  to facilitate bladder emptying, 2116-2117
  uropharmacology of, 1955
Prostaglandin E$_1$, for erectile dysfunction
  intracavernous injection of, 779-780
  intraurethral, 781
Prostaglandin E$_2$
  in renin secretion, 1162
  inhibition of T cell activity by, 497-498
Prostaglandin F$_{2\alpha}$, in male sexual function, 728
Prostaglandin I$_2$
  in male sexual function, 728
  in renin secretion, 728
Prostanoids, uropharmacology of, 1955
ProstaScint scan, of prostate cancer, localized vs. metastatic, 3072
Prostasoft 2.5 protocol, clinical studies of, 2817
Prostasoft 3.5 protocol, clinical studies of, 2817
Prostate, 61-63
  abscess of
    Candida causing, 460, 462f
    drainage of, 325
  anatomic relationships of, 61
  anatomy of
    arterial, 2956-2957, 2956f
    ultrasonographic, 2883, 2884f, 2885

Prostate (*Continued*)
  apex of, 61
    dissection of, in robotic-assisted laparoscopic radical prostatectomy, 2995
  arterial supply to, 63, 63f
  basal cells of, 2682-2683
  benign hyperplasia of. *See* Benign prostatic hyperplasia.
  biopsy of, 2887-2892
    contraindications to, 2889
    extended core, 2890, 2890f, 2890t
    fine-needle aspiration, 2891
    indications for, 2887-2889, 2887t
    patient preparation for, 251-252, 2889
    positive
      after cryotherapy, 3045, 3047
      in intermediate-risk patients, 3007-3009, 3008f
      in low-risk and favorable intermediate-risk patients, 3009, 3009f-3011f
    post-brachytherapy, 3023, 3024t
    post-radiotherapy, 3013-3014, 3013t
    repeat and saturation, 2890-2891, 2891t
    repeated, 2955
    rising PSA levels and, 3072
    risks and complications of, 2892
    sextant, 2890
    systemic results of, 2951
    transperineal, 2891-2892
    transrectal
      antibiotic prophylaxis for, 251-252
      techniques of, 2889-2891
      ultrasound-guided, 2923
        recommendations for, 2925
        techniques of, 2889-2891
    transurethral, 2892
  calculi in, 2670
  cancer of. *See* Prostate cancer.
  candidiasis of, 460, 468f
  cell types in, 2680-2683, 2680t
  central zone of, 63
  computed tomography of, 133
  cystic lesions of, transrectal ultrasonography of, 2886, 2886f
  development of, 3137-3139, 3139f
  dissection of, posterior, in robotic-assisted laparoscopic radical prostatectomy, 2990-2991, 2990f, 2991f
  embryonic development of, 2678-2679
  epithelial cells of, 2680-2681, 2680t
  examination of, 94
  exposure of
    in perineal prostatectomy, 2980-2981, 2980f, 2981f
    in retropubic prostatectomy, 2847, 2847f
      radical, 2960
    in suprapubic prostatectomy, 2850, 2850f
  expressed secretions from, in urinary sediment, 109, 109f
  fibromuscular stroma of, 61, 63, 64f
  glandular elements of, 61
  growth factors in, 2705-2711. *See also* Growth factors.
  growth of
    endocrine control of, 2684-2689
      androgen production in, 2685-2686, 2686t, 2687f
      androgen-binding proteins in, 2688-2689
      estrogens in, 2679-2680, 2686t, 2687f, 2688
      overview of, 2684-2685, 2685f
      prolactin in, 2689

Prostate (*Continued*)
  regulation of
    androgen action in, 2690-2691, 2691f
      nuclear matrix in, 2703-2705
    androgen receptor-dependent chromatin remodeling in, 2702-2703
    androgen receptors in, 2697-2701, 2697f, 2698f
    apoptosis in, 2714-2715
    balance of cell replication and death in, 2711-2715
    by steroids and protein growth factors, 2689-2696
    cell adhesion molecules in, 2694-2696
    cell aging, senescence, and immortality in, 2713-2714
    cell-adhesion molecules in, 2694-2696
    chromatin in, 2712-2713
    DNA damage in, 2714
    DNA synthesis and cell cycle control in, 2711-2712
    estrogens and estrogen-androgen synergism in, 2693
    interactive types of, 2690, 2690f
    5α-reductase and androgen metabolism in, 2691-2693, 2691t, 2692f
    steroid receptors in, 2696-2705
    stromal-epithelial interactions in, 2693-2694
    vitamin A in, 2705
    vitamin D in, 2705
  hormonal imprinting of, 2679-2680
  in exstrophy patient, 3504, 3505f
  in prune-belly syndrome, 3484
  inflammation of. *See* Prostatitis.
  innervation of, 63
  irradiation of, treatment effects of, 2880
  lobes of, 63
  localization of, in diagnosis of urinary tract infection, 242
  lymphatic drainage of, 63
  magnetic resonance imaging of, 135, 138, 138f, 139f
  massage of, for prostatitis, 323
  neuroendocrine cells of, 2680t, 2681
  pain in, patient history of, 83
  peripheral zone of, 63
  periurethral zone of, in benign prostatic hyperplasia, 2734
  postnatal development of, 2679-2680
  resection of. *See also* Prostatectomy.
    efficacy of injectable therapies after, 2281
  secretions of. *See* Prostatic secretions.
  size of, in benign prostatic hyperplasia, 2742-2743, 2742f
  smooth muscle of, adrenergic regulation of, 2737
  sparing of, in laparoscopic radical cystectomy, 2519f, 2520
    clinical outcome data on, 2531
  stem cells of, 2682-2683
  structure of, 61, 62f, 63
  tissue matrix of, 2683-2684, 2683f
  transit-amplifying cells of, 2680t, 2681-2682, 2682f
  transition zone of, 61, 62f, 63
    in benign prostatic hyperplasia, 2734
  transperineal biopsy of, 2891-2892
  transurethral biopsy of, 2892
  transurethral resection of, antibiotic prophylaxis for, 252
  trapped, 2039
  TRUS-guided biopsy of, 2887-2891
    contraindications to, 2889

Renovascular hypertension *(Continued)*
   phases of, 1165t
    two-kidney, one-clip model in, 1164
   historical background of, 1156-1157
   laboratory investigations in, 1167
   natural history of, 1157t
   pathology of, 1157-1161
    atherosclerosis in, 1157-1159, 1157t, 1158f, 1158t
    fibromuscular hyperplasia in, 1157t, 1161
    intimal fibroplasia in, 1157t, 1159, 1159f, 1160f
    medial fibroplasia in, 1157t, 1159-1160, 1160f
    perimedial fibroplasia in, 1157t, 1160-1161, 1160f, 1161f
   pathophysiology of, 1164-1165
   renal artery reconstruction in, 1733
   renin-angiotensin-aldosterone system in, 1161-1164
   symptoms of, 1167
   trauma-induced, in children, 3935
   treatment of
    endovascular stenting in, 1184-1187
     complications of, 1186-1187, 1186t
     indications for, 1185
     patient selection for, 1173-1174
     results of, 1185-1186, 1185t, 1186f
     technique of, 1185
    percutaneous transluminal angioplasty in, 1180-1184
     atherosclerotic renal artery stenosis and, 1182, 1183f, 1183t, 1184, 1184t
     children and, 1184
     complications of, 1181
     fibrous dysplasia and, 1181-1182, 1181t, 1182f
     inflammatory renal artery stenosis and, 1184
     mechanism of, 1181
     technique of, 1180-1181
    surgical, 1177-1180
     patient selection for, 1173-1174
     results of, 1179-1180, 1179t
     secondary revascularization in, 1180
     techniques in, 1177-1179
   vs. renal arterial disease, 1157
Renovascular injury, as complication of post-chemotherapy surgery, 956
Reproduction. *See* Fertility; Infertility; Pregnancy.
   assisted techniques in. *See* Assisted reproductive techniques (ART).
Reproductive axis, male, 577-580, 578f. *See also specific reproductive organ.*
   development of, 579
   physiology of, 577-607
   steroid feedback in, 578-579
   tiers of organization in, 577
Reproductive cloning, in tissue engineering, 571
"Rescue" therapy, with testosterone, for erectile dysfunction, 776
Resection
   endoscopic, of urothelial tumors, 1647-1648, 1648f
    percutaneous approach to, 1648, 1648f
    results of, 1648, 1648t
   in partial nephrectomy
    transverse, 1724-1725, 1727f
    wedge, 1724, 1726f
   segmental, of urothelial tumors, 1649, 1649t
Resectoscope, spring-loaded, 2480-2481, 2481f
Reservoir insertion, safe, in penile prosthesis placement, 793-794, 794f

Residual mass, post-chemotherapy
   in nonseminomatous germ cell tumors, 922
    indications for resection in, 922-923
   in seminomas, 912-913
Resiniferatoxin
   beneficial effects of, 2107
   for incontinence, 2072
   for painful bladder syndrome/interstitial cystitis, 362t, 364
   intravesical therapy with, 2106-2107
   uropharmacology of, 1958
Resistive index
   definition of, 3364
   in obstructed kidney, 3364-3365
Resorptive hypercalciuria, 1375-1377, 1402
Resource utilization, in health care, 145
Respiration, effects of, on pneumoperitoneum, 200-201
Respiratory acidosis, 1154
Respiratory alkalosis, 1154
Respiratory distress syndrome, as complication of post-chemotherapy surgery, 956
Responsiveness, of HRQOL instruments, 155
Resting membrane potential, of ureteral smooth muscle, 1892-1893, 1893f
Retinitis pigmentosa, in juvenile nephronophthisis, 3327
Retinoblastoma, familial, 516t
Retinoblastoma gene. *See* RB gene.
Retinoblastoma protein, G_1S checkpoint and, 524
13-*cis*-Retinoic acid, for neuroblastoma, 3877
Retraction, in laparoscopy, 196-197, 197f
Retrocaval ureter. *See* Ureter(s), circumcaval (retrocaval).
Retrograde pyelography. *See* Pyelography, retrograde.
Retroperitoneal fibrosis
   causes of, 1215t
   diagnostic biopsy of, 1216-1217
   diagnostic imaging of, 1215-1216, 1216f, 1217f
   drug-induced, 1270
   etiology of, 1270-1271
   evaluation of, 1271, 1271f
   gross appearance of, 1215, 1271
   idiopathic, 1270
   in ureteral obstruction, 1215-1218
   incidence of, 1215
   management of, 1271-1273
    initial, 1271
    laparoscopic ureterolysis in, 1273
    pharmacologic, 1217, 1271-1272
    ureterolysis in, 1217-1218, 1272-1273, 1273f
   membranous glomerulonephritis associated with, 1270-1271
   presentation of, 1270
Retroperitoneal hemorrhage, during radical nephrectomy, management of, 1710-1712, 1713f
Retroperitoneal ligation, for varicocele, 3796
Retroperitoneal lymph node dissection (RPLND)
   for testicular germ cell tumors
    anatomic considerations in, 939, 939f
    nonseminomatous
     stage I and stage IIA, 913, 915, 915f, 916f, 948
     stage IIB, 919, 919t, 949
      adjuvant chemotherapy after, 919, 949
     rationale for, 939

Retroperitoneal lymph node dissection (RPLND) *(Continued)*
    surgical technique of, 941-945
     intraoperative neurostimulation in, 945
     laparoscopic. *See* Laparoscopic retroperitoneal lymph node dissection.
     lymphadenectomy in, 943-944, 944f
     retroperitoneal exposure in, 941
     setting up for, 943
     thoracoabdominal approach in, 941-942
     transabdominal approach in, 942-943, 942f, 943f
    surgical templates in, 940-941, 940f, 941f
   laparoscopic, 945-948. *See also* Laparoscopic retroperitoneal lymph node dissection.
   postchemotherapy, for testicular tumors, 954-955
Retroperitoneal space, access to, for ureteropelvic junction obstruction repair, in children, 3376-3378, 3376f-3379f
Retroperitoneoscopy
   closed (Veress) technique in, 183
   gasless assisted, 182
   limitations and advantages of, 219
   open (Hasson) technique in, 183, 183f, 184f
Retroperitoneum, 3-19, 4f-5f, 6f
   colon in, 19, 20f
   duodenum in, 19, 20f
   exposure of
    in left-sided laparoscopic RPLND, 946
    in retroperitoneal lymph node dissection, 941
   innervation of, 14-19
    autonomic, 15, 16f, 17, 17f
    somatic, 17-19, 17f, 18f, 19t
   lymphatics of, 14, 15f
   pancreas in, 19, 20f
   posterior abdominal wall of, 3, 6f-9f, 8-9, 9t
Retropubic suspension surgery, for female incontinence, 2168-2185, 2170, 2171f
   bladder drainage in, 2174
   bladder overactivity after, 2183
   choice of technique in, 2169-2170
   complications of, 2182-2184
   contraindications to, 2172-2173
   definition of cure in, 2172
   dissection in, 2174
   drains in, 2174
   duration of follow-up in, 2171
   hypermobility in, contribution of, 2170
   indications for, 2172-2174, 2173f
   intrinsic sphincter deficiency in
    contribution of, 2170
    issue of, 2171-2172
   laparoscopic, 2180, 2182
   options in, 2168-2169, 2169t
   outcomes of, 2170-2172
   paravaginal repair in
    results of, 2179-2180
    technique of, 2178-2179, 2179f
   patient's vs. physician's perspective in, 2172
   postoperative voiding difficulties after, 2183
   procedures for, 2170, 2171f. *See also* Burch colposuspension; Marshall-Marchetti-Krantz procedure.
    comparison of, 2184-2185
   suture material in, 2174
   vaginal prolapse after, 2184
   vagino-obturator shelf repair in, 2180, 2181f
   vs. vaginal surgery, 2173-2174
Retroviral agents, erectile dysfunction caused by, 746
Retroviruses. *See also specific virus or infection.*
   RNA, 507

Revascularization
  penile. *See also* Penile vascular surgery.
    arterial, 802-812
    venous, 812-816
  renal, "no-reflow" phenomenon after, 1306
Reverse transcriptase inhibitors, for HIV
    infection, 401, 403t
Reverse transcriptase polymerase chain reaction
    (RT-PCR), in diagnosis of oncology, 548
Reverse transcription, of retroviruses, 389
Reye's syndrome, aspirin associated with, 3206
R-factor resistance, of bacteria, to antibiotics,
    244-245
Rhabdoid tumor, of kidney, in children, 3898
Rhabdomyolysis, after laparoscopic surgery, 218
Rhabdomyosarcoma, 3878-3885
  alveolar, 3879
  clinical grouping of, 3879, 3879t
  embryonal, 3879
  etiology, epidemiology, and genetics of, 3878-
    3879
  of bladder, 2446
  of prostate, 2881
  of testicular adnexa, 933
  of vagina, 3846, 3846f
  pathology of, 3879
  patterns of spread of, 3879
  staging of, 3879-3880, 3879t
  treatment of, 3880-3885
    for bladder tumors, 3880-3883, 3881f,
      3882f
    for nephrogenic adenoma, 3883
    for paratesticular tumors, 3883-3884
    for prostate tumors, 3880-3883, 3881f,
      3882f
    for transitional cell carcinoma of bladder,
      3883
    for uterine tumors, 3885
    for vaginal tumors, 3884-3885, 3884f
    for vulvar tumors, 3884-3885
    risk assignments in, 3880, 3881t
Rhizotomy, sacral
  for bladder denervation, 2289-2290
  for bladder storage disorders, 2152-2153
RhoA/Rho kinase, in penile smooth muscle, 732,
    732f
Rib cage, lower, 9, 11f
Ribonucleic acid. *See* RNA *entires*.
Rice bran, for nephrolithiasis, 1419
Rickets, hereditary hypophosphatemic, in
    hypercalciuria, 1375
Rifampin, for genitourinary tuberculosis, 443,
    445t
RigiScan studies, of nocturnal penile
    tumescence, 763-764, 764f
RNA
  interference, 510-512
  messenger, 509, 509f
    translation of, 511-512
  post-transcriptional modification of, 510
  ribosomal, 512
  transfer, 512
RNA viruses, 507
  oncogenes identified in, 513
RNASEL gene, in hereditary prostate cancer, 518
Robinson catheters, 161-162, 162f
Robotic-assisted laparoscopic surgery, 173-174
  for adrenalectomy, 1884
  for pyeloplasty, 1250
  for radical prostatectomy, 2985-3002. *See also*
    Laparoscopic radical prostatectomy,
    robotic-assisted.
  in children, 3927-3928, 3928f
  of seminal vesicles, 1124

Robson's staging, of renal cell carcinoma, 1600,
    1600f
  5-year survival and, 1604t
Rollerball, in transurethral vaporization of
    prostate, 2839
Rotating disk flowmeter, 1989
Rotoresection of prostate, for benign prostatic
    hyperplasia, 2843
Round cell(s), in semen, 625
Round ligament, of uterus, 3145
RPLND. *See* Retroperitoneal lymph node
    dissection (RPLND).
RT-PCR (reverse transcriptase polymerase chain
    reaction), in diagnosis of oncology, 548
Rubber bands, in penile strangulation injury,
    2652

S

S phase, of cell cycle, 524-525
Saccular aneurysm, of renal artery, 1187, 1188f
Sacher shunt, for priapism, 847f, 848
Sacral agenesis
  definition of, 3644
  diagnosis of, 3644-3645, 3645f, 3646f
  familial, Currarino triad associated with,
    3644
  findings in, 3645, 3647f
  management of, 3645, 3647
Sacral artery, 11f, 13, 13t
  middle, 46, 48t, 50f
Sacral colpopexy, in apical vaginal prolapse
    repair, 2228, 2229f
  laparoscopic, 2229-2230, 2230t
  vs. sacrospinous ligament fixation, 2190
Sacral evoked response-bulbocavernosus reflex
    latency test, in erectile dysfunction, 766
Sacral nerve electrostimulation
  for painful bladder syndrome/interstitial
    cystitis, 365
  responses to, 2148t
Sacral nerve neuromodulation
  complications of, 2160-2163
    published reports of, 2160-2162, 2161f,
      2162f
    troubleshooting algorithm for, 2162-2163,
      2163f
  for bladder emptying disorders, 2166-2167
  for bladder storage disorders, 2153-2158
    outcome of, 2155
    special populations and, 2155-2158
    technique of, 2153-2155, 2153f-2155f
  for incontinence, 2073
  mechanism of action of, 1947-1948, 1947f,
    1948f, 2149-2150
    in overactive bladder, 2150, 2150f
    in urinary retention, 2150, 2151f
Sacral plexus, 53
Sacral rhizotomy
  for bladder denervation, 2289
    selective, 2289
  for bladder storage disorders, 2152-2153
Sacral spinal cord injury, voiding dysfunction in,
    2012t, 2024, 2025f
Sacral vein, 13, 14f
Sacroiliac joint, defects of, in exstrophy patient,
    3501, 3501f
Sacrospinalis muscle, 8, 9t, 10f
Sacrospinous ligament, 38, 39f
  fixation of, in apical vaginal prolapse repair,
    2225-2226, 2226f
    vs. sacral colpopexy, 2229
Sacrum, 38, 39f
Safety, of injectable therapies, for incontinence,
    2284-2285

Safety guide wires, for ureteroscopy, 1515-1516
  cystoscopic placement of, 1515
Salmonella infection, in schistosomiasis, 453
Salvage chemotherapy. *See* Chemotherapy,
    salvage.
Salvage cryotherapy, for prostate cancer, 3039-
    3040
  outcomes after, 3047-3048, 3047t
Salvage metastasectomy, for renal cell
    carcinoma, 1632
Salvage procedure(s)
  for metastatic bladder cancer, 2478
  for penile prosthesis infections, 796
  for refractory disease, in non–muscle-invasive
    bladder cancer, 2460-2461
  for ureteropelvic junction obstruction, 1249
  tension-free vaginal taping in, 2256
Salvage radiation therapy, for prostate cancer,
    3048
Salvage radical prostatectomy, 2936, 2977-2978,
    3048-3049
  vs. other salvage therapies, 3047-3048
Salvage ureteroscopy, after failed shockwave
    lithotripsy, 1519
Sarcoidosis, hypercalcemia associated with, 1376
Sarcoma(s). *See also specific type, e.g.,* Kaposi's
    sarcoma.
  of kidney, 1632-1634, 1633f
  of penis, 990
  of prostate, 2881
    transrectal ultrasonography of, 2887
  of seminal vesicles, 1116
  of upper urinary tract, abnormal urothelium
    in, 1643
  renal clear cell, in children, 3898
Sarcomatoid variants, of renal cell carcinoma,
    1596, 1596f
Sarcoptes scabiei, 383, 425
Saturation states, in stone formation, 1366-1367,
    1366f
Saw palmetto berry. *See* Serenoa repens (saw
    palmetto berry).
S-bladder, for orthotopic urinary diversion,
    2634-2635
Scabies, 383, 383f, 425, 426f
Scalp, pediculosis of, 384
Scalpel, laparoscopic, 191
Scar, definition of, 4336
Scardino-Prince vertical flap technique, of
    pyeloplasty, 1245, 1246f
Scarpa's fascia, 38, 40, 40f, 1032f, 1036
Schafer nomogram, for outflow obstruction,
    1998-1999, 1999f
Schiller-Duvall bodies, in yolk sac tumors, 3901
Schistosoma haematobium, 448
  biology and life cycle of, 448-449, 448f
  in urinary sediment, 109
  infection with. *See also* Schistosomiasis.
    bladder cancer associated with, 2415, 2421
Schistosoma japonicum, 448
Schistosoma mansoni, 448
Schistosomal myelopathy, voiding dysfunction
    in, 2036-2037
Schistosomiasis, 448-455
  clinical manifestations of, 450, 452-453
  contracted bladder syndrome in, 452
  diagnosis of, 453-454, 453f
  epidemiology of, 449
  history of, 448
  hydronephrosis in, 450
  inactive, 450, 451f
  pathogenesis of, 449-450
  pathology of, 449-450, 450f, 451f
  prevention and control of, 455

Stent (stenting) *(Continued)*
  placement of, before shockwave lithotripsy, 1501-1502
  urethral
    for stress incontinence, 2140
    prosthetic, 2303-2304
Steroid(s)
  anabolic, abuse of, 611
  in regulation of prostate growth, protein growth factors and, 2689-2696
  natural and synthetic, half-life and biologic activity of, 1846t
Steroid feedback, on hypothalamus and pituitary, 578-579
Steroid receptor(s), in regulation of prostate growth, 2696-2705
Stevens-Johnson syndrome, 409-410, 410f
Stoma, abdominal, 2551-2553, 2552f, 2553f
Stomach. *See also* Gastric *entries.*
  anatomy of, 2533-2534, 2534f
  selection of, for urinary diversion, 2535-2536
Stomal stenosis, 2553
  after appendicovesicostomy, 42
Stone(s). *See* Calculus(i); *specific type.*
Straddle fractures, of pubic rami, 2658, 2658f
Straining, when voiding, 84
Strangulation injury, to penis, 2652
Strawberry hemangioma, of male genitalia, 3759
Streptococcal infection, glomerulonephritis after, 3226
Streptomycin, for genitourinary tuberculosis, 444, 445t
Stress, in painful bladder syndrome/interstitial cystitis, 348-349
Stress incontinence, 86. *See also* Incontinence.
  clinical evaluation of, 2202-2203
  clinical test for, 2206
  definition of, 2047, 2057
  diagnosis of, leak point pressures in, 2242
  female, 1977
    retropubic suspension surgery for, 2168-2185. *See also* Retropubic suspension surgery, for female incontinence.
  hammock theory of, 2051-2052, 2051f, 2052f
  in children, 3612
  in elderly, 2310
  in neurospinal dysraphism, 2029-2030
  integral theory of, 2052-2053
  male, 2314
    post-prostatectomy, sling for, 2392-2393. *See also* Perineal sling, for male incontinence.
  paraurethral tissue and, 1937
  risk factors for, 2128, 2128t, 2189-2190
  treatment of, 2074-2077, 2318
    behavioral therapy in, 2143
    injectable therapies in, 567-569, 2272-2287. *See also* Injection therapy, for incontinence.
    pelvic floor muscle in, 2142
    pharmacologic, 2075, 2109-2113, 2109t, 2110t
    rehabilitation techniques in, 2074-2075
    sling procedures in. *See* Sling procedures; *specific procedure.*
    surgical
      in females, 2076-2077, 2142-2143. *See also* Retropubic suspension surgery, for female incontinence; Stress incontinence, vaginal surgery for.
      in males, 2077
    tension-free transvaginal taping in, 2251-2266. *See also* Vaginal tape procedure, tension-free.

Stress incontinence *(Continued)*
  therapeutic options in, 2168-2169, 2169t
  urethral bulking agents in, 2075-2076
  urethral inserts in, 2138, 2140, 2140f
  urethral meatal occlusive devices in, 2138
  urethral stents in, 2140
  vaginal pessaries in, 2137-2138, 2138f, 2139f
  vaginal support prosthesis in, 2137, 2137f
  vaginal surgery for, 2212-2215
    complications of, 2214-2215
      intraoperative, 2214
      postoperative, 2214
    preoperative and intraoperative management in, 2212
    technique(s) of, 2212-2214
      Gittes bladder neck suspension, 2212-2213
      modified Pereyra, 2212
      Raz bladder neck suspension, 2213-2214, 2213f
      Raz vaginal wall sling, 2214
      Stamey needle bladder neck suspension, 2212
  vs. urgency incontinence, 2083
Stress relaxation, of ureter, 1902-1903, 1903f
Stress testing, 2313
Stress urethral pressure profilometry, 2007
Striated muscle
  fiber types in, 1936-1937
  vs. smooth muscle, 1928t
Strickler technique, of ureterocolonic anastomosis, 2556-2557, 2556f
Stricture. *See at* anatomic site.
String, in penile strangulation injury, 2652
Stroke
  after renal transplantation, 1324
  brain stem, voiding dysfunction after, 2016
  voiding dysfunction after, 2012t, 2014-2016
Stromal cell(s)
  epithelial cell interactions with, 2693-2694, 2706, 2707f
    in benign prostatic hyperplasia, 2731
  of bladder wall, 1931-1932
    nonfibrillar matrix of, 1932
  of prostate, 2683-2684, 2730
Stromal tumor(s), testicular, 927-928
  in children, 3904-3905
Strontium 89, clinical experience with, therapy, 3029
Struma lipomatodes aberrata renis, of tumors, 1567
Struvite calculi, 1407-1408, 1407f, 1408f
  in children, 3223
  urea-splitting bacteria causing, 261
Studer ileal bladder substitute, for orthotopic urinary diversion, 2635, 2636f
Sturge-Weber syndrome, pheochromocytoma associated with, 1861
SU11248, for renal cell carcinoma, 1630, 1630t
Subarachnoid block, for bladder denervation, 2289
Subcostal incisions, in adrenal surgery, 1874, 1875f
Subcostal nerve, 18, 18f
Subcutaneous fascia, of abdominal wall, anterior, 38, 40, 40f, 41f
Subcutaneous (dartos) flap. *See also* Flap(s).
  in hypospadias repair, 3716, 3716f
Subcutaneous (cavernous) hemangioma, of male genitalia, 3760
Subinguinal ligation, for varicocele, 3797

Substance P
  in pain transmission, 1959
  renal nerve activity responses to, 1906
Substitution cystoplasty, for painful bladder syndrome/interstitial cystitis, 367
Sulfisoxazole, prophylactic, for pediatric urinary tract infections, 3250t
Superfocusing mechanism, of stone fragmentation, 1476
Supernumerary kidney(s)
  associated anomalies with, 3277
  diagnosis of, 3278
  embryology of, 3277
  features of, 3277, 3277f, 3278f
  incidence of, 3276-3277
  symptoms of, 3277-3278
Supernumerary nipple(s), in children, 3207
Supernumerary ureter(s), 3417
Support devices, for bladder filling/storage disorders, 2291-2292
Supracostal puncture, for percutaneous nephrolithotomy, 1490, 1490f, 1490t, 1491f
Suprapubic cystostomy, for urethral injury, 2659
Suprapubic pain, patient history of, 82-92
Supraspinal pathways, in penile erection, 725-728, 726t, 727t
Supratrigonal cystectomy, for painful bladder syndrome/interstitial cystitis, 366-367
Suramin, for hormone-refractory prostate cancer, multidrug regimens with, 3107t
Surgery. *See also specific procedure.*
  antibiotic prophylaxis for, 253, 253t
  for genitourinary tuberculosis, 444-447
    reconstructive, 446-447
  for neuroblastoma, 3875-3877
    in high-risk disease, 3876-3877
    in low-risk disease, 3875-3876, 3876f
  for painful bladder syndrome/interstitial cystitis, 366-368
  for Peyronie's disease, 829-831, 831f-836f, 833, 836
    candidates for, 828-829
  for prostatitis, 325
    minimally invasive, 324
  for schistosomiasis, 454
  for sexual health problems, in females, 887-889, 887f, 888f
  for stress incontinence
    in females, 2076-2077
    in males, 2077
  laparoscopic. *See* Laparoscopic *entries.*
  organ-preserving, for testicular tumors, 908-909
  previous, patient history of, 88
  reconstructive. *See* Reconstructive surgery; *specific procedure.*
Surgical compression, for bladder filling/storage disorders, 2293-2294
Surgical templates, in retroperitoneal lymph node dissection, 915, 915f, 916f, 940-941, 940f, 941f
Surgical wounds, classification of, 253t
Surveillance studies
  after nonseminomatous germ cell tumor therapy, for stage I and stage IIA disease, 916-918, 917t
  after seminoma therapy, for stage I disease, 911-912, 911t
Survival pathways, in hormone-refractory prostate cancer, 3115-3116
Survivin, in bladder cancer, 2435-2436
Susceptibility gene(s), in prostate cancer, 2858, 2858t
Suspensory ligament, of clitoris, 67

Suture (suturing)
in hypospadias repair, 3719
in laparoscopy, 193-194
material for, in retropubic suspension surgery, 2174
sling, determination of tension in, 2244
traction, 3372f, 3377, 3378f
Sutured anastomosis, 2540-2542, 2540f-2542f
ileocolonic
end-to-end, 2542, 2542f
end-to-side, 2541-2542, 2541f, 2542f
single-layer, 2541, 2541f
two-layer, 2540-2541, 2540f
Sweeteners, artificial, bladder cancer associated with, 2415
Switch therapy, for pediatric urinary tract infection, 3249
Sympathectomy, for painful bladder syndrome/interstitial cystitis, 366
Sympathetic nervous system
degeneration of, in transurethral microwave therapy, 2815
increased activity of, in painful bladder syndrome/interstitial cystitis, 346-347, 346t
of lower urinary tract, pathways in, 1938
role of, in ureteral function, 1905-1906
Sympathetic skin response, in erectile dysfunction, 766-767
Sympatholytic agents, affecting lower urinary tract function, 3628t
Sympathomimetic agents
affecting lower urinary tract function, 3628t
for priapism, 845-846, 846t
Syndrome of inappropriate ADH secretion, 1147
disorders associated with, 1149t
Synthetic grafts. See also Graft(s).
in vaginal prolapse surgery, 2216, 2216t
Synthetic materials, injection of, for incontinence, 2274-2275, 2275f
Syphilis
chancre with, 420f
diagnosis of, 375-377, 375f, 376f
in HIV patients, 395
latent, 375
rates of, 372
secondary, 375-376, 376f
tertiary, 376
treatment of, 377
Syringomyelia, voiding dysfunction in, 2036
Systemic inflammatory response syndrome, 287
biologic effects of, 288
clinical presentation of, 288
Systemic lupus erythematosus
painful bladder syndrome/interstitial cystitis and, 336
renal manifestation of, in children, 3227
voiding dysfunction in, 2037
Systemic sclerosis (scleroderma), voiding dysfunction in, 2042
Systemic therapy, for cutaneous diseases, of external genitalia, 406

T

T cell(s), 476-477
activation of, 480-481, 480f
NFAT in, 483
signal 1 in, 480
signal 2 in, 481
signal 3 in, 481
signaling events in, 482-483, 482f
upregulated adhesion molecule expression in, 492-494, 493t

T cell(s) (Continued)
antigen-specific
activation of, 484-488
clonal expansion in, 485, 485f
cytokine production in, 486-487, 486f, 486t
cytolysis of target cells in, 487-488, 487f
development of memory cells in, 488
phenotypic changes in, 488
CD4+. See CD4+ T cell(s).
CD8+. See CD8+ T cell(s).
clonal anergy of, 491
endothelial cell interaction with, 493, 493f
in painful bladder syndrome/interstitial cystitis, 341
induction of apoptosis of, mechanism of tumor escape in, 498-499
memory, 488
naive, trafficking of, 492
peripheral deletion of, 491
regulatory, 491-492
in lymphocyte tolerance, 491-492
role of, in tumor immunology, 495
tumor antigens recognized by, 496t
T pouch ileal neobladder, for orthotopic urinary diversion, 2638, 2639f-2640f, 2640
Tabes dorsalis, voiding dysfunction with, 2030
Tachykinin(s), 1954-1955, 1954t
effect of, on ureteral function, 1906
Tachykinin receptors, 1954-1955, 1954t
Tacrolimus
as immunosuppressant, 1316, 1316f, 1316t
drug interactions with, 1317, 1317t
Tadalafil
adverse effects of, 776-777
clinical response of, 776
efficacy of, 775
for erectile dysfunction, 773-775
onset of action of, 776
patient satisfaction with, 776
starting dose of, 777
structure of, 774f
vasodilator effects of, 778
vs. sildenafil and vardenafil, 774t
Tail stents, 1517
Takayasu's arteritis, in children, 1184
Tamm-Horsfall protein, 100, 3219, 3234, 3260
as calcium oxalate crystal inhibitor, 1367, 1370
in renal casts, 107
renal excretion of, loop of Henle in, 1144
Tamoxifen
for male infertility, 646
for Peyronie's disease, 827
for retroperitoneal fibrosis, 1217
Tamsulosin
for benign prostatic hyperplasia, 2783-2784
dosage of, 2778t, 2784
efficacy of, 2784t
for prostatitis, 321, 327t
uropharmacology of, 2119
vs. other α-adrenergic blockers, 2787
Tanagho technique, of bladder outlet reconstruction, 2294
Tanner classification, of sex maturity stages, in boys, 3745, 3746t
Tape erosion, intravesical, 2262-2263, 2262t
Tapering procedure, for megaureter, 4379, 4379f
Target cells, cytolysis of, 487-488, 487f
Target populations
prostate cancer screening in, 2867-2868, 2868t
renal cell carcinoma screening in, 1599, 1599t
Targeted agents, for metastatic renal cell carcinoma, 1629-1631, 1630f, 1630t

TATA box, 2703
Taxanes
for bladder cancer, non–muscle-invasive, 2459-2460
for locally advanced prostate cancer, before radical prostatectomy, 3060-3061
Taxol. See Paclitaxel.
Taxotere. See Docetaxel.
T-cell receptor
in immune response, 479-480
signaling events transmitted via, 482-483, 482f
Tea consumption, bladder cancer associated with, 2415
TEBS. See Transurethral electrical stimulation (TEBS).
Technetium-99m-mercaptoacetyltriglycine (Tc-99m-MAG3) scintigraphy, of kidneys, 140f-142f, 142, 1335
Technical process, in quality of health care, 148
TEF3 protein, overexpression of, in renal cell carcinoma, 1583
Telomerase, 533, 534f, 2713
in bladder cancer, 2435, 2465
in renal cell carcinoma, 1590
in urothelial tumors, 1644
prostate cancer and, 2866
Telomerase reverse transcriptase, 2713
Telomerase RNA component, 2713
Telophase, in mitosis, 2712
Temperature, in transurethral microwave therapy, 2814-2815
Templates, brachytherapy-like, for cryotherapy, 3038, 3038f
Tendon reflexes, depression of, after sacral spinal cord injury, 2024
Tenesmus, 2204
Tenets of treatment, in cryptorchidism, 3775
TENS (transcutaneous electrical nerve stimulation), for painful bladder syndrome/interstitial cystitis, 364-365
Tension pneumothorax, laparoscopic renal surgery causing, 1808
Tension-free vaginal tape procedure. See Vaginal tape procedure, tension-free.
Teratoma(s), testicular, 895
in children, 3901
immature, 3903
mature, 3902-3903
incidence, pathology, and presentation of, 898t
resection of, 951-952
Teratospermia, evaluation of, 623
Terazosin
for autonomic hyperreflexia, 2027
for benign prostatic hyperplasia, 2779-2780, 2779f, 2780t, 2781f
dosage of, 2778t, 2780
efficacy of, 2779t
for prostatitis, 321, 327t
uropharmacology of, 2119
vs. other α-adrenergic blockers, 2787
Terbutaline, for overactive bladder/detrusor overactivity, 2093t, 2103-2104
Terfenadine, for Peyronie's disease, 827
Testicular adnexa tumor(s), 931-934, 932t
adenomatoid, 931-933, 932t
cystadenoma as, 933
epithelial, 931
mesothelioma as, 932
paratesticular, 932t, 933-934
leiomyosarcoma as, 934
management of, 933-934
rhabdomyosarcoma as, 933

Ureteral stricture (Continued)
ureteral stent placement for, 1255
ureteroscopic management of, 1521-1522
ureteroscopy causing, 1524
Ureteral valves, 3410-3411, 3410f, 3411f
Ureterectomy
distal, 1658-1662
intussusception technique of, 1659, 1662f
laparoscopic ligation and detachment technique of, 1662, 1663f
total laparoscopic, 1662, 1664f
traditional open, 1659, 1660f, 1661f
transurethral ureteral orifice resection in, 1659, 1661f
with bladder cuff excision, 1666
open segmental, 1667-1672
subtotal, 1671-1672, 1672t
ureteroneocystostomy with Boari flap in indications for, 1667
technique of, 1667-1668, 1669f-1671f, 1671
ureteroureterostomy in, 1667, 1668f
segmental, 1649
results of, 1649, 1649t
Ureteric bud, 3384-3387, 3385f-3387f
dichotomous branching of, 3126, 3127f, 3129-3130
division of, 3124-3125, 3125f
interaction of metanephric mesenchyme with, 3125, 3125f
outgrowth of, toward metanephric mesenchyme, 3127, 3129, 3129f
Ureteritis, tuberculous, 438
Ureterocalycostomy, for ureteropelvic junction obstruction, 1247-1249, 1248f, 1253
Ureterocele, 3312, 3397-3412
classification of, 3384
diagnosis of, 3397-3401
ectopic
dilated, 3399
prolapse of, 3194
embryology of, 3397
intravenous pyelography of, 3399-3400, 3399f
intravesical, 3384, 3385f
definition of, 3384
single-system, 3384, 3385f
prenatal diagnosis of, 3181-3182, 3182f
prolapsed, 3398, 3398f, 3409, 3845, 3845f
simple, definition of, 3383
single-system, 3408-3409, 3409f
sphincteric, 3383, 3384f
definition of, 3383
terminology for, 3383-3384
treatment of, 3402-3404, 3406-3408
cystoscopic incision in, 3407-3408, 3407f, 3408f
endoscopic, 3406
excision in, 3404, 3405f, 3406
ultrasonography of, 3398-3399, 3399f
voiding cystourethrography of, 3400-3401, 3401f, 3402f
Ureteroenteric fistula, 2353
Ureteroenteric stricture, anastomotic
etiology of, 1267-1268
evaluation of, 1268
incidence of, 1267
percutaneous treatment of, 1557
radical cystectomy and, 2472
surgical management of, 1269-1270
indications for, 1268-1269
Ureterography, of ureteral injury, 1276

Ureterointestinal anastomosis, 2554-2563
antireflux valves in, 2561-2562, 2561f, 2562f
complications of, 2556t, 2562-2563
ureterocolonic
complications of, 2556t
Cordonnier and Nesbit technique of, 2557
Leadbetter and Clarke technique of, 2555-2556f
Pagano technique of, 2557, 2557f
Strickler technique of, 2556-2557, 2556f
transcolonic Goodwin technique of, 2556, 2556f
Ureterolithotomy, laparoscopic, 1776, 1778
for ureteral calculi, 1455
Ureterolysis, for retroperitoneal fibrosis, 1217-1218, 1272-1273, 1273f
laparoscopic, 1273
Ureteroneocystostomy
antireflux, in renal transplantation, 1310, 1313f-1314f
for lower ureteral injuries, 1288
for ureteral stricture, 1261
laparoscopic, 1261
laparoscopic
extravesical, 2506, 2507f
intravesical, 2506, 2508f
results of, 2506-2507
with psoas hitch or Boari flap
indications for, 1667
technique of, 1667-1668, 1669f-1671f, 1671
Ureteronephrectomy, proximal, laparoscopic, 1665-1666, 1666f
Ureteropelvic junction
disruption of, trauma-induced, 1283, 1283f
in children, 3936
kinking at, 3361, 3361f
physiology of, 1907, 1908f
Ureteropelvic junction obstruction, 1227-1253
acquired, 1228
cautery wire balloon endopyelotomy for
complications of, 1238-1239
indications for and contraindications to, 1237, 1237f
postoperative care following, 1237
results of, 1237-1238
technique of, 1237, 1238f
congenital, 1227. See also Urinary tract obstruction, congenital.
progressive renal dysfunction in, 3164, 3164f
diagnosis of, 1228-1231
computed tomography in, 1229, 1230f
radiographic studies in, 1228, 1229f, 1230f
radionuclide renography in, 1229-1230, 1231f
ultrasonography in, 1228-1229
etiology of, aberrant vessels in, 1228
in children, 3359-3382
associated anomalies in, 3362, 3363f
biochemical parameters in, 3369-3370
diagnosis of, 3363-3370
etiology of, 3359-3362
evidence of, 3359
extrinsic narrowing contributing to, 3361, 3361f
intrinsic narrowing contributing to, 3360, 3360f, 3361f
lower pole, 3361-3362, 3362f
magnetic resonance imaging of, 3367-3368, 3368f, 3369f
presentation of, 3362-3363, 3364f
pressure flow studies of, 3368-3369
radionuclide renography of, 3365-3367, 3366f-3367f

Ureteropelvic junction obstruction (Continued)
secondary, 3361, 3362f
surgical repair of, 3370-3380, 3370f-3372f
Davis intubated ureterotomy in, 3370, 3371f
dismembered pyeloplasty in, 3370, 3372f, 3373
Anderson-Hynes modified, 3373-3374, 3373f, 3374f
endoscopic approaches to, 3374-3375, 3375f
flank approach to, 3374
Foley Y-V plasty in, 3370, 3370f
laparoscopic pyeloplasty in, 3375-3376, 3376f
minimally invasive techniques in, 3374-3376
outcome of, 3380, 3380t, 3381f
posterior lumbotomy in, 3374
retroperitoneal access in, 3376-3378
laparoscopic retroperitoneal pyeloplasty in, 3377-3378, 3378f, 3379f
lateral approach to, 3376-3377, 3376f, 3377f
prone posterior approach to, 3377
transperitoneal approach to, 3377, 3378f
special situations in, 3378, 3380
spiral flap technique in, 3370, 3371f
traction sutures in, 3372f, 3377, 3378f
vertical flap technique in, 3370, 3372f
ultrasonography, 3364-3365
in multicystic dysplastic kidney, 3335
intervention in
endourologic, 1232-1241
indications for, 1231-1232
laparoscopic, 1249-1253
open operative, 1241-1249
options for, 1232-1253
intubated ureterotomy for, 1245, 1247, 1247f
laparoscopic calicovesicostomy for, 1253
laparoscopic dismembered tubularized flap pyeloplasty for, 1253
laparoscopic pyeloplasty for, 1249-1252
anterior extraperitoneal approach to, 1250
complications of, 1252, 1252f
indications for and contraindications to, 1249-1250
postoperative care following, 1250, 1252
results of, 1252
robotic-assisted approach to, 1250
transperitoneal approach to, 1250, 1251f
with concomitant pyelolithotomy, 1253
laparoscopic ureterocalicostomy for, 1253
pathogenesis of, 1227-1228
percutaneous antegrade endopyelotomy for, 1233-1237
complications of, 1236-1237
indications for and contraindications to, 1233, 1233f
patient preparation in, 1233
postoperative care following, 1234, 1236
results of, 1236
simultaneous nephrolithotomy with, 1234
technique of, 1233-1234, 1235f, 1236f
prenatal diagnosis of, 3180
presentation of, 1228
pyeloplasty for
Culp-DeWeerd spiral flap technique of, 1245, 1246f
dismembered, 1242-1243, 1243f, 1244f
flap procedures in, 1243-1245, 1245f

Volume I: pp 1-1128 • Volume II: pp 1129-1888 • Volume III: pp 1889-3118 • Volume IV: pp 3119-3946